DICTIONARY OF CANADIAN BIOGRAPHY

DICTIONARY OF CANADIAN BIOGRAPHY

DICTIONNAIRE BIOGRAPHIQUE DU CANADA

GENERAL EDITORS

GEORGE W. BROWN

1959–1963

DAVID M. HAYNE

1965–1969

FRANCESS G. HALPENNY

DIRECTEUR ADJOINT

ANDRÉ VACHON

UNIVERSITY OF TORONTO PRESS

LES PRESSES DE L'UNIVERSITÉ LAVAL

DICTIONARY
OF CANADIAN
BIOGRAPHY

VOLUME X

1871 TO 1880

EDITOR
MARC LA TERREUR

UNIVERSITY OF TORONTO PRESS

STAFF OF THE DICTIONARY

TORONTO
MARY McD. MAUDE textual editor

DIANE M. BARKER, HENRI PILON manuscript editors

QUEBEC
GASTON TISDEL directeur des recherches

HUGUETTE FILTEAU, JOHANE LA ROCHELLE chargées de recherche

ENGLISH TRANSLATION OF FRENCH BIOGRAPHIES
JOHN S. WOOD

FRENCH TRANSLATION OF ENGLISH BIOGRAPHIES
J.-M. LACROIX   CLAIRE WELLS

© University of Toronto Press and
Les Presses de l'université Laval, 1972
Printed in Canada
Regular Edition: ISBN 0-8020-3287-7
Laurentian Edition: ISBN 0-8020-3288-5
Microfiche Edition: ISBN 0-8020-0206-4

CONTENTS

GENERAL INTRODUCTION

VOLUME X is the third volume of the *Dictionary of Canadian Biography/Dictionnaire biographique du Canada* to be published. Volume I, devoted to persons of Canadian interest who died between the years 1000 and 1700, inaugurated the programme of publication in 1966. It was followed in 1969 by volume II, containing the biographies of persons having died between 1701 and 1740. The introductions to those volumes contain an account of the generous bequest of James Nicholson (1861–1952) by means of which the DCB was founded, and of the establishment of the DBC with the support of l'université Laval; the principles of operation and selection for the DCB/DBC are also described therein. The present volume, dealing with persons who died between 1871 and 1880, does not follow volumes I and II in numerical or chronological sequence. Its appearance at this stage has both a historical and a practical explanation.

In 1967 Canada celebrated 100 years of confederation. The government of Canada, as one of its first contributions to the events of the year, created the Centennial Commission, which helped in a variety of ways to ensure the undoubted success of this significant anniversary. The DCB/DBC, a major historical undertaking in Canada's two languages, was privileged to receive one of the commission's early awards, a grant of $160,000, designated especially for biographical research in the years 1850–1900. Research in this period brought under scrutiny many of the figures involved in the confederation era. The grant has also assisted the work of the DCB/DBC in the 18th century. The first general editor of the DCB/DBC, George W. Brown, was greatly interested in the extension of its research to the 19th century and it is fitting that his contribution to this period at an early stage should be recorded here.

In July 1965 a research office for the DCB/DBC was opened in Ottawa, directed by Marc La Terreur from 1965 to 1967, and by Bernard Pothier from 1967 to 1969. This office built up a large file of biographical information for the 19th century (now assimilated into the files at Toronto and Quebec), and as the work progressed it became clear that a delay in the preparation of volumes based on its findings would be unfortunate. Moreover, it was desirable not to postpone taking advantage of the activity of historians and other scholars who have of recent years been making important contributions to knowledge of 19th century Canada. The organization of the DCB/DBC allows preparation and publication of volumes as chronological units but does not require publication of volumes in chronological sequence, and in 1967 the decision was taken to begin preparation of 19th century volumes. Persons dying between 1871 and 1880 were the first group to be assembled, and volume X contains, therefore, many of the figures and events associated with confederation. Mr La Terreur took on the responsibility of editing the first 19th century volume. The volumes between II and X will be prepared and published next.

Volume X covers only one decade, as compared with 700 years for volume I, 40 years for volume II and 30 years for volume III (now in preparation). With the growth in the population of Canada through the 18th and 19th centuries, the number of possible candidates for inclusion increases, and, although criteria for inclusion become more stringent, the time span to be covered by individual volumes gradually contracts.

The 256 contributors to volume X, who submitted manuscripts in either English or French, are listed on pages 767–74. The *Directives* they were given include this key paragraph:

> Each biography should be an informative and stimulating treatment of its subject, presented in readable form. All factual information should be precise and accurate, and be based upon reliable (preferably primary) sources. Biographies should not, however, be mere catalogues of dates and events, or compilations of previous studies of the same subject. The biographer should try to give the reader an orderly account of the personality and achievements of the subject, *against the background of the period in which the person lived and the events in which he or she participated.* It is evident that such biographies cannot be written to any one specification, but it is expected that the biographer will attempt, within the space available, to appraise the circumstances shaping his subject's character and career, enumerating the parts played by ancestry, parentage, education, physical and social environment, and other formative influences; that he will make discreet use of relevant anecdote; and that he will conclude his biography by an equitable and discriminating evaluation of the subject's strengths and weaknesses, successes and failures, and probable place in Canadian history.

After submission, the articles for a volume are reviewed by the DCB/DBC editors, and correspondence between them and the contributors takes up points of style, fact, and coverage in text and bibliography. Lastly, each biography is translated into the other language, and final copy of the two parallel volumes is prepared for the printer.

Volume X includes an introduction by the volume editor, tracing the scope of the biographies as a collection, and also a general bibliography and full nominal index with cross-references to other volumes to come. The glossary of Indian tribal names which appeared in volumes I and II was not thought to be necessary for volume X.

The names of members of the staff who have been engaged upon volume X in Toronto and Quebec are recorded on page v. The description of their responsibilities given in the paragraph above indicates the extent of their contribution to the DCB/DBC, but not the competence, devotion, and enthusiasm with which it has been made.

At the time volume X was inaugurated, and for the first two of its four years of preparation, Dr David Hayne was general editor of the DCB/DBC. Volume II had his supervision as general editor throughout, and for volume I he served as chairman of the Toronto Translation Committee. All those who have been associated with the DCB/DBC in any capacity and at any time would wish that tribute be paid here to Dr Hayne's wise and considerate guidance, to the variety of knowledge at his command, to the standards of scholarly and editorial execution he set, and to the contribution he made to the happy association of our two language groups in this important bilingual undertaking.

FRANCESS G. HALPENNY
ANDRÉ VACHON

INTRODUCTION TO VOLUME X

MARC LA TERREUR

The aim of the *Dictionary of Canadian Biography/Dictionnaire biographique du Canada* is to provide "a complete record of the activities of all noteworthy inhabitants of Canada from earliest times to the ultimate date of publication." The philanthropist who made this undertaking possible had stipulated in his will that the persons whose biographies were to be included should be "noteworthy from all points of view." The task assigned was therefore to create the Canadian equivalent of the *Dictionary of National Biography* and the *Dictionary of American Biography*: a venture bordering on temerity in a country with resources so inferior to those of Great Britain and the United States. But, through the extraordinarily close collaboration afforded by many scholars, the first volume, containing the biographies of persons of primary and secondary importance who died before 1700, was produced, and established criteria of research and presentation of such a kind that comparison with these other works of reference no longer appeared presumptuous. The enthusiastic reception given to its first volume prompted the DCB/DBC, already concerned with preparing volume II (for persons whose deaths occurred between 1701 and 1740), to "open a second front" by beginning a study of the 19th century. Such an activity would be nearer to the present time, and the numerous specialists whose work did not bear on the French colonial period could be called upon; moreover, with at least two volumes always in preparation, the speed at which the whole undertaking could be completed would be increased.

A timely grant from the Canadian Centennial Commission made possible a preliminary study of the period 1851–1900. General works, specialized studies, and archival sources were consulted in order to draw up a rough list of persons who might be included in the volumes for this half century. Numerically, the results were frightening. Whereas for the volumes of the French regime it had almost been necessary to use a magnifying glass to discover a full complement of men and women who would have a biography, now politicians and business men, engineers and administrators, judges and journalists, ecclesiastics and artists came into view, all bearing credentials for posterity. The editorial task was no longer searching, but pruning. The large first list was broken up by grouping explorers and fur-traders, important people of British Columbia, the Prairies, Ontario, Quebec, New Brunswick, Nova Scotia, Prince Edward Island, and Newfoundland, and a "special list" of those not easily classified. There were then ten lists of persons who had died between 1851 and 1900. A decision now had to be made about the decade to be covered by the first published volume.

Each decade offered attractions and disadvantages from the point of view of the number of significant individuals who died within it – a somewhat cynical criterion, we admit, by which to judge the importance of a period, but a convenient one, in conformity with the general policy of the DCB/DBC by which each volume covers "a specific number of years . . . with the contents arranged alphabetically. . . ." The years 1871–80 were finally adopted for several reasons: though they were an indirect preparation for the volumes of later decades, they necessarily contained the major themes of 19th-century Canadian history; they furnished an opportunity to study men such as Paul KANE, Louis-Joseph PAPINEAU, James DOUGLAS, William LOGAN, and John Sandfield MACDONALD; and through the study of politicians such as George-Étienne CARTIER, George BROWN, and Joseph HOWE, it was possible to follow the stages leading to the British North America Act and thus to comply with the implicit intention of the Centennial Commission.

This decision taken, the provisional lists for 1851–1900 were reviewed and the names belonging to the 1870s were extracted. The ten regional lists were further broken down into professions or activities as an aid to verification and the results were submitted to various experts. Their advice was highly valuable: they supplied missing dates of births and deaths, pointed out omissions, indicated the relative importance of persons, and made recommendations about possible biographers. The staff of the DCB/DBC had to make sure for its part that any person dying between 1 Jan. 1871 and 31 Dec. 1880 who had had a definite role in some sector of Canadian life appeared on these lists; to try to ensure that no person of note had escaped attention, a number of newspapers were scrutinized. Then, again in conjunction with experts, the persons actually to be included in the volume were selected, and the importance to be attached to them was determined, the categories of length extending from short factual notes to major studies of 10,000 words. At this point in the process of cutting down and classifying, the differences between the volumes for the French regime and the present volume really became apparent.

The geographical borders of 17th century New France and the Canada of the last third of the 19th century have some similarity, but there the resemblances between an embryonic colony and a partially industrialized country appear to end. The sedentary white population of New France consisted of a few score of persons in 1625 and of about 2,000 in 1660, whereas in 1870 Canada could count nearly 4,000,000 and its principal city, the former Ville-Marie, could boast of 107,225 inhabitants and the famous Victoria Bridge, then the largest tubular bridge in the world. What had been an immense, unknown territory, explored only along its waterways – a testimony to the boldness and endurance of missionaries and voyageurs – was now in many regions marked out by roads, lined with sections of iron track soon to be transformed into a transcontinental railway, and traversed by boats that almost mocked natural obstacles, thanks to the canals that were being built. The New World, which had been virtually cut off from all communication with the Old from November to May, was linked to it definitively in 1866 by submarine cable, so that news of any event was no longer delayed by frontiers or ice-floes. Whereas New France depended on the mother country for every manufactured article, Canada possessed a number of industries that could transform raw materials locally. The old colony, with an essentially autocratic regime the head of whose supreme and omnipresent authority resided beyond the seas, had become a country with a number of governments, in which functions were becoming more and more complex, most of which had two houses and also a ministry responsible to the elected representatives of the population, judicial systems, and a host of civil servants to assist legislators and ministers. There had once been a single institution of secondary teaching and a few primary schools; now the country had universities, with some specialized faculties, colleges, and systems of secondary and primary education. The religious and linguistic unity of the French regime had become linguistic and cultural dualism, as well as religious pluralism. The microcosm of the old regime, without lawyers and printers, had become a varied community endowed with newspapers and literary or scientific journals which were kept supplied by a pleiad of journalists, artists, scientists, and men of letters; professional and bourgeois classes instead of seigneurs were the unofficial leaders of this diversified society, which was more and more receptive towards the outside world but still much occupied in building a country in which industrialization was increasing and resources were being more fully exploited.

These fundamental changes suggest the pitfalls that have made the selection of the 574 persons in this volume a large task. To the difficulties inherent in any choice, and multiplied here by the number of individuals, were added those created by the immense size of the territory in which they lived and the need for regional representation.

Because date of death determines the contents of any volume, each covers a considerable period of time. The important activities of most men coincide with their maturity, and their old age is often not active. A person who died in the 1870s may have made his place in history through actions 20 or 30 years before, or even earlier. There is, for example, François BEAULIEU, who in 1791 accompanied Alexander Mackenzie* on his journey overland to the Pacific Ocean; yet on the next page one may find discussed the contract finally granted in 1880 to the company which was to build a railway to that same Pacific Ocean. Another good example of longevity is Étienne MAYRAND (1776–1872), who in the days of the North West Company went out to grow rich in the fur trade, returned to put his capital to work in "the old province," was elected to the Legislative Assembly, and finally sat in the Legislative Council. As his biographer points out, he had served "his country loyally under four sovereigns, George III, George IV, William IV, and Queen Victoria, no less than 19 governors general, and 21 lieutenant governors." Born at the time the Quebec Act was becoming effective, he lived under the constitution proclaimed in 1791 and under the union, and finally was a witness of the first five years of the federation of 1867. These instances are, of course, extreme, but none the less this volume, from the standpoint of biography, does describe in a fairly continuous fashion three-quarters of a century rich in events. In that sense, it does not mark a pause in time, but rather is the portrayal of an evolution.

The geographic factor that had to be taken into account was closely linked with the demographic factor alluded to above. The considerable size of the Canadian population necessitated the rigorous elimination of persons who are of secondary importance for our undertaking. Among some 20 judges, for example, we selected one who had distinguished himself in politics before acceding to the magistrature, or who had stood out among his colleagues because of his legal writings, or who had delivered judgements in noteworthy cases. In addition, we endeavoured to make a place for at least one person from the principal spheres of activity, and to have representatives of workers, craftsmen, farmers, fishermen, surveyors, etc. Indeed it is figures like these, often without precise outline or relief, and almost forgotten by history, who have ensured the stability of the family and who from day to day have fashioned Canadian society. For this reason the volume has itinerant missionaries defying distance and bad weather to sow the seeds of faith [*see* MILNER], and an Antoine LÉGARÉ teaching for 50 years at the little school of Saint-Roch in Quebec, reminding us of the "half century of servitude" that Flaubert speaks of in connection with the servant Catherine Nicaise. These humble people deserve their chronicles as much as politicians, artists, businessmen, scientists, doctors, and bishops. Thus the volume tries to present a faithful picture of a past when there were still numbers of dwellings of squared logs, when the pioneers' furniture was rudimentary, when hours of work were long and reward was slight. And is not history a description of past life? Despite the alphabetical arrangement of the biographies, a reader should not forget that volume X presents a full perspective of Canadian life, a life that, even allowing for the extent of the territory, shows certain common currents.

That immense expanse, which was to become Canada, begins at its eastern extremity with Newfoundland. Inhabited seasonally by fishermen, divided into six districts in 1792, Newfoundland changed its appearance in the 19th century, when English merchants gradually set up operations in such centres as St John's and Harbour Grace, and thus dominated still more closely the island's economic life. Its institutions were transformed, and, bit by bit, the mediaeval vestiges of the old judicial regime disappeared. In 1824 Newfoundland acquired the status of a colony, and in the following year received its first resident governor, the ostentatious but effective COCHRANE, who was instructed to divide its territory into three districts and who governed with the approval of a docile council. Pressures were such that in 1832 a civil government was established, although the seven executive councillors, appointed by Cochrane, did not sit in the assembly of 15 elected representatives. But quarrels flared: merchants against officials, immigrants against islanders, Catholics against Protestants, fishermen against suppliers, bankers and merchants of St John's against the rest of the island. The embryonic political parties collapsed, and in 1842 a new constitution was adopted by which the representatives, elected or appointed, theoretically worked on an equal footing in an assembly that was always exposed to the restlessness of a population swayed by many fluctuating influences. Finally, in 1855, Great Britain granted responsible government to Newfoundland, and a more modern if often still tumultuous political era began. This was the setting in which toiled a small population – 75,000 inhabitants in 1836 and 120,000 in 1857. On the island, where everything functioned in terms of the sea and its resources, the decline of the fisheries at the end of the 1850s and during the 1860s had disastrous consequences, but they were not enough to bring the independent islanders to accept union with Canada.

Also washed by the ocean but very different from Newfoundland, were the three Atlantic provinces. Their history, economy, expansion, and life were intimately linked, even if they preserved their individuality. Prince Edward Island experienced a population explosion during the 19th century: from 4,000 inhabitants in 1798 to 47,000 in 1814 and to 87,000 in 1864. But one problem predominated: the land question. The

Island, a French possession until 1763, was shortly after divided into 67 lots – long belts of land, each of about 20,000 acres, stretching from north to south. The concession holders, mostly British and Protestant, did not live on their properties and were unable to attract a stable population to them; they entrusted the administration to agents, who attempted to extract as much money as possible. In 1841 less than a third of the farmers owned the soil they tilled. The absenteeism of the owners was a cause of division among the Island's population, and numerous but vain attempts were made to change the system of tenure. Steps taken by the government of Prince Edward Island to buy the lands were frustrated by the influence the owners had with the British authorities and their desire to keep their domains; on the other hand, in the 1860s, the farmers' refusal to pay their rents only resulted in armed repression [see HODGSON]. This phenomenon poisoned political life [see COLES, POPE], and also affected daily living. A case in point is Father John MCDONALD, parish priest and landowner at the same time, a man divided between his duties and his interests, torn between God and Mammon, who, suffering the reproaches of his bishop and the ire of his flock, finally left lands and parish but did not give up his rents.

Conflicts of this kind did not exist in Nova Scotia, the first colony on Canadian soil to have a legislative body, and which, with the annexation of Cape Breton Island in 1820, had its frontiers set. Coal and iron mines gave rise to small industries, so that it did not depend solely on fisheries, lumbering, or agriculture. Commerce, moreover, played a major role. Merchants, chiefly British, sent to Nova Scotia supplies for fishing and manufactured articles, and loaded their vessels with fish which they sold in the West Indies and Brazil in exchange for sugar and rum. These slow, heavy cargo boats, built in Nova Scotia and often commanded by Nova Scotians, could also transport wood to Great Britain or coal to the United States. Local financiers shared more and more in this kind of trading. Shipbuilding, which was often a family undertaking [see CHURCHILL], prospered during most of the 19th century, but declined in the 1870s and 1880s because of a falling off in trade and the use of iron vessels, and because of the lack of cooperation from local banks. For as early as 1825 – thanks to enterprising businessmen such as Enos COLLINS, Samuel Cunard*, and H. H. Cogswell* – this colony possessed a bank, the Halifax Banking Company. Having no competition, and with five of its directors in the Legislative Council, it strove persistently, but in vain, to block the founding of the Bank of Nova Scotia in 1832. This rival, under the control of Tories such as M. B. ALMON and J. W. JOHNSTON, made a breach in the Halifax Banking Company's monopoly. The competition between these two establishments of the Nova Scotian oligarchy weakened the economy of the province, brought about a depreciation of the currency, and supplied the Reformers, who used every means to attain their ends, with weapons by which to attack the ruling class. Nevertheless, the impression of the province that remains is of an industrious population – nearly 400,000 inhabitants in 1870 – in which Acadians, British, Germans, loyalists had all been concerned with progress, where there prevailed an atmosphere of activity and prosperity, and where interest in common welfare was often intense.

The image is somewhat different in the case of New Brunswick, a territory detached from Nova Scotia in 1784. At that time it was a homogeneous colony: 20,000 loyalists easily submerged 1,500 Acadians. This homogeneity disappeared with the arrival of other English-speaking immigrants (the population passed the quarter-million mark in 1867). Social and geographical cleavages were to persist in the colony, and local problems monopolized all political activity. But larger issues of responsible government and confederation were nevertheless fought out here in much the same way and as vigorously as in the other colonies [see WILMOT, FISHER, and CHANDLER]. The basis of the economy was lumbering; agriculture and fishing seem poor juniors when compared to the seemingly inexhaustible resources of the forests. Until 1840, Great Britain drew from New Brunswick her supplies of timber for building ships; the preferences granted made possible the creation of "forest empires" in the valley of the Miramichi. The removal of preferences later did not prove disastrous, for the New Brunswick lumbermen early "discovered" the American market. It was the timber trade over which bitter struggles were fought at the beginning of the century. Its control passed from the officers of the crown to the legislative body [see Robert GOWAN and Wilmot], but the change proved difficult, and could not erase the memory of certain rather unsavoury deals involving "patronage." Yet it was by means of these forest resources used for shipbuilding at Saint John and in several other Bay of Fundy ports that New Brunswick became famous in the 19th century. The ships thus built were durable, and remarkable for their burden, which in certain cases almost reached the figure of 2,400 tons; they were the biggest sailing ships built in British North America [see HARLEY, HILYARD, WRIGHT].

Different from the Atlantic provinces, and enjoying a diversified economy, was the immense area whose development and population were related to the St Lawrence. It became the Province of Canada in 1841, in a union of the former Lower Canada and Upper Canada, but none the less remained divided: on the one hand there was Canada East, which continued to be called Lower Canada and in 1867 was to become the province of Quebec; on the other, Canada West, which was commonly known as Upper Canada and in 1867 was to be the province of Ontario.

The province of Quebec – it had already had that name before 1791, when the two Canadas were formed out of its territory – was the old "Canada," which had been conquered by force of arms, and it was the watchful guardian of the French and Catholic heritage. The French had eyed with distrust the British immigrants, who even if few in number were active, who tended to group together, and who showed both business sense and suspicion of the state, accustomed as they were to freedom of the press, freedom of speech, and free enterprise. For their part, the French had lived under the arm of the state or the church, and had not known a democratic tradition; individualistic as they were, they kept to areas with which they were familiar, agriculture and the fur trade. The loyalist immigration that followed the American revolution disturbed this society. The demographic transformation of the province of Quebec brought about changes in its political institutions, and the introduction of parliamentarianism into the two new provinces. Lower Canada, with 150,000 inhabitants of whom some 10,000 were Anglophones, was enabled officially to remain loyal to its traditions, but would have to adapt itself to this minority, which was different in its language and religion, and above all economically and financially powerful. At the beginning of the 19th century, Lower Canada's traditional sources of livelihood, agriculture and the fur trade, began to diminish in alarming fashion. The decline in the harvest continued unabated, but the revenues obtained from pelts were to be replaced by those from the export of lumber, facilitated again by the preferential tariffs of Great Britain. But lumbering benefited particularly the Anglophones, for it supplied the requirements of shipbuilding and the export trade. The Sharples [see John SHARPLES] and John GILMOUR are symptomatic. They bought their lumber to the east and west of Quebec, cut it at Sillery, and used their own ships to transport pine and oak in the form of square timber, and planks for construction, to England and Scotland.

The decline of prices after 1815, the vexatious practices of the seigneurs, who now were not controlled in civil matters, and the economic inferiority of the French Canadians, led the latter to transpose their frustrations and resentments to the political plane, so greatly had the old order changed. The bourgeoisie engaged in business and the bureaucrats, grouped under the generic term "English," were attacked by Francophones of the professional classes. The rebellion followed [see Papineau and NELSON]. Durham made his report, and in 1841 the two Canadas, almost by nature in opposition, were united.

Upper Canada had been created by the Act of 1791; it had given the loyalists, whose main concern was then agriculture, a constitution that allowed them to live under the shelter of the British institutions and flag they cherished. A local aristocracy, which was not, however, exclusively loyalist, assumed the lead, socially and politically, in the majority of institutions, and was able to boast of its defence of British territory in 1812–14. But the social stratification that it wanted, perhaps unconsciously, to create in the province could not resist the growing influence of Jacksonian democracy after 1820, or the spirit of enterprise shown by numerous immigrants. Upper Canada, an agricultural province, but one supported by the forest industry and strengthened by the creation of small undertakings involving some skilled labour, succeeded fairly well in providing a system of communications for the transporting of its products. The social confrontation which the 1837 uprising represented, Francis Bond HEAD's ephemeral victory, and the union with Lower Canada in no way diminished the progressive spirit of Upper Canada; all these events served rather as a stimulus.

After the union of 1841, the two colonies had willy-nilly to keep in step, with numerically equal representation in a parliament that continually changed its seat, and despite the demographic disproportions which first worked in favour of Upper Canada, whose population in 1841 was 455,000 in comparison with the 700,000 of Lower Canada. Ten years later, Upper Canada numbered 952,000 persons and Lower Canada 890,000. Since at that time equal representation bore unjustly upon Upper Canada, the latter raised the cry of injustice, gave out on every occasion its slogan "rep by pop" [see Brown], and reacted in varying ways to those who recommended double majority [see J. S. Macdonald]. This situation did not, however, prevent the economic development of the Province of Canada from entering a new phase.

In the 1840s, the popularity of free trade in Great Britain resulted in the virtual abolition of the preferential tariffs favourable to Canadian products, in particular those of the forest. This occurred at the time when a persistent agricultural crisis was forcing Lower Canada to turn to Upper Canada for its grain, and when businessmen and merchants were looking more and more to the United States, with the thought of annexation [see

HOLTON]. But the beneficial reciprocity treaty and an increase in customs duties on British products restored a certain balance. The abolition of the seigneurial regime and the settlement of the clergy reserves extinguished servitudes of the past and were an augury of a new age. It was marked by a revolution in transportation [see KILLALY], which threw the economy into confusion and gave it a different orientation, by enabling it to reach previously inaccessible markets rapidly; it was marked also by the appearance of entrepreneurs capable of adapting themselves to changes and even of anticipating them. The Torrances [see David TORRANCE] come to mind: wholesale merchants and owners of steamships that plied between Montreal and Quebec, they rivalled the Molsons on the St Lawrence [see William MOLSON], and organized a more rapid and less costly method of shipping merchandise. John YOUNG, importer, turned his attention with foresight and success towards railways, and even obtained a charter to link Canada to Great Britain and then to Asia by cable. These businessmen possessed a common spirit of enterprise, but diversified their interests [see WORKMAN], and did not hesitate to enter the political arena in order to promote the country's prosperity, and consequently their own. French Canadians took little or no part in these great ventures, with the exception of a few such as Jean-Baptiste PRAT (John Pratt), Jacques-Félix SINCENNES, and Marc-Damase MASSON; they confined themselves to embryonic manufacturing activity in textiles, furniture, and footwear, without attaining a level at which exporting was really profitable.

Upper Canada was more open to industrialization; it had many imaginative entrepreneurs who directed their capital away from progressive family industries into insurance companies and railroad and banking operations. They took precautions to safeguard their manufactured products from American competition, and the words protection and reciprocity were to constitute the poles of attraction of Canadian political economy in the second half of the century. All politicians dreamed, at one time or another, of renewing the beneficial reciprocity treaty abrogated in 1866. Meanwhile, through confederation, efforts were made to find new markets for the surpluses of United Canada, and later, in 1879, the protectionist budget of S. L. Tilley* gave if not prosperity to Canada at least success to the party of John A. Macdonald*.

The country situated to the west of the Great Lakes and bordering on the Arctic and the Pacific was to be one of these outlets. At the beginning of the period represented in volume X, it was theoretically under the control of the Hudson's Bay Company. From its trading posts on the bay whose name it had adopted, the company easily drained off the furs of Rupert's Land (from Labrador to the Rockies and from Red River to Hudson's Bay), for the Indians came to it to barter. But the North West Company, whose headquarters were at Montreal and not in London, made its way into this empire of ill-defined frontiers. A relentless struggle went on at the beginning of the century, and the merchants of the HBC had to leave their trading posts and go to meet the Indians. In 1821, Great Britain forced the two rivals to join together, the North West Company being taken over by the HBC; from that time the latter enjoyed the monopoly of trade from Labrador to the Oregon and from Red River to the Yukon. Through this huge territory, sparsely populated by Indians and Métis, with symbolic agricultural settlements on the Red River, travelled Protestant and Catholic missionaries; in bringing the succour of their religion, they tried to instil the rudiments of civilization, which for them meant the white man's way of life. To accomplish their ends, they learned Indian dialects, built chapels and schools with their own hands, followed hunting expeditions, even took the side of the Métis against the powerful company [see BELLECOURT]. The HBC ran up against not only the Red River Métis, who obtained freedom of trade in 1849, but also the Americans, who wanted to break its monopoly, and the Ontarian immigrants, whose violent spokesman was the *Nor'Wester* [see James ROSS]. The new dominion was anxious to acquire the Hudson's Bay Company's territories [see Cartier], and in 1869 bought the rights of the company. The assumption of authority was carried out clumsily, causing an insurrection [see BUNN, O'DONOGHUE] and resulting in hasty concessions to Bishop Taché* and Louis Riel* that the government subsequently wanted to attenuate or challenge. The creation of a new province, Manitoba, gave form to a tiny part of this immense territory, namely the Assiniboia and the Portage region, which had a population of about 10,000. The birth of this fifth province came about amid dissension; the transition from a nomadic life to a civilization based on colonization and agriculture contained within it the source of educational, religious, and ethnic problems that were later to shake the whole country.

Out of the former territory of the Hudson's Bay Company were also carved, in 1905, two other provinces: Saskatchewan and Alberta. Their history prior to the creation of Manitoba is indistinguishable from that of the trading posts of the HBC. The life of its employees, especially the juniors, was rough, and the isolation was hard to bear; the distances to be covered were enormous, and trips to the home land were rare. But the profits compensated for "the humdrum life we led there," to use the expression of one of these traders. Some, however, turned to experimental agriculture, others tried painting, like A. H. MURRAY, or botany, like B. R. ROSS. The company's interest in the aborigines was particularly as purveyors of furs in exchange for manufactured goods: a contact for them with a different culture was the work of the missionaries. This volume does not contain the biographies of the great Oblate propagators of the faith, such as Albert Lacombe* and Vital Grandin*, but in it will be found Brother REYNARD, who was paradoxically deemed too good to be ordained priest and to direct a mission. He was a skilful carpenter, sparing of neither time nor effort; he put up buildings, and relieved the missionaries of material concerns. For James NISBET, the first Presbyterian minister in this region, agricultural preoccupations even prevailed over the concern for spreading Christianity; G. M. McDOUGALL, a Methodist, arrived at a more felicitous balance, rather like that of the Catholic missions. All of them witnessed the migrations of the Métis, the epidemics that decimated the Indian population, the often dubious contributions from a lay society tainted by a ruthless pursuit of gain and tarnished by the trade in spirits. At least the zeal of the missionaries added a moderating touch of humanity to the penetration of whites, and their influence was a considerable help to the government in the settling of the problem of the Indian reserves [see WIKASKOKISEYIN and SOTAI-NA]. In that way they contributed to the development of the territory.

Beyond the Rockies the characters of the volume tread a soil that Russia and Spain once fought over, and that was mapped by Captain George Vancouver* at the end of the 18th century. The HBC established itself there after taking over the North West Company, which, thanks to Simon Fraser* and David Thompson*, had explored the rivers and set up trading posts. The HBC headquarters was first situated at Fort Vancouver, on the Columbia River, but in the 1840s, when the American government established control of Oregon, it transferred the seat of its operations to Victoria. The fur trade at such forts as Macleod, St James, and George still remained the company's predominant interest, but gradually it extended its activity to farming, timber, and mines. Immigrants were still coming in mere handfuls – less than 100 per year up to 1858 – at the time James Douglas, while remaining chief HBC officer west of the Rockies, was appointed civil governor of Vancouver Island. The discovery of gold in 1858, in the sands of the Fraser and the valley of the Thompson, threw the life of the colony into a turmoil; Douglas left the company to become governor of both Vancouver Island and British Columbia. Rapidly the miners crowded in; at the height of the rush, Barkerville and its vicinity numbered 25,000 inhabitants. Douglas enacted regulations and the "hanging judge" Matthew Begbie* saw to it that they were obeyed by the throng of prospectors and profiteers; justice was done, often of a spectacular kind, despite its lack of orthodoxy [see Cox]. Few miners got rich, but the government ran into debt endeavouring to build roads; the population decreased rapidly and the government kept its debts. In 1866 the two colonies were joined and in 1868 Victoria became the capital. When sawmills were being set up, when wood from British Columbia was on its way to Peru, California, Great Britain, Australia, and China [see Moody and Stamp], when the first salmon canneries were being established [see Deas], thought was also being given to railroads for this colony of about 20,000 inhabitants and to its political status. Promises that its debt would be absorbed, and that it would be linked by rail to Canada, convinced British Columbia of the advantage in becoming the sixth province of the Canadian confederation. Delays almost led it to withdraw from the union, and not until nine years after its entry was the railway really begun. A new era of development, less ephemeral than the one spawned by the gold rush, opened for British Columbia.

This bird's-eye view of the territory would be incomplete without mention of the Arctic, whose vastness haunts the mind and has the same appeal to the imagination as the exploration of America and the Pacific Ocean in the 15th and 16th centuries and the conquests of space in the 20th. "Terra incognita" was sufficient reason for the search for a northwest passage which would connect the Atlantic and the Pacific. At first, it was thought that it would be a shorter route to the Orient, and the charter of the HBC enjoined the "honourable" merchants to discover this passage. At the end of the 18th century, the voyages of Samuel Hearne* and Alexander Mackenzie pointed to a conclusion that this passage did exist, somewhere to the north of the mouths of the Coppermine and the Mackenzie, and the outlets from Hudson Bay, and that it must lie ice-bound in the wastes of the Arctic. Commercial ambitions faded, but the desire to make a last major geographical discovery remained. For the British navy, the most powerful of the day, it was a challenge to be taken up. Geographical knowledge could be perfected: mapping of localities, observation of air and water temperatures, study of maritime currents and variations of the magnetic needle, gathering of new geological and botanical species. The voyages took place under indescribable conditions, and the courage of captains and crews is sometimes beyond comprehension. Their expeditions lasted for years, and the wintering-over periods in the ice-fields exceeded ten months, for three of which they did not directly see the sun. The travellers were never assured of returning, and accidents could be tragic: 19 people swept away on an ice-floe went 1,300 miles in 6 months [*see* C. F. HALL]. Exposed to intense and sustained cold, these men became the prey of scurvy and of an immense boredom described by Sir John Ross*: "We were weary for want of occupation, for want of variety, for want of the means of mental exertion, for want of thought, and (why should I not say it?) for want of society. Today was as yesterday, and as was to-day, so would it be to-morrow: while if there was no variety, as no hope of better, is it wonderful that even the visits of barbarians were welcome, or can any thing more strongly show the nature of our pleasures, than the confession that these were delightful. . . ."

From 1819 to 1825 William Edward Parry* – whose mission was to explore Lancaster Sound thoroughly and to proceed as directly as possible, if he found a way through, to Bering Strait – discovered Prince Regent Inlet, Wellington and Barrow straits, and Bathurst and Melville islands. He was the first explorer to penetrate so deeply to the west within the Arctic Circle. From the expeditions of John Franklin*, John Ross, and George BACK some plausible hypotheses could be made: that the eastern entry to the famous passage was Lancaster Sound and the western entry was probably somewhere along Barrow Strait, with Bering Strait necessarily the western exit. Franklin, entrusted with localizing the passage, was lost with his crew in 1845. Forty expeditions searched for him, and scoured the entire Arctic except the region where he had actually perished [*see* Jane GRIFFIN and Richard KING]. One of these included Robert MCCLURE on the *Investigator* and Robert Collinson* on the *Enterprise*. They made their way into the Arctic through Bering Strait and went towards Melville Island, while Henry Austin* and then Edward BELCHER used Lancaster Sound. Finally, McClure passed Cape Bathurst on the starboard side, took possession of Nelson Head, discovered Prince of Wales Strait between Banks and Victoria islands, and proceeded up it to ascertain whether it communicated with Melville Sound. He had discovered a northwest passage. The date was 1851. Stefan Zweig would have called this a "great starlit hour." Only later was it learned that Franklin also had discovered a northwest passage, by way of Victoria Strait.

The geographical space covered by volume X appears, therefore, immense: immense and so varied that its regions seem to have been assembled at the whim of nature. The links between these different regions were tenuous, even non-existent, and it might be wondered whether any kind of unity would ever be realized. A world separated the fisherman of Newfoundland from the miner of Cape Breton, the parish priest of Quebec, the merchant of Toronto, or the lumberman of British Columbia. In the 1870s, when a central government succeeded in placing seven provinces in its orbit, regional aspirations rather than national sentiments became evident. "Our country is too divided and split by the barriers of divergent opinions; in reality, around each province there is a *Dixie line*," a Manitoban representative ruefully put it in the commons in 1885. A federal election represented a total of seven local elections; the campaigns were conducted separately, on issues often contradictory from one province to another, and with regional factors outweighing national considerations. Governing thus became a perilous art, based almost exclusively on a system of regional, ethnic, and religious adjustments, an art of adapting to conflicting pressures as varied as they were numerous. These regional differences merely prolonged in a more visible fashion the situation prevailing before 1867. All the same, amid the diversities one does find common features, even if they occur only in relation to problems attending the formation or evolution of the pieces on the chessboard.

The first is the state of dependency that over a long period characterized a number of aspects of the life of these different regions. A dependency on natural forces, and on rudimentary means of transportation. Dependency also because of the structure of land rights: much of Prince Edward Island was in the hands of absentee landlords; the Province of Canada had to grapple until 1854 with the enclaves of the seigneurial regime and the clergy reserves; until 1869 the west was entirely the domain of the HBC. Politically the dependency showed itself more sharply. Administrators and sometimes judges were given appointments by the British government, often through political or family influence [*see* LE MARCHANT], and their stay on Canadian soil was only a stage in their careers. Some wanted to domineer over "their" colonials [*see* Cochrane], others embarked on risky initiatives [*see* Head], or took advantage of their position to exercise favouritism or nepotism. To assess in any comprehensive way the contributions they made to Canada would not be easy: suffice it to say that their presence and their actions readily engendered unrest, whose source was eliminated with the granting of responsible government, but at the price of political agitation and even open insurrection.

The notion of responsible government haunted the minds of those preoccupied with reform during the first half of the century. The extreme limits of the country may be mentioned briefly: in Newfoundland responsible government was granted in 1855; for British Columbia, the departure of James Douglas – who hated the very notion, "the term is associated with revolution," he said – and later entry into the Canadian confederation were accompanied quite naturally by the application of the principle. But the Atlantic colonies had governments established by the ruling classes; the local aristocracy constituted the executive and monopolized the posts centring around it. Joseph Howe was undoubtedly the leader in the struggle for ministerial responsibility; he wanted for Nova Scotia a regime similar to that of Great Britain. In his twelve resolutions of 1837 he demanded only that the Legislative Council be elective, but when subsequently the group of Reformers he had brought together won the 1847 election, they were invited to form a government. The Reformers of Prince Edward Island proposed to Great Britain that they would meet the costs of the civil list, on condition that they have the benefit of ministerial responsibility [*see* Coles]. Their election victory in 1851 prompted Great Britain to grant their request. The administration was also monopolized by a local élite in New Brunswick, but the opposition to it was less clear cut than in Nova Scotia. E. B. Chandler, with reservations about political parties and their alternation in power, accepted a diluted form of ministerial responsibility, and directed affairs effectively in a paternalistic way. Charles Fisher's party was to acquire a certain cohesion, and finally formed a government in 1854 [*see* MANNERS-SUTTON and Wilmot]. Three years later the secretary of state for the colonies officially recognized the right of New Brunswick to responsible government. In the Atlantic provinces the acquisition of responsible government was thus brought about against local oligarchies, but without violence other than verbal.

Such was not the case in the Canadas, where there were rebellions against the power of the cliques. These revolts were, however, preceded by a series of claims put forward by the representative legislative assemblies, which, desirous of more or less radical changes, and aware of the necessity of fostering economic and social progress in the colonies [*see* Papineau, PARENT, BIDWELL], came up against the die-hard character of the executive councils. In Lower Canada, ethnic differences accentuated this fundamental problem; in each colony, Reformers were divided as to the means of obtaining more power for the elected representatives, the moderates wanting to exhaust all legal methods, the extremists precipitating armed insurrection. The union of the two colonies under the aegis of one parliament was the end result. It was the former moderate Reformers who, forgetting their ethnic differences and their reservations in regard to the new province, made responsible government a reality in United Canada [*see under* DRAPER]. Characteristically enough, in this achievement the mutual understanding that had existed among these moderate Reformers disappeared, and their spokesmen, Robert Baldwin* and Louis-Hippolyte La Fontaine*, chose to leave to others the task of administering the province with the type of government they had finally secured. That responsibility brought about the appearance of political parties. During the 1850s, John A. Macdonald and George-Étienne Cartier succeeded in creating if not in establishing the Liberal-Conservative party, made up of Tory elements and moderate Reformers [*see* J. H. CAMERON]. Former extremists of both sections found it extraordinarily difficult to decide upon a durable basis of ideological agreement; their history, under the union, was that of their prejudices, susceptibilities, and incompatibilities. The ministry that best maintained itself in power was the one that made most use of compromise; the most intransigent members constituted an opposition party, often sufficiently cohesive to bring about political instability in United Canada [*see* David CHRISTIE, George Brown, J. S. Macdonald, Holton]. To remove this danger, a number of politicians abandoned for a time their partisan concerns and tried to shape a new country by uniting the British colonies of North America. One great theme, the struggle to obtain responsible government, thus preceded another, that of federal union.

It is unnecessary here to go into the details of the achievement of union, which favoured the Liberal-Conservative party and excluded the French Canadian Liberals. Ultimately democratic process gave way before the will of men holding office [*see under* Cartier, Brown, Médéric LANCTOT, LABERGE, and Howe]. The participation of the Maritimes in confederation was achieved with difficulty (that is the very least one can say!), but the artisans of federation, Macdonald, Cartier, Tilley, and Tupper*, knew that in order to create any common identity the geographical elements had to be fused together. This desire for unity was a characteristic of the period: the acquisition of the HBC's territories, the entry of Manitoba [*see* A. H. SCOTT], of British Columbia [*see* CARRALL], and of Prince Edward Island [*see* Pope] into confederation, and likewise the almost obsessive urge to link the two oceans by a railway, are all illustrations of it.

Already other similarities had begun to appear in the colonies: the urgent need for railroad construction and the fear of American influence. The two phenomena were, indeed, connected. The Americans had begun early to build their network of railways, and their neighbours to the north saw in this the source of their great prosperity. The British colonies began to dream of similar accomplishments, and to get more and more into debt as they tried to realize their dreams. Prince Edward Island is a good example, for debts occasioned by railway building were by no means irrelevant to its entry into confederation. Nova Scotia and New Brunswick hesitated for a while between a line that would link them with the United States and one that would link them with Canada, but the latter choice prevailed. Many plans for an intercolonial were drafted. Meetings were held in 1851–52 and in 1861–62 [see Howe, McCully, Chandler]; all of them ran up against the problem of the route through New Brunswick: should it follow the valley of the Saint John or the east and north coasts? Businessmen favoured the first route for commercial reasons, the British government inclined towards the second for military ones. The provinces fell back on building local roads, until confederation held out the dazzling hope of an intercolonial line. United Canada also experienced its fever of railroad construction, with the Grand Trunk, the cause of numerous headaches for politicians [see Holton, Cartier]. The departure and terminal points of this line were at Detroit and Portland, which stressed in too obvious a fashion the subordinate position of United Canada with regard to its great neighbour; the latter did not fail to give itself – at least in the eyes of Canadians – arrogant or protective airs.

The proximity of the United States emphasized all the ways in which Canada was a British dependency. In that country the routed or exiled *Patriotes* and followers of W. L. Mackenzie* took refuge [see O'CALLAGHAN and Édouard-Élisée MALHIOT], and from it the luckless Fenians set out [see O'NEILL and O'Donoghue]. Canada feared the United States, while she continually cast longing glances in her direction. Thus J. W. Johnston, in the 1850s, reflected on the benefits a form of commercial union with the Americans might bring to Nova Scotia. An important annexationist movement developed in Lower Canada [see Holton, LYMAN, SANBORN], in which French Canadian Liberals joined Anglophone merchants, and Alexander Tilloch Galt* rubbed shoulders with Jean-Baptiste-Éric Dorion*; the movement also found some support in Upper Canada [see H. B. WILLSON]. A group of Americans from Pembina tried to bring the Red River Settlement under their flag [see STUTSMAN]; in the 1860s, in British Columbia, annexation to the United States appeared to some preferable to union with Canada or to continuance as a British colony. All these developments, however important or serious, had little chance of success. For the colonies had a common denominator: their sentimental attachment to Great Britain, an attachment that among Francophones was rather in the nature of a loyalty.

All the changes mentioned took place in a society where political manners were somewhat primitive, and fairly similar from one region to another. Violence at elections was common. In 1840, at Conception Bay, a magistrate who tried to re-establish order during a by-election barely got away with his life [see RIDLEY]; an Ontario representative, T. R. FERGUSON, who had endeavoured to part belligerents after a political meeting, never recovered from his physical and mental injuries. Open voting allowed intimidation and corruption. The 1841 election in Lower Canada, the "Sydenham election," provides a good illustration. Major T. E. CAMPBELL, an "agent" of the governor, placed polling booths so as to be particularly accessible to supporters of the union, and for still further surety his troops forbad opponents to come near. Alexandre-Maurice DELISLE, one of the few French Canadians to stand as a governor's man, took the precaution of getting himself made a police magistrate. Money was vital when each person knew for whom his neighbour voted: it was said of a millionaire candidate that his principal drawing cards were his money and his mortgages [see STREET]. The secret ballot and simultaneous elections only refined the tactics employed, for behaviour was rapidly adapted to the twists and turns of electoral laws. Already the avenging voice of Richard Cartwright* denounced the cynicism of John A. Macdonald, who gave votes to the dead and spent astronomical sums to win his elections.

In this age of virulent politics, when duelling had not disappeared (Howe fought for political reasons, Ogle Robert GOWAN called out Francis Hincks*, Cartier sent out seconds almost at random, J. W. Johnston wounded an adversary in the foot to end his career as a dancer!), the task of a member of parliament was hardly restful. J. A. BARRY was imprisoned for a whole session because he accused a colleague of smuggling; a speaker of the Legislative Assembly of Manitoba, who had given a decision against certain local interests, was trapped and doused with hot oil [see BIRD]; an inebriated legislative councillor of British Columbia had the lenses pushed from his glasses by his seat-mate, and, being shortsighted, had perforce to break off his speech [see Cox]. Personal antagonisms were numerous, and a widespread lack of sobriety did not restrain the expression of personal or ideological differences.

Accompanying the many events in the physical expansion and political development of the country were a variety of other movements and changes related to religion, education, the arts, and social life in general. A large number of the biographies of volume X present people who were noteworthy in such areas, from leaders of denominations and churches to teachers and scientists, painters, musicians, and writers.

The influence of the church was general at the time, and not merely confined to Quebec as some might be inclined to think. It is true that in Quebec relations between the religious power and one particular political group were especially difficult. The Ultramontanes [see LA ROCQUE], partisans of a theocratic system, saw in the proclamation of the dogma of papal infallibility a striking confirmation of the veracity of their doctrine. In their adversaries, particularly those of the Institut Canadien, they detected more anticlericalism and atheism than there really was. Bishop Ignace Bourget* wielded the weapon of excommunication with as much assurance and conviction as he handled the sprinkler. Gonzalve DOUTRE, for example, was refused the sacrament, which was equivalent to being banned from society. Sadly, Doutre pleaded for "graciousness" from his bishop, and was anxious to know whether "in order to be a Catholic one must strip off the inalienable attributes of man." After Bishop CONROY's visit, Ultramontane rigidity was gradually eased, and the interference of the Catholic clergy in politics grew less marked. On Prince Edward Island, the question of whether reading of the Bible should form part of the daily programme of every pupil divided politicians and their supporters for 20 years along religious lines [see Coles]. Extraordinary controversies filled the newspapers; they might even publish a list of the prices of indulgences [see Pope]. In Newfoundland, the Catholics favoured responsible government, but the Protestants rejected it. In Nova Scotia, in the 1840s, Howe received the support of the Catholics, and Conservatives raised the cry of "Catholic supremacy"; ten years later the Catholics changed their political allegiance, and Howe's Liberals styled their opponents "Romo-Johnstonites." Edward John HORAN, bishop of Kingston, was a fervent supporter of John A. Macdonald, and acted as his promoter in exchange for small favours for his friends: he could allow himself to urge "the Catholic vote in a proper direction." The development of the Orange lodges constituted another force with which politicians had to reckon. The Conservatives were able to accomplish the unparalleled feat of obtaining the backing of the Ultramontane Catholics and the Orangemen [see O. R. Gowan, J. H. Cameron]; to retain it required constant attention.

The activities of the churches were not primarily political: they resorted to politics in order to defend principles they deemed essential, or to develop institutions they considered necessary, in a period when their social and educational role was of great importance, though supplementary to their main task.

In the middle years of the century the various denominations extended the geographical range of their work by means of missions or preaching stations or itinerant circuits, not only in the west but in more remote areas of the older colonies, often with support from overseas organizations such as the Society for the Propagation of the Gospel in Foreign Parts, and often requiring heroic service from those appointed to the scattered posts [see ELLIOT, MIERTSCHING]. At the same time, parishes and congregations in the settled areas and in the towns and cities multiplied, and ecclesiastical structures became more complex. All denominations give evidence of this growth in volume X: larger bodies such as the Roman Catholics (see CHAREST, DEMERS, GUIGUES), Church of England (A. N. BETHUNE, CRONYN, FEILD), Methodists (GREEN, RICHARDSON, John and William RYERSON), and Presbyterians (JENNINGS, TOPP), and a variety of smaller groups, often fragments of the larger denominations, and characteristic of the intense religious feeling of this century in North America: Bible Christians (METHERALL), Primitive Methodists (LAWSON), Secession Presbyterians (SMART, William TAYLOR), Free Church of Scotland (STEWART and Michael WILLIS).

Strong religious convictions were significant not only in their relation to the spiritual needs of believers. They also contributed impetus to social causes such as temperance (J. G. MARSHALL, QUERTIER) and to many philanthropic efforts in a period when private charity was an essential means of alleviating the distress caused by epidemics, fire, economic depression, and personal afflictions such as deafness and leprosy (BERTHELET, COGSWELL, GADBOIS, GAUVREAU, MALLET, RODIER).

In their concern for the development of education, the churches were often involved in decisions about its administration and its guiding principles from the elementary school to the university. Large questions about the roles of church and state in education were debated vigorously throughout the century (Robert BELL, Brown, CONNOLLY, Howe, Draper, HATHEWAY), and often marked the activities of schools or school districts or institutions of higher learning.

Founders and teachers and administrators from Canadian educational history are numerous in volume X, as one would expect in a century when patterns of Canadian education were largely developed or instituted (BARBER, Mathilda DAVIS, W. A. JOHNSON, MACALLUM, MEILLEUR), and a number of universities were passing through their first years marked by difficulties of finance and jurisdiction. The early history of many of the institutions we know today is represented: Bishop's University (NICOLLS), Dalhousie University (REID), King's College (McCAWLEY), McGill (John BETHUNE), McMaster (FYFE), University of New Brunswick (MARSHALL d'Avray), Queen's College, Newfoundland (GREY), Queen's University (LIDDELL), St Francis Xavier University (MacKINNON), and the University of Toronto (HINCKS, SOULERIN, Michael Willis).

In the years covered by volume X the life of the mind was certainly not confined to the realm of education. Eclectism might still exist, but men like William Logan, Elkanah BILLINGS, and Charles SMALLWOOD stand out as genuine scientists, pioneers who trained followers in their own fields and established solid professional bases for their successors. Regular training for the professions developed at the same time, particularly in medicine [*see* PAINCHAUD, BOVELL, HODDER], and around these representatives of a new social élite appropriate structures began to form. It was to be expected that a need to preserve for the future a world already fading should have been felt in this period: hence Paul Kane applied himself to painting Indians still living in accordance with their traditional customs, and AUBERT de Gaspé described the seigneurial way of life as he set down "some episodes of the good old days." Cornelius KRIEGHOFF, in contrast, took the peasantry around him as the main theme of his work, and acquired thus a fame that eluded the economic theories of John RAE, too advanced for his day. Intellectual discussion was lively in the back-shop of a bookstore in Quebec, even if its prime inspirer, Octave CRÉMAZIE, died a sad death in exile. May Agnes FLEMING published popular novels, which may not have opened to her the gates of literary glory but which enriched her annually to the tune of $10,000. Meanwhile, newspapers increasingly better edited and informed [*see* Brown, Parent], if often violent, were a strong influence on community life and spread new ideas.

In all this one can see an active society, open to progress, in which individuals rejected the accustomed and feared adventure neither for themselves nor for those they led.

ACKNOWLEDGEMENTS

THE *Dictionary of Canadian Biography/Dictionnaire biographique du Canada* receives assistance, advice, and encouragement from many institutions and many individuals. They cannot all be named nor can their kindness be acknowledged adequately. None are forgotten in our consciousness of what we owe to those who have supported our endeavours in a multitude of ways.

The DCB/DBC owes its founding to the generosity of the late James Nicholson; it has been sustained over the years by its parent institutions, the University of Toronto and University of Toronto Press and the Université Laval and Les Presses de l'université Laval. Its work in the 19th century has been materially assisted by the Centennial Commission; this volume has been aided by grants from the Canada Council and the Ministère des Affaires culturelles du Québec. To all of these our debt is immediate and is gratefully acknowledged.

Our contributors form a large and distinguished company, and they have been especially helpful in assisting us with this first volume in the 19th century to be published. We have had the benefit of special consultation over a long period with a number of individuals, some of them also contributors: A. S. Abel, Frederick H. Armstrong, Louis-Philippe Audet, Roland-J. Auger, Mrs Zilda Barker, J. Murray Beck, Phyllis R. Blakeley, J.-C. Bonenfant, John A. Bovey, Hartwell Bowsfield, J. M. S. Careless, Gaston Carrière, O.M.I., Alan G. R. Cooke, Andrée Désilets, R. B. Donovan, C.S.B., C. Bruce Fergusson, Eugene Forsey, Armand Gagné, Henri Gérin-Lajoie, F. Burnham Gill, Jean Hamelin, J. Russell Harper, J. L. H. Henderson, Clive A. Holland, Mme Françoise Caron-Houle, Barry Hyman, Alice M. Johnson, J. K. Johnson, Frederick Jones, W. Kaye Lamb, Jean-Jacques Lefebvre, Douglas Leighton, George MacBeath, Ian McDonald, W. S. MacNutt, George Mainer, André Martineau, J. S. Moir, Jacques Monet, S.J., Marjorie G. Morley, George R. Newell, G. D. O'Gorman, C.S.B., Margaret A. Ormsby, Bruce B. Peel, K. G. Pryke, H. Keith Ralston, J. E. Rea, Mrs M. Robertson, Yves Roby, G. O. Rothney, G. F. G. Stanley, Mrs Carole B. Stelmack, Norah Story, Donald Swainson, Philippe Sylvain, Émile Tardif, O.M.I., L. G. Thomas, L. H. Thomas, Gerald Tulchinsky, Allan R. Turner, Mrs Elinor Vass, Nive Voisine, Peter B. Waite, Carl M. Wallace, and Brian J. Young.

Throughout the preparation of volume X we have enjoyed the most willing cooperation from the libraries and archives of Canada and other countries. We are particularly grateful to the administrators and staffs of those institutions to which we have most frequently appealed: in Toronto, the University of Toronto Library, the Metropolitan Toronto Central Library, the Ontario Legislative Library, and the Ontario Department of Public Records and Archives; in Quebec, the Bibliothèque générale de l'université Laval, the Bibliothèque and the Archives du séminaire de Québec, the Bibliothèque de l'Assemblée nationale, the Archives nationales du Québec, and the Archives de l'archidiocèse de

ACKNOWLEDGEMENTS

Québec; in Montreal, the Archives de la ville de Montréal, the McCord Museum, and the Archives judiciaires de Montréal; in Ottawa, the Public Archives of Canada. We are also indebted to other archives and libraries across Canada: the Provincial Archives of Newfoundland and Labrador, the Public Archives of Nova Scotia, the Provincial Archives of New Brunswick, the New Brunswick Museum, the Public Archives of Prince Edward Island, the Public Archives of Manitoba, the Saskatchewan Archives Board, and the Provincial Archives of British Columbia.

In our own offices we have had working with us at various times a number of persons who have contributed in important ways to the preparation of volume X. Marc La Terreur and Bernard Pothier directed the Ottawa office and in it compiled information on the 19th century which will serve as background material for a number of volumes; on their staff over the four years of its operation were: Fernande Blondeau, Louis Garon, and Mme Yvette Thériault. In Toronto, research assistance has been given at different times by Phyllis Creighton, Mme Évelyne Gagnon, Maud M. Hutcheson, Catherine Lane, Louise Trottier, and S. A. Barker; secretarial services have been provided by Mrs Paula Brine Reynolds, Anita Noel, Mrs Inez Woodhouse, and Mrs D. A. Sutherland. In Quebec, Michel Paquin and Jean-Pierre Asselin were a constant help during the last stages of the volume; Mme Marika Cancelier was in charge of the secretariat, assisted successively by Mme Céline Massicotte and Pierrette Desrosiers; Louise-Hélène Boileau and Mme Gilberte Massey provided assistance to the manuscript editors. We should also like to recognize the guidance and encouragement we have received at all times from the two presses with which the DCB/DBC is associated, and in particular Marsh Jeanneret, Eleanor Harman, Harald Bohne, and H. Van Ierssel at University of Toronto Press; Georges Laberge, Lucien Zérounian, and Roch-André Rompré at Les Presses de l'université Laval.

DICTIONNAIRE BIOGRAPHIQUE DU CANADA   DICTIONARY OF CANADIAN BIOGRAPHY

Editorial Notes

PROPER NAMES

Persons have been entered under family name rather than title, pseudonym, popular name, nickname, or name in religion. Where possible, the form of the surname is based on the actual signature. In the case of French family names "Le," "La," "Du," and "Des" (but not "de") are considered as part of the name and are capitalized. When both parts of the name are capitalized in the signature, French style treats the family name as two words, e.g. Louis-Hippolyte La Fontaine. Some compound French names occur in this period: Philippe-Joseph AUBERT de Gaspé; cross-reference is made in the text from the compound to the main name entry: from Gaspé to Aubert.

Married women and *religieuses* have been entered under their maiden names, with cross-references from their married names or their names in religion: Rosanna Eleanora MULLINS (Leprohon); Marie-Julie-Marguerite CÉRÉ de La Columbière, *dite* Soeur Mance.

Indian names have presented a particular problem, since an Indian might be known by his Indian name (spelled in a variety of ways by the French or English unfamiliar with Indian languages), by a French or English nickname, and often by a French or English baptismal name. An effort has been made to include the major variants of the original name, as well as the nicknames, with appropriate cross-references in the text. Since it is impossible to establish the original spelling of the Indian name the form chosen is that which appears in the major sources. E.g. Abraham WIKASKOKISEYIN (Sweet Grass, Herbe odoriférante).

CROSS-REFERENCES

The first time that the name of a person who has a biography in volume X appears in another biography his family name is printed in capitals and level small capitals: e.g. James DOUGLAS, Louis-Joseph PAPINEAU.

An asterisk following a name indicates either that the person has a biography in a volume already published or that he will receive a biography in a volume to be published: e.g. John A. Macdonald*, Antoine-Aimé Dorion*. Birth and death (or *floruit*) dates for such persons are found in the index as an indication of volume.

PLACE-NAMES

Place-names are generally given in the form used at the contemporary time of reference with the modern name included in parentheses. The modern name is based whenever possible on the *Gazetteers of Canada* issued by the Canadian Board of Geographical Names, Ottawa, and on the *Répertoire géographique du Québec*, published by the Ministère des Terres et Forêts du Québec, Québec, 1969.

Many other sources have been found useful as guides in establishing 19th century place-names: *Lovell's gazetteer of British North America . . .* , ed. P. A. Crossby (Montreal, 1881); Hormidas Magnan, *Dictionnaire historique et géographique des paroisses, missions et municipalités de la province de Québec* (Arthabaska, Qué., 1925); *Manitoba historical atlas . . .* , ed. John Warkentin and R. I. Ruggles (HSSM pub., Winnipeg, 1970); *Municipalités et paroisses dans la province de Québec*, C.-E. Deschamps, compil. (Québec, 1896); *Place names of Nova Scotia* (Fergusson); W. H. Smith, *Smith's Canadian gazetteer comprising statistical and general information respecting all parts of the upper province, or Canada West . . .* (Toronto, 1846; repr. Toronto, 1970); Walbran, *B.C. coast names*. The Geography Division, Surveying and Mapping Branch, Department of Energy, Mines and Resources of the government of Canada was helpful in establishing Arctic place-names.

QUOTATIONS

Quotations have been translated when the language of the original passage is different from that of the text of the biography. All passages quoted from government documents and works published in both languages are given in the accepted translations of these works.

BIBLIOGRAPHIES

Each biography is followed by a bibliography. Sources frequently used by authors and editors are cited in shortened form in individual bibliographies, and the general bibliography (pp. 733–65) gives these sources in full. Many abbreviations are used in the individual bibliographies, especially for archival sources; a list of these can be found on p. 2.

The individual bibliographies are generally arranged alphabetically according to the five sections of the general bibliography – manuscript sources, primary printed sources (including a section on contemporary newspapers), reference works, studies, and journals. Wherever possible, references to manuscript material give the location of the original documents, rather than copies. In general the items in individual bibliographies are the sources as listed by the contributors, but these items have been supplemented by bibliographical investigation in the DCB/DBC offices. Any special bibliographical comments by contributors appear within square brackets.

TRANSLATION INTO ENGLISH (a note by the translator of the French biographies)

In general the translator has followed the principles

that the Translation Committee adopted for previous volumes. The policy of the committee was to avoid any temptation to elaborate on the text, and to admit amplification or modification of the original, however slight, only in the interest of clarity. Certain 19th century terms, no longer in current usage, have been used: e.g. *bâtonnier*, clerk of the peace, etc. There are a number of distinctly Canadian words, usually relating to the fur trade or to lumber operations: see: *A dictionary of Canadianisms*, ed. W. S. Avis *et al.* (Toronto, 1967).

OFFICIAL NAMES

An effort was made throughout the volume to use the official names of organizations: companies, institutions, societies, religious bodies, etc. Many Roman Catholic institutions were international in operation during this period, and their English names were therefore used where it was appropriate. Canadian companies sometimes incorporated with both a French and an English name (though more often with one or the other), and again the form of the name appropriate to the text has been used.

BIOGRAPHIES

List of Abbreviations

AAQ	Archives de l'archidiocèse de Québec
ACAM	Archives de la chancellerie de l'archevêché de Montréal
ADB	*Australian Dictionary of Biography*
AHO	Archives historiques oblates
AHSJ	Archives générales des Religieuses hospitalières de Saint-Joseph
AJM	Archives judiciaires de Montréal
AJQ	Archives judiciaires de Québec
AJTR	Archives judiciaires de Trois-Rivières
ANQ	Archives nationales du Québec
APQ	Archives de la province de Québec. Now ANQ
AQ	Archives du Québec. Now ANQ
ASGM	Archives des sœurs grises de Montréal
ASHS	Archives de la Société historique du Saguenay
ASJ	Archives de la Société de Jésus
ASJCF	Archives de la Société de Jésus, province du Canada français
ASN	Archives du séminaire de Nicolet
ASQ	Archives du séminaire de Québec
ASSM	Archives du séminaire de Saint-Sulpice de Montréal
ASTR	Archives du séminaire de Trois-Rivières
AVM	Archives de la ville de Montréal
AVQ	Archives de la ville de Québec
BCHQ	*British Columbia Historical Quarterly*
BNQ	Bibliothèque nationale du Québec
BRH	*Bulletin des recherches historiques*
CCHA	Canadian Catholic Historical Association
CHA	Canadian Historical Association
CHR	*Canadian Historical Review*
DAB	*Dictionary of American Biography*
DCB	*Dictionary of Canadian Biography*

DNB	*Dictionary of National Biography*
HBC	Hudson's Bay Company
HBRS	Hudson's Bay Record Society
HSSM	Historical and Scientific Society of Manitoba
JALPC	*Journal de l'Assemblée législative de la province du Canada*
JIP	*Journal de l'Instruction publique*
MTCL	Metropolitan Toronto Central Library
PABC	Provincial Archives of British Columbia
PAC	Public Archives of Canada
PAM	Public Archives of Manitoba
PANB	Provincial Archives of New Brunswick
PANL	Provincial Archives of Newfoundland and Labrador
PANS	Public Archives of Nova Scotia
PAO	Ontario Department of Public Records and Archives
PAPEI	Public Archives of Prince Edward Island
PRO	Public Record Office
RHAF	*Revue d'histoire de l'Amérique française*
RSCT	Royal Society of Canada *Transactions*
RUL	*Revue de l'université Laval*
SAB	Saskatchewan Archives Board
SCHÉC	Société canadienne d'histoire de l'Église catholique
SGCF	Société généalogique canadienne-française
SH	*Social History*
SHQ	Société historique de Québec
SHS	Société historique du Saguenay
SPRI	Scott Polar Research Institute
USPG	United Society for the Propagation of the Gospel
UCA	United Church Archives

BIOGRAPHIES

A

ABBOTT, WILSON RUFFIN, businessman; b. of a Scotch-Irish father and a free Negro mother in Richmond, Virginia, in 1801; d. in Toronto Ont., in 1876.

Wilson Ruffin Abbott was in his youth apprenticed as a carpenter but left home at 15 to work on a Mississippi River steamer as a steward. Seriously injured when cord wood fell upon him, he was nursed by a Boston traveller's maid, Ellen Toyer, whom he later married. He then moved to Mobile, Alabama, where he opened a general grocery store. The Abbotts were indignant when the city required all free Negroes to provide bonds signed by two white men in pledge of their good behaviour. In 1834, receiving an anonymous warning that his store was to be pillaged, he withdrew his savings, put his wife and two children aboard a steamer for New Orleans, and slipped away alone on the night his store was attacked. After a brief sojourn in New York, the Abbotts moved to Toronto in late 1835 or early 1836, one of hundreds of American Negro families to seek a greater degree of freedom in Upper Canada at this time.

After a false start as a tobacconist, Abbott became a dealer in properties and increasingly made his mark in real estate; although he could not read until his wife taught him, he was known for an unusual ability to do complex calculations in his head. By 1871 Abbott owned 42 houses, five vacant lots, and a warehouse, largely in Toronto, but also in Hamilton and Owen Sound. He helped purchase freedom for fugitive slaves, kept his wife's sister, Mary, as a housekeeper on wages, and aided another sister-in-law, Jane, who married A. H. Judah in Toronto.

As the Abbotts' fortunes grew, they took an increasing interest in public affairs. Abbott served in the militia during the rebellion of 1837. In 1838 he was one of six organizers of the Colored Wesleyan Methodist Church, aiding in the purchase of property for it. He supported the Anti-Slavery Society of Canada under the Reverend Michael WILLIS, was elected to the city council from St Patrick's ward, which he carried by some 40 votes, and served as a member of the central committee established in 1859 by the Reformers in Canada West. In 1840 Mrs Abbott helped organize the Queen Victoria Benevolent Society to aid indigent black women, and in later years she was active in the British Methodist Episcopal Church.

The Abbotts had four sons and five daughters. One son, Anderson Ruffin, would become the first Canadian-born Negro to receive a licence to practise medicine. Through him, the Abbott family would become linked with another distinguished Toronto Negro family, the Hubbards, and it would be Anderson who would urge William Peyton Hubbard to enter politics, in emulation of his own father.

Wilson Ruffin Abbott was unusual in being a successful black businessman and politician in the late 19th century. Toronto, and Ontario, had once had a substantial Negro population, but this had fallen off after the American Civil War until there were perhaps not more than 2,000 Negroes in Toronto where once there had been reported to be three times as many. By the latter part of the century, prejudice had expressed itself against black men in a variety of ways in the province, and most Negroes went to segregated schools and separate churches. In Toronto, however, the virus of anti-black prejudice spread less deeply: Knox Presbyterian Church would place a visiting Negro in the pulpit, on occasion other black men would achieve at least modest successes in business, and Toronto's schools were never segregated. Abbott did not encounter any serious discrimination, even though Negroes elsewhere in the province did; thus, his experience was not a typical one. His undoubted abilities no doubt helped offset most of the residual prejudice he may otherwise have met.

ROBIN W. WINKS

MTCL, Hubbard-Abbott collection. *Evening Telegram* (Toronto), 17 May 1911. *Globe* (Toronto), 11 Dec. 1847. R. W. Winks, *The blacks in Canada; a history* (Montreal, 1971). D. G. Hill, "Negroes in Toronto; a sociological study of a minority group," unpublished PHD thesis, University of Toronto, 1960; "Negroes in Toronto, 1793–1865," *Ont. Hist.,* LV (1963), 73–92.

ALDER, ROBERT, Methodist minister and Anglican priest; b. in England in 1796; d. at Gibraltar, on 31 Dec. 1873.

Alder

A compositor in his early years, Robert Alder volunteered in 1816 to become a Wesleyan Methodist missionary, evidently hoping that he would be stationed in Ceylon. Instead he was sent as the first ordained Methodist minister to Yarmouth, Nova Scotia, to whose 5,000 citizens, bedevilled by New Light teaching, he proclaimed a "free, full and present salvation." He then served on several circuits in the Maritime provinces and Lower Canada before returning to England in 1827. Alder was resident in London as one of the secretaries of the Wesleyan Methodist Missionary Society from 1833 to 1851. In this post he was responsible specifically for the supervision of the Wesleyan missions in British North America and thus exercised a strong influence on their development.

Before becoming a secretary, Alder helped in 1832–33 to effect a union between the Methodist Episcopal Church in Upper Canada and the English Wesleyan Methodist Conference. He visited Upper Canada in 1834 and again in 1839 to consolidate the union and to iron out differences between the two conferences. These latter efforts were largely unsuccessful; his intransigence on the points at issue precipitated an epic clash with the Ryerson brothers – WILLIAM, Egerton*, and JOHN – which was one factor in the dissolution of the union in 1840. In the ensuing seven-year period he supervised the operations of a separate Wesleyan district in Canada West. When his brethren decided in 1846–47 to make a settlement with the Canadian conference, he fell into line. As the representative of the parent conference, he forced the Wesleyans in Canada West to accept reunion. Ironically but fittingly he was designated as the first president of the Canada Conference after the union was re-established in 1847.

In this same period Alder watched vigorously over the growth of the Methodist organization in the Maritime provinces. Apart from regular and detailed correspondence, he visited the area in 1839 and in 1847. On the first occasion he presided at a special meeting of the missionaries from the four provinces, in which they decided to seek permission to found an academy (later Mount Allison University) and agreed to support publicly the principle that a Christian government has a responsibility to provide for the religious needs of its subjects. Ill health prevented him from holding extended meetings in 1847, but he did press directly for the formation of a Maritimes conference; the creation in 1855 of the Conference of Eastern British America owed much to his initiative and persuasion.

Similarly, although he never travelled to the immense territories of the Hudson's Bay Company, he participated in the negotiations with that body which led to the inception in 1840 of the Wesleyan mission in the North West. So long as he was in office he guided and encouraged the missionaries – men such as James Evans*, Robert Terrill Rundle*, and the Indian minister, Peter Jacobs*. When Jacobs visited London in 1842 he lived in Alder's home and was introduced by him to English customs and churches. It is noteworthy that Jacobs held Alder in great esteem, as did the Wesleyans in the eastern provinces.

In his limited ecclesiastical sphere, Alder played a role analogous to that of the colonial officials in the broader secular context, and, like them, he brought ambivalent attitudes to his tasks. His legacy was in consequence equally mixed. A man of vision, who, with his associates, was continuously challenged by the disparity between the magnitude of the missionary task and the society's limited income, he sought from the outset to foster self-reliance among his brethren in British North America. The Methodists in the Maritime provinces, especially, were pressed to organize their work efficiently, to recruit lay and clerical leaders, and to raise their own funds. Yet independent initiatives on their part were regularly criticized by Alder as insubordinate or imprudent.

Underlying his curious behaviour was not only the natural paternalism and caution of the parent organization, but a concern lest Methodism in British North America not develop on sound lines. What was required, in Alder's view, was continued deference to the Anglican establishment, a friendly relationship with the Church of England, and a strong bias toward the liturgical element in the Wesleyan tradition. This orientation was reinforced by his conservative political ideas; for him, as for many in his generation, democracy and infidelity were intimately related. Not surprisingly, therefore, he regarded the Upper Canadian Methodists as Yankees in disguise and sought to bring them fully into the Wesleyan orbit. He was strongly critical of their independent stand on the clergy reserves and on political change, and, as has been indicated, for some time tried to undermine their conference by fostering a rival Wesleyan organization in Canada West.

The tension generated by Alder and his like-minded associates was often a source of concern to his brethren, but its effects were instructive. Out of it came a deeper awareness among Canadian Methodists of the need for religious and thus secular independence. Conversely, the restraints that were imposed and the attitudes that were transmitted by the English conference helped to maintain continuity between the religious traditions of England and British North America and hence between the two cultures.

Although he was greatly respected in England and America, as indicated for example by the conferring on him in 1839 of an honorary doctorate of divinity by Wesleyan University in Middletown, Connecticut, Alder resigned his position as a missionary secretary in 1851. This decision was doubtless precipitated by the deepening conflict between the Methodist reformers and the Wesleyan leaders, and the consequent discrediting of the latter. Two years later he left the Methodist ministry and was ordained in the Church of England. His effulgent oratory and measured zeal brought him prompt recognition in that body. He became a canon of Holy Trinity Cathedral in Gibraltar. It was fitting that his career ended in this great outpost of the Victorian empire.

G. S. FRENCH

Methodist Missionary Society (London), records of the Wesleyan Methodist Missionary Society (copies at UCA). *Christian Guardian* (Toronto), 1832–47. *Minutes of the Methodist conferences, from the first, held in London by the late Rev. John Wesley, A.M., in the year 1744* (12v., London, 1812–55), IV, VII, XII. *Wesleyan Methodist Magazine* (London), 3rd ser., XLV (1822)–LXVII (1844). Carroll, *Case and his cotemporaries*. G. G. Findlay and W. W. Holdsworth, *History of the Wesleyan Methodist Missionary Society* (5v., London, 1921–24). G. S. French, *Parsons & politics: the rôle of the Wesleyan Methodists in Upper Canada and the Maritimes from 1780 to 1855* (Toronto, 1962). Anson Green, *The life and times of the Rev. Anson Green, D.D.* ... (Toronto, 1877).

ALEXANDER, JAMES LYNNE, teacher, writer of verse, and Church of England clergyman; b. Glenhead (Cairnalbana), County Antrim, Ireland, 23 Oct. 1801; d. Grimsby, Ont., 22 Aug. 1879.

James Lynne Alexander emigrated to Upper Canada with his parents when he was 16 years of age. He taught at the Markham school and the district grammar school at York (Toronto) before he became an assistant teacher in the district school at Niagara.

The history and scenery of the Niagara frontier provided the setting and descriptive passages for Alexander's *Wonders of the west, or a day at the falls of Niagara, in 1825, a poem,* which was printed by Charles Fothergill* at York in 1825. This long poem, in a form imitative of Walter Scott's metrical romances, tells a conventional bitter-sweet love story about French tourists. It is noteworthy only because it contains descriptions of local scenery and because it was one of the first books of verse printed in Upper Canada.

When Bishop Charles James Stewart* opened a

seminary at Chambly, Lower Canada, in 1828, Alexander left Niagara, took up a scholarship, which had been awarded to him by the Society for the Propagation of the Gospel, and enrolled for theological studies under Joseph Braithwaite. He was ordained deacon on 13 Sept. 1829 and became assistant at Cornwall to the Reverend Salter Jehoshaphat Mountain*. In January 1831 the SPG appointed him a travelling missionary, and at about the time of his ordination as priest, on 7 Jan. 1832, he went to Leeds, Megantic County, Lower Canada, to open a mission. He served there until late in 1843.

In 1844 he began his work in the mission of Binbrook and Saltfleet, near Hamilton, Canada West, and on 15 August of that year he married Emelia, youngest daughter of Colonel Robert Nelles of Grimsby. Binbrook received most of his attention in the early years of his ministry in this parish, but later he served chiefly in Saltfleet and lived at Stoney Creek. His home was in Grimsby from the time of his retirement in August 1873 until his death in 1879.

CARL F. KLINCK

[J. L. Alexander], *Wonders of the west or a day at the falls of Niagara, in 1825, a poem, by a Canadian* ([York, Upper Canada], 1825); *Ontario's oldest poem, a day at Niagara in the year 1825 by the Rev. James Lynne Alexander, Anglican vicar,* ed. R. L. Denison (Toronto, 1952).

USPG, C/CAN/Que., f.368, f.399; Tor., f.559; E, Toronto, 1854–55. Upper Canada, House of Assembly, *Journal,* 1828, app., "Common school returns." *Examiner* (Toronto), 4 Sept. 1844. *Weekly Globe* (Toronto), 29 Aug. 1879. *Dom. ann. reg., 1879,* 382. T. R. Millman, *The life of the Right Reverend, the Honourable Charles James Stewart, D.D., Oxon., second Anglican bishop of Quebec* (London, Ont., 1953), 90, 94, 143, 180, 187. Pascoe, *Two hundred years of the S.P.G.,* 869, 873.

ALLARD, OVID, HBC clerk; b. 11 July 1817 in Montreal, Lower Canada, of French extraction; d. 2 Aug. 1874 at Fort Langley, B.C.

According to family tradition, Ovid Allard joined the Hudson's Bay Company at Lachine in 1834 and was immediately sent west with the party of traders and trappers who later established Fort Boise, where he is said to have been second in command. In 1839 he was transferred to the headquarters of the Columbia Department at Fort Vancouver, and thence to Fort Langley, New Caledonia, the first HBC post established on the lower mainland of what is now the province of British Columbia. Toughened by his five years on the buffalo plains and well versed in Indian ways, Allard was a useful member of the Fort Langley establishment. When on 11 April 1840 the fort burned to the ground he helped to rebuild it on the same site; he is also said to have acted as Indian trader and supervisor. James Murray YALE reported to Sir George Simpson* on 17 Dec. 1845: "Ovid Allard otherwise called Chatelain, is still here, and acts as Interpreter &c, his habits were not very praiseworthy when he first came here but he has reformed much of late, and was always a smart fellow." During this period, he married an Indian woman, Justine, who, according to family tradition, was a sister of the chief of the Cowichans. They had four children.

When the Oregon boundary treaty of 1846 made inevitable the withdrawal of the HBC from the Columbia to the Fraser, Allard helped to establish the new brigade route from Fort Kamloops to Fort Langley. In November 1847 he was sent with a party of six men to build Fort Yale and was afterwards placed in charge of the store; there he seems to have displayed considerable courage and resource in his dealings with the Indians. Allard was a member of the party which constructed Fort Hope during the winter of 1848–49 and again he was given charge of the store. He remained there until at least 2 June 1850, when he reported to Yale that he was "near out of all Articles of Trade." Subsequently he returned to Fort Langley as Indian trader and supervisor, but after an acrimonious dispute with Yale, he was transferred to Fort Victoria late in 1852. The next year Allard was sent to Nanaimo where the HBC was developing its coal deposits. He remained there for five years, superintending the Indian labourers, who, according to his superior officer, Chief Trader Joseph W. McKay*, were "worse than useless if not kept under strictest surveillance."

When the Fraser River gold rush began in the spring of 1858, Governor James DOUGLAS sent Allard to reopen Fort Yale, which had been abandoned on the completion of Fort Hope nearly ten years before. Now an experienced man was again needed there to trade with the Indians and avert clashes with the miners pouring into the area. Allard remained at Yale until 1864, when business had so far declined that he was sent to take charge at Fort Langley. There he spent the remaining ten years of his life, looking after the affairs of the HBC farm and trading with the Indians for salmon, cranberries, and furs. He seems to have given satisfaction in this post, though he never attained a rank higher than that of clerk. Presumably his lack of education held him back. His letters are ungrammatical, and he admitted to his supervisors in Victoria that he did not feel himself competent to open a new set of books, for "your system of accounts confuses me much."

This "faithful servant of the HBC" also took an interest in the affairs of the little community outside the fort. He served as chairman of the school board in the 1870s and was postmaster from 2 Sept. 1870 until his resignation early in 1871. It would seem that his health began to fail in 1867, but he was still in charge at Fort Langley when he died. He was buried in the old HBC graveyard near the fort, and his name is perpetuated on the cairn erected to mark this pioneer cemetery by the government of British Columbia. The fort he helped to rebuild in 1840 was restored in 1958 and is now the Fort Langley National Historic Park.

DOROTHY BLAKEY SMITH

HBC Arch. B.113/b/2, ff.2–6, 6–6v, 18, 25v–26, 36; B.113/b/3, ff.44v–45, 60v; B.113/c/1, f.3. PABC, Jason Ovid Allard, "Biographical notes on Ovid Allard"; "Reminiscences," undated; "Sketches of early life in British Columbia," copied and annotated by George Green, 1942; Fort Nanaimo correspondence, August 1852–September 1853. *Colonist* (Victoria), 1858–74. *Gazette* (Victoria), 1858–74. *Mainland Guardian* (New Westminster, B.C.), 5 Aug. 1874. Denys Nelson, *Fort Langley, 1827–1927, a century of settlement in the valley of the lower Fraser River* (1st ed., Vancouver, B.C., 1927; 2nd ed., 1947). George Green, "The fort builder," *Vancouver Province*, 24 Jan. 1953. F. W. Howay, "The raison d'être of Forts Yale and Hope," *RSCT*, 3rd ser., XVI (1922), sect.II, 49–64. B. A. McKelvie, "Jason Allard: fur-trader, prince, and gentleman," *BCHQ*, IX (1945), 243–57.

ALMON, MATHER BYLES, banker, politician, and philanthropist; b. at Halifax in 1796, son of William James Almon* and Rebecca Byles; d. at Halifax, 30 July 1871.

Mather Byles Almon was a member of a prominent Halifax family; his father was a loyalist and his mother was a daughter of Mather Byles Jr., a loyalist. Almon may have been educated privately for there is no record of his having attended the University of King's College in Windsor, N.S., or of his having been educated abroad. On 31 Jan. 1825 he married Sophia, fourth daughter of John Pryor, a loyalist, a member of the assembly of Nova Scotia, and a merchant. Mather Byles and Sophia Almon had 14 children, of whom five died at a relatively early age.

The Almon family's numerous social, political, and ecclesiastical connections undoubtedly aided Mather Byles Almon throughout his career. He set up his own general and wholesale firm in Halifax in the 1820s and continued to operate this business, which may have been financed by his family or with money from his wife, until he became active with the Bank of Nova Scotia. He was subsequently an insurance agent for the Halifax Fire Insurance Company and for the Halifax Marine Insurance Association, which he helped establish in 1838. He also acted as agent for several British firms including the Colonial Life Assurance Company, the Pelican Life Insurance Company, and the Phoenix Fire Insurance Company. In addition, he was associated with the Halifax Water Company and was particularly active, after 1836, with the Halifax Steamboat Company.

In 1832 Almon joined William Lawson*, William Blowers BLISS, Andrew Belcher, James William JOHNSTON, James Boyle Uniacke*, and others to establish the Bank of Nova Scotia; Almon became a member of its first board of directors and in 1837 became its president. The bank established a branch in Windsor in 1832 and branches in Pictou, Yarmouth, Annapolis, and Liverpool in 1839. During this period the bank also made financial arrangements with the Baring Brothers in London and with the Merchant's Bank of Boston, as well as with banks in New York, Portland, Maine, Saint John, N.B., and Montreal. This proved to be the limit of its expansion; during the depression of the early 1850s the bank closed its branches in Windsor, Annapolis, and Liverpool. One reason for its failure to grow was revealed by Almon on 28 July 1870 when he disclosed that James FORMAN, cashier of the bank since 1832, had embezzled $315,000 from the bank during a lengthy period of time. Evidence produced in a suit brought by the bank against Forman's sureties indicated that Forman had carried out his defalcations since 1844. Almon, who was ill and virtually blind, had probably been unable to provide much leadership for some time. In September 1870 he resigned on the grounds that he was unable to sign the notes of the bank as required by law. It would seem obvious that he was incapable of handling any problems created by the loss of funds and any resulting loss of public confidence. The possibility exists that the bank might have been better served if he had resigned before 1870.

During his lifetime Almon built up an estate which, at his death, was evaluated at $616,000. Of this sum, $152,735 was invested in the United States, particularly in government bonds, and in insurance and banking stocks. He also held stock in several banks and public utilities in Newfoundland, Prince Edward Island, New Brunswick, and Quebec. Of the sum invested in his own province, $261,000 was in the form of mortgages and notes of hand. His chief investment in provincial manufacturing was through an American company which operated a coal mine in Pictou County and in a British firm, the Acadia Iron Company. The range of his investments indicates that he wanted an assured return which would provide protection against fluctuations in the provincial economy. His own reluctance to invest directly in provincial companies probably helps explain why the Bank of Nova Scotia did not become involved in the growth of the provincial economy in the mid-1850s.

In political life, Almon took some part in the administration of Halifax in the 1830s but withdrew from civic affairs after Halifax was incorporated in 1841. In October 1838 Almon, as a representative of the mercantile community, along with James B. Uniacke, James W. Johnston, and George Renny Young*, was appointed as a Nova Scotia delegate to meet Lord Durham [John George Lambton*] in Quebec. Charles Buller* thought this group to be "not only of striking ability, but of a degree of general information and polish of manners which are even less commonly met with in colonial society." Almon became the centre of a political controversy in Nova Scotia in 1843 when Lieutenant Governor Falkland [Lucius Bentinck Cary*] named him to the Legislative and Executive Councils. He presented his mandamus as a member of the Legislative Council on 19 Feb. 1844. Lord Falkland told the colonial secretary, "I have admitted Mr. Mather B. Almon to the seat at the board which became vacant in February last [1843] by the retirement of Mr. [Thomas Andrew Strange] De Wolf"; thus Almon was probably a temporary member of the council in 1843 but it was not until after the election of 1843 that he was officially appointed. In December 1843 Joseph HOWE and two supporters resigned their seats on the Executive Council accusing the governor and the Tory attorney general, J. W. Johnston, who was Almon's brother-in-law, of weighting the council in favour of the Tories.

Almon and several other directors of the Bank of Nova Scotia played a prominent role in the Tory party. This political tie helped the bank, but it also gave the party a commercial tone. Almon, like other wealthy merchants of the day, probably gave financial contributions to the party. In 1864 Almon broke with the Conservatives and their new leader, Charles Tupper*, over the issue of confederation and became a prominent anti-confederate. In the critical year of 1866, however, failing health prevented his attending the Legislative Council. He remained a supporter of the anti-confederate provincial government until his death.

Almon was deeply interested in education, being a governor of Dalhousie University (1842–48) and a governor of King's College (1854–68 and 1869–71). He became a member, and generous

Alsop

supporter, of almost every Protestant charitable society in Halifax; he was also a life member of several Church of England colonial missionary bodies. A great deal of his time, however, was devoted to St Paul's Church. He was one of the faction which opposed the doctrinal changes proposed by Bishop Hibbert Binney*, who had been influenced by the Oxford movement. After several years of dissension, part of the congregation moved to St Luke's in 1858, and the bishop followed in 1864. St Paul's, which in the 1830s had been the dominant church in the province, retreated, under the leadership of men such as Almon, into respectable obscurity and parochialism. Thus, Almon's religious beliefs, like his political ideas, failed to play a significant role in the changing community. Although he did help adapt Tory attitudes to a commercial, Victorian society, he was forced to watch as St Paul's, the missionary societies, and the Legislative Council all lost their dynamic role in provincial affairs.

K. G. PRYKE

Bank of Nova Scotia Archives, Toronto, letter book, 1832–40; president's memoranda and bank note issue book, 1856–71; Mather Byles Almon letters. PANS, Mather Byles Almon papers; "Senator William Johnson Almon and his descendants," comp. by C. S. Stayner; "The Almons," comp. by K. A. MacKenzie. Halifax County Court of Probate, will of M. B. Almon. *Acadian Recorder* (Halifax), 31 July 1871. *Morning Chronicle* (Halifax), 31 July 1871. *Novascotian* (Halifax), 1838, 1843–44. Harris, *Church of Saint Paul*, 206–9. *History of the Bank of Nova Scotia, 1832–1900; together with copies of annual statements* ([Toronto, 1900]), 45–51.

ALSOP, ROBERT, merchant and politician, b. in 1814 to a prosperous Newfoundland merchant family; d. 25 March 1871 at St John's, Nfld.

Nothing is known of Robert Alsop's upbringing or education. He became a principal in the merchant and shipping firm of R. Alsop and Company, which in the 1840s and 1850s was one of the most extensive trading out of St John's, Newfoundland. Like many of the older firms, it suffered severely during the late 1850s and 1860s because of the failure of the fisheries. After the decline of the firm Robert Alsop was induced to enter political life. In September 1866 he ran in a by-election in Trinity Bay as a supporter of a coalition government headed by Frederic Bowker Terrington Carter*. He won the election and was named chairman of the Board of Works, thus entering the Executive Council. His entry to the council was opposed by the Liberal newspaper, the *Patriot*,

whose editor, Robert John Parsons*, while affirming his support of the coalition, asserted that John Kavanagh, a Catholic who had been elected in 1859 and 1861, had a better claim to the post. However Alsop's victory in the Trinity Bay riding was acclaimed by the *Patriot*, which rejoiced to see "a liberal Protestant, as is Mr. Alsop" returned.

The path of Alsop, a Liberal in the coalition government which had seen the coalescing of confederation forces under the Tory Protestant, F. B. T. Carter, and the Liberal Catholics, Ambrose* and Edward Dalton Shea* and John KENT, was to prove thorny. Carter's victory at the polls in 1865 had not really been a triumph for the confederate forces; many of his supporters had made pledges to their constituents not to support the union. As a new election campaign approached in 1869 the confederates tried to stem the mounting wave of opposition being organized by Charles Fox Bennett*. The government was, however, having trouble controlling its own members, including Robert Alsop, who received a terse communication from the colonial secretary, John Bemister*, on 7 Sept. 1869 asking "what course you [intend] to adopt at the approaching election on . . . confederation, it being, as you are aware, a government measure." This was the second such query to Alsop.

Alsop, like most of the St John's mercantile class, was hostile to confederation. He openly declared his opposition to it when he sought re-election for Trinity Bay as a Bennett supporter; he won by 22 votes. He was named colonial secretary in Bennett's new government on 5 March 1870. Alsop sought re-election in Trinity in the autumn of 1870, when, during a particularly bitter campaign, he was accused of turning "Catholic," and opposition manifestos warned voters that Alsop had "put the Queen and the British Government against us and made them take away the troops who were the people's protectors against the St. John's rowdies." He was also branded as one who would haul down the "Old Flag and put up the Stars and Stripes." Such abusive electioneering devices had their desired effect on the outport fishermen. Alsop was defeated by a narrow margin, but he continued to serve as colonial secretary until the time of his death and was given the consolation of being named to the Legislative Council though he never occupied his seat because of ill health.

Sometime prior to his death Alsop was converted to Roman Catholicism. He was described as a man of honour and integrity, and he served efficiently as colonial secretary. His entry into political life had not been without misgivings as he was by nature a retiring person preferring a contemplative life to the excitement and hazards of politics.

ELINOR SENIOR

PANL, Newfoundland, Department of the colonial secretary, letter books, 1867–1934, John Bemister to Robert Alsop, 7 Sept. 1869. *Courier* (St John's), 21 Sept. 1870. *Newfoundlander* (St John's), 27 Sept. 1870, 28 March 1871. *Newfoundland Patriot and Terra Nova Herald* (St John's), 15, 22 Sept., 17 Nov. 1866. *Royal Gazette* (St John's), 28 March 1871. *St John's Daily News*, 14 Oct., 18 Dec. 1869. Prowse, *History of Nfld.*, 706.

ALSTON, EDWARD GRAHAM, lawyer and public servant; b. 6 Sept. 1832 at Cambridge, England, second son of the Reverend George Alston and Anne Charlotte Oxenden; m. at Victoria on 2 Sept. 1861 Elizabeth Caroline Abbott (d. 1865) by whom he had two children, and on 6 Feb. 1867 Anna Maria Tuzo by whom he had three children; d. 12 Nov. 1872 at Freetown, Sierra Leone.

Edward Graham Alston was educated at St Paul's School, London, and Trinity College, Cambridge (BA, 1855), and was called to the bar at Lincoln's Inn in 1857. Arriving in Victoria by way of the Panama on 26 May 1859, he was admitted to the bar of Vancouver Island on 15 June 1859 and on 14 Feb. 1861 was appointed registrar of titles for Vancouver Island, a position he held until 1 June 1870, when he became registrar general of the united Colony of British Columbia. He was one of three commissioners who drew up the *Consolidated statutes of British Columbia* (Victoria, 1870) and he acted as attorney general from 12 May to 23 Aug. 1871, during which period British Columbia officially entered confederation.

Alston was a member of the Legislative Council of Vancouver Island, 1861–62; a commissioner of the Indian reserve and a member of the General Board of Education of Vancouver Island, he resigned these offices in 1865, when after the death of his first wife he went to England for a year. Following his return he was appointed a member of the Legislative Council of British Columbia, 1868–71; justice of the peace (3 Dec. 1868); commissioner of savings banks (15 April 1869); registrar of joint stock companies (26 Aug. 1869); and inspector general of schools (6 May 1870).

Outside his official duties Alston took an active interest in community affairs. A member of the Church of England, he was appointed registrar of the diocese in 1866 and he contributed an "Historical and political summary for . . . 1858–1868" to the *Report of the Columbia Mission* for 1868. He held office in the Mechanics' Literary Institute and

as a freemason was the prime mover in establishing the benevolent fund of the Victoria Lodge no.1085, A.F. & A.M. During the Fenian scare of 1866 he was "idiot enough to join the *corps* [Vancouver Island Volunteer Rifles] & go into camp & sleep out & make myself very juvenile & foolish." In 1868 he accompanied the expedition which crossed Vancouver Island from Nootka Sound to the east coast, a region whose exploration had been left unfinished by Dr Robert Brown*'s party in 1864; "Mount Alston" at the head of the Nimpkish River still commemorates his journey. In the 1870 edition of the *Hand-book to British Columbia and Vancouver Island* Alston himself comments on this 1868 expedition and affirms his belief that "this colony, with its latent wealth and splendid climate, has a rich – though it may be distant – future before it. . . ."

In this future, however rich, Alston himself had no wish to share. He was quite out of sympathy with the growing trend in British Columbia toward a more democratic form of government. When the colonies were united in 1866 he was privately delighted to have "got rid of the House of *Apes*" on Vancouver Island, and when the united colony joined confederation in 1871 he asked the imperial government for a transfer since he could see "no hope of preferment within the Colony, inasmuch as a Responsible form of Government has been established, in which all vacancies will be filled by the political friends of the ministry of the day." A month after British Columbia had officially become a province of Canada, Alston left Victoria to take up his appointment as queen's advocate in Sierra Leone where his career was cut short by African fever the following year. Evidently, as his son said, Alston found himself "more at home" in a colony like Sierra Leone where he was a member of the Legislative and Executive Councils and served as acting governor, and where the local newspaper bore witness that "his abilities and high character gave him a foremost place in the staff of officials."

DOROTHY BLAKEY SMITH

PABC, Alfred Edward Alston papers; Edward Graham Alston correspondence, 1860–71; diary, 1859–60, 1865; Crease papers, correspondence inward, 1862–70. E. G. Alston, "Historical and political summary for ten years – 1858–1868," in *Report of the Columbia Mission, 1868* (London, 1869) and reprinted in E. G. Alston, *A hand-book to British Columbia and Vancouver Island* . . . (London, 1870), 3–5.

British Columbia, *Blue Books*, 1859–70 (copies in PABC); Legislative Council, *Journals*, 1868–71. *British Columbia Government Gazette* (Victoria), 1871. *Colonist* (Victoria), 1859–68. *Gazette* (Victoria), 1858–72. *Government Gazette* (New Westminster and Victoria),

Anderson

1868–70. *Negro* (Freetown, Sierra Leone), 20 Nov. 1872. *Victoria Daily Standard*, 23 Aug. 1871. *Alumni Cantabrigienses . . .*, comp. John Venn . . . and J. A. Venn, PT.2, I (Cambridge, 1940), 47. S. D. Scott, "The attitude of the colonial governors and officials towards confederation," in *British Columbia & confederation*, ed. W. G. Shelton (Victoria, 1967), 143–64.

ANDERSON, THOMAS BROWN, merchant, banker, member of the Special Council for Lower Canada; b. June 1796 in Edinburgh, Scotland; d. 28 May 1873 in Montreal.

Little is known of Thomas Brown Anderson's early life. Sometime before 1827 he came to Montreal and worked as a clerk in the commercial firm of Forsyth, Richardson and Company, which in copartnership with Forsyth, Walker and Company of Quebec, traded in furs, wholesale provisions, and real estate, acted as the East India Company's Canadian agent, and served as the financial repository for the receiver-general's department of Lower Canada. Anderson's marriage on 12 Dec. 1827 to Ann Richardson (widow of David Ogden), eldest daughter of John Richardson*, a senior partner in Forsyth, Richardson and Company, undoubtedly assisted his business career; he became the company's last president. His only child, Elizabeth Magdalene, became the wife of Lieutenant-Colonel Joseph Bell Forsyth.

In 1847, when the major shareholders in Forsyth, Richardson and Company withdrew their capital, Anderson dissolved the copartnership with Forsyth, Walker and Company and reorganized the Montreal business under the name of Anderson, Auldjo and Company. Anderson's partners, Louis Auldjo, William Evans, and Thomas Forsyth, had also been clerks with Forsyth, Richardson and Company. In 1852 Auldjo left the company to establish his own business, and Anderson's firm became Anderson, Evans and Company, hardware merchants and importers. In 1858 Thomas and Samuel Evans joined the company and its name was changed to Anderson, Evans and Evans. This partnership was dissolved in 1861 and Anderson thereafter devoted his full time to banking.

Anderson, the son-in-law of one of the Bank of Montreal's most prominent founders and shareholders, served as a director of this bank from 1830 until 1834 and again from 1835 until his retirement in 1869. In 1837 he worked on a directors' committee to determine the bank's policy toward the exchange crisis of that year. In 1840 he supported the efforts of Peter McGill*, the bank's president, to extend its operations into Upper Canada; and a year later he represented the Bank of Montreal before the Legislative Assembly's committee on money and banking to request stronger legislation to facilitate branch banking in Canada. On 8 June 1847 Anderson succeeded Joseph Masson* as vice-president of the Bank of Montreal and, on 5 June 1860, when old Peter McGill retired, Anderson was unanimously elected to succeed him.

Although Anderson has been described as "one of the old race of Canadian merchants" he readily recognized the change in the country's economy away from its old mercantile base to a more sophisticated corporate structure, and he reorganized the Bank of Montreal's business and administration to profit from this change. From 17 April 1855 he had served as chairman of the Canadian board of directors for the Liverpool, London Fire and Life Insurance Company. (This position he retained until 20 July 1872; thereafter he remained a director of the company, at the board's request, until his death.) When he became president of the Bank of Montreal he authorized branch bank managers and agents to represent insurance companies and other corporate interests. In 1862 Anderson created the post of general manager and selected a clever Scottish banker, David Davidson, as its first occupant. When Davidson retired a year later Anderson promoted Edwin H. King*, later known as "the king of Canadian bankers," to fill Davidson's place; this young, shrewd, and skilful Irish banker, who succeeded Anderson as president, soon justified Anderson's confidence. During the American Civil War, the north's chronic need for credit, Canada's ready access to English gold, and King's knowledge of the American money market enabled the Bank of Montreal to exploit the situation to its advantage.

In November 1863 the Bank of Montreal wrested the Canadian government's account from its chief rival, the floundering Bank of Upper Canada. This account, owing to the government's extravagant financial commitments, seemed at times a dubious asset, but provided the Bank of Montreal with a position of valuable influence, which it rarely hesitated to use. In 1866, for example, the bank, despite the opposition of its rivals, persuaded the government to enact legislation enabling banks to convert specie and government debentures into provincial notes, legislation from which it, as the government's banker, stood most to gain. The next year, John A. Macdonald*, upon E. H. King's advice and contrary to that of his minister of finance, Alexander Tilloch Galt*, refused to assist the faltering Commercial Bank of the Midland District, the Bank of Montreal's chief rival following the failure of the Bank of Upper Canada. Consequently "one of the most powerful and seemingly most substantial institutions in the country" failed.

Despite Anderson's cautious and, at times, pessimistic annual reports, the Bank of Montreal thrived under his administration. In nine years deposits trebled, owing, in part, to the flight of American capital during the Civil War; gold, silver, and coin holdings and government debentures increased, adding to the stability of the institution. On 20 Oct. 1869 Anderson retired from the Bank of Montreal for reasons of health. He had developed a speech impediment probably caused by a slight stroke. The bank directors voted him a stipend of $2,000 in recognition of his faithful services.

Although Thomas Anderson retained a lively interest in British politics, remaining a devoted Tory, he, unlike many other prominent Montreal merchants of his day, played a relatively inconspicuous part in municipal or provincial politics. On 2 April 1838, the governor, the Earl of Gosford [Acheson*] appointed Anderson to the Special Council for Lower Canada, a position he retained only until 1 June 1838. In 1849 Anderson joined the Annexation Association, became one of its eight vice-presidents, and signed the Annexation Manifesto.

Anderson readily supported a variety of civic, charitable, religious, and educational organizations. In 1829 he joined the executive of the recently organized Montreal Committee of Trade, which in 1842 became the Montreal Board of Trade. Although he was never president of the Board of Trade, in 1849 he was chosen vice-president and he served on the executive council and board of arbitration continuously from 1842 until 1850. He acted as treasurer of the Montreal General Hospital, an institution to which his father-in-law had contributed liberally. He supported the Longueuil Mission. His wife also assisted charitable works; her principal interests were the Lying-in Hospital and the Ladies Benevolent Society, which her mother had reorganized in 1832. Although not of the Presbyterian faith, Anderson, like many Scottish Montreal merchants, retained a pew in the St Gabriel Street Church. A devoted Anglican and member of the Christ Church Cathedral congregation, and later of St James the Apostle, he actively participated in parish and diocesan work. In 1856 he joined a committee of 11 to draw up plans for the construction of the new Christ Church Cathedral. He also served as the financial secretary of the parochial endowment fund, investing some of its money in Bank of Montreal shares. From 2 May 1845 until his death Anderson was a member of the board of governors of McGill University, during which time he served on many committees and contributed generously to the original McGill endowment fund. From 1851

until 1852 he was vice-chairman of the board and thereafter first member of the finance committee.

Thomas Brown Anderson, through cautious methodical management and a fortunate marriage, enjoyed a successful business career in Montreal and made a definite if moderate contribution to its public life.

CARMAN MILLER

AJM, Registre d'état civil, Christ Church parish, 12 Dec. 1827; Registre d'état civil, St James the Apostle parish, 1873. PAC, MG 24, I79 (T. B. Anderson papers). McGill University Archives, Dawson papers; Minutes of the board of governors, 1851–74. *Annual report of the governors, principal, and fellows of McGill University, Montreal . . .* , 1851–73. [Bruce and Grey], *Elgin-Grey papers* (Doughty), IV, 1493. Canada, Province of, *Sessional papers,* XVIII (1860), PT.1, no.5; XXI (1863), PT.3, no.9. *Canada Gazette* (Quebec), 15 May, 3 July 1847. *Gazette* (Montreal), December 1827, 17 May–4 Aug. 1847, May 1873. *Montreal Herald,* May–June 1873. *Montreal Transcript,* May–November 1836. *Montreal Witness,* May 1873. *L'Opinion publique* (Montréal), 27 mai–11 juin 1873.

Canada directory, 1851–73. *The Canadian men and women of the time: a handbook of Canadian biography,* ed. H. J. Morgan (1st ed., Toronto, 1898). Desjardins, *Guide parlementaire. Montreal directory* (Mackay), 1842–50. *McGill University calendar,* 1856–73. *Canadian banking and monetary policy: recent readings,* ed. J. P. Cairns and H. H. Binhammer (Toronto, 1965). Denison, *Canada's first bank,* I. W. R. Graham, "Sir Richard Cartwright and the Liberal party, 1863–1896," unpublished PHD thesis, University of Toronto, 1950. Cyrus Macmillan, *McGill and its story, 1821–1921* (London, New York, Toronto, 1921), 207. G. H. S. Mills, "The annexation movement of 1849–1850 as seen through Lower Canadian press," unpublished MA thesis, McGill University, 1947. O. D. Skelton, *The life and times of Sir Alexander Tilloch Galt* (Toronto, 1920). F.-J. Audet, "Membres du Conseil spécial," *BRH,* VII (1901), 82–83. J. I. Cooper, "The origins and early history of the Montreal City and District Savings Bank, 1846–1871," *CCHA, Report,* 1945–46, 15–25. George Hague, "The late Mr. E. H. King, formerly president of the Bank of Montreal: some personal reminiscences," *Journal of the Canadian Bankers Association* (Toronto), IV (1896–97), October 1896, 20–29. D. C. Masters, "Toronto vs. Montreal; the struggle for financial hegemony, 1860–1875," *CHR,* XXII (1941), 141–42. Adam Shortt, "Founders of Canadian banking: the Hon. John Richardson, merchant, financier and statesman," *Journal of the Canadian Bankers Association* (Toronto), XXIX (1921–22), October 1921, 17–27; January 1922, 165–78.

ANDERSON, THOMAS GUMMERSALL, Indian agent; b. at Sorel, Province of Quebec, 12 Nov. 1779, sixth son of Captain Samuel Anderson, loyalist, and Deliverance Butts; d. at Port Hope, Ont., 10 Feb. 1875.

Anderson

Thomas Gummersall Anderson was taken to New Johnstown (Cornwall) when the Anderson family settled there in 1783. In 1795 he was apprenticed for five years to Thomas Markland*, a Kingston merchant. Robert Mackenzie of Montreal, half-brother of Markland, induced young Anderson to accompany him in 1800 to the American post of Mackinac (on Mackinac Island, later in the state of Michigan) to trade with the Indians. For the next 14 years Anderson traded in the upper Mississippi valley in what is now the state of Wisconsin. He was usually based at Prairie du Chien on the Mississippi, a general depot for Mackinac traders, but also became familiar with such places as Milwaukee (where he sometimes wintered), when they were small pioneer settlements. The items he traded for buffalo and beaver furs included pots and pans and ball shot. He worked with Jacob Frank for a number of years and was an independent trader by 1810, gaining a reputation for honourable dealing among the Indian tribes of the region – Sauks, Winnebagos, and Potawatomis, and later principally the Santees.

In one of the first actions of the War of 1812 Mackinac was captured by the British. Anderson learned there that the Americans had captured Prairie du Chien and had built a fort. Anderson immediately raised a company of volunteers and, with the aid of the commanding officer at Mackinac, Robert McDouall*, hastened to Prairie du Chien and captured the fort. Until the end of the war he remained in charge of Fort McKay, so named for an old Norwester, William McKay*, who accompanied the expedition. In 1815, through McDouall's recommendation, Anderson was given employment at Mackinac in the Indian Department as storekeeper, interpreter, and clerk. The department remained under military jurisdiction from 1816 to 1830, and Anderson had the rank and allowance of captain.

By the time he returned to Mackinac in September 1815, however, it had been given up by the British to the Americans, and the garrison, still under McDouall, had moved to Drummond Island. Anderson followed and remained there nine years as agent. Another move was made late in 1828 when Drummond Island was transferred to American sovereignty and the Indian agency was moved to Penetanguishene, Upper Canada.

Anderson had married in 1820 Elizabeth Ann Hamilton, eldest daughter of Captain James Matthew Hamilton of the 5th regiment of foot, by whom he had seven children. One son, Gustavus Alexander, was ordained priest in the Church of England; like his father, he devoted much of his life to the welfare of the Indians and was for several years incumbent of the Mohawk Church at Tyendinaga in Hastings County.

Until 1830 the objectives of the Indian Department were mainly political; its policy was essentially to retain the friendship of the Indians because of their usefulness as military allies. A change towards a more humanitarian attitude was indicated in the winter of 1829–30 when Anderson was summoned to York (Toronto) by Sir John Colborne* and ordered to undertake the settlement and civilization of three tribes of Chippewa Indians under chiefs Yellowhead*, John Aisance, and Snake at Coldwater and The Narrows (now Orillia). At these places Anderson, with the title of superintendent, built mills, houses, and schools for the Indians. His activities were hampered by a shortage of funds and the two Indian settlements were eventually abandoned in 1837. The initial success of the settlements, however, had led to an expansion of the plan in 1833. After an extensive search for a suitable locality had been conducted by Anderson and the Reverend Adam ELLIOT, it was determined to form a general establishment on Manitoulin Island with a view to drawing there most of the Indians from the settled parts of the province.

The Anderson family remained on Manitoulin Island for nine years. Although Anderson was tireless in his efforts to promote the settlement and although there was this time no shortage of funds, his stay at Manitoulin was marked by failure. Few Indians came because of the remoteness of the island, and it was eventually opened, in 1862, to settlement by whites. In 1845, Anderson was transferred to Toronto where he succeeded Samuel Peters Jarvis* as chief superintendent and was also named visiting superintendent. He moved his office to Cobourg in 1847 and retained the government post, one which required much travelling, until his resignation, 30 June 1858. His wife died the same day. The rector of Cobourg, Archdeacon Alexander Neil BETHUNE, preached a memorial sermon, later privately printed, on the Sunday following her funeral. T. G. Anderson's later years were spent for the most part in Cobourg and Port Hope, with shorter periods of residence at Tyendinaga and Toronto. He died at Port Hope where his old friend of Manitoulin days, Frederick Augustus O'Meara*, was rector of St John's Church.

As trader and government employee, Anderson had close contact with Indians for 58 years. He was a shrewd judge of their character, was devoted to their interests, and was highly regarded by them. He wrote copious journals and reports, a number of which were printed after his death.

T. R. MILLMAN

The Thomas G. Anderson papers at MTCL consist of copies of family papers in private hands. Material from this collection has been published by Sophia Rowe as "Anderson record, from 1699 to 1896," including "Reminiscences of Capt. Thomas Gummersall Anderson," in *Ont. Hist.*, VI (1905), 109–35, as well as in *Loyalist narratives from Upper Canada* (Talman) and in the *New Dominion Monthly* (Montreal), November 1874. The State Historical Society of Wisconsin has a collection of Thomas G. Anderson papers (copies at PAO), part of which has been reproduced in the Wis. State Hist. Soc. *Coll.* as "Personal narrative of Capt. Thomas G. Anderson, early experiences in the North-West fur trade – British capture of Prairie du Chien," in IX (1880–82), 137–206; "Prairie du Chien documents, 1814–'15," in IX (1880–82), 262–81; and "Papers of Capt. T. G. Anderson, British Indian agent," in X (1883–85), 142–49. The society's journal also published "Capt. T. G. Anderson's journal, 1814; journal of the proceedings at Fort McKay, from the departure of Lieut. Col. McKay, for Mackinaw, comprehending the particulars of every occurring circumstance in and out of the fort within the vicinity of Prairie du Chien," Wis. State Hist. Soc. *Coll.*, IX (1880–82), 207–61; the original of Anderson's journal is at PAC, MG 24, F19 (Thomas Gummersall Anderson papers).

See also: *Fifth annual report of the Society, for Converting & Civilizing the Indians, and Propagating the Gospel, among Destitute Settlers in Upper Canada; for the year ending October, 1835* (Toronto, n.d.). *The Stewart missions; a series of letters and journals, calculated to exhibit to British Christians, the spiritual destitution of the emigrants settled in the remote parts of Upper Canada . . .*, ed. W. J. D. Waddilove (London, 1838), 42, 43, 49, 53, 75ff.

ANDERSON, WILLIAM JAMES, physician, amateur geologist, and historian; b. 2 Nov. 1812 at sea off the Danish coast, to Scottish parents; d. 15 May 1873 in Quebec City of tuberculosis. He was married and makes reference to a daughter.

William James Anderson studied medicine at Edinburgh, and held the degree of MD and a LRCS. In the 1830s as a young emigrant doctor in the Maritimes, he fostered his taste for history by exploring Nova Scotia. At Chignecto Bay and South Joggins he investigated mining operations. Anderson's health collapsed during a typhus epidemic in Pictou in 1847. He left the Maritimes and the medical profession and operated a sawmill in Borelia, Upper Canada. In the 1850s he moved on to Toronto.

After a brief return to mining districts in the Maritimes, he settled in Quebec City in 1860, resuming his profession. There his other interests took much of his attention. In 1862, through newspaper articles on gold-mining, he became acquainted with Dr James Douglas*, a fellow mining enthusiast and member of the Literary and Historical Society of Quebec. Dr Anderson led a group of members who revived the society, re-animated its interest in securing and publishing documents on Quebec, and re-established its library and museum. He himself first reported to the society in November 1863; his first papers in its *Transactions* were on the gold-fields of Nova Scotia and of the world, and the bitumen of Point de Lévy. He continued to publish in this subject area. On a visit to Nova Scotia in 1862 he had toured Acadian regions and inspected the Provincial Archives at Halifax.

In 1866 he began a series of major historical contributions in the *Transactions* of the Literary and Historical Society, with historiography a particular theme; these papers dealt with the life of the Duke of Kent, including letters from him held by the de Salaberry family (the son of Charles-Michel d'Irumberry* de Salaberry, the "Victor of Châteauguay," had been one of Anderson's patients); Evangeline (his paper's subtitle, "The poetry and prose of history," is an indication of the author's approach); the capitulation of J.-B.-N.-R. de Ramezay* in 1759 (the essay explores closely differences between French and English accounts of the incident); and the siege of Quebec by Richard Montgomery* and Benedict Arnold* in 1775–76. In writing these essays Anderson made use of archival papers in Halifax, arranged for the transfer of others from Halifax to Quebec, and got archival materials transferred to Canada from Britain. While on the executive of the Literary and Historical Society, he fostered publication of two series of *Historical documents* (1866, 1871) and his last publication in 1872 advocated an archives for Canada. He was a friend of other historians of the confederation years: François-Xavier Garneau*, Jean-Baptiste-Antoine Ferland*, Philippe AUBERT de Gaspé, and James MacPherson Le Moine*. As president of the society he brought it into contact with Francis Parkman*, Joseph HOWE, and Louis-Joseph PAPINEAU.

Obituaries refer to Anderson's "dignified mien," his "long beard frosted by suffering," his "utterance measured slow," and his Scottish humour. His many publications attest to his energy, his breadth of interest, and his penchant for historical research.

ELIZABETH WATERSTON

W. J. Anderson, "The archives of Canada," and "Canadian history, the siege and blockade of Quebec, by Generals Montgomery and Arnold in 1775–1776," in Lit. and Hist. Soc. of Quebec, *Trans.*, new ser., IX (1872), 117, 49 (the second appeared as an off-print, Quebec, 1872); "Curiosities of Canadian literature: Washington and Jumonville," *Canadian Monthly and*

Andrews

National Review (Toronto), III (1873), 55; "Evangeline and the archives of Nova Scotia," Lit. and Hist. Soc. of Quebec, *Trans.*, new ser., VII (1870), 5; "Gold fields of Nova Scotia," Lit. and Hist. Soc. of Quebec, *Trans.*, new ser., II (1864), 35; *The gold fields of the world, our knowledge of them, and its application to the gold fields of Canada* (Quebec, 1864); *The life of F.M., H.R.H. Edward, Duke of Kent, illustrated by his correspondence with the de Salaberry family, never before published, extending from 1791 to 1814* (Ottawa and Toronto, 1870); *The lower St. Lawrence, its scenery, navigation and commerce, forming a complete tourist's guide* (Quebec, 1872); "Military operations at Quebec from the capitulation by De Ramesay on 18th September, 1759, to raising the siege by De Levis between the night of the 17th and the morning of the 18th May, 1760," Lit. and Hist. Soc. of Quebec, *Trans.*, new ser., VII (1870), iii; "On Canadian history and biography, and passages in the lives of a British prince and a Canadian seigneur," Lit. and Hist. Soc. of Quebec, *Trans.*, new ser., V (1867), 15; "On the coal-like substance or 'altered Bitumen' found in the excavations at Fort no. 3, Point Levis, and the presently accepted theories on the origin of coals, bitumens and petroleum springs, with an account of the 'Carboniferous system' of British North America," Lit. and Hist. Soc. of Quebec, *Trans.*, new ser., IV (1866), 19; "Opening address – 'Review of the past year, moving accidents by flood and field'," Lit. and Hist. Soc. of Quebec, *Trans.*, new ser., VIII (1871), 5.

[James Murray], *Journal of the siege of Quebec, 1759–1760, by General Jas. Murray* (Lit. and Hist. Soc. of Quebec, Historical Documents, D.6., 3rd ser., Quebec, 1871). *Recueil de ce qui s'est passé en Canada au sujet de la guerre, tant des Anglais que des Iroquois, depuis l'année 1682* (Lit. and Hist. Soc. of Quebec, Historical Documents, D.6., 3rd ser., Quebec, 1871). *Morning Chronicle* (Quebec), 18 May 1873. *Quebec Daily Mercury*, 18 May 1873. *The centenary volume of the Literary and Historical Society of Quebec, 1824–1924*, ed. Henry Ievers (Quebec, 1924). *Index to the lectures, papers, and historical documents published by the Literary and Historical Society of Quebec . . .*, ed. F. C. Wurtele and J. W. Strachan (Quebec, 1927), 30, 46, 47. *List of historical documents and new series of "Transactions" published by the Literary and Historical Society of Quebec* (Quebec, 1927). Morgan, *Bibliotheca Canadensis*. "Les disparus, William-James Anderson," *BRH*, XXXV (1929), 620.

ANDREWS, ISRAEL DE WOLFE, United States consul, special agent, and lobbyist; b. at Eastport, Maine, in May 1813; d. 17 Feb. 1871 in Boston, Mass.

Although an American, Israel de Wolfe Andrews had close family ties with British North America through his grandmother and father. As a youth he engaged in a trade "which consisted more or less of smuggling," and its inconveniences impressed him with the desirability of moulding North American economic relations in conformity with geography.

Appointed United States consul in Saint John, New Brunswick, in 1843, Andrews observed the problems of trade and fishing which were plaguing Anglo-American relations, and which were not ameliorated until the passing of the reciprocity treaty of 1854. Andrews was instrumental in shaping that treaty by defining what was eventually its content, by assisting its negotiation, and by working for its ratification. The basic American demands which later formed the matrix of the treaty were elaborated by Andrews as early as 1848 in a letter addressed to the American secretary of state, James Buchanan. When the *projet* for the treaty was finally drawn up in 1853 by Secretary of State William L. Marcy and the British minister in Washington, Sir John F. T. Crampton, Andrews was present. His most vigorous efforts were devoted to getting the treaty ratified. He sought to mould a favourable attitude in Congress through two reports on trade which, as a special agent to the Treasury Department, he was commissioned to compile. He endeavoured to affect relevant segments of opinion by seeing that articles sympathetic to reciprocity were placed in key journals, and by exercising his persuasive efforts with influential members of the executive branch of the American government. When the treaty was ready for ratification, he exerted pressure on persons in the Maritime provinces, including William Hayden NEEDHAM and Moses Henry Perley*, whose willingness to accept American fishing demands would be crucial. He also worked indefatigably to marshal support for ratification of the treaty by the U.S. Senate during the summer of 1854.

Andrews' extravagant expenditures in encouraging the treaty – supposed to be between $50,000 and $60,000 on behalf of the American government and $40,000 for the Canadian government – earned him an unenviable reputation both among contemporaries such as Lord Elgin [James Bruce*] and among historians. However, his actions, if unwise, were based upon strong convictions. His own writings and the maps he submitted with his second report reveal that he was a continentalist who believed that geography had created two great outlets, the Mississippi and the St Lawrence, for the heartland of North America. The accidents of politics had placed these two continental arterials in separate hands. Recognizing the political barriers inherent in the provincial attachment of the colonies to Great Britain, Andrews sought to encourage economic cooperation.

On 10 March 1855 Andrews was appointed American consul general to the British North American provinces, a new office deriving from the treaty. He held the post until his resignation on 11 July 1857. Thereafter he continued his lobbying activities, which included sending a memorial to Congress in 1860 protesting the possible termination of the reciprocity treaty, submitting a history of the treaty's negotiations to the secretary of state, William H. Seward, in 1862, and corresponding from 1861 to 1863 with John A. Andrew, then governor of Massachusetts, on the strains placed upon Anglo-American relations by the American Civil War. Israel Andrews apparently also attempted to encourage North American unification during the Civil War. His enthusiasm and devotion to the ideal of continentalism may seem bizarre today, for history has failed to vindicate that cause. Had the outcome been different, Andrews might have been hailed as a visionary rather than damned as a knave.

IRENE W. D. HECHT

PAC, MG 24, A16 (Elgin papers), correspondence concerning the reciprocity treaty of 1854. *Diplomatic correspondence of the United States, Canadian relations, 1784–1860*, ed. W. R. Manning (4v., Washington, 1945), III, IV. T. C. Keefer, *A sketch of the rise and progress of the reciprocity treaty; with an explanation of the services rendered in connection therewith* (Toronto, 1863). United States, Treasury Department, *Report of the secretary of the treasury in answer to a resolution of the Senate calling for information in relation to the trade and commerce of the British American colonies with the United States and other countries since 1829 . . .* ([Washington, 1851]); *Communication from the secretary of the treasury, transmitting, in compliance with a resolution of the Senate of March 8, 1851, the report of Israel D. Andrews, . . . on the trade and commerce of the British North American colonies, and upon the trade of the Great Lakes and rivers; . . .* (Washington, 1853). I. W. D. Hecht, "Israel De Wolfe Andrews and the reciprocity treaty of 1854," unpublished MA thesis, University of Rochester, 1961. D. C. Masters, *The reciprocity treaty of 1854: its history, its relation to British colonial and foreign policy and to the development of Canadian fiscal autonomy* (London, New York, and Toronto, 1936). C. C. Tansill, *The Canadian reciprocity treaty of 1854* (Johns Hopkins University Studies in Hist. and Pol. Sci., XL, Baltimore, 1922). R. W. Winks, *Canada and the United States: the Civil War years* (Baltimore, 1960). I. W. D. Hecht, "Israel D. Andrews and the reciprocity treaty of 1854: a reappraisal," *CHR*, XLIV (1963), 313–29. T. H. Le Duc, "Correspondence – I. D. Andrews and the reciprocity treaty of 1854," *CHR*, XV (1934), 437–38. D. C. Masters, "A further word on I. D. Andrews and the reciprocity treaty of 1854," *CHR*, XVII (1936), 159–67. W. D. Overman, "I. D. Andrews and reciprocity in 1854: an episode in dollar diplomacy," *CHR*, XV (1934), 248–63.

ARCHAMBAULT, PIERRE-URGEL, legislative councillor, one of those responsible for founding the École d'Agriculture de L'Assomption; b. 11 Jan. 1812 at L'Assomption, L.C., of the marriage of Pierre-Amable Archambault and Madeleine Bruguière; d. 19 Aug. 1871 in the same municipality.

Pierre-Urgel Archambault was one of the descendants in the imposing line of Archambaults that sprang from Jacques Archambault and Françoise Toureault (Thoureault), who came to Canada from Dompierre-sur-Mer in 1645. A merchant's son, Pierre-Urgel Archambault continued his father's business at L'Assomption, which was important as a commercial centre to the northeast of Montreal before the railways were built. He was mayor of his town from 1847 to 1854, was elected legislative councillor for the division of Repentigny in 1858, and remained a councillor until 1867. Like several members of his family he joined the militia. He became major of the 1st battalion of L'Assomption in 1851, then lieutenant-colonel in 1859.

Pierre-Urgel Archambault played an important part in the establishment of an agricultural school at the college of L'Assomption. In 1866 the agricultural societies of the counties of L'Assomption, Montcalm, and Joliette requested the college authorities to establish a school of agriculture. Pierre-Urgel Archambault, president of the Société d'Agriculture of L'Assomption, and Louis Archambault*, MLA for the county and in 1868 minister of agriculture and public works at Quebec, sought government support for this purpose. Their action was successful, and the superior of the college, Abbé Pierre-Férréol Dorval, was able to announce at prize-giving that the college would undertake the organizing of this school. (This prize-giving was in 1867, according to Dr Jean-Baptiste MEILLEUR, but Marc-A. Perron, in his book on Édouard-André Barnard*, claims it was in 1868.) One of the most distinguished teachers of the school was Isidore-Amédée Marsan*, who taught there from its inception until 1899.

The curriculum of this agricultural school was almost the same as that of the college of Sainte-Anne-de-la-Pocatière: it included theoretical and practical courses. The courses lasted two years for those who came with sufficient education. From 1864 on, the Board of Agriculture offered 20 scholarships of $50 each, which starting in 1868 were divided equally between the schools of Sainte-Anne-de-la-Pocatière and L'Assomption. In addition the government assisted in the payment of teachers' salaries as well as with running costs. The members of the Conservative party who had helped to found the agricultural school, particularly Pierre-Urgel Archambault, continued to take a keen interest in the work, and this interest explains in great part the prosperity of the early years. One should doubtless add the active sympathy of Pierre-Joseph-Olivier Chauveau*, the superintendent of education at that time and subsequently the minister of public instruction, who gave every kind of encouragement to the establishing of professional schools, especially those designed to prepare young French Canadians for their rural vocation. Serious difficulties, however, were to arise for the school at L'Assomption when the Parti National, with Honoré Mercier*, came to power in 1887: Mercier advocated the maintenance of a single school of agriculture for the whole of Quebec. This policy was taken up in 1897 by the Liberal party, under Félix-Gabriel Marchand*, and resulted in the closing of the École d'Agriculture de L'Assomption in 1899.

In 1835, at L'Assomption, Pierre-Urgel Archambault had married Joséphine Beaupré. They had two sons and three daughters; one of the daughters, Georgine, married twice, her second husband being Louis-Olivier Taillon*, prime minister of Quebec for a few days in 1887 and from 1892 to 1896, and postmaster general of Canada in 1896. Pierre-Urgel Archambault remarried about 1862, his second wife being Louise Poulin. He was first cousin of Louis Archambault, who had six children, one being Urgel-Eugène*, the organizer of the Montreal Catholic school commission and the founder of the Académie du Plateau and the École Polytechnique of Montreal. Pierre-Urgel Archambault died on 19 Aug. 1871 at L'Assomption; he was 59 years old.

LOUIS-PHILIPPE AUDET

AJM, Registre d'état civil (notes biographiques fournies par J.-J. Lefebvre). J.-B. Meilleur, *Mémorial de l'éducation du Bas-Canada* (2e éd., Québec, 1876), 171–72. Anastase Forget, *Histoire du Collège de L'Assomption* (Montréal, [1933]). M.-A. Perron, *Un grand éducateur agricole, Édouard-A. Barnard, 1835–98; étude historique sur l'agriculture de 1760 à 1900* (n.p., 1955), 52–56. L.-P. Audet, "Urgel-Eugène Archambault (1834–1904)," *Cahiers des Dix*, XXVI (1961), 143–75. J.-J. Lefebvre, "Les Archambault au Conseil législatif," *BRH*, LIX (1953), 25–29.

ARMSTRONG, JAMES ROGERS, merchant, foundry owner, and politician; b. 17 April 1787 at Dorchester (Iberville), Que., son of an Irish father, John Armstrong, and Mary Rogers, oldest daughter of loyalist Major James Rogers* who commanded a battalion of King's Rangers during the American Revolution; d. 13 July 1873 at Whitby, Ont.

After the early death of both his parents, James Rogers Armstrong was in 1796 sent to school in Vermont. He was living in Upper Canada by 1807, when on 9 October he married, at Hallowell (later part of Picton), Hannah Dougall, daughter of William Dougall, a pioneer Prince Edward County doctor. Armstrong acquired land in Hallowell Township (and, as the son of a loyalist, in Vaughan Township, York County) and farmed in Hallowell for a short time. He then became a merchant, first in Picton, then in Kingston about 1822, and finally in York where he opened a dry goods store in 1828. Some time in the 1840s he established the Toronto firm of J. R. Armstrong and Company, Toronto City Foundry, which specialized in the manufacturing of stoves, some of them of Armstrong's own design. At the age of 69 he moved to Whitby, where he spent the rest of his life, leaving the management of the company to his son James Rogers Armstrong.

During the 1830s he played some part in public life. He served briefly on the first York Board of Health during the cholera epidemic of 1832. He was elected to the House of Assembly of Upper Canada for Prince Edward County in 1836 as a Conservative but he was not a candidate in the election of 1842. In 1837 he was appointed a justice of the peace for the Home District.

Armstrong was a prominent member of the Wesleyan Methodist Church, a fact evidenced by the marriage of his daughter Mary to the Reverend Egerton Ryerson* (as his second wife) and of his daughter Eleanor to Dr John Beatty, professor at Victoria College. A third daughter, Phoebe Anne, married George DUGGAN, recorder of Toronto and judge of the county of York.

J. K. JOHNSON

PAC, RG 1, L3, A15/10, 31; RG 68, 1. PAO, James Dougall papers, J. R. Armstrong to the electors of Prince Edward County, 11 June 1836. "Assessment of the township of Hallowell for the year 1808," *Ont. Hist.*, VI (1905), 168–70. *J. of Education for Ont.*, XXVI (1873), 140. "Marriage register of Stephen Conger, J.P., Hallowell," *Ont. Hist.*, I (1899), 109–12. *Town of York, 1815–1834* (Firth). Upper Canada, House of Assembly, *Journals*, 1837–40. *The Canada directory . . . 1851*, ed. R. W. S. Mackay (Montreal, 1851). *The Canada directory for 1857–58 . . .* (Montreal, 1857). Chadwick, *Ontarian families*, II, 7–10. Canniff, *Medical profession in Upper Canada*, 223–24, 241–42, 344–45.

ARRAUD, JACQUES-VICTOR, priest, Sulpician, procurator, chaplain; b. 8 Sept. 1805 at Blaye, diocese of Bordeaux (department of Gironde), France, son of Augustin Arraud and Marguerite Florence; d. 22 March 1878 at Montreal.

Jacques-Victor Arraud was only a subdeacon when he was admitted to the *solitude* (noviciate) at Issy-les-Moulineaux (department of Hauts-de-

Seine) during the year 1828. He had been there only a few weeks when Jean-Henry-Auguste Roux*, the superior of the Sulpician seminary at Montreal who was passing through Paris, obtained authorization from both the English government and the superior general of Saint-Sulpice to take him to Canada with three other French Sulpicians. A recruiting of this importance had not been seen for more than 30 years. As soon as Arraud arrived he was given a class at the Sulpician college of Montreal, then, after his ordination on 26 July 1829, he became curate of the parish of Notre-Dame.

In 1844, after three years of negotiation, Bishop Ignace Bourget* persuaded Rose-Virginie Pelletier, *dite* Marie de Sainte-Euphrasie, superior general of the Good Shepherd Nuns of Angers (department of Maine-et-Loire), to establish her nuns at Montreal. Arraud was instructed to arrange accommodation, provide for their immediate needs, and work for the development of the community. First a residence suitable for their charitable works had to be found. The community wanted to set up a place of refuge for unfortunate women, and a needlework school and teaching establishment for poor girls. It was Arraud who, out of his own pocket and from the alms he collected, paid for their first house and had the necessary repairs and enlargements carried out. In addition, as the nuns were near to being completely destitute, he became their almost daily providence. He played the part of a beggar for their sake, even to the extent of himself conveying, in a cart, the clothes, small items of furniture, and provisions that he collected from door to door. After a few years, when the community began to grow and was in a position to assume total responsibility for its charitable undertakings, Arraud concerned himself with finding the necessary funds and supervising new buildings, for example, in 1870 when a boarding-school was founded at Saint-Hubert (Chambly County), and in 1872 when the community took charge of the women's prison. For all these services and for many others the Good Shepherd Nuns always looked upon M. Arraud as their second founder.

At the same time as he applied himself to providing for the nuns' most urgent needs, Arraud had to give his attention to another institution of a very different kind. In 1844 Joseph-Vincent Quiblier*, the superior of Saint-Sulpice, founded the Oeuvre des Bons Livres and chose Arraud as its administrator. The latter thus became the first director of the first French public library in Montreal. During the five years of his term of office, from 1844 to 1849, he succeeded in placing the institution on a solid base by recruiting about 150 subscribers, installing the library in more than adequate premises, and raising the number of volumes from 2,400 to 12,000.

M. Arraud's abilities, demonstrated in his various occupations, led his superiors to entrust important administrative offices to him, including that of procurator of the seminary from 1863 to 1876. He died suddenly on 22 March 1878, on his return from the Hôpital Général, of which he had been the ecclesiastical superior since 1876.

Antonio Dansereau

ASSM, Biographies, Jacques Victor Arraud; Oeuvres et institutions diverses. "Correspondance de Mgr Ignace Bourget pour 1842 et 1843," L.-A. Desrosiers, édit., APQ *Rapport*, *1948–49*, 438. "Correspondance de Mgr Jean-Jacques Lartigue de 1827 à 1833," L.-A. Desrosiers, édit., APQ *Rapport*, *1942–43*, 23, 34, 52. Allaire, *Dictionnaire*. Gauthier, *Sulpitiana*. *Annales des religieuses de Notre-Dame de Charité du Bon-Pasteur d'Angers* (2v., Montréal, 1895), I, 5, 12–16, 151, 156–59, 367–69. *Au soir d'un siècle, le Bon-Pasteur d'Angers à Montréal, 1844–1944* (Montréal, 1944). Édouard Gouin, *Le Bon-Pasteur d'Angers et ses œuvres à Montréal* (Montréal, 1916). Olivier Maurault, "L'Oeuvre des bons livres," *Revue trimestrielle canadienne* (Montréal), XII (1926), 152–77; "Vieux cahiers, vieux journaux," *Revue canadienne* (Montréal), 3e sér., XVIII (juill.–déc. 1916), 209–31.

ATWATER, EDWIN, landowner, businessman, alderman; b. 14 Sept. 1808 at Williston, Vt., son of Linus Atwater; d. 18 June 1874 at Montreal.

Edwin Atwater emigrated to Canada around 1830. He took up residence at Montreal and carried on his trade as a painter. Together with his elder brother Albert, he founded a business in paints, varnish, and plate-glass. The Atwater brothers were the first importers of glass in Canada, and their varnish factory was to reduce considerably the imports of this product on the national market. Edwin was active and enterprising, and soon rose to become one of the important figures of Montreal.

In 1846 he took part in the founding of the Montreal City and District Savings Bank [*see* Marc-Damase Masson]. Bishop Ignace Bourget* of Montreal deserves the credit for the idea of creating this mutual institution, dedicated to the best interests of the depositors. Edwin was an honorary director from 1846 to 1871, a director from 1848 to 1874, vice-president from 1852 to 1859, and president from 1859 to 1861. After a difficult beginning, the bank was obliged to close its doors from 1847 to 1849 because of local and international crises; it resumed its advance at the start of 1850. From 1850 to 1873 it held the confidence and esteem of the public by overcoming all

Aubert de Gaspé

the difficulties brought about by an unfavourable economic situation. In 1871 it received a new charter, under the jurisdiction of the Dominion of Canada.

To meet another pressing need, Atwater in 1846 went into partnership with some prominent people of Montreal to establish the Montreal Telegraph Company. Already, in 1844, the first telegraphic message had been transmitted from Baltimore to Washington, and Montreal, a great North American city, could not remain cut off from the rest of the world. In 1847 the company established a telegraph service between Montreal and Toronto and between Montreal and Quebec; on 17 April 1849 it received its official charter. In the same year Atwater took part in the founding of the Montreal and Troy Telegraph Company.

Not content with the services he gave to the Montreal community as a financier, Edwin Atwater entered municipal politics: he was elected to the city council of Montreal as a councillor (1850–51), then as an alderman (1852–57). He represented the Saint-Antoine ward, and stood out because of his energy and dynamism. He was a member of numerous committees created by the council to find solutions to the city's problems. From 1851 to 1857 he was president of the aqueduct commission, and it was under his direction that a new, more modern service was established. In 1865, as a delegate from Montreal, he attended an important assembly of municipalities at Detroit, Michigan.

An ambitious and hard-working man, Atwater was made president of the Montreal Board of Trade in 1861, and thereby became a member *ex officio* of the Harbour Commission, according to the practice in force from 1855 to 1873. He was also on the board of directors of the Merchants' Bank, which had been started by Hugh Allan* in 1861, and of the Citizens' Insurance Company of Canada; he later became vice-president of both undertakings. He was in addition an active member of the American Presbyterian Church.

After an illness of some weeks, Edwin Atwater died on 18 June 1874, leaving one of the largest fortunes of Montreal, the fruit of 40 years of unremitting toil. In 1871, to thank him for his devotion to the progress of the Montreal community, the city council gave the name of Atwater to a street in Saint-Antoine ward. On 23 May 1833 Edwin Atwater had married Lucy Huntington Greene, of Vergennes, Vermont, who gave him four sons and four daughters.

PIERRE LANDRY

Canada, Province of, Legislative Assembly, *Journals*, 1841–51. "The manufactures of Montreal," *RHAF*, VI (1952–53), 138. *La Minerve* (Montréal), 19 juin 1874. E. J. Chambers, *The book of Montreal; a souvenir of Canada's commercial metropolis* ([Montreal, 1903]), 63–65. Denison, *Canada's first bank*, II, 73, 152, 175. T. T. Smyth, *The first hundred years; history of the Montreal City and District Savings Bank, 1846–1946* (n.p., n.d.). *Storied Quebec* (Wood et al.), IV, 428–29. *Toponymie* (Service d'urbanisme de Montréal, Bulletin d'information, 4, [Montréal], 1966), 10. M.-C. Daveluy, "Un Canadien éminent: Raphaël Bellemare (1821–1906)," *RHAF*, XII (1958–59), 539–40.

AUBERT DE GASPÉ, PHILIPPE-JOSEPH, lawyer, writer, fifth and last seigneur of Saint-Jean-Port-Joli (L'Islet County); b. 30 Oct. 1786 at Quebec; d. 29 Jan. 1871 at Quebec, and buried in the church of Saint-Jean-Port-Joli.

Philippe-Joseph Aubert de Gaspé was the eldest son of Pierre-Ignace Aubert de Gaspé, a legislative councillor, and Catherine Tarieu de Lanaudière. His father had distinguished himself at the siege of Quebec in 1775, as had his grandfather, Ignace-Philippe*, throughout the Seven Years' War. The founder of the line, Charles Aubert* de La Chesnaye, an important figure in the fur trade, had arrived in New France in 1655, became subsequently a member of the Conseil souverain, and was ennobled by Louis XIV in 1693. One of his sons, Pierre, was the first to adopt the name Gaspé, in 1709. By his ancestors on both his mother's and his father's side, Philippe Aubert de Gaspé belonged to the most illustrious families in Canada bearing names such as Coulon de Villiers, Legardeur de Tilly, Jarret de Verchères, and Le Moyne de Longueuil. He also numbered among his forbears Robert Giffard* de Moncel and Pierre Boucher*.

At an early age Philippe was sent to Quebec; he boarded first with the Misses Cholette (1795–98), then at the seminary of Quebec, where he received his classical education (1798–1806). Louis-Joseph PAPINEAU and the doctors Joseph PAINCHAUD and Pierre-Jean de Sales Laterrière* were his fellow-students. From 1804 to 1806, while taking philosophy at the seminary, he lived at the boarding-school of the Reverend John Jackson, Church of England minister, where he was, he said, the only French Canadian. Afterwards he studied law first under Jonathan Sewell*, the future chief justice, then under Jean-Baptiste-Olivier Perrault*. He was called to the bar on 15 Aug. 1811. On 25 September of the same year, at Quebec, he married Susanne Allison, daughter of Thomas Allison, a captain in the 5th regiment of foot, and Thérèse Baby. Thirteen children were born of their marriage.

The young Gaspé, with a generous and enthusiastic disposition, had every advantage at the beginning of his career: high birth, financial sufficiency, an excellent education, advantageous connections in political, judicial, military, and social circles. He took part in a host of cultural, sporting, and even financial ventures. He was vice-president of the first literary society of Quebec in 1809, and a founding member of the Jockey Club in 1815 and of the Quebec Bank in 1818. In addition, in 1804 he had received a commission as lieutenant in the Quebec and District militia; in 1812 he became a captain in the 1st Battalion of Quebec District, and in the same year was promoted to the general staff of Lower Canada, as deputy judge advocate. He practised law at Quebec and "on the Kamouraska circuit" until 9 May 1816, when he received a commission as sheriff of the district of Quebec. In this capacity it was he who had the responsibility or the honour of proclaiming in the streets of the town, on 24 April 1820, the announcement of the recent accession of George IV to the throne.

Until that time success had thus come readily in everything to this man now in his thirties, who no doubt on that account had lived in the most easy-going contentment. However, by his liberality and want of foresight he had gradually brought himself to the brink of ruin. That ruin was startlingly revealed when "the iron hand of misfortune" descended upon him. In debt to the crown for a large sum of money and unable to reimburse it, he was relieved of his office as sheriff on 14 Nov. 1822. Shortly afterwards, on 13 Feb. 1823, his father died. It was then that he was forced to seek refuge, with his large family, which already numbered seven children, in the manor-house of his mother, the seigneuress of Saint-Jean-Port-Joli.

This forced retirement lasted 14 years, during which he lived in the midst of his family, continually haunted by fear and the threat of creditors who might some day have him imprisoned for debt. And this is what finally happened, on 29 May 1838. To extricate him from this predicament, in a troubled period, required as many negotiations and legal proceedings as had been necessary to get him implicated. They are summarized in a report which a special committee of nine members presented to the Legislative Assembly on 3 Aug. 1841, when commenting on the petition that Gaspé had presented on the previous 18 July. The report shows that he was put in prison in conformity with a judgement delivered against him on 20 June 1834, on behalf of the crown, for the sum of £1,169 14s.; that subsequently, in May 1836, he had attempted to avail himself of the provisions of the law respecting insolvent debtors by transferring all his personal and landed property, an expedient which the Court of King's Bench had endorsed; but that

the Court of Appeal had reversed its decision in November 1836, on the grounds that this statute did not extend to debtors of the crown. The report ended thus: "Considering the long period during which Mr. De Gaspé has been imprisoned, his advanced age [55], and that his health is impaired by his long confinement, and that he has 'given unto Court, upon Oath, a faithful statement of all the property and estate he possessed in the world,' with a view to the discharge of his debts, they [the members of the committee] respectfully recommend that an Act be passed for his relief, and accordingly report a Bill for the purpose."

This bill, ratified by both houses, was passed without amendment on 18 Sept. 1841, and received royal sanction some days later. At the beginning of October Gaspé was therefore enabled to regain his liberty, after a captivity of 3 years, 4 months, and 5 days.

The long period of misfortunes since his dismissal in 1822 does not show items solely on the debit side. True, he was kept apart from public life, where he doubtless might have played an eminent role, but his withdrawal to the country, followed by his seclusion, was a splendid preparation for the literary career that was to add lustre to the last part of his life. First of all, his tribulations made him a wiser man. They led him to look into himself and to reflect deeply upon his past conduct and his family memories. Furthermore, the solitude of the long winters allowed him, while he saw to the education of his numerous children, to complete his own literary education by steady association with authors, both ancient and modern, English and French, through contact with whom his taste was refined. An outcast as it were from urban society, he appreciated all the more the frank, simple companionship of the farmers, the *censitaires* of the seigneury. He found pleasure in associating with them, and accompanied them on hunting and fishing trips, lending an attentive ear to their talk and their stories, and recording in his prodigious memory the legends, tales, and songs that were to provide material for his books.

More especially, without being clearly aware of it, he acquired his first experience as a novelist through that of his eldest son and namesake. In 1837 the latter published, under his name alone, *L'Influence d'un livre*. But there is no doubt that the first French Canadian novel bears in more than one place the mark of the father, and not only, according to a tradition that is related by Philéas Gagnon* and Abbé Henri-Raymond Casgrain*, in the legend of Rose Latulipe (chapter five, "L'Étranger"). To support this new interpretation, it is necessary to retrace briefly the career of the son.

Aubert de Gaspé

Young Philippe-Ignace-François Aubert de Gaspé (1814–41) was tutored by his father before entering the seminary of Nicolet in 1827. Once his studies were completed, or broken off, in 1832, he was for several years a stenographer and journalist with the *Quebec Mercury* and *Le Canadien*. Following an altercation with Dr Edmund Bailey O'CALLAGHAN, member of the assembly for Yamaska, who questioned his professional integrity, he was sentenced in November 1835 to a month in prison. In February 1836, to avenge himself, the turbulent protester placed in the hall of the House of Assembly a bottle of asafoetida, which forced the members to evacuate the building. The situation was serious. To escape another warrant for his arrest, he left town and sought refuge in the manor-house at Saint-Jean-Port-Joli, where nobody worried him further. It was there, under his father's watchful eye, that he composed his novel.

This book recounts the misfortunes of an overcredulous peasant under the spell of *Le Petit Albert*, a collection of magical recipes by means of which he hopes to acquire wealth. Hence the justification for the title *L'Influence d'un livre*. The main theme also includes the story of a quack hanged at Quebec for a murder that was actually committed at Saint-Jean-Port-Joli in 1829. The whole is embellished with a little love plot, as well as with legends and folksongs. Absurd though the novel may appear at first sight, and despite many borrowings from books, it is none the less based on the attentive observation of many customs of the time, and on anecdotes some of which the son could have learned only through his father. An example is the hero's visit to the sorceress Nolet from Beaumont in chapter eight. This is a transposition into the novel of a recollection of 1806 belonging to Gaspé Sr. As the old woman Nolet died in 1819, his son was certainly not able to question her himself. In this way one can establish a series of significant rapprochements between the memories and works of the father and the novel of the son. These cross-checks are in no sense intended to deprive the son of his title of first French Canadian novelist, but rather to emphasize that by 1837 the father had acquired a certain amount of experience in the writer's trade.

We know that *L'Influence d'un livre* appeared at a most unfavourable moment, when all people were concerned more with politics and rebellion [see PAPINEAU] than with literature. The author was even the object of sharp criticism. He had stated in his preface: "Public opinion will decide whether I should go no further than this first venture," and he found he had to defend himself against the attacks of *Le Populaire*. There was no one to bring him the slightest word of encouragement. On the contrary, a correspondent of *La Gazette de Québec* concluded, on 10 Feb. 1838, that "great was the disappointment of the subscribers over M. de Gaspé's historico-poetic mish-mash." This total lack of comprehension eventually discouraged the young novelist and destroyed his career. Subsequently he went to Halifax to try his luck, and died there suddenly on 7 March 1841, while his father was in prison at Quebec.

It is not impossible that even at this time Gaspé Sr thought of accepting the challenge and taking up the pen that his son had broken. This hypothesis is confirmed to some degree by a contemporary testimony. Aimé-Nicolas, *dit* Napoléon Aubin* relates in his prison memories (*Le Fantasque*, 8 May 1839) that "there, buried in his black thoughts, lay Mr Hunter, who, like the old Indian, considered that not enough beavers were being killed in prison." The allusion to Gaspé is transparent, if we recall that it was precisely around this anecdote that the author of *Les Anciens Canadiens* was to build the speech for his own defence which he attributed to one of his characters.

But before carrying out the plan that was to rehabilitate him in his own eyes and in those of his compatriots, Gaspé had to wait some 20 years for favourable circumstances. In the meantime his existence returned to normal. In October 1841 he was restored to his family, who during his captivity had found shelter at the house of his mother, the seigneuress Aubert de Gaspé, a few steps away from the prison on Rue Sainte-Anne. The seigneuress died shortly afterwards, on 13 April 1842, only a week after her sister, Louise Tarieu de Lanaudière. A double inheritance then brought Philippe Aubert "the usufruct and possession of the fiefs and seigneuries of Port Joly and La Pocatière," as well as the "other lucrative and honorary rights" that were attached to them. He now went to take up residence on Rue des Remparts at Quebec, and resumed his summer trips to Saint-Jean.

For several years there is nothing noteworthy in his biography except for the succession of intimate events that are particularly frequent in a large family. His children got married, his daughters making the most advantageous matches available in Lower Canada: Susanne was married to William Power*; Adélaïde, to Georges-René Saveuse de Beaujeu; Elmire, to Andrew Stuart*; Zélie, to Louis-Eusèbe Borne; Zoé, to Charles Alleyn*; Atala, to J.-Eusèbe Hudon; and Wilhelmine-Anaïs, to William Fraser. The youngest girl, Philomène, became a nun in France. As for his son Thomas, he became a priest in 1847, the same year that his mother died. Philippe Aubert also discovered and practised early the art of being a grandfather. With his numerous descendants around him, he was able once more to enjoy respect.

Around 1850 and even before, he had begun to frequent Quebec society once more. He was a regular visitor to the Club des Anciens, which met each afternoon during the off season at Charles Hamel's store on Rue Saint-Jean. There he met the historians and archeologists of the old capital, among others François-Xavier Garneau*, Georges-Barthélemi Faribault*, and the commissary general James Thompson Jr The conversation of all these veterans usually turned on the antiquities of Quebec. Gaspé more than any others, because of his lengthy absence, was able to gauge the manifold changes that had taken place in the old capital since the beginning of the century. It was before this circle, as well as in family reunions, that he related his memories before writing them down.

From the first, no doubt thinking of his son, he was minded to give them the form of a novel and to place them at the most crucial moment in the history of New France. A witness of three generations, he had been in his childhood the recipient of the direct memories of the survivors of the old régime. The historical novel, a type of literature conceived after the manner of Walter Scott, one of his favourite authors, offered him the advantage of painting a general picture and at the same time using precise details of seigneurial life as he had lived it at the end of the 18th century or as it had been recounted to him in his family.

Hence the rather simple plot of *Les Anciens Canadiens*. The spatial setting of the novel is the very places where the author had had his own personal experiences; the main centres of the action are the town of Quebec and the manor-house of Haberville (slight modification for Aubert), to which must be added the picturesque trip along the south shore, with the old servant José Dubé as a mentor. The first part, which covers a good half of the novel (11 chapters), describes at some length seigneurial customs in 1757, at the end of the French régime. Traditional elements are deliberately given first place: the legends of the sorcerers of the Île d'Orléans and the appearance of "la Corriveau" [Marie-Josephte Corriveau*], the spring break-up, the popular feasts of the first of May (the planting of the fir-tree) and Saint-Jean, elaborate meals served as occasion requires, the paying of the seigneurial rents, etc. The protagonists are two young men who on leaving college propose to follow a military career: Jules d'Haberville, the seigneur's son, in the French army, and

Archibald Cameron of Locheil, a Scottish orphan brought from France to New France by the Jesuits after the disaster at Culloden in 1746, in the English army. They are given a warm welcome at the Haberville manor-house before they leave for Europe.

The action of the second part (three chapters only) takes place during the war of 1759. It is the climax of the collective and individual drama. The workings of destiny have brought the two young officers back to New France, but in opposite camps. Archy receives from the invader a ruthless order to burn the dwellings on the south shore, including the manor-house of his former protectors. The dictates of military discipline and honour prevail over his reluctance to carry out this sinister plan. But, taken prisoner by the Indians, the young officer escapes torture and death only because of the gratitude of Dumais, a Canadien whom he had formerly rescued from certain drowning. A little later, on the Plains of Abraham, at the time of the battle of Sainte-Foy, Archy comes face to face with his former comrade and friend. He magnanimously spares Jules d'Haberville's life, when he has him at his mercy.

The third part, also short (four chapters), tells the story of slow reconciliation after terrible years of anguish. In it Gaspé makes a critical assessment, as it were, of the misfortunes that befell New France after the shipwreck of the *Auguste*; then he shows the changes that occurred around 1767 in the environment in which his characters move. As wounds are not entirely healed, Blanche d'Haberville refuses the hand of her suitor Archy, but Jules marries an English girl. And the final episode of the novel portrays a typical scene of the times, with songs, dances, and mirth bringing back gaiety to the Haberville manor-house.

This not improbable plot was only a pretext for Gaspé, whose ambition was above all to "set down some episodes of the good old days." He received, he said, the encouragement of "some of our best writers, who begged me to omit nothing concerning the customs of the Canadians of old"; he was referring to such men as Faribault, his lifetime friend, Octave CRÉMAZIE, who wrote a prefatory poem on Quebec specially for Gaspé's book, and Joseph-Charles Taché*, whom he entrusted with his first chapters for publication in *Les Soirées canadiennes*. But he was none the less fearful of unkindly criticism. Consequently he informed purists that he was more aware than anybody of the weaknesses of his book. Let them, he exclaimed, "call it a novel, memoirs, a chronicle, a mish-mash, a hotch-potch: I care little!" The last two expressions, which do not strictly speaking represent literary categories, were without a

Aubert de Gaspé

doubt recalled to his mind by the unfavourable reception given earlier to *L'Influence d'un livre*.

But his fears were exaggerated. On 3 Jan. 1863 he read the manuscript to Abbé Casgrain; he had already published two chapters in January and February 1862. Casgrain immediately took it to Georges-Pascal Desbarats*, the publisher of *Le Foyer canadien*, where it appeared at the beginning of April. It was an immediate success. In 1864 there was a second edition "revised and corrected by the author," as well as an English translation, *The Canadians of old*. In 1865 the novel was adapted for the stage. One can say after more than a century that the popularity of this work has never declined. To the present time there has been a total of some 20 editions, including three English translations and one Spanish. The work's popularity is due not so much to the Corneille-like dilemma that faces the principal characters as to the personal recollections of the author, which abound on each page and even overflow into notes and explanations every bit as worthy of attention as the plot itself. This is because the writer of memoirs is everywhere present behind the novelist. The characters themselves are all identifiable prototypes in the family circle or among the former relations of the Gaspé family. For example, José is an old servant the author actually knew in his youth. Archy was suggested to him by an episode in the life of Lieutenant-Colonel Malcolm Fraser*. Moreover, he depicted himself at two periods of his life, first through the impulsive, spirited nature of young Jules d'Haberville, then in the person of Monsieur d'Egmont, an old man grown wise through trials similar in every respect to those Gaspé had experienced himself during his years of tribulation.

The *Mémoires* published by Gaspé in 1866 are the natural sequel to the notes and explanations in *Les Anciens Canadiens*. Once freed from the limitation of the novel form, the old author – he was then 80 – allowed his pen to run on at the command of his memory, which he himself called outstanding. He also had a high opinion of his propensity for always telling the truth. "I was born naturally truthful," he stated. Indeed, these are two qualities in which he is rarely found wanting. But there is another of which he does not boast, although he finds a way to praise it in others. That is the kindness, accompanied by a touch of humour, with which he surrounds the persons of whom he speaks. As their number exceeds a thousand, the effect is the more remarkable.

It is not easy to summarize the *Mémoires*, which do not unfold in a strictly chronological order. Roughly speaking, the author lingers more over the years previous to 1822, except in so far as his friends, the *habitants* of Saint-Jean-Port-Joli, are concerned. If he makes only brief mention of his helpmeet, "beautiful among the beautiful," and speaks only a little of his children, it is because he is writing for them. On the other hand, he never ceases to talk about the early generations of his ancestors, the families friendly with his own, and in general the society he frequented: students of the seminary of Quebec, lawyers, judges, doctors, military men, ecclesiastics, and politicians.

About each of the names he mentions he recalls anecdotes, a little at random, as he must have done during casual conversation. In short, his art is that of a brilliant conversationalist, and therefore of a story-teller. The anecdotes contained in the *Mémoires*, taken as a whole, constitute one of the best pictures we possess of Canadien society, both urban and rural, at the beginning of the 19th century. Above all Gaspé, although an aristocrat, was the first to make heard through a written work the pleasing voices of the *habitants* of the country. For his period, his work provides an unrivalled description of popular traditions of all kinds.

In a word, on many events and on a vast number of people, Gaspé sheds a light resulting from a balanced judgement, which makes the *Mémoires*, as also the posthumous fragments collected under the title of *Divers* (1893), a human testimony of major importance for Canadian history and literature. By his irreplaceable work the author of *Les Anciens canadiens* and *Mémoires* thoroughly redeemed the errors of his youth. He became the most illustrious of his line to bear the name of Gaspé. Like Alfred de Vigny he might have said, paradoxically, had it not been for his modesty: "My ancestors will spring from me."

LUC LACOURCIÈRE

AQ, Autographes, ff.68–73. Archives de l'université de Montréal, Collection Baby, Correspondance générale, dix lettres de Philippe Aubert de Gaspé. Archives du collège Bourget (Rigaud, Qué.), Philippe Aubert de Gaspé, Les Anciens Canadiens. Archives judiciaires de Montmagny (Qué.), Greffe Simon Fraser, 17 juin 1841. ASQ, Cartons, S, 110; Cartons, T, 128, 130; Fonds Casgrain, I, 115, 118–19; Fonds Casgrain, II, 17, 20.

Philippe-Joseph Aubert de Gaspé, *Les Anciens Canadiens* (1re éd., Québec, 1863; 2e éd., revue et corrigée par l'auteur, 1864; 16e éd., 1970); *The Canadians of old*, trans. G. M. Pennée (1st ed., Quebec, 1864), trans. C. G. D. Roberts (3rd ed., New York, 1898); *Divers* (1re éd., Montréal, 1893); *Mémoires* (Ottawa, 1866). Philippe Aubert de Gaspé (fils), *L'Influence d'un livre; roman historique* (1re éd., Québec, 1837).

D. M. Hayne et Marcel Tirol, *Bibliographie*

critique du roman canadien-français, 1837–1900 (Toronto and Quebec, 1968), 42–59. H. R. Casgrain, *Philippe Aubert de Gaspé* (Québec, 1871). V. I. Curran, "Philippe Aubert de Gaspé; his life and his works," unpublished PHD thesis, University of Toronto, 1957. [François Daniel], *Histoire des grandes familles françaises du Canada ...* (Montréal, 1867), 347–70. P.-G. Roy, *A travers les « Anciens Canadiens » de Philippe Aubert de Gaspé* (Montréal, 1943); *A travers les « Mémoires » de Philippe Aubert de Gaspé* (Montréal, 1943); *La famille Aubert de Gaspé* (Lévis, Qué., 1907). André Bellessort, "Les souvenirs d'un seigneur canadien," *Reflets de la vieille Amérique* (Paris, 1923), 216–58. Narcisse Degagné, "Philippe Aubert de Gaspé, étude littéraire," *Revue canadienne* (Montréal), 2e sér. XXI (1895), 456–78, 524–51. Charles ab der Halden, "Philippe Aubert de Gaspé," *Études de littérature canadienne-française* (Paris, 1904), 43–52. Luc Lacourcière, "L'enjeu des *Anciens Canadiens*," *Cahiers des Dix*, XXXII (1967), 223–54; "Philippe Aubert de Gaspé (fils)," *Livres et auteurs canadiens, 1964; panorama de la production littéraire de l'année* (Montréal, [1965]), 150–57. Camille Roy, "Les Anciens Canadiens," *Nouveaux essais sur la littérature canadienne* (Québec, 1914), 1–63.

AUMOND (Aumon), JOSEPH-IGNACE, lumber merchant; b. 21 March 1810 in L'Assomption, L.C., son of Ignace Aumon and Euphrosine Robichaud; m. Jane Cumming, 21 April 1833, by whom he had five sons and three daughters; d. 9 Nov. 1879, in Ottawa, Ont.

Joseph-Ignace Aumond went to Montreal as a clerk in the store of J. D. Bernard after having attended local schools. He then moved to the site of Bytown (Ottawa) as a storekeeper in a store opened by Bernard. A few years later he set up a general store of his own in Bytown.

Aumond entered the Ottawa valley timber trade about 1830. Within a few years he was a major figure in this trade, and in 1844 sent about 40 rafts annually to Quebec, representing nearly 2,000,000 feet of timber. He employed as many as 1,000 men and did business of more than £100,000 a year. The areas he exploited, mainly on his own account but also in conjunction with John Egan*, were along the upper Ottawa River and its tributaries. He held licences for cutting timber along the Madawaska, Petawawa, and Gatineau rivers, and in 1849 he acquired timber limits as distant from Bytown as Lake Timiskaming.

Although Aumond's business was damaged in the late 1840s by the removal of imperial preference, he remained one of the most important producers in the Ottawa valley and constructed in these years one of the largest steam sawmills in Canada. Yet by the mid-1850s he was in severe financial difficulties, and claimed to have lost £40,000 and to have been "all but ruined." How-ever, he continued in the lumber trade, on a much smaller scale, until his death and saw his son Charles established in it at Ottawa.

Aumond played a prominent part in advancing the interests of the Ottawa valley lumber trade and its focal point of Bytown. He was a member of the Ottawa Valley Lumber Association when it was formed in 1836, and two years later he was promoting the construction of an iron suspension bridge across the Ottawa. In 1846, Aumond and Egan purchased two steamers at £10,000 from John Molson* of Montreal, one to ply Lake Deschênes, east of the Chats falls, and the other Lac des Chats, west of the falls, on the Ottawa River. The two routes were linked by a horse-drawn railway constructed by Aumond, Egan, and Ruggles Wright*.

Aumond was the first president of the Bytown and Montreal Telegraph Company in 1849, and was director (Egan was president) of the Bytown and Aylmer Union Turnpike Company which completed the road between the two towns in 1850. He participated in the formation of the Bytown and Prescott Railway (later the St Lawrence and Ottawa) in 1851 and was on the first board of directors. He was also a trustee of the Consumers Gas Company formed in 1854, and a member of the first board of directors of the City Passenger Horse Railway in 1866.

As one of the principal industrialists in the community, Aumond participated actively in Ottawa's civic life. He was one of the organizers of the first regular fire company in Bytown in 1838, was on the first board of school trustees in 1842, and was appointed to the original Board of Health in 1847. He was also prominent in the Mechanics' Institute and the Board of Trade, as well as the Ottawa Association of Lumber Manufacturers. In 1874 he was persuaded to run along with J. M. Currier* in Ottawa City, a two member riding, as a Conservative supporting Sir John A. Macdonald*, but he was defeated. He had been appointed major in the 4th Battalion of Carleton militia in 1847, but was dismissed in 1850 after his name appeared, without his knowledge, on the Annexation Manifesto. He was reinstated as a major in 1856, and promoted lieutenant-colonel later that year and colonel in 1869.

The "reverses of fortune" which Aumond suffered in his long career only made it representative of the careers of many other early lumbermen in the Ottawa valley. His standing in the trade made him one of the "lumber kings," and his activities in the development of Ottawa entitle him to be called one of the area's most important founders.

HENRI PILON

PAC, MG 24, D8 (Wright papers), 12155, 12412, 12465, 17340–41, 17351; I9 (Hill collection), 8572–73, 8707; MG 30, D62 (Audet papers), 2, pp.768–829. *Ottawa Citizen*, January 1874, 10 Nov. 1879. *Ottawa Free Press*, 25 Oct. 1878. *Packet* (Bytown), 1846–51. Canada, Province of, Legislative Assembly, *Journals*, 1844–45, app. O.O., "Report of the select committee to which were referred the petition of John P. Waterston and others . . . and various other petitions, for amendments to the lumber act . . ."; 1849, app. P.P.P.P., "First report of the select committee on the lumber trade"; 1850, app. P.P., "Return to an address of the Legislative Assembly . . . regarding the setting apart of a tract of land in the valley of the river Gatineau for the use of certain Indians." [W. S. Hunter], *Hunter's Ottawa scenery, in the vicinity of Ottawa city, Canada West* (Ottawa, 1855), 12–17. *Dom. ann. reg., 1879*, 383. A. H. D. Ross, *Ottawa, past and present* (Toronto, 1927), 49, 82, 99, 139, 155–56.

AVRAY. *See* MARSHALL

AYLWIN, THOMAS CUSHING, lawyer, politician, and judge; b. 5 Jan 1806 at Quebec, son of Thomas Aylwin, merchant, and of Louise-Catherine Connolly; d. 14 Oct. 1871 at Montreal and was buried in Mount Hermon cemetery at Quebec.

Thomas Cushing Aylwin's education was at first entrusted to the Reverend Daniel Wilkie*, a Presbyterian minister, then, after a brief stay at Harvard University, Aylwin studied law with Louis Moquin, a Quebec lawyer. He was called to the bar of Lower Canada in December 1827, and rapidly acquired a reputation as an excellent criminal jurist. The young lawyer entered the rough-and-tumble of political life on the side of the *Patriotes*, and in the thick of the fight took up the defence, in the press of Lower Canada, of the prisoners whose cases he had argued.

However, it was not until after the union of the Canadas that Aylwin appeared in the assembly: he was member for Portneuf in 1841, and held the office of solicitor general for Canada East during the first government of Robert Baldwin* and Louis-Hippolyte La Fontaine*. His English Canadian origin and the fact that he represented a county in the Quebec area were largely responsible for his appointment. La Fontaine thus hoped to win over in that region the elements hostile to the Union. The control of patronage for that locality was, moreover, left in Aylwin's hands. In 1843 he was among the ministers who resigned because they did not agree with the governor, Sir Charles Theophilus Metcalfe*, on the question of the use of political patronage. Aylwin was elected member for the City of Quebec in the general elections of 1844 and 1847, and in the assembly he led the attacks, sometimes with violence according to *Le Canadien*, against the various Conservative ministries: "Short, nearsighted, and (at this time at least) never quite sober, Aylwin commanded not by his physical presence as much as by his charming, genial bluffness and, above all, by his prodigious bilingual gift for words."

When Baldwin and La Fontaine were recalled to office in March 1848, Aylwin was appointed solicitor general with William Hume Blake*, but he was the only one to hold a seat on the Executive Council. On the suggestion of Francis Hincks*, La Fontaine offered him a post as judge to make room for Blake: ". . . if Aylwin were to go on the bench," wrote Hincks, "I think it would remove the difficulty with Blake. . . ." On 26 April 1848 Aylwin became a judge in the Court of Queen's Bench, and declared himself happy to have given up political life. His electors thought otherwise: Aylwin's appointment, wrote Joseph-Édouard Cauchon*, "was censured by almost everybody, because he was too quick to get himself settled even though his services were needed." Aylwin seems, however, to have discharged his duties as judge satisfactorily; in 1854 he formed part of the Seigneurial Court responsible for instituting the transformation of the seigneurial régime. In 1868 he retired, for reasons of health.

On 2 June 1832, at Quebec, Thomas Cushing Aylwin had married Margaret Nelson Hanna; after her death, he married Eliza Margaret Felton of Sherbrooke on 14 May 1836; having become once more a widower, he married Ann Blake on 7 Sept. 1850. No child was born of any of these marriages.

ANDRÉ GARON

BNQ, Société historique de Montréal, Collection La Fontaine, Lettres, 480, 484, 491 (copies in PAC). *Le Canadien* (Québec), 16 déc. 1844. *Gazette* (Montreal), 16 Oct. 1871. *Political appointments, 1841–1865* (J.-O. Coté). P.-G. Roy, *Fils de Québec*, III, 126–28. Wallace, *Macmillan dictionary*. Dent, *Canadian portrait gallery*, IV, 105–7. Monet, *Last cannon shot*.

B

BACHAND, PIERRE, lawyer and politician; b. 22 March 1835 at Verchères, L.C., son of Joseph Bachand, a farmer, and Josephte Fontaine; d. 3 Nov. 1878 at Saint-Hyacinthe, Que.

After spending his youth at Saint-Damase, where his family lived, Pierre Bachand entered the college of Saint-Hyacinthe, but had to leave the institution before the end of his classical studies. He then began to study law under the direction of Louis-Victor Sicotte*, who had a strong influence upon his professional and political career; he was called to the bar on 3 Dec. 1860. While studying law, Pierre Bachand held at Saint-Hyacinthe the posts of deputy protonotary of the Superior Court and assistant clerk of the Circuit Court; he gave up these offices in 1862 when he entered into partnership with a lawyer of his own age, Jean-Baptiste Bourgeois, who became a judge of the Superior Court in 1876. In 1859 Bachand had married Delphine Dufort, who died in 1864, and in 1868 he remarried, his second wife being Marie-Louise Marchand, daughter of Louis Marchand, a Montreal broker. According to contemporary descriptions, Bachand was a dark-haired man, rather slender, calm, serious, active, and loquacious.

Bachand built up a large clientele for himself throughout the whole county, among both the agricultural population and the industrialists. With the advantage of railways and a number of plants using water-power, Saint-Hyacinthe experienced rapid growth, especially after 1870; its principal industries were shoe, furniture, and carriage factories, tanneries, some foundries, a brewery, and an organ works [see Joseph CASAVANT]. At the end of August 1871, with a view to promoting this industrial development, Bachand and a few prominent citizens set up the Chamber of Commerce of the district of Saint-Hyacinthe. But it was by starting the Banque de Saint-Hyacinthe that Pierre Bachand took the greatest part in the economic development of his region; this bank, which officially began financial operations on 27 Jan. 1874, made rapid progress despite the economic crisis. Bachand was its president until his death, and when in February 1878 he presented his annual report, he was able to compare the bank favourably with several much older ones. He was also active in the Société Saint-Jean-Baptiste of Saint-Hyacinthe, and was a member of its executive committee for several years.

A pupil of Louis-Victor Sicotte, Pierre Bachand, while still young, had a hand in partisan struggles. Although he shared the fears of the Rouges about confederation, he avoided identifying himself with the radical group of this party. The creation of a provincial government marked the beginning of his parliamentary career; he canvassed successfully for the provincial mandate of Saint-Hyacinthe, triumphing over Magloire LANCTÔT, a supporter of the government and a lawyer highly regarded by the bishopric of Saint-Hyacinthe. In 1867 the majority of radical Liberals aspired to a seat in the House of Commons, whereas the moderate Liberals, including Bachand, turned rather towards the provincial house. Bachand rallied to confederation and, influenced by Félix-Gabriel Marchand* of Le Franco-Canadien, for a while urged that an end be put to the partisan struggles in the Legislative Assembly of the province of Quebec. In 1871 and 1875 his mandate as an MLA was renewed without opposition.

In the house, Bachand stood out as one of the chief critics of the members of the government. During the first two sessions he was spoken of as one of the possible leaders of the opposition; it was not until March 1869 that the Liberals constituted themselves the official opposition, and they chose Henri-Gustave Joly* as their leader; Bachand and Marchand were his principal lieutenants. Throughout his parliamentary career, Bachand stressed the necessity of a reduction in the expenses of the provincial government, which had limited sources of revenue at its disposal; only a prudent budgetary policy could avoid too frequent recourse to direct taxation, the surest road to legislative union. On several occasions Bachand outlined the dangers that threatened the province's autonomy. A tenacious adversary of the double mandate, he considered the power of disallowance vested in the federal government baneful and urged the provincial cabinet to free itself from the tutelage of the central government. Bachand was interested in modernizing agriculture, was alarmed at the disastrous emigration of French Canadians to the United States, demanded that justice be administered in a less costly way and made more accessible, and argued that greater attention should be given to primary education and to "industrial and commercial education."

Although a provincial representative, Bachand did not remain aloof from the political struggles on the federal scene. Thus, on the occasion of the "Pacific Scandal" [see CARTIER], he was a leading figure on the hustings in the Saint-Hyacinthe region, together with his associate, Jean-Baptiste Bourgeois, the "Danton of the Reform party," and Honoré Mercier*, whose reputation as an orator already extended beyond the frontiers of the county. Bachand took part in the organization of the Parti National at the end of 1871 [see Cartier] and was a member of the council of the reform association of the Parti National of Montreal.

During the session 1877–78, Charles-Eugène Boucher* de Boucherville's government had to face the violent attacks of the opposition, who criticized the laying of the railway between Quebec and Montreal and the famous bill of the attorney general, Auguste-Réal Angers*, which forced

Back

municipalities to pay the subsidies promised for the building of the railway; on this occasion, Joly entrusted Bachand with the task of leading the Liberal troops in the attack. Following Lieutenant Governor Luc Letellier* de Saint-Just's "coup d'état," which dismissed the administration of Boucherville, Joly offered Bachand the post of provincial treasurer; it was the first time a Liberal and a Francophone had held this office. He defended the lieutenant governor's position vigorously, and assumed such an importance in the Liberal cabinet that the newspapers spoke of the "Joly-Bachand administration."

In the 1878 election Bachand had to face an outstanding candidate in his county: Antoine Casavant, a farmer from Saint-Domingue, nephew of Joseph, a member of the agricultural council of the province, and active in several industrial undertakings. Casavant could appeal to the solidarity of the agricultural class, and bank on a certain rivalry between the town of Saint-Hyacinthe and the surrounding country districts; Bachand, however, won with a majority of 68 votes. On 18 June 1878, during the stormy session of that year, he made his financial report, and set at $2,334,041 the financial estimates for the following year: it was the first time the budget speech was delivered in French in the Legislative Assembly of the province of Quebec. Ill and exhausted, Bachand found it difficult to take part in the business of the session, and the preparation of the budget required considerable effort on his part. On 3 Nov. 1878, after an illness of some months, he died at the age of 43. His funeral took place on 6 Nov. 1878 at Saint-Hyacinthe.

MARCEL HAMELIN

PAC, MG 30, D62 (Audet papers), 3, pp.131–32. *Le Courrier de Saint-Hyacinthe*, 31 août, 14 sept. 1867; 31 déc. 1869; 16 févr., 22 juin, 5 nov., 7 nov. 1878. *L'Événement* (Québec), 1er mai 1868, 13 déc. 1869, 13 mars 1878. *L'Opinion publique* (Montréal), 14 nov. 1878. *Le Pionnier de Sherbrooke*, 8 nov. 1878. *Can. parl. comp., 1878.* Auguste Achintre, *Portraits et dossiers parlementaires du premier parlement de Québec* (Montréal, 1871), 24–26. C.-P. Choquette, *Histoire de la ville de Saint-Hyacinthe* (Saint-Hyacinthe, Qué., 1930), 292–96. Rumilly, *Hist. de la prov. de Québec*, I, II.

BACK, Sir GEORGE, naval officer, Arctic explorer, and artist; b. 6 Nov. 1796 in Stockport, England, second son of John and Ann Back; d. 23 June 1878 in London.

The heroic exploits of the Royal Navy during the Napoleonic wars stimulated George Back's desire to go to sea, and a visit to Liverpool confirmed it. His father therefore took him to London and, with the help of a relative, he joined HMS *Arethusa* as first class volunteer on 15 Sept. 1808. Shortly afterwards, *Arethusa* joined battles off Cherbourg and along the north coast of Spain. In April 1809, when serving near San Sebastian in one of the boats seeking prizes, he was captured by French soldiers. From there he travelled to Verdun, where he spent the next five years as a prisoner of war. Although he began to "associate with dissolute characters and see something of vice and roguery," he soon settled down to resume his education in drawing and French. He was released early in 1814 and returned to England in May.

On 4 July 1814 he joined HMS *Akbar*, stationed at Halifax, Nova Scotia, as midshipman. He saw plenty of action before his ship returned to Portsmouth in December 1816. On 5 March 1817 Back was appointed passed Admiralty midshipman on board HMS *Bulwark*. This ship remained at Chatham, where, by his own account, he spent his time "drawing, reading and studying." After a request for promotion was refused, he volunteered for service under Commanders John Ross* and David Buchan* in an expedition that opened a new era of British Arctic exploration. He was appointed midshipman on board HM brig *Trent* in the expedition's eastern branch under Buchan, who was ordered to sail *Dorothea* and *Trent* across the Arctic Ocean from Spitsbergen to Bering Strait. Ross, commanding the western branch, was to attempt a northwest passage by way of Davis Strait. *Dorothea* and *Trent* left the Thames on 25 April 1818 and returned on 22 October, having spent a perilous three weeks beset in the ice off Spitsbergen, their only success being a record latitude of 82°34′N.

Although the expedition itself was a failure, it provided Back with the key to his future by bringing him into contact with Lieutenant John Franklin*, commanding officer of the *Trent*. Franklin's flattering report of Back's conduct, and particularly of his usefulness as an artist, was to make him a natural choice for the overland expedition that Franklin himself led in 1819 to explore the north coast of America from the mouth of the Coppermine River to Repulse Bay.

Back returned to *Bulwark* for a short time, then, on 23 May 1819, set out with Franklin for York Factory on the Hudson's Bay Company ship *Prince of Wales*. Dr John Richardson*, a naturalist, Robert Hood*, another midshipman, and John Hepburn*, a seaman, completed the party from England. The expedition passed one winter at Cumberland House, and a second at Fort Enterprise, a base camp they had built by Winter Lake, between Great Slave Lake and the Coppermine River.

Soon after their arrival at Winter Lake, Franklin asked Back to return south to hasten the passage of essential goods expected from Cumberland House. He set out on 18 Oct. 1820, and on 2 Jan. 1821 arrived at the trading posts on Lake Athabasca. Here, George Simpson*, who had recently taken charge of the HBC's Athabasca department, was justifiably irritated by Back's rudeness and impatience. "That Gentleman," he wrote of Back, "seems to think that every thing must give way to his demands." A month later the goods arrived, and Back returned with them to Fort Enterprise, saving the expedition from early failure.

On 14 July 1821 the party left their base in two canoes, descended the Coppermine River to the sea, then explored the coast as far east as Bathurst Inlet. Here, short supplies, the approach of winter, and unrest among their Canadian voyageurs obliged them to abandon hope of reaching Repulse Bay. Dogged by starvation and increasing debility, the party struggled back overland across the barren tundra towards Fort Enterprise. Half the party was saved when Back, who had gone ahead to search for Indians, located a tribe and sent them to the main group with supplies. Ten men, including Hood, died before he could send help.

These two courageous life-saving journeys, together with his numerous fine paintings of northern scenes, leave a strong impression of Back's contribution to this ill-fated expedition, but indications are that he did not always live up to a hero's reputation. A number of fur-traders spoke critically of him, but charges made years later by John Hepburn are probably the most reliable and are supported by similar accusations levelled at Back by others through much of his life. Hepburn recalled a quarrel between Back and Hood over an Indian woman, which nearly ended in a duel – behaviour in line with Back's later reputation as a dandy and a womanizer. He also held that "Back is not very brave . . . he is charming to those from whom he hopes to gain something." There are echoes of this remark in the description of Back that Sophia Cracroft, Franklin's niece, gave to Henry Grinnell in 1856: "He is never the man to originate a handsome act, but if he finds it popular, and that it will be successful, he steps in to take as much of the credit as he can secure. You must not think it harshness or severity when I describe him as intensely selfish, sly, and sycophantic."

Back was promoted lieutenant on 1 Jan. 1821 when the expedition was still in progress. Soon after his arrival in England in October 1822, he returned to service at sea to gain the qualifications necessary for promotion to commander. During his absence on HMS *Superb*, which was stationed in the West Indies, appointments were made for Franklin's second overland expedition to explore the coast eastwards and westwards from the mouth of the Mackenzie River. The Admiralty apparently wanted to reappoint Back, but Franklin had been poorly impressed by Back's conduct during the first land expedition and encouraged them to appoint Lieutenant John Bushnan instead. However, Bushnan died before the expedition left, and Back was then invited to take part. He readily accepted the offer and joined Franklin in London in December 1824.

By contrast with the first overland expedition, this one went ahead smoothly and almost without incident. The newly reorganized HBC was better able to fulfil its promise of assistance. The planning was better in London also; supplies were sent out well in advance, and British seamen replaced Canadian voyageurs who, the explorers felt, were less reliable.

The party arrived by packet in New York in March 1825 and travelled to Great Bear Lake, where they built Fort Franklin on the western shore. After a winter there, they set out for the Mackenzie delta on 22 June 1826. At Point Separation the party divided. Richardson and Edward Nicholas Kendall*, the surveyor, in the 24-foot boats *Dolphin* and *Union*, explored the coast eastward to the mouth of the Coppermine River; Franklin and Back, in the 26-foot boats *Lion* and *Reliance*, set their course westward towards Bering Strait where HMS *Blossom* (Capt. Frederick W. Beechey*) was awaiting them.

Soon after reaching the sea, on 7 July, Franklin and Back spent an exhausting day fighting off Eskimos who tried to raid the boats, but the main impediment was poor weather and ice conditions. Six weeks' coasting brought them to Return Reef, only half-way to Icy Cape, so, with winter fast approaching and supplies dwindling, Franklin decided to turn back. They reached Fort Franklin on 21 Sept. 1826, three weeks after Richardson and Kendall, who had completed their survey [see BEAULIEU]. During the winter Back learned he had been promoted commander on 30 Dec. 1825.

By the end of this second expedition, Franklin, Back, and Richardson had explored along half the length of America's northern coast – from Kent Peninsula to Prudhoe Bay, Alaska. The prospect of completing this north coast survey – from Kent Peninsula to Melville Peninsula – remained on Back's mind for many years; it was partly for this reason that he undertook his 1833–35 expedition, and it was the sole object of his abortive 1836–37 voyage.

Franklin made free use of Back's watercolours and drawings to illustrate his published narratives of both land expeditions. As the products of one

Back

of the first competent artists to penetrate into the Canadian Arctic, these illustrations are now considered an invaluable record of early northern history. Those which Franklin published are still used to illustrate books on northern exploration, but many other fine drawings, watercolours, and sketch-books from Back's three land expeditions, still preserved in the Public Archives of Canada, in the Scott Polar Research Institute, and elsewhere, remain unused and virtually unknown.

After his return to England on 10 Oct. 1827, Back tried for nearly three years to obtain another appointment. At the same time his health began to fail and he decided to restore himself by making a tour of Europe. Setting out on 3 Aug. 1830, he travelled up the Rhine to Switzerland, then spent more than a year visiting the artistic centres of Italy. In January 1832, when he was in Naples, he was disquieted by rumours about John Ross, who had not been heard of since he had set out on an attempt at a northwest passage in 1829. Back returned to England at once and offered to command a search. He learned that Dr Richardson had already submitted a plan for reaching Ross by way of the Thlew-ee-choh or Great Fish River (Back River), a river known only by Indian report, which was supposed to rise somewhere near Great Slave Lake and flow northwest into the Arctic Ocean. Richardson had received insufficient support and stepped down. Back adopted the same plan and raised enough support from the government, the HBC, and public subscription to go ahead with the expedition under the direction of the Colonial Office.

Taking with him Dr Richard KING as naturalist, Back left Liverpool by packet for New York on 17 Feb. 1833. In June he was at Fort Alexander on Lake Winnipeg, where George Simpson, now governor of all the HBC's activities overseas, greeted him cordially, apparently having forgotten their brush in 1821. From Fort Resolution Back set out to search for the Thlew-ee-choh and located it on 29 August. He then returned to the expedition's wintering station, Fort Reliance, at the eastern end of Great Slave Lake. When news reached him in spring 1834 of Ross's safe return to England, it only remained for him to explore the Thlew-ee-choh and the seacoast adjoining its mouth.

On 7 June 1834 his party left the fort for their depot on Artillery Lake, and, travelling by Clinton-Colden Lake and Aylmer Lake, reached the Thlew-ee-choh on 28 June. The descent of this river took them one month, after which they spent three weeks exploring Chantrey Inlet. Poor weather prevented their making a more extensive survey of the sea-coast, and they were back in Fort Reliance on 27 September. On 21 March 1835 Back left for England, leaving King to follow with the men and equipment.

Arriving in England on 8 Sept. 1835, Back received a hero's welcome. He was promoted captain on 30 Sept. 1835 by order in council, an honour that had only one precedent and that was necessary in Back's case because he had not served the prescribed year at sea since being made commander. Among other honours he received the royal medal of the Royal Geographical Society, and, on 8 Feb. 1836, was elected a fellow. The Thlew-ee-choh gradually became known as the Back River.

Richard King was noticeably absent from the throng of Back's admirers. He evidently believed that the expedition might have achieved much more and his narrative shows that his opinions frequently differed from Back's. Like HBC employee Thomas Simpson*, who met the expedition in 1833, he considered Back a weak leader, but above all he resented Back's interference with his duties as a naturalist.

King, however, had a way of making himself unpopular, and little notice was taken of his complaints. The high regard with which Back was generally held enabled him to dictate terms for a further expedition. On his behalf the Royal Geographical Society approached the government with a scheme that Back had had in mind since 1828: to take a ship to Repulse Bay or Wager River, and then trace the coast by boat as far as Point Turnagain, the farthest point reached by Franklin on the first land expedition. Back was given command of HMS *Terror* and the expedition set out in June 1836. Among the officers of the *Terror* were mates Graham Gore, who later perished in the ill-fated Franklin expedition, and Robert McCLURE, who in 1850–54 commanded *Investigator* in search of Franklin. The year was notoriously bad for ice throughout the whole of the eastern Arctic and the 325-ton *Terror* with her crew of 60 men was beset in August on entering Frozen Strait. She drifted throughout the winter in the pack off northeast Southampton Island and suffered heavy damage. When freed in July 1837, Back had no alternative but to turn homeward. He landed with his ship in a sinking condition at Lough Swilly in Ireland on 3 Sept. 1837.

Further honours followed this expedition, among them the gold medal of the Société de Géographie de Paris and a knighthood on 18 March 1839. Although Back was now only 40 years old, this voyage proved to be the last of his naval career. His health had weakened during the expedition and it continued to deteriorate. In July 1839 he took the cure at Marienbad (Mariánské Lázně), a fashionable German spa. Finding this treatment ineffective, he travelled to Italy, where he remained until 1842. In 1844 Francis Rawdon Moira Crozier*, who was to die on the Franklin expedition, wrote to James Clark Ross* from Florence that Back had not left a good impression behind him, and that he had gained a reputation for vanity. "He was a very pleasant fellow," one man told Crozier, "but if he was in love with himself he had no right to suppose every lady he met was the same."

Returning to England, Back led a comfortable life in London society and maintained an active interest in Arctic exploration, which was again entering the news. He opposed the choice of Franklin as commander of the 1845 expedition on grounds of age and encouraged James Ross to accept the appointment. On 13 Oct. 1846 he married Theodosia Elizabeth Hammond, a widow, spent six months with her in Italy, and returned in August 1847 to take an active part in the preparation of expeditions in search of Franklin. He served with a number of other Arctic veterans on the Arctic council which advised the Admiralty about preparing search expeditions. Unhappily Back and nearly all other members of the council were completely wrong in their opinions on the whereabouts of the missing men, and their advice resulted in the Admiralty's sending expeditions to all the wrong places. In 1851 he served on the Admiralty's Arctic committee, which met to investigate the conduct of Horatio Austin* and William Penny* on their respective expeditions. In 1856 the Admiralty made its final decision to abandon the Franklin search, and Back, almost alone among the Arctic veterans, agreed with them. He was forcibly condemned by Sophia Cracroft, who had for some time disliked him. "That miserable Sir G. Back," she wrote, "will say anything that a Lord of the Admiralty tells him, and is held in contempt or something worse by all who have served with him" [see Jane GRIFFIN].

With the end of the Franklin search, Back withdrew again into quiet retirement, receiving promotion to rear-admiral on the reserve list on 19 March 1857. He had been made an honorary doctor of civil law at Oxford University in 1854. Until the end of his life he participated actively in the Royal Geographical Society, of which he was vice-president for seven years and a member in council for many more. He was promoted vice-admiral on 24 Sept. 1863 and admiral on 18 Oct. 1876. One of his last acts in public life, on 6 Dec. 1876, was to preside over a meeting of Arctic veterans who had gathered to greet the returning expedition commanded by George Strong Nares* in *Alert* and *Discovery*. Thus this man who had been a leading figure from the first of Britain's great 19th century expeditions to the Canadian Arctic survived just long enough to witness the return of the last.

CLIVE A. HOLLAND

SPRI, MS 248/249/2 (letter from Sophia Cracroft, 8 April 1857); MS 248/250/4 (letter from Sophia Cracroft, 4 July 1856); MS 248/364/22 (letter from F. R. M. Crozier to James Clark Ross, 31 Dec. 1844); MS 395 (George Back papers including most of his journals and diaries, correspondence with the Admiralty, Sir John Franklin, and other Arctic officers, and official certificates, all on loan from J. Pares). McCord Museum, McGill University, Montreal, George Back papers (two journals and some correspondence, not used in the preparation of this biography). Royal Geographical Society (London), Back papers (a large collection not used in the preparation of this biography).

George Back, *Narrative of the Arctic land expedition to the mouth of the Great Fish River, and along the shores of the Arctic Ocean, in the years 1833, 1834, and 1835* (London, 1836); *Narrative of an expedition in HMS* Terror, *undertaken with a view to geographical discovery on the Arctic shores, in the years 1836–7* (London, 1838). *Les bourgeois de la Compagnie du Nord-Ouest; récits de voyages, lettres et rapports inédits relatifs au Nord-Ouest canadien,* L.-F.-R. Masson, édit. (2v., Québec, 1889–90; New York, 1960), I, 130–50. John Franklin, *Narrative of a journey to the shores of the polar sea, in the years 1819, 20, 21 and 22 . . .* (London, 1823); *Narrative of a second expedition to the shores of the polar sea, in the years 1825, 1826 and 1827 . . .* (London, 1828). HBRS, I (Rich), 205–61, 313–14. Richard King, *Narrative of a journey to the shores of the Arctic Ocean, in 1833, 1834, and 1835, under the command of Capt. Back* (2v., London, 1836).

The author also had access to manuscripts in the possession of Mrs Cell (Hopton Hall, Wirksworth, Derbyshire, Eng.), letters from John Franklin to John Richardson, 1823–24.

BADDELEY, FREDERICK HENRY, soldier and geologist; b. in London, England, 4 Dec. 1794; d. at Havre des Pas, Island of Jersey, 4 May 1879.

Frederick Henry Baddeley was commissioned 2nd lieutenant in the Royal Engineers from the Royal Military Academy, Woolwich, England, on 1 Jan. 1814. He served in Europe during the Napoleonic wars and was present at the capture of Paris in 1815. He was in the West Indies from 1817 to 1819, and in 1821 was posted to Quebec in Lower Canada. On 9 March 1822 he married Susan Green; the first six of their seven children were born at Quebec, and the last in Madras, India.

Baddeley was one of the original members of the Literary and Historical Society of Quebec in

Baddeley

1824 and served as its president in 1829. He read numerous papers before the society describing exploring expeditions he undertook in Canada and giving his observations on the geology of the country. In 1827 he reported to Colonel Elias Walker Durnford*, the commanding officer of the Royal Engineers at Quebec, on a possible "extensive formation of limestone" on the Rivière Saint-Maurice suitable for quarrying, and in that year was chosen a member of an exploring expedition in the area of the "King's Posts," lying north of Quebec and including the head waters of the Saguenay and Lac Saint-Jean. While Joseph Bouchette* led one party up the Rivière Saint-Maurice, Baddeley accompanied Andrew Stuart*, chief commissioner of the expedition, and Joseph Hamel to Tadoussac and up the Saguenay before exploring the shores of Lac Saint-Jean and then the area behind Baie-Saint-Paul. Baddeley's attention was focussed mainly on "mineralogical inquiries," but he also reported extensively on the area around Baie-Saint-Paul and its suitability for settlement.

In 1831 Baddeley explored the Îles de la Madeleine "for the purpose of reporting on the resources, localities, capabilities . . . ," as well as on the military significance of the area. Although he stayed only five days he presented an exhaustive paper on the islands to the Literary and Historical Society of Quebec. Two years later he again joined Hamel in exploring the interior of the Gaspé peninsula.

Baddeley was promoted captain on 25 June 1835, shortly after being chosen to accompany John Carthew on an expedition to explore the country north of the dividing line between the Home and Newcastle districts in Upper Canada, towards Lake Nipissing, and to report on the natural features of the area and its capacity to support settlement. On this venture into the Muskoka district, which he described as "slightly dangerous," Baddeley went primarily as a geologist, but his report is also of interest to naturalists and historians. He returned to Quebec but in 1837 he was posted to Kingston, Upper Canada. He was also appointed in that year a commissioner, along with John Macaulay* and John Solomon Cartwright*, to superintend a survey for a useful link by water between the Ottawa River and Lake Huron. He was troubled from the outset of the project; he resigned at one point because he felt that his other duties would not leave him sufficient time to carry out the functions of commissioner, but he later withdrew his resignation. He was unhappy too with the choice of David Thompson*, the first white man to descend the Columbia River, to lead one of the survey's three exploring parties, claiming that "there are rumours about that

Mr. T. is not trustworthy as to reporting of facts" and that "he would please me better if he had a more humble opinion of his woodland lore."

Baddeley was transferred to Toronto in late 1837, and the aftermath of the rebellion of that year led him to inquire into the defences of the colony. For much of the next two years he reported on the protection afforded to such places as Cornwall, Kingston, and the southwestern peninsula. He was commanding royal engineer at Toronto when, in September 1839, he sailed for England and brought his Canadian career to an end.

Baddeley lived for some time in Glasgow before going to serve in Ceylon in 1842. He was posted in New South Wales from 1849 to 1851 and in New Zealand from 1853 to 1856. He was promoted major in 1846 and major-general in 1856 when he retired and returned to England. His last years were spent in Jersey. He had been a member of the British Association for the Advancement of Science and the Société géologique de France.

The geology of much of southeastern Canada was first studied extensively by British military officers. Baddeley, a well-trained and meticulous observer as well as an ambitious man, was one of the pioneers, and the value of his work was recognized by later geologists such as William Edmond LOGAN. Richard Henry Bonnycastle* considered him the "most active and best geologist then in Canada."

HENRI PILON

F. H. Baddeley was the author of the following papers in the Lit. and Hist. Soc. of Quebec *Trans.*: "Additional notes on the geognosy of Saint Paul's Bay," II (1830), 76–94; "An essay on the localities of metallic minerals in the Canadas, with some notices of their geological associations and situation . . . ," II (1830), 332–426; "A geological sketch of the most southeastern portion of Lower Canada," III (1833), 271–81; "Geology of a portion of the Labrador coast," I (1824–29), 71–79; "On the geognosy of a part of the Saguenay country," I (1824–29), 79–166; "On the Magdalen Islands, being the substance of four reports," III (1833), 128–90. He was also author of "Discovery of gold in Lower Canada" and "Waterline made from the rock of Quebec," *American Journal of Science* (New Haven, Conn.), XXVIII (1835), 111–14, and "On the geology and mineralogy of Canada," British Association for the Advancement of Science, *Report*, X (1840), Notices and abstracts . . . , 114–15.

PAC, MG 24, F53 (Sir William Henry Clinton collection); RG 1, L3ᴸ, 27, 14767–984; RG 4, B48; RG 8, I, A1, 370, 441–47, 601, 612–14, 1406. PAO, Macaulay family papers, 1837; Misc. 1835, F. H. Baddeley, "Exploring report in Upper Canada in 1835 (north west of the Matchedash, in the direction of the French River)" (printed in Upper Canada, House of Assembly, *Appendix to journal*, 1836–37, app.37, "Report of Lieut. Baddeley, R.E. ...," pp.8–42). PRO, WO 25/3913. R. H. Bonnycastle, *The Canadas in 1841* (2v., London, 1842), I, 58; II, 18–19, 149–50, 319. Lower Canada, House of Assembly, *Journal*, 1828–29, app.V, "Report of the commissioners for exploring the Saguenay." *Muskoka and Haliburton* (Murray). *The centenary volume of the Literary and Historical Society of Quebec, 1824–1924*, ed. Henry Ievers (Quebec, 1924), 18, 96, 104–5. Christie, *History of Lower Canada*, III, 202–5.

BAGG, STANLEY CLARK, notary, large landowner, justice of the peace, president of the Numismatic and Antiquarian Society of Montreal and of the English Workingmen's Benefit Society; b. 23 Dec. 1820 at Montreal, only son of Stanley Bagg*, an important businessman, and of Mary Ann Clark; d. 8 Aug. 1873 in his birth-place.

The Bagg family claimed to be of Norman descent. At the end of the 18th century Stanley Clark's grandfather emigrated from England to America. At his death he left large estates in Durham County, England, to his son Stanley. The latter then launched out into business and took part in the political life of Lower Canada; he was one of the principal figures in the Montreal West election of 1832 [*see* MONDELET].

Stanley Clark Bagg began his studies under the direction of a Church of England minister, and completed them at McGill University. He became a notary on 31 May 1842, and carried on his profession for 14 years; then, following the death of his father, gave it up to devote himself to managing his property. He was at that time the largest landowner on Montreal Island after the Sulpicians. He was to give the town the land necessary for the building of several streets and squares.

A die-hard Conservative, Bagg was a close friend of John Alexander Macdonald*. He refused to run for parliament but none the less worked for the party. During the insurrection of 1837 he had shown his loyalty to the crown by enlisting as a standard-bearer, and he took part in the battle of Saint-Eustache. The fact that he was chosen to fill the post of justice of the peace for the district of Montreal in 1859 is evidence of his capability, and of the respect in which he was held by the civil authorities. In the following year he took an active part in Montreal's reception of the Prince of Wales, on the occasion of the opening of Victoria Bridge [*see* HODGES]. In January 1865 a deputation of seven representatives, from each district of the town of Montreal, asked him to stand as a candidate for the mayoralty, but he refused, since he was more concerned with various philanthropic projects and with the cultural progress of his fellow-citizens.

Stanley Clark Bagg was interested primarily in numismatics and archaeology. Adélard-Joseph Boucher*, Joseph-Amable Manseau, and he met at the houses of one or the other to discuss their favourite occupation and to share their discoveries. From these small gatherings grew the idea of a society. The Numismatic Society of Montreal, already with 20 members, was in actual fact founded on 9 Dec. 1862. The object of the new association was to study numismatics and to set up both a collection of medals and coins and a library. In 1866 it became the Numismatic and Antiquarian Society of Montreal, giving an important place to the study of archaeology. In 1872 the society started a journal, entitled *Canadian Antiquarian and Numismatic Journal*, which was intended to make its principles and its activities more widely known. The society's main task was, however, to establish a museum of Canadian archaeology and numismatics in the building known as the Château de Ramezay, whose construction went back to the year 1705. Bagg was president of the society in 1866–67.

Being anxious to share his knowledge with his fellow-citizens, Bagg published numerous scientific articles in the local newspapers. The English and American press also published his research, which they considered to be of great value. Among his principal writings may be mentioned: *Notes on coins* ... (1863), *Coins and medals as aids to the study and verification of holy writ* (1863), *A chronological numismatic compendium of the twelve Caesars* ... (1864), *Archæologia Americana* (1864), *Canadian archaeology* (1864), and a lecture, *The antiquities and legends of Durham* ... (1866). His insatiable liking for new discoveries, his spirit of initiative, and the need to exchange his knowledge with other scholars, led Bagg to join various local or international scientific associations, and to remain in contact with foreign researchers. He became a life member of the British Association for the Advancement of Science, the Natural History Society of Montreal, the Mechanics' Institute, and numismatic societies in London and Philadelphia. He was in addition a corresponding member of the Wisconsin State Historical Society.

Stanley Clark Bagg also took an interest in several philanthropic organizations. He was one of the founders of the English Workingmen's Benefit Society, and its first president. This benevolent society rendered inestimable service to hundreds of families who were forced to have recourse to it. A life member of the Young Men's Christian Association, founded in 1851 at Montreal, Bagg also accepted the responsibilities of the vice-presidency of the Montreal dispensary and the office of governor of the Protestant House of

Baptist

Industry and Refuge. Furthermore, he was the author of a number of hymns composed specially for Christmas, Good Friday, Easter, and Ascension Day.

In 1844 Stanley Clark Bagg had married Catharine, eldest daughter of Robert Mitcheson and Frances MacGregor, who was descended from the chief of the MacGregor clan and the old Scottish kings. They had one son, Robert Stanley*. Stanley Clark Bagg died on 8 Aug. 1873 at the family manor-house, Fairmount. His family was one of the oldest English families on Montreal Island, and one of those whose members were prominent in social, financial, religious, and intellectual circles. Stanley Clark Bagg was a worthy representative of what one might call the Anglo-Saxon "establishment" of Montreal. The names of Clark, Bagg, and Fairmount streets were chosen by the municipality of Montreal in his honour.

PIERRE LANDRY

S. C. Bagg, *The antiquities and legends of Durham, a lecture before the Numismatic and Antiquarian Society* (Montreal, 1866); *Archæologia Americana* (Montreal, 1864); *Canadian archaeology* (Montreal, 1864); *A chronological numismatic compendium of the twelve Caesars, and a summary of remarkable events from the birth of Julius Caesar, B.C. 100, to the death of Saint John the Evangelist, A.D. 100* (Montreal, 1864); *Coins and medals as aids to the study and verification of holy writ* (Montreal, 1863); *Notes on coins: being the first paper read before the Numismatic Society of Montreal* (Montreal, 1863).

AJM, Greffe de Stanley Clark Bagg, 1842–1856. *Can. biog. dict.*, II, 43–45. Morgan, *Bibliotheca Canadensis*, 15. Atherton, *Montreal*, III, 406–10. Borthwick, *Montreal*, 42. Lareau, *Hist. de la littérature canadienne*, 352–53. *Toponymie* (Service d'urbanisme de la ville de Montréal, Bulletin d'information, no.4, [Montréal], 1966), 35. "In Memoriam, Stanley Clark Bagg, esq., J.P., F.N.S.," *Canadian Antiquarian and Numismatic J.*, II, no.1 (1873), 73–78. Victor Morin, "Clubs et sociétés notoires d'autrefois," *Cahiers des Dix*, XIV (1949), 212–13. Léon Trépanier, "L'historique de nos noms de rues," *La Patrie* (Montréal), 22 mai 1949.

BAPTIST, GEORGE, logging contractor; b. 7 Jan. 1808 at Coldstream, a small town in Berwickshire, Scotland; d. 11 May 1875 at Trois-Rivières, Quebec.

Nothing specific is known about George Baptist's childhood and adolescence. In 1832 he emigrated to Canada, and first went to live near Lake Etchemin (Dorchester County, Quebec); he was employed in the sawmills of Sir John Caldwell* and acquired valuable experience for his future career. In 1834 he was at Pointe de Lévy, where he worked in the flour-mills. He apparently combined this occupation with the management of a similar mill on the Rivière Jacques-Cartier (Portneuf County). These activities did not in the end take him away from the logging business, since in 1846 he bought the sawmill on the Rivière Cachée, in the Saint-Maurice region; this mill had lain abandoned for two years following the death of its owner, the assemblyman Edward Greives*.

By the time George Baptist settled in the Saint-Maurice region, several inventories of its economic resources had already been made. In 1829, as a result of the preliminary inquiry by Joseph Bouchette* in 1828, the government of Lower Canada had entrusted to Lieutenant F. L. Ingall the mission "of exploring more thoroughly a certain part of the province between the Saint-Maurice and Ottawa Rivers that was still barren and uncultivated." Ingall stressed in his report that the rocky, sandy soil of the Saint-Maurice area was not suitable for agriculture; the forests, however, were rich in red and white pine, although spruce was the most common.

Ingall's team had noticed logs floating on the Rivière Bostonnais; already, in this period, men were cutting down trees on the upper Saint-Maurice. It is probable that the owners of the ironworks claimed exclusive rights for themselves, particularly on the Saint-Étienne fief. The fruitless petitions of Peter Patterson* (1831) and John Thompson (1836) to obtain cutting rights on these lands are suggestive in that respect. This situation forced less wealthy entrepreneurs to go higher up the river, and delayed the real exploitation of the enormous lumber potential of the Saint-Maurice basin. Furthermore, the Saint-Maurice appeared to be a "detestable timber route": its difficult course became unnavigable between Les Piles and Shawinigan, where it was interrupted by numerous falls.

Government action for the purpose of harnessing the Saint-Maurice became apparent only towards the end of the 1840s. During this period the Quebec economy was marked by a flow of capital into logging operations. The government, spurred on by the action of the contractors, ordered a systematic survey to be made of the Saint-Maurice region in 1847–48; in 1851 it started on the construction of slides and booms; finally, in 1852, the commission headed by Étienne PARENT proposed a policy of making grants of crown lands. This clearing of the way made it possible for Trois-Rivières to emerge from the lethargy that had beset it since the end of its fur-trading era, and to share once more in economic growth, which was now symbolized by lumber camps, cribs, and sawmills.

It is in these changes in economic structure,

which began to take shape at the dawn of the second half of the 19th century, that the origin of the formation of the "brotherhood of the Saint-Maurice barons" is to be found. The Gilmours, Halls, Studders, Norcrosses, Philippses, and Baptists were its principal representatives. Baptist was going to compete seriously with these logging entrepreneurs. Georges Gouin, one of the rare French Canadians operating in this sector on a commercial basis, had great difficulty in surviving; according to him the Baptist undertaking was the cause of his disappointments, since it controlled "almost all the Saint-Maurice, now that Norcross, Hall [George Benson HALL] and the others have gone bankrupt or have withdrawn."

In 1847 George Baptist built a mill at Les Grès. His employees came to live in progressively greater numbers in the neighbourhood of the establishment; this led to the formation of the parish of Saint-Étienne-des-Grès in 1859. Ten years later the notary Petrus Hubert*, when describing George Baptist's holdings (sometimes called the "domain of Les Grès"), enumerated a mill, houses, stables for horses, shops, sheds, and other outbuildings; the estate stretched the length of lots 42 to 47 inclusive, which were situated in the first range of the township of Saint-Maurice. Baptist also owned, in the same range and in the same township, lots 34, 35, and 36 on the Gabelle, plus the south-east half of lot 62. It was probably on these lots that he constructed a "dalle" which allowed his logs to bypass the falls on the Gabelle and continue their journey towards Trois-Rivières and Quebec in cribs. Pierre Dupin estimated that in 1852 the mill's production was "25,730 logs for which he [Dupin] paid $2,124.00, a little more than nine cents a log." Although this estimate did not take into account all the production costs, Baptist none the less had a comfortable profit margin.

George Baptist, like the bourgeois of this period, thought that profits must increase. For a year he had been the owner of part of the Île Saint-Christophe, and as early as 1854 he considered constructing a second mill at Trois-Rivières itself. This desire did not take concrete form until 1866, when he built a magnificent one on the Île de la Potherie. This modern mill, worked by steam and fitted with circular saws, contrasted with that at Les Grès; there, the energy produced by a paddle-wheel was transmitted to the alternating saws, which were mounted on crank-arms. Finally, the purchase of the steamboat *Arthur* completed the new equipment. The site of this mill was exceptional; not only was its builder the exclusive owner of the Île de la Potherie, which was situated at the mouth of the Saint-Maurice River, but he

also owned two stretches of land on either side of the river. The site offered the advantage of reducing costs of transportation and maintenance, since boats took on their cargoes of lumber practically at the doors of the mill. This strategic position, added to a technical innovation, influenced the production of the mill and conferred on the Baptist firm a prime place among the "brotherhood of the barons."

The governing body is the cornerstone of an undertaking of this type. When he started in the Saint-Maurice region, Baptist collaborated with Thomas and John Gordon; soon the latter withdrew from the company. In 1853, at least, Baptist and Thomas Gordon were partners under the name of George Baptist and Company. For some time Baptist directed affairs alone, before becoming president, in 1869, of a new company. By the provisions of the latter, the father held half the shares of the firm of George Baptist and Sons; his two sons, Alexander* and John, owned a quarter each. Following Alexander's defection in 1875, a new company, George Baptist, Son and Company, was formed, and James Dean, George's son-in-law, joined it. In addition to the directors were the managers; the elder son, Alexander, was manager at the lumber camps, and his brother John at the mill at Les Grès. Finally foremen and workers are essential to the smooth running of an undertaking, at the mill and on the farms as well as in the lumber camps. John Skroeder, for instance, was a foreman who hired 30 individuals, on condition that they complied "with any order given to them on behalf of their Foreman or other persons acting for the said George Baptist." These indentured employees were to receive "eight dollars a month"; any absence from the place of work would result in the deduction of "one dollar a day" from the monthly pay. These men, whose task was not specified, were certainly paid for their work in the lumber camps.

Every autumn, Baptist hired teams of voyageurs for the job of tree-felling during the winter months. The farms at the Matawin and Rat rivers, which were at the rear of the Baptist empire, were specifically detailed to provide the lumber camps with supplies. The cuts carried out on his limits were the chief source of supply for his two mills. But in addition, every autumn, George or Alexander Baptist signed "logging contracts" with small lumbermen (these were a kind of sub-contractor), who undertook to provide in the spring, from their own timber limits, a cargo of logs cut to such and such a length, width, etc.

In 1869, perhaps for health reasons, George Baptist expressed the desire to give up the business gradually, and he allotted himself ten years before he finally retired. He died on 11 May 1875. The long obituary notice *Le Constitutionnel* devoted to him stressed that "For several years, Mr Baptist has been manufacturing about 25 to 30 million feet of lumber per year." This production was thought to result from the exploitation of vast stretches of territory in the Saint-Maurice region. "Mr Baptist," wrote the journalist, "possessed about 2,000 miles of the best territory in the Saint-Maurice area. In a period when every one believed that timber limits were worthless, he only had to choose; these limits, obtained for nothing or next to nothing, are worth today at least half a million."

These figures, which would require checking, nevertheless give an insight into Baptist's financial position. In 1869, he himself estimated his share in the company of George Baptist and Sons at $200,000; but Alexander, who held only a quarter of the shares, sold them in 1875 for the sum of $150,000. The amounts are no more than suggestive. Besides his capital equipment, George Baptist, Son and Company shares, and his properties on Rue Boulevard and Rue Bonaventure, George Baptist bequeathed to his heirs shares worth $34,550. It was divided up as follows: Bank of Montreal, 131 shares at $200 each; Montreal branch of the Ontario Bank, 125 shares at $40; Dominion Telegraph of Toronto, 5 shares at $50; Eastern Townships Bank, Sherbrooke, 62 shares at $50. This list, which shows how diversified his portfolio was, in addition to his stupendous capitalist organization, is symptomatic of the qualities of George Baptist the industrialist.

In 1873, shortly before Baptist's death, the mill at Les Grès was swept away when the Saint-Maurice flooded, but it was immediately rebuilt, and kept in operation until 1883. The Union Bag and Paper Company purchased it at the beginning of the 20th century, and in 1922 the Shawinigan Water and Power Company became its owner. As for the mill on the Île de la Potherie, it was sold to the Wayagamack Pulp and Paper Company by George Baptist's descendants.

The industrial empire created by Baptist in the Saint-Maurice region, the success he enjoyed, his sense of organization and spirit of competition made of him one of the outstanding examples of the bourgeois class of Trois-Rivières. To any definition one might attempt of this bourgeoisie, the extension of the Baptist family connections adds a further element. Indeed, of Baptist's marriage with Isabella Cockburn, solemnized at Pointe de Lévy in 1834, were born three boys, and five girls who all married businessmen. Phillis married a Quebec merchant, James Dean; Isabella, George Baillie Houliston, a lawyer of Trois-Rivières, a banker, and a broker; Margaret, William Charles Pentland, an accountant of Trois-Rivières; Jane, Robert Mackay*, a Montreal merchant. Finally, the most important union was that of Helen Oliver Baptist and Thomas McDougall, since in this way relations were established between two distinguished families of the Saint-Maurice region, one engaged in the lumber business, and the other in metallurgy.

GEORGES MASSEY

AJTR, Greffe de Petrus Hubert, timber contract between Duncan McDonald and George Baptist, 26 Sept. 1862; deed of partnership between George Baptist and his sons Alexander and John Baptist, 15 Nov. 1869; will of George Baptist, 17 Nov. 1869; will of Isabella Cockburn, wife of George Baptist, 17 Nov. 1869; summary statement and rendering of account by Isabella Cockburn, 6 Sept. 1875; Greffe de F.-L. Lottinville, bill of sale between Georges Badeaux and John Gilmour, 6 Oct. 1852; bill of sale between Georges Badeaux and Baptist and Gordon, 31 Dec. 1853; déclaration de Georges Badeaux à George Baptist, 14 déc. 1855; Registre d'état civil, St Andrews Presbyterian Church, 1846–75. ASTR, Papiers Mgr Albert Tessier, contrat d'engagement, 15 oct. 1858.

Le Constitutionnel (Trois-Rivières, Qué.), 19 mai 1875. *Cyclopædia of Can. biog.* (Rose, 1888), 771. Raoul Blanchard, *Le centre du Canada français; province de Québec* (Publ. de l'Institut scientifique franco-canadien, 3, Montréal, 1947). Pierre Dupin, *Anciens chantiers du Saint-Maurice* (Pages trifluviennes, sér. B, 7, Trois-Rivières, Qué., 1935). *Storied Quebec* (Wood *et al.*), V, 809–10. Sylvain [Auguste Panneton], *Horizons mauriciens* (Trois-Rivières, Qué., 1962); *Par les chemins qui marchent* (Trois-Rivières, Qué., 1965). Albert Tessier, *Les forges Saint-Maurice, 1729–1883* (Coll. L'histoire régionale, 10, Trois-Rivières, Qué., 1952); *Trois-Rivières, 1535–1935; quatre siècles d'histoire* (2e éd., [Trois-Rivières, Qué.], 1935).

BARBER, GEORGE ANTHONY, educator, auditor, and sportsman; b. in 1802 at Hitchin, Hertfordshire, England; d. on 20 Oct. 1874, at Toronto.

Almost the only certain piece of evidence on George Anthony Barber's early life in England is an entry in the Hitchin baptismal register for 1803: "May 18th George Anthony, son of Anna Barber, illegitimate." If he attended Oxford briefly, as his obituaries state, he did not matriculate. Presumably he acquired some training as a teacher, perhaps at London, and he assisted the Reverend Thomas Phillips* for three years at a private school possibly at Whitchurch in Herefordshire, before coming to Canada in 1826 as assistant to Phillips at the Home District grammar school in York (Toronto). Barber married Lucinda Shortiss (b. *c.* 1811; d. 23 Jan. 1893) before 1829 and they had several children.

When Upper Canada College was formed in 1829, both Phillips and Barber joined the staff. Barber was the writing master and his duties included instruction in English and arithmetic. He was a popular teacher; the college records describe him as "a great character with much charm of manner but also a little pomposity." He also became collector of the college whose finances were interconnected with those of King's College (University of Toronto); he was therefore drawn into the scandal involving Colonel Joseph Wells* in 1839, was forced to put up £1,500 to cover shortages in the college accounts, resigned the collectorship, and was dismissed as writing master. The basic cause seems to have been poor accounting practices at both the college and the university; Barber admitted to "not having kept a set of books during any part of the time I held the office of college collector." The whole affair, however, which involved such prominent people as Bishop John Strachan* and Allan MacNab*, remains somewhat obscure.

Barber began three new careers at about this time. While still at Upper Canada College he had established a public auditing business which he continued for the rest of his life. After 1840 he was also auditor to the city of Toronto; in 1873 the junior auditor tried to oust him when he was ill and an uproar resulted. In addition, a group of anti-Sydenham [Thomson*] interests, who favoured the old Family Compact toryism, hired him by 1841 as editor of the Toronto *Commercial Herald* (later *Toronto Herald* and *Herald*). He became its proprietor and operated the paper until it ceased publication on 30 June 1848.

In 1844 Barber's third concurrent vocation began when he was appointed first superintendent of common (public) schools for Toronto. After a board of education was established for the entire city in 1847 he continued as superintendent and also became the board's secretary. Initially Barber faced an acute lack of funds and in both 1848 and 1849 the schools were closed for six months. With the establishment of an elected board in 1850 conditions improved, and eight schools were built in the mid-1850s. His term of office saw the beginning of the practice of saying regular prayers in schools in 1854 and the establishment of evening schools in 1855 and school libraries in 1857. Except for the calendar years 1852 and 1853, Barber held the superintendentship until 1858, when he resigned because he believed it was illegal to combine compulsory assessment with voluntary attendance. He felt that the cost of providing free schools on this basis was not justified by the low attendance. He continued as secretary of the board of education until his death in 1874 and, in 1859,

prepared a 131-page *Report of the past history, and present condition, of the common or public schools of the city of Toronto.*

Barber had a great interest in sports; he was extremely knowledgeable in sporting history and devoted many of the *Commercial Herald* editorials to the subject. He was particularly interested in cricket. Soon after coming to Canada he organized the game among his pupils and later acted as coach of the Upper Canada College teams for many years. He helped establish the Toronto Cricket Club in 1832 and became well known as "the Father of Canadian Cricket." He was also a founder and first secretary of the St George's Society in 1835. In politics he was a Conservative, in religion an Anglican. He attended St Stephen-in-the-Fields in his latter years and was buried in St James' Cemetery.

FREDERICK H. ARMSTRONG

Hertfordshire County Record Office (Hertford, Eng.), Hitchin parish baptismal register, 18 May 1803. PAC, RG 5, A1, 94, pp.52157–62. *Final report of the commissioners of inquiry into the affairs of King's College University, and Upper Canada College* (Quebec, 1852), 360. *Report of the past history, and present condition, of the common or public schools of the city of Toronto* (Toronto, 1859). Toronto City Council, *Appendix to minutes*, 1873, nos.126, 161, 167, 208; *Minutes of proceedings*, 1874, 215, 224–25. Upper Canada, House of Assembly, *Appendix to journal*, 1839–40, 349–90. *J. of Education for Ont.*, XXVIII (April 1875), 59. *Mail* (Toronto), 21, 24 Oct. 1874.

Early Toronto newspapers, 1793–1867: a catalogue of newspapers published in the town of York and city of Toronto from the beginning to confederation, ed. E. G. Firth (Toronto, 1961), 13. J. R. Robertson, *Landmarks of Canada, a guide to the J. Ross Robertson Historical Collection in the Public Reference Library, Toronto, Canada* (Toronto, 1917), 560. *The roll of pupils of Upper Canada College, Toronto, January, 1830, to June, 1916*, ed. A. H. Young (Kingston, Ont., 1917), 44, 96–97. *Centennial story, the board of education for the city of Toronto 1850–1950*, ed. H. M. Cochrane (Toronto, 1950), 16–24, 30–31, 38–40, 112. J. G. Hodgins, *The establishment of schools and colleges in Ontario, 1792–1910* (3v., Toronto, 1910), I. Scadding, *Toronto of old*.

BARRY, JOHN ALEXANDER, merchant and politician; b. *c.* 1790 at Shelburne, N.S.; d. 1872 at La Have, N.S.

John Alexander Barry was the son of Mary Jessop and Robert Barry, an early loyalist who came to Shelburne in 1773. Barry's first wife, by whom he had one son and four daughters, was Mary, daughter of the Reverend William Black*, a noted Methodist minister. After her death in

1833, Barry was married twice more: to Eliza J. Mercier, by whom he is thought to have had one son, and to Sophia Pernette.

For a brief time in 1829, while serving as a member of the assembly for the township of Shelburne, Barry was a popular hero and the most talked-of Nova Scotian. After he had intimated that a fellow assemblyman, Colonel Joseph Freeman, had engaged in smuggling, Barry refused to submit to the assembly's orders to retract and pursued a course so impetuous and uncompromising that eventually he was expelled as a member and imprisoned by order of the assembly for the rest of the session. When the assembly reprimanded the editors of the *Acadian Recorder* and the *Free Press* of Halifax for affording Barry an opportunity to defend himself, Joseph Howe warned that "if Editors are brought for offences to the Bar of the House, Legislators may depend upon this – that they will be brought, individually and collectively, to a bitter expiation before the bar of the public."

Sympathy for Barry and the unpopularity of the assembly led to a number of assemblymen being "hooted and hissed along the streets, pelted with snow, mud, stones and other missiles, and assailed by every opprobrious expression that could be vented by a heedless and unthinking rabble." The assembly quickly reasserted its authority, but the "Barry riots" became part of the folklore of the province. Upon his release Barry did extensive research in the *Journals* of the British House of Commons and published 25 letters in the *Acadian Recorder* seeking to demonstrate that British precedents could justify neither his imprisonment nor his expulsion.

Having taken the Tory side in the celebrated "Brandy Dispute" of 1830 [*see* COLLINS], Barry failed in his subsequent attempts to be elected to the legislature. Thereafter he gained public attention only through his lectures, principally to Halifax audiences, on the customs, artifacts, and chiefs of the Micmac and other North American Indians. In this capacity he aroused none of the excitement of 1829.

J. MURRAY BECK

Acadian Recorder (Halifax), 1829–30. *Novascotian* (Halifax), 1829–30. J. M. Beck, "Privileges and powers of the Nova Scotia House of Assembly," *Dal. Rev.*, XXXV (1955–56), 351–61. George Cox, "John Alexander Barry and his times," N.S. Hist. Soc. *Coll.*, XXVIII (1949), 133–46.

BAUDRY. *See* BEAUDRY

BEAUBIEN, JOSEPH-OCTAVE, doctor and politician; b. 22 March 1824 at Nicolet, L.C., son of Louis Beaubien and Élizabeth Manseau; d. 7 Nov. 1877 at Montmagny.

The Beaubien family, like the Pomberts and La Bissonnières, descended from Jules Trottier, who was born in 1590 in the little town of Igé in Perche (France) and who emigrated to New France about 1650. Joseph-Octave Beaubien was educated at the college of Nicolet, then went for a year to Rochester, U.S.A., to study English. When he returned to Canada, he decided to take up medicine, and studied in turn under two distinguished doctors, William Marsden* and Jean-Étienne Landry. He qualified as a doctor in 1847 and went to live first at Sainte-Élisabeth, then at Montmagny, on the invitation of his uncle, the parish priest Jean-Louis Beaubien. On 24 July 1849, at Cap-Saint-Ignace, he married Catherine-Élisabeth-Aglaé Chenet, daughter of Antoine Chenet, notary and seigneur of Vincelotte.

Joseph-Octave Beaubien soon embarked on a fairly long political career. In 1857 he was elected a Conservative member of the assembly for Montmagny County, and having been re-elected in 1861 and 1863, he sat in the Legislative Assembly of the Province of Canada until confederation. In 1867 he was elected federal member of parliament for Montmagny County by acclamation, and sat in the House of Commons until defeated in 1872. From 15 July 1867 to 23 Feb. 1873 he formed part of the cabinet of Pierre-Joseph-Olivier Chauveau* in the province of Quebec, as commissioner for crown lands. In addition, on 2 Nov. 1867 he was appointed to the Legislative Council, where he represented the division of La Durantaye until 1877. As a minister, Joseph-Octave Beaubien introduced a number of bills, among them one concerning the sale and administration of public lands, and others amending the gold mines act, the law on surveys, and those on colonization. However, his administration was violently criticized in the house by the opposition. During the sessions of 1872 and 1873, MPs Henri-Gustave Joly* de Lotbinière and Pierre-Alexis TREMBLAY endeavoured to prove that important concessions had been made to persons who were in no way involved in the timber trade, and called, in vain, for a commission of inquiry on this subject.

Joseph-Octave Beaubien had a veritable passion for agriculture. Having become co-owner of the seigneury of Vincelotte, he developed magnificent farms at Montmagny and Cap-Saint-Ignace; he was also a member of the agriculture council of the province of Quebec, which replaced the Board of Agriculture in 1868. He was lieutenant-colonel of the 61st Battalion of the Montmagny and l'Islet militia, and from February 1873 was one of the directors of the Canadian Pacific Railway.

He died at Montmagny on 7 Nov. 1877, leaving two children: a son who died without issue, and Caroline-Alix who married Jules-Joseph-Taschereau Frémont*, lawyer, professor of law at Université Laval, and MP for the county of Quebec in the House of Commons.

CLAUDE VACHON

AJTR, Registre d'état civil. Archives judiciaires de Montmagny (Qué.), Registre d'état civil. Quebec, Legislative Council, *Journals*, 1867–77. *Le Courrier du Canada* (Québec), 15 juill., 3 nov., 1867. *Journal de Québec*, 23 nov. 1872; 8 déc.–13 déc. 1873. *La Minerve* (Montréal), 20 juill., 3 nov. 1867; 8 nov. 1877. *Le Nouveau Monde* (Montréal), 8 nov. 1877. *Le Pays* (Montréal), 18 juill. 1867. *Can. directory of parliament* (Johnson), 27. *Can. parl. comp.*, *1862*; *1863*; *1864*; *1867*; *1873*; *1874*. Desjardins, *Guide parlementaire*. *Political appointments and judicial bench* (N.-O. Coté). P.-G. Roy. *La famille Boisseau* (Lévis, Qué., 1907). Rumilly, *Hist. de la prov. de Québec*, I. "Mémorial nécrologique; l'hon. Joseph-Octave Beaubien," *La Gazette des familles acadiennes et canadiennes* (Québec), III (1876–77), 362–63.

BEAUDRY (Baudry), JOSEPH-UBALDE, jurist, codifier of laws, and author; b. 15 May 1816 at Montreal, son of Louis Beaudry (Baudry) and Félicité Dubreuil; d. 11 Jan. 1876 at Montreal.

Joseph-Ubalde Beaudry received his classical education at the college of Montreal, where he excelled in languages and the exact sciences. He even defended a thesis on the theories of Euclid. As a clerk – it was before the institution of the faculties of law – in the office of Côme-Séraphin Cherrier*, one of the great figures of the bar at that time, he received his lawyer's commission in March 1838. He practised for some time at Montreal, but it was not long before he entered judicial administration.

First a clerk of the Court of Requests at Saint-Hyacinthe, Beaudry then returned to Montreal, where he served on the city council for three years as a councillor, from 1847 to 1849, and as an alderman, in 1850. During this period of serious epidemics he advocated various measures for improving sanitation. In 1850 he became clerk of the Court of Appeal, and five years later added to this office that of clerk of the Seigneurial Court, presided over by Sir Louis-Hippolyte La Fontaine*. This court concerned itself with changing the system of land tenure in Lower Canada. In 1859 Beaudry was appointed joint clerk of the commission for the codification of laws, which had been created in 1857. This measure, made necessary by the diversity of sources from which laws were derived, had been championed by George-Étienne CARTIER. Three commissioners and two secretaries were to classify and coordinate the laws in force, then to submit their work to the judges and the government [see René-Édouard CARON]. After being a secretary for more than six years, Joseph-Ubalde Beaudry succeeded Judge Augustin-Norbert Morin*, who died in 1865, as a commissioner. His part was a notable one, and he is considered one of the principal drafters of the first edition of the *Code de procédure civile du Bas-Canada*. . . . He was an assistant judge in the Superior Court in December 1868, and was promoted titular judge, with jurisdiction over the district of Montreal, 12 months later. He dispensed justice there for eight years.

Joseph-Ubalde Beaudry was one of the founders, in 1869, of the *Revue légale*, and one of the compilers of the *Lower Canada Reports/Décisions des tribunaux du Bas-Canada*. His major work is probably his *Code des curés, marguilliers et paroissiens*, published in 1870 and considered to be the first real treatise on parish law in Quebec. A founding member in 1859 of the Société Historique de Montréal, which did so much at that time to unearth and make public documents, still scattered, relating to the past of Canadian institutions, Joseph-Ubalde Beaudry was vice-president at the time of his death. He was also on the Catholic school commission of Montreal, and gave strong guidance to the Académie Commerciale Catholique of Montreal, better known later as the École du Plateau. Finally, he had been one of the founders, in 1852, of the Institut National, later reconstituted as the Institut Canadien-Français. This society began as a split from the Institut Canadien of some 135 members who were opposed to political discussions within the walls of the institute; it was chiefly literary [see CASSIDY]. Joseph-Ubalde Beaudry drew up its constitution.

Judge Beaudry was carried off by pneumonia after a few days illness. He died on 11 Jan. 1876; nearly 2,000 persons assembled at the parish church of Notre-Dame de Montréal for the impressive funeral. His colleagues of the court, including the chief justice of the province, Sir Antoine-Aimé Dorion*, the judges Charles-Elzéar MONDELET, Joseph-Amable Berthelot*, Samuel Cornwallis Monk*, Vincislas-Paul-Wilfrid DORION, and Robert Mackay*, accompanied him to his last resting place on the Côte-des-Neiges.

In 1841, at Montreal, Joseph-Ubalde Beaudry had married Caroline Beaudry. He left two sons, one, Pierre-Janvier, who was a lawyer, a protonotary of Beauharnois, and deputy clerk of the privy council of Canada, and another, his namesake, who was a civil engineer.

JEAN-JACQUES LEFEBVRE

Beaulieu

J.-U. Beaudry, *Code des curés, marguilliers et paroissiens accompagné de notes historiques et critiques* (Montréal, 1870).

AJM, Registre d'état civil. PAC, MG 30, D62 (Audet papers), 3, pp.611–12. *La Minerve* (Montréal), 12 janv. 1876. P.-G. Roy, *Les juges de la province de Québec*, 37. Lareau, *Hist. de la littérature canadienne*, 411–17.

BEAULIEU, FRANÇOIS, chief of the Yellowknife tribe, Arctic guide, and interpreter; b. 1771, son of Jacques Beaulieu and an Indian woman of the Montagnais tribe; d. in November 1872 at Salt River, North-West Territories.

François Beaulieu, a Métis, grew up among the Indians of the far northwest. According to John Franklin* he was raised by the Dogribs, but this may be an error as Beaulieu was later the bitter enemy of that tribe. He was one of the party that accompanied Alexander Mackenzie* overland to the Pacific in 1793. He first met the noted Arctic explorer, John Franklin, at Fort Wedderburn in 1820, and advised him that what is now the Dease Arm of Great Bear Lake, which Beaulieu knew well, afforded the best base for his projected journey to the mouth of the Coppermine River. Problems of supply compelled Franklin to reject this advice, which, had it been adopted, might well have averted the hardship and loss of life which were to attend his first "journey to the shores of the polar sea" [*see* George BACK].

On his second expedition (1825–27), by way of the Mackenzie River, Franklin employed Beaulieu as guide and interpreter, set up base at Fort Franklin on the west side of Great Bear Lake in the autumn of 1825, and the following summer sent Dr John Richardson* and the mate E. N. Kendall* down the Mackenzie to map the coast eastward to the mouth of the Coppermine by boat. Richardson completed this commission too late in the season to return the way he had come. He therefore travelled overland, as prearranged, to the Dease Arm of Great Bear Lake, where Beaulieu met him and took the whole party to Fort Franklin by boat. No writer, French or English, has properly stressed Beaulieu's share in the planning and execution of this trip, the most successful boat journey made by naval personnel in the Canadian Arctic.

As a chief of the Yellowknife tribe, Beaulieu "became the terror" of Dogribs, Slaveys, and Sekanis; he is said to have killed 12 of the last group with his own hand. He lived the life of a "sultan" with three wives and other casual relationships. In his later years Beaulieu settled on the Salt River, a tributary of the Slave, with his family and some Indian followers. There he developed a trade in salt obtained from the river and was granted a monopoly by the Hudson's Bay Company with which he enjoyed great prestige.

In 1848 he was baptized by Father Alexandre-Antonin Taché*, whereupon he dismissed (with adequate provision) two of his wives, and lived "ever faithful" with the third. He was nearly 80 when he made this act of renunciation. The energetic old man was no passive communicant: he was precise in religious observances, generous in aiding the church, and exerted himself "to open the eyes of those Indians who had been led astray by the Protestant minister." He was still active as a hunter at the age of 85 and lived to be just over 100.

A son, Étienne Beaulieu, was guide to the American traveller, Warburton Pike*, in 1889, and his descendants still live in the Great Slave Lake area.

LESLIE H. NEATBY

John Franklin, *Narrative of a journey to the shores of the polar sea in the years 1819, 20, 21 and 22 . . .* (London, 1823); *Narrative of a second expedition to the shores of the polar sea in the years 1825, 1826 and 1827: including an account of the progress of a detachment to the eastward, by John Richardson* (London, 1828). [Alexander Mackenzie], *First man west, Alexander Mackenzie's journal of his voyage to the Pacific coast of Canada in 1793*, ed. Walter Sheppe (Montreal, 1962). Morice, *Dict. hist. Can. et Métis*. Joseph Tassé, *Les Canadiens de l'Ouest* (2ᵉ éd., 2v., Montréal, 1878). Giraud, *Le Métis canadien*. É.-F.-S.-J. Petitot, *En route pour la mer glaciale* (Paris, 1887). Guy Blanchet, "Exploring with Sousi and Black Basile," *Beaver*, outfit 295 (autumn 1964), 34–41.

BEAUMONT, WILLIAM RAWLINS, surgeon; b. 1803 in Marylebone, London, England; d. 12 Oct. 1875 in Toronto.

William Rawlins Beaumont received his medical education at St Bartholomew's Hospital in London where he served as dresser to the distinguished surgeon, John Abernethy, whose teaching established the modern medical school in this ancient hospital. There Beaumont was a fellow-student of James Paget. He continued his training in Europe, studying for ten months in Paris under the anatomist Jean Amussat, who stimulated his interest in mechanical instruments. Returning to London, Beaumont commenced practice and was appointed a surgeon to the Islington Dispensary. He qualified as a member of the Royal College of Surgeons of England in 1826 and became a fellow of the Royal Medical and Chirurgical Society of London in 1836 and of the Royal College of Surgeons in 1844. Beaumont's hopes of receiving a commission in the Army Medical Service had been disappointed, and he came instead to Canada in 1841. He was already a highly competent surgeon when he established himself in Toronto in that year.

A faculty of medicine was established at King's College (later the University of Toronto) in 1843, and Beaumont was appointed professor of surgery by the chancellor, Governor General Sir Charles Bagot*; he became a member of the college council in 1848. He was also an attending physician and surgeon to the Toronto General Hospital, and in 1845 he was appointed to the Medical Board, the body responsible for the examination and licensing of candidates for medical practice in Canada West. The University of Toronto conferred a doctor of medicine on Beaumont in 1850. He was dean of the faculty of medicine at the university when the legislature abolished it in 1853, but continued clinical teaching at the Toronto General Hospital and became its consulting physician and surgeon when Christopher Widmer* died in 1858. In 1870 and 1871 he lectured on ophthalmic surgery at the Toronto School of Medicine, and was appointed professor of surgery at the University of Trinity College in 1871. He retired in 1873 and was made professor emeritus at Trinity College.

Beaumont established an outstanding reputation in Toronto as a teacher and a surgeon. After Widmer's death he was probably the doyen of the surgeons of Toronto. Younger surgeons sought his support and he was closely associated in his practice with James BOVELL and Edward Mulberry HODDER. Beaumont's published articles illustrate the broad scope of his practice and discuss such varied subjects as aneurism, ophthalmic surgery, and urology. He had particular skill in designing surgical instruments. One of these, designed for the passing of continuous sutures in deep-seated parts, is said to have embodied the concept later applied in the original Singer sewing machine.

Beaumont lost the sight of his left eye in 1865, but continued to practise until he became totally blind in 1873. He died in his home in Toronto on 12 Oct. 1875. Sir William Osler* recalled him as one who "by examplifying [sic] those graces of life and refinement of heart which make up character" contributed to "the leaven which has raised our profession above the dead level of business."

W. G. COSBIE

W. R. Beaumont, "Cases of operations for cataract, chiefly at the Toronto General Hospital," *Upper Canada Journal of Medical, Surgical, and Physical Science* (Toronto), I (1851–52), 329–32, 361–65, 407–11, 510–15; [ ], "A description of a new instrument for closing the vesico-vaginal and recto-vaginal fistulae, and fissures of the soft palate . . . ," *Medico-Chirurgical Transactions* (Royal Medical and Chirurgical Society of London), XXI (1838), 29–32; "Lithotrity," *Canada Lancet* (Toronto), III (1870–71), 35; [ ], "Rough notes of a clinical lecture, delivered by Dr Beaumont, F.R.C.S., London, and one of the surgeons to the Toronto General Hospital, on a case of false aneurism. Reported from memory," *Upper Canada Journal of Medical, Surgical, and Physical Science* (Toronto), III (1853–54), 251–58.

MTCL, typescript by J. H. Richardson, "Reminiscences of the medical profession in Toronto," 5–7. University of Toronto Archives, Office of the Chief Accountant financial records (117, King's College Council minute book, III, 1842–48). *Canada Lancet* (Toronto), VIII (1875–76), 92–93.

Canniff, *Medical profession in Upper Canada*, 183–96, 199, 204–6, 214, 242–45. C. K. Clarke, *A history of the Toronto General Hospital, including an account of the medal of the Loyal and Patriotic Society of 1812* (Toronto, 1913), 52, 62, 81, 103. William Osler, *Aequanimitas, with other addresses to medical students, nurses and practitioners of medicine* (London, 1904), 175–76, 369. G. W. Spragge, "The Trinity Medical School," *Ont. Hist.*, LVIII (1966), 63–98.

BEAVEN, JAMES, Church of England clergyman, theologian, and author; b. 9 July 1801 at Westbury, Wiltshire, England, second son of Samuel and Mary Beaven; d. 8 Nov. 1875, at Niagara, Ont.

James Beaven entered St Edmund Hall, Oxford, on 4 Nov. 1820. He received a BA in 1824 and an MA in 1827, and a BD and a DD in 1842. He was ordained deacon in 1825 and priest in 1826. His longest ministry in England was spent at Leigh in Staffordshire, and he was vicar of Welford in Northamptonshire when he received the appointment of professor of divinity at King's College in Toronto.

Beaven arrived in Toronto in February 1843. During his years at King's he was resident professor for a time and also had charge of chapel services. With the new professor ripples of the High Church Tractarian movement came to Toronto. It was observed that Beaven preached in the college chapel in the surplice and intoned the service, two usages not widely followed at that time. The frequent references in his writings to the desirability of improving the architecture and furnishing of churches illustrate his attention to another aspect of the revived churchmanship of the mid-19th century. King's College was officially closed in 1849 and Beaven was appointed in 1851 to the chair of metaphysics and ethics, first in the University of Toronto and then in University College. He resigned in 1871, lived for a brief time at Port Whitby where he was incumbent of the local church, and then moved to Niagara where he died.

James Beaven was prominent in church affairs. The scattered records of his life indicate that his interests lay in his church work rather than in the university, particularly after the secularization of King's College. He aided the building of churches at King and Oak Ridges, both north of Toronto, in the 1850s. From 1850 to 1868 he ministered to a congregation at Berkeley, and later, concurrently, to another at Chester (both of which are now part of the city of Toronto), and he built the first St John's, Norway, and the first St Barnabas'. He served the Church Society and the diocesan synod as chairman of the book and tract committee and of the church music committee. As chairman of the committee on canons he produced an important report in 1858.

From 1862 to 1873 Beaven was precentor of synod, in charge of music at synod services. In 1867 he was made a canon of St James' Cathedral. He was prolocutor or chairman of the lower house of the first four provincial synods of Canada, meeting in Montreal. Beaven, who favoured retaining the close connection between the Church of England in Canada and the mother church in England, chaired in 1865 a committee of the provincial synod which produced a memorial addressed to the convocations of Canterbury and York urging the calling of a general council of the Anglican communion. This event took place in 1867 with the assembling of the first Lambeth Conference.

James Beaven was the author of at least 16 publications. Three were sermons, one of which, remarkable for its ecumenical spirit, was preached to the synod of the diocese in 1859. He was an accomplished classical scholar and produced in 1853 a book of selections from Cicero. His *Account of the life and writings of St Irenaeus* and *Elements of natural theology* were both substantial volumes. His best known work is, however, *Recreations of a long vacation*, describing a diocesan tour in 1845 on which he accompanied Bishop John Strachan* as far as Sault Ste Marie. Beaven travelled with the bishop on other shorter tours in 1847, 1848, and 1854 and wrote a description of the latter which appeared in the *Church*.

In 1826 James Beaven married Elizabeth Speed, eldest daughter of John Speed Frowd of Croscombe House, Somersetshire. They had four sons and three daughters, and one son, Robert*, became prime minister of British Columbia, 1882–83. Mrs Beaven wrote *Private devotions and rules of conduct for young ladies* in 1845. She died in Toronto in her 76th year, 14 Sept. 1871.

Differing estimates of James Beaven were made by his contemporaries. Ernest Hawkins*, secretary of the Society for the Propagation of the Gospel, wrote in his journal, 24 Aug. 1849: "The worthy Dr. B[eaven] rather bored me with his slow prosaic manner, but he is, I am sure, a good and amiable and well principled man." Daniel Wilson*, president of the University of Toronto, in a moment of irritation, once described his colleague as "a stupid dry old stick that we would be well rid of." A former student, John Campbell*, remembered him as tall and angular, severe in aspect, but with integrity "written on every line of his unbending form." Among his clerical brothers he was given great respect for his learning, balanced judgement in times of ecclesiastical party strife, and long-continued and generous services to his church in many parts of the diocese.

T. R. MILLMAN

British Museum catalogue lists a number of James Beaven's publications. Others are: "*Ask for the old paths*"; *a sermon preached at the opening of the new church of St. James, at Dundas, in Upper Canada, on Sunday, December 31st, 1843* (Cobourg, Ont., 1844); *A brief catechism on confirmation, with prayers to be used before and after confirmation* (Toronto, 1878); *Elements of natural theology* (London, 1850); *Private devotions for schoolboys; together with some rules of conduct given by a father to his son on his going to school* (Toronto, 1845); *Recreations of a long vacation; or a visit to Indian missions in Upper Canada* (London and Toronto, 1846); "*That they all may be one*": *a sermon preached before the synod of the diocese of Toronto, on the 7th of June, 1859* (Toronto, 1859).

St John the Baptist Church (Norway (Toronto)), notes by D. M. Hayne, 1949–50, for a parish history. University of Toronto Archives, Daniel Wilson, "Journal," typescript; Office of the Chief Accountant financial records (41, university quarterly accounts, Sept.–Dec. 1871); Office of the Chief Accountant financial records (117, King's College Council minute book, 1842–48). *Church* (Cobourg, later Toronto), especially 23 June 1842, 22 Sept. 1843, 17 Sept. 1847. *Globe* (Toronto), 14 Sept. 1871, 10 Nov. 1875. Church of England, Church Society of the Diocese of Toronto, *Reports* (Cobourg, Toronto), 1843–69; Provincial Synod, *Journals of proceedings* (Montreal, Quebec), 1861–68; Synod of the Diocese of Toronto, *Journals* (Toronto), 1853–76. *Final report of the commissioners of inquiry into the affairs of King's College University, and Upper Canada College* (Quebec, 1852). John Campbell, "The Reverend Professor James Beaven, D.D., M.A.," *University of Toronto Monthly*, III (Dec. 1902), 69–72.

BECKET, JOHN C., printer; b. 14 May 1810 at Kilwinning, Scotland; married, but his wife's name is not known; d. 5 Sept. 1879 in Montreal.

John C. Becket was trained as a printer. In 1831 he emigrated and followed his trade for some months in New York. In 1832 he came to Montreal, where he lived for the remainder of his life. In his *Introduction of printing into Canada*,

Ægidius Fauteux* describes Becket and four contemporary printers as "ancestors of the profession" in Montreal, but not members of the true pioneering period, which closed by 1825. The importance of their craft in the growing metropolis (about 30,000 in 1832) is clear. Becket had an additional importance as an outstanding trainer of printers.

Until 1843 Becket was in business with a partner, Rollo CAMPBELL; thereafter, by himself. He did job-printing, for example the annual reports of the French Canadian Missionary Society and of the Montreal Sunday School Union. He printed a number of periodicals, such as the *French Canadian Missionary Record*, the *Canada Miscellany*, and the *Canada Temperance Advocate*. He conducted a stationery and book store as well. When John Dougall* gave up the editorship of the *Advocate* and established the *Montreal Witness* in 1846, Becket printed that paper also (at a later time the *Witness* took over its own printing). Dougall and Becket shared the same interest in furthering moral causes.

Becket was deeply concerned in religious issues and in various charitable enterprises, for example the Montreal Protestant House of Industry and Refuge, of which he was a governor. He was a life-long member of Erskine Presbyterian Church (whose pastor was William TAYLOR) and served as elder and clerk of session. "A prominent teetotaller," he frequently lent his business premises for the meetings of temperance societies. He was interested also in national and fraternal organizations. A member of the St Andrew's Society from 1835, he became its president in 1866. He was a founder of the first Montreal lodge of the Independent Order of Odd Fellows and for many years was a senior officer. "[His] kindly disposition and many charities prevented his ever becoming rich."

JOHN IRWIN COOPER

St Andrew's Society of Montreal, Minutes, 1834–79. Erskine and American United Church (Montreal), Erskine Church records, Minutes of the Board of Trustees, 1833–79; Minutes of the session of the church, 1833–79. *The Presbyterian Record for the Dominion of Canada* (Montreal), IV (October 1879). *Dom. ann. reg., 1879*, 384–85. Ægidius Fauteux, *The introduction of printing into Canada, a brief history* (Montreal, 1930), 110–11.

BECKWITH, JOHN ADOLPHUS, engineer, businessman, civil servant, and politician; b. 1 Dec. 1800 at Fredericton, N.B., one of six children of Nehemiah Beckwith and Julie-Louise Le Brun; d. 23 Nov. 1880 at Fredericton.

The son of a well-known early settler, John Adolphus Beckwith was educated at Fredericton grammar school and in Montreal and Quebec, and became a professional surveyor and engineer. He had one son and two daughters by his first wife Ann Jouett (Jewett) whom he married in 1822; he married his second wife, Marie Ann Berton of Saint John, in 1837 and had three more daughters.

Beckwith's career was long and active. He and his brother were in partnership in the lumber firm of J. A. and F. E. Beckwith, which was moderately successful until ruined in the depression of the 1830s. He served as deputy surveyor in the Crown Lands Office until 1840 when he became first clerk in the audit office, a position he held until 1860. In 1860 he became commissioner, or manager, of the New Brunswick and Nova Scotia Land Company – a speculative company, organized by Thomas Baillie* to sell colonial lands especially in York County, N.B. Beckwith held this position until his death, when his son Harry succeeded him, and was "more familiar with the business of the Crown Land department probably than anyone who has occupied a seat in the Provincial Government."

From his youth John Beckwith was interested in the militia, and rose to the rank of major in command of a battalion of the 1st York Battery (1860), but then resigned resentfully when Lemuel Allan WILMOT was promoted colonel over him. In 1846 Beckwith began an association with the York County Agricultural Society and remained a member until his death; he received much of the credit for its vitality. In the Orange order he was at one time the most worthy grand master for New Brunswick. As a sportsman Beckwith excelled in wrestling, boxing, and skating, and he was called "the father of cricket in New Brunswick."

Except for an unsuccessful attempt to enter the House of Assembly in the election of 1830, Beckwith, considered a "strong conservative," was not involved in politics for the first 60 years of his life. His entry into it was at the municipal level in Fredericton where he served frequently on the council and was twice mayor. In the confederation election of 1866 Beckwith was elected to the Legislative Assembly as a supporter of union, and when the provincial government was reorganized in 1867 he was named provincial secretary and registrar of the province by the government leader Andrew Rainsford Wetmore*. He held this position until 1871 when he was one of the members of the Executive Council eliminated in the realignment over the New Brunswick School Law. In 1874 he was appointed to the Legislative Council. Never an exciting man, nor an innovator, Beckwith passed his life as a dull, but competent, public

Belcher

servant, and in his later years was "a sort of an Encyclopaedia" on the old days of Fredericton.

C. M. WALLACE

Daily Sun (Saint John, N.B.), 24 Nov. 1880. *New Brunswick Reporter* (Fredericton, N.B.), 1867, 1870–71, 1880. *Can. parl. comp., 1870; 1873; 1878; 1880. Cyclopædia of Can. biog.* (Rose, 1888), 88. *Dom. ann. reg., 1880–81*, 392. Lawrence, *Judges of New Brunswick* (Stockton), 460–62. MacNutt, *New Brunswick*, 231–32, 305.

BELCHER, Sir EDWARD, naval surveyor and explorer; b. in Halifax, N.S., on 27 Feb. 1799, son of Andrew Belcher and Marianne Von Geyer; d. in London, England, on 18 March 1877.

Edward Belcher, a grandson of Jonathan Belcher*, chief justice of Nova Scotia, moved from Halifax to England with his family in November 1811. On 9 April 1812 he entered the Royal Navy as a first class volunteer, a rank which indicated that he was destined for an officer's career. He was promoted midshipman on 2 Dec. 1812 and lieutenant on 21 July 1818. During this period he served on a number of ships on the Atlantic coast of North America, in the West Indies, and on the African and Home stations. In September 1821 he was posted to the *Salisbury*, on the Halifax station. He had meanwhile been studying surveying and natural history, equipping himself to take part in the navy's extensive 19th-century surveys of the world's oceans which were to result in the famous Admiralty charts.

Belcher's first major assignment was as assistant surveyor on the *Blossom* commanded by Frederick William Beechey*, which sailed for Bering Strait by way of Cape Horn on 19 May 1825. The voyage had two purposes: to come to the relief of William Edward Parry* and John Franklin* should they reach the strait in their separate attempts to discover a northwest passage; and to conduct surveys of uncharted areas along the ship's route. Belcher returned to England in October 1828 for other duties, was raised to the rank of commander on 16 March 1829, and given his first ship, the *Ætna*, on 27 May 1830. With the vessel's return to England from surveying the West African coast on 19 Aug. 1831, Belcher and his officers laid a number of charges against one another, arising out of his alleged abusive treatment of the crew. Belcher was acquitted and sailed for Africa on 21 Dec. 1831. When the *Ætna* returned to England on 19 Aug. 1833, crew members again laid charges against Belcher. This time the Admiralty posted him in disgrace to the *Lightning*, surveying the Irish Sea. In 1836 the navy hydrographer, Francis Beaufort, who appears to have been Belcher's

patron, persuaded the Admiralty to give Belcher another command, and he replaced the ailing Captain Beechey on the *Sulphur* which was to undertake surveys of the west coasts of North and South America. This voyage lasted for almost six years; Belcher did not return to England until 19 July 1842. In the interim he had undertaken surveys of the Americas and the South Pacific islands, and on the return voyage by way of China he participated valiantly in the battles at Canton which ended in the ceding of Hong Kong to Great Britain. For his performance he was made a companion of the Order of the Bath on 14 Oct. 1841 and subsequently knighted on 21 Jan. 1843. The crew of the *Sulphur* complained of ill-treatment but Belcher was again exonerated by a court of inquiry and placed in charge of another surveying vessel, the *Samarang*, which left England on 26 Jan. 1843. He conducted surveys in the South China Sea and returned to England on 31 Dec. 1846.

On 11 Sept. 1830 he had married Diana Jolliffe, stepdaughter of Captain Peter Heywood. After the *Ætna* returned in August 1831, they lived together again at Portsmouth until he left in December. Shortly before the end of his second tour in 1833 she informed him that she would not live with him again, claiming that he had twice infected her with venereal disease. Then began a protracted legal struggle which Belcher spitefully prolonged. Despite the bitterness of the separation, his wife was content to call herself Lady Belcher after Belcher was knighted a decade later.

Daring and able though he was, Belcher had earned a wide reputation for harshness in command. After 1846 the Admiralty chose not to give him another command until 1852 when he was put in charge of an expedition of five ships to search in the Canadian Arctic for the missing ships and men of Sir John Franklin who had not been heard from since 1845. Belcher split his forces, sending the *Resolute* under Henry KELLETT and its tender, *Intrepid*, west through Barrow Strait to Melville Island. The only real accomplishment of this western division was the rescue in 1852 of Robert McCLURE and the men of the *Investigator* from their trap in Mercy Bay; in the summers of 1853 and 1854 ice conditions prevented much progress and Kellett's ships were not even capable of returning to Belcher's base on Beechey Island. Belcher's own ship *Assistance* and its tender *Pioneer* under Sherard OSBORN comprised the northern division, which in August 1852 went north through Wellington Channel. They did some survey work and made some discoveries but, like the western division, became enmeshed in heavy ice in 1853 and were unable to break free in 1854.

Belcher must take part of the blame for this outcome himself, for he refused to take the advice of skilled Arctic navigators such as Sherard Osborn and as a result blundered into the heaviest ice.

Finally, in the summer of 1854, Belcher ordered the abandonment of all the vessels, ignoring Kellett's strenuous objections. As a result the ships were deserted and the crews returned home on transport ships waiting at Beechey Island. On their return to England, Belcher was court-martialed for leaving his ships in the Arctic but he was acquitted when he was able to show that his orders gave him complete discretion. In spite of the acquittal, he continued to be criticized severely in England. The outcry against Belcher became even greater after Kellett's *Resolute* broke free from the ice and was salvaged in Baffin Bay by James Buddington, an American whaling captain. He towed her to New London, Conn., where she was bought by the United States Congress, refitted, and presented to Queen Victoria as a gift from the American people in December 1856.

In his retirement Belcher occupied himself with writing and scientific inquiry. Despite the numerous failures of his career and principally because of his advanced age and seniority, he became a rear-admiral on 11 Feb. 1861, was promoted vice-admiral on 2 April 1866, made a knight commander of the Order of the Bath on 13 March 1867, and finally raised to the rank of admiral on 20 Oct. 1872.

During his career, Belcher was one of the most controversial figures in the Royal Navy. As an officer he had many desirable attributes: scientific curiosity, technical competence, inventiveness, physical energy, and sometimes reckless bravery. However, he suffered from an irritable, quarrelsome, and hypercritical nature which made relations with superiors and subordinates alike extremely difficult. Although he was in many ways a capable officer, his record remains blighted by his ignominious failure as commander in chief of the Franklin search expedition, an appointment which has been described as "unfortunate" since Belcher's temperament did not enable him to function as the situation demanded.

BASIL STUART-STUBBS

University of British Columbia, Special Collections Division, Belcher papers. Edward Belcher, *Horatio Howard Brenton: a naval novel* (3v., London, 1856); *The last of the Arctic voyages; being a narrative of the expedition in H.M.S.* Assistance *under the command of Captain Sir Edward Belcher, C.B., in search of Sir John Franklin, during the years 1852–53–54* (2v., London, 1855); *Narrative of a voyage round the world, performed in Her Majesty's Ship* Sulphur, *during the years 1836–1842 ...* (2v., London, 1843); *Narrative of the voyage of H.M.S.* Samarang *during the years 1843–46; employed surveying the islands of the Eastern Archipelago ...* (2v., London, 1848); *A treatise on nautical surveying ...* (London, 1835).

F. W. Beechey, *Narrative of a voyage to the Pacific and Beering's Strait to co-operate with the polar expeditions: performed in His Majesty's Ship* Blossom *... in the years 1825, 26, 27, 28* (2v., London, 1831). [McClure], *Discovery of the north-west passage* (Osborn). Joseph Phillimore, *A report of the judgement delivered by Joseph Phillimore, in the cause of Belcher, the wife, against Belcher, the husband* (London, 1835). *The zoology of the voyage of H.M.S.* Samarang *during the years 1843–1846,* ed. Arthur Adams (London, 1850). *The zoology of the voyage of H.M.S.* Sulphur, *under the command of Captain Sir Edward Belcher, R.N., C.B., F.R.G.S., etc. during the years 1836–42,* ed. R. B. Hinds (2v., London, 1843–44). *Times* (London), 3 Oct. 1831, 7 Oct. 1854, 20 March 1877.

DNB. O'Byrne, *Naval Biog. Dict.,* 68–69. E. S. Dodge, *Northwest by sea* (New York, 1961), 304–8. A. G. L'Estrange, *Lady Belcher and her friends* (London, 1891). G. E. Fenety, *Life and times of the Hon. Joseph Howe, (the great Nova Scotian and ex-lieut. governor); with brief references to some of his prominent contemporaries* (Saint John, N.B., 1896). Harris, *Church of Saint Paul,* 187. M. A. Lewis, *A social history of the navy, 1793–1815* (London, [1960]). Beamish Murdoch, *A history of Nova-Scotia or Acadie* (3v., Halifax, 1865–67), III, 313. G. S. Ritchie, *The Admiralty chart: British naval hydrography in the nineteenth century* (London, 1967), 221–37. Noel Wright, *Quest for Franklin* (London, 1959), 206–14. Rutherford Alcock, "Address to the Royal Geographical Society ...: obituary," Royal Geographical Soc. *J.* (London), XLVII (1877), cxxxvi–cxlii. C. J. Townshend, "Jonathan Belcher, first chief justice of Nova Scotia," N.S. Hist. Soc. *Coll.,* XVIII (1914), 25–57. W. H. Whitmore, "Notes on the Belcher family," *New Eng. Hist. and Geneal. Register* (Boston), XXVII (1873), 239–54.

BELCOURT. *See* BELLECOURT

BELFORD, CHARLES, journalist and publisher; b. Cork, County Cork, Ireland, 25 April 1837 of Irish Protestant parents; m. in Toronto, Jennie Thomas, 11 Nov. 1864; d. Ottawa, 19 Dec. 1880.

Charles Belford came to Toronto with his two younger brothers, Alexander and Robert J., in 1857. Charles had been trained in Ireland as a draftsman but he turned to newspaper work in Toronto and went on the staff of the *Leader,* published by his great-uncle, James Beaty*. In 1867 he succeeded Charles Lindsey* as editor-in-chief of the newspaper, which ceased publication shortly before the end of 1871. Belford was a vigorous writer and in March 1872 he became editor of a more outspoken Conservative organ, the newly formed Toronto *Mail.* This was the

Bell

Toronto mouthpiece of Sir John A. Macdonald*, whose fortunes were soon to be overshadowed by the Pacific scandal in 1873 but whose loyal supporter Belford nevertheless remained. In 1876, while continuing his editorial duties with the *Mail*, Belford entered into partnership with his two brothers to establish the publishing firm of Belford Brothers. Their stock-in-trade was the publication of cheap, pirated reprints of popular British and American authors, notably Mark Twain.

The first Canadian Copyright Act of 1872 had been disallowed, but the act of 1875 made it legal to reprint in Canada any American book not coming under the imperial copyright act of 1842, which protected editions published first in the British Isles, or not registered in the Department of Agriculture, Ottawa, within 30 days of publication in the United States. The Belfords' publishing venture was within the law. At the same time, however, it was in part a reprisal against American publishers who pirated British authors and harmed their Canadian counterparts by flooding the market with cheap reprints. Belford Brothers published unauthorized editions of American subscription books which did not conform to the Canadian act of 1875 and sold them to retail outlets by mail order at prices undercutting the American editions. Thus they turned the tables on American publishers who indignantly accused them of sharp practice. Other Canadian publishers soon followed the Belfords' lead.

Belford Brothers operated from 1876 to 1878, during which time the firm published, in addition to pirated reprints, a journal of literature and art, *Belford's Monthly Magazine*, and a few Canadian books. Among the authors published were Twain, W. D. Howells, Harriet Beecher Stowe, Anthony Trollope, May Agnes Fleming [EARLY], Jean Talon Lesperance*, and G. M. Grant*. Children's books, religious tracts, reference works, books of travel and adventure, biographies, and autobiographies appeared in rapid succession.

Charles Belford withdrew from the firm in 1878 and his brothers reorganized the business with a new partner, G. M. Rose*, as the Rose-Belford Publishing Company. Within a year there was another shake-up: Alexander and Robert Belford withdrew, and with James Clarke formed Belfords, Clarke, and Company with headquarters in Chicago where Alexander married a daughter of Walter McNally of the publishers, Rand McNally Company.

It was a physical breakdown that made it necessary for Charles to dissociate himself from his brothers' publishing activities and to give up, at the same time, his editorship of the *Mail*. An able organizer whose counsel was highly regarded by

the Conservative party, he had worked to a state of exhaustion during the federal election campaign of 1878, and collapsed on the night of the Conservative victory. By autumn 1879 he was sufficiently recovered to accept an appointment as secretary to the Dominion Board of Appraisers and move with his family to Ottawa. He was still in frail health, however, and died the following year, survived by his wife, two sons, and four daughters.

H. P. GUNDY

Globe (Toronto), 22 Dec. 1880. *Ottawa Citizen*, 20, 22 Dec. 1880. *Dom. ann. reg.*, *1880–81*, 392–93. H. P. Gundy, *Book publishing and publishers in Canada before 1900* (Toronto, 1965). Gordon Roper," Mark Twain and his Canadian publishers: a second look," Bibliographical Society of Canada *Papers* (Toronto), V (1966), 30–89.

BELL, HERBERT, merchant, farmer, shipbuilder, and politician; b. 30 Nov. 1818 in Middlebie Parish, county of Dumfries, Scotland; d. 15 Feb. 1876 at his home in Alberton, P.E.I.

After being educated in his native Scotland, Herbert Bell immigrated to Prince Edward Island in the 1840s. He settled at Alberton in western Prince County, where he established himself as a farmer, merchant, and shipbuilder. In 1849 he married Jane Bowness; she bore him no children but they adopted a daughter.

Bell entered politics in 1867 and was elected to the assembly for Prince County, First District. During the next three years, the new Liberal government, which he supported, had a succession of three leaders and was sharply divided by the land and school questions. On the latter issue, Bell, a Presbyterian, openly opposed public grants to Roman Catholic denominational schools; however, First Prince was two-thirds Roman Catholic in population, and Bell was defeated by a Catholic Liberal in the election of 18 July 1870. Later in the same year, he successfully contested a seat in the Legislative Council, where he reiterated his views on the school question. He became president of the upper house in 1874, and held that position until his death.

Bell was a strong advocate of "temperance" and served as a grand worthy patron of the Sons of Temperance for several years. As a merchant with considerable trading interests, he vigorously supported the idea of free trade between P.E.I. and the United States. On most other issues his views were quite conventional; he opposed leasehold tenure and confederation.

IAN ROSS ROBERTSON

Prince Edward Island, Supreme Court, Estates Division, will of Herbert Bell, 7 Feb. 1876. Prince Edward

Island, House of Assembly, *Debates and proceedings*, 1867–70, especially 1868, 171; 1870, 64–65; *Journals*, 1867–70. Prince Edward Island, Legislative Council, *Debates and proceedings*, 1871–75, especially 1873, 80–82; 1874, 237–39; *Journals*, 1871–75. *Examiner* (Charlottetown), 21 Feb. 1876. *Patriot* (Charlottetown), 18 Feb. 1876. *Can. parl. comp., 1874*, 515. Robertson, "Religion, politics, and education in PEI," 195–96.

BELL, ROBERT, surveyor, journalist, and politician; b. in 1821, probably in Strabane, County Tyrone, Ireland, son of Robert Bell and Catherine Wallace; m. in 1849 Margaret Waugh Buckham by whom he had two daughters; d. 25 Feb. 1873, in Hull, Que.

Robert Bell's parents emigrated to New York when he was still young, and in 1832 the family settled on a farm near Kemptville in Upper Canada. He attended local schools and on 16 June 1843 qualified as a provincial land surveyor.

Bell moved to Bytown (Ottawa) and quickly established a sound reputation as a surveyor. He worked at first largely in the immediate Bytown area but in 1847 he undertook a survey of the Chalk River and its branches. In the same year he was chosen to head a party to survey a base line from the Madawaska River at Bark Lake to the northeastern limit of the Home District near the site of Bracebridge, while another party, under John James Haslett, continued the line eastwards to the Bathurst District. The government's object in ordering the surveys was to open the lands beyond the Midland, Victoria, and Colborne districts for settlement, and Bell was instructed "to project the best site for the road line." He set off on his difficult journey along what came to be known as Bell's Line in August 1847 and returned to Bytown in March 1848. He considered the "chief part" of the country he crossed, most of it in present-day Muskoka District and county of Haliburton, as "quite fit for settlement," but he acknowledged that "the greatest objection that at all exists in respect to the whole territory is the great abundance of Rocks."

Bell's last important survey again brought him into the area west of Bytown. In November 1850 he was asked to survey a line for a road from the Ottawa River in Horton Township to Opeongo Lake, a road which, it was hoped, would be continued to Georgian Bay near the mouth of the French River and would open up "the interior of the Ottawa and Huron country, benefitting equally the farmer and the lumberer." On this expedition, which took from January 1851 to April 1852, Bell found "many tracts of excellent land" and "remarkably well timbered" regions.

He retained an interest in surveying and often advised the assistant commissioner of crown lands, Andrew Russell, on the subject, but Bell's energies had shifted to journalism. In 1849 he purchased the Bytown *Packet* from Henry J. Friel* and John Gordon Bell, and in it he expounded his ideas for promoting the settlement of the waste lands between Bytown and Lake Huron and for advancing the interests of Bytown and the Ottawa lumber trade. In February 1851 the newspaper became known as the *Ottawa Citizen*.

Bell also undertook to promote the construction of a railway from Bytown to Prescott where it would connect with the railway at Ogdensburg, New York. Ottawa valley lumbermen would thus be provided with easier means of transport to the increasingly important American market. Bell was named secretary of the provisional committee of the Bytown and Prescott Railway (later the Ottawa and Prescott Railway) in 1850. When the railway was chartered in 1851 he was named its secretary, and he, more than anyone else, saw to its completion. He was later president of the line for many years.

After serving on the Bytown town council, Bell ran in Russell for the Legislative Assembly as a Reformer in 1854. He was defeated then and again in 1857, but he was successful in 1861. He spoke mainly on railways, acting as a spokesman of the Grand Trunk Railway, and on opening up the area west of Ottawa, and strongly supported Ottawa's claim for the seat of government. In 1866, however, he became the centre of a bitter controversy. Alexander Tilloch Galt* had promised to extend the educational privileges of the Protestant minority in Canada East. Although he was himself a Presbyterian, Bell brought in a bill to extend to the Roman Catholics of Canada West educational privileges equal to those obtained by Galt, "a proposition so fair," he thought, "that no man, whether Catholic or Protestant, would object to it." There were loud cries of outrage from Protestants in Canada West who saw Richard William Scott*'s bill of 1863 as the final compromise on the separate school question in Canada West. Egerton Ryerson*, the superintendent of education in Canada West, stated that the bill was "the most disingenuous, partial and execrable that can be conceived." Thomas SCATCHERD and George BROWN fought it in the assembly, and Hector Langevin*, who had introduced Galt's bill, privately considered it "the stupidest imaginable from a parliamentary point of view. . . ." When the French members from Canada East threatened to vote against Galt's bill unless Bell's was also passed and the members from Canada West threatened to do the same if Bell's was passed, both

Bellecourt

bills were withdrawn. Galt resigned from the ministry and the Protestants of Quebec entered confederation with a constitutional protection, added at the London conference in late 1866, "the precise terms of which had not the benefit of discussion and sanction of parliament."

Bell ran for the House of Commons for Ottawa City in 1867 but his wife was ailing and he was kept from the hustings and defeated. He had given up the editorship of the *Citizen* to I. B. Taylor in 1861 and had sold the newspaper to him in 1865, the same year that the Ottawa and Prescott Railway, of which he was still president, was foreclosed by the bondholders. Disheartened he retired. After his wife's death in 1868 he went to live with a daughter in Hull, "sunk altogether out of the ken of the world," and died there at the age of 52.

HENRI PILON

Ontario, Department of Lands and Forests, Surveys office, field note books, nos.86, 1895, 2202, 2203; Instructions to land surveyors, from 6 Nov. 1844 to 24 Oct. 1861, pp.93–96, 171–73; map no.020–24, B38. PAC, RG 31, A1, 1851, Ottawa City, West Ward, 270. PAO, RG 1, A-I-6, 22, 24–29; A-V, 9. Canada, Province of, *Parliamentary debates*, 1861–66. *Muskoka and Haliburton* (Murray). *Packet* (Bytown), 1849–51. R. W. Scott, *Recollections of Bytown; some incidents in the history of Ottawa* (Ottawa, [1910]), 3–9. *Times* (Ottawa), 26 Feb. 1873.

Can. parl. comp., *1864*. *Mitchell & Co's county of Carleton and Ottawa city directory, for 1864–5* (Toronto, 1864). *"The Ottawa Citizen" directory of Ottawa ... 1863* (Ottawa, n.d.). *Ottawa city and counties of Carleton and Russell directory, 1866–7,* comp. James Sutherland (Ottawa, 1866). H. R. Cummings, *Early days in Haliburton* (Toronto, 1963), 3–4, 7–13, 178–80. Andrée Désilets, *Hector-Louis Langevin, un père de la confédération canadienne (1826–1906)* (Les cahiers de l'Institut d'histoire, 14, Québec, 1969), 153–55, 226. J. L. Gourlay, *History of the Ottawa valley, a collection of facts ... events and reminiscences for over half a century* (n.p., 1896), 124–26. C. B. Sissons, *Church & state in Canadian education; [an historical study]* (Toronto, 1959), 138–41. "Robert Bell," Ont. Land Surveyors Assoc., *Annual Report* (Toronto), no.40 (1925), 106–9. "William Bell," Ont. Land Surveyors Assoc., *Annual Report* (Toronto), no.38 (1923), 135–38.

BELLECOURT (Bellecours, Belcourt), GEORGE-ANTOINE, priest and missionary, b. 22 April 1803 in Saint-Antoine-de-la-Baie-du-Febvre (Baieville), L.C., son of Antoine Bellecourt and Josephte Lemire; d. 31 May 1874 at Shediac, N.B.

George-Antoine Bellecourt studied at the seminary of Nicolet, and was ordained into the Roman Catholic Church on 10 March 1827. After serving as assistant in various parishes, he was installed in Sainte-Martine, Châteauguay County, in 1830, where he became attached to the parish and its people. He begged to be excused when in 1831 Mgr Bernard-Claude Panet* asked him to go to remote Red River. He went, however, and at Saint-Boniface began his work by mastering Chippewa (Sauteux), a form of the Algonkian tongue, which he had previously studied at the mission of Lac-des-Deux-Montagnes. Knowledge of the language gave him an advantage over the other missionaries who had to rely on interpreters. In 1839 his little grammar, *Principes de la langue des sauvages appelés Sauteux* was published in Quebec; he prepared a *Dictionnaire sauteux*, later printed by Father Albert Lacombe* in 1874, and is said to have translated the catechism of the diocese of Quebec into Chippewa.

In 1832–33 Bellecourt began his mission to the Chippewas on the Assiniboine River, west of the Métis mission of Saint-François-Xavier, on land given by the Hudson's Bay Company. He strove to persuade the Chippewas to build a village there like the one established by the Anglican missionaries at St Peter's (near present-day Selkirk) on the lower Red River. He himself laboured as farmer, builder, and carpenter. By 1839 the mission village, Baie-Saint-Paul, with tiny fields along the river, was well established.

He then decided, however, to return to his native province, and Archbishop Joseph Signay* recalled him to work with the Indians at Lac Témiscamingue. But Bellecourt, apparently an emotional and impulsive man, soon returned to the west. In 1840 the tireless priest started missions at Wabassimong (White Dog) Falls on Winnipeg River, at Rainy Lake (Lac La Pluie), and at Duck Bay (Baie des Canards) on Lake Winnipegosis, but Baie-Saint-Paul and its people remained his chief care. Support for his work came from the Société de la Propagation de la Foi, the diocese of Quebec, and the bishop of Quebec.

In 1844 trouble began to develop in the Red River Settlement when an American at Pembina, Norman Wolfred Kittson*, attempted to challenge the legality of the HBC monopoly by trading furs with the Indians, and Bellecourt joined in the agitation to destroy the company's position. He had not been hostile to the company itself, indeed his assistance in troubles between the Métis and the company in 1834–35 had been sought and was remembered by the HBC, and it is improbable that a man of his character was interested in the fur trade. He was, however, warmly committed to the cause of the Métis. Bellecourt believed that the Métis title to their land should be recognized, that they should be allowed a voice in government, and that "free trade" in furs was their right as natives of the northwest. Contemporaries said that he approved the claims for the Métis against the company listed in Alexander Kennedy Isbister*'s pamphlet, *A few words on the Hudson's Bay Company . . .*, and that he supplied much of its argument. He was a leader at meetings held in February 1846 at the house of Andrew McDermot* in Red River and he drew up a petition in French, setting out the claims of settlers, Indians, and Métis. This petition, with 977 signatures, was dispatched to London, where it precipitated an extensive inquiry into the position of the HBC.

By participating in the agitation Bellecourt made himself a marked man and anathema to Governor George Simpson*. Simpson requested that the archbishop of Quebec, Mgr Signay, recall Bellecourt, but this action had already been taken. In the fall of 1847, after suffering the indignity of having his luggage searched for furs, Bellecourt went back to Canada. A petition was organized, however, requesting his return to Red River, and Bellecourt was anxious that his mission to the Indians and Métis should not be ended. Simpson learned that there was a possibility that Bellecourt might re-establish himself at Pembina, a base for the buffalo hunt and a Métis settlement on American soil, 60 miles south of Upper Fort Garry (Winnipeg), and he invited Bellecourt to come back to Red River, provided that he undertook "not to interfere in the politics of the country." Bellecourt refused. In 1848, however, he did begin a mission at Pembina, a refuge outside the control of the HBC. In a sense Bellecourt had gone into partnership with Kittson against the company.

Simpson's only recourse was to have the new governor of Assiniboia, Major William Bletterman Caldwell*, write in 1849 to the British chargé d'affaires at Washington protesting Bellecourt's counselling the Métis to resist the authorities in Red River. There was some justification for the protest. Not only was Bellecourt attempting to draw off the Métis from Red River and assisting Kittson in making Pembina a centre of the fur trade, but he was also counselling the Métis in their continuing struggle with the government of Assiniboia. It was in fact Bellecourt who advised Jean-Louis Riel* and other Métis leaders on their resistance to the trial of Pierre-Guillaume Sayer who had been accused of illegal trade by the company. He may also have advised them in their petition for representation on the Council of Assiniboia and for the removal of Adam Thom*, recorder of Rupert's Land. From his base in Pembina Bellecourt was thus able to participate in the controversies far more effectively than he had been allowed to do while residing in British territory.

The coming of free trade in 1849 made removal to Pembina unnecessary for the Métis, and the United States treaty of 1850 which arranged transfer of lands to Minnesota treated the Métis as whites, thus denying them a share in the Indian title. The great flood of 1852 overwhelmed Pembina as it did Red River, and the new cart brigades of the free trade went through to St Paul [*see* Joseph ROLETTE]. The mission did not flourish. In 1853 Kittson moved his headquarters to St Joseph (Walhalla, North Dakota) and in the same year Bellecourt took up residence there, on an escarpment to the west where a small Métis settlement began. But the Métis and the HBC had come to terms in the new era of free trade, and Bellecourt was once more a humble missionary. At St Joseph he served with his usual zeal, but difficulties developed both with his helpers and with his superiors, perhaps because of the habit of working alone which he had formed over the years.

Bellecourt left the northwest in 1859 on vacation and was not allowed to return. At the request of Bishop Bernard Donald MacDonald* of Charlottetown, he was sent to serve in the parish of Rustico among the Acadians of Prince Edward Island. There he tried to improve the material lot of his people, as he had done by introducing agriculture to the Chippewas. He inspired the founding of the Farmers' Bank of Rustico which was incorporated in 1864 and lasted until 1894. This was a genuine "people's bank": the directors and the first president, Jérôme Doiron, were all farmers; the first cashier, Marin Blanchard, was a school-teacher. The initial capital was set at £1,200. J. T. Croteau writes: "It was by far the smallest bank, measured by share capital, ever to operate in Canada, it was the first people's bank in Canada, and it was the precursor of the North American credit union movement through its influence upon the pioneer credit union organizer," Alphonse Desjardins* of Quebec. Bellecourt also established a school and a library. Through his friend, the historian François-Edmé Rameau* de Saint-Père, he received an annual gift of 1,000 francs from Napoleon III for the library. Bellecourt gave up his parochial duties in 1869, but two years later he was sent to Havre-aux-Maisons (Îles-de-la-Madeleine) where he served until his final illness.

Bellecourt's tenacity and courage in his work as a missionary are admirable. But his career perhaps exemplifies the difficulty of using someone trained to be a parish priest as a missionary. Bellecourt's fundamental error was that, like so many before him, he attempted to use agriculture and its sedentary life as a means to convert nomads. Father Lacombe may have been wiser in attempting to make the faith itself nomadic.

Belvèze

After a brief illness, Bellecourt died at a farm he had acquired near Shediac, and was buried at Memramcook.

W. L. MORTON

[A complete list of Bellecourt's writings, both in English and in Algonkian, is found in B. B. Peel, *A bibliography of the Prairie provinces to 1953* (Toronto, 1956). References to manuscript sources can be found in J. M. Reardon, *George Anthony Belcourt, pioneer Catholic missionary to the northwest 1803–1874, his life and times* (St Paul, Minn., 1955), 205–17, which is the most complete study of G.-A. Bellecourt's life to date. W.L.M.]
HBC Arch. A.11/95 (Caldwell to the British chargé d'affaires, Washington, 31 July 1849); D.4/35 (Simpson to Christie, 18 Dec. 1849); D.4/37, D.4/45 (Simpson to the archbishop of Quebec, 3 March 1848); D.5/20 (Christie to Simpson, 30 Nov. 1847); D.5/21 (Bellecourt to Simpson, 28 Jan. 1848); D.5/25 (Christie to Simpson, 29 May 1849). G.B., CO, *Hudson's Bay Company. (Red River Settlement.) Return to an address of the Honourable the House of Commons, dated 9 February 1849 . . .* ([London, 1849]). HBRS, XIX (Rich, Johnson, and Morton), xlix, lxxxviii-ix. A. K. Isbister, *A few words on the Hudson's Bay Company with a statement of the grievances of the natives and the half-caste Indians, addressed to the British government through their delegates now in London* (London, 1847). J.-H. Blanchard, *The Acadians of Prince Edward Island, 1720–1964* (Ottawa, Ont., and Hull, Que., 1964). MacMillan, *Catholic Church in PEI*, 115–16, 264–65, 305–6. Morice, *Hist. of the Catholic Church*, I. J. T. Croteau, "The Farmers' Bank of Rustico: an early people's bank," *Dal. Rev.*, XXXVI (1956–57), 144–55.

BELVÈZE, PAUL-HENRY DE, French sailor, commander of *La Capricieuse,* descended from an old family of Languedoc; b. 11 March 1801 at Montauban, son of Antoine-Jean-François de Belvèze and Marie-Josèphe-Jeanne Garrigues de Saint-Fauste; d. 8 Feb. 1875 in his mansion at Toulon.

A former pupil of the École Polytechnique, young Paul-Henry de Belvèze joined the navy in 1823 and was subsequently put in charge of various expeditions, notably to South America, Europe, and the Holy Land. In 1855, while he was cruising in the Gulf of St Lawrence as "commander of the French forces in the waters of Newfoundland," Napoleon III's government decided to entrust to him the mission of renewing relations with Canada, a mission which, in the terms of the official mandate, was to be above all "commercial, with no diplomatic character." This objective was exceeded: in Canada East where deeply moved spectators watched the return of the French colours, the sailor's passage was a triumph; towns such as Ottawa, Kingston, and Toronto, despite some reservations, felt obliged to extend a welcome to the French delegation, which was invariably correct and sometimes warm. The moment seemed well chosen: Great Britain had just abolished the former customs duties which hitherto had made trade between Canada and abroad impracticable. Moreover, relations between France and England had never been better; the French sovereigns had been the guests of Queen Victoria in 1850, and the latter, in that same year 1855, was to return their visit on the occasion of the universal exposition in Paris, at which Canada had an exhibit.

The mission's success must be attributed to a large extent also to the personality of the commander – a "very well educated, extremely capable" man, as one of his superiors had said of him in 1831. In 1848 he was judged to be "one of the captains best fitted to command." A true meridional, Belvèze had the natural gifts of a brilliant speaker, but in him spontaneity was held in check by a wisdom and tact worthy of a professional diplomat. A detailed report of his observations appeared later and was reproduced in the newspapers. The introduction to this report is to be found at the end of his *Lettres choisies . . .,* published in 1882 through the good offices of his widow.

The commander was retired in 1861 without obtaining the promotion to which he thought he was entitled. One of the practical results of his mission was the establishment, in 1859, of a consulate at Quebec, where France had been represented only by an agent named Edward Ryan.

ARMAND YON

[C.-L.] de Beauvau-Craon, *La survivance française au Canada; notes de voyage* (Paris, 1914), viii. [P.-H. de Belvèze], *Lettres choisies dans sa correspondance, 1824–1875,* Hubert et Georges Rohault de Fleury, édit. (Bourges, France, 1882). *Le Canadien* (Québec), 10 juin–15 sept. 1855. *Journal de Québec,* 10 juin–15 sept. 1855. *La Minerve* (Montréal), 10 juin–15 sept. 1855. *Ottawa Tribune,* 3, 10, 17 Aug. 1855.
Henri Cangardel, "Voyage de *La Capricieuse* au Canada," *La Revue maritime* (Paris), nouv. sér., no.3 (juill. 1955), 865–83; "Voyage de « La Capricieuse » dans les eaux du Saint-Laurent en 1855," *Communications et mémoires* (Académie de Marine, Paris), nouv. sér., no.24 (juin 1947), 1–32. Jacques Gouin, "Un agent français « plus ou moins secret » à Ottawa en 1855: la visite du commandant Belvèze dans la future capitale du Canada," *Asticou,* no.2 (janv. 1969), 5–14. R. D. L. Kinsman, "The visit to Canada of 'La Capricieuse' and M. le Commandant de Belvèze in the summer of 1855 as seen through the French-langue press of Lower Canada," unpublished MA thesis, McGill University, 1959. Armand Yon, "Les Canadiens français jugés par les Français de France, 1830–1939," *RHAF,* XVIII (1964–65),

48

517–33; "L'Odyssée de la « Capricieuse », ou comment la France découvrit de nouveau le Canada en 1855," *Le Canada français*, 2ᵉ sér., XXIII (1935–36), 837–56.

BENNETT, GEORGE, convicted of the murder of George BROWN; hanged in Toronto, Ont., 23 July 1880.

George Bennett's early life is obscure. By his own account, written on the eve of execution, he was born of good Roman Catholic parents, but they died while he was young, leaving him prey to evil companions, infidelity, and alcohol. His is a fairly typical statement, though it accords with his later dissolute behaviour; however, it throws no light on the literate, if not literary, quality of the letters and verse he had written which were found on him at his arrest.

What is clear is that he had worked for the Toronto *Globe* between 1875 and 1880, and by the latter date was night engineer in the boiler room. By this time, moreover, he was in recurrent domestic – and police – trouble. He drank heavily; he was arrested for wife-beating and non-support. He felt himself friendless, except for "Dear Annie" McGovern to whom he wrote letters asserting that he had dragged her name "into the dirt" through his association with her. Several times he had been reprimanded by the chief engineer of the *Globe*, James Banks, for neglecting his work. Then on the night of 4 Feb. 1880 he was drunk on duty. Banks had to be called in to avert a dangerous accident to the boiler; on his report, Bennett was dismissed the next day. Bennett made attempts to gain reinstatement from Brown, proprietor of the influential *Globe* and leading Liberal party figure, who had authorized his dismissal. But the facts of drink and danger told too strongly against him. Over the next few weeks he drank and brooded on his wrongs, writing letters to himself projecting suicide or swearing vengeance and death to his enemies. On 25 March Bennett went to the *Globe* office again, this time with a fully loaded revolver in his pocket – telling his hotel-keeper he was "going to Leadville" from which there was no easy return. He had been drinking, but was apparently more agitated and obsessive than drunk.

He seemed to have no clear intent, but roamed the press and boiler rooms, at one time talking amicably to employees, at another threatening them. "You are an enemy of mine," he told Banks. About four-thirty in the afternoon he went to Brown's editorial office, to ask him to sign a statement that he had worked five years at the *Globe*; evidently he wanted a reference in the police courts for he was still out on bail. Brown refused to sign, telling him to see Banks or the *Globe* treasurer, who would have the facts. An argument ensued, then Bennett suddenly drew and cocked his gun. Brown grabbed for it, trying to deflect it. It fired in the brief scuffle. Hearing the noise, members of the editorial staff rushed down and easily secured the under-sized, and dazed, Bennett. Brown had suffered a flesh wound in the thigh. Bennett was taken into custody and on 27 March charged with shooting with intent to kill. He pleaded not guilty.

There was general expectation of Brown's recovery, but, as the weeks passed, the wound became inflamed and his condition gradually grew worse. Business problems, along with his worries and exertions over them, undoubtedly severely taxed Brown's strength; and medical knowledge then could not cope with the "blood poisoning" that set in. By late April he was weak and feverish, and gangrene was spreading. He lapsed into a coma, and died on 9 May. An inquest was immediately held. On 11 May it reached the verdict that Bennett had been responsible for Brown's death, "with malice aforethought."

In the shocked state of public feeling at the time, little other verdict might be expected. George Bennett was charged with murder. His trial opened on 23 June, and concluded in one day. His counsel, the able and eloquent Nicholas Flood Davin*, stressed that Brown's own exertions had rendered his wound fatal; that Bennett had been unbalanced by drinking and had never premeditated killing or even shooting him. But the weight of medical evidence was given on the other side, in testimony that the wound, inflicted by Bennett, had actually killed Brown, and the damning letters found on the prisoner at his arrest were taken as demonstrating premeditation (although one might wonder whether they had not pointed more at Banks than Brown). Bennett was swiftly found guilty and sentenced to death. At his execution one month later, Bennett said, as he had throughout, that he had never meant to shoot George Brown: "I was in liquor or I would not have done it."

J. M. S. CARELESS

[The best source for this article was found to be the *Globe* (Toronto) of 1880. Quotations are taken from its full reports of the police examination, inquest, trial, and execution of Bennett. The *Globe*'s record of these transactions has been checked with the *Mail* (Toronto) and the *Evening Telegram* (Toronto); that check shows it to be factually presented as well as providing the fullest account. The judge's notes on Bennett's trial are at the SAB. See also Careless, *Brown*, II, 368–73. J.M.S.C.]

BENNETT, THOMAS, merchant, politician, and

stipendiary magistrate; christened 15 Oct. 1788 in the parish of St James, Shaftesbury, Dorset, England, son of Thomas and Leah Bennett; d. 12 Feb. 1872 in Shaftesbury.

Thomas Bennett's first position was in the British Commissariat Department just before the end of the Napoleonic wars. A few years later, probably in the early 1820s, he came to St John's, Newfoundland, as a partner in the mercantile business that his brother, Charles Fox Bennett*, had just established. Charles Fox, the head of the firm, was the wealthier brother and an arch conservative. Thomas, perhaps more moderate in politics, also became a prominent member of the mercantile community in St John's. In 1831 he signed a petition asking for representative government. When the system was introduced the following year, he was elected to the House of Assembly as the first member for Twillingate and Fogo. In 1834 when John Bingley Garland, first speaker of the house, was appointed to the council, a sharp contest for the speakership took place between the Liberal Dr William Carson* and the Conservative Thomas Bennett. Bennett won. Although in 1836 he was again returned for Twillingate and Fogo, the whole election was invalidated, after which Bennett, like many of his party, chose not to stand for re-election.

He had been appointed a commissioner of lighthouses in 1834, and in 1837 was appointed to the Board of Control to regulate road-building. Before the introduction of the Amalgamated Legislature [see John Kent] in 1842, Governor Sir John Harvey* was careful to assure the services of both Bennett brothers, whom he described as "intelligent and highly reputed." An election had been called for December and Charles Fox had already announced his candidacy for St John's, when Harvey, reasoning that the more moderate Thomas would stand a better chance of winning a seat in Liberal Catholic St John's, promised Charles Fox a seat in the Legislative Council and urged Thomas to run in his stead. Once elected, Harvey would appoint him to the Executive Council as a representative from the assembly. Accordingly C. F. Bennett was appointed to the Legislative Council in January 1843 and Thomas, although defeated at the polls along with the other Conservative candidates, was appointed to the Executive Council in August 1843.

Bennett remained a member until the restoration of the usual form of representative government in 1848. Thereupon he retired from an active role in C. F. Bennett and Company and was appointed stipendiary magistrate at St John's. He continued to be a prominent figure in the city, with a residence known as Mount Dorset, was an active member of the Church of England, a director of the St John's Academy and of the St John's Hospital. He was appointed by the governor in 1859 to investigate election disturbances at Harbour Grace. Following a riot in St John's at the opening of the legislature in 1861, the Liberals blamed the two magistrates Peter W. Carter and Thomas Bennett for causing violence by calling out the troops to disperse the mob. In 1870, after his brother became prime minister, Bennett was pensioned off from the magistracy and retired to Dorsetshire.

ELIZABETH A. WELLS

Dorset County Record Office (Dorchester, Dorset, Eng.), records for the parish of St James, Shaftesbury. PANL, Newfoundland, Dept. of the Colonial Secretary, letter books, December 1832 – June 1835, September 1836 – June 1838. PRO, CO 194/83, 194/114. Newfoundland, House of Assembly, *Journals*, 1834, 87; 1871, app.9. *Newfoundlander* (St John's), 6 Oct., 15, 22 Dec. 1842; 14 May 1861. *Newfoundland Patriot* (St John's), 5 Oct. 1842; 30 Aug., 6 Sept. 1843. *Public Ledger* (St John's), 2 Dec. 1836, 20 June 1837, 15 Feb. 1872. *Hutchinson's Newfoundland directory for 1864–65*, comp. Thomas Hutchinson (St John's, 1864), 73, 338, 339.

BERCZY, WILLIAM BENT, painter, farmer, politician, and soldier; b. in London, England, 6 Jan. 1791, son of William Berczy* von Moll and Charlotte Allemand; d. at Sainte-Mélanie-d'Ailleboust, Que., 9 Dec. 1873.

William Berczy Jr, son of a pioneer Canadian painter and land developer, came to Upper Canada with his parents by way of Genesee County, New York, arriving at York (Toronto) in 1794. His father's complex business affairs required numerous family moves, with the result that William lived in York 1794–98 and 1802–4, in Montreal 1798–1802, and in Montreal and Quebec 1804–12. He served in the War of 1812. From 1818 to 1832 he resided intermittently at Sandwich, U.C., on a 2,400-acre tract awarded to him by the Upper Canadian government in some compensation for his father's losses on land settlement. On this property he was a pioneer cultivator of tobacco. After 1832 he lived at Sainte-Mélanie-d'Ailleboust, Joliette County, on the seigneury of his wife, Louise-Amélie Panet, a talented amateur artist, daughter of Pierre-Louis Panet*, whom he had married in 1819.

Berczy was an apprentice to his father in painting, and continued to paint for many years although probably never professionally. His water colours, the medium he seems to have favoured, deal with a variety of subjects usually from the life around him. They range from miniature portraits to camp scenes of the War of 1812; *trompe l'œil* studies of insects (in the "Album" collected by Jacques Viger*, Montreal Municipal Library); a painting, *Huron Indians leaving residence near Amherstburg* (in the National Gallery of Canada); and a landscape, with figures, of the *Blessing of the Fields* (also in the National Gallery of Canada). All are characterized by great delicacy and attention to detail, and they echo his father's instruction.

Berczy's varied activities are evidence of broad interests. In addition to cultivating tobacco, he was a ship owner and a contractor to the government for supplies for troops. From 1828 to 1834 he was member for Kent County in the Upper Canada House of Assembly and spent much time in Toronto. As a military man he progressed from cadet to captain of the Corps of Canadian Chasseurs during the War of 1812, and was present at the battle of Crysler's Farm in 1813. From 1845 to 1863 Berczy was active in the militia at Berthier, Que., rising from the rank of lieutenant-colonel to that of colonel commanding the 8th Military District (militia), Lower Canada. He died without issue.

JOHN ANDRE and J. RUSSELL HARPER

ANQ, Fonds Berczy (collection privée). Archives de l'Université de Montréal, Collection Baby, Correspondance générale. ASQ, Fonds Verreau, Ma Saberdache; Fonds Verreau, 19, liasse 2. Bibliothèque municipale de Montréal, Jacques Viger, Souvenirs canadiens. PAC, MG 23, I6 (Samuel Waldo papers). PAO, William von Moll Berczy papers. *Canadian Illustrated News* (Montreal), 21 Feb. 1874. John Andre, *William Berczy, co-founder of Toronto; a sketch* (Toronto, 1967). F. C. Hamil, *The valley of the lower Thames, 1640–1850* (Toronto, 1951), 123, 125, 126, 222, 223, 224, 318.

BERNARD, ALDIS, dentist, mayor of Montreal; b. *c.* 1810; d. 3 July 1876 at San Jose, California, and buried 15 July at Montreal, Que.

Aldis Bernard, probably the son of loyalists, was born perhaps at Beebe Plain, in the Eastern Townships, as certain newspapers indicated at the time of his death; however, there is nothing to confirm this statement. After studying dentistry at Philadelphia, Bernard practised his profession in the southern states, where he married Mary Webb Meredith, who came from Maryland. He stayed for a year in the Niagara region, and then in 1841 took up residence at Montreal. Four years later his wife died, leaving him one child.

In 1847, Bernard tried unsuccessfully to get his profession included in the bill whose aim was to create the College of Physicians and Surgeons of Lower Canada. The fact that this profession was in ill repute among doctors perhaps explains why he failed in his attempt. In 1869, however, when

the number of dentists in Quebec had increased, they united, backed by the prestige of this veteran practitioner, and formed the Dental Association of the Province of Quebec. Bernard was its president until his death.

He was a liberal in politics, and was elected municipal councillor by the property holders of the district of Montreal Centre for 1858 to 1861, then for 1866 to 1873. As chairman of the committees on public order and health, he proposed regulations allowing the creation of the City Passenger Railway Company of the City of Montreal, providing for the inspection of milk, and forbidding the sale of spirits on Sundays. In 1872, while he was chairman of the finance committee, he successfully negotiated the first city loan on the London market, after the treasurer of Montreal, who had been sent to England for the purpose, had failed in face of various difficulties. In 1868 he was appointed alderman by the municipal council, and in June 1873, after some 10 ballots, his colleagues elected him acting mayor to succeed Francis CASSIDY, who had died in office. The following year he was re-elected to this post by popular vote.

The municipal administration, under Mayor Bernard, laid out Mount Royal Park, rented Île Sainte-Hélène from the federal government for a park, acquired the former Protestant cemetery, which subsequently became Dufferin Park, and began the construction of the city hall. In 1875 Bernard did not stand for the mayoralty; he retired from public life, and went to California a few months before his death.

In 1852, in the parish of Notre-Dame, Bernard had married Sarah Couch. As Bernard's wife was Catholic and he was Protestant, she received dispensation from the reading of the bans. However, their seven children were baptized at the St James Methodist Church. Bernard was a member of the Grand (Orange) Lodge of Canada, in which he certainly held a high position; for proof one has only to look at the impressive list of officers of Canadian and American lodges who attended the demonstration in his honour at the time of his burial at Montreal.

LÉON LORTIE

AJM, Registre d'état civil (notes biographiques fournies par Jean-Jacques Lefebvre). AVM, Procès-verbaux du conseil municipal, 87, pp.209, 210–11; Procès-verbaux du conseil municipal, 92, pp.169–74; Procès-verbaux du comité des finances, année 1872, pp.365–66, 369–72, 381–83. Institut généalogique Drouin (Montréal), Aldis Bernard. *Gazette* (Montreal), 12 Dec. 1845; 6, 17 July 1876. *L'Opinion publique* (Montréal), 3 août 1876. *Histoire de la Corporation de la Cité de Montréal, depuis son origine jusqu'à nos jours . . .*, J.-C. Lamothe *et al.*, édit. (Montréal, 1903),

Berry

213, 297, 299. "His worship, the mayor," Canadian Dental Assoc. *J.* (Toronto), XXXIII (1967), no.11, 30–40.

BERRY, JONATHAN, pioneer settler and sawyer; b. in England in 1787 and emigrated to New Brunswick in 1826; d. 26 Aug. 1878 at Berry's Mills, N.B.

Where Jonathan Berry first settled in New Brunswick is not known. His wife Mary (Tingley?) was born in New Brunswick; it would appear from the birth dates of their children that he married sometime after his arrival. By the year 1840 he was living on a small tract west of the tiny settlement now known as Lutes Mountain (near Moncton). In 1844 a survey, under the direction of Sir James Edward Alexander*, for a proposed military road in New Brunswick passed through this region. Although the road did not materialize, the mountain settlements began to prosper. Shipbuilding in the area was expanding rapidly and the railways were soon to come. Berry received title to 100 acres, a portion of which he had already cleared and on which he had built a house. On 9 Jan. 1846 he petitioned for 200 acres adjoining his land and received the grant on 4 Feb. 1847.

Sometime after 1851, Berry established a sawmill driven by water power; the venture proved successful and later a grist mill was added by his son Thomas Berry. The Berrys' customers were the other settlers in the area, all of whom were building wooden houses, the shipbuilders in Moncton, and, later, the railways. As always in pioneer days, it was not long before a settlement developed near these convenient mills, and, in deference to the man who had established them, the settlement took the name of Berry's Mills, which it retains to this day. In 1870 the tracks of the Intercolonial Railway were laid across Berry's property and Berry's Mills became a station on the new line.

When Jonathan Berry died in 1878, he left as a permanent epitaph the prosperous farming settlement which bears his name and which was established because of his pioneering skill and foresight.

C. ALEXANDER PINCOMBE

New Brunswick Crown Lands Office (Fredericton), Memorials and grants, 3721. PAC, MG 9, A12, 11, Census of the parishes of Botsford and Moncton, 1861. *Hutchinson's New Brunswick directory for 1867–1868* (2nd ed., Saint John, N.B., [n.d.]), 559. C. A. Pincombe, "The history of Monckton Township (ca. 1700–1875)," unpublished MA thesis, University of New Brunswick, 1969, 150–51.

BERTHELET, ANTOINE-OLIVIER, businessman, MHA, and philanthropist; b. 25 May 1798 at Montreal, son of Pierre Berthelet*, a doctor who had become wealthy through trade, and Marguerite Viger; d. 25 Sept. 1872 in the same town.

Antoine-Olivier Berthelet was educated at the college of Montreal, where his fellow-students included Côme-Séraphin Cherrier*, John Donegani*, and Édouard-Raymond Fabre*. On his father's death in 1830, he launched out into business. He had foreseen that the town of Montreal would develop rapidly eastwards, and he bought up huge stretches of land which he sold again at a profit or made over as outright gifts to charitable institutions. As member of the assembly for Montreal East from 1832 to 1834, Berthelet realized that politics was not the field in which he could most usefully serve his compatriots. He did however lend his name and prestige to patriotic organizations. Thus he was one of the members of the Fils de la Liberté in 1837; however, he does not seem to have favoured recourse to arms. Berthelet likewise joined the Institut Canadien in Montreal, but he resigned after the intervention of Bishop Ignace Bourget*, who in 1858 condemned the institute and its liberalism. He belonged to a generation among whom by far the most widely held opinion was that Catholicism was one of the elements essential to French Canadian patriotism.

His great-grandson, the engineer Alfred Larocque, has demonstrated that during the last 25 years of his life Antoine-Olivier Berthelet lived in retirement from business and devoted himself entirely to charitable works. According to statistics prepared by Larocque, he gave more than $400,000, an incredible sum for the period, to charitable and educational institutions. In addition there were other acts of generosity of which the extent is not known. There was virtually no community in Montreal that did not benefit from his liberality: Sisters of Providence, Society of Jesus, Oblates of Mary Immaculate, Sisters of Mercy, Good Shepherd Nuns, Sisters of St Ann, Society of the Sacred Heart, Brothers of Charity, and so on. All these religious groups still exist today, and several owe their survival to the timely bounty of Antoine-Olivier Berthelet. In 1868, when Zouaves were being recruited to defend the papal states, he contributed personally as president of the committee, and from his own funds assumed the travel and maintenance costs for 20 soldiers of the pope.

The flourishing development of charitable works that marked Bishop Bourget's episcopate has been rightly admired, but it is fair to say that this success would have been neither so spectacular nor so durable if the bishop had not had the full collaboration of someone who might be called his minister of finance; a finance minister of a rare kind who did not seek to get the money from the pockets of others, but who taxed himself. Indeed, in his last years Antoine-Olivier Berthelet reduced his style of living in order to be able to give more.

In 1844, Cardinal Joseph Fransoni, prefect of the Propaganda, addressed a letter of thanks to him for his services to the church, and sent him a medal bearing the effigy of Gregory XVI; in 1864, Father Pierre Beck, general of the Society of Jesus, granted him the title of distinguished benefactor; and in 1869 he was named commander of the Order of Pius IX, in recognition of the outstanding part he had taken in the recruitment and organization of the Zouaves.

Antoine-Olivier Berthelet died on 25 Sept. 1872; his funeral took place at Notre-Dame, and attracted a large crowd. It was the collective farewell of all Montreal to a man who had only friends and who had given happiness to many. His body was placed in the church of Saint-Joseph, which he had built in Rue Cathédrale and which he had subsequently made over to the Grey Nuns. When this church was demolished in 1930 his remains were moved to the cemetery of the Grey Nuns' mother house.

On 30 Oct. 1822 Berthelet had married Marie-Angélique Chaboillez, by whom he had a daughter, Amélia, who married François-Alfred-Chartier Larocque. Of his second marriage with Charlotte, Louis Guy's daughter, there were no children.

LÉON POULIOT

[At the time of Berthelet's death many biographical sketches were published by the newspapers. The most important is the one which appeared in *Le Nouveau Monde* (Montreal) between 27 Sept. and 8 Oct. 1872. L.P.]

ASJCF, 2286, 5; 3098; 3175, 15. F.-J. Audet, *Les députés de Montréal*, 107–12. Borthwick, *Montreal*, 49. *L'Institut de la Providence; histoire des Filles de la Charité Servantes des Pauvres dites sœurs de la Providence* (6v., Montréal, 1925–40), VI, 265–313. É.-Z. Massicotte, "Un philanthrope canadien-français, M. A.-O. Berthelet," *BRH*, XXII (1916), 183–85. Léon Trépanier, "Un philanthrope d'autrefois: Antoine-Olivier Berthelet," *SCHÉC Rapport, 1961*, 19–25.

BETHUNE, ALEXANDER NEIL, Church of England clergyman and bishop; b. 28 Aug. 1800 at Williamstown, Charlottenburg Township, U.C., son of the Reverend John Bethune*, a loyalist, and Véronique Waddin; m. Jane Eliza, daughter of James Crooks*, and they had ten children, including Robert Henry, a founder and, for more than 20 years, cashier of the Dominion Bank, and Charles James Stewart*, who became headmaster of Trinity College School, Port Hope; d. 3 Feb. 1879 at Toronto, Ont.

A clergyman of the Church of Scotland, John Bethune emigrated to the Carolinas to be chaplain of a regiment of the Royal Militia. Captured soon after the outbreak of the American War of Independence, he made his way to Halifax and then lived for a number of years in Montreal, where he established its first Presbyterian church, the St Gabriel Street Church. In 1787 he moved to Charlottenburg; there Alexander Neil, the eighth of his nine children, was born. Other children were James Gray*, Angus*, and John BETHUNE.

From 1810 to 1812 Alexander Neil was a student at the grammar school run by the Reverend John Strachan* at Cornwall, Upper Canada. It was probably owing to Strachan's influence as well as that of Bethune's mother, who had a Reformed Church background, that both John and Alexander Neil entered the ministry of the Church of England. Alexander Neil's movements from 1812 to 1819 are not known for certain; he may have continued his schooling under his older brother John, incumbent in Elizabethtown and Augusta Townships from 1814 and then at Montreal from 1818, for in the autumn of 1819 Alexander Neil wrote from Montreal that he had determined to go to York (Toronto) "to place himself under the care and direction of Dr. Strachan, as a Student of Divinity, and to connect with this pursuit, such assistance in the Grammar School as a youth of nineteen could be expected to render."

From 1819 to 1823 Bethune remained at York as a student of divinity supported by the Society for the Propagation of the Gospel. He also assisted Strachan at St James' Church as an usher. On 24 Aug. 1823 Bethune was made a deacon by Bishop Jacob Mountain* in Quebec City. The following year, on 26 September, he was ordained a priest by Bishop Mountain. He had charge of the parish of The Forty (Grimsby), where he had served his diaconate, and was also responsible for an out-station at Twelve Mile Creek (St Catharines). In 1827 Bethune became the incumbent of the parish of Cobourg; he was later its rector and served there until 1867. In 1831 he made the first of a number of trips to England on behalf of the Church of England in the colony, on this occasion as secretary to Bishop Charles James Stewart* of Quebec, in support of the University of King's College at York and the Church of England's rights to the clergy reserves in Upper Canada, questions on which his views resembled closely those of Strachan.

While at Cobourg, Bethune also became first editor of the *Church*, a weekly newspaper that commenced publication 6 May 1837. He retained this position until 1841 when he resigned it to a layman, John Kent*, but in 1843 he once again

Bethune

became editor, commenting that "the excitement . . . amidst the clash and din of party strife, was too much for [Kent]." The decision to found a newspaper to represent "Church" opinion in the province came from the need to rally church support for its stand on the clergy reserves. Bethune, a man of not inconsiderable learning, had made a careful study of the whole question, and Strachan, chairman of the newspaper's committee, found in Bethune a man whom he could trust and in whom he could confide. Indeed Strachan directed much of the editorial policy.

At the beginning the newspaper had the respect of all sides of church opinion, for then, Bethune recalled, party spirit within the church was hardly known. But opposition was not long in developing: in 1841 Featherstone Lake Osler* noted that the *Church*, "Though not advocating the errors of the Oxford heresy, continually excuses them and sets forth the Church instead of Xt [Christ] set forth by the Church. The Editor . . . like the Bishop with whom he is an especial favourite is ultra high Church." In the next 30 years, during which more than half a million Irish poured into Canada West, the Church of England acquired a pronounced evangelical, low church flavour. To men of this persuasion, Bethune was a high churchman. There were two influences on Bethune in this regard. In reaction partly to the Methodists, he saw the Church of England as "the acknowledged bulwark of the Protestant faith, against Papal despotism and superstition, and the safe-guard of Gospel truth and order against the heretical and disorganizing principles of many modern dissenters." The other influence was Strachan, who had little respect for low churchmen. In the eyes of the Methodists and the steadily growing number of evangelicals within the church, Bethune came to be identified with the Anglo-Catholic movement which arose during the period of his editorship. His desire to be moderate and fair in assessing its leaders only exacerbated these feelings. When he wrote a balanced editorial on Henry Newman, who had gone over to the Roman Catholic Church, even Strachan admonished him.

The chief opponent of the *Church* was the Methodist newspaper, the *Christian Guardian*, edited by Egerton Ryerson*, which stoutly resisted the exclusive claims of the Church of England in the colony to the clergy reserves. Ryerson reflected the opinion of the Methodists and other bodies dissenting from the eligible established churches in objecting to government support of religious groups, on the grounds that it favoured some to the disadvantage of others and that the revenue would be better spent in such fields as public education and roads. He spoke against the bill of 1840 which proposed that the land be sold after existing obligations were honoured and the proceeds distributed to the various churches, but eventually resigned himself to the measure. Strachan, on the other hand, opposed the bill because it deprived "the national church of nearly three-fourths of her acknowledged property," and declared that "it attempts to destroy all distinction between truth and falsehood . . . its anti-Christian tendencies lead directly to infidelity, and will reflect disgrace on the Legislature, I give it my unqualified opposition." As for Bethune, he wrote in the *Church*: "we shall feel it a duty to inculcate obedience to it as the law of the land, and to render it as beneficial as possible for the object intended. It is with all wel -disposed persons a subject for congratulation that a topic of grievance has thus been removed."

Though Bethune had regarded the lands and revenues of the clergy reserves not merely as the unquestioned gift of a sovereign to his church in the colonies, but also as the only safeguard against the dissidence of many competing religious bodies, he was not built to relish the noise of battle and was visibly relieved at what he thought was a final settlement of such a vexatious issue. Bethune was a man of peace, one who wanted stability and who in the interests of quiescence would attach his loyalty to the settlement. He gladly followed the lead of Strachan, but would have been content to settle for less than his master.

When the diocese of Toronto was carved out of that of Quebec in 1839, Strachan became its first bishop and he appointed Bethune as one of his chaplains. In October 1841 Strachan asked his chaplains, Bethune, Henry James Grasett*, and Henry Scadding*, to draw up a plan for training divinity students pending the establishment of a regular college. The plan was submitted, and on 27 November Strachan announced the appointment of Bethune, though he did not have a degree, as professor of theology. The Diocesan Theological Institution opened in Cobourg in January 1842 with 15 students but was attended by indifferent success. There were complaints about both the quality of the students and their training; for the first three years Bethune was both principal and staff, and this together with the many other demands on his time helps to explain the low academic standards. But the greatest problem Bethune encountered had to do with churchmanship. As the decade wore on there appeared increasing opposition to the school on the part of the low churchmen, particularly in the western part of the province. Its opponents referred to it as a "hot bed of Tractarianism," an accusation Strachan in particular resented as false and malicious. This difficult and often stormy part of Bethune's ministry was brought to an end when the school was merged with the University of Trinity College, opened in Toronto in 1852.

Strachan had appointed Bethune his ecclesiastical commissary for the archdeaconry of York in 1845 with the title of "the Reverend Official." Though burdened with responsibilities, Strachan had felt unable to relinquish the post of archdeacon of York for financial reasons, and this arrangement permitted him to devote his time to his duties as bishop. Then, in 1847, the bishop collated Bethune into the archdeaconry of York upon his own resignation from that position. Bethune gave up the editorship of the *Church* and became the chief administrative assistant of Bishop Strachan while remaining principal of the college. He made regular visitations of the parishes, checking church buildings and rectories, reviewing parish registers, advising on pastoral problems, and making reports to the bishop. From 1847 to 1850 he visited about 127 churches and mission stations, in an area that extended westward through the province from Oshawa. The archdeaconry was a post Bethune filled with diligence, and it immersed him in the day-to-day problems of the diocese.

Strachan prevailed upon King's College, Aberdeen, of which both he and Bethune's father were graduates, to confer upon his archdeacon the degree of doctor of divinity in 1847, and ten years later Trinity College conferred upon him the honorary degree of Doctor of Canon Law. In the spring of 1852 Bethune went to England at Strachan's bidding to raise financial support for Trinity College, founded after Strachan's former creation, the University of King's College, had been secularized into the University of Toronto. Bethune was also his church's spokesman in England during the final battle over the clergy reserves. He met with limited success in both tasks. He was unable to shake the determination of the Lord Aberdeen ministry to comply with the demand from the administration of Francis Hincks* in Canada that an imperial act be passed enabling the provincial legislature to make a final settlement on the clergy reserves. Nor did he receive the response to his appeal for funds which he had expected: he often felt "baffled and disappointed," but considered that "fully £5,000 [would] be realized in all."

In July 1857 the first subdivision of the diocese of Toronto took place when the diocese of Huron was carved out of its southwestern portion. Bethune entered the first of his three episcopal elections and lost to Benjamin CRONYN, the Irish rector of London. When the diocese of Ontario was created from the eastern portion of the diocese of Toronto in 1862, Bethune was again a candidate but withdrew before the certain success of another Irishman, the 36-year-old rector of Brockville, John Travers Lewis*. In both elections, Bethune lost to local candidates with strong popular support. In addition, however, the growing strength in numbers and influence of the evangelical, low church wing was an obstacle to Bethune; he was regarded by many of its sympathizers as a high churchman, and by some as a Tractarian. Moreover, the opposition to Strachan, fostered by his dislike of low churchmen and by his driving personality, spilled over onto Bethune, popularly regarded as the bishop's favourite.

On 21 Sept. 1866, however, Bethune came into his own when Strachan at 88 requested a coadjutor to assist him. The synod elected Bethune on the ninth ballot, but only after Provost George Whitaker* of Trinity College, who had consistently led in the voting, asked after the eighth ballot that his name be withdrawn. Bethune had ranked third in both clerical and lay voting, taking about one-quarter of the clerical votes but one-fifth of the lay vote, trailing Whitaker and Thomas Brock Fuller*. The only other serious contender was Grasett, now rector of St James' Cathedral in Toronto. Bethune took the title of bishop of Niagara and was consecrated by Strachan in St James' Cathedral, 25 Jan. 1867.

Later in 1867 Bethune represented the diocese of Toronto in place of the failing Strachan at the first Lambeth Conference, in England. He returned to Toronto just before Strachan's funeral on 5 November. Bethune had succeeded his mentor on 1 Nov. 1867, and adopted as his signature "A. N. Toronto." He resigned both the rectory of Cobourg and the archdeaconry of York. He continued as bishop of Toronto until his death in 1879.

Bethune's tenure as second bishop of Toronto commenced with a memorial from his clergy expressing their "dutiful submission; of sincere regard for your person and office; and of our purpose, by God's help, to do all we can to render your Episcopate a blessing to yourself and to the Diocese." Events, however, proved the contrary. An articulate, powerful, low church laity fought the reverberations in Canada of the Oxford movement and Tractarian influence. There was a controversy over vestments with William Arthur JOHNSON, the most advanced of the Tractarians in the diocese. On the other hand, Grasett was asked to answer charges of "depraving the doctrine and discipline of the Church" by setting up a rival Church of England Evangelical Association in 1868 which drained off support of missionary efforts of the official Church Society. The low

Bethune

churchmen in 1873 created the Church Association to maintain Reformation principles, founded a rival newspaper, the *Evangelical Churchman*, in 1876, and established the Protestant Episcopal Divinity School (later Wycliffe College) in 1877 as a rival seminary to Trinity College for training divinity students. Finally, in 1878 the low church party thwarted Bethune's attempt to gain the assistance of a coadjutor bishop when the laity prevented the election of Whitaker. Bethune dismissed the synod, resigned to go to the end alone. He protested, in vain, against the rival associations, but they were symptomatic of the deep divisions within the diocese.

During his episcopate the Church of England in Ontario continued to grow with the expanding population. In 1869 the question of a division of the diocese of Toronto was raised once more. The proposal was a fourfold split, with the diocese of Toronto retaining the counties of Peel, York, Halton, Ontario, and Wellington, and the remainder being divided into three districts: Northern (Simcoe County and Algoma District west to the diocese of Rupert's Land), Western (to include the counties of Welland, Lincoln, Haldimand, and Wentworth), and Eastern (Peterborough, Northumberland, Durham, and Victoria counties). There the proposal rested until 1872 when Bethune announced that the SPG was prepared to help endow the proposed diocese of Algoma, on condition that in Canada a sum of at least £4,000 was raised for the same purpose before the end of 1875. In November 1872, Bethune, who had accepted the SPG's offer, attended an informal meeting with the other bishops in Ottawa where it was decided to raise a new bishop's salary immediately by assessment. The following month an election for Algoma was held but the bishop-elect declined the post. Nothing was done until the Toronto synod met in June 1873 and authorized the provincial synod to proceed to the election of a bishop for "the Northern and Missionary Diocese of Algoma." Bishop Bethune was empowered to appoint a clergyman to supervise the work until an election was held. Frederick Dawson Fauquier*, who had studied under Bethune at Cobourg, was consecrated first bishop of Algoma in October 1873. In 1875 the diocese of Niagara was also created out of the western district, and Fuller became its first bishop.

Alexander Neil Bethune was pre-eminently a gentle and mild individual, and a contrast to Strachan, the first bishop. The Reverend John Langtry* commented: "no two men could be more unlike than they. Bishop Strachan was a man of war from his youth. . . . The ideal of Bishop Bethune's life, whether consciously or not, was

that of one who was trying above all things to live peaceably with all men. He was a man of high intellectual gifts, and of extensive reading, of gentle and refined disposition, but of a reserved and unemotional character. . . . Bishop Bethune seldom or never got angry. He was distressed by the waywardness and rough tempers of others; but as the result of it all, he lived an unruffled life."

Bethune, without Strachan's fearless abilities as a strategist, inherited in no small measure the opposition which Strachan's methods and policies had stirred up. It was his misfortune to be bishop at the height of the storm, and his episcopate might have appeared more successful under other circumstances.

Bethune did not show the antipathy Strachan did toward low churchmen, but he did feel them to be deficient in a sense of beauty in worship and in obligation to maintain church order and discipline. He was a "high" churchman in the sense that he maintained a high estimate of the church, its ministry, and its sacraments. He had a high (and somewhat exclusive) interpretation of the church and would never allow the doctrine of justification by faith, on which the evangelicals laid so much stress, to be divorced from Christ's body the church. He was particularly distressed when the visible expression of the church's unity in the diocese was rent by the creation of rival organizations to official bodies.

Bethune was an example to all in his industry, his integrity, his loving manner, and his impartiality. He possessed conviction, but was an intensely humble man. His love of beauty and correctness in worship was interpreted by many in those unsettled times simply as a sign of "high church," and his humility was taken by many for weakness. His message was largely lost on his generation.

ARTHUR N. THOMPSON

A. N. Bethune, *The clergy reserve question in Canada* (London, 1853); *Memoir of the Right Reverend John Strachan, D.D., LL.D. . . . first bishop of Toronto* (Toronto, 1870); *Sermons, on the liturgy of the Church of England; with introductory discourses on public worship and forms of prayer* (York, 1829).

PAO, A. N. Bethune papers; John Strachan letter books, 1827–39, 1854–62; John Strachan papers. Trinity College Archives (Toronto), Bethune papers. A. B. Jameson, *Winter studies and summer rambles in Canada*, ed. J. J. Talman and E. M. Murray (Toronto, 1943). Susanna Moodie, *Roughing it in the bush or forest life in Canada* (Toronto, 1913). [Ryerson], *Story of my life* (Hodgins). Henry Scadding, *The first bishop of Toronto; a review and a study* (Toronto, 1868); *Toronto of old.* Henry Scadding and J. C. Dent, *Toronto: past and present: historical and descriptive; a memorial volume for the semi-centennial of 1884*

(Toronto, 1884). John Strachan, *A letter to the Rev. A. N. Bethune, rector of Cobourg, on the management of grammar schools* ([York], 1829).

Church (Cobourg; Toronto; Hamilton), 6 May 1837 to 1856. *Church Chronicle* (Toronto), 1863–70. Church of England, Synod of the Diocese of Toronto, *Journal . . . adjourned meeting of the fourteenth session* (Toronto), 1866; *Proceedings* (Toronto), 1853–64; *Journals* (Toronto), 1865–79. *Cobourg Star*, 1831, 1837–50, 1851, 1861. *Dominion Churchman* (Toronto), 1875–79. Society for the Propagation of the Gospel in Foreign Parts, *Reports* (London), 1819–60.

W. P. Bull, *From Strachan to Owen: how the Church of England was planted and tended in British North America* (Toronto, [1937]). J. G. Harkness, *Stormont, Dundas and Glengarry: a history, 1784–1945* (Oshawa, Ont., 1946). *History of the separation of church and state in Canada*, ed. E. B. Stimson (Toronto, 1887). *A history of the University of Trinity College, Toronto, 1852–1952*, ed. T. A. Reed (Toronto, 1952). *The jubilee volume of Wycliffe College* (Toronto, 1927). T. R. Millman, *The life of the Right Reverend, the Honourable Charles James Stewart, D.D., Oxon., second Anglican bishop of Quebec* (London, Ont., 1953). O. R. Rowley, *The Anglican episcopate of Canada and Newfoundland* (London and Milwaukee, Wis., 1928). *Trinity, 1852–1952* (Toronto, 1952). R. J. Powell, "The coming of the loyalists," *Annals of the Forty* (Grimsby, Ont.), I (1950). A. H. Young, "The Bethunes," *Ont. Hist.*, XXVII (1931), 553–74.

BETHUNE, JOHN, Anglican clergyman, dean of the diocese of Montreal, acting principal of McGill University; b. 5 Jan. 1791 at Charlottenburg (Williamstown), U.C.; d. 22 Aug. 1872 in Montreal, Que.

John Bethune, brother of Alexander Neil BETHUNE, was the third son of Véronique Waddin and the Reverend John Bethune*, a minister of the Church of Scotland. During the American Revolution, the elder Bethune served as chaplain in the 84th Regiment (Royal Highland Emigrants). Upon its demobilization he took up residence in Montreal, and in March 1786 organized that city's earliest Presbyterian congregation (later First Presbyterian Church of Montreal). In 1787 he moved to the Scots and American royalist settlement in Glengarry, west of Lake St Francis.

John Bethune the younger was schooled by the Reverend John Strachan* at Kingston and Cornwall, and later taught under him. Having been received into the Church of England, he studied for holy orders under Strachan's direction. He was the first product of the Church of England's "Experiment in Home Education," the training of Canadians for the ministry. He served the Cornwall Anglicans as a layreader between 1812 and 1814, when he was ordained in Quebec's Holy Trinity cathedral by Bishop Jacob Mountain*.

He was then posted to the mission of the townships of Augusta and Elizabethtown, the latter of which contained the substantial settlement of Brockville, and was "adopted" by the Society for the Propagation of the Gospel. An active missionary, he served his own district and itinerated widely beyond it among the Rideau River settlements. At the same time, he taught in the Eastern District grammar school, Cornwall. At this stage of his career Bethune appears as the protégé of Strachan, like the master "rather sanguine and partial in views" on the status of the Church of England.

In 1818 Bethune was posted to Montreal as minister of Christ Church and first rector of the Anglican parish of Montreal, which the provincial government had set up that year, its boundaries to be coterminous with those of the Roman Catholic parish of Notre-Dame. The parishes included all of the city of Montreal and its suburbs. As rector, Bethune made his presence felt. The new Christ Church, begun on Notre-Dame Street in 1805, was completed and freed of debt. It was consecrated in 1830 by Bishop Charles James Stewart*. Bethune multiplied agencies depending on Christ Church, many of which, though operated by that church, performed services open to all Montrealers. He organized a Sunday school, which also supplied secular instruction for adults. Aided by the National School Society, in 1819 he established a monitorial school (one in which the senior pupils taught the younger). The Pastoral Aid Society collected money to provide religious ministrations in outlying parts of Montreal. The Committee of Managers for the Poor was reorganized to cope with destitution. Poverty had been greatly aggravated by the termination of the War of 1812–14 and the Napoleonic wars in 1815, bringing a dislocation of the economy and adding large numbers of immigrants. The magnitude of the problem drove Bethune into active cooperation with interdenominational groups: the Montreal Dispensary, the Ladies Benevolent Society, and the Montreal General Hospital (1822). In 1828 Bethune acted as editor of the Montreal Anglican newspaper, the *Christian Sentinel and Anglo-Canadian Churchman's Magazine*. He was among the founders of the Montreal St George's Society and the German Society; the latter claimed his interest through his mother, who was of Swiss descent.

In November 1835 Bethune was appointed principal *pro tem.* of McGill University. He pressed at once for the erection of suitable buildings and for the teaching of disciplines other than medicine, the only faculty with which the college had opened in 1829. (Medicine at that time occupied quarters in the lower town.) Bethune's proposals involved him with the Royal Institution for the Advancement of Learning. This was the body that held in trust the property left by James McGill* in 1813 to endow a university or college. It named the governors of the college, principal, and staff, all subject to the approval of the secretary of state for the colonies. Though over 20 years had passed since McGill's death, and six since the college had opened, much of the money was still held up in litigation, and the governors of the college were still not free of the supervision of the Royal Institution. In spite of the battle with the Royal Institution for funds, the governors, led by Bethune, succeeded in getting plans approved and building under way. By September 1843 the central section of the arts building and the principal's residence were completed. Teaching, chiefly in classical languages and mathematics, began with three students, two of them nephews of the principal, who acted as professor of divinity as well. These achievements were suitably recognized in the same year by the awarding to Bethune of an honorary DD by McGill University. He had received a similar award from Columbia University in 1837.

Ironically, the president of the Royal Institution was Bethune's own bishop, George Jehoshaphat Mountain*. He not only shared the Royal Institution's alarm at the unauthorized, mounting debts of the governors, but he distrusted Bethune's claim to exclusive Anglican control over McGill. This claim to exclusiveness also alienated non-Anglicans and encouraged rival institutions, the Canada Baptist College and the High School of Montreal. Within McGill, friction developed between Bethune and the vice-principal, the Reverend Francis James Lundy*. Lundy was dismissed, but Bethune's own position was in jeopardy. On 3 April 1846 he too was dismissed by the secretary of state for the colonies, William Ewart Gladstone, acting in large measure on the advice of Bishop Mountain.

Interacting with Bethune's McGill principalship was a phase of his masonic life. He was a prominent member of the senior lodge in Montreal, Saint Paul's, and deputy grand master of the Provincial Grand Lodge of Montreal and William Henry (Sorel) from 1824 to 1846. Lundy was also a member of Saint Paul's (by affiliation), and when the feud between the two men developed, Saint Paul's Lodge appears to have tried to mediate. It was unsuccessful, the lodge itself tending to divide. The controversy may have had some bearing on the determination to establish an autonomous grand lodge for Canada. The Provincial Grand Lodge, which was subordinate to the United Grand Lodge of England, was not competent to deal with all questions referred to it. The Grand Lodge of Canada was set up in 1850.

The erection in July 1850 of the diocese of Montreal brought Bethune fresh responsibilities. He became rector of Christ Church Cathedral, and, in 1854, dean, the first in Canada to receive that dignity. He fully supported Bishop Francis Fulford* in the building of the second Christ Church Cathedral, 1856–59, and was his commissary during the bishop's frequent absences. He presided over the special synod 1868–69 that chose Fulford's successor, Ashton Oxenden*. Bethune's ministry in Montreal extended over 54 years and ended only with his death.

He was predeceased by his wife, Elizabeth Hallowell, whom he had married on 28 Aug. 1816. The couple had 11 children, five of whom survived infancy. The eldest son, Strachan Bethune* QC, was chancellor of the diocese of Montreal, 1868–1910.

JOHN IRWIN COOPER

McCord Museum (McGill University, Montreal), Masonic collection, letters and memoranda. McGill University Archives, Minutes of the board of the Royal Institution for the Advancement of Learning, 1835–46; Principal's records, accession nos.447–94. Masonic Memorial Temple (Montreal), Grand Lodge of Quebec, "Masonic membership in Quebec, 1760–1960," comp. A. J. B. Milborne. Montreal Diocesan Archives (Anglican Church of Canada), Francis Fulford papers. Church of England, Church Society of the Diocese of Montreal, *Annual Reports* (Montreal), 1850–58; Church Society of the Diocese of Quebec, *Annual Reports* (Quebec), 1842–50; Synod of the Diocese of Montreal, *Proceedings* (Montreal), 1859–73. *History and by-laws of Saint Paul's Lodge, no.374...* (Montreal, 1876), 183.

F. D. Adams, *A history of Christ Church Cathedral, Montreal* (Montreal, 1941), 64–65. Newton Bosworth, *Hochelaga depicta; or, a new picture of Montreal, embracing the early history and present state of the city and island of Montreal ...* (1st ed., Montreal, 1839), 124–27, 185–86. Campbell, *Hist. of Scotch Presbyterian Church*, 21–31. J. I. Cooper, *The blessed communion; the origins and history of the diocese of Montreal, 1760–1960* (Montreal, 1960), 83–85. J. H. Graham, *Outlines of the history of freemasonry in the province of Quebec* (Montreal, 1892), 193. J. G. Hodgins, *The establishment of schools and colleges in Ontario, 1792–1910* (3v., Toronto, 1910), II, 199, 200, 202, 204. T. R. Millman, *Jacob Mountain*, 147; *The life of the Right Reverend, the Honourable Charles James Stewart, D.D., Oxon., second Anglican bishop of Quebec* (London, Ont., 1953), 69, 80, 92, 190; "The Very Reverend John Bethune, D.D., LL.D.," *McGill News* (Montreal), XXIV, no.4 (1942–43), 16–18, 57. A. H. Young, "The Bethunes," *Ont. Hist.*, XXVII (1931), 553–74.

BÉTOURNAY, LOUIS, lawyer and judge;

b. Saint-Lambert, Chambly County, L.C., 13 Nov. 1825; d. Saint-Boniface, Man., 30 Oct. 1879.

Louis Bétournay was the son of Pierre Bétournay (who died before his birth) and Archange Vincent, and fifth-generation descendant of Adrien Bétourné, *dit* La Violette, soldier of the Carignan-Salières regiment, and Marie Deshaies. Educated at the college of Montreal, Bétournay subsequently studied law with the future judge Joseph-Ubalde BEAUDRY. He was called to the bar in February 1849 and practised law in Saint-Lambert and later in Montreal in a legal firm with George-Étienne CARTIER and François-Pierre Pominville. He served on the Montreal city council from 1870 to November 1872. Created a QC in 1872, he was appointed, on 31 October of that year, through the influence of his law partner, Cartier, puisne judge of the Court of Queen's Bench in the newly formed province of Manitoba, the first French Canadian to be appointed to a superior court west of Lake Superior. Leaving Montreal on 10 December, in company with Captain, the Viscount Louis Frasse de Plainval, chief of the Manitoba constabulary, he reached Fort Garry (Winnipeg) ten days later.

Bétournay's duties were not limited to those of a judge of the Court of Queen's Bench, but included those of a county court judge and police magistrate as well. He was a member of the court which ordered Ambroise-Dydime Lépine*, Louis Riel*'s principal lieutenant, to stand trial in 1873 for the execution of Thomas Scott* during the Red River troubles. In accordance with the bilingual character of Manitoba at this time, Bétournay addressed the jury in French, and his colleague on the bench, James Charles McKEAGNEY, spoke in English. As a result of his role in the Lépine trial, Bétournay gained the ill will of many of the French-speaking inhabitants of the province. In consequence, little mention was made of his activities in the local French-language newspaper, *Le Métis*.

Louis Bétournay was an urbane gentleman, who had a fine library. He was fond of horses, even though on several occasions he suffered injury while riding or driving. He possessed a strong sense of duty, and despite the fact that he suffered from dropsy in his later years, did not neglect his judicial responsibilities. He finally succumbed to his affliction at the age of 54.

On 3 March 1859 Bétournay had married Marie Mercil (Mercille) of Saint-Lambert. There were ten children by the marriage, the eldest of whom was 16 at the time of the father's death. Madame Bétournay survived her husband by 43 years, dying in Saint-Boniface in 1922.

GEORGE F. G. STANLEY

Archives de l'archevêché de Saint-Boniface (Man.), Correspondance de l'archevêché. *Le Métis* (Saint-Boniface), 21 déc., 28 déc. 1872; 3 nov., 11 nov. 1879. *La Minerve* (Montréal), 3 nov. 1879. *Ottawa Daily Free Press*, 4 Nov. 1879. *Dom. ann. reg.*, *1879*, 386. Stanley, *Louis Riel*, 193, 194, 210. J.-J. Lefebvre, "Louis Bétournay (1825–1879), premier juge canadien-français d'une Cour supérieure dans l'Ouest canadien," BRH, LVIII (1952) 29–31. E. K. Williams, "Aspects of the legal history of Manitoba," HSSM, *Papers*, 3rd ser., no.4 ([1948]), 59–60.

BETTRIDGE (Betteridge), WILLIAM CRADDOCK, soldier and Church of England clergyman; b. Warwickshire, England, 30 Aug. 1791; d. Strathroy, Ont., 21 Nov. 1879.

William Craddock Bettridge joined the 81st foot as an ensign, 7 April 1813, and saw service in the Low Countries; he was town adjutant of Brussels during the battle of Waterloo. He became a lieutenant, 31 Aug. 1815, and was retired on half-pay, 25 Feb. 1816. After the war he travelled in Europe and was, by his own account, a student at the University of Jena (where he matriculated on 24 Oct. 1817), a soldier in the employ of Ferdinand I, king of the Two Sicilies, and an aide to General Sir Richard Church.

When Bettridge returned to England, he was made deacon by the archbishop of York, 18 July 1824, and was appointed assistant curate of Ecclesfield, near Sheffield, Yorkshire, where he had married Mary Hounsfield in 1823. He was admitted to St John's College, Cambridge, on 15 June 1824 without coming into residence and was ordained 18 Dec. 1825, the day he went to his second curacy at Elvington, near York. From 1828 to 1833 he was in charge of the newly opened St Paul's Church, Southampton. He was accepted in 1834 as a missionary for Upper Canada by the Society for the Propagation of the Gospel and went out that spring with Admiral Henry Vansittart* and the other military and naval personnel who were founding the town of Woodstock. In 1836 he became rector of the parish and remained so until his death in 1879.

Determining to go home on private business in 1837, Bettridge accepted the additional duty of forming a deputation, along with Benjamin CRONYN, from the church of Upper Canada to the English people. He arrived in Liverpool 18 March 1837 and for the next 17 months toured England and preached the cause of the Canadian church. His *A brief history of the church in Upper Canada*, published in 1838, is less a history than a compilation of the deputation's letters and appeals. While in England he paid the fees of £40 and proceeded to the degree of Bachelor of Divinity in the University of Cambridge in 1837.

Bidwell

The SPG and the newly formed Upper Canada Clergy Society both attested to the interest Bettridge was able to arouse in England. Collections in excess of £3,000 were received. Six months after his return to Canada, however, Bettridge reported that the sums raised were more than swallowed by his expenses. John Strachan*, just appointed bishop of Toronto, set up a commission of inquiry headed by George Okill Stuart*, archdeacon of Kingston, and weighted by the inclusion of William Henry DRAPER, attorney general of Canada West. Bettridge appeared before the commission in Toronto on and after 10 June 1840, and admitted the irregularity of his accounts, but "he had sufficient else to do, and . . . account keeping was and is his antipathy." The commission found that he had made no distinction between church expenses and his own and that he could give no proper account of a sum in excess of £1,000.

The commission's findings were reported to William Howley, archbishop of Canterbury, who stated that Bettridge "[had] not acted in such a manner as to bring himself under the cognisance of the Ecclesiastical or Civil Law." Bettridge was not, therefore, disciplined, except by Strachan who refused to include the parish in his visitation for one year. After that, Bettridge made his peace with his bishop, and remained the respected rector of Woodstock. Bishop Cronyn appointed him rural dean in the diocese of Huron after its creation, and canon of St Paul's Cathedral, London. He was an able clergyman, "very rubrical," and of robust health. He retired in 1874 and died in Strathroy in 1879 at the home of his son, Dr William Bettridge.

J. L. H. HENDERSON

W. C. Bettridge, *A brief history of the church in Upper Canada . . .* (London, 1838).

PAO, John Strachan papers, "Bettridge case," 10–18 June 1840, papers in connection with the commission appointed to enquire into and report upon charges against the Rev. Wm. Bettridge of Woodstock. *Dom. ann. reg., 1879,* 386–87. [John Morris], *Old St. Paul's Church, 100th anniversary, 1834–1934* ([Woodstock, Ont.], 1934]).

BIDWELL, MARSHALL SPRING, lawyer and politician; b. 16 Feb. 1799 in Stockbridge, Mass., son of Barnabas Bidwell* and Mary Gray; m. Clara Willcox of Bath, near Kingston, U.C., and they had four children; d. 24 Oct. 1872 in New York City, N.Y.

Marshall Spring's father, Barnabas Bidwell, who had been attorney general of Massachusetts, a member of Congress, and an ardent Jeffersonian, was forced to leave his home state in 1810 after he had been accused of malversation of funds. The family settled in Upper Canada at Bath just before the War of 1812. The young Bidwell was educated in the local schools and at home by his father who laid the foundation of his profound legal learning. When he was about 17 Marshall Spring was articled as a student to Daniel Washburn and Daniel Hagerman, barristers and attorneys-at-law in Kingston, where the Bidwell family soon moved, and in 1821 he was called to the bar. From the beginning he had outstanding and continuous success as a courtroom lawyer.

Marshall Spring Bidwell and his father first came into public prominence in Upper Canada in the early 1820s in connection with the "alien question": whether Americans who had come into the colony in the previous quarter century must undergo a complicated naturalization procedure before they could enjoy political and civil rights as British subjects. In 1821 the House of Assembly voted to expel Barnabas from the seat he had won a few weeks earlier, on the grounds that the charges earlier made against him in Massachusetts rendered him unfit to hold his seat. A law was subsequently passed obviously intended to exclude the elder Bidwell from membership. Thereupon Marshall Spring offered himself as a candidate at the ensuing by-election, but the returning officer declared him ineligible to be a candidate. Again in 1823 the matter came before the assembly, which now declared that the younger Bidwell was eligible for membership so far as allegiance was concerned. In a second by-election in 1823, however, he was again excluded by the returning officer, and again the assembly declared the election void. Finally, in the general elections of 1824, the returning officer allowed votes to be counted for him; he was elected and took his seat, despite a ruling by the British law officers that he as well as his father was not qualified for membership. He represented Lennox and Addington until defeated in 1836.

The assembly of 1824, for the first time in Upper Canada's history, contained a majority of members highly critical of the executive branch of government – that is, of the group soon to be known as the "Family Compact" – and determined to seek reform through new legislation. At the outset, the young Bidwell, still in his midtwenties, took front rank as a leader of the assembly, working closely with his colleague from Lennox and Addington, Peter Perry*, and with Dr John Rolph*. Bidwell in the years 1825–28 moved the adoption of bills on such subjects as allowing benefit of defence counsel for persons tried for felony, providing for more equal distribution of the property of persons dying intestate, the abolition of imprisonment for debt and of punishment by whipping and the pillory, wider control by the assembly over the revenue and the post office, and the broadening of the law governing the solemnization of marriage. He also supported bills for the sale of the clergy reserves, with the proceeds to be used for erecting schools, and for the regulation of juries. These bills passed the assembly session after session but were as regularly thrown out by the Legislative Council. Bidwell also played a leading role in the protracted alien controversy, which resulted, in 1828, in the passage of a naturalization act acceptable to the American-born element in the province.

Party feelings and alignments were further inflamed and sharpened in 1827 by the Reverend John Strachan*'s "Ecclesiastical Chart," which inflated the strength of the Church of England in the province and accused Methodist clergymen of being agents of Americanization, and by the university charter, secured in England by Strachan, which reserved seats on the council of King's College to Anglicans. In response, the assembly set up a select committee, chaired by Marshall Spring Bidwell, to look into the danger of "ecclesiastical domination." Its report of 1828 is probably an accurate reflection of Bidwell's political outlook. It stated that the people of Upper Canada had a "strong aversion" to an established church and to "artificial distinctions between men of the same rank," that they demanded an educational system free of distinction based on "religious profession or belief," and that the university should not be "a school of politics or of sectarian views." On 28 May 1828 Bidwell wrote to his fellow Reformer, William Warren Baldwin*, that the affairs of the province were in a state of crisis because the government held "power, unaccompanied by any real responsibility, any practical accountability" and that "power, under such circumstances, will always be abused and its possessors corrupted." On the following 8 September, he assured Baldwin: "I shall be happy to consult with yourself and Mr. Rolph on the measures to be adopted to relieve the province from the evils which a family compact have brought upon it. . . . The whole system and spirit of the present administration need to be done away with." He also wrote on 7 Jan. 1829 to John Neilson*, the Quebec newspaperman and moderate Reformer, that changes would come about, not by making appeals to the British government, but by the people of Canada acting "with union and concert and tak[ing] such ground only as can be maintained by reason and truth."

In the elections of 1828 the Upper Canadian Reformers strengthened their majority in the assembly and proceeded to elect Bidwell speaker.

At this time, before the advent of cabinet or responsible government, the speaker was not an impartial presiding officer; instead, he was an active, partisan politician. Bidwell's election, like that of Louis-Joseph PAPINEAU as speaker of the Lower Canadian assembly, marks him as the leader of his party. As speaker, however, he did not make motions or vote, and it is not possible to identify him directly with the work of the short parliament of 1829–30. It can be assumed, however, that he was a strong supporter of such bills as those to abolish imprisonment for debt, to sell the clergy reserves, and to broaden the law governing solemnization of marriage, as well as of numerous resolutions sharply critical of Lieutenant Governor Sir John Colborne* and the executive government.

In the 1830 elections enough seats changed hands to place the Reformers in a minority, and Bidwell resumed his role as Reform floor leader. Although outnumbered, he and his followers were often able to carry their measures, such as the intestate estates bill, through the house. A Tory newspaper explained the situation as follows: "Mr. Bidwell, notwithstanding the inferiority of his party both in talent and numbers, has acquired an influence in the present House, beyond any other member in it. . . . The ministerial party . . . have no acknowledged leader – no mutual understanding – and no common or uniform system of action . . . while the party of which Mr. Bidwell is the head . . . is a well-drilled and compact little body – always at their post, and always ready to follow their leader." Nevertheless, the Reformers were often outvoted, particularly in the matter of the several expulsions of William Lyon Mackenzie*, when Bidwell argued that "the utmost latitude [should be] given to the freedom of the Press" in a province where the executive had such "great influence." At the time of the last expulsion he accused the conservative majority of "making Mr. Mackenzie a man of the greatest importance in the eyes of the freeholders, who look on him as a martyr in the cause of their civil rights. In doing this what a spectacle you make of this House! You are injuring its character, preventing those enquiries to which its attention ought to be directed, conducting the most important matters in the most careless and hasty manner, and trifling with the important duties you were sent to fulfil." Bidwell's greatest coup in this parliament was his moving, early in 1834, an address to the king protesting against the British government's disallowance of banking bills passed by the legislature of Upper Canada; the address, which Mackenzie called "The Latest Declaration of Independence," passed with only one negative vote.

Bidwell

In the elections of 1834 the Reformers were again victorious and again Bidwell was elected speaker, despite Christopher Hagerman*'s charge that he was "a disloyal man . . . politically connected with persons desirous of separating this Province from the Mother country." As in the 1820s the assembly passed the usual bills on the reform programme, and added to them one to legalize voting by ballot, all of them being again thrown out by the Legislative Council. But as the province moved in to the boom years of the mid-1830s there were signs of a growing split between the Reform majority led by Bidwell and Perry and a small group of agrarian radicals, led by Mackenzie. The majority supported bills to build canals and to charter banks and insurance companies which Mackenzie vehemently opposed. After Mackenzie had brought in his bulky and indiscriminate *Seventh report on grievances* in 1835, Perry sought to dissociate himself from it, and it is probable that he was also speaking for Bidwell. The year before, at a political meeting, Perry had said that "no two persons disapproved more at times of Mr. Mackenzie's occasional violence, than Mr. Bidwell and himself."

At the beginning of 1836 the provincial political scene was quickened by the arrival of a new lieutenant governor, Sir Francis Bond HEAD, sent out by the Colonial Office to deal with the grievances listed in Mackenzie's *Seventh report*. Inexperienced in politics, of a volatile temperament, and totally ignorant of Upper Canada, Head was astounded when, in a personal interview, he was informed by Bidwell that the people had grievances not mentioned in Mackenzie's 553-page *Report*. From that time forward Head was suspicious of Bidwell, not understanding the growing rift between the latter and Mackenzie and the different approaches to reform of the two men.

Finding it necessary to enlarge the Executive Council, Head, in February 1836, appointed three new members: J. H. Dunn* and two well-known Reformers, Robert Baldwin* and John Rolph. Reform hopes were soon dashed, however, when in less than a month the entire Executive Council resigned on the ground that they were not being adequately consulted by the lieutenant governor. There then followed a bitter quarrel between Head and the Reform-dominated assembly. The latter adopted addresses to the king and to the British House of Commons, each signed by Mr Speaker Bidwell and each denouncing the lieutenant governor as despotic and deceitful. The assembly then voted to stop the supplies and shortly afterward Bidwell entered on the *Journals* of the house a letter from Mr Speaker Papineau, asserting that "The state of society all over continental America

requires that the forms of its Government should approximate nearer to that selected . . . by the wise statesmen of the neighbouring Union." For his part, Head dissolved the legislature and plunged the province into one of the hottest election campaigns in its history. He was convinced that he "was sentenced to contend on the soil of America with Democracy," and that the leader of his "republican" opponents was Marshall Spring Bidwell.

The Reformers were routed in the 1836 elections, and among those not returned was Bidwell. In addition to the general swing against his party, there were probably some personal reasons for the speaker's defeat in Lennox and Addington. He had recently moved to Toronto as a better site for his growing law practice, and Canadian voters have often resisted non-resident candidacies. And Bidwell apparently did not campaign very hard in a heated political atmosphere that was not to his liking. At any rate he wrote to Robert Baldwin that "twelve years hard labour have exhausted my hopes, my strength . . . and I was unwilling to incur expence or trouble." Also, like other Reformers, Bidwell attributed his downfall to unfair tactics used by the other side. He now resolved to retire from politics, and he played no part in the events of the next year and a half culminating in the rebellion of December 1837.

While he was in political retirement, Bidwell, unknown to himself, was a central figure in a clash between Head and the Colonial Office that eventually led to the governor's resignation. In a dispatch of 5 April 1837, Head refused to restore George RIDOUT to offices from which he had been dismissed, and he also refused to appoint Bidwell to a judgeship. He stated that Bidwell's "legal acquirements are . . . superior to at least one of the individuals whom I have elevated. His moral character is irreproachable. . . . But, anxious as I am to give talent its due, yet I cannot but feel that the welfare and honour of this province depend *on his Majesty never promoting a disloyal man*." On 14 July Lord Glenelg insisted that Bidwell be offered the next vacancy on the Court of King's Bench, and on 10 September Head "determined to take upon myself the serious responsibility of positively *refusing* to place Mr. Bidwell on the Bench, or to restore Mr. George Ridout to the Judgeship from which I have removed him." On 24 November Glenelg informed Head that his resignation had been accepted. The colonial secretary regarded Head's disobedience in the Ridout affair as the more serious, but clearly Bidwell had, unwittingly, played a part in the recall of the lieutenant governor.

But Head was to have his revenge. Before

Glenelg's dispatch reached Toronto, Mackenzie's attempt at armed rebellion had been made and easily put down. Among the items left by the rebels as they scattered was a flag bearing the inscription "BIDWELL, AND THE GLORIOUS MINORITY! 1837, AND A GOOD BEGINNING." This was, in fact, an election banner dating back to 1831, with the date altered. A day or two later Head confronted Bidwell with the flag, stated that he could not guarantee him security of person or property in the existing excited state of feeling, and that he would give him a letter of protection if he would leave the province. Bidwell, later described by Egerton Ryerson* as having a "retiring, timid and even nervous" temperament, denied that he had had any part in the rebellion but nevertheless agreed to the governor's proposal that he leave Upper Canada forever. On 9 Dec. 1837 he crossed Lake Ontario to New York State. He carried with him a hastily written note from his old antagonist Christopher Hagerman which stated: "I have known you long and in some respects intimately and my respect for your private character as a neighbour and a friend arising from a knowledge of your amiable disposition in those relations of life which do not involve political controversy has impressed me so strong with feelings of friendship and esteem that I cannot now part with you perhaps forever without emotion."

This personal note did not prevent Hagerman, some weeks later, from stating in the Toronto *Patriot* that Bidwell had left Upper Canada after Head had offered him a choice between having letters addressed to him in the Toronto post office opened and read or having them returned to him unopened and leaving the province. The accusation brought Ryerson, the province's most powerful controversialist, into the lists on Bidwell's behalf. Ryerson had been Bidwell's political opponent from 1833 to 1836, but he was now convinced that the former speaker had "been banished for his talents and opinions," not his actions, and that whenever a people allowed their rulers to attach "pains and penalties . . . to opinions . . . that very moment they sign the death warrant of their own liberties, and become slaves." Ryerson's condemnation of Head has become the verdict of history.

Although most of the leading exiles of 1837 eventually returned to live in Canada, Bidwell never did. On at least two occasions in the 1840s attempts were made to secure his return but they came to nothing. He kept in touch with many Canadians and his later New York associates always regarded him as an authority on Canadian affairs. In 1872, shortly before his death, he paid a brief visit to Toronto, sharing a pew one Sunday morning with Ryerson.

Not long after he left the province Bidwell had two final contacts with its governors. In March 1838, when he was in Albany applying for admission to the New York bar, he accidentally met Sir George Arthur*, Head's successor, who had stopped to pay his respects to Governor William L. Marcy before continuing to Toronto. His finding Bidwell in the governor's residence immediately convinced Arthur that the former speaker must be an untrustworthy character, while his conversation with Arthur convinced Bidwell "that there will be no liberality under him." Shortly afterward, as he was passing through New York City on his return to England, Head invited Bidwell to call on him. At first their conversation was politely formal, but when Head informed him of the exchanges with Lord Glenelg about a judgeship, the usually mild Bidwell exclaimed that his banishment had been "exceedingly arbitrary, unjust and cruel." He probably now believed that Head had forced him to leave in order to score a point against the Colonial Office.

When Bidwell left Upper Canada more than two-thirds of his career still lay before him. At first he was despondent and pessimistic, writing to friends that he was too old "to get into business . . . in a strange land" where he had never practised his profession. Nevertheless, he was soon admitted to practise by both the state Supreme Court and the Court of Chancery, and after moving to New York City was taken into partnership in George W. Strong's law firm. After Strong's death Bidwell continued as its senior figure in partnership with Strong's son, George Templeton, later joined by the latter's cousin, Charles Edward. The firm of Strong, Bidwell and Strong became one of the most eminent in the metropolis, and Bidwell was soon known as one of the most learned lawyers practising before the American courts, with an unrivalled knowledge of the law of real estate. In his diary, George Templeton Strong states that "we all leaned on him, too much for our own good. Instead of studying up a question, I usually went to Bidwell and received from him an off-hand abstract of all the cases bearing on it and of all the considerations on either side. He loved law as a pure science." Another associate remarked that Bidwell had "often said that he found far more entertainment in tracing some legal principle back through the Reports of the seventeenth century, than in perusing the most attractive work of fiction." He lectured frequently at the Columbia Law School, and in 1858 Yale University conferred on him the degree of Doctor of Laws.

According to William M. Evarts, Bidwell decided that "the circumstances which withdrew

Billings

him" from Upper Canada must cause him "to abstain from any participation in active political affairs" in the United States. G. T. Strong also noted at Bidwell's death that it was "strange that this family, after so many years in New York, should have formed no positive friendships or alliances, especially considering poor, dear old Bidwell's warm-heartedness, geniality and strong social instincts. . . . I suppose poor Bidwell's Puritanic convictions led him to look on 'calls', tea parties, and all the little two-penny machinery of 'social' life as of the nature of evil, in spite of his own natural impulses." Throughout his life Bidwell was a devout Presbyterian and a temperance advocate, and in his New York years a faithful supporter of the American Bible Society and of other religious and charitable organizations and institutions.

Of his career in Upper Canada, Bidwell himself wrote the best evaluation in a letter dated 29 April 1838: "All my offence consisted in a faithful, honest, disinterested attempt by constitutional means, in the discharge of public duties, to improve the conditions and support the rights of the people of Upper Canada. If my views had prevailed, there would have been no rebellion."

G. M. CRAIG

MTCL, Baldwin papers. PAC, MG 24, B1 (Neilson family papers). PAO, Marshall S. Bidwell papers. *Arthur papers* (Sanderson). Head, *Narrative. In memoriam, Marshall Spring Bidwell* (New York, 1872). [A. E. Ryerson], *Sir F. B. Head and Mr. Bidwell: the causes and circumstances of Mr. Bidwell's banishment . . . by a United Empire Loyalist* (Kingston, U.C., 1838). *The seventh report from the select committee of the House of Assembly of Upper Canada on grievances . . .* (Toronto, 1835). [G. T. Strong], *The diary of George Templeton Strong*, ed. Allan Nevins and M. H. Thomas (4v., New York, 1952). Upper Canada, House of Assembly, *Journals*, 1821–36.

J. G. Brown, "Marshall Spring Bidwell and the reform movements in Upper Canada, 1822–1837," unpublished MA thesis, Queen's University, 1934. *Canadian portraits; C.B.C. broadcasts*, ed. R. G. Riddell (Toronto, 1940). Craig, *Upper Canada*. Dent, *Upper Canadian rebellion*. Sister Dominic (Genevieve Slawuta), "Marshal [*sic*] Spring Bidwell, a Reform leader in Upper Canada," unpublished MA thesis, University of Ottawa, [1968]. Aileen Dunham, *Political unrest in Upper Canada, 1815–1836* (London, 1927). Sissons, *Ryerson*. W. R. Riddell, "The Bidwell elections: a political episode in Upper Canada a century ago," *Ont. Hist.*, XXI (1924), 236–44. C. B. Sissons, "The case of Bidwell; correspondence connected with the "withdrawal" of Marshall Spring Bidwell from Canada," *CHR*, XXVII (1946), 368–82.

BILLINGS, ELKANAH, lawyer, journalist, official paleontologist of the Geological Survey of Canada, and member of the Natural History Society of Montreal; b. 5 May 1820 at Gloucester, U.C., son of Bradish Billings and Lamira Dow; d. 14 June 1876 at Montreal, Que.

The Billings family was Saxon by name and English by origin. It moved from New England into Canadian territory at the end of the 18th century, after the War of American Independence. Elkanah Billings was therefore the first of the line to be born in Canada. His maternal ancestors came from Wales; they had lived in the United States before establishing themselves in Canada with the loyalists.

Elkanah Billings was born on his father's farm at Gloucester. At the gates of Ottawa, an urban centre named Billings' Bridge recalls the site of the Billings' family home. The second son of a family of nine children, but coming from a well-to-do and socially privileged environment, Billings received an extensive education. He first attended the schools at Gloucester and Bytown (Ottawa), then, after a break of four years, the St Lawrence Academy, at Potsdam, New York State. In 1839 he registered as a student at the Law Society of Upper Canada, and in the autumn of 1844 was allowed to practise law. On 31 July of the following year he married Helen Walker Wilson, the sister of a Toronto colleague.

The young lawyer carried on his profession, alone or in partnership with Robert Hervey, at Bytown until 1849, then at Renfrew. He returned to Bytown on 10 June 1852 and opened a new office. But he soon abandoned law and found his real vocation in geology and its auxiliary, paleontology. In the autumn of 1852 he apparently became editor of the *Ottawa Citizen*, a position he may have occupied until 1855. While he was publishing in the columns of the *Citizen* articles of a popular scientific nature relating to geology, and acquiring a basic knowledge of physics, trigonometry, and zoology, Billings was studying the fossils preserved in the rock formations along the banks of the Rideau River. At the same time he was collecting the Crinoidea, Cystoidea, and Asteroidea of which he was later to offer a rich collection to the museum of the Geological Survey of Canada.

On 7 Jan. 1854 Billings made his official début in the scientific world: he was appointed a member of the Canadian Institute of Toronto. In the same year he published his first paleontological study in the institute's journal: "On some new genera and species of Cystidea from the Trenton limestone." In 1855, for the universal exposition in Paris, he wrote an essay entitled *Reddit ubi cererem tellus inarata quotannis*, which won him a prize of $100. February 1856 was witness to an epoch-making event in the life of Billings and in the history of scientific research in Canada. The young paleontologist launched the first number of a monthly review, the *Canadian Naturalist and Geologist*, in which for 20 years he was to publish his scientific studies. He immediately won the admiration and support of experts, and particularly of Sir William Edmond LOGAN, the director of the Geological Survey of Canada. The latter applied to the Canadian government for the services of Billings, who on 1 Aug. 1856 became the official paleontologist for the surveys, with residence at Montreal. Except for a few months which he devoted to a study trip in England and Paris between February and June 1858, Billings spent the rest of his life studying and describing the fossils preserved in the museum of the survey. He communicated to researchers the results of his intelligent and persistent labour, namely 93 articles in the *Naturalist*, the official reports of the Geological Survey of Canada, and studies published by the *Canadian Journal* . . . , the *American Journal of Science and Arts* of New Haven, and the *Geological Magazine* of London.

At the time when Billings joined the Geological Survey of Canada in 1856, to become its first paleontologist, paleontology was a recent branch of knowledge. To appreciate his contribution to science, two things must be remembered: Georges Cuvier and Jean-Baptiste de Lamarck [Monet] had died 25 years earlier, and it was only three years later, in 1859, that Charles Darwin published *On the origin of species by means of natural selection* . . . , a work that was to revolutionize the contemporary scientific world. Billings was therefore a pioneer. He was not alone, however; other names were already adding lustre to the paleontology of invertebrates: Joachim Barrande, James Hall, Jacob Green, Carl Eduard von Eichwald, James de Carle Sowerby, Constantine Samuel Rafinesque, and Roderick Impey Murchison, to mention only a few.

Billings had grasped immediately the importance of biology and geology for satisfactory work in paleontology. Moreover, he was a born naturalist, as is evidenced by his numerous monographs, particularly those describing recent animals, such as the bear, wolf, stag, otter, carcajou, caribou, lynx, beaver, and a number of birds. All these works appeared between 1855 and 1857. During the same years Billings also published numerous articles describing the fossils of Trenton (Ordovician), Potsdam (Cambrian), and Niagara (Silurian). He himself collected many of these fossils, including those of Trenton from the regions of Ottawa and Montreal, those of Niagara in the southwest of Ontario, and those of Potsdam

from the border region near Montreal and the state of Vermont.

When one looks at Billings' work, one is astonished at its extent. He has to his credit more than 200 articles, totalling some 3,000 pages. Among his important works must be cited some 500 pages of paleontology, which are contained in the famous *Report* of the Geological Survey presented by Logan in 1863 and known under the title of *Geology of Canada*, and his writings on the Paleozoic and Silurian fossils. It was the fossils of the Paleozoic age that he described in particular. To the description of the Silurian of Anticosti Island, which appeared about 25 years after Murchison's authoritative work on the Silurian of Great Britain, and which W. H. Twenhofel was to utilize much later for his classic work on Anticosti Island, must be added those of the Silurian of Port-Daniel (Gaspé Peninsula, Quebec) and of Arisaig (Nova Scotia), and of the Devonian of Gaspé. If Billings described above all the fossils of the Paleozoic period and particularly those of the east of Canada, it was because Logan had first established its geology. However, Billings was not prevented from describing the corals of the Canadian west, or from touching on the Mesozoic period of British Columbia, and the Tertiary, even the Quaternary eras, when he described the mammoth and the mastodon. But in the case of the Paleozoic period he described fossils belonging to all zoological groups: brachiopods, cephalopods, pelecypods, gasteropods, trilobites, annelids, Bryozoa, echinoderms, Porifera, and Cœlenterata. He created hundreds of new species and dozens of new genera, consequently modern treatises on paleontology, particularly those of North America, quote him abundantly.

Billings always described new species and new genera in a concise and exact manner. Knowing what written material was available, he made all the necessary comparisons with the species already described and known, according to modern rules of the subject, but he also knew how to stress any truly distinctive feature. In dealing with the group of the echinoderms, when he described a whole new fauna of Crinoidea, Cystoidea, and Blastoidea, he perhaps best displayed his qualities as an observer and a scrupulously careful analyst. On occasion, he knew how to defend his opinions. When Addison E. Verrill and W. H. Niles, in a statement to the Boston Natural History Society, asserted that Billings had seen a family relationship between the genus *Pasceolus*, which he had created, and the *Sphæronites*, he replied: "Mr. Niles is quite mistaken in supposing that I ever believed in the Ascidian affinities of the Sphaeronitidae. I was the first to point out the occurrence of that family in the palæozoic rocks of America. I discovered and described the genera *Comarocystites, Amygdalocystites* and *Malocystites*. In all that I have written on the subject I cannot find a single remark from which it could be supposed that I ever entertained such an idea."

He was conscious of very modern problems in paleontology, such as one related to systematics. "I think . . . the number of species is becoming so great that, sooner or later, *Conocephalites* will be broken up into a number of genera." He was already giving thought, therefore, to the tendencies of what are called, in the jargon of the science, the "lumpers" and the "splitters." Finally, he concerned himself with stratigraphic correlations and synchronism, for example when he compared the Silurian of Anticosti Island with that of Great Britain, or the calcareous rocks of Pointe de Lévy with the groups of Potsdam (Cambrian), Chazy, and Black River.

Elkanah Billings died on 14 June 1876 at Montreal, after suffering for three years from a severe illness, Bright's disease. His name was known to the scientific world: he had been a member of the Geological Society of London since 1858, and had been awarded medals by the International Exhibition of London in 1862 and by the Natural History Society of Montreal and the universal exposition in Paris in 1867. The journal Billings had founded, which he had kept supplied with his scientific studies for 20 years, survived him. An achievement that his critical eye, his researcher's mind, and his love of science and of the soil of Canada had rendered imposing and durable continued to perpetuate his memory.

In his report for 1876–77, the director of the Geological Survey of Canada, Alfred Richard Cecil Selwyn*, underlined Billings' disappearance thus: ". . . the country has . . . been deprived of the services of one who had for more than twenty years ably and efficiently fulfilled the duties of this important branch [paleontology] of the Geological Survey."

ANDRÉE DÉSILETS and YVON PAGEAU

A complete list of Billings' writings while he was a member of the Geological Survey of Canada will be found in D. B. Dowling, *General index to the reports of progress, 1863 to 1884* (Geological Survey of Canada, Ottawa, 1900). However, his most important works are the following: Elkanah Billings, *Catalogues of the Silurian fossils of the Island of Anticosti, with descriptions of some new genera and species* (Geological Survey of Canada, Montreal, London, New York, and Paris, 1866); *Palaeozoic fossils* (2v., Montreal, 1865–74). *Canadian Naturalist* (Toronto and Montreal), 1856–76. [Logan *et al.*], *Geology of Canada.* Canada, Geological Survey, *Report of progress for 1876–77* (Montreal, 1878). *Gazette* (Montreal), 15 June 1876. Le Jeune, *Dictionnaire*, I, 185. R. I. Murchison, *The Silurian system, founded on geological researches in the counties of Salop, Hereford, Radnor, Montgomery, Caermarthen, Brecon, Pembroke, Monmouth, Gloucester, Worcester, and Stafford; with descriptions of the coalfields and overlying formations* (2v., London, 1839). W. H. Twenhofel, *Geology of Anticosti Island* (Geological Survey of Canada Memoir, 154, Ottawa, 1927). H. M. Ami, "Brief biographical sketch of Elkanah Billings," *American Geologist* (Minneapolis), XXVII (1901), 265–81. J. F. Whiteaves, "Obituary notice of Elkanah Billings, F.G.S., paleontologist to the Geological Survey of Canada," *Canadian Naturalist and Quarterly Journal of Science* (Montreal), new ser., VIII (1878), 251–61.

BINNEY, STEPHEN, merchant, politician, shipbuilder, businessman; b. 24 March 1805 at Halifax, N.S., seventh child of Hibbert Newton Binney and Lucy Creighton; m. on 15 Oct. 1828 Emily Pryor, daughter of a Halifax merchant, and had a large family; d. 17 Jan. 1872 at Moncton, N.B.

Stephen Binney's father was collector of impost and excise at Halifax, and Stephen soon became a well-known figure in the business life of the city. When the first civic elections were held on 15 May 1841, Binney was elected a councillor; the councillors subsequently chose him as the city's mayor. Offended by the minor role assigned to him at a reception in September 1841 for a French prince, Binney clashed with the lieutenant governor, Lord Falkland [Lucius Bentinck Cary*]. The resulting clamour had not died down when a new crisis arose. The citizens of Halifax heard the news of the birth of a son to Queen Victoria early in December 1841. Binney immediately proposed that, since he planned to visit England on private business, he, as mayor, should lay at the foot of the throne a congratulatory address from the council and citizens. This should have been presented through the lieutenant governor, but the council, after consulting Falkland, allowed Binney to carry the address to England. Binney sailed on 3 Jan. 1842; in March his leave of absence expired and another councillor, Edward Kenny*, was appointed to complete his term.

When Binney returned to North America and decided to leave Halifax is not known, but on 20 Nov. 1843 he purchased for £600 half an acre of land with a wharf and shipyard in Lewisville, one mile northeast of "The Bend" (now Moncton), where his home, luxurious for the day, still stands. As well as being active in shipbuilding, Binney owned a wholesale business in lumber, flour, and feed. He was largely responsible for the establishment of St George's Anglican parish, of which he and Bliss Botsford*, a noted lawyer and politician, became first wardens in 1852. Binney also took an active interest in railways; he, Edward Barron CHANDLER, and Amos Edwin Botsford* were delegates at the Portland railway convention in 1850, and Binney backed those who wanted the Intercolonial Railway to pass through Moncton.

Stephen Binney, scion of a prominent Nova Scotia family, was unsuccessful as the first mayor of Halifax, but later made a valuable contribution to the religious, cultural, and mercantile life of his adopted community.

C. ALEXANDER PINCOMBE

St Paul's Church (Halifax, N.S.), Baptismal register, 1791–1816. Westmorland County Registry Office (Dorchester, N.B.), libro V, 297. Canada, *Sessional papers*, III (1870), PT.5, no.13, app.C, 27–28. *Moncton Daily Times* (special edition for the diamond jubilee of confederation), 15 June 1937, 12–13, 20, 39. W. C. Borrett, *East coast port and other tales told under the old town clock* (Halifax, 1944), 81–88. C. A. Pincombe, "The history of Monckton Township (ca. 1700–1875)," unpublished MA thesis, University of New Brunswick, 1969, 157, 161, 167. S. T. Spicer, *Masters of sail: the era of square-rigged vessels in the Maritime provinces* (Toronto, 1968), 97. F. E. Crowell, "Binney family," *Yarmouth Herald*, 25 July 1933.

BIRD, CURTIS JAMES, doctor and legislator; baptized 1 Feb. 1838, in St John's parish, Man.; d. in London, England, 13 June 1876.

Curtis James Bird was the son of James Curtis Bird*, former chief factor of the Hudson's Bay Company, and his second wife, Mary Lowman, a widowed teacher at the Red River Academy (Winnipeg), and was born at his father's estate (present-day Birds Hill). Curtis James was educated at St John's College (Winnipeg) and later studied medicine at Guy's Hospital, London. He returned to the Red River to practise medicine and in 1862 married Frances, a daughter of Donald Ross* who had been a chief trader in the HBC. By Frances, Dr Bird had four children. After her death, he married his sister-in-law, Annabella Ross McDermot, the widow of Charles Edward McDermot, and they had two children.

Following the death of Dr John Bunn* on 31 May 1861, Dr Bird served as coroner of the District of Assiniboia; at the meeting of the Council of Assiniboia, 8 and 11 April 1862, he received formal appointment as coroner. He held this position successively under the Council of Assiniboia, Louis Riel*'s provisional government, and the province of Manitoba. At one point during the period of the provisional government, concerned over the loss of life among the poor in the Red River Settlement, he proposed a crude medicare programme whereby two publicly supported surgeries would be established in the settlement.

Dr Bird's political career began with his appointment to the Council of Assiniboia, 23 Jan. 1868. He served on the council until its dissolution at the outbreak of the Red River disturbances in the fall of 1868. During the disturbances he was elected twice to represent the people of St Paul's parish. In the fall of 1869 he was chosen to meet with representatives of the other communities to decide whether or not a provisional government should be formed; in January 1870 he was a delegate at the meeting that decided that a "list of rights" should be presented to the government of Canada. In the convention that met from 25 Jan. to 11 Feb. 1870, Dr Bird was selected to serve on a committee of six to draft such a list.

After the creation of the province of Manitoba in 1870, Dr Bird continued to be interested in politics. He was nominated for the federal constituency of Lisgar in opposition to Dr John Christian Schultz*; he was also nominated for the provincial constituency of Baie de Saint-Paul. Following his victory in the provincial election of 30 Dec. 1870, Dr Bird withdrew from the federal campaign. He was re-elected in the same constituency in 1874 and remained a member of the Legislative Assembly of Manitoba until his death.

On 5 Feb. 1873, Dr Bird was elected speaker of the assembly and held this position until 1874. While he was speaker, a bill to incorporate the city of Winnipeg was introduced into the assembly [see Francis Evans CORNISH]. To this bill the Legislative Council attached amendments which impinged upon the provincial government's taxing powers; Dr Bird, as speaker, declared the bill out of order. Since a new bill could not be presented in that session of the legislature, the proponents of the bill were infuriated by Dr Bird's action. Early in the morning of 7 March, Dr Bird was lured from his house on the pretext that a patient needed immediate medical attention. While driving in his cutter to the patient's home, Dr Bird was attacked, dragged from his cutter, and soaked with heated oil. Though the government of Manitoba promptly offered a reward of $1,000 for information leading to the arrest of the offenders, they were never discovered.

In the spring of 1876 Dr Bird was in poor health; in the hope that a visit among old friends in England would improve it, he travelled to England. Instead of improving, his health worsened and he died in London on 13 June.

W. D. SMITH

PAM, Church of England registers, St John's Church (Winnipeg), baptisms, 1828–79, no.1077. Begg and

Birrell

Nursey, *Ten years in Winnipeg*, 19–20, 22, 41, 47, 49, 79–80. *Begg's Red River journal* (Morton). *Canadian North-West* (Oliver), I, 71, 485, 582. Hargrave, *Red River*. *Manitoba Free Press* (Winnipeg). *Manitoban* (Winnipeg). *Nor'Wester* (Winnipeg). R. B. Mitchell, *Medicine in Manitoba; the story of its beginnings* ([Winnipeg, 1955]), 47–48, 49, 54, 68–69, 107.

BIRRELL, JOHN, merchant and entrepreneur; b. 6 April 1815, at Lerwick, Shetland Islands, son of Ralph Birrell and Eliza Thompson; d. 12 Feb. 1875, at London, Ont.

John Birrell was raised at Lerwick and at Oban, Argyllshire, where his father was stationed as collector of excise. He was trained in business and worked as a clerk in Glasgow until about 1835 when he emigrated to Montreal. He then moved to Hamilton, where he worked for Isaac Buchanan and Company, and finally settled in London around 1840. There he formed a partnership, Angus and Birrell, which lasted three years. In 1845 Birrell established a new partnership with Adam Hope* – Hope, Birrell and Company – which operated stores selling hardware, groceries, and dry goods. In 1851 this partnership was amicably dissolved, Birrell taking the dry goods as John Birrell and Company. In spite of a fire in 1863, he developed a flourishing wholesale dry goods business with his own extensive warehouses. Stock was imported from England, France, Germany, and the United States, partly through the firm of Isaac Buchanan*, and sold over a territory that included Sarnia, Goderich, Stratford, and St Thomas. He also acquired John McMechan's boot and shoe store. In 1876 his business was valued at between $100,000 and $150,000. He was described as "a man who watched his business very carefully and pushed ahead, his trade expanding as the country settled up."

Birrell was prominent in the transformation of London into a railway and financial centre. He was a director of the London and Port Stanley Railway and later became president of the London, Huron, and Bruce Railway (1871–75), playing a leading part in its financing and construction, although he did not live to see the line completed. In addition, Birrell was an incorporator of the Board of Trade in 1857, a member of its council (1857–62), and a director of the Isolated Risk Insurance Company. In 1862 he became vice-president of the new London Permanent Building Society, which in 1865 amalgamated with the Huron and Erie Savings and Loan Society (now the Huron and Erie Mortgage Corporation). In 1864 Birrell chaired the inaugural meeting of the Huron and Erie, was elected a director, and served as president from 1871 until his death.

In politics Birrell was a Conservative and, though he refused to run for election himself, was president of the local organization from at least 1873. A Presbyterian, he was an active member of St Andrew's Church, sat on various boards, and donated liberally to the building fund. Birrell's suburban residence, "Beechwood" (built in 1854 and still standing in 1971), was one of the first estates in Westminster Township (South London). He was a popular figure in the city and an obituary stated that "he probably had not an enemy."

Before he left Hamilton, Birrell married Maria Louisa Sunley (1822–91), a native of England; they had ten children. A son, George Sunley Birrell (1842–1926), was a leading businessman in London, an alderman, and a president of the Board of Trade. Under his management the value of the family firm increased to between $200,000 and $300,000 by 1888. In 1891 he sold out, moved to New York City, and became a real estate agent. A daughter Elizabeth married Charles Smith Hyman*, son of Ellis Walton Hyman.

FREDERICK H. ARMSTRONG

Middlesex County Registry Office (London, Ont.), Register of partnerships, Liber A (1870–85), no.14. PAC, RG 30, 401–2. *Bradstreet's reports of the Dominion of Canada, February 1, 1876* (New York, 1876), 243, 247. *London Advertiser*, 12, 13, 15 Feb. 1875. *London Free Press*, 12, 13, 16 Feb. 1875; 16 Feb. 1891. *Can. biog. dict.*, I, 270–72. *Cyclopædia of Can. biog.* (Rose, 1886), 521–22. [Archie Bremner], *City of London, Ontario, Canada; the pioneer period and the London of today* (2nd ed., London, Ont., 1900), 92, 104, 108–9, 129. C. T. Campbell, *Pioneer days in London: some account of men and things in London before it became a city* (London, Ont., 1921), 93–94. *History of the county of Middlesex*, 371, 378, 387.

BLACK, HENRY, judge of the Vice-Admiralty Court, MHA; b. 18 Dec. 1798 at Quebec, of the marriage of James and Margaret Black; d. 16 Aug. 1873 at Cacouna, Que.

After studying at the school of Dr Daniel Wilkie* at Quebec, Henry Black became a law student, and was called to the bar on 20 March 1820. He practised his profession at Quebec in partnership with Andrew Stuart*. On 28 Sept. 1836 he was appointed judge of the Vice-Admiralty Court to replace Judge James Kerr*, who had been dismissed as a result of accusations levelled against him by the House of Assembly. Black was president of this tribunal for 37 years, and he acquired a fine reputation for impartiality, honesty, and exquisite kindness. On 18 April 1840 he had been appointed to the Special Council, while retaining his post as a judge, and he was confirmed in his duties at the Vice-Admiralty Court on 10 Feb. 1841.

On 29 March of the same year, Henry Black was elected member of the assembly for the city of Quebec, thanks to the substantial support given by public servants. On the occasion of the famous motion made by John Neilson* on 23 June 1841 condemning the Union, and throughout the whole of the first Union parliament, he consistently voted with the Tories. He supported the constitutional option proposed by governor Charles Theophilus Metcalfe* on 2 Dec. 1843, when a vote was taken following the resignation of the executive councillors who were supporters of ministerial responsibility [see DRAPER].

Even though he had the support of the newspaper *Le Canadien*, Black decided not to resubmit his name as a candidate in the general elections of 1844. Furthermore, during the 30 years or so that followed he seems to have limited his activity almost exclusively to his tribunal. Learned in maritime law, he enjoyed undisputed authority. He was named a CB, and Harvard University conferred on him an honorary degree of doctor of laws. After his death, which occurred with an attack of erysipelas at Cacouna, where he had gone to take the baths, *L'Événement* of Quebec paid him this tribute: "He was a man of profound learning, and on no subject was his erudition found wanting. The oldest lawyers consulted him, and his advice was law. He showed great kindness and interest in his dealings with young people who had recourse to his superior knowledge."

JACQUES MONET

Le Canadien (Québec), 18 août 1873. *L'Événement* (Québec), 16 août 1873. *La Minerve* (Montréal), 20 août 1873. P.-G. Roy, *Fils de Québec*, III, 96–97; *Les juges de la province de Québec*, 57. Cornell, *Alignment of political groups*. Monet, *Last cannon shot*. I. M. Abella, "The "Sydenham Election" of 1841," *CHR*, XLVII (1966), 326–43. F.-J. Audet, "Membres du Conseil spécial," *BRH*, VII (1901), 82–83.

BLACK, JOHN, recorder of Rupert's Land; b. 11 March 1817 at Edinburgh or St Andrews, county of Fife, Scotland; d. 3 Feb. 1879 at St Andrews, Man.

Little is known of John Black's childhood and youth; reserved by nature, he was silent about his early years, even with close friends. After completing his elementary education, he was employed for seven years in the office of an Edinburgh solicitor. He came to Red River in 1839, having been appointed clerk to the General Quarterly Court of Assiniboia. His duties as deputy to

Adam Thom*, the recorder of Rupert's Land, were soon superseded by his active employment in the offices of the Hudson's Bay Company. In 1845 he married Margaret, daughter of Alexander CHRISTIE, governor of Assiniboia, and three years later the company appointed him chief trader.

According to Governor Eden Colvile*, one of Christie's successors, Black was not too popular, except with the religious authorities – Black was almost a minister himself, the governor commented – and he was not a remarkable businessman either. All the same, in 1850 Black was appointed chief accountant of the Upper Red River district, with residence at Fort Garry (Winnipeg). The appointment did not prevent the governor from charging him with being as stupid as an owl. Black was given to arrogance, and people were put off by it. Colvile, however, gradually changed his opinion, and noted that Black was becoming less unpopular; nevertheless, having appointed him unwillingly, he continued to seek a replacement for him. On 21 July 1852 Black lost his post as chief accountant.

The following winter Black and his family visited Scotland. They came back to Red River in the spring. In 1854, after his wife's death, Black decided to leave the company. He returned to Scotland, stayed there for some time, then went to Australia, where he made a career for himself in the public service. He went back to England, and in the spring of 1861 was appointed president of the General Quarterly Court of Assiniboia. He was assuming what had previously been the office of recorder: its title had been changed solely to facilitate the appointment of Black, who had never been a member of the bar although he possessed a certain legal training. On 4 June 1862 the new president was introduced to the Council of Assiniboia.

During the eight years that he presided over the tribunal at Assiniboia, Black proved to be a conscientious judge, and rarely received anything but praise. He was well prepared for his role, and had a thorough knowledge of the people of Red River and their habits. He displayed untiring patience as he listened to illiterate plaintiffs. He was upright and understanding, but was none the less uncompromising. To the consequences of his decisions, and to the ways in which they were applied, he gave scant heed. Yet at a period when the company's authority was declining, it was desirable that the judge, an employee of the company, should take the new circumstances into account, for the company could no longer enforce unpopular sentences. In the summer of 1868 Black decided to resign; the company, foreseeing the end of its reign at Red River, asked Black to remain in office for another year. It was not until March 1870 that he left the colony.

Meanwhile, Black witnessed the Métis' sharp opposition to the plan to annex the west to Canada. He even played a part in the affair. As acting governor – William Mactavish* was seriously ill at the time – Black presided over the Council of Assiniboia on 23 Oct. 1869, when Louis Riel* appeared before it to explain why a group of Métis had prevented William McDougall*, the lieutenant governor appointed by the Canadian government, from entering Red River. The letters relating to this matter that were signed by Mactavish were drafted by Black. They clearly reflected the latter's moderate attitude.

Indifferent to the events taking place, Black continued to live several miles from the seat of government and the centre of affairs. He was, however, secretary of the public meeting held on 19 Jan. 1870 to which Donald Alexander Smith*, the Canadian government's representative, reported. From 25 January to 10 February of the same year he also presided over the convention during which a list of rights of the people of Rupert's Land was drawn up. Black represented the parish of St Andrews, and said little throughout the whole convention except on 4 and 5 February, when, in a tone that showed his slight respect for the assembly and its deliberations, he spoke at considerable length against the immediate creation of a province. He saw the necessity of replacing the company's paternalistic government by a representative one, but he advocated for the first years of the annexation an appointed and not an elected council. On 11 February the provisional government set up by the convention appointed Black one of three delegates (the two others were Alfred Henry Scott and Noël-Joseph Ritchot*) to the Canadian government at Ottawa; he was to be the spokesman for the English-speaking element. He accepted at the request of Bishop Alexandre-Antonin Taché*. The three delegates took with them the final version of the list of rights for the people of Rupert's Land.

Black arrived in the capital after the other two, and was lodged in the Russell House; in the next room was D. A. Smith, to whom the Canadian government had entrusted the task of winning Black over. It was to no avail, since throughout the discussions Black maintained the same opinion as at the convention, and accepted only tacitly the positions taken and the conditions laid down by the Canadian representatives. On 27 April 1870 discussion was begun on the question of lands, and Black agreed that Canada should keep control; to him the notion that the settlers of Red River should claim them as theirs was absurd. Subsequently, he considered that the compensatory offer of 150,000 acres made by the Canadian representatives to the Métis was reasonable, whereas the other two members of the delegation aimed at getting three million, and ultimately received a million and a half.

When the talks were finished, Black contemplated returning immediately to London. He was offered the position of lieutenant governor or of recorder of Manitoba, but he declined, and in the summer of 1870 took up residence in Scotland for good.

A conscientious judge, Black had been "a man of very great integrity, in whom the entire settlement had absolute confidence." However, according to D. A. Smith, his lack of firmness, courage, and boldness during the events of 1869–70 undermined the efforts of those who were endeavouring to reduce the issue involving the Métis to less significant proportions.

LIONEL DORGE

Archives paroissiales de Saint-Norbert (Man.), Journal tenu par le Rév. Mons. N.-J. Ritchot, ptre. HBC Arch. A.6/27, 31 March 1848; A.6/37, 17 April 1862; A.12/45, 11 Aug., 11 Nov. 1868; 23, 24 March 1869. *Correspondence relative to the recent disturbances in the Red River Settlement* (London, 1870). Hargrave, *Red River*. HBRS, XVI (Rich and Johnson), 241, 244, 245, 248; XIX (Rich, Johnson, and Morton), 154, 192, 195, 197, 200, 203, 216. [Mactavish], *Letters of Letitia Hargrave* (MacLeod), 208. *Manitoba; birth of a province* (Morton), 9–11, 21–23, 30, 34, 42–50, 77, 140–43, 209. F. E. Bartlett, "William Mactavish, the last governor of Assiniboia," unpublished MA thesis, University of Manitoba, 1964. Roy St George Stubbs, *Four recorders of Rupert's Land; a brief survey of the Hudson's Bay Company courts of Rupert's Land* (Winnipeg, 1967), 135–85. A.-H. de Trémaudan, *Histoire de la nation métisse dans l'Ouest canadien* ([Montréal, 1935]), 221.

BLANCHARD, HIRAM, lawyer and politician, son of Jonathan Blanchard and Sarah Goggins, b. in West River, N.S., 17 Jan. 1820, brother of Jotham Blanchard* founder and editor of the *Colonial Patriot*; m. in 1842 Eliza Cantrell of Guysborough, and had one son, who died young, and four daughters; d. in Halifax, 17 Dec. 1874.

Descendant of a New England family, Hiram Blanchard received his education at Pictou Academy, studied law with William Frederick DesBarres* in Guysborough, and was admitted to the bar as attorney in November 1841 and as a barrister in April 1843. Soon after his admission to the bar he opened a law office at Port Hood, and he practised on the Cape Breton circuit and also in the courts of Antigonish and Guysborough counties. In a short time he won a lucrative business and also achieved a high reputation; he was respected by judges, other barristers, and juries for his candour and fairness, his clear presentation of facts, and his skill in examining witnesses.

In 1860 he moved to Halifax and formed a partnership with Jonathan McCULLY, then solicitor general and railway commissioner in Joseph HOWE's Reform government. In many courtroom encounters his opponent was James MacDonald*, later federal minister of justice and chief justice of Nova Scotia. An observer of their legal jousting, Charles James Townshend*, also a chief justice, wrote, ". . . it was delightful and instructive to listen to [their] forensic battle. Both were men of high and honourable character, incapable of any unworthy schemes to win their cases." After McCully was appointed to the bench in 1870, Nicholas H. Meagher became Blanchard's partner.

Blanchard refused to become a political candidate until just before William Young* left politics in 1860 to become chief justice of Nova Scotia. The election of 1859 was influenced by quarrels between Protestants and Roman Catholics, but Blanchard, a Presbyterian from Catholic Inverness County, was elected as a Reformer upon his promise of "equal rights to all, proscription of none, favouritism to none." He was re-elected in 1863 and 1867, and in the assembly showed particular concern over the treatment of the insane and the deaf. Although he supported Charles Tupper*'s free school act, Blanchard opposed his idea that the schools be directed by a council of public instruction made up of members of the Executive Council [see Thomas Louis CONNOLLY].

Blanchard became a supporter of confederation, and was sworn in as attorney general of the province and leader of the government on 4 July 1867 in succession to Tupper after Nova Scotia became part of Canada. In the provincial election of September 1867, the question of Nova Scotia's entry into confederation was the dominant issue and the government was swept from office. In the new assembly only Blanchard and Henry Gesner Pineo, representing Cumberland County, supported confederation, and the Blanchard government was replaced on 7 Nov. 1867. The following year Blanchard's personal re-election in Inverness was declared invalid because he had been appointed legal adviser for the federal government in Nova Scotia; he suffered defeat from the anticonfederates in the subsequent by-election. Elected again in 1871, he served as leader of the opposition from 1871 to 1874. On his death the Liberal *Morning Chronicle* described him as a lawyer of "high reputation . . . a useful legislator, well-informed in public matters and an industrious worker."

WILLIAM B. HAMILTON

[There are scattered references to Blanchard in PAC, MG 24, B29 (Howe papers), 8; MG 26, A (Macdonald papers), 115, pp.130–38; 116, pp.325–31; MG 26, F (Tupper papers), 1. Thomas Miller, *Historical and genealogical record of the first settlers of Colchester County* (Halifax, 1873), 254–58 contains a complete genealogy of the Blanchard family. A short biographical sketch may be found in John Doull, "Four attorney-generals," N.S. Hist. Soc. *Coll.*, XXVII (1947), 2–4. *See also*: J. M. Cameron, *Political Pictonians; the men of the Legislative Council, Senate, House of Commons, House of Assembly, 1767–1967* (Ottawa, [1967]). J. W. Longley, *Sir Charles Tupper* (Toronto, 1926). C. J. Townshend, "The Honourable James McDonald," N.S. Hist. Soc. *Coll.*, XX (1921), 139–53. The *Morning Chronicle* (Halifax), 1859–74, records many of Blanchard's assembly speeches. His obituary notice is to be found in the issue of 18 Dec. 1874. W.B.H.]

BLISS, HENRY, author, lawyer, and provincial agent for New Brunswick and Nova Scotia; b. 1797 at Saint John, N.B., youngest son of Jonathan Bliss*, chief justice of New Brunswick, and Mary Worthington; d. 31 July 1873 at London, England.

Henry Bliss, with his brother William Blowers BLISS, was educated at King's College, Windsor, Nova Scotia, where he received a BA in 1816. In 1819, after legal training in Saint John, his father appointed him clerk of the pleas for the Supreme Court of New Brunswick. After his father's death in 1822, he was dismissed from this office by the lieutenant governor, George Stracy Smyth*, who appointed his aide-de-camp, Captain George Shore*, to the position. A bitter dispute over patronage ensued; Bliss travelled to England where he won the support of the colonial secretary, Lord Henry Bathurst. Bathurst in 1824 ordered that Bliss be reinstated; the latter, however, did not return to New Brunswick to take up the position, but was admitted to the English bar and later became a queen's counsel. In 1826 he resigned as clerk of the pleas.

In 1824, Bliss and John Bainbridge, a London merchant, had been appointed joint agents for the province of New Brunswick in London at a salary of £200 a year. Bainbridge died in 1836, but Bliss continued to represent the province and, for a number of years, also served as agent for Nova Scotia. The agent's task was to support legislation favourable to the colony, to oppose unfavourable legislation, and to try to see that the views of the provincial assembly were known at the Colonial

Bliss

Office. By 1846 the work of the provincial agent had declined in importance, and Bliss requested that his salary be discontinued but that he be allowed to continue to represent the province. He corresponded with the provincial government for several more years and there is no record of his appointment ever having been cancelled.

Bliss published a number of pamphlets on colonial questions, which caused considerable discussion in English and colonial journals. The most important of these were: *On colonial intercourse* (1830), in which he argued that new trade agreements with the United States were not in the best interests of Britain and the colonies, and *On the timber trade* (1831) and *Letter to Sir Henry Parnell . . . on the new colonial trade bill* (1831), in which he attacked free trade and the proposal to remove the preference given to colonial timber in British markets. The pamphlets of Bliss and the attitudes of others such as Sir Howard Douglas*, who resigned as lieutenant governor of New Brunswick in 1831 because of the proposed changes in colonial trade regulations, may have influenced the decision of the British parliament to reject the bill of 1832 proposing changes in the regulation of the timber trade. However, Bliss and Douglas were fighting a losing battle as the British government continued to move toward free trade. In *The colonial system . . .* (1833) Bliss stated that through the loss of protective markets "the seeds of disunion" had been sown and would eventually explode and "scatter through the world the fragments of the mighty, the rich, and prosperous Empire of Great Britain."

Another pamphlet presented *Considerations of the claims and conduct of the United States respecting their north eastern boundary . . .* (1826). In *An essay on the re-construction of her majesty's government in Canada* (1839), he pointed out the dangers of a union of British North America modelled on American principles of federalism and set forth measures he felt necessary to secure satisfactory union. He apparently approved of confederation when the issue arose in 1864.

In his later years Bliss published a number of works (including three under the pseudonym of Nicholas Thirning Moile) which were based on history and written in verse form: *State trials* (1838); *Cicero; a drama* (1846); *Philip the second; a tragedy* (1849); *Ideas seldom thought of, for extending knowledge* (1851); *A history of the lives of the most heroic martyrs . . .* (1853); *Robespierre; a tragedy* (1854); and, *Thecla; a drama* (1866). There is no evidence that his plays were ever produced.

In his own time Bliss was said to have been one of the best known colonial writers in England. He was a spokesman for shipowners and merchants involved in the colonial trade.

W. A. SPRAY

Some of Henry Bliss' pamphlets include: *The colonial system, statistics of the trade, industry, and resources of Canada and the other plantations in British America* (London, 1833); *Considerations of the claims and conduct of the United States respecting their north eastern boundary, and the value of the British colonies in North America* (London, 1826); *An essay on the re-construction of her majesty's government in Canada* (London, 1839); *Letter to Sir Henry Parnell, Bart., M.P., on the new colonial trade bill* (London, 1831); *On colonial intercourse* (London, 1830); *On the timber trade* (London, 1831). For a listing of his dramatic works see: Allardyce Nicoll, *A history of English drama, 1660–1900* (6v., Cambridge, 1952–59), IV, V.

N.B. Museum, Fairweather papers, copy of will of Henry Bliss, July 1873; Hazen coll., Chipman papers, Bliss to Chipman, 27 May 1823; Scrapbook 38, extract from *Saint John Daily Sun*, 26 April 1892. PRO, CO 188/29, ff.85–86; CO 189/12, ff.95–96, 113–16, 118–22, 181–83, 260–61. New Brunswick, House of Assembly, *Journals*, 1824, 51–52; 1846, 10–11. W. G. MacFarlane, *New Brunswick bibliography; the books and writers of the province* (Saint John, N.B., 1895), 11–12. Wallace, *Macmillan dictionary*, 64. Hannay, *History of New Brunswick*, I, 436–37. K. E. Knorr, *British colonial theories, 1570–1850* (1st ed., Toronto, 1944; 2nd ed., London and New York, 1963), 326, 327, 329–30, 331, 341. J. W. Lawrence, *Footprints; or, incidents in early history of New Brunswick* (Saint John, N.B., 1895), 75, 103; *Judges of New Brunswick* (Stockton), 413–14.

BLISS, WILLIAM BLOWERS, barrister and judge; b. 24 Aug. 1795 at Saint John, N.B., son of Massachusetts loyalists Jonathan Bliss*, attorney general of New Brunswick, 1785–1809, chief justice, 1809–22, and Mary Worthington; brother of HENRY; d. 16 March 1874 at his residence, Fort Massey, Halifax, N.S.

As a loyalist William Blowers Bliss was part of the group which ruled the colony of Nova Scotia and had tremendous social prestige. After graduating from King's Collegiate School, he received a BA in 1813 and an MA in 1816, both from King's College where he was recognized as a classical scholar and poet. Thomas Chandler Haliburton*, creator of "Sam Slick," was among his classmates. Bliss was admitted to the bar of Nova Scotia on 9 April 1818, then went to England where he spent several years at Westminster Hall and at the Inner Temple under Sir William Wightman, afterwards an eminent English judge. On 24 Aug. 1823 at St Paul's Church, Halifax, he married Sarah Ann Anderson, adopted daughter of Sampson Salter Blowers*, a Harvard classmate of Jonathan Bliss and chief justice of Nova Scotia from 1797 to 1833. Bliss had seven children; his three sons moved to England and three of his daughters married eminent men of the Atlantic provinces: the eldest, Elizabeth Ann, was married to William Odell* of New Brunswick, Mary to Bishop Hibbert Binney*, and Louisa to Bishop James B. Kelly* of Newfoundland.

In 1830 Bliss was elected to the Nova Scotia assembly for Hants County. In keeping with his family tradition and social position he was a Tory, but he expressed independent opinions by supporting the demand for the separation of the executive and legislative functions in the council and by backing a group of Halifax businessmen seeking a charter for the Bank of Nova Scotia in 1832. He was elected to the first board of directors of the bank on 10 May 1832 and remained in that capacity until 1835. Other directors of the bank included his brother, Lewis Bliss, Mather Byles Almon, James Boyle Uniacke*, James William Johnston, William Murdoch, and William Lawson*, the first president.

When S. S. Blowers resigned the office of chief justice in 1833, he strongly recommended that his son-in-law and protégé be appointed to the bench of the Supreme Court, but there were other candidates with more seniority. However, upon the death of Richard John Uniacke* II, Bliss was appointed by royal mandamus of Queen Victoria a puisne judge of the Supreme Court of Nova Scotia on 15 May 1834, at an annual salary of £540 and fees. Mr Justice Bliss was strict in upholding the dignity of the court and was respected for his industry, his legal knowledge, and the logical expression of his opinions. He had been appointed when it was customary for puisne judges to rise by seniority to be chief justice, but was disappointed in this expectation because responsible government made this position a prize of the political party in power. In 1860 the Liberal government by-passed Judge Bliss when their leader, William Young*, left politics; he became chief justice. Ill health forced Bliss to resign from the court in January 1869. Sir Charles Hastings Doyle*, lieutenant governor of Nova Scotia, requested that Queen Victoria confer "the honour of Knighthood or some other marks of Her Royal favour on her old Servant on his retirement from the Bench," but this request was never granted. A portrait of Mr Justice Bliss hangs in Halifax County Court House.

Bliss acted as one of the governors of King's College at Windsor from 1848 to 1853, and as one of the trustees of the Halifax grammar school from 1847 to 1868. He was president of a short-lived historical society formed at Halifax in 1863. A devoted member of the Church of England, he served for several years as a member of the vestry

of St Paul's Church in Halifax and later attended St Luke's Cathedral when his son-in-law Bishop Binney moved his episcopal chair there in 1864. He was one of the first contributors to All Saints' Cathedral in Halifax.

When Judge Bliss died in 1874, he left an estate valued at $536,725. Authors have assumed that he inherited Judge Blowers' fortune, but it was left to Bliss' wife, Sarah. It is known that Bliss inherited about $20,000 in 1818 from his American grandfather, Colonel John Worthington; he also received a bequest from his father. Bliss seems to have been shrewd enough to invest his capital in bank and railway stocks rather than in shipping. Certainly his position on the board of the Bank of Nova Scotia and his social contacts with the Halifax business élite provided him with useful financial information which enabled him to make astute and lucrative investments.

Phyllis R. Blakeley

Halifax County Court of Probate, will of S. S. Blowers, 1842; will of W. B. Bliss, 1874. PANS, Anderson family papers; Bliss family papers. PRO, CO 217/114, 97–99, 125–26; 217/155, 43, 55. *Morning Chronicle* (Halifax), 17, 20 March 1874. R. V. Harris, *Catalogue of portraits of the judges of the Supreme Court of Nova Scotia and other portraits*, Law Courts, Halifax, N.S. ([Halifax], n.d.), 45–47, 59. F. E. Crowell, "Bliss family," *Yarmouth Herald*, 9 Aug. 1932. J. W. Lawrence, *The first courts and early judges of New Brunswick* (Saint John, N.B., 1875), 17–19. C. J. Townshend, "Memoir of the life of the Honourable William Blowers Bliss, with portrait," N.S. Hist. Soc. *Coll.*, XVII (1913), 23–46.

BOOKER, ALFRED, merchant, auctioneer, and militia officer; b. in 1824 in Nottingham, England, son of the Reverend Alfred Booker, a Regular Baptist clergyman; d. 27 Sept. 1871 in Montreal, Que.

The Booker family had been in Hamilton, Canada West, for eight years when, in 1850, Alfred Booker Jr established a business which he conducted until 1867. At his sale rooms he auctioned real estate, horses, dry goods, and the stock of merchants going out of business. He became wealthy and was a respected member of the freemasons (being a founder of St John's Lodge of the Irish registry in 1852), of the St George's Society, and of the Regular Baptist Church.

On 16 May 1851 Booker was commissioned ensign in the 1st Wentworth militia. He transferred as 2nd captain to the 1st Hamilton Independent Artillery company in 1853; he claimed to have helped outfit this company. In 1855 he was gazetted captain of the Volunteer Militia Battery of Artillery of Hamilton, which he organized.

Booker

He was promoted major in 1857 to command the volunteer (or active) militia artillery and rifle companies of Hamilton, and lieutenant colonel in 1858 to command the volunteer force in Hamilton. On 15 June 1861, shortly after the outbreak of the Civil War in the United States, Booker was appointed a staff officer to provide information on local conditions to imperial troops.

In 1862 formation of the 13th Battalion (later the Royal Hamilton Light Infantry) was authorized and the command was given to Isaac Buchanan*. Booker took it over in 1865 in preference to another officer, James Atchison Skinner, while retaining over-all command of the active force in Hamilton. In the same year he commanded several volunteer companies on the Niagara frontier following the St Alban's raid by a group of Southerners in October. He had been examined by a board of three imperial officers in 1864 and received the first 1st class certificate of military qualification ever granted by the Department of Militia Affairs. His strenuous voluntary services brought some rewards: he was wont to refer to "the special approval and personal commendation" of the Prince of Wales in 1860 and to his presentation to Queen Victoria in 1864.

The event with which Booker's name is chiefly connected is the battle of Ridgeway fought on 2 June 1866 between Canadian volunteers under his command and the Irish Republican Army under John O'Neill. On 1 June, when news of a Fenian invasion was received by British military officials, Booker was instructed to call out the 13th Battalion and take it to Port Colborne. He picked up two additional volunteer companies (the York and Caledonia) en route, and found the 2nd Battalion of Toronto already there when he arrived late the same day. Because he was senior to the 2nd Battalion's temporary commander, John Stoughton Dennis*, Booker took command of the whole force.

The volunteers under Booker were to act in conjunction with imperial troops commanded by Lieutenant-Colonel George J. Peacocke; both were under the orders of Major General George Napier. Peacocke was to meet Booker in Port Colborne but the place was changed to Stevensville. Booker, however, had better knowledge of the whereabouts of the Fenians than Peacocke, and he suggested that he take his column to Fort Erie and attack them at Frenchman Creek; the scheme was vetoed by Peacocke.

Booker considered that to "keep my appointment at Stevensville was my obvious duty," and accepted Napier's expectation that the Fenians would not attack until the two columns had arrived there. Booker's force reached Ridgeway by train and began the march to Stevensville. His troops – young, inexperienced, and ill trained – consisted of 480 men in the 2nd Battalion under Charles Todd Gilmor, 265 in the 13th under J. A. Skinner (in temporary command as Booker had taken command of the whole column), and about 50 in each of the York Company and the Caledonia Company. Gilmor's advance guard, however, met the Fenians under O'Neill about midway between Stevensville and Ridgeway, and became heavily engaged. Booker then learned that Peacocke had been delayed at Chippawa; there was now no hope that the imperial troops would hear the fighting and come to Booker's aid. According to Gilmor, "the situation of the Volunteers was thereby rendered most critical, as it seemed improbable we would hold our position for the two hours we were thus left unsupported." Neither side had artillery or cavalry.

Booker drove back the Fenians, but when he ordered parts of Skinner's 13th to replace the companies under Gilmor which were low in ammunition, O'Neill counterattacked. "A scene of confusion ensued" and Booker's force was routed. Booker was unable to regroup his men at Ridgeway, and retired to Port Colborne, while O'Neill, wishing to return to the U.S.A., and unable to take advantage of his military success, moved to Fort Erie. In all, nine of Booker's men were killed in action. Peacocke's column, which had artillery, was never engaged. Subsequently it was hinted that Peacocke should be court-martialed, but Sir John Michel* (commander of the forces) let it be known that the volunteers' weapons were such that "at present the unfortunate Canadians fight at a disadvantage" and that if the Canadian government had authorized money for a dozen mounted volunteers Peacocke's force would have been warned in time to destroy the Fenians.

The British military placed responsibility on the Canadian government, but a court of inquiry demanded by Booker and presided over by George Taylor Denison II failed to assign blame at the same time indicating Booker's personal courage. The officers of the 13th, however, showed no intention of letting matters lie. Skinner and others hired a former protégé of Isaac Buchanan, Alexander Somerville*, to write a malicious account of the battle. Somerville later admitted that the officers were "hostile to Colonel Booker and blind to fair play" and that the book was "doing the work of Col. Booker's personal enemies."

Booker's resignation on 30 July 1866 from command of the 13th Battalion was followed by permission to retire from the militia in 1867; he retained his rank, a virtual vindication of his

Boucher-Belleville

actions by the Canadian government. The reasons for the defeat were, however, too deeply entwined with imperial and Canadian attitudes to defence to allow Booker's comeback in the volunteer movement. In 1867 he left Hamilton and reopened his shop in Montreal, where he died four years later, survived by a son.

GEO. MAINER

PAC, MG 27, I, D4 (Cartier papers), 4, p.1792; RG 7, G10, 2; RG 8, I, A1, 185; D5, 1672; RG 9, I, C1, 265–67, 270; C8, 6, 8; II, A1, 2, f.145; 6, f.501; 36, f.3923. *Canada Gazette* (Ottawa), 23 June 1866. *Evening Times* (Hamilton), 1864–66. *Gazette* (Montreal), 28 Sept. 1871. *Montreal Herald*, 5, 7 Nov. 1870. G. T. Denison III, *History of the Fenian raid on Fort Erie; with an account of the battle of Ridgeway* (Toronto, 1866). Alexander Somerville, *Narrative of the Fenian invasion of Canada* (Hamilton, C.W., 1866). *Hutchinson's Hamilton directory for 1862–63 . . .* (Hamilton, C.W., 1862).
E. A. Cruikshank, *The origin and official history of the Thirteenth Battalion of infantry, and a description of the work of the early militia of the Niagara peninsula in the War of 1812 and the rebellion of 1837* (Hamilton, Ont., 1899). J. A. Macdonald, *Troublous times in Canada; a history of the Fenian raids of 1866 and 1870* (Toronto, 1910). J. R. Robertson, *The history of freemasonry in Canada from its introduction in 1749 . . .* (2v., Toronto, 1899), II. E. A. Cruikshank, "The Fenian raid of 1866," Welland County Hist. Soc., *Papers and Records* (Welland, Ont.), II (1926), 9–49. F. M. Quealey, "The Fenian invasion of Canada West, June 1st and 2nd, 1866," *Ont. Hist.*, LIII (1961), 37–66.

BOUCHER-BELLEVILLE, JEAN-BAPTISTE, called **Jean-Philippe,** teacher, newspaper owner and editor, *Patriote*, civil servant, and linguist; b. 8 Sept. 1800 at Quebec, son of Pierre Boucher-Belleville and Louise Belleau; d. 1874 at Saint-Michel-de-Napierville, Quebec.

Boucher-Belleville, who signed himself "J.-Philippe," received a classical education at the college of Montreal from 1814 to 1825, and was first a teacher with Siméon Marchessault* at Saint-Charles-sur-Richelieu. In 1831 he published at Montreal *Les Principes de la langue française, en deux parties, suivis des règles de la versification française,* which ran into several editions, and in 1832, *Les Principes de la langue latine, en deux parties, suivis des règles de la versification latine.* He then tried journalism, and wrote numerous articles in the Montreal newspapers on subjects related to religion, politics, and agriculture.

In 1835 or 1836 Boucher-Belleville became the owner and editor of *L'Écho du Pays* (Saint-Charles-sur-Richelieu), a political weekly favouring the *Patriote* party that had been started by Pierre-Dominique Debartzch* in 1833 and first edited by

the lawyer Alfred-Xavier Rambau*. The paper devoted numerous articles to primary education and to the debates in the House of Assembly and the Legislative Council. Boucher-Belleville published the last issue in June 1836. He then launched another periodical, *Le Glaneur,* which lasted only a short time (December 1836 to September 1837). This was a newspaper concerned with literature, agriculture, and industry, which endeavoured to carry on the work of *L'Écho du Pays,* although stressing agriculture. Boucher-Belleville attributed the slump in agriculture in Lower Canada to the unenterprising methods of the French Canadians. Under the pen-name of "Jean-Paul Laboureur" he published articles on modern agricultural techniques, types of ploughing, the utilization of potash, and the function of crop rotation. He even adapted to agriculture a work by Dr Jean-Baptiste MEILLEUR, *Cours abrégé de leçons de chymie . . . ,* published at Montreal in 1833, and gave extracts of it in his journal.

During the 1830s Boucher-Belleville corresponded fairly regularly with Ludger Duvernay*. In a letter dated 11 April 1834 he stated "that there is nothing to be expected of priests, . . . they are a privileged caste like the ministerial tribe." On 4 April 1835 he opposed sending Louis-Joseph PAPINEAU to England to defend the requests of the House of Assembly, because no one, he thought, could replace him at home.

Boucher-Belleville was caught up in the turmoil created by the disturbances of 1837–38. On 22 Nov. 1837 Papineau presided over the meeting at Saint-Charles, where he arranged for officers to be chosen for the defence of the country: Boucher-Belleville was appointed quartermaster. On 7 December, after the defeat, he was taken prisoner. On 28 Feb. 1838 he wrote from Laprairie to Duvernay to tell him that he had come out of prison penniless, and that no one in the Richelieu valley had been willing to help him.

On 15 Jan. 1839 appeared the first number of *L'Aurore des Canadas* (Montreal), a political, literary, and commercial newspaper started by François Cinq-Mars; Boucher-Belleville was its first editor, probably until 1845. The paper endeavoured to find a basis of agreement between the French Canadians and their governors, to stress understanding between the two races, and to defend the Catholic clergy. This last aim scandalized Dr Antoine-Pierre-Louis Consigny, who wrote to Duvernay, saying that Boucher-Belleville "has never been the unquestioning friend of priests, and yet he is now coming to their defence!" Indeed, in a letter to Ludger Duvernay dated 3 Aug. 1841, Boucher-Belleville declared: ". . . religion is necessary for the mass of the

75

Boucher de La Bruère

people, . . . the priests acted badly in 1837, but . . . they have realized their error, in short . . . the clergy are powerful."

Around 1850 Jean-Philippe Boucher-Belleville was the secretary of the Department of Education at Montreal. Dr Jean-Baptiste Meilleur made it clear, in his *Mémorial de l'éducation du Bas-Canada*, that from 1846 on he was allowed a secretary and a clerk whose chief occupation was to keep the accounts, analyse the various documents, classify them, and index them; one of the two clerks was a copyist in the education office. We do not know how long Boucher-Belleville held this position. It was no doubt in this period that he published his *Dictionnaire des barbarismes et des solécismes . . .* (1855).

In 1835, at Terrebonne, Jean-Philippe Boucher-Belleville had married Marguerite Porlier, daughter of Jacques Porlier, a voyageur; he had one daughter, who died with her mother in 1841. Boucher-Belleville was the nephew of Jean-Baptiste Boucher-Belleville*, the parish priest of Laprairie from 1792 to 1839. The latter published a collection of canticles and a *Manuel abrégé de controverse*.

At the end of his life Boucher-Belleville was the owner of a farm at Saint-Michel-de-Napierville; he died there in 1874, at 74 years of age.

LOUIS-PHILIPPE AUDET

J.-P. Boucher-Belleville, *Dictionnaire des barbarismes et des solécismes les plus ordinaires en ce pays, avec le mot propre ou leur signification* (Montréal, 1855); *Les principes de la langue française, en deux parties, suivis des règles de la versification française* (Montréal, 1831); *Les principes de la langue latine, en deux parties, suivis des règles de la versification latine* (Montréal, 1832).
"Papiers Duvernay conservés aux archives de la province de Québec," APQ *Rapport, 1926–27,* 145ff. "Les Patriotes de 1837–1838 d'après les documents J.-J. Girouard," P.-A. Linteau, édit., *RHAF,* XXI (1967–68), 281–311. *L'Aurore des Canadas* (Montréal), 15 janv. 1839–1845. *L'Écho du Pays* (Saint-Charles-sur-Richelieu, Qué.), 1835–36. *Le Glaneur* (Saint-Charles-sur-Richelieu, Qué.), déc. 1836–sept. 1837. Beaulieu et Hamelin, *Journaux du Québec.* Morgan, *Bibliotheca Canadensis,* 41. Joseph Tassé, *Les Canadiens de l'Ouest* (2e éd., 2v., Montréal, 1878), I, 137. Gérard Filteau, *Histoire des Patriotes* (3v., Montréal, 1938–39), III, 33–34. J.-B. Meilleur, *Mémorial de l'éducation du Bas-Canada* (2e éd., Québec, 1876), 354. L.-P. Audet, "Jean-Baptiste Meilleur était-il un candidat valable au poste de surintendant de l'Éducation pour le Bas-Canada en 1842?" *Cahiers des Dix,* XXXI (1966), 179.

BOUCHER DE LA BRUÈRE, PIERRE-CLAUDE, doctor and public servant; baptized 28 Sept. 1808 at Boucherville, eldest son of Colonel René Boucher de La Bruère and Marie-Julie Weilbrenner; d. 19 May 1871 at Saint-Hyacinthe, Que.

Almost nothing is known about Pierre-Claude Boucher de La Bruère's youth. On 11 March 1829 he was licensed to practise medicine. On 3 Oct. 1836, at Boucherville, he married Marie-Hippolyte de La Broquerie. He carried on his profession at Saint-Hyacinthe, where he lived for some years prior to the disturbances of 1837, and where he was to end his life.

The troubled period that Lower Canada went through during the decade after 1830 was certainly the fullest one in his life. In 1838, suspected of being in sympathy with the *Patriotes,* he was arrested and taken to prison. Two years earlier nobody would have believed such an event possible. He was the parish organist, he loved sketching and the theatre, and he spent his leisure time talking with the teacher-priests and students of the college of Saint-Hyacinthe, who spoke highly of his sensibility and sense of humour. Before the resolutions of Lord John Russell, in the spring of 1837, La Bruère scarcely ever took part in the demonstrations that brought together the *Patriotes* of Saint-Hyacinthe and the surrounding districts. He was none the less greatly exercised over the turn of events.

As a citizen of Saint-Hyacinthe he found himself at the centre of the storm that burst upon Lower Canada. As a doctor, he shared with too many *confrères* a clientele whose incomes were low. As a friend of the college of Saint-Hyacinthe, where five members of the Papineau family and two sons of Wolfred Nelson* were studying, he exchanged and shared with young teachers his hopes and fears as to the nation's future. No doubt it was recalled to him that his grandfather had fought at Châteauguay, and that heroes' blood flowed in his veins.

During the pre-revolutionary period, from April to November 1837, Boucher de La Bruère's restraint progressively gave place to impatience and exasperation. He was to be found at the different charivaris inflicted upon the opponents of the *Patriotes,* he took part in the planting of the fir-tree in May before the church at Saint-Hyacinthe, in honour of Louis-Joseph PAPINEAU, and he walked through the streets of the municipality dressed in homespun. In October 1837 he was present at the assembly of the six counties. He is said to have taken up arms in November, although we do not know the exact role he played in the events at Saint-Charles and Saint-Denis.

A year later, when renewed restlessness occurred in connection with the secret association of

Frères-Chasseurs [*see* NELSON], Boucher de La Bruère was apprehended and taken to prison in Montreal. His arrest is no doubt explained by the fact that on 2 November of the preceding year he had met Édouard-Élisée MALHIOT, one of the *Patriote* leaders who had arrived from the United States. Furthermore, he was suspected of assisting the *Patriotes* by using the funds of the Banque Canadienne, which he had established at Saint-Hyacinthe in 1835–36, in partnership with one of his brothers-in-law, Charles-Adrien Pacaud, who was himself a supporter of the *Patriotes*. This bank was to cease operation in 1839. On 29 Dec. 1838 La Bruère was released without trial.

After the rebellion it seems that the doctor reverted to a more moderate line of political thinking, one that was, indeed, more in conformity with his temperament. On 15 Sept. 1847 he was appointed major of the 5th battalion of the Saint-Hyacinthe militia. In 1849 he took a vigorous stand against the agitation for annexation to the United States. After that we know nothing further about his political ideas and activities.

On 22 Dec. 1862 he was appointed by the government to the post of inspector of crown land offices, and on 29 Oct. 1867 to that of director of colonization in Lower Canada. In 1869 he accepted in addition the office of inspector of prisons [*see* Terence Joseph O'NEILL]. Despite his duties he nevertheless continued to concern himself with the life and future of his region. In 1853 he had been president of the Saint-Jean Baptiste society of his municipality. He took part in the organization of the Société de Colonisation de Saint-Hyacinthe, which directed a number of families towards Compton County.

La Bruère died at Saint-Hyacinthe, and was mourned by his wife and only son, Pierre-René-Joseph-Hippolyte*, who later became a member of the Legislative Council and superintendent of public instruction.

YVES ROBY

"Inventaire des documents relatifs aux événements de 1837 et 1838, conservés aux archives de la province de Québec," APQ *Rapport*, 1925–26. C.-P. Choquette, *Histoire de la ville de Saint-Hyacinthe* (Saint-Hyacinthe, Qué., 1930). Fauteux, *Patriotes*, 123–24.

BOUCHETTE, ROBERT-SHORE-MILNES, lawyer, cartographer, *Patriote*, and civil servant; b. 12 March 1805 at Quebec, L.C., fourth son of Joseph Bouchette*, surveyor general of Lower Canada, and of Marie-Louise-Adélaïde Chaboillez; d. 4 June 1879 at Quebec.

At his baptism Robert-Shore-Milnes Bouchette received the names of his godfather, Sir Robert Shore Milnes*, the lieutenant governor at the time. He studied under the Reverend Daniel Wilkie*, and began to read law as a clerk in the office of Andrew Stuart*, a friend of his father. Although specializing in maritime law, he had a predilection for the study of Italian, history, the humanities, and mathematics: "a relaxation," he wrote in his *Mémoires*. Tempted by his "natural liking for drawing and cartography," and by his "desire to travel," he temporarily broke off his studies in December 1823 to go to New York as assistant to Lieutenant Henry Piers of the Royal Staff Corps and copy maps of the common border of the United States and Canada. On 15 March 1826, when he was barely 21 years of age, he was admitted to practise law.

Robert Bouchette devoted himself "with ardour" to his new profession until 1828; the following year he was attached to the surveyors' office, and helped his father to publish his geographical and cartographical work. He went to London and worked at drafting the maps and putting together the topographical and historical description of Canada; the result was two publications by Joseph Bouchette, which appeared in 1831. Thanks to the official position occupied by his father in Canada, Robert Bouchette was able to associate with the English nobility and bourgeoisie, and through this association to meet many important personages of the time. At Dover, when he was returning from a trip to France and Italy, he met Mary Ann Gardner, whom he married on 6 March 1834. On 27 July, a few months after they arrived in Canada, the young Englishwoman died, a victim of the Asiatic cholera epidemic.

This sudden bereavement, added to the political situation, was a decisive turning-point in Bouchette's life. He came round "without hesitation to the side of the Liberals, although," he said, "it was very painful for me to break off from my family and many of my personal friends, who sympathized with the party that had adopted, quite wrongly, the title of *constitutional*." Robert Bouchette stood as parliamentary candidate for Saguenay County in February 1836, but his opponent, Charles DROLET, also a Liberal, gained the victory, thanks to Louis-Joseph PAPINEAU's influence. The defeated candidate subsequently took an active part in the meetings held in the Quebec region to protest Lord John Russell's resolutions. On 17 June 1837 he founded at Quebec a bilingual newspaper, *Le Libéral/The Liberal*, the editing of the English part of which he entrusted to his friend Charles Hunter*.

As Bouchette came within the provisions of warrants for arrest issued against chairmen of the *Patriote* committees, the Quebec editor was arrested, then let out on bail shortly afterwards. He quickly left Quebec and headed for the Richelieu valley, finally reaching Swanton in Vermont. On 6 Dec. 1837, as an officer under the command of Édouard-Élisée MALHIOT, Robert Bouchette led the advance-guard of the little band that encountered the enemy at Moore's Corner (Saint-Armand-Station) [see Philip Henry MOORE]. He was wounded, and put in prison at Montreal, and on 28 June 1838 was condemned to exile in the Bermudas with seven other *Patriotes*, from whom Durham [Lambton*] had extracted the semblance of a confession of guilt. Bouchette left Quebec on 4 July on board the frigate *Vestal*, and arrived in the Bermudas on the 28th, after a crossing that gave him time, in collaboration with Wolfred Nelson*, to write an account of the Canadiens' grievances. After the abrogation of Durham's ordinance, Bouchette left his place of exile and headed for the American coast. In 1839 he was called to the bar in Vermont, and in the same year married Caroline-Anne Berthelot.

He returned to Canada in 1845, after the *nolle prosequi* of 1843, and three years later was appointed court clerk of the attorney general for Canada East; in March 1851 he was named to the post of collector of customs. In addition to looking after the organization of this department, Robert Bouchette was a member of several government commissions, including those responsible for studying the results of the treaty of reciprocity with the United States (1860), the organization of the civil service (1862), Canada's participation in the universal exposition of 1867 in Paris – Joseph-Charles Taché* and he were Canada's official representatives there – and the repercussions of the new civil service law (1868).

Having become a widower for the second time on 28 Jan. 1858, Robert Bouchette married again on 11 June 1861; his third wife was Clara Lindsay, by whom he had, among other children, Robert-Errol*. He withdrew from the civil service in 1875, and died at Quebec. He was buried at Saint-Colomb-de-Sillery.

In the forefront of the *Patriote* movement, for which he bore arms and wielded the pen with spirit and enthusiasm, Robert Bouchette caused a scandal by breaking with the environment of his family and its bureaucratic allegiance. This same enthusiasm was apparent when he was collector of customs: he built up this department and defended its organization by presenting a personal report different from that of the commission responsible for studying the repercussions of the new civil service law. This zeal did not prevent him from entertaining some aesthetic pretensions when he turned to drawing and cartography, and when he enlivened his prison cell at Montreal, decorating it with his guitar and with drawings from his portfolios.

YVES TESSIER

PAC, MG 24, D8/1 (Wright papers), 4503, 4504, 12139–42, 12334–36, 12391, 12392, 12420, 12421, 12570, 12571, 13611, 13612, 16379–82, 17276; MG 29, G27 (Morgan papers), 3, pp.937–44; Map Division, various manuscript maps copied by Robert-Shore-Milnes Bouchette. [R.-S.-M. Bouchette], *Mémoires de Robert-S.-M. Bouchette, 1805–1840; recueillis par son fils Errol Bouchette et annotés par A.-D. Decelles* (Montréal, [1903]); R.-S.-M. Bouchette "Weights and measures," Lit. and Hist. Soc. of Quebec, *Trans.*, new ser., I (1863), 1–33. R.-S.-M. Bouchette and Wolfred Nelson, "Brief sketch of Canadian affairs," *Canadian Antiquarian and Numismatic J.* (Montreal), 3rd ser., XIII (1916), 21–29. "Inventaire des documents relatifs aux événements de 1837 et 1838, conservés aux archives de la province de Québec," APQ *Rapport, 1925–26*, 188–89, 272–73, 283, 327. "Papiers Duvernay conservés aux archives de la province de Québec," APQ *Rapport, 1926–27*, 147–252. Canada, *Sessional Papers*, II (1869), PT.5, no.19, 39–40. *Standard dict. of Can. biog.* (Roberts and Tunnell), I, 62–63. Fauteux, *Patriotes*, 126–28. P.-G. Roy, *La famille Taschereau* (Lévis, Qué., 1901), 35–36. "Robert-Shore-Milnes Bouchette," *BRH*, XXXII (1926), 563.

BOULTON, D'ARCY, lawyer, politician, and Orangeman; b. 29 March 1825, at Perth, U.C., grandson of D'Arcy Boulton*, and son of James Boulton and Susan Beman, half-sister of Sir John Beverley Robinson*; m. in 1856 Louisa Charlotte Corbett; d. at Toronto, Ont., 16 Feb. 1875.

Educated at Upper Canada College in Toronto, D'Arcy Boulton then studied for the legal profession. He was admitted to the bar in 1847 and became a member of the law firm of Boulton, Lount, Boys, and Stewart of Barrie. He soon laid the foundation for a career as a Conservative politician and Orangeman; to offset the influence of Reform newspapers in the Barrie area, he formed in 1857, with D'Alton McCarthy Sr and others, a company to establish a newspaper called the *Spirit of the Age*. Designed to defend Orange and Conservative interests in Barrie, the newspaper lasted about five years.

Boulton ran unsuccessfully for the Simcoe North seat in the Canadian assembly in 1861, and was again defeated in the dominion elections of 1867 in Grey North and of 1872 in Muskoka. In 1873 he entered the Ontario legislature as the member for Simcoe South in a by-election following Thomas Roberts FERGUSON's resignation, and he retained the seat in the elections of 1875. But Boulton's real career was within the Orange Order, which he seems to have joined in the 1850s. He rose through private and district lodges to become deputy grand master of British North America in 1864 and provincial grand master of Ontario West in 1870. At the Imperial Grand Council of Orangemen held in Glasgow, Scotland, in 1873, he represented the Orangemen of the province of Ontario; he was unanimously chosen president at Glasgow of the Triennial Orange Conference of the British Empire, the highest office in the Loyal Orange Association. Boulton was also prominent in the Grand Black Lodge Chapter of Canada West, a more exclusive order of Orangeism, whose members were required to pass through a variety of degrees before initiation. As grand master of the chapter in western Ontario, he was active in promoting amalgamation with the chapter for eastern Canada in 1874 to form the Grand Black Chapter of British America. He was named its first grand master.

D'Arcy Boulton died at the age of 50, ending a promising political career as a Liberal Conservative: his influence within the Orange movement would probably have assured him of a prominent place in provincial and, perhaps, national politics. In his lifetime, however, he remained a minor political figure, and his correspondence with John A. Macdonald* deals largely with legal matters and patronage. He was described as a tactful man and seems to have had few enemies. His funeral, held at the Anglican St James' Cathedral, was the largest in Toronto up to that time, an indication of his popularity but also of the efficiency of the Orange organization in securing the attendance of its members.

HEREWARD SENIOR

PAC, MG 26, A (Macdonald papers). *Globe* (Toronto), 17, 20, 25 Oct. 1856; 19 Feb. 1875. *Leader* (Toronto), 19 Feb. 1875. *Mail* (Toronto), 19 Feb. 1875. *Lovell's Canadian dominion directory for 1871* ... (Montreal, [1871]). Hunter, *Hist. of Simcoe County.*

BOULTON, WILLIAM HENRY, lawyer, politician, and Orangeman; b. 19 April 1812 at York (Toronto), U.C., eldest son of D'Arcy Boulton Jr and Sarah Ann Robinson; m. Harriette Elizabeth Dixon who, in 1875, married Professor Goldwin Smith*; d. 15 Feb. 1874, at Toronto, Ont.

Grandson of Chief Justice D'Arcy Boulton*, as was his cousin D'Arcy BOULTON, and nephew of Sir John Beverley Robinson*, George Strange Boulton*, and Henry John Boulton*, William Henry Boulton belonged to the third generation of what was popularly known as the "Family Compact." He became an attorney at the age of 23 and began practising law in the partnership Gamble and Boulton. Matthew Crooks Cameron* articled with the firm and Boulton later entered into a partnership with him. In 1840 Boulton was treasurer of the annual Toronto races, one of the most important sporting events in the city, and in the next few years he emerged as an important figure in politics, making use of his considerable family influence and acquiring popular support through association with the rising power of the Orange movement.

Boulton was first elected alderman for St Patrick's ward on the Toronto City Council in 1838. He retained his seat until 1843, was re-elected in 1844 and 1852, and re-entered the council as alderman for St Andrew's ward in 1858. From 1845 until 1847 and again in 1858 he was selected by the council to serve as mayor of Toronto. He resigned as mayor on 8 Nov. 1858, after a quarrel with the chief of police. Boulton contested the election in January 1859, the first in which the electors voted directly for the mayor, but was defeated by Reform lawyer Adam Wilson* who was supported by George BROWN's Municipal Reform Association.

Boulton lent dignity to the office of mayor by his family prestige and by his impressive residence known as the "Grange" where he entertained the governor general, Lord Elgin [Bruce*], during his tour of Canada West in 1847. As mayor he was himself a colourful figure with varied interests. Once, when councillors debated whether his salary should be £400 or £450, Boulton, on being informed that there were back streets in town that could not be paved for want of funds, told the council to "leave the money in the chamberlain's hands for the benefit of the community." Perhaps it was this apparent indifference to money that surprised and pleased his electors and it may explain the financial difficulties he experienced in 1851 when his property qualifications for nomination were questioned. One of Boulton's major interests while mayor was the Provincial Agricultural Association. He played a leading role in the decision of the city council to vote $20,000 towards a permanent exhibition building for agricultural and industrial arts. This building, known as the Crystal Palace, was opened in 1858 and annual exhibitions were held there until 1866.

Boulton's career as a representative for Toronto in the Legislative Assembly began in 1844 when he was pressed to stand for the Tories along with Henry Sherwood*. The Tory *British Canadian* stated, "Mr Boulton . . . is just the man of firmness and resolution that the times call for . . . he is shrewd, prompt, and persevering." The two Toronto seats were being contested by one Reformer, John Henry Dunn*, and two other

Boulton

Tories. Boulton's support came largely from the working classes (Brown complained in the *Globe* that the "Labourers were under the influence of the Corporation and the Family Compact"), and he was to continue to hold this support throughout his parliamentary career.

When Boulton entered the assembly in 1844, he joined the Conservative ranks under William Henry DRAPER, whose administration he was later to describe as the "weakest government that ever held power." The major issue facing the assembly was the Reformers' bill making King's College secular, and on it Boulton was firm; coming from a strong Church of England family, he tried consistently to protect what he considered the rights and privileges of the church. In 1845 Draper attempted to settle the university question, and Boulton, as one of Bishop John Strachan*'s spokesmen in the assembly, opposed his bill and moved a six-month delay; the motion eventually carried. Again in 1849 when Robert Baldwin*'s university bill, which removed all denominational distinctions, was being debated, Boulton led the opposition; however, the act was passed. King's College was completely secularized, but Queen's and Victoria, both sectarian colleges, refused to be affiliated with it. In 1851 Boulton unsuccessfully proposed a university plan of his own. It was comparable to one proposed earlier by Sherwood and had Strachan's approval. The University of Toronto would adopt the University of London's system; that is, it would become the examining board for denominational colleges. A new institution, University College, was to retain the endowment of King's College and the teaching functions.

One of Boulton's first acts in the assembly had been to present a petition asking that the portion of the clergy reserves set apart for the Church of England be given up to it. In 1845 he spoke out against an amendment by Baldwin which would prevent Church of England clergymen from voting by providing that a clergyman would have to prove that he possessed a 40 shilling freehold. Boulton declared that it was a "stab at the Church and he was surprised to find Mr. Baldwin, who was a member of the Church, among its bitterest enemies."

In his defence of the church, Boulton was acting on principle or, at least, following a family tradition, but on other issues he appears to have accepted the role of demagogue in his bid for popular support. Having retained his seat in the Conservative debacle of 1847–48, when he warned electors that their interests would be sacrificed to the "Tobacco-smoking, Dram Drinking, Garlick Eating Frenchmen," Boulton surprised his Con-servative colleagues in 1850 by proposing amendments to the constitution to develop more fully the "elective system" and in particular to make the Legislative Council elective. Answering objections that his proposals were "revolutionary and republican," Boulton replied, "Our institutions are republican . . . so are those of Great Britain." His Toronto colleague, Henry Sherwood, strongly condemned Boulton's proposals and said they were not the sentiments of his Toronto constituents, but Boulton campaigned in 1851 on the need for "radical changes in the working of the Government," and won his seat, although with a reduced majority.

Boulton was able to boast in that year that "he owed his election to . . . the bone and sinew of the country, the mechanics, the artisans, and labourers," and to the Orange association. In fact, much of Boulton's popular support came from Toronto Orangemen who were grateful to him for his efforts in having the act of 1843 restricting party processions repealed. They wanted Boulton as their candidate along with Henry Sherwood during the 1851 elections, which saw two other Conservatives and two Reformers in the contest. At the stormy nomination meeting, a "knot of young lads, the roughest and most noisy of our population," according to the *Globe*, shouted down not only Reformers Frederick Chase Capreol* and Terence Joseph O'NEILL, but also Orangeman Samuel Thompson* who persisted in running even after an Orange delegation asked him to retire from the contest. Boulton was elected, along with George Percival RIDOUT, but his election was declared invalid in March 1853.

In his role as an Orangeman, Boulton had risen from the mastership of a Toronto lodge to become deputy grand master of British North America in 1854. During the schism in the Orange movement from 1853 to 1856, Boulton supported the more Protestant and vocal wing of Orangeism led by George Benjamin* in opposition to Ogle Robert GOWAN.

After his expulsion from the assembly, Boulton left Canada to travel in England and on the Continent. He again made a bid for his former Toronto seat in the 1857 election but was defeated by George Brown. This set-back, coupled with his resignation as mayor in 1858 and his subsequent defeat in the mayoralty contest in 1859, led to his retirement from politics. He continued practising law in Toronto.

Boulton was a son of the Family Compact with a sympathy for tradition, but he had at the same time an instinct for popular politics. He early grasped the political importance of the Orange movement, and he was never disturbed by the views or methods of Orangemen. His defence of clergy reserves was consistent with his traditionalism and his advocacy of elective institutions consistent with his "popularism." Understandably, he was disliked and feared by Reformers such as Baldwin and Brown who disapproved of his essentially popular and non-intellectual approach to politics. But he had an affable personality; he was able to enjoy both a dinner in the officers' mess of the garrison after a day's race over "Boulton's Course" and electioneering on a platform that was flanked by "Boulton's Brigades" who applauded his promises to vote for "rep by pop" and to defend Protestantism.

HEREWARD SENIOR

Evening Telegram (Toronto), 12 July 1910. *Globe* (Toronto), 8, 15 Oct., 10 Dec. 1844; 14 Jan., 11 Feb., 11 March 1845; 27 June, 6 July 1850; 24 June, 20 Nov., 2, 9, 11, 18, 23, 25 Dec. 1851; 15 Dec. 1857; 13 July, 9 Nov. 1858. *The hand-book of Toronto; containing its climate, geology, natural history, educational institutions, courts of law, municipal arrangements* . . . , [comp. G. P. Ure] (Toronto, 1858), 175. Loyal Orange Association of British North America, Grand Lodge, *Annual Report*, 1854, 5–7. *Mail and Empire* (Toronto), 4 Nov. 1936. *Montreal Gazette*, 20 June 1840. J. R. Robertson, *Old Toronto: a selection of excerpts from Landmarks of Toronto*, ed. E. C. Kyte (Toronto, 1954), 59–60, 69. Scadding, *Toronto of old.*

Chadwick, *Ontarian families*, I, 58; II, 57. Dent, *Canadian portrait gallery*, III, 101. Wallace, *Macmillan dictionary*, 73. Careless, *Brown*, I, 245–46, 291; *Union of the Canadas*, 118. Creighton, *Macdonald, young politician*, 109–10, 161–62. *Landmarks of Toronto* (Robertson), II, 630, 754–55, 1089; VI, 191–92. Moir, *Church and state in Canada West*, 96, 110, 113.

BOURBOURG, CHARLES-ÉTIENNE BRASSEUR DE. *See* BRASSEUR

BOURGEAUX (Bourgeau), EUGÈNE, botanical collector; b. 20 April 1813 at Brizon, France (department of Hautes-Alpes), son of Jacques Bourgeaux and Françoise Missilier; d. in February 1877 in Paris.

Nothing precise is known about Eugène Bourgeaux's youth, except that he acquired a liking for botany while tending his father's herds. He seems to have received little education, to judge by his correspondence. Nicolas-Charles Seringe and Alex Jordan, of Lyons, taught him the rudiments of the science of botany. In 1843 Bourgeaux went to Paris where Philip Barker Webb employed him to assist in the conservation of his herbarium. For this purpose, in 1845 and 1846 Bourgeaux

travelled over all the Canary Islands. In the following year the Association Botanique Française d'Exploration appointed Bourgeaux a botanical collector. In this capacity he travelled until 1856, for the association or for other scientists, throughout Spain, the south of France, the Canary Islands, and Algeria.

In 1857, at the request of Sir William Jackson Hooker, who had known him in the French botanical association and who considered him "the prince of botanical collectors," Bourgeaux took part as a collector in the expedition led by John Palliser*. This expedition, financed by the British government, was to explore British territory between latitudes 45° and 50°N and longitudes 100° and 115°W, with a view to assessing the possibilities of settling the region. Thus its members were expected to provide impartial and complete scientific information on the topography, routes, soil, and climate of the prairies. Bourgeaux was engaged by John Ball, under-secretary of state for the colonies, and was to receive £150 per season. On 16 May 1857, together with Palliser and two other members of the expedition, he sailed for New York, and on 10 June the explorers set off on their first stage, to Fort William (Thunder Bay, Ont.).

"My botanical illusions have diminished a lot since arriving in these vast regions," he wrote to Hooker in typically misspelt French. "The forests and prairies are magnificent, and so is the vegetation, but one of my first observations is that the same plants occupy a large geographical territory, and the number of species is not related to the vastness of the country." This discovery in no way prevented Bourgeaux from gathering specimens in the vicinity of Lake Superior, Red River, and Lake Winnipeg, in the valley of the Saskatchewan River, around Carlton House (near Prince Albert, Sask.) and Edmonton, then in the Rockies. After that, according to his correspondence with Hooker, he followed the Bow River from old Fort Kananaskis to the head-waters – Bow Lakes, to the northeast of the present Yoho Park (British Columbia). In the Rockies he collected several examples of about 229 species. All the plants and seeds had to be carefully dried so that they would not mildew, and Palliser helped him in this task.

The leader of the expedition admired the collector's tenacity and courage. James Hector*, one of the members of the team, emphasized that Bourgeaux was everybody's friend: he was jovial, and quick to assist anybody who sought his aid. In particular he helped Thomas Wright Blakiston, who was responsible for astronomical and meteorological readings. Bourgeaux, who knew no English, was popular with the Métis because of

Bourgeaux

his language and personal qualities, and he became a friend of Father Albert Lacombe*. It was with regret that the expedition parted company with Bourgeaux in the spring of 1859. He had to leave them to discharge a previous commitment.

He went to the Royal Botanic Gardens at Kew in London, and there for some weeks he sorted his specimens. These were subsequently identified and classified by the Royal Botanic Gardens. He had collected altogether about 1,200 species, in 10–12 duplicates. Unfortunately his habitat notes were not retranscribed for each specimen. All that was done was to print a label: "Palliser's Brit. N. Am. Expl. Expedition. Saskatchewan. Coll. E. Bourgeau 1858–59." Yet the majority of the specimens did not come from Saskatchewan. Consequently Bourgeaux's North American collections can scarcely be utilized. This is a pity, the more because all the plants classified by Bourgeaux up to then were remarkable for the quality of the labels. However, the carices he had gathered on the prairies have been identified by the famous Francis Boott, and some are quoted in his classic work *Illustrations of the Genus Carex*.

This great North American expedition did not exhaust Bourgeaux. He had barely finished his task of classifying in London when Edmond Boissier, the Swiss botanist, commissioned him to explore Lycia so that he could complete his documentation on Asia Minor, whose flora he was engaged in describing. Bourgeaux devoted the year 1860 to this task, then he explored the county of Nice, and the following year Boissier sent him back to Asia Minor to explore the Pontic Alps (Turkey). On his return, Bourgeaux continued his botanical excursions, this time in Spain (1863–64). In 1865, on the proposal of the Muséum National d'Histoire Naturelle in Paris, Bourgeaux was attached to the scientific mission that was to explore Mexico in the wake of the French armies. There he spent the years 1865 and 1866. Asa Gray and Sereno Watson were often to speak in their publications of certain of Bourgeaux's Mexican collections. Some herbarium specimens indicate that Bourgeaux was on the Island of Rhodes in 1870, but his activities after his return from Mexico in 1867 until his death cannot be reconstructed.

In 1877 Édouard André paid tribute to Bourgeaux: "[He] was one of the most remarkable collectors of dry plants in this period. He embarked upon journeys that took in France, Spain, Asia Minor, the Canaries, the Rocky Mountains, and finally Mexico, which he explored as part of the French scientific commission, and the results of these have enriched all the herbariums in Europe. M. Bourgeau, who had been named knight of the Légion d'Honneur after the last

campaign, was occupied with the sorting of his collections at the Muséum d'Histoire Naturelle when death overtook him last February."

All in all, Eugène Bourgeaux classified for botanists more than 15,000 species, which were identified by authorities of his day such as Boissier, Webb, Cosson, Boott, and Hooker. Ernest Cosson dedicated to him a genus of compositae, the *Bourgaea*; in botanical literature occur, among others, *Astragalus bourgovii* Gray, *Statice bourgiaei* Webb, and *Saxifraga bourgaeana* Boissier and Reut. His contribution to the botanical exploration of western North America is noted by the *Rosa bourgeauiana* [François] Crépin, and his name deserves an honourable place in Canadian history among the great explorers of the last century.

The practical knowledge that Bourgeaux acquired of the Canadian prairies enabled him to draw the attention of the British government "to the eventual advantages of setting up agricultural centres in the vast plains of Rupert's Land, and particularly in Saskatchewan in the vicinity of Fort Carlton. [For] this region is much more suitable for the [large-scale] farming done in temperate climates (wheat, rye, barley, oats, Indian corn, etc.) than one would be inclined to believe." In his opinion, the prairies would, moreover, be ideal for stock-breeding, and would provide all the materials necessary for the establishment of a settlement. Through its produce, the latter would ensure "the subsistence of the Indians, whose sources of food, provided exclusively by hunting, tend to diminish daily." The only real difficulty the settlers would encounter would be "the immense distance to be covered in lands at present devoid of roads and almost uninhabited."

Although the Savoyard Bourgeaux signed no written work, he was such a keen and prolific collector, in so many diverse countries, that he is remembered in the history of botanical exploration. A mountain peak in the Banff area bears his name.

MARCEL RAYMOND

Palliser papers (Spry). Édouard André, "Nécrologie," *L'illustration horticole* (Ghent), XXIV (1877), 71–72. Ernest Cosson, "Notice sur les voyages et collections botaniques de M. Eugène Bourgeau," *Bulletin de la Société botanique de France*, XIII (1866), l–lvii. W. J. Hooker, "*Statice bourgiaei*, Bourgeau's Statice, Tab-5153," *Curtis's Botanical Magazine* (London), LXXXV (1859). Marcel Raymond, "Bourgeau en Amérique du Nord," *Les botanistes français en Amérique du Nord avant 1850* (Colloques internationaux du Centre national de la recherche scientifique, LXIII, Paris, 1957), 189–92.

BOURNEUF, FRANÇOIS-LAMBERT, sailor, school-teacher, farmer, merchant, shipbuilder, and politician; b. 20 Oct. 1787 at Rénéville, France (department of Manche), son of François Bourneuf and Michelle Énolle; d. 16 May 1871 at Grosses Coques, St Mary's Bay, N.S.

In 1808, after three years' service in the French imperial navy, François-Lambert Bourneuf signed on with the frigate *Furieuse*, trading to the French West Indies. During a voyage in 1809 he was taken prisoner by the English, and brought to Halifax. He managed to escape in 1812, after two attempts. Bourneuf then became a school-teacher at Pombcoup (Pubnico), N.S. He later went to St Mary's Bay, where on 20 May 1813, before Father Jean-Mandé Sigogne*, he took the oath of allegiance to the British crown. He taught for another year and then turned his attention to farming. In November 1815 he was again at sea as second in command on a schooner. Two years later he bought his own schooner and began to sail the trading route between Saint John, New Brunswick, and Nova Scotia. By 1830 Bourneuf was also doing well as a shipbuilder; from 1830 to 1855 he built some 30 vessels.

In the Nova Scotia elections of 1843 Bourneuf entered politics as a reform candidate and was elected MLA for Digby County, N.S.; his mandate was renewed in the elections of 1847, 1851, and 1855. In the same period he was appointed a member of the first schools commission for Clare (Church Point), N.S.; his name also appears among the first magistrates of that county.

In November 1855 the firm of Allison and Spur of Saint John, N.B., with which Bourneuf did business and for which he built ships, was forced by a series of bankruptcy actions to close its doors. The closure reduced Bourneuf's firm to bankruptcy – an experience from which neither Bourneuf nor his business ever recovered.

In 1859 at the end of his fourth term as MLA for Digby, Bourneuf retired from both provincial and municipal politics. He then began to write his memoirs, which he never completed.

In 1818 François-Lambert Bourneuf had married Marie Doucet, by whom he had ten children.

GÉRALD G. OUELLET

Archives acadiennes, Université de Moncton, Fonds de Placide Gaudet, 43–24; Mémoire de François-Lambert Bourneuf. Beck, *Government of Nova Scotia*. Alphonse Deveau, *La ville française* (Québec, 1968), 189, 202, 245–66. I. W. Wilson, *A geography and history of the county of Digby, Nova Scotia* (Halifax, 1900), 319–30. "François Lambert Bourneuf," *Le Petit Courrier* (West Pubnico, N.S.), 18 mars – 10 juin 1948. "Francois Lambert Bourneuf," *L'Évangéline* (Moncton, N.B.), 10 déc. 1891 – 2 juin 1892. J. W. Comeau, "François Lambert Bourneuf," N.S. Hist. Soc. *Coll.*, XXVII (1947), 147–72.

BOVELL, JAMES, physician, Church of England clergyman, theologian, and educator; b. 28 Oct. 1817, in Barbados, West Indies, eldest son of John Bovell, a wealthy banker, and Sarah Applewaite; m. at age 18 Julia Howard App-Griffith of Barbados who survived him by 11 years; of their six children, two died in infancy; d. 15 Jan. 1880, at Charlestown, Nevis, West Indies.

James Bovell received private schooling in Barbados, before going to England at age 17 for further education. He decided to study medicine, and in November 1834 entered Guy's Hospital, London, where he was Sir Astley Cooper's dresser, and was taught by Richard Bright, Thomas Addison, and other distinguished physicians. He later studied pathology at Edinburgh and Glasgow while awaiting admittance into the Royal College of Physicians of London as an extra-licentiate in 1839. He then worked for a few years under Robert Graves and William Stokes in Dublin, until stricken with typhus fever. When he recovered, he returned to Barbados and took up practice in Bridgetown. Bovell has been credited with medical degrees from London, Edinburgh, Glasgow, and Dublin universities, but official records do not confirm these additional qualifications.

In 1848 Bovell emigrated to Canada and began practising in Toronto, where he became one of the most prominent physicians. His broad training and questing spirit engaged him in such ventures as the treatment of cholera victims with milk transfusions, the practice of clinical microscopy, and the study of comparative pathology. In 1851 he was co-founder and editor of the *Upper Canada Journal of Medical, Surgical and Physical Science* (Toronto), and his personal contributions to medical journals totalled nearly 30 papers, on topics ranging from the anatomy of the leech to a uterine tumour as a complication of parturition. His writings often displayed both a reforming zeal and keen observation. He connected the unhealthiness of Barbados with "innumerable swarms of insects" (1848); and advocated health committees for Toronto that should order "the removal of all nuisances and filth," since "cholera delights in filth and moisture." Later, in *A plea for inebriate asylums*, he deplored the general indifference towards drunkenness, which led "the unfortunate victim to look on his state rather as a weak fault or excusable failing than a great sin, and so perpetuat[ed] a degrading vice to his utter destruction and eternal ruin."

Bovell

Bovell was a dedicated educationist and was one of the original councillors of the Canadian Institute in 1852. He, along with Edward Mulberry HODDER and four other colleagues, helped to organize the medical faculty of the new Trinity College in November 1850. He was dean from 1851 until 1856, when the faculty resigned and the school was dissolved following disputes with the council, headed by John Strachan*, bishop of Toronto. Friction arose initially because the faculty, whose services were freely given, resented the council's restrictions on expenditures and its exercise of authority over such matters as the advertisements for medical courses inserted in the press by the dean. The final break came after the faculty opened direct negotiations with the government to forestall a threatened reinstitution of the former King's College medical school. When Bovell's conciliatory efforts failed, he joined the Toronto School of Medicine as lecturer in physiology and pathology. In 1864 he also became lecturer in physiology to the Upper Canada Veterinary School (later the Ontario Veterinary College), established in 1862 by Andrew Smith*.

From 1857 until he left Canada in 1870, Bovell was at various times designated professor of physiology, of physiology and chemistry, and of natural theology in the faculty of arts at Trinity College. For several years he was also lay secretary to the diocesan and provincial synods. He was deeply religious and published about a dozen devotional or exegetical works presenting High Church beliefs. His physiology lectures to third-year arts students were based on his *Outlines of natural theology*, which illustrated divine goodness and wisdom through natural objects and phenomena and sought to reconcile recent geological discoveries with the Book of Genesis. Rejecting the doctrines of Sir Charles Lyell and Charles Darwin, he espoused the high sacramental teachings of John Keble and Edward Bouverie Pusey, leaders of the Tractarian movement at Oxford. In 1860, his views on the real presence of Christ in the Eucharist were denounced as "Romish" by the bishop of Huron, Benjamin CRONYN, whose evangelical convictions had involved him in open conflict with Trinity College authorities. To Bovell's distress, a commentary on his privately circulated denial of this allegation appeared in the *Globe* newspaper on 15 Nov. 1860. When the corporation of Trinity College (of which he was a member) disavowed and repudiated his doctrinal statements *in absentia*, he resigned his cherished chair, but Bishop Strachan persuaded him to retain it.

James Bovell strongly influenced William Osler*. In 1866, when Osler, at 17, was head prefect at Trinity College School, the founder and warden of the school, William Arthur JOHNSON, was Bovell's close friend and fellow-microscopist, and Bovell was himself medical superintendent and a governor of the school. Osler accompanied the two men on specimen-hunting expeditions, from which stemmed his deep interest in microscopy. When Osler decided upon a medical career, he became Bovell's unofficial apprentice, and between 1868 and 1870 frequented his house, attended his lectures, browsed in his library, and shared his hobbies, from natural history to the classics. Many years later, when Sir William Osler was Regius professor of medicine at Oxford, he publicly acknowledged owing his start in the profession to James Bovell. On a previous occasion, paying a "tribute of filial affection" to his old teacher, Osler summed him up in these words: "Only men of a certain metal rise superior to their surroundings, and while Dr. Bovell had that all-important combination of boundless ambition with energy and industry, he had that fatal quality of diffuseness, in which even genius is strangled."

When Bovell revisited the West Indies in 1870, he was persuaded to take holy orders by Bishop W. W. Jackson of Antigua, who ordained him in 1871, and he decided to remain in the West Indies. After serving as curate, then rector, at the united parishes of St George's and St John's, Nevis, moved to Charlestown in 1873, where he took charge of the less demanding combined parishes of St Thomas' and St Paul's. In 1875 his health began to fail and he died five years later following a stroke.

CLAUDE E. DOLMAN

Selected writings by James Bovell are: "Apparatus for the exhibition of vapour," *Upper Canada Journal of Medical, Surgical and Physical Science* (Toronto), I (1851–52), 59–60; "Clinical remarks on two cases of tumour of the uterus complicating parturition," *British American Journal of Medical and Physical Science* (Montreal), V (1849–50), 1–5, 29–32; *Constitution and canons of the Synod of the Diocese of Toronto, with explanatory notes and comments* (Toronto, 1858); *Defence of doctrinal statements, addressed to the right rev. the lord bishop of Toronto, the right rev. the lord bishop of Huron, and the Corporation of Trinity College, with the hope that the explanations now given may remove erroneous impressions, and satisfy the church at large that I am loyal and true to her* (Toronto, 1860); *Letters, addressed to the Rev. Mr. Fletcher and others, framers of a series of resolutions on "ritual"* (Toronto, 1867); "Note on the preservation of some infusoria with a view to the display of their cilia," *Canadian Journal*, new ser., VIII (1863), 341–42; "Notes on some points in the anatomy of the leech," *Canadian Journal*, new ser., I (1856), 27–33; "Observations on the climate of

Barbadoes and its influence on disease: together with remarks on angioleucitis or Barbadoes leg," *British American Journal of Medical and Physical Science* (Montreal), IV (1848–49), 113–16, 141–45, 169–72, 197–201, 225–28, 261–66; "On the transfusion of milk, as practised in cholera, at the cholera sheds, Toronto, July, 1854," *Canadian Journal*, III (1854–55), 188–92; "On the white globules of the blood in disease," *Upper Canada Journal of Medical, Surgical and Physical Science* (Toronto), II (1852–53), 48–50, 65–69, 128–37, 150–56, 182–89, 210–14; *Outlines of natural theology for the Canadian student, selected and arranged from the most authentic sources* (Toronto, 1859); *Passing thoughts on man's relation to God and on God's relation to man* (Toronto, 1862); *A plea for inebriate asylums; commended to the consideration of the legislators of the province of Canada* (Toronto, 1862); *Preparation for the Christian sacrifice, or holy communion* (Toronto, 1859); *The world at the advent of Jesus Christ* (Toronto, 1868).

Bishop of Antigua's Lodge, Bishop's diary, visitation of Nevis, 1872. PAO, Strachan letter books, 1854–62, John Strachan to James Bovell, 29 Nov. 1860. St. George's, St. John's, St Paul's, and St Thomas' Churches (Nevis, W.I.), Baptism, marriage, and burial registers. *Globe* (Toronto), 15, 17 Nov. 1860. [William Osler], "James Bovell, M.D.," *Canadian Journal of Medical Science* (Toronto), V (April 1880), 114–15. University of Trinity College (Toronto), *Calendars*, 1853–70. *Standard dict. of Can. biog.* (Roberts and Tunnell), II, 40–42.

Canniff, *Medical profession in Upper Canada*, 257–58. Harvey Cushing, *The life of Sir William Osler* (2v. Oxford, 1925). *A history of the University of Trinity College, Toronto, 1852–1952*, ed. T. A. Reed (Toronto, 1952). C. E. Dolman, "The Reverend James Bovell, M.D., 1817–1880," in *Pioneers of Canadian science*, ed. G. F. G. Stanley (Royal Society of Canada "Studia Varia" series, IX, Toronto, 1966), 81–100, 136–46. N. B. Gwyn, "Details connected with the evolution of medical education in Toronto," University of Toronto *Medical Journal*, VIII (1930), 224–29; "The early life of Sir William Osler," International Association of Medical Museums, *Bulletin IX*, and *Journal of Technical Methods* (Montreal, 1926), 109–49. A. J. Johnson, "The founder of the medical faculty, Dr. James Bovell," *Trinity University Review* (Toronto), XV (1902), 104–6.

BOYD, JOHN, teacher, publisher, and pharmacist; b. at South River, Sydney County, N.S., to John Boyd and Mary MacDonald in 1823; m. Ann MacDonald and had one son and three daughters; d. in Boston, Mass., on 28 Dec. 1880.

John Boyd, who apparently had little formal education, became a school-teacher in Pictou County in 1848. He prepared a Gaelic-English speller to which he added a short history of the "45" in Gaelic. This history was also printed by the Pictou *Eastern Chronicle*. Returning to Sydney County in 1849, he designed a primitive press which was built by Angus MacGillivray, a local carpenter. In 1850 he taught school at Broad Cove, at the same time continuing his interest in printing. In January 1851 he began a journal, *An Cuairtear og Gaelach*, which contained material that was mostly copied from Tormad MacLeod's *Cuairtear*, published in Scotland.

In June 1852 Boyd began the Antigonish *Casket*, a small Catholic newspaper, which appeared weekly. Two of its four pages had material written in Gaelic. The use of Gaelic was probably due less to a sense of ethnic pride than to the fact that many of the potential readers were Highland Scots. The Gaelic content was gradually reduced and by 1857 it had virtually disappeared from the paper. When he began his paper, readers "like the visit of angels," were few and far between. To keep the paper alive, Boyd turned to job printing, opened the first Catholic book-store east of Halifax, and, although he had no training, also operated a pharmacy. The lack of proper communication and transportation facilities posed a continuous difficulty in bringing in supplies for his enterprises and in obtaining information for the paper. In July 1852 a telegraph office was opened in Antigonish, but this was expensive, and a twice-weekly coach service, begun in 1841, was unreliable. To develop circulation for his paper on Cape Breton Island, which was particularly deficient in communication facilities, Boyd sent out agents who toured the island selling books, pills, and the *Casket*. By 1858 the paper was sold by four agents in the peninsula, 13 on Cape Breton, and three in Prince Edward Island. No figures on actual sales have survived but circulation never matched his expectations.

In content the *Casket* brought its readers a wide mixture of current events, theology, poetry, and literature, much of it written especially for the paper. Its editorials, principally by Dr William Currie, supported the Liberal party and unsuccessfully favoured such local reforms as the adoption of municipal institutions. The growing quarrel between the Catholics, particularly the Irish, and the Liberal government posed a difficult problem for the *Casket*. The paper, either because of devotion to reform principles or because of a lack of affinity with the Irish of Halifax, tried to continue supporting the Liberal government of William Young* despite Joseph HOWE's attacks on the Catholics. Its tactics merely brought a series of bitter attacks from the Halifax *Catholic*. Boyd capitulated and the *Casket* gradually became a staunch supporter of the Conservative party.

Boyd was always ambitious to play a prominent part in the colony's affairs and, in January 1861, moved his newspaper office to Halifax. This venture failed and Boyd returned to Antigonish; in

July 1861 he sold the *Casket* to his half-brother, Angus Boyd, and devoted himself to his book- and drug-store. In September 1862, after suffering further business reverses, he moved to Boston. Angus Boyd later stated that John Boyd was "the author of several ingenious inventions" and he may have been the John Boyd who had an American patent on a combination cane-umbrella. But Boyd, through his optimism and vision, had undoubtedly helped to build a newspaper which served its readers well.

K. G. PRYKE

Casket (Antigonish, N.S.), 1852–61 (broken run), 1943. D. J. Rankin, *A history of the county of Antigonish, Nova Scotia* (Toronto, 1929). D. G. Whidden, *The history of the town of Antigonish* (Wolfville, N.S., 1934), 113–15. D. M. Sinclair, "Gaelic newspapers and prose writings in Nova Scotia," N.S. Hist. Soc. *Coll.*, XXVI (1945), 105–14.

BRASSARD, LOUIS-MOÏSE, secular priest, bursar of the seminary of Nicolet, and parish priest; b. 25 Oct. 1800 at Nicolet, L.C., son of Jean-Baptiste Brassard and Marie-Josephte Manseau; d. 21 June 1877 at Longueuil, Que.

Louis-Moïse, grand-nephew of Louis-Marie Brassard*, the founder of the school that became the seminary of Nicolet, came from a family that provided many priests and nuns. He was a pupil at the seminary of Nicolet from 1811 to 1820, and was ordained priest at Quebec on 4 Jan. 1824. Having been assistant priest at Les Cèdres, in Soulanges County, parish priest of Saint-Timothée de Beauharnois, Saint-Polycarpe, and Sainte-Elizabeth de Joliette, he returned to the seminary of Nicolet as bursar for the period 1836 to 1840. In particular he sought to find ways of improving cultivation on the farms. The chronic deficit of the institution led him to doubt his ability for this kind of work, and he asked his bishop for permission to return to the care of a parish.

As parish priest of Saint-Antoine de Longueuil from 1840 to 1855, he displayed great activity, particularly in the field of education. He had a boys' secondary school built, on which work was almost finished when he left the parish. He founded the convent of Longueuil. His costly ventures drained the treasury of the parish council, and he did not succeed in having a new church built.

His dealings with the sisters of the Holy Names of Jesus and Mary are famous. After vainly trying to obtain the services of the nuns of the Congregation of Notre-Dame for his future school, Brassard, through the intermediary of the Oblate Pierre-Antoine-Adrien Telmon, had asked for some of the sisters of the Holy Names of Jesus and Mary. In 1846 he prevailed upon the parish council of Longueuil to build a spacious house and to put it at the disposal of the sisters. Soon the parish council was trying to dictate to the sisters' school. For his part, the Canadian priest considered that the nuns were too receptive to the directives given by the French Oblates, their spiritual advisers. He even threatened to withdraw his material assistance from the sisters. In 1849 the Oblates left Longueuil, and shortly afterwards Brassard assumed the spiritual direction of the community. Historians have not failed to stress that the difficult relations between the parish priest, the sisters, and the Oblates began when Charles-Paschal-Télesphore Chiniquy*, who had left the noviciate of the Oblates in November 1847, took refuge with Brassard; the parish priest had been Chiniquy's friend and protector since the latter's brief stay at the seminary of Nicolet.

In 1857, after residing two years in Europe, Brassard was appointed parish priest at Saint-Roch-de-l'Achigan. He built a convent there, which he entrusted to the sisters of the Holy Names of Jesus and Mary, and a college, intended for the Clercs de Saint-Viateur. He was also interested in encouraging settlement on the land. In September 1862, with this end in view, he explored the valleys of L'Assomption and La Mataouin (Matawin), together with the parish priests Théophile-Stanislas Provost* and Thomas-Léandre Brassard, his brother.

In 1874 L.-M. Brassard retired to Longueuil, and for some time lived in the residence of the sisters of the Holy Names of Jesus and Mary. He died at Longueuil at the age of 77. His body rests in the cemetery of the sisters.

PIERRE SAVARD

Allaire, *Dictionnaire*. Carrière, *Histoire des O.M.I.*, I, 133–41, 303–20; V, 41–82. J.-A.-I. Douville, *Histoire du collège-séminaire de Nicolet, 1803–1903, avec les listes complètes des directeurs, professeurs et élèves de l'institution* (2v., Montréal, 1903), I, 250. Stanislas Drapeau, *Études sur les développements de la colonisation du Bas-Canada depuis dix ans, de 1851 à 1861* (Québec, 1863), 425–31. Fidelis [J.-H. Prétot], *Mère Marie-Rose, fondatrice de la congrégation des SS. Noms de Jésus et de Marie au Canada* (Montréal, 1895). Alexandre Jodoin et J.-L. Vincent, *Histoire de Longueuil et de la famille de Longueuil* (Montréal, 1889), 410–12. Paroisse de Saint-Roch de l'Achigan, *Annuaire de Ville-Marie* (Montréal, 1871), 57–80. Marcel Trudel, *Chiniquy* (2e éd., [Trois-Rivières, Qué.], 1955).

BRASSEUR DE BOURBOURG, CHARLES-ÉTIENNE, secular priest, historian, specialist in American studies; b. 8 Sept. 1814; d. 8 Jan. 1874 at Nice, France.

Brasseur de Bourbourg

Charles-Étienne Brasseur was born at Bourbourg, a small town, Flemish in appearance, 18 kilometres from Dunkirk. He studied philosophy and theology first at Ghent, Belgium, then at Rome, where he was ordained priest in 1845.

While still a student, Brasseur gave indications that he was destined to be a writer. In 1837 he contributed to the journal *Le Monde* (Paris), directed by Félicité-Robert de La Mennais; then, under the pseudonym of Ravensberg, he published historical accounts, such as *Jérusalem, tableau de l'histoire et des vicissitudes de cette ville célèbre . . .*, or novels inspired by primitive Christianity, such as *Le Sérapéon. . . .* A contributor to *L'Univers* (Paris) pointed out, in the issue dated 8 Aug. 1839, that the latter contained "unfortunate reminiscences" of Chateaubriand's *Martyrs*; this kind of criticism, with its allegation of plagiarism, was to be levelled on many subsequent occasions against Brasseur de Bourbourg's works.

These first publications had however won him a flattering reputation at Rome, where the Canadian Abbé Léon Gingras made his acquaintance in 1844. To his friend Abbé Charles-Félix Cazeau*, vicar general of Quebec, Gingras wrote of his enthusiasm for the "famous writer," and of the desire he had soon come to feel, that Brasseur should be brought to Quebec: "It is to Quebec," he wrote on 28 Oct. 1844, "that he must be attached by all possible means." A month later, on 23 November, Gingras returned to the charge: "Once more, my dear Cazeau, move heaven and earth to ensure that such a splendid bird does not escape us and fly to Montreal, where it would be so highly thought of." Finally, on the reiterated invitation of one of the superiors of the seminary, Abbé Brasseur arrived at Quebec in the autumn of 1845, after a brief stay at Boston. The directors requested him to undertake a course in ecclesiastical history, which, according to Abbé Jean-Baptiste-Antoine Ferland*, he did not continue beyond the eighth lesson.

Enjoying a period of enforced leisure, Abbé Brasseur busied himself with historical researches in the archdiocesan archives at Quebec. At the beginning of 1846 he published an *Esquisse biographique sur Mgr de Laval. . . .* The French abbé antagonized the priests of the seminary by the publication of this pamphlet, and in the spring he left Quebec to return to Boston, where for some months he served as a priest to the great satisfaction of the bishop, John Bernard Fitzpatrick, who conferred upon him the title of vicar general of his diocese when he left for Mexico the following summer.

Brasseur returned to Europe in 1851, and concerned himself particularly with the writing of an *Histoire du Canada. . . .* The work was dedicated "to His Excellency Jean-Bernard Fitzpatrick, bishop of Boston," who had taken the author under his protection "when climate and circumstances had caused him to cross over from Quebec into his diocese." Instead of a mere *imprimatur*, Abbé Brasseur had received from his hierarchical superior, Bishop Pierre-Louis Parisis, ultramontane bishop of Arras and a friend of Louis Veuillot, a warm letter stating that his book offered "a description of the highest interest" of the work of the missionaries who had spread the gospel in Canada, of the courage and wisdom of the first governors who had been sent by France to found and organize that distant colony, and finally of the vicissitudes which that country, having become Christian and French, had undergone during three centuries. To stress further the merits of the work, if that were possible, the bishop added that "the historian had had at his disposal precious documents, which no writer before him had been in a position to examine," a circumstance which gave "to his accounts a character of truth" that was "the first and principal interest of the history."

As soon as the first copies of this work reached Quebec, curiosity was rapidly followed by indignation, for in the words of Henri d'Arles [Beaudé*] "our history was subjected to a veritable act of sabotage." Abbé Ferland, who had recently been attached to the archbishopric of Quebec, set to work to point out the gross mistakes of every kind with which this strange historian, in an apparently gratuitous fashion, had embroidered his pages: errors of date, names misinterpreted, geographical absurdities, texts truncated or misquoted, faulty translations, obvious plagiarisms. Ferland's work first appeared in the *Journal de Québec* on 22, 25, and 29 Jan. and 1 Feb. 1853, then as a pamphlet under the title *Observations sur un ouvrage intitulé Histoire du Canada, etc., par M. l'abbé Brasseur de Bourbourg*.

Pierre-Flavien Turgeon*, the archbishop of Quebec, after sending a copy of Ferland's opuscule to Bishop Parisis and another to Louis Veuillot, asked the editor in chief of *L'Univers*, in a letter dated 18 Feb. 1853, to be good enough "to insert a few lines" in his journal, "to avenge the Church in Canada for the insults it had received from an unjust detractor." Thanks to the good offices of Henry de Courcy, the New York correspondent of *L'Univers*, Abbé Ferland's brochure, in an improved form, was republished in Paris by Charles Douniol, publisher of the liberal Catholic review *Le Correspondant*. Bishop Parisis, by a letter published in *L'Univers* on 3 March 1854, withdrew the approval he had given to Abbé Brasseur's work.

But among the French public as a whole, the author of this history of Canada so hotly debated in Catholic circles had none the less established the basis of his reputation as a specialist in American studies. After 1852 he returned four times to America, on one occasion as chaplain of the French legation at Mexico City, on another as ecclesiastical administrator for the Indians of Rabinal, Guatemala, and finally as a French government envoy charged with scientific missions. He studied on the spot the primitive Mexican civilizations, collected important material on the geography, antiquities, and ethnology of Mexico and Central America, edited numerous curious texts such as the *Manuscrit Troano* . . . , and published works which, like the *Lettres* . . . , but especially the *Histoire des nations* . . . , assured him of a fine reputation as a scholar of America. In 1869, in an article in the *Revue des questions historiques*, Henry de Charencey placed Brasseur de Bourbourg "in the first rank among the learned men who have most contributed to reviving among us a liking for American studies." But later specialists were not slow to expose the unsound elements in this literary production. The contrary would have been surprising, for if Abbé Brasseur, according to the author of the biographical notice devoted to him in *La Grande Encyclopédie*, worked with "extreme fervour," "he often showed, in his hastily drafted works, a lack of the prudence and sagacity" that would have ensured for his writings less fragile foundations.

Brasseur de Bourbourg died on 8 Jan. 1874 in Nice at 59 years of age.

PHILIPPE SYLVAIN

[The different travel accounts sent by Abbé Brasseur de Bourbourg to the minister of education and religion from Mexico, Central America, and Spain are found in Archives Nationales (Paris), F¹⁷, 2942. Biographical details are found in Brasseur de Bourbourg, *Histoire des nations civilisées* . . . , and it provides the main biographical source for Justin Winsor, *Narrative and critical history of America* (8v., Boston, 1884–89), I, 170–72; *The Catholic encyclopedia; Dictionnaire d'histoire et de géographie ecclésiastique* (16v. parus, Paris, 1912–); *La grande encyclopédie* (31v., Paris, [n.d.]). P.S.]

Bibliotheque Nationale (Paris), Z. Renan, 7829. C.-É. Brasseur de Bourbourg, *Esquisse biographique sur Mgr de Laval, premier évêque de Québec* (Québec, 1864); *Histoire des nations civilisées du Mexique et de l'Amérique Centrale, durant les siècles antérieurs à Christophe Colomb* . . . (4v., Paris, 1857–59); *Histoire du Canada, de son Église et de ses missions depuis la découverte de l'Amérique jusqu'à nos jours, écrite sur des documents inédits compulsés dans les archives de l'archevêché et de la ville de Québec, etc.* (2v., Paris, 1852); *Lettres pour servir d'introduction à l'histoire primitive des nations civilisées de l'Amérique* . . . (Mexico, 1851); *Manuscrit Troano, étude sur le système graphique et la langue des Mayas* (2v., Paris, 1869–70); *Le Sérapéon, épisode de l'histoire du IVᵉ siècle* (Paris, 1839); *Sommaire des voyages scientifiques et des travaux de géographie, d'histoire, d'archéologie et de philologie américaines* (Saint-Cloud, France, 1862). Étienne de Ravensberg [C.-É. Brasseur de Bourbourg], *Jérusalem, tableau de l'histoire et des vicissitudes de cette ville célèbre depuis son origine la plus reculée jusqu'à nos jours* (Lille, France, 1843).

Journal de Québec, 22 janv., 25 janv., 29 janv., 1ᵉʳ févr. 1853. *Le Monde* (Paris), 1837. *L'Univers* (Paris), 8 août 1839, 18 fév. 1853, 3 mars 1854. J.-B.-A. Ferland, *Observations sur un ouvrage intitulé Histoire du Canada par l'abbé Brasseur de Bourbourg* . . . (Paris, 1854). Robert [Philippe] Sylvain, *La vie et l'œuvre de Henry de Courcy, premier historien de l'Église catholique aux États-Unis* (Québec, 1955), 189–224. Henri de Charency, "L'histoire et la civilisation du Mexique d'après les travaux de M. l'abbé Brasseur de Bourbourg," *Revue des questions historiques* (Paris), VII (1869), 283.

BRAUNEIS, JEAN-CHRYSOSTOME, musician; b. Quebec, 26 Jan. 1814; son of Jean-Chrysostome Brauneis and Christine Hudson; m. Jeanet Johnson by whom he had several children; d. Montreal, Que., 11 Aug. 1871.

Jean-Chrysostome Brauneis' father was a German-born bandmaster and music teacher who gave his son his first music lessons. Probably the first Canadian to go abroad to further his musical education, young Brauneis studied in Europe from 1830 to 1833. Upon his return he was offered the position of organist at Montreal's Notre-Dame Church and occupied it until 1844. He re-applied for this post unsuccessfully in 1849. He was also organist at St James Cathedral until fire destroyed the building in 1857. He held various teaching positions, for 30 years at the Institut des Sœurs de la Congrégation Notre-Dame and for shorter periods at the residential school of the sisters of the Sacred Heart at Sault-au-Récollet and at the École Normale Jacques-Cartier in Montreal.

In 1837 Brauneis founded the Société de Musique, which apparently was short-lived. Five years later he established courses in vocal music – sacred, drawing room, and operatic – for students aged 15 to 25 (males and females separated) and a mixed class for children from 10 to 15. Brauneis' skill in handling beginners made the course a success and an expansion was soon planned. An advertisement which appeared in *La Minerve* on 3 Nov. 1842 reveals Brauneis' vocal method as the standard German one which he learned from a distinguished European artist; he claimed perfect knowledge of French, English, German, and Italian and singled out Mozart, Haydn, Beethoven, and Handel as the masters represented in his collection of music. Brauneis' love of the great classics also pervaded his work as organist and piano teacher. His colleague Gustave Smith, who first met him in 1856, has credited Brauneis with introducing the piano study pieces of Czerny, Cramer, and Clementi to Montreal and with turning out well-trained pupils who were good sight-readers.

Like any other pioneer musician, Brauneis had to be versatile, both to obtain a living and to make up for the lack of specialists. At one time or another he advertised as an instrument importer and piano tuner and teacher of theory, harp, guitar, and violin. He was also a composer. A mass, dedicated to the Reverend Joseph-Vincent Quiblier*, was reviewed at length in *La Minerve* of 16 July 1835. Brauneis' first work to be heard in Montreal, at Notre-Dame Church on 12 July, it was praised for the skill of its part-writing and many other virtues. The singers were accompanied by five instruments although the work was scored for a larger orchestra. Three of his compositions have been traced: the *Marche de la St. Jean Baptiste*, published in Montreal in 1848, dedicated to the members of the Société Saint-Jean-Baptiste of Montreal; *The Montreal Bazaar Polka*, published not later than 1848; and *Monklands Polka*, published in Philadelphia, New York, and Montreal in 1849.

When a youth Brauneis is said to have considered a medical career, an ambition fulfilled by one of his grandsons, Louis de Lotbinière* Harwood. But as a musician he has left his name in the history of the arts in Canada. Gustave Smith described Brauneis as a man with "a stern appearance and a bantering manner"; the obituary in *La Minerve* (14 Aug. 1871) stresses his unselfish devotion to his pupils, his honest and humble personality, and his industriousness.

HELMUT KALLMANN

AJM, Registre d'état civil. AJQ, Registre d'état civil, Paroisse Notre-Dame. *Le Canadien* (Québec), 10 avril 1837. *L'Encyclopédie canadienne* (Montréal), janv. 1843. *La Minerve* (Montréal), 18 nov. 1833; 14 mai, 16 juill. 1835; 3 nov. 1842; 3 août 1843; 25 mai 1844; 26 sept. 1864; 14 août 1871. Helmut Kallmann, *A history of music in Canada, 1534–1914* (Toronto and London, 1960), 84–85, 188. O.-M.-H. Lapalice, "Les organistes et maîtres de musique à Notre-Dame de Montréal," *BRH*, XXV (1919), 243–49. É.-Z. Massicotte, "Les deux musiciens Braunies," *BRH*, XLI (1935), 641–43. Gustave Smith, "Du mouvement musical en Canada," *L'Album musical* (Montréal), févr. 1882.

BRAY, ÉMILE-FRÉDÉRIC DE (sometimes spelled **Debray**), French naval officer and participant in the Franklin search; b. 9 March 1829 in Paris, France, first of three children of Achille-Hector-Camille de Bray, landscape painter, and of Théophile-Marie-Louise Borrel; d. 19 March 1879 at Brest, France.

On completing his education at the École Navale in 1846, Émile-Frédéric de Bray embarked on the corvette *La Galathée* for a three-year voyage to the Pacific. He then served two years in France and Italy, and on 2 April 1851 was promoted sub-lieutenant in the navy. At this time French interest in the search for the missing ships and men of Sir John Franklin* was heightened by the participation of the French naval officer Joseph-René Bellot* in William Kennedy*'s 1851–52 expedition, and de Bray felt encouraged to volunteer for the search expedition commanded by Sir Edward BELCHER. The British Admiralty accepted his services and appointed him to HMS *Resolute* (Capt. Henry KELLETT) which sailed from London on 21 April 1852 and wintered at Dealy Island. De Bray commanded several sledge expeditions during his two years in the Arctic: in the autumn of 1852 he set up a depot at Cape Providence, Melville Island, and between 4 April and 18 May 1853 he surveyed the northwest coast of Melville Island while leading a party auxiliary to Francis Leopold M'Clintock*'s sledge expedition to Prince Patrick Island. On 8 May 1854 he left *Resolute*, which was shortly to be abandoned, and led a party of invalids to *North Star* anchored at Beechey Island. Four months later he departed for England on board *Phoenix*.

De Bray was a popular and energetic member of the expedition, and Kellett, M'Clintock, and Belcher praised him warmly for his services. He is the only Frenchman to receive the Arctic Medal. France rewarded him with nomination to knight of the Légion d'Honneur, back dated to 12 Aug. 1854, and promoted him lieutenant-commander on 5 Oct. 1855.

On his return to France, de Bray served in the Baltic. After his marriage on 20 May 1856 to Loetitia-Constance-Marie Le Bléis, he was stationed at Saint-Pierre and Miquelon and in Iceland. On 22 May 1869 he was promoted commander in the navy, and on 23 Jan. 1871 was made an officer of the Légion d'Honneur for his role in the defence of Paris in 1870 during which he had commanded a marine battalion and an army brigade. He spent the remainder of his career on shore service in France.

De Bray's early death at 50, only 6 months after retirement, was attributed in part to his prolonged service in cold regions, which, it was remarked, had worn down his energy and enthusiasm. He survived his wife by six years and left four children; two others had died in infancy. Unlike Bellot, who died a hero's death, de Bray never won widespread recognition for his role as a representative of France in the Franklin search, and his journal of the expedition has not been published. However, his friend Jules Verne made extensive use of de Bray's knowledge of Arctic regions in *Voyages et aventures du capitaine Hatteras: les Anglais au pôle nord – le désert de glace* (Paris 1867), a novel inspired by the Franklin search.

CLIVE A. HOLLAND

SPRI, MS 864/1 (Émile-Frédéric de Bray, "Journal de bord de l'enseigne de vaisseau Émile-Frédéric de Bray à bord de la frégate anglaise 'La resolue'. Expédition polaire de 1852–1853 envoyée à la recherche de Sir John Franklin," typewritten copy of the original, which has not been found); MS 864/2–4 (George de Bray, "Notice sur la participation de l'enseigne de vaisseau de Bray à l'expédition britannique de 1852–1854 envoyée à la recherche des navires de Sir John Franklin perdus dans les mers polaires," typewritten notes, La Rochelle, 1926; copies of documentary and genealogical material relating to Émile de Bray). G.B., Adm., *Further papers relative to the recent Arctic expeditions in search of Sir John Franklin and the crews of H.M.S. "Erebus" and "Terror"* (London, 1855). G. F. M'Dougall, *The eventful voyage of H.M. discovery ship "Resolute" to the arctic regions in search of Sir John Franklin and the missing crews of H.M. discovery ships "Erebus" and "Terror", 1852, 1853, 1854 . . .* (London, 1857).

Jules Rouch, "Deux officiers de marine français Joseph Bellot et Émile de Bray, à bord de navires de S.M. Britannique dans les mers polaires (1852–1854)," *France–Grande Bretagne: Bulletin des relations franco-britanniques* (Paris), no.194 (mars 1945), 1–12; "Émile de Bray," *La Géographie* (Paris), LXIX (1938), 257–63; "Le journal inédit d'Émile de Bray, explorateur polaire français," *Bulletin de la Section de géographie* (Paris), LIX (1944, pub. in 1951), 61–69.

BRENAN, DANIEL, land surveyor, merchant, banker, and politician, b. 1796 at Ballinakill, Queen's County (now Leinster Province), Ireland; d. 1 March 1876 in Charlottetown, P.E.I.

Daniel Brenan received his education in Ireland and at the age of 27 immigrated to Prince Edward Island. He immediately began work as a land surveyor, and a few years later became a merchant in Charlottetown. By the end of the 1820s he was one of the leading importers on the Island and was able to branch out into other fields – the carrying trade, real estate, insurance, and banking. Nonetheless, his main concern was his retail business; he built new brick stores in 1845 and 1866.

Brenan was a Roman Catholic, and as such was relieved of his civil disabilities by Catholic emancipation on the Island in 1830. Within a few months, he successfully contested an assembly seat for Kings County, and he was re-elected in 1834. In the assembly Brenan acted as a staunch Tory, and declared that the radical Escheators were "ignorant and designing men who choose to impose on the credulity of the country people." After the session of 1835, he resigned, having accepted the position of commissioner for ascertaining the boundary lines of counties and townships. His vacated seat was won by an Escheator, John Macintosh*.

Although he did not hold a seat in either branch of the legislature, Brenan was called to the Executive Council in 1849 by the lieutenant governor, Sir Donald Campbell*, who adamantly opposed responsible government. Brenan retained his seat on the council until the Reformers came to power two years later. Despite the sharp rise of religious tensions in the Island politics of the 1850s, 1860s, and 1870s, Brenan remained within the predominantly Protestant Conservative party, one of the few Roman Catholics to do so.

Daniel Brenan was one of the Island's best-known citizens throughout most of his life. When the Irish-Scottish relief fund was established in 1847, he was named treasurer. He was a prominent Roman Catholic layman, a successful businessman, and a frequent public lecturer at the Mechanics' Institute and the Catholic Young Men's Literary Institute. When he died in 1876, leaving a widow, Margaret, but no children, he bequeathed much of his estate to various Roman Catholic institutions.

IAN ROSS ROBERTSON

PAPEI, Prince Edward Island, Executive Council, Minutes, 16 Feb. 1849. Prince Edward Island, Supreme Court, Estates Division, will of Daniel Brenan, 20 Sept. 1872. Prince Edward Island, House of Assembly, *Journals*, 1831–35. Daniel Brenan, *Remarks on education, with suggestions for the improvement of the present system* (Charlottetown, 1856), copy in PAPEI. *Island Argus* (Charlottetown), 7 March 1876. *Patriot* (Charlottetown), 3 March 1876. *Prince Edward Island Register* (Charlottetown), 29 May 1824. *Royal Gazette* (Charlottetown), 28 Sept., 12, 19 Oct. 1830; 7 Feb. 1832.

BRIDGLAND, JAMES WILLIAM, surveyor and civil servant; b. 9 April 1817 at or near York (now Toronto), U.C., second son of James W. Bridgland and Eleanor Beaton; d. 22 Oct. 1880, at Toronto, Ont.

James William Bridgland's parents came to York from Kent County in England in 1816. For some years the family remained in York, the father having obtained the position of keeper of the Court of King's Bench, and young James attended Thomas Appleton's common school. In 1828 the family purchased property at Downsview (now in Metropolitan Toronto), where the sons and daughters grew up. Young James decided to become a land surveyor, and in 1842 attended the summer term at Victoria College, Cobourg. He was apprenticed to John Stoughton Dennis* and qualified as a provincial land surveyor on 6 May 1844.

Soon after he commenced to practise, James Bridgland was employed by the Crown Lands Department in making surveys in Canada West, and he became a member of the staff of the Crown Lands Office on 22 Jan. 1856. His more important surveys were in the townships of Mornington (1848), Kincardine (1850), and Carden (1852); along the Muskoka River (1852) and Indian River (1853); on Rama Island (1860); and in the Huron and Ottawa territory (1861–62). His reports frequently have a distinct literary flavour. To describe land near the Muskoka River, he wrote, "would only be to repeat the tedious monotony, of rocky barrens, swamps, marshes, and burnt regions; destitute of good water, good timber, in short of every-thing, necessary to make settlement desirable, or life supportable; regions where even the foraging partridge, and the provident squirrel, seem from their scarcity – scarcely able to exist." These reports were eminently sensible and won the approval of his superiors, as did no doubt his attitude towards employees who attempted to gain an increase in pay. To one of his subordinates he wrote: "The *Strike* you speak of should have been the immediate occasion for you to have discharged every man . . . , *I will not sanction a farthing of increase in wages.*"

After 1860 Bridgland's duties lay chiefly in the field of colonization roads, roads built by the government to attract settlers to the Georgian Bay–Ottawa area. His duties led him also to the mining districts and Indian lands north of Lake Superior. In 1864, when the superintendent of colonization roads in Canada West, David Gibson*, died, that office was discontinued but the duties were transferred to Bridgland. After confederation Bridgland continued to perform the duties connected with the oversight of colonization roads in Ontario – duties he could be relied on to perform with diligence and economy.

Bridgland married 16-year-old Maria Dennis, sister of John, in 1849. After her death in 1857 he married Martha Anne Jones. There was one daughter from his first marriage, and there were four children from the second.

GEORGE W. SPRAGGE

Ontario, Department of Lands and Forests, Surveys Office, instructions to land surveyors, 1848; reports of surveys, 1848–62. PAC, RG 1, E1, 88, pp.504–5 (copy at PAO in State and Landbooks of Upper Canada and Canada, Z, pp.504–5). PAO, RG 14, A, ser. V(b), 5 (J. W. Bridgland, memoranda, statements, and letters, 1862–67). *Christian Guardian* (Toronto), 23 Oct. 1844; 28 Oct., 9 Dec. 1857; 13 Jan. 1858; 27 Oct. 1880. *Colonial Advocate* (York), 20 Sept. 1827. *Muskoka and Haliburton* (Murray). W. P. Bull, *From Oxford to Ontario: a history of the Downsview community* (Toronto, [1941]), 72. "James W. Bridgland," Ont. Land Surveyors Assoc., *Annual Report* (Toronto), no.42 (1927), 94–96. G. W. Spragge, "Colonization roads in Canada West, 1850–1867," *Ont. Hist.*, XLIX (1957), 1–17.

BROWN, GEORGE, journalist and politician; b. at Alloa, Clackmannan, Scotland, 29 Nov. 1818; d. at Toronto, Ont., 9 May 1880.

George Brown was the elder son in the family of six children of Peter Brown* and Marianne, daughter of George Mackenzie, gentleman, of Stornoway on the Isle of Lewis. Peter ran a prosperous wholesale business in Edinburgh, but he also spent periods at Alloa up the Firth of Forth helping to direct a local glassworks. Thus George Brown's life began in the placid little Forthside port though the family returned to Edinburgh before he was eight. He attended Edinburgh's celebrated High School and its Southern Academy, and he was always proud to link himself with Scotland's national capital. After leaving school with prizes and honours, he joined his father's business, and began to settle into a life in well-to-do Edinburgh commercial society.

George was very close to his father. Peter Brown was a convinced Whig-Liberal and evangelical Presbyterian, an ardent believer in civil and religious liberty, progress, the economic liberalism of Adam Smith, and the destruction of Tory aristocratic privilege. Moreover, he set a strong political example by actively sharing in the struggle for borough reform in Edinburgh and the larger campaign that won the parliamentary reform bill of 1832. In 1836, however, Peter was involved, as collector of assessments in Edinburgh, in a loss of nearly £2,800 of municipal funds, which had somehow mixed with his private accounts. There was no charge against him and his guarantors made good the loss, but he strove urgently to redeem the money and his name. With the onset of the depression of 1837 he saw nothing else to do but try a new start in America. And so, on 30 April 1837, George Brown, aged 18, set out from Liverpool with his father for New York.

Within weeks of landing there in June, they had opened a small dry goods shop, in which George

Brown

was the only assistant. It thrived sufficiently that they could send for the family the next year. The business apparently continued to do moderately well, but Peter Brown was turning to other interests. In the next few years he became a contributor to the New York *Albion*, the weekly paper of the British emigrant community. Once more his son would acquire from him both a fervent abolitionism and a rooted preference for the British parliamentary system over the American republican model. Yet more than that, Peter Brown published his views in a book early in 1842, *The fame and glory of England vindicated* . . . (New York and London), and the ready reception of this work, at least by British emigrants in the United States and in neighbouring English Canada, stirred its author to turn fully to journalism. Again assisted by his willing son, he began the *British Chronicle* in New York on 30 June 1842, a little weekly more political and less literary in content than the *Albion*.

The new paper soon started noting Canadian affairs, as circulation spread in that quarter. It commented on the course of the union that had been set up in 1841 between the former provinces of Upper and Lower Canada, and approved the plan of responsible government which was backed by the existing Liberal or Reform leaders there, Robert Baldwin*, Francis Hincks*, and Louis-Hippolyte La Fontaine*. George Brown, moreover, began to travel up to Canada in the service of his father's paper. His role was growing, as he finished his apprenticeship in journalism. In March 1843, when he was still only 24, he was denominated in the *Chronicle* as "Publisher," his father as "Editor." That spring he spent some time in Canadian centres such as Toronto, Kingston, and Montreal, talking with politicians and editors and acquiring considerable knowledge of the prospects of the country.

Meanwhile, Peter Brown had thoroughly committed the *British Chronicle* on an issue that had recently come to a head in Scotland. There the evangelical element in the established Church of Scotland had decided to withdraw from the state Presbyterian church altogether, in the cause of religious freedom as they saw it. Thus occurred the "Great Disruption" of May 1843, and the birth of the Free Church of Scotland. Inevitably Peter Brown's sympathies were with the new Free Kirk. Indeed, there was considerable support for the movement throughout Scottish communities in America. Moreover, it grew evident that the conflict within Presbyterianism could also erupt in Canada because of colonial Scottish feelings for one or the other party in the homeland.

In this circumstance, Free Kirk sympathizers in

Canada looked to the *British Chronicle*, which spoke so warmly for their side. In the summer of 1843 a group of leading Free Church supporters in the Toronto area signed an invitation and put up a bond to persuade Peter Brown to move his paper to Canada. This invitation they passed through the Reverend William Rintoul* to George Brown on his travels through Toronto. He was already interested in a move himself, partly because of friendly contacts he had made with leading Canadian Reformers, partly because he felt that British Canada would be far more congenial than the American republic and that in its youth and sparse development it offered much better possibilities for getting ahead than crowded New York. He put these arguments forcefully to his father and won his consent. On 22 July the *British Chronicle* made a last appearance, announcing that its editor would henceforth publish a weekly paper in Toronto named the *Banner*, expressing a Presbyterian interest and upholding "Reform principles" on all great public issues.

On 18 August the first issue of the Browns' Toronto *Banner* came out. The editorial columns – which dominated the little four-page papers of the day – were divided between the "Religious Department" and the "Secular Department," the provinces of Peter and George Brown respectively. The first department at once took up the Free Church cause; the second was slower to commit itself. But before the end of 1843, the resignation of the chief Liberal ministers, Baldwin, La Fontaine, and Hincks, from the government of Sir Charles Metcalfe* provided a major public issue on which George Brown soon began to speak out in the name of Reform principles.

It appeared to him that Governor Metcalfe's insistence on controlling the power of patronage himself, the question on which his Liberal ministers had resigned, was a repudiation of the principle of responsible government. Metcalfe's dismissal of the Reform-dominated assembly that December fully decided him. He made the *Banner* the forceful champion of the Reform leaders as the political crisis continued.

But that paper, with its own sectarian cause to pursue, could only be a part-time champion at best. And George Brown's own interests were becoming wholly centred in politics. Recognizing his journalistic powers, moreover, a group of prominent Toronto Reformers approached him to found a new party paper; four of them offered to provide £250 starting capital. The sum meant more then – but also indicates how relatively simple it was to equip a small colonial weekly newspaper. Though they would continue the *Banner*, the Browns decided to establish the

Toronto *Globe*. It first appeared on 5 March 1844, and it was really George Brown's from the start. He above all was to make it the most powerful newspaper in British America.

He did so through his strong and stirring editorials, by pushing always for the latest and most detailed news reports (so that the *Globe* would be read, reluctantly, even by political enemies), and by seeking constantly to increase circulation through providing ever better press facilities. He introduced the new Hoe rotary press to Upper Canada before his paper was even three months old, and the greater production this permitted enabled the *Globe* to set up a book and job printing office also. In 1845 he established the *Western Globe*, to serve Reformers in the rising southwestern regions of the province, with its own sub-office in London to which material from the Toronto edition was regularly conveyed by road. The Toronto *Globe* itself advanced from weekly to semi-weekly; by 1849 it had triweekly issues, reflecting its expanding circulation, and a weekly edition specifically intended for the countryside was added. It was a further sign of the success of Brown's "forward policy" that the *Globe* in October 1853 became a daily, printed by a steam press. By that time Brown's paper had already become a province-wide institution, and soon could claim – with few to deny it – the largest circulation in all British North America.

As the *Globe*'s external influence expanded, it naturally grew internally as well. It had begun in the 1840s with a staff composed of George and Peter Brown, a printer, and a boy apprentice or two: one of them, according to tradition, George's young brother, Gordon*. In the 1850s the paper acquired a whole staff of printers (with union aims expressed in strikes in 1853 and 1854), pressroom and engine hands, reporters, and parliamentary correspondents; and the day had passed when George Brown would write the bulk of the editorials himself. He still kept a tight control over business affairs and the main lines of editorial policy, so that the popular presumption that he and the *Globe* were synonymous was not entirely wrong. But regular editorial management passed to his brother Gordon, named sub-editor in 1850 at the age of 22 – Peter Brown having then retired at 66, after closing down the *Banner* in 1848.

In short, within a few years of establishing his newspaper, George Brown had moved it from the day of personal journalism to the era of big newspaper business in Canada. He made himself a leading Toronto businessman in the process and also shaped a formidable political power. But though he was to enter politics himself, his strongest concern would always remain with the *Globe*, just as it did at its beginning, in March 1844.

He gave his first significant political speech in that very month on 25 March, to the Reform Association of Canada, at a meeting held in Toronto to protest Sir Charles Metcalfe's attempt to carry on government with but a trio of ministers, W. H. DRAPER, Dominick Daly*, and Denis-Benjamin Viger*, who had not yet managed to fill up the other ministerial offices. The young *Globe* editor's ringing denunciation of such an un-British and illiberal practice roused warm response. From that time onward, his fervent, powerful oratory was often called upon at party gatherings and public meetings. Meanwhile, he vigorously engaged the *Globe* in the Reformers' battle against Metcalfe and the Tory-Conservative forces that were rallying to the governor general's side. There was, indeed, a growing reaction in English-speaking Canada against what seemed excessively partisan Reform insistence on removing the governor's power over patronage. Hence, in the elections held that autumn, pro-Metcalfe forces carried Canada West (popularly still called Upper Canada), though the victory of La Fontaine's Liberals in Canada East, the largely French-speaking Lower Canadian section, meant that the new Conservative ministry had only a bare majority over all.

Many Canadian electors had apparently not fully understood the requirements of responsible government exercised through party rule. In the next few years of Tory-Conservative administration George Brown worked diligently to enlighten the public, and thus to strengthen the Reform party under Baldwin and Hincks in Upper Canada. By 1847, when the weak Tory-Conservative ministry failed to improve its position through a reconstruction, the chance for a resurgence of Reform seemed at hand: especially when Britain now accepted the full principle of responsible rule for Canada and sent a new governor general, Lord Elgin [Bruce*], instructed to put that principle decisively into effect.

In the elections of 1847–48 the *Globe* trumpeted the Liberal cause once more. But further, its editor personally entered into the contest in the western county of Oxford, where Baldwin asked him to conduct a campaign for Hincks who was away in Britain. This was Brown's first full-fledged election campaign, even though he was not a candidate himself. Undoubtedly his enthusiasm and untiring efforts in speaking across the riding did a good deal to win the seat for Hincks – though it also left a heritage of jealousy between two strong-minded men. The Reformers swept into power in both sections of Canada, and in March 1848 the

Brown

La Fontaine–Baldwin government took office as a wholly Reform cabinet embodying the principle of responsible rule.

This new administration, developing a broad programme of reforms, had a task for the editor of the chief party journal in the west. He was named secretary of a commission of inquiry to investigate alleged abuses in the provincial penitentiary at Kingston. The commission began hearings there in June and proceeded through the rest of 1848 as Brown worked zealously in a role which his energy and ability made markedly influential. This exhaustive inquiry produced voluminous evidence of brutality and maladministration, and the existing warden, Henry Smith*, was removed from office. The commission's report, which Brown drafted as secretary early in 1849, passed withering judgement on "most frightful oppression – revolting inhumanity." It also projected major forward steps in Canadian penology; for example, in recommending the separation of hardened criminals, first offenders, and juveniles, in making provisions for rehabilitation and after-care, and in urging the appointment of permanent, salaried prison inspectors.

Otherwise, in 1849, Brown's role was still essentially that of *Globe* editor. But his paper was now the official organ for the government in Upper Canada and he stood high in party circles. Accordingly, he was closely identified that spring with the La Fontaine–Baldwin ministry in supporting their contentious rebellion losses bill against angry Tory protests, which included an attack on his own home in Toronto. Later in that year of depression and turmoil he worked still more ardently to combat the movement for annexation to the United States that focussed on the Montreal Annexation Manifesto of October, but had lesser repercussions in Upper Canada as well. Through the *Globe* Brown strongly backed Baldwin's efforts to dissociate the Upper Canadian Reform party from annexationism, particularly in a by-election in December 1849 when the Reform candidate, Peter Perry*, an old radical, displayed unfortunate annexationist leanings.

Despite pressure from the party leadership and the party organ, however, Perry was elected without having fully disavowed annexation, at least as a future possibility. Yet his victory was more indicative of local left-wing Reform discontent with central party direction than of any real support for annexationism, now fast disappearing. In fact, Perry's success spurred radical elements, soon termed "Clear Grits" in the *Globe*, to shape a new movement by early 1850, which sought to push the party onward to "advanced" reforms in the belief that the leaders and their more moderate supporters had grown altogether too content with office. They demanded cheap and simple government close to the people and, above all, a fully democratic constitution on the American elective model. George Brown's own commitment to the Baldwin ministry and his distrust of American written constitutions and egalitarian democracy made him a determined foe of Clear Grit radical proposals. His journal urged the superiority of British responsible cabinet government, so recently won for Canada. But the Clear Grits held local conventions, adopted a thoroughgoing democratic platform, and established a new organ of their own in Toronto, the *North American*, edited by William McDougall*, a clever young radical lawyer.

Furthermore, the Grits took up another reform cause with wide popular appeal in Upper Canada: the secularization of the clergy reserves set up by imperial statute at the founding of the province in 1791 to support a Protestant clergy. The Anglicans still received the major share of the funds from the sale of reserve lands, but this situation was sharply questioned, both by those who sought a more equitable division and by those who wanted the reserves abolished altogether as an improper endowment of churches by the state.

George Brown himself naturally agreed with the latter stand. For him the state should know no church, and churches should be voluntarily sustained by their adherents. On this "voluntary principle" he was in accord with the Clear Grits and various evangelical Protestant bodies as well as his own Free Kirk supporters. But he rejected the Clear Grits politically for their constitutional views, and relied on the declared intentions of the Baldwin government to settle the reserves – deeming the radicals' demand a mere attempt to make political capital for themselves. The parliamentary session of 1850 gave him doubts, however. Resolutions were passed asking for an imperial act to authorize the Canadian legislature to deal with the reserves themselves. Yet James Price*, the minister who moved them, did so only as a private member, and La Fontaine and the French Canadian Reformers he led were plainly reluctant to tamper with a religious endowment. As Roman Catholics accepting ties of church and state, they approved of state support for religion – the antithesis of Brown's own position.

Another measure of the session further aroused his concern about Catholic influence on government policy. This, the Upper Canada school act introduced by Hincks, enlarged provisions for separate denominational schools in the western system of public education, so that Catholic schools, specifically, could more readily be organized to receive state support. Brown saw this enlargement as an alarming inroad into the maintenance of one non-sectarian public system. His *Globe* called it "the entering wedge." Then, as he and other voluntaryists were becoming increasingly exercised over "state church" influences on public affairs, the papal aggression question burst in England in the fall of 1850.

The root of the issue was a papal brief recreating a Roman Catholic hierarchy in England for the first time since the Reformation. The brief was at least unwise in declaring this realm of Anglicanism, Puritanism, and Methodism to be now returned to an "orbit" around Rome. There was strong response from Protestants, already reacting to the resurgent ultramontane and anti-liberal zeal of the papacy under Pius IX. Brown's *Globe* was only one of numerous liberal or voluntaryist-minded journals in Canada that commented severely on these papal and Catholic presumptions, but its power and vehemence involved it in a bitter exchange of doctrinal arguments and name-calling with the local Catholic press. Inevitably, by the spring of 1851, Brown had emerged as either a potent voluntaryist champion or an arch anti-Catholic in a country deeply divided by religious passions.

Meanwhile he had decided to try for parliament himself, to strengthen the cause there of non-sectarian public education and the separation of church and state. He stood in a by-election for Haldimand County in April 1851. His chief opponent was William Lyon Mackenzie*, now back, amnestied, from his long American exile and a rather obstreperous ally of the Grit radicals. The power of Mackenzie's name among western Grit farmers, the half-hearted support which the Reform leaders gave their own somewhat troublesome candidate, Brown, and, in particular, a powerful Catholic appeal to Irish Reformers to reject the sworn enemy of their faith, all combined to give the victory to Mackenzie. Brown's growing breach with the ministry widened and his concern over Catholic influence in politics was only reinforced.

Then in parliament that June Baldwin resigned from office when Clear Grit objections to his reconstruction of the Court of Chancery produced a temporary Upper Canadian majority against him. His chief lieutenant, Francis Hincks, became the western head of the government – a man to whom Brown had never been as loyal as he had been to Baldwin, and whose motives he distrusted as more concerned with keeping office to promote the new era of railways than with upholding true liberal and voluntaryist principles. Early in July, the *Globe* editor brought his paper out against the

ministry, on a path of independent Reform: the "one course for the opponents of priestcraft and state churchism." His judgement that a Hincks government would prove an unprincipled office-holding combination seemed to be borne out when it speedily came to terms with the Grits. McDougall's *North American* now became a government paper, and two Clear Grits, Malcolm CAMERON and John Rolph*, entered the cabinet. The Grits still hoped to impel the ministry on to radical reform, but Brown was right in predicting that they would be swamped in the combination by the more conservative-minded forces of the railway builders following Hincks and the French Canadians now led by Augustin Morin* as successor to La Fontaine.

The new Hincks–Morin Liberal government successfully appealed to the country in the autumn of 1851. Brown ran as an independent Reformer in the southwestern county of Kent. This time he was elected easily, thanks to the strength of voluntaryism there and effective work by prominent local Reformers, one of whom, Alexander Mackenzie*, was to become his closest supporter. The elections were over by early January 1852, but parliament did not meet till August. The provincial offices first had to be transferred from Toronto to Quebec; it was a sign of the sectional division in the Canadian union that the seat of government had to shift between the former capitals of Upper and Lower Canada, no one permanent seat having yet been found.

Sectionalism had been embedded in the very constitution of the union, since the two Canadas had been given equal representation in its parliament. Underlying this political division, however, was the deeper division between two cultural communities: that of Upper Canada, English-speaking and mainly Protestant; that of Lower Canada, largely French-speaking and Roman Catholic. The distinction could only be sharpened by the different aims of zealous western voluntaryism, striving to end state support and recognition of religion, and equally zealous French Canadian Catholicism, seeking to establish new religious corporations for educational and welfare purposes or to back demands from the Upper Canadian Catholic minority for further separate school rights. Sectional strains mounted when the reserves question and ecclesiastical corporations bills came up, and when a new separate school measure for the west was carried through by Lower Canadian votes. It was charged that a "French domination" was imposing its will on Upper Canada. George Brown was in the forefront of debate, clearly representing a broader constituency in the west than just his own riding of Kent.

Brown

As parliament went on into 1853, he made himself still more prominent in Upper Canada by moving a resolution in March for representation by population. This would give the western section a preponderance of parliamentary seats for its population had now outstripped the east's. French Canadians naturally feared being swamped by a western, English ascendancy, and held to the bulwark of equal sectional representation. In any case, Brown's motion did not win many adherents as yet in English Canada, which was more divided politically between Reform and Tory parties than the more compact, ethnically united French Canadian minority. The idea of "rep by pop," not originally Brown's, would become strongly associated with him, and would increasingly gain western support as sectional strife continued in the union.

Indeed by 1854 it threatened to break up the Reform party and topple the Hincks–Morin government. In June the failure of that government to settle the reserves – though they now had imperial authorization to act – was a major factor in creating a sudden combination of dissentient groups that defeated Hincks in parliament and led to elections that summer. Brown was handily returned for Lambton, a constituency newly divided off from Kent. Out of the party turmoil he hoped to shape a new alignment to advance voluntaryism and secularize the reserves, composed of non-radical Reformers and moderate Conservatives, many of whom were now ready to support secularization.

The governing coalition that emerged when parliament met in September dashed Brown's hopes. It combined Hincks' former following of moderate Liberals and the French Canadian group still under Morin with the Tory-Conservative forces led by Sir Allan MacNab*. In this new MacNab–Morin regime, Tories and Conservatives would accept the need to abolish the reserves; and they and the followers of Hincks could foster railway development in the alliance, which upheld the French Canadians' cultural interests. In short, this Liberal-Conservative coalition represented a fresh attempt to bridge sectional divisions, leaving in opposition George Brown and some western voluntaryists, the Clear Grit radical wing, and the smaller, largely French Canadian eastern radical faction, termed the Rouges, under Antoine-Aimé Dorion*.

Among these fragments of Reform there was no recognized opposition leader, but Brown increasingly took a prominent role, thanks to his parliamentary prowess and the strength of the Globe. When the government's promised measure to abolish the reserves came up in October 1854, he

and his former Clear Grit foes could vote together in criticizing loopholes in the bill, though they accepted its main tenor. Brown could also at least cooperate with the Lower Canadian Rouges in attacking alleged governmental waste and corruption in railway schemes, especially in regard to the costly Grand Trunk then building the main line across the province. In fact, he also might reach common ground with Rouges on many "state church" issues, since they had inherited the French Canadian strain of anti-clericalism. Nevertheless, any Liberal opposition front could only be a loose working alliance of sectional elements at best, and Brown's prime effort was to form a coherent Reform party within the western half of the union.

He achieved a good deal of progress during 1855. The Globe made overtures to the Clear Grits, urging the need for Reform unity. Leading Grit radicals were ready to sink their differences with Brown and put by their hopes of sweeping elective constitutional reforms in the more urgent need to fight revived Conservative power and the dangers of "French Catholic domination." It was an important sign, therefore, when Brown bought out the Grit North American in February and its editor, McDougall, joined the Globe staff. Then in May a new bill for Upper Canadian separate schools brought still more important developments. The act of 1855 introduced by Étienne Taché* was suddenly put through parliament in its last days at Quebec, when many Upper Canadian members had left for home. It was passed, moreover, by an eastern majority over the votes of those westerners still on hand, including Brown. This event seemed hard proof of Lower Canadian domination of the union, and of the Liberal-Conservative ministry's connivance in that domination.

In the indignation that swept Upper Canada many Grit adherents called for dissolution of the union. But Brown, the Toronto businessman, was perhaps more conscious of the commercial values of the Canadian union than embattled western farmers. He and the Globe argued for representation by population instead: to remake rather than destroy the union, assure justice for Upper Canada but maintain the unity of the St Lawrence transport system and the broad economic development that would be lost by separation. They waged a campaign for rep by pop through Upper Canada in the summer of 1855. By autumn Grittism had been largely won to it, and Brown had supplied a powerful policy on which to focus the reunification of Upper Canadian Reform.

He made further gains the next year. In parliament in the spring of 1856, the Liberal-Conservative regime, facing sectional discords and internal divisions itself, lost some of its Liberal supporters to the Reform forces in opposition. The ministry was reconstructed in May, when MacNab was replaced by the far more able John A. Macdonald* as western leader – and still only narrowly avoided defeat in the assembly. During heated debates earlier in the session Brown and Macdonald had had a sharply significant personal encounter. Macdonald, who had always supported the cause of an old family friend, Henry Smith, the ex-warden of the Kingston penitentiary, was carried away in anger to accuse Brown as secretary of the 1848–49 commission of having falsified evidence and suborned witnesses. The committee of inquiry, which the latter immediately requested, heard a mass of testimony that palpably exonerated Brown; but it produced only a non-committal verdict, being politically weighted against him. A proud and sensitive man, he was left with the grave charges unretracted, which put more than political barriers between him and his great Conservative rival.

In August 1856, Brown began a new campaign through the *Globe*, calling for the annexation to Canada of the vast British territories beyond the Great Lakes, still the preserve of the fur-trading Hudson's Bay Company. He had long been interested in the potentialities of the North-West. Now they were attracting widespread attention in Upper Canada, both from land-hungry farmers seeking new frontiers to settle and from Toronto businessmen hoping to direct new flows of trade to their fast rising metropolis. Brown and his brother Gordon were closely identified themselves with Toronto efforts to open communications with the North-West. And northwestern expansion was another powerful policy for a resurgent Upper Canadian Reform party, on which commercial and agrarian interests could unite. The time seemed ripe to cement party unity, when in December 1856 the emerging Toronto business and professional leadership group (with George Brown at its core) issued a call for a Reform convention to gather in the city.

The convention held on 8 Jan. 1857 brought together 150 Brownites, Clear Grits, and Liberals who had formerly followed Hincks. It readily adopted a platform that marked successful Reform reunion and included representation by population, annexation of the North-West, national non-sectarian education, and free trade. It was Brown's platform; he dominated the proceedings and his friends made the central party structure. He had remade the party in a Brownite image. Its opponents still might dub it "Clear Grit" – and "Grits" the Brownite Liberals would long be termed. But the old Clear Grit radicalism of American elective democracy had really been submerged within Victorian British parliamentary Liberalism.

The reorganized party faced its test when elections were announced in November by the government, now led by Macdonald and his powerful French Canadian ally, George-Étienne CARTIER. Brownite Reform forces won a clear majority in Upper Canada, and Brown himself was triumphantly returned for both Toronto and North Oxford, but in Lower Canada the Rouges under Dorion were decisively defeated by Cartier's large Bleu Conservative contingent. Hence the Macdonald–Cartier regime was able to continue in office when the new parliament opened at Toronto in February 1858. But Brown pressed hard on the ministry's weakness in Upper Canada; by mid-summer it was in trouble, meeting dissension in its ranks and minor defeats in the house. Accordingly, the Macdonald–Cartier cabinet decided to resign when a vote of 28 July rejected the choice of Ottawa as future permanent capital, a choice with which the cabinet was identified.

The governor general, Sir Edmund Head*, called on Brown as the leading figure in the opposition to form a new government. The danger for Brown was obvious, since his side had no real majority in the house. Yet if he refused, he would virtually endorse the constant Conservative charge that he was a "governmental impossibility." He worked closely with Dorion, and succeeded in constructing an able cabinet, dedicated to establishing representation by population, but with constitutional guarantees for French Canada. As might be expected, this Brown-Dorion ministry was nevertheless defeated when it met parliament on 2 August; but Brown had then hoped to go to the country and win a new general election. Head refused his request, on the ground that elections had been held so recently. Brown could only resign, as he did on 4 August.

His "Short Administration" would become a standard item of political comic relief thereafter. Still, one can scarcely see that he had a better course. Furthermore, his Conservative foes revealed their own insecurity on resuming office in the narrowly divided house. They were sworn into one set of posts, then promptly switched them for another, which let them take advantage of a legal technicality and avoid having to withdraw from parliament to undergo by-elections, as the Brown-Dorion ministers had had to do. This "Double Shuffle" both added salt to Brown's wounds and reinforced his belief that, under the existing sectionally divided union, government had become hopelessly unprincipled and venal. The failure of the courts to condemn the double shuffle in December 1858 [*see* Draper] further increased his bitterness, and a bad-tempered parliamentary session at Quebec in the spring of 1859 left him in a deeply despondent mood. The fact was that, for all his abundant physical energy, he was exhausted after two years of unrelenting political effort. In this state he let the *Globe* play with radical notions of dissolution of the union and written, American-style-constitutions – chiefly through the agency of an able *Globe* editorial writer, George Sheppard*, with strong American constitutional preferences of his own.

During the summer of 1859, Brown largely recovered his spirits and his hold over his journal. In fact, he launched the *Globe* on a new campaign, for a federal union to settle the ills of the two parts of divided Canada, so that each could govern its own sectional interests, under one general government based on representation by population for matters of common concern. In September he laid plans for a new Upper Canada Reform convention to reinvigorate his disheartened party. Plainly, he meant to bring it to adopt federation: a constitutional remedy which could appeal to both sections of Canada, if rep by pop alone could not, and one – as he made clear – which would be a step toward "a great confederation" of all British America and the incorporation of the North-West as well. He and his Toronto leadership group worked carefully to arrange the key convention committees to ensure that any dissolutionist radical opinions would be outweighed at the grand party gathering.

The convention of 570 delegates met in St Lawrence Hall, Toronto, on 9 Nov. 1859. Again Brown's presence, and engineering, dominated its affairs. Sheppard spoke powerfully for "simple dissolution," reflecting a widespread agrarian Grit suspicion of political complexity. Then William McDougall offered a usefully vague compromise term, "some joint authority," for the federal power to link two sectional governments; Brown made an eloquent appeal to national aspirations in urging federal union. Federation effectively gained the day. Thereafter the *Globe* boomed it exultantly across the west as chosen party policy.

Brown intended to move the convention programme early in the legislative session of 1860. But soon dissent appeared within his own parliamentary ranks, arising from moderate elements this time. Notably exemplified in John Sandfield MACDONALD, they held that it was still possible to gain power in the existing union by winning more support in Lower Canada from ministerialists who were tired of extravagant, Grand Trunk–influenced government, and that a proposal for sweeping constitutional change would simply frighten them away. Brown, however, argued that an attempt at still another coalition merely for office would settle nothing. He won his point, but only by threatening to resign as party leader. When he finally did bring forward the convention policy, it was about 30 April and late in the session, and backing for it was visibly uncertain. It was easily defeated. Nevertheless Brown had recorded a party stand on federalism of much future consequence.

Meanwhile his health was suffering. He had evidently not fully recovered from his earlier strains – and these were financial as well as political, going back to the depression that had begun in 1857. By that date Brown had become an entrepreneur with sizeable investments in Upper Canada, quite apart from maintaining his large newspaper business. In the early 1850s he had acquired extensive lands in Lambton County, and when the new Great Western Railway was built across them in 1855 the village of Bothwell had risen on his estate. The "Laird of Bothwell" sold farm and town lots, built roads and mills, cut lumber, and operated a cabinet factory. But this was in boom time, in a country that virtually ran on credit. When the depression of 1857 brought swift contraction, Brown was soon in difficulties, with Bothwell mortgaged, and funds again committed to *Globe* improvements in advance of circulation and advertising revenues.

He struggled through several bad years, surviving without a serious loss of property. But the struggles – and his creditors – were particularly demanding in 1860. As a result, his health collapsed completely in the winter of 1861, and he was sent to bed for more than two months. He thus missed the parliamentary session of 1861, and was still weak in June when a general election was called. Brown did his best; but he was beaten in his Toronto seat and was out of parliament for the first time in ten years. At any rate, business conditions were at last improving because of rising American demands for lumber and other Canadian products, stemming from the onset of the Civil War that year. But more than that, oil fields were being developed in the vicinity of Bothwell; by the fall of 1861 it stood to become a boom town. Brown held on to his own estate and bought more land. His financial prospects now looked excellent. Meanwhile his *Globe* was warmly supporting the northern cause in the Civil War – Brown's strong abolitionism made him a firm opponent of the slave-owning South – and no less warmly attacking the Grand Trunk railway influence and eastern power behind the Cartier-Macdonald regime in Canada.

In 1862, with his health still uncertain, he decided to take a long recuperative holiday in

Great Britain. He landed in Liverpool on 23 July, his first return in 25 years. After a month in London, he moved on to Edinburgh, and there saw such old friends as William and Thomas Nelson, of the Nelson publishing family, who had been his school mates at the High School. Above all, he met their sister, Anne Nelson, lively, intelligent, and cultivated. He fell deeply in love at 43, and on 27 November, he and Anne were married at Abden House, the Nelson home.

They returned to Canada in late December, to receive a tumultuous mass welcome in Toronto. But soon, despite George Brown's whole-hearted affection for his new domestic life, he felt the pull of unfinished political business. With his health fully restored and his horizons undoubtedly broadened by viewing colonial sectional politics from the centre of empire, he decided on another try: a man no less vigorous and resolute than before, but somehow more detached and judicious – perhaps the mellowing result of marriage.

Brown easily won a by-election in South Oxford in March 1863. He found himself in a parliament both altered and much the same. A moderate Liberal government under Sandfield Macdonald had replaced a crumbling Conservative regime in 1862, but Sandfield's ministry was just one more attempt to keep the existing union running without dealing with underlying sectional and constitutional problems. Sandfield, in fact, had pinned his faith to the double majority principle, whereby neither section of the union would be governed against the will of its own parliamentary majority. But that principle had foundered shortly before Brown rejoined parliament at Quebec in April, when another separate school bill had been passed for Upper Canada without having received western majority support. The discredited government was thereupon recast to give it a firmer Reform character, Brown playing a prominent part as he reasserted his old influence in his party even though he preferred to stay outside the ministry. Dorion and his Rouge friends replaced moderate eastern Liberals in the cabinet; associates of Brown, such as Oliver Mowat*, entered its western half. This new Macdonald–Dorion ministry then went to the polls in July 1863. The Reformers won in Upper Canada emphatically (as Brown again did in South Oxford), but Cartier's Conservatives equally swept the east. The two sides were practically in balance. Deadlock was approaching.

The fruitless power struggles in parliament that autumn showed that no real change had been made in the political situation. Brown, however, acting as a private member, disclosed a significantly new approach. He announced his intention to move for a select committee to inquire impartially into the sectional problems of Canada and report on the best means of remedying them. It was a constructive proposal, carefully worded to be non-partisan. But his motion did not come to a vote until the spring session of 1864, as the house battled on through more bitter, barren factional contests. The Sandfield Macdonald ministry, unable to govern, gave up in March. The Conservative cabinet that replaced it, under John A. Macdonald and Sir Étienne Taché, had no greater chance of achievement, or even survival. Brown's single-minded aim was to settle the constitutional impasse and retire from the burden of parliament to the warm family world he longed for – his first child, Margaret, had been born that January. Finally, on 19 May 1864, his motion passed. He became chairman of a select committee drawn from leading members of all parties; he put it industriously to work. And on 14 June it reported to parliament "a strong feeling" in favour of "a federative system."

This was only a general statement in a brief progress report. Yet it supplied the essential basis for a way out when, on the very day of that report, the Macdonald–Taché government collapsed. Brown moved decisively to use this latest crisis: he let the Conservative leaders know that he would support theirs or any other ministry if they would act to solve the constitutional problem. They were ready to respond. On 17 June, John A. Macdonald and Alexander Tilloch Galt*, a leading proponent of British North American federation, met with Brown in his room at the St Louis Hotel. Cartier later joined the discussions. It was soon decided that the only solution lay "in the federative principle suggested by the report of Mr. Brown's committee," and that an approach should first be made to the Atlantic provinces to seek a general British American federal union. Brown had looked ultimately toward this larger goal, but he had deemed earlier Conservative advocacy of it to be premature and mainly used as a red herring to evade action on Canada's own internal constitutional problem. But since the Conservatives had now agreed to federate the Canadian union, he could only see a great gain if the other colonies could also be included. He agreed, though reluctantly, to enter the government with two Reform supporters. The new coalition to seek a confederation would thus have overwhelming strength in the house, backed both by the Brownite Grit western majority and Cartier's Bleu eastern majority. Deadlock was over. George Brown had initiated the breakthrough, and the movement to a whole new union.

On 22 June 1864 the "Great Coalition" was

announced to a wildly jubilant house. Brown joined Macdonald and Cartier and their colleagues in the cabinet as president of the council, along with Mowat and McDougall as his Reform associates; all under Taché as prime minister. During the summer this strong new government developed the outlines of a federal scheme to lay before representatives of the Maritime provinces at a meeting in Charlottetown in September. Among the eight Canadian cabinet members who went to the Charlottetown conference, Brown took an important role, on 5 September presenting to it the constitutional structure proposed for federal union. After the conference unanimously endorsed confederation in principle, he went on to meetings at Halifax and Saint John.

In October came the larger Quebec conference to work out detailed terms for confederation. Again Brown took a leading part in this critically important gathering – being, after all, the strongest representative there of the most powerful provincial interest, that of the future Ontario. Yet his own interest was not just sectional, but national. For example, it was he who moved the essential resolution stipulating central and provincial governments for the union, with provision for the admission of the North-West, British Columbia, and Vancouver Island. He took a stand against an elected senate in the new federal parliament, as he had previously against the elective upper house introduced in the province of Canada, because of the problem of basing British responsible government on the confidence of two representative bodies, particularly if they were of different party complexion. And he wanted simple, non-political new provincial authorities, since they were to be left only "insignificant" matters to deal with. Brown believed that the establishing of representation by population in the central government (another resolution which he moved) would give Upper Canada its due voice in important national matters, and that the provincial regimes would take the divisive, but essentially local, sectional issues out of high politics. It was a clouded vision, but at least a well-meaning one for this "sectional" politician become a confederation statesman.

After the conference closed, Brown was one of the spokesmen who first presented the actual plan for confederation embodied in the 72 Quebec resolutions to the Canadian people, in his case, through a major speech in Toronto on 3 November. Later that month he set out for England. He had been chosen to open discussions with the imperial government on the project of union, and also to discuss the transfer of the North-West from the HBC to this grand new design. During December he went into these questions with British government and opposition leaders in London, as well as the question of British North American defence, made urgent by strained relations with the United States arising out of the Civil War, now hastening towards a northern victory. He returned early in 1865, sure of imperial approval for the confederation project, hopeful of progress on the transfer of the North-West, but worried by apparent British readiness to see the still weak colonies "shift for themselves" in the face of American danger.

The Canadian parliament met again in February, to debate the Quebec conference scheme and to give the approval to be expected from the government's big majority. Still, the confederation debates of 1865 were no mere rubber stamp; they expressed doubts and penetrating criticism, national hopes and powerful arguments for union. In the latter regard, Brown's own speech of 8 February was perhaps his greatest, and one of the strongest in support of confederation. Before the vote was taken, however, the plan had met reverses in the Maritimes, where the pro-confederation government of Samuel Leonard Tilley* had lost an election in New Brunswick in March, and the Charles Tupper* regime had not even dared to introduce the Quebec scheme in the Nova Scotian assembly.

Another Canadian mission was accordingly sent to England to discuss the future of confederation, this time composed of Brown, Macdonald, Cartier, and Galt. After busy meetings and much social life in London in May and June, they succeeded handsomely, gaining imperial assurance of cooperation in forwarding the project and of the defence of Canada in event of war, though now that the Civil War had ended any American military threat seemed fast receding. The British government also promised aid in negotiating a new trade agreement with the United States, since the existing reciprocity treaty was to end the following year. While in Britain, Brown was fully involved in the working out of these vital concerns of the confederation movement. The remaining essential was winning back the Maritimes. After the mission returned he played a part here also.

In September 1865 he and Galt represented Canada at the Confederate Trade Council in Quebec, a smaller meeting of the provinces to consider their commercial future now that their reciprocity agreement with the United States was to be terminated. The common approach to trade the council sought, and the Maritime contacts Brown made, stood him in good stead afterwards when the Canadian government sent him to the Maritimes to try the climate anew on confederation. He marked a hopeful trend in New Brunswick, and dealt with Tilley and Lieutenant Governor Arthur Hamilton Gordon* on ways to advance it. On his return in mid-November, however, he found the Canadian government had decided on a policy of their own for seeking reciprocity with the United States, by joint legislative action rather than by treaty, and this he firmly opposed.

Brown had long upheld reciprocity, as an economic liberal seeking to remove, not raise, the barriers of tariffs, and as an Upper Canadian who had seen his own section benefit from it. But he did believe its price might come too high. Legislative reciprocity, virtually open to change at the will of an American congressional lobby, would, he thought, place Canadian prosperity at the mercy of American dictation. He fought the proposal through tense cabinet discussions, yet failed to convince his colleagues. At length, on 19 December, he resigned. There is no doubt that the issue was crucial to Brown, though it is also true, of course, that strains had long been rising in the cabinet between two strong chieftains and old opponents, Macdonald and himself. Moreover Brown was still uneasy in a coalition, however great its purpose, and felt he was unduly committed in an old game of power-building and office-dealing. Hence he was emotionally ready to resign over an issue as important as reciprocity. There was meaning in the telegram he sent his wife: "I am a free man once more."

In any case, confederation now was well in train. Brown continued wholeheartedly to support it, in the *Globe* and at the next session of parliament in 1866. He had the satisfaction of seeing New Brunswick elect Tilley's pro-confederates in the spring, and Nova Scotia reopen the quest for union – not to mention, meanwhile, the failure of the legislative reciprocity approach to a scarcely interested United States. Towards the close of the year the final confederation conference met in London to draft the imperial bill, still fundamentally embodying the Quebec resolutions Brown had helped to formulate. It was passed as the British North America Act in March 1867.

By this time Brown was deep in party politics again, renewing contact with former Rouge friends such as Dorion and Luther HOLTON, who had opposed the confederation ministry, and striving to strengthen Reform party lines in Upper Canada, eroded by the years of coalition. Brown felt that any need for coalition would end with the inception of confederation and that party politics should reassert themselves in the new federal Canadian state. On the other hand, Macdonald Conservatives and some Liberals held that the new era should be instituted by a broad, non-partisan administration. Pressed by friends to take the lead for Reform again, challenged by the coalitionist stand, Brown overcame his sincere desire to be done with parliamentary life, and, as before, made one more try.

There was another large, excited Reform convention in Toronto in June 1867 to reaffirm party unity. There Brown virtually read from the party William McDougall and William Howland*, the two leading Liberals who still sat firmly in the coalition cabinet, Mowat having long since withdrawn to a judicial post. But the elections for the new union legislatures, held later in the summer, soon proved that the Reform convention had by no means overcome the wide popular appeal of the "patriotic" no-party cry. In August, Brown was beaten himself in South Ontario, a far from safe seat. By September it was clear that sufficient Reformers had joined with the Conservatives to give a majority in Ontario to the new federal regime of Sir John A. Macdonald and to a similar coalition government for the province led by Sandfield Macdonald. Brown himself was offered safer seats; but his feelings against parliamentary life had only been confirmed. In October 1867 he left Canada for an extended family holiday in Scotland: out of politics before he had turned 49.

In the next few years he gave himself largely to his growing family, now including two more children, Catherine Edith and George Mackenzie, to the *Globe*, his first love, and to his considerable business interests. He had sold his Bothwell properties to an oil syndicate in 1865 for $275,000, making him decidedly wealthy. But in 1866 he had bought a brand new estate at Bow Park near Brantford, where he began to develop a large herd of prime shorthorn cattle. Bow Park grew from a family country home to a cattle breeding enterprise that took much of his time. Nevertheless, he did not seek to escape from politics, only from public life. His journal was as potent a Reform organ as ever. Its owner, and former party leader, was regularly consulted by the Grit inner circle, whether in the provincial capital, Toronto, or the federal at Ottawa. Furthermore, he had a particularly close connection with Alexander Mackenzie, leader of the federal Liberal opposition in all but name, who had once been his election agent in early days in Kent and Lambton and later his trusted lieutenant in the old Canadian assembly.

Through the *Globe* he worked to bring about the end of Sandfield Macdonald's "Patent Combination" in Ontario. In the spring of 1871 the second Ontario election gave the Reformers the balance of power in the provincial house, possibly helped by the fact that Brown in his paper had made peace with Roman Catholic voters, declaring that divisive sectarian issues had now been "banished." Sandfield held on in office till December, but then a Liberal government under Edward Blake* replaced him. The next year, when Blake decided to move to the federal sphere, Brown helped persuade an old friend, Oliver Mowat, to leave the judicial bench and head the ministry, thus opening the long Mowat era in Ontario government in October 1872.

Meanwhile Brown had had his troubles as *Globe* proprietor, having faced a major printing strike by the Toronto typographical union from March to June of 1872. The strike ended in mutual concessions, but not before Brown and other "master printers" had had 18 printers arrested for intimidation, though they were released on bail and never brought to trial. The next year there was the very different excitement of the "Pacific Scandal." Here the *Globe* was on the side of the angels, as it denounced the corrupt payment of election funds to the chief Conservative ministers by Sir Hugh Allan*, who had been granted the Canadian Pacific Railway charter. The Macdonald federal government fell; the Liberals under Mackenzie won a sweeping election victory early in 1874. The Mackenzie government then asked Brown to undertake a mission to the United States to seek a new reciprocity treaty.

He readily accepted the task of negotiating for the kind of reciprocity he supported. Moreover there seemed to be some hope that the Americans would now agree to a treaty, in order to avoid having to pay a cash settlement for access to the Canadian Atlantic fisheries. Brown arrived in Washington in February, officially to serve as joint commissioner with the British minister in Washington, Sir Edward Thornton, but really to carry the weight of the work himself. For several months he fenced and bargained with the American secretary of state, the affable but wily Hamilton Fish. An extensive treaty gradually was drafted, providing for reciprocal free admission of many manufactures as well as natural products. On 18 June the draft treaty was finally sent to Congress for approval. Fish had so delayed, however, that there was not time for it to be considered before the adjournment four days later. The Senate simply set it aside; there was little chance it would be revived since any American interest by now had waned. In fact, for Brown's draft treaty of 1874 one well may use the dictum, the operation was successful but the patient died.

He played a declining part in political affairs after his Washington mission though he never entirely left them. He had been appointed a senator in 1874 but did not take his seat in Ottawa until the next year. Indeed, his attendance at the Senate was generally sporadic, and not a major return to politics. Still, Brown maintained his link with Mackenzie and the very core of stout Victorian Grittism. In this respect, he supported Mackenzie in 1874–75 against the passing discontents of the able Edward Blake, and the young Canada First idealists who temporarily gathered to him, finding Mackenzie's rule too stale and uninspired. Blake was to be won back, but Brown and the *Globe* also joined battle with the redoubtable Goldwin Smith*, the sharp-tongued intellectual publicist who for a time was allied with the short-lived Canada First group. Indeed, there began a long feud with Smith, largely because of his presumption that Canada was doomed to partisan excesses and colonial inferiority until it breathed the pure air of independence, which to him seemed to mean annexation to the United States.

From 1875, however, Brown was spending his time increasingly on affairs at his Bow Park estate. There his neighbour's son, Alexander Graham Bell*, offered him and his brother Gordon a share in the rights to the "sound telegraphy" system Bell had invented if they would advance $600 and patent the device in England. Both agreed to advance the money, and George Brown undertook to apply for a British patent for Bell in a forthcoming visit to Britain. But when the senator arrived in London in February 1876, the technical advice he received there discouraged him as to the value of Bell's invention. He did not proceed, the agreement lapsed, and Brown did not become part-owner of a future Bell empire. He was more concerned with his plan to launch a joint-stock company in Britain to build Bow Park into a major pedigreed cattle-raising venture. Already well known to leading British stockbreeders and aristocratic fanciers alike, he succeeded in raising close to $400,000 of capital, and returned to Canada in May to obtain his charter.

Under these new auspices Bow Park grew much larger, and it became a show-place for agriculturalists visiting Canada. Yet by 1877 the country was deep in a world depression, and the market for pedigreed stock was not growing as anticipated. Brown's enterprise was already heading into difficulties when the next year he turned his attention back to politics, to support the Liberal cause in the federal election of September 1878. He spoke through southern Ontario against the Conservative call for a "National Policy" of tariff protection. But after the National Policy, and the depression, swept Macdonald back into office, Brown returned to the mounting financial troubles of Bow Park.

In 1879 the British stockholders of his company

sent over an expert manager, John Clay, to try to save the situation. By early December Clay's work of reorganizing was beginning to bring an improvement, when a fire destroyed most of the estate's main buildings. Then on Christmas day another blaze, almost certainly of incendiary origin, burned out the stables. George Brown's pioneering venture into pedigreed stock raising in Canada seemed ruined. Moreover, early in 1880 he was facing problems at the *Globe*, where he had again invested heavily in improvements to produce a new multi-page machine-folded edition; delays in installation had held back its appearance.

On 25 March 1880, at the *Globe*, a former worker in the engine room, George BENNETT, discharged by his foreman for intemperance, came into Brown's office to seek a certificate that he had served five years. Brown tried to send the man, whom he did not know, to see the foreman. There was an argument; Bennett, who had been drinking, suddenly pointed a gun. As Brown grasped for it, it fired, inflicting a flesh wound in his thigh. His assailant was quickly secured. Brown's injury was pronounced slight, and he left thankfully for Lambton Lodge, his Toronto home. But while he stayed at home, calling meetings there on *Globe* business and worrying incessantly over the losses at Bow Park, the wound, far from healing, grew inflamed. During April his financial outlook brightened, as a good cattle sale was made in Chicago and the new *Globe* edition came out. But by this time his leg was badly infected and he had too greatly taxed his strength. Gradually he gave way to fever and delirium, then coma. Early on 9 May he died at Lambton Lodge, at the age of 61.

His life was saddened at the end by a sense of failure. Yet actually Bow Park recovered under new direction, and the *Globe* assuredly continued to flourish. Above all, there remained Brown's achievements in journalism, the Liberal party, and Canadian confederation itself. Lord Monck*, governor general in the confederation years, termed him "*the* man whose conduct in 1864 had rendered the project of union feasible." A man, also, who refused the lieutenant governorship of Ontario in 1875 and a knighthood in 1879, he preferred always to remain George Brown of the *Globe* – which was distinction enough in itself.

J. M. S. CARELESS

[This piece is essentially derived from my biography, *Brown of* The Globe. Little new research material on Brown has turned up since the writing of this biography. The main primary source was, and is, the Brown papers in the PAC. Some secondary works of value have certainly appeared since *Brown of* The

Globe was written. They offer useful related and background information, though they do not deal centrally with Brown or alter my interpretation of him in any significant way. A selection of such works is given below, along with some older volumes. But with respect to the latter, *Brown of* The Globe, of course, utilized many more, and again provides the fullest references to them. J.M.S.C.]

Alexander Mackenzie, *The life and speeches of Hon. George Brown* (Toronto, 1882). Careless, *Union of the Canadas*. Charles Clarke, *Sixty years in Upper Canada, with autobiographical recollections* (Toronto, 1908). Creighton, *Macdonald, young politician*; *Macdonald, old chieftain*; *Road to confederation*. Dent, *Last forty years*. John Lewis, *George Brown* (Toronto, 1906). Morton, *Critical years*. Waite, *Life and times of confederation*. James Young, *Public men and public life in Canada, being recollections of parliament and the press, and embracing a succinct account of the stirring events which led to the confederation of British North America into the Dominion of Canada* (Toronto, 1902).

BROWN, ROBERT CHRISTOPHER LUNDIN, Church of England clergyman, missionary, and author; b.c. 1831 in England, son of the Reverend Robert Brown; d. a bachelor either at Patras, Greece, in the spring of 1876 or in London on 16 April 1876.

Robert Christopher Lundin Brown received his MA from the University of Edinburgh in 1854 and was ordained into the Church of England in 1858. During the next two years he served as curate of St Mark, North Audley St, London, and published several English translations of German theological works. In 1860 the Society for the Propagation of the Gospel sent Brown to British Columbia as a missionary. He visited Barkerville in the Cariboo and became the first missionary in the Lillooet district. He was thus the first incumbent at St Mary's Church, Lillooet, the third Anglican church on the mainland of British Columbia, which had been founded in 1861 and consecrated in 1862. In addition to his work at St Mary's, Brown made several missionary visits to the Cariboo goldfields. According to his own account, he was rather given to lecturing the miners on their sinfulness: "A sermon was preached ... on the prevailing vice, concubinage with native females.... Once the preacher [Brown referring to himself] was interrupted by someone instancing Solomon as having many wives, and yet didn't the Bible say he was a man after God's own heart? ... The Sunday following that sermon not a soul came to service." One of Brown's letters on the shortage of women among the Cariboo miners had a part in bringing about the foundation of the Columbian Emigration Society (supported by the SPG and other missionary groups) which sent bride ships

Browne

to Victoria in 1862 and 1863. Brown also did some missionary work among the Indians, making himself understood through translators.

In March 1864 the Reverend Mr Brown was not well; he did not preach at St Mary's again and left there in 1865. Upon his return to England, Brown held two posts briefly and then was appointed vicar of Lineal-cum-Colmere, Salop (1869–74), and of Rhodes near Manchester (1874–75). In May 1875 he emigrated to Cape Town, South Africa. Sometime in the remaining 11 months of his life Brown became English chaplain at Patras, Greece.

Brown is best known in Canada for his prize essay entitled *British Columbia*, published by the newly established press of the Royal Engineers at New Westminster in 1863. Designed to encourage immigration, it is a valuable, if rather enthusiastic and occasionally misleading, account of the resources and life of the mainland colony. In 1870 Brown published in London a pamphlet called *British Columbia: the Indians and settlers at Lillooet: appeal for missionaries*. One of its most interesting anecdotes tells of the Lillooet chief Shiheileedza and his daughter Kanadqua. The chief with half of his tribe was killed in a war with California miners, probably about 1850; his daughter was sold by an uncle to a miner, but under the influence of Christianity broke free of her concubinage. Brown published in 1873, also in London, *Klatsassan, and other reminiscences of missionary life in British Columbia*. Klattsasine* was the Chilcotin chief who in 1864 led a rising against the attempt initiated by Alfred WADDINGTON to build a road from the coast across his tribe's territory, and the book gives a valuable contemporary account of an event on which firsthand evidence is scarce. Brown's writing is equally interesting in its revelation of the motives and limitations of a British cleric among Indians and miners. Other publications by Brown include religious writings and translations.

V. G. HOPWOOD

R. C. L. Brown, *British Columbia, an essay* (New Westminster, B.C., 1863); *British Columbia: the Indians and settlers at Lillooet: appeal for missionaries* (London, 1870); *Klatsassan, and other reminiscences of missionary life in British Columbia* (London, 1873); "Lillooet mission," *Mission Life* (London), 1870, 561–69; "The Thompson River Indians," *Mission Life* (London), 1872, 95–107, 153–55, 227–29.

PABC, R. C. L. Brown correspondence, 1862–63; St Mary's Church (Lillooet, B.C.), Register (original in possession of the government agent at Lillooet, B.C.; copy also at University of British Columbia); Society for the Propagation of the Gospel, "Papers relating to the Diocese of Columbia, 1858–1868," typescripts in 3 vols. "British Columbia prize essay," *Daily British Colonist* (Victoria), 10 Sept. 1863. "The prize essay on British Columbia," *Daily British Colonist* (Victoria), 25 Sept. 1863. "The British Columbia essay," *Daily British Colonist* (Victoria), 29 Jan. 1864. "Farewell address," *Daily British Colonist* (Victoria), 18 April 1865. "People's magazine," *Daily British Colonist and Victoria Chronicle*, 21 July 1872. Columbia Mission, *Annual Reports* (London), 1860–66. Boase, *Modern English biography*, I, 438. *The clerical directory, a biographical and statistical book of reference for facts relating to the clergy and the church* (London, 1858). *Crockford's clerical directory for 1860* (London, 1860). M. L. Murray, *St. Mary's of Lillooet* ([Lillooet, B.C.], 1935). F. A. Peake, *The Anglican Church in British Columbia* (Vancouver, B.C., 1959).

[The author also received information in a letter from C. A. Johnson, "Summymead," Welshampton, Ellesmere, Shropshire, Eng., 27 Aug. 1969. v.g.h.]

BROWNE, FRANCES (Stewart), pioneer; b. in Dublin, Ireland, 24 May 1794, daughter of Francis Browne and Anna Maria Noble; m. Thomas Alexander Stewart; d. 24 Feb. 1872, near Peterborough, Ont.

Francis Browne, the son of a Church of England clergyman, was himself dean of Elphin, Roscommon County, when he died in 1796. His wife was paralysed at about the same time and Frances was then adopted by a great-uncle. In 1800 she went to live with another great-uncle, Dr Daniel Augustus Beaufort, rector of Collon in Louth County, and was privately educated by the rector's daughter. Although they were never published, Frances' father had written books and Dr Beaufort, one of the founders of the Royal Irish Academy, was a man of literary tastes.

On 17 Dec. 1816 Frances married Thomas Alexander Stewart of Wilmont, County Antrim. In the six years in which the Stewarts lived in Ireland three of their 11 children were born. After the failure of the manufacturing firm in which Thomas Stewart and Robert Reid, who had married Stewart's sister, were junior partners, the two men decided to emigrate to Upper Canada with what small capital they had. In August 1822 they arrived at York (Toronto), welcomed by the former adjutant-general, Colonel C. L. L. Foster*, who was connected by marriage with Frances Stewart. Receiving large grants of land (1,200 acres for the Stewarts), the two families set out for Douro Township in Peterborough County.

The Stewarts' house, Auburn, was built on the Otonabee River, a short distance northeast of the present town of Peterborough. The Reids were their only neighbours until 1825, when they welcomed Peter Robinson*'s Irish immigrants and gladly released their claim to control of settlement in the whole township. The story of the Stewarts is typical of those of middle-class families, who, with limited capital, migrated to Upper Canada in the 1820s and 1830s in the hope of improving their economic positions, and who faced – in this case with goodwill – rather more problems than they had anticipated. Like many of her contemporaries, Mrs Stewart described for her friends at home the life on a pioneer farm, a life completely different from theirs. Some of her letters were later published under the characteristic title of *Our forest home*; although unskilfully edited, the book is one of the best in the long list of accounts by immigrants and travellers.

True to her ancestry and to her environment in Ireland, Frances Stewart was deeply religious and of cultivated tastes. The first trait enabled her to face hardships and sorrows with resignation if not equanimity. In the early years her life in Canada was a lonely one, with all too little chance, she remarked, of rest for mind and body, and her husband, a justice of the peace and a member of the Legislative Council, died young in 1847. She received books from friends in Ireland and treasured a piano which had survived a fall through the ice.

In her later years Frances Stewart spent some time in another family house, Goodwood, but always returned to her own Auburn, though leaving the management of the farm to a son. In the 1860s the property, because of mismanagement, failed as a strong economic base for a large family. Mentally undefeated, Frances Stewart continued to write her engaging letters and to follow the lives of children and grandchildren until her death in 1872.

G. DE T. GLAZEBROOK

[Frances Stewart], *Our forest home, being extracts from the correspondence of the late Frances Stewart*, ed. E. S. Dunlop (Toronto, 1889; 2nd ed., Montreal, 1902). *Valley of the Trent* (Guillet). G. H. Needler, *Otonabee pioneers, the story of the Stewarts, the Stricklands, the Traills and the Moodies* (Toronto, 1953).

BRUNET, LOUIS-OVIDE, priest, botanist; b. 10 March 1826 at Quebec, son of Jean-Olivier Brunet, merchant, and Cécile Lagueux; d. 2 Oct. 1876 at Quebec.

In 1835 Louis-Ovide Brunet entered grade VIII at the Petit Séminaire of Quebec; Octave CRÉMAZIE was one of his fellow-pupils. Abbé Edward John HORAN, the future bishop of Kingston (Ontario), introduced him to natural history. Brunet spent part of his holidays with his uncle, the notary Louis-Édouard Glackmeyer*, an ardent collector of plants, who was assembling a herbarium. Brunet entered the seminary in 1844, and was ordained priest on 10 Oct. 1848; after being a missionary for two years at Grosse Île, he was a curate from 1848 to 1851 and again in 1853 and 1854, and was parish priest of Saint-Lambert-de-Lévis from 1854 to 1858.

When in 1856 Abbé Horan was appointed principal of the École Normale Laval at Quebec, his post of professor at the seminary and at the young Université Laval became vacant. In considering a replacement, the names of Abbé Léon Provancher* and Louis-Ovide Brunet came up; they had not as yet published anything, but were actively engaged in botanical pursuits and each was preparing a description of Canadian flora. Brunet was chosen. From 1858 to 1861 he devoted himself at the seminary to the teaching of botany, at the same time giving a course in dogma to the theology students. In 1862, the mineralogist Thomas Sterry Hunt* having left the Université Laval for McGill, Brunet succeeded him in the chair of natural history, which he occupied from 1863 to 1871. He was appointed titular professor in 1865.

Meanwhile, according to Georg August Pritzel, Brunet had published a short paper on Canadian woods (1857), and a first study (1861) on the voyage of the botanist André Michaux* in the direction of Hudson Bay in 1792. The latter's diary being at that time unpublished – it was not published until 1888 – Brunet worked with fragmentary notes, whose deficiencies no doubt explain errors of interpretation in his text.

His botanical excursions at Petit Cap (Montmorency County), near Cap Tourmente, enabled him to meet Abbé Léon Provancher, at that time parish priest of Saint-Joachim. In 1861 they made botanical expeditions to various places: Petit Cap, Île d'Orléans, Saguenay, and Lac Saint-Jean. Between them there soon developed a stubborn enmity, of which their correspondence and writings preserve traces: it reached the point of Brunet's refusing to contribute to the *Naturaliste canadien*, which was owned by Provancher. In 1860 the professor of the Université Laval had gone to Niagara on his first journey in Upper Canada. The following year, alone, or with T. S. Hunt or Abbé Jean-Baptiste-Antoine Ferland*, he gathered more specimens at Quebec, Montreal, Saint-Hyacinthe, Drummondville, in Lotbinière County and along the Rivière Sainte-Anne.

A plan was put forward at this time to set up a botanical garden at Quebec under the auspices of the seminary, with the collaboration of the municipality and the government. To prepare himself for the task of future director of this undertaking, Brunet travelled in Europe for a year

Brunet

(1861–62), associating with botanists of repute, visiting Regent's Park in London, the Jardin des Plantes in Paris, the botanical gardens of Liverpool, Kew, Montpellier, Florence, Pisa, Rome, Brussels, Louvain, Bonn, Düsseldorf, Utrecht, Amsterdam, Leyden, Rotterdam, and a Danish nursery.

At the Sorbonne, Brunet attended the lectures of Pierre-Étienne-Simon Duchartre, and at the Jardin des Plantes those of Adolphe-Théodore Brongniart and of Joseph Decaisne. With the latter he visited the gardens of Nantes and Angers, and again Kew Gardens. At the Muséum National d'Histoire Naturelle, where he worked freely, in the company of some remarkable scientists, he undertook a study of the Canadian plants of Michaux, which were preserved in the herbarium of that institution, and of the Canadian species mentioned in the *Canadensium plantarum . . . historia*, by Jacques-Philippe Cornut. The identification of these species was assuredly a valuable help to Abbé Joseph-Clovis Kemner* Laflamme, his pupil and then his successor, when the latter presented a communication on this work to the Royal Society of Canada.

Once back in Quebec, Brunet resumed his teaching and research. He went to Boston, New York, Philadelphia, and Washington in 1864, and Anticosti Island and the Strait of Belle-Isle in mid-summer 1865. And according to his travel diaries, he was on botanical expeditions in 1866 at Ottawa, London, Belleville, Hamilton, Brockville, Chatham, and Newbury in Canada West, and at Montreal, Trois-Rivières, Rimouski, and Rivière-du-Loup in Canada East.

Before his return from Europe, Brunet had already begun to prepare a study on the flora of Canada. The notes he amassed from 1860 to 1866 cover 582 pages, and have remained unpublished, no doubt because in 1862 Léon Provancher published his *Flore canadienne*. In a letter to Asa Gray, Brunet deemed the publication of his rival's work to be too hasty. Other manuscripts of Brunet would be worthy of publication if they were accompanied by the commentaries of a sagacious botanist. The only work on flora that Brunet published, *Éléments de botanique et de physiologie végétale . . .* (1870), deserved a better fate. But Provancher's *Flore*, and the Sulpician Jean Moyen's *Cours élémentaire de botanique . . .* published in 1871 at Montreal, stole the market from him. Brunet's work comprises numerous accounts of what he had observed, lists of popular names, and the description of five botanical entities new to the science. Several vegetable species will recall to botanists the active life of this man that was too early cut off, in particular

the *Crataegus brunetiana* Charles Sprague Sargent and the *Astragalus brunetianus* (Merritt Lyndon Fernald) Jacques Rousseau*.

Apart from his courses, his publications, the founding in 1862 and the organization of the herbarium of the Université Laval, Brunet prepared collections of Canadian woods for exhibitions in Dublin (1865) and Paris (1867). The plan for a botanical garden at Quebec absorbed part of his energies from 1861 to 1870. In the latter year he thought of creating a school of forestry, in reality simply an arboretum, for want of a more elaborate undertaking. This project, like that of the botanical garden, did not come to fruition: the seminary struck it off its programme in 1879.

In 1870 the government of Quebec invited the Université Laval to give a course in applied sciences and offered to subsidize it. Entrusted to Louis-Ovide Brunet and Dr François-Alexandre-Hubert La Rue*, the course began, but after a few lessons the rector of the university, fearing that politics would push its way in, terminated the project.

At the age of 44, a sick man, disappointed by repeated failure to achieve success, Louis-Ovide Brunet retired to the home of his mother and sister, where he lived until his death. Self-taught, like all scientists in Quebec before 1920, Louis-Ovide Brunet none the less proved to be the best French Canadian botanist of the last century. His contemporaries, who lacked the necessary training to judge him, were not capable of seeing in him the scientist who might have brought great lustre to his milieu. Working with minute care and unobtrusively, he was not one of those who seek to be first at all costs in the field of publishing. Furthermore, as Brunet did not receive the necessary encouragement, the major part of his work, and the most interesting, remains unpublished.

JACQUES ROUSSEAU

[L.-O. Brunet, *Catalogue des plantes canadiennes contenues dans l'herbier de l'université Laval et recueillies pendant les années 1858–1865* (Québec, 1865) (The complete catalogue was to contain more than 200 pages and several plates; however, only the first section was published. The four plates cited by Brunet do not appear in the copies which were consulted; were they ever published?); *Catalogue des végétaux ligneux du Canada pour servir à l'intelligence des collections de bois économiques envoyées à l'exposition universelle de Paris, 1867* (Québec, 1867); *Éléments de botanique et de physiologie végétale, suivis d'une petite flore simple et facile pour aider à découvrir les noms des plantes les plus communes au Canada* (Québec, 1870); *Énumération des genres de plantes de la flore du Canada précédée des tableaux analytiques des familles . . .* (Québec, 1864); *Histoire des Picea qui se rencontrent* dans les limites du Canada (Québec, 1866); [ ], "Journal de voyage en Europe de l'abbé Ovide Brunet en 1861–1862," Arthur Maheux, édit., *Le Canada français* (Québec), 2ᵉ sér., XXVI (1938–39), 591–99, 681–90, 783–90, 886–92, 983–87; [ ], *Manière de préparer les plantes et autres objets de musée* (n.p., n.d.); "Michaux and his journey in Canada," *The Canadian Naturalist and Geologist* (Montreal), new ser., I (1864), 325–37; "Notes sur les plantes recueillies en 1858, par M. l'abbé Ferland sur les côtes du Labrador, baignées par les eaux du Saint-Laurent," *La littérature canadienne de 1850 à 1860* (2v., Québec, 1863), I, 367–74; *Notice sur le musée botanique de l'université Laval ...* (Québec, 1867); *Notice sur les plantes de Michaux et sur son voyage au Canada et à la baie d'Hudson, d'après son journal manuscrit et autres documents* (Québec, 1863); "On the Canadian species of the genus Picea," *Canadian Naturalist and Geologist* (Montreal), new ser., III (1868), 102–10; *Voyage d'André Michaux en Canada, depuis le lac Champlain jusqu'à la baie d'Hudson* (Québec, 1861). J.R.]

Frère Marie-Victorin [Conrad Kirouac], *Flore laurentienne* (1ʳᵉ éd., Montréal, 1935), 15, 308, 356. Jacques Rousseau, *Les Astragalus du Québec et leurs alliés immédiats* (Contributions du laboratoire de botanique de l'Université de Montréal, 24, New York, Montréal, Leipzig, 1933). Arthur Maheux, "Louis-Ovide Brunet, botaniste, 1826–1876," *Le Naturaliste canadien* (Québec), LXXXVII (1960), 5–22, 53–57, 120–64, 149–64, 228–36, 253–68, 277–86; LXXXVIII (1961), 78–83, 149–60, 324–36; LXXXIX (1962), 265–78. Jacques Rousseau, "Les entités botaniques nouvelles créées par Brunet," *Le Naturaliste canadien* (Québec), LVII (1930), 132–35; "Provancher et la publication des Éléments de botanique de Brunet (accompagné d'une lettre inédite)," *Le Naturaliste canadien* (Québec), LVII (1930), 196–202; "Un travail de l'abbé Brunet," *Le Naturaliste canadien* (Québec), LVIII (1931), 69; "Un travail oublié de l'abbé Ovide Brunet," *Le Naturaliste canadien* (Québec), LXVII (1940), 200; "Le voyage d'Asa Gray à Québec en 1858 (lettres inédites)," *Le Naturaliste canadien* (Québec), LVII (1930), 202–4. Jacques Rousseau et Bernard Boivin, "La contribution à la science de la *Flore canadienne* de Provancher," *Le Naturaliste canadien* (Québec), 95 (1968), 1499–530.

BRUYÈRE (Bruguier), ÉLISABETH, founder and first superior of the Sisters of Charity of Bytown (Ottawa); b. 19 March 1818 at L'Assomption, L.C.; d. 5 April 1876 at Ottawa, Ont.

Élisabeth's father, Charles Bruguier, was the eldest son of Jean-Baptiste Bruguier, who came originally from Pont-Saint-Esprit in Provence and arrived in Canada in 1756; Charles Bruguier's second wife was Sophie Mercier. Élisabeth's baptismal certificate gives the name Bruguier, but the spelling was later changed to Bruyère. From 1830, six years after her father's death, Élisabeth received a religious, intellectual, and domestic training of the highest quality under the protection of a cousin, Abbé Charles-François Caron, the parish priest of Saint-Esprit (Montcalm County). In 1834 she taught at the local school; she continued teaching at Saint-Vincent-de-Paul (Laval) when her benefactor was transferred there in 1836.

Élisabeth was easily moved by the sufferings of others, and in 1839 entered the order of the Sisters of Charity of the Hôpital Général of Montreal, commonly called the Grey Nuns. She professed in 1841 and was placed in charge of a ward of 40 orphan girls, whom she strove to train according to the principles she had received.

In the autumn of 1844 the community was invited by Patrick Phelan*, coadjutor to the bishop of Kingston, to establish itself at Bytown (Ottawa), an important centre of the timber industry, where the Catholics had no schools, hospitals, or relief organization for the needy. In the face of so many needs the community agreed to cooperate, and entrusted responsibility for the undertaking to Mother Marguerite-Dorothée Beaubien*. She became ill, and Sister Élisabeth Bruyère, despite her youth, was asked to succeed her.

On 12 Feb. 1845 Ignace Bourget*, bishop of Montreal, gave Sister Élisabeth Bruyère and her three companions a letter of authorization allowing them to set up one or several communities in Bishop Phelan's diocese, provided that they conformed in every respect to the rule followed by the mother house, the Hôpital Général of Montreal. For his part Bishop Phelan welcomed them officially to his diocese, and by a canonical order issued on 11 April 1845 he instituted the community of the Sisters of Charity of Bytown. The community was to be entirely autonomous except for the act of fidelity to the rule of the mother house. When the latter adopted a new rule in 1851, which prohibited the running of boarding-schools and fee-charging schools, Joseph-Bruno GUIGUES, who had been bishop of Bytown since 1848, was unable to agree to it; paid teaching had already been authorized at Bytown, and the poverty of the diocese did not make it possible to give financial support to another exclusively teaching community. In 1854 the Montreal house recognized the complete independence of the Ottawa community, which obtained its own rule in 1856.

The founders of the community had reached Bytown by 20 Feb. 1845, ready to assist the parish priest, Adrien Telmon; within three months they had established their chief projects. On 3 March one of the first so-called "bilingual" schools in Upper Canada was inaugurated. On 10 May a small seven-bed hospital opened its doors. In June an organization to care for the poor and the sick was set up. A noviciate began to take shape in the

Budd

summer with the admission of four aspirants, three of them from Bytown.

The typhus epidemic of the years 1847 and 1848 was for the young institute its initiation to heroism. With none but themselves to tend more than 600 patients sent to them by Dr Edward Van Cortlandt, the sisters saved some 475. In addition they were entrusted with the care of about 15 infant orphans. The epidemic overcome, they returned to their labours. In 1850 a capacious stone house replaced the cramped dwelling of the early days. This building housed the nuns, the orphans, the aged, and a girls' boarding-school which subsequently became the convent of Notre-Dame-du-Sacré-Cœur. A hospital was also equipped, and a school erected at Bishop Guigues' expense.

Apart from the founding of a boarding-school and a parish school at St Andrews West, near Cornwall, in 1848, the community did not go beyond the confines of Bytown until 1857, when it opened a school at Buffalo, New York. Under Mother Bruyère's direction, the community also concerned itself with missions; in 1866 sisters were sent to the Timiskaming district (Canada West), to assist the Oblates of Mary Immaculate among the Algonkins and the Crees in the region that is now northern Quebec and Ontario.

Mother Élisabeth Bruyère directed the community until her death, on 5 April 1876. During her long administration the community had opened some 25 houses in Ontario, Quebec, and New York State; all were under the direct control of the mother house at Ottawa. The majority were intended for teaching, and some concerned themselves with orphans, Indians, the aged, and the sick. It was an impressive achievement on the part of Mother Élisabeth Bruyère, who from the very beginning sought to make of her trainees workers who were deeply religious, zealous, and competent.

Sœur Paul-Émile (Louise Guay)

Archives des Sœurs Grises de la Croix d'Ottawa, Annales de l'Institut, I (1845–1875), II (1875–1886); Correspondance Bruyère, communauté, affaires, famille; Correspondance relative à la fondation de l'Institut, dossiers Bourget, Phelan, Telmon, McMullen; Louis Richard, "Notes généalogiques de la famille Bruguier-Bruyère, en France et au Canada"; Registre de l'admission et de la décharge des malades de l'Hôpital Général d'Ottawa, 1845–1866, pp.12–99; Statistiques générales de l'Institut. Sœur Paul-Émile [Louise Guay], *Mère Élisabeth Bruyère et son œuvre* (Ottawa, 1945); "Mère Élisabeth Bruyère, fille de l'Église et femme d'œuvres," SCHÉC *Rapport, 1962*, 51–58. Stanislas Drapeau, "Simple coup d'œil sur la communauté des Sœurs de la Charité d'Ottawa," *Album des familles* (Ottawa, 1880), 398–401.

BUDD, HENRY, HBC clerk, farmer, teacher, and first Indian Anglican minister; b.c. 1812 of an unknown Indian and a Métis woman; d. 2 April 1875 at The Pas, North-West Territories (Man.).

On 15 Oct. 1819 the Hudson's Bay Company appointed John West* as its first Church of England chaplain in Rupert's Land. West also made arrangements with the Church Missionary Society to do what he could for the education of Métis and Indians at the company's posts and he took George Harbidge, a trained schoolmaster, with him to Rupert's Land. They arrived at York Factory in August, and when they left they took the young son of Chief Withewacapo with them. At Norway House West secured an orphan boy for education. This was Henry Budd whom West baptized with the chief's son on 21 July 1822; West's register has an entry, "Henry Budd an Indian boy about ten years of age taught in the Missionary School and now capable of reading the New Testament and repeating the Church of England Catechism correctly."

John West returned to England in 1823 but Harbidge stayed on to teach in the Church Missionary Society school at Red River. Henry Budd remained there for a number of years and was highly respected by his teacher as "amiable" and "thoughtful." Budd left the school about 1827 to become a clerk for the HBC. It seems that he went to the Columbia River area, a region of open warfare and violence in the fur trade. On 2 Feb. 1836 he married Betsy, apparently a daughter of Chief Factor John Work*. Since his contract with the HBC was completed, Budd and his wife returned to Red River and bought farm land near St Andrews. In 1837 he was persuaded by David Thomas Jones* and William Cockran* to teach at the Upper Church (St John's) parish school.

Budd showed ability, and in 1840 Cockran and John Smithurst* asked him to go to the Cumberland House District to begin a new school and mission for the Indians. On 22 June he set out for this place, his wife and mother with him. Cochran and Smithurst had made the request on their own responsibility "because everything had been prepared," they thought, between the HBC and the Church Missionary Society for assistance at this mission. But a difference of opinion developed between the company and the society. Hence after a short time at Cumberland House, Henry Budd moved down the Saskatchewan River to W'passkwayaw (The Pas) and built there a house in which he taught and held services. In June 1842, Smithurst went to The Pas for the baptismals of 39 adults, 27 infants, and 22 schoolchildren, the result of Budd's work, and was pleased with the tidiness and productivity of the mission.

Bishop David Anderson* made his first visit to The Pas in 1850, and referred to the establishment as the Devon Mission. Henry Budd had then been assisting the Reverend James Hunter* as catechist, schoolmaster, and in the study of Cree for six years; he also had been given what he thought the undignified task of selecting timber for the parsonage and church. The bishop took Henry and Henry junior back to the Red River, and coached the father in theology. On 22 December Henry Budd was ordained as a deacon in St Andrews Church; he was the first Indian in North America to be admitted to the ministry of the Church of England. When he had been ordained a priest in the new Christ Church, The Pas, on 10 June 1853, he was sent to Nepowewin (Nipawin, Sask.) and appears to have remained in charge there until 1867, when he returned to minister at The Pas. He was also expected to oversee the church's missionary endeavours at Nepowewin, Cumberland House, and Carlton House where there were catechists as well. He remained at The Pas until his unexpected death; he was buried in the old churchyard there and a monument of granite marks his grave.

Henry Budd is said to have been a big man of fine appearance; he was an eloquent preacher in Cree, and his letters to the society are in fine script and excellent English. He was much loved by his own people, one of whom remarked at the time of Budd's death that he had only then known what it was to lose a father although his real father had died several years before. Henry Budd, however, had qualities not usually ascribed to his race: he was methodical and thrifty, his mission stations were models of neatness, his gardens, livestock, and management a constant object lesson to his people. His work has endured through the years.

T. C. B. BOON

Church Missionary Society Archives (London), Henry Budd papers, correspondence, 1822–73; Henry Budd papers, journal, 1850–75. Hargrave, *Red River*, 103–26. John West, *The substance of a journal during a residence at the Red River colony . . . British North America; and frequent excursions among the North-West American Indians, in the years 1820, 1821, 1822, 1823* (London, 1824), 16. Boon, *Anglican Church*, 6, 15, 45, 49–50, 66, 83, 99, 102. W. B. Heeney, *John West and his Red River mission* (Toronto, 1920). M. E. J., *Dayspring in the far west, sketches of mission-work in north-west America* (London, 1875). Robert Machray, *Life of Robert Machray, D.D., LL.D., D.C.L., archbishop of Rupert's Land, primate of all Canada . . .* (London, 1909). [J. A.] Mackay, "Henry Budd," *Leaders of the Canadian Church*, ed. W. B. Heeney (2nd ser., Toronto, 1920), 65–72. Sarah Tucker, *The rainbow in the north; a short account of the first establishment of Christianity in Rupert's Land by the Church Missionary Society* (London, 1851).

BUELL, ANDREW NORTON, lawyer, businessman, politician, journalist, and office-holder; b. 20 April 1798 at Elizabethtown (Brockville), U.C., the second son of William Buell*, loyalist and founder of Elizabethtown, and Martha Naughton; d. 9 Nov. 1880 at Toronto, Ont.

Andrew Norton Buell was educated at Pointe-Claire, Lower Canada (where he acquired a fluency in French), and at Brockville, Upper Canada. In 1816 he became a student-at-law and clerk in the office of David Jones of Brockville. He was admitted to the bar of Upper Canada on 6 Nov. 1821 as a barrister and attorney-at-law, and solicitor in chancery.

Beginning in 1821 Buell undertook an active career in journalism and politics on behalf of the Reform cause. He was instrumental in the founding of the Reform-oriented *Brockville Recorder*, and contributed the introductory address which appeared in the first number in 1821. Two years later he negotiated the purchase of the *Recorder* by his elder brother William*, who remained its editor and publisher for 28 years. Andrew Norton contributed innumerable editorials, communications, and addresses to its pages.

Buell was prominent locally in temperance societies and in the militia, but in politics he concentrated most of his efforts on behalf of his brother William who was elected to the Upper Canadian House of Assembly in 1828, 1830, and 1836. Local tradition has it that A. N. Buell was the first politician to organize a regular Reform political convention in Upper Canada as a means of securing the election of sympathetic candidates. During the 1825–37 period he carried on an active correspondence with other leading Reformers, such as Marshall Spring BIDWELL, William Lyon Mackenzie*, and Robert Baldwin*. He was also instrumental in drawing up several bills which brought about local reforms; one was a law allowing polls to be held at four locations in Leeds, supplanting the single poll which could be dominated by the Orange and Tory supporters of Ogle Robert GOWAN and Robert Sympson Jameson*. Both were unseated in 1835 as a result of their supporters' violence in the election of 1834.

Because of his political activity, Buell neglected both his business interests and his law practice to such an extent that in 1836 he was forced to undertake canal building contracts in New York State in hopes of recouping his fortunes. Thus he was living there when the Upper Canadian rebellion occurred in December 1837. Buell returned to

Bullock

Brockville in 1840 and was charged with treason by Gowan, his political enemy of long standing. He was able to clear himself only by obtaining numerous affidavits to his innocence. Equally distressing to Buell, the canal contracts had proven unprofitable with the result that he was forced to sell most of his patrimony to settle his debts, and finally had to apply for a government position to support his family.

Robert Baldwin, recognizing Buell's efforts on behalf of the Reform cause, appointed him registrar of Johnstown District (Leeds and Grenville counties) in 1842, a position he held until 1849. In 1849 he was offered two judgeships by Baldwin, but was forced to decline because of deafness. Instead, he was made clerk of the crown and pleas in the Court of Common Pleas, and registrar of the Court of Chancery at Toronto. In 1850 he became master in chancery, a position that he filled with distinction for 20 years. In 1870 he became accountant-general in chancery, from which position he retired in 1878 to his farm at Brockville. He died at Toronto two years later.

Buell was twice married, to Calcina Richards of Brockville, then to Ann Eliza Thorp. There were four daughters and two sons from his first marriage and no issue from his second.

LEO A. JOHNSON

MTCL, Baldwin papers, especially vols. 36, 64, 68, 73, 78. PAO, Harry D. Blanchard papers; A. N. Buell papers; Cartwright family papers; Frederick John French collection; Sir James R. Gowan and Ogle R. Gowan papers; Solomon Jones papers; Mackenzie-Lindsey collection; James Reynolds papers; Frederick Peter Smith collection. Ruth McKenzie, *Leeds and Grenville: their first two hundred years* (Toronto and Montreal, 1967), 65, 68, 120–21, 153. G. R. I. MacPherson, "The code of Brockville's Buells," unpublished MA thesis, University of Western Ontario, 1966.

BULLOCK, WILLIAM, naval officer, Church of England clergyman, and hymn-writer; b. 12 Jan. 1797 at Prittlewell, Essex, Eng.; d. 7 March 1874 at Halifax, N.S., and was buried in Camp Hill Cemetery.

William Bullock was educated at Bluecoat School in London. He entered the navy as a midshipman on the *Mutine* 15 Dec. 1815, and served at the bombardment of Algiers under Lord Exmouth [Edward Pellew] in 1816. Later, he joined the *Snap* as sailing-master's mate and assistant surveyor. The ship did extensive hydrographic surveys around the coasts of Newfoundland, where Bullock was disturbed by the apparent neglect of the spiritual needs of the people. On 4 Nov. 1821 he was officially discharged from the navy for reasons of health, and immediately offered to

serve in Newfoundland as a missionary for the Society for the Propagation of the Gospel. Bullock was ordained deacon on 31 March 1822 by George Henry Law, bishop of Chester, and raised to the priesthood two weeks later by George Pelham, bishop of Lincoln. He was appointed missionary at Trinity Bay, Newfoundland, in 1822. In 1823 he married Mary Clinch, daughter of John Clinch*, the former missionary at Trinity; they had ten children. Bullock was extremely popular with the people of his extensive mission, serving them as pastor, doctor, and magistrate until 1840.

After a brief period in St John's, he left for the mission of Digby, N.S., in the summer of 1841. Here he set to work with his usual energy and zeal, building four new churches and establishing several preaching stations. The latter were usually points at some distance from the main mission where the missionary occasionally held services. To hold the congregation together, he appointed some worthy layman, frequently the schoolmaster, to read prayers on the Sabbath. These centres often obtained the services of a regular minister and built churches of their own. Four preaching stations, Sandy Cove, Briar Island, South Range, and Roseway, which Bullock established, later built churches.

Bullock went to Halifax in 1847 for temporary duty, and in June of that year Bishop John Inglis* appointed him curate of St Paul's Cathedral; he also assisted in the work of supplying outlying missions. In 1848 he was placed in charge of St Luke's Chapel of Ease in addition to his work at St Paul's. When St Luke's became a separate parish in 1858, he was appointed its first rector, and under his leadership St Luke's became a very active church. On the death of Bishop Inglis in 1851, Hibbert Binney* had been appointed to the bishopric. In 1864, on Binney's urging, letters patent from Queen Victoria made St Luke's the cathedral church of the diocese of Nova Scotia. And since Bullock sincerely believed in the catholicity and mission of the Anglican Church, views totally in accord with the beliefs of the new bishop, Bullock's appointment as first dean of the new cathedral was not unexpected. He was assisted at St Luke's by George McCAWLEY, president of King's College. During much of his life Bullock was obsessed with the fear that he would leave his wife and children destitute, but his appointment to St Luke's removed this problem.

In 1854 William Bullock published a collection of 166 hymns, *Songs of the church*, which he dedicated to the SPG. The best-known of these, "We love the place, O God," composed for the opening of a new church in Trinity Bay, was later inserted in the official hymnbook of the Church of England. He frequently contributed devotional poems to the *Church Times* and sent birthday and anniversary greetings in poetic form.

Bullock was a man of tremendous energy and enthusiasm. He had a strong sense of duty to his parishioners, and was highly respected by his contemporaries.

C. E. THOMAS

Chester Records Office, EDA/1/10, Bishop of Chester's act book 1809–25. Lincolnshire Archives Office, Ord. Reg., I, f.7. PRO, Adm. 37/5904 (muster book of HMS *Mutine*); 37/6760 (muster book of HMS *Snap*). USPG, Journal of SPG, 33, p.254, 15 March 1822; SPG, C/CAN/NS, letter of William Bullock, 13 Sept. 1841; letter of John Inglis, 17 May 1847. R. H. Bullock, *A memoir of the very Rev. William Bullock, D.D., dean of Nova Scotia* (Halifax, 1899), 5, 25, 33. Harris, *Church of Saint Paul*, 207.

BUNN, THOMAS, lawyer, legislator, and politician; b. 16 May 1830 in the Red River Settlement, eldest son of Dr John Bunn* and Catherine Thomas; m. Isabella Clouston in 1854, and Rachel Harriott in 1859; d. 11 April 1875 at St Clements, Man.

Thomas Bunn was raised in the parish of St Paul (Middlechurch) and educated at the Red River Academy, and he settled in the parish of St Andrews. Bunn's mother was of part-Indian blood; his father was a local doctor and councillor of Assiniboia; Bunn himself became a member of the Church of England and a freemason. He was able, therefore, to have some influence in the Indian community and to enter English society in Red River. In January 1868 Bunn was appointed a member of the Council of Assiniboia and held this office until the council ceased to function in September 1870. On 17 Dec. 1869 he succeeded W. R. Smith as executive officer of the council with a salary of £100 per year.

In 1869 Louis Riel* had begun to organize resistance to the transfer of the North-West to the dominion of Canada without prearranged terms. Bunn was elected a representative from St Clements to the council of English and French parishes convened on 16 Nov. 1869 to draw up terms for entry. He hoped for a united front to negotiate these terms of union with Canada. Most English settlers, however, were disposed to think that Canada would be just, and if it were not, that Great Britain would ensure a fair settlement. Many English were willing to support Riel's policy of union through negotiation, not so much because they thought negotiation was necessary, but because they hoped thus to preserve peace in the Red River Settlement. Bunn tried indeed to pursue an intermediate position, and the strains were sometimes great. By accepting Riel's policy, Bunn, in a sense, made himself Riel's English half-breed lieutenant, despite the fact that there was no bond between the men.

On 19 and 20 Jan. 1870, a mass open-air meeting was held to hear Donald Alexander Smith*, commissioner of the Canadian government. Bunn was chairman of the discussion. It was decided that a convention should be held to prepare terms for negotiations with Canada, and that delegates should be elected. Bunn was one of those appointed to a committee to arrange the elections. He himself became a delegate from St Clements. From 27 January to 3 February, the convention prepared a second list of rights and approved the formation of a provisional government. Riel made Bunn secretary of state in the provisional government.

On 24 August the military forces of the crown under Colonel Garnet Joseph Wolseley* reached Upper Fort Garry (Winnipeg) and the provisional government was swept from power. Bunn survived its fall and may have been present at a meeting of the Council of Assiniboia which Wolseley revived in an attempt to settle the situation. Indeed, Bunn continued as usual in Red River society and set out to establish himself in the new order. As a man of some education and a fluent speaker with a judicious cast of mind, he decided to go into law. He was called to the bar of the new province of Manitoba in 1871, and was clerk to the First General Quarterly Court held in the new province on 16 May 1871. St Clements returned him as its first member to the provincial Legislative Assembly on 30 Dec. 1870. Thus Bunn's career decidedly bridged the way from the old order to the new. His early death in 1875 cut short his passage into it.

W. L. MORTON

Begg's Red River journal (Morton). *Canadian North-West* (Oliver), I, 71, 582, 620. *Rapport du comité spécial sur les causes des troubles du Territoire du Nord-Ouest en 1869–70* (Ottawa, 1874), 114–19. R.B. Mitchell, *Medicine in Manitoba; the story of its beginnings* ([Winnipeg, 1955]), 42. J. H. O'Donnell, *Manitoba as I saw it from 1869 to date, with flash-lights on the first Riel Rebellion* (Winnipeg and Toronto, 1909), 60.

BURNABY, ROBERT, commission merchant and legislator; b. 30 Nov. 1828 at Woodthorpe, Leicestershire, Eng., fourth son of the Reverend Thomas Burnaby and Sarah Meares; d. a bachelor, 10 Jan. 1878, at Woodthorpe.

Robert Burnaby came to British Columbia at the end of 1858 as an experienced civil servant

Bushby

from Her Majesty's Customs Office in London, and with a personal introduction to Governor James DOUGLAS from Sir Edward Bulwer-Lytton. Burnaby's first year on the Pacific coast was a busy one: he spent a short time as private secretary to Richard Clement Moody*, commander of the Royal Engineers at New Westminster; he explored for coal with Walter Moberly* at Burrard Inlet; and he made a short visit to San Francisco.

During this year he also founded the firm of Henderson and Burnaby, commission merchants, in partnership with Edward Henderson, an old school friend from Christ's Hospital and a man of means, who managed the London office. This type of business was precarious since the distance from sources of supply and risks in transportation encouraged overtrading and excessive speculation. The death of Henderson in 1865 and the general economic depression in Vancouver Island and British Columbia brought the firm to an end – a failure caused in part apparently by unwise investment in real estate. Burnaby then embarked upon a real estate and insurance business of his own. The exigencies of a mercantile career seem to have overwhelmed this man who, by upbringing and training, was more suited to a position in government service.

Robert Burnaby was intensely interested in the welfare of Vancouver Island and British Columbia, and did all in his power to promote stable economic conditions. Before the end of his second year in Victoria he was elected to the Legislative Assembly of Vancouver Island for the districts of Esquimalt and Metchosin, and he served his constituents well for five years. He was one of the founders of the Victoria Chamber of Commerce. During an 1866 visit to London on private business he attended a meeting of prominent Victoria merchants and officials who strongly favoured the union of the two colonies and other measures for developing and improving their economic prospects. This group carried its resolutions to the secretary of state for the colonies.

Burnaby was an active freemason and helped found the First Victoria Lodge in 1860. Among his recreational pursuits was a love of drama, and in 1863 he served as president of Victoria's Amateur Dramatic Association. Burnaby numbered among his intimate friends Colonel Moody, Arthur Thomas BUSHBY, Henry Pering Pellew Crease*, Judge Matthew Baillie Begbie*, Edward Graham ALSTON, and Thomas Elwyn*. In 1869 severe ill health caused Burnaby's retirement and five years later his return to England. Friends arranged for him to travel in the Hudson's Bay Company bark *Lady Lampson*; they later presented her captain, James Gaudin, with a generous purse in gratitude

for the attention he had paid the ailing Burnaby during the voyage.

Early in 1878 news reached Victoria that this "prominent and much respected merchant" had died. An honest, conscientious man of spirit, a clear-headed thinker, a "power" in his masonic lodge, a lucid speaker, full of fun, and clever, Burnaby has been fittingly commemorated in a number of place names in British Columbia including a lake, a strait, an island, a municipality, two mountain ranges, and finally Burnaby Mountain, the seat of Simon Fraser University.

MADGE WOLFENDEN

PABC, Robert Burnaby correspondence; Edward Bulwer-Lytton to James Douglas, letter of introduction, 8 Oct. 1858, testimonial re: Robert Burnaby. "Robert Burnaby and municipality," Art, Historical, and Scientific Assoc. of Vancouver, B.C., *Museum and Art Notes*, I (September 1949), 19–21. W. M. Draycot, "Early history of the Burnaby family," Art, Historical, and Scientific Assoc. of Vancouver, B.C., *Museum and Art Notes*, I (September 1949), 11–14; "The early history of the Burnaby family," *Burnaby Advertiser*, 17, 24, 31 July, 7 Aug. 1947. George Green and G. H. Slater, "The biography of Robert Burnaby," *Burnaby Advertiser*, 21, 28 Aug., 4 Sept. 1947. "Journal of Arthur Thomas Bushby" (Blakey Smith). R. L. Reid, *Grand Lodge of British Columbia A.F. & A.M.: historical notes and biographical sketches, 1848–1935* (Vancouver, n.d.), 7–8. G. H. Slater, "Robert Burnaby . . . ," Most Worshipful Grand Lodge of Ancient, Free and Accepted Masons of British Columbia, *Proceedings, 1944*, 137–53.

BUSHBY, ARTHUR THOMAS, public servant and amateur musician; b. 2 March 1835 in London, England, younger son of Joseph Bushby and Anne Sarah Stedman; d. 18 May 1875 in New Westminster, B.C.

Arthur Thomas Bushby's father was a highly respectable London merchant with West Indian estates. His mother, an accomplished linguist, was responsible for the first English translation (1863) of Hans Christian Andersen's *The ice maiden*, besides many other translations from Danish and Spanish, and was a frequent contributor of fiction to the *New Monthly Magazine*. Educated in England and on the continent, Bushby had become an exceedingly well trained and versatile amateur musician before he left London in 1858 to seek his fortune in the gold colony of British Columbia; it would seem indeed that he felt more at home in the musical world than in the business pursuits in which he had been employed under his father's direction. When he arrived in Victoria by way of Panama on Christmas Day 1858, he intended to establish himself as a merchant; but after one abortive attempt to set up a steam sawmill he entered government service where he proved himself "an upright, consistent and fearless public officer."

On 8 Feb. 1859 Governor James DOUGLAS (to whom he had brought a letter of introduction from the governor and committee of the Hudson's Bay Company in London) appointed him private secretary to Judge Matthew Baillie Begbie* – "just the thing I want," says Bushby's journal – and he was delighted to accompany Begbie on his first strenuous circuit on the mainland, acting as "clerk of the court, assize clerk, registrar, clerk of the arraigns &c" though he admits that he had never even been in a court of justice before. On 4 May 1859 he was officially appointed registrar of the Supreme Court of B.C., and on 8 May 1862, "in consequence of high testimony borne to his character & services by the Judge," Douglas appointed him registrar general of deeds for British Columbia at a salary of £500 a year. This promotion enabled him to marry, on 8 May 1862, the governor's third daughter, Agnes, to whom he had been unofficially engaged since 1859. He built a house for her in New Westminster, then the capital of British Columbia, and here the couple spent what seems to have been an unusually happy married life until "dear Arthur's" untimely death 13 years later. There were five children, four daughters (one of whom died in infancy) and one son.

Bushby held the office of registrar general until 1 June 1870, when he was replaced by Edward Graham ALSTON and himself became postmaster general (he had been appointed acting postmaster general on 12 April 1866). He was also registrar of joint stock companies (14 May 1866), justice of the peace (11 Jan. 1867), a commissioner of savings banks (18 June 1869), and a member of the Legislative Council (1869–70). He remained postmaster general until confederation when the dominion government took over the postal service of the province. In the meantime however Bushby had received his commission as county court judge (20 July 1869) and stipendiary magistrate (1 Aug. 1869) and had taken full charge of the District of New Westminster. As resident magistrate he was concerned with the administration of the jail, and both his humane feelings and his conscientious discharge of his duty are evidenced in his various representations to the government. He was indeed, as Douglas said, "a most worthy man, careful and attentive to the duties of his office," and he was both respected and loved wherever he went. In the fall of 1864 he travelled on horseback with the colonial secretary over the roughest of trails to the newly discovered Kootenay mines, and the party brought back safely from Wild Horse Creek (now Wild Horse River) what he calls "the treasure – some 70 lbs weight of gold dust." In the winter of 1872–73 he took the place of the resident magistrate in the Cariboo, winning the goodwill of all in his official capacity and the warm thanks of the Cariboo Amateur Dramatic Association at Williams Creek for his musical help in their charitable benefits. In December 1874 he went to Jervis Inlet, where he managed to settle a dispute with the Seechelt (Sechelt) Indians to the satisfaction of all concerned.

Bushby also played a prominent part in community affairs in New Westminster. He served on the Royal Columbian Hospital Board, 1860–71, and was appointed to the board of the public library in 1868. He was on the first board of school trustees, 1867, and was appointed inspector of schools for the District of New Westminster on 2 May 1870. He was also elected the first ensign of the New Westminster Volunteer Rifle Corps in 1863. In more purely social matters he was equally in demand, especially, of course, because of his musical abilities and his generous disposition. On 26 Jan. 1859 he had helped some 40 music lovers including Lumley FRANKLIN to found the Victoria Philharmonic Society, the first amateur musical organization west of the Canadian Rockies, and his fine tenor voice continued to be heard at concerts for worthy causes until the end of his life. At the New Westminster local dances he played violin or piano, occasionally even cornet and drum, and in the May Day celebrations for which the city was already becoming known he took an active part, being immensely popular with the children. In 1873 he tried acting for the first time, and was promptly elected president of the dramatic club. In a more serious vein Bushby was an exceedingly valuable supporter of Holy Trinity Church (Church of England). As his journal demonstrates, the firm foundation of his life was a simple Christian faith which expressed itself in all manner of good works, from acting as churchwarden, 1860–71, superintending the Sunday school and training the choir, to "pulling a bell" when needed and collecting pew rents.

Bushby's journal makes abundantly clear that he never spared himself, either in his official or in his private life, and he was only 40 when he died. He was buried in the Church of England cemetery at Sapperton (now part of New Westminster) with every possible mark of respect, and a memorial window was erected in Holy Trinity Church with the inscription "The memory of the Just is blessed."

DOROTHY BLAKEY SMITH

PABC, Bushby family papers; Arthur Thomas Bushby

Calf Shirt

papers; James Douglas, "A confidential report upon the character and qualifications of the principal officers of this government," Douglas to the Duke of Newcastle, 18 June 1863. British Columbia, *Blue Books*, 1859–70 (copies in PABC); Legislative Council, *Journals*, 1869–70. *British Columbia Government Gazette* (Victoria), 1871. *Colonist* (Victoria), 1858–75. *Government Gazette* (New Westminster, Victoria), 1866–70. *Mainland Guardian* (New Westminster, B.C.), 22 May 1875. *Victoria Daily Standard*, 20 May 1875. *Victoria Gazette*, 1858–59. R. E. Gosnell, "Sixty years of progress; British Columbia, portraits of some of those who laid its foundations . . . ," in E. O. S. Scholefield and R. E. Gosnell, *A history of British Columbia* (Vancouver, Victoria, 1913). "Journal of Arthur Thomas Bushby" (Blakey Smith).

C

CALF SHIRT. *See* ONISTAH-SOKAKSIN

CAMERON, ANGUS, North West Company partner and HBC chief factor; b. in 1782 or 1783 in the parish of Kirkmichael, Banffshire, Scotland, elder son of James Cameron and Janet Farquharson; d. at Nairn, Scotland, 11 Aug. 1876.

Although his uncle, Æneas Cameron*, was a partner of the North West Company in command of the Timiskaming District, Angus Cameron came to Canada on his own in the spring of 1801, engaging as a clerk with the company on 2 June. He arrived at Fort Timiskaming with the June canoes, surprising his uncle, who sent him a few months later to Matawagamingue, a frontier post on present-day Mattagami Lake, Ont. Apart from his being "an indifferent schollar and not very eager to improve himself," Æneas found him entirely satisfactory "in every other respect." Angus soon became master of Matawagamingue, remaining there until he succeeded to Fort Timiskaming in 1822.

During these years Cameron acquired tremendous influence over the Indians, whom he ruled autocratically but with genuine sympathy and understanding. After 1813 the Hudson's Bay Company had only one post in the Timiskaming District – Kenogamissi Lake, some 30 miles below Matawagamingue – and Cameron's outstanding success in opposing them there was no doubt chiefly responsible for his becoming commander of the district when Alexander McDougall* retired from Fort Abitibi in 1816. A few years later William McGillivray* was to describe Cameron as "the best trader" in the Southern Department, asserting that even as late as 1821 the combined Timiskaming and Lake Superior returns were valued at £20,000. Unlike the English servants, the Timiskaming traders remained for long periods at the same posts, and the loyalty of the Indians to them contributed greatly to the defeat of the HBC in that district and also slowed Timiskaming's orientation to Moose Factory after the union of 1821. The Indians' personal attachment to Cameron himself – and later to his nephew James Cameron* – also largely accounts for the failure in the area of early independent traders from Canada.

Cameron became a partner in the NWC about 1816. His contempt for his English neighbours made it hard for him to accept the union in 1821; his resentment doubtless was increased by his restriction, as a recent partner, to a chief tradership, despite the Montreal agents' preference for him over many of his seniors. Subsequently the agents' failure to notify him of Timiskaming's transfer from their control to the Southern Department led this proud, uncompromising man into a dispute with the governor and council at Moose Factory. He won his battle to retain command of Fort Timiskaming but, after inheriting a considerable fortune from Æneas in 1822, he apparently decided to retire on becoming eligible for a chief trader's interest. With this in mind he bought the late Alexander McDougall's farm at Lachine. Going to Montreal in the summer of 1826, however, he was faced with the bankruptcy of the agents with whom Æneas' legacy and all his own savings were deposited. Governor George Simpson*, not yet personally acquainted with him but aware of his importance to Timiskaming, suggested that he cancel his resignation. This Cameron was not inclined to do but, at Simpson's request, he did return to Fort Timiskaming for the 1826–27 season.

The following summer brought further troubles; the McDougall heirs, who had discovered they were not credited in the agents' accounts with the money Cameron had paid them, sued him, and the affair dragged on until settled out of court in 1835. Allowed bail within Lower Canada, Cameron re-entered the company's service and Simpson appointed him to Lac des Deux Montagnes, where trading opposition was rampant. His energy, skill, and amicable relationship with both the Iroquois and the Algonkin villages, as

114

well as with the Roman Catholic clergy, soon led to improvement and by 1831 his principal competitors had given up. Three years later, after petty traders had settled on Lake Timagami, Simpson sent him back to Timiskaming, giving him "carte blanche" in its direction. Again he quickly disposed of opposition, and continued progress in the district spoke, in Simpson's own word, "volumes" in his favour. Nevertheless since the preferment list was crowded with the overflow of the union he had to wait until 1838 to become chief factor.

By this time lumberers had reached Timiskaming's borders and in 1840, in an effort to discourage them, Simpson and Cameron began lumbering for the company on Lake Timiskaming. This experiment terminated on Cameron's retirement three years later, the losses having outstripped any possible value. Cameron himself now felt that the sooner the company exhausted Timiskaming the better, although in fact the post was to remain profitable longer than he seems to have anticipated.

Cameron returned to Scotland in the autumn of 1843; his three children preceded him but their mother, probably an Indian woman, of whom nothing is known, remained in Timiskaming. The following spring he bought the estate of Firhall, near Nairn, abandoning all thoughts of settling in Canada. In April 1845 he married Elizabeth Morison, who died in August 1846 after giving birth to a son. Like his uncle Æneas, Cameron suffered greatly from rheumatism, apparently a legacy of their years in "the wilds of Canada." Despite the affliction he was the longest surviving of the NWC partners.

When Angus Cameron, the most important of the succession of Camerons to command Timiskaming, went to the fort at the turn of the 19th century, the district was isolated by its geographical situation and by the deliberate policy of the NWC agents even from the rest of the Montreal trade. When he retired 42 years later, the Canadian presence was making itself felt; Roman Catholic missionaries were visiting the posts and lumberers had pushed beyond Lake Timiskaming. Like the best fur trade officers, Cameron combined initiative, managerial ability, and understanding of the Indians with the virtues of economy, honesty, and sobriety, and he played a decisive role in Timiskaming's most prosperous years, under both the NWC and the HBC. Even after he retired, his influence lingered on, to the company's advantage, for a decade or more.

ELAINE ALLAN MITCHELL

Cameron family papers, in possession of the author with restricted copies in PAO. HBC Arch. B.99/a/1–23 (Kenogamissi journals); B.99/e/1–8 (Reports); B.239/c/1 (York Factory correspondence); D.4/5–127 (George Simpson's correspondence outward); D.5/2–52 (George Simpson's correspondence inward).

CAMERON, DAVID, first chief justice of the Supreme Court of the colony of Vancouver Island; b. autumn 1804 in Perthshire, Scotland; d. 14 May 1872 near Victoria, B.C.

David Cameron spent his youth in Perth, Scotland, where relatives financed him as a cloth merchant in 1824. Cameron was "too liberal in giving credit" and the business failed. In 1830 he left for Demerara where he became the overseer of a sugar plantation, and in 1838 he acquired a small property of his own on the Essequibo River. He suffered serious losses, which he blamed on the effects of emancipation. He surrendered his property, and in 1851 applied to the courts for a legal discharge from his liabilities. Cameron was by then managing a sugar plantation "with a fair income, and every comfort consistent with [his] position," yet this application was unopposed. During his residence in Demerara, Cameron married Cecilia Eliza Douglas Cowan, James DOUGLAS' sister, whose first husband had evidently deserted her. Douglas seems to have been involved in the offer to Cameron of an appointment as Hudson's Bay Company agent at the Nanaimo coal mines on Vancouver Island, which HBC Governor Andrew Colvile made in a letter of 1 March 1853. Principally because his wife's failing health required a more temperate climate, Cameron accepted the position, at £150 yearly plus board. The Camerons, with their daughter Edith Rebecca, who was about ten years old, arrived in Victoria aboard the *Vancouver* in July 1853.

In September 1853 the Legislative Council of Vancouver Island authorized the creation of a Court of Common Pleas with jurisdiction in civil cases involving claims between £100 and £2,000; their action followed complaints by Governor Douglas of improper decisions by the Justice's Court. The council appointed Cameron judge for the new court at £100 per annum and requested him to draw up its rules and regulations. On 2 December the council established a Supreme Court of Civil Justice for the colony, to deal with cases of £50 or more, and right of appeal to governor and council. Cameron was appointed judge, his salary of £100 to be paid from duties on licensed ale-houses.

Opponents of the dominant "Family-Company Compact" at once seized upon Cameron's appointment, complaining that the council members were mostly HBC servants, that Cameron was an HBC employee and personally tied to Douglas, and

Cameron

that he lacked legal training. They were led by Thomas Skinner* and Edward Edwards Langford*, two of the four appointees to the first Justices' Court, and by James COOPER, a member of the council who had originally supported Cameron, and the Reverend Robert John Staines*, chaplain to the HBC and Victoria's schoolmaster.

On 5 December Cameron heard a complaint by Emanuel Douillet against Staines, who, with a magistrate's warrant from Skinner, had entered his premises to remove pigs which Staines said had been stolen (or strayed) from his Metchosin farm. Finally, on 2 Feb. 1854, Staines was exonerated and Douillet was fined and imprisoned; but Staines felt that by acting on Douillet's complaint Cameron had attempted "to convict the innocent and screen the guilty." Meanwhile, on 10 January, 90 settlers had signed a petition to Douglas protesting the establishment of the Supreme Court and particularly Cameron's appointment. But on the following day 54 freeholders protested against the petition, urging Douglas not to comply with the wishes of those who, having "little or no vested interest in the island," sought "to rescind important enactments framed expressly to protect property" thereby jeopardizing law and order. On 4 February a public meeting, chaired by Cooper, subscribed $480 to send Staines to England. The petitions he was to carry to Queen Victoria and the Duke of Newcastle [Henry Pelham Clinton], secretary of state for the colonies, were signed by James Cooper and 69 others on 1 March. Her majesty was requested to launch a strict inquiry into the establishment of the court and the appointment of Cameron. The petition to the Duke of Newcastle cited Cameron's "improperly close family connexion with the Governor," his lack of legal training, his "notorious and gross partiality, acrimony, malice and indecorum," his position as HBC clerk at Nanaimo, and his strenuous effort "to defeat the ends of justice" and "most vehement exertions on the side of knavery" (references to the recently concluded case of *Douillet* v. *Staines*). Staines died en route in a shipwreck, but on 20 April 1854 the petitions were sent to England.

In December Douglas received a letter from Sir George Grey, Newcastle's successor, requesting a report. Douglas staunchly defended both the establishment of the court and Cameron's temporary appointment, and concluded that the petitioners' "grievances were less real than imaginary." There matters rested until by order in council of 4 April 1856 the Supreme Court of Civil Justice of the Colony of Vancouver's Island was established, and on 25 April Cameron was confirmed as chief justice without jurisdiction in criminal cases. Soon after receiving his warrant, Cameron resigned his HBC office. The HBC properly felt colonial officials should be paid by the local legislature, but as the latter did not act Cameron continued at his 1853 salary until 8 Aug. 1860 when the assembly awarded him £800 annually, payable from the colony's land revenues.

On 17 Feb. 1857 the Legislative Council gave unanimous consent to Cameron's "Rules and Manner of Proceeding to be observed in the Supreme Court of Civil Justice of Vancouver's Island." The Victoria *Gazette* published the "Rules" in book form in 1858, the first book to be printed in the colony. Cameron was a member of Governor Douglas' party which proclaimed the establishment of the Colony of British Columbia at Fort Langley on 19 Nov. 1858. On 6 July 1859 Douglas appointed the chief justice to the Legislative Council of the Colony of Vancouver Island where at the time of his retirement he was serving as president.

The reform party had not rested in its efforts to embarrass Cameron. In London in May 1857 James Cooper testified before the parliamentary committee investigating HBC affairs that Cameron was unqualified for his post because "before he can decide upon a case, he has to refer to his books even in the most common case." Demands for his removal increased after Amor De Cosmos* began publishing the *British Colonist* in December 1858. De Cosmos, who relished the courtroom "rows" between the attorney general and the chief justice, was particularly alarmed in June 1861 when Cameron stated his opinion that certain acts of the assembly were contrary to law. The legislature sought to force Cameron's removal by refusing to permit bills to go to a third reading, and a motion to inquire into Cameron's seeming threat to legislative independence lost narrowly.

Cameron, with Douglas' support, withstood these attacks, but E. E. Langford was to cause special difficulties in the 1860s. At the opening session of the first Legislative Assembly of Vancouver Island on 12 Aug. 1856, Governor Douglas had appointed Cameron to administer the oath. Langford, after receiving the oath, protested the property qualifications for office holding. Unable to produce certification of qualification he was denied a seat in the assembly. In late 1859 he stood again and in his election address made ill-considered attacks on the governor, the council, and particularly the chief justice. A biting parody of Langford's address, possibly written by Judge Matthew Baillie Begbie*, was printed and widely distributed on New Year's Day 1860. It so discredited Langford that he withdrew from the election on 5 January and initiated a libel suit for

£2,000 damages against the printer. The suit was heard before Cameron on 16 and 17 April and a nonsuit was entered. But Cameron charged Langford with contempt for refusing to answer relevant questions and ordered a 24-hour imprisonment and a £10 fine. On the following day Cameron received a threatening letter from Langford describing the proceedings as "vile and illegal." Langford returned to England in January 1861; in June he submitted a complaint to the Duke of Newcastle in which he made charges against government officials on Vancouver Island and characterized his trial as "improper, illegal and vexatious."

In May and June 1862 Langford forwarded letters to Newcastle concerning Cameron's early financial difficulties and charged that Cameron was a man of obscure origins, without legal training, and an "uncertified bankrupt." Douglas, on request, in February 1863 forwarded statements from those charged, and explained that in 1853 he had chosen Cameron in preference to Langford, the senior magistrate, because the latter was "singularly deficient in judgment, temper, and discretion, and was much inferior both in legal and general knowledge to Mr. Cameron." He repeated an earlier statement that Cameron's appointment was originally to be temporary, and he offered to ask for the chief justice's resignation if the colonial secretary desired it. Cameron's own explanation of his personal affairs was accepted by Newcastle as "very straightforward and satisfactory," but he was not prepared to say whether Cameron should continue in office. Langford's complaint against Cameron did not proceed any further with the government and he next tried the House of Commons. The Colonial Office was asked for the relevant correspondence but no other action was taken and Langford was finally defeated in his efforts to obtain redress from what he considered to be arbitrary government and political privilege.

The reform party of the colony had again failed to dislodge Cameron, who emerged from the sordid affair with his dignity and his job. However, it was clear that a professionally qualified judge was needed as the affairs of the courts became more complex. Amor De Cosmos introduced a motion before the assembly on 4 Feb. 1864 requesting the governor to pension Cameron, who was to be replaced as chief justice by a qualified barrister from England. The motion passed, with Cameron's pension to be £500 yearly. Cameron's opinions were solicited by the colonial secretary, William Alexander George Young, the husband of his step-daughter Cecilia Eliza Cowan, and Cameron assented to the resolution provided that

its terms were embodied in an act of the legislature. The act was passed in March, and upon the arrival of his successor, Joseph Needham, Cameron tendered his resignation to Governor Arthur Edward Kennedy* on 11 Oct. 1865.

On 2 Jan. 1867 it was announced that Governor Frederick Seymour* had appointed Cameron a justice of the peace, a position he held until January 1871. He served on the Board of Education for Vancouver Island, as a road commissioner for the districts of Esquimalt and Sooke, and as one of three commissioners appointed to carry out the provisions of "The Tax Sale Repeal Ordinance, 1867, Amendment Act." For the third time in his life, Cameron faced severe financial difficulties, and on 20 Jan. 1871 he filed a petition of bankruptcy in the Supreme Court of British Columbia. Cameron's debts totalled $22,055.08, and the creditors received an assignment of £150 from his £500 pension as well as his life assurance policy and a large portion of his properties in the Esquimalt District. In October 1871 Cameron was one of eight candidates nominated to represent Esquimalt in the legislature. He came forward, he said, to assist in working out responsible government and to promote the transition from the provincial to the Canadian tariff, which he felt would lower the cost of wheat and flour. He ran third in a final field of six candidates, losing the second seat for the district by only three votes. De Cosmos, now editing the *Victoria Daily Standard*, renewed old animosities in an editorial entitled "The Living and the Dead Politicians" in which he accused Cameron of being "up for sale again," resurrected by the "ring," and of coming forward "to fill Mr. Cameron's empty pocket; not to serve the country."

This was the last public outcry against Cameron, for on 14 May 1872 he died at his home, Belmont, after a severe attack of gout from which he had suffered for at least a year. Too late, the *British Colonist* faintly praised Cameron as "a man respected by all who knew him – a man without an enemy, and one who may be considered one of the founders of the prosperity of the Province."

WILLIAM R. SAMPSON

PABC, British Columbia, Supreme Court, Orders in Bankruptcy, March 1870–May 1875, "In the Supreme Court of British Columbia, in bankruptcy in the matter of David Cameron a bankrupt"; David Cameron papers; Colonial correspondence, David Cameron files. G.B., Parl., House of Commons paper, 1863, XXXVIII, 507, pp.487–540, *Miscellaneous papers relating to Vancouver Island, 1848–1863.* ... *Minutes of the Council of Vancouver Island, commencing August 30th, 1851, and terminating ... February 6th, 1861,* ed. E. O. S. Scholefield (Archives of

Cameron

British Columbia, Memoir no.2, Victoria, 1918). *Daily British Colonist* (Victoria), 1 Jan., 12, 19 Feb., 10 June, 21, 29 Nov. 1859; 26 April, 4 Aug. 1860; 22 Jan., 6, 7 June, 2, 3, 12, 16 July 1861; 16 Feb., 17 March, 21 April, 27 May, 8 Oct. 1864; 12 Oct. 1865; 2 April, 6 Aug. 1866; 9 Nov. 1868; 27 May 1869; 15 June, 10 Aug., 13, 19, 28 Oct. 1871; 15 May 1872. W. K. Lamb, "Some notes on the Douglas family," *BCHQ*, XVII (1953), 41–51. S. G. Pettit, "The trials and tribulations of Edward Edwards Langford," *BCHQ*, XVII (1953), 5–40. G. H. Slater, "Rev. Robert John Staines: pioneer priest, pedagogue, and political agitator," *BCHQ*, XIV (1950), 187–240.

CAMERON, JOHN HILLYARD, lawyer, businessman, politician, Orangeman, and prominent Church of England layman; b. at Blendecques, France, 14 April 1817, son of Angus Cameron; d. at Toronto, Ont., 14 Nov. 1876.

Angus Cameron, a soldier in the 79th Highlanders during the Napoleonic wars, remained after 1815 with the British forces in France, where his son John Hillyard was born. In 1825, when Angus was posted to Kingston, the family emigrated to Upper Canada. Hillyard attended Kilkenny College in Ireland, then at Kingston the Midland District grammar school and a co-educational school, operated by the Reverend John Cruikshank. He was briefly a schoolmate of Oliver Mowat* and John A. Macdonald*.

Angus was posted to York (Toronto) in 1831, and John Hillyard was sent to Upper Canada College. He then began the study of law under Henry John Boulton*, a Family Compact Tory. The rebellion of 1837 broke out as his legal training was coming to an end; he was a captain in the Queen's Rangers, and on 4 Dec. 1837 Colonel James FitzGibbon* sent him to Toronto to warn of the approach of William Lyon Mackenzie*'s forces. After serving briefly in the Toronto area he helped guard the Niagara frontier. Cameron was only 20 at the time, and the rebellion almost certainly helped to strengthen his conservative outlook.

Cameron returned to Toronto and was called to the bar of Upper Canada in 1838. He immediately formed a partnership with J. Godfrey Spragge*. In the 1840s Cameron built a lucrative law practice and a province-wide reputation. His work included criminal cases, and he produced two legal compendia. In 1840 he was a commissioner for the revision of the statutes of Upper Canada, and, as reporter to the Court of Queen's Bench in Canada West (still popularly called Upper Canada) from 1843 to 1846, he was responsible for inaugurating the *Upper Canada Law Reports*; he was appointed a QC in 1846. He was chairman of the 1856–57 commission for the consolidation of the statutes of Upper Canada. In 1860 he was elected treasurer of the Law Society of Upper Canada, and was called to the bar of Quebec in 1869. In 1843 he had married Elizabeth, the third daughter of H. J. Boulton. She died in 1844, leaving a son, and in 1849 Cameron married Ellen Mallet, daughter of an American general. They had two sons and two daughters.

Politics, a sure route to public recognition, was an easy one for a lawyer to take, and Cameron entered both municipal and provincial politics in 1846. In Toronto he was elected alderman for St Andrew's ward for 1846–47 and 1851–52, and for St John's ward in 1854 (when his ward colleague was Ogle Robert Gowan) and 1855.

In the provincial sphere, Cameron gravitated naturally to the Conservative group. William Henry Draper, a "moderate Conservative," was government leader, but only by maintaining a precarious balance in the Legislative Assembly. Draper was dependent upon the Upper Canadian moderates and Tories elected after Lord Metcalfe*'s emotional appeals in the election of 1844, and they were far from a homogeneous group. The moderates refused to follow the Tories, and the Tories in turn bitterly resented Draper's support for the union of Upper and Lower Canada in 1841. The Tory faction was largely unrepresented in the Executive Council in order to retain the moderates' support; it stood by Draper, but only because to desert him would be to betray Metcalfe and his policies. Moreover, Draper had virtually no personal following, and attracted few French Canadians.

Within this near-vacuum of leadership Cameron seemed an attractive young politician. Reasonably moderate, he was respected as a lawyer and an able administrator. His popularity in Toronto might be sufficient to check the Tories within their stronghold. Although Cameron, as counsel to the Corporation of King's College, had opposed Draper's university bill of 1845, he was immediately offered the non-ministerial post of solicitor general for Upper Canada. His acceptance on 1 July 1846 was a move hardly calculated to please the Tory faction: Draper had just dismissed a Tory leader, Henry Sherwood*, from that post "because he [had] not given the administration his whole-hearted support." In later years Cameron was taunted with the epithet, "extreme Conservative," but in 1846 he clearly regarded himself as a follower of Draper, not of Sherwood. Cameron was asked to prepare two bills, one for a "uniform system of trying contested Elections," the other for the "better administration of Justice in Upper

Canada." He had to be in the assembly in order to present his bills: the constituency of Cornwall was opened and Cameron was elected in August 1846.

With Sherwood, his potential successor, removed, Draper turned to a personal objective – the post of puisne judge of the Court of Queen's Bench in Upper Canada. On the anticipated death of the incumbent, Christopher Hagerman*, Draper promptly resigned as attorney general, and was appointed judge on 28 May 1847. Draper had hoped to choose his own successor and first asked Cameron to take over as government leader and attorney general west. He declined, arguing "that retaining [the] position of solicitor-general of Upper Canada will best serve the interests of the Province." Sherwood then became Draper's successor. Cameron consoled himself with promotion to a seat on the Executive Council, obtained on 22 May 1847.

The invitation to lead the Upper Canadian Conservatives was the peak of Cameron's political career. But he was not, in fact, in a position to succeed Draper. Cameron was asked because Draper was reluctant to surrender to Sherwood without at least token resistance. Draper's following was small and his choice limited to a handful of men, notably Cameron, John A. Macdonald, and William Morris*. None of these had the identification with Metcalfe's policies that enabled Draper to exercise some control over the Tories. Led by Allan MacNab* and Sherwood, the Tory members, the largest group of government supporters, were, consequently, now in control.

The political outlook, however, was unpleasant for the Conservatives. The new governor general, Lord Elgin [Bruce*], had no intention of bolstering up Sherwood's regime when the assembly was dissolved late in 1847. In the ensuing elections the government suffered overwhelming electoral defeat by the Reformers under Robert Baldwin* and Louis-Hippolyte La Fontaine*. Cameron lost in Kent to Malcolm CAMERON and retained Cornwall by only 16 votes amid "evidence of gross irregularities." With his colleagues he left office on 10 May 1848.

Cameron was one of the few Conservative leaders to survive the election, and in 1850 George Duck described him as "the great gun of the Tories. . . ." But with the Conservatives virtually obliterated in Lower Canada and reduced to a small rump in Upper Canada, revival would require an alliance with French Canadians and policies attractive to moderate opinion in Upper Canada. Cameron could not provide this kind of leadership – he had no important ties with French Canada or its leaders, and his prominent role in

the Church of England as a close colleague of Bishop John Strachan* and a strong defender of the church's claims to the clergy reserves alienated moderate opinion in Upper Canada. Dedicated to his church's claims to sectarian educational rights and closely identified with MacNab and Toronto conservatism, Cameron, though able, energetic, and popular in many quarters, was not palatable to most Upper Canadian moderates.

Confusion within Reform ranks after 1849, moreover, did not assist the Conservatives. Instead, new Reform leaders, Francis Hincks* and Augustin-Norbert Morin*, won an easy electoral victory in 1851. Cameron was not a candidate. He may have wanted rest, having been ill several times during the 1840s. The less taxing municipal sphere occupied him politically until 1854. In that year he obtained control of the Toronto *British Colonist* from Samuel Thompson*, whom he retained as editor. According to Thompson, "It had been a semi-weekly paper; he [Cameron] offered to furnish five thousand dollars a year to make it a daily journal, independent of party control; stipulated for no personal influence over its editorial views, leaving them entirely in my discretion. . . ." The arrangement continued until 1857.

Cameron contested the Toronto seat in 1854. He and John George Bowes* won, defeating Henry Sherwood, William Henry BOULTON, and George Percival RIDOUT. Cameron was now the senior member for Upper Canada's largest and wealthiest town. His return coincided with the formation of the Morin–MacNab–Macdonald Liberal-Conservative administration, and Macdonald, who had earlier dismissed Cameron as lacking in "general intelligence, and . . . [as] altogether devoid of political reading," successfully excluded him from the ministry.

Yet, in the crucial question facing the ministry, that of the clergy reserves, Cameron, striving to save as much as possible for the Church of England, differed from Macdonald only in degree. Macdonald was willing to see the favoured churches retain much of their income, and, in the settlement of 1854 whereby clergymen with recognized rights to income agreed to commute their claims, the Church of England, though losing its reserve lands, acquired a large capital fund which accrued to its benefit as the annuitants died. Cameron was given considerable credit for his church's success; he had worked closely with Strachan, and during the protracted and delicate negotiations with many of the annuitants he represented both the government and the church. His vigour in upholding the vested rights of privilege, and his refusal to support the coalition in the introduction of an elective upper house, however, lumped him in many minds with the "old Tories." His stand on these issues alienated Macdonald, who was further irritated in 1856 when Cameron supported George Brown in the latter's dispute with Macdonald over the results of the committee Brown had chaired in 1849 investigating conditions at the Portsmouth Penitentiary.

The "Corrigan Incident" gave Cameron an opportunity to intensify his campaign against the coalition. In February 1856 a jury found seven Roman Catholics not guilty of Robert Corrigan*'s murder at Lotbinière, and many Upper Canadian Protestants screamed indignation. Cameron took their lead and on 7 March moved in parliament a resolution asking for publication of Judge Jean-François-Joseph Duval*'s charge to the jury, which many Protestants felt had been irregular. It carried but the government, after winning a vote of confidence, refused to resign or to produce Duval's charge. The damage had nevertheless been done: divided internally and battered from without by Cameron, Brown, Grits, and Rouges, MacNab's government was disintegrating. MacNab was forced out as premier in May 1856 and Macdonald became leader of Upper Canada's Conservatives. John Charles Dent* was doubtless correct when he commented that "Mr. Cameron was very willing to have greatness thrust upon him. . . ." Cameron was not, however, a viable alternative to MacNab. The considerations that militated against his success in 1847–51 remained factors of real importance. The "Corrigan Incident" indicated the extent to which he would make use of religious and racist passion to build a regional following in Upper Canada. French Canada was outside his range of potential appeal. Cameron now "went into continuing opposition," with an occasional and small following of disgruntled backbenchers. Whatever leadership aspirations he retained were smashed by the financial panic of 1857.

Like many of his contemporaries, Cameron had developed an interest in transportation ventures. He served as a director of the Toronto and Guelph Railway (absorbed in 1856 by the Grand Trunk Railway) and as solicitor for the Great Western Railway, and was part-owner of the Niagara Falls Suspension Bridge Company. He was also heavily involved in insurance. He helped found the Canada Life Assurance Company in 1847 and was elected a director. He was chosen president of the Provincial Insurance Company in 1859, a position he held for many years, and later served as chairman of the Canadian board of the Edinburgh Life Insurance Company, and director of the Canadian Life Assurance Company and the Beaver Mutual Fire Insurance Association.

Among his earliest business ventures was the purchase of large tracts of land in the Toronto area, but it was heavy investments in speculative English securities, through the brokerage firm of Duncan Sherman and Company of New York, that made him a wealthy man. His paper profits in the boom of the mid-1850s were enormous. But in the fall of 1857 investment money dried up after a financial panic and an international depression followed. Canada was hard-hit because of her orgy of land and railway speculation during the early 1850s and a crop failure which coincided with the business crisis. Duncan Sherman and Company collapsed, and as Samuel Thompson explained: "Drafts on London were dishonoured, and Mr. Cameron's bankers there, to protect themselves, sold without notice the securities he had placed in their hands. . . ."

Cameron's losses reached the staggering sum of £100,000. Although he must have realized the futility of his decision, he promised to repay his debts pound for pound. What assets remained were liquidated or mortgaged, and much of his land was sold. Using Toronto properties as collateral, he borrowed large sums from the Church Society, in transactions later attacked as too much in his favour, and from the Commercial Bank. For the remainder of his life Cameron carried the burden of these heavy debts. All other interests suffered as he strove, chiefly through the practice of law, to raise large sums of money. When he died his liabilities still exceeded his assets by $200,000.

His political career also suffered immediate decline. The *Colonist* could no longer be supported; instead it became an organ of the Macdonald–George-Étienne Cartier regime. Much of his political independence vanished; within a few months he started to receive legal patronage from Macdonald.

One of Cameron's strongest political bases had been his connection with the Church of England. Deeply committed to its welfare, and through it to education, he had served both causes in a variety of ways. With an early law partner, James McGill Strachan, the bishop's son, he represented the missionary service and the Society for the Propagation of the Gospel in Upper Canada. A representative Church of England leader, he was appointed to the first senate of the University of Toronto in 1850, and served on the University Visitation Commission in 1850, "to report a code of proper Statutes, Rules and Ordinances for the Government of the University [of Toronto]," and on the endowment board of the university and of Upper Canada College in 1850; he was a member of the council of the latter. When John Strachan established an Anglican university in the province following the creation of the University of Toronto, Cameron introduced Trinity College's incorporation bill in the assembly in 1851. After several years on the council of Trinity College (and as a professor of law from 1852), he was elected to succeed Sir John Beverley Robinson* as second chancellor of the college in 1863, a post he held until his death. Cameron took these educational duties seriously; he founded scholarships and involved himself in financial management. Cameron was also sufficiently influential within the church to overcome Strachan's reluctance to have a successor bishop appointed in the see of Toronto; at the diocesan synod in 1865 he moved the resolution that in 1866 permitted Alexander Neil BETHUNE to be elected coadjutor.

But grief as well as satisfaction came from his church connection. Division had been growing within the Church of England between the low church and high church parties. The rupture was made open in the election of the bishop of the new diocese of Huron in 1857. Trinity College became a focal point of accusations from the low churchmen, especially Bishop Benjamin CRONYN of Huron; in 1863 Huron College was founded in opposition to Trinity. Cameron's close identification with Trinity College, and his association with Strachan and Bethune, both regarded as high churchmen, linked him with that group, and he lost his position as a representative churchman.

His association with the church's investment fund also proved damaging. In 1861 the Toronto *Globe* charged that he could not account for the money from the clergy reserves commutation fund entrusted to him by the Church Society for investment. It claimed that he handed over instead "a quantity of land which though not of the full value of the monies placed in his hands was apparently accepted by the Church Society." J. W. GAMBLE, chairman of the committee which administered the commutation fund, and C. J. Campbell of the executive committee, immediately issued "a flat denial" of the charges. The *Globe*, doubtless influenced by the fact that Gamble and Campbell were well-known Conservative stalwarts, stuck by its charge.

More serious was the accusation in May 1865 by W. H. Boulton, a cousin of Cameron's first wife, that large sums administered by the Church Society had been manipulated by Cameron for his personal benefit, and that the Church Society, leading members of which were Cameron's friends and political colleagues, camouflaged the situation through an inadequate auditing arrangement. The society's management committee exonerated Cameron, but nonetheless his reputation suffered. The *Globe* pointed out that the Church Society

refused to approve a full and competent audit, and it in fact established a strong case that Cameron had borrowed more than $40,000 from church funds on "insufficient" security.

With this series of reversals in business and church connections, and Macdonald confirmed as Conservative leader, Cameron, to retain any independent political authority, needed another power base. He had found it in the Orange order. During the 1840s and 1850s the Orange order had gained both in numbers and in respectability. It had moved, under Ogle R. Gowan's leadership, into a continuing alliance with Conservative moderates like Macdonald. But George Benjamin* became grand master in 1846 and he tended towards Upper Canadian sectionalism, suspicious of any Conservative alliance with French-speaking Catholics and not unwilling to work with Reformers. A schism occurred in 1853 when Gowan attempted to unseat Benjamin as grand master. Cameron, who joined a Toronto lodge, no.507, in 1856, was given much credit for the reunion in that year of the two grand lodges, under George Lyttleton Allen*. Cameron was a follower of Benjamin, but, although willing to oppose the Cartier-Macdonald government on regional and racial issues, he was not in favour of an alliance with the Reformers. He was elected grand master in 1859 and served until 1870, when he was succeeded by Mackenzie Bowell*.

The Orange order became the backbone of lower class support for the Conservative party. Although Cameron's role as leader of this group has sometimes appeared to be anomalous, he was doing what the Duke of Cumberland, a grand master of the British lodges, had done earlier in Britain. He might be using the order for his own political ends, but Orangemen would also benefit in obtaining a leader who was a member of the social élite – a man who combined prestige with organizational ability. As grand master, Cameron quickly undertook a major reorganization, establishing three grand lodges in the Canadas, for Western Canada, Central Canada, and Eastern Canada, in 1859. A grand lodge was provided for each of the Maritime colonies, and each of the three western districts of Saskatchewan, British Columbia, and Vancouver Island was given permission to form a separate grand lodge as soon as it had ten primary lodges; by 1863 organizational work was under way in both Newfoundland and British Columbia. Cameron also involved himself in international Orange activities.

A crisis involving the order was occasioned in 1860 by the visit of the Prince of Wales to Canada. Because the Orange order was banned in Britain, the prince was advised by the Duke of Newcastle

Cameron

to give no official recognition to the order in Canada. Orangemen were infuriated by what they regarded as a slur on their loyalty. In a series of comic-opera incidents at Kingston and elsewhere, Orangemen strove to have the prince pass under an Orange arch or to recognize the order in some equivalent manner. Newcastle was generally successful in avoiding official contact with the Orangemen, who directed much of their anger at the Canadian government, and at Macdonald in particular. Cameron muted Orange fury with Macdonald while collecting signatures for a petition, protesting Newcastle's advice and affirming Orange loyalty, which he took to London in 1861. His motivation is difficult to assess. Perhaps it was to prevent the "Orange Order from breaking completely away from Sir John Macdonald," as Richard Cartwright* thought, but his massive petition has been seen by a modern historian, D. G. Creighton, as a threat to the Conservative ministry: "Acclaimed once more, brought suddenly back to something like his old prominence, Cameron was virtually leading an anti-ministerial wing of Conservative Orangemen. . . ." Certainly Cameron sought more influence, which would add to his prestige and give him additional patronage power and a voice in making policy. Consistent with his Benjaminite views, he was a strong supporter of representation by population, and by advocating regional policies he was strengthening his political position in Upper Canada. But his personal financial struggles precluded the accepting of office. What Cameron wanted was influence, not formal leadership. His new base could possibly give him such influence within the Conservative party as Macdonald's ally, if Macdonald could accept the fact that Cameron was no threat to his leadership.

Cameron ran against George Brown in the Toronto by-election resulting from the accession to power of the Reformers in 1858, but lost in this endeavour, which was probably not very serious. In the general election of 1861, with his finances improving, he successfully contested Peel, an Orange stronghold, and held the seat until 1867. Back in the assembly after an absence of four years (he was not a candidate in 1857), he found a troubled ministry. The cabinet underwent chronic reorganization in 1861–62, and Macdonald had difficulty maintaining his position. Representation by population had become so popular in Upper Canada that many Conservatives espoused it in spite of Macdonald's stubborn refusal to endanger his alliance with the French Canadians by it. Conservative advocates of rep by pop would have to be admitted to the cabinet, but Macdonald would not have Cameron. There is no conclusive evidence, however, that Cameron wanted to enter the cabinet in 1861. The next year he claimed that he was asked but this claim too is unsupported. Cameron did cooperate with Macdonald in the delicate task of cabinet reorganization in 1862, as intermediary between Macdonald and Thomas Clark Street, a rep by pop Tory from Welland.

After the fall of the Cartier-Macdonald government in 1862, Macdonald overcame his old suspicion that Cameron was a rival for leadership, and Cameron in turn was willing to accept a minor position in Canadian public life. Their *rapprochement* was sealed at a public dinner in February 1863, when Cameron affirmed his loyalty to Macdonald and assured Conservatives that their differences had been resolved. Differences of view could now prove useful rather than harmful; in 1863, for example, when Cameron voted against third reading of Richard Scott*'s education bill, he helped soothe militantly Protestant Conservatives who saw the bill as a manifestation of "French domination." So firm was the reconciliation that Macdonald attempted to bring Cameron into the short-lived Macdonald–Sir Étienne-Paschal Taché* government of 1864. Unable to have the attorney generalship, Cameron refused, "as I would never take any office in any Ministry which was outside of my profession." Yet Cameron knew that as leader Macdonald must be attorney general west; he himself could not give up the full-time practice of law. But he would support the ministry: "I must show myself in the House . . . or my friends here will think that there is something wrong, and that I am not giving the government the support which they ought to receive."

Cameron supported confederation in 1865, but with reservations. He was enthusiastic about transcontinental expansion and anxious to see rep by pop effected; he also felt that the alternative to confederation was annexation to the United States. He preferred legislative union, but he was confident that it would come. His main objection was to the lack of public involvement in the confederation movement. He wanted "a constitutional appeal . . . to the people," but was resigned to the failure of a resolution to that effect. When the new constitution for Ontario was debated, Cameron moved for a two-house legislature; this motion too was lost.

The Fenian troubles of 1866 illustrated Cameron's usefulness to the regime; Lord Monck* asked him to assist in muting Orange–Catholic hostility, as "there is a certain amount of bad feeling beginning to exhibit itself between Protestants and Roman Catholics . . . in connection with the late Fenian raids. . . ." Later in 1866 and in 1867 he was associated with Robert Alexander HARRISON in the prosecution of many Fenian invaders. In 1868 he displayed his professional independence by defending Patrick James Whelan*, the murderer of D'Arcy McGee*.

In 1867 Cameron contested Peel for the House of Commons. He was out of the country for most of the campaign, attending the founding meeting of the Imperial Grand Orange Council at London, and he needed assistance from Macdonald in a contest so doubtful that Macdonald postponed it for as long as he could (a practice made possible by not holding simultaneous elections). Cameron ultimately won a narrow victory.

Cameron's political standing declined rapidly after 1867. In 1856 Macdonald had offered Cameron a judgeship; when a judicial appointment for Cameron was mooted in 1867, Macdonald dismissed it. Later in 1867 Cameron wanted the speakership of the House of Commons and "pressed" his claims "vigorously"; James Cockburn* obtained the post. As his independence declined, Cameron's loyalty to the ministry increased. He sometimes assisted the prime minister in drafting legislation, and often acted for Conservatives in contested election cases. Liberal leader Edward Blake* regarded Cameron as a ministerial tool, describing him in 1873 as "the gentleman who had never hesitated to come to the front on doubtful and desperate issues. . . ."

Cameron's involvement in the Pacific scandal dramatically reveals his political decline. In 1873 he became chairman of the parliamentary committee appointed to investigate Lucius S. Huntington*'s charge of a causal tie between the grant of the transcontinental railway charter to Hugh Allan* and Allan's massive contributions to the Conservative campaign in 1872. Cameron assisted the ministry's delaying tactics by moving on 5 May 1873 the postponement of the committee's proceedings until 2 July, when parliament would be in session. The grounds he gave for the delay were specious: the impossibility of proceeding with the investigation in the absence of Cartier and John Joseph Caldwell Abbott*. The Liberals regarded him with suspicion, and Alexander Mackenzie* believed that Cameron himself had obtained a $5,000 "indefinite loan" from Allan – "such is the Chairman of the investigating Committee." Macdonald claimed that he had not consented to Cameron's appointment to the parliamentary committee, and had not suggested his name.

Cameron had in fact obtained $5,000 from Allan, through Macdonald, to finance his 1872 election campaigns in Peel and Cardwell. He lost Peel in 1872 but was elected for Cardwell, a safe Orange and Conservative seat, where he had asked for Macdonald's assistance to obtain the nomination. He retained Cardwell in 1874 in spite of the Liberal sweep, and was still a member when he suffered a heart attack and died at "The Meadows," his Toronto home, on 14 Nov. 1876.

Well educated, a gifted lawyer, and with close ties to the provincial élite, John Hillyard Cameron showed considerable promise during his early career. His initial political base – Toronto conservatism, the Church of England, and the business community – was not strong enough to propel him into a position of power in a party dominated after 1856 by John A. Macdonald, and his situation was badly compromised when his large fortune vanished in 1857. His later association with the Orange order and with sectional and regional policies such as representation by population failed to overcome the crippling effects of these losses. Thus his political position was never strong, and has probably been overestimated by both his contemporaries and historians. He was nevertheless essentially a political man, who remained in parliament until his career there had come to involve both pain and humiliation.

DONALD SWAINSON

MTCL, John Hillyard Cameron papers. PAC, MG 26, A (Macdonald papers); B (Mackenzie papers), ser.2; MG 27, I, D8 (Galt papers); RG 33, 1, vol. 2. PAO, A. N. Buell papers; John Hillyard Cameron papers; Sir Alexander Campbell papers; Sir John A. Macdonald letters, 1855–1891, copy of letter, J. A. Macdonald to J. G. Moylan, 9 Aug. 1867; John Strachan letter book, 1844–1849; John Strachan papers; Samuel Street papers. *Globe* (Toronto), 1846–76. *Mail* (Toronto), 1872–76. Canada, Province of, *Parliamentary debates*, 1846–65; *Confederation debates*. Canada, House of Commons, *Debates*, 1867–68 (Ottawa, 1967); *Journals*, 1873, app.1, "Report of the Royal Commission. . . ." Edward Blake, *Address by Mr. Blake at Bowmanville* (n.p., 1873). *Documentary history of education in Upper Canada* (Hodgins), III, V, VII–XVIII, XX. [J. A. Macdonald], *Letters* (Johnson), I. Samuel Thompson, *Reminiscences of a Canadian pioneer for the last fifty years: an autobiography* (Toronto, 1884). *Can. directory of parliament* (Johnson). *Can. parl. comp.*, 1873. Morgan, *Sketches of celebrated Canadians*. Notman and Taylor, *Portraits of British Americans*, III. *Political appointments, 1841–1865* (J.-O. Coté). Wallace, *Macmillan dictionary*.

W. P. Bull, *From the Boyne to Brampton, or John the Orangeman at home and abroad* (Toronto, 1936). Careless, *Brown*. Richard Cartwright, *Reminiscences* (Toronto, 1912). Cornell, *Alignment of political groups*. Creighton, *Macdonald, young politician*; *Macdonald, old chieftain*. Dent, *Last forty years*. J. L. H. Henderson, *John Strachan, 1778–1867* ([Toronto], 1969). *A history of the University of Trinity College, Toronto, 1852–1952*, ed. T. A. Reed (Toronto, 1952).

Cameron

William Leggo, *The history of the administration of the Right Honorable Frederick Temple, Earl of Dufferin, K.P., G.C.M.G., K.C.B., F.R.S., late governor general of Canada* (Montreal and Toronto, 1878). Moir, *Church and state in Canada West.* Joseph Pope, *Memoirs of the Right Honourable John Alexander Macdonald G.C.B., first prime minister of the dominion of Canada* (2v., Ottawa, [1894]). Sissons, *Ryerson*, II. F. A. Walker, *Catholic education and politics in Upper Canada: a study of the documentation relative to the origin of Catholic elementary schools in the Ontario school system* (Toronto and Vancouver, 1955). Wilson, *Clergy reserves of Upper Canada.*

D. R. Beer, "Transitional toryism in the 1840's as seen in the political career of Sir Allan MacNab, 1839–1849," unpublished MA thesis, Queen's University, 1963. "The clergy commutation fund," *Church Chronicle Extra* (Toronto), September 1865. D. G. Creighton, "An episode in the history of the University of Toronto," *University of Toronto Quarterly* (Toronto), XVII (1947–48), 245–56. F. J. K. Griezic, "An uncommon Conservative: the political career of John Hillyard Cameron, 1846–1862," unpublished MA thesis, Carleton University, 1965. B. W. Hodgins, "The political career of John Sandfield Macdonald to the fall of his administration in March 1864: a study in Canadian politics," unpublished PHD thesis, Duke University, 1964. George Metcalf, "Draper Conservatism and responsible government in the Canadas, 1836–1847," *CHR*, XLII (1961), 300–24; "The political career of William Henry Draper," unpublished MA thesis, University of Toronto, 1959. W. J. S. Mood, "The Orange Order in Canadian politics, 1841–1867," unpublished MA thesis, University of Toronto, 1960. V. M. Nelson, "The Orange Order in Canadian politics," unpublished MA thesis, Queen's University, 1950. "Portraits of the Canadian parliament of 1850," ed. N. F. Morrison, *Ont. Hist.*, XLII (1950), 153–58. Hereward Senior, "The character of Canadian Orangeism," in *Thought, from the Learned Societies of Canada* (Toronto, 1961), 177–89. M. H. Small, "A study of the dominion and the provincial election of 1867 in Ontario," unpublished MA thesis, Queen's University, 1968. Swainson, "Personnel of politics." *Trinity University Review* (Toronto), XV (1902), 96–97.

CAMERON, MALCOLM, businessman, politician, and temperance advocate; b. at Trois-Rivières, L.C., 25 April 1808, son of Angus Cameron, a hospital sergeant in a Scottish regiment, and Euphemia McGregor; d. 1 June 1876, at Ottawa, Ont.

Malcolm Cameron, the son of Presbyterian Scots, spent his early years in Lanark County, Upper Canada, where his father settled after the disbanding of his regiment. Angus Cameron established a tavern beside the Mississippi River between Lanark and Perth, and Malcolm, "the barefoot ferry boy," carried travellers across the river. At 15 he took a position in a store in Laprairie, then worked as a stable boy in Montreal.

He returned to Perth where he attended the local school and eventually obtained employment as a clerk in a brewery and distillery.

In 1828 Cameron entered into a short-lived partnership in a general store at Perth with his brother-in-law, Henry Glass. Four years later he, John Porter, and Robert Gemmell set up as general merchants. This business prospered, and while on a purchasing trip to Scotland in April 1833 he married a cousin, Christina McGregor.

Cameron's business interests expanded in the 1830s. He began dealing in real estate around Perth. In August 1834 he joined with his brother John in establishing the *Bathurst Courier*; it was to be an independent weekly, the "slave or the tool" of no party, but it was sold one year later because the wealthy and Tory merchants of the area would not advertise in it. Malcolm's attention had meanwhile moved westward to the St Clair region which had impressed him during a trip in 1833. He established in 1835 a general store at Port Sarnia, which he put under the management of an agent, and purchased 100 acres of what is now downtown Sarnia for £400 from Elijah Harris, deputy of the local Indian agent. The land was divided into lots, some of which he sold in the 1830s and 1840s and at a large auction in April 1857. Conspicuous among those he encouraged to settle were half-pay officers and Scottish weavers who had originally established themselves in Lanark.

Cameron himself moved to Port Sarnia in 1837; on 4 Aug. 1837 the partnership of Porter, Gemmell and Company was dissolved. At Port Sarnia he set up lumber and flour mills and he built ships to transport merchandise along the lakes from Chicago to Quebec City. He also acquired good wooded land in the interior away from Lake St Clair and established a timber business. In 1847 he was a contractor in the building of the Great Western Railway.

Cameron was greatly influenced by Scottish "Radicals" who had settled around Lanark, and in 1836 his interest in politics had led him to run as a moderate Reformer for Lanark. He was elected although he had made no clear statement of his intentions other than to support the connection with Britain and act in the interests of the constituency. He generally sided with Robert Baldwin*, Marshall Spring BIDWELL, and other Reformers in opposing Sir Francis Bond HEAD during the session of 1837. He was in Hamilton when rebellion broke out and he volunteered under Allan MacNab*; 16 days later he resigned when he considered his services no longer necessary. At the end of the 1839 session Cameron exhibited the temper which, along with an unwillingness to commit himself and a tendency to impulsive action, would characterize his later career. On the last night of the session a bill was rushed through to sell the clergy reserves and to place the proceeds in the hands of the imperial government for it to apportion. Judging this action to have been accomplished by force and drunkenness, with "every rule of the House, every pledge of members, every principle of honour in man trampled under foot," he swore never to enter the house again.

In fact, Cameron did not attend the next session. However he accepted the invitation of a group of friends in Lanark to stand again in the anticipated elections, the first after the union of Upper and Lower Canada (now Canada West and Canada East). He continued his independent stand, making vague promises to support the institutions on which the happiness of the province depended, although he did say he saw in the policies of Lord Sydenham [Thomson*] liberal tendencies he might endorse. He won the seat, and during the session of 1841 supported the administration formed by Sydenham. He had not agreed with Baldwin when the latter resigned, just as the assembly was to convene in 1841, over Sydenham's refusal to take other Reformers such as Louis-Hippolyte La Fontaine* into the government. Cameron now consistently voted with the majority against Baldwin, and was placed on a committee to prepare and report on a draft speech in answer to the speech from the throne. It was later said that in 1841 Cameron was offered but refused the post of inspector-general; no proof of this offer seems to exist and observers such as Francis Hincks* questioned the truth of the story. By 1842, however, Cameron returned to his support of Baldwin, and in that year was appointed inspector of revenue under the Baldwin–La Fontaine ministry. He resigned in September 1843 when he could not approve the government bill to move the capital to Montreal instead of retaining it at Kingston. Yet he had not considered that a political principle was involved and he thought that the ministry had been wrong in making it a government question. He felt no reluctance in continuing to recognize Baldwin's leadership.

Cameron again represented Lanark in 1844 although life now centred on Sarnia. In the 1847 elections he ran in Kent, defeating John Hillyard CAMERON, member of William Henry DRAPER's Executive Council, by a large majority. When the second La Fontaine–Baldwin ministry was formed in March 1848, Malcolm Cameron became assistant commissioner of public works. He nevertheless continued his pattern of independence, and as early as May 1848 Baldwin was forced to write him a stern letter demanding his immediate presence in Montreal and an explanation of why he had not yet appeared in the assembly. The alternative, he intimated, was dismissal. Then, in April 1849, having prepared a school bill at Baldwin's request, Cameron tabled it, in the midst of the furor over the rebellion losses bill and before informing Egerton Ryerson*, superintendent of education in Upper Canada, of its contents. Ryerson objected strongly, particularly to clauses forbidding the clergy to act as visitors in the common schools and banning the use of all books containing "controversial theological dogmas or doctrines," a phrase which he feared could mean the exclusion of the Bible from the schools. The bill passed and Ryerson resigned. Later, however, Baldwin and Hincks, in a calmer atmosphere than had prevailed in April, reconsidered the question; in late December Ryerson was asked to continue in his post as though the act of 1849 had never existed.

Cameron's unpredictable behaviour was not confined to politics; on one occasion while travelling with Baldwin he disappeared, and when the latter began to search, he was horrified to find his colleague stripped to the waist in an empty bar room having a thorough wash, claiming it was among the best he'd ever had. But Cameron's reaction to annexation talk was doubtless less awkward for Baldwin. Immediately after the Annexation Manifesto was issued in October, he denounced the movement as a treasonous conspiracy "by a set of disappointed and disloyal men to dismember the Empire."

Early in December 1849, however, Cameron resigned his cabinet seat, accusing his colleagues of not consulting him on cabinet changes, of not accepting his policies for retrenchment, and of refusing to allot funds for local improvements. He also declared that his post was a useless one. Others saw the affair differently; Baldwin stated that the first time Cameron had spoken of his resignation, he had mentioned only pressing business interests. As for retrenchment, Baldwin, La Fontaine, and James Hervey Price* all attested to the fact that Cameron had found the assistant commissioner's salary too low. Denying the charge that Cameron had not been consulted on cabinet changes, they concluded, as did many, that his resignation was "the result of personal spleen and mortified vanity," when he hadn't been offered the much-desired commissionership of crown lands.

Cameron's resignation did not remove him from the public eye. Almost immediately he began to act with a new radical faction in Upper Canada – with William McDougall* and those who were becoming known as the "Clear Grits." He had become restive under discipline and under Baldwin's leadership. He had also a common interest with the Grit faction. In 1840 he had felt that state support should be removed from all religions or apportioned equally to all that had a regularly constituted ministry. Now, he came out strongly for the Grit position against any church-state relationship at all. When John Wetenhall*, his successor in the cabinet, presented himself for re-election in Halton in 1850, Cameron successfully championed the anti-government Grit candidate, Caleb HOPKINS. With his bluff manner and hearty enjoyment of debate, Cameron assailed the new minister on numerous occasions with criticisms of the ministry, and relentlessly overpowered the mentally unbalanced Wetenhall.

Later at the founding meeting of the Toronto Anti-Clergy Reserves Association in May 1850, he moved with the support of Grit journalist James Lesslie* that the administration make the settlement of the reserves a ministerial question. The reserves and rectory lands, and the funds derived from them, should, he proposed, be devoted to education "or to such other objects of public utility as may be in accordance with the well understood wishes of the community." The association, wishing to avoid an anti-ministerialist cast, rejected the proposal, but on it Cameron based his own position in the house. When no reference to the clergy reserves or seigneurial tenure was made in the speech from the throne in May, Cameron moved an amendment that the house regretted the omission; the motion was decisively defeated. He continued to play a prominent role as radical opposition to the ministry developed. In June he proposed that the assembly act on the clergy reserves question first and seek British sanction later. Although the motion was defeated, it and other resolutions drew the support of a large proportion of the Reform element of the Upper Canadian section of the province, demonstrating the growth of opposition in the assembly to the Baldwin–La Fontaine ministry not only from the right but also from the left.

In November 1850 Cameron announced his intention of resigning his seat. His stated reason was his wish to devote more time to business concerns, but privately he seemed disenchanted with parliamentary life. On the one hand the ministry showed no signs of dealing with the reserves, while on the other he had begun to fear that Clear Grit principles would lead to annexation. As a lumberman and a shipper he was naturally interested in expanding business opportunities, and in February 1850 he had been sent to Washington by a group of Toronto merchants in an unsuccessful attempt to interest various congressmen in reciprocity. He was utterly opposed, however, to annexation. He did not resign but he attended the 1851 session only infrequently.

By the time the Hincks–Augustin-Norbert Morin* ministry succeeded Baldwin and La Fontaine in 1851, George BROWN's *Globe* in Toronto had adopted an independent stance, fearing that Hincks would favour closer church-state relations in order to retain the support of the Roman Catholic Lower Canadian Reformers. Hincks needed a new organ in Toronto; McDougall of the *North American* saw his chance to advance Grit fortunes and a deal was made. According to McDougall, the arrangement was that two Grits, Cameron and John Rolph*, would join the ministry which would proceed with "all reasonable progressive measures"; the *North American* would support it, abandoning for the time being the full Grit platform. Hincks' version differs slightly: he said he asked Rolph first but that Rolph refused to enter without Cameron; when moderate Reformer Sandfield MACDONALD declined to accept the post of commissioner of crown lands an opening was available which Cameron could fill. No specific portfolio, it appears, was mentioned when Cameron agreed to take office, but he went home to Sarnia in October 1851 thinking he would become postmaster general. When details of the new cabinet were announced, however, he found himself president of the council. This office he had frequently declared superfluous, and he immediately resigned.

Cameron ran as an independent in Huron in the elections of December 1851 and won, but it is for his activities in neighbouring Kent that he is best remembered. Here Brown, supported by Alexander Mackenzie* and the Central Reform Association of Lambton, was running as an independent. In 1849–50, Brown and Mackenzie had considered the survival of the ministry essential for any Reform progress, and Cameron had aroused their enmity by resigning from it, out of, Brown maintained, bad temper. The animosity remained. Cameron thundered onto the scene in Kent hoping to achieve the same success on behalf of the ministerial candidate, Arthur Rankin, as he had for the anti-ministerial Hopkins in Halton in 1850. He promised Brown a "coon hunt on the Wabash," circulated letters urging his friends to attend Brown's meetings to show him what real Reformers were made of, and appealed to the local Irish to drive out the man who had so often taken anti-Catholic stands in the past. Cameron taunted Brown about changing sides and withdrawing support from the ministry, accused him of trying to split the Reform movement and of sowing discord between Catholic and Protestant, and called him a "liar" and a "political prostitute." Brown, however, was more than able to hold his own. As to the charges of inconsistency, hadn't Cameron himself, a leader of the Clear Grit movement, suddenly joined a ministry most of whose members he had recently opposed? Brown repeatedly outscored Cameron and won the election; "the Coon" acquired a name which stuck for years.

Although Cameron had run as an independent in the election, Hincks was still anxious to have him in the ministry. As he saw it, Cameron wanted more work for the same pay, and arrangements were made to create a bureau of agriculture and attach it to the presidency of the council. Cameron was offered the position, and in early February 1852 he accepted. Life during the sessions of 1852 and 1853 must have been uncomfortable for Cameron, who was repeatedly put in the position of voting with the ministry against principles he had previously supported. When a government proposal to increase representation within the two sections of the province came up for debate in March 1853, Brown proposed an amendment for representation by population without regard to any division between Upper and Lower Canada. Cameron voted against the amendment, and the *North American* explained that Grit advocacy of representation by population had referred to redistribution within the sections only. A government-sponsored school bill, passed in June 1853, enlarged the separate school rights in Upper Canada; in the voting only ten Upper Canadian members, including Cameron, supported the measure and 17 went against it. The ecclesiastical corporations question increased the discomfort of the Grit ministers: after a number of bills had been passed incorporating hospitals and charitable, religious, and educational institutions in Lower Canada, the administration introduced a general bill to cover all cases. As for the opposition, neither the Conservatives, under the leadership of MacNab, nor Brown hesitated to point out inconsistencies and to enjoy themselves at the Grit ministers' expense. And among their Grit allies, disillusionment about Cameron and Rolph was growing; Lesslie asked Alexander Mackenzie in May 1853 if he regarded them as traitors or as men overwhelmed by influences they hadn't anticipated.

Cameron became postmaster general in August, replacing James Morris*. As such, he automatically served on the Board of Railway Commissioners, and he was named a government director for Canada West when the Grand Trunk Railway Company was formally organized. In November 1853 he was instrumental in persuading J. R.

Gemmill, publisher of the *Lanark Observer*, to establish the *Lambton Observer and Western Advertiser* (later the *Sarnia Observer*). During that winter Cameron was also involved in a libel suit brought on when Mackenzie insinuated in the *Lambton Shield* that he had attempted a shady land deal when a member of the La Fontaine–Baldwin government. Baldwin, Price, and William Hamilton Merritt*, Cameron's colleagues in that ministry, foiled Mackenzie by declaring themselves bound by an oath of cabinet secrecy. The jury decided for Cameron, but the publicity attracted by the case did him no good.

When the elections were called for July 1854, Cameron accepted invitations to run in both South Lanark and Lambton. His campaigning was restricted to Lambton, however, where a second instalment of the "Coon chase" was taking place between himself and Brown. Brown accused Cameron of engaging in underhanded railway and land deals, using his position as postmaster general to mail election literature, holding out advantageous offers to lumbermen for staves, arranging for jobs, bringing in boatloads of French and Irish-Catholic lumbermen to swell his cheering section on nomination day (in fact opening a tavern for them), and belonging to a corrupt ministry. Cameron protested that he was being slandered, played up his role in the temperance movement, and defended the ministry, saying that it was being as progressive as circumstances permitted. Again Cameron's temper displayed itself: at one meeting he warned Mackenzie and a friend that they would go to hell with their associates "unless they repented of their slanders against the Ministry." In the end Cameron was defeated in both Lambton and South Lanark and was out of the assembly for over three years.

During this period Cameron appears to have withdrawn from some of his commercial enterprises. He had acted in 1853 with the Baron van Tuyll* van Serooskerken in selling lots in the Bayfield Estate in Huron County, and in 1857 he was selling town lots in Sarnia. He remained a large land owner but retired from the shipping business and appears to have sold his store. By February 1857 it was rumoured that his finances were "irretrievably embarrassed."

When it became known that elections would be held in the late fall of 1857, Brown intimated to Mackenzie that he would run in Lambton if the Reform committee wanted him to, but suggested that they consider a local candidate. "If Cameron were only repentant & thoroughly convenanted to go for the points [of the Reform Alliance of 1857] & against the Ministry," wrote Brown, "it would be no loss to let him in." At Brown's suggestion

Cameron

Mackenzie and Archibald Young sought out Cameron to discuss his views, but negotiations failed when tempers flared. Cameron entered the campaign in Lambton as an independent, refusing to support or condemn the moderate Conservative ministry of John A. Macdonald* and George-Étienne CARTIER, and promising to judge it on its actions. An anti-ministerial candidate would also be in the fight; when it became evident Brown would not run, Hope Mackenzie was nominated. With few fundamental differences between Hope Mackenzie and Cameron other than support of the ministry, the campaign assumed a bitter personal character. Cameron was narrowly elected amid much hard feeling on all sides.

For the first year after his re-entry into the assembly Cameron voted almost consistently with the government of Macdonald and Cartier, because it was untried, he said, and should be given a chance to prove itself. When Brown proposed a resolution calling for representation by population in March 1858, Cameron voted against it, although he proposed a similar move himself in June. He then defended this apparent inconsistency by saying that he hadn't wanted to vote a want of confidence in the ministry. Others explained it as a desire to "gratify his spleen" against Brown. In early August he voted against the short-lived Liberal ministry of Brown and Antoine-Aimé Dorion*, claiming that Brown had violated his political principles in his greed for office. It was not until March 1859 that he executed a complete *volte-face*, removed his support from the government of Cartier-Macdonald, and joined Brown in vigorously condemning Alexander Tilloch Galt*'s higher tariff legislation. He had earlier objected, he said, to William Cayley*'s dismissal and the increase in members' salaries, but the new tariff had been the last straw. The *Globe* remarked, "There is one good thing about the member for Lambton – he never does things by halves, and having resolved to go into opposition, he took his stand accordingly." This stand was reaffirmed in April when he spoke out strongly against government proposals for financing seigneurial reimbursements in Lower Canada.

In September 1859 the western parliamentary opposition met in Toronto to discuss future policy; it was decided that constitutional changes were necessary for the country and that a large convention should be held to consider these and to revive interest and enthusiasm for their cause. "Malcolm was there," Brown wrote, "and behaved like a Trump. Took capital views & showed a workable spirit." Mackenzie and the Central Reform Committee, remembering old animosities and Cameron's erratic political record, were not so enthusiastic. They decided, however, that although they would not commit themselves for the future they would cooperate with Cameron now, "in view of the alarming state of the country." When the Reform Convention met in November 1859, Cameron served on two committees and led off the debate. After praising the present unanimity of feeling he explained his conversion from ministerial ranks. He had always supported union, he said, but it had become unworkable and with representation by population apparently a remote possibility under the existing system, a federal scheme was the only solution. Here he looked beyond Upper and Lower Canada and advocated a platform on which other territories could enter the federation; they would be creating "the nucleus of an empire extending from the Atlantic to the Pacific."

Cameron's last major activity in the assembly was the chairmanship in 1860 of a select committee to consider the University of Toronto. In June of that year he was offered and accepted the Reform nomination for the Legislative Council seat for St Clair; he won by acclamation. For two and a half years in the council he continued to urge federation and expansion. He advocated the construction of railways across the continent, and in 1862 visited British Columbia. Arriving in New Westminster in August, he carried from there to Great Britain a petition of a committee, with William James Armstrong* as chairman, formed by persons on the mainland who wanted their own government. He was considered an ideal delegate because of his political experience and connections, and because of his disinterestedness; however, he had already, in fact, asked the Duke of Newcastle in 1861 to remove Sir James DOUGLAS as governor of the colony.

In 1863 Cameron was appointed queen's printer jointly with Georges-Pascal Desbarats*, and for six years was out of politics altogether. In 1869 he surprised the people of the federal riding of Renfrew by announcing that he would run there in a by-election. He was defeated by John Lorn McDougall*, and was again defeated in the Ontario election for South Lanark in 1871 when he campaigned for an extension of the franchise and against the coalition government of Sandfield Macdonald. He tried again in the federal election of 1872 in Russell, but lost to James Alexander Grant*. In 1874 he was elected as a Liberal for South Ontario over Thomas Nicholson Gibbs* and sat in the federal house for two years. He died at Ottawa on 1 June 1876, survived only by an unmarried daughter. At the time of his death he was deeply in debt. His taxes were in arrears, and he owed money to several banks, trust and loan companies, and individuals. In his last years he was a director of the Ontario and Quebec Railway and the railway linking the Marmora Iron Works to Colborne, and of the Royal Mutual Life Assurance Company, and president of the Ontario Central Railway.

Although his political career was erratic, there was one cause to which Cameron was devoted throughout his life, that of temperance. He was on the executive of many societies, including the Sons of Temperance, and introduced a number of bills on the subject in parliament. He is, however, probably best remembered as a businessman, a founder of Sarnia, and an independent and quick-tempered politician, one of the early leaders of the Clear Grit movement in Canada West.

MARGARET COLEMAN

MTCL, Baldwin papers, 35, no.107; 38, nos.5, 8, 11, 13, 24, 39–63; 54, nos.68, 69; 55, no.56; 56, no.56; 58, no.94; 61, no.91; 65, no.86; 70, no.72; 73, no.71; 78, nos.18, 19, 20; 87. PAC, MG 24, B40 (Brown papers), pp.58–60, 147, 167, 195, 202, 206, 283, 443–44, 456, 519–20, 929–30, 1094, 1787, 1791, 1798, 1799. PAO, Charles Clarke papers, William McDougall to Clarke, 25 July 1851, 2 Feb. 1853; Mackenzie-Lindsey collection, William Spink to W. L. Mackenzie, 29 Jan. 1852; Cameron to Mackenzie, 2 April 1852; Spink to Mackenzie, 22 April 1852; Cameron to Mackenzie, 30 April 1852; Spink to Mackenzie, 7 May 1852; Cameron to Mackenzie, 10 May 1852; Thomas Webster to Mackenzie, 4 Oct. 1852; John Scott to Mackenzie, 27 Oct. 1852; James Lesslie to Mackenzie, May 1853. Queen's University Archives, Alexander Mackenzie papers, George Brown to Mackenzie, 11 Oct. 1851, 17 March 1853, 16 April 1854, 17 Oct., 25 Nov. 1857, 29 Jan. 1858; Brown to Luther Holton, 24 Sept. 1859; Brown to Mackenzie, 28 March 1860; Mackenzie to Mary Thompson, 29 April 1876.

Canada, Province of, Legislative Assembly, *Journals*, 1841–60. Charles Clarke, *Sixty years in Upper Canada, with autobiographical recollections* (Toronto, 1908), 76–78. Francis Hincks, *Reminiscences of his public life* (Montreal, 1884), 252–56, 263–65, 272. Upper Canada, House of Assembly, *Journals*, 1836–39. *Canadian Illustrated News* (Montreal), 2 Oct. 1875, 213. *Examiner* (Toronto), 5 Dec. 1849; 13, 20 Feb., 13 March, 13 Nov. 1850. *Globe* (Toronto), 1 Oct. 1844; 1847–60; 2 June 1876. *Lambton Observer and Western Advertiser* (later *Sarnia Observer and Lambton Advertiser*), 1853–63; 2, 9 June 1876. *North American* (Toronto), 1850–52. *Perth Courier* (titled *Bathurst Courier*, 1834–57), 1834–41; 8 Nov. 1844; 30 June, 14 July, 4 Aug. 1854; 16 June, 9, 16 July 1869; 21 Oct. 1870; 6 June 1876; 7 Jan. 1943.

C. D. Allin and G. M. Jones, *Annexation, preferential trade and reciprocity; an outline of the Canadian annexation movement of 1849–1850, with special reference to the questions of preferential trade and reciprocity* (Toronto and London, 1912), 97, 332–33, 336–38, 345, 348. Careless, *Brown*; *Union of the Canadas*. Dent, *Last forty years*. Victor Lauriston, *Lambton's hundred years, 1849–1949* (Sarnia, Ont., 1949), 91–99, 224–27. J. S. McGill, *A pioneer history of the county of Lanark* (Toronto, 1968), 147, 156–61, 186–87, 191. Moir, *Church and state in Canada West*. Sissons, *Ryerson*, II. D. C. Thomson, *Alexander Mackenzie, Clear Grit* (Toronto, 1960).

CAMPBELL, ROLLO, printer, newspaper publisher, politician; b. 18 Dec. 1803 at Dunning-Mason, Perthshire, Scotland, son of John Campbel (*sic*) and Nelly Smith; d. 2 Jan. 1871 at Montreal, Que.

In May 1822 Rollo Campbell emigrated to Montreal from Greenock, Scotland, where he had learned his printer's trade with several small weekly newspapers. In Canada he was employed as a printer by the *Montreal Gazette* and then by the *Morning Courier*, a Conservative commercial paper which he printed from its establishment in 1835 until 1836 or 1837. He was first a partner in the firm of John C. BECKET, then on his own, and he soon nurtured his printing business into one of Canada's biggest. He maintained branches in Toronto and Quebec in addition to his Montreal headquarters. Campbell printed the assembly's *Sessional papers* from 1842 to 1859, and he often won contracts to print its *Journals* and the reports for almost every administrative department and agency. He also published the *Weekly Register* from 1844 to 1847 and the monthly *Colonial Protestant* during 1848. Besides government documents and newspapers, Campbell printed "Books, Pamphlets, Catalogues, Cards, Cheques, Funeral Cards, Circulars, Auction Bills, Railroad do., Steamboat do., Programmes, Bill Heads, Posters, and Labels." He guaranteed his workmanship would be "equalled by few, surpassed by none, and on moderate terms." Campbell's business soon made him wealthy enough to own valuable real estate and to satisfy certain political ambitions, common enough to contemporary printers.

Campbell participated in Reform politics for years, and in 1844 was printer for Francis Hincks*' newspaper the *Pilot* until it got its own print-shop. In the same year Campbell also founded his own paper the *Gazetteer*, of which nothing is known except that it ceased publication after only a few issues. Campbell re-entered the newspaper business in 1849 when on 20 April, "entirely ruined" by a £500 libel verdict, the *Pilot*'s proprietors auctioned off their business. Campbell bought it and was officially endorsed by Montreal's Reform party. He described his political convictions as reform, progress, equality, utility, and the voluntary principle. "Give the people as much liberty as they are able to enjoy and turn to good account," he urged. "Educate them for self government, and let the power be enlarged as their capacity to use it beneficially increases." From his Place d'Armes office Campbell published the *Pilot* on Tuesdays, Thursdays, and Saturdays; the *Weekly Pilot and Journal of Commerce*, for outlying areas, was printed on Wednesdays. One of Campbell's editors was the Reverend John Mockett Cramp*, later president of Acadia College. Another was William Bristow*, after 1854 publisher of the *Argus*. With such editorial assistance, Campbell had time for other political ventures.

In March 1851 he ran for the Montreal city council seat for Saint-Laurent. The main campaign issue was the proposed suburban "Boulevard job." Campbell and such supporters as Jean-Baptiste-Éric Dorion* believed that after the central city's citizens were provided with essential services there would "be time enough to talk of Boulevards, in the suburbs, at the city cost." In the turbulent elections Campbell lost to Tory Joseph Russell Bronsdon, 111 to 124, though most wards elected Reformers. He failed in two bids to unseat incumbent mayor Charles WILSON in 1852 and 1853, but he won the Saint-Laurent council seat in 1852. He held this post until 1856 when he was elected an alderman for Saint-Laurent. The next year he retired from politics. He had worked diligently on the council; he wanted respite from work, and he planned to visit his native land.

In 1857, in Scotland, Campbell gave two talks, later published as *Two lectures on Canada*, in which he encouraged prospective Scottish emigrants to settle in Canada. Back home, Campbell's Montreal printing business continued to thrive, but his once informative and provocative *Pilot* floundered along with the Reform party. Its news was mainly sensational, it contained little political commentary, and it was crowded with advertisements. Campbell's financial difficulties in the spring of 1862 forced the *Pilot* to shut down. Afterwards he ventured into other fields. In the 1864–65 city directory he listed his occupation as "city assessor," and in 1865–66 "Customs House Officer." He had earlier held the unpaid customs post of deputy master of Montreal Trinity Board. From 1866 to 1867 he was again described as a "printer." Upon his death in 1871 he was survived by his wife Elizabeth Steel, and a son, Dr Francis Wayland Campbell*.

Rollo Campbell was one of those successful Scottish immigrants absorbed into Montreal's solid Protestant middle class. His career in business and his son's entry into a profession were typical. Even his tenure in public office was not unusual since municipal politics attracted many such participants. Campbell's main distinction was his politically committed *Pilot*, unfortunately acquired when his party's work was almost finished, and when new leaders, new problems, and new solutions thrust aside the old.

ELIZABETH NISH

[Rollo Campbell's *Two lectures on Canada* (Toronto, 1857) are interesting since they give an idea of his deep devotion to Canada and of his confidence in her future. The *Pilot* (Montreal), 1849–62, is the best source of information for Campbell, giving as it does all sorts of information about him, as well as expressing his political convictions. O. B. Bishop, *Publications of the government of the Province of Canada, 1841–1867* (Ottawa, 1963) never discusses Campbell, but this book is an excellent one for studying anyone such as Campbell who did so much government printing. E.N.]

General Register Office (Edinburgh), Register of births and baptisms for the parish of Dunning. St Catherine Street Baptist Church (Montreal), Register of births, marriages, and burials, 2 Jan. 1871. Beaulieu et Hamelin, *Journaux du Québec. Canadian newspapers on microfilm/Catalogue de journaux canadiens sur microfilm. Montreal directory* (Mackay), 1864–73. Wallace, *Macmillan dictionary*, 110. W. H. Kesterton, *A history of journalism in Canada* (Carleton Library series, 36, Toronto, 1967).

CAMPBELL, THOMAS EDMUND, military officer, secretary, politician, seigneur of Rouville; b. in London, Eng., perhaps in 1809, probably in 1811; d. in 1872, probably at Saint-Hilaire, Que.

Captain Thomas Edmund Campbell arrived in Canada in 1837 after 14 years of service in the British army (which included numerous postings in the Near East), and soon came into the limelight when, on 10 Nov. 1838 as commander of the Mohawks at Caughnawaga, he took part with the volunteers of the Lachine brigade in the attack on the rebels at Châteauguay. Afterwards the volunteers set fires and began to pillage a number of houses and terrorize the habitants; he sought out the ringleaders, who were all white, placed them under arrest in Lachine, and conducted the Indians back to Caughnawaga. For their part in the capture of 75 *Patriotes*, the Indians were congratulated and mentioned in dispatches by Sir John Colborne*.

A year later, Major Campbell (as he now was) became aide-de-camp and military secretary to Governor Charles Edward Poulett Thomson*. In this office he played a decisive role in the election of 1841, acting as "election agent" in Lower Canada for Thomson, now Lord Sydenham, and being, as the governor himself averred, his "sole reliance" for victory. He it was who formulated the strategy of placing the polling stations in areas where they would be most convenient to "loyal" voters who would support the union, and of making sure any troops which might be dispatched to "check violence" would be available only to sympathizers with the governor. In Beauharnois he personally led the military into their positions around the poll to prevent the anti-unionists from voting. His advice and tactics won an unexpected 20 out of 42 seats for Sydenham in Canada East.

Sometime about 1840 he had married Henriette-Julie Juchereau Duchesnay, and four years later acquired the seigneury of Rouville. (He was survived by one son, Bruce.) In 1846, having retired from the army, he settled in Saint-Hilaire to become almost wholly involved in developing his land. He set apart over 150 acres as a model farm, and took a deep interest in the growing of trees. In the mid-1850s, when he heard of Principal John William Dawson*'s work at McGill in natural history, he sent him a carload of spruce trees and the saplings which apparently became the great elms bordering the campus's central avenue. In 1848, Lord Elgin [Bruce*] described Campbell as "one of the most enterprising seigneurs in the province."

Perhaps because of his success, certainly because of his compatibility with both linguistic groups (all the transactions of Major Campbell's seigneury were conducted in French), Lord Elgin prevailed upon him to become his civil secretary. As such, he was also *ex officio* superintendent-general of Indian affairs, for between 1844 and 1860 all civil secretaries automatically served in this capacity. Having taken office on 31 March 1847, he resigned on 30 Nov. 1849 because of Lord Elgin's (and the capital's) move to Toronto. Once again he retired to Saint-Hilaire, whence he re-emerged in the winter of 1854–55 on a commission appointed to consider military defence. He sat with Sir Allan Napier MacNab* and Colonel Étienne-Paschal Taché*, their report resulting in the Militia Act of 1855 with its double system of sedentary militia and "volunteers."

In the general election of 1857 he was elected as member of parliament for Rouville, and in the house voted consistently with the Conservatives of Canada East. In 1861 he was defeated by the Liberal Lewis Thomas Drummond*, and retired from politics. He continued his interest in defence, however, and when the American Civil War and the *Trent* crisis provoked increasing anxiety in the colony, he agreed to sit on another commission formed in January 1862. In addition to Colonel Campbell (as he now was), who spoke for the military forces of the province, the commission was composed of George-Étienne CARTIER, John A. Macdonald*, Alexander Tilloch Galt*, and Sir Allan MacNab acting for the political interests, and Colonel Daniel Lysons*, a regular British officer who represented imperial concerns. The report of this commission, dated 15 March 1862, was a strong plea for the old sedentary system, from which a force could be trained to constitute the real defence of the Province of Canada. It was on the bill resulting from this plan that the Cartier-Macdonald government was defeated.

Although he became a director of the Bank of Montreal and of the Grand Trunk Railway, Colonel Campbell always maintained that the development of his seigneury was his central interest. He greatly enjoyed the rural life of French Canada. On 12 Oct. 1855, at a banquet in Cobourg to honour Sir Edmund Walker Head*, he is said to have declared about the habitant: "I have now lived nine years among the French Canadians, and I believe I can honestly claim to have learned something about them, and speak about them with some authority. Believe me, Jean-Baptiste, as the French-Canadian is often called, is an honest and good subject. He is hard working and kind.... I have never lived among better people."

JACQUES MONET

[Bruce and Grey], *Elgin-Grey papers* (Doughty), I, 20, 28, 54, 66, 134, 387; II, 810–11. [C. E. P. Thomson], *Letters from Lord Sydenham governor-general of Canada, 1839–1841, to Lord Russell*, ed. Paul Knaplund (London, 1931), 110. *Canada and its provinces* (Shortt and Doughty), VII, 396–401. Cornell, *Alignment of political groups*. E. J. Devine, *Historic Caughnawaga* (Montreal, 1922). E. A. Collard, "Popular Major Thomas Campbell," *Gazette* (Montreal), 11 Feb. 1943. P.-G. Roy, "Le major Thomas-Edmund Campbell," *BRH*, XI (1905), 359–61.

CANTERBURY, Viscount. *See* MANNERS-SUTTON.

CARON, RENÉ-ÉDOUARD, jurist, politician, second lieutenant governor of Quebec; b. 21 Oct. 1800 at Sainte-Anne-de-Beaupré, L.C., son of Élisabeth Lessard and Augustin Caron, a well-to-do farmer and MHA for Lower Canada; d. 13 Dec. 1876 at Quebec.

René-Édouard Caron was educated at the college of Saint-Pierre-de-la-Rivière-du-Sud (Montmagny County), where the rudiments of Latin were taught; with this preparation he was admitted to the Petit Séminaire of Quebec in September 1813 as a boarder. He took the full classical course there, and left in 1820 after two years of philosophy. He studied law in André-Rémi Hamel's office, was called to the bar on 7 Jan. 1826, and carried on his profession at Quebec. There he was not long in building up a good reputation as a jurist, at the same time acquiring a fairly well-paying clientele. In 1844 he went into partnership with Louis de Gonzague Baillargé*, who had studied under him; six years later the two lawyers were jointly appointed lawyers of the city of Quebec. The archives of the Petit Séminaire of Quebec also show that Caron was legal adviser to his Alma Mater. The firm of Caron et Baillargé was dissolved when Caron was appointed judge of the Superior Court in 1853.

It was by way of municipal institutions that Caron entered politics. On 31 March 1831 the House of Assembly of Lower Canada passed the bill that incorporated the city of Quebec and conferred on it the right to administer itself through an elected body. This law received royal sanction on 5 June 1832 (1 Wm IV, c.52). The city was divided into 10 wards, each having the right to elect two councillors. The councillors were to choose the mayor from among themselves at their first meeting. The new law was to remain in force until 1 May 1836. The first elections took place in 1833, and Caron became one of the representatives for the Palais district. Elzéar Bédard* was elected mayor, but in March 1834 the majority of the councillors voted in favour of Caron. He became second mayor of Quebec and remained so until 1 May 1836, when, the law not having been renewed, justices of the peace once more assumed direction of the city [see Hippolyte DUBORD]. Quebec had a second experience of a municipal system in 1840, as the result of an ordinance of the Special Council (4 Vict., c.35) by virtue of which the governor appointed the mayor. Lord Sydenham [Thomson*] chose Caron, and the latter was elected at the end of two years, when the office again became an elective one. He relinquished it in 1846.

In the summer of 1834, during the period of Caron's first administration, cholera ravaged the town of Quebec and claimed more than 2,000 victims. He organized the struggle against the epidemic and was not afraid to expose himself to the disease. He was again mayor when two successive fires, in May and June 1845, destroyed the greater part of the town. Appointed chairman of the relief committee, he gave proof of firm devotion to duty and great organizing ability.

In 1834 Caron was elected MHA by acclamation, for the Upper Town of Quebec, and from the beginning he was one of the French Canadian moderate liberals in the assembly of Lower Canada. He adopted the ideas defended by Étienne PARENT in Le Canadien and was not slow to oppose the radical wing led by Louis-Joseph PAPINEAU. Though he voted for the Ninety-two resolutions, he was soon identified with a small group of assemblymen, "the Quebec party," which favoured a policy of conciliation. Caron and his friends tried to give concrete form to this policy in March 1836 when Papineau was refusing to agree to vote supplies. Caron voted against the French Canadian leader, who triumphed in his no-compromise policy. On 6 March a large number of Caron's electors presented an address to Papineau approving his action, and by implication censuring their representative, and Caron judged it necessary to resign.

On 22 Aug. 1837 the Colonial Office authorized the governor, Lord Gosford [Acheson*], to appoint at one time ten legislative councillors, including seven French Canadians. Caron was one. The council was to disappear following the suspension of the constitution in 1838. In 1837 Caron refused to sit on the Executive Council. In January 1840, when the plan of union that had been adopted by the legislature of Upper Canada became known, Caron was one of the most active members at Quebec of the movement led by John Neilson* which opposed it. During a meeting held on 17 January, at the home of the notary Louis-Édouard Glackmeyer*, the first stages in the struggle were organized. A few days later Caron took part in a popular gathering at which a petition "against Union and for the constitution of 1791" was read. With Étienne Parent and François-Xavier Garneau*, he was a member of a committee of some 40 prominent citizens who in April managed to collect 38,928 signatures against the proposed union; a Quebec merchant, Vital Têtu, agreed to present them to the British parliament. The new constitution was none the less adopted, and ratified by Queen Victoria on 23 July 1840. In common with the majority of French Canadians, Caron deplored the new regime, but he had to accept it and before long was participating in its institutions. On 14 June 1841 he was appointed a member of the Legislative Council of United Canada, and was its speaker from 8 Nov. 1843 to 19 May 1847, and from 11 March 1848 to 14 Aug. 1853.

Caron took over as speaker of the council from Robert Sympson Jameson*, who had resigned in protest against the decision, backed by the government and accepted by parliament, to move the seat of the capital from Kingston to Montreal. The choice of Caron by Governor Sir Charles Theophilus Metcalfe*, who had first bargained with Peter McGill* and John Neilson, was initially regarded by the government of Louis-Hippolyte La Fontaine* and Robert Baldwin* as another move taken by the governor without consulting his ministers, but it was rather difficult for La Fontaine to oppose it because of the personal qualities of Caron, whom *La Minerve*, on 9 Nov. 1843, called "one of ours."

The 10-month break in Caron's speakership was occasioned by his taking part in political negotiations in 1845, 1846, and 1847. The negotiations, which aroused much strong feeling at the time, resulted from the desire to introduce Lower Canadian representatives into the Tory government, and were indeed the prelude to the recognition of responsible government in the Province of Canada. Already, on 10 March 1844, Denis-Benjamin Viger*, who was attempting to form a ministry following the resignation of the La Fontaine–Baldwin government, had offered Caron the post of attorney general for Canada East. He would have had to seek election to the assembly, but he was promised that if defeated he could resume his seat on the Legislative Council. Caron refused the offer. He was nevertheless considered a moderate who was easier to deal with than La Fontaine. At the beginning of July at Quebec, and at the beginning of August at Montreal, the first talks took place between Caron and William Henry DRAPER, who was regarded as a Conservative and on the whole opposed to La Fontaine's Lower Canadian Reformers. Draper made known to Caron his wish that other French Canadians as well as those who were in it already would join the administration. He is thought to have mentioned Augustin-Norbert Morin* in particular, expressly ignoring La Fontaine because of the personal difficulties between the latter and Governor Metcalfe. Caron, loyal to his moderate sentiments, agreed to serve as intermediary, but it was not until 8 September that he wrote to La Fontaine to convey to him Draper's offers of some portfolios for the Lower Canadian Reformers. Caron ended his letter with these revealing lines: "I must tell you that in my opinion our present situation cannot last. What we are offered is little enough, but it might be the beginning of something better. It is very possible that I see things wrongly, but it seems to me that this opening is well worth thinking about; I am informing you of it for this reason, so that you may consider it and be free to act, but the matter should be dealt with carefully." Two days later La Fontaine replied; his letter, according to historian Thomas Chapais*, "constitutes a document of capital importance for the constitutional history of this period." "What is proposed to us," wrote La Fontaine, "is a repudiation of the principle of responsibility, in so far as it applies to Lower Canada. Since Mr Draper admits that the Lower Canadian section of the ministry does not represent Lower Canada, why keep it? Why not, in accordance with your principles, form a new administration for Lower Canada, with the help

of some one who would be instructed to do it constitutionally?" On 17 September Caron wrote to Draper, to convey to him what could be regarded as La Fontaine's refusal, and in his letter he was one of the first to state what was to be recognized later as the principle of the "double majority." "The principle has been established," he wrote, "that the direction of affairs should be in the hands of the two dominant parties in each of the sections of the province, that the government should not run Lower Canada by means of a majority obtained from Upper Canada, nor should it impose laws on the majority in Upper Canada as a result of the assistance given to it by Lower Canada, and that a government should last only so long as it is supported by a majority in each of the sections of the province." The negotiations went on and ended fruitlessly in November 1845, when Draper informed Caron that, as Metcalfe felt obliged by illness to relinquish his post, the situation had changed, from which we may presume that the governor was not unacquainted with the actions of the Upper Canada politician.

At the beginning of April 1846 the Draper-Caron negotiations, which had been more or less secret, were the subject of a parliamentary debate during which La Fontaine read out all the correspondence between Draper, Caron, and himself: this conduct cast a chill on the relations between Caron and La Fontaine. In *Dix ans au Canada de 1840 à 1850 . . .*, Antoine Gérin-Lajoie* wrote: "What some of M. Caron's friends regretted, when all the correspondence was published, was to see that in a letter to Mr Draper, dated 8 Sept. 1845, he showed himself desirous of seeing a reaction in favour of Sir Ch. Metcalfe's government, a feeling that he concealed from M. La Fontaine. The latter could not but say publicly that if he had been aware of this letter his correspondence with M. Caron would have been discontinued immediately."

In August 1846, two months after Viger's resignation, Draper tried again, but unsuccessfully, to persuade Caron and Morin to enter a coalition analogous to the one he had proposed the preceding year. In a letter addressed to *La Revue canadienne* on 28 Aug. 1846, Morin wrote: "I must say unreservedly, on the subject of the recent negotiations between the provincial government on the one hand and M. Caron and myself on the other, that in this whole affair the steps taken by M. Caron, and my own, have been as honourable as I desired my own to be."

The third attempt at negotiations with Caron took place in April 1847, when Lord Elgin [Bruce*], who had been appointed governor the preceding year, sought to regulate the strange

Caron

situation whereby French Canadians were represented in the government only by Denis-Benjamin Papineau*, to whom the majority of Lower Canadian MLAs were hostile. Papineau and William Cayley*, the inspector general in the government, offered Caron the presidency of the Executive Council. The latter nearly succumbed to the invitation, but he seems to have been prevented from doing so by the advice of his friend Morin, and by the desire to see La Fontaine come to power, as is revealed by a letter dated 11 April 1847 from Thomas Cushing AYLWIN to La Fontaine: "I sincerely believe that Caron wants to do something worth while, and that he desires to see you recalled to power."

However that may be, Caron was relieved of the speakership of the Legislative Council, after he had been made to understand that the post had to be held by a politician who enjoyed the government's confidence, and he was replaced by Peter McGill. In the following session, in June 1847, Caron made a long speech in support of a series of resolutions put forward by John Neilson, in which it was argued that the French population was not sufficiently represented in the cabinet. He recalled all the dealings in which he had been involved, and concluded: "I am certain I have done nothing for which I should lose my seat; if I can reproach myself with anything, it is that I put my trust in the ministry. If the government had acted in this way for the good of the country, or even if it had acted in a polite manner, I should have been satisfied; but so long as it will not show that it had good reasons to treat me as it did, I shall say that its conduct was unjustifiable. When I accepted the position of Speaker of the Council, I stipulated that it should not be a political one. For four years I gave up my profession, and I consider that the ministry has no right to take this office from me without offering me what it gives to every official of the government who is deprived of his employment."

During the summer after the 1847 session a political association was formed at Quebec called the "Comité constitutionnel de la réforme et du progrès," and Caron was elected president of it. At the beginning of November the association launched a manifesto against the government; one of its resolutions demanded that the chief advisers of the governor should be "men enjoying the confidence of the people's representatives." In the elections of December 1847, which ended at the beginning of January 1848, the Reform party obtained a majority in the two parts of the country. Caron recovered his post as speaker of the Legislative Council, and at the same time entered the La Fontaine–Baldwin ministry. In the 1849 session

he was among those in the upper house who warmly supported the rebellion losses bill. On the occasion of a ministerial reshuffle in November 1849, Caron ceased to be the representative for the Quebec region and was replaced by a Quebec lawyer, Jean Chabot*, as chief commissioner of public works. However, he remained speaker of the Legislative Council. A few weeks before, he had signed the loyalist manifesto, published by La Minerve on 15 October, which opposed the Annexation Manifesto; the loyalist manifesto began by the following declaration of faith: "Sincerely attached to the institutions that the mother country has recently recognized, and convinced that these institutions are enough to assure us, through wise and judicious legislation, of a prompt and effective remedy for all the wrongs of which our province may complain, we believe it our duty to protest without delay, publicly and solemnly, against the opinions expressed in that document [the Annexation Manifesto]."

On 28 Oct. 1851, Caron, still in his capacity as speaker of the Legislative Council, entered the government of Francis Hincks* and Morin. He remained in it until 15 Aug. 1853, when he was appointed judge of the Superior Court to replace the late Jean-Baptiste-Édouard Bacquet. On 29 Jan. 1855 he became a judge of the Court of Appeal, following the death of Judge Philippe Panet*.

Judge Caron was a member of the Special Court which was created under the authority of the seigneurial act of 1854, and presided over by the chief justice, Louis-Hippolyte La Fontaine. On 11 March 1856, with other judges of the Court of Appeal and the Superior Court, he gave his verdict on the legal problems that had been submitted to him. Each judge had the right to formulate his observations separately, which Judge Caron did; his remarks were published in 1856 in the Lower Canada Reports; seigniorial questions. In this collection he made a fairly detailed study of three problems: the nature and extent of the right of ownership of the local seigneurs over their fiefs and seigneuries; the nature and extent of their right of banalité; the ownership of rivers and running water, whether navigable or not.

Caron's name has remained closely linked with the codification of civil law in Lower Canada. On 27 April 1857 George-Étienne CARTIER introduced before the Legislative Assembly of United Canada the "Act to provide for the Codification of the Laws of Lower Canada relative to Civil matters and Procedure." The bill became law on 10 June (20 Vict., c.43). It provided for the appointment by the governor of three persons as commissioners, to "reduce into one code to be called the

Civil Code of Lower Canada, those provisions of the Laws of Lower Canada which relate to Civil Matters and are of a general and permanent character, whether they relate to Commercial Cases or to those of any other nature." Once this task was completed, the commissioners were to reduce to "another Code, to be called the *Code of Civil Procedure of Lower Canada*, those provisions of the Laws of Lower Canada which relate to Procedure in Civil Matters and Cases, and are of a general and permanent character." The two codes were to be patterned as far as possible on the structure of the French codes "known as the *Code Civil*, the *Code de Commerce*, and the *Code de Procédure Civile*." The preamble to the act recalled the reasons for undertaking the codification. The civil laws in force in Lower Canada derived for the most part from the Custom of Paris, which had been applied in New France and of which the Quebec Act had ensured the continuance. These laws had, however, been modified by laws of English origin, so much so that there were not always good comparable versions in the two languages utilized before the courts. France, by codifying its law at the beginning of the century, had set an example for Lower Canada, as had Louisiana in its last civil code, adopted in 1825. Moreover, the French codification had suppressed the commentaries pertaining to those laws that pre-dated the Revolution, and in certain cases it seemed necessary to modify the old rules.

On 28 Nov. 1857 Cartier first approached the chief justice of Lower Canada, Louis-Hippolyte La Fontaine, to ask him to direct the commission, but La Fontaine refused: "there are too strong reasons against it; the first, the only one I need give, is the state of my health." On 4 Feb. 1858 three commissioners were appointed by the government: René-Édouard Caron, Augustin-Norbert Morin, and Charles Dewey Day*, the latter two being judges of the Superior Court. In the letters of appointment the provincial secretary asked them to devote all their time to the task of codification, starting from 1 April, which meant that they had to give up the cases they had heard. Judge Caron was not officially appointed president of the commission, but he acted as such. The commissioners met for the first time at Quebec, on 20 May 1858, and were authorized to rent an office in a house belonging to Caron. On 10 June another meeting took place "to determine the best plan to follow," and the work was apportioned between the commissioners and the secretaries.

The appointment of Caron touched off a brief controversy, reported in the Quebec papers of March 1859. The judge claimed that he had agreed to be a member of the commission only on con-dition that he could deliver judgements in the cases he had heard. His two colleagues maintained that he did not have the right to sit, and he finally yielded to their arguments. When Morin died in 1865, Joseph-Ubalde BEAUDRY replaced him as commissioner, and Louis-Siméon MORIN succeeded Beaudry in the post of secretary. In 1862 Thomas Kennedy Ramsay*, a secretary of the commission, was dismissed from his post for political reasons, and was replaced by Thomas McCord*.

Caron drafted "Notes on the plan to be followed in the preparatory work of codification," but Judge Day was entrusted with writing the first report, dealing with obligations. On 12 Oct. 1861 the commissioners submitted it to the government. The other reports appeared at intervals until 25 Nov. 1864, at which date the report on commercial law was delivered. The codifiers' recommendations were then brought before parliament by the government, and were the object of a law adopted in 1865 (29 Vict., c.41). Caron and his colleagues next devoted their attention to drafting the code of civil procedure, which came into force on 28 June 1867. The two codes were not solely Caron's work, but of the codifiers it was certainly he who by his knowledge of law and the equitable quality of his judgement left the deepest imprint upon them.

Caron then resumed his duties as a judge, and on 14 Feb. 1873 was appointed lieutenant governor of Quebec in succession to Narcisse-Fortunat Belleau*, the first holder of the position. He took as his motto the following Latin words, "suaviter in modo fortiter in re." In this office he acquitted himself with great dignity. He gave the residence of Spencer Wood, which his predecessor had hardly lived in, an air of vice-regal grandeur. A pious man, he decided to establish a chapel there, and mass was celebrated in it for the first time on 23 Oct. 1873. Caron died on 13 Dec. 1876, and his funeral took place in the basilica of Quebec on 20 December. The papers were happy to stress that the city of Quebec had not witnessed the funeral of a head of state for over a century. The funeral oration was delivered by the vicar general Thomas-Étienne Hamel*, who recalled the piety of the deceased and emphasized that at Spencer Wood "the evening prayer and the rosary were recited by the lieutenant governor," probably as it was done at Sainte-Anne-de-Beaupré during the young peasant's childhood. Caron had remained deeply attached to his native village, a celebrated place of pilgrimage, and on 26 July 1875, not long before his death, he had presented a processional banner to the church of Sainte-Anne-de-Beaupré in the name of several subscribers, and in the presence of

7,000 pilgrims. He was buried in Belmont cemetery.

On 10 July 1865 Caron had received from Université Laval the degree of doctor of laws *honoris causa*. On 24 Nov. 1875 he had been promoted to the rank of grand cross of the order of St Gregory the Great. On 20 June 1848 he had been made a queen's counsel. He had been an officer in the militia, becoming a lieutenant on 6 Dec. 1825 and a captain in the Quebec artillery on 30 Dec. 1837. On 15 Sept. 1853 the Société Saint-Jean-Baptiste of Quebec had thanked him for the important services he had rendered as its second president from 1842 to 1852.

On 16 Sept. 1828, at Notre-Dame de Québec, Caron had married Marie-Vénérande-Joséphine Deblois, daughter of Joseph Deblois and Marie-Vénérande Ranvoyzé. They had several children, including Joseph-Philippe-René-Adolphe*, a minister in the governments of John A. Macdonald*, John Joseph Caldwell Abbott*, and Mackenzie Bowell*; Corine, wife of Sir Charles Fitzpatrick*; and Marie-Joséphine, wife of Jean-Thomas Taschereau* and mother of Louis-Alexandre*, the future prime minister of Quebec.

Among the secondary personages of the union period, Caron occupied one of the first places. To a certain extent, he represented moderate sentiments in his region, with his sincere desire to reach compromises in order to benefit from the union, but he never yielded on the principles he regarded as essential. He was one of those who brought about responsible government, and, furthermore, his legal knowledge enabled him to carry through to a successful conclusion the important task of codification. Louis-Philippe TURCOTTE seems to have aptly expressed the judgement of his contemporaries when he wrote at the time of his death: "His career has been useful to his country. He has always followed a straight course, guided solely by his conscience and his conception of duty."

J.-C. BONENFANT

[The Caron papers are found in the ANQ and the ASQ, Fonds Caron, 1–4; MSS, 764–817. They consist of a certain number of private and official letters, account books, and especially documents he used in the codification. A concise inventory of the latter is found in a study by Professor J. E. C. Brierley, "Quebec's civil law codification; viewed and reviewed," *McGill Law Journal* (Montreal), XIV (1968), 521–89.

The correspondence between Caron, Draper, and La Fontaine is published: *Correspondance entre l'Hon. W. H. Draper et l'Hon. R.-É. Caron; et entre l'Hon. R.-É. Caron, et les honorables L.-H. Lafontaine et A.-N. Morin, dont il a été question dans un débat récent dans l'Assemblée législative* (Québec, 1846). It also appeared in English: *Correspondence between the Hon. W. H. Draper & the Hon. R. E. Caron . . .* (Montreal, 1846).

No real biography of Caron has been written. The one published by the *Journal de Québec* on 14 Dec. 1876, the day after the death of the lieutenant governor, over the initials L.T. was only a copy, with a few variants, of a pamphlet by L.-P. Turcotte, *L'honorable R.-É. Caron, lieutenant-gouverneur de la province de Québec* (Québec, 1873). The biography of Caron in Le Jeune, *Dictionnaire*, I, is often referred to but is quite incomplete. However it is patterned after a more complete biography, found in Dent, *Canadian portrait gallery*, I.

General works on the union are full of material on Caron: Chapais, *Histoire du Canada*, V, VI; Dent, *Last forty years*; Antoine Gérin-Lajoie, *Dix ans au Canada de 1840 à 1850; histoire de l'établissement du gouvernement responsable* (Québec, 1888); Turcotte, *Canada sous l'Union*; Monet, *Last cannon shot*. The last of these is the most recent and gives a more balanced view of Caron. J.-C. B.]

CARON, THOMAS, secular priest, teacher at the seminary of Nicolet; b. 19 June 1819 at Saint-Antoine-de-la-Rivière-du-Loup (Louiseville), L.C., son of Louis Caron, farmer, and Euphrosine Béland; d. 24 Sept. 1878 at Nicolet, Que.

Like many young men of his parish and the surrounding area, Thomas Caron enrolled at the seminary of Nicolet in 1831 for his classical education. Seven years later he began the study of theology, at the same time teaching the adolescents of the seminary. He was ordained priest in 1842, lived in the institution that had trained him, and was at first a teacher of rhetoric and theology there. Subsequently he was in turn director of students, teacher of theology, and director of seminarists. His bishop appointed him three times superior of the seminary of Nicolet (1855–59, 1861–68, 1871–77), and in 1857 chose him as vicar general of the diocese of Trois-Rivières.

As a priest Thomas Caron was profoundly imbued with the evangelical spirit. Always ready to give of himself ungrudgingly, and of exemplary goodness, he was loved by all those who lived near him. It was no doubt for this reason that pupils called him "papa Thomas." When he was teaching the seminarists, he drew up courses which have survived in manuscript form and which are a sound synthesis of the numerous theological treatises that were to be found in his personal library. He was most careful to provide teaching of good quality.

As a member of the corporation of the seminary of Nicolet, Caron worked towards the affiliation of the seminary with the Université Laval. In 1863 he succeeded in smoothing away the difficulties that had been delaying the realization of this project for ten years. The authorities of the seminary of Nicolet had indeed feared to lose their independence to the seminary of Quebec, whose priests directed the Université Laval. This question had barely been settled before he had to take up the problem of the poor results of the Nicolet students in the university examinations.

The finest moment of his life was probably in 1869, when his bishop, Thomas Cooke*, chose him to accompany Bishop Louis-François Laflèche* to the Vatican Council; Laflèche and Caron were friends of long standing. But on his return Caron had to defend his college against the inhabitants of Trois-Rivières, who insisted that the seminary of Nicolet close its doors. He opposed this demand with all his strength, so much so that his health was affected. According to Bishop Joseph-Antoine-Irénée Douville, who knew him well, this affair was one of the reasons for his premature death.

CLAUDE LESSARD

ASN, Boîte I; Boîte II; Polygraphie, V, 19, 21–24, 32–33; Séminaire, VII, 56; Séminaire, IX, 39–51. *L'Écho de Saint-Justin* (Louiseville, Qué.), 2 mars 1925. J.-A.-I. Douville, *Histoire du collège-séminaire de Nicolet, 1803–1903, avec les listes complètes des directeurs, professeurs et élèves de l'institution* (2v., Montréal, 1903), I, 409; II, 115–21. Germain Lesage, *Histoire de Louiseville, 1665–1910* (Louiseville, Qué., 1961), 170.

CARPENTER, PHILIP PEARSALL, Presbyterian minister, conchologist, and social reformer; b. 4 Nov. 1819 in Bristol, Eng., youngest of six children of Lant Carpenter and Anna Penn; d. 24 May 1877 in Montreal, Que.

Philip Pearsall Carpenter attended Bristol College, 1833–36, and then Manchester College, York, 1837–40; that college became affiliated with the University of London and he received a BA degree in the same year, 1841. In that year also he was ordained a Presbyterian minister. His first ministry was at Stand (Lancashire), 1841–46, where on 1 Dec. 1841 he became an avowed teetotaller. The period 1841–50 was one of distress and discontent in the manufacturing areas, and there were riots and burning. Carpenter was much concerned with these social problems. In his ministry at Warrington (Lancashire), 1846–58, where his religious commitment became Unitarian in emphasis, he tried to alleviate unemployment and ill health from lack of sanitation; he started a day and night school for men, an industrial school for women, was secretary of a working men's sanitary association, taught swimming to working people, and helped to establish an industrial school in 1847. In this latter school, printing was used as a means of encouraging literacy and teaching a trade to the unemployed. Subsequently a cooperative printing business, the Oberlin Press, was established, and it printed religious publications.

In his youth Carpenter had helped to arrange shells in the Bristol museum and he kept his interest in collecting. In 1855 he was helped by a relative to purchase a famous collection of west Mexican sea shells, made by Frederick Reigen. Carpenter reviewed over 100,000 shells in this collection, and gave two reports on it to the British Association for the Advancement of Science in 1856 as well as publishing at the Oberlin Press a 552-page *Catalogue*. From this collection, sets were given to the British Museum and sent abroad; one was accepted by the State Cabinet of Natural History in Albany (New York) on condition that Carpenter be its curator. Many scientific publications by Carpenter followed between 1855 and 1873, principally on living mollusks from British Columbia to Panama; he also participated in meetings of the British Association for the Advancement of Science.

Carpenter was given leave of absence at Warrington in 1858, and went to Albany. The visit to America was all the more welcome as his lack of sympathy with dogma and his belief in "the right of any member of the Church to search freely after the truth, and to hold and teach whatever appears to him to reveal the will of God" had set him apart in Warrington and were to lead to a final disassociation with the church there in 1862.

After arranging the Mazatlan shells at Albany, he went to arrange and catalogue the shell collection of the Smithsonian Institution, Washington, and when he returned to England the collection was sent to him so that he could continue. His strong views against slavery in the critical period before the Civil War made it necessary that he remain in the Smithsonian during his work in Washington. Carpenter travelled over 12,000 miles in America, meeting with temperance and anti-slavery groups. He attended many Roman Catholic services, with which he found himself in "religious sympathy" and whose music he greatly enjoyed. On three visits to Montreal he lectured on sanitary reform and at McGill University on his scientific work, becoming a friend of Sir John William Dawson* and Sir William Edmond LOGAN. He collected natural history specimens, and became a corresponding member of a number of scientific societies in the United States and England. In 1860 he received a PHD degree from the University of the State of New York, the first such degree granted by that body.

Carpenter returned to Warrington in 1860, and ministered there for another year and a half. On

Carrall

1 Oct. 1860 he married Minna Meyer, formerly of Hamburg, Germany, a friend of long standing; they adopted a young American orphan boy whom Carpenter had befriended in the Smithsonian Institution. He continued his arranging of shells and writing of scientific articles.

The Carpenters left for Montreal on 26 Oct. 1865. Believing that McGill University was the best place in British North America for natural history, he had given his large shell collection to McGill University, to be called the Carpenter Collection. In Montreal he continued to look after it and he gave lectures at various times, but he did not have a formal position at McGill. He opened West-End Select School for boys, often from Montreal's best families, in 1866. His preoccupation with social welfare continued, and he was involved in several citizens' committees endeavouring to combat the high death rate in Montreal and the unsanitary conditions which made attacks of pestilence a danger. Among his associates were William Hales Hingston*, Alexander Vidal*, William Bennett Bond*, and William WORKMAN. He was an indefatigable worker, lecturing and publishing pamphlets on temperance and on vaccination, and he continued his scientific work and writing, particularly a monograph on Chitons. Poor health gradually sapped his energy, and he died of typhoid fever.

Carpenter was a natural and persistent lecturer, with a sincere love of humanity, who strove in his ministry to follow the teachings of Jesus Christ. Prohibitionist, abolitionist, vegetarian, a supporter of reform in the living conditions of the poor and illiterate, he was respected and loved by all, whether they agreed with his doctrines or not. His chief personal delights were music and the collecting of shells, and from the latter enthusiasm he made himself an outstanding authority among the conchologists of his day by his careful and persevering habits of analysis and comparison.

KATHERINE V. W. PALMER

[P. P. Carpenter wrote two reports for the British Association for the Advancement of Science on west coast Mollusca. The second, "Supplementary report on the present state of our knowledge with regard to the Mollusca of the west coast of North America," *Report of the British Association for the Advancement of Science for 1863* (London, 1864), 517–686, is still one of the best compendiums in molluscan literature, particularly in reference to the west coast, from Linnaeus to Carpenter's day. It has a wealth of data and concise evaluation. Carpenter's principal works are: *Catalogue of the collection of Mazatlan shells in the British Museum: collected by Frederick Reigen, described by P. P. Carpenter*, ed. J. E. Gray (London, 1857); "Description of (supposed) new species and varieties of shells, from the Californian and west

Mexican coasts, principally in the collection of Hugh Cuming," Zoological Society of London, *Proceedings*, XXIII (1855), 228–35; *Memoirs of the life and work of Philip Pearsall Carpenter . . . chiefly derived from his letters*, ed. R. L. Carpenter (1st ed., London, 1879; 2nd ed., 1880); *The mollusks of western North America . . . embracing the second report made to the British Association on this subject with other papers . . .* (Smithsonian Miscellaneous Collections, X, Washington, 1873). K.V.W.P.]

K. E. H. Palmer, *Type specimens of marine Mollusca described by P. P. Carpenter from the west coast (San Diego to British Columbia)* (Geological Society of America, Memoir 76, [New York], 1958).

CARRALL (Carroll), ROBERT WILLIAM WEIR, doctor and politician; b. 2 Feb. 1837 at Carrall's Grove, near Woodstock, U.C., son of James and Jane Carrall; d. 19 Sept. 1879 at Carrall's Grove, Ont.

Robert William Weir Carrall, the grandson of a United Empire Loyalist, described himself as "a patriotic Canadian, descended from a race of patriotic Canadians – one of the oldest families in Canada." He is said to have been educated at Trinity College, Toronto, though he did not graduate, and he received his MD from McGill University in 1859. He practised for a short time in his native country, but late in 1862 he became a "contract" surgeon with the Union forces of the United States and served during the Civil War as acting assistant surgeon. He was on duty first at Emory Hospital, Washington, D.C., from 12 Dec. 1862 to 12 Sept. 1863, and subsequently at the Marine United States General Hospital at New Orleans, La., from 5 Dec. 1863 until his contract was cancelled at his own request on 8 July 1865.

By the end of October 1865 Carrall was established as a medical doctor in Nanaimo, Vancouver Island, where he took an active part in community affairs. He was elected ensign of the Nanaimo Volunteer Rifle Corps and was one of the "musical amateurs" who attempted to organize a brass band. He appears to have also been a freemason, a charter member of the Nanaimo Lodge no.1090, A.F. & A.M.

In 1867 Carrall left Nanaimo for Barkerville, where he practised his profession and also invested in various mines. The mining records for 1868 show that he had an interest in two companies on Williams Creek, and he is said to have been "the lucky owner of two shares in the rich Minnehaha claim." Confederation was now in the air, and Carrall, from the first "a zealous advocate" of the scheme, was chairman on 23 Nov. 1867 of a large meeting at Barkerville which passed a resolution in favour of confederation. He was reported as declaring that "we will span the continent with a

138

cordon of thinking, energetic, pulsating humanity, and a railroad will follow as a consignment [*sic*] to their necessities." For Carrall had returned from his 1862–65 sojourn in the United States "a greater Canadian than ever," and he could foresee his native Canada stretching from ocean to ocean, still part of the British empire and enabled by means of a transcontinental railroad "to compete with the United States for the European immigration." Carrall reported the feeling in the Cariboo to Sir John A. Macdonald*, whom he was later to eulogize as "a mighty Prince" and "the great father of this young Dominion . . . one of the nation-makers." Macdonald urged him to "keep the Union fire alight until it burns over the whole Colony," and Carrall did his utmost.

In the October 1868 election, in which confederation was the main issue, he gained a seat on the Legislative Council, on which he served until 1871. In January 1870 Governor Anthony Musgrave*, taking every precaution to ensure confederation and well aware of the doctor's correspondence with Sir John, gave him a seat on the Executive Council, and on 20 April he was appointed one of the three delegates to Ottawa to discuss the terms of British Columbia's union with Canada. In Ottawa, Carrall was the only delegate to have an interview with Macdonald, who was too ill to take part in the general negotiations, in which Carrall's role was to "make the most" of the interior of British Columbia and its economic value to Canada. After the triumph of the British Columbia delegation Carrall remained for a time in his native province, and on 31 Dec. 1871 he was appointed to the Senate.

He took his seat on 11 April 1872 as one of the three senators from British Columbia and made his maiden speech on 22 May on the insolvency laws. His most notable achievement came in 1879, during the last session before his death, when he introduced the bill "to make the first day of July a Public Holiday by the name of Dominion Day." He had made the proposal, apparently, as soon as he entered the Senate, but such a measure was deemed inexpedient at that time, for "some of the provinces were new in the harness of Confederation, and were restive – Nova Scotia to wit." In 1879 it was B.C. which was "irritated and restive," as Carrall admits. Nevertheless, he thought, "now is the time to legislate for a complete crystallization of the factions of the Dominion into one harmonious whole," by establishing one particular day as a national holiday, as every other country has done. He himself, he adds, has "always loved the Dominion dearly. I helped to bind it together, and I have worked since with all the energy I possessed by vote and voice, to consolidate it." In spite of the opposition of his fellow senator from British Columbia, Clement Francis Cornwall* (who felt that the union of his province with Canada had "not been so consummated as to render it expedient that we should establish any particular day as a recognition of Confederation"), Carrall's bill was passed.

A "good natured, sociable and companionable" bachelor, who "knew everybody almost between Halifax and Cariboo," Carrall seems to have thoroughly enjoyed his life in Ottawa, though he complained privately in 1872 that he was "worked to death *socially* – Dinners or Dances every night, and all the next day the anguish of having lost my heart which I invariably do from *one* to *four* times every night, oh! why was I created with such susceptibilities? or why on earth [are] the girls so sweet!!!" Just a few months before his death Carrall was married in Ottawa on 8 May 1879 to Mrs Elizabeth Amelia Macdonald Gordon, daughter of a former sheriff of Goderich, who survived him. Local tradition has it that Carrall married the widowed sweetheart of his youth so that he could leave her his property.

He is said to have died of "ulceration of the stomach." This was probably a condition of long standing, for George A. Walkem*, then premier of British Columbia, wrote privately to Sir John from Victoria on 29 Nov. 1878 that he was "afraid poor Carrall's days will be numbered. Liver, kidneys, & stomach are all badly affected & the doctor considers his recovery hopeless. He is of course in bed." Nevertheless Carrall rallied sufficiently to return to Ottawa to take part in the session of 1879 and to carry through with fortitude and spirit his cherished bill to establish Dominion Day.

DOROTHY BLAKEY SMITH

PABC, Robert William Weir Carrall correspondence, 1866–76; J. S. Helmcken, "Reminiscences" (5v. unpublished typescript, 1892), V. PAC, MG 26, A (Macdonald papers), correspondence with R. W. W. Carrall, 1868–78; correspondence regarding R. W. W. Carrall, 1870–87. National Archives (Washington), Old Military Records Division, Bureau of Medicine and Surgery, Medical officers file, R. W. W. Carrall. British Columbia, Legislative Council, "Debate on the subject of confederation with Canada," *Government Gazette Extraordinary* (Victoria), March 1870. Canada, Senate, *Debates*, 1872–79. *Cariboo Sentinel* (Barkerville, B.C.), 1868–71. *Colonist* (Victoria), 4 Oct. 1879. *Nanaimo Gazette*, 1865–66. *Victoria Daily Standard*, 4 Oct. 1879. *Can. directory of parliament* (Johnson). *Can. parl. comp., 1873*; *1874*; *1875*; *1878*; *1879*. M. A. Ormsby, *British Columbia*, chap. 9; "Relations between British Columbia and the Dominion of Canada," unpublished PHD thesis, Bryn Mawr College, [1934]. *British Columbia & confederation*,

Carter

ed. W. G. Shelton (Victoria, 1967), especially Brian Smith, "The confederation delegation," 195–216.

CARTER, Sir JAMES, lawyer and judge; b. in Portsmouth, Eng., 25 Jan. 1805, son of Captain James Carter of the British army, one-time mayor of Portsmouth; d. at Mortimer Lodge, Berkshire, Eng., 10 March 1878.

James Carter went to school in Walthamstow, one of his schoolmates being Benjamin Disraeli, and continued his education at Manchester College, York, and at Trinity College, Cambridge. He then studied law at the Inner Temple under his cousin, John Bonham Carter, was called to the bar in 1832, and served on the western circuit until 1834. With the aid of his cousin's political influence he was appointed in 1834 to the New Brunswick bench by the secretary of state for the colonies, Thomas Spring-Rice.

Carter's appointment, coming at a time when the province was in the throes of political excitement over crown lands and quitrents, caused an uproar especially among the legal profession who were educated to believe that judicial honours would fall to them in strict line of seniority. There were many outbursts in the press against the appearance on the New Brunswick bench of a 29-year-old stranger from England; a meeting of the New Brunswick bar passed a resolution protesting the appointment. The historian James Hannay* correctly interprets their reaction as one against "a gross insult" to the people of the province. A new colonial secretary apologized and promised that in the future judicial appointments would go to natives of New Brunswick.

Yet Carter's character and presence on the bench were so impressive that the heated reaction against him quickly abated. Lemuel Allen WILMOT wrote a panegyric on him in the press on 25 Feb. 1835, concluding the piece with the quotation, "O wise and upright judge, how much older art thou than thy looks." Approval grew stronger as the presence of a judge who was free of the family connections and alliances that explain New Brunswick politics at the time became more appreciated. Probably the most famous case he heard was that of the libel action against James Doak and Thomas Hill*, two journalists who in 1844 were jailed for contempt of the House of Assembly. Carter's award of a *habeas corpus* brought to an end the assembly's old custom of imprisoning those who offended its "privileges."

The second occasion on which Carter unwittingly became a principal in a constitutional quarrel was in 1851 when he was appointed chief justice. Renowned for an ability to keep out of politics, he found his name a subject for political speculation, each time with fortunate results. The lieutenant governor, Sir Edmund Head*, confronted by a divided government who refused to give collective advice on a successor to the chief justice, Ward Chipman*, unilaterally made the recommendation that Carter receive the appointment. The reasons Head gave were Carter's superior legal education, his aloofness from politics, and his private fortune. Charles FISHER led a powerful agitation in the assembly and the press against the appointment. The cry arose that the lieutenant governor had violated the principle of responsible government and that New Brunswick had slipped back under the complete control of Downing Street. Sir Edmund Head was called a tyrant, but Carter was serenely unaffected.

Having served as a referee in the Ryland case, a contentious affair in Anglo-Canadian relations, Chief Justice Carter was knighted in 1859. Eager to strengthen ties between the mother country and colonies, the British government had previously suggested awarding honours to eminent citizens of the province. The lieutenant governor, John Henry Thomas MANNERS-SUTTON, replied that honours would not produce the political result intended and that public opinion would be hostile. He would name but one man, Carter, as worthy of knighthood. Nothing was done until public opinion abruptly changed with news that the award had been conferred on Brenton Halliburton*, justice of Nova Scotia. Carter then became the first resident of New Brunswick to receive the honour of knighthood.

Suffering from failing health, Carter resigned in 1865. By arrangement with the lieutenant governor, Arthur Hamilton Gordon*, the withdrawal was carefully timed so that a place on the bench could be offered to the leader of the anti-confederate government, Albert James Smith*, thus easing the way for New Brunswick to accept confederation. Smith, however, refused.

In 1866 Carter left for England, where he died 13 years later at the residence of his son. He had been married three times: in 1831 to Emma Wellbeloved; in 1844 to Mary Ann Elizabeth Miller, by whom he had two sons; and in 1852 to Margaret Spencer Coster, by whom he had one daughter. Although he occupied a leading place in the more intellectual areas of Fredericton society, Carter enjoyed the wild life of the wilderness, keeping a bear and a beaver in captivity on his premises at Frogmore. He is invariably described as a highly cultivated man, gifted with a melodious singing voice, who for many years played the organ at St Anne's Church in Fredericton. A man of mild temperament and retired habits, his prominence as a figure of controversy in New

Brunswick's public life was quite unsought. The province discovered, however, that he had served it well.

W. S. MacNutt

[There is no collection of Sir James Carter's private papers in New Brunswick. Summaries of his judicial cases can be found in the Public Archives of New Brunswick. PRO, CO 188/105–188/132 contain numerous references to Carter. The Robb Letters at the University of New Brunswick Library, Archives and Special Collections Dept., contain many flattering allusions to him. For a biography see: Lawrence, *Judges of New Brunswick* (Stockton), 339–70. Also see Hannay, *History of New Brunswick*, II, 88, 94, and MacNutt, *New Brunswick*, 242, 342, 378–79, 437. w.s.m.]

CARTER, ROBERT, naval officer, magistrate, and politician; b. at Ferryland, Nfld., in 1791, son of William Carter*, judge of the Vice-Admiralty Court, and Anne Weston; m. to Anne Hutchings by whom he had one son and three daughters; d. in St John's, Nfld., 25 May 1872.

Robert Carter was the grandson of the first Carter to settle in Ferryland, where the family were prominent merchants and holders of the magistracy. He appears to have joined the navy at an early age, and was retired soon after the peace of 1815 with the rank of lieutenant. In 1843 he was promoted commander (retired). After the death of his elder brother William in 1815, Robert Carter was appointed surrogate magistrate in his place, probably early in 1817. He served in that capacity at Ferryland until early in 1826, when he retired amid subsequently unsubstantiated accusations of improper judicial behaviour. The first general election in Newfoundland was held in 1832, and Carter won the Ferryland seat. From that time his career was largely politically oriented and he moved to St John's.

The years between 1832 and 1836 saw the rise of denominationalism in local politics, and Carter, a member of the Church of England, was defeated in the Catholic district of Ferryland in 1836. From 1842 to 1852 and again from 1855 to 1859 he represented Bonavista Bay, and from 1859 to 1865, Fortune Bay. Both these districts were largely Protestant. Throughout his time in the assembly, Carter was a prominent member of the Protestant Conservative party, which was, however, in a minority from 1836 to 1861. But since, before the introduction of responsible government in 1855, patronage lay in the hands of the governor and council, Carter received several appointments of ascending importance. He remained a justice of the peace for the Ferryland area and served as a road commissioner there in the late 1830s. Following the fire that devastated St John's in

June 1846, he was appointed supervisor of streets, an important post which he held until the replanning of the town was completed in 1848. In October 1849 Carter became colonial treasurer and a governor of the Savings Bank. The tenacity with which he held to these posts slightly impeded the transition to responsible government in 1855. His demand for a retirement allowance being disallowed, Carter refused to resign. He argued that he had not been appointed as treasurer under the conditions imposed by the resolution, passed by the assembly in April 1849 and later approved by the Colonial Office, which stated that all executive appointees after that date would be liable to removal without compensation upon the introduction of responsible government. He received neither pension nor sympathy, and finally in May 1855 Governor Sir Charles Henry Darling* had to order him from office.

Carter's resistance to the change was typical of many of his class, who feared not only the loss of their positions but also a Roman Catholic political ascendancy. In 1861 a crisis within the largely Catholic government party led by John Kent enabled the Conservatives under the leadership of Hugh Hoyles*, openly backed by the governor, Sir Alexander Bannerman*, to seize power. Carter became colonial secretary in the Hoyles ministries of 1861 and 1861–65. When Hoyles resigned as premier in the summer of 1865 to become chief justice, Carter lost his post, but he remained a member of the Executive Council until just before the election that fall. The Conservatives were again victorious under the leadership of his nephew, Frederick B. T. Carter*. Carter retired from public life at the same time and lived in St John's until his death.

Never of outstanding importance in the political life of his time, Carter was a prominent member of, and spokesman for, the local establishment. Unlike his peers, however, Carter was neither in trade nor in the law; he had an economic dependence on political office which reinforced his resistance to responsible government but hastened his adaptation to the new order.

J. K. Hiller

PANL, Newfoundland, Dept. of the Colonial Secretary, letter books, 1815–27; Newfoundland, Executive Council, minutes, 1865. Newfoundland, *Blue Books*, 1832–65 (copies in PANL); House of Assembly, *Journals*, 1836, 1837, 1838, 1840. Gunn, *Political history of Nfld*. J. R. Smallwood, "The history of the Carter family in Newfoundland," unpublished typescript, 1937 (copy at PANL). E. A. Wells, "The struggle for responsible government in Newfoundland, 1846–1855," unpublished MA thesis, Memorial University of Newfoundland, 1966.

Cartier

CARTIER, Sir GEORGE-ÉTIENNE, lawyer, politician, prime minister of the Province of Canada; b. 6 Sept. 1814 at Saint-Antoine-sur-Richelieu (Verchères County, L.C.), son of Jacques Cartier (1774–1841) and Marguerite Paradis; d. 20 May 1873 in London, Eng.

Cartier's family made no claim to have descended from the discoverer of Canada, who had no children, but they were content to believe, without seeking proof, that a distant ancestor had been a younger brother of the Saint-Malo navigator; they were wrong, although he may have belonged to the same family. All the same, George-Étienne Cartier was coquettish enough to call the country house that he owned near the village of Hochelaga "Limoilou," after Jacques Cartier*'s manor.

In 1738 Jacques Cartier, *dit* l'Angevin, of Prulier in the diocese of Angers, France, set out for New France. In 1744 he married Marguerite Mongeon at Beauport, and became a salt and fish merchant at Quebec. In 1772 one of his sons, Jacques, settled at Saint-Antoine-sur-Richelieu, about 36 miles from Montreal. There he engaged in the grain trade and from 1804 to 1809 represented the constituency of Surrey, later Verchères, in the House of Assembly of Lower Canada. He left his son Jacques a sizeable fortune, which allowed him to lead the agreeable and easy life of a wealthy country squire. Eight children were born of the marriage of Jacques Cartier and Marguerite Paradis in 1798; George-Étienne was the seventh. Another son, François-Damien, also practised law, and was the professional partner of the politician.

Cartier, baptized on the day of his birth at Saint-Antoine-sur-Richelieu, received the name of George in honour of the reigning sovereign George III, hence the English spelling. As there was no school at Saint-Antoine, the boy was first educated by his mother. In 1824 he entered the college of Montreal, directed by the Sulpicians, with whom he retained connections all his life. He was a diligent and brilliant pupil. He completed his secondary education in 1831, and then started his legal training in the office of Édouard-Étienne Rodier*, a Montreal lawyer, who was favourably disposed towards the demands of the *Patriote* party. Called to the bar of Lower Canada on 9 Nov. 1835, he began to practise his profession with his former employer, also continuing to take an active interest in the struggles that marked these years of great excitement, especially in the region of Montreal.

While he was a student Cartier had worked during the 1834 elections on behalf of Louis-Joseph PAPINEAU and Robert NELSON. On 24 June of the same year, at a banquet in Montreal which heralded the birth of the Société Saint-Jean-Baptiste, he had sung a song that he had just composed and that was to survive him, *O Canada, mon pays, mes amours*. At the 1835 banquet he sang another patriotic song he had composed, *Avant tout je suis Canadien*, which later became a rallying-call for the Fils de la Liberté, an association of French Canadian militants, to which Cartier belonged [*see* LEBLANC]. Furthermore, in May 1834 he had been one of two secretaries of a political organization set up under the name of the Comité Central et Permanent du District de Montréal, which demanded that the government respect civil liberties. During the autumn of 1837, when the situation worsened in Lower Canada and rumbles of revolution were heard in assemblies [*see* Papineau], Cartier took part in the events in circumstances which, although unclear, enable us to situate him among those called *Patriotes*. Later on, his participation in the 1837 disturbances did not seem to him a gesture against England, even if he took pleasure in recalling with a smile that he had been a "rebel"; he claimed that it was, rather, a youthful escapade in which, as he wrote on 20 Sept. 1838 to Charles Buller*, the secretary of Lord Durham [Lambton*], he had not "forfeited his allegiance to the government of Her Majesty in the province of Lower Canada." It was, he said, against an oppressive minority rather than against the crown that he had fought, as is shown by these words uttered on 24 Sept. 1844 in a speech at Saint-Denis: "There is no longer any danger of a return to the events of 1837, caused by the actions of a minority which desired to dominate the majority and exploit the government in its own interests. The events of 1837 have been badly interpreted. The object of the people was rather to reduce this oppressive minority to nothingness than to bring about a separation of the province from the mother-country." However that may be, Cartier, who was probably not present at the assembly of the six counties, held at Saint-Charles on 3 October, was at the battle of Saint-Denis on 22 November, and far from deserving the accusations of pusillanimity heaped upon him by some of his opponents, he seems to have acquitted himself bravely. In his speech at Saint-Denis in 1844 he was able to exclaim without being contradicted: "I was of your number, and I do not think I showed lack of courage."

After the *Patriotes*' defeat at Saint-Charles, Cartier, who had remained at Saint-Denis, had to hide, with his cousin Henry Cartier, at Verchères, where he spent the winter with a farmer. His death was announced in the papers, but in reality he had to flee to the United States after his hiding place was discovered. He lived at Plattsburgh and

Burlington (Vermont) from May to October 1838. A proclamation of 9 Oct. 1838 annulled Durham's ordinance, by which on the preceding 28 June Cartier had been included among those accused of treason. He then returned to Montreal and took the authorities to witness that his conduct was "the most pacific and the most irreproachable."

The following year Cartier returned to the practice of law with his brother François-Damien. His great period of activity as a lawyer extended from this year until 1848. After he became a minister, in 1854, he no longer had the time or the opportunity to concern himself personally with his clientele. He had as partners later François-Pierre Pominville, Louis BÉTOURNAY, and Joseph-Amable Berthelot*, and his office numbered among other clients the Grand Trunk and the Sulpicians. In 1852 Cartier introduced in parliament the bill creating the Grand Trunk Railway Company. On 11 July 1853 he was appointed its legal adviser for Canada East. His opponents were quick to accuse him of collusion with the biggest railway company of the day. In 1854, to an MLA who accused him of being an agent of the Grand Trunk and receiving money from it, Cartier replied: "But I do not depend upon the company. I am independent, my private clientèle renders me so . . . the public has had sufficient confidence in me as a lawyer to render me independent of all emolument I may receive from the Grand Trunk company." One must nevertheless note that according to the deed of partnership between Cartier and Pominville, the politician was entitled to only one fifth of the income received, and that this restriction did not apply to the business of the Grand Trunk Company.

While carrying on his profession, Cartier continued to take an interest in public affairs. At the time of the reorganization of the Société Saint-Jean Baptiste in 1843, he became its secretary. In the political sphere, he accepted the union, became a supporter of Louis-Hippolyte La Fontaine*, and demanded the application of the principle of responsible government. On 18 Sept. 1842, immediately following the formation of the first ministry of La Fontaine and Robert Baldwin*, Cartier wrote to La Fontaine to congratulate him and tell him of his enthusiasm: "Your appointment has electrified our hearts and our spirits." Cartier seems to have quickly accepted the idea that armed resistance to authority was useless, and that it was better to seek to bring about constitutional reforms. In 1844, when the La Fontaine–Baldwin ministry resigned as a result of the refusal of the governor, Sir Charles Theophilus Metcalfe*, to accept its recommendations, Cartier campaigned in favour of ministerial responsibility

in the general elections that followed. Because he did not feel sufficiently established in his profession, he rejected a number of proposals that he should himself be a candidate, but finally agreed to stand against Amable Marion in a by-election in Verchères; on 7 April 1848 he was elected a member of the Legislative Assembly of United Canada. It was then that his true political career began; it continued uninterrupted until his death.

Cartier took his seat at the session that began at Montreal on 18 Jan. 1849, and that was marked at the end of April by the adoption of the rebellion losses bill and by the ensuing riot. He was in favour of the measure, although he did not take part in the debate. He also sided with La Fontaine in the debate that pitted the latter against Papineau. To the former leader who had returned to politics after his years of exile and who asked for the repeal of the union, La Fontaine replied that the regime had been planned in order to crush the French Canadians, but that the latter had succeeded in utilizing it for their own benefit, and they must continue to extract every advantage from it. Cartier was to put this idea into practice. Only one of his speeches during this session has been preserved, one dealing with the St Lawrence and Atlantic Railway and delivered on 15 Feb. 1849; in it all the interest he was to take in railway development, to which he was accused of being slavishly devoted, is already apparent. That same year, as an MLA, he protested against the movement started among politicians and businessmen, particularly of English origin, in favour of the annexation of Canada to the United States, and the subsequent published Annexation Manifesto [see HOLTON]. Cartier all his life had an almost morbid fear of the United States, and was always strongly opposed to its republican institutions. He continued to dread annexation, and in 1870, in a speech against a possible customs union with the United States, he went so far as to say: "Individually, the Americans are good neighbours, but as a nation, there are no individuals in the world who are less liberal towards other peoples, except the Chinese."

Cartier soon showed himself to be one of the most important French Canadian MLAs. He was re-elected by acclamation in Verchères in the general election of December 1851, and in 1852 took his seat at Quebec, now once more the capital. La Fontaine had just retired, and power was held by the moderate Reformers, led by Augustin-Norbert Morin* and Francis Hincks*. In general, Cartier supported the two men, but he refused to join the government they directed; he frankly admitted, in a speech on 22 Sept. 1852, that the inadequate stipend attached to the post offered was one of the reasons that prevented him from accepting. Cartier defended the government's policy, nevertheless, against the opposition, which reproached it for postponing the discussion of important questions, such as the secularization of the clergy reserves and the abolition of seigneurial tenure. The government was however in a minority, and it decided to appeal to the governor general, Lord Elgin [Bruce*], to dissolve parliament and call a general election. In August 1854, Cartier was re-elected in Verchères over L.-H. Massue. Of the three groups of representatives returned – the moderate Reformers of Lower and Upper Canada who supported the Hincks–Morin government, the radical Reformers of Upper and Lower Canada, and the Conservatives – none possessed an absolute majority, and none could form a stable government. From the first day of the session, when the speaker was elected, the Hincks–Morin ministry saw how precarious its position was. The Reformers had decided at a general meeting that Cartier should be their candidate for this post. For their part, the Clear Grits and the Conservatives of Upper Canada were in favour of John Sandfield MACDONALD, who had already held the post, and the Lower Canadian opposition wanted Louis-Victor Sicotte*, the MLA for Saint-Hyacinthe. Cartier was proposed on 5 Sept. 1854, but only collected 59 votes against 62, and it was Sicotte who was finally elected. Despite its weakness, the government continued to sit until 7 September, when it was defeated on a question of privilege. The Hincks–Morin government resigned, and an alliance of the Conservatives and moderate Reformers then took place; it was the origin of the Liberal-Conservative party. This coalition supported the ministry of Allan Napier MacNab* and Augustin-Norbert Morin, who was replaced on 27 Jan. 1855 by Étienne-Paschal Taché*. When the MacNab–Taché government was set up, Cartier was called upon to assume the office of provincial secretary for Canada East. As the law required that a minister should have his mandate renewed by his electors, Cartier stood again in Verchères. His opponent was Christophe Préfontaine, and he emerged victorious from a violent struggle waged against him by the radical Reformers, the Rouges, with whom he would have to contend from then on. On 24 May 1856 the MacNab–Taché ministry was replaced by that of Taché and John A. Macdonald*, and Cartier became attorney general for Canada East. On 26 Nov. 1857, as Prime Minister Taché had decided to give up active politics, John A. Macdonald, with Cartier, formed a government; in this government, which was called Macdonald–Cartier until 1 Aug.

1858 and then, from 23 May 1862, Cartier–Macdonald, Cartier remained attorney general.

Since La Fontaine had departed and Taché was growing old, Cartier had become the most influential man in the Lower Canadian section. At the elections held at the end of 1857, following the formation of the ministry, Cartier was re-elected in Verchères over his former opponent Préfontaine but was defeated in Montreal, where he had also stood, by Antoine-Aimé Dorion*. (In the general election of 1861, Cartier stood only in the newly created riding of Montreal East, and this time he emerged victorious from the battle against A.-A. Dorion.) For some years the assembly had been discussing the selection of a permanent capital: the cities of Quebec, Montreal, and Bytown (Ottawa) had been suggested. In 1857, nonplussed by varying opinions, the Macdonald–Cartier ministry obtained approval for an address to the queen in which she was requested to choose a capital. On the advice of her Canadian ministers, she decided on Ottawa. At first a supporter of Montreal, Cartier had finally come round to Ottawa, a choice which at the time seemed surprising, but which was consistent with the development of Canada westwards. In July 1858, when the royal decision was made known, a motion passed by a vote of 64 for and 50 against stating that "in the opinion of this House the City of Ottawa should not be the permanent seat of the government of this province." The Macdonald–Cartier ministry decided to resign and was replaced for two days by a ministry led by George BROWN and Antoine-Aimé Dorion; it was unable to preserve the majority required to remain in power because of the necessity for the new ministers to be re-elected. To avoid this difficulty the Cartier–Macdonald ministry, which replaced it, resorted to a device that has remained in history under the name of "double shuffle." Interpreting strictly the law that dispensed with re-election for a minister called to another ministerial post within a period of one month after his resignation, the ministers first accepted portfolios different from those they had held in the former government, and the next day resumed their former offices, thus being freed from the obligation to be re-elected. The Cartier–Macdonald ministry did, however, have to resign in May 1862, after being defeated in the house on the second reading of the Militia Bill: several supporters of Cartier deserted him on the grounds that the new law would result in excessive expenditure.

During this period from 1857 to 1862, Cartier gave evidence of great activity. In the autumn of 1858 he went to London with Alexander Tilloch Galt* and John Ross to put before the English government a plan for the federation of the provinces of British North America. Cartier had expressed approval of such a measure in August 1858, when Galt had entered the government on condition that it accept his plan of federation. However, in the face of the reticence of the other provinces, the English government did not deem it wise to put the plan into effect. Cartier was received by Queen Victoria, and it was on this occasion that he stated that an inhabitant of Lower Canada was an Englishman who spoke French. In the summer of 1860, in his capacity as prime minister, he accompanied the Prince of Wales during his visit to Canada and with him, on 25 August, officiated at the opening of Victoria Bridge, of which he had encouraged the construction [see HODGES].

As a minister and prime minister, Cartier was the guiding spirit behind many legislative measures; these measures contributed, in the middle of the last century, to the development of United Canada, and established institutions out of which have grown those that still govern Canada, and more particularly Quebec. In 1855 the government of which Cartier was a member had passed the Lower Canada Municipal and Road Act of 1855 (18 Vict., c.100), which created municipalities corresponding to the church parishes and grouped them in county municipalities; it was the basis of the system still to a great extent in force in Quebec. In 1860 Cartier had this law reshaped, and on 6 March declared that "our municipal system is one of the principal institutions in Lower Canada." He was also a supporter of the organization of primary education in Lower Canada. In 1856 he completed the fundamental 1846 Act (9 Vict., c.27), which established schools in all parishes and confirmed the principle of the religious duality of these schools, by having parliament decree that a council of public instruction be formed, made up of Catholics and Protestants (19 Vict., c.14), and that there be established some training schools for male and female teachers (19 Vict., c.54). He was not a member of the government when, on 18 Dec. 1854, an act for the abolition of feudal rights and duties in Lower Canada (18 Vict., c.3) was ratified, but he had long been in favour of this measure, and in 1853 he had declared categorically: "The seigniorial tenure retards the progress of the country." In 1859, he was to have a law passed which Upper Canada scarcely liked, and on which discussion was lengthy – one sitting lasted 39 hours – to increase the compensation to be paid to former seigneurs, a law that in Cartier's words "will satisfy all the large interests and ... do justice to the seigniors as well as to the *censitaires*" (22 Vict., c.48). In 1856 he took part in a reform of

the Legislative Council, accepting with some reservations, its elective basis.

It was in the sphere of the administration of justice, and in that of law, that Cartier was to accomplish his greatest reforms. In 1857 he got parliament to enact that in the Eastern Townships, populated mainly by Anglophones, French laws would apply as elsewhere in Lower Canada (20 Vict., c.43). The uncertainty that had hitherto prevailed threatened to create a system of personal law under which persons of the same territory were judged according to different law, by reason of their origins. In the same year, going against old traditions, he brought about the decentralization of the judiciary (20 Vict., c.44). By this measure, the number of judges in Lower Canada was considerably augmented, and new judicial districts were instituted outside the large towns. The work of which he was most proud was the codification of civil law. In 1857 he had an act passed "to provide for the codification of the laws of Lower Canada relative to civil matters and procedure" (20 Vict., c.43). To this end provision was made for the setting up of a commission; its president was Judge René-Édouard CARON, who did excellent work during the period 1859 to 1865. Cartier had parliament approve the plan that was drafted (29 Vict., c.41), and the civil code of Lower Canada came into operation on 1 Aug. 1866. The commission then codified the rules of civil procedure, and they were given effect on 28 June 1867. Cartier also, with John A. Macdonald, initiated the great legislative compilations which in 1859 made it possible to publish, in English and French, *The consolidated statutes of Canada*, and, in English, *The consolidated statutes for Upper Canada*; in addition, in 1861 *The consolidated statutes for Lower Canada* appeared in French and English. Hence *La Minerve* was able to write on 21 May 1873, at Cartier's death: "Besides what he has done for the advancement and material prosperity of our country, M. Cartier can claim the honour of having remoulded the legislation of Lower Canada, and of having endowed us with a code of laws which, in this respect, raises us to the level of the most civilized nation in Europe."

Standing out as he did against the ministry of John Sandfield Macdonald and Louis-Victor Sicotte from 24 May 1862 to 15 May 1863, and that of J. S. Macdonald and Antoine-Aimé Dorion from 16 May 1863 to 29 March 1864, Cartier was the government's chief opponent. In the general election of July 1863, he again was a candidate in Montreal East, where he defeated Antoine-Aimé Dorion. The latter had for several years been Cartier's principal opponent in Lower Canada. The liberal ideas that he defended were

Cartier

precisely those that Cartier despised. Dorion's alliance with George Brown harmed him in the minds of the Catholic hierarchy, with which Cartier was on good terms, and despite his great qualities he was forced to spend almost all his life in the opposition.

The session that opened at Quebec on 19 Feb. 1864 was to return Cartier to power and bring about the birth of confederation. At the beginning of the session, Cartier violently criticized the government of J. S. Macdonald and Dorion, which enjoyed only a slight majority. On 25 February he began one of the most fiery and lengthy speeches of his career, which went on for 13 hours and throughout several sittings, and in which he attacked the entire policy of the government. Finally, on 21 March, without waiting to be overthrown, the government resigned. The governor general, Lord Monck*, then called on Cartier to take office, but the latter refused, alleging as a pretext that in the circumstances it was better to put at the head of the administration a man less involved in the political struggles of the last few years. The governor followed his advice, and asked Étienne-Paschal Taché, a legislative councillor and former prime minister, who had almost entirely retired from political life in 1856, to form a ministry. Taché accepted, with John A. Macdonald as his counterpart for Upper Canada, and Cartier entered the government as attorney general for Canada East.

On 14 June 1864 the Taché–Macdonald government was defeated as a result of a vote of censure in the house for neglecting to give effect to a loan previously promised to the City of Montreal. In six years, it was the sixth ministry overthrown; no group seemed capable of taking hold, and a general election, the third in three years, did not seem to be a solution. Then on 16 June after some days of manœuvring, discreetly directed by Lord Monck, a coalition ministry was formed; its leader was theoretically Taché, but the real leaders on the Conservative side were John A. Macdonald and Cartier, with whom George Brown had agreed to ally himself on condition that the constitutional difficulties of the past few years be settled. Like Cartier, the political leader of Upper Canada set aside his personal antipathies for the sake of a national objective. All groups, except the radical liberals of Lower Canada, whom Cartier did not need and whom he regarded as his irreconciliable enemies, were represented in the coalition, which was given its essential character by the presence in the same ministry of Cartier and Brown. Up to then they had been unyielding adversaries, but they agreed to unite in order to bring about the federation of Upper and Lower Canada, or, if

possible, the confederation of all the colonies of British North America. Indeed, the new government undertook to "bring in a measure during the next session for the purpose of removing existing difficulties by introducing the federative principle into Canada, coupled with such provisions as will permit the Maritime provinces and the North-West Territories to be incorporated into the same system of government."

Within the coalition ministry, Cartier was one of the men chiefly responsible for the birth of confederation. After the setback of 1858, he was convinced that a plan emanating from a coalition government would be more acceptable to the mother country. The British government was moreover now in favour of such a plan, as a result of the inquiry that the secretary of state for the colonies, the Duke of Newcastle [Clinton], had circumspectly conducted when he had accompanied the Prince of Wales to Canada in 1860. Cartier became the advocate of a federation of the provinces of British North America because it appeared to him the best way of extrication from the political difficulties of the period, created especially by the question of representation by population. Lower Canada, which in 1840 had received representation equal to that of the less populous Upper Canada, now was favoured by the subsequent reversal in proportions. Cartier realized that Lower Canada could not hold out indefinitely against rep by pop, and that acceptance of it would not have as many disadvantages in a federative state: several areas important for French Canadians, such as education and justice, would be dependent on a local legislature. Cartier also feared annexation to the United States, and in 1865 he declared: "We must either have a Confederation of British North America or else be absorbed by the American Confederation." In order to consolidate the federation of the provinces, and ensure their expansion and economic development, Cartier strongly encouraged the building of the Intercolonial, which was to make Canada one country from east to west. His connections with the railway companies, and the fact that his legal office represented the Grand Trunk – which would gain from the extension of the line towards the Atlantic ports – had no doubt prompted him to favour such a programme, necessary, he felt, for the development of the south shore of the lower St Lawrence. Finally, it was natural that as a politician he should desire to play a role on a larger stage. From June 1864 to 1 July 1867, Cartier bent his energies and intelligence to the realization of the federative project.

Cartier was a member of the United Canada delegation that took part in the Charlottetown conference at the beginning of September 1864, and he was one of the principal speakers who succeeded in convincing the representatives of the other colonies of the advantages of a confederation. By his speeches in favour of the plan, he also participated in the publicity that marked the delegates' return journey via Halifax and Saint John, N.B. At the Quebec conference, held behind closed doors from 10 to 27 October and for which no official account exists, Cartier seems to have remained on the whole silent. This attitude is explained by the fact that the delegates from the colonies were studying John A. Macdonald's proposals, which had been prepared beforehand by the cabinet of United Canada; Cartier had preferred to defend there the measures he believed necessary to safeguard the interests of his Lower Canadian compatriots. At the session of February and March 1865, the Quebec resolutions, containing the details of the plan for federalism, were discussed and approved. Cartier defended them in a long speech on 7 Feb. 1865, first quoting certain texts at length, to prove that the French Canadians had preserved their institutions, their language, and their religion by their adhesion to the British crown, and that furthermore, by not responding to invitations from Washington at the time of the revolution, they had made it possible for British power to continue in America. He concluded: "These historical facts teach us that French-Canadians and English-speaking Canadians should have for each other a mutual sympathy, having both reason to congratulate themselves that Canada is still a British colony." "If we unite," he added, "we will form a political nationality independent of the national origin and religion of individuals." He was opposed to the "democratic system which prevails in the United States," proclaiming that "in this country we must have a distinct form of government in which the monarchical spirit will be found." He asserted that the clergy were in favour of confederation. "The clergy in general," he said, "are opposed to all political dissension, and if they are favourable to the project, it is because they see in confederation a solution to the difficulties which have so long existed." Subsequently he intervened several times during the debate in the house to answer the arguments of the project's opponents. In particular he opposed an appeal to the people that Antoine-Aimé Dorion wanted to make in order to ascertain popular feeling towards this measure. On 13 March he even went so far as to admit formally, half seriously and half in jest: "It is true, I consult no one when I want to make a decision." He alleged as a pretext the urgency that there was to submit the project to the British government once the assembly had

approved it, in accordance with the agreement with the other colonies, even if the latter had not approved in their turn. Indeed, it became evident that the Newfoundland and Prince Edward Island legislatures would not adopt the plan that had been conceived at Quebec. Furthermore in the general election of March 1865 in New Brunswick the supporters of confederation were defeated, and in Nova Scotia the legislature showed some reserve. Despite this situation, Cartier went to London in April, after the session, to present to the government the plan for federalism conceived at the Quebec conference and approved by the legislature of United Canada.

Having returned to Canada at the beginning of July 1865, Cartier continued to play the part of the real leader of the French Canadian majority in the ministry directed by Sir Narcisse Fortunat Belleau*, after Taché's death in July 1865. He took part in the last session held at Quebec, from 8 Aug. to 18 Sept. 1865, and in the first held at Ottawa, from 8 June to 15 Aug. 1866. During the latter session Cartier won acceptance of the plan for the future constitution of Quebec, which provided for the existence of an upper, non-elective chamber; such a chamber was not proposed for Ontario. According to Cartier, economic considerations were not a reason for refusing to give more dignity to our legislative institutions. In reality, a Legislative Council had been established in Quebec for another more precise motive, which his contemporaries stressed: it was intended to protect the Anglo-Saxon minority from the possibility of being harmed by any measure emanating from a lower chamber that represented the popular feeling of the French Canadian majority. It was also during this session that the government of which Cartier was a member suffered a reverse, while attempting to settle the problem of minority rights in education. On 31 July, Hector-Louis Langevin*, solicitor general for Canada East, introduced a bill, inspired by Galt, the object of which was to ensure more rights for Protestants in Quebec. The natural reaction of the Catholics in Upper Canada was to ask that they be granted similar rights, and on 1 August the MLA for Russell, Robert BELL, whose riding on the borders of French Canada was inhabited by many Catholics, introduced on behalf of the separate schools of Upper Canada a bill corresponding to Langevin's. As the MLAs for Upper Canada were opposed to the measure, the government withdrew Langevin's bill, and Bell did the same with his. Galt resigned from the ministry, and Cartier felt obliged to declare, in a speech given at Montreal on 30 Oct. 1866: "After telling you that the Protestants of Lower Canada will have all possible guarantees,

Cartier

I must add that the Catholic minority in Upper Canada will have the same guarantees." While the opposition newspapers highly approved of such a declaration, they expressed scepticism about this promise of Cartier's, and asked what would be the concrete solutions. Cartier and his supporters never gave any precise details.

The fate of the Protestant and Catholic minorities under a future federation was to be discussed again and decided at the London conference. Cartier left Montreal for London on 12 Nov. 1866, and from 4 December on he took part in the work of the conference. The delegates from Canada, New Brunswick, and Nova Scotia approved, with a few changes, the Quebec resolutions; these became the London resolutions, and finally the British North America Act, which was ratified by Queen Victoria on 29 March 1867. According to testimony published on 26 May 1873 in *Le Constitutionnel* of Trois-Rivières by Elzéar Gérin*, who was in London, John A. Macdonald tried to transform the federative system that had been accepted at Quebec into a much more centralized union. George-Étienne Cartier allegedly opposed it, and threatened his colleague that he would wire Prime Minister Belleau and ask for the ministry to be dissolved. Macdonald did not insist. This version has been accepted by some historians, without serious proof, but it remains true that Cartier continued in London, as he had at Quebec, to protect the interests of Lower Canada. He won for his French Canadian compatriots living in Quebec rights that he believed essential at the time. He wanted a Quebec that was master of its destiny in the matter of education, common law, and local institutions. Furthermore, he endeavoured to protect the religious rather than linguistic rights of the minorities in other provinces. One may even wonder whether Cartier believed in a veritable Canadian duality which would allow French speaking Canadians to enjoy their rights fully throughout the country from the point of view both of education and of the use of their language. On 15 January Cartier left London for Rome, where he was given an audience by Pope Pius IX. By the end of the month he was back in the British capital, where he took an enthusiastic part in social activities. He returned to Canada in the middle of May.

On 1 July 1867, the day of the official birth of the dominion of Canada, Cartier was at Ottawa. He entered the cabinet, formed by John A. Macdonald at the request of the governor general, Lord Monck, as minister of militia and defence. When the governor announced that Macdonald had been created by Queen Victoria a knight of the Order of the Bath, and that a number of other politicians, including Cartier, were made companions of the same order, a dignity inferior to the first, the French Canadian leader refused the distinction. In the spring of 1868 Cartier was created a baronet, which conferred on him the title of "Sir" and gave him a rank equal to that of the prime minister. At the end of August and beginning of September 1867, elections were held to choose representatives to the House of Commons and to the Legislative Assembly of Quebec. Cartier stood in Montreal East as candidate for both houses, as the law allowed. He was elected to Ottawa after a hot fight against the labour and liberal candidate Médéric LANCTOT, and he was elected to Quebec against Ludger Labelle. His party gained a resounding victory in the federal and provincial elections. Out of 65 members from Quebec elected to the House of Commons, there were only 12 opponents of confederation. At Quebec, Cartier officially played a somewhat unobtrusive role, content to be merely a member of the house supporting the government of Pierre-Joseph-Olivier Chauveau*, which in fact was strongly under the influence of the federal body. In the general election of 1871, Cartier again managed to get elected to the Legislative Assembly of Quebec, over Célestin Bergevin, but, fearing the voting in Montreal, he stood in Beauharnois.

In August 1872, in the federal general election, Cartier was again a candidate in Montreal East. His Liberal opponent was Louis-Amable Jetté*, and he was defeated by a crushing majority, thus meeting what was called his "political Waterloo." Instead of seeking election in another Quebec riding, which would have required the resignation of a Conservative member and probably resulted in a contested election, Cartier agreed to stand in Provencher, Manitoba, where Louis Riel* and Henry James Clarke* were contestants. The latter gave up his candidacy at the request of the lieutenant governor, Adams George Archibald*. As for Riel, he withdrew after much hesitation, acceding to the earnest requests of Alexandre-Antonin Taché*, archbishop of Saint-Boniface, who was happy to avert in this way the complications that the presence of the Métis leader would certainly have brought about at Ottawa. Cartier therefore had no opponent and was elected in September 1872 without even going to the riding, which he was never to see.

Cartier's defeat in the riding of Montreal East which he had represented for 11 years, and in a town for which he had worked diligently, occasioned surprise and even regrets among his opponents. The governor general, Lord Dufferin [Blackwood*], even wrote to Cartier to express his complete sympathy, and Ignace Bourget*, bishop of Montreal, offered him his condolences. Worn down by illness, Cartier had aged, and had lost his erstwhile ascendency over his supporters; the temporary rise of the Parti National, and to a certain extent the setback that the New Brunswick school question might have seemed to be for Cartier, explain his defeat. At the end of 1871 a certain number of young Liberals, particularly from the Montreal region, among them Louis-Amable Jetté, had attempted to make a synthesis of the best ideas of the two great parties, and had started the Parti National in order to transform the political atmosphere. They were rapidly to return to the Liberal party, but they had time, with their aggressive spirit, to contribute to Cartier's defeat. Furthermore, during the 1871 session the New Brunswick legislature had passed a law declaring that in order to obtain state aid schools must be neutral, which to all intents and purposes made it impossible for the Catholic schools to operate. The latter existed in New Brunswick by virtue of custom, not of law, and thus they could not avail themselves of the protection afforded by article 93 of the British North America Act. In the 1872 session the federal parliament was asked to intervene, and Cartier, in a speech delivered on 29 April, while deploring that New Brunswick had passed the law which had come under attack, admitted that it was valid, and that the protection of minorities at the beginning of federalism was proving to be weak. He was seriously reproached in Quebec.

From 1867 until his death, Cartier was Macdonald's principal lieutenant, and often replaced him as prime minister and leader of the government in the House of Commons. He was a kind of co-prime minister, practically the equal of Macdonald. Officially, he was minister of militia, and attached much importance to this task. He proposed, as a Quebec newspaper put it at the time, to take his "revenge for 1862." He brought before the House of Commons what he regarded as one of the most important measures in his political career, a militia bill that set up a theoretical force of 700,000 men, authorized the formation of numerous regiments, and was the basis of the Canadian system of defence until the war of 1914 (31 Vict., c.40). In the speech that he delivered on 31 March 1868 to introduce the bill in the House of Commons, Cartier explained that he was establishing an active and a reserve militia comprising all the male residents of Canada, from the ages of 18 to 60. "The measure which he was about to introduce ... would have afforded," he was reported to say, "the means of protection and defence required during the last three years, but at a greatly reduced expenditure. Should there be an-

other Fenian invasion they should be met with still stronger force than on the previous occasion. They would make known by their fortifications and militia measure that they were determined to be British...."

Among Cartier's achievements immediately following confederation, may be placed the negotiations that conducted and the measures he had passed to extend Canada from the Atlantic to the Pacific. It was mainly Cartier who was the moving spirit behind the advance westwards; this was something in which he took great pride, but in which, in retrospect, he also saw a few flaws. In October 1868 Cartier and one of his government colleagues, William McDougall*, went to London to negotiate the acquisition of Rupert's Land and the North-West Territory. As McDougall fell ill, the whole burden of the discussions with the British government and the Hudson's Bay Company fell on Cartier alone. He remained in London until April 1869, and had the opportunity to mingle in the political and social life of the capital. Finally, at the beginning of spring, the British government made the company a proposal by which it would receive £300,000 for its territory and retain one-twentieth of the fertile belt. The shareholders accepted the offer, and Cartier returned to Canada in triumph, his negotiations having added more than a quarter of North America to the territory of Canada. At the end of May Cartier had approved by parliament the agreement concluded with the imperial government and the Hudson's Bay Company (32–33 Vict., c.3); when the imperial parliament had in its turn ratified the agreement, the territories were officially joined to Canada on 23 June 1870. It was then necessary to organize these vast spaces, and create political and administrative cadres for the some 10,000 Métis, the descendants of Indians and French and Scotch white people, who lived in the Red River region. The Canadian government had made a clumsy attempt to occupy the new territory and already in the autumn of 1869 had found itself up against resistance from the Métis and from a provisional government directed by Louis Riel. It was Cartier who succeeded in negotiating a solution with Bishop Taché that satisfied most of the Métis' requests, and that took concrete shape in May 1870 with the creation of a new province, Manitoba, which was given a political and administrative system analogous to that of Quebec (33 Vict., c.3). The Métis were guaranteed land; the rights of the two languages were recognized, and the schools of the religious minorities, whether they existed by virtue of law or of custom, were authorized.

It is also to Cartier that we owe in large part the entry of British Columbia into the Canadian

Cartier

confederation. During the spring of 1871, in the absence of John A. Macdonald, who was sick, he obtained the Canadian parliament's approval for the address seeking the establishment of a sixth Canadian province, in return for the promise that it would be linked with the rest of Canada by a railway through the Rockies. "Before very long," Cartier exclaimed prophetically, "the English traveller who lands at Halifax will be able within five or six days to cover half a continent inhabited by British subjects." This became possible in 1885. The government, not wishing itself to build the railway, decided to entrust the responsibility for it to a company, to which in return it would ensure subsidies and grant blocks of land. In the spring of 1872, Cartier introduced a bill in the House of Commons that provided for the building of the Canadian Pacific Railway (35 Vict., c.71). It was at the time of the adoption of this bill that Cartier gave the exultant cry: "All aboard for the West!"

To carry out such a gigantic undertaking, the government had to choose between two financial groups that were competing for its favours. The Canadian Pacific Railway Company, headed by Sir Hugh Allan*, president of a large shipping concern, obtained the contract at the beginning of 1873. It was known that Allan was a political friend of Macdonald and Cartier, but it was none the less a surprise when, at the beginning of April 1873, the Liberal member Lucius Seth Huntington* rose in the House of Commons not only to expose the American origin of the capital of Allan's company, but in particular to assert that the financier had in some sort purchased his contract by paying $350,000 into the Conservative party's funds during the 1872 elections. In the inquiry that ensued, it was proved that Cartier had written to Allan, promising to allow him to build and run the railway, and that he had asked Allan in other letters for sums of money, which were in fact paid: Cartier himself had received $85,000. Such practices were part of the political customs of the day, but this time they were somewhat less than prudent. They are explicable in Cartier's case only by the habit of power, the belief that the good of the party was identified with that of the country, and perhaps also by the beginning of an illness to which he was to succumb at the moment when what has been called the "Pacific Scandal" burst.

At the end of September 1872, after his defeat in Montreal East, Cartier had sailed for England to get treatment in London: he had been suffering since 1871 from chronic nephritis, known as Bright's disease. He had spent the winter in England with his wife and his two daughters. On 20 May 1873 the transatlantic telegraph – Cartier had hailed its inauguration in July 1866 joyously –

transmitted from London a telegram in which Sir John Rose*, the former Canadian minister of finance, then acting as a kind of semi-official representative of Ottawa to the imperial government, announced that Sir George had died that morning at 6 o'clock, and that his body would leave on the 29th for Quebec. The news reached Ottawa in the beginning of the afternoon, and John A. Macdonald, after announcing it to the House of Commons, burst into tears; incapable of continuing to speak, he remained with his right arm extended in a dramatic gesture over the empty seat of one who had been his companion for nearly 20 years. The *Prussian*, which was transporting Cartier's remains, arrived at Quebec on 8 June. A *Libera* was chanted in the basilica at Quebec, and the coffin was then taken to Montreal. He lay in state in the Palais de Justice, then was conveyed, in the midst of a crowd such as Montreal had never known, to the church of Notre-Dame, where the funeral took place. Cartier was buried in the cemetery at Côte-des-Neiges, where a monument still recalls his memory.

Benjamin Sulte*, a journalist and historian, who during Cartier's last years was one of his associates, has left a portrait of him that his contemporaries considered accurate: "Sir George," he wrote, "was of medium height, even a little short, but one's first impression was of a man of unusual vigour. Without being fat, he was somewhat plump and chubby, so much so that his nerves and muscles were so to speak hidden under this covering. His hands and feet were small, superbly moulded. His head, set straight on his neck, was extremely mobile. . . . The very French liveliness that one noticed immediately one approached him had nothing of that importunate character that the English say is peculiar to the French temperament." The French writer Prosper Mérimée, who had met the Canadian statesman in Paris in 1858, wrote to one of his English correspondents: "I have seen M. Cartier. I was delighted to make his acquaintance. It seems as if I saw a Frenchman of the 17th century returned to visit the country which he had left two centuries before." Cartier was not a great speaker. He spoke with precision and logic in French and in English, sometimes making a few mistakes in the latter. He was a great worker, a strong-willed man, sure of himself, almost overweening. He was a leader who imposed his will somewhat brutally. He could also be genial, particularly at the numerous gatherings held in his home at Ottawa during the last years of his life.

Cartier had a profoundly conservative mind. True, he accepted discoveries and progress; he understood better than some others the transformations that the acceleration of communications would bring about, and it was not out of mere personal interest that he was in favour of railways. But, in the realm of ideas, he feared innovations, and particularly those advocated by liberals inspired by the 1848 revolution and by American republicanism. He was attached to British institutions, which, in conferring responsible government, seemed to him to guarantee sufficiently the triumph of a democracy tempered by a non-elective upper chamber. From the religious point of view, he was not a mystic but a sincere Catholic. Among his possessions, after his death, was found an *Imitation de Jésus-Christ* in Latin, which he seems to have consulted frequently and in which he had underlined the conclusion of chapter XXIX, book 3; in English it reads as follows: "He who does not desire to please men nor fear to displease them will enjoy great peace." For Cartier, to be a French Canadian was to be a Catholic. He was respectful of the clergy, to whom, according to him, French Canadians owed great gratitude, but he none the less preserved his full freedom of judgement and decision in temporal matters, so much so that he was regarded as a gallican. Immediately after confederation, he supported his former masters, the Sulpicians, in their opposition to the archbishop of Montreal, Ignace Bourget, who wanted to divide the parish of Montreal. He showed his gallican convictions on that occasion by claiming that it was the job of the state and not of the bishop to intervene in the civil organization of parishes.

By his marriage, which was solemnized on 16 June 1846 in the church of Notre-Dame at Montreal, Cartier had become allied to an excellent bourgeois family of Montreal. He had married Hortense Fabre, who was born on 28 Feb. 1828. She was the daughter of a wealthy merchant, Édouard-Raymond Fabre*, and the sister of Édouard-Charles Fabre*, the future bishop of Montreal, and of the journalist Hector Fabre*. Cartier and his wife had three daughters: Reine-Victoria, Joséphine, and Hortense. After Cartier's death, Lady Cartier never returned to Canada, and died at Cannes in 1898. Cartier's relations with his wife and her family were not always good. This situation was made public when some time after the statesman's death his will was published; certain provisions of it revealed some mistrust with regard to Lady Cartier and her family. Its publication revived political quarrels, and *La Minerve* of 7 July 1873 contented itself with saying: "We ask only one thing of our friends, that is to study the testator's intentions with impartiality and to take note of the expression of his religious sentiments which it contains."

Cartier's disappearance changed Canadian political life a great deal. For the Conservative party in Quebec it was one of the first blows that shook the omnipotence it had known at the beginning of confederation, and which it was not able subsequently to recover. In practice Cartier and Macdonald had been equal political leaders for more than a decade, and the former was never replaced in the search for a Canadian equilibrium. After La Fontaine and Morin, who in a brief period in power gave a new direction to politics, Cartier was the most illustrious of a long line of French Canadian politicians who were determined rightly or wrongly to play a role within institutions which, at first sight, seemed foreign to their spirit and their interests. When we judge him, we must place him in his time, and avoid condemning him in the light of the events that have taken place in the last 100 years, and that he could not reasonably have foreseen.

J.-C. BONENFANT

[The most complete biography of George-Étienne Cartier is by H. B. M. Best, "George-Étienne Cartier," unpublished PHD thesis, Université Laval, 1969. In his introduction, Best gives a list of the archival repositories he consulted, the main ones being the PAC, ANQ, and ASSM. The papers of the Cartier estate (property of the Succession Cartier, Montreal) also contain interesting information.

Best's thesis has lessened the importance of other works as sources of information on Cartier. The main ones are: [G.-É. Cartier], *Discours de sir Georges Cartier* . . . , Joseph Tassé, édit. (Montréal, 1893); Cartier's major speeches between 1844 and 1872 are found in this collection. There is no critical editing but it includes notes which place the speeches in the political context. The *Parliamentary debates on confederation* (Province of Canada) contain the speeches of politicians during the debate on the plan for confederation. They give a good picture of the various opinions held by the population as expressed by Cartier's supporters and opponents. John Boyd, *Sir George Etienne Cartier, Bart., his life and times: a political history of Canada from 1814 until 1873* (Toronto, 1914). By a journalist strongly sympathetic to Cartier but without a historian's craft, this work leaves much to be desired, but for a long time it was the most complete study of Cartier. It was translated into French by Sylva Clapin and includes a fairly extensive bibliography. Chapais, *Histoire du Canada*, IV–VIII; by a historian of Canadian parliamentary life, these volumes cover the period 1833–67 and provide a good background to Cartier's career. Alfred Duclos de Celles, *Cartier et son temps* (Collection Champlain, Montréal, 1913); a brief, rather laudatory biography. J.-L.-K. Laflamme, *Le centenaire Cartier, 1814–1914; compte rendu des assemblées, manifestations, articles de journaux, conférences, etc., qui ont marqué la célébration du centenaire de la naissance de sir George-Étienne Cartier et l'érection de monuments à la mémoire de ce grand homme d'état*

Casault

canadien (Montréal, 1927). Rumilly, *Hist de la prov. de Québec*, I. The first volume in this long series deals primarily with Cartier's influence on the government of Quebec, although he was then a minister in Ottawa. Benjamin Sulte, "Sir George-Étienne Cartier," *Mélanges historiques*, Gérard Malchelosse, édit. (21v., Montréal, 1918–34), IV contains some interesting personal details on Cartier. J.-C. B.]

CASAULT, LOUIS-ADOLPHE, soldier, deputy adjutant-general of the Canadian militia; b. 21 Oct. 1832 at Saint-Thomas de Montmagny, L.C., son of Louis Casault and Françoise Blais; d. 2 July 1876 at Quebec.

Louis-Adolphe Casault's ancestors had come originally from Saint-Pierre-Langers, Lower Normandy, and settled at Saint-Thomas de Montmagny in 1759. Louis-Adolphe was the 13th child of the family; one of his brothers, Louis-Jacques*, became founder and first rector of the Université Laval, and another, Louis-Napoléon*, chief justice of the Superior Court of Quebec. At the age of 12 Louis-Adolphe was enrolled as a boarder at the Petit Séminaire of Quebec and subsequently attended the college of Sainte-Anne-de-la-Pocatière. After his college course, he entered the firm of Casault, Langlois et Angers of Quebec, headed by his brother, Louis-Napoléon, where he studied law for three years.

The legal profession did not, however, appeal to his restless spirit and, in a burst of patriotic enthusiasm, he enlisted in the French army on the outbreak of the Crimean War in 1853. He later wrote: "young and enthusiastic, I was unable to resist wanting to play a part in this event which was already stirring up so much interest in both hemispheres." He had hoped to join the Zouaves in France, but because he was a foreigner he was sent to the Foreign Legion. He served in the Crimea, 1854–55, and was present at the battle of Chernaya and at the capture of the Malakoff at Sebastopol. In June 1856 he went to Algeria with the legion, and took part in the bitter campaign against the Berbers in 1856–57. Although in the Crimea he had become a corporal of grenadiers despite his small stature, and had been promised advancement, Casault lacked the necessary political connections in France to gain promotion. Accordingly, when his enlistment expired in March 1857, he took his discharge and returned to Canada where he wrote a series of articles describing his experiences in the Crimea and Algeria; these were published in 1857 by his cousin, Joseph-Charles Taché*, in *Le Courrier du Canada*. He intended to resume the study of law, but, when the 100th Regiment of Foot (Prince of Wales's Royal Canadians) was raised in Canada for the British army in 1858, Casault once more found himself in uniform. On 29 June he received a commission as lieutenant and served with his new regiment in England, Gibraltar, and Malta.

Following his retirement from the British army in 1868, he entered the Canadian service, was promoted lieutenant-colonel and became deputy adjutant-general of the militia in Military District 7, with headquarters at Quebec. In 1870 he raised and commanded the Quebec Regiment, one of the two militia regiments which formed part of Colonel Garnet Joseph Wolseley*'s Red River expedition, sent to maintain peace and order in the newly formed province of Manitoba. The militia were in garrison in the winter of 1870–71, the Quebec Regiment being stationed at Lower Fort Garry (Winnipeg). In the spring of 1871 Casault resumed his appointment at Quebec. On the recommendation of Wolseley, he was made a CMG on 16 Dec. 1871.

Lieutenant-Colonel Casault retained his appointment as deputy adjutant-general at Quebec until 16 May 1876, when he was obliged to retire owing to ill health and was succeeded by Lieutenant-Colonel Henri-Théodore Juchereau Duchesnay. At 43 years of age, he died at Quebec, where he was buried with full military honours.

Louis-Adolphe Casault was not long survived by his wife, the former Julie-Cimodecée Cauchon, daughter of the Honourable Joseph-Édouard Cauchon*, whom he had married in 1868. They left two children.

GEORGE F. G. STANLEY

L.-A Casault, "Trois ans dans l'armée française," *Le Courrier du Canada* (Québec), sept. et oct. 1857. Canada, *Report on state of militia*, 1869–76. *Le Canadien* (Québec), 6 juill. 1876. *Journal de Québec*, 4 juill. 1876. *Morning Chronicle* (Quebec), 6 July 1876. Hart, *New army list*, 1859–69. Le Jeune, *Dictionnaire*, I, 323. P.-G. Roy, *Les juges de la province de Québec*, 103.

F.-É.-J. Casault, *Notes historiques sur la paroisse de Saint-Thomas de Montmagny* (Québec, 1906). Benjamin Sulte, *Histoire de la milice canadienne-française, 1760–1897* (Montréal, 1897), 60, 74, 80, 84 F. E. Whitton, *The history of the Prince of Wales's Leinster Regiment (Royal Canadians)* (2v., Aldershot, Eng., 1926). F.-J. Audet, "Officiers canadiens dans l'armée anglaise," *BRH*, XXIX (1923), 91. "Les trois frères Casault," *BRH*, XLVI (1940), 141–42.

CASAVANT, JOSEPH, organ-builder; b. 1807 at Saint-Hyacinthe, L.C., son of Dominique Casavant and Marie-Desanges Coderre; d. 9 March 1874 in the town of his birth.

Joseph Casavant first became a blacksmith. He sometimes liked to abandon the music of the anvil to listen to the only piano in his village, which was in the house of Jean Dessaulles, seigneur of Saint-Hyacinthe. Of an inquiring and enterprising spirit, Casavant gave up the trade of blacksmith at the age of 27 and went to Sainte-Thérèse, with $16 in his pocket, to study under the direction of the parish priest Charles-Joseph Ducharme*, who had just founded a classical college. Although he lived in the village, Casavant studied at the presbytery. He had lost nothing of his taste for music, and he spent hours "drawing sounds from an old piano and from a violin of his own contriving." His natural ingeniousness led Ducharme to advise his pupil to study the mechanism of the organ. The parish priest lent him the works of Dom François de Bédos de Celles, one of which was an enormous treatise, *L'art du facteur d'orgues*; through the latter Casavant obtained his initiation into manufacturing instruments and learned his new trade. Soon success came his way, for he managed to finish a partially built organ which was in the presbytery and to give it life. The result was that by 1840 he was able to undertake, in his workshop at Saint-Hyacinthe, the building of an organ for the parish church of Saint-Martin on Île Jésus.

In 1843 he offered for sale another instrument, with 12 stops, and in 1844 the parish council of Saint-Jean (Laval County) wanted to have its Casavant organ. It was probably at this period that he took into partnership Augustin Lavallée, father of Calixa Lavallée*, and previously a blacksmith like himself. Casavant's growing fame soon brought him an order for an organ for the church at Bytown (Ottawa). He went to this town to live temporarily, and it was there that on 19 June 1850 he married Marie-Olive Sicard de Carufel. Two sons were born of this marriage: Claver on 16 Sept. 1855, and Samuel on 5 April 1859.

Meanwhile Joseph was receiving more and more orders, and producing an increasing number of fine instruments; for example, those of Kingston (1854), Longueuil (1860), and Saint-Jérôme (1861). In 1866 Joseph who, following the custom of the time, considered himself old at an early age, made over his establishment to his assistant, Eusèbe Brodeur. But he was mindful of his sons' future, and he came to an understanding with the new owner so that the latter would take in Claver and Samuel as soon as they were old enough to learn the trade.

History shows that he was right to steer his sons towards organ-building. Indeed, they became masters of their craft, and their reputation spread throughout America and even to Europe. If the name of Casavant still inspires respect, it is surely because of the company started by the brothers Samuel and Claver. But if they have acquired fame, it is because Joseph, their father, was able to transmit to them creative genius and the love of their art. We can only regret that nothing exists today of those instruments built a century ago by a blacksmith with music in his soul.

ANTOINE BOUCHARD

Cyclopædia of Can. biog. (Rose, 1888), 590. *Encyclopedia of Canada*, II, 10. Émile Dubois, *Le petit séminaire de Sainte-Thérèse, 1825–1925* (Montréal, 1925), 53–54. Frère Élie [J.-S. Phaneuf], *La famille Casavant; histoire, généalogie, documents, portraits* (Montréal, 1914). Gérard Morisset, *Coup d'œil sur les arts en Nouvelle-France* (Québec, 1941), 116, 118–19. Léonidas Bachand, "L'orgue et les frères Casavant," *La Vie canadienne* (Montréal), I (1929), 588–92. Antoine Bouchard, "Casavant Frères; facteurs d'orgues depuis un siècle," *Forces* (Montréal), no.2 (1967), 28–33. Victor Morin, "L'orgue, ce merveilleux instrument," *Les conférences du club musical et littéraire de Montréal* (Montréal), 1re sér., I (1941–42), 93–105.

CASSIDY, FRANCIS, lawyer, president of the Institut Canadien and of the St Patrick's Society of Montreal, member of the provincial parliament, and mayor of Montreal; b. 17 Jan. 1827 at Saint-Jacques-de-l'Achigan (Montcalm County, L.C.), of Irish parents, Francis Cassidy and Mary McPharlane, who had left County Cavan, Ireland, to emigrate to Canada; d. 14 June 1873 at Montreal, Que.

A Celt to his finger-tips, young Francis Cassidy soon revealed the distinctive qualities of his race, which would enable him to carve out an enviable place for himself in the country chosen by his parents as their second fatherland. "He was," as Laurent-Olivier David* described him, "a little Irish red-head, with a merry eye, a sprightly air, a precocious mind, and lively as a cricket."

His intellectual alertness and eagerness to learn led him, once through primary school in his native parish, to the college of L'Assomption, where he was admitted in 1838 to the first year of the classical course. Despite his family's poverty, he managed to complete the full course of classical studies thanks to the moral and financial support given by Abbé Étienne Normandin, who was director of the college and teacher of philosophy there from 1839 to 1846. Francis Cassidy never forgot that it was this remarkable benefactor who enabled him to finish his studies at the college, particularly after he had lost his father.

Armed with a letter of introduction from his rhetoric teacher, Pierre Garnot, he went to Montreal in 1844 to study law, and entered the office of lawyers Pierre Moreau and Charles-André LEBLANC, on the corner of Craig and Saint-Gabriel streets, as a clerk. He had only $60 a year to live on.

Cassidy

As this sum was clearly insufficient even for an ascetic's existence, he began to give French lessons. He liked to recount that at that period it was his lot to wear the same pair of cotton trousers summer and winter, and in severely cold weather to remain in bed on Sundays to save the cost of a fire in his room.

Cassidy qualified as a lawyer on 18 Aug. 1848, and soon entered into partnership with his employers. When Moreau retired, Cassidy shared with Leblanc the responsibility for a large clientele, attracted by a competence that soon made Cassidy, "in criminal and civil proceedings . . . one of the most brilliant lawyers of the Montreal bar," according to David. The latter indicated the reason for this success: "His pleas were concise, terse, and sound; he did not speak for the sake of speaking, to produce an effect on his audience, but only to win his case and convince his judge." On 5 Aug. 1863, at the age of 36, Cassidy was appointed queen's counsel. On many occasions he was called upon to be a member of the council of the Montreal bar. He was elected *bâtonnier* in 1871, the first Irish Catholic to obtain this distinction.

Cassidy had now become a person of note. His compatriots had chosen him president of the St Patrick's Society, founded in 1834. Profoundly Irish, but brought up in a French-speaking environment and counting a large number of French Canadians among his clients, he was considered to be the embodiment of the entente cordiale that his illustrious compatriot Thomas D'Arcy McGee* wished to see between the Irish and the French Canadians.

It was precisely because of Cassidy's racial origin that the Institut Canadien, of which he was a founder – he was also its secretary and archivist in May 1849 and its president from November 1849 to November 1850 – abolished one of the basic clauses of its constitution. Hitherto, only a French Canadian could belong to it. On 26 Feb. 1862 a friend of Louis-Antoine Dessaulles*, who at that time was disputing with Hector Fabre*, wrote in *L'Ordre*: "In 1850 the Institut Canadien was presided over by Mr. Cassidy, an Irishman on both sides of his family, and we thought . . . that it was time to do away with this contradiction between fact and law."

Francis Cassidy was elected president of the Institut Canadien a second time, for the period May 1857 to May 1858. Before the end of his term as president, some 135 members resigned on 22 April, under the leadership of Louis LABRÈCHE-VIGER and Hector Fabre, and founded the Institut Canadien-Français on 10 May. The Institut Canadien having been the object of episcopal censure, Fabre's group wanted "to remove from

the library a certain number of immoral and irreligious books, applying to this reform the greatest degree of liberalism compatible with the moral interests of the population and public security." The majority of the members, however, refused to allow anyone the right of supervision and of prohibition of books and reading material. Since agreement did not prove possible, the supporters of Fabre's temperate argument left the institute.

Although the Institut Canadien was attacked by Bishop Ignace Bourget* in pastoral letters of 10 March, 30 April, and 31 May 1858, Cassidy remained a member of the association until May 1867. Consequently, when in 1870 he was chosen to be one of the defence lawyers in the lawsuit over the burial of Joseph Guibord* [see TRUTEAU], one of the lawyers on the other side, Joseph Doutre*, his former *confrère* at the Institut Canadien, took malicious delight in pointing out to him on one occasion that from 1858 to 1867, i.e. for "nine years," he had lived "in that leprosy of impenitence" which he himself "so energetically condemned" in his plea. For in this famous case, according to Cassidy, the opposing parties were not Henriette Brown and the parish council of Notre-Dame, but the Institut Canadien and "the Church of Canada herself, threatened in her most essential immunities." Cassidy, "obeying life-long convictions" and fulfilling "a sacred duty" required of him in his "double capacity as an English subject and a Catholic," defended in his plea, step by step, the stand taken by the bishop of Montreal, as it was set out before Judge Charles-Elzéar MONDELET on 10 and 11 Jan. 1870 by the administrator of the diocese, the vicar general Alexis-Frédéric TRUTEAU.

In the following year his friends persuaded Cassidy to try politics by standing as a provincial candidate in the electoral district of Montreal-West. He was elected by acclamation, and sat in the house at Quebec throughout one parliament. This "likable character" "cut the most curious figure possible" according to Alexandre Lacoste*, who described his interventions as follows: "If the fire of discussion, fanned by party spirit, broke out in the Legislative Assembly, Mr. Cassidy hurled himself into the fray, challenging the right and the left in turn; he accused contestants of exaggeration, asked his friends the Liberals to abandon some of their pretensions, entreated the Conservatives not to misuse their power, and tried to bring about a reconciliation based on mutual concessions. One could divine in Mr. Cassidy the lawyer who had had to reconcile many litigants, but the situation was quite different in the house, where this role of adjudicator and arbitrator was not understood. Needless to say, the sceptre of this new-style Neptune never succeeded in calming the storm."

At the time when Cassidy was endeavouring to play a part for which he was obviously not destined, the illness that was to carry him off prematurely was beginning to undermine his strength. Nevertheless, once more he allowed himself to be persuaded, and stood for the mayoralty of Montreal, to which he was elected by acclamation in February 1873. But he was not able to discharge his new duties for more than a few months, since he died on 14 June 1873 at the age of 46.

His funeral was an impressive one. By a strange coincidence it took place at Notre-Dame two days after that of Sir George-Étienne CARTIER, whose candidature in the district of Montreal-East he had fought the previous year on behalf of his friend and colleague in the Guibord case, lawyer Louis-Amable Jetté*.

Francis Cassidy had remained a bachelor. According to David he regretted not having married, being of the opinion "that marriage alone gives youth its strength and maturity its joy."

PHILIPPE SYLVAIN

Plaidoirie des avocats in re *Henriette Brown* vs *la Fabrique de Montréal; refus de sépulture* (Montréal, 1870), 1–13. *L'Ordre* (Montréal), 26 févr. 1862. Pierre Beullac et É.-F. Surveyer, *Le centenaire du Barreau de Montréal, 1849–1949* (Montréal, 1949), 85–90. L.-O. David, *Biographies et portraits* (Montréal, 1876), 168–80. A. D[uclos] de Celles, "Sir Alexandre Lacoste," *Men of the day, a Canadian portrait gallery*, ed. L.-J.-C.-H. Taché (Montreal, [1890–94]), 273–81. J.-B.-É. Dorion, *Institut canadien en 1852* (Montréal, 1852). Anastase Forget, *Histoire du collège de l'Assomption* (Montréal, [1933]). J.-L. Lafontaine, *Institut canadien en 1855* (Montréal, 1855). Sylvain, "Libéralisme et ultramontanisme," *Shield of Achilles* (Morton), 111–38, 220–55. É.-F. Surveyer, "Two of the early English-speaking Bâtonniers of the Montreal bar," *RSCT*, 3rd ser., XLIII (1949), sect.II, 45–55.

CAUCHON, *dit* LAVERDIÈRE, CHARLES-HONORÉ. *See* LAVERDIÈRE

CAWTHRA, WILLIAM, capitalist; b. Yeadon, Yorkshire, Eng., 29 Oct. 1801, son of Joseph Cawthra* and Mary Turnpenny; d. Toronto, Ont., 26 Oct. 1880.

Joseph Cawthra came to Canada in 1803 and settled near the present Port Credit on Lake Ontario. Limited financial resources led him to enter retail trade, one of the few business opportunities of that time. Before long Cawthra broadened his shop into a general store.

His son William was educated by the Reverend G. Okill Stuart* at the Home District grammar school, which was open to children of all ages. William then went into his father's shop, which, like many others in York (Toronto), had profited from heavy British purchasing during the War of 1812. After his father died in 1842, William closed the shop, having inherited it and the greater part of a substantial estate. In 1849 he married Sarah Ellen Crowther, sister of James Crowther, a lawyer, and lived in a brick cottage in Yorkville village, at Bloor and Jarvis Streets in present-day Toronto.

While living there he built a large and handsome house at Bay and King streets. It was completed in 1853 and there he passed the rest of his days. Designed in classical style by Joseph Sheard*, it was constructed of cut stone, with roof timbers hand-hewn and fastened together by wooden pegs. The house was in the area of Cawthra's principal business interests, for he owned downtown property bought by his father or himself. The rents in that district rose in value and no doubt constituted the greater part of Cawthra's income. He also, however, made loans of a conservative character, on the security of real estate or of bank and government bonds and was a large holder of bank stocks. He was a director of the Bank of Toronto and of one or two companies. He had at least one secretary or agent, but as he does not appear to have had a business address he evidently conducted his affairs from his house.

Cawthra was alderman for St Lawrence ward in the first Toronto City Council of 1834, and again in 1836 after a conservative reaction had eased. In 1847 he was appointed by council to the Board of Trustees for common schools. He was an active worker in the House of Industry and a contributor to the building of the Toronto General Hospital. He died, without issue and intestate, leaving an estate of more than $2,000,000. His beautiful house long remained as his monument, but he is a shadowy figure of whom there is little record.

G. DE T. GLAZEBROOK

York County Surrogate Court (Toronto), will of William Cawthra. *Past and present, notes by Henry Cawthra and others*, comp. A. M. Brock, ed. A. H. Young (Toronto, 1924), 32–36. Middleton, *Municipality of Toronto*, I, II. Ross and Trigge, *History of the Canadian Bank of Commerce*, III, 356–57, 384.

CÉRÉ DE LA COLOMBIÈRE, MARIE-JULIE-MARGUERITE, *dite* Soeur Mance, Religious Hospitaller of St Joseph of Montreal, superior of her community 1851–57 and 1863–69; b. 29 June 1807 at Longueuil (Chambly County), L.C., daughter of François Céré de La Colombière,

Chandler

farmer, and Ursule Brin; d. 6 Dec. 1876 at Montreal, Que., and buried on the 9th in the vault of the monastery.

Marie-Julie-Marguerite Céré de La Colombière entered the Hôtel-Dieu of Montreal on 19 Feb. 1825 and on 17 March 1827 made her solemn profession of poverty, chastity, and obedience. She held various posts before assuming the headship of her community. Between 1851 and 1869 she was four times elected superior of the Hospitallers. The 12 years of her administration are particularly noteworthy for three projects: St Patrick's Hospital, assistance to orphans and the aged, and the lazaret at Tracadie (New Brunswick) for the care of lepers.

On 21 June 1852, in the old Baptist college, Sister Mance founded St Patrick's Hospital, intended for the Irish. She enlarged the sphere of activity of the Hospitallers in 1856; to the care of the sick she added help to orphans, and she admitted old men to the Hôtel-Dieu. St Patrick's Hospital and the orphanage, which was just beginning, were combined with the Hôtel-Dieu when it was moved in 1860 from Rue Saint-Paul to the domain of Mont-Sainte-Famille, on the slopes of Mount Royal.

On 12 Sept. 1868 Sister Mance sent some of her nuns to take over the direction of the lazaret at Tracadie, in New Brunswick, and look after the lepers there [see Ferdinand-Edmond GAUVREAU]. In reality Sister Mance was founding a new independent community of the Institute of Religious Hospitallers of St Joseph. Out of the lazaret was to grow the Hôtel-Dieu of Tracadie; the former disappeared in 1965.

The annals of the Hôtel-Dieu of Montreal say of Sister Mance: "Great and memorable events took place under her administration and are associated with her memory to remind us continually of her name and her good deeds." By extending both spiritually and materially the activities of the Hôtel-Dieu of Montreal, Sister Mance gave new impetus to the first charitable work of the Hospitallers of Ville-Marie. Julie Céré, *dite* Sœur Mance, therefore nobly bore the name of Jeanne Mance*, the founder of the Hôtel-Dieu of Montreal, and kept intact the spirit of charity that animated Mothers Judith Moreau* de Brésoles, Catherine Macé*, and Marie Maillet*, the first Hospitallers who came from La Flèche (department of Sarthe) to Ville-Marie on 20 Oct. 1659.

ANDRÉE DÉSILETS

AHDM, Actes de décès, 1681–1890, 9e feuillet, 77; Annales, II, 260–347; Annales, III, 216, 228–320; Lettres circulaires, nécrologies, 1861–1884, X, 226–36; Obédiences des religieuses hospitalières de Saint-Joseph de l'Hôtel-Dieu de Montréal, 1827–1876; Procès-verbaux, vêture et profession, 1787–1847, 99, 104; Registre des entrées et professions. Jeanne Bernier, *Trois siècles de charité à l'Hôtel-Dieu de Montréal, 1642–1942* (Montréal, 1949). *L'œuvre de trois siècles à Ville-Marie, 1659–1959; les Religieuses hospitalières de Saint-Joseph* ([Montréal], 1959).

CHANDLER, EDMUND LEAVENS, merchant and politician; b. 21 Dec. 1829 at Frelighsburg, Missisquoi County, L.C., son of Horace Mitchell and Lydia Leavens; d. 21 Aug. 1880 at Brome Corner (Brome, Que.).

Daniel Chandler, grandfather of Edmund Leavens, was born in East Hartford, Connecticut, and came to Canada in 1799, settling with his wife, Dolly Ayer, in "Slab City," an early local name for Frelighsburg. There Edmund Leavens was born. After receiving an "Academical education," he taught school, and at age 21 went to Lowell, Massachusetts, where he was secretary in a company of real estate dealers. In 1855 he moved to Brome Corner where he became a partner of Henry Rogers Williams, dealer in dry-goods, hardware, groceries, etc. At this time Brome Corner, although only a village of about 150, was the centre of a prosperous dairy-farming region and "the chief seat of business in the township." In the same year Chandler was elected secretary-treasurer of the Brome County council, and he held this office for 13 years. In 1856 he was elected chairman of the board of school commissioners of the township and served for six years. Three years after his arrival he was erecting a brick dwelling (still in use) and a small brick store adjoining it, in which he ran a general business until his death. He married, on 9 April 1860, Amanda Jane Darling, a teacher in the village's select school. His wife long survived him, but their only son died in 1878 at age 17, the year his father was elected to parliament.

Chandler's public career included serving as mayor of the township of Brome (1868–72) and as warden of Brome County (1868–72). "He was one of the original and most influential promoters of the South-Eastern Railway, of which corporation he was elected Secretary-treasurer, holding that office from the formation of the company in 1867 'til 1876." This railroad (later to be taken over by the Canadian Pacific Railway) was of great importance in the development of Brome County; at Brome Corner the first sod for it was turned in August 1871 and the first train arrived in Knowlton in 1875; regular service from Sutton Junction to Sorel started in 1879.

"Although [Chandler was] an active and earnest supporter of the Liberal party all his life, this gentleman's aversion to pushing himself forward kept him many years in the background of politics." On 17 Sept. 1878, however, he became the Liberal member of parliament for Brome County in the House of Commons in the general election. He defeated, by a large majority, Judge Samuel Willard Foster of Knowlton, although the Liberal government under Alexander Mackenzie* was defeated by John A. Macdonald*. Chandler remained the sitting member until his death in 1880. By his death "Brome County lost one of its most highly esteemed citizens."

H. B. S.

Bishop Stewart Memorial Anglican Church Cemetery (Frelighsburg, Que.), Daniel Chandler. Brome County Historical Society Museum Archives (Knowlton, Que.), Genealogical records, Mrs. A. J. Patten Chandler to H. B. Shufelt, 9 Sept. 1933. St John's Anglican Church Cemetery (Brome, Que.), Chandler family. St Paul's Anglican Church (Knowlton, Que.), Registers. *Guide to Canadian ministries since confederation, July 1, 1867–January 1, 1957* (PAC pub., Ottawa, 1957), 12. *Illustrated atlas of the Dominion of Canada...* (Toronto, 1881), xviii. George Chandler, *The Chandler family: the descendants of William and Annis Chandler, who settled in Roxbury, Mass. 1637* (1st ed., Boston, 1872; 2nd ed., Worcester, Mass., 1883). Cyrus Thomas, *Contributions to the history of the Eastern Townships: a work containing an account of the early settlement of St. Armand, Dunham, Sutton, Brome, Potton, and Bolton...* (Montreal, 1866), 256–58.

CHANDLER, EDWARD BARRON, lawyer, judge, politician, and administrator; b. 22 Aug. 1800 in Amherst, N.S., son of Charles Henry Chandler and Elizabeth Rice; d. 6 Feb. 1880 in Fredericton, N.B.

Edward Barron Chandler's grandfather, Colonel Joshua Chandler, had been a member of the Connecticut legislature and a relatively wealthy man before joining the loyalist ranks and settling in Nova Scotia in 1783. One of Joshua Chandler's sons, Samuel, took an active part in the public life of Nova Scotia; two of his daughters married into influential New Brunswick families: Mary married Joshua Upham*, a puisne judge of the Supreme Court and an early member of the Legislative and Executive councils of New Brunswick, and Sarah married Amos Botsford*, first speaker of the New Brunswick assembly. Edward Barron Chandler claimed that he had experienced hardships in his youth; but even if this were the case, his wealth of proper family connections was to prove compensation for any loss of family fortunes.

Chandler's father was sheriff of Cumberland County, N.S., and he was brought up and educated in Amherst. Later he studied law with his cousin, William Botsford*, at Westcock, near Sackville,

N.B., wrote bar admission examinations in Nova Scotia in 1821, and was admitted to the bar of New Brunswick in 1823. In the same year he was appointed judge of probate and clerk of the peace for Westmorland County, N.B., positions which he held until 1862. Chandler resided at Dorchester and within a few years had built his family residence, Rocklyn, a "home of lavish hospitality even for a Colonial magnate." His law practice and judicial appointments must have been lucrative for Chandler was soon thought to be a man of considerable wealth. In 1822 he had married Phoebe Millidge, a descendant of the Botsfords; they had 11 children, seven of whom lived to maturity.

Chandler's long association with New Brunswick politics began when he was elected to the House of Assembly in 1827 to represent the county of Westmorland. From his first session in the assembly in 1828, he took an active part in deliberations and, despite his youth, he was soon regarded as one of the leading members of that body. The first issue in which he became involved concerned the control of crown lands and the disposition of the customs revenue in the province. Both were directed by personnel appointed by the Colonial Office, which administered all revenues. To Chandler this arrangement denied the people of the province one of their basic freedoms. During his first year in the assembly he sat on a committee to consider these problems, and in 1833 he and Charles Simonds* went to London as a committee on grievances in an attempt to solve the conflict. The delegation nearly realized its objectives and Chandler gained a great reputation as a champion of the people. He later advocated the granting of a permanent civil list in return for complete control of the casual revenues by the assembly – a step which was taken in 1837.

While he sat in the assembly, Chandler continued to play the role of the tribune, becoming involved in such questions as the quitrents, Catholic emancipation, the rights of the Acadian population, school administration, the revision of provincial laws, and immigration. In all of these issues he adopted a progressive and enlightened attitude to problems and continually pleaded with his colleagues for a rational, calm, and dispassionate approach. During the 1830s, for example, Chandler warmly supported measures which would exempt Acadians from being taxed for poor relief since they cared for their own poor. In addition Chandler argued in favour of a grant for an Acadian school in Kent County to be administered by the Roman Catholic bishop. As might be expected, such a proposal was bitterly opposed by some members of the assembly. In giving the measure his continued support, Chandler displayed a keen insight into the way of life of the Acadian people. Because of their "peculiar habits and manners," he acknowledged that the French could not send their children to the public schools. It would be in vain, he said, for legislation to endeavour to assimilate them with other groups.

An advocacy of this kind gained for him the reputation of a moderate reformer, although such labels must be read carefully in the context of New Brunswick politics of that period. It would be a mistake, for instance, to compare his role with that played by the principal reformers in the other provinces. The casual revenues–civil list issue illustrates perhaps better than any other Chandler's theory of government. In his view, democracy would be served when complete control of the provincial revenues was turned over to the assembly, with the important qualification that the initiation of money bills be left with individual members of that body. He felt strongly that the power of the people's representatives should not be diminished by placing this all-important responsibility with the executive which, in New Brunswick, the assembly could not remove by a want-of-confidence motion. He consistently opposed, during this early period, the principle of party government and cabinet responsibility. Thus, although he was a moderate and responsible representative of the people, and although he advocated a basic form of democracy, he clearly did not accept responsible government in the sense in which it was advocated by Joseph Howe and the Canadian reformers.

Despite his interest in the affairs of the assembly, Chandler aspired to higher things and in 1834, at the age of 34, he applied directly to the Colonial Office for a position on the bench of the Supreme Court of New Brunswick. The application was not successful, but in 1836 he was appointed to the Legislative Council where he remained until 1878. In the upper house, Chandler, despite his youth, played the part of an elder statesman. Whether by accident or design, his appointment came just as the casual revenues–civil list bill was being debated, and he took a strong stand in favour of the measure. He was opposed by men with obvious vested interests such as Thomas Baillie* and Joseph Cunard*, but the bill eventually passed by a vote of eight to five. Chandler's presence seems to have had a levelling influence on the council whose members were traditionally supporters of the *status quo*.

In 1843 Chandler joined the Executive Council of Sir William Colebrooke* and, with one brief interruption, remained the acknowledged leader of the "compact" government until 1854. In this position of power he was able to impose his version of responsible government on the province. In November 1846 and March 1847 Lord Grey [Henry George Grey] made his attitudes on colonial government clear. The essence of his policy was that the government of the provinces must not be carried on in opposition to the wishes of the people, and that there should be no obstacle placed in the way of a responsible cabinet system. By 1848 the actual colonial administration of British North America was changing, and Chandler was aware of these events. But such radical change did not seem to be practical given the situation in New Brunswick. With no municipal government and with the assembly's control of public moneys, the members commanded the powerful tool of patronage, and were not anxious for change. In effect this was a rather benevolent patriarchal form of government in which the great power of the Legislative and Executive Councils was balanced by the assembly's power over funds. Such a system allowed the members of the "compact" to control major government policy, while leaving to individual members in the assembly the care of matters of purely local interest. Change was counselled from without, but there was no broadly based demand for it within the province.

Into this climate in 1848 came a new lieutenant governor, Sir Edmund Head*, determined to carry out the instructions of Lord Grey. It is significant that the man he chose to lead his government was Edward Barron Chandler. By this time Chandler was publicly supporting the principle of responsible government, and he did make a sincere effort to choose as executive councillors members of the assembly who could be said to enjoy the confidence, if not the active support, of the majority of the elected members. The new government contained an interesting mixture of old "compact" hold-overs, "conservative" members, and two of the most prominent reformers – Lemuel Allan Wilmot and Charles Fisher. It represented the best of the talent available, enjoyed the confidence of the assembly, and was heralded as a "responsible" administration. Beneath the surface, however, little had changed; during the six years in which this government remained in power, the administration of the province was carried on much as it had been in the past. Members of the assembly sacrificed little for they retained the right to initiate money bills and they were not subject to party discipline of any kind. In all of this Chandler emerges as the eternal pragmatist.

During the years when Chandler led the government, New Brunswick was caught up in the great era of railway building, and Chandler became a leading advocate of an improved system of transportation within the province and with its neighbours. Of immediate interest was a line which would connect the east coast of the province with the port of Saint John and the western counties. The proposal had been studied in the late 1840s and in 1850 it received a boost when railway promoters in Maine expressed an interest in tying in to a New Brunswick–Nova Scotia system [see John Poor]. In the summer of that year Chandler and several other legislators from New Brunswick and Nova Scotia attended a great railway convention in Portland, Maine [see J. W. Johnston and Howe]. It was at this meeting that the foundation was laid for the European and North American Railway Company.

At the same time discussions were carried on concerning a railway between Halifax and Quebec running through New Brunswick, but Chandler and his colleagues were sceptical about that scheme. In the first place, this line was being proposed primarily for military and political rather than economic reasons. Secondly, the British government, which would have to bear the brunt of the financing, supported the Intercolonial route, along the east coast and north shore of the province, whereas the majority of influential New Brunswickers favoured a Saint John River valley route. Nevertheless, in 1851 Chandler and Joseph Howe went to Toronto to meet the members of the Canadian legislature, and there they agreed in principle to build the railway. Early in 1852 a delegation of Canadians headed by Francis Hincks* met with Chandler in Fredericton and later, accompanied by Chandler, went on to Halifax to meet with Howe. In these meetings they agreed upon the Saint John valley route and discussed the financial arrangements, taking for granted that the British government would assume its share. They were greatly disappointed, however, when a delegation headed by Hincks and Chandler met the colonial secretary in London in the spring of 1852 and were informed that the British would give no financial support to a line running through the Saint John valley because such a route would not give the military advantages of a coastal railroad.

Chandler was disappointed to see his plans dashed by a stubborn British government, but he stayed on in England in an attempt to salvage something. As far as the New Brunswickers were concerned, the essential part of the scheme was a line to the American frontier, and before returning home Chandler negotiated with the firm of Peto, Brassey, Betts, Jackson, and Company for its construction. Negotiations were completed and approved by September 1852 and work began the following year. Although it would be many

years before adequate railways were built in the province, the era of railway construction had at least commenced, and the man primarily responsible for it was Edward Barron Chandler.

The question of a reciprocal trade agreement with the United States was discussed periodically while Chandler was government leader. Many New Brunswickers, including Saint John businessman John Robertson, Wilmot, and John R. Partelow*, a leading Saint John MLA, favoured such a proposal in the 1840s and early 1850s. By 1854 there was a certain scepticism that the province would receive sufficient compensation – free admission to the United States of processed lumber, fish, and other natural products, and, most of all, permission for New Brunswick ships to participate in the American Atlantic coastal trade – for its loss of exclusive rights to the inshore fisheries. During that year Chandler, Francis Hincks, and Lord Elgin [James Bruce*] went to Washington for negotiations, and, as a result, signed the reciprocity treaty of 1854. When Chandler returned home, however, he found considerable opposition to the terms of the treaty being expressed by some of the province's newspapers. Immediately he and Partelow went to Quebec to confer with Elgin and returned with renewed conviction of the potential value of the treaty. By November they succeeded in having it ratified by the legislature.

An election in 1854 heralded great changes in New Brunswick and marked the end of the most active part of Chandler's career. A relatively cohesive group of opposition members had formed in the assembly under the liberal banner of Charles Fisher, and early in the session Chandler's "compact" government was defeated. The government resigned, recognizing for the first time the truly responsible nature of the executive, and the new lieutenant governor, John Henry Thomas Manners-Sutton, called upon Fisher to form a government. Chandler, of course, retained his seat in the Legislative Council; he continued to take an active part in provincial affairs as the most prominent member of the "Dorchester Clique" and as leader of the opposition in the upper house. It was in this capacity that he became intimately involved in the confederation movement.

When the conference on Maritime union was convened in 1864, Chandler was appointed as one of the New Brunswick delegates, and he attended the conference in Charlottetown and further meetings in Halifax and Saint John. He had never taken a strong stand on the issue, and from the outset he adopted a questioning attitude. Thirty-seven years' experience in the political life of New Brunswick had taught him that Maritime politicians would not act contrary to the dictates of local pride and jealousies, which caused disagreement on such an elementary question as the location of a capital. When the possibility of a broader British North American union was raised, however, Chandler warmly supported it and fought strongly for a preliminary union of the Maritime provinces on the grounds that, as a unit, their position in the wider union would be more powerful. Chandler's enlightened arguments were not popular, and the cause of Maritime union was forgotten, much to the disgust of the lieutenant governor, Arthur Hamilton Gordon*.

In the fall of 1864, Chandler went as a New Brunswick delegate to the Quebec conference and participated in the drafting of the 72 resolutions. He made ardent representations against John A. Macdonald*'s case for a strong central authority, though he soon recognized that he was fighting a losing battle. Faced with the defeat of his stand on provincial rights, Chandler nevertheless acknowledged the inevitability of confederation and took comfort in the strong Maritime representation in the Senate, which he interpreted as an absolute guarantee that the Upper Canadians would not dominate the new union.

During the following year the confederation scheme encountered great opposition among the electorate in New Brunswick and for a time it appeared that achievement of it might be destroyed, or at least indefinitely postponed. Throughout the war of words waged during 1865 and 1866, Chandler, ignoring new political alignments, remained consistent in his support. He taunted the anti-confederates with statistics on the financial situation in the province and warned of the dire consequences of remaining outside confederation. The position of this respected member of the old establishment was simply another factor which militated against the anti-confederation cause. Albert James Smith* and his followers failed to find a viable alternative to confederation and in June 1866 Samuel Leonard Tilley* and the confederates were returned to office. Later that year Chandler went to London for the conference which was to weld the 72 resolutions into legal form. His opposition to investing the residual power in the central government had not changed but the Canadian delegates were irrevocably committed to the Quebec scheme and would allow no major revisions.

Confederation did not bring an end to Chandler's public career, despite his advanced age. He was offered a seat in the Senate of Canada, but throughout the confederation debate he had maintained that he was not interested in public office for himself and, true to his word, he declined the appointment. In 1868, however, he was asked to become one of the commissioners appointed to oversee the construction of the Intercolonial Railway and he accepted the position. Ten years later, at the age of 78, he received his final public appointment – as lieutenant governor of New Brunswick, succeeding Tilley.

Edward Barron Chandler's career in the public life of his province must be unique, if only because of its longevity. Between 1823 and 1880 he held public offices continuously in positions ranging from a county clerk of the peace to lieutenant governor. This long experience and a wealth of family, business, and political connections made him one of the most powerful public figures in New Brunswick in the 30 years preceding confederation. Throughout his career, Chandler does not seem to have been motivated by any overriding political principle. A loyalist and a member of the Church of England, he was always identified with the establishment or the "compact," and yet he displayed democratic tendencies. He was constantly concerned that the will of the people should be upheld, and he consistently supported the rights of the minority Acadians and Irish Catholics at a time when such advocacy demanded a certain amount of courage. It is in this respect more than any other that Chandler, as a representative of the "compact," differed from his counterparts in Upper Canada. In spite of these tendencies, however, he was not an innovator. His watchwords were reason and caution. In essence, he was a practical man living in a climate that did not produce, or even gladly suffer, novel political theories.

The fact that his views on the nature of responsible government and the party system prevailed for so long in the province is a commentary on the lack of political sophistication in New Brunswick in the first half of the 19th century. The province either did not produce or did not want a Howe, a Robert Baldwin*, a William Lyon Mackenzie*, or a Louis-Joseph PAPINEAU. Responsible government did come, however, and the fact that it came without bloodshed is to some degree attributable to the stability of Chandler's leadership.

MICHAEL SWIFT

N.B. Museum, Hazen family papers, E. B. Chandler to Sir John Harvey, 3 Feb. 1840; W. C. Milner coll., Chandler correspondence; Tilley family papers, correspondence between E. B. Chandler and S. L. Tilley; Ward family papers, John Ward and Sons letter book, 1832–36; Webster coll., Chandler correspondence. PAC, MG 27, I, D15 (Tilley papers), 1864–67. PANB, New Brunswick, Executive Council Draft minutes, 1843–56 (microfilm in PAC, MG 9, A1). PRO, CO 188/54–188/55, 188/84–188/85, 188/94,

188/104–188/106, 188/127. New Brunswick, House of Assembly, *Journals*, 1828–36; Legislative Council, *Journals*, 1836–67. *Speeches delivered in the Legislative Council, New Brunswick, on confederation and the resignation of the government, and correspondence connected therewith*, reporter, Samuel Watts (Fredericton, 1866).

Colquhoun, *Fathers of confederation*. M. O. Hammond, *Confederation and its leaders* (Toronto, 1917). James Hannay, *History of New Brunswick*; *The life and times of Sir Leonard Tilley: being a political history of New Brunswick for the past seventy years* (Saint John, N.B., 1897). Lawrence, *Judges of New Brunswick* (Stockton). MacNutt, *Atlantic provinces*; *New Brunswick*. G. E. Rogers, "The career of Edward Barron Chandler – a study in New Brunswick politics, 1827–1854," unpublished MA thesis, University of New Brunswick, 1953. Waite, *Life and times of confederation*. Edward Whelan, *The union of the British provinces*, intro. D. C. Harvey (Gardenvale, P.Q., and Toronto, 1927). W. M. Whitelaw, *The Maritimes and Canada before confederation* (Toronto, 1934). A. G. Bailey, "Railways and the confederation issue in New Brunswick, 1863–1865," *CHR*, XXI (1940), 367–83. D. G. G. Kerr, "Head and responsible government in New Brunswick," *CHA Report, 1938*, 62–70. W. S. MacNutt, "The coming of responsible government to New Brunswick," *CHR*, XXXIII (1952), 111–28.

CHANTER, THOMAS BURNARD, merchant, shipbuilder, and landed proprietor; b. in 1797 (baptized 6 April) at Great Torrington, Devon, Eng., only son of Moses Chanter and Elizabeth Burnard; d. 17 March 1874 at Bideford, Devon.

Thomas Burnard Chanter's uncle Thomas Burnard, a successful English merchant and shipbuilder, established a shipbuilding settlement, New Bideford (later Bideford), on the eastern end of Lot 12, Prince Edward Island, in 1818. A year later, Chanter, who had been trained in England to be a merchant and shipbuilder, assumed charge of the venture. Shortly afterward he took over a farm on Penman Point, P.E.I., which he named Port Hill; here he built a house and a store to serve the extensive settlement on the eastern part of Lot 13; he also established a fishing industry out of Richmond Bay. Chanter became a justice of the peace and captain of the 5th Battalion of the Island militia, and was an unsuccessful candidate for the colony's assembly in 1823.

He returned to England to live in Bideford in 1829 and Thomas Heath Haviland* (d. 1867) became agent on the Island for Chanter's financial interests in the timber trade, land, shipbuilding, and shipping. In 1835 Chanter acquired extensive landholdings, stores, and shipbuilding sites in the area of present-day Alberton, P.E.I. These he ran from England in association with Lemuel Cambridge of Charlottetown. Through the years

Chanter's money built at least 35 ships on the Island, and he was responsible for the settlement there of a number of skilled shipbuilders. His ships brought hundreds of immigrants from Britain to Quebec and to P.E.I. On the island these settlers provided labour and a market for his stores.

Thomas Chanter never returned to Prince Edward Island but remained at Bideford, where he and his wife Isabella Scott, whom he had married in 1829, had a fine estate. Chanter played a prominent role in the business and political life of the west of England until his death. He was survived by several children including Robert Campbell Chanter who settled on the Island at Mount Stewart Bridge. Thomas Chanter played a significant part in the establishment of shipbuilding in P.E.I., and this industry was to become one of the Island's most important. His settlements on Lots 12 and 13 also played an important role in populating the western part of the Island.

BASIL GREENHILL

Private Archives, Lot 13, Prince Edward Island, Port Hill papers, especially letters from Thomas Chanter to William Ellis, 31 Oct. 1831 – 10 Aug. 1836. *North Devon Journal* (Barnstaple, Devon), 23 Jan., 16 Oct. 1828; 24 June 1830; 4 April 1831; 31 March 1836; 29 Dec. 1842; 26 Jan. 1843. *Prince Edward Island Register* (Charlottetown), 13 Nov., 29 Dec. 1824; 27 May 1825; 7 Aug., 19 Sept. 1826. Basil Greenhill and Ann Giffard, *Westcountrymen in Prince Edward's Isle, a fragment of the Great Migration* (Newton Abbot, Eng., and Toronto, 1967). *Past and present of Prince Edward Island . . .*, ed. D. A. MacKinnon and A. B. Warburton (Charlottetown, [1906]).

CHAREST, ZÉPHIRIN, parish priest; b. 21 Feb. 1813 at Sainte-Anne-de-la-Pérade, L.C., son of Antoine Charest and Marie-Anne Marchand; d. 7 Dec. 1876 at Saint-Roch de Québec.

Zépharin Charest was born of well-to-do farmers, and was one of a large family; one brother was a doctor, and Bishop Louis-François Laflèche* was a relative. He was a pupil at the seminary of Nicolet, and, thanks to an outstanding memory, he was brilliantly successful. He completed his theological studies at Quebec, where on 11 Dec. 1836 he was ordained a priest. He was then appointed curate of Saint-Roch de Québec, and there he was to spend the remainder of his life. At the time of the events of 1837 and 1838, the parish of Saint-Roch was one of the most disturbed areas in the Quebec region. The parish priest and his curates were required, when called upon by the bishop, to preach against the revolutionary movement. On these occasions some of the inhabitants of the district even uttered threats against the priest and his curates. In 1839 Charest succeeded the parish priest David-Henri Têtu.

Chaussegros de Léry

During the second third of the 19th century the Saint-Roch area developed with great rapidity; from less than 8,000 inhabitants in 1831 it went up to nearly 25,000 in 1871. Country dwellers who had come there to work at shipbuilding on the St Charles River were particularly numerous. Charest took an interest in the material as well as the spiritual condition of this population, whose way of life was crude and who had little education. Since the schools run by laymen were too few in the area [see Antoine LÉGARÉ], he appealed to the religious communities to lend a hand. In 1841, following the wish of Bishop Joseph-Octave Plessis*, he asked the sisters of the Congregation of Notre-Dame, who were already in residence in Lower Town, for their services. He had a spacious convent built in which the nuns went to live in 1844, and he made himself their chaplain. The convent of Saint-Roch, which took in boarders and day-pupils, was the object of his tender care and his favourite refuge. The sisters left to the parish priest the task of dealing with many material as well as spiritual questions. The convent had 1,000 pupils at the time of Charest's death.

In 1852 the priest installed at Saint-Roch, in a school first called the École du Sacré-Cœur then the École Lagueux, the Brothers of the Christian Schools, who had arrived at Quebec in 1842. The Saint-Roch parish council, prompted by Charest, assumed the costs of building and maintaining the establishment. When Charest died, there were 800 children in the school run by the brothers.

A number of misfortunes, such as the fires at Saint-Roch in 1845 and 1866, made apparent the charity of Charest, whom contemporaries likened to St Vincent de Paul. Moreover, in 1866, as the shipbuilding which had brought prosperity to his parish was declining before his eyes, he assumed the leadership of a committee to establish the basis for the Shipbuilding Association of Quebec. This company of small shareholders wanted to revive the shipbuilding industry. It seems to have produced meagre results, for shipbuilding continued to decline and emigration from Quebec increased until 1872. The parish of Saint-Roch thus lost much of its drive and vitality.

In 1853 a church was opened for worship at Saint-Sauveur, under the religious leadership of the Oblate fathers [see Flavien DUROCHER]. Saint-Sauveur, which was served by Saint-Roch, developed rapidly, and soon its worshippers asked to be detached from the mother parish. The complete autonomy of the parish of Saint-Sauveur, obtained in 1867, seems to have been accepted regretfully by Charest, who was growing old.

On 7 Dec. 1876 he died at the age of 63. He was given an impressive funeral, attended by 7,000 people and some 50 priests. A few days later he was buried in the church of Saint-Roch. Shortly before that the authorities had changed the name of Rue Saint-Antoine to Rue Charest. Today Boulevard Charest is one of the main arteries of the capital of Quebec.

PIERRE SAVARD

Archives paroissiales de Saint-Roch (Québec). *Le Canadien* (Québec), 22 janv. 1866. Raoul Blanchard, *L'Est du Canada français, province de Québec* (2v., Montréal et Paris, 1935), II, 202ff. Carrière, *Histoire des O.M.I.*, III, 137–46. Drolet, *Ville de Québec*, III, 63–66. J.-C. Gamache, *Histoire de Saint-Roch de Québec et de ses institutions, 1829–1929* (Québec, 1929). *Histoire de la Congrégation de Notre Dame de Montréal* (10v., Montréal, 1941–   ), VII, 122, 124; IX, 141. P.-G. Huot, *Éloge du Rév. M.Z. Charest, curé de St. Roch de Québec* (Québec, 1876). *L'Œuvre d'un siècle; centenaire des Frères des écoles chrétiennes au Canada* (Montréal, 1937). P.-G. Roy, *Les cimetières de Québec* (Lévis, Qué., 1941), 199; *Les rues de Québec* (Lévis, Qué., 1932), 43.

CHAUSSEGROS DE LÉRY, ALEXANDRE-RENÉ, lawyer, legislative councillor, and senator; b. 26 March 1818 at Quebec, son of the Honourable Charles-Étienne Chaussegros* de Léry, seigneur of Rigaud-Vaudreuil, and Josephte Fraser, daughter of Judge John Fraser*; d. 19 Dec. 1880 at Quebec and buried at Saint-François-de-la-Beauce (Beauceville) on 23 December.

After finishing his classical studies at the Petit Séminaire of Quebec, Alexandre-René Chaussegros de Léry received instruction in law from Louis de Gonzague Baillargé*. On 28 July 1842 he was admitted to the bar of Lower Canada. Barely two years later, on 12 Feb. 1844, he married Catherine-Charlotte-Élise Couillard, by whom he had three sons, including William-Henri-Brouage*. Those who knew him are agreed that he gave scant thought to his profession. Law interested him a great deal, but only as it helped him to run his own affairs efficiently.

Alexandre-René Chaussegros de Léry owned properties in Rue d'Auteuil and Rue Sainte-Famille at Quebec, at Sainte-Marie, and at Saint-François-de-la-Beauce. He had also inherited two seigneuries, Rigaud-Vaudreuil and Sainte-Barbe-de-la-Famine. On 10 Aug. 1864 he sold his house in Rue Sainte-Famille to the seminary of Quebec: four years of discussion had been necessary for the two parties to reach an agreement on the price. This sale was probably occasioned by his activities after the discovery in 1846 of gold nuggets in the bed of the Rivière Chaudière. At that time Chaussegros de Léry hoped to become rich by engaging actively in the mining of gold deposits. Everything

162

25

was in his favour, for around the same period gold was found on his Rigaud-Vaudreuil seigneury. The crown, by letters patent dated 18 Sept. 1846, had recognized him from then on as owner of all the "gold and silver mines, surface mines and ores" on this seigneury. In 1865, with the fever of gold in his blood, he took part in the founding of the De Léry Gold Mining Company. His profits as a shareholder in this project are not known. There is reason to believe, however, that at that time his financial position was good, since in 1867 he was one of a group promoting the plan for a railway to link the towns of Lévis and Portland (Maine). A company was formed on 24 Feb. 1869, under the name of Compagnie de Chemin à Lisses de Lévis à Kennebec; it was also called the Levis and Kennebec Railway Company (now Quebec Central Railway Company). Chaussegros de Léry was its president, but Joseph-Goderic Blanchet* and Louis-Napoléon Larochelle* seem to have done much more than he for this undertaking.

His somewhat inconspicuous role might perhaps be explained by his appointment on 2 Nov. 1867 to the Legislative Council to represent the constituency of Lauzon. Four years later, on 13 Dec. 1871, he became a senator, replacing Elzéar-Henri Juchereau Duchesnay, but he found it difficult to discharge all his obligations adequately; hence he resigned from this post on 11 April 1876.

Chaussegros de Léry was a kindly and affable man, according to Narcisse-Henri-Édouard Faucher* de Saint-Maurice; he always had a friendly word or an excuse for others. The impression left is that he was in his time representative of the perfect Canadian gentleman. He was a charitable man, and made a number of gifts to the parish council of Sainte-Marie-de-la-Beauce. In business, however, he could drive a hard bargain and did not readily give ground before a competitor. He lived comfortably but was careful not to let any of his wealth slip out of his hands.

Claude Lessard

ANQ, Famille Chaussegros de Léry, Alexandre-René. ASQ, Lettres, X, 39, 119; Seigneuries, LXVIII–LXX; Séminaire, XXXIV, 32–38; LXXII, 19a; LXXXI, 71–71c; CCII, 123–24; S.M.E., 12 juill. 1864; Université, LXXV, 102. *L'Écho de Lévis*, 1869–76. *L'Opinion publique* (Montréal), 27 janv. 1881. Pierre Fontanel, *Minéraux et roches du Canada* (Montréal, 1924). Honorius Provost, *Sainte-Marie de la Nouvelle-Beauce; histoire religieuse* (Québec, 1967), 391–92. P.-G. Roy, *La famille Chaussegros de Léry* (Lévis, Qué., 1934), 33–36; *Fils de Québec*, IV, 22–23.

CHESLEY, SOLOMON YEOMANS, public servant and politician; b. 29 April 1796 at Shodack (now Castleton-on-Hudson), Rensselaer County, N.Y., son of All Saints Chasley (Chassley, Chesley) and his wife Lené Yeomans; m. 18 Aug. 1825 Margaret Ann Vankoughnet, by whom he had a large family; d. 5 Nov. 1880, in Ottawa, Ont.

Solomon Yeomans Chesley's parents left Shodack "for the wilds of Canada" in 1800, settling in Cornwall, Upper Canada. In February 1806 he went to live on the Iroquois lands at St Regis, where the border divides Canada and the United States. By November 1813 he was so fluent in Mohawk that he was appointed interpreter in the Indian Department, and on 25 July 1814 he was commissioned lieutenant in the St Regis Company of Indian Warriors. His services in the War of 1812–14 at Fort Covington, Châteauguay, Four Corners, and Plattsburgh earned him a grant of land and an appointment on 1 Aug. 1815 as agent at St Regis. Aided by 12 chiefs and warriors nominated by the band, Chesley managed about 50,000 acres in Upper and Lower Canada and nine islands in the St Lawrence; the Iroquois leased much of this land to tenants. In 1832 Chesley, who could speak Iroquois, French, and English, succeeded J.-B. de Lorimier as resident or superintendent at St Regis, while remaining as agent. Chesley's residency began at about the same time as the appointment of the Reverend François-Xavier Marcoux, a French-speaking Roman Catholic, as government missionary to the band.

Chesley along with Major William Plenderleath [Christie*], also of the Indian Department, and the Reverend George Archbold, Anglican rector at Cornwall, induced Lord Aylmer [Whitworth-Aylmer*] to allow an annual stipend for a schoolmaster at St Regis, and the Reverend Éléazar Williams*, an Iroquois educated at an Episcopal seminary in Connecticut, was hired. His school, in which he taught from English books, opened in July 1835 and attracted 40 students before Father Marcoux learned of the school in September. Roman Catholic Bishop Jean-Jacques Lartigue* wanted the Indian parents to withdraw their children from the school, and Lord Gosford [Acheson*] removed government support but declined to eject Williams from St Regis. The school closed, and when, in 1847, another school was planned the bishop was asked to name the schoolmaster.

The controversy caused embarrassment to the government which had not wanted to question the position of the Roman Catholic Church at St Regis. Perhaps as a result of Chesley's activities in the matter, his post was slated for abolition in 1837. However, his experience at the exposed Iroquois lands made him useful during the disturbances in

Chevalier

Lower Canada later the same year, and he was retained. He kept his life-long interest in the education of the Indians, supporting the manual labour schools pioneered by Plenderleath in Lower Canada.

Chesley had run in the Cornwall riding for the House of Assembly in the election of 1836, as a Tory, but was defeated by George Stephen JARVIS. He took the seat in 1841, but lost it to Rolland Macdonald* in 1844. In the assembly, Chesley opposed Hamilton Hartley KILLALY's selection of the south side of the St Lawrence as the site of the Beauharnois Canal, claiming that the soundings on charts drawn by Frederick Preston Rubidge* were misleading; the canal was built, flooding some of the St Regis lands.

The Indian Department was reorganized soon after his electoral defeat in 1844, and Chesley left the residency on 8 July 1845 to become second clerk at Montreal under the new chief clerk, George Vardon. As a result of a further reorganization in the department, Chesley was appointed accountant in 1851. He was now the most senior departmental official with continuous service since 1813. It was Chesley rather than the chief clerk who acted as superintendent-general briefly in 1852, until a former superintendent-general, Major Thomas Edmund CAMPBELL, was appointed *pro tem.*, and in 1854 until Laurence Oliphant* was appointed. Thereafter, Chesley was in fact, if not title, assistant superintendent-general and, on occasion, for example in 1856, acting superintendent-general.

Learning that the Indian Department was to be taken over by the colonial government, Chesley on 18 Jan. 1859 asked for a pension. On 1 December he retired and moved to Cornwall after having lived in the capital of Canada since 1845. He was elected mayor of Cornwall in December 1860. He later moved to Ottawa and in 1872 he was elected a member of the New England Company, an Anglican society which fostered Indian education.

GEO. MAINER

PAC, RG 7, G1, 87, p.78; RG 8, I, D2, 1171, p.334. PAO, Diary collection, S. Y. Chesley diaries, 1851–54; MS 155, St Regis mission papers (microfilm copy). PRO, CO 42/503, 71; 42/515, 51, 94; 42/516, 36, 607; 42/599, 371; 42/617, 42. *British Colonist* (Toronto), 21 Jan. 1845. Canada, Province of, Legislative Assembly, *Appendix to journals*, 1846, app.V, "Report. The select committee to which was referred the petition of Wishe Tegaréhontie and others . . ."; *Sessional papers*, XVIII (1860), PT.3, no.40, "Return to an address . . . for statements of appointments to public office since July, 1860." *Chronicle & Gazette and Kingston Commercial Advertiser*, 28 Oct. 1843. *Ottawa Citizen*, 6, 8 Nov. 1880. *Peterborough Examiner*, 17 Jan. 1861.

CHEVALIER, HENRI-ÉMILE, journalist and man of letters; b. 13 Sept. 1828 at Châtillon-sur-Seine, Côte-d'Or, France; d. 25 Aug. 1879 in Paris.

Scarcely anything is known about Chevalier's early years except that he enlisted in a regiment of dragoons in 1847, and that he stayed in it three years, at the same time contributing to various newspapers. The liking that he developed for this sideline prompted him to leave the army in order to devote himself full time to republican political journalism, which was then an occupation as hazardous as soldiering. An article he published in the newspaper he had just started, *Le Progrès de la Côte-d'Or*, landed him in Dijon prison. Republicans were sentenced to exile in great numbers by Charles-Louis-Napoléon Bonaparte [Napoleon III], after his coup d'état of 2 Dec. 1851. Victor Hugo, young Chevalier's idol, went to Guernsey; his distant disciple chose to continue in the United States, the land of liberty, a career that he had barely started. He landed at New York in the spring of 1852, worked for the *Courrier des États-Unis* there, and left it after a few months because the director, Eugène Masseras, turned over the journal to the Bonapartist cause. At the end of 1852 or beginning of 1853 he came to Montreal, where he knew he would find affinities of language and where he hoped to find affinities of thought. His hopes were not to be disappointed.

In February 1853 he became editor of *La Ruche littéraire et illustrée*, started by George-Hippolyte Cherrier with the object of publishing exclusively Canadian works in monthly instalments of 64 pages. But *La Ruche littéraire* – starting with the March issue, it ceased to be illustrated, for want of good sketchers – could never be kept supplied with strictly Canadian material: until it finally disappeared in 1859 it reproduced French writings and translations of foreign works. Moreover, from August onwards, Chevalier and his contributors, mostly exiles like himself, could not resist the desire to give "an account of the diplomatic events of the two continents." Entitled from then on *La Ruche littéraire et politique*, the paper published poems and *pensées* of Voltaire and Victor Hugo, gave generous place to romantic poetry, was a medium for republican and antibonapartist ideas, and condemned the intolerance that marked the tumultuous visit of Alessandro Gavazzi* to Canada [see Charles WILSON]. Chevalier, now co-owner of *La Ruche*, published in this journal instalments of his own novels which had an historical flavour, for instance "L'Héroïne de Chateauguay," "L'Iroquoise de Caughnawaga," and "Le Pirate du St Laurent," in which are to be found episodes taken from *L'Histoire . . .* by

François-Xavier Garneau*, and "Les Mystères de Montréal," a rather obvious imitation of the *Mystères de Paris* by Eugène Sue. The liberal character of *La Ruche* no doubt impressed contemporaries as much as did the ungainly manner of these first novels of Chevalier. A proof is that one reader even deplored the "pitiful political chronicles of a blood-red *rougisme*" that he read there. However, it was lack of funds that brought about the disappearance, in June 1859, of *La Ruche*, which the preceding month was said to be "at the peak of prosperity," and not the "blood-red *rougisme*." In the latter respect Chevalier had truly found in the Canada of the 1850s a well-disposed environment.

The Institut Canadien was showing itself at the time in its true colours: the divorce between its thinking and that of the church under Bishop Ignace Bourget* was pronounced, and the clash of uncompromising attitudes was sure to come into the open. Certainly the members of the Institut Canadien, a sort of popular university in Philippe Sylvain's words, had a keen sense of material and social progress which they wanted to communicate to the country, as well as a desire to help the French Canadian community. They waged their fight to the beat of a drum; they blazoned forth to the world their leitmotiv of "light, progress, knowledge." They glorified revolutions and their "immortal principles," they protested against the authoritarianism preached by the church and against the temporal power of the pope, they advocated the separation of church and state and even the neutrality of teaching, and, in the name of the right of peoples to decide their own fate, they heartily approved of Italian unification, which was in process of being realized. In their battle they faced the undisputed champion of the most stringent ultramontanism, Ignace Bourget, archbishop of Montreal, who waited for them with vizor lowered. For him, the church represented the supreme authority, and all Catholics owed obedience to its overriding power in religious, scientific, and political matters. This theocratic system, according to which revolution constituted the "absolute evil," could not therefore accommodate a single one of the positions taken by the liberals of the Institut Canadien [*see* DOUTRE].

It can readily be guessed with what faction Henri-Émile Chevalier would side, especially since the church rallied whole-heartedly to Napoleon III, and since in Canada this sympathy continued until 1859. Shortly after his arrival in 1853, Chevalier was admitted into the Institut Canadien, which that year numbered 499 members. The library contained 2,701 volumes, and its reading room was stocked with 66 newspapers, Canadian, American, and European. The new arrival, full of fervour, used his persuasive powers to get the institute to receive French republicans who were passing through Montreal. In 1854 he gave two "lectures" there (and the apostate, Narcisse Cyr*, three), was entrusted with a course of 18 lessons on French history and literature, and, an important point, was made librarian of the institute. He was still directing *La Ruche*, and found time to contribute to *Le Moniteur canadien*, *La Patrie*, and *Le Pays*. Moreover, in June 1859 he was to become editor of this last paper, which was the official organ of French Canadian liberalism. All his activities bore the stamp of *rougisme*, and Chevalier defined himself as follows: "What am I? A socialist republican. What do I want? Social reforms. What do I aspire to? The abolition of nationalities."

This credo did not fit in at all with Bishop Bourget's now belligerent ultramontanism. In 1858 the latter decided to curb the diffusion of revolutionary ideas by the Institut Canadien, and to proscribe books and papers which infected people with this poison. "Impious books" and "bad newspapers" (meaning *Le Pays*) were to disappear, and it rested with the bishop, backed by the decrees of the Council of Trent, to judge the nature of the works harboured by the institute's library. The liberals saw in this a direct attack on their liberty, and one can ill imagine "citizen" Pierre Blanchet* and Louis-Antoine Dessaulles* having their reading censured by the archbishop of Montreal. So the Institut Canadien kept its few hundreds of volumes deemed harmful by the Congregation of the Index, but lost 135 members who did not want to incur the anathema of their bishop [*see* CASSIDY].

Chevalier did not appear among the dissidents. He had given up his post as librarian, but none the less continued to take part in the life of the institute. A proof of this is the lectures that he gave there in 1857 on "the history, climate, and produce of the Hudson Bay territory." He held his meetings at the "café de la mère Lepère," in the Ruelle des Fortifications, when his numerous activities permitted. For as well as directing *La Ruche*, working at the institute, and contributing to various newspapers, Chevalier wrote novels, translated others, translated also the reports of the Canadian Geological Survey, and even, for a fee, gave French lessons. It is not surprising that his health was undermined. (It seems that his financial situation was always precarious, but we do not know whether family obligations were a burden on his budget. We know that he married a Miss Sophronie Rouvier and that they had a still-born child at Saint-Rémi-de-Napierville.) Wearied by this

Chevalier

toil, conscious perhaps that even beyond the ocean he could not compete with Louis Veuillot, he took advantage of the amnesty granted to political exiles by Napoleon III on 16 Aug. 1859. Less stiff-necked in his antibonapartism than Louis Blanc and Victor Hugo, Henri-Émile Chevalier left Canada on 17 March 1860. An old enemy, *L'Ordre*, exclaimed with a sigh of relief: "May the winds be propitious to him!"

Chevalier was only 31, but he was rich with an experience that he would try to turn to account in his own country. He worked on the staff of *Le Progrès*, and of *L'Opinion nationale*, a journal of left-wing Bonapartists. He also dabbled in politics, and represented the district of Grenelle on the Paris city council from 1871 to 1875. But it was the literary aspect of his career that was connected with Canada, and that consequently interests us.

James Fenimore Cooper's success in France was sensational; the South American reminiscences of Gustave [Olivier Gloux] Aimard, dressed up in fictional form, still enjoyed great popularity. Chevalier, in a society where romantic literature was out of date and where his radicalism closed the doors of the great newspapers against him, quickly found the course to take: he would turn his American experience into cash. His drawers contained nothing suitable. Never mind about that! He dug up *Les Trappeurs de la baie d'Hudson*, a translation he had made himself of a work by J. H. Robinson and had published in *La Ruche*, changed the title and a few of the translator's notes, and resolutely offered *Les Pieds-Noirs* by Henri-Émile Chevalier to the French public; it went through six editions in two years. In 1861, the same year, appeared a French translation of the *Wanderings of an artist among the Indians of North America . . .*, by Paul KANE. Given such an opening, he decided to write a series of novels, titled *Drames de l'Amérique du Nord*, of which *Les Pieds-Noirs* would be the first instalment. *La Huronne* would be the second stage. This *Huronne* is a queer medley: the first two chapters of the "Mystères de Montréal" formed the prologue, eight chapters of "La Huronne de Lorette" were added as they stood, and the rest was borrowed fairly liberally from Paul Kane. The plot is simple (in 1841 two young men leave Montreal for the west coast, to rescue the fiancée of one of them), and is a pretext for describing the geography and customs of Canada and for evoking its history. The two travellers meet a Métis, Poignets d'Acier, a central figure of the succeeding volumes (*La Tête Plate, Les Nez-Percés, Les Derniers Iroquois, Poignets d'Acier*), who is going to get rich in the gold mines, fight the Indians, direct the Fils de la Liberté during the 1837–38

insurrection, and undertake to drive the English out of Canada and Hudson Bay. The intrigue lacks probability, the figures do not stand out, characters get forgotten during the course of so many wanderings, and each heroine is carried off by Indians, but there is a profusion of "local colour," and the volumes proved successful. By this time an authority on Canada, Chevalier published an historical novel on Jacques Cartier*, produced a very presentable edition of *Le Grand Voyage . . .* by Brother Gabriel Sagard*, and began another series of Canadian novels, this time without links between them. Examples are *Le Chasseur noir, Les Requins de l'Atlantique, Peaux-Rouges et Peaux-Blanches*, and *La Fille des Indiens rouges* (the story of a French explorer who preceded the Cabots in Labrador and Newfoundland in 1494).

It must be allowed that Chevalier has a brisk, lively style, and a fiery imagination, which unfortunately is spoiled by the absence of any kind of discipline in the construction of the plots. His characters act under the impulse of some vague caprice on the part of their creator, and often serve only to express his opinions and prejudices. Chevalier is not sparing of historical facts and details, but his concern for exactitude is too often akin to that of his illustrious predecessor Chateaubriand. His feverish urge to publish harmed the quality of his work and even adversely affected his intellectual honesty. "He writes at the dictates of the moment," Edmond Lareau* said, speaking of his literary contributions to *La Ruche*, "at top speed, to fill the pages of the issue. You would think the publishers were wrenching the manuscript from his hands." This judgement may also be applied to his later work.

In short, Henri-Émile Chevalier was one of the group of French republicans who came, as exiles from their country, to the banks of the St Lawrence, where they disseminated their ideas and set passions afire at the Institut Canadien. Having returned home, they held learned discourse on a country that they knew superficially. Not over scrupulous, but hard-working, scamping what he did but conforming to the taste of the time, Henri-Émile Chevalier was not out of place in this context.

MARC LA TERREUR

The principal fictionalized works of Henri-Émile Chevalier are: *L'héroïne de Chateauguay; épisode de la guerre de 1813* (Montréal, 1858); *Le pirate du St Laurent* (Montréal, 1859). In the series entitled *Drames de l'Amérique du Nord* are: *Les Pieds-Noirs* (Paris, 1861); *La Huronne*, (Paris, 1861); *Les Nez-Percés* (Paris, 1862); *Les derniers Iroquois* (Paris, 1863); *Les requins de l'Atlantique* (Paris, 1863);

Peaux-Rouges et Peaux-Blanches; ou, Les douze apôtres et leurs femmes (Paris et Toulon, 1864); *La fille des Indiens rouges* (Paris, 1866).

AJM, Registre d'état civil (notes biographiques fournies par J.-J. Lefebvre). F.-X. Garneau, *Voyage en Angleterre et en France dans les années 1831, 1832 et 1833*, Paul Wyczynski, édit. (Coll. Présence, sér. A : Le Saint-Laurent, Ottawa, 1968). *La Ruche littéraire* (Montréal), févr. 1853–1859. Pierre Larousse, *Grand dictionnaire universel du XIXᵉ siècle* . . . (17v., Paris, 1865–90), XVI. Gustave Vapereau, *Dictionnaire universel des contemporains* . . . (5ᵉ éd., Paris, 1880). Théophile Hudon, *L'Institut canadien de Montréal et l'affaire Guibord; une page d'histoire* (Montréal, 1938). Lareau, *Hist. de la littérature canadienne*, 286–89. Sylvain, "Libéralisme et ultramontanisme," *Shield of Achilles* (Morton), 111–38, 220–55. Beatrice Corrigan, "Henri-Émile Chevalier and his novels of North America," *Romanic Review* (New York), XXXV (1944), 220–31. É.-Z. Massicotte, "Émile Chevalier et Montréal en 1860," *La Revue populaire* (Montréal) (oct. 1910), 92–97. Robert [Philippe] Sylvain, "Lamartine et les catholiques de France et du Canada," *RHAF*, IV (1950–51), 375–97.

CHISHOLM, GEORGE KING, politician, militia officer, and farmer; b. 4 Sept. 1814 in Nelson Township, U.C., eldest son of William Chisholm*, founder of Oakville, and his wife Rebecca Silverthorn; d. 14 April 1874, Oakville, Ont.

George King Chisholm was educated at the Nelson common school, at Gore District grammar school in Hamilton, and at Upper Canada College in York. He married Isabella Land, granddaughter of Robert Land*, the founder of Hamilton, in 1840. They lived in Hamilton for nine years before moving to Oakville; they had several children.

On 21 June 1841 Chisholm was appointed serjeant-at-arms in the Legislative Assembly of the Province of Canada. His duties were mainly ceremonial, especially to attend the speaker with the mace, but they also required him to expel disorderly and irregularly admitted persons from the house. While performing these functions in April 1849 in Montreal, he was injured in the riots over the rebellion losses bill. In 1854 he resigned his post and successfully contested an election in Halton County as the Conservative candidate.

Chisholm was instrumental in organizing Trafalgar Township and the town of Oakville. He helped found the White Oak Chapter of freemasons at Oakville and for years headed the town's school board. When the town of Oakville was incorporated in 1857, he was chosen as its first mayor. Chisholm was equally active in the militia. Commissioned captain in the 2nd Regiment of Gore militia in 1830, he saw active service during the 1837 rebellion. When the Gore District was abolished in 1849 and the militia of Halton

County was organized into battalions, Chisholm was gazetted major of the 1st Battalion of Halton (formerly the 2nd Gore). He was promoted on 11 Dec. 1857 to the rank of lieutenant-colonel and was placed in command of the 1st Halton. During the period of the Fenian raids, he stationed companies to guard the shore of Lake Ontario; in 1866 he proceeded to Fort Erie with 52 men but arrived too late to participate in the battle.

Four years later Chisholm retired from public life; he died at Oakville on 14 April 1874. A copy of a photograph of Chisholm can be seen at the Old Post Office Museum in Oakville.

HAZEL C. MATHEWS

PAO, Misc. 1850, letter of G. K. Chisholm to J. S. Macdonald, 16 March 1850. *Can. biog. dict.*, I, 408–10. H. C. Mathews, *Oakville and the Sixteen: the history of an Ontario port* (Toronto, 1953).

CHRISTIE, ALEXANDER, HBC chief factor and administrator; b. 1792 in Scotland; d. 9 Dec. 1872 in Edinburgh, Scotland.

Alexander Christie, said to be from Glasgow, joined the Hudson's Bay Company in 1809 and was sent to Moose Factory to investigate the possibilities of the lumber trade. He returned to Britain in 1810 but was back in Moose Factory the following year to establish a sawmill. In 1817 he was in charge of the company's Eastmain business and made his headquarters at Rupert's House. One of his major duties at the time was the supervision of the company's whale fishery business. At the time of the union of the HBC with the North West Company in 1821, he was listed in the Deed Poll as a chief factor. Christie was on furlough in 1824, and in charge of Moose Factory from 1826 until 1830 when he was transferred to York Factory. Three years later he was placed in charge of Red River and appointed governor of Assiniboia.

On 10 Feb. 1835, at Red River, Christie's marriage with Anne Thomas, daughter of Thomas Thomas* Sr, was confirmed by the Church of England. Like many company employees, Christie had married according to "the custom of the country" since in remote areas of the HBC's territory clergymen were seldom present to perform the ceremony. Formal marriage ceremonies and baptism of children took place when a missionary visited the area or when the couple reached a settlement where a church had been established. Two of Christie's sons, Alexander and William Joseph, and a grandson, Alexander, entered the company's service.

While he was in charge at Red River, Alexander Christie supervised the building of Lower Fort Garry, which had been begun about 1831 some

Christie

20 miles north of present-day Winnipeg; he also began construction of Upper Fort Garry on the site of an earlier company post of the same name at the confluence of the Red and Assiniboine rivers. Between 1839 and 1844 he was in England on furlough and at Moose Factory.

During his second term as governor of Assiniboia – from 1844 until his retirement in 1848 – Christie was forced to take strong measures against free traders in the Red River Settlement who challenged the HBC's legal right to a fur trade monopoly. Individual traders and small merchants, led by Andrew McDermot* and James Sinclair*, sought an unrestricted trade with American settlements to the south. The problem became particularly acute after 1843 when Norman Wolfred Kittson*, an agent for Henry H. Sibley* of St Paul, established an American trading post at Pembina just across the international boundary. Christie attempted to limit such trading by threatening to inspect the mails and seize goods imported by merchants and traders engaging in illicit trade. He issued a proclamation on 7 Dec. 1844 stating that the company's ships would not receive, at any port, goods addressed to anyone unless that person lodged at the company's office at Upper Fort Garry (Winnipeg) a declaration to the effect that he had neither directly nor indirectly trafficked in furs. On 20 December he ordered that all letters be sent to Fort Garry for inspection.

Christie, however, had no adequate force to support his authority, and his efforts were unsuccessful. It was his opinion that only a military force could maintain law and order in the settlement. As a result of HBC requests to the imperial government (and the possibility of war with the United States over Oregon), a force of approximately 350 men of the 6th Royal Regiment of Foot was sent to Red River in 1846 under Colonel John Folliot Crofton*. These troops were replaced two years later by 56 army pensioners under Major William Bletterman Caldwell*. The latter group proved ineffective, and illegal trading continued. Following the trial of Pierre-Guillaume Sayer in 1849 on a charge of illicit trade, the company abandoned all legal means of enforcing its monopoly [see George-Antoine BELLECOURT].

Alexander Christie was considered one of the most influential chief factors in the company during his career, and in recognition of his services was granted a half share in the company's profits for two years beyond the normal retirement period.

HARTWELL BOWSFIELD

Canadian North-West (Oliver). *Hargrave correspondence* (Glazebrook). HBRS, XXIV (Davies and Johnson). [Mactavish], *Letters of Letitia Hargrave* (Mac-Leod). J. S. Galbraith, *The Hudson's Bay Company as an imperial factor, 1821–1869* (Toronto, 1957). J. P. Pritchett, *The Red River Valley, 1811–1849, a regional study* (New Haven, Conn., and Toronto, 1942). "The Christie family and the HBC," *Beaver*, III, no.11 (1923), 417–19.

CHRISTIE, DAVID, politician and farmer; b. in Edinburgh, Scotland, in October 1818, son of Robert Christie; d. at Paris, Ont., 14 Dec. 1880.

David Christie was educated at Edinburgh High School; he was a good student, particularly well versed in Latin literature. In 1833 he came to Canada with his family. The next year his father took up a farm near St George in the southern part of Dumfries Township (in what is now South Dumfries Township), an area of largely Scottish settlement in the Grand River valley of Upper Canada. The Christie family was closely connected with the Dumfries Secessionist Presbyterian congregation, especially through David's uncle, the Reverend Thomas Christie, a Presbyterian missionary in the district for the United Associate Secessionist Church, a fragment split from the established Kirk in Scotland. David was certainly exposed to the Dumfries church's strongly held doctrine of voluntaryism – that churches should be voluntary organizations, not established, aided, or in any way interfered with by the state.

In the following years he also gained a strong interest in the improvement of agriculture, as he became an experienced farmer in his own right. By 1846 he was actively engaged in the movement to encourage better farming in Canada West through the holding of regular agricultural exhibitions. In August he was delegate to a meeting at Hamilton which set up the Provincial Agricultural Association. This in turn organized the first of an annual series of provincial fairs, held in Toronto that October. Christie again was a member of the committee that arranged the second provincial exhibition at Hamilton in 1847. He practised what he preached about agricultural improvement; in 1850 his own wheat won first prize at the fifth provincial fair in Niagara (-on-the-Lake).

Christie was emerging as a well-established, well-known member of the farming community, a fact signalled when, under the act of 1850 that incorporated the semi-official Board of Agriculture of Upper Canada, he was named one of its first members. He also served as reeve of Brantford Township in 1850, following the inception of the newly organized system of local municipal government for Canada West. And during the next decade he particularly gained a reputation as a stock breeder on the extensive new farming property he acquired between Brantford and

Paris, though he was still engaged as well with the Dumfries farm. Further, he continued to be active with the Provincial Agricultural Association, becoming its second vice-president in 1851 and first vice-president in 1853, and being elected president in 1855 – at which time he gave an eloquent presidential address on the theme of agricultural education.

Christie had developed still another keen interest, provincial politics. He was a staunch Reformer in background and temperament; indeed, his political and religious views had much in common with those of his old Edinburgh schoolmate, George BROWN, now editor of the Toronto *Globe*. The two Scots were in frequent contact by the late 1840s, and may well have been from Brown's own arrival in Canada in 1843. Brown did not, however, share Christie's enthusiasm for reforming the constitution along fully elective lines, once responsible government had been achieved in Canada by 1849; in supporting a British parliamentary pattern Brown stood with the main, moderate Reform group associated with Robert Baldwin*. But David Christie, full of zeal for democratic progress, turned toward a more radical element, concerned by the apparent tendency of the party to rest on its laurels, now that Reform had gained office as well as responsible rule.

The feeling that ministerial leaders were growing fat, if not unprincipled, in power was particularly likely to bring a response from Reform grassroots in agrarian Canada West. And Christie assuredly shared the rising demand among the farming community for cheap and simple government close to the people – not to mention the demand to abolish the clergy reserves system that gave churches (chiefly the Church of England) public funds from reserved lands. Accordingly, in the fall of 1849, he became engaged with a small but vigorous coterie who sought to remake the Reform party in a more radical image. This group, which included experienced politicians such as Malcolm CAMERON and later Caleb HOPKINS, as well as younger idealists such as Christie and William McDougall*, were quickly denominated the "Clear Grits." There are several possible origins for the name, but "the best authenticated version," according to John Charles Dent*, traces it to a discussion between Brown and Christie in the autumn of 1849 over the emerging radical movement, wherein Christie rejected any who might hang back like Brown, declaring, "We want only men who are *clear grit*."

Although it is impossible now to document that origin, the *Globe* certainly began applying the term to the radicals in December 1849. Moreover, it was evidently accepted by them, connoting as it did thoroughgoing reform integrity: in early 1850 they formulated a "clear grit" platform calling for elective institutions throughout, universal suffrage, and secularization of the reserves. By the following summer they had made sufficient impact in parliament to cause Baldwin to resign as premier. The Francis Hincks*–Augustin-Norbert Morin* Liberal regime that succeeded had to admit two Clear Grits, Cameron and John Rolph*, to the cabinet, a bargain worked out in July 1851 by McDougall and Christie. And in the ensuing general elections at the close of the year, Christie successfully ran for Wentworth County, which then included the Brantford area, to enter parliament at the age of 33.

Brown had meanwhile broken with the Reform ministry, because it had failed to settle the reserves question and had fostered Roman Catholic separate schools, but he continued to oppose the Clear Grits because of their advocacy of elective institutions and because they themselves, as he saw it, had now sold out for office. Undoubtedly Christie found himself in a difficult position after parliament opened in August 1852. The Hincks government showed more interest in promoting the new railway era than in taking up basic constitutional reform. Besides, not only did it still hang back on the reserves, but it also supported further enlargements of Catholic separate school rights in Canada West and incorporations of Catholic religious bodies in Canada East, thanks largely to the powerful French Canadian influence in its midst. These proceedings were sorely compromising for Grit ministerial supporters such as Christie, scarcely less voluntaryist on church-state issues than Brown. Indeed in January 1853, during the parliamentary recess, Christie met Brown in a grand public debate back in his constituency at Glen Morris, and, despite bold efforts to justify his support of the ministry, came off second best.

Nevertheless, Christie continued to hold a prominent place within Grit circles, a fact displayed when McDougall, voicing his own discontent with the Hincks government in a letter to Charles Clarke* in September 1853, even suggested that Christie might replace Hincks as leader. By 1854 the mounting strains between the eastern and western sections of the existing Canadian union and the unrest within Reform itself in Canada West, threatened to upset the government. In June it was beaten in the house, and elections were quickly called. This time, Christie stood for East Brant, one of two constituencies in the new county of Brant which had recently been divided off from Wentworth. He was narrowly defeated by a Conservative candidate, Daniel McKerlie – because, he said, "I had the whole Brown influence

Christie

against me." Still worse, when parliament met in September, the Hincks and Morin Liberals joined with Conservative forces to establish the Sir Allan MacNab*–Morin Liberal-Conservative government ("Awful treachery" to Christie). At least the new coalition was committed to secularize the reserves. Christie himself had hopes of overturning McKerlie's one-vote lead through contesting the electoral verdict. He still affirmed, "I have full confidence in Democratic principles. . . . The people will be brought to see their duty."

The electoral commission decided in Christie's favour in March 1855, and he was again seated in the Legislative Assembly. Here he found the Reform factions left in opposition beginning to form a common front against their Liberal-Conservative foes. In particular, the Clear Grits and Brown were moving together, as the former set aside their demand for elective institutions, at least for the present, and the latter concentrated on representation by population, to overcome eastern Conservative and French Catholic power in the Canadian union.

Like many Clear Grits, Christie was inclined to favour the outright repeal of the union of the Canadas, considering representation by population "a just and righteous thing" but "too slow a remedy." He nevertheless gradually came around in response to Brown's and the *Globe*'s forceful appeals for Reform unity. By September 1856 he could write: "Our friend Brown is wrong on many points. I suspect he will never go the length of constitutional changes and repeal. . . . He is a powerful man [however]. . . . We did right in standing by him." This knitting up of party ties, qualified as it might be, was symbolized by the Reform Convention of January 1857 in Toronto, which Christie attended. Indeed, he was one of the signers of the requisition calling it.

The reunited Reform forces carried Canada West in elections held late in 1857. Christie, returned again for East Brant, was on hand for the major debates on the ills of the union in the session of 1858 and the hectic summer change from the John A. Macdonald*–George-Étienne CARTIER Conservative government to Brownite Liberals, and swiftly back to Macdonald and Cartier again. In the autumn, however, he campaigned for a seat in the upper house, the Legislative Council. This had been made elective in 1856, and it was a less demanding arena than the assembly. Hence he would have more time for his growing farm outside Brantford; and he was also involved in local railway development: earlier in promoting the Buffalo and Brantford line (which became the Buffalo and Lake Huron Railway), and now in negotiating with Buffalo interests for a bridge to give direct rail access over the Niagara River. He was elected for the Erie division (which included his home territory) of the Legislative Council, and in December resigned his seat in the assembly.

He continued to be prominent in the Reform party. At the grand Reform Convention of November 1859, in Toronto, he was one of the vice-chairmen and a member of the key committee that controlled the structure of the sessions – although Brown's close associates still kept an effective grip upon them. At the convention, indeed, Christie seemed to have dropped some of his earlier outright radicalism. He did not support a demand for repeal of the union, and instead endorsed the Brownite call for a federation of the two Canadas as a step towards a future general British North American federation. Yet the next year he was informing one enduring radical associate, William Lyon Mackenzie*, that the convention's federal scheme would not do: "I now see that the only thing to save Upper Canada is a Simple Dissolution of the Union." In any case, Christie's role was now more one of prestige than of party influence. His political activities had less significance in the upper house, and old Grit radicalism had largely been tamed within the Brownite Liberal party. Accordingly, he played no very weighty part in politics in the early 1860s, as the Canadian union wound through mounting crises to complete deadlock in 1864. But when out of deadlock came the coalition of Brown, Cartier, and Macdonald to seek confederation, Christie gave it earnest support from his place in the Legislative Council. At the same time he advised the government on patronage questions in the Brant area as a leading Reform figure there.

During the confederation debates of 1865, when the plan for federal union was put to parliament, Christie spoke strongly in the council in favour of the scheme. True to his past, he did criticize the proposed federal Senate because it was to be an appointed, not an elected body: "I have always been an advocate of the elective principle." Still, he said, "I shrink from the responsibility of voting against the scheme because of that objection." And the next year, when it was enacted that existing members of the Legislative Council of Canada should be appointed to the Senate of the new confederation, Christie, at the end of his eight-year elected term, proceeded to accept a life position in the future federal upper house.

With the coming of confederation he remained actively involved in Liberal affairs. He attended the Reform Convention of June 1867 in Toronto; he worked faithfully in the party interest in the elections that followed, both in the federal sphere and in that of the new province of Ontario; and he sought to maintain his strong political influence in Brant County. Yet, as Sir John A. Macdonald shrewdly pointed out to a disconsolate local Conservative in October 1867, having become a senator had really greatly reduced Christie's importance: "the fact of being a nominee of the Crown instead of the choice of the people deprives him of any real hold."

In the following years David Christie nevertheless remained to the fore in the Senate itself; he had become one of the patricians of Liberalism. Thus, when Alexander Mackenzie* formed a Liberal government in November 1873, he was named secretary of state in the cabinet. But after the government won a sweeping election victory he was moved to the post of speaker of the Senate in January 1874, a post more honorific and less onerous, which he held with distinction until his resignation in October 1878 when the Mackenzie government fell. Although not an eloquent orator, Christie had forceful dignity, straightforward logical clarity, and a judicious choice of words that earned him respectful attention. After he left the speakership at the age of 60, he virtually withdrew from public life. Still, even in the years before, much of his most significant activity had not been in the Senate at all.

He had especially kept his interest in agricultural development; for example, he had served in various capacities in the Provincial Agricultural Association, and was its president again for the last time in 1870–71. In 1873 the Liberal government of Oliver Mowat* in Ontario named him a member of the commission which was responsible for setting up the Ontario School of Agriculture (later part of the University of Guelph). Subsequently, in 1880, he was president of the Dominion Council of Agriculture and of the American Shorthorn Breeders Association, an international body. He also sat on the Senate of the University of Toronto from 1863, and briefly in 1875 was administrator of the province of Ontario, during the illness of Lieutenant Governor John Willoughby CRAWFORD.

Meanwhile, he had continued to make his own estate, "The Plains," an agricultural showplace. The Dumfries property was also held until 1871, and by 1868 Christie already had, by deed, some 540 acres in his Brantford Township estate, on which he built a handsome mansion. He had married Isabella Turnbull of Dumfries in 1848. She died in 1858, and in 1860 he was married again, to Margaret Telfer of Springfield in Elgin County. The Christies had a large family at their Plains residence, where they frequently housed friends, political allies, and visiting agriculturalists. Moreover, from 1866 onward, a one-time schoolfellow

become political enemy and now again an increasingly close friend, George Brown, had been developing his own extensive farming estate at Bow Park on the other side of Brantford. In the 1870s the two became frequent visitors, happily reminiscing about past political battles. Christie, in fact, became vice-president of the cattle company which Brown incorporated for his large-scale pedigreed stockbreeding enterprise at Bow Park.

Like Brown's, however, Christie's final years were clouded by financial troubles. The deep depression of the later 1870s, the venture into the costly business of raising pedigreed cattle for a Canadian market not yet ready for it, undoubtedly had as much to do with his difficulties as with Brown's. But Christie had no powerful *Globe* to fall back on, and he was much more seriously overextended. He went bankrupt. His household goods were sold at auction in Brantford in December 1879; he had to leave the Plains for quarters in nearby Paris. And there the next year he suffered a trivial wound in his foot which refused to heal. His exhausted state forbade the operation needed for gangrene. He died on 14 Dec. 1880, aged 62 – only months after George Brown: their two interconnected lives thus having coincided in the year of both birth and death.

J. M. S. CARELESS

Blue Lake and Auburn Women's Institute (Paris, Ont.), "Tweedsmuir history" (copy in PAO). PAC, MG 24, D16 (Buchanan papers); MG 26, A (Macdonald papers), 339. PAO, Charles Clarke papers; Mackenzie-Lindsey collection. *Brantford Weekly Expositor*, 17 Dec. 1880. Canada, Province of, *Confederation debates. Globe* (Toronto), 10 Dec. 1849, 10 Jan. 1850, 22 Aug. 1851, 9 Jan. 1857, 11 Nov. 1859, 16 Dec. 1880. *Weekly Globe* (Toronto), 19 May 1876. *Dom .ann. reg. 1880–81. Encyclopedia of Canada*, III.
Careless, *Brown*. Cornell, *Alignment of political groups.* Dent, *Last forty years.* C. M. Johnston, *Brant County: a history, 1784–1945* (Toronto, 1967). W. J. Rattray, *The Scot in British North America* (4v., Toronto, 1880–84), II. James Young, *Public men and public life in Canada ...* (2v., Toronto, 1912), I; *Reminiscences of the early history of Galt and the settlement of Dumfries, in the Province of Ontario* (Toronto, 1880).

CHURCHILL, EZRA A., merchant, shipbuilder, and politician; b. 1804 at Yarmouth, N.S., to Ezra Churchill and Elizabeth Trefry; d. 8 May 1874 in Ottawa, Ont.

Ezra A. Churchill's father, a mate on a Yarmouth brigantine, was lost with his ship, *Hibernia*, in 1806, and his mother returned to her home in Hantsport, where she remarried and raised her son. On 10 Nov. 1824 Ezra Churchill married Ann Davidson of Falmouth, N.S., and they had two sons and several daughters. Following the death of his first wife, he married Rachel Burgess of Billtown, N.S., by whom he had four children; only one son lived beyond infancy.

Ezra Churchill began his career in Hantsport. In 1841 he bought shares in a small brigantine, and in 1844 he commissioned the building of another brigantine of 128 tons. In the 1850s he bought shares in at least two more vessels and owned the controlling interest in five others. One of these, the 697-ton *Morning Star*, launched in 1856, was the first ship built by Churchill; it was followed by such large vessels as the 1,138-ton *La Gloire*, built in 1862, the 1,383-ton *Marlborough*, built the following year, and the 1,050-ton *British America*, launched in 1869. Like other vessels built in the province, they were cargo ships with the blunt lines of the work ship rather than the sleek lines of the clipper ships which were designed for speed. Churchill differed from other builders at the time because he left much of the construction to his master builder, Robert Fuller. His yards continued to build smaller vessels suitable for the coastal trade long after other major yards had ceased this practice. At his death, his fleet and yards, among the foremost in the province, were taken over by his two sons, John and George. In the mid-1880s the Churchill yards, like other shipyards in the provinces, began to decline.

Churchill, who was obviously interested in the commercial and financial aspects of shipping, became involved with an attempt to establish a new provincial bank. A charter was granted in 1864 by the legislature for the Mutual Bank of Nova Scotia. The project did not develop any further, however, despite the support of the finance minister, Isaac LeVesconte, and other prominent Conservative assemblymen including H. A. N. Kaulback of Lunenburg and Peter Smyth of Inverness.

In 1855 Churchill was elected to the assembly as the member for Falmouth Township. When this seat was abolished in 1859, he sat as a member for Hants County, North Division, from 1859 until 1867. He was a relatively quiet supporter of the Conservative party but withheld support from Charles Tupper* by abstaining in the 1866 vote on confederation. He did not take part in the 1867 general election but joined with Jeremiah North-up to help elect Joseph Howe in the "better terms" by-election of 1869. Churchill was appointed, probably on Howe's recommendation, to the Senate in February 1871.

K. G. Pryke

PANS, Scrapbook 109, 134–35. *Directory of N.S. MLAs* (Fergusson). J. V. Duncanson, *Falmouth – a New England township in Nova Scotia, 1760–1965* (Windsor, Ont., 1965), 208. Wallace, *Wooden ships and iron men . . .*, 131–35, 204–5. [The author was also given significant aid by G. V. Shand of Windsor, N.S. k.g.p.]

CLARKE, JAMES PATON, musician; b. 1807 or 1808, probably in Scotland; m. Helen Fullerton 25 Dec. 1831, by whom he had several children; d. 27 Aug. 1877, at Yorkville (Toronto), Ont.

James Paton Clarke, the son of a musician, is first reported as a music seller's assistant in Edinburgh. In 1829 he was a musician at St George's Church in Glasgow and, in 1834, became organist at St Mary's Episcopal Chapel in Glasgow. Several of his songs appeared in British periodicals about 1832.

Clarke came to Canada in 1835. He may have settled at Elora, Upper Canada, as a farmer, but his first documented position in Canada was that of organist at Christ's Church in Hamilton in 1844 and 1845. In 1845 he gave two concerts in Toronto: in one he led a choir at the opening of St George's Church, and later he conducted a concert planned by John McCaul*, vice-president of King's College and an ardent promoter of fine music. McCaul probably induced Clarke to move to Toronto, where the latter became conductor of the Philharmonic Society (McCaul was president) from 1845 to 1847, in 1855, and in 1872–73, and of the Toronto Vocal Music Society from 1851 to 1853.

Under McCaul's influence Clarke usually featured music by Mozart, Haydn, or Beethoven in his concerts. He presented several symphonies by Mozart and Beethoven, although perhaps not in their entirety and hardly in their full instrumentation. He also conducted overtures and excerpts from oratorios, as well as some national, sacred, operatic, and humorous songs, and his own vocal pieces. Many of these performances were local premières. As was then usual, programmes were nearly always mixtures of orchestral pieces, vocal solos, choral music, or instrumental virtuoso display, performed by an equally mixed array of amateur and professional musicians. Clarke was not always a conductor: he also appeared as piano accompanist and as singer in ensembles. He was organist in Toronto at St James' Cathedral from 1848 to 1849, and probably at St Michael's Roman Catholic Cathedral.

Clarke became part of the local cultural élite as a composer as well. His songs were written to texts by Samuel Thompson*, the Reverend Robert Jackson MacGeorge*, Catharine Parr Traill [Strickland*], and other Canadian writers. This activity culminated in 1853 in the *Lays of the maple leaf, or songs of Canada*. It was the longest composition yet published in Canada and one inspired entirely by the country's scenery and its pioneers, hunters, and woodsmen. It was well received, and one contemporary hoped that he would "ere long again . . . gratify the public by other strains of that harp, which he touches with so masterly a finger. . . ."

Clarke obtained the Bachelor of Music degree from King's College (University of Toronto) in 1846, almost certainly the first such degree to have been granted by a Canadian university, and he may also have become an honorary music adviser at the college. In 1848 William Henry DRAPER presented him with three special university prizes for his compositions, the results of a contest. In 1856 he was to receive a degree of Doctor of Music, the first in Canada, from the university but it may not actually have been granted.

The years 1853–56 mark, in fact, the end of Clarke's brilliant career and the beginning of two decades of rarely interrupted obscurity. He was replaced as the conductor of the Toronto Vocal Music Society in 1853 and was an unsuccessful candidate for a professorship at Trinity College. He is not known to have published any music after 1853 or to have occupied any church or school position. In 1854 his songs were criticized as being "sadly deficient in both design and originality." He also seems to have left Toronto, but he had come back by 1861 when he co-edited *A selection of chants and tunes* for the Church of England Diocesan Synod of Toronto.

One more return to prominence occurred when the Philharmonic Society was revived in 1872 with McCaul president and Clarke conductor. The *Messiah* was performed on 28 Feb. 1873 with 160 singers and 30 orchestral players. Though uneven in quality the performance was judged "exceedingly creditable" in view of the inexperience of the singers. Clarke's health was failing and the Philharmonic Society continued under other leaders, notably Frederick Herbert Torrington*. Clarke's death came suddenly four years later.

Clarke was considered a "conscientious and earnest musician, a clever composer, and an able and successful teacher of the piano forte." Half a century after his emigration, his "reputation of being an excellent musician and vocalist" was still remembered in Scotland. Extremely versatile, as a musician in a pioneer country had to be, Clarke also tuned and repaired organs, and participated as a violinist and violist in several short-lived string quartets during his later years.

In Toronto Clarke had at least 15 vocal compositions published and another ten are known to have been performed, but only one instrumental work has been discovered. His musical invention is rooted in folk song and the idiom of the turn of the 18th century. His better melodies have a fresh outdoor quality; their simplicity is deliberate. The sincerity and clean harmonies of Clarke's unsophisticated songs stand in contrast to the flood of more pretentious music with feigned emotions which began to be produced in Canada after 1850. His most famous pupil was his son, Hugh Archibald, who made his debut as a pianist in 1854 and was trained entirely by his father. He was appointed in 1875 to the University of Pennsylvania staff, and was one of the first two university professors of music in the United States.

HELMUT KALLMANN

Christ's Church (Hamilton, Ont.) account book. MTCL, minute book of the Toronto Choral Society, 1845, and of the Philharmonic Society, 1846–47. St James' Cathedral (Toronto), churchwardens' register and minute book, 1842–1908.

Canadian church psalmody: consisting of psalm tunes, chants, anthems, etc., with introductory lessons and exercises in sacred music, ed. J. P. Clarke (Toronto, 1845). J. P. Clarke, *Lays of the maple leaf, or songs of Canada* (Toronto, [1853]). *Parochial psalmody: a new collection of the most approved psalm tunes . . . ,* ed. J. P. Clarke (2nd ed., Glasgow, 1831). *A selection of chants and tunes, made by the committee of the Toronto Diocesan Synod . . . ,* [ed. J. P. Clarke et al.] (Toronto, 1861; 2nd ed., Toronto, 1867).

Anglo-American Magazine (Toronto), II (1853), 648. "Music and composers," *Leader* (Toronto), 31 May 1854. "Music in Toronto, reminiscences of the last half century," *Mail* (Toronto), 21 Dec. 1878. "The Philharmonic Society: first public concert – the *Messiah*," *Mail* (Toronto), 1 March 1873. *A biographical dictionary of musicians,* ed. Theodore Baker (New York, 1900). Helmut Kallmann, *A history of music in Canada, 1534–1914* (Toronto and London, 1960). James Love, *Scottish church music, its composers and sources* (Edinburgh and London, 1891), 320. W. H. Pearson, *Recollections and records of Toronto of old, with references to Brantford, Kingston and other Canadian towns* (Toronto, 1914), 149, 214. D. J. Sale, "Toronto's pre-confederation music societies, 1845–1867," unpublished MA thesis, University of Toronto, 1968.

CLARKSON, THOMAS, merchant; b. Susworth, parish of Scotter, Lincolnshire, Eng., 26 Jan. 1802, son of John and Elizabeth Clarkson; d. 4 May 1874, at Toronto, Ont.

Thomas Clarkson apparently emigrated to York (Toronto) in 1832, where he appears as a storekeeper in 1837 and in the 1840s as an auctioneer. He also began in the 1840s to deal in produce and handle goods on commission, specializing in the grain trade; these two types of business were to occupy his attention for the rest of his life.

Clerk

For some time prior to the beginning of 1845 he was in partnership with Thomas Brunskill of Thornhill.

Clarkson soon became active in the financial development of the city, where his position does not seem to have been hurt by the fact that he was prepared to accept the presidency of the local Annexation Association in December 1849. He was one of the incorporators of the Toronto Board of Trade in 1845; as its president from 1852 to 1859 he supported reciprocity, pressed for changes in the usury laws, and opposed tariff increases. He was also a founder and president of the Commercial Building and Investment Society (incorporated in 1851), helped establish the Bank of Toronto (and was one of the first directors in 1856–58), and was active in the Toronto Exchange, established in 1854 "for commercial business." Like many other members of the Board of Trade, Clarkson was closely associated with the unsuccessful Toronto and Georgian Bay Canal Company, chairing, in September 1855, a Toronto meeting of delegates from both Canada and such American centres as Chicago, Milwaukee, and Oswego. In 1856 he appeared at the head of the list of incorporators of the company.

The panic of 1857, with the depression that followed, put a stop to such expensive ventures and led to a general decline in trade. Clarkson's speech on his retirement as president of the Board of Trade in January 1859 concentrated on the problems of trade in Canada. The next year he moved to Milwaukee, then the centre of a rapidly developing region. There, with his sons Benjamin Reid and Robert Guy (1841–89), he established a produce and commission business known as T. Clarkson and Sons. Thomas and Benjamin returned to Toronto in 1864, but Robert remained in Milwaukee and carried on the business until his death. He became well known through his articles in the *Evening Wisconsin*, written under the pseudonym Tommy Dodd.

In Toronto Thomas re-established his business which had been discontinued after operating briefly as Clarkson, Hunter and Company. He also became an official assignee in bankruptcy for the province, thus assuming responsibility for the storage and sale of goods of bankrupts. In 1869 he took over the lease of a large grain storage elevator which he renamed Clarkson's Elevator, and he was active in the Produce Merchants Exchange in the city.

Clarkson was forced to retire in 1872 because of a paralytic stroke. On his death two years later his business was divided: Benjamin, who was already a partner, took over the elevator and grain business; the assignee business passed to his other partners, Thomas Munro and another son, Edward Roper Curzon Clarkson (1852–1931), who later developed the auditing firm which is now Clarkson, Gordon and Company.

An Anglican and parishioner of St James Cathedral, Clarkson was also a sabbatarian. In 1858 he was elected president of a revived Toronto Sabbath Alliance which supported the exemption of civil servants from Sunday work. He was active in the St George's Society of Toronto and joined the York Pioneer Society in 1871. He married first, Elizabeth Farnham (d. 1829) in 1821, by whom he had two children; secondly, Carrie Brunskill in 1834, after he had come to Canada, by whom he had four children; and thirdly, Sarah Helliwell (1824–78), in 1844, by whom he had ten children. One son, John Brunskill Clarkson (1835–1903), became a Methodist minister, and a grandson, John Reed Teefy*, was superior of the Roman Catholic St Michael's College in Toronto.

FREDERICK H. ARMSTRONG

PAO, W. H. Merritt papers, 22 Nov. 1854; Toronto city council papers, 6, 18 July 1836. *Commercial Herald* (Toronto), 6 March 1845. *Globe* (Toronto), 17 Jan. 1859; 26 June 1860; 21, 28 May 1866. *Mail* (Toronto), 5, 6 May 1874. "The annexation movement, 1849–50," ed. A. G. Penny, *CHR*, V (1924), 236–61. Canada, Province of, *Statutes*, 1856, c.118. *Directory of the city of Milwaukee . . . 1860–61* (Milwaukee, 1860). *Milwaukee city directory for 1863 . . .*, comp. A. Bailey (Milwaukee, 1863). *Edwards' annual director to . . . the city of Milwaukee for 1865*, ed. Richard Edwards (Milwaukee, 1865). Toronto, *Directories*, 1837–73. *The roll of pupils of Upper Canada College, Toronto, January 1830, to June 1916*, ed. A. H. Young (Kingston, Ont., 1917), 170–71. [A. J. Little], *The story of the firm, 1864–1964: Clarkson, Gordon & Co.* (Toronto, 1964), 3–13. Middleton, *Municipality of Toronto*, I, 488, 504. Joseph Schull, *100 years of banking in Canada: a history of the Toronto-Dominion Bank* (Vancouver, Toronto, Montreal, 1958). Douglas McCalla, "The commercial politics of the Toronto Board of Trade, 1850–1860," *CHR*, L (1969), 51–67.

CLERK, GEORGE EDWARD, journalist; b. 18 March 1815 at Penicuik House, near Penicuik, county of Edinburgh, Scotland; son of Sir George Clerk, 6th Baronet of Penicuik, and Marie Law; d. 26 Sept. 1875 at Montreal, Que.

George Edward Clerk was born of an aristocratic but poor Scottish family whose manor was Penicuik House (to be devastated by fire in 1899). The barony of Penicuik, of which his father was the sixth holder, had become in 1646 the property of the Clerk family; earlier it had been distinguished by its attachment to the Stuart cause.

George Clerk, born in 1787, had married Marie, daughter of Ewan Law, in August 1810; she bore him eight sons and four daughters.

George Edward was the second of the eight sons. He studied at Eton, then, thanks to political backing, entered the Royal Navy as a midshipman; by this means he had an opportunity to sail along the west coast of Africa and witness many moving episodes of the slave trade. Early in the 1830s, he also formed part of the crew of a warship placed at Sir Walter Scott's disposal for a Mediterranean cruise.

Politics had put him into the navy; politics took him out of it after two years, a change of ministry having occurred. One of the openings available to a young Scottish aristocrat was therefore closed to him. There remained the army and the church, but neither offered enough attraction to a young man fired by the thought of a life of adventure. He therefore decided to emigrate to Australia, where for 14 years he was a sheep-farmer. An affliction of the eyes, caused by the intense reflection of sunlight on dry and sandy soil, forced him to return to Scotland.

In the meantime an important event had occurred in his life: he had been converted to Catholicism through reading a book by Nicholas Wiseman. Hitherto he had been somewhat indifferent to the question of religion; his one desire henceforth was to make his life conform as exactly as possible to the creed which he had espoused with one single surge of heart and mind.

On 7 Oct. 1847, while on his way to visit Australia a second time, he came to Montreal. He intended to stop there only for a short time, but an attack of rheumatic fever brought on by dampness first made him prolong his stay; then conjugal and paternal love – on 27 Nov. 1849, at Laprairie, he married Marie-Louise-Élisabeth Dupuis – introduced into this wanderer's existence an exemplary stability, by giving him permanent roots in the Canadian metropolis.

To earn a living, Clerk first tried his hand at being a notary. He then got in touch with Bishop Ignace Bourget* and Abbé Joseph Larocque*, editor of the *Mélanges religieux*. Thanks to them he had access to the library of the bishop's palace, and this allowed him to establish the bases of the philosophical and theological culture that was to ensure his success and authority as a journalist.

But it was only after the American Orestes Augustus Brownson, on 2 May 1850, had declined the invitation of Bourget and Larocque to become editor of a paper they had intended to entrust to his experience as a Christian publicist, that they turned to Clerk. Warmly encouraged by two spokesmen of the Irish Catholics of Montreal and

Quebec, the bookseller James Sadlier and the parish priest Patrick McMahon*, the Scotsman accepted. On 8 May he laid before the bishops a rough draft of a paper, and they agreed to it. Three days later a circular informed the public that the English-speaking Catholics would soon be provided with a publication dedicated to the defence of their faith and their rights: "Impelled by the needs of the day, and at the request of several laymen who are deeply distressed that Catholicism in Canada does not have a single organ in the English language to repel the ceaseless attacks of Protestant journals, we have reached the following decision. We fully approve, as being an undertaking beneficial to religion, of the publication of a religious newspaper in English, provided that it is attached to no political party."

From then on it was a highly intriguing spectacle for Montrealers to watch the brisk campaigns conducted by this authentic Scotsman who became, with no ulterior motive, the herald and acknowledged defender of the largest English-speaking Catholic group in Canada, the Irish. Clerk, as a personality as well as a journalist, did not lack the characteristics, even the peculiarities, which arouse and retain the curiosity of the public, always partial to those men whose appearance and behaviour strike a note of originality in the monotony of the mass. With broad shoulders, eyes of a deep blue usually concealed behind glasses that were equally blue, hair brushed well back from his forehead, sidewhiskers and moustache trimmed in the style of the period, a cleanly chiselled mouth, original in his dress to the point of eccentricity, Clerk, although an unflagging worker, abandoned his pen and his books as often as he could to stroll through the streets in all weathers, carrying his inseparable cotton umbrella which he had brought from Australia, accompanied by friends, and followed by two or three dogs.

He entitled his paper, the first number of which appeared on 16 Aug. 1850, the *True Witness and Catholic Chronicle*. This title indicated a whole programme. It was also a declaration of war on John Dougall*, of the *Montreal Witness*, and George BROWN, the founder and editor-in-chief of the Toronto paper the *Globe*. An emigrant Scotsman was wielding the claymore against two other Scotsmen, emigrants like himself. With truly Caledonian fervour on both sides, a struggle then began on the shores of the St Lawrence which certainly lost none of its fire for not being waged on the banks of the Clyde.

As well as being the uncompromising champion of the Catholic faith, Clerk showed himself the determined opponent of the Liberals, especially when they belonged to the Institut Canadien.

Cochran

To the great satisfaction of the clergy, his preferences inclined him towards the Conservative party. Bishop Bourget wrote to him on 3 Oct. 1860: "When one looks through your columns with a modicum of attention, one is soon convinced that you are a true conservative, working at full strength to link this colony firmly with the mother country; and to succeed in this undertaking you are setting powerfully in motion, with your irresistible logic, the religious principle, which is indeed the one solid basis of civil and political society."

It was only when he thought that the interests of Catholicism were at stake that Clerk deviated from this political line, as he did for example over confederation. "In 1865," Laurent-Olivier David* wrote, "a public meeting called by the opponents of the plan for confederation took place in one of the rooms of the Institut Canadien-Français. During the discussion a man got up and began to speak in English; he declared emphatically against this change of constitution, and quoted as an example of the dangers that it contained for the French Canadian Catholic minority the history of the Catholics in Scotland and Ireland. His powerful build, his military bearing, and his incisive, energetic manner of speaking gave the impression of great physical and intellectual vitality." David, who did not yet know him, learned then that the speaker was George Edward Clerk, "the famous editor of the *True Witness*." And David added: as Clerk "had always given evidence of independence in politics, the opponents of Confederation were happy to have such a powerful assistant in their struggle against the new constitution."

The journal of which Clerk was the owner and practically the sole editor appeared every Friday. It was printed by John Gillies, who saw to its circulation. In 1858 the *True Witness* had 2,837 subscribers and was distributed by agents in 21 areas. In the following year Clerk transferred the ownership to Gillies, who made many trips to Canada West, the Maritimes, and Nova Scotia to increase the number of subscribers.

Despite Gillies' efforts, the financial situation of the *True Witness* always remained precarious. From the time the paper was started, Bishop Bourget had assured Clerk that he could count on an annual sum of $600, $200 coming from the bishopric, $200 from the Sulpicians, and $200 from the diocese of Quebec through the intermediary of the vicar general, Charles-Félix Cazeau*. If by chance one of these sources happened to dry up, Clerk did not fail to approach the bishop of Montreal and remind him of his initial promise. Thanks to this meagre subsidy, Clerk held on heroically to his post as editor,

although there remained "very scanty means with which to support his large family," as vicar general Alexis-Frédéric Truteau wrote to Bishop Bourget on 18 Feb. 1870. Indeed, of the Clerk-Dupuis marriage 11 children had been born; nine of them, six boys and three girls, reached adult age. The youngest of the sons, Jean-Pio-Robert, was to marry a daughter of Senator Laurent-Olivier David, who expressed his warm admiration for Clerk in some well-informed pages later published in *Les gerbes canadiennes*.

A quarter of a century of exhausting work and militant journalism had undermined Clerk's health, and he was finally struck down by a severe attack of angina pectoris in February 1875. Surrounded by his family, and having received the last sacraments of the church, he passed away on 26 Sept. 1875.

Philippe Sylvain

ACAM, RLB, 11, p.450. *Mandements des éveques de Québec* (Têtu et Gagnon), III, 571–72. L.-O. David, *Les gerbes canadiennes* (Montréal, 1921), 67–80. Robert [Philippe] Sylvain, *Clerc, garibaldien, prédicant des deux mondes : Alessandro Gavazzi (1809–1889)* (2v., Québec, 1962), II, 323–29. Agnes Coffey, "George Edward Clerk, founder of the 'True Witness'; a pioneer of Catholic action," CCHA *Report, 1934–35*, 46–59; "*The True Witness and Catholic Chronicle*; sixty years of Catholic journalistic action," CCHA *Report, 1937–38*, 33–46.

COCHRAN, JAMES (he signed Cochran, but his family in Ireland used Cocoran or Corcoran), merchant and politician; b. 1802 at Granard, County Longford, Ireland, son of Timothy Cocoran (or Corcoran) and Margaret Flood; d. at Camp Hill Cottage, Halifax, N.S., 6 March 1877.

In 1825, when he was 23, James Cochran emigrated from Ireland to Halifax, where he was employed by the ship chandlery firm of Temple Piers* and his brother Lewis. The firm sold sailcloth, cordage, nails, spikes, and supplies needed by sailing ships; it also owned a ropewalk. Later Cochran operated as a commission merchant dealing in tobacco, tea, flour, sugar, and brandy. Cochran married Catherine Walsh at St Mary's Roman Catholic Cathedral on 28 Sept. 1829; they had four children, all of whom died without issue.

The accumulation of capital in Halifax during the American Civil War led to the incorporation of the People's Bank in 1864. George H. Starr was the bank's president with James Cochran, William J. Coleman, Benjamin Wier*, John Doull, and others serving as directors. By 1868 the bank had agencies at Wolfville and New Glasgow, and in 1875 established a branch at Lockeport, centre for the West Indies trade. In 1870 James Cochran also became one of the directors of the Acadia Fire Insurance Company which paid dividends as high as 15 per cent. Always an astute investor, Cochran died with a personal estate valued at $202,508 mostly in bank stock and debentures of the city of Halifax.

In 1835 James Cochran was admitted to the Charitable Irish Society, an organization founded in 1786 by prosperous Irish (both Protestant and Catholic) to help immigrants and to assist the poor and indigent among their countrymen in Nova Scotia. Cochran served as president of the society in 1853 and 1867; he was a generous contributor to its charities until his death. The Irish Roman Catholic population of Halifax had trebled before the influx caused by the potato famine of 1846, and continued to increase in succeeding decades. Cochran belonged to the influential class of Irish Catholics who acted with the Reform party and continued to support the Liberals after the Gourley Shanty Riots, but he took no active part in public life until 1867 when he was persuaded by his fellow anti-confederates to accept a nomination as one of the local candidates for Halifax County. Although he was in Europe for part of the campaign, he was elected to the assembly.

On 18 Feb. 1868 Cochran became a minister without portfolio in William Annand*'s anti-confederate government; in the assembly he served as chairman of the committee on trade and manufactures, where he worried about the adverse effect of higher federal tariffs on Maritime business. Annand's government was concerned with efforts to obtain the repeal of the British North America Act, but reluctantly accepted better financial terms from the Canadian government in 1869. Although Cochran favoured Nova Scotia's returning to independent colonial status, he refused to support annexation to the United States, and said that "the man who would not be loyal to this country [Britain] must be a fool or an idiot." He was a member of the education committee when the assembly considered separate schools, but "believed that the temper of the country would not admit of separate schools, and therefore I took but little trouble in the matter." He decided not to contest another election, and on 6 June 1871 was appointed to a seat in the Legislative Council to replace William James Stairs*. Cochran continued as a member of the Executive Council in Philip C. Hill*'s government where his opinions were valued because of his sound judgement and his integrity.

James Cochran was respected in the community for his benevolence, for his shrewd common sense

in business and politics, and as an example of a poor, Roman Catholic, Irish immigrant who had become a financially successful, influential citizen.

PHYLLIS R. BLAKELEY

Archdiocese of Halifax, Chancery Office, marriage registers of St Mary's Roman Catholic Cathedral, 28 Sept. 1829. Halifax County Court of Probate, will of James Cochran. PANS, Charitable Irish Society, Minutes, 1850–66; Halifax County death registrations, June quarter, 1874; March quarter, 1877. *Acadian Recorder* (Halifax), 25 July 1872, 4 April 1874, 6 March 1877. *Morning Chronicle* (Halifax), 7 March 1877. Nova Scotia, House of Assembly, *Debates and proceedings*, 1868–71. George Mullane, *Charitable Irish Society of Halifax, Canada, founded 1786; sketch of some of the foundation members of the Charitable Irish Society, including remarks on the "Morris family": being a paper read at a meeting of the society on November 20th, 1918* ([Halifax, 1918]), 8–9.

COCHRAN, JAMES CUPPAIDGE, clergyman and editor; son of Dr William Cochran* and Rebecca Cuppaidge, b. at Windsor, N.S., 17 Sept. 1798; d. at Halifax, N.S., 20 June 1880.

James Cuppaidge Cochran was born within the walls of King's College, Windsor, Nova Scotia, where his father Dr William Cochran was vice-president. Following a brief period in business he decided on the ministry as a career and entered King's College in 1821. He completed the requirements for the BA in 1824, but the degree was not conferred until 1825. Ordained a priest of the Church of England on 23 Aug. 1824, Cochran served the first 28 years of his ministry in Lunenburg, N.S. He married Anna Mathilda Power on 15 Dec. 1826, and had 12 children. From 1835 until 1840, Cochran was editor of the *Colonial Churchman*, a fortnightly newspaper published in Lunenburg. Always a keen student, he qualified for an MA from King's College in 1835. Throughout his lifetime he demonstrated great interest in his alma mater and served for 25 years as secretary of the board of governors. From 1850 to 1852 he undertook a successful canvass of the diocese of Nova Scotia to raise an endowment fund for King's College.

In 1852 Cochran moved to Halifax and for the next three years was editor of the *Church Times*. Here he strove "to make the paper not only the channel of information on all topics ecclesiastical and secular but also to give profitable instruction in righteousness." His editorials in both the *Colonial Churchman* and the *Church Times* exhibit strong views on a wide variety of issues such as temperance, education, and railway policy. These journalistic efforts provide a valuable commentary

Cochrane

on social and political conditions in mid-19th-century Nova Scotia. Cochran also gave leadership in various humanitarian and philanthropic endeavours. These included waging a successful campaign to establish an institution for the education of the deaf and dumb and voluntarily serving as chaplain in both the Halifax asylum for the poor and the city prison.

In 1855 he was appointed rector of Salem Chapel, a former Congregational church leased by the Church of England for work among the poverty stricken in Halifax. A successful ministry of 11 years was climaxed by a dispute with Bishop Hibbert Binney* which led to his dismissal in 1866. The controversy stemmed from Cochran's insistence on wearing a black geneva gown while preaching. Following this incident he and his followers organized Trinity Church – a free-pew church – where he remained until his retirement in 1875. His long career was recognized in 1872 when King's College conferred upon him the degree DD, *honoris causa*.

WILLIAM B. HAMILTON

[There are numerous references to Cochran in USPG, SPG, D10, 1, 2. The Andrew William Cochran papers in PAC, MG 24, B16, contain some correspondence between James Cuppaidge Cochran and his brother Andrew William Cochran*. "Recollections of half a century," a lecture delivered by James C. Cochran at Halifax, 26 Jan. 1864, in manuscript form, is in PANS. His published works consist mainly of collections of sermons; a number of these are in PANS, the Library of King's College, Halifax, and Acadia University Library, Wolfville, N.S. The pamphlet [Hibbert Binney], *Correspondence between the bishop of Nova Scotia and the Reverend Canon Cochran, M.A., touching the dismissal of the latter from the pastoral charge of Salem Chapel, Halifax, N.S.* (Halifax, 1866) is in General Synod Archives, Church House, Toronto. W.B.H.]

See also: *Colonial Churchman* (Lunenburg, N.S.), 1835–40, and the *Church Times* (Halifax), 1852–55. T. R. Millman, "Canadian Anglican journalism in the nineteenth century," Can. Church Hist. Soc. *J.* (Toronto), III (1959), 1–19.

COCHRANE, Sir THOMAS JOHN, officer in the Royal Navy and colonial administrator; b. in England on 5 Feb. 1789, eldest son of Admiral Sir Alexander Forrester Inglis Cochrane and his wife Maria Shaw, widow of Captain Jacob Wheate; m. on 6 Jan. 1812 to Mathilda Ross by whom he had two sons and two daughters; d. in England in 1872.

During their careers both Thomas John Cochrane and his father excited a great deal of envy and provoked considerable acid comment against themselves. Earl St Vincent [John Jervis] stated that the "Cochranes are not to be trusted. They are all mad, romantic, money-getting and not truth-telling." Reputedly Sir Alexander practised nepotism unduly, as when he entered his seven-year-old son on the books of his ship *Thetis* as a volunteer in 1796 and kept him under his pennant until 1805, when Thomas was promoted lieutenant on *Jason*. He became its captain in 1806 and saw service on it in the West Indies until 1809. By 1825 Thomas Cochrane had put in 26 years of service in the Royal Navy, including eight years on the North American Station, which were presumed to have been useful experience for his appointment as governor of Newfoundland on 16 April of that year.

Cochrane ushered in a new era for Newfoundland. He was the first resident governor, ending over 100 years of naval administration of an island long considered by the Admiralty as a ward of its own policy – a "great ship" anchored off the Grand Banks – and by the West Country merchants as their special area of commercial exploitation. Tory and authoritarian by upbringing and profession, Cochrane was fond of ceremony and preferred good living; he brought to Newfoundland enough household effects to equip a palace and, according to Sir Richard Henry Bonnycastle*, he "displayed a magnificence in his vice-regal function before unknown" in the poor colony. To fit his ideas of good living, Cochrane had a new residence built for the governor. It stood on a ridge between Fort William and Fort Townsend far away from the dangerous fire area of the lower town. Designed in England, it was originally estimated to cost £8,778; increased size and frequent alterations at Cochrane's wilful discretion brought the final costs in 1831 to £36,000, a most embarrassing sum which provoked a court of inquiry. Government house, now surrounded by the burgeoning city of St John's, remains as a memorial to Cochrane. To add to his comfort and enjoyment he purchased land about three miles from the city where, beside a private lake, he built an ornamental retreat, Virginia Cottage, joined by a special road to government house. Despite his love of luxury, however, Cochrane was extremely energetic and dedicated to his duties.

By royal charter of 2 Jan. 1826 a change was made in the administration of Newfoundland. Cochrane was to divide it into three districts – northern, central, and southern – over which he was to place a chief justice and two puisne judges for whom ample salaries were to be provided. The Supreme Court was to be given power to admit a sufficient number of qualified solicitors and attorneys to practise in the courts. Richard Alexander Tucker* became chief justice with John W. Molloy and Augustus W. DesBarres the assistants, following this charter. The extension of a civil court system was not, however, matched by the introduction of a more customary form of civil government. In fact the Colonial Office refused to consider representative government and imposed a system similar to that just prepared for New South Wales, by which Cochrane ruled over Newfoundland with a nominated council, composed of the three judges and the commander of the garrison. As A. H. McLintock puts it, "this council was strictly advisory in its functions, for it was to be summoned by the governor to discuss only questions proposed by him, and as it was entirely official, the executive powers of the governor differed little from those under the old order." The differences, however, were there; the political climate in England was changing and in the colony there were men able and willing to challenge an indefinite continuation of oligarchical rule.

Despite the restraints of the new order, Cochrane took up the solution of the colony's problems, including its depressed economic situation, with enthusiasm. He countered the unconditional pauper relief, which he believed encouraged idleness and dependence upon the government, by providing employment on road-building projects to connect the capital with some of the adjacent outports; he encouraged agriculture by making small holdings available at nominal quitrents, though he believed that, because of the nature of the land, farming could only be complementary to the fishery; he stopped the practice of deporting the most destitute. He also sought to classify the application of the laws of England to Newfoundland, but this effort was interrupted. Cochrane attempted as well to set up a system of municipal government in St John's. In 1826 a group was called together to devise a municipal system for the city, but he failed to get unanimity. Political cabals, Protestant and Catholic dissension, English and Irish antagonisms, and mercantile resistance all worked against him. Finally in 1827 he requested that the Colonial Office coerce the city into accepting a plan of local government, but London refused. During Cochrane's regime St John's was therefore ruled by the council.

Conspicuous among Newfoundlanders in their support for a representative assembly, a problem that engrossed the colony, were Patrick Morris*, born in Waterford, Ireland, and Dr William Carson* of Kirkcudbrightshire, Scotland. Cochrane was opposed to an assembly; his reasons were cogent and, in the light of later developments, justified if not completely valid. He was well aware that the reformers' case for representative government had the support of some important mer-

chants, although a not inconsequential number, resident and absentee, stood firmly against change. He had also been warned by the Colonial Office that the colony's population (approximately 60,000) had reached a size where its pressure against authoritarian rule could not be withstood. The governor, however, argued that among this substantial population only a small merchant class had the wealth, education, and respectability to take places in the legislature, and this group, along with their agents, were already fully occupied in their mercantile affairs. Even if the small professional class were considered along with the merchants, St John's alone would be well served. The lack of roads, the hostile climate, and a paucity of able men would leave the outports neglected. Cochrane was fully convinced that the existing form of government, with some innovations such as municipal governments for larger communities, was best suited for the mass of uneducated, politically innocent fishermen.

Sir James Stephen probably turned the scales in the reformers' favour when on 17 Dec. 1831 in his position as legal adviser to the Colonial Office he made a report on the suggested form of legislature for Newfoundland. He observed that "in every colony where the population is homogeneous, ... a Legislative Assembly is an inestimable benefit; that it executes its proper functions with a degree of ability for which it rarely obtains sufficient credit; that it either prevents discontents or gives them a safe direction; that it creates more useful exercise of the understanding; affords much innocent pleasure; and creates a subject of permanent interests in societies which would otherwise stagnate in a listless unconcern about all questions of a public character." In the House of Commons George Robinson, member for Worcester, and long acquainted with Newfoundland through trade and residence, had already pressed the case for an assembly in September by relating that issue to the British reform bill. When Cochrane was advised in July 1832 by the home government that he had lost the argument, he did not resign but promised to further the new constitution as if he had thought of it himself. This resolve was not easily made for Cochrane's voice on the needs of the colony had not been heeded by Viscount Howick [Henry George Grey], the under secretary for the colonies, a Whig and an enthusiast for representative institutions.

In August 1832 Cochrane obtained a new commission, and in fact became the first civil governor of the island. He was empowered to create a legislature with an executive council of seven members subject to his suspension for any just

Coffin

cause, and to divide the island into nine districts from which a 15-member assembly was to be elected on a franchise so wide that it amounted to manhood suffrage. Cochrane retained the usual negative voice with power to adjourn, prorogue, and dissolve the legislature. His two years under the new constitution were far from happy. Troubles, which Lord Goderich [Frederick John Robinson] had sought to prevent when he was colonial secretary, fell with a vengeance upon the infant legislature: despite warnings from Goderich and James Stephen, the council and assembly were not cojoined, hence there were no councillors in the lower chamber to check the radicalism of the more vociferous members; equally the separate council was an open invitation for the entrenchment of privilege. Quarrels between the council and assembly were constant, violent, and even undignified. The assembly bickered with Cochrane, fought with the public over privilege, and at times sought to browbeat the judiciary into compliance with its wishes. Strong, irascible personalities on either side of the contest both in and out of the legislature embittered the public and private debates, and newspapers argued blatantly with no attempt to cover their bias.

Factionalism in high places was exemplified in two persons particularly. Henry John Boulton*, lately dismissed by Goderich from his office as attorney general of Upper Canada and appointed chief justice (and thus a member of the council) in Newfoundland in 1833 by Goderich's successor Lord Stanley, was far from impartial in his legal office and overbearing in his political position. The Roman Catholic bishop, Michael Anthony Fleming*, did not hesitate to play a role in politics, especially in support of the Catholic John KENT, and set a pattern for clerical involvement in politics. A running feud developed between Cochrane and Fleming and culminated in a libel action brought by the governor against the bishop's chaplain, Father Edward TROY, for allegedly writing a series of articles against the governor in the local press.

Cochrane's removal from office in 1834 was the result not only of his embroilment with the colony's reformers and the bishop, but also of an accumulation of grievances against him and the disappearance from office of Goderich, who, according to Cochrane, had promised him a longer period than two years under his commission of 1832. To add to Cochrane's discomfiture, Lord Stanley's successor, Sir Thomas Spring-Rice, reminded him of his past extravagant expenditures and criticized his tardiness in writing dispatches to London. Only partially justified was the Colonial Office's criticism that Cochrane was to blame for

the mob violence against the Protestant editor, Henry D. Winton*, late in 1833 in St John's, and the unpreparedness of the garrison to suppress such violence. Cochrane suspected that his dismissal was also hastened by the constant complaints against him to the Colonial Office by the Catholic party and the reformers. To fill his cup of humiliation, he and his daughter Mary were reviled and pelted with filth on their way down Cochrane Street (named in his honour) to the ship ready to take him back to England.

Cochrane was never again employed in a colony, but he did re-emerge briefly in Newfoundland's affairs when he appeared before a select committee appointed in 1841 to enquire into the continuing legislative problems. On this occasion he reiterated his original belief that the colony was not ready for the constitution granted in 1832, and indicated that political events under Sir Henry PRESCOTT's governorship had served to strengthen his conviction. His opinions, along with others, persuaded the British government to modify a constitution they could not revoke, and led to the introduction of the Amalgamated Legislature the following year.

Cochrane served as the Conservative MP for Ipswich between 1839 and 1841, and in the latter year was promoted rear admiral; between 1842 and 1847 he was successively second in command and commander-in-chief of the China Station, and, from 1852 to 1855, commander-in-chief for Portsmouth. He ultimately rose to admiral of the fleet in 1865.

Though the events of his administration may not suggest a favourable verdict, Judge Daniel Woodley Prowse*, writing in the latter years of the 19th century, pronounced that "Sir Thomas Cochrane is now universally admitted to have been the best Governor ever sent to Newfoundland." Before his departure in 1834, England's oldest colony had been set on the rough and rocky road to representative government.

FREDERIC F. THOMPSON

PRO, CO 194/80–194/88. *DNB.* John Marshall, *Royal naval biography . . .* (2v. and supps., London, 1823–30), I. O'Byrne, *Naval biog. dict.* Gunn, *Political history of Nfld.* A. H. McLintock, *The establishment of constitutional government in Newfoundland, 1783–1832: a study in retarded colonisation* (Royal Empire Society imperial studies, 17, London, 1941). Prowse, *History of Nfld.* Thompson, *French shore problem in Nfld.*

COFFIN, WILLIAM FOSTER, soldier, author, and civil servant; b. at Bath, Eng., on 5 Nov. 1808, son of an army officer and grandson of John Coffin*, a loyalist from Boston who moved to

Quebec in 1775 and played a distinguished part in its defence against the Americans in 1775–76; d. at Ottawa, Ont., 28 Jan. 1878.

In 1813, William Foster Coffin's family came to Quebec. His father being in the army, Coffin was aware as a child of the echoes of the War of 1812. He learned French at this time, at the home of the parish priest of Beauport. In 1815, with the war at an end, the Coffins returned to England and William spent the next nine years at Eton. Perhaps because his uncle Thomas* was living at Quebec and had become a member of the Legislative Council of Lower Canada, William looked to the colony for a career. In 1830 he came to Canada, articled in Montreal, and, after reading law with Charles Richard Ogden* and Alexander Buchanan*, was called to the bar of Lower Canada in 1835. Two years later, he was active among the volunteers organized against the *Patriotes*, serving as an interpreter and intervening to protect the habitants and church property from pillaging by these volunteers.

This background of law and loyalty helped to shape Coffin's career in the ensuing years. In 1838 he was chosen by Sir John Colborne* to be assistant civil secretary for Lower Canada – an office created with a view to organizing a police force for the province – and in 1839 he became a police magistrate. In 1840, Coffin became commissioner of police for Lower Canada; two years later he was named joint sheriff of the District of Montreal, a post he resigned in 1851 when the legislature suddenly cut in half the income of the office. Coffin was frequently called on as a commissioner to investigate matters of law and order. In 1840 he looked into the state and condition of the Montreal jail; in 1841 he inquired into troubles on the Indian reserve at Caughnawaga and into election riots at Toronto [see George MONRO]. In 1854 he investigated accidents on the Great Western Railway and, in the following year, he studied the affairs of the University of Toronto. In 1855 also, he was sent to maintain order on the Gatineau "then seriously threatened by refractory characters to the great disquietude of the lumbering interest." Meanwhile, Coffin was acquiring land, wealth, and important interests in railways linking Montreal and New York.

In 1855, as a result of the Crimean War, Britain reduced her garrison in Canada to its lowest level in decades. Patriotic enthusiasm and anxiety at the possibility of war with the United States combined to persuade the government of the united province to revise the Canadian militia system. For the first time, formal authority was granted for the creation of units of volunteer militia. Coffin, a major in the older militia organization, was one of many who took advantage of the new legislation, forming the only militia field battery in Montreal. Since organizing field artillery involved hiring horses, recruiting men, and storing equipment, as well as mastering relatively complex training, only a man of enthusiasm and wealth could have managed so difficult a task.

To encourage Canadians to make permanent provision for their own defence, the British government decided to hand over, in 1856, most of its ordnance lands in Canada to the provincial authorities. With some misgivings, the Canadian government accepted the gift. At the suggestion of the governor general, Sir Edmund Walker Head*, Coffin was appointed commissioner for ordnance lands, a position he was to hold for the rest of his life. Choosing to establish himself in Ottawa, Coffin resigned his command of the Montreal battery, and received promotion to lieutenant-colonel as a final reward for his services.

Predictably, Coffin struggled hard to make Canadian government policy fulfil British expectations. The ordnance lands, he claimed, "represent a capital, the annual interest of which, if estimated as proposed, will exceed the present requirements of the militia of the Province." Rent from land and buildings in Ottawa alone would yield a million dollars a year for defence purposes. Coffin's efforts to secure the ordnance funds for Canadian defence were unavailing and his office and its revenues were soon swallowed up in the massive Crown Lands Department. For 18 more years he continued as a civil servant of first the provincial and later the dominion government.

Throughout his life, Coffin elaborated his claim that his grandfather had played the key role in saving Quebec in 1775 and, consequently, British power in North America. In the 1860s, with new threats of war with the United States, Coffin turned to a wider patriotic task in publishing *1812, the war and its moral*. Although his younger contemporary, John Charles Dent*, condemned the book's unflagging patriotic bias, he merely underlined Coffin's own purpose: to combat the sensational American versions of the war and to offer "an antidote to the American literature of the day." The heroism of Sir Isaac Brock*, Tecumseh*, Laura Secord [Ingersoll*], and the Canadian militia is presented with enough fervour to contribute significantly to a mythology known to a century of English Canadian schoolchildren. By accentuating the significance of Charles-Michel d'Irumberry* de Salaberry and the battle of Châteauguay, Coffin did his best to provide both the founding races of Canada with the heroic legends he felt were necessary for their common nationalism.

Cogswell

After his first book, Coffin continued to write, chiefly lectures. Those which survive in print, such as *Thoughts on defence, from a Canadian point of view* and *Quirks of diplomacy*, exhibit an increasing sense of Canadian nationalism. Even after the withdrawal of British troops from central Canada in 1870–71, Coffin argued that Canadians could defend themselves from the United States. If the British chose to be generous at Canada's expense in their diplomacy with the United States, Canadians should be recompensed.

In 1873, Coffin declined the appointment of lieutenant governor of Manitoba. Five years later he died at his home, "Aux Écluses," near Ottawa. In Boston, on 6 July 1841, he had married Margaret Clark, herself of loyalist and military stock. She and one son, Thomas, survived him.

DESMOND MORTON

PAC, MG 30, D62 (Audet papers), 8, 565–69. W. F. Coffin, *1812, the war and its moral; a Canadian chronicle* (Montreal, 1864); *Memorial of William F. Coffin to His Excellency Sir Edmund Walker Head* (Montreal, 1855); *Quirks of diplomacy; read before the Literary and Scientific Society of Ottawa, January 22, 1874* (Montreal, 1874); *Thoughts on defence, from a Canadian point of view . . .* (Montreal, 1870). *Dom. ann. reg.*, 1878, 333–34. E. J. Chambers, *The origin and services of the 3rd (Montreal) field battery of artillery, with some notes on the artillery of by-gone days, and a brief history of the development of field artillery* (Montreal, 1898). Dent, *Last forty years*, II, 566. Hodgetts, *Pioneer public service*.

COGSWELL, ISABELLA BINNEY, philanthropist; b. 6 July 1819 in Halifax, ninth child of Henry Hezekiah Cogswell* and Isabella Ellis; d. 6 Dec. 1874 in Halifax.

Isabella Cogswell's parents were born in the Nova Scotia outports; the Cogswells had emigrated from New England in the 1760s and the Ellis family were immigrants from Ireland. Henry Cogswell, an attorney, was first president of the Halifax Banking Company, an MLA, and member of the provincial Legislative Council. Isabella inherited her father's business instincts and carried on numerous property transactions in Halifax after his death. She also inherited his broad humanitarianism which was reinforced by the evangelical influence of her brother William Cogswell, curate of St Paul's Church. When her father's death left her free of family responsibilities, Isabella, who never married, devoted the rest of her life to bettering the educational and living conditions of the Halifax poor.

In the 1850s Isabella began assisting at Sabbath services at the Ragged School for pauper children. In the early 1860s she organized a ladies' committee to revive the faltering school; from it emerged, in 1863, the Halifax Protestant Industrial School, a home "for the reclamation of boys to the paths of industry and virtue." She headed a group of women who provided religious instruction at the school, entertained the teachers and boys at her residence, "Jubilee," and contributed financial aid, particularly for steam power in the workshop and for an endowment. She was also a founder and committee member of St Paul's Alms House of Industry for Girls, to which she granted a bequest for the carrying on of its work. To aid Christian women of inadequate means, Isabella participated in the founding, operation, and endowment of a home for the aged. Tirelessly, she laboured for St Paul's Parochial District Visiting Society and the Halifax branch of the Colonial Church Society which established Anglican schoolmasters and missionaries in Nova Scotia. With a bequest to Trinity, the free-pew church, and her assistance to interdenominational missions, she encouraged religious instruction for the poor. To aid them further, she endowed an orphans' home and served as first president of the Women's Christian Association.

Miss Cogswell's wealth encouraged not only philanthropic activity but also commercial transactions. Property was the principal field of investment, and in 20 years of substantial purchases and sales she demonstrated the same good business sense as her competitors. Her mortgage holdings, the customary instruments of her purchases, were valued in excess of $95,000 at the time of her death. But the main directing force in her life was her belief that the body was the home of the soul. Her most consuming efforts were devoted to the moral improvement of her fellow citizens – never ostentatiously, never condescendingly, but always persistently.

S. BUGGEY

Halifax County Court of Probate, will of Isabella Binney Cogswell. *Christian Messenger* (Halifax), 9 Dec. 1874. *Daily Acadian Recorder* (Halifax), 7, 8, 9 Dec. 1874. PANS, Beech Street Mission, *Report, 1882*; Halifax branch of the Colonial and Continental Church Society, *Reports, 1862–74*; Halifax Protestant Industrial School, *Reports, 1865–76*; Halifax Ragged and Industrial Schools, *Report, 1864*; St Paul's Alms House of Industry for Girls, *Reports, 1868–75*. Harris, *Church of Saint Paul*, 245–46. E. O. Jameson, *The Cogswells in America* (Boston, 1884), 388–89.

COLES, GEORGE, farmer, merchant, brewer, distiller, and politician, b. 20 Sept. 1810 in Prince Edward Island, son of James Coles and Sarah Tally; d. 21 Aug. 1875 in Charlottetown Royalty, P.E.I.

George Coles spent his early years on his father's

farm in Charlottetown Royalty. The Island was then at a primitive stage of development, and young George, not born into the local élite, received little formal education. At the age of 19 he went to England, where, on 14 Aug. 1833, he married Mercy Haine, who was to bear him 12 children. Later in the same year, he returned with his bride to Prince Edward Island.

On 29 Oct. 1833 Coles advertised that he had for sale, at his father's residence, several items, such as pipes and silverware, which he had brought back from England. By June of the following year he could announce that he had opened a "New and Cheap Store" in Charlottetown, selling imported manufactured goods and liquor. Eighteen months later he was advertising the products of a brewery and distillery which he had founded. He appears to have been successful in his new venture, for in May of 1836 he publicly thanked his patrons for their "kind and unexpected support." As the 1830s wore on, the production of beer and liquor became the focus of his business activities, and he advertised for the purchase of increasing quantities of barley and oats. Nevertheless, he did not restrict his talents to brewing and distilling. In 1840 he acquired a steam mill, in 1843 he announced that he had imported modern carding machines, and by the mid-1840s he was renting houses in Charlottetown. In addition, Coles managed a farm which the editor of the *Islander* described in 1843 as being "for its size . . . one of the best managed and most productive in the Island . . . in fact, a specimen on a small scale, of what may be seen as the effects of the most scientific husbandry in England." In all his ventures, George Coles was employing between 20 and 30 men, and had a capital outlay estimated as being between £7,000 and £8,000.

By this time, Coles had entered public life. In 1842 he had contested the rural constituency of New London and had been elected to the House of Assembly. The electoral card he distributed was non-committal as to party affiliation, but Coles was generally understood to be opposed to the radical escheat policies espoused by many of the Reformers. Escheat concerned the land question, the major issue in Prince Edward Island in the early 1840s, and indeed throughout Coles' career. In 1767 the Island had been divided into 67 lots, of approximately 20,000 acres each, which were parcelled out to various persons with claims upon the generosity of the crown. By the beginning of the 19th century there had been much consolidation of holdings, with the result that a few magnates, mostly absentees, came to own huge tracts. The owners often refused to sell their lands, and instead leased them, creating a neo-feudal system of tenure. In 1841, for example, fewer than one-third of the occupiers of land were freeholders. The landowners had received the lots under the stipulation that they fulfill certain requirements for settlement of the Island and that they pay quit-rents to the crown. In many cases, the obligations had been neglected, and the escheators advocated the establishment of a court of escheat to investigate non-fulfillment. The lands of the defaulting proprietors would be returned to the crown for distribution to the tenantry on a freehold basis. The escheators' plan, however, would require the consent of the Colonial Office in London, where the landlords' influence was paramount. Thus there were two possible grounds for opposition to the escheat agitation: that property rights should not be violated, and that the scheme was impractical and would never get the approval of the British government.

In speaking of the land question during his first term in the assembly, Coles usually chose the argument that escheat was impractical. But although he voted as a Tory regular, he did not take a reactionary position. He repeatedly made suggestions for the clarification and extension of the rights of tenants and squatters – this latter group composed 11.6 per cent of the occupiers of land in 1841. Coles was also pressing for the ultimate liquidation of leasehold tenure. This budding conflict of opinion between Coles and the rest of the established élite had strong roots in an inherent conflict of interest: Coles represented a different sort of capitalism than did a man like James Yeo*. The latter assemblyman had made his fortune mainly through his activities as a land agent, merchant, and carrier. Men in Yeo's position were concerned with extending their profits as middlemen in the established order, rather than seeing its stability disrupted. Coles more than once remarked that the land agents were more determined than the proprietors themselves to maintain the *status quo*.

Coles, on the other hand, was by this time primarily a manufacturer, whose prosperity as a producer of a consumer good depended upon the development of a healthy internal market with widespread purchasing power. As a distiller and brewer, he had no interest in seeing the tenants and squatters impoverished and capital exported *en masse* to absentee proprietors. Hence, his statement in the assembly in 1846 that conversion of the estates to freehold tenure would bring about "a greater consumption of manufactured articles" reflected an expectation growing logically out of his class interests; these, and not disrespect for the rights of property (as land agent and assemblyman William Douse had suggested), lay at the base of

Coles

Coles' increasing concern for the abolition of leasehold tenure. The archaic productive relations which nurtured men like Douse and Yeo would have to be abandoned if Coles' style of capitalism were to flourish.

Thus Coles spoke out often and forcefully in these years; even in his first session he did not hesitate to oppose Tory leaders such as Edward Palmer* on small matters. Unfortunately for the young assemblyman, he became embroiled in a feud with the speaker, Joseph Pope*. Several times in the session of 1845 they exchanged harsh words; Pope even alleged that a young man had died from the effects of Coles' whiskey – a charge which the latter angrily and effectively refuted. In 1846 Coles refused to obey an order of the house to retract his description of a statement by Pope as "false," and as a result spent the rest of the session, 31 days, in the custody of the serjeant-at-arms. He had evidently not endeared himself to the Tory leadership, for only two assemblymen had opposed his disciplining, and they were Reformers.

The obtaining of responsible government, which Coles supported, dominated the late 1840s, and thrust him into the forefront of Island politics. The struggle was prolonged and intense, for the resident establishment and the Colonial Office were reluctant in the extreme to grant the change: not only was there a small population, but the interests of many members of the establishment were bound up in the land system, which they feared would be the first target of a popularly elected administration. However, Coles, as an entrepreneur without a vital stake in the retardation of the Island economy, was receptive when, two days after the close of the session of 1847, the governor, Sir Henry Vere Huntley*, invited him to join the Executive Council. The governor had his own feud with Joseph Pope and the local family compact, and desired a Reformer on his council in the place of Pope, who had resigned. Coles had broken with the Tories by this time, and in the session just ended he had explicitly endorsed the general positions of Alexander Rae, then the acknowledged leader of the Reformers in the house. Huntley had first approached Rae with the offer of a seat on the council, but the latter declined, and in so doing recommended Coles. Thus Coles became the first self-avowed Reformer to sit on the Executive Council of the Island. But the alliance between government house and the Reformers did not endure; in December of 1847, a new governor, Sir Donald Campbell*, who had no motives for combining with the insurgents against the compact, arrived to replace Huntley. One year later Coles resigned from Campbell's Executive Council, declaring that he lacked confidence in the administration. Campbell, for his part, advised the Colonial Office that, with Coles' departure, he expected less trouble from his council.

The problems of the governor, who had no sympathy with the movement for responsible government, had only begun. A new weapon had been given to the Reformers. In the same month that Coles resigned from the Executive Council, the Colonial Office decided that the Island was sufficiently prosperous to pay for its own civil list. In return for discharging this financial obligation, the Reformers demanded responsible government. As the struggle grew in intensity through the session of 1849, Coles clearly emerged as the leader of the Reform forces. The movement was also gathering general support outside the house: an election held in February 1850 resulted in an 18 to 6 victory for Coles' party.

When the new house assembled, it was at once apparent that Coles had the full support of the majority of assemblymen in demanding responsible government, and in expressing want-of-confidence in the Tory Executive Council. Nonetheless, Campbell refused to acquiesce in the Reform programme. Throughout two sessions called in the spring of 1850, the governor and the house failed to come to a *modus vivendi*; consequently, the Reformers refused to vote supply. After the sessions, Campbell, realizing that he would ultimately have to give in, suggested to the imperial government that they pass a statute placing new restrictions on the franchise to curtail any impulse to radicalism. But Lord Grey [Henry George Grey], the colonial secretary, had decided that the election of 1850 had clearly indicated that the Island electors desired responsible government and therefore should have it. He bluntly rejected the governor's proposals and, when Campbell died in October 1850, Grey gave the new governor, Sir Alexander Bannerman*, explicit instructions to accede to the wishes of the Reformers.

On 25 April 1851, Coles rose in the assembly and reported that he had formed a new Executive Council, possessing the confidence of the house. Coles was the predictable choice as premier: he had led the movement in the assembly, on the hustings, and as chairman of a five-man committee of the house formed in 1850 to correspond with sympathetic British parliamentarians. In all cases, he had refused to compromise with Campbell and the local Tories – he would have responsible government, or the wheels of government on Prince Edward Island would not turn.

Donald Creighton once wrote that "responsible government was a method, not a measure" – it was a system of political relationships which derived its real significance not from the bare fact of its establishment, but from the substantive changes which its advent facilitated. Such a government would only acquire meaning for colonial citizens if its inauguration were marked by new and more democratic policies. Coles and his colleagues recognized this. They did not rest upon their laurels, but followed up their struggle for responsible government with a vigorous legislative programme.

The first great measure of Coles' government was the Free Education Act of 1852. A visit to Massachusetts and Ohio in the autumn of 1848 had inspired this legislation; there Coles had observed the benefits of state-paid education, and had been told by former Islanders of the disadvantages they faced without at least primary education. With the act, the Island became the first Maritime colony in which the government paid the entire salaries of district school teachers. Previously, the districts had been obliged to raise part of the stipends by local assessment and tuition fees. After 1852, local taxes were to be used only for the erection and maintenance of school buildings, and tuition fees were abolished. Within two years the number of students enrolled in Island schools doubled, and by 1855 the Island's proportion of students in relation to the total population was reputedly one-third greater than that of either Nova Scotia or New Brunswick. The second major reform was of a similar nature – the franchise was broadened to become almost universal.

The most intractable problem confronting the reform government was the land question. Coles rejected escheat and other drastic solutions, although the Liberal caucus contained two or more radicals when he was in power in the 1850s. As Coles articulated his policy, it consisted of ameliorative legislation in the short run, and a programme of purchasing estates over a period of years. These transactions, on a voluntary basis, would involve "fair compensation" for the landlords, and would result in resale of the lands to their occupiers at minimal rates. Examples of the ameliorative measures were the rent roll bill, the one-ninth bill, and the tenants' compensation bill. The first of these would have imposed a small tax per acre on estates in excess of 500 acres. The Colonial Office disallowed it outright. The one-ninth bill was intended to regulate the extraction of rents from the tenantry. Although it failed to gain the assent of the British government when first passed in 1851, an amended version was eventually accepted. The purpose of the tenants' compensation bill was to indemnify ejected

tenants and squatters for improvements made by them prior to ejectment. It too met obstruction from entrenched interests, and in 1855 Coles introduced a measure which was rigidly confined in scope: it applied only to those squatters who had been in use and occupation of their lands for a minimum of five years, and to those tenants who held leases for limited periods and were ejected before their leases expired. The squatters with less than five years on their lands, the tenants with 999-year leases (which were common), and the tenants ejected upon completion of, for example, seven-year leases, were left unprotected. "By asking too much," Coles said, "we shall, I fear, lose all." The Colonial Office refused to confirm even this bill.

The major component of Coles' land policy was the Land Purchase Act of 1853. Under its provisions, the government was empowered to buy estates in excess of 1,000 acres and to sell them to tenants and squatters in units up to a maximum of 300 acres. In 1854, the Liberals purchased the 81,000-acre Worrell estate, and began its resale [see William Henry POPE]. It was the first and last large purchase made in the 1850s: when the Island government passed a loan bill in 1857 to raise £100,000 for further purchases, the imperial government disallowed the legislation; and even if London had desired to cooperate, many proprietors, such as Sir Samuel Cunard*, had no intention of selling. Thus, Coles failed to liquidate leasehold tenure on Prince Edward Island.

Coles was the unchallenged leader of his party throughout this period of forward-looking government. He was the most effective defender of Liberal policies in the assembly, and his speeches reveal a thorough familiarity with all the major issues which were debated. He spoke directly to the point, and was able quickly to seize upon the weaknesses in his opponents' arguments. The only Liberal whose prestige approximated his was the brilliant journalist, Edward Whelan*. However, Whelan was often absent from his seat in the house, as he had little taste for the routine of party management and public administration – matters which he left by and large to Coles. Hence the energies of the two men were complementary rather than competitive.

Coles and his party remained in power until 1859, with the exception of some six months in 1854. In July 1853, largely because of the sudden rise in taxation occasioned by the Free Education Act, they had lost an election in which even Coles had been defeated. However, the partisanship of Governor Bannerman kept them in office until February 1854. After one session of Tory government, Bannerman dissolved the assembly over the objections of his new Executive Council, and called another election. His reasoning was that since the Franchise Act of 1853 had just become effective, the house had been rendered unrepresentative of the actual electorate. The new and enlarged body of voters gave the Liberals an 18 to 6 majority; Coles returned to the assembly, and assumed the additional duties of colonial secretary.

But, somewhere along the line, the Coles government had lost its edge. When the Bible question arose in late 1856, Coles badly underestimated its explosive potential. The controversy began at the inauguration of the Island's Normal School, when school visitor John Stark, who was also superintendent of the new institution, stated that reading and exposition of the Bible would be a part of the daily programme of all student teachers. The Board of Education quickly repudiated Stark's position, but this action did not become public knowledge. As a result, the Roman Catholic bishop of Charlottetown, Bernard D. MacDonald*, sent a protest against Stark's words to the secretary of the board. Coles soon learned of the bishop's letter, and arranged an interview, at which he explained that the school visitor's remarks did not represent government policy. The bishop then wrote a short letter to Coles, stating his satisfaction that he had been labouring under a misunderstanding, and authorizing the premier to show his retraction "to all whom it may concern." Coles neglected to do so, with disastrous consequences for his party. The bishop's first letter, which had not been temperately worded, went before a meeting of the board. A Protestant minister sitting on the board then published it, and began a campaign for the legal authorization of Bible reading in the district schools. Previously, the position of the Holy Scriptures had been governed by an informal system of local option; the bishop's letter, whose scope had not been limited to the Normal School, was held to be a threat to this extra-legal policy of permissiveness.

Religion in education became the prime determinant in Island politics for the next two decades. This was unfortunate for Coles, as he was vulnerable on issues such as the Bible question. He was an Anglican leading a party whose main electoral support came from the minority Roman Catholic community. By the time of his retirement, he had been denounced at various times by the militants of both denominational camps. The Bible question was the major factor in the defeat of his government at the end of the 1850s, as the Protestant electors deserted the Liberals en masse. More than once Coles misjudged the potency of the issue and the depth of the passions it could inspire, with the

result that opportunities to allay them were missed. In addition, the Liberals were faced with claims that their land policy had reached a dead end, and that a modified system of responsible government known as "non departmentalism" was better adapted to the small population of the Island [see POPE]. At the election of 24 June 1858, the Coles government was sustained by the narrow margin of 16 to 14. The resignation in February 1859 of one Liberal member and the resulting confusion ended the session begun that month after only three days. A second election ensued, and although Coles indicated his willingness to resort to escheat in order to resolve the land question, his party was decisively defeated by the Tories led by Edward Palmer.

As leader of the opposition, especially in the first two years, Coles more than bore his share of the responsibility of criticizing the Tory government. Palmer and his colleagues settled the Bible question to the general satisfaction of both parties in 1860, by simply giving a statutory basis to the status quo. But, in the same year, a new Roman Catholic bishop of Charlottetown, Peter MacIntyre*, took office. He was a vigorous man, and was determined that the Roman Catholic St Dunstan's College should get public financial support equal to that of the newly established, secular, and public Prince of Wales College. His attempts to gain this and other ends in matters relating to education, and the controversial public writings of the Catholic college's rector, Father Angus MacDonald*, eventually led to a public vendetta between William Henry Pope, the colonial secretary, and the rector. This provided the Tories with another occasion to campaign against "Romish aggression," and to unite the Protestant majority against Coles and the Roman Catholic population. Again the strategy was successful, and, largely over the college question, Palmer's government was sustained at the polls in 1863 by an 18 to 12 margin.

When confederation of the British North American colonies became a topic for public discussion, Coles declared that he would support any plan of union which would guarantee the liquidation of leasehold tenure. The implication was that if this condition could not be met, union would not be acceptable. Coles adhered to this policy on confederation throughout his public career. At both the Charlottetown and the Quebec conferences, he insisted in vain on this point. The answer of the Canadians was that the Islanders were already promised more than their fair share of financial subsidies. When he returned home, Coles successfully led the Liberal party (with the exception of Whelan) into adamant opposition to the

Quebec resolutions. In contrast, the Tory government split sharply over this issue.

Thus the Tories, like their predecessors in office, failed to resolve the land question. They had appointed, in 1860, a distinguished commission of investigation, whose recommendations had been disallowed by the imperial government; they had sent a delegation consisting of Palmer and W. H. Pope to London, and it had been stymied by the intransigence of a group of proprietors led by Cunard; and now the Canadian government had shown an equal lack of sympathy. The farmers of Prince Edward Island proceeded to take matters into their own hands: they formed Tenant Leagues whose members were sworn to resist the collection of rents. By the summer of 1865, class tensions were so sharp on the Island that the administrator, Robert HODGSON, called in troops from Halifax in order to prevent serious disorders. The unpopularity of this move and the deep Tory divisions over confederation determined the election of 1867 – the Liberals won by a majority of 19 to 11.

Coles resumed his position as premier and colonial secretary on 14 March 1867. At first it appeared as though there would be a complete restoration of the Liberal hegemony as it had existed prior to 1859. The government immediately returned to the principles of the Free Education Act of 1852, which the Tories had abrogated in 1863. After his brief flirtation with escheat, Coles had gone back to his programme of voluntary purchases of estates. Consequently, he had little use for the Tenant League movement; their "open defiance of the law" was "the disgrace of the Colony." He was proud that the leading Liberals "had taken every fitting opportunity to denounce the illegal organization, and to caution the tenantry against associating themselves with it." The mistake of the Tories was not in repressing the movement but in not acting sooner: if they had made use of the civil authorities, they would have avoided the recourse to troops. This position was consistent with Coles' class interests as an entrepreneur; just as in the 1840s he had had no interest in seeing the Island's farmer-consumers impoverished, he now had no interest in seeing the legal rights of property disregarded – even if it was property belonging to his political enemies. It was not the formation of a union, he said, which disturbed him – it was the refusal of its members to pay legally collectable rents.

Coles, however, was not fated to play his old role in Island public life for any length of time. His mind had begun a rapid deterioration; by the session of 1868, the attorney general, Joseph Hensley*, was the real Liberal house leader. By

August, Coles had formally resigned as premier and during the next session he spoke rarely. In 1870 he was absent from the house for the entire session. His premature senility was commonly attributed to overwork and anxiety. In 1866 there had been a wave of incendiarism in Charlottetown, and Coles' business premises had had at least one narrow escape; a further factor was probably the untimely death of Edward Whelan on 10 Dec. 1867 in unhappy circumstances. Whatever the causes, Coles did not recover his mental capacities, although he lived until 1875.

By 1868 Coles had reached the effective end of his brilliant career. For over 20 years he had been at the very centre of Island public life. Throughout this time he had been a controversial figure: he had been subjected to more than one attempt to exclude him from the deliberations of the assembly in the 1840s and 1850s; he had reputedly duelled with Edward Palmer in 1851; he had been convicted of and fined for assault in the mid-1850s; and, on the floor of the house in 1861, he had challenged James Colledge Pope* to a duel "with sword or pistol." His political trajectory had been that of a vigorous and progressive entrepreneur in a colony laden with a neo-feudal land system. The major task which he had set for himself, in alliance with the bulk of the farm population, was the breaking of the power of the landlords and their agents; his means to this end included responsible government, an expanded franchise, a universal education system, and a voluntary land purchase act.

Coles' success was incomplete, partially because of the limitations which he and Whelan had been able to enforce within the Island's reform movement. Coles refused to sanction the radicalism of the Tenant Leaguers although his ideological position and theirs were basically similar. Coles and the Leaguers opposed the outside domination exercised by the proprietors, not property itself – after all, the farmers were demanding the right to become property owners. The difference was that Coles, as a man of substance, was not inclined to lend approbation to any programme of forcible seizures, whereas the tenants, as men of poverty, had fewer inhibitions. Whether Coles' leadership would have resulted in the League's success is an unanswerable question. The fact remains that he did not live to see the final resolution of the land issue.

When Coles died, the newspaper columns of the Island overflowed with praise. The *Argus* described him as "the brightest star that illumines the pages of the political history of his native province," and the *Examiner*, at that time a Conservative paper, wrote that "we, unhesitatingly, say no man in this Colony so honestly earned the respect

Collins

and esteem of its people." George Coles, the father of responsible government, free education, a widened franchise, and land reform, had outlived all the animosity against him, and had become a bipartisan folk hero.

IAN ROSS ROBERTSON

[No collection of George Coles' papers has been found to date. All the manuscript sources mentioned here were read for the whole period of Coles' career; of special importance to the preparation of the text were: PAPEI, Henry Jones Cundall, letter book, 27 March 1867–26 May 1871, pp.137, 155; *Report of the speeches and proceedings at the inauguration of the Normal School in Charlottetown . . .*, reporter R. B Irving (Charlottetown, 1856), 27–29; Prince Edward Island, Executive Council, Minutes, 1847–48, 1851–59, 1867–68. Prince Edward Island, Supreme Court, Estates Division, will of George Coles, 3 July 1865. Prince Edward Island Libraries (Charlottetown), Dr John Mackieson diaries, 25 June 1851. PRO, CO 226/71, 259–61, 265–68, 287–300, 306–17, 328, 331, 332, 348–53, 358–68, 378, 451–58, 478; 226/73, 88–89; 226/83, 88; 226/90, 89–90; 226/105, 233.

The most important sources for Coles' career are the reports of the Prince Edward Island assembly and contemporary newspapers. The following are valuable for explaining Coles' early career, his positions on the land question, on an elective Legislative Council, and on trade with the United States, and his mental disability in later years: Prince Edward Island, House of Assembly, *Debates and proceedings*, 1855, 17, 20, 29–30, 52; 1857, 128; 1859, 10, 75, 84, 90; 1860, 11–14, 68; 1861, 88, 121; 1862, 29; 1863, 33; 1864, 18; 1865, 9, 67; 1866, 7–8, 9–13, 28–29, 46–47; 1868, 72, 224; 1869, 45, 200; 1870, 239, 241; 1873, 283–85, 287. For the assembly's punishment of Coles in 1846, his quick temper, the vacating his seat in 1848 and the subsequent by-election, and his disputed election defeat of 1853, *see*: Prince Edward Island, House of Assembly, *Journals*, 1846, 43–46, 98; 1848, 6–14, 58, 166–67; 1854, 8, 43, 58, app. L.

For aspects of his business career, his political affiliations, his opinions on the land question, his interest in education, his views on widening the franchise and on trade with the United States, his feud with Joseph Pope, the struggle for responsible government, and the by-elections of 1847 and 1848, *see*: *Colonial Herald* (Charlottetown), 21 Oct. 1843. *Examiner* (Charlottetown), 28 Aug. 1847; 8, 15, 22, 29 Jan., 18 March, 17 July, 7 Dec. 1848; 1 Jan. 1849; 14 Aug., 30 Oct. 1850; 3, 31 July, 7, 14 Aug. 1865. *Islander* (Charlottetown), 24 Nov., 1 Dec. 1843; 1, 8, 15 May 1846; 4 June 1852; 10 March 1854; 11 June 1869. *Morning News* (Charlottetown), 19 Oct., 11 Dec. 1844. *Patriot* (Charlottetown), 12 Nov. 1868, 27 April 1871. *Royal Gazette* (Charlottetown), 29 Oct. 1833; 17 June, 22 July, 25 Nov. 1834; 27 Oct., 8 Dec. 1835; 10 May 1836; 5 Sept. 1837; 1 Sept., 15 Dec. 1840; 7 June 1842; 7, 14, 21 Feb., 14 March, 4, 11, 18 April 1843; 5, 12 March, 20 Aug. 1844; 18 March, 1, 15, 22 April 1845; 24 Feb., 10, 17, 31 March 1846; 16, 23 March, 24, 27 April, 11 May, 15 June 1847;

15 Feb., 7 March 1848; 9 May 1850; 8 April 1851; 29 Jan., 23, 26 Feb., 5, 16 April, 17 May 1852; 7 March, 4, 11 April, 6 June 1853. Obituaries for Coles are in *Examiner*, 23 Aug. 1875, *Island Argus* (Charlottetown), 24, 31 Aug. 1875, and *Patriot*, 3 Sept. 1875.

There is no single comprehensive study of 19th-century Prince Edward Island. For the major issues and problems of Coles' era, the most relevant secondary sources are: Bolger, *PEI and confederation*. Duncan Campbell, *History of Prince Edward Island* (Charlottetown, 1875), 200. Clark, *Three centuries and the Island*, chap. 5, 6; p.95, table 3. MacKinnon, *Government of PEI*, chap. 3, 5, 6, and pp.296–99. MacNutt, *Atlantic provinces*, 210–12, 231–34, 252. George Sutherland, *A manual of geography and natural and civil history of Prince Edward Island for the use of schools, families, and emigrants* (Charlottetown, 1861), 132–35. D. C. Harvey, "Dishing the Reformers," *RSCT*, 3rd ser., XXV (1931), sect.II, 37–44. W. R. Livingston, *Responsible government in Prince Edward Island: a triumph of self-government under the crown* (University of Iowa studies in the social sciences, ed. Louis Pelzer, IX, no.4, Iowa City, 1931). Robertson, "Religion, politics, and education in PEI," chap. 1–7.

Additional works which have been useful in preparing this study are: Creighton, *Road to confederation*, 155–57, 171, 179–80. Greenhill and Giffard, *Westcountrymen in PEI*, especially chap. 7, 8. Waite, *Life and times of confederation*, 82–83, 96. H. R. Matthews, "Education in Prince Edward Island," unpublished MA thesis, Mount Allison University, 1938, 8. I.R.R.]

COLLINS, ENOS, seaman, merchant, financier, and legislator; b. at Liverpool, N.S., 5 Sept. 1774, first son of Hallet Collins and Rhoda Peek; d. at Halifax, N.S., 18 Nov. 1871.

Hallet Collins was a merchant, trader, and justice of the peace in Liverpool, N.S. He married three times, and was the father of 26 children; when he died in 1831 he left an estate of £13,000. His second child, Enos Collins, received little formal education, but went to sea at an early age probably as a cabin boy on one of his father's trading or fishing vessels. Before he was 20, he was captain of the schooner *Adamant*, sailing to Bermuda; in 1799 he served as first lieutenant on the famed privateer *Charles Mary Wentworth*. An ambitious young man, Enos Collins soon obtained part-ownership in a number of vessels trading out of Liverpool. During the Peninsular War he made a large profit by sending three supply vessels to break the Spanish blockade and replenish the British army at Cadiz.

Soon Enos Collins' ambitions outgrew the opportunities offered even by the thriving seaport of Liverpool, and he moved to Halifax where, by 1811, he was established as a merchant and shipper. During the War of 1812 he was an astute partner (with Joseph Allison*) in a firm which bought captured American vessels from the prize courts and sold their cargoes at a profit. Probably the firm prospered too by illegally including New England in the war trade between Nova Scotia and the West Indies. Collins was part-owner of three privateers, including the *Liverpool Packet*, the most dreaded Nova Scotian vessel to ply New England waters during the war.

In the decade after the war Collins participated in numerous business enterprises. He was successful in currency speculation, backed many trading ventures, carried on his mercantile activities, and entered the lumbering and whaling businesses. Like most of his contemporaries, he invested in the United States; it was rumoured that his American investments equalled his holdings in Nova Scotia. By 1822 Collins' ambitions seem once more to have outgrown his surroundings. Sir Colin Campbell* wrote to the colonial secretary, Lord Glenelg (Charles Grant), in 1838, "Sixteen years ago he [Collins] was about to remove from the Province for ever but was induced to remain by an offer made to him . . . of a seat in the council."

Collins' move into the principal governing body of the colony, the Council of Twelve, indicated the extent of his success. In 1825 he reinforced his position as a member of the ruling élite by marrying Margaret, eldest daughter of Brenton Halliburton*. In keeping with his social and economic position Enos Collins built a fine estate, Gorsebrook, where he and his wife entertained the governor and other leaders of the community. Collins and his wife had nine children, of whom one son and three daughters lived beyond childhood.

In 1825, after several unsuccessful attempts to gain a banking charter from the government, Enos Collins and a group of merchant associates – Henry H. Cogswell*, William Pryor*, James Tobin*, Samuel Cunard*, John Clark, Joseph Allison, and Martin Gay Black – formed a partnership and founded the Halifax Banking Company. The banking venture was the natural outgrowth of successful mercantile activity which provided each partner with the necessary capital to finance the new enterprise. Although Cogswell was president of the company, Collins was the dominant partner; the bank's transactions were conducted in the building which housed Collins' firm and the venture soon became known locally as "Collins' Bank."

One of the least attractive events of Enos Collins' career concerns the brandy dispute of 1830. In 1826 the assembly had imposed a tax of 1*s.* 4*d.* on foreign brandy in addition to the 1*s.* imposed by the imperial government. The customs collector decided that a duty of 2*s.* was sufficient, but he

failed to inform the assembly of his decision. In 1830 E. Collins and Company petitioned the assembly demanding a refund on their duty, arguing that the customs collector had given them an unfair rate of exchange on the doubloons with which they paid the tax. Their petition provided the assembly with the information that the full tax was not being collected. The assembly immediately passed a bill restoring the full tax, but the council, controlled by Enos Collins and his associates, refused to accept the bill. For some time no tax was collected on imported spirits, and Collins, taking full advantage of the situation, proceeded to sell his stocks of brandy without paying a penny into the treasury. His behaviour provoked an angry reaction in the assembly and from the local press. Unfortunately for Collins and the other importers, George IV died, causing an election in Nova Scotia. The brandy election of 1830, fought on the issue of the tax, resulted in the return of an assembly which quickly reimposed the duty; the council accepted their decision. Not only did this dispute tarnish Collins' name, but it also provided an issue around which criticism of the Council of Twelve could be concentrated.

During the 1830s Collins continued to expand his business activities and to participate in governing the colony. In 1832, despite Collins' objections, the council granted a charter to the Bank of Nova Scotia and destroyed the monopoly of the Halifax Banking Company. Soon the two banks were involved in a currency battle which weakened the financial stability of the colony and gave Reformers another point of departure for attacks upon the ruling oligarchy. The decade witnessed growing discontent with the rule of the Council of Twelve, until, in 1837, the British government decided that reorganization was necessary. The new Executive Council of Nova Scotia did not originally include Enos Collins, but, at Governor Colin Campbell's insistence, Collins became a member on 8 May 1838. He continued in the position until 6 Oct. 1840, when a second reorganization necessitated his resignation. During the turbulent 1840s and 1850s Collins refrained from active politics, but he was a financial backer of the Conservatives.

Enos Collins spent the last 30 years of his life in partial retirement keeping a close eye on his investments but withdrawn mainly to the privacy of Gorsebrook. The battle against confederation provided the last fighting ground for the old man. Breaking a lifetime allegiance with the Conservatives, Collins threw his whole-hearted financial support behind Joseph Howe, Mather Byles Almon, and other members of the anti-confederation league. The vehemence with which Collins opposed the scheme is best expressed by Howe: "Enos Collins who is now ninety years of age . . . declares that, if he was twenty years younger, he would take a rifle and resist it."

Enos Collins was an astute, hard headed, and even progressive businessman. With an estate estimated at $6,000,000, he was rumoured to be the richest man in British North America. He belonged to the Church of England and supported it financially. Like his contemporaries, Collins recognized that the ruling class was responsible for the less fortunate and less successful members of society. He was a member of the Poor Man's Friend Society and gave generously to the blind and to other philanthropic ventures which were common in 19th-century Halifax.

Collins' life, however, does not represent a complete success story. He strove to become a member of the ruling oligarchy in a period when the changing times were giving political and social power to a much broader segment of the community. Long before Collins died, the way of life which he wanted and had achieved through his material success was disappearing. His stand against confederation was the last losing battle of a man who failed to recognize the vast changes occurring in British North America between 1840 and 1870.

DIANE M. BARKER and
D. A. SUTHERLAND

PANS, "Collins family," compiled by T. B. Smith; Log book of the privateer *Charles Mary Wentworth*. PRO, CO 217/115, 75–76. *Acadian Recorder* (Halifax), 8 Jan. 1898. *Novascotian* (Halifax), 1830, 1835–36, 1942. [Enos Collins], "Letters and papers of Hon. Enos Collins," ed. C. B. Fergusson, PANS *Bull.*, XIII (1959). J. F. More, *The history of Queen's County, N.S.* (Halifax, 1873), 161–68. Ross and Trigge, *History of the Canadian Bank of Commerce*, I, 25–123. L. J. Burpee, "Joseph Howe and the anti-confederation league," *RSCT*, 3rd ser., X (1917), sect.II, 409–73. Peter Lynch, "Early reminiscences of Halifax – men who have passed from us," N.S. Hist. Soc. *Coll.*, XVI (1912), 171–204. G. E. E. Nichols, "Notes on Nova Scotian privateers," N.S. Hist. Soc. *Coll.*, XIII (1908), 111–52.

CONILLEAU, CHARLES, priest, Jesuit; b. 4 Aug. 1811 at Martigné, diocese of Mans, France; d. 1 April 1879 at Victoriaville (Arthabaska County), Que.

Charles Conilleau, the son of an ex-soldier of Napoleon Bonaparte, entered the Society of Jesus in 1846, after 12 years in the priesthood. In 1854 he was nominated to the New York–Canada mission, which was subject to the ecclesiastical province of France. He went to New York, and for a year devoted himself to studying English before going to Canada West.

From 1855 to 1859 he was at the Jesuit residence at Sandwich (Windsor, Ont.), where, under the immediate direction of the famous Father Pierre Point*, he had exclusive responsibility for English-speaking Catholics, who were already numerous in Windsor and Maidstone. To him goes the credit for the erection, in 1858, of the first church of the mother parish of Windsor, Saint-Alphonse. In the same year he reconstructed the church at Maidstone. At both places he established sound bases for religious development, and prepared the way for the canonical erection of both to parishes. In 1857, when the first bishop of London, Pierre-Adolphe Pinsonnault*, decided to bring all his seminarists together in the college at Sandwich, Conilleau became their teacher of theology, the first, it is thought, to hold this position within the confines of the present diocese of London. He watched closely the events that led Bishop Pinsonnault to transfer his episcopal seat from London to Windsor in 1859. The Jesuits at this point closed their house at Windsor and thus put an end to their evangelizing ministry in this historic place.

Father Conilleau was then appointed to the residence at Quebec, and nominated to the ministry, at that time an important one, in charge of parish missions and retreats for the priesthood. From 1862 to 1870 he was superior of the Jesuits at Chatham (Ont.), who worked throughout the region on behalf of English-speaking Catholics. In 1871 he was appointed superior and parish priest of the important parish of Guelph. Two years later, having returned to the province of Quebec, and despite failing health, he gave full attention to hearing confessions and preaching at Montreal and especially at Gésu. He had barely finished a parish retreat at Victoriaville when he died of a heart attack there on 1 April 1879. The clergy and congregation asked that burial be at this place where Conilleau had last preached the faith; he is thus one of the few Jesuits who were not buried in the cemetery of the community.

Father Conilleau's letters reveal a man who was disinclined to self-display, but conscientious and effective in carrying out the tasks assigned to him. He belongs to the heroic history of the beginnings of the diocese of London. Revered by his congregation, respected and esteemed by those who did not share his religious beliefs, he rendered great services to the Catholics of southern Ontario.

LÉON POULIOT

ASJCF, 1636–37; 5115, 2; A-1-7, p.66; A-2-4; D-7.

CONNELL, CHARLES, lumberman, magistrate, and politician; b. in 1810 in Northampton, N.B., one of 12 children of Charles Connell Sr, a

Connecticut loyalist, and Mary Palmer; d. 28 June 1873 at Woodstock, N.B.

Charles Connell received a public school education in Northampton and later embarked on a career as a general businessman. He moved to Woodstock, New Brunswick, where he soon became one of Carleton County's leading lumbermen. In 1835 he married Ann Fisher, sister of Charles FISHER; they had four sons and three daughters. Connell took an active interest in local affairs and was justice of the peace for many years; he later became a justice of the Inferior Court of Common Pleas for Carleton County

Connell's career as a politician began in 1846 when he was first elected to the assembly. In 1849 he was appointed to the Legislative Council, but resigned in 1851 and was subsequently returned as a member of the lower house. In 1858 he became postmaster general in Charles Fisher's government and held this position until his defeat in the election of 1861. Connell's chief claim to fame lies in an incident which occurred while he held the cabinet post. A new issue of stamps was needed in 1860. When the stamps were released one bore the likeness of Connell rather than that of Queen Victoria or some other member of the royal family. There was a storm of protest, the issue was withdrawn, and Connell resigned. The Connell stamp went on to become a collector's item among philatelists and a mint copy is now valued at $1,000.

Charles Connell returned to the assembly in 1864 and was re-elected in the confederation elections of 1865 and 1866. He was a supporter of Samuel Leonard Tilley* and his efforts to have New Brunswick enter confederation. For a short time in 1866 and 1867 Connell served as surveyor general in Robert Duncan Wilmot*'s cabinet. Eager to broaden his field of political endeavour, Connell sought election to the first dominion parliament and won in Carleton County by acclamation. In the general election of 1872 he was again returned by acclamation, which attests both to his personal influence and to the apathy of the opposition.

Because party lines were not sharply drawn in New Brunswick during the early years of the confederation period, it is difficult to give Connell a political label. In New Brunswick politics he was a Liberal. As a supporter of confederation, he initially voted with Sir John A. Macdonald* and his coalition in the House of Commons, but thereafter generally supported Alexander Mackenzie* and the Liberals. However, as with many New Brunswick politicians, parochial sentiments rather than party affiliation usually decided his vote.

Charles Connell, an MP until his death, was survived by his wife, three sons, and three daughters. As a loyalist, a lumber merchant, a man of little education but a host of political connections, Connell epitomized the New Brunswick politicians of his era.

CHARLES F. MacKINNON

PAC, MG 24, A20 (Edmund Head papers), letter book, 3, p.622; MG 27, I, D15 (Tilley papers), Charles Watters to S. L. Tilley, 23 April 1860; Charles Connell to Tilley, 27 April 1860; A. J. Smith to Tilley, 27 April 1860. *Morning Freeman* (Saint John, N.B.), 25 July, 10 Sept. 1867; 9 July 1872. *New Brunswick Reporter* (Fredericton), 24 July 1872. *St Croix Courier* (St Stephen, N.B.), 14 June 1867. *Saint John Daily News*, 12 Aug. 1872. *Can. parl. comp., 1869.* Waite, *Life and times of confederation*, 233.

CONNOLLY, THOMAS LOUIS, priest, Capuchin, vicar general of the diocese of Halifax, bishop of Saint John, archbishop of Halifax; b. 1814 at Cork, Ireland; d. 27 July 1876 at Halifax, N.S.

Thomas Connolly's father, a Cork retail dealer, died when Connolly was three years old and he was reared by his mother, an innkeeper. Influenced by Father Theobald Mathew, a renowned apostle of temperance, Connolly entered the Capuchin order and in 1832 went to Rome to complete his studies for the priesthood. After his ordination at Lyons in 1838, he worked briefly at the Capuchin Mission House in Dublin and then as chaplain of the Grange Gorman Lane Penitentiary. When Father William Walsh*, a fellow Capuchin, was appointed bishop of Halifax in 1842, Father Connolly accompanied him to Nova Scotia as his secretary.

Father Connolly served as a parish priest at St Mary's Church, Halifax, and, in 1845, was appointed vicar general of the diocese. In 1852 he was appointed to succeed William Dollard* as bishop of Saint John. During his seven years in Saint John he encouraged the building of Catholic schools, oversaw the opening of a Catholic orphanage run by the Sisters of the Sacred Heart, and brought a group of Sisters of Charity to Saint John to teach. He also organized the construction of a cathedral for the city.

When Archbishop Walsh died in 1858, Bishop Connolly was named as his successor. His nomination was strongly supported by church leaders on both sides of the Atlantic including Archbishop Paul Cullen of Dublin and Archbishop John Hughes of New York. The four dioceses of Halifax, Arichat, Charlottetown, Saint John, and the newly created diocese of Chatham were under

Connolly

Archbishop Connolly's jurisdiction. The religious unrest created in Nova Scotia in the mid 1850s by the controversy over enlistment in the Crimean war, by the Gourley Riots, and by William Young*'s abortive education bill of 1856, was beginning to wane; Connolly's tolerance and moderation did much to prevent any further incidents. [*See* Joseph HOWE and James W. JOHNSTON.]

The education bills of 1864 and 1865 brought Archbishop Connolly into conflict with Charles Tupper*. The archbishop strongly opposed the free school system based on compulsory taxation, and demanded instead a system that included separate schools for Roman Catholics. He feared that the school curriculum, which, under the new law, was to be controlled by the Council of Public Instruction, would not satisfy the educational demands of Catholics. When Tupper pointed out that the council was to consist of the entire Executive Council and that the number of Catholics in the province would ensure their adequate representation on it, Connolly assured Tupper that the bill ". . . shall have my support." His sensible and realistic attitude towards Tupper's ideas prevented a major conflict between the Roman Catholics and the provincial government. The agreement between the two led to the achievement of separate schools in practice if not in theory – an arrangement which has continued to the present without the conflicts that have plagued more formal arrangements in other parts of the country.

Archbishop Connolly was a strong supporter of confederation. He firmly believed that union of the British North American colonies was necessary and would be beneficial to Nova Scotia. He hoped that confederation would be a means whereby Maritime Catholics might obtain a legal recognition of separate schools similar to that given the Catholic minority in Canada West. In public debates on the subject of union he used the common arguments for the scheme. His first public utterance appeared in a letter to the editor of the Halifax *Morning Chronicle* on 13 Jan. 1865, in which he stressed the commercial advantages Nova Scotia would have as part of a larger community. At the end of the year he wrote an open letter to the lieutenant governor of New Brunswick, Sir Arthur Gordon*, by means of which he reassured non-Catholics that the Irish Roman Catholics of British North America had nothing to gain from the Fenians, "that pitiable knot of knaves and fools." He also used the Fenian threat as an indirect appeal in support of confederation for defensive purposes. He recognized that the life of Irish Catholics in British North America left much to be desired because of Protestant and Orange sentiment, but felt that their position was still superior to that of Irish Catholics in the United States.

Connolly's efforts to obtain educational concessions for the Catholics in the Maritimes took him to the London conference of 1866–67. The colonial secretary, Lord Carnarvon [Henry Herbert], Hector Langevin*, and many other Canadian delegates sympathized with his requests but the final initiative lay with the Nova Scotia delegates. Tupper remained firm in his opposition to separate schools, and the archbishop's demand was not granted. His attempt to have Tupper introduce separate school legislation in the House of Assembly in April 1867 also failed. Nevertheless, prior to the federal and provincial elections of 18 Sept. 1867, Connolly used an open letter to urge the Catholics of Halifax to vote: "The Whole Union Ticket – The Whole Five and Nothing but the Five." The city, with its large Roman Catholic population, voted for the union candidates, but the county polls overwhelmingly endorsed the Nova Scotia party candidates, giving them a sweep of the two federal and three provincial seats.

Despite this set-back Connolly continued to labour on behalf of confederation. His correspondence with John A. Macdonald* and Tupper is filled with his impressions of various personages and advice on how to enlist their support. He was constantly seeking favours for those who had served the cause of confederation, regardless of their religious affiliations. During the election campaign of 1872 he was the subject of a bitter attack by the *Morning Chronicle* because of a letter he wrote to Tupper in which he not only endorsed the policies of the Macdonald government but also gave Tupper permission to use the letter as he saw fit. In his reply to the *Morning Chronicle* editorial Archbishop Connolly defended his right as a citizen to take part in politics and accused the editors of trying to promote religious unrest. After this episode, however, he never again became publicly involved in politics.

In his efforts to promote the Catholic faith in the archdiocese he built numerous schools, churches, and a seminary where young men were trained for the priesthood. He also brought the Christian Brothers (Brothers of the Christian Schools) to teach in the diocese and increased the number of Sisters of Charity teaching in the schools.

Archbishop Connolly joined Bishop John Joseph Lynch* of Toronto and Coadjutor Bishop Louis-François Laflèche* of Trois-Rivières as Canadian representatives to the Vatican Council of 1869–70. Connolly was a member of the minority who opposed the infallibility definition introduced at the council. He firmly believed in the principle of papal infallibility but felt that the political climate was not right for the church to confirm the doctrine. Connolly left Rome before the final vote was taken, but he quickly acquiesed in the majority decision.

Thomas Connolly's greatest contribution to his country was his avid support of confederation. His influence upon the other bishops of Nova Scotia and New Brunswick led many of them also to become ardent supporters of the scheme. D'Arcy McGee* ranked Connolly and Oliver Mowat* of Ontario as two of the prime builders of confederation. His endeavours to heal the rift between confederate and repeal elements, and between Catholics and Protestants over the Fenian troubles, make him deserving of the eulogy of the Reverend George Grant*, a long-time friend: "He was a man of peace – ever seeking to build bridges rather than dig ditches between men of different creeds."

DAVID B. FLEMMING

[At one time there was reported to be a substantial collection of Connolly's correspondence at the archives of the archdiocese of Halifax. Supposedly this collection was stolen by "an Englishman" nearly 20 years ago, and the authorities have never recovered it. The largest collection of Connolly's letters was discovered at the archives of the diocese of Bathurst, N.B. (over 60 letters to one of his closest friends, Bishop James Rogers*). Another equally large and important collection was found among the papers of Abbot Bernard Smith, a Benedictine and member of the faculty of the American College in Rome. Smith was Connolly's contact in Rome and represented him at the Vatican. A smaller collection was found among the papers of Bishop John Sweeney* of Saint John, N.B.

Letters dealing with Connolly's political involvement are found in ANQ, Sir Hector-Louis Langevin, L12; PAC, MG 24, B29 (Howe papers), 17, 32; MG 26, A (Macdonald papers), 116, letter books, 11–13, 16, 18, 20; F (Tupper papers), 1–4; PRO 30/6 (Carnarvon papers), 137. The Vatican Archives contain letters and documents relating to the archdiocese of Halifax in the 1860s and 1870s, but these are mainly concerned with purely religious matters. Saunders, *Three premiers of N.S.*, and [Charles Tupper], *The life and letters of the Rt. Hon. Sir Charles Tupper*, ed. E. M. Saunders (2v., London, 1916) contain correspondence between Tupper and Connolly about the school question. Many of these letters are not in the Tupper papers, but have often been quoted, and are generally accepted as valid. D.B.F.]

Public letters are in: [T. L. Connolly], "The archbishop of Halifax on the Irish in British and in republican America," in T. D. McGee, *The Irish position in British and in republican North America: a letter to the editors of the Irish press irrespective of party* (2nd ed., Montreal, 1866), app.B; *Morning Chronicle* (Halifax), 14 Jan. 1865; *Evening Express* (Halifax), 16 Sept. 1867; *British Colonist* (Halifax), 30 Aug. 1872. An obituary is found in *Acadian Recorder* (Halifax),

28 July 1876. *See also:* "The late archbishop of Halifax, Nova Scotia," *Catholic World* (New York), XXIV (1876–77), 136–42. F. J. Wilson, "The Most Reverend Thomas L. Connolly, archbishop of Halifax," CCHA *Report, 1943–44*, 55–108.

CONROY, GEORGE, priest, Catholic bishop, and apostolic delegate to Canada; b. 31 Dec. 1832 at Dundalk, County Louth, Ireland; d. 4 Aug. 1878 at St John's, Newfoundland.

Born of a northern Irish family of modest means, George Conroy went to primary school in the primatial town of Armagh, then, at 17, went to Rome to complete his studies at the College of the Propaganda. On 6 June 1857 he was ordained priest at the church of St John Lateran by Cardinal Constantin Patrizi; in the same year he returned to his native country and was appointed to All Hallows' College, which was situated near Dublin and had been founded for the education of priests intending to serve with foreign missions. In 1866 Cardinal Paul Cullen of Dublin, who had known him at the college of Armagh, appointed him his private secretary; the young Father Conroy was also teacher of theology at Holy Cross College in Clonliff and editor-in-chief of the theological review, *Irish Ecclesiastical Record* (Dublin). After Bishop Cornelius MacCabe's death, Conroy was appointed to the combined sees of Ardagh and Clonmacnois, with residence at Longford, and on 11 April 1871 was consecrated bishop by Cardinal Cullen. It was from this post that he was summoned by Pope Pius IX to be the first apostolic delegate to Canada.

Bishop Conroy arrived at Halifax on 22 May 1877, and immediately set to work. His instructions, which remained secret until 1881, specified that he was to repair the divisions among Canadian bishops "in regard both to the political question and to other questions which are being heatedly discussed in Canada at the moment," such as the Université Laval, the Catholic Programme, and "undue influence." He was to put an end to "the excessive intervention of the clergy in political affairs," and to exhort the bishops to prudence in their relations with the state. Whereas the ultramontanes – bishops such as Ignace Bourget* of Montreal and Louis-François Laflèche* of Trois-Rivières, laymen such as François-Xavier-Anselme Trudel* and Joseph-Israël Tarte* – wanted to see the liberals condemned once and for all, Bishop Conroy endeavoured to make it clear "that the Church, in condemning liberalism, did not wish to censure all and each of the political parties who chanced to be called *liberal*." To this end he travelled through all the dioceses, met clergy and lay personalities, and presided over several meetings of Canadian bishops.

One of the first results he obtained was the publication, on 11 Oct. 1877, of a collective pastoral letter which recalled the various condemnations pronounced against Catholic-liberal doctrines, but which left "to the conscience of each to judge, under God's eye, what sort of men may be the subject of these condemnations, quite apart from the political party to which they belong." Soon the bishops appeared to be more united, the clergy was instructed no longer to interfere in political questions – there were, however, a few difficulties at the provincial elections of 1878 – and peace between church and state seemed to have returned in Canada. But it was precarious, for the ultramontanes, headed by Bishop Jean-Pierre-François Laforce* Langevin, argued that Bishop Conroy had been taken in by the liberals and had dangerously throttled "the salutary influence of the clergy." And they prepared to counter-attack. The aged Côme-Séraphin Cherrier* was not mistaken in saying to the delegate when he left: "Do you not know, Your Excellency, that they are only waiting for your departure to disobey you?"

Bishop Conroy set off from Canada for Rome, via Newfoundland, in June 1878. He left the memory of a "high-minded and conciliatory person," possessed of "an evangelical prudence" and admirable wisdom. The announcement of his illness created consternation among those who knew him; greater still was the surprise when news came of his death on 4 August. As a Quebec liberal paper, *L'Événement*, said: "This death is a public affliction, and affects us as if it were striking down one of our own priests."

NIVE VOISINE

ASTR, Fonds Louis-François Laflèche. *Le Journal des Trois-Rivières*. *Mandements des évêques de Québec* (Têtu et Gagnon), VI. Robert Rumilly, *Monseigneur Laflèche et son temps* (Montréal, [1945]), 128–46. Savaète, *Voix canadiennes*, X.

CONROY, NICHOLAS, farmer and politician; b. 1816 at Rathdowney, Ireland, youngest son of Thomas Conroy and Christine Le Herron; d. 13 Oct. 1879 at his home in Tignish, P.E.I.

Nicholas Conroy was educated in Ireland before immigrating to northwestern Prince Edward Island with his father in 1835. He took up farming, and as a comparatively educated man he often acted as an intermediary between his French-speaking Acadian neighbours and the land agents employed by the Cunards, the proprietors of his district. In 1842 he entered politics and was unsuccessful in contesting an assembly seat; four years later he was elected for Prince County, First District, and joined the Tory caucus. At this time he was not a moving force in the House of Assembly, and took little part in its debates.

Conroy did not run in the election of 1850, although he continued to be known as a Tory. He took an active part in public life again only when the Bible question arose late in the 1850s [see George COLES]. The Tories, in opposition, were demanding that "the open Bible" be legalized in the district schools, which were religiously mixed. The Liberal government, with the support of Bishop Bernard Donald MacDonald*, refused to give this statutory basis to permissive daily reading of the Bible fearing the supposed rigidities this would involve. Conroy, a prominent Catholic layman, supported the bishop and the government. He left his old party, and in 1859 successfully contested First Prince as a Liberal; William Henry POPE's *Islander* reported him as having said in June of the previous year: "THAT AS AN IRISHMAN AND A CATHOLIC HE WAS BOUND TO SUPPORT THE [Liberal] GOVERNMENT."

The Tories won the election, and Conroy found himself in opposition. He may have felt uncomfortable with the Liberals, for he soon attempted to bring about a reconciliation between the Conservatives and the Roman Catholic hierarchy. He was well suited for this task: not only was he a former colleague of the premier, Edward Palmer*, and of other Tory leaders, but in 1851 he had married Catherine McDonald, a niece of his parish priest, Father Peter MacIntyre*, who had become the new bishop of Charlottetown. These negotiations failed, and resulted in even more sectarian animosity. When the election of 1863 was held, the voters divided on religious lines; all Protestant districts returned Conservatives and all Catholic ones returned Liberals. In First Prince, MacIntyre and Conroy combined to oust the latter's running-mate of the previous campaign and to have George Howlan* elected in his place. Conroy lost his own seat in 1867, and remained out of politics for seven years, until he won a by-election following the appointment of Howlan to the federal Senate.

Conroy re-entered the assembly in 1874 virtually as a spokesman for Bishop MacIntyre. In a pastoral issued a few months earlier, the bishop had adopted a "centrist" position, and declared it the duty of Catholic electors to withhold support from all parties that would not grant the church its demands in matters of education. Conroy agreed with MacIntyre: "Catholic members [of the assembly] should not associate with any party who had the power to do right, and yet did wrong."

The correct course, he said, was to establish a separate school system in which religion and education would "go hand in hand." He often called upon Catholic assemblymen to desert the Conservative government, which was heavily dependent upon their support, and become "centrists." He was unsuccessful, however, as only one assemblyman and one legislative councillor joined him.

The election of 1876 provided a final settlement of the school question. The campaign was waged entirely upon the one issue, and the result was a victory for the "Free Schoolers" of Louis Davies* over the "Denominationalists" led by James Colledge Pope* and William Wilfred Sullivan*. Following the passage of the Public Schools Act in the next year, Conroy gave up the struggle for separate schools, and even became a trustee of the public school in Tignish. The school question had been the basis of Davies' coalition, and with its liquidation his government disintegrated. In September 1878 the premier attempted in vain to have Conroy and some other Catholic assemblymen return to the Liberal Party. When Sullivan formed a new Conservative administration in March of the following year, Conroy joined the Executive Council. However, ill health forced his resignation on 11 June, and two days later he was appointed registrar of deeds. He died of brain disease, leaving his wife and several children.

Nicholas Conroy was neither a brilliant man nor by nature a leader of men. On most issues he held the views of a conventional Island politician of his period; for example, he opposed confederation in the 1860s and advocated the abolition of leasehold tenure. He nevertheless also represents in its sharpest form a trend of fundamental significance in the social and political history of 19th-century Prince Edward Island: over the years, he became increasingly clerically oriented in matters of church and state. The mood of reaction within the Roman Catholic Church throughout the world, with which his friend Bishop MacIntyre agreed entirely, provides a partial explanation, but undoubtedly the death of his brother, Dr James Herron Conroy*, as an apostate also affected him deeply. Thus Conroy was basically a conservative man whose alignments were determined more by the interests of his church than by secular considerations; his three shifts in party allegiance reflect the instability of Island political parties in his time.

IAN ROSS ROBERTSON

[The author is indebted to Miss Margaret Conroy, a granddaughter of Nicholas Conroy, for an interview on 30 July 1969. PAPEI, Prince Edward Island, Executive Council, Minutes, 1879. Prince Edward Island, House of Assembly, *Journals*, 1847–49, 1859–66, 1874–79; *Debates and proceedings*, 1859–66, 1874–79; Supreme Court, Estates Division, will of Nicholas Conroy, 23 Sept. 1879. *Abstract of the proceedings before the Land Commissioners' Court, held during the summer of 1860, to inquire into the difficulties relative to the rights of landowners and tenants in Prince Edward Island*, reporters J. D. Gordon and David Laird (Charlottetown, 1862), 49–53. Obituaries will be found in *Examiner* (Charlottetown), 14 Oct. 1879, *Patriot* (Charlottetown), 16 Oct. 1879, and *Pioneer* (Montague, P.E.I.), 17 Oct. 1879. *Can. parl. comp., 1875*, 639. "Peter Conroy," *Past and present of Prince Edward Island . . .*, ed. D. A. MacKinnon and A. B. Warburton (Charlottetown, [1906]), 670–71. MacMillan, *Catholic Church in PEI*, 372–77. Robertson, "Religion, politics, and education in PEI." I.R.R.]

COOK, JAMES WILLIAM, lumber merchant and politician; b. in Williamsburgh Township, U.C., 11 Jan. 1820, son of George Cook and Sarah Casselman, and grandson of John Cook (Van Keugh), loyalist; d. at Morrisburg, Ont., 21 May 1875.

As the oldest of five brothers, James William Cook succeeded his father and his uncle, John Cook (1791–1877), in the management of the family's square timber business (to become known as Cook and Brothers), which began on the Castor and South Nation rivers in eastern Upper Canada. The firm had its headquarters at Morrisburg, but by the 1870s it had expanded to include operations in pine forests centring on Belleville, Toronto, Barrie, and Quebec City, and was claimed to be the largest square timber business in Canada. The principal office of the firm, however, was maintained by J. W. Cook at Morrisburg during his lifetime, with his two younger brothers, George J. (1824–1902) and John L., managing the branch offices. The firm continued to have a prosperous existence into the 20th century, when its operations reached into the Muskoka and Algoma districts.

James William Cook represented Dundas County in the Legislative Assembly of the Province of Canada, 1857–61 – as had his uncle John Cook in the assemblies of Upper Canada and the Province of Canada, 1830–45. Two of his brothers were also politicians: Simon Sephrenus (1831–92), MLA of Ontario for Dundas, 1867–75; and Hermon (Herman) Henry*, MP 1872–78 and 1882–91, MLA of Ontario 1879–82. The three brothers, as well as John Cook, were all Reform or Liberal politicians.

J. K. JOHNSON

PAC, Map division, S/420 (1862); RG 31, A1, 1851, Williamsburgh Township, Canada West; 1861, Williamsburgh Township, Canada West; 1871, Williamsburgh Township, Ontario. PAO, Legislative

Cooper

Assembly papers, biographical sketches of members of the assembly, 1792–1840, comp. J. S. Carstairs and W. D. Read. *Can. biog. dict.*, I, 35–38. *Lovell's Canadian dominion directory for 1871 ...* (Montreal, [1871]). J. S. Carter, *The story of Dundas, being a history of the county of Dundas from 1784 to 1904* (Iroquois, Ont., 1905). Cornell, *Alignment of political groups.* James Croil, *Dundas; or, a sketch of Canadian history, and more particularly of the county of Dundas, one of the earliest settled counties in Upper Canada* (Montreal, 1861), 280. J. E. Defebaugh, *History of the lumber industry of America* (2v., Chicago, 1906–7). J. G. Harkness, *Stormont, Dundas and Glengarry: a history, 1784–1945* (Oshawa, Ont., 1946), 218. Hunter, *Hist of Simcoe County.*

COOPER, JAMES, HBC employee, master mariner, politician, and public servant; b. 1821 at Bilston, Wolverhampton, Staffordshire, Eng.; date and place of death unknown.

James Cooper joined the Hudson's Bay Company in August 1844, and in 1845 was appointed first officer on *Vancouver*, of the Columbia Shipping Department. In 1846 he was given a command, and in 1847 he sailed *Mary Dare* to Fort Victoria for the north Pacific trade. He took a cargo of flour and deals to the Sandwich Islands, and the opportunities in the expanding Pacific trade impressed him. In 1848 he became captain of *Columbia*, the annual supply ship for Fort Vancouver. On his first voyage he violated company regulations by carrying goods to trade on his own account at Honolulu.

Visiting Fort Victoria on 16 Oct. 1849, Cooper decided to leave the company and emigrate as a "free settler" to Vancouver Island, the new colony in which the company had proprietary rights. In England he obtained an appointment as Lloyd's agent on the island but could not raise capital for a sawmilling venture. With his wife, four children, and workmen, Cooper came supercargo on *Tory*, arriving at Victoria on 9 May 1851, and having met his future farm superintendent, Thomas Blinkhorn, on board.

An enterprising colonist, Cooper at first prospered. Then misfortunes, which he blamed on the HBC and James DOUGLAS, befell him. The 385-acre farm at Metchosin, on which he had paid a deposit to the company, was nine miles by water from Fort Victoria and the lack of a road became a grievance. He depleted his capital by purchasing two properties at Esquimalt and a part-interest in a tavern at Victoria. In 1852, his 45-ton iron schooner *Alice*, brought with him on *Tory* in sections, began to carry potatoes and cranberries to San Francisco. Douglas at first assisted him, but became less amiable when he learned that Cooper had not paid Fort Langley for the potatoes and that his cranberries were obtained from Indians of the Fraser River delta against the company's monopoly on the mainland.

Cooper, however, had won the trust of the island's first governor, Richard Blanshard*, and was named on 27 Aug. 1851, with Douglas and John Tod*, to the island's ruling council. On his departure, Blanshard carried a petition signed by Cooper and the other independent settlers opposing the selection of Douglas as the new governor. Even so Douglas obtained the appointment. When, in 1853, he and the council imposed licence fees for the sale of spirits, and Douglas forbade members of the council to sell liquor, Cooper, a man of "an irascible, grumbling disposition," complained bitterly. His business affected and his shipping restricted, he prepared an attack on Douglas.

His excuse came with Douglas' appointment of David CAMERON, the governor's brother-in-law, on 2 Dec. 1853 as judge of the Court of Common Pleas. Supported by the HBC chaplain, the Reverend Robert J. Staines*, and by Captain Edward Edwards Langford*, a disaffected Puget's Sound Agricultural Company bailiff, Cooper organized the settlers to petition London to revoke the company's grant and put the colony under imperial control. Two further petitions were presented to the two houses of parliament in March 1854.

In June 1856, "in circumstances of some [financial] embarrassment," Cooper returned to England to become a merchant at Bilston. In 1857 his testimony before the House of Commons Select Committee inquiring into the administration of the HBC corroborated that given by Blanshard, Rear Admiral Fairfax Moresby, and Charles W. Wentworth-Fitzwilliam, MP. Their evidence was so damaging that the company's crown grant to Vancouver Island was revoked in 1859.

Cooper was still in England in August 1858, when Douglas was appointed governor of the new colony of British Columbia. But on 25 Dec. 1858 Cooper returned to Victoria with a commission from Sir Edward Bulwer-Lytton appointing him harbour master at Esquimalt, "chiefly for the purposes of British Columbia." Douglas protested: "Mr Cooper's office is a sinecure, there is literally nothing for him to do."

Once again, Cooper became politically active. He allied himself with Amor De Cosmos* and, though a public servant, stood twice for election to the Assembly of Vancouver Island. On 12 Jan. 1860 he was elected as a "reformer" for Esquimalt and Metchosin district. The Colonial Office intervened: he was ordered on 17 March 1860 to reside at New Westminster, the capital of B.C. In October Cooper resigned his seat.

Douglas and Cooper engaged in a bitter dispute

in 1861 when Cooper employed a coxswain without authorization. Cooper continued to make unwarranted appointments and expenditures and interfered with the duties of the collector of customs. He also associated with the element which pressed for Douglas' removal as governor, demanding representative government in the gold colony.

After Douglas' retirement in 1864, Cooper was less closely supervised, though the colonial secretary suspected him on occasion of sharp practice. With the union of the seaboard colonies, he returned to Victoria in 1867 to take on additional duties as harbour master of Victoria and Esquimalt. On 27 Jan. 1869 he resigned, with the promise of 18 months' salary in lieu of service. He became a hotel-keeper and wine merchant in Victoria. In 1870 he engaged briefly in a salmon fishing venture on the Fraser River six miles below New Westminster.

After B.C. entered confederation in 1871, Cooper was appointed on 17 Oct. 1872 dominion agent for the Department of Marine and Fisheries, inspector of lights, and inspector of steamboats. In 1876 a royal commission investigated charges that he had obtained money under false pretences while holding public office. Nothing was proven, and in December 1878 he won a lawsuit for slander against a lighthouse keeper who had branded him a "d---d old thief." His appointment, however, was cancelled by order in council on 25 June 1879 on evidence that he had been guilty of fraud. In October he was charged at Victoria with obtaining $95 unlawfully on 29 June 1876 while acting as dominion agent. Cooper failed to appear before a higher court in December. His bail was estreated and a bench warrant sworn out. Cooper then disappeared. He is believed to have drifted to California, though no proof has been obtained.

Cooper was the first political agitator in British Columbia and the first leader of a political faction. In part he was motivated by unsatisfied political and social ambitions, as well as by economic distress, but by conviction he was the foe of autocracy and privilege. He saw more clearly than the officers of the HBC the opportunity for trade created by the California gold boom and was prepared to challenge its trading privileges.

MARGARET A. ORMSBY

Bancroft Library, University of California, Berkeley, James Cooper, "Maritime matters on the northwest coast and other affairs of the Hudson's Bay Company in early times" (photocopy in PABC). HBC Arch. B.226/b, B.226/c, B.239/k. PABC, Edgar Crow Baker diary, 1879; British Columbia, Governor Frederick Seymour, Dispatches to London, 1864–69; David Cameron papers; James Cooper papers; Henry Pering Pellew Crease, Correspondence inward, 1869; James Douglas, "A confidential report upon the character and qualifications of the principal officers of this government," Douglas to the Duke of Newcastle, 18 June 1863; Governor James Douglas, Correspondence inward, 1830–68; Governor James Douglas, Dispatches to London, 1851–55, 1855–59 (letter book copies); Fort Vancouver, Correspondence outward (letter book copies); Fort Victoria, Correspondence outward to HBC, 1850–55, 1855–59 (letter book copies); Vancouver Island, Governors Richard Blanshard and James Douglas, Correspondence outward, 22 June 1850–5 March 1859 (letter book copies); Vancouver Island, Governor James Douglas, Correspondence outward, 27 May 1859–9 Jan. 1864 (letter book copies); J. S. Helmcken, "Reminiscences" (5v unpublished typescript, 1892), II. PRO, CO 60; CO 305.

Canada, *Sessional papers*, XIII (1880), PT.6, no.9. G.B., Parl., House of Commons paper, 1857 (Session II), XV, 224, 260 (whole volume), *Report from the select committee on the Hudson's Bay Company; together with the proceedings of the committee, minutes of evidence, appendix and index*; Parl., House of Commons paper, 1863, XXXVIII, 507, pp.487–540, *Miscellaneous papers relating to Vancouver Island, 1848–1863. . . . Minutes of the Council of Vancouver Island, commencing August 30th, 1851, and terminating . . . February 6th, 1861*, ed. E. O. S. Scholefield (Archives of British Columbia, Memoir no.2, Victoria, 1918). *Colonist* (Victoria), particularly 8 June 1859 – 10 Jan. 1860; 19 Dec. 1878 – 15 Oct. 1879. HBRS, XXII (Rich).

First Victoria directory . . . 1874, comp. Edward Mallandaine (Victoria, 1874). Walbran, *B.C. coast names*. H. H. Bancroft, *History of British Columbia, 1792–1887* (San Francisco, 1890). Morton, *History of the Canadian west*. Ormsby, *British Columbia*. "The diary of Robert Melrose," ed. W. K. Lamb, *BCHQ*, VII (1943), 119–34, 199–218, 283–95. "Journal of Arthur Thomas Bushby" (Blakey Smith). W. K. Lamb, "Early lumbering on Vancouver Island. Part I: 1844–1855," *BCHQ*, II (1938), 31–53; "The governorship of Richard Blanshard," *BCHQ*, XIV (1950), 1–41. S. G. Pettit, "The trials and tribulations of Edward Edwards Langford," *BCHQ*, XVII (1953), 5–40. G. H. Slater, "Rev. Robert John Staines: pioneer priest, pedagogue, and political agitator," *BCHQ*, XIV (1950), 187–240.

CORNISH, FRANCIS EVANS, lawyer, legislator, civic official; b. 1 Feb. 1831 in London, U.C., son of William King Cornish; d. 28 Nov. 1878 in Winnipeg, Man.

The family of Francis Evans Cornish had settled in the London District of Upper Canada in 1819; he was educated at the London grammar school and called to the bar of Upper Canada in 1855. A conservative and a member of the Orange order, Francis Cornish was an alderman in London from 1858 to 1861, and was elected mayor of the city in 1861. Cornish had a popular following but

Cox

gained a reputation as the "rowdy" mayor, being charged by opponents with bigamy, assault, drunkenness, and boisterous public disputes. He was defeated in 1864, it is said, when members of the city council called out the militia to ensure an honest election. In 1860 he had sought unsuccessfully a seat in the Legislative Assembly of Canada for the constituency of East Middlesex. He failed also in 1871 to win the city of London constituency in the Legislative Assembly of Ontario.

In 1872 Cornish moved to Winnipeg, where he set up a law practice and became active in civic and provincial politics. One of the leaders in the movement for the incorporation of the city of Winnipeg, he was elected its first mayor in 1874 and served for one year. The most important result of his administration was the enactment of a by-law providing for the beginning of municipal services. The same year he became a member of the provincial legislature for the constituency of Poplar Point, which he represented until his death.

Cornish was a genial and colourful figure, whose name both in London and in Winnipeg is associated with a series of flamboyant political antics. His success in mayoralty campaigns in London is attributed to smooth organization of the voters. He had even arranged, it is said, for British soldiers quartered in the area to take up residence for 24 hours at election time and vote for him. In Winnipeg in 1876 he was arrested and fined for stealing a poll-book on election day. On another occasion, the story goes, he kidnapped his opponent on the eve of an election, brought charges of corruption against him, and then stated that the failure of his opponent to come forward to answer the charges was tantamount to a confession of guilt.

In Winnipeg, Cornish was associated with the group opposed to the policy of reconciliation among the divisive forces engendered during the Red River disturbances of 1869–70. He assisted individuals seeking the arrest of Louis Riel*. He was partially instrumental in arranging for the arrest of Riel's adjutant-general, Ambroise-Dydime Lépine*, in 1873; the following year he assisted Stuart Macdonald, prosecutor, in the trial of Lépine. The judgement in this case allotted the reward offered by Ontario for the arrest of those responsible for the death of Thomas Scott*, and Cornish received $400 of it.

Cornish died at the age of 47 of cancer of the stomach. In the last year of his life he re-entered civic politics as an alderman in Winnipeg. On 31 Oct. 1853 he had married, in London, Victorine Clench, who survived him.

HARTWELL BOWSFIELD

Begg and Nursey, *Ten years in Winnipeg. Manitoba Free Press* (Winnipeg), 29 Nov. 1878. *Dom. ann. reg.*, *1878*. Orlo Miller, *A century of western Ontario; the story of London, "The Free Press", and western Ontario, 1849–1949* (Toronto, [1949]). Stanley, *Louis Riel*, 187, 191, 193, 210–11.

COX, WILLIAM GEORGE, magistrate, justice of the peace, gold commissioner, and artist; b. in Ireland in 1821 or 1822, son of Charles Cox; d. in California, 6 Oct. 1878.

Late in 1857 William George Cox ended a 12-year banking career in Dublin and emigrated to New York with his bride, Sophia Elizabeth Webb, whom he had married in Donnybrook, Ireland, on 6 November. When his wife returned to Ireland in August 1858, Cox proceeded to British Columbia, arriving in December. He became a constable at Fort Yale the following February; three months later he was appointed a deputy collector of customs, and then, on 26 Oct. 1860, assistant gold commissioner and justice of the peace for the Rock Creek district. He continued to perform the functions of these offices in the Cariboo mines from 1863 until 1867, and in the Columbia and Kootenay district in 1867 and 1868. He was made a county court judge in 1866, and was appointed to the Legislative Council in 1867 and 1868.

In performing his official duties Cox was a capable, if unorthodox, public servant. Governor James DOUGLAS thought him "Peculiarly well adapted for frontier service, where tact and a resolute will are indispensable qualities in managing the rough characters met with there." Dr Walter Butler Cheadle* described him as a "Fat, tall, thick set fellow . . . delicately polite, gentlemanly and jolly." In 1864 he distinguished himself by leading a party of men from the Cariboo to capture some Chilcotin Indians who had massacred one of Alfred WADDINGTON's road parties and were threatening a widespread uprising. Among the miners themselves Cox was popular. His sometimes unconventional "legal" decisions added a lighter tone to the otherwise sombre official duties; on one occasion he required the disputants over a mining claim to settle their difference by a foot race from the court house to the disputed claim; on another he assisted in the ceremony of drumming out of Rock Creek an Englishman who had been robbing the sluice boxes. Court procedures he adapted as circumstances warranted; Chinese were sworn in by chopping off a cock's neck or breaking a plate.

But Cox had his problems. His wife, abandoned in Ireland while he enjoyed the attentions of an Indian woman, demanded support, through official channels; the reluctant Cox was obliged to comply. Governor Frederick Seymour* reported that Cox resented authority, and his glib admission that he had "omitted some entries [in an official return] through my usual carelessness" was met by the cold charge that he endeavour to perform his duties "with care and attention, and not with admitted 'Carelessness.' "

Unfortunately his most celebrated escapade was to contribute to his undoing. During the discussion in the Legislative Council over the site of the capital of the united colonies, Cox's neighbour, magistrate William Hayles Franklyn of Nanaimo, a supporter of New Westminster, read his opening words three times since Cox had shuffled his papers after each reading. Then, when the inebriated Franklyn laid his glasses on the desk, Cox pressed the lenses from them and poor Franklyn could not see to read his notes. Amid pandemonium a recess was called, and when the council reassembled Franklyn was prevented from making a second speech. A short time later Seymour, a strong advocate of New Westminster, abolished Cox's position and Cox angrily refused the new office offered to him. In 1869 he moved to San Francisco where he planned to earn his living as an artist, a calling which may, indeed, have been closer to his heart. He is reported to have had little financial success.

Cox was one of several Irishmen who played prominent roles in developing British Columbia and who, at the frontiers of the colony, helped to establish the nascent communities and to secure British institutions.

G. R. NEWELL

PABC, Sophia E. Cox correspondence; William George Cox correspondence; John C. Haynes correspondence; British Columbia, Colonial Secretary, correspondence outward, 1859–69; British Columbia, Dispatches to Colonial Office, 1859–69. St Mary's Church, Donnybrook, Ireland, marriage certificate of William George Cox and Sophia Elizabeth Webb (copy in PABC). *Daily British Colonist* (Victoria, B.C.), 13 Nov. 1878.

CRATE, WILLIAM FREDERICK, miller, millwright, and HBC employee; b. between 1807 and 1813 at London, Eng.; d. 1 Oct. 1871 at Cowichan, Vancouver Island, B.C.

William Frederick Crate was engaged by the Hudson's Bay Company at Lachine, Quebec, in April 1834 for three years at an annual salary of £150 Halifax currency. His contract was cancelled at York Factory in July 1834 and he spent the winter of 1834–35 in the Red River Settlement. He was then re-engaged at £100 sterling plus house and board for service in the Columbia Department, where he was placed in charge of the mills at Fort Vancouver, the company's headquarters

for its operations west of the Rocky Mountains. By 1843 Crate had rebuilt and expanded the company's sawmills and supervised the construction of the first water-driven grist mill; all were built on streams to the east of Fort Vancouver. The grist mill, completed in 1839, could grind about 20,000 bushels of grain a year; from it came flour for the HBC's western posts and supply ships and for sale to the Russian American Company.

Crate did not renew his contract in 1843 but returned to England to marry on 29 Feb. 1844. He and his wife Sarah spent several years in Vermont where two of their four children were born. John Fenton, who had succeeded Crate as miller at Fort Vancouver, resigned in 1849 and Crate resumed his former duties. During his second employment at Fort Vancouver, Crate completed a new and larger grist mill and constructed a third sawmill which would cut between 3,000 and 4,000 feet of timber in 12 hours.

Following the Oregon Treaty of 1846, Fort Vancouver ceased to be the chief post of the HBC in the Pacific northwest. However, the fort continued as the major distribution and collecting point for the posts south of the 49th parallel, and Crate was in charge of the five-man crew which kept the buildings of the fort in repair. The Oregon Treaty confirmed the "possessory rights" of the HBC to its land and property north of the Columbia River. Nevertheless, the company had continuous trouble with Americans who took up claims to its lands surrounding Fort Vancouver. To protect the grist mill, Crate and his wife filed for a donation land claim of one square mile in 1849 and in 1850. Crate recognized that the mills still belonged to the company, and until 1860 he received wages for running them. But his claim did not include the site of the sawmills, which he also operated for the company. In 1853, Ervin J. Taylor and his wife filed a claim to the half-section of land on which the sawmills stood, and about 1856 Taylor took possession of the mills during Crate's absence. Despite an injunction drawn up by Dugald MACTAVISH, then in charge of Fort Vancouver, Taylor remained in possession.

In June 1860 the HBC finally abandoned Fort Vancouver, and employees and equipment were removed to Fort Victoria. Crate, however, chose to leave the company and remain on the Columbia River. He was ordered to send all of the milling machinery to Victoria, but he kept what was fixed to the mills and later sold it as his own before moving to Victoria in 1863.

Crate occupied a lot on Government Street near Fort Victoria until 1866 or 1867, when he took a farm in the Somenos District near Quamichan Lake in the Cowichan Valley. Denied permission to build a wharf at Maple Bay, he sought permission in July 1868 to build a small, water-powered grist mill on Somenos Creek on the Quamichan Indian Reserve. Officials of the colonial government were sympathetic to his application because such a mill would serve the Indians and would promote the sowing of cereals and grains by white settlers in the district. In August 1869, after consultation with the Indian owners, Crate was finally given a seven-year lease to two and a half acres for the mill site at an annual rent of $15. The government showed its support for Crate's mill by approving his request for free transport of machinery and building material on the government steamer *Sir James Douglas*. In return, Crate was to grind the chief's corn without charge, and all of the wheat required by the Quamichan Village Indians at half the price he charged other customers.

This mill proved to be the restless Crate's last effort to make a new life for himself and his family. Having outlived two of his four children, he died "in very indifferent circumstances."

WILLIAM R. SAMPSON

British Columbia, Department of Lands, Forests, and Water Resources, Lands Administration Branch, Crown grants, XIV, 2713. PABC, William Frederick Crate correspondence. "Disposition of W. F. Crate, Victoria, V.I., 26 August 1865," *Evidence on the part of the Hudson's Bay Company claimants* (British and American Joint Commission for the settlement of claims of the Hudson's Bay and Puget's Sound Agricultural companies, [*Papers*] (14v., Washington, Montreal, 1865–69), II), 104–18, 229. HBRS, VI (Rich), 23, 157–58, 229; VII (Rich), 122–23, 199–200. National Archives (Washington), Microfilm Publications, Microcopy no.432, *Population schedules of the seventh census of the United States, 1850, Roll 742, Oregon, Oregon Country* (Washington, 1964), 73, f.37. J. A. Hussey, *The history of Fort Vancouver and its physical structure* ([Tacoma, Wash., 1957]), 110, 151, 198–206. W. E. Ireland, "Early flour-mills in British Columbia: part I – Vancouver Island and the lower mainland," *BCHQ*, V (1941), 89–109.

CRAWFORD, JOHN WILLOUGHBY, lawyer, businessman, and politician; b. at Manorhamilton, County Leitrim, Ireland, in 1817, son of George Crawford* (later a member of the Canadian Senate) and Margaret Brown; d. in Toronto, Ont., 13 May 1875.

John Willoughby Crawford came to Canada with his parents in 1824. He was raised in Brockville, Upper Canada, where the family had settled and prospered, but was educated at York (Toronto). Called to the bar in 1839, he practised in Toronto and identified himself with that community. In 1845 he married Helen, daughter of Judge Levius Peters Sherwood* of Brockville. They had one son and five daughters.

Although he was in partnership with Ernestus Crombie* in a law firm, Crawford's business activities were so broad that he is more accurately described as a businessman than as a lawyer. His legal specialty was the law of property, banking, and commerce. Associated with numerous business establishments, he served as president of the Royal Canadian Bank, the Imperial Building, Savings and Investment Society, and the Canadian Car Company. He became the first president of the Toronto and Nipissing Railway in 1868 and was a director of the Toronto, Grey and Bruce Railway; both lines were closely involved with Toronto's metropolitan thrust northward. Crawford was also a director of several other firms, and acted in parliament for the Dominion Express Company and the Empire Fire and Marine Insurance Company.

Relatives and business associates tied Crawford to the politically sensitive Grand Trunk Railway. His father was a director, and his brother James (also an MP, 1867–72) was a contractor to the railway; its long-time president – John Ross – was both a brother-in-law and a business associate; its chief engineer was James Keefer, half-brother of Samuel Keefer*, another brother-in-law; George Sherwood*, a third brother-in-law, was also connected with the line. During the 1860s Crawford served the Grand Trunk as a solicitor.

Crawford's family was also closely involved in politics. His father-in-law was an important eastern Ontario Conservative, and a brother-in-law, Henry Sherwood*, had been a leading Tory politician in the 1840s. Crawford himself entered politics and, although manifesting occasional signs of independence, was a reliable Conservative. His début in politics was dramatic: in 1861 he contested East Toronto against George BROWN, arguing that he was an "independent": "I think it unworthy of the intelligence of an enlightened electoral body to require, as it is unworthy of the self-respect of the candidate entering political life to give, an express pledge of general opposition to or support of, any particular Government." Crawford wanted the seat of government moved to Toronto and promised that the headquarters of the Grand Trunk would be moved there. Like most people who lived west of Oshawa, however, he disclaimed, albeit disingenuously, any connection with the Grand Trunk. He also declared himself a supporter of representation by population. John Crawford was a powerful businessman, but George Brown was the editor of the *Globe* and the sitting member. Consequently there was considerable surprise when Crawford defeated Brown

1,135 to 944. He became a loyal and important backbencher.

In 1863 the most significant measure was Richard William Scott*'s bill codifying for the Roman Catholic minority in Canada West most of the educational rights later entrenched in Ontario's constitution by section 93 of the British North America Act. The bill was vehemently opposed by the bulk of the Canada West members, was a burning question during the 1863 election, and was the main issue in East Toronto. The act was especially important to John Crawford. Although himself a member of the Church of England, he was sensitive to Catholic interests in his constituency, and he supported the act with some courage, one of the few members from Canada West to do so. His associates, according to the *Globe*, constituted a "motley Catholic crowd," and his supporters were described as examples of "animal man" – "a credit to the ould sod." The phrases indicate the tenor of the campaign; Crawford was defeated by 489 votes.

Crawford was ready and anxious to run in the federal election of 1867. In South Leeds, where he had once lived, he won a narrow victory over Albert Norton Richards*. When Toronto was allotted a third seat before the election of 1872, Crawford left South Leeds and easily won West Toronto. Then, on 5 Nov. 1873, the day his government resigned, the prime minister, Sir John A. Macdonald*, announced the appointment of John Crawford as lieutenant governor of Ontario. His term was both short and uneventful, and he died at government house, Toronto, in 1875.

John Crawford combined business and public life. His contemporaries assumed that he was a wealthy man, the *Ottawa Citizen* commenting that "his ventures in landed speculation were very profitable, and at the age of forty [1857] he was independent financially. . . ." He made Toronto's concerns his own, championing that city even as a member of parliament for South Leeds, and zealously supported its economic interests. He also became a lieutenant-colonel in Toronto's 5th militia battalion. He was made a QC in 1867 and was elected a bencher of the Law Society of Upper Canada in 1871.

The openness and volatility of 19th century Ontario are illustrated by the Crawford family. In fewer than 50 years the Crawfords moved from the status of an immigrant family to the pinnacle of social leadership involving membership in a tightly knit élite. This was the achievement of a family, but also of an open and receptive society.

DONALD SWAINSON

PAC, MG 26, A (Macdonald papers), 228, 266; B (Mackenzie papers), ser.2, 1. PAO, Sir Alexander Campbell papers, 1872. Canada, *Parliamentary debates*, 1873. *Globe* (Toronto), 1861–75. *Leader* (Toronto), 1875. *Mail* (Toronto), 1875. *Ottawa Citizen*, 1875. PANS, *Report, 1952*, app. B. *Can. biog. dict.*, I, 23–26. *Can. parl. comp., 1873*. D. B. Read, *The lieutenant-governors of Upper Canada and Ontario, 1792–1899* (Toronto, 1900).

Careless, *Brown*. D. C. Masters, *The rise of Toronto, 1850–1890* (Toronto, 1947). M. H. Small, "A study of the dominion and the provincial elections of 1867 in Ontario," unpublished MA thesis, Queen's University, 1968. F. A. Walker, *Catholic education and politics in Upper Canada; a study of the documentation relative to the origin of Catholic elementary schools in the Ontario school system* (Toronto, 1955). D. W. Swainson, "Business and politics: the career of John Willoughby Crawford," *Ont. Hist.*, LXI (1969), 225–36.

CRÉMAZIE, JACQUES, lawyer, author of lawbooks, journalist; b. 10 Oct. 1810 at Quebec, of the marriage of Jacques Crémazie and Marie-Anne Miville; eldest brother of the poet Octave CRÉMAZIE whom he helped considerably with his financial difficulties and during his exile; d. 11 July 1872 at Quebec.

In 1818 Jacques Crémazie entered the Petit Séminaire of Quebec, where he completed his classical studies in 1828. After thinking for some time of becoming a priest, he studied law, and on 4 Feb. 1835 was called to the bar. He practised his profession for some years with Jean-Baptiste-Édouard Bacquet. On 26 April 1845 he was appointed inspector of the registry offices, in the districts of Quebec and Gaspé; these offices had been created in 1841, by a decree of the Special Council, for the registration of acts and particularly mortgages on real estate in Canada East, and government-appointed inspectors were responsible for maintaining efficient operation.

When the faculty of law was opened in 1854, shortly after the founding of the Université Laval, Jacques Crémazie became its first secretary and taught civil law there. In 1866 he succeeded Augustin-Norbert Morin* as dean of the faculty, a post which he held until his death and which made him a pioneer in French Canada in the teaching of law at a university. In 1860 he was appointed also recorder of Quebec City.

Having a keen interest in primary instruction, Crémazie submitted to the Legislative Assembly's committee on the state of education in Canada East, set up in 1853, an important document which prompted the committee's report and the educational reforms of 1856. Crémazie considered that the backwardness of education in Canada East resulted chiefly from "the failure to take any steps to train teachers, and to establish and fix at

Crémazie

a proper rate the salary which should be granted to them." He called for the setting up of normal schools. Crémazie found other causes of backwardness, in the lack of uniformity in teaching, the endless variety of school texts, and the absence of any supervision of the schools. He asked that the state, through a ministry of public instruction, intervene to determine salaries, publish a journal, and concern itself with all problems of education. When the Council of Public Instruction was formed in 1859, he became a member of it. Ten years later the council was reorganized, and he was appointed chairman of the Catholic committee. He was also secretary of the Catholic School Commission of Quebec City. He was a man of great charity, and paid particular attention to the Asile du Bon-Pasteur at Quebec. He even gave lessons to the teaching sisters and to poor pupils, and acted without payment as the community's legal councillor.

Jacques Crémazie published three works: in 1842, *Les lois criminelles anglaises* . . . , the first compilation in French outlining criminal law as it applied in the Province of Canada; in 1852, *Manuel des notions utiles sur les droits politiques, le droit civil, la loi criminelle, et municipale, les lois rurales, etc.*; and in 1867, *Notions élémentaires de cosmographie et de météorologie accompagnées de leçons sur l'usage des globes*. The first two do not display great originality of thought, but they served a useful purpose at the time by diffusing legal knowledge among French-Canadian readers. The third work shows that the author was interested in all subjects; it was composed chiefly to be of assistance to teachers. Crémazie edited *L'Ami de la religion et de la patrie*, a paper published by Stanislas Drapeau* from 18 Dec. 1847 to 13 March 1850. It appeared weekly, then twice and finally three times weekly. It styled itself "ecclesiastical, political and commercial," and its aim was to help develop popular instruction. This newspaper was replaced by *L'Ordre social*, which appeared from 28 March to 26 Dec. 1850 and which was also directed by Crémazie. He wanted to complete as a journalist the work he was doing as an educator, by defending what he regarded as the "eternal values of civilization," religion, property, and family.

After an illness of several months, Jacques Crémazie, a bachelor, died on 11 July 1872. The next day *Le Canadien* wrote: "A great Christian and a distinguished citizen has just died."

J.-C. BONENFANT

Jacques Crémazie, *Les lois criminelles anglaises, traduites et compilées de Blackstone, Chitty, Russell et autres criminalistes anglais, et telles que suivies en Canada: arrangées suivant les dispositions introduites dans le Code criminel de cette province par les statuts provinciaux 4 et 5 Victoria, chap. 24, 25, 26 et 27; comprenant aussi un précis des statuts pénaux de la ci-devant province du Bas-Canada* (Québec, 1842); *Manuel des notions utiles sur les droits politiques, le droit civil, la loi criminelle, et municipale, les lois rurales, etc.* (Québec, 1852); [Jacques Crémazie], *Notions élémentaires de cosmographie et de météorologie accompagnées de leçons sur l'usage des globes* (Québec, 1867).

L'Asile du Bon-Pasteur de Québec d'après les annales de cet institut (Québec, 1896), 132–37. Canada, Province of, Legislative Assembly, *Journals*, 1852–53, app.J.J., "Education, Lower Canada: report of the superintendent of education. . . ." *Le Canadien* (Québec), 15 juill. 1872. *Le Courrier du Canada* (Québec), 12 juill. 1872. *Annuaire de l'université Laval pour l'année académique 1873–74* (Québec, 1873), 51–55. Beaulieu et Hamelin, *Journaux du Québec*, 175–205. Audet, *Histoire du conseil de l'Instruction publique*, 40–41. André Labarrère-Paulé, *Les instituteurs laïques au Canada français, 1836–1900* (Québec, 1965), 156–61. P.-G. Roy, *A propos de Crémazie* (Québec, 1945), 17–28.

CRÉMAZIE, OCTAVE (baptized **Claude-Joseph-Olivier**), bookseller, writer, and poet; b. 16 April 1827 at Quebec, 11th child of Jacques Crémazie and Marie-Anne Miville; d. 16 Jan. 1879 at Le Havre, France.

Of the 12 children born to Octave Crémazie's parents, eight died in infancy, so that Octave, the youngest of those who survived, spent his early years in the company of three brothers: JACQUES, Joseph, and Louis. At the seminary of Quebec, where he was admitted as a day-pupil in 1836, Octave, under the influence of Abbé John Holmes*, acquired a liking for literature. Holmes introduced him particularly to the French romantics, who were subsequently a predominant influence on the poet, as the style of his poems shows and as he himself states. Musset and Lamartine were soon his literary gods, together with the Victor Hugo of the period prior to 1850.

When Octave had finished his studies in 1844, he went into partnership with his brother Joseph at the head of a small bookshop, which had been established in 1833, and which thenceforth bore the sign "J. et O. Crémazie." More venturesome than his elder brother, Octave worked to develop the business; in 1847 it was installed at 12 Rue de la Fabrique, and soon became one of the most important centres of French culture and refinement in Quebec City. Crémazie, a great reader, the first to use the classical and modern books he sold, quickly acquired a reputation as an intellectual and scholar. Thus on 2 Dec. 1847, at the age of 20, his name appeared among the founders at Quebec of the Institut Canadien, in which he subsequently held various positions on the governing body, including that of president in 1857–58. On the other hand, the company of ladies did not interest him; he was even perhaps a bit of a misogynist. The question of marriage was one he never entertained.

On 1 Jan. 1849 *L'Ami de la religion et de la patrie*, edited by his brother Jacques, published as a New Year's offering one of Octave Crémazie's first poems. From that time on, almost every year, at the same date and then on other occasions determined always by a particular event or circumstance, the papers of Quebec City published poems by Crémazie that earned him a certain fame until, in 1858, his *Drapeau de Carillon* established him as "national poet."

As 1860 approached, the back of the Crémazie bookstore became a kind of club, where those who took part in the literary movement later known under the rather too formal title of the Quebec school dropped in and sometimes assembled. Chance brought together there Étienne PARENT, François-Xavier Garneau*, Abbé Jean-Baptiste-Antoine Ferland*, Pierre-Joseph-Olivier Chauveau*, Joseph-Charles Taché*, Antoine Gérin-Lajoie*, Abbé Henri-Raymond Casgrain*, François-Alexandre-Hubert La Rue*, Alfred Garneau, Léon-Pamphile Le May*, Louis-Honoré Fréchette*, and a number of others, all friends of books and of Crémazie. It was the initiative of some members of this group that brought about the launching of two literary magazines *Les Soirées canadiennes* and *Le Foyer canadien*.

To enhance the quality of his commercial imports, and no doubt also through a desire to go to the sources of culture, Crémazie felt a need to travel to France himself. He made his first trip at the end of 1850 and stayed the whole month of January 1851 in Paris, and he apparently returned there each year from 1853 to 1860. Even when his bookshop was growing in importance and approaching its zenith, and at the same time his popularity as a poet was becoming established, during the years 1855–57 and after, Crémazie had not changed his reserved and somewhat austere habits. At Quebec, where success seemed to smile on his every undertaking, people remarked on his modesty. But in Paris he appeared to be quite a different person. Perhaps despite himself, he played the comedy of the rich man of the world, so much so that he literally took leave of his senses. To maintain this absurd reputation, he placed extravagant orders with his suppliers for goods as costly as they were unusual: books, of course, of all kinds and prices, but also wines, cheeses, toys, religious objects, work boxes, and even umbrellas. A number of these articles, unsaleable because they were so expensive, could not even be displayed, for want of space.

Meanwhile, under its prosperous and opulent exterior, the Crémazie firm was already experiencing serious financial difficulties. To quiet his creditors the bookseller-poet first obtained bank loans, then had recourse to the reasonable security guaranteed to him by three of his friends in particular: Joseph-Édouard Cauchon*, Augustin Côté*, and François Évanturel*. But after some time, for lack of authentic notes properly endorsed, Crémazie began to forge bills on which he counterfeited his friends' signatures and which he went to usurers to get changed. In the long run sums were involved which are impossible to specify but which were certainly astronomical for the period. This incredible game – which constitutes the enigma of Crémazie's otherwise likeable personality – lasted several years, until catastrophe came in the autumn of 1862. In the evening of 10 November some ten friends, along with the poet's two brothers, met to try to save him. But Crémazie knew that salvation was materially impossible, and did not appear at the meeting. The next day he secretly fled his native town and his country for a destination that long remained unknown outside the limited circle of his family. He took refuge in France, concealing his identity under the assumed name of Jules Fontaine. We do not know what sum Crémazie's frauds totalled. At the time of proceedings instituted against the broker John R. Healey, who had put some of the former bookseller's notes into circulation, the figure of $100,000 was mentioned, but it was not certain that this was correct, for Crémazie had acted in an incredibly chaotic fashion. What was certain was that the notes were numerous, "as numerous," Judge Lewis Thomas Drummond* said, "as the waves of the St Lawrence breaking against the sidewalks of Rue Saint-Pierre."

Having been so happy on each of his preceding voyages, finding in France as it were the ideal country, the source and model of his cherished Canada, Crémazie lived all the more wretchedly when he saw himself stranded there as an exile and separated completely from his own country. He entered France with his health already impaired by the nightmare years he had endured. Despite the help and affection he received constantly from a few French friends – in particular the Bossange family – he fell prey to sickness, poverty, solitude, and boredom, and was reduced to complete apathy toward poetic creation. The modest position he held in the business house of Hector Bossange, then in the shipping agency of Gustave Bossange, required him to live in turn in Paris, Bordeaux, and Le Havre. In 1870–71, during the

Crémazie

Franco-Prussian War, he experienced the siege of Paris, and he made a detailed account of it in the form of a diary; during the Commune he was at Orléans.

Except during the few weeks he spent in the company of his friend Abbé Casgrain, in 1873–74, and the short visits he received from the occasional Canadian traveller, Crémazie's contacts with his native land were maintained through correspondence with his mother and brothers, or, through the intermediary of his family, with a handful of old friends. Although he was the sole author of his misfortune, his reputation among his compatriots never lost its lustre. In 1862, at the very time when he disappeared from the local scene, he was at the height of his glory in Quebec as a poet. *Les Soirées canadiennes* had just published, at the end of October, the first part of a long poem entitled *Promenade de trois morts*, and promised for the next number a sequel, which was always hoped for and never written. The bankruptcy of the bookshop and the loss of the poet were a veritable thunder-clap in the Quebec sky. However guilty he might be, Crémazie, in the eyes of the public, appeared rather as an unfortunate victim. During the proceedings of 1864 he was never directly attacked. The tendentious pamphlet prepared by Louis-Michel DARVEAU which was published at that time, called *Cause célèbre; procès de J.-R. Healey, en juillet 1864 . . . affaire Crémazie*, questioned not the conduct of the poet but that of his alleged accomplices. In 1868, 75 prominent ecclesiastics and laymen addressed a petition to the Canadian government requesting royal pardon for Crémazie; from 1869 to 1872 a committee was engaged in seeking funds to pay off the exile's debts. But all these steps were futile, either because of the inextricable disorder in which Crémazie had kept his affairs, or because of the fatal powerlessness of the law: not only was the royal pardon not necessary, but it was legally impossible, for no proceedings had been instituted against the poet. Other efforts – those of Luc Letellier* de Saint-Just in 1874–75 and Gédéon Ouimet* in 1877 – not to repatriate Crémazie but to provide him with material assistance on a proper scale – could not be given concrete form because of the accidents of political life. Fate willed both that the poet should be the object of national veneration and that he should lead a tragic existence until the end. In profound isolation, after more than 16 years of exile, he died at Le Havre, and was buried in the cemetery of Ingouville, where there exists no trace even of his remains.

For a century Octave Crémazie's fame has been interpreted in diverse ways, but it has known no decline. His contemporaries and the generations following have long continued to admire and extol some of his ringing stanzas. But for the man of today, touched more by the exemplary misfortune of the poet and by the weaknesses of work brutally interrupted at a time when it should have begun to emerge from its stumbling beginnings, Crémazie is pre-eminently the literary symbol of French Canadian estrangement.

Whatever may be the variety and sometimes the exoticism of the subjects with which chance or circumstance inspired him, the basic incentive behind Crémazie's poetic writings is the expression of a certain national identity. To this is due the fact that he is considered the sonorous echo of his people. Indeed his most justly famous poems belong in a characteristic fashion to what the critic Gilles Marcotte calls the poetry of exile. Exile in time, for the poet, unable to accept fully the material conditions of a thankless, disappointing age, cultivates a longing for a glorious past, irretrievably gone. Like his *Vieux soldat canadien*, Crémazie compared "the happiness of yesteryear with the sorrows of today." He exclaimed: "Who will give us back that heroic age?" Exile also in space, for the spiritual country is France, with which one vainly tries to identify oneself through the bookish, poorly assimilated image one has of it. Like his hero in the *Drapeau de Carillon*, "he was exiled in his own native land." The Canadian reality, even the landscape, is described by means of commonplaces, in tones that betoken artificiality and contrivance. Thus, in this country where two centuries have established them, Crémazie and the Canadien of whom he is the voice lead only an illusory existence: their soul is elsewhere. It is therefore not surprising that the *Promenade de trois morts*, the longest and most original – although unfinished – poem of Crémazie should concern itself in morbid complacency with a macabre and tormenting obsession for death. With an expressive sincerity, and probably without realizing it, the poet grasps only the dark side of life or shadows that cannot endure.

Certainly the tribulations Crémazie experienced in his last years at Quebec must have aggravated his fundamental melancholia. He exercised his ingenuity to banish from his poetry any direct allusion to his personal sufferings – yet they are nevertheless to be found there. In any case his poems are truly a mirror held up to the generations who have recognized themselves in them. When he was in his beloved France, uprooted and withdrawn into his private drama, he wrote no more verses.

The 40 or so poems of unequal quality composed between 1849 and 1862, which constitute his work, reflect his somewhat chance apprenticeship to the poet's trade. The awkwardness and heaviness of the best pieces are due in part to the author's curious method: he would elaborate the poems at full length in his head and write them down only when they were complete. But it is clear also that Crémazie, imbued like his contemporaries with the most superficial rhetoric of French romanticism, could not, consciously or by instinct, conceive of poetry as being above all a creation in language. A sincere rimester visited by an eloquent muse, he remained throughout his active career as much exiled from true poetry as he was subsequently to be from his country. When, able to profit by sufficient perspective, he passed severe judgement on the *Drapeau de Carillon*, his most admired poem, no doubt he saw better what he should have done. But the sentence he wrote on 27 Jan. 1867 to his friend Abbé Casgrain, when the latter urged him to take up his pen again, expresses in the most poignant way the destiny that is acknowledged today to be his, that of the *poète maudit*, inevitably condemned to silence: "The finest poems are those that one dreams of but does not write."

On the other hand, his work in prose, fragmentary though it is, reveals an authentic writer. The *Journal du siège de Paris* is a spontaneous document of great psychological value, showing the quality of soul and intelligence of the person who kept it during those historic months. Without affectation – for these 200 pages were not in any way destined for publication – Crémazie succeeds in communicating in the most concrete and convincing fashion the distress and privations that a simple, lucid, and magnanimous man experienced in a daily tragedy. Furthermore, his correspondence with his family, which is only partially known and which one hopes will some day be discovered in its entirety, is direct, natural, moving, and touching. Finally, in his letters to Abbé Casgrain, Crémazie, engaging in lively and candid criticism of himself and others, or airing his views in random fashion on the cultural problems of his country, displayed a literary sensitivity unlike any other to be found in French Canada in the whole of the 19th century.

Thus Crémazie, a mythical figure among poets, remains for posterity a skilful prose-writer, living still despite his place in the span of time.

RÉJEAN ROBIDOUX

[Crémazie's poems, which first appeared in newspapers or as leaflets, were collected in two publications by the efforts of Abbé H.-R. Casgrain: 25 poems appear in the 2nd volume of *La littérature canadienne de 1850 à 1860, publiée par la direction du "Foyer canadien"* (2v., Québec, 1863–64), II, 9–122; and in the *Œuvres complètes de Octave Crémazie publiées sous le patronage de l'Institut canadien de Québec* (Montréal, 1882). The latter, prepared by Casgrain in collaboration with H.-J.-B. Chouinard*, does not include all Crémazie's poems. In fact, P.-G. Roy*, in *A propos de Crémazie* (Québec, 1945), lists the titles and publication data of four pieces which appeared in newspapers and are not in *La littérature canadienne* or *Œuvres complètes*. In addition, Roy reproduces in full *Le premier de l'an 1849*, the first poem Crémazie published. To this list must be added the poem which serves as an epigraph to *Les Anciens Canadiens* by Philippe AUBERT de Gaspé and which Casgrain maintains was written by Crémazie.

Crémazie's correspondence with his family is found in part in the *Œuvres complètes*, which includes 37 letters; in *A propos de Crémazie*, Roy adds to these certain others, including an important one from the poet to his mother, dated 6 Aug. 1872. The letters Octave Crémazie wrote to Casgrain and drafts of the latter's to Crémazie are found in the ASQ, Fonds Casgrain, Lettres, III, VII, IX. In his introduction to the *Œuvres complètes*, Casgrain published these letters, omitting some details. Finally, the last prose narrative by Crémazie, the *Journal du siège de Paris* is included in the *Œuvres complètes*. R.R.]

[H.-R. Casgrain], *Œuvres complètes de l'abbé H.-R. Casgrain* (4v., Montréal, 1896), I, 353–75. *Cause célèbre; procès de J.-R. Healey, en juillet 1864, sous la présidence de l'hon. juge Drummond; affaire Crémazie* ([Québec, 1864]). H.-R. Casgrain, *Octave Crémazie* (Bibliothèque canadienne, Collection Montcalm, Montréal, 1912). Michel Dassonville, *Crémazie* (Classiques canadiens, 6, Montréal et Paris, 1956). Gilles Marcotte, *Une littérature qui se fait, essais critiques sur la littérature canadienne-française* (Collection Constantes, 2, Montréal, 1962), 65–70, 71–83. Séraphin Marion, *Les lettres canadiennes d'autrefois* (9v., Hull et Ottawa, 1939–58), V. Fernand Rinfret, *Études sur la littérature canadienne-française; première série, les poètes: Octave Crémazie* (Saint-Jérôme, Qué., 1906). H.-R. Casgrain, "Le mouvement littéraire en Canada," *Le Foyer canadien, recueil littéraire et historique* (Québec), IV (1866), 1–31. Jeanne Le Ber, "L'amitié littéraire de Crémazie et de Casgrain," *Archives des lettres canadiennes* (Ottawa), I (1961), 184–208. Réjean Robidoux, "*Les Soirées canadiennes* et *le Foyer Canadien* dans le mouvement littéraire québécois de 1860, étude d'histoire littéraire," *Revue de l'université d'Ottawa*, XXVIII (1958), 411–52. G.-A. Vachon, "L'ère du silence et l'âge de la parole," *Études françaises, revue des lettres françaises et canadiennes-françaises* (Montréal), III (1967), 309–21.

CRONYN, BENJAMIN, Church of England clergyman and first bishop of Huron; b. at Kilkenny, Ireland, 11 July 1802, son of Thomas Cronyn, of Kilkenny, and Margaret Barton; d. at London, Ont., 21 Sept. 1871.

Benjamin Cronyn was educated at Kilkenny College, and at 15 entered Trinity College in Dublin where he received his BA in 1822, MA in

Cronyn

1825, and, later, DD in 1855. He was divinity prizeman in 1824. In 1825 he was ordained deacon and served as curate at Tunstall, Kirkby Lonsdale, in Lancashire, England, until 1827 when he was ordained priest. He was then curate until 1832 of Kilcommock, Longford, in the diocese of Ardagh, Ireland.

In 1832 the archbishop of Dublin wrote to Archdeacon John Strachan* in York (Toronto) inquiring about openings in Canada for Protestant clergymen who "are thinking of emigration from finding themselves destitute thro' the existing troubles of the Church." Cronyn and his family were among the many Irish Protestants who decided to emigrate to Upper Canada. They sailed in the summer of 1832 on the *Anne of Halifax* chartered by a group of friends. Among them were Anne Margaret Hume, widow of the Reverend Dominick Edward Blake of County Wicklow, with her two sons, the Reverend Dominick Edward and William Hume*, and her daughters Frances Mary and Wilhelmina, wife of the Reverend Charles Crosbie Brough.

Cronyn had married in Ireland Margaret Ann Bickerstaff of Lislea, Longford, in December 1826. Of their seven children, Margaret married Edward Blake*, son of William Hume Blake; Verschoyle married Edward's sister, Sophia; Rebecca married Edward's brother, Samuel Hume Blake*; Benjamin married Mary G. Goodhue, daughter of George Jervis Goodhue*. Margaret Ann Cronyn died 29 Oct. 1866, and Benjamin was married again at Dublin, Ireland, on 16 March 1868, to Martha Collins; there were no children from this marriage.

Arriving in York, Cronyn met Strachan and Bishop Charles James Stewart* of Quebec, who licensed him to Adelaide. This township was then being settled by many of Cronyn's Irish friends, and there had apparently been an understanding that Cronyn would minister to them. On their way to Adelaide in November, Cronyn and his family were overtaken by darkness in London. He preached there on the following day, and, so effective was his sermon, he was persuaded to remain. Stewart subsequently authorized the change, appointing Cronyn to London and parts adjacent and Dominick Blake to the Adelaide charge.

London at this time was a settlement six years old. The Reverend Benjamin Lundy*, a pioneer abolitionist, visited the village in 1832, and told of the recently finished court house, two houses of public worship being built, three hotels, and six general merchant stores; he enumerated its variety of craftsmen, who were necessary in a new community. He estimated that there were about 130 buildings, nearly all frame, in the village. There were two doctors and two lawyers, and one weekly newspaper, the *Sun*. By this time there were Methodist, Presbyterian, and Church of England congregations in the community, which had a population of about 300.

One of Cronyn's first actions was to move and complete, during the winter of 1832–33, the unfinished church building begun by his predecessor, the Reverend E. J. Boswell. This had been erected on an unsatisfactory site and he located St Paul's Church (which burned in 1844 but was rebuilt in 1846) where St Paul's Cathedral now stands. Cronyn held services in London and at various stations in London Township. His son, Verschoyle, wrote that he was a "fearless horseman" and "expert swimmer," necessary attainments for travelling in his extensive field.

Under the terms of the Canada Act of 1791, the British government had power to authorize the erection of rectories in the province endowed with glebe lands. Implementation was delayed until 1836 when Sir John Colborne*, acting on an 1832 dispatch from the colonial secretary, Lord Goderich, ordered the preparation of patents setting up 57 rectories (Colborne actually signed only 44 before leaving the colony). Both London and London Township were among the rectories established. Cronyn thus held and received the income from two rectories, the only clergyman in Upper Canada to do so. He gave up the township rectory (now St John's, Arva) in 1841. In 1838 he was able to augment his income by taking on the duties of chaplain at London: the War Office had deemed it expedient in 1832 to discontinue the appointment of chaplains to the forces at certain Canadian posts and to employ a resident "Clergyman of the Established Church." (When Archdeacon Alexander Neil BETHUNE preached in St Paul's in 1848, the military constituted most of the congregation.)

Support from overseas for the church in Upper Canada was vital in these years, and in January 1837 Cronyn accompanied William BETTRIDGE to England to solicit aid. They separated in July when Cronyn went to Ireland to deal with family affairs and to carry on there the campaign for men and money.

The population in the western parts of Upper Canada increased rapidly and by 1847 it was clear that the diocese of Toronto should be divided. Legal and financial obstacles stood in the way. Strachan took the lead in overcoming the former, by obtaining an act in 1857 which resolved any doubt as to the right of the Canadian church to meet in synods to elect bishops rather than having appointments made from England. Cronyn took care of finance. With other clergy and laity in the western part of the diocese, he organized an episcopal fund committee which raised the £10,000 endowment stipulated by the crown, and he must be given credit for the success of this campaign. With all barriers removed, the synod of Toronto met on 17 June 1857 to set up the present diocese of Huron (a name chosen and applied by Strachan in May), comprising the 13 counties in the southwestern part of the province.

The choice of a bishop precipitated an unseemly, if not scurrilous and libellous, controversy in the pages of the *London Free Press* and other newspapers of the region (the documents were reprinted in a pamphlet a few days before the election). The names of A. N. Bethune and Cronyn were put forward, and lines were drawn between high and low church. Bethune, the candidate favoured by Strachan, was challenged for his support of Puseyism and Tractarianism and tenets which led "downward to Rome"; Cronyn was identified with "Calvinistic cliqueism." The theological arguments degenerated into a personal attack on Cronyn, who was accused of neglect of his duties to his parishioners, to prisoners in the jail, and to the troops when he was chaplain. He was also accused of being a speculator in land and "an appropriator to his own use, of the property of his parish."

Cronyn had, it is true, taken on many responsibilities in his early days in London. He ministered to those who had been condemned to death for their part in the events of 1837–38, and the troops of the garrison attended his church while stationed in London. How far he carried out the other duties associated with the work of a chaplain cannot be shown. His land transactions were complicated, profitable, and, according to some, devious. In a letter to the *London Free Press* the churchwardens of St Paul's discussed the accusations, and strongly claimed that church welfare rather than speculation was his motive in negotiations over land which later became valuable.

On 8 July 1857 the delegates met in St Paul's Church. There were 42 clergy licensed in the 39 parishes in the new diocese, and two laymen from each parish (with one vote; if they did not agree they would not vote). Bishop Strachan presided over the election, which resulted in 22 of the clergy and 23 of the laity voting for Cronyn, and 20 clergymen and ten laymen for Bethune. Six parishes had not voted, presumably because the two lay delegates could not agree. Thus Cronyn was elected on the first ballot.

Many explanations of the result have been given. The clerical vote was greatly influenced by the number of Irish clergy serving in the new diocese. Of the 42 clergy voting, nine were Trinity College, Dublin, men, and at least another six had been born in Ireland or had an Irish background. The low church Irish clergy had more sympathy for Cronyn's religious views than those of Bethune. Furthermore, the endowment had been raised locally, and the lay contributors also preferred the churchmanship of Cronyn whom they knew and who had led the campaign for funds.

Cronyn was consecrated at Lambeth on 28 Oct. 1857 by the archbishop of Canterbury acting under Queen Victoria's mandate, the last Canadian bishop required to go to England for consecration. He also visited Ireland where he recruited Edward Sullivan*, later bishop of Algoma, James Carmichael*, later bishop of Montreal, and John Philip DuMoulin*, later bishop of Niagara. After his return he was enthroned in St Paul's Cathedral on 24 March 1858.

In his charge delivered to the clergy of the diocese at his first visitation in June 1859, Cronyn told something of his activities as bishop: "Since April, 1858, I have visited eighty-four congregations in the Diocese, and preached 130 sermons; I have confirmed 1,453 candidates, consecrated five churches and two burial grounds, ordained fifteen Deacons and three Priests, and travelled in the discharge of these duties 2,452 miles." At the same time he made clear his evangelical views. He emphasized the importance of preaching, saying that "Amongst the many means of grace which God has appointed in the Church . . . the preaching of the word stands pre-eminent. The pulpit is the Ministers' great battle-field." He condemned "auricular confession and priestly absolution," "penances and self-inflicted torments," and "purgatory, with its thousands of years of torment," stressing instead the need of conversion. The 39 Articles to him were the "*ultima ratio* in all questions of doctrine," and "where any of our formularies are expressed in ambiguous language and appear inconsistent with the plain statements of the articles, we are bound to interpret the former by the latter."

His evangelical views soon involved him in a serious difference of opinion with Strachan. In 1858 some graduates of Trinity College in Toronto, a college instituted by the bishop, expressed views concerning the character and doctrines of the Roman Catholic Church which disturbed Cronyn. He concluded that these views were traceable to the teaching they had received. In April 1860 he wrote to Strachan expressing his disapproval of the college "in many things" and declined to nominate the five councillors whom he had the right to name. At the June 1860 synod of Huron one of Cronyn's own clergy, the Reverend Adam

Cronyn

Townley* of Paris, proposed a resolution which stated in part: "this Synod respectfully requests the Lord Bishop [Cronyn] to adopt such means as in his wisdom he may see good as shall tend to secure the hearty co-operation of all Churchmen in support of Trinity College, Toronto." A lay representative asked Cronyn to give his opinion on the motion and he replied that he could not approve of it: "I think it dangerous to the young men educated there, more particularly if they are educated for the ministry." He also said that he would not for any consideration send a son of his to the institution nor could he see any prospect of effecting a change in the teaching there.

In a pastoral letter in July 1860 Cronyn gave his recollection of what he had said at the June synod of that year, and attacked "The Provost's Catechism" which he claimed was placed in the hands of every student entering Trinity College. The views put forth in the catechism were to him "unsound and un-Protestant" and dangerous in the extreme. This attack launched a lengthy controversy between Cronyn and Provost George Whitaker* of Trinity College, which was fully canvassed by the press and in many pamphlets. The Corporation of Trinity College eventually submitted the documents in the dispute to the bishops of the church in British North America, requesting them to declare whether they found any of the doctrines of the provost "unsound or unscriptural, contrary to the teaching of the Church of England, or dangerous in their tendency, or leading to the Church of Rome." The judgement of the bishops, with Cronyn dissenting, was that several of the points in the provost's teaching had reference to matters about which the church is silent, but which a theological professor might well discuss. Such statements, however, were private opinions.

Cronyn's distrust of Trinity College, as well as the urgent need for more clergy in his diocese, had suggested to him the desirability of establishing his own college in which young men might be trained for the ministry under his eye. In his charge to the synod in 1862 he admitted that he had entertained the idea for some time. In 1863 there were only 76 clergy in the diocese and more than 50 townships were without the ministrations of a clergyman. The need for a theological college was clear.

He had already secured in 1861 the services of Dr Isaac Hellmuth*, a man ideally suited for his purposes, to solicit aid in England for the erection of his projected school of theology. In 1862 Hellmuth persuaded the wealthy Reverend Alfred Peache of Downend, Bristol, to contribute £5,000 as an endowment for a divinity chair in the new college, to be called the "Peache chair." The appointee, the first being Hellmuth himself, was required to "be a Clergyman of the United Church of England and Ireland of strictly Protestant and Evangelical principles and of approved learning ability piety and holiness of life holding and continuing to hold the same as expressed in the Thirty-nine Articles interpreted in their plain and natural sense." The Colonial and Continental Church Society, with which Hellmuth had been associated, also proved to be a friend to the college from the first. The accent on "Protestant and Evangelical principles" produced financial support in England which almost certainly would not otherwise have come. Cronyn applied to the legislature for a charter and on 5 May 1863 the act to incorporate Huron College received royal assent. The college opened on 2 December.

Such was the uncompromising theology of Cronyn that when he received an invitation from the archbishop of Canterbury to attend the first Lambeth Conference in September 1867, he viewed it with suspicion. The conference had developed from a suggestion of the provincial synod of Canada, that a "Pan-Anglican Conference of Bishops" be called to discuss common problems [see James BEAVEN]. One was the privy council decision of 1865 in the case of Bishop Colenso, which had put the validity of all documents appointing the bishops in self-governing colonies in doubt; another was the effect of the publication in 1860 of the theologically controversial *Essays and reviews*.

Cronyn gave his opinion of the proposed gathering in no uncertain terms in his charge to synod in 1867: "It is evident that his Grace intends that all should understand that the meeting is to be regarded merely as a social gathering. . . . Of course, all shades of opinion, recognised or not recognised in the church, would be represented there, from the almost full-blown Romanism of those who boldly profess to celebrate the mass in our churches, with incense and the idolatrous worship of the consecrated elements, to the feeble, timid and dishonest efforts of incipient innovators, who are endeavoring, bit by bit, to introduce the exploded and condemned ritual of former days, and thus in time to effect the unprotestantizing of our church, by accustoming the people to the ritualism of Rome, and thus undoing the work of the Reformation." Nor was he alone in his opposition, for the archbishop of York and the dean of Westminster also would not cooperate.

The synod nevertheless requested Cronyn to attend the conference, which he did "with much diffidence and hesitation." He was not unhappy over the proceedings, and on the invitation of the

Colonial and Continental Church Society he preached "in the two English Churches" in Paris. He visited the Paris exhibition of that year and was surprised to find that the "circulation of God's Holy Word, and of religious publications of various kinds" was being extensively carried on. He was not so happy with what he saw at St Alban's, Holborn, London. He left that church humiliated and grieved, and more than ever convinced of the necessity of guarding against the introduction "even of the smallest things savouring of those superstitious observances which can hardly be distinguished from the ceremonial of the Church of Rome."

While in England, Cronyn interviewed the secretary of the Society for the Propagation of the Gospel, who told him that the society had decided to reduce its annual grant to the diocese from £1,200 to £800. The reduction meant that assistance to ten missionaries had been withdrawn. In order to make up the deficiency Cronyn suggested at the 1868 synod that a general appeal should be made throughout the diocese. The synod responded to the proposal by launching a "Sustentation Fund" appeal which by 1869 had reached nearly $30,000. Cronyn advocated making the fund sufficiently large to provide "a moderate endowment in the Diocese for all time to come," as the voluntary system had never been found sufficient to supply the spiritual wants of the people; by 1871 the fund had reached $68,000. Cronyn had again shown his ability for fund raising, as he had in 1854.

A measure of Cronyn's contribution to the diocese is provided by his report to his final synod in 1871. At that time there were 88 active clergymen and one superannuated. During the preceding year he had confirmed 1,371 candidates, preached 65 sermons, delivered 43 addresses to candidates, ordained seven priests and six deacons, consecrated six churches, opened two churches for divine worship, visited 67 congregations in ten counties, and travelled 3,355 miles.

Cronyn's evangelical views, maintained by the early Irish clergy in the diocese and by the many who followed them, were sustained by the teaching at Huron College. They coloured the theology of the diocese of Huron for many years after his death. He must not, however, be judged by his theological views alone. His practical contributions were lasting and incalculable. The number of clergymen in the newly formed diocese had more than doubled by 1871. He had opened no fewer than 101 churches. Parishes in the same period increased in number from 39 to 160. Of the latter 15 were vacant, suggesting a need for perhaps an additional eight clergy. Huron College, the institu-

tion which Cronyn had founded on his own initiative, supplied over the years many clergy not only for his own diocese but for the Canadian church at large and the mission field. From Huron College, through the efforts of Hellmuth, grew the present University of Western Ontario, which became non-denominational in 1908.

Cronyn was pre-eminent as a judge and recruiter of men. Six of the clergy he ordained during his episcopate (they numbered at least 83) were destined to become bishops: in addition to the three volunteers he brought from Ireland following his consecration he ordained John McLean*, Maurice Scollard Baldwin*, and William Cyprian Pinkham*. He was also a most indefatigable and successful raiser of funds. Philip Carrington was to say: "The new Diocese of Huron, under its energetic and forceful bishop, became a powerhouse for the whole Canadian Church. He was a great fighter, and a great fisher of men."

JAMES J. TALMAN

[The only collection of Cronyn papers is in the library of Huron College, London, Ontario. It is a small collection of documents and letters dealing with the every-day life and business of four generations of the family. The synod office of the diocese of Huron possesses a Cronyn letter book, covering the period 1858–67, which deals with diocesan matters. The John Strachan papers and letter books at PAO contain material from Cronyn between 1840 and 1865. Cronyn was a prolific pamphleteer, and his addresses to synod, although not always printed, give his views and describe his activities in great detail. J.J.T.]

Benjamin Cronyn, *The bishop of Huron to the clerical and lay gentlemen composing the Executive Committee of the Synod of the Diocese of Huron* (n.p., 1860); [ ], *Bishop of Huron's objections to the theological teaching of Trinity College, as now set forth in the letters of Provost Whitaker . . .* (London, C.W., 1862); *A charge delivered to the clergy of the Diocese of Huron, in St. Paul's Cathedral, London, Canada West, at his primary visitation, in June, 1859* (Toronto, 1859). *The bishop of Huron and Trinity College, Toronto* ([London, C.W., 1860]). *The bishop of Huron's objections to the theological teaching of Trinity College, with the provost's reply* (Toronto, 1862). James Bovell, *Defence of doctrinal statements; addressed to the right rev. the lord bishop of Toronto, the right rev. the lord bishop of Huron, and the Corporation of Trinity College . . .* (Toronto, 1860). *The episcopal controversy; being a series of letters written by the respective friends of the Ven. Archdeacon Bethune, D.D., and Dr. Cronyn, rector of London; the two candidates for the bishopric of the western diocese* (London, C.W., 1857). *The gospel in Canada: and its relation to Huron College . . .* (London, C.W., [1865?]). *The judgments of the Canadian bishops, on the documents submitted to them by the Corporation of Trinity College, in relation to the theological teaching of the college* (Toronto, 1863). [J. T. Lewis], *A letter to the right rev. the lord bishop of*

Cunningham

Huron by the lord bishop of Ontario ([n.p., n.d.]).
[A Presbyter], *Strictures on the two letters of Provost Whitaker in answer to charges brought by the lord bishop of Huron against the teaching of Trinity College* (London, C.W., 1861). *The protest of the minority of the Corporation of Trinity College, against the resolution approving of the theological teaching of that institution* (London, C.W., 1864). Adam Townley, *A letter to the lord bishop of Huron: in personal vindication; and on the expediency of a new diocesan college* (Brantford, C.W., 1862). George Whitaker, *Two letters to the lord bishop of Toronto, in reply to charges brought by the lord bishop of Huron against the theological teaching of Trinity College, Toronto* (Toronto, 1860).

Church of England, Synod of the Diocese of Huron, *Minutes*, 1858–71 (London, Ont., 1862–71). *London Free Press*, 8–10 July 1857, 23 Sept. 1871. Upper Canada, House of Assembly, *Appendix to journal*, 1836, app.106, p.60. R. T. Appleyard, "The origins of Huron College in relation to the religious questions of the period," unpublished MA thesis, University of Western Ontario, 1937. A. H. Crowfoot, *Benjamin Cronyn, first bishop of Huron* (London, Ont., 1957). C. H. Mockridge, *The bishops of the Church of England in Canada and Newfoundland ...* (Toronto, 1896), 150–62. J. J. Talman, *Huron College, 1863–1963* (London, Ont., 1963) J. J. and R. D. Talman, *"Western" – 1878–1953* (London, Ont., 1953). Verschoyle Cronyn, "The first bishop of Huron," London and Middlesex Hist. Soc., *Trans.*, III (1911), 53–62. S. W. Horrall, "The clergy and the election of Bishop Cronyn," *Ont. Hist.*, LVIII (1966), 205–20.

CUNNINGHAM, ROBERT, journalist and politician; b. 12 May 1836 at Stewarton, near Kilmarnock, Ayrshire, Scotland, son of John Cunningham and Barbara Newlands; d. 4 July 1874 at St Paul, Minnesota.

Robert Cunningham grew up in Scotland and was educated there. He took a degree in arts at Glasgow College, and then proceeded to the University of London from which he graduated in science. In 1862 he married Annie Brown of Aberdeen, Scotland, and they were to have three daughters and one son. Six years after his marriage Cunningham decided to emigrate to Canada; he settled first in Toronto where he found employment as a journalist. In the winter of 1869 he was sent west as a special correspondent for the Toronto *Globe*, and subsequently the Toronto *Telegraph*, to cover the disturbances at Red River.

The new province of Manitoba seemed to offer ample opportunity to Cunningham, and he quickly determined to locate there permanently. With William Coldwell*, he became, and remained until his death, joint editor and proprietor of the independent Liberal *Manitoban* in Winnipeg; in 1870 he and his partner received the appointment of queen's printer, which may have helped their financial situation. In 1871 Cunningham was named a justice of the peace; he took an active and leading part in the Fenian excitement [*see* O'DONOGHUE], summarily ordering the arrest of two suspects without any real evidence.

Cunningham's newspaper supported the Liberals politically, and he formed a close association with Joseph Dubuc*, member of the Legislative Assembly for Baie de Saint-Paul, and other leaders of the French-speaking community; in this community he saw a reliable political base. At their urging, Cunningham stood for election, successfully, in the federal constituency of Marquette in 1872. One of his agents was Louis Riel*, who served as a returning officer in a poll that went solidly for Cunningham.

As a member of parliament, Cunningham assumed the obligation of representing the interests of the Manitoba Métis community. He assured Riel he would support a general amnesty for all those involved in the Red River disturbance of 1869–70. He was also instrumental in the settling of the Métis land claims; the old settlers were assured of 160 acres plus their rights to the hay privilege on the outer two miles of the river belts, under the terms of the Dominion Lands Act of 1874. That same year he was involved in the scheme to have Riel, elected for the constituency of Provencher, take his seat in the House of Commons despite the charges against him arising from the Red River disturbances.

Devoted as he was to the interests of his constituents, Cunningham was much less attached to the Liberal party. His tendency toward political independence was so obvious that Sir John A. Macdonald* invited him to the Conservative caucus in the autumn of 1873. Cunningham had no intention of being trapped in the aftermath of the Canadian Pacific Railway scandal, and ignored Macdonald's offer. He ran again as a Liberal in 1874, and was returned handily. With his party in power, Cunningham found it a distinct advantage to vote regularly with the Liberals. On 7 May 1874, Antoine-Aimé Dorion* announced Cunningham's appointment to the Council of the North-West Territories, but he did not take up his new appointment. He died in July of that year in St Paul, Minnesota, while returning to the west.

Cunningham's career reflected the instability of a new province. His tendency toward independent action, and his concern for the Métis community for which he spoke, made him a somewhat difficult colleague in his political party. His sudden death deprived Manitoba of an effective representative and journalist.

J. E. REA

PAM, Adams George Archibald, 1870–74; Alexander Morris, Ketcheson collection, correspondence, 1872–74; Louis Riel papers, correspondence and papers, 1870–74; Settlement and pioneers, Robert Cunningham, 1872–74. Begg and Nursey, *Ten years in Winnipeg*, 4, 6, 51–52, 56, 59, 68, 71, 96, 99. *Manitoba Free Press* (Winnipeg), 1872–74. *Manitoban* (Winnipeg), 1870–74. *Can. parl. comp.*, *1874*, 159–60.

CURRIE, DONALD, educator, journalist, and civil servant; b. between 1831 and 1834 at West River, P.E.I.; d. 9 March 1880 in Charlottetown, P.E.I.

After completing his education at the Central Academy, Charlottetown, and the Free Church Academy, Halifax, N.S., Donald Currie became a teacher in the public schools of rural Prince Edward Island. On 1 Feb. 1859 he was appointed assistant master of the Central Academy, a position he held until the new Conservative government replaced the academy with Prince of Wales College 16 months later. Currie then turned to journalism, first writing for James Barrett Cooper* of the *Monitor*, whom he left in 1861 for David Laird* of the *Protestant and Evangelical Witness*. The role of religion in education was a dominant issue in the early 1860s, and Laird's paper was the most strident of the Conservative and Protestant camp. Many years later, James Hayden Fletcher, a fellow editor, recalled that at this time Currie was a rabid partisan, and "could see nothing good in a political opponent."

When controversies with less sectarian content arose, Laird changed the name of his paper to the *Patriot*, and placed more emphasis upon secular affairs. Currie became his associate editor in 1865, and after 18 months they were able to make the *Patriot* into the first successful semi-weekly journal on the Island in many years. By 1871 it was probably the leading newspaper in the colony; its editorial policy was strongly anti-confederation, and the two editors eventually left the Conservative party because of the strength of pro-confederate elements within it. They opposed the railway legislation of the premier, James Colledge Pope*, on the grounds that the consequent financial burden would force the colony into confederation.

In a by-election held on 5 July 1871, Laird defeated James Duncan, the newly appointed chairman of the Railway Commission. Currie's role became that of an aide to Laird both in politics and in journalism. When the latter was made by Alexander Mackenzie* federal minister of the interior in late 1873, Currie, who had occupied minor bureaucratic posts, was appointed collector of customs for Charlottetown. He con-

tinued to hold the office until a few months before his death from consumption in 1880. He was survived by a wife and several children.

Currie's main contribution to Island public life, particularly after the founding of the *Patriot*, was his work as a journalist. He was generally admitted to be an able writer, and was reputed to have played an indispensable role in the anti-railway campaign of 1871 and 1872 which propelled Laird into a successful political career. When Currie died, Henry Lawson, who was then editor and proprietor, wrote that "as editor of the *Patriot* he made this journal a power in the land."

IAN ROSS ROBERTSON

[PRO, CO 226/89, 212. Currie's editorials appeared regularly in the *Monitor* (Charlottetown), 1860–61, the *Protestant and Evangelical Witness* (Charlottetown), 1861–65, and the *Patriot* (Charlottetown) 1865–80. Unfortunately there is no way of knowing which commentaries were written by him and which by his associates. For particular details of his journalistic career *see: Presbyterian and Evangelical Protestant Union* (Charlottetown), 30 March, 20 April 1876, and *Patriot*, 21 April 1876. For obituaries *see: Examiner* (Charlottetown), 10 March 1880, and *Patriot*, 11, 13 March 1880. *See also*: J. H. Fletcher, "Newspaper life and newspaper men," *Prince Edward Island Magazine* (Charlottetown), II (May 1900), 74–75. Robertson, "Religion, politics, and education in PEI," especially 228–46. S. N. Robertson, "The public school system," in *Past and present of Prince Edward Island . . .*, ed. D. A. MacKinnon and A. B. Warburton (Charlottetown, [1906]), 370a. I.R.R.]

CUSHING, LEMUEL, pioneer of the Ottawa valley, businessman of Chatham, Que., volunteer militiaman during the 1837 insurrection; b. 29 April 1806 at Trois-Rivières, L.C., eighth child of Job Cushing and Sarah (Sally) Rice; d. 18 May 1875 at Montreal, Que., and was buried in Chatham.

Lemuel Cushing belonged to an illustrious English family which crossed to America in the 17th century, in the wake of the *Mayflower*. On 10 Aug. 1638 Matthew Cushing had taken up residence at Hingham in Massachusetts, not far from Boston. His descendants emigrated to Canada when the government of Lower Canada opened the Eastern Townships to settlement. In the autumn of 1798 Elmer and Job Cushing received uncleared land in Shipton Township, which today forms part of Richmond County. Six years later Job moved to Trois-Rivières, where Lemuel was born.

Lemuel was eight years old when his family went to live in Montreal. On his father's death, 21 Jan. 1821, he set out for the United States,

Daly

where he apparently lived for some months at Peacham, Vermont. But at the time of the American infiltration into the Ottawa valley he returned to Canada, to take part in the settling of Chatham Township. Although he was only 16 and had little capital, Lemuel Cushing started a retail business on his own account, at the very place where the municipality of Cushing is today, between Carillon and Grenville. Thanks to his energy, perseverance, and strong constitution, he triumphed over seemingly insurmountable odds and became very rich. On three occasions he was the owner of the famous Caledonia Springs. In 1859 he bought an island in the country of his ancestors, in the harbour of Portland, Maine; Cushing Island became a renowned tourist centre because of Ottawa House, which Cushing built there.

As a rich businessman, Cushing naturally enjoyed great prestige in Chatham Township. For more than 40 years he was one of its justices of the peace, with a jurisdiction extending for a time to the town of Montreal. He was successively mayor of the municipality of Chatham Township, from 1861 to 1872, and warden of the electoral constituency of Argenteuil until his death.

At the time of the 1837 insurrection Cushing had armed a group of volunteers, and with them went to the defence of the English flag. His intervention prevented the pillaging of Saint-Eustache and the destruction of the registry office of Saint-Benoît, where precious documents were held.

On 25 Aug. 1836 Lemuel Cushing had married Catherine Hutchins, of Lachute. Thirteen children were born of this marriage, among them eight sons, who were all active and powerful businessmen. Moreover, one of these sons, Lemuel Cushing (1842–81), won distinction in the parliament of Canada and at the bar of Montreal.

Lemuel Cushing died on 18 May 1875; he had contributed substantially to the development of the Ottawa valley, and the considerable influence that this development has had on the economic destiny of the province of Quebec is well known.

ANDRÉE DÉSILETS

AJTR, Registre d'état civil. Archives de la municipalité du canton de Chatham (Saint-Philippe-d'Argenteuil, Qué.). Private Archives, Bruce Wright (Fredericton, N.B.), 30, pp.13327, 13333; 37, pp.17127–28 (microfilm at PAC). PAC, MG 30, D62 (Audet papers), 9, pp.400–4; RG 1, L3, C bundle 3, no.110; L3ᴸ, pp.66528, 66556; L1, 42, p.423. *Argenteuil Advertiser* (Lachute, Que.), 9 June 1875. *Montreal Herald*, 20 May 1875. P.-G. Roy, *Les noms géographiques de la province de Québec* (Lévis, Qué., 1906), 142–43. Lemuel Cushing, *The genealogy of the Cushing family* (Montreal, 1877). Cyrus Thomas, *History of the counties of Argenteuil, Que., and Prescott, Ont., from the earliest settlement to the present* (Montreal, 1896), 297–99.

D

DALY, JOHN CORRY WILSON, merchant, office-holder, and politician; b. in Liverpool, Eng., 24 March 1796; d. at Stratford, Ont., 1 April 1878.

John Corry Wilson Daly, born into "the better class of Irish society" (his birth occurred in Liverpool while his parents were visiting that city), received a sound education in Ireland before serving in the Royal Navy as a surgeon's assistant. He then emigrated to Cooperstown, New York, and, in 1826, to Hamilton, Upper Canada. There he began a 30-year association with the Canada Company, in 1831 acting as its land agent in what later became the Huron District. In 1833 he moved to Stratford where the Canada Company had already built some shanties; his house was the second frame building in the settlement. He opened the town's first store, and became its first postmaster. By 1841 he had purchased for himself the Canada Company's mill dam and sawmills in the area. Daly also became agent for the Bank of Upper Canada in Stratford.

A Conservative, Daly was much involved in public life. Prior to 1842, Daly was a member of the local Board of Magistrates for the London District. He was elected in 1842 to the Huron District Council as the representative for Downie, Blanshard, and Fullarton townships for a term of three years. In 1845 he decided not to seek another term. His departure from the council was part of a dramatic incident, the "Stratford Riot." The new councillors were chosen on 6 Jan. 1845 at a township meeting attended heavily by both Catholics and Orangemen. Daly, a member of the Church of England, was popular with the Roman Catholic minority in the district, where political and religious animosities had become acute, and, without his knowledge or consent, he was nominated for another term by his Catholic supporters. He was defeated. As justice of the peace, Daly had attempted to ensure order at the meeting by appointing special constables, but after the vote members of the two sides withdrew and began to drink. The result was a riot involving some 80 men, the majority of them Irish Catholics. Daly, summoned to restore order, arrested several rioters and one-month prison terms were eventually meted out to five of the Catholics. Religious tension persisted, but riot was avoided at later township meetings.

Daly was Stratford's first mayor; indeed he held "all the important offices of honour and trust in the town: mayor, coroner, magistrate, militia officer." In 1849 he was instrumental in the establishment of Perth County. He was a lieutenant-colonel in the militia and he helped to set up the first school district in the county. Though often regarded as "the founder of Stratford, Ontario," he was not the first to arrive: the first known settler in Perth County itself was Sebastian Fryfogle. Nonetheless, J. C. W. Daly was a Huron District pioneer whose biography indicates the opportunities available to a man of ability and drive in early settlement days.

Daly married three times. A son, Thomas Mayne*, born to his wife Leonora Mayne, and a grandson, also Thomas Mayne*, were politicians.

DONALD SWAINSON

Illustrated historical atlas of county Perth, Ont. (Toronto, 1879). *Dom. ann. reg., 1878,* 339–40. Wallace, *Macmillan dictionary.* H. F. Gardiner, *Nothing but names: an inquiry into the origin of the names of the counties and townships of Ontario* (Toronto, 1899), 349–50. William Johnston, *History of the county of Perth from 1825 to 1902* (Stratford, Ont., 1903). Robina and K. M. Lizars, *In the days of the Canada Company: the story of the settlement of the Huron tract and a view of the social life of the period, 1825–1850* (Toronto, Montreal, 1896). Swainson, "Personnel of politics." P. E. Lewis, "When orange and green united – the Stratford riot of 1845," *Western Ontario Historical Notes* (London), XX (September 1964), 1–5.

DARVEAU, LOUIS-MICHEL, notary, journalist, and literary critic, b. 29 Sept. 1833 at Quebec, son of Grégoire Darveau and Marie Simpson; d. 24 Aug. 1875 in his native city.

Louis-Michel Darveau entered the Petit Séminaire of Quebec in 1845 and finished his classical education six years later. On 5 May 1856 he became a notary. He seldom acted in this capacity, preferring the more exciting career of a journalist. On 9 March 1858, at Quebec, he started a weekly *L'Observateur*, which had as its motto: "I observe everything; I support the good; I fight the bad and with a laugh I tell each person the truth about himself." Darveau regularly used banter as an antidote for the ridiculous in his contemplation of the world and the life of men. He published the last number of *L'Observateur* on 17 May 1860, and 33 days later started a more moderate weekly *La Réforme*, in which he undertook the defence of the Rouge party.

In May 1863, a new political team headed by John Sandfield MACDONALD and Antoine-Aimé Dorion* came into power; the Liberals were seeking an organ to represent their ideas and approached Darveau with a view to making *La Réforme* a party newspaper. As they considered the weekly a little too radical, Antoine-Aimé Dorion and Luc Letellier* de Saint-Just, the minister of agriculture, negotiated with its owner to get him to change his attitude. They asked him to let them choose another name for the journal, as well as a new editor. Darveau accepted these two conditions, but refused a third: that of allowing the name of a figure-head to appear as owner in place of his. An agreement was finally reached in August: Darveau assumed all the costs of publication in exchange for a promise of political patronage. The last number of *La Réforme* appeared on 18 August, and the first issue of *La Tribune* seven days later. But contrary to the promises they had made, the governing party did not reimburse the owner for the sums spent in maintaining the Liberal paper. This situation irritated Darveau. On 19 September, to force the government's hand, he announced the discontinuance of *La Tribune* as a daily paper speaking for the party in power. He resumed publication five days later, however, after reaching an understanding with Napoléon Aubin*. Aubin induced Darveau to sign an agreement to sell, which was realized on 9 Nov. 1863. Frustrated, the Quebec journalist left for Montreal, where he wrote for a number of papers. He contributed in particular to *Le National*, a paper with liberal and democratic leanings.

In 1864, at the time of an action brought against the broker John R. Healy [see Octave CRÉMAZIE], Darveau prepared a pamphlet, *Cause célèbre; procès de J.-R. Healy, en juillet 1864 . . . affaire Crémazie*, in which he attempted to disparage Joseph-Édouard Cauchon*, François Évanturel*, and Augustin Côté*, his political enemies; these three had stood surety for loans contracted by Octave Crémazie.

Darveau belonged to the school of Louis-Joseph PAPINEAU, Antoine-Aimé Dorion, and Louis-Antoine Dessaulles*. He was a Rouge: an idealist, a patriot, and a democrat. He had close ties with the nationalists of the Saint-Jean-Baptiste societies and the radical liberals of the Institut Canadien of Montreal. He even delivered lectures to these associations, and *L'Observateur* published two of them. In the first, given before the Société Saint-Jean-Baptiste of Quebec on 15 Jan. 1858, he declared his nationalist and

Davis

democratic stand: "we are Catholics and French; we must always be so. We have two principles to defend: Catholicism and democracy; they constitute our nationality. We cannot defend one and deny the other: they are identical." On the national level, Darveau considered the independence of the United Canadas as "the supreme end towards which the destiny of the country is bent." As a French Canadian nationalist, he propagated a veritable mystique of the *Patriotes* of 1837–38. But, for him, the real value of a people is revealed in its literary accomplishments.

Afflicted with partial paralysis in 1867, Darveau was unable to walk and remained tied to an armchair until his death. Despite his illness, he found the courage to become a literary critic and to write several biographies. He published the first portion of them in 1873 in his volume *Nos hommes de lettres*. Although he put into it all his talent and effort, this work is not a masterpiece of literary criticism; he accepted or rejected an author's opinion to the extent that it resembled his own patriotic and democratic ideal. Death struck him down on 24 Aug. 1875 and prevented him from publishing a second volume. On 7 Jan. 1857, at Saint-Roch in Quebec, he had married Henriette Giguère; they had no children.

Louis-Michel Darveau was above all a radical journalist, a supporter of democratic ideas and freedom of expression. Unfortunately, at that period there was no place for independent journalism. Papers that wished to survive had to remain strictly tied to political parties.

PIERRE LANDRY

AJM, Greffe de Louis-Michel Darveau, 1871–1874. AJQ, Greffe de Louis-Michel Darveau, 1856–1868. Archives paroissiales de Saint-Roch (Québec), Registre des baptêmes, mariages et sépultures. ASQ, Fichier des anciens du séminaire. L.-M. Darveau, *Nos hommes de lettres* (Montréal, 1873). *L'Observateur* (Québec), 9 mars 1858–21 mars 1860. *La Réforme* (Québec), 9 juin 1860–18 août 1863. *La Tribune* (Québec), 25 août–15 sept. 1863. Beaulieu et Hamelin, *Journaux du Québec*, 204, 215, 223–24. P.-G. Roy, *Fils de Québec*, IV, 133–35. Lareau, *Hist. de la littérature canadienne*. J.-P. Tremblay, *A la recherche de Napoléon Aubin* (Vie des Lettres canadiennes, 7, Québec, 1969).

DAVIS, JOHN, Baptist minister and author; b. 7 or 8 Nov. 1802 at Liverpool, Eng., son of Richard Davis (or Davies); d. 14 Aug. 1875 at Charlottetown, P.E.I.

John Davis' father was a prominent Baptist clergyman and four of his sons followed in his footsteps. John received his theological education at Horton College, Bradford, Yorkshire, and was ordained at Portsea, Hampshire, probably in 1829. When Richard Davis died in 1832, John wrote *A brief memorial of the Reverend Richard Davis of Walworth* (1833), his first published work.

After serving in several English churches, Davis came to North America, probably in 1845. Following a brief ministry in New Jersey, he became an agent for the American and Foreign Bible Society, which shared his belief in the folly of infant baptism. This belief he later developed in *Circumcision and baptism*, published in Charlottetown in 1867. His work with the society brought him to Yarmouth, N.S., in 1852; he was eventually persuaded to become co-pastor there with the aging Harris Harding*. During his pastorate two additional churches were established in Yarmouth when he sent his own members out to form "colonies" of his church.

In 1855, the year after Harding's death, John Davis resigned to move to New Brunswick. He visited Prince Edward Island as a representative of the New Brunswick Home Mission Board, and was invited to become pastor of the First Baptist Church in Charlottetown. At first he declined, but in 1858 he was persuaded to accept the position to represent both the Nova Scotia and the New Brunswick Home Mission boards on the Island. There he continued his work of colonization by establishing at least two more churches – St Peter's Road and one called North River (West and Clyde River). Davis published *The patriarch of western Nova Scotia: life and times of the late Rev. Harris Harding . . .* in Charlottetown in 1866. He was instrumental in separating the churches in P.E.I. from those of Nova Scotia – a split designed to make work more effective and probably to provide some financial relief to Nova Scotia churches.

John Davis was noted among his contemporaries as a man of vigorous intellect, more interested in truth than in feeling; his preaching was instructive rather than emotional. He was described as an enthusiastic friend of liberty, of conscience, of trade, of the constitution, and of the press. A prominent member of Maritime Baptist circles, he was awarded an honorary MA by Acadia University in 1870. He resigned his pastorate in 1873 and died two years later, having outlived all his children.

MINERVA TRACY

Acadia University Library, "Historical sketch (1836–1874) of the Charlottetown Baptist Church," W. B. Haynes MS; Zion United Baptist Church, Yarmouth, N.S., Notes from the records, 1814–56. John Davis, *Circumcision and baptism* (Charlottetown, 1867); *The patriarch of western Nova Scotia: life and times of the late Rev. Harris Harding, Yarmouth, N.S.,* intro.

214

J. W. Nutting (Charlottetown, 1866). I. E. Bill, *Fifty years with the Baptist ministers and churches of the Maritime provinces of Canada* (Saint John, N.B., 1880), 330–32. J. A. Clark, *A history of the First Baptist Church, Charlottetown* ([Charlottetown, 1959]). W. E. McIntyre, *Baptist authors, a manual of bibliography, 1500–1914* (3v., Montreal and Toronto, [1914]), III, 190. *One hundred and fiftieth anniversary, Zion Baptist Church, Yarmouth, Nova Scotia, 1797–1947* ([Yarmouth, N.S., 1947]). *A short history of the Baptist Church of Charlottetown, Prince Edward Island* (Sunnyside (Charlottetown), [1904]), 9, 10.

DAVIS, MATHILDA, teacher; b. *c.* 1820 in the parish of St Andrews, Red River Settlement, daughter of John Davis, a retired officer of the Hudson's Bay Company; d. 1873 at St Andrews, Man., and buried on 10 December.

Mathilda Davis' parents sent her to England to be educated and upon her return to Red River she devoted her life to teaching. The settlers and HBC families were at this time obliged to have their daughters educated in England as she herself had been. Now, through the efforts of influential citizens, HBC families, and Dr John Bunn*, physician for the company, a young ladies school was started at Red River about 1840, with Mathilda Davis as the teacher. The company provided some assistance and students paid fees: full board and instruction in English, French, and music, $132 per annum; weekly board and instruction, $105; day pupils (who received lunch at the school), $50.

The school was first located in a frame house in St Andrews, the property of Mathilda Davis' brother, an HBC employee at Lower Fort Garry. A stone house (still standing) was completed in front of the wooden one around 1858 and provided living quarters for the staff and students; the latter numbered about 40 in the mid-1850s.

Some letters from pupils to their parents in Red River have been preserved. They show that the students "like school very much, particularly geography, music and French," and that they were using Pinnock's *History of England* and Reid's *Dictionary* since they ask their parents to bring these books when they next visit the school. In addition to music, drawing and dancing were taught.

Miss Davis was assisted in her teaching by several women prominent in the colony and by her sister Nancy (d. 1893) who also helped with the arduous household chores. These chores necessitated rising every morning at 4:00 AM to light the inevitable Carron stove, carry water, and milk the cows.

After Mathilda Davis' death, education in the new province of Manitoba was supported mainly by ecclesiastical bodies. The name Mathilda Davis will long be remembered in Red River for the pioneer educational work she did and loved so well.

MARJORIE G. MORLEY

PAM, Church of England registers, St Andrews Church, burials, 1870–84, no.154; Miss Davis' school, Correspondence, accounts and miscellaneous papers, 1837–76; Miss Davis' school, note books, 1840–72; Red River Settlement, Red River Census, 1870, no.1125, 1127; Red River Settlement, Samuel Taylor diary, II; Alexander Ross family papers, 284, 474, 476, 477. W. J. Healy, *Women of Red River: being a book written down from the recollections of women surviving from the Red River era* (Winnipeg, 1923), 159. Lillian Gibbons, "Early Red River homes," HSSM, *Papers*, 3rd ser., [no.2] (1945–46), 26–42.

D'AVRAY. *See* MARSHALL

DAY, SAMUEL STEARNS, Baptist clergyman and missionary; b. in 1808 on a farm in Leeds County, U.C., near the village of Delta, son of Captain Jeremiah Day; d. at Homer, N.Y., in 1871.

In his early twenties Samuel Stearns Day decided to study for the ministry and entered the Hamilton Literary and Theological Institution in Hamilton, New York (later Colgate University). Before graduating he volunteered for foreign mission work, and after his ordination at Cortland, N.Y., on 3 Aug. 1835, the American Baptist Missionary Union sent him and his wife to India. They arrived in February 1836 and went first to Chicacole to study the Telugu language. In 1837 Day became the pastor of a small mixed English-speaking congregation in Madras. He moved from Madras to Vellore in February 1840, to minister solely to the Telugu people. Illness forced the Days to return to their home at Homer, N.Y., in 1845. After recovery, Day went back to Vellore, arriving in April 1849, but this time he left his wife and small family in the United States. In 1853 sickness required him to leave India again.

The growth of the mission in Vellore was painfully slow, and the American board had considered abandoning it. However, it was kept alive until the first Canadian-supported missionaries, the Reverend A. V. Timpany and his wife, were sent to the Telugu mission in 1867.

In his later years, Day travelled among churches in the United States and Canada as an advocate for foreign missions. His influence played an important role in inspiring Canadian Baptists to support the work in India, which evolved into the

Deas

principal foreign mission endeavour of Canadian Baptist churches.

F. T. Rosser

S. S. Day was the author of "Extracts from a letter of Mr. Day ...," and "Another letter from Mr. Day ...," in *Baptist Missionary Magazine* (Boston), XXI (1841), 297–99 and 299–301 respectively. It also published an obituary of Day in LII (1872), 22–24. A. V. Timpany, "The Gospel to the outcasts," *Canadian Baptist* (Toronto), 15 Feb. 1872. *The Baptist encyclopædia ...*, ed. William Cathcart (Philadelphia, 1881), 319. G. W. Hervey, *The story of Baptist missions in foreign lands, from the time of Carey to the present date* (St Louis, Mo., 1892). Stuart Ivison and F. T. Rosser, *The Baptists in Upper and Lower Canada before 1820* (Toronto, 1956).

DEAS, JOHN SULLIVAN, tinsmith and salmon canner; b.*c.* 1838 in South Carolina; m. 4 Sept. 1862 at Victoria, Vancouver Island, to Fanny Harris by whom he had at least eight children; d. 22 July 1880 in Portland, Ore.

John Sullivan Deas, described as a mulatto, was a tinsmith in Charleston and San Francisco before moving to Victoria, Vancouver Island, probably in 1861 or 1862. He may have come to Vancouver Island to work for Martin Prag, a hardware and tinware dealer, who had previously employed him in San Francisco. By 1866 Deas was a manufacturing tinsmith and hardware dealer in Yale, and from about September 1868 he was established in his trade in Victoria under the name Birmingham House.

In Victoria Deas joined a black community of several hundred, started in 1858 by organized migration from San Francisco. The black migrants were spurred by fear of attempts by the California legislature and judiciary to worsen their already unequal position in the state, and by the attraction of the Fraser River gold rush. In British territory they did not find the equality they sought, although discrimination was social rather than legal, private rather than official. Deas, for instance, was able to carry on several businesses, to buy property, and eventually to exercise the rights and privileges of a natural-born British subject, including obtaining a crown grant of land and becoming a registered voter. But he and his family were on one occasion held up to ridicule in a Victoria newspaper as stereotype members of their race.

Deas started in salmon canning in 1871 by making the tins for Captain Edward STAMP. In 1872, after Stamp's death, Deas canned salmon on his own, leasing the saltery built in 1870 for Captain James COOPER. In 1873 he pre-empted near this site on what is now Deas Island. By 1874 his cannery on the island consisted of three substantial buildings, surrounded by a dyke which enclosed about seven acres, together with smaller buildings, a wharf, and sheds. Deas operated it until the end of the 1878 season, marketing the product under the label "Fresh Salmon, John S. Deas, Frazer [*sic*] River, British Columbia." He then sold to his Victoria agents, commission merchants Findlay, Durham and Brodie, his interest in the plant which was shortly thereafter valued at between $13,000 and $15,000. After the sale, Deas settled in Portland, Oregon, where his wife had bought a rooming house in November 1877.

During the first years of his operation, Deas could claim to be the largest canner on the river. But in 1877 vigorous new competitors entered the business. Deas felt that the salmon potential of the Fraser was limited, as compared with that of the Columbia River, by irregular runs and the scarcity of good salmon "drifts" in the main channel. When another cannery was planned close to his plant, he applied for an exclusive lease of the drifts near Deas Island, thus provoking opposition in both the provincial and the federal legislatures. Yet his fear of competition seems justified; in 1878 the new cannery put up twice as many cases as Deas, whose pack in his last season was the smallest of the eight canneries operating on the Fraser River that year. Nevertheless, seven seasons in salmon canning during the first decade of continuous operation on the Fraser River entitle John Sullivan Deas to a prominent place among the founders of the canning industry in British Columbia.

H. Keith Ralston

British Columbia, Central Microfilm Bureau (Department of the Provincial Secretary), Chief commissioner of lands and works, Correspondence inward, 3116/74, 3117/74. British Columbia, Department of Finance, Assessment rolls for New Westminster District, September–December 1879, 26–27. British Columbia, Department of Lands, Crown grant records, no.1381 G, v.3; 1556/3; Original field survey book, 37/74, P.H. 2, group 2, New Westminster District. Multnomah County Department of Records and Elections (County Courthouse, Portland, Ore.), Multnomah County, Deed records. National Archives (Washington), United States, 10th Census, Oregon, Multnomah County, Original enumerator's sheets, 425 (microfilm available).

PABC holds copies of two books which published samples of the labels used by British Columbia canners. They are: *Salmon labels ...* (n.p., n.d.) and *Specimens, label printing, Victoria, B.C.* (n.p., n.d.). *British Columbia Examiner* (New Westminster, B.C.), 4 April 1868. *British Columbia Examiner* (Yale, B.C.), 17 Aug. 1868. *British Columbia Tribune* (Yale, B.C.), 16 April 1866. *Daily British Colonist and Victoria Chronicle*, 8 Sept. 1868; 20, 21, 22 Oct. 1870; 3 March 1871; 25 July 1872; 6 May 1874. *Mainland Guardian*

(New Westminster, B.C.), 18 June 1870; 20 June 1871; 21, 28 Aug. 1878. *Morning Oregonian* (Portland, Ore.), 23 July 1880. *Pacific Appeal* (San Francisco, Cal.), 27 Sept. 1862. *Victoria Daily Standard*, 15 Sept. 1870; 6 March, 9 June 1871. British Columbia, Legislative Assembly, *Journals*, 1878; *Sessional papers*, 1878, 210. Canada, Senate, *Debates*, 1878, 287–92; *Sessional papers*, X (1877), PT.5, no.5, supp.4, 339–40; XI (1878), PT.3, no.1, supp.5, 287, 306–7; XII (1879), PT.4, no.3, supp.4, 292, 302; XV (1882), PT.4, no.5, supp.2, 223.

Charleston city directory ... for 1856, comp. R. S. Purse (New York, 1856). *First Victoria directory ... 1871*, comp. Edward Mullandaine (Victoria, 1871). *List of voters in the several electoral districts in British Columbia in force on the first August 1874* (Victoria, 1874). *Portland directory for 1879 ...; 1880; 1881; 1882* (Portland, Ore., [1879], 1880, 1881, 1882). *The San Francisco directory for ... 1860 ...; 1861;* comp. H. G. Langley (San Francisco, 1860, 1861). "Victoria assessment roll, 1868," *Daily British Colonist, Supplement* (Victoria), 14 Nov. 1868. F.W. Howay and E. O. S. Scholefield, *British Columbia from the earliest times to the present* (4v., Vancouver, B.C., 1914), II, 585. James Pilton, "Negro settlement in British Columbia, 1858–1871," unpublished MA thesis, University of British Columbia, 1951. R. M. Lapp, "Negro rights activities in gold rush California," California Hist. Soc. Q., XLV (1966), 11–15.

DEIGHTON, JOHN, steamer captain and hotel-keeper; b. in November 1830 at Hull, Yorkshire, Eng.; d. 29 May 1875 at Burrard Inlet, B.C.

Information on John Deighton's early life is scanty but he probably began his career as a merchant seaman. He came to California in 1849, but soon returned to the sea, sailing between London, the British colonies, and China. In 1858, the year of the Fraser River gold rush, Deighton arrived in British Columbia. After trying prospecting, he entered the river steamer services, piloting vessels and sometimes commanding steamers that ran between Victoria, New Westminster, and Fraser River points. There is substantial evidence that in 1862 Deighton was briefly captain of James Irvine Bramley's ship, *Union*.

After a lengthy illness and with the decline in traffic on the Fraser, Deighton turned to hotel-keeping. In September 1867 he moved to Burrard Inlet where Captain Edward STAMP had recently opened a sawmill. Although the population of the area was sparse, thirsty mill-workers and visiting sailors provided a steady trade for Deighton's Globe Saloon, the first enterprise of its kind on Burrard Inlet. Two other public houses were soon established in the area but Deighton, who was "celebrated for his good table and his warm hospitality," did most of the business. In 1870 he replaced the original saloon with the more spacious Deighton House. In 1873 he was able to open the commodious Deighton's Hotel which he placed under the management of his brother and sister-in-law, Thomas and Emma Deighton. The hotel was advertised as a resort for invalids and sportsmen.

Deighton's success is explained by the increasing activity in the area's lumber mills and by his affectionate and generous personality. He was well respected for his political opinions although his language was occasionally uncouth. According to local legend, the townsite of Granville, later Vancouver, received its unofficial but well-known name of Gastown from Deighton's sobriquet, "Gassy Jack," a tribute to his loquacity.

Deighton's prosperity was short-lived. He quarrelled with his brother and sister-in-law, probably as a result of complications caused by his "klootchman," an Indian woman, Qua-hail-ya, known as Madeline or Matrine, the mother of his illegitimate son. In 1874 Deighton returned briefly to steamboating on the Fraser as captain of John Irving*'s steamer, *Onward*. When his brother and sister-in-law left his employ he returned to hotel-keeping. He began to expand Deighton House but took ill and died. His son, and sole heir, died before the estate, which yielded little more than $300, was probated.

PATRICIA E. ROY

PABC, John Deighton correspondence. *Mainland Guardian* (New Westminster, B.C.), 9 June 1875. F. W. Howay, "Early settlement on Burrard Inlet," *BCHQ*, I (1937), 101–14. Raymond Hull, "Sailor at the bar," *British Columbia Library Quarterly*, XXVII (January 1964), 22–26.

DELAGRAVE, CYRILLE, lawyer, member of the Council of Public Instruction for Lower Canada; b. 25 Nov. 1812 at Sainte-Marie-de-Monnoir (Rouville County), L.C., of the marriage of François Delagrave and Geneviève Amiot; d. 15 Sept. 1877 at Quebec.

Cyrille Delagrave was educated at the Petit Séminaire of Quebec and received his legal training in the office of René-Édouard CARON. He was called to the bar on 8 Aug. 1838, and practised in partnership with the future judge Jean Chabot*. In 1854 he was appointed secretary of the commission responsible for applying the law that abolished seigneurial rights in Lower Canada; he became a member of this commission in 1859, and shared in its activities until its dissolution [see Edward SHORT]. In 1868 he was offered the opportunity of succeeding Judge John Gawler Thompson on the bench of the Superior Court for the Gaspé district, but he declined for reasons of

Delaney

health. However, on 22 Oct. 1872 he agreed to replace Jacques CRÉMAZIE as recorder of the town of Quebec, a post he held until his death.

Cyrille Delagrave had always an intense interest in the education of the young; it is one of the remarkable aspects of his career. On 26 May 1862 he was appointed a member of the Council of Public Instruction for Lower Canada (or Canada East), in place of François-Xavier Garneau*. He took his task seriously, attending 17 of the 20 sessions of that body from 1862 to 1869. On 11 Nov. 1862 he supported the superintendent, Pierre-Joseph-Olivier Chauveau*, who proposed holding sessions of the council only twice a year (in May and November). At the same meeting Delagrave was appointed inspector of the Board of Examiners [see Jean-Baptiste MEILLEUR], with the duty of submitting reports. The ensuing accounts, which appeared in the *Journal de l'instruction publique*, show that he performed his task conscientiously.

In 1869, when the Council of Public Instruction was reorganized and divided into two committees, Cyrille Delagrave was nominated to the Catholic committee. In 1871 Bishop Jean-Pierre-François Laforce* Langevin suggested forming a commission, with Cyrille Delagrave as a member, which would be responsible for preparing a series of French reading texts for schools. Final approval of five books written by André-Napoléon Montpetit* was granted by the council on 12 May 1875.

On 9 June 1875 the prime minister, Charles-Eugène Boucher* de Boucherville, consulted Cyrille Delagrave about reorganization of the Ministry of Public Instruction and changes to be made in the composition of the denominational committees of the council. The 1875 law implemented the suggestions formulated by the bishops of Quebec and the members of the council. Once more Cyrille Delagrave was named as a member of the reorganized Catholic committee, which included all the bishops whose dioceses were situated entirely or partly in the province, and an equal number of laymen. He was still a member of it at the time of his death on 15 Sept. 1877 at Quebec. It was at Quebec that on 6 Nov. 1844 he had married Louise Mason, by whom he had at least three children.

LOUIS-PHILIPPE AUDET

AJM, Registre d'état civil (notes biographiques fournies par J.-J. Lefebvre). ANQ, PQ, Éducation, Registre de copies de lettres envoyées 1868–1919, XVI, 506. PAC, MG 30, D62 (Audet papers), 10, pp.277–81. *JIP* (Montréal), nov. 1862, 190; oct. 1863, 153. *Le Courrier du Canada* (Québec), 15 sept. 1877. P.-G. Roy, *Les avocats de la région de Québec*, 121–22. Audet, *Histoire du conseil de l'Instruction publique.* Pierre Boucher de La Bruère, *Le conseil de l'Instruction publique et le comité catholique* (Montréal, 1918).

DELANEY, PATRICK, teacher; b. 1829 in County Armagh, Ireland; d. 18 Sept. 1874 at Montreal, Que.

We know nothing about Patrick Delaney's life before 1857, the date at which he was appointed schoolmaster at the model school for boys [see Jean-Baptiste MEILLEUR], as well as assistant master and usher at the École Normale Jacques-Cartier, at Montreal. This French normal school was primarily intended to train teachers for the Roman Catholic population of the districts of Montreal, the Ottawa valley, and Saint-François, and of the town of Trois-Rivières and the part of the district of Trois-Rivières to the west of the town.

Since 1826 the organizers of the normal schools, conscious of the two ethnic groups in Lower Canada, had maintained as an essential part of the curriculum the teaching of the mother tongue and of the second language, English or French, as the case might be. To make clear the seriousness of such a decision, Pierre-Joseph-Olivier Chauveau*, the superintendent of public instruction, and Abbé Hospice-Anthelme Verreau*, the principal of the École Normale Jacques-Cartier, decided that "English literature, and elocution and declamation in that language, shall be entrusted to Mr. Delaney, who has studied in the national schools of Ireland." It was considered desirable, therefore, that future teachers should know French, their native language, but also English, the second language, of which the French-speaking milieu of Montreal realized the full importance.

On 16 June 1857, at the time of the first prize-giving at the École Normale Jacques-Cartier, Delaney made a speech in English, stressing "the difficulties that had to be surmounted last spring to organize the school and, taking into account each one's level of instruction, to place the young pupils of the model school, who came for the most part from the different schools of the town."

In November 1860, the principal, Verreau, solemnized the marriage of Patrick Delaney and Mary Ann Kennedy at Montreal. From 1857 on, Delaney had been a member of the Association des Instituteurs for the École Normale Jacques-Cartier district. He does not seem to have attended the meetings of this association with much regularity, since his name is mentioned only twice in the minutes.

On 23 July 1867, Delaney was appointed English language secretary to the minister of public instruction and assistant editor of the

Journal of Education, in place of James Julien Theodore Phelan, a lawyer, who had been called on to undertake other duties.

Delaney died seven years later, and was buried in the cemetery at Côte-des-Neiges.

LOUIS-PHILIPPE AUDET

AJM, Registre d'état civil. *JIP*, 1857–1874 (Procès-verbaux de l'Association des instituteurs de la circonscription de l'école normale Jacques-Cartier de Montréal); mars 1857, 31; juin 1857. Adélard Desrosiers, *Les écoles normales primaires de la province de Québec et leurs œuvres complémentaires, 1857–1907* (Montréal, 1909).

DELISLE (DeLisle), ALEXANDRE-MAURICE, public servant, member of the assembly, and businessman; baptized 21 April 1810 at Montreal, L.C., third son of Jean-Baptiste Delisle, a public servant, and Mary Robinson; d. 13 Feb. 1880 at Montreal, Que.

After studying at Montreal, Alexandre-Maurice Delisle was admitted to the bar in 1832, and on 29 April the following year he married Marie-Angélique Cuvillier, daughter of Augustin Cuvillier*, member of the assembly, merchant, and well-known financier. In 1833 also Delisle had begun his *cursus honorum* in the public service at Montreal. First a clerk of the peace (8 Jan. 1833), then clerk of the crown (February 1833), he was nominated as commissioner (April 1838) to receive the oath of members of the Special Council. Shortly afterwards he again became clerk of the peace (25 May 1838), and then, on 13 April 1843, clerk of the crown. He was appointed harbour commissioner on 27 May 1859, and also accepted the post of sheriff in March 1862. It was in this last capacity that he presided over the reorganization of the Montreal prison; but it was during this year that he suffered the worst setback in his career.

In February 1863 he was publicly accused, by his brother Michel-Charles, of having perpetrated sizeable frauds when he was clerk of the crown. The investigators, Pierre-Richard Lafrenaye and Marcus Doherty, appointed by the ministry of John Sandfield MACDONALD and Louis-Victor Sicotte*, concluded that Delisle, his fellow clerk William-Henry Bréhaut, and their deputy Charles Schiller, had obtained considerable sums by means of false returns and overcharges on the cost of *subpoenas*, which had permitted them to carry through some attractive speculations. On 19 Dec. 1863 Delisle was therefore relieved of his duties as sheriff, and in January 1864 of his post at the harbour commission. The inquiry had produced lively excitement in Montreal, and as it was directed by Delisle's political enemies, it brought him

the warmest sympathy from Conservatives. The procession of witnesses who had come forward to support him comprised almost the entire élite of the party: Henry Hague Judah*, Charles-Elzéar MONDELET, William Badgley*, Lewis Thomas Drummond*, Charles-Joseph Coursol*, Louis-Siméon MORIN, William WORKMAN, Jean-Louis Beaudry*, Thomas Cushing AYLWIN, and Sir Louis-Hippolyte La Fontaine*. Delisle claimed that the whole inquiry was a plot organized by Joseph Doutre*, a rabid Liberal. In any case, after the Conservatives had regained power, he was reinstated on the harbour commission (22 Aug. 1866), and later became its president. On 20 Aug. 1866 he had already accepted the post of collector of customs at Montreal, an office he held until 1874, the year of another Liberal victory. He then resigned; at the same time the ministry of Alexander Mackenzie* requested him to relinquish his presidency of the harbour commission.

Clearly the vicissitudes of Delisle's career in public administration had a direct relation to the role he played in political circles. Even before the birth of the Bleus he behaved like a Conservative. In 1841, yielding to the request made by Lord Sydenham [Thomson*], he had stood against James LESLIE in Montreal County. The better to ensure his victory, and the more readily to command the electors' respect, he had had himself appointed a police magistrate a few days before. It was an unnecessary precaution, for after a few scenes of violence in the course of which two of his Irish supporters were killed, a riot broke out and Delisle was proclaimed elected. At Kingston he regularly gave his support to the governor's party, and on 23 June 1841, when John Neilson* made his famous motion condemning the Union, he was one of the two French Canadians who refused to support him. In July 1843 he resigned when he became clerk of the crown. He never returned to active politics, but none the less continued to show himself a person of strong views.

In March 1844 Delisle was a returning officer for a Montreal by-election, a violent election during which Lewis Thomas Drummond won against William MOLSON, the candidate of the governor Charles Theophilus Metcalfe*, to whom Delisle had given his unqualified support. After that, and until his death, he was one of the most prominent figures in the Bleus. He subscribed regularly to the party treasury, and in the counties where he owned property he exercised an influence on the electors that was often decisive. For example, in Argenteuil County in 1854 he paid out several thousands of dollars to get his friend Sydney Robert Bellingham* elected. Furthermore, he always kept the close and devoted

Delisle

friendship of George-Étienne CARTIER, who is said to have set great store by his judgement and his discerning and practical advice. At the time of his death, rumour had it that he would soon have been appointed a senator.

It was particularly as an entrepreneur and a businessman that Delisle made his mark – and his fortune. According to an obituary in *La Minerve* of 16 Feb. 1880, "he was the practical man par excellence, always ready to meet and solve a difficulty, always equal to a situation. . . . He was therefore always able to achieve his aim, through his enlightened will and the inexhaustible resources of a subtle, sharp, and shrewd mind." For example, he made several successful speculations in land in the Rimouski and Pointe-au-Père areas, and notably, in 1864, in partnership with William Workman, he bought an expanse of 78 acres which in a few years became the flourishing town of Sainte-Cunégonde (later annexed to Montreal). He was appointed in 1850 one of the directors, and later the president, of the Montreal City and District Savings Bank. He was likewise a director of the City Bank. During the 1840s, working with Wilfrid-Antoine Masson, Henry Hague Judah, and 35 other associates, of whom 22 were French Canadians, he became one of the most enthusiastic promoters of the Montreal and Bytown Railway, to which he subscribed £1,000. This company, of which he was president in 1854, went bankrupt in 1859, but not before the completion of the portion of line from Carillon to Grenville, which particularly concerned Delisle and his partner Bellingham. He was also a director, then president, of the Champlain and St Lawrence Railway Company, until it was combined with the Grand Trunk in 1872. In 1857 he joined with 32 of the principal capitalists of Montreal to place at the disposal of this company, and of the Montreal and New York Railway Company, a sum amounting to £40,000. At his death he was still a director of the Gulf of St Lawrence Steamship Company, and it was to extend the operations of this undertaking that he had visited the West Indies during the summer of 1878. In 1865 he had, moreover, been a member of the commission responsible for establishing commercial relations with Latin America, and in 1866 he had gone to the West Indies for the first time, before visiting Mexico, Brazil, and several other countries of South America. He also owned bridges over the Rivière des Prairies and several toll-roads on Île Jésus.

Delisle's will, of which the last codicil is dated 24 Jan. 1880, gives an idea of the extent of his fortune. After bequeathing $2,000 to a priest of Saint-Sulpice for charitable works, and some $300 to religious foundations, he gave instructions that following the death of his wife his assets should be divided in equal parts among his children, and that the sum of £70,000 should be deducted from the portion allotted to his two sons, Maurice-Nolan and Charles-Alexandre; they had had interests in the iron trade and in their collapse (before 1862) their father had lost this sum.

Influential, well-to-do, and always very much in evidence because of his social connections, Alexandre-Maurice Delisle was naturally called upon to assume many honorary positions. On 11 Dec. 1837 he was elected churchwarden of the parish council of Notre-Dame, and in 1841 he was credited with having induced Lord Sydenham – a remarkable feat at the time – to be present at the sermons of Bishop Charles-Auguste-Marie-Joseph de Forbin-Janson*. On 21 Oct. 1854 he was appointed a member of the provincial committee responsible for seeing that the industry and resources of the province were properly represented at the universal exposition in Paris. Finally, in 1860, the city council of Montreal appointed him president of the committee entrusted with arranging the decorations and preparing for the reception of the Prince of Wales in the capital. Such positions, which brought him consideration and respect, no doubt compensated for the insults, political persecutions, and denunciations to which he was exposed. These passions, current at that time in the worlds of politics and business, never succeeded in bringing him down.

Delisle was a man of sturdy build and tall stature; he had keen eyes that sparkled with intelligence; a staunch defender of his nationality, he knew himself to be respected by his friends, and, because of his resources and successes, to be above the common level. He was one of the most remarkable French Canadians of the second third of the 19th century, both because of the social position that his spirit of enterprise and great political activity earned for him and because of the fortune he was able to acquire. He lies at the top end of the cemetery at Côte-des-Neiges, beside Louis-Adélard Sénécal* and Sir George-Étienne Cartier.

JACQUES MONET

A.-M. Delisle, *General rules and regulations for the interior order and police of the common gaol of the district of Montreal* ([Montreal?], 1864).

PAC, MG 24, B103 (Delisle papers); MG 30, D62 (Audet papers), 10, p.286–88. Archives de l'université de Montréal, Collection Baby, 108, 114. BNQ, Société historique de Montréal, Collection La Fontaine, Lettres, 237, 276, 652, 656, 660, 663, 665, 666, 667, 669, 670, 678, 682, 685, 686, 689. *Correspondance, documents, témoignages et procédés dans l'enquête de Messrs Lafrenaye et Doherty, commissaires, dans le bureau du greffier de la couronne et greffier de la paix, Montréal, suivis des remarques de Messrs Delisle et Schiller sur cette partie du rapport des commissaires qui a pu être connue et les remarques de Mr. Bréhaut sur la lettre annonçant les causes de sa démission* (Montréal, 1864). *Railroad between Quebec, Montreal, Bytown and Georgian Bay; great public demonstration; presentation by A.-M. Delisle of the petition of the citizens of Montreal to the common council of Montreal, praying for aid to said railroad ...* (Montreal, 1853). *La Minerve* (Montréal), 1864, 16 févr. 1880. *Montreal Gazette*, Dec. 1863. *Dom. ann. reg.*, 1880–81, 405. Cornell, *Alignment of political groups.* Monet, *Last cannon shot.* T. T. Smyth, *The first hundred years; history of the Montreal City and District Savings Bank 1846–1946* (n.p., n.d.). G. R Stevens, *Canadian National Railways* (2v., Toronto, 1960), I, 39–43. F.-J. Audet, "1842," *Cahiers des Dix*, VII (1942), 216–18. É.-Z. Massicotte, "La famille de Jean De Lisle de La Cailleterie," *BRH*, XXV (1919), 175–86. Jacques Monet, "*La crise Metcalfe* and the Montreal election, 1843–1844," *CHR*, XLIV (1963), 1–19.

DEMERS, MODESTE, Roman Catholic priest and missionary, bishop of Vancouver Island; b. 11 Oct. 1809 at Saint-Nicholas-de-Lévis, L.C., son of Michel Demers, farmer, and Rosalie Foucher; d. 28 July 1871 at Victoria, B.C.

Modeste Demers was educated at the seminary of Quebec and ordained priest in 1836 by Bishop Joseph Signay*. After serving briefly as priest at Trois-Pistoles, Demers was accepted by Signay in 1837 as a missionary and sent to work under Bishop Joseph-Norbert Provencher* at the Red River Settlement. The following year he was selected by Signay to accompany the Reverend François-Norbert Blanchet* in answer to the calls of the Roman Catholics of Oregon for their own missionaries and priests.

Demers and Blanchet found much work to occupy them among the settlers and the French Canadian servants of the Hudson's Bay Company in the Oregon country posts. But Signay had indicated that their primary duty was to be to the Indians and had instructed them to learn the native languages as quickly as possible. Demers' facility with languages had already attracted attention at Red River, and after 12 months on the Pacific coast he had compiled a dictionary, a catechism, a prayer book, and hymns in the Chinook jargon and had acquired an elementary knowledge of more than one of the Indian languages of the area. His good knowledge of English was also useful, particularly in dealing with the HBC which held the economic and political power in the Oregon country and whose patronage was essential to any missionary who hoped to travel beyond the confines of their main post, Fort Vancouver.

Demers' work in the Oregon country was characterized by arduous and extensive travel, large scale baptisms, and elementary religious instruction of the Indians, often using Blanchet's Catholic ladder, a graphic representation of the historic progress of Catholic Christianity. He was particularly active in the establishment of a mission at Cowlitz and later made two notable missionary journeys to the north. He was the first Christian missionary to reach the mainland of the present British Columbia. In September 1841 he visited Fort Langley in the Fraser Valley and made contact with and baptized many of the Indians assembled there. The following year, Demers extended his mission to the Carrier Indians of New Caledonia, travelling with the HBC caravan to Fort Alexandria. Here he wintered, built a small chapel, and made several expeditions to Fort George, to Stuart Lake, and to the Atnan people.

Returning to the Oregon country, Demers, after 1844, served as pastor in Oregon City under Bishop Norbert Blanchet. With the elevation of Oregon to an ecclesiastical province in 1846, Blanchet became the first metropolitan, and his fellow missionary from Quebec, Modeste Demers, who had retained his interest in and concern for the northern Indians, was appointed bishop of Vancouver Island and administrator of the diocese of the Princess Charlotte Islands (Queen Charlotte Islands) and New Caledonia, being consecrated as such on 30 Nov. 1847. The new bishop of Vancouver Island was reluctant to accept his burden, feeling that Blanchet had been too hasty in recommending the establishment of a bishopric in a region with apparently such sparse resources and so little touched by Christianity. Vancouver Island itself had been visited briefly by Spanish priests in the late 18th century and in 1843 by Father Jean-Baptiste-Zacharie Bolduc*, who had accompanied James DOUGLAS to the site of Fort Victoria as the HBC began its withdrawal from the Columbia. On the mainland of British Columbia only Demers himself, Father Pierre-Jean DE SMET SJ, and Father John Nobili* SJ had visited the Indians. Outside the fur-trading posts of the HBC virtually no white settlement existed.

Before taking up residence in his new diocese, Demers directed his energies towards acquiring funds and mission personnel to help cope with the vast task that lay before him. Travelling extensively in Europe, particularly in France, Demers managed to find several missionaries for his diocese, but was sadly disappointed with the response to his appeal for funds. Arriving at his episcopal seat in 1852, Demers confessed that "now I am the village priest, I sing mass on Sundays and

Demers

feast-days, and also preach from time to time [and] as for resources, you know that I do not hold them in my hand." The slender means of his diocese, his dependence upon unpredictable sources of financial aid from Quebec and Europe, and his at times desperate need for competent English-speaking priests were problems which were to remain with Demers until his death.

During the Fraser River gold rush of 1858, greater attention was focused on the distant Pacific colonies and Demers was able to persuade the relatively new order of the Sisters of St Ann of Montreal, led by Sœur Marie du Sacré-Cœur [Salomé Valois*], to commit themselves to work in his diocese, and to convince the missionary order of the Oblates of Mary Immaculate to establish their headquarters at Esquimalt under the Reverend Father Louis d'Herbomez*. A girls' school, orphanage, and later a hospital were established for the population of Victoria under the aegis of the sisters. The Oblates established a school for boys in Victoria and continued Demers' own work of missions to the Indians both on Vancouver Island and on the Fraser River. The bishop himself was thus able to begin construction of his cathedral in Victoria, to give more attention to the organization and supply of his diocese, to extend his charitable works, and to visit the miners and others in the distant parts of his diocese.

The departure of the Oblates for the mainland in 1865, with the appointment of d'Herbomez as vicar apostolic of British Columbia, was a serious loss to Demers' work, in spite of the fact that relations between the bishop and the order had never been smooth. Since 1863, however, Demers had been applying to the American College at Louvain, Belgium, for English-speaking priests, and it was fortunate that this institution was now able to fill the void left by the withdrawal of the Oblates.

Demers himself was becoming increasingly sickly, and in 1865 retired temporarily to San Francisco for medical care. The following year he again left Victoria for a three-year extended tour of South America, the eastern United States, Quebec, and France, soliciting men and money for his diocese. He came back to Victoria briefly in 1869, only to return to Europe with Father Charles John Seghers* to attend the œcumenical council at the Vatican in 1870. In France en route to Rome the bishop was badly injured in a train accident, from which he never fully recovered. He died a year later at his residence in Victoria, only a few days after British Columbia entered the Canadian confederation.

The days of the fur trade empire and of the crown colony had ended, and the character of the Pacific province was soon to be radically changed. It was perhaps fitting that during his last illness Bishop Demers "frequently expressed a desire to see and converse with Sir James Douglas, who was often found at his bedside." It was Douglas who had first greeted the young Demers at Fort Vancouver, and whose role in the fur trade and as a colonial governor had brought him into continuous contact with the bishop for over 30 years. It was their world of trading posts and Indians, of civilization in the wilderness, of company government, and of the close contacts of a small colonial society which had now passed.

JEAN USHER

AAQ, Colombie anglaise, I–III (letters from Modeste Demers to the archbishopric). Archives de la Congrégation pour l'évangélisation des peuples (Vatican City), Lettere e Decreti; Udienze di Nostro Signore; Lettere della S. Congregazione e Biglietti di Monsignore Segretario, Scritture riferite nelle Congregatzioni, America Centrale. Archives de la Propagation de la Foi de Paris (France), F.202 (Vancouver, reports of the missions, 1847–1922). Archives de l'archevêché de Rimouski, Lettres de Mgr Modeste Demers à l'abbé Edmond Langevin, 1848–1866. Archives Deschâtelets (Scholasticat Saint-Joseph, Ottawa), Dossier Orégon, I, A–XI, 1–3 (Modeste Demers to Father Pascal Ricard, O.M.I., Superior, St Joseph Mission, Olympia, W.T., 1853–56); B–IX, 2 (Miscellaneous correspondence of Modeste Demers with Father Louis d'Herbomez, O.M.I., 1860–65). Archives générales O.M.I. (Rome), Dossier Modeste Demers (microfilm at the Archives Deschâtelets, Scholasticat Saint-Joseph, Ottawa). Archives of the Archdiocese of Portland (Portland, Ore.), Letters of Modeste Demers to Mgr N. Blanchet. PABC, Modeste Demers correspondence, 1860–71.

Modeste Demers, J.M.J. Chinook dictionary, catechism, prayers and hymns. Composed in 1838 & 1839 by Rt. Rev. Modeste Demers. Revised, corrected and completed, in 1867 by most Rev. F. N. Blanchet. With modifications and additions by Rev. L. N. St. Onge ... (Montreal, 1871). P. M. Hanley, "The Catholic ladder and missionary activity in the Pacific northwest," unpublished MA thesis, University of Ottawa, 1965; "Frs. Blanchet and Demers and missionary preaching in Oregon," unpublished PHD thesis, Pontifical Georgian University, Rome, 1965. Morice, History of northern interior of B.C. M. L. Nichols, The mantle of Elias; the story of Fathers Blanchet and Demers in early Oregon (Portland, Ore., 1941). A. E. Oksness, "Reverend Modeste Demers, missionary in the northwest," unpublished MA thesis, University of Washington, Seattle, 1934. J. M. Hill, "The most Reverend Modeste Demers, D.D., first bishop of Vancouver Island," CCHA Report, 1953, 29–35. Émilien Lamirande, "L'implantation de l'Église catholique en Colombie-Britannique 1838–1848," Revue de l'université d'Ottawa, XXVIII (1958), 213–25, 323–63, 453–89.

DE MILLE, JAMES (the family used DeMill, but he wrote under De Mille, and used this name after 1865), author and professor; b. at Saint John, N.B., probably on 23 Aug. 1833, third child of loyalists Nathan Smith DeMill and Elizabeth Budd; d. at Halifax, N.S., 28 Jan. 1880, at the age of 47.

Nathan DeMill was a prosperous merchant, ship-owner, and lumberman in Saint John, N.B. He was a man of strong principles and a strict abstainer, called "cold-water DeMill" by his contemporaries. He left the Church of England to become a Baptist, and was active on the board of governors of Acadia College which was chartered in 1841. James De Mille and his brothers were educated at Horton Academy, Wolfville, before continuing at Acadia. Their adventures at the academy, real or imaginary, form the substance of an excellent set of boys' books, The *"B.O.W.C."* *Series*. Taking place in and around Minas Basin or celebrating great Maritime events such as the Miramichi fire, these adventures of the Brothers of the White Cross were published between 1869 and 1873.

James matriculated at Acadia College in 1849. The following year he and his elder brother Elisha Budd DeMill set off on a year's travel, going by boat to Boston, overland to Quebec, and there boarding one of their father's ships for England. They went on a walking trip in England and Scotland, crossed to France, and spent several months in Italy. The experiences of this year profoundly affected James – most of his many novels reflect a knowledge of places, people, and languages not his own – and left him with a life-long love of Italy.

On his return to North America he transferred to Brown University, Providence, Rhode Island, and graduated with an MA in 1854. Then followed some eventful but frustrating years. He travelled to Cincinnati to wind up a wildcat mining concern in which Acadia College money was involved; in 1856 in Saint John he and a partner started a book business, which failed leaving many debts; his father, too, suffered business reverses.

In 1859 James De Mille married Elizabeth Ann Pryor, daughter of Dr John Pryor*, first president of Acadia College. He was appointed professor of classics at Acadia in 1860, thus beginning a career as an outstanding teacher and scholar. He instituted the classical honours course and is supposed to have encouraged his students to use Latin as a language of conversation. He also taught Italian to interested students. The first of his books, *Martyrs of the Catacombs*, about first-century Rome, which he had written in 1858, was published in 1864.

In 1865 he moved to Halifax to become professor of history and rhetoric at Dalhousie College, having in the same year refused an appointment as superintendent of education for Nova Scotia. After moving to Halifax, he returned to his father's first affiliation, the Church of England, and published a pamphlet on its early history. He spent the rest of his life in Halifax, enhancing his reputation as a teacher and publishing, at the rate of about two a year, a long series of books. Obviously he wrote his novels under tremendous pressure, perhaps driven by the debts incurred during his business venture. During this time he also wrote *The elements of rhetoric* (1878), a well-planned and gracefully executed textbook.

His novels originally appeared serially in American magazines before being published as books in New York or Boston by Harper, Appleton, and other publishers. The majority of the novels show signs of haste and of a desire to satisfy the demand of readers of popular fiction for mystery and high adventure. *Helena's household*, an early novel that De Mille had the leisure to write with care, was much admired as giving an accurate picture of Roman family life. Almost all his novels show a delightful sense of humour and parody and a good eye for national absurdities as well as national characteristics. His merry story, *The Dodge Club*, published in 1869, and anticipating Mark Twain's *Innocents abroad*, splendidly caricatures a group of American travellers (the Dodge Club of the title), exposed to stock continental situations; a scene in which a senator woos a countess by reading Isaac Watts' poetry is magnificent. De Mille's second series of boys' books, *The young Dodge Club*, also exploited this vein. In *Lady of the ice* he enjoys equally the foibles of the young officer class stationed in Quebec. The posthumous, anonymously published, and probably unfinished book, *A strange manuscript found in a copper cylinder*, has been much admired as a Swiftian satire. A long mystical poem called *Behind the veil* was edited by Archibald MacMechan* and published in 1893.

James De Mille must have been a delightful person: extremely intelligent with artistic and literary abilities of a high order. The story told of his fishing trips with another Dalhousie professor on which they conversed in Latin as the only language that would not "profane the mysteries" of fishing, is typical of the reminiscences of students and friends. His interests were varied: he wrote and delightfully illustrated a translation of Homer for his four children; he owned books printed in nearly a dozen languages, from Sanskrit to Icelandic; and he expressed a deep concern for the future of higher education in his community.

Denison

De Mille has been generally too much forgotten. During his lifetime he was one of Canada's few well-known writers, but today he is perhaps best known for a poem, "Sweet maiden of Passamaquoddy," that first appeared in a serialized story, "Minnehaha Mines," and has since been reprinted in many anthologies. Although many of his writings are of little interest except as examples of 19th-century adventure stories, a few – *The Dodge Club*, for example – deserve to be reprinted and read. His books for boys would still delight a young reader.

MINERVA TRACY

[James De Mille's birth date has been the subject of disagreement among various authors. The year 1833 was chosen for several reasons: 1836, the year usually used, would have made De Mille too young to matriculate from Acadia in 1849 since the college required a minimum age of 15; 1833 is quoted on De Mille's tombstone; Archibald MacMechan, who knew the De Mille family, used 1833. M.T.]

Some of James De Mille's works include: *The "B.O.W.C.": a book for boys* (Boston, 1869); *Behind the veil, a poem* (Halifax, 1893); *The boys of Grand Pré School* (Boston, 1871); *A comedy of terrors* (Boston, 1872); *The Dodge Club; or, Italy in 1859* (New York, 1869); *The early English church* (Halifax, 1877); *The elements of rhetoric* (New York, 1878); *The lady of the ice* (New York, 1870); "Minnehaha Mines," *The Dominion: True Humorist* (Saint John, N.B.), 16 April 1870; *An open question, a novel* (New York, 1873); *A strange manuscript found in a copper cylinder* (New York, 1889; Toronto, 1910); "Professor De Mille's inaugural address," *Dalhousie Gazette* (Halifax), 15 Nov. 1873.

Dalhousie University Library (Halifax), Special Collections, James De Mille, Family correspondence and business papers, 1856–80; Journal of Elisha B. De Mille, 1850–51; Notebook of James De Mille when attending Brown University; manuscripts of several of James De Mille's works. Acadia College (Wolfville, N.S.), *Catalogue of the officers and students* (Halifax), 1861–62, 3–4, 9, 20; 1863–64, 11. L. J. Burpee, "Who's who in Canadian literature, James De Mille," *Canadian Bookman* (Toronto), VIII (1926), 203–6. R. W. Douglas, "James De Mille," *Canadian Bookman* (Toronto), IV (1922), 39–44. A. M. MacMechan, "De Mille, the man and the writer," *Canadian Magazine* (Toronto), XXVII (1906), 404–16. George Patterson, *More studies in Nova Scotian history* (Halifax, 1941), 120–48.

DENISON, GEORGE TAYLOR (sometimes designated as George T. Denison Jr, George T. Denison II, or George T. Denison of Rusholme, to avoid confusion with his father and eldest son), lawyer, landowner, farmer, and militia officer; b. 17 July 1816 at York (Toronto), U.C., second son of George Taylor Denison* and Esther Borden Lippincott, loyalist; m. Mary Anne Dewson of West Gwillimbury Township and had nine children, the eldest being George Taylor Denison* of Heydon Villa; d. 30 May 1873 at Toronto, Ont., and was buried with military honours in the family's private cemetery, St John's-on-the-Humber, Weston, Ont.

George Taylor Denison's grandfather, John*, was among the first inhabitants of York. He established the family's position as minor landed gentry, a status that was enhanced by his son G. T. Denison of Bellevue who, at his death in 1853, was reputedly the wealthiest private landholder in Canada West. G. T. Denison I also secured the family's place among Tories influential in Toronto affairs. A vigorous proponent of the loyalist ideal of creating a British nation in North America, he had used his wealth and position to promote the growth of the volunteer militia as a necessary adjunct of Tory social and political leadership and as Upper Canada's first line of defence against both external and internal threats. In 1822 he created the York Dragoons, one of the first cavalry troops attached to the York militia.

George Taylor Denison of Rusholme was cast in the mould established by his father and grandfather. After receiving his formal education at Upper Canada College, he articled under George Cartwright Strachan, son of John Strachan*, and was admitted to the bar of Upper Canada in 1839. He was actively engaged in legal practice only until 1856, however, having amassed extensive landholdings which required all his energies. Rusholme, his estate in west Toronto, was itself a farm where Denison raised field crops and tobacco for export, cattle, swine, and thoroughbred horses. Surrounding Rusholme were the farms of Denison's tenants whose rents were partially commuted into labour on the estate. In addition, Denison leased land from the city of Toronto for development as residential sites, and as Toronto spread westward to the edge of his estates he subdivided much of his land into fashionable "park lots." These and other commercial ventures (such as contracts for the resurfacing of Toronto's major thoroughfares) provided Denison with a fortune of almost $200,000 at middle age, and an income permitting him to accept the heavy social, political, and military responsibilities that were assumed by his family.

Denison represented Saint Patrick's ward as alderman from 1843 until 1853 when he led seven other councillors in resigning over the admitted complicity of Toronto's mayor, John G. Bowes*, in Francis Hincks*' "£10,000 job," which involved many public officials who profited privately from the Northern Railway scheme. A member of the Toronto Turf Club, Denison was among those men responsible for establishing the "Queen's Plate" racing classic. He was also a founder of the Upper Canadian (later Dominion) Rifle Association in 1861 and was an officer of the St George's Society. In every respect Denison was characteristic of the generation of vigorous young businessmen whose enthusiasm propelled Toronto into commercial and cultural rivalry with Montreal.

But it was Denison's commitment to his family's adopted function as soldiers dedicated to the survival of the loyalist ideal in North America that led to his most lasting contribution. First gazetted as an officer in the 1st Regiment of West York militia in 1834, Denison joined his father's cavalry troop in 1838. He rose to the rank of full colonel and commandant of the 5th and 10th military districts in 1860, and at his death was the senior militia officer in Ontario. He saw action at the battle of Gallows Hill in 1837 when William Lyon Mackenzie*'s rebels were routed, and was later attached to Sir Allan MacNab*'s force which pursued the insurgents in the London area and which laid seige to Navy Island in the Niagara River. During the Fenian invasions of 1866 Denison was in command of the Toronto garrison.

His main contribution, however, was his activity on behalf of an indigenous Canadian military establishment during the critical period of responsible government in Canada when the institutions of nationhood were being forged. A viable native defensive force was one of the prerequisites of self-determination in British North America after 1846. Nevertheless, successive governments in the Province of Canada, especially during the troubled years between 1854 and 1866, consistently refused to provide adequately for local defence in spite of the dangers of open Anglo-American hostilities. The militia was in a state of stagnation, offset partially by the volunteers who maintained themselves in readiness. George Denison and his brothers Richard Lippincott and Robert Brittain set an early precedent in 1839 when the disbandment of the active force threatened the demise of the Queen's Light Dragoons (an honorary designation conferred on the York Dragoons during the campaigns of 1837–39); their equipment was to be returned to imperial stores. The Denisons purchased all of the necessary equipment themselves, renamed the troop "Denison's Horse," and continued to drill the men. When the Militia Act of 1846 failed to provide funds for the maintenance of troops of volunteer cavalry, considered by the Denisons to be the crucial element in local defence strategy, George Denison of Rusholme, now commanding officer of Denison's Horse, regazetted the troop

as the 1st Toronto Independent Troop of Cavalry (it became the York Light Dragoons in 1853 and was designated the Governor-General's Body Guard in 1866) and thereafter maintained it out of his private fortune. In 1853 he also organized the first field battery to be integrated with the Mounted Force of the York militia (9th Field Battery), and he reorganized several independent infantry companies to create the 2nd battalion, Queen's Own Rifles. Meanwhile, Denison and his son, George Taylor, campaigned by pamphlet, letter, and personal pressure on senior officials and officers to promote more vigorous policies in support of the militia as the mainstay of provincial and, ultimately, national defence.

It is impossible to assess with accuracy the impact of Denison's individual effort, but it is clear that, with others like him, he aided the development of a Canadian military tradition, especially the volunteering spirit, through difficult and trying times.

DAVID GAGAN

G. T. Denison II was the author of "The burning of the *Caroline*," *Canadian Monthly and National Review* (Toronto), III (1873), 289–92; *Chronicle of St. John's Cemetery on the Humber* (Toronto, 1868).

MTCL, Denison family papers. PAC, MG 29, F13 (George Taylor Denison III papers); RG 7, G12, 74; RG 9, I, C1, 291, 292. PAO, MS 58, Percy C. Band collection (microfilm copy). F. C. Denison, *Historical record of the Governor-General's Body Guard and its standing orders* (Toronto, 1876). G. T. Denison III, *The national defences; or, observations on the best defensive force for Canada* (Toronto, 1861); *Soldiering in Canada* (Toronto, 1900). *Globe* (Toronto), 31 May 1873. *Leader* (Toronto), 31 May 1873. Chadwick, *Ontario families*, I, 108–10.

E. J. Chambers, *The Governor-General's Body Guard: a history of the origin, development and services of the senior cavalry regiment in the militia service of the Dominion of Canada* (Toronto, 1902). R. L. Denison, *The Canadian pioneer Denison family of county York, England and county York, Ontario* (4v., Toronto, [c.1951–c.1953]), IV. Scadding, *Toronto of old* (Armstrong). C. P. Stacey, *Canada and the British Army, 1846–1871* (2nd ed., Toronto, 1963). G. F. G. Stanley, *Canada's soldiers: the military history of an unmilitary people* (Toronto, 1960). Samuel Thompson, *Reminiscences of a Canadian pioneer for the last fifty years; an autobiography* (Toronto, 1884). C. F. Hamilton, "Defence, 1812–1912," *Canada and its provinces* (Shortt and Doughty), VII, 379–468.

DEROME, FRANÇOIS-MAGLOIRE, lawyer, writer, journalist, protonotary, and clerk of the crown and of the peace; b. 1821 at Montreal, L.C., son of François Derome and Éléonore Pagé; d. 30 July 1880 at Rimouski, Que.

From 1830 to 1835 François-Magloire Derome

De Smet

was a brilliant student at the college of Sainte-Anne-de-la-Pocatière, and already showed his literary talents by winning French essay prizes and writing for newspapers. On 19 Oct. 1842, after studying law under Augustin-Norbert Morin*, he was called to the bar; he carried on his profession at Montreal and at the same time contributed to newspapers.

As a writer Derome first attracted attention by his poetry. Particularly during his youth, he published poems in the press; with its nationalist themes, this poetry placed him among the French Canadian pre-romantics, and, though somewhat dull, it won him the honour of appearing in the *Répertoire national.* . . . One of his poems, "Le Lendemain," published in *Le Canadien* in 1841, caused a certain stir, especially among the Anglophones, when it was translated in the *Quebec Mercury.* In it Derome denounced the loss of liberty:

> Non, le bonheur, ni les chants qu'il inspire,
> N'existe point où meurt la liberté

> No, neither happiness nor the songs that from
> it spring,
> Can exist where liberty is no more,

and in particular he heralded a resurgence of the Canadiens:

> Le peuple un jour aura son lendemain!

> The people one day will have its tomorrow!

His career as a journalist was longer and more brilliant. After writing several articles for various journals while he was studying law, Derome was editor of the *Mélanges religieux* in 1851 and 1852; in 1854 he replaced Ronald MacDonald* at the head of *Le Canadien,* and remained in this post until 1857. He accepted and continued the paper's moderate tendency, and supported the Liberal-Conservative coalition of 1854. When introducing Derome to its readers, *Le Canadien* portrayed him accurately as a well-informed man of rare talent, who wrote his language with an elegance and purity uncommon in Canada.

In 1857 Derome gave up active journalism to become protonotary of the crown and clerk of the peace at Rimouski. He continued to contribute to the *Foyer canadien* and the *Revue canadienne,* but he gave more of his time to the study of law, and was of great service to his colleagues at the bar on difficult questions. He left this post only in 1878.

On 30 July 1880 François-Magloire Derome died of pneumonia at his residence at Rimouski. He had been married twice: first to Théotiste Labadie, in September 1848; secondly, in 1869, to Malvina Langevin, sister of Jean-Pierre-François Laforce* Langevin, bishop of Rimouski, and of Sir Hector-Louis Langevin*. In 1876 his daughter Malvina married Louis-Napoléon Asselin, who was the father of a "dynasty" of Rimouski lawyers.

NIVE VOISINE

Le Canadien (Québec), 1854–57. *Le Courrier du Canada* (Québec), 9 août 1880. *Le Nouvelliste de Rimouski,* 1876–80. *Catalogue des anciens élèves du collège de Sainte-Anne-de-la-Pocatière, 1827–1927* (Québec, 1927). Morgan, *Bibliotheca Canadensis,* 101–2. Tanguay, *Dictionnaire,* III, 355. *Le répertoire national, ou recueil de littérature canadienne,* James Huston, édit. (4v., Montréal, 1848–50), II, 205.

DE SMET, PIERRE-JEAN, priest, Jesuit, missionary; b. 30 Jan. 1801 at Dendermonde, diocese of Ghent, Belgium, fifth child and second son of Josse De Smet and his second wife, Marie-Jeanne Buydens; d. 23 May 1873 in St Louis, Missouri.

Pierre-Jean De Smet's father, primarily a chandler, was a merchant of considerable means. De Smet's early education was at home and in various colleges; in his 19th year he entered the Petit Séminaire at Mechlin. In August 1821 he sailed for the United States to begin his noviciate at White Marsh, a Jesuit estate near Baltimore. Eighteen months later he was transferred to Florissant, just north of St Louis, Missouri, where he was ordained on 23 Sept. 1827. As a prefect in St Regis Seminary, a school for Indian boys, 1824–30, he learned something of Indian customs and ways before he was sent to St Louis as treasurer of the college in that city (now St Louis University).

Father De Smet was for some years plagued with an irritating skin infection, and he was advised by local physicians to visit his native country for a period. Accordingly, he left the United States for Belgium in September 1833 and did not return to St Louis until November 1837. While abroad he found his true *métier* – as a recruiter of men, supplies, and money for the Missouri mission. Soon after his return to America he was sent as a missionary to the Potawatomi Indians at Council Bluffs (Iowa); he also visited the Yankton and Santee Sioux with a view to negotiating peace between these tribes.

De Smet returned to St Louis from Council Bluffs in February 1840, and between 30 April and 31 December of that year made his first journey to the Rocky Mountains to spy out the land, that is to ascertain the prospects for missions among the Indians in those parts, especially among the Flatheads. His plan, a chimerical one, was to establish a *reduction* such as the Jesuit fathers of the 17th century had established in Paraguay, a mission wherein a white man would never set foot. In 1841, with two fathers and three brothers, he reached the Bitterroot Valley where he founded the mission of Sainte-Marie (Stevensville, Mont.) 35 miles south of present-day Missoula. In the following spring he visited the missionaries at Fort Vancouver (in present-day Vancouver, Wash.), François-Norbert Blanchet* and Modeste Demers, to concert plans for the propagation of the faith in the Oregon country. Between them it was decided that, since assistance in personnel and material was necessary for the success of the mission, Father De Smet should return to the central states and seek permission to visit Europe to obtain these ends. Accordingly, before the close of that year he again crossed the Atlantic, and he returned to the Pacific northwest via Cape Horn, reaching the Columbia River on 31 July 1844 with five additional Jesuits and a group of sisters of Notre-Dame de Namur. The following 12 months were spent in founding new missions and in visiting Sainte-Marie. But, convinced that the very existence of these new missions depended upon a permanent peace with the Blackfeet, the traditional enemies of the Flatheads, he determined to visit the country of the former.

In August 1845 he began a momentous journey which was to take him into Hudson's Bay Company territory. From the north end of Pend d'Oreille Lake he cut across country to the valley of the Kootenay River, followed along it to *la haute traverse*, whence he crossed over to the sources of the Columbia River. Moving down this valley he entered Sinclair Pass, recrossed the Kootenay and by White Man's Pass reached the Bow River valley near the site of present-day Canmore, Alberta. Thence he travelled northward to Rocky Mountain House which he reached on 4 October. He was there until the end of the month. Here it was that he met bands of Crees, Chippewas, and Blackfeet. He then set out to visit other Blackfoot bands, wandered aimlessly for days – apparently to the east of the area he had just passed through – and was fortunate to get back to Rocky Mountain House, whence he was conducted to Fort Edmonton, where he spent the winter of 1845–46 as a guest of the HBC. This long trek in the wilderness constitutes De Smet's significant connection with Canadian history. He had, however, not succeeded in his purpose inasmuch as he had met only one small band of Blackfeet.

In the spring he set out with a party over the company trail via the upper North Saskatchewan River to Jasper House, where they spent Easter Sunday, 12 April 1846. From there by way of the Wood River they reached the Columbia after terrible sufferings. Three weeks later, on 29 May, they were at Fort Colvile (near present-day Kettle Falls, Wash.) and before the end of June arrived at Fort Vancouver. After a quick visit to the religious houses on the Willamette River, De Smet set out for the upper country with supplies for the missions there; he was back at his first foundation, Sainte-Marie on the Bitterroot, on or about 8 August. He then returned to St Louis. These long journeys of 1845–46 had been made at about the same time and over much of the same territory as the travels of the artist Paul Kane in search of Indians of the west. De Smet did some sketching himself as he journeyed.

De Smet's days as a missionary to the Rocky Mountains were over. During the years that were left to him, he made numerous trips to Europe (in all he crossed the Atlantic Ocean 19 times) and, though he was not actually serving on missions, he was deeply involved with them. Between 1851 and 1870 he also journeyed to the upper Missouri River many times in the interest of the American government. Perhaps his finest hour was in 1868 when, accompanied only by a squaw-man as interpreter and a few friendly chiefs and braves, he entered the camp of Sitting Bull* and persuaded him to accept the subsequent treaty of Fort Rice, "the most complete and wisest thus far concluded with the Indians of this country." De Smet visited the Sioux for the last time in 1870. He died three years later and was buried at Florissant where he had completed his noviciate 50 years before.

Wm. L. Davis

[The following depositories hold De Smet's papers: General Archives of the Society of Jesus in Rome. ASJ, Province belge du nord (Bruxelles), papiers De Smet; Missouri Province (St Louis University), Pius XII Library, Desmetiana section. Holland Library (Washington State University, Pullman), De Smet family papers.

Although there is no complete bibliography of Father De Smet's published works in one place, two are useful: Augustin et Alois de Backer, *Bibliothèque de la Compagnie de Jésus; première partie: bibliographie, par les Pères Augustin et Aloys de Backer; seconde partie: histoire, par le Père Auguste Carayon,* ed. Carlos Sommervogel (11v., Bruxelles, Paris, 1890–1932), VII, 1307–10; and *Bibliographie nationale: dictionnaire des écrivains belges et catalogue de leurs publications, 1830–1880* (4v., Bruxelles, 1886–1910), I, 536–37. To date, only two biographies of De Smet have been published and neither of these is adequate: Eugène Laveille, *Le P. De Smet (1801–1873)* (1re éd., Liège, Belgique, et Arras, France, 1912; 2e éd., Liège et Lille, France, 1913); [P.-J. De Smet], *Life, letters, and travels of Father Pierre-Jean De Smet, S.J., 1801–1873 . . . ,* ed. H. M. Chittenden and A. T.

Dessane

Richardson (4v., New York, 1905). In the latter, facing p.150, is a youthful portrait of Father De Smet; another, done after he was made a chevalier of the Order of Leopold on 18 June 1865, faces p.839. He himself prepared the most exact map of his travels in Alberta and British Columbia, and it is reproduced in his *Missions de l'Orégon et voyages aux montagnes Rocheuses aux sources de la Colombie, de l'Athabasca et du Sascatshawin en 1845–1846* (Gand, [1848]). W.L.D.]

DESSANE, MARIE-HIPPOLYTE-ANTOINE, musician; b. Forcalquier (Basses-Alpes, France), 10 Dec. 1826; son of Louis Dessane and Marie Maurel; m. in 1847 Irma Trunel de la Croix-Nord by whom he had nine children, with three boys and four girls surviving infancy; d. Quebec, 8 June 1873.

Marie-Hippolyte-Antoine Dessane's father was a music teacher, and two of his brothers became musicians. They moved to Billom, Auvergne, in 1828, and the father gave Antoine his first music lessons. In 1837 the family went to Paris where Antoine studied at the Conservatoire until October 1841. He is said to have had the sympathy of Luigi Cherubini, the director, who was ordinarily a gruff person. Cherubini called him his "Benjamin" as Dessane was one of the youngest students. Dessane had contact with such fellow students as César Franck and Jacques Offenbach. He studied piano, organ, and violoncello and on two occasions was one of the few successful applicants for classes with limited enrolment. However, he did not graduate or obtain a prize from the Conservatoire. About 1842 Dessane, his father, and his eldest brother set out on a concert tour which lasted a year and a half. It began in France, continued through northern Italy to Trieste, and through Austria and southern Germany. Dessane then taught for a year at the Jesuit college in Billom and in 1845 moved to Clermont-Ferrand. There he associated with a friend of his family, the composer Georges Onslow. In an informal workshop atmosphere they tried out and discussed each other's compositions and performed music. In Clermont-Ferrand Dessane also taught piano; one of his pupils became his wife.

Living conditions for artists in France after the revolution of 1848 influenced his decision to accept a position as organist and choirmaster at the Quebec basilica, offered to him through a friend of his wife's and Abbé Pierre-Henri Bouchy of the college of Sainte-Anne-de-la-Pocatière. The Dessanes arrived in Quebec in July 1849. About 18 months later Antoine and his wife, a soprano or mezzo-soprano, took part in a Quebec concert for the first time. He soon rose to a leading role in musical circles and in the mid-1850s led the Société Harmonique. Operatic music was emphasized in its concerts. In 1855 Dessane conducted the first act of *La Dame blanche* by Boieldieu. In 1857 and 1858 he participated in concerts of the Septette Club featuring excerpts from several Beethoven symphonies and music by Haydn, Rossini, Schubert, Weber, and others. In 1860 Dessane briefly engaged in polemics with Ernest Gagnon* on the theory of plain-chant accompaniment, provoked by the publication of P.-M. Lagacé*'s *Chants liturgiques*, based on the ideas of Louis Niedermeyer, a prominent church musician in France. Niedermeyer's views did not win much acceptance, but partly as a result of the controversy Dessane resigned from the cathedral a few years later. About 1861 he formed an orchestra of some 60 players, including regimental musicians, but this proved a financial failure.

In September 1865 the Dessanes moved to New York where Antoine became organist at St Francis Xavier Church, connected with a Jesuit institution. In New York he participated as cellist in a series of string quartet recitals but also appeared as conductor and pianist. A highlight was the performance of his Mass no.4. The decline of his health influenced a decision to return to Quebec where Dessane became organist at Saint-Roch Church in November 1869. Once again he assumed a central position in musical life. He founded the choral Société Sainte-Cécile in 1869 and together with Frederick W. Mills served as conductor of the newly revived Société Harmonique.

In 1870 Dessane announced plans for a Conservatoire National de Musique, scheduled to open in November 1871. The school was to offer courses in orchestral playing, theory, and voice and present six concerts each season. It does not appear to have become a reality, but on 28 June 1871 Dessane conducted a concert demonstrating what the conservatory might accomplish. The program was mostly operatic but also included the funeral march from Beethoven's *Eroica* and Berlioz' *Les Francs Juges* overture. In May and November of that year Dessane presented Adam's one-act operetta *Farfadet* and in June 1872 Boisselot's opéra-comique *Ne touchez pas à la reine*. Already a sick man, he had to curtail his activities, making a single return to the Saint-Roch organ on 1 June 1873, a week before his death. On 7 Oct. 1872 the leading citizens of Quebec had organized a concert to pay homage to Dessane.

Dessane's motto was "Alterius non honoris." A product of the strictly disciplined training of the Paris Conservatoire, he was himself a strict teacher and a hard worker. According to Gustave Smith he raised the level of musical instruction and established the study of solfège in the Quebec convents. Nazaire Le Vasseur* has stated that in contrast to his organist predecessors, who knew little besides plain-chant and operatic music, Dessane introduced the great classical tradition. This view is open to doubt. Dessane's predecessor as organist of the basilica, Theodore Frederic Molt*, was familiar with classical music and had even paid a visit to Beethoven. On the other hand Dessane's performances themselves were heavily slanted towards opera. The few pieces of his church music available for inspection appear to be rooted entirely in the early 19th century and reflect little of tradition. All his music examined, whether sacred or secular, shows a theatrical quality, for example, strong dynamic contrasts. The harmonies are euphonious. Within a basically homophonic style the composer knew how to give each vocal part independence. His dance music, for example *Le Galop de Pégase*, conveys a genuine sense of fun.

Dessane's more than 50 compositions include about equal amounts of sacred and secular music. The former category includes four settings of the mass (at least two of these with orchestra), several settings each of the *Regina Cœli*, *Dominum Salvum*, *Ave Maria*, and *Tantum Ergo* as well as other choral settings to Latin words and sacred songs with French texts. The larger instrumental works include a symphony in C, a Suite for orchestra (1863) and a Fantaisie-Sonate for flute and strings (1858). The titles of his instrumental music often refer to Canada: *Quadrille sur des airs canadiens* (1854), *La Québecoise* (polka), *La berceuse indienne* (rêverie for violoncello) and the same is true of such songs as *La Mère canadienne* (chant patriotique, by Emmanuel Blain de Saint-Aubin) and three to words by Octave Crémazie: *Le chant des voyageurs*, *Chant du vieux soldat canadien*, *Hommage à la France* (chant canadien). Some of these songs enjoyed a measure of popularity. To the list of compositions should be added a didactic work on the theory of orchestration, written in 1869. Dessane set up his own lithographic workshop in which he prepared reproductions of some of his works.

Dessane's contribution was reinforced by his wife, who is said to have introduced the French romance to Quebec ("ou pour mieux le dire le *chansonette* de bon ton," G. Smith), and at least three of their children became musicians.

HELMUT KALLMANN

Catalogue of Canadian composers, ed. Helmut Kallmann (Toronto, 1952). Sœurs de Sainte-Anne, *Dictionnaire biographique des musiciens canadiens* (2e éd., Lachine, Qué., 1934). Helmut Kallmann, *A history of music in Canada, 1534–1914* (Toronto and London, 1960), 91–92, 93, 106, 124, 126, 181, 188. Nazaire Le Vasseur, "Musique et musiciens à Québec," *La Musique* (Québec), I (1919), 126 – II (1920), 123. Irma Michaud, "Antonin Dessane — 1826–1873," *BRH*, XXXIX (1933), 73–76; "Madame Dessane, née Irma Trunel de la Croix-Nord, 1828–1899," *BRH*, XXXIX (1933), 76–79. Gustave Smith, "Du mouvement musical en Canada," *L'Album musical* (Montréal), 1882.

DEVLIN, BERNARD, lawyer and politician; b. 15 Dec. 1824 at Roscommon, in Ireland, son of Owen Devlin, a rich landowner, and of Catherine Mellany; d. 8 Feb. 1880 at Denver, Colorado.

Bernard Devlin began his medical studies under the direction of his uncle, Dr Charles Devlin, a famous practitioner of Ballina, County Mayo, and he went to Dublin to complete them. In 1844 he arrived at Quebec with his father, who was emigrating as a result of financial misfortunes. Since he was still a minor, the medical board at Quebec refused to allow him to practise medicine, and he founded a weekly paper with a liberal bias, the *Freeman's Journal and Commercial Advertiser*, which survived from 1844 to 1847, and which he directed until he left for Montreal, where he continued his activity as a journalist and studied law with Edward Carter. He was called to the bar of Lower Canada in October 1847. He rapidly acquired a large clientele, particularly as a criminal jurist. For some years he was also one of the lawyers of the municipal corporation of Montreal, and, from 1863 to 1870, councillor and alderman; it was partly through him that Mount Royal Park was created. In 1868 he was called to the bar of Ontario.

In 1864 the United States government engaged his services in the legal action taken at Montreal against the Confederates who had been involved in the St Albans raid. Bernard Devlin was an officer of the militia for 15 years, and in June 1866 commanded the 1st regiment of the Prince of Wales Rifles against the Fenians. He was active in Irish circles, taking part in a meeting advocating the repeal of the union of England and Ireland in 1848, and being on several occasions president of the St Patrick's Society of Montreal, the patriotic centre of a group which had become powerful.

In 1867 Bernard Devlin stood in the federal election as Liberal candidate against Thomas D'Arcy McGee* in the riding of Montreal West. He was unsuccessful. The struggle was a violent one among Irishmen. McGee and his supporters represented the moderates, who were afraid of the Fenians, whereas Devlin was accused of being secretly well disposed towards them. Devlin managed to reduce his adversary's majority to a handful of votes. He was defeated in Montreal Centre in 1874 by Michael Patrick Ryan*, but the latter's election was annulled and Devlin was elected in 1875 by acclamation. He sat in the House of Commons until the 1878 election, when he was defeated by his former opponent, Ryan. An excellent speaker, popular with crowds, he addressed the house on a number of occasions. His first speech was delivered on 12 Feb. 1875 in support of the amnesty for Louis Riel* and Ambroise-Dydime Lépine*. On 8 March 1875 he took an important part in the debate on a motion by John Costigan* in favour of the separate schools of New Brunswick, and he was specially thanked by the Catholic bishop of Saint John, John Sweeney*. One of his most famous speeches was given on 19 March 1877; in it he proposed that a study be made of the feasibility of giving better representation to minorities through a transformation of the electoral system. He died on 8 Feb. 1880 at Denver in Colorado, where he was staying because of his failing health.

In 1848 Bernard Devlin had married Anna Eliza Hickey, of Brooklyn, New York. At his death he left two daughters and one son. His funeral, which was held at Montreal, attracted thousands of people, and the burial took place on 16 Feb. 1880 at the cemetery of Côte-des-Neiges.

J.-C. BONENFANT

[Bruce and Grey], *Elgin-Grey papers* (Doughty), I, 163–64. Canada, House of Commons, *Debates*, 1875, 108–11; 1877, 814–34. Canada, *Sessional papers*, I (1867–68), PT.8, no.41; VI (1873), PT. 6, no.60; VII (1874), PT.6, no.59; XII (1879), PT.9, no.88. *True Witness and Catholic Chronicle* (Montreal), 11, 18 Feb. 1880. *Can. parl. comp.*, 1875, 207–8. *Dom. ann. reg.*, 1880–81, 405–6. T. P. Slattery, *The assassination of D'Arcy McGee* (Toronto and New York, 1968).

DIAMOND, ABRAHAM, lawyer, journalist, and police magistrate; b. 7 May 1828, Fredericksburgh Township (in present-day South Fredericksburgh Township), U.C., second son of John Diamond and Elizabeth Jeffers; m. Louisa Coleman in 1860, by whom he had several children; d. 24 July 1880, Belleville, Ont.

Abraham Diamond, a Wesleyan Methodist of loyalist descent, graduated from Victoria College in Cobourg and was a governor general's prize winner at the Toronto Normal School. He taught school in Thornhill, Bloomfield, and Belleville before beginning the study of law in the office of Caleb P. Simpson in 1858. He was admitted to the bar in 1859 and began practising with W. W. Dean's firm. He was called to the bar in 1862 and was later in partnership with George D. Dickson; he eventually formed a partnership in 1868 with a brother, Wellington Jeffers, later mayor of Belleville.

From 1856 to 1868 Abraham Diamond edited Elijah Miles' Reform paper, the Belleville *Hastings Chronicle*. An effective speaker and writer, Diamond's reasoned pragmatic approach made him seem less forcible but also less erratic than many of his better known journalist contemporaries. An enthusiastic supporter of constitutional change in Canada, Diamond was active in the Reform Convention of 1859. Besides being a member of the credentials committee, he moved the key fifth resolution, speaking in favour of a practicable, efficient, and beneficial federal union of the two sections of the Province of Canada. In the election of 1867 Diamond made a sharp and effective break with Reform leader George BROWN by actively supporting in West Hastings two Conservative candidates, James Brown in the federal election and Ketchum Graham in the provincial.

Diamond was police magistrate of Belleville from 1868 until his sudden death, from an overdose of hydrate of chloral. He was active in community life as a town councillor, school trustee, notary public, and militia officer. He was a director of the Grand Junction Railway Company. A mason and the secretary of the Literary Association in Belleville, he was also the first president of the town's Native Canadian Association.

ELWOOD JONES

Hastings County Museum (Belleville, Ont.), files on Abraham Diamond and on the Belleville Printing and Publishing Company. PAC, MG 24, K19 (Peter Robertson papers), James Ross to Robertson, 28 Feb. 1854; RG 31, A1, 1861, no.43, f.99. *Canada Gazette* (Quebec), 1 March 1862, 15 May 1863. *Globe* (Toronto), 9–11 Nov. 1859, September 1867. *Hastings Chronicle* (Belleville), 1859, 1867. *Intelligencer* (Belleville), 26 July 1880. *London Free Press*, 14 Nov. 1859.

Canada directory, 1857–58, 55. *The Canadian legal directory: a guide to the bench and bar of the Dominion of Canada*, ed. H. J. Morgan (Toronto, 1878). *Directory of the county of Hastings ... 1860–61* (Belleville, 1860), 118, 160. William Canniff, *History of the settlement of Upper Canada (Ontario), with special reference to the bay Quinté* (Toronto, 1869). *City of Belleville history*, comp. W. C. Mikel (Picton, Ont., 1943). *Pioneer life on the Bay of Quinte including genealogies of old families and biographical sketches of representative citizens* (Toronto, n.d.). E. H. Jones, "Ephemeral compromise: the Great Reform Convention revisited," *J. of Canadian Studies* (Peterborough, Ont.), III (February 1968), 21–28.

DICK, THOMAS, shipbuilder, shipowner and captain, and hotelier; b. 1809 in Scotland; d. 7 Nov. 1874 in Toronto, Ont.

Thomas Dick went to sea as a youth and earned his master's certificate. He emigrated to Upper Canada about 1833 and took employment in Niagara-on-the-Lake at the Niagara Harbour and Dock Company, which commenced operations in that year. Dick was sailing the schooner *Fanny* by 1835, and he commanded HMS *Experiment* at the battle of the Windmill, 12 Nov. 1838.

During the 1840s and 1850s Dick had command of several popular passenger steamers, some of which are said to have been built under his supervision. In 1850 he purchased the *City of Toronto*, the first of a number of ships he was to own and command in a day when steamboat skippers enjoyed considerable prestige in the community. He and his brother James are said to have inaugurated in 1858, with the steamer *Rescue*, the first mail service between Collingwood and Fort William (Thunder Bay).

Dick also built a contiguous row of four large houses in 1844 on property now the site of the Royal York Hotel in Toronto. These were occupied by Knox College and the Toronto Academy before becoming Sword's Hotel and, later, the Revere House. Famous in its time, the row was further enlarged and, in 1862, opened under Dick's management as the Queen's Hotel, which became one of Canada's leading hostelries.

Dick served as alderman for St George ward, 1871–72, and as a director of the St Lawrence Bank and the Toronto, Grey and Bruce Railway. He died in 1874 at the Queen's Hotel.

K. R. MACPHERSON

Canada, Province of, *Statutes*, 1853, c.148; 1857, c.168; 1858, c.122. *Globe* (Toronto), 7 Nov. 1874. *Mail* (Toronto), 7 Nov. 1874. *Patriot* (Toronto), 25 July 1837, 6 April 1838. *Weekly Leader* (Toronto), 13 Nov. 1874. *Cherrier, Kirwin & McGown's Toronto directory for 1873* ... (Toronto, 1873), 291. *Fisher & Taylor's Toronto directory for the year 1874* ... (Toronto, 1874), 374. *Rowsell's city of Toronto and county of York directory for 1850–1* ... ed. J. Armstrong (Toronto, 1850), 37. *Landmarks of Toronto* (Robertson), II. Middleton, *Municipality of Toronto*, I, 212, 487; II, 742, 802. Scadding, *Toronto of old*. A. G. Young, *Great Lakes' saga; the influence of one family on the development of Canadian shipping on the Great Lakes, 1816–1913* (Owen Sound, Ont., Toronto, and Montreal, 1965), 96–98.

DIXON, WILLIAM, public servant; b. in Ireland *c.* 1825, second son of Alexander Dixon and Esther O'Dwyer; m. Clara Rowsell by whom he had several children; d. London, Eng., 27/28 Oct. 1873.

William Dixon was brought to Canada in 1830, and in 1835 the family settled in Toronto where his father opened the British Saddlery Warehouse. William was educated at Upper Canada College in Toronto, but nothing else is known of his early career. About 1859 he went to England where he travelled widely and engaged in business.

In February 1862, on the recommendation of Philip Michael Matthew Scott Vankoughnet*, the chief commissioner of crown lands in Canada, Dixon was put in charge of exhibits arriving from Canada for the London International Exhibition. Because of his efficient discharge of his duties he was kept on as curator of the Canadian court at the exhibition later that year.

It is as Canada's chief emigration agent in England that Dixon is mainly known. In 1859 the Canadian Bureau (later Department) of Agriculture had begun sending Canadian agents to Europe on temporary missions to promote emigration, a policy which received its most enthusiastic support from Vankoughnet and Thomas D'Arcy McGee*. In January 1866 McGee, as minister of agriculture, appointed Dixon temporarily Canada's emigration agent for the United Kingdom. The agency proved so useful and Dixon so capable that McGee continued the office on a temporary basis and Dixon was stationed in Liverpool, then in Wolverhampton (1867–68). Finally, in January 1869, Dixon went to London to establish a permanent office. His duties as emigration agent included distributing publicity, supervising the work and accounts of other Canadian emigration agents throughout Europe, cooperating with provincial emigration agents, and reporting to Canada on the conditions affecting European emigration. He also undertook such general duties as providing information about Canada and assisting Canadian visitors.

Dixon was agent until his death in 1873, and during his tenure was established the basic framework for the Canadian emigration agency, which lasted until the appointment of Alexander Tilloch Galt* as high commissioner in 1880. Dixon advocated strengthening the agent's authority, particularly as regards the agents in the dominion, a reform achieved under his successor, John Edward Jenkins*, who was also given the title of agent general. Dixon was frequently recalled to Canada for consultation with the Canadian government, and had official contact with McGee, and with the deputy minister of agriculture, Joseph-Charles Taché*. He did not, however, have the influence on Canadian government policies enjoyed by the chief agent at Quebec until 1868, Alexander Carlisle Buchanan*.

From 1869 to 1873 there was a considerable increase in emigration to Canada from the British Isles and western Europe over the previous years.

Dodd

Economic and political conditions in Europe and North America were chiefly responsible for the increase but Dixon deserves some credit because of his vigorous efforts in the promotion of emigration. His honesty, courtesy, and competence helped ensure the permanence of the Canadian agency in London and set a high standard for future agents.

WESLEY B. TURNER

PAC, MG 24, B19 (Brown Chamberlin papers), 7, 10; MG 29, B13 (John Lowe papers), 4, 13; RG 2, ser.1, 14, 17, 20, 54; RG 7, G1, 172; RG 17, AI, ser.1, 3, 8, 11, 12, 17–19, 21, 26, 46, 96, 97, 103, 105; ser.2, 4, 6, 8, 10, 13, 14, 16, 18; ser.4, 1, 2; ser.5, 2, 5; ser.6, 1. Canada, Province of, *Sessional papers*, 1866. Canada, House of Commons, *Journals*, 1867–74; *Debates*, 1875; *Sessional papers*, 1867–74. Ontario, *Sessional Papers*, III (1870–71), PT.2, no.28, "Annual report of the commissioner of agriculture and public works for the province of Ontario, on immigration, for the year 1870." *Daily Colonist* (Toronto), 29 June 1855. *Gazette* (Montreal), 30 Oct. 1873. *Mail* (Toronto), 30 Oct. 1873. *Times* (London), 30 Oct. 1873. *Commemorative biog. record, county York*, 26. *Cyclopædia of Can. biog.* (Rose, 1886), 428–29.

W. A. Carrothers, *Emigration from the British Isles, with special reference to the development of the overseas dominions* (London, 1929). H. I. Cowan, *British emigration to British North America; the first hundred years* (Toronto, 1961). D. C. Harvey, *The colonization of Canada* (Toronto, 1936). S. C. Johnson, *A history of emigration from the United Kingdom to North America, 1763–1912* (London, 1966). Norman Macdonald, *Canada: immigration and colonization, 1841–1903* (Aberdeen, Scot., and Toronto, 1966). H. G. Skilling, *Canadian representation abroad from agency to embassy* (Toronto, 1945). Samuel Thompson, *Reminiscences of a Canadian pioneer for the last fifty years; an autobiography* (Toronto, 1884). P. W. Gates, "Official encouragement to immigration by the Province of Canada," *CHR*, XV (1934), 24–38. Hugh Morrison, "The secret passenger warrant system of 1872," *CHR*, XVIII (1937), 406–13. Roland Wilson, "Migration movements in Canada, 1868–1925," *CHR*, XIII (1932), 157–82.

DODD, EDMUND MURRAY, lawyer, politician, and judge; b. at Sydney, Cape Breton, 9 Jan. 1797, son of Archibald Charles Dodd and Susannah Gibbons; d. at Cow Bay (Port Morien), N.S., 27 July 1876.

Edmund Murray Dodd served as a midshipman in the British navy during the War of 1812 and was a prisoner of war for a time. During the 1820s he practised law in Sydney. In 1826 he married Mary Ann Sarah Weeks, who died within a few years, and in 1830 he was married again, to Caroline Maria Ritchie, by whom he had several children.

Dodd was elected to the Legislative Assembly of Nova Scotia in 1832 as the first member for Sydney Township. He soon joined Tories James William JOHNSTON, Mather Byles ALMON, Alexander Stewart*, and Simon Bradstreet Robie* in their opposition to the attempts of Joseph HOWE and Herbert Huntington* to introduce a system of party government. Despite their political differences Dodd and Howe appear to have been personal friends. Howe sought his advice when threatened with a duel in 1838 – perhaps because Dodd had taken part in a bloodless duel in Halifax not long before.

Dodd's appointment to the Executive Council in 1838, and his elevation to the post of solicitor general six years later, cemented his alliance with the Tories. During the ill-fated coalition government of Lieutenant Governor Falkland [Lucius B. Cary*], Dodd's relations with Howe and the Reformers deteriorated steadily. In 1842 Dodd attempted to heal the breach between the Tories and Reformers in the Executive Council when he declared that the council was responsible to both the governor and the assembly. In spite of this "Confession of Faith," as the Reformers labelled it, Dodd was soon leading the Tory attack on the Reformers whom he regarded as a group of place-hunting trouble-makers. With savage humour Howe returned the attack, lampooning Dodd as an obsequious lackey of the governor and as one of the "geese" whose "cackling" had wrecked the coalition.

From 1842 to 1848 Dodd was a judge of probate as well as solicitor general. With his elevation in 1848 to puisne judge of the Supreme Court of Nova Scotia, he left the political arena. Despite his acknowledged ability as a lawyer, he was not a particularly successful judge. Increasing deafness combined with a tendency toward tedious and verbose explanation handicapped him on the bench. His family life was marred with tragedy: a lawyer son was shot to death in Sydney by the father of a girl whom he had raped but refused to marry. The physical infirmities of old age hampered Dodd's activity during his last five years in the Supreme Court. The Liberal legislature, resenting the pro-confederation stand taken by most of the province's judges and lawyers, refused to appoint new judges. Dodd remained on the bench until 1873 when he was finally allowed to retire.

A. A. MACKENZIE

[Joseph Howe], *Speeches and letters* (Chisholm), II, 160, 210, 387, 456–59, 467–68, 515–17, 522. *Directory of N.S. MLAs* (Fergusson). David Allison, *History of Nova Scotia* (3v., Halifax, 1916), II, 704. Beck, *Government of N.S.*, 288. [Joseph Howe], *Joseph Howe, voice of Nova Scotia*, ed. and intro. J. M. Beck (Toronto, 1964), 87. George Patterson, *Studies in*

Nova Scotian history (Halifax, 1940), 78; More studies in Nova Scotian history (Halifax, 1941), 65, 87. Benjamin Russell, "Reminiscences of the Nova Scotia judiciary," Dal. Rev., V (1925–26), 499, 509.

DOEL, JOHN, brewer, businessman, and politician; b. in 1790 in Wiltshire, Eng.; d. in Toronto, Ont., 9 Feb. 1871.

John Doel emigrated about 1817 to Philadelphia, where he may have become a bookseller. He had married Hannah Huntly in England three years earlier, and they were to have five children. The family arrived in York, Upper Canada, on 5 Nov. 1818. For a time Doel was employed to deliver uncalled-for letters but he soon established a brewery at the rear of his home. This, along with profitable investments in real estate, provided him with a comfortable living.

A radical Reformer in politics, Doel was a critic of Sir Peregrine Maitland*'s administration of 1818–28 and in 1828 was a supporter of Judge John Walpole WILLIS in the controversy surrounding him. St Andrew's ward elected him in 1834 to the Toronto City Council, where he voted for William Lyon Mackenzie* as mayor; he was re-elected in 1835. Doel refused to sign the council's complimentary address presented to Lieutenant Governor Sir John Colborne* when Colborne retired the next year, and he did sign a sarcastic protest delivered to Lieutenant Governor Francis Bond Head in 1836 after the latter had replied in an insulting manner to an address from the House of Assembly.

Doel was a close associate of Mackenzie. When the latter needed to borrow from the Bank of the People to sustain his second newspaper, the Constitution, Doel endorsed one of his notes and subsequently lent him other sums. On the eve of the rebellion, the Reformers held several important meetings at Doel's home and at his brewery. There he signed the declaration of the Toronto Reformers drawn up on 28 July 1837, and moved the resolution that Reformers refrain from the consumption of dutiable imports so as to diminish the government's revenue. He was a member of the vigilance committee named on 31 July. It is usually stated that when, in October, Mackenzie presented his plans for seizing the lieutenant governor and establishing a provisional government, Doel would not assent to them and took no part in the uprising. There is some evidence, however, that Mackenzie's supporters in Toronto used Doel's brewery as a gathering place as late as 5 December. Doel was arrested three times, and on each occasion imprisoned for several days; his home was subjected to repeated searches and soldiers were billeted with the family.

After Mackenzie's flight from the province, Doel had to make good on his note held by the Bank of the People. Mackenzie's property was attainted, but the crown permitted his creditors to make good their claims against him. In 1839 James Lesslie*, on behalf of himself and other creditors, obtained a judgement in the Court of Queen's Bench against Mackenzie. In 1845, after the crown granted Mackenzie's lands to Lesslie in trust to sell so that the proceeds could liquidate the judgement, Doel bought Mackenzie's two town lots in Dundas and his lot in Garafraxa Township (now East and West Garafraxa) for £81. When Mackenzie returned to Canada in 1850, Doel sold him the property back for £200. This was a generous settlement, being less than the total sum Doel had spent for the property, interest, and taxes, as well as the original loan and the debts to other creditors of Mackenzie which he had paid. Doel indeed accepted £50 in cash and a note on the balance. He thus helped Mackenzie meet the property qualifications for a member of the Legislative Assembly.

Doel remained a Reformer after the rebellion although he did not take an active part in politics. He did, however, sign the resolutions critical of Sir Charles Metcalfe*'s administration drawn up by the Reform Association of Canada in 1844. He continued to operate his brewery until it was burned on 11 April 1847. He had been a member of the first Methodist Episcopal church erected in York in 1818, and he was a trustee of the Toronto General Hospital. When he died in 1871 his funeral was attended in a body by the York Pioneer Society of which he had been a member.

LILLIAN FRANCIS GATES

PAO, Mackenzie-Lindsey collection, especially f.2540; Misc. 1896, "Rev. John Doel's recollections of the rebellion of 1837 and '38." Globe (Toronto), 10 Feb. 1871. Charles Lindsey, The life and times of William Lyon Mackenzie; with an account of the Canadian rebellion of 1837, and the subsequent frontier disturbances, chiefly from unpublished documents (2v., Toronto, 1862), II, 52. Town of York, 1815–1834 (Firth), 118. T. E. Champion, The Methodist churches of Toronto (Toronto, 1899). Dent, Upper Canadian rebellion, I. E. C. Guillet, The lives and times of the Patriots; an account of the rebellion in Upper Canada, 1837–1838, and the Patriot agitation in the United States, 1837–1842 (Toronto, 1938), 192. Landmarks of Toronto (Robertson), I, 50–55. Scadding, Toronto of old, 309–10. Sissons, Ryerson, II, 59. Bruce West, Toronto (Toronto, 1967), 111, 113.

DOHERTY, PATRICK J., secular priest, teacher, writer; b. 2 June 1838 at Quebec, L.C., son of Patrick Doherty, gardener, and Bridget Byrns;

d. 21 May 1872 in Quebec in the parish of Saint-Roch.

The son of Catholic Irish immigrants, Patrick J. Doherty received his education first from an English tutor, Patrick Kennedy, then from the Brothers of the Christian Schools at Quebec. He entered the Petit Séminaire in 1852, and completed his classical education in 1861. In the same year he began his theological studies at the seminary, and on 11 March 1865 was ordained priest.

In 1861 Doherty had started work as a teacher and supervisor at the Petit Séminaire; he taught chiefly the English language. He had a good mastery of French and a talent for oratory, and even in his school days had delivered speeches in public and also contributed to the student journal *L'Abeille*. After he became a priest, he preached at the cathedral and elsewhere on various occasions, in French or in English. Witty, jovial, and voluble, he was popular with students, but his poor health forced him to leave the seminary for a parish ministry. In the autumn of 1869, before receiving a parish, Doherty undertook a six months' trip to Europe and the Holy Land. At Rome, he struck up a friendship with the Canadian Zouaves [*see* Hugh MURRAY], and in April 1870 returned to Canada via New York with their first detachment.

After 10 months as curate at Sainte-Catherine (Portneuf County), he was assigned by his bishop to the large parish of Saint-Roch and the chaplaincy of the Marine and Emigrant Hospital [*see* Joseph PAINCHAUD]. This assignment asked too much of him, despite his exuberant temperament, and his health suffered. On 16 March 1871 he left for Georgia and spent three months there resting. He returned to Saint-Roch but was unable to complete another full year of active ministry, and after a short relapse he died on 20 May 1872. Since he had celebrated his first mass at the convent of the Ursulines, where he had a sister, he was buried there, and in the following autumn a marble tablet was placed in the chapel in his memory.

"Mr. Doherty was a man of great talent and tremendous wit." He left "some remarkable writings, particularly from the point of view of style and composition; they bear the stamp of the most piquant originality."

HONORIUS PROVOST

ASQ, Journal du séminaire, XI, 90, 119, 128, 130, 139, 210, 437, 490; M 211; M 775; MSS, 26; MSS, 611; MSS, 626; MSS, 627; MSS, 651; MSS, 676; MSS, 677; Université, LXXXIV, 24. [P. J. Doherty], *L'abbé Doherty; ses principaux écrits en français, précédés d'un portrait et d'une notice biographique, par un ami*, [L.-H. Paquet] édit. (Québec, 1872); *Principal English writings of the late Rev. P. J. Doherty, prefaced by a sketch of his life*, ed. [L.-H. Paquet] (Québec, 1873).

DONNELLY, JAMES, farmer; b. 7 March 1816 in County Tipperary, Ireland; murdered 4 Feb. 1880, near Lucan, in Biddulph Township, Ont.

James Donnelly emigrated from Ireland in 1844 and settled with his family in Biddulph Township, Canada West, in 1847. By 1857 Donnelly and his wife Johannah Magee had a family of seven boys, but had been able to purchase only half of the 100 acres they had been living on; in 1856 they had been ejected from the south 50 acres. Somewhere at the bottom of what later came to be known as the "Biddulph Tragedy" lies this divided farm; it may also lie behind Donnelly's quarrel with neighbour Patrick Farrell at a logging bee on 25 June 1857, when he threw "a certain wooden handspike of the value of one penny" at Farrell and killed him. After hiding out for a year, Donnelly was eventually tried and on 5 Aug. 1858 for this "unlucky stroke" given "in liquor" was sent down to Kingston Penitentiary for seven years.

But the "Roman Line" where Donnelly lived was already notorious for darker, more premeditated crimes than his. And in contrast too, unsolved and unpunished. Arson, a secret society with a hate target, faction fighting, and assassination are in evidence, some as early as the mid-1840s. Tipperary had been like this for years; it was once written that its inhabitants "look with indifference upon the most atrocious acts of violence, and by screening the criminal, abet and encourage the crime." The Roman Line settlers had come from County Tipperary; the trouble was they still dreamed there. All this made the Roman Line a very dangerous community to live in; when Donnelly came back from prison in 1865 he was to survive its growing hatred and violence for only 15 more years.

But the rest of Donnelly's story is really that of his seven sons and their defiance, sometimes of the law, frequently, some would say, of the neighbourhood's secret power structure. In 1867 the Donnelly barn is burnt down; in 1874, since the Thompsons would not let her marry him, Will Donnelly twice attempts to abduct Maggie Thompson; in 1875 the Donnelly stage coach line is in such fierce competition with a rival line that stables on both sides eventually go up in flames; at the beginning of the next year Will's elopement with Norah Kennedy makes for himself and his family one more determined enemy – the girl's brother John who develops a mania about Will disinheriting him. To a community that was dangerous to live in, the Donnelly boys (some of them dangerous enough already) replied by being dangerous themselves, and extremely independent.

For, in the federal election of 1878, the family voted against their Conservative Catholic candidate; after this action their ability to hold their own on the Roman Line seems to weaken, partly because two sons are dead, partly because their opponents suddenly become well organized. In 1879 the Donnellys are denounced by the new parish priest and a mob riots at the homestead in daylight. January 1880 brings charges of incendiarism against the Donnelly parents, charges intended to climax a long and skillful campaign of dignity-erosion and slander. After the harassment and boycotting the Donnellys had suffered, any other family would have left the community; the Donnellys would not and so, on 4 Feb. 1880, with a well-planned attack, another mob, at night this time, effected a final solution. For this date a diarist noted "... news of a most atrocious murder ... perpetrated last night at Lucan 17 miles from London the victims were the Donnelly family. Father Mother two sons and one niece and then their house had been set afire to cover the crime four of the bodies were burnt to a cinder. The people in the city were terrified to hear of such a diabolical and lawless crime."

But "Others again go so far as to say that the Donnellys were so bad that it would be better to leave things alone; that it was a good riddance...." Prejudice such as this probably influenced a jury to acquit their alleged murderers even in the face of strong evidence. As one notes, however, the large amounts of hearsay behind the evidence of this prejudice, perhaps one should hear Will Donnelly: "My mother told him [the parish priest] that there were worse than her sons in the neighbourhood, but that the biggest crowd was against them, and that herself and her family was persecuted."

In any case one would still have to admit the magnetism of the love the Donnellys showed for each other and the typical aplomb old Donnelly displayed early one September morning in 1879 when he awoke to find his yard filled with a mob carrying clubs: "I told them I would be there if the devil would burn the whole of them, I was not in the least afraid of them."

JAMES REANEY

Middlesex County Registry Office (London, Ont.), land records, 1800–48 (copies at PAO). PAC, RG 5, C1, 529, no.1653. PAO, Sir Aemilius Irving papers, package 25, no.12. University of Western Ontario Library, Huron County, Ont., clerk of the peace, assessment rolls for Huron District, 1843–45, 1847–48; 13–15 (Huron County, Ont., clerk of the peace, coroner's inquests, 1841–1904); 25 (John B. Cox diaries, 1878, 1880); 28 (Donnelly family papers); 49–72 (Huron County, Ont., clerk of the peace, criminal cases, 1841–1933); 73–79 (Huron County, Ont., clerk of the peace, criminal justice accounts, 1840–1928); 292–331 (Middlesex County, Ont., clerk of the peace, criminal records, 1844–1919); 368–405 (Middlesex County, Ont., Court of Chancery, cases); ULM 56–44 (Biddulph Township, Ont., assessment rolls; collectors' rolls for 1853.

The Biddulph tragedy (London, Ont., 1880). *London Advertiser*, 17 May 1880. *Weekly Globe* (Toronto), 20 Feb., 12 March 1880. *City of London and county of Middlesex general directory for 1868–9 . . .*, ed. James Sutherland (Toronto, 1868), 8. Thomas Laffan, *Tipperary's families: being the hearth money records for 1665–6–7* (Dublin, 1911). W. P. Burke, *History of Clonmel* (Waterford, Ire., 1907). T. P. Kelley, *The black Donnellys* (Winnipeg, 1954). Orlo Miller, *The Donnellys must die* (Toronto, 1962).

DORION, EUGÈNE-PHILIPPE, lawyer, translator, and man of letters; b. 6 Aug. 1830 at Saint-Ours, of the marriage of Dr Jacques DORION and Catherine-Louise Lovell; d. 1 July 1872 at Ottawa and was buried at Saint-Ours.

Eugène-Philippe Dorion completed his secondary education at the seminary of Saint-Hyacinthe, which he had entered in 1841. He was called to the bar on 5 Dec. 1853, and two years later was appointed a translator to the Legislative Assembly of the Province of Canada. In 1859 he was invited to direct its office of French translators, a post he afterwards held at Ottawa in the House of Commons. His contemporaries spoke highly of his knowledge of classical languages, English, French, and some Indian languages. Dorion considerably improved the French text of laws, but he sometimes had to bow to the wishes of the politicians. Thus George-Étienne CARTIER is said to have compelled him to translate the word "dominion," in the British North America Act of 1867 as "puissance" (power).

In 1862 Dorion had published at Quebec a pamphlet entitled *Historique des fonds de retraite en Europe et en Canada*, in which he asked that a pension fund be set up for civil servants. After describing the pension systems in France and England, the author analysed the schemes that had been submitted to the parliament of the Province of Canada in 1860 and 1861, and concluded that it was in the interest of the state to create a pension fund rather than to continue to pay old and inefficient civil servants.

In the last years of his life in Ottawa, he was president of the Société Saint-Jean-Baptiste and of the Institut Canadien-Français. He was a tall man, eloquent, and much admired for his impromptu speeches.

In 1855 he had married Marie Panet, daughter

Dorion

of Charles Panet, a lawyer and MLA for Portneuf. In 1876 their daughter Eugénie married Alfred Duclos* de Celles, parliamentary librarian at Ottawa.

J.-C. BONENFANT

E.-P. Dorion, *Historique des fonds de retraite en Europe et en Canada* (Québec, 1862). *La Minerve* (Montréal), 3 juill. 1872. P.-G. Roy, *Les avocats de la région de Québec*, 136. C.-P. Choquette, *Histoire du séminaire de Saint-Hyacinthe depuis sa fondation jusqu'à nos jours* (2v., Montréal, 1911–12), II, 280. [Azarie Couillard-Després], *Histoire de la seigneurie de Saint-Ours* (2v., Montréal, 1915–17), II, 426–31. Fauteux, *Patriotes*, 217–18.

DORION, JACQUES, doctor, MHA, *Patriote*; b.*c.* 1797 at Quebec, son of Pierre Dorion, butcher, and Jane Clarke; d. 29 Dec. 1877 at Saint-Ours, Richelieu County, Que.

Researchers place Jacques Dorion's birth around 1797, although only one son of Pierre, born on 18 Sept. 1796 and baptized Pierre, is entered in the registers of the parish of Notre-Dame at Quebec. Jacques Dorion began his studies at the Petit Séminaire of Quebec in 1810 and abandoned them in 1816 after completing the fourth year of his classical course, as was common at the time. According to written tradition he studied medicine in Paris under Guillaume Dupuytren and Marie-François-Xavier Bichat, but his name appears neither in the registration book nor in the list of doctors of the faculty of the Université de Paris. No doubt he was one of the 15 Canadians who studied medicine in Paris between 1816 and 1822. On his return to Canada he took up residence at Saint-Ours, where he practised his profession competently and with dedication for more than 55 years. In 1835 he founded the Société Saint-Jean-Baptiste of Saint-Ours.

As MHA for Richelieu County from 26 Oct. 1830 to 27 March 1838, he was associated with the *Patriotes*; he took part in the great assembly of the six counties, signed the Ninety-two Resolutions, and played an active role in the 1837 rebellion. He was arrested on 12 December for high treason by the sheriff Édouard-Louis-Antoine Juchereau Duchesnay, and imprisoned at Montreal, during which time Charles Stephen Gore* had Dorion's house ransacked. Dorion was accused of having given orders to fire on the boat *Varennes* between Saint-Denis and Saint-Ours; it may have been bringing supplies to Gore's troops. Thanks to the influence of his friends, notably François-Roch de Saint-Ours, sheriff of Montreal and his wife's cousin, he was set free on 3 March 1838 after paying bail of £1,000.

Jacques Dorion offers a fine example of social advancement in the 19th century. A butcher's son, he was nonetheless able to get a classical education, and even to travel to France to learn medicine. Having gone to live in the prosperous Richelieu region, he married, on 30 Jan. 1824, Catherine-Louise Lovell, niece of the seigneur Charles-Louis-Roch de Saint-Ours*, was elected a member of the assembly, and led his children to the top of the social and professional hierarchy. Edmond-Jacques was a doctor and journalist; EUGÈNE-PHILIPPE was head of the French translators in the House of Commons; Joseph-Adolphe, married to Henriette-Amélie de Saint-Ours, was a notary, coroner, justice of the peace, MHA, and legislative councillor; Charles was a lawyer at Sorel and a district judge.

CLAUDE GALARNEAU

Archives de l'université de Paris, Faculté de médecine, Catalogue des docteurs en médecine, I; Faculté de médecine, Registre des inscriptions, 1816–1822. Archives paroissiales de Notre-Dame (Québec), Registres des baptêmes, mariages et sépultures, 1795–1796, 1797–1798, 1799–1800. ASQ, Fichier des anciens du séminaire; Séminaire CIII, 56, 61; Séminaire CIV, 3, 6. Desjardins, *Guide parlementaire*. [Azarie Couillard-Després], *Histoire de la seigneurie de Saint-Ours* (2v., Montréal, 1915–17), II, 285–94. Fauteux, *Patriotes*, 217–18. [L.-O. David], "Les hommes de 37–38, le Dr Jacques Dorion," *L'Opinion publique* (Montréal), 7 févr. 1878.

DORION, VINCISLAS-PAUL-WILFRID, lawyer, journalist, politician, and judge; b. 2 Oct. 1827 at Sainte-Anne-de-la-Pérade, L.C., son of Pierre-Antoine Dorion* and Geneviève Bureau; d. 2 June 1878 at Montreal, Que.

Vincislas-Paul-Wilfrid Dorion's father was a merchant, a member of the assembly in 1829–38 for Champlain County, and a staunch supporter of Louis-Joseph PAPINEAU. His remarkable family included Antoine-Aimé*; Hercule*, destined to die as parish priest of Yamachiche; Louis-Eugène; Nérée; Jean-Baptiste-Éric*, nicknamed "l'enfant terrible"; Edmond; Célina; and Cyphise, who became Sœur Amable, superior general of the convent of La Providence at Montreal.

Because the financial situation of the family had seriously deteriorated, Wilfrid, unlike his elder brothers Antoine-Aimé and Hercule, did not have the advantage of a regular classical education at the college of Nicolet. After attending the primary school in his parish, he became a clerk at age 13 in a small country store. In 1842 he went to Montreal, where he found employment in the bookstore of Édouard-Raymond Fabre* and J.-A. Gravel. Eager for knowledge, he utilized the leisure left him in his work to satisfy his passion for reading. Soon he began to study law under the direction of Côme-Séraphin Cherrier* and his eldest brother Antoine-Aimé Dorion, who were in a law partnership. In the words of Laurent-Olivier David*, "Never was a clerk more studious and diligent."

Wilfrid qualified as a lawyer in 1850 and soon joined the Cherrier-Dorion partnership. He was launched. It was not long before he was commanding attention at the bar. His success was due to his obvious natural gifts, but also to an unremitting effort designed to develop his talents as a speaker and journalist. He was one of the founders of the Institut Canadien, and he contributed to L'Avenir. His confrères of the institute recognized this young man's worth by appointing him their librarian in August 1845, and by electing him their president for the period November 1848 to November 1849. It was on behalf of Louis-Joseph Papineau that Wilfrid Dorion first appeared on the political stage: in 1851 he went to Saint-Eustache to support the candidature of the great leader in the county of Deux-Montagnes. From then on he was the favourite speaker of the Rouge party.

Of medium height, with a large head joined by a short neck to a thick chest and with an inexhaustible supply of breath, Dorion possessed "a sonorous and indefatigable voice which dominated every noise and triumphed over every hubbub," wrote David, who characterized his oratorical talent thus: "His eloquence, essentially popular, lacked the polish and the correctness conferred by a study of the classics, but it was vigorous, practical, and solid, devoid of the ornaments and flowers of rhetoric, of philosophical considerations or literary digressions, but full of facts and clear, formidable arguments, of warm appeals to the intelligence and reason of his listeners. A little embarrassed in a gathering of men of letters, and even within the precincts of the Palais de Justice, it needed air and space, the liberty and independence of the forum."

As well as helping the Rouge party by his oratory, Wilfrid Dorion continued a participation in journalism that had begun with his collaboration in L'Avenir. When this paper temporarily ceased to appear in 1852, he helped to start Le Pays and became one of its owners in June 1858; its printer, Jacques-Alexis Plinguet*, had resigned from the Institut Canadien on 22 April of that year to found with 135 of his confrères the Institut Canadien-Français [see Francis CASSIDY], and had made over his rights in the journal to Dorion et Cie. Wilfrid Dorion was a director of Le Pays with his brother Edmond until the latter's death on 8 June 1862; he engaged the services of

two eminent liberal journalists, Charles Daoust* and Henri-Émile CHEVALIER, and subsequently secured the collaboration of Louis-Antoine Dessaulles* from 1 March 1861 to the end of December 1863. He wrote to his cousin Napoléon Bureau* of Trois-Rivières, a few days after Dessaulles' acceptance: "I think you will be pleased to learn that Mr. Dessaules has undertaken the editorship."

When Dessaulles declared himself for Italian unification, the greatest concrete realization of political liberalism in the 19th century, Le Pays incurred the censure of the ultramontanes, and especially of Bishop Ignace Bourget*, who, to refute the liberal arguments, composed seven lengthy letters, which he demanded should appear in the paper. Wilfrid Dorion and his partners vigorously claimed the right of journalists and politicians to dissociate religion and politics. In a letter – one of the essential documents of French Canadian liberalism – that Dorion et Cie, owners and directors of the journal Le Pays, addressed to Bishop Bourget on 4 March 1862, they set forth their position without restraint: " 'Le Pays' represents in the Canadian press a political party formed apart from any religious controversy, and its sphere of action embraces only the material and moral concerns of the country to which we all belong. Never has it presumed to set itself up as being a tribunal for dogma; it leaves to the competent authorities the entire domain of faith and religious doctrines, it addresses itself solely to the intelligence, reason, and conscience of the people in matters concerning the conduct and administration of their temporal affairs. The liberal institutions we enjoy, the form of our government, authorize and justify this attitude, whatever may be the political direction in which this freedom of examination and discussion, one of the most precious attributes of constitutional governments, finds expression. We have always believed and we continue to believe that this position is completely compatible with the status of a Christian, a Catholic, and a good citizen." Bishop Bourget finally desisted, and called no longer for the insertion of his letters in Le Pays. On 15 August Wilfrid Dorion reported to Napoléon Bureau: "There is nothing new here. Politics are a matter of course. Our former adversaries leave us a clear field."

Following the example of his brothers Antoine-Aimé and Jean-Baptiste-Éric, Wilfrid vehemently opposed the projected confederation of the provinces of North America. Writing to Napoléon Bureau on 11 June 1866, he branded as infamous the "scourge" of "Confederation": "It appears that we must submit to it willy-nilly. Our people are so demoralized that they no longer feel anything." He attributed this lethargy in great part to the clergy, who had shown themselves favourable to the government bill and who supported the candidates of the Conservative party. Consequently he had published in *Le Pays*, from mid-September 1867 to mid-January 1868, a series of articles intended to prove that in the various counties of the province the clergy had made every effort to prevent the election of Liberal candidates. On 12 Oct. 1867 he thanked Napoléon Bureau for the "electoral documents" he had just received: "Some of them are excellent. We want to publish enough of them to put the clergy to shame and kill their political influence in the future." Delighted with the success of these articles, he thought of putting them together into a pamphlet. He wrote to the same correspondent on 14 November: "The clergy must bitterly regret having drawn such a broadside on themselves, the more because people are avidly reading it. The number of our subscribers is increasing daily in extraordinary fashion. The bishops in council at Toronto have decided to wage war against *unholy* journals. I suppose that *Le Pays* will come in for its share. It is up to those who are determined not to let themselves be hoodwinked not to abandon us. It will be hard for the clergy to make us lose subscribers now, for over a number of years they have taken away from us all those upon whom they exerted some influence."

Dorion never relented in his opposition to confederation, which he regarded as a political system with little prospect of surviving: "I cannot believe," he wrote on 10 Feb. 1870 to Napoléon Bureau, "that it is possible for us to remain long in the state of humiliation in which we find ourselves." The Liberal party's victory in the federal elections of 1874, despite opposition from the clergy, gave him a satisfaction which he communicated on 2 Feb. 1874 to his habitual correspondent: "The clergy has waged war on our candidates while accepting the government. Happily we have been successful on the whole. It is true that we have lost some good soldiers, but one does not go to war without its costing something."

In 1875, at the age of 48, Wilfrid Dorion was appointed judge of the Superior Court; he no doubt owed this appointment to the fact that the Liberal party was in power. According to Laurent-Olivier David, he "had all the qualities necessary for him to become one of the most distinguished judges in the country": "less scholarly and less studious" than his eldest brother Antoine-Aimé, "with an intelligence and character not so finely moulded, he was superior in the clarity and alertness of his mind, the vigour of his thought, and the power of his oratory."

Wilfrid Dorion had married a Miss Trestler, sister of his eldest brother's wife. Seven children, three boys and four girls, were born of this marriage. He died suddenly on Sunday, 2 June 1878, at Montreal.

PHILIPPE SYLVAIN

ASTR, Papiers Napoléon Bureau, Correspondance. *L'Opinion publique* (Montréal), 13 juin 1878. *Le Pays* (Montréal), 1852–71. J.-B.-É. Dorion, *Institut canadien en 1852* (Montréal, 1852). Sylvain, "Libéralisme et ultramontanisme," *Shield of Achilles* (Morton), 111–38, 220–55.

DOUGLAS, Sir JAMES, HBC officer and governor of Vancouver Island and of the crown colony of British Columbia; b. 5 June or 15 Aug. 1803; d. at Victoria, B.C., 2 Aug. 1877.

A "Scotch West Indian," as he was known in the fur trade, James Douglas was the son of John Douglas and nephew of Lieutenant-General Sir Neill Douglas. John Douglas and his three brothers, merchants in Glasgow, held interests in sugar plantations in British Guiana. At Demerara John Douglas seems to have entered into a liaison with a "Creole," possibly a Miss Ritchie, by whom he had three children, Alexander, b. 1801 or 1802, James, b. 1803, and Cecilia Eliza, b. 1812. John Douglas' second family were the children of Jessie Hamilton whom he married in Glasgow in 1809. For one of these, Jane Hamilton Douglas, James Douglas developed an affectionate regard.

Placed at an early age in a preparatory school in Scotland, James Douglas learned "to fight [his] own way with all sorts of boys, and to get on by dint of whip and spur." He received a good education at Lanark, and probably further training from a French Huguenot tutor at Chester, England. During his early years in the fur trade he was singled out for having a sound knowledge of the French language and "possessing a clear and distinct pronunciation."

At the age of 16 both Alexander and James Douglas were apprenticed to the North West Company. After sailing on 7 May 1819 on the brig *Matthews* from Liverpool, bound for Quebec, James Douglas proceeded to Fort William, arriving on 6 August. That winter he applied himself to accounting, learning business methods, and studying the Indian character. It is not unlikely that he already displayed those characteristics for which he became noted: industry, punctuality, observance of the smallest detail, and a determination amidst the most pressing business to acquire knowledge of literature and history, politics and public affairs.

In the summer of 1820 he was transferred to

Île-à-la-Crosse. There he threw himself into the struggle between the North Westers and the Hudson's Bay Company men, fighting a duel with Patrick Cunningham and engaging in military manoeuvres and threatening appearances. He was one of four Nor' Westers specifically warned on 12 April 1821 to desist from parading within gunshot of the neighbouring HBC post with "Guns, Swords, Flags, Drums, Fifes, etc., etc."

On the union of the two companies in 1821, Douglas entered the employ of the HBC as a second class clerk. In 1822, though only 18 years old, he was regarded as "a very sensible young man" and a good Indian trader, who could be trusted to take charge that summer of the Island Lake post.

On 15 April 1825, Douglas left Île-à-la-Crosse by way of Lake Athabasca to take charge of Fort Vermilion in Peace River during the summer. He wintered at McLeod's Lake on the east side of the Rocky Mountains with John Tod*. The next spring he was at Fort St James, Stuart Lake, headquarters of the New Caledonia district. Douglas had now completed the first of seven crossings of the Rocky Mountains, and the experience had left an imperishable memory "of fresh scenes, of perilous travel, of fatigue, excitement and of adventures by mountain and flood."

That spring (1826) he visited the Pacific seaboard for the first time. It had been decided to supply New Caledonia from Fort Vancouver, built in 1824 on the north bank of the Columbia River, and to ship its returns round Cape Horn to England. Chief Factor William Connolly*, finding Douglas a "Fine steady active fellow good clerk & Trader, well adapted for a new country," chose him to assist in opening the overland brigade route for pack-horses from Fort Alexandria on the upper Fraser to Fort Okanagan at the junction of the Okanagan and Columbia rivers. The brigade left Stuart Lake on 5 May, and, travelling 1,000 miles, reached Fort Vancouver on 16 June. With the outfit in nine boats, Connolly started the return journey on 5 July. Douglas, who had been sent with John Work* and Archibald McDonald* to obtain horses from the Nez Percés Indians, joined him at Fort Okanagan. They arrived back at Fort St James on 23 September. In October Douglas was sent on a trading mission to the Secanni Indians, and with its success he was dispatched on 15 May 1827 to establish Fort Connolly on Bear Lake.

During the winter of 1827, at Fort St James, Douglas decided to retire from the fur trade at the end of his three-year contract. By March 1828, discouraged by the isolation of his life, the lack of companionship and of good books, the hostility of the Indians, and the danger of starvation after the salmon run failed, he was "bent on leaving the country." His employers, however, were willing to renew his contract and increase his salary from £60 to £100.

On 27 April, according to the custom of the country (confirmed in a Church of England ceremony at Fort Vancouver in 1837), Douglas took Amelia Connolly, half-Indian daughter of the chief factor, as his wife.

During the time Connolly left him in charge of Fort St James while he himself took out the 1828 returns to Fort Vancouver, a "tumult" with the Indians erupted. Following the execution of an Indian who had been involved in a murder at Fort George in 1823, Carriers invaded the fort to avenge his death and threaten Douglas' life. James Douglas could be "furiously violent when aroused," and the Indians had taken an inveterate dislike to him. In November he was again assaulted, near Fraser Lake. There was further trouble at Fort St James on New Year's Day, 1829. "Douglas's life is much exposed among these Carriers," Connolly reported to Governor George Simpson* in February 1829, "he would readily face a hundred of them, but he does not much like the idea of being assassinated."

Connolly's recommendation that Douglas be transferred to Fort Vancouver, where extensive coastal trading and farming operations were under way, was accepted by the Council of the Northern Department. On 30 Jan. 1830 Douglas left Stuart Lake to become accountant under Dr John McLoughlin*, superintendent of the vast Columbia Department.

"James Douglas is at Vancouver and is rising fast in favour," a fur-trader reported in 1831. Simpson, who had met Douglas at Île-à-la-Crosse in 1822 and at Fort St James in 1828, was convinced that Douglas "is a likely man to fill a place at our Council board in course of time." McLoughlin entrusted him in 1832 and 1833 with taking the accounts to York Factory. In 1835, as McLoughlin's chief assistant, he attended the council meeting at Red River Settlement. There, on 3 June, he was given his commission as chief trader. During McLoughlin's absence in England in 1838–39, Douglas had charge of Fort Vancouver, the coastal posts, the trapping expeditions, and the shipping. Finally, in November 1839, he was advanced to chief factor.

Douglas' promotion gave him financial security. As chief trader he had earned 1/85 of the company's net profits, about £400 annually. As chief factor he was entitled to 2/85. Totally dependent on his salary, he practised frugality. As a young clerk earning £60 a year, he had put aside

Douglas

half that amount; as chief trader in 1835, when he received £406 in annual dividends, he kept his expenses at a little over £30. That year he began to support his sister Cecilia, and pay his mite to charity – the Bible Society and the Christian missions in Oregon. By the spring of 1850 he had accumulated savings of nearly £5000.

As the officer responsible in McLoughlin's absence for the Columbia headquarters, Douglas sought to elevate moral standards. He was disturbed by the presence of slavery. "With the Natives, I have hitherto endeavoured to discourage the practice by the exertion of moral influence alone," he informed the company in London. "Against our own people I took a more active part, and denounced slavery as a state contrary to law; tendering to all unfortunate persons held as slaves, by British subjects, the fullest protection in the enjoyment of their natural rights." In 1849 he ransomed a slave with goods worth 14 shillings. He entrusted the moral and religious improvement "of our own little community" to the fort's Church of England chaplain, but his support was withdrawn when the Reverend Herbert Beaver* proved to be a religious fanatic. "A clergyman in this country must quit the closet & live a life of beneficent activity, devoted to the support of principles, rather than of forms; he must shun discord, avoid uncharitable feelings, temper zeal with discretion, [and] illustrate precept by example." These standards of behaviour had, in fact, become his own.

During this period, when McLoughlin was working to eliminate American competition on the northwest coast and Simpson was expanding the company's activities in the whole Pacific area, Douglas was adjudged the most reliable man for important missions. In April 1840 he was sent north to Sitka, where he was received with "the most polite attention" by the Russian authorities and where he arranged to take over Stikine under the agreement of 1839 with the Russian American Company. He also selected the site for, and commenced building, Fort Taku in Alaska. In December he went to California to investigate trade prospects, buy cattle, and negotiate with the Mexican authorities for the opening of trade with California. On his advice, the HBC built the post of Yerba Buena at San Francisco.

On these delicate missions, Douglas displayed his talent as negotiator. Like Simpson, he had learned to take the measure of a man with whom he dealt; like McLoughlin, he presented a dignified and self-confident appearance. No detail of government policy, business practice, or social value escaped his attention. The officers and men of the Russian American Company lived in what

he considered idleness, and the naval officers employed by the company were "the most unqualified men to manage commercial undertakings." In Spanish California, in contrast to John Bull's territories, he found the government arbitrary and the law feebly administered.

At Sitka, treating the Russian governor with firmness, tact, and concession, Douglas negotiated the boundary between Russian and British posts. In their daily conferences he spoke "in a frank and open manner so as to dissipate all semblance of reserve and establish our intercourse on a basis of mutual confidence." For the Indian trade he obtained an equal tariff at every post. Implementing the 1839 agreement, Douglas promised to supply articles needed by the Russians in this trade, and a quantity of butter and other provisions from Fort Langley. "Honesty is found to be in all cases ultimately the best policy," he wrote, "but in our intercourse with our Russian neighbours, it will be found so from the first day to the last of our intercourse."

In California, Douglas found himself received "with a sort of reserved courtesy" by Governor Juan B. Alvarado. His first impulse was to resent such behaviour, but knowing that "second thoughts are best," he restrained himself and, again making concessions, succeeded in obtaining permission for trapping expeditions, commercial rights, and the right to purchase at a fair price sheep and cattle needed for the HBC farms on the Columbia.

In August 1841 Douglas welcomed Simpson to Fort Vancouver in the absence of McLoughlin and travelled with him to Sitka to negotiate once more with the Russians. Simpson arrived at decisions which were to anger McLoughlin: the far northern posts were to be abandoned, the trading operations of the steamboat *Beaver* expanded, and a new port was to be established at the southern end of Vancouver Island. Douglas made a reconnaissance of the tip of Vancouver Island in July 1842 and in March 1843 started the construction of Fort Victoria.

The building of Fort Victoria signalled the approach of the last great days of the Columbia District. Though Americans and Britons had enjoyed equal rights west of the mountains since 1827, the great company had virtually eliminated competition in the fur trade between 54°40′ and 42°. Its provisions contract with the Russians, however, had necessitated diversification of operations. Farming at Fort Vancouver and in the Cowlitz Valley had been expanded, and settlers brought in from Red River. In the 1840s American settlers began to trickle into the area, and in 1843 people, according to Douglas "of a class hostile to British interests," arrived in such numbers that a provisional government was set up in Oregon. Faced with the presence of the American immigrants led into the Willamette Valley in 1842 by Dr Elijah White and by the arrival in 1843 of 120 wagon-loads of settlers, McLoughlin made a virtue of necessity. The new settlers were well armed but they lacked money and supplies. McLoughlin provided seeds and other necessities, and also extended credit at the company's stores.

Douglas knew that McLoughlin and Simpson were now moving towards a complete break in their personal relations. He remained loyal to the doctor. He agreed with McLoughlin that the Americans might be induced to move to California, but he was alarmed at the sacrifice of the company's commercial rights, and was convinced that American pressure would increase. He viewed with grave concern the interest of the United States government in additional good ports on the Pacific coast. "An American population will never willingly submit to British domination," he wrote to Simpson, "and it would be ruinous and hopeless to enforce obedience, on a disaffected people; our Government would not attempt it, and the consequence will be the accession of a new State to the Union." If the United States gained an advantage on the coast, "Every sea port will be converted into a naval arsenal and the Pacific covered with swarms of Privateers, to the destruction of British commerce in those seas."

As American immigration swelled the white population in Oregon to 6,000 in 1845, the provisional government extended its jurisdiction north of the Columbia River. The British government showed little concern about defending its claim to the river. With foresight, Douglas put forward the idea of "possessory rights" to permit the company to occupy its posts and farms north of the river, should British territorial claims be surrendered.

In 1845 the company, recognizing that the situation in Oregon had reached a critical stage, replaced McLoughlin's rule with a board of management consisting of Dr McLoughlin, Peter Skene Ogden*, and James Douglas. On McLoughlin's retirement in 1846, Douglas was selected as the senior member, and John Work was added. McLoughlin and Douglas would now go their separate ways: McLoughlin had decided to throw in his lot with the Americans; without wavering for a moment, Douglas remained loyal to the company and to Britain.

When, in 1846, the British government relinquished its claims to the north bank of the Columbia River and accepted the 49th parallel as the boundary, Douglas reorganized the brigade

routes from New Caledonia to make them converge at Fort Langley on the lower Fraser River. In 1848 he investigated the market at Honolulu for salmon and lumber. At last, in 1849, he moved the company's headquarters, shipping depot, and provisioning centre from the Columbia to Fort Victoria.

To prevent American expansion northward, the company on 13 Jan. 1849 accepted a royal grant to Vancouver Island for ten years. A colony was to be set up within five years, and Douglas expected to be chosen governor of "the real ultima thule of the British Empire." But to avert "the jealousy of some parties, and the interested motives of others," he was passed over in favour of Richard Blanshard*. Preparations for the governor, the colonists, and the farm bailiffs sent from England were incomplete when Blanshard arrived at Fort Victoria in March 1850. Workmen were deserting for the California goldfields. "The affairs of our nascent Colony on Vancouver's Island are not making much progress," Douglas admitted in November. Blanshard had already sent in his resignation. Awaiting its acceptance, the governor became attentive to complaints that too much power was vested in Douglas, that land prices were too high, and that prices at the company store were exorbitant. Settlement was so impeded by the selective immigration policy of the Colonial Office that when Blanshard set up a council on 27 Aug. 1851, he was forced to appoint Douglas and Tod, company men, and Captain James COOPER, a former HBC employee.

On 16 May 1851 Douglas had been appointed governor and vice-admiral of Vancouver Island and its dependencies. The news did not reach him until 30 October. "I am again appointed Governor pro tempore" he had complained on Blanshard's departure in September, "this is too much of a good thing. I am getting tired of Vancouver's Island." His appointment confirmed, however, he entered into his dual capacity of governor and chief factor with enthusiasm. The gold discovered on Queen Charlotte Islands was protected from the American grasp, the company was advised to purchase the Nanaimo coalfield, Indian lands near Fort Victoria were bought and reserves laid out, roads were built, and schools established.

No matter concerned Douglas more than Indian policy. Towards the Indians, his attitude was one of benevolent paternalism, though he followed the HBC rule that outrages must be speedily punished. To hunt a Cowichan murderer in 1853, he organized among the company servants the Victoria Voltigeurs – a small group of volunteer militiamen – enlisted the services of the Royal Navy, and, for the trial, empanelled a jury on

Douglas

board the *Beaver*. The same year he had the bastion built at Nanaimo.

In laying out reserves, he left the choice of the land and the size to the Indians. Surveyors were instructed to meet their wishes and "to include in each reserve the permanent Village sites, the fishing stations, and Burial grounds, cultivated land and all the favorite resorts of the Tribes, and in short to include every piece of ground to which they had acquired an equitable title through continuous occupation, tillage or other investment of their labour." At first the Indians' requests were moderate, not exceeding ten acres per family, but later in the pastoral country in the interior, where they needed range land for their cattle and horses, the reserves were much larger. Title remained vested in the crown "as a safeguard and protection to these Indian Communities who might, in their primal state of ignorance and natural improvidence, have made away with the land." As his total land policy evolved, Douglas, certain that the time would arrive "when they might aspire to a higher rank in the social scale and feel the essential wants of and claims of a better condition," permitted the Indians as individuals to acquire property by direct purchase from government officers or through pre-emption, "on precisely the same terms and considerations in all respects, as other classes of Her Majesty's subjects."

As senior company officer west of the mountains, Douglas encouraged the traders at Fort Langley to supplement fur exports with farm produce and other commodities. Knowing that the innovations on Vancouver Island would in time destroy the fur trade, he jealously guarded the company's rights in New Caledonia, on the mainland. He scrutinized the company's civil and military expenditures in the island colony, and paid into a trust fund all revenues from sales of land, timber, and mines.

In his new authority as governor, he experienced resentment. Colonists expected more than he could provide in the way of improvements, and accused him, when he appointed two old associates to the council, of desiring oligarchic control. In 1853 his old friends, Tod, Dr William Fraser Tolmie*, and Roderick Finlayson*, influenced by the views of Captain Cooper, the Reverend Robert J. Staines*, company chaplain, and Edward E. Langford*, farm bailiff, permitted representations against him to be made to a visiting English MP, C. W. Wentworth-Fitzwilliam. At Lachine, Sir George Simpson, hearing complaints about neglect of the fur trade from Tod and Ogden, questioned his loyalty to the company, and spread a report that Douglas was "always personally vain and ambitious of late years. His advancement to the

prominent position he now fills, has, I understand, rendered him imperious in his bearing towards his colleagues and subordinates – assuming the Governor not only in tone but issuing orders which no one is allowed to question." "Douglas appears anxious to keep us in the dark relative to affairs in Vancouver Island," Ogden informed Simpson. "From what I can learn some of the Settlers say Cooper and Tod speak the words of truth which he does not find very palatable and very soon the Fur Trade will find an advocate to speak the truth also. The present system will never answer, too much *power* placed in the hands of one Man must and will cause a clashing of Interests. . . ."

Settlers like Cooper claimed that neither the company nor Douglas had carried out the obligation to settle the island. They demanded that the colony revert to the crown and a governor be chosen who would be independent of the company and who would not rely on company officers for advice and the enforcement of governmental policies.

The basic grievance, Douglas felt, was the land policy. Neither the company nor the Colonial Office had accepted his advice that free grants of 200 or 300 acres be allowed. Instead, the price of land was set at £1 an acre, the minimum holding was 20 acres, and settlers who bought 100 acres were required to bring out labourers. In addition, the company, by setting aside an HBC reserve of nearly six square miles near the fort, and by locating its farms in the other good agricultural areas, had caused the settlers to disperse to inferior farming districts.

Douglas himself was convinced that a settlement was being effected and that the colony had a future. Though other company men were, he said, "scared at the high price charged," he commenced in December 1851 to purchase land at the regular price as an investment. To 12 acres he acquired adjacent to the fort, he soon added other properties: at Esquimalt, 418 acres in 1852, 247 acres in 1855, and 240 acres in 1858. At Metchosin he bought 319 acres. His most valuable properties were at Victoria – Fairfield Farm and a large holding at James Bay adjoining the government reserve.

Memorials prepared in the colony in 1854 were brought before both houses of parliament through Fitzwilliam's efforts. To previous complaints was added the charge of nepotism – Governor Douglas, having found his magistrates, E. E. Langford, Thomas Blinkhorn, Kenneth MCKENZIE, and Thomas James Skinner*, ignorant and unreliable, had appointed David CAMERON, who arrived from Demerara in 1853 with his wife Cecilia Eliza

Douglas Cowan, to the position of chief justice of the new Supreme Court of Justice.

Before parliament made any decision about renewing the monopolistic trading rights on the Pacific slope granted to the company for 21 years in 1838, it would have to examine its record. Its performance as colonizing agent would also be assessed. In the interval, the Colonial Office retained Douglas in his position, but curtailed his executive power. On 22 May 1856 he was ordered to establish an assembly. He complied, though, as he said, he had "a very slender knowledge of legislation, and was without legal advice or intelligent assistance of any kind."

A fur preserve boasting a single stockaded fort only a few years before, Vancouver Island was now a colony with limited representative government. Compared with neighbouring Washington Territory where land was free, the colony's population was small, but it lived in peace without Indian warfare. Through Douglas' efforts, large-scale farming, saw-milling, coal-mining, and salmon fishing had been established. He had plans for government buildings for his diminutive capital, and was endeavouring to have Esquimalt become a naval base. His accomplishments offset the criticism of his rule by Blanshard, Cooper, and Admiral Fairfax Moresby before the select committee of the British House of Commons in 1857. When the government converted Vancouver Island into a crown colony in 1859, the governor it chose was James Douglas. It was already known in London in 1857 that gold had been discovered on the mainland, still under HBC control. A colonial officer of Douglas' experience would be a good man to have standing by.

In July 1857 Douglas had reported to London that Americans were mining on the Thompson River and an officer was needed to maintain law and order. By December a rush impended. Left without instructions, he seized the initiative as he had done at the time of the Queen Charlotte Islands' gold discovery. As the nearest representative of British authority, on 28 Dec. 1857 he proclaimed the crown's control of mineral rights and required miners to take out licences. He was still without instructions when the first shipload of California miners landed at Victoria on 25 April 1858. "If the Country be thrown open to indiscriminate immigration, the interests of the empire may suffer," he warned London. Equally concerned about the company's private trading rights, he enlisted the aid of Captain James Charles Prevost* of the British Boundary Commission, and had him station his gunboat at the mouth of the Fraser to collect licences from all ships and boats entering the river.

Once before Douglas had experienced the results of American penetration. Now he saw danger of repetition of the Oregon story. American squatters were on San Juan Island, close to Victoria and the sandheads of the Fraser River, and 8,000 miners had travelled the old brigade trail up the Okanagan valley. The English hamlet of Victoria, transformed into a tent-city, was filled with American merchants, brokers and jobbers, land agents, and speculators. In the wild and empty country across the Gulf of Georgia, foreign prospectors had made the Indians restive and were threatening to take the law into their own hands. As Douglas saw it, Victoria, rather than San Francisco, must become the supply centre for the mines; the Fraser, rather than the Columbia, the artery of commerce and traffic. To protect British sovereignty, a military and a naval force were needed. The British rule of law would have to be imposed on "the lawless crowds."

Twice during the summer of 1858 he visited the diggings. Some miners, discouraged by the high waters of the spring freshet, had already abandoned the river-bars and left the country. But between Fort Langley and Fort Yale over 10,000 men were panning gold. A few had pushed along the precipitous river banks beyond Yale and the big canyon to Lytton. River transportation and roads were required. So were mining regulations and policing. In July Douglas permitted two American stern-wheelers to supplement the company boats on the navigable 100 miles to Yale. Volunteers were called for to build a road by the Harrison River route to Lillooet and a mule track from Yale to Lytton. Mining regulations were drawn up, constables were hired, and Indians were appointed as magistrates to bring forward natives who broke the law. To prevent squatting Douglas had townsites surveyed near the company posts at Langley and Hope and lots were offered for sale.

"I spoke with great plainness of speech to the white miners who were nearly all foreigners representing almost every nation in Europe," he reported to the Colonial Office on 15 June 1858 after his first visit to the goldfields. "I refused to grant them any rights of occupation to the soil and told them distinctly that Her Majesty's Government ignored their very existence in that part of the country, which was not open for the purpose of settlement, and they were permitted to remain there merely on sufferance, that no abuses would be tolerated, and that the Laws would protect the rights of the Indians no less than those of the white men."

After his authority had been confirmed in August he vested title to land in the crown. It was opened to settlement slowly, and, in the hope of attracting British immigrants, it was priced low. Only British subjects could purchase land, but all those who applied for naturalization could obtain it.

Douglas' initiative had at first aroused enthusiasm in London. Then a new colonial secretary, Sir Edward Bulwer-Lytton, a severe critic of the HBC monopoly, read into his preliminary measures an intention to keep the whole trade of the country for "the HBCo's people as far as possible." He reprimanded Douglas, then took steps to terminate the company's rights and to open the Pacific slope to settlement. On 2 Aug. 1858 parliament, on his advice, converted the territory of New Caledonia into the crown colony of British Columbia.

Douglas was offered the governorship of the new colony on condition that he sever his connection with his old company. In Simpson's opinion, he was unquestionably the best man for the office, and his salary would help "to carry him through his difficulties, aided by personal vanity of which he has a fair store combined however with a good deal of determination and tact." The two interests Douglas represented had become antagonistic, and although there would be general regret at his quitting his old concern, his "ostentatious style of living" as governor and his liberality in entertaining all comers had been saddled on the fur trade "whose interests benefitted very little by it."

The salary offered Douglas as dual governor was only £1,800, but he obtained solace from a Companionship of the Order of the Bath, conferred for his administration of the company-sponsored colony of Vancouver Island. At Fort Langley on 19 Nov. 1858, divested of his commission and supposedly of his interests in the HBC, James Douglas, CB, took the oath of office as governor of British Columbia.

By the spring of 1859 Douglas had not succeeded in persuading the company to purchase his retiring rights. The company was pressing its own claims for compensation for expenditures in the colony of Vancouver Island, and its headquarters was disturbed by reports from Alexander G. Dallas* in Victoria who was investigating Douglas' accounts. Instances had been found when "fur trade" funds had been used for colonial purposes. In addition, £17,000 had been taken from the fur trade account in 1858 "under the pressure of the moment" to buy provisions for the miners flocking into British Columbia. Simpson confided in Dallas that "the conviction has been most unwillingly forced upon me, that Mr. Douglas has been making an unjustifiable use of the authority with which he is invested for the

promotion of his private interests and the benefit of his Family and retainers. . . . I presume there will be difficulty in putting a detainer on his funds in the Company's hands; but his retired interest is under their control, and I think it might very fairly be held in suspense until the Colonial account is settled." The company shared this view. No action was taken when in May 1859 Douglas tendered his rights for the sum of £3,500.

His legitimate expectations destroyed, and his salary as governor inadequate, Douglas threatened to resign. "As a private individual I can live in a style befitting the fortune I possess," he informed the Colonial Office, "but as Governor for the Crown there is no choice, one must live in a manner becoming the representative of the Crown." Though the government regarded him as the indispensable man, all it would give was a vague promise that his salary would be augmented as proceeds from land sales in British Columbia increased.

Until the crown decided to establish a legislature in British Columbia, absolute power had been given to the governor to administer justice and to establish laws and ordinances. It would not be fair to the grand principle of free institutions, Lytton had declared in July 1858, "to risk at once the experiment of self-government among settlers so wild, so miscellaneous, and perhaps so transitory, and in a form of society so crude." The plan satisfied Douglas, who believed that "the best form of government, if attainable, is that of a wise and good despotism," and that "representative Governments cannot be carried on without recourse directly or indirectly to bribery and corrupting influences." He took the opportunity to determine policy and announce it in the form of proclamations.

Because the gold colony was richly endowed by nature, the British government, other than bearing military costs, intended only to provide a tiny civil list for a judge and a few officials. It did instruct Rear-Admiral Robert Lambert Baynes of the Pacific fleet to assist Douglas, but his flagship, the 84-gun *Ganges*, did not reach Esquimalt until October 1858, after most of the miners had left to winter in California. In February 1859 a frigate and a corvette with 164 supernumerary marines arrived from the China waters. A detachment of 165 Royal Engineers was also sent from England; the main body arrived in April 1859.

During the critical period of the first mining season there had thus been neither civil power nor military aid. Unarmed with political authority, Douglas was accompanied only by a bodyguard of 20 sailors and 16 Royal Engineers seconded from the boundary commission when in August

1858 he had made his sortie to the mining camps to suppress disorder and announce his intention to consolidate the goldfields as an integral part of the British empire. He wrote to Herman Merivale on 29 Oct. 1858 that he had never before seen "a crowd of more ruffianly looking men," but at his command they gave three cheers, "with a bad grace," for the queen.

Nothing like the 1858 influx of 25,000 prospectors occurred in 1859. Some of the miners preferred the freer atmosphere of the American mining-fields; others followed rumours of fresh finds on American soil. The Royal Engineers, sent to plan a communications system, survey townsites, and provide military protection, could concentrate on these tasks. Colonel Richard Clement Moody*, officer commanding the troops and commissioner of lands and works, selected, with defence against the Americans in mind, a site near the mouth of the Fraser River for a colonial capital, later called New Westminster. The sappers and the marines were put to work to cut down the giant timbers on the steep hillside.

The governor, too, was concerned about security. When an American military force landed on San Juan Island on 27 July, it took both the Legislative Assembly of Vancouver Island and Rear-Admiral Baynes to restrain him from using force to expel it. Until its sovereignty could be decided, the island was put under joint military occupation. When he heard of the *Trent* incident in 1861, Douglas longed to use the naval force in the north Pacific, the Royal Engineers, and the Royal Marines stationed on San Juan Island to seize San Juan, take possession of Puget Sound, and push overland to the Columbia: "With Puget Sound, and the line of the Columbia in our hands, we should hold the only navigable outlets of the country – command its trade, and soon compel it to submit to Her Majesty's rule." To his disappointment a damper was put on this proposal by the British government.

In 1860 the provisioning of the inland mines became an acute problem. To encourage importers, Victoria was declared a free port, and, to stimulate farming in the interior, a pre-emption system was introduced. When rich strikes were made at distant Antler Creek in 1860, it became evident another rush was impending. Wagontrains would have to replace pack-trains, and the cost of transporting goods through the rugged mountain passes would have to be reduced. For improving roads Douglas employed civilians as well as sappers, and when the British government refused financial assistance, he raised funds by tonnage duties, road tolls, mining licences, and, in 1861, a bank loan of £50,000.

In 1862 the Cariboo goldrush attracted 5,000 miners. On this occasion, Governor Douglas produced his plan for a major wagon road, 18 feet wide, to run 400 miles from Yale, beyond the river's gorge northward to Quesnel, and eastward to Williams Creek. The Great North Road, to be built by Royal Engineers and civilian contractors, was to end the threat of American economic domination by making the Fraser River, despite its obstacles, the commercial and arterial highway of British Columbia. He hoped that the road could be extended to link British Columbia with Canada. "Who can foresee what the next ten years may bring forth," he wrote in 1863, "an overland Telegraph, *surely*, and a Railroad on British Territory, *probably*, the whole way from the Gulf of Georgia to the Atlantic."

Since the discovery of the first heavy gold nuggets at Williams Creek in Cariboo in 1861, the population had changed. On his visits in 1862 to Barkerville and the other towns along the creek, it seemed to Chief Justice Matthew Baillie Begbie*, the stern and haughty judge sent from England, "as though every good family of the east and of Great Britain had sent the best son they possessed for the development of the gold mines of Cariboo." In the overland party from Canada in 1862 were farmers who intended to reside permanently in the colony. At last there was that infusion of "the British element" so much desired by Douglas.

New Westminster, the gold colony's capital city, already had its full complement of Canadians. Many of them were merchants and speculators who became malcontents as their hopes for prosperity dwindled. Business languished in New Westminster with Victoria emerging as the commercial and banking centre, and with Yale becoming the river-landing for transshipment to the inland mines. A bitter jealousy of the island colony developed, and Douglas came under criticism for continuing to reside, along with his officials, at Victoria. His unpopularity grew as he became increasingly dependent on assistants sent from England and as John Robson*, the fiery editor of the *British Columbian*, disseminated evidence of his authoritarianism.

To the first request for popular government at New Westminster, Douglas had responded by granting on 16 July 1860 incorporation as a city and the election of a municipal council. In forwarding the demand for an assembly made in 1860 he had expressed the opinion that the British element in the gold colony was still too small to justify this concession. Four later memorials requesting popular government were forwarded to the Colonial Office; three of these remained unacknowledged

Douglas

by the Duke of Newcastle [Henry Pelham Clinton].

The calling of a convention at Hope in September 1861 to demand responsible government aroused the governor's ire: "The term is associated with revolution and holds out a menace – the subject has an undoubted right to petition his sovereign, but the term 'convention' seems something more, it means coercion." The principle of representative government he recognized: in 1862, anticipating the reorganization of the colony's government in 1863, for which provision had been made in the founding act, Douglas recommended a small chamber, one-third nominated by the crown and two-thirds elected.

Douglas was aware that "the New Westminster radicals" had enlisted the support of a Canadian politician, Malcolm CAMERON, and that Cameron had been applying pressure on Newcastle since 1861 for his removal. After a visit to New Westminster in 1862, Cameron called on Douglas to show him a petition he intended to present to the queen. Douglas dismissed him, curtly informing him that he himself was the proper guardian of the people's rights and liberties, and that if he could not grant relief, he would lay the grievances "in a proper manner" before her majesty's government. In reporting the incident to the Colonial Office, he insisted that the community in British Columbia was prosperous and content. "A petty Californian-Canadian clique about New Westminster, the authors of all the clamour about 'Responsible Government,' form the only exception. That party is composed of men utterly ignorant of the wants and conditions of the Country; who never have done anything, and never will do anything for it, but complain; and who are, not unjustly, the objects of its derision."

In London, in February 1863, Cameron presented to the authorities the memorial signed by "certain inhabitants of British Columbia." "I cannot help thinking," Newcastle told him, "that they are a little unreasonable in complaining of their appeals for a complete change of their present form of Government. . . . They call that form 'Anti-British' and 'anomalous' but they forget that their Colony is hardly five years old, – that the form was established by Act of Parliament in 1858, and that this year, – 1863 – was fixed in that act as the period at which the question of any change of government should again come under consideration."

One month later the Duke sent a dispatch to Douglas: "As you have now ruled over Vancouver Island for twelve years – twice the usual period of Governorship – and as I do not think it would be desirable to replace you by a new Governor there and leave you to take up your abode in New Westminster as Governor of British Columbia alone, I intend to relieve you of both Governments. . . . It may be assumed however that I shall not carry out this decision in any way that can be disagreeable to you or shall give a triumph to those who have desired your recall. . . . I have now recommended to the Queen your Successor in the two Governments, and I have accompanied the recommendation with one that you shall be raised to the second rank in the Order of the Bath."

In order to finance his great arterial highway, Douglas had not waited for formal authorization before borrowing £100,000. On this score he had been criticized in London. Newcastle had learned that somehow Douglas had increased his salary from £1,800 to £3,800. Old and new enemies made in the course of a long career had also turned up at Whitehall; one was Langford who long ago had attacked Douglas for creating on Vancouver Island a "Family-Company Compact"; another was Captain William Driscoll Gosset, an officer in the Royal Engineers who had proved incompetent as treasurer of British Columbia. It was known that Douglas' relations with Colonel Moody, who with the Royal Engineers was recalled in 1863 from the colony, had not been cordial, and some credence was put in the assertions of the newspaper editors, Amor De Cosmos* in Victoria and John Robson in New Westminster, that he was despotic.

As he prepared to step down from office in the spring of 1864, Sir James Douglas had the satisfaction of knowing that he had ended the alien threat and protected the British foothold on the Pacific seaboard. His road was built, Cariboo was at the height of gold production, towns were laid out in the interior, and law and order prevailed in the mining fields. In 1864 the colonial revenues rose to £110,000; Victoria was a city of 6,000 persons, and Barkerville almost as large. Douglas' last task for British Columbia, now a stable community, was to set up a legislative council. "Sir James Douglas's career as governor has been a remarkable one," an official at the Colonial Office acknowledged. "He now quits his two Govts. leaving them in a state of prosperity, with every prospect of greater advancement."

To Douglas, it seemed that, whatever the character of his administration, the queen's grace in knighting him and the honours tendered him by the colonists on his retirement left only one opinion: his driving purpose had been "to promote the public good and to advance the material interests of the colonies." He continued to urge on Newcastle the building of a practicable road to connect British Columbia and Canada: if this step were taken, "trade would find an outlet, population and settlement would follow."

During his long service in the fur trade Douglas had never taken a furlough nor been absent one day from duty. As colonial governor, he had dedicated himself to responsibility and toil. His manner was singular and pompous, but he could never consent "to represent her Majesty in a shabby way." "All people speak with great admiration of the Governor's intellect – and a remarkable man he must be to be thus fit to govern a Colony," Sophia Cracroft, the travelling companion of Lady Franklin [Jane GRIFFIN], noted in 1861. "He has read enormously we are told & is in fact a self educated man, to a point very seldom attained. His manner is singular, and you see in it the traces of long residence in an unsettled country, where the white men are rare & the Indians many. There is a gravity, & a something besides, which some might & do mistake for pomposity, but which is the result of long service in the H.B. Co's service, under the above circumstances. . . ." The governor's wife they found to be a woman with a gentle, simple, and kindly manner. "Have I explained that her mother was an Indian woman & that she keeps very much (far too much) in the background, indeed it is only lately that she has been persuaded to see visitors, partly because she speaks English with some difficulty, the usual language being either the Indian, or Canadian French wh. is a corrupt dialect."

The British government allowed Sir James the usual perquisite of office and paid his passage "home." On 14 May 1864, after welcoming his successors, he set out on a voyage to London. His sickly son James had already been sent home to be educated, and living in Scotland was his daughter Jane, wife of A. G. Dallas. He would also make the acquaintance of his half-sisters and others of his father's relatives.

Sir James was in Paris in 1865, returning from a grand tour of Europe, when he received news that his daughter Cecilia, wife of Dr John Sebastian Helmcken*, had died. It was the first break in a family circle which had included six children (seven of the 13 children born to Douglas' wife at a fur trade post had not lived to maturity).

A devoted family man, and one with strong puritanical instincts, Douglas treated his wife with the same respect and affection he had seen Dr McLoughlin display for his half-Indian wife. "I have no objection to your telling the old stories about 'Hyass'," he gently reprimanded his youngest child, Martha, "but pray do not tell the world they are Mammas." Perhaps because of their background, he had watched the development of his children with the greatest solicitude. His son James, too delicate to live long, died in 1883. Of Sir James' three remaining daughters, Agnes was married to Arthur T. BUSHBY, an officer in the colonial service of B.C., and Alice to Charles Good, another of the young men who had arrived during the first gold-rush seeking employment. Alice's marriage, an unhappy one, ended in separation in 1869 and there was a divorce after her father's death. Martha would eventually marry Dennis Harris.

Except for his grand tour of 1864–65 and another brief trip abroad, Douglas spent his retirement years in Victoria. Martha was the consolation of his last days. He and Lady Douglas could hardly bear to part with her when she was sent to England for schooling in 1872. Martha was to be his "learned daughter – the veritable Blue-stocking of the family," and she responded dutifully to his admonitions: "You have plenty to say, and you must learn to say it well, for that is a necessary accomplishment to young Ladies as to others – therefore study to express your meaning with ease, without prolixity and without Tautology." "You must be very careful about your personal expenses, studying a proper economy in every way. Sheer extravagance is a sure road to poverty and ruin."

In his retirement Sir James seldom commented on political affairs to anyone but Martha, or to his sons-in-law, Dr J. S. Helmcken, one of the three delegates who negotiated British Columbia's entry into confederation, and A. G. Dallas, by this time well known in London financial circles. Bemoaning the union of the seaboard colonies in 1866 and the loss of Victoria's free port, Douglas inscribed in Martha's diary: "The Ships of war fired a salute on the occasion – A funeral procession with minute guns would have been more appropriate to the sad melancholy event." In 1872 he lamented to her: "The Island of San Juan is gone at last. I cannot trust myself to speak about it and will be silent." "We are now in hourly expectation of hearing how Sir John [Macdonald*'s] Ministry are faring at Ottawa," he wrote at the time of the Pacific Scandal, "if the want of confidence is carried against him by the Grits, Sir John will have to resign and there will be no end of trouble and delay about the construction of the Railway. The Grits as the opposition faction is termed are a low set and nothing good is to be expected from them."

His little family, with his respectable connections in England and Scotland, had grown dearer to him with the passing of the years. His visits abroad seemed to increase his determination to

Douglas

leave his children "a competence" so that they could take their place in society. "Friend Douglas . . . ," old John Tod wrote in 1870, "as he gets older, seems more and more engrossed with the affairs of this world notwithstanding his ample means, he is as eager and grasping after money as ever, and, I am told, at times seized with gloomy apprehensions of dying a beggar at last. . . ." Douglas practised economy to the end of his days: in 1869, when his income from land and investments was $27,300, his expenses were only $5,000. In addition to establishing a trust fund and annuity for Lady Douglas, his will amply provided for his son James, as well as for legacies for his small family circle amounting to nearly $70,000. His valuable properties remained almost intact during Lady Douglas' lifetime. (Her death occurred on 8 Jan. 1890.)

As the result of a heart attack Sir James Douglas died at Victoria on 2 Aug. 1877. His funeral was public; in Victoria and throughout B.C. there was a great outpouring of grief, affection, and respect for the man who had become known as "The Father of British Columbia."

A man of iron nerve and physical prowess, great force of character, keen intelligence, and unusual resourcefulness, Douglas had had a notable career in the fur trade. As colonial governor his career was even more distinguished. Against overwhelming odds, with indifferent backing from the British government, the aid of a few Royal Navy ships, and a small force of Royal Engineers, he was able to establish British rule on the Pacific Coast and lay the foundation for Canada's extension to the Pacific seaboard. Single-handed in the midst of a gold-rush he had forged policies for land, mining, and water rights which were just and endurable. He had kept the respect of the individualistic, competitive, and wasteful miners. His great Cariboo road had served their purpose, but it had served a still greater purpose: it permitted trade and commerce to be kept in British hands and British law and justice to be more easily upheld. As the gold of Cariboo flowed into British coffers, the links with the mother country were strengthened; as travel on the Cariboo road increased, the possibility seemed less remote that transcontinental travel routes could be practicable.

A practical man, but yet a visionary, Sir James Douglas was also humanitarian. He treated individuals, including Negro slaves and Indians, with a respect that few of his contemporaries showed. The majesty of his bearing aroused criticism, but that same bearing made him the symbol, in the motley crowd attracted to the two British seaboard colonies, of the fact that the British presence was firmly established on the northwest coast.

Margaret A. Ormsby

Archives of the ecclesiastical province of British Columbia (Vancouver, B.C.), George Hills diary, 27 June 1838–17 Nov. 1895. Gregg M. Sinclair Library, University of Hawaii, Hawaiian coll., Sophia Cracroft journal, 15 Feb.–3 April 1861. HBC Arch. A.7/2 (London locked private letter book, 1823–70); A.8/8; B.89/a, B.89/b, B.223/b, B.226/a, B.226/b, B.226/c; D.5/30, D.5/32, D.5/36 (George Simpson, Correspondence inward, 1822–60). PABC, Fort Vancouver, Correspondence outward to HBC, 1832–49 (letter book copies); Fort Vancouver, Correspondence outward, 1840–41 (letter book copies); Fort Victoria, Correspondence outward to HBC, 1850–55, 1855–59 (letter book copies); Vancouver Island, Governors Richard Blanshard and James Douglas, Correspondence outward, 22 June 1850–5 March 1859 (letter book copies); Vancouver Island, Governor James Douglas, Correspondence outward, 27 May 1859–9 Jan. 1864 (letter book copies); British Columbia, Governor James Douglas, Correspondence outward, 27 May 1859–9 Jan. 1864 (letter book copies); Governor James Douglas, Dispatches to London, 1851–55, 1855–59 (letter book copies); Governor James Douglas, Correspondence inward, 1830–68; James Douglas, Account and correspondence book, 1825–72; James Douglas, Correspondence outward, private, 22 May 1867–11 Oct. 1870 (letter book copies); James Douglas, Diary of a trip to the northwest coast, 22 April–2 Oct. 1840; James Douglas, Diary of a trip to California, 2 Dec. 1840–23 Jan. 1841; James Douglas, Diary of a trip to Sitka, 6 Oct.–21 Oct. 1841; James Douglas, Diary of a trip to Europe, 14 May 1864–16 May 1865; James Douglas, Letters to Martha Douglas, 30 Oct. 1871–27 May 1874; David Cameron papers; Jane Dallas letters; J. S. Helmcken papers; J. S. Helmcken, "Reminiscences" (5v. unpublished typescript, 1892); Archibald Macdonald, Correspondence outward, c.1830–1849; John McLeod, Correspondence inward, 1826–37; Donald Ross papers. PRO, CO 60, CO 305. University of Nottingham Library, Newcastle MSS, Letter books, 1859–64 (microfilm in PAC).

G.B., Parl., Command paper, 1859, XVII, [2476], pp.15–108, *Papers relative to the affairs of British Columbia, May to November 1858*; Parl., Command paper, 1859 (Session II), XXII, [2578], pp.297–408, *Further papers relative to the affairs of British Columbia, October 1858 to May 1859*; Parl., Command paper, 1860, XLIV, [2724], pp.279–396, *Further papers relative to the affairs of British Columbia, April 1859 to April 1860*; Parl., Command paper, 1862, XXXVI, [2952], pp.469–562, *Further papers relative to the affairs of British Columbia, February 1860 to November 1861*; Parl., House of Commons paper, 1849, XXXV, 103, pp.629–50, *Papers relating to Vancouver Island and the grant of it to the HBC . . .*; Parl., House of Commons paper, 1857 (Session II), XV, 224, 260 (whole volume), *Report from the select committee on the Hudson's Bay Company; together* with the proceedings of the committee, minutes of evidence, appendix and index; Parl., House of Commons paper, 1863, XXXVIII, 507, pp.487–540, Miscellaneous papers relating to Vancouver Island, 1848–1863. . . . British Columbian (New Westminster, B.C.), 1861–77. Colonist (Victoria), 1858–77. Victoria Gazette, 1859–60. HBRS, IV (Rich); VI (Rich); VII (Rich); XXII (Rich). James Douglas in California, 1841: being the journal of a voyage from the Columbia to California, ed. Dorothy Blakey Smith (Vancouver, B.C., 1965).

H. H. Bancroft, History of British Columbia, 1792–1887 (San Francisco, 1890). Coats and Gosnell, Douglas. F. W. Howay, The work of the Royal Engineers in British Columbia, 1858 to 1863 · · · (Victoria, 1910). F. W. Howay and E. O. S. Scholefield, British Columbia from the earliest times to the present (4v., Vancouver, B.C., 1914). J. S. Galbraith, The Hudson's Bay Company as an imperial factor, 1821–1869 (Toronto, 1957). Morton, History of the Canadian west. Ormsby, British Columbia. W. N. Sage, Sir James Douglas and British Columbia (Toronto, 1930). W. E. Ireland, "James Douglas and the Russian American Company, 1840," BCHQ, V (1941), 53–66. "Journal of Arthur Thomas Bushby" (Blakey Smith). W. K. Lamb, "The founding of Fort Victoria," BCHQ, VII (1943), 71–92; "The governorship of Richard Blanshard," BCHQ, XIV (1950), 1–41; "Sir James Douglas goes abroad," BCHQ, III (1939), 283–92; "Some notes on the Douglas family," BCHQ, XVII (1953), 41–51. W. N. Sage, "The gold colony of British Columbia," CHR, II (1921), 340–59; "Sir James Douglas, K.C.B.: the father of British Columbia," BCHQ, XI (1947), 211–27.

DOUTRE, GONZALVE, lawyer, professor, author of literary, historical, and legal works, and president of the Institut Canadien; b. in Montreal, L.C., 12 July 1842, son of François Doutre and Élisabeth Dandurand; m. Laura Brunelle, by whom he had at least one son; d. 28 Feb. 1880 in Montreal.

The first years of Gonzalve Doutre's life remain obscure. The youngest son of an illustrious family, he was also the brother-in-law of two distinguished men, Charles Daoust* and Médéric LANCTOT. In 1861 he obtained his baccalaureate in law at McGill University. As he had not yet attained his majority, he had to wait two years before being called to the bar (August 1863). Meanwhile he spent his leisure time frequenting the literary and legal organizations of Montreal. In April 1862 he gave a lecture at the Institut des Lois, an association where law students got together, on "the utility of a course in civil procedure" for law students; the following month his confrères elected him their president.

Gonzalve Doutre still had no more than his baccalaureate when he started a movement that resulted in an important reform of the Canadian bar. In February 1863, at the young candidate's suggestion, the Institut des Lois discussed a petition to be presented to the council of the bar for the purpose of "changing the present type of examinations for those aspiring to the study and practice of the profession of lawyer." Three years later (1 May 1866), Gonzalve Doutre laid a series of concrete proposals before a general meeting of lawyers; the latter entrusted the study of them to a committee made up of George Washington Stephens, Robert Mackay*, Charles-André LEBLANC, Thomas Weston Ritchie, Pierre-Richard Lafrenaye, and Gonzalve Doutre. "It is not the first time that I take the trouble to ask for reforms within the bar," he wrote in La Minerve of 29 May 1866. "In a period when I had everything to gain from the present system I wanted to try to have it changed, at the risk of suffering myself as a result. I hope therefore that no one will reproach me with waiting until I cleared the obstacles in order to pull up the ladder behind me." On 9 June Doutre submitted the committee's report to the assembled lawyers "in the form of a precise and detailed bill"; this bill became law on 15 Aug. 1866.

In the course of a meeting on 5 Oct. 1866, the lawyers' association elected Gonzalve Doutre secretary-treasurer of the general council, whose president was then William Locker Pickmore FELTON. At the end of his mandate, on 30 May 1868, the council presented Doutre with a silver inkwell as a tangible sign of its gratitude. It was a significant gesture, for already this young man of 25 had a remarkable achievement to his credit: he had initiated a reorganization of the Quebec bar, shepherded through parliament the 1866 law, watched over the application of this law, prepared rules governing the profession, and begun the publication of his principal legal works: all this despite failing health.

On 6 June 1867, wanting "to put an end to the permanent violation of the law that was occurring at the Jesuit College," where diplomas were conferred sometimes without due regard for the requirements of the law and for the proper duration of the course, the Institut Canadien set up a law faculty, affiliated to Victoria University at Cobourg; Gonzalve Doutre taught civil procedure for it. The new faculty conferred its first diploma on Jean-Baptiste Doutre, who subsequently entered the law office of his two brothers.

McGill University engaged Gonzalve Doutre in September 1871 as professor "of civil procedure, legal medicine, and forensic logic." On 28 March 1873 he received his doctorate in law from the same university, and on 3 Jan. 1879 the Quebec Liberal government made him a queen's counsel;

Doutre

finally, on 1 May 1879 he was elected a member of the council of the Montreal bar.

Gonzalve Doutre already belonged to the Institut Canadien when on 30 April 1858 Bishop Ignace Bourget*, the promoter of religious restoration and revival, issued his comminatory decree censuring the institute and instructing confessors to refuse the sacraments to its members [see Charles-Joseph LABERGE]. At its elections of 5 May 1859 the institute entrusted him with the office of secretary-archivist, a duty he was to take on several times until he became treasurer in 1863; in 1865 he became corresponding secretary, and finally president in 1871 and 1872.

Within the institute itself, Gonzalve Doutre's great activity was evident in his regular attendance at meetings and his numerous lectures. As a member of the governing body, he placed at the disposal of the association his eagerness and his intelligent zeal. It was in large measure thanks to the approaches he made to Canadian and foreign authorities that the museum of the institute, founded in 1864, was enriched with objects of art of real value; he himself, on 17 March 1866, gave to the museum a precious collection of coins and medals.

Gonzalve Doutre had a likeable personality, he was sincere and deeply religious, and during the disturbed years from 1858 to 1866 he had the benefit of the clergy's benevolence and indulgence. Bearing a note delivered to him on 3 April 1865 by the administrator of the diocese, Alexis-Frédéric TRUTEAU, he made his Easter communion. In December 1865 he received absolution from Léon-Alfred Sentenne, and was admitted to the special jubilee communion decreed by Pius IX. An event occurred, however, which upset everything. On 16 Oct. 1865, 17 members of the institute decided to appeal to the pope, "less in order to complain than to ask the common father of the faithful for a reconciliation with their bishop," as Louis-Antoine Dessaulles* wrote in 1868. When Bishop Bourget, who had just returned from Rome, was informed of this move, he stormed more than ever. He called the action "a sham appeal," and assured Rome that "the so-called sentence of excommunication" was, when all was said and done, "only a pastoral letter to the people to forewarn them against the dangers to which this evil institution exposed their faith." But on 1 Dec. 1865 the bishop none the less asked confessors to apply rigorously the rules concerning the institute and secret societies.

On 25 March 1866 Gonzalve Doutre followed the exercises of a retreat held by the Jesuits. When he presented himself before Abbé Sentenne to receive absolution, the latter insisted upon a formal authorization from Bishop Bourget. Forthwith, Doutre asked the bishop for this "permission to receive absolution and be admitted to the paschal communion." A letter dated 28 March, from Joseph-Octave PARÉ, informed him that Bishop Bourget, in the discharge of a "rigorous duty," found himself obliged to refuse Doutre access to the sacraments so long as he remained a member of the censured institution. Then came news that Bishop Bourget had allowed a member to receive the sacraments without requiring him to leave the institute. Doutre therefore took up his pen again on 12 April 1866. The bishop's severity towards him, he wrote, had not prevented him from performing his religious duties punctually, even if he regretted "being excluded from the number of Catholics admitted to the paschal communion"; however, he was anxious to know the particular reasons that excluded him "from the favours that Your Excellency extends to other members of the Institut Canadien." The next day, Bishop Bourget gave an answer to Doutre's question: the bishop had indeed authorized a member of the institute to receive the sacraments, but on the express condition that he would use his influence to turn his associates away from this dangerous organization.

In an exchange of letters that went on until 22 May 1866, Gonzalve Doutre undertook the defence of the institute in a plea characterized by unusual deference and pained sincerity. He had never thought, he said, of casting doubt on the obedience he owed his bishop; but for all that he did not accept his harshness and injustice. In the first place, Doutre rejected the term "rebel," which had been applied to him as one of the signatories of the petition sent to the pope to ask him to intervene between the bishop of Montreal and the members of the institute, who in Doutre's opinion had been victims of an unjust censure. Furthermore, he disapproved of the bishop's conduct, which was a cause of vexation to an institute that brought together Catholics and Protestants. "Certain Catholics," he noted, "are members of associations composed of a majority of Protestants and possessing libraries that are worse than ours; we observe that they have not come under censure." In the matter of the institute's library, which had been condemned more than once, Doutre reminded the bishop of the directors' promise to put offending books under lock and key; as for himself, he had not read a single book from the banned library for more than two years.

What were the reasons behind this special intransigence towards the institute? Doutre asked. "That Your Excellency is not strictly obliged [to give the reasons], I admit; but it also seems to me that a small gesture of graciousness, on behalf of those whose salvation may be in question, would not be out of place on the part of a bishop, and that this would have a better effect on the institute's members than an unbending rigour." Doutre ended his last letter with these severe words: "I shall never be convinced that in order to be a Catholic one must strip off the inalienable attributes of man, and be nothing but a kind of jelly-fish, delivered to the whims of a man who has not become God just because he has been consecrated bishop."

Gonzalve Doutre was living out a painful drama. On the one hand, he revolted against the bishop's arbitrariness and injustice, on the other his soul was wracked by agony and dread. Consequently, on 11 Nov. 1866 he confided his personal case to Charles-François Baillargeon*, administrator of the archdiocese of Quebec. Because of the danger in which he would find himself in the event of unexpected death, he entreated the archbishop, who had "jurisdiction over the bishop," to allow him to receive the sacraments in spite of the episcopal censures. Archbishop Baillargeon confessed his helplessness; he could only advise a reconciliation "with your worthy bishop. The bishop, and yours in particular, is a father. And such a father is always ready to give the kiss of peace to his child. . . . Why should you fear to go and cast yourself in his arms?" The letters received from Bishop Bourget, Doutre wrote subsequently, "scarcely allowed me to maintain this great confidence in the goodness and charity of the bishop of Montreal, who has never required from me anything less than a blind submission to his wishes, whether or not they have any connection with his episcopal powers."

On 1 Jan. 1868, in the hope of learning the opinion of the Roman authorities, Gonzalve Doutre sent a letter to the vicar general of Montreal, Abbé Truteau, who had just returned from Rome: "I anxiously await the final decision, and I assure you that I for one am desirous of seeing a prompt settlement of these difficulties, one way or the other." To Doutre's profound consternation, Abbé Truteau replied that the matter had never been discussed. "I believed until now that the mission of a priest was to work for harmony and concord among Catholics, and to seize the slightest opportunity to end any cause of dispute or hatred. Unfortunately this has not been the case with His Excellency and his vicar general. Each time one of them has been in Rome, he has taken care to make no mention to anyone of the affairs of the institute, hoping to drag the question out so that the bishop may harass the institute with fresh

censures, more threats, excommunications, or refusals of burial."

In 1869 disasters beset the Institut Canadien: on 7 July, a decree by the Inquisition condemned the doctrines "contained in a certain year-book"; on 14 July, a decree by the Index banned the *Annuaire de l'Institut Canadien pour 1868.* . . . Gonzalve Doutre reassured the members of the institute. According to him, the aim of the decree by the Index was merely to withdraw the 1868 year-book from circulation; it was no more an attack upon the institute than upon "the person of the writer whose work is often condemned with so much thoughtlessness." Furthermore, he went on, the court of the Inquisition, which "has judged without us, unknown to us and without consulting us," has not passed any judgement on the merit of our appeal: "our appeal has never been heard by the Inquisition, and only the year-book has served as grounds for the decree." The bishop of Montreal did not see the situation this way. On 29 August a statement was read in the churches of the diocese, requiring members to leave the institute under pain of being refused sacraments even at the point of death. But, having submitted purely and simply to the decrees, the institute came up against the intransigence of the religious authorities of Montreal, who demanded in particular that its constitutions and regulations be revised by the ordinary, in order that the latter might eradicate from them "false principles." Four members, including Gonzalve Doutre, then had recourse to Cardinal Alessandro Barnabo, and on 12 Oct. 1869 complained bitterly to him about the stiffness and inflexibility of the bishop of Montreal, "a man of great piety, but somewhat lacking in enlightenment, and consequently ill equipped for debate."

On 16 October Gonzalve Doutre left Canada to go to plead the institute's case before the authorities in Rome. He arrived there on 6 December. He met the prefect of the Sacred Congregation of the Propaganda, and then Lorenzo Nina, the assessor to the Holy Office, with whom he entered into "a long conversation" on the whole issue. Bishop Nina declared that one must not expect "censure to be passed on the bishop of Montreal; for to censure him would be a cause of scandal." He therefore recommended that Doutre prepare for him a "concise report with conclusions embodying an acceptable method of settlement." On 20 December Doutre submitted his report. After relating the salient facts in the painful dispute, the author proposed in conclusion that the bishop of Montreal's jurisdiction should be exercised only over the Catholic members of the institute, and that equally Catholics should be allowed to belong

Doutre

to it provided they submitted to the church's directives.

Subsequently Gonzalve Doutre made two attempts to smooth away the difficulties "without anyone making unworthy concessions." The first was on 18 Oct. 1873, when Canon Édouard-Charles Fabre* became coadjutor to Bishop Bourget; the second was on 2 June 1879. A plan took shape: to create a literary and scientific institution grouping together "all Canadian and Catholic youth." Gonzalve Doutre was not to see his project through: he died on 28 Feb. 1880, fortified with the last sacraments and assisted by Bishop Fabre and the parish priest Sentenne.

The originator of a major reform of the bar, the author of important legal works, a dedicated teacher respected by his students, Gonzalve Doutre lived through a grievous spiritual experience that commands the highest respect. The painful battle between ultramontanism and liberalism in Canada, which began in 1848 and occupied the remainder of the century, reached its climax around 1870. Bishop Bourget and his clergy wanted to build a kingdom with a theocratic emphasis, and did not shrink from means to crush the opposing camp: accusations of malicious intent, insinuations, and invectives were mingled with condemnations and excommunications. More adept in hurling anathema than in refuting the boldest arguments of the liberals, and ill adjusted to the times, the ecclesiastics stirred up confused currents within the liberal bourgeoisie. Some people submitted uncomprehendingly, others preferred to revolt, for example, Jean-Baptiste-Éric Dorion*, Pierre Blanchet, Toussaint-Antoine-Rodolphe Laflamme*, and Doutre's brother Joseph*, who could not "pardon the clergy for the harm it has done us." Were they, as their opponents claimed, ungodly men? To probe the intimate lives of human beings in an endeavour to determine what they are, or to interpret incidents and statements that put their deepest beliefs in question, is not easy. One fact stands out, however: in the period that concerns us, the most uncompromising of the liberals still remained attached to the Catholic religion.

Amongst these harried liberals, Gonzalve Doutre appears as a unique case. He entered the institute at the moment when the struggle was approaching its decisive phase, and lost no time in measuring himself against the leader of ultramontanism in person. To blind obedience, even to easy and fruitless revolt, he preferred combat, conducted with moderation, courtesy, and sincerity. As a profoundly religious man he would no doubt not have sacrificed his faith; but neither was he in any way disposed to submit blindly. He

waited for a decision which never came, and even when death was drawing nigh he was at grips with an internal drama whose intensity is difficult to estimate.

More than once Doutre betrayed his impatience, and that is understandable. "There is hatred in the bishop's heart towards us," he wrote in 1870. Indeed, at Rome Doutre tried three times to meet the bishop of Montreal, who avoided him; at Rome, Bishop Bourget refused to support a Canadian's request to attend a papal audience because Gonzalve Doutre was one of those applying; again at Rome, a single Canadian was excluded from a celebration organized in honour of a friend, the Chevalier Joseph-Édouard Lefebvre de Bellefeuille* – that Canadian bore the name of Gonzalve Doutre.

It is difficult to resist the feeling of sympathy this man inspired. He died very young, without having time to give full development to his great talent.

JEAN-ROCH RIOUX

Gonzalve Doutre, *Conseil général du Barreau du Bas-Canada; assemblée annuelle tenue à Québec le 28 mai 1867; rapport officiel* (Québec, 1867); *Loi du Barreau du Bas-Canada, suivie des règlements du conseil général et des sections de Montréal, Québec, Trois-Rivières* (Montréal, 1867); *Les lois de la procédure civile; savoir: texte du code, rapport des codifacteurs, autorités par eux citées, lois de faillite, règles de pratique des différents tribunaux, principes et formules de procédure, etc., etc., etc.* (2v., Montréal, 1867); *Règles de la profession d'avocat* (Montréal, 1868); *Tableau des avocats du Bas-Canada pour 1867* (Montréal, 1867); Gonzalve Doutre et Edmond Lareau, *Le droit civil canadien suivant l'ordre établi par les codes; précédé d'une histoire générale du droit canadien* (1v. paru, Montréal, 1872).

Gonzalve Doutre, "Cours d'histoire du Canada; cours donné à l'institut à partir du 13 octobre 1870," *Le Pays* (Montréal), 12 oct., 20 oct. 1870 and later numbers; [ ] "Discours de M. Gonzalve Doutre; sur les affaires de l'Institut canadien à Rome, prononcé à l'institut le 14 avril 1870," *Le Pays* (Montréal), 14 juin, 15 juin, 17 juin, 18 juin 1870; "Du principe des nationalités; lecture faite à l'Institut canadien, le 1er décembre 1864," *Le Pays* (Montréal), 15 déc., 17 déc., 20 déc. 1864; "Étude critique médico-légale: procès Provencher-Joutras," *La Minerve* (Montréal), 2 mars–31 mars 1868; "Musée de l'Institut canadien; lettre destinée à Alphonse Lusignan," *Le Pays* (Montréal), 20 mars, 22 mars, 24 mars, 30 mars 1866; "Procès Ruel-Boulet: étude critique médico-légale: conférence prononcée devant les membres de l'Institut médical de la faculté de médecine de l'université du collège Victoria, le 23 janvier 1869," *Le Pays* (Montréal), 10 févr.–18 févr. 1869; "Profession d'avocat," *La Minerve* (Montréal), 29 mai 1866; "Recherches dans les vieilles archives françaises appartenant à l'État; conférence prononcée à l'institut, le 23 février

252

1871," *Le Pays* (Montréal), 22 févr., 28 févr. 1871; "Vaccination," *Le National* (Montréal), 16 juill. 1872.

Gonzalve Doutre, "Administration de la justice," *Revue canadienne* (Montréal), X (1873), 762–70; "Code des curés, marguilliers et paroissiens, par l'Hon. J.-U. Beaudry, un des juges de la Cour supérieure, 1870," *La Revue légale* (Montréal), II (1870), 473–89; [ ], "Discours prononcé par M. Gonzalve Doutre, D.C.L., professeur de procédure à l'université McGill de Montréal, lors de la distribution des diplômes le 30 mars 1874," *Revue canadienne* (Montréal), XI (1874), 280–85; "La profession d'avocat et de notaire en Canada," *Revue canadienne* (Montréal), X (1873), 840–48; XI (1874), 58–68, 134–42; "Québec: la législation de la session 1869–1870," *La Revue légale* (Montréal), II (1870), 78–90.

Gonzalve Doutre gave many speeches on the most varied subjects; the texts of many do not seem to be extant, and in some cases all that remains is the announcement made in the newspapers at the time: "Un avocat plaidant sa propre cause, a-t-il droit à des honoraires contre la partie adverse qui a perdu sa cause? Conférence prononcée à l'Institut des lois, en février 1862," *Le Pays* (Montréal), 12 févr. 1862; "Considérations sur le procès Connol jugé le 13 janvier 1860; essai prononcé à l'institut, le 15 mars 1860," *Le Pays* (Montréal), 26 déc. 1860; "Les dîmes, essai donné à l'institut, le 22 septembre 1859," *Le Pays* (Montréal), 11 oct. 1859; "L'encombrement des professions; conférence prononcée à l'institut, le 30 janvier 1862," *Le Pays* (Montréal), 6 févr. 1862; "Essai sur les romans et les romanciers; conférence prononcée à l'institut, le 9 février 1860," *Le Pays* (Montréal), 17 avril 1860; "La guerre américaine; conférence donnée en avril 1863," *Le Pays* (Montréal), 18 avril 1863; "L'influence des maisons d'éducation et des institutions littéraires sur la jeunesse; conférence prononcée à l'Institut canadien, le 26 novembre 1863," *Le Pays* (Montréal), 28 nov. 1863; "L'Institut canadien en 1859; conférence prononcée à l'institut, le 30 mars 1859," *Le Pays* (Montréal), 31 mars 1859; "Le passé, le présent et l'avenir de l'Institut des lois; conférence prononcée en novembre 1862," *Le Pays* (Montréal), 8 nov. 1862; "L'utilité d'un cours de procédure civile; conférence prononcée à l'Institut des lois, en avril 1862," *Le Pays* (Montréal), 8 avril 1862.

ACAM, 901.135, pp.866–901. Bibliothèque municipale de Montréal, Fonds Gagnon, Institut canadien. Pierre Beullac et É.-F. Surveyer, *Le centenaire du Barreau de Montréal, 1849–1949* (Montréal, 1949). Lareau, *Hist. de la littérature canadienne; Histoire du droit canadien depuis les origines de la colonie jusqu'a nos jours* (2v., Montréal, 1888–89). Sylvain, "Libéralisme et ultramontanisme," *Shield of Achilles* (Morton), 111–38, 220–55. Maréchal Nantel, "Les avocats à Montréal," *Cahiers des Dix*, VII (1942), 185–213; "L'étude du droit et le barreau," *Cahiers des Dix*, XIV (1949), 11–40. Léon Pouliot, "Le cas de conscience de Gonzalve Doutre," *RHAF*, XXIII (1969–70), 231–45. É.-F. Surveyer, "Une école de droit à Montréal avant le code civil," *Revue trimestrielle canadienne* (Montréal), VI (1920), 140–50.

DRAPER, WILLIAM HENRY, politician, lawyer, and judge; b. near London, Eng., 11 March 1801, son of the Reverend Henry Draper; d. at Yorkville (Toronto), Ont., on 3 Nov. 1877.

Educated by private tuition, William Henry Draper ran away to sea at age 15. He made at least two voyages to India with the East India Company, and in the spring of 1820 emigrated to Upper Canada. Settling in Hamilton Township, he lived with John Covert*, a prominent Orangeman of the Cobourg area. He appears to have intended at one point to return to England, but he moved to Port Hope, taught school briefly, then began to study law. After a period in the office of George Strange Boulton*, Draper was called to the bar in 1828. He was also for a time assistant registrar for Durham and Northumberland. In 1829 he was given a position in the York (Toronto) office of John Beverley Robinson*, who was soon to be chief justice, then entered into a legal partnership with Solicitor General Christopher Hagerman*. He was also appointed reporter for the Court of King's Bench and named a bencher of the Law Society of Upper Canada. His reputation as a particularly fluent Tory barrister grew rapidly. He early achieved considerable success in the courtroom, and his eloquence gained him the sobriquet "Sweet William."

Good fortune, ability, and a pleasing personality thus brought Draper quickly into the society of the group so influential in governing the colony – the "Family Compact." He was soon also acquainted with the most formidable man of them all – John Strachan*, later the first Church of England bishop of Toronto. It was Robinson, however, who actively persuaded Draper to enter politics; this course was directly against the young lawyer's wishes, but it was no doubt suggested to him as the quickest route to the judiciary where his ambitions lay.

Draper's political *début* was made in the election of 1836 when he handily defeated the Reform candidate in Toronto, James Edward Small*. He took his position among the Tory majority gained in Upper Canada that year through the unprecedented intervention in party politics of the governor, Sir Francis Bond HEAD. In his first session in the House of Assembly, Draper was active, and his position on such thorny problems as the clergy reserves and the charter of King's College early indicated a man less intransigent than the majority of his Tory colleagues. In matters pertaining to the Upper Canada Academy (later Victoria College) in Cobourg his favourable report gained him the friendship of Egerton Ryerson* and the Wesleyan Methodists, which was to be one of the constants

Draper

of his political career. Yet Draper was by no means alienated from his Family Compact friends, and because of their influence with Head his rise was swift. In December 1836 he was made a member of the Executive Council, and in the following March, solicitor general. Shortly afterwards, Head dispatched him to London to present the governor's position in the acute financial crisis of 1836–37. This, however, was a painful episode: Draper's awkward reception by the Colonial Office officials possibly reflected their dislike of Head.

Shortly after Draper's return, the colony was immersed in the rebellion of 1837. It was to his house, on the night of 4 December, that Head brought his wife and other women and children of the little colonial *élite* to seek refuge from the expected assault of William Lyon Mackenzie*'s "army." After the failure of the rebellion Draper organized many of the prosecutions which took place in the next two years when raids by rebels kept the border in constant turmoil. The internal political situation of Upper and Lower Canada was going through an even more basic upheaval with the arrival of Lord Durham [Lambton*] and the British government's decision to implement that part of his Report recommending a union of the two Canadas, the appointment of Charles Poulett Thomson* to make that union a reality, and Lord John Russell's dispatch of 16 Oct. 1839 which meant in effect that executive councillors could be removed at the will of the governor.

It was during this period of trouble that Draper first began, consciously or not, to tread the pathway towards what was to be the cherished, though unfulfilled, goal of his political career – the formation of a new political party. A conservative party, it would stand ideologically between the old Family Compact Tories, whose system was failing, and the Reformers under Robert Baldwin*, whom Draper believed were endangering the connection with Britain. It was a course that would lead to much vilification. Most of it was undeserved, but Draper soon found himself in an undoubtedly compromising position.

He supported the union of the two Canadas in the Upper Canadian assembly on economic grounds. This action alienated many Tories, but he defended his position by pledging himself to the resolutions introduced by John Solomon Cartwright* in March 1839 which would have heavily weighted the union against the French Lower Canadians and assured a loyal and probably Tory majority in the assembly. Draper ultimately gave up his adherence to the resolutions in the face of Thomson's determination to force through the union without any such restrictions.

However, the publication soon afterwards of Russell's dispatch of 16 October led most of Draper's enemies, Tory and Reformer, to look upon it as an explanation of his conduct in changing his position – he was now simply a placeman of the governor. Draper's denials were not particularly convincing. Though never politically ambitious, he did hope to preserve his place in the government as a route to the judiciary and there seems little doubt that he bent his principles under Thomson's iron pressure.

Yet Draper, who succeeded Hagerman as attorney general for Upper Canada in February 1840, did not gain real credit with the governor for his performance. Once Thomson had pushed through the union of the Canadas by February 1841 (and been created Baron Sydenham), he was determined to act as his own prime minister and to destroy the old political groupings, forming a "moderate" party devoted to himself. In the election held in March and April (in which Draper was returned for Russell) Sydenham was successful. The French Canadians stood out against him, but in Canada West (still popularly called Upper Canada) both the old Tories and Baldwin's Reformers were reduced to a handful of seats by the Moderates committed to the governor. Draper continued as attorney general west and, as head of the conservative Moderates, was co–government leader with Samuel Harrison* in the assembly. But Draper had only four or five real followers, and Sydenham privately considered him a "poor creature." It was in Harrison, provincial secretary and leader of the liberal Moderates, that the governor placed his confidence. Unable to comprehend Sydenham's curious blend of liberalism and autocracy, Draper felt baffled and isolated; he had just written a letter of resignation in the autumn of 1841 when he was informed of the governor's death.

The arrival of Sir Charles Bagot* as governor in January 1842 marked a new phase in Draper's career. The two men found both their political views and their personalities compatible, and Draper rapidly replaced Harrison as the governor's chief Canadian adviser. Also, Draper's own political philosophy had clarified, and his appreciation of political realities sharpened.

In September 1841, Baldwin had moved resolutions calling for responsible government. These had been parried by Sydenham when Harrison had moved counter-resolutions, ostensibly promising responsible government, in a much vaguer form. It was the Harrison resolutions that were passed, and Draper had supported them. Though he would not have argued that a governor was ever bound to take the advice of his councillors, he now felt himself committed to the principle that executive councillors must have the confidence of a majority of the assembly. This did not necessarily mean a two-party system in the way that Baldwin foresaw; it could also mean a multi-party or a no-party government, and there is no doubt that Draper favoured the last. Now, however, as he began to realize that party government was inevitable, he hoped for a great, loyal Conservative party embracing both French- and English-speaking Canadians – for by now he believed the French to be naturally conservative. He was becoming more convinced that if government were not to founder completely, the French must be brought quickly into it even if they stood by their alliance with Baldwin and the price was a Reform ministry.

It was Bagot who eventually took responsibility for the generous offer to the French that led to the formation of the first Baldwin–Louis-Hippolyte La Fontaine* government in September 1842. Acclaim for the governor from the French and Reformers, and disapproval from the British government and the Canadian Tories, resulted. Draper's role in this upheaval was critical: in July he had begun urging Bagot that La Fontaine's French bloc must be brought into the ministry if the governor were not to be placed in an untenable position by being unable to maintain a council acceptable to the assembly. Other councillors, such as Harrison and Robert Baldwin Sullivan*, were urging this course, but Draper's advice was the most persuasive. Draper knew that if the French remained committed to Baldwin their accession to power would necessitate his own resignation. This he magnanimously offered, and advised as well that other Tory councillors be forced out. When Bagot still wavered, Draper and Harrison led the Executive Council in forcing his hand by threatening a mass resignation on 12 September. The following day, to La Fontaine, Bagot made his ultimate offer, to place four French Canadians and Baldwin on the council and to retire councillors in whom they did not have confidence. When Baldwin caused further difficulties, Bagot empowered Draper to read out in the assembly the extent of this offer. Most of the French members had not previously known of the magnitude of the concessions, and La Fontaine's hold on his party was briefly shaken. A compromise was worked out and the new Baldwin–La Fontaine ministry formed in a way least damaging to the governor's prestige. Draper resigned from the Executive Council (on 15 September) and from the assembly, and was promised a seat on the judiciary by Bagot.

Draper retired from active politics altogether,

taking no great interest in the Legislative Council, to which Bagot appointed him shortly before he died in 1843. Late the same year, however, a crisis erupted under Bagot's successor, Charles Metcalfe*, and, led by Baldwin and La Fontaine, the whole of the Executive Council, except Dominick Daly*, resigned. When Metcalfe could not form an administration that had a majority in the assembly he summoned Draper and gave him a seat in the Executive Council. With only Daly and Denis-Benjamin Viger*, he carried on the administration for nearly a year though he did not hold any portfolio. The non-responsible government of this "triumvirate" was loudly condemned as autocratic, yet Draper was working towards a broadly based "Ministry of Moderates," like the one that had worked under Sydenham. He failed. In Lower Canada, Viger brought over a few individuals, including Denis-Benjamin Papineau*, to his cause, but no mass support. In Upper Canada, Draper's appeals to such prominent moderates as Harrison, William Hamilton Merritt*, and Ryerson all foundered, and William Morris*, who wielded great influence with the Presbyterians, was the only notable accession to the Executive Council (as receiver general) that Draper was able to secure.

Yet a government was somehow patched together in time for the general election in the autumn of 1844. A number of factors – the removal of the seat of government from Kingston to Montreal, the secret societies bill, which had outraged the Orangemen under Ogle Robert GOWAN, and a general feeling that the French Canadians were being pandered to – had turned much public opinion in Upper Canada against the Reformers before their resignation and Metcalfe was able to capitalize on this discontent when he entered the campaign and denounced the Reformers as traitors. The result was that, though defeated in the lower half of the province, the government triumphed in Upper Canada and Draper's ministry had a small majority of four or five.

Draper was now in a curious position for one who had resisted so long the doctrines of Baldwin. From late 1844 until his resignation in May 1847 he was virtually prime minister of Canada, and as he had a majority in the assembly, the Reformers could no longer term his administration irresponsible. At the same time, the rapidly failing health of Metcalfe and the lack of interest in domestic politics shown by Lord Cathcart [Charles Murray Cathcart*] who succeeded him, meant that Draper saw hardly any interference from above. Yet this was not the greatest anomaly in his situation. He was also a party leader without a party, a prime minister without a following.

Draper

His majority in the assembly was made up mainly of Tories who had little love for Draper but had been elected to support the governor, and who were largely excluded from the Executive Council. They endured the attorney general as leader because there was no one else to take his place – he had the support of the governors, and the Tories themselves were split into factions led by Henry Sherwood* and Sir Allan MacNab*.

Under the circumstances, Draper envisaged a period of retrenchment with few controversial issues. In fact, despite the weakness of his position, the last two sessions of the assembly he faced as attorney general saw several important measures. A schools act for Lower Canada drafted by Augustin-Norbert Morin* was passed in 1845. The Upper Canada common school act of 1846, drawn up by Ryerson at Draper's behest, has been termed the first really workable settlement of that troublesome problem. The voting of a permanent civil list firmly established the principle that it was the Canadian legislature only that had the right to tax Canadians. Perhaps more significant were Draper's efforts to lay the spectre of the rebellion of 1837. On 17 Dec. 1844 the house addressed the queen, unanimously asking her to pardon all former rebels; two months later, an amnesty was granted. Early in 1845 D.-B. Papineau moved a successful rebellion losses bill for Upper Canada, although the more controversial subject of indemnifying Lower Canadians was not solved until later. Nevertheless, the French Canadians welcomed the repeal of restrictions on the French language, moved by Papineau on behalf of the government, in February 1845. It proved a coup for Draper who had persuaded Metcalfe to disobey his instructions on the subject in order to forestall an address the Reformers were planning to make on the subject of the French language.

Despite such successes, Draper's government gave an appearance of chronic weakness. It was defeated frequently on minor issues and retreated ignominiously over the university bill. This measure, which Draper considered important enough to warrant his leaving the Legislative Council and seeking a seat in the assembly (for London), was introduced by him on 4 March 1845. It called for a University of Upper Canada to which Queen's College at Kingston and Victoria College would be affiliated, as well as the Church of England King's College (which later became the University of Toronto). Acceptable to the Methodists and the Church of Scotland, the bill aroused the ire of the Church of England, and Strachan managed to rally many of the Tory assembly members against it. Draper persisted, saying he would stand or fall by the measure, and he forced the resignation of his own recently named inspector general, William Benjamin Robinson, on the floor of the house when the latter supported Strachan. Perhaps Draper was hoping for aid from Baldwin's Reformers who had previously framed a similar bill; it was not forthcoming. In the end, a group of Tories, led by Sherwood, threatened to bring down the government if the bill had a third reading. This was too much for the ailing Metcalfe who felt that he would not be able to form a new ministry. Following a plea from the governor, Draper's measure was withdrawn.

From an administrative or legislative point of view, Draper's ministry could hardly be termed more than a limited success. Politically, it seemed to be a complete failure. Yet the attorney general was working towards something important which would bear fruit after his own political retirement: a modern Victorian conservative party. His plan was twofold – to placate the leading English-speaking Tories while he replaced them with Moderates, and to win the French bloc, or a substantial part of it, away from its alliance with the Reformers.

In this last task Draper came remarkably near to success. There was no longer any hope that Viger or D.-B. Papineau would bring in any mass support, so Draper struck shrewdly at the weakest link of La Fontaine's supporters, the Quebec City wing, which felt neglected by their Montreal leaders. Negotiations with René Caron, the mayor of Quebec and speaker in the Legislative Council, broke down when Metcalfe refused to eject Daly from the Executive Council and when the correspondence fell into the hands of La Fontaine who read it in the assembly in April 1846. Further negotiations conducted in the autumn of 1846 again came to nothing, but on this occasion Draper managed to drive a wedge between La Fontaine and his chief lieutenant, Morin. In the spring of 1847 approaches were again made to Caron and the Quebec wing of the party, which in turn applied pressure on Morin; in his last approach Draper came closest to success. A substantial section of the French bypassed La Fontaine and empowered Caron to enter the administration if the "double majority" principle was offered. Acceptance, however, would have given four out of the seven seats on the council to the French, and it seemed a prohibitive demand. Draper was well content to wait.

The negotiations were never again to be taken up. Draper's failure to break the French bloc was matched by a more disastrous failure to contain rising Tory opposition to himself. The departure in 1845 of Metcalfe, whom the Tories had pledged to support and who had himself fully supported

Draper, was a serious blow. Nevertheless, factions led by Sherwood and MacNab kept the Tories disunited and provided Draper with the opportunity to pursue his hope of filling the Upper Canadian section of his Executive Council with moderate Conservatives. William Morris, John Hillyard CAMERON, John A. Macdonald* – these were the stamp of men Draper wanted and ultimately brought into his ministry. William Badgley* became attorney general east. But they were too few. Attempts to placate the Tories with positions failed. Sherwood and W. B. Robinson had been brought into office but both had to be ejected, and dealings with MacNab proved disastrous. Only a few men such as William Cayley* were acceptable to both right and left wings of the party. The Tory members of the assembly increasingly chafed under the leadership of men many of them despised.

That Draper, who had always disliked politics, should begin to look towards retirement under such discouraging conditions was natural. A further inducement came with the appointment of Lord Elgin [Bruce*] as governor in 1847. Since Draper had answered Metcalfe's desperate summons to office in 1843 he had assumed that British governors would be interested, above all, in avoiding a Baldwin administration. But Elgin and Lord Grey in the Colonial Office were quite willing to accept both responsible government and Baldwin. It was becoming apparent to Draper that he was in the way of everyone – governor, Tory, and Reformer. On 28 May, following the death of Christopher Hagerman, Draper resigned as attorney general and became puisne judge of the Court of Queen's Bench of Upper Canada. His ministry fell into the hands of Sherwood until the subsequent election returned Baldwin and La Fontaine.

Draper's legislative accomplishments were real but modest, his efforts to form a moderate Conservative party in alliance with French Canadians failed, and he swam clearly, if obliquely, against the historical tide of responsible government and reformism. Yet it was he, along with Baldwin and La Fontaine, who really dominated the 1840s. Moreover, the formation of a Conservative party linked to the French Canadians was to become a reality in 1854. It was the creation of Draper's ablest follower, Macdonald, who clearly had the political gift in which Draper was most lacking – the ability to organize a national party with wide popular support.

There are other important aspects to Draper's political career that have rarely been appreciated. Following the racial conflicts of the 1830s, the 1840s were comparatively quiet, owing partly to a reaction against the rebellion, partly to the Baldwin–La Fontaine alliance. Giving the French Canadians their fair share of political power was a factor and Draper's critical part in that episode is clear. Similarly his efforts to form a coalition with the French Canadians between 1844 and 1847 undoubtedly helped to convince them that their claims for office would eventually be met.

Draper's role in the evolution of responsible government was an unwitting one, but perhaps his most important. After the rebellions and the era of Durham and Sydenham, the tide was moving towards acceptance of responsible government. But between 1841 and 1846, when Sir Robert Peel's Conservative ministry was in power in England, particularly when Stanley held sway in the Colonial Office, a different view prevailed there. An unremitting clash between a Canadian legislature championing responsible government and a British Colonial Office and governor could have had serious consequences in this period, and such a clash appeared about to develop in December 1843 with the resignation of Baldwin and La Fontaine. Draper stepped into the breach, first by supporting Metcalfe with his temporary government, and then from 1844 to 1847 by carrying on a full administration which stood on a majority in the assembly after the election of 1844. Thus he neatly bridged the transition between the era of Metcalfe and Stanley and that of Elgin and Grey. In doing so he helped allow responsible government to evolve peacefully, and was thus one of the many architects in the development of commonwealth from empire.

Following his retirement from politics, Draper was at last given the opportunity to advance in what had always been his chosen field of endeavour – the judiciary. After sitting on the Court of Queen's Bench for nine years, he was created chief justice of the Court of Common Pleas of Upper Canada in 1856, succeeding James Macaulay*. In 1863 he was named chief justice of the Court of Queen's Bench for Upper Canada; in 1868 he was appointed presiding judge of the Court of Error and Appeal in Ontario, succeeding Archibald McLean*, and the next year became its chief justice.

Though eminently distinguished, Draper's later career saw none of the turbulence, nor indeed of the constructive innovations that had marked his political life. To Draper himself it was the consummation of a personal preference for a tranquil and ordered existence. He did, however, make two brief reappearances in the public eye in the 1850s – in the question of transferring the Hudson's Bay Company territories, and as presiding judge over the "double shuffle" trials.

Draper

The HBC question arose when problems concerning the colony of Vancouver Island prompted Henry Labouchere, colonial secretary in Lord Palmerston's administration, to undertake an investigation in 1857 of the company's charter by a select committee of the British House of Commons. In the Canadas, the Macdonald–George-Étienne CARTIER government was weak, and the Clear Grit opposition, led by George BROWN, had just hammered "western expansion" into its platform. Though Macdonald was happy to pre-empt an attractive Grit policy, he knew the difficulties of occupying and defending the lands, and therefore had to pursue a policy combining aggressive expansionism with prudent realism. He chose Draper to represent Canada before the select committee, with no powers to commit the province but with wide latitude of argument. It was a task suited to Draper's broad legal knowledge and persuasive powers of argument. Labouchere claimed that Draper, who favourably impressed the committee, was one of the ablest men he had ever met. Concentrating on the necessity of preserving the west from American encroachments, Draper argued that only settlement could achieve this but that the company's interests were inimical to settlement. He suggested that an appeal to the Judicial Committee of the Privy Council might be the best way to test the company's chartered territorial rights.

The work of the select committee bore no immediate fruit, but Draper's arguments had made their mark and the principle that Canada would likely be the ultimate legatee of the HBC's territorial rights became more and more taken for granted.

Draper's next appearance on the political scene in 1858 was a good deal more controversial. In August the Cartier–Macdonald ministry came back into power after a defeat which had resulted in the famous two-day Brown–Antoine-Aimé Dorion* administration. The new ministers did not resign their seats and face by-elections as was normal procedure. Instead they swore the oaths for one office, resigned, and swore again for another office. The manœuvre was soon dubbed the "double shuffle," and Brown bitterly attacked both the governor, Sir Edmund Head*, who had accepted it, and the government. Another Reformer, Adam Wilson*, tested the legality of the issue by starting proceedings against Macdonald and two of his colleagues, and the case was heard before Draper. Despite the fact that all the judges involved in the hearings were Conservatives, the Grits appear to have hoped for victory. However, it was on the letter of the law that Draper stood in giving judgement for the defendants on 18 Dec. 1858. Yet, though disclaiming any right of the judiciary to guess what the legislators intended in framing the original act [see HARRISON], Draper did interpret what they had "meant" in dealing with another, more minor point in the issue. This lent some credence to the charges Brown and his allies soon made that both the governor and the judiciary were in an unholy alliance to subvert the constitution at the behest of the corrupt Macdonald. Draper was singled out for particular contempt, and the *Globe* expounded: "Mr. Draper has mistaken his place and age. He would have made a very fair Jeffreys and might have served for the Bloody Assize." The charges by the Grits of a conscious conspiracy were unfounded and unfair, but the whole episode of the "double shuffle" was hardly edifying. The bias in Macdonald's favour and against Brown must, unconsciously at least, have influenced Head and Draper in making their otherwise unexceptionable decisions.

If the remainder of his years on the bench were quiet, Draper was active in many civic and religious organizations, being at one time president of the St George's Society in Toronto, of the Canadian Institute (from 1856 to 1858), of the Toronto Cricket Club, and of the Philharmonic Society. He was president of the Church Association of the Diocese of Toronto, formed in 1873 and including as members William Hume Blake*, Casimir Stanislaus Gzowski*, and Daniel Wilson*, which led to the founding of Wycliffe College in Toronto. In 1854, he was made a CB. He maintained a lifelong passion for exercise but became increasingly infirm in the last decade of his life, and he died on 3 Nov. 1877. He had married Mary White in 1827. They had several children, one of whom, William George*, became well known as a lawyer.

GEORGE METCALF

MTCL, Baldwin papers. PAC, MG 24, A13 (Bagot papers); E1 (Merritt papers); MG 26, A (Macdonald papers). PAO, John George Hodgins collection; John Strachan letter books; John Strachan papers. PRO, CO 42/437–42/550; CO 537/140–537/143.

Arthur papers (Sanderson). [Bruce and Grey], *Elgin-Grey papers* (Doughty). Canada, Province of, Legislative Assembly, *Journals*, 1841–47. *Correspondence between the Hon. W. H. Draper & the Hon. R. E. Caron; and between the Hon. R. E. Caron, and the Honbles. L. H. Lafontaine & A. N. Morin* (Montreal, 1846). [C. T. Metcalfe], *The life and correspondence of Charles, Lord Metcalfe, late governor-general of India, governor of Jamaica, and governor-general of Canada . . .*, ed. J. W. Kaye (2v., London, 1854). [Ryerson], *Story of my life* (Hodgins). [C. E. P. Thomson], *Letters from Lord Sydenham, governor general of Canada, 1839–1841, to Lord John Russell*, ed. Paul Knaplund (London, 1931). Upper Canada, House of Assembly, *Journals*, 1836–40. *British Colonist*

(Toronto), 1838–47. *Christian Guardian* (Toronto), 1836–47. *Examiner* (Toronto), 1838–47. *Globe* (Toronto), 1844–47.

Cyclopædia of Can. biog. (Rose, 1886). Dent, *Canadian portrait gallery*, II. Careless, *Union of the Canadas.* Creighton, *Macdonald, young politician.* G. P. de T. Glazebrook, *Sir Charles Bagot in Canada; a study in British colonial government* ([London], 1929). George Metcalf, "The political career of William Henry Draper," unpublished MA thesis, University of Toronto, 1959. Moir, *Church and state in Canada West.* Monet, *Last cannon shot.* Ormsby, *Emergence of the federal concept.* D. B. Read, *The lives of the judges of Upper Canada and Ontario, from 1791 to the present time* (Toronto, 1888). Sissons, *Ryerson.* George Metcalf, "Draper Conservatism and responsible government in the Canadas, 1836–1847," *CHR*, XLII (1961), 300–24.

DREW, ANDREW, naval officer; b. at London, Eng., 27 Nov. 1792, son of John and Mary Drew; m. in 1832 Mary Henderson by whom he had five sons and one daughter; d. in England, 19 Dec. 1878.

Andrew Drew entered the Royal Navy as a first class volunteer in May 1806. He took part in operations at Boulogne, Copenhagen, and Walcheren Island and was promoted lieutenant in 1814. He remained on active duty until 1824, when he was promoted commander for distinguished service during the Ashanti War and placed on half-pay.

In 1832 Drew entered into a partnership with Vice-Admiral Henry Vansittart* to develop a farming estate in Upper Canada. Under the terms of the partnership Vansittart supplied capital of £1,800, one half on his own account and one half as an interest-free loan for Drew's share of the capital. Drew took up land in Blandford Township in July and played a leading part in developing the district. His efforts led to the laying out of the town of Woodstock, which he had Charles Rankin* survey; he erected the first church, with money supplied by Vansittart, and built some of the first houses.

When Vansittart arrived in 1834, he and Drew quarrelled. There were several reasons for Vansittart's dissatisfaction: all the land was held in Drew's name; Drew refused to hand the church over to the parish because, he claimed, there was money owing to him for construction costs; and certain investments made by Drew on Vansittart's behalf did not meet the latter's approval. As a result the partnership was dissolved, on terms arbitrated by Christopher A. Hagerman*.

Drew devoted himself to improving the land he retained – about 350 of the 700 acres originally granted, including 40 in the town plot – until the outbreak of the rebellion in Upper Canada. He was appointed to command a naval brigade attached to the force raised and led by Allan MacNab* to expel William Lyon Mackenzie* and a party of Americans from Navy Island in the Niagara River. Mackenzie's supporters hired a steamer, *Caroline*, to carry supplies to the island, and on 29 Dec. 1837 MacNab ordered Drew to cut out the vessel. That night he led a naval expedition to Fort Schlosser on the American side of the river, seized the ship after a fight in which one of her crew was killed, set her on fire, and cut her adrift to burn in the river.

This affair embittered relations between England and the United States for many years. The Americans regarded the deliberate attack on an American ship in an American port and the death of an American citizen as acts of piracy and murder. In Upper Canada the attack was regarded as proper punishment for bandits who were trying to overthrow the government of the province and who should have been restrained by the American authorities. An American jury indicted Drew for murder. The American government demanded compensation for the loss of the ship, and the incident formed the excuse for the outrages of the Patriot Hunters.

Drew remained on duty during the winter of 1838, and, when Captain Williams Sandom* was sent to command the naval forces in the province, acted as naval adviser to the lieutenant governor, Sir George Arthur*. In the summer of 1838 he was ordered to prepare plans for a provincial marine which Arthur intended to use, if needed, to defend the upper lakes in the event of an American invasion of the province. In November Drew was asked to raise the force and proceed to Amherstburg to help repel a threatened attack. Damage to his two ships as a result of a fire stopped him, however, and he spent the winter at Dunnville.

He continued to serve until the summer of 1839, during which time he was employed by Arthur in various other matters, including preparations to capture Fort Niagara in the event of war with the United States. In July he was relieved of his command by Sandom on charges of being absent without leave and of signing a false muster roll. Drew requested a court martial and was acquitted but was not employed again in Canada.

In 1842 Drew left Canada, as a result, he claimed, of attempts to murder him for his part in the *Caroline* affair, and he never returned. In England he went back to active duty in the navy, serving in the West Indies. In 1843 he was promoted captain on half-pay and at his death was an admiral.

M. L. MAGILL

Andrew Drew, *A narrative of the capture and destruction of the steamer 'Caroline' and her descent over the*

Driard

falls of Niagara on the night of the 29th of December, 1837 (London, 1864).

MTCL, Robert John Turner papers. PAO, Marston collection, Andrew Drew papers, 1836–1839; RG 1, A–IV, 44 (Blandford); RG 1, C–IV, Oxford East Township, Vansittart family papers. PRO, CO 42/459, 144; 42/465, 160, 166; 42/473, 41; 42/474, 134, 138. *Arthur papers* (Sanderson). O'Byrne, *Naval biog. dict.* John Ireland, "Andrew Drew and the founding of Woodstock," *Ont. Hist.*, LX (1968), 229–45; "Andrew Drew: the man who burned the *Caroline*," *Ont. Hist.*, LIX (1967), 137–56.

DRIARD, SOSTHENES MAXIMILIAN, hotelier; b. 1819 at Chapelle-la-Reine (Department of Seine et Marne), France; d., probably a bachelor, on 15 Feb. 1873 at Victoria, B.C.

Sosthenes Maximilian Driard was one of those Frenchmen who, as a result of the revolution of 1848, the downfall of Louis-Philippe, and the ensuing economic depression in France, decided to emigrate to the "New World." Driard is said to have settled initially in New Orleans but in 1853 he was certainly in San Francisco. At that time, in association with Jules Rueff and others, Driard founded a charitable organization called Maison d'Asile, designed to assist Frenchmen not eligible for help from the French Benevolent Society. Driard, and also Rueff (who later moved to Victoria, B.C.), were among its first directors.

Driard, according to his obituaries, was attracted to British Columbia in 1858 by news of the Fraser River gold rush; the first mention of his presence in Victoria is in 1859 when he advertised the Colonial Restaurant in the *Victoria Gazette*. Edgar Fawcett, a well-known pioneer, described the Colonial Hotel in the 1860s as "one of the swell places of that day" and its owner as "very corpulent and asthmatic." In 1871 Driard purchased the St George Hotel on View Street. With two additional storeys, numerous alterations, and new furnishings, the hotel, renamed Driard House, was opened in May 1872, advertising accommodation for 100. Driard died nine months later at the age of 54; the hotel, luxurious and with a fine cuisine, was subsequently owned by his nephew Louis Lucas and a partner, Louis Redon, eventually passing to the Hartnagles.

Driard was a member of the French Benevolent Society of Victoria, formed early in 1860. The society founded a hospital in Victoria and initiated a system of medical benefits at a low monthly fee. There were no restrictions as to the nationality of its subscribers. Driard was also a member of Victoria Lodge, Free and Ancient Masons (an unusual proceeding for a Roman Catholic), probably drawn to freemasonry by his benevolent and charitable disposition. He was also one of the charter members and a director of the British Columbia Pioneer Society. In his will he remembered relatives (most of whom were in France), the sisters of St Ann, and the French Benevolent Society; if he died in B.C., four baskets of champagne were to be given to his brother masons. At his death he was described in one account as "intelligent and assiduous at his business," in another as "much esteemed and respected for his charitable nature and many other good qualities."

MADGE WOLFENDEN

British Columbia Law Courts (Victoria), will of Sosthenes Driard (no. 1804). PABC, letter of S. Driard to the governor, 27 Oct. [1868]. *Daily British Colonist and Victoria Chronicle*, 10 Aug. 1870; 4 May 1872; 16, 17, 18 Feb. 1873. *Victoria Daily Standard*, 15, 17, 18 Feb. 1873. *Victoria Gazette*, 3 Sept. 1858, 29 Oct. 1859. Daniel Lévy, *Les Français en Californie* (San Francisco, Calif., 1884), 201. A. P. Nasatir, *French activities in California, an archival calendar-guide* (Stanford, Calif., London, [1945]), 37. W. E. Ireland, "The French in British Columbia," *BCHQ*, XIII (1949), 67–89.

DROLET, CHARLES, lawyer, politician, officeholder; b. in Quebec, 8 May 1795, son of Charles Drolet and Angélique Hill; d. in Quebec, 22 Sept. 1873.

Charles Drolet was admitted to the bar of Lower Canada on 28 April 1827 and practised at Quebec. There on 27 July 1830 he married Marguerite Quirouet; they do not seem to have had any children. In February 1836, Drolet, assisted by Louis-Joseph PAPINEAU, defeated Robert-Shore-Milnes BOUCHETTE, who was a *Patriote* friend, in a by-election for Saguenay County. As a member of the Association des Frères-Chasseurs, Drolet was in favour of armed rebellion but he did not participate in the first uprising. On 1 July 1838, just before the exiles to Bermuda sailed from Quebec, Drolet smuggled supplies to their ship. After Lord Durham [Lambton*] resigned in October 1838, Drolet disturbed the authorities by calling a public meeting in Saint-Roch, Quebec City, to thank Lord Henry Peter Brougham and John Temple Leader, the British politicians believed responsible for the resignation.

On 16 Nov. 1838, Drolet executed his boldest scheme, the escape from the Citadel of two prominent *Patriote* prisoners, Edward Alexander Theller* and William W. Dodge [see John G. HEATH]. Sir John Colborne* issued a warrant for his arrest, and Drolet fled Quebec for the United States border. He stopped for a night in Saint-Gervais with his first cousin (also his wife's uncle), legislative councillor François Quirouet, and was arrested there by a militia squad on an order signed by his host. Near Quebec, Drolet cleverly persuaded a guard to permit him to visit his mother, and he escaped to the United States. At Rouses Point, Drolet joined *Patriote* friends and on 5 December Robert NELSON named him one of 12 councillors of the proposed republic of Lower Canada.

When the *Patriote* cause, in which Drolet had played a useful but limited part, collapsed in 1839, Drolet was admitted to the bar of New York at Buffalo, then moved to Detroit where he practised for eight years. After the general amnesty of 1849 Drolet returned to Montreal. In August 1850 he moved to Quebec where, upon the recommendation of Louis-Hippolyte La Fontaine*, Drolet, an unpopular choice among many government supporters, received a minor imperial judicial appointment, clerk of the Court of Vice-Admiralty, Quebec. Soon after La Fontaine moved to the Court of Appeal in July 1854, Drolet received his second appointment, deputy clerk of the Court of Appeal. He retained both positions until his death.

CARMAN MILLER

[R.-S.-M. Bouchette], *Mémoires de Robert-S.-M. Bouchette, 1805–1840; recueillis par son fils Errol Bouchette et annotés par A.-D. de Celles* (Montréal, [1903]), 40, 85. "Papiers de Ludger Duvernay," *Canadian Antiquarian and Numismatic J.* (Montreal), 3rd ser., VII (1910), no.2, 94. *Le Canadien* (Québec), janv., mars 1836; janv., mai 1850. *Mélanges religieux* (Montréal), 27 août 1850. *Montreal Gazette*, 1 Jan., 16 Feb., 15 March 1836; 10, 16 Oct., 15 Nov. 1838. *Le Nouveau Monde* (Montréal), 4 sept., 27 sept. 1873. *L'Opinion publique* (Montréal), août, 3 oct. 1873. *Canada directory, 1857–58.* Desjardins, *Guide parlementaire.*
L.-N. Carrier, *Les événements de 1837–1838* (Beauceville, Qué., 1914). Christie, *History of Lower Canada.* Fauteux, *Patriotes,* 220–21. E. C. Guillet, *The lives and times of the Patriots; an account of the rebellion in Upper Canada, 1837–1838, and the Patriot agitation in the United States, 1837–1842* (Toronto, 1938), 128. P.-G. Roy, *Fils de Québec,* III, 70. Télesphore St-Pierre, *Histoire des Canadiens du Michigan et du comté d'Essex, Ontario* (Montréal, 1895). E. A. Theller, *Canada in 1837–1838, showing by historical facts, the causes of the late attempted revolution, and of its failure; the present condition of the people, and their future prospects, together with the personal adventures of the author, and others connected with the revolution* (2v., Philadelphia, 1841). Tremblay, *Histoire du Saguenay.* [J.-.B.-H. Brien], "Un document inédit sur les événements assez obscurs de l'insurrection de 1837–1838," *Canadian Antiquarian and Numismatic J.* (Montreal), 3rd ser., V (1908), no.1, 13. Victor Morin, "La 'république canadienne' de 1838," *RHAF,* II (1948–49), 483–512. Antoine Roy, "Les Patriotes de la région de Québec pendant la rébellion de 1837–1838," *Cahiers des Dix,* XXIV (1959), 247–48. P.-G. Roy, "L'évasion de Dodge et Theller de la citadelle de Québec," *Cahiers des Dix,* V (1940), 121–44.

DUBORD, HIPPOLYTE, shipbuilder, politician, and justice of the peace; b. 25 Nov. 1801 at Bonaventure, L.C., son of Louis Dubord and Marie-Antoinette Bourdages; d. 9 Oct. 1872 at Quebec.

The son and grandson of a navigator, Hippolyte Dubord seems to have developed early a liking for things of the sea. When he was quite young he came to Quebec with his parents, and was initiated in shipbuilding. In 1827 he launched a brig of 133 tons, the *Bonaparte*: it was a time when the Napoleonic legend, long repressed, was finding its way into French Canada. Nine years later he built two barks christened *Papineau* and *Jean-Baptiste*; patriotic fever was at its height, and Dubord seems to have associated himself with the demands then being made. He launched a ship again in 1840, but it was particularly after 1845 that his reputation as a shipbuilder became established. In ten years he built some 23 ships, including brigantines, brigs, and barks. From 1856 to 1869 he launched 25 others, 12 of them in 1864 and 1865. Among his most important ships may be mentioned the *Pemberton*, 1,253 tons (1846), the *Crown*, 1,284 tons (1851), the *Julia*, 1,070 tons (1852), the *Stambord*, 1,272 tons (1853), the *Maldon*, 1,187 tons (1855), the *Québec*, 1,257 tons (1860), the *Calumet*, 1,628 tons (1863), the *François Dumas*, 1,208 tons (1864), the *Steward Lane*, 1,180 tons (1864), the *Lena*, 1,061 tons (1865), and the *Algonquin*, 1,499 tons (1867).

Setbacks and the generally bad state of his business made him give up shipbuilding around 1869. This industry had been the most important economic activity in Quebec since the end of the 18th century. More than 5,000 vessels had been built there, and during the good years, between 1842 and 1876, more than 5,000 workers were employed. Competition from iron ships, a rise in production costs, due in large measure to an upward movement of salaries, a fall in the prices of ships on the British markets, the lack of capital on the part of Quebec contractors, who operated on a family basis: all these are reasons that help to explain the decline of shipbuilding, and no doubt Dubord's difficulties at the end of his career.

Dubord had taken part in the political life of Quebec on the municipal and provincial levels. In 1836 he was active as one of the justices of the peace responsible for the administration of the town of Quebec. Five years earlier the city had received a charter by a law passed by the House of Assembly, and therefore the right to administer

Duchesnay

itself through an electoral body. From 1833 to 1836 the charter had been applied, but when it expired at the end of three years it had not been renewed. The town was then governed by justices of the peace, a regime that had existed between 1764 and 1833. The jurisdiction of the justices of the peace extended in principle to all that concerned the peace and good order of the citizens; it applied to areas as diverse as trade, public works, protective services against fire and disease, and police forces. In 1840 the town reverted to government according to the terms of the charter of 1833, amended.

Dubord represented Quebec Lower Town in the House of Assembly from 1834 to 1838. In 1836 he voted in favour of the famous motion calling for an elected Legislative Council. In 1851 he was MLA for the town of Quebec, which he represented until 1854. He returned to the assembly in 1857 and remained there until 1860; at the election of 16 April 1860 Dubord, who contested the election as a Liberal-Conservative, had to yield to a Liberal, Pierre-Gabriel Huot*. In the house Dubord kept his distance from the Rouges, and seems to have been concerned above all with local interests, which led him to adopt a line of action that was scarcely partisan. It is, of course, true that all political life in this period was characterized by the absence of party discipline and consequent ministerial instability.

On 31 Jan. 1870, at Quebec, Dubord married Bridget Furlong from Neuville, where he lived at least from then on. He died in dramatic circumstances less than two years later. On a brief visit to Quebec, where he was brought by a lawsuit that could not help but worry him, he put up at the Hôtel Fréchette on the Côte de la Montagne. During the night he fell from his fourth floor window and succumbed as a result of multiple fractures. It appears that Dubord, who was accustomed at home to take the air at night, wanted to step out of his room, thinking he was in his own house where the window of his room gave on to a gallery. At the coroner's inquest the jury returned a verdict of accidental death.

The reporter of the *Journal de Québec* praised his excellent spirit and great generosity. The reporter of *L'Événement* (perhaps Hector Fabre*) described him as "a man whom one could not approach without taking a strong liking to him. To an individual turn of mind, as original as it was piquant, was allied an excellent heart. His conversation was full of quips, a mixture of amusing anecdotes and half jocular, half serious admissions.... Like all sincere people he did not spare himself any more than he did others, and when he acknowledged his own mistakes and commented

on his contemporaries it was something worth hearing: he was able to etch with one stroke the things in his memory."

PIERRE SAVARD

AJQ, Registre d'état civil, paroisse Notre-Dame, paroisse Sainte-Jeanne de Neuville. *Le Canadien* (Québec), 11 oct. 1872. *L'Événement* (Québec), 10 oct. 1872. *Journal de Québec*, 10 oct. 1872. *Morning Chronicle* (Quebec), 10 Oct. 1872. Desjardins, *Guide parlementaire*, 152, 163, 178. Chapais, *Histoire du Canada*, IV. Cornell, *Alignment of political groups*. Drolet, *Ville de Québec*, II, III. Fernand Ouellet, *Histoire de la Chambre de commerce de Québec* (Publ. du Centre de recherche de la faculté de commerce de l'université Laval, série: histoire économique, 1, Québec, [1959]). Narcisse Rosa, *La construction des navires à Québec et ses environs; grèves et naufrages* (Québec, 1897).

DUCHESNAY. *See* JUCHEREAU

DUGGAN, GEORGE, lawyer, judge, and politician; b. August 1812, at Mallow, County Cork, Ireland, son of John and Mary Duggan; d. at Toronto, Ont., 14 June 1876.

George Duggan came to Canada as an infant with his parents. They joined John's brother George*, in York (Toronto), Upper Canada, then settled in Hamilton. The younger George went to York about 1828 and studied law in the office of Simon Washburn. He was licensed attorney and notary public in 1833, and called to the bar in 1837 after an unusually lengthy apprenticeship. On 19 Nov. 1839 he married Phoebe Anne, daughter of James Rogers ARMSTRONG and sister of Mary, wife of Egerton Ryerson*. When his brother John was admitted to the bar in 1840 they formed the partnership of Duggan and Duggan.

The Duggan family was exuberant in its opposition to the rebels of 1837, and George Jr more than the others; he succeeded in being captured by William Lyon Mackenzie*'s men. His uncle George, a Tory and office-seeker of long standing, had risen in Toronto from carpenter to coroner and the younger George, his protégé, showed similar ambition. He must early have been an Orangeman, and was district master by 1840. He sat as alderman in Toronto twice, 1838–40 and 1843–50. In 1840, 1848, 1849, and 1850, he aspired unsuccessfully to the mayoralty.

In January 1838 Duggan attempted to fill the vacant assembly seat in the 1st riding of York, and polled strongly behind John William GAMBLE, a Tory. A full year before the election of March 1841 his electoral address was out for the 2nd riding of York. The other five seats within the county fell to candidates of Lord Sydenham [Charles Poulett Thomson*]. Duggan sought but did not receive

Sydenham's backing; nevertheless his boisterous loyalism, his Orange order ties, his links with the Methodists through his marriage, and the Roman Catholicism of his opponent gave him an easy victory, and he immediately assured the administration of his goodwill. Election irregularities compelled him to fight the seat again in 1842; this time he decisively defeated Robert Baldwin* himself. In November 1844 he won again as a supporter of Sir Charles Metcalfe* "for British Hearts and Liberal Measures" against the low, scheming, Reform "oligarchy." His most conspicuous parliamentary activity was in opposition to the bill, directed against the Orange order, outlawing party processions. Conservatives in the riding jockeyed for the nomination in December 1847. Duggan, the city lawyer, was thrust aside. Provincial party leaders then entered him belatedly in Durham against the county's leading Reformer, James Smith, but he lost decisively.

Duggan hoped to be appointed recorder of Toronto through the offices of the city council and a Tory government, but the incoming Reformers in 1848 refused him patronage despite his assurance, made in confidence, that his lodge membership had lapsed three years before. He made an identical assurance, of his membership having lapsed three years earlier, when he again applied in 1850, even though he had been deputy county master for East York in 1848–49, and junior deputy grand master for British North America in 1849–50. Nevertheless, the Reform government, on the city council's recommendation, and perhaps trying to buy Orange neutrality if not support, grudgingly appointed him recorder from January 1851.

The recorder tried minor civil cases. In fine judicial tradition Duggan shed much of the partisanship which petitioners had claimed disqualified him for the post. As one of Toronto's police commissioners *ex officio* from 1858, he helped to enforce a new policy of refusing employment to all members of secret societies (such as the Orange order), and during the Fenian scares of the 1860s he worked to contain Protestant animus. In 1868 he was promoted judge of the York county court, and he remained in this post until his death in 1876.

By learning effacement and observing decorum in routine magisterial tasks George Duggan reached the lower level of the judiciary, and the two sons who survived him were lawyers. He had not attained the mayor's chair and could not ensure his renomination as a parliamentary candidate. He was only a makeweight on a number of company boards and was not a member of synod (though churchwarden of St James' in Toronto, 1862–69). His funeral nevertheless brought out the city's dignitaries and 70 carriages, and encomiums from newspapers of all political leanings on a man "not brilliant but kind and conscientious."

BARRIE DYSTER

City of Toronto Archives, Toronto city council, Minutes, 1838–50. MTCL, Baldwin papers, index entries for Duggan and Gurnett; George Duggan Jr, a.l.s. to J. C. Morrison, 20 March 1848. PAC, MG 26 A (Macdonald papers), 237, G. McMicken to Macdonald, 18 March 1866; RG 5, A1, 30 Sept. 1837; C1, 1850, no.2167. PAO, Toronto city council papers, 1838–50. PRO, CO 42/456, 417–21. *Christian Guardian* (Toronto), 9–23 Nov. 1842; 9 Oct., 6 Nov. 1844. *Evening Telegram* (Toronto), 15, 16 July 1876. *Globe* (Toronto), January 1848; 15 July 1876. *Mail* (Toronto), 15–17 July 1876. *Patriot* (Toronto), 30 Jan. 1838.

Arthur papers (Sanderson). British American League, *Minutes of the proceedings of a convention of delegates* ... (Kingston, 1849); *Minutes of the proceedings of the second convention* ... (Toronto, 1849). Loyal Orange Association of British North America, Grand Lodge, *Annual Reports*, 1849–50. *Town of York, 1815–1834* (Firth). *Commemorative biog. record, county York*, 397–98. *Landmarks of Toronto* (Robertson), III, 469. Middleton, *Municipality of Toronto*.

DUNCANSON, ROBERT STUART, artist; b. in 1817 or 1822 in New York State of a Scottish-Canadian father and Negro mother; d. on 21 Dec. 1872 in Detroit, Mich., leaving a wife.

Robert Stuart Duncanson, who was given at least a primary school educaton by his father, spent his childhood in Montreal. He was sent abroad to study by the Anti-Slavery Society. In 1842 he joined his mother in Cincinnati, working as a daguerreotypist, and there also painted and exhibited some works. Duncanson went to Europe in 1853 for the customary tour of art centres in Italy, France, and England, in the company of William Sonntag, a painter of the Hudson River school. He returned the following year: "I was disgusted with our Artists in Europe. They were mere copyists." He was living in Montreal in 1861 (and possibly earlier), but went abroad late in 1861 or 1862, spending much of his time in Scotland; he was evidently greeted with enthusiasm abroad. Two of his landscapes in oil, "The Lotus Eaters" and "Chaudière Falls," were in the Canadian display at the Dublin exhibition, 1865. The date of his return to America is unknown. It seems probable that he again spent some time in Montreal and associated with artists connected with William Notman*'s photographic studios. He was in Detroit from 1871 until his death. In Detroit he exhibited with considerable success, one of his best known canvases, "Ellen's Isle, Loch Katrine," going into the possession of Charles Sumner, a

Dundas

prominent abolitionist senator. Before his death, Duncanson suffered a mental breakdown.

The subject-matter of Duncanson's paintings was varied. His earlier works included portraits of leading citizens of Cincinnati and Detroit, and *genre* paintings. Later he had affinities with the romantic realists of the Midwest who were linked with the Hudson River school of landscape painting. Noteworthy among his landscapes in this manner were murals commissioned by Nicholas Longworth I for his home in Cincinnati (now the Taft Museum). Exotic subjects with lakes and palm trees appear in his canvases. He was most eclectic in his later years. Among his works are a number of Canadian landscapes showing scenes of autumn and of winter snow somewhat in the manner of Cornelius KRIEGHOFF. His painting is represented in the collection of the Montreal Museum of Fine Arts as well as in American galleries.

J. RUSSELL HARPER

Canada, an encyclopædia, IV, 357. G. C. Groce and D. H. Wallace, *The New York Historical Society's dictionary of artists in America, 1564–1860* (New Haven, 1957). J. R. Harper, *Early painters and engravers in Canada* (Toronto, [1971]), 98. *The Negro in art; a pictorial record of the Negro artist and of the Negro theme in art*, ed. A. L. Locke (Washington, 1940). *Ten Afro-American artists of the nineteenth century, an exhibition commemorating the centennial of Howard University* (Washington, 1967). A. S. Cavalla, "Uncle Tom and Little Eva, a painting by Robert S. Duncanson," Detroit Institute of Arts, *Bull.*, 30 (1950–51), 21–25. E. G. Porter, "Robert S. Duncanson, midwestern romantic-realist," *Art in America; an illustrated magazine* (New York), XXXIX (Oct. 1951), 99–154.

DUNDAS, GEORGE, army officer, politician, and colonial administrator; b. 12 Nov. 1819 in England, first son of James Dundas of Dundas, Scotland, and Mary Tufton Duncan; d. 18 March 1880 on St Vincent in the Windward Islands.

Following completion of his education, George Dundas entered the British army in 1839. He served for five years and during that time was posted to Bermuda and Nova Scotia. After resigning his commission, he was elected as a Tory to the British House of Commons where he sat for Linlithgow from 1847 to 1858. He married Mary Clark in April 1859 (they did not have children), and in the same year embarked upon a new career, as colonial administrator.

When Dundas arrived in Prince Edward Island on 7 June 1859 to take up his duties as lieutenant governor, he was stepping into a delicate position. His four predecessors in office had become openly identified with one party or the other in local politics, with the result that they had been un-reservedly abused by whatever section of the factious Island press felt itself to be out of favour. A few months before Dundas' arrival, the Tories under Edward Palmer* had defeated the Liberals led by George COLES. In his early dispatches to the Colonial Office, the new governor sometimes betrayed a partiality towards the Palmer government and a corresponding irritation with the opposition. He confidently described the Tories as having the support of "far the greatest proportion of the educated and the most respectable classes." In contrast, he portrayed the Liberal legislative councillors as "obscure, uneducated, and ignorant, selected from the lower classes, irresponsible for their actions."

In late 1860 Dundas became embroiled in a public controversy with William McGill, a militia officer and former Liberal assemblyman. A group of Roman Catholic volunteers had resigned from their company because of a dispute with their commanding officer, a Captain Murphy, also a Catholic, and had requested that McGill, a Presbyterian, command a new company. Dundas refused to give arms to the new company. McGill took the issue to the public, and chaired a meeting at which Dundas was censured. When the governor, through his adjutant general, Lieutenant-Colonel P. D. Stewart, asked for a retraction, and was refused, he stripped McGill of his rank. McGill responded by publicly accusing Dundas, as an Anglican and a former Tory member of parliament, of having acted out of religious prejudice and political partisanship. Dundas then struck McGill's name from the list of justices of the peace. In taking these actions, Dundas was widely considered to have exceeded his authority; whether he had done so or not, the whole affair was unfortunate for him, as he subsequently became a target for abuse in the Liberal press.

Edward Whelan*'s *Examiner* and Edward REILLY's *Vindicator* were especially critical of Dundas in 1862 and 1863, when he was caught in the middle of polemical battles between William Henry POPE, the colonial secretary, and Father Angus MacDonald*, the rector of St Dunstan's College. In June 1862 MacDonald wrote to Dundas and demanded that he dismiss Pope from office for his offensive writings on the Roman Catholic religion. When Dundas, a personal friend of Pope, refused, the rector sent the same request to the secretary of state for the colonies, the Duke of Newcastle [Henry Pelham Clinton]. The latter also declined to intervene officially but did, however, write a private letter to Dundas referring to Pope's conduct as "disgraceful" and asking the governor to "do all in your power" to terminate the controversy. The vendetta was renewed in early

1863, when MacDonald wrote two more letters to Newcastle, in which he attacked both Pope and Dundas; the secretary of state, weary of the "quarrelsome priest," again refused to become involved. Although these differences with Mac-Donald, and related episodes, apparently did not affect Dundas' standing with the Colonial Office, they led to an intensification of the attacks upon him in the *Examiner* and the *Vindicator*. These did not slacken until a general political calm descended late in 1863.

Dundas took an active part in attempts to settle the Island's land question. In his first year as governor, he intervened personally to ensure that the Selkirk estate was sold to the government rather than to private individuals. George Coles stated in 1869 that "Mr. Dundas had more influence with the proprietors in inducing them to sell, than any Lieut. Governor we ever had." Nonetheless, in the mid-1860s Dundas was repelled by the radicalism of the Tenant League whose members were pledged to refuse payment of rents. He called the league a "contemptible" organization, led by "senseless demagogues." He was on leave in Britain when in 1865 the administrator, Robert Hodgson, called in troops to deal with disorders caused by the league. Dundas heartily approved of this vigorous action, and wrote to Edward Cardwell, the secretary of state for the colonies, telling him that he had more than once urged his constitutional advisers to take legal action against *Ross's Weekly*, the organ of the league.

When the confederation issue arose, Dundas privately urged the Quebec resolutions upon Island politicians. He fully agreed with his superiors in London in their hope that Prince Edward Island would join the other British North American colonies, and in May 1866 he reported to Cardwell that "at one time I even indulged in the hope that if the other Colonies agreed to terms of Union, I should be able to form a Party [on the Island] to carry it." This was a vain hope, for in the election of 1867 the Island population strongly supported the anti-confederate candidates running for assembly seats.

George Dundas returned to Britain in October 1868. He never came back to Prince Edward Island, although the decision to transfer him to another posting was not finally taken until the end of 1869. Dundas died in 1880 on the Island of St Vincent where he had been governor for several years.

Dundas' decade as governor of Prince Edward Island was eventful. He was the object of much criticism, and even abuse, in the early 1860s. This may have been inevitable, considering the verbal violence of Island public life at that time,

and the role which his predecessors in office had played in local politics. He failed in his efforts to further the cause of confederation, but public opinion was almost totally opposed to the measure. Despite his hysterical reaction to the challenge of the Tenant League to established authority, he nevertheless appears to have been genuinely concerned with the plight of the tenantry. The judgement rendered in 1863 by Arthur Hamilton Gordon*, then lieutenant governor of New Brunswick, that "Dundas though no Solomon has some quiet sense" seems valid; by the time he left the Island, he had few enemies. Placed in a difficult position, with many pitfalls, Dundas had done a competent job and had won the respect of both Liberals and Conservatives.

IAN ROSS ROBERTSON

University of Nottingham Library, Newcastle MSS, Letter books, Colonial correspondence, 1859–64 (microfilm in PAC). PAC, MG 27, I, F2 (Pope papers), George Dundas to James Dundas, 1 Sept. 1863. PRO, CO 226/91–226/104, especially 226/91, 156–63; 226/100, 153–55, 463–66; 226/101, 664–67; 226/102, 160–63; 226/103, 138–39; 226/105, 513–14. Prince Edward Island, House of Assembly, *Debates and proceedings*, 1869, 131–38, 142–46, 154, 160–61. *Examiner* (Charlottetown), 13 April 1880. *Vindicator* (Charlottetown), 1863 – especially important are 6, 13, 20 March, 3, 17, 24 April, 22 May. Bernard Burke, *A genealogical and heraldic history of the landed gentry of Great Britain* (12th ed., London, 1914), 572. Bolger, *PEI and confederation.* MacKinnon, *Government of PEI.* MacMillan, *Catholic Church in PEI*, 193–206, 231–33. Robertson, "Religion, politics, and education in PEI," 78–91, 94–143, 150–54, 157–60.

DUPUIS, NAZAIRE, founder of one of the great Montreal business undertakings; b. 1843 at Saint-Jacques-de-l'Achigan (Saint-Jacques, Montcalm County), L.C., son of Joseph Dupuis, a merchant, and Euphrasie Richard, of Acadian ancestry; d. 24 Aug. 1876 at Montreal, Que.

On his father's death in 1864, Nazaire Dupuis came to Montreal with his family in order to try his fortune there and support his dependants. In 1868, after acquiring a working knowledge of business as an employee for four years, he opened a fancy goods shop at the corner of Sainte-Catherine and Montcalm streets, in the east end of town. The business, a modest one, occupied a building 25 feet by 50. Two years later, success obliged him to enlarge his undertaking, and he established himself on the corner of Sainte-Catherine and Amherst streets.

At this period the population of Montreal was nearing 100,000. Full of initiative, Nazaire Dupuis crossed the Atlantic no less than five times for his

Dupuy

business affairs, and established profitable contacts with European industrialists, particularly with those of Lancashire, England. He had gradually got his numerous brothers interested in his firm, which, despite the economic crisis that struck the continent after 1872, continued to prosper. But in August 1876 Nazaire Dupuis died prematurely. He was only 32.

The legal proceedings which ensued nonetheless indicated that, thanks to his shrewdness, Nazaire Dupuis had already acquired substantial assets, valued at more than $215,000. Fortunately his estate, properly administered, ensured the continuation of the firm. It was reconstituted shortly afterwards as a limited liability company, and in 1882 was moved to the spot occupied today by the large store known as Dupuis Frères Ltée. With varying fortunes, the company remained under the management of the brothers, the nephews, and a great-nephew of the founder until 1961.

In 1870, at Montreal, Nazaire Dupuis had married Alphonsine Saint-Onge. She survived him by 40 years. At his death he left several children, the eldest being Joseph-Nazaire-Odilon Dupuis*, who became parish priest of Saint-Eusèbe-de-Verceil and a distinguished personality in Montreal life during the first third of the 20th century. The name of Nazaire Dupuis has its place on the list of those creative spirits who, in each generation, make an appearance in the economic and social history of Canada.

JEAN-JACQUES LEFEBVRE

AJM, Greffe de J.-L. Coutlée, succession Nazaire Dupuis, 7 sept., 16 sept. 1876; Procédures non-contentieuses, sept.–déc. 1876; Registre d'état civil. Guy Courteau et François Lanoue, *Une nouvelle Acadie, Saint-Jacques de l'Achigan, 1772–1947* ([Montréal, 1947]), 321–24. Roger Duhamel, *Une grande aventure commerciale* (Montréal, [1963]). "Canadian Chamber's executive faces year of surging growth and activity," *Canadian Business* (Montreal), XXIX, no.11 (1956), 18–19. Noella Desjardins, "Dupuis et Frères un centenaire canadien-français," *Le Magazine de La Presse* (Montréal), 24 févr. 1968.

DUPUY, JEAN-BAPTISTE, Catholic priest, editor, and educator; b. 15 Sept. 1804 at Contrecœur (Verchères County), L.C., son of Joseph Dupuy, militia captain, and Françoise Richard; d. 13 Oct. 1879 at Saint-Antoine-sur-Richelieu, Que.

While continuing his studies at the college of Montreal, Jean-Baptiste Dupuy taught there from 1829 to 1832. He was ordained priest on 2 Sept. 1832, and was first a curate in different parishes for about four years. On 28 Oct. 1836 he was appointed first parish priest of Saint-Aimé (Richelieu County), and held this post until 1841. Then he was made responsible for the parish of Saint-Jean-Baptiste (Rouville County) until 1843. In that year Bishop Ignace Bourget* entrusted him with the editorship of the periodical *Mélanges religieux*, which was then the organ of the bishopric of Montreal. He carried out this duty for two years and then again became a parish priest.

During the many years he devoted to ministering to a parish, Dupuy liked to bring together the poorest and most intelligent of the children, in order to teach them and prepare them for classical studies. He had stayed for a short time at the college of Chambly in September 1836; in 1846 he was appointed director of the college of L'Assomption. Founded by Dr Jean-Baptiste MEILLEUR, Dr Louis-Joseph Cazeneuve, and the parish priest François Labelle, this college had opened its doors in 1833. In 1846 it offered two programmes: a preparatory course which emphasized practical subjects, and the classical course proper. Two years after Dupuy's arrival the only teaching staff left were priests and seminarists. The lay teachers assigned to the French and English classes had been let go, for it was considered that only ecclesiastics could be good educators, with the qualities and the special grace necessary for training youth. In addition, the laymen had to be paid much more than the churchmen; the latter received board and lodging at the college, and their salaries were paltry.

In 1850 the college and its director were the victims of a somewhat curious occurrence. A group of pupils formed a kind of secret society, adopting a code language, dressing in a weird fashion, and playing at being revolutionaries. They were called the "Flambards." They started a clandestine paper, part playful, part scientific, and uniformly mocking and disrespectful towards the authority of the institution. Dupuy had to take the blame for this affair, whose echoes penetrated to the ears of Bishop Bourget of Montreal.

At the college of L'Assomption, Dupuy preserved and established a number of customs relating to piety, studies, hygiene, and festivals. In his *Histoire du collège*, Anastase Forget sums up Dupuy's work, saying that he understood young people, re-established authority, and made himself well liked. The pupils he trained remembered him with extraordinary affection.

Another incident is a good example of Jean-Baptiste Dupuy's zeal for education. In 1849 the parish of L'Assomption, with the authorization of the superintendent, Meilleur, decided to open a bilingual school and to stress the teaching of English; the commissioners went further, and

266

asked for two schools to be opened, one English and the other French. Dupuy then offered to set up a French model school free of charge. The aim of the programme was "to teach, within three years, gradually and as the children [acquired] ability, French grammar, arithmetic, double entry bookkeeping, Canadian history, Biblical history, geography, the art of letter-writing, a little zoology and ornithology, particularly the part that [might] be helpful for domestic economy and agriculture, a small manual of agriculture, the understanding of [A. Gérin-Lajoie*'s] political catechism, and even, if it [were] possible, as an experiment, a small manual of the humanities and rhetoric."

Dupuy became a parish priest again in 1852, and was appointed to the parish of Saint-Antoine-sur-Richelieu in 1858. Always held in high esteem by the bishops of the diocese of Saint-Hyacinthe, he accompanied them on their pastoral visits in 1856, 1859, and 1861. In 1866 he was appointed a member of the diocesan council, and in 1873 went with Bishop Charles La Rocque as a theologian to the Quebec council.

In an obituary article, *La Minerve* testified eloquently in Jean-Baptiste Dupuy's favour: it stressed his extraordinarily honest judgement, his enlightened mind, his warm heart, his detachment from earthly possessions, his spirit of charity, and his love and generosity towards the poor, whom he assisted to the extent of being continually in want. Study was always one of the passions of his life, and this enabled him to be a preacher as serious as he was interesting, and a theologian whose counsel and opinions were always received with profit.

Louis-Philippe Audet

Mélanges religieux (Montréal), 1843–1845. Allaire, *Dictionnaire*. Alexis de Barbezieux, *Histoire de la province ecclésiastique d'Ottawa et la colonisation dans la vallée de l'Ottawa . . .* (2v., Ottawa, 1897), I, 187–89. Anastase Forget, *Histoire du collège de L'Assomption* (Montréal, [1933]), 95–98, 151–56, 251–52. J.-B. Meilleur, *Mémorial de l'éducation du Bas-Canada* (2e éd., Québec, 1876), 156, 171.

DUROCHER, FLAVIEN, Sulpician, Oblate of Mary Immaculate, missionary, parish priest; b. 7 Sept. 1800 at Saint-Antoine-sur-Richelieu (Verchères County), L.C., son of Olivier-Amable Durocher and Geneviève Durocher; d. 6 Dec. 1876 at Quebec.

After studying at the college of Montreal from 1818 to 1820, Flavien Durocher taught there until 1823; on 20 September of that year he was ordained priest. He was appointed assistant priest at Notre-Dame de Montréal, then at Trois-Rivières,

and in 1827 he joined the Sulpicians, who received him as a member the following year. He resumed teaching at Montreal (1827–29), then became assistant priest on the Indian reserve of Lac-des-Deux-Montagnes (Oka); there until 1843 he gave his services to the Algonkins, for whom he had some religious works printed.

As he wanted to devote his efforts more completely to spreading the gospel among the Indians, he entered the noviciate of the Oblates at Longueuil (Chambly County) in 1843, and was sent a year later to the residence of Saint-Alexis in Grande-Baie (Grande-Baie, Chicoutimi County). Appointed superior in 1849, he was entrusted with the supervision of 14 missions among the whites and eight among the Montagnais at Chicoutimi, at Lac-Saint-Jean, and at the king's posts on the banks of the St Lawrence and as far as Labrador. He had thus to cover a territory of more than 200 leagues. For these Indians he composed books of prayer and built chapels, particularly at Bersimis.

At this time the Oblates considered that they would be better situated at Quebec, even for spreading the gospel among the Indians. They left their Saguenay residence in 1853 and took over the Saint-Sauveur chapel, which had been built by Abbé Zéphirin Charest and which was inaugurated on 29 June 1853. Durocher was appointed director of the new residence (1853–73). Following the fire of 14 Oct. 1866 the mission of Saint-Sauveur was made into a parish, and by the efforts of Flavien Durocher, who was nominated parish priest, the church and the schools rose once more from their ashes.

This work did not prevent him from retaining his interest in the Indian missions – the residence of Escoumains, and that of Bersimis, which was controlled by Quebec. Almost every year he visited the Lac-Saint-Jean mission, and worked towards the establishment of missions among the Naskapis in the interior of Labrador and on Ungava Bay.

Durocher was a high-spirited, persistent, and devout man, and was regarded as a zealous minister by several generations of worshippers at Saint-Sauveur, of which he was parish priest from 1867 to 1876. A lake and township in the province of Quebec bear his name, and a monument has been erected in his honour in the city of Quebec.

Gaston Carrière

[The AHO hold several works by Father Flavien Durocher; the main manuscripts are: "Anicinâbe aiamie Kikkinwa' amigusi kiwek'amang Kanactogeng," 1842; "Dictionnaire français-montagnais," [1846–47]; "Instructions sur le sacrement de pénitence," [algonquin], 1834; "Kikijeb gaie onaguci

Duval

aimaianiwang. Manadji'ata K.M.," 82–121; "Tebeni-minang Jezos ka iji-pimâtisigubanen akking ij onbi-winitagogubanen wakwing Kikkinawâcijikâtêm ka on dimikâtênik o miniwadjimowiniwang Kwa Mattieu, Kwa Mark, Kwa Luk, Kwa Jan"; Pierre Cholenec, "Vie de Catherine Tekakwita appelée en algonquin Mitakwenibekwe, morte en odeur de sainteté au Sault St Louis en 1680, à l'âge de 24 ans," traduit de l'algonquin par Flavien Durocher. The main printed works are: *Aiamie kushkushkutu mishinaigan* ([Québec], 1847); *Ir mishiniigin*. *Eku omeru tshe apatstats Ishkua-mishkornuts, Uiapokornuts, Uashaornuts, Mashkua-rornuts, Shikotimiornuts kie Piokuakmiornuts* ([Montréal], 1852). [Pierre Cholenec], *Catherine Tekakouita* (traduit de l'algonquin par Flavien Durocher, [Montréal], 1876). G.C.]

AAQ, PP. Oblats; Registres des lettres des évêques de Québec. Archives générales des O.M.I. (Rome), Dossier Flavien Durocher (copie aux AHO). Archives provinciales O.M.I. (Montréal), Dossier Flavien Durocher; Dossier Québec; Dossier Saguenay (copies aux AHO). Marcel Bernad, *Bibliographie des missionnaires Oblats de Marie-Immaculée; I: Écrits des missionnaires Oblats, 1816–1915* (1v. paru, Liège, 1922). *Notices nécrologiques des O.M.I.*, III, 301–31. A.-L. Bertrand, *Bibliothèque sulpicienne ou histoire littéraire de la Compagnie de Saint-Sulpice* (3v., Paris, 1900), II, 376–77. Gaston Carrière, *Un apôtre à Québec; le père Flavien Durocher, o.m.i. (1800–1876), premier curé de Saint-Sauveur* (Montréal, 1960). Adrien Valiquette, *Biographie du révérend père Flavien Durocher, premier curé de Saint-Saveur de Québec* (Québec, 1911).

DUVAL, EDMUND HILLYER, educator and philanthropist; b. February 1805 at London, Eng., third child of Peter Duval and Elizabeth Wood; m. 28 Sept. 1828 to Sarah Turner by whom he had eight children although only four lived to maturity; d. 17 Sept. 1879 at Saint John, N.B.

During most of his life Edmund Hillyer Duval was a teacher. Between 1835 and 1845 he was in charge of a large school at Bristol, England, sponsored by the British School Society. The society founded such schools to bring at least a rudimentary education to the working classes. The teaching method consisted of gathering a large number of pupils together with one teacher and several of the better students acting as sub-teach-

ers. In 1845, upon invitation, Duval came to Saint John and established a "British School," the first classes apparently being held in the Mechanics' Institute. Conscious of the extreme shortage of teachers, Duval promoted his school to a model school for the training of teachers. In 1849 he visited teacher-training schools in New England and Toronto; his report of the trip stressed the need to raise substantially the miserable wages paid New Brunswick teachers. As master of the model school (after the Fredericton normal school was destroyed by fire in 1850, it was for almost two decades the sole institution for the training of teachers) and as inspector of schools after 1858, Duval returned repeatedly to the wage issue in his official reports. He was also author of a pamphlet published in 1858 which advocated reforms in New Brunswick education.

Duval's efforts to raise the standards of life were not limited to formal education. As a young man he is said to have worked for the benefit of the Jews of East London. He was an active Christian, gaining a licence to preach from the Germain Street Baptist Church of Saint John in 1870. In the last years of his life he worked hard to improve the deplorable lot of the Negroes in Saint John, not through missionary zeal, as might have been expected, but by trying to induce the spirit and practice of self-help.

RICHARD RICE

N.B. Museum, Edmund Hillyer Duval papers, transcripts, and genealogy; Tilley Papers, Edmund Hillyer Duval to S. L. Tilley, 16 June 1860. E. H. Duval, *Suggestions on the improvement of our common schools* (Saint John, N.B., 1858). *Daily Telegraph* (Saint John, N.B.), 19 Sept. 1878. New Brunswick, Chief superintendent of schools, *Fourth annual report* (Fredericton, 1855), *Sixth annual report* (1857), *Seventh annual report* (1859), *Reports, 1861–68* (1862–69). New Brunswick, House of Assembly, *Journals*, 1847–50. I. E. Bill, *Fifty years with the Baptist ministers and churches of the Maritime provinces of Canada* (Saint John, N.B., 1880). K. F. C. MacNaughton, *The development of the theory and practice of education in New Brunswick, 1784–1900: a study in historical background*, ed. with intro. by A. G. Bailey (University of New Brunswick Hist. studies, I, Fredericton, 1947), 129, 130, 137, 139–42, 173, 174.

E

EARLY, MAY AGNES (Fleming), novelist; b. 15 Nov. 1840 in Saint John, N.B., daughter of Bernard and Mary Early; d. 26 March 1880 in New York, N.Y.

May Agnes Early was educated in Saint John at the Convent of the Sacred Heart. While still a school girl, and an avid reader of fiction, she sold her first story to the *New York Mercury*; she then devoted herself to the writing of short stories and serial novels. These, published for some years under the name of Cousin May Carleton, appeared in such papers as the *Western Recorder and Weekly Herald* (Saint John), the *Mercury*, the *Pilot* (Boston), and the *Metropolitan Record* (New York). She appears to have taught school for a short time near Saint John, and on 24 Aug. 1865, after an acquaintance of three weeks, she married a machinist, William John Fleming. Her fiction from then on appeared under the name by which she is best known, May Agnes Fleming.

A prolific and popular writer, Mrs Fleming was offered exclusive contracts, first with *Saturday Night* (Philadelphia), and then with the New York *Weekly* and the London *Journal*. Her serials for periodicals later appeared in book form, running to a long list of novels. From all sources her yearly income in the depressed 1870s was in excess of $10,000 a year, making her Canada's first outstanding success as a professional novelist. In the Maritimes at that time this term could be applied accurately only to one other writer, James DE MILLE. Indeed so valuable was the name May Agnes Fleming on a title-page that after her death it was given not only to her own writing but to the work of others with the approval of her publishers, the most active of them being Street and Smith.

Mrs Fleming and her family went to the United States about 1875, living briefly in Boston apparently and then in Brooklyn (New York). At her death from Bright's disease at the age of 40, she and her husband were estranged, and she left a controversial will drawn up in 1876 which was intended to ensure that her children – two sons and two daughters – should be brought up as Roman Catholics and that her husband should have as little as possible to do with them or their inheritance.

May Agnes Fleming was a master of the minor convention in which she wrote: the suspense-laden serial tale of high life in England and America. Her characters and incidents were simple and stereotyped, but her plots were as ingenious and satisfying as those of Wilkie Collins, and her writing style was vigorous and direct. Typical of her work published in the 1870s are *Guy Earlscourt's wife*, *A terrible secret*, *A wonderful woman*, *A mad marriage*, *Kate Danton*, *One night's mystery*, *The rival brothers*, *The heir of Charlton*. Although her fiction was primarily designed for a British and American audience, Mrs Fleming remembered her Canadian readers and took pains to introduce Canadian episodes and characters into most of her novels, at times with considerable ingenuity. The fact that her novels were written for and published by firms in the United States and Britain is to be explained, not only by the larger market in those countries whose literary fashion she followed, but also by the state of copyright law at the time, which gave scant protection to works by Canadian authors published in Canada.

FRED COGSWELL

For a listing of May Agnes Early's books *see*: W. G. MacFarlane, *New Brunswick bibliography: the books and writers of the province* (Saint John, N.B., 1895), 31–32 and Watters, *Check list*, 207–8.

N.B. Museum, Macbeath papers, E. T. C. Knowles scrapbook, assorted newspaper clippings. *Daily Sun* (Saint John, N.B.), 1880. *Daily Telegraph* (Saint John, N.B.), 13 Dec. 1878. H. P. Gundy, *Book publishing and publishers in Canada before 1900* (Toronto, 1965). *Lit. hist. of Can.* (Klinck), 111.

ELLIOT, ADAM, (Elliott), Church of England clergyman; b. at Nicholforest, Cumberland, England, baptized 19 Dec. 1802, son of Adam Elliot and Margaret Little; d. at Grand River (Tuscarora) Reserve, Ont., 4 June 1878.

The Elliot family came to Upper Canada and settled in York (Toronto). Adam Elliot Jr presented himself to Archdeacon John Strachan* in 1828 asking for help in pursuing studies for the ministry. Strachan was impressed with Elliot's earnestness and directed his reading until his ordination to the diaconate in November 1832. Adam Elliot then immediately began a five-year term of service as a travelling missionary in the Home District north and east of York. He received financial support from a local missionary society in Upper Canada and from the Reverend William James Darley Waddilove* in England.

Elliot's journals describe vividly the pioneer conditions of the time, and his registers of baptisms and marriages reflect the faithfulness and untiring energy of the young missionary. He ministered to the Ojibwa Indians, who had been concentrated in 1830 by the government at Coldwater and The Narrows (Orillia) under the charge of Captain Thomas Gummersall ANDERSON. A proposal by Anderson in 1835 to settle the scattered tribes of the north shore of Lake Huron on Manitoulin Island was approved by the lieutenant-governor, Sir John Colborne*, and Elliot obtained the consent of Bishop Charles James Stewart* of Quebec to be the resident missionary in the infant establishment in 1836. When the plan was temporarily shelved in 1837, Elliot returned to the Home District but was soon stationed for a short time at Beckwith in the Bathurst District (now in Lanark County).

Elliot accepted a request in 1838 to work at the New England Company station near Brantford.

Ellis

The company had begun to take an interest in the Six Nations Indians on the Grand River in 1827. They appointed Robert Lugger* their first missionary at Brantford in that year, and he was later joined by Abraham Nelles*. Lugger died in 1837 and in March 1838 Elliot took over at Tuscarora, where he carried on pastoral and educational work until his resignation in 1875. He died 4 June 1878 and was buried in the cemetery of Holy Trinity Church, Onondaga, Ontario.

Shortly after moving to the Tuscarora mission Adam Elliot married Eliza Beulah Howells. Four children were born to them but none survived their parents. Emily Susanna Howells, Eliza's sister, came to live with the Elliots in 1845 and helped to care for the children; that same year she married George Johnson*, Elliot's Indian interpreter who also lived at the parsonage. Their daughter was Pauline Johnson*, the poetess. Eliza Howells died in 1849 and Adam Elliot married Charlotte Racey in 1856.

Adam Elliot enjoyed the confidence of the New England Company throughout his long service with them. He retained the approving friendship of his former instructor John Strachan and was highly regarded by the first bishop of Huron, Benjamin CRONYN, in whose diocese the Tuscarora mission was located after 1857. His quiet and effective labours among the Indians never ceased to arouse interest among visitors, one of whom, James BEAVEN, wrote of Elliot in his *Recreations of a long vacation*: "I was gratified to observe his peculiar adaptation of character to the simple people amongst whom he dwells, and the entire confidence which subsists between him and his flock."

T. R. MILLMAN

The Elliot family papers are in the possession of Mrs Lawrence Crumb, Nashotah, Wisconsin. James Beaven, *Recreations of a long vacation; or a visit to Indian missions in Upper Canada* (London, Toronto, 1846), 30–55. New England Company, *Report, 1840* (London, 1840); *Report, 1868* (1869); *History and report, 1869–70* (1871); *Report, 1871–72* (1874); *Six years' summary, 1873–78* (1879). *Dominion Churchman* (Toronto), 23 June 1878. *The Stewart missions; a series of letters and journals, calculated to exhibit to British Christians, the spiritual destitution of the emigrants settled in the remote parts of Upper Canada ...*, ed. W. J. D. Waddilove (London, 1838), 29–96. W. P. Bull, *From Strachan to Owen; how the Church of England was planted and tended in British North America* (Toronto, 1937). *A sketch of the origin and recent history of the New England Company by the senior member of the company* (London, 1884). Dorothy Keen and Martha McKeon, "The story of Pauline Johnson, Canada's passionate poet," as told to Mollie Gillen, *Chatelaine* (Toronto), XXXIX (February, March 1966), 25f, 39f.

ELLIS, JOHN, printer and musician; baptized 21 Jan. 1795, at Cley-next-the-Sea, Norfolk, Eng., son of Anne Ellis; d. 19 Nov. 1877, near Toronto, Ont.

John Ellis was apparently comfortably established in London, England, by 1836. He had a business in the City in Old Broad Street and was a freeman of the Goldsmiths' Company; he owned two country properties in Essex; his wife of eight years, Rhoda Anne Benton, had just had their first child. But in that year he sold the London property and in August the family sailed for British North America, reaching Toronto in October. For a year or two Ellis "bushed it" west of the city on land adjoining that of John George Howard*.

In the early 1840s Ellis opened an office in Toronto as an engraver, eventually extending into lithographic printing of substantial projects, including the *Plan of Toronto* in about 1858. Probably the main line of business was stationery. In 1867 the firm was bought by Joseph T. Rolph and, with mergers, has since grown into the modern lithographic house of Rolph-Clark-Stone, Limited.

Ellis was an enthusiastic, and reportedly an accomplished, amateur cellist, prominent in the city's young musical life. With the Reverend John McCaul* he organized the Toronto Philharmonic Society in 1845 and served on its committee for many years. He was also a founder, and the orchestra leader, of the Toronto Vocal Music Society.

Ellis was Anglican, Conservative, and an early member of the St George's Society in Toronto. After retiring from business he lived at his old home overlooking Humber Bay, where he died in 1877.

IAN MONTAGNES

MTCL, Plan of Toronto, surveyed and compiled by W. S. and H. C. Boulton, Toronto, 1858(?). A xerox of a manuscript, "R.C.S. LTD," with additional comments by Arthur Alder can be found at Rolph-Clark-Stone, Limited, Toronto. *Globe* (Toronto), 21 Nov. 1877. *The Toronto directory and street guide for 1843–4*, ed. Francis Lewis (Toronto, 1843), 35. *Brown's Toronto city and Home District directory, 1846–7* (Toronto, 1846), 23. *City of Toronto directory for 1867–8* (Toronto, 1867), 380. *W. C. Chewett & Co's Toronto city directory for 1868–9* (Toronto, 1868), 399. *Commemorative biog. record, county York*, 519–20. Helmut Kallmann, *A history of music in Canada, 1534–1914* (Toronto and London, 1960), 98. Middleton, *Municipality of Toronto*, I, 525. W. H. Pearson, *Recollections and records of Toronto of old, with references to Brantford, Kingston and other Canadian towns* (Toronto, 1914), 213–14.

END, WILLIAM, lawyer, politican, magistrate; b.c. 1800 in Limerick, Ireland; m. in 1827 to

Lucy Morse in Amherst, N.S.; assassinated on 14 Dec. 1872 at Bathurst, N.B.

Nothing is known of the circumstances under which William End immigrated to New Brunswick, or the date. He studied law with William Botsford* in Dorchester and became an attorney on 20 Feb. 1823. He worked first in Saint John; following his admission to the bar on 17 Feb. 1825, he moved to Newcastle. End served as clerk of the peace for Gloucester County from 1827 to 1847, and as registrar from 1837 to 1841, the year he was appointed queen's counsel. He was appointed prosecuting officer for Gloucester in 1848.

William End was elected to the New Brunswick assembly in 1830. He represented Gloucester County until 1850, and again from 1854 to 1861. End's notoriety as "a loquacious and impetuous partisan of the common people" arose from his first campaign, during which he made astute use of the religious and patriotic emotions of the county's Acadian and Irish population. End allegedly called the powerful magistrates' courts "a scandalous, corrupt and rotten system packed up by Mr. [Hugh] Munro," his opponent and the leading magistrate. He likewise "foamed and raged in the most furious manner" against the tyranny of such influential merchants as Robert Ferguson* and Alexander Rankin* who, in league with the justices, were inclined to trample on the susceptibilities of Gloucester's indigent majority.

In the assembly, however, End generally "worked and voted with the 'compact' side of the House," prompting the liberal James Hannay* to see in him "a man of no principle, who took the side of those in authority because he thought it would be to his own personal advantage." Thus End supported the administration on the explosive crown lands issue and William Colebrooke*'s rash appointment of his son-in-law Alfred Reade as provincial secretary in 1845, and he strongly sustained the prerogative of John Henry Thomas MANNERS-SUTTON to dissolve the assembly in 1856.

Though in 1846 End enthusiastically supported the appropriation of £1,000 for a loyalist monument, he had protested the fanfare bestowed in 1833 upon the 50th anniversary of the loyalist arrivals, reminding people of the labours of the English, Scots, and Irish. It is perhaps indicative of the over-all climate of New Brunswick that it did not occur to the member for Gloucester to include the Acadians, who comprised the majority of his own constituents. Before the 1860s, the Acadians as a group virtually never came up in debates on the politics of New Brunswick. Indeed, it was only when End's career was near its end

that this group ventured their first timid steps on the main road of provincial life.

End suffered defeat in 1850, but ran again in 1854. Despite his strong conservatism (he was vehemently opposed to the transfer of money grants to the executive), End kept in mind his recent defeat, supported the return to power of Charles FISHER, and was himself elected. In the "Rum" election of 1856, End, who supported the repeal of prohibition, was returned, but lost his seat when his opponents successfully contested the result. He returned to the assembly in the election of 1857, and sat until dissolution in 1861. In all, William End represented Gloucester for 26 years. In 1862 former colleagues appointed him law clerk to the House of Assembly.

Little information is available about End's private life. There seems to be no record of children of his own (his wife had a daughter from a previous marriage). The details of his law practice are vague. It is known that he had profitable property holdings and other investments, and that he lived in Saint John from 1841 to 1843, and in the United States from 1850 to 1854. At confederation he became the first county clerk, and at the time of his death he was a stipendiary magistrate and a director of the Bathurst grammar school.

William End died tragically in his burning office in Bathurst at the hands of a young man, James Meahan Jr, whom he had recently sentenced to four months in the county jail. Though the incident outraged the public, newspaper commentary suggests that by 1872 End's political career had been all but forgotten. Sir Howard Douglas* had felt End, though "very clever," was "disposed to be troublesome and factious. . . ." George Edward Fenety* saw in him "a man of superior parts . . . who seemed to want judgment at the right time."

BERNARD POTHIER

Gloucester County Court (Bathurst, N.B.), Gloucester County records, 1–21. N.B Museum, Folder 58, deeds to land in Westmorland County, 1784–1828; Folder 64, item 37 (William End to Sir John Harvey, 25 June 1838); Folder 90, original appointments; New Brunswick, Gloucester County land grants; "Linking the past with the present," a series of articles by E. S. Carter which began in the Saint John *Telegraph-Journal*, 6 Nov. 1929; New Brunswick Historical Society papers, Packet 4 (Steeves coll.), item 10; Howard P. Robinson papers, "History of Albert County," typescript by W. C. Milner, c.1933. PAC, MG, 24, A17 (Harvey papers), ser.1, 1; ser.2, 6. PRO, CO 188/41, 188/43, 188/71, 188/72, 188/91, 188/104.

Fenety, *Political notes and observations*. New Brunswick, House of Assembly, *Journals*, 1831–62. *New Brunswick Courier* (Saint John, N.B.), 1830–65. *New Brunswick Royal Gazette* (Fredericton), 1830–70. *Morning Freeman* (Saint John, N.B.), 17 Dec. 1872,

Erlandson

15 Feb. 1873. *Saint John Daily Telegraph and Morning Journal*, 16, 26 Dec. 1872; 15 Feb. 1873. *Telegraph-Journal* (Saint John, N.B.), 17 March, 16 June 1931. *An almanack for the year of our Lord, 1828 ... for ... Saint John, N.B. ...* (Saint John, N.B.). *Lovell's province of New Brunswick directory for 1871* (n.p., n.d.). *The New Brunswick almanac and register for ... 1849* (Saint John, N.B., 1848). Hannay, *History of New Brunswick*, II. Lawrence, *Judges of New Brunswick* (Stockton). MacNutt, *New Brunswick*.

ERLANDSON, ERLAND, HBC clerk and the first European to travel overland from Hudson Strait to the Atlantic coast; b. *c.* 1790 in Denmark; d. at Port Hope, Ont., 23 Jan. 1875.

Erland Erlandson was "bred a ship carpenter in the dock yard of Copenhagen." In December 1813, while apparently serving as a Danish seaman, he was taken prisoner by the English in the Kattegat and sent to a prison ship at Chatham, Kent. Early in the following year, at the end of the war between Great Britain and Denmark, the Hudson's Bay Company recruited a number of Scandinavians, including Erlandson, for service in Hudson Bay. At this time he was described as a stoutly built man of 5 feet 9½ inches, with a pale, oval, pock-marked face, hazel eyes, and light brown hair.

Erlandson began work in 1814 as a sailor attached to Eastmain House on the east shore of James Bay. He had then only a slight knowledge of English, but his correspondence and journals of a later date show that he gained a good command of the language. He quickly earned the reputation of being "an excellent servant . . . strictly honest, sober, and active, and very intelligent," and was rewarded with promotion. In 1817 he was transferred to the Moose Factory district where he was in charge of workmen engaged in carpentry and various routine duties. Two years later he became a clerk, and in 1822 took charge of Eastmain House. He remained there until 1830 when he accompanied Nicol FINLAYSON as second in command "on dangerous service" to Ungava.

After an overland journey from Richmond Gulf (Lac Guillaume-Delisle) to Ungava Bay, they built Fort Chimo about 27 miles from the mouth of the South (Koksoak) River and near an anchorage for the vessels which were to bring supplies to this most isolated of all HBC posts. An early breakdown of the sea-link with Hudson Bay emphasized their hazardous position in an inhospitable country and this, coupled with their concern about the meagre trade, caused Finlayson, in February 1831, to send Erlandson overland with letters to Governor George Simpson*. These were lost, however, when Erlandson's canoe was wrecked near the head of Michipicoten River. But

he reported to Simpson in person at York Factory and arrived back at Fort Chimo in the sloop *Beaver* in the following September.

In 1832 Erlandson built South River House on the Kaniapiskau River about 130 miles south of Fort Chimo. After suffering great hardship and gaining only a small trade at the expense of Finlayson's, he abandoned his post in 1833 and returned to Fort Chimo. His experience convinced both Finlayson and himself that any post inland from Fort Chimo should be situated near the height of land, and that communication with the company posts on the Gulf of St Lawrence was essential. Erlandson, therefore, under instructions from Finlayson, prepared to travel overland to Mingan and eventually five somewhat reluctant Indians agreed to guide him. The party left Fort Chimo on 6 April 1834 and travelled south via Whale River to Lake Petitsikapau (near present-day Schefferville, Que.). There Erlandson realized that the Indians' firm intention, suspect from the start, was to travel towards the Atlantic coast. The party crossed Lake Michikamau and continued east, following a chain of small lakes to Naskaupi River and Grand Lake. On 22 June they reached the western end of tidal Lake Melville (in the area of present-day Goose Bay, Labrador) and Erlandson thus became the first European to travel overland from Hudson Strait to the Atlantic coast. On the return journey, beyond the height of land, he used a more westerly route through Lakes Wakuach and Chakonipau to reach Kaniapiskau River and Fort Chimo, where he arrived on 17 July. His report on the promising fur country of the interior led Simpson to adopt a new policy for Ungava. In future Fort Chimo and interior posts were to be linked with a depot on Esquimaux Bay (Hamilton Inlet) which would be supplied by ship from Quebec.

On Finlayson's departure in 1836, Erlandson had charge of Fort Chimo until John McLean* arrived in the following year. In spite of his undoubted abilities Erlandson had not been promoted and he was now a disappointed man. Simpson recognized his claims, but thought that the vote-casting commissioned officers would be unwilling to elect to a chief tradership one who was "a foreigner and raised from the ranks." Erlandson's health was deteriorating but in 1838 he built Fort Nascopie on an arm of Lake Petitsikapau. From there, in 1839, he accompanied John McLean on a journey to Esquimaux Bay during which they became the first Europeans to see the Grand (Churchill) Falls of the Grand (Churchill) River. Before leaving Ungava in 1840, Erlandson spent the winter at Fort Trial on George River.

In 1841, after many delays while travelling,

Erlandson reached the company's Lake Superior district to which he had been assigned. The posts of which he had charge there, Long Lake (1841–43) and Pic (1843–48), did not offer enough scope for his abilities and so enable him to press for promotion. His dissatisfaction grew and he retired voluntarily in 1848.

In "easy circumstances, without a family," he settled near retired chief trader George Gladman* in Port Hope, Canada West. He visited London and Denmark in 1853–54, and apparently in 1855 stayed for a while with John McLean, who was then agent for the Bank of Montreal in Guelph, C.W. Two sums of money disappeared in mysterious circumstances during his visit, and because, on his death in 1875, he left an estate of some $14,000 (most of which he bequeathed to the Toronto General Hospital), he has been accused of having stolen the missing money. No accusation was made against Erlandson during his lifetime and in the interests of justice an examination should be made of his financial transactions in Canada, in London, and possibly in Denmark, before judgement is passed on one who always bore an exemplary character.

ALICE M. JOHNSON

HBC Arch. G.1/62, G.1/64, G.1/236 (three MS charts). HBRS, III (Fleming); XXIV (Davies and Johnson). *McLean's notes of twenty-five year's service* (Wallace).

ERMATINGER, EDWARD, fur-trader, businessman, politician, and writer; b. in February 1797 on the island of Elba, son of Lawrence Edward Ermatinger, assistant commissary general in the British army, and grandson of Lawrence Ermatinger*, merchant of Swiss origin who married a sister of fur-trader Forrest Oakes*; d. in October 1876 at St Thomas, Ont.

Edward Ermatinger's mother, an Italian, died when he and his younger brother Francis* were infants. Their father – "indeed a good-hearted man – but what a strange Father" – apparently took only a casual interest in their upbringing, but Edward received in England a good education in languages and music. Several members of the family were fur traders – an uncle, Charles Oakes Ermatinger*, established the important trading post at Sault Ste Marie – and Lawrence Edward Ermatinger arranged for his sons' entry into the service of the Hudson's Bay Company as apprentice clerks. The brothers sailed from London on *Prince of Wales*, arriving at York Factory on 14 Aug. 1818.

Edward Ermatinger remained in the company's service until 1828, at Island Lake, Oxford House, York Factory, Red River (all in present-day Manitoba), and for three years in the Columbia district. His "York Factory express journal," covering his travels between Fort Vancouver and York Factory, 1827–28, has been published, along with a diary of his canoe journey out to Lachine in 1828. He had, however, little enthusiasm for the life of the trade. "I have long sought to get out of this Country but never could manage it before – now I must struggle once out of it to keep so." Though there is reason to believe that he was diappointed in his hopes that Governor George Simpson* would promote his advance in the company, he accepted a reverse with equanimity: "I never heartily desired to return." He was to remain on friendly terms with many former colleagues in the trade, including John Work*, some of whom unburdened themselves freely to this sympathetic correspondent and often asked him for advice on their establishing themselves after retirement. He seems to have had no regrets about leaving the northwest and the "humdrum life we led there."

Ermatinger visited England in 1828, where he saw his father, but returned to Canada in 1829. He made several journeys through Upper Canada and his diaries suggest that he was seeking a new way of life. He finally settled in St Thomas where he thought he saw opportunities for the profitable employment of his small capital. There, as postmaster from at least 1842 to 1876, banker, and merchant, he remained until his death. He opened a general store, and was successively manager of the Bank of Upper Canada, the Commercial Bank, and for 14 years the Bank of Montreal. When Elgin County was established in 1851 he was the moving spirit in the formation of the Bank of the County of Elgin and was chairman of the board.

Ermatinger contested the Middlesex seat in the Legislative Assembly. In 1844 he was elected as a Conservative. He was defeated in 1847 and by 1851 he had withdrawn from politics: "What I gained in wisdom I lost in pocket." He did not find congenial a political climate in which "some of the advisers of Her Majesty's Representatives were the rebels of '37." He obviously found more enjoyment in literary composition, writing several pamphlets, many letters to the press, particularly to the Hamilton *Spectator* under the pseudonym of "British Canadian," and a biography of Colonel Thomas Talbot*. He also founded the *St. Thomas Standard* about 1843–44, and edited it for two years before selling it. He married Achsah Burnham, daughter of Zaccheus Burnham* of Cobourg and sister of the Church of England rector at St Thomas. They had seven children.

Edward Ermatinger appears from his correspondence to have been a man of attractive personality,

Evans

who cherished his friendships. He devoted himself indefatigably to his business, but his diary of a trip to New York records a nightly visit to a theatre or other entertainment. He took great pleasure in music and his proficiency with the flute and violin provided him with enjoyment long after he had left the fur trade. He made a collection of the words and music of French Canadian folksongs, which survives, and one of his friends refers to a "Red River March" he composed. An active man, though introspective, he displayed a lively interest in affairs at home and abroad and held vigorous opinions on the issues he discussed in his letters and published writings. In spite of his freely expressed dislike of the life of the fur trade, he preserved no animus against the HBC and defended it against its critics.

Deeply concerned with religion, Ermatinger was a staunch adherent of the Church of England. He was, as a Mason and an anti-Catholic, no sympathizer with the more conciliatory views espoused by Toronto bishop, John Strachan*, noting that "the vigilance of the laity is required to expurgate the leaven of popery with which [the church] is infected." He seems early to have won the "estimation of all the most respectable" and to have retained it until his death.

L. G. THOMAS

Edward Ermatinger was the author of *The Hudson's Bay territories; a series of letters on this important question* (Toronto, 1858), and of *Life of Colonel Talbot, and the Talbot settlement, its rise and progress ...* (St Thomas, C.W., 1859). There is also: "Edward Ermatinger's York Factory express journal, being a record of journeys made between Fort Vancouver and Hudson Bay in the years 1827–1828," ed. C. O. Ermatinger and James White, *RSCT*, 3rd ser., VI (1912), sect.II, 67–132.

PABC, Edward Ermatinger papers, 1828–49. PAC, MG 19, A2 (Ermatinger family papers), ser.2; A21 (Hargrave papers); MG 24, D16 (Buchanan papers); MG 25, G, 107 (Ermatinger family papers). University of Western Ontario Library, 27 (Ermatinger papers), boxes 1–3. HBRS, II (Rich and Fleming); IV (Rich); VI (Rich); XVIII (Rich and Johnson). *Vignettes of St. Thomas, an anthology of the life and times of its first century*, ed. W. C. Miller (St Thomas, Ont., 1967). C. O. Ermatinger, *The Talbot regime; or the first half century of the Talbot settlement* (St Thomas, Ont., 1904).

EVANS, JOHN, miner and MLA; b. 25 Jan. 1816 at Machynlleth, north Wales; m., in Wales, first, on 1 June 1840, Martha Evans (who died young) and secondly, in November 1842, Ann Thomas (d. 1866) by whom he had three sons and two daughters, and at Victoria, B.C., on 24 April 1877, Catherine Jones; d. 25 Aug. 1879 at Stanley, B.C.

Born and brought up in a Welsh village, John Evans worked as a young man in Manchester, but in 1854, in order to give his children a "pure Welsh" upbringing, he moved to Tremadoc, where he had interests in several small quarries. In 1863 he emigrated to British Columbia in charge of "one of the better organized attempts to secure gold in the Cariboo." Henry Beecroft Jackson, a wealthy Manchester cotton manufacturer, offered to finance the project for two years, all profits to be divided: one half going to the men in equal shares; the other half to Evans and his patron. Evans personally selected 26 respectable north Welsh miners including his second son Taliesin, and on 22 Dec. 1862 the men sailed aboard the *Rising Sun* for Victoria *via* Cape Horn. Evans himself went by the shorter Panama route. Leaving Liverpool on 17 Feb. 1863 he arrived on 15 April, and thus had time to examine various mining possibilities on the mainland before the *Rising Sun* docked on 10 June.

Having applied for a mining lease on Lightning Creek, "Captain" Evans, as his men called him, left Victoria at the head of the Welsh company on 16 June, and after a gruelling journey over the Harrison-Lillooet trail established on 21 July the "Basford Mines," at the junction of Last Chance and Lightning creeks, the site of the present settlement of Stanley. Capital, skill, and energy were not wanting; nevertheless the venture failed. The glowing descriptions of the Cariboo by the Victoria correspondent of the London *Times* had ignored the exorbitant price of provisions, as well as the need for more efficient machinery than wooden pumps and waterwheels to control the water which flooded into the shafts. By the time the men's contract expired on 1 Oct. 1864 eight rebels had already left the enterprise and Evans had recovered only $450 worth of gold for an expenditure of over $26,000. Most of the Welsh company returned home, but their leader stayed on until he died, trying to develop claims on Antler and Davis creeks, acting as a mining and land surveyor in the Cariboo district, and cherishing the vain hope that "sooner or later something may turn up." But he was never able to send for the wife or the "dear children" left behind in Wales.

Almost as soon as he arrived on Lightning Creek, Evans was asked to stand for election to the first Legislative Council of the mainland colony. He consented, chiefly in order to press for the amendment of the existing mining laws which gave no protection to the man who had sufficient capital to embark on a large-scale venture. A claim could be staked only by an individual miner, who was then free to dispose of it as he chose. Thus Evans had been compelled either to place himself at the mercy of his workmen by recording titles in their names, or to lease ground abandoned by individual miners. He was defeated in the elections of 1863, 1965, and 1871. Finally in 1875 he was elected to the Legislative Assembly of the province, and re-elected in 1878. He declared himself to be "no party man," but voted as his conscience bade him, and "his energetic and eccentric manner in urging his views on the House" was long remembered.

A strict Nonconformist, who had hoped to give part of his mining profits to the Booth Street Welsh Congregational Chapel in Manchester, Evans did his best to improve manners and morals in the Cariboo. He frowned on drinking, gambling, and swearing and would not allow his men to work or travel on Sunday. In 1866 he and other Welshmen built the Cambrian Hall in Barkerville, where religious services, literary meetings, and celebrations of St David's Day were held until the great fire of 1868. Evans had no great success as a miner, but he was loved and respected throughout the Cariboo for his generosity, his scrupulous integrity, and his courage in maintaining the principles he believed to be right. For the simple wooden head-board of his grave in the Stanley cemetery his friends chose the fitting epitaph: "Blessed are the dead who die in the Lord."

DOROTHY BLAKEY SMITH

PABC, John Evans papers. British Columbia, Legislative Assembly, *Journals*, 1876–79. *Cariboo Sentinel* (Barkerville, B C.), 1865–75. *Colonist* (Victoria), 1863–79. *Victoria Daily Standard*, 28 Aug. 1879. *Can. parl. comp.*, 1876; 1877; 1878; 1879. Alan Conway, "Welsh gold-miners in British Columbia during the 1860's," *BCHQ*, XXI (1957–58), 51–74. R. L. Reid, "Captain Evans of Cariboo," *BCHQ*, II (1938), 233–46.

EYNARD, MARIE-GERMAIN-ÉMILE, Oblate of Mary Immaculate, missionary; b. 28 May 1824 at Genoa, Italy, son of Jacques Eynard and Marie-Anne-Agathe Lévêque, who came originally from Embrun (department of Hautes-Alpes), France; d. 6 Aug. 1873 at Fort Chipewyan, N.-W.T.

Marie-Germain-Émile Eynard began his studies at the classical college of Embrun and completed them at the college of the university, where he obtained his baccalaureate in arts and also in mathematics. After studying at the École Polytechnique, he joined the roads department.

In 1847 he was at Longuyon (department of Moselle) as acting inspector of rivers and forests. He soon left this post and entered the seminary of Metz; he was then admitted into the noviciate of the Oblates at Notre-Dame de l'Osier (department

of Isère), and made his profession on 1 Nov. 1854. He completed his training at the theological college of Montolivet, near Marseilles, and there, on 24 March 1855, holy orders were conferred on him by Bishop Charles-Joseph-Eugène de Mazenod.

The following year Eynard was living in the presbytery of Notre-Dame de Cléry (department of Loiret), where because of his frail health and innate timidity he seldom officiated as a priest, but acted as tutor for the Marquis de Poterat's sons. From there he went to Dublin to study English for some months, before leaving for the missions in the Canadian northwest.

He arrived at Saint-Boniface (Manitoba) in 1857, and during the winter of 1857–58 was curate of Saint-Norbert; he then set out for the missions of the Athabasca-Mackenzie district, together with Archdeacon James Hunter* of the Church of England. He was intended for the poor but important mission of St Joseph, at Fort Resolution on the shore of Great Slave Lake. The missionary was exposed to hunger and solitude, and the employees of the mission put endless difficulties in his way. In addition to looking after his flock, Eynard studied the Montagnais language and taught French and the catechism to the children at the Hudson's Bay Company post. Despite feeble health and weak eyesight, he visited and ministered to the posts at Fort Rae and Fort Providence. His numerous and arduous journeys caused his bishop, Henri Faraud*, to remark that he spent "the greater part of his winters with snow-shoes on his feet, and sleeping on the snow."

From 1863 until his death in 1873 he served at the mission of La Nativité (Fort Chipewyan, N.-W.T.), on the shores of Lake Athabasca, and at the chapel of Notre-Dame-des-Sept-Douleurs (Fond du Lac). From there he went out to various parts of the region, and each year was to be found at different forts: Providence, Resolution, as well as at Salt River. On 15 Aug. 1867, while living at Fort Chipewyan, he was one of the two assistant priests on the occasion of the modest ceremony at which Bishop Isidore Clut* was consecrated.

Timid and not much of a talker, Eynard always experienced considerable difficulty in learning and speaking the Montagnais language, which he styled "unmanageable"; he nevertheless continued to study it until the end of his life. The Indians with whom he dealt considered him a "good man," and one of them was prompted to say: "With Father Eynard one speaks less, but one prays with more fervour." His spiritual influence was unrivalled; but because of his absentmindedness he was always deemed unsuited to take on the practical direction of a mission. However, his superiors and his *confrères* sought

275

out his company and held him in high esteem. He was a level-headed and sagacious man, and became a member of the vicariate council of the Mackenzie district. Moreover, his conciliatory spirit enabled him to act as an agent for peace between the Catholic missions and the officers of the HBC. He maintained relations of real friendship with Lawrence Clarke, a bourgeois of Fort Rae, and with Roderick MacFarlane, of Fort Chipewyan. In conformity with the attitudes of the time, Eynard deplored the arrival of Protestant ministers in the district, and was ready for any sacrifice to defend his flock.

Father Eynard died while bathing in Lake Athabasca. His body was recovered thanks to his friend MacFarlane. In accordance with the desire he had expressed before his death, he was buried in the old Indian cemetery of the mission of La Nativité. It is said that he was keenly missed by all, Protestants as well as Catholics.

GASTON CARRIÈRE

Archives of the archbishopric of Grouard-McLennan (McLennan, Alta.), Mémoires de Mgr Isidore Clut. Archives de l'archevêché de Saint-Boniface (Man.), Germain Eynard, Histoire de la mission de Saint-Joseph du Grand lac des Esclaves. Archives générales O.M.I. (Rome), Dossier Germain Eynard; Histoire de la mission de Notre-Dame-des-Sept-Douleurs établie au fond du lac Athabasca (copies in AHO). *Notices nécrologiques des O.M.I.*, II, 423–29. [P.-J.-B.] Duchaussois, *Aux glaces polaires; Indiens et Esquimaux* (1re éd., Lyon, [1921]), 230–33. Morice, *Hist. de l'Église catholique*, II. Henri Faraud, "Nécrologie," *Les missions catholiques* (Lyon), VI (1874), 21–23.

F

FALCON, PIERRE (or jocularly Pierriche – Pierre the rhymer), poet and song-writer, a Métis of Red River; b. 4 June 1793 at Elbow Fort (near present-day Swan River, Manitoba), in the Swan River Department of the North West Company; d. 26 Oct. 1876 at Saint-François-Xavier, Man.

Pierre Falcon was named after his father, an employee of the North West Company. His mother was an Indian woman said by early historians to have been from the Missouri country but believed by her descendants to have been a Cree. As a child Pierre was taken to Lower Canada and baptized at L'Acadie (Saint-Jean County) on 18 June 1798. He apparently lived with relatives, and although early historians described him as unlettered, he learned to read and write. At the age of 15 young Falcon returned to Red River to become a North West Company clerk. In 1812 he married Mary, daughter of the Métis Cuthbert Grant* Sr; the couple had three sons and four daughters. After the amalgamation of the Hudson's Bay Company and the North West Company in 1821, Falcon served the new company until 1825.

With a number of other Métis families, he then followed Cuthbert Grant* Jr to Grantown (Saint-François-Xavier) on the White Horse Plain. There the group settled, and the 1838 census listed Falcon as having 30 acres of land under cultivation. By 1849 he was shown with only 15 acres since the remainder had been divided among his sons. He was a justice of the peace for the settlement.

Pierre Falcon, described by his descendants as an excitable and quick-moving man, had a poet's feeling for words and a musician's sense of rhythm, and he used them to put local incidents into songs. An armed clash between a party of mounted Métis under Cuthbert Grant Jr and the Selkirk settlers under Governor Robert Semple*, at Seven Oaks (in present-day Winnipeg) on 19 June 1816, was the subject of his best known song, "La Chanson de la Grenouillère." Another Métis ballad, entitled "Le Lord Selkirk au Fort William, ou La danse des Bois-Brûlés," tells a further part of the story of Seven Oaks. In retaliation for events at Red River, Lord Selkirk [Douglas*] and his soldiers, en route to the settlement, seized the Nor'Westers' headquarters at Fort William in August 1816. A ball held there later by Selkirk is what is described in this ballad, attributed to Falcon. A third song to survive is "Ballade du général Dickson," describing the departure from Grantown in 1837 of an American adventurer, James Dickson*, who dreamed of setting up an Indian kingdom in California.

During the Red River troubles of 1869–70, Falcon, though advanced in years, wished to accompany the party of Métis going to the boundary to stop Governor William McDougall*'s entry into the settlement in October 1869. He protested: "While the enemy is occupied in despatching me, my friends can strike hard and get in many good blows." Prevented from participating he wrote instead a song of mockery, "Les tribulations d'un roi malheureux," which was set to the tune of "The wandering Jew."

Pierre Falcon is said to have composed many other songs describing the daily life of the voyageurs on the rivers and the hunters on the plains. Agnes Laut's "The buffalo hunt" is believed to be a romanticized free translation of the lyrics of a song by Falcon. The bard's songs were carried by the voyageurs from the St Lawrence to the Mackenzie, and Lake Falcon in Manitoba was named by them in his honour. His ballads were also sung by the Métis to the accompaniment of the fiddle around prairie camp fires. Regrettably, the words of many of Falcon's songs were never written down and have been lost.

BRUCE PEEL

[Pierre Falcon's extant songs are given in M. A. MacLeod, *Songs of old Manitoba; with airs, French and English words, and introductions* (Toronto, [1960]), 1–40. The following three articles by Mrs MacLeod each give one of Falcon's songs with its background; the first article has biographical information on Falcon, and the second includes a picture of him: M. A. MacLeod, "Bard of the Prairies," *Beaver*, outfit 286 (spring 1956), 20–25; "Dickson the liberator," *Beaver*, outfit 287 (summer 1956), 4–7; "Songs of the insurrection," *Beaver*, outfit 287 (spring 1957), 19–23. For variants in the tune of "Chanson de la Grenouillère," and biographical information on Falcon *see:* Margaret Complin, "Pierre Falcon's 'Chanson de la Grenouillère' " *RSCT*, 3rd ser., XXXIII (1939), sect.II; 49–58. B.P.]

FARRELL, JOHN, Roman Catholic priest and bishop; b. 2 June 1820, at Armagh, Ireland, son of James Farrell and Joan Patterson; d. 26 Sept. 1873, at Hamilton, Ont.

John Farrell emigrated to Canada with his parents, who settled in Kingston, Upper Canada, in 1830. He was educated in Kingston and at the seminary of Saint-Sulpice at Montreal, ordained in October 1845, and named pastor at L'Orignal. He later taught at Regiopolis College in Kingston for a few years before taking on the duties of pastor at Peterborough, Canada West. On 11 May 1856 Farrell was consecrated first Roman Catholic bishop of Hamilton.

One of Bishop Farrell's first tasks in the newly created diocese was to provide for the needs of its many German-speaking Roman Catholics. To this end he brought from Europe in 1857 two brothers, Fathers Eugene and Louis Funcken of the Congregation of the Resurrection of Our Lord Jesus Christ, who laid the foundations for the education of a native clergy, one of Farrell's principal objectives. The fruit of these efforts was St Jerome's College, located in Berlin (Kitchener) and incorporated by provincial statute in 1866.

In the summer of 1862 Farrell became involved in a local controversy when the dying Sir Allan MacNab*, long the leading political figure in Hamilton and a member of the Church of England,

requested the bishop to receive him into the Roman Catholic Church. In the furore that ensued, George BROWN, the powerful publisher of the Toronto *Globe* and an opponent of Catholic interests in the province, claimed, over Farrell's strong denials, that MacNab had been duped into this "remarkable" death-bed conversion. The heated exchange was symptomatic of the deeper conflict then raging in the province.

Farrell, who had been lauded for his efforts to "educate his people" in both Peterborough and Hamilton, urged politicians, especially those in Canada East (Quebec), to defeat attempts by Brown and other Reformers to block effective school legislation for Roman Catholics in Canada West. The bishop repudiated his fellow-Irishman, Thomas D'Arcy McGee*, in 1859 for contemplating a political alliance with Brown and he criticized Brown's programme of representation by population in the fear that it might unduly strengthen the Protestant segment of the province. Later he was gratified when McGee rejected the friendship of Protestant Reformers who were opposed to separate school legislation, particularly the bill first introduced in 1860 by Richard William Scott*. A modified version of this bill received royal assent in 1863, after protracted debates, and "quite satisfied" Farrell. On the eve of confederation, Farrell, in company with other Canadian bishops, urged the government of John A. Macdonald* to embody the principles of Scott's act in the constitution of the Dominion, a course of action subsequently provided for in the British North America Act.

Farrell augmented the educational facilities of his diocese, notably by supporting the work of the Ladies of Loretto, who established schools for young women in Guelph and Hamilton, and of the Congregation of Notre Dame which founded academies at St Agatha, Formosa, and Waterdown. He combined his efforts on behalf of Catholic education with a "loathing and contempt for American Fenianism." Throughout his career he was, it would appear, "an uncompromising foe" of the "agitators who trade[d] upon Irish patriotism and Irish generosity."

C. M. JOHNSTON

Berliner Journal (Berlin (Kitchener), Ont.), 2 Oct. 1873. *Canadian Freeman* (Toronto), 29 July 1859. *Catholic Citizen* (Toronto), 5 June 1856. *Gazette* (Montreal), 29 Sept. 1873. *Globe* (Toronto), 27 Sept. 1873. *Hamilton Spectator*, 26 Sept. 1873. *Mail* (Toronto), 29 Sept. 1873. *Documentary history of education in Upper Canada* (Hodgins), XIX.
The golden jubilee of the diocese of Hamilton and consecration of St Mary's Cathedral, ed. M. J. O'Reilly (Hamilton, [1906]). J. G. Hodgins, *The*

Feild

establishment of schools and colleges in Ontario, 1792–1910 (3v., Toronto, 1910), I, II. Moir, *Church and state in Canada West.* Theobald Spetz, *The Catholic Church in Waterloo County* ([Toronto], 1916). F. A. Walker, *Catholic education and politics in Upper Canada: a study of the documentation relative to the origin of Catholic elementary schools in the Ontario school system* (Toronto and Vancouver, 1955). Brother Alfred [A. J. Dooner], "The conversion of Sir Allan MacNab, Baronet (1798–1862)," CCHA *Report, 1942–43,* 47–64. T. F. Battle, "The Right Reverend John Farrell, D.D., first bishop of Hamilton," CCHA *Report, 1942–43,* 39–45. A. P. Monahan, "A politico-religious incident in the career of Thomas D'Arcy McGee," CCHA *Report, 1957,* 39–51.

FEILD, EDWARD, Church of England clergyman, inspector of schools, bishop of Newfoundland; b. 7 June 1801 at Worcester, England, third son of surgeon James Feild; m. in 1867 Sophia Bevan of Rougham Rookery, Suffolk, England, the widow of the Reverend Jacob Mountain; d. 8 June 1876 at Bishop's Court, Hamilton, Bermuda.

Edward Feild was educated at Rugby, where he gained distinction in Latin composition, and at Queen's College, Oxford, graduating BA in 1823, MA in 1826. He became a fellow of his college and after his ordination he served as curate at Kidlington, near Oxford, from which parish he rode into Oxford to attend to his university duties, thus reversing the practice of clerical fellows by lodging in his curacy instead of living in college and going out to his parish. At Kidlington, as at Bicknor, Gloucestershire, where he served from 1834 until 1844, Feild combined his parish duties with an interest in schools and teaching. Of this period a friend wrote, "He readily made up his mind, and was firm in execution; he was no talker, made no display, and all proceeded from him earnestly from the sober temperament and habit of his mind."

Partly through the influence of Dr Charles James Blomfield, the reforming bishop of London, who was impressed by Feild's reports in 1840 and 1841 as an inspector of schools for the National Society (a society for promoting the education of the poor in the principles of the established church), Feild was appointed bishop of Newfoundland in 1844. His consecration took place at Lambeth on 28 April 1844 at the hands of William Howley, archbishop of Canterbury, assisted by the bishops of London and Worcester. Upon his arrival in St John's on 4 July, he was greeted aboard ship by the two Church of England clergymen of St John's, their wardens, and other church officials, as well as by the son and private secretary of the governor, Sir John Harvey*. On the wharf were the Royal Newfoundland Companies with their officers, and the carriage of Lady Harvey took him to his temporary residence at government house. Of his reception, Bishop Feild wrote, "I should have preferred a procession with litanies and holy services attended by priests and choristers leading me to church ... yet the mixture of secular and ecclesiastical respect was not to be contemptuously rejected ... though to me, personally, the whole proceedings were as distasteful as they were unsought for and unexpected."

His dislike for secular display was soon forgotten in the larger task he found in Newfoundland. Some 24 clergymen of the Society for the Propagation of the Gospel together with perhaps some 12 or 15 others were coping with the 43 churches scattered along its eastern and southern coasts. On the western French shore and Labrador coast were some settlements never visited by a clergyman. The area from Cape Ray on the southwestern corner of Newfoundland along the western coast to Cape St John near the port of Twillingate was treated as one of "non-settlement" by the government in keeping with a treaty with France, and no magistrates, excise officers, laws, or police were provided. Thus the settlers there, by their remoteness from any source of authority, tended to licentiousness in conduct and conversation. According to Archdeacon Edward Wix*, who visited the western coast and Labrador in 1830 and 1836, "acts of profligacy were practised at which the Micmac Indians expressed to me their horror and disgust. ... I met with more feminine delicacy in the wigwams of the Micmac and Canokok Indians than in the tilts of many of our own people." Archdeacon Wix warned that "unless some sympathy be excited for the improvement of our people in this and like places, they must fast merge into a state similar to that in which the first missionaries found the inhabitants of the islands in the South Seas."

The new bishop's diocese included not only Newfoundland and the coast of Labrador, but also the Bermudas. During his 32-year episcopacy, Feild consistently protested against this arrangement as it added immeasurably to his problems by forcing him to divide his time between two areas some 1,200 miles apart, whose problems were completely different. The difficulties of travel in Newfoundland were alleviated by the Reverend Robert Eden, the rector of Leigh in Essex, later bishop of Moray and primus of Scotland, who presented an 80-ton brig to the diocese to be used as a church ship. As this vessel proved too large, the donor permitted it to be sold. A smaller ship, *Hawk,* was purchased, and became a familiar sight along the coasts of Newfoundland and

Labrador. Each summer Bishop Feild spent three to four months visiting fishermen in the isolated outports where he regularized marriages, baptized children, and consecrated graveyards and churches. Often he travelled as much as 1,600 miles each year, and continued to do so until a coadjutor was appointed in 1867.

Gradually, under Bishop Feild's powerful influence, the character of the church in Newfoundland changed. Most of the clergy, influenced by Feild's predecessor Aubrey George SPENCER, had inclined towards the low church; by the close of Bishop Feild's long episcopacy, as D. W. Prowse* noted in his history of Newfoundland, "one of this school is now a *rara avis* in the diocese." Bishop Feild's firmness, or what some considered his intransigence, paralleled a similar hardening of feeling under the Roman Catholic bishops, Michael Anthony Fleming* and John Thomas Mullock*. The latter had forbidden the practice of "Catholics . . . going to Church in the evening . . . to compliment their Protestant friends," after attending mass in the morning. Bishop Feild's attitude towards Wesleyans and other Protestants was uncompromising. In a charge to the clergy in 1858 he warned of the "increase of the Wesleyans, now assuming the name and functions of a church, which makes but too manifest their desire and endeavour to draw away disciples after them." His fear of Wesleyan activities amongst Church of England members was reinforced by reports from clergymen in the outports. At Moreton's Harbour in Notre Dame Bay, he was told, the "Methodists, by their class-leaders and prophetesses, are busy everywhere, and have made such havoc in this mission, driving some out of their senses and many out of the Church."

His attitude towards Roman Catholicism was indicated in a letter to the bishop of London, to whom he described his first visitation along the Labrador coast in 1848. He observed that there were as many as 1,000 permanent settlers and some 10,000 temporary fishermen during the four summer months, and he spoke of the "wolves . . . among them, not sparing the flock"; "had a Roman Catholic priest come along the shore before me, many would have sought baptism, at least for the children . . . this danger is always imminent." He urged that a French-speaking clergyman be secured as "many of the men understand little English."

Both Church of England and Catholic feeling increased in the controversy that arose over the General Academy, established in 1845 under a grant from the provincial legislature. Even though the headmaster of the new academy was a Church of England clergyman nominated by the bishop,

Feild was far from satisfied with it. He continued his own school, which he had established immediately upon his arrival in Newfoundland, "to mitigate," as he said, "the evil of a public academy established under liberal principles" that is, one having no religious instruction. Bishop Feild's hostility to the new academy was shared by Roman Catholics and other Protestants. The teaching staff was composed of the Anglican headmaster, two Irish Roman Catholic masters, and an Irish Episcopalian secretary. Native-born Newfoundlanders objected that there should have been a Newfoundland master and other Protestant denominations were irritated by the Church of England and Catholic monopoly on the staff. An additional objection was the fee of £8 per child. By 1850 the General Academy was dissolved and three separate academies formed, one of which was a Church of England academy directly under the bishop's control.

The same fears that led to the closing of the General Academy influenced Feild in his disapproval of the manner of distribution of the legislature's educational grant of £5,100. This was divided between Catholics and Protestants in proportion to population, which meant, in effect, that half of it went to the Catholics and the other half was awarded to the Protestants with no special reference to the Church of England. Feild complained that "We are fighting the battle of Education . . . and the Church (as between Romanists and Dissenters is usually the case) is jostled out of her rights." He also resented the share of the grant which was allotted to the schools of the Newfoundland School Society, a Church of England organization, but one which permitted Wesleyans on the staff of its schools. To Feild "Education could not be carried on without religion, and religion can never be truly and honestly taught without frequent recurrence to . . . those distinctive matters of faith . . . which each church recognizes." For these reasons, Feild sought and eventually secured a subdivision of the Protestant educational grant according to denominations. Each denomination gained more direct control over its allotment, but the result was a proliferation of denominational schools and, in some cases, a lowering of teachers' salaries.

Bishop Feild had incurred unpopularity by his uncompromising attitude towards any joint Protestant endeavours. In the spring of 1846 he refused an invitation to be a vice-patron of the newly formed Newfoundland branch of the British and Foreign Bible Society – an organization not exclusively Church of England. He claimed that there was no need for such a society in Newfoundland as Bibles could be procured

Feild

already at the cheapest rate. Bishop Feild's action was not popular with low church members of his flock and it produced dismay among many Protestants in St John's who "lamented that the new Bishop . . . had made a terrible mistake, for they [Protestants] cried for unity as regards religion, the more so, indeed, as unhappily, by party strife, their [Protestants'] religious and political positions could not be separated."

Since the introduction of representative government in Newfoundland in 1832, political parties had tended to reflect denominational differences. The Liberal party was almost exclusively Catholic, although its leadership contained a sprinkling of Protestants; the Conservative or Tory party was solidly Protestant. Any religious conflict among Protestants tended to weaken their political position, thus many Protestants were anxious to promote religious harmony and to have Bishop Feild assume the leadership of the British and Foreign Bible Society branch. But Feild preferred to confine his activities strictly within the Church of England.

To help alleviate the lack of clergy in the diocese, Bishop Feild concentrated on building up the theological college which had been begun by Bishop Spencer. In 1844 the college consisted of a poor wooden building in which six students met daily to receive instruction from the clergy of St Thomas's Church. Bishop Feild required these students to attend daily prayer and to be instructed in church music, and he hoped for a theological college where the students would live under collegiate discipline. By 1847 he had formulated plans for Queen's College (named for his Oxford college) and for a collegiate school, both to be endowed. Each was to have accommodation for 12 resident students, and by 1850 the bishop had expended some £3,000 towards the purchase of buildings and had secured the services of the Reverend William GREY as principal. Lack of funds made it difficult for him to secure a vice-principal or tutor.

From the beginning of his work in Newfoundland, Bishop Feild stressed the importance of church people in the colony contributing towards the upkeep of the clergy and parsonages, rather than depending entirely upon the generosity of members of the parent church in England. In 1846 the usual SPG stipend for a clergyman was £100 with another £100 raised locally. Bishop Feild contemplated trying to raise an additional £200 or £300 in the hope that "two or three might be found who would be ready to endure hardness for these poor fishermen and for Christ's sake." As an agency for organizing the financial basis of the church, he supported the Newfoundland Church Society, but his attempt to make a pledge to contribute to the Church Society the sign of church membership met with much opposition. Lieutenant-Colonel Robert Barlow McCrae, the commanding officer of the garrison in St John's in the 1860s, reported that "year by year the Bishop has to go down to the annual meeting [of the Church Society] and sorrowfully announce the amount of the subscriptions, in a place where the exports and imports of commerce amount to more than 3,000,000£ (the greater part of which is in the hands of Protestants) to be something over or under 800£, dividing some 40£ or 50£ a year among a number of half-starved clergymen, and leaving a pitiful balance in his hands for churches and parsonages."

The 1860s saw the fisheries fail season after season, and in 1863 Bishop Feild asked the legislature to appoint a day of special "humiliation in which Christians of all denominations would unite in supplication for Divine favour . . . for the removal of these afflicting dispensations." He observed that many of the old fishing establishments of the northeast coast, originally founded by Church of England people from Dorsetshire and Poole, had failed and "the owners have let their houses to young adventurers, who generally are dissenters . . . which is one of the ways in which our Church is now divided and desolated."

In 1869, after a decade of severe depression, Bishop Feild published one of his most powerful pastorals in which he condemned the "supply system" by which fishermen were given provisions at exorbitant prices by suppliers in the expectation that payment would be made out of the season's catch. This system, he claimed, led to recklessness and dishonesty on the part of many fishermen who tended to sell their catch to other suppliers for cash and evade payment to their own supplier by saying they had had a poor season. Bishop Feild not only deplored the dishonest practices of both fishermen and suppliers, but also regretted what he called the "continual withdrawal from the colony, every year, of wealth . . . to be wholly spent in other countries, cruelly hindering all material progress and improvement here." No less caustic were his references to the moves towards confederation with the new dominion of Canada. "He must have greater faith in Dominion politics and politicians than I have, who expects to obtain much relief from that quarter."

In spite of the financial and other difficulties which beset him during the 32 years he spent in Newfoundland, Bishop Feild could recount an increase of SPG clergy from 24 in 1844 to more than 50 in 1876, a large number of whom were trained under his close supervision. Of the 100 churches in existence in 1876, more than one half had been consecrated by Feild. In addition to the theological college and the collegiate school for which he had succeeded in raising endowment funds, he had also established schools for boys and girls, created a widows' and orphans' fund for the benefit of clergy, and built two partly endowed orphanages. In the last five years of his episcopacy, steps were taken to organize a synod to encourage the laity to take an interest in the affairs of the church.

Feild was largely responsible for financing the construction of the cathedral in St John's, which was consecrated and opened for service on 21 Sept. 1850. The foundation stone had been laid as early as 21 Aug. 1843 by Bishop Spencer. In 1846 Feild journeyed to England to obtain consent to the appropriation of £15,000 towards the completion of the cathedral, and much of the money was collected in English churches. Copied from a design of Sir George Gilbert Scott, the cathedral was built of grey cut stone in the Gothic style with a tower and spire 130 feet high. At its opening in 1850 only the nave was completed, but when finished the cathedral was considered one of the finest in British America.

Feild's great contribution to the church in Newfoundland was in administration. Like his Roman Catholic contemporary in Montreal, Bishop Ignace Bourget*, Feild laid the groundwork for a firm church establishment, backed by a financial arrangement no longer dependent upon the bounty of the mother church in England. His was an uncompromising spirit in matters of church doctrine and discipline, which led to the accusation that he was "wanting in Christian charity towards ministers of other denominations." This was too harsh a judgement. Rather, he permitted no compromise in matters which seemed to him to threaten the religious or financial position of the Church of England. A high churchman, Feild gradually influenced the character of the church and clergy in the colony away from the low church tendencies which had previously prevailed. For many years he was distrusted by a large section of Protestants, but eventually he won the esteem of all classes by his uprightness, modesty, and piety. In religious matters, he was not a controversialist. When refusing to join the British and Foreign Bible Society, he preferred to rest his case on the reasons given by the bishop of Salisbury for withdrawing from the society rather than to elaborate his own. In social life, he was described as a delightful companion, full of humour and pleasantness, and a great lover of children.

ELINOR SENIOR

[There are neither Edward Feild papers nor memoirs, but many of his journals of visitations along the coasts of Newfoundland and Labrador were published in their entirety. These include: *Diocese of Newfoundland. A journal of the bishop's visitation of the missions on the western and southern coast, August and September, 1845 ...* (Church in the Colonies series, X, London, January 1846). *Diocese of Newfoundland. Part II. A journal of the bishop's visitation of the missions of the northern coast, in the summer of 1846* (Church in the Colonies series, XV, London, November 1846). *Journal of the bishop of Newfoundland's voyage of visitation and discovery on the south and west coasts of Newfoundland and on the Labrador in the year 1848* (Church in the Colonies series, XXI, London, March 1849). *Journal of the bishop of Newfoundland's voyage of visitation on the coast of Labrador and the north-east coast of Newfoundland, in the church ship, "Hawk," in the year 1853* (Church in the Colonies series, XXX, London, [1854]). Some letters from Feild to the secretary of the Society for the Propagation of the Gospel in Foreign Parts are in the *Report of the incorporated Society for the Propagation of the Gospel in Foreign parts ...* (London) for the years 1845–76. The biography of Feild by H. W. Tucker, *Memoir of the life and episcopate of Edward Feild, D.D., bishop of Newfoundland, 1844–1876 ...* (London, 1877), is well written and valuable for its many extracts from his letters to clergymen in England and for its appendices which include his "Poor pastoral" of 1869. A number of his charges to his clergy and many of his pastorals exist in printed form; a partial list can be found in the *British Museum catalogue.*

Accounts of Feild's life are found in: *DNB.* John Langtry, *History of the church in eastern Canada and Newfoundland* (Colonial church histories of the Society for Promoting Christian Knowledge, London, 1892), 87–116. C. H. Mockridge, *The bishops of the Church of England in Canada and Newfoundland: being an illustrated historical sketch of the Church of England in Canada as traced through her episcopate* (London and Toronto, 1896), 101–11. O. R. Rowley, *The Anglican episcopate of Canada and Newfoundland* (London and Milwaukee, Wis., 1928), 217.

Other sources include: PANL, Morine papers; Alfred Morine's unpublished history of Newfoundland including his memoirs; Newfoundland, Executive Council, Minutes, 14 Dec. 1861; Returns of an address to the House of Commons, 15 May 1862. *Newfoundlander* (St John's), 16 June 1876. *Royal Gazette* (St John's), 1843–76. M. F. Howley, *Ecclesiastical history of Newfoundland* (Boston, Mass., 1888). R. B. McCrae, *Lost amid the fogs; sketches of life in Newfoundland, England's ancient colony* (London, 1869). Charles Pedley, *The history of Newfoundland from the earliest times to the year 1860* (London, 1863). Prowse, *History of Nfld.* Philip Tocque, *Newfoundland: as it was and as it is in 1877* (London, 1878). E.S.]

FELTON, WILLIAM LOCKER PICKMORE, lawyer and politician; b. 6 April 1812 at Mahon, Minorca, eldest of a family of 12 children, son of

Ferguson

William Bowman Felton*, who had distinguished himself in the navy during the Napoleonic wars, and of Anna Maria Valls; d. 12 Nov. 1877 at Sherbrooke, Que.

In 1815 William Locker Pickmore Felton came to Canada with his parents, who settled at Belvedere, near Sherbrooke (then called Hyatt's Mill). He attended Mr Johnson's school at Hatley, then that of Mr Dricoll at Saint-Jean-Baptiste-de-Nicolet. After studying law at Quebec in the firm of Andrew Stuart* and Henry BLACK, he was admitted to the bar on 21 Nov. 1834; he then took up residence at Quebec, where he practised for three years. It was in this town that on 6 Aug. 1835 he married Clara Lloyd, daughter of Thomas Lloyd, a surgeon in the English army.

In 1837 Felton was attached to the judicial district of Saint-François; he was first appointed a queen's counsel, became president of the Court of Sessions before 1854, then crown attorney (1853–61), and was elected *bâtonnier* of the district (1861–75). He was the MLA for Sherbrooke-Wolfe from 1854 to 1857, and as a candidate in Sherbrooke in 1861 against Alexander Tilloch Galt* was defeated by a slight majority. The prestige of Galt, who for 20 years had directed the colonizing company known as the British American Land Company, and who had obtained passage of the St Lawrence and Atlantic Railroad through Sherbrooke in 1853, explains Felton's defeat. At this time Galt was also solicitor general in the cabinet of George-Étienne CARTIER and John A. Macdonald*. As a Liberal-Conservative deputy, Felton had concerned himself with questions relating to seigneurial rights and municipal laws. Furthermore, at his wife's suggestion, he had defended the cause of the separate schools in Upper and Lower Canada when Joseph Papin* made a proposal recommending the establishment of a general and uniform system of elementary schools maintained by state support. At the local level, Felton, although a Protestant, encouraged his wife to contribute to religious and educational causes in the parish of Saint-Michel at Sherbrooke. Thus in 1857 Clara Lloyd was to make possible the founding of Mont Notre-Dame, which was administered by the sisters of the congregation.

William Locker Pickmore Felton died at Sherbrooke, in Villa Belvedere, on 12 Nov. 1877. He left one son, William Hughes, who had been called to the bar on 8 April 1862 and who was practising at Arthabaska. The respect in which Felton was held can be judged through a significant incident: on the day of his death, his colleagues at the bar of the district of Saint-François decided to honour his memory by wearing mourning for a month. Felton was a prominent man in the region of Sherbrooke, and people of high social standing were often to be found at his house. Nevertheless he does not seem to have exercised as great an influence in the community as his father or to have made as lasting a contribution to its causes as his wife, who outshone him in this regard.

MAURICE O'BREADY

The author had access to the family papers of Mrs H. S. Horsfall (Lennoxville, Que.). Archives du Mont Notre-Dame (Sherbrooke, Qué.), letters of William Locker Pickmore Felton to the superior. *Gazette* (Montreal), 15 Nov. 1877. *Le Pionnier de Sherbrooke*, 16 nov. 1877. *Le Progrès* (Sherbrooke), 16 nov. 1877. *Annuaire du séminaire Saint-Charles-Borromée, Sherbrooke, 1882–1883* (Sherbrooke, Qué., 1883), 28, 48. *Can. biog. dict.*, II, 249–50. P.-G. Roy, *Les avocats de la région de Québec*, 162. Maurice O'Bready, *La première messe à Sherbrooke* (Sherbrooke, Qué., 1933), 14–16.

FERGUSON, THOMAS ROBERTS, merchant, soldier, Orangeman, and politician; b. December 1818, at Drumcor, County Cavan, Ireland, son of Andrew Ferguson; d. 15 Sept. 1879, in Innisfil Township, Ont.

Thomas Roberts Ferguson's parents left Ireland for Upper Canada during the late 1830s; his father died en route. After a brief stay in Montreal, the family settled near Cookstown in 1842 where Ferguson became a farmer. He bought more property in Innisfil Township and established each of his brothers on a farm before becoming a merchant in Cookstown. In 1856 he married Frances Jane Gowan, daughter of Orange leader Ogle Robert GOWAN, and they had three sons and six daughters. Ferguson had joined the Orange order in 1847 and he became a prominent member. In 1852 he was master of the Loyal Orange Lodge no.1580 and in June 1858 he was elected one of the deputy grand masters of the order. From 1867 to 1873 he was a director of the Northern Railway, and in 1872 he became a provisional director of the Huron and Ontario Ship Canal Company.

Ferguson served from 1847 as an officer with the 4th Battalion and then the 7th Battalion Simcoe militia. In 1861 he was instrumental in the establishment of the 1st Rifle Company of volunteer militia of Cookstown, to which he was appointed captain on 13 June 1862. He rose to the rank of lieutenant-colonel by 1865. The next year he led his company against the Fenians at Fort Erie; in the engagement Ferguson accompanied John Stoughton Dennis* on the tug *W.T. Robb* and met the Fenians under John O'NEILL as the latter was leaving Canada. Lieutenant Christopher Cook later charged Ferguson with misconduct in matters of morale and money. He was acquitted of the charges, and on 25 June 1869 he was provisionally appointed major with the "Simcoe Foresters," the 35th Battalion of the Volunteer Infantry. He held this post until his retirement in 1873.

When the first council of Innisfil Township had been formed in 1850, Ferguson was elected a councillor. From 1852 to 1873 he served on the council, four years as councillor and 18 years as reeve. He was also warden of Simcoe County in 1858 and from 1862 to 1867.

A Conservative, Ferguson first ran for a seat in the Legislative Assembly in the election of 1858 against Tory William Benjamin ROBINSON. In this election, and subsequently in 1861 and 1863, he was returned for Simcoe South. In 1867 and 1872 he was elected by acclamation to represent Simcoe South in the Legislative Assembly for Ontario. He also campaigned successfully in Cardwell in 1867 for a seat in the House of Commons but did not run in 1872.

Ferguson was a strong advocate of representation by population and during his first term in the assembly he moved for the adoption of a bill to introduce it into law. On 19 Oct. 1860, Ferguson was appointed arbitrator on behalf of Simcoe County to see to the maintenance and repair of the Holland River bridge at Bradford. As a politician, he was concerned about local and county affairs and about the people he represented. He wrote letters supporting their petitions on a wide variety of subjects, including the release of prisoners whom he felt had been punished too severely by lengthy sentences for minor crimes; he was often actively involved on their behalf, for example in 1857 and 1859 when he attempted to prevent the incorporation of a section of the Innisfil Township into Barrie.

In 1872 at a political meeting in Bradford, Ferguson frustrated the intention of its sponsors to condemn acts of the federal government. When the meeting was over and the majority of people had left, however, a fight broke out; in attempting to stop it, Ferguson suffered a serious blow to his head which caused permanent physical and mental damage. As a result, he resigned his seat in the Ontario legislature in 1873 and he was prevailed upon to accept the office of collector of customs at Collingwood. Shortly after the Liberal government of Alexander Mackenzie* came to power in 1873, Ferguson was moved to Toronto. In 1876 he was dismissed without compensation or apology. He spent his remaining years at his home in Cookstown where he died of paralysis at 60 years of age.

CAROLE B. STELMACK

PAC, MG 26, A (Macdonald papers), entries for T. R. Ferguson; MG 27, I, E30 (T. R. Ferguson papers); RG 5, C1, 557, no.906; 587, no.2026; 613, no.597; 636, no.1580; 680, no.558; 681, no.585; 682, nos.595, 617; 683, no.652; 706, no.489; 742, nos.639, 640; 772, no.391; 779, nos.781, 795; 782, no.908; 804, nos.507, 508; 851, nos.853, 854; 868, no.54; RG 9, I, C1, 19, 20; C3, 11; C6, 7; 174, no.1002; RG 30. [G.-É. Cartier], *Discours de Sir Georges Cartier ...*, Joseph Tassé, édit. (Montréal, 1893). *Can. directory of parliament* (Johnson). *Can. parl. comp.*, 1867; 1869; 1871; 1872. Hunter, *Hist. of Simcoe County. Innisfil Township centennial, 1850–1950, June 23–24, 1951; a record of 100 years of progress, historical review* ([Barrie, Ont., 1951]).

FIFE, DAVID, farmer; b. 1805, third son of John Fife and Agnes Hutchinson; m. about 1826 Jane Beckett by whom he had eight children; d. 9 Jan. 1877, near Peterborough, Ont.

John Fife brought his family from Kincardine, Fifeshire, Scotland, to Canada in 1820, and cleared a farm in the newly opened Otonabee Township, Peterborough County. After David married, he settled nearby in Otonabee Township, where he lived the rest of his life.

In 1842 Fife received through a friend a small sample of wheat taken from a cargo from Danzig (now Gdańsk, Poland) as the ship was unloaded in Glasgow. David sowed the sample in the spring, but not many heads developed as it contained only a few grains of spring wheat – later identified as Galician. However, these were carefully harvested and multiplied. The new wheat yielded well, notably on heavy clay soils, was free of rust, threshed well, and produced flour of excellent quality, although it matured eight to ten days after the currently grown varieties.

Until 1848 Red Fife, as it came to be known, was grown by Fife and his neighbours in Otonabee Township, but in 1849 cultivation of it spread first into the adjacent townships and then "rapidly throughout Upper Canada so that by 1860, it had almost completely superseded other varieties of spring wheat." It spread to New York State and Wisconsin, then to Minnesota and the Dakotas. By 1870 small amounts were grown in Manitoba and from 1882 to 1909 it was the leading variety in the province. However, as the prairies were opened to agriculture to the west and north of the Red River valley, an earlier maturing variety was needed to escape damage from frost. On account of its high quality, Red Fife was chosen as the male parent of the famous Marquis wheat and it enters into the pedigree of most spring wheat varieties now grown on the western prairies.

I. L. CONNERS

PAC, RG 31, A1, 1851, Peterborough County, Otonabee Township; 1861, Peterborough County,

Finlayson

Otonabee Township; 1871, Peterborough County, Otonabee Township. Henry Bawbell, "Fife's spring wheat," *Canadian Agriculturist* (Toronto), I (1849), 302–3. *Peterborough Examiner*, 25 Jan. 1877, 31 Dec. 1929, July 1945, 12 June 1950, 24 Nov. 1958, 22 Sept. 1962, 15 Nov. 1963. A. H. R. Buller, *Essays on wheat* (New York, 1919), 206–15. R. L. Jones, *History of agriculture in Ontario 1613–1880* (Toronto, 1946), 103–4.

FINLAYSON, NICOL, HBC chief factor; b.*c.* 1795 at Loch Alsh, Ross-shire, Scotland; d. at Nairn, Scotland, 17 May 1877.

Nicol Finlayson and a younger brother, Duncan*, joined the Hudson's Bay Company as writers in 1815. Nicol's early experience was gained at Albany Factory on James Bay and at subordinate inland posts as far west as Lac Seul in present day northwestern Ontario. Although he was first considered frivolous and inattentive to business, he became efficient both as a trader and as an accountant. Being a good-natured man, he was liked by his Cree customers and in time acquired an exceptional knowledge of their language and customs.

On 10 June 1830 Finlayson left Moose Factory for Ungava Bay to execute Governor George Simpson*'s plans for trading with the Eskimos of Hudson Strait, who usually visited the Moravian missions on the northern part of the Labrador coast, and with the wandering Indians of the interior, who obtained their few necessities either from opposition traders on Esquimaux Bay (Hamilton Inlet) or from traders, HBC and others, on the Gulf of St Lawrence. Formerly the Ungava Bay area had been known to the HBC only from the journeys of the Moravians, Benjamin Gottlieb Kohlmeister* and George Kmoch, and its own employees, James Clouston* and William Hendry*.

Finlayson followed Hendry's overland route of 1828 and built Fort Chimo on the east bank of the South (Koksoak) River about 27 miles from its mouth. The site was almost destitute of wood and clay for building purposes but it provided a convenient berth for the vessel which was expected to keep Fort Chimo regularly supplied with trading goods and provisions from York Factory on the west coast of Hudson Bay. Because of its extreme isolation, both from York Factory and from the posts on James Bay, it proved impossible to maintain regular communication with Fort Chimo. Consequently Finlayson faced not only danger from the age-old enmity between Eskimos and Indians but also the problem of survival in a grim, barren land. In spite of all his efforts and those of his "second," Erland ERLANDSON, business was unprofitable, the Eskimos having but little to spare and the Indians being more concerned with following the herds of caribou which supplied food and clothing (as well as the means for trading guns, ammunition, and tobacco) than with trapping furs, which were much more profitable for the company. John McLean*, who succeeded Finlayson, suffered less patiently the frustrations endured in trying to carry out Governor Simpson's over-optimistic plans for exploiting the trade of a region he (McLean) described as presenting "as complete a picture of desolation as can be imagined."

Finlayson, who had been a chief trader since 1833, left Fort Chimo for Moose Factory in July 1836. He was granted extended furlough and visited Scotland in 1837–38 before returning to duty. For the remainder of his career he was employed at Michipicoten and York Factory, and in the HBC districts of Rainy Lake, Saskatchewan, Swan River, Île-à-la-Crosse, and Cumberland. His promotion in 1846 to the rank of chief factor entitled him to a seat on the Council of the Northern Department of Rupert's Land. His health, impaired in Ungava, never fully recovered, and in 1855, at the end of his fourth visit to Scotland, he was retired by the company. He moved to Nairn, where he died in 1877.

Finlayson had four sons and a daughter by an unidentified "native woman," and two sons and a daughter who survived childhood by Elizabeth, a daughter of chief factor Alexander Kennedy*, to whom he was married by Governor Simpson at Moose Factory on 10 Aug. 1829.

ALICE M. JOHNSON

HBRS, III (Fleming); XIX (Rich and Johnson); XXIV (Davies and Johnson). R. M. Ballantyne, *Ungava, a tale of Esquimaux-land* (London, 1857).

FISHER, CHARLES, lawyer, politician, and judge; b. 15 Aug. or 16 Sept. 1808 at Fredericton, N.B., eldest son of Peter Fisher and Susanna Williams; d. 8 Dec. 1880 at Fredericton.

Peter Fisher, a merchant and lumber operator of loyalist ancestry, is noted for his *Sketches of New Brunswick* (1825), the first historical study published in the province. More a description than a history, the book was highly critical of those big businessmen who exploited the province while contributing nothing to its progress. Charles Fisher seems to have been influenced by his father's point of view on this subject.

Charles Fisher was educated at the Fredericton Collegiate School and at King's College (University of New Brunswick), where he received a BA in 1830. He turned to the study of law under the attorney general, George Frederick Street*, was admitted attorney to the New Brunswick bar in

1831 and, after a stay at one of the Inns of Court in England, became a barrister in 1833. He started his practice in Fredericton where, in September 1836, he married Amelia Hatfield, by whom he had four sons and four daughters.

Almost as soon as he was admitted to the bar, Fisher turned to politics, running unsuccessfully for York County in the 1834 election. Three years later he entered the assembly as a colleague of Lemuel Allan WILMOT, also from York. For the next 10 or 12 years these two were the backbone of the New Brunswick reform movement, working mainly for responsible government. Wilmot has gone into the history books as the great man in the movement, but Joseph W. Lawrence*, an acute contemporary observer, quotes with approval the widely held view that "Fisher made the balls and Wilmot fired them." Fisher certainly understood the issues behind the constitutional changes being demanded, and may well have worked out the arguments which the more volatile Wilmot presented.

Following his election in 1837, Fisher worked diligently, often in cooperation with the government. A moderate reformer, he attempted to effect innovations in the fluid non-party structure of the day. New Brunswick was governed, often well but frequently injudiciously, by the lieutenant governor and the executive councillors, none of whom had a seat in the assembly in the 1830s. Not content to exist in what he considered an imperfect system, Fisher demanded improvements. In 1842 he introduced a bill requiring that assemblymen resign and seek re-election when appointed to the Executive Council or to an office with remuneration. He introduced another resolution calling for the initiation of money bills by the executive – an essential practice for efficient government; it was defeated 23 to 12, apparently because the members were not yet ready for such a sacrifice. Fisher also pressed for bills to fix the property qualification of legislative councillors at £500, to reduce the charges on the province under the civil list bill, to limit the salaries of department heads to £600, and to have all fees placed in the public treasury, not in the pockets of office-holders. His reform proposals reveal a deep streak of parsimony.

During the 1840s Fisher's relationship with Edward Barron CHANDLER and Robert Leonard HAZEN, the leaders of the government, was most amicable. They appointed him registrar at King's College in 1846 knowing full well that the move was probably "distasteful" to the college council. Fisher wrote to his friend Joseph HOWE on the evil ways of the "family compact" and on the irresponsible nature of the government and its politics. "Till this Election," he wrote in 1843, "I could not believe that respectable people would resort to such lies as have been made use of in this community to carry a point & the acrimony they evince exceeds anything to be conceived." At the same time Fisher hoped to avoid party strife in the small province of New Brunswick even though he praised it elsewhere. In one breath he could exult in "the general liberal triumph" of 1847 in Nova Scotia. In another: "He would regret to see the day when the organization of violent antagonistic political parties would be found necessary in this province" where "there was little talent enough for one good Government."

Fisher divorced the concept of responsible government from party considerations. He wrote of New Brunswick: "We are *too loyal* and *too ignorant* to put down the old [compact]." The best approach was a coalition which "with the growing influence of the liberals would in ten years give the liberals all without any violent movement." It was with this point of view that Fisher, fully aware of the theoretical ramifications of responsible government, moved his resolution of 1848 "that the House should approve of the principle of Colonial Government contained in the despatch of the Right Honorable Earl Grey [Henry George Grey] ... and of their application to this province." The motion was carried 24 to 11 and within three months Fisher entered the government formed by the new lieutenant governor, Sir Edmund Walker Head*. For taking this step both Fisher and L. A. Wilmot, who was appointed attorney general, have been accused of desertion and lack of principles. Fisher's defeat in the election of 1850 is offered as proof of public indignation. If the partisanship of the party system was required to attain responsible government, for which Fisher had been chief advocate and theoretician, then he had committed an indefensible act. If it could be achieved by coalition and collaboration without loss of integrity, then Fisher was wrongly accused. In his own defence he said: "In accepting office, I have compromised no principles; I have neither changed nor surrendered any opinion which I have heretofore advocated in Trade [in particular] nor Politics in general."

Fisher was not prominent in the council: Hazen, Chandler, John R. Partelow*, and even Wilmot tended to dominate. He wrote to Howe asking him about the operation of the council. "Does the Governor take the opinion of the whole Council and act upon the recommendation of a majority?" Fisher thought the appointment of persons to the Legislative Council was "a Branch of patronage indispensable to the well working of an Executive Council" and that the decision of that council must prevail. Lieutenant Governor

Fisher

Head, however, was not a man who would be ruled by his council.

Fisher's defeat in the election of 1850 should have been followed by his resignation as a matter of course, but he stayed in the council until January 1851. Governor Head had just before this date appointed a new chief justice, James CARTER, and had filled the vacancy on the Supreme Court with L. A. Wilmot. Both appointments were made in spite of the advice of the Executive Council. Fisher resigned, he stated, because the governor had not acted "consistent with my ideas of Responsible Government." Since his resignation was overdue, the sentiment has a hollow ring, yet Fisher realized better than anyone that Head had crippled responsible government for the time being. Its resurrection became his goal. By this time Fisher had lost faith in a coalition system; from being an opponent of the party system, he became its champion, and set about to weld together a party that would gain power and control all aspects of government, especially the actions of the governor.

Fisher's status as a constitutional lawyer and the respect he enjoyed from the "compact" council resulted in his serving, from 1852 to 1854, with William B. Kinnear* and James Watson Chandler* on a commission appointed to consolidate and codify the provincial statutes and to examine the courts of law and equity and the law of evidence. The results of the study were published in many volumes in 1854.

The year 1854 was an election year in New Brunswick and Fisher returned to the house. There was a new lieutenant governor, John Henry Thomas MANNERS-SUTTON, and reciprocity with the United States provided a new political issue. When the house was called together to ratify the reciprocity treaty in the fall of 1854, Fisher, fully aware that he controlled a majority in the house, rose on 20 October to introduce an amendment to the fifth paragraph of the address in reply to the speech from the throne. He stated "that your Constitutional Advisers have not conducted the Government of the Province in the true spirit of our Colonial Constitution." Should the governor believe, declared Fisher, "that the Bluenoses had no pluck, that the New Members were divided and split into sections with internal jealousies and disputes, and could be easily beaten in detail . . . , it was only fair to disabuse his mind." The amendment was carried on 28 October by a vote of 27 to 12, and Fisher was called upon to form a government. The compact council was finally removed from office; responsible government had been rescued by the creation of a political party.

Fisher, who became attorney general, proceeded to form a government that ranks with the best in the history of the province. Young and talented, it included men of such future prominence as Samuel Leonard Tilley*, Albert James Smith*, William Johnstone Ritchie*, John Mercer Johnson*, James Brown*, and William Henry STEEVES. When the extensive legislative record that followed is considered, the old saw that New Brunswickers were unfit for responsible government before 1854 may well deserve retirement. The new council contained no member of the historic families, and represented, for the most part, the middle class. Levelling, anti-establishment, commercially oriented, the new government meant a "social as well as political" change.

Fisher immediately set about his programme of reform. First the Legislative Council, formerly the preserve of the establishment, was shorn of its power. Its president was included in the Executive Council, and thereby lost his independence. About the same time the bishop of the Church of England was induced to give up his seat in the upper house. Of greater importance than these changes was the "Reform Bill of 1855," calling for "an extension of the franchise . . . to secure the fair representation of intelligence and property at the Polling booths." Fisher pressed for the removal of the £25 property qualification, but, not a supporter of universal manhood suffrage, he wanted to retain the requirement that each voter have a yearly income of £100. Vote by ballot was also introduced. The Liberal party, Fisher maintained, would always be "practical . . . progressive . . . conservative of everything good . . . destructive of everything evil in the political and social condition of the people of this country." With this aim in mind an act was later presented to prevent any person who conducted business with the government from being elected to the assembly or holding a seat in the upper house

Sound financing had always been one of Fisher's themes, and, in 1856, the government supported a private member's bill to the effect that "the right of initiating money grants should be conceded to the Executive government and the practice of the imperial parliament in this respect adopted." A new department of public works was created to carry out government projects, especially the building of highways and railways. New municipal institutions were set up, to "train men in the principles of self-government." Other reforms sought to limit the interest rate to 6 per cent, to introduce decimal currency, to regulate the qualifications of members of the medical profession, and to simplify legal procedures. Fisher supported a public school system but he was unable to push it through; he did establish an improved teacher training system, and named his brother, Henry Fisher, chief superintendent of education for the province.

Two pieces of legislation – the Prohibition Act and the University of New Brunswick Act – require some elaboration. S. L. Tilley, Fisher's provincial secretary, introduced a private member's bill on 3 March 1855 to prohibit the manufacture and sale of alcoholic beverages after 1 Jan. 1856. Passed by a vote of 21 to 18, it received royal assent, and the members of the government, although divided on the issue, became responsible for upholding the act. The law was not and apparently could not be enforced, and the public outcry for repeal was so great that Manners-Sutton seized on the issue as a way to escape from the Fisher government, which he did not like. When it refused to repeal the law, he forced its resignation, and in the ensuing election had the pleasure of seeing his unconstitutional methods justified. The John Hamilton Gray*–Robert Duncan Wilmot* government received a majority and repealed the law (1856). Within a year, however, Fisher was back in power. With the prohibition issue out of the way it became clear that Fisher and his supporters were more in tune with New Brunswickers than Manners-Sutton's carefully chosen men.

King's College was another contentious issue. People like A. J. Smith and Charles CONNELL repeatedly pressed for its abolition on the grounds that it was a plaything for the privileged subsidized by yeoman labour. Fisher, as a graduate and long time registrar, defended the college but in 1858 he could not stop a bill to abolish it. British disallowance of the act and the inclusion of Connell in the Executive Council as postmaster general brought the college issue up for reconsideration, and in 1860 the University of New Brunswick Act became law. Fisher's bill, based on a commission report, set up a non-sectarian university with a much broader curriculum than in the old classical college.

During these years Fisher was actively supporting railway construction. Though once burned in effigy in Saint John for opposing the Saint John to Shediac line, he was a solid supporter of the European and North American Railway as well as the Intercolonial. After consulting Joseph Howe, Fisher, accompanied by John ROBERTSON, held discussions in London in 1855 on the Saint John to Shediac line, then partly finished. The line was taken over completely by the government. When the Intercolonial project was again revived in 1858, Fisher, full of hope, went to London only to see both the railway project and the union of British North America dismissed as impractical.

Despite some rebuffs Fisher appeared, as the 1860s dawned, to be in complete control of New Brunswick. His government was successful and popular. Tilley, the provincial secretary, was doing most of the administrative work and looking after the affairs of state in general. When he wrote to Fisher in 1859 about serious financial problems, Fisher replied "dont be disheartened. It will all turn out for the best. . . ." He let Tilley find solutions while he concerned himself with crown cases in the law courts of the province. As attorney general that was his responsibility, but it seems that he left far too much to Tilley. For reasons that are unclear, some members of the council, especially A. J. Smith, wanted to be rid of Fisher. Perhaps his leadership was not strong enough. Perhaps he looked too much to the needs of his family and of Fredericton rather than the province. Perhaps it was his personality. One contemporary remarked on Fisher's "want of . . . frankness." "Privately he was not always to be understood – there was a non-commitalism about him, even in important matters, which many of his friends could not account for, as though he always felt that his best counsellor was himself, and the least he divulged to others it would be all the safer for his side." Whatever the reason, a tide began to swell against Fisher in 1858, and when he was implicated in a crown lands scandal of 1861, his colleagues dumped him immediately. Undeniably he used his position to exploit the crown lands for himself, his friends, and his relatives, yet he claimed he was taking the brunt of an attack which should have been more widely spread. He refused to admit a misdeed and he refused to resign as attorney general and thus "compromise his character and independence." Tilley, who emerged as leader, eventually had Fisher removed from the council and induced him to resign as attorney general rather than face further humiliation.

Thus ended Fisher's career as leader of the government. Its record was one of which he could be proud, for it covered constitutional, political, social, and economic reforms that were badly needed. The extent of Fisher's success can be gauged by the complete disintegration of the old "compact" and of all party opposition.

Following his removal in 1861, Fisher remained in the House of Assembly and was easily re-elected in the general election later that year. His constituents apparently believed he had not been treated fairly as did long-time friends such as Joseph Howe and George E. Fenety*. Fisher's personal following in the province and in the assembly posed a serious threat to Tilley. Certainly Tilley feared that Fisher might control the

Fisher

balance of power, and in February 1862 believed he faced an attempt to overthrow him, but this either failed or did not take place. For the next few years Fisher waited, looking forward, he claimed, "to uniting with Tilley" and to again becoming attorney general "at no distant day." Little separated them for they agreed completely on railway policy, especially the Intercolonial. It was confederation that was to reunite them.

Tilley went to the Charlottetown meeting of 1864 on Maritime union expecting little. Fisher was opposed to a Maritime union but supported a British North American federation. The totally unexpected conclusion of the Charlottetown conference and Tilley's commitment to confederation required remodeling of the Liberal party into a union movement, for the issue was so contentious that it required more support than Tilley had. Charles Fisher was therefore invited to join the New Brunswick delegation to the Quebec conference. His contribution does not seem to have been significant. He "preferred a legislative union if it were feasible," but said little except to complain that Canadian domination was excessive and unwarranted. Whatever his apprehensions, he agreed with the over-all conclusions of the conference and returned to New Brunswick confident that the province would follow the lead of the delegates.

New Brunswick was the only province in which the Quebec scheme was voted on in an election. In March 1865 the Tilley government and the confederation project were overwhelmingly defeated. Tilley and Fisher suffered personal defeat and all but six of their supporters fell before the anti-confederation platform of their old colleague, A. J. Smith. Fisher had concentrated his efforts in York County; there as elsewhere the suspicions of New Brunswickers that confederation was a plot originated in "the oily brains of Canadian politicians" could not be allayed.

Charles Fisher's role in reversing the decision of 1865 was central. The death of the chief justice, Robert Parker*, in November 1865 created a vacancy on the bench that was filled by John Campbell Allen*, MLA for York County. A by-election was called immediately, and Charles Fisher offered: "The strong feeling evinced for me . . . leave[s] me no honourable alternative but to step into the arena and throw myself upon you, my fellow subjects." It is unlikely that Fisher's motives were entirely altruistic and it is true that he treated confederation as a minor issue in the campaign, but in the final analysis this by-election was a key to the success of the movement. Confederation desperately needed a boost in the fall of 1865, and a defeat might have discouraged the

confederates into giving up. However from the moment of Fisher's victory over John Pickard by a two-thirds majority until Smith's resignation, forced upon him by an unconstitutional action of the lieutenant governor, Arthur H. Gordon*, the pressure in favour of confederation mounted steadily. Fisher's part in Smith's defeat centred on an amendment to the speech from the throne which he introduced on 12 March 1866 and which led to a four-week debate. The governor eventually forced Smith out of office, and Fisher became attorney general in the S. L. Tilley–Peter Mitchell* government that was to carry confederation. He had, as he predicted, returned to his position. It may be that he forestalled Smith's move because he did not wish Smith to claim any rewards – the *New Brunswick Reporter*, a Fisher paper, said as much, and John A. Macdonald* certainly suspected it.

One of Fisher's rewards was the voyage to England as a delegate to the London conference. There he was thought to be "a good fellow, who talks a good deal and has only a mediocre capacity." Following the success of the London conference and the creation of the new nation, Fisher was one of the first to present himself as a candidate for election to the dominion parliament. He was unopposed. Fisher definitely entertained hopes of being included in Macdonald's first cabinet; Tilley wanted him, but geographic considerations excluded two Saint John River men. After considerable hesitation Tilley selected Peter Mitchell as his fellow cabinet member. Fisher was left with much of the responsibility of reorganizing the New Brunswick government which had many problems caused by the mass exodus to Ottawa.

Because of his distinguished career and his Maritime origin, Fisher was selected to move the address in reply to the speech from the throne – the first speech in the new dominion parliament. That speech, which was received indifferently, marked the highlight of his federal career. As new tariffs and other policies were introduced, mostly over the objections of the New Brunswick members, Fisher recoiled into a defensive position. The selection of the north shore route for the Intercolonial was typical of the decisions he disliked: "*If you prefer the longest, the most expensive and the least productive line*, then by all means build the Northers; but do not flatter yourself with the belief that it will command much travel and traffic." Defeated on this as on other issues, Fisher, for the first time, seems to have lost interest in politics. With the appointment of his old associate, L. A. Wilmot, as lieutenant governor of New Brunswick in 1868, he sought the vacated judgeship. He was appointed after Tilley warmly supported him in a strong memo to Macdonald in September 1868, "I consider Mr. Fishers claims superior to any other man in New BN except Mr [John Hamilton] Gray." On 3 Oct. 1868 Fisher was appointed puisne judge of the Supreme Court of New Brunswick and on 14 October judge of the Court of Divorce and Matrimonial Causes.

As a judge Fisher was considered thorough and conscientious rather than profound. His devotion had been to politics more than to the law and the change of pace was extreme. Yet he was considered the leading constitutional lawyer of the day.

In his years as a judge Fisher found that most of the old bitterness of the early struggles disappeared, and he became a respected elder statesman. He and his wife Amelia were at the centre of Fredericton society and were especially active at the university which had awarded him a DCL in 1866 and which Fisher served as a member of the senate. Little is known of Mrs Fisher except that she was inarticulate. An apocryphal story is worth repeating because it may contain a germ of truth. On the occasion of Fisher's elevation to the bench Mrs Fisher asked "You'll be 'Your Honour' and what will I be?" He replied instantly, "You will be the same damned old fool you always were." Fisher remained alert and active until the end. On Saturday, 5 Dec. 1880, he was well; on Tuesday, 8 December, he was dead, apparently from an inflammation of the lungs.

Of all those who participated in the struggle both for responsible government and for confederation, Fisher has received the least attention and has never had a biographer. Historians have been content to incriminate the "corrupt Charles Fisher" with his "bad reputation, deserved or not." One statement is quoted widely as the final word on Fisher. The Duke of Newcastle [Henry Pelham Clinton] wrote: "I am not ignorant that Mr. Fisher is one of the worst public men in the British North American provinces and his riddance [1861] is a great gain to the cause of good government in New Brunswick." This statement, the crown lands scandal, and his apparent willingness to disregard principles in 1848 seem to be the major reasons for the denigration of Fisher. His not entirely attractive personality may also have contributed.

A more favourable interpretation is reached if one considers Fisher's attitude to parties on the one hand and the nature of colonial politics on the other. It seems clear that politics in New Brunswick differed little from politics in Nova Scotia or Canada. The "spoils" of office was an integral part of the system both in British North America and in Britain. Fisher got caught in the crown lands scandal, yet his exclusion from office was only temporary. His constituents and friends honestly believed he was treated unjustly, and S. L. Tilley, whose probity as a politician ranks as high as any, did not hesitate to recommend Fisher to the bench. Fisher's reputation was set by the opinions of young, inexperienced, and frequently arrogant individuals of the British colonial system such as Manners-Sutton, Gordon, and the Duke of Newcastle. Their views of either the people or the society in the colonies can hardly be accepted as definitive. Fisher in particular refused to defer to these officers and was singled out for this reason. A gentleman, by their definition, he may not have been, but a close examination of his career leads to the conclusion that he was a better man than most. A few years before his death he stated what might well have been his obituary: "My object is not personal aggrandizement; and I do not regard the gathering together of money as important, except for the sake of my family. I want to live and to act so, that when I die men may say of me, 'he left the impress of his mind on the institutions of his country.'"

C. M. WALLACE

[There is no Charles Fisher manuscript collection, but useful material is available in: N.B. Museum, Edward Barron Chandler papers; Tilley family papers. PAC, MG 24, B29 (Howe papers); MG 26, A (Macdonald papers); MG 27, I, D15 (Tilley papers). PRO, CO 188 (letters of Edmund Walker Head, John Henry Thomas Manners-Sutton, and Arthur Hamilton Gordon). University of New Brunswick Library, Archives and Special Collections Dept., Arthur Charles Hamilton Gordon papers, 1861–66.

Among the contemporary printed sources are: New Brunswick, House of Assembly, *Journals*, 1834–68; *Synoptic reports of the proceedings*, 1834–68. *Globe* (Saint John, N.B.), 1858–68. *Morning News* (Saint John, N.B.), 1839–65. *New Brunswick Reporter* (Fredericton), 1844–80. *Saint John Daily Telegraph and Morning Journal*, 1869–73. *Saint John Morning Telegraph*, 1862–68.

There is no biography of Fisher except for the short and inadequate ones in J. C. Dent, *Canadian portrait gallery*, IV, and *Biographical review, this volume contains biographical sketches of the leading citizens of the province of New Brunswick*, ed. I. A. Jack (Boston, 1900). Other sources include: G. E. Fenety, *Political notes and observations*, and his "Political notes," *Progress* (Saint John, N.B.), 1894, collected in scrapbooks in N.B. Museum and PAC.

Lawrence, *Judges of New Brunswick* (Stockton) is of some use for information on Fisher as is Hannay, *History of New Brunswick*, II. The latter has been largely superseded by MacNutt, *New Brunswick: a history*. D.G.G. Kerr, *Sir Edmund Head, a scholarly governor*, with the assistance of J. A. Gibson (Toronto, 1954) should be consulted along with J. K. Chapman,

Fisher

The career of Arthur Hamilton Gordon, first Lord Stanmore, 1829–1912 (Toronto, 1964). See also the following articles: A. G. Bailey, "The basis and persistence of opposition to confederation in New Brunswick," *CHR*, XXIII (1942), 374–97. J. K. Chapman, "The mid-nineteenth-century temperance movement in New Brunswick and Maine," *CHR*, XXXV (1954), 43–60. W. S. MacNutt, "The coming of responsible government to New Brunswick," *CHR*, XXXIII (1952), 111–28.

By far the most valuable study of Fisher is E. D. Ross, "The government of Charles Fisher of New Brunswick, 1854–1861," unpublished MA thesis, University of New Brunswick, 1954. C.M.W.]

FISHER, THOMAS, merchant miller; b. 3 March 1792 in Pontefract, Yorkshire, Eng., son of John Fisher and Mary Colley; d. 23 July 1874, in Toronto, Ont.

Thomas Fisher, who received a good education, was a merchant in Leeds, Yorkshire, by 1813 when he married Sarah Sykes. Three sons and one daughter were born to them in England, and three daughters in Upper Canada.

Leaving his family in England, Fisher emigrated to North America in 1819. He landed in New York, and spent three years partly in the United States and partly in Upper Canada looking for a good investment. In May 1820 he was given the right to locate 200 acres in Upper Canada as a farm. In 1821 he selected 100 acres in Nissouri Township (now East and West Nissouri), but did not receive the grant until 1823. Meanwhile, his family had joined him at York (Toronto) in 1821, and in 1822 he settled down as tenant of the King's Mill on the west bank of the Humber River, Etobicoke Township. The Nissouri lands were still undeveloped when he sold them in 1827.

The King's Mill was a saw mill, with a timber reserve of 1,100 acres, built in 1793 by the Queen's Rangers at the head of navigation, about 2½ miles above the mouth of the river. The Humber flooded each year making repairs to the dam costly and government policy towards the mill's tenants was so niggardly that few did more than patchwork. The property was dilapidated when Fisher took it over.

By 1829 Fisher had turned the mill into a profitable business. He had paid off back rent and other debts incurred by his predecessor, Josiah Cushman, and had begun to manufacture nails; he was also a merchant miller: a designation given to millers who acted as traders, shippers, storekeepers, and frequently as innkeepers, and who performed other services for their customers, labourers, and neighbours.

Fisher surrendered the timber reserve in 1834 and most of it was assigned for a rectory for Christ Church, Mimico. He had been a major contributor to the building of the church. He retained the King's Mill and was granted 100 acres of land with a mill site on it about 1½ miles south of Dundas Street. In 1835 he sold the King's Mill to William Gamble*, who added a grist mill, and on his own property Fisher built Millwood House, a grist mill, a store, and cottages for his labourers. As Millwood was hemmed in by the rectory, Fisher built roads north to Dundas Street and south to Milton Mills (the former King's Mill) where, under arrangement with Gamble, he sent his flour in summer. In winter he teamed his flour to Toronto. He was active in 1844 in the organization of the parish of St George's-on-the-Hill (Islington), as a contributor to its building in 1847, and as a parish officer until 1864.

In the prosperous 1840s Fisher began to mortgage his property and engage in speculative ventures, partly in properties and partly in expansion of his mill after a fire in 1847. He was unable to meet his commitments in 1849 when a number of export firms failed after the repeal of the British corn laws, and mill credits were tightened. A disastrous flood in 1850 washed out the dams on the Humber. Fisher got so into debt that in 1860 the mill was bought for a fraction of its value by Edward William Thomson* whose daughter Sarah Maria had married Edwin Colley Fisher, now working with his father.

After the flood Fisher left management of the mill mostly to his son, and took up another career. He had bought land at a crossroad where the village of St Andrews (now Thistletown) was taking shape. Here he built a store which he sold at a profit in 1857. He then retired from business.

Fisher had performed a number of public duties. As an officer of the West York militia, he had turned out with the regiment during the rebellion of 1837. He had been given responsibility for road improvements. He was appointed to the Court of Requests in 1836, made a justice of the peace in 1837, and a coroner in 1838.

NORAH STORY

Borough of Etobicoke, Clerk's Office, assessment rolls, 1851–60. Middlesex County Registry Office (London, Ont.), deed of sale, lot 11, concession 2, Nissouri Township, 16 Jan. 1827. Ontario Provincial Secretary's Office (Toronto), patent, 5 Jan. 1835, east half of lot 9, concession C, Etobicoke. PAC, RG 1, E3, 10, pp.169–72; 29, pp.12–15; 30, pp.156–57; 31, pp.60–63; 34, PT.3, p.28ff; L1, 29, p.412; 35, p.353; L3, 130, p.494; 190, no.136; 191, no.13; 196a, years 1822–25; RG 7, G16, C, 30, p.21; 36, p.51; RG 9, I, B5, 2, list of 1824; 3, list of 1827; 6, list of 1838; RG 31, A1, 1851, Etobicoke Township; 1861, Etobicoke Township; RG 68, 151, p.47. PAO, RG 1, C–IV, Etobicoke Township papers, Fisher to J. W. Gamble, 12 Dec.

1832; J. W. Gamble to [the civil secretary], 24 Dec. 1832; Nissouri Township papers, certificate of 4 Oct. 1826; RG 22, ser.7, 20, 28 May 1840; 25, 9 June 1858. St George's-on-the-Hill Church (Toronto), minutes of the vestry, 1848–64. York County Registry Office (Toronto), deeds relating to land sales and transfers, 1835–60. York County Surrogate Court (Toronto), will of E. W. Thomson, 1865.

Courier of Upper Canada (Toronto), 17 Sept. 1835. *Globe* (Toronto), 1 Nov. 1848, 23 July 1874. *Landmarks of Toronto* (Robertson), II, 771–72. *Toronto Mirror*, 12 July 1843, 15 Dec. 1845. *Toronto Patriot*, 1 Sept. 1835, 20 Sept. 1837, 17 May 1849. Upper Canada, House of Assembly, *Journals*, 1828, app.21, "Revenue accounts. Upper Canada. Names of persons licenced as innkeeper...." Edna-Mae Pickering, *Through the years at St. George's-on-the-Hill, Islington, Ontario, 1844–1969* (n.p., n.d.).

FLEMING, JOHN ARNOT, surveyor, artist, draughtsman, and topographer; b. 5 Dec. 1835 in Kirkcaldy, Scotland, youngest son of Andrew Greig Fleming and Elizabeth Arnot and brother of Sandford Fleming*; d. unmarried on 8 Jan. 1876 in Toronto, Ont.

John Arnot Fleming was educated in Kirkcaldy and came to Canada in 1847 with his parents. He attended the Toronto Academy under Thomas Henning. In 1861 he qualified as a provincial land surveyor and began his brief career in surveying.

Already, however, he had taken part in the events for which he is chiefly remembered. In 1857 he accompanied Henry Youle Hind* as his assistant on the expedition sent out to explore the routes to Red River. He was again Hind's assistant the following year on the expedition to the Assiniboine and the Saskatchewan rivers to explore the agricultural and settlement possibilities of the prairies. In the course of this expedition Fleming led a small party down the Saskatchewan River from Fort-à-la-Corne to the Red River Settlement by way of the Grand Rapids of the Saskatchewan and of Lake Winnipeg, enduring much bad weather and near starvation. His account of the journey is printed in Hind's report for 1859, and he also left sketches in pencil and water-colour.

Fleming was a cheerful and steady person. His work is distinguished by the clarity and accuracy of his pencil sketches, which have been described as "models of draughtsmanship," and the limpid beauty of his water-colours of the falls between Lake Superior and Red River and the great valleys of the plains west of Red River. These charming relics are a moment of vision in Canadian history, last glimpses of the prairies before settlement.

His family believed that Fleming's health never recovered from the hardships of the western expeditions. Between 1862 and 1870, however, he was engaged, under Sandford Fleming's supervision, in surveys on the Northern Railway in Ontario, and on the reconnaissance survey of the Intercolonial Railway, 1863–1864. In 1865 he was draughtsman in the office of the city engineer of New York. In 1870 and 1871 he explored a route for the Canadian Pacific Railway along the north shore of Lake Superior, his last recorded employment.

W. L. MORTON

Fifty-four sketches by John Arnot Fleming, 25 in water-colour and the rest in pencil, are in the John Ross Robertson Collection at the MTCL. His report on the journey he undertook in 1858 is printed in H. Y. Hind, *North-West Territory: report of progress, together with a preliminary and general report on the Assiniboine and Saskatchewan exploring expedition ...* (Toronto, 1859), 72–84.

PAC, RG 5, C1, 523. J. R. Harper, *Early painters and engravers in Canada* (Toronto, 1970). "John A. Fleming," Ont. Land Surveyors Assoc., *Ann. Report* (Toronto), no.35 (1920), 121–23.

FLEMING, MAY AGNES. *See* EARLY

FLETCHER, HENRY CHARLES, soldier, private secretary, and author; b. 28 April 1833 at Sussex Place, Regent's Park, London, Eng., son of Major-General Edward Charles Fletcher, magistrate of Kent, deputy-lieutenant for Kirkcudbright County, Scotland, and the Hon. Ellen Mary Shore, daughter of John, 1st Lord Teignmouth; d. 31 Aug. 1879 at Putney, Eng.

Henry Charles Fletcher's mother died when he was two years old and three years later his father married Lady Frances, daughter of Charles, 2nd Earl of Romney. In November 1850 Henry Charles obtained a commission as ensign in the Scots Fusilier Guards (and as lieutenant in the army). He saw active service in the Crimea in 1856, and promotion to captain (and lieutenant-colonel in the army) came in June 1859. He travelled to Canada with the 2nd Battalion in the Guards brigade at the end of 1861, when troops were sent out during strained relations between Great Britain and the United States following the *Trent* incident. He took the opportunity to see the American Civil War and was present at the battles of Williamsburg, Fair Oaks, and the Seven Days. General George Brinton McClellan showed him "every courtesy," had him pitch his tent near his own, and invited him to stay as long as he wished. Fletcher thus learned the power of the new American armies. His reports to General Sir William Fenwick Williams*, the commander-in-chief in North America, were brought to the notice of the Duke of Cambridge at the Horse

291

Guards. Returning home before his regiment, Fletcher married Lady Harriet, second daughter of Charles, 3rd Earl of Romney, on 24 Sept. 1863. He also published a three-volume *History of the American war*.

Fletcher appeared before the commission on military education of 1868–69, presided over by Lord Dufferin [Blackwood*], and there advocated that British infantry and engineer officers should be trained together as in the United States. This proposal was not accepted by the commission but Dufferin invited Fletcher to join it as a member for the second part of its investigation, the education of other ranks.

In 1872 Dufferin was appointed governor general of Canada. Because there were no troops in central Canada, he was not given a military secretary and therefore took an officer, Fletcher, as his private secretary to Ottawa. Fletcher's wife was considered a suitable companion for the Countess of Dufferin [Hariot Georgiana Hamilton*] in the bourgeois society of North America, and the Fletchers enjoyed the gay social life of Rideau Hall. The secretary's chief task was to develop a military spirit in Canada so that the Canadian government might be induced to make adequate provision for defence. He lectured to militia officers and others on the theme that the peaceful attitude of the United States, which then only had forces scattered along the Indian frontier, might change overnight and that every nation must have military forces at its disposal if it wished to survive. Dufferin forwarded Fletcher's memorandum on this subject to his ministers and to the War Office, and Fletcher published his lecture at his own expense. He suggested Canada should train its militia officers in permanent schools.

In 1869 Dufferin had obtained a report on the United States Military Academy for his commission on military education. Colonel Sir Patrick Leonard MacDougall*, its author, had stressed West Point's high moral qualities, which contrasted strongly with what the commission heard about the Royal Military College at Sandhurst. In April 1874, sent by Dufferin, Fletcher visited West Point and supplemented MacDougall's report to the effect that the great contribution West Point had made could be duplicated in Canada by a similar institution in which officers of all arms would be trained together. Fletcher's report was important in influencing Alexander Mackenzie* to establish the Royal Military College of Canada at Kingston in 1875.

The Canadian government offered Fletcher £80 as an honorarium for the report, but he courteously refused it. He had been promoted colonel in the army in 1874 and was considered for appointment as GOC Canadian Militia, but he preferred to return to his regiment in 1875 as major lest his professional career be jeopardized by long absence. Dufferin reported to the colonial secretary and the commander-in-chief that Fletcher had contributed substantially to the revival of the military spirit in the dominion; he was decorated with the CMG.

After his return to England, Fletcher was aide-de-camp to the Duke of Cambridge and a justice of the peace in Kent. He lectured to the Royal United Service Institution on the use of colonial forces in imperial wars. But he retired on half-pay in March 1879 and died at his residence, Spencer House, at the comparatively early age of 46, a few days after he had sold his commission. He left a son, and "other issue."

In Dufferin's opinion Fletcher was "not particularly brilliant or quick," but he was "sensible and trustworthy. . . . Everybody . . . liked him." Fletcher's *History of the American war*, although sound, shows little insight into the revolutionary changes taking place in warfare. Nevertheless Fletcher did much to foster the development of suitable military institutions in Canada and a comment in an obituary, that by his death the army lost an able and zealous soldier, is fully justified.

RICHARD A. PRESTON

H. C. Fletcher, *The defence of Canada; a lecture delivered at the Literary and Scientific Institute* (Ottawa, 1875); *History of the American war* (3v., London, 1865–66); *Memorandum on the militia system of Canada* (Ottawa, 1873); *Report on the Military Academy at West Point, U.S.* ([Ottawa, 1874]); "A volunteer force, British and colonial in the event of war," Royal United Service Institution, *J.* (London), XXI (1877), 631–58.

PAC, MG 26, A (Macdonald papers), 100, pp.39616–35; RG 9, II, A1, 85, f.9053; 604, pp.211–514. Public Record Office of Northern Ireland (Belfast), Dufferin papers, D 1071/H2/4, 16; D 1071/H2/5, 107; D 1071/H3/1, 8–10, 120–24, 182–86. [Blackwood and Herbert], *Dufferin-Carnarvon correspondence* (de Kiewiet and Underhill), 141–42, 157. Edward Walford, *The county families of the United Kingdom or royal manual of the titled and untitled aristocracy of England, Wales, Scotland and Ireland* (London, 1875), 361. *Gentleman's Magazine and Historical Chronicle* (London), CIII (1833), I, II. *Journal of the Household Brigade for . . . 1879* (London), XVIII (1879), 309.

FORMAN, JAMES, merchant and banker who was accused of embezzlement; b. in May 1795 at Halifax, N.S., eldest son of James Forman (1763–1854) and Mary Gardner; d. early 1871 in London, Eng.

James Forman was probably educated at the

Halifax grammar school. His father was a successful merchant in partnership with George Grassie, and it is likely that James was trained in the family business and worked with the Grassie family after his father's retirement in 1820. On 5 March 1821 Forman married Margaret Ann Richardson at St Matthew's Church, Halifax; they had two, perhaps three, sons.

James Forman was one of the men who petitioned the Nova Scotia assembly on 31 Jan. 1832 requesting incorporation of the Bank of Nova Scotia. The incorporation was granted on 30 March, and William Lawson* became the bank's first president; on 24 May the bank appointed James Forman its first cashier – a position equivalent to general manager. After a period at the Bank of New Brunswick in Saint John, where he studied its accounting system, Forman took up his new duties. When Forman's friend, Mather Byles Almon, succeeded Lawson in March 1837, the cashier was placed in a position of great trust which he maintained throughout Almon's 30-year presidency. During these years Forman was active in the community as a member of the Nova Scotia Literary and Scientific Society, treasurer of the Halifax Mechanics' Institute, a trustee for the Provincial Building Society, a member of the council of the Horticultural Association and International Show Society, and president of the North British Society of Halifax.

Although the Bank of Nova Scotia opened several new branches during Almon's presidency and Forman's tenure as cashier, its annual statements showed little progress. A partial explanation for this lack of success came to light in 1870 with the discovery by the accountant, J. C. Mackintosh, that over a period of many years James Forman had embezzled about half the bank's capital of £140,000 – a theft of $314,967.68. After his actions came to light, Forman transferred property worth $179,296.45 to the bank as partial coverage for the theft. Because of Forman's social position and the collapse of his health, the bank did not prosecute, despite an uproar in the local press. A rumour at the time said that Forman had taken the money to help his son who was in financial difficulty, and this supposedly brought public opinion to Forman's side. He quickly left Halifax and went to London where he died a few months later, probably early in 1871.

PHYLLIS R. BLAKELEY and DIANE M. BARKER

PANS, Nova Scotia House of Assembly petitions, Trade and Commerce, 31 Jan. 1832. St Matthew's Church (Halifax, N.S.), records, 1795, 1821, 1854, 1858. *Acadian Recorder* (Halifax), 14 Jan. 1878, 27 April 1925. *British Colonist* (Halifax), 6, 11 Aug. 1870. *Morning Journal* (Halifax), 9 April 1860. *Novascotian* (Halifax), 6 Nov. 1854. *Belcher's farmer's almanack*, 1864. *McAlpine's Nova Scotia directory, 1868–69. Annals of the North British Society of Halifax, Nova Scotia, for one hundred and twenty-five years ...*, comp. J. S. Macdonald (Halifax, 1894), 378, 388, 395, 396. *History of the Bank of Nova Scotia, 1832–1900; together with copies of annual statements* ([Toronto, 1900]), 43, 44, 46, 48, 50–51.

FOSTER, ASA BELKNAP, railway contractor and politician; b. at Newfane, Vermont, 21 April 1817, son of Stephen Sewell Foster*, a physician and politician, and Sally Belknap; d. at Montreal, Que., 1 Nov. 1877.

Asa Belknap Foster came with his parents to Frost (near Waterloo, Lower Canada), in 1822 and was educated in the village. In 1837 he returned to the United States where he joined his uncle, S. K. Belknap, a railway contractor, and for 15 years built railways in New England. He married Elizabeth Fish of Hatley, Lower Canada, in 1840; they had ten children.

Foster returned to Canada in 1852 and settled in Waterloo. He became both a merchant and an immensely successful contractor, building railways throughout Quebec and bordering areas. Foster served as president of the South Eastern Counties Junction Railway (later the South Eastern Railway), vice-president and managing director of the Canada Central Railway, managing director of the Brockville and Ottawa Railway, and director of the Bedford District Bank, and he attained prominence in Montreal business circles.

Foster entered politics in 1858 as a follower of George-Étienne CARTIER when he was elected in a by-election to the Legislative Assembly for Shefford. He had received the support of Lucius Seth Huntington*, a Liberal, both of them being opposed to the custom of non-resident members in the Eastern Townships. Huntington was elected for Shefford when Foster resigned in 1860 to run for the Legislative Council. Acclaimed for Bedford, Foster held the seat until 1867 when he entered the dominion Senate. Also in 1867 he was chosen the first mayor of the municipality of Waterloo, and from 1857 to 1869 was a lieutenant-colonel in the Shefford militia.

Foster was involved in the "Pacific Scandal," partly through his friend, George W. McMullen, the Canadian-born businessman from Chicago. McMullen, acting for a group of American businessmen bitter over their exclusion from the transcontinental railway company being formed in Canada in 1872, attempted to redeem some of the money they had advanced through Sir Hugh Allan* to the Conservatives (including Sir John A. Macdonald* and Cartier) during the 1872 election.

Franklin

The expedient tried was blackmail: on 31 Dec. 1872, McMullen visited Macdonald and demanded business concessions connected with the railway in exchange for not publishing incriminating documents concerning the 1872 campaign. Macdonald refused. Charges of corruption based on the documents were soon after made in the House of Commons by Huntington and the documents were later published.

Foster had been aware of the dealings between Allan and Macdonald and Cartier in 1872, and revealed this knowledge in a letter meant for publication which he wrote to McMullen, who was being much abused, in July 1873. The angry Conservatives assumed that it was Foster who gave McMullen's evidence, which helped to destroy Macdonald's government, to his friend Huntington and the Liberals. Foster, a provisional director of Allan's Canada Pacific Railway, refused to testify – as did the Liberals – before the royal commission investigating the scandal.

Belief in the apostacy of the Conservative senator was intensified by two agreements made by the new Liberal government under Alexander Mackenzie* in 1874 and 1875 under the authority of the Canadian Pacific Railway act of 1874. The first agreement, with the Canada Central Railway of which Foster was a leading figure, provided a subsidy of $12,000 per mile for the construction of the link between the village of Douglas, near Renfrew, Ontario, and the Georgian Bay branch of the Canadian Pacific Railway. The latter was to be constructed, under the second agreement, from Lake Nipissing to Georgian Bay. Although it was to "be considered as forming part of the Canadian Pacific Railway," it would "upon its completion be the property of the Contractor...."; the subsidy per mile was $10,000 and 20,000 acres of land. Senator Foster thus contracted to build and operate some 200 miles of line, from the C.P.R. terminus at Lake Nipissing to Georgian Bay as well as into the Ottawa valley. According to Alexander Mackenzie these lines would provide "the most direct line from . . . Georgian Bay to Montreal. . . ." Provision was made for cooperation between Foster's system and such north-south lines as the Northern Colonization Railway (which formed part of the Canada Central Railway) and the Kingston and Pembroke Railway. Foster had earned the epithet: "Canadian Railway King."

The Conservatives were convinced that these railway transactions were venal. Senator Robert Read* charged: "Now what is this for? Simply to pay the Northern Pacific [to which McMullen was connected] for their assistance through McMullen to defeat the late Government, and also Mr. Foster for the part he took in that transaction." According-

ing to J. G. Haggart*: "It was a notorious fact that the information used to turn out the late Government was furnished by the Hon. A. B. Foster, and everybody in the country expected that [he] would receive his reward. . . . And he did."

By the mid-1870s Foster was in financial trouble. In 1871 he had purchased major portions of the Brockville and Ottawa Railroad and of the Canada Central. He also bought a huge quantity of rails. His debt of $2,000,000 was to be paid in instalments, but by 1877 he was bankrupt, and at the insistence of the American competitors of his South Eastern line in Vermont he was briefly imprisoned in Vermont for debt. So vicious was competition, that in 1877 parts of that line were sabotaged and had to be "guarded by a sheriff and posse." The bankrupt promoter died of heart disease at Montreal. He had resigned his seat in the Senate in 1875, ending an undistinguished legislative career.

The Montreal *Gazette* commented: "He devoted himself to the construction of railways with an ardor which did not spring from any mere desire of pecuniary profit, but from enthusiasm in his profession." This assessment can be faulted without accepting the strictures of the Conservatives. Nineteenth-century railway promotion in Canada reveals little selfless idealism; David Mills* pointed out that "Corruption taints the majority of railroad enterprises from their inception to completion." Evidence in this area concerning Asa Belknap Foster is both documentary and circumstantial; he sometimes used the aphorism: "It is no good having friends if you can't use them." He was doubtless not an untypical railway man, although his career juxtaposes failure and success in an unusually dramatic manner.

DONALD SWAINSON

PAC, MG 26, A (Macdonald papers), 125. Canada, House of Commons, *Debates*, 1877; *Sessional Papers*, VIII (1875), PT.8, no.44. *Gazette* (Montreal), 1877. *Globe* (Toronto), 1873, 1877. *Montreal Witness*, 1877. *Can. biog. dict.*, II, 75–76. *Can. directory of parliament* (Johnson). *Can. parl. comp.*, 1873. *Dom. ann. reg.*, 1878. Creighton, *Macdonald, old chieftain*. H. A. Innis, *A history of the Canadian Pacific Railway* (Toronto, 1923; Toronto, 1971). Gustavus Myers, *History of Canadian wealth* (Chicago, 1914). J. P. Noyes, *Sketches of some early Shefford pioneers* ([Montreal], 1905), 7–90.

FRANKLIN, Lady JANE. *See* GRIFFIN

FRANKLIN, LUMLEY, businessman and amateur musician; b. probably *c.*1820 in England, son of Lewis Franklin, a Liverpool banker, and

Miriam Abraham; d. 3 Aug. 1873 in San Francisco, Calif.

At least as early in 1857 Lumley Franklin was in San Francisco, where his brother Selim had been in business since 1849, and in July 1858 he followed Selim to Victoria, Vancouver Island. Here the brothers established the firm of S. Franklin and Company, auctioneers and land agents, and were soon recognized as among the most able and highly respected members of the Jewish business community, whose growth had been stimulated by the gold rush to the Fraser River. In 1863 Lumley was president of the short-lived Eureka Copper Company. Both Franklins were active in the Victoria Philharmonic Society, which was organized at their place of business, the "Anchor Rooms," on 26 Jan. 1859. Lumley is said to have "had the advantage of an Italian musical education" and was a composer as well as a performer: at a concert in 1865 he sang his own setting of Byron's "Adieu, adieu my native shore." He was also active in masonic circles. While in San Francisco he had been a member of the Occidental Lodge no.22, A.F. & A.M., and in 1865 he became worshipful master of Victoria Lodge no.1085 of which he was considered a founding member.

In November 1865 Lumley Franklin was elected mayor of Victoria, and when the laying of the Atlantic cable was completed in July 1866 he signed the city's telegram of congratulation to the mayor of London. Urged to seek a second term he declined, but continued to take an active interest in public affairs, serving on the board of education for Vancouver Island and as president of the Mechanics' Literary Institute, and advocating the removal of the capital from New Westminster to Victoria. In October 1871 he left for England and returned a year later, after "a lengthened tour of Europe and Canada." In 1873 he was in San Francisco administering the estate of his brother Edward when he had a paralytic stroke; he died soon after, leaving a reputation as "a most amiable gentleman . . . always foremost in good works."

DOROTHY BLAKEY SMITH

PABC, Colonial correspondence, Lumley Franklin correspondence, 1863–71. *Colonist* (Victoria), 1858–73. *Daily Alta California* (San Francisco), 5 Aug. 1873. *Victoria Daily Standard*, 11 Aug. 1873. *Victoria Gazette*, 1858–59. R L. Reid, *Grand Lodge of British Columbia, A.F. & A.M.: historical notes and biographical sketches, 1848–1935* (Vancouver, B.C., n.d.), 9. David Rome, *The first two years: a record of the Jewish pioneers on Canada's Pacific coast, 1858–1860* (Montreal, 1942), 51–52. "Journal of Arthur Thomas Bushby" (Blakey Smith), "Biographical appendix," 177.

FYFE, ROBERT ALEXANDER, Baptist clergyman and educator; b. on 20 Oct. 1816, in the parish of Saint-Philippe, in the seigneury of Laprairie, L.C.; d. at Woodstock, Ont., on 4 Sept. 1878.

Robert Alexander Fyfe was the son of Scots who had emigrated from Dundee in 1809. He grew up on the farm, later learned the art of shoemaking and worked in lumber camps, and, in his late teens, moved with his family to the town of Laprairie where he clerked in a store. On 27 April 1835 he was baptized by the Reverend John Gilmour* and joined the Laprairie Baptist Church. Soon after, he determined to devote his life to the Baptist ministry.

His formal education was so limited that it took four years of arduous work for him to qualify for entrance into a theological college. The first year of this preparation was spent at the Hamilton Literary and Theological Institution in Hamilton, New York; the second, in the Baptist College in Montreal. In June 1837 he journeyed to Massachusetts hoping to enter the Newton Theological Institution, but he was advised to take more preliminary training, and this he received at the Manual Labor High School of Worcester, Massachusetts. Overcoming severe financial and health problems, he entered the Newton institute in October 1839, graduated in 1842, and was ordained to the ministry at the Brookline Massachusetts Baptist Church on 25 Aug. 1842.

Fyfe immediately left for Canada. In previous summers he had served as student pastor in the Ottawa valley with the Reverend Daniel McPhail. He went now to Perth, Canada West, where a church was organized on 31 Oct. 1842, and on 23 Feb. 1843 he married Jane Thomson, also the child of a Scottish immigrant, of Laprairie.

That fall Fyfe was prevailed upon by the governing body of the Montreal Baptist College to accept its principalship on an interim basis. He was deeply interested in education, but he did not feel prepared at that stage of his career to accept permanent charge of the college, although it was offered to him. After the arrival of a new president, John Mockett Cramp*, in the fall of 1844, Fyfe accepted a call to the March Street Baptist Church (later Bond Street, and then Jarvis Street) in Toronto, where he laboured with great success until 1848. During his term a new church was erected on Bond Street.

A son had been born in 1844, and a second son in June 1845. Fyfe experienced great tragedy when in June 1846 the two boys died within 17 days of each other and when a year later, in June 1847, his wife died after a long illness. In September 1848, in Massachusetts, he married Rebecca S.

Kendall of Brookline. They had no family and she survived him, living until May 1884.

Fyfe left Toronto in October 1848 to begin a second pastorate at Perth. After three successful years as pastor he resigned, having become discouraged over his failure to bring about closer cooperation between the Baptists of the eastern and western portions of the Province of Canada. The Baptists of the Ottawa valley and Montreal were mainly immigrants from Great Britain with traditions that differed from those of the Baptists farther to the west who were largely of American origin. The fundamentalism of the latter led to differences on a number of doctrinal questions between the two groups which were hard to reconcile. In December 1851 Fyfe accepted a call to the Baptist church in Warren, Rhode Island, and in November 1853 he became the minister of the First Baptist Church in Milwaukee, Wisconsin. Two years later he returned to the Bond Street Church in Toronto for a second pastorate.

After the failure of attempts to operate Baptist theological schools in Montreal (where the Baptist college had closed in 1849), and later in Toronto, Fyfe advocated the founding, for men and women, of a school for advanced literary education of which theological education would form a part. His plan was accepted, and he became the first principal of the Canadian Literary Institute at Woodstock, which opened in September 1860. Through the institute, he exerted great influence on all aspects of denominational life. After Fyfe's death, the theology department was moved in 1881 to Toronto as the Toronto Baptist College; in 1887 it was incorporated as McMaster University. The Canadian Literary Institute, which had remained in Woodstock, was in affiliation and it was renamed Woodstock College.

In 1859, with a friend, Fyfe had purchased the *Christian Messenger*, a denominational paper published in Brantford, and made its place of publication Toronto, renaming it the *Canadian Baptist* in 1860. He provided outstanding editorship until 1863 when he was succeeded by the Reverend Hoyes Lloyd. Fyfe was a champion of civil rights, and from the earliest days of his ministry was concerned with questions of public interest. He was a prolific writer and a forceful speaker. With vigour and clarity he entered into public discussions on clergy reserves, endowed rectories, the desectarianism of King's College, and, in later years, reform in the management of the University of Toronto even though he was then a member of that university's senate.

Fyfe was the leading Baptist of his time in Ontario and Quebec. He was a sincere Christian gentleman, respected by old and young alike. His ability as a pastor and evangelist is attested by the fact that two of the four congregations he served recalled him for a second term. He had a broad outlook and everything connected with the prosperity of his denomination was of interest to him. After his return to Canada in 1855 he did more than anyone else to unite the heterogenous body of Baptists in the two sections of the province. He gave leadership on boards, committees, and societies covering almost every activity connected with the organization of the Baptist churches. At the same time he was the wise counsellor of the small rural churches, the sincere friend and helper of missionaries, and the confidant of distraught pastors.

F. T. ROSSER

The Baptist encylopædia ..., ed. William Cathcart (Philadelphia, 1881) J. E. Wells, *Life and labors of Robert Alex. Fyfe, D.D.* ... (Toronto, n.d.). John McLaurin, "Robert Alexander Fyfe," *McMaster University Monthly* (Toronto), III (1893–94), 1–9.

G

GABOURY, MARIE-ANNE (Lagemodière), first white woman resident in the west, grandmother of Louis Riel*; b. 2 Aug. 1780 in Maskinongé, diocese of Trois-Rivières, Que., fifth child of Charles Gaboury (Gabourie) and Marie-Anne Tessier (Thésié); d. 14 Dec. 1875 at Saint-Boniface, Man.

Following the death of her father on 7 Dec. 1792, Marie-Anne Gaboury went into domestic service as the assistant housekeeper to the parish priest of Maskinongé. She remained there until her marriage, on 21 April 1806, to Jean-Baptiste Lagemodière (sometimes written Lagimonière, Lajimodière, and Lagimidière), a fur-trader from the Hudson's Bay Company territories, formerly from Maskinongé.

Immediately following her marriage she travelled with her husband by canoe from Montreal to Fort Gibraltar, at the junction of the Red and Assiniboine rivers in present-day Winnipeg. It was a long and arduous journey for a young woman and did not end until her arrival at a Métis encampment on the Pembina River in the autumn. At Fort Daer (Pembina, N.D.), on 6 Jan. 1807, her first child was born. The date being the church festival of the Epiphany, the baby girl was named Reine in honour of the Magi.

In the following spring the Lagemodières left Fort Daer for the Saskatchewan valley. At Cumberland House, Marie-Anne and her daughter were welcomed as the first white females to have penetrated thus far into the interior of the company's territories. Finally, at the end of August, they found themselves in the North Saskatchewan region, where they remained from 1807 until 1811. In 1810 Alexander Henry Jr met Lagemodière with his family at Paint Creek (Vermilion River). During these years Marie-Anne accompanied her husband on the many hunting expeditions which were the way of life of the free-trader in the west, thus experiencing to the full the hardships and privations that were the lot of the pioneer woman. Several more children were born to them.

When news arrived that a permanent colony was to be started under the initiative of Lord Selkirk [Douglas*] along the Red and Assiniboine rivers, Lagemodière and his family returned to Red River. They reached Red River towards the end of August, before the colony had really got under way, and continued their journey to Fort Daer. In the spring they returned to the newly established Red River Settlement. The North West Company, looking upon the establishment of the settlement as a scheme on the part of the HBC to cripple its trade, undertook to destroy the colony. Marie-Anne and her husband witnessed but took no part in the struggle between the Nor'Westers and the Selkirk settlers. However, in October 1815 Colin Robertson*, the HBC representative in the region, anxious to communicate with Lord Selkirk, employed Jean-Baptiste Lagemodière to carry dispatches to the earl in Montreal. He made the journey during the winter of 1815–16, on foot and unaccompanied, travelling over 1,800 miles and successfully completing his mission. On the return journey, however, he was taken prisoner by Indians acting in the interests of the North West Company. He was imprisoned in Fort William and detained there until August 1816, when he was released following the capture of the fort by Lord Selkirk.

Meanwhile Marie-Anne had been compelled to take refuge with the Indians. On the arrival of Selkirk, she was once more reunited with her husband in September 1816. For his services to the earl, Lagemodière was rewarded with a grant of land lying between the east bank of the Red River and the Seine in the vicinity of present-day Winnipeg. Here he built a frame house in which he, Marie-Anne, and their expanding family lived for many years. To the children already

mentioned, the Lagemodières added five others, one of whom, Julie (b. 1822), became the mother of Louis Riel.

On 7 Sept. 1855 Marie-Anne's husband died. She, however, lived to the advanced age of 95. Deprived though she so often was of comforts and necessities, her life had been one of selflessness and devotion, and she survived long enough to see the settlement of the west grow in strength and numbers, and her grandson become the father of the province of Manitoba.

GEORGE F. G. STANLEY

AJTR, Registre d'état civil. Archives de l'archevêché de Saint-Boniface (Man.). Archives de la Société historique de Saint-Boniface (Man.). *L'Écho de Louiseville*, 4 févr. 1970. HBRS, II (Rich and Fleming), 229. Morice, *Dict. hist. Can. et Métis*, 116–17. J. M. Gray, *Lord Selkirk of Red River* (Toronto, 1963), 124–26, 136, 170, 273, 284. Georges Dugas, *La première Canadienne du Nord-Ouest ou biographie de Marie-Anne Gaboury, arrivée au Nord-Ouest en 1806, et décédée à Saint-Boniface à l'âge de 96 ans* (Montréal, [1883]).

GADBOIS, ALBINE, *dite* **Marie de Bonsecours,** Sister of Providence of Montreal, foundress and directress of the Institution des sourdes-muettes de Montréal; b. 22 Jan. 1830, daughter of Victor Vandandaigue, *dit* Gadbois, of Belœil (Verchères County), L.C., and Angélique Daignault, of Longueuil (Chambly County), L.C.; d. 31 Oct. 1874 at Montreal, Que., and buried 3 Nov. 1874 in the cemetery of the community at Longue-Pointe.

Albine Gadbois belonged to a family that came from French Flanders to Quebec around 1675. Her father cultivated a rich, spacious farm at Belœil, bordering on the Richelieu River and at the foot of Mont Saint-Hilaire. He had a fortune which allowed him to give his eight children a private education in French, English, and deportment. As the children grew up, Victor Gadbois kept them informed of his affairs. Unknown to himself, he thus contributed to the establishment of a charitable institution for deaf and dumb girls. The story of Albine Gadbois and of three of her sisters who joined the Sisters of Providence is identified with that of the Institution des sourdes-muettes de Montréal.

In 1846 Abbé Charles-Irénée Lagorce, parish priest of Saint-Charles-sur-Richelieu, through the help given by Mother Marie-Émélie-Eugénie Tavernier*, foundress of the Sisters of Providence, opened a school for the deaf and dumb of both sexes in a room of the Asile, then the mother house of the sisters at Montreal. With the members of the house, Albine Gadbois, who was

Gadbois

still a novice, attended the Sunday catechism lessons, and showed a particular interest in them. She remembered a deaf-mute whom her parents had welcomed to their home, and the keen desire she had experienced to help children afflicted with deaf-muteness; she had said: "I will become a nun and care for these unfortunate ones." She joined the Sisters of Providence on 17 March 1847, and made her profession on 31 March 1849. Appointed then to the boarding-school at Longue-Pointe, Marie de Bonsecours found there quite by chance a deaf and dumb girl eight years old, and was appointed to devote herself exclusively to her education and that of the daughter of a friend of her family. On 19 Feb. 1851 the charitable organization for deaf and dumb girls was thus started.

As she saw her activity on a large scale, the foundress asked to go to study at L'Industrie (Joliette), where the Clercs de Saint-Viateur had just set up a class for deaf-mutes. This was in 1852, when Abbé Lagorce, who had recently joined the Clercs de Saint-Viateur, was returning from a study leave in France. Seven weeks later the young schoolmistress returned to Longue-Pointe with a third pupil. Then in 1853, when there were 10 deaf and dumb girls at the institution, she left for New York. As an ordinary student, in secular costume, she spent a year at the Peet Institution (New York School for the Deaf). With new theoretical and practical knowledge, Marie de Bonsecours resumed her teaching at Montreal in July 1854. She brought new pupils back with her, and thus increased the number to 20. She spent eight more months in New York in 1858, and went to the United States for several more study leaves.

The growing institution was already suffering from its inadequate quarters at Longue-Pointe. On 8 July 1858 her 32 pupils were therefore transferred to Saint-Joseph house, the community house of the Sisters of Providence, near the Asile. A government grant of $480 had by now been obtained, as well as contributions from some municipalities. The public responded generously to the institution's annual collection, but during its first 30 years it lived above all on the generosity of the parents and friends of the foundress. It is therefore true to assert that the Institution des sourdes-muettes owes its existence to the Gadbois family. Following their sister, Azilda, Malvina, and Philomène Gadbois gave to it the best part of their lives. The parents assigned all their wealth to it, even converting their farm, which had become a burden with the entry into religion of their seven daughters and the accidental death of their only son, into a branch establishment. The hospice La Providence Saint-Victor, at the foot of Mont Saint-Hilaire, still stands as a testimony to a family's generosity.

In its turn, Saint-Joseph house became too small. On 17 July 1863, a Montreal lawyer, Côme-Séraphin Cherrier*, gave it a piece of land in Rue Saint-Denis, in the Saint-Jacques district, on the edge of his property. The community of the Sisters of Providence was in poverty; Marie de Bonsecours had only $300 with which to put up a building. Fortunately, a gift of a few thousand dollars enabled her to meet the legitimate requirements of the undertaking. In July 1864 a house of rough stone opened its doors to deaf and dumb girls, at the spot where the present Institution des sourdes-muettes de Montréal stands.

Marie de Bonsecours spared no effort to forward her endeavours. At the beginning, under the influence of the Clercs de Saint-Viateur, she had adopted the mimic method of Abbé Charles-Michel de l'Épée. This famous 18th-century French educator had created for deaf-mutes a language of conventional signs. But Sister Marie de Bonsecours went to Europe in May 1870, to study a method of teaching which had been developed in Germany. This so-called oral method is based on the principle that the mutism of deaf-mutes is most often due to inability to hear, and not to lack of vocal organs. It is therefore possible to enable a deaf-mute to perceive speech through sight and touch, and thus to teach him gradually to pronounce sounds, syllables, words, and sentences. From May to July 1870, Sister Marie de Bonsecours visited institutions similar to her own in Belgium, France, England, and Ireland. In the autumn of 1870, in her own institution, she gave priority to the oral over the dactylological method, keeping the sign method for extreme cases only.

Sister Marie de Bonsecours' establishment was improved and expanded. In January 1872 a wing was added to the house in Rue Saint-Denis. It was the last building operation supervised by the foundress. In August 1874 she came back ill from a mission at Missoula (Montana), afflicted with cancer of the throat. She returned only to die at home, at the Institution des sourdes-muettes de Montréal, an establishment she had herself created, organized, and developed with tenacious will power and indefatigable charity. Of the 44 years of her life, Albine Gadbois, *dite* Sister Marie de Bonsecours, had devoted 24 to the education of deaf and dumb girls. By bringing them out of their intellectual and moral isolation she had restored them to themselves and to Canadian society.

ANDRÉE DÉSILETS

Nécrologies des Filles de la Charité Servantes des Pauvres, dites sœurs de la Providence de Montréal

Gamble

(1847–1891) (2e éd., Montréal, 1921), 124–43. Institution des sourdes-muettes (Montréal), *Au pas de la Providence; les étapes d'un centenaire, 1851–1950* (Montréal,[1950]). "L'Institution des sourdes-muettes, à Montréal," *La Semaine religieuse de Montréal*, 20 févr. 1892. *La Minerve* (Montréal), 5 nov. 1874 (obituary of S. Marie de Bonsecours).

GAMBLE, JOHN WILLIAM, manufacturer and politician; b. 5 July 1799, in the garrison at York (Toronto), U.C., eldest son of John Gamble*, loyalist and army surgeon, and Isabella Elizabeth Clarke of Connecticut; m., in 1822, Mary, daughter of James Macaulay* of York, by whom he had five children; in 1834, Matilda Atkinson, by whom he had three daughters; and thirdly the widowed Minerva Anne Niles; d. 12 Dec. 1873 at Pine Grove, Ont.

John William Gamble was brought up in Kingston but returned to York about 1815 because the family lands were concentrated in Etobicoke Township. He kept a store, first with his brother-in-law William Allan* and, from about 1822, with his own brother, William*, to whom he left most of the responsibility until the arrangement was dissolved in William's favour in 1827. By 1823 J. W. Gamble had settled on Mimico Creek in Etobicoke to engage in farming, milling, and management of his inheritance. He became a magistrate in 1827 and was chairman of General Quarter Sessions of the Home District from 1836 to 1842. In the absence of Church of England clergymen he read services in Mimico (now in the borough of Etobicoke) until Christ Church was built on land he gave in 1833.

In 1843 Gamble moved up the Humber to Pine Grove in Vaughan Township. Here he resided the rest of his life and built up a manufacturing complex: grist and flour mill, sawmill, distillery, and a cloth factory. He served 14 active terms on the district (later county) council as reeve of Vaughan Township from 1846, but, a Tory among Reformers, was only twice warden of York County. He supervised the Vaughan Plank Road Company and was parliamentary spokesman (1853–56) for the farmers, millers, and merchants who formed the Bank of Toronto. Gamble helped establish Christ Church, Woodbridge, on land he gave in 1851, and was an influential layman on the synod of the Church of England.

Gamble entered politics in 1838 when he ran as a "Constitutional" Tory and defeated George DUGGAN to represent the 1st riding of York in the assembly; his electorate, despite later changes, always included both Mimico and Woodbridge, and his political stronghold was Etobicoke. He opposed the union of the Canadas as threatening to extend Catholic influence, and stood in the election of 1841 for "attachment to the Throne and reverence for the Altar." The Reformer James Hervey Price* defeated him in the brawling poll, and again in 1847. Though returned comfortably in a swing against the followers of Robert Baldwin* in 1851 and 1854, Gamble was unsuccessful in 1857 against William Pearce Howland*, also prominent in milling and the grain trade. Tory and Orange interests brought him forward for the Legislative Council in October 1860, but he suffered a heavy defeat.

Gamble accepted "absolute Free Trade" in December 1847 but by February 1849 he had made protection his central political concern. The threat he saw to Canadian produce and manufacturing came from Britain which, with its overwhelming economic superiority, would keep Canada a permanent "plantation," a primitive source of raw materials and a helpless dumping ground for British products. Capital must be built up in Canada behind tariff walls, he felt, and not be allowed to leave the country as profit for British capitalists. Under tariffs the United States had grown rapidly, Gamble believed, and he admired Yankee enterprise which he knew from his early business connections with his mother's relatives in Boston. The annexation movement later in 1849 was viewed by Gamble as a serious threat to Canadian nationality and the British connection, and he feared it could lead to civil war. He joined the executive of the British American League and held the floor (flanked by Ogle Robert GOWAN) during much of its second convention. He made proposals for an elective governor and upper house. A pamphlet of his at this time concluded that *"To continue British, Canada must possess a prosperity as great and rapid in its growth as that of its neighbour, and with institutions not less favourable to popular liberty."*

From 1851 to 1857 Gamble fought in the legislature against reciprocity with the United States, and also against undiscriminating tariffs that would penalize American raw materials the province could never itself produce but would not protect it from Britain. He also stood for the clergy reserves and against fullblown separate schools. Nevertheless, he deplored, at this period, those Tories who refused to concede that theirs was an age of democracy. His faith in the basic common sense of the mass of the people came from his work on the county council and his views on education showed a loyalty to the local schools. His advocacy of protection, above all, fitted not only his own interests but his vision of a complex, self-reliant, close-knit Canadian society.

Gamble saw himself the squire of a god-fearing

Garvie

parish, a thriving village, to which his own industries were crucial, and a trusty yeomanry. He looked the squire too, broad and tall with a strikingly handsome head and a decisive manner. By the 1860s, however, Gamble had lost his last election, some of his chief causes had been overthrown or bypassed, and various family enterprises had crumpled in the depression of the late 1850s. He turned to genealogy for solace and compiled *Family records*. Its epigraph revealed a retreat to hard-shelled Toryism: "My son, fear thou God and the King, and meddle not with them that are given to change."

BARRIE DYSTER

J. W. Gamble edited *Family records of the Gambles of Toronto* (Toronto, 1872), and was the author of *Letter on Lord Grey's despatch of 31st March, 1848, relative to Canadian customs duties* (Toronto, 1849); *Memoir of Isabella Elizabeth Gamble* (Toronto, 1859); *Produce tables, showing the value of any quantity of grain, the standard weight of which is sixty pounds to the Winchester bushel* (Toronto, 1844); *Speech on the commercial policy of the country* (Toronto, 1852); *To the members of the Yorkville branch of the British American League* (n.p., [1850]).

MTCL, Baldwin papers, entries for J. H. Price; Boulton papers, Gamble to G. S. Boulton, 15 April 1853. PAC, MG 24, D16 (Buchanan papers), pp.23129–40. *Globe* (Toronto), July 1854, December 1857, 3–6 Oct. 1860. *Leader* (Toronto), July 1854, December 1857, 28 Sept. 1860. *Mail* (Toronto), 13 Dec. 1873. *Patriot* (Toronto), 30 Jan. 1838, January 1848, December 1851. *Arthur papers* (Sanderson). British American League, *Minutes of the proceedings of the second convention . . .* (Toronto, 1849). *J. of Education for Ont.*, XXVII (1874), 9. *Town of York, 1815–1834* (Firth). *Christ Church, Woodbridge, Ontario, 1842–1967* (n.p., [1967]). Creighton, *Macdonald, young politician*. *Landmarks of Toronto* (Robertson), I, 16; V, 321. Joseph Schull, *100 years of banking in Canada, a history of the Toronto-Dominion Bank* (Vancouver, Toronto, Montreal, 1958). Samuel Thompson, *Reminiscences of a Canadian pioneer for the last fifty years; an autobiography* (Toronto, 1884). H. O. Tremayne, *One hundred years old; a sketch of the history of Christ Church, Mimico, 1827–1927* (n.p., [1927]).

GARVIE, WILLIAM, journalist, scholar, and lawyer; b. in the West Indies in 1837, son of John Garvie, came to Halifax, N.S., with his Scottish parents; d. at Hyères, France, 15 Dec. 1872.

Garvie was probably educated at King's College, Windsor, Nova Scotia, and at the University of Edinburgh. His initial training was in classics, and upon his return to Halifax from Scotland he became a private tutor at the newly revived Dalhousie College. Garvie's interests soon took a different turn; he was one of those rare spirits endowed with intelligence, humour, and sensiti-

vity, from whom the role of tutor never required, nor commanded, his full energies. In 1863, with Edmund M. MCDONALD, he founded the *Halifax Citizen*, a tri-weekly newspaper.

Halifax at that time had a constellation of able newspapers and editors, but even among these the *Citizen* was conspicuous. It came into its own in 1864 with confederation, an issue which first appeared upon Nova Scotia's horizon in July 1864. The *Citizen*'s editorials (probably Garvie's) against the federal principle were the paper's main weapon in opposing the Quebec resolutions, and were used with considerable effect in November and December 1864. Even more effective was Garvie's famous satire, *Barney Rooney's letters on confederation, botheration and political transmogrification*. Like all satire, *Barney Rooney's letters* have an evanescent quality, much depending on personal knowledge that only contemporaries could have. But the *Letters* make lively reading even now as can be seen in the following attack on Charles Tupper* and Jonathan MCCULLY:

"'Sir,' sez Tupper, as he dried the bottom iv his tumbler, and held it handy to D'Arcy's ladle, 'the well understood wishes iv the people are so notoriously in favor iv this scheme that it would be a reckless and infamous policy to put them to the trouble of expressing themselves in a special vote upon it. . . . My dear McCully, I am sure you will agree with me. . . .'

"'My dear Tupper,' sez McCully, 'yes – no – that is, I mean yes, – or rather no; but I want to see you privately about it. . . .' "

In 1866 Garvie gave up his interest in the *Citizen*, and, at the age of 29, went to Lincoln's Inn to study law. He won a first prize and an exhibition in constitutional and legal history which he held 1868–70, and was called to the bar in Lincoln's Inn in 1869. He was still a strong anti-confederate, and while in England supported with all his energy the Nova Scotian anti-confederate missions to London in 1866, 1867, and 1868.

He returned to Nova Scotia in 1870 to establish a legal practice in Halifax, and in 1871 was appointed to the Executive Council of the province as commissioner of public works and mines. He was returned for Halifax County in the provincial election of May 1871. When the new assembly opened, 22 Feb. 1872, Garvie was too ill to attend, but an attack on the government in the house brought him from his bed despite the expostulations of friends. There he made an impassioned and powerful speech in support of the government on 24 Feb. 1872. It was the first and last day he was ever in the house. Already ill with consumption, a disease that had struck down three others of his family, he went to the south of France later in 1872 in the vain hope of arresting the disease. He died at Hyères, 15 Dec. 1872. "Everyone who stood in the presence of William Garvie," wrote the *Acadian Recorder*, "felt the power of the man." The *Morning Chronicle* added, "Nil tetigit quod non ornavit."

P. B. WAITE

PANS *Report, 1948*, app.C, 35–56. *Acadian Recorder* (Halifax), 16 Dec. 1872. *Morning Chronicle* (Halifax), 17 Dec. 1872. Benjamin Russell, "Reminiscences of a legislature," *Dal. Rev.*, III (1923–24), 5–16. M. J. Shannon, "Two forgotten patriots," *Dal. Rev.*, XIV (1934–35), 85–98.

GASPÉ, PHILIPPE-JOSEPH AUBERT DE. *See* AUBERT

GAUTHIER, AMABLE, sculptor and architect; b. 11 Nov. 1792 at Saint-Jean-Baptiste-de-Nicolet, L.C., son of Antoine Gauthier and Gosephte Girardin; d. 30 June 1873 at Maskinongé, Que., and buried 3 July at Saint-Barthélémi (Berthier County).

Amable Gauthier was orphaned as a boy, and his uncle found work for him at the studio of the sculptor, Louis-Amable Quévillon*, the head of Les Écorres (an art studio) at Saint-Vincent-de-Paul (Laval). According to tradition the young apprentice, receiving free board and lodging while learning his trade, shared with his companions in the master's undertakings. In this studio, the largest in the region, they were trained in sculpture, but also in the art of ornamentation by which an architectural creation is embellished and completed. Several of the apprentices, under Quévillon's influence, were also to take up architecture. Thus Gauthier, with his master's direction, worked on the churches at Lavaltrie, Saint-Ours, and Maskinongé.

After the master's death in 1823, Gauthier took up residence at Saint-Barthélémi, near Berthier, and opened his own studio. In his turn, he developed around him a group of bright young architects and sculptors. He remained at Saint-Barthélémi until about 1850, and then went to Maskinongé to live. During the first years of his career he devoted himself to sculpture, and at the same time engaged in business. It was only after 1844 that he adopted the title of architect and contractor.

During half a century of work as a sculptor and architect, Gauthier, whom Gérard Morisset* has called the "prince" of Quévillon's pupils because of the quality and quantity of his production, completed innumerable undertakings. Among the best known are the church of Sainte-Élisabeth at Berthier; the churches of Saint-Viateur and Saint-Paul at Joliette; the church at Berthier, which he restored and decorated with Alexis Milette; the famous statue of St Cuthbert, the altars of the church of Saint-Isidore at Laprairie, and the pulpit of the church of Saint-Barthélémi, sculpted at the age of 80.

Amable Gauthier had been promoted to the rank of militia captain in 1833, which did not prevent him from devoting himself to the nationalist cause: in 1837, for example, he hid two refugees in his own house.

Gauthier had married Euphrosine Gendron before his arrival at Saint-Barthélémi. They had at least 15 children, several of whom died in infancy. Their son Agapit, a sculptor of promise, died at the age of 25. Louis-Zéphirin, who was also trained in his father's studio, became known particularly for his extensive work as an architect. He built more than 100 churches, among them those of Hull and Aylmer in Gatineau County.

JEAN COUTU

AJTR, Registre d'état civil, paroisse Saint-Jean-Baptiste-de-Nicolet, 1792. Archives judiciaires de Nicolet (Qué.), Registre d'état civil, paroisse de Saint-Barthélémi. PAC, MG 30, D62 (Audet papers), 13, p.766. Gérard Morisset, *Coup d'œil sur les arts en Nouvelle-France* (Québec, 1941), 35–39. Émile Vaillancourt, *Une maîtrise d'art en Canada* (Montréal, 1920).

GAUTHIER, FÉLIX-ODILON, lawyer, recorder for Quebec City, judge of the Superior Court; b. 18 Aug. 1808 at Quebec, son of Augustin Gauthier and Marie Trudelle (Trudel); husband of Marie-Sophie Lapane; d. 29 April 1876 at Montmagny, Que.

Félix-Odilon Gauthier, whose father was the treasurer of Quebec City from 1851 to 1868 and one of the founders of the society of St Vincent de Paul in Canada, studied at the Petit Séminaire of Quebec, and then received legal training under Jean-Baptiste-Édouard Bacquet. He was called to the bar in 1833, and for 23 years carried on his profession at Quebec. In 1847 he was a captain in the 3rd Battalion of Quebec militia.

In 1856 the town prevailed upon the legislature to create a recorder's court, the recorder's role being to ensure the collection of debts and fines and to judge certain offences committed in the town. The court sat every day in a room in the town hall. The recorder was therefore a highly placed municipal official, appointed by the crown, and he drew a salary greater than that of the mayor. Félix-Odilon Gauthier was the first to hold the office, from 1856 to 1860. At a time when Quebec was the principal port of entry into Canada, his post was not a sinecure. Each summer brought its procession of unruly sailors.

In 1860 Gauthier accepted the post of judge of the Superior Court for the newly created district of Montmagny. For 10 years he discharged his duties, and earned the respect of the population. When he retired on 27 May 1870 he remained at Montmagny, where he died six years later. He was buried in the cemetery of that town.

PIERRE SAVARD

ASQ, Fichier des anciens du séminaire. Drolet, *Ville de Québec*, III, 17–19. P.-G. Roy, *Les juges de la province de Québec*, 235.

GAUVREAU, FERDINAND-EDMOND, Roman Catholic priest; b. 12 Sept. 1806 at Quebec, L.C., son of Louis Gauvreau and Marie-Anne Barbeau; d. 2 May 1875 at Saint-Flavien, Quebec.

Ferdinand-Edmond Gauvreau studied theology at the seminary of Nicolet and was ordained on 20 Sept. 1828. Almost immediately he was appointed curate at Memramcook, New Brunswick, where he arrived in October. He was parish priest of this large mission from June 1829 until July 1832, when, exhausted physically and emotionally, he returned to Quebec. In October he was appointed parish priest at L'Ange-Gardien (Montmorency County). In November 1833 he became the first parish priest of Saint-Sylvestre, Lotbinière County, and while there he founded the neighbouring parish of Saint-Ferdinand (now Bernierville) in Megantic County in 1834. Gauvreau returned to the Memramcook mission in December 1836 and remained there until his appointment to Tracadie, N.B., in January 1852.

At Tracadie, during the following 20 years, Gauvreau accomplished the most significant work of his career among the 25-odd inmates of a leprosarium transferred from nearby Sheldrake Island in 1849. The plight of the lepers had improved, thanks in part to the newly built institution and the proximity of the inmates to family and friends in Tracadie. Nevertheless, discontent and insubordination, engendered by insufficient, untrained, and poorly motivated staff, as at Sheldrake, soon turned to open hostility, evasion, and violence. Gauvreau became intensely preoccupied not only with the physical condition of the lepers, but also with the despair which consumed their minds and spirit. As chaplain of the institution and as a member and later chairman of the Board of Health for Gloucester and Northumberland counties, he pleaded, in correspondence with government officials and in the newspapers, for more humane treatment and improved general conditions. His efforts were finally rewarded in

1868 when the provincial government agreed to transfer the administration of the leprosarium to six nuns of the Hôtel-Dieu of Montreal [*see* CÉRÉ]. Contemporary views attribute the new hope and dignity which henceforth emanated from the inmates of the institution to the work of this group of dedicated women.

Gauvreau's health began to fail him soon after this achievement at Tracadie, and worsened during 1870. In September 1871 he returned once more to Quebec. He spent his final years as parish priest at Saint-Flavien (Lotbinière County).

BERNARD POTHIER

Archives acadiennes, Université de Moncton, Archives paroissiales de Saint-Thomas (Memramcook, N.B.), 1828–52. Gloucester County Court (Bathurst, N.B.), Gloucester County records, 21 (1969). N.B. Museum, Edward Barron Chandler papers, political correspondence, 1829–65; New Brunswick, Gloucester County land grants, 1842. *Lovell's province of New Brunswick directory for 1871* (n.p., n.d.). Allaire, *Dictionnaire*. R.-É. Casgrain, *Histoire de la paroisse de l'Ange-Gardien* (Québec, 1902). F.-M. Lajat, *Le Lazaret de Tracadie et la Communauté des religieuses hospitalières de Saint-Joseph* (Montréal, 1938). MacNutt, *New Brunswick*. L.-E. Cousineau, "M. l'abbé François-Xavier Lafrance, fondateur du Lazaret de Tracadie et 'préfondateur' du collège Saint-Joseph de Memramcook," *Revue canadienne*, new ser., XVI (1915), 481–95. Édouard Lefebvre de Bellefeuille, "Les lépreux de Tracadie," *Revue canadienne*, VII (1870), 545–74. P.-G. Roy, "Saint-Ferdinand d'Halifax," *BRH*, III (1897), 17. "Saint Ferdinand d'Halifax," *BRH*, XXXVI (1930), 606. F. L. Whitehead, "Leprosy in New Brunswick: the end of an era," CMA *Journal*, 97, no.21 (1967), 1299–1300.

GEDDIE, JOHN, Presbyterian clergyman and missionary; b. 10 April 1815 in Banffshire, Scotland, only son of John Geddie and Mary Menzies; d. 14 Dec. 1872 at Geelong, Australia.

John Geddie's family immigrated in 1817 to Pictou, Nova Scotia, then the centre of the timber trade in the province. There they joined the Secession Church under Dr Thomas McCulloch*. John was educated at the Pictou grammar school and Pictou Academy. During his formative years the young man worked with his father as a clockmaker, but spent many hours reading books sent by the London Missionary Society. When he was 19 he made a public profession of religion and enrolled in theology courses under Dr McCulloch. Geddie was licensed to preach by the presbytery of Pictou on 2 May 1837. After working in various congregations he was called to Cavendish and New London, Prince Edward Island, on 13 March 1838 and was ordained there. On 21 Sept. 1839 at Antigonish, N.S., he married Charlotte Lenora

Harrington MacDonald, who was to bear him eight children.

The young minister longed to undertake missionary work although, at that time, no branch of any Presbyterian church in the British colonies was actively involved in missions. Geddie organized a missionary society in his own church and persuaded other congregations to do the same. He also wrote letters to the local Island papers and to the *Presbyterian Banner*, and brought his suggestions for missionary work before the presbytery of P.E.I. and the synod of Nova Scotia. Finally a board of foreign missions was appointed with the Reverend James Waddell as recording secretary and John Geddie as corresponding secretary. At a synod meeting in July 1845 the board reported that $1,000 had been collected; the synod, by a vote of 13 to 12, decided that the board should select a field "and negotiate with candidates for occupying that field as soon as possible." The New Hebrides was chosen and John Geddie, who had volunteered, was selected as the potential missionary.

Geddie spent the next year preparing himself for the new life. At the offices of the *Eastern Chronicle* in Pictou, he learned to operate a printing press, which he would take with him; he studied the rudiments of house building and shipbuilding; he learned to identify and treat tropical diseases. Shortly after their designation service at Pictou on 3 Nov. 1846, Geddie, his wife, and their two small children sailed from Halifax. They spent eight months in Samoa learning the language, then settled in July 1848 at Aneiteum, the most southerly of the New Hebrides. There they encountered tropical storms, strange new diseases, and suspicious natives, described as heathen cannibals. By the end of the second year Geddie reported that ten people were attending his services, but signs of success began to increase rapidly thereafter.

Geddie organized a school which the natives began to attend, and he printed school books in their language on his press. His wife, a doctor's daughter, dispensed medicines and attempted to discourage the natives from following some of their old customs. To prevent the habit of strangling widows, she took the women into her home. In 1857 the Geddies were joined by the Reverend George N. Gordon* and his wife, who were killed by natives in 1861. In 1863 a mission vessel, *Dayspring*, was sent from Pictou to assist in the work. The money to build her had been raised mainly from Sunday school collections and mite boxes, one of which was in practically every Presbyterian home in the area. Aboard *Dayspring* were more missionaries including the Reverend James Douglas GORDON, to carry on the work of his slain brother, the Reverend Donald Morrison and his wife, and the Reverend William McCulloch, son of Thomas McCulloch.

After 15 years at their post Geddie and his wife returned to Nova Scotia on furlough. While in Canada Geddie received a DD from Queen's University at Kingston, but he spent most of his time in Nova Scotia visiting churches and recounting the dramatic tale of the mission. He also worked at revising his translation of the Book of Psalms into Aneiteumese.

The Geddies were back in Aneiteum on 5 Sept. 1866, but the missionary's health was deteriorating. He spent the remaining years of his life in the New Hebrides and in Australia mainly working on his translations of various books of the Bible into Aneiteumese. He finished a translation of the New Testament, and at the time of his death was working on the Old Testament.

John Geddie's death was widely reported in the Nova Scotia press where his work had been greatly admired. As a memorial a fund of $6,000 to assist the widows and orphans of missionaries was announced by the *Home and Foreign Record of the Presbyterian Church of the Lower Provinces* in May 1873.

PHYLLIS R. BLAKELEY and DIANE M. BARKER

Maritime Conference Archives of the United Church of Canada, Pine Hill Divinity Hall (Halifax, N.S.), Dr John Geddie scrapbook, letters of the Reverend John Geddie, 14 Jan. 1845–May 1870, extracts from his journal; Presbyterian Church of Nova-Scotia (Secession), Minutes of the proceedings of the synod, 3 July 1817–15 July 1842; Presbyterian Church of Nova Scotia, Minutes of the proceedings in the synod, 4 July 1843–4 Oct. 1860; Presbyterian Church of the Lower Provinces of British North America, Minutes of the synod, 4 Oct. 1860–1875.
Acadian Recorder (Halifax), 12 March 1873. *Christian Instructor, and Missionary Register, of the Presbyterian Church of Nova Scotia* (Halifax, then Pictou, N.S.), I (1856)–V (1860). *Eastern Chronicle* (Pictou, N.S.), 1843–65. *Home and Foreign Record of the Presbyterian Church of the Lower Provinces of British North America* (Halifax), I (1861)–XV (1875). *Missionary Register of the Presbyterian Church of Nova-Scotia* (Pictou, N.S.), 1 (1850)–7 (1856). J. W. Falconer, *John Geddie, hero of the New Hebrides* (Toronto, [1915]). J. P. MacPhie, *Pictonians at home and abroad* (Boston, Mass., 1914). George Patterson, *Missionary life among the cannibals: being the life of the Rev. John Geddie, D.D., first missionary to the New Hebrides; with a history of the Nova Scotia Presbyterian mission on that group* (Toronto, 1882).

GÉLINAS, ÉVARISTE, journalist, federal civil servant; b. 1840 at Saint-Barnabé, Saint-Maurice

Gélinas

County, not far from Yamachiche, L.C., of the second marriage of Joseph Gélinas, with Théotiste Hudon-Beaulieu; d. 7 Jan. 1873 at Ottawa, Ont.

According to Benjamin Sulte*, Évariste Gélinas' family was descended from Étienne Gélineau (he signed Gellyneau or Gélineau), who was born at Saintes, the capital of Saintonge, and who had emigrated to Canada with his son Jean in 1662. His grandsons were among the first to make their home at Yamachiche, where they had numerous descendants with the names Gélinas, Gérin, Lacourse, and Bellemare.

In his 13th year, in October 1852, Évariste Gélinas entered the college and seminary of Nicolet to receive a classical education, which he completed in 1860. A philosophy student, he had been elected president of the college in 1859, the same year the establishment acquired a distinguished superior in Abbé Louis-François Laflèche*. Since his return from the Canadian west in July 1856 Laflèche had had unrivalled influence on the students, thanks to his lively eloquence and fluency as a teacher and his ascendancy as a priest who for 12 years of his life had been a missionary engaged in spreading the gospel.

Shortly after leaving the college, and following in the footsteps of Antoine Gérin-Lajoie* and Raphaël Bellemare, both inhabitants of Yamachiche and his relatives, Gélinas joined *La Minerve*, and was responsible for almost all the editorial work from 1861 to 1865. Being at the head of the principal Lower Canadian newspaper, a Conservative party organ, he had to manœuvre in difficult circumstances: not the least of these were three general elections, three changes of ministry, and particularly the alliance that George-Étienne CARTIER, then at the height of his political power and enjoying the clergy's support, made, to the stupefaction of his opponents, with George BROWN, in order to prepare the way for confederation. The Liberal journals such as *Le Défricheur*, directed by Jean-Baptiste-Éric Dorion*, *Le Pays* under Charles Daoust* (in December 1863 he had succeeded Louis-Antoine Dessaulles* as editor), Médéric LANCTOT's *L'Union nationale*, and finally *L'Ordre* denounced this alliance, and sought to win the clergy's trust. "It is our right," the journalist of *L'Ordre* wrote on 4 July 1864, "to make a proud appeal to the sympathies of the clergy of the country. To wish to deny the enormous influence the clergy has exercised for some years in our country's political affairs would be to lie to our conscience, and an act of the most cowardly hypocrisy. Without a doubt, this influence has been exerted on the side of the Conservative party only under the honest and patriotic impression that thereby the preserva-tion of religion and consequently of nationality was being assured. Today all is unmasked!"

Évariste Gélinas replied in his best vein to this self-seeking invitation. In *La Minerve* of 9 July 1864 he gave an example of his style, and of the level of polemics at that time: "The Rouge press . . . finds itself suddenly smitten with a noble passion for what was previously the butt of its sarcasm. It becomes national, patriotic, nay, religiously minded. Behold, it is now *the high-principled press*! Why, it even goes so far as to woo the clergy; it no longer fears either the stole or the holy water!" Attacking at the same time Dessaulles and the other liberal journalists who, logically to them, favoured Italian unification and consequently wished to see the disappearance of the Pope's temporal power, which Catholics as a whole then considered essential for the country's spiritual independence, Gélinas added vehemently: "You, the supporters of Catholicism, nonsense! But are you even Catholics? How long have you ceased to be free thinkers? And dear Garibaldi, you would abandon him outright! Thankless individuals!"

These four years of intense labour in the field of journalism had impaired his health. In 1865, for a rest, Gélinas went to Europe to travel. On his return some months later, he obtained from the Conservative party, which he had served loyally, the post of supernumerary first class in the Department of Militia at Ottawa. During the leisure that his occupation as a public servant left him, Évariste Gélinas returned to journalism, but as a freelance writer; he wrote witty articles for *La Minerve* and *L'Opinion publique* which he signed with the initials C. T. or the pseudonym Carle Tom or as "Un Solitaire." These sparkling *causeries* raised him straightway to the level of a Hector Fabre*, who on Gélinas' death at the young age of 33 rendered homage in *L'Événement* of 10 Jan. 1873 to his rival's talent as a humorist: "A collection of his chronicles would form a piquant volume to which one might give the title of *Comédie humaine*."

On 3 Sept. 1862, at Quebec, Évariste Gélinas had married Mathilde, the second daughter of Étienne PARENT; she bore him four sons.

PHILIPPE SYLVAIN

ANQ, Collection Chapais, Fonds Langevin, É. Gélinas à H.-L. Langevin, 8 nov. 1864. St Joseph's Church (Ottawa), Register of burials. *Le Canadien* (Québec), 10 janv. 1873. *Le Constitutionnel* (Trois-Rivières), 8 janv. 1873. *Le Courrier de l'Outaouais* (Hull), 8 janv. 1873. *L'Événement* (Québec), 10 janv. 1873. *Le Journal des Trois-Rivières*, 9 janv. 1873. *L'Opinion publique* (Montréal), 30 janv. 1873. *L'Union des Cantons de l'Est* (Arthabaska), 9 janv. 1873. Tanguay, *Diction-*

naire, IV. F.-L. Desaulniers, *Les vieilles familles d'Yamachiche* (4v., Montréal, 1898–1908), II, 197, 237. J.-A.-I. Douville, *Histoire du collège-séminaire de Nicolet, 1803–1903, avec les listes complètes des directeurs, professeurs et élèves de l'institution* (2v., Montréal, 1903), I, 323, 454; II, 180. Benjamin Sulte, "Nos écrivains d'il y a cinquante ans," *Le Bien public* (Trois-Rivières), 5 Sept. 1918.

GERMAIN, CÉSAIRE, notary and school inspector; b. in 1808 at Saint-Vincent-de-Paul (Laval), L.C., son of Jean-Baptiste Germain and Marie Dusablé; d. 16 April 1874 in the same municipality.

Césaire Germain received his legal training from Jean-Baptiste Constantin, and was admitted to the profession of notary on 6 April 1830; an active scrivener, he practised at Saint-Vincent-de-Paul and signed his last act on 17 March 1874. His registry is deposited in the Palais de Justice at Montreal.

On 2 March 1852, when the first school inspectors were appointed, Césaire Germain was named inspector for the counties of Laval, Terrebonne, Deux-Montagnes, and for part of Argenteuil, at a salary of $600 per year; in 1855 this salary was raised to $875. At that time his area contained 110 schools divided among 38 municipalities. On 1 April 1858, at a meeting held in his house at Saint-Vincent-de-Paul, Césaire Germain established a society of the schoolteachers of his district. He gave a talk on the progress made in public instruction in the country and the advantages of teachers' associations [*see* KÉROUAC].

It was not long before the inspectors' influence and their pedagogical action had results. Inspector Germain, in a report that reveals his learning, estimated the progress made: "The number of children who have attended school," he wrote, "is far superior to that of preceding years. The commissioners are showing more zeal in their efforts to secure the services of better qualified teachers, both male and female. The secret of the perfect teacher lies in creating a love of school and in making lessons interesting, thus putting in an attractive light what is by nature arid." In the *Journal de l'instruction publique* for the year 1870–71, Inspector Germain gave as his opinion that the salaries of women teachers, which varied between $72 and $80, were inadequate, and he voiced his astonishment that so much devotion, self-denial, and toil should be offered so cheaply. On 19 Aug. 1873 Césaire Germain took part in the first congress of school inspectors held at the École Normale Laval, at Quebec, under the chairmanship of the minister of public instruction, the Honourable Gédéon Ouimet*.

Césaire Germain, postmaster, notary, and school inspector, was a citizen of amazing activity. He seems to have succeeded in reconciling his profession as a notary with the regular visiting of 110 schools. In 1830, at Saint-Vincent-de-Paul, he had married Zoé Pépin; he had several sons: one, Césaire-Ernest, became a notary in 1862 and practised at Montreal, signing nearly 12,000 acts. It is possible that Édouard-Pépin Germain, a notary at Sainte-Thérèse-de-Blainville, and Joseph-Gérasime, an Ottawa doctor, were also Césaire Germain's sons.

LOUIS-PHILIPPE AUDET

AJM, Registre d'état civil (notes biographiques fournies par J.-J. Lefebvre). Canada, Province of, Legislative Assembly, *Journals*, 1852–53, app. J.J., "Education, Lower Canada: report of the superintendent of education...." *JIP*, avril 1858, 66; juill. 1858, 124; févr. 1861, 35; mai 1863, 76; oct. et nov. 1872, 149. André Vachon, *Histoire du notariat canadien, 1621–1960* (Québec, 1962).

GILMOUR, JOHN, timber merchant, shipbuilder; b. 31 Oct. 1812, at Craigton, Mearns, in Renfrewshire, near Glasgow, Scotland, fourth child of John Gilmour (d. 1841–42) and Margaret Urie; d. 25 Feb. 1877 in Montreal, Que.

John Gilmour came with his brother David (b. 20 Aug. 1815) to Quebec about 1832 to work for the Glasgow timber firm of Pollok, Gilmour and Company. The three partners who made up this firm, John and Arthur Pollok and Allan Gilmour Sr (1775–1849), all of whom came from Mearns and lived in Glasgow, had started in 1804 as importers of timber, tar, hemp, and flax from the Baltic. When Napoleon forced the British timber trade to shift from the Continent, Allan Gilmour* Jr, a nephew and namesake of the partner in the firm, was sent to British North America and established the family business in New Brunswick, first on the Miramichi and then at Saint John. Allan Jr, the older brother of John and David, came to Lower Canada in 1828 to tap the timber trade coming down the St Lawrence and managed the office in Quebec.

John and David Gilmour were put to work at the booms of the timber storage ground and pond, or at the company shipyard, all located at Wolfe's Cove (Anse au Foulon); they also worked in the office. In the winter they went up the river valleys on snowshoes, to inspect the camps of the timber-cutters on the lands leased by the firm on the Ottawa River and its tributaries. Of wiry constitution, they adapted quickly to Canada, became great hunters, particularly of moose, and could sleep in the snow in the coldest weather. In the 1830s and 1840s the firm had an expanding

Globensky

timber business and some 130 ships were built for the trade. When Allan Gilmour Sr retired in 1838 his namesake left the Quebec business in the hands of John and David Gilmour and moved to Glasgow; the latter two were admitted into the firm. John married Caroline White and David married her sister Matilda. About 1856, David Gilmour died suddenly in Rutland, Vt., on his way to New York, and John became the resident partner in Quebec the next year. The other partners in 1857 were Allan Gilmour Jr of Glasgow – the Polloks had retired in 1852 – Robert Rankin* of Liverpool and a third Allan Gilmour* (1816–1895), known as "Shotts Allan," of Ottawa, another nephew of Allan Gilmour Sr.

John Gilmour was elected to the council of the Board of Trade of Quebec in 1843 and re-elected in 1844, 1845, and 1846; in 1848 he was elected to its board of arbitration and in 1849 again to the council. He remained a member of the board, but without holding office.

John Gilmour was a reserved man, a "good-humoured, honest farmer type." In July 1848 he bought a residence "Marchmont" with property on the high ground just above the Gilmour timber depot at Wolfe's Cove; it became the Maison Généralice of the Ursulines of Quebec. John Gilmour was active from 1847 with the St Andrew's Society and he was founder of the Mount Hermon Cemetery in 1848; his wife was a director of the Quebec Protestant Ladies' Asylum in 1859. Otherwise Gilmour "immersed himself in his work," which centred on the Rue Saint-Pierre office in the Lower Town; there he "seemed somewhat careworn, severe and suspicious," according to the reminiscences of an employee.

The Gilmour shipyard was active in the 1850s and continued to produce until 1870; among the more notable vessels built there were the *Advance*, 1,466 tons, and in 1855 the *Illustrious*, a clipper of 1,200 tons. As many as four ships at a time were often on the stocks and over a thousand men were employed in the shipyards and at the timber-handling. A shipping-point was established at Indian Cove (Anse aux Sauvages) on the Lévis side, to which timbers were towed from Wolfe's Cove. Prominent employees of the shipyard were naval architects Robert McCord, James Dodds, and Captain John Dick, and the woodcarver John Penney. Two paintings of the timberyard and ships by Robert Clow Todd* survive in the possession of a relative in England.

John Gilmour of Quebec received a severe blow when Thomas McDuff of Edinburgh, who had taken over the family interests in Montreal from a younger brother James Gilmour (b. 1818), abused his trust, speculated in pork, lost large

sums of money, and absconded. Deeply affected by this event, John disappeared early in 1877. His body was found under the ice in Montreal harbour in the spring. The date of his death is recorded as 25 February. Liquidation of his former business interests in Quebec followed quickly. John's sons and their cousin, David's son, were to continue the family tradition in their timber interests on the Ottawa and Gatineau rivers.

COURTNEY C. J. BOND

ANQ, Quebec Board of Trade, minute book, 5, 6. PAC, MG 28, III, 6 (Gilmour and Hughson Limited). *Quebec Daily Mercury*, 3 May 1832, 12 June 1838, 1 March 1877. Borthwick, *Hist. and biog. gazetteer.* George Gale, *Quebec twixt old ... and ... new* (Quebec, 1915), 45, 64, 66, 68, 230, 241–42. J. W. Hughson and C. C. J. Bond, *Hurling down the pine; the story of the Wright, Gilmour and Hughson families, timber and lumber manufacturers in the Hull and Ottawa region and on the Gatineau River, 1800–1920* (Historical Society of the Gatineau pub., Old Chelsea, Que., 1964). John Rankin, *A history of our firm; being some account of the firm of Pollok, Gilmour and Co., and its offshoots and connections, 1804–1920* (2nd ed., Liverpool, Eng., 1921), 12–40, 90, 94, 103–5, 245, 254, 287, 303.

GLOBENSKY, HORTENSE (Prévost), known as Chevalière des Deux-Montagnes and Héroïne du Nord; b. 1804 at Saint-Eustache, daughter of Dr Auguste-France Globensky and Marie-Françoise Brousseau, *dit* Lafleur de Verchères; d. 29 April 1873 at Montreal.

Of Polish ancestry, Hortense Globensky's father was born in Berlin. He came to Canada in 1776 as a surgeon in the Brunswick-Hesse regiment. On 7 Jan. 1829, at Saint-Eustache, Hortense married the notary Guillaume Prévost, son of Guillaume Prévost and Josephte Quévillon, of Sainte-Anne-des-Plaines, by whom she had at least two children.

In the election of 1834 Hortense's brother, Frédéric-Eugène Globensky, stood as Tory candidate in the county of Deux-Montagnes. Many times Hortense, with her usual fieriness, publicly championed his cause. But it was the representatives of the *Patriote* party, William Henry Scott* and Jean-Joseph Girouard*, who were elected. Hortense, having made no secret of her attachment to the government, could not expect, when the insurrection came, to escape the attacks of the young *Patriotes* of the county of Deux-Montagnes. On 6 July 1837 friends advised her to seek refuge with neighbours, since the *Patriotes* intended to come and attack her house. But Hortense, who had just lost one of her children, aged three and a half, decided not to abandon its body. At nightfall some 50 *Patriotes* approached the house with the purpose of sacking it. Dressed in her husband's garb and wearing his characteristic blue cap, Hortense stationed herself at a window with all the firearms she had been able to muster. The *Patriotes* saw her, with a gun levelled straight at them, and chose to run. As a memento of this event, loyalist admirers made Hortense a gift of a silver teapot bearing the following inscription: "Presented to Madame G. Prévost, of Sainte-Scholastique, by several loyal persons of Montreal, in testimony to her heroism, greater than that expected of a woman, on the evening of 6 July 1837."

Subsequently Hortense Globensky often got herself talked about, and what people said was not always flattering. Coming from mass on 15 Oct. 1837, at a moment when *Patriotes* were inciting the parishioners to rebellion, Hortense began to speak and asked them to remain loyal to the government. When the *Patriotes* made a move to silence her, she took out a pistol and threatened to shoot the first one who came near. As a result of this incident she had to answer a charge of illegally carrying firearms. In November she repeated the action, once more against the *Patriotes*, who never lost an opportunity to provoke her. Amury Girod*, an associate of Dr Jean-Olivier Chénier*, organized an expedition one day to try to bring Hortense to heel, but it had no result.

After the battle of Saint-Eustache, several people of Sainte-Scholastique and the neighbourhood are believed to have gone to Hortense's house to express their regret for not having listened to her wise advice, and to entreat her to intercede with her brother, Colonel Maximilien Globensky*, on behalf of *Patriotes* who had been arrested by John Colborne*. Hortense agreed, and obtained the release of several prisoners.

Brave to the point of recklessness, Hortense Globensky-Prévost had an impetuous temperament, or at least an exceptional one. She was called Chevalière des Deux-Montagnes and Héroïne du Nord by newspapers at the time.

YVON GLOBENSKY

La Minerve (Montréal), 17 juill., 20 juill. 1837. *La Patrie* (Montréal), 11 nov. 1933. *Le Populaire* (Montréal), 12 juill., 6 oct., 22 déc. 1837. Ludwik Kos-Rabcewicz-Zubkowski, *The Poles in Canada* (Canada Ethnica, VII, Ottawa and Montreal, 1968), 17. *The Polish past in Canada; contributions to the history of the Poles in Canada and of the Polish-Canadian relations*, ed. Wiktor Turek (Toronto, 1960), 119–21. Michèle Lalonde, "La femme de 1837–1838: complice ou contre-révolutionnaire?" *Liberté* (Montréal), VII (1965), 155–57. Jacques Prévost, "Les Globensky au Canada Français," SGCF *Mémoires*, XVII (1966), 160–62.

GORDON, Lord GORDON (alias **Hon. Mr Herbert Hamilton, Lord Glencairn, George Gordon, George Herbert Gordon, John Herbert Charles Gordon**), adventurer and swindler; b. 184?; d. 1 Aug. 1874, Headingley, Man.

Gordon's career is first documented in 1868 when, using the name of Glencairn, he leased a shooting estate in Scotland after convincing London solicitors and Edinburgh jewellers that he would fall heir to the title and fortune of Lord Glencairn on 25 March 1870. He vanished from the British Isles shortly before that date.

In 1871 he appeared in Minneapolis, Minnesota, with the name Gordon. There he convinced the Northern Pacific Railroad that he was about to buy a vast acreage. He moved to New York in January 1872 and rapidly, but briefly, convinced the notorious financier Jay Gould that he held 60,000 shares of Erie Railway stock. Gould began court proceedings against Gordon when the deception was revealed, but his lordship fled to Canada leaving his bondsmen to pay $37,000 bail.

As Mr Gordon Gordon he arrived at Fort Garry (Winnipeg) in October 1872, posing as a British gentleman in search of sport. In Manitoba he lived quietly, enjoying frequent shooting expeditions, until 2 July 1873. On that evening he was seized by a party of Minnesotans, acting as agents of one of the bondsmen for his bail. The kidnappers attempted to abduct him to the United States, but were arrested the next day at Pembina, 100 yards north of the international border, on the ground that they had no legal authority on Canadian soil. They were returned to Fort Garry where stormy legal proceedings ensued. Throughout the remainder of the summer Manitoban, Canadian, Minnesotan, United States, and British officials angrily contested the legality of the abductions, arrests, and court proceedings within their respective authorities. By September 1873 the Manitoba courts had restored international calm but Gordon's American accomplishments had been fully exposed.

On 1 Aug. 1874 his lordship's British past also caught up with him. At the home of Mrs Abigail Corbett, where Gordon was boarding, he was arrested under a warrant issued at Toronto on the instance of an Edinburgh jeweller to whom he was in debt. Apparently deciding that the best of his days were now over, Lord Gordon Gordon shot himself through the head and died immediately, carrying with him to a Manitoba grave the truth of his origin and identity.

JOHN A. BOVEY

PAM, Alexander Morris, Ketcheson collection, correspondence, telegram book; Alexander Morris, Lieutenant Governor's collection, Lord Gordon Gordon

Gordon

papers. *Manitoba Free Press* (Winnipeg), 12, 19, 26 July, 2, 9 Aug., 20 Sept., 22 Nov. 1873; 8, 15 Aug. 1874. W. W. Folwell, *A history of Minnesota* (4v., Minnesota Historical Society pub., ed. S. J. Buck, St Paul, 1921), III, 362–88. J. L. Johnston, "Lord Gordon Gordon," HSSM *Papers*, 3rd ser., no. 7 (1952), 7–20.

GORDON, JAMES DOUGLAS, Presbyterian clergyman, author, and missionary; b. 1832 at Cascumpeque (Alberton), P.E.I., son of John Gordon and Mary Ramsey; d. 25 Feb. 1872 at Eromanga, New Hebrides.

James Douglas Gordon was born into a large family; they were tenants on the estate of Samuel Cunard* in Prince Edward Island. In 1850, after years of battle against Cunard's "unrighteous" high rents, his father was forced to give up his land. James Gordon's education included some years of study in arts at the Presbyterian Theological Seminary in Truro, Nova Scotia, where one of his classmates was David Laird*; Gordon and the future P.E.I. editor and politician became lifelong friends. For several years Gordon worked as a journalist on the Island, and, at one time, was legislative reporter for the P.E.I. assembly. In 1861, his brother, George N. Gordon*, and his sister-in-law, Ellen, were martyred at the Presbyterian mission which had been established by John GEDDIE in 1848 in the New Hebrides. James Gordon was studying theology at the Presbyterian College in Halifax, N.S., at the time of his brother's death. He completed his studies, and in 1863 published a eulogistic volume, *The last martyrs of Eromanga; being a memoir of the Rev. George N. Gordon and Ellen Catherine Powell, his wife.*

In 1864 James Gordon followed in his martyred brother's footsteps and became a missionary in Eromanga. During his first four years in Eromanga Gordon represented the Presbyterian Church of the Lower Provinces of British North America; for the next two, he represented the Presbyterian Church of New South Wales. He resigned the latter tie in 1870, and henceforth served on his own authority although he made frequent trips to New South Wales. During his eight years at the mission, Gordon became an accomplished linguist, translating the Book of Genesis, the Gospel of St Matthew, hymns, and primers into the local language. He also helped to establish a mission station on the larger island of Espiritu Santo.

On 25 Feb. 1872 a native arrived at the mission sub-station at Portina Bay requesting urgent medical help for his ailing sons. Gordon accompanied the man to his hut only to find the two children dead. The distraught father accused the missionary of witchcraft and immediately killed him

with his hatchet. James Gordon's body was buried at Dillon's Bay, the main mission on the island; the Martyr's Church there was opened in 1879 and restored in 1968.

James Gordon had remained unmarried and had insisted on working and living alone, a tendency which friendly critics thought "greatly impaired his happiness and his usefulness." He was described as a man of "singular piety, somewhat eccentric in his way, self-denying to an extreme."

BRUCE W. HODGINS

J. D. Gordon, *The last martyrs of Eromanga; being a memoir of the Rev. George N. Gordon and Ellen Catherine Powell, his wife* (Halifax, 1863). *Patriot* (Charlottetown), 3, 8 Aug. 1872. "Sad report confirmed: death of Rev. James D. Gordon," *Home and Foreign Record of the Presbyterian Church of the Lower Provinces of British North America* (Halifax), XII (1872).

GOSSELIN, SCHOLASTIQUE, Grey Nun of Montreal, missionary; b. 11 June 1806 at Sainte-Famille, Île d'Orléans, L.C., daughter of Joseph Gosselin, farmer, and of Josephte Pageot; d. 5 Oct. 1876 at Saint-Boniface, Man.

Scholastique Gosselin received a good education as her elegant writing shows. She entered the Congregation of the Grey Nuns of Montreal and took her vows on 8 July 1828. After making her profession, she was for 18 years in charge of the education and care of orphans at the mother house. In 1844 the Grey Nuns of Montreal, in response to the request of Bishop Joseph-Norbert Provencher*, founded their Red River mission. Sister Gosselin joined the third group of nuns nominated to it. She set out from Montreal on 10 July 1846 and travelled, by steamboat and railway, via Lake Ontario to Buffalo, Detroit, and Chicago. From Chicago the last stage was covered in what were known as prairie wagons. The party reached its destination on 5 September.

When Sister Gosselin arrived the community was still in its heroic period. The sisters, lodged at Saint-Boniface in a small tumble-down house where everything froze hard in winter, had to adapt themselves to a pioneer's existence, tilling the fields and weaving their clothes. They had already begun to educate Indian children; they travelled about the countryside to help the poor and care for the sick, some of whom were brought under their roof, where the sisters organized a small hospital. For her part, Sister Gosselin was responsible for domestic matters at the bishop's palace and for the upkeep of the cathedral sacristy. When the cathedral burned down in December 1860 she displayed remarkable coolness; making her way three times into the flaming building, she managed to save the sacred vessels.

Sister Gosselin's courage is also revealed by her correspondence; speaking of difficult days, she wrote: ". . . I did all I could to appear cheerful." As a counsellor, Sister Gosselin assisted the superior and also took part in the expansion of the Red River mission; she was closely associated with the founding of the boarding-schools of Saint-Boniface (1849), Saint-François-Xavier (1850), Saint-Norbert (1858), and Saint-Vital (1860), and of the Saint-Boniface hospital (1871). When a septuagenarian, she was still said to be "the most sprightly of them all." On 5 Oct. 1876, pleurisy terminated her 30 years of missionary life. Sister Gosselin was buried at Saint-Boniface.

LÉONIE FERLAND

Archives paroissiales de Sainte-Famille, Île d'Orléans, Registres des baptêmes, mariages et sépultures, 1806, B, no.7. ASGM, Ancien Journal, II, 132; Chapitre des fondations, 1843–1872, 17; Chroniques de Saint-Boniface, I, II; Correspondance de Saint-Boniface, 147, 224, 246, 256, 260; Registre des admissions, vêtures et professions, I, f.27. Morice, *Dict. hist. Can. et Métis*, 125–26. David Gosselin, *Figures d'hier et d'aujourd'hui à travers Saint-Laurent, I.O.* (3v., Québec, 1919), II, 18–19. Raoul Raymond, "Gosselin," SGCF *Mémoires*, XIII (1962), 243.

GOWAN, OGLE ROBERT, Orangeman, journalist, farmer, and politician; b. at Mount Nebo, County Wexford, Ireland, 13 July 1803, sixth son of John Hunter Gowan, a prominent landlord, magistrate, and captain of the Wexford yeomanry, and of his second wife, Margaret Hogan; d. at Toronto, Ont., 21 Aug. 1876.

Ogle Robert Gowan was raised at Mount Nebo and educated at home. The son of an important Wexford Orangeman and a godchild of George Ogle, one of the early grand masters of the Irish Orange Order, he was initiated as an Orangeman in 1818 in County Wicklow. He later moved to Dublin where he published, in collaboration with George Perkins Bull*, a small political newspaper called the *Antidote*. Gowan also wrote several tracts hostile to Roman Catholicism, including a lengthy address to the lord lieutenant of Ireland, the Marquis of Wellesley; these were undoubtedly printed in the *Antidote* and some may have been published in pamphlet form. His major work during this time was a book entitled *The annals and defence of the Loyal Orange Institution of Ireland*, published in 1825.

When the Irish Orange lodges were dissolved temporarily in 1825, Gowan became assistant grand secretary of the Benevolent and Loyal Orange Institution of Ireland, which was organized by Sir Harcourt Lees, a prominent Orangeman. Although this society received only limited support in Ireland, it carried on correspondence with Orangemen in Canada. Gowan was thus known to many Canadian Orangemen before he arrived in 1829.

Orangeism in Upper Canada was firmly established at this time in centres such as York (Toronto), Kingston, Perth, and Brockville. Orangemen numbered perhaps several thousands and had already attracted unfavourable attention because of riots in Perth and Kingston. In politics, the Orangemen of York supported William Lyon Mackenzie*, and elsewhere many supported local Tories who would not acknowledge Orange support. Most Orangemen felt the need for a grand lodge to provide central leadership and for an able spokesman who would act as their political champion. Gowan may have come to Canada with this possibility in mind, particularly as he had incurred the enmity of the reconstituted Irish Grand Lodge by his efforts to continue the Benevolent and Loyal Orange Institution as a separate organization, but his departure from Ireland may also have been influenced by the passage of the Roman Catholic emancipation act and by the general prospects of better opportunities in the new world.

Gowan settled in Escott Park, Leeds County, Upper Canada, with a household of nine, including two servants. Although he soon became a substantial "gentleman" farmer in the community, his real interest was in politics, and the obvious means of entering Canadian politics was by providing the Canadian Orangemen with a leader and a grand lodge. As a young gentleman who had played an active part in the Irish Orange movement (his quarrel with the Irish Grand Lodge was not generally known in Canada at the time of his arrival) and who was able to talk and write in a manner comprehensible to plebeian Orangemen, Gowan's talents were ideally suited to the needs of the Canadian movement. He was able to call a meeting of representatives of most existing lodges in Upper and Lower Canada at the Brockville courthouse on 1 Jan. 1830. The Grand Orange Lodge of British North America was founded and Gowan was chosen deputy grand master. The Duke of Cumberland was invited to become grand master but he declined, and after several years of negotiations Gowan became the first Canadian grand master. The movement was dedicated to the defence of the Protestant religion and the preservation of the British connection, but it owed much of its vitality to its function as a fraternal society. Although it was potentially an

Gowan

agency of anti-clericalism, this aspect of Orange-ism was overshadowed by its loyalism during the 1830s.

As the leader of the Canadian Orangemen, Gowan was a person of some consequence in the province. He therefore decided to run as an independent "immigrant" candidate in the election of 1830, appealing to Roman Catholics as well as Protestant Irish. His refusal to run in partnership with the Tory candidate, Henry Sherwood*, seems to have upset the Perth Orangemen, and he was denounced in the Tory *Brockville Gazette* in letters which were strongly nativist in tone.

Although defeated in the election, Gowan had established a position in provincial politics. This he sought to consolidate by founding a small newspaper in 1830 called the *Brockville Sentinel* (named the *Antidote* in 1832), but it did not flourish. His efforts with the *Brockville Gazette*, which had been founded in 1828, were no more successful: after Gowan took it over in December 1831 it appeared for a few issues and then ceased publication until July when it was acquired by Orangeman Arthur McClean.

While engaged in these journalistic ventures, Gowan, with the support of the Tory families of Ephraim Jones* and Solomon Jones*, attempted to found "independent" clubs and later "patriot" clubs; these were, in most respects, similar to the Constitutional Clubs that flourished later at the time of the 1836 elections. Although Gowan undoubtedly profited by his connection with the Joneses, he seems to have been embarrassed by this association. In an encounter with Mackenzie he felt it necessary to deny that he served either the Joneses or the Sherwoods, and during a Grenville by-election he denounced as calumny rumours that he had instructed the Orangemen to vote for the Joneses' candidate. Mackenzie commented at the time that "Mr Gowan's general manner of speaking pleased me much, and I really regretted to see an Irishman of his abilities acting the humble part of a deputy assistant to such as the Jones and Sherwoods." Mackenzie's comments were hardly a fair commentary on Gowan's relations with the Compact families in Brockville, but Gowan was obviously sensitive to such criticism. He nevertheless continued to cooperate with the Jones and Sherwood families in 1832 in support of the immigrant societies of Sir John Colborne*, which were opposed by the Reformers.

In 1833, however, Gowan became involved in feuds with the Tory families in the Brockville area which had their origin in the refusal of Sheriff Adiel SHERWOOD to release an Orangeman convicted of arson. Relations further deteriorated when Gowan attacked members of the Family Compact for their outspoken criticisms of the Colonial Office at the time of the dismissal of Christopher Hagerman* and Henry John Boulton* in 1833. Relations between the Orangemen and the Family Compact at this time are indicated by a resolution of the grand lodge which declared that "The policy of W. L. Mackenzie is the one which should prevail," although the grand lodge stated its disapproval of Mackenzie's methods and suspected him of secret republicanism. At this time, Andrew Norton BUELL of the Reform newspaper the *Brockville Recorder*, wrote, "Gowan was coming around to the liberal side and with a little management could be brought fully over."

In 1834 Gowan stood for election in company with the attorney general, Robert Sympson Jameson*, who was a government rather than a Tory candidate. Jameson's willingness to run with Gowan is a measure of the degree to which Gowan's influence was supplanting that of the Compact families in Leeds County – influence gained to a large extent by his efforts to secure title deeds for immigrants, thus enabling them to vote. He was elected for Leeds in 1834 and in 1835, but his election was declared invalid each time because of Orange violence at the polls. In a by-election early in 1836 he was defeated, but was re-elected along with Jonas Jones* in the summer of 1836 after Lieutenant Governor Sir Francis Bond HEAD had dissolved the House of Assembly.

During the general election of 1836, Gowan had arranged an alliance with Roman Catholics which he had always sought and which had been maturing since 1832. Under his leadership the grand lodge of British North America welcomed "the manifestations of loyalty on the part of the Roman Catholics and their Venerable Bishop," and in an election address to the free-holders of Stormont and Glengarry, the Roman Catholic bishop, Alexander Macdonell*, acknowledged "having received from Orangemen unequivocal and substantial proof of disinterested friendship." The alliance provided a combination of the bloc votes of Catholics and Orangemen in favour of candidates who supported Head. Before the election Gowan had also toured the Toronto area in company with the Tory journalist, George Gurnett*, helping to win Toronto Orangemen away from the lingering influence of Mackenzie. By 1836, Gowan was already a figure of consequence in provincial politics, and he consolidated his position by founding the *Brockville Statesman* in 1836, his first successful venture in journalism.

With the outbreak of the rebellion in Lower Canada in the late autumn of 1837, Gowan inspired the raising of a volunteer company named the Brockville Invincibles. He was made a captain in the 2nd Regiment of Leeds militia, and later given a company of the Queen's Own Rifles which he led during the capture of Hickory Island near Gananoque in 1838. He was then given command of a provisional battalion of militia of Upper Canada as lieutenant-colonel. At the battle of the Windmill near Prescott, where he was wounded twice, he was thanked for his services in general orders, and his provisional battalion was honoured with the name of Queen's Royal Borderers.

Before his brief career of active service had come to an end, Gowan was directing criticism at the policies of Head, and of his successor, Sir George Arthur*. The Orange lodges in the United Kingdom had been dissolved in 1836 under threats of anti-Orange legislation and Head had expressed the hope that the Canadian Orangemen would also dissolve. Although a few Orangemen severed their connection with the movement in deference to Head, the grand lodge, led by Gowan, refused to disband. As Head and Arthur were unwilling and unable to make any public acknowledgement of the services performed by the Orangemen during the rebellion, the Orangemen were prepared to introduce their own reform programme.

There is a tradition that Gowan had written a letter on responsible government in 1830, and he always described himself as an independent rather than a Tory. In 1839 he published a letter on responsible government in the *Statesman* which Francis Hincks* reprinted in pamphlet form. As a result of this letter Gowan was removed from his post as agent of crown lands in the Johnstown District (which included Leeds and Grenville counties) and there was Tory pressure within the Orange lodges for his removal as grand master. Gowan placed still greater strain on the unity of the lodges and on his relations with the Tories by introducing on 8 April 1839 in the House of Assembly a bill for dividing clergy reserves among all legally recognized denominations. Under pressure from Tory Orangemen and the threat of the proposed union with Lower Canada, Gowan turned to other issues, without repudiating his stand on clergy reserves and responsible government.

In his views on the union of Upper and Lower Canada, Gowan differed little from the Tories in that he expressed fear of a combination of Upper Canadian Reformers with the French majority of Lower Canada. His opportunities to impose these views were limited as he failed to win a seat in the first election after the union in 1841. This defeat forced him to seek consolation in the politics of the Johnstown District. Here he became involved in a dispute with one of the Reformers, Buell, whom he accused of treason during the 1837 rebellion. Buell retaliated by charging that Gowan over-stated his property qualifications when seeking election. Gowan also had to bear the brunt of the attack on the Orange lodges launched by the administration of Robert Baldwin* and Louis-Hippolyte La Fontaine*, with the moral support of the governors, Sir Charles Bagot* and then, for some time, Sir Charles Metcalfe*.

The ministry's attacks reached a climax in 1843 when a bill, introduced by Baldwin, was passed which was intended to prevent Orangemen from holding office under the crown and sitting on juries, and which endangered the liquor licences of taverns where Orange meetings were held. As the passage of the bill coincided with a cabinet crisis involving disputes between Metcalfe and Baldwin over patronage, the governor reserved it for the consideration of the imperial parliament, where it was subsequently disallowed, but he permitted the passage of a bill against Orange processions. Metcalfe's action was undoubtedly undertaken as a concession to Gowan, whom he had consulted at this time on the prospect of forming an alternative ministry.

Gowan was returned as representative for Leeds and Grenville in the 1844 election and soon won the respect of his friends and enemies for his abilities as a parliamentarian. La Fontaine declared that Gowan was the most accomplished speaker in the house; Hincks found him formidable and the possessor of a "greater amount of tact and general information than any man engaged in public affairs." His skill was demonstrated in 1846 when during the debates on clergy reserves, Gowan opposed Henry Sherwood's motion calling for the division of the reserves among interested denominations on the grounds that it would lead to the establishment of a tenant system in Canada. He followed these comments by an amendment calling for the sale of the reserves at the least expense and as quickly as possible, an amendment which passed with a substantial majority.

During this period, Gowan formed a close association with John A. Macdonald* and was credited by the Montreal *Pilot* with leading the popular wing of conservatism against the Family Compact interest represented by Sir Allan MacNab*. It has been said that it was John A. Macdonald's association with Gowan which influenced the leader of the government, William Henry DRAPER, in his decision to offer Macdonald the post of attorney general shortly before Christopher Hagerman's death. Moreover, Draper urged Macdonald to visit Lord Elgin [Bruce*] in the

Gowan

company of Gowan to persuade the new governor that Conservatives were not ultra-Tories. The nature of Gowan's relationship with Macdonald and the Draper administration is indicated by a letter which Macdonald wrote in May 1847, stating, "We cannot expect to obtain his [Gowan's] services and refuse the reward and highly as I appreciate his powers of benefiting us, I confess I fear his means of doing mischief more." The reward under consideration was the appointment of Gowan as assistant commissioner of crown lands, but Gowan's prospects in this regard vanished with the fall of the Draper ministry.

The administration's neglect of Gowan can be attributed partly to his position as Orange grand master, a position he was unwilling to renounce, but was more the result of the continued influence of Compact Tories who distrusted and disliked Gowan as a demagogue and a political manipulator. Gowan was inclined to blame Macdonald for not pressing his claim to office with sufficient force, and this conviction was strengthened by Macdonald's neglect of him when the Conservatives were returned to office in 1854. Gowan seems to have nursed his grievances in private as he accepted the relatively minor post of supervisor of tolls on the canals west of Lachine, a post from which he was dismissed in 1849 by the Baldwin-La Fontaine government. Although it is possible that Macdonald might have pressed Gowan's claims more vigorously, he would have done so without much support from other Liberal Conservatives, who felt no need to have Gowan in the inner circles of Draper's administration from 1844 to 1847.

The growing political influence of Gowan did not help secure his hold on the Orangemen; he lost the office of grand master to George Benjamin* of Belleville in 1846. Benjamin, and later John Hillyard CAMERON, represented a new type of Orange grand master, better able to conciliate vested interests and more acceptable to conventional Conservatives. But they were wanting in Gowan's powers as a popular leader, and consequently they were less able to control the militant Protestantism of the lodges which so often posed a threat to Conservative political alliances.

In the elections of 1847–48 Gowan was defeated by a narrow majority by the Reformer, William Buell Richards*, and he suffered further loss of prestige when he led the Orange opposition to the rebellion losses bill. In the demonstrations against Lord Elgin during his visit to Canada West (still popularly called Upper Canada), Gowan took a prominent part and he attacked the governor viciously in the *Statesman*. These actions resulted in his removal from the commission of the peace

for Brockville, to which he had been appointed in 1845, and the loss in 1849 of his commission as a lieutenant-colonel in the militia.

In 1849 Gowan was active along with the new Orange grand master, George Benjamin, in organizing the British American League, which was designed to rally public opinion against a supposed threat to the British connection. At the Kingston convention of the league in July 1849, Gowan introduced a motion calling for Canadian "protectionism," which was supported by Macdonald. When the question of the federation of the British North American provinces was raised, Macdonald criticized it as premature whereas Gowan declared himself opposed to a federal union of the provinces on the grounds that it would leave the English in Lower Canada under French domination. He proposed instead a scheme for redividing the counties of Lower Canada (Canada East) which would give the river-front counties to the French and the back counties to the English. At the Toronto convention of the British American League in November, which was held after the Montreal Annexation Manifesto had appeared, Gowan took a strong stand against annexation, but announced his support of an elective Legislative Council, pointing out that the last of the 13 American colonies to revolt had had an elective Legislative Council.

Gowan remained active in the local politics of the Johnstown District and appears to have continued as a gentleman farmer since he was prominent in the local agricultural society. In 1851 he was again defeated in the Leeds election by the Reformer, W. B. Richards. Early in 1852 he ceased publication of the *Statesman* and moved to Toronto where he acquired the former Compact newspaper, the *Toronto Patriot*, and entered municipal politics, being elected a Toronto alderman in 1853 and again in 1854.

While engaged in these journalistic and political activities, Gowan challenged Benjamin's leadership of the Orange lodges at the Kingston meeting of the grand lodge in 1853. Benjamin had become a formidable rival as he had gained credit with Orangemen for the repeal of the anti-Orange processions act. Yet Gowan's supporters were more aggressive and better organized, and they succeeded in electing Gowan grand master. In the course of the contest and its aftermath Benjamin's supporters made use of charges which had been brought against Gowan by Orangeman G. P. Bull, with whom Gowan had earlier quarrelled in Ireland. Bull had come to Canada in 1832 and had attacked Gowan, accusing him of being an imposter on the grounds that he had not been a member of the Grand Lodge of Ireland, reconstituted in 1828 on the eve of Gowan's departure. As Gowan had been assistant grand secretary of an institution recognized by the British Grand Lodge, Bull's charge had little substance. Bull also circulated a transcript of an Irish court case, *Hopkins v. Gowan*, involving a quarrel over a family will, during the course of which doubts were raised about Gowan's legitimacy and one witness declared that Gowan had been a shoemaker's apprentice. Although Bull had made careless statements before (he was imprisoned in Ireland for libel against a Roman Catholic priest), his charges seem to have induced Montreal Orangemen to repudiate Gowan's leadership in the 1830s and the charges were from time to time circulated by Gowan's enemies in Upper Canada. Yet they seem to have made no impression on his friends and little on the general public.

After its defeat, the minority supporting Benjamin formed a separate grand lodge which they claimed was the only authentic grand lodge of British North America. Although they charged Gowan with making the lodges subservient to political interests, the schismatic leaders were equally political and merely stood for a more consistently anti-clerical policy. Yet their accusations became more pointed when Gowan, after some wavering between a Protestant alliance with Reformers and a Conservative alliance with the French *Bleus*, chose the latter, leaving the Benjamin followers to support the "rep by pop" campaign of George BROWN. Gowan sought the aid of Roman Catholics by arguing, in company with other Conservatives, that the complete secularization of clergy reserves would endanger the special position of the Roman Catholic church in Quebec and the aspirations of Catholics throughout the province. Gowan was able to rally most of the Orange vote for Conservative candidates, but he himself failed to win a seat in the new riding of Ontario North in 1854, and was compelled to sell the *Patriot* to James Beaty* who merged it with the *Leader*.

Gowan conducted a vigorous campaign against the schismatic Benjamin faction, which he accused on occasion and without evidence of attempting to create a nativist movement in Canada. Of the 563 lodges in Canada, only 106 adhered to Benjamin and all the Maritime lodges supported Gowan. Yet the schism was unpopular with the average Orangeman and Gowan agreed to step down as grand master in 1856, thus permitting a reunion under the leadership of George Lyttleton Allen* who had been grand secretary for a number of years.

The following year Gowan again ran for the riding of Ontario North and again suffered defeat,

as local Orangemen accused him of "being sold to the Pope." He received some compensation for this humiliation in the spring of 1858 when he won a by-election in the riding of North Leeds. During these campaigns, Gowan infuriated George Brown by adapting his slogan of rep by pop, to "rep by pop and territory." Brown denounced Gowan as an "uncompromising adherent of the priest party, whilst all the time professing to be an Orangeman and extreme Protestant," and declared that no constituency would return him.

After Gowan's victory in the by-election, Brown attacked him again, asserting that the ministry would regret his presence in the assembly and that he was more dangerous to his friends than to his enemies. But when Gowan retired from provincial politics in 1861, he was regarded as "the father of the House." There is no obvious motive for Gowan's retirement from politics at the age of 58, except a need for rest and possibly greater financial security. He accepted the office of inspector in the money order department of the post office in Upper Canada, an office he held for a number of years before becoming issuer and inspector of licences for the city of Toronto from 1869 until 1874. During the 1860s much of his attention was devoted to the Orange movement, particularly the founding of the Imperial Grand Council in Belfast in 1867. As early as 1855, Gowan had written to the Irish grand master, the Earl of Enniskillen, suggesting periodic meetings of Orangemen from different parts of the empire. He attended a preliminary conference at Belfast in 1866 as the representative of the Provincial Grand Lodge of Western Canada and there he proposed that an Imperial Grand Council be held annually "for the consideration of the state of Orangeism and Protestantism generally, with the view of devising means for the extension of Orangeism."

Gowan was married to Francis Anne Turner of Wexford who died in 1852. Of his 11 children, two sons, the eldest, Nassau, who became a clergyman of the New Connexion Methodist Church, and Harcourt, were prominent Orangemen. Of his daughters, Aliza Amelia married the Reverend William Peck of Lansdowne and Frances Jane married Thomas Roberts FERGUSON. Gowan married Alice Hitchcock in 1866.

In many respects Gowan resembles the Irish Chartist leaders such as Feargus O'Connor and Bronterre O'Brien. Like them he learned the art of popular politics in the Ireland of the 1820s when Daniel O'Connell's Catholic Association dominated politics. Like them, too, he was an effective orator with a flair for popular journalism and a master of machine politics and he went as far as

Gowan

these abilities could take him. Gowan differed from the Chartists in being more conventional in his politics; his views on general questions did not differ much from those of John A. Macdonald. After 1850 being an Orangeman no longer barred a man from high office, yet, though men such as Mackenzie, Hincks, and Macdonald could appreciate Gowan's abilities as a popular leader, he was kept from it because most Reformers and nearly all compact Tories did not consider him "respectable."

This impression of Gowan was largely the result of his style and manner, but it was enhanced by his continual involvement in private disputes which often resulted in legal action, the first and most serious of these being his long quarrel with G. P. Bull. But Gowan was undoubtedly the most impressive of all Canadian Orange grand masters, and he gave the movement the kind of prestige and energetic leadership it required during its formative years in the 1830s. By the 1850s the lodges had gained a secure place in Canadian society and could be better served by the more conventional leaders such as Benjamin and Cameron.

In his political writings Gowan offers shrewd commentary on contemporary affairs, spiced with quotations from Viscount Bolingbroke and Edmund Burke. The most influential was his letter on responsible government, published in 1839. His major literary work, however, was a multivolume history entitled *Orangeism, its origin and history*, of which three volumes were published in Toronto in 1859–60. The fourth volume, dealing with the Canadian Orange movement, was never published and the manuscript has been lost. The published volumes provide much useful information on Irish Orangeism, but this is blended with Orange folklore and the Orange interpretation of history.

HEREWARD SENIOR

[O. R. Gowan was the author of *The annals and defence of the Loyal Orange Institution of Ireland* (Dublin, 1825); *An important letter on responsible government* (Toronto, 1839); and *Orangeism; its origin and history* (Toronto, 1859–60). His other writings are listed in Morgan, *Bibliotheca Canadensis*.

The principal manuscript sources are MG 27, I, E30 (T. R. Ferguson papers) and RG 5, A1, at the PAC, and the A. N. Buell papers, the Sir James R. Gowan and Ogle R. Gowan papers (which are disappointing as they contain only a few letters exchanged mainly by Gowan and his cousin James R. Gowan* between the years 1825 and 1843), and the Mackenzie-Lindsey collection at PAO. A Gowan scrapbook, compiled by his daughter Mrs Emily Ferguson, and now in the possession of Colonel Ashmore Kidd, Kingston, Ontario, contains many interesting notes and clippings. A series of letters written by one of Gowan's granddaughters was published in the *Mail and Empire* (Toronto), 15 March 1930, 12 July 1934, and in the *Globe and Mail* (Toronto), 12 Oct. 1938; they give valuable details on Gowan's life.

The most extensive sources are the newspapers, especially Gowan's *Brockville Statesman*, 1836–51, and *Toronto Patriot*, 1852–54. Also useful are the *Colonial Advocate*, 1829–34, *Constitution*, 1836–37, *Examiner*, 1838–55, and *Globe*, 1844–61, of Toronto; *Pilot and Journal of Commerce*, 1844–62, and *Vindicator and Canadian Advertiser*, 1828–37, of Montreal; *Orange Lily and Protestant Vindicator*, 1849–54, of Bytown (Ottawa); and *Brockville Gazette*, 1831–32, and *Brockville Recorder*, 1830–49. The Loyal Orange Association of British North America, Grand Lodge, *Annual Reports*, include some of Gowan's addresses, and those for 1853–56 contain long accounts of the schism in the movement. *Interesting trial: Hopkins against Gowan, Wexford spring assizes ...* (Dublin, 1827; Kingston and Toronto, 1837) is the most important pamphlet.

Creighton, *Macdonald, young politician*, discusses Gowan's relations with John A. Macdonald; [Walter McCleary], *One man's loyalty; background of first grand master, Ogle R. Gowan ...* (History of the Orange Association in the Dominion of Canada, no.1, n.p., 1953) is an attempt at an official history of the Orange order and has a somewhat sketchy biography of Gowan. W. B. Kerr's three articles on Orangeism, "The Orange order in Upper Canada in the 1820's" and "The Orange order and W. L. Mackenzie in the 1830's" in the *Sentinel and Orange and Protestant Advocate* (Toronto), 19 Jan., 2, 16 Feb., 2, 16 March, 6, 20 April, 4, 18 May 1939, and "When Orange and Green united, 1832–9; the alliance of Macdonell and Gowan" in *Ont. Hist.*, XXXIV (1942), 32–42, present thoughtful narratives by an Orangeman and professional historian.

Brief but not always accurate summaries of Gowan's life can be found in the obituary notices in the Toronto *Globe*, *Leader*, and *Mail*, in August 1876. There are also biographical sketches in *Encyclopedia Canadiana*, V, 5; Morgan, *Sketches of celebrated Canadians*, 777–79; *Sketches of the 13th parliament in Upper Canada* (Toronto, 1840); Wallace, *Macmillan dictionary*, 274; and Davin, *Irishman in Canada*, 411. H.S.]

GOWAN, ROBERT, banker, journalist, and civil servant; b. in Scotland, c. 1800; d. 30 Jan. 1879 at Fredericton, N.B.

Robert Gowan came to Fredericton about 1816 as a drummer-boy in the 74th Regiment and later became a hospital sergeant. He entered civilian life as an accountant in the firm of Robert Rankin*, lumber merchant and shipbuilder. Gowan took a leading part in the founding of St Paul's Presbyterian Church in Fredericton and in the organization of freemasonry in New Brunswick. In association with Henry Garrett Clopper, Gowan was a founder of the Central Bank of New Brunswick, which opened in 1834. This bank was a Fredericton corporation capitalized at £15,000 which helped break the monopoly of the Saint John-based Bank of New Brunswick.

His experience with Rankin and Company in the timber trade gave Gowan a powerful bias against the authoritarian control exercised by the commissioner of crown lands, Thomas Baillie*, who levied heavy charges on the timber trade in the hope of creating a giant fund that would make government independent of the legislature. In 1832 and 1833 Gowan wrote a series of letters, under the *nom de plume* of John Gape, to the *New Brunswick Courier*. These letters concentrated on attacking the inefficiency of the Crown Lands Office and the arrogance and alleged graft of Baillie. They hardened public opinion against the government in power and gave impetus to the movement led by Charles Simonds* and Edward Barron CHANDLER that in 1837 resulted in the surrender of the crown lands to legislative control. Witty and homespun and reflecting the libertarian prejudices of the timbermen against overbearing bureaucracy, these letters could scarcely be described as literary, but they were influential. "He wielded a facile and sprightly pen; and his Johnny Gape letters to the St John *Courier* have created a wider influence in the province than any letters before or since. . . . What old resident of New Brunswick has forgotten those famous letters?" Perhaps the most impressive of his journalistic contributions was a drama in three parts, commencing in the *Courier* 23 Feb. 1833 and entitled "The triumph of intrigue." This depicts Baillie and his father-in-law, William F. Odell*, presiding over the crown lands after the fashion of Scottish lairds.

Probably as a reward for political service Gowan became chief clerk in the Crown Lands Office in 1840, and held the position until his retirement in 1870. Among the freemasons he was notable for a determination to maintain the independent jurisdiction of the Scottish lodges.

W. S. MacNUTT

New Brunswick Courier (Saint John, N.B.), 1832–33. *New Brunswick Reporter* (Fredericton), 5 Feb. 1879. W. F. Bunting, *History of St John's Lodge, F. & A.M. of Saint John, New Brunswick together with sketches of all Masonic bodies in New Brunswick, from A.D. 1784 to A.D. 1894* (Saint John, N.B., 1895), 21, 358, 378. MacNutt, *New Brunswick*, 234, 236, 476. *The old grave-yard, Fredericton, New Brunswick: epitaphs copied by the York-Sunbury Historical Society Inc.*, ed. L. M. Beckwith Maxwell (Sackville, N.B., 1938), 139.

GREELEY, HORACE, journalist and American politician; b. 3 Feb. 1811 near Amherst, New Hampshire, son of Zaccheus Greeley and Mary Woodburn; d. 29 Nov. 1872.

The eldest of five sons of a poor farmer, Horace Greeley received a rudimentary education, then was apprenticed to a Vermont printer. As soon as he was 20 he set out for New York, where, while endeavouring to complete his education, he concerned himself with ways of developing a cheap newspaper.

On 11 April 1841, after starting some short-lived papers, he founded the *New York Tribune*, a daily which from 500 subscribers at the beginning numbered 11,000 only seven weeks later, and which in 1854 reached a circulation of 112,000 copies. Thanks to this newspaper, Greeley became a political power to be reckoned with. The *Tribune* was the spokesman for his firm anti-slavery opinions and for his social views, inspired chiefly by Charles Fourier, whose doctrine had been popularized in the United States by Albert Brisbane.

Alert to all the liberal movements shaking the Old World, Horace Greeley placed at the service of his convictions the influence of his pen or of his word – for he was a speaker sought after as much for the impetuous quality of his utterance as for the extreme originality of dress that made him an eminently picturesque personage. Thus, on 29th Nov. 1847, "to the accompaniment of thunderous applause," he read before an assembly of more than 6,000 persons an address of congratulations to Pius IX, who was considered at that time a liberal pope. When the same pontiff withdrew from the Italian national movement, the *Tribune* was not slow to condemn him.

It was not surprising that in 1868 the Institut Canadien should have thought of inviting as a speaker this eminent American liberal, then at the height of his fame as journalist and lecturer. At this time the institute found itself the object of a renewed outburst of severity on the part of episcopal authority. Bishop Ignace Bourget* did not believe in the sincerity of the members who had applied to Rome to obtain the lifting of censures pronounced against them [see Gonzalve DOUTRE]. On the contrary, he was convinced that "The Institute is not waiting for Rome's reply in order to reform itself in submission to its judgement," and he offered proof to his correspondents: "At present it [the institute] is reviewing the bishops and priests of the country, and giving them sharp rebuffs for having concerned themselves with Confederation."

Ten days earlier, 17 Dec. 1868, Greeley had addressed the Institut Canadien, on the 24th anniversary of its founding. One of the speeches was by Louis-Antoine Dessaulles*, on "tolerance,"

Green

but the lecturer had set himself to analyse an example of intolerance that each of his listeners had been easily able to identify. Greeley exalted "the truly liberal man," who had "only one country: the world; one religion: love; one patriotism: to civilize and improve the human family," and whose adversaries were: "tyranny, ignorance, superstition, in a word all that is degrading."

One of the members of the institute, a lawyer, Christophe-Alphonse Geoffrion*, then made himself the interpreter of the "keen enthusiasm" that Greeley's words had aroused in the audience, taking good care to specify that "all liberties are of the same family": "The enemy of corporal slavery is necessarily the irreconcilable adversary of intellectual slavery: soldiers under the same flag, we are indebted to him [Greeley] for the harmony of feeling which is being demonstrated for him at this moment. . . . Your presence here," Geoffrion added, addressing himself directly to Greeley, "is a solemn approval of the path the Institute has followed ever since its foundation, without deviating from it by one iota, despite the countless obstacles amassed on that path." The texts of Dessaulles, Greeley, and Geoffrion were reproduced in the *Annuaire de l'Institut canadien pour 1868*. This 30-page pamphlet was put on the Index in July 1869.

The firmness with which Greeley had all his life defended liberal principles, and the talent he had displayed as a journalist and lecturer, led the liberal Republicans and the Democrats to put him forward in 1872 as a candidate for the presidency. But despite more than 150 speeches in a ruthless electoral campaign, he had the mortification of being defeated by his adversary General U. S. Grant, who was re-elected by a large majority. Horace Greeley died on 29 Nov. 1872 of the double grief caused by this failure and the loss of his beloved wife, Mary Youngs Cheney.

PHILIPPE SYLVAIN

Many archives in the United States hold Greeley papers; the most important collections are in the following: Calais Free Library (Calais, Me.); Denver Public Library; Library of Congress (Washington); New Hampshire Historical Society (Concord, N.H.); New York Historical Society; New York Public Library; Western Reserve Historical Society (Cleveland, Ohio).

The main printed works by Greeley are: *The American conflict: a history of the great rebellion in the United States, 1860–1865 . . .* (2v., Hartford, Conn., and Chicago, 1864–66); *A history of the struggle for slavery extension or restriction in the United States, from the Declaration of Independence to the present day . . .* (New York, 1856); *Recollections of a busy life: including reminiscences of American politics and politicians, from the opening of the Missouri contest to the downfall of slavery . . .* (New York and Boston, 1868).

ACAM, RLB, 17, p.73; 901.059. *Annuaire de l'Institut canadien pour 1868; célébration du 24e anniversaire de la fondation de l'Institut canadien, le 17 décembre 1868* (Montréal, 1868). *DAB.* W. G. Bleyer, *Main currents in the history of American journalism* (Boston, 1927), 211–38. Robert [Philippe] Sylvain, *Clerc, garibaldien, prédicant des deux mondes: Alessandro Gavazzi (1809–1889)* (2v., Québec, 1962), I, 221–22; *La vie et l'œuvre de Henry de Courcy, premier historien de l'Église catholique aux États-Unis* (Québec, 1955).

GREEN, ANSON, Methodist clergyman; b. 27 Sept. 1801 at Middleburgh, Schoharie County, New York, one of a large family born to Joseph Green and Lydia Vorce; d. 19 Feb. 1879 at Toronto, Ont.

Anson Green was raised on the family farm in the Catskills and sent to school for only a short period each year. He had little interest in religion until his mother died in 1816 and he was seriously ill for several months in 1818. He was then led to read the Scriptures and attend prayer meetings, and to a growing conviction of personal sin. In 1819, after he had discovered his brother praying privately in a field for his conversion, Green passed through a spiritual crisis. He felt that his burden of guilt had been removed and he soon joined the Methodist Episcopal Church and was licensed as an exhorter.

Green came to Upper Canada in 1823 while *en route* to Ohio, decided to remain, and, although largely self-educated, obtained a teaching post at West Lake in Prince Edward County. He was licensed to preach in 1824 by the Canada Conference of the Methodist Episcopal Church and was received into the ministry on trial the next year. He was ordained deacon in 1827 and elder in 1830. In 1828 he had married Rachel, second daughter of Caleb HOPKINS, a Reform politician who was later a founding member of the Clear Grit party.

As a saddle-bag parson responsible for a 400-mile frontier circuit, Green preached on an average of once a day. Methodist itinerants were posted to different circuits at least every second year but most of Green's early circuits were in the eastern Lake Ontario–upper St Lawrence region. Green soon earned the reputation of being a fiery preacher, but he also displayed administrative talents which quickly led to his promotion to positions of authority within his church. From 1832 to 1835 he was chairman of the Augusta District in eastern Upper Canada and, from 1836 to 1839, chairman of the Bay of Quinte District. He left this area in 1839 and until 1844 was chairman, first of the Toronto District, later of the

Hamilton District, before returning to the Toronto District.

In 1833 the Canadian conference of the Methodist Episcopal Church had united with the more conservative British Wesleyan Methodist Church (this name being retained), at the instigation and with the financial encouragement of the Colonial Office and the Upper Canadian government [*see* Robert ALDER]. However, many members of the British conference disapproved of the voluntaryism and liberal political sentiments of their Canadian colleagues, particularly as publicly expressed by Egerton Ryerson*, and the union was dissolved in 1840. Some of the Canadian itinerants went to the British body, but Green remained with the Wesleyan Methodist Church in Canada.

Green deplored the disruption of 1840, however. When he was elected president of the Canadian conference in 1842, after having been secretary in the previous year, he and John RYERSON were sent to New York to seek the aid of the American Episcopal Church in healing the breach. They were unsuccessful, but in 1846, when Green went to England with John Ryerson to attend the meeting which resulted in the formation of the Evangelical Alliance, they also formulated the terms which led to the reunion of the Canadian and British churches in 1847.

Green also played a prominent part in promoting the union of the several Methodist denominations in Canada. He was active in the events that led to union of the Wesleyan Methodist conferences of Canada East and Canada West in 1855. He served on a joint committee from 1871 to 1874 when the union of the Canadian Wesleyan Methodist Church, the Methodist New Connexion Church, and the Wesleyan Methodist Church in Eastern British North America was effected.

In 1844 Green had succeeded Alexander McNab* as steward of the conference Book Room and printing establishment (later the United Church Publishing House and its subsidiary, the Ryerson Press) in Toronto, an appointment that marked his effective separation from circuit work and his entry into the central administrative offices of the church. He expanded the operations of the Book Room by making a highly favourable trade arrangement for books with the American conference's Book Room in 1848 and by opening a branch in Montreal in 1849. He also introduced the first steam newspaper press to Canada in 1851 for the use of the Methodists' weekly, the *Christian Guardian*.

Green was concerned with regularizing the institutional life of the church. He was responsible for the incorporation in 1851 of the Wesleyan Methodist Church in Canada and of its Book Room, Annuitant Society, and Superannuation Fund Society. He was involved in the reorganization of the church's temporalities in 1855 when the conference provided increased pecuniary benefits to its preachers. It was also resolved at this conference to appoint equal numbers of laymen and preachers to all committees dealing with finance, the first time laymen were given a role in the government of the Canadian Wesleyan Methodist Church. Green was also named chairman of the church's Board of Superannuation.

Although he himself was superannuated in 1855, Green returned to service in 1856 as a delegate to the British conference, and supervised the transfer of the Methodist missions in the north-west to Canadian jurisdiction. He served as book steward from 1859 to 1862 and in 1864, and he became, in 1863, the first Canadian to be appointed president of the Canadian conference by the British conference under the terms of the 1847 union. He was again placed on the superannuated roll in 1865.

Green had a long connection with Victoria College, particularly with its financial administration. As chairman of the Bay of Quinte District in 1836 he had presided at the opening of the conference's educational institution, the Upper Canada Academy at Cobourg. As treasurer and member of the academy's managing committee he negotiated with Lieutenant Governor Sir Francis Bond HEAD for the payment of the royal grant. When the academy was reopened as Victoria College in 1841 to teach university subjects, Green was chairman of the college board and delivered the address at the installation of its first principal, his friend Egerton Ryerson. In 1858 he became bursar of the college and in 1860 appeared along with Samuel Sobieski Nelles* and Joseph Stinson* before a parliamentary committee which was investigating the claims of denominational colleges to share in the provincial university endowment. In 1868 he was secretary of a joint committee of Queen's University at Kingston and Victoria College, appointed to study the questions of their finances and their proposed affiliation to the University of Toronto.

Over a period of years Green was active in a variety of social and religious agencies, including the provincial asylum and the Toronto House of Industry; he helped organize Canadian Indian and Japanese missions, build Toronto's Metropolitan Methodist Church, and found the Dominion Evangelical Alliance.

In an age when the laity played little part in the government of the Wesleyan Methodist Church, Green acquired a reputation among his fellow clergy of being a successful seeker of offices of power. In every position he occupied he showed

317

managerial talents of a high order and seemed to achieve satisfaction through controlling much of the inner operations of the church rather than in creating a public image as a prominent preacher. In addition to having been three times a delegate to both the English and the American conferences and twice president of the Canadian conference, he held virtually every senior administrative post in his church and served on many of its committees.

Anson Green died in Toronto in 1879 and was survived by his widow and one son, Columbus H. Green, a barrister. His married daughter, Eliza, had died in 1863. Green's autobiography refers in the 1870s to a son, Anson, but this may have been a family name for Columbus.

JOHN S. MOIR

[Anson Green wrote his autobiography, *The life and times of the Rev. Anson Green, D.D. ...* (Toronto, 1877), at the request of the Canadian Wesleyan Methodist Conference. The book is both readable and reliable, but the personal papers on which it was obviously based do not appear to have survived. A few of his letters are in the A. E. Ryerson papers at the United Church of Canada Archives, Toronto, and have been quoted in Sissons, *Ryerson.*

Christian Guardian (Toronto), 26 Feb. 1879. *The minutes of the annual conferences of the Wesleyan Methodist Church in Canada, from 1824 to 1857* (2v., Toronto, 1846–63). [A. E. Ryerson], *My dearest Sophie, letters from Egerton Ryerson to his daughter,* ed. C. B. Sissons (Toronto, 1955). Cornish, *Cyclopædia of Methodism,* I. Carroll, *Case and his cotemporaries. The chronicle of a century, 1829–1929, the record of one hundred years of progress in the publishing concerns of the Methodist, Presbyterian, and Congregational churches in Canada,* ed. Lorne Pierce (Toronto, 1929), 78–85. J.S.M.]

GREY, WILLIAM, Church of England clergyman, missionary, educator, architect, and artist; b. 27 Oct. 1819 in England, second son of the Reverend Harry Grey and Frances Elizabeth Ellis; m., on 25 July 1849, Harriet White by whom he had one son, William, 9th Earl of Stamford; died 1 Sept. 1872 in Exeter, England.

William Grey graduated in classics with a BA in 1842 and an MA in 1845 from Magdalen Hall, Oxford, where he also studied church architecture and ecclesiology. Having been ordained by the bishop of Salisbury, in 1843 Grey became curate of Allington and Amesbury, Wiltshire, where he surprised his neighbours and shocked his relatives by lodging with an old farmer. "His quarters did for him, for he was content with the smallest attendance and the simplest fare," observed a neighbour.

Late in 1848 Edward FEILD, bishop of Newfoundland, who considered Grey to be "a very valuable acquisition" with "qualities eminently serviceable to St John's," engaged him to serve as his secretary and chaplain on a visitation of Bermuda and Newfoundland. Heir presumptive to the earldom of Stamford for the greater part of his life, Grey, unlike most of the men who became missionaries, was in no need of preferment or social advancement. Together with a few others, he is an example of the exceptional type of missionary whom Feild inspired to serve in Newfoundland.

In 1849 Grey's offer to begin a mission on the Labrador coast was refused by Bishop Feild who felt that Grey's talents were more needed in St John's. Feild instead appointed Grey as the principal of Queen's College, St John's – the remodelled version of the theological institute founded by Bishop Aubrey George SPENCER in 1841. There students were hardened for work in Newfoundland by a semi-monastic discipline, were taught theology, and, since the college was Tractarian in tone, could make their confessions to the principal.

After a year as principal, Grey, probably because he wanted a more distinctly missionary existence, moved to Portugal Cove, near St John's. In 1849 he had become diocesan architect, and, as well as designing numerous new churches, such as St Peter's, Portugal Cove, he spread the principles of the Gothic Revival by regular lectures to students and clergy. As colonial correspondent of the Oxford Architectural Society, he contributed an article on "The ecclesiology of Newfoundland" to the *Ecclesiologist.* In it he bemoaned the lack of good church architecture in Newfoundland, and praised Feild's campaign against high pews and galleries.

His wife being ill, Grey left for England in 1853 but returned to Newfoundland in 1857 to accompany Feild on a voyage of visitation of Newfoundland and Labrador. During the voyage, he designed churches at Battle Harbour and Tilt Cove, and, feeling that the quality of sketches published by the Society for the Propagation of the Gospel was too low and that Newfoundland, a "country little known and often very under-rated," deserved better publicity, he made sketches of the colony's churches and scenery which he published in England.

On his return to England late in 1857 or early in 1858 he took charge of the parish of Milford, Whitley, from which he retired in 1865 to live in Exeter. He was in poor health but occupied himself by decorating the roof of St Mary-Steps, a project which may have expedited the throat cancer which caused his death.

William Grey brought to Newfoundland the ideas of the Gothic Revival, and by his sketches and writings helped his bishop to publicize in England the Church of England in Newfoundland.

FREDERICK JONES

USPG, C/CAN/NFL, 7; D, 9A, 9B. William Grey, "The ecclesiology of Newfoundland," *Ecclesiologist* (London), XIV (new ser., XI; 1853), 151–61; [ ], *Sketches of Newfoundland and Labrador* (Ipswich, Eng., [1858]). *Burke's peerage* (1967), 2357. Thomas Mozley, *Reminiscences, chiefly of towns, villages and schools* (2v., London, 1885), II.

GRIFFIN, JANE (Lady Franklin), world traveller, organizer of Arctic expeditions; b. 1792 in London, one of three daughters of John Griffin and Mary Guillemard, both of Huguenot stock; d. 18 July 1875 at London.

Jane Griffin was educated at home and at a small boarding school in Chelsea. She was a close friend of the poetess, Eleanor Anne Porden, first wife of John Franklin*, who died in 1825, only six days after Franklin had left England on his second Arctic overland expedition. When Franklin returned in 1827, he renewed his acquaintance with the Griffin family and in November 1828 he and Jane were quietly married. Five months later he was knighted.

During her youth, Jane had travelled throughout Britain and had frequently visited the Continent with her widowed father, a wealthy silk weaver, and with her sisters or friends. Now, as Lady Franklin, she continued to travel and to describe the events of a crowded life in voluminous journals and long letters. Between 1830 and 1833, when Franklin had command of a frigate on the Mediterranean station, she visited many parts of North Africa, Syria, and Asia Minor. From 1836 to 1843, when Franklin was lieutenant governor of Van Diemen's Land (now Tasmania), she toured the island and took a lively interest in promoting the social and cultural life of the young settlement. She is said to have been the first woman to go overland from Melbourne to Sydney, Australia, and she also visited many parts of New Zealand.

On his return to England in 1844, Franklin, despite his age (nearly 60), sought and obtained the command of a naval expedition then being outfitted to find a northwest passage. In May 1845 he sailed with *Erebus* and *Terror*, provisioned for three years. When in 1848 no word had been received from the expedition, five relief and searching expeditions were sent out. Other expeditions followed every year until 1854, when Dr John Rae* learned from Eskimos near King William Island details of the expedition's tragic fate.

Lady Franklin took a leading part in the organization of the searching expeditions. Between 1850 and 1857 she outfitted five ships wholly or mainly at her own expense, and she inspired substantial contributions to her cause from other persons and from other nations. This work involved her with many leading personalities of her time and she became as learned in Arctic geography as any authority of the day. By returning again and again to the orders Admiralty had given her husband and to her knowledge of his invincible sense of duty, she was, as events proved, in general more nearly correct about his route and where his ships should be sought than anyone else except, perhaps, Dr Richard KING.

In 1857, at personal expense, she sent the yacht *Fox* (Capt. Francis Leopold M'Clintock*), in a final search for survivors, records, and other evidences of the expedition's fate. Three years later M'Clintock returned with numerous relics, among them a record that gave news of the discovery of a northwest passage, of Franklin's death in 1847 and of other deaths, of the abandonment of the ships in 1848, and of the survivors' intention to head for Back River, on which journey, as later searches revealed, the last of the men must have died.

Exhausted by the dramatic events of the previous 12 years, Lady Franklin now turned with relief to her passion for foreign travel. She and her secretary-companion, Sophia Cracroft, her niece by marriage, accepted a long-standing invitation to visit Henry Grinnell, a wealthy New York merchant who had personally supported two expeditions in the Franklin search. Lady Franklin had visited North America in 1846, and she was eager to return. In August 1860, after an enthusiastic reception in New York, she and Sophia travelled to Montreal, where their reception was hardly less royal than that accorded the young Prince of Wales, who was then touring the Canadas. They visited Quebec and cruised up the Saguenay River, then stopped at Ottawa, Kingston, Toronto, and Hamilton on their return to New York, where they sailed for San Francisco by way of Cape Horn.

They reached California early in 1861 and pressed northward to British Columbia, reaching Esquimalt on 24 February, delighted, according to Sophia, to be "once more among our own people only, after many months of residence with Americans." Lady Franklin was more than somewhat anti-American and objected especially to American accents. They spent a month in Victoria, during which they crossed to the mainland to ascend the Fraser River, first by commercial vessel as far as Yale, then in a canoe paddled by 12 Indians up to the Fraser's first falls. On their return, they discovered hanging over a narrow canyon a white banner with "Lady Franklin Pass" lettered on it, a tribute from the citizens of Yale that has not, as a place-name, endured. After a short return visit to California, they continued their journey by way of the Sandwich Islands (Hawaii), Japan, and India. During the rest of the decade, Lady Franklin frequently visited Europe and made a long tour of India.

In October 1865 she first heard rumours that Charles Francis HALL believed, on the basis of Eskimo reports, that there might still be survivors of Franklin's expedition. She wished to question him personally and, when she learned in September 1869 that he had come back from King William Island with numerous relics of the expedition, she and Sophia set out, by a circuitous route, to meet him in the United States.

They rounded Cape Horn once more, stopped again at San Francisco, then, in late April 1870, travelled farther north on the steamer *Newborn*. After a few days among old friends in Victoria, they continued up the west coast to Alaska. On 10 May they stopped at Tongass and two days later reached Sitka, where they spent a month. Sophia's 16-page letter home and her illustrated journal of their residence in Sitka are a valuable description of Alaska in its first years of occupation by the United States. In July they travelled by rail from San Francisco to Salt Lake City, where they stopped to disapprove of the Mormons on their home ground. Brigham Young himself came to visit them, which prompted Sophia to suppose "it was the first time in his life, that the President [Young] had ever paid a visit of ceremony or respect to any woman." In Cincinnati, Ohio, and later in New York they achieved the great object of their journey, interviews with Hall. Unfortunately, no record of what passed between them has been preserved. At the time of their meetings, Hall's plans to try for the North Pole had been formed, but he evidently agreed to renew later his search for survivors on or near King William Island.

Even when she was in her eighties, Lady Franklin's attention was still firmly fixed on Arctic matters and in 1875 she took an active interest in the preparations of the expedition by George Strong Nares* toward the North Pole and, especially, in Allen Young*'s proposed search for Franklin's records. Among her very last concerns was the erection in Westminster Abbey of a monument to her husband, which was unveiled a fortnight after her own death. It bore, in part, these words: ". . . erected by Jane, his widow, who, after long waiting, and sending many in search of him, herself departed, to seek and to find him in the realms of light. . . ." She was buried in Kensal Green, west London, beside her sister, Lady Mary Simpkinson.

Lady Franklin never allowed herself to be photographed, she published no books, she did not lecture, and her campaigns were mainly conducted through others. But, in a period when popular sentiment was greatly influenced by the example of Queen Victoria mourning her consort, Lady Franklin's steadfast loyalty to her husband's memory and her own impressive dignity in adversity gave her, despite her reserve, a firm hold on the public's imagination and sympathy, and her name was a household word throughout the world.

It has often been said that the loss of Franklin's expedition achieved more for the exploration of the Canadian Arctic than its success could have done. To the extent that this generalization is true, the credit is due to Lady Franklin, who would not rest nor would she let those in authority rest until the whole truth of the expedition's fate, so far as it could be ascertained, had been found out and the achievements of her husband and his men fittingly acknowledged.

ALAN COOKE

SPRI, MS 248/121, 248/122 (Jane Franklin's two-volume journal, August–September 1860, 1–5 Jan. 1861); MS 248/160 (Jane Franklin's journal, July–August 1846); MS 248/163/3 (Jane Franklin's journal notes, July–August 1860); MS 248/242 (Sophia Cracroft's journal at Sitka, 12 May–14 June 1870); MS 248/247/73–83 (Sophia Cracroft's letters, 13 Dec. 1860–9 June 1862); MS 248/247/84–96 (her letters, 23 Jan.–18 July 1870); MS 695 (Sophia Cracroft's journal letter, February–April 1861).
Times (London), 19 July 1875. *DNB*. Kathleen Fitzpatrick, *Sir John Franklin in Tasmania, 1837–1843* (Melbourne, Aust., 1949). A. L. Korn, *The Victorian visitors: an account of the Hawaiian kingdom, 1861–1866, including the journal letters of Sophia Cracroft, extracts from the journals of Lady Franklin, and diaries and letters of Queen Emma of Hawaii* (Honolulu, 1958). F. L. M'Clintock, *The voyage of the "Fox" in the Arctic seas: a narrative of the discovery of the fate of Sir John Franklin and his companions* (London, 1859). W. F. Rawnsley, *The life, diaries, and correspondence of Jane, Lady Franklin, 1792–1875* (London, 1923). F. J. Woodward, *Portrait of Jane: a life of Lady Franklin* (London, 1951).

GUGY, BARTHOLOMEW CONRAD AUGUSTUS, soldier, MHA, seigneur; b. 6 Nov. 1796 at Trois-Rivières, eldest son of Louis Gugy*, member of the assembly, seigneur, and legislative councillor, and of Juliana O'Connor; d. suddenly on 11 June 1876 at his residence of Darnoc, at Beauport, near Quebec.

A Huguenot by birth, and the son of a Swiss colonel who was a French royalist before entering the service of Great Britain, Bartholomew was educated at the school of the Reverend John

Strachan* at Cornwall, and enlisted in the Canadian Fencibles as soon as war was declared in 1812. He fought beside his father, was promoted lieutenant, and distinguished himself at the battle of Châteauguay. He then studied law and was called to the bar on 7 Aug. 1822. He was not long in acquiring a numerous and lucrative clientele, but his subsequent career was above all political and military.

In 1831 Gugy was elected to the assembly for Sherbrooke, and was re-elected until the period of the 1837–38 disturbances. As he was one of the small number of Tories who could express themselves readily in French, he had frequent and stirring verbal bouts with Louis-Joseph PAPINEAU. Gugy fought with supple oratory, using irony, banter, sarcasm, and insolence. He had the knack of finding the best way to exasperate the speaker, and the latter would respond loudly. (According to certain champions of Papineau, it was this same Gugy who was chiefly responsible for the improprieties of language of the *Patriotes* and their leader.)

In 1837, at the first echo of the revolt, Gugy volunteered for the militia. With the rank of colonel, he led the cavalry at Saint-Charles, and it may have been he who personally seized the "column of liberty" the *Patriotes* had erected in honour of Papineau, and carried it in triumph (with two subalterns) to Montreal. At Saint-Eustache he again distinguished himself by his enthusiasm. He is said to have led his horse into the church in order to water it at the stoups. He was accused of cruelty, and even of walking knee deep in the blood of French Canadians. But a pamphlet, *Attestation de six curés au sujet de la conduite du colonel Gugy en 1837–1838*, re-establishes the truth in his favour. Later, having billetted his troops at Saint-Hyacinthe, Gugy stayed at the Dessaulles' house, where the Papineau children had taken refuge. He gave a wax doll to Ezilda and two picture books to Gustave.

From 22 Nov. 1838 to 2 Jan. 1839, Gugy held the position of police magistrate at Montreal, and on 14 March 1841 he agreed to become adjutant-general of militia for Lower Canada. Until his resignation on 30 June 1846 he was one of the favourite targets of the Liberal party of Louis-Hippolyte La Fontaine*, which accused him of not appointing enough French Canadians to the higher ranks of the militia. After the Union in 1841, Gugy had stood as a Tory candidate in Saint-Maurice County, but had been defeated despite the scrutineer's efforts on his behalf. In fact, the supporters of his opponent, Joseph-Édouard Turcotte*, had seized the polling booth. He had also been a candidate in Sherbrooke but was de-

feated by Edward HALE. In 1848 he was elected by acclamation in the town of Sherbrooke. In the house, Gugy voted regularly against La Fontaine's ministry, and during the famous debate on the rebellion losses bill, Gugy, with Sir Allan Napier MacNab*, was the principal leader of the opposition. His speeches contributed not a little to the almost electric tension that finally exploded during the riots following the burning of the parliament building in 1849. He reacted with his customary spirit and impetuosity, and began to fight with the very people who had been aroused by his speeches. During the night the parliament was set on fire, he seized several of the agitators to stop them from setting upon the speaker, Augustin-Norbert Morin*; the next day, 26 April, on the Champ de Mars, when the rioters were assembling to launch an attack on the homes of Francis Hincks*, Benjamin Holmes*, and La Fontaine, Gugy climbed a lamp-post and harangued the crowd for two hours, trying in vain to persuade them to disperse. These pirouettes (physical and political) led *Le Canadien* of 9 May 1849 to portray the colonel as "a hitherto undescribed variety of the species, one who belongs to no nation in particular . . . being part Swiss, part Irish, part French, part Indian, and we believe part ——." After 1850, through fear of the annexationists, Gugy gradually drew away from the Montreal Tories. This is perhaps why he did not venture to become a candidate in the 1851 election.

That year Colonel Gugy was nevertheless appointed one of the Canadian representatives to the universal exhibition in London. In 1853 he received another civil post as inspector and superintendent of police at Montreal, but resigned the same year to retire to the estate at Beauport that he had inherited in 1840 from his father, together with the seigneuries of Yamachiche, Rivière-du-Loup, Grandpré, Grosbois, and Dumontier. After a stinging defeat in 1854 at the hands of another Tory, James Moir Ferres, in Missisquoi-Est, he retired from politics for good.

Hot-headed, irascible, endowed with a colourful nature, the bulky, loud-voiced colonel was not vindictive, or intolerant, or sectarian. As a seigneur, he collected his rents with regularity, but never resorted to vexatious measures. He liked lawsuits. In 1844, for example, he had given a thrashing to a young delivery-boy who, on Francis Hincks' orders, persisted in leaving the *Pilot* at the colonel's door. Hincks had prosecuted him, and Gugy had particularly enjoyed his victory. Later, he brought actions against a certain William Brown which lasted 22 years, and which were ended only by the fire that destroyed the Palais de Justice at Quebec in 1873. Towards the end of his life Gugy

Guigues

often returned to Quebec, riding erect on horseback despite his 78 years, to ensconce himself in the library of the Palais de Justice and regale the young of all ages with the details of his former litigations and addresses to the court. He does not seem to have had a fanatical temperament. If he was never popular among French Canadians, it is because he too often upheld principles which they rejected.

By his two marriages, with Louise Duchesnay and Mary McGrath, he had one son and three daughters.

JACQUES MONET

B. C. A. Gugy, *How I lost my money: an episode in my life* (Quebec, 1859); *Letters originally published in the "Quebec Gazette," addressed to His Excellency Sir E. W. Head, Bart, governor-general of B.N. America, &c.* (Quebec, 1855). PAC, MG 30, D62 (Audet papers), 14, pp.641–762. *Certaines attestations, dédiées au jury éclairé qui a décidé la cause Gugy vs Brown* (Québec, 1871). *Le Canadien* (Québec), 9 mai 1849, 12 juin 1876. *Montreal Standard*, 3 Feb 1912. Morgan, *Sketches of celebrated Canadians*, 517–28. *Political appointments, 1841–1865* (J.-O. Coté).

Raphaël Bellemare, *Les bases de l'histoire d'Yamachiche 1703–1903; commémoration des premiers établissements dans cette paroisse; ses fiefs, ses seigneurs, ses premiers habitants, ses développements, son démembrement en plusieurs paroisses et autres renseignements tirés de manuscrits inédits conservés dans les vieilles archives du Bas-Canada* (Montréal, 1901), 100–1. Cornell, *Alignment of political groups*. Dent, *Last forty years*, II, 616. Gérard Filteau, *Histoire des Patriotes* (3v., Montréal, 1938–39). Monet, *Last cannon shot*. D. R. Barry, "An eminent Quebec lawyer of the last century," *Canadian Law Times* (Toronto), XXXII (1912), 427–38. É.-Z. Massicotte, "Les tribunaux de police de Montréal," *BRH*, XXVI (1920), 180–83. P.-G. Roy, "Bartholomew-Conrad-Augustus Gugy," *BRH*, X (1904), 333–36.

GUIGUES, JOSEPH-BRUNO, priest, Oblate of Mary Immaculate, bishop, and educator; b. 26 Aug. 1805 in the hamlet of La Garde, in the commune of Gap (department of Hautes-Alpes), France, son of Bruno Guigues, army officer and goldsmith, and Thérèse Richier; d. 8 Feb. 1874 at Ottawa, Ont.

Joseph-Bruno Guigues, to whose first name Eugène is sometimes added, began his studies at Gap and continued them at the classical college at Forcalquier. On 2 Aug. 1821 he entered the noviciate of the Oblates at Notre-Dame-du-Laus (Hautes-Alpes). Because of his youth he did not make his profession until 4 Nov. 1823, at Aix-en-Provence, and he remained in this town to complete his theological studies.

While still just a deacon, Guigues was appointed professor of philosophy (1827–28) and bursar (1827–29) at the seminary of Marseilles. On 31 May 1828 he was ordained priest by Charles-Fortuné de Mazenod, bishop of Marseilles. Shortly afterwards he was appointed novice-master at Saint-Just, near Marseilles, but was obliged to give up his post for reasons of health, and he then spent some years at Notre-Dame-du-Laus and at Aix. In 1834 Guigues became first superior and parish priest *ex officio* at Notre-Dame de l'Osier (department of Isère), and raised this ancient place of pilgrimage from its material and spiritual ruins. At the same time he devoted himself to preaching retreats in the dioceses of Grenoble and Valence, and contributed to the regional Catholic journal.

In 1844, after 10 years of steadfast service during which he won the confidence of the French bishops, he was appointed "visitor," or acting superior, in Canada, where the Oblates had been working since 1841. He arrived at Longueuil on 18 Aug. 1844, and immediately began organizing his congregation. During his stay at Longueuil he sent missionaries to relieve secular priests; the Indians of the Saguenay and Timiskaming regions thus received visits. Then, in 1845, Fathers Alexandre-Antonin Taché* and Pierre Aubert* set off for the Red River missions. Guigues endeavoured also to send missionaries to Oregon: in 1847 Father Pascal Ricard, together with three priests and a brother, left France for this mission. In addition, the Oblates concerned themselves with a number of houses in the United States. While directing missionary activities, Guigues was also superior of the new community of sisters of the Holy Names of Jesus and Mary.

The Canadian bishops, Ignace Bourget* in particular, were not slow in recognizing the qualities of the superior of the Oblates and obtained his appointment as first bishop of Bytown (Ottawa) on 9 July 1847. Not being familiar with the English language, Guigues withdrew to the parish of Saint-Colomban in the diocese of Montreal (now in the diocese of Saint-Jérôme) to learn it, as it was indispensable for his new sphere of activity. On 30 July 1848 he was consecrated bishop in the Bytown cathedral by Rémi Gaulin*, bishop of Kingston.

The new bishop continued to direct the Congregation of the Oblates, first as "extraordinary visitor" until 1851, when Father Jacques Santoni* succeeded him, and again from 1856 when he was appointed provincial. He was replaced by Father Joseph-Henri Tabaret* in 1864. This position with the congregation did not prevent him from giving serious attention to the affairs of his vast diocese, with a population of 35,000 to 40,000 persons, a good many of whom were Protestant. On his arrival he found an unfinished cathedral, three stone churches, and some 15 chapels made of wood; seven secular priests and seven Oblates made up his whole clergy. He set to work resolutely, and at the time of his death 67 churches, 48 chapels, and several schools were in existence; he had under him 53 secular priests and 37 Oblates. In 1871 the population of the diocese reached a total of 182,171, of whom 96,548 were Catholics.

The bishop took a keen interest in the missions among the Indians and in the lumber camps. He even worked towards setting up an apostolic vicariate for the Indians located between James Bay and Labrador, but this plan was realized only in the 20th century. Guigues also devoted his efforts to the task of settlement; to ensure its success, he started a settlement society on 3 Sept. 1849 and took on the presidency himself. The purpose of this society was to supply useful information to new settlers, and to get the government to open roads and survey land. He wrote numerous letters on this subject to various authorities. He was of the opinion that the clergy must take an interest in this work, but he considered that it was "essentially a laic" enterprise and that the direction of it was better left to laymen. For the work to make headway, he judged it expedient to steer the Quebec settlers towards the Gatineau region and the townships situated between Rigaud and Bytown. "It is better to begin with these," he said, "for Canadiens are troubled when they are alone; it is preferable to put them in groups." As for the Irish settlers, he encouraged them to settle between Ottawa and Lake Huron.

Education of youth was one of his first concerns. As early as September 1848 he opened a college and a seminary at Bytown. In 1856 a new stone college was erected on the present site of the University of Ottawa. Father Joseph-Henri Tabaret was its superior, and the Oblates were entrusted with directing it. They continued to do so until 1965. The seminary provided the bishop with some priests, but, to fill his needs, he had to recruit several from his native diocese.

Bishop Guigues was a perspicacious man, who grasped immediately the special character of his diocese and introduced bilingualism into the ministry and into education. He was also active on behalf of Catholic schools, and fought for a long time to obtain justice for Catholics and French Canadians. He offered to have given free at the college in Ottawa "a course of instruction designed to provide complete education and result in the qualifications necessary for teaching." He presided over several citizens' meetings to encourage them to support and defend Catholic and French schools. He was in constant touch with the episcopate of Ontario, in particular with Armand de Charbonnel*, bishop of Toronto, as well as with Richard William Scott*, a member of the Legislative Assembly, in order to obtain a law favourable to separate schools. It was passed in 1863. In his letters to Egerton Ryerson*, the superintendent of education for Canada West, Guigues denounced mixed schools (common schools), which he considered as one of the greatest threats to family peace and the future of the whole country. Finally, he helped the Ottawa schools by lending them sums drawn from the episcopal treasury. He supported the Grey Nuns, who were already established at Ottawa, and their superior, Mother Élisabeth Bruyère, and had the Brothers of the Christian Schools and the sisters of the Congregation of Notre-Dame come to Ottawa. The latter organized a boarding-school.

A friend of the poor and forsaken, Bishop Guigues gave his support to the setting up of an old people's home, and recruited the Good Shepherd Nuns of Angers who came from Buffalo to open a house for the protection of young girls. The bishop also encouraged the Institut Canadien-Français of Ottawa, the Union Saint-Joseph (which has become the Union du Canada), the Institute of Young Catholic Irishmen, the Cercle Littéraire de la Jeunesse Catholique, and the St Vincent de Paul Society.

The bishop of Ottawa had the interest of the Canadian church at heart, and regularly attended the provincial councils of Quebec. In 1870 he went to the Vatican council, where he received the title of Roman count, and visited several general chapters of his congregation in France. His attachment to the universal church had led him to propose a plan for the support of the Zouaves when the papal states were invaded in 1867. As early as 1860 he had recommended that each bishop support one or more Zouaves.

By nature of great gentleness and charm, Bishop Guigues possessed unusual energy and knew how to circumvent obstacles to attain his ends. He was a simple man; until the end of his life he discharged the duties of parish priest or vicar, he regularly heard confession in his cathedral, and he often preached and visited the sick. He made a tour of his diocese each year, and these visits constituted veritable retreats during which the bishop was accessible to all.

GASTON CARRIÈRE

Ten registers of Bishop Guigues' correspondence are found at the Archevêché d'Ottawa; other letters are in the Archives provinciales O.M.I. (Montreal) and the Archives générales O.M.I. (Rome). A copy of each of these documents is at the AHO. A copy of Dossier F. 182 (Ottawa, mission reports, 1848–76), Archives

Gunn

de la Propagation de la Foi de Paris, can be found at the Research Centre in Canadian Religious History at St Paul's University Seminary (Ottawa).

[Louis Gladu], *Monseigneur J.E.B. Guigues, 1er évêque d'Ottawa: sa vie et ses œuvres* (Ottawa, 1874). *Notices nécrologiques des O.M.I.*, III, 89–130. Alexis de Barbezieux, *Histoire de la province ecclésiastique d'Ottawa et de la colonisation dans la vallée de l'Ottawa* (2v., Ottawa, 1897), I, 241–609. Carrière, *Histoire des O.M.I.* Pierre Hurtubise, "Mgr de Charbonnel et Mgr Guigues; la lutte en faveur des écoles séparées à la lumière de leur correspondance (1850–1856)," *Revue de l'université d'Ottawa*, XXXIII (1963), 38–61. Henri Morisseau, "Mgr Joseph-Eugène Guigues, oblat de Marie-Immaculée, premier évêque d'Ottawa," *Revue de l'université d'Ottawa*, XVII (1947), 136–80. Albert Perbal, "Mgr Guigues . . . ," *Petites annales de la Congrégation de missionnaires oblats de Marie-Immaculée* (Paris), XIX (1909), 139–45. Edgar Thivierge, "A la naissance du diocèse d'Ottawa," *Revue de l'université d'Ottawa*, VII (1937), 424–40; VIII (1938), 6–30.

GUNN, DONALD, educator, scientist, historian, and politician; b. at Halkirk, Caithness-shire, Scotland, September 1797, youngest son of William Gunn, a tenant farmer in the strath of Braeholme; d. at St Andrews, Man., 30 Nov. 1878.

Donald Gunn was educated in the parish school of Halkirk. In 1813 he entered the service of the Hudson's Bay Company and spent ten years at York Factory, Severn Fort, and Oxford House successively, earning promotion to lesser postmaster. In 1819 he married Margaret, eldest daughter of James Swain, a company officer; between 1822 and 1849 they had seven sons and two daughters. In 1823, his services not being required after the union of the HBC and the North West Company, he settled at Red River in "Little Britain," later the parish of St Andrews. His farm prospered and after ten years the assistance of his growing family enabled him to take charge for the next 18 years of the Church Missionary Society's parish school. He also acted later in his substantial stone house as custodian and librarian of the only public collection of books in Red River.

A critic of the company and a leader of the settlers in the demand for a greater degree of self-government, Gunn was never appointed to the Council of Assiniboia, but he early became a magistrate and president of the Court of Petty Sessions in his district. He served as foreman of the jury at the trial of Pierre-Guillaume Sayer in 1849. In 1870 he was chosen as delegate from St Andrews to the provisional assembly, although he was an advocate of the entry of the northwest into confederation. The Gunns seem to have been on friendly terms with John Christian Schultz* and his wife. Subsequent to the establishment of Manitoba as a province, Gunn was appointed police magistrate, justice of the peace, postmaster, and inspector of fisheries. On 10 March 1871 he was appointed to the Legislative Council of Manitoba and remained a member until its abolition, which he supported, in 1876.

Gunn played an important part not only in public affairs but also in the cultural and intellectual life of Red River. As an outspoken opponent of the HBC and as a leading Presbyterian layman, he was frequently involved in controversy with the authorities of the colony. Nevertheless he retained the respect of the majority and the personal esteem of many. He was a member of the Council of the Institute of Rupert's Land of 1862. His interest in natural history was reflected in his experiments with new methods of tillage and new strains of wheat and led to his long-standing connection with the Smithsonian Institution, of which he was one of the earliest meteorological correspondents. He earned a tribute from its secretary for the reliability of his observations of the weather and the importance of the objects he contributed in nearly every branch of natural history as well as archaeology and ethnology. In 1866 he made a special exploration for the Smithsonian of the region west of Lake Winnipeg to collect skins and birds' eggs, "among the latter several previously entirely unknown in museums."

Gunn disputes with Alexander Ross* the title of father of the history of Canada's prairie west. As an historian he was primarily concerned to provide for his readers all the available information. At the same time he by no means ignored the historian's duty of critical evaluation of his sources. An eye-witness of many of the events described in his posthumously published *History of Manitoba*, he was aware of the danger of "depending for our knowledge of past events on the special pleading of others." Though his history is essentially a narrative of events he did not avoid problems of interpretation. His sympathies clearly lie with the settlers rather than with the HBC. A staunch Presbyterian and an elder of his Kirk, he was not illiberal in religious outlook, though often critical of the Anglican and Roman Catholic clergy of the colony. His attitude to those he saw as representative of an unjust order, from Lord Selkirk [Douglas*] to Bishop David Anderson*, was tinged with an acerbity by no means characteristic of the relations with others of this genial and humorous man.

L. G. THOMAS

Smithsonian Institution, *Annual report, 1878* (Washington), 63–64. Donald Gunn, "Indian remains near Red River settlement, Hudson's bay territory," Smithsonian Institution, *Annual report, 1867* (Washington), 399–400; "Notes of an egging expedition to Shoal lake, west of lake Winnipeg. Made under the direction of the Smithsonian Institution in 1867 . . . ," Smithsonian Institution, *Annual report, 1867* (Washington), 427–32. Donald Gunn and C. R. Tuttle, *History of Manitoba from the earliest settlement to 1835 by the late Hon. Donald Gunn, and from the admission of the province into the Dominion by Charles R. Tuttle* (Ottawa, 1880). Begg, *Hist. of North-West*, I, 393ff., 450; II, 35. Morton, *Manitoba, a history*.

GWYNNE, WILLIAM CHARLES, physician and educator; b. at Castleknock, Ireland, April 1806, son of the Reverend William Gwynne, of the Church of Ireland, and of Eliza Nelson; d. on board ship, 1 Sept. 1875.

William Charles Gwynne followed the eight-year programme in arts and medicine at Trinity College, Dublin, becoming a Bachelor of Medicine in 1831, and earned certificates of surgical competence in both Dublin and Edinburgh. Early in 1832 he sailed for Quebec as ship's surgeon and by June had established himself in York (Toronto). His scholarly antecedents ensured a respectable practice, which was strengthened socially by his marriage in 1835 to Anne Murray Powell, granddaughter of William Dummer Powell*. His combativeness, however, drove him immediately to oppose the Tory clique which controlled medical teaching, licensing, and hospital attendance for Toronto and Upper Canada. He convened meetings and circulated petitions in this cause during the late 1830s; in October 1838 he took his place on the enlarged and reformed Medical Board of Upper Canada. By 1839 Gwynne was also deputy grand master of the Grand Orange Lodge of British North America, but left the order after an unsuccessful attempt in that year to depose and succeed Ogle Robert GOWAN as grand master.

Gwynne was ready to admit his involvement in politics, his special enemies being "the Ultra-Canadian party" or Compact Tories. He considered himself "liberal conservative," and the appointment of Charles Poulett Thomson* as governor cheered him. He was at first the only doctor named to the new commission of management for the Provincial Lunatic Asylum in 1841. In November 1842 Governor Sir Charles Bagot* appointed him professor of anatomy and physiology in the projected King's College, Toronto, with precedence over the other medical professors. (He was later Bagot's physician during his last illness.) Sitting on King's College council from September 1843, Gwynne led minority opposition to High Church and clerical dominance there, and precipitated prolonged inquiries into the manage-

ment of the college's rich endowment. He continued his campaigns (usually in association with Christopher Widmer*, the city's senior doctor) against both Tory and Radical factions seeking sole and statutory control over the medical profession. In all these matters Gwynne, like many other whiggish, low church Anglo-Irish gentlemen, found Robert Baldwin*'s parliamentary group congenial spokesmen, and Baldwin's bill of 1849 reconstituting the University of Toronto met his wishes. Under it he remained professor of anatomy.

When a political deal involving John Rolph*, leader of the Radical doctors in Canada West and a minister in Francis Hincks*' administration, abolished the university's medical school in 1853, Gwynne, incensed, retired to Britain, but he returned to Toronto in 1856. He neglected both politics and medicine (except for his continued membership on the Medical Board) for farming and the study of insects. Gwynne had various landholdings which were always entangled by mortgage and debt; he had only one other business interest: a directorship in the Toronto and Goderich Railway for 1846–49 and for 1851–53 in the railway that succeeded it in 1851, the Toronto and Guelph, both short-lived promotions of his brother, the lawyer John Wellington Gwynne*.

Gwynne's strong sense of intellectual and social self-esteem had drawn him first to combat on many fronts. Then, on his own defeat, and the eclipse of his allies, he was condemned to a stubborn inner exile. Wracked by long frustrations, Gwynne died from "an ulcer in the stomach" on board the *Miramichi* on 1 Sept. 1875 while travelling to New Brunswick for his health. Three sons had died in infancy; only an unmarried daughter and his shrewish wife survived him.

BARRIE DYSTER

Academy of Medicine (Toronto), 920 (Local biography), (Gwynne, certificates and testimonials, 1829–31); AM 360 (Bagot to Gwynne, January 1843). MTCL, Baldwin papers, entries in the index for Gwynne, Croft, and Crooks; typescript by J. H. Richardson, "Reminiscences of the medical profession in Toronto." PAC, MG 24, A13 (Charles Bagot papers), 2, Christopher Widmer to Bagot, 10 Nov. 1842; Gwynne to Bagot, 25 Nov. 1842; 5, Bagot to Gwynne, 21 Nov. 1842; Bagot to Widmer, 6 Nov. 1842; Bagot to John Strachan, 9 Dec. 1842; RG 5, A1, 17 Nov. 1835, 29 Jan. 1836, 5 March 1836; C1, 1841, no.1434; 1842, no.2723. PAO, Jarvis-Powell papers, 1842, 1843, 1853, 1854; Ridout papers, G. Powell to Charlotte Ridout, 10 Feb. 1873. St James' Cemetery (Toronto), record book and monument. University of Toronto Archives, Office of the Chief Accountant financial records (109, Final report of the commission of inquiry of 1848 into the affairs of King's College and Upper Canada College); Office of the Chief

Hale

Accountant (117, King's College Council Minute Book, III, 1842–48); University of Toronto Senate minutes, 1850–53.
Examiner (Toronto), 8 May 1850. *Globe* (Toronto), 4 May 1850, September 1875. Toronto, *Directories*, 1833–75. Canniff, *Medical profession in Upper Canada*, 86–89, 402–7. *Institutional care of the insane in the United States and Canada*, ed. H. M. Hurd (4v., [Baltimore, 1916–17]), IV, 131. *Landmarks of Toronto* (Robertson), III, 13–14.

H

HALE, EDWARD, businessman, MHA, and legislative councillor; b. 6 Dec. 1800 at Quebec, second son of the Honourable John Hale* and Elizabeth Frances Amherst, sister of Lord William Pitt Amherst; d. 26 April 1875 at Quebec.

Edward Hale is sometimes confused with his uncle and namesake, the seigneur of Portneuf, who died in 1862. His father was a member of both the Legislative and the Executive councils of Lower Canada; his brother, Jeffrey Hale*, was an important figure at Quebec, where a hospital still bears his name. Edward Hale was educated at Kensington, England, in a private school, where he seems to have attained a level of knowledge equivalent to that of today's secondary schools. His voluminous correspondence, in which he expresses himself with elegance, precision, and humour, gives evidence of remarkable learning. In 1820 he returned to Quebec, where he was appointed a secretary in the office of the auditor general of the province of Lower Canada.

Edward Hale spent the years 1823 to 1828 in India as private secretary to his uncle, Lord Amherst, who was then its governor general. On 10 March 1831, having returned to Quebec, he married Eliza Cecilia Bowen, daughter of Edward Bowen*, chief justice of the Superior Court of Lower Canada; they had seven children, one of whom, Edward John, married the granddaughter of Jonathan Sewell*.

Life as a public servant does not seem to have appealed strongly to Edward Hale. As early as the summer of 1833 he thought of settling in the Eastern Townships, and gathered information from compatriots already established at Drummondville, Sherbrooke, and Richmond. On 18 Feb. 1834 his uncle Edward Hale, of Portneuf, congratulated him on having bought a farm at Sherbrooke, sent him seed, and discussed the timber trade with him. Hale built a house on the banks of the Rivière Saint-François, probably during 1834. On 14 October of the same year, Peter McGill* asked him for information about the Eastern Townships, on behalf of immigrants who wanted to buy land from the British American Land Company: Hale eventually became one of the shareholders of this company, of which for a time Alexander Tilloch Galt* was secretary. Hale spent the years after 1834 developing his holdings.

During the 1837–38 disturbances, Hale served "for some weeks" with the Sherbrooke volunteers as the colonel's secretary. He was considered an important citizen of the Eastern Townships and was nominated to the Special Council. Thomas Leigh Goldie informed him of the appointment on 27 Aug. 1839, and on 2 September he accepted. He voted for the resolutions on the union of Upper and Lower Canada on 13 November.

On 6 Aug. 1840 the governor general, Lord Sydenham [Thomson*], divided Lower Canada into 22 municipal districts and appointed wardens for each of them. Edward Hale was chosen to preside over the district council of Sherbrooke. The new officials found themselves charged with important responsibilities both for the municipalities and for education. Edward Hale's correspondence with Dr Jean-Baptiste MEILLEUR, concerning the schools in his district, showed that he carried out his task conscientiously.

In 1841, at the time of the elections for the new parliament, Edward Hale was asked to stand in Sherbrooke. His opponent was Colonel Bartholomew Conrad Augustus GUGY, who had already represented this constituency in the House of Assembly of Lower Canada from 1831 to 1838. Gugy even wrote to Hale on 21 March 1841, to ask him to withdraw from the electoral struggle, but Hale refused to do so. Gugy was defeated, disputed the election, and lost his appeal.

Edward Hale went to the sessions of the assembly regularly, whether at Kingston or Montreal. His correspondence with his wife shows that he was most assiduous in attending the sittings of the house and interested in the different questions debated there. But these duties were prejudicial to his business, and on 17 Nov. 1847 he informed William Badgley*, who had just been appointed attorney general for Lower Canada, of his intention not to stand at the next elections. His successor as MHA for Sherbrooke was Colonel Gugy. In 1867, when the province of Quebec was set up, Edward Hale agreed to sit on the Legislative

Council for the division of Wellington, and remained a member until his death.

Edward Hale was a businessman of some standing: in the three townships of Shipton, Eaton, and Simpson alone he owned nearly 4,000 acres of land; in that of Brompton, he owned seven lots "in good condition." His correspondence reveals him as a man much taken up with the sale of land, mortgages, loans, the negotiating of interest, and farm activities; farmers would write to borrow money, buy pieces of land, pay their interest, or request extensions of time. Hale was often urged to establish a branch of the Bank of Montreal at Sherbrooke, but none was opened in the town until 1908. He placed funds in the Eastern Townships Bank; when it was amalgamated with the Canadian Bank of Commerce in 1912, the Hale estate still had $12,000 in it. He also had an interest in the Stanstead and Sherbrooke Mutual Fire Insurance Company, of which he was president from 1865 until his death, and gave much attention to the Sherbrooke Agricultural Society. Finally, Hale was associated with the project, proposed in 1843 by A. T. Galt, for the construction of a railway linking Montreal and Boston and passing through the Eastern Townships; he was a member of the sub-committee responsible for drawing up plans. In 1845 the St Lawrence and Atlantic Railway received a charter, the railhead decided on being Portland (Maine) rather than Boston [see POOR]. Hale was on the provisional committee formed to supervise the undertaking.

In 1866 Edward Hale was appointed chancellor of the University of Bishop's College, in recognition of his services to the Church of England in the Eastern Townships. He died at his son's residence at Quebec, and was buried at Sherbrooke.

LOUIS-PHILIPPE AUDET

ANQ, Famille Hale. PAC, MG 23, G II, 18 (John Hale papers). Bishop's University Archives (Lennoxville, Que.), Minutes of the corporation, 1866–75. Holy Trinity Cathedral (Quebec), marriage registers, 1831. McCord Museum (McGill University, Montreal), Hale family papers. St Peter's Church (Sherbrooke, Que.) burial registers, 29 April 1875. Stanstead and Sherbrooke Insurance Company (Sherbrooke, Que.), Minutes, 1865–75. *Cyclopædia of Can. biog.* (Rose, 1888), 518–20. Turcotte, *Conseil législatif de Québec*, 9, 298. Chapais, *Histoire du Canada*, V. O. D. Skelton, *The life and times of Sir Alexander Tilloch Galt* (Toronto, 1920). L.-P. Audet, "La surintendance de l'éducation et la loi scolaire de 1841," *Cahiers des Dix*, XXV (1960), 147–69.

HALL, CHARLES FRANCIS, Arctic explorer; b. 1821; d. 8 Nov. 1871.

Charles Francis Hall was born in the state of Vermont in 1821, but while he was still a child his family moved to Rochester, New Hampshire, where he spent his boyhood and received what little formal schooling he was given. In the 1840s he married and drifted westward, arriving in Cincinnati, Ohio, in 1849. There he established a small seal-engraving business and, in the late 1850s, two small newspapers, the *Cincinnati Occasional* and the *Daily Press*.

During Hall's years in Cincinnati, he developed a passionate interest in the Arctic, reading widely in its geography and history. Always driven by boundless energy and an inquiring mind, he decided in 1859, at the age of 39, that he was destined to find survivors of Sir John Franklin*'s expedition, which had disappeared almost 15 years before. The discovery in 1859 of bodies and relics of the Franklin expedition on King William Island by Francis Leopold M'Clintock* did not deter Hall or change his belief that there might be survivors living with the Eskimos.

Although his businesses had been moderately successful, Hall had little money. Furthermore, he knew nothing about navigation. Early in 1860 he went to the east coast and there met the founder of the American Geographical and Statistical Society and patron of United States Arctic exploration, Henry Grinnell. Grinnell gave him introductions to whaling firms in New London, Conn., one of which offered Hall free passage to Baffin Island. Hall sailed north for the first time on 29 May 1860 on the bark *George Henry*, Sidney O. Budington, captain.

Hall's plan was to put ashore at "Frobisher Strait," hire Eskimos, navigate through the so-called strait to Foxe Basin, and from there make his way to King William Island. His expedition boat was destroyed, he discovered that the strait was actually a bay, and he did not even approach King William Island, but his first expedition was not a complete failure. He not only proved that the strait was a bay but also, by finding relics of Sir Martin Frobisher*'s attempts to mine gold on his third expedition, that it was indeed the site of the Elizabethan's 16th-century explorations. Hall also hardened himself to living in the Arctic environment, helped by a remarkable English-speaking Eskimo couple, Ebierbing and Tookolito, known to whalers as "Joe" and "Hannah." They had been taken to England by a British whaler in the early 1850s, and according to legend enjoyed tea with Queen Victoria.

After two years in Frobisher Bay, Hall returned to the United States, bringing Joe and Hannah with him. He virtually ignored the war between the states, which was at its height, to devote all his energy to gathering money for his next expedition.

Hall

He lectured, using the Eskimos in their native costumes as an attraction, and worked on a book about his first expedition, *Arctic researches and life among the Esquimaux* ... (New York, 1865, published in London in 1864 as *Life with the Esquimaux*).

Hall still insisted that even after almost 20 years there might be survivors of the Franklin expedition living in the area of King William Island, and he persuaded Grinnell and the American Geographical and Statistical Society to help him on his next venture. In July 1864, still accompanied by the loyal Joe and Hannah, he sailed again with Captain Budington in the whaler *Monticello* to northern Hudson Bay. In the four years that followed, he led a life of hardship and frustration in the area of Roes Welcome Sound. Except for occasional visits to whaling ships, he stayed with Eskimos, trying unsuccessfully to persuade them to accompany him to King William Island. For a brief time, despairing of their help, he hired some whalemen, but this experiment ended violently when he shot and killed one for threatening mutiny. Finally in the spring of 1869 he made his way to King William Island, helped by Joe, Hannah, and several other Eskimos. In spite of rumours that there were white men living in the area, all he found of the Franklin party was more relics and skeletal remains.

During this expedition, he determined to try to reach the North Pole on his next venture. Soon after his return to New Bedford, Mass., in September 1869 he gained the attention of President Ulysses S. Grant and of some powerful men in Congress. Fifty thousand dollars were appropriated, and Hall was put in command of what became known as the Polaris expedition (named after his ship, the 387-ton *Polaris*).

At last Hall had a large-scale, well-financed expedition, but the Polaris expedition proved to be ill fated. Sailing early in July 1871, the *Polaris*, captained by Budington, easily set a record farthest north of about 82°11' by September, cruising up the narrows between Ellesmere Island and Greenland. Turned back by ice at the edge of the Lincoln Sea, Hall had Budington put the ship into a shallow harbour on the northwest shore of Greenland, which he called "Thank God Harbour." There they prepared to winter. In October Hall made a two-week sledge journey to the north. When he returned to the ship, he became violently ill after drinking a cup of coffee. For two weeks he was sick, apparently paralysed on one side and sometimes demented. In his dementia he accused many of the officers of murdering him. He died on 8 Nov. 1871 and was buried ashore.

After Hall's death, the morale of the expedition deteriorated and little was accomplished. In the fall of 1872, when Budington tried to sail the badly damaged *Polaris* southward, a party of 19 men, women, and children – the Eskimos had their families with them – were separated from the ship on an ice floe during a storm in Smith Sound. After six months during which they drifted some 1,300 miles on the floe, the party (which included George E. Tyson*) was rescued by a sealer off Labrador. In the meantime, Budington had run the *Polaris* aground near Etah, Greenland, where he and the rest of the expedition spent the winter. They were picked up by Captain William Allen of the Scottish whaler *Ravenscraig* in the spring.

A navy board of inquiry cleared Budington of any serious charges and reached the conclusion that Hall had died of apoplexy. The transcript of its investigation, however, shows that the expedition had been seriously weakened by hostilities among the officers. Budington had been drinking heavily and had quarrelled with Hall. Dr Emil Bessels, the expedition's surgeon and naturalist who had treated Hall in his final illness, also had quarrelled with him.

In August 1968 Hall's well-preserved remains were exhumed by a party of investigators, and a graveside autopsy was performed. Neutron activation tests run by Toronto's Centre of Forensic Sciences on his hair and fingernails proved that during the last two weeks of his life he had received large amounts of arsenic (76.7 ppm at the base of his fingernail). That the cause of his death was arsenic poisoning cannot be conclusively proved although the dosage he had received was very large. Nor can it be proved that he was murdered: he owned a medical kit of his own and, distrusting Dr Bessels, he may have overdosed himself with an arsenical patent medicine. In spite of the new evidence, Hall's death must remain a mystery forever.

The irony of the Polaris expedition is that, although Hall had always wished to command a large-scale expedition, he was far more successful as a lone-wolf explorer than as an expedition leader. His greatest contribution to Arctic exploration was perhaps in proving that a white man living as the Eskimos lived could survive for long periods of time in the Arctic free from ships or other sources of civilized supplies. In his adaptability to the Arctic environment, he was the predecessor of Vilhjalmur Stefansson*. And like Stefansson he was a propagandist for the Arctic, enthusiastically praising its beauty and its potential value for the civilized world. In one of his typical lectures, delivered just before the departure of the Polaris expedition, he said: "Many who have written to me, or who have appeared to me personally, think that I am of an adventurous spirit and of bold heart to attempt to go to the North Pole. Not so. It does not require that heart which they suppose I have got. The Arctic Region is my home. I love it dearly; its storms, its winds, its glaciers, its icebergs; and when I am there among them, it seems as if I were in an earthly heaven or a heavenly earth."

ERNEST S. DODGE and C. C. LOOMIS

Smithsonian Institution (Washington), Division of Naval History, Charles Francis Hall papers. C. F. Hall, *Arctic researches and life among the Esquimaux: being the narrative of an expedition in search of Sir John Franklin, in the years 1860, 1861, and 1862* (New York, 1865); [C. F. Hall], *Life with the Esquimaux; the narrative of Captain C.F. H. . . . from the 29th May, 1860, to the 13th Sept., 1862; with . . . the discovery of actual relics of Martin Frobisher . . . and deductions in favour of yet discovering some of the survivors of Sir J. Franklin's expedition* (2v., London, 1864). *Narrative of the second Arctic expedition made by Charles F. Hall: his voyage to Repulse Bay, sledge journeys to the Straits of Fury and Hecla and to King William's Land, and residence among the Eskimos during the years 1864–'69*, ed. J. E. Nourse (Washington, 1879). *Narrative of the north polar expedition: U.S. Ship* Polaris, *Captain C. F. Hall, commanding*, ed. under the direction of G. M. Robertson by C. H. Davis (Washington, 1876). "Report of the reception, by the American Geographical Society, of Captain Hall and his officers, previous to their departure for the Arctic regions, held June 26th, 1871," American Geographical Society of New York, *Journal*, III (1870–71), 406. [G. E. Tyson], *Arctic experiences: containing Capt. George E. Tyson's wonderful drift on the ice-floe, a history of the Polaris expedition, the cruise of the* Tigress, *and rescue of* Polaris *survivors*, ed. E. V. Blake (New York, 1874). *DAB*.

HALL, GEORGE BENSON, lumberman and businessman of the region of Quebec; b. 1810 at Amherstburg, U.C., son of George Benson Hall, an officer in the Royal Navy, and Angelica Fortier; d. 4 Sept. 1876 at Montmorency, Que., and buried 7 September in Mount Hermon cemetery at Quebec.

George Benson Hall was of Irish descent and was an Anglican; his father had come to Canada with the British troops sent to defend the colonies during the Anglo-American War of 1812, and had assumed command of one of the ships under General Isaac Brock*'s orders in the Great Lakes.

The circumstances that brought his son to the Quebec region are unknown. It seems that Hall merely wanted to take advantage of the commercial exploitation of timber, which in the 19th century was being carried out on a large scale in the province of Quebec. But when in 1842 Great Britain revoked the preferential customs tariff formerly granted to the Canadas, and began to buy Baltic timber which was sold more cheaply, Hall was one of those who saw the expansion of the lumber industry as the answer. And Hall was doubly served by circumstances. The 1854 reciprocity treaty created favourable conditions for sawmill owners by opening to them a large, safe market in the United States. Furthermore, in 1843 Hall had married Mary Jane Patterson, only daughter of Peter Patterson*, from whom he inherited an important business undertaking. By harnessing the power of the Montmorency Falls, Patterson had started the lumber-milling industry in the Quebec region. Conducted on profitable lines, the exploitation of commercial lumber had been so extensive that on 27 May 1844 Patterson had been able to purchase the seigneury of Beauport for £8,300.

Thus favoured, Hall increased his commercial activities in the Quebec region and beyond. Over a period of 25 years, using his intelligence and energy, he bought sawmills which he made prosperous, and obtained new land grants in all the regions of Canada East, even on the upper Matawin River where in 1869 he set up a farm to supply his lumber camps with agricultural produce. At his death in 1876 he was acknowledged to be one of the most active and one of the richest lumbermen in Canada. According to *The storied province of Quebec*, "The Hall Mills at Montmorency were the greatest in the world." His business then passed into the hands of his son, Peter Patterson Hall (1851–1910), one of his ten children born between 1843 and 1863.

For Quebec City, Hall was a valuable citizen: he opened a lumber business there in 1851, and, as an alderman, took part in the government of the town from 1853 to 1862. But it was the region of Montmorency Falls and the parish of Beauport that particularly benefited from Hall's activity. In 1876, 800 families of this region owed their livelihood to his lumber business. Consequently, immediately after his sudden death the municipal council of Beauport held a special meeting, and, in the form of unanimous resolutions, the citizens of Beauport acknowledged George Benson Hall as "one of the greatest benefactors of the parish," and "the protector and father" of all the socially underprivileged of Beauport. In the opinion of the editor of the *Morning Chronicle* of Quebec, Hall was "one of Quebec's most prominent and enterprising citizens . . . particularly esteemed for the benevolence and kindness of his character."

ANDRÉE DÉSILETS

AJQ, Greffe de E. G. Meredith, acts de vente des héritiers Hall à L.-A. Sénécal, 7 juin 1883. AVQ, Procès-verbaux du conseil. *Documents concernant la*

Haly

construction, la pose de la pierre angulaire et l'inauguration solennelle du nouvel hôtel-de-ville (Québec, 1896). Le Canadien (Québec), 7 sept. 1876. L'Événement (Québec), 7 sept. 1876. Morning Chronicle (Quebec), 6 Sept. 1876. Raoul Blanchard, Le Canada français; province de Québec; étude géographique (Montréal, 1960). Storied Quebec (Wood et al.), I, 402; IV, 400. P.-B. Casgrain, "Le Kent-House; rectification historique," BRH, XIX (1913), 5–9.

HALY, Sir WILLIAM O'GRADY, soldier, general officer commanding British forces in North America; b. 1810, son of Aylmer Haly of Wadhurst Castle, Sussex, Eng.; d. Halifax, N.S., 19 March 1878.

William O'Grady Haly joined the army in June 1823 when he was 13, became an ensign in the 4th Foot on 17 June 1828, and a captain in April 1834. Between 1828 and 1854 his regiment served in Scotland, Ireland, Australia, and India as well as in England. Haly fought in the Crimean War, 1854–55, won a medal with four clasps, and was awarded the CB on 5 July 1855 and also the Third Order of the Medjidie and the Turkish Medal. He was appointed lieutenant-colonel of the 38th Foot, then stationed in India, on 4 Feb. 1859 and served in the East Indies from 1861 to 1870; he was promoted major-general in January 1865 and lieutenant-general, May 1873.

From 6 May 1873 he was general officer commanding the British forces in North America, stationed at Halifax. The governor general, Lord Dufferin [Blackwood*], wanted the Halifax garrison to come under the command of the GOC Canadian militia, a new appointment in 1874, but the War Office feared it would thereby lose control. Major-General Sir Edward Selby Smyth*, the first incumbent of the new appointment, was junior to Haly, who had to be reminded by Dufferin that the GOC militia was not under his command and would not report to the War Office through him.

In 1877 Haly's independence of Ottawa, combined with negligence in the offices of the governor general and the prime minister, Alexander Mackenzie*, led to a confrontation when Haly arbitrarily ordered the stopping of traffic on the Intercolonial Railway because it had failed to build a tunnel across War Department land near a powder magazine in Halifax, as promised by Mackenzie. Instead it had made a cutting, and the War Office had already refused to approve an iron roof over this as a substitute. Dufferin protested emphatically against Haly's action, which he said was "too violent a proceeding even for a lieutenant-general." He sent Haly a telegram "couched in sufficiently strong language" to make it possible for Haly to back down and postpone the carrying out of the War Office's orders. Shortly after this incident Haly asked for a recommendation to the vacant governorship of Gibraltar.

As GOC British North America Haly was appointed administrator to act as head of government during the absences of the governor general. He served in this capacity from 12 Oct. to 2 Nov. 1874, from 15 May to 21 Oct. 1875, and from 21 Jan. to 3 Feb. 1878. But Dufferin thought it "a good deal of bother" to bring the GOC British North America all the way from Halifax especially as he was likely to know little of Canadian affairs and might be "a headstrong soldier unused to civil life and anxious to 'make a splash.'" He found Haly "fidgetty and incompetent." He suggested that the GOC militia would be a more suitable administrator. During Haly's service Dufferin succeeded in postponing the introduction of a Colonial Office arrangement for the administrator to receive one-fourth of the governor general's allowances; at Mackenzie's suggestion, he did not call upon Haly to act as his deputy during short periods of leave in remote parts of Canada but appointed the chief justice of the Supreme Court, with somewhat circumscribed powers.

In 1875, Haly's incompetence led to a virtual diminution of the governor general's prerogative of pardon. A Canadian minister had told a prisoner that he would be reprieved from a death sentence at a time when the administrator had not made a decision about the minister of justice's recommendation. The colonial secretary, the Earl of Carnarvon [Herbert], said Haly should have stood firm and used the telegraph to obtain instructions instead of backing down.

Haly was appointed colonel of the 106th Regiment in 1874, was knighted (KCB) on 29 May 1875, transferred to the command of the 47th Regiment on 2 Nov. 1875, and was promoted brevet-general on 1 Oct. 1877. He died in office in 1878 as a result of an attack of "gout of the stomach." He had married Harriett Hebden, and their eldest son, Major-General Richard O'Grady Haly, was GOC Canadian militia, 1900–2.

RICHARD A. PRESTON

Royal Archives, Windsor Castle, Cambridge papers, Dufferin to Cambridge, 11 Dec. 1874. [Blackwood and Herbert], Dufferin-Carnarvon correspondence (de Kiewiet and Underhill), 156, 164, 283, 346–48, 384, 419. The annual register: a review of public events at home and abroad for the year 1878 (London, 1879), 142. Boase, Modern English biography, I, 1297.

HAMILTON, WILLIAM, iron founder, machinist, and inventor; b. in 1810 in Lasswade,

Midlothian County, Scotland; d. 28 Nov. 1880 in Toronto, Ont.

After a seven-year apprenticeship with an iron founder in Scotland, William Hamilton moved to England in 1834 and worked in the shops of the Liverpool and Manchester Railway in Manchester, the Bridgewater Foundry at Patricroft, and the Great Western Railway at Swindon. He was a pattern maker for James Nasmyth and after 1840 for Daniel Gooch, learning from them the techniques of steam-driven machine-making tools.

With 23 years experience in "mechanical engineering," Hamilton arrived in Toronto in October 1850 with his wife and their two sons and two daughters. He worked for James Good and then for James Rogers ARMSTRONG before establishing in 1851 or 1852, in partnership with his son William, the St Lawrence Foundry, Engine Works, and Machine Shop. The shop offered castings and steam engines. The latter were then in great demand in the province: 340 were imported from 1853 to 1857, half of them railway locomotive engines. The foundries of Toronto had, however, to be content with producing castings primarily. The Ontario, Simcoe, and Huron Union Railroad (later the Northern Railway) gave the contract for the first locomotive to be built in Toronto to James Good in 1852, and William Hamilton secured only the contract for iron chairs and other accessories. Yet, despite considerable competition, Hamilton's assets doubled from 1856 to 1857, in 1858–59, and again in 1860–61. In 1861 he employed 40 men and produced $37,000 worth of castings, nuts, and bolts for the railways.

With the outbreak of the Civil War in the United States in 1861, American shops turned to war production and Canadians had to make more of their own machinery. Hamilton acquired a larger power plant, and his became one of the first Canadian shops to produce whole systems of steam-driven tools. In the Civil War years he manufactured the power plant and hammer-rollers for the Steel, Iron, and Railway Works Company in Toronto, and the power plant and machinery for the Toronto Knitting and Yarn Factory. In the mid-1860s he invented and began manufacturing his "fish-plate bolt" which reduced railway accidents caused by rails shaking loose from their ties.

Hamilton's production techniques differed markedly from those then most current in Toronto. Good, for example, had been producing what were virtually handmade machines since the 1830s. Hamilton used a larger number of machine tools while retaining numerous well-trained artisans; his techniques attracted machinists, inventors, and moulders of high calibre, including James Martin Sr. He produced such diverse items as the fence for Osgoode Hall in Toronto, railway cars and wheels, steam engines with boilers for factories and boats, and steam dredges for clearing harbours.

Hamilton, however, rarely owned the land on which his machines were housed in wooden buildings, and he was hard hit by business slumps. A fire on his major site in 1876 almost ruined him. He lost control of the St Lawrence Foundry in 1879 but continued to work the Don Foundry in Toronto.

Hamilton married twice, his second marriage being to a young widow, Anne Kilgallen Erlan, on 21 October 1865; he adopted her two sons. A daughter married the distiller Henry Gooderham.

GEO. MAINER

City of Toronto Archives, Toronto assessment rolls, 1849–80. Little Trinity Church (Toronto), records of baptisms, marriages, and burials. PAC, RG 31, A1, 1861, Toronto, St Lawrence's ward; 1871, St Lawrence's ward. St James' Cemetery (Toronto), records of burials, 1880. *Daily Colonist* (Toronto), 3 Feb. 1852. *Globe* (Toronto), 1 Dec. 1880. *Mail* (Toronto), 30 Nov. 1880. *City of Toronto directory, for 1867–8 ...*, comp. James Sutherland (Toronto, 1867), 328, 384. *Hist. of Toronto and county of York*, I, 386.

HANRAHAN, EDMUND, politician and public servant; b. in 1802 at Carbonear, Nfld.; d. at Ferryland, Nfld., on 6 Feb. or 13 Feb. 1875.

Edmund Hanrahan, a man of "humble origins," entered Newfoundland politics in December 1840 by contesting a by-election in Conception Bay. Both Hanrahan and his opponent, James Luke Prendergast, were Roman Catholics; Prendergast was backed by the Protestant merchants including John MUNN, and Hanrahan was actively supported by the Roman Catholic clergy. The election was rendered abortive "by the ferocious conduct of a mob at Carbonear." Rowdyism at elections was, indeed, known for a time in Newfoundland as "Carbonearism," for it was at Carbonear that rioting occurred with regularity. Hanrahan was returned for Conception Bay in the general elections of 1842, 1848, and 1852; and, following the 1854 sub-division of districts, for Carbonear in 1855, 1859, and 1861. In the House of Assembly he was among the more radical of the Liberals and after 1850 supported Philip Francis Little* in the struggle for responsible government.

In 1855, on the introduction of responsible government, he was appointed to Little's cabinet as surveyor general. After Little's retirement, Hanrahan was continued in John KENT's cabinet until its dismissal by Governor Alexander Bannerman* in 1861. The weak and divided Liberal party lost the general election in May 1861. Although

Harding

Hanrahan was re-elected as a Liberal for Carbonear, where there was again violence, he accepted the appointment of acting appraiser to the General Water Company from the Conservative government of Hugh Hoyles*. Hanrahan's resignation from his House of Assembly seat caused a by-election in Carbonear in November 1862 in which, for the first time in more than 20 years, a Conservative candidate, John Rorke*, was elected. The following year Hoyles rewarded Hanrahan with the appointment of stipendiary magistrate at Ferryland, necessitating the retirement of the incumbent Peter Winser. The Liberal *Record* reported that "Hanrahan sold Carbonear . . . at the expense of an honest man . . . Peter Winser." In 1872 Hanrahan was elevated to the position of sheriff of the Southern District.

Hanrahan was married and the father of an apparently large family; four sons died young. After Hanrahan's death his widow Mary unsuccessfully petitioned the assembly for a pension in consideration of her husband's long service.

ELIZABETH A. WELLS

PANL, Newfoundland, Executive Council, Minutes, 1 March 1862. Newfoundland, *Blue Books*, 1842–74 (copies in PANL); House of Assembly, *Journals*, 1863, 8, 931. *Courier* (St John's), 20 March, 25, 29 Oct. 1862. *Newfoundlander* (St John's), 18 Oct. 1872, 17 Jan. 1873, 26 Feb. 1875. *Newfoundland Patriot* (St John's), 27 Feb 1875. *Pilot* (St John's), 8, 22 Jan. 1853. *Public Ledger* (St John's), 30 Oct., 14 Nov., 15 Dec. 1840; 28 Jan. 1862. *Record* (St John's), 8 March 1862, 15 Dec. 1863. *Times and General Commercial Gazette* (St John's), 4 Jan. 1843. E. A. Wells, "The struggle for responsible government in Newfoundland, 1846–1855," unpublished MA thesis, Memorial University of Newfoundland, 1966.

HARDING, FRANCIS PYM, army officer and administrator; b. *c.* 1821 in England; d. at the Grove, Lymington, Hampshire, England, 25 Feb. 1875, aged 54 years.

As an officer of the 22nd Foot (Cheshire Regiment), Francis Pym Harding not only saw more active service than most of his contemporaries, but also distinguished himself on several occasions. Gazetted ensign in 1836, he was posted to India and, in 1850, was Persian interpreter to Sir Charles Napier. A major in 1854, Harding served in the Crimea as aide-de-camp to General John Lysaght Pennefather; there he took part in the battles of Alma, Balaklava, and Inkerman, when he was severely wounded and mentioned in dispatches. He was commandant of Balaklava from January 1855 until the evacuation of the Crimea. He received the CB and other decorations and was promoted colonel in 1858. By 1866 he was commanding the first battalion of the 22nd Foot in Malta.

At this time the Fenian threat was troubling New Brunswick and the governor, Arthur Hamilton Gordon*, had been energetically deploying the military resources at his disposal to counter it. Colonel Harding and the 22nd Foot were brought from Malta to stiffen the defence and reinforce the 15th Foot whose commander, Lieutenant-Colonel John Ambler Cole, did not have Harding's experience. Harding and his men appear to have arrived in New Brunswick in April 1866 by which time Gordon had sailed for England. Major-General Charles Hastings Doyle*, administrator of the province, appointed Harding commanding officer of the exceptionally large garrison serving there at the time. Harding proved himself most efficient in his duties, worked well with the local militia, and was much concerned about the comfort of his troops, housed in the Fredericton Exhibition Building.

On 12 Oct. 1867, Hastings Doyle sent a telegram to Sir John A. Macdonald* stating that Harding was the senior military officer in New Brunswick. Sir John promptly recommended Harding's appointment as lieutenant governor; it was confirmed on a provisional basis later the same month. Doyle himself was then appointed lieutenant governor of Nova Scotia, which meant that these two experienced soldiers and administrators were able to provide effective continuity during the period of administrative transition and military reorganization caused by confederation.

In March 1868 Harding was promoted major general; in February of the following year, the garrison was reduced and the 22nd Foot transferred home. Harding sailed for England with his regiment and retired on half pay for the few remaining years of his life.

HUGH A. TAYLOR

Lymington, England Registration District, entry of death, 1875, no.407. PAC, MG 26, A (Macdonald papers), 126070; RG 2, ser.2, 1, file 14A; RG 7, G1, 68, ff.351–52; G17, A, 9, f.20; RG 8, I, A1, 37, ff.25, 184; 186A; C18, 1681–88 1690; C20, 1689. PANB, Lieutenant governor's letter book, 1867–74. PRO, CO 42/663, 337–38. Hart, *New army list*, 1867; 1875.

HARLEY, JOHN, shipbuilder, inspector of lights, buoys, and beacons, and harbour master; b. in 1800 at Courtmacsherry, County Cork, Ireland, second son of a schoolmaster; d. 16 Sept. 1875 at Chatham Head, Miramichi, N.B., and buried in St Andrew's Churchyard, Newcastle, N.B.

John Harley's older brother, William, emigrated

from Ireland to Miramichi, New Brunswick, about 1820 and quickly found employment as a government land surveyor. William Harley encouraged his sister Mary Ann to follow him in 1822; the next year a third member of the family, John, also came to Miramichi. On his arrival John Harley went to work for William Abrams*, who was a prosperous merchant and shipbuilder at Rose Bank (Nordin) both before and after the great Miramichi fire of 1825. "By his faithfulness and industry," said the *Union Advocate* in an 1875 obituary, "he [John Harley] in a short time reached the responsible post of foreman of the yard, and soon after rose to the position of master builder." At Miramichi, in 1829, John Harley married Ann Coughlan by whom he had three sons and two daughters.

After Abrams' death in 1844, John Harley became master builder for Joseph Russell at Beaubair's (Beaubear's) Island. When Russell, a devout Mormon convert, left Miramichi for Salt Lake City, Utah, in 1849, John Harley with a partner, George Burchill, of Nelson, bought the island and the shipbuilding plant. This partnership was dissolved in 1857, and Harley continued on his own until 1866 when his last craft were built. At this time he stated that he had been responsible for the building of 62 sailing vessels on the Miramichi River.

John Harley had been appointed one of two commissioners for the lighthouse at Escuminac in 1853. After confederation he was appointed inspector of lights for New Brunswick, a position he held until his superannuation in 1871. He continued as inspector of buoys and beacons for Miramichi River and Bay as late as 1873; in that year he was also harbour master, a post he had held for some years.

John Harley's successful career as a shipbuilder is a notable example of what could be achieved in the 19th century by industry and ability. His 62 well-built vessels, mostly large barks and full-rigged ships, found a ready market in the Old Country. They were sound and durable and had no difficulty in maintaining the Lloyd's classifications for which they were built. William Abrams' *Phoenix*, built the year after the Miramichi fire and so aptly named, was still registered at Lloyd's in 1850. Other Harley vessels reached the age of 21 years – the *Royal Adelaide* (built in 1830), the *Romulus* (1831), the *Kalodyne* (1856), the *Sandringham* (1864), and many more. Fast passages of the Harley vessels between Miramichi and Liverpool were often recorded in the *Gleaner* (Chatham); in 1864 the bark *Sea Mew* took 16 days from Miramichi to Liverpool and equalled that speed on her return trip.

John Harley's 50 years in Miramichi were well spent. When he died the *Union Advocate* said a host of friends mourned him for "his warm and loving disposition, and for his integrity and sterling character."

LOUISE MANNY

Lloyd's register of British and foreign shipping (London), 1839–71. *Gleaner* (Chatham, N.B.), 1833–73. *Mercury* (Chatham, N.B.), 1829. *Union Advocate* (Newcastle, N.B.), 23 Sept. 1875, 16 Feb. 1898 (this issue contains a reprint from the *Press* (Portland, Me.) of family traditions related by Mrs John Henry (Mary Ann Harley) when she was 99 years old). Louise Manny, *Ships of Miramichi: a history of shipbuilding on the Miramichi River, New Brunswick, Canada, 1773–1919* (N.B. Museum Hist. Studies, 10, Saint John, N.B., 1960).

HARPER, JEROME, cattle rancher, flour mill and sawmill owner; b. in Tucker County, West Virginia, in 1826; d. a bachelor 27 Nov. 1874, at Santa Barbara, Calif.

Little is known of Jerome Harper's youth. He is reported to have been involved in a rebellion in Chile, and in 1852, with his younger brother Thaddeus*, he was farming in Santa Clara County, California. The two brothers probably came to British Columbia in 1858 with the great rush of gold miners to the Fraser River. By 1859 they were operating a sawmill in Yale. Jerome took an active interest in the Cariboo mines and bought and sold several mining claims there, but by the autumn of 1862 he had entered the cattle business and had stock on a ranch east of Kamloops. In 1862 or 1863 Jerome began to purchase cattle in Washington and Oregon and import them into British Columbia. After wintering the cattle south of Osoyoos, B.C., he would drive them in herds of about 450 head along the old fur brigade trail through the Okanagan Valley to Kamloops and from there on to the Cariboo where they were held in the mountains to be slaughtered as required. The success of these operations provided the miners with inexpensive beef and the Harper brothers with increased wealth. Jerome, pursuing the business with great energy, soon won a dominant position in the cattle importing industry and diversified his activities by building a sawmill at Quesnellemouth late in 1863 and, five years later, a flour mill north of Clinton.

In 1871 Jerome signified his intention to retire, and advertised his mills for sale. He moved to San Francisco for health reasons in March 1872, but in February 1873 was reported to be "hopelessly insane." He drowned in his bath tub in November 1874. His estate, valued at $150,000, passed to Thaddeus but only when the will had

Harris

been upheld in court after relatives maintained Jerome had been insane.

Jerome Harper never changed his citizenship and was a strong supporter of the Confederate states; to him, Robert E. Lee was the equal of Napoleon or Wellington. In 1862–63 he was connected with a plot to outfit a Confederate privateer at Victoria, but the scheme failed and only the plotters were discomfited. Harper was widely known and respected. The lavishness of his entertainment was celebrated – champagne lunches at the Clinton mill were not unknown. Jerome was always the leader of the two brothers; it was his initiative that laid the foundations for the giant cattle ranches later owned by Thaddeus at Kamloops, Cache Creek, Clinton, and in the Chilcotin.

G. R. NEWELL

PABC, Jerome Harper correspondence; F. W. Laing correspondence. *Cariboo Sentinel* (Barkerville, B.C.), 1865–74. F. W. Laing, "Some pioneers of the cattle industry," *BCHQ*, VI (1942), 257–75.

HARRIS, ALEXANDER, writer; b. 7 Feb. 1805, London, Eng., eldest of 11 children of the Reverend William Harris and Mary Redford; d. Copetown, Ont., 1 Feb. 1874.

Alexander Harris was educated privately at Windsor and Wallingford. He moved to London in 1823 to work as a proof-reader, later enlisted in the Horse Guards, deserted, and in 1825 set sail for Australia. Here, chiefly in the Goulburn-Taralga-Crookwell district of New South Wales, he spent the next 16 years as an itinerant sawyer, carpenter, and clerk. He returned to England late in 1840 and married Elizabeth Atkinson, who died five weeks after the marriage; he subsequently married, in 1842, Ursula Sarah Carr, by whom he had three sons. Harris separated from his wife in 1847, and emigrated in 1851 to the United States where he settled eventually at Sturgeon Bay, Wisconsin; it was in this area that he was to spend most of the years between 1854 and 1872 as a teacher and free-lance writer. He was joined at Sturgeon Bay by his family in 1858, but with the outbreak of civil war in 1861 his wife and children moved to Berlin (Kitchener), Canada West, and here Harris spent varying periods of time between 1861 and 1863. By the latter date the attempted reunion had failed. Ursula and the children left for Nova Scotia and Harris returned to the United States, where he became an American citizen in 1870. By July 1872, however, he was writing to his wife from Copetown, a small settlement not far from Hamilton, on the Great Western Railway. Two years later he died and was buried at Copetown.

Harris' best-known work is *Settlers and convicts, or recollections of sixteen years' labour in the Australian backwoods*. It was first published in 1847, anonymously, but *A guide to Port Stephens in New South Wales*, published in 1849, identified the author of the earlier work as "Alexander Harris." His writings, which also include *Testimony to the truth* (1848), a three-volume novel entitled *The emigrant family* (1849), and a number of pamphlets, draw heavily on his Australian experiences and are almost obsessively autobiographical. It is clear, however, that Harris made no sharp distinction between fact and fiction, creating his own image of himself and his environment according to his mood at various stages of his career. A mission worker in London in the 1840s and a devout nonconformist to the end of his life, his work is pervaded by an evangelical concern for soul salvation: he is pursued by the hound of heaven. Subsidiary themes are the ideal nature of woman, the evils of drink, and the iniquity of flogging. He belongs to the ranks of the itinerants of empire of the 19th century along with Sir George Arthur*, William Dunlop*, and Samuel Butler. A descriptive artist of the first order, his *Settlers and convicts* has become an Australian classic.

In 1953 an Australian edition of *Settlers and convicts* was published with a foreword by Australian historian C. M. H. Clark, who raised doubts as to whether Harris had actually existed, a wide search of primary documents, chiefly Australian, having yielded no evidence. The entry on Harris in the 1958 edition of *The Australian encyclopædia*, which took note of the controversy, was read by a grandson of Harris, Grant Carr-Harris of Ottawa; in 1961 Carr-Harris produced *The secrets of Alexander Harris*, a book based on a series of articles contributed by his grandfather, under the title "Religio Christi," to the *Saturday Evening Post* (Philadelphia) in 1858, and containing, in an introduction, extensive biographical information about him. In a third Australian edition of *Settlers and convicts* (1964), Professor Clark took note of the new evidence.

ROBERT L. McDOUGALL

Alexander Harris, *The emigrant family* (3v., London, 1849); new ed. with intro. W. S. Ramson (Canberra, 1967); *A guide to Port Stephens in New South Wales* (London, 1849); new ed. with intro. Grant Carr-Harris (Sydney, Aust., 1961); [ ] *The secrets of Alexander Harris, a frank autobiography . . .*, ed. Grant Carr-Harris ([Sydney, Aust.], 1961); *Settlers and convicts, or recollections of sixteen years' labour in the Australian backwoods* (London, 1847; Carlton, Aust., 1953, 1954; Parkville, Aust., 1964); *Testimony to the truth* (London, 1848). Works by Harris, who wrote also under the epithets "An emigrant mechanic" and "A working hand," are listed in the *British Museum catalogue*; it gave Harris' name as a pseudonym in 1963, but the entry was corrected in 1968. *ADB. The Australian encyclopædia* (10v. Sydney, Aust., [1958]).

HARRIS, THOMAS DENNIE, merchant and office-holder; b. 30 Oct. 1803, of English parents, at Boston, Mass.; m. Lucy (Lucille, Lucinda) Charles of Montreal in 1827, by whom he had 12 children; d. 18 Jan. 1873, at Toronto, Ont.

Thomas Dennie Harris emigrated to Montreal in 1817 and worked in John Frothingham's hardware store. In 1825 he moved to Kingston, and in 1829 he went to York (Toronto) as manager of a branch hardware store for John Watkins of Kingston. He entered into a partnership with Watkins for operating the store in 1832. It was dissolved in July 1838 and Harris continued as a wholesaler and retailer, later in partnership with William Robert, his first-born, as Harris and Son. Harris was retired by 1859 but the firm continued for about seven more years as Harris, Evans and Company, William Robert Harris joining with John J. Evans who had earlier been an assistant in the store.

Harris had joined volunteer fire companies in Montreal and Kingston. He did the same on arrival at York, and with the reorganization of the Toronto Fire Brigade in March 1838 he was appointed its chief engineer. The post was unpaid but required supervision at every fire and detailed reports. These he presented with characteristic thoroughness until he retired exhausted and amid much regret in 1841. In the next few years he formed and led new fire and hose companies and was president of the Home District Mutual Fire Insurance Company. In the mid-1860s Harris was Toronto agent for the Home and Colonial Life and Fire Insurance Company. Fire had also made a massive intrusion on Harris' time in the great blaze of April 1849 when he lost his own store. St James' church, where he was rector's churchwarden, was levelled, and he managed its reconstruction. He also oversaw the establishment of St James' cemetery from 1844 and imported its iron chapel in 1861.

A member of the Toronto Board of Trade from the 1830s, and its president in 1864, Harris served as the board's representative on the Toronto Harbour Commission from 1854 to 1864 and again from 1866 to 1869. In 1863–64 he was the commission's president. He was harbour master of Toronto from 1870 to 1872, when he resigned through ill health. In the 1830s he had also become treasurer of the Commercial Newsroom, a meeting-place and reading-room mainly for merchants. He was later treasurer of the Toronto Athenaeum from its founding in 1845 (it soon absorbed the Newsroom and in turn merged with the Canadian Institute in 1855).

Harris helped inaugurate or sustain many enterprises. He was president of Canada's first telegraph company, the Toronto, Hamilton, Niagara, and St Catharines Electro-Magnetic Telegraph Company, from the year of its formation in 1846 until it was swallowed by the Montreal Telegraph Company in 1852. He served long periods on the boards of the British America Assurance Company, the Colonial Life Assurance Company, the Toronto Building Society, and the Canada Permanent Building and Savings Society. He was frequently called in to adjudicate commercial disputes.

Harris' most distinctive contribution to the city's commercial life, however, came in 1838 and 1839 when the banks suspended specie payment causing trade to limp for lack of ready cash. Harris issued handsome printed notes for small denominations, "the Harris shinplasters," which circulated as change and could, in aggregates worth a dollar or more, be exchanged for bank bills at par. Several thousand dollars worth came into use. He was the only person to make such an issue and one of only three merchants at this time who manufactured special metal tokens to do duty as pennies.

Harris was a manager rather than a speculator, supervising rebuilding or harbour maintenance, and keeping trade open with his "shinplasters." He eschewed notoriety in any guise, including the offer of a magistracy, and every temptation to speechmaking. His church work did not extend to a seat on synod and he was never a candidate for city council. An admirer of another native of Boston, Ben Franklin*, he presented a portrait of him to the Toronto Mechanics' Institute on its formation, and in his constant busyness, severe practicality, and sense of civic responsibility there are echoes of Franklin's Poor Richard.

BARRIE DYSTER

Metropolitan Toronto Board of Trade, Council, minute books. MTCL, Consumers' Gas Company papers, lists of shareholders, 1855; Toronto, Mechanics' Institute papers, 1832. PAC, RG 5, A1, 17 Aug. 1836. PAO, Toronto City Council papers, 1838–46. St James' Cemetery (Toronto).

Church Herald (Toronto), 23 Jan. 1873. *Globe* (Toronto), 25 Jan., 27 Nov. 1860; 20 Jan. 1873. *Mail* (Toronto), 20 Jan. 1873. *Patriot* (Toronto), 30 Jan., 4 Sept. 1838. *Town of York, 1815–1834* (Firth). *Brown's Toronto general directory, 1856 . . .* (Toronto, [1856]). *Brown's Toronto general directory, 1861 . . .* (Toronto, [1861]). *Caverhill's Toronto city directory, for 1859–60 . . .*, ed. W. C. F. Caverhill (Toronto,

Harrison

n.d.). *Landmarks of Toronto* (Robertson), I, 300–1; II, 575–76. F. H. Armstrong, "The first great fire of Toronto, 1849," *Ont. Hist.*, LIII (1961), 201–21; "The rebuilding of Toronto after the great fire of 1849," *Ont. Hist.*, LIII (1961), 233–49. Ernest Green, "Canada's first electric telegraph," *Ont. Hist.*, XXIV (1927), 366–72.

HARRISON, ROBERT ALEXANDER, lawyer, author, politician, and judge; b. 3 Aug. 1833, at Montreal, Lower Canada, son of Richard Harrison and Frances Butler; d. 1 Nov. 1878, at Toronto, Ont.

Robert Alexander Harrison's parents emigrated to Canada from Skegarvey, County Monaghan, Ireland, shortly before his birth. Soon after his birth, the family moved to Cookstown and then settled in Toronto where Harrison received his education. He attended Upper Canada College and Trinity College, obtaining a BCL in 1855 and DCL in 1859. In June 1859 he married Anna E. Muckle; she died in March 1866, leaving one daughter. Harrison was married again in January 1868, to Kennithina Johana Mackay, and they had one daughter.

Harrison began his law studies with the Toronto firm of Robinson and Allan when he was 17 and completed them in the office of Crawford and Hagarty. He was called to the bar of Upper Canada in 1855, and in 1867 became a QC. From 10 Sept. 1854 to 28 Feb. 1859 he was chief clerk of the Crown Law Department, having been appointed by the attorney general, John Ross, and retained by Ross's successor in 1854, John A. Macdonald*. Harrison left this position to go into private practice with James Paterson, and they were later joined by Thomas Hodgins* and then John Bain. When Paterson died, Harrison established the firm of Harrison, Osler and Moss, with Thomas Moss* and Featherston Osler*. Harrison was a successful lawyer and rapidly acquired a brilliant reputation. He was industrious and conscientious, "a gentleman of ability," as Macdonald said. His connection with the Crown Law Department had provided him with important contacts, and the firms he was associated with frequently acted as agents for crown business. Harrison was often himself a counsel for the crown. One of his more notable cases was the successful defence of the ministers of the crown accused of violating the Independence of Parliament Act in 1858 by the "double shuffle." The defence was based on an act passed in 1857, which said in effect that any person could vacate an office and be appointed to another within a month without having to resign and be re-elected; the defendants were exonerated from liability in respect of the statutory penalties and it was declared that the letter of the law had not been violated [*see* DRAPER]. During the Fenian trials in 1866–67, he and John Hillyard CAMERON conducted most of the cases for the crown. In 1871, Harrison was elected a bencher of the Law Society and on 8 Oct. 1875 he was appointed chief justice of the Court of Queen's Bench of Ontario. His appointment was generally regarded by the legal profession as a "reward [which] had been fairly and justly earned, and had been bestowed on one who would bring to bear on the administration of justice. a wide experience and tireless energy."

Harrison's contribution to jurisprudence was not confined to his work as a lawyer and judge. He was also an eminent author in the field, contributing works of learning and practical value. He began writing as an 18-year-old law student and published *A digest of reports of all cases . . .* , with James Lukin Robinson. Harrison was also an active contributor to various periodicals and newspapers, including the *Merchants' Magazine and Commercial Review* (New York) and the *Daily Colonist* (Toronto). In Toronto he was one of the founders and editors of the *Local Courts' and Municipal Gazette*, a joint editor of the *Upper Canada Law Journal*, and an editor of *Poker*, a humorous journal, in 1859–60.

Although for most of his career he was involved in jurisprudence, Harrison did serve in other positions at various times. He was a member of the Corporation of the City of Toronto, and a director of the Royal Canadian Bank and of the Life Association of Scotland. In 1876 he was appointed one of the arbitrators to decide the northwestern boundary of Ontario. He also managed to entertain a brief political career, serving as an alderman for Toronto in 1867 and 1868 and as the representative for Toronto West in the House of Commons, 1867–72. Preferring to devote himself to his extensive legal practice, he did not stand as a candidate in the 1872 election. As a member, he was chairman of the Committee on Miscellaneous Private Bills for two sessions. He was associated with several measures of some importance, including bills for amending the law as to stamping promissory notes and bills of exchange and for the collection of criminal statistics. He was a strong supporter of the extension and consolidation of the dominion, and to this end favoured the widening and deepening of canals and the building of railways. Because of his interest in the latter, he became a director of the Toronto, Grey, and Bruce Railway in 1869. He was a Conservative and a staunch supporter of Macdonald.

CAROLE B. STELMACK

R. A. Harrison was the editor of *The Common Law Procedure Act; and other acts relating to the practice of the superior courts of common law; and the rules of court* (Toronto, 1858; 2nd ed., 1870); *A digest of reports of all cases determined in the Queen's Bench and practice courts for Upper Canada, from 1823 to 1851 inclusive* . . . , ed. under the supervision of J. L. Robinson (Toronto, 1852); *The new municipal manual for Upper Canada, containing notes of decided cases . . .* (Toronto, 1859; 2nd ed., 1867; 3rd ed., 1876); *The statutes of practical utility in the civil administration of justice, in Upper Canada, from the first act passed in Upper Canada to the Common Law Procedure Acts, 1856* (Toronto, 1857); and. with Henry O'Brien, *Queen's Bench, Common Pleas, and Chancery, in Upper Canada . . .* (Toronto, 1863).

PAC, MG 26, A (Macdonald papers); RG 1, E7, 46, 67; RG 5, C1, 562, f.1137; 607, f.370; 658, f.844; 672, f.103; 673, f.130; 879, f.541; RG 10, A8, 254; RG 19, A1, 1, PT.3. *Globe* (Toronto), 8, 11 Oct. 1875; 2 Nov. 1878. *Mail* (Toronto), 2, 4 Nov. 1878. *Can. biog. dict.*, I. *Can. directory of parliament* (Johnson). *Can. parl. comp., 1867.* Dent, *Canadian portrait gallery*, IV. Morgan, *Bibliotheca Canadensis; Sketches of celebrated Canadians.* Wallace, *Macmillan dictionary.*

HART, ADOLPHUS MORDECAI, lawyer and author; b. 11 April 1814 in Trois-Rivières, son of Ezekiel Hart* and Frances Lazarus, grandson of Aaron Hart*; d. 23 March 1879 in Montreal and buried in Trois-Rivières.

Adolphus Mordecai Hart took up the study of law and spent part of his time as a law clerk in the office of the attorney general of Lower Canada, Charles Richard Ogden*. He was admitted to the bar of Lower Canada on 19 May 1836. Along with his uncle Benjamin Hart* and Benjamin's son Aaron Philip Hart, Adolphus Hart took part in the movement of the 1830s to obtain equal rights for Jews in Lower Canada, in particular to make it possible for Jews to take the oath as a justice of the peace by omitting the phrase "on the true faith of a Christian." A law of 1832 granting Jews rights and privileges came under question, and the House of Assembly in 1834 formed a special committee to consider this legislation; Hart submitted evidence to it, which appears in the committee's report.

While he was still a student, Hart also lodged a complaint in 1836 before the assembly, through Bartholomew Conrad Augustus GUGY, against the conduct of Judge Edward Bowen*. His complaint had some justification but was said to have been presented in such an exaggerated manner that the assembly would not pursue the case. Louis-Michel Viger* and Amable Berthelot* were authorized to make an inquiry; on 10 March 1836 the committee on grievances found the judge guilty. Hart's family home was in Trois-Rivières.

Louis-Joseph PAPINEAU came there to dinner in 1836, a significant occasion for nearly all the respectable English citizens of the town refused the invitation. Hart established a practice in the aftermath of the disturbances of 1837–38, and he defended several persons associated with them. In 1837, during the trial of "a rebel," he was fined for contempt of court. In 1839 he pleaded for Joseph-Guillaume Barthe*, law student and journalist, and Richard Cook, saddler, both of Trois-Rivières, who were arrested for publicizing an address to the exiles of Bermuda.

In the early 1840s Adolphus Hart was living in Montreal and is recorded as a member of the Jewish synagogue. In 1846 he appears as an ensign in the 3rd battalion of militia. On 12 Dec. 1844 he had married Constance Hatton Hart, daughter of his uncle Benjamin Hart; they had three daughters and two sons, one of whom, Gerald Ephraim Hart*, became known as a historian, bibliophile, and numismatist. Constance Hatton Hart was the author of *Household receipts; or domestic cookery* by "A Montreal Lady" which had a second edition in 1867.

Hart went to the United States in 1850. He was active in the Democratic party in New York State, assisting with literature for the gubernatorial campaign of Horatio Seymour in 1854. He also wrote a number of works from 1850 onwards. Among these was a *History of the discovery of the valley of the Mississippi* (1852), one of the early discussions of this subject. Written for the general reader, and presenting events up to 1748, it had two editions in 1852; the story was extended in another edition in 1853. In 1854 came *Uncle Tom in Paris; or views of slavery outside the cabin.* He wrote also, under his own name or pseudonymously, on such topics as paper money and the liquor question. This writing activity was continued after he returned to Canada in 1857 and resumed his legal practice in Montreal. He wrote *Practical suggestions on mining rights and privileges in Canada . . .* in 1867. *The political state and condition of her majesty's Protestant subjects in the province of Quebec . . . ,* 1871, has been ascribed to him; the edition is reported to have been purchased and destroyed by the government.

Adolphus Hart suffered a stroke while pleading a case in court and died a few days later. The entire Montreal bar and most of the bench joined the escort for the body to the station, and the bar observed a month of mourning for him. At his funeral in Trois-Rivières, Alexander Abraham de Sola* officiated.

D. ROME

Adolphus Mordecai Hart published three works under the pseudonym of "Hampden": *A few thoughts on the liquor question* (New York, 1854); *The impending crises* (New York, 1855); *The political state and condition of her majesty's Protestant subjects in the province of Quebec (since confederation)* (Toronto, 1871). He also wrote *History of the discovery of the valley of the Mississippi* (1st ed., St Louis, Mo., 1852; rev. ed., Cincinnati, Ohio, 1853); *History of the issues of paper-money in the American colonies, anterior to the revolution, explanatory of the historical chart of the paper-money of that period* (St Louis, Mo., 1851); *Life in the far west; or, The comical, quizzical, and tragical adventures of a Hoosier* (Cincinnati, Ohio, [1850]); *Practical suggestions on mining rights and privileges in Canada; with an appendix containing the gold mining regulations . . .* (Montreal, 1867); *Uncle Tom in Paris; or, Views of slavery outside the cabin* (Baltimore, Md., 1854).

McCord Museum, Hart papers. Lower Canada, House of Assembly, *Journal*, 1834, app.GG. *Le Journal des Trois-Rivières*, 31 mars 1879. Morgan, *Bibliotheca Canadensis*. P.-G. Roy, *Les avocats de la région de Québec*. M. H. Stern, *Americans of Jewish descent; a compendium of genealogy* (Cincinnati, Ohio, [1960]). Wallace, *Macmillan dictionary*. Fauteux, *Patriotes*. V. B. Rhodenizer, *Canadian literature in English* (Montreal, 1965). David Rome, *Jews in Canadian literature; a bibliography* (2nd ed., 2v., Montreal, 1964), I, 1–3. Benjamin Sulte, *Pages d'histoire du Canada* (Montréal, 1891), 401–32. J.-P. Tremblay, *A la recherche de Napoléon Aubin* (Vie des lettres canadiennes, 7, Québec, 1969), 41–43.

HARTT, CHARLES FREDERICK, geologist and paleontologist; b. 23 Aug. 1840 at Fredericton, N.B., eldest son of Jarvis William Hartt and Prudence Brown; m. in 1869 Lucy Lynde of Buffalo, N.Y., by whom he had two children; d. in Rio de Janeiro, Brazil, 18 March 1878.

Charles Frederick Hartt's father was principal of the Baptist seminary in Fredericton, New Brunswick, when his son was born; he soon joined the staff of Horton Academy, Wolfville, Nova Scotia. Charles Frederick was educated at the academy and at Acadia College, receiving his BA in 1860. In that year his father moved to Saint John, N.B., and established a young ladies' high school, where his son taught for a year.

From an early age C. Fred Hartt (as he was usually known) manifested a great interest in the natural sciences, especially geology and paleontology, and he made extensive collections in both Nova Scotia and New Brunswick. Several species new to science which he had collected were described by Sir William Dawson* in *Acadian geology* (Edinburgh, 1855). From 1861 to 1864 Hartt studied under Professor Louis Agassiz at the Museum of Comparative Zoology at Cambridge, Mass. Hartt was a founding member, along with Moses H. Perley*, George Frederick Matthew*, and others, of the Natural History Society of New Brunswick in 1862; the society bought his fossil collections to assist in financing his studies under Professor Agassiz. In 1864 he and G. F. Matthew assisted Professor Loring Woart Bailey* of the University of New Brunswick in a government-instituted survey of southern New Brunswick.

In 1865 when Professor Agassiz was organizing the Thayer Expedition to Brazil, Hartt was appointed one of the two geologists. The expedition returned to the United States in 1866 but Hartt went back in 1867 for further study of the geology of the Bahia region and the coral reefs. In 1868 he became professor of natural history at Vassar College but soon resigned to become head of the department of geology at Cornell University.

Brazil was, however, his great interest. In 1870 he organized the largest of his expeditions, taking with him another professor and 11 Cornell students. On this and a subsequent expedition he worked in the Amazonas. In 1874 he submitted a proposition to the Brazilian government for a geological survey of Brazil, and in 1875 the Geological Commission of the Empire of Brazil was organized with Professor Hartt as its chief. For the next three years he directed expeditions working in many parts of the country and set up a museum to house all the scientific specimens collected. Then in the spring of 1878, when he returned to Rio de Janeiro after an exhausting inland expedition, he died of yellow fever at the age of 38, cutting short a brilliant career.

Hartt's contribution to scientific research in Brazil did not end with his own outstanding geological work. Inspired by his example the students whom he had taken to Brazil continued the research long after his death. Dr John Casper Branner, who had been personally associated with Hartt, wrote: "It is not difficult to sum up Hartt's influence upon geological work in Brazil, for with very few exceptions all the work of this character which has been done in that country since 1874 is traceable, either directly or indirectly, to the impetus given it by Hartt . . . as he was not a narrow specialist but a broad-minded naturalist, his students have also done other than purely geological work."

W. AUSTIN SQUIRES

J. C. Branner, "Prof. Hartt in Brazil," *Cornell Magazine* (Ithaca, N.Y.), February 1890. G. U. Hay, "Memorial sketch of the life and work of Prof. Ch. Fred. Hartt," New Brunswick Natural History Society, *Report, 1881* (Saint John, N.B.), 3–14; "The scientific work of Prof. Chas. Fred. Hartt," *RSCT*, 2nd ser., V (1899), sect.IV, 155–65. G. F. Matthew, "Charles Frederick Hartt," Natural History Society of New Brunswick, *Bull.* (Saint John, N.B.), IX (1890), 1–24.

HASZARD, JAMES DOUGLAS, printer, journalist, farmer, and businessman; b. 27 June 1797 at Charlottetown, P.E.I., eldest son of Thomas Rhodes Haszard and his wife Jane; d. 17 Aug. 1875 at his home in Charlottetown, P.E.I.

James Douglas Haszard was the son of Rhode Island loyalists who immigrated to Prince Edward Island in 1785. At an early age James was apprenticed to his uncle, James D. Bagnall*, who was king's printer. When Bagnall was absent from the Island for three years, his young apprentice took over the task of printing royal notices and proclamations. With his uncle's return in 1811, Haszard resumed his role as apprentice. He broadened his experience by attending school in Halifax from 1816 to 1817, and by working as a printer in Rhode Island.

In 1823, two years after his return from the United States, Haszard established the *Prince Edward Island Register*, which because of the lack of printed matter on the Island was used as a reading text as well as a newspaper. The 11 Oct. 1823 issue was strongly critical of the Island's lieutenant governor and chancellor, Charles Douglas Smith*, whose actions as governor were described as "highly oppressive and illegal." Haszard was called before the governor in his capacity as chancellor, sternly lectured, but discharged, ostensibly because of his "youth and inexperience."

In 1825 Haszard married Sarah Sophia Gardiner who died within the next decade; then in 1835 he married Susanna Jane Nelmes. His second wife survived him as did at least four of his children.

Haszard continued to publish the *Register* until 1830 when he was appointed king's printer, a position he held until 1851. During those 21 years he published the *Royal Gazette*, which carried local and foreign news, and letters to the editor, as well as official notices and proclamations. After Edward Whelan* displaced him as queen's printer, Haszard began to publish *Haszard's Gazette*, which his son George continued after the father's retirement in December 1852.

Haszard was involved in several other enterprises. He established the first clothing mill in the colony, had interests in the insurance business, and owned a store which carried a wide selection of books, stationery, and Protestant religious tracts. He rented a number of houses in Charlottetown, and several farms around the Island, which a lieutenant governor, Sir Henry Vere Huntley*, described in 1844 as "extremely good" in quality. In a letter to the Colonial Office three years later, Haszard portrayed himself as "holding a large and important stake in the country." He also took an active part in community institutions such as the Royal Agricultural Society, Temperance Hall, and the Mechanics' Institute.

James Haszard was the first native Island journalist. He was not a gifted writer, and when Governor Huntley was about to strip him of a minor office he wrote that there was nothing to fear from Haszard: "he is without talent of his own, too penurious to pay for that belonging to others, and moreover, he will do nothing to endanger his possession of the office of Queen's Printer." Nonetheless, Haszard did introduce several important Island newspapermen, such as John Ings and James Barrett Cooper*, to their future profession, and in late 1852 he and his son George imported the colony's first power printing press. In politics, he was closely associated with the Tory élite which ruled the Island prior to responsible government. It was but natural that he should be displaced when this era came to an end. He appears to have aged prematurely, and not to have taken an active part in public life in his declining years.

IAN ROSS ROBERTSON

PAPEI, Henry Jones Cundall, letter book, 27 March 1867–26 May 1871, p.111. PRO, CO 226/67, 16–20; 226/71, 288, 361, 367; 226/75, 18; 226/98, 336–38. Prince Edward Island, Supreme Court, Estates Division, will of James Douglas Haszard, [21 April 1868]. *Examiner* (Charlottetown), 23, 30 Aug. 1875. *Haszard's Gazette* (Charlottetown), 1852. *Patriot* (Charlottetown), 3 Sept. 1875. *Prince Edward Island Register* (Charlottetown), 1823–30. *Royal Gazette* (Charlottetown), 1830–51.

Duncan Campbell, *History of Prince Edward Island* (Charlottetown, 1875), 201. R. L. Cotton, "Early press," in *Historic highlights of Prince Edward Island*, ed. M. C. Brehaut (P.E.I. Hist. Soc. pamphlet, Charlottetown, 1955), 42–43. W. L. Cotton, *Chapters in our Island story* (Charlottetown, 1927), 92–93, 125–28; "The press in Prince Edward Island," *Past and present of Prince Edward Island . . .*, ed. D. A. MacKinnon and A. B. Warburton (Charlottetown, [1906]), 112–21. T. R. Millman, *A history of the parish of New London, Prince Edward Island* (n.p., 1959), 6–7. J. B. Pollard, *Historical sketch of the eastern regions of New France, from the various dates of their discoveries to the surrender of Louisburg in 1758; also Prince Edward Island, military and civil* (Charlottetown, 1898), 200–1.

HATHEWAY, GEORGE LUTHER, farmer, merchant, lumberman, and politician; b. at Musquash, Sunbury County, N.B., 4 Aug. 1813, son of Calvin Luther Hatheway and his wife Sarah; m. in June 1840 to Martha Slason of Fredericton (there were no children); d. 5 July 1872 at Fredericton, N.B.

George Luther Hatheway attended school in Saint John, New Brunswick. He settled at Durham

Hatheway

Bridge, York County, where he became a farmer, country merchant, and lumber operator. He later moved to Saint Mary's across the Saint John River from Fredericton. At the time of his death he owned large areas of timber land.

Hatheway, a born politician, entered politics in 1850 as a reformer. Loud and boisterous, he was also warm-hearted, yet a formidable adversary in any debate. He was the central figure at any social gathering and he appealed to rural voters who felt he was one of them. He was able to do things which would have ruined other politicians. During his election campaigns he frequently dispatched messengers to the nearest tavern for brandy which he drank in full view of his audience. One story tells that he was surprised to receive the votes of a man and his three sons with whom he had quarrelled. He offered to shake hands with the head of the family saying he was glad their differences had apparently been resolved. The man refused, replying that there were two places for which he felt Hatheway was suited – Hell and the legislature – and that he would do his best to see him in both.

Hatheway, a supporter of responsible government, was elected in 1850, 1854, and 1856. He advocated in 1851 a bill to make the Legislative Council elective. In 1856 he introduced perhaps the most important legislation passed that year – a bill giving the Executive Council the sole right to initiate money grants. He was defeated in the 1857 election but in 1861 was back in the house and became chief commissioner of public works.

In 1865 Hatheway objected to the terms under which it was proposed that New Brunswick enter confederation. These terms were accepted by the majority of Samuel Leonard Tilley*'s government and Hatheway was the only member who decided to resign, which he did in January 1865, thus weakening the government. Hatheway has been criticized for his apparent lack of political conviction and his willingness to change sides when an issue seemed doomed to failure, yet, in deserting the Tilley government in 1865, he appears genuinely to have believed that the terms discussed at the Quebec conference of 1864 were not advantageous to New Brunswick. He demonstrated his sincerity in later years when he fought for better terms.

It has been said that during the debate over confederation "party politics was completely set aside . . . and personal advantage in the public area became the guiding spirit" of New Brunswick politicians. This may be so but after the government's defeat in the 1865 election, Hatheway, who had been re-elected as an anti-confederate, turned down an opportunity to form the new government.

He was the first man approached by Lieutenant Governor Arthur H. Gordon*, despite the fact that Gordon considered him "destitute of principle, as well as of education." Instead Hatheway became chief commissioner of public works in the government formed by Albert James Smith*. In the election of 1866, probably because he sensed a major upset coming at the polls, Hatheway withdrew from the contest a few days before the end of the campaign. His desertion weakened the anti-confederates' chances of regaining power.

Hatheway was re-elected in 1870 to the provincial assembly and in February 1871 he was one of the men responsible for ousting the government of George Edwin King*. King was not a strong leader and many considered his government to be a creature of Ottawa. Hatheway was again accused of office seeking and in this case the charge had more validity. He deserted those who had helped him defeat King, and formed a new government including King and some of the ablest men from both parties.

Hatheway became premier and provincial secretary of a government organized primarily to pass the controversial school law bill of which King had been the architect. In his views on educational reform, Hatheway followed a consistent policy. As early as 1852 he had supported direct taxation for school purposes, pointing out that higher wages were paid to men working in the woods than to teachers. He realized that assessment would be unpopular but argued that "every child had a right to an education." He also supported the appointment of additional school inspectors and in 1854 he defended King's College (University of New Brunswick) against the attacks of A. J. Smith and others who wanted it closed. In the election of 1871 he declared that his government would stand or fall on the issue of the school bill and the principle of direct taxation for school purposes. He won the election and the bill was passed.

The school act of 1871 called for "free, tax supported, non-sectarian schools" and was opposed by those who felt that direct taxation was unnecessary and by the clergy, particularly Roman Catholics. The opponents of the bill carried the fight to the New Brunswick Supreme Court and the dominion parliament, and the government of Sir John A. Macdonald* referred it to the Judicial Committee of the Privy Council. All attempts to overthrow the bill failed and the higher courts declared it to be constitutional and within the jurisdiction of the province. This act, for which Hatheway deserves much of the credit, "laid the foundation of a free school system" when it went into effect in January 1872 and was "the most significant educational advance in New Brunswick during the nineteenth century."

On 25 June 1872 Hathaway badly damaged his left hand when he jumped from a moving train; he died as a result of blood poisoning from the injury. Hatheway was an able politician and a colourful individual though with many faults. Much more than a "loud-mouthed demagogue" or an unprincipled opportunist, he worked for reform both in government and in education and was never afraid to state his views, no matter how unpopular, to the house or to the people he represented.

W. A. SPRAY

N.B. Museum, Hatheway papers, F28, draft of a short history of the Hatheway family by W. F. Hatheway; "New Brunswick biographies," unpublished MS by G. H. Markham, 94–95. York County Court of Probate (Fredericton), IV (1866–77), 216–19. Fenety, *Political notes and observations*, 405, 474. New Brunswick, House of Assembly, *Debates*, 1866, 91. *Morning Freeman* (Saint John, N.B.), 6 July 1872. *New Brunswick Reporter* (Fredericton), 10 July 1872. *Saint John Daily News*, 6 July 1872. *Saint John Daily Telegraph and Morning Journal*, 6 July 1872. *Telegraph Journal* (Saint John, N.B.), 1 March, 28, 29 April, 6 May, 15, 16 June 1932. *Can. parl. comp., 1871*, 258, 267. Wallace, *Macmillan dictionary*, 305.

Creighton, *Road to confederation*, 200, 231. Hannay, *History of New Brunswick*, II, 140, 178–79, 234–37, 252–53, 293–301; *Wilmot and Tilley* (Toronto, 1907), 228, 233, 250. K. F. C. MacNaughton, *The development of the theory and practice of education in New Brunswick, 1784–1900: a study in historical background* ed. with intro. A. G. Bailey (U. of New Brunswick Hist. Studies, 1, Fredericton, 1947), 143–47, 155–263. MacNutt, *New Brunswick*, 365, 427–32. Waite, *Life and times of confederation*, 242, 245. C. M. Wallace, "The life and times of Sir Albert James Smith," unpublished MA thesis, U. of New Brunswick, 1959, 111–12, 122–31. A. G. Bailey, "The basis and persistence of opposition to confederation in New Brunswick," *CHR*, XXIII (1942), 374–97. James Hannay, "The premiers of New Brunswick since confederation," *Canadian Magazine* (Toronto), IX (1897), 213–21.

HAZEN, ROBERT LEONARD, lawyer, judge, and politician; b. 15 Oct. 1808 in Fredericton, N.B., son of William Hazen* Jr and Deborah Murray, a daughter of Colonel John Murray*; d. at Saint John, N.B., 15 Aug. 1874.

Robert Leonard Hazen's grandfather, William Hazen* Sr, had been one of the original members of the Council of Twelve which administered the province of New Brunswick before the appointment of the first governor, Thomas Carleton*, in 1785. After studying law in the office of Robert Parker* in Saint John, Robert L. Hazen was called to the bar of New Brunswick when he was 23 years old. In 1837 he married his cousin Sarah Ann, a daughter of William Botsford*, a provincial politician and judge; they had three children of whom one son survived the father. Hazen had a successful career in law; in 1843 he was named a queen's counsel, a considerable honour at that time, and three years later he was appointed a judge of the Court of Vice-Admiralty and recorder of the city of Saint John. At one time he served as a director, and at another as solicitor, for the Commercial Bank of New Brunswick.

In the general election of 1837 Hazen was elected to the assembly as one of the members for Saint John; he was re-elected in 1843 and 1846. In 1844 he was taken into the government, which included Edward Barron CHANDLER and Lemuel Allen WILMOT, as a member of the Executive Council and minister without portfolio. He resigned from the council in 1845 over a controversy involving the prerogative powers of the lieutenant governor, Sir William Colebrooke*, and became after this time one of the proponents of responsible government in New Brunswick. Once the controversy had been settled to his satisfaction, Hazen re-entered the Executive Council in 1846 where he remained until 1854; he was again a member from 1856 to 1857. As a member of the council, Hazen fought the government's battles in the assembly with conspicuous success. He resigned the assembly seat in 1848, however, to become a member of the Legislative Council; since he was popular in Saint John he could have retained his assembly seat for many years, but not being an ambitious man he chose to retire to the ease of the Legislative Council.

Robert Leonard Hazen exercised power and influence in New Brunswick politics for many years. His obvious talent and sterling honesty made him a man who commanded great respect among his fellows. When the union of the British North American provinces took place on 1 July 1867, Hazen was appointed, by royal proclamation, to a seat in the Senate of Canada. He remained a senator until his death, but did not participate actively in the debates. In the early 1860s his health had deteriorated and he partially lost his voice. He retired from the bar, practising only when, as recorder, he had to appear in court on behalf of the city.

P. R. LINDO

N.B. Museum, Hazen coll., Robert Leonard Hazen papers; Hazen family estate papers, 1852–92; Hazen family papers, 1720–1889. T. E. Hazen, *The Hazen family in America, a genealogy*, ed. D. L. Jacobus (Thomaston, Conn., 1947). J. W. Lawrence, *Footprints; or incidents in the early history of New Bruns-*

Hazlewood

wick, *1783–1883* (Saint John, N.B., 1883); *Judges of New Brunswick* (Stockton). MacNutt, *New Brunswick*, 285–94, 299, 318, 340, 343, 360, 430.

HAZLEWOOD, SAMUEL, civil engineer and surveyor; b. in 1822 at Newtonbarry, Wexford, Ireland; d. 11 Jan. 1878, at Brockville, Ont.

Samuel Hazlewood was a land surveyor in Ireland, and had worked on the Ordnance Survey as well as on other public and private projects. This background meant that when he emigrated to Canada at the age of 29 he had little difficulty in finding employment in a country just beginning its era of railway expansion.

It is likely that Hazlewood first settled in the vicinity of Brockville, Canada West. On his arrival he worked on a survey of a projected railway from Prescott to Georgian Bay, and shortly afterwards on the proposed Grand Junction Rail-Road between Belleville and Peterborough. In 1852 Hazlewood was employed on the first survey of the Grand Trunk Railway. Various employments in his profession followed, including time spent with the private contracting firm of Peto, Brassey, and Betts.

Hazlewood again became involved in a major work in 1864. He worked on both the exploratory survey and the preliminary survey of the Intercolonial Railway, and acted as one of the four district engineers during the construction of the road between 1868 and 1874. After its completion he was appointed district engineer for a portion of the Canadian Pacific Railway route under construction between Thunder Bay and Rat Portage (now Kenora). This was to be an "amphibious route," so named because it would use a combined water and rail system along the "Dawson Road," which had been explored and surveyed by Simon J. Dawson* and used as a route for immigrants and soldiers. Hazlewood was specifically in charge of the Fort Frances Canal Works located at the foot of Rainy Lake. In 1878, the year of Hazlewood's death, the route was abandoned, although the canal was almost finished, in favour of the present more northerly route.

ANNE E. F. SNIDERMAN

PAO, Historical Branch, "Historical plaque to commemorate the Fort Frances Canal." *Revised record, engineers and their assistants employed on public works, Canada, 1779 to 1890* ([Ottawa], n.d.). *Dom. ann. reg.*, 1878.

HEAD, Sir FRANCIS BOND, soldier, author, and colonial administrator; b. 1 Jan. 1793, at The Hermitage, Higham, Kent, Eng., son of James Roper Mendes Head and Frances Anne Burges; m. his cousin, Julia Valenza Somerville, in 1816,

and they had four children; d. at his home, Duppas Hall, Croydon, Eng., 20 July 1875.

Francis Bond Head was descended from Dr Fernando Mendes, a Spanish Jew who accompanied Catherine of Braganza to England in 1662 as her personal physician. Francis' grandfather Moses married Anna Gabriella Head, the heiress of a Kentish gentry family; his father took the Head name on inheriting Anna's estates.

Francis Head was commissioned a lieutenant in the Royal Engineers upon passing out of the Royal Military Academy, Woolwich, in 1811. He saw service in Malta, at Waterloo, and as engineering officer in the Edinburgh garrison, retiring as a major on half-pay in 1825 to take a position as mining supervisor for a company with South American interests. Loss of the company's concession rendered the expedition a costly failure, for which Head indicted his employers in *Reports relating to the failure of the Rio Plata Mining Association* (1827).

Head had already begun in 1826 a lifelong connection with the publishing house of John Murray with *Rough notes taken during some rapid journeys across the pampas and among the Andes*, a book which reveals his talent for graphic description, his love of nature, his interest in primitive peoples, his deep suspicion of things un-English, his erratic and impulsive bent, and his penchant for self-dramatization. Both his books and his exploits brought him to public notice. He was nicknamed "Galloping Head" for his feat in riding twice across South America between Buenos Aires and the Andes; and his demonstration of the military usefulness of the lasso brought him a knighthood from William IV in 1831. A number of other writings followed, including articles for the *Quarterly Review* and his most successful book, *Bubbles from the Brunnens of Nassau* (1834), a travel book of ingratiating superficiality which went through six editions. In 1834 as well he was named assistant poor law commissioner for Kent under the new poor law of that year, a preferment he is said to have owed to Lord Brougham's influence.

In December 1835 came a more surprising appointment. Head was named to succeed Sir John Colborne* as lieutenant governor of Upper Canada. Lord Glenelg, the colonial secretary, selected Head not because he had confused him with his cousin Edmund Walker Head*, or because of Lady Head's exalted family connections, but because the strongly reformist members of the cabinet, especially Lord Howick (later 3rd Earl Grey), were convinced by Head's vigorous administration of the new poor law and his writings on the subject that he was the conciliator needed in Upper

342

Canada. It was for the same reason that the puzzled Head, on his arrival in Toronto in January 1836, found himself welcomed as "a Tried Reformer." The cabinet had made an astonishing choice. Head had so little political experience that he had never voted in an election; he had displayed no interest whatever in colonial policy; and even his essay on the poor law, though couched in the rhetoric of reform, was based upon the deepest social conservatism.

Head's first moves as lieutenant governor were promising. Though his publication in full of his instructions from Glenelg embarrassed both the commission under Lord Gosford [Acheson*] in Lower Canada and the home government, and showed his insubordinate attitude towards Glenelg as well as his political innocence, to many Upper Canadians his action seemed an augury of change. Then, after a round of conversations with leading Reformers, Head succeeded in persuading John Rolph* and a reluctant Robert Baldwin*, as well as John Henry Dunn*, the receiver general, to join the Executive Council. Within two weeks, however, Head's coup led to a crisis when all six councillors formally protested his failure to consult them on all matters relating to the government of the province. Head's reply, an able document often attributed to Chief Justice John Beverley Robinson*, was constitutionally unassailable. Since, under the Constitutional Act, the lieutenant governor alone was responsible for the conduct of government and was bound to consult his council only on certain specified matters, Head demanded that his councillors either alter their views or resign. They chose to resign, on 12 March, after having held office for three weeks. The Tory members of the council, George H. Markland*, Joseph Wells*, and Peter Robinson*, though now ready to retract, went out with the new councillors, Head arguing that the council must act as a body though he wished also to avoid the unpopularity that a dismissal of the new councillors alone would have brought him.

The controversy between Head and the council had been conducted temperately; the assembly's reaction, however, was violent. Reformers and Conservatives, with but two dissenting votes, demanded more information from Head on the controversy; on its production a select committee was set up to investigate and report. While it was sitting, the political climate worsened sharply with the disclosure of Colborne's 11th-hour endowment of 57 Anglican rectories. In consequence the committee's report, given the house on 15 April, was extremely harsh. Head was termed a deceitful despot whose conduct dishonoured the king he represented. On adopting the report, the assembly voted also to stop supply, thereby depriving government of £7000 for official salaries. Head, deeply angered by the personal attack upon him, reacted disproportionately by reserving all money bills passed during the session and proroguing the legislature. A month later, on 28 May, he dissolved it and ordered writs to be issued for an election.

Head's pose during these events was that of a man above party, unjustly accused by a faction of partiality to the Conservatives. Far from being captured by the Family Compact, however, he had quite independently made up his mind about the nature of provincial politics almost as soon as he had arrived, and never changed his ideas thereafter. As early as 5 February he had told Glenelg that the Whig policy of conciliation was wrong, that the Reformers – all Reformers – were "The Republican party," and that their aim was to use responsible government to sever the imperial connection.

His private intention of February of "throwing himself on the good sense and good feeling of the people" was carried out during the most bitter election in the province's short history, when he campaigned openly against the Reformers. Many factors caused their overwhelming defeat, but Head's electioneering skill was certainly an important one. His direct and vivid language transformed the complexities of provincial politics into a simple confrontation between the forces of loyalty, order, and prosperity and those of a selfish and disloyal faction. He managed to conjure up the menace of outside intervention (whether French Canadian or American he left unsaid) in support of provincial democrats, and trumpeted, in the name of the loyal militia, "Let them come if they dare!" Such tactics were "not exactly according to Hoyle," he admitted to Glenelg, "but, Mon Seigneur, do you think that Revolutions are made with Rose water," he wrote in French. What Head called his "plain homely language" may have astonished the Colonial Office, but gained him "herds of friends." Conservatives, moderates, and recent immigrants alike responded to his appeals and combined to defeat not only such prominent Reformers as William Lyon Mackenzie*, Marshall Spring BIDWELL, and Peter Perry*, but the bulk of their followers as well.

For Head, the result of the election was a vindication of his views, and the year that followed was a relatively quiet and happy period for him. During the summers of 1836 and 1837 he toured the province informally, meeting many settlers, visiting Indian bands, and acquiring the fund of anecdote that gives piquancy to his books on

Head

Upper Canada. His relations with his new legislature went smoothly enough, Head encouraging the conservative majority in the assembly in its ambitious programme of public improvement.

But during the same period, Head dissipated much of the moderate support he had gained during the election and at the same time lost the prestige his victory had momentarily given him at the Colonial Office. Dismissing from office a number of men, including Dr William Warren Baldwin* and Judge George RIDOUT, who had shown Reform sympathies during the election, he embarked at the same time on an extraordinary correspondence with Glenelg in which he urged the abandonment of the policy of conciliation. Although it was plain to Glenelg that Ridout had been unjustly treated, Head refused to reinstate him, nor would he appoint Bidwell to the bench. To Head, Bidwell was a "disloyal man" though he admitted him to be much abler than those raised to judgeships in the province. The strong personal animus Head felt towards Bidwell probably had its origin in the part Bidwell had played as speaker of the Reform assembly. Whatever the reason, Head was so blinded by it that he did not see how valuable a judgeship for Bidwell would have been in cementing the temporary alliance of conservatives and moderates formed during the election campaign. His quixotic response to the bank crisis of early 1837 (he refused to allow provincial banks to suspend specie payments, as banks in the United States and Lower Canada had done) was vigorously attacked in a special session of the legislature called to resolve the crisis. Deadlock between the House of Assembly and the Legislative Council, though eventually broken on Head's terms, showed the extent to which his popularity had diminished.

Head's weakening grip upon provincial politics was soon overshadowed by the events that were to lead to armed revolt in December, a revolt for which he has traditionally been held largely responsible. Yet the origins of the rebellion of 1837 lie in political and religious antagonisms that predate his arrival in the province, and with social tensions engendered by the flood of British immigration that was changing the composition of the province's population. Agrarian economic distress and the swift movement towards revolt in Lower Canada were specific causes of the rebellion in Upper Canada; so too was the personality of Mackenzie. For none of these can Sir Francis be held responsible.

But he was hardly blameless. Although he had not "stolen" the election of 1836 in the corrupt sense alleged by Mackenzie and others, his unprecedented intervention had shattered the old politics and created deep disaffection among a minority; his uncompromising hostility toward Reformers after the election, with the apparent backing of the home authorities, had extinguished for many what hopes they had held for gradual change. More immediately, his deliberate stripping of regular troops from the colony in November 1837 to help Colborne meet the Lower Canadian emergency was most provocative, especially in the light of his foreknowledge of the martial preparations of Mackenzie and his followers. In his *Narrative* (1839) Head explained that "the more I encouraged [the rebels] to consider me defenceless the better"; he wished "to await the outbreak, which I was confident would be impotent," in order to prove the loyalty of the mass of the people. As J. B. Robinson remarked upon reading this passage, "any quiet Englishman will be apt to say, that man would make a rebellion anywhere." Public criticism prompted Head to change his story in *The emigrant* (1846). There he alleged that Colborne had withdrawn the troops without consulting him, a statement for which there is no foundation. As late as 20 Nov. 1837 Head told Colborne that he was releasing troops to Lower Canada "as nothing more or less than a challenge to the rebels to change agitation into attack," while at the same time fatuously assuring him (in the face of repeated warnings from Colonel James FitzGibbon* and others) that "nothing can be more satisfactory than the present political state of this province."

It was precisely the defencelessness of the government that led Mackenzie first to propose, and then, on the night of 4 December, to attempt to carry out an armed coup. When Head was awakened with the news of the revolt, he appears to have been thrown into a state of shock, judging from his erratic and indecisive behaviour in the ensuing days. On 7 December the militia had dispersed the rebels on Yonge Street north of Toronto and Head (like Mackenzie before the battle) indulged his talent for excess by ordering burnt both John MONTGOMERY's tavern and the home and buildings of David Gibson*, a rebel leader, though at the same time granting immediate clemency to prisoners from the rebel rank-and-file. He had already settled another score by persuading Marshall Spring Bidwell, who was not involved in the revolt, to go into voluntary exile.

After the suppression of armed risings in the province, Head, his confidence restored, threw himself with characteristic energy into the task of supervising the movements of the militia on the frontiers in order to counter the threat posed by Mackenzie and his new-found American adherents. In the midst of these activities he learned, in a dispatch from Glenelg, that the resignation he had proffered some months earlier had been accepted because of his refusal either to reinstate Judge Ridout or to acquaint him with the grounds of his dismissal. Almost the last accomplishment of Head's administration was the acceptance by the Colonial Office of his recommendation, against the advice of his council, that the special authority under which Thomas Talbot* had for many years controlled settlement in the western part of the province be terminated "without loss of time."

Head departed Upper Canada convinced that he had saved it for the empire, and for several years tilted unavailingly against the colonial policies of such men as Durham [Lambton*], James Stephen, Lord John Russell, and Sir Robert Peel whom he considered were squandering the fruits of his work. Had Francis Head never come to Upper Canada he would still be remembered as a minor and rather engaging member of the gallery of 19th-century English literary eccentrics; Lord Melbourne, who gave Head an interview on his return from North America, could only reply to his catalogue of grievances by observing, "But Head, you're such a damned odd fellow." His selection as lieutenant governor was a singularly unfortunate one, for the implementation of the policy of the Whig government and the state of the province demanded the stabilizing arts of the political healer, not the melodramatics of a literary man turned polemicist with a romantic yearning for the hero's role.

Head never again held a government post. During the remaining years of his long life, his fluent pen produced a series of books and articles, the mixed and ephemeral character of which is indicated by the following titles: *Stokers and pokers* (1849), *Hi-ways and dry-ways* (1849), *The defenceless state of Great Britain* (1850), *A faggot of French sticks, or Paris in 1851* (1852), *A fortnight in Ireland* (1852), *The horse and his rider* (1860), *Mr. Kinglake and his history of the Crimean War* (1863), *The life of Field Marshal Sir John Burgoyne* (1872), and his collected essays, published in two volumes in 1857.

In confederation year Sir Francis petitioned the cabinet for recognition of the contribution he had made to the development of Canada. On 21 Dec. 1867 Queen Victoria made him a member of her Privy Council, an honour termed by the prime minister, Lord Derby, "a tardy act of justice."

S. F. WISE

A complete list of F. B. Head's works can be found in the *British Museum catalogue* but the following are of interest here: F. B. Head, *Descriptive essays contributed to the Quarterly Review* (2v., London, 1857); *The emigrant* (London, 1846); *A narrative* (London, 1839), repub. as *A narrative with notes by William Lyon Mackenzie*, ed. with intro. S. F. Wise (Carleton Library series, no.43, Toronto, Montreal, 1969); *Rough notes taken during some rapid journeys across the pampas and among the Andes* (London, 1826).

PAC, MG 24, A25 (Francis Bond Head papers); A40 (Colborne papers); RG 5, A1, 160–80; RG 7, G1, 75. PAO, Macaulay family papers; Mackenzie-Lindsey collection; Sir John Beverley Robinson papers; John Strachan papers. PRO, CO 42/429–42/431, 42/437, 42/439, 42/444. Charles Lindsey, *The life and times of William Lyon Mackenzie; with an account of the Canadian rebellion of 1837, and the subsequent frontier disturbances, chiefly from unpublished documents* (2v., Toronto, 1862), I, 355–401; II, 5–132. [A. E. Ryerson], *Sir F. B. Head and Mr. Bidwell . . .* (Kingston, U.C., 1838).

J. C. Dent, *The story of the Upper Canadian rebellion; largely derived from original sources and documents* (2v., Toronto, 1885). M. A. FitzGibbon, *A veteran of 1812, the life of James FitzGibbon* (Toronto, 1894), 184–235. S. W. Jackman, *Galloping Head; the life of the Right Honourable Sir Francis Bond Head, bart., P.C., 1793–1875, late lieutenant governor of Upper Canada* (London, [1958]). J. A. Gibson, "The 'persistent fallacy' of the Governors Head," *CHR*, XIX (1938), 295–97. H. T. Manning, "The colonial policy of the Whig ministers, 1830–37," *CHR*, XXXIII (1952), 203–36, 341–68. H. T. Manning and J. S. Galbraith, "The appointment of Francis Bond Head: a new insight," *CHR*, XLII (1961), 50–52. C. B. Sissons, "The case of Bidwell; correspondence connected with the withdrawal of Marshall Spring Bidwell from Canada," *CHR*, XXVII (1946), 368–82. William Smith, "Sir Francis Bond Head," *CHA Report, 1930*, 25–38.

HEATH, JOHN, *Patriote*, notary, and registrar; b. *c.* 1808 in Ireland, son of a regimental captain William Heath and Elizabeth Allen, originally from London, Eng.; d. 16 Nov. 1874 at L'Isle-Verte, Que.

John Heath arrived in Canada when he was still young. A family named Bâcon, probably that of François Bâcon of Quebec, took him in and gave him an education which enabled him to acquire a notary's commission on 17 Nov. 1834. John Heath followed his profession successively at Saint-Charles, county of Saint-Hyacinthe, from 1834 to 1836, at Quebec from 1838 to 1842, at Saint-Germain-de-Rimouski from 1842 to 1849, then at L'Isle-Verte from 1852 until his death. But his registry contains no acts from September 1836 to February 1838 and from November 1838 to the end of August 1840.

For these last four years, John Heath abandoned the profession of notary in order to support the cause of the Quebec *Patriotes*. He won renown in an unusual way in October 1838, when he engineered the escape from the Quebec citadel of the

Heavysege

Americans William W. Dodge and Edward Alexander Theller*, who had been condemned to be hanged for taking part in the Upper Canada insurrection. The fugitives hid for some weeks in the city of Quebec, thanks to Charles DROLET's assistance; then Jean-Baptiste Carrier and John Heath undertook to conduct them across the American border. In the night of 4–5 November the travellers, taking circuitous routes, reached Saint-François-de-la-Beauce (Beauceville). After a rest, they managed to get past three sentinels' posts without attracting attention, and to reach the border. John Heath had the police at his heels when he got back to Canada and stayed in the woods at some distance from Quebec City.

The proclamation of the amnesty allowed him to take up his profession again. He then settled at Saint-Germain-de-Rimouski, where on 11 July 1842 he married Émilie Reeves; they had two children, one being James William Adhémar who also became a notary. John Heath ended his career at L'Isle-Verte, after receiving a commission as registrar for the county of Rimouski in August 1849. When the county of Témiscouata, formed from part of the county of Rimouski, was set up in 1853, John Heath was assigned to it as registrar.

JACQUES MATHIEU

AQ, John Heath; QBC, Procureur général, Événements de 1837–1838, nos.3363, 4136; P.-G. Roy, Dossiers de recherche, Heath. *Le Monde illustré* (Montréal), 19 févr., 12 mars 1898. *La Quotidienne* (Montréal), 28 oct. 1838. P.-G. Roy, "L'évasion de Dodge et Theller de la citadelle de Québec," *Cahiers des Dix*, V (1940), 121–44.

HEAVYSEGE, CHARLES, poet and dramatist; b. 2 May 1816 in Huddersfield, Yorkshire, England; m. Mary Ann Oddy in 1843, by whom he had seven daughters; d. in Montreal, 14 July 1876.

There is little verifiable information on the early life of Charles Heavysege, and we must depend to some extent on his own accounts of his childhood, especially those appearing in an article by Lawrence Johnston Burpee*, a report of an address by G. H. Flint, and an unpublished thesis by T. R. Dale. Heavysege said, in a letter to Charles Lanman* (Montreal, 1860): "I was born in England, as I believe you are aware; my ancestors on the paternal side being of Yorkshire. . . . I was what is usually styled religiously brought up, and, though my works are dramatic, taught to consider not only the theatre itself, but dramatic literature, even in its best examples, as forbidden things. Hence, when a boy, it was only by dint of great persuasion that I covertly obtained from my mother some few pence weekly for a cheap edition of Shakespeare. . . ." According to the same source,

Heavysege left school at nine, to return only briefly later. He wrote in another letter that his father, through romantic idealism, had sold his patrimony and divided the money among relatives, but Dale could find no evidence of a Heavysege family holding land in England. In the same letter Heavysege said he was proud to belong to the working class. G. H. Flint adds the following information, probably obtained from Heavysege himself or some friend: "He [Heavysege] was apprenticed to a woodcarver and soon became a first-class workman. On completing his apprenticeship, he started business for himself and employed several men. But he did not seem to have the necessary business tact to compete with the world, and, having married ten years previously, he came to Montreal in 1853, on the invitation of a gentleman here, and followed his occupation as a journeyman carver. . . ."

John Reade*, in a letter to Burpee, writes: "I first met Charles Heavysege in the summer of 1858. He was then living on St. Constant Street, Montreal, and pursuing his occupation as a carver in the firm of J. & W. Hilton, cabinet-makers and upholsterers. . . . Heavysege told me that he was accustomed to compose while he was engaged at work, the occupation of his hands not interfering with the efforts of his mind. Speaking especially of *Saul*, he said that in this way he had elaborated some of the liveliest scenes." In 1860, according to Heavysege, he became a reporter for the *Montreal Transcript*; Flint maintained this move was "on the advice of his friends," who hoped it "would stimulate his poetic ability, but, instead, the endless grind and routine almost ruined it." Heavysege apparently remained with the *Transcript* a short time, and returned briefly to woodcarving. He then joined the *Montreal Daily Witness*, where he remained until he retired. The report of Flint's address says: "Some two years before his death, his health failing, he resigned his post as City Editor of the *Witness*, and again turned his thoughts to poetry. He often expressed his desire to review *Count Filippo* and leave it perfect . . . but he was cut down before the work was fairly begun, on July 14, 1876."

As to the man himself, Burpee quotes a letter from Dr Samuel Edward Dawson*: "The Bible and Shakespeare were his two books. He had a high opinion of his own work, and was obstinate about having anything cut out by his friends. Being a man without general culture, he could not well distinguish . . . between what was good and what was bad. He knew what cost him a long time to do, and he was apt to overvalue that." Heavysege's daughter, Harriet Pettigrew, characterized her father in these words: "He had all a poet's intense

346

love and appreciation of nature. He fairly revelled in the changes in the autumn season." Another daughter, in a letter to Burpee, described him as a sensitive person, who sometimes played his violin with his family. Heavysege seems to have become part of a small literary circle in Montreal which included John Reade and George Martin, and was also, for a time, honorary member of the Montreal Literary Club, which broke up upon the death of Thomas D'Arcy McGee*. Thus he had sympathetic friends, even though, as he remarked, Canada was not a country where circumstances favoured the writer.

Heavysege's first published work is *The revolt of Tartarus*, a poem in six parts which takes up Milton's *Paradise Lost* where Lucifer leaves Pandemonium for his mission on the newly created Earth. Upon Lucifer's departure, a group of the fallen angels, despairing and desiring God's forgiveness, decide to disobey Lucifer. Heavysege, wryly, has Jesus, on instructions from God, condemn them once more to eternal punishment although they had begged forgiveness. The machinery for forgiveness had not yet been instituted through the death of Jesus on the cross, but Heavysege shows the same uneasy attitude to the Old Testament God in other works. The dates of the composition and publication of *The Revolt* remain a mystery as yet. Burpee gives London, 1852, as place and date, which would mean the poem was composed in England. Other sources give other information. Two copies of the work actually obtainable today indicate the poem was published in London, but give no date; it also appeared in Montreal in 1855.

Sonnets "by the Author of 'The Revolt of Tartarus' " was also published in Montreal in 1855. Its 14-line poems only loosely fit the sonnet pattern. They deal with nature, fate, death, and the lessons of history, and contain many Shakespearean echoes.

In 1857 *Saul: a drama in three parts* appeared in Montreal. This long verse drama, never intended for the stage, deals with Saul's failure to carry out God's commands, and is Heavysege's most notable work. A copy found its way to Nathaniel Hawthorne, then in England, and was passed on by him to the *North British Review*. The author of its review, Coventry Patmore, said, in part: "In it the greatest subject, in the whole range of history, for a drama, has been treated with a poetical power and a depth of psychological knowledge which are often quite startling, though, we may say, inevitably, below the mark of the subject-matter, which is too great to be done full justice to. . . ." Patmore also speaks of the author's knowledge of the Bible, Shakespeare, and human nature, and of

the oddity, subtlety, and originality of his language. Even by modern standards, Patmore's comments are fair and just, though perhaps a little too laudatory. They touch directly on the truth about all Heavysege's works – grand (mainly) in conception, full of a keen understanding of human nature, having fine passages, but spoiled often by the author's lack of self-criticism, which led him from beauty to incongruity. Two short quotations, one from *Saul* and one from *Count Filippo*, will serve to show the two extremes: these ridiculous lines from *Saul*,

Mew, mew, a cat did mew,
That a cat was in the vault is true,
The vault that Saul's his wine in, . . .

and this beautiful passage, which would grace any poet's name:

So often the indulgent moon allows
The tide come kissing up the wet-lipped sands.

The friendly reception abroad, as usual, sharpened appreciation of Heavysege's works in North America; other reviews appeared in the New York *Evening Post*, the *Atlantic Monthly*, *Galaxy*, etc. *Saul* was revised and reprinted in Montreal in 1859 and again in Boston in 1869. There is a hint that Heavysege prepared a stage version, never produced, but evidence is conflicting.

Count Filippo; or, the unequal marriage (Montreal, 1860) "By the Author of 'Saul' " is based on the trials of a May and December marriage. This verse play seems the best sustained of Heavysege's efforts, and its topic suited to his taste for the incongruous, for bawdy puns and racy dialogue. It is a Boccaccio-Chaucer crossbreed, overlaid with Shakespearean language.

Heavysege produced three shorter poems in 1864 and then *Jephthah's daughter*, which appeared in London and Montreal in 1865. It was composed, according to a letter that year from the author to Charles Lanman, in the interval between his working for the *Transcript* and the *Witness*. A dramatic poem of about 1,200 lines, it tells the tragic story of Jephthah's vow to God, fulfilment of which means the killing of his daughter. Jephthah's moral dilemma is explored. The daughter's final acceptance of her fate means her father's promise will be fulfilled and he will be at peace with his God, if not with himself. The work is marked by the same faults and strong points as earlier writings.

Heavysege's only novel, *The advocate*, a melodramatic tale which makes use of English and French antagonisms in Lower Canada, was a disaster by any standards. After its appearance in Toronto and Montreal in 1865, the author is reported to have tried to destroy all copies of it. "Jezebel", which appeared in the *New Dominion*

Herbert

Monthly in 1867, is apparently Heavysege's last written work. Again a biblical story is used to exhibit his obvious ability to portray moral agony in the face of God's punishment; it is not a great work though he does succeed in portraying a spicy, lively Jezebel.

It is difficult to assign a place to the works of Charles Heavysege in the perspective of Canadian literature. He is one of those mysterious figures who often turn up in Canada, produce literature which has little, if any, Canadian flavour, and then perhaps move on to another country; they leave behind works to be examined anxiously for possible literary value, and to be claimed loudly as Canadian if any value, no matter how small, be found. Heavysege's works did not receive wide acclaim or recognition outside of Canada, except for *Saul*; he never achieved popularity in Canada, and it cannot be said with certainty that his works influenced any other poet. The nature and the quality of his works would hardly seem to merit their republication. Still the works do exist. The product of a circumscribed mind in a circumscribed environment, they contain flashes of acute human insight into moral problems and passages of great beauty. They are a monument to Heavysege's perseverance; more than this cannot be safely said.

J. C. STOCKDALE

Charles Heavysege, *The advocate, a novel* (Toronto, Montreal, 1865); [ ], *Count Filippo; or, The unequal marriage, a drama in five acts* (Montreal, 1860); *The dark huntsman (a dream)* (Montreal, 1864); *Jephthah's daughter, a poem* (London, Montreal, 1865); "Jezebel," *New Dominion Monthly* (Montreal), 1867; *The owl* (Montreal, 1864); [ ], *The revolt of Tartarus* ([London, 1852]; Montreal, 1855); [ ], *Saul: a drama in three parts* (Montreal, 1857); [ ], *Sonnets* (Montreal, 1855).

AJM, Registre d'état civil, Dominion Square Methodist Church (Montreal), 1876. Morgan, *Bibliotheca Canadensis*. Watters, *Check list*. Watters and Bell, *On Canadian literature*. T. R. Dale, "Charles Heavysege," unpublished PHD thesis, University of Chicago, 1951. L. J. Burpee, "Charles Heavysege," *RSCT*, 2nd ser., VII (1901), sect.II, 19. G. H. Flint, "Charles Heavysege," *Dominion Illustrated Monthly* (Montreal), 27 April 1889, 263–66. *North British Review*, XXIX (August 1858), 143–47.

HERBERT, MARY ELIZA, author and magazine editor; b. at Halifax, N.S., c. 1832, second daughter of Catherine and of Nicholas Michael Herbert, shoemaker and blacking manufacturer, who had emigrated from Ireland; d. in Halifax at her father's home, Belle Aire, 15 July 1872, after a long illness, of "chronic gastroses."

Mary Herbert's early poems were published in 1857 with those of her elder sister, Sarah Herbert* in *The Aeolian harp: or, miscellaneous poems*, a collection on religious, moral, and temperance themes. Both women belonged to the Wesleyan Methodist evangelical group and were active in the temperance movement; these interests provided the main themes for their poetry. Mary Herbert later published a volume containing her own poetry, *Flowers by the wayside . . .*, written on more romantic themes. In the preface "she trusts that the unassuming flowers thus gathered, may be instrumental in instructing, cheering and comforting some weary traveller in life's rugged way."

Mary Herbert was the first woman in Nova Scotia to edit and publish a magazine: the *Mayflower, or Ladies' Acadian Newspaper*, a small 32-page volume. It included works partly selected and partly original, and was devoted to literature for those who wished "to roam a while in the flowery fields of romance, – to hold communion with the Muses." The magazine began publication in May 1851, in the year the *Literary Garland* of Montreal ceased, and was a Maritime example of the North American and English fashion for genteel periodicals with many lady contributors and a literary content which displayed sentiment, piety, and propriety. Printed at the Athenaeum, the official press of the Sons of Temperance, the *Mayflower* continued for at least nine monthly numbers, but failed to obtain enough support even from those eager to encourage native literature. The outcome is not surprising as the intense competition among Nova Scotia periodicals during this period led to many financial failures.

Mary Herbert also wrote tales and essays for Nova Scotia newspapers and several of her tales were published separately, at her own expense, because the province had no book publishing firms. The tales have little merit, and the poems show a morbid concern with death, but a few have vivid descriptions of nature or poetic mood.

PHYLLIS R. BLAKELEY

M. E. Herbert, *Belinda Dalton; or scenes in the life of a Halifax belle* (Halifax, 1859); *Flowers by the wayside, a miscellany of prose and verse . . .* (Halifax, 1865); *Woman as she should be; or Agnes Wiltshire* (Halifax, 1861); *The young men's choice* (Halifax, 1869). Sarah and M. E. Herbert, *The Aeolian harp; or, miscellaneous poems* (Halifax, 1857). *Mayflower, or Ladies' Acadian Newspaper* (Halifax), May 1851–February 1852.

Acadian Recorder (Halifax), 16 Oct. 1830, 16 July 1872. *Novascotian* (Halifax), 28 May 1835. *Presbyterian Witness* (Halifax), 20 July 1872. Morgan, *Bibliotheca Canadensis*, 183. Watters, *Check list*, 162, 223.

HILYARD, THOMAS, shipbuilder and lumberman; b. October 1810 at Saint John, N.B., son of Thomas Hilyard and Margaret Miles; m. Matilda Dyer and had 13 children; d. 22 June 1873 at Saint John.

Only a few details of Thomas Hilyard's activities prior to 1852 are known. In 1842, described as a shipwright, he is listed in the Saint John shipping register as the owner of a minute schooner, the *Nevermind*. From 1848 to 1850 Hilyard owned the large new ship *Patriarch*. With the construction of two big ships in 1852 he started building on a large scale. He obtained, first by lease and later by purchase, a shipyard in Portland, N.B. At the end of 1854 he bought the adjoining steam sawmill which would give him not only cheap supplies of shipbuilding timber and ready cargoes for his new ships on their maiden voyages, but also the means to maintain his business during the frequent ebbs in shipbuilding. The latter aspect must have been particularly important because Hilyard, unlike most of the long-term successful shipbuilders of Saint John, did not invest to any extent in shipowning. In 1856 or 1857 he further expanded by initially leasing and subsequently purchasing a neighbouring shipyard from John Haws*, for decades a leading shipbuilder in the area.

Hilyard launched at least 48 vessels – a number surpassed by few Canadian builders. An early vessel laid down at Portland in 1853 was his largest, the three-decked ship *Clas-Merden* of 1,768 tons. Most of his 28 or more large ships, from about 900 tons upward, were sold to major shipowners at Liverpool, England. These ships went into service in the 1850s carrying emigrants to Australia and later as merchantmen in the bulk trades. Hilyard's smaller vessels were generally sold locally, some for use in the West Indian trade. Near the end of his life Hilyard extended his business to include ship repairing. For that purpose he constructed in 1870 a marine railway to carry vessels out of the water.

Hilyard gained a high reputation as a shipbuilder. The *Canute*, 1,391 tons, built in 1863, was advertised for sale 16 years later by one of England's most reputable shipbrokers as "The very fine St. John built ship . . . built under special survey, by Hilyard. . . ." The ship was still afloat in 1905 in the United States as the barge *Nyack*. The quality and quantity of his ships and the extent of his sawmilling operations made Thomas Hilyard a leading figure in the economic life of the Saint John region. The business continued under two sons, Thomas K. and Henry, until 1915.

RICHARD RICE

N.B. Museum, Hilyard family papers, 1788–1955; Ward family papers, 1755–1850. Registry of British Ships, HM Customs and Excise, Custom House (Liverpool, Eng.), Liverpool Registers, 1850–52. *Daily Telegraph* (Saint John, N.B.), 23 April 1874. *Liberal Review* (Liverpool), 4 Oct. 1879. *Biographical review: this volume contains biographical sketches of leading citizens of the province of New Brunswick,* ed. I. A. Jack (Boston, 1900). *Census of Canada, 1870–71* (5v., Ottawa, 1873–78), III. F. W. Wallace, *Record of Canadian shipping: a list of square-rigged vessels, mainly 500 tons and over, built in the eastern provinces of British North America from the year 1786 to 1920* (Toronto, 1929). A. B. Lubbock, *The colonial clippers* (new ed., Glasgow, 1948). J. R. Rice, "A history of organized labour in Saint John, New Brunswick, 1813–1890," unpublished MA thesis, University of New Brunswick, 1961. Donald Ross, "History of the shipbuilding industry in New Brunswick," essay awarded the James Simonds prize in history by University of New Brunswick, 1933 (copy in N.B. Museum). S. T. Spicer, *Masters of sail: the era of square-rigged vessels in the Maritime provinces* (Toronto, 1968). Wallace, *Wooden ships and iron men*.

HINCKS, WILLIAM, Unitarian clergyman, theologian, and university professor; b. 16 April 1794, Cork, Ireland, second son of the Reverend Thomas Dix Hincks and Anne Boult; d. 10 Sept. 1871, Toronto, Ont.

William Hincks was born into a distinguished family. He was educated for the Presbyterian ministry, and served at Cork in 1814 and at Exeter, England, from 1816 until 1822 when he joined the Unitarian Church and became minister of Renshaw Street Unitarian Church, Liverpool.

His interests having shifted to science, he began a teaching career in 1827 and was tutor in mathematics and philosophy at Manchester College, York, until 1834. There he also became associated with the political school known as Philosophical Radicals and argued for the extension of popular rights. In 1839, in London, he resumed his ministerial work, and served as well from 1842 to 1847 as the first editor of the *Inquirer*, a Unitarian weekly journal. In it Hincks showed a special interest in education, peace, and temperance, and favoured the abolition of slavery and of the death penalty, the shortening of hours of labour, and the rational use of leisure. He obtained in 1849 the appointment of professor of natural history at Queen's College, Cork. Four years later at nearly 60 years of age Hincks came to Canada as the first professor of natural history at University College, Toronto.

Hincks' appointment has attracted more than passing attention because he was chosen in preference to the young, but later famous, Thomas Henry Huxley. The preliminary selection committee did not fix upon one person but placed Hincks, Huxley, and one Dr Ayres on an equal footing. Huxley had already an impressive list of zoological publications to his credit and had the support of 16 prominent British and French biologists including Charles Darwin. Success, however, fell to Hincks, probably "through the influence of his brother," Francis Hincks*, at that time premier of the Province of Canada, a "qualification," Huxley remarked, "better than all the testimonials in the world." Such political interference with university appointments was a long-standing problem.

In Toronto William Hincks served as president of the Canadian Institute (now the Royal Canadian Institute) from 1869 to 1871. For several years he was editor of its *Canadian Journal* and contributed 24 articles on subjects ranging from botany and zoology to economics and psychology. He also published in British journals and was a fellow of the Linnean Society in Great Britain. He was a prominent member of Toronto's Unitarian congregation and occasionally conducted its services.

Hincks was a gentleman beloved by his students, who nevertheless spoke of his ideas as "antiquated" and of his methods of teaching as out of date and "leaving much to be desired." "We learned to know his ways," asserted one student, "and to make our papers suit his peculiar taste." Another, James Loudon*, later president of the University of Toronto, commented that in Hincks' department "success . . . depended largely on memorizing."

Hincks married in 1817 Maria Ann Yandell by whom he had eight children; she died in 1849. The maiden name of his second wife, Sarah Maria, whom he married before leaving England, is not known.

J. DONALD WILSON

PAC, RG 5, C1, 375, 386. York County Surrogate Court (Toronto), will of William Hincks. "The late Professor Hincks," *Canadian Journal*, new ser., XIII (1871–73), 253–54. *Inquirer* (London), 30 Sept. 1871. *J. of Education for Ont.*, XXIV (1871), 155. *DNB* (entry for Thomas Dix Hincks).

E. H. Craigie, *A history of the department of zoology of the University of Toronto up to 1962* ([Toronto, 1966]). John King, *McCaul: Croft: Forneri, personalities of early university days* (Toronto, 1914). R. S. Longley, *Sir Francis Hincks; a study of Canadian politics, railways, and finance in the nineteenth century* (Toronto, 1943). Herbert McLachlan, *The Unitarian movement in the religious life of England; its contribution to thought and learning, 1700–1900* (London, 1934). *The Royal Canadian Institute, centennial volume, 1849–1949*, ed. W. S. Wallace (Toronto, 1949), 197. W. S. Wallace, *A history of the University of Toronto, 1827–1927* (Toronto, 1927). C. R. W. Biggar, "The Reverend William Hincks, M.A.," *University of Toronto Monthly*, II (1901–2), 232–33.

HODDER, EDWARD MULBERRY, physician, surgeon, and educator; b. 30 Dec. 1810, at Sandgate, Kent, Eng., son of Edward and Mary Hodder; d. 20 Dec. 1878, at Toronto, Ont.

Edward Mulberry Hodder was educated on the island of Guernsey and at Saint-Servan, France. At 12 he became midshipman under his father, a captain in the Royal Navy, but he left the service within a year, and went to study medicine in London, under Joseph Amesbury and James Blundell, and in Paris and Edinburgh. He became a member of the Royal College of Surgeons in 1834, and practised at London and later at Saint-Servan. In 1834 he married Frances Tench by whom he had several children.

About 1838 Hodder immigrated to Upper Canada, which he had visited three years before, and settled near Queenston. He moved to Toronto during 1843, and soon established himself as one of its leading medical practitioners. He was granted a CM by King's College (later the University of Toronto) in 1845. In 1850 he and James BOVELL founded the Upper Canada School of Medicine, and after Bishop John Strachan* returned that year from England – he had gone there to obtain support for the establishment of a Church of England university – they offered to have the school constitute the medical faculty of the proposed university. Introductory lectures in the medical faculty of Trinity College were given in November, and Hodder lectured on "Midwifery and Diseases of Women and Children." In 1851 he established with Bovell the *Upper Canada Journal of Medical, Surgical, and Physical Science* to which he contributed several articles.

Hodder continued to teach at Trinity College (which granted him an MD in 1853) until the closing of the medical faculty in 1856. He then became professor of obstetrics at the Toronto School of Medicine, affiliated since 1854 with Victoria College. When the medical faculty at Trinity College was re-established in 1871, Hodder returned to it. He was unanimously elected its dean, a position he held until his death in 1878.

As perhaps "the acknowledged leader of the profession in Toronto and in the Province of Ontario" Hodder was active in numerous medical institutions and societies. He was appointed the representative of Trinity College on the board of trustees of the Toronto General Hospital in 1853, and was for a long time associated with it as a consulting physician and with the Burnside Lying-in Hospital as the senior physician. He was made an associate member of the Medical Board of Upper Canada in 1853, and in 1858 was appointed its president to succeed Christopher

Widmer*. In 1862 he was chosen president of the Toronto Medico-Chirurgical Society and, in 1875, of the Canadian Medical Association at their meeting in Halifax. He was elected a fellow of the Royal College of Surgeons in 1854, and of the Obstetrical Society of London in 1865. At the time of his death he was an honorary local secretary of the latter. He had also served as vice-president of the Canadian Institute in Toronto for 1868–70.

Hodder was an imaginative and respected medical practitioner. During the cholera epidemic of 1854 in Toronto he and Bovell made transfusions of milk into the veins of some patients – with mixed results. Hodder was one of the first to report the use of carbolic acid as an antiseptic in surgery. It was mainly, however, as an obstetrician and gynaecologist that he was prominent, and it was said that "as an ovariotomist he was admittedly the most successful in Canada." He has been called the "Father" of these two branches of medicine in Ontario.

Hodder retained a love for boating all his life. He was a founder in 1852 of the Toronto Boat Club, which became the Royal Canadian Yacht Club, and participated in many regattas. He published *The harbours and ports of Lake Ontario* in 1857, a useful compilation for sailors.

HENRI PILON

E. M. Hodder, *The harbours and ports of Lake Ontario, in a series of charts, accompanied by a description of each* ... (Toronto, 1857); "A case of apoplexy, terminating fatally, in which the Caesarean operation was performed with a favourable result to the child," *Upper Canada Journal of Medical, Surgical, and Physical Science* (Toronto), I (1851–52), 4–7; "On the poisonous plants which are indigenous to, or which have become naturized in the neighbourhood of Toronto," *Canadian Journal*, I (1852–53), 204–7, 218–19; "Transfusion of milk in cholera," *Practitioner* (London), X (1873), 14–16.

MTCL, V. M. Roberts papers, memorabilia, 14. *Canada Lancet* (Toronto), X (1877–78), 215–16. *Canada Medical and Surgical J.* (Montreal), VI (1878), 428–31. *Cyclopædia of Can. biog.* (Rose, 1888), 647. Canniff, *Medical profession in Upper Canada*, 432–34. Middleton, *Municipality of Toronto*, II, 576, 618–22, 625, 634, 751. W. G. Cosbie, "J. Y. Simpson oration: Simpson and some Toronto contemporaries," Royal College of Obstetricians and Gynaecologists (London), *Report, 1968*, 73–80. G. W. Spragge, "The Trinity Medical School," *Ont. Hist.*, LVIII (1966), 63–98.

HODGES, JAMES, engineer; b. 6 April 1814 at Queenborough, Kent, Eng.; d. 28 May 1879 on his estate of Penny-Hill at Bagshot, Surrey, Eng.

In Queenborough James Hodges received only an elementary education, and he took advantage of the industrial revolution to carve out a place for himself. He was apprenticed to a Brompton contractor at the age of 17, and soon turned to railway construction, taking part in some ten important projects and becoming works manager of the South-Eastern Railway Company. After that, as Sir Samuel Morton Peto's agent, he worked at the building of the suspension bridges at Norwich, Needham, and Somerleyton, accepted a post as engineer, and then undertook the construction of 50 miles of track for the Great Northern Railway.

With this valuable experience to help him, Hodges arrived in Canada in 1853 to represent the firm of Peto, Brassey, and Betts, which had just signed a contract with the Grand Trunk Railway Company. Until 1860 he directed the gigantic task of building a bridge (Victoria Bridge) over the St Lawrence near Montreal. He had to tackle numerous technical problems resulting from the speed and strength of the current and the intense cold of the winters. Furthermore, he could not count on a stable work force. The fitters and labourers, dissatisfied with the wage offers made them, periodically went on strike; some were signed on by other contractors who offered them better wages. Drownings occurred; cholera and blindness due to the reflection of the sun on the ice affected a considerable number of workmen. However, thanks to the assistance given by five doctors, the number of deaths among the 3,040 men employed during these six years was kept down to 26. The workers lived on the banks of the river, and had the advantage of a chapel, a school, and a library of some 1,000 volumes.

The Grand Trunk Railway Company wanted to do away as soon as possible with the ferry linking the two banks, which would lighten its annual budget by about £2,500. The contractors therefore decided in June 1858 to try to open the bridge to traffic by the following year. To meet this objective, Hodges used the support of the ice to place in position during the winter of 1858–59 the central deck of the bridge and its tubular structure, which measured 330 feet in length and weighed 771 tons. By this daring operation he completed his task before the time provided for in the contract. This achievement earned him the honour, on 25 Aug. 1860, of welcoming the Prince of Wales, the future Edward VII, who had come specially to open the bridge, named Victoria after the reigning sovereign.

His work ended, Hodges returned to England. But he soon found himself alone once more, as a result of his wife's death. In 1863 he came back to Montreal as the agent of the Grand Trunk, and endeavoured to obtain a cheap form of fuel for Canadians, who lacked coal. He developed a peat-bog on a 25,000 acre tract of land near the railway

Hodgson

in the township of Bulstrode (Arthabaska County), which had been granted to him in May 1869. He met with little success and shortly before 1871 he returned to England to his estate in Surrey, where he died in 1879.

JACQUES MATHIEU

James Hodges, *Construction of the great Victoria Bridge in Canada* (2v., London, 1860). Langelier, *Lands granted in Quebec, 1763–1890*, 65, 1465. *Le Courrier du Canada* (Québec), 31 août 1860. *Morning Chronicle* (Quebec), 27 Aug. 1860. Morgan, *Sketches of celebrated Canadians*, 706–8. Notman and Taylor, *Portraits of British Americans*, I, 267–92. A. W. Currie, *The Grand Trunk Railway of Canada* (Toronto, 1957), 51. Raphaël Bellemare, "Inauguration du pont Victoria," *BRH*, V (1899), 189–90.

HODGSON, Sir ROBERT, lawyer, land agent, politician, judge, and administrator; b. 1798 in Charlottetown, P.E.I., eldest son of Robert Hodgson and Rebecca Robinson; d. 15 Sept. 1880 at his home in Charlottetown.

Born into an Anglican family of comfortable circumstances, Robert Hodgson completed his education at King's College, Windsor, Nova Scotia. He studied law with Simon Bradstreet Robie* and James W. JOHNSTON in Halifax and was called to the bars of Nova Scotia and Prince Edward Island in 1819. He then took up residence in Charlottetown and pursued an active career as a lawyer, land agent, and politician. He married Fanny McDonell in 1827, and they had two sons and one daughter. Hodgson did not remarry after she died on 2 May 1832.

Hodgson entered public life in 1824 by successfully contesting an assembly seat for Charlottetown. He rapidly became an integral part of the local élite. Sometimes in partnership with John Lawson, he acted as land agent for such leading proprietors as Robert Cundall, the Earl of Westmoreland, the Montgomerys, the Stewarts, and the Douglases. When William Johnston*, the attorney general of the colony, died in May 1828, Hodgson was named his successor on an interim basis. A year later, the appointment became permanent, and Hodgson resigned his assembly seat. He was then appointed to the Executive Council and the Legislative Council, becoming president of the latter body in 1840. An investigation carried out by the assembly in the following year revealed that Hodgson had close family connections with no less than three of his eight fellow executive councillors.

Hodgson nevertheless enjoyed bipartisan prestige among Island politicians. In 1846 the lieutenant governor, Sir Henry Vere Huntley*, described him as "clever and professionally well informed ... [and] uniformly popular from his kind-heartedness." Four years later, during a crisis in the struggle for responsible government, when it seemed as though the Reformers might assume office, they offered to allow Hodgson to retain the office of attorney general and his seat on the Executive Council if he would join them. He declined, and when the Reformers did take power in 1851 he resigned the two positions. He remained president of the Legislative Council for another year.

In consideration of his long tenure as attorney general, Hodgson was granted an annual pension of £200, conditional upon his not accepting any office of emolument "under the Government of this Island." Stating that "the pension of that Gentleman ... will be saved to the Colony," the Executive Council of George COLES appointed Hodgson to the vacant chief justiceship in 1852. He was an appropriate choice, as he had been the senior practising barrister on the Island for some years, and because, in the estimation of the governor, Sir Alexander Bannerman*, he had "a thorough knowledge of Colonial & Constitutional law." He held the position for 22 years, and three times within that period (July to December 1865, October 1868 to October 1870, and August 1873 to July 1874) acted as administrator when the governor was absent. In January 1869 both he and the chief justice of Nova Scotia, William Young*, were knighted.

Serious problems arose over the land question when Hodgson was administrator in 1865. The new and radical Tenant League, whose members were pledged to refuse payment of rent to landlords, caused such disorders in Queens County that Hodgson sent to Halifax for two companies of soldiers to restore order. The military presence was effective, and the administrator's action brought approval from London, from most of the Island press, and from the lieutenant governor, George DUNDAS.

Although Hodgson asked to be appointed lieutenant governor in 1869, he was maintained in his office as chief justice, and William Robinson* became lieutenant governor. Robinson left the Island in 1873, Hodgson was again appointed administrator, and was named lieutenant governor the following summer. Since his salary was now paid by the government of Canada, Hodgson demanded resumption of the pension granted in 1851 and withdrawn in 1852. Despite considerable criticism from members of both houses of the local legislature, he was successful in his claim. As a result, he was receiving one salary and two pensions (as retired attorney general and chief justice) during his tenure as lieutenant governor. He retired in 1879 and died the following year, leaving a considerable estate in land and money.

Sir Robert Hodgson was a life-long office-seeker; in fact, his indefatigable quest for offices, honours, and pensions more than once betrayed a lack of taste. Nonetheless, he was undeniably a man of distinction in the history of Prince Edward Island: he was the first native chief justice, the first native lieutenant governor, and the first Islander to be knighted. For most of his public career, he was also a very popular man. When he died, the *Patriot* described him as "an excellent specimen of the English gentleman. . . . He will be long remembered as the Good Sir Robert."

IAN ROSS ROBERTSON

PAC, MG 26, A (Macdonald papers), p.48274; RG 6, A1, 4, f.1465. PAPEI, Robert Bruce and David Stewart letter book, I (16 March 1821–21 Aug. 1834), 355, 359–60; Prince Edward Island, Executive Council, Minutes, 21 May 1852, 1 Aug. 1865. PRO, CO 226/78, 111–12, 158; 226/79, 192–94; 226/80, 183–86; 226/91, 48–51, 178–80; 226/101, especially 329–39, 345–63, 380–88, 664–67; 226/104; 226/105, especially 216–17; 226/106; 226/109. Prince Edward Island, Supreme Court, Estates Division, will of Robert Hodgson, 31 March 1879.

Prince Edward Island, House of Assembly, *Journals*, 1825–29; *Debates and proceedings*, 1875, 101–8; Legislative Council, *Journals*, 1830–52; *Debates and proceedings*, 1875, 231–32. *Examiner* (Charlottetown), 16 Sept. 1880. *Patriot* (Charlottetown), 16 Jan. 1869, 18 Sept. 1880. *Pioneer* (Summerside, P.E.I.), 22 Sept. 1880. *Prince Edward Island Register* (Charlottetown), 13 Nov. 1824. *Royal Gazette* (Charlottetown), 11 June 1850. *Can. parl. comp.*, *1874*, 513. MacKinnon, *Government of PEI*, 38, 145. T. R. Millman, *A history of the parish of New London, Prince Edward Island* (n.p., 1959), 7. J. B. Pollard, *Historical sketch of the eastern regions of New France from the various dates of their discoveries to the surrender of Louisburg, 1758; also Prince Edward Island, military and civil* (Charlottetown, 1898), 200.

HOLMES, JOHN, politician; b. March 1789 in Ross-shire, Scotland, son of John Holmes and Christy Monroe; d. 3 June 1876 at Springville, N.S. John Holmes married Christina Fraser in 1814; they had several children including Simon Hugh Holmes*, premier of Nova Scotia from 1878 to 1882.

In 1803 John Holmes and his parents migrated from Scotland to a farm in the East River area of Pictou County. The family became prominent as leaders in the religious life of the developing community; John Holmes Sr organized a congregation of Church of Scotland adherents, and his son later served for 50 years as a Kirk elder. By 1836 the younger Holmes was an officer in the Pictou militia and a justice of the peace. Maturing in a society torn by sectarian rivalries, Holmes took the side of the Church of Scotland, which was continually being challenged from within by a group of stern Calvinists (commonly known as Antiburghers) led by Thomas McCulloch*. In the early 19th century, Pictou's politics were, indeed, essentially an extension of the county's religious quarrels. In 1836 the Kirk Council named John Holmes as a candidate for election to the assembly, and, after complicated manœuvring, secured his return by acclamation.

Within the new assembly Holmes soon emerged as an opponent of Joseph HOWE's reform movement. Holmes' Toryism predictably had its roots in sectarian antagonisms: the Church of Scotland was an integral part of the Nova Scotian oligarchy and Kirkmen identified reform with the activities of the Antiburghers. This attitude on Holmes' part was reinforced during the brief coalition government of 1840–43 when Howe was able to influence the distribution of patronage in favour of his Antiburgher allies. Understandably, Holmes' attacks on reform increased until at one point Howe was provoked to describe him as a "political Rip Van Winkle" who had slept so long in the Sleepy Hollow of reaction as to be ignorant of the new world taking shape around him.

After the collapse of the coalition Holmes aligned himself with the attorney general, James W. JOHNSTON. Holmes lost his assembly seat in the 1847 provincial election, but was returned as member for Pictou in 1851 when disputes over railway policy had weakened his Liberal opponents. In the 1850s Holmes concentrated his efforts on the economic development of his constituency and urged the construction of an Atlantic seaboard railway which would pass through Pictou county. Holmes' identification with the business community proved politically costly, however. His close relations with the General Mining Association, an English corporation with monopolistic control over local coal deposits, helped secure his defeat in the 1855 general election.

After a mass defection of Roman Catholics from the Liberals restored the Conservatives to power in 1858, J. W. Johnston rewarded Holmes with a seat in the Legislative Council (1858). Holmes' loyalty to Charles Tupper* through the crisis over confederation resulted in his appointment to the first dominion Senate. Age had drained Holmes' energies by then and he contributed little to the federal scene. His death concluded a long political career which reflected faithfully the ideals of Nova Scotia's Conservative tradition.

D. A. SUTHERLAND

Belcher's farmer's almanack, for . . . 1837 (Halifax, [1837]). *Acadian Recorder* (Halifax), 1858–67. *British Colonist* (Halifax), 1866. *Colonial Standard* (Pictou, N.S.) 1876. *Eastern Chronicle* (New Glasgow, N.S.),

Holton

1843–55. *Novascotian* (Halifax), 1837–67. *Pictou Bee*, 1836–37. *Pictou Observer*, 1840. *Directory of N.S. MLAs* (Fergusson), 162. J. M. Cameron, *Political Pictonians; the men of the Legislative Council, Senate, House of Commons, House of Assembly, 1767–1967* (Ottawa, [1967]). George Patterson, *Studies in Nova Scotian history* (Halifax, 1940). G. G. Patterson, *A history of the county of Pictou, Nova Scotia* (Montreal, Pictou, Halifax, Saint John, N.B., and Toronto, 1877). H. L. Scammell, "The rise and fall of a college," *Dal. Rev.*, XXXII (1952–53), 35–44.

HOLTON, LUTHER HAMILTON, Montreal businessman, civic leader, and politician; b. 22 Jan. 1817 at Sheffield's Corners (now Soperton), Leeds County, U.C., the second son and fourth child of six children of Ezra Holton and Anner Phillips, who had migrated from Brandon, Vermont, to Sheffield's Corners in 1811; d. 14 March 1880 in Ottawa, Ont., and was buried in Mount Royal Cemetery, Montreal, Que.

When Luther Hamilton Holton was seven years old, his father, a poor farmer, died, and in 1826 he went to Montreal to live with his uncle, Moses Gilbert, a Vermont-born general merchant, who enrolled him in the Union School. A bright and determined student, he remained in this private institution for four years and received a good elementary education. In the 1830s and 1840s Montreal was an important centre for the growing western wheat trade with the United Kingdom and offered young men profitable mercantile opportunities. At the age of 12 Luther Holton started as a clerk in his uncle's counting house and quickly mastered the principles of book-keeping. In 1836 he left his uncle's business and was made a clerk in the forwarding and commission house of Henderson and Hooker. James Henderson of Montreal and Alfred Hooker of Prescott had founded this enterprising partnership in January 1825 and had built wharves and warehouses at Montreal, Prescott, and Kingston. On 27 April 1839 the tall, stern-visaged, industrious, and shrewd Luther Holton married his first cousin Eliza Forbes. They had three sons and three daughters, two sons and one daughter dying in infancy. His employers had a high opinion of Holton's ability and accepted him as a junior partner in their firm on 1 April 1841. With the death of Henderson on 22 March 1845, Holton became a senior partner and the firm adopted the name of Hooker and Holton.

The firm was a major participant in the carrying trade on the upper St Lawrence and Lake Ontario and Lake Erie, and it reflected entrepreneurial problems of capital formation, maximizing profits, competition, navigation, and the marketing of wheat. An owner-manager of the firm, Holton provided working capital by using the firms' schooners, steamboats, wharves, and warehouses as collateral for short-term bank loans. He borrowed money from the Commercial Bank of the Midland District and the City Bank of Montreal and was careful to preserve the good credit relations that his partners had established with these banks. In 1842 the firm's property was valued at about £20,000 and by the early 1850s it amounted to about £50,000. An efficient and hardheaded merchant, Holton increased profits through expansion of the firm's freight and passenger business, prudent outlays for additional steamboats, tight control of operating expenses, and effective advertising. In order to counteract the threat of ruinous competition Hooker and Holton cooperated with their principal rivals such as Macpherson and Crane and H. and S. Jones in a Montreal steamboat combination that maintained high freight rates, monopolized the upper St Lawrence carrying trade, and drove individual forwarders out of business. Hooker and Holton's solution to the problem of the unimproved St Lawrence waterway between Montreal and Prescott was to ascend by the indirect Ottawa-Rideau route, to trans-ship their cargoes at Kingston, and to descend to Montreal by running the St Lawrence rapids. After the completion of the St Lawrence canals in 1848 the firm acquired large, screw-propelled steamers for its new through line between Montreal and Port Stanley on Lake Erie and thus tapped the lucrative traffic of the west. The firm was strong enough to survive the commercial depression of 1848–49, and as a major exporter of wheat and flour and small importer of general goods Holton helped to build an impressive mercantile establishment.

With Britain's gradual abandonment of the imperial preference on Canadian wheat in the period between 1846 and 1849, Holton became prominent in the economic affairs of Montreal. In March 1846 he was made vice-chairman of the Montreal Free-Trade Association [*see* John YOUNG] and on 5 April he was elected to the council of the Montreal Board of Trade. He was an ardent free-trader and saw a flexible economy as a means of providing the St Lawrence commercial community with new markets for its export trade in bread-stuffs and as a way of lowering the cost of the necessaries of life. Working through the Free-Trade Association and the Board of Trade, Holton and other Montreal free-traders successfully sought the support of merchants in Quebec, Kingston, Toronto, and Hamilton, and they exerted enough pressure on the Canadian and imperial governments to secure the repeal of Canada's tariff on American wheat in 1846, the removal of the Canadian preference on British manufactures in 1847, and the establishment of free navigation on the St Lawrence in 1849. But Holton was dismayed by the failure of the Canadian government's attempt at reciprocity with the United States in 1848, and the upsurge of protectionism in the Montreal Board of Trade between 1847 and 1849 led to his resignation from the council.

On 15 Nov. 1849 Holton became a vice-president of the Montreal Annexation Association and during the next few months believed that in the scheme for the annexation of Canada to the United States he had the answer for the slump in his forwarding business and Montreal's commercial ills. On 24 Dec. 1849 the government punished him for becoming an annexationist by depriving him of his lieutenant's commission in the Canadian militia. This event made him lose his zest for annexationism. The revival of the St Lawrence economy and his re-election to the council of the Board of Trade early in 1850 provided him with a fresh sense of civic purpose. As president of the Board of Trade and as a harbour commissioner from 1856 to 1859 and from 1862 to 1863, Holton was attuned to the metropolitan aspirations of Montreal and carried through a St Lawrence improvement programme that helped to stimulate commerce and lift the level of affluence of the city's acquisitive business class.

Between 1852 and 1854 Holton gradually transferred his capital from forwarding and overseas trade to railway development and on 12 Jan. 1854 withdrew from the partnership of Hooker and Holton. In the 1850s the St Lawrence trade was still expanding, but railways became the focus of entrepreneurial activity and opened more attractive fields of investment. On 10 Aug. 1852 Holton was made head of the projected Montreal and Kingston Railroad, capitalized at £600,000 and designed to give Montreal command of east-west traffic. As he did not want the road to fall into the hands of the construction firm of William Jackson and associates of the United Kingdom, Holton, together with the other directors, bought control of the railway and raised £60,000 in Montreal but were beaten by the difficulty of obtaining the state aid and English capital that were necessary for construction and forced to surrender the railway charter to the Canadian government. Holton was a key figure in the negotiations that led to the consolidation of the St Lawrence-Atlantic, Montreal-Kingston, Toronto-Kingston, and Toronto-Sarnia roads as the private-public Grand Trunk Railway of Canada. On 10 Nov. 1852 he became a director of

the Grand Trunk and in the same month joined Alexander Tilloch Galt*, David Lewis Macpherson*, and Casimir Stanislaus Gzowski* in forming the construction firm of C. S. Gzowski and Company. On 12 April 1853, shortly after Holton had resigned from the Grand Trunk, the firm contracted to build the 167-mile Toronto-Sarnia road for £1,376,000.

On 5 Sept. 1854 Holton entered the Canadian assembly as a representative for Montreal and as a principal member of the Liberal opposition from Canada East (Lower Canada). In the 1840s he had eagerly identified himself with the cause of responsible government and such Reformers as Francis Hincks*, but in 1854 he found Hincks too conservative and became a strong supporter of Antoine-Aimé Dorion*, who had succeeded Louis-Joseph PAPINEAU as the leader of the Lower Canadian Liberals. Holton proclaimed himself a progressive Liberal and called for an elective Legislative Council, secularization of the Upper Canadian clergy reserves, abolition of seigneurial tenure in Lower Canada, and reform of the financial machinery of government. He drew immense satisfaction from the success of these reform measures in the mid-1850s and continued to emphasize the importance of individual, religious, and economic freedom. Fundamentally, however, he was a moderate Liberal who displayed little radical fervour. He believed in free public education but felt that it was politically inexpedient to criticize the confessional schools of Lower Canada. Though he was distressed by the lack of unity between the Upper and Lower Canadian Liberals, his Lower Canadian sectionalism and his intimate business connection with the Montreal-oriented Grand Trunk Railway between 1854 and 1857 vitiated his attempts to build a provincial Liberal party out of the two sectional groups.

In fact, until 1857 Holton's railway business occupied most of his time. The main entrepreneurial problems confronting the Gzowski group from 1852 to 1857 were those of fostering good public relations, raising capital, keeping down costs, and dealing with the Grand Trunk. Holton and Galt as members of the Canadian assembly between 1854 and 1857 were under public attack for securing the Toronto-Sarnia contract through government favouritism and for influencing legislators to provide their firm with indirect financial assistance. In attempts to conciliate public opinion Holton drew attention to the importance of the railway as an agent for the economic development of Canada and the metropolitan expansion of Montreal and persuaded the editor of the *Montreal Herald*, Edward Goff Penny*, with whom he had close political and

Holton

social relations, to give the Gzowski group favourable publicity. Although the capital required for building the Toronto-Sarnia line came largely from English investors and the state, Holton made a substantial contribution by channelling his money from steamboating into railway construction and borrowing for his firm from the Commercial Bank. Fearing that the rising prices of labour and building materials would wipe out the firm's profits, Holton made a convincing case for rapid construction, a reduction in the engineering staff, and speculation in land at Sarnia. With the outbreak of the Crimean War and the tightening of the London money market, the Grand Trunk was unable to sell sufficient stock to cover the cost of construction, fell behind in its cash payments to the Gzowski firm, and suspended all work on the line between St Mary's and Sarnia. Expecting a downturn in the business cycle, Holton was anxious to wind up his affairs with the Grand Trunk. According to its agreement with the railway on 4 Feb. 1857, the Gzowski group realized a net profit of £120,000, and on 12 March Holton withdrew from the firm and retired a rich man.

After his retirement from active business in 1857, Holton wished to turn his full attention to parliamentary politics and his defeat in the general election in December of that year left him deeply disappointed. From 1858 to 1862 Holton remained outside parliament but kept a watchful eye on the activities of the George-Étienne CARTIER– John A. Macdonald* Liberal-Conservative government and the Liberal opposition. In these years Holton's close relationship with George BROWN, editor of the Toronto *Globe* and leader of the Upper Canadian Liberals, was of considerable significance in the politics of the legislative union of Canada and represented an important link between the two parts of the province. Holton always admired Brown's talents for leadership and his effective oratory, although their divergent sectional loyalties often imposed a severe strain on their friendship. In February 1858 Holton was a chief participant in the discussions that became the basis of the union of the Upper and Lower Canadian Liberals in the common agitation for representation by population, constitutional safeguards for the Catholic religion and the French language, and a provincial school system that would meet the needs of both Protestants and Catholics. Holton became minister of public works on 2 Aug. 1858 when the Brown–Dorion Liberals came into office. But on the same day, before he had a chance to seek a parliamentary seat, the ministry was defeated. He was angered by the refusal of the governor general, Edmund Walker Head*, to dissolve parliament and believed that the very existence of responsible government was threatened.

Holton continued to stress the need for Liberal unity and in October 1859 he drafted a manifesto that appealed to the Liberals of Upper and Lower Canada to accept federalism as the remedy for the political instability of the Canadian union. When the majority of the Lower Canadian Liberals rejected Holton's scheme for a Canadian federation, he urged Brown to try to destroy the Cartier–Macdonald administration on a financial issue. In November 1860 he failed to persuade Brown to condemn the Bank of Upper Canada, the government's fiscal agent, as a corrupt institution for keeping the Liberal-Conservatives in power but was himself unwilling to find fault with the government-subsidized Grand Trunk Railway for buying costly land in Sarnia from the Gzowski firm. In the June 1861 general election Holton declined the Montreal Liberals' invitation to become a candidate for Montreal Centre because of his fear of being beaten by the Conservatives. On 11 Sept. 1862 the Montreal Liberals and Conservatives joined forces and elected him to the Victoria seat in the Legislative Council, where for a short time he enjoyed his work on the banking and commerce committee but had little scope for partisan action.

On 16 May 1863, when a reconstructed Liberal government under the leadership of John Sandfield MACDONALD and Antoine-Aimé Dorion took office, Holton resigned from the Legislative Council and became the minister of finance. In the general election in June 1863 Holton was defeated in the prized constituency of Montreal Centre but was then victorious in Châteauguay. Painfully conscious of the ministry's slender parliamentary majority, he did not dare to call upon the legislature to carry burdensome financial measures. With no provision for higher taxation and only a small reduction in total expenditures, his budget in October 1863 did not offer a solution to a deficit of $1,500,000. Holton paid the interest on the Canadian debt in London with the help of new loans, but his failure to achieve a budget surplus made a net repayment impossible. His desire to save public money largely closed his mind to the need for railway expansion to the Maritime provinces and for economic development in general. In his view his main task lay in providing the government with a reliable fiscal agency in Canada. The Bank of Upper Canada, which was in serious trouble because of its heavy involvement in land and railway speculation, could not lend money to the government. At Holton's urging the government transferred the public account from the

Bank of Upper Canada to the Bank of Montreal on 1 Jan. 1864 [see Thomas Brown ANDERSON]. Though Holton sought to keep the Bank of Upper Canada alive, the removal of the government deposit contributed to the loss of public confidence in the bank and to its collapse two years later. As the new public banker, the Bank of Montreal gave strength to the ministry. But George Brown's dissatisfaction with the ministry for adopting a bank policy that favoured Montreal, combined with Dorion's inability to secure more Lower Canadian followers, led Holton to withhold his 1864 budget and insist on a reconstruction of the government. Depressed by the cares of the finance office, he was actually relieved when the unsuccessful attempt at reconstruction resulted in the resignation of the ministry on 21 March 1864.

From June 1864 until early in 1867 Holton opposed the coalition ministry's programme for the federal union of British North America and grimly clung to the unsatisfactory constitutional system of the Canadian union. His opposition to confederation in part derived from his party prejudice and his myopic view that the coalition ministers were politicians more interested in power than in improving the political system and providing new economic opportunities. His opposition also arose from his fundamental desire to preserve the integrity of the English and French societies of Lower Canada. He was sensitive to their cultural and religious needs and wanted to ensure that they would not suffer under a highly centralized government. Above all, he believed that the confederates had gone much too far in their plans for territorial expansion with all the financial burdens such expansion entailed. He thus found himself estranged from the Upper Canadian Liberals and many Montreal businessmen. He did not promote his Canadian federation scheme of 1859 as a counterweight against general union. Indeed, he himself was unable to provide a solution to the complex political and constitutional problems of the Canadian union. It was undoubtedly his realization of his inability to find an answer, combined with a warming in his relations with George Brown in mid-1866, that made it easier for him to change his mind about confederation. Once confederation became a reality, he began to appreciate its advantages and persuaded Antoine-Aimé Dorion and other Lower Canadian Liberals to accept the new political order.

Between 1867 and 1880 Holton gave some attention to the politics of the province of Quebec but devoted most of his time to federal politics in Ottawa. He represented Montreal Centre in the Quebec Legislative Assembly from 1871 to 1874 and was the member for Châteauguay in the Canadian House of Commons from 1867 to 1880. Though an infrequent and laconic speaker in the commons, Holton followed the debates closely and was a willing worker on the committees for banking and commerce; railways, canals, and telegraph lines; and public accounts. During the Liberal administration of 1873–78, he was a chief adviser to Prime Minister Alexander Mackenzie* but declined the finance office in 1873 as well as a second cabinet offer in 1875. Holton shrank from responsibility but wanted to exercise power, and was quickly offended when he was not taken into the confidence of the government.

Holton's conception of the new Canadian nation reflected the basic aspects of his Liberalism after 1867. He was against the repeal of confederation but was anxious to see that Nova Scotia obtained better terms than those under which it had entered the union. This anxiety was related to his aim of establishing a national Liberal party that would be sympathetic to provincial problems. He favoured amnesty for Louis Riel*, leader of the Red River Rebellion, deplored the Protestant attack on the Quebec Catholic clergy for their involvement in politics, and advised Alexander Mackenzie to accept the scheme of the colonial secretary, Lord Carnarvon [Herbert], for compensating British Columbia for the delay in the construction of the Canadian Pacific Railway. Though an ardent advocate of Canadian autonomy in domestic matters, Holton stressed that confederation was founded on imperial policy and legislation and felt that it was appropriate for Carnarvon to mediate between the federal government and British Columbia in order to settle the dangerous dispute over the railway. Holton opposed the Liberal proposals for complete Canadian independence and emphasized the necessity of maintaining the imperial connection and preserving British parliamentary institutions.

Concerned as Holton was about his business ventures, he did not let them dominate his life. He had a great deal of civic pride and combined community activity and private interest, a mixture that helped to build both Montreal and his own fortune and prestige. In 1850 he was a municipal councillor. He played a leading part in founding the Unitarian Society of Montreal on 6 June 1842. His Unitarianism sprang from his association with his uncle, Moses Gilbert, who was one of the earliest Unitarians in Montreal. As a member of the society's managing committee in the 1840s and 1850s, Holton participated in preparing the constitution of the society, installing the Reverend John Cordner* of Newry, Ireland, as the pastor, building a new church on Beaver Hall Hill, and

Hopkins

securing legal status for the small congregation in spite of considerable opposition from the other Protestant denominations in Montreal. Though zealous in claiming the unity instead of the trinity of God, Holton was tolerant, refined, and more concerned with philanthropic endeavour than religious doctrine. He assisted in organizing the Montreal City and District Savings Bank on 23 May 1846 [*see* Marc-Damase MASSON]. As a director from 1846 to 1873, he encouraged workingmen to deposit their savings in the bank in order to improve their standard of living, and until 1871 invested these funds in profitable bonds and stocks for the exclusive benefit of the depositors. He received no remuneration before 1862 and used his own money and credit to help extricate the bank from difficulties in 1848–49. In 1871, when the savings bank became a joint-stock corporation, Holton was made president and during the next two years his investment in the reorganized bank brought him good returns. Holton resigned from the bank in 1873. From 1876 to 1880 he expressed his concern for the social growth of the city by serving as a governor of McGill University.

When Luther Holton died on 14 March 1880, he left a large fortune and his commodious Sherbrooke Street house to his family.

H. C. KLASSEN

AJM, Greffe de Charles Cushing, no.16403; Greffe de W. M. Easton, nos.4076, 4272; Greffe de I.J.Gibb, nos. 5643, 11051, 12133, 15257, 15281; Greffe de William Ross, no.275. Glynn Mills and Company (London), Incoming correspondence, Official letters, 1850–59, 1860–61, 1862–74 (microfilm in PAC). Montreal Board of Trade Archives, Minutes of the general meeting, 1842–63; Minutes of the council, 1843–63. Montreal City and District Savings Bank Archives, Minute book, 1846–62. PAC, MG 24, B40 (Brown papers), 1–11; D16 (Buchanan papers), 15, 18, 25, 27, 30, 31, 37, 46, 63, 94, 99; D21 (Baring Brothers and Company), 1–4; D36 (Glynn Mills and Company), 8; E9 (Gzowski papers), 1–3; MG 26, B (Mackenzie papers), ser.2, 1–6; MG 27, I, D8 (Galt papers), 1–4; I, E5 (Holton papers). PAO, Edward Blake papers, 1, 2, 3, 4, 9; Francis Shanly papers, 41, 42, 81, 85. Queen's University Archives, Alexander Mackenzie papers, general correspondence, 1–4. Unitarian Church Archives (Montreal), Minute book, A (1842–56); Minute book, B (1856–74).

Canada, House of Commons, *Debates*, 1867–80. Canada, Province of, Legislative Assembly, *Journals*, 1841–67; *Parliamentary debates*, 1858–67. *Canadian Economist* (Montreal), 1846–47. *Globe* (Toronto), 1844–67. *Montreal Herald*, 1863–80. *Montreal Witness*, 1846–54, 1857, 1860–67. *Le Pays* (Montréal), 1852–71. Dent, *Canadian portrait gallery*, II, 193–98.

The ancestry of Ezra Holton of Northfield, Mass., and Soperton, Ont., 1785–1824; twenty-eight "stories" edited and correlated by Geoffrey Gilbert, comp. E.L. Moffat (Victoria, 1953 (copy in University of Toronto Library)). Careless, *Brown*, I, II. H. C. Klassen, "L. H. Holton: Montreal businessman and politician, 1817–1867," unpublished PHD thesis, University of Toronto, 1970. J. R. A. Pollard, "Luther Hamilton Holton, 1817–1880," unpublished MA thesis, University of Toronto, 1928.

HOPKINS, CALEB, farmer and politician; b. 1785 or 1786 in New Jersey, ninth of 13 children of Silas Hopkins and Mary Swayze; d. 8 Oct. 1880, in Toronto, Ont.

Of "late Loyalist" parentage, Caleb Hopkins farmed in Nelson Township, Halton County, Upper Canada. With three brothers, he founded the settlement of Hannahville. He played a major role in local affairs, establishing the area's first school in 1828, chairing the first township meeting for Nelson in 1836, serving as a district councillor in 1842, and as a prominent layman in the Wesleyan Methodist Church. He married Hannah, daughter of John Green, UEL, of Grimsby, Upper Canada; they had several children, and one of their daughters, Rachel, married Anson GREEN.

Halton County was a radical stronghold by the late 1820s and Hopkins was returned there in 1828 as a Reform member of the Upper Canadian House of Assembly. He was one of the few members consistently radical enough to be endorsed by William Lyon Mackenzie*'s *Colonial Advocate*, but he chose not to stand for re-election in 1830. However, he was again returned for Halton in 1834. Unlike so many of his radical colleagues he was not implicated in the rebellion of 1837; as a result, he rose by elimination, along with a number of other second rank Upper Canadian politicians, to a position of leadership in the Reform party. In the first election under the union of the Canadas, in 1841, he was one of the few to resist the pressure of the new governor, Lord Sydenham [Charles Poulett Thomson*], and was returned as an anti-Sydenham Reformer for the East Riding of Halton.

In Canada West the only effective parliamentary opposition to Sydenham was offered by six "ultra-Reformers" led by Robert Baldwin*. Hopkins was one of this obstructive six, but already he was demonstrating the maverick quality which would mark his later career. His first break with the Reform leadership came in 1841. As chairman of the house committee on the municipal corporations bill for Canada West, he consistently supported the measure against the vigorous opposition of Baldwin and other Reform leaders.

Hopkins returned to liberal orthodoxy and supported the Reform administration of 1842–43.

However, when Louis-Hippolyte La Fontaine* and Baldwin proposed moving the capital from Kingston to Montreal, the staunch Upper Canadian Hopkins in November 1843 joined the Tories in opposing the measure. More serious was his public disapproval of the resignation of the Reform ministers after their dispute over patronage with the governor, Sir Charles Metcalfe*, in November 1843. Hopkins' behaviour isolated him from the Reform party at both the local and the provincial levels, and in the election of 1844 he was rejected by the Reformers of East Halton who nominated John Wetenhall* at a highly disputed convention. But Hopkins refused to withdraw from the campaign. To avoid a split in the Reform vote Baldwin had to intervene. He sent two agents to East Halton in October 1844, George BROWN and Thomas Ewart. Far from neutral in the local dispute, they were there to dispose of the troublesome Hopkins. As Brown reported to Baldwin, ". . . we found it necessary to blackball Mr. Hopkins. . . ." It was all to no avail. Hopkins stayed in the race, splitting the Reform vote and allowing a Tory to be elected in this liberal stronghold.

Hopkins was now an enemy of the party. His sense of grievance was strong but he would wait five and a half years to find his revenge. The opportunity came with the rise of a splinter group of radical Reformers, the "Clear Grits." Although there is no evidence that Hopkins was involved in the founding of the Grit movement, he was one of a group of "old Reformers" – men with lingering, if fading, reputations from the glamorous period before 1837 – whom the young Grit intellectuals adopted both as symbols and as political instruments. When Malcolm CAMERON, another pre-union radical, bolted the "Great Ministry" of La Fontaine and Baldwin in 1849 and joined the new movement, he was replaced in the cabinet by Wetenhall. Required by law to seek re-election, Wetenhall faced a by-election in Halton County in March 1850. Hopkins announced that he would run against him, and Cameron and the Grits rallied to Hopkins, in hope of embarrassing the government. Under attack for its conservatism since the achievement of responsible government, the ministry found itself in serious difficulty in Halton. The task was further complicated by Wetenhall's poor health and apparent mental instability. To buttress the cause, James Durand, former member for West Halton, was drafted to manage Wetenhall's campaign, and the party press, notably the *Globe* of Toronto, was mobilized on his behalf. The candidates were shoved to the side as Cameron and Durand fought it out. The *Globe* description of the campaign was savage but accurate: ". . . Mr. Cameron . . . pinned this wretched Caleb to his coat-tails, and told off *ex cathedra* a catalogue of the iniquities of which his late colleagues had been guilty." Cameron's effective campaigning and the voters' resentment against the *Globe*'s vicious abuse of Hopkins settled the issue: on 11 March 1850 Hopkins won a resounding victory. The shattered Wetenhall came out of the contest completely mad, and finished his days in an insane asylum.

The Halton by-election further embittered relations between the Grits and the Baldwinites. Hopkins was a special target of Reform abuse: ". . . that old Hypocrite Hopkins" as James Durand called him. Picturing him as a doddering old fool, the *Globe* derided the Grits as the "Calebites." But the ministry would find that there was much vigour yet in the "wretched Caleb." One of five Clear Grits in the assembly, Hopkins helped harass the government at every turn. Never a true leader, he nevertheless made an effective follower. Joining with Henry John Boulton*, W. L. Mackenzie, and Cameron, Hopkins in 1850 and 1851 helped put before the house a series of resolutions demanding basic democratic reforms and the separation of church and state.

The high point in the career of the Grits, and of Hopkins, came on 26 June 1851. Mackenzie moved a resolution, seconded by Hopkins, for the abolition of the Court of Chancery in Canada West. They had chosen their target well, for the recently restructured court was dear to lawyer Baldwin's heart. The resolution was defeated but a majority of members from Canada West had voted for it. Weary and angry, Baldwin resigned from the government, soon to be followed by his colleague La Fontaine.

It was the last hurrah for the Grits, who moved into an alliance with the new premier, Francis Hincks*. And for Caleb Hopkins. He did not contest the election of 1851, retiring into respectable obscurity on the farm in Nelson. About 1870 he moved to more comfortable surroundings in the city of Hamilton, Ontario. Time would heal the wounds of 1850 as the Reform party gladly accepted the once hated sobriquet of Clear Grit, and Hopkins lived long enough to become a grand old man of Ontario Liberalism. He died, aged 95, on 8 Oct. 1880 at the Toronto home of his son-in-law, lawyer and author William Leggo*. The party leadership, once so hostile, attended his funeral in strength: this congenial independent was carried to his grave in Toronto by a group of pall bearers which included the recently retired national Liberal leader, Alexander Mackenzie*, and the premier of Ontario, Oliver Mowat*.

Caleb Hopkins was a political curiosity. Never a

Hopper

leader, innovator, or thinker, he nevertheless played a significant role in many of the major political controversies of the Province of Canada. His career was, in microcosm, the story of the cross-currents in Upper Canadian Reform, and a vivid demonstration of the rugged independence, the maverick quality, which so often split the Liberal party in 19th-century Canada.

MICHAEL S. CROSS

MTCL, Baldwin papers, 35, nos.103–4; 43, nos.20, 59–63; 47, no.7; 49, no.15; 52, nos.25–28; 65, no 1; 76, no.35. PAC, RG 31, A1, 1851, Halton County, Nelson Township, 78–79. PAO, Mackenzie-Lindsey collection, 2482; William Reid collection, data on the United Empire Loyalists. Canada, Province of, Legislative Assembly, *Debates* (Nish), 1841, 618–36; *Journals*, 1841–51. Upper Canada, House of Assembly, *Journals*, 1828–36. *Colonial Advocate* (York, U.C.), 1828–34. *Examiner* (Toronto), 1840–51. *Globe* (Toronto), 1850–51; 9–11 Oct. 1880. *Arthur papers* (Sanderson), II, 161, 325, 334. [Bruce and Grey], *Elgin-Grey papers* (Doughty), II, 604, 690, 742, 836. Chadwick, *Ontarian families*, I, 25. *Hamilton directory for 1872–3* (Montreal, 1872), 145.

Careless, *Brown*, I, 56–57, 112–13, 134. Charles Clarke, *Sixty years in Upper Canada, with autobiographical recollections* (Toronto, 1908), 78–79. Cornell, *Alignment of political groups*, 6, 15–17, 28–29, 93–97, 102. Dent, *Last forty years*, I, 137–38; II, 186. C. D. Emery and Barbara Ford, *From pathway to skyway; a history of Burlington* (Burlington, Ont., 1967), 53, 97, 125. L. A. Johnson, "The Halton by-election, March, 1850: a politician's view," *Ont. Hist.*, LX (1968), 147–48.

HOPPER, ARTHUR, Orangeman, merchant, and farmer; b. Roscrea, County Tipperary, Ireland, in 1784, son of Arthur Hopper, a substantial farmer and landowner, and his wife Sara; d. Merivale, Ont., 14 Nov. 1872.

Arthur Hopper left Roscrea for Dublin, where he was living at the time of the union of the British and Irish parliaments in 1801. He became an Orangeman in 1802 and served in a yeomanry corps in 1803. Some time after, he returned to Tipperary where he became deputy grand master of the Orange order in County Tipperary. On 27 July 1807 he married Anna Sparling. Hopper left Ireland in 1821 although he retained land in Tipperary and continued to receive revenue from it.

Hopper with his wife and four children (three more were born later) settled in Montreal, where he opened a jewellery shop. Shortly after his arrival he organized, in company with several other Montreal Orangemen, what was possibly the first civilian Orange lodge in the Canadas. Moving to Huntley in the Dalhousie District,

Upper Canada, in 1825, he opened a store, and established the first post office and the first Orange lodge in the township (first known as Hopperville, now Huntley). Two years later he settled at Bytown where he ran a jewellery shop for five years. He then acquired 600 acres of land in Nepean Township; the village that was established there was called the Hopper Settlement until 1864 when the name was changed to Merivale.

Hopper was instrumental in founding a number of Orange lodges in the Ottawa valley, the last being number 85, in Nepean, of which he was master. The authority to found such lodges came from a warrant which William Burton of Montreal had secured during a visit to Ireland in 1827, and it was over Hopper's signature that several of the warrants founding lodges in the Ottawa valley were issued, thus earning him a claim to the title of father of Canadian Orangeism. Hopper was among those who met with Ogle Robert GOWAN in Brockville in 1830 to form the Grand Orange Lodge of British North America, and he was elected to the grand committee in 1838. Throughout his life he remained an active Orangeman. Yet Hopper was on good terms with the Roman Catholics in the Ottawa valley and was never a violent partisan in politics. For him the Orange lodges were primarily fraternal societies, useful in providing social life in frontier communities.

HEREWARD SENIOR

The most extensive source of information on Arthur Hopper is a collection of papers privately held by his grandson, Henry Hopper, of Merivale, Ontario. *Ottawa Citizen*, 15 Nov. 1872. *Times* (Ottawa), 16 Nov. 1872. Davin, *Irishman in Canada*, 323–25. R. B. Sibbett, *Orangeism in Ireland and throughout the empire* (2v., Belfast, [1914]), II, 522. Harry and Olive Walker, *Carleton saga* (Ottawa, 1968), 146–52.

HORAN, EDWARD JOHN, Roman Catholic priest and bishop, scholar, and educator; b. 26 Oct. 1817, Quebec, son of Gordian Horan and Eleanore Cannon; d. 15 Feb. 1875 at Kingston, Ont.

Edward John Horan was born into an English-speaking family but received his early education in French. He entered the Petit Séminaire in Quebec in September 1830, where he had an excellent academic record. After then completing his course at the seminary of Quebec, he joined its faculty in 1839 as an instructor in English, a post he held until 1848. His scholarly interest, however, was in the sciences, then called natural history, a new subject in which he had been an apt pupil. He was especially concerned with scientific agriculture, seeking in technological advances some solution to the agricultural depression which had persisted in the St Lawrence valley through the 1830s. In 1843 he was appointed professor of natural history at the seminary.

His superiors encouraged his work and, in February 1848, agreed to send him to Harvard University in the United States for further training. Horan had hoped to study under the naturalist Louis Agassiz at Harvard but, unfortunately, Agassiz presented only infrequent lectures. Life in Boston, however, fascinated Horan; his letters reveal a wide circle of acquaintances, including publicist Orestes Brownson, then a Roman Catholic and in his conservative phase, who seems to have influenced the young cleric strongly. At the end of March 1848, Horan decided to transfer to Yale to follow the lectures of the celebrated scientist, Benjamin Silliman, and of his son Benjamin. The scholarly environment proved congenial, but the community of New Haven, where anti-Catholicism flourished in those early days of American nativism, did not. Horan wrote anxiously to his superior in Quebec that he "would be happy when the moment arrived when I can leave the United States, and exchange their vaunted *liberty* for the *slavery* of Canada, where at least one can serve God according to his conscience without fearing the torch of the incendiary."

Returning to Quebec in the autumn of 1848, Horan resumed his teaching duties at the seminary in the sciences, and conducted geological field trips down the St Lawrence River. He worked closely with Louis-Ovide BRUNET and Elkanah BILLINGS. Increasingly he became involved in the administrative life of his institution. He was a director of the Petit Séminaire and secretary of the Université Laval council in 1855, and in 1856 the first superior of the École Normale Laval. These careers came to an end in 1858 when he was appointed fourth bishop of Kingston to succeed Patrick Phelan*. He was consecrated on 1 May at St Patrick's Church in Quebec and moved immediately to his new diocesan seat. A continuing interest in the Université Laval was recognized in 1867 when he was named a director.

Bishop Horan was as efficient and firm an administrator in his diocese as he had been at Quebec. In the 17 years of his episcopate there was little disruption in its religious life. The surviving evidence of his social philosophy indicates that he had a conservative cast of mind, although his correspondence with the archbishop of Baltimore reveals a sympathetic attitude toward the trade union movement. In 1861 he introduced the Sisters of Providence of St Vincent de Paul who established the first house of providence in Canada West.

As bishop of Kingston, however, Horan's principal concern was Catholic education in Canada West, and he took a great satisfaction in the passage of Richard William Scott*'s act in 1863 which provided for the extension of public aid to separate schools. Horan had played his part well in obtaining this legislation although he had worked behind the scenes, preferring, for obvious reasons, lay leadership in the cause of Catholic education.

Horan almost inevitably became involved in the web of patronage and politics that characterized public life in Canada in the late 19th century. He established a firm relationship with John A. Macdonald* and other prominent Conservatives. Yet he had a curious correspondent in Edmund Bailey O'CALLAGHAN, once a Lower Canada rebel, and then the archivist of the state of New York. In a letter accompanying a new edition of the *Jesuit Relations*, which Horan was sending to O'Callaghan, there is evidence of a long and warm friendship between the two men. The major criteria for the bishop's political support were soundness on the school question and allegiance to Macdonald. In 1861, a year that was not untypical, he wrote to Macdonald, George-Étienne CARTIER, and Joseph Cauchon* (who had been a class-mate at the Petit Séminaire), seeking positions for various people, including his own brother-in-law. As the expected *quid pro quo*, Horan urged his parish priests to support the Conservative cause, writing, for example, to one correspondent, "I trust you will use your influence in this matter and direct the Catholic vote in a proper direction." Locally, he exerted himself in Macdonald's own riding. The Catholic vote of Kingston required careful cultivation and Macdonald relied heavily on the bishop through the years.

Horan retired in 1874 and was succeeded by John O'Brien. His death the following year prompted many laudatory obituaries, but perhaps his most significant accomplishment was the degree to which he furthered the integration of Roman Catholics into the public life of the province.

J. E. REA

Archdiocese of Kingston, Archives, E. J. Horan papers. P.-G. Roy, *Le vieux Québec* (2v., Québec, 1923–31). Arthur Maheux, "L'abbé Edward John Horan (1817–1875)," *Le Naturaliste canadien* (Québec), LXXXVI (1959), 77–92.

HOW, HENRY, chemist, mineralogist, and educator; b. 11 July 1828 in London, England, son of Thomas How; d. 28 Sept. 1879 at Windsor, N.S. He married, probably in Great Britain, Louisa Mary Watkins, and they had five children.

Educated at a private school in Beaconsfield and

Howe

at the Royal College of Chemistry, Henry How then became assistant to Dr Lyon Playfair, professor of chemistry at the College for Civil Engineers, Putney. How was analytical chemist for the Admiralty Steam Navy Coal Enquiry; he also worked with Dr Thomas Anderson first at the University of Edinburgh and then at Glasgow university. In 1854, on Dr Anderson's recommendation, he was appointed professor of natural history and chemistry at King's College, Windsor, N.S. He was given an honorary DCL by King's in 1861, and appointed vice-president of the university in 1877; he also served as librarian and curator of the university museum.

In 1861 How was appointed to the Nova Scotia Board of Commissioners responsible for arranging displays at the London International Exhibition of 1862, and was selected to make an illustrative collection of Nova Scotia minerals. He was one of the organizers in 1862 (with John Matthew Jones, Dr Alexander Forrester*, Dr J. B. Gilpin*, John R. WILLIS, R. G. Haliburton*, Captain Campbell Hardy*, and others) of the Nova Scotian Institute of Science, an organization which grew out of the interest aroused by the display of the province's natural resources at the London Exhibition. Over the years he contributed ten papers to the *Transactions* of the institute.

How also prepared a collection of minerals for the Paris Exposition of 1867, and this collection became the basis of the Nova Scotia Museum, founded in 1868. He brought the most recent chemical techniques from Europe to Nova Scotia and provided Nova Scotia students with an alternative to classical studies. In addition to his 25-year career as a teacher, he constantly corresponded with learned men in Great Britain, carried on original research in both analytical chemistry and mineralogy, and served as a consultant to government and industry. Through his pupils and his writings, he strongly influenced science in Nova Scotia in the 19th century. His chief work was *The mineralogy of Nova Scotia* (1869), consulted and used for many years. He discovered and named several Nova Scotia minerals; "howlite" was named in his honour by one of his students. He contributed at least 44 papers on chemistry, analytical chemistry, mineralogy, and botany to British, American, and Canadian periodicals.

PHYLLIS R. BLAKELEY

Henry How, *Sketch of the mineralogy of Nova Scotia, as illustrated by the collections of minerals sent to the Paris Exhibition, 1867* (Halifax, 1867); *The mineralogy of Nova Scotia: a report to the provincial government* (Halifax, 1869).

PANS, Nova Scotia provincial secretary's papers, 1867, 3189. *Morning Herald* (Halifax), 29 Sept. 1879. King's College (Windsor, N.S.), *Calendars*, 1855–80; *Record*, I (1879), 73–74. F. W. Vroom, *King's College: a chronicle, 1789–1939, collections and recollections* (Halifax, 1941). Harry Piers, "A brief historical account of the Nova Scotia Institute of Science, and the events leading up to its formation; with biographical sketches of its deceased presidents and other prominent members," N.S. Inst. of Sci., *Proc. and Trans.*, XIII (1910–14), liii–cxii.

HOWE, JOSEPH, journalist, politician, and public servant; b. 13 Dec. 1804 at the Northwest Arm in Halifax, N.S., son of John Howe and Mary Edes; d. 1 June 1873 at government house in Halifax.

The most lasting influence upon Howe was exercised by his father, loyalist John Howe, whom he once described as "my only instructor, my play-fellow, almost my daily companion." The one member of his family who sided with Britain in revolutionary times, John Howe had a reverent, almost mystical, attitude towards the British connection, and he passed this attitude on to his son; indeed, it was one of two qualities which, more than any others, determined the son's conduct and shaped his career. The second quality was "a restless, agitating uncertainty" which made an ordinary, humdrum existence intolerable. "If I could be content," Joseph Howe wrote, "to go along quietly and peaceably like my neighbours and at the end of some fifty or sixty years tumble into my grave and be dust, I should be happy – very happy." But that was not to be.

Because his formal education was limited by impecunious circumstances, Howe was largely self-educated: he read late into the night "if the book is amusing and the fire does not go out"; he was an acute observer of the circumstances around him. "My books are very few, but then the world is before me – a library open to all – from which poverty of purse cannot exclude me – and in which the meanest and most paltry volume is sure to furnish some thing to amuse, if not to instruct and improve." To his Sandemanian father he owed not only his familiarity with the Bible and his "knowledge of old Colonial & American incidents and characteristics," but also the moral and physical courage which later stood him in good stead.

At the age of 13 Howe was already assisting his father in his duties as postmaster general and king's printer. Since these offices would eventually go to his older half-brother John Jr, he had to seek other employment. The fateful decision was made early in 1827 when he and James SPIKE purchased the *Weekly Chronicle* and began to publish it as the *Acadian*. However, within less than a year – in December 1827 – Howe took over the *Novascotian* from George R. Young* and soon made it the most influential newspaper in the province.

Joseph Howe married Catherine Susan Ann McNab on 2 Feb. 1828. Between 1829 and 1848 they had ten children; of these only five lived to become adults, and none achieved the preeminence of the father. Howe's enemies implied that he fathered numerous illegitimate children, but these implications were based more on rumour than on fact. His letters suggest that he was very close to his wife and that he greatly missed his family during the long periods when his political career took him away from home.

Howe, as Daniel Cobb Harvey* pointed out, did not spring Minerva-like from the waters of the Northwest Arm. Rather his career took the direction it did because of an intellectual awakening in Nova Scotia which he in turn did much to promote. In his hands the *Novascotian* became an instrument both for his own self-education and for the education of his readers. In the early years he personally reported between 150 and 200 columns of debate during each session of the assembly. By 1834 he could boast that he had written as much manuscript as he could carry and that without it the people would have been "about as incapable of judging of the conduct of their Representatives, as if they had assembled in the moon."

Each session concluded, he turned with zest to the books, magazines, pamphlets, and newspapers which had accumulated on his desk, and the columns of his paper attested to his thorough acquaintance with British, European, and North American affairs. Wanting to observe at first hand, he explored every nook and cranny of large sections of his native province. The fruits of these travels – the "Western Rambles," which appeared in the *Novascotian* between 24 July and 9 Oct. 1828, and the "Eastern Rambles," appearing between 16 Dec. 1829 and 4 Aug. 1831 – concentrate on the physical features of the regions and the social characteristics of their people. Occasionally Howe would publish verses of his own, some of which appeared in *Poems and essays*, published the year after his death. Commenting on his poetry, Professor J. A. Roy has said that although "he had the urge towards poetry and poetic expression . . . his ear was defective; he was imitative and trite, and ignorant of the most elementary prosodic principles." Howe sought also to "elevate the character of the country . . . and lay the foundation of a Provincial Literature" by printing such works as Beamish MURDOCH's *Epitome of the laws of Nova Scotia* and Thomas Chandler Haliburton*'s *The clockmaker* and *The historical and statistical account of Nova Scotia*; these ventures provided an important service to the province but greatly increased the financial difficulties that perennially embarrassed Howe.

Although Howe turned out to be a political animal, it was not his original intention to seek the improvement in all aspects of colonial society that he wanted through direct political action. Not inaccurately he has been described as a mild Tory at this stage. What people, he asked on 17 Jan. 1828, have "a government which sits lighter on the people, or under which they may enjoy more of rational freedom"? He stood for "the Constitution, the *whole* Constitution, and *nothing but* the Constitution."

Even the Brandy Dispute of 1830, in which the council prevented the assembly from correcting an error in the revenue laws at the cost of defeating the entire appropriation act [*see* Enos COLLINS], did little to change his opinion. Apparently he felt that an assembly which opposed one outrageous action would also intervene in less extreme cases. Furthermore, he still considered parties to be factions operating against the public interest; personally he wanted to belong to only one party, "the party of Nova Scotia." It took another series of issues to make him appreciate the complex forces at work in Nova Scotian society and realize that the machinations of the true possessors of power were not disinterested.

In 1832 and 1833 Nova Scotia's banking and currency problems showed the assembly's weakness and the council's power. The five councillors who were directors of the Halifax Banking Company first delayed the incorporation of a second bank and then whittled down its powers. The manipulations of the two banks soon led to a depreciated currency, and the assemblymen, moving like puppets controlled by wires from the council, did not demand the action that would restore the currency to a sound basis. In 1834 Howe denounced an assembly which seemed willing to negotiate with the British government for the commutation of quitrents on land in return for a suitable establishment for the public officials. The quitrents, he insisted, should be commuted unconditionally; Nova Scotia would do justice to its public servants without having a club held over its head.

In 1835 an even more belligerent Howe dared to publish a letter alleging that, in the previous 30 years, the magistracy and police of Halifax had "by one stratagem or other, taken from the pockets of the people, in over exactions, fines, etc., etc., a sum that would exceed in the gross amount £30,000." Though he had undoubtedly broken the law of criminal libel of the day, he pleaded his

Howe

own case before a jury, won an acquittal, and proclaimed that "the PRESS OF NOVA SCOTIA IS FREE." This was his first resort to the oratorical talents which placed him head and shoulders above his Nova Scotian rivals and, according to Professor Keith Thomas, above George BROWN and John A. Macdonald* in many respects: "he was a master of factual detail and its skilful presentation; in his smooth and effective transitions he possessed the last touch in structural skill; his astounding adaptability allowed him to persuade even a greater range and variety of audiences than those won over by the others; and his powerful rhythm could reinforce and make still more effective all his other qualities of persuasion."

Thus it was a transformed Howe who wrote on the state of the province and the prospects of Halifax in 1834 and 1835. As usual, he painted an idyllic picture of the sturdy agriculturist who had won a good living from the wilderness by the sweat of his brow. Nova Scotia, he warned, had no place for "gentleman merchants," "gentleman mechanics," and "gentleman farmers," but unfortunately the high salaries of the officials induced the industrious classes of Halifax to attempt a similar style of living, while each village contained "a little knot of traders, lawyers, and public officers, through whom the fashionable follies of the capital are reflected upon the surrounding country." Howe told the people to look at the faulty structure of the council, at the great string of public officers who took so much of the revenue that they were "in truth our masters", and at the assembly in which the lawyers led a time-serving majority, and then to adopt the only true remedy: elect a "public-spirited assembly" which would bring "the sentiments of the Country . . . to bear upon the rottenness of Denmark."

Thomas Chandler Haliburton warned Howe not to seek election to the assembly; the *Novascotian* "(always enough on one side of politics) will be thought after your election . . . a party paper altogether." But Howe felt the assembly would be "an admirable school" for his own development; besides, "being under great obligations to many thousands . . . I ought not to shrink from any sacrifice of time and labour to pay the debt." Accordingly he ran and was elected for the county of Halifax in the general election of 1836. His message to the voters was a simple one: ". . . all we ask for is what exists at home – a system of responsibility to the people."

But Howe was still not the typical colonial reformer. For, when he proposed his twelve resolutions to the assembly in 1837, instead of demanding a responsible executive council as Robert Baldwin* did in Upper Canada, he simply advocated an elective legislative council. Apparently he thought that an exact copy of British institutions was unsuited to a small colony like Nova Scotia and that two elective houses could keep in check the advisers of the governor and the provincial bureaucracy. Yet, when Lord Durham [John George Lambton*] recommended otherwise in his *Report*, Howe unreservedly accepted his conclusions. Indeed, to meet the objections of the colonial secretary, Lord John Russell, Howe addressed a series of letters to him in September 1839, which Chester Martin* describes as the colonial counterpart of the Durham *Report*. Howe told Russell that the remedy for colonial problems was the one prescribed by Durham: "the Colonial Governors must be commanded to govern by the aid of those who . . . are supported by a majority of the representative branch."

In his attitude towards political parties Howe still found it difficult to don all the trappings of the typical colonial reformer. Although he admitted that there were questions in the colonies that might "form the touchstones of party" much as in England, he could not dispel his earlier fears that parties would become selfish factions; he was also suspicious of highly disciplined parties that restricted their members' freedom of action. None the less, it was much of his doing that the assemblies which were elected in 1836 and 1840 contained majorities favouring Reform principles. His success so antagonized the official faction that he was forced to fight a duel with John Halliburton, son of the chief justice, on 14 March 1840; Halliburton missed and Howe fired his pistol into the air.

The strongest act in which Howe participated – an address to the crown in 1840 requesting the removal of Lieutenant Governor Colin Campbell* – brought Governor General Charles Poulett Thomson* (soon to be Lord Sydenham) to Halifax and led, in October 1840, to Howe's entering the Executive Council in a coalition with the Tory James W. JOHNSTON. Sydenham persuaded Howe that it was his duty to cooperate in reducing discord; he was wrong, however, in suggesting that Howe had "made the amende honorable and eschewed his heresies on Responsible Government publicly in his newspaper." Howe agreed for the moment that "the Queen's representative [could] devolve the responsibilities of his acts on no man"; but he felt there was little difference between Sydenham's and the Reformers' ideas of responsibility, since in the former's scheme the governor must depend upon public confidence and popular support, and would be foolhardy to refuse the advice of a council which had to defend his acts. Howe's conduct, wrote Chester Martin, was logical for one who "distrusted stark theories and relied ... upon the subtler accommodations of practice and experience." Indeed, during the election late in 1840, Howe argued that, if Nova Scotia were to be a normal school for the other colonies, it ought not to press organic changes too rapidly, but be content with steady, piecemeal progress. Naturally he regretted that such Reformers as Herbert Huntington*, the Robert Baldwin of Nova Scotia, refused to support the coalition, which they considered, at best, an ineffectual armistice, reversing the progress towards a well-disciplined Reform party.

During the coalition period Howe became speaker of the assembly (1841) and collector of excise at Halifax (1842). By the end of 1841 he had decided upon a full-time political career and sold the *Novascotian*. Meanwhile the coalition was experiencing rough weather. In early 1843 Howe told Lieutenant Governor Falkland [Lucius Bentinck Cary*], that something more was "required to make a strong Administration than nine men, treating each other courteously at a round table – there is the assurance of good faith – towards each other – of common sentiments, and kindly feelings. . . ." During the session of 1843 Howe's denunciation of grants to denominational colleges, particularly Acadia, exacerbated his relations with the Baptist Johnston. After the Tories assumed office in Britain in September 1841, the governor had relied more and more upon the Tory councillors. Towards the end of 1843, during Howe's absence from Halifax and against his advice, Falkland dissolved the assembly, supposedly to escape the party government which he said the Reformers were trying to force on him. He got what he wanted: a Tory majority, albeit small. Then, in December 1843, he weighted his ministry altogether in favour of the Tories by appointing Mather Byles ALMON, Johnston's brother-in-law, to the council, ostensibly to demonstrate his belief in mixed rather than party government. Howe and the two other Reform councillors resigned forthwith.

Until the election of August 1847 Howe devoted all his energy to undoing the effect of the coalition and reviving the Reform party. From May 1844 to April 1846 he assumed the editorship of the *Novascotian* and the *Morning Chronicle*, and "his armchair became the centre and rallying point of the whole party." Again the readers could say: "Why, here is Howe among us again; not Mr. Speaker Howe, not the Hon. Mr. Howe, but Joe Howe . . . making us laugh a good deal, but think a good deal more, even while we [are] laughing." Howe delineated the issues more clearly than ever before, and the election of 5 Aug. 1847 was as much a referendum on the single issue of responsible government as a British-style election is likely to be. The Reformers' margin in seats was only seven, but their victory was certain, for none of the new assemblymen fell into the category of "loose fish." It was simply a question of voting out the Tories on 26 Jan. 1848; a Reform administration was installed a few days later. Nova Scotia had become the first colony to achieve responsible government, and Howe boasted it had been done without "a blow struck or a pane of glass broken." Yet he was being somewhat sanctimonious, for external circumstances such as the rebellions in the Canadas played no small part in making it possible.

James Boyle Uniacke* rather than Howe, the architect of victory, headed the new administration. Howe was paying the price for his intemperate conduct. Unable to stand exaggerated criticism and invective for long, he had reacted violently to Falkland's conniving with Tory publicists behind the scenes. However, his lampoons and pasquinades reflecting on the governor – the "Lord of the Bed-Chamber" was the best known – not only horrified the colonial Tories but also hurt his reputation for moderation in England. Nevertheless, Chester Martin goes much too far when he suggests that this barbarous type of warfare "embittered [Howe's] most cherished memories, coarsened his nature, and stained his name; lost him perhaps the first premiership under responsible government overseas in 1848, and in the end contributed not a little to fasten upon him the cardinal sin of indiscretion that barred him from the career he coveted beyond his native province." Actually Howe's loss of the premiership was more in name than in substance, for to many it was his ministry all the same. Indeed, because of his friendship with Sir John Harvey*, some suggested he ran not only the government, but also the governor.

As provincial secretary, Howe played an active role in adapting the province's institutions to responsible government. But by March 1850 he had turned his chief attention to the idea of building a railroad from Halifax to Windsor, N.S. "It is the first duty of a government," he said, "to take the front rank in every noble enterprise; to be in advance of the social, political, and industrial energies, which they have undertaken to lead." In November he went to Britain to determine the conditions on which Nova Scotia might borrow money for the project. Then one of his so-called "flashes" transformed a purely pecuniary mission into a plan for the elevation of the empire. It included promoting vital public works through imperial credit, preparing crown lands for settlement, and encouraging the migration of the poor from Britain through cheap transportation. After an initial rejection of his plan, the colonial secretary let Howe come "face to face with the people of England"; his speech at Southampton on 14 Jan. 1851 drew wide and favourable attention in the British press.

By March he appeared to have won guarantees from the British government for lines from Halifax to Quebec and Portland, Maine. On his return he sought, in a speech-making tour, to educate the people of Nova Scotia, New Brunswick, and Canada to the value of the combined project. He told them that, as a political leader, he rejected the pageantry of sitting on gilded chairs and pocketing his salary; "those who aspire to govern others should neither be afraid of the saddle by day nor of the lamp by night." On the beneficence of his scheme he waxed especially eloquent: "Aid me in this good work, and the capital of England will flow into North America . . .; aid me in this good work, and the poor rates of Britain may be beaten down . . .; aid me in this good work, and . . . North America will rise to the rank of a second or third rate power, with all the organization and attributes of a nation."

By year's end the blow fell. The colonial secretary denied that he had intended to offer guarantees for the Portland branch and Howe's grandiose plan lay in tatters. At the time he personally accepted blame for the misunderstanding; later he attributed his failure to sinister influences operating on the British government. Howe was now determined that Nova Scotia should build its own railways as public works. Late in 1852 he arranged for adequate financing on favourable terms with Baring Brothers. Even then he had to accede to the demands of the opposition that private enterprise have the first opportunity. When it reneged he finally, in 1854, got railway legislation along the lines he wanted. Shortly afterwards he resigned as provincial secretary to become chief commissioner of a bi-partisan railway board. It is sometimes said that the only figures he understood were figures of speech, but he had no difficulties with the details of railway finance, and no scandal or bumbling occurred in railway building under his management.

In addition to the railway commissionership, Howe had the Crimean War to occupy him during 1855. Because of his attitude towards Britain, he accepted without question the British case in this conflict. Furthermore, during March and April 1855 he engaged in a "recruiting" mission to the United States; according to him, he simply made known the conditions of acceptance to those who voluntarily offered their services and he did not break the American neutrality laws. But he himself admitted that, if ordered to violate the policy of any foreign state in order to assist "the gallant fellows in the Crimea . . . , I would have obeyed without a moment's hesitation," and there is evidence to suggest that he did commit such violations even without express instructions from his superiors.

His American venture had unforeseen repercussions. It allowed him only 18 days to fight the general election of 22 May and he went down to personal defeat before Dr Charles Tupper* in Cumberland. Indirectly, but of greater significance, it led him into conflict with the Irish and other Catholics of Nova Scotia. He had noted that some Irish priests had recently founded the *Halifax Catholic* and were using it to gloat over British reverses in the Crimea. A little later the president of the Charitable Irish Society had met Irish volunteers from the United States on their arrival in Halifax and persuaded them not to enlist for Crimean service; he also publicized Howe's activities in a New York newspaper, forcing him to flee from the United States in fear of arrest. Finally, in May 1856, Irish navvies working on the Windsor railway, as a reaction to their being taunted about their religious beliefs, inflicted a merciless beating on their Protestant tormentors at Gourley's Shanty. For the moment Howe held himself in check. But when the alleged perpetrators of the crime went free in December 1856, and the *Halifax Catholic* warned Protestants not to ridicule Catholics – especially those of the "mercurial" Irish variety – about their beliefs, Howe was betrayed into saying that Protestants had the right to make fun of any doctrines that they found to be absurd.

The controversy led to the complete estrangement of all Catholics – Irish, Scottish, and Acadian – from the Liberal party. When the assembly met in February 1856, all the Catholic Liberals and two Protestant Liberals from Catholic counties deserted their party and brought the Conservatives to power. Howe resigned as railway commissioner and contemplated leading a Protestant alliance, but soon thought better of it. As one who had been foremost in advocating complete Catholic equality, he regarded this episode as one of the most regrettable of his life. He insisted, however, that the Catholics "left me foolishly and without cause, and like little Bo-peep in the nursery rhymes, I let them alone till they choose [to] come home, wagging their tails behind them."

Religion intruded itself strongly into the general election of 12 May 1859; the Liberals described their opponents as "Romo-Johnstonites" and were in their turn labelled "Proscriptionists."

The Liberals won by 3 seats, but half a dozen of their members were allegedly disqualified because they held offices of emolument under the crown. None the less, the assembly voted out the Conservatives in February 1860 and Howe, who had been elected again in Cumberland, became provincial secretary in William Young*'s administration. Eventually committees of the assembly confirmed all the Liberal members in their seats. This outcome of the "Disputed Election of 1859" exacerbated further an overheated political situation. Since January 1855 papers like the *Acadian Recorder* had been wondering if there were "any cogent reason for the division of the Representatives of Nova Scotia into two parties, regularly organized for the annihilation of each other, in the halls of our Legislature." Over the next few years things got worse, and this was the situation Howe inherited when Young became chief justice and Howe took over the government in August 1860.

Howe's premiership was an unending struggle to maintain his precarious majority against the out-and-out onslaught of Charles Tupper. More than once he told Tupper that he would "never command that influence which he wishes to attain until he learns to have more of . . . Christian charity in dealing with his fellow-men." In 1862 Howe almost got agreement upon an intercolonial railway, only to be defeated by the political difficulties in Canada. Generally, however, he was occupied with picayune, humdrum matters. On the basis of an occasional excerpt from his diary or letters, J. A. Roy pictures him as utterly despairing and disillusioned during this period, but this was not his typical state. None the less, he did welcome, in December 1862, his appointment as imperial fishery commissioner under the reciprocity treaty of 1854 although the position provided little scope for his talents. Almost against his will he contested the general election of 1863, in which a worn-out, leaderless Liberal party went down to overwhelming defeat, and he suffered personal loss in Lunenburg.

Howe's acceptance of an imperial office was the culmination of protracted activity which had begun in March 1855, when he made a request to the colonial secretary, Lord John Russell, for an under-secretaryship in his department. This desire for office fitted into his design for the organization of the empire first put forward in his second series of letters to Lord John Russell in the autumn of 1846 and unfolded in the legislature in February 1854. It included the representation of colonials in the House of Commons and the participation of leading colonials in the government of the empire. "What national distinction ever lights upon British America? Has she ever supplied a governor to the Queen's widely extended dominions, a secretary, or an under-secretary of state? . . . How long is this state of pupilage to last? Not long. If British statesmen do not take this matter in hand, we soon shall."

When, in November 1858, the two volumes of his speeches and letters (the so-called [William] Annand* edition) came off the press, he forwarded copies to many Britons of influence to demonstrate his own capacity for high public office. J. A. Roy describes Howe's pleas as "one of the most humiliating and self-abasing dunnings of Downing Street on record," but Howe's 15 letters over a six-year period during which the colonial secretaryship often switched hands hardly constituted a highly concentrated campaign of self-aggrandizement. In any case his requests were motivated by much more than personal ambition. To him responsible government had conferred on colonials only part of the rights enjoyed by Britons, and the empire should be organized to confer these rights in their entirety. To serve the empire, preferably at its centre in London, but alternatively even in so remote and primitive a region as British Columbia, was the noblest mission Howe could conceive.

Howe's ideas for the organization of empire cannot be divorced from his attitude towards intercolonial union. He has often been accused of being inconsistent in opposing the union he allegedly advocated over a long period. The record shows, however, that from 1838 he had been contending that an improvement in communications, especially in the form of an intercolonial railroad, was a necessary prerequisite to union. Only at a convivial affair in Halifax on 13 Aug. 1864 did he express himself otherwise and, as he himself put it, "Who ever heard of a public man being bound by a speech delivered on such an occasion as this?"

Howe declined Tupper's invitation to be one of the Nova Scotian delegates to the Charlottetown conference in September 1864. Apocryphally, he refused to "play second fiddle to that damn'd Tupper"; actually, he had been instructed by Russell to finish his work as fishery commissioner as quickly as possible, and did not have permission to accept Tupper's invitation.

Myth has it that it was Howe who roused Nova Scotian public opinion against the Quebec resolutions. But by November 1864 the governor of the province had found so many leaders of the community opposed to them that he doubted whether they could be carried. As a public servant, Howe did not participate in the confederation debate, other than to publish anonymously his "Botheration Letters" in the *Morning Chronicle* between 11 Jan. and 2 March 1865. Some have said that

Howe

they rallied opinion everywhere, but few knew their authorship, and their function, together with a mass of similar literature, was simply to reinforce existing opinions. Until March 1866 Howe played no further part in the discussions of confederation in Nova Scotia. Then Tupper's determination to use the Fenian scare to press a resolution favouring union through the legislature forced Howe to make a decision. Should he accept the editorship of the New York *Albion* and financial ease, or should he stay in his province now that the commission work was ended to assist "poor old Nova Scotia, God help her, beset with marauders outside and enemies within"? Why did he choose the second alternative? At one level there was the fear that implementation of union would deal a death-blow to his scheme for the organization of the empire. At another level his opposition was based on practical grounds: railroads, and social and economic intercourse, were needed first to make union a success; the Quebec resolutions, born of Canadian necessity, would lead to the loss of independence and the economic ruination of Nova Scotia. In providing specific evidence to demonstrate these points, Howe used too many arguments, some good, some bad, some indifferent. But his prediction that the tariff increases under the new order would be ruinous to Nova Scotia turned out to be all too correct, and his prophecy that it would take "the wisdom of Solomon and the energy and strategy of Frederick the Great" to weld the disparate people of the proposed union into "a new nationality" was not too far off the mark. However, the factor which more than any other propelled Howe back into active politics was Tupper's decision not to consult the people on union. As Howe's friend and admirer, George Johnson*, put it, a "firm, fixed passion for the people's rights was at the bottom of all Mr. Howe's opposition to the Union of the Provinces."

Howe could not prevent the Nova Scotian legislature from adopting Tupper's resolution in April 1866. The result, for him, was two years of frenzied activity. Almost immediately he embarked on a speaking tour of the western counties. Then from July 1866 to May 1867 he headed a delegation to England to oppose the passage of an act of union. During that time he published a major paper, *Confederation considered in relation to the interests of the empire* (September 1866), and interviewed or addressed letters to any man who might assist his cause, all to no avail. On his return home he campaigned actively to ensure that the British government appreciated the true state of feeling in Nova Scotia, and in the general election of 18 Sept. 1867 the Nova Scotian confederates returned only one member to the House of Commons and two to the House of Assembly. After participating actively, as the member for Hants, in the first session of the first dominion parliament, Howe led the Nova Scotia repeal delegation to London between February and July 1868. He got only one concession: the colonial secretary agreed to ask the dominion government to review the impact of its taxation, trade, and fishing policies on Nova Scotia with a view to their modification. Howe's participation in the two delegations left him – always a great admirer of British political institutions – highly disillusioned with British public men and the British political process. He noted that only ten peers were in their place when the House of Lords gave third reading to the British North America Act. "If disloyal men can be made at all it is by such treatment as that." Once he had felt that a man with an honest case would always get fair play from the independent English gentlemen in the House of Commons. "If you ask me if I feel that confidence now, I am sorry to say that I do not."

By mid-1868 Howe knew that the game was up, but he did not openly "accept the situation" until December 1868, when Gladstone's newly installed administration confirmed that the union was to remain as it was. Throughout the summer and autumn of 1868 Howe's main function was to keep in line the advocates of insurrection and annexation within the anti-confederate ranks. If the issue had been one simply between Canadians and Nova Scotians, he said, "I would take every son I have and die on the frontier before I would submit to this outrage," but he had been a loyal and devoted British subject all his life and would continue one to the end.

In January 1869 Howe and his fellow Nova Scotian MP, Archibald W. McLelan*, reached an agreement with the federal minister of finance, Sir John Rose*, for granting "better terms" to Nova Scotia and on 30 Jan. 1869 he entered the dominion cabinet as president of the council. The necessity of fighting a by-election in Hants in midwinter against determined opposition resulted in his complete physical breakdown, and, although he won the election, he never fully regained his health.

As a federal minister, he was the subject of controversy on two occasions. On 16 Nov. 1869 he became secretary of state for the provinces and in that capacity oversaw the arrangements for bringing Manitoba into Canada. Anxious as always to see things at first hand, Howe overtaxed his ebbing strength by a visit to the Red River. Later, when the lieutenant governor–designate, William McDougall*, could not enter the new province because of insurrection, he blamed his difficulties on the loose talk and anti-Canadian bias of Howe. But the House of Commons declined to go along with him.

Howe's disillusionment with the British government reached zenith when it failed to safeguard Canadian interests in the negotiations leading to the Treaty of Washington of 1871. In an address to the YMCA of Ottawa on 27 Feb. 1872, he suggested that if "Englishmen, unmindful of the past, repudiate their national obligations," Canadians had the ability to work out their own destiny by themselves. In any case he felt that the time was rapidly approaching when Canadians and Englishmen would have to reach "a clear and distinct understanding as to the hopes and obligations of the future." Sir John A. Macdonald was not amused: "although [Howe] had outlived his usefulness he has not lost his power of mischief."

In May 1873 Howe became lieutenant governor of his native province. He had held that office less than three weeks when he died at government house in Halifax on 1 June 1873.

For his part in the winning of responsible government Howe has received fair and judicious treatment at the hands of the historians, especially from Chester Martin in *Empire and commonwealth*. But he has fared badly on the confederation issue. The style was set by his contemporary, Presbyterian pastor G. M. Grant*, who attributed his position on the Quebec resolutions purely to egoism. "Was he to help, to be the lieutenant of Dr. Tupper, the man who had taken the popular breeze out of his sails . . . only a hero would have done his duty. . . . And Howe was an egotist . . . [possessed of an] egotism which long feeding on popular applause had developed into a vanity almost incomprehensible in a man so strong."

E. M. Saunders* in *Three premiers of Nova Scotia* and W. L. Grant* in *The tribune of Nova Scotia* accepted G. M. Grant's thesis at its face value. But more recently (1935) J. A. Roy went them one better in *Joseph Howe: a study in achievement and frustration*. A professor of English, he treated Howe as the protagonist of a Shakespearian tragedy whose fortunes proceeded inexorably downwards after reaching their apogee. "Once [responsible government] was achieved his main work was done. Dullness succeeded enthusiasm, cynicism, faith; and from now on, his story is one of fading day and falling night." In writing of Howe, most general historians and biographers of Howe's contemporaries have taken their cue from G. M. Grant or J. A. Roy or both.

None would deny that Howe was an egotist, but Grant adduces not a tittle of evidence to indicate that egoism determined his opposition to the Quebec resolutions. The fact is that Howe's

position was thoroughly consistent with the statements and activities of his past life and was entirely predictable, apart from considerations of jealousy or egoism.

Any suggestion that the later Howe was basically a disappointed, disillusioned, embittered, cynical man fails to take into account his irrepressible ebullience. Despite serious disappointments and disillusionment with institutions by which he set great store, he quickly rebounded with new ideas or, at least, with a renewal of faith. In any case, just because Howe was unsuccessful in his advocacy of some proposals and in his opposition to others, it ought not to be assumed – as some historians have done – that he was guilty of bad judgement or suffered from a deficiency of character. It was Howe's fate to have the soundness of his later political ventures judged by the criterion of success and, as Professor R. G. Trotter* indicated, there is "no justice in that sort of *ex post facto* verdict on political opinions." It would mean that a public man who craved favourable recognition in the history books would have to calculate the probabilities of alternative lines of action and act in accordance with the likely outcome rather than his own principles. But when Howe made his fateful decision in April 1866, could anyone have forecast the probable success of the union? Surely this kind of criterion for making judgements would "downgrade a person of unimpeachable motives who makes a strong fight against impossible odds and at the same time tend to enthrone Machiavellianism as a cardinal virtue of politics."

Howe, "a liberal imperial federationist" (to use Professor Donald Creighton's description), may be criticized because he failed to appreciate that his plans for the organization of the empire ran completely counter to the trend of thinking in Britain when he proposed them. He may have been altogether too unwilling to recognize the feasibility of a united British North America in the 1860s and he may have exaggerated the possible evil effects of that union on Nova Scotia. But he has suffered unfairly because the charges of inconsistency, precipitate intervention, and bad motives that were made against him by the partisanship of the confederation era were perpetuated in a hoary mythology that has been resistant to reinterpretation.

Throughout his career Howe exhibited failings and deficiencies of varying kinds: when it suited his own purposes he could be annoyingly ingratiating; although his diaries reveal him as humble and self-effacing, on occasion he was highly egotistical; in the matter of office-holding by members of his family, he permitted himself a line of conduct he would not tolerate in others; after putting up with abuse for a time, he might finally demonstrate an utter lack of moderation; self-educated in a hard school, he sometimes lacked refinement, as instanced by his off-colour allusions in the assembly and his stooping to outright vulgarity with less sophisticated audiences. But these are minor blemishes and they are more than counterbalanced by a basic consistency, an adherence to principles, which is uncommon.

None the less, Howe is a difficult man to categorize. Basically he was a conservative reformer, even though his name is primarily associated with radical, even revolutionary objectives. Although he personally thought of himself as a liberal, he outdid even the most ardent Tory in his devotion to Britain. As a man who felt that land, easily acquired in Nova Scotia, should be the basis of the franchise, and whose government abolished the universal suffrage which had been operative for a decade, he could hardly be labelled a democrat. Yet he did insist that the people had a right to be consulted directly on intercolonial union.

Time has vindicated Howe in the sense that the right of the electorate to give prior approval to radical constitutional changes has become an established convention of the British constitution. Furthermore, despite the impracticability of his ideas on the organization of the empire, the commonwealth has become what he hoped it would become: "a partnership, which may last for centuries, and need not terminate at all, so long as it is mutually advantageous." But perhaps Howe would like best to be remembered for his efforts to rescue his compatriots from the parochialism which besets a small community. When accused of "innoculating the public mind with extravagant and unrestrained ideas," he pridefully admitted that he was guilty of giving his countrymen enlarged views and concepts on many subjects. "I have striven," he said, "to elevate their eyes and minds from the little pedling muddy pool of politics beneath their feet to something more enobling, exacting and inspiring, calculated to enlarge the borders of their intelligence, and increase the extent and area of their prosperity."

J. MURRAY BECK

[PAC, MG 24, B29 (Howe papers); MG 30, D9 (Johnson papers). *British Colonist* (Halifax), 1848–73. *Morning Chronicle* (Halifax), 1844–73. *Novascotian* (Halifax), 1827–73. *Sun* (Halifax), 1845–67. *Times* (Halifax), 1834–48. Nova Scotia, House of Assembly, *Journals and proceedings*, 1837–68.

For older biographical material on Howe, *see*: G. M. Grant, *Joseph Howe* (1st ed., Halifax, 1904; 2nd ed., Halifax, 1906); G. E. Fenety, *Life and times of the Hon. Joseph Howe, (the great Nova Scotian and ex-lieut. governor); with brief references to some of his prominent contemporaries* (Saint John, N.B., 1896); Saunders, *Three premiers of N.S.*; Longley, *Howe*; and W. L. Grant, *Tribune of N.S.: Howe*. For more recent biographical material, *see*: J. A. Roy, *Joseph Howe, a study in achievement and frustration* (Toronto, 1935), and J. M. Beck, "Joseph Howe," *Our living tradition*, 4th ser., ed. R. L. McDougall (Toronto, 1962), 3–30.

For extracts from Howe's speeches and letters, *see*: [Joseph Howe], *The speeches and public letters of the Hon. Joseph Howe*, ed. William Annand (2v., Boston, 1858); *Speeches and letters* (Chisholm); *The heart of Howe, selections from the letters and speeches of Joseph Howe*, ed. D. C. Harvey (Toronto, 1939); and *Joseph Howe: voice of Nova Scotia*, ed. and intro. J. M. Beck (Toronto, 1964). For an account of Howe's early career, *see*: J. M. Beck, "Joseph Howe: mild Tory to reforming assemblyman," *Dal. Rev.*, XLIV (1964–65), 44–56. For his part in the movement for responsible government, *see*: Martin, *Empire and commonwealth*. For his recruiting activities in the United States, *see*: J. B. Brebner, "Joseph Howe and the Crimean War enlistment controversy between Great Britain and the United States," *CHR*, XI (1930), 300–27. For his efforts to secure imperial office, *see*: J. M. Beck, "Joseph Howe: opportunist or empire-builder?" *CHR*, XLI (1960), 185–202. For his participation in the confederation issue, *see*: J. M. Beck, "Joseph Howe and confederation: myth and fact," *RSCT*, 4th ser., II (1964), sect.II, 137–50; and J. M. Beck, *Joseph Howe: anti-confederate* (CHA hist. booklet, 17, Ottawa, 1965). For conflicting views of various aspects of Howe's career *see*: *Joseph Howe: opportunist? man of vision? frustrated politician?*, ed. George Rawlyk (Issues in Canadian History, ed. Morris Zaslow, Toronto, 1967). J.M.B.]

HUMPHREYS, JAMES DODSLEY, singer and music teacher; b. in Mansfield, Nottinghamshire, Eng., c.1811, son of Francis Humphreys and Mary Hardwick Unwin; d. in Toronto, Ont., 23–24 Feb. 1877.

Little is known of James Dodsley Humphreys' early life. He claimed at one time that he was "formerly of the Royal Academy of Music," but there is no evidence of this claim. He first comes to our attention in 1835 when he sang at two "Musical Meetings" in Toronto along with the famous English songwriter, Henry Russell.

Humphreys was considered by many as Toronto's "favourite tenor." He made more concert appearances, over a longer period, than any other Toronto artist in the second third of the 19th century. He appears to have been able to satisfy all the demands on a singer's repertoire made by Toronto audiences. Most often he performed songs, ballads, or, as part of a vocal ensemble, glees, but he frequently included Italian opera and oratorio music by Handel and Haydn. He sang in the first act of Donizetti's "Lucrezia Borgia" in 1853, although in a bass part, and in "Judas Maccabeus" and the "Creation" in 1858.

Humphreys was associated with many Toronto musical societies as performer or executive. He was a conductor of the Toronto Choral Society of 1845, president of the Metropolitan Choral Society (1858–60) and conductor of the Societa Armonica (1861–62) and the St Cecilia Society (1864–65). In 1850 he was singing master *pro tem* at Upper Canada College; he remained on its staff until 1854 and may have taught singing at that school until his death. He was also singing master at ladies' schools, a private teacher, and in the 1840s leader of the amateur choir of St James' Cathedral.

In 1843 Humphreys had a number of compositions published in New York by J. F. Nunns including four waltzes and several ballads; one ballad, "When we two parted," he dedicated to Mary Jane Hagerman, his best known pupil. When production of sheet music in Toronto began a year or two later, after Abraham Nordheimer* and his brother Samuel* had opened their music house, it was mentioned on their first publication, J. P. Knight's "Beautiful Venice," that it was "sung with much applause by Mr. Humphreys." Of later date, only one composition, the song, "The junior warden's toast," has been discovered.

Humphreys' last known concert appearance was in 1873, nearly 40 years after his Toronto debut; "and within a year of his death, his fine tenor had still much of its wonted power." In 1876 a concert was held for his benefit in which leading Toronto musicians including Frederic Herbert Torrington* and Waugh Lauder* participated. He was called "so skilled a musician, so genial a gentleman, and so true a friend" and "not only a good teacher but perhaps the best performer in our midst."

Humphreys' widowed mother had married the Toronto widower Samuel Smith Ridout* in 1838; Humphreys himself married Ridout's daughter, Caroline Amelia, and they had several sons and a daughter.

HELMUT KALLMANN

The Canadian Music Library Association (Canadian Library Association, Ottawa) is compiling a list of J. D. Humphreys' publications.

Anglo-American Magazine (Toronto), II (1853), 334. *Belford's Monthly Magazine* (Toronto), I (1876), 711. *Correspondent and Advocate* (Toronto), 31 Dec. 1835. *Globe* (Toronto), 26 Feb. 1877. *Mail* (Toronto), 26 Feb. 1877, 21 Dec. 1878. *Mail and Empire* (Toronto), 7 Nov. 1896. *Toronto Patriot*, 14 Feb. 1844. *Rowsell's city of Toronto and county of York directory for 1850–1* . . ., ed. J. Armstrong (Toronto, 1850).

C. C. Taylor, *Toronto "called back" from 1886 to 1850* . . . (Toronto, 1886). Samuel Thompson, *Reminiscences of a Canadian pioneer for the last fifty years; an autobiography* (Toronto, 1884).

Chadwick, *Ontarian families*, I, 39–40. J. R. Robertson, *Landmarks of Canada, a guide to the J. Ross Robertson Historical Collection in the Public Reference Library, Toronto, Canada* (Toronto, 1917), 562. D. J. Sale, "Toronto's pre-confederation music societies, 1845–1867," unpublished MA thesis, University of Toronto, 1968. F. N. Walker, *Sketches of old Toronto* (Toronto, 1965).

HUNKAJUKA (Little Soldier, sometimes cited as **Little Chief**), chief of a nomadic band of Assiniboine Indians of the North-West Territories; killed at Cypress Hills (Saskatchewan), May 1873.

Virtually nothing is known of Little Soldier prior to the significant event in which he lost his life. The incident has an explanation in social problems in the North-West Territories when the area was acquired by Canada in 1870: horse stealing was rife among the Indians and the southwestern region was demoralized by American whiskey traders infiltrating from posts on the Missouri River. The episode began with a band of "wolfers," traders and hunters who followed the buffalo hunt and poisoned carcasses to kill the scavenger wolves whose furs they sought. A mixed party of Canadian and American "wolfers" had their horses stolen while en route to Fort Benton, Montana Territory, in early spring 1873. Organizing an expedition to recover them, they rode into Canadian territory, and arrived at the whiskey-trading outpost of the Fort Benton merchants, operated by Abel Farwell and Moses Solomon in the Cypress Hills. There they found Little Soldier's band, whom they mistakenly suspected of the thefts. Little Soldier attempted to appease the "wolfers" but drunkenness on both sides contributed to the violence which ensued on a Sunday in early May (probably 4 May). Little Soldier and between 15 and 35 of his followers were wantonly slain.

The Canadian government had already introduced legislation to provide for policing the territories, but news of this massacre hastened the organization of the North-West Mounted Police. Dispatched to the area in 1874, the subsequent persistence of the NWMP in bringing the "wolfers" to trial demonstrated their resolve to administer justice in the North-West Territories without racial distinction and won them the respect of the native people.

ALLAN R. TURNER

SAB, Dan (Ochankugahe) Kennedy, Cypress Hill's massacre, 1873; Dan Kennedy, Easchappie's version of the massacre; Saskatchewan Historical Society, 100.

Hunt

P. F. Sharp, "Massacre at Cypress Hills," *Saskatchewan History* (Saskatoon), VII (1954), 81–99. J. P. Turner, "Massacre in the Hills," *Royal Canadian Mounted Police Quarterly* [Ottawa], VIII (1940), 302–9.

HUNT, CHARLES, miller and contractor; b. 5 March 1820, at Motcombe, Dorsetshire, Eng., eldest child of John Hunt and Mary Golpin; d. 2 Oct. 1871, at New York, U.S.A.

Charles Hunt received only one year's formal education because of his father's early death in 1827. He worked for a miller at Stalbridge and a grocer at Cranborne before emigrating. In 1842 he arrived in Windsor, Canada West, where he was employed in the provisions and shipping business of J. and J. Dougall until 1845. He next farmed at St Thomas for two years, and then returned to Windsor to begin a business career which, even for that period, was remarkable for its diversity.

In Windsor, Hunt rented the dock property of James Dougall* and began a forwarding and lumber business, later expanding into contracting and land speculation sometimes in partnership with Dougall. In 1854–55 Hunt built the Great Western Railway depot, including a dock, freight house, and some bridges. Then in 1856, in partnership with William Knight, he went into shipbuilding, contracting with the railway for the *Union*, a 750-ton ferry and icebreaker, which ran between Windsor and Detroit from 1857 to 1874. In 1857 he rebuilt the steamer *Transit*. When Windsor was incorporated as a village in 1854 he was elected to the first council.

Hunt decided, however, that London was the future commercial centre of western Ontario. He moved there in 1856 though he always retained interests in Windsor. In 1853 he had purchased land on the Thames River from John Kinder Labatt for a flour mill and, in 1854, he had begun to construct there the City Mills, which were operated by his descendants until 1957. The mill had four stones capable of grinding 123 barrels of flour a day. Grain was purchased at various Great Lakes centres and flour was supplied to western Ontario, the Great Lakes cities, New York, and Great Britain. Hunt also developed operations in commissions, coopering, groceries, lumber, wood, and coal (being the first London dealer in this last commodity, in 1868). In addition, he built the Bank of British North America in 1856 and his own block in 1866. Finally, in 1867 he added a 70,000-bushel grain elevator to his operation. His business flourished in spite of setbacks occasioned by floods, his backing of Dougall who ran into financial difficulties, and litigation over street closure.

In London Hunt also played a leading role in the financial and commercial community. He was president of the Board of Trade in 1861–63 and 1869–70, chairman of the group that briefly operated the London City Oil Refining Company in 1866–67, and from 1864 first president of the City Gas Company (now part of the Union Gas Company). He was a director of the Bank of British North America and of the Great Western Railway (1864–69), and was elected a director of the Detroit and Milwaukee Railway (later the Detroit, New Haven, and Milwaukee Railway) in 1863.

An Anglican, he was a warden of St Paul's Cathedral in 1861–62 and 1864–65, and in 1861 agreed to support a missionary in the north of the diocese of Huron. He was well known for his charity in the city, providing flour for the poor and helping to arrange the shipment of cheap wood during a firewood shortage in 1867.

On 19 May 1845, at St Thomas, he married Emma Brewer, a native of England (*c.*1822 – 1909), and they had a large family. Two sons, Charles Brewer and John Inkerman Alexander, carried on the business. Charles Hunt died at New York City while travelling to the West Indies for his health. He "was one of the best known men in Western Ontario; and by his energy and enterprise did much to stimulate a development of its resources."

FREDERICK H. ARMSTRONG

St Mary's Church (Motcombe, Dorsetshire, Eng.), Registers. [Charles Hunt], "Charles Hunt, 1820–1871," ed. G. W. H. Bartram, *Centennial review, 1967* (London and Middlesex Hist. Soc. pub., XVI, London, Ont., [1967]), 55–85. *London Free Press*, 6 Oct. 1871, 15 March 1917. "London: its manufactures and general progress," *Western Ontario History Nuggets* (London), no.13 (1947), 7. *City of London and county of Middlesex general directory for 1868–9 . . .*, ed. James Sutherland (Toronto, 1868), 277. [Archie Bremner], *City of London, Ontario, Canada; the pioneer period and the London of today* (2nd ed., London, Ont., 1900), 68, 143. *History of the county of Middlesex*, 251, 362–63, 369, 866–67. F. J. Holton et al., "History of the Windsor and Detroit ferries," *Ont. Hist.*, XVI (1918), 40–51.

HURLBURT, THOMAS, Methodist missionary, linguist and philologist; b. 3 March 1808, in the township of Augusta, Upper Canada, the fourth son of 16 children of Heman Hurlburt and Hannah Mosier; m. 1832, Betsy Almira, eldest daughter of the Reverend Ezra Adams; d. 14 April 1873, at Little Current, Ont.

Heman Hurlburt was a prosperous farmer and gave each of his children a good education; of his 11 sons, five became Methodist ministers. It is not known where Thomas received his formal education, and he does not appear to have attended university. However, although his 45-year career as a missionary, first of the Methodist Episcopal Church, then of the Wesleyan Methodist Church, was spent primarily in remote areas, he showed a thorough knowledge of many of the works of major scientists, philologists, and theologians, and produced some scholarly studies in geology and philology.

Hurlburt began teaching Indians at Muncey, Middlesex County, under Methodist auspices in 1828, and the next year was put in charge of a mission. In 1834 he was sent to the Indian village of Saugeen on Lake Huron, and in 1835 he was ordained. Moving to the St Clair mission in 1837, he came under the superintendency of James Evans* whom he assisted in the development of his recently invented orthography of the Ojibwa language. He continued to work closely with Evans in 1838 when they were sent to the outposts of the Lake Superior mission (later called Pic River) by the Methodist Missionary Society. Hurlburt remained at Pic River until 1843; in 1844, for the sake of his wife's health, he was given leave to work under the Indian Mission Conference of the Methodist Episcopal Church of the United States in Missouri and neighbouring regions in the Mississippi valley. He returned to Canada in 1851 and served in the Indian villages at Alderville and Rice Lake until 1854 when he was appointed chairman of the Hudson's Bay District. He travelled to his new post at Norway House accompanied by John RYERSON, who was on a tour of inspection of the Methodist missions in the northwest.

Hurlburt remained at Norway House until 1857 when he was sent to Garden River and, in 1858, to the St Clair mission. He laboured mainly at this post and on Manitoulin Island until his death on 14 April 1873, which resulted from injuries caused when he fell on the ice while building a boat for a missionary journey. Except for five years spent in pastorates among whites, he had served in almost all the Methodist Indian missions in Canada, and, for seven years, in missions in the United States.

Hurlburt's aim was to Christianize and civilize the Indians. Only their Christianization, he argued, could bring about their civilization, and the primary needs were "the Scriptures in the vernacular, and . . . a native agency, with day schools and preaching all in the language of the people." Hurlburt encouraged the training of Indian teachers and ministers; he made translations of scripture, catechisms, and hymns into Cree and Ojibwa and printed them. While stationed at the St Clair mission, he began to publish, in 1861,

Petaubun, Peep of Day (Sarnia), a monthly newspaper in Ojibwa and English. His mastery of several Indian dialects, won by an expert knowledge of the functions of the organs of speech and of Indian phonetics, was an outstanding achievement. He was the only Methodist missionary of his time who could preach to Indians without an interpreter.

In the 1850s, the government began to expropriate lands in the Bruce Peninsula claimed by the Indians, with a view to settlement by whites. Hurlburt did not oppose expropriation but did object to the unjust and unnegotiable compensation given the Indians and their relegation to a state of "perpetual minority." He decried the government's assumptions that the Indians were lazy and that they would soon be extinct and urged that the only good policy was to make the Indians "citizens in every respect."

Hurlburt's views went unheeded and, despite his work and that of his contemporaries, the churches and governments failed to conceive a viable way of life for the Indian in Canada.

ARTHUR G. REYNOLDS

Thomas Hurlburt was the author of *Evidences of the glories of the one divine intelligence as seen in his works* (Toronto, 1867); "A memoir on the inflections of the Chippewa tongue," in *Information respecting the history, condition, and prospects of the Indian tribes of the United States . . .*, ed. H. R. Schoolcraft (6v., Philadelphia, 1851–57), IV, 385–96; and "Review of Sir Charles Lyell on *The antiquity of man*," *Methodist Review* (New York), XLVII (1965), 559–82. His writings and translations in Cree and Ojibwa, as well as other writings attributed to him, have not been located.

UCA, John Maclean collection, material gathered for a biography of Thomas Hurlburt. *Christian Guardian* (Toronto), 1838–73. Carroll, *Case and his cotemporaries*, III, IV, V. John Maclean, *Vanguards of Canada* (Toronto, 1918), 66–83. Erastus Hurlburt, "Thomas Hurlburt, Indian missionary," *Methodist Magazine* (Toronto, Halifax), XXXIV (1891), 52–59

HURTEAU, ISIDORE, notary, company director, and mayor of Longueuil; b. 11 July 1815 at Contrecœur, Lower Canada, son of Gabriel Hurteau and Louise Duhamel; d. 16 Dec. 1879 at Longueuil, Que.

Isidore Hurteau completed his course of study at the age of 18. He received legal training from a practitioner whose name we do not know, and on 24 Dec. 1838 obtained a commission as notary. At this time, when the province was under martial law, he took up residence at Longueuil, where on 1 Feb. 1839 he signed his first act. He was to practise there for nearly 40 years, and in particular he was the notary and adviser of the Montenach

Hyman

family, which was closely related to Marie-Charles-Joseph Le Moyne de Longueuil, Baronne de Longueuil and seigneur of Belœil. The parish council of Saint-Antoine-de-Longueuil also called upon his services when it made over some land to the newly formed community of the Sisters of the Holy Names of Jesus and Mary.

In 1846, at Longueuil, Isidore Hurteau organized a brewery, which lasted only a short time. According to the *Gazette* (Montreal), "after the temperance lectures delivered by Father [Charles-Paschal-Télesphore Chiniquy*], Mr. Hurteau became convinced of the evils of the liquor traffic and preferred to lose the sum he had invested in the brewery and to destroy the business which he had inaugurated at so great an expense." In 1848 Isidore Hurteau became the first mayor of the municipality of the parish of Longueuil. During his period of office he obtained from the agent of the barony of Longueuil a grant of a piece of land for a public market. Thirty years later this site, "embellished with magnificent clumps of trees," received the name of Hurteau Place. Hurteau was elected mayor a second time in 1870, and held the same office once more from 1876 until his death, by which time Longueuil had become a town. In 1847 he was lieutenant and adjutant of the 4th Battalion of Chambly, in 1853 captain and major, and in 1862 he became lieutenant-colonel commanding the 3rd Battalion of militia in the Chambly division.

In 1865 Isidore Hurteau took part in instituting the Longueuil Shipping Company, which operated a ferry service between Longueuil and Montreal, and became its principal director. To his manifold activities he added that of co-owner and probably principal silent partner of the Montreal political daily, *La Minerve*. Precise details are not known but this development may have occurred around 1874–75, when Ludger Duvernay*'s son, Louis-Napoléon, ended his association with the paper on assuming other managerial responsibilities. Hurteau's son-in-law, Clément-Arthur Dansereau*, was at that time the senior editor. Hurteau was appointed arbitrator for the Canadian government in 1868, and held this important office for nearly ten years.

Isidore Hurteau passed away at Longueuil in December 1879, after long months of suffering. He was still mayor of his town, and was given an impressive burial. He was interred in the crypt of the church at Longueuil, the resting-place of so many members of its founding family, the Le Moynes de Longueuil. In February 1838, at Longueuil, Hurteau had married Françoise Lamarre, who survived him by 25 years. Of this marriage were born four girls, one of whom,

Cordélie, married Clément-Arthur Dansereau in 1866.

JEAN-JACQUES LEFEBVRE

"Les Grant de Longueuil," J.-J. Lefebvre, édit., APQ *Rapport, 1953–55*, 123–28. *La Minerve* (Montréal), 20 déc., 27 déc. 1879. *Dom. ann. reg., 1879*, 406. Alexandre Jodoin et J.-L. Vincent, *Histoire de Longueuil et de la famille de Longueuil* (Montréal, 1889), 221–650.

HYMAN, ELLIS WALTON, tanner and entrepreneur; b. Williamsport, Pennsylvania, in 1813, son of Jacob and Sarah Hyman; d. London, Ont., 12 April 1878.

Ellis Walton Hyman, the son of a builder of German descent, was trained as a tanner and currier, and emigrated to London, Upper Canada, in 1834. He became a British subject in 1850, "when political feeling ran high" following the movement in favour of annexation, along with Elijah Leonard*, the younger, and other Americans.

In 1835 Hyman established a tannery in partnership with David O. Marsh, and about 1838 they obtained the boot contract for the new British garrison at London. Marsh retired in 1845. Hyman's tannery was not reopened after a boiler explosion in 1873, but in 1867 he had built a second tannery which was later expanded. In 1874 he began a shoe factory in partnership with his son Charles Smith*, and in 1877 a pork-packing plant in London East (now in London) for the English export trade. He sometimes operated the firms in partnership and, at different times, had branches in Tillsonburg, in Centreville, Oxford County, and in Hamilton, where he and John McPherson operated a wholesale shoe business. In 1876 the total value of his London businesses was estimated at between $200,000 and $250,000; when he died there were 75 employees. The tannery remained in the family until 1947, and in operation until 1970.

A leading member of the small group of entrepreneurs under whose aegis London developed from an administrative centre into the economic metropolis of western Ontario, Hyman was an incorporator of the Board of Trade in 1857, a member of its council through most of the 1860s, and a founder of the Chamber of Commerce in 1875. He was instrumental in establishing the Huron and Erie Savings and Loan Society (now the Huron and Erie Mortgage Corporation), was its vice-president, 1864–67, president, 1867–71, and a director until 1876. He was also one of the incorporators of the London and Port Stanley Railway in 1853, of the City of London Oil Company in 1866, of the London, Huron and

Bruce Railway (of which he was treasurer in 1871–73), of the Bank of Hamilton (in which he was a provisional director in 1872), and of the London Life Insurance Company (in which he was a director from 1873 until his death). In a different field, he set up the first Music Hall in the town in 1866. A few years after his death it was averred that "everything he touched seemed to turn to gold"; except for his participation in the unsuccessful first Tecumseh Hotel syndicate in 1854, this claim would appear to hold true.

In politics Hyman was a Reformer, acting as organizer in London for Elijah Leonard in the 1862 election. Hyman himself was an alderman in 1853–54 and later was active in establishing a public water supply for London; he and Tory John Carling* were jointly elected first water commissioners in 1878. He attended St Paul's Anglican Cathedral and was an active freemason.

Hyman married, first, Frances L. Kingsley of New York, who died in 1848, and by whom he had one son. In 1850, he married Annie Maria Niles (1824–1901), daughter of William NILES; two of their sons succeeded Hyman in the businesses: Charles Smith, later federal minister of public works, and Jesse Willett. Ellis Hyman's mansion,

"Elliston," was later owned by Adam Beck* and has long been a London landmark.

FREDERICK H. ARMSTRONG

Middlesex County Registry Office (London, Ont.), Joint Stock Company register, Liber A (1851–66), 10–11. PAC, RG 31, A1, 1871, district 10, sub-district London, ward 1; RG 68, 1. *Bradstreet's reports of the Dominion of Canada, February 1, 1876* (New York, 1876), 246. *London Advertiser*, 17 Jan. 1878. *London Free Press*, 8 Feb., 5 March 1856; 13 April 1878; 28 July 1938; 22 Aug. 1947. *The Honourable Elijah Leonard, a memoir* (London, Ont., [1894]), 43.

Can. biog. dict., I, 673–74. *City of London and county of Middlesex general directory, for 1868–9 . . .* , ed. James Sutherland (Toronto, 1868), 283–84. *Dom. ann. reg.*, *1878*, 353–54. [Archie Bremner], *City of London, Ontario, Canada; the pioneer period and the London of today* (London, Ont., 1897), 84, 87, 90, 91; (2nd ed., London, Ont., 1900), 32, 34, 116. C. T. Campbell, *Pioneer days in London; some account of men and things in London before it became a city* (London, Ont., 1921), 6. *History of the county of Middlesex*, 362, 365, 374. J. E. Middleton and Fred Landon, *The province of Ontario: a history, 1615–1927* (5v., Toronto, [1927–28]), III, 18–20. Ross and Trigge, *History of the Canadian Bank of Commerce*, III, 67–68. "London, its manufactures and general progress," *Western Ontario History Nuggets* (London, Ont.), no.13 (1947), 13–14.

I

IFFLAND, ANTHONY VON (baptized **Antoine**), physician, surgeon, and epidemiologist; b. 3 March 1798 at Quebec, son of John (Johann) Iffland and Marie-Madeleine Bibeau, *dit* Portugal; d. 7 Dec. 1876 at Quebec.

Anthony Iffland's father was born in Germany in Hutten (county of Hanau, later integrated with Hesse-Cassel); he served with troops of Hesse-Hanau in America during the Revolutionary War, and settled in Quebec as a farmer and tavern-keeper. Anthony, though baptized in the Roman Catholic Church, opted for the Protestant religion of his father, and identified with the English-language community.

Soon after he started medical practice, Anthony added von (the German particle of nobility) to his name. Though he later also adopted the style of doctor of medicine, like most practitioners of his time he was licensed without a medical degree. He had apprenticed in surgery with the senior medical examiner for the district of Quebec, Dr James Fisher*, former chief surgeon at the garrison. Iffland completed his medical studies in England at the London Hospital, passed the examinations of the Royal College of Surgeons of England in

January 1818, and obtained his licence as physician and surgeon in Quebec in July. At that time, only five of 31 medical practitioners in the district of Quebec and 51 in the district of Montreal possessed the MD degree.

Iffland was secretary and lecturer in anatomy as well as general practitioner at the Quebec Dispensary, privately established toward the end of 1818 as a general medical centre and clinic for indigents and immigrants. His medical colleagues were Pierre-Jean de Sales Laterrière*, Charles-Norbert Perrault*, and Augustin Mercier*. When the dispensary failed in 1820 for lack of money, Iffland was unable to combine, as he had hoped, private practice with a clinic for the indigent sick. In 1821 he travelled on an arduous government assignment to vaccinate people for smallpox in the isolated, and therefore vulnerable, district of Gaspé.

In Quebec City Iffland had been harassed for his procurement of cadavers at a time before satisfactory legal provision of bodies for medical research, and he felt it impossible to continue his work in anatomy there. Also, with the closing of the dispensary he must have had serious financial problems. Consequently he spent many years in the garrison town of William Henry (Sorel), where there was only one other doctor, and the nearby parish of Saint-Michel-de-Yamaska. In 1836 he married Elizabeth Allen, daughter of a prominent merchant and landowner in William Henry, and sister of the town schoolmaster; they were to have three children. To supplement his income he served as commissioner of census for Richelieu County in 1831 and 1835, as well as preventive officer of customs from 1824 until 1832. Although from 1830 he continuously held a commission as justice of the peace, he appears not to have exercised the function.

Like many English Canadians, Iffland was an early supporter of the idea of the union of Upper and Lower Canada. But despite an effort, unsuccessful, to win election to the legislature for Gaspé in 1834, Iffland was not a political person. The campaign in Gaspé was widely cited in the press as an instance of corrupt electoral practice. Iffland and his electors arrived at the poll at the appointed day and hour only to discover, too late to intervene, that the venue had been changed, and they could not vote.

With recurrent epidemics of Asiatic cholera in Canada beginning in 1832, and later of typhus, Iffland became concerned with the care of the victims and generally with questions of public health when he moved back to Quebec. An important centre for sick travellers, who often brought epidemic diseases, was the Marine Hospital (later the Marine and Emigrant Hospital), where in the winter of 1836–37 Iffland became resident physician and resumed teaching. The hospital served as a focus for medical teaching and training until the incorporation in 1845 of the School of Medicine of Quebec [see Joseph PAINCHAUD]. This school was functioning in 1848 and was absorbed by the faculty of medicine of the Université Laval in 1852.

After a further stage as a country doctor at Saint-Michel-de-Yamaska, between 1838 and 1847, Iffland returned to Quebec to work closely with Dr James Douglas* for most of his subsequent career. First at the private hospital in Beauport set up by Douglas to care for typhus patients, he was then on the staff of the Lunatic Asylum that Douglas cofounded with Charles-Jacques Frémont* and Joseph Morrin* on government contract to provide modern progressive facilities for the insane. In 1852 Iffland moved to the Quarantine Station at Grosse Île (Montmagny County), about 33 miles downstream from Quebec to assist Douglas at the Quarantine Hospital. He succeeded him in the position of medical superintendent in 1860, until his own retirement to Quebec in 1867.

At his death he was the dean of physicians in the old capital.

He had been the secretary of various medical commissions, notably Dr Wolfred Nelson*'s commission on the state of hospitals and asylums held during 1848–49, and the committee to investigate the cholera epidemic of 1854. He became corresponding member of the Epidemiological Society of London in 1856, the year he served as vice-president of the College of Physicians and Surgeons of Lower Canada. He wrote minor articles on medical cases, the profession, and public health.

Although Iffland's long medical career was not in any sense outstanding, it is of interest because it spanned a period of considerable scientific and political change, and because of the variety of his preoccupations. As an epidemiologist he did not hesitate to risk his life in the care of cholera victims and of those suffering from the other contagious diseases that proliferated with increased immigration. Yet Iffland's early interests and talents were blunted for lack of consistent opportunities in his profession. Although his first love was anatomy, early in his career it proved impossible to continue research in that field openly. A devoted, though often disappointed practitioner, Iffland tended to resist a purely comfortable routine life. But, inevitably drawn to administrative tasks under financial pressure, he was overshadowed by more creative medical men who were his friends, and with whom he worked.

LEWIS HERTZMAN

Anthony von Iffland's writings include the following: "Apperçu d'un voyage dans le district de Gaspé pendant les mois de mai, juin, juillet et une partie d'août 1821, par le Docteur Von Iffland," *Revue d'histoire de la Gaspésie* (Gaspé), VII, no.1 (1969), 19–41; "The duties and responsibilities of physicians to insane asylums," *British American Journal of Medical and Physical Science* (Montreal), IV (1848–49), 154–57, 177–78; "Sheets from my portfolio," *British American Journal of Medical and Physical Science* (Montreal), IV (1848–49), 24–26, 109–11, 137–38.

PAC, MG 30, D62 (Audet papers), 16, pp.332–39. Canada, Province of, *Sessional papers*, XXI (1863), PT.5, no.66; XXV (1865), PT.1, no.14; XXVI (1866), PT.3, no.6. Canada, *Sessional papers*, I (1867–68), PT.8, no.40. *Quebec Mercury*, 27 Nov. 1834. Morgan, *Bibliotheca Canadensis*, 384. Abbott, *History of medicine*, 50, 54–55, 63. Ahern, *Notes pour l'histoire de la médecine*, 539–41. C.-M. Boissonnault, *Histoire de la faculté de médecine de Laval* (Québec, 1953). E. D. Worthington, *Reminiscences of student life and practice* (Sherbrooke, 1897).

INKSTER, JOHN (nicknamed Orkney Johnny), merchant, politician; b. 1799 in the Orkney

Islands, Scotland; d. 30 June 1874, at Kildonan, Man.

Nothing is known about the parentage or background of John Inkster. In 1819 he came to Rupert's Land as a stone mason in the service of the Hudson's Bay Company. On 20 Jan. 1826, in St John's parish, he married Mary Sinclair, daughter of Chief Factor William Sinclair. They had nine children, of whom the eldest, Colin*, was to become sheriff of Winnipeg. John Inkster did not serve out his contract with the HBC. In 1823 or 1824 he had joined an uncle, John Inkster, who had come to the country in 1797 and who owned land on both sides of Red River. John Inkster began farming on the west side of the river, but he was to win prosperity and respect as a freighter and one of the earliest independent merchants of the settlement. He dealt in a variety of goods ranging from pemmican to "plough irons," from shirts to shot and powder. Among his customers were numerous Red River worthies, other traders such as his brother-in-law James Sinclair*, missionaries, Indians, and tripmen. His dealings extended from Portage la Prairie to York Factory and St Paul (Minn.). Some produce came from local sources, such as wheat and potatoes; other goods were imported from Edinburgh, London, and Hamilton, Canada West. The HBC handled his overseas financial transactions and brought in a proportion of his supplies by the bay; others came via St Paul. After his death, his estate was evaluated at about $20,000.

In 1856 the settlers of Red River decided a steam grist mill was essential for a more reliable service than that given by the wind and water mills. Inkster, who already owned a water mill, became president of the Steam Mill Company, which brought components for a mill down-river by barge to be set up at Redwood (Kildonan Park) with a sawmill attachment. A fire destroyed the mill in 1860.

Inkster is said to have been the first teacher in the school organized in 1849 by the Scottish settlers in Kildonan. He attended St John's Cathedral and served as rector's warden. He served as magistrate for the Lower District from 1850 to 1858 and as petty judge with a salary of £5 a year. In 1863 he became auditor of public accounts and worked on committees dealing with the regulation of liquor imports and the marking out of public roads. He was concerned with such public matters as the provision and upkeep of bridges and postal services. A member of the Council of Assiniboia from 1857 to 1868, he attended 54 meetings. He was elected as one of the English-speaking members to a council convened by Louis Riel* in November 1869 but could not attend.

Of special interest is the imposing house he built, constructing the stone foundation himself in 1851. Work was interrupted by the flood of 1852; however, the nine-room, two-storey house, built of squared oak logs floated down from Baie Saint-Paul (Man.), was completed in 1853. A much smaller structure alongside served as a store and post office. Seven Oaks is today a museum.

IRENE M. SPRY

PAC, MG 19, E7 (John Inkster papers), account books, papers. PAM, John Inkster, correspondence, 1860–74; John Inkster, papers, 1862–73. Surrogate Court for the Eastern Judicial District (Winnipeg), will of John Inkster, 16 July 1874. *Begg's Red River journal* (Morton), 165, 357, 396. *Canadian North-West* (Oliver), I. J. W. Graham, *Winnipeg architecture; the Red River Settlement, 1831–1960* (Winnipeg, [1960]), 6. W. J. Healy, *Women of Red River; being a book written down from the recollections of women surviving from the Red River era* (Winnipeg, 1923), 46, 74, 86, 90–92, 95–96, 200. Martin Kavanagh, *The Assiniboine basin; a social study of the discovery, exploration and settlement of Manitoba* (Brandon, Man., 1966), 197.

IRVING, WILLIAM, master mariner and ship-owner; b. 10 March 1816 at Annan, Dumfrieshire, Scotland; d. 28 Aug. 1872 at New Westminster, B.C.

In William Irving's youth Annan was a ship-building centre and his father was a shipwright in one of the yards. He himself went to sea as a cabin boy in the locally built brig *Helen Douglas* in 1831. Later he served in ships on the New York run, and it is said that he had some steamboating experience in New Brunswick.

Attracted to the Pacific coast by the gold discoveries in California, Captain Irving and an associate bought the bark *Success* and arrived at San Francisco in May 1849. In August, Irving moved to Portland, Oregon, where he later acquired extensive properties; a suburb of the city is still known as Irvington. In 1851 he became part owner of the steamer *Eagle*, the first of several steamers operating on the Columbia and Willamette rivers in which he had an interest. The gold rush to the Fraser River lured him north and in 1859 he purchased a share in the British Columbia and Victoria Steam Navigation Company. This he soon increased to a controlling interest. The company was operating the *Governor Douglas*, the first steamer built in British Columbia, between Victoria and New Westminster, as well as the *Colonel Moody* and *Maria* up the Fraser from New Westminster to Yale and to Harrison Lake.

The years 1862–65, which saw the height of the Cariboo gold rush, were a period of intense and

Jackman

often unscrupulous competition on the Fraser. Rate wars were frequent; competitors who had been paid subsidies to take their steamers off the river often sold them, whereupon the new owners would put them back in service. Steamboat inspection was lax, and boiler explosions not infrequent. Irving himself had a narrow escape in April 1861, when an explosion demolished the *Fort Yale*, a rival of his own ships, on which he happened to be travelling.

Irving was not satisfied with the ships he had acquired and he sold all three in May 1862. He had decided to concentrate on the run between New Westminster and Yale and ordered a new vessel specially designed for the service. This was the sternwheeler *Reliance* of about 300 tons, launched at Victoria in October, which proved to be the most successful Fraser River steamer of her time. In spite of strenuous competition, she proved, under Irving's shrewd management, to be a consistent money-maker. In 1865 he built the 283-ton *Onward*, an improved version of the *Reliance* with more comfortable passenger accommodation, and she repeated the earlier ship's success. By 1866, however, the Cariboo mines were declining and traffic on the Fraser declined with them. Only one competitor of Irving's Pioneer Line had survived, and to cut costs the two companies agreed to operate their ships alternate years until trade improved.

Irving was by this time perhaps the most popular and prominent citizen of New Westminster. He served for several years on the city council and was its president in 1868. He had many business interests, including control of the Albion Iron Works in Victoria. A generous man, he would willingly carry free a passenger who was genuinely unable to pay his fare, but he was not one to be imposed upon. He was thus characterized by the Victoria *Colonist* at the time of his death: "An intrepid navigator, possessed of more than ordinary pluck and push, he had an open hand and a warm heart for the needy."

In 1851 Irving had married Elizabeth Jane Dixon, who was born in Indiana. They had four daughters and one son. The home Irving built in New Westminster in 1864 was purchased from his granddaughters by the city of New Westminster and is now Irving House Historic Centre.

For a dozen years William Irving was the leading figure in shipping on the Fraser River. Under his son, Captain John Irving*, the Pioneer Line united with the coastal shipping interests of the Hudson's Bay Company to form the Canadian Pacific Navigation Company which in 1901 became the British Columbia Coast Service of the Canadian Pacific Railway.

W. KAYE LAMB

Colonist (Victoria), 1859–72. M. A. [Irving] Cox, *Saga of a seafarer; the annals of Capt. William Irving* (New Westminster, B.C., 1966). *Lewis and Dryden's marine history of the Pacific northwest* (Wright). N. R. Hacking, "Steamboating on the Fraser in the 'sixties," *BCHQ*, X (1946), 1–41; "British Columbia steamboat days, 1870–1883. I: Fraser and Stikine River steamboats," *BCHQ*, XI (1947), 69–111.

J

JACKMAN, WILLIAM, sealing captain and sailing master; b. 20 May 1837 at Renews, Nfld., eldest child of Captain Thomas Jackman, a descendant of a native of the Isle of Wight who was shipwrecked on the southern shore of the Avalon Peninsula; m. Bridget Burbage by whom he had four children; d. 25 Feb. 1877 at St John's, Nfld.

William Jackman, like his celebrated brother "Viking Arthur" [Arthur Jackman*], entered the cod and seal fisheries as a boy with his father. He commanded sailing vessels on the Labrador and at the ice; between 1867 and 1876 he was in charge of Bowring Brothers' sealing steamers *Hawk* and *Eagle*. A man of immense energy and strength, Jackman was on 9 Oct. 1867 the hero of a striking sea rescue at Spotted Islands, Labrador. He had taken his vessel there for safety during fierce gales, and saw the fishing schooner *Sea Clipper*, with 27 persons aboard, run aground on a reef some 600 feet from the shore. With little more than two hours to effect a rescue, Captain Jackman swam through heavy seas to and from the vessel 11 times to carry 11 persons to safety on his back. Then, companions having fastened a rope around his waist, he made 16 more swims to bring the remaining men and women ashore. He was presented with the medal and diploma of the Royal Humane Society on 18 Dec. 1868.

His death at the age of 39 cut short a sealing career of great promise, and removed one who, as president of the Star of the Sea Society, had devoted exceptional energy to the improvement of the status of Roman Catholic fishermen and seamen.

C. W. ANDREWS and G. M. STORY

Newfoundlander (St John's), 29 Nov. 1867, 27 Feb. 1877. *Public Ledger* (St John's), 27 Feb. 1877. L. G. Chafe, *Chafe's sealing book; a history of the Newfoundland sealfishery from the earliest available records down to and including the voyage of 1923* . . . (3rd ed., St John's, 1923), 91–92. M. E. Condon, *The fisheries and resources of Newfoundland* . . . (St John's, 1925), 106–9, 113. J. R. Smallwood, "Stories out of our history," *The book of Newfoundland*, ed. J. R. Smallwood (4v., St John's, 1937–67), III, 457–58.

JACKSON, EDWARD, merchant, prominent Methodist layman, and philanthropist; b. 20 April 1799 at Redding, Conn.; d. 14 July 1872, at Hamilton, Ont.

Edward Jackson received his elementary schooling at Redding and was then apprenticed in the trade of tinsmith. After his marriage in 1826 to Lydia Ann Sanford of Redding he emigrated to Niagara, Upper Canada, moving shortly after to Ancaster, and, in 1830, to Hamilton. There he sold tinware and set up a tin factory which employed his nephew William Eli Sanford* and four other men, all of whom in time became partners in various branches of the business. Jackson held the controlling interest in these but preferred to remain anonymous. Thus, the Hamilton firm, under Dennis Moore*, was D. Moore and Company, and a foundry in London, Anderson, Sanford and Company. With industry and sound investment, Jackson eventually amassed a considerable fortune.

Jackson's parents were members of the Episcopal Church but his wife was a Methodist. He was converted to Methodism during revival services in 1832 and became a life-long class leader and Sunday school worker. Of his three children, only a daughter, Emmeline, survived infancy. She married her cousin, William Sanford, in 1856, but died 18 months later, only briefly survived by an infant daughter.

The effect of this double bereavement was to direct Edward Jackson's energies to religious and philanthropic works. He supported Methodist missions on the Pacific coast, was the main contributor to the founding of Wesleyan Female College in Hamilton, and served as president of the board of the college. He was also founder and principal supporter of Centenary Methodist Church, the corner-stone of which was laid by Mrs Jackson, 28 May 1866. He took an active part in the campaign to provide an endowment for Victoria College, Cobourg, and personally endowed the chair in theology in 1871. A year later, aged 72, he died at family prayer.

Edward Jackson was a man of handsome bearing and unimpeachable character, and was noted for his wit. He was highly respected as a public-spirited citizen, a successful businessman, and a sincere Christian.

H. P. GUNDY

A biography by Nathaniel Burwash in the *Canadian Methodist Magazine* (Toronto), III (1876), 7–10, 97–104, was later issued as *Memorials of the life of Edward and Lydia Ann Jackson* (Toronto, 1876). *Christian Guardian* (Toronto), 17, 24 July 1872. *Herald* (Hamilton), 11 Nov. 1910. W. H. Poole, *A sermon occasioned by the death of Edward Jackson, Esq., of Hamilton* (Toronto, 1872). *Can. biog. dict.*, I, 708–9. J. E. Middleton and Fred Landon, *The province of Ontario: a history, 1615–1927* (5v., Toronto, [1927–28]), III, 126. Mabel Burkholder, "Out of the storied past," *Spectator* (Hamilton), 8 Dec. 1956.

JARVIS, GEORGE STEPHEN BENJAMIN, soldier, judge, and politician; b. at Fredericton, N.B., 21 April 1797, son of Amelia Glover and Stephen Jarvis*, loyalist, of Danbury, Conn., who came to New Brunswick after the American Revolution and who in 1809 moved to York (Toronto), Upper Canada; d. at Cornwall, Ont., 15 April 1878.

George Stephen Jarvis attended schools at Fredericton and York but his education ended in 1812 when, at the age of 15, he enlisted as a "gentleman volunteer" in the 49th Regiment. He was commissioned an ensign in the 8th Regiment in 1813. His service during the War of 1812 was distinguished; he was present at most of the major engagements, including Queenston Heights (when he was mentioned in general orders), and Lundy's Lane, where he commanded a company at the age of 17.

After the war Jarvis remained in the regular forces as a lieutenant of the 104th Regiment (formerly the New Brunswick Fencible Infantry), but he returned to civilian life when the regiment was disbanded in 1817. He then studied law in the office of Jonas Jones* of Brockville, was admitted an attorney in 1820, and was called to the Upper Canada bar in 1823. Two years later, at age 28, he was appointed judge of the Ottawa District (Prescott, Russell, and part of Carleton counties), and for the rest of his life he held a series of appointments as a judge. He became judge of the Johnstown District (Leeds and Grenville) in 1837 and of the Eastern District in 1842; after the abolition of the districts in 1849 he continued as judge of the united counties of Stormont, Dundas, and Glengarry until his death. He was also appointed judge of the Surrogate Court of Stormont, Dundas, and Glengarry in 1858.

At various times he held a number of other public offices. He was collector of customs at Cornwall, 1836–41, and was twice, in 1835–36 and 1840, president of the board of police of Cornwall.

Jennings

In the general election of 1836 he was elected as a Conservative to the House of Assembly of Upper Canada for Cornwall Town (there not being any constitutional barriers preventing a judge from sitting in the assembly), but did not stand for re-election in 1841. During the period of the rebellions of 1837–38 he commanded a body of cavalry troops attached to the 1st Regiment of Stormont militia, as captain (1838) and major (1839). In 1850 he succeeded to the command of the regiment as lieutenant-colonel but he resigned in the same year, retaining his rank.

Jarvis married first Julia, daughter of Adiel SHERWOOD, sheriff of the Johnstown District, and second, Anna Maria Mountain, daughter of the Reverend Salter Jehoshaphat Mountain*, Church of England rector in Cornwall. There were ten children of the first marriage, and three of the second.

J. K. JOHNSON

PAC, RG 9, I, B5, 6; C4, 5; C6, 7; RG 68, 1. James Croil, *Dundas; or, a sketch of Canadian history, and more particularly of the county of Dundas, one of the earliest settled counties in Upper Canada* (Montreal, 1861). G.B., WO, *A list of the officers of the Army and of the Corps of Royal Marines*, 1815–17. Armstrong, *Handbook of Upper Canadian chronology.* Chadwick, *Ontarian families*, I, 126–33. *Dom. ann. reg.*, *1878.* L. H. Irving, *Officers of the British forces in Canada during the war of 1812–15* (Welland, Ont., 1908).

JENNINGS, JOHN, Presbyterian clergyman; b. near Glasgow, Scotland, 8 Oct. 1814, son of John Jennings, merchant of Glasgow; d. Toronto, Ont., 25 Feb. 1876.

John Jennings was raised by his maternal grandfather, the Reverend John Tindal (sometimes spelled Tindall), secession Presbyterian minister at Cupar, Fife, Scotland. He attended St Andrews University from 1828 to 1831 (receiving no degree), and the Theological Hall of the United Associate Synod. He was ordained by the secession presbytery of Cupar on 11 July 1838 to be a missionary to Canada. The next day he married Margaret Cumming of Cupar.

Jennings arrived in Canada in the fall of 1838, and during the winter of 1838 and 1839 he served as a missionary for the Missionary Presbytery of the Canadas, making extended tours into the area of lakes Simcoe and Huron, and organizing congregations in Vaughan and King townships. On 9 July 1839 he was inducted as minister of the United Associate Church in Toronto (later Bay St Church), where he remained until March 1874. Under his pastorate the congregation grew from seven members to 273, erecting in 1848 a large white-brick Gothic church costing £3,000.

Jennings took an active part in promoting the cause of education in Upper Canada. He was prominent in the agitation for the secularization of the clergy reserves, contributing many articles to the press on the subject, and drafting a petition sent to the British House of Commons 13 Feb. 1840 from the Canadian Synod of the United Associate Presbyterian Church calling for the secularization of the reserves for educational purposes. Again, in 1848, while moderator of the Synod of the United Presbyterian Church in Canada, he led in petitioning the government of Canada to devote the proceeds of the clergy reserves to educational purposes. A strong supporter of Robert Baldwin*'s university bill and of free public schools, and a firm believer in the complete separation of church and state, he opposed any division of the university endowment to provide state support for denominational schools or the establishment of a theological chair in the University of Toronto. He also took a prominent part in organizing the Toronto Society for the Instruction of the Deaf, and Dumb, and the Blind.

Jennings was a member of the Council of Public Instruction for Upper Canada (Ontario) from 1850 to 1875, serving on the standing committee on regulations and textbooks for many years, and working for the establishment of the Toronto Normal School and the Education Office in Toronto. He was also a member of the senate of the University of Toronto from 1851 to 1872, of the committee of the senate for Upper Canada College at various times during these years, and a trustee of the Toronto Grammar School. In the United Presbyterian Church, he took an interest in theological education, home and foreign missions, the union of the various Presbyterian bodies in Canada, and pensions for the widows and children of deceased ministers. He was editor in Toronto of the *Canadian Presbyterian Magazine* from 1851 to 1854. In the Canada Presbyterian Church formed in 1861, he served as a member of various standing committees, including those for the Kankakee Mission and the *Home and Foreign Record of the Canada Presbyterian Church* (Toronto), for both of which he was convener. He was a member of the senate of Knox College, and a lecturer there in 1867. He received an honorary Doctor of Divinity from New York University in 1857 and was the author of two books.

Jennings was described as a kindly, genial man, of strong physique, liberal in his views, and honest and wise in his judgement. He died in 1876 survived by his wife and five children.

C. GLENN LUCAS

John Jennings was the author of *Reason or revelation; or the religion, philosophy, and civilisation of the ancient heathen, contrasted with Christianity and legitimate consequences* (Toronto, 1852) and *Say no* (Toronto, 1865). His papers are in the possession of Douglas Jennings, Toronto.

General Record Office (Edinburgh), Minutes of the Synod of the United Associate Synod of Scotland, 1837–44. UCA, Minutes of the Missionary Synod of Canada, 1843–47; Minutes of the Synod of the United Presbyterian Church in Canada, 1848–61; Minutes of the Synod of the Canada Presbyterian Church, 1861–69; Minutes of the general assembly of the Canada Presbyterian Church, 1870–75; Minutes of the general assembly of the Presbyterian Church in Canada, 1875–80; Minutes of the Presbytery of Toronto, Presbyterian Church in Canada, 1875–80. *Banner* (Toronto), 1843–48. *Canadian Presbyterian Magazine* (Toronto), 1851–54. *Globe* (Toronto), 1876. *Presbyterian Record for the Dominion of Canada* (Montreal, Toronto), 1876. *United Presbyterian Magazine* (Edinburgh), 1847–77. *United Secession Magazine* (Edinburgh), 1833–45. *Cyclopædia of Can. biog.* (Rose, 1888), 462–63. Morgan, *Bibliotheca Canadensis*, 204–5. *Documentary history of education in Upper Canada* (Hodgins), V, 18; VI, 111; X, 277; XI, 206; XVII, 171.

JOB, THOMAS BULLEY, businessman and politician; b. near Teignmouth, Devon, in 1806, fifth son of John Job and Sarah Bulley; d. in Liverpool, England, 30 Nov. 1878.

Thomas Job's father was one of the founding partners of the firm of Bulley and Job, which had branches in St John's, Newfoundland, and Teignmouth, England; by 1809 the centre of the English branch had moved to Liverpool though strong links were maintained with Devon. The Bulley connection with the firm had ceased by 1839, and in that year four of John Job's sons formed a co-partnership – Samuel and John Jr in Liverpool, and Robert* and Thomas Bulley in St John's. The Liverpool house carried on a considerable timber trade with Canada, but the St John's branch – assuming its present name of Job Brothers and Company – continued its exclusive concern with Newfoundland. Among the largest in 19th-century Newfoundland, the firm supplied extensively for the cod and seal fisheries, and carried on a large export trade with Europe and Brazil.

Both Robert and Thomas Job were active in public affairs. Prominent members of the local merchant society, they were associated with the campaign to gain a constitution for the island – a concession made in 1832. The association is symbolized by Thomas' marriage on 8 July 1834 to Jessy Carson, daughter of one of the most radical agitators for this reform, Dr William Carson*. Job himself was not a radical, however, and from 1846 until his defeat in 1852 he sat in the assembly with the Conservative minority as a member for Trinity Bay, a constituency along the southern shore where his firm did a considerable business. Always a quiet Conservative never associated with the famous political battles of the period, Job was appointed to the council in 1852 and resigned on the introduction of responsible government in 1855.

In 1859 his only son Thomas Raffles Job joined the partnership and, together with the more experienced Stephen Rendell as co-partner and manager, took over the St John's business when his father with the rest of the family (four daughters) moved to Liverpool. Thomas Raffles joined his father in 1866, and it was another branch of the family which returned to run the Newfoundland business later in the century. Thomas Bulley Job became prominent in Liverpool as a town councillor from 1858 to 1864, and as a borough justice and member of the Dock Board. There, as in St John's, however, the activity of the firm was of more lasting importance than its senior partner.

J. K. HILLER

Newfoundlander (St John's), 12 Dec. 1878. Gunn, *Political history of Nfld.*, 129, 198. R. B. Job, *John Job's family: a story of his ancestors and successors and their business connections with Newfoundland and Liverpool, 1730 to 1953* ([2nd ed.,] St John's, [1954]), 33–47, 117, 119.

JOHNSON, WILLIAM ARTHUR, Church of England clergyman, biologist, and educator; b. 10 March 1816 at or near Bombay, India, the second son of Lieutenant-Colonel John Johnson and Dederika Memlingh; m. in the parish of Dunn, Upper Canada, 13 Dec. 1836, Laura Eliza Jukes; d. in Yorkville (now in Toronto, Ont.), 29 Dec. 1880.

Colonel Johnson retired from active service in 1819. His son William Arthur was educated at Addiscombe Military College at Croydon, near London, England. He was destined for the army, but abandoned that career, and in 1835 migrated with his father to Upper Canada to a settlement being formed near Port Maitland.

In his early twenties William Johnson became aware of the pressing need for Church of England clergymen in the colony. In 1848, when he was living in Yorkville, he was interviewed by Bishop John Strachan*. Strachan considered him " a very fine lad," and encouraged him to attend the Diocesan Theological Institution at Cobourg where A. N. BETHUNE was principal. Johnson did so, was ordained deacon on 26 Oct. 1851, and admitted to the priesthood on 10 Oct. 1852.

Meanwhile, in 1848, Dr James BOVELL had

Johnston

arrived in Toronto from the West Indies to practise medicine. Possibly he and Johnson had previously known each other for on 3 Sept. 1848 Bovell stood godfather to Johnson's second son, Arthur Jukes, and his third son was named James Bovell. Both men were skilled in the use of the microscope, and had similar interests, including religion; their close friendship continued for the rest of their lives.

After his ordination as deacon Johnson was appointed officiating minister at Scarborough. The next year he was sent to Cobourg, and remained there until March 1855. Returning to Yorkville, he assisted the minister of St Paul's, John George Delhoste MacKenzie, and agreed to act as assistant minister for one year. His appointment as minister of St Paul's was discussed but a few members of the congregation threatened to leave if Johnson was retained. An appeal was made to Bishop Strachan, who recommended that Johnson withdraw and appointed him incumbent of Weston. Johnson's removal to the village of Weston might be considered a demotion, but it afforded him scope to develop the talents by which he is chiefly remembered: the founding in 1865 of a well-known Canadian residential school, Trinity College School; and the guiding of one of its pupils, William (later Sir William) Osler*, into the field of scientific research.

In the early 1860s Johnson, with three sons to educate, started a small school for boys in Weston, at his own expense. In 1864 he proposed that it be placed under the control of the University of Trinity College and be known as the Trinity College School. Trinity agreed, appointed a headmaster, Charles Howard Badgley, and left Johnson to be responsible for the finances. The school, opened in May 1865 with nine pupils, was modelled on an English public school: the main subjects were classics and mathematics, and prefects were appointed from among the senior boys. Johnson taught French, drawing, and painting, without remuneration. The most popular sport was cricket.

Johnson's connection with the school was brief, ending in 1868 when the school was moved to Port Hope. The number on the roll from 1865 to 1869 was 131. The medical director of the school was Bovell, and he and Johnson, usually accompanied by William Osler who was one of the prefects, spent parts of many weekends at Weston collecting and mounting specimens for microscopic study. Throughout his life, Osler acknowledged that a large part of his success was due to the influence and friendship of Bovell and Johnson.

Johnson was also a hard-working and devoted pastor, and won the respect and affection of the majority of his congregations. However, because of his ritualistic views and practices he incurred the hostility of a small but vocal and determined number. For his part Johnson was outspoken and as determined as his opponents; he appears to have enjoyed the controversies which were occasioned by what his bishop called "errors in judgment."

Both Johnson's parents were artists of some note, and his inheritance of their artistic ability may be seen from his paintings, sketches, and wood-carving. A cabinet, Johnson's handiwork, containing a large number of his slides, is on view in the Academy of Medicine in Toronto.

GEORGE W. SPRAGGE

PAO, Strachan letter books, 1844–49, 8316. Anglican Church of Canada, Toronto Diocesan Archives, W. A. Johnson file, W. A. Johnson to Bishop Arthur Sweatman, 6 June 1879. Trinity College Archives (Toronto), Corporation minutes, 1850–68, 40, 52, 83, 324, 338–39. *A narrative of certain circumstances which took place at St Paul's Church, Yorkville; to which are appended all the correspondence and papers, which came to hand during the unhappy discussion* (Toronto, 1856). University of Trinity College, Toronto, *Calendar*, 1865–68. *Canadian Churchman* (Toronto), 14 Oct. 1852. *Church* (Toronto), 30 Oct. 1851. Harvey Cushing, *The life of Sir William Osler* (2v., Oxford, 1925). F. K. Dalton, "The Reverend William Arthur Johnson, clergyman, artist, architect, scientist, teacher, 1816–1880," Can. Church Hist. Soc. *J.* (Toronto), VIII (1966), 2–15. C. E. Dolman, "The Reverend James Bovell, M.D., 1817–1880," in *Pioneers of Canadian science*, ed. G. F. G. Stanley (Royal Society of Canada "Studia Varia" series, IX, Toronto, 1966), 81–100. J. B. Elliot, "The Johnson cabinets in the Osler collection at the Academy of Medicine," and N. B. Gwyn, "The early life of Sir William Osler," in International Association of Medical Museums, *Bulletin IX*, and *Journal of Technical Methods* (Montreal, 1926), 465–69, 109–49. [A. J. Johnson], "T.C.S. history, reminiscences of Dr A. Jukes Johnson (1865)," *Trinity College School Record* (Port Hope, Ont.), XLIII (1940), 45–50.

JOHNSTON, GEORGE MOIR, surgeon; b. 10 Oct. 1817 in Pictou, N.S., son of Dr George Johnston and his wife Sarah Hatton; d. at his residence, Hillside, in Pictou, 17 Jan. 1877. He married Sarah Mortimer Smith, daughter of George Smith, merchant and MLA for Pictou County, 1836–40; they had four sons and one daughter.

George Moir Johnston attended the University of Aberdeen in Scotland, where his father had been educated, and was admitted to the Royal College of Surgeons of England on 1 June 1838. Returning to Pictou, he established a medical practice, which he continued for 38 years. On 15 April 1841 Dr Johnston was appointed health officer for Pictou;

he was also on the Board of Health for that town. Pictou was then one of the most important ports in the province and its health officials sometimes had to care for sick and poverty-stricken immigrants. From 1843 to 1865 he served as surgeon to the 1st Regiment of Pictou County militia, and then as surgeon to the Militia Artillery Brigade. In 1867 he was elected one of the officers of the Pictou County Rifle Association.

Dr Johnston was a founding member of the Medical Society of Nova Scotia in 1854 and served as first president of the Pictou County Medical Society in 1864. He was a delegate to the Dominion Medical Association at Montreal in September 1868; the next year he was a member of the council of the Medical Society of Nova Scotia.

He took a deep interest in the advancement of agriculture and horticulture, and was an enthusiastic patron of the arts and sciences in Pictou County. When the Pictou Literary and Scientific Society was formed in 1834 he was one of the founding members. He was prominent in the freemasons, having been an officeholder in the New Caledonia Lodge of Pictou, where he was associated with Simon Hugh Holmes* who became premier of Nova Scotia, James MacDonald*, later chief justice, and Edmund Mortimer McDonald, of the *Eastern Chronicle*.

PHYLLIS R. BLAKELEY

PANS, Pictou County, death certificates for the quarter ending 31 March 1877; "Distinguished Pictonians of New Caledonia Lodge," compiled by E. T. Bliss, 1960; Halifax Medical Society, Minutes, 1853–61; Nova Scotia Medical Society, Minutes, 1861–68; "Pictou County Cemeteries' list," compiled by H. C. Ritchie, 1951, 1956. *Colonial Standard* (Pictou, N.S.), 23 Jan. 1877.

JOHNSTON, JAMES WILLIAM (the name is sometimes written Johnstone, but he signed Johnston), lawyer, politician, and judge; b. 29 Aug. 1792 in Jamaica; d. 21 Nov. 1873 at Cheltenham, England.

In the mid-18th century, James W. Johnston's grandfather, Dr Lewis Johnston, emigrated from Scotland to Georgia, where he became treasurer and president of the council at Savannah. Dr Johnston and his sons fought for the crown during the Revolutionary War and, in defeat, fled the colony. William Martin Johnston and his bride, Elizabeth Lichtenstein, eventually settled in Jamaica, where their youngest son, James William, was born. At the age of ten, the boy went to Scotland for several years' education under carefully selected tutors. In 1808, shortly after his father's death, James rejoined his mother and other members of the family in Nova Scotia. He settled at Annapolis Royal with his sister, Elizabeth, and her husband, Thomas Ritchie, a member of the provincial assembly. Ritchie assumed the role of James' guardian, placed him in his law office as a clerk, and enrolled him under his command in the local militia during the War of 1812. When he reached his maturity in 1813, James gained admission to the Nova Scotia bar and began practising law in Kentville.

Shortly after the restoration of peace in 1815, Mrs Johnston, who wished apparently to regain in Nova Scotia the prominence which the family had had in Georgia, brought James to live with her at Birch Cove on the outskirts of Halifax. James entered into a law partnership with Simon Bradstreet Robie*, then provincial secretary and speaker of the House of Assembly. Johnston was an imposing figure – over six feet tall, thin, with a Grecian nose, black hair and eyes, a large mouth, a well-defined chin, and skin which showed "a tint of the tropics." In 1821 he married Amelia Elizabeth Almon, daughter of an influential Halifax doctor.

At this time young Johnston appeared quick-tempered, proud and rash. Soon after arriving in Halifax he reacted to certain courtroom remarks of Charles Rufus Fairbanks* by challenging the man to a duel and then shooting him in the foot, allegedly to end his rival's dancing career. Johnston's letters from these years, however, indicate that he was experiencing deep intellectual and emotional turmoil. After a brief enthusiasm for Enlightenment rationalism, he moved increasingly towards a strong religious faith, perhaps influenced by his mother. Contacts with a group of evangelicals active in the Anglican community of Halifax were equally stimulating. Johnston began meeting on Sunday afternoons with other young members of the social élite for prayers, scripture reading, and hymn singing. He joined the Poor Man's Friend Society to work as a "visitor" among the destitute of Halifax.

In 1824 a crisis erupted in St Paul's, Halifax's Anglican cathedral, when Bishop John Inglis* blocked efforts to place the evangelically minded John Thomas Twining* in the recently vacated rectorship. Johnston was swept into the centre of the controversy when the parishioners of St Paul's called upon him to plead their case against the bishop in the Court of Chancery. The court upheld the bishop, but could not prevent a mass defection from St Paul's. Most of the dissidents withdrew to St George's Anglican church, but a small minority, including Johnston, set out in search of a new allegiance. They tried to establish a proprietary chapel, independent of the bishop,

Johnston

with Twining as their pastor, but Twining refused to sanction this defiance of ecclesiastical authority and left his erstwhile disciples to drift uncomfortably among Halifax's dissenting congregations. Their isolation ended in 1827 when Edmund A. Crawley*, who had studied law under Johnston, returned from Massachusetts with two leading Baptist clerics from Newton Theological Seminary. These men impressed Johnston and the others so favourably that they agreed to establish a Baptist church on Granville Street and appointed one of the men from Boston, Alexis Caswell, their first pastor.

The Granville Street converts quickly emerged as leaders among the Baptists. They provided recruits for the ministry, founded a newspaper, the *Christian Messenger*, and launched a drive to improve educational standards throughout the Baptist community. J. W. Johnston helped found an education society in 1828, and assisted in the management of the academy which was built that same year in the Annapolis valley. In 1841 he was instrumental in helping secure a charter for Queen's (Acadia) College at Wolfville, and sat on the new institution's board of governors.

Meanwhile, Johnston's career was steadily advancing. He was closely tied to Halifax's expanding business community, and belonged to a number of commercial societies. In 1832 he joined several of the capital's leading merchants in forming the Bank of Nova Scotia to break the monopoly of the Halifax Banking Company. In 1834 Johnston secured the appointment of provincial solicitor general, and in the late 1830s he began building, on the Dartmouth side of Halifax harbour, an estate, Mount Amelia, named in memory of his recently deceased wife.

At this point Johnston's career began to be influenced by the provincial reform movement, which, under Joseph HOWE's leadership, was starting to undermine the oligarchic power structure. In 1837 the British government, in response to the assembly's demands for change, dissolved the Council of Twelve and created separate Executive and Legislative councils. Because of his qualifications as a skilled administrator, a confidant of the business community, and a champion of the province's leading dissenting sect, Johnston was named to both councils. In the Legislative Council he occasionally supported the forces of change in the province, as when he urged that dissenters receive an equitable share of school lands which had been set aside for the Church of England. From time to time Johnston proposed other limited changes, always in the name of greater administrative efficiency. Only once did he decisively break from his normal

pragmatic approach. He was a member of the Nova Scotia delegation which visited Lord Durham (John George Lambton*) in Quebec during the autumn of 1838. Johnston returned to Nova Scotia an advocate of Durham's plan for the legislative union of British North America, which he persistently urged against the almost universal hostility of his colleagues.

Johnston's reservations about Joseph Howe's programme for reform remained private until 1840 when three years of agitation culminated in the assembly's demand for the recall of the governor, Colin Campbell*. Johnston's sense of duty drove him to speak out against what he considered an unjustified attack on the representative of the crown. On 30 March 1840 he angrily lectured Howe on the folly of political extremism. Johnston opposed responsible government, maintaining that Nova Scotia, which lacked England's social balance, could not successfully adopt the mother country's constitutional practices. He predicted that responsible government would destroy all prospects for administrative excellence by ushering in an era of "party struggling against party" for nothing but naked power.

The speech revealed the extent to which Johnston held to the traditional values of the old regime. His views reflected those prevailing in English ruling circles, and he was one of the first consulted by Governor Poulett Thomson*, who came to Halifax in July 1840 in search of a settlement to the crisis. Thomson's discussions with various leaders resulted in a compromise. Demands for the immediate granting of responsible government were set aside, and Howe and Johnston agreed to work together in a coalition Executive Council which would attempt to find solutions for pressing popular grievances.

Johnston's decision to cooperate with Howe set him apart from Tory die-hards; the gap widened as the exigencies of trying to keep the coalition together forced him to modify his anti-democratic sentiments. During an 1842 constitutional debate Johnston, who had been appointed attorney general in April 1841, agreed that no executive could govern in defiance of the expressed wishes of an assembly majority. Although he still urged that institutions must be "moulded and tempered according to the circumstances of the country," Johnston now recognized the need to make concessions to public opinion. The attorney general's change of position drew a tart comment from the *Pictou Observer*: "Alas! we find him today a schismatic – tomorrow the advocate of Conservatism – and the third day, he shines forth as the brilliant champion of Responsible Government."

Johnston's conciliatory attitude failed to secure harmony between Reformers and Tories. Howe's administrative reforms aroused the ire of vested interests, and the two factions were soon struggling for ascendancy. By 1843 enmity and mistrust so permeated the Executive Council that it was virtually useless as a decision-making body. Amid this confusion Johnston strove to preserve a position of neutrality and keep the coalition alive. He held aloof from ultra-Tory agitation and consistently supported the government's programme of administrative reconstruction.

If Johnston felt any uneasiness about Howe's intentions he kept these doubts to himself and might never have broken his silence had not Howe, during the 1843 legislative session, supported William Annand*'s motion to withdraw provincial grants from sectarian colleges and devote public funds to the creation of one non-denominational university. This move placed Acadia College in jeopardy, thereby providing the Tory-leaning Baptist leaders with a cry which could rally their rank and file against all Howe's policies. During that same session Howe had announced his intention to push ahead toward full responsible government, including "the formation of a cabinet composed of heads of departments." Johnston interpreted this as a demand for party government, and in a memorandum to the governor he argued that implementation of Howe's policies would introduce rule by political factions and "lead to the oppressive and corrupting use of patronage." The attorney general insisted that the executive power must be shared among a variety of groups acting in a coalition if abuses were to be avoided.

Fears of political dislocation and the introduction of a "godless" system of higher education finally persuaded Johnston to abandon non-partisanship. He attended the June 1843 annual meeting of the Baptist Association in Yarmouth, and delivered a rousing indictment of Reformers and their educational policies. Endorsed by the clergy, Johnston and Edmund Crawley held "educational meetings" throughout central and western Nova Scotia to rally popular support. By early autumn Howe was defending his anti-sectarian policies, and provincial newspapers teemed with arguments on higher education. Seeing his executive advisers out stumping in opposition to one another, a dismayed Governor Falkland [Lucius Bentinck Cary*] ordered dissolution of the assembly on 26 Oct. 1843 in the hope that an election might clear the air. Johnston greeted the news by resigning from the Legislative Council and entering the active political arena as candidate for Annapolis County. Simultaneously, the attorney general and his religious allies

broadened the basis of their campaign by attacking "party government." This shift brought them the support of Halifax Tories and other traditional foes of Howe. These allies apparently thought that with Johnston leading a sizeable bloc of votes in the new assembly, the pace of change could be slowed or made more amenable to their interests.

Johnston's strategic objectives in the campaign appeared to be maintenance of the status quo. The impossibility of stabilizing the situation on the basis of the 1840 compromise quickly became apparent, however. In December 1843, as final election returns were coming in, Governor Falkland was impolitic enough to appoint Mather Byles ALMON, a Tory and Johnston's brother-in-law, to the Executive and Legislative councils. Howe, James Boyle Uniacke*, and James McNab denounced the appointment as an intolerable display of favouritism toward the attorney general, and resigned from the coalition.

When the house met in 1844, Johnston assumed leadership of the "rump" administration and, after a hectic three weeks' debate, staved off an opposition non-confidence motion by a two-vote margin. The assembly's decision was essentially negative, more a hesitant withholding of support from Howe than an enthusiastic endorsement of Johnston. Recognizing this, Johnston tried to strengthen his position by negotiating for restoration of an all-party coalition. The opposition refused to cooperate. For three years Johnston struggled to maintain his slim majority. Although weak and generally indecisive, his government did enact a compromise settlement which preserved the principle of state-supported sectarian colleges, brought in a series of minor administrative reforms, authorized surveys for a Halifax to Quebec railway, and passed a simultaneous voting act decreeing that future elections take place on the same day throughout the province. Perhaps more significantly, Johnston used this period to consolidate his leadership, transforming the loose coalition of his supporters into a disciplined party with considerable popular support. Each autumn found him on the hustings trying to rally electoral support behind the gradualist policies of his administration. After a last futile attempt to reactivate the all-party coalition in 1846, Johnston secured dissolution of the assembly from the new governor, Sir John Harvey*, and led the Conservatives into an election.

Through a long, bitter campaign Johnston stumped the province, uttering dire warnings that Howe had abandoned the coalition ideal for "a system pregnant with all the elements of anarchy." Political antagonisms became intertwined with religious feelings as Conservative spokesmen, including Johnston, raised the cry of "Catholic Ascendancy," alleging that the Liberal party's Irish allies were plotting Protestantism's destruction. Racial tensions further confused the issues, and just before the campaign closed Halifax witnessed a minor riot between Negro Conservatives and Irish Liberals. Voting took place on 5 Aug. 1847, and as returns trickled in it became apparent that the Liberals had won, although their margin of victory remained uncertain. Johnston refused to accept this result as a clear mandate for change and stayed in office in the hope of reconstructing the coalition. Early in 1848 the assembly decisively voted non-confidence in the administration; Johnston resigned immediately.

Following the government's defeat, Governor Harvey offered to help his ex-attorney general find a place in the imperial service, but the idea quickly died, probably because Johnston had no desire to leave the province. Despite loss of office, his professional skills and business connections in Halifax provided him with position and material comfort. In addition, he had just settled into Mount Amelia with his new wife, Louisa Pryor Wentworth. He had not, moreover, appeared to enjoy being a partisan politician; certainly his temperament was not suited to the role. Volatile pride and a rather humourless sense of propriety made him vulnerable to criticism. Within the assembly Johnston's supporters found him aloof and withdrawn; he went into company rarely and then almost exclusively among Halifax's élite. He did keep his assembly seat, however, perhaps because of his sense of mission, his ambition, and an irascible refusal to admit defeat.

Johnston's early efforts as opposition leader were devoted to a defence of the existing social order. For example, he opposed any extension of the franchise for fear that influence be given to an "inferior class," who were without property and irresponsible. Although consistently conservative in motivation, Johnston frequently advocated radical measures. He urged replacement of the appointed Legislative Council and appointed justices of the peace by an elected upper house and elected municipal councils. He ultimately emerged as an advocate of manhood suffrage. Yet this zeal for franchise reform resulted from his conclusion that the rate-paying franchise was unsatisfactory because it could be used by the executive to manipulate the electorate to its own advantage. He openly predicted that an elected upper house would curb "the surges of popular opinion." Thus Johnston's principal objective in urging these changes was to hobble the reform-dominated Executive Council by decentralizing authority and restoring what he described as a "just balance" of power among the various branches of government.

Not surprisingly, the electorate did not regard Johnston as a champion of reform. He did briefly stir popular enthusiasm in the mid-1850s, when, as present worthy patriarch of the temperance movement, he rallied a bipartisan group of assemblymen behind a prohibition measure. The bill failed in its last stages because of Johnston's unwillingness to include Annapolis valley cider in the ban.

Railways preoccupied most Nova Scotians through the 1850s. Johnston emerged as a voice of caution, criticizing many suggested construction schemes and refusing to support a line from Halifax to Quebec without imperial financial backing. Early in the decade he appeared to favour a form of commercial union with the United States as the surest guarantee of provincial economic expansion. If railways must be built, he urged a line from Halifax to Windsor as a first step towards linking Nova Scotia and the New England states in an all-steam transportation system. In 1850 Johnston attended the Portland railway conference and pledged his support to an overland rail line from Maine to Nova Scotia [see POOR].

Shortly after the return of the delegates from Portland, Howe announced that a shortage of private capital necessitated government construction of Nova Scotia's section. Johnston immediately attacked Howe's policy, predicting that public railways would be ruinously expensive and patronage-ridden. Sectional and monied interests rallied to the Conservatives during the 1851 election, weakening the Liberal majority and delaying the start of construction. Meanwhile, Johnston had opened negotiations with William Jackson, agent of an English engineering firm involved in several North American rail projects, including the Grand Trunk. In 1853 Johnston announced that British capital was ready to finance railways in Nova Scotia and the assembly moved to suspend Howe's policy and await a firm offer from Jackson's principals.

The opposition leader appeared to have triumphed, and in September 1853 he and Jackson attended a railway celebration in Saint John, N.B., where Johnston boasted that modern means of transportation would enrich the British North American colonies and ultimately "unite them by iron bands into one great confederation." The bubble of optimism burst within weeks, however, when Jackson withdrew his offers, arguing that disturbed conditions in Europe made it impossible to secure the necessary private capital. The assembly met in 1854 and Howe easily gained permission to proceed with his plan. The affair seriously undermined Conservative unity and morale and led the *Novascotian* to comment that Johnston had "been used – sucked dry – and then thrown aside like a dry orange."

The opposition leader was again roused by the 1854 reciprocity treaty which threw open Nova Scotia's coastal fisheries to the Americans. Johnston told the assembly that this was a virtually gratuitous surrender of provincial resources resulting from Nova Scotia's isolation and consequent weakness. He used the occasion to reiterate his belief that the province's destiny lay in a union of British North America which would have an "acknowledged national character" and the strength to resist absorption into the United States. Johnston also advocated union as a means of escaping the rancour and corruption which had plagued local politics since the coming of responsible government.

The province continued to grumble about the reciprocity treaty but no support materialized for Johnston's union proposals. People increasingly tended to discuss the opposition leader as "the old man malignant" clinging to impractical and lost causes "like grim death to a dead nigger." After a disastrous Conservative showing in the 1855 election, Johnston announced that the "infirmities of age" had persuaded him to "leave the trials and responsibilities of statesmanship in the hands of more youthful and vigorous men." It was widely assumed that the informal mantle of party leadership had passed to Charles Tupper*, the newly elected member from Cumberland.

Johnston's status remained uncertain through the succeeding months of intrigue as religious antagonisms aroused by the Crimean War eroded the strength of William Young*'s Liberal administration. In 1857 the bloc of Roman Catholic assemblymen shifted their allegiance over to the Conservatives, and Johnston, who had just completed a successful courtroom defence of the Irish navvies accused of murder in the Gourley Shanty religious riots, returned to take office as attorney general and head of the new government. His leadership seems to have been nominal: he failed to prevent wholesale political purges in the civil service, and appears to have largely surrendered control of patronage to Tupper. Nevertheless, Johnston played a major role in terminating the General Mining Company's coal monopoly in Nova Scotia. After journeying to England and negotiating a preliminary agreement with the company in 1857, he returned to pilot a settlement through the assembly. Suspicions that Johnston, as the company's ex-solicitor, might have betrayed provincial interests were unfounded: a Liberal, Adams G. Archibald*, had participated in the negotiations and fully concurred in the terms.

The year 1859 brought another fierce electoral contest from which the Liberals emerged as apparent victors. As in 1847, Johnston refused to resign, maintaining that several of the Liberals were legally disqualified from sitting in the assembly. His critics, probably with cause, saw this as a desperate attempt to stay in power until the aged Sir Brenton Halliburton* died and cleared the path for Johnston's promotion to chief justice. After months of squabbling the Conservatives were driven from office. William Young, who became premier, shared Johnston's ambitions for the bench and shortly succeeded Halliburton. With unconcealed fury Johnston proclaimed the moral bankruptcy of responsible government in Nova Scotia.

Three years later, in 1863, Charles Tupper engineered a campaign which virtually annihilated a demoralized Liberal party, and the Conservatives returned to office under Johnston's nominal leadership. The new government had been formed amidst a renewed interest in colonial union, especially a union of the Maritime provinces. Early in 1864 Johnston told the assembly, "I look at a union of the Lower Provinces as a step toward a larger one. I have never favoured a union of the provinces by way of federation, for it did not appear to tend to the great object we had in view. What we want is to produce a real unity – make the parts that are now separate a homogeneous whole – give them a oneness of existence and purpose." A few weeks later he published a letter reiterating his preference for a legislative union, but saying that he was prepared to accept federation as a temporary expedient.

In May 1864 Johnston retired to the bench. Tupper's intention to create a second chief-justiceship had been blocked by the Liberals in the Legislative Council with the result that Johnston accepted office as judge-in-equity, a position subordinate to William Young. This appointment prevented him from actively participating in the conferences leading to confederation, but in 1867 he made several grand-jury addresses appealing for the calm acceptance of membership in the new dominion. His partisanship was rewarded in 1873 when John A. Macdonald* proposed that Johnston succeed Howe as Nova Scotia's lieutenant governor. The old man, who was in France at the time, initially accepted the offer. In June 1873, however, he wrote Tupper from London saying that poor health prevented his assuming new official duties. Johnston died in England a few months later.

In many ways Johnston always remained a figure of the old regime, adhering to an 18th-century view of society as a hierarchical order based on property rights. At the same time, however, evangelical zeal, which made him an ardent advocate of mankind's spiritual redemption, enabled him to go beyond the oligarchy and become a spokesman for alienated dissent. When he entered politics in the 1840s he drew together disparate interests into an alliance which ultimately emerged as the Conservative party. Under Johnston's leadership, party policy hovered precariously between reaction and reform. He never fully committed the Conservatives to responsible government, being more concerned to spread his view that Nova Scotia's prospects depended on her entry into a larger economic and political entity. After a brief flirtation with New England, he returned, in the mid-1850s, to his conviction that British North American union offered the best avenue for escape from provincial isolation and political frustration. Johnston, as a survivor of the old regime, could well have seen confederation as a final triumph over the volatile local democracy which had so disrupted his public career.

D. A. SUTHERLAND

PANS, Pierce Stevens Hamilton diary, 1861–78; James W. Johnston letters; Johnstone family papers; Simon Bradstreet Robie papers; Sir Charles Tupper papers; White family papers; Halifax Poor Man's Friend Society, Proceedings, 1820–26. PRO, CO 217/175; CO 218/115, 218/116, 218/119, 218/125.

Nova Scotia, House of Assembly, Debates and proceedings, 1856–61, 1864; Journals and proceedings, 1836–64; Legislative Council, Journals of the proceedings, 1836–43. [Joseph Howe], Speeches and letters (Chisholm). [E. L. Johnston], Recollections of a Georgia loyalist, ed. A. W. Eaton (New York and London, 1901). J. W. Johnston Jr, The Crawley memorial address . . . June 4, 1889 (Halifax, 1889). Commercial Society, Rules and regulations (Halifax, 1822). Society for the Encouragement of Trade and Manufactures, Rules and regulations with a list of subscribers (Halifax, 1838). E. M. Saunders, A sketch of the origin and history of the Granville Street Baptist Church (Halifax, 1877). Acadian Recorder (Halifax), 1850–73. British Colonist (Halifax), 1849–73. Christian Messenger (Halifax), 1840–73. Halifax Morning Post, 1840–48. Novascotian (Halifax), 1836–73. Pictou Observer, 1842. Royal Gazette (Halifax), 1838. Times (Halifax), 1840–48. Directory of N.S. MLAs (Fergusson).

Beck, Government of N.S. W. A. Calnek, History of the county of Annapolis . . . , ed. and completed by A. W. Savary (Toronto, 1897), and A. W. Savary, Supplement to the history of the county of Annapolis . . . (Toronto, 1913). Harris, Church of Saint Paul. G. E. Levy, The Baptists of the Maritime provinces, 1753–1946 (Saint John, N.B., 1946). R. S. Longley, Acadia University, 1838–1938 (Wolfville, N.S., 1939). MacNutt, Atlantic provinces. Martin, Empire and commonwealth. Saunders, Three premiers of N.S. [Charles Tupper], The life and letters of the Rt. Hon. Sir Charles Tupper, ed. E. M. Saunders (2v., London, 1916).

J. M. Beck, "The Nova Scotian 'Disputed Election' of 1859 and its aftermath," CHR, XXXVI (1955), 293–315. John Doull, "Four attorney-generals," N.S. Hist. Soc. Coll., XXVII (1947), 1–16. D. C. Harvey, "The age of faith in Nova Scotia," RSCT, 3rd ser., XL (1946), sect.II, 1–20; "The intellectual awakening of Nova Scotia," Dal. Rev., XIII (1933–34), 1–22. G. W. Hill, "History of St. Paul's Church," N.S. Hist. Soc. Coll., III (1883), 13–70. W. R. Livingston, Responsible government in Nova Scotia: a study of the constitutional beginnings of the British Commonwealth (University of Iowa studies in the social sciences, ed. Louis Pelzer, IX, no.1, Iowa City, 1930). Peter Lynch, "Early reminiscences of Halifax – men who have passed from us," N.S. Hist. Soc. Coll., XVI (1912), 171–204. D. J. McDougall, "Lord John Russell and the Canadian crisis, 1837–1841," CHR, XXII (1941), 369–88. J. Y. Payzant, "James William Johnston, first premier of Nova Scotia under responsible government," N.S. Hist. Soc. Coll., XVI (1912), 61–92. M. C. Ritchie, "The beginnings of a Canadian family," N.S. Hist. Soc. Coll., XXIV (1938), 135–54. Benjamin Russell, "Reminiscences of the Nova Scotia judiciary," Dal. Rev., V (1925–26), 499–512. Norah Story, "The church and state 'party' in Nova Scotia, 1749–1851," N.S. Hist. Soc. Coll., XXVII (1947), 33–57.

JUCHEREAU DUCHESNAY, ELZÉAR-HENRI (also called **Henri-Elzéar**), lawyer, seigneur, legislative councillor, and senator; b. 19 July 1809 at Beauport, son of Antoine-Louis Juchereau* Duchesnay, seigneur of Beauport, and of Marie-Louise Fleury de La Gorgendière; d. 12 May 1871 at Sainte-Marie-de-la-Beauce and buried in the parish church.

After receiving an excellent education within his family and through lessons from skilful tutors, Elzéar-Henri Juchereau Duchesnay completed his legal training and was called to the bar on 10 Jan. 1832. He married for the first time on 24 July 1834, and went to live at Sainte-Marie-de-la-Beauce, where his wife, Julie Perrault, daughter of Jean-Baptiste-Olivier Perrault*, bore him three children. At her death, on 22 Aug. 1838, she bequeathed to him part of the Sainte-Marie seigneury. Having been appointed stipendiary magistrate for the district of Montreal on 22 July 1839, then police magistrate on 8 April 1840, Juchereau Duchesnay took up residence at Sainte-Marie-de-Monnoir. But in 1843 he returned to the practice of law at Quebec. On 17 June 1844, he married his first wife's cousin, Élisabeth-Suzanne, daughter of the Honourable Jean-Thomas Taschereau* and sister of Cardinal Elzéar-Alexandre Taschereau*, and this marriage brought him back to Sainte-Marie-de-la-Beauce. They had seven children who, like their descendants, made their mark in the society of the time; one son was Charles-Edmond*, who was superintendent of the Canadian Pacific Railway Company in British Columbia.

In 1846, having received military training during his youth, Juchereau Duchesnay became lieutenant-colonel of the Dorchester, the 4th militia battalion of his region. His sympathies were with the Conservative party, and on 29 Sept. 1856 he was elected legislative councillor for the Lauzon division; he remained a councillor until confederation, and on 23 Oct. 1867 was named to the Senate of the dominion.

He was a great philanthropist, and a promoter and benefactor of education. The *guerre des éteignoirs* [*see* MEILLEUR] raged in his parish, as it had elsewhere since 1846, and the local scuool commission broke up, leaving education in utter neglect. On 28 Aug. 1849 Juchereau Duchesnay addressed to Lord Elgin [Bruce*] a petition signed by 42 notables requesting a new school commission for the village. On 24 September the governor replied favourably. The promoter of the commission, having become its president, assumed the thankless task of reviving the schools; he undertook all the correspondence with the superintendent of education, and personally drafted the contracts of appointment with the schoolmistresses. Louis PROULX, who became priest of the parish in 1851, gave him strong support. The two "friends of education" succeeded in putting 15 schools into operation again, and the report of

the superintendent for 1855 praised their tireless zeal. In August 1856 Juchereau Duchesnay handed over his responsibilities to his colleague.

Juchereau Duchesnay was also interested in agriculture. At the time the agricultural society of the county was revived, on 23 Feb. 1847, he became president. *Le Canadien* on 3 Feb. 1864 reported that at an annual meeting he was re-elected. It seems that in the interval he had continued to be president, and that in this way he championed the cause of agriculture in the county for at least 18 years; he was a farmer himself, and as a philanthropist took an interest in the bettering of the occupation of farming.

Juchereau Duchesnay was also mayor of Sainte-Marie-de-la-Beauce from 1868 to 1870. Finally, at his death he was still lieutenant-colonel of the reserve militia, division of La Beauce. At his funeral four farmers carried his coffin.

HONORIUS PROVOST

Archives de la Fabrique Sainte-Marie (Beauce, Qué.), Papiers des écoles. ANQ, QBC, Instruction publique, 28, 29, 35, 36, 37, 41, 42, 43, 50, 51, 55, 62, 64. Canada, Province of, Legislative Assembly, *Journals*, 1856, app.16, "Report of the superintendent of education for Lower Canada for 1855." *Le Canadien* (Québec), 3 févr. 1864. *La Gazette des familles acadiennes et canadiennes* (Québec), 15 juin 1871. Honorius Provost, *Sainte-Marie de la Nouvelle-Beauce; histoire religieuse* (Québec, 1967). P.-G. Roy, *La famille Juchereau Duchesnay* (Lévis, 1903); *La famille Taschereau* (Lévis, 1901).

K

KANE, PAUL (his name is spelled Kean on his baptismal certificate), artist; b. 3 Sept. 1810, probably at Mallow, County Cork, Ireland; d. 20 Feb. 1871 at Toronto, Ont.

Paul Kane was the fifth of eight children born to Michael Kane and Frances Loach. Michael Kane was a native of Preston, Lancashire, England, and served in Captain G. W. Dixon's troop of the Royal Horse Artillery from 1793 to 1801, when he was discharged with the rank of corporal. He had evidently been stationed in Ireland, where he married prior to his discharge. In 1805 he was living in Fermoy, County Cork, but some of his children were born in Mallow. It was repeatedly asserted by Paul Kane and his friends that he was a native of Toronto, but there can be no doubt that he was born in Ireland. About 1819 he immigrated with his parents to York (Toronto), where his father became a wine and spirits merchant.

Paul Kane is supposed to have been a pupil at the Home District grammar school at York though evidence is lacking. Thomas Drury (Drewery), a local painter and the art teacher at Upper Canada College, gave him painting lessons about 1830. When Kane decided to become a professional painter he followed a common practice among North American artists and worked briefly as a sign painter at York. Later he was a decorative painter of furniture in Wilson S. Conger's furniture factory, also at York.

In 1833 he met James Bowman, an American artist then at York, who persuaded him that study in Italy was necessary for an artist aspiring to be competent and professional. However, Kane did not go overseas immediately. He lived in Cobourg from 1834 to 1836, working as a decorative painter in F. S. Clench's furniture factory and painting portraits. His style in these portraits varied

Kane

greatly. Some, like those of Mrs F. S. Clench and Mrs William Weller (Mercy Willcox), are primitive in approach but have a direct appeal and a warm colouring that make them attractive.

In 1836 Kane went to Detroit, where Bowman was then living; they had intended to go to Italy with Samuel Bell Waugh, an American portraitist who had worked briefly in Toronto. Bowman, however, had married recently, and the trip was again postponed. Instead, Kane remained in the United States and painted portraits for the next five years in Detroit, St Louis, Mobile, New Orleans, and other cities of central United States. None of these works were signed and only one canvas, depicting a ship owner or master with a Mississippi River boat in the background, has been traced to this period.

Kane's passport documents his movements in the next two years. Leaving New Orleans by ship in June 1841, he arrived at Marseilles in September. A brief visit was made to Genoa where he saw his first gallery of old masters, and then he went to Rome for the winter. Along with many British and American art students in Rome he studied at the academies and copied paintings by Murillo, Andrea del Sarto, and Raphael. In the spring of 1842 he and a Scottish artist friend, Hope James Stewart, hiked to Naples. Several authors have stated that Kane went on to North Africa and the Near East but his passport does not bear out this claim. He remained with Stewart in northern Italy from May to September. In Florence Kane sketched the Donatello sculpture on Or San Michele and copied Raphael's "Pope Julius II" in the Palazzo degli Uffizi; in Venice he copied canvases in the Accademia delle Belle Arti. He went north that autumn, going by foot through the Great St Bernard Pass into Switzerland on his way to England. After spending about four days in Paris, he reached London in late October and stayed for the winter, living with an English artist, Stewart Watson.

While in London, Kane met the American artist George Catlin. Catlin was then exhibiting and also lecturing in northern England and at Egyptian Hall in Piccadilly, London, on his paintings of Indians from the American prairies and the foothills of the Rockies. In his book, *Letters and notes on the manners, customs and conditions of the North American Indians* (London and New York, 1841), published just before Kane's arrival in London, Catlin predicts the early disappearance of the North American Indian because of his contacts with Europeans. Thus, he argues, it is the artist's duty to record his features and customs for posterity, while this is still possible. Kane, obviously inspired by this argument, decided to do

in Canada what Catlin had done in the United States. He left London early in 1843, went first to Mobile, Alabama, where he had earlier been a popular artist, and set up a portrait-painting studio in April 1843. After working to repay money he had borrowed for his passage back from Europe, he returned to Toronto in late 1844 or early 1845.

Kane's own later writings record the next four years of his life until 1848. He left Toronto alone on 17 June 1845 with only his portfolio, sketching materials, and gun, intending to travel to the west coast. That summer he painted constantly in the Lake Huron and Lake Michigan region. In his account of the trip, Kane makes particular mention of his visits to the Saugeen Reserve on Lake Huron, to Sault Ste Marie, and to Fox River and Lake Winnebago, west of Lake Michigan. At Manitowaning on Manitoulin Island, he was present at an assembly of 2,000 natives from the whole area when the tribes received their annual presents. Later, at Mackinac Island, he attended an assembly where a payment for lands ceded to the United States government was made. Sketches were made among what Kane described as the Chippewas, Ojibwas, Ottawas, and Potawatomis, and among the Menominees.

A meeting with John Ballenden*, the Hudson's Bay Company chief trader àt Sault Ste Marie, changed Kane's immediate plan to continue west beyond the Lake Michigan area. The trader pointed out the difficulties such a trip involved and suggested that he first request assistance from Sir George Simpson*, the superintendent of the HBC in North America. Following this advice, Kane returned to Toronto that autumn and visited Simpson in Montreal. Kane received permission to travel with the company's fur brigades and was promised free lodging at company posts. That winter he remained in Toronto and painted canvases from the previous summer's sketches. The finest of this group are his "Encampment among the islands of Lake Huron" and "Sault Ste Marie."

Kane's second year of sketching began after he overtook the HBC spring fur-trade brigade at Fort William on 24 May 1846. He travelled westward with the fast moving canoes and sketched when they halted at portages. A brief stop at Fort Frances gave him the opportunity to meet Saulteux Indians. A series of sketches illustrating the annual Métis buffalo hunt and also Sioux was made during an excursion south from Upper Fort Garry. Continuing north with the brigade, he spent several weeks at Norway House as a guest of Donald Ross*. He then turned westward with the brigade to follow the Saskatchewan River past

Fort Carlton, where he sketched the Crees, to Fort Pitt. While riding overland from Fort Pitt to Fort Edmonton, he was accompanied by the Reverend Robert Terrill Rundle* and Chief Factor John Rowand*. His party crossed the mountains from Jasper House to the upper Columbia River, which they descended, stopping at Fort Colvile and at Walla Walla. On 8 Dec. 1846 they reached Fort Vancouver (now Vancouver, Washington), the principal HBC post west of the mountains, administered by Peter Skene Ogden* and James DOUGLAS.

Kane made Fort Vancouver his principal base, and from it he journeyed to Oregon City, visited the Clackama Indians, and sketched in the Willamette River valley. On 25 March he left Fort Vancouver to explore the lower Columbia area. He sketched the erupting Mount St Helens, the last active volcano in North America, and was fascinated by the canoe burials on the Cowlitz River and by the various head deformation practices of the Indians farther north.

Kane continued to Fort Victoria and arrived at a time of particular activity. Fort Vancouver was to be abandoned by the HBC when the Oregon country was transferred to the United States, and Fort Victoria was being enlarged to replace it. Here he sketched intensively, at the fort, along the Vancouver Island coastline, and on the mainland down to Puget Sound, among the Haidas and other west coast tribes. Returning to Fort Vancouver on 20 June 1847, he stayed only ten days before beginning the journey back to Toronto.

Along the way, Kane visited the Grand Coulee Lake region around Walla Walla and sketched among the Cayuse, Nez Percés, and other Plateau Indians. At Fort Colvile he was present at a Colville (Kane called them Chualpays) Indian scalp dance, and watched the Indians salmon fishing. The lateness of the season made crossing the mountains difficult and the small party of HBC employees accompanying Kane did not reach Fort Edmonton until December. This was Kane's headquarters until the following summer, providing him with the opportunity to sketch the Indians of the western plains and visit Rocky Mountain House. The Crees especially attracted him and he witnessed their medicine pipe-stem dance and other ceremonials. He left Fort Edmonton on 25 May travelling eastwards with the fall fur-trade brigade led by John Edward Harriott*. At Norway House he joined some British army officers also travelling to Sault Ste Marie. Here he boarded a steamship and reached Toronto in October 1848, after an absence of two and a half years.

Kane was but one of a group of painters who were discovering the emerging west, and several other artists visited the Columbia River during the 1840s. Henry James Warre*, a British army officer, sketched there and at Fort Victoria in 1845. John Mix Stanley, whom Kane had probably met at Detroit in 1836, did considerable work among the Columbia River Indians in 1847 and painted some subjects identical to those chosen by Kane; Kane missed meeting him by only a few days. Father Pierre-Jean DE SMET, a Jesuit, also sketched the Columbia Indians in 1845. Finally, in 1855 Gustavus Sohon worked among the Flatheads and other tribes east of Walla Walla, sketching some of the same individuals Kane had previously portrayed. Yet, although Kane is not the only artist to document the whole region artistically, he must be considered the most important because of the excellence of his work and the extensive and thorough treatment he gave his subject-matter.

Many of Kane's sketches are particularly important for the study of 19th-century Canada. His portrayal of the Métis buffalo hunt is detailed and his record of the HBC forts is of tremendous interest. Two of the Columbia River sketches are unique: that of the Whitman Mission, which was destroyed at the time of the massacre of 1847, and that of the church of Saint-Paul-de-Wallamette in the Willamette valley, the first brick building on the Pacific coast.

Ethnologists find a wealth of information in his portrayal of the life and customs of the native peoples. Of particular significance are sketches from Victoria of women spinning and weaving, and of Indian artifacts. Equally important are the sketches of fishing and of the scalp dance rituals on the upper Columbia, and of the rituals of the militarist society of the Indians of the plains. No other pictorial record of the early Canadian northwest even approaches the wealth or magnitude of that made by Kane.

Kane returned to the northwest in the spring of 1849, but only went as far as the Red River Settlement. On this occasion he guided Sir Edward Poore, a young officer, and two of his friends who were in search of adventure in the west. The trip was made almost entirely in American territory by way of the Mississippi River and Kane does not mention having done any sketching.

For the remainder of his life Kane was a painter in Toronto. He had made more than 700 sketches from 1845 to 1848, some carefully executed and others hasty pencil notes. They now became virtually the entire subject-matter for his canvases and he occasionally painted several versions of the same subject. He had already, in the winter of 1848, begun painting these canvases, including

Kane

14 destined for Sir George Simpson. The canvases, in oil, are stolid and dull compared to the brilliant and fresh water-colour and oil studies completed in the field. He was afraid, it would seem, to follow his own sketches literally; in them the colours are almost impressionistic. He later often substituted dull grey backgrounds for his portraits.

Kane has been criticized for the European characteristics found in these paintings. In some, for example, the clear Canadian skies of the sketches have been overlaid with European cloud formations. Other instances of this European influence may be simply the consequence of particular circumstances: trimmed greenswards may have resulted from the lack of detail in small spot sketches. However, it has been shown that a few compositions are actually based on European prototypes. Occasionally, the horses in his canvases have classical lines, modelled after Italian engravings. In his "Assiniboine hunting buffalo," Kane reinterpreted an Italian engraving of 1816 of two Romans hunting a bull. "The death of Big Snake" is inspired by a European romantic artist who painted like Théodore Géricault; it is an entirely imaginary work painted after Kane heard an incorrect report of the death of Big Snake [Omoxesisixany*]. The Indian actually died in 1858, several years after the execution of the painting. This painting was lithographed in Toronto under the supervision of the artist in the mid 1850s and is said to be the first coloured lithograph published in that city.

These "created" compositions are, however, exceptions to the rule. Most canvases were painted either from individual studies or from several studies which he combined onto a single canvas. His "Winter travelling in dog sleds" is based on a pencil sketch of the scene and on water colour studies of a sleigh, of two harnessed dogs, and of trees covered with snow.

Kane stressed that he strove for accuracy in recording his subject-matter but this assertion is only partly true for his canvases. His Indian portraits are often embellished with features such as hair ornaments and elaborate robes which do not appear in the field sketches but which produce a more exotic effect. Nor was any real attempt made to relate the artifacts reproduced on the canvas to the tribal designation of the sitter. The result is often confusing to the ethnologist.

Today's public will find many of Kane's field sketches his most attractive works. They were executed simply and precisely, their colours are fresh, and they make an immediate impact on the viewer. On the other hand, the canvases based on the sketches, which were intended for gallery display and on which Kane felt that his reputation would rest, lack the brilliance of the colour of the more intimate sketches; though many are impressive works, they are sometimes laboured, and often include too many embellishments.

Opportunities for the public exhibition of paintings in the Ontario of Kane's day were limited. His early canvases were shown at the exhibitions of the Society of Artists and Amateurs in York in 1834 and of the Toronto Society of Artists in 1847. A two-week exhibition of 240 sketches by Kane and of the Indian artifacts he had collected during his trips was held at the Toronto City Hall in November 1848, giving Canadian residents their first real opportunity to view the northwest. Newspaper publicity was extensive both on the subject-matter and on the value of the sketches to aspiring young artists for study purposes. Kane probably first met George William Allan*, a leading Canadian financier and politician who was to be his future patron, at this exhibition. The next year the governor general, Lord Elgin [James Bruce*], and his wife called at his studio to see his western sketches.

Between 1851 and 1857 Kane exhibited his western paintings and won awards at the annual Upper Canada Agricultural Society exhibitions held in various centres in Canada West. He was acclaimed a celebrity when he appeared at one of these in person. The excellent reviews of the canvases the Canadian government sent to the Paris exposition of 1855 reputedly much cheered the artist.

Until the 1850s only a portrait painter could hope to earn a reasonable income from artistic production in Canada. In 1851, Kane had applied to the Canadian government for monetary assistance to paint the canvases from his sketches, basing his claim on the national importance of his work. The government gave him a grant of £500 on condition that he deliver 12 canvases to the Library of Parliament, and several paintings were commissioned by private individuals. His most important work with his western sketches constitutes a cycle of 100 canvases painted for Allan for $20,000, and completed by March 1856. Kane intended illustrating the Canadian native peoples, their customs, and the scenery of the country in which they lived by this group of paintings. Catlin and Stanley had painted similar cycles, which they sold to the Smithsonian Institution in Washington as a permanent record of the American Indians. Similarly, Kane would undoubtedly have preferred to have had the government buy his works, and he wished to see the group preserved for the people of Canada.

As early as October 1848 Kane planned a book

describing his trips of 1845–48, based on the notes and diaries he kept en route. In the 1850s he began writing *Wanderings of an artist among the Indians of North America*. Although some chapters were delivered before the Canadian Institute (later the Royal Canadian Institute) in 1855, published in its annual proceedings, and republished in the *Daily Colonist*, the publication of the complete volume was long delayed. Finally, a visit by Kane to England in 1858 and, simultaneously, pressure from influential persons, presumably Simpson and his associates of the HBC, resulted in the publication of the volume in 1859. A pirated French edition appeared in 1861, and, in 1863, a Danish edition. When it was first published, the volume contained coloured lithographs and woodcut illustrations based on the sketches and canvases in the Allan collection. A German edition with newly prepared lithographs and woodcuts, and genre scenes by another artist, was published in several parts beginning in 1860 and as a complete work in 1862. Kane also intended publishing a book consisting of plates depicting the west. He prepared a portion of the text for such a volume but it was never published. Kane dedicated his *Wanderings* to George Allan. Simpson took umbrage at this and ordered the HBC staff neither to receive Kane at their posts nor to assist him in any way in the future. It was apparently for this reason that Kane abandoned a proposed sketching trip to Labrador in 1861.

Kane exerted a major influence on many people. Sir Daniel Wilson*, professor at the University of Toronto, became a close friend and relied heavily on Kane's information on the plains and Pacific coast Indians for his *Prehistoric man, searches into the origin of civilisation in the old and the new world*, the first major anthropological work written in Canada. Among Kane's later associates were men like Allan, Wilson, and Frederick A. Verner*. The last, in emulation of Kane, painted the Indians and buffalo of the prairies. Lucius Richard O'Brien* was also influenced in his early years as an artist by Kane.

Kane had married Harriet Clench of Cobourg, the daughter of his former employer, in 1853, and they had several children. After 1862 they lived in a house which they built on Wellesley Street in Toronto. The artist evidently maintained a studio on King Street until he was forced to retire because of his increasing blindness, which began to be apparent in 1858. He kept somewhat aloof in later life, possibly embittered by his bad sight (which he blamed on the glare from the snow in the Alps during his 1842 trip and also in the west), and by the lack of continuing interest in his work on the part of the general public.

He died suddenly at his Toronto home shortly after returning from his daily walk.

J. RUSSELL HARPER

[The great bulk of known sketches and paintings by Paul Kane is divided between three depositories. Of the 12 canvases he delivered to the Library of Parliament, 11 are now in the National Gallery of Canada in Ottawa. The cycle of 100 paintings completed in 1856 was purchased by Sir Edmund Boyd Osler* in 1903, and presented to the Royal Ontario Museum in Toronto, where they are now located. Most of the sketches made during the field trips are in the Royal Ontario Museum and with the Stark Foundation in Orange, Texas. Kane's collection of Indian artifacts was donated by the Allan family to the Manitoba Museum of Science and History in Winnipeg. A catalogue raisonné of Kane's sketches and paintings is in *Paul Kane's frontier; including* Wanderings of an artist among the Indians of North America *by Paul Kane*, ed. J. R. Harper (Toronto, 1971). Frederick A. Verner produced three portraits of Kane. The most important one is now in the collection of the Royal Ontario Museum. An early self-portrait is in the Weir collection in London, Ont. Another, painted during his first western tour, is in the Stark Foundation collection.

Paul Kane, "The Chinook Indians," *Canadian Journal*, new ser., II (1857), 11–30; "The Chinook Indians," *Daily Colonist* (Toronto), 6, 7, 8, 9 Aug. 1855; "Incidents of travel on the North-West coast, Vancouver's Island, Oregon, etc. The Chinook Indians," *Canadian Journal*, III (1854–55), 273–79; "Notes of a sojourn among the half-breeds, Hudson's Bay Company's territory, Red River," *Canadian Journal*, new ser., I (1856), 128–38; "Notes of travel among the Walla-Walla Indians," *Canadian Journal*, new ser., I (1856), 417–24; *Wanderings of an artist among the Indians of North America from Canada to Vancouver's Island and Oregon through the Hudson's Bay Company's territory and back again* (London, 1859); republished with intro. and notes by L. J. Burpee (Master-works of Canadian authors, ed. J. W. Garvin, VII, Toronto, 1925; repub. with intro. by J. G. MacGregor, Edmonton, 1968). The 1859 edition is included in *Paul Kane's frontier.... The Wanderings* has also been translated into French, German, and Danish: *Les Indiens de la baie d'Hudson, promenades d'un artiste parmi les Indiens de l'Amérique du Nord ...*, trans. Édouard Delessert (Paris, 1861); *Wanderungen eines Künstlers unter den Indianern Nordamerika's ...*, trans. Luise Hauthal (Leipzig, 1862); *En Kunstners Vandringer blandt Indianerne i Nordamerika ...*, trans. J. K. (Copenhagen, 1863).

Kane's writings were reviewed in: Charles Lavollée, "Un artiste chez les Peaux-Rouges," *Revue des deux mondes* (Paris), XXII (1859), 963–86. Daniel Wilson, "Wanderings of an artist," *Canadian Journal*, new ser., IV (1859), 186–94. *Athenaeum* (London), 2 July 1859, 14–15. Kane's work is mentioned in the following catalogues: *Catalogue of the first exhibition of the Society of Artists and Amateurs of Toronto* (Toronto,

Keefer

1834). *Catalogue of sketches and paintings by Paul Kane* (Winnipeg, 1922). *Catalogue, pictures of Indians and Indian life by Paul Kane* (property of E. B. Osler, n.p., [1904]). Paul Kane, *Catalogue of sketches of Indians, chiefs, landscapes, dances, costumes, etc.* (Toronto, 1848). National Gallery of Canada, *Catalogue of paintings and sculpture*, ed. R. H. Hubbard *et al.* (4v., Ottawa, 1959–65), III: *The Canadian school*, 151–56.

Art Gallery of Ontario (Toronto), Challener papers, notes on Paul Kane. Church Missionary Society Archives (London), Journal of the Reverend J. Hunter. HBC Arch. D.4/54, D.4/67, D.5/15, D.5/24. *British Colonist* (Toronto), 14 Nov. 1848. *Canadian Agriculturist* (Toronto), III (1851), 228; IV (1852), 292–93. Morgan, *Sketches of celebrated Canadians*, 731–33. *Oregon Spectator* (Oregon City), 11 Feb. 1847. "Paul Kane", *Anglo-American Magazine* (Toronto), VI (May 1855), 401–6. *Valley of the Trent* (Guillet), lvii.

W. G. Colgate, *Canadian art, its origin and development* (Toronto, 1943). Davin, *Irishman in Canada*, 611–17. J. R. Harper, *Painting in Canada, a history* (Toronto, 1966). W. H. G. Kingston, *Western wanderings or, a pleasure tour in the Canadas* (2v., London, 1856), II, 39, 42–47. A. H. Robson, *Paul Kane* (Toronto, 1938). Daniel Wilson, *Prehistoric man, searches into the origin of civilisation in the old and the new world* (2v., Cambridge and London, 1862).

D. I. Bushnell Jr, *Sketches by Paul Kane in the Indian country, 1845–1848* (Smithsonian Misc. Coll., XCIX, Washington, 1940). W. G. Colgate, "An early portrait by Paul Kane," *Ont. Hist.*, XL (1948), 23–25. J. R. Harper, "Ontario painters 1846–1867," National Gallery of Canada, *Bull.* (Ottawa), I (1963), 16–31. K. E. Kidd, "Notes on scattered works of Paul Kane," Royal Ontario Museum, Art and archaeology division, *Annual, 1962*, 64–73; "Paul Kane – a sheaf of sketches," *Canadian Art* (Ottawa), VIII (1950–51), 166–67; "Paul Kane, painter of Indians," Royal Ontario Museum of Archaeology, *Bull. 23* (Toronto, 1955), 9–13; "The wanderings of Kane," *Beaver*, outfit 277 (December 1946), 3–9. Daniel Wilson, "Paul Kane, the Canadian artist," *Canadian Journal*, new ser., XIII (1871–73), 66–72. Kathleen Wood, "Paul Kane sketches," *Rotunda* (Toronto), II (1969), 4–15. J.R.H.]

KEEFER, JACOB, merchant, miller, and notary; b. 8 Nov. 1800 in Thorold Township, U.C., the second son of George Keefer*, UEL, and Catherine Lampman; m. 8 June 1829 Christina Theresa Grant, and by her had nine sons and six daughters; d. 12 June 1874 at Thorold, Ont.

Jacob Keefer was employed in his youth by a druggist in Erie, Pennsylvania, where a brother-in-law practised medicine. After a few years he returned to Upper Canada and kept general stores at Mud Creek, Beaver Dams, the Deep Cut, and Thorold. In 1826 he was commissioned to receive affidavits and began to serve the community as a notary. From 1826 to 1832 he was postmaster at Beaver Dams and Thorold.

In 1828 Keefer was granted the right to erect a sawmill on the Welland Canal in Thorold. By 1843, he estimated, the sawmill had yielded him an average annual profit of more than £209 over the past 12 years. His major enterprise, however, was the Welland Mills which he decided to construct in Thorold in 1845 after the Welland Canal had been rebuilt. When the mills were completed by 1847 they were among the largest flour mills in Canada with a capacity to grind 200 to 300 barrels of flour per day, a ship elevator capable of discharging 1,000 bushels of wheat an hour, and storage space for 70,000 bushels of wheat and 5,000 bushels of flour. After he had invested $3,000 in labour and materials, Keefer learned of Sir Robert Peel's intention to repeal the corn laws and eliminate the preference Canadian flour had enjoyed in the British market. It was a serious blow to his financial prospects, but after considering the alternatives he concluded that the mills must be completed if loss was to be avoided. He was further disappointed when Robert Gillespie* of London, England, failed to purchase a partnership in the mills for his nephew, Alexander Gillespie Jr, as he had proposed. Faced with a shortage of funds, Keefer mortgaged the mills heavily. Scarcely had they begun operating when prices declined sharply. From 1847 to 1850 it was frequently necessary for him to obtain short term loans from the Bank of Montreal and the Bank of Upper Canada in addition to large advances from John Torrance*'s firm in Montreal with whom he did business. By 1850 he was faced with a debt of more than £8,000 and was unable to obtain further credit. He lost control of the mills in April 1850 when James Oswald and Samuel Zimmerman*, who held one of the mortgages, brought a suit of ejectment against him. He continued to hope that he would be able to repay his debts and regain possession of the mills but this hope vanished in December 1855 when Oswald and Zimmerman carried foreclosure proceedings through the Court of Chancery.

In addition to his milling operations Keefer had numerous other interests. He was president of the Thorold Joint Stock Cotton Company and, until 1847, of the Erie and Ontario Railroad. He was chairman of the common school commission for Thorold Township in 1842 and in 1846 he was superintendent of common schools in the Niagara District. After he lost control of his mills in 1850, Keefer purchased a partnership in W. H. Ward's lumber business in Thorold, but in less than a year the partnership was dissolved. Henceforth, he occupied himself mainly with notarial work and his duties as postmaster, which he resumed in 1851 and continued until his death. In 1851 he was appointed clerk of the 4th division court of the united counties of Lincoln and Welland and in 1853 he received a commission as a notary public.

Although he was not active in politics, Keefer generally supported moderate reform principles. In the 1820s he solicited subscriptions for William Lyon Mackenzie*'s *Colonial Advocate*, but in 1837 he served as a captain in the militia and participated in operations against Mackenzie on Navy Island. As a result of his financial experiences he had become convinced by 1849 that annexation to the United States was essential for the economic survival of Upper Canada. Beyond openly expressing his opinions in his correspondence, however, he did not agitate in favour of annexation.

Throughout his life Keefer was a staunch supporter of the temperance and sabbatarian movements, but he was not active in the leadership of either movement.

WILLIAM ORMSBY

PAC, MG 24, B18 (W. L. Mackenzie papers), 1; E1 (Merritt papers), ser.1, 20, pp.3288–91; 23, pp.3905–8; I33 (Keefer papers); RG 11, ser.2, 43, f.7539. PAO, W. H. Merritt papers, 12 July 1848. "The annexation movement, 1849–50," ed. A. G. Penny, *CHR*, V (1924), 236–61. *J. of Education for Ont.*, XXVII (1874), 107. Chadwick, *Ontarian families*, II, 92. [W. H. Wetherell], *Jubilee history of Thorold, township and town, from the time of the red man to the present* (Thorold, Ont., 1897–98).

KEITH, ALEXANDER, brewer and politician; b. 5 Oct. 1795 in Caithness-shire, Scotland, son of Donald Keith and Christina Brims; d. 14 Dec. 1873 in Halifax, N.S.

When Alexander Keith was 17, his father sent him to an uncle in northern England to learn the brewing business. Five years later, when Keith migrated to Halifax, he became sole brewer and business manager for Charles Boggs, and he bought out Boggs' brewery in 1820. On 17 Dec. 1822 he married Sarah Ann Stalcup, who died in 1832. On 30 Sept. 1833 he married Eliza Keith; they had six daughters and two sons. One son, Donald G. Keith, became a partner in the brewing firm in 1853.

In 1822 Keith moved his brewery and premises to larger facilities on Lower Water Street and in 1836 he again expanded, building a new brewery on Hollis Street. In 1863 he began construction of Keith Hall which was connected by a tunnel to his brewery. Keith Hall, now occupied by Oland's Brewery, is in the Renaissance palazzo style, with baroque adornments, pillars of no particular style, and a mansard roof. This peculiar combination of styles resulted from the fact that the designs were probably derived from books with plans of buildings in Great Britain and the United States. Keith's appointment as a director of the Bank of Nova Scotia in 1837 along with William Blowers BLISS is an indication of his importance in the Halifax business community. Beginning in 1837, he also served as a director, at various dates, of the Halifax Fire Insurance Company. In 1838 he helped found the Halifax Marine Insurance Association, and in the 1840s he was on the board of management of the Colonial Life Assurance Company. He was also a director of the Halifax Gas, Light, and Water Company, incorporated in 1840, and in 1844 helped incorporate the Halifax Water Company, becoming a director in 1856. By 1864 Keith was a director of the Provincial Permanent Building and Investment Society. At the time of his death his estate was evaluated at $251,000.

Keith's interest in utilities and insurance was but part of his general involvement in the public life of Halifax. He was unsuccessful in the general election of 1840 when he stood as a Conservative candidate for the town of Halifax but was elected to the first city council in 1841. In 1842 he served as a commissioner of public property and in 1843 was selected mayor of Halifax. He continued as a member of council until he again served as mayor, by election, in 1853 and 1854. In December 1843 he was appointed to the Legislative Council and in June 1867 he accepted the appointment of president of the council, declining a seat in the Canadian Senate. As a supporter of confederation and president of the council, he was helped at first by the fact that before 1 July 1867 Charles Tupper* had filled several seats in the upper house with known confederates. Although the premier, William Annand*, appointed to the upper house in November 1867, had complete control of the lower house, he did not dare introduce a resolution into the upper chamber in 1868 calling for repeal of union. The anti-confederates gradually secured control of the upper house, however, and Keith was unable to prevent passage, in 1871, of a particularly flagrant bill which took the vote from all federal officials in provincial elections. It was perhaps a commentary on Keith that he was not actively involved at this time with the Conservative party organization which was run by such party stalwarts as Philip C. Hill* and James MacDonald*.

Throughout his career Keith was connected with several charitable and fraternal societies. He served as president of the North British Society from 1831 and as chief of the Highland Society from 1868 until his death. In 1838 he was connected with the Halifax Mechanics Library and

Kellett

in the early 1840s with the Nova Scotia Auxiliary Colonial Society. Keith was perhaps best known to the Halifax public as a leader of the freemasons. He became provincial grand master for the Maritimes under the English authority in 1840 and under the Scottish lodge in 1845. Following a reorganization of the various divisions in 1869, he became grand master of Nova Scotia.

K. G. PRYKE

Halifax County Court of Probate, will of Alexander Keith. PANS, Keith family papers; "Masonic grand masters of the jurisdiction of Nova Scotia, 1738–1965," compiled by E. T. Bliss, 1965, 21. *Acadian Recorder* (Halifax), 15 Dec. 1873. *Morning Chronicle* (Halifax), 15 Dec. 1873. *Annals of the North British Society of Halifax, Nova Scotia, from its foundation in 1768, to its centenary celebration March 26th, 1868,* compiled by J. S. Macdonald (Halifax, 1868), 187. G. A. White, *Halifax and its business: historical sketch and description of the city and its institutions* (Halifax, 1876), 87–88.

KELLETT, Sir HENRY, officer in the Royal Navy, oceanographer, Arctic explorer; b. 2 Nov. 1806 at Clonabody, Tipperary, Ireland, son of John Dalton Kellett; d. 1 March 1875 at Clonabody.

Henry Kellett joined the navy in 1822. He served for five years in the West Indies before being appointed to survey vessels commanded by William Fitzwilliam Owen* and Edward BELCHER on the west coast of Africa and in the East Indies. Shortly after distinguishing himself in the Opium War with China (1840–41), Kellett attained the rank of post captain. In 1845 he was appointed to command the frigate *Herald* for survey work on the Pacific coast of Central America. In the summers of 1848, 1849, and 1850 he and his ship were detached from this service to cooperate with Commander T. E. L. Moore of the *Plover,* then based in Kotzebue Sound, Alaska, in the search for the lost ships of Sir John Franklin*. In pursuance of this duty, Kellett in 1849 discovered and landed on Herald Island in the Russian Arctic and obtained a distant view of Wrangel Island. The following year on 31 July, in the neighbourhood of Cape Lisburne (near the northern exit of Bering Strait), he met Commander Robert McCLURE, of the Franklin rescue ship, *Investigator,* who had become separated from his commanding officer, Captain Richard Collinson* of *Enterprise.* Kellett remonstrated against McClure's intention of going directly into the ice without waiting for his consort, but did not use his superior rank to forbid the action.

In 1851 *Herald* returned to England and the crew was paid off. Despite his strenuous cruise of six years, Kellett immediately accepted a posting to the command of HMS *Resolute,* and in the spring of 1852 sailed as second in command in the expedition led by Sir Edward Belcher, whose orders were to prosecute the search for Franklin by way of Lancaster Sound. Belcher stationed *North Star* as depot ship at Beechey Island, and took his ship *Assistance* and the *Pioneer* up Wellington Channel. He sent *Resolute* and its tender *Intrepid,* captained by the famous Arctic traveller Commander Francis Leopold M'Clintock*, to search for Franklin in the Melville Island area, and, if necessary, to give aid to *Investigator,* unreported for many months, but believed to be in that region.

Kellett berthed his ships for the coming winter at Dealy Island off the south shore of Melville Island. An autumn travelling party under Lieutenant Frederick Mecham* visited Winter Harbour, 50 miles to the west, and there discovered a record planted by McClure from which it was learned that *Investigator* had discovered a northwest passage and that it had later become icebound in the Bay of Mercy on the north shore of Banks Island. The Arctic winter was too far advanced for help to be sent until the following spring. In the bitter cold of March 1853, Lieutenant Bedford Pim* made the 160-mile journey by dogsledge across Viscount Melville Sound to bring McClure word of the rescue ships. *Investigator* was abandoned on Kellett's order and her starving and scurvey-ridden crew trekked over the ice to Dealy Island.

In the meantime, under Kellett's direction, M'Clintock and Mecham, on sledge journeys of great length, found no trace of Franklin, but added Eglinton and Prince Patrick islands to the map of the Arctic.

On the voyage home Kellett's ships were frozen in at the west end of Barrow Strait and passed the winter of 1853–54 near Cape Cockburn. In April, Belcher, who was still in Wellington Channel, sent orders to Kellett to abandon his ice-bound ships and take their crews, with the men of *Investigator,* on foot to the depot at Beechey Island. Kellett protested that his ships were not in enough danger to warrant this desertion but he had no choice but to obey. Belcher deserted his two ships as well; all crews were taken home on *North Star* and two summer supply ships. Belcher's written orders requiring Kellett to abandon his ships procured the latter a prompt acquittal by court-martial for their loss; Kellett also received a handsome compliment from the president of the court on the services he had rendered. Kellett's judgement was vindicated in the autumn of 1855 when James Buddington, an American whaling skipper, found *Resolute* drifting in Baffin Bay and sailed her, still seaworthy and manageable, to New London, Conn. The

United States Congress purchased the derelict and gave her, refitted, to Queen Victoria. A table from her oaken beams stands today in the White House to commemorate this act of generosity.

The British parliament voted £10,000 to McClure and his crew for the discovery of the northwest passage. (It was not positively known in 1855 that Franklin's lost crews had anticipated McClure by the discovery of an alternate passage by way of Victoria Strait.) Kellett's crews, but for whom the men of *Investigator* must inevitably have perished, expected a share of this bounty. McClure, however, secured the entire grant for himself and his crew by his blandly unscrupulous testimony before a parliamentary committee that he could have brought his men out alive without Kellett's aid. This ungrateful attitude was not endorsed by the petty officers and men of *Investigator*. At a meeting in honour of Dr Alexander Armstrong*, *Investigator*'s surgeon, they took the opportunity of voicing their thanks to Lieutenant Pim – and by implication to Kellett – but for whom "many of us would never have seen old England again." Kellett was hurt at the manner in which his services were neglected, especially for the sake of his men who had suffered much hardship during the last winter through sharing sleeping quarters and bedding with 60 additional hands from the *Investigator*.

Kellet subsequently held commands in the West Indies and on the China Station, and then retired to his native Clonabody, where he died in 1875.

In addition to the rescue of McClure and the survey work done by M'Clintock and Mecham under his command, Kellett is credited by Soviet writers with doing the first hydrographic work in the eastern Russian Arctic. The Canadian explorer, Captain Joseph-Elzéar Bernier*, paid a fine tribute to his professional character. There are numerous witnesses to his kindness and to the pains he took to keep up morale and good humour under trying conditions. The stormy "Jacky" Fisher, who served under Kellett in China, was at first repelled by him: "He hasn't a spark of religion about him, never goes to Church, and this, together with his being an Irishman, makes me distrust him," but soon yielded to his charm: "he is so full of kindness to me."

LESLIE H. NEATBY

Baker Library, Dartmouth College, Stefansson coll., Grinnell Scrap-Book, undated newspaper clipping, c. October 1854. A. A. Armstrong, *A personal narrative of the discovery of the north-west passage; with numerous incidents of travel and adventure during nearly five years' continuous service in the Arctic regions while in search of the expedition under Sir John Franklin* (London, 1857). Edward Belcher, *The last of the Arctic voyages; being a narrative of the expedition in H.M.S. Assistance, under the command of Captain Sir Edward Belcher, C.B., in search of Sir John Franklin, during the years 1852–53–54* (2v., London, 1855). J. A. Fisher, *Fear God and dread nought: the correspondence of Admiral of the Fleet Lord Fisher of Kilverstone*, ed. A. J. Marder (3v., London, 1952–59), I. [McClure], *Discovery of the north-west passage* (Osborn). G. F. M'Dougall, *The eventful voyage of H.M. discovery ship "Resolute" to the Arctic regions in search of Sir John Franklin and the missing crews of H.M. discovery ships "Erebus" and "Terror", 1852, 1853, 1854 . . .* (London, 1857). J. A. Miertsching, *Frozen ships; the Arctic diary of Johann Miertsching, 1850–1854*, trans. with intro. L. H. Neatby (Toronto, 1967). B. C. Seemann, *Narrative of the voyage of H.M.S. "Herald" during the years 1845–51, under the command of Captain Henry Kellett . . . being a circumnavigation of the globe and three cruizes to the Arctic regions in search of Sir John Franklin* (2v., London, 1853).

DNB. J.-E. Bernier, *Report on the dominion of Canada government expedition to the Arctic Islands and Hudson Strait on board the D.G.S. 'Arctic' [1908–1909]* (Ottawa, 1910). C. R. Markham, *Life of Admiral Sir Leopold McClintock* (London, 1909). L. H. Neatby, *In quest of the north-west passage* (Toronto, 1958). V. IU. Vize (Wiese), *Moria Sovetskoi Arktiki* (Leningrad, 1939). Noel Wright, *Quest for Franklin* (London, 1959). F. H. Burns, "H.M.S. 'Herald' in search of Franklin," *Beaver*, outfit 294 (autumn 1963), 3–13. L. H. Neatby, "McClure and the passage," *Beaver*, outfit 291 (winter 1960), 33–41.

KELLY, FRANCIS, land surveyor, business agent, farmer, and politician; b. May 1803 in Mullologhan, County Monaghan, Ireland; d. 19 April 1879 at Fort Augustus, P.E.I.

Francis Kelly completed his schooling in Dublin, where he worked as a teacher and law clerk. Sometime before he emigrated to Prince Edward Island in May 1835, he married Catherine Lennon of Tullycorbett. Upon arrival on the Island, Kelly settled at Fort Augustus in Lot 36. There a large landowner, the Reverend John MCDONALD, hired him to survey his estates and to serve as his business agent. This association lasted until 1 May 1846.

After two unsuccessful attempts in the 1840s, Kelly was elected to the House of Assembly for Queens County, Third District, in 1858 as a running mate of the Liberal premier, George COLES. With the exception of the 1872 session, Kelly held this seat until his death. A strong Catholic layman, he was often in the forefront of attempts by the church to gain educational concessions. In 1870 an internal crisis in the Liberal government over the granting of public funds to Catholic St Dunstan's College caused Kelly and six other Catholic assemblymen to leave the party and join the Tories led by James Colledge Pope*. Such a shift in an

Kent

assembly of 30 members was enough to bring the Tories to power, and as a reward Kelly was named chief commissioner of crown lands. He held the post until the government changed hands in 1872 and regained the position for 1875 and 1876.

On the other issues of his era Kelly took the position of most of his contemporaries. In the 1860s he ardently opposed confederation and voted for James Pope's "no terms" resolution in 1866; when union became a financial imperative seven years later, however, Kelly joined Pope to seek "better terms." On the land question he argued in favour of easier conditions for tenants wishing to purchase their farms.

Kelly's importance as an Island politician stems from his longevity and from his constant and forthright support for the educational demands of his church. It is this cause which motivated him and explains both his change in party allegiance and his about-face on confederation.

D. B. BOYLAN

PAPEI, Prince Edward Island, Executive Council, Minutes, 1858–79, especially 10 Sept. 1870. PRO, CO 226/82, 108–10; 226/106, 225–27. Prince Edward Island, House of Assembly, *Debates*, 1858–78, especially 1861, 126–27; 1871, 45–46, 57; 1872, Session 2, 237; 1875, 198, 359; *Journals*, 1858–79, especially 1860, 186–87; 1876, 86. *Colonial Herald* (Charlottetown), 9 July 1842. *Examiner* (Charlottetown), 4 Dec. 1871; 7 Aug. 1876; 19 April, 2 May 1879. *Islander* (Charlottetown), 15 July 1870. *Patriot* (Charlottetown), 21 July, 20, 25 Aug., 3, 17 Dec. 1870. *Royal Gazette* (Charlottetown), 21 April, 28 July 1846. *Can. parl. comp.*, *1874*; *1875*; *1876*; *1877*; *1878*; *1879*. Bolger, *PEI and confederation*.

KENT, JOHN, commission agent and politician; b. in Waterford, Ireland, in 1805; d. 1 Sept. 1872 in St John's, Nfld.

John Kent came to Newfoundland in 1820. He served for a time as clerk to his uncle, Patrick Morris*, who had emigrated to Newfoundland 20 years before, and whose impetuosity, wit, and belligerence Kent seems to have shared. By 1830 Kent was already established as an auctioneer and commission agent, and doing a business sufficient for him to be able to marry the sister of the Roman Catholic bishop of the colony, Dr Michael Anthony Fleming*. It was Bishop Fleming's influence that was largely instrumental in getting John Kent elected for St John's in the first Newfoundland assembly. This assembly was established by an imperial act in 1832, in the movement for which Kent had played an important role.

Kent's electioneering was a compound of his own strident vitality, intimidation, and clerical influence. Newfoundland in 1832 had virtually universal suffrage under a household franchise,

and it was not difficult to secure election by turbulent, and very effective means. Kent was of the school of Reformers who relished quarrels with authority. He was a democrat by instinct, hating irresponsible power, by which he meant any power unresponsive to popular demands. He had all of William Lyon Mackenzie*'s rabble-rousing facility, and a rich command of language, not to say invective; but he had other attributes Mackenzie had not, acquisitiveness, a driving ambition, and a real capacity for administration. One of Kent's most characteristic utterances was his address to a public meeting in St John's on 24 May 1848, in which he quoted George Canning: "inaction never yet begot repose, nor were the objects of human ambition ever yet attained but by human exertion."

Given principles and capacities like these, John Kent would go far as a popular demagogue. He seems never to have scrupled much about the means he used to get elected, and stay elected: he was never defeated in any election. But then Kent was no worse in this respect than many of his contemporaries. It was alleged by Protestants in 1836 that the Catholic population of Newfoundland (37,600 as against 36,000 Protestants) was controlled "by an ignorant, vicious and a political priesthood." The Protestant author of that statement, Henry D. Winton*, the editor of the *Public Ledger*, had had his ears cut off just the year before. But Protestants were no better. Not even an angel, wrote one exasperated governor of Newfoundland, Captain Henry PRESCOTT in 1839, could "still the storm of religious rancour. . . ." Kent made no attempt to do so. He enjoyed the storm and rode it to his own advantage, though as he grew older he developed a greater sense of responsibility and his youthful asperities softened somewhat.

In 1842 Kent was appointed to the new amalgamated legislature, made up of 11 elected members and 10 appointees of the crown; in 1849 he became speaker of the reseparated assembly. Later that same year he was given the post of collector of customs and resigned his seat in the assembly.

Kent had by this time become an enthusiast for responsible government. He had first proposed the system in 1846; he believed that the assembly could be made responsible by giving it responsibility, whereas without responsible government an opposition would remain permanently demagogic. This was an argument from Robert Baldwin* in Canada West; but the St John's *Morning Courier* asked (30 May 1848) if Newfoundland, lacking a cohesive population, did not need some solid institutional structures of local government first. To bring responsible government at this time would be folly. It would put it "on a rotten foundation . . . propped by needy partisans, who have not sufficient industry to earn their own substance. . . ." Governor John Gaspard Le Marchant believed that the agitation for responsible government, coming, as it did, nearly exclusively from the Reform or Liberal party, was simply a mask for Catholic striving for power. Kent may have been naive in believing that the circumstances that had justified, or had seemed to justify, responsible government in the provinces of Canada and Nova Scotia could apply in Newfoundland.

In 1848 the Liberals in the assembly controlled about 3/5 of the seats – a proportion continued by the general election of 1852. Nearly all of their holders were Roman Catholics, and all of these were pledged to responsible government. After many representations the British government agreed, reluctantly, to grant responsible government to Newfoundland. Elections to this end were held in May 1855, and in the same month the first cabinet was sworn in in Newfoundland, under the Liberal premier, Philip Francis Little*. John Kent, who had resigned his office as collector of customs and been elected in 1852, was made colonial secretary in an administration consisting of four Roman Catholics and two Protestants.

In 1857 the draft Anglo-French Convention signed by France and Britain in the spirit of cooperation engendered by the Crimean War threw all parties into one unanimous protest. The convention, on the question of the French Shore, which at this time ran from Cape St John (about 150 miles northwest of Cape Bonavista) to Cape Ray on the west coast (about 230 miles south of Pointe Riche), was subject, on the British side, to ratification by the Newfoundland legislature. Among other vital details, the convention proposed an extension of French fishing privileges into Labrador; it also gave the French an exclusive right (except for certain limited military and administrative purposes) to an important section of the existing treaty shore. Newfoundland, now under responsible government, reacted swiftly and violently.

In March 1857, Kent, with Frederic B. T. Carter* of the Conservative opposition, went to Halifax, N.S., thence to New Brunswick and to Canada, to drum up colonial support for the Newfoundland cause. They won support in all the colonies, Prince Edward Island included, an incident that may have influenced Newfoundland's willingness to at least consider confederation in 1864 and 1865. "We cannot soon forget," said the *Newfoundlander*, on 16 April 1857, "our obligations to our Sister Colonies . . . who have identified themselves with our struggle." As a result of these colonial representations Britain abandoned the

convention, and Kent subsequently served as one of two British delegates on a joint Anglo-French commission in 1859. He was dropped from the commission early in 1860. The suspicion was that he had not made much of a contribution to it; possibly he was too refractory.

Kent had become premier in 1858, following P. F. Little's appointment to the Supreme Court of Newfoundland. He was returned to power in the general election of November 1859, an election contested with more than the usual bitterness. In these years the sectarian rivalry had sharpened fiercely. The census of 1857 had shown a shift in the narrow balance between Protestant and Catholic in Newfoundland. In the census of 1845 the Protestants had had a slight edge – 49,500 to 47,000 – but now the margin had increased (the result of a considerable Methodist immigration) to 64,000 Protestants against 55,000 Roman Catholics.

The Kent ministry fell upon bad times. The early years of responsible government had gone well; as Kent put it, "the sunshine of prosperity" had beamed upon the Little government. In 1859 revenues dropped and in 1860 there was a partial failure of the fishery. This in turn necessitated consideration of direct provincial relief for the poor – a problem that had a splintering effect on Kent's party. The issue was whether poor relief moneys should be administered by local members (and thus become a form of patronage) or by a non-partisan committee. Kent was under some pressure from the bishop to opt for the latter solution, but his own party refused to accept it. The Roman Catholic church was in fact now turning against Kent. He had always enjoyed the confidence of Bishop Fleming, but Fleming had been succeeded in 1850 by Bishop John Thomas Mullock*, a man with even more Irish in him than his predecessor, and Kent never had the same rapport with Mullock. The new bishop seems to have gravitated toward Ambrose Shea*, member for Burin.

The quarrel about relief within the Liberal party broke into the open in 1861. The failure of the 1860 potato crop had made relief essential; but Kent believed, perhaps rightly, that the administration of poor relief had to be tightened. Early in 1861 regulations to this effect were published which aroused considerable popular resentment, and members of Kent's own party were not above capitalizing on it. In the assembly Kent defended himself and his government's action in his usual forthright style. He was being attacked, he said, by a "miserable faction who sought his political destruction; a set of frozen serpents which having been warmed into life had stung the breast which

Kent

gave it vitality." The cabal against him was engineered by a "designing, cozening, cunning rogue," whom Kent did not name, but whom everyone knew to be Ambrose Shea.

Kent succeeded in saving his ministry in January 1861, but within a month he was hit from another quarter. A bill had been introduced by the government authorizing the payment of public accounts, and official salaries, at a reduced rate of exchange – a loss of about 4 per cent. Strong protests came in from both officials and the Conservative opposition. Kent was angry. In the assembly he spoke darkly of a conspiracy against his Liberal government by the governor in league with the opposition. Perhaps the speech was one way, crude enough in all truth, of healing the rift within the ranks of the Liberal party. Governor Sir Alexander Bannerman*, who had resented Kent's dictatorial methods and disliked his administration, partly because he thought it corrupt and partly because he knew it was Catholic, asked Kent for an explanation of his words against the queen's representative. Kent imperiously replied that he need not account for his words in the assembly to anyone. Then Bannerman struck. Having ascertained that the opposition would be willing to form a government, he dismissed the Kent ministry early in March 1861. Bannerman's conception of his role as governor was clearly, in the context of responsible government, anachronistic. Kent moved and carried resolutions in the assembly protesting that his dismissal was a "gross act of treachery" to the people of Newfoundland; the house was then dissolved and the tumultuous election of the spring of 1861 began. Only the defeat of Kent and his party could save Governor Bannerman. The issue may account for some of the character of the 1861 election.

Kent and his Liberal party were defeated, though only narrowly; it was upon doubtful constituencies, where feeling had run high, that office and power turned. There had been rioting and loss of life; troops had had to be called in; but in the end was ameliorated the old habit of Catholics who were voting Liberal intimidating Protestant and Conservative voters, and *vice versa*. Most of the members of the legislature seemed ready to recognize that Newfoundland's own interest, to say nothing of her reputation, required that further disorders on this scale be avoided. Hugh W. Hoyles*, the Conservative premier, was able, with some important Roman Catholic support, to put measures through the legislature increasing the police establishment, and to secure more independence for jurors. Governor Bannerman was seen, by Daniel W. Prowse* in the perspective of later years, to have begun the trend

toward parties crossing religious lines and toward the lessening of electoral violence. Bannerman was much helped in this endeavour by the courageous and firm Hoyles government. Nevertheless there are many unanswered questions about this amelioration of Newfoundland politics. Some have suggested a private pact between Hoyles and Ambrose Shea; some that Bishop Mullock's withdrawal from active party politics – perhaps as a result of pressure exerted from Rome – was the reason for the change.

Kent had kept his own seat in St John's East in 1861, but he was ere long replaced as leader of the opposition by Shea. Kent never forgave Bannerman for the events of March 1861; on Bannerman's departure in September 1864, Kent denounced him fiercely in the pages of the *Newfoundlander*. The coalition government that came to power in the awful depression year of 1865 appointed Kent as receiver general, and he went to Ottawa as one of the Newfoundland delegates to discuss confederation in 1869. When, however, that government was defeated on the confederation issue in the general election in the autumn of 1869, Kent retired from politics. After an extended trip abroad, he returned to Newfoundland and died suddenly, in his sleep, at St John's on 1 Sept. 1872. He was survived by his wife and by at least two children.

Kent had developed his political career in a period of Newfoundland history notorious for its rabble politics; his régime as premier was weakened by the corruption within his own party, and by the consequent alienation of the Roman Catholic bishop who preferred Ambrose Shea. Kent's style was in fact outdated. There was still much rabble-rousing to be done in Newfoundland politics, but more skilful and more circumspect politicians were on the scene. Kent would have been much in sympathy with the *Newfoundlander*'s boredom before the prospect of the assembly that was about to meet in 1864: nothing interesting was to be expected from that assembly – only the "dull" dispatch of legislative business.

P. B. WAITE

There are no known collections of John Kent papers. Newfoundland newspapers, however biased, are the best contemporary source – notably the Liberal *Newfoundlander* (St John's), 1830–72, and the Conservative *Public Ledger* (St John's), 1830–72. Also useful is PRO, CO 194, the dispatches of the Newfoundland governors to the Colonial Office.

The most recent and most complete secondary work for the period is G. E. Gunn, *Political history of Nfld.*, which has a comprehensive bibliography. Also useful is A. H. McLintock, *The establishment of constitutional government in Newfoundland, 1783–1832: a study of retarded colonisation* (Royal Empire Society Imperial

Studies, 17, London, 1941). For the French Shore see F. F. Thompson, *French Shore problem in Nfld.* For Newfoundland and confederation see the chapter in P. B. Waite, *Life and times of confederation.* A still useful general account of Newfoundland by a Newfoundlander is D. W. Prowse, *History of Nfld.* P.B.W.]

KER, ROBERT (the family name is also spelled Kerr or Carr, but his branch used Ker), public servant; b. 14 Aug. 1824 in Dalkeith, Scotland, son of James Ker and Janet Ker; m. at Bathgate, Scotland, on 19 July 1855 to Jessie Russell by whom he had five sons and one daughter; d. 11 or 12 Feb. 1879 at Victoria, B.C.

Robert Ker belonged to a family long prominent on the Scottish border. He was educated in Scotland, presumably as an accountant, and is said to have become a freemason before he emigrated to Victoria, Vancouver Island, in 1859. He had intended to join the gold rush to the mainland colony of British Columbia, but instead he became a clerk in the Treasury Department of B.C. on 1 June 1859 and on 12 July 1860 was made chief clerk in the Department of the Auditor General. He was himself appointed auditor general of B.C. on 14 March 1865; he also acted as auditor for the colony of Vancouver Island from 31 Aug. 1861 to 21 April 1864, when the audit office of B.C. was moved from Victoria to New Westminster and he was obliged to resign the Vancouver Island appointment. On the union of the colonies in 1866 Ker was continued as auditor general, and when the capital was moved from New Westminster to Victoria in 1868 he returned to Victoria to live.

He remained in the service of the province until confederation, when he was given the office of dominion paymaster general, which the Victoria *Colonist* called "a responsible position, for which his tried integrity and past experience eminently fit him." He retired on pension on 1 Oct. 1874 and died of exposure in "the great snowstorm" of 1879. The 100th anniversary of Robert Ker's arrival in Victoria was commemorated in 1959 by his grandson, Robert Henry Brackman Ker, who donated the Ker Memorial Wing to the Greater Victoria Art Gallery.

DOROTHY BLAKEY SMITH

[Information on the family was received from R. H. B. Ker in an interview on 5 Aug. 1970. D.B.S.] General Register Office (Edinburgh), Parish registers, Register of proclamations and marriages for the parish of Bathgate. PABC, Robert Ker correspondence, 1861–71. British Columbia, *Blue Books*, 1859–70 (copies in PABC). *Colonist* (Victoria), 1859–79. *Government Gazette* (Victoria), 12 Aug. 1865. *Victoria Daily Times*, 6 Jan. 1960. R. E. Gosnell, *A history of British Columbia* (n.p., 1906), 588. S. D. Scott, "The attitude of the colonial governors and officials towards confederation," *British Columbia & confederation*, ed. W. G. Sheldon (Victoria, 1967), 159, 161.

KÉROUAC (Kirouac), LÉON, school-teacher; b. in 1805 at Saint-François-de-la-Rivière-du-Sud (Montmagny County), L.C., son of Charles de Kérouac and Josette Blanchette; m. on 11 April 1836 at Saint-Marc (Verchères County) Éléonore Létourneau; d. 21 Feb. 1880 at Montreal, Que.

Léon Kérouac was a school-teacher at Saint-Antoine-sur-Richelieu. On 23 July 1845 he was elected president of the Association des Instituteurs of the district of Montreal (Belœil section). *La Minerve* of 7 Aug. 1845 stressed the importance of this association, and Dr Jean-Baptiste MEILLEUR gave it resounding praise in his *Mémorial de l'éducation du Bas-Canada.* For many years Kérouac devoted himself to teaching the children of the Richelieu valley. On 4 March 1857, at a banquet which brought together the teachers of the École Normale Jacques-Cartier (Montreal), the superintendent of the Council of Public Instruction, Pierre-Joseph-Olivier Chauveau*, sat Kérouac beside him as the "senior among the schoolmasters present"; yet he was only 52.

On 28 Aug. 1857 Léon Kérouac was nominated as a member of the Association des Instituteurs of the district of the École Normale Jacques-Cartier. From the time of the creation of the first normal schools, the superintendent had strongly encouraged the formation of these associations "connected with the École Normale Jacques-Cartier or Laval." They met at the normal school at least four times a year: pedagogical questions were the principal topics of discussion, and teachers were invited to give lectures on methodology, pedagogy, psychology, and teaching methods. Matters relating to the welfare of the school-teachers were also talked over. The *Journal de l'Instruction publique* gave accurate reports of each of these meetings.

The same journal reports in 1857 that for nine years Kérouac had contributed to the teachers' pension fund (£1 a year). In 1856 a law had authorized the superintendent to deduct from his budget "a sum not exceeding 500 *louis* to help in forming a fund for the support of the teachers of the common schools of Lower Canada who had become old or exhausted by their work, provided always that no teacher [had] a right to a share of the said funds if he [had] not contributed to such a fund the amount of at least one *louis* a year." This contribution was optional, and a number of school-teachers, alleging their poor salary as a pretext, refrained from contributing to the pension fund. On several occasions Chauveau complained of the teachers' indifference in this respect.

Kerr

Kérouac was deemed to be a teacher of great experience, very attached to his profession, conscientious, a man who took on the duties and obligations prescribed by the school laws and who stood out among the teachers as a leader.

LOUIS-PHILIPPE AUDET

AJM, Registre d'état civil (notes biographiques fournies par J.-J. Lefebvre). *JIP*, mars 1857, 71; août 1857, 163; sept. 1857, 187. J.-B. Meilleur, *Mémorial de l'éducation du Bas-Canada* (2e éd., Québec, 1876), 280–82. *La Minerve* (Montréal), 7 août 1845. L.-P. Audet, "P.-J.-O. Chauveau, ministre de l'Instruction publique, 1867–1873," *RSCT*, 4th ser., V (1967), sect.I, 171–84.

KERR, JAMES HOOPER, staff commander in the Royal Navy and hydrographic surveyor; b. in 1828 in Jersey, Channel Islands; m. in March 1862 at Simonstown, Cape of Good Hope, to Mary J. Bull; d. 24 Aug. 1877 at Hammersmith, Eng.

James Hooper Kerr entered the Royal Navy at Portsmouth on 18 Oct. 1843 as a volunteer in the *Victory*. His mathematical ability must have been exceptionally high for he was soon rated acting master's mate in the navigating branch of the navy. In 1844 Kerr joined the *Flamer* in the Mediterranean and in the same year was promoted second master in the *Volage* on the same station. He was appointed in 1851 to the surveying ship *Pandora* for the New Zealand survey. Five years later he was promoted master in the *Actæon* for the survey of China and the Tartary coasts. The *Actæon* was engaged in operations against the Chinese and Kerr was awarded the China War Medal (1857–60).

James Kerr's work in the surveying service – to which so much is owed by all the maritime nations of the world – had been noted by the Admiralty, and in April 1864 he was appointed master in charge of the important Newfoundland survey. For nearly eight years, working both ashore and afloat, he surveyed and charted the coasts and harbours of Newfoundland. Lines of soundings, rocks, shoals, and other hazards to navigation had to be accurately fixed by compass bearings or sextant angles of special marks on the coast line; then they had to be plotted on charts. In 1867 Kerr was promoted staff commander.

Over 40 of Kerr's Newfoundland surveys, topographic maps, and sketches – including that of the telegraph cable in 1866 – are preserved in the archives of the Hydrographic Department. Current editions of Admiralty charts which still give credit to Staff Commander Kerr include *Gander Bay to Bonavista* and *Cape Bonavista to Bay Bull, including Trinity and Conception bays*.

In 1871 Kerr returned home to take charge of the survey of the west coast of England. He re-mained at that post until his retirement, shortly before his death. Staff Commander Kerr was one of the distinguished fraternity of seaman-scientists who have served in the Royal Navy down the ages. The work of surveying uncharted coasts was always arduous, often dangerous, and called for a high degree of professional skill. James Kerr was a man dedicated to his profession.

MICHAEL GODFREY

G.B., Ministry of Defence, Hydrographer of the Navy (Taunton, Somerset), Admiralty charts by J. H. Kerr, 1866–71. PRO, Adm. 38/2118 (*Victory*, muster books); Adm./Ind. 12568-57/1 (surveying officers services). G.B., Adm., *Navy lists* (London), 1844–77. Archibald Day, *The Admiralty hydrographic service, 1795–1919* (London, 1967).

KILLALY, HAMILTON HARTLEY, engineer and civil servant; b. in Dublin, Ireland, in December 1800, son of John A. Killaly and Alicia Hamilton; d. at Picton, Ont., 28 March 1874.

Hamilton Hartley Killaly graduated from Trinity College, Dublin, BA 1819 and MA 1832. He learned engineering from his father, a prominent engineer who worked on the extension of the Grand Canal in Ireland.

In 1831 he came into contact with Edward George Stanley and John Fox Burgoyne, who were to form good opinions of him and to influence the course of his life. In that year Stanley, as chief secretary for Ireland, formed the Board of Works, and he appointed Burgoyne as chairman: "Determined honesty," Stanley told Burgoyne, "and decision to check all *jobbing* (no very easy task in Ireland) are the first requisites." Killaly served the board "principally as a consulting Engineer" from its inception until 1833 by which time he had become discouraged by the proclivity of Burgoyne, a military engineer, for employing officers of the Royal Engineers. He was himself later to resist similar tendencies in Canada since he thought they would inhibit growth of its engineering profession. Nonetheless, Stanley stated that Burgoyne considered Killaly to be "a very clever Engineer, and a steady man of excellent character." Stanley was "at all times my [Killaly's] steady friend," and his good opinion was, according to Killaly, "above all" responsible for his receiving senior engineering employment in Canada. He was to need such a powerful imperial ally.

In 1833 Killaly married Martha Jane Handy and in the following year they moved to the New World, where they were to have three sons and two daughters who lived to maturity. The Killalys passed some time in New York State and in the Niagara peninsula before settling in the township of London in 1835. Though he kept possession of his land until November 1848, Killaly tried his hand at farming only until 1837, when he secured an engineering post.

Killaly's arrival in Upper Canada coincided with lively consideration of the merits of railways, giving year-round service, versus water routes, which might be iced for about five months of the year. Many engineers of the day believed that railways were unsuited to the terrain of North America and to long hauls. In the mid-1820s, the provinces north of New York had responded to the Erie Canal by investigating the potentialities of railways. By the late 1830s, a number of railway inventors had elaborated a railway technology. In 1840 the United Kingdom had 1,331 miles of railway, the United States had 3,328 miles, and the Canadas had "our solitary famed fourteen miles between Laprairie and St Johns" in Lower Canada. This line was constructed by two engineers of New York – William R. Casey and Robert R. Livingston – and was opened for traffic in July 1836. The Upper Canada legislature had incorporated a company in 1834 to construct a line from Burlington Bay through the town of London to the navigable waters of the Thames River giving access to Lake St Clair, but when the line was begun in 1836 it was to run from Burlington Bay to Port Dover on Lake Erie to "divert a portion of the trade from that job of all jobs – the Welland Canal," as a newspaper put it.

Both military and commercial men in the Canadas desired to move material quickly to and from the Atlantic and the lakes, but their opinions sharply clashed over the use of the St Lawrence route, most of which formed the frontier with the United States. In view of the experience of the War of 1812, and of the Richard Rush–Sir Charles Bagot* agreement, few soldiers and no sailors believed that Britain could maintain a naval supremacy on the lakes by use of the St Lawrence route. Army extraordinaries had financed, and military engineers had built, an alternative to the St Lawrence route. This alternative followed the Ottawa and Rideau rivers to Kingston (a section completed in 1832) and contemplated that supplies in wartime would pass into the Bay of Quinte and go by the Trent River to Lake Simcoe. From Lake Simcoe, the contemplated route might have three branches: to Lake Huron by the Severn River, to Lake St Clair by the Thames, and to Lake Erie by the Grand River. In 1819 Wellington had expressed a preference for linking Lake Simcoe by railroads or canals direct to the Rideau's confluence with the Ottawa River. Another alternative to the St Lawrence route would follow the Ottawa and Mattawa rivers and Lake Nipissing to Lake Huron. Killaly, who was to be largely concerned

with the building and improvement of canals, was to support for some 30 years the development of the St Lawrence route. This preference was to bring him into conflict with military men.

A lengthy association with the Welland Canal, an integral part of the St Lawrence route, began for Killaly in 1837. The Welland, opened in 1835 by the efforts of William Hamilton Merritt*, was now experiencing difficulties because of an urgent need for deepening and for repairs that could not be financed by private investors. The government of Upper Canada, preparing to step in, ordered a re-survey by (in the words of the act) "two scientific and practical Engineers." Nicol Hugh Baird* and Killaly reported early in 1838, whereupon Killaly again was unemployed. On 15 May of that year Killaly was appointed engineer of the Welland Canal Company, a post he kept until Lord Sydenham [Thomson*] appointed him chairman of the reorganized Board of Works of Lower Canada early in 1840. Killaly speedily prepared for Sydenham a master plan for public works in the two Canadas which he incorporated in a memorandum dated at Kingston on 12 August 1841. As early as May 1840 Sir George Arthur* was objecting to his scheme.

Killaly had become an executive councillor on 17 March 1841 and was also a member of the assembly. George Jervis Goodhue* had persuaded him to seek election in London and he had defeated John Douglas in the first union election on 8 April. Killaly professed to be out of his own milieu: "*politics*, politics – I had rather be a mason's attendant than have my brain confined in it – & every moment occupied in a manner so wholly contrary to my inclination," he wrote to Baird on 2 June 1841. Nor was his master plan for public works politically balanced: "You say I may expect a rowing for disposing so summarily of the Trent & Ottawa. I care not a cent for a rowing – nor do I consider how any report of mine will be received, favourably or otherwise. I act conscientiously – while I feel I do so, I care not what the world says." However, the major weakness of Killaly's master plan was that it under-estimated costs of construction, as was common before precise costing techniques were developed. It became known only in 1845 that his estimates fell far short of the costs.

On 17 Aug. 1841 royal assent was given to the statute by which the union Board of Works was established. Killaly fully understood that the act would centralize decision-making: "The truth is . . . now is a critical time for the profession in this country," he informed Baird on 23 July 1841, "for recollect I tell you that the establishment of the district councils & their district Engineers or Surveyors at 2 or 300 a year will use up all the

Killaly

business ex officis, which heretofore has been done by jobs and which has been some of the most profitable employment." Under the act only the board's chairman and secretary were salaried and they were forbidden to perform in other professions or callings. It was originally intended that the board would be composed of the principal officers of the government who would provide information "relating to the general bearing of the works," and the act authorized the governor general to appoint up to five persons to the board, one of whom would be chairman. Killaly acted as chairman even before his formal appointment on 29 Dec. 1841, along with Samuel Bealey Harrison* and John Davidson. All three were members of both the assembly and the Executive Council. Killaly's salary was lower than that of most of his council colleagues but the statutory basis of his post rendered him somewhat immune from politics. The secretary of the board was Thomas A. Begley. When the government assumed full control of the Welland Canal, Killaly, Harrison, and Dominick Daly* were appointed a board of directors on 16 Feb. 1842. Daly refused to serve and Davidson was appointed in his place. Finally, on 4 March 1842, the three were named commissioners for superintending and maintaining the Lachine Canal.

That October, a large loan guaranteed by the imperial government was made available for Canadian public works, including the six St Lawrence canals west of Lachine; these were, in Killaly's words about the Cornwall Canal, "so much exposed to annoyance from the American side, that it would not be possible, in the face of the enemy, to work a Boat. . . ." The St Lawrence canals competed with the four pre-existing canals on the Ottawa and Rideau rivers, and the strategists agreed that in wartime the St Lawrence canals would have to be destroyed to prevent them from falling to the Americans. Their value depended upon continuing peace.

Killaly's selection of the south side of the river St Lawrence for the Beauharnois Canal was one of the principal grounds of attack on Bagot's government in 1842; his tempo of work drew criticism in 1843 from his former patron, E. G. Stanley, now secretary of state for the colonies ("Lord Stanley thinks we are going *too fast*!!!").

In 1843, the governor general, Sir Charles Theophilus Metcalfe*, appointed Melchior-Alphonse d'Irumberry* de Salaberry to be aide-de-camp for Canada East without having first asked the opinion of his Executive Council. On plea of sustaining their influence by their having the final say on matters of patronage, and in furtherance of responsible government, on 27 Nov. 1843 Killaly

and all other councillors except Dominick Daly officially resigned. Killaly did not resign as chairman of the Board of Works, however. During the time that he was in the Executive Council, Killaly seems to have been regarded not as a politician but, in the words of a naval officer, Captain Williams Sandom*, as "a talented and persevering engineer." It was in that character that Metcalfe retained his services as chairman of the board. He did not stand for election thereafter.

Meanwhile, the imperial government's interest in Canadian defence and in development of colonial communications forced a review of Killaly's work. His memorandum of 12 Aug. 1841 had discouraged work on the Trent, saying that it would cost much more than the current estimate and would never be of more than local importance. Just a few months earlier, on 31 March 1841, the Duke of Wellington had, on the other hand, stated that "Its completion will facilitate, if not render certain, all military operations. . . ." The two conflicting opinions were to be resolved, it was imagined, by a military and naval commission appointed confidentially to determine "the best mode of protecting the general line of communication and rendering it available in case of war for military purposes." In June 1844, Metcalfe directed Killaly to give the commission all information and assistance in his power. It consisted of Captain (later rear-admiral) Edward Boxer and Lieutenant-Colonel William Cuthbert Elphinstone Holloway. Boxer and Killaly quarrelled. Echoing others, Boxer though that "our only safety valve" was uniting all the British North American provinces under one government; and he was "decidedly of opinion that our safety depends entirely on a Railroad from Halifax to Port Sarnia." If Boxer's view ultimately prevailed, it was largely because Killaly's works and the later railways running across the international border at many points rendered Canadian defence so expensive that the British could not afford to maintain their guarantee of it.

Killaly grew unhappy in his job: "I would most cheerfully tomorrow take a permanent situation of 400 a year in any line or in any part of the Province," he wrote to Baird on 15 July 1844, predicting that, once the loan money for public works ran out, civil engineers would have a hard time making a decent livelihood in Canada. While the loan lasted, Killaly's operations employed many notable engineers including Charles Atherton, Alfred Barrett, George W. Cattley, Casimir Stanislaus Gzowski*, John Jackson, Samuel Keefer*, James Lyons, John B. Mills, and Freeman Talbot.

Dissatisfaction with the Board of Works finally

led to a commission of inquiry, gazetted on 6 Sept. 1845, and consisting of William Cayley*, Frédéric-Auguste Quesnel*, George Sherwood* (who had earlier opposed Killaly's works and who did not sign the commission's report), Moses Judah Hays* and John Redpath*. The commission in effect recommended that the chairman be a politician to whom all engineers would be decidedly subordinate. On 9 June 1846, the soldier-governor Charles Murray Cathcart* assented to a statute which abolished the board and created instead the Department of Public Works. William Benjamin ROBINSON took over from Killaly, who had only sporadic appointments until June 1848, when Étienne-Paschal Taché*, chief commissioner of the department, invited him to accompany him on a tour to select projects for deletion in an economy drive. Though the measures taken included a reduction in staff, Taché recommended that Killaly take over superintendence of the Welland Canal from Samuel Keefer, Killaly's former subordinate in the Board of Works, who was now appointed to the departmental headquarters in Montreal. Killaly moved to St Catharines and sold his farm in London Township. In June 1849 and again in September Killaly took a leading part in founding the Canadian Institute (incorporated 5 November 1851) in the Toronto office of the architect Kivas Tully*.

On 15 Feb. 1851, Killaly was appointed assistant commissioner of public works and became virtually the department's permanent deputy head with no seat in the legislature or in the council. In 1858–59 he served under chief commissioners Louis-Victor Sicotte* and John Rose*, both of whom felt it necessary to reassert political supremacy; Killaly's position was abolished by legislation assented to on 26 March 1859. His competence as an engineer was widely recognized, but his judgement on matters of policy was open to fair criticism and his capacity for financial administration may be inferred from his remark in 1850 about the audit procedure (there was a departmental pre-payment audit followed by a post-payment audit by non-departmental auditors): "What earthly use there is in this Roundabout I never could see."

In consequence of the departmental reorganization of 1859, Samuel Keefer, of the Board of Railway Inspectors, was appointed deputy commissioner on 6 May 1859. Killaly's only public office was that of inspector of railways, but he seems to have devoted little time to this office for Keefer reported that during the years 1859 and 1860 he had himself inspected 149 miles of line (including the Victoria Bridge) while Killaly and the assistant inspector, A. De Grassi, had together inspected a total of less than 132 miles. Nonetheless, Killaly kept close records of changes in the system of transportation within the province, and referred to himself as "general Inspector of Railways."

In 1855, Killaly had taken up residence in Toronto in a commodious dwelling on Wellington Place. The property had been part of the ordnance lands, ownership of which was a contentious issue between the imperial and Canadian governments so that he never had clear title.

Similar confusion existed about the naval reserves – lands set aside for naval defence. The Admiralty had decided before the American Civil War broke out to investigate the status of its long-neglected naval reserves. However, its representative, Captain Richard Collinson*, R.N., did not arrive in Canada until after the war had erupted. The War Office's representative was Lieutenant-Colonel Bernard Whittingham, R.E., and on 18 July 1861 the Canadian government appointed Killaly to represent it on the commission of inquiry. To Killaly the officers "appeared ... to consider themselves confined strictly to reporting upon the simple matters of the Titles under which each Naval Reserve was held – its situation and extent – and its value; upon most of those ordinary points, full information could have been furnished, in a few hours, from the Crown Land Office here, without the appointment and expense of any Special Commission." Consequently, Killaly induced the officers to join him in a wide-ranging inquiry that took the three into the United States and its waters. Collinson submitted the information on naval reserves to the Admiralty; Killaly submitted his own report on defence to the Canadian government which was not, however, prepared to expend funds for this purpose (an imperial responsibility). Killaly's report nevertheless served to alert the government of Canada to the deplorable state of colonial defence.

Late in 1861 the *Trent* affair made relations between the United States and Great Britain especially tense. The commander of the forces in British North America, Sir William Fenwick Williams*, made a hurried trip to inspect the virtually non-existent defences west of Kingston. The Executive Council placed Killaly's services at Williams' disposal. The general's aide, Captain Francis W. De Winton, noted Killaly's usefulness to the hero of Kars: "no man knows the country better; he has a strong, clear, practical head." A number of erroneous deployments were made, but fortunately for British rule in North America the crisis cooled.

On 6 Feb. 1862, Lord Charles Stanley Monck*

King

appointed a royal commission to report on a system of fortification and defence. Colonel John William Gordon, R.E., was chairman, the members being Lieutenant-Colonel Henry Lynedoch Gardiner, R.A., and Killaly. Captain William Crossman, R.E., was secretary. Colonel Edward R. Wetherall (Williams' chief of staff) and Captain John Bythesea, R.N., were added on 31 March. Killaly was included because a civilian's presence would, according to the secretary of state for war, Sir George Cornewall Lewis, "be of value in conciliating the feelings of the colonists towards the commission and giving them confidence in its recommendations," the adoption of which (according to the imperial authorities only) "must in the main be matter for consideration and decision of the Provincial Authorities." Besides a fleet of 72 gunboats on Lake Ontario and the St Lawrence, the commission's report of 6 September recommended a new naval base to replace Kingston, 18,000 effectives in Canada East and 47,000 in Canada West, enlargement of canals and an Intercolonial Railway, and so many fortifications that one official asked: "What is the good of all these little forts? They can detain an enemy for a very short time, must eventually fall. Why waste troops to defend them and money to build them?" But the last word ought, perhaps, to be left to J. F. Burgoyne, then inspector-general of fortifications. When he read the Gordon report, Burgoyne concluded that the loss of Canada was certain. Loyally, he did not blame Killaly's canals. His analysis was that "the perpetual bugbear of the invasion of Canada" had induced imperial diplomacy to surrender "the most advantageous military positions" to the United States in order to placate the "arrogant bullying system" of the Americans.

From 1862 until 1874 Killaly seems to have lived in quiet retirement. He sold "his" house on Wellington Place and was making arrangements to build a new residence near Picton in March 1874, when he died and was buried in Toronto. The bane of John Langton*'s life as auditor-general, he was also a vividly remembered personality, a genial gentleman, and a superlative engineer.

GEO. MAINER

PAC, RG 4, B29, 6, 15 Sept. 1861; RG 7, G9, 38, pp.140–41; G19, 31; G21, 74, G. C. Lewis to W. F. Williams, 15, 28 Feb. 1862; 165, T. C. Weir to Sidney Herbert, 11 Feb. 1860, Newcastle to Head, 26 April 1860. PAO, W. H. Merritt papers, 13 May 1843, 1 April 1850. PRO, CO 42/492, 228–29, 230, 243–44, 253, 309; 42/496, 138–40, 202–5, 208–31, 288; 42/498, 1, 37; 42/504, 134; 42/509, 542; 42/524, 187–232; 42/532, 389, 395–405; 42/533, 378; WO 1/540; 55/1/551.

[J. F. Burgoyne], *Life and correspondence of Field Marshal Sir John Burgoyne, Bart.*, ed. George Wrottesley (2v., London, 1873), I, 389–90; II, 405–7. *Chronicle and Gazette and Weekly Commercial Advertiser* (Kingston), 5 March, 31 Aug. 1836; 25 Jan. 1837. *Examiner* (Peterborough), 22 Jan. 1943. *Examiner* (Toronto), 16 March 1842. *Pilot and Journal of Commerce* (Montreal), 22 July 1848. *Weekly Dispatch* (Peterborough), 7 Oct. 1847. *A catalogue of graduates who have proceeded to degrees in the University of Dublin ... with supplements to December 16, 1868*, ed. J. H. Todd (Dublin and London, 1869), 320.

KING, RICHARD, doctor, Arctic explorer, ethnologist, and writer; b. probably in 1810 in London, Eng., son of Richard King; m. in 1857 to Elizabeth Lumley by whom he had at least one son; d. in London on 4 Feb. 1876.

In 1820 Richard King entered St Paul's School in London; in 1824 he began a seven-year apprenticeship with an apothecary. The Society of Apothecaries granted him their licence in 1832. His medical degree is believed to have been granted by the University of St Andrews in Fife, Scotland; however, their records for that period are defective and the supposition cannot be proved. It was as a surgeon and naturalist that King set out in 1833 with Captain George BACK's Arctic land expedition in search of Captain John Ross*, then four years absent on a search for a northwest passage.

King, although second in command, was in large part responsible for the success of the expedition. The two men evidently worked well enough together in the field, even though Back created unnecessary difficulties in King's task of collecting natural history specimens. On the outward journey to the northwest, King had charge of the main party and the heavy supplies, while Back hurried ahead in a light canoe to prepare for the exploration of the Great Fish River (Back River). After his return, Back set out as early as possible for England again leaving King in charge of the main party with instructions that were all but impossible to carry out.

Back, of course, wrote the official narrative of the expedition, to which King contributed botanical and meteorological appendices. In addition, King published his own account which is, in many respects, the better book. King showed a deeper understanding of the Indians and, although his share of the work had been far more arduous than Back's, he did not exaggerate, as Back did, the hardships of the journey. He differed from Back on some material geographical points and he made it clear that he thought the expedition might have been better managed and might have accomplished much more – so much more that he had decided, "while yet tented on the shores of the Polar Sea, to form the project of returning to resume the search at the point where Captain Back had terminated his labours. . . ." For 22 years King attempted unsuccessfully to secure support for this project: principally because of Back's persuasive and unfriendly influence in higher places than those to which King had access, he always failed.

King considered the completion of the survey of the northern coast of North America to be the great geographical problem of the time, one that would help to settle the practicability of a north-west passage. In 1836 he proposed to solve the problem of Boothia Isthmus, a feature placed by John Ross on his map of the area on the basis of Eskimo report only. If the isthmus existed, then King thought – rightly, as it turned out – that the land north of it, named North Somerset (now Somerset Island) by Ross, was a part of the north-ern coast, and that Boothia Peninsula, rather than Melville Peninsula, was the most northeastern point of the continent.

When the colonial secretary refused his pro-posal, King opened a public subscription for the £1,000 he needed. Response was favourable until the Admiralty decided to send Back in *Terror* to the northwest coast of Hudson Bay with orders to cross overland to the Gulf of Boothia and explore the unknown territory by boat. At the same time the Hudson's Bay Company refused to support King but sent, instead, their own men, Peter Warren Dease* and Thomas Simpson*, to explore the other two unknown sections of the northern coast, one in Alaska, the other between Coronation Gulf and the Back River. King believed that his own initiative had stimulated both expeditions.

Back's expedition was a failure and he turned home after a winter beset in Hudson Bay. Dease and Simpson, using small parties of the kind King had advocated and with some of the same men he had wished to take, were entirely successful.

In 1842 King again submitted his proposal, still insisting on the importance of the coast between the Back River and Melville Peninsula. With a small expedition in canoes, he planned to work northward from Back River along the east coast of Chantrey Inlet. If Boothia proved to be an island, they would soon reach Fury and Hecla Strait and, by passing through it, quickly complete the north-ern configuration of the continent. But if the isthmus did exist, he planned to follow the land to its northern limit, to see how it connected with land to the eastward and, if he found it separated by a sufficient width, to solve at last "the grand problem of a practicable passage from the Atlantic to the Pacific. . . ." Once again, his proposal was refused.

When, in 1845, King first heard of the expedition planned by Sir John Franklin*, he strongly urged that a land party be sent in support of it. And when, in 1847, no word had been received from Franklin, King was one of the first to raise alarm for the expedition's safety. Although his under-standing of Franklin's orders was at that time im-perfect (they had not yet been made public), he declared without hesitation that Franklin's ex-pedition would be found on "the Western land of North Somerset." He reached the right conclusion, according to the historian R. J. Cyriax, from ex-tremely questionable premises. As better informa-tion became available, he argued the same points more firmly, insisting with his own peculiar vehemence that the only efficient means of reach-ing the lost expedition was by way of Back River. In 1847 he offered to lead an expedition there and to guide Franklin's men to depots of food that he wanted laid down in 1848. He was refused. In 1848 Admiralty sent out three relief expeditions, and many others followed in succeeding years, until nearly the whole Arctic – except where King said the expedition was to be found – had been combed. Among all the Arctic experts, only Sir Edward BELCHER, Frederick William Beechey*, and Lady Franklin (Jane GRIFFIN) supported King's views in any way. In 1850 Lady Franklin sent William Kennedy* in her ship *Prince Albert* to search near the mouth of the Back River, but he did not fully carry out his orders and the object of his voyage remained unattained. Finally, in 1854, John Rae* unexpectedly learned from Eskimos in Pelly Bay of the death of a large number of white men not far to the west, near the mouth of the Back River.

All this time, King had persistently and noisily urged, as a matter of logic as well as of life and death, the necessity of a search exactly where the tragedy took place. Although the authorities re-jected his opinions and proposals, the journals of the day took them up with enthusiastic sympathy. His appeal to the public – a thoroughly ungentle-manly thing to do – increased the animosity felt toward him by officers of the Admiralty, the Royal Geographical Society, and the HBC. In 1855 King reviewed his unwavering position in a book, *The Franklin expedition from first to last*, and, with a sarcastic wit that was frequently unpleasant, he spared none of his opponents. In 1856 he offered for the fifth time to descend the Back River, this time to search for Franklin's records, and, later in the year, he renewed the offer in a joint plan with Bedford Pim*. It was, however, only in 1859 that Sir Francis Leopold M'Clintock*, sent by Lady Franklin at her own expense on a final search, examined the right place, and it was he who brought home the single record found, together

Kirouac

with other evidences of the expedition's final distress. If any of King's many offers had been taken up, it is possible that more records might have been found. However, even if the Admiralty had acted on his first proposal in 1847, it is doubtful whether any of Franklin's men could have been saved. It has even been suggested that it may have been, in part, King's very insistence that discouraged the authorities from looking where he said to search.

The nearest to official acknowledgement that King had for his efforts and for the correctness of his views is an obscure reference in the revised third edition of M'Clintock's *The fate of Sir John Franklin: the voyage of the "Fox"* ... (1869; first ed., 1859). Sir Roderick Murchison, president of the Royal Geographical Society, observed in a footnote to his preface, "Amidst the various recent publications, it is but rendering justice to Dr. King ... to state that he suggested and always maintained the necessity of a search for the missing navigators at or near the mouth of the Back River."

Although King is chiefly remembered for his share in Back's land expedition, 1833–35, and for his polemical role in the Franklin search, he led an active and useful life in medicine and learned pursuits. In 1842 he issued a prospectus that resulted in the formation of the Ethnological Society of London, of which he was the first secretary. In 1871 the society amalgamated with the Anthropological Society to form what is today the Royal Anthropological Society of Great Britain and Ireland; King remained on the council. He wrote many ethnological and medical papers of considerable value. His two small books on cholera and on the cause of death in still-born infants were important in their time, and he received a number of medical appointments and honours.

ALAN COOKE

[George Back, *Narrative of the Arctic land expedition to the mouth of the Great Fish River, and along the shores of the Arctic Ocean, in the years 1833, 1834, and 1835* (London, 1836). Richard King, *Narrative of a journey to the shores of the Arctic Ocean, in 1833, 1834, and 1835, under the command of Capt. Back* (2v., London, 1836); *The Franklin expedition from first to last* (London, 1855); "On the industrial arts of the Esquimaux," Ethnological Society of London, *Journal*, I (1848), 277–300; "On the intellectual character of the Esquimaux," Ethnological Society of London, *Journal*, I (1848), 127–52; "On the unexplored coast of North America," *London, Edinburgh, and Dublin Philosophical Magazine and Journal of Science*, 3rd ser., XX (1842), 488–94. F. L. M'Clintock, *Fate of Sir John Franklin: the voyage of the "Fox" in the Arctic seas* ... (1st ed., London, 1859; 3rd ed., revised and enlarged, London, 1869), vii–xviii.

DNB: the biography of Richard King contains many inaccuracies including a confusion with another man of the same name who served as assistant-surgeon on *Resolute* during Horatio Thomas Austin*'s 1850–51 expedition, and who won the polar medal. R. J. Cyriax, *Sir John Franklin's last Arctic expedition ... a chapter in the history of the Royal Navy* (London, 1939). F. J. Woodward, *Portrait of Jane: a life of Lady Franklin* (London, 1951). R. J. Cyriax, "Sir James Clark Ross and the Franklin expedition," *Polar Record* (Cambridge, Eng.), III (1942), 528–40. This biography is also based on information supplied to the author by Mr Hugh Wallace from his personal correspondence. A.C.]

KIROUAC, LÉON. See KÉROUAC

KRIEGHOFF (Kreighoff), CORNELIUS, painter; b. 1815 at Amsterdam, Holland, son of Johann Ernst Krieghoff, a coffee-house servant, who in 1811, at Amsterdam, had married Isabella Ludivica Wauters; d. 9 March 1872 at Chicago, Illinois.

Cornelius Krieghoff, the third of four children, learned the rudiments of music and painting from his father. At the age of 16 he was sent to relatives at Schweinfurt, Bavaria, to study painting. He returned to Düsseldorf two years later, where his parents had been living since about 1815–20; he no doubt studied here the works of artists who had been trained at its academy. Under the direction of their professor, Wilhelm von Schadow, these artists devoted themselves to genre painting, and presented similar subjects: card-players, drunkards, tricksters, outings, and children's festivities. At the beginning of 1837 Krieghoff sailed for New York. There he enlisted as a volunteer in the American army, at a time of war against the Seminole Indians of Florida. On 5 May 1840, after three years in uniform as an artist, he was discharged at Burlington, Vermont. His services had earned him the rank of corporal. There is a record of his marriage, at Manhatten, to Louise Gauthier, *dit* Saint-Germain, a French Canadian. This is about all we know of Krieghoff before his arrival in Canada.

Anything else is a matter of hypothesis. His father, who apparently became a maker of carpets in Düsseldorf and also in Schweinfurt, was interested in arts and music. Young Cornelius is thought to have learned to play the violin, the guitar, the flute, and the piano. After his father's death, he travelled with a friend, probably an artist like himself. Little is known about his travels. He may have spent two years at Rotterdam with his mother's parents, and studied painting there. He was in Austria, Italy, and France, and then returned to Holland. His talents as a musician and painter do not seem to have been great enough to earn him a livelihood in Germany. He sailed for New York. For what reasons? To see his brother Ernst, who was settled at Toronto? To try his luck in America? Love of adventure? No doubt all of these. Unfortunately, the numerous pen and pencil drawings – about 100 – that he made while serving in the American army have been lost, and it is impossible to form an idea of this first artistic work. The circumstances attending his leaving the army and his marriage remain rather obscure. On the very day of his discharge, he rejoined the army, then deserted. The fact of his meeting Louise Gauthier perhaps explains his behaviour. Born at Longueuil, near Montreal, she had worked as a servant in New York. The reaction of her father, a fairly well-to-do farmer, to the announcement of the marriage is not known. Finally, there is no link which would make it possible to determine what influence American genre painting may have had on Krieghoff's work.

The young couple decided to leave the United States and settle in Canada. They went to Toronto. The reasons for their choice, and the length of their stay, are unknown. Ernst Krieghoff no doubt advised his brother to take up residence in Toronto because of its artistic activities. He owned a studio of photography, and was probably acquainted with the possibilities open to a young artist. Cornelius worked as a professional painter, belonged to an art circle, and exhibited at the Toronto Society of Artists in 1847. But all had not gone according to his wishes, since by that date he had already left Toronto for Longueuil; two years later he went to Montreal to live. In five years there he occupied four different dwellings.

Montreal did not bring good fortune any more than had Toronto or New York. His pictures would not sell: he went from door to door and offered his paintings for $5 or $10 each. The merchants and important businessmen had scant interest in painting, and furthermore Krieghoff's subjects held little attraction for them. They could not look too favourably upon scenes, costumes, and dwelling-places that reminded them of their peasant origins. He was expected rather to do paintings of horses imported from England, and signs for banks and stores. In fact Cornelius Krieghoff became more or less a housepainter in order to provide for his wife and their daughter Emily, who had been born in 1841.

The city of Quebec, however, possessed an aristocracy, formed of military men of a certain standing and other officers, who attached some importance to things of the mind. Moreover in the colleges and in society numerous literary, philosophical, and musical circles were being formed. At the Petit Séminaire of Quebec alone, more than

seven societies came into being. People liked to meet to discuss literature, hear a play, and also on occasion talk about painting [see Octave CRÉMAZIE]. But this discussion was hardly art criticism; the aesthetic concerns of European art centres were on a quite different level. The English officers liked to send their families a canvas on which was perpetuated some typical scene of the Canadian countryside or its people. The merchant wanted to have his own portrait, a tangible sign of his importance.

In 1851 Krieghoff had an opportunity to make contact with a representative of this society. John Budden, an auctioneer for A. J. Maxham and Company, met him at Montreal and bought some pictures from him. Did Budden make certain proposals to Krieghoff? Did he know him already or was this the first meeting? We do not know. But the pictures must certainly have captivated people in Quebec, for three years later Budden again met Krieghoff at Montreal and brought him to Quebec with his family. This new migration seems to have been carried out without much enthusiasm. Once more the family had to leave an environment to which they had become accustomed, and their relatives. Ernst had come to take up residence at Montreal with his wife and three children, and Cornelius would apparently have liked his brother to follow him to Quebec.

Cornelius Krieghoff resided at Quebec for 11 years: 11 years of intense productivity, 11 years of prosperity. Budden shared his house with the Krieghoff family, and introduced the painter to his friends and acquaintances. The artist met influential people, and was even host to the governor general, Lord Elgin [Bruce*]. Too much importance should not be attached to this visit, but undoubtedly such marks of esteem contributed greatly to the growth of Krieghoff's popularity. With Budden, he took numerous trips around Quebec, to see people and landscapes and to familiarize himself with ways of living. Two schools asked him to give a few hours' teaching: the Quebec School for Young Ladies and Miss Plimsoll's establishment. His teaching seems to have been confined to having his pupils copy his own paintings.

During the year 1854 Krieghoff went to Europe for six or eight months. Little has been discovered about this voyage. We do not know if he went alone, his reasons for going, or the countries he visited. To a desire to see once more the places of his youth were probably added practical reasons, such as the opportunity to make a show of his popularity and to meet the English publishers who had made engravings of his works. He may have stayed two months in Paris, where he sold a

Krieghoff

collection of Canadian plants assembled during his excursions in the woods. Of his alleged stay in Germany nothing is known. This voyage does not seem to have had great importance from the strictly artistic point of view, for Krieghoff's manner underwent no change during the succeeding years.

The same was apparently not true of his family life. His wife disappeared, but no one knows when or how. Some say that she left Krieghoff, discreetly, after they arrived at Quebec; others assert that she died at Longueuil in 1858 after a short illness. However, the Archives Judiciaires of Quebec and Longueuil possess no death certificate in the name of Louise Gauthier for the year 1858. Krieghoff may have had a second wife, about whom we are ignorant. His life is thus hardly known, and the most important sources of information about Krieghoff are indubitably his paintings.

Krieghoff's art found its inspiration in everyday life and in the countryside surrounding Quebec. No mythological painting came from his studio. Was it through ignorance of the ancient literatures? It does not seem so, for he possessed a well-stocked library and had seen European paintings in museums. There are also no nudes; the one he painted, around 1844, was a cause of some scandal in his entourage. Religious themes are rare too: no Pietà, no Madonna with child, no Vision. He did paint a few religious pictures, but they are really studies of manners with religion a pretext for a subject.

Cornelius Krieghoff was a genre painter. He was interested not in what had happened once at a given spot, but in what was going on every day around him. His characters are not important individuals in themselves; rather they present an image of a particular profession or social group, or of people of a particular age. The humour that breaks through in the majority of his canvases gives to his work an air of gaiety which recalls the great age of genre painting, the Dutch 17th century.

Genre painting in the 19th century is part of a wider phenomenon that René Jullian has rightly called *paysannerie*. The peasant world did occupy some place in the minds of artists and writers before this period, but it was not a major preoccupation. Even when they became interested in the peasant, they surrounded exact details with an idealized setting, as in the novels of George Sand. In painting, Millet directed his art exclusively towards *paysannerie*, as we see in "La Barateuse," "The Winnower," and many others. In the same way Courbet wanted "living art" in his "Stonebreakers," "Vendange à Ornans," and "Paysans de Flagey revenant de la foire." Novelists, such as Max Buchon and Balzac, described peasant customs at length, and showed various social groups in opposition. In Spain, Leonardo Alenza y Nieto, an admirable *costumbrista*, was untiring in his descriptions of the *maja*, the *casuchas*, the poor, and all the little people of Madrid. Krieghoff also made peasant life his principal theme. Without seeking to idealize, he depicted numerous scenes showing the customs and landscapes of a given region, and his regionalism thus linked him with this artistic movement of the 19th century. In the same way as Max Buchon and Courbet revealed Franche-Comté, and Alenza portrayed Madrid types, Krieghoff took the inhabitants of Quebec as his theme.

Krieghoff was interested in the imposing natural setting of the town of Quebec, and made it a favourite theme. The main subject of many of his pictures is the landscape. Landscape appeared tardily in Canadian painting with the first efforts of Joseph Légaré*. Krieghoff seems indeed to have been the first to take a constant interest in landscapes. Untiringly, he painted the rich colours of autumn at the moment when the forests are decked with the brightest vermilions, dazzling yellows, and deep greens. Many have taken him to task for using over-bright colours, without being aware of the brilliance of the Quebec forests in the autumn, when, for example, a sheet of water doubles their image. The mother-of-pearl whiteness of winter appealed to his palette just as strongly, and he has given us a great variety of landscapes in which firs and birches share the vast expanses of snow. Mountains pleased him equally, and serve as a backdrop for many compositions whose principal theme is the Canadian farm. Generally his attention was taken by a squalid looking dwelling. He has been reproached for painting tumble-down houses rather than the lavish seigneurial mansions of the Beaupré shore, and admittedly he has not left many pictures representing the aristocracy, but it is useless to hold this against him. His farms are pleasing because of their calm and realistic character. The little house with the pointed roof, the shelter where firewood and tools are to be seen, the shed some distance away, the sleigh pulled by a workhorse, the children playing in the snow: here was the spectacle that the Quebec countryside set before him. Often a stream runs through his paintings, or a lake occupies the centre of the composition. The river motif returns frequently, and he has left images of the Montmorency as well as of the lakes close to Quebec.

Krieghoff observed the work people did, and transposed its picturesque aspects to his canvas. He liked to represent the sugaring-off time, when the whole family shared in gathering the sap of the maple and the mother busied herself boiling the liquid under a shelter of planks. With tireless enthusiasm he repeated hunting scenes in the great forests. Wearing snowshoes and heavily clothed, the hunters pursue the stag and exhaust it in the soft snow before bringing it down. Sometimes it is their conquered victim that is the centre of the composition. He also portrayed trappers at work or workers busy laying in stocks of ice.

But Krieghoff's most engaging theme is perhaps that of people enjoying themselves. The inn scenes show gatherings of jolly fellows who are having a fling, dancing and drinking copiously. The canvas called "Merrymaking" is undoubtedly his greatest success with this group. Other scenes at the Jolifou Inn similarly delight by their spontaneity. The men have gone to get the horses from the stable, and harness them either to a heavy sleigh or to an elegant carriage. Meanwhile, the women are taking their leave on the inn porch or giving their husbands the blankets that have been carefully warmed to protect them from the cold during the journey. Others are adjusting their snow-shoes. The "fiddler" has come out, violin and bottle in hand, and takes the first step of a dance, to the amusement of the people around.

It is well known that at this period the French Canadians valued their horses greatly: the animal's beauty, and his skill and speed, were important to them. On many occasions Krieghoff depicted wild rides on the snow and ice, and the moment when two teams entered into competition. He often represents a low sleigh on which two or three men stand to travel over the countryside. At that time Montmorency Falls drew people of every class because of its varied attractions. The great frozen plain was eminently suitable for drives, and the women of fashion showed off their rich finery. The men guided their elaborate and high-spirited teams with an air of pride. The enormous ice cone at the foot of the falls delighted sliders, who found this place less formal than the slide before the citadel. Drinks were even served in a little room set up in the cone itself. The seminary of Quebec possesses an admirable print of Krieghoff's representing this place, with dozens of small figures enjoying themselves in a fairylike setting. Even the games of children – who are numerous in Krieghoff's work – captured his attention. They are most lively when they are coming out of school: they jostle each other, organize snowball fights, or slide on brightly coloured toboggans.

Travellers often appear in the artist's pictures. A canoe glides silently over the water or passes between banks covered with vegetation. Even in the 19th century the canoe was still a principal means of locomotion. There were portages around rapids

and dangerous spots; it might be necessary to risk paddling between blocks of ice, or to hoist the canoe onto a frozen surface and then put it back in the water: all this in icy temperatures. These were the conditions under which the mail was dispatched from Quebec to Lévis and travellers ventured the crossing. Each year the Quebec carnival revives these perilous scenes, which Krieghoff has immortalized. Other kinds of locomotion – horse and snow-shoe – offered material for interesting studies.

Paintings of the fur trade with the Indians and the transporting of pelts give an opportunity to observe men, rough and strong, who resemble the lumbermen of today. The pedlar, the timber merchant, the go-between, even customers of the general store appear in this world of tough, grasping individuals.

Religious scenes are infrequent in Krieghoff's work. The mystical aspect of convent life, the activities of clergy or nuns, interested him little. When he did portray a member of the clergy, Krieghoff sought rather to express a tension between two social groups. One thinks of "Le Carême": the parish priest calls on a family unexpectedly and finds that they are feasting away royally. This is a grave offence against religious precepts and against the priest, who expected every home to take his rigorous teaching seriously.

The Indians, also, are a rich source of inspiration for Krieghoff. No doubt he came into contact with them in the United States, during the expedition to Florida. At Montreal he painted the Indians of Caughnawaga, and at Quebec, those of Lorette. The majority of scenes are situated in the Laurentians, where the Indians are portrayed in habitual dress and their special way of life. He shows their sleighs, their mocassins, their great bright-coloured cloaks. Women place their children near a fire, in a basket made of branches or leather thongs, and prepare a meal, while the men smoke their long pipes. Or else we see Indians with baskets they have made for sale. This social group, still strongly individualized at the time, had in Krieghoff a sympathetic and prolific interpreter.

Krieghoff as a portrait-painter had a period of real celebrity. "He shows us the old Canadien, with keen, clear eye, slightly hooked nose, mat complexion, cheeks ruddy and brightened by the winter cold, and graying side-whiskers, which frame the face of a man wrapped and buttoned up to his neck in his cloak of local cloth." As well as these portraits, in which he reproduced the features of those who lived around him, he did others of important people, for example, Lord Elgin. The McCord Museum at Montreal possesses a fine portrait of this governor. Krieghoff has also left us

Krieghoff

an interesting portrait of his friend John Budden. Elegantly garbed in check trousers and a golden-brown jacket, he is in a restful pose, nonchalantly seated by a stretch of water. Behind him he has placed his tall hat, his gun, and his game-bag. Krieghoff did not miss the opportunity to recall his subject's partiality towards hunting. The scene stands out against a background of forest and heavy rocks.

Krieghoff painted an enormous number of pictures, and it is at present impossible to determine exactly the extent of his work. From the catalogue of 500 pictures established by Charles-Marius Barbeau*, a number must be removed. On the other hand, many should be added. He seems to have painted some 700 pictures. Nine were destroyed in the chamber of the Legislative Assembly when the parliament of Quebec was burned down in 1881, others have been stolen. A re-evaluation of Krieghoff's art would necessitate a systematic effort to establish an exact catalogue of his works. While this task remains to be done, fresh information may come to light but Krieghoff's work cannot be known in all its complexity.

Krieghoff does not seem to have done any engraving himself, but he may have had works lithographed during 1848, that is during his stay at Montreal. Lithography, a new technique, had been invented in 1796 and had become popular in Europe during the 1820s. In 1848 Krieghoff had four of his paintings lithographed by the firm of Borum in Munich. These lithographs, dedicated to Lord Elgin, were sold by subscription. Then a Philadelphia company published two prints representing beggars: "Pour l'amour du bon Dieu!" and "Va au Diable!" In 1860 John Weals of London published at least two engravings: "Passengers and mail crossing the river," and "Indian chief." The seminary of Quebec possesses an excellent coloured engraving representing "The Ice Cone at the Falls of Montmorency." This print was made by the lithographic studios of Day and Son of London, and published by the Ackermann Company.

Was Krieghoff a prolific sketcher? It seems not, since no known drawing of his now exists. For some years it was thought that an admirable book of 36 sketches, representing several sites at Montreal, was his work, but it has now been proved that these are by James Duncan*. Krieghoff's impulsive temperament was probably ill suited to lengthy study; he painted from life and without the help of preliminary sketches.

Krieghoff is perhaps one of the most controversial Canadian artists. Some praise him to the skies, others cannot find sufficiently uncomplimentary expressions to apply to his work. In the 19th century Krieghoff seems to have been much appreciated, and to have sold his paintings easily. At Quebec, the English officers, who liked to buy souvenirs for their families, were ready purchasers of his pictures, offered at trifling prices. This popularity can be confirmed from the auction sales organized by the firm of Maxham to which Budden belonged.

On 1 Aug. 1861, *Le Journal de Québec* announced for 7 August a sale of engravings collected by Krieghoff. On 21 December the same paper announced a sale of 100 of his works, mentioning "Divertissement" ["Merrymaking?"] and "The Alchemist." The lot included copies after English and other masters. It was stated that "this is the last and sole opportunity to procure works from the pencil of Mr. Krieghoff, since he is soon leaving for Europe." But the sale seems not to have taken place, for almost the same announcement appeared on 27 March 1862. This time the lot sold fairly well, since on 13 December the firm announced the sale of the remainder of the lot, that is 30 paintings with Canadian subjects and a few engravings. On 13 December also, *Le Journal de Québec* informed its readers of the sale of his collection of stuffed birds, of coins and Chinese curios, and particularly of his library, made up of 1,200 volumes, historical and scientific as well as classical. His library can therefore be considered among the large private libraries, the majority of which in the first half of the 19th century contained less than 500 volumes. This sale casts new light on the painter's personality. His vast curiosity and his collector's tastes prove indeed that Krieghoff was not the gay dog, the tippler and roisterer, that people have taken pleasure in presenting, by identifying him too readily with certain figures in his paintings.

After Krieghoff left Quebec, works still appeared on the market. Thus, on 18 Oct. 1870, *Le Journal de Québec* announced a sale of paintings from Europe and "some Canadian, Russian, and English subjects by Krieghoff." There was apparently no auction sale of Krieghoff's works before 1862, but before he left the artist wanted to sell off his works, his collections, and even his furniture. It would therefore be an exaggeration to say that it was the auctioneers of the firm of Maxham who launched Krieghoff, by ordering pictures from him which would fetch a good price thanks to skilful publicity. The truth seems simpler. Krieghoff sold his pleasing, lively canvases regularly to art lovers. On the eve of his departure, his friend Budden helped to sell his collections and works by putting them up for auction.

The announcement of his leaving Quebec in 1862 raises a few problems. The artist does not appear to have gone to Europe. It seems more likely that he rejoined his daughter Emily and lived with her from then on. Her first husband had been Lieutenant Hamilton Burnett, whom she had married at Quebec; her second was Count de Wendt, a Russian who had emigrated to Chicago. At the end of his life, Krieghoff may have visited Quebec and Montreal. On 9 March 1872 he died suddenly at Chicago.

In the 20th century two currents of opinion have formed, while the commercial value of his works continues to soar. In 1893 John George Bourinot* first praised Krieghoff in his volume *Our intellectual strength and weakness*. He commended him as the first painter to draw attention to the beauty of Canadian scenes, and George Moore Fairchild* corroborated this judgement in 1907. Henri-Arthur Scott exaggerated so grossly the value of this artist that it was easy to foresee an eventual reaction in the opposite direction. Scott, lost in admiration, exclaimed: "We have seen paintings of Krieghoff, sunsets of a brilliancy that truly recalls the marvellous splendours of the western sky, and permits us to affirm that the richness of his palette was in no way inferior to the finest examples of this genre in the museums of Europe. But why then is this painter not known over there, not placed among the great landscape-painters, the Corots, the Courbets, the Ziems, the Théodore Rousseaus? He painted our 'few acres of snow,' and this was not enough to stir up public opinion in Europe." In 1925 Newton McFaul MacTavish*, speaking of Krieghoff's talent for caricaturing the types that he encountered, compared him to William Hogarth.

But from 1922 on another current of opinion was appearing, a current created and fed by French Canadians alone. Pierre-Georges Roy* stated that Krieghoff's painting could not be valued highly as an artistic achievement. If his paintings sold well it was because he was a foreigner, and was the only one to have treated local subjects. These opinions have clashed and contradicted each other particularly since 1934, the year of the publication of Marius Barbeau's romanticized study. Numerous criticisms of Krieghoff have appeared in reviews and journals; some have been openly hostile. Jean Chauvin reproached him with liking "the common people, carousing, noisy merrymaking, and knock-about farce," and with putting his farmers "in huts that looked more like pigsties." Two years later Maurice Hébert derided Krieghoff's characters in violent language. "What Prussian faces they display, or should we say Bavarian or Dutch snouts! One of the men lifts a glass of spirits, rubs his belly, licks his chops, and slobbers, all in a grossly stupid manner." Gérard

Morisset* took up these judgements on his own account, and amplified them. According to him, "this painter is a gay dog who does not disdain to souse with his monied clientele; he turns out pictures, as a manufacturer would, which are within everybody's grasp because of the carousing that he depicts, the besotted faces of his figures, the rather crude comedy of his genre scenes, and his autumn landscapes with their violent and loud colours." It is true that his canvases please people. Since 1847 the majority of the exhibitions of traditional Canadian art have included pictures by Krieghoff. The 163 paintings exhibited in 1934 caused a stir of interest around Krieghoff, and the prices of his works have not ceased to rise. His paintings sell now for $8,000, $18,000, and even $45,000.

Misunderstandings have distorted many judgements passed on Krieghoff's art. Certain critics, aristocratic in their taste, wanted grand subjects, noble and worthy themes. Krieghoff, they say, ought to have used a bold brush to paint a complete panorama of French Canadian life in the 19th century. If he had depicted the aristocracy, the rich manor-houses and the stately ceremonies of the period, he would have been pardoned an occasional incursion into less exalted fields. But to devote his entire art to peasants, and to the humble setting in which their undistinguished life unfolded, was unthinkable. He is blamed in addition for not being a truly Canadian artist, and for drawing his inspiration too narrowly from the 17th century Dutch. Are we so certain that Krieghoff always wanted to be a "Canadian" artist? Did not his clientele like to buy "Russian and English" subjects, as we can see from *Le Journal de Québec* of 18 Oct. 1870? Numerous canvases certainly recall the Dutch, but the attitudes of the characters and the details of the composition are indeed Krieghoff's. Disappointed at not finding in him all the aspects they would like to see, certain people have come to the point of being unable to appreciate his art.

His themes have great interest in themselves and for their historical value. He is one of the first artists to draw his inspiration from the French Canadian milieu. He perpetuates customs and traditions which it would be hard to rediscover in another way. Krieghoff as a genre painter is undeniably pleasing, and his regionalism, far from lessening the value of his art, adds a component to the vast current of ideas centring around the peasant, both in Europe and in America. Certainly he is not a great master, but his technique is good, and his compositions are simple and firm. With deft touches he paints the face of an old man with graying hair, but he is just as adept at grouping several figures on a canvas, as his scenes of merry-

413

making prove. Thus, brought back to more accurate proportions, Cornelius Krieghoff's work occupies an important place in the evolution of the arts in Canada.

RAYMOND VÉZINA

AJQ, Registre d'état civil, mariage d'Emily Krieghoff. *Gazette* (Montreal), 23 June 1951; 16 March, 28 Oct. 1957; 19 March, 29 Nov. 1958; 13, 23 April 1959; 4 June 1963. *Le Journal de Québec*, 1er août 1861 (announcement of a sale of engravings by Krieghoff), 21 déc. 1861; 27 mars, 13 déc. 1862 (lists of paintings sold); 21 mai 1869 (list of paintings exhibited). *Montreal Star*, 22 May 1958, 12 March 1963, 19 Nov. 1966. *La Presse* (Montréal), 25 oct., 28 oct., 8 nov. 1957; 12 déc. 1958; 16 mars 1959. *Le Soleil* (Québec), 10 déc. 1966.

Edwy Cooke, *Cornelius Krieghoff, ca 1815–1872* (Fredericton, n.d.). *The development of painting in Canada/Le développement de la peinture au Canada, 1665–1945* (Toronto, 1945). *Encyclopedia Canadiana*, VI, 21. *Encyclopedia of Canada*, III, 348–49. *Exposition rétrospective de l'art au Canada/The arts in French Canada*, Gérard Morisset, édit. (Québec, 1952). R. H. Hubbard and J.-R. Ostiguy, *Three hundred years of Canadian art: an exhibition arranged in celebration of the centenary of confederation/ Exposition organisée à l'occasion du centenaire de la confédération* (Ottawa, 1967). Mexico, Museo nacional de arte moderno, *Arte Canadiense* ([Mexico City?], 1960). Ottawa, National Gallery, *Exhibition of Canadian painting to celebrate the coronation of Her Majesty Queen Elizabeth II* (Ottawa, 1953). *Le peintre et le Nouveau Monde; étude sur la peinture de 1564 à 1867 pour souligner le centenaire de la Confédération canadienne/[The painter and the New World]; a survey of painting from 1564 to 1867 marking the founding of Canadian confederation* (Montreal, 1967). A. H. Robson, *Catalogue of Toronto centennial historical exhibition, paintings by Cornelius Krieghoff* ... ([Toronto], 1934]). Toronto, Art Gallery, *Painting and sculpture; illustrations of selected paintings and sculpture from the collection* (Toronto, [1959]). *Treasures from Quebec; an exhibition of paintings assembled from Quebec and its environs/Trésors de Québec; exposition de peintures provenant de Québec et des environs* (n.p., [1965]). United States, National Gallery of Art, *Canadian painting, an exhibition arranged by the National Gallery of Canada* (Washington, 1950). Vancouver, Art Gallery, *The arts in French Canada/Les arts au Canada français* ([Vancouver], 1959). Wallace, *Macmillan dictionary*, 374–75.

[C.] M. Barbeau, *Cornelius Krieghoff, pioneer painter of North America* (Toronto, 1934). J. G. Bourinot, *Our intellectual strength and weakness; a short historical and critical review of literature, art and education in Canada* (Royal Society of Canada series, 1, Montreal, 1893). *Canadian painters, from Paul Kane to the Group of Seven*, ed. D. W. Buchanan (Oxford and London, 1945). Antonio Drolet, *Les bibliothèques canadiennes, 1604–1960* (Ottawa, 1965). G. M. Fairchild, *Gleanings from Quebec* (Quebec, 1908), 66–74. J. R. Harper, *Painting in Canada, a history* (Toronto, 1966). R. H. Hubbard, *The development of Canadian art* (Ottawa, 1963). J.-S. Lesage, *Notes et esquisses québecoises; carnet d'un amateur* (Québec, 1925), 52–57. N. M. MacTavish, *The fine arts in Canada* (Toronto, 1925), 15–20. Gérard Morisset, *Coup d'œil sur les arts en Nouvelle-France* (Québec, 1941), 85–87. A. H. Robson, *Cornelius Krieghoff* (Canadian artists series, Toronto, 1937). P.-G. Roy, "Les peintures de Krieghoff," in *Les petites choses de notre histoire* (7v., Lévis, Qué.), 1919–44), IV, 168–71. H. A. Scott, *Grands anniversaires; souvenirs historiques et pensées utiles* (Québec, 1919), 297–99.

[C.] M. Barbeau, "Krieghoff découvre le Canada," *RSCT*, 3rd ser., XXVIII (1934), sect I, 111–18 and 3 illustrations; "Kreighoff's [sic] early Canadian scenes. Varied, resourceful, embracing," *Montreal Daily Star*, 17 March 1934. Hébert Budden *et al.*, "Cornelius Kreighoff [sic]," *BRH*, I (1895), 45–46. Jean Chauvin, "Cornelius Krieghoff [sic] imagier populaire," *La Revue populaire* (Montréal), juin 1934. William Colgate, "Krieghoff, pictorial historian," *Mail and Empire* (Toronto), 8 Jan. 1935. E. A. Collard, "Krieghoff's beautiful oil-paintings," *Gazette* (Montreal), 14 March 1959. A. Ch. de Guttenberg, "Cornelius Krieghoff," *Revue de l'université d'Ottawa*, XXIV (1954), 90–108. Maurice Hébert, "Quelques livres de chez nous: Cornélius Krieghoff," *Le Canada français* (Québec), XXIV (1936–37), 162–65. "The Jolifou Inn by Krieghoff," *Weekend Magazine* (Montreal), V, no.52 (1955). Kay Kritzwiser, "Laing galleries," *Globe and Mail* (Toronto), 12 Feb. 1966. Michel Lapalme, "Krieghoff à l'encan," *Le Magazine Maclean* (Toronto), May 1969, 59–61. Gérard Morisset, "Cornelius Krieghoff. Réflexions en marge du livre de Marius Barbeau," *Le Canada* (Montréal), 19 janv., 21 janv. 1935. "Six Krieghoffs return to Canada," *Montreal Star*, 23 Nov. 1966.

[The author would like to thank Mr Luke Rombout, Dept. of Fine Arts, York University (Toronto), for information he supplied. R.V.]

L

LABERGE, CHARLES

LABERGE, CHARLES, lawyer, journalist, politician; b. 21 Oct. 1827 at Montreal, L.C., son of Ambroise Laberge, a merchant, and Rose Franchère, sister of the explorer Gabriel Franchère*; d. 3 Aug. 1874 at Montreal, Que.

Charles Laberge's mother, who early became a widow and had only limited means, gave music lessons for some time, in order to meet the needs of four children of tender years. Charles, whose health gave her cause for anxiety, was committed to the care of a farmer at Rivière-des-Prairies, so that the pure country air would strengthen his lungs.

He enrolled at the college of Saint-Hyacinthe in 1838 and completed his classical studies in 1845. All the evidence indicates that young Laberge at once impressed his masters and fellow-students by his intellectual liveliness and an aptitude for assimilating knowledge which won him, as Laurent-Olivier David* wrote, "effortlessly and without work successes that many others labour after in vain."

In the literary and oratorical assignments particularly his gifts showed themselves with the greatest felicity. A journalist in embryo, he founded at the college a journal with the predestined title *Le Libéral*, in which his waggish pen ran freely at the expense of teachers who displeased the pupils. While speaking one day before Lord Elgin [Bruce*], who was visiting the college, he earned the compliment that he would become a distinguished orator, a forecast which Louis-Joseph PAPINEAU, after his return from exile, said was already realized when he heard him during the literary exercises in 1845. "Frankly, M. Laberge, I have never spoken as well as you have just done; if I have had the title of *Speaker*, you have the speaker's talent."

At the end of his college years, Charles Laberge studied law at Montreal under René-Auguste-Richard Hubert*. He was called to the bar in 1848 and went into partnership with the lawyer Toussaint-Antoine-Rodolphe Laflamme*, but in 1852 he moved to Saint-Jean-d'Iberville, where in a short time he acquired a large clientele.

While still a law student, Laberge had been intensely active in the Institut Canadien, of which he was a founder. In November 1845 his *confrères* had elected him corresponding secretary of their association. When *L'Avenir* began to appear in November 1847 he was one of "thirteen" contributors whose average age was not more than 23. Both on the rostrum of the Institut Canadien and as a journalist, he tackled the most varied subjects, but he insisted above all that it was necessary for Canada to be annexed to the United States. In a series of articles that appeared in *L'Avenir* from 2 June to 30 Oct. 1849, signed "34 stars," he developed the following thesis: "We have reached the time when Canada must become a republic, when our star must go to take its place in the American sky." With Jean-Baptiste-Éric Dorion*, Joseph Papin*, and Charles Daoust*, some of his friends from the Institut Canadien and *L'Avenir*, he allowed himself to be carried into active politics in the wake of Louis-Joseph Papineau. In 1854 he was elected member for Iberville County; with 10

of his *confrères* of the Institut Canadien who had also been returned by their respective counties, he belonged to the constellation of young Liberals, headed by Antoine-Aimé Dorion*, whom two political adversaries, Joseph-Charles Taché* and Pierre-Joseph-Olivier Chauveau* under the pseudonym Gaspard Le Mage, endeavoured to ridicule in a pamphlet called *La pléiade rouge*.

In the house, according to Oscar Dunn*, Laberge "was on his own ground, in the element most suited to his abilities. Not sufficiently wily to be a first rate lawyer, or sufficiently profound to dominate on the bench, he possessed a natural gift of eloquence, a breadth of ideas, an uprightness of character which won him, without effort on his part, an exceptional place in a deliberative assembly." And Dunn added: "He had a fine turn of speech, a French of true quality; in this respect no one in our country was more gifted than he."

When the Conservative ministry fell in 1858, over the question of the seat of government, Laberge agreed to become solicitor general in the cabinet of George BROWN and Antoine-Aimé Dorion, which lasted only two days. Although ephemeral, this alliance with the Scotsman whom French Canada hated was certainly not calculated to increase his stature in his own eyes and in those of his friends.

Be that as it may, in 1860 he decided to leave active politics and devote himself exclusively to his family and his profession. Hence he refused to stand as a candidate in the 1861 general elections. He did allow himself to be appointed a judge at Sorel in 1863 by the Liberal government, but the Conservatives, back in power the following year, lost no time in getting him to return to private life. He accepted this situation philosophically, being thoroughly happy in the home that he had set up on 23 Nov. 1859, when he married Hélène-Olive Turgeon, daughter of the former legislative councillor, Joseph-Ovide Turgeon*.

Journalism always had a keen attraction for him. In 1860, with his friend Félix-Gabriel Marchand*, he established *Le Franco-Canadien* (Saint-Jean-d'Iberville), to which he contributed from time to time. He did the same for another liberal paper, *L'Ordre* (Montreal), in which he published articles signed "Liberal but Catholic."

Like the majority of his liberal friends, he took a stand against the projected confederation of the provinces of British North America. In 1865, replying in a public meeting at Montreal to those who said that the opponents of confederation offered no other remedy, he exclaimed: "I do not admit that a change of constitution has become necessary, but supposing it has, can we justifiably

Laberge

accept a political régime which will give us three or four enemies instead of one? If we already have so much difficulty in struggling against Upper Canada, what shall we do when we have to fight three or four other provinces?" He proposed the "separatist" solution: "If the constitution must be changed, let us separate since we cannot agree, and let us have the questions of customs and tariff that concern all the provinces settled by a small congress which will not have the right to deal with anything else."

It was no doubt at the repeated requests of his liberal friends that in 1872 he tore himself away from his little town of Saint-Jean-d'Iberville, where he was keenly appreciated by his fellow-citizens who had twice elected him mayor, to go back to live in Montreal and take on the editorship of *Le National*. In its first number, on 24 April 1872, this paper broke with the tradition of *L'Avenir* and *Le Pays*: "*Le National* will be a political and not a religious journal, but the special organ of a Catholic population, and, in conformity with the beliefs of those directing the journal, we shall when occasion arises adopt entirely the Catholic viewpoint; we disavow in advance anything which in the rapid compiling of a daily newspaper might slip through by inadvertence, and expressly declare our entire devotion and our filial obedience to the Church." Laberge, his health already seriously affected, was unable to show what he was capable of. His friend Oscar Dunn says that "it was only by dint of truly heroic efforts that he managed to write his articles, while in the grip of the disease that was eating him away." "Poor and burdened with a family, he silenced his tortures in order to accomplish his daily task; and his sense of duty was so developed that he drew from it the strength to master his sickness, so much so that sometimes he deceived his family and gave it fleeting periods of hope."

To physical suffering was added moral suffering. A firm Christian, he had always been distressed by the suspicions of some opponents and even some members of the clergy about his religious beliefs, because he professed himself a liberal. This suffering had been sharpened when the Institut Canadien, after being the object of episcopal censures in three pastoral letters issued by Bishop Ignace Bourget* on 10 March, 30 April, and 31 May 1858, lost some 135 of its members, who broke away to found the Institut Canadien-Français [*see* Cassidy]. When in 1867 conservative papers started to revile the members of the Institut Canadien by styling them "excommunicates," Charles Laberge was roused, and in a letter from Saint-Jean dated 16 Aug. 1867 he informed Bishop Bourget that as one of "the founders" of the institute, and

because he was "still a member" although he no longer took part in its meetings, he wished to be enlightened in the "cruel embarrassment" in which he found himself with regard to "the positive assertion of excommunication" directed against him and his *confrères*.

According to him, the differences of opinion that had resulted in the unfortunate scission of 1858 could have been avoided: "When, some years back, difficulties arose, I thought, and I still think, that the same resources and the same energy that founded the Institut Canadien-Français would have been more usefully employed in reshaping the Institut Canadien, and I have several times offered my services in order to achieve this result. It seemed to me that by bringing in a large number of new members one might give the institute a different orientation, and preserve an institution which is prosperous and has reached its 23rd year, a unique occurrence in Lower Canada. I am still ready to employ all my possible influence as founder to arrive at the same result, if it is still desirable."

Laberge had never actually read the pastoral letters of 1858 on the Institut Canadien. When he heard of them, he consulted his confessor, "a distinguished priest, who has since become a bishop, and who told me," wrote Laberge to Bourget, "that, as I was taking no active and public part in the work of the institute, I could without objection remain a member of it, reserving the right to withdraw when it became necessary." This "distinguished priest" was probably Charles La Rocque, parish priest of Saint-Jean-d'Iberville, 1844–66, and third bishop of Saint-Hyacinthe, 1866–75. Indeed, in the Bourget-La Rocque correspondence concerning the members of the Institut Canadien, one can sense how reticent the parish priest of Saint-Jean-d'Iberville and the future bishop of Saint-Hyacinthe was in face of the uncompromising and inflexible attitude adopted by the bishop of Montreal towards them.

Laberge therefore implored Bishop Bourget to extricate him from his perplexity: "Now, My Lord Bishop, I desire to know where I stand, and I am not sufficiently important to be granted the honour of an interview with Your Excellency at Montreal. Although a member of the institute, I continue to receive the sacraments, on the strength of the consultation reported above."

Whatever the bishop of Montreal's reply was – if he replied at all – Charles Laberge, although he ceased to be a member of the Institut Canadien, remained faithful to the last to the position that had made him, according to Oscar Dunn, "with due allowances," "the Montalembert of his party, associating modern ideas on Church and State with solid religious convictions, a democrat as much as a Christian"; "I do not know what the foundation of his liberalism was," Dunn added, "but he had the hopes of the convinced Catholic."

The day after his death, on 3 Aug. 1874, his successor in the office of *Le National* wrote in the paper that had received the last productions of his pen: "He remains a model politician, and he has always been the living proof that one could be a sincere liberal and a fervent Catholic."

PHILIPPE SYLVAIN

[The newspapers on which Laberge collaborated, *Le Franco-Canadien* (Saint-Jean-d'Iberville), *Le National* (Montréal) and *L'Ordre* (Montréal), must be consulted for any thorough study of him. *See also*: *L'Avenir* (Montréal), 2 juin–30 oct. 1849 and *L'Opinion publique* (Montréal), 27 août 1874. P.S.]
ACAM, 901.135. Borthwick, *Hist. and biog. gazetteer*, 220. L.-O. David, *Souvenirs et biographies, 1870–1910* (Montréal, 1911), 43–49. Oscar Dunn, *Dix ans de journalisme, mélanges* (Montréal, 1876), 229–41.

LABRÈCHE-VIGER, LOUIS, journalist and politician; b. 1824 at Terrebonne, L.C., son of Louis Labrèche and Marguerite-Julie Viger; d. 27 April 1872 at Montreal, Que.

Born of parents who were farmers, Louis Labrèche was educated at the college of Montreal, probably thanks to the patronage of Denis-Benjamin Viger*, who persuaded the youthful student to contribute to *L'Aurore des Canadas* for some months. Out of either gratitude or admiration, Louis seems from then on to have added his protector's name to his own. He spent two years at the seminary of Montreal, left it to study law in the office of Côme-Séraphin Cherrier*, another of Denis-Benjamin Viger's protégés, and was called to the bar at Montreal on 27 April 1848.

It was as a member of the group of young men belonging to the Institut Canadien that Labrèche-Viger began to make himself known. In 1848, when this group started the Association pour le Peuplement des Cantons de l'Est, he acted with Joseph Doutre* as one of its two secretaries. Its aim was to check the movement of emigration to the United States that followed the insurrection, and to open for settlement the undeveloped areas of the Eastern Townships. Then Labrèche-Viger worked as a journalist with *L'Avenir* until 1851, and for some months in 1852 was editor of *Le Pays*. This means that at that time he was an annexationist, and one of the most enthusiastic supporters of the liberalism of the Institut Canadien. Later, in 1858, when the institute came into conflict with Bishop Ignace Bourget*, Louis Labrèche-Viger

left it and drew up the declaration of the founders of the Institut Canadien-Français [*see* CASSIDY].

Meanwhile, around 1852, he had become a merchant. An employee, then in 1854 a partner of the grocer Ephrem Hudon, he was also a member of the Trust and Loan Company. He entered the political arena again: in 1861 he was elected at Terrebonne by a majority of 30 votes over the outgoing member, Louis-Siméon MORIN, and he was re-elected for the same county against the same opponent in 1863. He apparently made himself famous by never making a single speech in the house. However, he consistently voted on the side of the Rouge party. He also contributed to *L'Ordre*, and along with the editors of this paper he opposed confederation. At the time of the famous vote on 11 March 1865, he was one of the 21 French Canadian assemblymen who voted against the plan.

After 1867 Labrèche-Viger left politics in order to give his attention more and more to metallurgy, and to exploiting iron mines in the Rivière Moisie region [*see* MOLSON]. He incorporated a mining company, and became passionately absorbed in a search for the secret of the conversion of iron into steel. After three years of trials and tests, he thought he had found it, and obtained patents in Canada, the United States, and Great Britain. He also wanted to exploit the magnetic sands of the Rivière Moisie, and set up a laboratory on the banks of the Rivière Saint-Charles near Quebec. He died before learning the result of these experiments.

Louis Labrèche-Viger had married in 1852 a sister of Toussaint-Antoine-Rodolphe Laflamme*, Caroline, who bore him a son. According to contemporaries, he was a man of pleasing appearance, with an intelligent countenance and a shrewd mind. He was most affable in his demeanour and was always ready to be of service.

JACQUES MONET

PAC, MG 30, D62 (Audet papers), 8, p.81. *L'Avenir* (Montréal), 1848–49. *L'Opinion publique* (Montréal), 16 mai 1872. *Le Pays* (Montréal), 1851. Cornell, *Alignment of political groups*. L.-O. David, *Les gerbes canadiennes* (Montréal, 1921), 43–50. Monet, *Last cannon shot*.

LA BRUÈRE, PIERRE-CLAUDE BOUCHER DE. *See* BOUCHER

LA COLOMBIÈRE, MARIE-JULIE-MAR-GUERITE CÉRÉ DE. *See* CÉRÉ

LACOSTE, LOUIS, notary and politician; b. 3 April 1798 at Boucherville, L.C., son of Louis Lacoste and Joséphine Dubois; d. 26 Nov. 1878 at Boucherville, Que.

Lacoste

A descendant of Alexandre Lacoste, who came originally from the Department of Gard (France), Louis Lacoste received his secondary education at the college of Montreal, then studied law, and on 19 March 1821 was commissioned as a notary. He practised at Boucherville.

In 1834 he decided to launch out into politics. He was chosen as member for Chambly County in the House of Assembly of Lower Canada, a position he kept until the constitution was suspended in 1838. He was an ardent supporter of Louis-Joseph PAPINEAU, and on 23 Oct. 1837 took part in the assembly of the six counties held at Saint-Charles-sur-Richelieu. He delivered a violent speech there, and even proposed a resolution in which was stressed the urgency of replacing officers who had been appointed by an "administration hostile to the country" by trustworthy men. Therefore "all the parishes of the six counties are simultaneously invited, between the first of December and the first of January following, to elect justices of the peace, arbitrators, and officers of the militia." It was not long before this unequivocal commitment in the fight against the government brought reprisals upon him: on 8 Dec. 1837 a warrant of arrest was issued against him. He gave himself up to the sheriff, was put in prison in Montreal, and was not freed until 7 July 1838, on bail of £1,000.

Once the storm was over, Louis Lacoste returned to his profession, of which he was one of the most brilliant representatives. On 23 Oct. 1843 he was again elected MLA for Chambly, and remained its member until 6 Dec. 1847 (Ægidius Fauteux* states, however, in his work *Patriotes de 1837–1838* that Lacoste did not return to public life until 1849). He again represented the same county from 25 Sept. 1849 to 23 June 1854. After an absence of four years, he returned to parliament for the period 1858 to 1861. With George-Étienne CARTIER, Joseph-Édouard Cauchon*, and Joseph-Édouard Turcotte*, he was one of the last of the members who had been elected to the first parliaments of the Union. These liberals had evolved under Cartier's leadership, and around 1856 they were referred to as the Bleus, by contrast with the Rouges, or radical liberals. When the Legislative Council became elective, Louis Lacoste resigned as a member of the assembly and was elected legislative councillor for the division of Montarville, a post he held until confederation. In 1867 he was appointed a senator, and remained in the Senate until his death.

Louis Lacoste was called upon to play an important role in the field of education. On 22 Feb. 1853 the government set up a select committee "to inquire into the state of education in Lower Canada." This committee was presided over by Louis-Victor Sicotte*, MLA for Saint-Hyacinthe; Lewis Thomas Drummond*, William Badgley*, Cartier, Antoine Polette, Louis Lacoste, John Sewell SANBORN, Jean-Charles Chapais*, and Robert Christie* were assigned to assist him. The inquiry was made necessary by the sharp criticisms levelled against the school system in Lower Canada and by the friction which disturbed Dr Jean-Baptiste MEILLEUR's administration. The committee prepared a questionnaire which was addressed to all the parish priests or Protestant ministers, and to the secretary-treasurers of the municipalities. More than 400 persons replied, in particular Jacques CRÉMAZIE, lawyer and member of the Quebec Board of Examiners. The report of the inquiry had no immediate results: the principal consequence of the recommendations of the Sicotte commission was Dr Meilleur's resignation on 19 June 1855, and his replacement by Pierre-Joseph-Olivier Chauveau*, who thus became the second superintendent of education in Lower Canada. In the following year two important school laws were passed by the parliament of Canada, with Lower Canada expressly in mind: these laws set up a Council of Public Instruction, a *Journal de l'Instruction publique* (in both languages), and three normal schools. They were the logical outcome of the work of the Sicotte commission.

On 14 July 1823 Louis Lacoste had married Catherine-Renée Boucher de La Bruère, who died on 23 Aug. 1832. One son, Louis-René, was born of this marriage. A notary, he died at the age of 31, when he was showing great promise. On 28 Sept. 1836 Louis Lacoste married Charlotte Magenty Mount, but soon afterwards became a widower a second time. He took as his third wife Marie-Antoinette-Thaïs Proulx, on 17 Nov. 1838. Of this third marriage Alexandre Lacoste*, a chief justice of the province of Quebec, was born.

The historian of Boucherville, Father Louis Lalande*, wrote of Louis Lacoste that "he was the man who spoke for his country. For 50 years, in all the great events affecting his people, he was the guiding spirit of the large population spread out between the St Lawrence and the Richelieu and extending as far as the Chambly basin."

LOUIS-PHILIPPE AUDET

JALPC, 1852–1853, app. J.J., "Rapport du comité spécial de l'Assemblée législative nommé pour s'enquérir de l'état de l'éducation et du fonctionnement de la loi des écoles dans le Bas-Canada." *Dom. ann. reg., 1878*. Le Jeune, *Dictionnaire*, II, 21–22. *Political appointments, 1841–1865* (J.-O. Coté). P.-G. Roy, *Les juges de la province de Québec*, 283. Turcotte, *Conseil législatif de Québec*, 249.

L.-P. Audet, *Histoire du conseil de l'Instruction*

publique, 15–24. Dent, *Last forty years.* Fauteux, *Patriotes*, 280–81. Louis Lalande, *Une vieille seigneurie Boucherville; chroniques, portraits et souvenirs* (Montréal, 1890), 211–20. J.-E. Roy, *Histoire du notariat*, III. J.-J. Lefebvre, "Les députés de Chambly, 1792–1967," *BRH*, LXX (1968), 16–18.

LAGEMODIÈRE, MARIE-ANNE. *See* GABOURY

LAGIER, LUCIEN-ANTOINE, priest, Oblate of Mary Immaculate, preacher; b. 4 Oct. 1814 at Saint-André-d'Embrun, Hautes-Alpes, France, son of André Lagier and Marie-Madeleine David; d. 28 Feb. 1874 at Isle-Verte, Rivière-du-Loup County, Que.

After receiving a classical education at the "juniorate" of Notre-Dame-de-Lumières, Vaucluse, and at the Petit Séminaire of Embrun, Lucien-Antoine Lagier followed his brother Jean-Marie and on 14 Aug. 1834 entered the noviciate of the Oblates at Saint-Just, near Marseilles. On 25 May 1839, his theological studies completed, he was ordained priest there by Charles-Joseph-Eugène de Mazenod, bishop of Marseilles and founder of the Oblate fathers.

Lagier worked for two years in France, then joined the first group of Oblates to land at Montreal, on 2 Dec. 1841. He became the curate at Saint-Hilaire-de-Rouville and guardian of the cross that had been erected on Mount Beloeil (Saint-Hilaire) in memory of the great retreat preached by Bishop Charles-Auguste-Marie-Joseph de Forbin-Janson*, which was destined to become a place of pilgrimage. At the same time he continued his ministry in the Eastern Townships, where he served until 1843.

Father Lagier, who had been a preacher since his arrival, then spent some years at Longueuil, and after that resided at Montreal; in 1847 he stayed some time at Bytown (Ottawa) to give a helping hand to his *confrères* during the typhus epidemic. In 1853 he went to Detroit, Michigan, to found a residence there, but returned to Canada shortly afterwards. In 1858, at the request of Anthony O'Reagan, bishop of Chicago, he worked in association with Father Augustin-Albert Brunet in the region of Kankakee, Illinois, to combat the heresy that Charles-Paschal-Télesphore Chiniquy* was spreading there. As a result of the preaching done by the two Oblates, about 150 schismatics returned to the practice of the Catholic religion. On his return to Canada, Lagier continued his preaching and lived at Quebec from 1863 to 1868. In that year he helped to found the first French parish of Lowell, Mass.

His ministry was always sought after, for he was prudent, a good judge of men, and a preacher of distinction. During his 32 years in the missions he conducted more than 1,000 retreats. His death occurred during a mission at Isle-Verte; he was the only one of the first group of Oblates to die in Canada.

GASTON CARRIÈRE

Archives générales O.M.I. (Rome), Dossier Lucien Lagier (copy in AHO). Archives paroissiales de Saint-Sauveur (Québec), Codex historicus (copy in AHO). Archives provinciales O.M.I. (Montréal), Codex historicus; Dossier Lucien Lagier; Dossier Québec (copies in AHO). *Notices nécrologiques des O.M.I.*, III, 181–206. Carrière, *Histoire des O.M.I.*, I, III, IV, V, VI; "Une mission tragique aux Illinois; Chiniquy et les oblats," *RHAF*, VIII (1954–55), 518–55.

LAIRD, ALEXANDER, farmer, shipbuilder, and politician; b. in 1797, probably in Stirling, Renfrewshire, Scotland; d. 15 April 1873 at New Glasgow, P.E.I.

Alexander Laird immigrated to Prince Edward Island in 1819 as a member of a colonization party organized by William Epps Cormack*, a prosperous landlord in the New Glasgow area. While aboard ship, Laird met Janet Orr, whom he married; they had two daughters and six sons of whom Alexander* and David* were to become prominent public figures. Upon arrival on the Island, Laird bought a farm in New Glasgow where he continued to live for the rest of his life. A progressive farmer, he was a long-time member of the Royal Agricultural Society of Prince Edward Island.

Laird entered politics in 1850 when he successfully contested Queens County, First District, as a running mate of the Reform leader, George COLES. Both men lost their seats in the defeat of the Liberal government in July 1853 but were returned to the assembly in an election in June 1854. Although he was known to hold certain radical views, Laird acted as a loyal Liberal backbencher until the session of 1855 when, with escheators William Cooper and John Macintosh*, he began to assume an independent position on the land question. Specifically, he opposed the Coles government for purchasing the Worrell estate from William Henry POPE and his associates. Laird felt that the title of the estate should have been investigated in the hope of finding that at one time or another the landowners had failed to fulfil the requirements of the original grant. If they had so failed, the land could then have been escheated or returned to the crown by default rather than purchase.

As the struggle over the use of the Bible in the public schools developed in the late 1850s, Laird

Lanctôt

became increasingly immune to the discipline of the Liberal caucus. A prominent Presbyterian layman, he was disturbed by the government's apparent indifference about the place of the scriptures in the schools. By 1858 he had become so disenchanted with his former colleagues that he ran in Queens County, Second District, as a Tory. He was successful and, when the Tories under Edward Palmer* formed an administration in 1859, Laird was named to the Executive Council. Despite the fact that he was dropped from the cabinet in 1863, Laird remained with the Tories until his retirement in 1866. After withdrawing from politics he lived quietly on his farm.

Although Laird began his career as a Reformer and concluded it as a Tory regular, he was widely credited with basic integrity. Unlike other politicians, who were accused of capitalizing on the dispute over the Bible for reasons of political gain, Laird seems to have been sincere in his position.

D. B. BOYLAN

PAPEI, Prince Edward Island, Executive Council, Minutes, 1857–62. Prince Edward Island, House of Assembly, *Debates*, 1855, 57–58, 66, 69; 1860, 11; 1861, 25; 1864, 23; *Journals*, 1850–67. *Examiner* (Charlottetown), 28 June 1858, 11 April 1859. *Islander* (Charlottetown), 19 Nov. 1851, 10 Sept. 1858. *Patriot* (Charlottetown), 17 April 1873. *Royal Gazette* (Charlottetown), 23 Feb., 8, 15 March 1852. *Can. parl. comp., 1876*. Bolger, *PEI and confederation*. Frank MacKinnon, *Government of PEI*; "David Laird of Prince Edward Island," *Dal. Rev.*, XXVI (1946–47), 405–21.

LANCTÔT, MAGLOIRE, lawyer and judge; b. 4 March 1823 at Saint-Constant de Laprairie, L.C., of the marriage of Alexis Lanctôt and Agnès Boire; d. 18 April 1877 at Saint-Hyacinthe, Que.

On his father's death in 1834, Magloire Lanctôt was adopted by his uncle, the notary Pierre Lanctôt, who had him educated at the college of Montreal. He was admitted to the bar in 1847 and first practised at Montreal, where he specialized in criminal law – a field in which few French-Canadian jurists were interested at that time. In 1849 he was one of the signatories to the Annexation Manifesto, which proposed union with the United States as a solution to the economic and political problems of Canada. He was mayor of Laprairie from 1858 to 1862. In 1863 he took up residence at Saint-Hyacinthe, an important legal and political centre, and shared in the legal practice directed by Louis-Victor Sicotte*, who was head of the government of the Province of Canada with John Sandfield MACDONALD in 1862 and 1863. In the provincial elections of 1867 Lanctôt stood as Conservative candidate for Saint-Hyacinthe. He

campaigned in support of confederation, which had just come into being, and was defeated by Pierre BACHAND, one of the few Liberal candidates elected to the Legislative Assembly of Quebec, thanks to his great popularity. Lanctôt was crown attorney for the districts of Saint-Hyacinthe and Bedford and on 4 Nov. 1870 was appointed magistrate at Saint-Hyacinthe by the government of Quebec.

In 1874, at Montreal, Magloire Lanctôt published *Le livre du magistrat*, which was republished in 1896 by Benjamin-Antoine Testard* de Montigny. It describes the details of legal procedure and of the rules of evidence in criminal matters. An orator loved by the crowds, Lanctôt gave several speeches on official occasions, particularly at the festival of Saint-Jean-Baptiste. He died on 18 April 1877 at Saint-Hyacinthe. The same day, the members of the bar of Saint-Hyacinthe assembled to testify "that by his integrity, intelligence, and urbanity, M. Lanctôt [had] performed his judicial duties in the district with honour to himself and in the best interest of the public."

In 1850 Magloir Lanctôt had married Angélique Raymond, daughter of Jean-Moïse Raymond, member of the assembly for Laprairie from 1824 to 1838. They had several children.

J.-C. BONENFANT

Magloire Lanctôt, *Le livre du magistrat* (1re éd., Montréal, 1874).

Le Courrier de Saint-Hyacinthe, 19 avril 1877. *La Minerve* (Montréal), 20 avril 1877. Chapais, *Histoire du Canada*, VI, 307–25. Joseph Chevalier, *Laprairie; notes historiques à l'occasion du centenaire de la consécration de l'église* (s.l., [1941]). C.-P. Choquette, *Histoire de la ville de Saint-Hyacinthe* (Saint-Hyacinthe, Qué., 1930). Philippe Constant [J.-J. Lefebvre], "Famille Lanctot," SGCF *Mémoires*, X (1959), 27–48.

LANCTOT, MÉDÉRIC, lawyer, journalist, and politician; b. 7 Dec. 1838 at Montreal, L.C., son of Hippolyte Lanctot and Mary Miller; d. 30 July 1877 at Lucerne (Gatineau County), and buried 2 August in the cemetery at Côte-des-Neiges (Montreal), Que.

Médéric Lanctot was born when the turmoil of revolution was at its height. His father, a notary in the village of Saint-Rémi (Napierville County), had been stagnating in the prison at Pied-du-Courant since 14 November. He had been put behind bars for having stirred up rebellion in the Richelieu valley and taking part in the fight at Odelltown as a lieutenant under Charles Hindenlang*, commander of the rebels' right wing. On 19 March 1839 he was found guilty of high treason, and, in September of that year, deported to

Australia. He did not return to Canada until January 1845.

This incident profoundly affected the personality of young Médéric, who until the age of six was brought up by his mother. It has been said, although without proof, that she was a descendant of the French family of Janson, to which belonged Charles-Auguste-Marie-Joseph de Forbin-Janson*, bishop of Nancy, famous in the history of Quebec for the religious lectures that he delivered in the 1840s. It is not possible to follow the Lanctot family during the father's exile. Laurent-Olivier David*, who knew the Lanctots well, says that Mme Lanctot lived with her children at Montreal.

On his return in 1845, Hippolyte installed his family at Saint-Édouard, an agricultural parish in the Richelieu valley, and devoted himself to his profession. A courteous and hospitable gentleman, he deeply resented his years of exile, which had not shaken his convictions. He remained a democrat, a republican, and a nationalist. When Médéric and his brothers came home from school, their father's memories completed their history lessons. Médéric grew up in the "mystique of 1837–38." Later, he explained his political commitment by reference to his youthful memories: "I had only to follow my inclinations, and the feelings inspired by a political education drawn directly from the unshakeable patriotism of an exile who had returned to the family hearth."

Lucky speculations, the post of clerk of the Commissioners' Court, and his professional activities, gave Hippolyte Lanctot a comfortable income. In September 1849 he sent his two sons, Médéric and Edmond, to the college of Saint-Hyacinthe. They entered the third year of the classical course. Médéric was not yet 11 years old. He was said to be brilliant, but inattentive and refractory. Laurent-Olivier David reported that he was "in all the plots, all the revolts against authority, all the pranks against an unpopular teacher." Bishop Charles-Philippe Choquette*, historian of the college of Saint-Hyacinthe, numbered him among the four pupils who plotted to set fire to the institution in January 1851. It is difficult here to distinguish between history and legend, for the seminary's archives contain little about Médéric, except that he was a mediocre student, passionately interested in history and French. He was informed at the end of the fifth year of his classical course that he would have to repeat his year "until he had given satisfactory answers in Latin grammar." Médéric did not register at the beginning of the next school year. Presumably, therefore, he left the college in the summer of 1852.

Médéric was then faced with the dilemma of thousands of young men of his age: in what direction should he turn? There was no system of specialized or professional schools for those who, on leaving college, wanted to take up a trade, a profession, or some kind of artistic career. The schools of medicine at Quebec and Montreal were the only institutions of this type. Apprenticeship was the sole means of entry into the arts and trades. Médéric's father, who had connections in business and political circles, asked Augustin Cuvillier*, an influential financier of Montreal, to take his son as a clerk.

Médéric therefore moved to Montreal. Like the majority of apprentices of the period, he probably received board and lodging from his master, who undertook to initiate him into the mysteries of his calling. Médéric lived with the Cuvilliers for three years. This phase of his life is obscure. One may suppose that he spent his leisure time reading, and mingling with those of his own age who shared his liking for things of the mind and for politics. These young men had a meeting place: the Institut Canadien, which from its foundation on 17 Dec. 1844 had been called a "rallying-point for youth." The pleiad of well-known and distinguished men who frequented the institute attracted the young Médéric, steeped in the liberal and nationalist mystique. He was a reader and a diligent listener at the institute. Joseph Doutre*, a lawyer and journalist, and president of the institute, soon advised him to seek work with the *Courrier de Saint-Hyacinthe*, which had been started in February 1853.

It is difficult to give a date for Médéric's arrival at Saint-Hyacinthe, and to state precisely the role he played in the newspaper. It is said that he was assigned his new duties in the autumn of 1855. As journalists did not sign their articles at this time, it has not been possible to determine with certainty what was written by Médéric. Once more David must be trusted: "For two years he polemized in this newspaper with a vigour and skill which caused him to be thought of as a rising star of the Liberal party."

The period at Saint-Hyacinthe was only an interlude in Lanctot's life. Montreal, the centre of the principal ideological and political movements, attracted him. He returned there in 1858 to undertake the study of law. His friends of the institute, Joseph Doutre and Charles Daoust*, who had their office on Rue Saint-Gabriel, accepted him as a clerk to study law.

Médéric resumed his activities at the Institut Canadien at the time when Bishop Ignace Bourget* declared war on *rougisme*. He lost no time in making his presence known by creating an uproar. Around 3 o'clock in the night of 8–9 April,

Lanctot

together with Guillaume-Ernest Roy, a medical student, he shattered the windows of the Oeuvre des Bons Livres, on Rue Saint-Joseph. This library, organized by Bishop Bourget, made pious and edifying literature available to the public [see Jacques-Victor ARRAUD]. The affair gave rise to a law suit. Joseph Papin*, a prominent member of the Rouge party, defended the young fanatic. Judge Charles-Joseph Coursol* sentenced Médéric and his accomplice to a fine of $20, or, failing payment, to two months of hard labour in a reformatory. Médéric was quickly to forget that he had a judicial record; the Conservatives, on the other hand, remembered it.

Bishop Bourget's fulminations did not shake Médéric, who took part in all the institute's activities and gained a reputation as an eloquent lecturer and a skilful dialectician. He was invited to give a number of public lectures before the élite of Montreal. During the winter of 1859 he read an essay on electoral reform in England, and another on that country's social and political situation. On 2 May, thanks to the intellectual qualities and untiring energy that he placed at the service of the institute, he was elected its corresponding secretary. He was also asked to contribute to Le Pays, the institute's newspaper.

On 7 May 1860, with 11 other candidates, Médéric was authorized by the Montreal bar to practise law. His years of training were therefore over. Physically of small stature, thin and muscular, he had black, piercing eyes that reflected a tenacious will-power and a lively intelligence. His fertile imagination, ceaselessly in ferment, formed grandiose visions, devised expedients, and formulated syllogisms, which kept the writer and orator well primed. He derived his ideas from family tradition, the institute's library, L'Avenir, and Le Pays. English history revealed to him the social problems that sprang from the industrial revolution, and gave him a deep-rooted respect for individual rights. From the time of his birth he had thus lived in an atmosphere in which two ideological currents prevailed: nationalism and liberalism. Would he be able, having reached manhood, to make of them a fruitful synthesis, on which coherent and sustained action could be based?

The new lawyer set up his office first at 7 Rue Sainte-Thérèse, then around 1862 at 126 Rue Notre-Dame. He had specialized in no particular area, and accepted all the cases that came his way. His professional activities did not lessen his participation in the work of the Institut Canadien, but this feverish existence began to undermine his health, and he felt a need for rest. On 11 July 1862 he boarded a steamer for Liverpool. A maze of conjecture surrounds Lanctot's travels in Europe. From his later writings it can be deduced that he visited England, France, and the adjoining countries. On 16 Oct. 1862 Le Pays announced his return, and stated that he "has arrived from Europe in good health."

This voyage gave Lanctot an opportunity to determine where he stood. As a frequenter of the Institut Canadien he was in close touch with the Doutre family, particularly with Joseph, who seems to have been his counsellor at important moments of his life. At 16 Rue Saint-Gabriel, where Lanctot lived, Joseph Doutre also had his residence and here too was the office of the lawyers Doutre and Daoust. It was perhaps there that Lanctot made the acquaintance of Agnès, the sister of Joseph, Léon, and GONZALVE Doutre. He returned from Europe determined to make Agnès his life's companion. The marriage took place on 28 Oct. 1862.

The decision to marry was not the only one made during his stay in Europe. Because of his spirited and excitable nature, he felt too hampered within the confines of the courts, and decided to become a crusading journalist. Together with Toussaint Thompson and C.-E. Bouthillier he acquired the printing-shop of M. de Montigny, probably during the autumn of 1862. On 15 Sept. 1863 he issued the prospectus of a new newspaper, La Presse, which began to appear regularly on 5 October. He was its editor. The paper had original features: it was a daily and was independent of parties. This was a difficult challenge to maintain, for the cheap press financed by subscriptions and advertising did not yet exist. The majority of the papers of the time were party organs supported by party funds. Not only was La Presse independent of parties, it wanted them to disappear. It advocated a new formula: the union of all French Canadians within a national party. Claiming kinship with the Patriotes of 1837 and the intellectuals of the institute, La Presse was a nationalist organ.

The birth of La Presse occurred at a turning-point in Canadian history. In June 1864 John A. Macdonald*, George-Étienne CARTIER, and George BROWN announced the formation of a great coalition, aimed at bringing about a federal union of the colonies of British North America. Only the Rouges of the institute remained aloof from the coalition. Lanctot was dumbfounded by this news, for in his view federal union would endanger the future of the French Canadian people. Throughout the summer of 1864, he fired shafts against the coalition group in his paper. A few young Conservatives, such as Laurent-Olivier David and Joseph Leblanc, and some young

Liberals, among whom were Louis-Amable Jetté*, Wilfrid Laurier*, and Narcisse Valois, rallied to Lanctot to organize the struggle against the project of confederation. In August they formed a national committee and published a manifesto signed by 46 adherents, and on 3 September they launched the first number of a new journal, *L'Union nationale*, which replaced *La Presse*.

The young nationalists set in motion a vigorous press campaign against the plan of confederation and against the old parties. They favoured setting up an independent state of Quebec. Side by side with this press campaign, Lanctot organized a campaign of political agitation, which, conducted at a brisk pace by the team of *L'Union nationale*, took on the appearance of a crusade. Two phases can be distinguished. From August to November, the young nationalists held public meetings which brought together some hundreds of people; there they denounced the principle of confederation, then got resolutions passed condemning the plans of the coalition. From November on, they demanded an appeal to the people, and got petitions signed to this effect. They had the support of two liberal papers: *L'Ordre* and *Le Pays*.

The press campaign and the political agitation did not prevent the politicians from pursuing the plan of confederation. But while Cartier, one of the principal architects of confederation, was advancing towards a triumph on the parliamentary scene, Lanctot hoped to humiliate him electorally in Montreal East. Although in the winter of 1866 Médéric was only 28 years old, he had considerable prestige in Montreal. He was the leader of a group of young nationalists and he could count on numerous supporters in working-class circles, whom he defended unceasingly against employers, in particular the Canadian Grand Trunk, whose lawyer Cartier was. His gifts as a demagogue, his indomitable energy, and his ability for organization made him a dangerous opponent. He was thus a formidable political force in Montreal, and he was eager to tackle Cartier.

In February 1866, municipal elections gave him the opportunity to take the measure of his opponents. He stood in Montreal East against Alexis Dubord, Cartier's man of straw. He had a programme: installation of sewers, improvements to the Place Jacques-Cartier, and utilization of waste ground. Cartier himself came to Montreal to direct Dubord's campaign. It was to no purpose, since on 28 February Lanctot was elected by a majority of eight votes.

This victory filled him with wild enthusiasm, and convinced him that even in an election against Cartier himself he would win. However, he could leave nothing to chance. All his political activity from then on was directed towards the duel he would one day fight with Cartier. He utilized his post as councillor to undermine the prestige which the latter enjoyed with the city council. The riposte was not slow in coming: Alexis Dubord challenged the election of Lanctot, on the grounds that he did not fulfil the necessary property qualifications to sit in city hall. The hearing of the case took place at the end of November. Lanctot faced an annulment of the election, but he did not slow up his activities in any way. He began to draft a pamphlet in support of independence.

At the beginning of 1867 a great dream took shape: the union of all workers in one powerful association. Intuitively, Lanctot believed that national liberation would bring the improvement of the lot of the working classes. On 5 February his newspaper proclaimed: "Association is the salvation of the French Canadian nationality." On 27 March Lanctot summoned all workers to the Champ de Mars, and there, before 5,000 persons, he delivered a speech lasting several hours. The assembly formed a committee to prepare the founding of the Grande Association de Protection des Ouvriers du Canada. Each evening Lanctot held meetings in the working class districts. On 6 April he received the reward for his toil: in the great hall of Bonsecours Market 3,000 persons voted on statutes and rules. The Grande Association was born. Conceived as an instrument for the liberation of the working classes, the Grande Association, in the heat of action, became a political instrument for achieving the union of all French Canadians. The association was a federation of trade organizations. It was directed by a commission on which sat about 200 representatives of the various organizations, representation being proportionate to the numbers of their members. Each adherent paid a subscription of 10 cents a month to finance the movement. The founders established a triple function for the Grande Association: to ensure harmony between capital and labour, to improve the well-being of its members, and to stop emigration to the United States. On 9 May the commission elected an executive and appointed Lanctot to the presidency.

The new president made use of all his prestige to settle a conflict over wages and hours of work that divided the master bakers and their employees. He opened low-price bakeries to provide for the needy, asked people to buy bread only from the bakers who had negotiated with their employees, and on 10 June organized a great popular demonstration. That evening more than 8,000 workers, grouped by their trade associations, marched on the Champ de Mars, chanting slogans and holding aloft the green, white, and red flag of 1837–38.

Lanctot

Lanctot was at his zenith. Praised, greeted with cheers, he seemed to be advancing towards a resounding political victory, even though his opponents did not give up. Judge Samuel Cornwallis Monk* handed down a judgement in favour of Alexis Dubord on 10 June 1867, but this slap in the face was a stimulus to Lanctot, who was actively preparing his electoral campaign against Cartier in Montreal East.

The poll was to take place on 5 Sept. 1867. All summer long, Lanctot held public meetings. He experienced some difficulty, however, in maintaining the enthusiasm of 10 June, for the people's bakeries and consumers' cooperatives he had set up had gone bankrupt. These disappointments worked to the advantage of the Conservatives, who on 21 August, through the intermediary of *La Minerve*, launched a smear campaign against Lanctot. He was called "a breaker of windows, a Fenian, a violent anticlerical, an annexationist, an excommunicate, a revolutionary, a plague of Egypt, etc." *La Minerve* closed its campaign with a piece of scandal: Alderman Lanctot, it reported, had degraded himself by associating with a certain Jérémie Sinotte in order to obtain contracts from the municipality. On the evening of 6 September, Cartier was victorious by a majority of 348 votes.

Lanctot did not accept defeat. He was convinced that Cartier had "stolen the election." He began to busy himself again, hoping to stir up violent protest in working class districts. He held public meetings, had petitions circulated, and thundered in *L'Union nationale* against the priests who had supported Cartier and confederation. This agitation worried the Rouges, who felt uncomfortable in his company. Lanctot isolated himself by his excessive behaviour. He never recovered from the defeat that Cartier had just inflicted on him.

By the end of September 1867 Lanctot no longer had friends or political allies. He returned to his law practice to meet the needs of his family. The massive support of the parish priests for confederation led him to question his faith. He ceased to publish *L'Union nationale*; it no longer paid its way. But these difficulties did not prevent him from forming new plans, and from preparing a counterstroke.

On 15 Feb. 1868 Lanctot issued a prospectus for a new newspaper, *L'Indépendance canadienne*, the first number of which appeared on 22 April. He had found a new cause: the independence of Canada from England and annexation to the United States. According to him, confederation was a provisional situation. It would evolve towards a legislative union or a federation of states within a *zollverein*, or annexation to the United States. Canadians must therefore prepare themselves from now on to adopt one of these three options. He proposed annexation. Lanctot's appeal aroused no enthusiasm among French Canadians, and it irritated English Canadians. When in August he tried to organize an independence league, he received only gibes.

Ruined financially and politically, he decided to go to the United States where he hoped to find among Franco-Americans a more open mind about the annexation of Canada. He arrived at Detroit on 10 Sept. 1868. The Club Démocratique Français gave him a warm welcome. On the 22nd he gave a speech which was a manifesto, designed to launch "L'Association de l'Indépendance pacifique du Canada." Encouraged by his first success, he then went to New England, where he encountered nothing but indifference. In the spring of 1869, at Burlington, he started *L'Idée nouvelle* to propagate his movement, then, at Worcester, he launched *L'Impartial*. These papers touched off no response among Franco-Americans and went bankrupt.

In the autumn of 1869 Lanctot returned to Detroit, where on 13 October a Franco-American convention was held. He succeeded temporarily in setting up cells among the delegates and in getting his campaign for the independence of Canada endorsed by a majority. On 20 November he again began to publish *L'Impartial*, in which he idealized American society. A fleeting victory, obtained by intrigues at a convention! The content and tone of *L'Impartial* were displeasing. For want of money, Lanctot had to abandon publication of his paper with the tenth number.

The failure of *L'Impartial* meant the end of another dream for Lanctot. It gave rise to an internal crisis, about which little evidence exists. In a moment of despair and revolt, he rejected the faith of his forefathers and became a Baptist. Perhaps he hoped he had found a means of acquiring celebrity in the American republic, where it was good form, in certain circles, to attack Catholicism. In the defence of his new cause he displayed the ardour of a neophyte. He published a pamphlet whose very title was a declaration of war, *Rome, the great usurper. . . .* In March he began at Detroit the publication of a paper, the *Anti-Roman Advocate*, in which he denounced "the despotism, superstition and ignorance" of the Catholic Church. The Baptist religion awakened no response among Franco-Americans, any more than annexation had. The *Anti-Roman Advocate* foundered, swamped by debts if not by ridicule, barely five months after its first number appeared.

Ruined and discredited, Lanctot returned to Montreal in the autumn of 1870. He took up the practice of law again, in partnership with his brother Philéas. He waited for an opening. It occurred at the time of the provincial elections in the spring of 1871. Lanctot stood for Montreal East. He counted on the support of the Knights of St Crispin, a secret association that grouped workers of the boot and shoe industry, and that the church had denounced. The loyalty of these workers did not spare him a humiliating defeat. Lanctot did not give up. He hung on to the workers and attempted to revive the Grande Association. In March or April 1872 he published a 46-page pamphlet, *Association du capital et du travail*, in which he demonstrated that workers should share in entrepreneurial revenues by a system of dividends. In the federal elections of autumn 1872, Cartier, in difficulties in Montreal East because of the ultramontanist opposition, gambled on the working class issue, and made use of Lanctot's talents. The latter's about-face is largely explicable by his financial needs, even if he did try to justify it by the interest Cartier was beginning to take in the working class. This strategy profited neither Cartier nor Lanctot. The former was beaten in Montreal East, and the second, who had repudiated the ideas of his youth, was now merely "a dead leaf at the mercy of every wind."

Lanctot no longer had any following at Montreal. His lawyer's office was deserted. He learned what destitution was. David places his return to the bosom of the Catholic Church during these difficult months. Did Lanctot yield to popular pressure? Did he truly rediscover the faith of his forefathers? Had he even lost it? It would be fruitless to elaborate, for Lanctot entrusted his secret to no one.

Lanctot's life, from then on, was a succession of rebuffs. In 1873 or 1874 he tried in vain to make a new life for himself in the United States. In January 1875 his friend Alphonse Lusignan* got for him the post of editor of the *Courrier de l'Outaouais*, and a few months later that of stenographer in the House of Commons. Lanctot bought the *Courrier de l'Outaouais* in June 1875, and moved it to Hull. He launched out into municipal politics, and played the role of defender of the people. For a while he seemed to have struck a lucky vein. He was appointed lawyer of the town of Hull, and published a sort of unofficial paper of the town council, called *L'Écho de Hull*. But he misused his prestige, and revealed his personal interest too clearly. His supporters deserted him, and in their turn his enemies, once back in power, ostracized him. Exhausted, worn out physically, he already needed, at 38 years of age, to retire to a quiet place to recover his health. In the spring of 1877 he went to live on a farm at Lucerne. He died during the night of 30 July.

Lanctot belonged to his time. In more than one respect he was an embodiment of the French Canadians, ceaselessly torn between their admiration for British institutions and their situation as members of a colony, between their French origin and their North American environment. In particular, he was the embodiment of a city, Montreal, where in the second half of the 19th century problems were of two kinds: those related to national considerations and those related to social considerations. He was one of the first French Canadian ideologists to make a tentative beginning at a synthesis of them.

Lanctot left five daughters and one son. Two children had died in infancy. His wife, Agnès Doutre, survived him by less than two years. She died on 9 May 1879 and was buried in the cemetery at Côte-des-Neiges.

JEAN HAMELIN

[Lanctot's private papers have disappeared. To follow his intellectual development we must fall back on his printed writings, which are numerous: *La Presse* (Montréal), 5 oct. 1863 – 5 sept. 1864; *L'Union nationale* (Montréal), 3 sept. 1864 – 7 nov. 1867; *L'Indépendance canadienne* (Montréal), 22 avril – 3 août 1868; *Association du capital et du travail* ([1872]). Other works by Lanctot are known to have been published, but could not be consulted, usually because they no longer exist: *L'Idée nouvelle* (Burlington, Vt., et Worcester, Mass.), spring 1869; *L'Impartial* (Worcester, Mass., et Detroit, Mich.), autumn 1869; *Rome, the great usurper ... church and man* ([1870]); *The Anti-Roman Advocate* (Detroit, Mich.), March – August 1870; *Le Courrier de l'Outaouais* (Hull), janv. 1875 – avril 1876; *L'Écho de Hull*, 1876.

No one was indifferent to Lanctot; his enemies replied to his words. For this reason *La Minerve* (Montréal), Cartier's mouthpiece, *Le Pays* (Montréal), the Rouge party's organ, *L'Ordre* (Montréal), paper of the moderate liberals, *Le Nouveau Monde* (Montréal), the ultramontane tribune, *L'Opinion publique* (Montréal), the nationalist paper, provide further information.

Laurent-Olivier David, who knew the Lanctot family well, published a biography of Lanctot in *L'Opinion publique* on 23 Aug. 1877. Stripped of its romanticism, David's study remains a valuable source, which is full of details. In March 1968, Gaétan Gervais presented at the University of Ottawa a thesis entitled, "Médéric Lanctot et l'Union nationale," which analyses in depth Lanctot's political thought from 1864 to 1867. Philippe Constant [J.-J. Lefebvre] published a genealogy of the Lanctot family in SGCF, *Mémoires*, X (1959), 27–48.

Some references to Lanctot are found in the following more general works: Alexandre Belisle, *Histoire de la presse franco-américaine; comprenant l'historique de l'émigration de Canadiens français aux États-Unis, leur développement et leurs progrès* (Worcester, Mass., 1911), 21–77. J.-C. Bonenfant, *La naissance de la*

Landry

Confédération (Montréal, 1969), 136–43. Silas Farmer, *The history of Detroit and Michigan; or the metropolis illustrated; a chronological cyclopædia of the past and present, including a full record of territorial days in Michigan and the annals of Wayne County* (Detroit, 1884), 678. Fauteux, *Patriotes*, 284–85. Télesphore St-Pierre, *Histoire des Canadiens du Michigan et du comté d'Essex, Ontario* (Montréal, 1895), 234–49, 325–39. "Biographie de Médéric Lanctot," *La Minerve* (Montréal), 1ᵉʳ août 1877. Gustave Lanctot, "La fin d'une légende," *Revue franco-américaine* (Montréal), X (1912–13), 282–91. Télesphore St-Pierre, "Les sociétés et les conventions canadiennes aux États-Unis," Société Saint-Jean-Baptiste de Québec, *Annales*, IV (1902), 466–69. J.H.]

LANDRY, AMAND, farmer, teacher, and politician; b. 8 Dec. 1805 at Memramcook, Westmorland County, N.B., son of Allain Landry and Anastasie Dupuis (Dupuy), a descendant of Charles de Saint-Étienne* de La Tour; d. 12 July 1877 at Memramcook.

Amand Landry was educated at the Memramcook Public School; he taught school for a short time and then became a prosperous farmer and respected leader of the Acadian community of Westmorland County. In 1839 he married Pélagie Caissie (Casey) of Memramcook by whom he had seven children. The eldest son, Pierre-Amand Landry*, was an MLA in New Brunswick, a federal MP, and a judge of the Supreme Court of New Brunswick.

Amand Landry had a long career in New Brunswick politics. He was first elected to the assembly in 1846; in 1850 he was defeated by William Crane* but in 1853 he won a by-election called to fill the vacancy caused by Crane's death. He won re-election in 1854 and in 1856, was defeated in 1857, but returned to the house in 1861 and remained a member until 1870, when he retired from politics. Landry has been described as a Liberal; however, he had a mind of his own and always voted for what he considered to be the best interests of the Acadian people. He was a strong opponent of railway construction both in 1847 and in 1868 because he felt that the proposed line between St Andrews and Woodstock and the Woodstock branch railway would do nothing to benefit the Acadians.

Landry was a strong anti-confederate, and supported Albert James Smith* in the elections of 1865 and 1866. In the latter, which saw the defeat of Smith's government, Landry was one of the eight anti-confederates returned; of these, six came from constituencies with a large French population. In opposing confederation Landry expressed the fears of the Acadian community, which did not wish to be absorbed into a larger political entity. Anxious not to lose their identity and individuality, they were suspicious not only of English-speaking Canadians but also of French Canadians and spurned attempts by Roman Catholic officials sent from Quebec to persuade them to vote for confederation.

Amand Landry was the first Acadian political figure of any importance in New Brunswick. He understood the Acadians' problems, he spoke their language, and they, in turn, trusted him.

W. A. SPRAY

Archives paroissiales de Saint-Thomas (Memramcook, N.B.), Registres des baptêmes, mariages et sépultures. University of New Brunswick, Graves (New Brunswick) MSS, Westmorland County. *Chignecto Post* (Sackville, N.B.), 19 July 1877. *Le Moniteur Acadien* (Shediac, N.B.), 19 July 1877. *Morning News* (Saint John, N.B.), 21 June 1861. Hannay, *History of New Brunswick*, II, 107. MacNutt, *New Brunswick*, 354–55, 453–54.

LANE, RICHARD, HBC clerk, lawyer, and territorial official in Oregon and Washington; b.c. 1816 at Sandgate, Kent; d. 20 Feb. 1877 at The Dalles, Oregon.

Richard Lane was appointed apprentice clerk in the Northern Department by the Hudson's Bay Company in December 1837; the following June he sailed for York Factory aboard the company ship *Prince Rupert*. Lane moved to the Red River District in September 1838, where he served as accountant until 11 June 1845 when Governor Sir George Simpson* ordered his transfer to the Columbia Department. Four days later Lane departed for Fort Vancouver with Peter Skene Ogden* and Lieutenants Henry James Warre* and Mervin Vavasour*. The party reached its destination on 26 August, and Lane, whose original instructions were to take charge of a post to be established at Cape Disappointment at the mouth of the Columbia River, was made accountant at Fort Vancouver, replacing Dugald MACTAVISH. To protect the company's lands and improvements at Fort Vancouver, Lane was employed during the later summer in marking out the nine-mile-square claims around the fort which were then recorded with the Oregon provisional government. Lane himself took a claim beginning one-and-a-half miles west of the fort. The claims were abandoned on 4 April 1849 at the request of James DOUGLAS.

Simpson had promised Lane that he could return to Red River in 1846, and he accompanied Warre and Vavasour with the York Factory Express when it departed from Fort Vancouver on 25 March. Lane took with him the annual accounts of the Columbia Department, but his real purpose

La Rocque

for making the trip was personal. The express arrived at Fort Garry (Winnipeg) on 7 June, and on 13 June Lane married Mary McDermot, the "country-born" daughter of Andrew McDermot*. Accompanied by his bride and the artist Paul KANE, Lane took charge of the returning express, arriving at Fort Vancouver on 8 Dec. 1846 with confirmation of the final settlement of the Oregon boundary dispute, which had been concluded at Washington, D.C., in June.

The Oregon provisional government had organized the area north of the Columbia River as Vancouver County, and, on 16 Jan. 1847, Governor George Abernethy appointed Lane to the county judgeship which Dugald Mactavish had resigned. A change in the laws of the provisional government in 1846 required that justices of the peace or judges be elected, and on 7 June 1847 Lane was one of three justices elected for Vancouver County, but he did not stand again in 1848.

Although he evidently did not resign from the HBC until 1851, Lane moved to Oregon City in 1850 and became a merchant. At the same time he served, for about a year after his retirement, as the company's agent at Champoeg, where it had a granary and store. Lane seems to have conducted the business at Champoeg "most shamefully," and his operations were said "to savour of fraud" because of losses and bad debts. In the 1850 census Lane's personal real estate in Oregon City was valued at $20,000.

Mary McDermot Lane died at Oregon City after a long and painful illness on 10 May 1851, leaving Lane with two small children. He sent the children back to Red River where they were raised by Andrew McDermot. Early in 1853 Lane cleared land for a farm near Fort Vancouver, but in 1855 he was back in Oregon where he ran unsuccessfully for justice of the peace in Milton Precinct, Columbia County. During the Yakima Indian war (1855–58) he enlisted for nine months in the Lewis River Mounted Rangers. Following this service he moved to Olympia, capital of the Washington Territory, and in November 1857 he was appointed instructor for the Squaxin Indian Reservation and taught there until July 1858. That same month Lane returned to Olympia where he was elected auditor of Thurston County, an office which he held until 1862 and again from 1864 to 1866. Thereafter Lane was a servant of the territorial, county, and city governments until 1870, sometimes holding offices at all three levels concurrently. However there was small remuneration from such offices, and public office-seeking was uncertain, particularly in a time when the Democrats, who had long held a virtual monopoly of territorial offices, were being replaced by Republican appointees and candidates. With his years of experience as a justice of the peace and a clerk of the courts, Lane moved to the other side of the bench. On 20 May 1865 the *Washington Standard* announced that Lane, a "well qualified" and "affable gentleman," had been admitted to practise as an attorney. Lane was evidently too reticent to be a successful lawyer, and his habits and attitudes remained those of a competent, amiable, and meticulous clerk.

On 25 March 1873, Lane was declared "dangerous to himself and the community at large" because of "mental derangement produced by long continued use of alcoholic liquors." Judged insane, he was committed to the Territorial Asylum at Steilacoom for treatment which was expected to take two or three months, and his affairs were placed in trusteeship. Following his release from the asylum, Lane returned to Olympia and his law practice. But his affairs continued to decline. He had married Mrs Anna Gardiner on 9 Dec. 1858, but by 1875 he was listed in the county census as unmarried. In the late winter of 1877 he set out from Olympia en route for Yakima on legal business. Stopping in The Dalles, Oregon, he evidently became despondent and purchased ten grains of morphine. He was found dead in his bed on 20 February, and following a coroner's inquest which returned a verdict of suicide, he was buried at county expense as he had neither baggage nor funds.

WILLIAM R. SAMPSON

PABC, Thomas Lowe journal, 1843–50. "Documents relative to Warre and Vavasour's military reconnaissance in Oregon, 1845–6," ed. Joseph Schafer, *Oregon Hist. Q.* (Portland, Ore.), X (1909), 1–99. HBRS, VII (Rich). United States, Office of Indian Affairs, *Report of the commissioner of Indian affairs, accompanying the annual report of the secretary of the interior, for the year 1858* (Washington, 1858). *Daily Pacific Tribune* (Seattle, Wash.), 1 March 1877. *Pioneer and Democrat* (Olympia, Wash.), 10 Dec. 1858. *Washington Standard* (Olympia, Wash.), 29 March, 19 April 1873; 3 March 1877. H. H. Bancroft, *History of Oregon* (2v., San Francisco, 1886–88); *History of Washington, Idaho, and Montana, 1845–1889* (San Francisco, 1890). Mrs G. E. Blankenship [Georgiana Mitchell], *Early history of Thurston County, Washington, together with biographies and reminiscences of those identified with pioneer days* (Olympia, Wash., 1914). G. R. Newell, *So fair a dwelling place* (Olympia, Wash., 1950). J. C. Rathbun, *History of Thurston County, Washington* (Olympia, Wash., 1895). T. C. Elliott, "Peter Skene Ogden, fur trader," *Oregon Hist. Q.* (Portland, Ore.), XI (1910), 229–78.

LA ROCQUE (Larocque), CHARLES, Catholic priest, third bishop of Saint-Hyacinthe; b. 15 Nov.

La Rocque

1809 at Chambly-sur-Richelieu, L.C., eldest son of Henri La Rocque and Sophie Robert; d. 15 July 1875 at Saint-Hyacinthe, Que.

Charles La Rocque was still a child when the parish priest of Chambly, Abbé Pierre-Marie Mignault, detected in him aptitudes which he resolved to nurture. Charles' cousin, Joseph La Rocque*, who was to precede him in the episcopal see of Saint-Hyacinthe, was also noticed.

On 1 March 1821, at the initiative of Charles-Louis-Roch de Saint-Ours*, legislative councillor, an association to improve educational opportunities in the Chambly River area had been established. Its aim was to obtain – for gifted but poor children of the region – scholarships which would allow them to receive their full classical education at the college of Saint-Hyacinthe. Charles and Joseph La Rocque were chosen by Father Mignault to be among the first of the 30 students to receive the association's bursaries. The two La Rocque cousins vied with each other and were formidable rivals. Later Charles readily recalled these eager struggles, and added: "nature made us relatives, the college made us friends, and we have always cultivated our friendship as being one of the sweetest pleasures of life."

His classical education finished, Charles La Rocque donned the cassock, and in 1828 began to study theology. While preparing himself for the priesthood, he taught humanities at the college of Saint-Hyacinthe, of which the authoritarian Abbé Thomas Maguire* had been director since 1827. In the middle of 1831, Bishop Jean-Jacques Lartigue* summoned La Rocque to Montreal to complete his theological studies at the seminary of Saint-Jacques, which was established in the first floor of the bishop's residence. It was no doubt there that Abbé La Rocque was introduced to the propositions of ultramontanism, of which Bishop Lartigue was a firm supporter, and particularly to the doctrine of papal infallibility, which he was to see confirmed with great ceremony when he took part in the Vatican Council in 1870.

La Rocque, curate since 1832, was summoned to his native parish in 1835 to assume the direction of the classical college of Saint-Pierre, established ten years before by his childhood benefactor, the parish priest Mignault. The following year he began his own career as a parish priest at Saint-Pie (Bagot County), where he spent four years. In 1840 he became the sixth parish priest of L'Acadie (Saint-Jean County), and the first priest of this parish to be appointed by the bishop of Montreal.

It was at L'Acadie that Abbé La Rocque first encountered the Protestants of Swiss origin who were waging an intense campaign of proselytism in the region. These Protestants originally included Henriette Odin* Feller and the pastor Louis Roussy; they had taken up residence at Grande-Ligne in 1835, and were joined there, in 1840, by four ministers who were compatriots. One of La Rocque's confrères, Abbé Louis Normandeau*, whom he was lodging out of charity, even left him to take refuge among them and become a Baptist minister.

In 1844 Abbé La Rocque was transferred to the parish of Saint-Jean-l'Évangéliste (Saint-Jean). This parish formed part of the barony of Longueuil, of which Charles William Grant, 5th Baron of Longueuil, had held the title since 1841. A shipping and rail terminal, and a large commercial entrepôt between New York and Montreal, Saint-Jean was to see its population grow from 1,315 inhabitants in 1841 to 4,500 in 1858. Thanks to this growth, and to its commercial and industrial activity, Saint-Jean received its charter as a municipality on 15 Sept. 1856. The Civil War still further increased its prosperity, through the extensive growth of transit trade and the export of grain, hay, and manufactured products.

According to the 1851 census, out of a total of 3,215 persons there were 2,577 Catholics to constitute the flock under the care of La Rocque, who displayed the qualities of a born administrator in this rapidly expanding parish. In the spring of 1845 the church, whose construction had been finished in 1828, was provided with an organ built by Joseph Casavant. The financial state of the parish council was a thriving one. In 1848 La Rocque had a convent built for the sisters of the Congregation of Notre-Dame. Two years later he asked the college of Saint-Hyacinthe to set up a branch in his parish. In 1864 he renewed his request. This time the offer was accepted. On 29 September of that year, a teacher from Saint-Hyacinthe, two seminarists, and 85 pupils inaugurated the college of Saint-Jean, with a programme of two distinct courses, one commercial and the other classical.

La Rocque did not always have an easy time as the parish priest of Saint-Jean. He had had apprehensions about going there because of a population in which Catholics mingled with Protestants, and because the events of 1837–38 had left some open wounds. Indeed at Saint-Jean he encountered once more the "Swiss" who had greatly worried him at L'Acadie. Despite his pacific intentions – he wrote that "no bitter word" had ever left his mouth to "attack a Protestant of any denomination, because of his religious opinions" – he perforce engaged in polemics when in 1852 he published a controversial book which drew much attention at the time, and in which he deplored "the setting up of this *Branch of the Bible Society* specifically for Saint-Jean and Saint-Athanase, in the midst of a completely Catholic population, and with the firm intention of doing violence to their principles and conscience." In particular he blamed Normandeau, who had been sent to Saint-Jean "with the express purpose of having him preach there for my parishioners," Normandeau, "a poor wretched Canadian priest" who had "passed from the Catholic church to Protestantism by such a sorry path."

One of his own parishioners, the notary Pierre-Paul Desmaray, gave Abbé La Rocque no less trouble. Desmaray had drawn attention to himself during the rebellion by his zeal for the cause of Louis-Joseph PAPINEAU and had been one of the first to be arrested, on 17 Nov. 1837, with Dr Joseph-François Davignon. Some years later Desmaray had returned to Canada from the United States, and had taken up his profession again at Saint-Jean. He had not forgiven the clergy for its attitude towards the events of 1837, and contrived to harass La Rocque continually. On 7 Jan. 1844 he transmitted to him a petition to have the position of the pulpit changed, and the appointments of churchwardens made in future by a general meeting of the property owners resident in the parish. However, the affair of the seigneurial pew gave Desmaray the chance to flout the parish priest and the council even more effectively.

The seigneurial pew was reserved for the Baron de Longueuil. As the seigneur was a Protestant, the pew was left at the disposal of his representative, the notary Desmaray, who occupied it for nothing, thus getting out of paying the pew rent to which all other parishioners were liable. This awkward situation, which lasted for five years, ended with Desmaray's death on 17 Sept. 1854.

Abbé La Rocque maintained cordial relations with his bishop, Ignace Bourget*. The latter had requested him to pronounce Bishop Lartigue's funeral oration at the memorial service celebrated at the church of St James on 29 April 1841, and La Rocque had accompanied Bourget on his voyage to Rome in 1854, to be present at the proclamation of the dogma of the Immaculate Conception. But despite these relations, La Rocque kept his distance, for the bishop's intransigent ultramontanism sometimes clashed with La Rocque's sense of what was possible and his concern for pacifying by compromise. In 1857, when the Roman liturgy was adopted in the diocese of Montreal, La Rocque did not conceal from the bishop that he disagreed about the application of certain points of this liturgy. The bishop was obliged to admit the cogency of the reasons put forward by the parish priest of Saint-Jean, although holding firmly to his own line of conduct: "In one liturgy as in another," he replied to La

Rocque on 22 May 1857, "there are questions on which differences of opinion are permitted. . . . By consulting very skilful masters of ceremonies in Rome, I reached the conviction that all questions of liturgy were not yet clearly decided, at least for them. It must not appear surprising, therefore, that in a country like ours we should still find ourselves perplexed. Yet one must not remain in a state of indefiniteness, the worst state of all. But while settling many undecided cases, I conceived it my duty to leave to the discriminating conscience of good priests a way of avoiding needless worry."

Charles La Rocque had been parish priest of Saint-Jean for 22 years when, on the resignation of the second bishop of Saint-Hyacinthe, his cousin Joseph La Rocque, he was persuaded to agree to succeed him. Out of affection for his parishioners, he decided to receive the episcopal consecration in the new church of Saint-Jean, the building of which had been the object of his attentions since 1857 and which had scarcely been completed. On 29 July 1866 he was consecrated by Bishop Charles-François Baillargeon*, administrator of the archdiocese of Quebec, who was assisted by Bishop Bourget and Joseph-Bruno GUIGUES, bishop of Ottawa. One of those present in the congregation was George-Étienne CARTIER, who wanted to indicate by this gesture the friendship between himself and the new bishop.

It was not without distress that on 20 March 1866 La Rocque had agreed, at the request of the bishops of the ecclesiastical province, to be appointed by Pius IX bishop of Saint-Hyacinthe. He foresaw the financial difficulties and the political-religious conflicts in which he would wear out his health prematurely, and he is said to have confessed at that time to one of his close associates: "I accept this high position, because it is a veritable sacrifice that is imposed on me. I must not now expect to reach the age of my worthy old mother. This will give me 10 years, certainly not 15."

Indeed, the episcopal corporation was encumbered with a debt of $44,000, an enormous sum for the period. But the dissensions that split the town and the diocese were far more disturbing. Saint-Hyacinthe was probably at that time, after Montreal, the town of Canada East where partisan struggles were most bitter: the Papineau and Dessaulles families had their roots there; the college, whose superior was the vicar general Joseph-Sabin Raymond*, had been a target for the violent attacks of Louis-Antoine Dessaulles* ever since the Bleu candidate, Rémi Raymond, had won against Augustin-Cyrille Papineau, Dessaulles' cousin, in the 1863 elections. The first six months of 1867 were to see the opponents Sabin

La Rocque

Raymond and Dessaulles waging a savage paper war; each man put together some 20 interminable letters, Raymond's prose being reproduced by *Le Courrier de Saint-Hyacinthe*, which was edited by Oscar Dunn*, a brilliant former pupil of the college and an ardent supporter of Louis Veuillot into the bargain, and that of Dessaulles appearing in *Le Journal de Saint-Hyacinthe* and *Le Pays* of Montreal.

Bishop La Rocque therefore arrived in a diocese that was in complete ferment. His attitude towards confederation, an "occurrence of immense significance," an "achievement without parallel in the annals of our history," as he wrote in a pastoral letter of 18 June 1867, was not calculated to induce calm, as can easily be imagined. He acknowledged that through his letter he would show himself to be more a patriot than a bishop, for he feared above all annexation to the United States, which according to him would amount to the death of the French Canadian nation. At this time too Alexandre Dufresne, the MLA for Iberville, had introduced into his county a branch of the Société Saint-Jean-Baptiste, a centre of resistance to confederation, but also, to some extent, a secret society, and as such an object of suspicion to the church. In March 1867 Dufresne published a pamphlet reproducing his stormy correspondence with Bishop La Rocque; after his defeat Dufresne passed to Alphonse Lusignan*, editor of *Le Pays*, the documents relative to his quarrel with the bishop, and Lusignan gave them a wide publicity in the issues of *Le Pays* of 24 and 29 Oct. 1867.

To the vexations that his stand on political-religious matters brought him were added the financial straits of the diocese. To meet the debt and gradually pay it off, La Rocque appealed to each of his priests through a plan which he outlined in circular letters of 19 Sept. and 27 Dec. 1866, and expanded on in a pastoral letter of 11 May 1867. Abbé Isaac Lesieur-Desaulniers, on whom he conferred the title of vicar general, beggared himself for his bishop's sake. La Rocque reduced his own expenses by departing from Saint-Hyacinthe and going to live in the parish of Beloeil, leaving as locum tenens his secretary, Abbé Louis-Zéphirin Moreau*, who disposed of current business. After seven years of absence La Rocque returned to his bishopric, with the satisfaction of having liquidated by the beginning of 1875 the debt that had so concerned him at the start of his episcopate.

In 1870 he attended the Vatican Council. Unfortunately a serious illness forced him to leave Rome, "at the moment when the doctrine [of infallibility]," which he had advocated all his life, "was about to be made an article of faith by a solemn definition," as he wrote, on his return, in a pastoral letter of 15 Nov. 1870.

The following year, in a circular letter dated 28 April 1871 from Beloeil, he declared himself on the side of the archbishop of Quebec, Elzéar-Alexandre Taschereau*, and the bishop of Rimouski, Jean-Pierre-François Laforce* Langevin, who had just disavowed the *Programme catholique* – an ultramontane political programme – as having been "formulated without any participation by the episcopate." Taking an increasingly independent stand in relation to Bishop Bourget, La Rocque intervened in the affair of the keeping of the civil registers, when *Le Nouveau Monde*, semi-official organ of the bishopric of Montreal, was leading a ruthless campaign against the "gallican" George-Étienne Cartier. In a circular letter of 23 Jan. 1871 to his clergy, La Rocque exhorted his subordinates "to bless and praise God for the independence, the liberty, and the most ample and wide privileges enjoyed by our modest Church of the Province of Quebec, perhaps better endowed in this respect than any other Church in the world." These lines and many others in Bishop La Rocque's circular letter startled Bishop Bourget, who was struggling relentlessly "against the encroachments of civil law," and who, as he wrote to the bishop of Saint-Hyacinthe on 11 Feb. 1871, was "preparing to ask for the reform of the civil code at those points that are at variance with canon law and the authority of the Holy See." Bishop Bourget continued: ". . . that you should have rendered your circular letter public in the present circumstances, by placing it in the hands of your clergy, is in my opinion a great scandal. For the world will not fail to conclude that you are a slavish supporter of the secular authority; and that, to serve the cause of a few friends belonging to the world, who consider you their defender, you are turning your back on your colleagues and being evasive over principles that we are responsible for upholding at all costs."

Other incidents revealed to the public at large that the spiritual heads of the diocese of Saint-Hyacinthe did not concur with the extravagant arguments of Bishop Bourget and his friends. The one that created the most stir was probably the Raymond-Pinsonnault dispute. Bishop Joseph-Sabin Raymond stated in a lecture in 1872 that there were neither liberals nor gallicans in Canada in the religious sense of the term; Bishop Pierre-Adolphe Pinsonnault*, who had been attached to the bishopric of Montreal after a stay in the United States, his deafness and administrative follies having obliged him to resign as bishop of Sandwich, retorted that Bishop Raymond was precisely one of those Catholic liberals that Pius IX had condemned. The dispute was turning into a dialogue of the deaf!

Bishop La Rocque thought it advisable to set aside these polemics, in order to devote himself to more useful projects. In October 1873 he had the joy of welcoming to his episcopal town four French Dominicans, the forerunners of a permanent establishment; he had overcome the prejudices of the prior of the Dominican province of France, Father Bernard Chocarne, who after a first visit to Canada in 1868 had scoffed at those "half-savage Canadians, backward in politics, in philosophy, in literature, out and out preservers of a past that all peoples truly worthy of liberty and progress consider done away with." From Bishop La Rocque too came the plan of starting a new episcopal see in the Eastern Townships, using a part of the dioceses of Quebec and Trois-Rivières. He argued convincingly for this plan during the fifth provincial council of Quebec. At the request of the priests on this council, Pius IX created the diocese of Sherbrooke by a brief dated 28 Aug. 1874.

Exhausted by the opposition that had beset him, and by the work he had imposed upon himself during nine years of an episcopate notable, in addition to the achievements already described, for the founding of two missions, the erection of seven parishes, and the ordination of 55 priests, grievously distressed also by the death of his mother in the spring of 1875, Bishop La Rocque passed away on 15 July 1875 at the Hôtel-Dieu of Saint-Hyacinthe. His body was placed in the vault of this establishment, near his mother's.

Tall in stature, with regular features and a florid complexion, alert, searching eyes, a well-shaped, usually smiling mouth, and distinguished bearing, he was nicknamed "handsome La Rocque." To this impressive physique corresponded qualities of the heart, the chief of which was probably his capacity for warmth and understanding. The balance he maintained in the midst of the furious discords that troubled the second part of the 19th century made his role by no means a negligible one. We may conclude with Abbé Élie-Joseph-Arthur Auclair* that Bishop La Rocque "was an outstanding man of action, a zealous priest, devoted to his flock, a bishop of great distinction, a true leader of the Church."

PHILIPPE SYLVAIN

[Charles La Rocque], *Une autre récompense de 1 600 louis ou réponse au défi de Mr Atkinson avec la preuve des dogmes catholiques attaqués dans ce défi* (Montréal, 1852). ACAM, RLB, 10, pp.109–10; RLB, 19, pp.306–12. *Mandements, lettres pastorales et circulaires des évêques de Saint-Hyacinthe*, A.-X. Bernard, édit. (8v., Montréal, 1888–98), II, 313–27. *Le Courrier de Saint-Hyacinthe*, 16 juill. 1875. *L'Opinion publique* (Montréal), 22 juill. 1875. J.-P. Bernard, "La pensée et l'influence des Rouges (1848–1867)," unpublished PHD thesis, Université de Montréal, 1968, 343ss. J.-D. Brosseau, *Saint-Jean-de-Québec; origine et développements* (Saint-Jean, Qué., [1937]), 213–15. S.-A. Moreau, *Histoire de L'Acadie, province de Québec* (Montréal, 1908), 71–74. É.-J. Auclair, "Les trois évêques Larocque," SCHÉC *Rapport*, 1945–46, 11–17. Robert [Philippe] Sylvain, "Aperçu sur le prosélytisme protestant au Canada français," *RSCT*, LV (1962), 3rd ser., sect.I, 69–72. Armand Yon, "Les Canadiens français jugés par les Français de France, 1830–1939," *RHAF*, XIX (1965–66), 578.

LATERRIÈRE, MARC-PASCAL DE SALES, doctor, seigneur, and politician; b. 25 March 1792 at Baie-du-Febvre (Baieville, Yamaska County), L.C., son of Pierre Fabre*, *dit* Laterrière, and Catherine Delzenne; married Eulalie-Antoinette, daughter of Claude Dénéchaud*, who bore him four boys and two girls; d. 29 March 1872 at Les Éboulements, Que.

Originally from Languedoc, Marc-Pascal's father adopted the name of Jean-Pierre de Sales Laterrière after his arrival in Canada in 1766. Jean-Pierre practised medicine, engaged in commerce, and directed the ironworks at Saint-Maurice, before becoming seigneur of Les Éboulements. Concerned about his sons' education, he obtained admission for them to the Petit Séminaire of Quebec. When Marc-Pascal left this institution, in 1807, he studied medicine at Philadelphia. He was back in Canada in 1812 and took up residence at Quebec; when the war came, he served as surgeon of the 6th Battalion of militia of Lower Canada. After the war he carried on his profession in Lower Town, Quebec, until he received from his mother, in 1816, half of the seigneury of Les Éboulements; in 1829 he acquired the whole of it. His manor-house was situated in Northumberland County, which Laterrière represented in the House of Assembly from 1824 to 1830. He then became the member for Saguenay County. He was not identified with the members of the Tory party, but was rather considered as a politician sympathetic to the claims of the Parti Canadien. In 1832 he entered the Legislative Council, and from 1838 to 1841 was part of the Special Council, but attended none of its meetings.

From then until 1845 he kept apart from political life. "I am against Union," he explained to Louis-Hippolyte La Fontaine* on 29 Oct. 1842, "even with all the modifications that our enemies are today forced to concede." He had no faith "in that problematic justice" that the French-speaking leader sought to establish. Notwithstanding his opposition to union, he returned to the political

Laverdière

arena in 1845 as MLA for Saguenay County. The debates on the seigneurial régime might have prompted him to take this decision. In 1851 he sat on the parliamentary committee responsible for defining the terms and conditions governing the abolition of seigneurial tenure in Canada East. Laterrière abandoned politics again during the period 1854 to 1856. In the latter year he was elected legislative councillor for the Laurentians. He was an anti-confederate candidate in the federal elections of 1867, and was defeated.

Laterrière showed less interest in military life than in political life. In 1830 he refused an appointment as major in the militia of Lower Canada, for fear that the obedience due to a superior might endanger the "great privileges" inherent in the profession of doctor. In 1848 he accepted the position of adjutant-general of the militia of Lower Canada, but rapidly dissociated himself from it.

He led a peaceful existence on his seigneury of Les Éboulements, and played a rather unobtrusive role in politics. The rare sources that make mention of his career do, however, give an indication of his nationalist convictions.

JEAN-PIERRE GAGNON

BNQ, Société historique de Montréal, Collection La Fontaine, Lettres, 212, 707, 710, 717 (copies in PAC). PAC, RG 1, L1, 43, p.644; L3L, 121, pp.59135–36, 59138; RG 4, A1, 131, pp.41955–57; 190/2, p.108; 216, p.26; 247, p.1; 248, pp.114, 133; 266 (1831), pp.121–125A; 275/1 (1832), p.35; 392, p.396; 399, p.4; 410, p.26. *Journaux du Conseil spécial de la province du Bas-Canada*, 1838–1840. Turcotte, *Conseil législatif de Québec*, 233–34. Ahern, *Notes pour l'histoire de la médecine*, 351–52. H.-R. Casgrain, *La famille de Sales Laterrière* (Québec, 1870). Gérard Malchelosse, "Mémoires romancés," *Cahiers des Dix*, XXV (1960), 103–46.

LAVERDIÈRE (Cauchon, *dit* **Laverdière**), **CHARLES-HONORÉ**, priest, teacher, librarian, and historian; b. 23 Oct. 1826 at Château-Richer (Montmorency County), L.C., son of Charles Cauchon, *dit* Laverdière, farmer, and of Théotiste Cauchon; d. 11 March 1873 at Quebec.

Charles-Honoré Laverdière entered the Petit Séminaire of Quebec in the autumn of 1840 and proved to be a brilliant student; he notes himself that his name regularly appeared on the annual prize list. In September 1848 he was appointed assistant teacher at the seminary and taught physics until 1850, after which he completed his theological studies and was ordained a priest on 3 Aug. 1851.

After his ordination he was again appointed a teacher at the seminary, possibly through the influence of Thomas-Étienne Hamel*, who was one of the familiars of the superior, Abbé Louis-Jacques Casault*. Indeed, Hamel wrote to Laverdière on 1 Sept. 1851: "Your affair is settled. You remain at the seminary." From then on Laverdière held no further office as vicar or parish priest. On 8 May 1855, when he asked the superior for membership in the seminary, which he was to receive a month later, he explained that he felt himself called more strongly to a community life than to the discharge of the duties of the ministry. He first taught mathematics, and in 1854 history. Thirteen years later he succeeded Jean-Baptiste-Antoine Ferland* in the chair of history at the Faculty of Arts of the Université Laval.

From 1851 on, while continuing to teach, Laverdière occupied semi-officially the post of deputy to the librarian of the seminary. In 1858 he was appointed librarian of the university; on 13 June 1856, the Congregation of the Index had allowed him to read and keep censured books.

As well as discharging his duties as professor and librarian, Laverdière published several collections of profane and religious canticles, and in the field of history his name is attached as collaborator or editor to works important not because of their quantity but because of their quality. While he was studying at the Petit Séminaire he had taken part in the founding of *L'Abeille*, a students' journal to which he contributed until his death. In 1859 he brought out 26 successive instalments of hitherto unpublished documents on the history of Canada. In 1858, he had had a share in the publication of the *Relations des Jésuites*, which was edited under the direction of Abbé Édouard-Gabriel Plante and Abbé Ferland, by setting up the "table of contents"; Antoine Gérin-Lajoie* wrote to congratulate him, saying that his contribution "admirably completed the entire work." Furthermore, in 1869 he published his *Histoire du Canada*, a text which classical colleges were still using at the beginning of the 20th century. "This competent work," writes Pierre Savard, "which is very accurate in relation to the historical knowledge of the time, has been severely judged from a pedagogical and literary point of view."

In 1870 the first Canadian edition of the *Œuvres de Champlain* appeared. This edition, which Laverdière had been shaping and recasting since 1864, was according to Narcisse-Henri-Édouard Faucher* de Saint-Maurice a "masterpiece of Canadian typography"; moreover, it was one of the historical works of the period that attracted most attention. Its scientific value is still acknowledged today, despite reservations expressed by the Jesuits, whom Laverdière accused, wrongly according to Lucien Campeau, of having falsified those writings of Samuel de Champlain* that were

432

first published in 1632. Finally, in 1871, in collaboration with Abbé Henri-Raymond Casgrain*, Laverdière edited the *Journal des Jésuites*.

His career ended abruptly in 1873, in a place predestined by his veneration for the published word: on 10 March he was stricken with an attack of apoplexy in a printing house at Quebec when he was giving directions for a new publication. He died the next day, intestate. His creditors had difficulty in obtaining a settlement: to meet their credit of $1,640 there was only the sum of $503.

This man "of medium height, with keen black eyes, tanned complexion and square shoulders," was a tireless worker to whom his edition of the *Œuvres de Champlain*, his other historical publications, and an entire life devoted to the cause of the printed book bear eloquent testimony. Laverdière strove for scientific rigour; he would check the slightest details to make sure that the facts were exact. His works, like those of Louis-Philippe Turcotte, Benjamin Sulte*, Narcisse-Eutrope Dionne*, and Cyprien Tanguay*, marked the revival of an interest in history that characterized the years 1860–80.

Michel Paquin

[For additional bibliographic information on Laverdière's main publications see *DCB*, I, 199, 455–56, 694, 698, 702.]

ASQ, Carton Laverdière; mss, 26, 175; mss, 626; mss, 627; mss, 676, 38, 573–74; Polygraphie, V, 57; Polygraphie, XIII, 63, 79, 90; Polygraphie, XX, 8; Séminaire, IX, 34; Séminaire, CXI, 22, 72. *L'Opinion publique* (Montréal), 27 mars 1873. Le Jeune, *Dictionnaire*, II, 116. Provost, *Le séminaire de Québec: documents et biographies*, 476. Lucien Campeau, "Les Jésuites ont-ils retouché les écrits de Champlain?" *RHAF*, V (1951–52), 340–61. Auguste Gosselin, "Le vrai monument de Champlain: ses œuvres éditées par Laverdière," *RSCT*, 3rd ser., II (1908), sect.i, 3–23. Pierre Savard, "Les débuts de l'enseignement de l'histoire et de la géographie au Petit Séminaire de Québec (1765–1880)," *RHAF*, XVI (1962–63), 201.

LAW, ROBERT, army officer and colonial administrator; b.*c.* 1788 in England; d. 16 May 1874 in England.

When Robert Law was 20 years old he joined the British army in Spain as a volunteer just in time to take part in Sir John Moore's action at Lugo and the retreat from Corunna. He returned to Spain and until 1814 fought in numerous campaigns, receiving several serious wounds. In July 1814 he was embarked for New Orleans, but recalled and sent to Belgium where he served in the campaigns of 1815. He fought at Waterloo as a lieutenant in Sir Frederick Adair's brigade, was again seriously wounded, and was awarded the Waterloo Medal. Law remained in France with the army of occupation until 1818, and subsequently served 15 years in the colonies, including the West Indies, before being sent to Newfoundland. He became a captain in October 1821, a major in August 1834, and was promoted lieutenant-colonel in 1844.

Robert Law probably came to Newfoundland in 1834, the same year as Governor Henry Prescott, for he was reported to have held the post of commandant of the garrison for 25 years when he departed in 1859. Regular troops had been withdrawn from Newfoundland in 1825 following the arrival of replacements in November 1824. These replacements were the Royal Veteran Companies formed in 1824 from former servicemen – outpatients of the Royal Hospital for Invalid Soldiers at Chelsea. In 1827 they were renamed the Royal Newfoundland Veteran Companies and, in 1843, the Royal Newfoundland Companies. The main duties of the garrison were to bring some pomp and ceremony to the colony – especially under the governorship of Sir Thomas Cochrane – and to assist the civil power. This assistance was most essential before the establishment of an armed police force in the colony in 1871. Troops were called out to protect the court house in 1835 at the height of a political crisis relating to Chief Justice Henry John Boulton*. They were often in demand during elections to quell riots, such as at St John's in 1836 and during a by-election in Carbonear in 1840. In 1846 Law was commended for the part he and his men played in fighting the disastrous fire in St John's and for their later work of reconstruction and maintaining law and order in the stricken community. The fire, which began at 8:30 AM on 9 June in the east end of the town at a cabinet maker's shop, had by evening moved westward to destroy over one mile of shops, houses, and public buildings on the two main streets. The total loss was estimated at £890,000, and D. W. Prowse* considered it the worst of the great fires which devastated British North American towns such as Quebec and Saint John, N.B., during the period.

Apart from his military duties, which were only occasionally onerous, Law participated in the political life of the colony during different periods. When Governor Sir John Harvey* was transferred to Nova Scotia in August 1846, Law assumed the duties of administrator until the arrival of Sir John Gaspard Le Marchant in April 1847. Almost all of his tenure was taken up by the administration of relief. The problems of assistance and reconstruction after the June 1846 fire were compounded by a severe and destructive storm in September and by the blight that affected the potato harvest. Hence Law's political duties were made increasingly difficult because of social and economic distress.

Law was disturbed by the unseemly competition for the £102,500 granted from outside Newfoundland to relieve the fire victims. In November 1846 he reported to the Colonial Office that the principal uninsured sufferers had now received almost the whole amount of their losses, and advised against continuing direct relief which, he believed, was having a demoralizing effect upon the recipients. The balance of the fund ought to be retained and administered by the secretary of state; a portion should be set aside to rebuild the Church of England Cathedral, otherwise the cost of this project would fall mainly on the shopkeepers and merchants of the city who had not been reimbursed for the full amount of their fire losses. By and large these recommendations were followed by Lord Grey, but not without a great deal of grumbling among those adversely affected. In December Law called the Amalgamated Legislature [see Prescott] into its final session to pass a loan bill for the relief of outport fishermen and to ease the financial burden of the Rebuilding Act. This act, passed by a special session of the Amalgamated Legislature in 1846, provided for the rebuilding of St John's with the cost to be met by the legislature and the merchants and householders of the city. Subsequently, by the royal instructions of 19 July 1848, pertaining to another new constitution, Law was created president of the Legislative Council, which office he held until 1850, and again from 1853 to 1854.

On his promotion to major-general in 1859 Law was obliged to relinquish his command, and he returned to England. A subscription of £100 sterling was raised for a piece of plate which was presented to him by a group of prominent citizens with a commendation for his services to the colony. He was elevated to lieutenant-general in 1868.

FREDERIC F. THOMPSON

PRO, CO 194/126. *Royal Gazette* (St John's), 1834–59. Hart, *New army lists*, 1840–74. H. G. Grey, *The colonial policy of Lord John Russell's administration* (2v., London, 1853; 2nd ed., with additions, 2v., London, 1853), I. Gunn, *Political history of Nfld.* Prowse, *History of Nfld.*

LAWSON, WILLIAM, lay preacher and merchant; b. 27 Nov. 1793, at Wallholme, near Brampton, Cumberland, Eng., second son of William Lawson, a tailor, and Frances Bell; m. 25 June 1814 Ann Atkinson of Brampton, a bonnet-maker, by whom he had 11 children; d. 19 Feb. 1875 at Hamilton, Ont.

After a rudimentary education William Lawson entered his father's trade, but suffered financial losses and in 1829 emigrated to Canada with his family. He opened a shop in York (Toronto) as a tailor, draper, and hat-maker, and was joined by his former apprentice, Robert Walker, who bought the business in 1834. Lawson moved to Brampton, Upper Canada, then returned to Toronto, and finally settled in Hamilton in 1847.

Lawson's importance is not as a merchant but as a Primitive Methodist. His family belonged to the Church of England, but in 1813 he joined the Methodists and began preaching around Brampton. Although lacking formal training he was obviously a gifted preacher, arousing great feeling. He complained of the lukewarm attitudes of many Wesleyans, and in 1822 joined the Primitive Methodists, attracted by their enthusiasm and democratic organization, in which lay preachers played an important role.

Through Lawson's efforts the first Primitive Methodist congregation in Canada was formed at York in 1830. Toronto remained the centre of Canadian Primitive Methodism, which spread mainly into western Ontario. At its peak in 1882 there were 8,200 members; in 1884 the Primitive Methodists united with other Methodist bodies to form the Methodist Church of Canada. Besides his preaching, Lawson served his church as missionary secretary for many years, and in 1853 attended its English conference as the special delegate from Canada. He holds a pre-eminent place in the history of Canadian Primitive Methodism.

EDITH FIRTH

UCA Primitive Methodist Church (York), minute book. *Christian Journal* (Toronto), 26 March 1875. William Lawson, *The life of William Lawson, J.P., one of the builders of Canada . . .* , [ed. J. D. Lawson] (n.p., 1917). Jane Hopper, *Old-time Primitive Methodism in Canada, [1829–1884]* (Toronto, 1904).

LEBLANC, CHARLES-ANDRÉ, lawyer, civil servant; b. 18 Aug. 1816 at Montreal, L.C., of the marriage of Charles Leblanc, craftsman, and Louise Brien-Desrochers; d. 16 Aug. 1877 at Montreal.

Charles-André Leblanc was educated at the old college of Montreal, and had as fellow-students George-Étienne CARTIER, Joseph-Amable Berthelot*, and Joseph-Ubalde BEAUDRY; he studied law, and received his legal training under Pierre Moreau. During the troubled days of 1837, when he was 21 years old, he became the youngest member of the Fils de la Liberté. This association, set up on 5 Sept. 1837, comprised more than 700 young men of Montreal. Half civilian and half military, it had two sections which were to work, "one through speech and writing, the other by force of arms if necessary, for the progress and triumph of the people's cause." In November 1837 Leblanc was put in prison on a charge of high treason and spent the winter in jail, which did not prevent him from being called to the bar on 30 Sept. 1839.

As a partner first of his original employer Pierre Moreau, later of Francis CASSIDY who had become mayor of Montreal, and finally of Alexandre Lacoste*, Charles-André Leblanc had extensive experience at the bar. For 35 years he pleaded before all the courts in Montreal. He was one of the firm supporters of George-Étienne Cartier. Leblanc was a member of the Montreal council of the bar in 1855, syndic in 1858, examiner of candidates for admission to the profession in 1859, *bâtonnier* in 1863; he was also president of the Société Saint-Jean-Baptiste of Montreal in 1867, and churchwarden of the charitable organization and council of the parish (Notre-Dame) of Montreal, which before the subdivisions made in 1873 numbered nearly 100,000, that is, the entire Catholic population of the town.

Charles-André Leblanc had advocated the opening of a colonization road to the north of Montreal and, as representative of the provincial government, was one of its administrators. He contributed to the founding of the Reform School at Montreal, and also was a member of the Council of Public Instruction. In November 1872, towards the end of his life, he became sheriff of the district of Montreal, an office which consisted principally of seeing to the enforcement of summonses and writs of execution, safeguarding goods and possessions under distraint, having charge of the prisons of his district, and being present at executions. He still held this office when he passed away on 16 Aug. 1877 at Montreal.

In January 1837, at Montreal, while still in training, Charles-André Leblanc had married Julie Dumont, daughter of Philippe Dumont and Julie Valière. They had eight children; one, Elmire, married Mathias-Charles Desnoyers in 1865; another, Mathilde, became the wife of Oscar Dunn*, writer and journalist. Charles-André Leblanc married again, his second wife being Marguerite Wilson, Jean-Baptiste-Alexandre Couillard's widow.

JEAN-JACQUES LEFEBVRE

PAC, MG 30, D62 (Audet papers), 18, pp.71–77. *La Minerve* (Montréal), 17 août 1877. *L'Opinion publique* (Montréal), 23 août 1877. Fauteux, *Patriotes*, 291–92. Pierre Beullac et É.-F. Surveyer, *Le centenaire du Barreau de Montréal, 1849–1949* (Montréal, 1949), 61–64. Borthwick, *Hist. and biog. gazetteer*, 402–3.

LE BOUTILLIER (Le Bouthillier), JOHN, businessman and politician; b. 1797 in the family

home at La Chasse, on the Isle of Jersey; d. 31 July 1872 at Gaspé, Que.

After his arrival in the Gaspé peninsula, around 1815, John Le Boutillier worked for Charles Robin and Company, traders in fish, first as a clerk, then as a manager at Paspébiac and Percé. In 1830 he left the Robins to open his own business under the name of John Le Boutillier and Company. At the same period, he took up residence at Gaspé, where he was to spend the rest of his life.

His commercial activities consisted chiefly of exporting dried cod to different countries of Europe, the West Indies, and Brazil. He possessed establishments along the whole Gaspesian coast, from Paspébiac to Sainte-Anne-des Monts; in 1861 he owned 12 ships and 169 fishing boats, and had 2,500 employees settled along the coast. Soon after his death in 1872, his firm was, however, taken over by Charles Robin and Company.

John Le Boutillier devoted part of his life to politics. He represented Gaspé in the assembly from 1833 to 1838, and was then MLA for Bonaventure County from 1844 to 1847 and for Gaspé County from 1854 to 1867. On 2 Nov. 1867 he was appointed legislative councillor for the division of the Gulf, and continued a councillor until his death.

A Protestant, but married to a Catholic, Elizabeth Robin, the daughter of one of his former employers, Le Boutillier was converted to Catholicism shortly before his death. He was survived by four children.

ULRIC LÉVESQUE

Archives paroissiales de Saint-Albert-de-Gaspé (Qué.), Registres des baptêmes, mariages et sépultures, 2 août 1872. Private Archives, Mlle Gertrude Sutton–Le Boutillier (Gaspé, Qué.), Papiers Charles Sutton–Le Boutillier. PAC, MG 30, D62 (Audet papers), 18, pp.130–32. Desjardins, *Guide parlementaire.* H. A. Innis, *The cod fisheries; the history of an international economy* (The relations of Canada and the United States series, New Haven, Toronto, and London, 1940). C.-E. Roy et Lucien Brault, *Gaspé depuis Cartier* (Québec, 1934). Firmin Létourneau, "La Côte Nord de Gaspé," *Revue d'histoire de la Gaspésie* (Gaspé, Qué.), III (1965), 192, 203–4.

LEE, WILLIAM HENRY, civil servant; b. at Trois-Rivières, L.C., 26 June 1799, son of Dr William Lee, from Ireland, who was on the army medical staff in Upper Canada; d. Ottawa, Ont., 11 Sept. 1878.

William Henry Lee was educated in Montreal. In May 1821 he was appointed extra clerk in the office of the Executive Council of Upper Canada, and then junior (1828) and senior (1831) clerk. He became acting clerk of the Executive Council

Leeming

in 1839, and had the same position in the Province of Canada in 1841. In 1844 he married Harriet Louisa, daughter of Samuel Smith*, a leading Upper Canadian politician. Lee was made clerk of the Executive Council in 1853 and was clerk of the Privy Council from 1 July 1867 until his superannuation at his own request in 1872. Lee held several minor appointments connected with his regular work (for example, clerk to the Heir and Devisee Commission, 1839–53, and commissioner for sundry official purposes). Official papers were his only writing.

Lee's successor as clerk of the Privy Council was William Alfred Himsworth. Born 28 Aug. 1820 at Trois-Rivières, he had been educated at the college of Montreal and was called to the bar of Lower Canada in 1841; he had then practised law briefly at Aylmer (Gatineau County), until he entered government service. He was sessional clerk of the Legislative Assembly, Province of Canada, 1842–43, and became a full-time clerk in the office of the Executive Council in 1843. Thereafter he rose to be assistant clerk of the Executive Council, 1851; assistant clerk of the Privy Council for Canada from 2 July 1867; clerk from 1 July 1872 to 1880. He died in 1880, in Ottawa. He had married Louisa Morrison on 31 Dec. 1844, by whom he had one son.

Himsworth, like Lee, held a number of minor appointments supplementary to his major position (for example, as a deputy for signing money warrants, and commissioner for signing commitments under a habeas corpus suspension act) and was appointed justice of the peace for Carleton County on 6 Nov. 1875. The only literary work connected with his name is a doubtful attribution: he may have been the youthful author of a brochure, *La crise ministérielle*, published in 1844 under the name of Denis-Benjamin Viger*.

The duties of Lee and Himsworth throughout their careers were mainly secretarial. In their junior days (when both would travel with the peripatetic government of the Province of Canada) their clerical tasks included anything that might be assigned to them. As they rose in rank, they were increasingly concerned with the routine preparation of business for the cabinet, including receiving departmental applications which had to be passed on for executive decision, and the subsequent communication of decisions back to the departments. The duties have been authoritatively described as "menial," and they allowed for little initiative; the largest staff either ever supervised rarely exceeded a dozen clerks.

That both Lee and Himsworth served under more than one constitution and numerous governments, at a time when appointment and promotion depended on political superiors, is a mark of their capacity and integrity; but longevity in the public service was common even then, and no great significance can be attached to longevity alone. Both were held in high regard by their associates and Lee, who at his retirement was the dean of the public service, was honoured by a presentation from the cabinet.

NORMAN WARD

PAC, MG 24, I9 (Hill collection), 25, pp.6399–6400; MG 26, A (Macdonald papers), 82, pp.13184–85, 39678, 39679, 77048–49; RG 1, E14, 8–40. Queen's University Archives, Alexander Mackenzie papers, pp.327–28, 329–30, 851–54. *Can. parl. comp., 1872; 1874. Dom. ann. reg., 1880–81*, 411. Hodgetts, *Pioneer public service*, 52, 86–87, 94, 271.

LEEMING, RALPH, Church of England clergyman; b. 27 Jan. 1788, Blackburn, Lancashire, Eng.; d. 13 March 1872 at Dundas, Ont.

Ralph Leeming was educated at St Bees College in Cumberland and was ordained in 1812. He served two curacies and an endowed school in the diocese of Rochester, before asking, in 1816, to be sent as a missionary to the diocese of Quebec. His application was welcomed by the Society for the Propagation of the Gospel: at that time there were but six clergymen of the Church of England in all of Upper and Lower Canada, a situation created in part by the "higher advantages" offered by the older and more settled colony of Nova Scotia.

The SPG in September 1816 appointed Leeming the first resident clergyman of Ancaster Township, a "neat and rising" community of some 1,000 inhabitants (only 200 of whom, by Leeming's count, were members of the Church of England). The appointment, which reflected the growing promise of the upper colony after the War of 1812, also included "Barton and adjacent parts," a territory embracing most of what is now Wentworth County at the head of Lake Ontario. Four years after his arrival in the district Leeming married Susan, the daughter of Richard Hatt*, a prominent miller and supporter of the church in the village of Dundas.

Early in 1818, at the urgent request of the Reverend Robert Addison* of Niagara, Leeming broadened his activities by taking over from Addison the duties of serving the Mohawks and other converted members of the Six Nations Confederacy, who occupied lands granted them in 1784 on the Grand River. For nearly ten years Leeming periodically ministered to the spiritual and educational needs of these otherwise neglected Indian communicants. In the fall of 1818 he endowed a school in the Tuscarora village and over the next few years supported the educational work conducted by the SPG among the Mohawks. Following the appointment in 1827 of the Reverend Robert Lugger* by the New England Company as the Iroquois' resident clergyman, Leeming confined his attention to white communicants in his constituency. By that time, St John's Church, the headquarters of his mission, had been completed in the village of Ancaster.

In 1830, complaining of failing health, Leeming resigned his charge and sought lighter duties elsewhere. After briefly considering an English parish, he decided to remain with the society and move to a newly organized mission in the township of March, about 14 miles above Bytown (Ottawa) on the Ottawa River. He was appointed in 1833 to another mission in the township of Hamilton, but again ill health forced him after a brief tenure to resign this, his last living. In spite of his physical frailties, however, he lived a long life, travelling extensively for some years and apparently residing latterly in the Ancaster and Dundas area. He died in 1872, having survived both his wife and his missionary brother, the Reverend William Leeming, of Chippawa.

C. M. JOHNSTON

PAC, MG 19, F1 (Claus papers), 12; RG 5, A1, 44; RG 10, A1, 5. USPG, Journal of SPG, 31–37, 40–41. Robert Gourlay, *Statistical account of Upper Canada, compiled with a view to a grand system of emigration* (2v., London, 1822), I, 389ff. John Howison, *Sketches of Upper Canada, domestic, local, and characteristic: to which are added practical details for the information of emigrants of every class; and some recollections of the United States of America* (Edinburgh, 1821), 161–64. John West, *A journal of a mission to the Indians of the British provinces of New Brunswick, and Nova Scotia, and the Mohawks, on the Ouse, or Grand River, Upper Canada* (London, 1827), 276–89. *Church Herald* (Toronto), 21 March, 18 April 1872. *Gore Gazette* (Ancaster), 3 March, 14 April 1827. "Rev. Ralph Leeming; an address from his parishioners and friends," Wentworth Hist. Soc., *Papers and Records* (Hamilton), VIII (1919), 59–61. T. D. J. Farmer, *A history of the parish of St John's Church, Ancaster . . .* (Guelph, Ont., 1924), 53–61. W. B. and A. B. Kerr, "The Reverend William Leeming, first rector of Trinity Church, Chippawa," *Ont. Hist.*, XXXI (1936), 135–54.

LÉGARÉ, ANTOINE, teacher; b. 2 Oct. 1799 at Saint-Roch de Québec, son of Ignace Légaré, a tanner, and Marie Parant; d. 7 March 1873 at Saint-Roch de Québec.

After completing his senior class at the seminary of Quebec in 1820, Antoine Légaré took up a teaching career. He was the first layman, in Lower Canada, to devote himself to elementary teaching after having gone so far in his classical studies. At that period, a schoolteacher was regarded as an unfortunate person who had not succeeded in other professions, and who had turned towards teaching while waiting for better things. Even in the last years of Légaré's career, a teacher who earned $300 a year was considered to be very well paid. In the same period a coachman drew an identical salary, but received his board and lodging in addition. In 1872, Légaré received a pension of $35.

For Légaré and those like him, teaching was therefore a veritable vocation: he devoted all his talent and his whole life to it. In 1822 he started the first elementary school in the parish of Saint-Roch de Québec, where he taught for 50 years. Meanwhile a few courageous inhabitants of Quebec had followed in this pioneer's footsteps, and in 1845 they met, under Légaré's presidency, to form a school-teachers' association. Légaré was then chosen as vice-president of the first board of directors. Five years later the new society was incorporated under the name of the Association de la Bibliothèque des Instituteurs du district de Québec.

In 1846 Antoine Légaré had been appointed by the cabinet a member of the Catholic Board of Examiners of the district of Quebec City. This board preceded the founding of the normal schools, and its aim was to eliminate incompetent teachers. Légaré worked on it until 3 Jan. 1851.

Antoine Légaré's *confrères*, who considered him their model and dean, on 12 June 1872 celebrated his fiftieth year as a teacher. On this occasion, they entertained him at a banquet and literary meeting among the population of Saint-Roch whom he had loved so well; he had taught 4,000 children there.

Less than a year later he died, a bachelor, at Saint-Roch de Québec, after an illness of some weeks which he bore with resignation.

BÉATRICE CHASSÉ

ASQ, Lettres, Y, 113. *JIP*, 1872, 92–125; mars 1873, 35. *La Gazette des familles canadiennes et acadiennes* (Québec), 31 mars 1873. P.-G. Roy, *Fils de Québec*, III, 103–5.

LEMAIRE, FÉLIX-HYACINTHE, notary, legislative councillor; b. 14 March 1808 at the mission of Lac-des-Deux-Montagnes (which became the parish of Oka in 1910), L.C., son of Ignace Lemaire and Louise Gastonguay; d. 17 Dec. 1879 at Saint-Benoît (Deux-Montagnes County), Que.

Félix-Hyacinthe Lemaire became a notary in January 1836, and practised his profession until the last month of his life; he signed some 6,000 acts. His principal client was the seminary of Saint-Sulpice in Montreal (the Sulpicians were the

Le Marchant

seigneurs of the region); he was its agent for more than 30 years after 1842. As agent his chief duty was to collect seigneurial dues from the farmers. Félix-Hyacinthe Lemaire was a major in the militia battalion of Deux-Montagnes, and also clerk of the Circuit Court there.

In November 1867 he was appointed to the Legislative Council as representative for the division of Mille-Isles, which comprised Terrebonne and Deux-Montagnes counties. In September 1874, in his capacity as president of the Legislative Council, he was sworn in as a member of the Executive Council of the province in Charles-Eugène Boucher* de Boucherville's cabinet. The obtaining of this appointment was no doubt facilitated by the friendship between Boucher de Boucherville and himself. Less than two years later the state of his health obliged him to resign.

Félix-Hyacinthe Lemaire died in his village of Saint-Benoît, where he was buried. *La Minerve* of Montreal stressed that he had "a high sense of his family traditions, a lofty intelligence, a firm character allied to a strong underlying sense of moderation."

In January 1837, at Sainte-Scholastique, Lemaire had married Luce Barcelo, who survived him. She was the daughter of Jacob Barcelo, a merchant and *Patriote* of 1837, and of Luce Dorion. They had one son and one daughter.

JEAN-JACQUES LEFEBVRE

Archives judiciaires de Terrebonne (Saint-Jérôme, Qué.), greffe de Félix-Hyacinthe Lemaire. *La Minerve* (Montréal), 18 déc. 1879. *Can. parl. comp., 1877*, 289. Rosario Gauthier, "Les mariages du comté de Deux-Montagnes" (manuscript in the possession of the author). Turcotte, *Conseil législatif de Québec*, 242. Fauteux, *Patriotes*, 96. Rumilly, *Hist. de la prov. de Québec*, I, 123.

LE MARCHANT, Sir JOHN GASPARD, army officer and colonial administrator; b. in England in 1803, third son of John Gaspard Le Marchant and Mary Cary; m. 28 May 1839 to Margaret Anne Taylor by whom he had several children; d. in London, Eng., 6 Feb. 1874.

John Gaspard Le Marchant was a member of a distinguished Guernsey family. He entered the army at the age of 17 as an ensign, and made a series of moves upward, all by purchase. Within a dozen years he was a major serving in Cape Colony. In all he spent £10,000 to purchase commissions and was one of the youngest officers in the British army to command a regiment.

In 1846 he was, according to his own account, "unexpectedly" offered the lieutenant governor-ship of Newfoundland. Perhaps the influence of his brother, Denis Le Marchant, a prominent Whig who was appointed under-secretary of the Board of Trade by Lord John Russell's government in 1847, prompted the offer. John Gaspard Le Marchant had loved soldiering and left it only after positive assurance from the Duke of Wellington that the acceptance of the civil position would promote his prospects in the army. Le Marchant's appointment became official in February 1847 and he arrived in St John's in April succeeding Sir John Harvey*. Unlike Harvey, Le Marchant was devoid of experience in administering a government. He came at a difficult time. St John's had been devastated, on 9 June 1846, by a great fire that rendered 12,000 of its 19,000 people homeless. The potato crops of 1846 and 1847 were badly affected by the same blight that wrought such havoc in Ireland.

After these difficulties, Le Marchant, and Newfoundland, had a short run of good luck. By the end of 1849 he was able to report that political activity, the bane of the colony, as he believed, was at a low ebb. This subsidence did not last long. The Liberals, who were mainly Roman Catholics, produced a rancorous agitation for responsible government, something which the commercial classes of the colony, heavily Protestant, Le Marchant himself, and the colonial secretary in London all opposed.

Le Marchant deplored many local habits: those of the merchant princes wont to retire to England with their profits, those of improvident fishermen. The merchants devised ingenious schemes for dodging taxes, and the fishermen sought whatever forms of relief the government would provide. So great were the prejudices against direct taxation that the legislature was afraid to establish municipal organizations to raise money through rates for local charges.

In the summer of 1852 Le Marchant went to Nova Scotia as lieutenant governor. There, with James Boyle Uniacke*, William Young*, and Joseph Howe leading a responsible ministry, the lieutenant governor's position was different. Le Marchant's governorship was much less controversial than his tenure in Newfoundland; but impartiality, which was now the lieutenant governor's role, did not prevent his being criticized by those who were out of office and wanted to be in. The change of government from Liberal to Tory in 1857 was effected with some party bitterness; but when Le Marchant was finally to leave Nova Scotia, in February 1858, he was praised by Conservative papers for his judiciousness. The Liberals tended to be more critical (they were now out of office), but even they felt compelled to avoid acrimony. Le Marchant himself believed, or at least on 7 March 1856 he told Henry Labouchere, the secretary of state for the colonies, that in both Newfoundland and Nova Scotia he had lived "in the most *perfect harmony*, both with my Executive Councillors, as well as the two Houses of the Legislature. . . . At the present moment they [Nova Scotian affairs] are in every sense most satisfactory."

Le Marchant was governor of Malta from 1859 to 1864, and was commander-in-chief of Madras, 1865–68, after which he retired to England. He was given a KCB in 1865. He was an enthusiastic horseman and agriculturalist, who sought to encourage good farming practices in both Newfoundland and Nova Scotia. He was never a man to stay put in government house, but sought an over-all view of his constituency. Le Marchant also believed that a successful governor in British North America had to entertain frequently and liberally, even lavishly. Over and above his £3,000 income he spent some £4,000 to £5,000 outfitting himself for his North American missions and another £5,000 from his private purse for dinners and parties in the colonies.

It is fair to add that the Duke of Wellington's views were not justified in the event. The Crimean War saw Le Marchant left on the shelf in Nova Scotia, while officers who had been his contemporaries in the army went gloriously to war and became major generals, to Le Marchant's almost daily mortification.

P. B. WAITE

[There are a few interesting private letters from John Gaspard Le Marchant to Henry Labouchere, secretary of state for the colonies, in a small private collection owned by Professor R. L. Raymond of Dalhousie University (Halifax). Especially useful here were letters of 7 March 1856 (private and confidential) and 18 Dec. 1857 (private). I am grateful to Professor Raymond for placing these papers unreservedly at my disposal. P.B.W.]

Le Marchant's dispatches from Newfoundland are in PRO, CO 194/127–194/136; from Nova Scotia, PRO, CO 217/122–217/124. Secondary sources are: *Burke's peerage* (1967). *DNB.* Gunn, *Political history of Nfld.*

LÉPINE, JEAN-BAPTISTE, Métis leader, fl. 1869–71.

Jean-Baptiste Lépine was probably the son of Jean-Baptiste Lépine (1792–1876) and Julie Henry. In July 1869 he was appointed by a group of Métis in the Red River Settlement to organize with Baptiste Tourond a patrol whose duty was to scrutinize the movements of Canadians in the settlement and to warn of strangers suspected of designs on Métis lands. In March 1870 he was a member of the military council presided over by his brother Ambroise-Dydime*, which condemned Thomas Scott* to death for insubordination to Louis Riel*'s provisional government. Lépine was one of two members of the council of seven who opposed the death penalty.

At the time of the threatened Fenian invasion of the province of Manitoba in the autumn of 1871, the Métis leaders held a number of meetings at which Lépine was present. The purpose of these was to determine what action the Métis should take if the invasion materialized. At a meeting of 4 October Louis Riel reported that a messenger had come from William Bernard O'DONOGHUE, an associate of Riel in 1869–70, asking the Métis leaders to meet him at Pembina on the American side of the border. All of the leaders, Riel stated later, had refused to go with the exception of Lépine and André Nault*. These two, he said, had "gone in their own right" to determine what O'Donoghue wanted. On 6 October Lépine and Nault reported that O'Donoghue planned to seize the Hudson's Bay Company post at the border and wanted the Métis to join him in the invasion. The Métis leaders decided to hold meetings in all the French parishes of the settlement in order to decide what attitude to take. Lépine presided at a meeting at Pointe-Coupée (near present-day Sainte-Agathe) on 7 October at which it was resolved that the Métis would respond to the call to arms of the lieutenant governor, Adams George Archibald*, to repel the invaders. The same day Riel offered the lieutenant governor the services of his Métis followers, The Fenians were easily rounded up and returned to the United States without any force from the province, English or French, being required. Nothing is known of Lépine after 1871.

Jean-Baptiste Lépine had been closely associated with the Métis supporters of Riel, but in this role he was obviously overshadowed by his brother, Ambroise-Dydime.

HARTWELL BOWSFIELD

Morice, *Dict. hist. Can. et Métis*, 183. Begg, *Hist. of North-West*, II, 68–71. Stanley, *Louis Riel*, 55, 173. J. P. Pritchett, "The origin of the so-called Fenian Raid on Manitoba in 1871," *CHR*, X (1929), 23–42. A.-H. de Trémaudan, "Louis Riel and the Fenian Raid of 1871," *CHR*, IV (1923), 132–44.

LEPROHON, ROSANNA ELEANORA. *See* MULLINS

LÉRY, ALEXANDRE-RENÉ CHAUSSEGROS DE. *See* CHAUSSEGROS

Leslie

LESLIE, JAMES, merchant and politician; b. 4 Sept. 1786 at Kair, Kincardine, Scotland, son of Captain James Leslie, James Wolfe*'s deputy quartermaster at Quebec in 1759; m. in 1815 Julia, daughter of Patrick Langan, seigneur of Bourchemin and Ramesay; d. 6 Dec. 1873 at Montreal, Que.

Before emigrating to Canada in 1804, James Leslie completed his studies at Marischal College and at the University of Aberdeen. As owner of the firm of James Leslie and Company, which was set up at Montreal in May 1809 and which specialized in the wholesale trade in foodstuffs, James Leslie met with rapid success. The doors of the business world were open to him, and he contributed to the formation of one of the most important financial institutions of the time, the Bank of Montreal, of which he proved to be an energetic director from 1817 to 1829. With George Moffatt*, Horatio Gates*, and Thomas Torrance*, he formed part of the group that promoted strict business procedures and that did not consider the administration of the bank as a family undertaking.

Like the majority of the businessmen of his period, Leslie divided his other activities between his seigneuries of Bourchemin, Ramesay, and Lake Matapédia, and political life: from 1824 until the constitution of Lower Canada was suspended in 1838, he represented the county of Montreal East in the Legislative Assembly of that province. Increasingly he identified himself with the moderate wing of the *Patriote* party, and he was out of sympathy with the English merchants around him because of his support of this party. In December 1837, before the outbreak of armed disturbances, Leslie accompanied Louis-Hippolyte La Fontaine* to Quebec to ask the governor, Lord Gosford [Acheson*], to convene the houses of parliament, in the hope of avoiding recourse to other than constitutional means. Immediately after the failure of the 1837 rebellion, Leslie began to look favourably upon the possibility of a union of the two Canadas: ". . . a union of the Canadas will probably be proposed," he wrote to La Fontaine on 6 Jan. 1838, "if on fair and equitable principles, I see no serious objection to it"; but he added: "Care however must be taken that the representation is based upon population and that the heavy public debt of the Upper is not saddled upon the Lower Province. . . ."

Since the Act of Union went against these two principles, James Leslie stood as an anti-unionist candidate, and he met defeat in the county of Montreal at the first general election under the Union. A by-election in December 1841 enabled him to join the Reformers again in the following session, as MLA for Verchères. He was re-elected in the same county in 1844 and 1847, and from 1848 to 1851 formed part of the ministry of Robert Baldwin* and La Fontaine; he was president of the Executive Council from 11 March to 14 Sept. 1848, then became provincial secretary on 15 September and kept this post until 27 Oct. 1851. He was appointed legislative councillor on 23 May 1848, and kept his seat until confederation; he was then called to the Canadian Senate, where he sat until his death.

ANDRÉ GARON

BNQ, Société historique de Montréal, Collection La Fontaine, Lettres, 39 (copies in PAC). F.-J. Audet, *Les députés de Montréal*, 105–6. *Can. directory of parliament* (Johnson), 336. *Can. parl. comp., 1872*, 63–65. Turcotte, *Conseil législatif de Québec*, 145. Denison, *Canada's first bank*, I.

LEVESCONTE, ISAAC, merchant and legislator; son of Peter LeVesconte and Jane Malzard, b. at St Aubin's, Jersey, 12 Aug. 1822; educated at the Parsonage House Academy, St Helier, Jersey; m. Caroline Susan Jean, and had a daughter, Caroline; d. at Arichat, N.S., 26 Oct. 1879.

For many years the North Atlantic fishery had attracted the attention of the commercial and fishing interests of the Channel Islands. When he was 12, Isaac LeVesconte emigrated from Jersey to Arichat, Isle Madame, on the Strait of Canso, a centre for this trade, to work for the family firm of DeCarteret and LeVesconte. This firm shipped fishery supplies, salt, clothing, and manufactured goods from Europe for the use of the fishermen and families, exported dry fish to Brazil and the West Indies in the firm's own vessels, brought return cargoes of wines from Brazil to England, and carried molasses, sugar, and rum from the West Indies to Nova Scotia. When he was 17, LeVesconte captained one of the firm's ships to Puerto Rico. About 1855, when Peter DeCarteret returned to Jersey, Isaac LeVesconte was placed in charge of the business at Arichat.

Because of his business acumen and his knowledge of the Bible and the law, LeVesconte was often consulted by the fishermen of Arichat. He was elected as a Conservative to the Legislative Assembly in 1863 representing Richmond County. For a brief period (June 1863–December 1864) he held office as financial secretary in the James W. JOHNSTON–Charles Tupper* administration. LeVesconte, who was a Protestant representing a county with a majority of Roman Catholic voters, played a prominent part in the legislative debate on free schools in 1864, and in 1865 moved an unsuccessful amendment calling for the establishment of separate schools.

On 7 Dec. 1865 LeVesconte and his successor

as financial secretary, James MacDonald*, were appointed to represent Nova Scotia on a commission sent by the British North American colonies to open trade relations with the West Indies, Mexico, and Brazil. The report of the commission called for increased trade and improvement in communications with these areas; however, little was accomplished until after confederation. Elected to the House of Commons as member for Richmond in a by-election in April 1869, LeVesconte continued to represent this constituency until his retirement prior to the general election of 1874. He left no great mark in the annals of commons debates, but did prompt Joseph HOWE to comment that "he was a queer fish who drank too much." Later his grandson, Isaac Duncan MacDougall, served for ten years as federal member of parliament for Inverness.

WILLIAM B. HAMILTON

PAC, MG 24, B29 (Howe papers), 4, pp.787–89; 40, pp.21–22 (Joseph Howe to A. Campbell, 29 Jan. 1870). Canada, Province of, *Sessional papers*, XXVI (1866), pt.4, no.43, pp.1–180. Nova Scotia, House of Assembly, *Debates and proceedings*, 1864–65, 163–65; *Journals and proceedings*, 1866, app.9. Saunders, *Three premiers of N.S.* Sister Francis Xavier, "Educational legislation in Nova Scotia and the Catholics," CCHA *Report*, *1957*, 63–74.

LEWIS, JOHN BOWER, lawyer, politician, and land speculator; b. in France, 18 March 1817, son of Captain J. B. Lewis of the 88th Light Infantry; he was married three times, to Anna Eccles in 1840, to Helen Street in 1843, and to Elizabeth Susan Wilson in 1856, and had 11 children; d. in Ottawa, Ont., 24 Jan. 1874.

John Bower Lewis came to Canada with his parents and they settled near Bytown (Ottawa) in 1820. He studied law in Toronto with James Boulton, was admitted to the bar in 1839, and became a QC in 1867 and a bencher in the Law Society of Upper Canada in 1871. He practised law in Bytown and also bought and sold land in the area.

Lewis entered politics in 1847 when he was elected to the council of the district of Dalhousie (corresponding to the present county of Carleton) and to the first municipal council for Bytown. He contested the seat of Carleton unsuccessfully in the 1847–48 election for the Legislative Assembly but was later chosen as Bytown's second mayor, for 1848–49. Bytown became the city of Ottawa in 1854 and Lewis was chosen its first mayor in 1855. He was also appointed police magistrate in 1855 and served as city recorder from 1855 to 1869. He was appointed police commissioner in 1863 and was the city solicitor when he died.

John Lewis was normally a Conservative but placed community above party interests. Thus he braved Sir John A. Macdonald*'s wrath and supported the entry of Richard William Scott*, a powerful Ottawa Catholic, into Edward Blake*'s provincial Liberal government of 1871. In 1872 Lewis and Joseph Merrill Currier* both entered parliament following election by acclamation for the two-member seat of Ottawa. In 1873 he was considered a possible successor to Sir Francis Hincks*, minister of finance, but he left his party over the Pacific Scandal later in the same year. He indicated firmly, however reluctantly, that he would oppose Macdonald's government. Lewis either found the government's actions unacceptable in principle or he wished to protect the interests of the Ottawa valley, for, as Richard Cartwright* pointed out, "the Ottawa country . . . goes with the tide." In 1874, J. B. Lewis was again nominated for Ottawa, as an "Independent" but with Liberal support. He died during the campaign.

DONALD SWAINSON

PAC, MG 24, B40 (Brown papers), 8; MG 26, A (Macdonald papers), 194, 301; MG 27, II, D14 (R. W. Scott papers), 3–5. PAM, Alexander Morris papers, Ketcheson collection, Alexander Campbell to Alexander Morris, 29 Nov. 1873. PAO, Edward Blake papers; Cartwright family papers; Alexander Morris papers. *Globe* (Toronto), 1874. *Ottawa Citizen*, 1855–74. *Packet* (Bytown), 1847–49. PANS, *Report*, *1952*, app.B. *Can. biog. dict.*, I. *Can. parl. comp.*, *1873*; *1875*. A. H. D. Ross, *Ottawa, past and present* (Toronto, 1927). Swainson, "Personnel of politics."

LIDDELL (Liddle), THOMAS, Presbyterian minister and educator; b. St Ninian, Stirlingshire, Scotland, 18 Oct. 1800, son of John Liddell and Janet Martin; m. Susan Anne Jane Stewart, by whom he had two daughters; d. Edinburgh, 11 June 1880.

Thomas Liddell was educated at the universities of Glasgow and Edinburgh (receiving from the latter the honorary degree of DD in 1841). He was licensed to preach in 1827 and ordained two years later. In 1831 he became assistant minister, later minister, of Lady Glenorchy's Church, Edinburgh.

On 27 Oct. 1841 Liddell was nominated by the colonial committee of the Church of Scotland as principal of Queen's College at Kingston, Canada West. This Presbyterian foundation, established to break the monopoly of the Church of England in higher education in Canada West, was granted, by royal charter in 1841, full university powers as a liberal arts college and would be open to students of all denominations. Liddell's appointment was confirmed by the Board of Trustees of the college

Liddell

in Kingston at a salary of £400 per annum and he arrived in December 1841. He found, however, that no provision had been made for opening the new college and he was obliged to canvass presbyteries near Kingston for funds and students. The college opened on 7 March 1842 with one other professor, Peter Colin Campbell, later principal of the University of Aberdeen, and 12 students; Liddell himself taught Hebrew, church history, theology, logic, mathematics, and moral philosophy.

In 1842 Liddell conferred with Egerton Ryerson*, then principal of the Methodist Victoria College in Cobourg, about a plan to transform King's College, Toronto (due to open in 1843 after having obtained its charter in 1827) into a "University of Toronto" with Queen's, Victoria, and Regiopolis (the Roman Catholic college in Kingston) as affiliated theological colleges. These would be located in Toronto and would be represented on the council of the university. Canada West, Liddell argued, could support only one arts college, which should be open to all denominations each sharing in the endowment. Ryerson agreed that King's endowment should be shared, but would not consider moving to Toronto, and was not, in the least, willing to confine instruction at Victoria to theology. Bishop John Strachan* of the Church of England and president of King's College vehemently opposed any alteration in King's charter, and Regiopolis, not yet operating above the secondary school level, was unenthusiastic. Nevertheless, Liddell persuaded the trustees of Queen's and the synod of the Presbyterian Church in Canada to petition the government to alter the structure of King's College. A modified form of the plan was incorporated in Robert Baldwin*'s university bill of 1843, despite objections by Strachan, but Baldwin resigned before it came to a vote. When William Henry DRAPER's university bill was being prepared by the new government in 1845, Liddell renewed his agitation and tried in vain in a series of letters to Ryerson to win the support of Victoria College.

The defeat of Draper's bill was a disappointment to Liddell. In addition, his health had suffered following the death of an infant daughter in 1842, and he was unhappy with the slow progress of Queen's College. To make matters worse, the Free Church party in Scotland sent to Canada as an emissary the Reverend Dr Robert Burns* of Paisley, Scotland, who proceeded to disrupt the Church of Scotland in Canada. Although Dr John Machar*, incumbent of St Andrew's Church in Kingston, refused him the pulpit of the church, Burns so swayed the Presbyterians from Methodist pulpits in Kingston that Queen's College lost two-thirds of her students and supporters, including ten trustees. Liddell took up the challenge and preached against the secessionists, but his sermons were said to have been "especially noted for their length." The Free Church movement prospered and plans were laid to open a rival theological institution, Knox College, in Toronto. Adding insult to injury, Burns had accused Liddell of failure to acknowledge gifts of books to Queen's which he and a prominent benefactress in Edinburgh had made; he now threatened legal action to recover the books for Knox College.

Dissident students had departed and Liddell's class in divinity was reduced to one pupil. Utterly discouraged and pessimistic about the future, he resigned, 13 July 1846, and returned to Scotland, despite a plea from the moderator of the synod, George Romanes, that he reconsider. Machar was immediately appointed principal *pro tem*. At the end of the following academic year, the trustees invited Liddell to resume his duties but he replied that he saw no reason for changing his mind.

In 1849, when the fortunes of Queen's had somewhat improved, Liddell was again offered the principalship. By this time a third university bill had finally been passed, setting up the University of Toronto as a non-religious institution. Liddell strongly opposed this solution and agreed to return to exert all his influence in demonstrating the necessary connection between religion and higher education. His only conditions were that he should have at least six divinity students and the same salary as before. By the time negotiations were concluded, the last ship had sailed for Montreal. Liddell hoped to get a passage to Halifax and arrive in Kingston by late October. He failed to appear. Finally, in March 1850, after learning that only four students had registered for divinity and following the death of his father, he wrote to the chairman of the Board of Trustees announcing his decision to sever all connection with Queen's College. Before the end of the month, he had taken up an appointment at Lochmaben, Scotland, where he served acceptably but without distinction until his death.

As principal of Queen's College, Liddell was described by Machar as "a pious man possessing much energy, serious character, and practical wisdom and [he] seems zealously devoted to the work. . . . one better fitted to his office with all its difficulties and discouragements could not have been found." The portrait of Thomas Liddell gives the impression of an intellectual rather than a man of action, a character which Liddell's career in Canada and in Scotland would appear to sustain.

H. P. GUNDY

442

Queen's University Archives, Queen's University Records, correspondence series 1, Liddell correspondence; James Williamson papers. *Chronicle and Gazette* (Kingston), 1 Dec. 1841; 24 Apr. 1844; 5, 15, 19 March, 21 May, 3 Aug. 1845. *Documentary history of education in Upper Canada* (Hodgins), V, 4–9, 12–17; VI, 29. *Report of the discussion on the late disruption in the Presbyterian Church, which took place in St Andrew's Church, Galt between the Rev. Principal Liddell ... and the Rev. John Bayne* (Galt, C. W., 1845). Hew Scott, *Fasti ecclesiae Scoticanae, the succession of ministers in the Church of Scotland from the Reformation* (new ed., 9v., Edinburgh, 1915–61), II, 215. D. D. Calvin, *Queen's University at Kingston: the first century of a Scottish-Canadian foundation, 1841–1941* (Kingston, 1941). [John Machar], *Memorials of the life and ministry of the Reverend John Machar, D.D., late minister of St Andrew's Church, Kingston* (Toronto, 1873). C. B. Sissons, *A history of Victoria University* (Toronto, 1952).

LINDSAY, Sir JAMES ALEXANDER, soldier; b. 25 Aug. 1815 at Muncaster Castle, Cumberland, Eng., second son of James Lindsay, 7th Earl of Balcarres and 24th Earl of Crawford, and of the Hon. Maria Margaret Frances Pennington, daughter of John Pennington, 1st Baron Muncaster; d. 13 Aug. 1874, at Mitcham, Surrey, Eng.

James Alexander Lindsay was educated at Eton College and entered the Grenadier Guards by purchase on 16 March 1832. He advanced by purchase to the rank of lieutenant and captain in 1836 and then to captain and lieutenant-colonel in 1846. From 1838 to 1842 he was adjutant of the 3rd battalion of his regiment in Canada.

In 1845, James Lindsay entered parliament for the borough of Wigan, where the family seat was located. He supported Sir Robert Peel on free trade but remained a Conservative until he gave up his seat in 1865. Meanwhile, he rose steadily in rank, becoming lieutenant-colonel of the Grenadier Guards in 1860 and, on 12 March 1861, being promoted major-general. Advancement came apparently without his hearing a shot fired in anger. On 6 Nov. 1845, Lindsay married Lady Sarah Elizabeth Savile, daughter of John, 3rd Earl of Mexborough. Two sons died in infancy but three daughters survived. Lady Sarah became woman of the bedchamber to Queen Victoria.

In 1861, with the United States and Britain on the brink of war, General Lindsay accompanied the reinforcements rushed to the British garrison in Canada. He was given command of the troops in the lower province (Canada East). Colonel Garnet Joseph Wolseley*, then a staff officer at Montreal, remembered Lindsay as "an able, energetic soldier, whose heart was in his work, and one of the most charming men I ever knew," adding that he was "as great a favourite with the Canadians as he was with the troops."

In 1866 Lindsay returned to England, taking command of the battalions of foot guards in London and then receiving the appointment of inspector general of reserve forces. William Ewart Gladstone's government took office in England in 1868, and its secretary of state for war, Edward Cardwell, was bent on eliminating British garrisons in self-governing colonies. The task of dismantling more than a century of unbroken British military presence in Canada proved too much for the lieutenant-general commanding in British North America, Sir Charles Ash Windham*, who died on 2 Feb. 1870. Command devolved on Major-General Sir Charles Hastings Doyle*, the British commander at Halifax, but the War Office decided to send another officer to wind up the British garrisons in central Canada.

Lindsay accepted the task, was given local rank as lieutenant-general, and on 5 April 1870 arrived in Montreal to take command of the remaining troops in Ontario and Quebec. His first task, according to his instructions, was to cooperate with the Canadian government in providing a force to secure the transfer of the Red River colony to the dominion. The Canadians arranged supplies and transport, raised two battalions of militia, and paid three-quarters of the cost; Lindsay chose the commander, Colonel Garnet Wolseley, gave him his orders, and oversaw the arrangements. "I felt from the first," he explained to Cardwell, "that the Force, though mixed, was an Imperial one and that I was responsible for everything connected with it." The assumption led to friction with the Canadian authorities and to complaints from Lindsay of Canadian mismanagement and political interference, particularly in relation to the recruiting of a Quebec rifle battalion and the failure to make arrangements for transportation to Lake Superior.

Lindsay was also instructed to help the Canadians develop their own military institutions. He advanced a number of practical suggestions to the Canadian ministers: they could hire a British regiment; they could recruit their own force from disbanded British soldiers; they could organize mounted patrols and man gunboats to prevent Fenian attacks. Looking beyond the immediate problem, Lindsay wanted to guarantee that Canadian forces "would be organized upon the same system as those of the United Kingdom." His most insistent recommendation was the appointment of a British general to command the Canadian militia. Canadian ministers took little heed of Lindsay's advice, though many of his proposals were eventually adopted.

Lisgar

At the end of May 1870 the long-heralded Fenian threat manifested itself in two feeble thrusts across the Quebec border [*see* John O'Neill]. Though the Fenians were easily repelled, 13,489 Canadian militiamen were mobilized and placed at Lindsay's disposal.

By September Lindsay had closed most of the British military establishments in central Canada and had concentrated the remnants at Quebec. The British troops in the Red River expedition were returning from Fort Garry (Winnipeg). On 24 September, Lindsay's appointment ended with the closing of the British military headquarters at Montreal. The War Office was now anxious for him to return to his duties with the reserve forces. Both Cardwell and the colonial secretary, John Wodehouse, 1st Earl of Kimberley, were pleased with his service in Canada, and their satisfaction was demonstrated by a knighthood in the new order of St Michael and St George, confirmation in the rank of lieutenant-general, and the colonelcy of the 3rd Foot (The Buffs). Lindsay was still holding the appointment of inspector general of reserve forces when he died.

DESMOND MORTON

PAC, RG 8, I, A2, 1287, pp.419–503. PRO, CO 42/693, pp.230ff.; WO 32/813/058/316. *Returns of addresses of the Senate and House of Commons, relative to the withdrawal of the troops from the dominion and of the defence of the country and Honorable Mr Campbell's report* (Ottawa, 1871). Kenneth Bourne, *Britain and the balance of power in North America, 1815–1871* (London, 1967), 295–302. J. M. Hitsman, *Safeguarding Canada, 1763–1871* (Toronto, 1968), 133–43, 208–23. Desmond Morton, *Ministers and generals; politics and the Canadian militia, 1868–1904* (Toronto, 1970). C. P. Stacey, *Canada and the British Army, 1846–1871* (2nd ed., Toronto, 1963), 204–63. Desmond Morton, "French Canada and the Canadian militia," *SH*, no.3 (1969), 36.

LISGAR, Baron. *See* YOUNG

LITTLE CHIEF. *See* HUNKAJUKA

LITTLE SOLDIER. *See* HUNKAJUKA

LOGAN, Sir WILLIAM EDMOND, geologist and geological cartographer, founder and first director of the Geological Survey of Canada; b. 20 April 1798 at Montreal, L.C., third son of William Logan, a baker and owner of real estate, and of Janet Edmond, both from Scotland; d. 22 June 1875 at Cilgerran, Pembrokeshire, Wales.

William Edmond Logan's education was begun in Mr Alexander Skakel*'s school in Montreal, but at the age of 16 he was sent with his older brother Hart to high school in Edinburgh. In 1816 he registered as a medical student at Edinburgh University where his subjects included logic, mathematics, and chemistry. Although he may not have been impressed at the time, his lectures in chemistry probably provided his first exposure to theories on the formation of rocks and minerals: the professor of chemistry, Dr Thomas Charles Hope, was an ardent supporter of the Neptunian theory of rock formation – that all stratified rocks were formed in water.

Logan left the university at the end of his first year, even though his scholastic achievement was high, to enter the London business establishment of his uncle, Hart Logan, for whom he worked for over 20 years. The systematic procedures of accountancy undoubtedly were a training which influenced William's geological field measurements in later years; his geological maps and geological sections were drawn with a skill and accuracy far superior to those of his contemporaries. Logan probably became interested in geology because mining activity and construction materials such as building stone may have been a principal part of his uncle's business. After 1827 the management of the business was left to Logan, who devoted days and many evenings to his work. The social contacts with "much company, rich food, and rich wine" were not particularly palatable and were considered prejudicial to his health. During this period he took lessons in art and languages, and continued the study of mathematics. In 1829 he went to Italy, possibly as a tourist, for his diary records descriptions of numerous churches, palaces, gates, bridges, and other buildings; he was also most diligent in recording the types of rock in columns and other parts of the great edifices.

In 1831 Logan moved to Swansea, Wales, where he was appointed manager at the Forest Copper Works, Morriston, a copper smelting and coal mining establishment in which his uncle had invested a substantial sum of money. His prime task was to set up a proper system of accounts but Logan soon realized that a continuous supply of coal for the smelters had to be guaranteed, and that this could only be done with the help of accurate maps of coal seams from which reserves could be determined. Existing geological maps of Wales were highly generalized with too little detail to make them useful. Logan therefore set out to make field observations and to plot them on the available topographic maps of South Wales, recording the continuity of seams and the succession of rocks. A high degree of accuracy was obtained by using surveying instruments such as a compass, a theodolite, and probably barometers. His data included subsurface information from miners, and subsequently from drill cores. By these means he constructed, for the first time, true-scale horizontal cross-sections upon which the underground occurrence of the coal seams was mapped. The results allowed predictions about the depths of mines and the discovery of coal seams that were not exposed at the surface. In 1835 the Geological Survey of Great Britain was initiated and when its first director, Sir Henry Thomas de la Beche, saw Logan's maps for South Wales he adopted them, because "the work on this district [was] of an order so greatly superior to that usual with geologists." Logan's contribution is still recognized in that modern revisions of the geological maps for South Wales bear his name as an original co-author.

Geology had become a popular science in the early decades of the century, with the formation of the Geological Society of London in 1807, the publication of a geological map of England and Wales in 1815 by William Smith, and of a book on the geology of England and Wales by William Daniel Conybeare and John Phillips in 1822. In 1834, while on a business trip in France and Spain, Logan mentions in his diary the works of Charles Lyell who, at that time, was one of the principal authors in the field of geology. On such trips Logan carried painting supplies; some of his watercolours and sepias are held today in trust by the Geological Association of Canada. Logan helped to organize the Swansea Philosophical and Literary Institute in 1835 in order to encourage study of natural history and preservation of antiquities. Between 1836 and 1842, as honorary secretary of the institute and curator for geology, he organized an extensive collection of specimens, well labelled and displayed, including two fossil tree trunks which are still in the grounds of the institute's building in Swansea. He was elected to the Geological Society of London in 1837, and in 1840 presented to it a paper outlining his concept of the origin of coal. The rock succession, including the coal seams, in South Wales suggested that coal had accumulated *in situ*: below every bed, he found, there occurred persistently an underclay with numerous fossil tree stumps *Stigmaria*. He was further convinced of the theory's validity by finding later the same association of underclay and stumps at the bottom of coal beds in Pennsylvania, Nova Scotia, and Scotland. Logan's concept of the *in situ* formation of coal is still considered to be generally valid.

Logan's employment in Swansea ended in 1838 with his uncle's death but he continued to live there and to make geological maps of South Wales. In July 1841 the Natural History Society of Montreal and the Literary and Historical Society of Quebec petitioned the first united parliament of Upper and Lower Canada to allocate an amount not exceeding £1,500 sterling to defray the probable expense of carrying out a geological survey of Canada. Logan was immediately interested in the position of provincial geologist and requested the support of several eminent British geologists in his application. Canadian friends, principally in the Montreal and Quebec societies, also placed his name before the governor of the province. The reputation Logan had acquired from his skilful mapping of the geology of South Wales, and the fact that he was a native Canadian, obtained him the appointment in the spring of 1842 at an annual salary of £500, just half of what he had been receiving in Wales.

The task of the new Geological Survey was to furnish "a full and scientific description of the country's rocks, soils, and minerals, to prepare maps, diagrams, and drawings, and to collect specimens to illustrate the occurrences." These fundamental objectives were initiated by Logan in such a way that the Geological Survey still continues its work within a similar framework and on a similar pattern.

Logan recognized that a proper geological survey of the vast wilderness of Canada would require a permanent institution. At the same time he realized that the politicians who would have to provide money for his organization would only be impressed by practical results and by indications of both actual and potential mineral occurrences from which the country would benefit economically. His task was going to be a difficult one, and capable assistants would be required. Geological mapping would be hindered by the fact that topographic base maps were not available; Alexander Murray*, a retired naval officer with no previous geological experience, proved, however, to be a most able field mapper. Rock and soil specimens would need chemical analyses; the first chemist Logan engaged, Édouard-Sylvestre, Comte de Rottermond*, proved to be incompetent (and subsequently a considerable nuisance), but after 1847 a self-taught chemist and mineralogist named Thomas Sterry Hunt* pursued chemical investigations which gave him a world-wide reputation and added to the eminence of the Geological Survey. During his tenure as director, Logan was to engage capable field and laboratory assistants, such as James Richardson*, Robert Bell*, Edward Hartley, Thomas Macfarlane*, Charles Robb, and Henry George Vennor*. He recognized that Professor James Hall, of the New York Geological Survey, Albany, a renowned paleontologist, would

Logan

provide valuable advice on the geology of Canada. Hall declined an offer to join the survey in 1854 and so Elkanah BILLINGS, a lawyer and newspaper editor, became the survey's paleontologist. One of Logan's close associates in Montreal, and a leading authority on the geology of New Brunswick and Nova Scotia, was the influential John William Dawson*, principal of McGill University.

The first "office" of the Geological Survey was set up in the autumn of 1843 in a Montreal warehouse provided by Logan's brother. By the end of the year Logan was seeking continuance of the survey and urging government leaders to establish a more satisfactory and definite fiscal arrangement. He realized that if the results of his work were made obvious, they could have an influence on politicians and the public. He therefore rented a house in the spring of 1844 on Great St James Street, Montreal, to display his collections as well as for offices and laboratory. In April 1844 his "Report of progress for the year 1843" was submitted to the legislature, the first of a yearly series. He also took great care to talk and write to legislators and perform small tasks on their behalf. By 1845 Logan could demonstrate notable achievements in return for the original £1,500 grant, although he had spent an additional £800 from his own pocket. The Legislative Assembly in that year quickly passed a bill, which Logan himself had drafted, and £2,000 per annum became available for a period of five years.

The act of 1850 experienced opposition, and to ensure its passage Logan had to spend time reluctantly in Toronto, then the seat of government, and away from his field work. After some delay, the same financial support was provided for an additional five years. In 1854, however, the government created a select committee on the Geological Survey. It received evidence from Logan and Hunt along with numerous distinguished individuals including Professor James Hall, Albany, Professor Edward John Chapman*, Toronto, Alexander Jamieson Russell*, Quebec, and the Reverend Andrew Bell, L'Orignal. The select committee was sufficiently impressed to recommend an increase in the survey's facilities, the republication of all reports, and the compilation of a coloured map of Canada. In 1855 the legislature granted Logan $20,000 per year for five years along with $8,000 for reports and maps. From 1861 to 1863 annual appropriations were made. By January 1864 he had advanced $10,000 from his own resources to cover salaries and publication costs. During the spring the government changed, and a sympathetic legislature provided an annual grant for another five years.

Geological mapping of the Canadian provinces,

in which Logan himself participated actively, could be done in the mid-19th century only by a person with considerable physical strength and stamina, perseverance, unrelenting resourcefulness, and untiring enthusiasm. (The same qualities were necessary to obtain funds from a succession of governments which remained sceptical of the survey's worth.) Travel around the provinces was difficult. There were steamships on the Great Lakes and the Rideau Canal had been built between Bytown (Ottawa) and Kingston; but in the early years of the survey travel from Montreal to Canada West was by stage coach through the United States. Geological traverses were made by walking, with distances determined by counting paces, establishing lines laid out by compass. In the field, where he had an Indian guide, John Basque, Logan's tent was a blanket held up by two poles. He describes conditions as "living the life of a savage, sleeping on the beach in a blanket sack with my feet to the fire, seldom taking my clothes off, eating salt pork and ships biscuit, occasionally tormented by mosquitoes." More than once local inhabitants wondered about the sanity of this red-bearded individual dressed in a tattered and streaked jacket and patched grey trousers stuffed into large, torn, and roughened field boots, his hair matted with spruce gum, his spectacles cracked. The impression was heightened by his seemingly continuous mutterings, wanderings in a zig-zag fashion, and hammering on the rocks to obtain chips which he wrapped in paper with great care. In the field, Logan usually started at dawn and continued throughout the day and into the evening until he could no longer see distinctly. By the light of the campfire he would work until a late hour to ink-over the pencilled notes and figures made during the day and plot on field maps all the measurements and dimensions which had been recorded. His geological observations were authenticated by pen and ink sketches which clearly reveal his artistic talents. His note books, held by the Geological Survey, are exemplary models for recording field data.

By the end of the field season of 1843, Logan and Murray had established that the united Province of Canada could be divided into three well-defined geological areas. A division of folded rocks extended through the Eastern Townships and the Gaspé Peninsula. Between Montreal and the Detroit River were Paleozoic rocks, flat-lying but broken into two parts by a band of metamorphic gneisses and schists extending for several miles east of Lake Ontario. A northern division of complex metamorphic rocks would present a formidable task of understanding.

In order to justify the continued existence of the

survey, Logan immediately started a search for an obviously valuable mineral resource, coal. In the summer of 1843 he compiled for use in comparison a detailed section of the coal-bearing strata near Joggins, Nova Scotia. Subsequently he traversed the north and south shores of Chaleur Bay but he soon recognized that the exposed strata are geologically older than the Carboniferous strata, such as at Joggins, in which beds of coal occur. In the summer of 1844, Logan with Murray traversed the north shore of Gaspé, then went up the Cap Chat River to its headwaters and down the Cascapédia River to Chaleur Bay; the highest peak located on this traverse was named Mount Logan – against his wishes! The expedition, which provided both topographic and geological information, established that coal would not be found in the area.

In 1845 Logan made the first of several expeditions across the ancient rocks north of Montreal. He found evidence of glaciation in polished, scratched, and grooved rock surfaces. He commented on the numerous veins and dikes and especially the occurrences of metallic minerals which would provide an impetus for the development of a mining industry. His report included observations on iron, lead, and copper, and such building stones as marble and slate. The next year he examined the north shore of Lake Superior specifically for occurrences of copper, within a rock sequence he named the Upper Copper-bearing Series, a major discovery having been made on the south shore. In 1847 and 1848 additional occurrences, like that being mined at the Bruce Mines copper deposit, were sought along the north shore of Lake Huron. For each prospect he wrote a cautious report presenting factual observations in a carefully worded style. He pointed out that the high cost of transportation, machinery, and labour would make only the richest deposits suitable for economic development. His objective reports did not, of course, have a kind reception from mining promoters. (On several occasions during his tenure as director of the survey he was called upon to evaluate mineral occurrences. Whenever evidence of fraud by citizens became obvious, his reaction was dismissal of the perpetrators from his office bluntly and swiftly.) Apparently Logan did not observe any evidence of the deposits of silver near Cobalt, of nickel at Sudbury, and of uranium north of Blind River.

From 1847 to 1851 Logan turned his attention to the complex formations of the Eastern Townships, eventually tracing the geology from New York State nearly to the tip of the Gaspé Peninsula. He examined closely the copper occurrences in the vicinity of Sherbrooke, and the alluvial gold deposits of the Chaudière River. Deposits of serpentine found in the area would have had commercial value as a decorative stone except that the occurrences of asbestos, then considered a mineralogical curiosity, made it unusable. In 1860, near Quebec City, he recognized a major geological phenomenon when he realized, on the basis of fossils identified by Billings, that the folded rocks had been faulted and great masses had been thrust northward up and over younger formations. This break, which separates the folded rocks to the south from the flat-lying rocks to the north, is still known as Logan's Line.

In 1851 and subsequent years Logan's main attention was turned to the rocks north of the St Lawrence River primarily in the vicinity of Grenville, Quebec. In 1863 he defined the Grenville Series as a succession of gneisses and crystalline limestones intruded by dikes and granites. The limestones contain distinctive layerings and internal tubular structures which he concluded were the remains of fossils, and to them his friend J. W. Dawson applied the name *Eozoon Canadense*. To Logan these structures provided a strong argument for the occurrence of life in these very ancient rocks. Subsequent study has demonstrated that similar features can be formed by inorganic processes but other evidence for abundant life in the rocks of the Precambrian is now well established.

To the generally flat-lying rocks north of Lake Huron, resting on the Grenville Series, Logan in 1855 applied the name Huronian. In 1863 he applied the name Laurentian to the seemingly more ancient rocks north of the Ottawa River and in the Adirondack Mountains of New York; he considered them the oldest rocks in North America, perhaps influenced by the then accepted theory that granitic rocks formed the original crust of the earth. Modern scientific methods have proven his interpretation wrong but his names are still used though in a different sense.

In 1841 Logan became the first to recognize in North America the tracks of Carboniferous vertebrate animals in rocks at Horton Bluff, Nova Scotia. He found in 1851 distinctive trails of invertebrate animals in Cambrian rocks near Beauharnois, Quebec. His description in 1846 of the St Lawrence River ice pack near Montreal causing damage to buildings along the shore was subsequently used in the designing of the Victoria Bridge [*see* James HODGES]. He also was the first to give a scientific explanation of land slippages in clays along the St Lawrence River. Such failures still occur to this day.

The government of Canada was asked to participate in the Exhibition of the Industries of All

Logan

Nations in London in 1851 and Logan organized an extensive collection of Canadian minerals along with a geological map. The display was described as "superior ... to all countries that have forwarded their products to the exhibition." It did not receive an award primarily because Logan himself had acted as a juror in mineralogy and metallurgy, for which he received a medal from the Prince Consort. At the Paris Exposition of 1855 the collection of minerals displayed by Logan was awarded the Grand Medal of Honour and the emperor of France, Napoleon III, presented Logan with the Cross of the Legion of Honour. In 1862 Logan was again called upon to display Canadian materials at the International Exhibition in London. Although the collection was of high quality, Logan, because of administrative and publication problems within the Geological Survey, and his participation as a juror at the exhibition, responded with less than his normal enthusiasm. He was now 64 years old.

Logan's contributions to the geological literature are not particularly extensive, despite his diligence in assembling accurate data. The culmination of his years as director of the survey was, however, the publication in 1863 of the *Geology of Canada*, a volume of 983 pages with Murray, Hunt, and Billings as co-authors, which even to this day is a basic reference for geological work. The volume was followed in 1865 by an atlas of coloured geological maps covering the entire area from Newfoundland and Nova Scotia to the central United States and Canada. The publication of a larger geological map of Canada in 1869 required such diligent attention that it is said Logan's eyesight was impaired.

Logan's first major honour was election in 1851 as a fellow of the Royal Society; he was the first native Canadian so honoured for work in Canada. Queen Victoria bestowed a knighthood upon him in 1856; only two other Canadians had been distinguished in this manner. At the same time the Geological Society of London awarded him its distinguished Wollaston Medal. Upon his return to Canada after receiving these honours, McGill University conferred on him the degree of LLD. The Canadian Institute, which had been founded in 1850 with Logan elected its first president, gave a public reception in Toronto and commissioned his portrait in oil. The Natural History Society of Montreal gave a soirée in his honour. In anticipation of having to make a public address, he wrote "if speech-making is to become the consequence of distinction, I shall soon wish distinction far off." His contribution to the geological sciences was again recognized in 1867 when the Royal Society of London awarded him the Royal Gold Medal

with specific reference to his geological map of Canada.

Sir William Edmond Logan was indeed an extraordinary man. Starting a major career at the age of 44, he organized, directed, and contributed in a substantial way for more than a quarter of a century to the Geological Survey of Canada. Logan stated: "The object of the Survey is to ascertain the mineral resources of the country," and the survey still operates on this principle. Subsequent to 1855 he saw the development of a major copper-producing area in the Eastern Townships, where the Acton Mine was said to be the largest copper mine in the world in its time. The Geological Survey's greatest contribution during Logan's tenure as director was producing reports and maps, which established the fundamentals of Canadian geology; especially important were those for the north shore of Lake Huron and Lake Superior where rich beds of copper, nickel, uranium, iron, platinum, and other metals occur in the ancient rocks of the Precambrian.

During the middle part of the 19th century, the rigours of field work in the Canadian wilderness demanded exceptional physical strength and endurance, and the administrative problems of a government organization along with the arrangement of international exhibitions demanded political skill and a sense of dedication to profession and country. So determined was Logan to continue the Geological Survey that he was willing to provide financial support from his own funds when government money was not immediately available. He was a benefactor of the discipline of geology and McGill University in providing the bulk of an endowment of $20,000 for a chair in geology and a medal for the geology student with the highest academic standing. With all this he seems to have been a shy person, even an introvert, and was most uncomfortable at social gatherings. The diligent and strenuous effort he made as director of the Geological Survey placed him in the limelight and he was apparently prepared to endure some personal discomfort in it because he drew satisfaction from acquiring national and international recognition for Canada.

Sir William officially retired from the Geological Survey on 30 Nov. 1869, to be replaced as director by Alfred Richard Cecil Selwyn* who had previously directed the Geological Survey of Australia. Sir William took up residence with his sister, Elizabeth Gower, at Castle Malgwyn at Llechryd, Wales. He returned to Canada several times, however, and for a few months in 1871 assumed temporary directorship of the survey while Selwyn was in British Columbia doing field work. During the summer of 1874 Logan spent several weeks in the Eastern Townships and made plans for some further subsurface drilling in order to demonstrate that his geological interpretation of the complex structure was correct. But in the spring of 1875 his health was failing noticeably. He died on 22 June 1875 in Wales and is buried in the yard of the church of St Llawddog at Cilgerran, Pembrokeshire, Wales. Sir William had not married and had devoted long periods to geological field work as well as to being principal administrative officer of Canada's first government scientific organization; his life of loneliness, to some degree self-imposed, was culminated by burial remote from the land for which he had worked so diligently.

C. GORDON WINDER

Canada, Province of, Legislative Assembly, *Journals*, 1844–45, app.W, "Geological Survey: Report of progress for the year 1843." [Logan *et al.*], *Geology of Canada*. F. J. Alcock, *A century in the history of the Geological Survey of Canada* (Ottawa, 1947), 11–25. Robert Bell, *Sir William E. Logan and the Geological Survey of Canada* (Ottawa and Montreal, [1907]). B. J. Harrington, *Life of Sir William E. Logan, Kt., first director of the Geological Survey of Canada* (Montreal, 1883); "Sir William Edmond Logan," *American Journal of Science* (New Haven, Conn.), 3rd ser., XI (1876), no.61, 81–93. J. M. Harrison and E. Hall, "William Edmond Logan," Geological Association of Canada, *Proceedings* (Toronto), XV (1963), 33–42. A. H. Lang, "Sir William Logan and the economic development of Canada," *Canadian Public Administration* (Toronto), XII (1969), 551–65. C. G. Winder, "Logan and South Wales," Geological Association of Canada, *Proceedings*, XVI (1965), 103–24; "Where is Logan's silver fountain?" Geological Association of Canada, *Proceedings*, XVIII (1967), 115–18.

LORD, JOHN KEAST, veterinarian, naturalist, and author; b. 1818; d. a bachelor, 9 Dec. 1872, at Brighton, Sussex, Eng.

John Keast Lord, who was brought up in Tavistock, Devon, received his diploma from the Royal Veterinary College, London, in 1844, and returned to Tavistock to practise his profession, but his "convivial tastes led him astray" and he disappeared suddenly. No connected record of his subsequent movements can be formed, but his writings mention, among other experiences, a winter spent at the Bruce copper mines of Ontario, living and wandering with Indians "over the fur countries east of the Rocky Mountains," and "rambling about" in Arkansas.

After service as a veterinary surgeon in the Osmanli Horse Artillery during part of the Crimean War (1854–56), Lord became veterinary surgeon and assistant naturalist to the British North American Land Boundary Commission

which, during 1858–62, surveyed and marked the 49th parallel between the mainland of British Columbia and the United States. Lord's work of caring for the animals and arranging the transport of supplies, his journey to California in 1860 to buy pack-mules (which he drove 1,000 miles overland to the Columbia River), and his zeal in collecting zoological and other specimens, both when in the field and from winter quarters on Vancouver Island (1858–59 and 1859–60), earned high praise from the commissioner, Colonel John Summerfield Hawkins, Royal Engineers.

In 1863 Lord gave a series of lectures based on his experiences with the commission at the Egyptian Hall, London, and following a meeting there with the naturalist Francis T. Buckland, he became a frequent contributor to the *Field*, to *Land and Water* (established by Buckland in 1866), and to other periodicals. His travels in northwest America and California were also reported in *The naturalist in Vancouver Island and British Columbia* (1866) with interesting descriptions of animals and birds and a list of his zoological collections. *At home in the wilderness* (1867) contains "practical hints" based on Lord's experience in his wanderings: "I have . . . lived in a Sibley tent in North-west America, in a Bell-tent in the Crimea, in a Turkish tent with eight sides in Asia Minor, in a Bedouin Arab's tent, in Indian wigwams east and west of the Rocky Mountains, and in Palmetto shantees in the tropical world. . . ."

Lord spent 1868–69 carrying out scientific researches in Egypt, along the African shore of the Red Sea, and in Arabia, on behalf of the viceroy of Egypt. After his return to England he became the first manager of Brighton Aquarium, but he was already a sick man when it was officially opened in August 1872, and he died from "chronic disease of the brain" on 9 December.

ALICE M. JOHNSON

[The *DNB* called him William Keast Lord in the 1893 ed.; the name was corrected in the 1909 ed. A.M.J.]

PRO, FO 5/811, ff.1–377. Royal Veterinary College (University of London), Register of students, 1844. J. K. Lord, "Furs how trapped and traded," *Land and Water* (London), III (1867); *At home in the wilderness by "The Wanderer"* (*J.K.L.*) (London, 1867; 3rd ed., 1876); *List of coleoptera collected by J. K. Lord, Esq. in Egypt, Arabia and near the Arabian shore of the Red Sea, with characters of the undescribed species by Francis Walker* (London, 1871); *A list of hymenoptera collected by J. K. Lord in Egypt, in the neighbourhood of the Red Sea, and in Arabia, with descriptions of the new species by Francis Walker* (London, 1871); *The naturalist in Vancouver Island and British Columbia* (2v., London, 1866); "The traveller. The viceroy of Egypt's exploring expedition," *Land and Water* (London), V (1868).

Lyman

"The Brighton Aquarium, death of the manager," *Brighton Daily News and Sussex Gazette*, 12 Dec. 1872. F. T. Buckland, "Practical natural history. The late John Keast Lord," *Land and Water* (London), 14 Dec. 1872, 395. "Obituary," *Land and Water* (London), 14 Dec. 1872, 387. *Times* (London), 1863, 1872.

LYMAN, BENJAMIN, chemist, drug wholesaler, and manufacturer; b. in Derby, Vermont, 11 June 1810, son of Elisha Lyman, a farmer and tavern-keeper, and Hannah Stiles; d. at Toronto, Ont., 5 Dec. 1878.

The Lymans were a New England family descended from Richard Lyman of Essex County, England, who crossed the Atlantic in 1631. About 1816 Elisha Lyman moved to Montreal, where one of his brothers, Lewis, had founded a Montreal drug firm with George Wadsworth about 1800. This partnership, Wadsworth and Lyman, was the first of many drug businesses that were to be carried on in Montreal and Toronto by various branches of the Lyman family.

In 1819 Lewis Lyman moved to Syracuse, New York, and his store in Montreal passed to Benjamin's uncle, Samuel Hedge, and to his older brother William* (1794–1857), as Hedge and Lyman. In 1827 and 1829 respectively, Benjamin and his younger brother Henry* (1813–97) entered the firm, and in 1836 the partnership was reorganized; until William retired in 1855 the three brothers were proprietors, operating under the name William Lyman and Company. Alfred Savage then joined the firm, which became Lymans, Savage and Company until his retirement in 1860, when William H. Clare replaced him and the name was changed to Lymans, Clare and Company. Just before Benjamin's death his son Charles and Henry's son Roswell Corse were associated. In 1879 the name was changed to Lyman, Sons and Company, and in 1908 it became Lymans Limited; today the corporation is a division of the National Drug and Chemical Company Ltd.

The main operations of the firm as chemists and druggists were located on St Paul Street, where extensive premises were erected in 1855 (burnt 1888). Both wholesale and retail operations were carried on until about confederation, when the retail side was dropped. Manufacturing of pharmaceutical products, linseed oil, paints, and oils took place at a separate location on the south side of the Lachine Canal basin. These products won medals at several exhibitions including those in Paris in 1855 and 1878. In addition the Lymans were importers of drugs, seeds, oils, dye stuffs, and painters' colours.

In York (Toronto) the partnership opened a branch under J. W. Brent in 1832, which became Lyman, Farr and Company about 1835 with Timothy J. Farr as a partner. By that year a subsidiary had also been opened in London under the same name. This became Lyman, Moore and Company by 1840; the business apparently did not last long, but it was the first drugstore in that area of Upper Canada. There was also a Bytown (Ottawa) branch. In Toronto, the firm, which was kept separate from the Montreal business, underwent several changes in partnership: in 1850 it was operated with Richard Kneeshaw as Lyman, Kneeshaw and Company, then became Lyman Brothers and Company, and in 1855 Benjamin, who continued to live in Montreal, formed a partnership with William Elliot, as Lyman, Elliot and Company. Finally, in 1870, the Lymans bought out the Elliot family and again assumed the name Lyman Brothers and Company. As in Montreal separate manufacturing and warehousing operations were maintained. The firm had travellers in Ontario, Manitoba, and the western districts. At the time of Benjamin Lyman's death, in 1878, it was the largest wholesale drug company in Toronto and the estate valuation of the Ontario operation alone was $115,000. In the same year Bradstreet estimated the firm's total value at Toronto and Montreal as $250,000 to $300,000.

Benjamin Lyman demonstrated a great interest in improving the standards of the drug business generally. He was particularly active in this respect in Ontario, where he helped establish the Canadian Pharmaceutical Association in 1867; after it became the Ontario College of Pharmacy, he was elected president in 1873, holding that office for several years. He was also one of the founders of the *Canadian Pharmaceutical Journal*, designed to raise the level of the profession, in 1868. During the same period he helped form the Montreal Chemists' Association (1870), and attempted to found a Toronto pharmaceutical association (1872). In Ontario, at least, his firm was the first to use a bright red label to mark all dangerous preparations.

Lyman was also interested in manufacturing associations generally, attending an 1858 meeting at St Lawrence Hall, Toronto, to promote Canadian industry and being elected first vice-president of the Manufacturers' Association of Ontario (now the Canadian Manufacturers' Association) in 1875. He was a member of both the Montreal and the Toronto Boards of Trade and was a "strong advocate of protection for the industries of Canada." In addition he had financial interests: he was a director of the Federal Bank of Canada (organized 1872–74) and one of the

450

incorporators of the Royal Canadian Insurance Company in 1873.

When the second rebellion had broken out in Lower Canada in 1838, Lyman had been commissioned captain commanding the 5th Company of Montreal Rifles, "The Cold Water Company," on 5 November and remained on active duty with the militia for six months. He retained his captaincy in the company until 1847 when he transferred to the Montreal Fire Battalion on its formation. Like most of the leading Montreal merchants, however, he was one of the initial signatories of the Annexation Manifesto of 1849 and was briefly deprived of his commission in 1850. Reinstated, in 1854 he was promoted major and retired from the militia in 1862. In the municipal sphere he and his brother Henry organized in Montreal the volunteer Union Fire Company in 1840 and Benjamin became its captain. He also was a councillor of Montreal in 1845, 1847, and 1848, and an alderman in 1846, 1849, and 1850. In 1863 he was appointed warden of Trinity House at Montreal.

A trustee and elder of the American Presbyterian Church in Montreal, he laid the corner stone of the new church on Dorchester Street in 1865. As the *Montreal Daily Witness* stated in his obituary, he was "active in the promotions of nearly all benevolent enterprises in the city": a founder of the Mount Royal Cemetery Company, and its president in 1875–77; and a promoter of the Montreal Auxiliary Bible Society and the Montreal Temperance Society.

He married Delia Almira Wells (1810–83) of Waterbury, Vermont, in 1834 and they had 13 children of whom two sons and two daughters outlived him. Particularly in his last years, he spent a good deal of time travelling, and attending to business in Toronto, where he died of pneumonia. His entire estate was left to his widow. Lyman's obituary described him as a man of commanding presence, who, although not demonstrative, formed firm friendships; slow and careful of speech, he nevertheless put his conclusions into practice promptly once decided upon a policy.

FREDERICK H. ARMSTRONG

College of Pharmacy Library (University of Toronto),

Douglas Fatum, "Biography of Mr. Benjamin Lyman (1810–1878)"; T. I. Kahnykevych, "Benjamin Lyman, an outstanding figure in the history of pharmacy." PAC, RG 1, E1, 77, pp.534–35; RG 9, I, C4, 2. York County Surrogate Court, inventory of the estate of Benjamin Lyman, 22 Jan. 1879; will of Benjamin Lyman, 12 Aug. 1861. *Bradstreet's reports of the Dominion of Canada, February 1, 1876* (New York, 1876). Canada, *Statutes*, 1872, c.59; 1873, c.79, c.99; 1874, c.57. *Mail* (Toronto), 7 Dec. 1878. *Montreal Daily Witness*, 27 April 1865; 6, 9 Dec. 1878. *Montreal Herald*, 15 Oct. 1849. *The Canada directory for 1857–58 . . .* (Montréal, 1857). *Dom. ann. reg., 1879*, 356–57. *Montreal Directory* (Mackay), 1848, 1857, 1862. Toronto, *Directories*, 1850, 1856, 1861, 1873, 1879.

Atherton, *Montreal*, II, 278; III, 560–61. Campbell, *Hist. of Scotch Presbyterian Church*, 256–58. *Centennial/Anniversary souvenir; a commemorative volume celebrating Canada's centenary and National Drug's 60 years of service* (Montreal, 1967), 112. *Genealogy of the Lyman family in Canada; ancestors and descendants of Elisha Lyman (no.18) from the end of the 18th century to the present time (1943)*, ed. Arthur Lyman (Montreal, 1943), 30, 39, 72, 75. *Histoire de la Corporation de la Cité de Montréal, depuis son origine jusqu'à nos jours . . .*, J.-C. Lamothe et al., édit. (Montréal, 1903), 206–8. *Hist. of Toronto and county of York*, I, 408. F. W. Terrill, *A chronology of Montreal and of Canada from A.D. 1752 to A.D. 1893, including commercial statistics, historical sketches of commercial corporations and firms and advertisements . . .* (Montreal, 1893), 57–58.

"Editorial; the election for council," *Canadian Pharmaceutical Journal* (Toronto), VIII (1874–75), 436–37. "Editors of the journal from 1868–1942," *Canadian Pharmaceutical Journal* (Whitby), LXXV (15 June 1942), 26. George Hodgetts, "Minutes of the semi-annual meeting of the council of the Ontario College of Pharmacy," *Canadian Pharmaceutical Journal* (Toronto), VIII (1874–75), 40–47; "Ontario College of Pharmacy, council meeting," *Canadian Pharmaceutical Journal* (Toronto), VII (1873–74), 68–75; "Ontario College of Pharmacy; minutes of the semi-annual meeting of the council," *Canadian Pharmaceutical Journal* (Toronto), VIII (1874–75), 267–72. "Many important drug companies started in little back shops," *Canadian Pharmaceutical Journal* (Whitby), LXXV (15 June 1942), 82. "Obituary; Benjamin Lyman," *Canadian Pharmaceutical Journal* (Toronto), XII (1878–79), 190–93. "The story of Canadian pharmacy from 1868 to 1942 as it unfolded . . . in the C. Ph. Journal," *Canadian Pharmaceutical Journal* (Whitby), LXXV (15 June 1942), 12.

M

MACALLUM, ARCHIBALD, educator and author; b. 1 Aug. 1824, in Killmichell, Argyll, Scotland, son of Donald Macallum and Mary Macalpine Barramollach; m. Maria Adams and, after her death, Mary Biggar in 1859; d. 29 June 1879, at Hamilton, Ont.

Archibald Macallum was about six years old when his family came to Upper Canada and settled

Macaulay

in the township of East Hawkesbury. He received little formal education before entering, in 1847, the Normal School in Toronto where he obtained the first first-class certificate granted in Canada West. The next year he was appointed senior teacher at the Model School in Toronto. He received a BA from the University of Toronto in 1864, an MA in 1866, and an LLB in 1877.

In 1853 Macallum declined the principalship of the new Central School in Hamilton and recommended that his assistant, John Herbert Sangster*, be appointed. Macallum took instead the office of master of the Model School in Toronto, but in 1858, when Sangster resigned from the Central School, he accepted a second offer of the position. He became superintendent of schools in Hamilton in 1870 and inspector in 1871. During his term as inspector, the first collegiate institute (called at first the grammar school) and seven public elementary schools were constructed.

Macallum was one of the founders of the Teachers' Association of Canada West (later the Ontario Educational Association), in 1861, and served as its vice-president until 1865. He was recognized as a forward-looking teacher and he spoke against racial discrimination, gave support to equal opportunities for women, encouraged women teachers to join the Educational Association, and suggested the need for commercial education, sewing for girls, and other innovations regarded as "frills and fads." In an address in 1862 he also advocated the use of corporal punishment only as a last resort and instead of expulsion.

Macallum was the author of four textbooks which appear to have enjoyed considerable popularity although they do not seem to have been authorized. Nine editions of his *Literary extracts* were published in three years and the preface to the second edition states that 3,000 copies were sold in ten days. Active in the Centenary Church in Hamilton, he was one of the two Canadian members of the International Sunday School Lesson Committee formed in 1872 and was a member of the board of the Wesleyan Female College (later called the Hamilton Ladies College).

At the time of his death in 1879 Macallum was president of the St Andrews Society and he had been active in forming the Caledonia Society in Hamilton. He was a member of the Masonic order and an office-bearer in the Scottish Rite. He served as director of the Canada Fire and Marine Insurance Company, the Hamilton Street Railway Company, and the Canada Loan and Banking Company. He was survived by his wife, one son, and four daughters.

FREDA F. WALDON

Archibald Macallum, *An eclectic grammar, practical and analytical of the English language* . . . (Hamilton, 1867); *Manual of dates with brief notes, in Canadian, English, ancient and modern history, for the use of public schools in the Dominion of Canada* (Hamilton, 1870); *Synopsis of natural history; in explanation of the author's chart of natural history* (Toronto, 1857). Archibald Macallum and J. M. Buchan, *Literary extracts to aid pupils who are preparing for examination in English literature for admission to high schools* . . . (Toronto, [1878]; 9th ed. Toronto, 1881).

Hamilton Board of Education, Proceedings of the Board of Trustees for Common Schools for the City of Hamilton, I–IV. Hamilton Public Library, clipping from an unidentified Hamilton newspaper, 30 June 1879, obituary of Archibald Macallum. *Documentary history of education in Upper Canada* (Hodgins), VII, 283; VIII, 254; IX, 161–62; XI, 16, 168, 279, 282; XIV, 53. *Cyclopædia of Can. biog.* (Rose, 1888), 738–39. *Register of the University of Toronto for the year 1920* (Toronto, [1920]). E. C. Guillet, *In the cause of education; centennial history of the Ontario Educational Association, 1861–1960* (Toronto, 1960). J. G. Hodgins, *The establishment of schools and colleges in Ontario, 1792–1910* (3v., Toronto, 1910), I, 72–107. J. H. Smith, *1853–1903, the Central School jubilee re-union, August 1903; an historical sketch* (Hamilton, 1905). L. T. Spalding, *The history and romance of education (Hamilton), 1816–1950* ([Hamilton, 1950]). *Toronto Normal School, 1847–1897, jubilee celebration, 1897* . . . (Toronto, 1898).

MACAULAY, WILLIAM, Church of England clergyman; b. 9 Aug. 1794 at Kingston, U.C., son of Robert Macaulay*, loyalist, and Ann Kirby; d. Picton, Ont., 2 March 1874.

William Macaulay received his early education under John Strachan* at Cornwall and York (Toronto); from 1816 to 1818 he attended Queen's College, Oxford, but did not take his degree. He was made deacon in London, England, in July 1818 and received priest's orders from Bishop Jacob Mountain* at Quebec in October 1819. In the latter year he was licensed to Hamilton, now Cobourg, as missionary of the Society for the Propagation of the Gospel. Here he built the first St Peter's Church and served also in the adjacent townships. He visited England in 1827 and after his return he was appointed to the mission of Hallowell (Picton) in Prince Edward County where he owned property and had begun, in 1825, the building of a brick church, largely at his own expense. He itinerated in the Hallowell area until other missions were established. From 1821 to 1835 he was chaplain to the Legislative Council, succeeding John Strachan in that office.

William Macaulay was closely involved with the management of the clergy reserves. From 1820 he was a member of the Upper Canada Clergy Corporation established to manage the reserves in

Upper Canada. His mission of Hallowell was made into a rectory in 1836 and it was endowed with lands from the reserves. When the reserves were secularized in 1854 Macaulay was the only rector whom Strachan could not persuade to enter the commutation scheme, by which the funds received for the reserves would be placed by the bishop in an endowment fund; hence Macaulay received a government stipend until his death.

In 1871 Macaulay left Picton to live in England but he had returned to Picton by 1872 and he remained there in retirement until his death on 2 March 1874. In 1829 he had married Anne Catherine Geddes, who died 20 April 1849. He then married in 1852 Charlotte Sarah Vesconte (who died in 1884) and by his second marriage had two daughters.

William Macaulay's ambition was to become bishop. In a letter written to his mother, 18 Oct. 1837, his brother, John Macaulay*, then legislative councillor of Upper Canada, wrote frankly and, it appears, accurately of William: "He considers himself overlooked in the Church. He has very aspiring thoughts and a high opinion of himself but has always committed the fatal error of not endeavouring to impress others with a like opinion. . . . He thinks *he* should be Bishop. I'll venture to say not another clergyman has concurred in this." Macaulay's ambition was never attained, but it often strained his relations with John Strachan even before Strachan's appointment as bishop in 1839. The close connection of early years between the two men, however, was never entirely broken, and at the bishop's visitation in Toronto in 1844, Macaulay preached an eloquent sermon, printed in the *Church*, in the course of which he praised his former preceptor.

Although he was a gifted preacher William Macaulay did not gain wide repute outside the two communities in which he served for over half a century and to which he is said to have given their present names. His obituary notice remarked: "He was a sound and consistent Churchman of the old Anglican type, courteous and genial to all," and his kindness and generosity is attested to by Frances Stewart [Browne] in *Our forest home*. He was conservative, punctilious in the performance of duty, closely involved in local affairs, and independent in thought and action.

T. R. MILLMAN

PAO, Macaulay family papers; D. B. Stevenson papers; John Strachan letter books. Queen's University Archives, William Macaulay papers. Macaulay published three sermons: *The harvest blessing, or a word to prudent men, being a sermon preached . . . August 28th, 1853* (Kingston, n.d.); *The portraiture of a true and loyal Orangeman; as sketched in a sermon* (Toronto, 1854); *A sermon preached . . . on the occasion of the funeral of Mrs. Catherine Wright* (Picton, U.C., [1837]).

Scadding, *Toronto of old*. [Frances Stewart], *Our forest home, being extracts from the correspondence of the late Frances Stewart*, ed. E. S. Dunlop (2nd ed., Montreal, 1902), 17, 19. [John Strachan], *The John Strachan letter book: 1812–1834*, ed. G. W. Spragge (Toronto, 1946). *Church* (Cobourg), 4 Dec. 1841, 28 June 1844. *Church Herald* (Toronto), 6, 12 March 1874. *New Nation* (Picton), 7 March 1874. Wilson, *Clergy reserves of Upper Canada*, 65–67, 69, 154–55.

McCAWLEY, GEORGE, Church of England clergyman and educator; b. at St John's, Newfoundland, in 1802; d. at Halifax, N.S., 21 Dec. 1878.

George McCawley was educated at the University of King's College, Windsor, Nova Scotia, from which he was graduated with a BA in 1821 and an MA in 1824; he was granted his DD in 1835. From 1822 to 1828 he was headmaster of the grammar school at Fredericton, New Brunswick. He was ordained deacon by Bishop John Inglis* of Nova Scotia on 9 July 1826 at Fredericton, and was raised to the priesthood in 1827. He was appointed professor of Hebrew and mathematics at King's College (University of New Brunswick), Fredericton, in 1828, and the next year became chaplain to the Legislative Council of New Brunswick. Between 1831 and 1834 he also served as a visiting missionary for the Society for the Propagation of the Gospel. While in Fredericton he married Anne, the daughter of William Franklin Odell*, a loyalist who had been provincial secretary under the imperial government. They had one child, a daughter, who married the Reverend Charles Bowman.

When the Reverend Charles Porter* resigned as president of King's College, Windsor, in 1836, McCawley was chosen to succeed him. Both Bishop Inglis and William Howley, archbishop of Canterbury, highly approved the appointment; the former wrote: "he [McCawley] is a man of superior talents, an excellent scholar of great distinction, and a man of most pleasing address." McCawley's long tenure at King's can be called its second formative stage; the first was the period ending with Dr Porter's resignation. McCawley went to King's at a crucial time; there had been grave difficulties in 1835 when the government demanded the surrender of the college charter. In 1849 the government attempted to make King's a secular college by prohibiting the teaching of theology, and in 1850 the government grant was withdrawn when the college refused to conform to the new ruling. These problems could have brought

McClure

disaster, but McCawley met them resolutely, and the college continued.

Since the emoluments at King's were insufficient for his needs, McCawley was appointed rector of Falmouth in 1846. He held this office until his death, but retired from active parochial duties in his later years. In 1865 he was appointed archdeacon and senior canon to assist Dean William BULLOCK at St Luke's Cathedral in Halifax, and held these offices until 1874. He resigned the presidency of King's on 1 Oct. 1875, and retired on pension. He then moved to Halifax where he lived quietly until his death. McCawley was buried in the Old Burying Ground in Windsor, N.S., within sight of the college to which he devoted most of his active life.

C. E. THOMAS

PANS, John Inglis papers, Journal, 1806–7; letters to SPG, 19 Jan. 1827, 17 Nov. 1846. *Morning Chronicle* (Halifax), 23 Dec. 1878. *Encyclopedia of Canada*, IV, 158. Pascoe, *Two hundred years of the S.P.G.*, 867. F. W. Vroom, *King's College: a chronicle 1789–1939, collections and recollections* (Halifax, 1941), 96, 105, 123.

McCLURE, Sir ROBERT JOHN LE MESURIER (also spelled **M'Clure**), officer in the Royal Navy and Arctic explorer; b. 28 Jan. 1807 in Wexford, Ireland, son of Robert McClure and Jane Elgee; d. 17 Oct. 1873 in London, Eng.

Robert John Le Mesurier McClure's father, an army captain, died five months before his son's birth, and an old army comrade, John Le Mesurier, acted as his godfather and guardian. McClure was educated at Eton and Sandhurst and entered the navy in 1824. He had his first experience of the Arctic in 1836 when he served as mate of *Terror* under George BACK. This expedition reached Foxe Channel where *Terror* became frozen in the ice; eventually the ship, badly damaged, recrossed the Atlantic barely making the west coast of Ireland. Certainly McClure could have had no more severe initiation to the Arctic. His next service was on *Niagara*, flagship of Williams Sandom*, captain on the Great Lakes in 1838 during the Upper Canadian rebellion. He went next to the West Indian Station; he received the *Romney* at Havana and commanded it from 1842 to 1846. Then he went on coast guard duty for two years.

McClure's second visit to the Arctic lasted from 1848 until 1849 when he served as first lieutenant on *Enterprise* in an expedition commanded by Sir James Clark Ross* on *Investigator*. This was the first of many expeditions in search of Sir John Franklin*. The ships entered Lancaster Sound but were soon frozen in and further searches had to be

made by sledge; McClure, who spent a month on the sick list, took no part. Eventually *Enterprise* drifted back into Baffin Bay and returned to England with no information about the missing Franklin.

This failure caused an outcry in Britain where the public felt that the government must act resolutely to discover Franklin's fate. The two ships were recommissioned; Richard Collinson* was appointed to *Enterprise* as leader of the expedition, and McClure was given the command of *Investigator*. They were to rendezvous at Honolulu and approach the polar seas through Bering Strait. *Enterprise* arrived at the meeting point first, waited five days, and left; *Investigator* reached Honolulu on the day *Enterprise* had gone. McClure then took a dangerous short cut through the Aleutian Islands and arrived before his commander at Bering Strait. Although he must have known he was ahead, McClure continued. Thirty miles past Cape Lisburne, he met Henry KELLETT in *Herald*. Kellett, who outranked McClure, did not believe that Collinson had gone on ahead and thought that *Investigator* should await *Enterprise*, but he did not order McClure to stay and McClure sailed on. *Investigator* ran aground near Return Reef but was freed to continue her voyage in a northeasterly direction. McClure's route carried him to Banks Island and, almost immediately, he discovered Prince of Wales Strait between it and Victoria Island. He managed to sail part way up the strait before becoming frozen in for the winter; further exploration by sledge showed him that the strait led to Viscount Melville Sound and convinced McClure that he had discovered the northwest passage. His conviction was sound, but, unknown at the time, Sir John Franklin had found another route four years previously. McClure left on Banks Island a record of his achievement dated 21 April 1851 which was discovered in 1917 by Vilhjalmur Stefansson*. In 1851 ice blocked further travel up Prince of Wales Strait so McClure turned back and attempted to sail west around Banks Island. He succeeded in reaching the northern end of the island by entering Banks (now McClure) Strait and spent the winter in an inlet which he called the Bay of Mercy because it provided an escape from the crushing ice. In the spring of 1852 one of his sledge parties reached Winter Harbour on Melville Island and left a message on a rock on which was inscribed a record of Sir William Edward Parry*'s achievement in 1819.

Investigator was trapped in the ice in the Bay of Mercy throughout 1852; by spring the crew were suffering badly from malnutrition and scurvy. McClure made elaborate plans for evacuating the less healthy members who would be unlikely to stand the rigours of a third winter. He had always shown a great concern for their health, delighted in their amusements during the long hours of winter inactivity, and won their respect and affection. By the spring of 1853, however, help was at hand. The message which McClure had left at Winter Harbour in 1852 was found by members of Kellett's *Resolute*, one of the four ships of Sir Edward BELCHER's expedition. Lieutenant Bedford Pim* walked over the ice from *Resolute* and found *Investigator*. McClure wanted to keep enough men to try to get his ship back to England, but Kellett, who subsequently paid a high tribute to McClure, ordered him to abandon it. McClure and his men were forced to spend a fourth winter in the Arctic when *Resolute* became trapped in the ice. In April 1854 McClure and the crew were sent by sledge to Beechey Island where they boarded the transport *North Star*. They finally arrived in England on 28 Sept. 1854 along with the crews of Belcher's disastrous expedition.

McClure was court-martialed for the loss of *Investigator* but was honourably acquitted. He was promoted captain and knighted, and parliament voted £10,000 to the officers and men of his ship for finding the northwest passage. McClure served on the Pacific Station from 1856 to 1861, then returned to England. He was promoted rear-admiral in 1867 and vice-admiral on the retired list in 1873. During his years of active service he remained a bachelor but in 1869 he married Constance Ada Tudor.

McClure handed all his papers over to his fellow officer Sherard OSBORN who wrote an account of McClure's great voyage. This narrative makes clear that McClure took every opportunity to obtain information about the missing Franklin. He also left records of his own movements, as well as supplies for others who might be in need, in order that the Arctic could become fully known. Osborn said that he was "Stern, cool, bold in all perils, severe as a disciplinarian, self-reliant, yet modest as became an officer. With a granite-like view of duty to his country and his profession, he would in war have been a great leader, and it was his good fortune, during a period of profound peace, to find a field for all these valuable qualities." He will always remain one of the great leaders of Arctic expeditions.

J. N. L. BAKER

[McClure], *Discovery of the north-west passage* (Osborn). *DNB.* L. J. Burpee, *The discovery of Canada* (Toronto, 1944). E. S. Dodge, *Northwest by sea* (New York, 1961). Christopher Lloyd, *Mr. Barrow of the Admiralty; a life of Sir John Barrow, 1764–1848* (London, 1970). A. H. Markham, *Life of Sir John Franklin and the north-west passage* (London, 1891).

C. R. Markham, *Life of Admiral Sir Leopold McClintock* (London, 1909).

McCLURE, WILLIAM, Methodist New Connexion minister; b. in Lisburn, County Antrim, Ireland, June 1803, son of John McClure, a Methodist minister, and Sarah Trelford; d. Toronto, Ont., 19 Feb. 1871.

William McClure was apprenticed to a Belfast tradesman at the age of 14. In 1828 he became a preacher and a travelling agent for the Hibernian Bible Society. During the next 20 years he preached on the Dublin, Bangor, Lisburn, and Limerick circuits, acquiring a reputation as a powerful speaker, a tireless worker, and a resolute foe of both Roman Catholicism and strong drink. In 1848 conditions in Ireland and the wishes of his church brought McClure to emigrate to Canada, to become assistant superintendent of the New Connexion mission.

From 1848 to 1851 McClure served at the Temperance Street Church in Toronto, but he travelled throughout the province, preaching and lecturing on temperance and a variety of other subjects. He was a charter member of the Anti-Slavery Society of Canada along with Michael WILLIS, and he was active in the movement against the clergy reserves. From June 1851 to January 1854 he was in London, Canada West, after which he was transferred to Hamilton. Here he found a debt-ridden church and a small congregation, a situation he worked hard to remedy. He was then appointed in 1857 to Montreal; there he was disgusted by the prosperity of the Roman Catholic Church, which he called "the Roman Beast." He spent much of his time gathering funds for new churches, and saw two buildings completed. He frequently toured the Eastern Townships, and also began contributing to the struggling New Connexion paper in London, Canada West, the *Evangelical Witness*, of which he became an editor in 1865.

In 1860, McClure took charge of the important Toronto circuit. Despite his lack of formal education, he was appointed to a committee to train young men for the ministry. The year 1860 was also one of personal tragedy for McClure: his wife, Hannah Glynn, whom he had married in 1827, died on 19 July. He subsequently married Margaret Bussell of Oakville in December 1861; she died in 1865.

Although superannuated in 1865, McClure divided his time from 1861 until his death in 1871 between travelling, lecturing, and collecting money for the church and his interest in the education of the ministry. He worked on the Toronto, Galt, Hamilton, Aurora, and Montreal circuits during these years, and twice went on fund-raising and lecturing tours around Canada West. As a tutor with the Theological Institute, which had been established in 1861, he spent much of his time and energy training future ministers. He applied for a seat on the senate of the University of Toronto in December 1862, and was admitted to that body two months later.

William McClure was a sincere, hard-working humanitarian. His prime interests were the welfare of his church and the temperance movement, but he was possessed of sufficient breadth of spirit to endorse such projects as the Young Men's Christian Association, the Young People's Mutual Improvement Association, and the Canadian anti-slavery movement. He was truly an example of the spiritual philanthropist.

I. C. B. PEMBERTON

William McClure, *The character and fatal tendency of Puseyism, defined and exposed; being a course of lectures delivered in the Temperance Street chapel* (Toronto, 1850); *A charge to five ministers, who were set apart to the work of the ministry; delivered at the Whitchurch conference, June 8th, 1850* (Toronto, 1850); [ ], *Life and labours of the Rev. Wm. McClure, for more than forty years a minister of the Methodist New Connexion,* ed. David Savage (Toronto, 1872).

PAC, RG 5, C1, 729, f.1602. *Christian Guardian* (Toronto), 22 Feb. 1871. *Globe* (Toronto), 22 Feb. 1871. *London Free Press*, 3 March 1951. Methodist New Connexion Church, Canada, *Minutes of the annual conference* (Toronto; London, Ont.), 1849–71. S. R. Ward, *Autobiography of a fugitive Negro: his anti-slavery labours in the United States, Canada, & England* (London, 1855).

McCOUBREY, JOHN WILLIAMS, newspaper proprietor; b. of middle-class Protestant parents in Waterford, Ireland, in 1806; d. at St John's, Nfld., on 10 Oct. 1879.

In 1819 John Williams McCoubrey's family emigrated to St John's, Newfoundland, where he was apprenticed to a well-known printer, Robert Lee Jr. After his seven years as an apprentice he went to work for John Shea's newspaper, the *Newfoundlander*, apparently both as printer and as journalist, until 1832, when he founded his own newspaper, the *Times and General Commercial Gazette*.

McCoubrey had no trouble with the colonial authorities, despite the tight control of the Newfoundland press at the time. Throughout his career he avoided the political and sectarian controversies usual in the journalism of St John's, and achieved a reputation for impartiality and personal integrity. A rival newspaper, the *Public Ledger*, records his support for Conservative candidates in the 1842 election. The incident in his life most

celebrated by the obituarist in his own newspaper was his refusal to compound with his creditors, at great personal expense, after the fire of 1846, when his business was almost wiped out. Perhaps the most fitting last words on his career come from an anonymous correspondent to the *Times*, who wrote on 17 Oct. 1879 that he had never known McCoubrey "either through the press or otherwise utter one word to wound the feelings of any man, no matter to what creed or party he belonged."

E. J. DEVEREUX

Public Ledger (St John's), 4 Oct. 1842. *Times and General Commercial Gazette* (St John's), 1832–94. "Chronological list of Newfoundland newspapers in the public collections at the Gosling Memorial Library and Provincial Archives," 18-page typescript compiled by Ian McDonald (copy at the Reference Library, Arts and Culture Centre, St John's). E. J. Devereux, "Early printing in Newfoundland," *Dal. Rev.*, XLIII (1963), 57–66.

McCULLY, JONATHAN, lawyer, journalist, senator, and judge; b. on a farm in Cumberland County, N.S. (probably at Maccan), 25 July 1809, fifth in a family of nine children of Samuel McCully and Esther Pipes; d. at his home in Halifax, N.S., 2 Jan. 1877.

Jonathan McCully attended the usual one-room school until he had exhausted what it offered, then began work on his father's 150-acre farm. From 1828 to 1830 he taught school to earn money to study law, which at that time meant a five-year apprenticeship to a lawyer. He was admitted to the bar in 1837 at the age of 28. McCully enjoyed fighting his cases and put much hard work on them. He was not without elements for success in a colonial society: ambition, thoroughness, and, perhaps one can add, poverty. Yet he was one of those who succeed by grit rather than by brains. He was always a slow, rather unoriginal thinker. Nor was he a great orator. He spoke with force and directness, often with homely allusions laced occasionally with slang, but neither in force nor in metaphor, nor in his public presence, was he the equal of Joseph HOWE, whom McCully seems much to have admired.

By 1837 McCully was a convinced Reformer, despite Cumberland County's Tory preponderance, and had begun to write political articles in the Halifax *Acadian Recorder* in much the same terms as he conducted his law practice. He was a vigorous, slashing writer, who spared nothing and no one. Under the pseudonym, "Clim o' the Cleugh," he made some savage comments in the *Recorder* on Alexander Stewart* in 1839. His support of Howe in the 1847 election was repaid with his appointment in 1848 to the Legislative

Council, a position he continued to hold until 1867. McCully was appointed judge of probate in 1853, an office he held until after the change of government in 1857, when he was duly fired. He then opened a law practice with Hiram BLAN-CHARD, MLA, Inverness, a partnership which lasted until McCully left the bar for the bench.

In 1842 McCully married Eliza Creed of Halifax; they had three children, a son and two daughters. The son, Clarence, was ultimately to go into the Anglican Church, but it was a berth rather than a vocation; he was a continued disappointment to his father.

While in the probate court McCully had supported Howe's railway projects, one of which was to build, as a government work, a line from Halifax to Truro with a branch to Windsor. His reward was membership on Howe's railway commission from 1854 until Howe's government was replaced by the James W. JOHNSTON–Charles Tupper* government in 1857. It is remarkable that McCully acquired so many offices; in 1855, for example, he was a member of the Legislative Council, a judge of probate, and a railway commissioner.

He was by now beginning to write for the Halifax *Morning Chronicle*, the Liberal party's lighthouse in the capital. He rapidly became its leading editorial writer, a position he was to retain until 1865. McCully had the pleasure of seeing some of his efforts on behalf of William Young*, Howe, and the Liberals bear fruit, for in 1860 the Liberals (the name "Reformers" was falling out of use now) returned to power. McCully was promptly appointed solicitor general and also made the sole railway commissioner, while still keeping his hand on the editorial desk of the *Morning Chronicle*. McCully ran the Nova Scotia Railway from 1860 to 1863 with a ruthless eye to saving money. This, rather than that other touchstone, efficiency, guided him. He was in an excellent position for creating enemies and, being blessed with neither tact nor taste, made good use of his opportunities. A doggerel of the time ran:

> I am monarch of all I survey,
> My will there is none to dispute,
> Trains run when I want 'em to run
> And toot when I tell 'em to toot.

McCully's railway interests had also ramified into the Intercolonial Railway project. He had urged this in the *Chronicle* as early as 1855 and periodically afterwards. In September 1861 he was in New Brunswick for negotiations on the Intercolonial; partly as a result of these negotiations and partly as a result of reaction to the American Civil War, a conference on the Intercolonial Railway between Canada, New Brunswick, and

Nova Scotia was held at Quebec in October 1861; there McCully again represented Nova Scotia. At a similar conference in September 1862, McCully was replaced by William Annand*, the owner of the *Morning Chronicle*.

It is fair to say that McCully was a difficult man for Howe's Liberal government to carry. He had little popular appeal; there is good reason to doubt whether he could ever have been elected for a constituency, a fact that Howe was to throw at him in 1867. Howe blamed him, in part at least, for the Liberal defeat at the polls in the general election of 1863, especially because of his bullying administration of the government-owned railway. "Jonathan," said Howe, "is the kind of fellow that costs more than he comes to. I carried him as long as I could stagger under him."

In August 1864 the Tupper government chose both Liberal and Conservative delegates to represent the province at the Charlottetown conference. McCully was the leader of the Liberals in the Legislative Council; nevertheless his name was omitted. Only at the last minute, as a result of the withdrawal of John Locke, was McCully's name suggested by Adams G. Archibald*, leader of the Liberal party. McCully's contribution at Charlottetown and at Quebec was inconspicuous; it can be roughly documented, but it seems to have been unimportant. His real importance in the confederation movement was his attempt to popularize the Quebec resolutions in Nova Scotia, and to expand the political horizons of Nova Scotians to include the idea of a united British North America.

Up to this time union had not been a particular theme of McCully's. The *Morning Chronicle* in 1856 had praised colonial union as "a measure that every thinking man feels is essential. . . . We cannot remain as we are." But even Howe in those days would have agreed with that. By 1860 McCully was raising massive doubts about the value of a colonial union, as if he were already following Howe's ideas about some new reorganization of the empire. For McCully, Canada's expenditure on such projects as canals and the Grand Trunk Railway and her burgeoning population had, by 1860, made it obvious that this province was outdistancing New Brunswick and Nova Scotia, to say nothing of Prince Edward Island and Newfoundland; although the *Morning Chronicle* would not say flatly that it opposed a colonial union, it felt, on the whole, that Nova Scotia should leave well enough alone (1 Dec. 1860). In any case that project was soon overshadowed by the more immediate prospects (so it was thought) for the Intercolonial Railway, and by the American Civil War. When colonial union

457

appeared again in the *Chronicle*'s editorials, in 1864, it was still being regarded with distrust, especially so with Canadian talk of a *federal* union being noised abroad (30 June, 4 Aug., 1 Sept. 1864).

Within three weeks after 1 Sept. 1864, the position of the Halifax *Morning Chronicle* radically changed. The Charlottetown conference had converted McCully, and not a few others, to confederation. Howe made bitter sport of McCully's conversion. After Charlottetown, Howe said, McCully returned to Halifax as full of the glory of confederation as a girl newly proposed to. Indeed, Howe added, more than proposed to: seduced. St Paul, said Howe, had been converted by a flood of light; Danaë was converted from a virgin to a strumpet by a shower of gold: "you . . . can judge whether McCully was converted after the fashion of Danaë or St Paul." All through the autumn of 1864 (though editorials languished somewhat during McCully's absence at Quebec) the *Morning Chronicle* threw its heavy weight behind confederation, and especially so in the critical period after McCully had returned to Halifax from Quebec on 10 November. Then on 10 Jan. 1865 came the announcement that McCully was fired from the editorial desk of the *Chronicle*.

At once the *Chronicle* swung over on its anti-confederate tack. McCully bought out the old *Morning Journal and Commercial Advertiser*, christened it the *Unionist and Halifax Journal*, and for over two years laboured to sell confederation to the Nova Scotians. It was uphill work; and after confederation was approved by the Nova Scotia legislature, in April 1866, McCully gradually eased off. He was a delegate to the London conference of 1866–67, but his strength, as before, lay in his pen. In the pamphlet battle he and Tupper vigorously defended the course Tupper's government had taken in London in January and February 1867.

Jonathan McCully was appointed to the Senate of the dominion of Canada later that same year. From this point he is gradually overshadowed politically by Tupper, Archibald, and, in 1869, Howe. McCully was bound to support Tupper and the better terms of 1869, but he seems not to have been influential in the negotiations for Howe's entering the John A. Macdonald* government in 1869. McCully was shrewd enough however to perceive that Canada's acquisition of the North-West would impose tremendous tasks upon the new confederation. "It has come upon us," he said in the Senate, "before we are fully prepared for it. We are scarcely organized ourselves. Our own house is not [yet] set in order. . . ."

In 1870 McCully was appointed puisne judge on the Nova Scotia Supreme Court; he had obviously made his peace with Howe, since it was to Howe as well as to Tupper that he owed his appointment. McCully came comfortably to rest on the bench. Here his forthright manner and natural instincts for dispatching business crossed the penchant of Halifax lawyers for talk. McCully won. The backlog of court dockets was thus dispatched with some celerity, which did not endear him to the legal fraternity but won him golden opinions – a refreshing change for McCully – from the public at large. This firmness was joined, as it seemed appropriate it now should be, to a newer impartiality, something for which McCully had not always been conspicuous.

He died at his home on Brunswick Street, Halifax, at the age of 67, leaving a substantial estate of $100,000. He is buried in Camp Hill Cemetery.

McCully was not a remarkable man; one of those people who could not do things by halves, he climbed, not very elegantly, up through colonial society. He disliked humbug or pretence; he had none of those arts himself. He cared little for public opinion; his course on confederation took courage: there were not many who would have done what he did. Yet somehow he remains an unlovely figure. With McCully, instincts answered for ideas, and his advocacy did not always help a good cause. He was in this respect like Charles Tupper, but without Tupper's cleverness or agility. McCully's stubbornness and pugnacity, his capacity for work, took him a long way – farther perhaps than his talents really deserved. He was a successful man before confederation became an issue; but it was confederation that made him famous, and gave him the right to this long essay here.

P. B. WAITE

[Up to the present no major collection of McCully papers has been found. There are a few McCully letters in PAC, MG 24, B29 (Howe papers), 1–5, 30–31; MG 26, A (Macdonald papers), 51; MG 26, F (Tupper papers), 1–18; MG 27, I, D8 (Galt papers), 1–4. One can probably assume that most of the leading editorials in the Halifax *Morning Chronicle* between 1856 and 1865 were written by McCully, and the same can be said for the *Unionist and Halifax Journal* for 1865 and 1866. His speeches in the Legislative Council of Nova Scotia can be found in the *Journals of the proceedings* of that body; those in the Senate of Canada, for 1867–68, in *Senate debates, 1867–68*, ed. P. B. Waite (Ottawa, 1967). The later Senate debates to 1870 have not yet been reprinted and can best be read in the *Ottawa Times*. McCully's decisions in the Nova Scotia Supreme Court are in Nova Scotia Supreme Court *Reports*, VIII–XII (1869–79). For secondary sources see the following: Saunders, *Three premiers of N.S.*; P. R. Blakeley, "Jonathan McCully, father of confederation," N.S. Hist. Soc. *Coll.*, XXXVI (1968), 142–81; N. H. Meagher, "Life of the Hon. Jonathan McCully, 1809–1877," N.S. Hist. Soc. *Coll.*, XXI (1927), 73–114. P.B.W.]

McDONALD, DONALD (the family sometimes spelled their name **Macdonald**), surveyor and politician; baptized at Caledonia, N.Y., 7 April 1816, son of Alexander McDonald and Margaret McColl; d. Toronto, Ont., 20 Jan. 1879.

The McDonald family were residents of the Loch Ness region of Inverness. Donald's father, Alexander, was one of a group that left Inverness in 1803 and settled on the Holland Land Company's holdings at Caledonia (then called Northampton) a year later. In 1823 Alexander joined other Scottish families emigrating to Upper Canada. He settled first in the Niagara area, then moved to the township of Dumfries (now North and South Dumfries) near Galt.

Donald McDonald was registered at Upper Canada College in 1830 and in 1832–33, and was trained as a surveyor by his cousin John Macdonald (1794–1873). John, known as "Stout Mac" for his great strength, was the surveyor for the Canada Company before becoming sheriff of the Huron District in 1845 and later of Huron County. Donald worked with him on numerous surveys and "many of the standard maps of the Huron and neighbouring districts were prepared under his [Donald's] supervision."

McDonald joined in the defence of Toronto in the rebellion of 1837 and was present at the assault on John MONTGOMERY's tavern on 8 December. About 1838 he married Frances, daughter of James Mitchell, judge of the London District Court, and niece of Egerton Ryerson*; they had 14 children. A few years later McDonald had to give up surveying because of rheumatism and was transferred to the clerical staff of the Canada Company, working first at Goderich, then, from at least 1843, at Toronto where he rose to hold the post of assistant commissioner. He built a 26-room house which became one of the social centres of the city, for he and his wife were famous for their hospitality.

In 1858, when the first election was held for the new Legislative Council seat of Tecumseth (the counties of Huron and Perth), McDonald was nominated by the Reform party to run against his Conservative (ministerialist) opponent, Thomas Mercer Jones*, his former superior at the Canada Company. He won, his majority being obtained in Huron County. The *London Free Press* stated that he was opposed by the Canada Company; certainly from this time his connection with the company seems to have ended. Jones contested the election, claiming that McDonald had used bribes and had opened taverns to the voters. A hearing was held, at which McDonald's supporters objected that the presiding judge, Robert Cooper*, had campaigned for Jones. A report was forwarded but no action was taken by the government; McDonald was duly seated the next year.

McDonald was elected chairman of the committee on finance at the Reform convention of November 1859 [*see* George BROWN]. In a speech he stated that the best solution for Canada's constitutional problem was the establishment of two or more local governments in federation. He argued that "to be effective we must not be rash" but changes were needed in both government and the men in power. When the Constitutional Reform Association was established to follow up the work of the convention, he was elected treasurer, but he played little part in later events leading to confederation. He was appointed a senator in 1867; he held that office and remained a supporter of the Liberal party until his death.

McDonald became a fairly wealthy man, leaving an estate of $141,800, mostly in notes, mortgages, and cash. Although interested in the construction of the Buffalo and Lake Huron Railway and listed in 1873 as a provisional director of the Huron and Ontario Ship Canal Company, he seems to have had little connection with entrepreneurial activities. In 1865 he was elected a director of the Royal Canadian Bank and became vice-president, but in 1869 he got into an acrimonious dispute with some of the other directors over the policy they were pursuing; the subsequent ill-fated course of that corporation probably indicates that he was right. He also owned a 2,000-acre ranch in Kansas where he bred improved shorthorn cattle, and at the end of his life, along with Alexander Campbell* and others, he was speculating in lands in Michigan.

In religion McDonald was a Presbyterian, a member of St Andrew's Church in Toronto. He was a lay trustee of Queen's College at Kingston from 1868 until 1878. McDonald died in Toronto in 1879 after a year's illness; his wife and several of his children afterwards went to live in Los Angeles, California.

FREDERICK H. ARMSTRONG

First Presbyterian Church (Caledonia, N.Y.), "Records," I, baptismal entry for 7 April 1816. Huron County Surrogate Court (Goderich, Ont.), will of John Macdonald, 26 July 1873. PAO, A. N. Buell papers, 13 April, 1, 15 May 1869; 17 Sept. 1871; C. E. Macdonald papers. University of Western Ontario Library, ULM 56–107 (Minutes of the contested election case of Thomas Mercer Jones *versus*

McDonald

Donald McDonald). York County Surrogate Court, inventory of the estate of Donald McDonald, 17 May 1879; will of Donald McDonald, 14 June 1877.

Globe (Toronto), 10, 12 Nov. 1859; 22 Jan. 1879. *Mail* (Toronto), 21 Jan. 1879. *Dom. ann. reg., 1879,* 412. *The roll of pupils of Upper Canada College, Toronto, January, 1830, to June, 1916,* ed. A. H. Young (Kingston, Ont., 1917), 382–84. Wallace, *Macmillan dictionary,* 437. *Centennial book of the First Presbyterian Church, Caledonia, N.Y.* (Caledonia, N.Y., 1906), 16, 50. W. E. Elliott, *Huron early houses and their families; Book III* (Goderich, Ont., 1969), 12–17. *Landmarks of Toronto* (Robertson), I, 271; IV, 140–53. C. E. Macdonald, "The clans in Canada," *Scottish Canadian* (Toronto), VI (1901), 258–59. A. P. Walker, "John McDonald," Ont. Land Surveyors Assoc., *Annual Report,* no.53 (1938), 100–3.

McDONALD, EDMUND MORTIMER, journalist, politician, and civil servant; b. 29 Sept. 1825 at Pictou, N.S., son of George McDonald; d. 25 May 1874 at Halifax, N.S.

Edmund Mortimer McDonald was one of a number of young Maritimers who apprenticed with Joseph HOWE on the *Novascotian* during the early 1840s. In 1847 he purchased the New Glasgow *Eastern Chronicle,* which he used to further the interests of the Reform party in Pictou County. In 1860 his services to the party were recognized by his appointment as queen's printer for the province, a position he held until the Tories swept back into power in a provincial election in June 1863.

In November of 1863 McDonald joined with William GARVIE to found the *Halifax Citizen,* a tri-weekly, which, like the *Eastern Chronicle,* was in the Reform interest. The combination of McDonald's publishing expertise and Garvie's satirical pen thrust the *Citizen* to the fore in the busy newspaper world of Halifax in the 1860s. Generally speaking, the *Citizen* favoured the idea of a Maritime union; in 1864, however, it opposed the immediate union of all of British North America under the federal system proposed by the Canadians at the Quebec conference. Suspicious of Canadian politicians, McDonald led the *Citizen* into almost violent opposition to the Quebec resolutions, and it became the first important paper in Nova Scotia to take a stand in opposition to union.

After the initial opposition to confederation was side-stepped by the provincial government, McDonald and Garvie became founding members of the League for the Maritime Provinces (or the Anti-confederation League). In September 1867 McDonald contested the riding of Lunenburg in Canada's first federal election. He campaigned and was elected as a member of the Nova Scotia party, the political wing of the Anti-confederation League. In the commons he was a leading spokesman for the release of Nova Scotia from the terms of confederation. In the spring of 1868, while Howe was fighting the league's cause in London, McDonald introduced in the commons a series of resolutions formally demanding the repeal of the British North America Act for Nova Scotia, arguing: "The people of Nova Scotia disliked the Union, not merely because of itself or its financial consequences, but because of the mode in which it was thrust upon them."

Like Joseph Howe and many others McDonald soon realized the futility of continued opposition to confederation. When Howe negotiated better terms for Nova Scotia in 1869, McDonald was quick to lay down his arms. The *Citizen* thereafter supported confederation. McDonald also became a supporter of John A. Macdonald*'s government in the House of Commons. In 1872 he achieved his political reward by being named collector of customs for the port of Halifax, a post he filled without incident until his untimely death just two years later. McDonald was married and had one son who predeceased him by about a year.

McDonald possessed a facile pen and a shrewd political sense. His opposition to confederation struck a chord which many Nova Scotian politicians have played successfully since 1867. His turnabout in 1869 reflected his capacity to judge the political consequences of continued opposition to confederation from a small province.

D. A. MUISE

[PANS, *Report, 1948,* app.C, 35–56 contains two letters from McDonald to William Garvie justifying his political switch in 1868–69. *See also: Eastern Chronicle* (New Glasgow, N.S.), 1847–60. *Halifax Citizen,* 1863–69. Obituaries are found in the *British Colonist* (Halifax), 28 May 1874, and the *Morning Chronicle* (Halifax), 26 May 1874. The best secondary account of the confederation struggle in Nova Scotia is: K. G. Pryke, "Nova Scotia and confederation, 1864–70," unpublished PHD thesis, Duke University, 1962. D.A.M.]

McDONALD, JOHN, priest, landed proprietor, colonizer, and land agent; b. in 1796 or 1797 at Tracadie, P.E.I., third son of Captain John McDonald* and his second wife Margaret Macdonald; d. 12 Oct. 1874 at Brighton, Eng.

John McDonald was born into the Jacobite family of a Highland tacksman or laird who in 1772 sent 210 Roman Catholic Scots to the central part of the Island of St John (P.E.I.). John McDonald Sr arrived in 1773, established a large house, New Glenalladale, at Tracadie, and settled the "opprest people" on his estate. In September 1813 his widow sent her sons John and Roderick to Lower Canada where they studied at the college of Nicolet. In 1820 John proceeded to England and later to France for further study; he was ordained in Paris in May 1825, the second Island native to become a priest.

Family financial difficulties had compelled John McDonald to obtain assistance from a Scottish bishop to complete his education. In return he had agreed to do missionary work in Glasgow after his ordination, and he remained there until spring 1830. At that time Father McDonald departed for Prince Edward Island taking with him 206 Scots and Irish as tenants for the lands he had inherited. He settled the immigrants at Fort Augustus, and took up residence with his mother at Tracadie. In addition to being priest and landlord, he also acted as land agent for his brother Roderick. This accumulation of functions resulted in considerable discontent among the tenants in the area, most of whom were his parishioners. As a result he soon left for a position in Lower Canada but, after a brief stay, returned to Tracadie. In mid-1835 renewed conflict in Tracadie and the need for a Gaelic-speaking priest in eastern Kings County led Bishop Bernard Donald MacDonald* to transfer McDonald there. He was for a time more successful as a priest than he had been previously. However he was working in an area well known for its radical or escheat views on the land question [see George COLES], and it became apparent that he and his parishioners were in fundamental disagreement. The situation was aggravated by McDonald's attitude toward the people whom "he regarded as his inferiors in every respect," according to the Catholic historian John C. MacMillan*.

In March 1843 Sir Henry Vere Huntley* called out troops to enforce the legal rights of property on lots 44 and 45 of the Cunard estate. When they were given accommodation by Father McDonald many of the settlers suspected that his class position and sympathies had led the priest to concur in, or even suggest, the action. Local sentiment against him was so strong that the bishop, after a visit to the district, requested in September 1843 that Father McDonald leave the area within a month. He refused, with the result that his parishioners took matters into their own hands. On 1 Jan. 1844 under the leadership of their escheat assemblyman, John Macintosh*, they elected new elders (customarily appointed by the priest) and directed them to tell McDonald "to quit the Parish, in a fortnight, or month, as they might determine." At the next Sunday mass, McDonald refused to recognize the new elders; Macintosh rose demand-

ing a hearing and was only silenced when the priest knelt in prayer. The service then ended with Father McDonald retreating to the parochial house and Macintosh angrily berating him.

The priest took legal action against the assemblyman, and employed as his lawyers the Tory politicians Robert HODGSON and Edward Palmer*. Macintosh was acquitted by a jury, and the bishop, who had opposed the action, ordered McDonald to leave the parish. Although many of the congregation were now boycotting his church, the priest refused and did not withdraw to Tracadie until he was suspended from his duties late in 1844. After this reprimand, McDonald, who felt the bishop and neighbouring priests had conspired with the escheators against him, resolved never again to serve in the Island diocese. Leaving his estate on lots 35 and 36 in the hands of an agent, he went to Quebec City in 1845. After teaching church history at the seminary there, he proceeded to England where he held several charges near London until his health deteriorated. He then retired to a convent in Brighton where he died.

Father John McDonald appears to have been a man of considerable talent. According to MacMillan "he was a preacher of more than ordinary power," and the author of "a few minor works, one of which, a manual of devotion and an abridgement of Christian doctrine combined, had at one time a wide circulation among the people of eastern King's County." He was fluent in three languages – Gaelic, English, and French. Nevertheless, during his years in his native colony these abilities were largely negated by his class position and attitudes, and by his insensitivity to the antagonisms thus generated. By the mid-1840s John McDonald had outlived his usefulness as a pastor in P.E.I. and was virtually compelled to go where the performance of his religious functions would not be impaired by his social rank.

IAN ROSS ROBERTSON

Archives of the diocese of Charlottetown (Roman Catholic), Bishop Bernard D. MacDonald papers, letter book of bishops MacDonald and Peter MacIntyre; a tattered copy of a volume published by Father John McDonald containing reprints of documents relevant to his conflicts with John Macintosh, Bishop MacDonald, and his fellow priests (the first four pages are missing but the probable date of publication is 1845). Prince Edward Island, Supreme Court, Estates Division, will of John McDonald, 14 June 1872. *Examiner* (Charlottetown), 16 Nov. 1874. *Islander* (Charlottetown), 26 July, 16, 23 Aug. 1844. *Palladium* (Charlottetown), 25 July 1844. R. C. Macdonald, *Sketches of Highlanders: with an account of their early arrival in North America . . .* (Saint John, N.B., 1843).

The arrival of the first Scottish Catholic emigrants

Macdonald

in *Prince Edward Island and after, 1772–1922* (Summerside, P.E.I., 1922), 27, 37–40, 50–53, 110. James Donahoe, *Prince Edward Island priests who have labored or are laboring in the sacred ministry outside the diocese of Charlottetown* (St Paul, Minn., 1912), 3, 25–28. J. C. MacMillan, *The early history of the Catholic Church in Prince Edward Island* (Quebec, 1905), 43–44, 151, 189, 193, 208–9, 279–80, 292–93; *Catholic Church in PEI,* 3–5, 10–11, 45–52, 308. John Prebble, *The Highland clearances* (London, 1969), 12–19. A. F. MacDonald, "Captain John MacDonald, 'Glenalladale,'" CCHA *Report, 1964,* 21–37. Ada MacLeod, "The Glenaladale pioneers," *Dal. Rev.,* XI (1931–32), 311–24. J. F. Snell, "Sir William Macdonald and his kin," *Dal. Rev.,* XXIII (1943–44), 317–30.

MACDONALD, JOHN SANDFIELD, lawyer and politician; b. 12 Dec. 1812 at St Raphael West, Glengarry County, U.C.; d. 1 June 1872 at Cornwall, Ont.

John Sandfield Macdonald's father, Alexander, was a Roman Catholic Highland Scot of Clan Ranald. As a child Alexander had emigrated in 1786 with other Catholics from Scotland to settle in what was to become Upper Canada. He married Nancy Macdonald, the daughter of a distant cousin, and John Sandfield was the first of their five children.

Left without a mother at eight, Sandfield developed the independent and undisciplined character that marked his future political career as an "Ishmaelite." He seemed to dislike the confines of the parish school, attending it only for a few years and, at 16, he took his first job as a clerk in the general store in Lancaster. Later, he had a similar position in Cornwall.

Discontented with his prospects after several years as a clerk, Sandfield was encouraged by a local lawyer to enter the legal profession. In 1832 he enrolled in Cornwall's Eastern District grammar school, the famous training school of the Family Compact, then under the Reverend Hugh Urquhart of the Church of Scotland. Sandfield graduated in 1835 at the top of his class and was articled to Archibald McLean*, a lawyer and leading Tory in Cornwall.

McLean was elevated to the Court of the King's Bench in 1837, and Sandfield became his assistant on the western circuit. It was a position which enabled Sandfield to meet eminent men of the day, including Allan MacNab*, Thomas Talbot*, and William Henry DRAPER under whom he later articled. He was also given a commission as queen's messenger, charged with carrying dispatches between the lieutenant governor in Toronto and the British minister in Washington. On one of these missions the tall, gangling Glengarrian met Marie Christine Waggaman, daughter of George Augustus Waggaman, a former Whig senator from Louisiana originally from the Maryland gentry, and Camille Armault, who came from Louisiana's old French aristocracy. In 1840 Sandfield opened his own law office in Cornwall and in June of that year was called to the bar. Several months later, Christine eloped from her French finishing school in Baltimore with the adventuresome Scot. They were married in New York City in the fall of 1840.

In 1841 Sandfield was drafted by Colonel Alexander Fraser* and John McGillivray*, respectively the Catholic and Presbyterian political lairds of Glengarry, to stand for election to the first Legislative Assembly of the united Province of Canada. His patrons' control over the area was such that Sandfield won by a substantial majority over the Reformer, Dr James Grant, without delivering a single political address. Sandfield became known outside his district as a Draper Conservative but had at this point few fixed ideas on politics. He seemed at times closer to the old-line Tory position of Alexander McLean, MLA for Stormont and brother of his former tutor, Archibald, particularly when Draper's municipal reforms threatened the patronage system of Glengarry. Draper placated Fraser by appointing him first warden of the Eastern District, made up of the counties of Stormont, Dundas, and Glengarry, and Sandfield secured the privilege of delivering the speech of welcome at Cornwall to the new governor general, Sir Charles Bagot*, and of seconding the address-in-reply at the opening of the session of the assembly in 1842. He was jibed at by the old-line Tories for his alleged betrayal. He believed that it was they who made Draper's position untenable and he agreed with Bagot's policies. For these reasons he continued to support the government when it was reorganized along Reform lines with the coming of Robert Baldwin*, Louis-Hippolyte La Fontaine*, Augustin-Norbert Morin*, and others. Moreover, the new council was prepared to serve Glengarry well: a generous provincial grant for district education was obtained and patronage jobs were given to supporters. Sandfield himself became a lieutenant-colonel in the 4th Regiment of the Glengarry militia. Aided by his own and Christine's flair for entertaining, he was fast becoming his own master in Glengarry.

Sandfield went into opposition on the resignation of the Reform ministers in November 1846, following the dispute with Governor General Charles Metcalfe* over patronage. The Glengarrian thus took the decisive step in affixing to himself the label of Reformer and joined Baldwin's crusade for responsible government; he was to remain a self-proclaimed "Baldwinite" until his death. Despite Draper's successful attempt in most of Canada West (still popularly called Upper Canada) in the ensuing election to condemn Reformers as disloyal and inimical to British institutions, Sandfield was easily returned in Glengarry and helped defeat McLean in Stormont.

The tide began to turn to Reform and Sandfield's influence increased. He had his own weekly newspaper, the Cornwall *Freeholder*, and won re-election in 1848 despite the intervention of the Catholic bishop Patrick Phelan*, who implied that the faithful should vote for the Tories. The La Fontaine–Baldwin ministry was formed with a majority from both Lower Canada (Canada East) and Upper Canada and responsible government seemed secure. To Baldwin, patronage was its vital concomitant and, in and around Glengarry and Cornwall, Sandfield was its chief purveyor. He supported Baldwin's municipal reforms in 1849 (although securing the survival of the Eastern District as the United Counties of Stormont, Dundas, and Glengarry), and held Glengarry for Lord Elgin [Bruce*] during the crisis over the rebellion losses bill despite Fraser's objections. Late that same year, he became both a queen's counsel and Baldwin's solicitor general for Upper Canada. In 1850 Sandfield's followers made a clean sweep in the local municipal elections.

Sandfield's personal fortunes were also rising. He was steadily acquiring property and his legal practice had so expanded that he was forced to hire two assistants. "No barrister," claimed the *Globe*, later to be his most insistent critic, "stands higher in the estimation of mercantile men." In 1849 his family, then including three daughters and a son, moved into Ivy Hall, the stately residence that had once housed the imperial garrison in Cornwall. Later there were two more children.

Once formal responsible government was secure, Reform forces began to disintegrate, and in 1851 La Fontaine and Baldwin resigned. Francis Hincks* tried to reorganize the government and Sandfield now expected to succeed Baldwin as attorney general west. Hincks personally disliked Sandfield, however, considering him too independent-minded, and felt it essential also to regain the support of the Clear Grits, the Upper Canadian radical democrats. Using an unsuspecting Sandfield as a go-between, Hincks succeeded in bringing two Clear Grits into the cabinet and secretly asked William Buell Richards* to be attorney general. Knowing the effect it would have on Sandfield, Hincks wrote him a condescending letter blaming him for the Clear Grit demand for two cabinet positions rather than one. The enraged Glen-

garrian resigned as solicitor general. He never forgave Hincks for turning him out "to pasture like an old horse."

Sandfield had become essentially an independent Reformer but, after the elections of December 1851 and his own flattering return by acclamation, he had a considerable following in the assembly from eastern Upper Canada. In recognition of his power and, no doubt, to mute his voice, Hincks offered him the speakership. After considerable hesitation, he accepted. As speaker, however, he was unable to voice his and his constituents' dissatisfaction with the government's support of sectarian colleges and separate schools and with its hesitation in abolishing the clergy reserves and other examples of denominational privilege in Upper Canada. In Glengarry, the relationship between Protestant and Roman Catholic Scots was a friendly one. This experience, his own individualism, and the alienation of the Catholic Scots from the church hierarchy, securely in militant Irish hands, shaped Sandfield's highly secular attitudes toward church and state relations. He was himself only nominally Catholic.

The speaker was also greatly displeased with the profusion of railway scandals, some involving the premier himself. To increase his frustration, he was forced in 1853 to take a rest of six months in Europe because of lung trouble which was to leave him a semi-invalid. While in London, he made a dubious deal by which his brothers, Alexander Francis and Donald Alexander*, were to construct the portion of the Grand Trunk Railway between Farrans Point in Stormont and Montreal.

The speakership was a burden but it gave Sandfield one of his greatest moments. The government did not resign after defeat in the speech from the throne debate at the opening of the 1854 session. Instead of calling for a new ministry Elgin appeared two days after the vote to dissolve the house. Before he could read the closing address, an irate Sandfield delivered a stern rebuke, in English and French, questioning the constitutionality of Elgin's actions. Dissolution followed, but the outspoken speaker became overnight a popular hero as the defender of the constitution against tyranny. He was returned by acclamation in Glengarry, and George BROWN of the *Globe* even pledged support to any government he formed if it was dedicated to the separation of church and state and to representation by population. Sandfield could hardly have accepted the latter proposition; as a central Canadian with Montreal as his metropolis, he was dedicated to the dual nature of the united province. He believed that government should not be carried on against the wishes of a

463

Macdonald

majority from one or other of its two historic sections.

The election proved inconclusive but it seemed that Sandfield, with the backing of Brown, dissident Reform elements, and moderate Conservatives, would become premier of Canada. This did not happen. Although Hincks was defeated in the house, he and others were able to effect a coalition with the Conservative faction. Elgin summoned MacNab of the Tories, not Sandfield, and Morin and the rest of the Lower Canadian wing of the old government held firm.

Sandfield was left as the leader of a disunited Reform opposition made up of Brown, the Clear Grits, the Rouges or Lower Canadian radicals, Sandfield's own following, and a few other scattered Baldwinites. Sandfield refused to support Brown's policies, including representation by population, and relations between them deteriorated during the sessions of 1855 and 1856. Sandfield ceased to be leader of the opposition and their cooperation ended when Brown mounted a scathing personal attack in 1856 against a resolution by Sandfield favouring official endorsation of the principle of the double majority. Brown seemed, meanwhile, to be taking over and absorbing the more radical Clear Grits.

Sandfield's health was also declining and in 1857 he lost the use of one lung. Because of his weakened condition, he turned over his large rural constituency of Glengarry to his brother Donald Alexander, retaining the riding of Cornwall with its fewer than 700 voters for himself. Both brothers won in the elections of November 1857. With Reform victories elsewhere, the Conservative government failed to gain an Upper Canadian majority. In early 1858, John A. Macdonald*, now premier, offered Sandfield a ministerial post to gain support in the eastern counties. It was doubtful whether Sandfield ever intended to join the government. He took a tough line, demanding for Reformers three of the six Upper Canadian seats. John A. was unwilling to go that far. Sandfield then telegraphed a simple "No Go."

When the cabinet was defeated in July on the seat of government question, Sandfield reluctantly agreed to serve as attorney general west in the government formed by George Brown. This "most ephemeral government" met defeat in the house and, being refused dissolution, lasted less than 48 hours. The chief Reformers were out of the house seeking re-election, as they were required to do on accepting portfolios, and a somewhat strengthened old gang under George-Étienne CARTIER returned through the dubious manœuvre known as the "Double Shuffle." Sandfield took part in the ensuing opposition tour of the province

denouncing the actions of Cartier, John A. Macdonald, and Governor General Edmund Head*, but privately he was convinced that Brown's impatience to seize office had led to the Reform downfall. To Sandfield, Brown was a leader incapable of getting a Lower Canadian majority to accept him. He could not understand the adulation heaped upon Brown in the western peninsula and once snapped to Charles Clarke*, in Elora: "Can't you do anything without George Brown . . .?" Consequently, Sandfield gradually moved closer to Louis-Victor Sicotte* and other members from Lower Canada, who had become alienated from Cartier and might be termed "Mauves," and farther away from the Free Kirk, Toronto-based, Victorian Liberal George Brown.

The two great Reformers clashed bitterly and personally in 1859 and 1860 in the assembly and in the press over the source of compensation to the former seigneurs of Lower Canada for the loss in 1854 of their casual dues. Was this to come from general revenue or, as Brown claimed he had proposed, from some special levy on Lower Canada alone? In a dualistic country such as Canada, Sandfield argued, Brown could not be a leader, and did nothing now but disrupt Reform and prevent it from achieving power. In all this, Sandfield found a friend and ally in Josiah Blackburn*, influential owner and editor of the London Free Press.

Sandfield also became embroiled in the other major split within Reform. In the spring of 1859, when the Globe was temporarily under the editorial direction of George Sheppard*, the paper urged the dissolution of the union and the abandonment of the British parliamentary system for the republican version operating in some mid-western American states. This proposal was as unacceptable to Sandfield as was Brown's advocacy of the single majority in the assembly. In the fall, Brown called for a great Reform convention in Toronto to reassert his authority and to secure endorsement for "rep by pop" and Canadian federalism. Not happy with conventions, especially those held in Toronto under Brown's leadership, Sandfield refused to attend and few delegates were present from east of Cobourg. Division continued and, despite Brown's protestations of strength after the convention, Sandfield argued through the London Free Press that Brown's followers were the smallest faction of Reform, the dissolutionists second, and the Baldwinites the largest. He was willing to admit that rep by pop was perhaps desirable at some future date if Upper Canada continued to grow, but he emphasized that double majority was more important for harmony, goodwill, and necessary reform.

By March 1860, Sandfield had determined to

overthrow Brown as leader of Upper Canadian Reform and began again to attend Reform caucuses. Rumours of a Sandfield–Sicotte alliance increased as both men tried to form closer links with the Rouges and some restless Bleus. They would be "Baldwinite Reformers," and, like Baldwin, Sandfield argued that, to be viable, Reform had to avoid doctrinaire, sectarian, and sectional stands. The problems of the union were the agitation from the southwestern peninsula and unsuitable men in government, not the constitution.

Sandfield and Sicotte failed in their attempt at reconstruction. Michael Foley*, considered a potential rallying point in the west, succumbed to Brown's pressure by voting in May 1850 for his resolutions in the assembly declaring the union a failure and calling for a redivision, to be linked by "some joint authority." Foley attempted to reconcile Brown and Sandfield but their relations grew increasingly bitter. Sandfield stayed away from the caucus during the session of 1861, and continued to cooperate with Sicotte and other sympathetic French-Canadians. A small triumph came when his motion, seconded by Foley, criticizing the government for its failure to have an Upper Canadian majority, narrowly missed acceptance (49 to 64), and helped force the Conservatives to declare the basis of representation an open question. But if Reform was not able to unite on the constitutional question, it could on most non-sectional economic issues. A motion moved by Sandfield and seconded by Antoine-Aimé Dorion*, the Rouge chief, condemning the government for financial mismanagement, failed by only a few votes. Nevertheless, Reform disunity helped the Conservatives in the 1861 elections. Brown was personally defeated and his monopoly on rep by pop destroyed when some Conservatives adopted the programme. The *London Free Press* bluntly called him a "government impossibility." Sandfield was again on his way up.

It was true that John A. Macdonald gained in Upper Canada but Cartier lost ground to Sandfield's ally, Sicotte, in Lower Canada. When 16 more Lower Canadians switched over to Sicotte to defeat Cartier's militia bill, the governor general, Lord Monck*, summoned Sandfield who had stayed in the background during the defence debate. Sandfield accepted and was sworn in as attorney general west on 24 May 1862, with Sicotte as his associate (he had been passed over lest the British authorities be enraged because he had caused the militia bill to fail).

Premier Sandfield Macdonald's government was dominated by Baldwinites and Mauves, although it did contain Dorion and William McDougall*, and it was dedicated to the double majority. Difficulties were many: the province was torn by sectional and sectarian tensions, and a civil conflagration raging south of the border threatened Canada. At the same time Britain viewed the province with disdain and condescension. Sandfield secured approval of a measure that doubled the size of the provincial voluntary militia and provided for the encouragement of unpaid units. The defence budget was three times that of 1861 but less than one third that provided in Cartier's bill. After it completed routine business Sandfield had the restless assembly prorogued in June 1862 and did not have it reassembled until 1863. In that interval he prepared legislation and pared expenditures.

He also tried to cope with the Duke of Newcastle, the irate colonial secretary, in order to improve Anglo-Canadian relations. Reasserting the argument that the defence of Canada was primarily a Canadian responsibility, Newcastle virtually demanded an active Canadian militia of 50,000 trained men. On 24 Sept. 1862, in Sandfield's most important state paper, he and his cabinet informed Newcastle that Canada would support such a costly military force only during a state of war or imminent invasion. The province, it continued, had no quarrel with the United States; if war came, Canada would loyally respond, yet war would only come as the result of a British-American feud. Enlarging the militia would require direct taxation, which no Canadian government could sustain. The cabinet rejected Newcastle's suggestion that army funds be placed beyond the control of the Canadian legislature as totally unacceptable to "a people inheriting the freedom guaranteed by British institutions." It urged Britain to consider any Canadian expenditure on the construction of the Intercolonial Railway as expenditure for imperial defence. If he was unsuccessful with Newcastle, to whom the arguments were "buncombe," Sandfield gradually brought Monck to an understanding of the realities of Canadian politics, and the two men developed a close and lasting friendship.

Sandfield met the assembly with optimism in early 1863: internal divisions seemed to have subsided, the administration was going well, and he could report that the volunteer force had reached 25,000 men. Nevertheless, the old disruptive issues remained unresolved, and they appeared in the crucial debate over Richard Scott*'s government-supported separate school bill. The issue of separate schools for the Roman Catholic minority of Upper Canada had bedevilled Canadian politics since at least 1850. The Scott bill, in its final emasculated form, seemed aimed mainly at clarifying the Étienne-Paschal Taché* act of 1856, which had been passed against a majority from Upper Canada, and it only slightly extended the privileges of the minority. Sandfield personally opposed the religious segregation of children but accepted the bill to achieve educational tranquillity, as did Egerton Ryerson*, the chief superintendent of education in Upper Canada. Scott and the representatives of the Irish hierarchy agreed that it would serve as the final settlement of their demands.

Both the Clear Grits and the Orangemen were in an uproar. Two events now changed the whole political situation: Dorion's withdrawal from the cabinet because of his opposition to expenditures on the Intercolonial, and Brown's reappearance in the assembly after winning a by-election. The Scott bill, backed by Sandfield, John A. Macdonald, Sicotte, Cartier, and Dorion, carried but without a majority from Upper Canada. Sandfield was furious with Brown and the Grits and he vainly argued that the passage of Scott's bill did not really invalidate the double majority because his government retained the support of the two majorities. Sicotte's hold on the erstwhile Bleu supporters, however, was faltering and there was a drift back to Cartier. The government was defeated in the assembly on 8 May even though it regained its majority in Upper Canada when Brown declared that he preferred John S. to John A. and Cartier.

Monck granted Sandfield a dissolution and Sandfield began secret negotiations with Brown, Dorion, Luther HOLTON, and Oliver Mowat* aimed at a reconstruction. He and others kept the double majority as their personal conviction but the government had to declare the basis of representation an open question. Sicotte was dropped for Dorion as Sandfield's chief associate, and Sicotte, Michael Foley, D'Arcy McGee*, and other dropped ministers turned with a vengeance on their former chief. In the ensuing elections, "re-united" Reform swept Upper Canada but in the sweep Brown gained most. In Lower Canada the Mauves had already disintegrated, and although Dorion and his Rouges slightly improved their position, they could not win the majority. With a shaky lead of one, Sandfield could no longer govern in the image of La Fontaine and Baldwin.

Yet the régime survived through 1863 and made considerable progress. Plans for departmental and fiscal reforms matured. Sandfield secured the passage, with double majorities, of two defence bills which reorganized the militia, providing for service battalions, a volunteer force of 35,000, and a defence budget over twice that of 1862. Even the British press was impressed with these bills and with Finance Minister Holton's restrained, though still unbalanced, budget. Brown himself seemed mellowed as he and Sandfield even entertained each other. The survey of the Intercolonial, but not the construction, was undertaken by Sandford Fleming* at Canadian expense, despite Dorion's misgivings, alleviating somewhat Maritime distrust of Canadians, especially of Canadian Reformers. The government was also working on an unprecedented audit bill which would establish careful legislative scrutiny of departmental expenditures.

The old chronic deterioration then recommenced, and the tiny majority evaporated. Brown became hostile over cabinet changes, over Holton's Montreal orientation in fiscal policies, and finally over Sandfield's attempt to secure support from "loose fish" members in the Ottawa area. A vital by-election was lost. The assembly gathered in February 1864 with the opposition under Cartier eager and ready for the kill. It talked parliament to a standstill. Sandfield tried desperately to break loose from Brown by combining with Sir É.-P. Taché and other Bleus but failed and resigned on 22 March. The audit bill, his main legislative achievement, became law under his successor.

The régime which followed Sandfield's fared even worse, falling within three months. Canada had reached a political impasse which reflected the centrifugal forces within the province; the political problem was not deadlock arising from two solid, equally matched phalanxes facing one another in the assembly but the impossibility of forming an executive in this multi-party situation where every government was a coalition.

Sandfield, with Monck's backing, had attempted an unusual coalition with Taché that would consist of Reformers from Upper Canada and Bleus from Lower Canada. This was a precedent, but it failed, partly because it did not propose major constitutional change. In June, the "Great Coalition" involving Brown, Cartier, John A. Macdonald, and Alexander Tilloch Galt* was formed, dedicated to seek release from the impasse "by introducing the federal principle into Canada" and, if possible, by a linking of the Maritimes to the new system. Sandfield opposed federalism, which he considered a prodigal, divisive, and un-British system, one which would split "Central Canada" by cutting most of the upper St Lawrence off from its natural *entrepôt* in Montreal, but he did not necessarily disapprove of coalition or even British North American union. For the next three years he found himself on the side-lines leading a small disunited band of Upper Canadian Reformers, some of whom were Clear Grits, against union.

Sandfield expressed his viewpoint in the Canadian confederation debates in 1865. He was incensed by the haste with which a strange coalition, along with the British government and the Grand Trunk Railway, was demanding a major and indefinite constitutional rearrangement, even though the "disruption" of the union had not been an issue in the last election. The Canadian problem, he argued, was not really the present constitution but "demagogues and designing persons who sought to create strife between the sections." The assembly did nevertheless approve the Quebec resolutions by a double majority, and Sandfield and Dorion later failed in their attempt to secure referral of the Quebec or subsequent London scheme to the people through a general election. The expectant Canadian Fathers would brook no notions of popular sovereignty.

Sandfield was a realist and soon accepted confederation itself as inevitable. During the latter part of the 1866 session he concerned himself mainly with trying to nudge the proposed constitution of Ontario toward his line of thought. He fully accepted supervision of provincial legislation but opposed, as a violation of responsible government, the prohibition against provincial tampering with separate schools.

Where would he fit politically in the new scheme of things? Brown, his constructive work completed, had left the great coalition but John A. was determined to preserve it; without it, the Conservatives' extremely weak position in Ontario might prove his political undoing in the new dominion parliament. With Brown and most of the Grits in opposition denouncing continuing coalition, the two Macdonalds were drawn toward one another and had serious talks in mid-1867. Given Monck's enthusiastic approval, and counselled by John A. Macdonald's chief confidant in Toronto, Senator David Macpherson*, the provisional lieutenant governor of Ontario, Sir Henry William STISTED, asked Sandfield Macdonald to become the first premier of Ontario. His coalition government was sworn in on 15 and 20 July 1867; besides the premier, who became attorney general, the cabinet contained another Baldwinite, a coalition Grit, and two Conservatives.

The "royal choice" had now to be submitted to the verdict of the electorate. In Ontario this was a unique election: voting for federal and provincial candidates took place at the same time and the two first ministers, the two Macdonalds, "hunted in pairs," crossing and recrossing the province trying to work out compromises and deals so that Coalition Reformers and Conservatives would face only "factious" Grits. When the count for the Ontario legislature was in, it was clear that about 50 of 82 members, with more Conservatives than Reformers, were prepared to follow the "Patent Combination" led by the gaunt and sickly lawyer from Cornwall, himself elected to both parliaments.

With a great martial display, Sandfield had Ontario's first legislature opened on 27 Dec. 1867. The ensuing session went well and its greatest achievement was undoubtedly Stephen Richards*' homestead act. It was modelled on the American act of 1862 and provided for virtually free land for homesteaders on surveyed crown lands of Muskoka, Haliburton, and north Hastings. Another act encouraged the northern extension of railways into these "free land grant" areas, and during the next three years this policy of northern development was broadened, further liberalized, and extended to include growing concern for forestry and mining developments as well as for settlement.

Sandfield showed his predilection for the separation of church and state and for retrenchment by concentrating aid on the University of Toronto and cutting off the rather feeble denominational colleges, over Ryerson's and Sir John's objections, but with opposition approval. Sandfield later regained Ryerson's confidence by supporting his plan to reorganize the primary and secondary school systems: free schooling, compulsory attandance, standard teaching qualifications, more emphasis on science in the curriculum, and municipal financial support for both levels were all part of this proposal. The Liberal opposition, led by Edward Blake*, fought the bill, especially its compulsory and centralizing features, so vehemently that it was not passed until 1871. The same year enabling legislation was passed for the Ontario School of Agriculture, opened in 1874 (later the Ontario Agricultural College, now the University of Guelph), and a technical college (ultimately the Ryerson Polytechnical Institute).

Sandfield's other important legislation was the election act of 1868, which established "same day" elections throughout Ontario and considerably broadened the franchise, and in the field of social welfare institutions. His prison and asylum inspection act of 1868 and other subsequent measures gave his fighting inspector J. W. Langmuir* vastly increased powers to begin the long overdue task of prison and hospital inspection and reform. Large additions were begun on the Toronto Asylum for the Insane and an asylum was established in London. He also had constructed the Ontario Institution for the Deaf and Dumb in Belleville and the Ontario Institution for the Blind in Brantford.

Macdonald

Solid and substantial as these reforms were, they failed to capture the Ontario mind. Instead, Grit accusations that Sandfield was a kept man, vassal of the Canadian prime minister, gained more and more credence. There was little substance to the charge; surviving correspondence clearly shows this. Sir John's chief complaint was that Sandfield was too independent for his own good and for the proper operation of the new and, as Sir John vainly hoped, highly centralized system. In fact, Sandfield, like Sir John, really preferred United Kingdom–style legislative union but accepted the quasi-federalism of the British North America Act, which clearly seemed to provide for provincial subordination to the central government in Ottawa. Admitting this system, Sandfield was as much his own master as he dared, and he chafed when Sir John declined to consult him about senior Ontario appointments.

Despite disagreements, Sandfield and Sir John again "hunted in pairs" in 1868 and went to Nova Scotia to persuade Joseph Howe to accept confederation. Then, in the summer of 1869, the prime minister infuriated Sandfield by appointing his old enemy, Sir Francis Hincks, lately returned to Canada, as minister of finance and McDougall's replacement as Reform leader in the cabinet. To Sandfield, the old railway broker was neither a Reformer nor an honest man. Late in 1869 and early in 1870, Sandfield was involved in various schemes aimed at overthrowing Sir John and creating some new kind of combination, perhaps under himself or Cartier. At one point he even had discussions with Brown. Nothing came of these plots, and the Grits prepared instead to destroy Sandfield. They were assisted by the revival of anti-French feelings accompanying Louis Riel*'s adventures on the Red River, when Sandfield's identification with Sir John caused him to be included in accusations made against the latter.

Sandfield was vulnerable from the candid and rather crude way in which he used the patronage system, a system which he, like Baldwin, believed to be an essential aspect of responsible government. He did not regard the Ontario legislature as a sovereign parliament, moreover, and emphasized the role of the provincial cabinet. Though noted and abused for his personal parsimony, he had the legislature vote large, only vaguely appropriated amounts of money for governmental expenditure. When, in 1871, $1,500,000 from the huge provincial surplus was voted for purposes of aiding the northern extension of railways, the Grits had a popular issue although it has never been shown that any of the money was improperly expended.

The results of the spring election of 1871 were inconclusive. The Grits made the campaign for the defence of Ontario rights almost a holy crusade. Sandfield's efforts were seriously curtailed by his rapidly declining health. He had been suffering repeatedly from long "infernal colds" and had to spend most of the campaign in bed with rheumatic pains and high fever. Equally serious, Sir John, in Washington for the protracted negotiations which would lead to the Anglo-American treaty, was unable to pull the usual strings. But although the Grits swept most of the western peninsula with the exception of London they did not have a clear majority; a very ill Sandfield determined to carry on and meet the legislature even if he had "to be carried there in a blanket."

One of his own reforms proved his undoing. The Grits charged irregularities in the election of six Sandfield men but were themselves only charged for one. The Controverted Elections Act of 1871 took decisions on electoral irregularities out of partisan committees of the legislature to the courts; it also provided, unwisely, that while the matter was before the courts, the member whose election was being investigated could not take his seat. Under the stern provisions of the law, by-elections had also to be called, but they could only be called after parliament opened, which it finally did on 7 Dec. 1871.

With so many vacancies, Sandfield claimed that a non-confidence vote could not overthrow his government but Blake moved the motion nonetheless. He chose the issue of the railway appropriation, an astonishing motion because it really attacked the former legislature, not the cabinet. It carried by seven votes. Sandfield refused to resign, but the one Grit coalitionist in the cabinet, Edmund Burke Wood*, joined forces with Blake. The assembly was paralysed and the speaker, R. W. Scott, whom Sandfield had appointed in an attempt at mollification after the Sandfield Macdonald family had repeatedly clashed with him on social, economic, and political issues, appeared to act in support of Blake's position. All efforts at a compromise failed. Sandfield's support ebbed away and efforts to adjourn failed. On 19 February he announced the resignation of his government and Blake became premier in a cabinet which included Scott. Despite its fall from power, Sandfield's coalition, ironically, won all but one of the by-elections called.

Although Sandfield occasionally reappeared in the assembly, his health prevented him from acting as leader of the opposition, and this role was taken up by Matthew Crooks Cameron*. He also gave up law, which he had practised in partnership with John and Donald Ban MacLennan. He had concentrated on real estate law, and it had made him a wealthy man. He was, however, able to play the key role in securing the services of Thomas Charles Patteson* as editor of a new broadly financed daily, the Toronto *Mail*, to challenge the *Globe* and act as the Ontario spokesman for both the Ontario opposition and Sir John A.'s government.

Confined to bed in March 1872, Sandfield blithely wrote Patteson that he secretly believed that he had "a touch of the horse distemper." But in May doctors informed him that his heart was so "displaced and impaired" from previous illness that death was imminent; he took the news bravely and philosophically. On 1 June he died at Ivy Hall.

Throughout his career, John Sandfield Macdonald was enigmatic, and there is still no agreement among historians as to his stature. Usually a lighthearted and an affable man, he and his wife were famous for their gala entertaining. He could, however, when slighted or attacked, be vindictive and sustain a grudge. Although not a truly great man he did give Ontario four good years of service, efficiently establish the machinery of provincial government, and carefully and creatively begin the long process of reform and construction which the paralysis of pre-confederation politics had so long delayed. But Ontario was not really his focus; instead it was the old "central Canada," based on Montreal and expressed in the "bicultural" Province of Canada.

As premier of Canada, Sandfield had lowered the temperature of sectional, sectarian, and cultural conflict, though the specific constitutional details of his double majority were hardly realizable; he thus made the Great Coalition and confederation more attainable. His central concept of Canada as a land of two majorities has again now found increasing acceptance. Sandfield's opposition to the details of the Quebec scheme and to the procedures for implementing it might show some lack of realism or foresight but hardly, as has been claimed, a lack of vision. It was not union but the American kind of federalism which he opposed. On the other hand, as premier, he accepted the system established by John A. Macdonald and can therefore scarcely be accused of betraying Ontario because he did not endorse the new doctrine of provincial rights and coordinate federalism that the Grits were now successfully advancing.

As a political leader he was not able, as did George Brown or Sir John A. Macdonald, to secure a large body of geographically dispersed followers dedicated to him personally. He was essentially a central Canadian based in Cornwall, looking as much to Montreal as to Toronto, not

the best of places from which to lead Upper Canadian Reform.

BRUCE W. HODGINS

[A complete list of the sources, primary and secondary, used in the preparation of this biography for the period up to March 1864 in given in the author's "The political career of John Sandfield Macdonald to the fall of his administration in March 1864: a study in Canadian politics," unpublished PHD thesis, Duke University, 1964. A selective bibliography appears in the author's *John Sandfield Macdonald, 1812–1872* (Toronto, 1970). B.W.H.]

MTCL, Baldwin papers. PAC, MG 24, B30 (Macdonald-Langlois papers); B40 (Brown papers); MG 26, A (Macdonald papers); MG 27, II, D14 (Scott papers). Queen's University Archives, Alexander Mackenzie papers. Canada, Province of, *Confederation debates*; Legislative Assembly, *Journals*. Ontario, Legislative Assembly, *Journals*, 1867–72. *Globe* (Toronto), 1844–72. *Leader* (Toronto), 1852–72. *London Free Press*, 1849–64. *Mail* (Toronto), 1872. *Quebec Daily Mercury*, 1862–64. "A letter on the Reform party, 1860: Sandfield Macdonald and the *London Free Press*," ed. B. W. Hodgins and E. H. Jonse, *Ont. Hist.*, LVII (1965), 39–45.

Careless, *Brown*. Chapais, *Histoire du Canada*, VI–VIII. Cornell, *Alignment of political groups*. Dent, *Last forty years*. B. W. Hodgins, "Attitudes toward democracy during the pre-confederation decade," unpublished MA thesis, Queen's University (Kingston, Ont.), 1955. Morton, *Critical years*. Waite, *Life and times of confederation*. B. W. Hodgins, "Democracy and the Ontario fathers of confederation," *Profiles of a province: studies in the history of Ontario* (Ont. Hist. Soc. pub., Toronto, 1967), 83–91; "John Sandfield Macdonald and the crisis of 1863," CHA *Report, 1965*, 30–45.

MacDONELL, DONALD AENEAS, soldier, politician, and public servant; b. in Charlottenburg Township, U.C., 31 July 1794, son of Isabella McDonell and Miles Macdonell*, who came to Upper Canada from Schoharie County, N.Y., after the American Revolution and who was chosen by Lord Selkirk [Douglas*] to be the first governor of Assiniboia (1811–15); m. Mary McDonell, daughter of Archibald MacDonell of Leek, by whom he had several children; d. 11 March 1879, at Brockville, Ont.

Donald Aeneas MacDonell attended John Strachan*'s school at Cornwall. He then served during the War of 1812 in the British regular forces in Upper Canada. Commissioned an ensign in the 8th Regiment in 1813, he took part in the engagements at Stoney Creek, Lundy's Lane, Sackets Harbor, and York (Toronto). In 1815 he exchanged into the 98th Regiment as a lieutenant and served in England and in Nova Scotia. He was placed on half-pay in 1817 with the rank of lieutenant and returned to Stormont County,

MacDonnell

Upper Canada. He had also a long career in the militia, serving with the 1st Battalion of Stormont as an officer and ultimately (1846–50) as its commanding officer. During the uprising in Lower Canada in November 1838, he commanded the regiment on a special expedition to Beauharnois, where rebels had seized the manor house of the seigneury of Beauharnois and taken prisoner Edward Ellice Jr; when the force arrived, the rebels had already fled.

In 1834 MacDonell had been appointed a justice of the peace for the Eastern District (the counties of Stormont, Dundas, and Glengarry) and in the same year was elected to the House of Assembly of Upper Canada for Stormont as a Reformer. He was re-elected in Stormont in 1836 but was then defeated three times, in 1841, 1844, and 1847, in bids for a seat in the Legislative Assembly of the Province of Canada. In April 1848 he was appointed crown lands agent and sheriff of the Eastern District, but in November of the same year he became warden of the Provincial Penitentiary at Kingston, on the suspension of the then warden, Henry Smith*, as a result of the investigations of a committee of which George BROWN was secretary. In 1850 his position as warden was made permanent and he held this post until 1869. More humane (and economical) than Smith, he was personally popular with the staff and inspectors until increasing infirmity brought some complaints about his effectiveness toward the end of his career.

His last years were spent in Brockville, Ontario, in somewhat straitened circumstances and much of his time was devoted to an attempt to recover arrears in salary and a larger retiring gratuity to which he believed he was entitled.

J. K. JOHNSON

PAC, MG 26, A (Macdonald papers), 300/1, letterbooks 5–7; 276341–429; RG 5, Cl, 512, nos.818, 820; RG 9, I, B5, 6; C4, 5; RG 68, 1. G.B., WO, *A list of the officers of the Army and of the Corps of Royal Marines*, 1813–17. *Dom. ann. reg.*, *1879*. L. H. Irving, *Officers of the British forces in Canada during the war of 1812–15* (Welland, Ont., 1908). Cornell, *Alignment of political groups*.

MacDONNELL, ROBERT LEA, doctor, author, and professor; b. 1818 at Dublin, Ireland, son of Robert MacDonnell, a prominent Dublin doctor, and Margaret Lea; d. 31 Jan. 1878 at Montreal, Que.

Robert Lea MacDonnell was orphaned in infancy; he was entrusted, with his three sisters and his brother Richard, who later followed him to Canada, to the care of a paternal uncle, the Reverend George MacDonnell, rector of Trinity College, Dublin. Robert completed his elementary schooling in Scotland before registering, in 1835, at Trinity College, where he studied medicine. He passed the degree examinations in 1841 and was admitted to the Royal College of Surgeons of Ireland. The following year he married Margaret Croates, by whom he had three children. Shortly afterwards MacDonnell began to collaborate regularly in the editing of the *Journal of Medical Science*, published at Dublin, where he taught anatomy in a private school. In addition, he took part in the sessions of the Pathological Society of Dublin. He obtained another degree in 1844, from the King's and Queen's College of Physicians of Ireland.

During 1845 Dr MacDonnell took up residence at Montreal, after being nominated to the chair of medicine at McGill University. In the same year he was appointed secretary of the Montreal Medico-Chirurgical Society, and until 1847 collaborated in the editing of the *British American Journal of Medical and Physical Science*. In 1849 MacDonnell accepted the post of director of the Department of Clinical Medicine at McGill, while still retaining his positions as professor in the faculty and as practitioner attached to the Montreal General Hospital.

MacDonnell spent a few months at the University of Toronto in 1850, then returned to Montreal. He worked as a surgeon at St Patrick's Hospital, and in 1851 founded the St Lawrence School of Medicine. The following year the school went out of existence, and MacDonnell started the *Canada Medical Journal* . . . , a periodical which replaced the *British American Journal* but ceased to appear in February 1853. At this period Dr MacDonnell enjoyed an enviable reputation in the field of gynaecology.

In 1866, following the cholera epidemic that swept through Europe, the Canadian government created a board of health and entrusted the presidency of it to Dr MacDonnell. Robert Lea MacDonnell died on 31 Jan. 1878 of injuries received two days earlier in a road accident, on his way back from the funeral of his *confrère* Hector PELTIER.

JEAN-PIERRE CHALIFOUX

British American Journal of Medical and Physical Science (Montreal), 1845–47. *Canada Medical and Surgical Journal* (Montreal), VI (1878), 382, 422–27. *Canada Medical Journal and Monthly Record* (Montreal), 1 March 1852 – Feb. 1853. Abbott, *History of medicine*, 56, 67–69. J. J. Heagerty, *Four centuries of medical history in Canada and a sketch of the medical history of Newfoundland* (2v., Toronto, 1928), II, 71, 119–20. *Some historical and personal notes on the Tynekill branch of the MacDonnell family* (Dublin,

1892), 33–34 (copy in the Osler Library, McGill University).

McDOUGALL, GEORGE MILLWARD, Methodist clergyman and missionary, b. 9 Sept. 1821 at Kingston, U.C.; d. 25 Jan. 1876 near Fort Calgary.

George Millward McDougall's parents were Highland Scots. His father was stationed in Kingston as a non-commissioned officer in the Royal Navy during the War of 1812, and he himself, when a youth, served during the rebellion of 1837 in a militia unit, the Royal Foresters. Later he migrated with his parents to a farm near Barrie, Upper Canada. Though his elementary education was slight, he early learned the many pioneer skills needed in his future mission in the far west. On 10 Jan. 1842 he married Elizabeth Chantler, an English-born woman of Quaker parents. They had eight children, including John Chantler*, who became his father's assistant in missionary work, and David, a trader and rancher supplying the missions.

After religious conversion in meetings held by a Methodist lay preacher, Peter White, McDougall became a lay preacher also and offered himself for the ministry. He attended Victoria College, Cobourg, C.W., during the winter term of 1849–50, and then went to Alderville where he became assistant "on trial" to the veteran educator of Indians, the Reverend William Case*. McDougall's early service as missionary was at Garden River and at Rama, near Orillia. He was ordained by the Methodist conference at Belleville, C.W., in June 1854.

In 1860 McDougall was appointed to the Rossville mission, near Norway House, HBC territory, and made chairman of the Methodist district extending from Oxford House and Rainy Lake (Lac La Pluie) to the Rocky Mountains. After visits to the missions in the Norway House area, he undertook an exploratory trip into the Saskatchewan valley in 1862. He conferred with fellow missionaries and with the Crees, and promised to become resident there the following year. In 1863 he and his family did indeed travel in HBC York boats up the Saskatchewan River, perhaps the first family in the vanguard of Ontario pioneers who settled in Alberta in the 1860s.

McDougall established a mission, Victoria (Pakan), on the North Saskatchewan River about 80 miles east of Edmonton House. His immediate task was to reinforce the religious work begun by the English Wesleyan missionary Robert Terrill Rundle* in 1840–48 and being continued by Henry Bird Steinhauer* and Thomas Woolsey,

and to demonstrate to the Indians a way of life based on settlement and agriculture. On a fertile river bench, McDougall constructed the mission as the nucleus of a model pioneer settlement. Soon Indians and Métis (some of the latter from the Red River Settlement) took river lots on either side of the mission. With meagre equipment, seed grain and garden seeds were sown and agriculture taught, and homes and auxiliary buildings, a school and a church, were constructed. McDougall made numerous missionary journeys to his nomadic people in remote areas.

His son John was pressed into service to reopen a mission which they named Woodville, at the northwest end of Pigeon Lake. This mission was on an overland trail midway between Edmonton and Rocky Mountain Houses, accessible to both Stoney and Blackfoot tribes from the south.

The period from the transfer of the HBC territory in 1869 to the acquisition of the land by treaties with the Indians and the entry of the North-West Mounted Police in 1874, was one of distress and uncertainty in the North West. The buffalo migrated beyond the usual hunting ranges, crops failed, and game animals were visibly diminishing. The long-established authority of the HBC was set aside for a civil government previously unknown. The North-West Rebellion of 1869–70 made the procurement of food, goods, and mail service difficult for the missionaries. Then followed the smallpox epidemic of 1870. McDougall did his best with the remedies and medical knowledge he had. All his household were affected except his wife, and three of his daughters died. McDougall was appointed to a board of health, which reported that 3,512 persons died in the epidemic, approximately one-third of the native population. About this time McDougall built at the Victoria mission possibly the earliest hospital in present-day Alberta.

McDougall's administrative duties had been made lighter in 1868, when a Red River District was established to the east, centring in Upper Fort Garry (Winnipeg), with its own chairman, the Reverend George Young*. McDougall's western area was named the Saskatchewan District, and more missionaries were found to expand the work. Financial support then and later was largely supplied by the Missionary Society of the Wesleyan Methodist Church in Canada.

Because of the growing importance of Edmonton House as a transportation and trading centre, McDougall moved there to establish a permanent mission in 1871. He no doubt wished this mission to be a counterfoil to those of the Roman Catholics, by then well established at Lake Ste Anne and at St Albert under Father Albert Lacombe*, and

McEachen

at Edmonton with a church within the palisade. In 1873, authorized to begin a mission among the Blackfeet, McDougall and his son John located a site in the valley of the Bow River (Morley). This mission would be protected by the Mountain Stonies and within easy reach of the Blackfoot tribes on the prairies. Since the time of Rundle, the Stonies had remained staunch allies of the Wesleyans. The Blackfeet were the most intractable of the western tribes, and little missionary work had been done among them except when they had come to trade at the northern posts. McDougall appointed John to Morley as missionary in late October 1873, and his brother David went with him.

McDougall was involved in two pressing social problems, the illegal liquor traffic among the Indians [see ONISTAH-SOKAKSIN] and the demands of the Indian tribes for treaties with the Canadian government [see WIKASKOKISEYIN]. Feeling compassion for the many Indians, especially widows and orphans, made destitute by unrestrained tribal warfare, debauchery, and violence, often traceable to the rapacity of free traders, McDougall led the Indians to request the total prohibition of the sale of liquor in the territory. He voluntarily supported the new dominion government in persuading the native peoples to remain at peace and not to join the rebellious elements led by Louis Riel* in the Red River area. He was a "middleman" in communicating to the Indians the government's intention to treat with them fairly; he also encouraged the Indians to address their own petitions to the government urging that their rights be settled by formal treaty.

When McDougall returned from furlough in 1875, he was requested by Alexander Morris*, lieutenant governor of Manitoba and the North-West Territories, to assure the western Indians that commissioners would be sent to negotiate treaties. McDougall undertook to visit every Indian camp from Carlton House (near present-day Prince Albert) west to the Rocky Mountains bearing this message and listening to the Indians' addresses and requests. He carried this exacting assignment out satisfactorily, preparing the Indians for Treaties No. 6 and 7.

As the earliest Wesleyan clergyman to settle permanently on the prairies, McDougall advanced the cause of the Protestant church beyond the itinerancy of his predecessors. A man of his times, he was strongly sectarian in his church loyalties, but worked without stint to "christianize and civilize" his charges. His promotion of elementary education, agriculture, and health was outstanding, for the period and for the west. At his death he was planning a new mission station and an Indian orphanage on the Playground River (Oldman River). A strong stabilizing influence among the Indians and Métis, he was also a believer in confederation as a solution of the British North American problem and essentially nationalist in his sympathies. He warned church and state against separatist tendencies which he felt were supported by the Roman Catholic clergy, or which might be caused by the encroachments of the American free traders.

McDougall died of exertion while hunting buffalo. His body was found after a search and was buried in the Wesley Band cemetery (on the property of McDougall Memorial Church), near Morley. "Few men have passed away more deeply regretted by the Indian or white man, than this large hearted, courageous, laborious, and self-denying minister of Christ."

JAMES ERNEST NIX

Alberta Provincial Library, Journal of John Chantler McDougall, 1875–76. J. C. McDougall, *George Millward McDougall, the pioneer, patriot and missionary* (1st ed., Toronto, 1888; 2nd ed., 1902). Methodist Church of Canada, Missionary Society, *Annual Report*, 1875–76. *Missionary notices of the Methodist Church of Canada* (Toronto), 3rd ser., III (1875–78). Morris, *Treaties of Canada with Indians*, 168–276. Wesleyan Methodist Church in Canada, in connexion with the English conference, Missionary Society, *Annual Reports* (Toronto), 1865–74. *Wesleyan Missionary Society notices, Canada conference* (Toronto), I (1854–59); new ser., II (1868–74). John Maclean, *Vanguards of Canada* (Toronto, 1918), 119–38. J. E. Nix, *Mission among the buffalo; the labours of the Reverends George M. and John C. McDougall in the Canadian Northwest, 1860–1876* (Toronto, [1960]).

McEACHEN, EMANUEL, farmer and politician; b. in 1816 or 1817 at South Lake, P.E.I.; d. a bachelor, on 5 Nov. 1875, in Charlottetown, P.E.I.

Emanuel McEachen, an only son, was born four months after the death of his father, a farmer. He eventually became head of his family, taking possession of more than 100 acres of the farm and supporting his mother and sisters. Well known in his district, McEachen entered politics in 1853 when he was elected to the House of Assembly for Kings County First District. He was appointed to the Tory Executive Council, but, after one tempestuous session during which he became a centre of controversy and struck a Liberal assemblyman, William McGill, in an anteroom of the house, McEachen decided not to contest the election of 1854. He ran again in 1858 and 1863, but without success. A Roman Catholic of Scottish descent, McEachen had remained a Tory at a time when religious issues dominated Island politics and

McKay

induced most Tory Catholics to join the Liberals. In the 1863 election he was the only Catholic Tory running and was defeated by a margin of more than two-to-one in his constituency – the most Catholic on the Island.

In 1866, when religious passions had subsided, McEachen won a by-election against Benjamin Davies*, a Protestant Liberal. However, he was defeated in the general election the following year, and remained out of public life until 1870, when he was once again elected, and was named to the Executive Council of Premier James Colledge Pope*. Pope's government was swept out of office in 1872, and McEachen lost his seat to William Wilfred Sullivan*, then a Liberal. But the following year McEachen returned to the assembly and the new Tory government appointed him commissioner of public lands, a position he held until his death. In this period he forcefully advocated a system of publicly supported separate schools, declaring in the assembly that "it is better that Mormonism be taught to children, than no religion at all." McEachen, no friend of Mormonism, was emphasizing the faults of the existing system, which he accused of instructing the young in "the mysteries of heathen mythology."

As a politician, Emanuel McEachen was primarily distinguished by unswerving loyalty to his party when almost all his fellow Catholics had abandoned it. Known for vehemence in debate, he was generally considered to be a man who, while hot-tempered, bore few grudges.

IAN ROSS ROBERTSON

Prince Edward Island, Supreme Court, Estates Division, will of Emanuel McEachen, 22 Oct. 1875. Prince Edward Island, House of Assembly, *Debates*, 1866, 75, 105; 1871, 39; 1873, 31–32, 110; 1874, 291, 296, 448–50, 468–69, 494–95, 513–14; 1875, 173–74, 192–93, 196, 208, 312, 320, 322, 358. *Examiner* (Charlottetown), 26 Jan. 1863; 8 Jan., 5, 12, 19, 26 Feb. 1866; 27 Sept., 4, 18 Oct., 8 Nov. 1875. *Island Argus* (Charlottetown), 26 Oct., 9, 16 Nov. 1875. *Islander* (Charlottetown), 18 Jan. 1867. Bolger, *PEI and confederation*, 140. Robertson, "Religion, politics, and education in PEI."

McKAY, JAMES, fur-trader, guide, and politician; b. 1828 at Edmonton House, North-West Territories (present-day Alberta), son of the fur-trader James McKay; d. at St James, Man., 2 Dec. 1879.

James McKay was educated at Red River. In the employ of the Hudson's Bay Company, 1853–60, he advanced rapidly, serving as clerk and postmaster, principally in the Swan River district, and establishing posts on the Sheyenne and Buffalo rivers in American territory in 1859.

His facility in Indian languages, which he may have acquired through his mother who was either Métis or Indian, and his thorough knowledge of the prairies combined to make him a notable guide whose services were sought by distinguished travellers. He was responsible for meeting Sir George Simpson* on several of the trips made by the HBC governor from eastern Canada via the Mississippi en route to Upper Fort Garry (Winnipeg). "Jeemie McKay was proud of the fact that, always on the tenth day of their start from Crow Wing [Minn.] at the stroke of noon from the Fort Garry bell, he landed Sir George at the steps of the Chief Factor's House. Relays of horses enabled him to do this, rain or shine; and the slightest stoppage in muskeg or stream found McKay wading in to bring Sir George on his broad shoulders to dry land." In 1857 McKay guided the British expedition headed by Captain John Palliser* [*see* BOURGEAUX] from Fort Ellice (St Lazare, Man.) through the Saskatchewan plains to its winter quarters at Fort Carlton (Sask.). In 1859 when the Earl of Southesk [Carnegie*], on a western hunting trip, was in Simpson's party from Crow Wing to Upper Fort Garry, he described McKay: "Immensely broad-chested and muscular, though not tall, he weighed eighteen stone; yet in spite of his stoutness he was exceedingly hardy and active, and a wonderful horseman. His face – somewhat Assyrian in type – is very handsome: short, delicate, aquiline nose; piercing dark grey eyes; long dark-brown hair, beard, and moustaches; white, small, regular teeth; skin tanned to red bronze from exposure to weather. He was dressed in Red River style – a blue cloth 'capot' (hooded frock-coat) with brass buttons; red-and-black flannel shirt, which served also for waistcoat; black belt round the waist; buff leather moccasins on his feet; trowsers of brown and white striped home-made woollen stuff."

McKay left the service of the HBC – Simpson tried unsuccessfully to keep him – to engage on his own account in trading, freighting, mail transportation, and supervision of road construction. He had married Margaret Rowand in June 1859 and established a fine home at Deer Lodge. A son died in infancy; McKay had informally adopted a girl named Augusta whose parents had been killed by Sioux and who lived with the Grey Nuns.

McKay was appointed a member of the Council of Assiniboia in 1868, and president of the Whitehorse Plains District Court. When disturbances broke out in the Red River Settlement in 1869–70, McKay was prepared to accept the plans of the Canadian government for administration of the newly acquired territory, but he would not actively oppose his Métis friends and withdrew for a time to the United States. Subsequently, he averted a visit to the settlement by an armed band of Sioux Indians which might have provoked hostilities in the delicate situation. He was named one of the English councillors in the provisional government.

When, after the formation of the province of Manitoba, Lieutenant Governor Adams George Archibald* appointed his first council, on 10 Jan. 1871, he included McKay. McKay's addition to the two French and two English representatives, wrote Archibald, "would in no way disturb the delicate balance since his father was Scotch, his mother French Half-breed and though he himself [is] a Catholic he has two brothers Presbyterians." McKay occupied several important positions in the government of Manitoba until he was forced by ill health to retire in 1878. He was president of the Executive Council, 1871–74. He was a member of the Manitoba Legislative Council throughout its existence, 1871–76, and its speaker until 1874.

McKay was minister of agriculture in the Robert Atkinson Davis* government, 1874–78. The programme of the Bureau of Agriculture and Statistics over which he presided was confined, as were those of other departments of the Manitoba government of that period, by inadequate funds. However, the bureau did undertake the compilation of information for the advancement of agriculture and the encouragement of immigration, and supported the establishment of agricultural societies. McKay represented Lake Manitoba in the Legislative Assembly, 1877–78. Throughout his political performance, he was described by a contemporary as "cautious, of excellent judgment in some instances; but had implicit faith in the advice of the clergy and [was] not likely to oppose the views of the Archbishop [Alexandre-Antonin Taché*]. I must say in fairness he considered those opposed to him, and was at all times willing to discuss public questions with his opponent, with a degree of justice, and at times wonderful adroitness."

From 1873 to 1875 McKay had also been a member of the Council of the North-West Territories in which he concerned himself with problems affecting the native population, including the regulation of the buffalo hunt and the control of the liquor traffic. It was in the settlement of Indian claims that McKay made his most significant public contribution. He had assisted in the negotiation of Indian Treaties No 1 (Lower Fort Garry) and No 2 (Manitoba Post on Lake Manitoba) in 1871, and No 3 (North West Angle of Lake of the Woods) in 1873. He was one of the commissioners for Treaty No 5 (Winnipeg) in 1875

and for Treaty No 6, concluded at Forts Carlton and Pitt (near present-day Lloydminster) in 1876. As Alexander Morris*, lieutenant governor of Manitoba and the North-West Territories, pointed out, McKay on these occasions "had the opportunity of meeting with them [the Indians] constantly, and learning their views which his familiarity with the Indian dialects enabled him to do." He was both negotiator and interpreter. At Fort Carlton, in 1876, he said to the Indians: "I hope you will not leave until you have thoroughly understood the meaning of every word that comes from us. We have not come here to deceive you, we have not come here to rob you, we have not come here to take away anything that belongs to you, and we are not here to make peace as we would to hostile Indians, because you are the children of the Great Queen as we are, and there has never been anything but peace between us." Morris' observation that this "remarkable man, the son of an Orkneyman by an Indian mother . . . possessed large influence over the Indian tribes, which he always used for the benefit and the advantage of the government" must be coupled with other statements attesting to his generosity in treating with the Indians. He was associated with his fellow commissioners in Treaty No 6 in according additional benefits to the Indians, including provision for medical supplies and for assistance in times of epidemic and general famine, and during the initial period of establishment on reserves.

James McKay died at his estate in the parish of St James. "His career spanned the transition from a way of life based on the nomadic buffalo hunt and fur trade to one based on agriculture and settlement."

ALLAN R. TURNER

Archives des soeurs grises (Saint-Boniface, Man.), Chroniques de la Rivière-Rouge, 10 avril 1863, 10 août 1866; Registre des orphelines, 1846–1904, p.11, no.63. PAC, MG 26, A (Macdonald papers), correspondence with Adams George Archibald, 1870–72, and Alexander Morris, 1872–73 (copies in SAB). PAM, Alexander Morris, Lieutenant-Governor's collection, correspondence and papers, 1872–77; Alexander Morris, Ketcheson collection, 1869–77 (copies in SAB). SAB, Saskatchewan Historical Society, 37. Canada, Sessional papers, III (1870), PT.5, no.12, 93–95. Canadian North-West (Oliver), I, 71, 85, 125–26; II, 1011–75. Morris, Treaties of Canada with Indians, 195. Palliser papers (Spry). Southesk, Earl of [James Carnegie], Saskatchewan and the Rocky Mountains: a diary and narrative of travel, sport, and adventure, during a journey through the Hudson's bay company's territories, in 1859 and 1860 (Edinburgh, 1875). Manitoba, Statutes, 1873–78. Manitoba Free Press (Winnipeg), 3 Dec. 1879. Can. parl. comp., 1874, 481, 483; 1875; 1877, 363, 371. Donnelly, Government of Manitoba, 3–25. Margaret

McWilliams, *Manitoba milestones* (Toronto and London, [1928]), 106–12. Morton, *Manitoba, a history.* J. H. O'Donnell, *Manitoba as I saw it from 1869 to date, with flash-lights on the first Riel Rebellion* (Winnipeg and Toronto, 1909), 53–54. I. M. Spry, *The Palliser expedition; an account of John Palliser's British North America expedition 1857–1860* (Toronto, 1963). L. H. Thomas, *The struggle for responsible government in the North-West Territories, 1870–1897* (Toronto, 1956), 56, 64, 83. F. A. Milligan, "The establishment of Manitoba's first provincial government," HSSM, *Papers*, 3rd ser., no.5 (1948–49), 5–18. R. T. F. Thompson, "Deer Lodge through the century," HSSM, *Papers*, 3rd ser., no.22 (1965–66), 95–98

McKAY, JOHN RICHARDS, HBC employee; b. Rupert's Land, probably 10 Aug. 1792, eldest child of John McKay and Mary Favell; m. first Harriet Ballenden by whom he had seven sons and five daughters, second Catherine White by whom he had one son and two daughters; buried at St Clements Church, Mapleton, Man., 11 Dec. 1877.

John Richards McKay was sent to England to be educated and returned to Albany Factory in 1808 as a writer for the Hudson's Bay Company. Later he joined his father at Brandon House and was with him at the time of his death in 1810. During the next 14 years he served at various HBC posts. After the North West Company destroyed Qu'Appelle House in 1815 McKay was sent to rebuild it, but met with such strong opposition from the Nor'Westers' neighbouring post, under Alexander Macdonell*, that his senior officer, James Sutherland*, came to his assistance. At the time of the coalition of the HBC and the North West Company he was in charge at Brandon House.

In 1824 he retired to the Red River Settlement, but after the failure of several enterprises ending with an academy to teach "writing, arithmetic, reading, English French dancing fencing and the Graces," McKay joined the American traders on the Missouri River in 1830. The next year found him back with the HBC. In 1833 he was placed in charge of Fort Ellice (St Lazare, Man.), where his popularity with the Indians enabled him to extend the trade of that post. After another retirement in 1844 he again served the company at various posts from 1846 until his final retirement in 1859.

McKay was "very active and much beloved by the Indians" whom he understood and liked, and who admired his unusual skills as a horseman, swordsman, and marksman. He treated them justly and generously, sometimes to the annoyance of his superiors who considered him an extravagant trader.

T. R. McCLOY

PAC, MG 19, E1 (Selkirk papers), 6, pp.1946–59; 62, pp.16500–51. PAM, Church of England registers, St Clements Church (Mapleton), burials, 1862–91. Somerset House, London, Heathfield 147, will of John McKay. Isaac Cowie, *The company of adventurers: a narrative of seven years in the service of the Hudson's Bay Company during 1867–1874 on the great buffalo plains* (Toronto, 1913), 173, 180–81, 185. *Hargrave correspondence* (Glazebrook), 40, 61. HBRS, III (Fleming), 54, 446–47. M. A. MacLeod and W. L. Morton, *Cuthbert Grant of Grantown, warden of the plains of Red River* (Toronto, 1963), 11, 19, 32, 35, 38, 79, 81. Morton, *History of the Canadian west*, 437, 548, 573. W. B. Cameron, "Clan McKay in the west," *Beaver*, outfit 275 (Sept. 1944), 3–7.

McKEAGNEY, JAMES CHARLES, lawyer, politician, and judge; b. in 1815 in County Tyrone, Ireland; d. 14 Sept. 1879 in St Andrews, N.B.

James Charles McKeagney's family migrated to Nova Scotia in 1822, and he was educated in Baddeck, Cape Breton Island, and at McQueen's Academy in Halifax. On 20 Oct. 1842 he married Eliza Henry of Antigonish. Six years after her death in 1851, he married Eliza Hearne of Sydney.

McKeagney was called to the bar of Nova Scotia in October 1838 and appointed a QC in 1866. He was elected to the assembly for Richmond County in 1840 as a Reformer but was unseated on a technicality. In 1843 he successfully ran in Inverness County; McKeagney, however, was a non-resident and this fact was used by Peter Smyth, also a Reformer, to defeat him in the election of 10 Aug. 1847. Elected in Sydney Township in a by-election in 1848, he served in 1851 as minister without portfolio in the Liberal government until his defeat six months after his appointment. Re-elected in 1855, he was one of the Roman Catholics who helped bring the Conservatives to power when he crossed the floor in 1857 [*see* Joseph HOWE and James W. JOHNSTON]. In December 1857 McKeagney was appointed to the new position of inspector of mines and minerals, his principal duty being to carry out the terms of an agreement with the General Mining Association concerning the mineral resources of the province. In 1859 he declared that his heavy duties precluded his running for election again, but comments from the Antigonish *Casket*, which supported him, indicated that he was unhappy over not receiving a promotion.

In 1867 McKeagney was elected to the federal parliament for Cape Breton County as an anti-confederate, though prior to the election he had promised the bishop of Arichat, Colin Francis MacKinnon, to accept confederation. However, in 1868 he was forced by opposition within his own county to support the agitation for repeal of union,

475

McKenzie

although he assured John A. Macdonald* that, in a crisis, he would vote with the government. His tactics were unsuccessful and he was defeated in the general election in 1872.

Privately, however, McKeagney had been promised a judicial appointment in Manitoba by Charles Tupper* if he contested the election, thereby splitting the Nova Scotia Catholic vote. Macdonald was afraid that McKeagney was too old but Thomas Louis CONNOLLY, archbishop of Halifax, strongly supported the appointment. McKeagney, apart from his experience as a lawyer, had gained some judicial training as judge of probate for Cape Breton from 1848 until 1867 and also as a surrogate in the Court of Vice-Admiralty. He was appointed as a puisne judge of the Queen's Bench of Manitoba on 7 Oct. 1872. During his tenure, he served as administrator of Manitoba from 10 Jan. 1873 until 7 Sept. 1874. He was again administrator on 28 Feb. 1876, becoming acting lieutenant governor of Manitoba and the North-West Territories on 25 Aug. 1876. From 1873 until 1875 McKeagney also investigated claims arising from the uprising led by Louis Riel*. The most dramatic cases heard by McKeagney were the trials of Ambroise-Dydime Lépine* [see BÉTOURNAY] and of André Nault* in 1874 for the murder of Thomas Scott*; the trial of Nault ended in a split jury.

McKeagney's political career in Nova Scotia, often influenced by his defence of the Roman Catholic church, suggests that, though the religious issue disrupted party organization, it did not force a man to change his political principles. McKeagney's now faint reputation in Manitoba would indicate that he was barely competent either as a lawyer or as a judge during that phase of his career.

K. G. PRYKE

PAC, MG 26, A (Macdonald papers), pp.47030–40, 47069–72, 47124–26, 47357–58, 47401–3, 157564–67; letter books, 12, 20. *The Canadian legal directory: a guide to the bar and bench of the dominion of Canada*, ed. H. J. Morgan (Toronto, 1878), 238–39. *Directory of N.S. MLAs* (Fergusson), 223–24. D. G. Whidden, *The history of the town of Antigonish* (Wolfville, N.S., 1934), 101–3. F. J. Wilson, "The most reverend Thomas L. Connolly, archbishop of Halifax," CCHA *Report, 1943–44*, 55–108.

McKENZIE, GEORGE ROGERS, shipbuilder, sea captain, and politician; b. at Halifax, N.S., 12 Dec. 1798, son of John McKenzie and Elizabeth Grant; m. Sarah McGregor, daughter of Dr James McGregor*; they had two daughters; d. at New Glasgow, N.S., 12 March 1876.

Captain George Rogers McKenzie was a prominent shipbuilder in Pictou County, Nova Scotia. He started in a small way in 1821 at Boat Harbour, N.S., with a 45-ton schooner, named *James William* in honour of his nephew James William Carmichael*. Later he moved his yards to New Glasgow where he began to build much larger vessels, notably the 1,444-ton *Hamilton Campbell Kidston* and the 1,465-ton *Magna Charta*. Initially, his brother-in-law, the New Glasgow merchant James Carmichael, helped provide the capital required for McKenzie's shipbuilding and shared in the profits when the ships were sold. George McKenzie was known as the "father of shipbuilding" in Pictou County for he led the way in constructing vessels of a superior class which he owned and usually sailed himself. His business flourished during the 1850s and 1860s when wooden vessels from the Maritimes were needed for the timber trade to Great Britain, for the coal trade from Pictou to the United States, and for supplying the British and American armies during the Crimean War and the American Civil War.

An energetic and courageous man, Captain McKenzie divided his time between shipbuilding and seafaring; he was noted as the instructor of many skilful captains who sailed Nova Scotian ships on the seven seas. When the *Hamilton Campbell Kidston* made a voyage to Glasgow in the spring of 1852, Captain McKenzie sailed the ship up the narrow Clyde to the city. The arrival of this large vessel caused a sensation among Glasgow merchants who marked the event on 14 April 1852 with a presentation to the captain of a silver tea and coffee service.

McKenzie soon gained the attention of Joseph HOWE, who referred to his prowess as a shipbuilder in a speech on "The organization of the empire" delivered in the Legislative Assembly of Nova Scotia on 21 Feb. 1854. The following year McKenzie followed Howe into politics and was elected to the assembly as a Reform member for Pictou County. Although the two men shared the same political outlook, McKenzie was content to remain on the sideline in debate, but served on committees for trade and navigation. Despite the fact that he had decided views on many controversial issues, he won the respect and friendship of his political opponents. He was re-elected to the assembly in 1859 and represented Pictou County Eastern Division until 1863 when he retired from politics. McKenzie died 13 years later leaving an estate of $34,864 in property, notes, and shares in two ships.

WILLIAM B. HAMILTON

[Joseph Howe], *Speeches and letters* (Chisholm), II, 274–75. J. P. MacPhie, *Pictonians at home and abroad*

(Boston, 1914). G. G. Patterson, *A history of the county of Pictou, N.S.* (Montreal, Pictou, N.S., Halifax, Saint John, N.B., and Toronto, 1877). J. H. Sinclair, *Capt. George McKenzie: an appreciation* (n.p., n.d., copy at Acadia University Library, Wolfville, N.S.). Wallace, *Wooden ships and iron men.*

MacKENZIE, JOHN GEORGE DELHOSTE (he signed MacKenzie; Mackenzie and McKenzie are also frequently used), Church of England clergyman and educator; b. 22 April 1822, at St Ann's Garrison, Bridgetown, Barbados, son of Captain John MacKenzie, a Peninsular war veteran; d. 4 March 1873, at Stratford, Ont.

John George Delhoste MacKenzie came to Upper Canada in 1834 with his family, who settled near St Thomas. He attended schools in Trinidad, in England, and in Toronto (Upper Canada College). In 1839 he was tutor to the family of the Reverend Alexander Neil BETHUNE at Cobourg and assisted Bethune in editing the *Church.* He entered the Diocesan Theological Institution at Cobourg, was ordained deacon in 1845 and priest in 1846, received his BA from King's College, Toronto, in 1849, and in 1853 was granted the first MA degree conferred by Trinity College in Toronto. From 1845 to 1856 he was incumbent of St Paul's Church, Yorkville, and at the same time he was headmaster of St Paul's Grammar School. He laboured in the parish of Georgetown and Norval, 1856–1859, and then removed to Hamilton where he took charge of a school attached to Christ's Church.

John G. D. MacKenzie made solid contributions both to the church and to education. As a parish priest he gained the warm approval of Bishop A. N. Bethune, his lifelong friend, and of the congregations among whom he laboured. As a teacher he tried, in his two private schools, to incorporate religious with secular instruction at the secondary level. He was appointed inspector of grammar schools for Ontario in 1868. In this position, which he retained until his death, he earned praise from the Council of Public Instruction for his impartiality, faithfulness, and efficiency.

During his connection with the *Church,* MacKenzie wrote several sketches, one of which, "Paul of Samosata: a tale of the ancient Syrian church," appearing in the newspaper in 1844, combined elements of history and imagination. Two funeral sermons delivered in Toronto were printed in 1852, and selections from other sermons were published posthumously in 1882 with a memoir written by Bishop Bethune and an appendix composed of extracts from MacKenzie's reports to the provincial education department from 1868 to 1871. The sermons are scriptural

expositions of a high order; the reports illustrate his ideals in educational matters and his accurate observation of the schools which it was his duty to visit. Both sermons and reports are written in a lucid, polished English reflecting his classical training.

MacKenzie married in 1846 Catherine Eliza, eldest daughter of Marcus Crombie, headmaster of the Toronto grammar school, and they had several children.

T. R. MILLMAN

PAO, John Strachan letter books; John Strachan papers. J. G. D. MacKenzie, *A sermon, on the occasion of the death of Clarence Yonge Wells, preached October 20th, 1850, at St Paul's Church, Toronto* (Weymouth, Ont., 1852); [ ], *Selection from sermons of the late Rev. J. G. D. Mackenzie . . . with memoir* (Toronto, 1882). *J. of education for Ont.,* XXVI (1873), 58–59. Synod of the Church of England, Diocese of Toronto, *Journal,* 1876. *Church Herald* (Toronto), 13 March 1874. *The roll of pupils of Upper Canada College, Toronto, January 1830, to June 1916,* ed. A. H. Young (Kingston, Ont., 1917). *Trinity University Review* (Toronto), XV (1902), 85–86.

McKENZIE, KENNETH (in his youth he sometimes spelled his name Mackenzie), Puget's Sound Agricultural Company bailiff and agent on Vancouver Island, farmer, and provisions supplier; b. 25 Oct. 1811 in Edinburgh, Scotland, son of Dr Kenneth McKenzie, surgeon, and Janet Blair; d. at Lakehill Farm, Victoria, ·B.C., 10 April 1874.

Kenneth McKenzie spent his youth in Edinburgh where he attended the High School and College of Edinburgh. Probably in the late 1820s he moved to his father's estate of Rentonhall in the parish of Morham, Haddingtonshire, in the East Lothian District, where he managed the farms, sheep-runs, and a tile works. About 1841 he married Agnes Russell who bore him eight children, six before the family left Scotland.

In spite of his attested abilities in managing the estate, young McKenzie was unable to cope with the encumbrances left by his father. In 1848 he put the lands and estate up for auction, but a sale did not take place; and from 1848 to 1851 McKenzie applied unsuccessfully for positions as factor, bailiff, or land steward on estates in the British isles. Finally, in October 1851, he sold Rentonhall for £4,925, and, through his friendship with John Haldane*, was granted an interview by the Hudson's Bay Company. He was offered the position of bailiff or overseer on one of the four farms it projected under its subsidiary, the Puget's Sound Agricultural Company, in the Esquimalt district near Fort Victoria on Vancouver Island, and he spent the spring and summer

McKenzie

of 1852 recruiting labourers, blacksmiths, carpenters, and a schoolteacher for the venture.

McKenzie's five-year contract with the Puget's Sound Agricultural Company is dated 16 Aug. 1852. It was to provide a farm of 600 acres, livestock, seed, and implements, and to pay for all improvements. McKenzie was to receive £60 per annum and after three years share 1/3 of the profit or loss. The company stipulated that the relationship was that of master and servant, but in effect it sought to establish a landed gentry or squirearchy surrounded by small landholders, a paternalistic form which proved incompatible with conditions on the frontier of empire.

McKenzie and his party of 73 persons arrived at Vancouver Island on 16 Jan. 1853, and were temporarily accommodated at Fort Victoria. After viewing Craigflower, the farm allotted to him at Maple Point between Esquimalt Harbour and the Gorge, McKenzie moved the carpenters and blacksmiths to the site on 24 January. By 1 April preparations were sufficiently advanced for his family to move to a temporary dwelling; a large manor house resembling Rentonhall was ready on 1 May 1856. During the spring and summer of 1853 McKenzie and his men built additional houses, planted gardens and fields, set up the seven horsepower engine brought from England to run a sawmill and grind grain, and began a lime kiln and a brick works. McKenzie's men proved to be fractious with frequent instances of drunkenness and desertion. To augment his labour force, he used men from HMS *Trincomalee* then at Esquimalt and he hired several groups of Indians, but these too proved unsteady hands. Evidently in an attempt to provide a measure of authority and justice on the four farms of the Puget's Sound Agricultural Company, on 31 March 1853 Governor James DOUGLAS appointed McKenzie and three others to be magistrates and justices of the peace in the District of Victoria.

On 3 Feb. 1854 the HBC appointed McKenzie agent and superintendent for the agricultural company on Vancouver Island with a commission of ten per cent on the net profits of the four farms in addition to his regular salary from Craigflower. Wage disputes and unauthorized salmon trading with the Indians along the Fraser River led to Douglas' intervention in 1855; on McKenzie's appeal to London the HBC instructed him to follow the governor's advice. The company also found it necessary to complain to McKenzie about inadequate accounts and excessive expenses. When McKenzie proposed mills and a brewery, the HBC governor, Andrew Colvile, reminded him that bailiffs should devote their efforts to raising crops and making the farms self-sufficient. Colvile added that McKenzie was to be prepared for a precise limitation on his expenditures.

McKenzie as company agent was instructed to deal with Edward Edwards Langford*, the luxury-loving, lavish, and intractable bailiff of Colwood Farm at Esquimalt. In 1854 McKenzie received orders to terminate Langford's contract, but Langford refused to give up quietly and McKenzie was chastised for not taking "more active and effective measures for the protection of their [the company's] property." The troubles with Langford put McKenzie in an embarrassing position between company officials and the bailiffs, and he was further discredited in the eyes of the company. In 1857 Alexander Grant Dallas* was sent to Fort Victoria, and one of his responsibilities was the administrative supervision of the farms.

In 1855 hospital huts were erected at Esquimalt to receive the wounded from the battle of Petropavlovsk, and thereafter ships of the Pacific Squadron increasingly used the harbour as a base, particularly during the San Juan Island dispute [see Douglas]. Craigflower Farm was ideally situated to supply the naval squadron, and in September 1856 McKenzie reported that he had provided nearly 1,000 pounds of meat and 400 pounds of vegetables per day. Despite HBC opposition, McKenzie erected mills at Craigflower to provide flour for the navy's bakers, who frequently used his ovens. Continuing to supply the Royal Navy with meat and vegetables, McKenzie undertook to supply bread and biscuit in 1858, and in 1860 he entered into a regular contract with the commander-in-chief of HM Pacific Squadron to supply 10,000 pounds of biscuit within 24 hours of demand and an unlimited quantity within 14 days. The navy's demand for bread was so great that it took all of the wheat McKenzie could supply from his own farms, and he was forced to import wheat from Oregon. Despite protests from local bakers in Victoria, McKenzie continued to hold the navy's bread contract until his death in 1874 except for a brief period in the mid-1860s. He installed an engine and biscuit machines at Dallas Bank on Esquimalt Harbour. He also sold breadstuffs to the HBC for its ships, and during the British Columbia gold rush he advertised breads and crackers for sale at San Francisco prices when a loaf of bread sometimes sold for as much as $3 in Victoria.

During this period, Craigflower became a social centre for naval and colonial officials, and the McKenzie girls were much courted by visiting officers. When Lady Jane Franklin [Jane GRIFFIN] visited Victoria in the spring of 1861 the season's most colourful social event was the picnic in her honour at Craigflower.

478

The farm at Craigflower was not large enough for both cropland and pasturage for the sheep from which McKenzie hoped to get a profitable wool clip. In 1855 he established a sheep station at Lakehill, near Christmas Hill, north of Victoria; and in 1856 and 1857 he acquired lands there in his own name along with 825 acres for the Puget's Sound Agricultural Company's new Lake District farm known as Broadmead.

Craigflower began to show small and intermittent profits after 1857, but the agricultural company remained concerned by McKenzie's "confused and incorrect" accounts. Despite the fact that Craigflower was its only profitable farm, it became increasingly critical of the capital debt charged against the operations. In 1861 McKenzie's second five-year contract as bailiff was cancelled and he was given a two-year lease (renewable on a year-to-year basis for a total of five years) on the cultivated acreage of the farm with the rent set at £500 per annum so long as he held the naval bread contract. If McKenzie lost the biscuit contract, the rent was to be halved. The livestock and implements of husbandry at Craigflower were to be sold, and McKenzie's Lakehill farm was used as security for his purchase of the stocks of flour, biscuit, growing crops, and equipment. At the termination of this contract, McKenzie was to leave Craigflower. In 1864, McKenzie, still beset by financial problems, was notified that his lease on Craigflower farm would terminate on 31 Oct. 1865; on that date he mortgaged his Lakehill and Dallas Bank properties to the company to secure his indebtedness to them of more than £3,000. He moved his family to Lakehill during 1866. Although the company was patient, the burdensome debt plagued him for the remainder of his life.

Kenneth McKenzie's position and experience led him to accept minor legal positions and to assume leadership in the agricultural community. He served as a justice of the peace from 1853 to 1855 and again from 1867 until his death. During the 1860s he was a road commissioner for the Esquimalt District and for Victoria, and in 1871 was appointed to the Court of Appeal for the Esquimalt and Metchosin Road District. In 1861 he was a founder of the Vancouver Island Agricultural and Horticultural Association, serving at various times as director and president. In 1865 McKenzie, considered to be a protectionist, was a candidate for the legislature, but he stepped aside in favour of John Ash*, a free trader. Again in 1869 he supported protection and opposed confederation with Canada in seconding the nomination of James Lowe as a candidate for the Legislative Council.

McKenzie died at his home of heart disease. Beset by the effects of overcapitalization in a developing economy, he nevertheless had done a great deal to encourage agriculture and milling on Vancouver Island as the colony moved from the limitations of the fur trade to become the *entrepôt* for the mining rush and the base for Britain's Pacific naval operations. So far as the company was concerned, its agricultural enterprise on Vancouver Island was a "mistake" conducted at "fearful expense," but families such as the McKenzies "did much good to the colony in the shape of keeping it at a high standard of civilization. . . ."

WILLIAM R. SAMPSON

PABC, Kenneth McKenzie papers (catalogued collection and unsorted uncatalogued collection); Robert Melrose, "Royal emigrant's almanack concerning five years servitude under the Hudson's Bay Company on Vancouver's Island" (copy of a diary, August 1852–July 1857, handbound). *British Colonist* (Victoria), 21, 22 March, 8 June, 5 Sept. 1861; 10 March 1862; 24 July 1863; 11 June 1864; 6 June, 12 July, 29 Sept., 2, 21 Oct. 1865; 6 June 1866; 3 May 1867; 19 March, 29 July, 21 Oct., 30 Nov. 1869; 5 Feb., 26 March 1871; 11, 15 April 1874; 8 April 1884; 15 June 1897. N. de B. Lugrin, *The pioneer women of Vancouver Island, 1843–1866*, ed. John Hoise (Victoria, 1928). S. G. Pettit, "The trials and tribulations of Edward Edwards Langford," *BCHQ*, XVII (1953), 5–40.

MacKINNON, COLIN FRANCIS, priest and educator; b. at Williams Point, a sparsely settled rural area adjacent to the town of Antigonish, N.S., 20 July 1810, son of John MacKinnon and Una (Eunice) MacLeod; d. at Antigonish, 26 Sept. 1879.

Colin Francis MacKinnon's family emigrated from Scotland in 1791 and first settled at Parrsboro, Nova Scotia. His parents later moved to Williams Point to live among other Roman Catholic Highland settlers. The lack of educational facilities in the immediate area forced MacKinnon's parents to place him, in 1824, under the tutelage of the Reverend William B. MacLeod, parish priest at Grand Narrows, and later under Malcolm MacLellan at East Bay, Cape Breton. Following his completion of preparatory classical studies the young student enrolled at Urban College in Rome on 22 Jan. 1829. He remained there until 26 June 1837 and qualified for both his PHD and DD. MacKinnon was ordained into the priesthood at the College of the Propaganda in Rome by Archbishop Luigi Fransoni on 4 June 1837.

Father Colin Francis MacKinnon returned to Nova Scotia that summer and was appointed first resident pastor at St Andrews, Sydney (now Antigonish) County. His pastorate extended from 3 Nov. 1837 to 11 May 1853. In the summer of 1838 he established the St Andrews grammar school, the first school of its kind in the area, and one which gained a respectable reputation through the distinctions won by its graduates. It was probably through his efforts in this venture that Father MacKinnon became convinced of the need for an institution of higher learning in eastern Nova Scotia.

On 11 Nov. 1851, the Reverend Colin MacKinnon was appointed bishop of Arichat, at that time the ecclesiastical centre of eastern Nova Scotia. He was consecrated by Bishop William Walsh* on 27 Feb. 1852 and lived at Arichat from 11 May 1853 until 21 July 1858. Recognizing the religious needs and educational aspirations of the Roman Catholic Highlanders of his diocese, Bishop MacKinnon founded a minor seminary, St Francis Xavier College, on 20 July 1853, his 43rd birthday. When it opened the college had a staff of four professors and a student population of 40; instruction was given in mathematics, Latin, Greek, theology, philosophy, English, French, and Christian doctrine. In 1855 the college was moved to Antigonish where it grew into St Francis Xavier University. In an effort to improve the educational opportunities for young women, Bishop MacKinnon brought the sisters of the Congregation of Notre-Dame to Arichat in 1856; their superior was Mother Sainte-Élisabeth (Marie-Louise Dorval*), a former superior-general of the congregation.

Bishop MacKinnon lived at Antigonish from 21 July 1858 until his death in 1879. During that period he carried out his episcopal and educational duties aided by the Reverend John Cameron, DD, whom he had appointed as the first rector of the college when it transferred to Antigonish. In 1860 MacKinnon was able to write that St Francis Xavier "bade fair to realize to religion and to society all the benefits anticipated at its foundation." The recognition of its success came in 1866 when the college was granted, without any difficulty, full university powers by an act of the provincial legislature. From the evidence available, it is apparent that MacKinnon did not become seriously involved in any political controversies of the day. He was quite successful in increasing the number of churches and priests in his diocese, and between 1866 and 1874 he was largely responsible for the building of St Ninian's Cathedral, the present seat of the diocese.

During his later years he was again assisted by the competent and aggressive Cameron, who had been appointed coadjutor bishop in 1870. Forced by ill health to retire from active charge in July 1877, MacKinnon was made titular archbishop of Amida on 7 September. He died on 26 Sept. 1879 and was buried in the vault of St Ninian's Cathedral. His work in the promotion of higher education in Nova Scotia stands as his greatest achievement.

R. A. MacLean

Ronald MacGillivray, *Remember your prelates: a sermon, preached at the solemn requiem of Colin Francis MacKinnon, archbishop of Amydo, in St. Ninian's Cathedral, Antigonish, September 30, 1879* (Halifax, 1879), copy in PANS. *Casket* (Antigonish, N.S.), 27 June 1895; 17 June, 30 Sept., 25 Nov. 1943; 7, 14 July 1960. *Catholic encyclopedia* (1907–12), II, 563. *St. Francis Xavier's University, 1853–1920* (Antigonish, N.S., 1920). A. A. Johnston, "Antigonish diocese priests and bishops, 1790–1825," typescript in possession of the author, Antigonish, N.S. Sister St Miriam of the Temple [Eileen Scott], "The Congregation of Notre Dame in early Nova Scotia," CCHA *Report, 1953*, 67–80.

McLACHLIN, DANIEL (Donhuil), lumber merchant and politician; b. 1810, near Pointe-Fortune, Vaudreuil County, L.C., son of Hugh McLachlin; m. Maria Harrington in 1837, by whom he had four sons and two daughters; d. 6 Feb. 1872, at Arnprior, Ont.

Daniel McLachlin, the son of a Highland Scot Presbyterian, entered the Ottawa timber trade. The first record of his activity is in November 1834 when he and his brother William signed a contract with the timber exporting firm headed by William Sharples to deliver a raft of white pine timber to Quebec by 1 July 1835. Daniel may have been in the trade for some time before this: William Sharples and Sons, a large and successful house, would have been unlikely to deal with inexperienced timbermen.

The McLachlin business operated originally from Pointe-Fortune, Lower Canada. However, in 1837 Daniel moved to Bytown (Ottawa), Upper Canada, already the *entrepôt* of the Ottawa River timber trade. No longer working with his brother, he obtained extensive limits in the next decade on the Ottawa River, and on the Madawaska and Indian rivers. Restless and ambitious, he constantly expanded his business into new areas. He was among the first to employ the power of the Chaudiere Falls at Bytown, erecting saw and grist mills there with three run of stones. He was also a general merchant with his brother Hugh. Their store in central Bytown remained open until 1855 when they dissolved their partnership.

McLachlin truly began to build an empire in 1851 when he bought 400 acres of land along the Madawaska River near its junction with the Ottawa. This was the site of the near-ghost village of Arnprior, in Renfrew County. Founded in 1831, the settlement and its excellent millsites had languished for over a decade until McLachlin's purchase. Setting up his timber business there, he reconstructed the mills, built bridges, and laid out and peopled a village. He took the lead in promoting public improvements which made Arnprior more accessible, such as the Madawaska River Improvement Association (later Company) and a wagon road from Arnprior to the Long Rapids on the Madawaska River. He moved to Arnprior himself in 1857, settling his family in a substantial two-storey stone house popularly known as "The Hill." In this now-thriving community McLachlin built one of the largest and most prosperous firms in the Ottawa valley. By 1865, when his sons were brought into the business and it was given the name of McLachlin Brothers, his mills and timber operations employed 800 men and produced 25,000,000 feet of lumber, worth about $500,000 annually.

McLachlin combined his business ambition with a paternalistic concern for his settlement: he advanced adult education through the Mechanics' Institute and the Ottawa Natural History Society; he was generous to the poor and to churches; he showed a continuing concern for improvements as a director of projects such as the Upper Ottawa Steamboat Company and the Bytown and Prescott Railway (later the St Lawrence and Ottawa Railway). Nevertheless, he remained a typically rough-hewn timberman. He shared the lumber community's impatience with any restraints upon their business, their contempt for government attempts to regulate the trade. For instance, in 1856 McLachlin and several other major operators in the area found their logs caught in a jam on the Madawska River. In clearing the jam they calmly destroyed the recently completed Madawaska Bridge. There is a pathetic quality to the correspondence in which the Bureau of Agriculture attempted to convince McLachlin and his associates that it was their duty to rebuild the bridge or to pay for its replacement.

McLachlin entered politics in 1851 when the Reformers of Bytown chose him as their candidate. He ran as a moderate, "Baldwinite" Reformer, and on 10 Dec. 1851 was elected to the Legislative Assembly of the Province of Canada. He did not seek re-election in 1854, perhaps because he had been appointed the previous year as an associate justice in the Court of Oyer and Terminer for Carleton County. In 1861, by now a "Coalition Reformer" supporting the George-Étienne CARTIER–John A. Macdonald* government, he was unopposed for the Renfrew seat in the assembly. His move toward the business-minded Liberal-Conservatives was typical of the pragmatic politics of the Ottawa valley, where principles took second place to the interests of the timber trade. Indeed, the only factor which could compete with the staple was religious antagonism. McLachlin discovered this to his sorrow in 1863 when he decided to contest the riding of Carleton. Despite a sound, business-like platform, he was easily defeated by the prominent Orangeman and Protestant agitator, William Frederick Powell*. McLachlin returned to politics in 1867 when he was chosen by acclamation for South Renfrew to the first dominion parliament.

Daniel McLachlin was feeling the effects of his busy career. In June 1869 he resigned his seat in parliament. At the same time he retired from the lumber trade, turning the business over to his three older sons, Hugh, John, and Daniel. McLachlin himself retreated to the bucolic pleasure of his estate, happily listing himself as a "farmer" in the census of 1871. He could be well content with his life when he passed from it on 6 Feb. 1872.

McLachlin's chief importance is not as a politician, for his career though long was undistinguished. He is significant as an example of the entrepreneur-paternalists who did so much to develop and settle the commercial frontier in Canada.

MICHAEL S. CROSS

PAC, RG 31, A1, 1861, Arnprior village, 14; 1871, Arnprior village, 1, 41. PAO, McLachlin papers. *Ottawa Citizen*, 1851–72. *Can. directory of parliament* (Johnson), 422. *Arnprior centennial, 1862–1962 ...* (Arnprior, Ont., 1962), 17–22. Cornell, *Alignment of political groups*, 31, 48, 50, 103–4, 109. [Charlotte Whitton], *A hundred years a-fellin' ... 1842–1942* (Ottawa, n.d.), 62–63, 133.

MacLEAN (McLean), DONALD CHARLES, HBC employee, farmer, militia officer, and justice of the peace; b. 1786 in Argyllshire, Scotland, d. 1873 at Eardley, Que.

Donald Charles MacLean came to Hudson Bay in July 1813, having been contracted by the Hudson's Bay Company as a "shallop master." He served as mate of the schooner *Mainwaring* until it was decommissioned in 1815. Early in 1816, after the HBC ships had become ice-bound in Hudson Bay, he accompanied George Gladman*, the chief factor at Moose Factory, on a hazardous, two-month, overland journey to Montreal with the company "Indents and papers," which were destined for London. They started out with six others but four were forced to turn back within a week of their departure from Moose Factory. Alternate freezing and thawing conditions caused

McLeod

the travellers to become fatigued and frequently to lose their direction. MacLean fell through the ice on at least two occasions, but he and the other three men completed the trip with little or no adverse effects. Upon the expiration of his contract with the HBC in July 1816, MacLean joined the North West Company as a ship's master on the upper Great Lakes.

In 1820 he married Annie Warren of Fort Erie and within a year quit the company and journeyed to Scotland. He returned in 1824 accompanied by his wife, his son, his father, and ten brothers, sisters, and cousins. They all settled on a 1,500-acre grant in Eardley Township, Lower Canada. In the early 1830s MacLean left the family homestead and settled in Lochaber Township. He was appointed justice of the peace for Lochaber in 1833, a post which he held intermittently for about 15 years. In 1837 he was appointed captain of the Two Mountains Loyal Volunteer Cavalry. They were on call during the rebellion in Lower Canada, and in 1838–39 were paid for general service, mostly involving escort and dispatch duties. MacLean moved back to Eardley during the 1850s; there he farmed, operated a lumber mill, and served as justice of the peace for a short time. He and his wife raised ten children. Although a member of the Presbyterian Church of Scotland, he was buried in the cemetery of the Church of England at Eardley.

Donald MacLean was typical of thousands of courageous pioneers who left their homeland to immigrate to British North America and settle in the wilderness.

DAVID B. FLEMMING

HBC Arch. A.1/51 (Minute books, 1814); A.5/7 (London correspondence books outward, General series, 1824); A.16/17 (Officers' and servants' ledgers, Moose, 1791–1822); A.30/14 (Lists of servants in Hudson Bay, 1798–1816); A.32/18 (Servants' contracts, 1813); A.32/41–43 (Servants' contracts, MacE-MacV); B.3/a/119b (Albany, Post journal, 1815–16: "Journal of a journey from Albany and Moose Factorys in Hudson's Bay to London . . . by George Gladman"); B.135/e/3 (Report for Moose District, 1815–1816, by Joseph Beioly); C.1/298 (log of *Eddystone*, 1813); C.1/302 (log of *Eddystone*, 1815); F.4/32 (North West Company ledger, 1811–21). PAC, RG 4, B36 (Provincial Red Book, 1845); RG 8, I, B5, 1039, 1044. *Census of the Canadas, 1851–2* (2v., Quebec, 1853–55), I. *Census of the Canadas, 1860–61* (2v., Quebec, 1863–64), I. *Census of Canada, 1870–71* (5v., Ottawa, 1873–78). Langelier, *Lands granted in Quebec, 1763–1890*. *Lovell's Province of Quebec directory for 1871* (n.p., n.d.). *Mitchell's Canada Gazetteer and business directory for 1864–65* (Toronto, 1864). Cyrus Thomas, *History of the counties of Argenteuil, Que., and Prescott, Ont., from the earliest settlement to the present* (Montreal, 1896).

McLEOD, ALEXANDER, deputy sheriff and storekeeper; b. 17 Jan. 1796 at Carnoustie, Forfarshire (Angus), Scotland; m. Ellen Morrison by whom he had several children; d. 27 Sept. 1871.

After a brief, youthful career in the British army during the Napoleonic Wars – he was discharged as a sergeant from the 127th Lancers – Alexander McLeod emigrated to Upper Canada in the early 1820s. On two occasions he began a grocery business, first in Kingston and then in York (Toronto), with indifferent success. McLeod's relationship to the "Family Compact," and the web of local official groups which sustained it, is obscure. He did secure an appointment as deputy sheriff of the Niagara District, and turned out, in the defence of Toronto, for the skirmish at John MONTGOMERY's tavern in early December 1837.

It was in the aftermath of the rebellion that McLeod was thrust into prominence. His official duties often took him to the Buffalo, New York, area. Here he learned, on Christmas eve 1837, that the American steamboat *Caroline* was to be used to supply rebel William Lyon Mackenzie* and his followers who had established themselves on Navy Island in the Niagara River just above the falls. McLeod conveyed this information to the Upper Canadian authorities, and later accompanied the small party led by Commodore Andrew DREW which confirmed the report. On the night of 29 December, Drew took a raiding party across the river to the American side where the *Caroline* was moored at Schlosser's Wharf. The ship was seized after a brief scuffle in which one man, an American named Amos Durfee, was killed. The unmanned *Caroline* was towed into the river, set afire, and allowed to drift a short distance downstream where it sank. Despite the lurid accounts that still persist, especially in American textbooks, it did not go plummeting down Niagara Falls ablaze. There is no evidence that Alexander McLeod was involved in the raid.

Not surprisingly, American opinion, particularly in the northeast, was incensed at this violation of sovereignty. Great Britain and the United States were already at odds over the disputed boundary between New Brunswick and Maine, and tension increased. Protracted discussions between the two countries brought no resolution; and then, enter Alexander McLeod. In November 1840 he was arrested in Lewiston, New York. It was alleged (falsely) that he had boasted openly of his participation in the cutting out of the *Caroline*. McLeod was indicted by a state grand jury for arson and murder, and bound over for trial.

Lord Palmerston, the British foreign secretary,

482

demanded McLeod's release, arguing that the attack on the *Caroline* was authorized by the proper authorities in Canada and the unfortunate McLeod could not be held personally liable. If he were convicted and hanged, Palmerston thundered, his death would be avenged. Daniel Webster, the new American secretary of state, was prepared to accept the British interpretation, but he could not intervene directly. New York state refused to surrender its jurisdictional rights in the case, although it did agree to change of venue to Utica, some distance from the inflamed Niagara district. Opinion in England, however, viewed this step as so much federalist sophistry and the newspapers of both countries indulged in a fit of warlike bombast.

The administration of William Henry Harrison had no wish for hostilities. When Palmerston left office, the prospect for an amicable resolution improved. In any case, William H. Seward, governor of New York, informed Webster that if McLeod were convicted a pardon would be granted. The trial took place in October 1841, closely covered by the newspapers. McLeod was able to produce a satisfactory alibi and was acquitted.

The American Congress repaired the constitutional difficulty the following year with legislation which provided that in such cases involving aliens the federal government could claim jurisdiction. With the McLeod case settled, Webster and Lord Ashburton proceeded to resolve the *Caroline* affair itself by a diplomatic nicety. Ashburton did not, in fact, extend a formal apology for the violation of American sovereignty, but regretted that an apology had not been made.

As for Alexander McLeod, he returned to the relative obscurity from which he had so bizarrely emerged. Once again he became a store-keeper, this time in Drummondville (now part of Niagara Falls), Upper Canada. As a result of repeated petitions (he also went to England in the 1850s to press his claims), he was awarded a pension of £200 in 1855 to assuage his wounded feelings. He was further compensated in 1866 by an appointment as justice of the peace in Welland County.

J. E. REA

PAC, RG 5, A1, 1837–40; B43; RG 7, G1, 108–11, 226–27, 241, 244–49, 253–54, 454–56; RG 8, I, A1, 35, 610. PAO, McLeod-Morrison papers. PRO, FO 414. *Arthur papers* (Sanderson). Head, *Narrative. Trial of Alexander M'Leod, for the murder of Amos Durfee; and as an accomplice in the burning of the steamer Caroline, in the Niagara River, during the Canadian rebellion in 1837–8* (New York, 1841). Craig, *Upper Canada.* A. B. Corey, "Public opinion and the McLeod case," *CHA Report, 1936*, 53–64. Alastair Watt, "The case of Alexander McLeod," *CHR*, XII (1931), 145–67.

M'LEOD, DONALD, soldier and journalist; b. at Fort Augustus, Inverness-shire, Scotland, 1 Jan. 1779; d. at Cleveland, Ohio, 22 July 1879.

Donald M'Leod was educated for the ministry at the University of Aberdeen. He served, however, in the Royal Navy, 1803–8, and then in the British army, fighting as a sergeant in the Peninsular campaign, then in Canada in the War of 1812–14 at Queenston Heights, Crysler's Farm, and Lundy's Lane, and again in Europe at Waterloo in 1815. In 1816, after his discharge, he returned to Canada and settled on land in Augusta Township. Unsuccessful in farming, he taught school in Brockville and then moved to Prescott where he opened a classical school and was appointed clerk of the Court of Requests.

In 1832 M'Leod purchased the Reform newspaper, the *Grenville Gazette*, in Prescott. He also took an active part as a journalist in the politics of Grenville County in opposition to Jonas Jones*, the Tory member for Leeds and Grenville. With the outbreak of the rebellion in Upper Canada, in December 1837, a Tory mob seized his printing office and destroyed his property. M'Leod, who had been a major in the Grenville militia, fled to the United States, made his way to Navy Island where the "Patriots" had massed for an invasion of Upper Canada, and became a brigadier-general in the Patriot army.

After the Patriot withdrawal from Navy Island, General Rensselaer Van Rensselaer*, their military commander, directed M'Leod to lead the men to Detroit to join the western Patriots and their American supporters. His force occupied Fighting Island in the Detroit River on 24 Feb. 1838 but, being practically without arms, was forced to withdraw. M'Leod then went to the support of the Patriots who had occupied Pelee Island, only to learn that they had been defeated and driven off on 3 March. Later in March a committee of the Canadian refugees at Lockport, New York, including M'Leod, organized the party that burned the British vessel *Sir Robert Peel* in the St Lawrence River on 29 May. When the premature Short Hills affair of June threatened to render abortive a larger plan for coordinated Patriot raids on Canada on 4 July, M'Leod sent Linus MILLER to Canada in an unsuccessful effort to get the participants to withdraw.

M'Leod then established himself at Cleveland, the headquarters of the western division of the Hunters' Lodges, formed to transform Canada into a republic, and attempted to recruit men for the Patriot cause. He was now in financial need

McNeill

and resented the fact that the American Hunters kept control in their own hands and would give him no relief from the funds collected for the cause. M'Leod called the Cleveland committee a set of "speculators." He also stated that he had quarrelled with them over their intention to resort to "the midnight assassin business," by which leading Upper Canadian Tories would be seized and kept as hostages and their property burnt, and "threw . . . my commission . . . in their faces."

M'Leod was arrested on a charge of violating the neutrality laws of the United States and tried at Detroit on 25 June 1838. The jury acquitted him after deliberating all night. In 1840, after William Lyon Mackenzie*'s release from jail, M'Leod quarrelled with him, disappointed at Mackenzie's refusal to countenance more border warfare. M'Leod then announced his own withdrawal from Patriot activity.

In 1841, "driven by necessity," M'Leod published *A brief review of . . . Upper Canada . . .*, writing it in six weeks and copying freely from Mackenzie's *Caroline Almanack* and *Mackenzie's Gazette*. In 1846 he published his *History of Wiskonsan. . . .* This book was under way in 1843 but M'Leod has been accused of plagiarizing from Increase Allen Lapham's *A geographical and topographical description of Wisconsin . . .* (Milwaukee, 1844). He may have made free use of it, but he also gave considerable additional material on the soil and climate of Wisconsin; he praised its land system and constitution at the expense of Canada West.

M'Leod returned to Canada West in November 1846, after receiving a pardon, and settled in Sparta, Yarmouth Township. When Mackenzie was elected to the Legislative Assembly in 1851, M'Leod promptly renewed his correspondence with him. In the same year John Rolph*, who had also been implicated in the rebellion, became commissioner of crown lands; M'Leod solicited an appointment through him and was given a post in the Patent Office. He supported Rolph in the "Flag of Truce" controversy, over whether Rolph had played a treacherous part in agreeing to be one of Francis Bond Head's emissaries to the rebels in Toronto with a flag of truce, and while on this mission advising the rebels to march on Toronto without delay.

In his old age M'Leod was granted a pension for his services. Weakened by asthma and catarrh, but in possession of his faculties to the end, M'Leod died in Cleveland at the home of his daughter in 1879.

LILLIAN FRANCIS GATES

Donald M'Leod, *A brief review of the settlement of Upper Canada by the U.E. loyalists and Scotch Highlanders in 1783; and of the grievances which compelled the Canadas to have recourse to arms . . .* (Cleveland, Ohio, 1841); *History of Wiskonsan, from its first discovery to the present period; including a geological and topographical description of the territory with a correct catalogue of all its plants* (Buffalo, N.Y., 1846).

PAC, MG 24, B24 (Dr John Rolph papers). PAO, Mackenzie-Lindsey collection. Wisconsin Hist. Soc., a.l.s., M'Leod to L. C. Draper, 18 May 1879. *The Caroline Almanack, and American Freeman's Chronicle . . .*, ed. W. L. Mackenzie (Rochester, N.Y., [1840]). *Cleveland Herald and Gazette*, 5 Feb. 1838. *Cleveland Leader*, 19 July 1876. *Detroit Daily Free Press*, 28 July 1839. William Canniff, *History of the settlement of Upper Canada (Ontario), with special reference to the Bay Quinté* (Toronto, 1869). R. B. Ross, "The Patriot war," *Michigan Pioneer Collections* (Lansing, Mich.), XXI (1892), 509–609. O. E. Tiffany, "The relation of the United States to the Canadian rebellion of 1837–1838," Buffalo Hist. Soc., *Pubs.*, VIII (1905), 7–147.

McNEILL, WILLIAM HENRY, master mariner, HBC chief factor, and pioneer; b. in Boston, Mass., 7 July 1801, son of William Henry and Rebecca McNeill; d. at Victoria, B.C., 3 Sept. 1875.

William Henry McNeill, like many of his New England contemporaries, answered the call of the sea when young. In 1823 he became a master mariner, and at the end of the following year commanded the brig *Convoy* on a trip to the Sandwich Islands (Hawaii) and to the Queen Charlotte Islands. For some years he traded between Massachusetts and South America, West Africa, and the Sandwich Islands, but in 1830 he was on the northwest coast of America working for the Boston merchants Bryant and Sturgis. His energy soon established him as one of the more successful fur-traders, and he refused to be coerced by the powerful Hudson's Bay Company into abandoning the lucrative northwest coast. On one occasion, in April 1832, Captain Thomas Sinclair aboard the HBC brigantine *Cadboro* attempted to force McNeill to take his ship, the brig *Lama*, out of the competition; McNeill faced the challenge and Sinclair was obliged to back down.

Although Chief Factor John McLoughlin* of the Columbia District wanted to be rid of the competing American traders, he respected McNeill's experience and ability and, in August 1832, needing another ship for the coastal trade to replace the damaged schooner *Vancouver*, McLoughlin arranged through his assistant Duncan Finlayson* for the purchase of *Lama*. McNeill and his two mates entered the service of the company at the same time, although McLoughlin knew that the HBC committee would object to his employing Americans; not until 1834 did he receive approval of McNeill's appointment.

At first McNeill continued to command *Lama*, and in 1834 rescued three Japanese sailors whose junk had foundered off Cape Flattery and who were being held captive by Indians. Three years later, he received command of *Beaver*, first steamship on the Pacific coast. Although a mutiny of its crew early in 1838 marred his record, he was promoted chief trader in November 1839. The appointment meant that he would have to become a British subject and he travelled to London in 1842 for this purpose, but it does not appear that he changed his citizenship before 1853 when he took up land near Fort Victoria.

Back in the Columbia District in 1844, McNeill requested a transfer to a land establishment and in 1845 took charge of Fort Stikine. Three years later he moved to Fort George because of ill health, but in 1849 established Fort Rupert, on the north end of Vancouver Island, where he stayed one year. After a trip to the Sandwich Islands he took charge of Fort Simpson in 1851 and remained there till 1859. One of his more interesting experiences was a trip he made in 1851 in *Una* to investigate the gold deposits on the Queen Charlotte Islands. The local Indians were not cooperative; when the sailors set off blasts to loosen the gold-bearing rock, both Indians and sailors would rush in to recover the more valuable pieces. Since the Indians were bellicose, dragging the seamen from the holes by their feet and threatening them with knives, McNeill was obliged to withdraw. His main concern, however, was trading for furs, and his journals and letters written at Fort Simpson indicate that he found the men at the post difficult to manage and the Tsimshians and other Indians a constant threat. The sale of spirits by American traders aggravated his problems; he wanted a gun boat to bring them under control. In 1856 his labours were rewarded when he was appointed a chief factor, and after a furlough from 1859 to 1861 he returned to Fort Simpson where he remained until he retired to his farm at Victoria in 1863.

Even in retirement McNeill was active. He was appointed to the British Columbia pilot board in 1868, and from 1872 until 1874 he captained the steamer *Enterprise* which operated between Vancouver Island and the mainland. He was a signatory to the 1869 petition addressed to President Ulysses S. Grant requesting the annexation of British Columbia to the United States. McNeill was married twice – to Mathilda who died in 1850 leaving one son and five daughters, and to Martha who was probably of the Nass tribe.

McNeill's career with the HBC was long and distinguished. In the 1830s and 1840s he helped the company to overcome the tricky navigational problems of the coast. As master of a trading post he managed to establish with the Indians the relationship necessary for profitable trading.

G. R. NEWELL

PABC, W. H. McNeill journals and correspondence. *Daily British Colonist* (Victoria), 5 Sept. 1875. *Daily British Colonist and Victoria Chronicle*, 15 May 1868. HBRS, IV (Rich); VI (Rich); VII (Rich); XXII (Rich).

MACTAVISH, DUGALD (the name is frequently written MacTavish or McTavish, but his branch of the family used Mactavish), HBC officer; b. 10 Aug. 1817 at Kilchrist House near Campbeltown, Argyllshire, Scotland, second son of Dugald Mactavish Sr and Letitia Lockhart; d. a bachelor, on 24 May 1871, at Montreal, Que.

Dugald Mactavish and his elder brother William* were appointed as apprentice clerks in the Hudson's Bay Company on 2 Jan. 1833; they sailed for Hudson Bay in the summer, and Dugald was posted to Moose Factory in the Southern Department where his uncle, John George McTavish*, was in charge. Dugald was transferred to Michipicoten, 100 miles north of Sault Ste Marie, on Lake Superior in 1835; for outfits 1837–38 and 1838–39 he was a clerk at Lachine.

The Council of the Northern Department meeting at Red River in June 1839 ordered Dugald Mactavish to the Columbia Department as clerk at Fort Vancouver under Chief Factor John McLoughlin*. When he reached this post in October he found it "so very large that on first arriving a stranger is almost apt to imagine himself in the civilized world. . . ." In the spring of 1840 he accompanied the York Factory Express east with the Columbia Department's yearly accounts, and in June he was instructed to take charge of the Columbia Brigade from Edmonton to Fort Vancouver and to convey 3,000 prime otter skins to meet the company's contract with the Russian American Company. The brigade arrived safely on 31 Oct. 1840 and Mactavish received McLoughlin's praise.

In June 1841 Mactavish was promoted to the rank of clerk first class at £100 a year, and his engagement at Fort Vancouver was renewed for three years. In 1842 Dugald's sister Letitia*, wife of James Hargrave*, characterized him as "a distinguished voyageur & driller of unruly men but he appears to be a good accomptant [*sic*] – as they say the Columbia papers were never before in such order as since he went." Yet advancement was slow under McLoughlin, and Dugald considered leaving the company. His merits were not entirely unnoticed on the Columbia, however, for when he took the accounts to Red River in 1845,

Mactavish

Chief Factor James DOUGLAS urged Governor Sir George Simpson* to send Mactavish back to the Columbia "as there is no person here, capable of replacing him."

Mactavish, who went east with the accounts both in 1844 and in 1845 was, according to his sister Letitia, a slender, handsome, and intense youth of charming, buoyant manner dressed in expensive finery ordered out from England, including an embroidered black satin waistcoat in which he astonished some of the residents of York Factory. He was an indefatigable horseman, and rode at Fort Vancouver even on Sundays, when McLoughlin required all to walk. According to Edward Martin Hopkins, personal secretary and assistant to Sir George Simpson, who visited the post in 1841–42, Mactavish worked from 4:00 A.M. to 11:00 P.M. the entire year, but could be wild as well as serious. The American missionaries conducting Sunday services at the fort were apt to find themselves disconcerted by "a loud & curious chanting" from the next apartment, where lay Dugald "singing . . . voyageur songs with his head under the blankets, & this is his pastime every Sunday morn^g from 6 till 9. . . ."

Increasing American settlement south of the Columbia River in these years made the HBC's continued ability to retain its lands and investments in Oregon doubtful. Accordingly, McLoughlin and other company employees entered claims in their own names, attempting to secure the company's important site at the falls of the Willamette River (Oregon City). Mactavish entered a claim to part of the lands at the company's mill, which he registered with the provisional government of Oregon on 16 Dec. 1843. However Isaac W. Alderman, an American probably encouraged by the Methodist mission, forcibly took possession of the land and improvements arguing that Mactavish's claim was invalid since he was not an American citizen. Mactavish was successful in his suit for recovery of the land but soon sold the claim to McLoughlin for $900.

When Mactavish arrived back at Fort Vancouver from York Factory in October 1845 it was expected that he would soon leave to take charge of Fort Victoria, Richard LANE having been assigned to his post as accountant at Fort Vancouver. However, the suicide of McLoughlin's son-in-law, William Glen Rae*, at San Francisco in January 1845 had revealed that the company's affairs there had been poorly managed, and McLoughlin sent Mactavish to close its business. He sold the company's premises for $5,000 and appointed an agent for the collection of the $10,000 in accounts owed to the HBC. With David McLoughlin and Rae's family, Mactavish returned to Fort Vancouver on 11 July aboard the HBC barque *Vancouver*.

He spent the next six months getting his accounts in order, taking measures to keep American claim jumpers off lands held by employees for the company, and attempting to collect the debts of the Red River settlers who had left the company and taken up farms south of the Columbia. Beginning in September, he sat as one of two judges for Vancouver County under an appointment from Oregon's governor, George Abernethy. His most important case concerned the jumping of a claim of Chief Factor Francis Ermatinger*. Richard Lane arrived on 8 Dec. 1846 bringing Mactavish's long-sought commission as chief trader effective 1 June 1846, and orders to succeed George Pelly in the "principal management" of the company's business at Oahu (Hawaii). Mactavish turned his Columbia Department responsibilities over to Henry N. Peers* and Thomas Lowe*, resigned as judge, and left to join the barque *Toulon* for passage to San Francisco, where he boarded the *Currency Lass* for Oahu.

In August 1852 Mactavish took a long-deferred furlough in England and Scotland. He had been promoted chief factor in 1851, and upon his return to Fort Vancouver in September 1853 he acted jointly with Chief Factor Peter Skene Ogden* on the board of management of the company's newly created Oregon Department, comprising the lands and posts in the United States to which it retained possessory rights by the Oregon treaty of 1846. Ogden died on 27 Sept. 1854, and Mactavish had sole responsibility for the department until June 1857 when Chief Factor William Fraser Tolmie* joined him on the board, although Tolmie remained at Fort Nisqually on Puget Sound. During the Indian troubles of 1855–56, Mactavish had to abandon Fort Hall in present-day Idaho, and he was called on to advance supplies to the territorial volunteers of both Oregon and Washington. He estimated the total value of these supplies at $100,000, and as late as 1866 the bill remained unpaid. At Fort Vancouver itself he protested what he considered the premature survey of HBC lands by United States officials and the appropriation of company lands and buildings for the U.S. army's Columbia barracks. In June 1858, with the company's ability to maintain its operations at Fort Vancouver in doubt, Mactavish turned the fort over to Chief Trader James Allan Grahame* and moved to Fort Victoria where he replaced James Douglas. With the creation of the crown colony of British Columbia, the position of the HBC there became what it was in its last years on the Columbia. Mactavish and Chief Factor John Work* prepared a report on its claims to lands and posts in mainland British Columbia which governor Douglas transmitted to the Colonial Office. Douglas felt that the company had acquired rights to the soil by occupation, improvement, and public services, and he urged that its claims be met in a spirit of "judicious liberality" particularly as the decision of the British government would influence the settlement of the company's claims in Oregon. Mactavish's future with the company was determined in part by his work on the British Columbia claims.

From February 1859 to June 1860 Mactavish was in England on sick leave. He returned to serve as the senior member of the board of management for the company's posts in British Columbia until November 1863, when he again returned to England.

In the early months of 1864, the United States and Great Britain ratified a treaty which provided for a joint commission to make final settlement of the claims of the HBC and the Puget's Sound Agricultural Company arising from the Oregon Treaty of 1846. Mactavish left London on 28 Oct. 1864 for Washington, D.C., with orders to help prepare the company's memorial to the joint commission. From Washington, Mactavish went to Canada and in May 1865 he made his last trip to the northwest coast. Arriving in Victoria on 26 June he had a month to prepare for the arrival of the U.S. commissioner who was to take testimony. Mactavish was back in Montreal by Christmas, and in March and April 1866 he wrote his first deposition for the agents of the commission. Between April 1866 and March 1867 he moved between Montreal, New York, Washington, D.C., and North Carolina on business connected with the company's claims, and from 8 March to 1 May he gave many hours of testimony in Washington to the joint commission. On 10 Sept. 1869 the commissioners made their final awards, reducing the claims of the two companies from $5,449,936.67 to $650,000.

Mactavish left for London at the conclusion of the commission's deliberations, but his days as company trouble-shooter were not yet over. Scarcely a month after his arrival, Mactavish, "a man of great intelligence, plain and unpretentious in his manner, and possessed of sound common sense," was recalled to Montreal to take the position vacated by Chief Factor Donald A. Smith*. Mactavish took rooms at St Lawrence Hall, and there on 24 May 1871 he died on a reading room sofa of "disease of the heart" following a sudden seizure at Martineau's bathing rooms.

WILLIAM R. SAMPSON

PABC, Thomas Lowe journal, 1843–50. *Canadian North-West* (Oliver). *Evidence on the part of the Hud-son's Bay Company claimants* (British and American Joint Commission for the final settlement of the claims of the Hudson's Bay and Puget's Sound Agricultural companies, [*Papers*], 14 v., Washington, Montreal, 1865–69, II). *Evidence for the United States in the matter of the claims of the Hudson's Bay and Puget's Sound Agricultural companies. Miscellaneous* (British and American Joint Commission for the final settlement of the claims of the Hudson's Bay and Puget's Sound Agricultural companies, [*Papers*], 14v., Washington, Montreal, 1865–69, XI). *Hargrave correspondence* (Glazebrook). HBRS, VI (Rich); VII (Rich). [Mactavish], *Letters of Letitia Hargrave* (MacLeod). *British Colonist* (Victoria), 10 Oct. 1859, 23 June 1860. *Daily British Colonist* (Victoria), 27 June, 28, 31 July 1865. *Daily British Colonist and Victoria Chronicle*, 17 June 1871. *Gazette* (Montreal), 25 May 1871. *Montreal Herald and Daily Commercial Gazette*, 25 May 1871. *Treaties and other international acts of the United States of America*, ed. [David] Hunter Miller (8v., Washington, 1931–48). J. A. Hussey, *The history of Fort Vancouver and its physical structure* ([Tacoma, Wash., 1957]).

MAGUIRE, JOHN, lawyer, judge of the Superior Court; b. April 1810 at Maguire's Bridge in Fermanagh County, Ireland, son of Matthew Maguire and Catherine O'Hara; d. 5 July 1880 at Quebec.

John Maguire arrived in Canada in 1823 with his parents. He attended the Petit Séminaire of Quebec and completed his classical education there. He then received legal training in the office of William Power*, and on 20 Sept. 1834 became a member of the bar.

During the 1837 insurrection John Maguire marched under the standard of the *Patriotes*. He then rallied to the party of Louis-Hippolyte La Fontaine* and offered himself as a candidate on the Liberal-Conservative ticket for the city of Quebec, but was defeated. From then on he turned his talents to municipal politics. Maguire had been a member of the city council for the district of Champlain since 1846 and he occupied this post until 1854. In 1852 he also became inspector and superintendent of police for the city of Quebec. The following year, the English Protestants of Quebec accused him of negligence in carrying out his duty at the time of the riot caused by Alessandro Gavazzi*, a fanatical, anti-Catholic Italian who had come to Quebec to give lectures against "papism" [see Charles WILSON]. An inquiry conducted by two Protestant justices of the peace cleared Maguire of all blame. Still in the setting of municipal administration, he was active on the aqueduct committee, where he exerted all his influence to provide Quebec City with the water services it needed.

In 1852 Maguire was appointed judge of the

Maillet

Court of Sessions of the Peace for the district of Quebec. Sixteen years later he became judge of the Superior Court for the district of Bonaventure, and, from 1 Sept. 1873, for the district of Rimouski. In 1877, with two of his colleagues, Judges Thomas McCord* and Louis-Napoléon Casault*, he had the courage to deliver a judgement condemning the Catholic priests of Bonaventure County, who during the previous electoral campaign had supported the Conservative candidate by using their spiritual authority. As Judge Maguire refused to retract, he incurred the wrath of Bishop Jean-Pierre-François Laforce* Langevin, and the bishop excommunicated him. This sentence was lifted by Bishop George CONROY in the autumn of 1877.

At his death, on 5 July 1880, he left his wife, Frances Agnes Horan, sister of Bishop Edward John HORAN, the first principal of the École Normale Laval, and nine of his 14 children.

BÉATRICE CHASSÉ

Rapport des commissaires nommés pour faire une enquête sur la conduite des autorités de police lors de l'émeute de l'église Chalmers, le 6 juin 1853, avec les minutes des procédés et des témoignages rendus devant la dite commission (Québec, 1854). *Journal de Québec,* 25 oct. 1853; 6 juill., 9 juill. 1880. *Morning Chronicle* (Quebec), 6 July 1880. *Quebec Mercury,* 8 July 1880. F.-J. Audet, "Commissions d'avocats de la province de Québec, 1765 à 1849," *BRH,* XXXIX (1933), 587. P.-G. Roy, *Les juges de la province de Québec,* 335. Robert [Philippe] Sylvain, "Séjour mouvementé d'un révolutionnaire italien à Toronto et à Québec," *RHAF,* XIII (1959–60), 183–229.

MAILLET (Maillé), MARIE-ANNE-MAR-CELLE. *See* MALLET

MAILLOUX, ALEXIS, secular priest, vicar general, temperance advocate, and missionary in Illinois; b. 8 Jan. 1801 at Île-aux-Coudres (Charlevoix County), L.C., son of Amable Mailloux and Thècle Lajoie; d. 4 Aug. 1877 at Île-aux-Coudres, Que.

In the autumn of 1814 Abbé Jérôme Demers* made the acquaintance of the young Alexis Mailloux at Île-aux-Coudres, and because of his family's poverty offered him free instruction at the seminary of Quebec. In May 1825 Bishop Joseph-Octave Plessis* ordained him to the priesthood.

Abbé Mailloux began his pastoral life as chaplain (1825–29), then first parish priest (1829–33), of Saint-Roch de Québec. After some months officiating at Fraserville (Rivière-du-Loup), he was required by his bishop to go to work among the student body of the young college of Sainte-Anne-de-la-Pocatière (Kamouraska County). Ill

prepared to devote himself to education, opposed by temperament to the laxity of the founder-superior of the institution, Abbé Charles-François Painchaud*, in matters of discipline and administration, he went so far as to challenge the *promitto* of the priesthood (the vow of obedience to the bishop), in the hope of declining his superior's invitation. Consequently it was without enthusiasm, and even with the greatest repugnance, that he agreed to become director of the college, a post he held until 1838.

In that year, following the death of the founder, he received advancement, and became parish priest of Sainte-Anne and superior of the parish college. Also in 1838 he was appointed vicar general of the diocese. During the ten years or so that followed, his vocation as preacher and writer became clear. Indeed, from that time on his correspondence abounds in details about his pastoral concerns. The evils he castigated and fought were drunkenness, luxury, immorality in all forms, and especially neglect on the part of parents in bringing up their children properly and watching their associates. The remedies he advocated were temperance societies, an extension of the role of confraternities or pious associations, the use of indulgences, and the use of parish retreats, which he inaugurated in the diocese.

All the same, it was the setting up of retreats that he liked best, the more because a sedentary life did not suit his personality. During the decade 1840–50, he contemplated in turn joining the Oblates of Mary Immaculate, founding a society of preaching priests of which he would be the head, and becoming a missionary in British Columbia or the Saguenay. To satisfy these aspirations, Bishop Joseph Signay* finally agreed, in 1847, to release him from his parish, to enable him to give himself exclusively to preaching in the diocese. After ten years of an itinerant ministry as preacher and colonizing missionary, Mailloux left Canada to go to combat Charles-Paschal-Télesphore Chiniquy*'s schismatics in Illinois. Returning to Canada, he was parish priest of Saint-Bonaventure-d'Hamilton (Bonaventure County) from 1863 to 1865. After that, preaching and writing took up the rest of his life.

Mailloux's written work is extensive. Among the best known titles are: *La croix présentée aux membres de la Société de tempérance*; *L'ivrognerie est l'œuvre du démon ...*; *Essai sur le luxe et la vanité des parures ...*; and *Manuel des parents chrétiens ou devoirs des pères et des mères....* This last work reproduces the content of his first sermons given at retreats. Its distribution and therefore its influence – the fifth edition was in 1927 – did not diminish in the 20th century; indeed in 1945 the *Bulletin des recherches historiques* recommended it for French Canadian homes because it "is best adapted to our ideas and needs."

The ideas of Vicar General Mailloux were inspired by the rigorism that owed its prevalence to Jansenist ethics, as were those of the 19th-century French Canadian clergy as a whole. Hence there is nothing surprising in the fact that he felt little sympathy for his "materialistic and mechanistic century." As a whole his teaching was based on a rejection of the world and still more on a fear of God and hell. Furthermore, his impetuous temperament carried him away while he was preaching. In 1863, during a retreat of 40 hours at Sainte-Claire, Dorchester, his homily so scared the congregation that many complained and did not want to confess their sins. Consequently Bishop Charles-François Baillargeon* once deemed it expedient to say to Mailloux: "One must beware of arbitrariness; of the rigorism that damns many and saves no one; of the exaggeration that ... falsifies consciences; of the excess that finds sin where there is none."

SERGE GAGNON

Alexis Mailloux's writings are many; his best known titles are: *La croix présentée aux membres de la Société de tempérance* (Québec, 1850); *Essai sur le luxe et la vanité des parures spécialement dédié aux personnes de la campagne* (Sainte-Anne-de-la-Pocatière, Qué., 1867); *L'ivrognerie est l'œuvre du démon, mais la sainte tempérance de la croix est l'œuvre de Dieu* (Québec, 1867); *Manuel des parents chrétiens ou devoirs des pères et des mères dans l'éducation religieuse de leurs enfants* (Québec, 1851).

AAQ, Registres des lettres des évêques de Québec. Archives de l'évêché de Sainte-Anne (La Pocatière, Qué.), Paroisse de Sainte-Anne; Collège de Sainte-Anne (original letters of Mailloux, 1834–47). Archives du collège de Sainte-Anne-de-la-Pocatière (Qué.), Fonds Alexis Mailloux (large collection of original documents concerning Mailloux, 1834–47). ASQ, Polygraphie, L, LI, LII, LIII (Mailloux's correspondence during his years in the United States). Julienne Barnard, *Mémoires Chapais; documentation, correspondance, souvenirs* (4v., Montréal et Paris, 1961–64), I. N.-E. Dionne, *Sainte-Anne de la Pocatière, 1672–1910; l'Île-aux-Oies, 1646–1910* (Galerie historique, III, Québec, 1910), 82–85, 87–95, 129; *Vie de C.-F. Painchaud; prêtre, curé, fondateur du collège Sainte-Anne de la Pocatière* (Québec, 1894), 206–57. Wilfrid Lebon, *Histoire du collège Sainte-Anne-de-la-Pocatière* (2v., Québec, 1948–49), I, 39–79. Fernand Porter, *L'institution catéchistique au Canada; deux siècles de formation religieuse, 1633–1833* (Montréal, 1949). Marcel Trudel, *Chiniquy* (2e éd., [Trois-Rivières], 1955). "Le « Manuel des parents chrétiens »," *BRH*, LI (1945), 242.

MAKOYI-KSIKSINUM. *See* SOTAI-NA

MALCOLM, ELIAKIM, miller, farmer, politician, and rebel; b. 18 March 1801 in the township of Oakland, U.C., son of Tryphena and Finlay Malcolm, an early American settler in the area; d. 26 Sept. 1874, at Scotland, Ont.

A miller and "yeoman" like his father, Eliakim (or "Liak") Malcolm laid out the village of Scotland and served as surveyor and as a justice of the peace. He married Samantha Sexton in 1822 and became the father of eight children.

Malcolm was a vocal Reformer and opposed the administration at York (Toronto) in the 1830s because of its alleged neglect of remote communities such as Oakland and its awarding of lucrative monopolies in transportation and banking to its "extravagant" friends. Following the lead of Dr Charles Duncombe*, the principal Reformer in the London District, Malcolm and members of his family spoke at protest meetings in Burford and Oakland townships in 1837. When the rebellion broke out in December, Scotland was the gathering place for Duncombe's armed supporters, who included Malcolm. Following the defeat of William Lyon Mackenzie*'s force near Toronto, many loyal militiamen were released for duty in the west and they soon descended on Scotland, from which the disheartened rebels had already withdrawn. The militiamen uncovered on Malcolm's property incriminating correspondence and a muster-roll of local dissidents. A few days later, on 16 Dec. 1837, a proclamation offered a reward of £250 for his apprehension. He succeeded, however, like Duncombe, in escaping to the United States. On a list of rebels drawn up in October 1838 Malcolm's name still occupied a prominent place after that of Duncombe.

Yet he seems to have been able to return to Upper Canada about three years later. Resuming his life as a farmer and miller (he constructed the first sawmill in Scotland in 1848), Malcolm still found time for local politics. In the less turbulent political atmosphere of the mid-century his Reformist ideas were more acceptable. Malcolm was elected to Oakland Township's first council and was named its first reeve at the council's inaugural meeting in 1850. In 1853 when the county of Brant (of which Oakland formed a part) was separated from its neighbours, Halton and Wentworth counties, the one-time rebel was selected as its first warden. He strongly championed such "internal improvements" as navigation on the Grand River and the Buffalo and Brantford Railway (named, in 1856, the Buffalo and Lake Huron Railway Company), called for the effective use of the county's vaunted "hydraulic power," and promoted social improvements such as penal reform and public sanitation.

Malhiot

In 1855 Malcolm was defeated in a bid to serve a third term as warden and in 1857 stepped down as reeve of Oakland. He spent the remainder of his life farming and milling.

C. M. JOHNSTON

Oakland, Ont., Township offices, minutes of the Oakland Township Council, 1850–56. Brant County Council, *Minutes*, 1853–57. [George Coventry], "A contemporary account of the rebellion in Upper Canada, 1837," ed. W. R. Riddell, *Ont. Hist.*, XVII (1919), 113–74. J. H. Land, "The recollections of Lieut. John Land a militia man, in the rebellion of 1837," Wentworth Hist. Soc. *Papers and Records* (Hamilton), VIII (1919), 20–24. *Brantford Expositor*, October 1874. *Mirror* (Toronto), 26 Oct. 1838. *Upper Canada Gazette* (Toronto), 2 Dec. 1837, 25 Oct. 1838. J. K. Malcolm, *The history and genealogy of the Malcolm family of the United States and Canada* (Ann Arbor, Mich., 1950). Dent, *Upper Canadian rebellion*, II. *The history of the county of Brant, Ontario* (Toronto, 1883). Fred Landon, *An exile from Canada to Van Diemen's Land, being the story of Elijah Woodman transported overseas for participation in the Upper Canada troubles of 1837–38* (Toronto, 1960); *Western Ontario and the American frontier* (Toronto, 1941). F. D. Reville, *History of the county of Brant* (2v., Brantford, 1920), I. W. C. Trimble, "Historical sketch of the county of Brant," in *Illustrated historical atlas of the county of Brant, Ont.* (Toronto, 1875), iii–xvi.

MALHIOT, CHARLES-CHRISTOPHE, doctor, seigneur, member of the Legislative Council of the Province of Canada and of the Canadian Senate; b. 11 Oct. 1808 at Verchères, L.C., second son of François-Xavier-Amable Malhiot, seigneur of Verchères, member of the assembly and legislative councillor for Lower Canada, and of Julie Boucher de La Perrière; d. 9 Nov. 1874 at Pointe-du-Lac, Que.

After completing a classical education at the college of Montreal, Charles-Christophe Malhiot studied medicine under Dr Robert NELSON, considered a great surgeon at that time. Having qualified as a doctor, he first went to live at Yamachiche; on 20 Oct. 1835, at Pointe-du-Lac, he married Julie-Éliza Montour, daughter of Nicolas Montour*, seigneur of Pointe-du-Lac, member of the assembly for Saint-Maurice, and one of the pioneers of the North West Company. Nine children were born of this marriage, but they all died in infancy.

After his marriage Charles-Christophe established his office and took up residence in the parish of La Visitation-de-la-Pointe-du-Lac. In 1833 he had been appointed surgeon in the 3rd Battalion of Saint-Maurice County. Although a stranger to this region, Dr Malhiot, who was a great bene-

factor of the poor, rapidly won the respect of the people. The fact that he was seigneur of Pointe-du-Lac undoubtedly also brought him a good deal of prestige. Dr Malhiot's wife had inherited a joint third of this seigneury, of which Malhiot was to become owner on her death in 1865; a few years later, in 1873, he made an offer to purchase another third of the seigneury. As well as this land at Pointe-du-Lac, he possessed titles to other seigneuries: on the death of Joseph Boucher de La Perrière in 1819 he had become the owner, with his father and two brothers, of the seigneury of Contrecœur, and in 1854 his father bequeathed to him the seigneury of Verchères.

Even if the practice of medicine in this rural region interested him greatly, Dr Malhiot did not restrict his field of activity to his occupation. In 1847 he sat on the council of the College of Physicians and Surgeons of Lower Canada in his capacity as one of the governors of this organization, representing the district of Trois-Rivières and Saint-François. He had, moreover, supported with his signature a petition, presented that same year to the house, seeking legal recognition of the medical profession in Canada East.

Dr Malhiot, like several doctors in his day, was interested in political life. The son of an ardent *Patriote*, he had defended the cause of the *Patriotes* in the circles in which he moved, but does not seem to have taken part actively in the disturbances of 1837–38. He began his political career at the municipal level when he was elected mayor of Pointe-du-Lac in 1859; he held this office until 1864. At the same period, following in his father's footsteps, Dr Malhiot turned his attention to the national scene; he stood as candidate in the Shawinigan division for the elections to the Legislative Council of 1862. He was the Liberal candidate, and faced George BAPTIST, a merchant of Trois-Rivières. Baptist, less popular than his opponent, withdrew a few days before the election, and on 30 Sept. 1862 Dr Malhiot was elected by acclamation. He sat until confederation. In May 1867, by royal proclamation, he was called to the Senate as representative for the division of La Vallière. He remained a senator until his death. Malhiot was acknowledged as a loyal supporter of the Liberal party throughout his career. Although he took a fairly active interest in political life, he seems on the whole to have played only an unobtrusive part in it.

Charles-Christophe Malhiot, a great landowner and from a fairly well-to-do family, lived in comfortable circumstances. On his death he left a fortune estimated at about $60,000, which, after charitable donations to religious communities at Trois-Rivières and to the parish council of Pointe-du-Lac, he bequeathed to his brothers, chiefly to Adolphe.

LOUISE CRÊTE-BÉGIN

AJTR, Registre d'état civil, paroisse La Visitation-de-la-Pointe-du-Lac, 1834–1874. ASTR, Trifluviens du 19ᵉ et du 20ᵉ siècle, Charles Malhiot. Canada, Province of, Legislative Council, *Journals*, 1862–1866; *Statutes*, 1847, c.26. *Le Canadien* (Québec), 22 sept., 13 oct. 1862; 11 nov. 1874. *Le Constitutionnel* (Trois-Rivières), 11 nov. 1874. *L'Ère nouvelle* (Trois-Rivières), 22 sept., 2 oct. 1862. *Le Journal des Trois-Rivières*, 12 nov. 1874. *Le Pays* (Montréal), 18 sept., 27 sept. 1862. *Can. parl. comp.*, 1874, 61–62. *Political appointments, 1841–1865* (J.-O. Coté), 57, 60. *Political appointments and judicial bench* (N.-O. Coté), 3, 168. Turcotte, *Conseil législatif de Québec*, 275–76. Ahern, *Notes pour l'histoire de la médecine*, 399–400. F.-J. Audet, *Contrecœur: famille, seigneurie, paroisse, village* (Montréal, 1940), 44–46. *Deux siècles de vie paroissiale à La Pointe-du-Lac; compte-rendu des fêtes du deuxième centenaire de La Pointe-du-Lac le dimanche 31 juillet 1938* (Pages trifluviennes, sér. A, 21, Trois-Rivières, 1939), 23. Alexandre Dugré, *La Pointe-du-Lac* (Pages trifluviennes, sér. A, 15, Trois-Rivières, 1934), 23, 59. J.-J. Lefebvre, "La famille Malhiot, de Montréal et de Verchères," SGCF *Mémoires*, XII (1961), 153. Sœur Marie du Rédempteur, "La Pointe-du-Lac aux 19ᵉ et 18ᵉ siècles," *BRH*, XXXVIII (1932), 301–15. Albert Tessier, "Les Trifluviens s'échauffent . . . Le dernier demi-siècle des forges (1833–1883)," *Cahiers des Dix*, XV (1950), 168.

MALHIOT, ÉDOUARD-ÉLISÉE, *Patriote* and lawyer; b. around 1810 or 1814 at Saint-Pierre-les-Becquets (Nicolet County, Quebec); d. August 1875 at L'Assomption (Assumption), in Illinois.

Information about Édouard-Élisée Malhiot's childhood is totally lacking. We know, however, that he went to Montreal around 1830, and that he studied law there. At Montreal he adopted the *Patriote* cause with a kind of mystic fervour. He was a friend of Ludger Duvernay*, a keen supporter of Louis-Joseph PAPINEAU, and an active member of the Fils de la Liberté [*see* LEBLANC], and was to be found at all the meetings and demonstrations that took place repeatedly at Montreal between April and November 1837. On 6 November he took part in the brutal clash between the Fils de la Liberté and the members of the Doric Club, who supported the government's policies. This episode, as he told Duvernay in confidence, was for him the beginning of total commitment.

He threw himself into the battle like a crusader. He is thought to have commanded the small contingent that on 28 November, the day after the events at Saint-Charles, attempted to intercept Colonel George Augustus Wetherall* at Pointe-Olivier (Saint-Mathias), in Rouville County, as he was on his way to Montreal. Shortly afterwards,

with several of his compatriots, Malhiot reached the United States and took refuge at Swanton, Vermont. With the object of joining the *Patriotes* at Saint-Eustache he recrossed the border at the head of a group of 70 to 80 men, but was shortly, on 6 December, stopped at Moore's Corner (Saint-Armand-Station) by a party of Canadian volunteers [*see* MOORE]. He was wounded, and got back to Swanton the next day; then began for him a short but painful period of exile.

Malhiot passed through a stage of discouragement. During the first weeks of January his material situation was precarious. Above all, he dreaded the worst for the future. In his opinion, the Americans were too tardy in showing in a tangible way their sympathy and especially their support. Moreover, the dissensions among the *Patriote* leaders were in danger of compromising the cause of independence beyond redemption. Loyal to Papineau, he was angry with Robert NELSON and Cyrille-Hector-Octave Côté* for criticizing his leader in public. Only towards the end of May, impatient "with the unpopular and dishonest conduct of Papineau," did he make it up with Robert Nelson and come round to the idea of an invasion from the United States, as a means of facilitating the move to make Lower Canada an independent republic.

After the failure of a first attempt on 28 Feb. 1838, due it was believed to excessive rashness and to Washington's desire to keep a more careful watch on the observance of American neutrality, the *Patriotes* had decided to reorganize themselves in a secret society, the Frères-Chasseurs [*see* NELSON]. In this group Malhiot was to play an important role. Taking advantage of the general amnesty granted by Lord Durham [Lambton*] on 28 June 1839, he returned to Montreal in August of that year intending to remain there. He did not receive any unwelcome attention. He was appointed *Grand Aigle* of the Association des Frères-Chasseurs, and conducted a remarkable propaganda campaign in the Richelieu valley. Going round from parish to parish, the "Commandant du Sud," as he styled himself, set up lodges, initiated new members, and promised arms and munitions for the day of the general uprising. On that day, 3 November, the *Patriotes* of Lower Canada, assisted by the invasion army directed by Nelson, were to launch simultaneous attacks against Saint-Jean, Chambly, and Sorel and proceed towards Montreal, where the *Patriotes* would have risen. Sorel was Malhiot's objective.

The plan proved to be a total failure. Malhiot managed to assemble rapidly nearly 300 men at Saint-Ours, and set off towards his objective during the night of 3 or 4 November. Learning that

Mallet

Nelson had not moved from Napierville, he returned to Saint-Ours the same night. He was a helpless witness of Nelson's departure from Napierville, his defeat at Odelltown, and his flight to the United States. From 10 to 14 November, with about 200 *Patriotes*, 3 guns, and more than 100 rifles, he maintained a camp on the mountain of Saint-Bruno-de-Montarville, fully determined to hold out. To no avail. On the morning of the 14th, as the regular troops approached from Sorel, Malhiot, on whose head a price had been set, fled with a few comrades. They crossed the border after wandering for two weeks in the woods.

Malhiot was profoundly depressed and embittered by the turn of events. Few persons found grace in his eyes. He wrote to Duvernay expressing his contempt for the egoism and ignorance of the Americans, the ingratitude of his compatriots, and particularly the deceit and cowardice of some of those who preached revolution before November 1837 for the purpose of acquiring popularity or through personal interest. It is not impossible that his feelings, together with a certain uneasiness at the idea of seeing again those who had had faith in him, explain why he chose exile. In any case, he had not the kind of temperament which could accept a life of self-effacement.

After some hesitation he went to settle at L'Assomption (Assumption), in Louisiana. The French-speaking settlement that existed in Louisiana was now the home of other refugees of the 1837–38 period, for example Benjamin Ouimet and the doctors J.-Guillaume Beaudrieau and Pierre Damour*. Until 1856 Malhiot practised law with great success, acquiring fame and fortune. In 1856 a district elected him senator in absentia.

Malhiot had decided, in this year, to renew contact with his past. Abandoning his career, he bought some fertile land in Illinois. He had conceived the plan of starting there an agricultural settlement, where homes could be set up by some of the thousands of French Canadians who each year were forced to emigrate, and who preferred to work with the earth rather than in the brick-fields and textile factories of New England. About 50 families, some of whom came from his native parish, joined him there. His undertaking prospered. He obtained the services of a Canadian priest for his little community of L'Assomption (Assumption). In 1875 he died prematurely, stricken by cholera. He was mourned by his wife and two sons.

YVES ROBY

"Inventaire des documents relatifs aux événements de 1837 et 1838, conservés aux archives de la province de Québec," APQ *Rapport, 1925–26*, 172, 193, 210, 212, 217, 221, 224, 258, 259, 260, 272, 322. "Papiers Duvernay conservés aux archives de la province de Québec," APQ *Rapport, 1926–27*, 147–252. Fauteux, *Patriotes*. Ivanhoë Caron, "Édouard-Élisée Malhiot," *RSCT*, 3rd ser., XXII (1928), sect.I, 155–66.

MALLET (Maillet, Maillé), MARIE-ANNE-MARCELLE, professed religious of the Sisters of Charity of the Hôpital Général of Montreal, foundress of the Institute of the Sisters of Charity of Quebec, and superior of that community from 1849 to 1866; b. 26 March 1805 at Montreal, L.C., daughter of Vital Mallet, farmer and tanner, and Marguerite Sarrazin; d. 9 April 1871 at Quebec.

Marie-Anne-Marcelle Mallet's childhood was upset by her father's premature death on 23 April 1810, and by the disruptions that resulted. At the age of 10 she had to leave the village of L'Assomption, where her family had lived since 1806: faced with the problem of her children's education, the mother had resigned herself to giving them up to an aunt and uncle at Lachine. Each year the adolescent girl regretfully took leave of her brother and her adoptive parents and went for some months as a boarder to the sisters of the Congregation of Notre-Dame, probably at Pointe-Claire.

At 16 Marcelle Mallet was already sensitive to the disarray well known to the child without a family and the poor without a home. She therefore decided to join the religious daughters of Mother d'Youville [Dufrost* de Lajemmerais], who had founded the Institute of the Sisters of Charity of the Hôpital Général of Montreal, the earliest religious congregation that was strictly Canadian. Admitted first as a postulant because of her youth, Marcelle Mallet was permitted to enter the noviciate on 6 May 1824. She made her profession in the community on 18 May 1826, and was called upon to perform the most varied tasks, but above all to care for the sick. In 1846 she began the custom of home visiting as a charitable undertaking. In 1847 typhus struck Montreal, and she had an opportunity to display her organizational abilities as much as her zeal, when, in the capacity of assistant superior, she assumed entire responsibility for the hospital.

In the period 1840 to 1850 the community set up a number of foundations. After Saint-Hyacinthe, Saint-Boniface (Manitoba), and Bytown (Ottawa) [see Élisabeth BRUYÈRE], came Quebec. Selected as foundress-superior of this last mission, Sister Mallet left her religious family on 21 Aug. 1849 with five companions. It was an irreversible departure, according to the rule of the foundations of the time. On 22 Aug. 1849 the population of Quebec received its first Sisters of Charity. After two conflagrations and a terrible cholera epidemic, Quebec was then going through one of the most harrowing periods in its history. On their arrival, the sisters set themselves up in the orphanage-school in Rue des Glacis, on the boundary of the parish of Notre-Dame. On 5 November the members of the Société Charitable des Dames Catholiques de Québec entrusted to Mother Mallet an organization which they had founded in 1831 and maintained for 18 years; the ladies of the society remained associates of the Sisters of Charity.

Mother Mallet, who had come with her companions "to look after the sick, the education of needy young girls, and other requirements," concerned herself with answering the most pressing appeals of those in distress. In 1849 she instituted a relief service for poor schoolchildren. Then, in addition to the orphan girls, she took in women boarders in 1855, aged and infirm persons in 1856, and orphan boys in 1861. In 1866 she agreed to set up an out-patient service for the needy, and, during the 17 years that she directed the community, she established in the country, within the confines of the diocese of Quebec, five boarding-schools for girls, which were complementary to the local schools and served as training centres for schoolmistresses.

These charitable activities, which grew and became diversified, took their toll of Mother Mallet. She knew the ordeal of solitude: her early companions had either died soon after the founding of the institute, or, taking advantage of an invitation from the Hôpital Général of Montreal in 1854, had decided to return to Montreal despite their pledge in 1849; the epidemics of typhus in 1851 and of cholera in 1854 had reduced her work force while increasing her duties; on 3 May 1854 a fire had laid waste an orphanage that had just been built; and finally, quite unforeseen conflicts within the community she had started tried her sorely.

In September 1849 Mother Mallet had received four recruits for her charitable undertaking. She had thus established the bases of a new religious family. The Institute of the Sisters of Charity of Quebec received its official consecration in the church on 1 July 1866. On that day Pius IX approved its *Règles et constitutions*. Mother Mallet and several of her companions would have liked to remain loyal to the spiritual heritage of the Sulpicians bequeathed by Mother d'Youville and the Hôpital Général of Montreal. The foundress had refused a change in the legislation so long as she had been free to do so. But in 1863 Charles-François Baillargeon*, bishop of Quebec, had imposed on her a new rule which was the work of the Jesuit Antoine-Nicolas Braün, and which was essentially derived from the Society of Jesus.

When this new rule was put into force, the community of the Sisters of Charity of Quebec experienced a period of internal crisis. Although there was no conflict of principle between the two rules, all the sisters could not give their allegiance with equal freedom to the reorientation of the community. Mother Mallet herself, accustomed to the old rule, found it difficult to pass from the liberal atmosphere of the Sulpician school, in which her charity had flourished for 40 years, to this Ignatian framework, whose quality had proved itself but in which everything was more measured, more austere, and more rigorous. On the other hand the young nuns formed by Father Braün, the spiritual director of the community from 1856, enlisted boldly under the banner of the robust St Ignatius. Soon conflicting currents of ideas began to be apparent. In this drama of the *Règles et constitutions* Mother Mallet had the most difficult role. Ever since 1863 her attitude, conciliatory though it was, had been challenged by certain of the sisters. And Father Braün readily fostered this contention. In the 1866 elections the foundress was not re-elected as head of her community; she did not even have a place in the administration.

Mother Mallet then addressed herself to the humble task of a Sister of Charity, and, gently, reached her last days. She died at dawn on Easter Sunday, 9 April 1871. She was remembered as a woman of great activity and energy. Undaunted by time and space, her community in its vitality confirms her faith and justifies her work. Today, a century after her death, the community of the Sisters of Charity of Quebec numbers nearly 1,800 professed religious in the United States, Japan, Paraguay, Argentina, the Congo, and above all in the province of Quebec which gave it its corner-stone. "With no distinction of country, race, or culture" these nuns perpetuate Marcelle Mallet's consecration to childhood, sickness, and old age.

ANDRÉE DÉSILETS

[Sœurs de la Charité de Québec], *Actes du chapitre général, première session, juillet-août 1968* (n.d., 1968); *Statistiques de la congrégation des sœurs de la Charité de Québec* (n.d., 1968); *Dans le sillage de la charité* (Québec, 1959). *Une fondatrice et son œuvre: mère Mallet (1805–1871) et l'Institut des sœurs de la Charité de Québec, fondé en 1849* (Québec, 1939).

MANCE. *See* CÉRÉ

MANNERS-SUTTON, JOHN HENRY THOMAS, 3rd **Viscount Canterbury,** politician and

Manners-Sutton

colonial administrator; b. 27 May 1814 in London, Eng., son of Charles Manners-Sutton, 1st Viscount Canterbury, and Lucy Maria Charlotte Denison; d. 24 June 1877 in London.

John Henry Thomas Manners-Sutton was descended from a line of distinguished British Conservatives; his grandfather, Charles Manners-Sutton, had been archbishop of Canterbury; his great-uncle, Thomas Manners-Sutton, had served as lord chancellor of Ireland; his father was speaker of the British House of Commons for 18 years. He himself was educated at Eton and at Trinity College, Cambridge, where he received an MA in 1835; he entered Lincoln's Inn in that year but was never called to the bar. On 5 July 1838 he married Georgiana Tompson by whom he had five sons and two daughters.

The political career of Manners-Sutton began somewhat falteringly in 1839 when he won a Cambridge by-election for the Tories but was subsequently unseated for bribery. He won the seat again in 1841 and in September was appointed under-secretary for the Home Department in Sir Robert Peel's administration. He rarely took part in Commons debates and resigned his office when Peel was overthrown in 1846. Defeated in the 1847 election, Manners-Sutton retired from politics to devote much of his time to editing the *Lexington Papers* (8v., London, 1851) for publication.

On 1 July 1854 Manners-Sutton was appointed the eighth lieutenant governor of New Brunswick. According to W. S. MacNutt, he had been selected "by reason of a promising ability that had been displayed" at the Home Office and by reason of his family's "important connections." When he arrived to take up his post in October, a group of local politicians were concerned because responsible government had not become an accomplished fact and they believed Manners-Sutton had reservations on this score. On 20 Oct. 1854 the reform leader, Charles FISHER, introduced an amendment to the address in reply to the speech from the throne arguing that the government had "quailed" before the lieutenant governor, Sir Edmund Head*, in 1851, and that responsible government had, therefore, really not come in 1848 [see WILMOT]. Fisher also referred to rumours that Head had met his successor, Manners-Sutton, in Boston and told him how to run the Legislative Council and, through it, the colony. It was obvious that the new governor was not popular with the reform-minded members of the assembly. Eight days after Fisher's speech, the government, led by John Ambrose Street*, lost a division in the assembly. "Shortly after," as MacNutt has noted, "for the first time in New Brunswick history, a

government resigned because of an adverse vote in the house of assembly." Manners-Sutton then appointed Fisher attorney general, but in his dispatches to London the governor made no attempt to hide his distaste for the new government.

The main concern of the Colonial Office in 1854 was that the New Brunswick assembly pass the laws necessary for the success of the reciprocity treaty with the United States. A dispatch to Manners-Sutton in September expressed the hope that "the fruits of so much execution will not be thrown away." The British government felt that the treaty would bring "the greatest advantages to Her Majesty's North American subjects" but recognized that the colony had "the ultimate decision as to the deliberations of this legislation." Manners-Sutton was authorized to make changes in colonial trade laws in compliance with the council and to bring the question of reciprocity "in the fullest and fairest manner before the provincial legislature."

During the first year of his tenure, Manners-Sutton and the Colonial Office disagreed on several points. The governor was in favour of granting the title "honourable" to retiring members of the Legislative Council, but he was over-ruled by Sir George Grey at the Colonial Office who wrote to Sir Robert Peel that such a move threw "an invidious power into the hands of a Governor who has already for the most part sufficient danger of unpopularity." In January 1855 both Grey and Peel opposed Manners-Sutton's suggestion that New Brunswick's civil list be placed in the hands of the Executive Council. Six months later he seemed to be on better terms with his superiors: the legislature had made changes especially in the trade and fishing laws – a continued preoccupation of the imperial government.

Manners-Sutton's next test came in 1855. The New Brunswick assembly had passed a bill in 1853 prohibiting the importation of alcoholic beverages into the colony. This measure could not be enforced effectively, but the temperance adherents, led by Samuel Leonard Tilley*, wanted a more stringent bill. In 1855 a second prohibition bill was passed, and, despite the governor's objection, given royal assent. Manners-Sutton did, however, recommend to the Colonial Office in London that it disallow the bill, but the Colonial Office ignored the recommendation. After the controversial measure became law, Manners-Sutton advised his New Brunswick government either to enforce the law or to repeal it – advice intended to destroy Fisher's government. The government's failure to enforce the prohibition bill eventually forced its resignation, but a subsequent election saw most of the same men returned to the assembly. Many of those elected had changed their minds about prohibition during the campaign; they acknowledged the propriety of Manners-Sutton's actions by repealing the measure.

During the remaining four years of his term, amidst a period of unprecedented prosperity in the province, the secret ballot was introduced, the power of the Legislative Council was reduced, and some assemblymen were pressing Manners-Sutton to open negotiations enabling the executive to initiate money grants. In 1857 the Colonial Office recognized the principle of responsible government in the colony by stating that any bill which did not receive "the assent of the three branches of the legislature must be regarded simply in the light of a 'Dropped Bill.' " A prolonged controversy over government grants to King's College, later the University of New Brunswick, aided Fisher and his supporters in their persistent demand that the legislature be given the right to supervise the drafting of confidential dispatches sent by Manners-Sutton to London. The Colonial Office supported Manners-Sutton's right to give confidential and private advice but when word reached Fredericton that Sir Howard Douglas*, Bishop John Medley*, and Edward Barron CHANDLER all had called at the Colonial Office to make representations concerning King's College, the New Brunswick government successfully demanded that copies of the documents should be made available for rebuttal. Yet another inroad had been made on the powers of the lieutenant governor.

Manners-Sutton had many other differences with Fisher, but they did agree on one issue: they chose to ignore a resolution passed in Canada in 1858 urging talks about the union of the British North American colonies. Manners-Sutton feared that imperial trade might be hampered by a union, and he also predicted that the Maritime provinces might resent the loss of their autonomy. He was in favour of Maritime union, however, and, in 1858, reported to London that talks on the subject would shortly begin between New Brunswick and Nova Scotia. The news was premature, for when Manners-Sutton was succeeded in October 1861 by Sir Arthur Hamilton Gordon* the movement for union of any kind seemed dormant.

From New Brunswick, Manners-Sutton went to Trinidad where he was governor for two years, long enought to witness the nearby Jamaica Rebellion and its bloody aftermath. His last colonial appointment, as governor of the Australian colony of Victoria in 1866, was the most tranquil and hence the happiest. That colony had undergone significant and, at times, stormy changes during the term of the previous governor, Sir Charles Henry Darling*. Manners-Sutton had no serious confrontations with the assembly during his seven-year term, and was one of Victoria's most popular governors. He resigned in 1873 and returned to England to take his seat in the House of Lords, having become 3rd Viscount Canterbury on the death of his older brother.

Like many other British colonial administrators in the mid-19th century, Manners-Sutton was fighting a rearguard action against rising demands for local autonomy. His aristocratic upbringing and outlook contrasted sharply with the egalitarian and colonial mentality of men like Charles Fisher. Nevertheless, Manners-Sutton was able to work with these local politicians and to gain their grudging respect.

RICHARD WILBUR

PRO, CO 188/118, 188/122–188/135. New Brunswick House of Assembly, *Debates*, 1854–61. *DNB*. R. M. Crawford, *Australia* (rev. ed., London, 1963). Hannay, *History of New Brunswick*, II. MacNutt, *New Brunswick*, 353–93. Geoffrey Serle, *The golden age: a history of the colony of Victoria, 1851–1861* (Melbourne, Aust., 1963). E. E. Williams, *History of the people of Trinidad and Tobago* (London, 1964).

MANSON, DONALD, HBC chief trader; b. 6 April 1796 at Thurso, Caithness, Scotland, son of Donald Manson and Jean Gunn; d. 7 Jan. 1880 at Champoeg, Oregon.

Donald Manson was engaged by the Hudson's Bay Company in 1817 and stationed at Rock Depot (Gordon House) on the Hayes River in present-day Manitoba. From there he went to Fort Superior and various other posts including Ile-à-la-Crosse in the English River District. An 1822 report noted that he was a "fine powerful active young man [and a] tolerable Clerk & Trader." Manson, once described by John Tod* as a "ramping highlander," had already begun to show his penchant for a rugged outdoor life. In 1822 he participated in expeditions led by Chief Factor Donald McKenzie* to the headwaters of the Missouri and South Saskatchewan rivers. Later in the same year, Manson travelled with Francis Heron* to examine the Bow and Red Deer rivers for possible trading post sites.

A report of 1825 confirms Manson's reputation as a "Fine strapping fellow" who "would be thrown away at an Establishment, active service being his forte." Late that year he was transferred as a clerk to the Columbia District, where, under John McLoughlin*, he helped to supervise improvements at Fort Vancouver with James McMillan* and John Work*. Then Manson was

Marie de Bonsecours

sent to build Fort Langley on the Fraser River in 1827. In the season of 1829–30, he was stationed at Fort George at the mouth of the Columbia. There he tried to rescue from the "Graveyard of the Pacific" two company ships, the *William and Ann*, which had gone down in March 1829, and the *Isabella*, which sank in May 1830.

Manson took charge of Fort Simpson on the Nass River in 1831 and explored the stream during that season. He explored the Skeena River in 1832, finding not "one solitary spot" suitable for a post. The following spring, he constructed Fort McLoughlin on Millbank Sound. In George Simpson*'s words, "Besides blasting and levelling, Mr. Manson, without aid of horse or ox, had introduced several thousand loads of gravel, while, by his judicious contrivances in the way of fortifications, he had rendered the place capable of holding out, with a garrison of twenty men, against all the natives of the coast." Manson was promoted to chief trader in 1837 and remained at Fort McLoughlin until 1839, when he travelled to Scotland. During this trip Manson was presented to the governor and committee in London on 21 Oct. 1840.

Manson took over Kamloops Post on the Thompson River in 1841. During 1843–44 he was in charge of Stikine, a post established in territory leased from Russia. One of his duties was to investigate the murder there of young John McLoughlin, son of the departmental governor. The senior McLoughlin was upset by Manson's apparent lack of vigour in searching out the killers and handing them over to the Russian authorities for trial, but apparently there was no evidence on which he could act.

From 1844 until his retirement in 1857, Manson was based at Fort St James on Stuart Lake in New Caledonia. Unfortunately, the final part of his career was marred by complaints that he treated his subordinates roughly. More than once, Governor Sir George Simpson reprimanded Manson for his bad temper and his reputation for harshness, and warned that "club law" would not be tolerated. It would appear that Manson was denied promotion to chief factor primarily because of his rough and abrasive ways.

In October 1828 Manson had married Félicité Lucier and they had eight children. After his retirement from the HBC, he and his family moved to Champoeg, Oregon, where they bought a farm on the banks of the Willamette River. The farm was inundated by a flood in December 1861, but the house remained unscathed. After his wife's death in 1867, Manson lived on at the farm until his own death.

Donald Manson was one of the many capable individuals who manned the farthest outposts of the huge HBC empire. A recent biographer, Harriet Munnick, describes him as "a typical trader in the employ of a great monopoly – tough, obstinate, a little grim, honest, humorless, and a titan for work."

KENNETH L. HOLMES

PABC, "Biography of Donald Manson," typescript by J. A. Grant, 1938. Oregon State Library, Salem, Ore., Archives Division, U.S. Census Bureau, Population schedules, Oregon, 1860, Marion County, Champoeg Precinct, family no.2200; Oregon, 1870, Marion County, Champoeg Precinct, family no.961; schedules of mortality, Oregon, 1880, Marion County; Provisional Government recorder, Land claim records, 1845–49, 3, p.21. *Canadian North-West* (Oliver), II. Isaac Cowie, "The minutes of the Council of the Northern Department of Rupert's Land, 1830–1843," North Dakota State Hist. Soc. *Coll.*, IV (1913), 644–862. HBRS, III (Fleming); XVIII (Rich and Johnson). Morice, *History of northern interior of B.C.* F. W. Howay, "Authorship of traits of Indian life," *Oregon Hist. Q.* (Portland, Ore.), XXXV (1934), 42–49. H. S. Lyman, "Reminiscences: Mrs. Anna Tremewan," *Oregon Hist. Q.* (Portland, Ore.), IV (1903), 261–64. H. D. Munnick, "Donald Manson," *Mountain men and the fur trade*, ed. L. R. Hafen (7v., Glendale, Cal., 1965–69), VII, 217–25. W. H. Rees, "Donald Manson," Oregon Pioneer Assoc. *Trans.* (Portland, Ore.), VII (1880).

MARIE DE BONSECOURS. *See* GADBOIS

MARSHALL, JOHN GEORGE, lawyer, legislator, judge, author, and lecturer; b. at Country Harbour, N.S., in 1786; d. at Halifax, N.S., 7 April 1880, in full possession of his faculties.

John George Marshall was the son of Captain Joseph Marshall, a loyalist of the King's Carolina Rangers, and his wife Margaret. In 1794 the family moved to Guysborough where George received his early education before proceeding to Halifax grammar school. In 1803 he entered the law office of Judge Lewis Morris Wilkins* Sr, and was admitted to the bar of Nova Scotia in 1810. He first practised in Pictou, but later moved to Halifax where he built up a lucrative business. He married Catherine Jones on 26 Nov. 1809; they had several children.

In 1811 Marshall succeeded his father as representative for the county of Sydney (now Antigonish County) in the assembly, and held the seat until 1818. He was re-elected in 1820 and remained in the legislature until April 1823 when he resigned his seat. In the assembly he took great interest in bills which were designed to reform the social structure of the community. In 1823 he introduced a bill for the support of schools by local assessment and also backed a bill to give

Marshall de Brett Maréchal

all creditors equal claim in bankruptcy suits. Although both bills failed to pass the house while Marshall was a member, the former was accepted by 1825 and the latter many years later.

Marshall resigned from the assembly on his appointment as chief justice of the Interior Court of Common Pleas and president of the Courts of General and Special Sessions, Custos Rotulorum, and justice of the peace for Cape Breton. He lived in Sydney for the 18 years he was on the bench, administering justice in a manner which commanded the respect of all and doing what he could to improve social and moral conditions in the province. When the Court of Common Pleas was abolished in 1841, Judge Marshall retired on pension and devoted the rest of his life to a number of causes which he felt would better the lot of the common people. He was a prolific writer upon almost every topic that men of his day discussed – law, temperance, education, to mention only a few. Although not a brilliant writer, he studied his subjects carefully and wrote forcibly. His best-known work was *The justice of the peace, and county & township officer, in the province of Nova Scotia*, which became a standard textbook for local magistrates.

Marshall was a zealous temperance advocate; he travelled widely on this continent and in Europe lecturing on the topic. Politically he was an anti-confederate. He supported Joseph Howe with a zeal which prompted Howe to declare publicly in 1867, "When I think of a man of his age and intellect . . . aiding his countrymen in this struggle, I feel he has done that for us which hardly anyone else could have done so well. . . . The service which he has rendered his country will make me feel grateful towards him to the day of my death. . . ."

When Judge Marshall died, a personal friend, the editor of the *Acadian Recorder*, wrote: "A Puritan of the Puritans himself, he regarded worldly amusement in general as snares of the devil, and being utterly indifferent to popularity, he attacked right and left with a directness of speech in the cause of morality and righteousness. . . . He was a prodigious writer on a multitude of subjects, never hesitating to attack what he thought was wrong. He was stern and uncompromising, nevertheless he contributed of his limited means to all objects of charity and philanthropy, and he died as he had lived, in the midst of a true and noble fight."

C. E. THOMAS

A list of Marshall's publications appears in Morgan, *Bibliotheca Canadensis*. J. G. Marshall, *The justice of the peace, and county & township officer, in the province of Nova Socita; being a guide to such justice and officers*

in the discharge of their official duties (2nd ed., Halifax, 1846). *Acadian Recorder* (Halifax), 7 April 1880. *Morning Chronicle* (Halifax), 7 April 1880. *Morning Herald* (Halifax), 7 April 1880. *Directory of N.S. MLAs* (Fergusson). *Dom. ann. reg., 1880–81.* A. C. Jost, *Guysborough sketches and essays* (Guysborough, N.S., 1950). D. P. Floyd, "Jottings of Guysboro County happenings during the past centuries," *Canso Breeze and Guysboro County Advocate* (Canso, N.S.), 11 March 1921.

MARSHALL DE BRETT MARÉCHAL, JOSEPH, 2nd **Baron d'Avray,** professor, educator, and journalist; b. in London, Eng., 30 Nov. 1811, the eldest of 12 children of Joseph Head Marshall, 1st Baron d'Avray, and Elisabeth Golding Elrington; d. in Fredericton, N.B., 26 Nov. 1871.

Marshall d'Avray's early life was conditioned by the fact that his father was associated with Edward Jenner in the discovery of vaccination, and subsequently introduced the practice into Naples where he became physician extraordinary to King Ferdinand I and Queen Maria Carolina. The family lived much in France. Joseph Head Marshall warned the government of the impending escape of Napoleon from Elba, and he received his title as a reward for aiding in the restoration of the Bourbons in 1815. Marshall d'Avray was tutored by his father in company with the children of Louis-Philippe, and subsequently inherited his father's title at the latter's death in 1838. On the decline of the family fortunes, largely because of French dynastic changes, Marshall d'Avray found employment as a professor in the Royal College in Mauritius, but the climate there did not suit his wife, Margaret Emma Glenn. In 1848, he, his wife, and their daughter, Laurestine Marie, moved to Fredericton, N.B., where he had been appointed to found the first training school for teachers in the province.

As head of the normal school until it burned in November 1850, and later as chief superintendent of education (1854–58), d'Avray proceeded to institute a series of educational reforms which a modern student has characterized as "ultra-progressive." His policy was unjustly attacked by John Gregory*, secretary of the board of education, as undemocratic. Not unmindful of the importance of classical education, d'Avray nonetheless proposed the establishment of an agricultural college, to which a model farm would be attached. As an exponent of the philosophy of Johann Heinrich Pestalozzi and Philipp Emanuel von Fellenberg, he was the first in the province to perceive the need for a system of vocational education. During his tenure as chief superintendent of education, he defended King's College, Fredericton, where he had become professor of modern languages on

Masson

28 Oct. 1848, against the attacks of Albert James Smith*, member for Westmorland, and others in the legislature, who, largely for sectarian reasons, wished to deprive that institution of public support, and divert its grants to a denominational institution founded by the Methodists. With a view to making his defence of the college more effective, d'Avray assumed the editorship, in 1854, of a local newspaper, the Fredericton *Head Quarters*. Rough treatment at the hands of Smith and others on the floor of the assembly was the response to his mild editorial banter, and when the "Smasher" government succeeded to office in 1858, he, along with many others, lost his place, a circumstance that evoked a public outcry.

During the remainder of his life, he occupied himself exclusively with the duties of his professorship at King's College, Fredericton, and the University of New Brunswick, into which it was transformed in 1859. He was devoted to the teaching of English and French literature, but he opened to his students a wider spectrum than the university curriculum had hitherto provided, including, for the first time, works in political economy and modern history. Eldon Mullen, a former student of d'Avray and later deputy director of education in the Transvaal and Orange River colonies, wrote of him as "a thorough and elegant scholar with a keen appreciation of what was best and truest in literature." Bliss Carman* recalled Professor d'Avray and his wife as a most delightful couple: "he was a distinguished looking gentleman of the old school, with grey waxed moustache and a charming dry wit; she very animated, with sparkling dark eyes and an incessant fund of humour." At their home Carman first met George R. Parkin* who was to become, except for his parents, the chief influence on his life. Parkin and Canon George G. Roberts, the father of Sir Charles G. D. Roberts*, were two of Marshall d'Avray's most distinguished students and through them d'Avray became an influence upon the formation of the Fredericton school of poets, the first national movement in English-Canadian literature.

ALFRED G. BAILEY

[Many d'Avray family papers were destroyed in the great Fredericton fire of 1850; most of those remaining are with the Bailey papers in the University of New Brunswick Library. The family background is most fully treated by Marshall d'Avray's grandson, J. W. Bailey, in *The curious story of Dr Marshall, with a few side lights on Napoleon and other persons of consequence* (Cambridge, Mass., 1930). *See also*: Pietro Colletta, *History of the Kingdom of Naples, 1734–1825*, trans. by S. Horner (2v., Edinburgh, 1858), I, 403, and Sir Jonah Barrington, *Personal sketches of his own times* (3rd ed., 2v., London, 1869), II, 97–104, 145–50.

J. W. Bailey gives a brief chapter to Marshall d'Avray in *Loring Woart Bailey, the story of a man of science* (Saint John, N.B., 1925) D'Avray's role as founder of New Brunswick's first training school for teachers and as superintendent of education is most fully treated in K. F. C. MacNaughton, *The development of the theory and practice of education in New Brunswick, 1784–1900: a study in historical background*, ed. and intro. A. G. Bailey (U. of New Brunswick Hist. Studies, I, Fredericton, N.B., 1947), chapters 7 and 8. For references to his professorship at King's College, New Brunswick, see *The University of New Brunswick memorial volume*, ed. A. G. Bailey (Fredericton, N.B., 1950), 22–32, and J. S. Willison, *Sir George Parkin, a biography* (London, 1929), 13–16. A.G.B.]

MASSON, ISIDORE-ÉDOUARD-CANDIDE, businessman and legislative councillor; b. 4 May 1826 at Montreal, L.C., son of Joseph Masson*, seigneur of Terrebonne, and Marie-Geneviève-Sophie Raymond*, founder of Collège Masson at Terrebonne in 1847; brother of Louis-François-Roderick* (Rodrigue), lieutenant governor of the province of Quebec 1884–87; d. 5 Aug. 1875 at Montreal, Que., buried 7 August in the old church at Terrebonne, and reinterred in 1880 in the present church in the Masson family's vault.

Isidore-Édouard-Candide Masson's family was originally from Vendée. Gilles, the forbear, born at Luçon in 1630, was still young when he emigrated to New France. Édouard's father belonged to the fifth generation of the Masson family. Around 1805 he left Saint-Eustache, his birthplace, to try his hand at business in Montreal. It was there that Édouard was born, the fifth child of a family of 14, eight boys and six girls.

At six years of age, that is in 1832, Édouard Masson left Montreal. His father had just bought the seigneury of Terrebonne. The new seigneur, who was already "the largest and richest merchant in Montreal," was able to provide his family with a comfortable existence in an unpretentious house beside the Thousand Islands River, opposite Île Jésus.

Édouard Masson was educated at the college of Montreal, then studied literature and science in England from 1842 to 1846. After his father's death on 15 May 1847, he and his eldest brother Wilfred (Wilfrid) took over the management of the family business, which consisted chiefly of dealing in cloth and fabrics, as well as in potash. Joseph Masson left three commercial undertakings: Joseph Masson, Fils et Cie., in Montreal; Masson, Langevin et Cie., in Quebec; and Masson, Sons and Company, in Glasgow, Scotland. Édouard Masson was also president of the Montreal Gas Company and major of the 12th Battalion of militia. On 17 Jan. 1848 he married Marie-

498

Josephte-Caroline Dumas, who gave him three boys and two girls.

Following in his father's footsteps, Édouard Masson became municipal councillor for the eastern district of Montreal in 1855. On 31 Oct. 1856 he was elected legislative councillor for the division of Thousand Islands, which comprised the counties of Terrebonne and Deux-Montagnes. Politically he was opposed to the Rouges of the time, but he maintained an independent position in relation to the Conservative party, of which George-Étienne CARTIER, conjointly with John A. Macdonald*, had just assumed the leadership. Masson returned to private life on 28 Sept. 1864, after being defeated by Dr Léandre Dumouchel*, an avowed supporter of the Conservative party.

Édouard Masson then devoted his energy and his "very fine intelligence" to the settlement of the vast territories to the north of Montreal. He was the founder and organizer of a large French-Canadian settlement at Sainte-Marguerite, in the picturesque and untouched region of the Laurentians. A large number of settlers came from the Terrebonne seigneury and its vicinity. A mission was founded in 1864, and in 1871 a church was built on a piece of land given in 1869 by Édouard Masson. He had received by letters patent a grant of 1,646 acres of land, which took in the lake that bears his name today. There he erected a saw and flour mill on the outlet, right beside the village. In 1875 the parish of Sainte-Marguerite-du-Lac-Masson numbered 700 souls.

Lac Masson, and the municipality of the parish of Sainte-Marguerite-du-Lac-Masson, where Édouard Masson lived himself for some time, preserve the memory of what he did for colonization. To the homage represented by the Laurentian place-name can be added that of a contemporary and friend of Édouard Masson: "He was," wrote Laurent-Olivier David*, "one of the most spiritual, likeable, and generous men of his day."

ANDRÉE DÉSILETS

AVM, B 2735; Biographies de conseillers. Bibliothèque de l'université de Montréal, Collection Baby, Correspondance et papiers concernant la famille, XXIII, 14225–26 (copies in PAC). PAC, MG 24, D47 (Robertson collection); MG 30, D62 (Audet papers), 20, p.431; RG 4, B28, 138, no.5797. Private archives of Henri Masson (Montreal, Que.), family papers. "Correspondance de Jean Langevin avec son frère Hector (1843–1867)," Béatrice Chassé, édit., AQ *Rapport, 1967,* 51–55. "Lettres de Joseph-Adolphe Chapleau (1870–1896)," Fernand Ouellet, édit., APQ *Rapport, 1959–60,* 38–40. *La Minerve* (Montréal), 8 oct., 15 oct. 1856; 16 sept. 1864; 6 août 1875. *Le Nouveau Monde* (Montréal), 6 août 1875. Desjardins, *Guide parlementaire.* Raymond Masson, *Généalogie des familles de Terrebonne* (4v., Montréal,

1930–31). Turcotte, *Conseil législatif de Québec,* 241–42.

L.-O. David, *Mes contemporains* (Montréal, 1894), 261–68. C.-A. Gareau, *Aperçu historique de Terrebonne; 200e anniversaire de fondation et congrès eucharistique* (Montréal, 1927). J.-E. Garon, *Historique de la colonisation dans la province de Québec de 1825 à 1940* (Québec, 1940). B.-A. Testard de Montigny, *La colonisation, le nord de Montréal ou la région de Labelle* (Montréal, 1895). É.-J. Auclair, "Terrebonne, les Masson, leur château," *RSCT,* 3rd ser., XXXVIII (1944), sect.I, 1–14.

MASSON, LUC-HYACINTHE, doctor, businessman, and politician; b. 16 Aug. 1811 at Saint-Benoît (Deux-Montagnes County), L.C., son of Louis Masson, tavern-keeper and militia captain, and of Marie-Louise Choquet; d. 18 Oct. 1880 at Coteau-Landing (Soulanges County) and buried 20 Oct. 1880 at Saint-Anicet, Que.

Luc-Hyacinthe Masson belonged to the fifth generation of an Orléans family that emigrated to Quebec in the middle of the 18th century. He learned the rudiments of grammar and mathematics while living at home in the little village of Saint-Benoît. He continued his education at the college of Montreal, then turned towards medicine, which he studied under Dr Robert NELSON. An arbitrary action of the government had made the youth susceptible to the political influence of the famous Dr Nelson: on 12 July 1827 his father had been relieved of his post as militia capatin for "*Patriote* activity."

In the spring of 1832 the epidemic of Asiatic cholera that reached Lower Canada from Europe pushed major political and national questions into the background. Doctors were summoned to another kind of heroism than that of nationalist resistance. The young student went to the assistance of the immigrants of Pointe-Saint-Charles, replacing his master, who had just fallen ill; on 1 Aug. 1832, at Saint-Clément-de-Beauharnois, he took the place of Dr Charles Fleming, who had succumbed to the disease. Masson's strong constitution enabled him to emerge unscathed from this arduous experience, and the following year, 1833, he qualified as a doctor. He practised first at Saint-Clément-de-Beauharnois, then in his native village of Saint-Benoît, where on 28 Jan. 1835 he bought a piece of land in Rue Saint-Jean-Baptiste.

At this time was formed the famous triumvirate of Jean-Joseph Girouard*, Jean-Olivier Chénier*, and Luc-Hyacinthe Masson, which formed the basis of the resistance of the north to the "Red Coats." Luc-Hyacinthe Masson took part in all the meetings prior to the rebellion and showed himself to be a fiery orator. Lord Gosford

Masson

[Acheson*] as a result annulled his commission as justice of the peace. From words the young doctor quickly passed to action, and became closely involved in the organization of resistance on "military" lines. Arrested on 16 Dec. 1837, the day after the defeat at Saint-Eustache, he was exiled to the Bermudas by the proclamation of Lord Durham [Lambton*] on 28 June 1838. Luc-Hyacinthe obtained permission to practise medicine during his months of exile.

The disavowal of Lord Durham's proclamation by the British parliament allowed Luc-Hyacinthe Masson to leave the Bermudas. He entered the United States on 9 Nov. 1838. At Fort Covington, New York State, he opened a general store in partnership with his uncle, Eustache Masson, who, having been compromised and ruined by the rebellion, had resolved to take refuge in the United States with his family. The business was highly successful, and Luc-Hyacinthe married his uncle's daughter Cécile (Céline). But Eustache Masson died in 1840, and two years later Luc-Hyacinthe decided to return to Canada. His liking for trade prevailed over his liking for medicine, and, in partnership with his brother Damien, Luc-Hyacinthe Masson laid at Saint-Anicet the foundations of a general business under the name of Masson et Cie. Through his drive and spirit of initiative he stimulated the growth of the new village of Saint-Anicet.

In 1844 Luc-Hyacinthe became collector of customs in the port of Dundee, on the Canadian-American border. He also became involved in municipal politics as mayor of Coteau-Landing and in provincial politics as representative for Soulanges in the assembly of the Province of Canada from 31 July 1854 to 28 Nov. 1857. In parliament he completed the task to which he had given his energy since 1849: the obtaining of an indemnity for farmers on the two shores of Lac Saint-François for damage caused by floods resulting from the construction of piers at the head of the Beauharnois Canal. In 1860 he took up residence on the other side of the river, at Coteau-Landing, where he again devoted himself to business. After confederation, Luc-Hyacinthe Masson was the representative for Soulanges in the Canadian House of Commons from 3 Sept. 1867 to 8 July 1872. The fiery *Patriote* agitator of 1837 had become a fervent supporter of the Conservative party.

In 1872 Luc-Hyacinthe Masson returned to private life. He held the offices of registrar of the county of Soulanges and of clerk of the circuit court, with residence at Coteau-Landing. Having lost his wife on 3 May 1846, he had married on 12 June 1849 Odile (Élodie) Watier, daughter of

Joachim Watier of Coteau-du-Lac. Of his six children, only two survived him.

At the southwest corner of the monument to the *Patriotes* of 1837–38, erected in the cemetery of Côte-des-Neiges at Montreal, the name of Luc-Hyacinthe Masson bears witness to the tragic moments of a sometimes troubled life. His reputation as a philanthropist when he died on 18 Oct. 1880 is a testimony of another kind, to a life always well lived.

ANDRÉE DÉSILETS

AJM, Louis Richard, La famille Masson. AVM, B 2015. Archives paroissiales de Saint-Clément-de-Beauharnois (Beauharnois, Qué.), Registres des baptêmes, mariages et sépultures. Archives paroissiales de Saint-Ignace (Coteau-du-Lac, Qué.), Registres des baptêmes, mariages et sépultures. Archives paroissiales de Saint-Zotique (Coteau-Landing, Qué.), Registres des baptêmes, mariages et sépultures. ANQ, Jean-Joseph Girouard, Papiers personnels et lettres reçues, 17 août 1751; Ludger Duvernay, nos.292, 391; QBC, Procureur général, Événements de 1837–1838, nos.598, 669, 770, 803, 805, 845, 869, 3182, 4106, 4145. PAC, MG 30, D62 (Audet papers), 20, p.450. "Le journal de l'abbé N.-J. Ritchot, 1870," G. F. G. Stanley, édit., *RHAF*, XVII (1963–64), 537–64. "Les Patriotes aux Bermudes en 1838, lettres d'exil," Yvon Thériault, édit., *RHAF*, XVI (1962–63), 438; XVII (1963–64), 424–32. *La Minerve* (Montréal), 18 oct., 19 oct. 1880. *L'Opinion publique* (Montréal), 19 avril 1877. *Can. directory of parliament* (Johnson), 358. *Can. parl. comp.*, 1872. Desjardins, *Guide parlementaire*. Raymond Masson, *Généalogie des familles de Terrebonne* (4v., Montréal, 1930–31). R.-L. Séguin, "Biographie d'un patriote de '37, le Dr Luc-Hyacinthe Masson (1811–1880)," *RHAF*, III (1949–50), 349–66.

MASSON, MARC-DAMASE, merchant and businessman; b. 23 Feb. 1805 at Sainte-Geneviève on Montreal Island, L.C., son of Eustache Masson and Scholastique Pfeiffer (Payfer); d. 23 April 1878 at Montreal, Que.

Marc-Damase Masson's family came from Saint-Benoît parish in the town of Orléans (province of Orléanais). The first member of the family to take root in Canadian soil was Pierre, a manufacturer of pulleys (born in 1724). He married Marie-Louise Beaupré on 22 Feb. 1751 at Quebec, and their son Pierre-Marc was Marc-Damase Masson's grandfather.

Marc-Damase Masson spent the early years of his childhood on his father's farm at Sainte-Geneviève. He then lived at Saint-Clément-de-Beauharnois, where his father soon established a business. In 1829, after a good business training in the family environment, the young man became a merchant himself at Saint-Clément-de-Beauharnois. On 1 Feb. 1830 he married Virginie Jobin, daughter of the notary André Jobin* of Montreal.

Eight children were born of this marriage: three boys and five girls.

Marc-Damase Masson's business position was excellent when the 1837 rebellion broke out. The young merchant aligned himself with the *Patriotes*. His property was "destroyed by the soldiery," and he thereby lost the results of several years' work. In 1839 he moved to Montreal to re-establish himself, and thanks to his experience and unremitting toil he succeeded in becoming a leading Montreal businessman. At the corner of McGill and Notre-Dame streets he opened a wholesale and retail grocery, which, as the *Montreal Herald and Daily Commercial Gazette* was to write on 23 April 1878, "he carried on most successfully, making the house of D. Masson & Co. not only one of the largest, but one of the best known firms throughout the city and country." After his death his three sons, Damase, Alfred, and Adolphe, continued their father's large business.

Marc-Damase Masson's activities became more numerous and varied as his business grew. In 1846, a number of prominent Montreal citizens founded the Montreal City ond District Savings Bank. The majority of Montreal banks at that time were strictly commercial banks, that is, they met only the needs of trade. The basic principles of the Savings Bank were the value and necessity of saving and the need to popularize the habit. Together with a few of the most prominent Montreal citizens of the time, Marc-Damase Masson was elected a director of the new bank from 1846 to 1850. According to the official organ of the Savings Bank, "this was a judicious choice. Masson, an honest and prosperous merchant, put his experience at the disposal of his colleagues, so that the Savings Bank would be established on sound bases."

On 13 Dec. 1846 Marc-Damase Masson was chosen churchwarden of Notre-Dame. In February 1855 he was elected by popular vote to the council of the city of Montreal. He sat for three years as alderman for the St Lawrence district, and for some years was chairman of the finance committee. He contributed generously to the building of the aqueduct and to other improvements in the town. In 1858 he became president of the Société Saint-Jean-Baptiste, and in 1861 was among the businessmen who, with Hugh Allan* as president, founded the Merchants' Bank. Lacking sufficient capital, the bank did not open its doors until three years after receiving its charter. Masson was one of its directors until his death and one of its biggest shareholders. He took a great deal of interest in this institution and it largely owed to him its few years of prosperity, from the time of its purchase of the Commercial Bank of the Midland District in 1868 until 1873. The Merchants' Bank then suffered from the Canadian Pacific railway scandal in which Allan was implicated, as well as from the economic crisis that followed. But because it had been launched properly, the bank recovered after 1878 and extended its operations throughout the whole of Canada. It had acquired a valued place among Canadian banks by 1921, when it was taken over by the Bank of Montreal. Marc-Damase Masson was a director of the Richelieu Company, and also a member of the board of directors of several insurance companies, among them the North British and Mercantile Insurance Company [*see* SINCENNES].

On 23 April 1878 he died at Montreal, at the age of 73. His name was highly esteemed in the business world, where he had distinguished himself by his honesty in public and private dealings: "His word was above reproach, and he steadily tried by his example to instil into those who came in contact with him the same high principles."

ANDRÉE DÉSILETS

AJM, Louis Richard, la famille Masson. AVM, 3610.4, 3610.6; Biographies de conseillers. Archives paroissiales de Sainte-Geneviève (Pierrefonds, Qué.), Registres des baptêmes, mariages et sépultures, 23 févr. 1805, 14 sept. 1853. *Gazette* (Montreal), 23 April 1878. *La Minerve* (Montréal), 24 avril 1878. *Montreal Herald and Daily Commercial Gazette*, 23 April 1878. *Le National* (Montréal), 23 avril 1878. *Le Nouveau Monde* (Montréal), 23 avril, 26 avril 1878. *L'Opinion publique* (Montréal), 25 avril, 2 mai 1878. *The Canadian album* . . . , ed. William Cochrane *et al.* (5v., Brantford, Ont., and Toronto, 1891–96), V, 117. Raymond Masson, *Généalogie des familles de Terrebonne* (4v., Montréal, 1930–31). Tanguay, *Dictionnaire*, V. Denison, *Canada's first bank*. É.-Z. Massicotte, *Processions de la Saint-Jean-Baptiste en 1924 et 1925* (Montréal, 1926), 40–41. R.-L. Séguin, "Biographie d'un patriote de '37, le Dr Luc-Hyacinthe Masson (1811–1880)," *RHAF*, III (1949–50), 496.

MATHESON, RODERICK, merchant, militia officer, and politician; b. December 1793, in Lochcarron, Ross County (now Ross and Cromarty), Scotland, son of John Matheson and Flora Macrae; m. at Montreal, 5 Nov. 1823, Mary Fraser Robertson who died in 1825, then on 11 Aug. 1830 at Gavilock, Scotland, Annabella Russel by whom he had at least five sons, one of whom, Arthur James*, was treasurer of Ontario, 1905–13; d. Perth, Ont., 13 Jan. 1873.

Roderick Matheson moved to Lower Canada with a brother at the age of 12. He was a sergeant in the Canadian Fencibles when, on 12 Feb. 1812, he was named quartermaster of the Glengarry Light Infantry Fencibles. He was wounded during

Mayrand

the attack on Sackets Harbor, N.Y., on 29 May 1813, and promoted lieutenant on 21 August. He ended the war as the paymaster of the regiment and was placed on the half-pay list in 1816. He was granted land the following year in the military settlement at Perth, around which the rest of his life centred.

Matheson was named returning officer at Perth in 1820. The next year he was gazetted captain in the newly formed 2nd Battalion Carleton militia, and on 18 June 1822 major of the 4th Battalion. These positions were contrary to the rule that militia promotions were to be based on relative seniority in the British army and elicited remonstrances from several half-pay officers senior to Matheson. He was not present at the fray at Perth between a company of the 4th Carleton and the Irish immigrants at the militia muster in April 1824, but he was among the justices of the peace who restored order. He was promoted lieutenant-colonel of the 1st Regiment Renfrew militia in November 1846, and in the next month of the 2nd Lanark. On 14 Sept. 1855 he was made colonel and given command of the 1st military district of Canada West, a post he retained until 1863.

Matheson used his land grant and regular income from half pay wisely. He established a successful general store in Perth, bought land, and was a director in William Morris*' Tay Navigation Company. On 24 Aug. 1833, he was appointed one of ten commissioners of the court of requests for the 1st division of the Bathurst District, and he was a member of the board of education of Perth. He also took a lively interest in securing internal improvements in the Bathurst District. Sir Charles Metcalfe* put his name forward in 1844 as a possible nominee to the Legislative Council. In February 1847, William Henry DRAPER again placed Matheson on a list of nominations to Lord Elgin [Bruce*] for a seat in the Legislative Council. He was appointed on 27 May 1847. Matheson sat in the upper chamber as a conservative until 1867 when he was named a senator. He helped in 1855 to defeat a bill supporting an elective Legislative Council by introducing resolutions against the principle.

The first of a series of paralytic strokes in December 1867 disabled Matheson and another stroke on 7 Jan. 1873 caused his death at Perth one week later.

GEO. MAINER

PAC, RG 8, I, A1, 625, p.33; D2, 1168, p.93; RG 9, I, B1, 17, 4 Jan., 14 Aug. 1822; 18, 27 March, 5 July 1822. PRO, CO 42/519, index entry for missing p.310; 42/541, index entry for missing p.386; 42/542, index entry for missing p.453; 42/598, 142 (copies at PAC). *Bathurst Courier* (Perth), 5 Sept. 1834; 10 July 1840; 4 April 1842; 7 March, 22 May, 20 June 1843; 16 Jan. 1844. *Brockville Recorder*, 24 July 1845. *Canada Gazette* (Montreal; Quebec), 5 June 1847, 17 Oct. 1863. *Montreal Gazette*, 2 Nov. 1813, 8 Nov. 1823, 14 Oct. 1830. *Perth Courier*, 17 Jan. 1873. *Upper Canada Gazette* (York), 17 Sept. 1821. *Cyclopædia of Can. biog.* (Rose, 1888), 459.

MAYRAND, ÉTIENNE, businessman and politician; b. 3 Sept. 1776 at Montreal, Quebec, of the marriage of Jean-Baptiste Mayrand and Agathe Roy; d. 22 Jan. 1872 at Rivière-du-Loup (Louiseville, Maskinongé County), Que.

Young Étienne Mayrand's intellectual training was probably rather superficial, although elementary schools directed by the Sulpicians did exist at Montreal at that time. He early became interested in the fur trade and travelled in the Canadian west, working for the North West Company; he returned from this venture with a sizeable capital. While he was in the west, Étienne Mayrand had married an Indian; she bore him two daughters, whom he brought back with him to Lower Canada. The exact date of this return is not known, but it was certainly at the beginning of the 19th century, since Mayrand married his second wife, Sophie Héneau, of Berthier on 20 Aug. 1806; they had one child, who died young. He established himself at Rivière-du-Loup, where he made a fortune in the grain and hay business. His success enabled him to act as a moneylender and real estate agent. He built a comfortable stone house measuring 60 feet in length by 35 feet in width, with two large rooms serving as "salons," one for his family and the other for the master of the house. If an absent-minded visitor made his way into the latter without having been expressly invited, "he was withered with a look," Édouard-Zotique Massicotte* remarked, and he learned with brutal clarity that "the master was not receiving at the moment."

During the War of 1812 Mayrand served as an officer of the militia. He was promoted lieutenant in the 2nd Rivière-du-Loup Battalion in 1813, and then was appointed captain in the 8th Battalion of the Trois-Rivières division. He kept his interest in the military and, in 1846, was major of the 4th Battalion of Saint-Maurice County. He retired from the militia in 1855 at the age of 79.

Mayrand's remarkable success in business led him to take an interest in politics. In November 1809 he served as returning officer for Saint-Maurice County, when Louis Gugy* was chosen to represent this county in the House of Assembly. He also canvassed for votes himself in this constituency, which he represented from 1816 to 1820 (according to Édouard-Zotique Massicotte he was an MHA from 1816 to 1838). He was a believer in law and order, and in politics was always a thoroughgoing Conservative. On 2 April 1838 he was nominated a member of the Special Council that replaced the House of Assembly during the disturbances of 1837–38, and took part in the deliberations of that body until the setting up of the government of the Union in 1841. Finally, on 9 June 1841 he became a member of the Legislative Council, but resigned on the 22nd of the same month. He then gave his attention to finance and real estate.

In addition to his commercial and political activities, Étienne Mayrand also took on various important responsibilities in the public life of his region and even at the provincial level. He was appointed commissioner for internal communications in Lower Canada (12 Jan. 1818), commissioner for small causes (13 Nov. 1821), member of a commission instructed to make a hydrographic survey of Lac Saint-Louis with a view to improving its navigability (5 July 1836), and commissioner for the administration of the oath of allegiance (21 Dec. 1837).

Francis-Joseph Audet*, in his work on the members of the assembly for Saint-Maurice, states that Mayrand was a "school visitor" for his county (4 July 1826): the statement can only refer to the royal schools created by the school act of 1801, for the law establishing schools under public trustees was not passed until 1829. A royal school did exist at Rivière-du-Loup, and it is probable that Mayrand was named a visitor to it by reason of his social standing. "Visitors," according to the regulations of the Royal Institution, were to make a report to the corporation every six months, on "the number and progress of the pupils, the conduct of the master, his conformity or non-conformity with the directives of the Institution, any deficiencies in the provisions made for the education offered at the school, and any irregularity in the method of applying them." They were also to "make a formal inspection of the school . . . , they have the authority to determine the school hours, the number and duration of the holidays and the different feast-days it is appropriate to allocate, to establish the rate of tuition and to name the children who will be admitted free and those whose parents will be obliged to pay, all this being subject to the approval of the Institution."

Étienne Mayrand died at Rivière-du-Loup, at the venerable age of 96. On 30 Sept. 1811, at Montreal, after his second wife's death, he had married Thérèse Heney, who bore him eight children and died in 1825. On 2 Aug. 1827, at Quebec, he married again, his fourth wife being Félicité Le Maître-Bellenoix, Louis Gauvreau's widow. Étienne Mayrand served his country loyally under four sovereigns, George III, George IV, William IV, and Queen Victoria, no less than 19 governors general, and 21 lieutenant governors. He was a witness of three constitutions: 1791, 1840, and the confederation of Canada.

LOUIS-PHILIPPE AUDET

AJM, Registre d'état civil (notes biographiques fournies par J.-J. Lefebvre). Desjardins, *Guide parlementaire. Journal de la chambre d'Assemblée du Bas-Canada*, 1824, app.Y, "Règles et règlements pour les écoles de fondation royale dans la province du Bas-Canada sous la conduite de l'Institution royale." Turcotte, *Conseil législatif de Québec*, 134–35. Audet, *Le système scolaire de la province de Québec*, IV, 274–75. F.-J. Audet, *Les députés de Saint-Maurice, 1808–1838, et de Champlain, 1830–1838* (Pages trifluviennes, sér. A, 12, Trois-Rivières, Qué., 1934), 45–48; "Membres du Conseil spécial," *BRH*, VII (1901), 82–83. F.-L. Desaulniers, "Les députés de Saint-Maurice," *BRH*, V (1899), 284–85. É.-Z. Massicotte, "La famille de l'honorable Étienne Mayrand," *BRH*, XXXIII (1927), 708–12.

MEDCALF, FRANCIS HENRY, millwright, ironfounder, Orangeman, and politician; b. 10 May 1803 at Delgany, County Wicklow, Ireland, son of William and Martha Medcalf; d. 26 March 1880 at Toronto, Ont.

Francis Henry Medcalf's parents emigrated to Upper Canada with their eight children in 1819 and settled on the Big Otter Creek in Bayham Township on land bought from Thomas Talbot*. About 1823, Francis Henry moved to Philadelphia where he worked as a blacksmith and millwright. He returned to Upper Canada in 1839, living in Toronto, and by 1843 he had his own business as millwright and machinist. In 1847 he opened the Don Foundry and Machine Shop, specializing in agricultural implements and machinery, in steam engines, and in heavy castings for grist- and sawmills.

Philadelphia in the 1830s was a battleground between Irish Roman Catholics and Protestants; Medcalf was for the rest of his life the staunchest of Orangemen. He was several times master of Lodge 275 in Toronto, district (later county) master for Toronto from 1854 to 1862, and from 1862 to 1864 provincial grand master of Canada West. In 1860 Medcalf first ran for office and was elected alderman in Toronto; he sat again in 1863 and from 1867 to 1871. His lodge service took him into the mayoral election of January 1864. The separate school controversy was at its height in 1863 and a coalition of Liberals (marshalled by George BROWN's *Globe*), Orangemen, and Tories brought him forward to oppose Mayor John G. Bowes*. Bowes, a defender of separate schools,

Meilleur

was said to be too clever as well as too deceitful. Medcalf, a simple mechanic risen by hard toil, was pictured by contrast as honest and bluff, with no pretence to skill in argument or finesse in finance. He was also the adamant Protestant candidate. He deprived Bowes of a seventh term.

In 1865 Medcalf won the mayoralty overwhelmingly and in 1866 he was not opposed. So seriously did he take this mandate that in 1866 cooler heads had to restrain him from precipitating bloodshed on St Patrick's Day, when fears of a confrontation with Fenians were high. From 1867 to 1873 the city council chose the mayor, but when the system of popular election returned in 1874 Medcalf once again received most votes. By 1876, however, when even supporters acknowledged his torpor, he was heavily defeated. Already in March 1871 he had been beaten in the provincial constituency of East Toronto by Matthew Crooks Cameron*.

Medcalf married Mary Harrison of Philadelphia in 1831, and they had six children. The four sons were brought into their father's trade; the third son, Alfred, entered into a partnership with his father and took over the foundry after Medcalf's death in 1880.

A favourite with the ambitious and the common man alike, Medcalf was nicknamed "Old Squaretoes," pointing up his utilitarian boots, and he gloried in the name as a mark of his incorruptible ordinariness. The only matters which aroused him to anger and eloquence were Catholic assertiveness and slurs on the Orange order. He had been a man who joined fraternal societies, and his long funeral procession included Orangemen, freemasons, oddfellows, and foresters.

BARRIE DYSTER

MTCL, Toronto Public Libraries scrapbooks, II, especially election card for 1874. PAC, MG 26, A (Macdonald papers), 237, Gilbert McMicken to Macdonald, 18 March 1866. St James' Cemetery (Toronto). Loyal Orange Association of British North America, Grand Lodge, *Annual Reports*, 1847–57. Toronto, City Council, *Minutes of proceedings*, 1860–71, 1874–76. *Globe* (Toronto), 1860; January 1861; December 1863; January, December 1864; January, December 1865; January 1866; January 1874; 1875–76; 29 March 1880. *Leader* (Toronto), December 1863; January, December 1864; January, December 1865; January 1866. *Mail* (Toronto), 29 March 1880.

City of Toronto directory, for 1867–8 (Toronto, 1867). *Commemorative biog. record, county York*, 626–27. *Cyclopædia of Can. biog.* (Rose, 1886), 124. *The Toronto directory and street guide for 1843–4*, ed. Francis Lewis (Toronto, 1843). *Hist. of Toronto and county of York*, II, 108–9. *Landmarks of Toronto* (Robertson), VI, 153–64, 195. Middleton, *Municipality of Toronto*. S. B. Warner, *The private city: Philadelphia in three periods of its growth* (Philadelphia, 1968).

MEILLEUR, JEAN-BAPTISTE, doctor, educator, founder of the college of L'Assomption, MLA, first superintendent of education in Lower Canada; b. 8 May 1796 at Petite-Côte, in the parish of Saint-Laurent (Montreal Island), L.C., son of Jean Meilleur and Marie-Suzanne Blaignier; d. 6 Dec. 1878 at Montreal, Que.

An only son, Jean-Baptiste Meilleur was 14 months old when his father died. His mother remarried in 1798, and his paternal grandparents brought him up. It is not known what form his elementary education took. A family tradition has it that at 19 he came into his inheritance and registered at the college of Montreal, where he completed his classical studies among students younger than himself. He became acquainted at the college with a young American convert, John Holmes*, a native of Vermont and a future teacher at the Petit Séminaire of Quebec. Meilleur wanted to become a lawyer, but Holmes advised him to go to New England and study medicine.

Meilleur left the college, attended an English school at Montreal, enrolled in 1821 at Castleton Academy of Medicine (Vermont), which was affiliated to Middlebury College at Montpelier (Vermont), and followed the courses in science and medicine given at both institutions. Chemistry and botany were taught by a famous teacher, Amos Eaton, and experimental physics and mineralogy by Frederick Hall, who had a great influence on Meilleur. On 18 Nov. 1824 Meilleur defended a thesis, "On Scrofula," which earned him his doctorate in medicine; this was conferred on him in 1825 by Middlebury College, at the time when he was registered as a graduate student at Dartmouth College, Hanover (New Hampshire). During his stay at Middlebury and Hanover, Meilleur gave private French lessons, and in 1825 published *A treatise on the pronunciation of the French language* . . . , as well as several other short works which are today equally untraceable. His stay in the United States was beneficial for Meilleur. He noticed the enthusiasm displayed by the inhabitants of that country for public education in comparison with the little store set by it in Lower Canada. In addition, he acquired scientific knowledge which would help in the education of his fellow-countrymen.

In February 1826, on his return to Canada, Meilleur took up residence at L'Assomption. The following month the Medical Board granted him a licence, and he began medical practice, which he

504

carried on concurrently with his educational, scientific, and political activities. On 26 June 1827, at Repentigny, he married Joséphine Éno, *dit* Deschamps. Ten children were born of this marriage, one of them being Joséphine-Charlotte who married Georges-Isidore Barthe*.

During the 15 years he lived at L'Assomption, Meilleur practised medicine and took an active part in public life. He soon acquired a competency, and the various official positions in which he served gave him a firm reputation as an enlightened citizen. In 1827 he received a commission as lieutenant in the 1st militia battalion of Leinster (L'Assomption County), and five years later a commission as surgeon of the 2nd militia battalion of Berthier (Berthier County). After being named a member of the Medical Board in 1831, he was appointed census-taker and justice of the peace for Leinster County, and in 1834 became postmaster at L'Assomption. From 1827 on, he had been actively involved in the elections to the House of Assembly, and in November 1834 was elected, at the same time as Édouard-Étienne Rodier*, for L'Assomption County; he served until 1838.

Meilleur's political venture was a brief one, but he sat in the assembly amid the feverish atmosphere that preceded the 1837 rebellion. His colleague Rodier, one of the most prominent members of the *Patriote* party, endeavoured, unsuccessfully, to see that Meilleur, who was considered a moderate, did not follow those who broke away from Louis-Joseph PAPINEAU. When the orator came to harangue the students of L'Assomption, Meilleur replied tartly to his impassioned appeals. Although in sympathy with the *Patriotes*' cause, he disapproved of their appeals to violence, and he went through all the parishes in his county to exhort the population to obey the pastoral letter of Bishop Jean-Jacques Lartigue*.

As a member of the house standing committees on education, hospitals, and charitable institutions, Meilleur had a hand in the passing of a bill creating normal schools. But the opposition of the Legislative Council prevented the renewal of the 1829 primary schools act, thus forcing some 1,300 schools to close their doors. Meilleur got approval for the purchase of the museum established by Pierre Chasseur, and he was made responsible for classifying the collection of animals that Chasseur had placed in their natural habitat. This museum was almost completely destroyed in the fire that devastated the Quebec parliament in 1854.

Meilleur's interest in education and science was revealed also by the numerous letters and articles he published from 1826 on in *La Minerve* of Montreal, of which he was the correspondent, in Michel

Bibaud*'s *Bibliothèque canadienne*, and in *L'Écho du Pays* and *Le Glaneur* of Saint-Charles-sur-Richelieu. He wrote on chemistry, domestic economy, the salt-impregnated water of L'Assomption, geology, agriculture, and the Hessian fly; in 1826 and 1827 he published in the *Quebec Medical Journal*, the first Canadian medical journal, two articles, one "On prussic acid" and another "On scrofula," which was his doctoral thesis. In 1828, in *La Minerve*, Meilleur began to publish letters on education which gave rise to a long controversy; he kept it alive himself, signing some of his letters with various pseudonyms. In this way he prepared people's minds for the founding of a college at L'Assomption, where he had become a trustee of the parish schools established by the act of 1829. He undertook to give regularly each week in the village schools explanations and exercises relating to grammar, arithmetic, and geography. In 1833 he published a *Nouvelle grammaire anglaise*, and, at Montreal, his *Cours abrégé de leçons de chymie*. The latter work, intended for the youth of the schools, was the first of its kind written by a Canadian and published in Canada. Having finally won over the parish priest, Abbé François Labelle, and his *confrère*, Dr Louis-Joseph-Charles Cazeneuve, he founded with them the college of L'Assomption, which opened its doors in 1834. The founders, the priest's brothers, and some friends subscribed the funds required for its construction, and Meilleur obtained from the Legislative Assembly a grant for its operation. The teaching followed Lancaster's mutual system, which was popular at the time (under the master's direction, the most advanced pupils instructed the youngest). Except for the parish priest Labelle, the teachers were all laymen [*see* DUPUY]; the pupils who were boarders took their meals at the presbytery as did the teachers.

The deplorable state of education in Lower Canada and the ways to remedy it were one of the concerns of Lord Durham [Lambton*]. In July 1838 he issued letters patent, which were published in the papers, instructing Arthur Buller*, a member of his administrative staff, to "inquire and seek information as to the past and present methods of utilizing all moneys or funds intended for or applicable to education in the said province of Lower Canada." Meilleur replied to this invitation. An exchange of letters began on 3 Aug. 1838 in *Le Populaire* of Montreal; the first one, signed with the initials A.B., was followed by a reply signed C.D. of which Meilleur claimed the authorship; he also said that the one signed A.B. was by Arthur Buller. In four letters, printed in *Le Canadien* of Quebec, Meilleur outlined plans for

Meilleur

the organization and financial support of public instruction, from the primary school to the classical college. A.B. published three letters in this paper, and other correspondents took part in this interesting discussion, to which Meilleur replied in a fifth letter.

Meiller did not favour imposing a land tax because of the poverty and even destitution of the farmers and proposed in his letters that, at least at the beginning, primary education should be free. To balance the cost, the wealth of the Jesuits would be used, particularly to subsidize the classical colleges, where he wished to see the direction and teaching reserved for the clergy. He suggested increasing customs duties on tobacco and alcoholic beverages, and raising the amount charged for innkeepers' licences. Finally, the savings realized by reducing the enormous salaries of certain officials would be allocated for education.

In his second letter Meilleur analysed the causes of the sorry plight of education: the apathy, ignorance, and prejudice of too great a number of farmers, bad administration on the part of trustees who were sometimes illiterate, the incompetence and poor habits of too many teachers, and the beggarly emoluments of schoolmasters. In the third, he described the school organization he advocated. He visualized four levels, including classical teaching, leading to the priesthood and the professions; academic teaching, including model schools, analogous to the high schools he admired in the United States, and preparing for commerce, business, the classical course, and, as necessary, training future elementary school teachers; and normal schools for the training of secondary school teachers. The fourth level, primary school, would be obligatory, and Meilleur's wish was that after 10 years no one would be allowed to hold a public office if he had not at least this level of instruction. Boards of examiners would confer teachers' certificates, and visitors would see that the schools, administered by trustees elected by all groups of a parish, were pedagogically and financially efficient. Meilleur, firmly convinced that a law of this kind would be successful, was ready to assume full responsibility for it.

Meilleur's observations were well received by Lord Durham, who made favourable mention of them in his famous *Report*, but the plan did not correspond to his views. When the union of the two Canadas was an accomplished fact, a Montreal lawyer Charles-Elzéar MONDELET published in the *Canada Times* of November and December 1840 a series of letters. In them he proposed the setting up of communal schools, in which religious instruction would be given under the supervision of ministers of the various churches, and which would be financed by a land tax, and the creation of school districts administered by commissioners, of whom some would be elected and others nominated by the district inspectors, the whole being under the jurisdiction of a superintendent appointed by the governor. The plan was coldly received by the religious authorities; however, the education act of 1841 was partly based on Mondelet's proposals, and everyone thought he would be appointed superintendent of education. But when he was appointed a judge by the governor, Sir Charles Bagot*, Meilleur asked for the post of superintendent. In 1842 Bagot, judging that one man could not perform its duties properly, appointed an unpaid superintendent, responsible to parliament, and two deputy superintendents: Meilleur for Lower Canada and the Reverend Robert Murray* for Upper Canada.

Meilleur, who had been practising medicine in Montreal since 1840, was the obvious choice for the duties that were being entrusted to him. Bilingual, and a man of integrity, he had acquired valuable experience in the field of education. He had, however, to set in motion, in deplorable conditions and in the unhealthy political climate of the first years of the union, a law that went against his own convictions. The 1841 act related to both schools and rural municipalities, and in practice did not distinguish between the municipal councils and the school commissions that in a way emanated from them. The members of these commissions, elected by the taxpayers of the school districts, were to administer the schools, while the mayors and treasurers of the municipalities, appointed by the governor, received the grants paid by the superintendent of schools and were authorized to levy and collect school taxes as well as municipal taxes. The people, who had never paid any taxes, detested the school tax, the more because it was imposed on them by non-elected officials. The act did not provide for initial expenses, maintenance costs, or the payment of staff for the office of the deputy superintendent, who had furthermore to be content with a salary lower than that of his counterpart in Upper Canada. Under these conditions, about which Meilleur constantly complained, he had to revive schools which had been closed for six years and create others, knowing that there were not enough competent teachers to meet the demand. He had no real authority over school curricula and textbooks, any more than he had over the choice of schoolmasters.

During the 13 years of his administration, Meilleur had to apply seven different versions of the schools act. The 1845 version corrected a few anomalies of the original act: it made Meilleur the superintendent of education for Lower Canada, and put the parish rather than the municipality at the base of the school system. In addition, it replaced the obligatory tax by a voluntary contribution, collection of which, Meilleur foresaw, would be difficult and uncertain. In 1846 an act set up parish school commissions; their members, elected by the landowners, were to raise, through contributions, a sum equal to the grant made by the superintendent. A board of examiners was to approve the school textbooks and the teachers' certificates, but the commissioners hired the teachers and could decide upon the curricula to be used in their schools. It has been said of this act that it was the great charter of public instruction in Quebec, but contemporaries did not view it in this way. The habitants of the country districts, spontaneously or at the instigation of demagogues, many of whom were MLAs, saw in it nothing less than the dreaded spectre of taxation, and that is how what has been called the *guerre des éteignoirs* began. Parents withdrew their children from the schools; elections of commissioners were interfered with; prominent citizens and members of the clergy who supported the superintendent and the government were intimidated; schools were burned. In certain places the government had to be asked to call in the militia to re-establish order. These disturbances lasted until about 1850, at which time, in the face of the firm attitude of the superintendent, the clergy, and the civil authorities, the rural population calmed down and recognized the benefits that education could bring them. The acts of 1849 and 1851 brought Meilleur only part of what he had been seeking for a long time: visitors, then school inspectors, whom he had appointed immediately, and normal schools, which came into existence only under his successor's administration.

Meilleur, especially at the beginning of his administration, could well say that having had to struggle unremittingly against difficulties and obstacles not created by him, he had had more worries and weariness than success in the application of an unpopular act, and that no one seemed to know what the Department of Education was. Later he was able to congratulate himself on the ever growing number of schools and of pupils who attended them. This increase meant an added burden of work and responsibilities too heavy for one man, who was approaching 60 years of age. Meilleur's personality did not make things easier. He was a blunt man, who did not brook interference in his affairs. Portraits of him show a man with a high, broad forehead, thin lips, and a strong jaw; the look appears at first severe and inquisitive, but one detects a certain gentleness in it. His didactic writings testify to his respect for science as a source of certainty and to his sense of order and method, which often became dogmatic. His astounding memory and almost universal curiosity induced him, except when he was a superintendent, to give the newspapers his opinion on all manner of questions. But if he wrote a lot it was because, as a timid and uncommunicative man, he preferred the pen to the spoken word as a way of convincing people and if need be to justify himself.

His correspondence with Abbé Louis-Édouard Bois*, his only confidant, shows that in trying to escape the interventions of politicians Meilleur was uncompromising in the extreme. His letters are full of his complaints, his anxieties about his family, whom he accused himself of neglecting, but also of his suspicions concerning MLAs and ministers and of accusations against them. His distrust, not always justified, prevented him from associating with those who might have been able to help him.

When the government left Montreal, after the riots and the burning of the parliament buildings in 1849, Meilleur followed it neither to Toronto nor to Quebec, where it sat alternatively. Far from the centre of power, the superintendent found himself more and more isolated and overlooked. During this period, classical teaching in Lower Canada was at its peak, and the Institut Canadien was the focal point of renewed intellectual activity at Montreal and Quebec; younger men were entering parliament, and among the school commissioners were men better educated than others about whose competence he had complained. Those whom Meilleur called his adversaries cast doubt on the quality of the masters and the education they were dispensing. In 1853, to ascertain what the situation was, the Legislative Assembly appointed a special committee, presided over by Louis-Victor Sicotte*, the member for Saint-Hyacinthe, "to inquire into the state of education." Meilleur, who thought Sicotte was proud, vindictive, and arrogant, considered this inquiry a personal insult.

The Sicotte report brought out facts such as the illiteracy of half the commissioners, and the lack of qualifications of the majority of male and female teachers, of whom most were too young and all were badly paid. These were things that the superintendent, anxious to open schools and lacking teachers, had been unable to prevent, since the act gave him neither the authority nor the means to do so. The committee did not blame Meilleur directly, but concluded that the school system needed "a directorate that is active, energetic, and intelligent, and has the right to take

Meilleur

the initiative. . . ." However, the report recommended keeping the structure and principles of the 1846 act, while modifying its details and increasing the financial participation of the government, so that the plans the committee was submitting might be carried out. The most important were the appointment of competent inspectors, fewer and better paid, who would preside over the examiners' boards of the school districts and form, with the superintendent, the Council of Instruction; this council would be responsible for applying the schools act, and, among other activities, choosing and approving the school texts and having them printed, and ensuring the uniformity of teaching methods. Finally, the report recommended that normal schools be opened at Quebec and Montreal, that teachers be better paid, and that they be assured of a pension after 30 years of teaching.

The Legislative Assembly did not put this report into effect. For his part, Meilleur prepared a plan designed to correct a situation he deplored, but the government of Francis Hincks* and Augustin-Norbert Morin* did not deem it opportune to bring it before the assembly. Meilleur's position rapidly became untenable, and on 19 June 1855 the superintendent resigned. Pierre-Joseph-Olivier Chauveau* succeeded him. Chauveau was more fortunate than his predecessor, whom he praised in his first *Rapport annuel* for "the intelligent and continued efforts, the determined perseverance, the even superhuman patience required merely to manage to set in motion a law that was unfortunately unpopular." He had the support of a council and a department of education established in 1856. Meilleur never forgave Chauveau for not mentioning his name in this report, and in 1859 picked a useless quarrel with him in *La Minerve*, over a trifling botanical question.

Meilleur's career continued to wane, although on several occasions his fellow-citizens showed him their gratitude. Immediately after his resignation he was appointed director, then in 1861 inspector, of the post office at Montreal. He ran into serious difficulties in this appointment, being obliged to make good from his own pocket a cash deficit for which he was not responsible, and he left his employment. As he could not continue to live except by using up his slender resources, he accepted the office of justice of the peace, and, in response to a petition from 30 MLAs worried about his fate, the government appointed him temporarily a distributor of legal stamps. When confederation, which he had combatted, finally came into being, he became provincial deputy registrar, with residence at Quebec, and his salary was paid until his death.

In retirement, the former superintendent found new intellectual vigour. In 1857 he attended the congress of the American Association for the Advancement of Science held at Montreal, was a member of the local organizing committee, and deplored the apathy of his French-speaking fellow-citizens. The following year he disputed the validity of the opinion of those who claimed that French Canadians had no aptitude for sciences. The Société Saint-Jean-Baptiste of Montreal had elected him president "in recognition of the outstanding services he had rendered to the country in the cause of education," and he was president of the building society of the district of Montreal. During this period he wrote the work that was to be the crowning achievement of his career as an educator, and in a manner avenge his memory. The *Mémorial de l'éducation du Bas-Canada* appeared in Montreal in 1860; the first edition, which had a printing of 1,009 copies, was quickly exhausted, and a second, considerably larger, was published at Quebec in 1876. This is an indispensable work for anyone who wishes to know the history of education in Canada. The author gives an objective version of the events in which he was both actor and witness, without showing animosity against those who, he says nonetheless, thwarted his endeavour.

While he was living at Quebec, Meilleur became interested again in the natural sciences and collaborated actively with his friend Abbé Léon Provancher*, who in 1870 got him elected president of the Natural History Society of Quebec. He published several articles in *Le Naturaliste canadien*, which Provancher had started in 1868. In his old age Meilleur thus returned to his first love, after having devoted to education the 30 most fruitful years of his long career. His life was an example of persistent and unselfish determination in the service of his fellow-citizens.

Léon Lortie

Meilleur's writings are extensive His reports as superintendent of education for Lower Canada are published in appendices of the *JALPC* for 1843–55. In addition there are: "Agriculture et chimie," *Bibliothèque canadienne* (Montréal), VI (1828), 72ff. and VII (1828), 73ff.; "Analyse de l'eau saline de L'Assomption," *Bibliothèque canadienne* (Montréal), II (1826), 142, 199; *Cours abrégé de leçons de chymie, contenant une exposition précise et méthodique des principes de cette science, exemplifiés* (Montréal, 1833); "Dissertation on scrofula," *Quebec Medical Journal*, I (1826), 233 and II (1827), 81ff.; "Géologie; réponse à J.M.B.," *Bibliothèque canadienne* (Montréal), V (1827), 215; "Lettre à l'abbé Provancher au sujet du *Traité de botanique* de l'abbé O. Brunet," *Le Naturaliste canadien* (Québec), II (1870), 150–52; "Lettre au sujet des recherches du docteur J.A. sur la 'bufonine',"

Le Naturaliste canadien (Québec), II (1870), 239–41, 268–70; "Lettre de remerciement à l'abbé Provancher," *Le Naturaliste canadien* (Québec), IV (1872), 100–2; *Mémorial de l'éducation du Bas-Canada* (1ʳᵉ éd., Montréal, 1860; 2ᵉ éd., Québec, 1876); *Nouvelle grammaire anglaise … (1ʳᵉ éd., Saint-Charles-sur-Richelieu, Qué., 1833; 2ᵉ éd., Montréal, 1854); "On Prussic acid," *Quebec Medical Journal*, I (1826), no.3, 171ff.; "Quelques-unes de nos plantes les plus intéressantes," *Le Naturaliste canadien* (Québec), II (1870), 355–64; "Supplément critique au *Petit traité d'agriculture* de Valère Guillet," *Bibliothèque canadienne* (Montréal), IX (1829), 170–77, 189–95, 210–14; *A treatise on the pronunciation of the French language or a synopsis of rules for pronouncing the French language with irregularities exemplified* (2nd ed., Montreal, 1841).

There are also a number of articles either under his own name or under a pseudonym in the following newspapers, *L'Écho du pays* (Saint-Charles-sur-Richelieu, Qué.), 10 oct. 1833, 4 juill., 11 juill. 1833; *Le Glaneur* (Saint-Charles-sur-Richelieu, Qué.), avril, mai, juin, sept. 1837; *Mélanges religieux* (Montréal), 1841; *La Minerve* (Montréal), 1826, 1829, 9 juin 1831, 23 août 1832, 3 mars, 17 mars, 19 mars, 9 avril 1859; *Le Populaire* (Montréal), 6 août, 13 août, 17 août, 27 août, 3 sept., 5 sept., 7 sept., 26 sept. 1838.

AJM, Registre d'état civil. ASJCF, Collège Sainte-Marie, Fonds Meilleur (microfilm in the possession of Léon Lortie). ASN, Collection Bois, lettres de Jean-Baptiste Meilleur (microfilm in the possession of Léon Lortie). Audet, *Le système scolaire de la province de Québec*, I. Anastase Forget, *Histoire du collège de L'Assomption* (Montréal, [1933]). J. K. Jobling, "The contribution of Jean-Baptiste Meilleur to education in Lower Canada," unpublished MA thesis, McGill University, 1963. André Labarrère-Paulé, *Les instituteurs laïques au Canada français, 1836–1900* (Québec, 1965), 161ff. Léon Lortie, *Notes sur le « Cours abrégé de leçons de chymie » de Jean-Baptiste Meilleur* (Publ. du laboratoire de chimie de l'Université de Montréal, 1, Montréal, 1937). L.-P. Audet, "Index analytique du *Mémorial de l'éducation dans le Bas-Canada* du Dr Jean-Baptiste Meilleur," *RSCT*, 4th ser., II (1964), sect.I, 49–62; "Jean-Baptiste Meilleur était-il un candidat valable au poste de surintendant de l'Éducation pour le Bas-Canada en 1842?" *Cahiers des Dix*, XXXI (1966), 163–201. Léon Lortie, "Deux notaires amateurs de science; Jean De Lisle et son fils Augustin-Stanislas De Lisle," *RSCT*, 3rd ser., LV (1961), sect.I, 39–47; "L'étrange aventure de quelques documents officiels concernant Jean-Baptiste Meilleur," *Annales de l'ACFAS* (Montréal), IX (1943), 171–75; "Les lettres de J.-B. Meilleur sur l'éducation en 1838," *Revue trimestrielle canadienne* (Montréal), XXIV (1938–39), 251–71; "Le retour de Jean-Baptiste Meilleur au Canada," *RSCT*, 3rd ser., L (1956), sect.I, 69–83.

MERCER, ANDREW, issuer of marriage licences and office-holder; b. possibly in Sussex, Eng., *c.* 1778–84; d. Toronto, Ont., 13 June 1871.

The first certain fact about Andrew Mercer's early life is that he arrived at Quebec late in 1800, accompanying Thomas Scott*, the new attorney general of Upper Canada. Mercer once stated that his mother, Mary Mercer, was unmarried, and his intimacy with Scott led to gossip that he was Scott's illegitimate son.

They arrived at York (Toronto) early in 1801 and Mercer became Scott's secretary. He next held the junior clerkship in the Executive Council (1803–20), and the office of king's printer (1816), probably through Scott's influence. Mercer was paymaster for the Home District militia during the War of 1812 and was taken captive at the fall of York in April 1813, but was soon released. In 1833 he became a magistrate. Mercer also had business interests for some years after 1809, operating a general store in partnership with Samuel Smith Ridout*, and later developing an extensive mortgage and loan business.

Although much was later said about his philanthropy, it is known only that he made a gift of 1,000 acres of land, located in swampy townships, toward the endowment of the University of Trinity College in 1851. From 1827, although wealthy, he lived at Bay and Wellington streets in Toronto in a cottage later said to be "scarcely worth insuring," and he was described as "almost parsimonious."

Mercer was issuer of marriage licences in York by 1818 but never himself obtained one. In 1850 he acquired a violent-tempered, illiterate, and thieving housekeeper, Bridget O'Reilly, who seems to have terrorized him for the rest of his life. She gave birth in 1851 to a boy, christened Andrew Francis Mercer, and generally believed to be the son of septuagenarian Andrew, whom she threatened with seduction charges. He provided for the boy and gave him some land, but never made him his heir and on one occasion reportedly stated that he "would leave his money to the government."

Mercer died suddenly in 1871, intestate. As the estate would pass to the crown unless legitimate heirs were found, the provincial government immediately took over on a commission of escheat, and in 1872 the attorney general, Adam Crooks*, was appointed administrator. Mercer's household was allowed to remain in the cottage, a search for heirs was begun in Great Britain and Canada, and steps were taken to put the $180,000 estate in order, as the holdings, largely in the form of land, mortgages, loans, and stocks, were found to be in considerable disarray.

In 1875 Oliver Mowat*, appointed administrator the previous year, began arrangements for a hearing in the Court of Chancery to test the claims of the would-be heirs. At this point Bridget

Mercier

O'Reilly and her son suddenly produced a marriage certificate, dated a month before the latter's birth, and a will leaving them the entire estate. The hearing of all claims took place in January 1876 with John Beverley Robinson* acting for the crown. Roman Catholic Archbishop John Joseph Lynch*, John MONTGOMERY, and others supported young Mercer's claim, but he himself refused to enter the witness box for examination. Vice-Chancellor Samuel Hume Blake* declared both documents forgeries and decided in favour of the province.

Still, Mercer refused to vacate the Bay Street property and a series of law suits resulted. These developed into a constitutional test case over whether a province or the federal government had the right to escheat estates under sections 102 and 109 of the British North America Act. The Ontario courts decided in favour of the province, the Supreme Court of Canada supported the dominion claim, and a decision in favour of Ontario was finally handed down by the Judicial Committee of the Privy Council of Great Britain in 1884. The Bay Street property was then taken over and sold.

The rest of the estate had meanwhile been disposed of by the Ontario government. A sum of $10,000 was allocated for an Andrew Mercer Eye and Ear Infirmary for the Toronto General Hospital in 1878, and a total of $106,000 went toward the erection of the Andrew Mercer Ontario Reformatory for Females, opened in 1880 and used until 1969. Much of the money was swallowed up in legal costs, including a large portion of the $30,000 Mowat generously allowed young Mercer.

Andrew Mercer, albeit unwittingly, gained a certain immortality through the court cases and the institutions. To later generations, who knew the name but not the circumstances, he appeared a great benefactor of the cause of female reform.

FREDERICK H. ARMSTRONG

PAC, RG 1, E1, 47, pp.283, 291; E14, 10, pp.158–59; L3, M6/332, 37; RG 5, A1, 26, pp.12067–69; 27, pp.12563–64, 12799–800, 26686–87; RG 7, G16, C, 9, p.48; RG 8, I, A1, 690, pp.166–66a; RG 68, 1. PAO, Alexander Campbell papers, 18 Nov. 1881, 31 May 1883; Chancery Court files, 1875, 55, "Mercer v. attorney-general"; 1878, 526, "Attorney-general v. O'Reilly"; Misc. 1934, John Robertson, "Memorandum re A. Mercer and Thomas Scott"; RG 8, I-7-b-2, 1878, no.34; 1879, no.33; 1882, no.51; 1888, no.30; Ridout papers, 1809, agreement of partnership. Trinity College Archives (Toronto), Minutes of the council, 20 Feb. 1851, 27.
   Attorney general of Ontario v. *Mercer* (1883), 8 App. Cas. 767 (P.C.) reversing (1881), 5 S.C.R. 583, which reversed (sub nom.) *Attorney general of Ontario* v. *O'Reilly* (1880), 6 O.A.R. 576, which affirmed (1878), 26 Gr. 126 (Ch.). Ontario, *Sessional papers*, IX (1877), PT.2, no.7; X (1878), PT.4, no.38; XII (1880), PT.4, no.34; XIII (1881), PT.4, no.48. Ontario, *Statutes*, 1878, c. 1; 1879, c. 38.
   Globe (Toronto), 14 June 1871, 15 Nov. 1875, 14–22 Jan. 1876. Scadding, *Toronto of old*, 55, 84, 269, 363, 366. *Town of York, 1793–1815* (Firth), 140, 281. *Hist. of Toronto and county of York*, II, 109. J. E. Jones, *Pioneer crimes and punishments in Toronto and the Home District . . .* (Toronto, 1924), 46. *Landmarks of Toronto* (Robertson), I, 46–48, 433.

MERCIER, ANTOINE, priest, Sulpician, parish priest of Saint-Jacques-le-Majeur (Montreal); b. 14 May 1817 at Lyons, Department of Rhône, France, son of Antoine Mercier and Élisabeth Chirat; d. 12 April 1875 at Montreal, Que.

Antoine Mercier was ordained priest in 1842, and the following year entered the Society of Saint-Sulpice in Paris. His noviciate completed, he served for five years as bursar of the seminary of Clermont, Department of Oise; then, at his own request, his superiors allowed him to go to Canada, where he arrived on 10 Oct. 1849.

He was at first curate at Notre-Dame de Montréal, where he had several administrative responsibilities. Shortly before his installation as chief bursar of the seminary of Montreal, M. Mercier, on 26 April 1857, founded the institute of the Little Sisters of St Joseph; the founding was on the initiative of a pious young girl, Rose de Lima Dauth, and had the approval and consent of his superior and his *confrères*. The community's main object was to devote itself, through prayer and good works, to the material and moral support of seminarists and priests. Initially, in accordance with its founder's ideas, it had new features: it was an association of girls for whom no special dress, vows, or noviciate were required; they could join after a retreat of only three days. M. Mercier had scarcely laid the foundations of the new institute and drawn up its general regulations when he was replaced at the head of the undertaking by his *confrère* Damien-Henri Tambareau. Even if subsequently the functions entrusted to him did not allow him to direct the Little Sisters of St Joseph, he always remained keenly interested in the institute and ready to advise its members.

After a year's stay at the seminary, Mercier withdrew from the temporal administration of charitable works of the Society of Saint-Sulpice to give his attention almost exclusively to parish ministry. He was entrusted with the direction first of the dependent church of Notre-Dame-de-Grâces at Montreal, 1858–62, then of the Indian mission at Lac-des-Deux-Montagnes (Oka), 1862–68, and finally of the parish of Saint-Jacques-le-Majeur at Montreal, 1868–75. In 1864 he had brought the Little Sisters of St Joseph to Oka and allotted them various tasks among the Algonkins, the Iroquois, and the missionaries, including the upkeep of the mission church and the missionaries' residence, and the running of a needlework school for Algonkin women; one of the nuns learned enough of the Iroquois language to be able to teach the children.

In the different duties he had to perform, M. Mercier always distinguished himself by his great spiritual qualities, by his gentleness and benevolence, and especially by an irrepressible activity that never knew any respite. He died on 12 April 1875 at the seminary of Notre-Dame, after an illness of four months.

ANTONIO DANSEREAU

[Antoine Mercier], *Réflexions et retraites*, Émile Boucher, édit. (Montréal, 1964). This book contains the private notes of M. Mercier's spiritual retreats from the time of his ordination to the subdiaconate in 1840 until his death. The volume was not for sale but was designed for the religious community which he founded. A.D.]

Archives de l'Institut des Petites Filles de Saint-Joseph (Montréal). ASSM, Biographies, Antoine Mercier; Communautés religieuses. Allaire, *Dictionnaire*. Gauthier, *Sulpitiana*. A.-L. Bertrand, *Bibliothèque sulpicienne ou histoire littéraire de la Compagnie de Saint-Sulpice* (3v., Paris, 1900), II. René Labelle, *Les Petites Filles de Saint-Joseph; les origines de la communauté* (Montréal, 1923). Olivier Maurault, *Saint-Jacques de Montréal; l'église, la paroisse* (Montréal, 1923). L.-O. David, "Biographie du Révérend M. Mercier, s.s.," *La Minerve* (Montréal), 14 avril 1875.

METHERALL, FRANCIS, Bible Christian minister, founder of the Bible Christian mission in Prince Edward Island; b. December 1791 in North Devon, Eng.; d. 9 June 1875 at Cape Wolfe, P.E.I.

Francis Metherall experienced evangelical conversion in 1819 under the ministry of James Thorne, associate of William O'Bryan, founder of the Bible Christian movement, a Methodist sect which originated in Shebbear, Devon, in 1815. After being received into the Bible Christian ministry in 1822, Metherall served circuits in the Isles of Scilly, Monmouth, Jersey, Somerton, Guernsey, Portsea, and Penzance.

Metherall was appointed to Prince Edward Island in 1831 following a request by Bible Christian immigrants from the west of England for a minister of their own. He arrived at Bedeque on 26 May 1832, and soon founded his first congregation at Union Road six miles northeast of Charlottetown. Within a year he organized an 80-mile circuit including Wheatley River, Vernon

River, and Sturgeon track, with a total of 47 members. He also built a residence and mission house at Vernon River; his first wife was Mary Langlois, whom he had married in Guernsey on 22 Aug. 1826, and they had eight children. When Philip James arrived on the Island in 1834, the circuit was enlarged to include New London with an itinerary of 120 miles and 36 preaching stations. James served the eastern area, and Metherall extended the work westwards to St Eleanors, New Bideford, and West Cape, for several years travelling the rough terrain on foot. In an area settled largely by Roman Catholics and Presbyterians, the progress of the Bible Christians was slow, but widespread use of protracted meetings led to "the great revival" of 1843 when the church's membership increased to 400 in two years. With this increase, P.E.I. was designated a district of the English Bible Christian Church with Metherall as superintendent. Two additional ministers, William Calloway and William Harris, joined Metherall; James had by that time gone to the Cobourg circuit in Canada West.

In 1846 Metherall moved from Vernon River to the West Cape circuit. His first wife had died in 1841, and in 1853 he married Mary Nelson by whom he had four children. In that same year he took over the Union circuit, and in 1857 was succeeded as superintendent by Cephas Baker. At this time Metherall's poor health and his failure to secure additional help from England caused a recession in the work of the mission. Metherall retired from active ministry in 1869, but continued to serve on the West Cape circuit until his death. An obituary said of him, "His name on P.E. Island is, and will for many years be an household name, while the fruit of his Christian toil abides as a monument of indefatigable perseverance under the divine direction and blessing." In 1884 the Bible Christian Church in Canada became part of the Methodist Church of Canada.

ALBERT BURNSIDE

UCA, Francis Metherall papers, letters and diary. Francis Metherall family bible, in possession of Miss I. M. Metherall, Halifax, N.S. Bible Christian Church in Canada, Annual Conference, *Minutes*, 1857–84. Bible Christians, Annual Conference, *Minutes* (Shebbear, Devon; London), 1819–76. *Bible Christian Magazine . . . being a continuation of the Arminian Magazine* (Shebbear, Devon), 1831–84. *Observer* (Bowmanville, Ont.), 1867–84. Albert Burnside, "The Bible Christians in Canada, 1832–1884," unpublished DD thesis, University of Toronto, 1969. John Harris, *The life of the Rev. Francis Metherall, and the history of the Bible Christian Church in Prince Edward Island* (London and Toronto, 1883). J. E. Sanderson, *The first century of Methodism in Canada . . .* (2v., Toronto, 1908–10), II, 426–30. Thomas Shaw,

Middleton

The Bible Christians, 1815–1907 (London, 1965), 31, 52. George Webber, "The Bible Christian Church," *Centennial of Canadian Methodism* (Toronto, 1891), 205–27; "Prince Edward Island, No. II," *Observer* (Bowmanville, Ont.), 9 April 1873.

MIDDLETON, ROBERT, journalist; b. 1810 at Berwick-on-Tweed, Eng.; d. 27 Aug. 1874 in Quebec City.

After apprenticeship to a printer in Scotland, Robert Middleton married and emigrated. He arrived in Quebec City in 1832 during the Asiatic cholera outbreak, and at the height of a political crisis involving John Neilson*, owner and editor of the *Quebec Gazette*, the oldest and leading newspaper in the Canadas. Neilson, long the proponent in the assembly of French Canadian rights, had just broken with his former ally Louis-Joseph PAPINEAU, refusing to vote in censure of the governor general, Lord Aylmer [Whitworth-Aylmer*]. To clarify his position, Neilson in April 1832 began publishing a separate French version of his paper three times a week, at the same time continuing an English edition three times a week. The young Middleton took charge of the printing press and book shop while Neilson battled in parliament and in editorials. After Neilson lost his seat in the 1834 election, his sons Samuel and William successively took over ownership of the paper. Though Neilson still wrote articles, Middleton is listed until 1847 in Quebec City and Canada directories as "Editor." The paper published important accounts of constitutionalism and the insurrections, and of Neilson's opposition to the union of the two Canadas. From 1842 to 1847 the *Gazette* published only in English.

Middleton, Neilson's printer, writer, and bookseller, also became a lay preacher at Centenary Methodist Chapel in 1838, and by 1844 was superintendent of the Sunday schools in the Saint-Louis suburbs and corresponding secretary of the Quebec Auxiliary Bible Society.

In May 1847 there was a political crisis over the question of local responsible government in the colonies. Neilson battled against Francis Hincks* and Robert Baldwin*. On 18 May 1847, Middleton left Neilson's *Gazette* and with Charles Saint-Michel set up a rival publication, the *Morning Chronicle*, on the Côte de la Montagne, taking a stand for Canadian self-government and supporting the views of Lord Elgin [Bruce*], while attacking those of his predecessor Sir Charles Theophilus Metcalfe*. The new paper also announced its intention to emphasize commercial and shipping news, and to include more literary reviews than its rivals. Neilson, "Bookseller and Stationer," continued to publish the *Gazette*, also

at premises on Côte de la Montagne, writing fiery editorials till the eve of his death on 1 Feb. 1848. Neilson's third son, John, inherited, and hired Ronald MacDonald* as editor for the next three months. Then he invited Robert Middleton to rejoin the *Gazette* as a partner. Within a few months the younger Neilson retired, leaving Middleton as editor, and from May 1849 as proprietor. The stationery and bookselling shop had been suspended on the death of John Neilson, but was revived by Middleton.

Politically, Middleton swung the *Gazette* in the spring of 1849 into support of Baldwin and Louis-Hippolyte La Fontaine*, Hincks and Augustin-Norbert Morin*. *L'Avenir*, founded 1847 by Jean-Baptiste-Éric Dorion*, emerged as a rallying point for the late John Neilson's followers. During the Hincks-Morin administration, the *Gazette*, still liberal, became the official government organ. Middleton took John T. Dawson into partnership in paper and shop in 1856.

Middleton, who had written strong pleas for Quebec in the "seat of government question," found his paper diminishing in power when the capital shifted from city to city. In 1857 the *Gazette* dropped from daily to tri-weekly publication. Now politically independent and moderate, the *Gazette* gave more and more space to literary reviews, latest news from overseas and from the United States, news of ship arrivals, and good-humoured debate with its rival, the *Quebec Mercury*. In 1864, the centenary of the founding of the *Gazette*, Middleton was editorializing mildly about confederation, and more vehemently on civic questions such as the plight of victims of fire, the nature of Irish celebrations on St Patrick's day, and the good work being done by evangelical harbour missionaries. When the government moved permanently to Ottawa in 1866, the *Gazette*'s value as first-hand observer of day-to-day activities in the house ceased. During Middleton's last years, the now Conservative *Gazette* focused on business and shipping news. After his death the paper merged with the *Morning Chronicle* he had helped to found, and the successor was named the *Quebec Chronicle and Quebec Gazette* (1875).

Middleton's editorials, lively and direct, brought him wide respect as an accurate and impartial reporter. Like his predecessor, Neilson, whom he praised for being "always on the side of truth, honesty and virtue," he had an attractive ironic touch and a gusto in political reporting.

ELIZABETH WATERSTON

Morning Chronicle (Quebec), 1847–49. *Quebec Gazette*, 1833–74. Beaulieu et Hamelin, *Journaux du Québec.*

McLaughlin's Quebec directory . . . for 1855–1856, comp. Samuel McLaughlin (Quebec, 1855); *1857–1858* (Quebec, 1857). Morgan, *Bibliotheca Canadensis*. *The Quebec directory, and city and commercial register, 1847–1848*, comp. Alfred Hawkins (Montreal, 1847). *A history of Canadian journalism . . .* (2v., Toronto, 1908–59), I. *Canada, an encyclopædia*, V, 221, 226.

Careless, *Union of the Canadas*. Christie, *History of Lower Canada*, III, IV. Dent, *Last forty years*. Elzéar Gérin, *La Gazette de Québec* (Québec, 1864). W. H. Kesterton, *A history of journalism in Canada* (Carleton Library series, 36, Toronto, 1967). S. M. E. Read, "An account of English journalism in Canada from the middle of the eighteenth century to the beginning of the twentieth, with special emphasis being given to the periods prior to confederation," unpublished MA thesis, McGill University, 1925. Shortt, *Sydenham*. Waite, *Life and times of confederation*.

MIERTSCHING, JOHANN AUGUST, Moravian missionary to the Eskimos and Arctic explorer; b. 21 Aug. 1817 at Groeditz, Saxony, son of Johann Miertsching and Erdmuth Naacké; m. in 1856 C. A. Erxleben; d. 30 March 1875 at Kleinwelke, Saxony.

Born of German working-class parents, Johann August Miertsching was sent as a boy to the Moravian community at Kleinwelke, Saxony, where he became a shoemaker and eventually joined the Moravian Church. One of the oldest Protestant sects in Europe, the Moravians had established their headquarters at Herrnhut in eastern Germany in the 18th century after fleeing from persecution in Bohemia. The evangelical impulse to convert the Eskimos led them first to Greenland in 1733, then to Labrador in 1771. Miertsching was called to the service of the mission to the Eskimos in 1844 and spent the following five years at the Okak mission station on the northern Labrador coast. Here he learned the Eskimo language and gained experience in Arctic travel.

In 1849 the British Admiralty asked the Moravian Mission Board for the services of a Labrador or Greenland missionary to join the expedition then being fitted out to search for Sir John Franklin*. Miertsching, in Saxony on furlough at the time, accepted the assignment and joined HMS *Investigator* (Capt. Robert McClure) just before she sailed from Plymouth on 20 Jan. 1850. Sailing around Cape Horn, *Investigator* entered the Arctic seas from the Pacific, attempting to search out a northwest passage. Johann Miertsching and most of the crew did finally make their way across the Arctic and home to England, but only after enduring four Arctic winters and leaving *Investigator* and a rescue ship abandoned in the ice.

During this gruelling experience Miertsching kept a journal, which was published in abbreviated form in 1855 and translated into English and published in full in 1967. The journal is rich in topographical detail and in descriptions of the Eskimos tribes encountered, and relates in dramatic fashion the perils from ice and cold. Several times Miertsching, attired in native Eskimo dress, acted as the captain's "invaluable interpreter," drawing on the English he had learned in daily study sessions aboard ship. On more than one occasion, when the natives were armed and threatening, he took command of the situation, calmed the Eskimos by assurances in their own language, and left them as friends. He found that the Eskimos of the western Arctic were similar to those in Labrador in their features, dress, language, and tools. Through his efforts much valuable information was gained about the geography of the region, although, unfortunately, no trace of Sir John Franklin was found.

Miertsching preached to the Eskimos whenever possible, defended his religion to Captain McClure and other sceptics on *Investigator*, and made several converts among the ship's crew. He entered wholeheartedly into the sledge journeys and hunting expeditions that became the daily round of life in the Arctic winters. Through it all he regarded and recorded shipboard life with an observant and not unhumorous eye. Describing the "school" held aboard the ice-bound ship he remarks: "It is interesting to see a polar school: some of the bearded scholars writing on paper, others on a blackboard, others forming letters; some mending their clothes, while others in a half-reclining posture smoke their pipes of tobacco and play the silent spectator."

After this epic journey Miertsching never returned to Canada. Following his marriage in Saxony, he became a missionary to the Hottentots of South Africa, serving at the mission stations of Elim and Genadendal, east of Capetown. He retired to Kleinwelke in 1868 and died there. His daughter Marie married another Labrador missionary, Hermann Theodor Jannasch*, with whom she spent 24 years working on the Labrador coast. Descendants have settled permanently in Canada.

Johann Miertsching was in many ways a typical Moravian missionary – quiet, candid, and possessed of a deep religious faith. When he was seconded to the Arctic expedition he rose to the occasion, and, under exacting conditions, carried out his duties conscientiously and ably, leaving the mark of his personality on the whole of the ship's company.

WILLIAM H. WHITELEY

Miller

[McClure], *Discovery of the north-west passage* (Osborn). [J. A. Miertsching], *Frozen ships: the Arctic diary of Johann Miertsching, 1850–1854*, ed. and trans. by L. H. Neatby (Toronto, 1967); *Reise-Tagebuch des Missionars Joh. A. Miertsching welcher als Dolmetscher die Nordpol-Expedition zur Aufsuchung Sir John Franklins auf dem Schiffe Investigator begleitete* ([Gnadau], 1855; Gnadau, Leipzig, 1856). *Periodical accounts relating to the missions of the Church of the United Brethren, established among the heathen* (London), 1846–75. Daniel Benham, *Sketch of the life of Jan August Miertsching, interpreter of the Esquimaux language to the Arctic expedition on board H.M.S. "Investigator," Captain M'Clure, 1850, 1851, 1852, 1853* (London, 1854). H. W. Jannasch, "Grossvater Miertsching," *Herrnhuter Miniaturen* (Lüneburg, 1953), 80–96.

MILLER, LINUS WILSON, farmer and insurrectionist; b. 28 Dec. 1817 in Delanti (now Stockton), N.Y., son of Benjamin Miller, a pioneer settler in Chautauqua County, N.Y., and Laura Hamlin; d. 11 April 1880, at Jamestown, N.Y.

Linus Wilson Miller was among the Americans who strongly sympathized with the "Patriot" cause. He studied law with Judge James Mullett, and in early spring of 1838 he visited Upper Canada to verify the views he held on the situation in the colony. He returned to Canada in April as the emissary of the Canadian Refugee Relief Association in Lockport, New York, to abduct seven men who had been sentenced to die for their part in the rebellion and who were being held in the Hamilton jail. The scheme failed, as the result, Miller said, of the activities of the "*Prince of Traitors*, JACOB BEEMER." Miller himself narrowly escaped to the United States.

He again entered Upper Canada in June 1838, alone, as the staff officer of General Donald M'LEOD in the Patriot army. Major plans for an invasion by the Patriots on 4 July had been made, and M'Leod saw these jeopardized when news came that a small party of Patriots, under Colonel James Morreau and including Beemer, was in the vicinity of the Short Hills in the Niagara peninsula. Miller was sent with orders from M'Leod that they withdraw, but they refused. The border was too closely guarded for Miller's return to the United States, and he rejoined the raiders, but he was captured soon after. Miller and 15 others were tried at Niagara and received the death sentence, later commuted to transportation overseas. Confined in Fort Henry, they were later sent to England and were held in Newgate Prison for six months while the English Court of Queen's Bench examined the cases. The sentences of transportation were eventually confirmed for the 16 men, despite pleas made by Lord Brougham,

John Arthur ROEBUCK, Joseph Hume, and William Henry Seward, later a member of Abraham Lincoln's cabinet. Miller and his fellow prisoners were placed aboard *Canton* along with numerous English felons, and landed at Hobart, Van Diemen's Land (Tasmania), on 12 Jan. 1840.

For the next four years Miller was compelled to undergo the same hard labour and harsh treatment as the English felons. He was interned for some time with the other Canadian prisoners at Brown's River Road Station; after being transferred to Lovely Banks he attempted to escape in 1840 and was sent to the maximum security prison at Port Arthur. Only in his last year of exile did his condition improve. He received his pardon following the recall in 1843 of the lieutenant governor of Van Diemen's Land, Sir John Franklin*, and he became tutor to the family of Thomas James Lempriere, the colony's assistant commissary. He sailed for home in September 1845 and landed in the United States 25 Jan. 1846.

Linus Miller's account of his exile is recorded in a book he wrote and published in 1846 after his return. It is divided rather unequally between the record of his service with the Patriot force in Upper Canada, the review of his case before the English Court of Queen's Bench, and his days of exile between 1840 and 1844. Miller provides abundant detail of penal life. His style is bitter and bombastic, and a reader might doubt his mental balance. Despite the author's readily apparent prejudices, however, the narrative is one of the most informative of the memoirs written by men sent to Van Diemen's Land.

Miller was married on 10 Jan. 1850 to Anne Jeanette Curtis, to whom two sons and three daughters were born. Miller engaged in farming and dairying at Delanti. He moved to Jamestown, N.Y., shortly before his death.

FRED LANDON

L. W. Miller, *Notes of an exile to Van Dieman's Land: comprising incidents of the Canadian rebellion in 1838, trial of the author in Canada, and subsequent appearance before her majesty's Court of Queen's Bench, in London, imprisonment in England, and transportation to Van Diemen's Land . . .* (Fredonia, N.Y., 1846). *Fredonia Censor* (Fredonia, N.Y.), 21 April 1880, 7 April 1897. E. C. Guillet, *The lives and times of the Patriots; an account of the rebellion in Upper Canada, 1837–1838, and the Patriot agitation in the United States, 1837–1842* (Toronto, 1938). Fred Landon, *An exile from Canada to Van Diemen's Land; being the story of Elijah Woodman transported overseas for participation in the Upper Canada troubles of 1837–38* (Toronto, 1960), 178, 204–7, 212, 216, 255–56. A.W. Young, *History of Chautauqua County, New York: from its first settlement to the present time* (Buffalo, N.Y., 1875).

Mills

MILLER, MARIA FRANCES ANN. *See* Morris

MILLOY, DUNCAN, steamboat captain and owner; b. 1825 (perhaps in August), in Scotland, fourth son of Alexander Milloy; d. 20 Oct. 1871 at Niagara, Ont.

Duncan Milloy was raised in Oban, Argyllshire, Scotland, but left in 1843 with his widowed father and his six brothers to settle in Brant County, Canada West. All the brothers made their careers in inland shipping, Duncan immediately taking employment on Royal Mail Line steamers running between Hamilton and Montreal. On 25 Nov. 1851 he married Euphemia Thompson, who came from a shipping family; in 1862 they moved from Toronto to Niagara.

In 1853 Milloy took command of the passenger steamer *Chief Justice Robinson* running from Toronto to Niagara and Lewiston, New York, a route he was to travel most of his life. He transferred in 1854 to the opulently appointed sidewheeler *Zimmerman*, 475 tons, estimated cost $60,000, launched that year from Louis Shickluna's yards at Niagara for the Erie and Ontario Railroad Company with whose service it connected at Niagara. In 1858 he commanded the *Peerless* running from Toronto to Hamilton, but he bought the *Zimmerman* from Samuel Zimmerman*'s estate in time for the 1859 season and returned to the Toronto, Niagara, and Lewiston route. In 1863, however, the *Zimmerman* burned at its Niagara wharf, its steam-whistle shrieking mournfully. Milloy immediately handed a design of his own to Shickluna, and on 20 April 1864 the *City of Toronto*, 221 feet, 512 tons, and built of seasoned oak, slipped into the water. Railways ran around the head of Lake Ontario after 1855, and there was less need for passenger shipping; except for one year, Milloy was the only one making the journey from 1861 on.

Duncan Milloy appears to have been a handsome, genial, and even dashing figure – fitting the captain who travelled the route to the falls, at once a festive, a fashionable, and an international voyage. Canadians favoured his route as a link to the eastern seaboard and to Europe since it connected with the New York Central Railroad at Lewiston. A passenger skipper had standing in the community. Milloy, a Presbyterian and a freemason, appears to have been on familiar terms with Conservative leaders John A. Macdonald* and John Hillyard Cameron, but his affability had to extend the whole range of the social scale to cope with the holiday and moonlight excursions for which his vessel was often hired.

Milloy died in 1871 at "Oban House," his home at Niagara. In the last two seasons before

the *City* burned in 1883 it was owned and skippered by his eldest son William. One of Milloy's brothers, Donald*, at one time purser on the *Zimmerman*, later headed steamboat partnerships.

BARRIE DYSTER

Niagara Historical Society (Niagara), W. A. Milloy papers. PAC, MG 26, A (Macdonald papers), pp.258203–4; RG 5, C1, 1858, no.195. *Globe* (Toronto), especially 11 July 1867 and 21 Oct. 1871. *J. of Education for Ont.*, XXIV (1871), 187. *Caverhill's Toronto city directory, for 1859–60* ... (Toronto, [1859]). *Hutchinson's Toronto directory, 1862–63* ... (Toronto, n.d.). *Commemorative biog. record, county York*, 627. Erik Heyl, *Early American steamers* (5v., Buffalo, N.Y., 1953–67), II, 37; III, 353–54; V, 61–62. Janet Carnochan, *History of Niagara (in part)* (Toronto, 1914). Barlow Cumberland, *A century of sail and steam on the Niagara River* (Toronto, 1913). *History of the Great Lakes* (2v., Chicago, 1899), II, 4. *Landmarks of Toronto* (Robertson), II, 896, 915, 917.

MILLS, SAMUEL SYLVESTER, businessman and politician; b. at what later became Hamilton, U.C., 1 Dec. 1806, one of 11 children of James Mills and Christina Hesse; d. at Hamilton, Ont., 24 Jan. 1874.

Samuel Sylvester Mills' parents, born in the United States, pioneered on a farm in the Hamilton area in 1800. Available evidence does not support the claims that either his father or his mother were UEL. Samuel was educated at a Hamilton grammar school and went into the wholesale hardware business. Later he also involved himself in shipping, milling, real estate, and construction. He built and rented a large number of houses in workers' districts. He owned a sizeable amount of stock in insurance companies and banks, and served as a director of the Bank of Hamilton and of the Canada Life Assurance Company. For a short period he was president of the Gore Bank.

Described as one of "the three wealthiest men in Hamilton," Mills was generous with his wealth. An Anglican, he donated to his diocese the land and money required for the construction of All Saints' Church. He also presented land to Hamilton for use as a cemetery.

Samuel Mills served briefly as a Hamilton alderman and for several years was chairman of the board of commissioners of the Provincial Lunatic Asylum. In 1849 the government of Robert Baldwin* and Louis-Hippolyte La Fontaine* made him a life member of the Legislative Council, in which he served until 1867. Although one of Baldwin's local Reform lieutenants during the 1840s, he was a Conservative during the confederation period, a pattern of political evolution consistent with that of numerous Baldwinites. He

515

Milner

was called to the Senate on 23 Oct. 1867 but did not play a prominent role in the upper house.

He had married in 1831 Aurora Holton, an American, by whom he had eight children. He died in Hamilton in 1874.

DONALD SWAINSON

Hamilton Public Libarary, A. W. Roy, "Newspaper clippings scrapbook," 14. MTCL, Baldwin papers, A58, ff.32–41. PAC, MG 26, A (Macdonald papers), 508–10, 512–15, 518. *Can. directory of parliament* (Johnson), 367–68. *Can. parl. comp., 1873.* A. M. Brock, *The Mills, Holton and Smith families* (Toronto, 1927). M. F. Campbell, *A mountain and a city, the story of Hamilton* (Toronto, 1966). *Genealogical and historical records of the Mills and Gage families, 1776–1926, 150 years,* comp. Stanley Mills (Hamilton, Ont., 1926). Ross and Trigge, *History of the Canadian Bank of Commerce,* III. A. C. Cawthra, "The Mills family," UEL Assoc. of Ont., *Annual Trans.* (Toronto), I (1897–98), 46–48.

MILNER, CHRISTOPHER, Church of England priest and missionary, b. 28 Feb. 1787 at Hawxwell, Yorkshire, Eng.; d. 2 Nov. 1877 at Sackville, N.B.

Christopher Milner was ordained a Church of England deacon on 20 Dec. 1812 by Brownlow North, bishop of Winchester, and immediately appointed curate at Binstead, Isle of Wight. He was raised to the priesthood in the following year by George Henry Law, bishop of Chester. Late in 1817 he was accepted as a missionary by the Society for the Propagation of the Gospel, and was sent to Halifax where he arrived with his family on 18 May 1818. At the request of the governor, Lord Dalhousie [George Ramsay*], and with the approval of Bishop Robert Stanser*, he took charge of the collegiate school in Windsor, Nova Scotia, in June 1818.

In May 1820 Milner was appointed missionary at Sackville, New Brunswick, and, upon arrival, found himself the only Church of England missionary between Sussex Vale and Halifax. Making his headquarters at Fort Cumberland until a parsonage was built at Westcock in 1824, he served congregations at Amherst, Dorchester, Shediac, and several other settlements. Wherever he could find a congregation, Milner encouraged the people to build churches and schools. The church at Fort Cumberland, which had fallen into ruin through disuse, was rebuilt by March 1821, and a church and school were built at Shediac in 1822. He also encouraged the establishment of new schools under the Madras system which enabled one schoolmaster to teach a large number of children by employing the advanced students as "pupil teachers."

In 1836 he became missionary at Westfield,

N.B., and also took charge at Petersville and Greenwich until those parishes obtained resident ministers. Here, as elsewhere, he exhorted the people to build churches, taking an axe into his own hands and felling the first tree when he felt the congregation was moving too slowly. The churches constructed at Oke Point, Greenwich, and Nerpesis were a result of his endeavours.

The Reverend Mr Milner was an energetic and vigorous clergyman, who covered his large mission on foot, on horseback, and by rowboat. It was reported to the SPG that "[he] often rowed himself, in storms when no person would venture with him." Another report told how Milner's horse got its foot caught in the ice while crossing a river. The missionary freed his mount by cutting a hole with his pocket knife, but "his hands and arms . . . were completely frozen, like solid masses of ice, to his elbows, and were with great difficulty recovered by immersion in spirits." He often preached as many as four times on a given Sunday at points many miles apart. In July 1859, while rowing from Greenwich to Westfield after morning service, he suffered a sunstroke which completely incapacitated him and forced his retirement from the ministry after 42 years of service.

C. E. THOMAS

USPG, Journal of SPG, 31, letters of John Inglis, 19 May, 21 June 1818; 32, p.319, 19 May 1820; C/CAN/NS, letter of Christopher Milner, 7 Sept. 1824. G. H. Lee, *An historical sketch of the first fifty years of the Church of England in the province of New Brunswick (1783–1883)* (Saint John, N.B., 1880), 122. W. C. Milner, *History of Sackville, New Brunswick* (Sackville, N.B., 1934), 63–64. Pascoe, *Two hundred years of the S.P.G.,* 867.

MILTON, Viscount.
See WENTWORTH-FITZWILLIAM

MINIXI. *See* ONISTAH-SOKAKSIN

MOLESWORTH, THOMAS NEPEAN, surveyor and engineer; b. 24 June 1824 in Moy, County Armagh, Ireland, son of Arthur Nepean Molesworth and Harriett Hawkins; d. 24 April 1879 in Toronto, Ont.

Thomas Nepean Molesworth is said by earlier writers to have attended Trinity College, Dublin, but the college records do not bear out this claim. He was, apparently, apprenticed to Williby Hemans under whom he learned civil engineering. Having acquired a trade, and married Sarah Georgina Kertland, Molesworth in 1848 emigrated to Canada.

Molesworth's first employment in Canada was teaching school at Trafalgar, near Oakville,

Canada West. He soon moved to Goderich (the centre for the developing counties of Huron, Grey, and Bruce), qualified as a provincial land surveyor in 1851, and established a practice which he maintained until 1858. Molesworth was also retained for several public projects; in 1852–56 he surveyed parts of St Joseph and Bear islands in Lake Huron and laid out the town plots of Wingham and St Joseph. He formed a partnership in 1856 with Thomas Weatherald, which lasted about nine years, and the next year surveyed part of the north shore of Lake Superior.

In 1858 Molesworth became chief engineer of the Buffalo and Lake Huron Railway (which had its western terminus at Goderich) and he moved to Brantford, the company's headquarters, in 1859. He moved to Fort Erie in 1863, where he helped survey and plan the International Bridge, and went into the employ of the Grand Trunk Railway. His home at Fort Erie was damaged in a Fenian attack in 1866.

Molesworth was retained by the Department of Public Works of Ontario in 1868 and 1869 to survey swamp lands in Kent and Essex counties. In 1870 he became assistant engineer of the department and moved to Toronto. In his new capacity he was largely concerned with drawing up reports on the status of canal, road, and drainage projects. From 1874 until his death in 1879 he was chief engineer of public works for Ontario, concerned mainly with reports regarding the inspection of railways, which had to meet established standards of quality as well as specific construction deadlines to qualify for provincial aid.

Molesworth had seven children, one of whom, Balfour Nepean, also became a provincial land surveyor.

STEPHEN F. SPENCER

PAO, J. C. Bailey papers, 29 Nov. 1876, 27 Nov. 1877, 8 Jan. 1878; RG 15, ser. IV–2 (Assistant engineer's letter book, 1870–73). Ontario, Dept. of Public Works, *Annual Reports*, 1874–79. *Burke's peerage* (1924), 1596–97. H. L. Esten, "Balfour Nepean Molesworth," Ont. Land Surveyors Assoc., *Annual Report*, no.47 (1932), 123–25. "Thomas Nepean Molesworth," Ont. Land Surveyors Assoc., *Annual Report*, no.35 (1920), 109–10.

MOLSON, WILLIAM, brewer and distiller, merchant, and banker; b. 5 Nov. 1793 at Montreal, L.C., third and last son of John Molson* Sr and Sarah Insley Vaughan; d. 18 Feb. 1875 at Montreal.

Little is known about William Molson's childhood, except that it was spent amid the influence of a family of entrepreneurs. His father, who had arrived at Montreal in 1782, an orphan of 18 years of age, had immediately ventured with his friend James Pell into the lucrative trade in foodstuffs, especially meat, that was a feature of the years of high inflation caused by the American Revolution. He had also gone into the production of beer with his friend Thomas Loid. In 1785 he became sole owner of the brewery. John Molson Sr refused, however, to take part in the active fur trade on which, during these years when the North West Company was being formed and the Beaver Club instituted, Montreal's commercial activity was based. All his life he opposed by his activities this structure of a staple economy. He was above all an industrial entrepreneur, if we can agree not to consider this term an anachronism given the slow progress of manufacturing at that period. His three sons were to be profoundly marked by this pattern, William like the others, but in his own way.

William was only 16 when his father, having bought the shares of his two partners John Bruce and John Jackson, to whom he had given financial assistance for the building of a steamboat, launched the *Accommodation* on 19 Aug. 1809, the first steam vessel to ply the St Lawrence between Montreal and Quebec. William went to school at that time, but his interest and activity were already centred on the family enterprises. On 19 Oct. 1810, on the eve of a departure for England, John Molson prepared a will before a notary, in which he mentioned the activity of his two youngest sons, Thomas* and William, as brewers, and committed them to the care of John*, his eldest son. The latter, in a letter to his father on 6 Jan. 1811, wrote: "William is still at school and I believe he can go the whole season as we will endeavour to do without him. He is growing fast and is nearly as tall as I am."

When war broke out between England and the United States in 1812, young William, aged 19, entered the militia as a volunteer. By October 1812 he had obtained an ensigncy. The Molsons' shipping company profited considerably from this war, taking soldiers who had arrived at Quebec to the Upper St Lawrence with their arms and baggage. The writer Bernard Keble Sandwell* states that William, despite his youth, commanded the *Swiftsure* during the war. At the end of the war, during at least two shipping seasons, John Sr and Jr corresponded, each from the ship he commanded, and their letters show that both were engaged in transactions involving bills of exchange from Montreal to Quebec and London, a prelude to their future activity as bankers. The youngest son also profited from these transactions. In a letter of 24 June 1815 to his father, John Jr wrote: "I have also purchased a bill for William of 110

Molson

Pounds." At this period the eldest son was established at Quebec to direct the wharf and warehousing operations, with the double responsibility of handling general merchandise for the shipping business and of taking delivery of and selling beer in the Quebec area for the Montreal brewery.

The first contract of partnership between the father and his three sons, under the name of John Molson and Sons, was signed before a notary on 1 Dec. 1816. Each remained the owner of the assets that he contributed to the company, and received on their value an annual interest of 6 per cent. The capital of the company came from John Sr, except for the ship *Swiftsure*, which he had given to the eldest brother. The latter was responsible for all the business at Quebec, where he resided; Thomas and William would live at Montreal, where they would work under their father's direction. It was mentioned that Thomas would be in charge of the brewery. The company's profits would be divided equally between the four partners. The uncollected profits, which were left in the enterprise, were capitalized. A reckoning of capital, dated 1 April 1819, shows that William had already accumulated £7,165 12s. 8d.

We do not know when William moved to Quebec to replace his elder brother and assume responsibility for the business in that town, but in 1819, at the time of his marriage, he moved to a house at 16 Rue Saint-Pierre and was to remain there until 1823. On 7 Sept. 1819, in the Anglican Christ Church, Montreal, William married Elizabeth Badgley (1799–1887), daughter of Francis Badgley* and sister of John Thompson Badgley (of whom William became a partner in 1830) and Judge William Badgley*. Their first two children were born at Quebec.

William probably developed his liking for politics at this period. In fact it is more than likely that his father entrusted him with the task of carrying on certain lobbying activities that were concomitant, on the one hand with John Sr's shipping business, and on the other with his status as member of the assembly since his election in the county of Montreal East on 25 April 1815. In the eyes of the entrepreneurs it was urgent that authorization be granted to build a wharf on the beach at Montreal, near the new market, an authorization which up to then the colonial authorities had persistently refused, out of respect for the crown monopoly on beach right of way. John Molson Sr remained a member for Montreal East until he lost his seat in the election of 1827, a few months after he had been made president of the Bank of Montreal.

When Thomas, in the spring of 1822, after his first experiments with making whisky, decided to try to sell it in England, he sought help from his brother William at Quebec with the necessary customs formalities. Meanwhile, William continued to capitalize part of the income paid by John Molson and Sons to the four partners; a reckoning dated 9 Feb. 1822 indicates that William's share amounted to £10,813 8d.

In the same year an important event, with repercussions on the assets of the family firm, took place in the shipping company. In April 1822 the Molsons succeeded in obtaining control of the shipping undertakings that since 1815 had been competing with them on the St Lawrence. Thus, in addition to the ships they already owned were added the *Car of Commerce*, property of a group of men that included Horatio Gates* and Jabez Dean De Witt; Thomas Torrance*'s and David Munn's *Caledonia*; the *Telegraph* from Montreal; the *Québec*, owned by a group that included Noah Freer; and a few other ships.

The competition had entailed over-capitalization and a considerable wastage of resources. With the arrival of a period of stagnation and of serious and numerous economic crises, consolidation became essential. In April 1822 the St Lawrence Steamboat Company was formed; it brought together the vast majority of the steam navigation interests on the St Lawrence. The company was made up of 44 shares of £1,000 each, the four Molsons holding collectively 26 and individually 6 1/2 each. Furthermore, the firm of John Molson and Sons was appointed to manage the company. This new responsibility resulted in the separation of the shipping enterprise from the activities of the Molson family. In book-keeping terms, it implied the withdrawal of the most important components (ships, wharves, and warehouses) of the assets of the family enterprise.

According to certain documents, John Jr seems to have returned to Quebec, and worked there in 1822 together with William, while Thomas stayed at Montreal, in sole charge of the brewery for several months. Thomas did not have a marriage contract, and the difficulties this entailed in a country whose law was that of France's *ancien régime*, persuaded him to leave Montreal in 1824 for Kingston, Upper Canada, where he became a brewer and distiller. In fact, for an entrepreneur joint estate was unthinkable. When it came time to negotiate a new partnership, with the expiry after seven years of the 1816 contract, John Jr maintained that he could leave Quebec for Montreal and take the direction of the brewery from Thomas. The father intervened, however, and insisted that William should leave Quebec, move to Montreal near him, and take charge of the brewery. "John fansied he could manage the

Brewhouse himself," John Molson Sr wrote to Thomas on 4 January. "I told him not, have had William near a fortnight."

The new contract was signed at the beginning of 1824 but applied retroactively to 1 Dec. 1823, the date on which the previous firm's accounts were closed. The partners were John Molson Sr, John Jr, and William. The assets consisted of the property of John Sr: the brewery and hostelry establishments at Montreal and the businesses at Quebec. The firm had the same name as the previous one: John Molson and Sons. It was also in 1824 that William's third and last child, Anne, was born.

In 1828 the Molsons decided that the companies in which they participated should be diversified according to the nature of their undertakings. Thus the firm of John Molson and Sons became exclusively responsible for steam navigation, as an agent of the St Lawrence Steamboat Company. Around 1830 the firm took over control of the Ottawa Steamboat Company, which held the monopoly for steam navigation on the Ottawa River. In 1834, with the opening of the Rideau Canal, this company became the Ottawa and Rideau Forwarding Company and was to dominate steam navigation from Montreal to Kingston.

The other undertakings of the family were from 1828 managed by a new company, founded that year, that of John and William Molson, which brought together the father and his two sons, John and William. For reasons which remain obscure, John Jr withdrew from this company in April 1829, and thus brought about its dissolution. But a new company, John and William Molson, was immediately formed on 30 June 1829, bringing together this time the father and William, his youngest son.

During the next five years William was in sole charge of the brewery. In addition, he undertook the management and administration of St Mary's Foundry, a small metallurgical enterprise, probably originally called the Bennett and Henderson Foundry. As well as selling implements for the building of the Rideau Canal, William closely followed the foundry's work in 1831 on the *Royal William*, the first ship entirely powered by steam to cross the Atlantic.

At this period William launched out into commerce. From 1 May 1830 to 14 Feb. 1834 he worked in partnership with his brother-in-law, John Thompson Badgley, to set up, with the help of funds advanced by his father, a business for the importing and retail sale of all kinds of goods from England. They operated under the name of Molson and Badgley. According to newspaper advertisements of the time, it appears that William

was competing with John Jr, who on 1 May 1829, with George and George Crew Davies, had established the firm of Molson, Davies and Company, in exactly the same business.

However, it does not seem that the competition between the two brothers had any deep significance. Thus, when the Champlain and St Lawrence Railroad Company was founded in 1831, both brothers sat on the board of directors, together with Peter McGill* and Jason C. Pierce; John Jr was president. This company built the first Canadian railway, the one that in 1836 linked Laprairie-de-la-Madeleine on the St Lawrence with Saint-Jean on the Richelieu, a distance of 20 miles.

Both William's activities as an industrialist and his wealth continued to expand. The will that he prepared on 3 Aug. 1832 before the notary Henry Griffin permits us to evaluate the approximate extent of his fortune. He left an annuity of £400 to his wife which, at the then usual rate of interest of 6 per cent, represents a principal of nearly £7,000, and £6,000 to each of his two daughters. The will also directed that his sons (he had only one) be residuary legatees.

In contrast to his son's expanding activities, those of the father continued to decline. However, the latter became more active in political and social life. He was appointed a legislative councillor in 1832, and was a member of the Constitutional Committee of Montreal (in 1835, the Constitutional Association of Montreal), a political movement formed to defend the interests of the English-speaking bourgeoisie of Montreal against the activities, which it considered menacing, of the *Patriotes*. William played an important role within this organization. A letter he wrote to his father on 16 Nov. 1834 gives evidence about the unrest which was already prevalent in Montreal in 1834. "The election in the western ward [Louis-Joseph PAPINEAU was a candidate] still remains unsettled, but am sorry to say that every night there are disturbanses in the streets, people beaten, and glass or windows of houses broken." In 1835 he was named commissioner to hear minor cases (litigation involving amounts of less than £6 5s.).

In 1833, William Molson, then in the full vigour of manhood, had begun a new operation destined to become much more lucrative than brewing: distilling. He obtained the necessary equipment in the spring and began to purchase raw materials after the autumn harvests. In December 1833 or January 1834 distillation actually began. In January 1834 William asked Robert Shaw* of Quebec to be his agent in that town for his product. His partnership with his brother-in-law, John Thompson Badgley, came to an end in this period. On 14 Feb. 1834 an act by the notary

Molson

Henry Griffin dissolved the firm of Molson and Badgley.

The same year Thomas Molson decided to leave Kingston and return to Montreal to go into partnership with his father and his brother William. A new company was then formed bringing together the father, William, and Thomas. The contract was signed on 21 Feb. 1835, and was retroactive to 30 June 1834. The share capital of the firm of John Molson and Company was divided into eight portions: two for John Sr, three for Thomas, and three for William. The father contributed the physical capital, namely all his establishments, for which he drew an annual rent of £1,100, representing a rate of 6 per cent of their value. Profits and losses were to be distributed in proportion to the number of shares held by each partner.

This partnership began a close collaboration, which was to last nearly 20 years, between the two brothers. In a commercial economy, at grips with the considerable difficulties that inevitably accompanied frequent and also profound crises, William and Thomas Molson, with surprising persistence, identified themselves as industrialists. True, the products of their establishments met demands that economists call inelastic, that is to say a rise in prices or a fall in income did not lead to a diminution in production. Perhaps even the demand for spirits was at that period "counter-cyclical," in the sense that an economic crisis might make it go up. And a fall in the price of the raw materials might well have been more important than a fall in the price of the finished product, since it would enable the entrepreneurs, when the demand varied little, to increase their profits at the height of an economic crisis.

But the Molson brothers were in opposition to their society, both from the economic and from the social and cultural point of view. In a mercantile economy, the whole structure is centred on export and import trade. The principal source of public revenue is customs, customs duties on exports and on imports. A tacit agreement is established between the state and the large merchants, encouraging foreign trade and discouraging national production. Such is the "staple trap," as critics of this famous theory of economic development have called it.

Customs duties on the importation of spirits were an important source of fiscal receipts, the more because this revenue fluctuated little throughout the trade cycle and did not fall in a time of crisis, when other sources of income run dry. With the increase in the production of spirits, in the early 1830s began "the battle of whisky against rum," which brought into conflict industrialists who produced spirits and a coalition of large merchants and the state. The Montreal Board of Trade made itself the eloquent spokesman of the large merchants when the governor of the colony consulted it in order to ascertain the cause of a fall in treasury receipts. But it was also the whole puritanical society of the time that the producers of spirits were up against, because to their activity was imputed responsibility for popular behaviour. Consequently, in a period of flourishing evangelical revival, they were the prey of preachers of all sects. The decision of William and Thomas during the 1840s to build the church of St Thomas' in the district where their factories stood, did not, apparently, allay this animosity.

The partnership of William and Thomas was furthermore directed against their eldest brother. John Molson Sr died on 11 Jan. 1836. William exclusively received all the properties situated at Près-de-Ville (Quebec): wharf, warehouses, houses, other buildings, and all the land. St Mary's Foundry reverted to John Jr. The brewery, whose buildings also housed the distilling equipment, became the property of John Henry Robinson Molson, Thomas's eldest son. This clause thus enabled John Henry Robinson to avoid the risks involved in the system of joint estate that governed the marriage of Thomas and Martha Molson. But the boy was only nine. The will stipulated that until he reached his majority the brewery should be directed by Thomas and William, according to the terms of the company established in 1835. The three sons were in addition named residuary legatees. John claimed that as residuary legatee he had the right to share in the profits of John Molson and Company, and that the credits remaining, in the form of invested income, on properties sold at Quebec before their father's death, did not form part of William's personal endowment, but of the residuary legacy. The Honourable Peter McGill and George Moffatt*, who had been nominated by John Sr to act, with his three sons, as executors, withdrew when they saw dissensions arise, but in 1842 they agreed to act as arbitrators. They declared John to be right in the matter of sharing in the profits of the company, and William to be right in respect of the Quebec credits. In addition to the shares he already owned and those he received as residuary legatee, William may have had a third of the controlling shares held by the Molsons in the St Lawrence Steamboat Company.

The firm of John Molson and Company came to its scheduled end on 30 June 1837. A new company was formed under the name of Thomas and William Molson. On 5 Jan. 1838 fire destroyed a large part of the Montreal factories, and the

Molson brothers obtained a sum of money as compensation from their insurance company. The arbitration board of 1842 decided that this sum was to be used to restore the buildings. Meanwhile the two partners had agreed to form a second company, unrestricted by the difficulties involved in carrying out their father's will. On 25 April 1838 they founded the firm of Thomas and William Molson and Company. It is clear, from the various account books, that the sole object of the partnership of 1837 was to administer the brewery on behalf of young John Henry Robinson, whereas that of 1838 managed the distillery and brewery establishments, built after the fire, for the exclusive advantage of William and Thomas.

The combativeness of the two brothers in partnership did not stop there. Indeed, they ventured to attack the Bank of Montreal, the most powerful banking institution in the colony, by taking advantage of special circumstances to issue currency. Following their father's death, John had been appointed to the board of directors of this bank to replace him. During the economic crisis of 1837 and the rebellions of 1837 and 1838, the government decided to suspend specie payments, from 16 May 1837 to 23 May 1838 and from 5 Nov. 1838 to 1 June 1839. In times of suspension several business houses took advantage of the situation to issue their own paper-money, which was convertible, not into coin, but into notes of the best known banks. Some did so in good faith, but others acted in a completely fraudulent manner; yet the practice was tolerated, for it was a way of avoiding the difficulties created by the scarcity of specie. The Thomas and William Molson Company, like many others, issued in 1837 notes bearing in this case the words "Molsons Bank." Once specie payments had resumed, these "bills on sufferance" were supposed to be bought back by those who had issued them. William and Thomas abstained from withdrawing their notes from circulation and continued to issue new ones.

At the beginning of 1839, the Bank of Montreal and the Board of Trade prepared for the Special Council (of which John Molson had been a member since 1837) the text of a decree forbidding the circulation of private currency. On 1 March, the Molsons protested against the draft decree to the governor, Sir John Colborne*, and on 10 March they forwarded proposed amendments. The decree was none the less promulgated on 11 April 1839 and was to be in force by 1 June 1839, the date of the second return to specie payments. It provided in general terms that certain private banks could issue notes. On 18 May William and Thomas Molson asked that their enterprise be recognized as a private bank. The Special Council's refusal

was announced on 22 July. During all this time the two brothers continued to issue their private money illegally. On 8 November, the board of directors of the Bank of Montreal approved the managing director's decision to refuse deposits made by the firm of Thomas and William Molson, and on 19 November instructed him to close the account of this firm by forwarding to it the £1,600 that remained in its balance. The Molson brothers' situation was becoming precarious; for several months, no longer having any bankers, they had to do cash transactions with their suppliers and customers. In order not to lose credit with the public, they soon agreed to buy back the notes they had issued. After they had acquired a substantial block of shares in the Banque du Peuple, the latter agreed to receive them as customers. This institution was their banker from 1840 to 1844. When the new governor general, Lord Sydenham [Thomson*], who was known for his plans for monetary and banking reform, arrived at the end of 1839, the two brothers again attempted to obtain a private bank licence. On 22 Dec. 1840 they presented their petition, which was refused in its turn on 31 December.

Such were the relatively troubled beginnings of this long association of William with his brother Thomas. The years of depression (1837–42), followed by a short expansion (1842–45) and the great commercial crisis of 1845–50, do not seem to have affected too grievously the common undertaking of the two brothers. On the contrary, they modernized their factories, and continued to add more important and more productive pieces of equipment. They got rid of some of their competitors by buying their businesses, such as the Handyside brothers' in 1844, and John Michael Tobin's small distillery on the Rivière Saint-Pierre in 1848.

The correspondence of the Molson enterprise shows that William, among other activities, had developed a certain specialization in relations with competitors and with the state. Thus it was he who negotiated cartel agreements with companies, and who saw that they were respected. No doubt because of his skill in this area, he was chosen by the brewing and distilling industry as a whole to defend their interests by lobbying parliament and certain ministries; it was indeed necessary to see that any increase of taxes on production and consumption was constantly discouraged, and that the laws restricting or forbidding the consumption of spirits were delayed and rendered less severe.

Was it to defend more effectively the collective interests of the brewers and distillers that William entered politics? When the municipal council for Montreal was re-established in 1840 (the city

Molson

charter was not renewed in 1837) he accepted a nomination by the governor as councillor until 1 Dec. 1842. He was elected in December 1842 in Sainte-Marie ward and again in 1843. In April 1844, when the political "Metcalfe crisis" was at its height, William decided to stand for "the party of the governor," Sir Charles Theophilus Metcalfe*, against the Irishman Lewis Thomas Drummond*, of the Reform party, in a by-election in the constituency of the town of Montreal. On 26 March, his friend John Young wrote to tell him that groups of Irish and French Canadian workers employed on the Lachine Canal were banding together to attack his supporters on election day. He urged William to ask for the protection of the police and the army. It was one of the most violent elections in Canadian history. It had been set for 11 April, but in view of the violence it was broken off and postponed until the 16th and 17th. On those days there were clashes, and soldiers intervened. But the returning officer, Alexandre-Maurice Delisle, declared that the electors had nevertheless had the opportunity to vote, and announced the election of Drummond. According to Jacques Monet, the powerful Temperance Society had displayed strong opposition to William Molson.

William's solidarity with the Tory party explains why five years later he was closely involved in the annexationist movement, of which he was secretary, and why he signed the famous manifesto of 1849. Like all the signatories, William was the victim of repressive action by the colonial administration: he lost his rank, which he had obtained in 1847, as major in the 2nd Battalion of the Montreal militia, and it appears that he also lost his post as judge.

William's wealth continued to increase. The will that he made on 24 April 1840 made his wife the beneficiary of an annuity of £500 – a principal of £8,000 when calculated at 6 per cent interest – and his daughters the beneficiaries, in equal parts, of the interest on a capital sum of $10,000 which would itself be given over to them on their coming of age; his son was made residuary legatee.

At this period William's career as an entrepreneur underwent a profound change. Perhaps his activity as a banker at the end of the 1830s had produced a vocation that would now find expression: that of banker and financier. In 1843 he joined his eldest brother on the board of directors of the Bank of Montreal, on which the latter had sat continuously since their father's death in 1836. It was also at the beginning of the 1840s that he was elected to the board of directors of the Mutual Insurance Company of Montreal.

The family also underwent profound changes in this period. His only son, William, died on 22 Jan. 1843 from smallpox. The funeral took place at the Episcopalian St Thomas' Church, which William and his brother Thomas had just constructed. The marriage of his eldest daughter, Elizabeth Sarah Badgley, to David Lewis Macpherson* was celebrated at the same church on 18 June 1844. In 1845 it was the turn of his daughter Anne to leave the family circle and she married John Molson III, son of John Molson Jr. The *rapprochement* between the two brothers thus took on a new, deeper significance.

Around 1845 vast plans for railroad construction, which had been retarded by the economic crisis, began to be brought into effect in Canada, although it was not until 1850 that the building of the Grand Trunk was undertaken. But before 1850, some small railroads were built, radiating from Montreal in several directions. William Molson appeared on the boards of directors of a large number of these small companies, sometimes even as president. With him on the boards were often the Honourable James Ferrier* or his son-in-law David Lewis Macpherson. William was a director of numerous companies between 1845 and 1850: the Champlain and St Lawrence Railroad Company, the Champlain and New York Railroad Company, the Montreal and New York Railroad Company, the Montreal and Champlain Railroad Company, the Lake St Louis and Province Line Railway Company, the St Lawrence and Ottawa Grand Junction Railroad Company, the St Lawrence and Atlantic Railroad Company, and the Grand Trunk Railway Company. This list clearly contains a certain amount of duplication and repetition. Indeed, the railroad companies changed their names when some of them grouped together, or when they obtained from the government a supplementary tract of land over which they could extend their lines. And there is no proof all these legal entities actually built railways.

The extent of the sums William invested in these undertakings is not known. The Molson Archives contain numerous statements for purchased shares, but it is impossible to ascertain whether they are a complete inventory of his operations. It is known that on 12 March 1855 the board of directors of the Bank of Montreal advanced £3,000 to the Champlain and New York Railroad Company and that William alone personally guaranteed repayment of £1,000; this guarantee, by its size, is indicative. The significant thing, however, is that he took a close interest in the new forms that industrial capitalism was taking as it developed in Canada. Technological progress, and the increasingly large place the capital factor was assuming in the production process, were bringing about important shifts in the role of the entrepreneur, and leading to the formation of a capital market in Canada. At the same time the financiers in the mother country, particularly those of Baring Brothers, were beginning to show an interest in financing private companies in the colonies that were investing in the economic infrastructure.

William Molson was willing to adjust himself to the new capitalist structures. In future, a leading entrepreneur would no longer be a technician, who personally owned the means of production and administered an undertaking. It would from then on be too vast for individual or family ownership. Its large number of employees, and the complexity of the problems involved in organizing the work of factory and office, would no longer permit an entrepreneur to see to all the details of its daily running. The law would then adapt itself to the new economic structures and the joint-stock, limited-liability company would appear. The new entrepreneur was therefore no longer the exclusive owner of the means of production. Thanks to the control that he could exercise over the other shareholders, he did not even need to own a majority of the shares. From then on the top-ranking entrepreneur would be above all a financier. William Molson, in the new directions he gave to his activities, recognized the developments the Canadian economy, even western capitalism, was undergoing.

In 1847 William's name appears along with that of his brother Thomas among the first group of shareholders of the New City Gas Company. This company, formed to provide the city of Montreal with a proposal for gas street lights, was in competition with an existing company but would soon bring about its disappearance.

The new structures of Canadian capitalism, which had developed during the late 1840s with the railroads, were to grow more firm in the mining industry at the beginning of the 1850s. William Molson showed a great interest in this field also. In different capacities, he was a member of various companies, in particular the Montreal Mining Company, the Upper Canada Mining Company, the British North American Mining Company, and the Quebec and Lake Superior Mining Association. Here again it would be hard to specify to what extent all these mining companies were developed and the importance of William's participation.

While William was thus asserting new characteristics of his personality as a financier-entrepreneur, he was also preparing to break the long, close association with his brother Thomas. On 30 June 1848 Thomas and William Molson and Company, formed in 1838, reached the end of its

contract, and a new agreement had to be signed. This was done on 12 July before the notary Isaac Jones Gibb, and was retroactive to 1 July. A new partner joined the undertaking, John Henry Robinson Molson, Thomas' eldest son, who had reached his majority the previous year; he brought to the common undertaking the brewery he now owned. Each partner, as in the previous companies, remained the owner of the physical capital that he brought in and for which he drew an annual rent. From the brewery the young partner would get £500, and from the distillery William and Thomas would get conjointly £1,800. The profits would be distributed in the ratio of 10/24 for each of the senior partners and 4/24 for the youngest.

On 5 June 1847 John Henry Robinson had become 21. Normally, on that day he should have received possession of the brewery inherited from his grandfather, and the sum of £3,872 2s. 6d. from the insurance company in compensation for the damage that the business had suffered in the 1838 fire. On that day also William and Thomas should have handed him his indentures and taken him in at least as a salaried employee, by virtue of the articles of apprenticeship concluded between the youth and his two employers on 15 Nov. 1844, but which were retroactive to 1 Nov. 1843. The latter waited a year before delivering him his indentures and giving him the sum of money and possession of the brewery. The young man received no compensation for the interest that had accumulated for ten years on the sum paid by the insurance company and for the remuneration that had not been paid since the end of his apprenticeship. These actions would influence John Henry Robinson's behaviour towards his father and his uncle William.

According to the contract, the new company would come to an end in ten years. But special provision was made whereby William could withdraw from it after five (on condition that advance notice of one year was given to his co-partners) without detriment to the structure of the undertaking. No doubt the early foundation of Molsons Bank was anticipated, as well as the broad outlines of the bill the Legislative Assembly was to pass in 1850, which would authorize the formation of private banks but forbid a banker to engage in any other business than that of the bank.

And in fact, on 24 June 1852, William did give his brother Thomas advance notice in writing. During the months that followed, the two brothers attempted to reach an understanding as to the value of William's equity, which Thomas wanted to purchase. The latter offered £7,000; William demanded £8,000, and even threatened to sell to a

Molson

third party if he did not get his price. The final agreement came on 11 Dec. 1852, and the sale took place on 18 December: William sold his share in the distillery (£8,000), two pieces of land (£122), five lots and a house (£738 10s.); the sum was payable three years after the date of William's withdrawal on 1 July 1853, with an annual interest of 6 per cent. Even if the negotiations had sometimes been difficult, one cannot accept the hypothesis, suggested by Merrill Denison, of a quarrel between the two brothers. On 7 Jan. 1853 Thomas decided to leave for England, and gave his brother a general power of attorney for the administration of all his affairs. A rupture between the two brothers would have prevented such confidence.

In 1850, the Legislative Assembly had passed the bill authorizing private banks. On 1 Oct. 1853 William Molson went into partnership with his brother, John Molson, to set up the firm of Molsons and Company. The name of Molsons Bank was registered on 3 December. The correspondence of Thomas Molson's enterprises shows that during its first two years the new bank encountered certain difficulties in issuing and circulating its notes. In this period, when notes were convertible, it was permissible for a bank to accumulate the notes of a rival bank for a certain time, and to demand suddenly from that bank the conversion of the accumulated notes into coin; as a considerable sum might be involved, the stability of the latter's cash balance might thereby be endangered. The Bank of Montreal, despite the wishes for success addressed by the members of its board of directors to William and John Molson at the time of their resignation, exerted this pressure on Molsons Bank, sometimes in collusion with the Bank of Upper Canada in Toronto.

Difficulties of this kind perhaps underlay the decision of the Molson brothers to withdraw from the regime set up by the private banks' act, and to ask that their bank be placed under the system of charter banks, in operation since 1817. On 19 May 1855 Molsons Bank was legally constituted. It was to be directed, not by a company of individuals, but by a joint-stock company or "corporation." The persons who had submitted this request were John, Thomas, and William Molson, George and John Ogilvy Moffatt, Samuel Gerrard*, James Ferrier, William Dow*, and Johnson Thomson. The new charter bank began operations on 1 Oct. 1855. On 22 October, the shareholders named their first board of directors: John, Thomas, William, and John Henry Robinson Molson, and Ephrem Hudon. The next day, at the first meeting of the board, William was elected president and John Jr vice-president.

Thereafter, William Molson's career was to be characterized by his new activity as banker. Until his death he was the president of the family bank. However he continued to interest himself in one way or another in the mining and railroad companies of which he was a director. In addition he continued to direct certain small undertakings such as the Otterdorf and Heilman's Soap Factory at Place Papineau, in which, according to certain documents dated 1855, he had a substantial interest. He also had real estate investments in certain areas of Montreal, particularly in the Sainte-Marie district, where the brewery and distillery establishments were, and where he lived himself on Rue Sainte-Marie (now Rue Notre-Dame) until shortly before his death. The great fire of Montreal, on 9 July 1852, had affected this district seriously and had destroyed three of William's houses, one in Rue Sainte-Marie, the two others at Place Papineau.

Apart from the appreciation in the value of the shares that he held in the bank, and of the dividends that he drew from them, William received each year the sum of $2,000, not as a contractual payment but as a bonus voted by the shareholders at their annual meeting in recognition of his work. A few months prior to his death, at the annual meeting of 12 Oct. 1874, he refused to accept the sum, stating that he had not been able to concern himself with bank business during the previous year.

During the late 1860s and early 1870s, Molsons Bank developed considerably, and extended its operations in Quebec and Ontario. In February 1875, however, at the time of William's death, the Canadian economy was experiencing the effects of the great world crisis of 1873 and of the long depression that was to last until 1879. It is this that explains the financial disaster which befell one of William's last undertakings: the production of iron by the treatment of the magnetic iron sands found at the mouth of the Rivière Moisie, in Baie des Sept-Îles on the north shore of the St Lawrence. In this venture William had been closely associated with his nephew William Markland, Thomas's son. The two Molsons had controlled the Moisie Iron Works Company since 1867; their manager from 1867 to 1869 was Louis LABRÈCHE-VIGER. The bulk of the production was exported to the United States. The crisis of 1873 brought about a sudden drop in demand, and a change in the American government's tariff policy and the tariff structure placed Moisie iron in such a heavily taxed category that its price in the United States became prohibitive, and the Molsons were never able to sell their iron there again. A few months after William's death the enterprise had to close its doors and the company had to declare itself bankrupt.

During a great part of his life William showed much interest in McGill University and the Montreal General Hospital. As in every industrial and financial community, in a young country, certain large educational and health institutions derive financial resources and administrative competence from the generosity and initiative of entrepreneurs; one can go so far as to say that in defining an entrepreneur's place in society one must include almost of necessity an active interest in such institutions. In 1856, when a fund-raising campaign was started on behalf of McGill University, 50 donors paid £15,000, the three Molson brothers alone giving £5,000, the income from which was earmarked for the endowment of a chair of English language and literature. In 1861 William gave a sum large enough to cover the cost of constructing William Molson Hall, a wing added to the west end of the arts building. The obituary notices published in the Montreal newspapers stressed that he had made a gift of $5,000 to the Montreal General Hospital, and a few months before his death a further gift of $2,000 for the endowment of the convalescent home of the hospital. During much of his life he was a member of the boards of governors of these two large institutions. In 1868 he succeeded John Redpath* as president of the Montreal General Hospital. The *Saturday Reader* of 8 Sept. 1866 stressed that William Molson was one of those who promoted the founding of the Hospice de Montréal. In the same way he supported places of worship. In 1866 Mrs William Molson, at the cost of £2,000, had built the two stories of the tower and the spire of Trinity Church, at the northwest corner of Place Viger.

William Molson had prepared his last will on 18 May 1865. He completed it with two codicils, one dated 22 Nov. 1869 and the other 31 Jan. 1870. He left all his possessions to his wife, his two daughters, and his 12 grandchildren. It is interesting to note that by the codicil of 1870 he expressly named his successor to the presidency of Molsons Bank: his son-in-law John Molson III, the son of his brother, John Molson Jr.

William Molson died on 18 Feb. 1875 and was buried in Mount Royal cemetery where, after the death of John Jr in 1860, was erected a huge monument, topped by an obelisk. William's death was announced in all the newspapers of the time and in resolutions adopted by the shareholders' meetings and the boards of directors of the companies and institutions with which he had been the most closely connected. Each vied with the other in praising the dynamic nature of the entre-preneur and the humane qualities displayed throughout his life by the man William Molson.

Thanks to the perspective afforded by time, it is possible to look at William Molson within the society in which he lived and to compare him with other entrepreneurs, first with those who were closest to him: his father, his brothers, and his nephews. More than others, he had the flexibility required to adapt himself to the transformations that the Canadian economy and western capitalism were undergoing. The evolution of industrial technology, the rise in incomes, and the increase in savings encouraged entrepreneurs to look more and more towards financial operations, in order that the savings of individuals could be built up to proportions appropriate to the growth in the capital equipment of business enterprises. William Molson's career illustrates clearly that the first and indispensable condition for being an entrepreneur is to know how to take part in building up investment capital, either by acting on one's own, or through one's family, or – still better and more effectively – through the large financial institutions.

ALFRED DUBUC

Materials on William Molson are distributed in several archives. Among the most important sources are: the minutes of the board of directors' meetings and of the shareholders' meetings in the Archives of Molsons Bank (kept at the head office of the Bank of Montreal, Montreal) and in the Archives of the Bank of Montreal; the minutes of the board of directors' meetings in the Montreal Board of Trade Archives; the minutes of the municipal council at AVM; the registers of notaries Thomas Barron, Isaac Jones Gibb, Henry Griffin, John Carr Griffin, James Stewart Hunter, William Ross, and James Smith at AJM; the Molson documents at Château de Ramezay (Montreal) and at the McCord Museum (McGill University, Montreal); and the William Molson collection at the Redpath Library (McGill University).

Without doubt the most important repository is the Molson Archives at the Molson's Brewery, Montreal. This archives is described in an inventory prepared in 1955 for the Molson's Brewery (copy in PAC, MG 24, D1). The following volumes were consulted: 321–24, 327–29, 349–52, 356, 360–67, 370–74, 383–85, 388, 390–91. The Shortt papers at the PAC (MG 30, D45) also contain interesting information on Molson. See also: *Report of progress from 1866 to 1869* (Geological Survey of Canada, Montreal, New York, London, Leipzig, and Paris, 1870), 211–304. Merrill Denison, *The barley and the stream; the Molson story* . . . (Toronto, 1955); *Canada's first bank*. Alfred Dubuc, "Thomas Molson, entrepreneur canadien: 1791–1863," thèse de doctorat, Université de Paris, 1969 (in process of publication). *Father's Rest* (Montreal, n.d.). G. C. Mackenzie, *The magnetic iron sands of Natashkwan, county of Saguenay, Province of Quebec* (Ottawa, 1912). Georges Ripert, *Aspects juridiques du*

Mondelet

capitalisme moderne (Paris, 1946). B. K. Sandwell, *The Molson family, etc.* (Montreal, 1933). B. E. Walker, *A history of banking in Canada; reprinted from "A history of banking in all nations,"* ... (Toronto, 1909). F. W. Wegenast, *The law of Canadian companies* (Toronto, 1931). G. H. Wilson, "The application of steam to St. Lawrence valley navigation, 1809–1840," unpublished MA thesis, McGill University, 1961. René Bélanger, "Les forges de Moisie," *Saguenayensia* (Chicoutimi, Qué.), VI (1964), 76–79; "Moisie; peuplement – mouvement de la population de 1860 à 1895," *Saguenayensia*, VI (1964), 103–5. Alfred Dubuc, "Montréal et les débuts de la navigation à vapeur sur le Saint-Laurent," *Revue d'histoire économique et sociale* (Paris), XLV (1967), 105–18. Jacques Monet, "*La crise Metcalfe* and the Montreal election, 1843–1844," *CHR*, XLIV (1963), 1–19.

MONDELET, CHARLES-ELZÉAR, lawyer and judge; b. 28 Dec. 1801 in the parish of Saint-Marc, county of Verchères, L.C., son of Charlotte Boucher de Grosbois and Jean-Marie Mondelet*, notary, member of the Legislative Assembly from 1804 to 1809, and coroner of Montreal; d. 31 Dec. 1876 at Montreal, Que.

Charles-Elzéar Mondelet attended the college of Nicolet and the college of Montreal, and then studied law under the distinguished Michael O'Sullivan* and under Lower Canada's attorney general, Charles Marshall. He was admitted to the bar of Lower Canada on 30 Dec. 1822 and practised first in Trois-Rivières. On 21 June 1824, in Montreal's Christ Church Cathedral (Church of England), Charles married Mary Elizabeth Henrietta Carter. The Mondelets had 15 children; six reached adulthood.

In Trois-Rivières Mondelet immediately flung himself into the pro-assembly anti-administration politics of the period of Governor General Dalhousie [Ramsay*], which were at their most passionate in the years immediately after the 1822 union bill scare. Mondelet began with journalism, editing Ludger Duvernay*'s political and literary newspaper *Le Constitutionnel*, "the French gazette of Trois-Rivières," from its foundation in 1823 until 1825 when it was discontinued. In 1826 Mondelet founded the lively and more incisive *L'Argus*, "journal électorique," which was designed primarily to influence the electorate to choose radical members of parliament. Specifically, *L'Argus* supported the unsuccessful candidature of Pierre-Benjamin Dumoulin* against Solicitor General Charles Richard Ogden*, and then ceased to appear until it was revived a year later in Montreal by Augustin-Norbert Morin*. Mondelet was also active in a local constitutional committee which in association with committees in other districts had been formed to oppose union

with Upper Canada and which also protested against the policies of the governor and his legislative councillors generally. These activities cost Mondelet his militia commission in November 1827. His subsequent condemnation of Governor Dalhousie's militia policies in the *Quebec Gazette* earned him an indictment for libel in March 1828. After Dalhousie left Canada, these charges were dropped.

In 1829 or 1830 Mondelet moved to Montreal. There he practised law with his brother Dominique*, and worked for the latter's election to the assembly in April 1831. Under the signature "Pensez-Y-Bien" he also wrote letters to the editor of *La Minerve* demanding that the Legislative Council be abolished or made elective. The council declared this statement libellous and imprisoned the publisher, Ludger Duvernay, for about a month. Soon after Duvernay's release, Charles' close association with the *Patriote* party ended temporarily when personal loyalties and other circumstances persuaded him tacitly to renounce his political radicalism and to defend his brother's different politics.

In an 1832 by-election the Mondelets favoured the moderate candidate Stanley Bagg* over his radical opponent Daniel Tracey*. The *Patriote* party condemned the brothers for their support, and even more for avoiding the inquest after troops transformed the polling into the notorious "Massacre of Montreal" by killing three of Tracey's supporters. The Mondelets did wear mourning arm bands but their father, Jean-Marie, was after all the coroner and therefore deeply involved in the proceedings as a non-partisan official. Then on 27 Nov. 1832 the Reform-dominated assembly censured Dominique for becoming an honorary executive councillor, and the censure extended to the brother who supported him. Finally, in April 1834, when Charles publicly opposed the 92 Resolutions, Louis-Joseph PAPINEAU's young lieutenant Louis-Hippolyte La Fontaine* viciously attacked both brothers in *Les deux girouettes, ou l'hypocrisie démasquée*. He accused Charles of slavishly following Dominique in betraying his ideals and his party and added charges of personal hypocrisy and meanness.

Charles Mondelet nevertheless continued in close association with both moderate and radical politicians through the Comité Sanitaire de Montréal in which he was active during the cholera years. He also joined the politico-literary Aide-toi, le Ciel t'aidera club, whose radical members later transformed it into the militant Fils de la Liberté, which in its turn gave rise to the nationalistic Société Saint-Jean-Baptiste. On 2 Nov. 1837 he was unanimously accepted into the revolutionary Comité Central et Permanent du district de Montréal.

At the Montreal assizes in September 1838 Mondelet and two colleagues defended four *Patriotes*, François Nicolas, Amable Daunais, Joseph Pinsonnault, and Gédéon Pinsonnault, for executing loyalist Joseph Armand, *dit* Chartrand; the trial was noted for Charles' impassioned speech on behalf of Nicolas. In 1839 Charles defended François Jalbert* for killing Lieutenant George Weir while he was a prisoner in *Patriote* custody. In both cases Mondelet argued that his clients had committed political not criminal acts, and should therefore be treated as political prisoners: he even tried to have Jalbert freed under the amnesty granted by Lord Durham [Lambton*] on 28 June 1838. Mondelet also argued that an oppressed people should not suffer for acts committed during justifiable rebellions. In both cases the jury acquitted the prisoners. Ironically, Nicolas and the 20-year-old Daunais were later retried for their activities during the 1838 uprisings, with Dominique Mondelet one of the crown prosecutors, and they were sentenced to hang.

Between assizes, on 4 Nov. 1838, Charles Mondelet was arbitrarily arrested and thrown into the prison of Montreal where he renewed his friendship with La Fontaine. When they were finally released without trial, Mondelet returned to his law practice until his partner and brother Dominique was appointed to the Trois-Rivières Court of Queen's Bench on 1 June 1842. Then Charles practised briefly with his frequent legal associate Côme-Séraphin Cherrier*, Louis-Joseph Papineau's cousin.

After the rebellions Charles, who supported Union, had mingled with politicians but not politics, devoting himself to law and to education. His farsighted *Letters on elementary and practical education* greatly influenced the education act of 18 Sept. 1841 introduced by Sydenham [Thomson*]. Mondelet proposed English and French public schools for the united province, financed by direct taxes and legislative grants. The system would be headed by a powerful superintendent, officials appointed by the governor but responsible to the legislature, several elected officials, and all resident clergymen as *ex officio* school wardens. Thus in the control of public education there would be a nice balance between the people, the government, and the religious establishments. Mondelet's description of the almost autocratic powers of the proposed superintendent of education is interesting because Sydenham promised him the post. The latter died without a commission

having been issued; it may be that either the governor or Mondelet changed his mind.

Sydenham's successor, Sir Charles Bagot*, appointed Jean-Baptiste MEILLEUR deputy superintendent for education in Lower Canada and named Mondelet to the district bench instead, with a jurisdiction including the counties of Terrebonne, L'Assomption, and Berthier. In 1844 he became circuit judge at Montreal. On 24 Dec. 1849 he was appointed judge of the Superior Court and served until 1859 and from 1869 until his death. From 30 May 1859 to 31 Dec. 1869 he was judge *pro tem.* of the Court of Queen's Bench. It was as superior court judge that Mondelet became involved in the famous Guibord affair.

The battle raging between Quebec's clerical hierarchy and the politically radical Institut Canadien, whose 1868 and 1869 annuals were on the Papal index, culminated in a local parish's refusal to bury Institut member Joseph Guibord*, *dit* Archambault [*see* TRUTEAU]. In November 1869 in his decision on the suit brought against the parish of Notre-Dame by Guibord's widow, Henriette Brown, and later by her heir, the Institut, Judge Charles Mondelet instructed the parish to bury Guibord and to pay all court costs. This decision, reversed on 12 Sept. 1870 by the Court of Revision, was sustained on 28 April 1874 by the paramount judicial authority, the Privy Council. Mondelet's judgement was of great moment because of the issues involved: his selection of the custom of Paris as the relevant body of law and his interpretation of essentially ecclesiastical questions in defiance of contemporary ecclesiastical opinion. On 16 Nov. 1874 Guibord was buried but Bishop Ignace Bourget* declared his plot morally separate from the Catholic cemetery, and so it has remained. Thus the spirit of Mondelet's judgement was defied by the ecclesiastical authorities he had challenged.

Mondelet's *Essai analytique sur Le Paradis perdu de Milton* (1848), co-authored with William Vondenvelden*, and his *Address before the American Association for the Advancement of Science* (1857), indicate his diversified interests. He even translated Peter Parley's *Geography* and adapted it for use in Canadian schools, adding a supplement for small children explaining the operation of natural phenomena.

Mondelet, very much a free thinker, married an English Canadian in an Anglican church, despite his French-Canadian Catholic background, and defied not only his bishop but public opinion in the Guibord affair. A witty man, he was learned in the law and also in various aspects of education, its practical operation in many countries and its philosophy. In politics he was a radical, except for

Monro

one brief period, and it was these sympathies which dominated when he became a member of Aide-toi, le Ciel t'aidera, when he joined the revolutionary Comité Central et Permanent du district de Montréal, and when he defended *Patriote* prisoners. Immediately after 1834 Charles continued his close association with many of the radical politicians, and his youthful radicalism remained intact, for in the Guibord affair he sided with the most radical members of French Canadian society when he himself was an old man.

ELIZABETH NISH

[Mondelet's *Letters on elementary and practical education* (Montreal, 1841) gives his ideas on how a school system should be set up. *Documents relating to constitutional history, 1819–1828* (Doughty and Story) contains many extracts from the official correspondence relating to the decommissioning of the militia under Dalhousie and to the libel suits of that period. L.-H. La Fontaine, *Les deux girouettes; ou l'hypocrisie démasquée* (Montréal, 1834) is of great importance for anyone interested in the Mondelet brothers since the entire book is devoted to attacking them. Much of the available information about Charles' early political life in Montreal comes from this book. Christie, *History of Lower Canada*, III–V, and H. T. Manning, *The revolt of French Canada, 1800–1835: a chapter in the history of the British commonwealth* (Toronto, 1962), provide excellent surveys of the early period of Mondelet's life. Théophile Hudon's study of *L'Institut canadien de Montréal et l'affaire Guibord; une page d'histoire* (Montréal, 1938) is essential for an understanding of the intricacies of the situation, religious as well as legal. Hudon is prejudiced against Mondelet because of the latter's anti-clericalism; still the book is an excellent account of the Guibord case. P.-G. Roy, *Les juges de la province de Québec*, 379; F.-J. Audet, "Les Mondelet," *Cahiers des Dix*, III (1938), 191–216; L.-P. Audet, "Charles Mondelet et l'éducation," *RSCT*, 3rd ser., LI (1957) sect.I, 1–27; Gérard Malchelosse, "Généalogie de la famille Mondelet," *BRH*, LI (1945), 51–60, are factual notices of Charles Mondelet and his family and provide the bulk of the secondary material on Charles. E.N.]

Archives paroissiales de Saint-Marc (comté de Verchères, Québec), Registres des baptêmes, mariages et sépultures, 1801. BNQ, Société historique de Montréal, Collection La Fontaine, Lettres, 18, 215, 405, 554. Christ Church Cathedral (Montreal), Register of baptisms, marriages, and burials, 21 June 1824. P.-J.-O. Chauveau, *L'instruction publique au Canada, précis historique et statistique* (Québec, 1876). *Report of the state trials before a general court martial held at Montreal in 1838–9, exhibiting a complete history of the late rebellion in Lower Canada* (2v., Montreal, 1839). Beaulieu et Hamelin, *Journaux du Québec*. Chapais, *Histoire du Canada*. David, *Patriotes*. L.-P. Audet, "Jean-Baptiste Meilleur était-il un candidat valable au poste de surintendant de l'Éducation pour le Bas-Canada en 1842?" *Cahiers des Dix*, XXXI (1966), 163–201. Bernard Dufebvre, "Ludger Duvernay et

« La Minerve », 1827–1837," *RUL*, VII (1952–53), 220–29. Victor Morin, "Clubs et sociétés notoires d'autrefois," *Cahiers des Dix*, XV (1950), 185–218.

MONRO (Munro, Munroe), GEORGE, merchant and politician; b. in Scotland in 1801; m. about 1822 Christine Fisher of Montreal, and was survived by two sons and four daughters; d. 5 Jan. 1878 in Toronto, Ont.

George Monro came to Niagara, Upper Canada, as a child with his parents. He left for York (Toronto) in 1814 with his elder brother John and together they entered the retail grocery business. They separated in 1824, and George continued on his own to develop a successful wholesale enterprise, advertising himself as "Importer of British and India Goods." He also began to take part in the political life of the town.

Throughout his public career Monro was a weak pillar of the Toronto establishment. He attended the Church of England cathedral, St James', was a member of the Church Society and the Bible Society, was a director of the Home District Savings Bank and the British America Assurance Company, and in 1833 was appointed a magistrate. From 1834 to 1845 (except for 1836) he was elected to the city council from the St Lawrence ward. In 1841 he was chosen mayor, after the nomination of George Gurnett* had been successfully challenged on the grounds that he sublet a house for use as a brothel.

During his mayoralty Monro was the "Conservative and Constitutional Candidate" for Toronto's two-seat riding in the Legislative Assembly. He repudiated responsible government as "anti-British and unreasonable," and thought Toronto should have the "carrying trade of the St. Lawrence." When the poll closed after six days, Monro was last, and the other Conservative, Henry Sherwood*, second last; the two Reformers, John Henry Dunn* and Isaac Buchanan*, had to their surprise won.

Among those disappointed by this result was a man named Allen, who recruited some fellow-Orangemen to demonstrate against the Reformers' triumphal parade on Monday, 21 March 1841. The Orangemen gathered at the North of Ireland Coleraine Tavern; about noon they sallied forth to beat up a kilted piper on his way to join the parade and dismembered his instrument. On being told of the assault and asked to provide protection for the parade, Monro replied "You may go to the Devil." The mayor and magistrates had not been unaware that trouble was brewing: at a meeting earlier that morning Monro had suggested calling out the military, but the magistrates preferred to swear in special constables – mostly the same men

528

who had been notoriously partisan during the election of the week before. These constables do not appear to have gone far from the city hall, for it was realized that they were more likely to provoke trouble than to reduce it.

The parade started, but when it reached St James' Cathedral it was pelted with muck and stones and horses were clubbed. The attackers were beaten off and the parade continued. When the carriages bearing the successful candidates passed in front of the Coleraine inn, shots were fired from within and one bystander was killed and others wounded. Alderman John Powell arrived on the scene and read the riot act and Dunn sent two men to the Osgoode Hall barracks for military help. A request from the mayor was needed, so the men had to find Monro (who had mounted a feckless horse in order, he said, to get military help himself) and pressure him into going with them to the barracks and admitting that he was indeed the mayor. The troops then restored order. The provincial government ordered a commission of inquiry headed by William Foster COFFIN, which concluded that the "indecision and remissness evinced by the magistrates . . . amounts . . . to little less than connivance, if not to an actual collusion with the rioters. . . . [The Mayor] is amenable to a charge of dereliction of duty."

Monro petitioned for a committee to investigate the truth of the commission's report, but failed to get a hearing. He completed his year in office and, so little was his reputation apparently sullied by the events of the riot, was sent to England as the bearer of an address to Queen Victoria on the birth of the Prince of Wales. In 1844 Monro stood again as a Conservative candidate, this time in the east riding of York, where he was defeated by James Small*. Monro's supporters then claimed that Small's qualifications were defective, and the assembly found that Monro "was duly elected and ought to have been returned." He ran again in the general election of January 1848 in the same riding, but fell an easy victim to the Reformer, William Hume Blake*, who was in Europe at the time.

This defeat ended Monro's peppery political career, and he lived quietly thereafter. He gave up his business around 1856 and moved to the fashionable new district around the foot of Spadina, where he practised his life-long hobby of gardening. He sat amid his flowers listening to his gardener play the pipes and slowly passing, as the *Mail* said on his death, "beyond the recollection of the present generation."

R. I. K. DAVIDSON

Canada, Province of, Legislative Assembly, *Journals*, 1841, app.S, "Report of the commissioners appointed to investigate certain proceedings at Toronto connected with the election in that city. . . ." *Examiner* (Toronto), 1841. *Toronto Patriot*, 1841. *City of Toronto poll book: exhibiting a classified list of voters, at the late great contest for responsible government . . .* (Toronto, 1841). *Landmarks of Toronto* (Robertson), I. *Town of York, 1815–34* (Firth). *York commercial directory, street guide, and register, 1833–4 . . .*, comp. George Walter (York, [1833]). *Toronto city directory for 1872–73 . . .*, ed. and comp. W. H. Irwin (Toronto, 1872).

MONTGOMERY, JOHN, tavern-keeper; b. probably 29 Feb. 1788, at Gagetown, N.B., son of Alexander Montgomery; d. at Barrie, Ont., 31 Oct. 1879.

John Montgomery's parents left Stamford, Connecticut, for New Brunswick after the American Revolutionary War, and in about 1798 settled at York (Toronto), Upper Canada. John served in the War of 1812 as a York volunteer on the Niagara frontier, and was present at the battle at Queenston.

Alexander Montgomery had established a tavern at York soon after his arrival, and in 1828 John was keeping the Bird in Hand Tavern, also at York. In the same period he operated a tavern on Yonge Street near Newton Brook (now in the borough of North York). About 1830 he erected Montgomery's Tavern on Yonge Street, a few miles north of York.

Montgomery had sympathized with the Reformers in Upper Canada, perhaps as early as 1824. In 1832 he helped send William Lyon Mackenzie* to England to present petitions to the Colonial Office, and he was later among the Reformers who founded the Bank of the People. He was also a commissioner for the roads of York County and a director of the Mutual Insurance Company. In July 1837, on the eve of the rebellion in Upper Canada, he signed at John DOEL's brewery a declaration of Toronto Reformers and was a member of a vigilance committee named to carry out its resolutions aimed at creating "the effectual organization of the Reformers of Upper Canada." He appears, however, to have quarrelled with Mackenzie, disapproving of the latter's plans for open rebellion.

On 3 December he was informed that his tavern would be the headquarters for the rebels, and was asked to act as commissary. But Montgomery had leased his tavern to John Linfoot by this time. Linfoot was to take possession of the tavern on 1 Feb. 1838, but had moved in on 1 December. While the rebel forces were assembling, Montgomery continued living in one of the rooms of the tavern and was said to have been occupied mainly with moving furniture to his new home. Although

Moody

he apparently took no active part in the activities of the rebels and is said to have quarrelled at the tavern on one occasion with Mackenzie, his conduct was found at his trial to have been ambivalent.

On 7 December government forces reached the tavern and burned it on the orders of Francis Bond HEAD. Montgomery was arrested, and charged with high treason. Tried before John Beverley Robinson*, he was found guilty and sentenced to be executed, but this sentence was commuted to transportation for life. Montgomery was sent to Fort Henry; he escaped and made his way to Rochester, New York, where he kept a boarding-house, which became a rendezvous of Canadian Patriots, and a grocery store. He was again closely associated with Mackenzie at Rochester and was president of an association for Canadian refugees.

Montgomery was pardoned and returned to Toronto in 1843. He built a large new tavern on the site of the old on Yonge Street, and later operated taverns in Toronto itself; in 1858 he was proprietor of the Robinson House, a "temperance hotel" where liquor was not sold. In 1871 he moved to Headford, in Markham Township, where he was postmaster. Soon after his return to Canada he had submitted the first of a long series of petitions requesting compensation for the loss of his tavern in 1837. He enlisted Mackenzie's help, but only in 1873 was action taken; in that year, Oliver Mowat*'s government established a select committee of the Legislative Assembly which decided that Montgomery's losses had exceeded $15,000; it awarded him $3,000.

Montgomery was married three times, but only the name of Mary Wilmot, whom he married in 1835, is known. When he died in 1879 he was survived by his third wife and six children. He claimed that at his trial, when asked by Robinson if he had anything to say, he replied that he had been convicted by perjured evidence and that "These perjurers will never die a natural death; and when you, sir, and the jury shall have died and perished in hell's flames, John Montgomery will yet be living on Yonge Street." If the prophecy was made, parts of it did come true: two men killed themselves, and Montgomery outlived judge, jurors, witnesses, and prosecutors.

EDWIN C. GUILLET

PAO, Mackenzie-Lindsey collection, clippings, no. 305; Misc. 1959, E. A. Lacey, "John Montgomery, a miscarriage of justice." *Globe* (Toronto), 15 Jan. 1876. *Picton Times*, 29 Jan. 1880. Dent, *Upper Canadian rebellion*. E. C. Guillet, *The lives and times of the Patriots; an account of the rebellion in Upper Canada, 1837–1838, and the Patriot agitation in the United States, 1837–1842* (Toronto, 1938); *Pioneer inns and taverns* (5 v., Toronto, 1954–62), I. E. A. Lacey, "The trials of John Montgomery," *Ont. Hist.*, LII (1960), 141–58. Mrs O. B. Sheppard, "Incidents in the life of John Montgomery during the rebellion of 1837–38," York Pioneer and Hist. Soc., *Annual Report, 1926* (Toronto), 11–15.

MOODY, SEWELL PRESCOTT, lumberman; b. probably between 1835 and 1840, perhaps in Hartland, Maine, son of Joshua Moody; m. in 1869 Janet McAuslyn Watson by whom he had two children; drowned in the sinking of the steamer *Pacific* near Cape Flattery, 4 Nov. 1875, while bound for California on a business trip.

Sewell Prescott Moody is said to have crossed the American continent to San Francisco in the traditional covered wagon with his family when he was 14. He came to New Westminster, B.C., about 1861 and in 1862 formed a partnership with Moses Ireland, who had made a small stake in the Cariboo mines. Ireland later stated that his investment was $2,000 and Moody's, $600. They imported cattle and other supplies and prospered in a modest way. The Moody family had had a long association with the lumber trade in Maine, and in 1862 Moody formed a syndicate that included Ireland, Joshua Attwood Reynolds Homer*, and Captain James Van Bramer to build a steam sawmill at New Westminster. This was the first mill of any size on the mainland of British Columbia. Unfortunately the first vessel to load an export shipment stranded on a sandbar in the Fraser River and remained aground for six weeks. As a result other ships refused to load. Members of this syndicate later became interested in coal seams that had been discovered on Coal Harbour and English Bay, in Burrard Inlet. They incorporated the British Columbia Coal Mining Company in 1865, but nothing came of this venture.

Meanwhile Moody had decided to move his lumbering activities to Burrard Inlet. Late in 1863 he tried to purchase the Pioneer Mills, the first industrial plant on the inlet, but was outbid at the auction. A year later he succeeded in buying the mill, which was cutting lumber under his ownership by February 1865. Though greatly handicapped by the lack of marketing information and exchange facilities, Moody slowly built up the first substantial lumber export business from the British Columbia mainland, and sent shipments to California, Hawaii, Peru, China, Australia, New Zealand, and Great Britain.

In 1866 Moody entered into partnership with George Dietz and Hugh Nelson*, who had operated an express business serving the Fraser River mines. For a time the firm continued to be known as S. P. Moody and Company, but in 1870 the name was changed to Moody, Dietz and Nelson. The additional capital had made it possible to expand the mills. The original plant was driven by water-power, and in 1868 a larger steam mill was added. This was burned in December 1873 but was replaced at once by a new mill powered with the engines of HMS *Sparrowhawk*, a gunboat recently retired by the Royal Navy. Moody's mills then had a cutting capacity of 112,000 feet in 24 hours.

These mills were on the north shore of Burrard Inlet, within the limits of the present city of North Vancouver. First known locally as "Moody's Mills," the surrounding settlement was officially named Moodyville in 1872. Moody was an enterprising, astute, and perhaps occasionally sharp trader; but he had a puritanical streak and a liking for law and order. Moodyville was a company town, and he ruled it and his men with a firm hand. The sale of liquor was forbidden, and in large part owing to Moody himself Moodyville had the first school, the first religious service, the first library and reading room, and the first Masonic lodge on Burrard Inlet. He also extended the telegraph line from New Westminster at his own expense. Sewell P. Moody thus built a community as well as an important pioneer industrial enterprise.

W. KAYE LAMB

Daily Colonist (Victoria), 12, 13 Sept. 1901. W. A. Carrothers, "Forest industries of British Columbia," in A. R. M. Lower, *The North American assault on the Canadian forest: a history of the lumber trade between Canada and the United States* (The Carnegie Endowment for International Peace, Division of economics and history, Toronto, New Haven, Conn., London, 1938). J. S. Matthews, "Early Vancouver: narrative of pioneers" (unpublished typescript, 7v., 1932–56, IV, VI, copies in City Archives, Vancouver, and Library of Parliament, Ottawa). R. L. Reid, *Grand Lodge of British Columbia A.F. & A.M.: historical notes and biographical sketches, 1848–1935* (Vancouver, n.d.). F. W. Howay, "Early shipping in Burrard Inlet, 1863–1870," *BCHQ*, I (1937), 1–20.

MOORE, PHILIP HENRY, farmer, soldier, legislative councillor, and railroad president; b. at Rhinebeck, Dutchess County, New York, 22 Feb. 1799, the third son of Nicholas and Catherine Streit; m. Harriet A. Stone (b. at Fairfax, Vermont, in 1802), and they had six sons and two daughters; d. 21 Nov. 1880 at Saint-Armand-Station, Missisquoi County, Que.

Philip Henry Moore moved with his parents in 1802 to Moore's Corner (later known as Saint-Armand-Station). After attending the district school, he studied at an academy in St Albans, Vermont. As a young man he farmed for a short time and for some years was a merchant in Bedford, Missisquoi County. On 25 July 1829 he was appointed commissioner for the trial of small causes in the seigneury of Saint-Armand, along with Jonas Abbott; he was commissioned the first registrar of Missisquoi County at Frelighsburg on 19 June 1830. He retired from business in 1833 to the ancestral farm two and a half miles north of Moore's Corner and proved to be "a good intelligent farmer": his name appeared for many years on the annual prize list of the county. He served in the local militia, which formed a company of the 4th Bedford battalion, and he took a prominent part in the battle at Moore's Corner in the rebellion of 1837 for which he was officially thanked by Sir John Colborne*, commander in chief. Charged by some with taking too much credit for the success of the battle, he produced documents, printed in the *Montreal Herald* in March 1838, which confirmed that he had indeed directed his party to the extent he had claimed.

On the union of the provinces in 1841, Philip Henry Moore was called to the Legislative Council, a position he held until confederation. He was active in the council's debates and, with his colleague for Missisquoi, Paul Holland Knowlton*, laboured ardently for decentralization on behalf of their area. Before union the courts, both civil and criminal, had been in Montreal. That city was also the market for the products of Missisquoi County and it was hard to reach, except in winter; yet farmers of the area were unable to sell in the American market because of U.S. tariffs. By 1859 Moore could state that this situation had completely changed: new judicial districts, "municipal, county, township and parish councils," and "a corporate local Legislature" had been established, and by the reciprocity treaty of 1854 agricultural products were admitted into the American market free of duty. Moore insisted also that the Eastern Townships should send their own residents to parliament and "no longer submit to be used as trading capital by political demagogues."

In 1846 Moore had been chairman of the committee instructed to investigate losses of inhabitants of Lower Canada in the 1837–38 uprising. The commissioners' task was not easy. The claimants themselves chose the witnesses, who were often their wives, brothers, or sisters, to testify about the nature of their losses, their conduct during the rebellion, and the accuracy of the amount of reparation being applied for. However questionable this sort of testimony, it was the only evidence available. The investigations lasted until 1851, and Moore worked diligently, as he was in favour of compensation for all those who had suffered losses. In 1849 the parliamentary library had burned and he was deputed in 1857 to visit the United States to procure public documents to replace those lost. His efforts were highly successful.

At confederation he was offered membership in the Legislative Council of Quebec but declined in order to become a candidate for the federal House of Commons. Moore ran as an independent Conservative and was defeated by the Conservative candidate, Brown Chamberlin* of Frelighsburg.

Moore was instrumental in securing the charter for the Montreal and Vermont Junction Railway and gave the railroad the right of way to build across his property. He was president of this railroad until his death. In this activity as in others, he was untiring in promoting the interests and welfare of the people of the Eastern Townships.

MARION L. PHELPS

[The author had access to Moore family papers owned by Mrs Charles Moore, Stanbridge East, Que. M.L.P.] Archives judiciares de Bedford (Cowansville, Qué.), Registre d'état civil, 21 nov. 1880. Brome County Hist. Soc. Museum Archives (Knowlton, Que.), County papers, Missisquoi. Canada, Province of, Legislative Assembly, *Journals*, 1852–53, app.V.V., "Reports on the rebellion losses, 1837 & 1838." *Advertiser and Eastern Townships Sentinel* (Waterloo, Que.), 23 Feb. 1860. *District of Bedford Times* (Sweetsburg, Que.), 14 June 1867. *Montreal Herald*, 2 Jan., March 1838. *Illustrated atlas of the dominion of Canada . . .* (Toronto, 1881), iii. Cyrus Thomas, *Contributions to the history of the Eastern Townships: a work containing an account of the early settlement of St. Armand, Dunham, Sutton, Brome, Potton, and Bolton . . .* (Montreal, 1866), 35. "Honourable Philip Henry Moore," Missisquoi County Hist. Soc., *Report* (Saint-Jean, Que.), 1907, 51–52. "The Moore's Corner battle in 1837," Missisquoi County Hist. Soc., *Report* (Saint-Jean, Que.), 1908–9, 67–70.

MOREAU, HIPPOLYTE, secular priest, missionary, canon, vicar general; b. 8 March 1815 at Saint-Luc-sur-Richelieu, L.C., son of Raphaël Moreau and Marguerite Tremblay; d. 30 July 1880 at Montreal, Que.

Hippolyte Moreau received his classical education at the seminary of Saint-Hyacinthe. He was studying theology there, and at the same time teaching junior classes, when in 1838 Bishop Jean-Jacques Lartigue* judged him worthy of succeeding the Sulpician C.-L. Lefebvre* de Bellefeuille, missionary to the Indians of Lakes Timiskaming, Nipissing, and Abitibi. He was immediately elevated to the diaconate and sent to the mission of Lac-des-Deux-Montagnes (Oka) to study the Algonkin language under the direction of Flavien

DUROCHER. On 16 March 1839 he was admitted into the priesthood by Bishop Ignace Bourget*, and returned to Oka to continue his study of Algonkin. In 1840 he undertook his first journey as a missionary, to Timiskaming. From 1841 on he lived at Fort des Allumettes and travelled throughout the vast region of the Ottawas, carrying out his ministry among the Indians and scattered whites. He left this post on 14 Sept. 1844 and was appointed parish priest of Saint-Joseph-de-Soulanges.

During the typhus epidemic that raged at Montreal in 1847, he devoted himself, to the point of exhaustion, to tending the Irish who were relegated to sheds at Pointe-Saint-Charles (Montreal Island); he fell seriously ill with the disease. On 11 Feb. 1848 he became parish priest of Saint-Eustache (Deux-Montagnes County), in succession to Abbé Jacques Paquin. He applied himself particularly to bringing religious education to the poor and ignorant. He paid out of his own pocket for the completion of the presbytery and its outbuildings, and in 1850 he enlarged the convent of the Congregation of the Sisters of Notre-Dame. Two years later he started work on the vault of the parish church.

He left Saint-Eustache in 1853 and became titular canon of the cathedral at Montreal, where for 20 years he was archdeacon; in 1873 he was appointed vicar general, in place of Alexis-Frédéric TRUTEAU. He held this position until his death, which occurred on 30 July 1880 at the Hôtel-Dieu at Montreal, following a stroke he had had a month earlier. His body was buried in the cathedral.

In his *Mémoire pour servir à l'histoire du chapitre de la cathédrale . . .*, Bishop Bourget testified as follows: "Both as an archdeacon and as a vicar general M. Moreau showed himself skilful, prudent, and wise. In this respect he rendered real service to the bishop. Nor do the nuns of the Hôtel-Dieu forget the services he has rendered them by the skill and devotion with which he has straightened out the matter of their temporal possessions." In all the positions he held, Moreau displayed unusual dedication. He belonged to the class of unassuming workers who are vitally necessary to all institutions, religious or lay, if they are to live and develop.

LÉON POULIOT

ACAM, RCD, 94, 95. *Rapport sur les missions du diocèse de Québec . . .*, no.4 (janv. 1842), 67–74; no.6 (juill. 1845), 112–16. [Ignace Bourget], *Mémoire pour servir à l'histoire du chapitre de la cathédrale S. Jacques de Montréal* (Montréal, 1882), 180–81. Paroisse de Saint-Eustache, *Annuaire de Ville-Marie* (Montréal, 1871), 191–93.

MORIN, LOUIS-SIMÉON, lawyer and politician; b. 20 Jan. 1831 at Lavaltrie, Lower Canada, of the marriage of Joseph Morin, a farmer, and Félicité Peltier, niece of Salomon Juneau*, the founder of Milwaukee, Wisconsin; d. a bachelor on 7 May 1879 at Lavaltrie, Que.

From 1841 to 1849 Louis-Siméon Morin pursued his classical studies at the college of L'Assomption, then trained for the profession of lawyer in the office of Côme-Séraphin Cherrier* and Antoine-Aimé Dorion*. He was called to the bar of Lower Canada in 1853, and went into partnership at Montreal with Gédéon Ouimet* and Louis-Wilfrid Marchand*. While still young, he shone in the court-room by his eloquence and skill, especially in criminal cases. He contributed to *La Patrie*, a journal published in Montreal from 1854 to 1858 which gave moderate support to the Liberal-Conservative coalition.

In the general election of 1854, Louis-Siméon Morin waged a brilliant but unsuccessful struggle in the constituency of L'Assomption against Joseph Papin*, the distinguished Rouge party candidate; he was returned unopposed as MLA for Terrebonne in the general election of 1857, and in 1860 entered the cabinet of John A. Macdonald* and George-Étienne CARTIER as attorney general for Canada East. During the by-election which at that time was necessary after an MLA entered a cabinet, the government's opponents, represented by Godefroy Laviolette*, put up a stiff fight against Morin; he emerged victorious, but was defeated in the 1861 election in the constituency of Terrebonne by Louis LABRÈCHE-VIGER. He then stood in Laval, where he won out over Joseph-Hyacinthe Bellerose*. In 1863 Morin was again defeated in Terrebonne by Louis Labrèche-Viger.

In 1865 the government appointed him French secretary of the commission for the codification of the laws of Lower Canada relating to civil matters, replacing Joseph-Ubalde BEAUDRY, who had been raised to the position of commissioner following the death of Judge Augustin-Norbert Morin*. Morin held this office until the commission completed its task in 1867, on the eve of confederation [see René-Édouard CARON]. Afterwards he lived at Lavaltrie, out of public life. On 27 July 1871 the Quebec government appointed him joint protonotary, with Joseph-Octave Désilets, of the Superior Court, and clerk of the crown for the district of Joliette. He died on 7 May 1879 at Lavaltrie.

In *Souvenirs et biographies, 1870–1910*, Laurent-Olivier David*, while praising Morin's talents highly, judged him as follows: "He became a minister at the age of 28, he was surrounded by friends and admirers, but he had lost in the hurly-burly of politics the habits of moderation, work, and love of duty that were required if he was to continue to add lustre to his name and bring honour to his country. He showed that he had more talent than character; his best friends were dismayed, the people disappointed."

J.-C. BONENFANT

La Minerve (Montréal), 13 mai 1879. *La Patrie* (Montréal), 1854–58. Beaulieu et Hamelin, *Journaux du Québec*, 135. *Dom. ann. reg.*, 1879, 415–16. L.-O. David, *Souvenirs et biographies, 1870–1910* (Montréal, 1911), 49–54. Anastase Forget, *Histoire du collège de L'Assomption* (Montréal, [1933]), 541.

MORRILL, SIMEON, tanner, currier, and businessman; b. in Vermont, 11 Aug. 1793; d. London, Ont., 20 June 1871.

Simeon Morrill was raised in Maine and was a tanner in Kingston, Upper Canada, in September 1817. Nothing else is known about him until his arrival in 1829 in London, Upper Canada, where within a year he had established a tannery. He rapidly expanded this business by adding a factory for boots and shoes, and he was noted as the first businessman in this area to pay cash for hides and as wages. In 1861 he had approximately $20,000 capital involved in his tannery, employed ten persons, and had hides valued at $15,000. He was forced, however, to declare insolvency in 1868, and his affairs were finally wound up in 1876.

As the city grew, so did Morrill's other financial interests: he was a trustee of the London Savings' Bank, 1847–65; in 1853 an incorporator of the London and Port Stanley Railway (which he later served as director), and a trustee of the London Gas Company. He was also a founding member of the Board of Trade in 1857.

Like many other American emigrants to the area, Morrill was a Reformer in politics, and in December 1837 he participated in a midnight meeting of radicals supporting William Lyon Mackenzie*. In a by-election in 1844 he ran against a Tory, Lawrence Lawrason*, to represent London, but, to quote the *London Inquirer*, "the Reformers evinced great apathy" and he was forced to concede. He was more successful in municipal politics and represented St Andrew's ward on the council for several years. He was elected first town mayor in 1848 and held the office again in 1850 and 1851. As mayor Morrill broke a tie vote on the route of the Great Western Railway in 1851, and the line ran across his property next to his tannery. He was appointed a justice of the peace in 1841. In the 1840s he played an important part in reorganizing the Mechanics' Institute and in establishing the volunteer fire brigade and the Board of Health.

Morris

Morrill, a Wesleyan Methodist, was known as a generous contributor to a variety of educational and religious charities. He was particularly active in the London Temperance Reformation Society and his tombstone proclaims that he was "For forty years a consistent advocate of the cause of Temperance." He married first Margaret Andrews, by whom he had a large family, and secondly, Eleanor Beach (c. 1809–78). There were no children from his second marriage.

MADALINE RODDICK

Middlesex County Registry Office (London, Ont.), Joint Stock Company register, Liber A (1851–66), 6. PAC, RG 31, A1, 1861, London (City). University of Western Ontario Library, 234/2 (Proudfoot family papers, William Proudfoot journals, 1832–1850), entries for January 1844; 332/8 (Middlesex County, Ont., Court of Common Pleas, appearance and pleading books, 1874–75, and Insolvency Court register, 1865–81), p.19 and supporting papers. *J. of Education for Ont.*, XXIV (November 1871). *Kingston Gazette*, 25 Nov. 1817. *London Advertiser*, 23 June 1871. [Archie Bremner], *City of London, Ontario, Canada; the pioneer period and the London of today* (2nd ed., London, Ont., 1900), 35, 84, 105, 119, 132. C. T. Campbell, *Pioneer days in London; some account of men and things in London before it became a city* (London, Ont., 1921), 53, 92, 122, 125–27. *History of the county of Middlesex*, 62, 74, 196, 258, 268, 284, 285, 303, 321, 362. Fred Landon, *Western Ontario and the American frontier* (Toronto, 1941). Augusta Gilkinson, "The Great Western Railway," London and Middlesex Hist. Soc., *Trans.*, II (1909), 31–44. Fred Landon, "London and its vicinity, 1837–38," *Ont. Hist.*, XXIV (1927), 410–38.

MORRIS, MARIA FRANCES ANN (Miller), teacher, artist, and poet; b. in Halifax, N.S., 12 Feb. 1813, daughter of Captain Guy Morris and Sibylla Amelia Maria Sophia Leggett, and descendant of Charles Morris*, chief surveyor of land and second chief justice of the Nova Scotia Supreme Court; d. in Halifax, 28 Oct. 1875. On 7 July 1840 she married Garret Trafalgar Nelson Miller of La Have by whom she had several children.

Maria Frances Ann Morris received much of her training in art from W. H. Jones, an American who was teaching at Dalhousie College and giving lessons in Halifax, and from Professor L'Estrange, an English artist teaching in Halifax. About 1828 she painted Mount Uniacke; the picture is now owned by the Public Archives of Nova Scotia. During the early 1830s, at intervals between her studies, Miss Morris opened and closed three schools in Halifax for teaching drawing and painting to young ladies.

Encouraged by Titus Smith*, a talented local botanist, Maria Morris began to paint the wild flowers of her native land. In 1839 she announced the proposed publication of *Wild flowers of Nova Scotia* to be sold by subscription. A total of four series appeared comprising 99 sheets and representing 146 species; the third of the series was titled *Wild flowers of Nova Scotia and New Brunswick* and the fourth, *Wild flowers of British North America*. Specimens of her work, sent to London in 1862, arrived too late for the International Exhibition, but were praised by the London press. A collection of the paintings was shown at the universal exposition in Paris in 1867. Maria Morris was the finest artist among a group of Maritime ladies who made floral painting into a 19th-century phenomenon in the area. *Wild flowers of Nova Scotia* is a pleasing and valuable contribution not only to floral art but also to the study of botanical science.

Maria Morris' talent was not limited to painting, nor was she the only member of her family to possess creative ability. In 1856 she and her sister Catherine published a volume of poetry, *Metrical musings*, in New York.

CHARLES BRUCE FERGUSSON

[Maria Morris, *Wild flowers of Nova Scotia*. Parts i and ii of the first series appeared in 1839–40 under the patronage of Sir Colin Campbell* with descriptive texts by Titus Smith, lithographed and coloured in London, and published by C. H. Belcher, Halifax, and John Snow, London. A second series, under the patronage of Sir John Gaspard LE MARCHANT, with text by Dr Alexander Forrester*, and published by A. and W. Mackinlay, Halifax, and John Snow, London, appeared in 1853. A third series, under the patronage of Sir William Fenwick Williams*, with text by Professor George Lawson*, and published by M. L. Katzman, Halifax, and John Snow, London, was issued in 1866. The fourth series, again under the patronage of Lieutenant Governor Williams' patronage, and with text by Professor Lawson, was published by Reeve and Co., London, in 1867. C.B.F.]

PANS, "Collection of genealogies of Nova Scotian families (Cumberland County)," compiled by T. H. Lodge, 1954. St Paul's Church (Halifax, N.S.), Records. *Acadian Recorder* (Halifax), 11 July 1840, 30 Oct. 1875, 10 Jan. 1920, 13 Oct. 1924. *Christian Messenger* (Halifax), 3 Nov. 1875. *Colonial Churchman* (Lunenburg, N.S.), 23 July 1840. *Halifax Daily Reporter*, 29 Oct. 1875. *Novascotian* (Halifax), 23 Sept. 1830; 13 Jan., 24 Nov. 1831; 20 July 1832; 22 Aug. 1833; 25 Dec. 1834; 15 Sept. 1836; 19 Jan. 1837. *Times* (Halifax), 15 Oct. 1839, 9 June 1840. Exposition Universelle de 1867, *Catalogue of the Nova Scotian Department with introduction and appendices* (Paris, 1867). W. G. Colgate, *Canadian art, its origin and development* (Toronto, 1943). W. B. Tucker, *The romance of the Palatine Millers; a tale of Palatine Irish-Americans and United Empire Loyalists* (Montreal, 1929). E. S. Nutt, "An incident in the golden age of fine art in Nova Scotia," *Nova Scotia Journal of Education*, 4th ser., III (1932), 71–75. Harry Piers, "Artists in Nova Scotia," N.S. Hist. Soc. *Coll.*, XVIII (1914), 101–65.

MOUAT, WILLIAM ALEXANDER, master mariner and HBC employee; b. in 1821 in London, Eng., son of William Mouat; m. 8 Aug. 1854 at Stepney, England, to Mary Ann Ainsley, by whom he had seven children; d. 11 April 1871 at Knight Inlet, B.C.

William Alexander Mouat went to sea in 1835 and served three years as an apprentice before becoming an officer. He came to the Pacific coast of North America as second mate of the Hudson's Bay Company bark *Vancouver* (Capt. Andrew Cook Mott) arriving at Fort Vancouver on 27 March 1845. On 28 April he was transferred to the *Cadboro* as first officer and served in her until the end of February 1847 when Captain James Scarborough "put him off duty." He is believed to have acted as pilot for the Columbia River bar in 1848, and he himself says that in 1849 he was "master of an American vessel at California." In the summer of 1849 he was again serving as first officer under Scarborough, but this time in the *Mary Dare* at Beaver Harbour, where Fort Rupert was being established by Captain William Henry McNEILL of the *Beaver*. On 30 July 1849 an eye-witness (Charles Beardmore of the HBC) reported to Dr William Fraser Tolmie* that Scarborough had kept Mouat "under arrest during his whole stay here," and that by 25 July Mouat had been "so driven & bullied that he left the ship putting himself under Captain McNeil[l's] protection." Scarborough then "declared him a deserter & broke open his chest & proceeded to the extremity of the law." "We shall be anxious to hear how it is settled," added Beardmore, "as this officer is a favorite with us all." The HBC apparently found for Mouat, since in 1850 he was master of the *Mary Dare* and took her home in 1853, arriving in London on 27 May 1854. But Mouat was now himself accused by his own first officer of "disgraceful conduct" in making a physical assault on the second officer of the *Mary Dare* in the presence of the crew. Later episodes in Mouat's career would seem to indicate that although he was a kindly man, generous to the unfortunate, he had a quick temper and would brook no interference in what he considered the performance of his duty.

The outcome of the *Mary Dare* incident of 1854 is not known, but it was as a passenger on the *Marquis of Bute* that Mouat returned with a bride to Victoria on 1 April 1855. On 16 April he was given command of the HBC steamer *Otter*, then plying between Victoria and Fort Langley, and on 27 Feb. 1860 he was made a chief trader. He was master of the *Otter* until 3 April 1862 when he was transferred to the newly acquired *Enterprise* for her first trip to the Fraser. When in 1865 gold was discovered on the Big Bend of the Columbia River, he was sent to look into the possibility of steam navigation on the Kamloops and Shuswap lakes and the Thompson River which connected them. He reported the scheme "entirely practicable," and the HBC ordered the *Marten* to be built at Savona's Ferry.

Early in 1866 the HBC was awarded the contract for direct mail service between Victoria and San Francisco, and Captain Mouat, "one of the most careful and reliable men that ever handled a wheel," was given command of the *Labouchere*, which he took to San Francisco on 15 Feb. 1866 to be fitted out for the accommodation of passengers. On her second voyage after the refit, on 14 April 1866, the *Labouchere* was lost off Point Reyes, her captain displaying "admirable coolness, bravery and forethought" in saving his passengers. But the official inquiry censured Mouat for "very gross negligence . . . in not swinging the *Labouchere* to ascertain the deviation of the compasses before leaving San Francisco, the steering apparatus having been shifted from aft forward" during the refit, and also for not having taken sufficient care of her majesty's mails.

The HBC now placed Mouat in command of the *Marten*, which made her maiden trip on 26 May 1866, the first steamer to ply the Thompson River. But the Big Bend mines proved a failure, and at the close of the season the *Marten* was laid up and Mouat was posted to Fort Rupert, where he remained in charge until his death in 1871 while on a canoe trip from Knight Inlet to the fort. Mouat was buried in Victoria, and his tombstone, the inscription almost obliterated, may still be seen in Pioneer Square, adjoining Christ Church Cathedral.

DOROTHY BLAKEY SMITH

HBC Arch. A.33/4, f.413; B.113/c/1, f.16; C.1/459; C.1/462; C.1/625, f.208 (log of *Otter*). PABC, Charles Beardmore correspondence; Thomas Lowe journal, 1843–50; William Alexander Mouat correspondence, 1859–66. *British Columbian* (New Westminster, B.C.), 28 April 1866. *British Columbia Tribune* (Yale, B.C.), 28 April, 7, 21 May, 4 June 1866. *Cariboo Sentinel* (Barkerville, B.C.), 31 May 1866. *Colonist* (Victoria), 1863–71.
Lewis and Dryden's marine history of the Pacific northwest (Wright). Denys Nelson, *Fort Langley, 1827–1927, a century of settlement in the valley of the lower Fraser River* (Vancouver, 1927; 2nd ed., 1947), 15–26. Walbran, *B.C. coast names*. N. R. Hacking,

Mulkins

"Steamboating on the Fraser in the 'sixties," *BCHQ*, X (1946), 1–37.

MULKINS, HANNIBAL, Wesleyan Methodist minister and Church of England clergyman; b. in Upper Canada in 1811 or 1812; m. 19 May 1842, Jane Gray Dennis, by whom he had several children; d. 26 July 1877, at Stapleford, Nottinghamshire, Eng.

Hannibal Mulkins was received on trial in the Wesleyan Methodist Church in Canada in 1835 and was ordained in 1838. From 1835 to early in 1840 he served on the Yonge Street, Toronto Township, Whitby, Cobourg, Belleville, and Brockville circuits. He was described by John Carroll* as "a very gifted young minister." He was popular and successful, and Carroll mentions that he led "a good revival ... among the young people" in Brockville. However, in 1840, "taking umbrage at some slight disciplinary proceedings relating to himself," he went over to the Church of England. According to Carroll, he was a useful minister, who did not fall "into ritualistic folly" and always "exhibited a fraternal feeling towards his early fellow-laborers."

Mulkins prepared for orders in the Church of England with the Reverend Edward Denroch, clergyman in charge of the parish at Brockville, and the Reverend Henry Caswell, master of the grammar school. Made deacon by Bishop John Strachan* on 25 April 1841, and ordained priest 9 May 1842, he was appointed travelling missionary in Fitzroy and Pakenham, and was reported as itinerating in the area west of Bytown (Ottawa) along the Ottawa River in the townships of Torbolton, Fitzroy, Pakenham, McNab, and Horton and in some unsurveyed territory. On 1 Jan. 1851 he was appointed by Lord Elgin [Bruce*] to the chaplaincy of the Provincial Penitentiary in Kingston in the place of the Reverend Robert Vashon Rogers, with whom he was involved in a proposal in the mid-1850s to have the Reverend Thomas Hincks, brother of Sir Francis*, appointed to the see of Kingston.

During the years 1869–73 Mulkins spent some time acting as agent in England for John Travers Lewis*, bishop of Ontario, to arrange for the commutation of the grant made to the diocese by the Society for the Propagation of the Gospel. Superannuated from the penitentiary on 1 Nov. 1875, Mulkins left the chaplaincy and emigrated to England. He was appointed curate of Stapleford in the diocese of Salisbury in December 1875, and vicar in 1876.

JAMES J. TALMAN

Hannibal Mulkins was the author of *Report to the Canada Temperance Society on the workings and effects of prohibitory legislation to suppress intemperance in the New England states* (Kingston, C.W., 1855). *Church* (Cobourg; Toronto), 1 May 1841; 1, 29 July 1852; 17 May 1856. *Examiner* (Toronto), 25 May 1842. *Clerical guide and churchman's directory, an annual register for the clergy and laity of the Anglican Church in British North America, 1876,* ed. C. V. F. Bliss (Ottawa, 1876). Cornish, *Cyclopædia of Methodism*, I, 118. Carroll, *Case and his cotemporaries*, IV, 259–60. J. L. H. Henderson, "John Strachan as bishop," unpublished DD thesis, University of Western Ontario, 1956, 603–5.

MULLINS, ROSANNA ELEANORA (Leprohon), poet and novelist; b. in Montreal, L.C., 12 Jan. 1829, daughter of Francis Mullins, a well-known businessman, and Rosanna Connelly; d. 20 Sept. 1879 at Montreal, Que.

Rosanna Eleanora Mullins was educated at the convent of the Congregation of Notre-Dame in Montreal, which offered schooling and moral instruction to the daughters of the well-to-do. She remained there until some time after 1846 when she published her first poems. Judging from the religious themes, the moral tone, and the vocabulary employed in her poetry, she received a sound instruction in languages and religion. Her love for the teacher who recognized and encouraged her talent is obvious in a poem addressed to her.

At the beginning of her literary career, in 1846, much of Rosanna's prose and verse appeared in the *Literary Garland*, a small magazine dedicated to encouraging Canadian talent. It regularly published poetry, memoirs, essays, sketches, short stories, and serialized novels of an impersonal, wholesome, and uplifting kind, and was a magazine fit to appear in the parlour of the most demanding and cultivated Canadian family. Other well-known Canadians whose work appeared in the *Garland* included Susanna Strickland* Moodie, Catharine Parr Strickland* Traill, John Richardson*, William Dunlop*, Mary Anne Madden* Sadlier, and Charles Sangster*. Rosanna, who then signed herself "R.E.M.," published in other magazines and newspapers as well, for example the *True Witness* [see CLERK], the *Journal of Education*, and the *New Dominion Monthly*.

In 1851 Rosanna married Dr Jean-Lucien Leprohon, of an old French Canadian family, who was then practising medicine at Saint-Charles-sur-Richelieu. He was a man of culture, as well as of science, and a man of energy, who had found time to publish one of the first medical journals in Canada East, *La Lancette canadienne*. In 1855 they moved to Montreal, where he became surgeon to an army regiment, a city councillor, professor of medicine, member of the Catholic Committee of the Council of Public Instruction, and a leader in his social circle. He was also made Spanish consul in Montreal and was decorated by that country for his services. Through him, his family, and his friends, Mrs Leprohon came to know intimately the aristocracy of Quebec, and their values, hopes, and aspirations; much of the background for her later novels was gathered among them.

The marriage proved a fruitful one, and 13 children were born to the couple. From her portrait Mrs Leprohon appears an intelligent, self-possessed, handsome woman. Though her literary output was smaller after her marriage, her best work, the novels set in Quebec, was produced then. She died in September 1879, and was buried in Côte-des-Neiges Cemetery in Montreal.

Mrs Leprohon's poetry was collected after her death and published in 1881 in Montreal. It is touched with moral seriousness and didacticism, and the tone of much of it is summed up by a footnote to a poem called "The Boyhood of Jesus": "An old tradition avers that our Saviour was never seen to laugh during his mortal life." Besides many poems of Catholic inspiration, she wrote others describing family life – its happy and its sad moments – and her country. Her best poem, "A Canadian Snowfall" evokes a picture somewhat similar to that in Ralph Waldo Emerson's "The Snowfall," but the likeness may have been accidental. The influence of Thomas Gray is more easily identified, not only in the many morbid themes but in actual turns of phrase. Her nature poetry consists mainly of romantic descriptive lyrics depicting seasonal changes or giving impressions of vistas such as those at Murray Bay (Pointe-au-Pic) or the gorge of the Saguenay River. These poems are Canadian in the sense that they describe Canadian nature, but they are first of all romantic in tone. Her patriotism shows in "The Maple Leaf" and her intense interest in Canada's past in "Jacques Cartier's First Visit to Mount Royal," and others. A small number of poems on Indian themes are difficult to characterize. They deal mainly with death – the deaths of Indian maidens, who somehow assume the attitudes of romantic white heroines. In "The White Maiden and the Indian Girl," R.E.M. compares at length two life styles, and decides that the Indian leads the superior existence – a conclusion which, considering what R.E.M. must have known about the lives then led by Indian women, is romantically dishonest. R.E.M.'s poetry is good technically, and, in places, interesting in theme and content, but it must take second place to her novels of life in early Quebec.

Her first story, "The Stepmother," appeared serially in the *Literary Garland* in 1847, and the next year, in the same periodical, came "Ida Beresford," which was later translated by Joseph-Édouard Lefebvre* de Bellefeuille into French and ran serially in *L'Ordre* (1859–60). Other romantic serials appeared in the *Garland* in 1849, 1850, and 1851.

There appears to be a gap in Mrs Leprohon's output of fiction from 1851 (the year of her marriage and the year the *Garland* disappeared) until 1859 when "The manor house of Villerai" appeared in installments in the *Family Herald*. A French translation, by de Bellefeuille, *Le manoir de Villerai*, came out in book form in 1861. (It was published again in French in 1924.) The story is set in Quebec prior to the English conquest; in it Blanche de Villerai, heiress to a seigneury, finally renounces her aristocratic husband-to-be to a beautiful, saintly peasant girl, Rose Lauson, who has just nursed her through a case of small-pox. It is a romantic novel, marred by intrusions of large wedges of history and folk-lore. The second novel in this new series, which also shows the results of Mrs Leprohon's introduction into the upper levels of French Canadian society, was *Antoinette de Mirecourt* (published by John Lovell* of Montreal in 1864), which was translated into French and published in book form the following year. It also appeared serially in French in *Les Nouvelles soirées canadiennes* in 1886 and 1887. A well-to-do country girl comes to Montreal immediately following the British occupation. Her relatives welcome British officers into their society, and the heroine falls in love with one of them, who turns out to be a villain from whom she has to be rescued. This is a romantic, stilted novel, the worst of the later group. Four years later, *Armand Durand* appeared serially in the *Daily News* of Montreal. It was published in book form by Lovell in 1868, and in French the following year. This novel concerns two sons of a farmer, one of whom inherits the farm dishonestly; the other becomes a lawyer and he is made the centre of attention as he struggles first to qualify and then to support a silly wife. Mrs Leprohon's final full-length novel, *Ada Dunmore*, appeared in 1869 in the *Canadian Illustrated News* and was followed by several other stories in the *Canadian Illustrated News* and in the *Canadian Monthly*.

Mrs Leprohon's early fiction, and indeed almost all of it, is filled with tearful partings, broken engagements, timely and untimely deaths, chance meetings, and happy reconciliations: obviously the outpouring of a romantic fancy fed on the novels of her time. But though her novels have little appeal now, they retain some of their charm

Munn

if taken for what they were: amusement for women readers of early Canada. They are readable, if not believable, episodic (because of publishing demands), but not boring, especially *Armand Durand*. In her later novels more serious themes appear. Most common is love between people widely separated by background, temperament, or wealth. Her knowledge of Quebec and its history, and her psychological insight into strained domestic arrangements (both of which seem to have appeared after her own marriage) give a refreshing realism to many parts of these novels. She made shrewd use of her observation of her French in-laws, her own sense of class, and her talents as a story teller. In her major novels, she appears in the role of peacemaker between the French and the English, trying to make good manners smooth over ruffled feelings, seeking to explain the feelings of the French Canadian and to make the English appear in an acceptable light. The measure of her success in both languages is to be seen in the number of her publications and in the fact that her works were found worthy of translation and were being reissued as late as 1924. As the first Canadian widely read in both languages she is the precursor of William Kirby*, Horatio Gilbert Parker* and Hugh MacLennan.

J. C. STOCKDALE

Among the writings of Rosanna Eleanora Mullins are the following: *Antoinette de Mirecourt: or, secret marrying and secret sorrowing, a Canadian tale* (Montreal, 1864); *Armand Durand; or a promise fulfilled* (Montreal, 1868); "The manor house of Villerai," *Family Herald* (Montreal), 1859, published in French as *Le manoir de Villerai, roman historique sous la domination française* (Montréal, 1861; [1884?]; 1924); *The poetical works of Mrs. Leprohon (Miss R. E. Mullins)* (Montreal, 1881); and two works that she signed "R.E.M.": "Clarence Fitz Clarence," *Literary Garland* (Montreal), Jan.–May 1851; "Florence, or wit and wisdom," *Literary Garland* (Montreal), Feb.–Dec. 1849.

The following works provide a complete list of Mme Leprohon's writings: M. M. Brown, *An index to the* Literary Garland *(Montreal, 1838–1851)* (Toronto, 1962), 24. Morgan, *Bibliotheca Canadensis*. Watters, *Check list*. Watters and Bell, *On Canadian literature*.

Archives paroissiales de Notre-Dame (Montréal), Registres des baptêmes, mariages et sépultures. Morgan, *Sketches of celebrated Canadians*. A.-H. Deneau, "Life and works of Mrs. Leprohon," unpublished MA thesis, Université de Montréal, 1949. *Lit. hist. of Can.* (Klinck). Desmond Pacey, *Creative writing in Canada; a short history of English-Canadian literature* (2nd ed., Toronto, [1961]). V. B. Rhodenizer, *Canadian literature in English* ([Montreal, *ca* 1965]).

MUNN, JOHN, merchant and politician; b. in 1807 at Port Bannatyne, near Rothesay, Scotland, son of Stewart Munn and Isabella Fisher; m. in 1838 to Naomi Munden by whom he had one son and four daughters; d. at Southport, Lancashire, Eng., on 29 Sept. 1879.

John Munn was reared in Scotland. After arriving in St John's, Newfoundland, in 1825, he spent eight years in the general trading firm of Baine, Johnston, and Company as a bookkeeper. In 1833, with Captain William Punton, a Scottish master mariner trading out of Greenoch, he moved to Newfoundland's second city, Harbour Grace, purchased property for £515, and set up business as Punton and Munn. The firm started on a small scale with one vessel. After Punton's death in 1845 the firm continued as Punton and Munn until 1872, when the name was changed to John Munn and Company, Munn admitting his son William Punton Munn and his nephew Robert Stewart Munn as partners and transferring the more active duties to them.

Under John Munn's direction the firm had prospered and expanded until it was the colony's largest general supplying and mercantile business outside St John's. It was active in the seal fishery and the Labrador fishery and owned large shipping and other interests in the colony. The shipbuilding yard at Harbour Grace began production about 1838. After his partner's death Munn brought several relatives from Scotland into the business. They suffered a setback in 1858 when their large premises went up in smoke but there was no delay in rebuilding. John Munn and Company increased its business still further in the 1870s when Thomas Ridley and Sons, the other big mercantile house at Harbour Grace, was declared insolvent and the Munn firm bought out the Ridley estate and undertook to supply many of Thomas RIDLEY's former dealers. John Munn helped to found the Union Bank of which he was appointed a director in 1870. Munn's company also owned the *Harbour Grace Standard*.

Munn's influential position in the trade and fisheries of Newfoundland made him a power in the colony, especially in Conception Bay. Harbour Grace was often referred to as a pocket borough, "Munnsborough," since the Munn-approved candidate usually won an election. Munn himself took an active interest in politics, representing Conception Bay in the Amalgamated Legislature, 1842–48, as a Conservative. On the introduction of responsible government in 1855 he was appointed to the Legislative Council, but he resigned in 1869 when the question of confederation arose. Munn, a prominent confederate, contested the election in 1869 and succeeded in carrying the district of Harbour Grace, thus becoming one of a minority in the House of Assembly. At the dissolution of the house in 1873 he retired from politics.

The leading man in Harbour Grace for over 40 years, John Munn had won respect as an honourable and clearheaded merchant. A Presbyterian, he donated liberally to other churches and organizations, and was a member of the Protestant Board of Education and a director of the Harbour Grace grammar school. When news of his death at Southport, near Liverpool, reached the colony, Harbour Grace and much of Conception Bay put on mourning, with flags flying at half-mast, shops closed, and almost all work suspended for the day.

ELIZABETH A. WELLS

Department of Justice of Newfoundland and Labrador (St John's), Registry of deeds, companies, and securities, Registry of deeds for the Northern District, 1826–88. PANL, Family tree of Azariah Munden (1739–1827) showing descendants of William Azariah Munn, 1864–1940; Family tree of Stewart Munn showing descendants of William Azariah Munn, 1864–1940; Newfoundland, Harbour Grace Sessions Court, Records, 1834, 744. *Carbonear Herald and Outport Telephone*, 2 Oct. 1879. *Harbour Grace Standard and Conception Bay Advertiser*, 4 Oct. 1879. *Newfoundlander* (St John's), 3 Oct. 1879. Newfoundland, *Blue Books*, 1842–73 (copies in PANL). *The Newfoundland almanack, for . . . 1849 . . .*, comp. Philip Tocque (St John's, 1849). *The Newfoundland Almanac, for . . . 1858 . . .*, comp. Joseph Woods (St John's, 1857). W. A. Munn, "Harbour Grace history," chaps. 11–21, in *Newfoundland Quarterly*, XXXVI (1936–37)–XXXVIII (1938–39).

MUNRO (Munroe), GEORGE. *See* MONRO

MURDOCH, BEAMISH, writer, lawyer, and politician; b. to Andrew Murdoch and Elizabeth Beamish at Halifax, N.S., 1 Aug. 1800; d. in Lunenburg, N.S., 9 Feb. 1876.

Beamish Murdoch was raised and educated by a maiden aunt, Harriet Jane Ott Beamish, after his father, a merchant, became involved in an expensive lawsuit and was jailed as a debtor for seven years. In 1822 Murdoch was admitted to the bar of Nova Scotia and began a legal practice. He also began to contribute articles to the *Acadian Recorder*, which was owned by Philip J. Holland (d. 1839), and to the *Acadian Magazine or Literary Mirror*, which began publication in Halifax in 1826. Although his grandfather, the Reverend James Murdoch, had been a missionary in the Antiburgher wing of the Church of Scotland, Beamish Murdoch was raised in the Church of England and belonged to St Paul's Church. In the disruption of that church in 1824 he joined the faction which included Thomas Chandler Haliburton*, and moved to St George's Church in Halifax [*see* J. W. JOHNSTON].

In 1826, Murdoch, aided by his uncle, Thomas Ott Beamish, ran for the House of Assembly for Halifax Township. In spite of opposition from the city merchants, he had sufficient strength in the township to carry the election. Murdoch, who in 1824 and 1825 had been vice-president of the Charitable Irish Society, also received aid from the Irish, and in the assembly he worked to remove civil disabilities from the Roman Catholics. He quickly became an active member, generally following Haliburton's lead. Thus, in 1827, when a question arose concerning the right of the legislature to control customs revenue, Murdoch supported Haliburton's proposal that the assembly should petition the crown seeking a compromise measure which would give it some control over future revenue expenditures. Murdoch was irritated over the refusal of the Legislative Council, which included Hibbert N. Binney, the collector of customs, to support the move. He was further annoyed when the upper house failed to support his motion requesting that the crown reverse its decision to collect quitrents. He did not deny the constitutional right of Great Britain to enforce payment but argued that the measure was unjust. A real conflict with the upper house did not develop until 1830 when the two houses clashed over the duty on brandy [*see* Enos COLLINS]. Murdoch, who followed the lead of Samuel George William Archibald*, regarded the action of the council as unconstitutional and argued that the council's stand denied the lower house the authority which it should possess as the representative of the people.

In the election of 1830 Murdoch ran against Stephen Wastie DeBlois. He received support from Joseph HOWE and the *Novascotian* despite the fact that Howe had criticized Murdoch during the legislative session of 1830. Prior to 1830 Murdoch had supported public grants to Pictou Academy, but he, like Haliburton, apparently objected to attacks on Bishop John Inglis* by the academy's president, Thomas McCulloch*. Howe, in turn, felt that Murdoch had made unwarranted attacks on McCulloch. Any chance of Murdoch's carrying the election in 1830 was ended when he was provoked into complaining about so-called loyalists who fled the United States to escape bad debts and monopolized public offices in the province. After the election, Murdoch withdrew from public affairs until the campaign of 1836 when he ran, unsuccessfully, against a Reformer. In the 1840 election he ran against Joseph Howe and William Annand* and again was defeated. During the 1840 campaign, Murdoch complained that the

Reformers' demands for responsible government threatened the tie with England and would upset the balance in the British constitutional system. By the time he wrote his history of the province, however, he had come to regard cabinet government and self-government as being compatible with association in the British empire.

During his withdrawal from public affairs in the early 1830s, he prepared his four-volume *Epitome of the laws of Nova Scotia*, printed by Joseph Howe in 1832–33. This work, which involved a detailed study of the provincial and English law, was modelled after Sir William Blackstone's *Commentaries*. Murdoch's work was well received by the Maritime press and was apparently a significant contribution to both lawyers and law students until the growing body of provincial law made it obsolete and more specialized works made it unnecessary.

Throughout his life Murdoch showed a keen interest in education, in charitable institutions, and in moral issues. In January 1825 he was appointed joint secretary of the Poor Man's Friend Society and in the 1830s he served on the Nova Scotia Philanthropic Society. His interest may have been sparked by the experiences of his father and in 1826 he wrote a pamphlet in which he supported the introduction of a bankruptcy law. Murdoch was an early supporter of temperance and, by 1842, was president of the Halifax Temperance Society, which had been established in 1832. His concern with public education led him to serve on the Halifax Library Committee in the 1840s and 1850s. He assumed a more significant role in provincial education when he became clerk of the Central Board of Education in April 1841. As clerk, he earned an annual salary of £150 and played an important part in the board's attempts to establish a uniform school system in the province. He prepared a summary of the ordinances of the city of Halifax in 1851 and, in October 1852, was appointed recorder for the city with an annual salary of £200. As recorder he was required to offer legal advice to the city and to try cases before the mayor's court.

When he retired in 1860 Murdoch began to prepare *A history of Nova Scotia, or Acadie*, which was published in installments between 1865 and 1867. He originally intended the history to end with the year 1807 but extended it to the year 1827. He even considered going as far as 1867 but his energy, or perhaps the public response to the first three volumes, was not equal to the task. In his work he adopted a severely chronological approach, with extensive quotations from documents and earlier books. There was no critical appraisal of the documents, nor was there any

sense of development through time. Murdoch was so convinced of the universal truth of his beliefs that he expected his reader to perceive the real nature of liberty, loyalty, and progress merely by seeing the actual words of the pioneers. He felt no compulsion to expound on his beliefs, but assumed that they were inherent in the British race. Thus, according to his *History*, as soon as the English arrived in Nova Scotia, the province began to take on an English aspect. The British belief in law, freedom, and industry helped preserve the province from the convulsions of revolution which racked the United States and was gradually adapted to the local environment. Thus, he was able to reconcile a faith in a Nova Scotian nationalism with a continued loyalty to Great Britain. Intended as a delineation of the Nova Scotian character, Murdoch's work stands as a monument to chronology as history.

K. G. PRYKE

Beamish Murdoch, *The charter and ordinances of the city of Halifax in the province of Nova Scotia with the provincial acts concerning the city, collected and revised by authority of the city council* (Halifax, 1851); *An epitome of the laws of Nova Scotia* (4v., Halifax, 1832–33); *An essay on the mischievous tendency of imprisoning for debt* (2nd ed., Halifax, 1831); *A history of Nova Scotia, or Acadie* (3v., Halifax, 1865–67); *A narrative of the late fires at Miramichi, New Brunswick: with an appendix containing the statements of many of the sufferers, and a variety of interesting occurrences; together with a poem, entitled "The conflagration"* (Halifax, 1825).

PANS, Beamish Murdoch papers. Duncan Campbell, *Nova Scotia in its historical, mercantile, and industrial relations* (Montreal, 1873), 268–77. *Directory of N.S. MLAs* (Fergusson), 262. G. E. Hart, "The Halifax Poor Man's Friend Society, 1820–27. An early social experiment," *CHR*, XXXIV (1953), 109–23. D. C. Harvey, "History and its uses in pre-confederation Nova Scotia," *CHA Report, 1938*, 5–16. D. C. Harvey, "Nova Scotia's Blackstone," *Can. Bar Rev.*, XI (1933), 339–44. Gene Morison, "The Brandy Election of 1830," N.S. Hist. Soc. *Coll.*, XXX (1954), 151–83. H. L. Stewart, *The Irish in Nova Scotia: annals of the Charitable Irish Society of Halifax (1786–1836)* (Kentville, N.S., [1949]), 138–41. Norah Story, "The church and state 'party' in Nova Scotia, 1749–1851," N.S. Hist. Soc. *Coll.*, XXVII (1947), 35–57. K. N. Windsor, "Historical writing in Canada to 1920," *Lit. hist. of Can.* (Klinck), 208–50.

MURRAY, ALEXANDER HUNTER, HBC chief trader and artist; b. in 1818 or 1819 at Kilmun, county of Argyll, Scotland; d. on 20 April 1874 at his home near Lower Fort Garry, Man.

No fur-trader ranged farther over North America than Alexander Hunter Murray. According to his *Journal* of 1847–48 he had early been in the swamps of Lake Pontchartrain (near New Orleans,

La.) and along the Red River in Texas. It is difficult to determine exactly how or when he got there and nothing much is known about his life until he became an employee of the American Fur Company working out of St Louis, Mo. In 1844–45 he was on the upper Missouri River and there he sketched the fur posts of that region: forts Union, Pierre, Mortimer, and George.

Murray left the American Fur Company in 1846 and proceeded north to join the Hudson's Bay Company at Fort Garry (Winnipeg). Because of his experience he was appointed senior clerk and transferred to the Mackenzie River District under the chief factor Murdoch McPherson*. On his way there he met Chief Trader Colin Campbell* of the Athabasca District, whose daughter Anne he shortly married at Fort Simpson. Since there was no clergyman in the area, "McPherson and a Bible" had to serve and the marriage was registered at St John's Cathedral, Red River, on 24 Aug. 1846. The couple descended the Mackenzie River to the mouth of the Peel River, then went to Fort McPherson for the winter.

On 11 June 1847, after leaving his bride at Lapierre House on Bell River, Murray started out to establish Fort Yukon, the assignment for which he is chiefly known. Descending the Bell River to the Porcupine, Murray reached the Yukon River on 25 June and soon began construction just above the junction of the Yukon and Porcupine rivers, at a point slightly north of the Arctic Circle. The fort consisted of three large log structures surrounded by a stockade 100 feet square with a bastion at each corner. Murray and the leaders of the HBC seem to have known that the fort was inside Russian territory, contrary to an agreement between the HBC and the Russian-American Company. As a result, Murray feared an attack by the Russians, but Fort Yukon was beyond the sphere of their trading activity and no Russian made an appearance at the post until 1863, by which time Murray was serving elsewhere. In effect, Murray and the HBC developed and exploited an area where they had no right to be, and this occupation of a profitable territory continued until 1869 when the HBC was peremptorily ejected from Fort Yukon by the United States after the American purchase of Alaska. Their main trade was in marten pelts, but they also took out beaver, fox, and otter.

During the winter of 1847–48, Murray occupied himself with work on the fort buildings, and acquainted himself with the Kutchin or Yukonikhotana Indians who inhabited the area around the fort. He kept a daily journal of his activities which has been published by the Public Archives of Canada along with his sketches of the area and its people. On 5 June 1848, with the returns of the season, he set out for Lapierre House to rejoin his wife; later that year the couple returned to Fort Yukon where Murray was in charge until 1851. A letter from Chief Factor John Rae* to HBC Governor Sir George Simpson* dated 30 Aug. 1850 commented, "Mr. Murray is evidently an excellent manager and an interested person, but unfortunately his men will not stay any length of time with him." Simpson wrote Rae the following 10 December, "I have read a letter from Mr. Murray who gives a great deal of interesting information. . . . [From] his correspondence and the activity with which he conducts the affairs of that section of the business, I should judge him to be a very efficient and intelligent officer." However, by 1851 Murray's health was failing and he had to be relieved of his duties.

After a rest at Fort Garry with his wife and several small children, he was assigned to the post at Pembina and was in charge there for several years. Later he served at Rainy Lake and Swan River before being returned to Pembina where he was advanced to chief trader in 1856. Murray went home to Scotland on furlough in 1857, evidently partly for his health. Fully recovered, he returned to the Red River Settlement and was placed in charge of Lower Fort Garry where he remained until his retirement in 1867. From then until his death in 1874, he lived at his home, Bellevue, on the Red River.

Murray was a man of varied accomplishments. His sketches of fur trade posts and of people give an interesting picture of the times, and his *Journal of the Yukon, 1847–48* provides valuable insights into the manners and customs of the Indians of the Yukon, the difficulties of establishing a post, and the policies and methods of the fur trade.

KENNETH L. HOLMES

HBC Arch. B.240/a/1–8 (Murray's journal at Fort Yukon). Murray, *Journal of the Yukon* (Burpee).

HBRS, XVI (Rich and Johnson). J. S. Galbraith, *The Hudson's Bay Company as an imperial factor, 1821–1869* (Toronto, 1957). Richard Mathews, *The Yukon* (New York, 1968). J. E. Sunder, *The fur trade on the upper Missouri, 1840–1865* (Norman, Okla., 1965). M. M. Black, "Alexander Hunter Murray," *Beaver*, outfit 265 (June 1934), 29–32. Robert Watson, "Chief trader Alexander Hunter Murray and Fort Youcon," *Beaver*, outfit 260 (June 1929), 211–13. Clifford Wilson, "Founding Fort Yukon," *Beaver*, outfit 278 (June 1947), 38–43.

MURRAY, HUGH, Papal Zouave; b. 30 April 1836 at Montreal, L.C., son of Hugh Murray and Henrietta Horan; d. February 1874 at Manresa or Bilbao, Spain.

Murray

Hugh Murray, an Irishman, received his classical education at the Petit Séminaire in Quebec, probably attracted there by his uncle, Abbé Edward John HORAN, at that time a teacher in the institution. He took his baccalaureate in arts in 1856 and then became a student at the faculty of medicine, but according to the *Annuaire de l'université Laval* he had already discontinued his medical studies before the opening of the academic year in 1857.

Deeply affected in that year by the deaths of his mother and father within a few months, he planned for a while to become a priest, but grief and constant work weakened his health to such an extent that he had to give up theological studies. In 1859 he was attached to the editorial staff of the *Journal of Education* (Montreal), which for two years had been appearing under the direction of the superintendent of Public Instruction, Pierre-Joseph-Olivier Chauveau*.

Murray was still employed in this way when news reached Canada of the disaster at Castelfidardo on 18 Sept. 1860: the little papal army, commanded by Christophe-Louis-Léon Juchault de Lamoricière, had been vanquished by the Piedmontese troops. The ultramontanes of Canada were horror-stricken: "Piedmont, with unspeakable audacity," Cyrille Boucher wrote in *L'Ordre* (Montreal) on 5 October, "has invaded the Papal States, against all human and divine rights." The editor in chief of the *Courrier du Canada* (Quebec), the French legitimist Auguste-Eugène Aubry, prophesied in his journal on 5 Nov. 1860 that "Italian unity" having "never existed," "never will exist."

It was to oppose the progress of King Victor Emmanuel II's "sacrilegious usurpation" that the Papal Zouaves had come into being in March 1860, during a secret interview between the Belgian Redemptorist Victor-Auguste Dechamps, the French general Juchault de Lamoricière, and Bishop Xavier de Mérode, the Belgian minister of the papal arms. From the Catholic countries young men flocked to Rome, eager to place their valour at the service of Pius IX. *L'Ordre* of 13 Feb. 1861 informed its readers that the name of the first French Canadian to "enlist as a Zouave in the papal troops" was Benjamin Testard* de Montigny, "Montreal lawyer, former student of Université Laval."

Hugh Murray wrote at that time to his uncle Bishop Horan, who took the place of his father, to ask permission to follow Montigny's example. It was immediately granted. On 31 July 1861, having arrived at Rome, he donned the uniform of a Papal Zouave. On 21 Nov. 1866 he was appointed sergeant second class. At Mentana (Italy), in the victory of French and papal troops over the Garibaldians on 3 Nov. 1867, Murray truly distinguished himself by his courage and was one of 57 wounded whom, in addition to 24 dead, the papal column counted after the action. He was mentioned in regimental dispatches, soon received the cross of knight of the Order of Pius IX, and was promoted second lieutenant on 4 April 1868. The Canadian Zouaves presented him with a sword, bearing an inscription on its blade: "To Second-Lieutenant Murray, knight of the Order of Pius IX, first Canadian officer, his compatriots."

Back in Canada, Murray, after recovering from a serious operation, offered his services to the Veuillot of American journalism, James Alphonsus McMaster, owner and editor in chief of the *New York Freeman's Journal*. But it was not long before Murray the journalist abandoned the writing-desk to put on his Zouave's uniform again. His royal comrade in the Papal Zouaves, Don Alfonso de Bourbon, had offered his sword to his brother Don Carlos, who had proclaimed himself king of Spain as Charles VII but who had to win his throne away from a prince of Piedmont, Amadeo I, the choice of the Cortès. Since the fight was once more, in a way, against Piedmont, Hugh Murray hastened to Spain during the summer of 1873, and there, having soon obtained the rank of captain, he was second in command of a force of 400 Spanish, Dutch, and Belgian volunteers.

The Carlist Zouaves waged war for two years against the liberal troops of Amadeo of Savoy, then of Alfonso XII, distinguishing themselves in many engagements which caused them to be particularly dreaded. It was during one of them, in February 1874, that Murray met a glorious death, either during the siege of Manresa or under the walls of Bilbao.

With him disappeared "the perfect type of Papal Zouave." His generous commitment and courage in the service of the papacy must be praised unreservedly, but his political perspicacity, it must be admitted, was not equal to his warlike ardour. Indeed, Murray never understood the complexity of the Italian national problem; in this respect he was like his comrades, and also like the ultramontanes, whether European or American.

PHILIPPE SYLVAIN

L'Opinion publique (Montréal), 19 mars, 9 avril 1874. *Annuaire de l'université Laval pour l'année académique 1856–1857* (Québec, 1856); *1858–1859* (Québec, 1858). *Catalogue des officiers et des élèves du séminaire de Québec, 1851–1852* (Québec, 1852); *1852–1853* (1853); *1853–1854* (1854); *1854–1855* (1855); *1855–1859* (1856). Georges Cerbelaud-Salagnac, *Les zouaves pontificaux* (Paris, 1963). Paolo Dalla Torre, *L'anno di Mentana: Contributo ad una storia dello Stato pontificio nel 1867* (Milan, 1968), 314. G.-A. Drolet, *Zouaviana: étape de trente ans, 1868–1898* ... (2ᵉ éd., Montréal, 1898). Édouard Lefebvre de Bellefeuille, *Le Canada et les zouaves pontificaux: mémoire sur l'origine, l'enrôlement et l'expédition du contingent canadien à Rome, pendant l'année 1868* ... (Montréal, 1868). Roberto di Nolli, *Mentana* (Rome, 1865). Elio Lodolini, "I volontari del Canadà nell'esercito pontificio (1868–1870)," *Rassegna storica del Risorgimento* (Rome), LVI (1969), 641–87.

N

NEEDHAM, WILLIAM HAYDEN, lawyer and politician; b. 9 Dec. 1810 at Fredericton, N.B., son of Mark D. Needham and his wife, a Miss Fraser of Inverness, Scotland; d. 29 Sept. 1874 at Woodstock, N.B.

William Hayden Needham's father was widely known in Fredericton, both as a participant in municipal politics and as the city's quaint old legislative librarian. William was educated at the Fredericton grammar school and at King's College (University of New Brunswick), though he did not receive a degree. Instead, he turned to law and studied under George Frederick Street*. On 8 May 1832 Needham was admitted attorney and in 1834 he was called to the bar of New Brunswick. He practised in Woodstock, Fredericton, and for ten years in Saint John. On 20 Oct. 1835 in Saint John he married Mary Ann Gale. He settled permanently in Fredericton about 1853. Needham had a province-wide reputation as a lawyer of "much ability" and was, at one time, vice-president of the New Brunswick Bar Association.

Needham was rarely out of politics during his adult years. As a student in 1830 he had taken to the hustings in opposition to his Conservative patron, George Frederick Street; for this activity he was evicted from Street's law office. While in Saint John he struggled for the reform of the city charter. "Almost unaided he fought his measure through, against all the old toryism of the day in and out of Council." By 1850 "Billy" Needham was a popular hero, and in the election of that year, he and five other reformers were returned to the assembly for the Saint John district. A government reorganization in 1851 created a crisis among these reformers. Robert Duncan Wilmot* and John Hamilton Gray* accepted appointments to Sir Edmund Head*'s council. Needham, Samuel Leonard Tilley*, William Johnstone Ritchie*, and Charles Simonds* were indignant, and stated their determination to resign should Wilmot be returned to the house in the election necessitated by his becoming surveyor general. Wilmot's success brought immediate resignations from Tilley, Ritchie, and Simonds, but Needham decided not to follow their lead and remained in the assembly until 1854. The reform press of the time vilified him as a man without principles – a charge that has clung to him ever since.

The government of Edward Barron CHANDLER apparently rewarded Needham by appointing him, in 1853, to the well-paid post of secretary of the law commission which was drafting revised statutes for the province. His contribution to the consolidation and revision of the statutes was considerable. According to the commissioners, Needham was "most able and valuable. ... His assistance in the art of condensing has materially tended to the accomplishment of so much of our labours."

After his move to Fredericton, Needham entered municipal politics and was six times elected mayor between 1856 and 1868. He re-entered provincial politics in 1865 when he became convinced that confederation was a menace. A most effective speaker, he used colour, wit, and ridicule to destroy the arguments of the confederates – especially their idea that New Brunswick manufacturers could exploit the Canadian market. The move towards confederation meant defeat for Needham in 1866, but he was soon elected mayor of Fredericton again. On 19 May 1869 he was successful in a provincial by-election, but he was defeated in the general elections of 1870 and 1874. Few men, he often said, have "been so often beaten at the polls." On 2 April 1873 he was appointed queen's counsel.

William Needham deserves better treatment than he has received from the 19th-century liberal historians George Edward Fenety* and James Hannay*. His contributions to municipal government and his work for the law commissioners were of major significance. Perhaps most important, however, was his continuing struggle to advance the public school system of New Brunswick. "Educate your people and make them free," he cried in the assembly, "educate the people and make them happy; educate the people and keep them from crime and misery." For this cause he strove until his death. His interests did not stop with the public school system. He also gave continuing support to King's College as a public institution, and throughout the 1840s and 1850s the college needed friends. It had become the despised symbol of the privileged in the eyes of anti-establishment reformers such as Albert James Smith*. In 1854 Smith spearheaded a drive to abolish the institution and the outcome was still uncertain when Needham delivered his stirring "speech that saved the college," concluding that "the institution owed its want of success in a great measure to the hostile measures brought forward in the House year after year instead of assisting it by the proper application of their united individual intellect."

The ordinary people, with whom Needham sympathized, were never forgotten. In his last major speech in the assembly, he spoke in opposition to the practice of imprisonment for debt in a "speech which for earnestness, pathos and masterly eloquence has seldom if ever, been surpassed on the floor of the legislature."

Needham was typical of the politicians of the time who were unable to accept the partisanship of the party system that was evolving during his career. He chose his sides and causes for personal rather than party reasons. This attitude guaranteed him enemies, but even they regarded William Needham as a man of "wonderful versatility and ability."

C. M. WALLACE

N.B. Museum, Marriage register B, 1828–38. Fenety, *Political notes and observations*; "Political notes," *Progress* (Saint John, N.B.), 1894 (collected in a scrapbook in N.B. Museum and PAC). *Daily Telegraph* (Saint John, N.B.), 30 Sept. 1874. *Morning Freeman* (Saint John, N.B.), 1, 6 Oct. 1874. *New Brunswick Reporter* (Fredericton), 30 Sept. 1874. *Saint John Daily News*, 30 Sept. 1874. *Can. parl. comp., 1869.*

James Hannay, *History of New Brunswick*, II; *The life and times of Sir Leonard Tilley: being a political history of New Brunswick for the past seventy years* (Saint John, N.B., 1897). Lawrence, *Judges of New Brunswick* (Stockton), 502. K. F. C. MacNaughton, *The development of the theory and practice of education in New Brunswick, 1784–1904: a study in historical background*, ed. with intro. A. G. Bailey (University of New Brunswick Hist. Studies, I, Fredericton, 1947).

NELSON, ROBERT, doctor, member of the assembly, *Patriote*; b. January 1794 in Montreal, son of William Nelson and Jane Dies; d. 1 March 1873 at Gifford, Staten Island, N.Y.

William Nelson, the son of a commissary in the Royal Navy, and originally from Nesham, Yorkshire, was a teacher in New York, where he married Jane Dies, whose father owned large estates on the Hudson River. After the American Revolution (during which he was probably an officer in the

Royal Navy), he moved to Montreal. It was there that his younger son Robert was born.

Robert Nelson studied medicine, first at Montreal under the famous Dr Daniel Arnoldi*, then at Harvard University. On 15 April 1814 he received authorization to practise. War was at its height; the young doctor enlisted in the army and was immediately appointed surgeon in ordinary to the 7th Battalion, called Deschambault's force (after Colonel Louis-Joseph Fleury* Deschambault). Later, in 1824, with these wartime comrades, he was to sign a petition to Lord Dalhousie [Ramsay*], to obtain land that the veterans had been promised. On 26 July 1814 he was transferred to the corps of Indian braves, where an epidemic of what was apparently lithiasis was raging. Nelson retained his affection for the Indians after the hostilities were over. At least until 1826 he worked on a voluntary basis among the 3,000 inhabitants of the reserves at Caughnawaga, Lac-des-Deux-Montagnes (Oka), Saint-Régis, and Saint-François. Twice, in 1821 and at the time of a syphilis epidemic in 1826, he asked Lord Dalhousie, in vain, to appoint him surgeon to the Indians. He also spent some of his time assembling material to be used for a history of the aborigines of America, which he seems never to have completed.

Having gone to live at Montreal, the young doctor rapidly acquired an enormous clientele and a more than creditable reputation. Two of his students were Luc-Hyacinthe MASSON and Charles-Christophe MALHIOT. Nelson was said to be the man for difficult cases, for major operations. He is thought to have been the first man in the country to operate for stones (lithotritis). According to Laurent-Olivier David*, while on a journey in France he interrupted a surgeon who was "perplexed and in danger of following the wrong course," and completed a delicate operation "to the applause of the doctors and students present." In 1827 his brother Wolfred* brought him into politics. He was elected with Louis-Joseph PAPINEAU in Montreal West. In the house he did not particularly attract attention, and, judging that his political duties did not fit in with his profession, he resigned in 1830. Two years later, on the outbreak of the cholera epidemic, he gave his services especially to the immigrants at Pointe-Saint-Charles. In 1834, for reasons that have remained obscure, he returned to politics, representing Montreal West in the assembly. He joined with the members of the *Patriote* party who refused to vote supplies to the government so long as the latter did not meet their chief requests for reforms. Although Nelson was one of the most vehement speakers in the *Patriote* assemblies of the counties and one of the most active members of the Comité Central et Permanent du district de Montréal, he did not take part in the 1837 insurrection. He was none the less arrested on 24 November as a suspect, undoubtedly because of his close association with his brother Wolfred, who was present at the battle of Saint-Denis. The next day, however, he was released because of irregularities in the warrant for his arrest. He was indignant and furious. Louis-Joseph-Amédée Papineau*, in his diary, stated that Nelson wrote on the wall of his cell: "The English government will remember Robt. Nelson." It was in this state of mind that he went to the United States at the end of 1837.

Among the other leaders who succeeded in evading the English army were L.-J. Papineau, Edmund Bailey O'CALLAGHAN, the parish priest Étienne Chartier*, Édouard-Étienne Rodier*, Édouard-Élisée MALHIOT, Cyrille-Hector-Octave Côté*, Thomas Bouthillier*, Joseph-François Davignon, and Julien Gagnon. They all arranged to meet on 2 Jan. 1838 at Middlebury, Vermont, to discuss the possibility of another insurrection. The failure of 1837 had profoundly changed the alignments in the revolutionaries' camp. The radicals had taken over the leadership of the movement from the moderates. Among the radicals two tendencies appeared. The first favoured direct and immediate action: the setting up of a provisional government, the proclamation of a republic of Lower Canada, and the invasion of Lower Canada. Robert Nelson, supported by a group including Dr Côté and Julien Gagnon, represented this tendency. Other *Patriotes*, centring around Papineau, were opposed to any precipitate action without having previously obtained the assurance of formal aid from the government of the United States and the border states. The first group prevailed, and Nelson was elected general of the army and president of the future Canadian republic.

The extreme haste and enthusiasm of Nelson and his followers are no doubt to be explained by their revolutionary fervour and their indignation over recent events in Lower Canada. To these must probably be added their belief that large sectors of the American population would spontaneously support them, and that many would march by their side. This belief is understandable. The northwestern states had numerous reformers who were demanding the abolition of slavery and of imprisonment for debts, the emancipation of women, and the extension of liberty to oppressed peoples. Many of these reformers, imbued with the revolutionary excitement of 1776, were sympathetic to the cause of the Canadian political refugees. Moreover, thousands of American unemployed, who considered the Bank of England

responsible for the 1837 recession, were perhaps tempted to take advantage of an opportunity to avenge themselves on Great Britain. At least the *Patriotes* might believe they would be.

It was with these possibilities in mind that Nelson and his chief lieutenant, Dr Côté, prepared a first invasion for 28 Feb. 1838. After having "obtained" 250 rifles from the Elizabethtown arsenal, Nelson, at the head of 300 to 400 *Patriotes*, invaded Canada from Alburg, Vermont. As soon as it had cleared the border, the band distributed copies of a declaration of independence. The latter, drawn from the American Declaration of Independence, first enumerated the crimes that Great Britain had committed against Lower Canada, then set forth the right to overthrow the government. There followed 18 declarations, not untinged with propaganda, on abolition of the union of church and state, seigneurial tenure, and imprisonment for debts, the nationalization of the clergy reserves, and so on. The invasion proved to be a total failure. Scarcely had the *Patriotes* reached Canadian territory when they were attacked and pushed back into the United States. Nelson and others were put in prison for having infringed the American neutrality law. However, they were rapidly acquitted by a jury sympathetic to their cause.

Nelson and his friends realized that even if this failure could be imputed to a lack of preparation and organization, their own lack of discretion was also largely to blame. Hence the formation of a secret society, known as the Frères-Chasseurs. The decision to set this up was also taken with the object of getting round the new neutrality law passed by Congress in March 1838 (but requested two months earlier by the president), a law much more rigorous than the previous one.

The secret society was constituted on the model of an army. At the head of the association was the *Grand Aigle*, a sort of major-general; under his orders were *Aigles* of various districts, who were each to organize a company. To do this they chose two *Castors* – captains, as it were – who in their turn undertook to assume command over five corporals, commonly called *Raquettes*. The latter each had under their orders nine men, and these formed the corps of Chasseurs proper. The funds necessary for financing the movement were collected from among sympathizers in Lower Canada and the United States.

Nelson entrusted the recruiting to dynamic comrades such as John McDonell, Célestin Beausoleil, and Édouard-Élisée Malhiot, who travelled through Lower Canada setting up lodges and promising arms and ammunition for the great day of deliverance. The wildest and most

Nelson

improbable reports circulated as to the number of Frères-Chasseurs. Sir John Colborne* spoke of several tens of thousands; others commented that each parish in Lower Canada had its lodge.

Whatever the number of Frères-Chasseurs might have been, this army was hardly a disciplined one. Nelson's leadership was not very firm. Aloof, doctrinaire, uncompromising in his ideas, he did not have the unconditional support of those of his compatriots who were the most devoted to the cause. Édouard-Élisée Malhiot, among others, would not soon forget the fate in store for Papineau. Also, Nelson did not manage to eliminate among his associates the conflicts of personality, the personal rivalries, the ambitions that would forever be obstacles to effective action. Anarchy often prevailed in this association, where each member wanted to achieve the most lofty ends.

After long discussions and numerous compromises, Nelson succeeded in getting the date of the invasion and uprising fixed for 3 Nov. 1838. On the third, according to orders, the *Patriotes* began to assemble in the parishes along the border, Napierville, Lacolle, and Châteauguay, where arms and reinforcements were to reach them from the United States. Impatient, and without necessarily consulting Nelson, groups of *Patriotes* tried isolated actions. At Beauharnois some easily occupied the seigneury of Edward Ellice* [*see* D. A. MacDonell] and others seized the steamship *Henry Brougham*, with the intention of converting it into a war vessel.

An over-all strategy had, however, been worked out by Nelson and his principal lieutenants. It would seem that after launching an offensive on the American border, by prearrangement with the force of William Lyon Mackenzie*, the *Patriotes* were to start simultaneous attacks against Beauharnois, Châteauguay, Laprairie, Saint-Jean, Chambly, Boucherville, and Sorel. Nelson himself, at the head of 800 men, was to make use of the Richelieu valley, capture Saint-Jean, and proceed towards Montreal. Montreal, Trois-Rivières, and Quebec were then to be attacked successively. It was hoped that meanwhile the Chasseurs of these towns would revolt from within.

This fine plan was not put into effect. At Montreal the authorities reacted quickly, and arrested several ringleaders. A number of Chasseurs, seeing that the promised arms did not arrive, attacked the Indians of Caughnawaga, with the object of seizing their weapons and ammunition. This was unlucky for them, since many of them were taken prisoner. Meanwhile confusion reigned at Napierville, where Nelson had arrived in the night of 3 or 4 November, not at the head of a band of 800 men but with two French officers: P. Touvrey

and Charles Hindenlang*. There he found about 3,000 poorly armed men. And what was more, the American schooner that was coming to bring them arms and ammunition had been intercepted by Canadian volunteers. On the 5th, a detachment of about 400 *Patriotes* set off for Rouse's Point, to get arms and ammunition that had been hidden there. The American authorities had confiscated them. When they returned, they were thrashed by militiamen.

The operation was turning into a complete fiasco. Nelson, realizing the danger that these incidents represented, and the threat constituted by the movements of regular troops under Colborne's command, decided to direct his men towards Odelltown. It certainly seems that at this moment he contemplated flight. The *Patriotes* left Napierville on the morning of the 8th and arrived at Lacolle at the end of the afternoon. The story goes that Nelson tried to flee during the night, but that he was captured when he was preparing to get across the border and brought back bound hand and foot. He succeeded in convincing the discontented that he had set out on a tour of inspection. On 9 and 10 November the *Patriotes* attacked the militiamen at Odelltown. During the decisive engagement that followed the arrival of reinforcements for the militia, the Chasseurs lost 50 men; they then made their way back to the United States. Nelson had fled before the end of the fight.

It is harder to keep track of Nelson after these events. We know however that towards the end of 1838 he called Côté, Gagnon, Malhiot, Ludger Duvernay*, and Robert-Shore-Milnes Bouchette together at Swanton, Vermont. Faced with repression in Lower Canada, the firm opposition of the American government, and, within the last little while, of a large section of the American border population, the *Patriote* leaders had planned to modify their tactics. They decided to exploit or even provoke border incidents between the United States and Great Britain. They hoped to be able to achieve their ends during a conflict between the two countries. To no avail. The Aroostook "war," and the incident in which Alexander McLeod was implicated, gave them a faint hope, but London and Washington, eager for peace, settled their differences in 1842 by the Webster-Ashburton treaty.

Ruined, saddled with debts, Nelson decided to go to try his luck in California, where the goldrush was at its height: in a few weeks he acquired a large fortune. However, he lost it through the dishonesty of an agent to whom he had entrusted it. Refusing to return to Canada, where he had been pardoned, he practised his profession in the west until 1863, when he took up residence in New York, in partnership with his son, Eugène (the name of Nelson's wife is not known); Eugène, born on 28 March 1837, had just finished his medical studies in London. In 1866 Robert Nelson published, in New York, *Asiatic cholera: its origin and spread in Asia, Africa, and Europe, introduced into America through Canada; remote and proximate causes, symptoms and pathology, and the various modes of treatment analysed*. He also translated a medical text and several articles of interest to students of medicine.

According to David, "Robert Nelson was swarthy, of medium height, but vigorous; he had a piercing eye, a keen, searching glance, a severe cast of features. He was a man of few words; his speeches were concise but energetic, he went straight to the point, openly and without mincing matters. He had a forceful, bold, original, adventurous and independent nature, and was headstrong in his opinions and feelings." A portrait dating from the early 1870s shows him wearing a long beard.

RICHARD CHABOT, JACQUES MONET, and YVES ROBY

[The most important genealogical material on Nelson and information about his early career as a doctor and member of the assembly are found in: PAC, MG 30, D62 (Audet papers), 23; RG 8, I, A1, 507, pp.48, 71–72; I, D7 1694, pp.3–4; RG 10, A5a, 18, 19. *La Minerve* (Montréal), 10 avril 1873. Audet, *Les députés de Montréal*, 233–34. L.-O. David, *Biographies et portraits* (Montréal, 1876); *Patriotes*. Wolfred Nelson, *Wolfred Nelson et son temps* (Montréal, 1946). *L'Union médicale du Canada* (Montréal), II (1873), 188 (obituary). J.M.]

[Information on the events of 1838, the personal rivalries and intrigues that were a continual obstacle to coordinated and effective action, was drawn from ANQ, Collection Ludger Duvernay; the *Canadian Antiquarian and Numismatic Journal* (1908–1910); and the "Inventaire des documents relatifs aux événements de 1837 et 1838, conservés aux archives de la province de Québec," APQ *Rapport, 1925–26*, 179ff. Fernand Ouellet's article, "Papineau dans la révolution de 1837–1838," CHA *Report, 1957–58*, 13–34, also contains material.

Details concerning the period from Nelson's arrest in 1837 until his departure for the United States are found especially in Louis-Joseph-Amédée Papineau's journal, "Journal d'un Fils de la liberté, 1837–1840." The original is in the BNQ and there is a manuscript copy in the ANQ.

Accurate information on the establishing of the Frères-Chasseurs by Nelson is found in: A. B. Corey, *The crisis of 1830–1842 in Canadian-American relations* (New Haven, 1941). O. A. Kinchen, *The rise and fall of the Patriots Hunters* (New York, [1956]). Ivahoë Caron, "Une société secrète dans le Bas-Canada en 1838: l'Association des Frères Chasseurs," *RSCT*, 3rd ser., XX (1926), sect.I, 17–34. Victor Morin, "La « république canadienne » de 1838," *RHAF*, II (1948–49), 483–512; "Clubs et sociétés notoires d'autrefois," *Cahiers des Dix*, XV (1950), 199–203.

The Perrault papers in the State Historical Society of Wisconsin contain material on the invasion of 3 November, as do the following: *Report of the state trials before a general court martial held at Montreal in 1838–9: exhibiting a complete history of the late rebellion in Lower Canada* (2v., Montreal, 1839). L.-N. Carrier, *Les événements de 1837–1838* (Québec, 1877), 111–16. Fauteux, *Patriotes*, 65–74.

Carrier's study and the article by Victor Morin on the "republique canadienne" should be consulted also for the circumstances surrounding Nelson's flight. R.C. and Y.R.]

NICOLLS, JASPER HUME, Anglican clergyman and educator; b. 17 Oct. 1818 on the island of Guernsey, son of General Gustavus Nicolls and Heriot Frances Thomson; d. at Lennoxville, Que., 8 Aug. 1877.

Jasper Hume Nicolls spent a good deal of his early life in British North America where his father was Commanding Royal Engineer successively in Halifax and Quebec. He was educated at Oriel College, Oxford (BA 1840), and was made a fellow of Queen's College, Oxford, in 1843. He was ordained deacon in 1844 and priest in 1845. In 1845 Nicolls returned to Canada to become the first principal of Bishop's College, Lennoxville, incorporated in 1843 and about to open. Bishop George Jehoshaphat Mountain*, the president of Bishop's and Nicolls' uncle by marriage, was responsible for Nicolls' appointment, and from 1845 until Mountain's death in 1863, Nicolls had the benefit of his counsel and support.

For 32 years Nicolls successfully directed Bishop's as a liberal arts college and Anglican divinity school. He saw Bishop's as an institution that would provide clergy for the Church of England in Canada and would offer to the country at large a sound and liberal education upon reasonable terms. The institution was to be under Anglican control but open to students of all denominations. In his convocation address at Bishop's in 1860 Nicolls asserted, "We are not ashamed of being what is termed denominational; but we open our doors to all; we have no test on admission; we have no test in granting degrees." He developed a curriculum similar to that in other Anglican colleges in Canada, which consisted of instruction mainly in the classics, mathematics, and divinity.

Influenced by the Tractarian movement during his Oxford career, Nicolls remained throughout his life a high churchman. He showed his Tractarian sympathies in 1845 when William George

547

Niles

Ward, an associate of John Henry Newman, was tried by the Oxford University convocation for making an extreme Tractarian statement and was degraded from his degrees. Nicolls, a member of convocation, supported Ward. Nicolls' churchmanship helps to explain his relations with other Church of England bishops in Canada. He got on well with Francis Fulford*, the bishop of Montreal, who was a high churchman, and badly with Fulford's successor, Ashton Oxenden*, who was sympathetic to the Anglican evangelicals. Politically Nicolls was a Conservative; he strongly favoured English influences in Canada and was much opposed to American ideas and institutions. Like Bishop Mountain, Nicolls was prepared to work with either Conservative or Reform politicians provided they were willing to advance the interests of Bishop's College. Thus he enlisted the good offices of adherents of the Liberal-Conservative party such as Alexander Tilloch Galt* and Timothy Lee TERRILL, the MLA for Stanstead, but also Reformers such as Thomas Cushing AYLWIN and Antoine-Aimé Dorion*. In 1852 Nicolls made strong representations to Lord Elgin [Bruce*] and the Reformist administration of Francis Hincks* and Augustin-Norbert Morin* in his successful effort to secure a royal charter for Bishop's.

Nicolls was a strong believer in the principle that Christian thought should occupy a central position in education at all levels. In his convocation address at Bishop's in 1860, he said, "Let it be the University's privilege to demonstrate that – while man discovers, he discovers what God has made, what *God gives* him to understand. Universities let us remember are Christian Institutions." Nicolls was prepared to accept state supervision of secondary schools, but thought that the curriculum should contain religious instruction of a non-sectarian type.

Jasper Hume Nicolls was a man of fine character: sincere, straightforward, witty, with a fine sense of humour and great personal charm. In 1847 he had married his first cousin, Harriet Mary, daughter of Bishop Mountain; they had two sons and one daughter.

D. C. MASTERS

J. H. Nicolls, *An address delivered before the convocation of Bishop's College, Lennoxville, June 27, 1860* (Sherbrooke, Que., 1860); *An address to the teachers of academies in the district of Bedford . . . on the occasion of the formation of a teacher's association, October 29, 1858* (Burlington, Vt., 1859); *The end and object of education, a lecture* (Montreal, 1857); J. H. Nicolls and John Carry, *Essay on the subject of the restoration of the diaconate . . .* (Montreal, 1863).

Bassett Memorial Library, Bishop's University (Lennoxville, Que.), Nicolls papers. *Clerical guide and churchman's directory, an annual register for the clergy and laity of the Anglican Church in British North America, 1876*, ed. C. V. F. Bliss (Ottawa, 1876). D. C. Masters, *Bishop's University, the first hundred years* (Toronto, 1950), 3–63; *Protestant church colleges in Canada; a history* (Studies in the History of Higher Education in Canada, 4, Toronto, 1966), 4–5, 8, 15, 65–66, 211; "Bishop's University and the ecclesiastical controversies of the nineteenth century (1845–1878)," CHA, *Report, 1951*, 36–42; "The Nicolls papers; a study in Anglican Toryism," CHA, *Report, 1945*, 42–48.

NILES, WILLIAM E., farmer, businessman, magistrate, militia officer, and politician; b. 1799, Coeymans, New York, son of Henry Niles and Hannah Hicks; d. 17 Aug. 1873, London, Ont.

William E. Niles apparently first came to Upper Canada as a child with his brother Stephen to live with an uncle, Willet Casey, in Adolphustown Township. In 1820, Niles, then living at Detroit, was commissioned by Governor Lewis Cass of Michigan to purchase lumber from William Putnam of Putnamville, Middlesex County, Upper Canada. The following year he settled in Upper Canada near the present site of Nilestown, established a farm, erected a sawmill, and later operated a store. His sawmill was to supply "a large proportion of the lumber of which early London was built."

Throughout his life Niles was "a staunch and consistent Reformer." He was chairman on 8 Dec. 1837 of a meeting of leading Reformers in the London area, including John TALBOT, Charles Latimer, William Putnam, and Edward Allen Talbot*, but his political career survived the aftermath of the rebellion. He served on the District of London (later the County of Middlesex) Council from 1842 until 1854, and was warden, 1847–54. He was appointed justice of the peace in 1849 and was made a lieutenant-colonel in the militia in 1851. Niles represented East Middlesex in the Legislative Assembly from 1854 to 1857, elected as a moderate Reformer in support of Francis Hincks*. He upheld the government, which became progressively more conservative, until April 1856 when he crossed over to the opposition. He was not a candidate in 1857. Elected one of the delegates from Middlesex County to the Reform convention of November 1859, he served as chairman of the committee on procedure.

Niles was a strong advocate of the construction of the Great Western Railway and, while warden, was one of its directors. He served as director of the East Middlesex Agricultural Society, as vice-president of the Provincial Agricultural Association, and, in 1866, as trustee of the short-lived Nilestown Oil Company. A landowner in London and Dorchester Township and a contractor, he was also an active promoter of the Agricultural Mutual Assurance Association of Canada (formerly County of Middlesex Mutual Fire Insurance Company), later becoming inspector of agencies with it and with the Isolated Risk Fire Insurance Company of Canada.

In 1821 Niles married Gertrude Dykert (Daggart), also a native of the United States, and sister-in-law of William Putnam, and they had four children, one of whom Annie Maria, married Ellis Walton HYMAN. Raised as a Quaker, William Niles became a Presbyterian and later an Anglican. He was a prominent freemason.

DANIEL J. BROCK

Globe (Toronto), 10 Nov. 1859. *London Advertiser*, 18 Aug. 1873. *London Free Press*, 19 Aug. 1873. *J. of Education for Ont.*, XXVI (October 1873), 157. *Hudson-Mohawk genealogical and family memoirs, a record of achievements of the people of the Hudson and Mohawk valleys in New York State . . .*, ed. Cuyler Reynolds (4v., New York, 1911), I, 400–2. *Pioneer life on the Bay of Quinte including genealogies of old families and biographical sketches of representative citizens* (Toronto, n.d.), 594–99. *History of the county of Middlesex*, 74–79, 90, 115, 155, 283, 322–23, 332, 488. Fred Landon, "London and its vicinity, 1837–38," *Ont. Hist.*, XXIV (1927), 410–38.

NISBET, JAMES, first Presbyterian missionary to the Indians in the northwest, founder of the settlement at Prince Albert, Sask.; b. 8 Sept. 1823 in the parish of Gorbals, Glasgow, Scotland; d. 30 Sept. 1874 at Kildonan, Man.

James Nisbet was the son of Thomas Nisbet, a master shipbuilder of Rutherglen on the Clyde, who brought his family to Canada West in 1844 and settled at Oakville on the shore of Lake Ontario. James had served an apprenticeship as carpenter in Glasgow and he worked at this trade for a short time after coming to Canada. He then took the four-year course in theology at Knox College, Toronto, graduating in 1849. He was employed as agent and missionary of the Sabbath School Society of Montreal until January 1850 when he was ordained and inducted as pastor of the Oakville congregation. While at Oakville he did missionary work in winter in distant townships such as St Vincent, Artemesia, and Nottawasaga.

In 1862 Nisbet was selected by the Foreign Mission Committee of the Canada Presbyterian Church to assist the Reverend John Black* at the Red River Mission, and to make inquiries about where and how a mission might be established among the Indians in the Hudson's Bay Company territory. Nisbet reached Kildonan in July 1862 and readily adapted himself to his new work. In

1864 he married Mary, daughter of Robert MacBeth of Kildonan, a member of the Council of Assiniboia; they had four children.

In October 1862 Nisbet sent the Foreign Mission Committee an estimate of the cost of a mission to the Crees at Berens River on the east shore of Lake Winnipeg. Next he suggested the possibility of missions at the Saskatchewan mines near Fort Edmonton and in the Mackenzie River district. In June 1863 he made a personal appeal at the synod meeting in Hamilton but he could not persuade the delegates to incur new liabilities for an Indian mission. Black shared Nisbet's disappointment and he proposed to the synods of 1864 and 1865 that the church consider a mission to the Crees in the North Saskatchewan River valley. Finally the synod agreed that Nisbet be designated to the work of a Saskatchewan mission to be opened in 1866.

Nisbet wanted the mission to be "the itinerant kind" and in addition to an interpreter who would accompany him to different bands he needed a trustworthy person to take charge of the mission station. An ordained man was not available but Nisbet obtained the assistance of two first-rate interpreters. George Flett, brother-in-law of Mrs Black (Henrietta Ross), was to come from Fort Edmonton to Fort Carlton to help Nisbet find a site. Part Cree and interested in the welfare of the Indians, Flett promised to join the mission when his term of service with the HBC ended. John McKay, Mrs Nisbet's brother-in-law, was to act as guide and to supervise the erection of buildings. Like Flett he was part Cree, and he was also a noted buffalo hunter. Two hired men, one of them a brother of Mrs Nisbet, were to help with the work for a year.

The mission party set out from Kildonan by ox-cart on 6 and 7 June and 40 days later reached Fort Carlton on the North Saskatchewan River. There they learned that Flett had not been able to find a band of Crees willing to receive the mission. However, Flett had a farm on the river flats about 60 miles below Fort Carlton and he advised Nisbet to settle there. After inspecting the site Nisbet took his party to the place, which he named Prince Albert. The date of their arrival was 26 July 1866.

The Crees at Prince Albert did not want a mission there because they feared that settlers would come later to take their land and buffalo. Nisbet was patient and tactful, however, and under Flett's guidance he overcame the Indians' reluctance. Gifts of food and clothing completed the work of reconciliation. Land was cleared, hay was gathered for wintering the cattle, and log buildings were erected. In September Nisbet and Flett travelled upstream to hold services at the

HBC forts and the Cree camps between Fort Carlton and Fort Edmonton. This was to be the only "itinerating" that Nisbet could manage. Flett did not stay long at Prince Albert and McKay could not be spared from other work. Unfortunately Nisbet did not acquire the proficiency he needed for preaching in Cree.

Nisbet believed that permanent results could best be obtained by gathering the children in a school to be taught "the ordinary branches of a common and Christian education," and to be trained as farmers and skilled tradesmen. The expense of keeping the children in school would not be great once the farming operations were fully established. Indian families were to be encouraged to settle near the mission. In addition to a school for the Indian children Nisbet wanted a school for the children of HBC and mission employees, and he succeeded in getting Adam McBeth, an experienced teacher from Red River, to open the English school in 1867. Nisbet thought that the Indian children should be taught in Cree and only those showing aptitude for learning the language should be taught English. In the summer of 1866 Nisbet himself had tried to teach the syllabic characters to Cree children and he had McKay prepare a Cree reader. Before long, however, he noticed that the Indian children picked up English rapidly and he abandoned the plan of using Cree as a language of instruction. In 1871–72, 26 children were attending the school, but only eight were Indian boarders.

Church services were held in both Cree and English until 1871–72 when English was used exclusively in the morning and English and Cree in the afternoon. In 1872 the religious services were moved from the missionary's house to a church with seating for 120 persons.

The farm played an important role in the life of the mission. It was intended to serve as an example to the Indians and a source of supply for the mission and other stations to be established nearby. Wheat and barley were harvested in 1867 and in 1868 a crop of 600 bushels of wheat was produced from 17 bushels sown. By 1871, 40 acres were in crop and a threshing machine and small iron grist-mill were in use. In "starvation years," as Nisbet dryly reported, the produce from the farm was a greater attraction to wandering bands than the religious instruction available at the mission.

Nisbet continued to plead for the assistance of a second missionary but he did not get one until 1872. In that year also his work was unfairly attacked. On 2 Feb. 1872 the *Western Advertiser* of Winnipeg carried an article charging favouritism and mismanagement at the Prince Albert mission. The charges were said to be based on the state-ments of former employees and were serious enough for the Foreign Mission Committee to depute the Reverend William Moore to investigate. He arrived in Prince Albert in September 1872 and found that Nisbet, by his own modest standards, had achieved "a splendid success." However, in Moore's opinion, too much time and energy had been devoted to farming and not enough to evangelism. More teaching should have been done in Cree and more preaching of the Gospel to itinerant bands. Since the farm was no longer needed as a source of supply or for use as a training school he recommended that it be abandoned. The Foreign Mission Committee was already considering changes in the mode of conducting the work and, in full consultation with Nisbet, now decided to close the farming operations.

But this decision was too late to help Nisbet, who had to spend the winter of 1873 at his old home in Oakville. After his return to Prince Albert Mrs Nisbet's health rapidly deteriorated and she was taken east for medical attention. She died at her father's home in Kildonan and Nisbet, worn out by his arduous labours, fell ill and died a few days later.

Nisbet's main achievement was the establishment of a mission base from which evangelical work was carried on as opportunity offered. He was regarded by his contemporaries as "a singularly unselfish and devoted missionary." He did more, perhaps, to pave the way for white settlement in the Saskatchewan district than to prepare the Indians for the arrival of immigrant settlers.

JEAN E. MURRAY

McGill University Archives, James Nisbet, letters, accounts; James Nisbet, diary, Prince Albert, 1868–74; James Nisbet, statement of conditions in Prince Albert, 1875. *The Home and Foreign Record of the Canada Presbyterian Church* (Toronto), III–XIV (1863–75). G. W. D. Abrams, *Prince Albert; the first century, 1866–1966* (Saskatoon, 1966), 2–17. Hugh McKellar, *Presbyterian pioneer missionaries in Manitoba, Saskatchewan, Alberta and British Columbia* (Toronto, 1924), 13–15, 87–91. H. C. Mathews, *Oakville and the sixteen; the history of an Ontario port* (Toronto, 1953), 267–70. *Missionary pathfinders; Presbyterian laborers at home and abroad*, ed. W. S. MacTavish (Toronto, 1907), 83–93. E. H. Oliver, "The Presbyterian Church in Saskatchewan, 1866–1881," *RSCT*, 3rd ser., XXVIII (1934), sect.II, 61–94.

NOAD, JOSEPH, public servant and legislator; b. *c.* 1797 in England; d. 20 Feb. 1873 in Woodstock, Ont.

Nothing is known of Joseph Noad's background or his career before he arrived in Newfoundland. Just out from England, he was appointed surveyor general of Newfoundland on 20 Aug. 1832. Despite the criticism of a Liberal politician, Dr William Carson*, that Noad had no stake in the colony and could only be interested in his salary and fees, he was appointed by Governor John Harvey* in 1842 to the Executive Council. With the introduction of the new constitution the following year he also became an appointed member of the Amalgamated Legislature [see KENT], from which he resigned in 1845. He continued to sit in the Executive Council until the restoration of the older form of representative government in 1848; he was then appointed to the Council, a body that performed both executive and legislative functions by advising the governor and acting as an upper house. On the introduction of responsible government in 1855 Noad, along with other members of the local oligarchy, was forced to resign his government position.

Noad's major projects as surveyor general were probably street plans for Harbour Grace after the fire of 1832 (Noad Street in that town gets its name from him), and for St John's after the conflagration of 1846. In 1847 Governor John Gaspard LE MARCHANT wrote of him that "the zealous and indefatigable manner in which this officer has ever discharged his duties is deserving of the highest praise and encouragement." That summer Noad accompanied Le Marchant on a cruise along the south and west coasts of Newfoundland. His report of the survey stressed the importance to the colony of the west coast, then included in the French Shore, stating that the fertility of the soil and the valuable fisheries made the area desirable for settlement.

Noad was also a director of the Newfoundland Steam Navigation Company, a member of the St George's Society, and a leading figure in the small Congregational church to which he had been admitted in 1833. He was twice married. Two sons of his first marriage, both of whom were educated in England, survived him. On 7 July 1835, in St John's, he married his second wife, Emma Gaden Lilly; they had two daughters and one son. At the time of his forced retirement in 1855 Noad, like most of the other pensioned officials, left Newfoundland. He moved with his family to Woodstock, Upper Canada, where he died a poor man.

ELIZABETH A. WELLS

Congregational Church (St John's), John Jones' journal; register of baptisms. Ontario, Department of Provincial Secretary and Citizenship (Toronto), record of death of Joseph Noad. Oxford County Surrogate Court (Woodstock, Ont.), will of Joseph Noad. PANL, Newfoundland, Dept. of the Colonial Secretary, letter book, August 1830–November 1832, 367; Newfoundland, Governor's office, Dispatches to the Colonial Office, 1824–58, John Gaspard Le Marchant to Sir Henry George Grey, 27 Aug. 1847. PRO, CO 194/114, 73. St David's Presbyterian Church (St John's), Register of interments. Newfoundland, *Blue Books*, 1838, 1842, 1845, 1847, 1848, 1872 (copies in PANL). *The Newfoundland almanack . . . 1849 . . .*, comp. Philip Tocque (St John's, 1849). *Newfoundland Patriot* (St John's), 28 April 1835, 29 Sept. 1840. *Public Ledger* (St John's), 6 Nov. 1840. *Royal Gazette* (St John's), 1 Aug. 1843. *Times and General Commercial Gazette* (St John's), 2 April 1873. Ethel Canfield, "Record of people and personalities of Woodstock," unpublished MS in Woodstock Public Library (Woodstock, Ont.). W. E. Cormack, *Narrative of a journey across the island of Newfoundland in 1822* (St John's, 1856), app., "Remarks on part of the western shore of this island by the surveyor general after personal examination in 1847."

NORTHUP, JEREMIAH, merchant, shipowner, and politician; b. at Falmouth, N.S., in 1816, son of John Northup and Agnes Harvey; m. Emily Cochran on 3 Oct. 1848; d. at Halifax, N.S., 10 April 1879.

Jeremiah Northup began his mercantile career as a clerk in the Halifax firm of Charles R. Fairbanks* and Joseph Allison*. In 1837 he and his younger brother, Joseph, joined their father who operated a small grocery store in Halifax. Joseph Northup had a particular interest in agriculture. After the colony's economy improved about 1853, Jeremiah Northup, acting through the family firm, became involved in shipbuilding in the Maitland area of Hants County. He bought his first shares in ships in 1854 and acquired an interest in at least six more during his lifetime. One of his vessels was the schooner *Emily*, of 334 tons built in 1863; others were the barque *Eva*, 517 tons built in 1869, the barque *Lara*, 948 tons built in 1872, and the *Senator*, 1,474 tons launched in 1878. Unlike Ezra CHURCHILL or Thomas Killam, Northup did not build up a family fleet nor could he be considered a major shipowner of the period. His activities, however, provided connections not only with his fellow Halifax merchants but also with English firms. Thus the type of shipbuilding carried on by Northup maintained an important economic development and supported the general mercantile economy of the province.

Politically a supporter of Joseph HOWE, Jeremiah Northup was elected to the provincial house for Halifax as an anti-confederate in 1867. He broke with the provincial government when he supported the "better terms" arranged by Howe in 1869; he also assisted Howe in the campaign which led to the latter's victory in a federal by-election of that year. On Howe's recommendation

Nugent

Northup was appointed to the Senate in 1870. He did not make a major contribution to the Senate, perhaps because he was becoming increasingly hard of hearing. When he did appear in the chamber, he defended the commercial interests of Halifax and of the Maritimes. He was able to reconcile his political allegiance to the Conservative party and his interest in shipping to support the National Policy in 1878.

After 1870 Northup devoted himself to commercial affairs, particularly to the Ocean Marine Insurance Company, which he had helped establish in 1869. He was a partner in the private company that formed the Merchant's Bank in 1864, joined its board of directors in 1870, and became a vice-president in 1872. The family firm, John Northup and Sons, began to decline after the death of his brother in 1874, and closed at Jeremiah's death in 1879, perhaps because neither brother left children to carry on the business. Jeremiah Northup was reputed, probably with exaggeration, to be one of the richest men in the province, leaving an estate evaluated at $150,000. He ranks as one of the builders of the mercantile economy of Nova Scotia in the 19th century.

K. G. PRYKE

Royal Bank of Canada Archives (Montreal). *Acadian Recorder* (Halifax), 10 April 1879. *Morning Chronicle* (Halifax), 12 April 1879. *Morning Herald* (Halifax), 11 April 1879. *Memorials of the Messrs Northup (father and sons)* (Halifax, 1881). *Directory of N.S. MLAs* (Fergusson), 269. J. V. Duncanson, *Falmouth — a New England township in Nova Scotia, 1760–1965* (Windsor, Ont., 1965), 334–36. G. A. White, *Halifax and its business: historical sketch and description of the city and its institutions* (Halifax, 1876).

NUGENT, JOHN, journalist and U.S. government agent; b. in 1821? in County Galway, Ireland; d. 29 March 1880 in San Leandro, California.

John Nugent's parents brought him to the United States at an early age. In the 1840s he served in Washington as correspondent for the New York *Herald*. At the decade's end he travelled overland to California, and in 1851 became owner-editor of the San Francisco *Herald*. In 1856 he opposed the re-establishment of the Vigilance Committee, a business-supported, extra-legal organization for the preservation of law and order. His failure to support it was an unpopular move which led to his newspaper's collapse. It was a blow from which his career never recovered. He continued in journalism, however, and five years later he was Democratic runner-up in an election for the U.S. Senate. He tried, unsuccessfully, to re-establish the *Herald* in 1868 and, toward the end of the 1870s, worked on his memoirs.

In 1858 President James Buchanan, anxious to determine in what way the recently discovered Fraser River gold-fields affected American interests in the northwest and how Americans were being treated, appointed Nugent, whom he had known in Washington in the 1840s, special agent to New Caledonia (British Columbia). He was to report on the mining operations, assist American citizens, ascertain their number, discover whether they were subject to discrimination, and report what new settlements had been formed in adjacent American territories and what lines of communication existed between them and the British territories to the north. His instructions suggest an interest on the part of the United States government not only in determining whether the rights of American citizens were in need of protection but also in knowing how closely linked to the United States the gold-fields were. Nugent was in British territory from 20 September to 17 November. His first days there revealed no tension between Americans and British. Indeed, many of the restrictions on trade and the movement of personnel up the Fraser, which had concerned Americans and their government, had been removed.

Nugent had, however, a falling-out with Governor James DOUGLAS over the treatment of American citizens in the courts, and in a farewell speech to an audience of Americans in Victoria, he suggested that if the rights of American citizens in the area were ever in jeopardy, the American government would not hesitate to intervene. This provocative utterance reflected Nugent's own interest in the annexation of Vancouver Island and New Caledonia, which he thought would, in the course of time, naturally occur. The British ambassador at Washington reported, however, that the attitude of the American government had been quite correct. Nugent's visit did not have much of an impact on Victoria, and such bitterness as it did arouse was directed at him personally and not at the government he represented.

ALLAN SMITH

Daily Bee (Sacramento, Cal.), 24 Dec. 1884. H. H. Bancroft, *Popular tribunals* (San Francisco, Cal., 1887). Ormsby, *British Columbia*. R. L. Reid, "John Nugent: the impertinent envoy," *BCHQ*, VIII (1944), 53–76.

NUGENT, JOHN VALENTINE, educator, politician, newspaper editor and proprietor, sheriff; b. 1796 in Waterford, Ireland; m. Ellen Maria Creedon of Cork, Ireland, and had several children; d. St John's, Nfld., 12 June 1874.

There is no certain evidence concerning John

Valentine Nugent's early life in Ireland. He seems to have been well educated, having devoted four years to the study of law. According to his political enemies in Newfoundland, he was forced to leave Ireland because of his "violence in politics." After arriving in St John's in May 1833 he opened a private school. Because of his fluency in writing and speaking he soon became the spokesman for the liberal cause, and a man regarded by the conservative as a hot-headed, fiery, restless agitator who systematically attempted to array Catholics against Protestants. Soon after his arrival in Newfoundland Nugent applied unsuccessfully for permission to practise at the bar. He felt that his exclusion was based solely on religion and was therefore unjust.

In 1834 a series of letters signed by "Junius" accusing Governor Thomas COCHRANE of bigotry, injustice, and despotism appeared in the *Newfoundland Patriot*. Even though Father Edward TROY, chaplain to the Roman Catholic bishop, Michael Anthony Fleming*, admitted authorship, Cochrane attributed the letters to Nugent whose radical political views were already well known. During the 1830s Nugent did contribute much, under various signatures, to the liberal *Patriot*. Robert John Parsons*, the editor, was later to write that Nugent had been the sole cause of all the resentment against the *Patriot*, his anonymous letters having been "calculated to incite the people to discord."

In the invalidated general election of 1836 Nugent was elected to the assembly by acclamation for Placentia and St Mary's. In 1837 the fiery Irish schoolmaster was re-elected. Soon he became one of the leaders in the assembly, his radicalism doing nothing to decrease the violence of the struggle between the assembly and the council. He was a member of the delegation to London – with Patrick Morris* and William Carson* – which in 1838 secured the removal from Newfoundland of Chief Justice Henry John Boulton* and ensured that in future the chief justice would not be a member of the council. Unfortunately Nugent, a poor man, found himself stranded with no money to pay for his passage home. After the Colonial Office had refused him a loan, Bishop Fleming, who happened to be in London, helped him out of his difficulty. On his return to St John's, he was appointed solicitor to the House of Assembly. In the summer of 1841 Nugent was one of the delegates appointed by the house to appear in London before the parliamentary select committee on Newfoundland. Although the delegation failed to reach England before the inquiry adjourned, they did present the assembly's case in a series of letters to Lord John Russell.

During the 1842 general election campaign, in which Nugent was a candidate for St John's, he was arrested for non-payment of libel damages. The magistrate – a Protestant Conservative – was reprimanded by Governor John Harvey* for the timing of this arrest; the Liberals, enraged, raised the money for Nugent's bail and had him released; and the three Conservative candidates were defeated. From 1842 to 1848 John Valentine Nugent sat in the Amalgamated Legislature.

Meanwhile he had been combining politics with journalism. When R. J. Parsons of the *Patriot* was heavily fined and sent to jail for contempt in 1835, Nugent helped to set up the Constitutional Society whose purpose was to free the editor. Briefly in 1837 Nugent was the proprietor of the *Patriot*. Although Parsons resumed the responsibility of owner after a month, Nugent continued to own the press and types of the *Patriot* till 1840. Thereupon he became editor and later proprietor of the *Newfoundland Vindicator*. After the *Vindicator* collapsed he became editor of the *Newfoundland Indicator*. Both the *Vindicator* and the *Indicator* took an active part in politics supporting the Irish Catholic element.

J. V. Nugent's appointment in 1844 as Newfoundland's first inspector of schools caused much resentment among Protestant Conservatives. When, after a year, he was succeeded by a Protestant, he helped found the St John's Academy, a government-supported school. He was junior master and later head of the Roman Catholic division of the academy, 1845–56. His defeat in St John's district in the general election of 1848 was attributed to the fact that he held this government appointment.

After the introduction of responsible government in Newfoundland, with the Liberals finally in office, John Valentine Nugent was appointed in 1856 sheriff of the Central District, a position he filled until infirmity forced his retirement in 1871.

ELIZABETH A. WELLS

Newfoundland, Department of Provincial Affairs, "List of affidavits of proprietorship of newspapers," 1836–1900. PRO, CO 194/88, 70. Newfoundland, *Blue Books*, 1837–56 (copies in PANL). Newfoundland, House of Assembly, *Journals*, 1836–46. *Courier* (St John's), 9 Aug. 1871. *Newfoundlander* (St John's), 27 Oct. 1862. *Newfoundland Patriot* (St John's), 7 July 1835, 3 Feb. 1841. *Newfoundland Vindicator* (St John's), 1842. *Public Ledger* (St John's), 19 July, 2 Aug. 1844. *Telegraph* (St John's), 17 July 1874. *Times and General Commercial Gazette* (St John's), 21 Oct. 1848. Gunn, *Political history of Nfld*. Leslie Harris, "The first nine years of representative government in Newfoundland," unpublished MA thesis, Memorial University of Newfoundland, 1959.

O'Brien

O

O'BRIEN, EDWARD GEORGE, soldier, pioneer, and businessman; b. probably on 8 Jan. 1799, at Woolwich, Eng., son of Lucius O'Brien and Mary Callender-Campbell; d. 8 Sept. 1875 at Shanty Bay, Ont.

Edward George O'Brien spent his early boyhood at Cork, Ireland, and went to sea as a midshipman in 1810. He remained in the Royal Navy until 1815 when peace ended hope of promotion. In 1816 he became ensign in the 58th Regiment of foot and went with the regiment to Jamaica. Promoted lieutenant in 1820, he exchanged to the 29th Regiment in 1825, and retired on half-pay in 1826. He returned to sea in the merchant marine.

O'Brien emigrated to Upper Canada in 1829 and took up land near Thornhill. One year later he married Mary Sophia Gapper and, in 1832, left Thornhill and completed a new home, "The Woods," on Lake Simcoe at what came to be called Shanty Bay. O'Brien had been made emigrant agent for Oro Township in 1831. In this capacity he was entrusted with the supervision of a proposed Negro settlement, but the project attracted few settlers and was soon abandoned. As magistrate and commissioner of the Court of Requests, O'Brien played a leading role in the life of Shanty Bay, and he was also largely responsible for the building of St Thomas' Church (Church of England). Commissioned lieutenant-colonel in May 1838, he commanded the 3rd Regiment of Simcoe militia during the aftermath of the rebellion.

About 1845 O'Brien moved to Toronto and became secretary of the projected Toronto, Simcoe, and Lake Huron Union Railway (later the Northern Railway). He also served as secretary of the Provincial Mutual and General Insurance Company. In 1848 he bought a newspaper, the *Toronto Patriot*, edited first by his brother Lucius James O'Brien*, then by Samuel Thompson*, but he sold it after a few years to Ogle Robert GOWAN. About 1858 he retired from active business life and returned to Shanty Bay, where he died. He had several children, one of whom, Lucius Richard O'Brien*, became a prominent painter.

K. R. MACPHERSON

PAO, [Mary Sophia Gapper (O'Brien)], O'Brien journals, 1828–38. [Mary O'Brien], *The journals of Mary O'Brien, 1828–1838*, ed. A. S. Miller (Toronto, 1968). Chadwick, *Ontarian families*, II, 143–44. Davin, *Irishman in Canada*, 294–99. Henry O'Brien, "Reminiscences of Lake Simcoe," Simcoe County Pioneer and Hist. Soc., *Pioneer Papers* (Barrie, Ont.), no.3 (1910), 8–11. W. E. O'Brien, "Early days in Oro," Simcoe County Pioneer and Hist. Soc., *Pioneer Papers* (Barrie, Ont.), no.1 (1908), 22–27.

O'CALLAGHAN, EDMUND BAILEY (Baillie occurs sometimes), doctor, MHA, journalist, and archivist; b. probably on 27 Feb. 1797 at Mallow in Ireland; d. 29 May 1880 in New York, N.Y.

Edmund Bailey O'Callaghan studied medicine first at Dublin in 1820, then in Paris. He arrived at Quebec in 1823, continued his medical studies there, and received authorization to practise in 1827. It was particularly because of his political involvement that he attracted attention; indeed, even in his first months at Quebec he began to work with the earnest and express purpose of making the political and religious life of the capital aware of the Irish fact. As a member and then secretary (1829–33) of the Society of the Friends of Ireland, a founding member (1830) of the Quebec Mechanics' Institute, and president (1833) of the Quebec Emigrant Society, he seems to have devoted all his efforts to reconciling the Irish and the party of Louis-Joseph PAPINEAU. He also promoted a school for Anglophone Catholics in the Près-de-Ville district; and, in his capacity as secretary for the committee of stewards of St Patrick's Church, he was a principal founder of the Irish parish of Quebec.

Even though he had thus ensured for himself "a reputable existence" at Quebec, O'Callaghan, according to *Le Canadien* of 17 May 1833, decided to move to Montreal and accept the editorship of the *Vindicator and Canadian Advertiser*, owned by the famous *Patriote* bookseller Édouard-Raymond Fabre*. He was its editor for four and a half years. At the same time he continued to take an active part in Irish affairs: he joined the Montreal section of the Society of the Friends of Ireland, and was elected a member of the management committee of the normal school at Montreal. In 1834 he allowed himself to be persuaded by Papineau to stand in the county of Yamaska, where he was elected thanks to his leader's support. In the house, he made himself one of the most spirited and fiery defenders of the *Patriote* party. He was in fact Papineau's right-hand man. After the death of Louis Bourdages* on 20 Jan. 1835, O'Callaghan replaced him as chairman of the grievances committee. Then, at the opening of the 1836 session, when the members of the assembly who supported Papineau appeared at the bar of the council dressed in homespun after the Canadien manner, O'Callaghan was among those whose originality of costume drew the most attention. For several years speeches and writings had been making him just as conspicuous. He was an impassioned speaker, even a demagogue; he could give a fierce retort and wield a bitter and satirical pen. Lord Gosford [Acheson*] and especially Lord Aylmer [Whitworth-Aylmer*] had suffered through his Irish transports. Hence it was not surprising that a crowd of Doric Club members sacked the offices of the *Vindicator* on the night of 6 Nov. 1837.

O'Callaghan had incited his fellow-citizens to revolt. "Agitate! Agitate!! Agitate!!!" he had written in the autumn of 1837, "Destroy the Revenue; denounce the oppressors. Everything is lawful when the fundamental liberties are in danger." But when the riot broke out at Montreal (and against him!), he left immediately with Papineau for the Richelieu valley, and once a price was put on his head he made his way to the United States. Subsequently, even if he maintained a fairly regular correspondence with Canadian leaders such as Louis-Joseph Papineau, William Lyon Mackenzie*, Édouard-Raymond Fabre, and Louis Perrault, he never set foot again in British territory.

In April 1839, after a stay in New York, O'Callaghan took up residence at Albany. He practised medicine there until 1846, and was a member of the Albany County Medical Society. During this period he became an enthusiastic student of history. Between 1842 and 1844 he published several articles in the *Northern Light*, a newspaper that upheld the interests of the working class. His house became the meeting-place of the scholars and cultured men of the region. In 1848 he gave up medicine to accept the post of archivist of the state of New York. During the 22 years that followed, he devoted himself with indefatigable energy to the publication of documents relating to the colonial period. His principal works are: *History of New Netherlands . . .* (1846–48); *Jesuit relations of discoveries and other occurrences in Canada and the northern and western states of the Union, 1632–1672* (1847); *A list of editions of the Holy Scriptures, and parts thereof, printed in America previous to 1860* (1861); and *The register of New Netherland; 1626 to 1674* (1865). He edited the first 11 volumes of the *Documents relative to the colonial history of the State of New-York . . .* (1853–61), which contain valuable material on the history of the state and which are important in Canadian history as one of the earliest published sources of French documents (translated into English) relating to the frontier conflict of New France and New York and their rivalry over the Ohio country and the *pays d'en haut*. In addition to other works he edited *The documentary history of the State of New-York* (1850–51), and the *Calendar of historical manuscripts in the office of the secretary of state, Albany, N.Y.* (1865–66). He also wrote an introduction, outlining the history of New York from 1691 to 1775, for the *Journal of the Legislative Council of the colony of New York . . .* (1861).

In 1870, Mayor Abraham Oakey Hall of New York City commissioned him to prepare for publication the proceedings of the municipal council. O'Callaghan therefore moved to New York. Before his death he had succeeded in preparing the text of 15 volumes. Unfortunately, because of budgetary restrictions, these were never published. They are now the property of the New York Historical Society.

O'Callaghan was a serious, thin, pale man, totally lacking in elegance, and with nothing physically attractive about him. The electors of Yamaska had nicknamed him Doctor "qu'a la gale." But according to Joseph-Guillaume Barthe* he was bilingual, a man of great scholarship, who spoke easily and with a real flow of words, and who had a keen eye. His library was particularly well stocked, and he was a highly cultured man. In 1830, at Sherbrooke, he had married Charlotte Augustina Crampe, born in Ireland around 1800. She died on 17 July 1835 as a result of a disease of the lungs. She had given birth to a boy, who survived only a few days. On 9 May 1841, in the United States, O'Callaghan married again; his second wife was Ellen Hawe, who bore him a son; he also died at a very young age.

JACQUES MONET

Edmund Bailey O'Callaghan's main works are: *History of New Netherlands; or, New York under the Dutch* (2v., New York, 1846–48); *Jesuit relations of discoveries and other occurrences in Canada and the northern and western states of the Union, 1632–1672* (New York, 1847); *Laws and ordinances of New Netherlands, 1638–1674; compiled and translated from the original Dutch records in the office of the secretary of state* (Albany, N.Y., 1868); *A list of editions of the Holy Scriptures, and parts thereof, printed in America previous to 1860* (Albany, N.Y., 1861); *The register of New Netherland; 1626 to 1674* (Albany, N.Y., 1865).

The following are some of the works he edited: *Calendar of historical manuscripts in the office of the secretary of state, Albany, N.Y.* (2v., Albany, N.Y., 1865–66); *The documentary history of the State of New-York* (4v., Albany, N.Y., 1850–51); *Documents* relative to the colonial history of the State of New-York; procured in Holland, England and France, by John Romeyn Brodhead . . . ed. with Berthold Fernow (15v., Albany, N.Y., 1853–87), I–XI; Journal of the Legislative Council of the colony of New York . . . 1691; . . . 1775 (2v., Albany, N.Y., 1861).

PAC, MG 24, B50 (O'Callaghan papers). State Historical Society of Wisconsin (Madison), Perrault papers. L'Opinion publique (Montréal), 10 juin 1880. Vindicator and Canadian Advertiser (Montreal), 1833–37. J.-G. Barthe, Souvenirs d'un demi-siècle ou mémoires pour servir à l'histoire contemporaine (Montréal, 1885), 386. Fauteux, Patriotes. Gérard Filteau, Histoire des Patriotes (3v., Montréal, 1938–39). F. S. Guy, "Edmund Bailey O'Callaghan; a study in American historiography (1797–1880)," unpublished PHD thesis, Catholic University of America, 1935. H. T. Manning, The revolt of French Canada, 1800–1835: a chapter in the history of the British Commonwealth (Toronto, 1962). "M. O'Callaghan et les 'Relations' des Jésuites," BRH, XXXI (1925), 256. A. E. Peterson, "Edmund Bailey O'Callaghan, editor of New York historical records," New York State Hist. Assoc., Proceedings (New York), XXXIII (1935), 64–74. Léon Pouliot, "Note sur Edmund Bailey O'Callaghan (1797–1880)," BRH, XLVII (1941), 18–20. "La Quebec Mechanic's Institute (1830)," BRH, LII (1946), 217–18. P.-G. Roy, "L'auteur des 'Anciens Canadiens' en prison," BRH, XI (1905), 368–69. J. J. Walsh, "Edmund Bailey O'Callaghan, of New York; physician, historian and antiquarian, A.D. 1797–1880," American Catholic Hist. Soc. of Philadelphia, Records, XVI (1905), 5–33.

O'DONOGHUE, WILLIAM BERNARD, treasurer of Louis Riel*'s provisional government; b. 1843 in County Sligo, Ireland; d. 16 March 1878 in St Paul, Minnesota.

William Bernard O'Donoghue moved to New York while still a boy, having witnessed the Irish famine and the Young Ireland rebellion of 1848. He carried with him a strong antagonism towards Great Britain and an equally strong feeling of Irish patriotism. Whether O'Donoghue became an active member of the Fenian Brotherhood at this time, as some authorities suggest, is uncertain, but there can be no doubt that he sympathized with its aims.

In 1868 O'Donoghue met at Port Huron, Michigan, the Oblate Vital-Justin Grandin*, then coadjutor bishop of Saint-Boniface, and offered to serve in the western missions of the Catholic Church. Accordingly he accompanied Grandin to Red River where he became a teacher of mathematics at the college of Saint-Boniface and began to study for the priesthood. A year later he abandoned the soutane to take part in the Métis protest movement organized by Louis Riel in the autumn of 1869. On 16 November he was elected to the first convention of Red River as the representative of Saint-Boniface.

At first O'Donoghue adopted an attitude of moderation, supporting the English-speaking members of the convention in a proposal that the Hudson's Bay Company's Council of Assiniboia should be permitted to continue as the legislative body of the settlement; but on 22 December he helped Louis Riel seize the company's funds at Upper Fort Garry (Winnipeg) and on the 27th he became treasurer of Riel's provisional government. He was elected to the second convention in January 1870 and was confirmed in his appointment as treasurer on 10 February. On the 18th of the same month, he participated, along with Ambroise-Dydime Lépine*, in the capture of a number of Canadians from Portage la Prairie who had planned to overthrow the provisional government.

Nicknamed "Uriah Heep" by his enemies, O'Donoghue was, in fact, less emotional and less timid about bloodshed than Riel. He witnessed the execution of Thomas Scott* but refused to intervene on the condemned man's behalf. He assisted in drafting the first three versions of the Métis List of Rights, but apparently had no hand in the fourth list, carried by Riel's delegates to Ottawa in March 1870. During the remaining months of the provisional government in Red River, O'Donoghue became increasingly dissatisfied with Riel's leadership, which he regarded as too compromising and too pro-British. Nevertheless, he remained with Riel until 24 August, when both he and Riel were forced to flee to the United States, following the arrival of Garnet Joseph Wolseley*'s troops at Fort Garry.

At this point the breach between the two men became an open one. Riel believed that O'Donoghue was more concerned with striking a blow at Great Britain than with relieving the plight of the Métis. This belief seemed justified when, in January 1871, O'Donoghue carried a secret petition to President Ulysses S. Grant asking the United States to intervene in Red River. When Grant refused to act, O'Donoghue turned to the Fenian Brotherhood. He obtained only moral support from the brotherhood, but did succeed in enlisting the active help of two Fenian leaders, John O'Neill and J. J. Donnelly. Then he drew up a constitution for the proposed Republic of Rupert's Land naming himself as president, and, with O'Neill, led on 5 Oct. 1871 a small force of some 35 men, recruited among the unemployed labourers in Minnesota, across the Manitoba frontier. Riel's influence prevented the Métis from joining him and the so-called Fenian invasion of Manitoba collapsed. O'Donoghue was captured by a group of Métis and taken back to Minnesota.

No proceedings were taken against O'Donoghue in the United States for his filibustering expedition against Manitoba, but in Canada he was expressly exempted from the amnesty granted Riel and Lépine in 1875. As a result of the advocacy of John Costigan*, an Irish-Canadian member of the federal parliament, the Canadian government agreed to extend the clemency of the crown to O'Donoghue in 1877. Following his return to the United States, O'Donoghue had been employed as a teacher in District 13, Dakota County, Minnesota. In 1877 he moved to Rosemount where he ran unsuccessfully for the post of county superintendent of schools. Meanwhile he became engaged to Mary Callan, daughter of James Callan, county commissioner of Dakota County. They were, however, never married. In 1878 O'Donoghue was taken to St Paul where he died of tuberculosis on 26 March 1878. His fiancée died several weeks later on 3 May 1878. The former treasurer of the provisional government was buried in the old St Joseph's cemetery, three miles from Rosemount, the cost of the burial and headstone being borne by his American friends.

GEORGE F. G. STANLEY

Alexander Begg, *Begg's Red River journal* (Morton); *The creation of Manitoba; or, a history of the Red River troubles* (Toronto, 1871). "L'invasion fénienne au Manitoba, un journal contemporain," G. F. G. Stanley, édit, *RHAF*, XVII (1963–64), 258–68. *Dom. ann. reg., 1879*, 33, 40, 114, 361. Le Jeune, *Dictionnaire*, II, 377. J. K. Howard, *Strange empire; a narrative of the northwest* (New York, 1952). J. P. Robertson, *A political manual of the province of Manitoba and the North-West Territories* (Winnipeg, 1887), 152. Stanley, *Birth of western Canada*, 98–174; *Louis Riel.*

O'HARA, WALTER, soldier; b. about 1789 in Dublin, son of Robert O'Hara and Fanny Taylor; d. 13 Jan. 1874 in Toronto, Ont.

Walter O'Hara's family was from County Galway, Ireland. He graduated in 1806 from Trinity College, Dublin, and took up a military career, serving in the 91st and 47th Foot of the British army and in the 7th Caçadores and 1st Line Regiment of Foot of the Portuguese service. He was twice wounded in the Peninsular War and was perhaps captured after the battle of the Nive. He had "a respectable fortune to expend" in 1826 when he moved to Upper Canada with his wife Marian Murray and settled near York on a farm in what is now the Parkdale district of Toronto. They had a large family.

On 14 June 1827 Peregrine Maitland* appointed O'Hara assistant adjutant general of the Upper Canada militia with the rank of colonel after O'Hara had accepted Nathaniel Coffin*'s invitation to succeed James FitzGibbon*. The post that O'Hara held for 19 years had been created in 1816 when Coffin asked FitzGibbon to work as a clerk in the adjutant general's office. By the time O'Hara was appointed there had been a history of interest in this office and in the composition of the staff by the colonial politicians. When Coffin resigned the post of adjutant general in 1837 O'Hara expected to succeed him. FitzGibbon, however, followed Coffin as acting adjutant general, and in December Richard Bullock* Jr received the post. FitzGibbon and Bullock had wider contacts in the colony outside the militia than O'Hara, who was dismayed at the "anomalous peculiarities of Canadian patronage," by which persons professionally not as well qualified, he felt, but better assimilated into colonial life, were entrusted with the post. He conducted a lengthy correspondence with the imperial authorities in an unsuccessful attempt to redress his grievance. In early December 1837, when William Lyon Mackenzie*'s force gathered north of Toronto, O'Hara led part of FitzGibbon's force that headed north to meet the rebels. Two years later, he asked for a seat in the Legislative Council, but was rebuffed.

In 1846 an act established the province's militia and the post of assistant adjutant general was abolished. O'Hara was not seriously suggested for the new post of deputy adjutant general and appears to have gone into retirement. In 1861, however, when Duncan Macdougall acted as deputy adjutant general for Canada West, he made use of O'Hara's undoubted talents as a staff officer for a brief time.

O'Hara died in 1874 in Toronto, where he had lived from his arrival in Canada except for the years 1841–46 when he lived in Kingston. He was considered as a "chivalrous, high-spirited, warm-hearted gentleman," but he had felt himself victimized in the colony for not receiving the adjutant generalcy in 1837 and for not being regularly employed after 1846. He severely criticized the "exclusiveness of Canadian politics" which, in his opinion, had not allowed him to use his full talents.

GEO. MAINER

PAC, RG 9, II, A1, 2, f.195. PRO, CO 42/470, 119–53. *Arthur papers* (Sanderson), II, 94. *The Gentleman's Magazine: and Historical Chronicle* (London), LXXXII (1812), PT.1, 575; LXXXIV (1814), PT.1, 176. *Globe* (Toronto), 14 Jan., 24 Dec. 1874. *Upper Canada Gazette* (York), 16 June 1827. *Cyclopædia of Can. biog.* (Rose, 1886), 485–86.

O'Hea

O'HEA, TIMOTHY, soldier; b. 1846 in Bantry, County Cork, Ireland; d. November 1874, in the desert of Queensland, Australia.

Little is known of O'Hea's early life or parentage. He joined the 1st Battalion of the Prince Consort's Own Rifle Brigade as a private before the age of 20 and was sent to Canada with his regiment in 1866. On 9 June 1866, during the Fenian uprisings, O'Hea and three other men were guarding a munitions shipment attached to a passenger train carrying 800 German immigrants; the shipment was bound from Quebec to the Lake Erie front. En route, at Danville, in the Eastern Townships, a fire was discovered in the munitions car. The car was disconnected, and before a decision had been made about further action O'Hea took the keys to the burning car from the sergeant in command, opened it, and fought the fire for nearly an hour at great peril to his life. He singlehandedly put out the blaze. On 7 Jan. 1867, at Quebec, he was awarded the Victoria Cross. This was the only instance in which the VC was given for service within Canada and awarded for an act of valour not performed in the presence of an enemy.

Shortly afterwards O'Hea left the army and joined the New Zealand Mounted Police. In June 1874 he moved to Australia where he joined Andrew Hume and Lewis Thompson in a search party looking for a reported survivor of the Ludwig Leichhardt expedition lost some 20 years earlier in the interior of the country. The party set out from Nockatunga station in November, apparently inadequately supplied, and soon met with tragedy. O'Hea and Hume died of thirst; Thompson managed to return to Nockatunga with the report of their deaths. He afterwards led a search party, which found Hume's body but not O'Hea's. O'Hea's body was recovered sometime later apparently by aborigines.

O'Hea is buried at Nockatunga station in Queensland. His VC remained for many years in the National Art Gallery in Sydney, Australia. The gallery was to give it to Canada in 1950, but at the request of Field Marshal Lord Henry Maitland Wilson, Baron of Libya, Canada waived her claim and it was returned to the regimental museum in Winchester, England.

CHARLES A. THOMPSON

PAC, RG 8, I, AI, 1038, pp.47–53. *Town and Country Journal* (Sydney, Aust.), 9 Jan. 1875. *The Australian encyclopædia* (10v., Sydney, 1965), II, 331; V, 284; VI, 391. *Encyclopedia Canadiana*, VIII, 7. A. H. Chisholm, *Strange new world; the adventures of John Gilbert and Ludwig Leichhardt* (2nd ed., Sydney, 1955), 256–58. *"For valour": the V.C.; a record of the brave and noble deeds for which her majesty has bestowed the Victoria Cross from its institution to the present date*, ed. J. E. Muddock (London, 1895), 155. *Canadian Military Gazette* (Montreal), XV, no.19 (1900), 20. A. H. Chisholm, "The V.C. of Timothy O'Hea," *Sydney Morning Herald*, 25 Feb. 1950. Thomas Dunbabin, "Tim O'Hea's Canadian V.C.," *Ottawa Citizen*, 10 Aug. 1951.

O'NEILL, JOHN, Fenian leader; b. 8 March 1834 at Drumgallon, County Monaghan, Ireland; d. 7 Jan. 1878 at Omaha, Nebraska, U.S.A.

John O'Neill went to New Jersey in 1848, and after a year of schooling additional to what he had received in Ireland worked at a variety of employments until 1857, when he enlisted in the 2nd United States Dragoons for the "Mormon War." He seems to have deserted and gone to California, where he joined the 1st Cavalry and became a sergeant. He served with this regiment in the Civil War until commissioned in the 5th Indiana Cavalry in December 1862. He showed himself a daring fighting officer, but considered that he did not receive the promotion he merited, transferred to the 17th United States Colored Infantry in the rank of captain, and left the service before the war ended. His marriage to Mary Crow, by whom he had several children, took place about this time.

While working in Tennessee he joined the Fenian Brotherhood, adhering to the party led by William Randall Roberts*, which favoured attacking Canada. In 1866 as a Fenian colonel he led a group from Nashville to take part in the proposed invasion. The person intended to command the operation on the Niagara frontier did not appear and O'Neill took his place. Early on 1 June he led a force, which according to his own account numbered 600 men, across the Niagara River and occupied the village of Fort Erie. The next day he encountered north of Ridgeway a detached column of Canadian volunteers commanded by Lieutenant-Colonel Alfred BOOKER consisting mainly of the Queen's Own Rifles, of Toronto, and the 13th Battalion, of Hamilton. In a sharp little fight the Fenians (many of them, like O'Neill, certainly Civil War veterans) routed the inexperienced Canadians, who retreated on Port Colborne. O'Neill withdrew his own force to Fort Erie, where there was a sanguinary skirmish with a Canadian detachment, under John Stoughton Dennis*, which had been landed from a tug. That night, with superior British forces closing in, O'Neill successfully evacuated his men from Canada. Although arrested by an American gunboat which was patrolling the Niagara River, they were shortly released. O'Neill was charged with breaking the U.S. neutrality laws but the charge was dropped.

Ridgeway made O'Neill a Fenian hero. He had won the only success the Fenians ever achieved in their numerous enterprises against Canada. He had handled his force well, and it should be added that he had kept his men under strict control and that there was little looting or disorder. The episode shortly led to the Roberts party of the Fenian Brotherhood appointing him "inspector general of the Irish Republican Army." He took Roberts' place as president at the end of 1867. Negotiations for reunion of his branch of the brotherhood with that formerly headed by John O'Mahony and now led by John Savage failed, and O'Neill proceeded to collect funds and acquire and distribute arms for another Canadian adventure. These activities caused considerable alarm and much defensive preparation in Canada during 1868 and 1869. However, O'Neill's organization had been penetrated by Canadian agents, and in particular one of his staff, Henri Le Caron (Thomas Beach*), was in the employ of Gilbert McMicken*, chief of the Canadian detective police. Early in 1870 O'Neill quarrelled with his "Senate," losing much support. On 25 May, with those portions of the brotherhood still prepared to follow him, he attempted a raid at Eccles Hill on the border near Frelighsburg, Quebec. Ample warning had enabled the Canadian authorities to take precautions. The Fenian vanguard was fired on as soon as it crossed the border, and fled. O'Neill himself was arrested by a United States marshal. At the end of July he was sentenced to two years' imprisonment, but with other Fenian prisoners was pardoned by President Ulysses S. Grant in October.

O'Neill renounced the idea of further movements against Canada, but was sought out by William Bernard O'DONOGHUE, a former member of the provisional government headed by Louis Riel* at Red River, and accepted his proposal for an attack on Manitoba. The official Fenian organization rejected the plan; nevertheless on 5 Oct. 1871 O'Neill, with a small number of supporters, seized the Hudson's Bay Company post at Pembina, on ground then considered to be in dispute between Canada and the United States. He was at once arrested by U.S. troops, but was discharged by an American court on the ground that his offence had been committed in Canada. This was his last raid. Seven years later he died of a paralytic stroke while working for a firm of land speculators in Holt County, Nebraska.

It is hard to believe that O'Neill was a man of much intelligence, for the idea of righting Irish wrongs by attacking Canada, of which he was the most active exponent, was essentially stupid. He was egotistical and credulous. He seems however to have been a brave soldier and a sincere Irish patriot. Unlike many Fenian leaders, he was ready to risk life and liberty for the cause he believed in.

C. P. STACEY

John O'Neill was the author of *Address of Gen. John O'Neill . . . to the officers and members of the Fenian brotherhood, on the state of the organization, and its attempted disruption* (New York, 1868); *Message of Gen'l John O'Neill, president, F.B., to the seventh national congress* (Philadelphia, 1868); *Official report of Gen. John O'Neill, president of the Fenian brotherhood; on the attempt to invade Canada, May 25th, 1870; the preparations therefor, and the cause of its failure, with a sketch of his connection with the organization, and the motives which led him to join it: also a report of the battle of Ridgeway, Canada West, fought June 2d, 1866 . . .* (New York, 1870); and a letter in *Irish American* (New York), 28 Sept. 1867.

PAC, MG 26, A (Macdonald papers), 234–46. G. T. Denison III, *History of the Fenian raid on Fort Erie; with an account of the battle of Ridgeway* (Toronto, 1866). *Irish American* (New York), 19 Jan., 2 Feb. 1878. Henri Le Caron [T. M. Beach], *Twenty-five years in the secret service* (London, 1892). Gilbert McMicken, "The abortive Fenian raid on Manitoba," HSSM *Papers*, no.32 (1887–88), 1–11. John Savage, *Fenian heroes and martyrs* (Boston, 1868). *DAB*.

O'NEILL (O'Neil), TERENCE JOSEPH, soldier, civil servant; b. 1802 in Ireland; d. 21 July 1872 at Gaspé, Que.

Terence Joseph O'Neill arrived in Canada in 1829; he was serving in the British army, a member of the 30th infantry regiment. When he left the army in 1832, he was entitled as a former captain to a land grant. He settled at York (Toronto), and went into partnership with Patrick Burke in a firm of auctioneers.

In 1836 the St Patrick's Society was founded at Toronto, and O'Neill immediately became a member. During a meeting the following year, the president of the society refused to propose a toast to Daniel O'Connell, the Irish leader, and denounced him. O'Neill, after a violent controversy, "could no longer countenance the Orange hypocrites." He therefore left the society's ranks, and a few months later joined William Lyon Mackenzie* and the Reformers for a struggle against the Orangemen. During the election of 1841 he was a campaign worker for Isaac Buchanan*.

Having been appointed, on 14 Aug. 1861, inspector of prisons and asylums in the Province of Canada and in New Brunswick, O'Neill had to live at Kingston for some months each year, but he kept his house at Toronto. His role consisted of making the rounds of these establishments, the most important of which were the

Onistah-Sokaksin

Kingston penitentiary and the provincial mental asylum at Toronto.

At this period there was not one of these institutions "whose material resources were complete." Some were waiting for a proper building then under construction, others were occupying quarters ill suited to their purpose, with no hope of getting out of them rapidly. Furthermore, the administration of the penitentiaries lacked firmness: the prisoners bribed their warders, bought on the black market, and indulged in homosexuality. So long as he held the post of inspector, O'Neill made persistent efforts to ensure that work was given to prisoners and that defaulters were whipped.

On 22 May 1868, at the time when a federal commission of directors of penitentiaries was set up, O'Neill was chosen as one of the directors. His great problem was always "What must be done with the prisoners." He accepted the presidency of the commission in 1869, and the following year went to Ottawa to live, with his wife Anne. It was during this same year that the federal government decided to have prisoners work in return for pay; they were thus able to assist their families.

By the time O'Neill died, improvements had been made in the penitentiary system, in particular at Kingston: reforms in discipline and working conditions, improved sanitation in the quarters, separate cells, new buildings. In addition, a reduction in the number of recidivists was apparent. Obviously part of this success is attributable to O'Neill, though it also reflects the prosperity of the country. He was a hard working and well-intentioned official, who had the public interest at heart.

O'Neill died at Gaspé, probably during one of his numerous tours of inspection.

ANDRÉ MARTINEAU

PAC, RG 8, I, AI, 220–21. Canada, *Sessional papers*, III (1870), PT.1, no.2; IV (1871), PT.6, no.60; VI (1873), PT.6, no.75. *Rapport du bureau des inspecteurs d'asiles, prisons, etc., pour l'année 1863* (Québec, 1864), 1–30. *Constitution* (Toronto), 29 March 1837. Middleton, *Municipality of Toronto*, I, 181–212.

ONISTAH-SOKAKSIN (Calf Shirt; sometimes called **Minixi** or **Wild Person),** leader of the Nitayxkax (Lone Fighters) band of Blood Indians (a division of the Blackfeet), d. in the winter of 1873–74 at Fort Kipp (Alberta).

Calf Shirt was believed to have gained supernatural and ferocious powers from a grizzly bear. A chief who was held in awe by his followers, he, unlike other chiefs, was known for his constant hostility to white traders.

Calf Shirt's name appears first in 1855 when he signed a treaty with the American government on behalf of his band, who commonly wintered along the Belly River. This treaty attempted to establish peaceful relations between the Blackfeet and the United States government, and between the Blackfeet and their enemies, including the Flatheads, Pend d'Oreilles, Kutenais, and Amikwas (Nez Percés). It set aside an exclusive hunting area for the Blackfeet, allowed for the peaceful entry of missionaries and the building of military posts, and provided for an annual annuity of $20,000 for ten years.

In 1865, when two fellow chiefs were murdered by Americans, Calf Shirt led a war party which wiped out a number of pioneers who were establishing a town called Ophir, in Montana Territory. After the raid, plans for building the town were abandoned. Four years later, he tried to kill a Catholic missionary, Father Jean B. Imoda. By 1870, Calf Shirt had become a leading war chief of the tribe, with a personal following of 72 warriors and with 288 persons in his Lone Fighters band.

Initially he had traded with both the British and the Americans, but after his 1865 raid he did business primarily with the Hudson's Bay Company. In 1869, however, Americans built illicit trading posts in the heart of Blackfoot territory (southern Alberta), where they sold whiskey and repeating rifles. During the winter of 1873–74, Calf Shirt visited one of these establishments, Fort Kipp, and was killed by the proprietor, Joseph Kipp, during a dispute about liquor. Calf Shirt's wives, believing he had the power to come back to life as a grizzly bear, began the necessary rituals but were restrained from completing them by other Indians because of the fear they had had for him in human form.

After Calf Shirt's death his band was amalgamated with the Awaposo-otas (Many Fat Horses) band under the leadership of Akakitsipimi-otas (Many Spotted Horses), a wealthy and respected war chief; the new band kept the name of the largest group, Nitayxkax.

HUGH A. DEMPSEY

H. A. Dempsey, "Blood Indian bands; their identification and history" (unpublished MS in the possession of the author, 1955).

Montana Historical Society Collections (Helena, Mont.), Biographical files, John J. Healy. National Archives (Washington), Census of the Blackfeet Indians, Alfred Sully to E. S. Parker, 16 July 1870. *Forest and Stream* (New York), 18 July 1903. *Fort Benton Record* (Fort Benton, Mont.), 31 Jan. 1879. Montana Hist. Soc., *Contributions*, X (1940), 275. J. C. Ewers, *The story of the Blackfeet* ([Lawrence, Kansas, 1944]), 39. H. A. Dempsey, "The amazing death of Calf Shirt," *Montana; the Magazine of Western History*, III, no.1 (1953), 65–72.

O'REILLY, JAMES, lawyer and politician, b. in Westport, County Mayo, Ireland, 1823, son of Peter O'Reilly; m. Mary Jane Redmond in November 1850; d. at Kingston, Ont., 15 May 1875.

James O'Reilly came to Upper Canada in 1832 with his father, who settled in Belleville and there became a merchant before moving to Kingston in 1847. After attending the Hastings County grammar school, James began the study of law with C. O. Benson of Belleville. He continued his studies first with John Ross, then with John Willoughby CRAWFORD and John Hawkins Hagarty*, and was thus introduced to important public men during his training. Called to the bar of Upper Canada in 1847, O'Reilly moved to Kingston. He was a bencher of the Law Society of Upper Canada, became a QC in 1864, and in 1870 was admitted to the bar of Quebec. O'Reilly participated in several spectacular criminal cases and, in 1868, successfully prosecuted Patrick James Whelan*, the assassin of D'Arcy McGee*. This trial, a *cause célèbre*, in which John Hillyard CAMERON acted for the defence, revealed O'Reilly as an able, energetic, and vociferous attorney.

Religion largely explains O'Reilly's political career. President of the Kingston St Patrick's Society, he was an important Catholic layman whose close rapport with the bishop of Kingston, Edward John HORAN, and extensive law practice made him influential throughout eastern Ontario. In 1872, when Catholic leaders insisted on a greater political influence for Catholics, Sir John A. Macdonald* encouraged Catholic Conservatives to run for parliament. O'Reilly responded and was elected MP for South Renfrew in 1872. His term in parliament was uneventful, and in 1874 he declined to seek re-election, claiming that politics interfered too much with his law practice.

O'Reilly served as director of the Kingston and Pembroke Railway. He was an alderman in Kingston from 1850 to 1855, and was its recorder, 1865–69. The town honoured him for raising a militia company during the *Trent* crisis in 1861. He was anxious to become a judge, and but for his premature death in 1875 he would have preceded John O'Connor* as the first Irish Catholic appointed to an Ontario superior court judgeship.

DONALD SWAINSON

PAC, MG 26, A (Macdonald papers), 188, 194, 204, 228, 339; B (Mackenzie papers), ser.2, 1; MG 27, I, 117 (James O'Reilly papers). PAO, Sir Alexander Campbell papers, 1872. *Ottawa Citizen*, 1875. *Trial of Patrick J. Whelan for the murder of the Hon.* Thos. D'Arcy McGee ... (Ottawa, 1868). *Can. parl. comp.*, 1873. N. F. Davin, *Irishman in Canada.* Swainson, "Personnel of politics."

OSBORN, SHERARD, naval officer, Arctic explorer, and author; b. 25 April 1822 in England, son of Lieutenant-Colonel Edward Osborn of the Indian army, and of Eliza Todington; d. 6 May 1875 in London, Eng.

Sherard Osborn, nominated first class volunteer in the Royal Navy by Captain William Warren on 30 Sept. 1837, began his career with two long voyages. The first, in 1838–43, was on Warren's ship HMS *Hyacinth* to the Far East, where he took part in a campaign against Malay pirates in Siam (Thailand) and in Britain's first Chinese war at Canton and Shanghai. The second voyage, in 1844–48, took him to the Pacific on board HMS *Collingwood*. He was promoted lieutenant on 4 May 1846. Between the two voyages, he spent some months as mate on HMS *Excellent* at Portsmouth, where he studied gunnery. He profited greatly from these years; his commanding officers cultivated his enthusiasm and talents, and Warren in particular set him an example as a diligent officer and a sympathetic commander.

After leaving *Collingwood*, Osborn received command of a small steamer, HMS *Dwarf*, in which he patrolled the coast of Ireland during the insurrection of 1848. He was warmly thanked for his services by local authorities in Ireland and by his own commander-in-chief, and in 1849 he was reported to the Admiralty for gallantry "beyond all praise in remaining by his vessel, the Dwarf, in a sinking state in tempestuous weather."

He returned to England in 1849 to find anxiety about Sir John Franklin*'s missing expedition reaching its climax after the failure of Sir James Clark Ross* in 1848–49. Osborn immediately joined the campaign in favour of a further expedition and volunteered to serve. The Admiralty decided to send out four ships under Captain Horatio Thomas Austin*, and Osborn received command of the 430-ton steamer HMS *Pioneer*.

The expedition sailed in spring 1850; in the summer its members helped to locate and search the site of Franklin's first winter quarters at Beechey Island; in September the ships were beset and forced to winter off Griffith Island in Barrow Strait. Close at hand were two other expeditions, one commanded by Sir John Ross*, the other by the veteran arctic whaling master William Penny*, who soon became one of Osborn's closest friends. In spring 1851, Osborn led a sledge party southwestward to the western extreme of Prince of Wales Island. This 500-mile journey revealed no undiscovered coasts and other parties covered

Osborn

much greater distances. By far the most important of Osborn's contributions to the expedition were his untiring cheerfulness, and his skilful handling of *Pioneer*, which proved the superiority of steam over sail in ice navigation. He wrote a popular narrative of the expedition, *Stray leaves from an Arctic journal* . . . , in which his jovial good humour is everywhere present. Yet the expedition was not altogether a happy experience for Osborn. He often disagreed with Austin, and, when Austin quarrelled with Penny, Osborn made little effort to conceal his much greater respect for the latter. When the expedition returned to England in autumn 1851, Osborn was the only officer whom Austin did not recommend for promotion. A number of his friends, including Penny, wrote to the Admiralty to protest, and Lady Franklin (Jane GRIFFIN), was reported to be upset. Osborn himself remained unmoved, and received the news with a defiant forbearance that was typical: "I am young yet and have room & time enough to win a Post-Captain's commission in spite of Captain Austin or any other Liar in buttons." While the argument continued, Osborn was married, on 8 Jan. 1852, to Helen Harriet Gordon Hinxman.

Meanwhile, the Admiralty decided to send back Austin's four ships with one added vessel, HMS *North Star*, and they again gave Osborn command of *Pioneer*. Charge of the whole squadron went to Sir Edward BELCHER.

On arrival in Barrow Strait in summer 1852 the ships separated. Captain Henry KELLETT took two ships to Melville Island, *North Star* remained as base ship at Beechey Island, and Belcher and Osborn sailed *Assistance* and *Pioneer* up Wellington Channel to Northumberland Sound, northwest Devon Island, where they wintered. In spring 1853 Osborn sledged with an officer of *Assistance*, George Henry Richards*, along the north shore of Bathurst Island and the northeast coast of Melville Island, both previously unexplored. He then parted from Richards and, returning, explored the east coast of Bathurst Island. This journey lasted from 10 April to 15 July and covered more than 900 miles. During July and August the two ships sailed southward, but they were forced by ice to winter again in Wellington Channel. In September 1853 news reached Osborn from the supply vessel HMS *Phoenix* of his promotion to commander on 30 Oct. 1852. *Phoenix* also brought out Osborn's brother Noel, who spent the winter as mate on board *North Star*. In 1854, to Osborn's disgust, Belcher ordered all of his ships except *North Star* to be abandoned, and the men returned to England in her and in the supply vessels *Phoenix* and *Talbot*.

This voyage was undoubtedly the most depressing of Osborn's career. Many of Belcher's officers suffered under his humiliating and dictatorial treatment, but none more than Osborn. In 1853 he complained to Belcher of ill treatment and proposed to refer one difference between them to the Admiralty. From that moment, all the weight of Belcher's wrath fell on Osborn. Richards kept a private journal through 1853–54, which records little else but Belcher's "abuse & insult" and his "malignant hatred" of Osborn. Richards applauded Osborn for "the admirable way he has borne everything," but there is no doubt that the latter's good humour was sorely tested.

After the expedition, Osborn spent a short time in charge of the Norfolk coast guard while he recovered his health. He also began editing Robert MCCLURE's journal of his Franklin searching expedition on HMS *Investigator*, which was published in 1856 as *The discovery of the north-west passage*. . . . Early in 1855 he was sent in command of HMS *Vesuvius* to the Crimean War, where he was promoted captain on 18 Aug. 1855, decorated with the Order of the Bath, awarded the Turkish Medjidie, and made an officer of the Légion d'honneur by France.

The triumph of his return from the Crimea in 1856 was soon marred when his wife, by whom he had had two daughters, left him, or, as he defiantly expressed it, he "got clear of a bad wife by her absconding." (There is no evidence that they were ever divorced.) Yet Osborn was certainly distressed. He was in poor health at the time, and for once he fell to despair: "My Naval career I feel is over," he wrote to Penny. "I had an object and honourable ambition once – it's gone now. I live merely for myself now, and it is little I want." However, he was not yet 35 when he wrote these words, and his long career of naval achievements and unselfish public service had scarcely begun.

In 1857 he commanded HMS *Furious* and escorted a fleet of gunboats to China, where Britain was again at war. When peace had been concluded, he was active in the development of European trade with China and Japan, and performed, in the words of Lord Elgin [James Bruce*], British ambassador to China, "a feat unparalleled in naval history" by sailing *Furious* 600 miles up the Yangtze (Ch'ang) River to prove its navigability for much smaller trading vessels. His health deteriorated during this service, and in 1859 he was invalided home. For three years he was obliged to supplement his income by editing some of his journals for publication, and by writing on naval matters, Chinese politics, and Arctic exploration for *Blackwood's Magazine*. He also contributed papers to the Royal Geographical

Society of which he had become a fellow in 1856.

In 1861 he returned to the navy and subsequently began a period of varied activity. He commanded HMS *Donegal* off the coast of Mexico. In 1863 he took a fleet of ships to Peking in an unsuccessful attempt to cooperate with the Chinese government in the suppression of piracy. In 1865–66 he was agent for the Great Indian Peninsular Railway Company in Bombay; in 1867–73 he was managing director of the Telegraph Construction and Maintenance Company which laid a submarine telegraph cable from Britain to India and Australia. He stood unsuccessfully for parliament in 1868, was elected a fellow of the Royal Society in June 1870, and won promotion to rear-admiral on 29 May 1873.

Polar exploration continued to occupy his mind in this period, however, and he led a successful campaign for the renewal of British Arctic interests. He presented a paper to the Royal Geographical Society in January 1865 arguing for exploration of the unknown region surrounding the North Pole by way of Smith Sound. He repeated his case many times and steadily gained support until, in August 1874, the government agreed to finance the venture, and the expedition of 1875–76 was born. For nine months Osborn, whose health prevented his making the trip, worked with Francis Leopold M'Clintock* and Richards on the Admiralty's Arctic committee advising on preparations for the expedition. On 3 May 1875 he went to Portsmouth to visit George Strong Nares*, commander of the expedition, and his crew. Three days later he died in London, shortly before the departure of the expedition that he, more than anybody, had made possible.

Sherard Osborn was one of the most talented naval officers of his day. Those who knew him paid tribute to his outstanding professional abilities, his courage and determination, his sound judgement, his warm-hearted enthusiasm, and his tireless good humour. He was admired by his fellow officers and by those who served under him. He was steadfast in his opinions, and seldom allowed diplomacy to prevent his expressing them – a feature of his character that brought him into conflict not only with Austin and Belcher, but also sometimes with his closest friends. Lady Franklin, for instance, was deeply upset because he consistently proclaimed Robert McClure – not her husband – as the discoverer of the northwest passage. In addition to Osborn's accomplishments in the field of Arctic exploration, he was a capable administrator, a keen geographer, a prolific writer on many subjects, and an established authority on Chinese affairs; but most of all he was a highly gifted naval officer, a master of all aspects of seamanship.

CLIVE A. HOLLAND

SPRI, MS 116/57/1–10 (ten letters from Sherard Osborn to William Penny, 1850–56); MS 768 (private journal of George Henry Richards aboard H.M.S. *Assistance*, 17 Aug. 1853–28 May 1854). G.B., Adm., *Further papers relative to the recent Arctic expeditions in search of Sir John Franklin and the crews of H.M.S. Erebus and Terror* (London, 1855), 187–261. G.B., Parl., Command paper, 1852, [1436], L, 269–935, *Additional papers relative to the Arctic expedition under the orders of Captain Austin and Mr. William Penny*, 87–103. [McClure], *Discovery of the northwest passage* (Osborn). Sherard Osborn, *Stray leaves from an Arctic journal; or, eighteen months in the polar regions, in search of Sir John Franklin's expedition, in the years 1850–51* (London, 1852); "On the exploration of the north polar region," Royal Geographical Society, *Proceedings*, IX (1865), 42–70; "On the exploration of the north polar region," Royal Geographical Society, *Proceedings*, XII (1868), 92–112; "The routes to the north polar region," *Geographical Magazine* (London), I (1874), 221–25. "Obituary," *Geographical Magazine* (London), II (1875), 161–70. *Times* (London), 10, 14 May 1875.

P

PAINCHAUD, JOSEPH, physician and surgeon; b. 23 Jan. 1787 at Quebec, son of François Painchaud, a navigator, and Marie-Angélique Drouin; d. 24 Aug. 1871 at Quebec.

On 9 Jan. 1811, after serving his apprenticeship under Dr James Fisher*, a surgeon attached to the Quebec garrison, Joseph Painchaud was authorized to practise medicine. He was a popular practitioner with the people of Quebec, and from morning to night was to be seen travelling the streets of the city, "usually making his house calls on horseback and wearing long Wellington boots and silver spurs." On 5 June 1815, in the parish of Notre-Dame, he married Geneviève Parant.

In 1820 the Emigrant Hospital was opened in the Saint-Jean district. Painchaud was put in charge of the institution, and practised medicine and surgery there until 1834. In that year the hospital closed its doors, and the patients were transferred to the new marine hospital (called the Marine and Emigrant Hospital), where Painchaud, who had been taken on by James Douglas*, worked until his death [*see* IFFLAND]. Both by his teaching and by his monetary gifts, he contributed substantially to the progress of the hospital. Thanks to him and Dr Douglas, this institution became not only useful to all Quebec residents, but also "a school of surgery unrivalled on the North American continent." In 1833 Painchaud was named doctor to the community of the Hôpital Général of Quebec, in place of Dr William Holmes. On 29 March 1845, he was one of those who obtained from the government of the Province of Canada the right to establish a school of medicine at Quebec. Painchaud, who had professed obstetrics and epidemiology at the Marine Hospital, gave instruction at the new Quebec Medical School in "the obstetrical art, and [the treatment of] women's and children's diseases."

Throughout his whole career Painchaud endeavoured to develop a team spirit among his *confrères*. He took an active part in the founding of the Quebec Medical Society in 1826. He was noteworthy for the regular support he gave it, by publishing reassessments and periodical reviews of medical progress in Europe and the United States as well as in Canada. In the same period he was a member of a committee, probably the first, whose purpose was to recommend the setting up of a minimum schedule of medical fees, based on "three different rates for house visits, surgical operations, and deliveries and attendance on board ship." As he also had been on the Quebec Medical Board since 1831, and had presided over it for many years, he had considerable influence with his *confrères*, governments, and in councils and medical societies. On 31 July 1831, as the most senior "licensed" doctor present, Painchaud was invited to preside at "the general meeting of the licensed doctors, surgeons and midwives living in the district of Quebec, a meeting called by a proclamation of His Excellency the governor in chief." In 1837 the government of the country entrusted him with the post of commissioner responsible for supervising the application in the Quebec region of "the ordinance to prevent unlicensed persons from practising medicine and surgery in the province of Quebec or midwifery in the cities of Quebec or Montreal."

In 1844 Painchaud started a new medical association intended to "give assistance to needy doctors unable to practise their profession either because of advanced age or because of infirmities, or to aid the widows and children, the latter until the age of 21." This plan came to nothing, but in 1846 the doctors and surgeons of Lower Canada met at Trois-Rivières, to set up a society to ensure the regulation, control, and defence of medicine. Dr Painchaud argued vigorously in favour of such

an organization, and outlined the reasons for the creation of a college of physicians and surgeons, pointing out in particular that the city of Quebec possessed all the institutions necessary in this respect. "Our hospitals," he stated, "are open to students, and above all we have a Marine Hospital, the leader of the whole province, which for surgery is unequalled on this continent, and which alone attracts students from the four corners of the province." Finally Painchaud's initial proposal, that of 1844, was some years later to "give birth to the Canadian Medical Association."

Joseph Painchaud, an influential member of the most important medical associations in the province, enjoyed great prestige and made a substantial contribution to the evolution and development of Canadian medicine. To relieve the sick, to improve the teaching of medicine, to create and develop hospital establishments: these were his daily concerns.

CHARLES-MARIE BOISSONNAULT

PAC, RG 4, B28, 48, 9 June 1811. Ahern, *Notes pour l'histoire de la médecine*, 231, 237, 309, 421, 456. C.-M. Boissonnault, "Création de deux écoles de médecine au Québec," *Laval médical* (Québec), 39 (1968), 547–49. C.-A. Gauthier, "Histoire de la Société médicale de Québec," *Laval médical* (Québec), 8 (1943), 84–110, 117. Ignotus [Thomas Chapais], "La profession médicale au Canada," *BRH*, XII (1906), 147–50. Sylvio Leblond, "L'hôpital de la Marine de Québec," *L'Union médicale du Canada* (Montréal), mai 1951. P.-G. Roy, "L'Hôpital des émigrés du faubourg Saint-Jean à Québec," *BRH*, XLIV (1938), 200–2.

PAPINEAU, LOUIS-JOSEPH, lawyer, seigneur, politician; b. 7 Oct. 1786 at Montreal, son of Joseph Papineau* and Rosalie Cherrier; d. 25 Sept. 1871 at Montebello, Que.

The Papineau family had begun to emerge from obscurity with Louis-Joseph's father, Joseph Papineau, a surveyor and notary, who on occasion constructed mills and managed seigneuries. He was a politician who himself became a seigneur by purchasing the seigneury of Petite-Nation from the seminary of Quebec in 1802. This acquisition, which was to prove profitable, improved the social status of the Papineau family and coincided with the rise of the liberal professions in French Canadian society. It is therefore not surprising, in view of the central role played by the Papineau, Viger, Dessaulles, Cherrier, Bruneau, and other allied families in the society and politics of Lower Canada, that Louis-Hippolyte La Fontaine* should have denounced the political ascendancy of this family clan during the 1840s. Whether or not these family groups tended to form a "family compact," they none the less influenced the political destiny of Lower Canada and Quebec throughout the 19th century. The family was, after all, perhaps the most powerful institution in French Canadian society. Louis-Joseph Papineau was born at a time when the values attached to the monarchy and nobility still exercised a potent attraction, and when the acquisition of a seigneury remained a mark of social advancement. The transition from the position of his grandfather, Joseph Papineau, a farmer and cooper, to his own status as a dignified seigneur could not be achieved without a painful psychological adjustment.

A gradual penetration of bourgeois values into the society had its effect on Papineau. Towards the end of the 18th century certain groups, chiefly connected with trade, began to define political and social power in terms of economic criteria. Their attitude towards wealth – the authentic source of prestige and power in their eyes – differed fundamentally from that of the traditional élites, but as years went by it was to acquire an even greater vigour and appeal. It was also in this period that the inferiority of French Canadians in the commercial and industrial sectors really became apparent; the British had become the main holders of wealth and were responsible for the spread of bourgeois values. Papineau's formative years were thus lived amid a changing mentality. His contradictory attitudes, a blend of open hostility and fascination, towards the search for profit that characterized the businessmen and the British, certainly date from this time. "They alone," he wrote about the British, "have the breeding, the fortune necessary for entertaining. No Canadian family can do it. . . . The resources of the country are devoured by the newcomers. And although I have had the pleasure of meeting among them educated and estimable men, who are glad to see me, the thought that my compatriots are unjustly excluded from sharing in the same advantages saddens me when I am at their gatherings. . . ." His ambiguous attitudes with regard to capitalist and seigneurial ownership, individual and collective rights, also illustrate his profound ambivalence towards what the bourgeoisie represented. The son of the notary Joseph Papineau did not join the ranks of the bourgeoisie immediately.

In fact the young Louis-Joseph Papineau was subjected to social pressures of another order. In many respects his family differed little from most peasant families, where the importance of the clan predominates. The family not only provided values and attitudes, it was also a source of prestige. The bonds of affection between its members did not, however, prevent rivalries from abounding. Papineau was to be profoundly marked by this family climate, which he never questioned, at least consciously. In this domain he showed uncompromising loyalty to tradition. For him the family environment was one of affection and security, a refuge if need be from a hostile society. It did not stifle the individual or render him unproductive.

Among the strong influences on Papineau, that of his father and mother was particularly significant. In the few letters the latter has left, she appears strong-willed, cold, at least outwardly, authoritarian, and unswervingly devout. No doubt she loved her children, but her affection bore an austere mask. It was obvious that Papineau would react against the conception of life and religion exemplified by his mother. His subsequent break with Catholicism and his search for a more optimistic vision of the world would indicate as much. Nevertheless, he never succeeded, despite his efforts, in liberating himself from this basic pessimism, which was perhaps innate but which was fortified by his education. He remained all his life an austere man who never attained the moderation and smiling scepticism taught by certain writers whose works he read. His choice of a wife who projected an image rather like his mother's may be considered significant.

His father, a meticulous man, inclined to be gruff and uncommunicative, seems to have shown more benevolence and indulgence in his dealings with his children, particularly with Louis-Joseph, who was also his mother's favourite, according to John Charles Dent*. It is certain that Joseph Papineau did not possess great religious fervour. He renounced Catholicism, probably during the 1810s, and did not return to it until shortly before his death. It should be noted that in addition to having been among the minority who favoured establishing parliamentary institutions, he had proved to be one of the most influential members of the House of Assembly. His efforts to adapt to new institutions and his activity as a member of the house certainly influenced the subsequent choices made by his son. Joseph Papineau was not a radical: he was a monarchist who professed a very moderate liberalism.

Once his primary education was completed, Louis-Joseph Papineau entered the college of Montreal, directed by the Sulpicians. In 1802, following an incident that brought him into conflict with the authorities, his parents sent him to continue his studies at the Petit Séminaire of Quebec. This institution did not aim, any more than the previous one, at forming revolutionary minds, or even minds merely inclined to innovation. The teaching programme could not have been more traditional. The supremacy of Latin was maintained, and the teaching, by its content, was

Papineau

directed towards the rejection of the heritage of the 18th century. Fear of the French Revolution and of its ideas animated the teachers. The cult of authority and obedience sustained an aristocratic and hierarchical vision of society. In a period when parliamentary institutions were opening the way for changes in political behaviour, these clerical establishments imposed on their pupils the theory of the divine right of absolute monarchy. Despite their leniency towards him, it is unlikely that his masters allowed Papineau to make the works of Voltaire, or the *Encyclopédie* of Diderot and d'Alembert, habitual reading. These books were probably in his father's library. At the seminary, Papineau had the reputation of being a gifted pupil, not much of a worker but a great reader. He was even active within the Congrégation de la Sainte-Vierge. He was to state at the end of his life that he lost his faith at the seminary of Quebec. But in 1833 he praised his father "for the courage he showed in keeping me despite myself at the seminary"; and in 1804 he wrote to his young brother, Denis-Benjamin*, whom he urged to study: "Never have I felt more than I do now what I owe to the seminary." It does not seem that his stay at the seminary of Quebec was marked by open revolt and brutal ruptures. The truth is less obvious and more complex: neither on the religious plane nor elsewhere do his choices appear to have been clear and final.

When he left the seminary in 1804, Papineau hesitated long as to what career to choose; in that respect he was like many graduates of the time, who were ill prepared by the environment and by their education to adapt themselves to social change. In fact the choices were few: once a student had rejected the priesthood, only the liberal professions were open to him. But would Papineau's instability have allowed him to find full satisfaction in a profession even in a more diversified society? He first decided to become a notary, then, modifying his choice, he opted for the profession of lawyer. He received his legal training at Montreal, in the office of his cousin, Denis-Benjamin Viger*, complaining as he did so that he no longer had the time to read. Once authorized to practise law in 1810, he carried on his profession intermittently, and continued to make his dissatisfaction heard. In 1816 he wrote to his brother: "In truth, I am very much a slave at this moment, and that does not endear me over much to a condition with which I was disgusted, but what is to be done?" It was in this period that he began to celebrate the nameless hopes and joys of rustic life. In 1809 he had been elected to the assembly for the county of Kent, thus starting a long political career that was not to come to an end until after

1850: he represented the counties of Montreal West (1814–38), Surrey (1827–28), Montreal (1834–35), Saint-Maurice (1848–51), and Deux-Montagnes (1852–54). No doubt politics allowed him to express certain aspects of his personality, but they left him unsatisfied, eager for the day when he could live in the country with his family and books around him. Yet when he was confined to activities which up to then had been more means of escape than of personal development, the exalted seigneur of Montebello was not to find peace, any more than the disappointed lawyer and the flattered political leader. The sources of his fear were within him: Papineau was and remained an eternal discontent.

Papineau entered the assembly at the height of a political crisis, which had begun in 1805. This crisis, which was unquestionably new, had been marked by the emergence of French Canadian nationalism and political parties. The economic, demographic, and social changes of the first decade of the 19th century were felt as a mortal threat by the elements which were becoming conscious of the existence of a "Canadian nation." The liberal professions, in association with the small merchants, devoted themselves at that time to the defence of the traditional French Canadian institutions and opposed the English merchants, the public servants, the American immigrants, and the so-called "French Canadian traitors." The former, however, went beyond the stage of passive resistance, and, through the intermediary of a political party whose main base was at Quebec, they shaped a strategy and theories which were eventually to give them power and control of patronage. The idea of ministerial responsibility supported this intention, to which the clergy and the old seigneurial families took exception. During the 1810 crisis, a rift was opened between the clerics and the new political élites.

Although his father had warned him against the "so-called reformers" and the "demagogues," and had suggested that he vote on questions according to their merit, Papineau joined the Parti Canadien. The settling of the political crisis in 1810 precipitated the end of the leadership of Pierre-Stanislas Bédard*, and was the beginning of a period during which various claimants disputed for the right to lead this party. Bédard's protracted rancour against the Papineaus suggests that at bottom the latter had little interest in a comeback of the former leader. The conciliatory policy of the governor, Sir George Prevost*, would serve young Louis-Joseph Papineau's ambitions. Its aim was to silence the extremist elements or remove them from the direction of the party. François-Xavier Blanchet*, Gabriel-Elzéar

Taschereau*, Andrew Stuart*, Louis Bourdages*, and Jean-Baptiste-Amable Durocher* did not succeed in commanding attention at a time when Papineau appeared as a moderate. James Stuart*, the most serious candidate, came into direct collision with the governors, and, as Bédard said, could not claim to be a "true blue Canadien," although he was a friend of the "Canadiens." In 1815 Papineau was elected speaker of the House of Assembly, which gave him a salary of £1,000 a year. He was already appearing as the real successor to Bédard.

On 29 April 1818 Papineau married Julie Bruneau, daughter of Pierre Bruneau, a Quebec merchant and an MHA. In the preceding year he had bought the seigneury of Petite-Nation from his father. Despite the rivalries of all kinds which plagued the Parti Canadien, his authority continued to grow with the ever increasing concentration of problems in the Montreal region. The crisis of 1822 over union was to add to his prestige and authority. The merchants' party, previously in a minority in the house, had submitted to the London parliament a bill aimed at bringing about a political union of the St Lawrence valley, an essential condition for the launching of a programme of economic development, and the assimilation of the French Canadians. There was violent opposition in Lower Canada; Papineau and John Neilson* went to London in 1823 to prevent the adoption of such a measure. The groups opposed to the plan of union may have had varying motives, but Papineau and Neilson none the less appeared as the representatives of an extraordinarily large majority of the population. Their mission had relatively little effect on the course of events in England, where the government, in the face of the energetic opposition of certain members of the House of Commons, deemed it wise not to reintroduce the bill, but they nevertheless had the credit for the decision. Papineau, moreover, was able to exploit for political ends the fear generated by this plot, attributed to business circles. On his return he had no difficulty in resuming his position as speaker of the assembly, which Joseph-Rémi Vallières* de Saint-Réal had occupied during his absence.

In 1826 the Parti Canadien became the *Patriote* party. Not only did it reinforce its regional and local bases, while remaining first a Montreal party in which the Papineaus, Vigers, and Cherriers enjoyed great influence, but it also acquired an organ, the newspaper *La Minerve*, to be directed by Ludger Duvernay*. Papineau's authority, despite the rivalries that continued in the party, increased as the party's objectives became more extreme. The party brought together "the most

diverse elements: the French Canadian middle bourgeoisie, a few English liberals, the Irish, farmers of American origin who had settled in the [Eastern] townships, and the French Canadian peasant classes." Defections were severely punished, and rivals ruthlessly thrust aside. In this connection, Thomas Frederick Elliot wrote in 1835: "I have never seen anyone who appeared more skilled than this Canadian speaker in the contrivances and comportment by means of which a single man dominates the minds of a large number, and he becomes more rooted every day in his authority, as they in their obedience. Such is the man whom a small number of his supporters have the presumption to believe that they can discard when he is no longer useful to them. . . . One look from Papineau would subdue all his Canadian flock." Papineau had thus arrogated to himself the authority he enjoyed, but the authority itself rested on a consensus much less conscious than the one of which the *Patriote* Abbé Étienne Chartier* spoke in a letter written to Papineau in 1839: "Your misfortune, sir, is to have been spoiled as a result of the extraordinary influence and fame which the Canadiens have deliberately conferred on you, by all flocking round you, and by raising you upon their shoulders, in order that by this fictitious grandeur you might tower above all the Tory luminaries."

The practice, after 1830, of systematic obstruction, which was intended to force the English government to adopt the reforms sought, was imposed by Papineau. But within the *Patriote* party a wing of authentic liberals was talking about revolutionary action, and placing more and more emphasis on social transformation. La Fontaine, one of Papineau's lieutenants and already one of those aspiring to succeed him, had clearly felt the ambiguities in the ideology of the party and of its leader. In February 1837 he wrote to Henry Samuel Chapman*: "People have reconquered their natural independence by having recourse to arms, and by letting the earth drink the blood of their oppressors. . . . To stir up peoples, one must not rest content with debating purely abstract questions. Something more solid is required. One must touch the sentimental part: the purse. So long as a question of this nature is not raised, agitation cannot be constant and lasting. In the circumstances, I see no question more calculated to lead to this end than the abolition of seigneurial rights. Apart from the seigneurs and the government, everyone desires it, whatever their shade of political opinion. I am therefore firmly resolved to bring this proposal up for discussion at the opening of our next session. . . . The government, the seigneurs and the *hauts petits aristocrates* of

Papineau

both parties will no doubt oppose it; but the masses will unite and act in concert." Basically, the problem raised by La Fontaine revealed a conflict, still latent, between the dominant element, represented by Papineau, which wished to change the political system without interfering with the social structure, and an active but minority group seeking to bring about a political and social revolution. The Papineau group was firmly opposed to any institutional change, whether it concerned the seigneurial system, or the customary law of Paris, or even the status of the clergy. Thus, when the prospectus for the newspaper *Le Patriote canadien*, of which Duvernay was publisher, appeared, Papineau wrote to his wife on 29 April 1839: "So long as there is not national representation, which can remedy abuses in provincial, civil or ecclesiastical institutions, we are giving arguments to the government abroad so that it can abruptly destroy structures which, contained within proper bounds, will protect Canadien interests, and which, if overthrown by the fanaticism of Protestants or philosophers, will be so for the benefit not of the people but of those in power." The opposition between the two groups of *Patriotes* was due not only to differing views of strategies, but also to differing ideologies.

The thinking of a man so unstable as Papineau, and a politician into the bargain, is not easy to describe. If he tended to act as though moved by the most absolute disinterestedness, the purest patriotism, and rigid obedience to sacred principles, he was none the less inclined to present the image of the great democratic liberal battling against obscurantism, corruption, and the oppression exercised by reactionary colonizers greedy for wealth. It was for this cause that he would have willingly agreed to sacrifice his tranquillity and his happiness. This view of him – his own – which was accepted by many people at the time and subsequently, belongs more to myth than to reality. In Papineau, the nationalist, when he was not using new ideologies to support conservative objectives, was usually at war with the liberal and the democrat.

Papineau had taken up French Canadian nationalism as he had found it at the time of Bédard. This nationalism was at first pledged to the defence of linguistic rights and traditional institutions, which were in no way liberal and democratic, quite the contrary. In this connection Papineau, when weighing up the principal achievements of the House of Assembly, wrote: "The ecclesiastical institutions of the country would have been reduced to nothing, the notariat debased, not a single Canadien would be at the bar, and landed property would have been taxed to fatten a crowd of tax-collecting Europeans, if the administration had not been checked by the resistance of an elective Assembly." This judgement revealed more than a state of fact, it expressed a permanent element of Papineau's politics and thought.

Papineau had read the *philosophes* of the 18th century and the liberal thinkers of his day, and he declared himself a supporter of their doctrines. By his declamations against medieval feudalism, against nobles and aristocrats of all times, even on occasion against the descendants of the old French Canadian seigneurial families, Papineau might appear a bitter adversary of the old regime. His eulogies of the authors of the American Declaration of Independence and of the Declaration of the Rights of Man in France implied that he was in favour of a conception of property as individual and absolute and opposed to the feudal conception. In reality he remained throughout his life a supporter of the seigneurial regime. He would never admit openly that France had introduced feudal servitudes as well as seigneurial servitudes into Canada, and that the regime served as a support for a hierarchical and aristocratic society. This attitude might be explained by the fact that he was a seigneur himself. But Papineau saw in seigneurial tenure not only a traditional but also a national institution. Indeed in 1855 he wrote to Eugène Guillemot, the former French minister to Brazil: "My father had bought the seigneury sold to me, being prompted and impelled by the desire to save the remains of our Canadien nationality from being stifled by the English government. Systematically the latter denied land to the Canadiens and lavished it upon the men of their own race, but placing it under the operation of English laws, pettifoggers' traps that would have swallowed up our compatriots who were unfamiliar with them." A year earlier he had attacked the Rouges: "The Rouges are hastening their bondage by their anticlericalism and their antiseigneurial attitude, for the clergy and the seigneurs are the country's safeguard." According to him the role of the seigneurial system had been to procure land free for the French Canadians and to protect them against the British, particularly against the merchants, who considered land as property of the capitalist type. Seen in this light the seigneurial system was supposed to act as a brake on the mobility of landed property and on speculation. Instead of concentrating property in a few hands, this system, according to Papineau, tended to divide up the land equally between individuals. The seigneur was not therefore a large landowner to whom a mass of *censitaires* were subject, but the unremunerated architect of equality. If the enormous abuses committed by the seigneurs of Lower Canada were pointed out to him, Papineau replied that the system had deviated from its intentions, and that all that was necessary was to restore its original purity by legislative and judicial means.

After 1830 Papineau became a democrat. Influenced by Thomas Jefferson and by Jacksonian democracy, he considered North America the natural site for the development of a republic of small landowners. "Canada," he declared in 1833 in one of his speeches, "a country which is impoverished by the harshness of its climate, and in which laws and customs have always favoured the equal division of property, rejects substitutions, condemns the privileges of primogeniture, and should be the last place where such an inept measure should be attempted." Seeking to reconcile his democratic ideas and his attachment to the seigneurial system, Papineau tried to show that the Canadian temperament, the seigneurial system, and democratic ideology all pointed towards the same goal: equality of conditions. This rationalization concerning the seigneurial system and its social intentions was a pure creation of the mind, which was accepted by numerous supporters of the *Patriote* party. But the liberal wing of the party could not but come into conflict with Papineau on this point. The break occurred after the failure of the first insurrection in 1837. Robert NELSON wrote at that time: "Papineau has abandoned us, and has done so for personal and family motives related to the seigneuries and his inveterate love for old French laws." This uncompromising attachment for the seigneurial regime shows that Papineau was not prepared to consider a recasting of civil law. Despite the admiration that he professed for the Code Napoléon, it is clear that he could not accept the conception of property that had served as a basis for this legal revolution. Papineau recognized it himself: he was a liberal and democrat in politics but a conservative in regard to the "sacred right" of property. No better definition of economic and social conservatism can be found. By refusing to interfere with the seigneurial system, he sanctioned the status and economic privileges of the clergy.

Papineau's thought hardly obeys any formal logic. It fluctuates in accordance with his likings and aversions, conscious or unconscious, with his ambitions, his own interests and those of the people he represented. Canon Lionel Groulx* even speaks of a "nebulous incoherence of thought" that increased with age. All this tallies indifferently with the claims of Papineau, who posed as a rationalist philosopher and never missed an opportunity to point out the strictness and firmness of his principles. This rigid but poorly connected thought, which might be considered the product of conscious opportunism, reflects the complex personality of the man. His religious ideas in particular reveal his profound uncertainty. Gradually, after leaving the seminary of Quebec, Papineau drew away from Catholicism. While still believing in God, he finally rejected all revealed religions. It is obvious, although this is not the chief explanation for his religious evolution, that the influence of the 18th century *philosophes* and of the La Mennais of *Paroles d'un croyant* was of capital importance. He found in their works, as well as a stimulus to his anticlericalism, the kind of arguments that would confirm his religious, political, and moral attitude. Violently anticlerical, he showed himself to be also a sharp critic of religious education, the privileges of the church, and the union of church and state. Thus, in the 1831 session, Papineau strongly supported the "notables bill" introduced by Louis Bourdages, which proposed to allow almost all the inhabitants of a parish to share in the administration of the parish council. He denounced the attitude of the members of the clergy who "claimed that they constituted within the state, in civil society, among citizens who were all subject to the laws, a privileged, independent order . . . , and that they could dictate how a part of the fruits of the labour of citizens should be employed." Around 1836, he proposed to place university teaching within the responsibility of "national representation" (i.e., the state): "put under civil, lay control, with full and complete tolerance for all, this establishment [the university] will produce incalculable benefits; under the direction of ecclesiastics of one persuasion or another, such an establishment could not and will not be so liberal." When he returned from exile, he was to declare himself still more an enemy of nobles, priests, and kings, who were naturally in league against liberty and tolerance in all its forms. The Canadian clergy's attitude towards the Parti Canadien and the *Patriote* movement, and their close association with the state, no doubt helped to increase Papineau's anticlericalism. His religious experience was however accompanied by an authentic questioning of part of the Catholic heritage which had been handed down to every French Canadian of the period. To a certain extent, Papineau, as a political leader, attempted to adjust social institutions to his political and religious beliefs. He certainly envisaged society as a lay society, with churches separate from the state. He put forward and supported several measures with this design in mind. But in this domain he appears to have been surprisingly timid for an avowed liberal. In reality Papineau feared that by modifying the status of

Papineau

the Catholic Church he would play into the hands of the real or supposed enemies of the French Canadian nation.

Papineau saw in Catholicism a national institution, possessing, therefore, the same protective virtues as seigneurial tenure. If he saw the latter as French Canada's buckler against Anglo-Saxon capitalism, the Catholic Church appeared to him as the safeguard of this same nation against the Church of England – "the ally of the persecution that had been contrived against Canadiens" – and against a "Protestant" government. Thus, in 1826, when Papineau, in the debate on the bill that proposed to grant Protestant dissenters the right to keep registers of births, marriages, and deaths, took up the cudgel for the Presbyterians, Methodists, and Jews in the name of religious liberty, it was clear that his first object was to undermine the claims of the Church of England. In that connection, he wrote to his wife: "The fact is that there was an offensive and defensive alliance between Mr. Mountain [Jacob Mountain*, the Anglican bishop of Quebec], and Mr. Sewell [Jonathan Sewell*, the attorney general of Lower Canada], directed against the political and religious rights of Catholic Canadians and of all Protestants other than those who wanted to follow Mr. Mountain." A true liberal, in these matters, would rather have spoken of the responsibilities of the state than utilized arguments drawn from liberalism to defend and extend the privileges of the churches. The truth is that Papineau always closely associated Catholicism and the French Canadian nationality: "I admit, however," he wrote about his cousin in 1821, "that as a neighbour I should have little liking for Bishop [Jean-Jacques Lartigue*], for fear he . . . should take it into his head to preach at me. But as for the progress of the establishment of the Canadien clergy, since their interests are bound up with all other Canadien interests, I would resign myself to this inconvenience, as well as to all the others that I would not like to put up with as a private person but that I accept as a public figure."

Papineau was hurt by the incomprehension of the Catholic clergy, who saw in him only a liberal and a democrat dangerous for the church, and he reproached them for equating "sovereignty of the people" with the overthrow of catholicism, for confusing popular sovereignty and national sovereignty without realizing that their real influence must be based upon the support of the French Canadian nation. In a letter to his wife, dated 9 Nov. 1835, he said: "They [the priests] are either knavish or *irresponsible* when they fail to see that there is one maxim the English government will never give up, namely the need to de-

nationalize us in order to anglicize us, and that to accomplish this end they attack our church with no less ardour than they do our *laws, customs, and language.*" His obsession with England so obscured Papineau's thinking that he postponed until later, perhaps to the day of independence, the pursuit of his liberal objectives in politico-religious matters. Meanwhile the clergy, under the aegis of Bishop Lartigue, were adjusting their ideology to the new age, without liberalizing it, and undertaking a struggle that in a few decades was to ensure them social supremacy. Papineau did not understand these innovations. Even after his return from exile in 1845, he continued to make similar declarations which, it must be said, were not inspired only by the desire to take back power from La Fontaine. Thus, in 1848, he declared in a public speech: "Our clergy come from the people, live in and for the people, are everything for the people, nothing without the people. Here is an indissoluble alliance. Here is a unity that is strength. . . . Here is a pledge of indissolubility for a nationality. . . . As a politician, I repeat that the agreement and affection between our clergy and our people has been and always will be one of the most powerful elements in the preservation of our nationality." These words throw light on the social conservatism of Papineau, which was incompatible with his religious liberalism. It is here that the contradictions of the man really appear: a deist, he remained nevertheless a prisoner of the social institution, the Catholic Church.

To this social conservatism, of which the seigneur of Montebello, attending church to set a good example to his *censitaires*, was the symbol, was added an economic conservatism. Certainly Papineau had felt the influence of the French physiocrats, who, opposed though they were to the feudal system, had exalted the prime importance of agriculture in the French economy; but that is not enough to explain his particular emphasis. His economic conceptions were clearly dominated by the idea that the vast majority of French Canadians lived on the land and took a very small part in important commercial activities. For him, agriculture was the predominant economic activity, and any economic policy must proceed from that fact. In a word, the vital objective of French Canadians must be to acquire the land, making use of the framework most suited to its equal distribution and to a humane society: the seigneurial regime. His social ideal was the small farmer, virtuous and, perhaps, enlightened.

Papineau's hostility to commerce was no doubt rooted in tradition, but it also resulted from the fact that large-scale trading was controlled by the

British, who were promoters of capitalism in all its forms. He believed that they were endeavouring to build an economy and a society in which the mass of the French Canadian proletariat, both urban and rural, would be dominated by a minority of men of large property of British origin. It was against this eventuality that he fought. It would be pointless to see in him a socialist. When he criticized English tenure and English common law, it was these tendencies that he was condemning. When he objected to the establishment of government registry offices, it was always through fear of the same dangers. Papineau came to the point where he pictured the English business bourgeoisie as an aristocracy of wealth, and therefore an artificial one, which was aspiring to reinstitute in Canada a society founded on inequality. "It seems to me," he said during the debate on the Ninety-two Resolutions in 1834, "that there is nothing baser than the English nobility who come to us in this country, so eager are they to place themselves and to enrich themselves." As his democratic ideas became more deeply rooted, Papineau, the seigneur, saw the merchant classes more and more as the product of an aristocratic plot fomented by England herself. Thus, in objecting to the timber trade, to massive investments in transportation, which was undergoing a total upheaval, and to banks, he had the feeling that he was working against those responsible for the economic bondage of the French Canadians, and he believed also that he was doing away with a developing aristocracy. After recommending to the population that they withdraw their money from the banks, he declared in December 1834, before the electors of Montreal West: "They will call that destroying trade, whereas in reality it will merely be escaping from enemy hands to fall into friendly ones. Producers will continue their habits of work and economy, the only important sources of a country's wealth. Whether there are banks or not, there will not be one acre more farmed, or one acre less. From the moment that there is a surplus of exchangeable produce, the European capitalists, in view of the profit they would derive from it, will have it bought up." This attitude towards banking institutions recalls that of the Jacksonian democrats. In reality the resemblances are only superficial.

This stand is surprising in a man who professed to be the disciple of Adam Smith and Jean-Baptiste Say. In practice, Papineau had retained from his reading of the two economists only their philosophy of free trade. By taking fragments of their thought, he was able, in addition to acquiring allies in England, to combat the protective tariffs on Canadian timber and grain. He needed an effective weapon against the business world, where his chief political opponents were. Finally, even his belief in free trade reveals the ultra-conservatism of his economic thought.

Papineau's nationalism was therefore strongly rooted in his economic and social conservatism. Even on the religious plane, his aims and liberal aspirations were compromised by this dominant attachment to tradition. Seen in this perspective, his political liberalism and his adherence to democratic ideology raise similar questions, for it seems difficult to reconcile fundamental conservatism and doctrinaire liberalism. When we try to determine the roles that these two facets of his thought were called upon to play, the contradiction can be partly resolved. It is clear that in accepting French Canadian nationalism, such as it was at the time of Bédard, Papineau was at the same time endorsing the political strategy which, in order the better to protect the traditional institutional and cultural heritage, aimed at the assumption of power by a "truly national élite." Even if Papineau tended to present himself as the "national leader" and the authorized spokesman of the French-Canadian nation's aspirations and interests, he none the less remained the real representative of a more restricted section of society. His strong ties with the liberal professions, which were aspiring to power and the benefits of patronage, are in this respect most significant. His presentation of himself as a man of principle above factions, as a pure symbol of a will towards national regeneration that was beyond all the pettiness of daily action, came both from his personality and from the image of himself that he wished to project. Papineau, despite a gift for oratory which would have enabled him to put himself on the people's level, was not by inclination a popular speaker. The great majority of his speeches were intended for a more educated group. His political friends even reproached him with not maintaining steady contact with the populace. Thus, when he spoke of the "people" and the "nation," he referred more to a minority that knew the real needs of the worthy masses. His liberalism was therefore in the last analysis bourgeois or even aristocratic. In this sense he belonged to his century.

When Papineau entered politics in 1809, he shared the unbounded admiration of the Lower Canadian élites for British institutions. Montesquieu, Voltaire, and several other 18th century *philosophes* had already extolled the merits of the English constitution. The English were moreover the first to see in their political institutions a matchless achievement. Papineau wrote: "My education is more English than French. Indeed it is in the English publicists and in the writings of public

Papineau

men that I have studied the English constitution."
He took part in the war of 1812 as a militia captain, for at that period Papineau refused to accept republicanism and democracy after the French or American manner. He remained an ardent monarchist, although he had broken with the absolutist tradition. His attitudes towards the "aristocratic branch" may not be clear; on the other hand his belief in the primacy of the "popular branch" grew stronger over the years. From the beginning of his political involvement, his place was among the Reformers. Certainly one can see here the influence of John Locke in particular, but there were other and more varied influences working upon him. Basically, he looked to the constitutionalists and to active politicians, both in the colonies and in England, for the justification of political choices that he had already made. It is in his nationalism that one must seek the principal source of his reform attitudes. During the debate on the Ninety-two Resolutions in 1834, Papineau analysed the political evolution of the colony before the Quebec Act, and noted: "At that period, there were men who claimed their rights as men and as British subjects. It was recognized that there were principles conforming to the law of nations that could not be violated; that there was a population possessing laws, a religion, a language, customs, and institutions that must be preserved." His main interpretation of the granting of parliamentary institutions can be placed in exactly the same perspective: the English government, he declared in 1833, "had just published some sound maxims. They should have added practice to theory, and have given us a political structure by means of which we could have repulsed the assaults attempted against our institutions." According to him, the constitution of 1791 was supposed to give Canadiens a political instrument destined to ensure the survival of their culture and institutions. On the other hand, according to him, the working of these institutions after 1792 had attributed a kind of supremacy to the governors, the officials of British origin, and the English merchants, who had formed an alliance with the two French Canadian groups least conscious of national objectives: the clergy and the old seigneurial families. In his opinion, the political structures had been manipulated by elements that were hostile to or little aware of the real interests of the French Canadian nation. As to the actual representatives of the nation sitting in the assembly, their influence was almost nil. It was because of this subjective way of looking at the balance of political forces that Papineau accepted the idea of the responsibility of the executive. The aim of those who subscribed to this thesis was to get the real

power into the hands of those whom he was to call later "the national representation." After his rise to the leadership of the Parti Canadien in 1815, Papineau, always with this perspective in mind, brought the struggle to bear on the control of public funds. While attacking the French Canadian nation's enemies on all possible fronts, he made the voting of supplies the priority question in his political strategy. Behind the discussions of principles and constitutional theories, Papineau, whose interests were linked to those of the liberal professions, led the fight for the conquest of political power. His movement, which was based on liberal ideas, was in essence primarily nationalist. It was this surface liberalism that won him the cooperation of the English radicals.

Until around 1830, Papineau remained convinced the British institutions constituted a perfect framework for the survival and development of the French Canadian nationality. It was sufficient to model the local constitution on that of England, and allow it to evolve according to the same principles. Moreover, the fact of belonging to the empire was a guarantee against the United States, and in general against American influence. In his mind, the good faith of Britain could not be called in question. The opponents of the French Canadians, he thought, resided in Lower Canada. They were at times the governors, ill counselled by their entourage, but particularly the highly placed officials and the merchants. For him, certain groups within the French Canadian nation, such as clerics and nobles, represented a danger, for they did not understand their true interests. There were also those who, for personal motives, rallied to the side in power. If he thundered against all these types of people, he never questioned the validity of the bonds that united Lower Canada to the mother country. Already in 1823, however, on his trip to England, he was struck by the aristocratic character of English society and the poverty of the urban masses, and began to ask himself questions. In Lower Canada too, economic and social uneasiness was spreading discontent in the rural milieux. The overcrowding in the liberal professions, and the instability of the lower bourgeoisie in country districts and towns, also suggested the need for more radical political action. The influence of the Paris revolution of 1830 was another invitation to take a more extreme stand. Increasing social tensions were having a hardening effect in all sections of society. Papineau let himself be carried along by this prevailing mood, which worked in his favour. It must be said that the growth of his ambitions coincided with his successes. Despite the concessions made by England, the beginning of the 1830s saw the stepping-up of demands. Papineau's thought tended to turn in another direction.

From that time on Papineau believed in the existence of a plot between the mother country herself and the internal enemies of the French Canadians, the object being the complete subjection of the latter by the implantation of an aristocratic society in Lower Canada. In December 1834 he declared in Montreal West: "No nation ever knew how to govern another. The affection of the Bretons [affections bretonnes] for Ireland and the colonies has never been anything more than the love of pillaging Ireland and the colonies, which had been abandoned to exploitation by the Breton aristocracy and its creatures." This criticism of the aristocratic character of the British constitution, directed particularly against the Legislative Council, on which sat representatives of the business world, became more and more extensive as the struggle for power became more bitter. In March 1836, after William Lyon Mackenzie*, the leader of the Upper Canada Reformers, and Marshall Spring BIDWELL, the speaker of the House of Assembly of Upper Canada, had sent Papineau extracts of the instructions given to the commissioners made responsible for inquiring into the situation in Lower Canada, he violently attacked the English colonial system: "It is only to place in the colonies junior men whom they do not know what to do with in the mother country, it is only to ensure for itself a European influence, that the old colonial regime is preserved. . . . In the Canadas, as in all the other colonies of England . . . there cannot be elements from which to make up an aristocracy or seeds out of which to raise one." Quite obviously, Papineau was seeking to prove that the colonial system was an instrument, by which British institutions could be used to ensure economic, political, and social control for an aristocratic minority imported from Great Britain. His rejection of English institutions was only partial, and to the extent that they served his political objectives he was loyal to them. "There will be found," he wrote, "in the English publicists, in parliamentary histories, in the speeches of [Charles] Fox and others, sublime maxims concerning public law and liberty . . . the enemies of the Canadien name who want to give such narrow limits to English liberty would do much better to go and read them. . . . It is therefore essential for us to recognize in this source the institutions that suit us and that can never be taken from us. From the time that we have belonged to England, we have had the right to institutions as democratic as hers. An attempt has been made to give us an aristocracy, and the system has proved not to be applicable."

Papineau's past distrust of the United States now gave place to unstinted admiration for American institutions. In 1832 Papineau declared himself a republican. The influence of Jacksonian democracy on him is not in doubt; that of Jean-Jacques Rousseau and later of Charles-Alexis-Henri Clérel de Tocqueville is also present. American democracy was, according to him, the reflection of a sort of state of nature peculiar to America. After the American revolution, "pure republicanism" supposedly had flourished in New England, and subsequently spread to all the new states. "But what has been the progress of the United States?" declared Papineau in 1834 during the debate on the Ninety-two Resolutions. "As new agreements have been formulated everything has tended towards democracy. It is therefore in the nature of things that under a government where the influence of birth has been destroyed, where the influence of fortunes is weak . . . it is natural . . . that there should be no privileged classes. . . . If therefore all the changes in this part of the world have been conducive to the establishment of the democratic system, and if those states which have been the last to be established in the west are the most democratic of all, it is evident that this is an order of things special to America, and that one cannot create an aristocracy there."

At bottom Papineau, while retaining from the English constitution what served his political strategy, was to draw from the American model a theoretical justification for the radical transformation of the Legislative Council. The latter would need to be elective because of the fundamentally democratic character of the society of Lower Canada: "The ministers have tried to bring the aristocratic principle into full operation in the Canadas, whose social constitution is essentially democratic, where every one is born, lives and dies a democrat; because every one is an owner; because every one has a small piece of property; because we come into the world, live, and will die in a country that is side by side with the United States." By means of ministerial responsibility, the *Patriote* party and Papineau would have made sure of the control of the executive and the public service; through an elected Legislative Council and the extension of the elective principle to lower levels, the party would have dominated the second legislative branch and the other sources of power. In the light of this naturally democratic society, where the seigneurial regime, the customary law of Paris, and the privileges of the church would still exist, one can understand that Papineau's opponents should question his real objectives. They would certainly not feel that their economic interests and those of the country would

Papineau

be in good hands if Papineau gained his ends.

The idea of instituting by peaceful means a Lower Canadian republic, of which he would naturally be the president, took shape after 1830. By the practice of obstruction, and in particular by the systematic refusal to vote supplies, Papineau proposed to force the British government to bring about radical changes. Nevertheless, in 1834, as is shown by his speech to the electors of Montreal West, he would presumably have been satisfied with a statute allowing a large measure of autonomy, within the empire, for Lower Canada: "A local, responsible, and national government for each part of the Empire, as regards settlement of its local interests, with supervisory authority held by the imperial government, to decide on peace and war and commercial relations with foreign countries: that is what Ireland and British America ask for; that is what within a very few years they will be strong enough to take, if there is not enough justice to give it to them." The Ninety-two Resolutions introduced in the House of Assembly on 17 Feb. 1834 were intended to make clear Papineau's aspirations and political ideas. These resolutions, prepared by a small committee composed of Papineau, Elzéar Bédard*, Augustin-Norbert Morin*, and Louis Bourdages, contained a summary of the principal grievances of the house and of its most important requests: control of revenue by the legislature, responsibility of the executive, and the election of legislative councillors. In the following year, when a certain number of *Patriotes* contemplated without apprehension the possibility of a violent confrontation, Papineau wrote: "We will not withdraw the requests we have made for the full measure of our political powers and rights. . . . We hope, but with some unease, that the British government will give us justice. In this hope we will do nothing to hasten our separation from the mother country except to prepare the people and make them ready for an age that will be neither monarchical nor aristocratic." This weakening of the belief in normal political strategies on the part of the Montreal *Patriotes* continued until 1837, when London, by adopting the resolutions of Lord Russell, categorically rejected the *Patriotes'* requests, which it deemed excessive. This formal refusal precipitated a confrontation that rapidly took on the character of a revolutionary movement.

Papineau's behaviour during the 1837 insurrection is not very easy to explain. His conduct appeared more ambiguous than ever, and he also took care to destroy the documents that he knew to be compromising. He warned his subordinates to do likewise. After the event, he maintained the following argument: the *Patriotes* did not intend to revolt; the government, in order to crush them the more effectively, had forced them to defend themselves; and he himself had advised against any recourse to arms. He also declared that he had had no connection with the Banque du Peuple, thereby admitting the justice of the accusations made against that institution. He said that it was only on his way through Saint-Charles that he had gone to the assembly there, and that he had left Saint-Denis at the beginning of the fight only at the express request of Wolfred Nelson*. According to his interpretation, he was supposed to keep himself in a safe place in order to be able to act as a negotiator in case of a defeat. It is obvious that, taken as a whole, this explanation does not stand up against a serious examination of the facts.

During the months of April and May 1837 the *Patriotes* put their strategy into shape. Unanimity does not seem to have prevailed among them. The radical wing, dominated by people such as Nelson, Cyrille-Hector-Octave Côté*, Édouard-Étienne Rodier*, Amury Girod*, and Thomas Storrow Brown*, certainly opted for openly revolutionary steps. On his side, Papineau represented the more prudent and moderate elements, and appears to have favoured more complicated tactics: that while opinion was being prepared for an armed struggle, action should in the first stage be kept within the bounds of "constitutionality." He thought that by stirring up the population and boycotting taxed products, the English government would finally be forced to give way. Under Papineau's direction, the Comité Central et Permanent du district de Montréal, reorganized on 15 May 1837, was to coordinate the action of the *Patriotes* throughout the entire province. If however these methods proved ineffective, he would then agree to the use of force. In this contingency, armed revolt was not to take place until December, after the freeze-up. On 10 May 1837 Papineau drew up two wills. In 1839, Abbé Chartier wrote: "It is unfortunate that Lord Gosford [Acheson*] did not put off his attack until after 4 December, the day for which all the leaders received notice to be at Saint-Charles, and when you would have had to sign a declaration of independence: you would not have to defend yourself today against the charge of not wanting a revolution because no contradictory document exists." Abbé Chartier added that he had himself destroyed a note sent by Papineau to the *Patriote* Jean-Joseph Girouard*. As well as having been widely known among Lower Canadian *Patriotes* since at least June 1837, this plan had also been communicated to the revolutionaries of Upper Canada.

Similarly, the relationships between the Banque du Peuple, or certain elements of it, and the revolutionary movement are still less clearly established, but they seem more and more plausible. In November 1839 Abbé Chartier wrote: "As for money, was not the Banque du Peuple, which had been in existence barely a year, universally understood to have been established for the purpose of the revolution, and in order to help it? Is it not this motive, which the shareholders skilfully made known, that underlay the rapid success which came to this most patriotic establishment? The cowardly directors of this bank, they too, will have a terrible reckoning to face on the day when payments are due, and they do not seem even to suspect it." Several of the directors and shareholders, the majority friends and relatives of Papineau, were involved in one way or another in the revolutionary events. Before leaving Montreal, Papineau was in continuous contact with his cousin Louis-Michel Viger*, the president of the bank. Questioned in 1840 by Abbé Chartier on his relations with this institution, Papineau replied "that he had always been opposed to setting up the Banque du Peuple, and that he had predicted to Louis-Michel Viger that it would be the tomb of his popularity and even of his patriotism." In short, he did not deny the connections between the bank and the movement. Abbé Chartier ended with the words: "I was very glad to learn that he had nothing to do with this bank, which has so much disappointed the hopes of Canadians." It should also be noted that, during the insurrections, the rumour circulated that if the *Patriotes* triumphed this institution would become the "national" bank, and the other banks would be eliminated. Likewise, the sudden arrival of Édouard-Raymond Fabre*, one of the directors of the bank, at Saint-Denis, just before the battle, his conversation with Papineau, and his no less sudden departure, raise a number of questions. Charles Dansereau declared in 1840: "To the best of my knowledge, no one came to tell P. [Papineau] and O'Callaghan [Edmund Bailey O'CALLAGHAN] to slip away, and to say that it was Dr. [Wolfred] Nelson's orders. If there had been some one to send Papineau and O'Callaghan away, it could only be Mr Fabre. . . ." Truth to tell, all of this can only serve to supply material for a hypothesis which, if verified, would allow us to uncover certain minority but powerful interests that influenced the course of the revolutionary events, and most probably the supreme commander.

Once the series of great assemblies in the six counties got under way, Papineau quickly lost control of a number of the revolutionary leaders, who openly preached revolt and sought to direct the movement towards a revolution of a social character, which no doubt the directors of the Banque du Peuple and Papineau scarcely desired. For his part, Papineau, even if he recommended sticking to legal means, encouraged initiatives of a revolutionary character by what he said. This was how the Association des Fils de la Liberté came into being: divided into two sections, civil and military, it "reproduced the double intention of the plan of resistance" advocated by Papineau. This surge of agitation reached its highest point at the time of the great assembly at Saint-Charles, which on 23 Oct. 1837 issued a declaration of the rights of man. Papineau went to Saint-Charles accompanied by an armed escort. A few days earlier Papineau's wife had told her son Lactance, a student at Saint-Hyacinthe, that his father might visit him after the assembly. This assembly truly marked a turning-point. For the radical elements it constituted a virtual declaration of independence and the beginning of a trial of strength between them and the government. As for Papineau, he still urged the use of peaceful means. Forgetting the revolutionary nature of several resolutions passed on that occasion, he later reproached the radicals for having prompted the government, by their behaviour, to intervene before the moment appointed for the uprising.

After the Saint-Charles assembly, Papineau's behaviour appears more and more ambivalent. Indubitably he was afraid. In particular the way the liberals acted frightened him, but at the same time served his ends. His interviews with Denis-Benjamin Viger, before his forced departure from Montreal, are significant of the conflicts within the man himself. The government's decision to arrest the leaders and intervene militarily forced him to go to the Richelieu valley. Once he got to Saint-Denis, he acted both as supreme commander, distributing generalships, and as the leader of the civil section. It was probably at the time when these civil and military sections were set up that arrangements were made, perhaps at the direct or indirect suggestion of Papineau himself, to provide cover, in the event of an emergency of a military nature, for the two promoters of the civil section: Papineau and O'Callaghan. Seen from this angle, the visit, after the arrest of Louis-Michel Viger, of Édouard-Raymond Fabre, who no doubt had important news to transmit, may merely have hastened the departure of the two men. Once in the United States, Papineau travelled under an assumed name. Meanwhile he had forgotten his role as a negotiator.

The months that followed marked the break between Papineau and the extreme radical elements of the movement [see NELSON]. The *Patriote*

Papineau

leader had met influential Americans, who were ready to back a retaliatory expedition. This plan was not adopted at the assembly of refugees held at Middlebury, Vermont, because Papineau refused to accept a declaration of independence involving the abolition of seigneurial rights, customary law, and tithes. His intransigence, more than differences over strategy, explains the profound disagreement that gradually divided the refugees. It is possible that the religious question also counted for something in this conflict. Dr Thomas Fortier, of Gentilly, wrote to Duvernay in 1840: "I am neither a Jesuit nor a bigot; but when one wants to revolutionize an ignorant people, one must be acquainted with its spirit and not offend its prejudices, but rather utilize them as a stimulus – your railing against the clergy and the tithes has spread terror among this body, they have taken alarm; they have had the idea that you would follow the course of the French revolutionaries, that you would despoil them; [Robert] Nelson's proclamation did not reassure them." It is obvious that Papineau was linked with those *Patriote* elements, clerical or anticlerical, that closely associated religion and nationality. The attitude of Jean-Philippe BOUCHER-BELLEVILLE, who stated around 1840 that anticlericalism was no longer justifiable, since all the parish priests had become nationalists, is significant. That Papineau should have supported the endeavours of Abbé Chartier, who was seeking to modify the anticlerical fever among the refugees, is also revealing. Thus the gap widened more and more between the two groups. Papineau consequently kept aloof from any invasion plan, at the same time as he tried to obtain the support of the French, Russian, and American governments. The insurrection of 1838 took place without his participation. He was opposed to the venture, yet he did not protest when the leaders of the second rebellion used his name as a rallying cry to stir the population to revolt. His brother-in-law, Théophile Bruneau, wrote to Duvernay on 11 Oct. 1838: "I warned Papineau that I had taken the oath of allegiance to Nelson's provisional government, and that I was a member of the secret societies of Albany. . . . I told him further that we were going to use his name freely everywhere, except in the matter of money. . . . So use his name with discretion in New York, I am certain we shall not be disavowed by him."

From the spring of 1838 on, the refugees' hostility towards Papineau increased. Not only did they reproach him with having abandoned the cause, but they attributed to him more and more responsibility for the failure of 1837. Several went so far as to talk about his flight from Saint-Denis. Côté spoke of exposing him publicly. But several refugees tried to stop an action that would harm the movement, because of Papineau's extraordinary popularity among the people. In October 1839 Dr Antoine-Pierre-Louis Consigny wrote to Duvernay: "No one blames Papineau more strongly or detests him more heartily than I do; but for the sake of the cause, I believe it is better to keep silent than to try to lay low the arrant poltroon who is the principal source of all the evils that have weighed so heavily on the country since 1837." After the failure of the second insurrection, the refugees, convinced that Papineau's presence in the United States was a basic obstacle to any revolutionary plan, worked out a plot to get him away to France. Papineau was to win French sympathy for the Lower Canadian cause. On 8 Feb. 1839 he sailed from New York for Paris.

His stay in France, where his wife and three of his children went to join him, produced no political result. Until 1845, Papineau lived there poor and most often alone, but following Canadian events with great interest. He sometimes worked at the Bibliothèque Nationale or the archives, where he copied and had copied documents relating to the French period. He had contacts with liberals, socialists, and even Irish nationalists, and visited Italy and Switzerland. It was not until 1845, two years after his wife's return to Canada, and because of her insistence, that he finally decided to end his exile; he had obtained a full amnesty a year earlier. It was also because of pressure exerted by his wife, and by a certain number of his friends, that he turned towards politics again in 1848. For some time, once he had been elected MLA for the county of Saint-Maurice, he maintained friendly relations with the La Fontaine group. But soon the inevitable divergences came to the surface. Papineau did not readily tolerate being one man in a crowd, and his political beliefs appeared irreconcilable with those of his chief La Fontaine.

To begin with, Papineau refused to accept the union of the Canadas, which he regarded as a disgrace. For him the future, since the defeat of 1837, lay rather in the direction of annexation to the American republic. Though his nationalism remained as uncompromising as before, he proclaimed more loudly than ever the strength of his democratic beliefs. It is true that the notion of annexation to the United States occasionally led him to question himself as to the repercussions that this fusion into the great American universe might have on French Canadians. In this connection, he had written to his wife in May 1838: "But Canadiens are so much an unusual people on this continent, that it is painful to think of the necessity of a dispersal in which they would not recover the combination of circumstances that has given them their moral and religious habits, their language, their laws, and a nature as happy, gay and sociable as theirs is. There is no Englishman who does not derive the greatest advantage from settling in any part of independent America, or who has not the most legitimate reasons for doing so. For such people emigration leaves no true cause for regrets." But these momentary misgivings rapidly disappeared before the unbounded admiration that he had for American institutions, and before his hatred of "aristocratic England." Socially and even culturally, Lower Canada, once it had become an American state, would have in his estimation every chance of flourishing in this prophetic environment. Since Papineau could not approve of the abolition of the seigneurial system, which the supporters of La Fontaine demanded, his conflict with the latter gave rise to violent attacks on both sides. As for a number of Papineau's former collaborators, among them Wolfred Nelson and Duvernay, they now considered the future of Lower Canada to lie within the empire. What was more important, they commanded the support of public opinion, both from the élites and from the masses. Ministerial responsibility seemed to them the best solution to the French Canadian problem as a whole. Beaten, Papineau still supported the annexationist movement of 1849, but gradually withdrew from politics. From 1852 to 1854 he was an MLA for the county of Deux-Montagnes, but he did not stand in the election of 1854. During the last part of his life, he devoted his time to his seigneury at Montebello.

After his return from France, Papineau had renewed contact with his seigneury. The prospects of development had become good because of the growing number of *censitaires* and the possibilities in the area for lumbering. From then on Papineau took an active interest in his fief. Certainly he was not the seigneur that he dreamed of being: the protector of the good, happy peasant and the guardian of equality. He looked after his interests with care, prosecuted recalcitrant *censitaires*, and utilized for his own benefit the rich resources offered by the forests that covered a great part of Montebello's 178,000 acres. As one might expect, he objected with the utmost vigour to the movement in favour of the abolition of the seigneurial system. Just before 1854, disregarding his past prejudices because he was afraid to lose part of his possessions, he even went so far as to ask that his fief be converted into free and common socage.

Papineau had always wished to live in the country, with his wife and surrounded by his books. By his marriage with Julie Bruneau he had had three boys and two girls, but only the two latter remained by his side. Ezilda and Azélie, who

was to marry Napoléon Bourassa*, had like their mother no wish to live on the seigneury. In order to attract them, and perhaps imbued with the desire to project a magnificent image of himself, Papineau built a luxurious manor-house. Yet he did not succeed in conquering their repugnance. This last period of his life was marked by frustrations and domestic misfortunes.

Politically he changed little. He continued to denounce responsible government as a hoax, and the advent of confederation as one more attempt to perpetuate English monarchical and aristocratic institutions in Canada. The movement that produced the Institut Canadien, of which he was an honorary member, seemed to him more promising, but it did not satisfy him fully. He expressed his disagreement with the antiseigneurialism and anticlericalism of this movement, which in reality was only a small minority group, no doubt a very active and noisy one, but one that was incapable of making common cause with the great mass of people that bowed to the conservatism of the liberal professions and to an ultramontane clergy. From 1850 until his death in 1871, Papineau, without succeeding in solving his contradictions, remained the prophet of annexation and democracy. To the great indignation of the priest of the parish, the seigneur of Montebello refused to return to the faith of his youth and died loyal to his deist convictions.

FERNAND OUELLET

[An exhaustive bibliography of materials on Papineau would have to mention most of the large series of documents covering at least 1810–50. Only the most essential items are listed here. The best source is doubtless the ANQ. The Collection Papineau, which in 1961 was one of the richest private collections in Canada, provides the basis for any study of Papineau. His letters to his wife for the period 1820–62 have been published in APQ *Rapport, 1953–55,* 187–442; *1955–57,* 255–375. Julie Papineau's correspondence from 1823 to 1862 has also been published in APQ *Rapport, 1957–59,* 55–184. At the ANQ there is as well: QBC, Procureur général, Événements de 1837–1838; the papers of Ludger Duvernay; and a copy of the correspondence of Charles-Ovide Perrault* in the Édouard-Raymond Fabre papers. The National Library (Ottawa) and the PAC also have some Papineau papers, mostly correspondence. Other archival collections are also important.

At the ASQ, the Verreau collection includes the Viger papers which give much interesting information in the series of manuscript volumes by Jacques Viger* entitled "Ma Saberdache".

At the PAC, the following papers are useful: MG 24, B1 (Neilson collection); B6 (Denis-Benjamin Viger papers). The large series of official correspondence and correspondence of the bishops also provide information, and to trace the career of a man in public

Paré

life special attention must be given to the numerous newspapers of the period.

Papineau's "Histoire de l'insurrection du Canada," published in Paris in May 1839 in the *Revue du Progrès*, is also an important historical document. F.O.]

Several biographies of Papineau have been published: Eve Circé-Côté, *Papineau, son influence sur la pensée canadienne; essai de psychologie historique* (Montréal, 1924). L.-O. David, *Les deux Papineau* (Montréal, 1896); *L'honorable Ls.-Jos. Papineau* (Montréal, 1872). Alfred Duclos de Celles, *Papineau 1786–1871* (Montréal, [1905]). Robert Rumilly, *Papineau* (Montréal, [1944]). Benjamin Sulte, "Papineau et son temps," *Mélanges historiques*, Gérard Malchelosse, édit. (21v., Montréal, 1918–34), XIII.

For complementary information the following should be consulted: *Papineau; textes choisis*, Fernand Ouellet, édit. (Cahiers de l'institut d'histoire, 1, Québec, 1964). Gérard Filteau, *Histoire des Patriotes* (3v., Montréal, 1938–39). Lionel Groulx, *Notre maître le passé* (3 sér., Montréal, 1924–46), 1 (3ᵉ éd.), 189–213; 2 (2ᵉ éd.), 69–133; 3, 245–54. A. R. M. Lower, *Colony to nation; a history of Canada* (1st ed., Toronto, 1946). Edgar McInnis, *Canada, a political and social history* (new ed., New York, 1961). Monet, *Last cannon shot*. Fernand Ouellet, *Histoire économique*; *Louis-Joseph Papineau, a divided soul* (Canadian Hist. Assoc. Historical booklets, 11, Ottawa, 1961). Marcel Trudel, *L'influence de Voltaire au Canada* (2v., Montréal, 1945). Mason Wade, *Les Canadiens français de 1760 à nos jours* (L'Encyclopédie du Canada français, III, 2ᵉ éd., 2v., Ottawa, 1966), I. Fernand Ouellet, "Les insurrections de 1837–1838: un phénomène social," *SH*, no.2 (November 1968), 54–82; "Papineau dans la révolution de 1837–1838," CHA, *Report, 1957–58*, 13–34; "Papineau et la rivalité Québec-Montréal (1820–1840)," *RHAF*, XIII (1959–60), 311–27.

PARÉ, JOSEPH-OCTAVE, secular priest, canon, secretary of the bishopric of Montreal; b. 16 May 1814 at Saint-Denis-sur-Richelieu, L.C., son of Léon Paré and Marie-Angélique Grenier; d. 20 Jan. 1878 at Sault-au-Récollet, Que.

At his baptism Joseph-Octave Paré received the first name of Bishop Joseph-Octave Plessis*. In 1827 he began his classical studies at the seminary of Saint-Hyacinthe, and spent his last year at the seminary of Quebec. Having decided on the priesthood, he subsequently studied theology at Saint-Hyacinthe and taught at the same time, as was customary. He was pleased to be able to say that Alexandre-Antonin Taché*, the future archbishop of Saint-Boniface (Man.), was one of his pupils.

Joseph-Octave Paré had already become valuable to Bishop Jean-Jacques Lartigue* at the secretariat of the bishopric when he was ordained priest on 22 Sept. 1838. In 1841, when the cathedral chapter was instituted, he became its chief canon,

and in the same year accompanied the new bishop of Montreal, Ignace Bourget*, to Europe. Before returning to Montreal, Bourget made Paré and Michael Power* his chargés d'affaires, with the mission of obtaining from the Colonial Office a written statement that the secretary would undertake not to obstruct the steps being taken by Bourget to set up an ecclesiastical province in Canada. Having done this, Power and Paré went to Ireland to recruit English-speaking priests for the diocese and to consult the bishops on various points of discipline.

In 1856 Paré returned to Europe to visit the great basilicas of the old continent, and to determine which one might serve as a model for the future cathedral of Montreal. St Peter's in Rome was his choice. He then had the thankless task of collecting the funds for this undertaking.

Being solely responsible for the secretariat from 1845 to 1876, Paré knew Bishop Bourget more closely and over a longer period of time than did any other person. The two men were not always of the same opinion. If the bishop of Montreal accepted his secretary's views on singing, the liturgy, and the plan of the new cathedral, he disagreed with him as to the measures to be taken to finance the construction of the edifice. However, Paré always carried out Bourget's decisions with unimpeachable fidelity.

Joseph-Octave Paré was remarkable for the perseverance and good humour with which, for nearly 40 years, he served Lartigue and Bourget. He took an active part in the charitable work, the labours, and the successes of Bourget, whose humiliations he also shared. In the spring of 1877, when Bishop Bourget retired to the Saint-Janvier residence at Sault-au-Récollet, Paré went with him. It was there that on 20 Jan. 1878 he died, attended by his venerable friend; he was buried in the vaults of the cathedral at Montreal.

The chorus of praise that was heard at his grave, which Bourget has preserved for us in a biographical account, bears witness to the fact that his contemporaries had understood the magnitude of the services rendered by Joseph-Octave Paré to the cause of the church in Montreal.

Léon Pouliot

ACAM, RCD, 137; RDM, 7; RLB; 901.079. J.-B.-A. Allaire, *Histoire de la paroisse de Saint-Denis-sur-Richelieu (Canada)* (Saint-Hyacinthe, Qué., 1905). [Ignace Bourget], *Mémoire pour servir à l'histoire du chapitre de la cathédrale S. Jacques de Montréal* (Montréal, 1882), 157–70; *Notice historique sur la vie de M. Joseph-Octave Paré ...* (Montréal, 1878). Léon Pouliot, "Mgr Bourget et la reconstruction de la cathédrale de Montréal," *RHAF*, XVII (1963–64), 340–62, 471–89; XVIII (1964–65), 30–38.

PARENT, ÉTIENNE, journalist, lawyer, member of the assembly, public servant, and essayist; b. 2 May 1802 at Beauport, L.C., son of Étienne-François Parent and Josephte Clouet; d. 22 Dec. 1874 at Ottawa, Ont.

The name of Étienne Parent is less famous than those of political personalities who were his contemporaries, such as Louis-Joseph PAPINEAU or Louis-Hippolyte La Fontaine*. A few flattering terms applied to him are all that remain: the Victor Cousin of America, the Nestor of the press. Paradoxically, there is as yet no biography of him, and one can only speculate as to the reasons for this silence. Is it because the major part of Parent's work consists of innumerable newspaper articles, and that articles are less accessible to curiosity than books or texts of speeches? Or is it that the debates for which Parent's generation felt such passion have lost their brilliance, dimmed by the stormy ideological conflicts of the second half of the 19th century? Or is Parent's "moderation" responsible for the less arresting quality of his thought by comparison with the exalted rhetoric of the leaders of the 1837–38 rebellion? No doubt varying degrees of probability can be attached to each of these hypotheses, but it seems that the relative oblivion into which he has slipped is due above all to the fact that the essential function of his ideas was to give inspiration, and less credit has been accorded to them than to the political and social achievements of which they were the source.

In fact, Étienne Parent's thought dominated the first half of the French Canadian 19th century. This man incarnated as did no one else the ambitions of a new social type, that of the intellectual and political élite, which at the turn of the 19th century was replacing the gentleman class of landowning seigneurs, and, along with the ecclesiastical leaders, resolutely taking hold of the destiny of the French Canadian people. He was to be called "Père Parent," so much did he appear to be a prototype and an example.

Robust shoulders, a sturdy neck, a massive head with a high, broad brow framed in thick hair, an authoritative, even bitter mouth, clamped tight upon unshakeable convictions, eyes whose unwavering look passed beyond an invisible audience, preoccupied it would seem to outdistance his thoughts in order to hasten the affirmation of conclusions already foreseen, desired, and decided upon: such is the impression given by the clear lines of a portrait of Parent in his maturity. A mere glance at this face makes one forcibly aware of certain essential characteristics of the personality: assurance, sturdiness, and determination. One feels, before learning it through the written word, that Parent was a man of the soil; that before handling ideas he had handled oxen and plough; that this reflective look had long been accustomed to the horizons of a countryside full of promise. It is no surprise to learn through his son-in-law Benjamin Sulte* that he was "endowed with a Herculean constitution"; that he could "work 18 hours a day"; that "he produced by himself almost as much as all the journalists of Quebec put together." One may furthermore easily accept that all his gifts were intellectual, and that he was awkward or clumsy in society. Moreover, all his life he suffered from an inability to talk readily. The essence of Parent's life is that he transcends his period by his intelligence and frankness. He was one of the first to give thought to the destiny of French Canadians. With unrivalled lucidity and vigour, he defined "national" objectives which were to sustain not only his generation but succeeding generations for more than a century.

Through two centuries of ancestors, Parent had his roots in the soil of Quebec. He belonged to the sixth generation of Parents in Canada. The forebear, Pierre Parant, who came from Mortagne in Perche, France, emigrated to New France on 9 Feb. 1634 with a group of settlers brought by Robert Giffard*. Following him, an uninterrupted line of Parants or Parents farmed the land on which he had settled at Beauport, some miles down river from Quebec on the north bank of the St Lawrence.

Étienne Parent was the eldest of a family of 15 children, nine boys and six girls. As soon as his age permitted, he helped on the farm and attended a primary school at Quebec. His intelligence attracted attention. Although his parents were not rich, in 1814, when he was 12 years old, they sent him to the college of Nicolet for his secondary education. He had as fellow-students a future bishop, Charles-François Baillargeon*, 16th bishop of Quebec, and a future judge, Charles-Elzéar MONDELET. He spent five years at Nicolet. He was studious and methodical, and won several prizes. Each summer he became once more the young farmer turning his strength to the labours of the fields. In 1819 he left Nicolet, and went to the seminary of Quebec to continue his studies. The teaching at the seminary was strongly influenced by the Cartesianism perpetuated in a textbook of the old régime, *La Philosophie de Lyon*. The ideas of Bonald enjoyed great popularity there, and much store was set by Bossuet's *Discours sur l'histoire universelle*. Students' exercise books of the period reveal that instruction in history disparaged France and praised England. Young Parent read all the books available in the library, and those lent by certain teachers. His

Parent

memory was prodigious, and, according to one anecdote, he had among other feats learned a lecture on Bossuet by heart. He stood out from his comrades by the soundness of his judgement, his literary bent, and the precision of his ambitions. He was considered a young man who "gave promise of living by his pen" – an unusual phenomenon in his time.

The opportunity came his way when he was still at the seminary. Times were alarming for French Canadians. The threat of a union of the two Canadas had been voiced in 1805 and again in 1807; a first proposal had been put forward in 1810. Governor Sir James Henry Craig* had suspended the newspaper Le Canadien in 1810. About the same time Papineau and John Neilson* joined the Parti Canadien, and in 1817 Le Canadien was revived; it was called the "Petit Canadien" to distinguish it from the "Grand," which had existed from 1806 to 1810. At the seminary, Parent struck up a friendship with Augustin-Norbert Morin*, who contributed to the Petit Canadien. Morin obtained the collaboration of Parent, who published his first articles in the paper in 1819. Even before the end of his studies, Parent's career was under way. The seminary, however, had other ideas, and forbade this activity. For that reason or some other, we do not know, Parent left the seminary in 1821, on the eve of his final examinations. His family then offered him employment, which he accepted, with a maternal uncle, Michel Clouet, a hardware merchant on Rue Buade in Quebec. This task soon wearied him, and he decided to return to the family farm to help his father in the fields. There in August 1822 destiny came to seek him: the owner and the editor of Le Canadien, Dr François-Xavier Blanchet* and Flavien Vallerand, offered him the editorship of the newspaper; Augustin-Norbert Morin, who had held this position since December 1820, had had to leave Quebec to study law at Montreal. The two men stressed the political situation: a new threat of union of the two Canadas was worrying French Canadians; a bill to this effect had just been announced in London. Parent hesitated, reflected, accepted. At 20 years of age he became editor of Le Canadien.

The post was an enviable one, although not lucrative. Above all it was unstable, being threatened from both outside and inside. Le Canadien still opposed the dominant oligarchy, but no longer commanded the support of all members of the Parti Canadien. From his first appearance on this disputed tribune, Parent showed himself a fighting journalist. The characteristics that were to prevail throughout his life asserted themselves firmly: his astounding capacity for work, the rigour of his dialectic, the unshakeable persistence

of his convictions. In vehement articles he fought and helped to bring about the failure of the plan of union, withdrawal of which Papineau and Neilson were to try to obtain when they went to England in 1823. Parent insisted on complete respect for the constitution of 1791, and demanded recognition of political liberties that had been flouted. Then, in 1823, La Gazette de Québec (which had been started in 1764) became a political paper and an organ of the Parti Canadien. In March 1825 Le Canadien, deserted by its supporters, was forced to go out of circulation.

Parent set about consolidating his knowledge and at the same time varying his activities. From 1825 to 1829 he studied law as a student in the office of Joseph-Rémi Vallières* de Saint-Réal, and later in that of Charles-Eusèbe Casgrain*. To support himself he had to give French lessons. In the autumn of 1825 he was taken on as editor of the French section of La Gazette de Québec. He was soon holding a number of offices: in 1827 he was appointed deputy French translator and law officer of the assembly of Lower Canada. On 11 May 1829 he was called to the bar of Lower Canada. Shortly afterwards, on 30 June, he married Marie-Mathilde-Henriette Grenier, daughter of Gabriel Grenier, a Beauport cooper. Five girls and one boy were born of this marriage; Joséphine-Henriette was to marry Antoine Gérin-Lajoie*, Mathilde-Sabine was to marry first Évariste GÉLINAS on 3 Sept. 1862 at Quebec, then Guillaume-Sylvain de Bonald* on 17 Feb. 1885, and Marie-Augustine was to marry Benjamin Sulte on 3 May 1871 at Quebec.

Lower Canada experienced more and more difficult years. In the 1830s a generation of ardent young Patriotes threw themselves into the political struggle, several as members of the assembly, where they became rivals of their great elders. In 1826 Augustin-Norbert Morin had started the paper La Minerve, to support the Patriote party and teach French Canadians "to resist any usurping of their rights." The 1830 revolution in France kindled admiration for the Men of July. Ardent spirits were rallied by the person and the voice of O'Connell in Ireland. The names of La Mennais, Lacordaire, and Montalembert acquired a magical quality. It was said that La Gazette de Québec was no longer sufficiently alert, and an attempt was made to start a new newspaper. As Parent had been refused a salary increase at La Gazette, the decision was speeded up. With the help of René-Édouard CARON, Jean-Baptiste Fréchette, Elzéar Bédard*, and Hector-Siméon Huot, he collected the necessary capital and undertook to revive Le Canadien once again. The paper was to be a bi-weekly, and would have its office at the "political centre of the district of Quebec," on the Côte de la Montagne. The guiding spirit was to be Étienne Parent.

The first number of the third *Canadien* appeared on 7 May 1831. As a motto, Parent took the watchwords: "our language, our institutions, our laws," which, he wrote, would be all his life his own "polestar." His first article had the appearance of a manifesto: "It is the lot of the Canadiens to have not only to preserve civil liberty, but also to struggle for existence as a people. . . . No middle course, if we do not govern ourselves we shall be governed. . . . Our politics, our aims, our sentiments, our wishes and desires are to maintain all that constitutes our existence as a people, and, as a means to that end, to maintain all the civil and political rights that are the prerogative of an English country. . . ."

On 4 June Parent launched the idea of a national, political, and patriotic association that would be under the patronage of St John the Baptist. The association was founded a few years later (1834) by Ludger Duvernay*. In every manner and by every means Parent endeavoured to rouse the communities of Quebec. He also published poetry and songs that quickly became popular, particularly the song of the *Chouayen* which poured scorn on cowards and defeatists. As a result of articles criticizing the Legislative Council in the *Vindicator* and *La Minerve*, Daniel Tracey* and Ludger Duvernay were kept in prison at Quebec from 17 Jan. to 25 Feb. 1832; on their return to Montreal, it was Parent who presented Duvernay with one of the two medals struck to commemorate this imprisonment.

These were the most crowded years of Parent's career, during which he sought to give expression to the consciousness of the French Canadian people at the same time as he informed and guided it. A philosopher by training, a journalist by temperament, a fighter by necessity, he made the fervour of his convictions felt in the pages of *Le Canadien*. In an open, disinterested fashion, with independence and competence, he treated all the burning questions that the political events of the day gave rise to, pointing out dangers, demanding justice, and standing as an advocate of law and order. At this time Papineau was still a "constitutionalist," and Parent's views coincided with his. "Parent," Joseph-Guillaume Barthe* wrote, "is in journalism what Papineau is at the parliamentary tribune." Papineau was the political leader of the *Patriote* party, Parent its intellectual leader. His house in the Upper Town of Quebec, on Rue Saint-Joseph (now Rue Garneau), and later each of those he was to live in at Toronto, Montreal, and Ottawa, was the familiar meeting-

place of all those who had some standing in the political world.

The profession of journalist, however, was not in itself a sufficient source of livelihood. Parent had to accept other offices. Already a translator and legal officer of the assembly, he was appointed on 30 Jan. 1833 first titular librarian of that body. He was also made responsible for overseeing the printing and proof-reading of the *Journaux de la chambre d'Assemblée du Bas-Canada*. All these posts brought him the modest salary of $800. His two reports as librarian (7 Jan. 1834 and 27 Oct. 1835) described the deplorable state of the library, proposed purchasing volumes that were "urgently needed," announced that he had established a new catalogue, and recommended leaving the library open "until dusk" to help those who could not frequent it during the day. At the end of 1835, deeming his salary inadequate, he gave up his post as librarian, and shortly afterwards was appointed clerk of the assembly.

The political situation was deteriorating more rapidly. An economic crisis from 1833 to 1836 caused serious unrest, which was not unrelated to the agitation of the years 1837–38. A large number of the Ninety-two Resolutions presented to the assembly in 1834 by Papineau, Bédard, and Augustin-Norbert Morin were derived from Parent's *Le Canadien*. These resolutions prompted Britain to send a royal commission, in 1835, to inquire into the situation in Lower Canada. The report of this commission gave rise to Lord Russell's deplorable resolutions of May 1837. In August the last session of the House of Assembly of Lower Canada was held. Public protest meetings took place in increasing numbers from spring to autumn. Then occurred the bloody clash between the Fils de la Liberté and the Doric Club at Montreal (6 November), the six counties' address (13 November), the uprisings at Saint-Denis (23 November), Saint-Charles (25 November), and Saint-Eustache (14 December), and the flight of Papineau.

The stands Parent took and the statements he made in *Le Canadien* of that period, particularly during the grim year of 1837, would merit being reported month by month and day by day. He devoted earnest efforts to demanding changes in the constitution, supporting the struggle against established authority, and clarifying what form the necessary reforms should take. Like Dr Elzéar Bédard at Quebec, who was the political leader of the moderates, he advocated only legal courses of action against the government. In 1835 he had parted company with Papineau and Morin when they began to urge people to violence. He was a patriot, but he condemned agitation. "We are not

Parent

ready," he wrote on 24 April 1837, "for independence; let us have patience, let us prove ourselves, the law will resume its course; let us assure citizens that impartial juries will be maintained and protected; let us work for improvements in the common weal that have been suspended for years; let us educate the people in its affairs: let us open the schools that have been closed as a result of political upheaval." Again, in May of 1837: "We cannot follow them when they say that our submissiveness should henceforth be determined by our numerical strength, combined with the sympathies that we shall find elsewhere." And once more, in June 1837: "We in no way wish to share the terrible responsibility assumed today by our former brothers in arms and their partisans: we impute to them the blame for all the blood that will be shed . . . against them alone must rise the wailings of widows, mothers, and orphans, and the lamentations of a whole people brought to social abasement."

Parent incurred the reprobation of several Montreal *Patriotes*. *La Minerve* insulted him, and in the autumn of 1837 reproduced the decree of the Comité Central et Permanent which declared him a "traitor to the nation." He nonetheless persisted in denouncing excesses both on the governmental and on the *Patriote* side, and thus earned the ill feeling of every one. "There is no middle course left: either the leaders of the unrest of which we are beginning to taste the poisoned fruits knew that they would let loose in society the most disastrous passions, or they had not foreseen it; in the first case they have rendered themselves guilty of a great villainy, in the second, they have shown a great lack of foresight, which must cause them to be declared unworthy to guide the people's destinies" (25 Sept. 1837). After the battles at Saint-Charles and Saint-Eustache, Parent remained silent until the end of 1837. He was horror-stricken by the tragic events, whose consequences he had, alas, predicted.

When he took up his pen again it was to plead in favour of the exiles, who had nevertheless treated him as a renegade; it was to try to repair the evil and to urge Britain to understand the lesson of 1837. He demanded a responsible government, as the only means by which long-accumulated grievances could be met. "We have merely the name and shadow of a constitutional government," he wrote on 14 Feb. 1838. A few weeks after the departure of the governor, Lord Gosford [Acheson*], the 1791 constitution was suspended. Government was reduced to a Special Council directed by Sir John Colborne*.

Parent greeted hopefully the arrival of Lord Durham [Lambton*] on 27 May 1838. Despite everything he retained his faith in British justice. As soon as Durham left, at the beginning of November of the same year, a new insurrection broke out and was savagely put down by Colborne: villages were sacked, nearly a thousand persons were imprisoned, three French Canadian judges, Philippe Panet*, Elzéar Bédard, and Joseph-Rémi Vallières de Saint-Réal were suspended, 12 *Patriotes* were condemned to death. In the face of these outrages, Parent's voice became scathing. "The groans of the oppressed," he wrote on 24 Dec. 1838, "awaken remorse in the hearts of the oppressors, and bring a blush to their faces. . . . We should like to spare England the unenviable honour of seeing its name associated with that of Russia, the 'executioner of Poland.' There is all our crime. It is a great crime, we admit, in the eyes of all those who are plotting the annihilation of the Canadien people."

Two days later, on 26 Dec. 1838, he was arrested, at the same time as the printer of *Le Canadien*, Jean-Baptiste Fréchette. He was accused of "seditious schemings" and taken to the prison at Quebec. Despite his endeavours to obtain a trial, he remained there until 12 April 1839. His release was secured by a writ of *habeas corpus*. The cold and bad conditions in the prison made him almost deaf, and he was to remain afflicted with this infirmity until the end of his life. Even in prison he continued to direct *Le Canadien* and publish articles in it, thanks to an ingenious stratagem like that resorted to by the young Duc d'Orléans at Clairvaux: regularly a young messenger, Stanislas Drapeau*, brought to him in prison a faked tart that contained newspaper clippings, news, and messages; by the same means, Parent sent back outlines of articles and corrected proofs. When he came out of prison he did not regain his post as law officer, and concerned himself only with *Le Canadien*.

Durham's report was published in England on 8 Feb. 1839. Étienne Parent translated it and published it in sections in *Le Canadien*. The report left him disillusioned. He wrote in April 1839: "If the report has been drafted with as much good faith as is said, it is a fresh proof that the English cannot pronounce an impartial judgement between us, poor French Canadians, and our adversaries, who have the good fortune not to be stricken like us with original sin." The report proposed the union of the two Canadas, a measure that aimed at nothing less than the assimilation of the French Canadians. Faced with this almost inevitable eventuality as a result of union, Parent adopted a fatalistic attitude. In a series of articles that appeared in *Le Canadien* between May and November 1839, he set forth arguments in a pro-

582

cess of reasoning that took him from sorrowful resentment to resignation, and finally to a conditional confidence. "We invite our compatriots," he wrote on 13 May 1839, "to make a virtue of necessity, not to struggle wildly against the inflexible course of events. . . . We have always considered that our 'nationality' could be preserved only with the sincere tolerance, if not the active help of Great Britain, but efforts are being made openly to extirpate that nationality from this country. . . . [The task facing] us French Canadians, whom England is sacrificing to the demands of a favoured minority regardless of acts and guarantees that were equivalent to a sworn social contract, is to show, as one of the parties in the political marriage that is imposed on us, that we are prepared to bring to the proposed union all the goodwill necessary to make the alliance as profitable and as happy as possible, while expecting reciprocity from the other party."

Parent's dialectic was not without moments of stupefaction, even of revolt. In December 1839 and January 1840 he gave a bitter account of the debates in the assembly of Upper Canada on the plan of union proposed by the governor, Lord Sydenham [Thomson*]. He remarked on the distrust, even the contempt of the Upper Canadians, and noted the injustices and oppression that union might bring for his compatriots. For a while he was fiercely anti-unionist. In January 1840, with François-Xavier Garneau*, he headed a committee of 40 prominent citizens which was responsible for collecting signatures on a petition against union. They obtained 39,928 signatures [see Caron]. The Act of Union was, however, approved in England on 23 July 1840, and on 28 August Louis-Hippolyte La Fontaine, prompted by Parent's initial thesis, published in *L'Aurore des Canadas* his "Address to the electors of Terrebonne," a programme-manifesto that accepted the principle of union and recommended collaboration with the Upper Canadian Reformers, with the object of gaining ministerial responsibility. Parent published the address in *Le Canadien* of 31 August, and again began to hope for the possible effectiveness of union. On 20 October, with an electors' committee of Quebec, he contributed to an "Address to the electors of the whole province," which favoured union and endorsed La Fontaine's programme. Despite these political vicissitudes, he continued to concern himself with the intellectual progress of his compatriots. For a long time *Le Canadien* had been receiving newspapers from Paris, and had been reproducing numerous articles from them in its columns. In the autumn of 1840 Parent and Jean-Baptiste Fréchette decided to use these articles as material for a special journal, which would also publish Canadian works "bearing the mark of excellence." They launched *Le Coin du feu*, a weekly review that lived only a year, from 21 Nov. 1840 to 13 Nov. 1841.

The Act of Union was proclaimed in Canada on 10 Feb. 1841. In the first assembly elections for the new United Canada (or Province of Canada), Parent stood as a candidate in Saguenay County, and was returned by a majority of three votes on 8 May 1841. He attended the first two sessions of the new parliament at Kingston, from 14 June to 18 Sept. 1841, and from 8 Sept. 1842 to 12 Aug. 1843. In *Le Canadien* he persisted in his arguments that the greatest possible advantage should be taken of the union, pleaded for the equality "of the two populations and the two countries," and urged confidence in the government. He was the invited speaker on the occasion of the first celebration of Saint-Jean-Baptiste day at Quebec, on 24 June 1842. He submitted to the assembly a bill proposing that French be recognized as an official language. His partial deafness prevented him, however, from discharging his responsibility as a representative of the people in the way he would have liked. When the office of superintendent of public instruction was created, the governor, Sir Charles Bagot*, offered Parent the direction of the French section of the province, but Dr Jean-Baptiste MEILLEUR was finally chosen. La Fontaine, who had just formed a cabinet, invited Parent to assume another high public office: on 14 Oct. 1842 he was appointed clerk of the Executive Council. He had to leave *Le Canadien*, which he had directed for nearly 15 years. On 21 Oct. 1842 he published in it his last article, a "farewell to his readers." He was 40 years old. A second stage in his career was beginning: that of public servant, writer, and lecturer.

A nomadic existence also began for him, for he had to follow the shifts of the seat of government of the Province of Canada: Kingston until 1843, Montreal from 1844 to 1849, Toronto from 1849 to 1852, Quebec from 1852 to 1855, Toronto from 1855 to 1859, and again Quebec in 1859. His duties brought him into direct contact with the decisions and the trend of the union government. But though he observed the evolution of politics from close at hand, he remained an impartial critic. A friend of La Fontaine, he played the part of a mentor towards him. His existence was less agitated than before, but he continued to be the strenuous worker he had always been. He read copiously. He contributed occasionally to *Le Canadien* in 1847, and again from 1851 to 1854. He was a professor in so far as one could be at a time when the former Lower Canada did not yet

Parent

possess a university. The Institut Canadien was founded at Montreal in 1844 by enthusiastic young intellectuals (Parent's future son-in-law, Antoine Gérin-Lajoie, was its first secretary); the courses and lectures it offered and its library made it the equivalent of a French Canadian university. It was while the seat of government was at Montreal that Parent undertook, before the members of the institute, the series of lectures (or public addresses, as they were called) that constitute a major part of his work. His ideas were taking a different turn, and his style was changing. The journalist gave free rein to the philosopher. Now that the constitutional struggles were over, he concerned himself with the development of the French Canadian people. In his lectures to the Institut Canadien of Montreal he tackled the following subjects: "L'Industrie considérée comme moyen de conserver notre nationalité" (22 Jan. 1846); "Importance de l'étude de l'économie politique" (19 Nov. 1846); "Du travail chez l'homme" (23 Sept. 1847); "Considérations sur notre système d'éducation populaire, sur l'éducation en général et les moyens législatifs d'y pourvoir" (19 Feb. 1848); and "Du prêtre et du spiritualisme dans leurs rapports avec la société" (17 Dec. 1848). Before a literary society, the Club Social, he gave another talk, on "La presse."

In 1847 Parent advanced to further stages in the governmental hierarchy: on 22 May he was appointed assistant secretary of the Province of Canada, at the same time as an English-speaking colleague, Edmund Allen Meredith*. Later, at Quebec, in the winter and spring of 1852, he delivered four other lectures designed for various professional groups: "De l'importance du commerce" (15 Jan. 1852); "De l'intelligence dans ses rapports avec la société" (22 Jan. and 7 Feb. 1852); and "Le sort des classes ouvrières" (15 April 1852). In the same year *Le journal de l'instruction publique* published an article of his on "Pierre Bédard et ses deux fils." Through these audiences, as previously through those of Montreal, Parent spoke to the French Canadian people as a whole, solemnly calling on them to work for their material and intellectual advancement. He was already one of the most respected and heeded among the older members of the French Canadian élite. Since the ministry of La Fontaine and Robert Baldwin* and the actual recognition of ministerial responsibility in 1848, the struggles of even the recent past had grown blurred in people's memories. He was the friend of all of his contemporaries – journalists, politicians, civil servants – who had some standing in public life.

This phase of Parent's existence has no history other than that of a conscientious public servant.

In 1866 he once more accompanied the government, when it went to Ottawa for good. On 29 May 1868 – a new step upward in public administration – he was appointed undersecretary of state in the federal government, a post he was to occupy until retirement in 1872. He then lived two more years. Parent, who had never ceased to be a believer or to attend church, had nevertheless, in Benjamin Sulte's words, "long maintained a scepticism, which worried him." He edified his friends who visited him regularly during the three weeks of his last illness. He was already deaf, and a rapidly developing cataract made him almost blind. He spoke of nothing but the rebellion of 1837–38 and the prison where he had been detained. He passed away on 22 Dec. 1874 at Ottawa. His wife survived him by 16 years and also died at Ottawa, at the age of 86.

Étienne Parent's life is surprising in its continuity, despite its two phases marked by the activities of the journalist and those of the public servant, two phases which moreover coincide in a strange way with two periods in the evolution of the French Canadian people. As astonishing in their consistency are the dominant elements of his thought, which, enriched by the fuller information and the broadening and deepening influences brought to it by events, remained centred around one unshakeable preoccupation: his concern for the destiny of the French Canadians.

In seeking to determine the forms this concern took, one must not lose sight of the ecology, social structures, and mentality of Quebec society, and particularly the political situation, at the time when Étienne Parent was born. He was of the second generation after the conquest. When he was a student at the seminary (1820), Papineau, at 34, had been a member of the assembly for 11 years and speaker of the assembly for five. Papineau was at the pinnacle of his political glory. He was the most illustrious combatant in the epic parliamentary struggles which, over the almost 30 years the constitutional regime of 1791 had been in force, made the claim for redress of violated rights heard. The first period of Parent's professional life and ideology was marked by the bitterness, pugnacity, and aggressiveness that the continuation of these struggles required. However, once Parent became convinced, after the equivocations and dramas of conscience occasioned by the setting up of the union government, that the new regime allowed hope for political stability and self-government, he conceived his task and that of his compatriots to be to consolidate and use political power with an eye to the cultural autonomy and "national" interest of French Canadians.

Accordingly, Parent, the man who favours continuity, stands in contrast to Papineau, the man who chooses separation. In them also two mentalities are opposed, two visions of the French Canadian world that were associated with two regions, with two cities that had long been the poles around which the dialectical tensions of French Canadian society had been fashioned: Montreal and Quebec. Montreal was the commercial metropolis, the city of competition, the place of symbiosis where two Canadian peoples, the English-speaking and the French-speaking, confronted each other; Quebec was the fortress city, the political and religious capital, the "citadel of memory." Parent represented a certain Quebec way of being a French Canadian. More profoundly, and the one trait accentuated the other, he was a man of the soil. Without attaching undue importance to atavism or to environmental influences, it is impossible not to recognize in Parent a man who, born on the land, and having worked on the land, identified himself with the small paternal homestead that remained in his eyes a microcosm of the great.

Parent also owed to his country origin his physical attributes and several moral and intellectual characteristics. A desperately hard worker, he detested idleness. He was perseverance itself. Consequently he was opposed to any form of defeatism. If these attitudes are not taken into account, one can scarcely understand some of his ideological positions. He was sceptical of if not hostile to the seigneurs or the descendants of the nobles of the old regime, because he blamed them for having been idle, for having lacked the ability to be architects of social progress; it was they who must be held responsible for the backwardness and inferiority of French Canadians in the economic and industrial spheres. Likewise, Parent was ruthless towards all those who, taking their example from the seigneurs, made themselves the instruments or accomplices of the new master, those whom the people had christened *chouayens* and whom Parent lampooned in a scathing song. Finally, it is in this same light that one must interpret Parent's opposition to all those who after 1837 advocated the annexation of Canada to the United States: annexation appeared to him a solution of least resistance, a lack of faith in the national destiny.

Étienne Parent's thinking, it must be repeated, turned around an immovable centre: the "national" idea. Before him and at the same time, many other politicians, *Patriotes*, and publicists had spoken of the "nation," but beneath this concept was as a rule a lyrical, sacred entity, of a more or less abstract character. Parent's talent and originality lay in having been the first to be-come aware of the realities of the French Canadian nation, and to propound a definition of them in a coherent body of doctrine. The formulation of this doctrine was a gradual one, and reflected the two periods of his life. From the beginning, however, its elements were clearly defined.

It was a nationalism above all sensual, being anchored in the soil and in the past. It was also juridical and constitutional, like that of the first Papineau. By the Quebec Act, French Canada concluded with England a "true social contract," by the terms of which it was entitled to "self-government." Using the same logic as the first French Canadian assemblymen after 1791, Parent was convinced that French Canadians must have an effective share in the government of *their* Lower Canada. He knew the philosophy and recognized the value of the institutions of British parliamentarianism: he demanded that they be applied to the realization of the social contract, and that they not be vitiated by an immoderate oligarchy or by a discretionary power. It was on this that his acceptance of union was later to be postulated: the conviction that each of the two Canadian peoples would be able to govern itself within the same constitutional framework. To this extent, Parent's nationalism was loyalist, if one understands that this loyalism was a means towards the achievement of national survival. Furthermore, this nationalism had scarcely any link with France. Rather it was part of a conception of a natural right of a people to realize its own destiny. It belonged first and foremost to a theological and providentialist conception. It is God "who creates nationalities so that they may live." Parent's nationalist profession of faith was a cult, "a religion."

These basic ideas, latent in the articles of Parent's first period, became evident in the lectures of the second. In them the influences that had contributed to shaping his ideology also stood out more clearly. A variety of paths criss-cross in this ideology, yet they blend in sweeping designs often lyrically conceived. With the providentialist vision of history inherited from Bossuet, Parent combined philosophical credos from the age of enlightenment. A reader of Rousseau, he believed in the fundamental goodness of man. Having read the works of Condorcet and Buchez, he was convinced of the inevitability of an indefinite progress of human nature and of society, a progress and improvement that were "intended by God." From La Mennais he derived the titles and inspiration for at least two of his lectures. He was acquainted with the writings of the socialists, Saint-Simon, Fourier, and Louis Blanc, and not infrequently passages of his lectures bore the imprint of a

Parent

utopian ideal. In all that concerned economic matters, he was a disciple of the physiocrats and a determined supporter of free trade. A long thesis would be required to do justice to the whole of Parent's view of society, which led him to consider society as collective man in the service of individual man, actuated by a spirit of fraternity, whose progress was attainable only through an equilibrium that respected the double principle, material and spiritual, of human nature. In short, Parent's "moderate" thought looked for a harmony, analogous to the ambition of Comte's social view, between order and progress.

Parent wanted each of his lectures to bear on a theme "closely related to our nationality," and used his ingenuity to illustrate in them how this nationality should express itself and progress. Now that the house of government had "become habitable," politics must turn to the material and intellectual questions on which the social and economic advancement of a young country depended. Parent identified areas of disquiet, made diagnoses, and prepared plans of action. French Canadians must without delay initiate themselves in political economy: their elders had performed their task, and the younger must now perform theirs; the former had been orators defending popular rights and from now on "enlightened economists" were needed. The new age would be one of industry. The new nobles of America were the industrialists. French Canadians should pay honour to industry by their acts; if they did not "the mass of the people . . . exposed to the influence and denationalizing action of the leaders of industry of the rival race . . . will with time lose their national character." Hence the necessity for a system of education planned to meet the specific needs of the French Canadian people, and not "inspired by foreign canons," for like Montesquieu Parent knew that laws can neither be exported nor imitated from country to country. He proposed free compulsory education. A sometimes utopian intellectual, he put forward a general plan of education of which the aim was nothing less than the creation of "a class of intellectuals" to whom alone public administration would be entrusted. He spoke of popular education, and as he used it this term had a resonance very close to the one it has now: newspapers, "the people's book," must discuss economic questions and all the problems with which an enlightened social life requires familiarity.

Hence Étienne Parent was at one and the same time a realist, a utopian, a Cassandra, and a planner. Several of his prognostications and suggestions, particularly in the spheres of economics and education, have remained topical, without alas awakening much response until the end of the century, or even until the present day. His arguments were to be repeated by Robert-Errol Bouchette* and Édouard Montpetit*. With uncommon perspicacity, he was able to elaborate a nationalist doctrine that was complete even in its economic and cultural components. The style in which he expressed himself may seem today either too dry or too lyrical. The period rather than the man is responsible. It is remarkable that through the rhetoric of the day so much of his breadth of vision and originality appears. Few of his contemporaries could remain on his level. Few men could write, as he could: "For myself, I have never understood that God would have imposed work upon man as a punishment."

JEAN-CHARLES FALARDEAU

There are unpublished works of Étienne Parent at the PAC, ANQ, and ASQ. These archives, as well as the AAQ, AJQ, and ASN, have material on Parent. For more information on the documents in the archives, consult: Urbain Blanchet, "Étienne Parent, ses opinion pédagogiques et religieuses," unpublished DES thesis, Université Laval, 1965.

Interesting information on Parent is found in P.-E. Gosselin, "Étienne Parent et la question politique au Bas-Canada de 1836 à 1838" (unpublished typescript at the Bibliothèque du séminaire de Québec, Québec, 1939). [J. G. Lambton], Le rapport de Durham, M.-P. Hamel, édit. et traduct. ([Saint-Jérome], Qué., 1948). J.-G. Barthe, Souvenirs d'un demi-siècle ou mémoires pour servir à l'histoire contemporaine (Montréal, 1885). F.-X. Garneau, Histoire du Canada depuis sa découverte jusqu'à nos jours (4e éd., 4v., Montréal, 1882–83), III. Antoine Gérin-Lajoie, Dix ans au Canada de 1840 à 1850; histoire de l'établissement du gouvernement responsable (Québec, 1888). P.-E. Gosselin, Étienne Parent (1802–1874) (Classiques canadiens, 27, Montréal et Paris, 1964). Marc Lebel et al., Aspects de l'enseignement au petit séminaire de Québec (1765–1945) (SHQ, Cahiers d'histoire, 20, Québec, 1968). Monet, Last cannon shot. P.-E. Parent, Histoire généalogique des familles Parent-Grenier, Fournier dit Préfontaine et Lamarre ou Delamarre (Ottawa, 1931). Benjamin Sulte, "Étienne Parent," Mélanges historiques, Gérard Malchelosse, édit. (21v., Montréal, 1918–34). Turcotte, Canada sous l'Union. Mason Wade, Les Canadiens français de 1760 à nos jours (L'Encyclopédie du Canada français, III, 2e éd., 2v., Ottawa, 1966), I. Marcel Cadieux and Paul Tremblay, "Étienne Parent, un théoricien de notre nationalisme," L'Action nationale (Montréal), XII (1939), 203–19, 307–18. Bernard Dufebvre, "Étienne Parent, le « renégat »," RUL (Québec), VII (1953), 405–12. Roger Duhamel, "Le journalisme," Cahiers de l'Académie canadienne-française (Montréal) no.3 (1958), Essais critiques, 126–30. Fernand Ouellet, "Étienne Parent et le mouvement du catholicisme social (1848)," BRH, LXI (1955) 99–118. Gérard Parizeau, "Mon ami Étienne Parent," L'Action universitaire (Montréal), II (1935–36), 50–51, 64. Léon

Pouliot, "Une leçon d'histoire d'Étienne Parent," *BRH*, LX (1954), 71–73. Antoine Roy, "Les Patriotes de la région de Québec pendant la rébellion de 1837–1838," *Cahiers des Dix*, XXIV (1959), 241–54.

PARKIN, JOHN BUCKWORTH, criminal lawyer; b. 1816 at Dewsbury in Yorkshire, Eng., of the marriage contracted on 15 Sept. 1814 by the Reverend Edward Parkin and Sarah Cullen; d. 16 Dec. 1875 at Quebec.

John Buckworth Parkin arrived in Canada with his parents in September 1819. He attended the school at Chambly run by his father, the Church of England minister there; then in 1834 he went to England to study law and arts. Trained in classics and with a good knowledge of English and French literature, Parkin was called to the Quebec bar on 23 Feb. 1837, after working at Montreal in the office of the future judge William King McCord*.

For a short while Parkin was in turn a circuit court judge, a commissioner of bankruptcy, an acting judge in the superior court, and president of the Quebec bar (1862); above all he acquired a great reputation as a defence counsel in criminal cases. At Quebec, where he lived, his name was linked particularly with three trials. In January 1858 he managed to have Captain John Charles Rudolph cleared of a charge of manslaughter; Rudolph was in command of the *Montréal* on 26 June 1857 when it was destroyed by fire off Cap Rouge near Quebec causing the death of about 250 persons. Thomas Crozier, an English soldier who killed a sergeant in July 1862, was found guilty only of manslaughter. Parkin obtained the same verdict for Robert Murphy, a carter who had killed a policeman in 1875. This was his last victory. He died on 16 Dec. 1875 at Quebec.

He married Katherine Bradley, by whom he had seven children, among them a son, Edward Bradley Parkin, who also became a lawyer. A few days before his death Parkin was converted to Roman Catholicism, and received a Catholic burial in St Patrick's Church.

J.-C. BONENFANT

Le Canadien (Québec), 20 nov. 1875. *Morning Chronicle* (Quebec), July 1862, 17 Dec. 1875. *Quebec Mercury*, July 1857, January 1858. P.-G. Roy, *Les avocats de la région de Québec*, 339. *Storied Quebec* (Wood *et al.*), IV, 283–84. Charles Langelier, "J.-B. Parkin, c.r.," *BRH*, III (1897), 82–89, 98–106. T. R. Millman, "Edward Parkin, first S.P.G. missionary at Chambly, 1819–1828," *Montreal Churchman*, XXVII (1939), no.6, 16–17; no.7, 7, 19.

PEARKES, GEORGE, lawyer and public servant; b. in 1826 in Guildford, Surrey, Eng.; m. 30 April 1869 at Victoria, B.C., Mary Elizabeth Dorman; d. 18 March 1871 in Victoria.

Nothing is known of George Pearkes' family background or of his upbringing. His correspondence demonstrates, however, that he was a well-educated man with a gift for clear analysis. He probably studied law in England but does not seem to have been admitted to the bar there. Pearkes immigrated first to eastern Canada, later to California, and finally arrived in Vancouver Island in 1858. Here he became the colony's first practising solicitor and was appointed the first notary public by Governor James DOUGLAS on 3 Aug. 1858. On 28 August the governor named him the first crown solicitor and attorney (analogous to attorney general) for the colony. As such he accompanied Douglas to Fort Hope that year, where he and two others were commissioned by the governor as competent judges to hear a charge of murder.

George Pearkes spent most of his years on Vancouver Island in private practice. His original law partnership with Elisha Oscar Crosby was dissolved on 31 Jan. 1859; he was later associated with William Saunders Sebright Green, the arrangement ending 12 July 1866, and on 28 Oct. 1870 he formed his final partnership with Edwin Johnson. Probably arising from his early sojourn, Pearkes had a familiarity with the laws of California and on 27 Dec. 1859 he was appointed a commissioner for that state. For almost a year in 1865–66 he was acting registrar general for Vancouver Island while the permanent incumbent, Edward Graham ALSTON, was on leave.

At his untimely death the Victoria *Colonist* said of George Pearkes: "A prominent member of the Masonic Fraternity, and a zealous promoter of every public movement or patriotic enterprise, the earnest friend of every private charity, he has succeeded beyond what is the lot of most men in making himself useful and respected in this day and generation."

ALFRED WATTS

PABC, George Pearkes correspondence. PRO, CO 478/3. *Cariboo Sentinel* (Barkerville, B.C.), 8 April 1871. *Colonist* (Victoria), 27 Dec. 1859–21 March 1871. *Victoria Gazette*, 3, 28 Aug., 28 Sept., 4 Nov. 1858; 1 Feb. 1859.

PEDLEY, CHARLES, historian and Congregational clergyman; b. 6 Aug. 1820 in Hanley, Staffordshire, Eng., son of James Pedley and Alice Curtain; d. at Cold Springs, Ont., on 22 Feb. 1872.

Charles Pedley, whose father was an engraver, entered Rotherham College in Yorkshire in 1844. During his student years he spent a summer vacation as a supply minister in Hamburg, Germany.

In 1849 he married Sarah Stowell, the eldest daughter of his tutor at Rotherham. In the same year he received a call from the Congregational Church at Chester-le-Street, Durham. After nine years in Durham he was asked by the Colonial Missionary Society to go to St John's, Newfoundland; in 1857 he and his family moved there.

During his Newfoundland years he took an active part in the community and delivered a series of lectures on David Livingstone's travels, the proceeds from which he donated to the Colonial Missionary Society. He seems to have been popular with people of all faiths, and his engaging personality as well as his evident intellectual interests were probably responsible for the encouragement he received from Sir Alexander Bannerman*, governor of Newfoundland, when he undertook to write a history of Newfoundland. He returned to England in 1863 to oversee the publication of this work, which was dedicated by permission to the Duke of Newcastle [Clinton], principal secretary of state for the colonies.

Pedley's *History of Newfoundland . . .* is attractively written. He went to some pains to give due recognition to earlier writers on the subject, John Reeves* and Lewis Amadeus Anspach*, and criticized another whom he accused of "over credulousness." He shows considerable tolerance for other races and other beliefs. Bannerman had put at his disposal "many-thousand pages" of documents and, despite his period's limited knowledge of the early explorers, Pedley's book is generally useful. His interest in his subject was more than factual, which adds to the readability of the book, as may be seen from the following extract: "The French nomenclature is not confined to the South of the island, but is also found . . . scattered on the n. e. shore, and it must be confessed that the names thus derived are less coarse and homely than many which are of English origin, among which we meet with such as 'Old Harry,' 'Pipers-Hole,' 'Hell Hill,' 'Seldom-come-bye,' 'Come-by-chance' and other like suggestive, but unpoetic, sounds."

Whilst in Newfoundland Pedley travelled both in the United States and in Canada. He attended the ninth annual meeting of the Congregational Union of Canada in 1862. At that meeting he was invited to assist at the service and apparently decided that he would eventually settle in Canada.

When Pedley moved his wife and seven sons there in 1864 he did so with no certainty of a church. He was eventually appointed as a substitute in Guelph while the regular minister was on missionary service in British Columbia. When the incumbent returned, Pedley was once more out of work, with an ailing wife and a hungry family.

His son remembered that "there were times when we had little but turnips to eat . . . we boys were having the time of our lives but father was breaking his heart."

Finally in January 1866 a call came from Cold Springs. There his wife died leaving him with a large family to care for by himself. He undertook their education, and raised several ministers and missionaries, a school teacher, and a civil servant. At Cold Springs he was a vigorous and popular minister, and in May 1866 took on the church at Cobourg as well. During his ministry he made his church self-supporting.

Pedley seems to have been an unhappy and unfortunate man, his intellectual capacities not challenged enough by his work or by his associates. Although welcomed by the Congregational Union when he came as a visitor from Newfoundland, once he had moved to Ontario he was made to wait several years before he was accepted as a member. One wonders if this delay was the result of his showing impatience or arrogance. When finally accepted he seems to have been appreciated and was scheduled to lead the opening service at the next meeting of the Congregational Union of Canada when he died suddenly at the age of 51.

MINERVA TRACY

Charles Pedley, *The history of Newfoundland from the earliest times to the year 1860* (London, 1863). Congregational Church (St John's), Register of baptisms. UCA, Interview with the Reverend J. W. Pedley by C. E. Silcox, 16 Dec. 1930; letter from Miss Stowell, Charles Pedley's sister-in-law, to the Reverend A. M. Fenwick. Colonial Missionary Society, *Reports* (London), XXI (1857)–XXXVI (1872). Edward Ebbs, "Notes of missionary meetings, Western District, no. 2," *Canadian Independent* (Toronto), XI (1865), 286–89. *Morning Chronicle* (St John's), 4 April 1872. *Public Ledger* (St John's), 5 April 1872.

PELTIER, HECTOR, doctor and teacher; b. 15 Sept. 1822 at Montreal, L.C., son of Toussaint Peltier*, lawyer, and Émélie Herigault; d. 29 Jan. 1878 at Montreal, Que.

At the age of 16, Hector Peltier went to France to study philosophy at the Collège Henri IV in Paris. He began medical studies in Paris, went to Edinburgh to complete them, and after two years obtained his doctorate there. On 21 Feb. 1846, after his return to Canada, he received authorization to practise medicine, and was appointed professor of physiology in the new Montreal School of Medicine and Surgery, which had been established three years earlier.

No doubt because of his European training, Peltier was closely connected with the evolution of the medical profession in Montreal. For example, he was one of the 180 signatories who sought from the parliament of the Province of Canada official recognition of the study and practice of medicine; this was granted in 1847.

In 1849 Peltier was instructed, with Dr Louis Boyer, to present to the Hôtel-Dieu of Montreal a draft agreement, soon to be realized, for the organization of clinical instruction for the school's pupils. On 13 June 1850 the school delegated him to appear before the committee of parliament on private bills, in order to obtain amendments to its charter which would allow it to issue certificates to practise. This request was refused; indeed, in 1853, 27 Montreal doctors, joined by those of the Université Laval, presented to the assembly a report demonstrating that to grant to non-university institutions the authorization to issue licences to practise would be to lower the level of the profession.

Since 1847 McGill University had been giving the students of the school their final teaching and conferring diplomas on them. Consequently it did not appreciate the school's request to have its charter modified. Faced with the repeated annoyances created for it by McGill, the school decided to affiliate with some other better disposed university. After fruitless negotiations with the Université Laval and the University of Ottawa, the school, through the intermediary of Hector Peltier and Pierre Beaubien*, submitted to Victoria University (Cobourg) a draft agreement which was immediately accepted. On 10 Sept. 1866, the Montreal School of Medicine and Surgery became the Faculty of Medicine of Victoria University, which was Methodist. "A fine subject of scandal for which moreover the school would be blamed during conflicts with Laval," wrote Dr Roger Dufresne in 1946. "Some would then feign belief that under the Methodist dispensation the faith of the French Canadian Catholic students must certainly be endangered! Yet the only individuals exposed to this peril were the professors who were responsible for going, once a year, to have the names and official signatures affixed to diplomas printed beforehand at Montreal."

Their situation, however, did not entirely satisfy the directors of the school, who renewed their petition, through Peltier and Beaubien, to the Quebec MLAS, for a university charter for Montreal. In view of the opposition of Bishop Elzéar-Alexandre Taschereau*, of Quebec, this petition was dismissed. In 1872 the Jesuits presented a bill to found a university at Montreal, and the reply was again negative. These repeated and unavailing steps pitted against each other the cities of Quebec and Montreal, the politicians and the religious authorities, the Gallicans and the Ultramontanes. Therefore in 1872 Le Franc-Parleur published over the signatures of Beaubien, the president of the school, and Peltier, his secretary, the following declaration: "After all our previous steps and our dealings with the Université Laval, we have decisive reasons to wish never to have anything further to do with the Université Laval or with its teaching. . . . However, we feel the urgent need of a Catholic university for Montreal."

This struggle between Montreal and Quebec was taken to Rome, and Bishop Ignace Bourget* had to request the Jesuits to withdraw their bill. Dr Hector Peltier was a witness of part of this painful story: he learned of the decision to establish a branch of the Université Laval at Montreal and the first bargainings by the Quebec rector, Thomas-Étienne Hamel*, to get the teaching of medicine organized at Montreal.

On 6 Jan. 1878 the founding of a Catholic university at Montreal was celebrated. Dr Peltier attended the banquet; his confrères expected a speech from him, but he kept silent. Perhaps he had a presentiment of the cerebral haemorrhage that was to strike him down a few days later when he was finishing a class.

One of the leading figures of Montreal in his time, Peltier in 1852 had married, at Notre-Dame de Montréal, Suzanne Ellen Van Felson, daughter of a judge, George Van Felson*.

LOUIS-PHILIPPE AUDET

AJM, Registre d'état civil. Le Collège des médecins et chirurgiens de la province du Québec, 1847–1947 (Montréal, [1947]). Rumilly, Hist. de la prov. de Québec, I, 242–43. Roger Dufresne, "L'école de médecine et de chirurgie de Montréal, 1843–1891," L'Union médicale du Canada (Montréal), nov. 1946, 1314–26. L.-D. Mignault, "Histoire de l'école de médecine et de chirurgie de Montréal," L'Union médicale du Canada (Montréal), oct. 1926, 597–674.

PINSENT, ROBERT JOHN, magistrate and judge; b. in 1797 in the Conception Bay area of Newfoundland; d. 28 Nov. 1876 at Pimlico, London, Eng.

Robert John Pinsent's family was one of long standing in the Conception Bay area of Newfoundland. As the son of a prominent family he was probably sent to England to be educated. He married Louisa Broom; their only known child, Sir Robert John Pinsent*, played a distinguished role in Newfoundland's legal and political life.

Robert Pinsent was appointed a stipendiary magistrate at Brigus in 1836 and in 1843 received a similar appointment at Harbour Grace. In 1851 reports reached the Newfoundland government

Poor

that there were serious difficulties in St George's Bay on the island's western coast. Until 1850 St George's Bay had been within the area of "non-settlement" according to treaty arrangements with France, and Newfoundland had had neither magistrates nor excise officers there [*see* Kent]. In 1850 James Tobin became magistrate and collector of customs for the area and the people were called upon to pay taxes including boat and net taxes. The French, however, continued to fish alongside them without paying taxes; in fact they were paid a bounty for their catch by the French government. The people of St George's Bay protested; the resulting arrests, fines, and transportations to gaol in St John's provoked outbursts – the magistrate was stoned, public meetings were held, and petitions were signed. On 15 July 1851 the government appointed Robert John Pinsent and Captain George Ramsay as justices of the peace for Newfoundland and its dependencies, and sent them to St George's Bay on Ramsay's ship, *Alarm*, to investigate the disturbances. On Pinsent's appointment the Roman Catholic *Newfoundlander* commented, "We entirely concur in the fitness of the selection of Mr. Pinsent; the well-earned reputation of this gentleman being an excellent voucher for the impartial and efficient discharge of his responsibility."

Pinsent and Ramsay spent several weeks at St George's Bay and recommended that the Catholic magistrate, James Tobin, be replaced by a "Protestant of good plain sense, having a patient temper and a tolerable acquaintance with the law." Governor John Gaspard Le Marchant ignored the recommendation, stating that "although Tobin was not an over-judicious person, his removal would be the cause of a quarrel [as] he is a bitter Catholic and a friend of the Roman Catholic bishop who would espouse his cause."

In 1861 Pinsent was involved in a particularly difficult situation in Harbour Grace. On nomination day, 26 April 1861, after three controverted elections to the assembly since 1859, intense party strife, complicated by religious animosity, caused a serious riot, despite the presence of some 100 soldiers from St John's. Pinsent, having read the riot act to no avail, attempted to persuade the mob to disperse. An accusation of negligence was later brought against him by the Protestant inhabitants as a result of his refusal to request that the troops break up the armed crowd of between 300 and 400. Pinsent claimed that he understood his only alternative was to order the troops to fire "and that last and deadly resort I did not feel warranted in adopting . . . as although the damage to property was considerable, little or no personal violence

was inflicted on anyone." The Executive Council sent Joseph Peters, the stipendiary magistrate of Old Perlican, to Harbour Grace to act with Pinsent, but Pinsent refused to recognize Peters in his official capacity. The council then decided to remove Pinsent although "in view of his former services, he was to receive some other suitable appointment."

By 1862 Pinsent was a member of the Legislative Council and in 1863 he was named judge of the court of Labrador, a post he held until his retirement in 1874. In 1866 he took a leading part in organizing a meeting of St John's merchants and other citizens to prepare resolutions in opposition to the proposed confederation of Newfoundland with the other provinces of British North America.

Throughout his life Pinsent was an active member of the Church of England community and a member of the Newfoundland Church Society. As one of a family long established in the Conception Bay area and having connections with leading families in St John's, Pinsent fitted into the role of outport squire and magistrate, respected by both Catholics and Protestants. His unwillingness to take harsh measures during the riotous proceedings in Harbour Grace in 1861, although justly resulting in his removal as magistrate, indicates his humane attitude and his concern for the outport people.

Elinor Senior

PANL, Newfoundland, Executive Council, Minutes, 1861, 563–629. PRO, CO 194/133–194/134, 194/135–194/136. Newfoundland, House of Assembly, *Journal*, 1852, appendix. *Evening Telegram* (St John's), 28 April 1893. *Newfoundlander* (St John's), 10, 24 July 1851. *Newfoundland Patriot* (St John's), 30 June 1866. *Public Ledger* (St John's), 27 June 1865. *Royal Gazette* (St John's), 12 Dec. 1876.

POOR, JOHN ALFRED, lawyer, editor and pamphleteer, railway entrepreneur; b. 8 Jan. 1808 at East Andover, Maine, second son of Dr Silvanus Poor and Mary Merrill; d. 5 Sept. 1871.

The Poor family came to Massachusetts as Puritan immigrants in 1638. John Alfred Poor's father was a physician and he was raised in comfortable New England surroundings. After teaching school for one winter in Bethel, Poor entered the Bangor law office of his uncle, and was called to the Maine bar in 1832. Married three times (Elizabeth Adams Hill, 8 July 1833; Elizabeth Orr; and Mrs Margaret Robinson Gwynne, 19 July 1860) he had one daughter by his first marriage.

Over six feet tall and weighing 250 pounds, Poor impressed his contemporaries with his prodigious energy, his rapid manner of speaking, and his violent temper. As a young Bangor lawyer, Poor served as counsel for the great New England politician and family friend, Daniel Webster. He participated in city government and was a founder of the local literary and debating society and the Bangor Social Library. "I honor the men," he wrote in 1871, "who have acquired success in the useful arts, as the great benefactors of their age. I have honoured Watt, Arkwright, Stephenson, Fulton and Whitney more than any of the heroes of war."

Poor had been present at Boston in April 1834 when the first locomotive ran in New England. He did not forget that experience: "It gave me such a shock that my hair seemed to start from the roots rather than to stand on end; and as I reflected in after years, the locomotive engine grew into a greatness in mind that left all other created things far behind it as marvels and wonders." Railways became the great challenge of Poor's life. At this time his own state of Maine, looked upon as an appendage of Massachusetts, was undeveloped; Portland, its major city, had been bypassed in the commercial expansion that was bringing prosperity to Montreal, New York, and Boston. In 1844 Poor published a plan for a railway network, centring on Portland, which would provide Montreal with an ice-free port on the Atlantic and link Montreal and Halifax by a trunk line from Montreal to Maine intersecting in Portland with another trunk line following the New England–Maritimes coast from Massachusetts to Nova Scotia.

His first task was to convince Canadian entrepreneurs and politicians of the superiority of the port of Portland. Ice-free, it was 100 miles closer to Montreal than Boston and half a day closer to England by steamer. While the American portion of the route between Montreal and Portland was still being surveyed and a company organized and chartered (on 10 Feb. 1845), Poor spoke in Eastern Townships communities through which the railway would pass. With the support of Sherbrooke, the *Montreal Gazette* and *Herald*, and the new laws which permitted Canadian goods to cross American soil in bond, Poor hurried to Montreal in February 1845 to meet that city's Board of Trade. There he won support for his Portland project over a trunk line from Montreal through Vermont to Concord and Boston. In 1846 construction began on the St Lawrence and Atlantic Railroad and its American counterpart, the Atlantic and St Lawrence, of which Poor was one of the directors from 1846 until probably 1853.

In 1853 Poor and his Maine associates leased the entire railway to William Jackson, Thomas Brassey, Samuel Morton Peto, and Edward Ladd Betts, the English contractors. The Portland entrepreneurs considered the lease and the subsequent incorporation of the Atlantic and St Lawrence into the Grand Trunk Railway as a great coup since, as Poor's daughter explained, "the city retained both its road and its money." Portland was now the Atlantic terminus of an international system that would soon stretch to Detroit and Lake Huron. Reminiscing in later years, Poor took full credit for the success of the railway, which he called "the work of my own mind exclusively."

Poor was also instrumental in the choice of gauge for the Canadian trunk line. By the mid 1840s Boston entrepreneurs in Maine used a gauge of 4′6″. To ensure Maine's independence, Poor favoured a broad gauge of 5′6″. In 1847 he journeyed to Montreal and helped persuade the Canadian government to overrule its earlier commitment to the Boston interests and to accept the broad gauge. Again in 1851 he appeared before a parliamentary committee in Toronto and helped influence the choice of the broad gauge for the Great Western Railway. After his death, and at great cost, the Grand Trunk Railway adopted the narrow gauge of the American railroad system.

Poor's success in the trunk line to Montreal only heightened his interest in railways. In 1849 he moved to New York where he purchased the *New York Railroad Journal*. Returning to Portland in 1850, he became associated with a number of railways and to promote his projects he edited a newspaper, the *State of Maine*, from 1853 to 1859, when he merged it with the *Portland Daily Advertiser*. An active lobbyist, Poor was well known in Washington and corresponded with Canadian politicians such as Joseph HOWE and John A. Macdonald*. Poor developed close contacts with Montreal entrepreneurs such as George Moffatt*, Peter McGill*, John YOUNG, Alexander Tilloch Galt*, and John Torrance*. In 1854 he and his Portland associates joined with Allan Napier MacNab*, Augustin-Norbert Morin*, Jacob DeWitt*, Galt, Henry Smith*, Jean Chabot*, John Young, and Ira Gould to present a petition to the Legislative Assembly of Canada on behalf of the Northern Pacific Railroad Company for an international railway system from Portland to Montreal, Sault Ste Marie, and along the south shore of Lake Superior to the Missouri River.

With the beginning of construction in 1846 on the St Lawrence and Atlantic Railroad and on the Atlantic and St Lawrence, Poor turned to the proposed coastal trunk line, the European and North American Railway. To offset interest in

Poor

Britain and the Maritimes in a railway from Halifax to Quebec, having defence as its primary purpose and running far from the American border, Poor proposed an international line from Halifax to Truro, Moncton, Saint John, Bangor, and Danville Junction, Maine, where it would join the trunk line between Portland and Montreal. To promote it, in July 1850 he organized an international convention in Portland [*see* Edward Barron CHANDLER]. Steamships and railways, he wrote in the invitations, have made the citizens of Montreal, Portland, Halifax, Boston, Saint John, and New York "to all intents and purposes one people, speaking a common language and struggling for the same destiny. National hostility has given way to commercial and social intercourse and under whatever form of government they may hereafter exist, they can never again become hostile or unfriendly."

With international cooperation and the unity of Anglo Saxons his political theme, Poor promoted his railway commercially by advocating it as the shortest route to Europe. He proposed a port on the Cape Breton coast and steamship service to Galway, Ireland. The Cunard or Collins steamers and the Midland Railway of Ireland would form part of a system to reduce the passage to London. Poor communicated with both the British and the American governments concerning mail contracts.

Poor's dream of a commercial empire centred on Maine never materialized. Political instability in the Maritimes, and the failure of Joseph Howe to win guarantees from the British government for lines from Halifax to Quebec and Portland in 1851, made progress difficult. With the lapsing of British interest the Intercolonial Railway rose as another competitor for Poor's international railway. Nor did Poor have great success in promoting the railway in his native state; as one scribe noted, the Poor plan, "though it might dazzle talkers, did not convert investors." Before 1863 some 200 miles of railway had been constructed by the governments of Nova Scotia and New Brunswick. In that year the railway was granted a loan of 800,000 acres from Maine and a $500,000 loan from Bangor; New Brunswick granted a charter the same year and a subsidy of $10,000 a mile to build from Saint John to the Maine boundary. Construction finally began in Maine in 1867 and the railway was completed in 1872. Poor had been president of the European and North American Railway since 1853, but in 1866 he was forced out of the presidency on a question of contracts and because of opposition from Bangor's citizens.

Poor's attitude to British North America must be interpreted in terms of his determination to advance the interests of Maine. A strong supporter of reciprocity, he proposed its expansion into a North American Zollverein with the Great Lakes as an "open Mediterranean Sea." The Civil War and confederation soured Poor's hopes of achieving the European and North American Railway by cooperative measures. Abandoning the rhetoric of continental goodwill, Poor urged the American government to build the railway from Bangor to the international boundary as a defence project. As an alternate, he appealed for federal assistance to the European and North American Railway as Maine's compensation for its losses in the Maine–New Brunswick boundary dispute of 1842.

Poor's attitude to confederation reflected his growing animosity to Britain and his feeling that British North America would ultimately join the United States. Again his railway interests were a determining factor. Alice Stewart's interpretation that Poor assessed the anti-confederate group in New Brunswick as more favourable to his railway interests seems valid. Certainly, the Intercolonial Railway promised in the confederation agreement would provide vigorous competition to his international trunk line along the coast. After confederation Poor again favoured amicable relations between Canada and the United States. However, his resources were failing by this time; partially blind and unable to write after 1866, he died of a heart attack on 5 Sept. 1871.

John Alfred Poor's efforts to promote his state had a great influence on the pattern and gauge of Canadian railways. A continentalist, he considered politics and nationalism to be secondary factors that could be supported or abandoned as his business interests demanded. His career raises the question of whether his Canadian counterparts and Canadian railway entrepreneurs in general have in fact been the great proponents of "the national dream."

BRIAN J. YOUNG

[Primary material on John Alfred Poor consists of five boxes of letters, receipts, and clippings held by the Maine Historical Society (Portland). Scattered letters of Poor are at the PAC, in the Galt papers (MG 27, I, D8), Macdonald papers (MG 26, A), and Howe papers (MG 24, B29).

Poor wrote a large number of pamphlets, and most of these are available in his private papers at the Maine Historical Society. An inventory of these pamphlets was prepared by Poor's daughter, Laura Elizabeth, in *The first international railway and the colonization of New England; life and writings of John Alfred Poor* (New York, 1892). The most important of the pamphlets are the following (place of publication not always known): *Extracts from report of directors of St Lawrence and Atlantic Railroad Company in favor of a line to the east from Danville Junction to Bangor, and St John, New Brunswick* (1848); *The* first colonization of New-England: an address, delivered at the erection of a monumental stone in the walls of Fort Popham, August 29th, 1862, commemorative of the planting of the Popham colony of the peninsula of Sabino, August 19, O.S. 1607, establishing the title of England to the continent (New York, 1862); The future of North America: a letter to the Chicago Ship-Canal Convention suggesting a Zoll-verein with Canada (1863); Memorial of John A. Poor in behalf of the European & North American Railway Co., and for a state policy favorable to immigration and the encouragement of manufacturers . . . (Augusta, 1861); Memorial to thirty-first legislature of Maine in relation to the European and North American Railway for shortening the transit of mails between New York and London (1852); No restriction on railway transit. Argument of John A. Poor before the joint standing committee on railroads, ways, and bridges, delivered in the Senate chamber of Maine, Feb. 14, 1865 (Bangor, 1865); Petition to the parliament of Canada praying for a charter for the Northern Pacific Railway Company, Quebec (Portland, 1854); Plan for shortening the time of passage between New York and London, with map: petition to the legislature of Maine in aid of the European and North American Railway (1850); Proceedings of Portland convention, etc., European and North American Railway (1850); "Project of a railway from Montreal to the Atlantic coast at Portland, Maine," Sherbrooke Gazette, 5 Sept. 1844; Report to the legislature of Maine of commissioners on the coast defences of Maine, and documents relating thereto, in favor of building the European and North American Railway as a military railroad (1862); The trans-continental railway. Remarks at Rutland, Vermont, June 24, 1869 (Portland, 1869).

The only substantial biography of Poor is in the book edited by Laura Elizabeth Poor. Important references to Poor are found in the transportation studies: E. C. Kirkland, Men, cities and transportation; a study in New England history, 1820–1900 (2v., Cambridge, Mass., 1948); S. H. Holbrook, The story of American railroads (New York, 1947); and G. P. de T. Glazebrook, A history of transportation in Canada (The Relations of Canada and the United States, Toronto, 1938).

Of direct interest but limited value are two theses: Elda Gallison, "The short route to Europe, a history of the European and North American Railroad," unpublished MA thesis, University of Maine, 1950. D. B. Pillsbury, "The history of the Atlantic and St Lawrence Railway Company," unpublished MA thesis, University of Maine, 1962.

Poor's role in the confederation period is treated by A. R. Stewart, "The State of Maine and Canadian confederation," CHR, XXXIII (1952), 148–64.

E. E. Chase, Maine railroads; a history of the development of the Maine railroad system (Portland, 1926). A. G. Bailey, "Railways and the confederation issue in New Brunswick, 1863–1865," CHR, XXI (1940), 367–83. B.J.Y]

POPE, WILLIAM HENRY, lawyer, land agent, journalist, politician, and judge; b. 29 May 1825 at Bedeque, P.E.I., elder son of Joseph Pope* and Lucy Colledge; d. 7 Oct. 1879 at St Eleanors, P.E.I.

William Henry Pope received his early education in Prince Edward Island and proceeded to higher studies in England, from which his father had emigrated in 1819. William read law at the Inner Temple in London, then returned to his native colony to article in the office of Edward Palmer* in Charlottetown; he was called to the bar in 1847. He married Helen DesBrisay in 1851, and they had two sons and six daughters; their elder son, Joseph Pope*, became private secretary to and biographer of Sir John A. Macdonald*.

Like many contemporary lawyers in the colony, William Pope also became a land agent. His legal practice and his land business remained his principal activities until he entered journalism and government office in 1859. His father, a shipbuilder and politician, was a prominent member of the local élite which originally served primarily as an intermediary between the absentee landowners of the Island and their tenants; consequently, William Pope gained important clients, such as Captain Cumberland, Lady Cecilia Georgiana Fane, and Charles Worrell. It was as Worrell's agent that Pope acquired lasting unpopularity on Prince Edward Island. In 1854, after the Liberal government had passed a land purchase act, Worrell's trustees, on the Island, decided to advise him to sell. They delegated one of their members, Theophilus DesBrisay*, Pope's father-in-law, to gain Worrell's acquiescence. DesBrisay persuaded Worrell to give up his estate to the government for £10,000, but withheld this news from the other trustees. He then, apparently with no justification, informed Worrell that the government no longer wished to buy the property. Worrell now suggested that the estate be offered to a certain potential buyer for £9,000, but DesBrisay failed to make the offer. Having thus by his own authority suppressed both possible transactions, he next advised Worrell to discuss the matter with Pope – who happened to be on his way to England.

Worrell, impatient to be rid of his debt-encumbered and far-away estate, readily accepted Pope's offer of £14,000. On 28 Dec. 1854 Pope and his financial backers – his father, his father-in-law, and one George Elkana Morton of Halifax – resold the property to the government for £24,100. The Liberals had been persuaded to pay what they knew to be an exorbitant price by Pope's thinly veiled threats to take the tenantry on his new estate to court for payment of arrears in rent. The property consisted of five adjacent townships, numbers 38 to 42, in northern Kings County, and such a proceeding would have caused riots. In

Pope

addition, DesBrisay allegedly extorted £1,700 from Worrell for his "services." However, the failure of Pope and his associates to transfer all of the promised 81,303 acres to the government led to the refusal of the latter to pay the final £3,000 of the purchase-price. Although his actions became public knowledge, Pope never took the trouble to deny vigorously the essentials of the case against him; as he was capable and politically ambitious, it is probable that he would have contested them could he have done so successfully. The result of this jobbery, unique in its magnitude for this period on the Island, was that his public reputation was permanently scarred.

As the 1850s progressed, William and his younger brother James Colledge Pope* became increasingly active in the Conservative party, which was then in opposition. When the Liberal government under George COLES was defeated in 1859, James, an assemblyman, was named to the Executive Council, and William, who was a member of neither branch of the legislature, was appointed colonial secretary. William's appointment was in accord with the policy of "non-departmentalism" practised by the new government. The Tories claimed that the Liberals had instituted a "spoils system," with the legislators themselves as the prime recipients of patronage, and they had promised to exclude representatives of the people from public offices of emolument, which were supposedly to be filled by non-partisans. Pope was immediately recognized by the Liberals as the most influential of the new government's public officials. Two months earlier Edward Whelan* had written that "Mr. Pope is a man whom the Tories rather fear than respect . . . he has more cunning, more perseverance in pursuit of his object (no matter what it is,) and more real talent than any other man in his party."

William Pope had already assumed a strategic position within the ruling élite. Shortly after the election of 1859, Duncan MacLean, the editor of the *Islander*, the leading Conservative newspaper in the colony, had died, and Pope had been appointed his successor by John Ings, the *Islander*'s publisher and the new queen's printer. As an editor, Pope maintained the important position of his paper, and, in the tradition of MacLean, carried on a running battle with Whelan, the publisher and editor of the *Examiner*. Pope and Whelan were controversialists by nature, and they exhibited an interesting contrast in abilities: Whelan was a master of literary style and the pungent epigram; Pope, whose style was more laboured, exhibited precise logic and flawless argument. Together, they provided the Island public with an invaluable political dialogue.

The most momentous and lingering issue in Island politics prior to confederation was the land question. Pope's position was that although leasehold tenure was "obnoxious" and had "injurious" effects upon the colony, whatever was to be done must be done "without infringing the rights of property." The absentee landlords were "not blamable for the existence of the leasehold system"; rather, the "great injustice" had been inflicted by the imperial government in 1767 when it imposed the system upon the Island. The current owners had full legal title to their holdings, and hence all benefits to their tenants must come "by the *favor* of the Proprietors." Radical schemes such as escheat were out of the question: "the rights of property – sacred in all civilized countries – will be inviolably preserved." The proper course for the tenantry was to enter into "friendly negociation [*sic*] with the Proprietors." The new Tory government, intimately connected with men of position and wealth, was ideally suited to play the role of mediator between landlord and tenant.

But it was not over the Worrell estate, or the land question in general, that Pope gained his greatest fame – or notoriety – on the Island. The Conservative victory of 1859 had been accomplished largely through skilful exploitation of Protestant anxieties over the Bible question, in which Pope himself had not taken an active part, and the result had been division of the electorate almost entirely on religious lines. Although William Pope had been born into a Methodist family, he was widely known to be an "infidel" – the contemporary Island name for atheists, agnostics, Unitarians, and apostates – and he did not have strong convictions about the intrinsic rightness or wrongness of either Protestantism or Roman Catholicism. After 1860, or when the role of the Bible in the district schools had been defined to the general satisfaction of all concerned, Pope and the premier, Edward Palmer, saw no reason for the estrangement between their party and the Roman Catholic Church to continue. In early 1861 Palmer and his chief lieutenant in the cabinet, Colonel John Hamilton Gray*, made two clandestine attempts to gain the friendship of the Catholic hierarchy by offering certain concessions in the field of education; both efforts failed, largely because of ill fortune.

Meanwhile, William Pope stumbled upon a third opportunity for reconciliation. By chance, Bishop Peter MacIntyre* mentioned to him that he planned to present a petition to the government asking for endowment of the Roman Catholic St Dunstan's College. Pope then promised to approach the government and its friends, in order to canvass support for the grant in advance,

594

if the bishop would postpone presentation of his petition. MacIntyre agreed, and Pope proceeded to consult with the Executive Council, the caucus, and members of the Protestant clergy. With the exception of Palmer and Gray, no one gave him much encouragement; indeed, most of those with whom he spoke said they would oppose the endowment under any circumstances.

When Pope reported his bad news to MacIntyre, the latter became angry, and declared that in the next election he would mobilize the Island's Roman Catholics as never before in order to defeat the all-Protestant government. Pope apparently believed that the bishop was in earnest, and consequently changed his mind about the direction that relations between the Conservatives and the Catholic population should take. The Tories, it seemed, would have to rely upon a purely Protestant appeal if they were to retain the support of a majority of Island electors. In the summer of 1861, Pope published a series of "Letters to the Protestants of Prince Edward Island." His political message, expressed in the first letter, was that "*as parties now stand*, ANY GOVERNMENT OTHER THAN AN EXCLUSIVELY PROTESTANT ONE, MUST OF NECESSITY BE VIRTUALLY A ROMAN CATHOLIC ONE." The letters that followed became abusive of Catholic beliefs, referring to the Real Presence as "a God made of a little flour and water," and warning Protestants that the Council of Trent had pronounced non-believers in the Eucharist "accursed." "Pope's Epistles against the Romans," as Whelan labelled the series, marked the beginning of 18 months of religious disputation in the Island press. The main protagonists were Pope and the rector of St Dunstan's, Father Angus MacDonald*. A formidable polemicist, who always acted in full consciousness of his objectives rather than an excess of zeal, Pope was rapidly becoming the most controversial public figure in the colony, and the *bête noire* of the Liberals.

Father MacDonald and William Pope had already clashed in public concerning the temporal powers of the papacy, and now, in the latter part of 1861, the rector took up the defence of his church. Matters became more serious in February 1862 when MacDonald, in referring to some abusive anonymous correspondence in David Laird*'s *Protestant*, declared that the letters in question were obviously written "by some low rabid character who holds the same position in the literary world, that a rowdy, blackleg, or pimp does in the social one." Such a person, said the rector, was W. H. Pope. This prompted Pope to write an open letter to MacDonald, in which he quoted St Jerome to show that Roman Catholicism

and ignorance were natural concomitants, cited Baronius to prove that the early popes were "harlot chosen," and finally asked whether, like the augurs of ancient Rome, Father Angus laughed at the credulity of those who believed that "a little wheaten flour" could become God. In the same number, "A Protestant," who in reality was William Pope, submitted a price-list of indulgences and dispensations, dated 1514. After these inflammatory epistles, Pope retired from the quarrel.

MacDonald added a new dimension to the feud in the summer of 1862 by asking both the lieutenant governor, George DUNDAS, and the secretary of state for the colonies, the Duke of Newcastle [Henry Pelham Clinton], to dismiss Pope from office because of his attacks upon Roman Catholic beliefs. The attempt was unsuccessful, and after the furor surrounding it had subsided – MacDonald published his letters and Pope replied – the vendetta dropped out of public sight for two months. Then in September Pope wrote an editorial claiming: "The grand aim of the Roman Catholic Clergy on this Island is to obtain a grant for their College of Saint Dunstan. This they cannot procure unless the present Government can be ousted." The Liberal press and MacDonald replied by asserting that the government itself had intended to endow the college. Pope denied this, and gave his full version of the conversations of the spring of 1861, which had hitherto not been made public.

In the course of his disclosures, Pope drove his accusers from the field; it was a devastating display of the logical powers of his mind, and it meant that the Palmer government retained the confidence of Island Protestants. The results of the controversies generated by the revelations of September and October were momentous: an ultramontane newspaper was founded, the militant Presbyterians and Orangemen were mobilized against "Romish aggression," and the Conservatives won the general election of January 1863 on the religious-educational issue. William Pope entered the lists, and successfully contested Belfast, the most Presbyterian constituency in the colony. Once elected to the assembly, Pope joined the Executive Council, and remained colonial secretary, as non-departmentalism was abandoned after a trial of four years.

The session following the election was tempestuous from start to finish. William Pope, at the apex of his power and influence in Island politics, was brimming with calm spite, for he was aware that MacDonald was again writing – although in vain – to London to have him removed from office. On St Patrick's Day, Pope introduced a bill to incorporate the colony's Grand Orange Lodge, and the

Pope

ferocity of the debate which followed has probably never, before or since, been equalled in the legislative history of the Island. The nadir was reached when George William Howlan*, a Catholic Liberal, accused Pope of having said outside the house "that a Catholic woman going to confess to a priest was the same as taking a mare to a stallion." But the "religious question" had by this time reached a peak in intensity; within a few months it appeared to have burned itself out.

In the meantime, the land question remained unsolved. The Palmer government had in 1860 arranged for the appointment of a distinguished three-man commission, whose recommendations had been disallowed by the London government, at the urging of the proprietors. In the summer of 1863, the Island government, now led by Colonel Gray, renewed its efforts to settle the issue, and delegated two leading cabinet members, Pope and Palmer, to go to England to confer with the Colonial Office and the landlords. The two delegates proceeded to London, and on 13 October presented Newcastle with a new set of proposals; he immediately passed them on to Sir Samuel Cunard*, who at that time owned one-sixth of the land in the colony, and who was acting on behalf of a group of proprietors. Since it appeared that the negotiations would be lengthy, Palmer sailed for the Island in early November, leaving Pope alone to deal with the British government and Cunard. The Colonial Office expected little difficulty in handling Pope for they had formed an unflattering opinion of him through the unseemly vendetta with MacDonald; on 14 September the permanent undersecretary had written that "the appointment of Mr. Pope does not look as if this matter [the delegation] could come to much."

However, when Cunard and his associates refused the October proposals, Pope responded vigorously. He wrote detailed and well-documented replies to Cunard's statement, and declared that "high as may be the respect entertained for the legal rights of the land owners, there are cases in which they should give way to the requirements of 'public policy.' " For example, there was no possibility that full arrears in rents could be collected; the whole purpose of the delegation was to get the landlords to consent to a compromise. The consequence of intransigence, Pope predicted on 13 Jan. 1864, would be "those much to be dreaded evils, which necessarily result from wide-spread agrarian agitation." Events soon proved him correct: the tenants of the Island were already forming a new and militant organization, the Tenant League, whose members were pledged to resist payment of rents. The commission and the delegation had failed, and by August 1865 troops were required to

maintain the legal rights of property in Prince Edward Island [see HODGSON].

When the question of a union of the British North American colonies arose in 1863 and 1864, William Pope was one of the very few Islanders to advocate it enthusiastically. He attended both the Charlottetown and the Quebec conferences, and was an honorary secretary of the latter. Soon after the Quebec Conference, he found himself at odds with Palmer, who opposed confederation, and who attempted to regain the premiership at the expense of Colonel Gray. In mid-December 1864, Gray resigned under pressure; but Palmer failed to become president of the Executive Council, because William Pope came to the defence of the colonel. At issue was Palmer's consistency on the confederation question, and Pope pursued him with the cold fury and relentless logic which he had unleashed upon MacDonald in September and October 1862. Pope won the argument, but in the longer perspective Palmer could claim a considerable victory: the Conservative party would not now lead the Island into confederation. With this in mind, and aware that public opinion supported Palmer rather than himself and William Pope, Gray refused to resume the premiership or a seat on the Executive Council.

A makeshift government, led by James Pope, took office. Although his brother was now premier, William became increasingly isolated within the cabinet. During the 1865 session, when James was on the point of moving the house into committee on the Quebec terms, William presented eight pro-confederation resolutions before his younger brother could speak. James accused William of having, "to say the least of it, acted most uncourteously." The defeat of William's resolutions, and the acceptance of James's counter-resolutions, were foregone conclusions, but the incident served to widen the breach between the colonial secretary and his colleagues. The finishing blow came in the 1866 session, when William was absent on a trade delegation to Brazil: James Pope presented the "No terms Resolution" on confederation, expressing the belief that union with Canada was not a foreseeable possibility. Shortly after his return, William resigned as executive councillor and colonial secretary, in protest against this position.

The rest of William Pope's public career is anti-climactic when contrasted with the immense power and influence which he had wielded in the first half of the 1860s. He remained editor of the *Islander* until Ings sold the newspaper in October 1872, but he did not even contest the election of 1867 which the Tories lost badly. The party was hopelessly fragmented by the confederation question; Gray and James Pope also declined to run.

From this time until his appointment to the bench in 1873, William Pope concentrated upon two objectives: the entry of the Island into confederation, and, as the means to this end, the rebuilding of the Conservative party on a strong confederate base.

The Tories were in a sad state, but the Liberal government was vulnerable because they had their own serious divisions over the land and school questions. The session of 1868 revealed a deep fissure in their ranks over whether to give public aid to Roman Catholic schools, including St Dunstan's, under the control of Bishop McIntyre. William Pope had already shown renewed interest in the college's financial problems; in February he had declared in favour of a grant, without mentioning any conditions to be met. He warned of the tendency of the age to infidelity, and recommended that Roman Catholics "force" the school question upon the government.

Pope – who had with his usual coolness and deliberation changed his political strategy, not his religious convictions – kept constant pressure on the government throughout early 1868, and eventually published a draft bill that embodied the amendments he desired in the education act. In November 1868 James Pope contested a by-election in Prince County, Fifth District, on the promise to give public aid to all "efficient" schools. Despite the active support of MacIntyre, the *Islander*, the leader of the opposition (T. H. Haviland* Jr), and the approval of Gray, James lost badly. Consequently, the Popes decided to let the school question stand for the present. Their attempt to inaugurate a new party system on the basis of a partnership between the Conservative confederates and the Roman Catholic Liberals had been premature.

Nonetheless, William Pope did not give up his advocacy of confederation. He continued to write editorials on the subject, gave public lectures, kept in contact with John A. Macdonald, and sent memorials and pamphlets to London. The election of 1870 provided the opportunity for forging the new alliance. Palmer and David Laird, the leaders of the anti-confederate faction within the Conservative party, were defeated, and James Pope, now ambivalent on the confederation issue, was returned to the assembly as leader of the party. The Liberals had won by the margin of 17 to 13, but they immediately shattered on the rock of the school question, largely owing to the inept leadership of Robert P. Haythorne*.

Soon after the Liberals split, James Pope joined with George Howlan and his followers to form a coalition government. But in the meantime, William Pope had prepared a rationale for his brother to refuse the Roman Catholic demands, which, if met, might have split Pope's group: no Protestant Conservative had submitted the subject of denominational grants to his constituents at the late election, and nothing, William said, could be done without a mandate from the people. Yet the Popes did not follow the example of the Protestant Liberals, and close the door for all time – denominational grants were not rejected in principle. The basis of the new alliance was mutual self-denial: no action would be taken on the confederation or school questions until they had been presented to the electorate. The Tories had won over the Roman Catholic legislators and returned to power; one of William Pope's objectives had been accomplished.

Less than three years after its formation, the Pope-Howlan coalition led the Island into confederation. In early 1871 a sudden desire for a railway swept the Island, and the coalition responded by passing appropriate legislation. The new project, which William Pope had been advocating for several years, drove the colony to the brink of bankruptcy; by early 1872 public alarm was so great that James Pope was forced to call an election, in which his government was badly defeated. However, the damage to the Island's finances was irreparable: Haythorne and Palmer, the strongly anti-confederate leaders of the new government, conceded defeat in February 1873 and delegated Haythorne and David Laird to go to Ottawa to negotiate terms. When they returned, a new election was called, which was won by James Pope on the promise of better terms.

With the coming of confederation in July 1873, the Macdonald government appointed William Pope judge of the Prince County Court. He had an outstanding record on the bench: of several thousand decisions, only two were appealed, and in both cases he was upheld by the provincial Supreme Court. During his career as a lawyer and jurist he was twice (in 1861 and 1878) asked to undertake the revision and consolidation of the Island's statutes.

William Henry Pope died on 7 Oct. 1879 as the result of a stroke suffered a few days earlier. He had been a truly remarkable Islander. As well as being an outstanding member of his chosen profession, he had a wide variety of interests and connections. At the time of his death he was planning to write a history of the Island; he had done primary research in the archives of the Colonial Office and elsewhere during trips to the mother country. In London itself, he was three times (in 1863, 1866, and 1870) elected as one of the 15 honorary non-British members of the Athenaeum Club; he was also a friend and correspondent of some of the most distinguished Englishmen of the period.

Pope

By the standards of the day, his tastes were quite extravagant, and despite his shrewdness, he was a poor manager of his personal finances. His sudden death left his family in difficult circumstances.

William Pope's principal vocations were politics and journalism. With undoubted abilities he was for years considered to be the most influential member of his party. When his brother was premier, it was often said that "William made the snowballs and James threw them." William was at the centre of the bitter religious-educational controversies of the early 1860s. He was also the Island's most forceful and persistent advocate of confederation, and he masterminded the creation in 1870 of a new Tory party, which was destined to be the vehicle for the entry of the Island into confederation. Most famous off the Island as a father of confederation, it was, nevertheless, in the role of political manipulator that Pope was best known at home. In short, from the late 1850s to the early 1870s, William Henry Pope was the *éminence grise* of the Conservative party of Prince Edward Island.

IAN ROSS ROBERTSON

[There are two collections of W. H. Pope papers; the larger is in PAC, MG 27, F2, and the other in the possession of General Maurice Pope of Ottawa to whom the author is indebted for his permission to examine the material and for a helpful interview on 20 May 1968. PAC, MG 26, A (Macdonald papers), includes a number of Pope-Macdonald letters written between 1870 and 1876. Pope appears to have been Macdonald's closest ally on P.E.I. Letters referring to Pope's financial problems can also be found in PAPEI, Henry Jones Cundall, letter books, 1874–78. The papers of administration for Pope's estate are in Prince Edward Island, Supreme Court, Estates Division. Prince Edward Island, Executive Council, Minutes, 1863–66, the years during which Pope was a member of the Executive Council, can be found at PAPEI. The Grand Orange Lodge of Prince Edward Island allowed the author to examine its records. Its *Annual Report, 1865*, refers to Pope as "Brother, the Honorable W. H. Pope," indicating that he was, at least temporarily, an Orangeman. Scattered references to Pope can also be found in PRO, CO 226, throughout the volumes covering the years 1857 to 1873. For details of the sale of the Worrell estate *see* CO 226/88, 248–69, 446–65; for Pope's views on the defences of P.E.I. *see* CO 226/102, 294–97. *See also*: Prince Edward Island, House of Assembly, *Debates and proceedings*, 1856, 61; 1857, 105; 1863–65, especially 1864, 16; *Journals*, 1863–65, especially 1864, app.W. *Abstract of the proceedings before the Land Commissioners' Court, held during the summer of 1860 to inquire into the differences relative to the rights of landowners and tenants in Prince Edward Island*, reporters J. D. Gordon and David Laird (Charlottetown, 1862), 13, 30, 237 (copies in PAC, PAPEI, and Redpath Library at McGill University).

Islander (Charlottetown), 1859–71, provides the most comprehensive picture of the political positions and attitudes of W. H. Pope. The most valuable source for tracing the progress of the Pope-Palmer delegation of 1863–64 is a series of 19 letters written between September 1863 and February 1864 and published in the issue of 26 Feb. 1864. Pope's own description of the objectives of the delegation is given in the issue of 21 Aug. 1863. For examples of Pope's efforts on behalf of confederation see *Islander*, 10 Feb. 1865, in which he published a lecture he had given on the subject. The issue of 21 June 1867 gives Pope's opposition to the efforts of the Coles government to obtain a loan in aid of settling the land question. The issues of 24 Nov. and 1 Dec. 1865 explain Pope's purposes as a member of the 1865–66 delegation to Brazil; see also 18 May 1866 and 19 Feb. 1869.

In 1862 and 1863 the *Examiner* (Charlottetown) and the *Vindicator* (Charlottetown) published a considerable number of anti–W. H. Pope articles. Some are interesting and useful for the factual material they contain on Pope's life, for example, *Vindicator*, 27 March and 26 June 1863. Its 7 Nov. 1862 issue carried the proceedings of a libel suit launched by Pope against Edward Whelan.

Obituaries of William Henry Pope will be found in *Examiner*, 7 Oct. 1879; *Patriot* (Charlottetown), 9 Oct. 1879; *Pioneer* (Montague, P.E.I.), 10 Oct. 1879; *Gazette* (Montreal), 20 Oct. 1879 (reprinted from *Island Argus* (Charlottetown), 14 Oct. 1879, which does not survive).

The main studies of interest include: Bolger, *PEI and confederation*, which gives a full account of Pope's role as a father of confederation: *see* especially 90–99, 113–14, 155–60. Duncan Campbell, *History of Prince Edward Island* (Charlottetown, 1875), 163–66. Careless, *Brown*, II, 155, gives George Brown's impression of the W. H. Pope household. W. L. Cotton, *Chapters in our Island story* (Charlottetown, 1927), 80, briefly mentions one of Pope's early business ventures. Creighton, *Road to confederation*, 13. MacKinnon, *Government of PEI*. MacMillan, *Catholic Church in PEI*, chap. 13–17, 20, 23, and 24, give a partisan and sometimes misleading account of Pope's involvement in the church-state issue. *Past and present of Prince Edward Island . . .* , ed. D. A. MacKinnon and A. B. Warburton (Charlottetown, [1906]), contains three relevant articles: "The Pope family" (which does not include a consideration of W. H. Pope but provides valuable background material on his family), "W. H. Pope," and W. L. Cotton, "The press in Prince Edward Island." *Pioneers on Prince Edward Island*, ed. Mary Brehaut (Charlottetown, 1959), 13. J. B. Pollard, *Historical sketch of the eastern regions of New France, from the various dates of their discoveries to the surrender of Louisburg, 1758: also Prince Edward Island, military and civil* (Charlottetown, 1898), 200. [Joseph Pope], *Public servant: the memoirs of Sir Joseph Pope*, ed. and completed by Maurice Pope (Toronto, 1960), contains several interesting personal sidelights on W. H. Pope. Waite, *Life and times of confederation*, 8, 51–52, 180. W. M. Whitelaw, *The Maritimes and Canada before confederation*, with intro.

by P. B. Waite (Toronto, 1966), 198. D. C. Harvey, "Dishing the Reformers," *RSCT*, 3rd ser., XXV (1931), sect.II, 37–44, gives an account of the genesis, growth, and eventual death of the system of "non-departmentalism" under which Pope held office for four years. Robertson, "Religion, politics, and education in PEI," assesses Pope's role in the issues centring on religion and education in chap. 4–8; see also 153–54, 166, 167 174, 289. I.R.R.]

PORTER, JAMES, Congregational clergyman and educator; b. at Highgate (in London), Eng., 16 May 1812; d. at Toronto, Ont., 18 April 1874.

James Porter studied in London at University College and at Coward Theological School, graduating in 1836. In the same year he married Agnes Dryden, by whom he had several children, and entered the ministry of the Independent (Congregational) Church, serving in Lancashire, Dorsetshire, and Devonshire successively.

In 1843 he was called by Dr Henry Wilkes* of Montreal, the superintendent of missions for Canada East and Canada West for the Colonial (later Commonwealth) Missionary Society, to the oldest church of that society in New Brunswick, that of Sheffield. After nine years in Sheffield he became the superintendent of education for the colony. A year and a half later, in 1853, he left this post to found a newspaper in Saint John, the *Saint John Free Press*. When that failed in 1854 he went back to preaching, lecturing, and writing, particularly for the temperance cause. He supplied the Congregational church in Windsor, Canada West, for six months, but returned to Saint John and again vacillated between the ministry and secular work. In 1857 he received a call from the London Congregational Church, Canada West, and moved there with his family. A year later, in June 1858, he became superintendent of public schools for the city of Toronto, succeeding George Anthony BARBER.

As superintendent (later inspector), Porter was responsible for examining prospective teachers, and for the appointment and inspection of teachers. He also oversaw the curriculum of the schools and their erection and maintenance. He retained the post until his death, 16 years later, and saw his charge grow from 35 teachers and 2,500 pupils to 65 teachers and 8,500 pupils. Many innovations in the curriculum were made, including the introduction of music, drawing, the military cadet system, and night classes. He remained a minister in the Congregational Church, worshipping in Zion Church, Toronto, and later in Bond Street Church.

He was a devoted and "a sound and accurate scholar," sensitive to the task of his teachers and with a high regard for the responsibilities of public office. He won the esteem and respect of all. His obituary contains this fine tribute: "He was a scholar, a Christian and a gentleman."

EARL B. EDDY

Canadian Independent (London; Toronto), XX (1874), 352–54. *Harbinger* (Montreal), II (1842), 181. Toronto, Local Superintendent of Public Schools, *Reports*, 1859–70; Inspector of Public Schools, *Reports*, 1871–74. Middleton, *Municipality of Toronto*, I, 541–43.

PRAT, JEAN-BAPTISTE, (also known as **John Pratt),** businessman, industrialist, and financier; b. 20 July 1812 at Berthier (Berthier County), L.C., son of Jean-Baptiste Prat, a merchant, and Louise Paillé (Paillard); d. 22 July 1876 at Montreal, Que.

Jean-Baptiste Prat's forefather Jean Duprat was originally from Agenais, France. In 1833, after attending a commercial school at Berthier, Jean-Baptiste Prat rejoined his elder brother Charles-Ferdinand, who was running a general store at Quebec. In the same year they went into partnership, and their firm took the name of C.-F. Pratt & Frère; Jean-Baptiste was also responsible for opening a branch at Trois-Rivières. In 1839 he established himself at Montreal, and launched a third firm there, which traded in wholesale leather under the name of John Pratt & Cie. Success was not long in coming. From then on the Prat brothers specialized in leather goods. They started a tannery, which employed several dozen men, at Roxton Falls (Shefford, Que.). Leather was widely used at that time, particularly for footwear, harnesses for draught-animals, parade-horses, the cavalry and the mounted police, and seats for cabs and carriages.

As time passed Jean-Baptiste, or John Pratt, closely involved as he was in the city's business life, became a member of the boards of directors of several important companies, which were generally set up under English names, such as Canadian Rubber (today Dominion Rubber Company), Montreal Weaving, Citizens' Insurance Company, Montreal Cotton, and finally Dominion Oilcloth and Linoleum. He was also president of the Banque du Peuple, a truly French Canadian institution, which was founded in 1833 and remained in operation until 1895, and presided over the destinies of the Richelieu and Ontario Navigation Company, which in 1913 became the Canada Steamship Lines [see SINCENNES]. Jean-Baptiste Prat was a Montreal harbour commissioner in 1863, and again in 1874 under Alexander Mackenzie*'s government, and was still holding this office at the time of his death. He was a liberal in politics, and a loyal supporter of Antoine-Aimé Dorion* and his group.

Prat assigned part of his fortune to charitable institutions, and paid for the education of several young people. Thus he supported a school of elementary and industrial draughtsmanship, founded and directed by Abbé Joseph Chabert, a Frenchman who had taken refuge at Montreal and who, despite his title, was not a priest.

According to *Le National*, Prat's opinion, in Canada, "enjoyed unquestioned authority wherever business dealings were involved. He was one of the most outstanding businessmen in his country and even in North America." The journalists of the day said that he was a millionaire. However, the inventory of his possessions drawn up in November 1876 by the notary Léonard-Ovide Hétu shows that in reality his fortune amounted to $625,000; it was divided between real estate – more than a half – and shares in banks or commercial companies. Half of these shares were American securities, which were at that time devalued by two thirds because of "the prevalent commercial and financial crisis," as the attesting notary recorded.

In 1840, at Montreal, Jean-Baptiste Prat had married Mathilde Roy, widow of the unfortunate Charles-Ovide Perrault*, lawyer and assemblyman for Vaudreuil, who was killed in November 1837 at the battle of Saint-Denis. They had four daughters and three sons. In 1861 the eldest girl, Mathilde, married Désiré Girouard*, an eminent jurist.

JEAN-JACQUES LEFEBVRE

AJM, Greffe de L.-O. Hétu, 27 nov. 1876 (inventory of John Pratt's estate). *Journal de Québec*, 25 juill. 1876. *L'Opinion publique* (Montréal), 3 août 1876. Atherton, *Montreal*, III, 120–24. L.-A. Rivet, "John Pratt: artisan de l'essor économique des nôtres au siècle dernier," *La Presse* (Montréal), 30 mars 1950.

PRESCOTT, Sir HENRY, officer in the Royal Navy and colonial administrator; b. at Kew, England, on 4 May 1783, son of Admiral Isaac Prescott; m. in July 1815 to Mary Anne Charlotte d'Auvergne by whom he had at least one daughter, the poet Henrietta Prescott Lushington; d. in London on 18 Nov. 1874.

Henry Prescott entered the Royal Navy in 1796 aboard *Formidable*; he was commissioned lieutenant in 1802 and promoted commander in 1808. Most of Prescott's naval service during the Napoleonic wars was in the Mediterranean; in fact his rapid elevation to post rank in 1810 was a reward for gallantry at Amantea, Italy, in the same year. Captain Prescott was on naval duties in Brazilian waters and in the Pacific until 1825 when he returned to England and was paid off.

The last of the 19th-century naval governors of Newfoundland, Henry Prescott received his appointment in 1834. He arrived in St John's on 3 Nov. 1834, the week of Thomas COCHRANE's departure, an exodus which must have warned him that the eminence of his position would not necessarily protect him against mud-slinging opponents. Prescott inherited from Cochrane a disturbed social and political situation. It was scarcely possible for the new governor to set a foot in the right place in a colony where Anglo-Irish quarrels were complicated by Catholic-Protestant enmity, and which was embittered by disagreements between merchants and fishermen and by West Country *versus* native rivalry for public office.

Prescott immediately sought ways to reduce the political and religious tension in the colony; he discontinued the libel case which Cochrane had begun against Father Edward TROY, and tried deperately to play the role of a disinterested administrator between the opposing factions in church and state affairs. His neutral position was soon compromised, however, by the unseemly quarrels between the Catholic bishop, Michael Anthony Fleming*, and Chief Justice Henry John Boulton*, the uncompromising spokesman of the establishment. Boulton, a Protestant, urged a revision of the laws governing fishermen and merchants which would be favourable to the merchants, whereas Bishop Fleming supported the local fishermen. A quarrel between a Protestant firm, Slade, Elson and Company, and Catholic fishermen at St Mary's in 1835 precipitated an open conflict between the chief justice and the bishop. Prescott, a man of compromise, considered both dangerous. He had at first established friendly relations with the bishop but within a year of his arrival he was embroiled with him and was openly accused of being a captive of the merchants who dominated the colonial economy and the Executive Council, such as John MUNN, Thomas BENNETT, and William Thomas*. The judgement of D. W. Prowse* that Prescott "disliked Boulton, but appears to have been either unable or unwilling to control him" is far from accurate, for the governor with a letter to the colonial secretary, Lord Glenelg [Charles Grant], on 5 Jan. 1838 initiated proceedings leading to the removal of the fractious chief justice from the bench and the council on 5 July. Prescott also encouraged the home government to seek the removal of Bishop Fleming. In the latter attempt he was unsuccessful and the attempt increased his disfavour among Catholic radicals. Prescott nevertheless participated in later efforts of the home government to induce the pope to remove Fleming. In 1840 only the spiritual accomplishments of the bishop saved him from dismissal, and it appears that following his summons to Rome in that year his political influence declined.

Prescott's administration must be judged within the context not only of the problems which troubled all British North American colonies in the 1830s, but also of Newfoundland's limited experience in constitutional government. A legislature had been functioning for barely two years when Prescott arrived, and the problems which bedevilled his rule were part of the warp and woof of the colony's life. He was damned by either side for his part in the removal of Boulton and the silencing of Fleming; by the Catholic-controlled assembly (after 1837) for his partiality .to the Protestant-controlled council, and by the latter for his appointment of the Catholic radical, Patrick Morris*, to the council in 1840 in an effort to improve the Catholic position on that body. He was criticized by the Colonial Office for advocating an improvement of the garrison to aid the civil power (although there was a lack of police and a continuing situation of danger), and yet also for not sending troops to Bay Roberts during the highly disturbed election of 1840 in time to prevent an outbreak of violence. There were certainly achievements in his régime: the setting up of the first non-denominational elementary schools in 1836 by the first education act in Newfoundland, a continuation of Cochrane's road-building efforts and in 1837 the appointment of the colony's first road commissioners, and the encouragement of agriculture to supplement the unpredictable fisheries. But these were supported, opposed, or evaluated on narrow political and religious grounds. That Prescott was not a trained colonial administrator is obvious, but that he possessed considerable sagacity and judgement is indicated by his important dispatch of 4 July 1839 to Lord Normanby [Sir Constantine Henry Phipps], in which he set forth what was, on the whole, a prudent policy to meet the degenerating political situation. Prescott called for an imperial act to enforce the provisions of the Newfoundland Representation Act of 1834, so that Newfoundland would be divided into more districts and a property qualification for representatives in the assembly would be established. By a supplementary letter he recommended simultaneous nomination and polling days throughout the colony.

In the summer of 1838 events occurred in St John's which finally caused Prescott to attempt to resign. John KENT, member of the amalgamated legislature, and Edward Kielly, government medical officer, had a disagreement on the streets of St John's which led Kent to complain to the assembly that Kielly had been guilty of a "gross breach" of its privileges. Dr William Carson*, the speaker of the assembly, called Kielly before the house demanding an apology. The ensuing dispute over the jurisdiction of the assembly went to the Supreme Court of Newfoundland in the autumn, which ruled against Kielly and therefore in favour of the assembly. Prescott, appalled at the overbearing conduct of the assembly in defence of its privileges, had earlier prorogued the house for a week, and in January 1839 resigned. Glenelg did not accept his resignation, and later backed his action. (The whole case was finally settled before the Privy Council on 11 Jan. 1843 when the queen was asked to reverse the decision of the Newfoundland Supreme Court.)

In 1841 Prescott was in England to participate in a parliamentary inquiry, which subsequently led to a modification of Newfoundland's constitution. The Colonial Office did not accept his advice on the reform of the constitution, and on principle Prescott resigned again in May. This time his resignation was accepted, partly as a result of the home government's agreement with Sir Richard Henry Bonnycastle*, who supported the appointment of a civil administrator. Prescott was succeeded by Sir John Harvey*, and returned to naval life.

Prescott was awarded the captain's good service pension in 1841, promoted rear-admiral in 1847, and for a few months was a lord of the Admiralty until in December he accepted the post of admiral-superintendent of the Portsmouth Dockyard, which he held until 1852. He became a vice-admiral in 1854, an admiral in 1860, and admiral of the blue in 1862; he was nominated KCB in 1856 and GCB in 1869, and for a time was JP for Surrey.

FREDERIC F. THOMPSON

PRO, CO 194/90–194/111. *Times* (London), 20 Nov. 1874. *DNB.* G.B., Adm., *Navy lists* (London), 1844–74. John Marshall, *Royal naval biography* . . . (2v. and supps, London, 1823–30), supp. 2, 197. O'Byrne, *Naval biog. dict.* Gunn, *Political history of Nfld.* Prowse, *History of Nfld.*

PRÉVOST, HORTENSE. *See* GLOBENSKY

PRICE, WILLIAM EVAN, businessman and politician; b. 17 Nov. 1827 at Quebec, son of William Price*, the first of his family in Canada, and Jane Stewart; d. 12 June 1880 at the family residence of Wolfesfield, at Quebec, and buried in Belmont cemetery.

When he was still young, William Evan Price

Proulx

joined the enterprise for the commercial exploitation of timber that had been established by his father in the Saguenay region, and comprised numerous centres of production spaced out between Lac Saint-Jean and Sault-au-Cochon (today Forestville), on the north shore of the St Lawrence. He was a bachelor and his usual pied-à-terre was at Chicoutimi; from there he went to the various lumbercamps, sawmills, and ships' loading points where his presence was required.

Less of a hustler than his brother David Edward*, who concerned himself with organization and numerous external activities, William Evan concerned himself particularly with maintenance of the undertaking and effective supervision of operations. However, he allowed himself to be drawn towards politics, like his brothers David Edward and Evan John*. In the federal election of 1872 he stood as Conservative candidate against Pierre-Alexis TREMBLAY, in Chicoutimi-Saguenay County. A circular sent to his electors recalled discreetly the part he had taken in social works, stressed the economic importance of the Price firm for the region, and promised to press for the building of the railway that was to link this region with the capital of the province; representing an almost entirely Catholic population, although Protestant himself, he undertook furthermore to support Catholic schools with his influence, and to follow "always and above all, in politics, the advice of the bishops and priests." He was elected on 10 September, and was a member of the House of Commons until the dissolution of parliament on 2 Jan. 1874.

On 20 July 1875 William Evan was elected as a Conservative to the Legislative Assembly of Quebec to represent the same county. He did not attend the 1875 session, but from 1876 to 1878 he served on several special committees, in particular the committee on railways, canals, telegraph lines, mines, and manufactures, and the committee on agriculture, immigration, and colonization. In 1878 and 1879, when the ministry of Henri-Gustave Joly* stayed in power only by a slim majority, Price's vote with the liberals was sometimes decisive. Because of ill health, which obliged him to make protracted stays in Georgia, he resigned on 13 Feb. 1880; he died four months later.

William Evan Price, who was cultured and benevolent, and a man of refined behaviour, received French language newspapers, was a member of the Mechanics' Institute and of the Chicoutimi library, and director of the Agricultural Society. In addition he maintained friendly relations with the bishop and the majority of the priests in the region,

and enjoyed the respect of his employees and of the people. He showed himself generous and ready to help the unfortunate. The old folk who knew him called him "the best of the Prices." In 1882 a monument was raised to him at Chicoutimi; it also bore the name of his father, who had died in 1867.

VICTOR TREMBLAY

The Price papers, property of the Price Company Limited (Quebec), contain valuable information on the activities of the Price family; they are being reclassified by the company at this time and the author was unable to consult them.

ASHS, Documents, adresse aux électeurs, 1872; Documents, témoignage de J.-A. Gagné, 22 août 1872; Documents, Institut des artisans de Chicoutimi; Dossiers Price, nos.4, 6, 16, 17, 70, 325; Mémoires d'anciens. Quebec, Legislative Assembly, *Journals*, 1875–80. *Le Canadien* (Québec), 28 août, 27 oct., 30 oct. 1872; 20 oct. 1873; 14 juin, 16 juin 1880. *Le Courrier du Canada* (Québec), 4 oct. 1872; 14 juin, 6 août 1880; 5 juill. 1881; 7 juill. 1882. *L'Électeur* (Québec), 25 juill. 1881. *Journal de Québec*, 7 juin 1870; 24 sept., 4 oct., 7 oct., 28 oct. 1872. *Le Nouvelliste* (Québec), 26 févr., 14 juin 1880; 7 mai 1881. Desjardins, *Guide parlementaire*, 188, 223, 281. *Dom. ann. reg., 1880–81*, 426–27. P.-G. Roy, *Fils de Québec*, IV, 94–95. *Inauguration du monument érigé à Chicoutimi à la mémoire de William Evan Price, 24 juin 1882* (Québec, 1882), A. R. M. Lower, "Lumbering in eastern Canada; a study in economic and social history," unpublished PHD thesis, Harvard University, 1928. Rumilly, *Hist. de la prov. de Québec*, I, II. *Storied Quebec* (Wood et al.), I, 384–85; IV, 403–5. Tremblay, *Histoire du Saguenay*. "Les disparus," *BRH*, XXXII (1926), 126.

PROULX, LOUIS, secular priest, educator, writer, parish priest, and vicar general; b. 10 April 1804 at Baie-du-Febvre (Baieville, Yamaska County), L.C., son of Louis Proulx and Élisabeth Grondin; d. 6 July 1871 at Sainte-Marie (Beauce County), Que.

After completing his classical education at the seminary of Nicolet, Louis Proulx taught from 1826 to 1830 at the seminary of Saint-Hyacinthe, where he even assumed responsibility for the direction of studies and discipline. Meanwhile, on 28 Sept. 1828, he was ordained priest at Boucherville (Chambly County). His wise leadership, as well as his brilliant talents, led his superior at Nicolet, Abbé Jean Raimbault, to send him in 1830 to assist Abbé Charles-François Painchaud*, the founder of the college of Sainte-Anne-de-la-Pocatière, and to restore discipline there; the unskilful leadership given by the famous Abbé Étienne Chartier* had reduced the institution to a state of indescribable chaos. Proulx was successful, but remained there only three years.

He was parish priest of Saint-Pierre-les-Becquets (Nicolet County), also serving Deschaillons (Lotbinière County), from 1834 to 1835, and parish priest of Saint-Antoine-de-Tilly (Lotbinière County) from 1835 to 1847. He was then summoned to the archbishop's palace at Quebec by Archbishop Pierre-Flavien Turgeon*, to be his adviser and perhaps eventually his coadjutor. Indeed he possessed the qualities necessary in a great bishop, but, as he was also outspoken, opponents ready to divert him from this path were not lacking. In 1850 he was made parish priest of Notre-Dame de Québec, an office which had become vacant through the departure of the future coadjutor, Bishop Charles-François Baillargeon*.

During his stay at Quebec, Proulx became aware of a new talent, that of writer and polemicist. Under the pseudonym of Marteau, in the *Journal de Québec*, he attacked the radical ideas of *L'Avenir*. He also complained about the Irish immigrants, who had found shelter in large numbers in the parish of Notre-Dame de Québec; he taxed them with being ungrateful and unduly demanding in the matter of the services he or the curate rendered them at their mission in Rue Champlain. These difficulties with the Irish increased his sensitivity, and the slightest opposition from the archbishop's palace became to him hostility and ostracism. Fourteen months after becoming parish priest of Quebec, feeling himself misunderstood, he asked for "a humble post in the country." Shortly afterwards, the parish priest of Sainte-Marie de Beauce, Abbé Joseph Auclair*, was replaced by Proulx; this replacement, a distinctly surprising one, weighed as heavily upon Proulx as if it were a banishment. At that time the prejudices against Beauce were such that it was a long while before the parish priest could accept his exile and resign himself finally to it.

While at Quebec, Louis Proulx had contributed to the founding of two religious communities. In 1849 he helped to establish, at Quebec, the congregation of the Sisters of Charity, of the Hôpital Général in Montreal, under the direction of Mother Marie-Anne-Marcelle MALLET; he was their first chaplain and director. In the same year he persuaded Marie Fitzbach, later Mother Marie du Sacré-Cœur, to found a house of refuge for female prisoners; on 12 Jan. 1850 the house of the Bon-Pasteur admitted its first boarder, and six years later the congregation of the Sisters of the Immaculate Heart of Mary was established by canon law.

In 1857, at Sainte-Marie, following plans of the architect Charles Baillargé*, Proulx began the construction of a new stone church with Gothic lines, which everybody regarded as a folly. It was blessed on 20 Oct. 1859, and the interior was completed during the period 1862 to 1864. A new sacristy was built at the same time, and in it were placed an organ and altars carved by François-Xavier Berlinguet*.

Louis Proulx was a great builder and also a great educator. As soon as he arrived at Sainte-Marie he found himself involved, together with Elzéar-Henri JUCHEREAU Duchesnay, in the difficult task of reviving the schools (1850–55), after the crisis that was known as the "guerre des éteignoirs" [*see* Jean-Baptiste MEILLEUR]. To satisfy the important persons of the region, Proulx raised the level of study and introduced the teaching of music into the convent for girls, which was directed by the nuns of the Congregation of Notre Dame. In 1855 the size of the convent had to be doubled. In the same year, after obtaining a grant through Jean-Baptiste Meilleur's influence – obtaining a grant was no easy matter then – he enlarged the old school for boys, making of it a college which he entrusted to the Brothers of the Christian Schools.

In May and June 1871 Louis Proulx was deputed by the archbishop of Quebec, Elzéar-Alexandre Taschereau*, to go to settle the financial difficulties of the college of Sainte-Anne-de-la-Pocatière. He did so, but it cost him the remainder of his strength, which was already undermined by toil and sickness. On his return to Sainte-Marie he took to his bed and died a month later; he was buried in the parish church. He had been appointed vicar general in 1867 under Bishop Baillargeon.

Louis Proulx was intelligent and had an open mind. He was outspoken with everybody, even his superiors. But he was apt to take offence and to be contradicted was almost unbearable to him.

HONORIUS PROVOST

AAQ, Registres des lettres des évêques de Québec, 24, 25, 28, 29; Sainte-Marie, II. ANQ, QBC, Instruction publique. Archives de la Fabrique Sainte-Marie (Beauce, Qué.), Cahiers de prônes; Comptes et délibérations, II, III. *L'Asile du Bon-Pasteur de Québec d'après les annales de cet institut* (Québec, 1896). *Une fondatrice et son œuvre: mère Mallet (1805–1871) et l'Institut des sœurs de la Charité de Québec, fondé en 1849* (Québec, 1939). Wilfrid Lebon, *Histoire du collège de Sainte-Anne-de-la-Pocatière* (2v., Québec, 1948–49), I, 431–34. Honorius Provost, *Sainte-Marie de la Nouvelle-Beauce; histoire religieuse* (Québec, 1967).

Quertier

QUERTIER, ÉDOUARD, Catholic priest, temperance advocate; b. 5 Sept. 1796 at Saint-Denis-sur-Richelieu, L.C., the second of 17 children of Hélier Quertier, a sacristan, and Marie-Anne Ariail; d. 17 July 1872 at Saint-Denis-de-Kamouraska, Que.

Édouard Quertier studied at the seminary of Nicolet from 1809 to 1815, and in Abbé Paul-Loup Archambault's words he was "the best in his class." In 1815 he enrolled for theology at the seminary of Quebec, which he left three years later. In 1820 he was at Sainte-Marie-de-la-Nouvelle-Beauce, where he was working as a tutor. He then decided in favour of law and in 1822 went to work in Charles Panet's office at Quebec. Two years later, being destitute, he was forced to abandon his legal training and asked to return to ecclesiastical life. Bishop Joseph-Octave Plessis* decided to admit Quertier only after he had had two years for reflection; during this period the young man directed the parish school of Saint-Antoine at Rivière-du-Loup (Louiseville). Finally, on 9 Aug. 1829, on the threshold of his 34th year, Édouard Quertier was ordained priest at Quebec by Bishop Bernard-Claude Panet*.

With "an athlete's build, a rugged face, heavy and prominent features, an imperious look, hair flowing from under the black skull-cap," Abbé Quertier was a remarkable man. In October 1831, after 26 months as a curate, he was appointed first resident parish priest of Saint-Antoine, on Île aux Grues (Montmagny County). "A charming little spot," Quertier wrote. "An old hovel for a lodging, the only trouble being that as it had to be half repaired twice in three years, I had to retire to the attic of my little sacristy. If I was not able to build a presbytery, everyone knows who thwarted my endeavours at that time, and everyone also knows that for the sake of peace I gave in and withdrew." The parish priest was in conflict with Abbé Charles-François Painchaud*, the owner of the site where the parish church and presbytery were built, who fiercely upheld his rights. "All the trouble ... falls on the great benefactor of the island [Painchaud]," the parish priest wrote to Charles-Félix Cazeau*.

In the spring of 1833 Abbé Quertier visited the Mingan missions (Saguenay County); he returned to his island and lived there, grumbling the while, until 1834, when Bishop Joseph Signay* yielded to his complaints and appointed him parish priest of Saint-Georges de Cacouna. Would he be there "the angel of peace and the agent of reconciliation" that his bishop hoped for? At this period the civil and ecclesiastical powers were continually at variance. A bill designed to modify the composition of the parish council assemblies, by giving more representation to the important persons of the parish, had been presented to the Legislative Assembly during the session of 1831 and rejected by the Legislative Council; it had set the state against the church, at least in the minds of the public, by the stir it had created. Quertier was warned that at Cacouna he would be caught between two opposing groups: one in favour of building in the village itself a church intended to replace the old chapel, the other of building this new church in the country. "It is only a matter of softening and overcoming the prejudice of the people far removed from the place decided upon ... [which is] so difficult, especially when one proceeds legally." Quertier did partly satisfy his bishop's expectations: after seven years as parish priest he had to his credit a new presbytery in the village and a renovated chapel.

As early as 1835, while he continued to assure Bishop Signay that "peace is made and almost solidly established," the priest was seeking his recall. Every now and again, in pages of bitter claims and mocking insinuations, the prolific letter-writer renewed his pleas. Finally in 1841 he received a reply, but not to his liking. In September 1841, for the second time in 12 years of ministry, Abbé Quertier was called upon to set up a new parish, that of Saint-Denis-de-Kamouraska. "How did I accept this arid rock? ... When I arrived [in October], there was not even a piece of board on which to place a bed or a table. I had to go down the slope and rent a small house, or rather a cabin. No matter! I waited there until my lodging was acceptable."

It was however from this isolated corner that Quertier's fame was to spread. At Saint-Denis he was to realize the greatest achievement of his career, the founding of the Société de Tempérance, or Société de la Croix Noire. Since 1839 outstanding preachers, including Bishop Charles-Auguste-Marie-Joseph de Forbin-Janson* and Charles-Paschal-Télesphore Chiniquy*, had been protesting against the scourge of alcoholism. But it was Quertier who could claim the credit, in 1842, of drawing up the statutes of the temperance society, formulating the oaths of its new crusaders, and setting up as a symbol a bare black cross. The following year Quertier was able to write: "Temperance prevails everywhere. Each house is decorated with a blessed cross, the reminder of our undertakings." In 1844, the same happy affirmation: "Everything is peaceful here. I can attribute only to our society of the cross our real tranquillity, in the midst of the discords of our neighbours. . . . This blessed cross . . . must speak with its mighty language."

From 1847 on, Abbé Alexis Mailloux assisted Quertier. He came to be considered his most powerful collaborator, even his master. Gradually, through Quertier's action, the preaching of total abstinence spread far beyond the confines of Saint-Denis and even of the diocese of Quebec. Quertier's marvellous eloquence made him famous: in the pulpit he became in turn "the man of fire," the passionate orator, the suave preacher or the learned catechist: "There were often more people at catechism than at mass . . . ," noted the minister. "The church is often so crowded that one can barely get through." Popular belief attributed miraculous virtue to the black cross, and the Quertier rosary was thought to have extinguished fires and cured sick people.

Although the priest's memory is still revered, history must perforce acknowledge that the man was difficult: unstable and always fretful, violent by nature, given to finding fault with the neighbouring parish priests, and unreliable in his estimation of the politicians of the time. Quertier had his knuckles rapped many times by the heads of the diocese, and he made life hard for certain of his contemporaries, including the seigneur of La Bouteillerie, Pierre-Thomas Casgrain, the MLA

Pierre Canac, *dit* Marquis, and the merchant Jean-Charles Chapais Sr.

After 15 years of parish ministry at Saint-Denis, Abbé Quertier, "old [and] worn out," obtained his retirement, which was spent in calm and serenity. As his hair whitened, the violence of the man lessened, but the faith and zeal of the priest did not decline. He died in Saint-Denis and was buried under the sanctuary of the church. Today his statue looks down from the bare hill that he climbed more than 100 years ago.

JULIENNE BARNARD

AAQ, Cahier Signay, p.196; Registres des lettres des évêques de Québec, 15, f.295; 16, f.260; 19, f.252; Séminaire de Nicolet, I, 217, 238. Archives de l'évêché de Sainte-Anne (La Pocatière, Qué.), Isle aux Grues, I, 10; Saint-Denis, I, 66, 71, 82, 100. AJQ, Greffe d'Étienne Boudreault, 9 sept. 1822. Archives paroissiales de Saint-Denis (comté de Kamouraska, Qué.), Registre des baptêmes, mariages et sépultures, 1872. Archives paroissiales de Saint-Denis (comté de Saint-Hyacinthe, Qué.), Registre des baptêmes, mariages et sépultures, 1872. "Inventaire de la correspondance de Mgr Bernard-Claude Panet, archevêque de Québec," Ivanhoë Caron, édit., APQ *Rapport, 1934–35*, 350.

J.-B.-A. Allaire, *Histoire de la paroisse de Saint-Denis-sur-Richelieu (Canada)* (Saint-Hyacinthe, Qué., 1905), 256. Julienne Barnard, *Mémoires Chapais; documentation, correspondance, souvenirs* (4v., Montréal et Paris, 1961–64), I, 191–237; II, 17–22, 36–39, 60, 191–92, 321–24, 346–49. N.-E. Dionne, *Vie de C.-F. Painchaud; prêtre, curé, fondateur du collège Saint-Anne de la Pocatière* (Québec, 1894), 399–404. J.-A.-I. Douville, *Histoire du collège-séminaire de Nicolet, 1803–1903, avec les listes complètes des directeurs, professeurs et élèves de l'institution* (2v., Montréal, 1903). *Inauguration du monument Quertier; quatrième croisade de tempérance* (Québec, Kamouraska, 1925).

R

RAE, JOHN, economist and author; b. 1 June 1796 in Footdee, a suburb of Aberdeen, Scotland, son of John Rae and Margaret Cuthbert; d. 12 July 1872 at Staten Island, New York.

John Rae, the second youngest of seven children, was the son of a well-to-do merchant and shipbuilder who suffered financial reverses and became bankrupt in 1820. Rae's childhood was marred by marital discord in his family, and some undefined mental or physical problem barred him from normal activity and encouraged his interest in intellectual pursuits very early.

Rae entered Marischal College in 1809 or 1810

and in 1815 was granted an MA. In this period he was keenly interested in science and invention, and he invented a number of devices including an apparatus for measuring ocean currents and a device for feathering paddle wheels on steamboats. He became a medical student at the University of Edinburgh in 1815 and continued his studies there until 1817. His dissertation, entitled "De vita," expounded some novel views on human society and natural science. Rae's opinion was that the medical and physiological theories of the time were irrational and burdened with traditional non-scientific notions. His theories of the origin and

Rae

development of man – based on his understanding of the extreme antiquity of the earth – his experimental bias, and his belief in the virtues of comparative studies, placed him in opposition to established doctrines. He recognized that it would be imprudent to challenge the medical profession in Edinburgh and, as a result, postponed the presentation of his thesis pending further study. It was never presented and he never received his medical degree. Rae toured Norway in 1818 and probably spent some time in Paris pursuing his interest in the study of natural science. He married at about this time but all that is known of his wife is that her name was Eliza.

Rae had expected that he would inherit one of his father's estates and be able to devote his life to study. His father's bankruptcy and the loss of the property changed his plans; in the spring of 1822 he and his wife emigrated to Canada. He later wrote: "I exchanged the literary leisure of Europe for the solitude and labors of the Canadian backwoods." Rae went first to Montreal where his older sister, Ann Cuthbert*, was living. She had published two books of poetry, in 1815 and 1816, and through her second husband, merchant James Fleming, provided Rae with an *entrée* into the intellectual and commercial life of Montreal. He doubtless knew John Fleming*, the brother of James, an author and political commentator of some force who was an early president of the Bank of Montreal. He soon left Montreal, however, to open a boys' school in Williamstown, Upper Canada, in 1822, giving as his references the Reverend Henry Esson*, of the St Gabriel Street Church in Montreal, Alexander Skakel* of the Royal Grammar School in Montreal, and the Reverend John Mackenzie*, Presbyterian minister in Williamstown.

Williamstown had the largest Presbyterian congregation in Canada at that time and Rae became a spokesman for the Presbyterian Church in Canada in Connection with the Church of Scotland. He was intimately involved in the clergy reserves controversy, and in 1828 he published a long open letter in the *Canadian Miscellany* to E. G. Stanley (later the 14th Earl of Derby) on the disputes between the Church of England and the Presbyterians in Canada. Rae argued that the revenue from the clergy reserves, if managed properly and supplemented by modest public contributions, would provide ample support to both the Church of England and the Presbyterians. He also claimed that the use of 21-year leases was unsuitable in an undeveloped country and proposed instead leases extending from 70 to 100 years. This would provide an inducement for the heavy investment in clearing wild lands. Rae served briefly

as one of the coroners of the Eastern District (Stormont, Dundas, and Glengarry counties), and may have practised medicine in Williamstown.

While living in Williamstown Rae travelled extensively throughout Upper Canada investigating its geology and economic prospects. In 1832 he petitioned the lieutenant governor of Upper Canada, Sir John Colborne*, for financial support for his explorations and research and announced his intention of publishing a work on the present state and resources of the colony. He intended initially to include an appendix dealing with the theoretical aspects of economic development and with Upper and Lower Canada's economic relations with England.

In 1832 and 1833, Rae contributed a number of polemical letters to the *Montreal Gazette* on current affairs. A vigorous letter on colonial policy late in 1832 attacked the faction which would destroy the ties between Canada and Britain. This was an emotional appeal for loyalty which buttressed his view that the economic development of the colony depended on the maintenance of the close commercial relations. Shortly after, he wrote two letters vigorously supporting high levels of immigration and attacking the anti-British group who were fearful of the effects of pauper immigration. Rae also contributed a bitter essay on the inadequacies of the educational system of Lower Canada early in 1833: he denounced the education bill of 1832 for its restrictive and parochial character and for its completely inadequate provisions for encouraging the supply of competent teachers.

Rae continued the work on his book meanwhile. He visited Boston in 1834 and with the encouragement of a number of Boston literati, including Alexander Hill Everett, the editor of the *North American Review*, decided to issue the appendix first as a separate publication. It appeared in 1834 with the title *Statement of some new principles on the subject of political economy exposing the fallacies of the system of free trade, and of some other doctrines maintained in the "Wealth of Nations."*

The main achievement of this remarkable and brilliant book was to present a theory of economic development and to analyse the influences governing the accumulation of capital. Rae's view was that individuals could become rich by acquiring greater shares of existing wealth but that nations had to create new wealth before they could become richer. They could only do so with the help of the "inventive faculty." It was thus of cardinal importance to encorage invention and to facilitate the transference of new industrial techniques from one country to another. His concept of external economies could be used to justify the adoption of protective duties, bounties, and other forms of

606

state intervention. Rae's analysis of capital accumulation rested heavily on his concept of the "effective desire of accumulation," governed by the following influences: first, "the prevalence throughout the society, of the social and benevolent affections, or, of that principle, which, under whatever name it may be known, leads us to derive happiness, from the good we communicate to others"; second, "the extent of the intellectual powers, and the consequent prevalence of habits of reflection, and prudence, in the minds of the members of the society"; and third, "the stability of the condition of the affairs of the society, and the reign of law and order throughout it." Rae's analysis of the role of invention, of durability in capital formation, and of the economic role of the state was admirable from both a technical and a literary point of view. Many of the ideas he advanced remain applicable to the problems of developing countries in the mid-20th century.

Rae's book was not an easy one to understand and attacked the entrenched views of the followers of Adam Smith. As a result it did not achieve any popular success and did not bring Rae the acclaim he had hoped for. In England, Rae's criticism of some of the established economic doctrine and his espousal of state intervention to foster new technologies were received coldly and he was, for the most part, dismissed as presumptuous. So far as Rae's protectionist sponsors in the United States were concerned, they found his arguments too moderate and reasoned, and unsuited to the shrill and simple-minded controversy in which he had become involved. This cool reception was matched by indifference in Canada, not surprising in view of the colonial mentality and primitive economic ideas which prevailed at the time. There were two favourable references in the *Montreal Gazette* but this is the only direct and recognizable impact which Rae's book had on economic thought in Canada in the 19th century. Twenty years after its publication Rae wrote to John Stuart Mill about his book, "I have not looked at it for many years, and have no copy of it." His disappointment with the reception of his book was great but, having to earn a living, he turned again to schoolteaching and, late in 1834, was appointed headmaster of the Gore District grammar school in Hamilton. He remained in this position until 1848.

Rae was active in the work of the Hamilton Literary Society, which was one of the centres of intellectual life in the community. He began a lifelong friendship with Hugh Bowlby WILLSON after moving to Hamilton. Roderick William Cameron*, the son of Duncan Cameron*, and at one time a pupil of Rae's in Williamstown, moved to Hamilton to begin a distinguished mercantile career; their friendship was to last until Rae's death. Rae was also well known to Sir Allan Napier MacNab* and claimed the acquaintance of Sir Francis Bond HEAD. Rae's loyalist sentiments remained firm in the face of the reform agitation of the mid-1830s. During the armed insurrection in December 1837 Rae joined the militia to help suppress the rebels and participated in a number of skirmishes on the Niagara frontier.

During his life in Hamilton, Rae's intellectual activities continued unabated. In the summer of 1840 an announcement appeared in several newspapers that Rae's book "Outlines of the natural history and statistics of Canada" would be published in England. The manuscript was evidently rejected and later submitted for publication in New York where it was lost. He experimented with balloons using solar heat (the first recorded aeronautical experiment in Canada) and published the results in the *American Journal of Science and Arts* (New Haven) in 1838. He became involved in the educational and religious controversies which bedevilled Upper Canada in the 1840s and wrote a number of spirited articles in this field. He also contributed several graceful essays to the *Literary Garland* of Montreal and entered into a controversy in 1845 over the geology of North America with the Reverend William Turnbull Leach* in the *British American Journal of Medical and Physical Science*.

Beginning in 1832, the Presbyterians were concerned about the lack of a theological seminary in Canada. In 1837, as a stopgap, arrangements were made to have four young candidates for the ministry begin their studies under John Rae at the Gore District school. In 1842, when Queen's College at Kingston opened, four of Rae's students were among those enrolling in theology. On two occasions, in 1841 or 1842 and in 1845, Rae applied for a teaching post at Queen's but was turned down.

In the late 1840s Rae's relations with the trustees of the Gore District school became strained. He had become involved in the controversy with the educational authorities, spearheaded by Church of England Bishop John Strachan*, concerning the attempts to impose centralized control over the operations of the grammar schools. The board of trustees of his school, at one time dominated by Presbyterians, had changed as a result of the disruption of 1844 and Rae found himself under the control of an unsympathetic board consisting of the Reverend John Gamble Geddes*, a Church of England minister in Hamilton, and Dr William Craigie*. There were allegations about Rae's "inefficiency" as a teacher, as well as disagreement over religious matters and accommodation. The

Rae

upshot was that the trustees closed the school, effectively dismissing Rae. Rae moved to Boston and then to New York where he took a teaching post. In August 1849, Rae's wife, who had stayed behind in Hamilton, died of cholera and in December Rae set off for the gold fields in California. He spent some time in Panama en route and remained in California until the spring of 1851 when, finding the gold fields unrewarding, he sailed to the Hawaiian Islands.

At some time prior to 1847, Nassau William Senior, the English political economist, acquired a copy of Rae's book and praised it highly to John Stuart Mill. Mill recognized Rae's significant contribution to the theory of capital and incorporated some of Rae's views in his *Principles of political economy*. Mill wrote: "in no other book known to me is so much light thrown, both from principle and history, on the causes which determine the accumulation of capital." Professor Francesco Ferrara of the University of Turin also recognized the quality of Rae's work and translated it into Italian in 1856. Copies of Rae's *Statement of some new principles* were scarce and its general theme was known mainly because of Mill's copious quotations. Rae himself learned of Mill's interest in 1853 and exchanged some interesting correspondence with him in 1853 and 1854.

Not long after Rae's arrival in the Hawaiian Islands he settled down on the island of Maui and began to operate a small school. He was appointed medical agent of the Board of Health in 1853 and acquired a farm in Hana. Late in the 1850s Rae was made district judge of Hana, a notary public, and a coroner. He became a close friend of Robert Crichton Wyllie, a fellow-Scot and the Hawaiian minister of foreign relations, and strongly supported Wyllie in his contests with the American missionaries. Early in 1861 he completed a long and profound article on the legislative system of the Hawaiian Islands, published in six instalments in the *Polynesian*. In the fall of 1862 Rae also contributed to this newspaper an essay on the "Polynesian languages," in which he developed the theory that human speech originated in facial gestures. The essay was praised by Mill, who felt that the paper would "place Dr. Rae very high among ethnologists and philologists," and by Friedrich Max Müller. Rae continued to develop his ideas on this subject and a long manuscript on languages was found among his papers. It was so badly mixed up that it could not be properly assembled and it has since been lost. He wrote voluminously on the geology of the Hawaiian Islands and enunciated some novel views on tides and volcanoes.

In the summer of 1871 Rae returned from Maui to spend his remaining years on Staten Island with his lifelong friend, Roderick William Cameron. The next summer, in his 77th year, Rae died and was buried on Staten Island in an unmarked grave.

In 1897, Charles Whitney Mixter, a student at Harvard University, published an article in the *Quarterly Journal of Economics* on Rae in which he ascribed to Rae some of the views of Eugen von Böhm-Bawerk set forth in the *Positive Theorie des Kapitals*. The resemblance was exaggerated but stimulated Böhm-Bawerk's interest and led him to include a long chapter on Rae in the second edition of his *Geschichte und Kritik der Capital-zins-theorien* (1900). Irving Fisher wrote an appreciative note about Rae in 1897 and dedicated his book *The theory of interest* (1930) "To the memory of John Rae and Eugen von Böhm-Bawerk who laid the foundations on which I have endeavoured to build." He described Rae's *Statement of some new principles* as "truly a masterpiece, a book of a generation or a century."

R. WARREN JAMES

[John Rae's principal work is *Statement of some new principles on the subject of political economy exposing the fallacies of the system of free trade, and of some other doctrines maintained in the "Wealth of Nations"* (Boston, 1834). Other works are "Letter to the Honourable Mr. Stanley, on the relative claims of the English and Scotch churches in the Canadas," *Canadian Miscellany* (Montreal), I (August 1828), 129–60; "How ought the clergy reserve question to be settled?" *Canadian Christian Examiner and Presbyterian Magazine* (Niagara, Toronto), III (1839), 217–23, 237–42, 269–74; "Thoughts on the system of legislation which has prevailed in the Hawaiian Islands for the last forty years; on the evils that have arisen from it; and on the possible remedies for these evils," *Polynesian* (Honolulu), 2, 9, 16 Feb., 16, 30 March, 20 April 1861; "Polynesian languages," *Polynesian* (Honolulu), 27 Sept., 4, 11 Oct. 1862; and "Laiei-kawai: a legend of the Hawaiian Islands," *J. of American Folk-lore* (Boston), XIII (1900), 241–60.

The following works which were signed "J.R." have been attributed to John Rae: "Loyal address to the king," *Montreal Gazette*, 24 Dec. 1832; "The opposition to emigration," *Montreal Gazette*, 19 Jan. 1833; "Emigration – Mr. Evans' letter," *Montreal Gazette*, 26 Feb. 1833; "Remarks on the education bill," *Montreal Gazette*, 19 March 1833; "Plagiarism," *Literary Garland* (Montreal), I (1838–39), 561–62; and "Genius and its application," *Literary Garland* (Montreal), II (1839–40), 33–36.

The following unsigned writings have been attributed to John Rae: "Sketches of the origin and progress of manufactures and of the policy which has regulated their legislative encouragement in Great Britain and in other countries," *Canadian Review and Literary and Historical Journal* (Montreal), II (1825), 122–33; and "On the state and prospects of education

608

and learning in the Canadas," *Canadian Miscellany* (Montreal), I (May 1828), 33–45.

Rae's *Statement of some new principles* was translated into Italian by Francesco Ferrara as *Dimostrazione di taluni nuovi principii sull'economia politica . . . (Biblioteca dell'economista*, 1st ser., XI, Turin, 1856). C. W. Mixter republished Rae's book as *The sociological theory of capital; being a complete reprint of the new principles of political economy, 1834* (New York, London, 1905). The biographical preface was very valuable but unfortunately Mixter edited and rearranged Rae's text clumsily and produced a distorted version of it. The *Statement of new principles* was reprinted in its original form and Rae's other writings collected and edited by R. W. James in *John Rae, political economist; an account of his life and a compilation of his main writings* (2v., Toronto, 1965), which also includes a study of Rae's life and work and extensive bibliographical references.

John Rae's manuscripts on geology are deposited with the National Library, Ottawa. C. D. W. Goodwin, *Canadian economic thought: the political economy of a developing nation, 1814–1914* (Duke University Commonwealth-Studies Center pub., 15, Durham, N.C., London, 1961). Helmut Lehmann, *John Raes Werk, seine philosophischen methodologischen Grundlagen . . .* (Dresden, 1937). J. A. Schumpeter, *History of economic analysis; edited from manuscript by Elizabeth Boody Schumpeter* (New York, 1954). R.W.J.]

RAINY CHIEF. *See* SOTAI-NA

REBOUL, LOUIS-ÉTIENNE-DELILLE, priest, Oblate of Mary Immaculate, and missionary; b. 4 Dec. 1827 at Saint-Pons (department of Ardèche), France, son of Louis-Antoine Reboul and Augustine-Marie Guillon; d. 2 March 1877 at Mattawa (Nipissing District), Ont.

Louis-Étienne-Delille Reboul, son of one of the most well-to-do and reputable families at Saint-Pons, studied at the Petit Séminaire of Bourg-Saint-Andéol and at the seminary of Viviers (1847–50), then entered the noviciate of the Oblates at Notre-Dame-de-l'Osier in the department of Isère, where he made his profession on 8 Dec. 1851. He finished his studies at Marseilles, and on 27 June 1852 was ordained priest by Bishop Charles-Joseph-Eugène de Mazenod.

Reboul worked for some months at Notre-Dame-de-la-Garde at Marseilles, then left for Canada. He was sent to Bytown (Ottawa), was assistant to Bishop Joseph-Bruno GUIGUES in the surrounding missions, and devoted himself to ministering to a parish at South Gloucester (Russell County) from 1853 to 1855 and at Rivière-du-Désert (Maniwaki, Gatineau County) in 1855 and 1856. During the summers of 1854 and 1855 he worked in the Indian missions of Témiscamingue, Abitibi, and James Bay.

In the winter of 1854 Reboul undertook his first mission to the lumbercamps. He went as far as the Creuse (Deep River, Ont.) and Noire (Black River) rivers, visited the various camps of young lumber-cutters, and offered them the help of religion. He went through some 60 lumbercamps, occupied by more than 1,500 persons. In the summer, the missionary would meet these men again in the Ottawa region. Reboul became head of the mission to the Ottawa lumbercamps in 1858, and continued its work for several months each winter until his death, which occurred during one of his trips.

The rest of the year he lived at Ottawa, where he devoted himself to ministering to a parish and to the spiritual and temporal care of travellers, to whom he became a legendary apostle. He denounced unscrupulous innkeepers, and worked to break up brawls among the members of his flock and preserve peace between Catholics and Protestants. He also served the little chapel of Notre-Dame-des-Voyageurs, which had been set up at Hull for the men of the lumbercamps.

Hull grew in size after 1860; a great number of the loggers lived there with their families. The Oblates made the village a mission, and Reboul was entrusted with ministering to all the Catholics there. In 1868 he undertook the construction of a spacious church, a presbytery, and some schools. He completed all these projects without going into debt, through his ability to obtain gifts by subscription and with the help of Bishop Guigues and money from the parishioners.

In 1871 the Oblates agreed to look after the parish, and sent Reboul to reside there. He was the heart of the locality, and its father; he took an interest in everything and shrank from no task; he became president of the school commission, promoted the building of a bridge, and had an active part in obtaining a charter for the town in 1875. From 1866 to his death, Reboul also exercised his ministry at the monastery of the Good Shepherd Nuns at Ottawa.

An upright, frank, and honest man, Reboul won the affection and respect of all. Lac Reboul (Winawiah), in the region of Grand Lac de Victoria (Témiscamingue County), a school, a street, and a park in Hull recall his name.

GASTON CARRIÈRE

Archives générales O.M.I. (Rome), Dossier Louis-Étienne Reboul; Dossier Florent Vandenberghe (copies in AHO (Ottawa)). Archives provinciales O.M.I. (Ottawa), Dossier Ottawa; Dossier 1ʳᵉ maison; Dossier Hull; Dossier Université d'Ottawa (copies in AHO (Ottawa)). *Journal de l'Ardèche* (Privas), 11 avril, 12 avril 1877. *Notices nécrologiques des O.M.I.*, III, 353–81. Carrière, *Histoire des O.M.I.*,

Rees

V, VII; *Le père Louis-Étienne Reboul, oblat de Marie-Immaculée; organisateur de la vie religieuse à Hull et apôtre des chantiers* (Ottawa, 1959). J. K. Foran, "In the path of the pioneer priest," *The Owl* (Ottawa), VII (1893), 126–28.

REES, WILLIAM, physician and surgeon; b. *c.*1800, son of Evans Rees of Bristol, Eng.; d. unmarried 4 Feb. 1874 in Toronto, Ont.

William Rees studied medicine in England under Sir Astley Cooper and came to Canada in 1819. He was assistant health officer at the port of Quebec until 1822 when he was commissioned to take medical charge of transport to England. In 1829 he moved to York (Toronto) and, after examination by the Medical Board of Upper Canada in January 1830, he purchased the practice of John Porter Daly. With the exception of a brief sojourn in Cobourg in 1832 Rees lived the rest of his life in Toronto. In 1834 he advertised a course of lectures which he hoped would form the beginning of a school of medicine. He ran unsuccessfully in the first riding of York for election to the Legislative Assembly in that year. During the Upper Canadian rebellion he was appointed surgeon to the guard-ship at Toronto and assistant surgeon to the regiment of Queen's Rangers.

Rees advocated throughout his career numerous measures for social reform and the development of public service. When he began his practice in Toronto he advertised that he would vaccinate the poor and give them medical advice free of charge. In 1837 he constructed a wharf and public baths on the waterfront at Toronto for the use of immigrants. At various times he promoted the establishment of an orphans' home, a female aid society, sailors' homes, a juvenile reformatory, an industrial farm, an institution for the treatment of alcoholics, a military and marine frontier force for defence and to provide training for indigent juveniles, a humane society to reward heroic rescue acts and to punish cruelty to animals, a medical dispensary and vaccine institution for the poor, a provincial board of prison and sanitary inspectors, a provincial museum with botanical and zoological gardens, and new waterworks and a street railway for Toronto. Primarily as a result of his efforts, the Provincial Lunatic Asylum was established in 1841 and he was appointed its medical superintendent.

Before taking up his appointment Rees toured Europe at his own expense consulting authorities on institutions for the care of the insane and on the latest methods of treatment. Until an asylum could be built an old jail was used to house the insane under Rees' care. The number of inmates was initially 17 but it grew rapidly, and a wing of the vacant parliament buildings and a house had to be used until the asylum was ready for occupation.

In the course of his duties Rees received a blow on the head from one of the inmates, an injury which left him with greatly impaired eyesight and incapable of performing his duties or returning to private practice. He was replaced as superintendent of the asylum by Dr Walter Telfer in 1844 and thereafter lived in semi-retirement in his cottage on the waterfront adjacent to his wharf. He wrote frequently to the government seeking a pension in compensation for the time spent in organizing the asylum and for the injury he had suffered, or proposing administrative reforms and an appointment for himself in connection with the proposed changes. Although he had the support of a majority in the legislature, his efforts to obtain a government appointment were unsuccessful and the only compensation he received was a lump sum of $1,000 in 1864.

Many of the administrative reforms he suggested were ultimately implemented. His contemporaries, however, held divided opinions about him. Dr Christopher Widmer* was opposed to his appointment as superintendent from the outset and informed Robert Baldwin* that Vice Chancellor Robert Sympson Jameson* of the Court of Equity had "smuggled him into office." "The cure of the insane," Widmer asserted, "should certainly be consigned to a practical man with a philosophic knowledge of the treatment of insanity." Even before Rees' injury, Widmer was urging his dismissal and in 1851 opposed the attempt to obtain a pension for Rees as "the most impudent effort ever projected." In a memorandum prepared for William Canniff*, Clarke Gamble stated that Rees "was a learned man on some things, but an eccentric and most sanguine man," and added "he was appointed to the superintendence and management thereof upon the principle, I suppose, of setting a madman to watch a madman." On the other hand, Rees' superintendence of the asylum was commended by a number of British and American medical authorities and Henry Scadding* informed Canniff that "he was of a speculative disposition, and a man of unusual intelligence." In supporting his application for a pension the *Dominion Medical Journal* referred to him as "one of the oldest and most respected practitioners in this Province."

WILLIAM ORMSBY

William Rees, *The case of Doctor William Rees, late physician to the Provincial Lunatic Asylum, Toronto, C.W.: memorial to his excellency the governor general in council . . .* (Quebec, 1865).

MTCL, Baldwin papers, entries for Christopher Widmer. PAC, RG 5, C1, 1841–42, nos.1982, 2392,

2642, 2884, 3418, 3424, 4167, 4505, 4643A, 5095, 5120; 1846–47, nos.16587, 17398; 1847–48, nos.17997, 18467, 18817, 19837, 20053; 1849, no.467; 1850, nos.602, 669; 1851, nos.1506, 1667; 1852, no.1032; 1853, no.540; 1854, no.1528; 1857, nos.613, 1086; 1858, no.811; 1860, no.889; 1861, nos.229, 513, 682, 1004; 1862, nos.987, 1042, 1091, 1264, 1484; 1863, no.1470; 1864, nos.444, 819; RG 7, G20, 1843, no.2719; 1844, no.3473; 1855, no.6261; 1862, no.10139; 1865, nos.969, 1009, 1297, 12036, 12039; 1866, nos.575, 933; 1869, no.979 1/2. PAO, Toronto City Council papers, 1 June 1837; 5 June, 12 July 1843; 26 Dec. 1848; 3, 26 Nov. 1849. Canniff, *Medical profession in Upper Canada*, 570–73.

REGNAUD, FRANÇOIS-JOSEPH-VICTOR, teacher, surveyor; b. 1799 in France; d. 28 Feb. 1872 at Montreal, Que.

Nothing is known of François-Joseph-Victor Regnaud's childhood and adolescence. In a speech at the opening of the École Normale Jacques-Cartier at Montreal on 3 March 1857, he recalled that he had been appointed by the minister of Public Instruction in France to set up and direct, at Montbrison, one of the first normal schools for primary teachers. The subjects taught there were reading, writing, grammar, arithmetic, the metric system, surveying, the history and geography of France, and geometrical drawing.

Regnaud's success no doubt prompted the minister of Public Instruction, François Guizot, to recommend him to Abbé John Holmes*, who in 1836 was looking for a teacher for the normal school that Lower Canada wanted to establish at Montreal. After an interview with the candidate, Holmes concluded that he possessed "merit, capability, experience, an excellent character, unwavering virtue, and unshakeable principles of uprightness and religion." He gave him an examination, and noted that he was not "sufficiently well grounded in mechanics, chemistry, natural history, agriculture and horticulture, civil law, and religious instruction." François Regnaud arrived at Montreal on 15 June 1837, and was appointed head teacher of the new École Normale de Montreal for a period of five years at the annual salary of £245, plus accommodation.

The normal school opened its doors on 5 September, and after a fashion courses were given there for five years. The political events of the time did not unduly interfere with the school's activities; it seems however that the moment was scarcely auspicious for the setting up of a normal school which would have some prospects of surviving, at least according to the formula of 1836 – a two-denominational school open to both Catholics and Protestants.

When the school was closed on 23 Feb. 1842,

Regnaud became a government surveyor. In 1857 the new École Normale Jacques-Cartier entrusted him with giving a course in pedagogy and applied mathematics. However, he did not abandon surveying, since his reports show that he carried on this profession until 1870.

François Regnaud understood the cardinal importance of normal schools; he stated that these "institutions were the corner-stone, the foundation stone of primary teaching." He gave his complete support to the Association des Instituteurs de l'École Normale Jacques-Cartier, attended its conferences regularly, and presented reports on the best method of teaching history, the advantages of teachers' associations, and the importance of using the same books in all normal schools.

Canada was for François Regnaud a second country, towards which he displayed affection and where he gave the best of himself. What judgement of him can be made? According to Auguste Gosselin*, Regnaud "was a skilful teacher, a distinguished man, especially in mathematics. He was also a perfect Christian. He lacked only one thing, apparently, the ability to keep discipline, the principles of which he had, moreover, himself established at the school."

In France, François Regnaud had married Antoinette Gay, who died in Montreal at the age of 88. They had three children.

LOUIS-PHILIPPE AUDET

AJM, Registre d'état civil. Institut pédagogique national (Paris), Lucien Simiand, Monographie de l'école normale d'instituteurs de Montbrison. *JIP*, 1857, 63–64; 1858, 11; 1859, 25–26, 57–58, 70–73, 95–98, 135–38; 1860, 49; 1866, 128; 1867, 106; 1868. Audet, *Le système scolaire de la province de Québec*, VI, 115–80. P.-J.-O. Chauveau, *L'instruction publique au Canada, précis historique et statistique* (Québec, 1876), 71. Adélard Desrosiers, *Les écoles normales primaires de la province de Québec et leurs œuvres complémentaires, 1857–1907* (Montréal, 1909). André Labarrère-Paulé, *Les instituteurs laïques au Canada français, 1836–1900* (Québec, 1965), 49–117. Robert Rumilly, *Henri Bourassa, la vie publique d'un grand Canadien* (Montréal, 1953), 9–10. Auguste Gosselin, "L'abbé Holmes et l'instruction publique," *RSCT*, 3rd ser., I (1907), sect.i, 127–72.

REID, HUGO, educator and author; b. 21 June 1809 in Edinburgh, Scotland, third son of Dr Peter Reid and Christian Arnot; d. 13 June 1872 in London, Eng.

Hugo Reid spent an active and useful life in Great Britain and North America lecturing in science, language, and logic and writing on a wide variety of subjects. A distinguished alumnus of the High School in Edinburgh, he lectured in Glasgow, Carlton, Mile End, Brighton, and Liverpool and

Reilly

became principal of People's College, Nottingham. He was a member of the Lothian and Philosophical societies of Glasgow and of the Hunterian Society of Edinburgh. In 1839 he married Marion, eldest daughter of James Kirkland, a Glasgow merchant. They had one child, a daughter.

In November 1855 Hugo Reid went to Halifax where he became principal of the high school and of the junior school which began in Dalhousie College on 15 Jan. 1856. He was also professor of logic, general grammar, and English, dean of the faculty, and chairman or principal of Dalhousie when it resumed university courses in October 1856. The university then had a faculty of five and a student enrollment of 15. By 1857 two of the professors had resigned and again the decision was made to discontinue university work. Reid remained as principal of the Collegiate School until 26 Jan. 1860 when he resigned. At this point the governors of Dalhousie, who were receiving no cooperation from the community, decided to give the one remaining professor six months notice and to cease operations completely, "perhaps the darkest period in the history of Dalhousie."

While in Halifax Reid wrote and published several works including *Elements of geography adopted for use in Br. America . . .* and *Remarks on university education in Nova Scotia.* He was a founding member and secretary of the Nova Scotia Literary and Scientific Society and a frequent contributor to its *Transactions.* In 1858 he gave a series of lectures to the Halifax Mechanics' Institute, and later prepared and published a map of Nova Scotia. Following a visit to relatives in the United States, he returned to Great Britain where he continued to write and publish until his death.

CHARLES BRUCE FERGUSSON

A list of Hugo Reid's works can be found in *British Museum catalogue. See also*: PANS, Correspondence of Hugo Reid, 1856–59. *Edinburgh Courant*, 21 June 1872. *Morning Chronicle* (Halifax), 18 Dec. 1855; 1 Jan., 26 June, 16 Sept. 1856; 23 Jan. 1858. D. C. Harvey, *An introduction to the history of Dalhousie University* (Halifax, 1938). G. G. Patterson, *The history of Dalhousie College and University* (Halifax, 1887).

REILLY, EDWARD, journalist and politician; b. 1839 or 1840 in Prince Edward Island; d. 29 March 1872 in Charlottetown, P.E.I.

After a brief career as a teacher in the rural schools of Prince Edward Island, Edward Reilly became a journeyman printer in Charlottetown in the offices of David Laird*'s *Protestant* and Edward Whelan*'s *Examiner*. On 17 Oct. 1862

he founded the militantly ultramontane *Vindicator,* which was to provide an alternative to other Island newspapers – reading matter "of a dangerous character, filled with moral poison." Although Reilly was the publisher of the *Vindicator,* in later years he denied having been the editor; it was widely suspected at the time that this position was held by Father Angus MacDonald*, rector of St Dunstan's College. The *Vindicator,* a weekly, specialized in vitriolic denunciations of various public figures, such as William Henry POPE, David Laird, the Reverend George Sutherland*, and the lieutenant governor, George DUNDAS. In 1864, Joseph Webster, master of the Normal School, brought Reilly to court for an article which suggested that Webster had had improper relations with his female students. The case ended with a full apology by Reilly in October 1864. He discontinued publication of the *Vindicator* at that time, but one week later founded another weekly, the *Herald,* of which he was both editor and publisher. In 1870 he took partners into the venture, one of whom appears to have been John Caven, a professor at St Dunstan's.

Although Reilly remained sympathetic to the demands of the Roman Catholic hierarchy in educational matters, he began to seek a wider base of support. He adopted a vigorously pro-tenant position on the land question, and denounced the Quebec resolutions of 1864 as a "scheme of spoliation" for the Island. He claimed that union would make Islanders pay for expenses such as continental defence and the Intercolonial Railway without commensurate benefits. In particular, he objected to the failure of the confederation proposals to provide for the liquidation of leasehold tenure, agreeing with George COLES and others that resolution of the land question was a *sine qua non* of entry.

Reilly's adamant opposition to confederation brought him into conflict with Edward Whelan, the leading Roman Catholic public man of the colony, who ardently supported the Quebec plan. The two men also clashed on the explosive subjects of Fenianism and the Tenant League. Whelan utterly condemned both movements, but Reilly was non-committal. The younger man was clearly challenging Whelan's hold on the Catholic population, particularly those who were tenants, or Irish immigrants, or both. When a general election took place in February 1867, Reilly ran against Whelan in Kings County, Second District, although both were Liberals; Reilly lost, but greatly reduced Whelan's majority. After the election, which the Liberals won, Whelan was appointed queen's printer and was obliged to face the electorate again in a by-election. This time,

Reilly dealt Whelan his first defeat in 21 years of politics. Eight days after Whelan's death on 10 Dec. 1867, Reilly succeeded him as queen's printer; he won the by-election called in early 1868.

Reilly remained queen's printer until 1870, when the Liberals split over the school question. He then followed George Howlan* and all but one of the Roman Catholic Liberal assemblymen into a coalition led by Conservative James Colledge Pope*. The basis of the alliance was a mutual self-denying pledge signed by the Catholic Liberals and the Conservative leaders, some of whom were confederates: nothing would be done on the school or confederation questions until they were submitted to the people at the polls. In the change of government, Reilly lost the queen's printership because a prominent Tory, Frederick de St Croix Brecken*, threatened to resign should he retain the office. A year later, Reilly left the coalition and returned to the Liberals in protest against the government's railway policy. Although he had supported the legislation when it was first introduced, he now feared it would be the means of forcing the Island into confederation. As it turned out, he was correct, although he did not live to see his prophecy fulfilled. On the morning of 29 March 1872 at his house in Charlottetown he died suddenly of heart disease, leaving his wife Hannah.

Edward Reilly was a controversial person, particularly in his early years as a journalist. After entering the assembly, he became more restrained and employed milder language in the *Herald* editorials. When he died, at the age of 32, he was one of the most effective debaters in the assembly, as well as a prominent journalist. On the day before he died, he had been nominated for the election of 4 April, which his party won. There can be no doubt that had he lived he would have been a leading public figure for many more years.

IAN ROSS ROBERTSON

Prince Edward Island, Supreme Court, Estates Division, will of Edward Reilly. Prince Edward Island, House of Assembly, *Journals*, 1867–72; *Debates and proceedings*, 1867–72. *Examiner* (Charlottetown), 9 Jan., 24 July 1865. *Herald* (Charlottetown), 1864, 1866–68, 1870–71. *Island Argus* (Charlottetown), 2 April 1872. *Patriot* (Charlottetown), 30 March, 4 April 1872. *Vindicator* (Charlottetown), 1862–64. MacMillan, *Catholic Church in PEI*, 219–20, 260–61, 271–75. Robertson, "Religion, politics, and education in PEI," chapt. 6–8.

RENAUD, LOUIS, merchant and member of the Legislative Council; b. 3 Oct. 1818 at Lachine, near Montreal, L.C., son of Jean-Baptiste Renaud, a voyageur, and Marie-Reine Garriépy; d. 13 Nov. 1878 at Sainte-Martine (Châteauguay County), Que.

After a brief primary education, and when he was quite young, Louis Renaud had to work to support his sick father. With his brother Jean-Baptiste, he first became a carter. The two Renauds were still plying their trade, the registers of Notre-Dame de Montréal testify, when they were married at the same wedding service, 18 Jan. 1841. Jean-Baptiste married Sophie Lefebvre, daughter of Jean-Baptiste Lefebvre and Appoline Abraham, and Louis (to whom the registers add the name Paul, which is not found on his baptismal certificate) married Marie-Anne Pigeon, daughter of Félix Pigeon and Véronique-Aimée Trudelle. By the age of 20 Louis had saved up enough to enter business, and at 30 he possessed a sizeable fortune. He went into partnership with his brother Jean-Baptiste, who was later to set himself up at Quebec and establish there the firm of J.-B. Renaud and Company, and exported on a large scale to the English market and to the United States, where their company had agents in most large towns. Around 1856 he became a partner of John YOUNG, an important politician from 1851 to 1872 and one of the most influential businessmen in British North America. The two men engaged in commercial operations that were extensive for the period. Their dealings in England, France, and the United States rivalled those of the largest British and American firms. It is recorded that in certain years they amounted to 20 million "piastres."

Renaud specialized in the grain trade, and the majority of the merchants in Lower Canada to whom he advanced money and goods became his agents. The master of the grain and flour trade in Lower Canada, he was able to set prices. He was at the height of his career when unfortunate transactions by one of his agents in the United States compromised his credit, and forced him to sell depreciated American shares at a loss. An immense fortune disappeared, but he succeeded in meeting all the demands of his creditors. He lived out his life in moderately easy circumstances at Sainte-Martine, where he owned a great amount of land.

In politics Louis Renaud played a discreet role, which his contemporaries considered important. The Legislative Council of united Canada having become elective, he was returned in 1856 for the division of Salaberry by a majority of 1,200 votes over his adversary, Joseph Doutre*, a lawyer and one of the leaders of the Rouge party. In the autumn of 1864 he was re-elected by acclamation. When in 1867 confederation came into being, he was summoned by royal proclamation to sit in

Reynard

the Senate. The poor state of his health and in particular his failing eyesight forced him to resign in 1873, and he was then replaced by his son-in-law. By his first marriage he had had 11 children; his only daughter, Zoé-Aimée, married François-Xavier-Anselme Trudel*, and one of his sons, Napoléon, after serving as a papal Zouave, succeeded him at the head of his business. In March 1864 he married again, his second wife being Hélène Chicoux-Duvert, widow of Charles-Joseph-René Drolet; she survived him. Louis Renaud's funeral was held at the church of Notre-Dame de Montréal, and the burial took place at Côte-des-Neiges.

At the time of his death *La Minerve* wrote on 15 November: "He made the name of Canada known to advantage on the English and French markets, through commercial operations that revealed him as a man of exceptional genius." In 1875, a few years before his death, one of the principal chroniclers of Montreal, the Reverend John Douglas Borthwick*, devoted a highly laudatory biography to him, containing these words: "Although his childhood was lacking in any form of instruction, he succeeded, thanks to superior intelligence, indomitable energy, a very strong constitution, and almost superhuman labour, in acquiring knowledge and experience which soon made him a master in the realm of commerce. Few have equalled and perhaps none have surpassed him as far as accuracy in sizing up a situation, speed of conception, and rightness of judgement are concerned." Throughout his whole career Renaud was a friend of George-Étienne Cartier, whose politics he supported and who used to consult him; Borthwick was thus led to write: "Although he was a man of little culture, his experience, advice, firmness, and energy have often exercised a decisive influence on the politics of his time."

J.-C. Bonenfant

La Minerve (Montréal), 15 nov. 1878. Borthwick, *Montreal*, 110. É.-Z. Massicotte, "Deux grands négociants," *BRH*, XLII (1936), 339–40.

REYNARD, ALEXIS, missionary lay brother of the congregation of the Oblates of Mary Immaculate; b. in Castillon, diocese of Nîmes, France, 28 Sept. 1828, son of Alexis-Joseph Reynard and Victoire Dugas; d. at House River, a tributary of the Athabasca, about 20 July 1875.

Alexis Reynard had an elementary schooling and worked as a vine dresser on the family farm. He made his vows with the Oblate congregation on 9 May 1852, and was appointed in 1853 to the missions of Athabasca. The 1850s were a period of expansion of Oblate missions in the North-West, culminating in the establishment of Saint-Cœur-de-Marie at Fort Good Hope near the Arctic circle on the lower Mackenzie River.

Brother Alexis served under Mgr Vital-Justin Grandin*, Mgr Henri Faraud*, and Mgr Isidore Clut*. He became a skilled carpenter, stoneworker, voyageur, and gardener. All the buildings at La Nativité mission, Lake Athabasca (today Fort Chipewyan) and at Providence mission (on the present-day Mackenzie Highway near Yellowknife, Northwest Territories) were built by him. His performance of these duties permitted the priests to devote themselves to their spiritual duties. Along with his great strength and vigour, he "had the gentleness and guilelessness of a child."

From the time he joined the order, Brother Alexis hoped to be ordained a priest. He frequently approached his superiors, at first without success. Then he received permission to study Latin under Father Grandin at La Nativité. But on the advice of his superiors, he finally withdrew his request for ordination. It was concluded in 1861 that his very goodness would make it impossible for him to direct a mission. This was a bitter disappointment to Brother Alexis.

During the last decade of his life Brother Alexis was in poor health, yet he continued with his usual arduous duties and in 1868–69 assisted in constructing the buildings at Providence for the Grey Nuns. From 1870 to 1874 he served at Notre-Dame-des-Victoires mission at Lac la Biche.

In 1875 another group of Grey Nuns left Saint Boniface to serve in their northern establishments, and Brother Alexis was sent from La Nativité to prepare transportation and accompany them north from Lac la Biche. His companions on the way south were two Métis families and an orphan, Geneviève Duquette, whom the Grey Nuns were sending to Lac la Biche. The guide was an Iroquois Métis, Louis Lafrance, a servant of La Nativité. Although professing to be a good Catholic he had an uncontrollable and vengeful temper. Even Brother Alexis had reprimanded him.

The party left La Nativité on 1 June and after a difficult trip reached Grand Rapids on the Athabasca about 18 June. Here the Métis families refused to go farther until the river subsided. But Brother Alexis was determined. He would have left the orphan with the Métis, but Lafrance insisted that he would guide them both to the mission, about 100 miles south. In August, at the House River, a short distance above Grand Rapids, the remains of Brother Alexis were discovered by a party from the Lac la Biche mission. There was unmistakable evidence that Lafrance had murdered the brother, dismembered the body, and eaten it. Lafrance had then proceeded with the orphan to the Peace River, where she suffered the same fate. Retribution followed. One night a camp of Beaver Indians shot a marauder – Lafrance.

Thus ended Brother Alexis' long and arduous career in the service of the missions of the North West. His remains were buried at Lac la Biche, but were later removed to be with those of other martyrs at the Oblate mission in St Albert, Alberta.

LEWIS H. THOMAS

[P.-J.-B.] Duchaussois, *Apôtres inconnus* (Paris, 1924), 220–27. Morice, *Hist. de l'Église catholique*, II, 54, 193, 379–82. A. Philippot, *Une page d'histoire des missions arctiques: le frère Alexis Reynard O.M.I. (1828–1875), premier "apôtre inconnu" du Grand Nord canadien* (Lablachère, France, 1931).

RICHARD, LOUIS-EUSÈBE, merchant, legislative councillor; b. 1 March 1817 at Saint-Grégoire-le-Grand (Nicolet), L.C., son of Charles-Auguste Richard, merchant, and of Marie Hébert; d. 13 Nov. 1876 at Princeville, Que.

In 1840 Louis-Eusèbe Richard came to settle in the township of Stanfold, to the west of the road leading to Saint-Norbert-d'Arthabaska, and opened a general store there; he thus became the second merchant of the township. He had foreseen the importance which the spot he had chosen would assume, and he placed himself at the head of a movement that brought about a modification in the route of the Grand Trunk Railway (from Richmond to Lévis) in the Arthabaska region. As he also traded in wood, the building of this line allowed him to enlarge his fortune appreciably. Thus, according to the notary François-Xavier Pratte's registry, in 1844 Richard began to "lend money" on recognizance, and until 1871 he arranged purchases, sales, transfers, conveyances, and other remunerative contracts.

In 1862 Louis-Eusèbe Richard, at the request of a large number of influential electors in the division of Kennebec, stood as a candidate for the office of legislative councillor against Charles Cormier*, the first mayor of Plessisville. Having to contend with the influence of the representatives of three counties, Henri-Gustave Joly* de Lotbinière (Lotbinière), Noël Hébert (Mégantic), and Jean-Baptiste-Éric Dorion* (Drummond-Arthabaska), and being up against a very highly regarded and respected man, he was defeated by a majority of 275 votes, even though he obtained the greatest number of votes in the two counties of Arthabaska and Lotbinière. In 1874 he accepted the seat left vacant by the resignation of the Honourable Isidore Thibaudeau*, the Legislative Council having ceased to be elective in 1867. Richard does not seem to have concerned himself very actively with politics, but he was known to be a Conservative.

On 15 Jan. 1841, Louis-Eusèbe Richard had married Hermine Prince, of Saint-Grégoire-le-Grand. After raising a large family, he left a sizeable fortune to his wife and four children, among them Édouard*, who was MLA for Mégantic from 1872 to 1878 and author of *Acadie, reconstitution d'un chapitre perdu de l'histoire d'Amérique.*

Louis-Eusèbe Richard belonged to one of the most highly respected families in old Acadia. "A man of uncommon vigour, of great intelligence, of proverbial honesty, he won the esteem of all those who, through ties of kinship, or business relationships, or friendship, were fortunate enough to know him." It was in his honour that in 1848 St Eusèbe was given to the parish of Stanfold as its patron saint.

ALCIDE FLEURY

Archives judiciaires d'Arthabaska (Qué.), Registre d'état civil, Saint-Eusèbe-de-Stanfold, 13 nov. 1876. AJTR, Registre d'état civil, paroisse Saint-Grégoire-le-Grand, II, 99; IV, 147. C.-É. Mailhot, *Les Bois-Francs* (4v., Arthabaska, Qué., 1914–25), II, 308–15.

RICHARDSON, JAMES, naval officer, office holder, Methodist minister, and bishop; b. 29 Jan. 1791 at Kingston, province of Quebec, son of James Richardson, a naval officer, and Sarah Ashmore, both from England; d. 9 March 1875 in Toronto, Ont.

James Richardson, who became a leading Methodist and a staunch Canadian, was born, appropriately, in the year of John Wesley's death and of Upper Canada's formation. He was educated in the Kingston schools, and in 1809 entered the Provincial Marine, receiving a lieutenant's commission in 1812. He served with distinction during the War of 1812–14, losing his left arm in 1814 at the battle of Oswego. In 1813 he had married Rebecca, daughter of John Dennis, a York (Toronto) loyalist; two children survived him.

A veteran and an Anglican, Richardson was appointed after the war as a magistrate and collector of customs at Presqu'ile. He might well have remained there, an honoured citizen and a useful functionary, but along with many others he was swept up in the post-war resurgence of Upper Canadian Methodism. He was converted at a quarterly meeting held in Haldimand Township in 1818: "God shone into my heart and I saw light in his light, 'My chains fell off, my heart was free.'" He concluded at once: "This people shall be my people, and their God my God," a conviction from which he never wavered throughout his life, and one which led him quickly into a new and difficult career.

The Methodist leaders, always alert to recruit men of character and education for lay and ministerial office, pressed Richardson to become a local preacher in the conference year of 1822–23 and in 1825 he was taken on trial for the itinerant ministry. Without hesitation he gave up his appointments and his comfortable life to minister in company with Egerton Ryerson* to his first circuit, that of Yonge Street and York (Toronto), stretching from Lake Ontario to Lake Simcoe. But he was not destined to continue long in this humble role. Well before his ordination in 1830 he had emerged as an important figure in a religious community that had reached a critical stage in its development.

In the late 1820s and early 1830s Canadian Methodists, who began as a part of the Methodist Episcopal Church in the United States, were obliged to reshape their relationship with their British and American brethren, and to play an active part in the political controversies besetting Upper Canada. Although Richardson believed, and evidently continued to believe, that the episcopal polity of American Methodism was the nearest to Wesley's design, he agitated vigorously for the establishment of an autonomous Canadian conference in 1824. He also seems to have supported the move to independence in 1828 when the Methodist Episcopal Church in Canada was formed. Conversely, he was reluctant, along with many of his colleagues, to accept the union with the British conference in 1833 because it would break the continuity between American and Canadian Methodism, and, more significantly, because he anticipated that the Tory proclivities of the Wesleyans would undermine the Canadian conference's political credibility.

Richardson's attitude toward the position of his church in society was probably not untypical among native Canadian Methodists. A fervent patriot – ready to enlist against the Fenians in 1866 – who did not wish to weaken the British connection, he was nevertheless convinced that Canadians should settle their own problems in their own ways. An evangelical Christian, his primary concern was not the pursuit of ecclesiastical or political goals but the salvation of souls, an end which he believed could best be achieved through the complete separation of church and state and the full acceptance of the voluntarist position. As editor of the *Christian Guardian* he upheld this view; he would later also welcome the secularization of the clergy reserves and oppose the commutation clause in the act of 1854 by which the Wesleyan Methodist Church, along with others, was paid a lump sum in return for surrendering its claims on the reserves fund.

Richardson became the editor of the Methodists' *Christian Guardian* for 1832–33, but declined re-election as editor in 1834. He continued to hold other important offices in the conference between 1833 and his resignation from the conference in 1836, and he was a member of the committee which drafted plans for and initiated the building of the Upper Canada Academy (later Victoria University). In the interval, however, the conference had restricted the privileges of the local preachers, a group for whom Richardson felt much concern and sympathy. Moreover, at the behest of their Wesleyan associates, it had begun, in sharp contrast to its previous course, to curry favour with the local goverment and to equivocate on the vexed question of public grants to religious bodies. This change of front, coupled with the realization that the parent Wesleyan conference had accepted such assistance, exposed the Canadian conference to much abuse from the Reform press and politicians. Richardson and others who were convinced that their church should adhere to the voluntarist position and at least maintain political neutrality were humiliated by this course of action. His determination to put integrity above denominational unity produced increasingly strained relations between him and such senior colleagues as JOHN and Egerton Ryerson and Ephraim Evans*. Hence by 1836 he no longer felt at home in the conference and decided to leave quietly. He was already so alienated by 1835 that he refused to contribute to the funds of the Upper Canada Academy.

In the year following his resignation Richardson apparently considered a career in American Methodism and to that end he held a temporary pastorate in Auburn, N.Y. Upon his return to Upper Canada he became a minister in the newly constituted Methodist Episcopal Church (the earlier church of this name having become the Wesleyan Methodist Church), the haven of those who for various reasons refused to accept the 1833 union. From 1840 to 1852, however, he was chiefly employed as agent of the Upper Canada Bible Society. It was not until 1858 that he was ordained a bishop to assist his aged friend, Bishop Philander Smith*. Despite growing infirmity he retained this office until his death; one of his last acts was to ordain Albert Carman* as his assistant and eventual successor.

Bishop Richardson presided over an important branch of Canadian Methodism at a significant point in its evolution, and thus helped to determine

Ridley

the shape of such influence as Methodism had on the broader growth of his country. In 1867 the Methodist Episcopal Church was the second largest Methodist body, but it was essentially confined to Ontario. It was if anything more evangelical than the larger Wesleyan denomination, strongly anti-liturgical, and possibly less sophisticated generally. It continued to oppose state support for religious enterprises and in particular separate schools. Despite its episcopal polity, the line between Methodist Episcopal laymen and clergy was drawn as imprecisely as in the earlier days of Methodism. Above all, the Episcopal Methodists considered themselves *the* Canadian Methodists as indeed they were in background and outlook in so far as Ontario was concerned.

Richardson's principal contribution was to maintain the distinctive features of Methodist Episcopal organization and teaching, and at the same time to encourage those in his church whose interest was the constructive dissemination of their views rather than destructive opposition to the dominant Wesleyan Conference. Thus, by 1875, the two churches were growing together, as was symbolized by the holding of a memorial service for the bishop in the Wesleyans' Metropolitan Church in Toronto. Bishop Carman, whose orientation was akin to his predecessor's, would bring about formal union in 1884 and in so doing would infuse the new Methodist Church with many of the values cherished by his brethren.

In his church and in the community, James Richardson was held in high esteem as a humble, kindly, and saintly individual whose life was "manly and devoid of display." He impressed on his countrymen that distinctive mixture of religious, moral, and patriotic values cherished by so many native Canadian Methodists. Neither a great scholar nor a great preacher, he had nonetheless the gift of "plain yet forcible and majestic speech." He detested "sham everywhere" and "could not for a moment bear it in religion." To Carman, "If James Richardson was a man of God, he was also a man for the world," an "advocate and defender of the rights of man." "Liberty of conscience and liberty of worship were cardinal doctrines of his religious and political faith," as was concern for the moral character of society. Hence he promoted the work of the Bible Society, and vigorously supported the Temperance Reformation Society. As president of the York Pioneer Society he helped to arouse interest in the historical development of that Upper Canada whose life was almost coterminous with his own.

G. S. FRENCH

[There is no collection, unfortunately, of James Richardson papers. For his letters and statements one must look to the *Christian Guardian* (York) in the year of his editorship, 1832–33, and to the *Canada Christian Advocate* (Hamilton, Ont.) in the period of his episcopate, 1858–75. Thomas Webster, *Life of Rev. James Richardson, a bishop of the Methodist Episcopal Church in Canada* (Toronto, 1876), is naturally highly partisan, as is its introduction by Richardson's successor, Albert Carman. As a corrective, one should consult John Carroll's lengthy review in the *Canadian Methodist Magazine* (Toronto), IV (1876), 513–23. G.S.F.]

James Richardson, *Incidents in the early history of the settlements in the vicinity of Lake Ontario* (n.p., n.d.). *Canada Christian Advocate* (Hamilton, Ont.), 17 March 1875. *Globe* (Toronto), 13 March 1875. *The minutes of the annual conferences of the Wesleyan Methodist Church in Canada, from 1824 to 1857* (2v., Toronto, 1846–63), I. Dent, *Canadian portrait gallery*, III, 60–65. Carroll, *Case and his cotemporaries*. Anson Green, *The life and times of the Rev. Anson Green, D.D. . . .* (Toronto, 1877). Sissons, *Ryerson*.

RIDLEY, THOMAS, merchant and politician; b. in England or Ireland in 1799; d. Upper Tooting, Surrey, Eng., 20 March 1879.

Thomas Ridley came to Newfoundland to work for his uncle William Bennett, a merchant with premises at Adams Cove, Carbonear. By 1824 they had formed a partnership, Bennett and Ridley, which lasted until the late 1820s. Ridley, having married a daughter of a well-to-do Liverpool family, was joined by her relative Thomas Harrison in the firm of Thomas Ridley and Company, with headquarters at Harbour Grace but with stores as well at Carbonear and Western Bay. In spite of the fire of 1832 which destroyed much of Harbour Grace, Ridley built up a flourishing business. In the late 1830s Ridley established a partnership with Gilbert Henry Harrison and James Harrison – Ridley, Harrison and Company. After the death of Gilbert H. Harrison in 1849 this partnership was dissolved and Ridley took his two sons, Thomas Harrison and William, into the business as Ridley and Sons.

Several incidents in the 1830s, a decade marked by bad feeling between fishermen and merchants, show that Thomas Ridley was especially unpopular. In February 1832 after the sealers' strikes and riots at Harbour Grace and Carbonear, all the merchants made concessions except Ridley. As a result a mob of fishermen boarded and partially destroyed Ridley's schooner, the *Perseverance*. In the 1836 general election Ridley was forced to withdraw as a candidate because of violence and intimidation. Then in the Conception Bay by-election of December 1840, while trying in his capacity as a magistrate to keep order, Ridley was hit over the head and nearly killed. The times, nevertheless, were changing. In 1842 Ridley was elected to represent Conception Bay in the

617

Ridout

Amalgamated Legislature. From 1843 to 1848 he also sat as a member of the Executive Council.

After 1850, with Thomas Harrison Ridley emerging as the most prominent member of the family, Ridley and Sons expanded and played a leading role, second only to that of John MUNN's firm, in the development of Harbour Grace as the commercial centre of Conception Bay. They set up a branch at Catalina, took part in the seal hunt, carried on extensive operations on the Labrador, and began to develop the winter codfishery at Rose Blanche. In the fall of 1870 the news that Ridley and Sons were in trouble came as a shock both to their creditors and to the many fishermen who were depending on them for winter supplies. In spite of efforts to keep the business going, Ridley and Sons were declared insolvent in 1873. They sold out to the Munns and moved back to England where Thomas Ridley died.

ELIZABETH A. WELLS

PANL, Harbour Grace Sessions Court, Records, 1825–35. Department of Justice of Newfoundland and Labrador (St John's), Registry of deeds, companies, and securities, Registry of deeds for the Northern District, 1826–88, I, II, IX, X, XI, XIII, XVIII, XIX; Registry of deeds for the Central District, XXII, 341. Newfoundland, *Blue Books*, 1842, 1843 (copies in PANL). *Conception-Bay Man* (Harbour Grace, Nfld.), 7 April 1858. *Newfoundlander* (St John's), 29 April 1879. *Newfoundland Patriot* (St. John's), 12 Dec. 1840. *Royal Gazette* (St John's), 24 Aug. 1843. *Times and General Commercial Gazette* (St John's), 11 Nov. 1848. Leslie Harris, "The first nine years of representative government in Newfoundland," unpublished MA thesis, Memorial University of Newfoundland, 1959, 114.

RIDOUT, GEORGE, lawyer and judge; b. Quebec, 1791, second son of Thomas Ridout*, surveyor general of Upper Canada, and of Mary Campbell; d. at Clinton, Ont., 24 Feb. 1871.

George Ridout attended John Strachan*'s school at Cornwall from 1805 to at least 1807, in company with the sons of many other families prominent in early York (Toronto). He subsequently studied law in the office of John Macdonell*, who was appointed attorney general in 1812, and was admitted to the bar 4 Jan. 1813. The next year he attended the court at Ancaster as acting solicitor general. In 1820 he became a bencher of the Law Society of Upper Canada and continued to serve in this capacity for the next 50 years until his death. He succeeded Dr William Warren Baldwin* as treasurer of the law society in 1829 and served in this position until 1832, during this time presiding over the planning and construction of the original building of Osgoode Hall, perhaps the most important of the early buildings still surviving in Ontario. He also took a lead in establishing the library of the law society. Ridout was appointed judge of the Niagara District Court in April 1828, and reappointed to this office in April 1832.

Ridout served with the York volunteers during the War of 1812–14, and took part in the battle of Queenston Heights as 3rd lieutenant in the grenadier company of the York militia. He was taken prisoner of war on 27 April 1813 when the Americans occupied York. He maintained his interest in military matters in subsequent years and served as colonel of the East York militia.

Ridout took an active part in the social life of York. Dorset House, the substantial home he built about 1820, was long a landmark of the community. However, although the Ridouts were one of the oldest families in York, their frequently independent views were suspect to some of the other early established families. This rivalry and tension, in particular between the Ridouts and the families of William Dummer Powell* and William Jarvis*, found expression in the duel between John Ridout, George's brother, and Samuel Peters Jarvis*, son of William, in 1817, in which John was killed, and it was a factor throughout the social and political career of George Ridout.

In politics Ridout was a moderate, in general supporting constitutional reform and the position of W. W. Baldwin and his son Robert*; his family was connected with the Baldwins by marriage. He was defeated in his own attempts at office: in the elections for the legislature in 1816 when he sought to succeed his father as the representative of Simcoe and the East Riding of York and was beaten by Peter Robinson* who had the support of Strachan; and in the elections for city council in Toronto in 1837 at the time of his dispute with the lieutenant governor. However, he often gave active and effective support to the candidacy of others: for example, to Robert Baldwin in his successful attempt to unseat Sheriff William Botsford Jarvis* in the elections for the House of Assembly in 1830, and to Robert Baldwin Sullivan* in 1835 in his successful campaign to replace William Lyon Mackenzie* as mayor in Toronto's second municipal election.

Ridout was dismissed on 12 July 1836 from the offices of judge of the Niagara District Court, colonel of the East York militia, and justice of the peace by Sir Francis Bond HEAD, who "as Lieutenant-Governor, by the advice of my Council, deliberately selected him for punishment, as the most intemperate of my opponents." The charges, which Ridout denied, were insult to the person and office of the lieutenant governor and disloyalty to the policies of the crown. The dismissal became a *cause célèbre* in the colony and at the Colonial Office, and it was one of the major political issues in Upper Canada during the subsequent 18 months leading up to the outbreak of rebellion in December 1837. Responding to a petition from Ridout, the colonial secretary, Lord Glenelg, ordered his reinstatement. Head declined and submitted his resignation rather than comply with this instruction, "it being utterly impossible for me to obey this order, and retain my authority in the province." The resignation of the lieutenant governor, primarily on this issue, and on the related issue of his refusal to name Marshall Spring BIDWELL a judge as Glenelg wished, was in fact accepted in a dispatch from London, dated 24 Nov. 1837, a week before the rebellion broke out in Upper Canada, where people were still unaware of this development. The dispute over Ridout's appointments, rather than the rebellion, was thus the main cause of Head's resignation, and, as such, a significant episode in Canadian history.

Ridout also played an active part in municipal affairs. He was a prominent member of the York Board of Health, proposing the establishment of a receiving house for cholera patients during the epidemic of 1832, and presenting a report in the same year which focussed public attention on the weakness of the board because of its lack of funds and insufficient legal authority. He was a strong advocate of the merits of retaining York as the capital of the province and helped to draft legislation to incorporate and enlarge York as a city under the name of Toronto. The choice of the name Toronto in 1834, in preference to the name of York, reflected the long-standing preference of the Ridouts for the original Indian name and was one of the bones of contention between them and some of the more Tory pioneer families.

Ridout's varied business interests included participation in 1822 in the founding of the Bank of Upper Canada, of which he became a director. He was elected a member of the board of the City of Toronto and Lake Huron Railway in 1845.

George Ridout married twice: first, Dorothy McCuaig of Boston; secondly, Belle Nelson. He had one daughter by his first marriage and four daughters and four sons by his second. His older brother Samuel* was sheriff of the county of York and his younger brother Thomas Gibbs* was for many years cashier of the Bank of Upper Canada.

THOMAS H. B. SYMONS

MTCL, Baldwin papers. PAO, Ridout papers; Sir John Beverley Robinson papers; John Strachan papers. Head, *Narrative. Ten years in Upper Canada in peace and war, 1805–1815; being the Ridout letters . . . ,* ed. Mathilda Edgar (Toronto, 1890). *Town of York, 1793–1815* (Firth). *Town of York, 1815–1834* (Firth). Chadwick, *Ontarian families,* I, 36–43. W. R. Riddell, *The legal profession in Upper Canada in its early periods* (Toronto, 1916), 68–85.

RIDOUT, GEORGE PERCIVAL, merchant and politician; b. Bristol, Eng., 21 Aug. 1807, son of George Ridout and Mary Ann Wright; d. unmarried, in Toronto, Ont., 28 June 1873.

George Ridout, Sr, emigrated from Bristol in 1820, going first to Philadelphia, then in 1826 to York (Toronto), where his uncle Thomas Ridout*, the surveyor general, secured for him a position in the government service. His two oldest sons, George Percival and Joseph Davis, remained in the United States; by 1826 they were employed there by Tarratt's, iron and hardware merchants of Wolverhampton, England. G. P. Ridout, after joining Tarratt's in Philadelphia, had moved to New York, where Joseph Davis joined him. G. P. Ridout moved to York in 1828 and began legal studies. Tarratt's sent J. D. Ridout to Boston in 1830, but in 1831 he moved on to York. There, in 1832, with the support of Tarratt's, the two brothers opened Ridout Brothers and Company, wholesale and retail iron and hardware merchants. Wholesaling was just developing in Toronto in the early 1830s, and the Ridouts were the first specialized hardware merchants there. Their mercantile training and British backing, linked to the rapid growth of the market, enabled them to build one of Toronto's largest hardware houses in the next two decades.

G. P. Ridout soon became active in local politics. A moderate conservative, he often fought with Toronto's more extreme Tories, including William Henry BOULTON and Henry Sherwood*. He captained a company of York volunteers in 1837 and in the 1840s opposed the rebellion losses bill and also British free trade, along with many other Tories and moderates who feared the breaking of the British connection. Nevertheless, he worked energetically in 1841 to elect two Sydenham [Thomson*] Reformers, Isaac Buchanan* and John Henry Dunn*, in Toronto. Three years later he stood for Toronto himself as a moderate supporter of Sir Charles Metcalfe*, but opposition from extreme Tories forced his withdrawal before polling day. In 1844 he was elected president of the Toronto Board of Trade, a post he held until 1852. He now pursued his public career vigorously. He was president of the St George's Society from 1845 to 1847; in 1851 he secured election to the Toronto City Council and the board of trustees for Toronto public schools and was narrowly defeated when he ran for mayor in 1851.

In 1851 he won a Toronto seat in the assembly,

Robertson

where he acted as an independent Conservative and took a particular interest in issues concerning Toronto's trading community. Thus he sought amendments to the Upper Canada assessment act, the Grand Trunk Railway charter, and the usury laws; and he opposed Francis Hincks*' tariff and efforts of Montreal interests to promote a commercial empire focussed on Montreal. He also advocated the abolition of Sabbath labour. In the 1854 election, though he won the support of Conservative businessmen, he found this too narrow a political base and was defeated in Toronto by two other Conservatives, John George Bowes* and John Hillyard CAMERON. He did not seek election again.

Unlike his brother, Joseph Davis, and many other Toronto merchants in these years, Ridout did not play a central role in forming new companies, but in 1853 he did become governor of Toronto's British America Assurance Company, a post for which his mercantile and political positions qualified him well. He retired from the hardware business in 1866, leaving his brother to carry it on, and devoted himself wholly to the insurance company. In 1871 he became its manager as well and held both posts until his death.

DOUGLAS MCCALLA

Canada, Province of, Legislative Assembly, *Journals*, 1852–53. [Hugh Scobie], "Letters of 1844 and 1846 from Scobie to Ryerson," ed. C. B. Sissons, *CHR*, XXIX (1948), 393–411. *Town of York, 1815–1834* (Firth). *Globe* (Toronto), 1850–60. *Rowsell's city of Toronto and county of York directory, for 1850–1 . . .*, ed. J. Armstrong (Toronto, 1850). *Brown's Toronto general directory, 1856 . . .* (Toronto, 1856). *Brown's Toronto general directory, 1861 . . .* (Toronto, 1861). *Hist. of Toronto and county of York*, II, 137–39. D. C. Masters, *The rise of Toronto, 1850–1890* (Toronto, 1947). Douglas McCalla, "The commercial politics of the Toronto Board of Trade, 1850–1860," *CHR*, L (1969), 51–67.

ROBERTSON, ANDREW, lawyer, author and compiler of legal works, governor of McGill University; b. 1815 at or near Stuartfield, in Aberdeenshire, Scotland, son of James Robertson; d. 21 March 1880 at Côte-Saint-Antoine, Montreal, Que.

Andrew Robertson was 17 when his father decided to leave Scotland with his family and emigrate to the United States. The Robertsons lived for some time at Derby, in Vermont, before crossing the border and settling at Sherbrooke, where James Robertson acted for more than 25 years as minister of the Congregational Church.

On 28 Sept. 1841 Andrew Robertson was called to the bar at Montreal, after working as a clerk in the office of the future judge Charles Dewey Day*. Two of Andrew's brothers, George R. and William Wilcox*, followed his example and became lawyers; another, Joseph Gibb*, held the post of treasurer of the province of Quebec. Their sister Margaret* followed a literary career.

Andrew Robertson took up residence at Montreal, where, with his brother George and then with his brother William Wilcox, he conducted a prosperous legal practice (A. and W. Robertson), and for a period of nearly 20 years (1852–71) was an active member of the council of the bar. He held in succession the offices of council member, examiner, treasurer, and *bâtonnier* (1866–67). On 12 Feb. 1864 he was appointed queen's counsel. From 1856 to 1867 he collaborated with Judge Joseph-Ubalde BEAUDRY in the compiling of the *Lower Canada Reports/Décisions des tribunaux du Bas-Canada*. This collection sought to make known to lawyers and to the public the most important rulings in civil matters; it constituted a valuable reference work for members of the bar, who were able to base their cases or judgements on precedents. In 1864 Andrew Robertson brought out an important work entitled *A digest of all the reports published in Lower Canada to 1863*, which contained a summary of all legal rulings published up to that time.

Andrew Robertson, a governor of McGill University, bequeathed part of his estate to the library of the Faculty of Law, to enrich its collections. After several years of intensive work and research, he gradually lost his sight. He died at Montreal at the age of 65. It is not known whether he married.

JEAN-PIERRE CHALIFOUX

Andrew Robertson, *A digest of all the reports published in Lower Canada to 1863* (Montreal, 1864). PAC, MG 30, D62 (Audet papers), 26, pp.40–43. *Dom. ann. reg., 1880–81*, 428. Pierre Beullac et É.-F. Surveyer, *Le centenaire du Barreau de Montréal, 1849–1949* (Montréal, 1949), 69–71. Lareau, *Hist. de la littérature canadienne*, 389–91.

ROBERTSON, JOHN, businessman and politician; b. in Perthshire, Scotland, in 1799; d. at Lawford Place, Mannington, Essex, Eng., on 3 Aug. 1876.

Before immigrating to Saint John, New Brunswick, in 1817, John Robertson married Sophia Dobie of Lancashire; they had six children. Starting as a clerk in Saint John under his uncle, Robert Robertson, he later became a super-cargo for Thomas Millidge* on vessels trading from Saint John to Newfoundland and the West Indies. When Millidge retired, Robertson joined Angus M'Kenzie to form the company of M'Kenzie and Robertson and to continue the business. Robertson formed partnerships with one or two others and by mid-century had become an independent entrepreneur in a variety of pursuits, not only in Saint John but throughout the province and internationally.

Early in his career Robertson became interested in the prosperity of Saint John and the province of New Brunswick. He ran unsuccessfully for the New Brunswick assembly in 1832. In 1836 he was appointed mayor of Saint John, and from 1837 to 1867 he was a leading spokesman for the city in the New Brunswick Legislative Council. He was, at the same time, a magistrate for Saint John. He was active in the Chamber of Commerce, often as president or a member of the council. He supported numerous projects such as the 1835 harbour bridge and the Saint John to Shediac railway. In 1859 he was one of the commissioners who recommended the removal of the provincial capital from Fredericton to Saint John. That same year he castigated the government for eliminating winter dredging in the harbour.

Robertson's own businesses were thriving all the while. Typical of his operations was a sawmill at Saint John which was "one of the most complete on the continent." It was destroyed in a spectacular fire on 5 May 1852. His interests included extensive mercantile transactions, lumbering, shipbuilding, shipping supplies, banking, insurance companies, and railways. He was president of the Victoria Coal Mining Company, a director of the Maritime Bank of the Dominion of Canada, local director of the Bank of British North America, and a director of the European and North American Railway Company. He was, in addition, the honorary New Brunswick director of the Atlantic telegraph company of 1858. He supported this project because he did not want it to bypass New Brunswick, a circumstance, he wrote, "I would think a great pity." Because of such international contacts he was appointed consul in Saint John for Uruguay and Argentina.

Robertson was also active in the New Brunswick militia. He served in several regiments and rose to the rank of lieutenant-colonel of the Saint John City Light Infantry. When the British were preparing to send troops to Canada following the *Trent* affair, he was in London where he presented the advantages of using Saint John as their eastern terminal. Not the least of these was the New Brunswick militia, and the facility with which British troops were cleared through New Brunswick on their way to Quebec was in large part the result of careful planning and coordination by the local organization. The high regard in which Robertson was held can be measured by the support he received from the officers and men for promotion over a senior officer in 1863.

In New Brunswick Robertson was regarded as a competent and indefatigable Scot who exhibited all the hospitality and independence usually associated with the type. A letter he wrote to Samuel Leonard Tilley* illustrates the point: *"The taking of a man's property without his consent, yea against his will, is a violation of his just right."* This was a firm comment on the method of government expropriation for railway purposes. Yet he saw the necessity for government regulations, especially of "banks and other corporations to ascertain the true state of such institutions." In some respects he exhibited the paternalism of the laird, both in the hospitality he extended to his guests and in his real concern for the downtrodden. In 1862 he spearheaded a drive to raise money for Lancashire workers who were put out of work through lack of American cotton for the mills. His sympathy did not extend, however, to the owners and their *"over-speculation in mills and manufacturing."* The real enemy to him was "the unmitigated selfishness of the Manchester School" who "expect the world to consume their cotton output [on] such terms as they would dictate – but besides and beyond all this they *expect the Country to find their Raw Materials* – to keep their mills going on terms that would leave them a profit no matter who suffers." He was particularly aware of the dangers this system held for the colonies which "have suffered . . . by the Manchester School Legislation *more than once.*" Robertson's efforts were directed toward increasing the trade of the colonies, even if it meant protection or closer integration into the American economy.

In 1867 Robertson was appointed to the Canadian Senate. He retired to Great Britain in 1874 and there served as a director of the Imperial Bank at Lothbury. He kept close contact with Canada, especially with St Andrew's Church in Saint John where he had been an active layman and to which he continued to extend financial aid. At his death he left a North American estate alone of $390,000, and part of this was bequeathed to St Andrew's.

Robertson's career had been long, active, and prosperous. "His great success made his opinion a law to others on more matters than those of business."

C. M. WALLACE

N.B. Museum, John Robertson estate papers, 1877–93; Tilley family papers, 1854–67. PAC, MG 27, I, D15 (Tilley papers), 1854–67. *Saint John Daily News*, 5 Aug. 1876. *Can. directory of parliament* (Johnson). *Can. parl. comp., 1873.* D. R. Jack, *History of Saint*

Robinson

Andrew's Church, Saint John, N.B. (Saint John, N.B., 1913).

ROBINSON, WILLIAM BENJAMIN, politician; b. 22 Dec. 1797 in Kingston, U.C., youngest son of loyalists Christopher Robinson* and Esther Sayre; d. 18 July 1873 in Toronto, Ont.

In the year after William Benjamin Robinson's birth the family, which included two older brothers, Peter* and John Beverley*, moved to York (Toronto); the father died when the youngest son was less than a year old. The family seems to have lived in scanty comfort but in 1802 Esther married Elisha Beman, a mill-owner and merchant in Newmarket who had earlier been a tavern-keeper in York. It was at Newmarket that William was brought up and educated by his mother.

In his youth William was influenced by his brother Peter who took a special interest in him. Peter wrote in 1816 that "William is a very steady good lad, is with me now, and I mean to give him every opportunity of improving himself." When Peter moved from Newmarket to Holland Landing, William took over the mills and stores built by their stepfather, and on 5 May 1822 he married Elizabeth Ann Jarvis, daughter of William Jarvis*, provincial secretary of Upper Canada. They had no children. In 1833 they moved to Holland Landing, taking over the house that Peter had built there. It became the usual stopover for travellers north.

William also followed Peter into the fur trade, in the firm P. and W. Robinson. He established two trading-posts in the Muskoka district, one on an island, later called Yoho, in Lake Joseph, and the other on Georgian Bay at the mouth of the Muskoka River. He was described as being "one of the chief Indian traders throughout northern Ontario, a most intelligent and well-informed gentleman," and his reputation for fair dealing gave him a position of influence among the Indians.

In 1828 William, who like his brothers was strongly Tory in his sympathies, contested the first election for the Legislative Assembly in Simcoe County after its separation from York County. He lost to John Cawthra by nine votes, but won in the elections of 1830 and 1834. Lavish grants of lands in Medonte and Nottawasaga townships to Tory supporters just before Francis Bond HEAD's "bread and butter" election of 1836 were credited with helping Robinson defeat Samuel Lount*, who soon after supported the agitations of William Lyon Mackenzie*. In the assembly Robinson succeeded in having passed an act for macadamizing the York roads and in raising a loan of £10,000 for improvements in his constituency.

A new sphere of activity had opened for Robinson in 1833 when the assembly appointed him with Absalom Shade* and John Macaulay* as commissioners to superintend the expenditure of a grant voted for the improvement of the Welland Canal. Robinson acted in a supervisory capacity for the canal for many years, his instructions being "to give his personal attendance on the canal until it was rendered navigable." He carried out his duties with vigour (living in St Catharines from 1837 to 1843), and took charge of all contracts and disbursements.

In the first election after the union of Upper and Lower Canada in 1841 Robinson was defeated in Simcoe by Elmes Steele* of Medonte in a bitter contest in which the militia was notified to stand by. Out of the assembly, he negotiated in 1843 the first of the "Robinson Treaties" with the Indians, whereby over 700 acres of the District of Simcoe were "set aside to be held in trust for the use of the Chippewa Tribe of Lake Simcoe." Chief William Yellowhead* was a signatory.

In 1844 Robinson was re-elected to the assembly for Simcoe, and he held this seat until 1854. On 20 Dec. 1844 he became inspector-general in the government of William Henry DRAPER, with a seat on the Executive Council. Robinson, however, strongly opposed Draper's bill in 1845 to establish a provincial "University of Upper Canada," endowed partly from the grants made to King's College, the Church of England university. Although Draper was willing to postpone the bill, Robinson resigned from the Executive Council in March 1845 as a matter of principle, an action which gained him praise from the *Globe* and other Reform newspapers as "the only *honest* politician" in the ministry. After the failure of Draper's university bill Robinson refused to re-enter the Executive Council, but in 1846 accepted the post of chief commissioner of public works which he retained until the formation of the Reform ministry of Robert Baldwin* and Louis-Hippolyte La Fontaine*. His position enabled him to push forward many improvements in his constituency, such as the important road to Penetanguishene in 1846, the Ridge Road between Barrie and Orillia in 1848, and surveys of the county.

In 1850 Governor General Lord Elgin [Bruce*], prompted by Chief Justice John Beverley Robinson and by Bishop John Strachan*, was anxious to appoint William assistant commissioner of public works to help relieve his financial difficulties, but Baldwin rejected the suggestion as a violation of his principle of giving patronage only to his supporters. Instead, the ministry commissioned Robinson, who was already well known to the Indians, by order in council on 11 Jan. 1850 to negotiate "for the adjustment on [the Indians'] claims to the lands in the vicinity of Lakes Superior and Huron, or of such portions of them as may be required for mining purposes." In the late 1840s the Indians living on the northern shores of lakes Huron and Superior had become concerned that, although the government had not arranged treaties with the tribes, location tickets were being issued to mining companies. An armed skirmish in 1848 at one of the Quebec Mining Company's locations forced the government to act, and Alexander Vidal* and Thomas Gummersall ANDERSON reported on a proposed treaty in December 1849.

Robinson, who had earlier submitted a memorandum to the government on possible ways of settling the issue in the region of the upper lakes, made two trips to the Sault Ste Marie and Michipicoten areas in April and May 1850 to sound out Indian leaders and Hudson's Bay Company officials. Final negotiations took place at Sault Ste Marie and two treaties were signed; on 7 September the Indians of Lake Superior surrendered the land from Batchawana Bay to Pigeon River, and on 9 September the Indians of Lake Huron under Chief Shinguacouse gave up the area between Batchawana Bay and Penetanguishene. The Robinson treaties ended the difficulties on the upper lakes and were later used as models, but Robinson himself looked upon them as being "based on the same conditions as all preceding ones." The treaties included provisions for the traditional "treaty money" cash payments (£2,000 in each of these cases), payments of annuities of £1 per Indian per year, the setting aside of reserves, and the retention of hunting and fishing rights throughout the surrendered tracts. The Indians would not interfere with mineral exploration and were to be entitled to royalties from any mineral deposits found on their own reserves. An "escalator" clause provided for an increase in the annuity payments should the value of the surrendered lands increase considerably; this was a unique feature of the treaties of 1850.

After 1845 Robinson's attention in the assembly centred on the affairs of the Church of England and on measures to improve transportation facilities in the colony. He opposed Baldwin's 1849 University of Toronto Act which secularized King's College, and the following year he signed a petition to Queen Victoria requesting a royal charter for a new Church of England college. In 1850 and again in 1851 he voted against resolutions put forward by the Reform government to secularize the clergy reserves; and in the latter year he took an active part in proposals to construct an intercolonial railway linking Canada and the Maritimes. When the first separate school act for Canada West, introduced in 1855 in the Legislative Council by Étienne-Paschal Taché*, reached the assembly, Robinson voted with other Tories and with George BROWN and Mackenzie in opposing it, even though he gave nominal support to the Liberal Conservative ministry of Allan MacNab* and Taché. He was a consistent supporter of the British connection. Although he had spoken against the union of Upper and Lower Canada both before and after the visit of Lord Durham [Lambton*], and voted for dissolution of the union in 1851, he moved resolutions in the assembly expressing loyalty to the crown and the constitution during the annexation crisis of 1850. He became one of the commissioners of the Canada Company in 1852 and senior commissioner in 1865 on the death of Frederick Widder*.

The representation act of 1853 divided the Simcoe County seat; Robinson was elected by acclamation in Simcoe South in 1854, but in 1857 was defeated by an opponent of long standing, Thomas Roberts FERGUSON. He did not run again. After the death of his wife in 1865 he travelled abroad and on his return in 1867 lived in Toronto.

William Benjamin Robinson did not achieve the prominence of his two elder brothers but he carried out the various responsibilities that came his way with energy and ability, and honourably stuck to his convictions. He shared what came to be known as "the Robinson charm," a rare humour, and a zest for living that made him a delightful companion.

JULIA JARVIS

PAC, RG 10, A8, 266, 511–14. PAO, Charles Clarke papers; Sir Aemilius Irving papers; Jarvis-Powell papers; Sir John Beverley Robinson papers. *Barrie Herald*, 12 July 1854. *Christian Guardian* (Toronto), 26 March, 17 Sept. 1845. *Church* (Toronto), 3 July 1851. *Cornwall Observer*, 10 April 1845. *Globe* (Toronto), 25 March 1845, 22 May 1855. *Kingston Herald*, 25 March 1845. *Mail* (Toronto), 19 July 1873. *Toronto Herald*, 31 March, 3 April 1845. *Toronto Mirror*, 20 June 1856. [Bruce and Grey], *Elgin-Grey papers* (Doughty). *Canada: Indian treaties and surrenders . . .* (3v., Ottawa, 1891–1912), I, II. Robina and K. M. Lizars, *In the days of the Canada Company: the story of the settlement of the Huron tract and a view of the social life of the period, 1825–1850* (Toronto, Montreal, 1896). Upper Canada, House of Assembly, *Appendix to journal*, 1836. Armstrong, *Handbook of Upper Canadian chronology. Political appointments, 1841–1865* (J.-O. Coté). Wallace, *Macmillan dictionary.*

Dent, *Last forty years.* R. K. Gordon, *John Galt* (University of Toronto Studies, Philological series, 5, Toronto, 1920). Hunter, *Hist. of Simcoe County.* Julia Jarvis, *Three centuries of Robinsons: the story of a family* (Toronto, 1967). C. W. Robinson, *Life of Sir John Beverley Robinson, bart., C.B., D.C.L., chief*

Roblin

justice of Upper Canada (Toronto, 1904). *The University of Toronto and its colleges, 1827–1906*, ed. W. J. Alexander (Toronto, 1906). [Julia Lambert], "An American lady in old Toronto: the letters of Julia Lambert, 1821–1854," ed. S. A. Heward and W. S. Wallace, *RSCT*, 3rd ser., XL (1946), sect.II, 101–42.

ROBLIN, JOHN PHILIP, farmer, politician, and public servant; b. in Sophiasburgh Township, U.C., 16 Aug. 1799, son of Prudence Platt and Philip Roblin, loyalist, who came to Adolphustown Township from New Jersey in 1784 and who later settled on Long Reach in Sophiasburgh at a place which became known as Roblin Mills; d. at Picton, Ont., 12 Nov. 1874.

John Philip Roblin was educated at the local school taught by Jonathan Greely. As a young man he cleared and farmed land in Ameliasburgh Township, but he moved to Hallowell Township in 1847 and in 1858 to the town of Picton. From an early age he took an active part in public life in Prince Edward County. He was appointed a justice of the peace in 1834. As a captain of the 2nd Battalion of Prince Edward militia he commanded a troop of cavalry during the winter of 1837–38. From 1848 to 1856 he was lieutenant-colonel commanding the battalion. He was first warden of the district of Prince Edward, 1841–42.

Roblin represented Prince Edward in the House of Assembly of Upper Canada from 1830 to 1836. Defeated in 1836, he again sat for Prince Edward in the Legislative Assembly of the Province of Canada from 1841, when he defeated David Barker Stevenson*, to 1846. In the latter year he resigned his seat to become registrar of Prince Edward County, crown lands agent, and collector of customs at Picton.

Roblin began his political life as a Reform supporter of Marshall Spring BIDWELL and Peter Perry*, but, like his younger cousin David Roblin*, he eventually became somewhat disillusioned with the Reform Party of the 1840s and 1850s, and especially with the policies of George BROWN whom he considered too moderate and to be "working for the Tories."

He was a staunch Wesleyan Methodist. From at least 1848 until 1863, he was a member of the senate of Victoria College at Cobourg, Ontario.

J. K. JOHNSON

Lennox and Addington Hist. Soc. (Napanee, Ont.), III (Thomas Willet Casey papers), 2, pp.11585–600; IV (Roblin family papers) 1, pp.14993–15002 (copies at PAC). PAC, RG 9, I, B5, 6; C4, 4; C6, 8; RG 68, 1. PAO, Legislative Assembly papers, biographical sketches of the members of the assembly, 1792–1840, comp. J. S. Carstairs and W. D. Read. *J. of Education for Ont.*, XXVIII (1875), 12. Armstrong, *Handbook of Upper Canadian chronology*.

RODIER, CHARLES-SÉRAPHIN, merchant, lawyer, philanthropist, mayor of Montreal, and legislative councillor of Quebec; b. 4 Oct. 1797 at Montreal, L.C., son of Jean-Baptiste Rodier, blacksmith, and Julie-Catherine Le Jeune; d. 4 Feb. 1876 at Montreal, Que.

Charles-Séraphin Rodier was the grandson of Pierre Rodier, a native of the Dauphiné, who fought in the Seven Years' War and remained in Canada after 1759. One of 16 children, he was born in the Saint-Joseph section of Montreal, and was baptized as Charles only, the Séraphin being added at a later date. Of his early life little is known; he attended the Sulpician college of Montreal, 1809–10, and entered the dry goods business about 1816, opening a shop on St Paul Street. He was the first merchant in the city to import his own goods direct from Great Britain and France, working through agents in London and Liverpool, and also making regular trips across the Atlantic to obtain the lowest prices. He crossed the ocean some 40 times between 1819 and 1832. Before long he branched into the wholesale trade and by the time he retired in 1836, evidently anticipating the coming troubles, he had amassed a considerable fortune.

Rodier then began a new career: along with the future judge, Samuel Cornwallis Monk*, who became a lifelong friend, he studied law under Alexander Buchanan*. Rodier was admitted to the bar in 1841, but did not practise to any great extent except to appear for friends or in charity cases. Instead he turned to various speculations; in these he was generally successful, for he left an estate that was estimated to be worth over half a million dollars. His first speculative venture, during which he nearly ran into great difficulties, was his acquisition of the Hotel Rascoe. Rodier was also a director of the Banque Jacques Cartier.

He was one of those who petitioned for Montreal's first municipal charter of 1831 and was an elected councillor while it was in force, 1833–36. Although he was the only member of the council to vote for open meetings he was not a political radical, unlike his cousin Édouard-Étienne Rodier*. As he said in private, "You are wrong, my friends, the time is not ripe." After the first charter was allowed to lapse, he was appointed one of the justices of the peace to administer the city in 1837 and served as president of that body. In February 1839 he was further commissioned as one of the investigators "Concerning losses sustained during the Rebellion," in which capacity he decided some 400 cases [*see* Philip Henry MOORE].

When Governor Charles Edward Poulett Thomson* appointed a council to administer Montreal under the revived municipal charter of 1840, Rodier was again a member, serving until a council was elected in 1843. He was then out of municipal government for some years. Nevertheless, he served as a harbour commissioner from 1840 to 1850, and as such was responsible for consolidating and refinancing the debt in 1845. For some years after 1844 he was also one of the commissioners who arranged for the foundlings and indigent sick in the Montreal district.

In 1858, when Henry Starnes* retired from the office of mayor, Rodier contested the election against John James Day, one of the aldermen. Day had alienated some of his potential voters by supporting Thomas D'Arcy McGee* in the provincial election of 1857–58 and Rodier was elected by 3,132 votes to 2,329. He was re-elected in 1859, 1860, and 1861. In 1859, he defeated Côme-Séraphin Cherrier* easily by 1,558 to 194; however, there was a major effort by Benjamin Holmes*, supported by the *Montreal Gazette*, to unseat him in 1860 and he won by only 24 votes. In 1862 he was defeated by Jean-Louis Beaudry* by 1,235 to 903 in a light vote in a "dull and flat" contest.

As mayor, Rodier was particularly proud of the improvement he made in the city's financial position and of the role he played in having new docks built. Rodier's mayoralty further saw the completion of the Victoria Bridge (1859) [*see* James HODGES], the beginning of a public transportation system (1861), and the building of the Crystal Palace. On the other side of the balance was the great flood of April 1861, when the water rose 24 feet above average and a quarter of the city was inundated. Rodier himself distributed food for the stranded from a skiff. The major social event of his mayoralty was the arrival of the Prince of Wales in August 1860, on his tour of Canada. The city was refurbished and Rodier greeted the prince in new robes, chain of office, and sword, copied from those of the lord mayor of London; his attire won him the nickname "The Peacock" from his political opponents. Afterwards he renamed his Rue Saint-Antoine house "Prince of Wales Castle" and had a statue of the prince erected on a turret. Later he also received François d'Orléans, Prince de Joinville, and Prince Alfred of Saxe-Cobourg-Gotha, another son of Queen Victoria. The *Montreal Daily Witness*, in evaluating his career, said that "as Mayor he kept firm control on the reins of power, and made himself respected in the Council."

After his defeat in 1862 Rodier retired from politics until 1867, when he was appointed to the new Legislative Council of Quebec as member for the De Lorimier division. There he sat as a Conservative and gained a reputation for both eloquence and financial acumen. Throughout his life he was connected with the militia, being commissioned ensign and acting as quartermaster of the Montreal 2nd Battalion in 1821, rising to lieutenant in 1828, captain in 1831, major in 1847, and finally lieutenant-colonel of the 7th Montreal Battalion in 1862.

He was also active in religious charities. In 1843, a year after the Jesuits had returned to Canada, he provided them, without charge, with their first Montreal noviciate in a portion of his own Rue Saint-Antoine mansion, which they used until 1851. In 1868 he turned part of his premises over to the Grey Nuns as the Bethlehem Asylum for orphans and in 1872–73 he built them a larger building on Richmond Square. He presented them with this property, valued at $35,000, and also endowed the orphanage both then and in his will. Further he arranged for the Sulpicians to provide aid and medical treatment for the poor in part of the orphanage, and endowed the Good Shepherd Nuns. It was at his suggestion that St James Cathedral was located in Dominion Square.

On 8 Sept. 1825, at Notre-Dame Church, he had married Marie-Louise (d. 14 April 1879), the daughter of Paul Lacroix. The family were Alsatians whose original name was Von Kreuz. Two sons and a daughter died young, but two daughters outlived him. Senator Charles-Séraphin Rodier* (1818–90), an industrialist and a leading figure in Montreal, was his nephew.

A man who made a success of several careers, and was famous in the city for his correctness of dress and his courteous manner, Rodier often had an original way of doing things and could be eccentric. His long and varied career provides a good example of how the conservative businessmen of the pre-rebellion days could adapt themselves to new circumstances, and play an important role in the era after responsible government: the *Patriotes* of 1837 would have seen him as a traitor, but one of his pallbearers was Antoine-Aimé Dorion*. As *Le Nouveau Monde* stated in his obituary, he was "one of Montreal's most respected citizens; his fine and charitable nature has long earned him the esteem of his fellow citizens."

FREDERICK H. ARMSTRONG

AJM, Greffe de A.-C. Décary, testament de C.-S. Rodier, 22 janv. 1876. AVM, Biographies de maires. *Gazette* (Montreal), 5 Feb. 1876. *Montreal Daily Witness*, 12 Feb. 1862, 5 Feb. 1876. *Montreal Gazette*, 6 March 1858; 13 Jan. 1860; 24, 25 Feb. 1862. *Le Nouveau Monde* (Montréal), 5 févr., 9 févr. 1876;

Roebuck

15 avril 1879. *L'Opinion publique* (Montréal), 24 févr. 1876.

Can. parl. comp., *1875*, 458–59. Turcotte, *Conseil législatif de Québec*, 239. *A la mémoire de l'honorable Charles-Séraphin Rodier, avocat, ex-maire de Montréal, membre du Conseil législatif de la province de Québec, lieut.-colonel du 7ᵉ bataillon, fondateur de l'asile de Bethléem* (s.l., s.d.). Atherton, *Montreal*, II, 208; III, 85–86. *Histoire de la Corporation de la Cité de Montréal, depuis son origine jusqu'à nos jours* . . . , J.-C. Lamothe *et al.*, édit. (Montréal, 1903), 58–59, 161, 200–1, 204, 207, 281, 283, 286. F. W. Terrill, *A chronology of Montreal and of Canada from A.D. 1752 to A.D. 1893, including commercial statistics, historical sketches of commercial corporations and firms and advertisements* . . . (Montreal, 1893), 230, 236–67. E. A. Collard, "Mayor's house," *Gazette* (Montreal), 25 Jan. 1969. J.-J. Lefebvre et Thérèse Cromp, "Nos disparus," *La Revue du barreau de la province de Québec* (Montréal), XVIII (1958), 407–9. É.-Z. Massicotte, "Deux Rodier," *BRH*, XLIV (1938), 120–22.

ROEBUCK, JOHN ARTHUR, politician; b. 28 Dec. 1802 at Madras, India, fifth son of Ebenezer Roebuck, civil administrator in India, and Zipporah Tickell; d. 30 Nov. 1879 in London, Eng. In 1834 he married Henrietta Falconer, who, with a daughter, survived him.

On his father's early death, John Arthur Roebuck's mother took him to England in 1807; she made a second marriage there to John SIMPSON and members of the family emigrated to Upper Canada in 1815, where they initially owned an estate at Augusta, on the St Lawrence between Prescott and Brockville. In 1824 John Arthur returned to England and entered the Inner Temple, being called to the bar in 1831 and eventually appointed QC in 1843. He became MP for Bath in 1832 and, as a disciple of Jeremy Bentham, adopted radical views, supporting vote by ballot, an elective magistracy, a national system of secular education, disestablishment of the Church of England, the removal of all civil and religious disabilities, and a reduction in the powers of the House of Lords. Although his radicalism mellowed in later years, he remained strongly out of sympathy with the Whigs, denouncing them as an exclusive aristocratic faction that insincerely employed democratic slogans for party purposes.

In 1834 Roebuck moved in the House of Commons for the appointment of the committee which inquired into the affairs of Canada in that year. He did not speak on Canadian affairs on any other occasion between 1832 and 1835, when, perhaps because of Louis-Joseph PAPINEAU's connection with the radical Joseph Hume, he became agent in England for the assembly of Lower Canada and, acting in effect as Papineau's personal representative, advanced in parliament and in the press the demands of the Canadian reformers for an elective legislative council and for local control over all provincial revenues and crown lands. Despite Papineau's appreciation of his efforts, the assembly did not meet his expenses and a debt lasted for some years. One of a small group of outspoken radicals, Roebuck vigorously condemned Whig policy towards Canada as embodied in Lord John Russell's resolutions in March 1837, and, though he had lost his parliamentary seat in an election later that year and was no longer Lower Canada's agent, he was allowed in 1838 to speak at the bar of both houses in opposition to the bill to suspend the Canadian constitution. Roebuck never doubted the value of colonies to Britain, but he demanded the reform of the existing system of imperial administration at home and overseas. Fearing also the annexation of the Canadian provinces by the United States, he advocated that Britain grant the colonists a greater degree of self-government and form a North American federation, views he set out in *The colonies of England*, published in 1849.

Roebuck was again returned to parliament by Bath, 1841–47, and by Sheffield, 1849–68 and 1874–79. In 1855 he was appointed chairman of a parliamentary select committee whose report condemned ministerial incompetence in the conduct of the Crimean War. To the annoyance of his friends and supporters, he championed the south in the American Civil War and defended Austrian rule in Italy. In 1878 he was made a privy councillor by a Conservative government.

Roebuck, short in stature, was self-confident and impulsive in expressing his opinions. The destructive criticism and bitter invective of his speeches were appreciated more by popular audiences than by the House of Commons, where the strength of his language tended to harm rather than promote the causes he espoused and his irritability was reputed to be more in evidence than his undoubted intellectual powers. His independence of party ties and conscientious exposure of shams and abuses suggested to the English public a person of great integrity, but he remained one of the most wayward politicians of his time.

PETER BURROUGHS

J. A. Roebuck, *The colonies of England: a plan for the government of some portion of our colonial possessions* (London, 1849); *History of the Whig ministry of 1830 to the passing of the Reform bill* (2v., London, 1852); [   ] *Life and letters of John Arthur Roebuck* . . . , ed. R. E. Leader (London and New York, 1897); *Radical support to a Whig ministry* (n.p., 1836). *Pamphlets for the people*, ed. J. A. Roebuck (2v., London, 1835).

PAC, MG 24, A19 (Roebuck papers), 1. *Times* London), 1 Dec. 1879. *DNB*.

ROGER, CHARLES, historian and journalist; b. Dundee, Scotland, 14 April 1819, son of Charles Roger and his first wife Ann Cruikshank; d. perhaps in 1878.

Charles Roger Sr moved from Perthshire to Dundee where he was successively a tobacco merchant and city librarian. His son, Charles, matriculated at St Salvator's College in St Andrews University in 1832–33 and studied first for the ministry and then for the medical profession. In September 1835, however, he gave up his studies and enlisted in the Royal Artillery at Perth. He was first enrolled as a gunner in the 7th Battalion, but in 1836 was transferred to the 4th Battalion where he was promoted bombardier in 1839 and corporal in 1841. From 1836 to 1839 he was stationed at Halifax, Nova Scotia, and from then until 1842 he was at Quebec City. When he was discharged, at his own request, in July 1842, his conduct was shown as "exemplary" and he was allowed £25. (He should not be confused with the Charles Rogers of the 95th Foot who was cashiered by court martial in 1842.)

Roger, a Presbyterian, married Dorothy MacRobie at Quebec on 29 Feb. 1840; they had at least five sons and four daughters. He apparently remained in Quebec City after he left the army, and by 1847 he was superintendent of the library for the Quebec Library Association. In 1849 he left this post to work for the *Morning Chronicle* (1849–53) and then briefly for the *Quebec Gazette*. Although he is often given as an editor of the papers, he was not the editor-in-chief for either. On 30 March 1854, with the help of subscriptions raised by friends, he began his own paper, the *Observer*, which expired in 1855. By 1856 he was back working for the *Quebec Gazette*, but in the next year he was again superintendent for the Quebec Library Association before moving to Port Hope, Canada West.

It was in Quebec that Roger began writing works on Canadian history. His first and best known work was *The rise of Canada, from barbarism to wealth and civilisation* (1856), of which only one volume covering the period 1534 to 1824 was ever published. The projected second volume, which would have brought the history up to 1837, was apparently never written, probably because of the appearance of John Mercier McMullen*'s history in 1855. Roger worked in haste, relying on only a few sources, particularly Robert Christie*'s history of Lower Canada; he has received more credit from the critics for his energy than for his merits. Yet the work is well written. It concentrates most

heavily on the modern period, and as the title indicates, it is a tale of progress. The next year he wrote *Stadacona depicta; or Quebec and its environs*, the title obviously influenced by the Reverend Newton Bosworth*'s study of Montreal. Roger's work is a history and description of the city as it was in 1842, based on *Hawkins's picture of Quebec; with historical recollections* (Quebec, 1834), by Alfred Hawkins*, along with further information on conditions in 1857. Roger probably also prepared an historical guide *Quebec: as it was, and as it is*, of which there were five editions between 1857 and 1867, the first four appearing under the name of Willis Russell*.

Once resident at Port Hope, Roger founded another newspaper, the *Atlas*, which was described succinctly as "a venture of C. Roger & Co., in 1858 which stood a short battle." He then moved to the small village of Millbrook, some 15 miles to the north, where he apparently published a newspaper, again called the *Observer*, for some years.

Roger next turned up in Ottawa where he was a clerk in the post office from about 1866 to 1874. He resumed his literary efforts, and in 1871 produced another historical guide book, *Ottawa past and present*. He also wrote a series of letters to the Ottawa *Times* describing a visit to England in 1872–73, which were later reprinted in pamphlet form as *Glimpses of London, and Atlantic experiences*. It was while in England in 1873 that he was elected a fellow of the Royal Historical Society, probably under the aegis of its secretary, his cousin the historian Charles Rogers, who was the most important of the several members of his family with literary interests.

What happened to Roger after his return from England is obscure; he disappears from the Ottawa city directories after 1874. W. S. Wallace* shows the date of his death as 1878, but Roger continued to appear as a correspondent of the Royal Historical Society until 1880. He disappears after this date.

Although a minor figure Charles Roger is interesting as one of the earliest Canadian historians and as an example of the type of wandering, unsuccessful newspaper editor who appears so frequently in 19th century Canada.

FREDERICK H. ARMSTRONG

Charles Roger was the author of *Glimpses of London and Atlantic experiences; or, an account of a voyage to England . . . in the winter of 1872–73* (Ottawa, 1873); *Ottawa past and present, or a brief account of the first opening up of the Ottawa country, and incidents in connection with the rise and progress of Ottawa city and parts adjacent thereto . . .* (Ottawa, 1871); *The rise of Canada, from barbarism to wealth and civilisation* (Quebec, 1856); *Stadacona depicta: or Quebec and its*

Rolette

environs historically, panoramically, and locally exhibited (Quebec, [1857]); and was probably the author of *Quebec: as it was, and as it is, or, a brief history of the oldest city in Canada, from its foundation to the present time, with a guide for strangers to the different places of interest within the city and adjacent thereto,* prepared for Willis Russell (1st ed., Quebec, 1857; 3rd ed., 1860; 4th ed., 1864; 5th ed., 1867). *Morning Chronicle* (Quebec), 1849–53. *Quebec Gazette*, 1853, 1856. No copies of the newspapers Roger edited are known to exist.

PAC, RG 31, A1, 1871, Ottawa city, Wellington ward. PRO, WO 69/107; WO 71/314. Beaulieu et Hamelin, *Journaux du Québec*, 204. Boase, *Modern English biography*, III, 254; VI, 493. *Canada, an encyclopædia*, V, 161. *Illustrated historical atlas of the counties of Northumberland and Durham, Ont.* (Toronto, 1878), x. Morgan, *Bibliotheca Canadensis*, 324. Norah Story, *The Oxford companion to Canadian history and literature* (Toronto, London, New York, 1967), 723. Wallace, *Macmillan dictionary*, 642. Lareau, *Hist. de la littérature canadienne*, 181–83. *Lit. hist. of Can.* (Klinck), 215–16. Horace Têtu, *Historique des journaux de Québec* (2e éd., Québec, 1889), 41. Charles Rogers, "Notes on the history of the Scottish branch of the Norman house of Roger," Historical Society *Trans.* (London), I (1872), 357–88. F. C. Wurtele, "Our library," Lit. and Hist. Soc. of Quebec, *Trans.*, new ser., XIX (1889), 31–73.

ROLETTE (Rollette), JOSEPH, fur-trader and legislator; b. 23 Oct. 1820, Prairie du Chien, Wisconsin, son of Jean-Joseph Rolette* and Marguerite Dubois; d. 16 May 1871, Pembina, North Dakota.

Joseph Rolette Jr was the son of a pioneer French Canadian fur-trader of the upper Mississippi River region. After his education in New York under the guardianship of Ramsay Crooks, the president of the American Fur Company, for whom his father worked, he returned west to Fort Snelling (St Paul), Minnesota. In 1840 he was employed by the American Fur Company in the Pembina area under the supervision of one of its partners, Henry Hastings Sibley*, who was in charge of the fur trade of the northern Minnesota district. With his uncle, Henry Fisher, Rolette established a cart route between Pembina and St Paul as part of a plan of drawing furs from the Hudson's Bay Company territories to the St Paul market.

By 1844 Sibley had formed new business associations, including a partnership with Norman Wolfred Kittson*. A post was established at Pembina, and Rolette, both clerk and trader, was placed in charge of it and several other posts along the international frontier. Three years later, during the fierce competition between American traders and the HBC for the border fur trade, he burned a post which the latter's traders had established near Pembina. In 1853 Kittson moved his headquarters west to St Joseph (Walhalla), North Dakota. Rolette remained at the Pembina post, and when Sibley and Kittson withdrew from the border area the following year because they could not compete with the high prices which the HBC offered in its campaign to defeat them, he was left in charge as a semi-independent trader. By this time he had invested his own money in the fur trade as well as in land speculation in the Pembina area. Rolette lost heavily in both enterprises and by 1857, a year of depression, he was almost penniless.

In 1852 Rolette had been elected one of two representatives of the Pembina district to the territorial legislature of Minnesota and in 1856–57 was a member of the territorial council. He served later as postmaster at Pembina and from 1866 to 1870 was a United States customs officer. Throughout his life he was associated with this border community, and was a well-known and hospitable host to travellers in the Red River valley, as well as a familiar figure in the Red River Settlement where his children were educated. In 1845 he had married at Saint-Boniface Angélique Jérôme, a French-Chippewa woman; they had 11 children.

During the Red River disturbances of 1869–70 Rolette was one of a group of "correspondents" forwarding information on the events at Red River to the St Paul newspapers. They sought to make the disturbances a movement which had as its purpose independence or annexion to the United States. Along with other Americans in the Red River Settlement and at Pembina, including Enos STUTSMAN, he endeavoured to induce Louis Riel* to bring the settlement into the American union.

Rolette is remembered as a jovial and spirited frontier figure of enterprising and aggressive methods. Whether in an Indian fight, in relations with the Métis population, or in the highly competitive fur trade, he was both a capable and a daring adventurer.

HARTWELL BOWSFIELD

Begg's Red River journal (Morton), 9, 86, 165, 349. Minnesota Hist. Soc. *Coll.*, XXIV (1912), 654. *Manitoban* (Winnipeg), 27 May 1871. Joseph Tassé, *Les Canadiens de l'Ouest* (2e éd., 2v., Montréal, 1878), I, 211; II, 31–40. A. C. Gluek, *Minnesota and the manifest destiny of the Canadian northwest; a study in Canadian-American relations* (Toronto, 1965), 85, 116–17. J. P. Pritchett, "Some Red River fur-trade activities," *Minnesota History Bulletin* (St Paul), V (1923–24), 401–23. G. B. Winship, "Early politics and politicians of North Dakota," University of North Dakota, *Quarterly J.* (Grand Forks), XIII (1923), 254–67.

ROSS, BERNARD ROGAN, HBC chief trader and naturalist; b. 25 Sept. 1827 at Londonderry, Ireland, son of James Ross and Elizabeth Rogan; d. 21 June 1874 while visiting Toronto, Ont.

Bernard Rogan Ross was educated at Royle College, Londonderry, and entered the service of the Hudson's Bay Company at the suggestion of Sir George Simpson* who had met him at the Londonderry home of his uncle, Dr Frank Rogan. Coming to Canada too late in the season to proceed to the northwest, Ross taught school in Cornwall until the spring when he went to Norway House. His posting to that place as an apprentice clerk is listed in the minutes of the Council of the Northern Department of the company held at the Red River Settlement in June 1843. While with the company Ross served at many posts including Norway House, York Factory, Fort Simpson, Fort Norman, and Fort Resolution. In 1856 he was appointed a chief trader and from 1858 to 1862 was at Fort Simpson in charge of the Mackenzie River District. He retired in 1871. In 1860 he had married Christina Ross, daughter of chief factor Donald Ross*; they had three children.

Ross was in the Red River Settlement at the time of the disturbances of 1869–70 and according to Alexander Begg*, the diarist, was one of an unofficial group which advised against the formation of a provisional government. This group suggested that the HBC continue to govern and that the people elect an executive council to negotiate with Canada the terms by which they should enter confederation.

Ross's primary significance is in the field of natural history rather than the fur trade. Like many company men he contributed much to the early scientific knowledge of the northwest. While at Fort Simpson he made valuable collections of mammalia, insects, and birds, forwarding specimens to the Smithsonian Institution in Washington, the Royal Scottish Museum in Edinburgh, and the British Museum in London. Ross's Goose was named after him in 1861. He was a foundation fellow of the Anthropological Society in 1863, and became a fellow of the Royal Geographical Society the following year. In addition he was a corresponding member of the New York Historical Society, a correspondent of the Academy of Natural Sciences of Philadelphia in 1861, and of the Natural History Society of Montreal. A list of some of his scientific papers is found in the *Catalogue of scientific papers (1800–1863)* compiled by the Royal Society of London and published in 1871. A short essay on the fur trade and transportation in the north, which he wrote when he was 18, was published in the *Beaver* in 1955.

HARTWELL BOWSFIELD

PAM, Biographical files. *Begg's Red River journal* (Morton). HBRS, XVI (Rich and Johnson). [B. R. Ross], "Fur trade gossip sheet," *Beaver*, outfit 285 (spring 1955), 52 (originally published in the Fort William *Daily Times-Journal*, 27 Dec. 1928). B. W. Cartwright and Angus Gavin, "Where the Ross' Geese nest," *Beaver*, outfit 271 (Dec. 1940), 6. Robert Kerr, "For the Royal Scottish Museum," *Beaver*, outfit 284 (June 1953), 32. J. M. Sherk, "HBC pioneer Bernard Rogan Ross," *Beaver*, outfit 257 (Dec. 1926), 25.

ROSS, JAMES, teacher, public servant, journalist, and lawyer; b. 9 May 1835 at Colony Gardens, the family house in Red River Settlement, son of Alexander Ross*, former chief trader of the Hudson's Bay Company, and Sarah, who may have been a daughter of an Okanagan Indian chief; d. 20 Sept. 1871 probably at Colony Gardens.

James Ross was educated at Red River and at Toronto. The Reverend David Anderson*, bishop of Rupert's Land, later wrote that Ross was "a distinguished scholar at the Red River College of St. John's . . . who afterwards went through a very creditable academic career at the University of Toronto." He entered the university on a scholarship in 1853, received awards each year, and upon graduation in 1857 won three medals, two gold and one silver. For a brief time after graduation Ross seriously considered entering the Presbyterian ministry, but an opportunity to teach at Upper Canada College changed his mind. However, the death of an older brother, William, in 1856, followed by the death of his father in the same year, left the affairs of his family in a tangled condition. Ross and John BLACK, the two executors, disagreed about the settlement of the estates and Ross was forced to return to Red River. Before leaving Toronto, Ross married Margaret Smith on 18 May 1858; five children were born of this marriage. Upon his arrival at Red River Ross found himself confronted by extremely complex family problems and, though he did his best to resolve them, these problems plagued Ross and complicated his relations with other members of the family until his death. Shortly after his return, on 12 May 1859, Ross was appointed postmaster of the Assiniboia at a salary of £10 per annum.

In 1860, Ross joined his brother-in-law, William Coldwell*, and William Buckingham*, two former Toronto journalists, as part owner and an editor of the *Nor'Wester*, the first newspaper in the Red River Settlement. In October 1860 Buckingham withdrew and Ross' interest in, and work for, the *Nor'Wester* increased. During 1861 the *Nor'Wester* published, in 16 instalments, "History of the Red

Ross

River Settlement," written by Ross, a work of considerable interest for it contains much information about the settlement which is not readily accessible elsewhere. Not long after Ross joined the *Nor'Wester*, the paper carried an editorial criticizing the Hudson's Bay Company and the system of government at Red River. As a result, Ross and the paper were identified with the "Canadian party." This did not, however, prevent the Council of Assiniboia from appointing Ross sheriff and governor of the gaol in the spring of 1862. But Ross continued to antagonize the local authorities.

During the summer of 1862 the Sioux massacred many American settlers; to avoid reprisals by American troops they fled into British territory and encamped not far from the Red River Settlement. Their presence caused much alarm in the settlement. Under these circumstances the Council of Assiniboia circulated a petition calling for the imperial government to send out troops for the protection of the settlers. In the *Nor'Wester* Ross immediately launched a counter-petition, not only calling upon the imperial government to dispatch troops to Red River but also requesting "such changes in the system and administration of the local government as will remove the present discontent and dissatisfaction. . . ." This was too much; by a unanimous vote of the council on 25 November, Ross' appointments as postmaster, sheriff, and governor of the gaol were terminated. Ross, however, continued his attacks; a number of meetings were held at which he denounced the local government and urged the settlers to sign the counter-petition. Eventually Sandford Fleming* forwarded the counter-petition to the colonial secretary, the Duke of Newcastle [Henry Clinton].

Ross again identified himself with the anti-government forces during the trial of the Reverend Griffith Owen Corbett*. Corbett, who had supported the counter-petition, was brought to trial on the charge of having attempted to perform an illegal operation upon his maid servant. Ross saw in this the persecution of Corbett for the latter's opposition to the government and consequently played a leading role in the defence of Corbett, thereby adding to his reputation as an opponent of the existing government.

Ross' association with the *Nor'Wester* had placed him squarely among the members of the Canadian party. When Ross withdrew from the *Nor'Wester* late in 1863, in anticipation of his return to Canada, the manner in which he withdrew reinforced his connection, for his place was soon taken by Dr John Christian Schultz* who was regarded by many as the leader of the Canadian faction at Red River.

Leaving his wife and children behind him, Ross departed from the settlement in the spring of 1864 and returned to Toronto to study law. Margaret and some of the children joined him when it became evident that his stay in the east would be a long one. On 5 July Ross became a clerk for John McNab, attorney, and in August of the same year he wrote and passed examinations for admission to the Law Society of Upper Canada. Ross pursued other studies also and in June of 1865 he received an MA from the University of Toronto.

While carrying on his studies Ross had to support his wife and family; not unnaturally he turned to journalism. Given his association with the *Nor'Wester*, Ross had little difficulty in establishing a connection with George BROWN and the *Globe*; he maintained this connection until September 1864, when he accepted a position with the *Hamilton Spectator* which he held until the spring of 1865. At that time, having decided to settle permanently in Canada, Ross returned briefly to the Red River in order to clear up his personal affairs. Upon returning to Toronto in the late summer of 1865, Ross bought a house and went to work for the *Globe*. As a journalist in Canada from 1865 to 1869, Ross continued his attacks upon the HBC, and became known as a staunch proponent of the annexation of the company's territories by Canada.

As his stay in Canada lengthened it became increasingly evident that Ross was unhappy; he was cut off from most of his family and from many of his friends; moreover, as his letters indicate, he became more and more concerned over the cost of living in Toronto. Then too, there were still disputes over his father's estate which could only be resolved in the Red River Settlement. Late in the summer of 1869 Ross sold his house in Toronto and, accompanied by his family, he set out for the Red River. The early fall saw Ross back in Colony Gardens and thus in a position to play an important role in the dramatic events of 1869–70.

After Louis Riel* and his followers forced William McDougall*, the governor from Canada, to return to Pembina on 21 Oct. 1869, elections were held in all the Red River communities to choose representatives to consider Riel's proposal for establishing a provisional government. James Ross was elected to represent the people of Kildonan. In the meetings which followed, Ross became "the spokesman for the English as definitely as Riel was for the French." Ross and the majority of the English representatives did not sanction the establishment of a provisional government because they believed that such an act would be illegal. Instead they proposed that a more representative government, under the authority of the HBC, should be established. However, while Ross differed from Riel on the course of action to be taken, he firmly believed that it was essential for the English settlers to cooperate with the French in order to prevent the outbreak of civil war in the Red River. It is evident that his was a wise and statesmanlike position, and in adopting it Ross helped to prevent disaster overtaking the people of the settlement. But by taking this stand Ross found himself diametrically opposed to his former friends in the Canadian party; from their point of view Ross' action was little short of treason, and they never forgave him for it.

Following the intervention of Donald Alexander Smith*, special commissioner from the Canadian government, it was proposed that a convention, composed of representatives from each part of the settlement, should meet to discuss the terms on which the people of Red River would enter confederation. Ross was the unanimous choice to represent the parish of St John's. The delegates met from 26 Jan. to 11 Feb. 1870, and selected Ross as a member of the committee of six chosen to draft the List of Rights. Throughout the debate which followed the presentation of the committee's report, Ross was not only the leading spokesman for the English representatives, but served as translator of the speeches of the French delegates. Often he led the opposition to the proposals stemming from Riel's suggestion that Red River should enter Canada as a province. Ross argued that it would be more in the interest of the people of Red River to enter as a territory and the convention supported him on this issue. But though the debate was often heated and emotional Ross' efforts helped to prevent a complete break between the English and French representatives. Riel, as president of the provisional government, recognized the value of Ross' efforts and appointed him chief justice in his administration.

It appears that Ross had been drinking heavily for some time and during this tense period his drinking increased; consequently for weeks in the late spring of 1870 Ross did little and he had no impact upon developments. In the late summer he went to Toronto, ostensibly on personal business, but his letters reveal that he wanted to be absent from the settlement when Colonel Garnet Joseph Wolseley*'s expeditionary force arrived. He was afraid that his actions during the previous winter might be misunderstood by the Canadians. He wrote his wife that he would return only after things had settled down and he suggested she state that his actions had been determined by his efforts to prevent bloodshed. While in Toronto, Ross took every opportunity to explain the policy he had followed during the critical days at Red River.

When Ross finally returned in the middle of October 1870, the newly established province was relatively peaceful. This was only a momentary lull before it was disturbed by both provincial and federal election campaigns in 1870 and 1871. Dr John Schultz was a candidate for the federal constituency of Lisgar, and Ross, convinced that the actions of Schultz during the winter of 1869–70 had nearly provoked civil war, threw himself into the campaign to oppose his election. First Ross supported Dr Curtis James Bird and campaigned vigorously to rally the old settlers behind Dr Bird. When the latter withdrew from the contest after being elected to the provincial assembly, Ross gave his support to Bird's replacement, Colin Inkster*. All Ross' efforts were in vain, for Dr Schultz won an easy victory.

Courts were soon established in Manitoba, and Ross decided to return to the legal profession. On 8 May 1871, he became the third man to be admitted to the bar of Manitoba, but he had little opportunity to practise in the new province. In the tension of the election campaigns Ross had again taken to drink and during the summer his health began to decline rapidly. Pulmonary disease, of which there was a history in the family, may have caused his death.

W. D. SMITH

PAM, Alexander Ross family papers; Church of England registers, St John's Church (Winnipeg), baptisms, 1828–79, no.885. *Begg's Red River journal* (Morton). *Canadian North-West* (Oliver), I, 442, 505–8. Hargrave, *Red River. Manitoban* (Winnipeg), 23 Sept. 1871. *Nor'Wester* (Winnipeg), 1860–63. *The Canada directory, for 1857–58* . . . (Montreal, 1857), 808. Begg and Nursey, *Ten years in Winnipeg*. Careless, *Brown*, II, 7–8.

ROSS, JOHN, lawyer, politician, and businessman; b. in County Antrim, Ireland, 10 March 1818; d. 31 Jan. 1871, at Toronto, Ont.

John Ross was brought to Canada as an infant and was educated in Johnstown District (Leeds and Grenville counties) and Brockville. At 16 he was articled to Andrew Norton Buell* and later to George Sherwood*. He was called to the bar of Upper Canada in 1839 and set up practice at Belleville. The roots of both his business and his political career lay in Belleville and the surrounding Hastings County, but acquaintance with the families of Levius Peters Sherwood* and George Crawford* and with William* Jr and A. N. Buell in Brockville introduced Ross to a circle of political, legal, and financial connections that he constantly enlarged. Alexander Tilloch Galt*'s brother

Ross

Thomas* was for a time a partner of Ross. God-parents of his sons included Robert Baldwin*, David Lewis Macpherson*, Philip VanKough-net, and A. T. Galt. In September 1855 he wrote of Francis Hincks*: "He and I have been like brothers for so many years that I find it hard to part from him." Because of his work for the Grand Trunk Railway Company his associations also extended to the financial interests of London, England.

Business affairs had prospered sufficiently by early 1847 to allow Ross to marry Margaret, the daughter of George Crawford. She died before the year was out, and on 4 Feb. 1851 he married Robert Baldwin's daughter, Augusta Elizabeth, at St James' Cathedral in Toronto; they had three sons. They resided in Belleville for several years; by 1857 they were established in Yorkville near Toronto. Here Ross practised law in partnership with Abram William Lauder* and Thomas Charles Patteson*, but he continued his practice in Belleville with John Bell and later Thomas Holden.

In a letter of 1867 to John A. Macdonald*, Ross wrote: "my politics can best be described according to the facts. Up to the year 1854 I was follower first of Mr. Baldwin and then of Mr. Hincks. I then joined the coalition government with you, and have supported you and your policy ever since." When just 23 Ross had campaigned vigorously for Baldwin's election to the Legislative Assembly in 1841 and had persuaded him to stand for Hastings. A special confidence grew up between the two men, based in part on an identity of political views but reinforced by mutual sympathy in widowerhood and later in the relationship of father and son-in-law. From 1841 to 1848 John Ross was Baldwin's loyal aid and adviser in the area from Hastings to Grenville counties. He was rewarded on 1 Dec. 1848 with a seat on the Legislative Council. Ross did not treat the appointment as a sinecure, but continued to lead an active political and official career from the "Upper House."

John Ross' service in public office extends from late 1851 to early 1862. He was appointed solicitor general for Canada West without a seat in the cabinet on 12 Nov. 1851. Hincks brought him into the cabinet as attorney general for Canada West on 22 June 1853. When Hincks was defeated and withdrew from politics in the late summer of 1854, his mantle fell upon Ross who entered the Allan Napier MacNab*–Augustin-Norbert Morin* government as leader of the moderate Reformers. His presence in the cabinet as speaker of the Legislative Council was viewed as a pledge that a number of measures advocated by the Hincks-Morin government would be carried into law by the new coalition government. In the next years the political tensions apparent in the Legislative Assembly were echoed within the cabinet. John Ross repressed the full measure of his frustration in the meetings of the executive, but wrote of them privately. He distrusted Lewis Thomas Drummond*, and lacked sympathy for Joseph-Édouard Cauchon* and François-Xavier Lemieux*. He felt that MacNab was not effective and seemed always to be dealing with a mob of hangers-on. By 18 April 1856 the moderate Reformers had lost confidence in MacNab and were drifting into opposition. Ross resigned his speakership in the Legislative Council and strove to rally the moderate Reformers to support John A. Macdonald who was emerging as the new leader of the government. Macdonald brought Ross back into the government on 2 Feb. 1858 as receiver-general and member of the Board of Railroad Commissioners. Following the brief interlude of the George Brown–Antoine-Aimé Dorion* administration of 2–4 August, George-Étienne Cartier appointed Ross president of the Executive Council and minister of agriculture on 7 Aug. 1858. He continued in these offices until his resignation from government 26 March 1862.

Ross was an effective administrator as well as an astute politician. His official correspondence reveals a clear concise mind, and the long continuity of his service in office confirms that he was reliable. Much of his correspondence to Baldwin and Macdonald is filled with well-founded speculation about contemporary political affairs. He was a trusted lieutenant of Hincks, serving at times as his special "trouble shooter" in Washington and London in the 1850s, and there making use of his political as well as administrative and financial talents. His role is one of the antecedents of the office of high commissioner in London. Cartier took Ross along as well as Galt when he went to London in October 1858 to press for British North American federation. On 5 November Ross had an audience with Queen Victoria and spoke of the possibility of a royal visit to Canada. A part of Ross' usefulness to the mission of 1858 was that he was well regarded in some influential British financial circles.

Hincks appointed Ross one of the six government directors of the newly projected Grand Trunk Railway on 11 Nov. 1852, and dispatched him immediately to London. There, in the next months, Ross was at the centre of the intricate negotiations that brought together financial resources and experienced contractors and resulted in the Grand Trunk Railway prospectus of 12 April 1853. At the request of the British financial interests Ross was then appointed president of the railway. His effectiveness as president was in maintaining the legal and administrative machinery of the company and in coordinating in one policy the disparate pressures of various financial interests, the contractors, and the Canadian government. At the same time he fended off threats from competing railroads and the opposition in the Canadian parliament. On 20 Feb. 1857 he was the first witness to give evidence before the select committee of the House of Commons enquiring into the future of the Hudson's Bay Company. He appeared as a former Canadian minister and an expert witness concerning the development of railroads to the west. He remained president of the Grand Trunk until 1862 when the company was reorganized and Sir Edward W. Watkin* succeeded to the office.

After 1862 John Ross receded from public attention into private business, but his attendance in the Legislative Council was regular. In 1867 he was appointed to the Senate. He was a director of the Northern Railway Company of Canada, a charter member of the Dominion Bank in 1869, and from 1862 to 1869 lieutenant colonel in the 2nd Battalion of Toronto militia. He died in Toronto in 1871 "after a long painful illness."

PAUL CORNELL

MTCL, Baldwin papers. PAC, MG 24, B11 (Baldwin papers), ser.2, 5; B40 (George Brown papers), ser.1, 2; D16 (Buchanan papers), 53; MG 26, A (Macdonald papers), 260. St James' Cathedral (Toronto), baptismal and marriage registers. G.B., Parl., House of Commons paper, 1857 (Session II), XV, 224, 260 (whole volume), *Report from the select committee on the Hudson's Bay Company ...*, "Minutes of evidence ...," 1–357. *Robert Ross, friend of friends; letters to Robert Ross, art critic and writer, together with extracts from his published articles*, ed. Margery Ross (London, [1952]). *Canada, an encyclopædia*, I. *The Canada directory ... 1851*, ed. R. W. S. Mackay (Montreal, 1851). *Can. directory of parliament* (Johnson), 508–9. *Encyclopedia of Canada*, V. *Mitchell & Co.'s Canada classified directory for 1865–66* (Toronto, n.d.). *Mitchell's Toronto directory for 1864–5* (Toronto, 1864). Morgan, *Sketches of celebrated Canadians*, 612–14.

Careless, *Brown*, I; *Union of the Canadas*. Creighton, *Macdonald, young politician*. R. S. Longley, *Sir Francis Hincks; a study of Canadian politics, railways, and finance in the nineteenth century* (Toronto, 1943). Sissons, *Ryerson*, II. O. D. Skelton, *The life and times of Sir Alexander Tilloch Galt* (Toronto, 1920). G. R. Stevens, *Canadian National Railways* (2v., Toronto, 1960), I. D. W. Swainson, "Business and politics: the career of John Willoughby Crawford," *Ont. Hist.*, LXI (1969), 225–36.

ROUSSY, LOUIS, Protestant missionary, b. at Vevey, Switzerland, in 1812; d., a bachelor, at Grande Ligne (Saint-Jean County), Quebec, in November 1880.

Louis Roussy, of Huguenot descent, was educated in the Swiss school system, and then served a mason's apprenticeship. At 19 he began religious work as a colporteur in France, and two years later, in Lausanne, entered a missionary seminary supported by the Independent Swiss Protestant churches. Here he became acquainted with Madame Henriette Odin* Feller, a prominent member of an independent Protestant group. In 1835 Madame Feller decided to join missionary friends in Montreal, Henri Olivier and his wife; Roussy volunteered to go with her. Proselytizing was next to impossible in Montreal because of the hostility shown to it, and Roussy went immediately to the country, where he was engaged to teach school in the parish of L'Acadie in a settlement called Grande Ligne [see Charles LA ROCQUE].

After two months Roussy had to quit teaching because of objections to his preaching on Sundays. He apparently had some private means in addition to support from the Swiss church and perhaps local donations. Roussy's evangelistic efforts were successful in winning a few converts, and Madame Feller joined him in 1836, to teach in a rented house. In this newly opened section of the province they taught both children and adults, using the Bible as their textbook. By midsummer of 1837, Roussy had organized his converts into the first independent French Protestant church in Canada. When the rebellion of 1837 broke out, the *Patriotes* identified the two missionaries with English Protestants and harassed them until they fled to Champlain, New York. Here Roussy met Dr Cyrille-Hector-Octave Côté*, a leader of the rebellion, whom he converted and who later became an able member of the mission.

When Roussy and Madame Feller returned to Grande Ligne after two months, they were welcomed by their flock and the people of the district. Their work became better known, and financial aid came from Switzerland and other parts of Canada and the United States. The first large mission building was opened for occupancy in August 1840.

Under the sponsorship, after 1845, of the Canadian Baptist Missionary Society, Louis Roussy remained until his death in 1880 the esteemed pastor of the Grande Ligne church and an occasional teacher in Feller College. As a colporteur he travelled on horseback distributing literature and Bibles; he held meetings and preached in houses or on street corners in many villages of southern Quebec and northern Vermont, meeting often with rebuffs. His main work was in his church, however, which grew to include 30 or more

Rowan

families. It is called today Roussy Memorial Church.

F. T. ROSSER

Canadian Baptist Archives (Hamilton, Ont.), [A. de L. Therrien,] "Pastors of the past in G.L.M." (handwritten MS). *The Baptist encyclopædia* . . . , ed. William Cathcart (Philadelphia, 1881). E. R. Fitch, *Baptists of Canada; a history of their progress and achievement* (Toronto, [1911]). Théodore Lafleur, *A semi-centennial, historical sketch of the Grande Ligne Mission read at the jubilee gathering, Grande Ligne, Oct. 18th, 1885* (Montreal, [1886]). M. J. Milne, *In the shadow of Mt. Royal: Madame Henrietta Feller* (New York, [1958]). E. A. Therrien *et al.*, *Baptist work in French Canada* (Toronto, n.d.). Théodore Lafleur, "Louis Roussy," *McMaster University Monthly* (Toronto), III (1893–94), 49–58.

ROWAN, Sir WILLIAM, field marshal and administrator of the Province of Canada; b. Isle of Man, 18 June 1789, eighth son of Robert Rowan of County Antrim, Ireland, and of Mary Wilson of County Down; m. Martha Sprong in 1811 (d. 1874), they had no children; d. at Bath, Eng., 26 Sept. 1879.

At the age of 14, William Rowan became an ensign in the 52nd Light Infantry, a regiment in which his uncle Charles Rowan and two older brothers, Charles (later Sir Charles, the first commissioner of the London Metropolitan Police) and Robert, also served. The renewal of the war with Napoleon brought the boy opportunities for active service and quick promotion. He became a lieutenant within a year and served in Sicily, 1806–7, and Sweden, 1808. Before he was 20 he commanded a company in the 2nd Battalion of the regiment and went with Robert Craufurd to Vigo (1808). He was also present at the capture of Flushing (1809). From 1811 to the end of the war Rowan took part in a number of engagements in the Peninsula and France; his conduct on the field at Orthez won him his brevet-majority. Rowan fought for the third time on a birthday (his 26th) at Waterloo, taking part in the 52nd's famous charge under Sir John Colborne* against the Imperial Guard, an attack which some have said brought Wellington the victory. Rowan then went with the occupying force to Paris and was put in charge of the 1st *arrondissement*. On 21 Jan. 1819 he became a lieutenant-colonel in the army (he was a captain in his regiment).

In 1823 Rowan was posted with his regiment to New Brunswick, and in 1826 he transferred to the 58th (which was not stationed in Canada) with the rank of major in the regiment. Leaving Canada in 1829, he went on half-pay on 22 July 1830.

Sir John Colborne, Rowan's war-time chief and life-long friend and patron, had come to Upper Canada in 1828 as lieutenant governor. Four years later Rowan joined him there as his military secretary (1832–39) to handle his correspondence on military matters. He also served him as civil secretary for Upper Canada from 1832 to 1836. The civil secretary, a personal appointee, conducted the whole internal management of the province, initiating or handling all public business and dealing with petitions for favours and appeals from decisions made by subordinate authorities. Colborne retired as lieutenant governor in 1836, but a year earlier he had been appointed commander-in-chief of the forces in Canada. Rowan thus served as Colborne's military secretary when he dealt with the uprisings of 1837 and 1838. Rowan was made a colonel in 1837, and the next year was awarded the CB for his services during the rebellions. He served as civil secretary in Lower Canada in 1838, and returned to England in 1839.

Promoted major-general on 9 Nov. 1846, Rowan was granted the Distinguished Service Award on 1 April 1848 and returned to Canada a year later as commander of the British forces there. On 30 May 1849, when there was a possibility that the governor general, Lord Elgin [Bruce*], might be insulted if he appeared in public since the violent disturbances in Montreal provoked by the rebellion losses bill had only recently abated, Rowan was sent to prorogue parliament, which he did with a conciliatory speech. Lord Elgin was on leave from 23 Aug. 1853 to 10 June 1854, and Rowan became administrator of the province. Ten days after Elgin returned, Rowan was promoted lieutenant-general and in that same year was appointed colonel of the 19th Regiment.

Rowan left Canada in 1855 and took up residence at Bath. He was knighted a year later (Military Knight Grand Cross of the Bath), and in 1861 became a colonel of his old regiment, the 52nd. On 13 Aug. 1862 he was promoted general and on 2 June 1877 field marshal. His death was occasioned simply by "a decay of nature."

It was Rowan's delight in his old age to claim that he had never purchased a commission or a promotion, a rare boast for that era and one which testified not only to his courage in the field but also to his abilities. He was entitled to wear a war medal with six clasps, but he marked a memorandum recounting his war services "strictly private" and during his long retirement at Bath was loath to talk about them. By contrast with his war record, Rowan's years in Canada appear unexciting, but he brought with him the prestige of a distinguished military career and rendered good service in three different roles.

RICHARD A. PRESTON

Illustrated London News, LXXV (1879), 322, 335, 337. *The annual register: a review of public events at home and abroad for the year 1879* (London, 1880), 221. Boase, *Modern English biography*, III, 322. *DNB*. J. T. Haydn, *The book of dignities, containing lists of official personages of the British empire ...* (3rd ed., London, 1894), 770, 778, 856, 882. Morgan, *Sketches of celebrated Canadians*, 549–50. Edward Walford, *The county families of the United Kingdom or royal manual of the titled and untitled aristocracy of England, Wales, Scotland and Ireland* (London, 1875), 843. Dent, *Last forty years*, II, 171, 280; *Upper Canadian rebellion*, I, 152.

ROY, LOUIS-DAVID, lawyer, man of letters, and judge; b. 9 June 1807 at Quebec, son of Joseph Roy and Marie Brunet; d. 31 July 1880 at Quebec.

Louis-David Roy studied at the Petit Séminaire of Quebec from 1818 to 1827, and was called to the bar of Lower Canada in 1832. While carrying on his profession, he used his spare time to publish, with François-Xavier Garneau*, a literary and scientific journal, *L'Institut ou Journal des étudiants*; it had no more than a fleeting existence, since publication, which began on 7 March 1841, had to be suspended on 22 May of the same year. The purpose of this undertaking was to ensure a wider reading public for reports on the literary and scientific societies of Canada and abroad, and to publish bibliographical articles on education, industry, and the arts. It was an ambitious project, and as Pierre-Joseph-Olivier Chauveau*, one of Roy's friends, wrote, a "noble effort to provide the country with a useful and serious publication, and to direct the ambition of our youth along a new path."

After this excursion into the realm of letters, Louis-David Roy devoted his time and energies to his profession. In 1842 he was appointed assistant to the chief justice, with jurisdiction in the lower district of Kamouraska. On 24 Dec. 1849 he became judge of the Circuit Court at Chicoutimi; he took the oath of office on 2 Jan. 1850 and had his first hearing on 24 May. He took up residence in what was then called "the village of Chicoutimi," and lived there from 1850 to 1858. As the first law courts were not built until 1862, the hearings of the court were held first in private houses, then in the town hall. One of the first cases to come before Judge Roy was that of a Métis Peter McLeod*, the associate of William Price*, against a certain Thiboutot, over a "scuffle." On 25 Nov. 1857, Louis-David Roy was appointed judge of the Superior Court for the new districts of Saguenay and Chicoutimi, with residence at La Malbaie; his house was situated at Pointe-au-Pic, near the present church. The government decided to hold three sessions of the Superior Court and

the Circuit Court at Chicoutimi, and Judge Roy was instructed to preside over them. He dispensed justice for 14 years to the satisfaction of all. Furthermore, he took an interest in the natural sciences, and wrote 13 letters to Abbé Léon Provancher* concerning them. The two correspondents exchanged several plants, and Abbé Provancher, in his preface to *Flore canadienne ...*, made a point of stressing the collaboration of Judge Roy, who had provided him with a list of plants at Chicoutimi and La Malbaie and in the surrounding area.

On 7 Jan. 1871 Judge Roy retired; he returned to Quebec to live, and died there on 31 July 1880. He was buried in the chapel of the Hôtel-Dieu. On 11 Sept. 1832, at Quebec, he had married his first wife Adeline Masse, by whom he had at least one daughter, Adeline, who married Montreal lawyer Alexandre de Lusignan. Widowed, on 19 Aug. 1839 he married again, his second wife being Hélène Parent, who gave him six boys and one girl.

LOUIS-PHILIPPE AUDET

Archives du séminaire de Chicoutimi, Fonds Victor-Alphonse Huard, Scrap-book, I, f.234; Fonds Léon Provancher, Correspondance, lettres de Louis-David Roy, 1860–1873. ASQ, Fichier des anciens du séminaire. PAC, MG 30, D62 (Audet papers), 26, pp.701–4. *Le Canadien* (Québec), 3 avril, 8 avril, 15 avril 1844; 1er mars, 13 mai 1850. *Dom ann. reg., 1880–81*, 428. Frère Éloi-Gérard, *Recueil de généalogies des comtés de Charlevoix et Saguenay depuis l'origine jusqu'à 1939* (Publ. de la SHS, 5, La Malbaie, Qué., 1941), 448. *Inventaire des contrats de mariages au greffe de Charlevoix accompagné de documents précieux se rapportant à l'histoire de Charlevoix et du Saguenay*, Frère Éloi-Gérard, édit. (Publ. de la SHS, 8, La Malbaie, Qué. 1943), 257–61; P.-G. Roy, *Les juges de la province de Québec*, 481. Léon Provancher, *Flore canadienne ou description de toutes les plantes des forêts, champs, jardins et eaux du Canada donnant le nom botanique de chacune, ses noms vulgaires français et anglais, indiquant son parcours géographique, les propriétés qui la distinguent, le mode de culture qui lui convient ...* (2v., Québec, 1862), I, iv. Percy Martin, "Le premier juge à Chicoutimi," *Saguenayensia* (Chicoutimi, Qué.), I (1959) 81–82.

RUBIDGE, CHARLES, naval officer, settler, and emigration agent; b. 30 April 1787, and baptized at London, Eng., second son of Robert Rubidge and Margaret Gilmour, and half-brother of Frederick Rubidge*; m. Margaret Clarke 20 Jan. 1810, by whom he had three sons and three daughters; d. 5 Feb. 1873.

Charles Rubidge's mother died when he was eight, and one year later he entered the Royal Navy as a volunteer first class on an uncle's ship. His far-flung naval service took him to the West

Ruttan

Indies and, in 1812, to Annapolis, Maryland. He served with the Mediterranean and Atlantic fleets in the Napoleonic campaigns, was commissioned a lieutenant in 1812, and was twice wounded on active service.

Rubidge was placed on half pay in 1815. By 1819 he saw no hope of resuming active service and emigrated to Cobourg, Upper Canada. In the spring of 1820 he took his wife and three small children to the bush to become one of the first settlers in Otonabee Township. He settled on a 200-acre lot and acquired three other lots to make up the 800 acres allowed a naval officer of his rank. As a backwoods farmer Rubidge was one of the more successful of the half-pay officers who settled in the Peterborough district. He attributed his success in the early years to a cautious beginning, to "doing little, and that partly with my own hands," until he gained experience.

It is for his connection with emigration, which began in 1825 with the arrival of Peter Robinson*'s settlers from southern Ireland, that Rubidge is best known. He assisted Robinson on a voluntary basis by placing the emigrants destined for Otonabee Township on their lots and directed the cutting of ten miles of bush road, briefly named after him, to serve as a winter supply route to the depot on the townsite of Peterborough. In common with several others he received a town and a park lot in Peterborough for his exertions.

From 1831 until August 1832 Rubidge held a temporary appointment as a crown land agent at Peterborough with responsibility for seven townships in neighbouring parts of Newcastle District; he claimed that 4,000 new emigrants came to the district while he held this office. His duties as agent included supervision of the assistance given poor settlers at Lieutenant Governor Sir John Colborne*'s direction.

In 1838 Rubidge visited England and wrote *A plain statement of the advantages attending emigration to Upper Canada*, in which he stated that improvements over the past few years had demonstrated "that Canada is destined to become the comparatively rich as well as the poor man's country," and offered practical advice to those who decided to emigrate. The following spring Colonel G. F. Wyndham employed Rubidge to superintend the voyage of 181 emigrants from his Irish estates to Cobourg and to find work for them in Upper Canada.

Rubidge played an active role in the community that grew up around him: he was appointed a justice of the peace in 1820, with his neighbours he petitioned for local improvements and helped raise funds for the Church of England, and he was chosen as a returning officer in four elections. He gave up active farming in 1841 when he was appointed registrar for the county of Peterborough, a post he held for more than 30 years. He was also promoted retired commander in the Royal Navy on 12 Oct. 1841, and in 1853 he received a Greenwich Hospital out-pension.

Rubidge's experience enabled him to speak with authority to those interested in assisting the emigration of paupers. Sir Robert John Wilmot-Horton printed information and opinions supplied by Rubidge in his *Ireland and Canada* (1839). Eight years later Rubidge gave evidence on backwoods settlement and assisted emigration to the 1847 select committee of the House of Lords on colonization from Ireland.

Rubidge indirectly influenced the writing of the history of his district. Thomas Poole* set a pattern in 1867, followed by others, when he relied on Rubidge for material describing Robinson's emigrants and when he reflected Rubidge's opinion in assessing the manner in which they were settled.

WENDY CAMERON

Charles Rubidge was the author of *An autobiographical sketch* (Peterborough, Ont., 1870); *A plain statement of the advantages attending emigration to Upper Canada* (London, 1838); "Report of Lieutenant Rubidge," *Canadian, British American and West Indian Magazine* (London), I (1839), 375–78.

PAO, RG 1, A-I-6, 6, 8–9, 11–13; RG 21, sect.A, Census and assessment rolls, Newcastle District, Otonabee Township. PRO, CO 42/393, 42/394. G.B., Adm., *Navy list* (London), 1813, 1863. G.B., Parl., House of Lords paper, 1847, VI, 737, pp.547–62, *Report of the select committee of the House of Lords on colonization from Ireland*. . . . Basil Hall, *Travels in North America, in the years 1827 and 1828* (3v., Edinburgh, 1829), I, 325–39. *Valley of the Trent* (Guillet). R. J. Wilmot-Horton, *Ireland and Canada; supported by local evidence* (London, 1839). *Directory of the united counties of Peterborough & Victoria for 1858 . . .* (Peterborough, C.W., [1858]). T. W. Poole, *A sketch of the early settlement and subsequent progress of the town of Peterborough, and of each township in the county of Peterborough* (Peterborough, Ont., 1867).

RUTTAN, HENRY, soldier, businessman, legislator, author, and inventor; b. 12 June 1792 at Adolphustown, U.C., son of William Ruttan, a United Empire Loyalist of French ancestry, and of Margaret Steele; d. 31 July 1871 at Cobourg, Ont.

Henry Ruttan's formal schooling, which was obtained at Adolphustown, ended at 14 when he left home to become a store assistant in Kingston. His boyhood on a farm being developed from the wilderness was, he later wrote, remarkably healthy and provided him with a robust constitution. During the War of 1812 Ruttan joined the militia, was commissioned, and served in Upper Canada. In 1814 he was severely wounded in the bitter fighting at Lundy's Lane, but he returned to active service before the war ended. He continued to serve in the militia, in the 1st Battalion of Northumberland and after 1825, when he became colonel, in the 3rd Battalion. He left the active militia in 1846 but was recalled in 1860 to command the 4th Military District until 1862.

In 1815 Ruttan went into business in Cobourg. He was elected to the House of Assembly in 1820 as the representative for Northumberland, and served until 1824. During his second term, 1836–40, he was influential in having the Trent Canal started, and he replaced Allan MacNab* as speaker of the house from 28 Dec. 1837 to 24 Jan. 1838. Appointed in 1827 sheriff of the Newcastle District (which became in 1849 the United Counties of Northumberland and Durham), he held that office for 30 years; he also served on the Board of Agriculture for Upper Canada.

His autobiography, written in 1861, deals with the history of his family and with his experiences in war and in politics. It unaccountably makes no mention of his studies, perhaps the most comprehensive hitherto undertaken, of problems in the heating and ventilation of buildings or of his related inventions.

The conservation of fuel and the proper ventilation of houses were impossible to achieve with the inefficient fireplaces and stoves then in use. Ruttan began to design air heaters and ventilating equipment, for which he was granted seven patents between 1846 and 1858. His method, extensively used, for the combined heating and ventilation of buildings involved drawing in outside air through a duct. The air then passed by natural flow through a heater and circulated by convection through the various rooms, finally to flow through a duct to a foul-air shaft which sent it outside.

Ruttan also devised a system for the heating and ventilation of railway coaches. Outside air, forced through ducts into the cars by means of the train's motion, passed through a wash tank which cleaned, humidified, and cooled it. In the winter the system was modified to heat the air entering the cars. Ruttan's system, probably the first to provide an air-conditioned vehicle, was used by several railways in Canada and the United States.

In 1816 Ruttan married Mary Jones. They had nine children of whom Henry Jones continued his father's interests in ventilation and was editor of the Cobourg *Star* from 1846 to 1855. In his 68th year Henry Ruttan was thrown from a carriage and suffered injuries from which he never fully recovered. Stricken six years later by a disease which gradually undermined his health, he died in his 80th year, thus ending the many-faceted and useful life of an intelligent man of good character.

T. RITCHIE

PAC, MG 24, K2 (Coventry papers), 11, "Reminiscences of the Hon. Henry Ruttan of Cobourg," pp.361–82. Other versions, with some changes, of this autobiography are: "Autobiography of the Honorable Henry Ruttan of Cobourg, Upper Canada," copied by C. E. Thomson, United Empire Loyalists Assoc. of Ont., *Trans.*, II (1899), 75–84; and *Loyalist narratives from Upper Canada* (Talman), 296–311. Henry Ruttan, *Lectures on the ventilation of buildings, delivered at the Cobourg Mechanics' Institute* (Cobourg, C.W., 1848); *Lecture on ventilation, delivered before the Cobourg Mechanics' Institute ... Feb'y 22, 1858* (Cobourg, C.W., 1858); *Ventilation and warming of buildings ...* (New York, 1862). *Cobourg Sentinel*, 12 Aug. 1871.

Armstrong, *Handbook of Upper Canadian chronology. Can. biog. dict.*, I, 729–30. Morgan, *Bibliotheca Canadensis*, 329. *Patents of Canada*, I, nos.210, 222, 225, 244; II, no.311. Wallace, *Macmillan dictionary*, 659. E. C. Guillet, *Cobourg, 1798–1948* (Oshawa, Ont., 1948), 23–25, 56.

RYAN, JAMES, labour leader; fl. 1872.

James Ryan was corresponding secretary and moving spirit of the Nine Hour League in Hamilton when, on 20 Feb. 1872, 120 men struck a Hamilton sewing-machine factory, Wilson, Lockman and Company, over demands for a nine-hour day. Ryan had probably been named to this position at a mass meeting of delegates from various Hamilton shops on 1 February to appoint officers and adopt a constitution for the league, the first in Canada. On 24 February he spoke to another mass meeting of "sixteen or eighteen hundred men" in support of the strike. He said that the workingmen were willing to settle by arbitration, but that they would resort to other means if forced to do so. The strike ended on 27 February by a "mutual understanding," which Toronto *Globe* editor George BROWN called a victory for the employers. Ryan's actions in Hamilton and his correspondence with the Toronto Trades Assembly encouraged that group to start its own nine-hour movement, which resulted in a printers' strike throughout Toronto in March 1872.

Ryan held a "Council of deliberation" in Hamilton on 3 May to gain support for a proposed demonstration on 15 May. There were 12 delegates from Hamilton, three from Toronto, and one each from Montreal, Brantford, and Dundas, as well as supporting letters from several other Ontario communities; a Toronto delegate called it the first labour convention in Canada. The council formed the Canadian Labor Protective and Mutual Improvement Association with the purpose of forming "similar local organizations throughout the Dominion for the purpose of uniting all classes of workmen for mutual benefit." Ryan was made recording secretary of the new association. Nothing further is known about his life.

BERNARD OSTRY

Canadian Labour Congress Library (Ottawa), Toronto Trades Assembly minutes, 18 April 1872–27 March 1873. *Globe* (Toronto), 1 Jan.–1 July 1872. *The Hamilton and District Trades and Labor Council, T.L.C.–A.F. of L.; 60th anniversary, diamond jubilee, 1888–1948* (n.p., n.d.). Eugene Forsey, "The Toronto Trades Assembly, 1871–1878," *Canadian Labour* (Ottawa), X (July–August 1965), 21–22; X (September 1965), 32–33. Bernard Ostry, "Conservatives, Liberals, and labour in the 1870's," *CHR*, XLI (1960), 93–127.

RYERSON, JOHN, Methodist minister; b. at Charlotteville, Norfolk County, U.C., 12 June 1800, fourth son of Colonel Joseph Ryerson*, a loyalist of Dutch and Huguenot ancestry, and of Sophia Mehetabel Stickney; m. Mary Lewis in 1828 by whom he had a son and a daughter; d. 8 Oct. 1878, at Simcoe, Ont.

Five of Colonel Ryerson's six sons entered the Methodist ministry despite his strong disapproval. After serving with his father as a volunteer on special service during the War of 1812, John was converted to Methodism in the evangelical awakening which followed the war in Upper Canada as were his two older brothers George* and William RYERSON and, subsequently, his two younger brothers Egerton* and Edwy. In 1820 he began preaching as supply and in 1821 he was received on trial on the Ancaster circuit. Two years later, on the Yonge Street circuit, he was ordained deacon and in 1825, on the Perth circuit, elder. In the ensuing years he served as presiding elder, chairman, or superintendent of almost every circuit or district in the province, and in 1843 he was elected president of the Wesleyan Methodist Church in Canada. Subsequently, for nine consecutive years from 1849 to 1857, he was elected co-delegate, or vice-president, of the church, which was then, under the terms of reunion with the British conference, the highest post to which his colleagues in the Canadian conference could elect him.

John took, with his brothers William and Egerton, an active part in resolving many of the issues which confronted the Methodists in Upper Canada, particularly during the period from the mid-1820s to the mid-1850s. He was a leader in the fight, which he described as "a desperate struggle,"

against the schismatic body of Methodists, led by Henry Ryan*. At the same time, he advocated the separation of the church in Upper Canada from the American Methodist Episcopal Church of which it was then a part; as one of five delegates from the Canada conference to the American general conference in Pittsburgh in 1828, he was instrumental in bringing about the amicable separation that year which resulted in the establishment of an independent Methodist Episcopal Church in Canada [see RICHARDSON]. In 1832 he proposed a union with the British conference of the Wesleyan Methodist Church to avoid wasteful competition and duplication of effort, and to affirm the essential loyalty of the Canadian Methodists. The Wesleyan Methodist Church in Canada was formed but the union collapsed in 1840. He again expressed concern at the harm done by having two rival Methodist bodies and urged another attempt at union. In 1846 he and Anson GREEN were chosen delegates to the British conference where they successfully advocated this cause.

John, William, and three others were asked in 1829 to study the advisability of establishing a Methodist seminary of higher learning and, in 1830, he and William were named to a new committee to further the project. It selected Cobourg as the site for the Upper Canada Academy, which later became Victoria College. In 1835 John was made one of the first five visitors to the college; they were given the responsibility of working with the trustees in appointing the principal and teachers, drafting regulations, managing the affairs of the institution, and reporting upon its academic and financial state each year to the conference. In 1841 he was, with William and Egerton, among those who petitioned the Legislative Assembly for a charter and an endowment for the college. Throughout these years, when the college was in financial difficulties and its survival sometimes in doubt, John signed notes on its behalf, borrowing money on his personal credit to meet its indebtedness even though these debts were incurred against his advice. He continued for more than three decades to work actively for the college, serving terms as treasurer and chairman of the board.

The modest extent of John's own formal education is reflected in his remarkably colourful and imaginative spelling. But his qualities of intellectual distinction and his feeling for language are unmistakable. At the 1837 conference John was named, as were William and Egerton, to the Book and Printing Committee, forerunner of the Ryerson Press, which supervised the publishing of the *Christian Guardian*, in that period the most widely read and influential newspaper in Canada, and of other productions, as well as overseeing the sale of books from Britain and the United States of interest to Upper Canadian Methodists. John served as book steward from 1837 to 1841.

The range of John's intellectual and literary interests is, however, more substantially indicated by his own writing which included an extensive correspondence, diaries and journals, and numerous notes and papers on Methodist history and policy. Although much of this material remains unpublished, or has been misplaced, a good deal of his writing was apparently published without attribution, perhaps because of an aversion which John had to seeing his own name in print. His name appears, however, at the head of five of the 18 chapters of *Canadian Methodism; its epochs and characteristics*, and it may well be that this book was really the work of John, annotated by Egerton and published in his name in compliance with his brother's wishes. John's book, *Hudson's Bay; or, a missionary tour in the territory of the Hon. Hudson's Bay Company . . .*, published in 1855, which records the perilous expedition he led the previous year from Sault Ste Marie to Hudson Bay, *via* Red River, and from there to England, furnishes the most accurate and reliable account available of this early trade route. The expedition was made with a view to the assumption by the Canadian Methodist Church of responsibility for missionary activity in the area. He described the promise of parts of this land and, in contrast to some other writers of the period, looked ahead to its settlement and development with confident enthusiasm.

It was characteristic of John to undertake so difficult a journey in his 55th year. Throughout his life he worked to excess and he was frequently exhausted by these exertions, with a consequent strain on his health. This strain and chronic ill-health led him to some dependence at times, in particular immediately following his journey, upon opium and brandy, which aroused acute concern amongst his Methodist brethren. At the conference of 1858, which had in any case an under-current of hostility towards the Ryerson brothers, a committee of ten was appointed to investigate his character and its report resulted in his being "left without a station" and his name being "dropped from the Minutes of Conference for One Year." In the following year he was restored to his accustomed place, however, and chosen a member of the special committee entrusted with conference business between the annual sessions. From 1860 until his death he was superannuated at Brantford and at Simcoe, continuing an active work in the ministry despite his precarious health.

John was in age and affection the brother nearest to Egerton who, in the years when his career was in the making, never took a step without consulting "this brother who commanded his entire respect and affection." Egerton, writing in 1843, records that he regarded John as "for many years the most cool and accurate judge of the state of the public mind" of any man he knew in Canada. Described by Egerton as "a life-long Conservative," John was the principal architect of the strategy advocated by Egerton and, in general, followed by the Methodists, of support for loyal reform, within the constitution, aimed at civil and religious liberty. In the difficult period before the 1837 rebellion he cautioned Egerton constantly to "take good care not to lean a hair's breadth toward Radicleism." He repeatedly expressed concern that the Methodists had become too much associated with extreme Reformers, "a banditti of compleat vagabonds," so that it was "absolutely necessary to disengage ourselves from them entirely. You can see that it is not Reform, but Revolution they are after." He rejoiced that in the critical 1836 elections not "a ninny of them was elected in the Bay of Quinte District" where "the preachers and I laboured to the utmost extent of our ability to keep every scamp of them out and we succeeded."

Nevertheless John was far from being a stern and unbending Tory. Once the rebellion had been coped with, he renewed his advocacy of constitutional reform and urged the Methodists to pursue "the enlightened, just and liberal course we have been wont to persue." He signed and presented to Lieutenant Governor Sir George Arthur* a petition, on behalf of some 4,000 signators, asking that the lives of the rebels Samuel Lount* and Peter Mathews* be spared and when the petition was rejected he followed the two men to their execution. Similarly, in the wake of the rebellion, he protested arbitrary measures including the indiscriminate keeping of scores of persons in prison awaiting trial. He felt it necessary for "the friends of Civil and Religious liberty" to remain vigilant, noting that "it is a great blessing that Mackenzey [William Lyon Mackenzie*] and Radicalism are down, but we are in immediate danger of being brought under the domination of a military and high-church *oligarchy*, which would be equally bad if not infinitely worse."

Often seemingly aloof, austere, and taciturn in public, John was in the privacy of his family and friendships warm, kindly, and forthcoming. In C. B. Sissons*' assessment, "Seldom has a Canadian home produced four such men as George, William, John and Egerton Ryerson. Differing in character and talent, they all had upon them the

Ryerson

mark of greatness." Of the brothers, John was pre-eminently the statesman and the practical man of public and ecclesiastical affairs. He was for several decades probably the most influential man in the councils of the Methodist Church in Upper Canada.

THOMAS H. B. SYMONS

John Ryerson, *Hudson's Bay; or, a missionary tour in the territory of the Hon. Hudson's Bay Company* . . . (Toronto, 1855).

Methodist Missionary Society (London), Correspondence, continent of America. UCA, A. E. Ryerson papers. John Carroll, *Case and his cotemporaries*; [ ] *Past and present, or a description of persons and events connected with Canadian Methodism for the last forty years* (Toronto, 1860). *Christian Guardian* (Toronto), 1829–78. [Ryerson], *Story of my life* (Hodgins). Cornish, *Cyclopædia of Methodism*, I. *Dom. ann. reg.*, 1878, 364–65.

G. S. French, *Parsons & politics: the rôle of the Wesleyan Methodists in Upper Canada and the Maritimes from 1780 to 1855* (Toronto, 1962). G. F. Playter, *The history of Methodism in Canada: with an account of the rise and progress of the work of God among the Canadian Indian tribes, and occasional notices of the civil affairs of the province* (Toronto, 1862). A. E. Ryerson, *Canadian Methodism: its epochs and characteristics* (Toronto, 1882). A. W. Ryerson, *The Ryerson genealogy; genealogy and history of the Knickerbocker families of Ryerson, Ryerse, Ryerss; also Adriance and Martense families; all descendants of Martin and Adriaen Ryerz (Reyerszen), of Amsterdam, Holland*, ed. A. L. Holman (Chicago, 1916). Sissons, *Ryerson*. Clara Thomas, *Ryerson of Upper Canada* (Toronto, 1969).

RYERSON, WILLIAM, Methodist minister; b. at Maugerville, N.B., 31 March 1797, third son of Colonel Joseph Ryerson* and Sophia Mehetabel Stickney; m. Mary Griffen, and they had three sons and three daughters; d. 15 Sept. 1872 at Salt Springs near Brantford, Ont.

William Ryerson's formal education was confined to the log schoolhouse near the family farm in Norfolk County, Upper Canada. He served as a volunteer on special service with his father during the War of 1812, and was converted to Methodism by David Youmans in the religious awakening which followed the war. His conversion incurred the strong displeasure of his father and he left home, moving to Oxford County where he started bush farming. He was received on trial as a preacher at the Methodist Episcopal conference of 1823 and was ordained deacon on the Queenston circuit in 1825.

William rapidly assumed responsibility in his church, serving as a presiding elder, chairman, and superintendent in various districts throughout the province. The outline of powers given to quarterly meetings in all matters of general importance which he prepared with his brother Egerton* in 1828 was adopted by the church conference and remained in use with little change for decades. In the same year he was chosen a delegate to the conference of the American church at Pittsburgh, where he argued successfully for the separation of the Canadian church from its American parent. He collected funds for Egerton's trip to England in 1833 to arrange the union between the Canadian church and the British Wesleyan Methodist Church; when this union disintegrated he made, with Egerton, a trip to England in 1840 in a final attempt to salvage it, and presented to the British conference, to no avail, the address and resolutions of the Canada conference. While in London, William and Egerton also met with Lord John Russell to remonstrate unsuccessfully against his clergy reserves bill.

Collapse of the union with the British church opened the way for the Canada conference to choose its own head, and William was elected the first Canadian president of the Wesleyan Methodist Church in Canada in 1840. He was chosen president a second time at the annual conference of 1847 which approved reunion with the British church, subsequently yielding the office to Robert ALDER, the first appointee by the British conference under the terms of the reunion. He was thus both the first and the last of the presidents elected by the Canadian church during its period of autonomy between 1840 and 1847.

Despite frequent ill-health, including periodic bouts with "bleeding of the lungs," William worked prodigiously throughout his life. During the early years of his ministry he was particularly interested in the Indian peoples, assisting with the planning and operation of special Indian schools and often joining with the Reverend Peter Jones* in missions to the Indians at which he preached and Jones acted as interpreter. He was instrumental in arranging for the Bible to be translated into Chippewa and for the preparation of spelling and hymn books in several Indian tongues. In 1829 he was named to the committee which oversaw the establishment of the *Christian Guardian*. In the same year, he and his brother JOHN were put on a committee to study the advisability of establishing a Methodist seminary of higher learning. The following year the two brothers were named to a committee given the task of establishing the Upper Canada Academy (later Victoria College).

William's relations with Egerton were not as close as those of John. Nonetheless, he was an influential mentor to Egerton in his earlier years.

His political views, as a constitutional liberal leaning somewhat towards radicalism, more nearly coincided with those of his fellow Methodist ministers than did those of either John or Egerton. Though William helped defend Toronto at John MONTGOMERY's tavern against William Lyon Mackenzie* and the rebels in December 1837, he asked that the punishment of Samuel Lount* and Peter Mathews* be mitigated, and he deplored the role of Sir Francis Bond HEAD, noting that "the *most* guilty author of these miseries is to escape without punishment, yes, with *honour and praise* . . . !" Weary of political and religious factionalism, he briefly contemplated emigration to the United States after the suppression of the rebellion.

William was, however, always interested in politics, and in 1861 he ran as an independent candidate for the West Riding of Brant in response to appeals by members of his church who were anxious that his views should be expressed in the legislature on the question of university reform. He won, defeating Herbert Biggar, despite the vigorous opposition of George BROWN and the *Globe*. He was, however, badly beaten in the next election, in 1863, by Edmund Burke Wood*, probably because of the support he gave to Richard William Scott*'s separate school bill, for which he was again bitterly denounced by Brown. He had retired to his farm at Salt Springs, superannuated, in 1858, and he continued to live there until his death.

William was the orator of the Ryerson brothers and indeed was one of Canadian Methodism's most renowned preachers. His forthright manner and strength of feeling, coupled with his wit and good humour, enabled him to establish a powerful sympathetic bond with his listeners. In many ways the prototype saddle-bag preacher of pioneer Upper Canadian Methodism, he excelled in the setting of the camp meeting, and was gifted in organizing these gatherings.

THOMAS H. B. SYMONS

Methodist Missionary Society (London), Correspondence, continent of America. UCA, A. E. Ryerson papers. John Carroll, *Case and his cotemporaries*; [ ], *Past and present, or a description of persons and events connected with Canadian Methodism for the last forty years* (Toronto, 1860). *Christian Guardian* (Toronto), 1829–72. [Ryerson], *Story of my life* (Hodgins). Cornish, *Cyclopædia of Methodism*, I. *Dom. ann. reg., 1878*, 364–65.

G. S. French, *Parsons & politics: the rôle of the Wesleyan Methodists in Upper Canada and the Maritimes from 1780 to 1855* (Toronto, 1962). G. F. Playter, *The history of Methodism in Canada: with an account of the rise and progress of the work of God among the Canadian Indian tribes, and occasional notices of the civil affairs of the province* (Toronto, 1862). A. E. Ryerson, *Canadian Methodism; its epochs and characteristics* (Toronto, 1882). A. W. Ryerson, *The Ryerson genealogy; a genealogy and history of the Knickerbocker families of Ryerson, Ryerse, Ryerss; also Adriance and Martense families; all descendants of Martin and Adriaen Ryerz (Reyerszen), of Amsterdam, Holland*, ed. A. L. Holman (Chicago, 1916). Sissons, *Ryerson*. Clara Thomas, *Ryerson of Upper Canada* (Toronto, 1969).

S

SAINCENNES, JACQUES-FÉLIX. *See* SINCENNES

SANBORN, JOHN SEWELL, teacher, politician, and judge; b. 1 Jan. 1819 at Gilmanton, N.H., ninth and youngest child of David Edwin Sanborn, farmer and teacher, and Hannah Hook; d. 17 July 1877, at Asbury Park, N.J.

In 1842 John Sewell Sanborn graduated from Dartmouth College, New Hampshire, where his brother, Edwin David, was professor of Latin language and literature. He later received the degrees of AM (1845) and LLD (1874) from Dartmouth, and of MA (*ad eundem*, 1854) and DCL (1873) from the University of Bishop's College, Lennoxville. After 1842, Sanborn was for three years principal of the Sherbrooke Academy (now high school). He then read law in Sherbrooke with Edward SHORT and in Montreal with ANDREW and George Robertson; he was admitted to the bar in 1847 and, returning to Sherbrooke, married in July Eleanor Hall Brooks, daughter of Samuel Brooks, Conservative member of the Legislative Assembly for the old Sherbrooke County. Throughout his political career he continued to practise law.

Brooks died in March 1849, and the parliamentary vacancy was filled by Alexander Tilloch Galt*, commissioner of the British American Land Company in the Eastern Townships. In November Galt proclaimed himself an annexationist, and in January 1850 resigned his seat, implying that his attitude had been criticized by his company and that he disapproved of moving the seat of government from Montreal to Toronto. Sanborn was nominated to contest the by-election as an annexationist, both he and Galt believing that annexation would bring greater prosperity to the Eastern Townships. Their agitation undoubtedly influenced the ministry to give strong backing

Sanborn

to the projected railroad, pushed by Galt and Sanborn, from Montreal through Richmond and Sherbrooke to Portland, Maine, thus promising the region the advantages of annexation without the political formality.

Sherbrooke County in 1850 included not the town but the present counties of Richmond, Wolfe, Compton, and Frontenac; only 15 per cent of the population was French Canadian. Sanborn was opposed by Chester B. Cleveland of Shipton, who was nominated by John Henry Pope*, at this time an anti-annexationist farmer in the southern part of the county and now beginning his long political career. Both candidates were born in the United States and had had personal connections with members of the Tory party, but whereas Sanborn was a liberal Congregationalist living amidst the business "aristocracy" of the town, Cleveland was a rural "Episcopalian" (Church of England), residing in the constituency. The Reform ministry of Louis-Hippolyte La Fontaine* publicly supported Cleveland the "Loyalist," and during the campaign stripped the county's annexationists of their public commissions. Privately, however, Sanborn, as a promoter with Galt of the St Lawrence and Atlantic Railroad, had business connections with the speaker of the assembly, Augustin-Norbert Morin*, and his friend, George-Étienne Cartier. Sanborn appealed for Liberal support.

At the by-election, on 5 and 6 March 1850, Sanborn obtained 51 per cent of the vote. Lord Elgin [Bruce*] reported that "this is the first instance in which a person avowing these doctrines has been elected to the Canadian Parliament," and explained it by the number of American settlers in the area and the activities of Galt, chief agent "of a body of absentee English proprietors," the "selfish traitors" of the British American Land Company.

Sanborn was introduced to the house in Toronto on 14 May by two Eastern Townships oppositionists, who had also introduced Galt in 1849 – William Badgley*, the former Tory attorney general, and John McConnell of Stanstead, a Conservative turned annexationist. On 17 May, Sanborn, McConnell, and Louis-Joseph Papineau were among seven members who voted against Robert Baldwin*'s motion not to receive a petition brought by John Prince*, member for Essex, calling upon Canada "to become an Independent Sovereignty." In the general election of 1851 Sanborn was opposed by John Henry Pope himself, but greatly increased his majority. A month before the election the new railroad had been opened to Richmond. At his nomination he stated that the annexation question was "nowhere mooted in the

Province," and added "requiescat in pace." In an 1853 by-election he helped secure the election of Galt for Sherbrooke Town.

No longer opposed by the ministry, who were prepared to forget the annexationist agitation, Sanborn supported advanced liberal proposals, but not radical opposition for its own sake. In June 1854 he voted against the vague motions by which Conservative and Liberal opposition members combined to defeat the Francis Hincks*– Morin government. An immediate dissolution followed. In the election, Sherbrooke County having been divided, Sanborn contested Compton, bordering on the United States. But in Compton lived his relentless Tory opponent, John Henry Pope, who ran as a farmer, denouncing the Sherbrooke "family compact and the oppression of the British American Land Company." Sanborn won but only by eight votes.

In September 1854, Galt and Sanborn voted for Cartier, ministerial candidate for speaker. But upon his defeat they joined the section of the opposition led by William Lyon Mackenzie* and George Brown. They participated in the final destruction of the Hincks-Morin administration but denounced the succeeding Allan Napier Mac-Nab*–Morin (or Liberal-Conservative) combination as "an utter abandonment of principle."

Upon the creation of elective seats for the Legislative Council in 1856, Sanborn and Pope each nominated a candidate for Wellington, a new division including the town of Sherbrooke and a surrounding area even larger than the original county. Sanborn's man, Hollis Smith, won for the Liberal opposition in spite of a bitter personal attack on Sanborn by the provincial secretary, Timothy Lee Terrill.

In the general election of 1857, Sanborn and Galt parted company politically. Galt suddenly dissociated himself from the Grit-Rouge party, promised not to endeavour to overthrow the administration, and was re-elected by acclamation in Sherbrooke. But Sanborn remained in opposition, and allowed Compton to go by acclamation to Pope. In contrast to 1854, George-Étienne Cartier's party would this time have helped Sanborn's Tory opponent in the closely balanced constituency.

The death of Hollis Smith enabled Sanborn to enter the Legislative Council for Wellington by acclamation on 8 May 1863. The John Sandfield Macdonald–Antoine-Aimé Dorion* government, formed a few days later, offered Sanborn the post of solicitor general east, but he declined; he preferred to remain a private member and a practising advocate. On 15 Aug. 1863, he was created queen's counsel by the same ministry, and was re-elected by acclamation to the Legislative Council on 27 Sept. 1864 for a regular term.

In the confederation debate of 1865, Sanborn proposed an amendment calling for an elective senate, which was defeated 18–42. Although he viewed confederation favourably, he would not vote for the measure "unless after it had been submitted to the country." He abstained on the main motion, warning that "the power of the local governments" (that is, provincial governments), which might not respect their minorities in matters of property and civil rights, was "an apple of discord which our posterity might gather in fruits of the most bitter character." However in 1867 he was almost automatically appointed to the Senate for Wellington, and on 1 July was the official orator in Sherbrooke.

In July 1872 his law partner since 1858, Edward Towle Brooks, brother of his first wife, succeeded Galt as Conservative member for the federal constituency of Sherbrooke, and on 12 Oct. Sanborn's political career ended with his appointment by the Conservative government to the Superior Court for the district of Saint-François, at Sherbrooke; he was proud of the fact that this nomination had been made by his political opponent, Sir John A. Macdonald*. On 6 March 1874 his old friend, A.-A. Dorion, in the new Liberal government, promoted him to the Court of Queen's Bench in Montreal. He died while vacationing in the United States and his funeral service, appropriately for the only person ever elected to the Canadian parliament as an annexationist, was held at the American Presbyterian (now Erskine and American United) Church in Montreal.

Sanborn was a characteristic New England Calvinist – a deacon in the Congregational (now Plymouth United) Church in Sherbrooke, president of the Temperance and Prohibitory League of Quebec, full of good works and charity towards the poor, president of the Sherbrooke Library Association, thoroughly democratic in outlook, highly successful in business, a champion of the rights of private property and throughout his life a progressive continentalist. A Liberal living until 1874 in a town which after 1854 was overwhelmingly Conservative, he was fortunate in having close personal connections in both parties.

John Sewell Sanborn's first wife died in 1853, leaving three children; their only son died unmarried. His second wife, Nancy Judson Hasseltine, of Bradford, Mass., whom he married in 1856, died in 1874, leaving one daughter.

GORDON O. ROTHNEY

PAC, RG 4, B37, 5, A.-N. Morin to B. C. A. Gugy, 19 Feb. 1852; RG 31, A1, 1851, no.423, ff.2, 13. PRO, CO 42/565, 42/662. University of Bishop's College, Registrar's Office, official records of degrees granted. [Bruce and Grey], *Elgin-Grey papers* (Doughty), II, 604. Lower Canada, *Statutes*, 1829, c.73. Canada, Province of, Legislative Assembly, *Journals*, 1848, 1850, 1854, 1854–55. Canada, Province of, *Statutes*, 1853, c.152. *Montreal Courier*, 9 Nov. 1849; 16, 30 Jan., 8, 13, 18, 22 Feb., 4 March 1850. *Montreal Daily Witness*, 28 Dec. 1874; 18, 19 July 1877. *Montreal Gazette*, 7, 18 Jan., 13 Feb., 1 March 1850; 17 Dec. 1851; 8 Aug., 18 Sept. 1854; 19 July 1877. *Montreal Herald*, 28 May 1863, 19 July 1877. *Montreal Transcript*, 21 May 1850; 23 Sept., 1 Oct. 1856; 8, 28 Dec. 1857. *Pilot and Journal of Commerce* (Montreal), 18 May 1850, 26 Dec. 1854. *Le Pionnier de Sherbrooke*, 6 juill. 1867. *Quebec Gazette*, 16 Sept. 1854. *Sherbrooke Gazette*, 8 Jan. 1853; 22, 29 July, 23 Sept. 1854; 26 Jan. 1861; 10 Sept., 1 Oct. 1864.

Appleton's cyclopædia of American biography, ed. J. G. Wilson *et al.* (10v., New York, 1887–1924), V. *The Canadian men and women of the time: a handbook of Canadian biography*, ed. H. J. Morgan (1st ed., Toronto, 1898). *A catalogue of the officers and students of Dartmouth College, September 1838* (1st ed., Windsor, Vt., 1838). *A catalogue of the officers and students of Dartmouth College, 1838–39* (2nd ed., Concord, N.H., 1838). *DAB. Political appointments, 1841–1865* (J.-O. Coté). P.-G. Roy, *Les juges de la province de Québec*, 81, 493. Turcotte, *Conseil législatif de Québec*, 297.

C. D. Allin and G. M. Jones, *Annexation, preferential trade and reciprocity; an outline of the Canadian annexation movement of 1849–1850, with special reference to the questions of preferential trade and reciprocity* (Toronto and London, 1912), 193–95, 266–327. L. S. Channell, *History of Compton County and sketches of the Eastern Townships, district of St Francis, and Sherbrooke County* (Cookshire, Que., 1896). G. T. Chapman, *Sketches of the alumni of Dartmouth College, from the first graduation in 1771 to the present time, with a brief history of the institution* (Cambridge, Mass., 1867). Edward Cleveland, *A sketch of the early settlement and history of Shipton, Canada East* (Sherbrooke, C.E., 1858). *Plymouth Church, past and present; a brief history of Plymouth United Church, Sherbrooke, Quebec* (Sherbrooke, Que., 1956). L. B. Richardson, *History of Dartmouth College* (Hanover, N.H., 1932), 573. J. G. Robertson, *Sketch of the formation of the Congregational Church at Sherbrooke and Lennoxville* (Sherbrooke, Que., 1890), 4–6. V. C. Sanborn, *Genealogy of the family of Samborne or Sanborn in England and America, 1194–1898* (Concord, N.H., 1899). O. D. Skelton, *The life and times of Sir Alexander Tilloch Galt* (Toronto, 1920).

SAUNDERS, JOHN SIMCOE, lawyer, legislator, and public servant; b. in 1795 at Fredericton, N.B., son of John Saunders*, a judge of the Supreme Court and later chief justice of New Brunswick, and Arianna Margaretta Jekyll Chalmers; d. 27 July 1878 at Fredericton, N.B.

John Simcoe Saunders' father had distinguished himself in the American Revolution as an officer of the Queen's American Rangers under the command of Colonel John Graves Simcoe*; he consequently enjoyed the benefit of high official connections in England. With this patrician background, young Saunders was a scion of the slender loyalist aristocracy of the new province of New Brunswick. In his youth he received many benefits from his family's position; in his later years his career can be explained by the declining importance of the colonial aristocracy.

Young Saunders was sent to school in England under the supervision of his maternal grandfather, James Chalmers, who had commanded the Maryland loyalists during the American Revolution. After a higher education at Oxford and Lincoln's Inn, Saunders returned to Fredericton where he was called to the bar in 1817. Finding his profession unrewarding, he returned to London and studied law with the eminent pleader, Joseph Chitty. In 1828 he published *The law of pleadings and evidence in civil actions*, a work that enjoyed rapid sale and was reprinted several times in the United States. In New Brunswick there was a rumour, probably caused by envy, that the work was really Chitty's, that for some unknown reason the teacher preferred to publish the book under the pupil's name. Sometime during this period Saunders married his first cousin, Elizabeth Sophia Storie of Camberwell, Surrey; they had a son and a daughter.

During this London residence Saunders conducted an interesting correspondence with friends and relatives in Fredericton. His exchanges with his boyhood friend, Henry BLISS, reveal a sophisticated amusement with, and a mild contempt for, the decaying rural aristocracy of his native province. His letters to his father, who was the greatest landowner in the colony, poke fun at the judge's conviction that real estate eventually would produce a fortune and that a great agricultural property, fashioned after the family's lost estate in Princess Anne County, Virginia, could be created. More abreast with current commercial development than his father, Saunders believed that agriculture in New Brunswick had no future. One of his prophecies was that by 1947 New Brunswick would be Acadian once again.

In 1830 he again returned to Fredericton and, favoured by family connection, enjoyed for many years a number of public offices. Because of his superior education, he was at once appointed master of the rolls, but the legislature would provide no salary for the post. In 1833, when the government was reorganized, he was made a member of both the Executive and the Legislative Council, and in 1834 became advocate general.

None of these appointments gave much financial reward, but from 1840 to 1843, during the temporary disgrace of Thomas Baillie*, Saunders held the lucrative post of surveyor general. After the death of the provincial secretary, William Franklin Odell*, and during the controversy over Sir William Colebrooke*'s appointment of his son-in-law, Alfred Reade, to the vacant post, Saunders fell heir in 1845 to the office of provincial secretary. He was the last man to hold this position before it became subject to political tenure with the advent of responsible government in 1848.

Saunders' resignation in 1848 provides the key to his character. According to the testimony of the lieutenant governor, Sir Edmund Head*, Saunders was a scholarly man who could not bring himself to the disagreeable necessity of fighting a popular election. Since the fortunes of the new government would depend on its ability to keep the confidence of the House of Assembly, he could not be a source of strength. Until his death he continued to play a minor official and political role, serving as clerk of the circuits until 1867 and president of the Legislative Council until 1878.

Saunders was an astute man financially; his estate included stock in several banks and insurance companies as well as property in New Brunswick and England. He also left a collection of "minerals and geological specimens" to his son. Able, scholarly, and somewhat cynical, the product of an era of aristocratic domination, John Simcoe Saunders was not equipped temperamentally for the period of greater popular participation in government.

W. S. MacNutt

University of New Brunswick Library, Archives and Special Collections Department. Saunders papers, correspondence and papers of John Simcoe Saunders; journal of John Simcoe Saunders, 1871–77. York County Court of Probate (Fredericton), V, 18–22. J. S. Saunders, *The law of pleadings and evidence in civil actions, arranged alphabetically, with practical forms: and the pleadings and evidence to support them* (2v., London, 1828). Lawrence, *Judges of New Brunswick* (Stockton), 274–75, 359, 423, 440. MacNutt, *New Brunswick*, 164, 178, 288–89, 318, 480.

SCATCHERD, THOMAS, lawyer and politician; b. at Wyton (Station), U.C., 10 Nov. 1823, eldest of 12 children of Anne Farley and John Scatcherd, who emigrated from Yorkshire in 1821 and became member for Middlesex West in the Legislative Assembly of the Province of Canada, 1854–58; d. at Ottawa, Ont., 15 April 1876.

Thomas Scatcherd attended the London District grammar school, then articled in London with William Horton and in Toronto. He was town clerk for London, 1845–46, and began the practice of law in London in 1848. In 1849 he became solicitor for the town, a post he held for the rest of his life. In partnership, first with Ephraim Jones Parke and from 1861 with William Ralph Meredith*, he established an extensive legal practice. In 1851 he married Isabella Sprague, and they had two sons.

In politics, Scatcherd's unbroken record of electoral success began when he ran in Middlesex West in 1861, returning to the Reform cause the seat which had been lost to the Conservative party after his father's death in 1858. Re-elected in 1863, he supported the Clear Grit positions developed in the 1850s. He broke party ranks on the coalition of 1864, opposing the Quebec resolutions on the grounds that they did not provide for the type of federation agreed to in the Reform convention in 1859. He regarded confederation as primarily "a scheme to construct the Intercolonial Railway" and "to benefit the Lower Provinces at the expense of Upper Canada," whose true interests were to be found in the development of the northwest territories. In his view, the new constitution should not become law until it had been "submitted to and pronounced upon by the people."

In 1866, Scatcherd played a leading role in opposing a private bill introduced by Robert BELL designed to extend to Roman Catholic schools in Canada West the privileges then being proposed for the Protestant minority of Canada East in a government bill sponsored by Alexander Tilloch Galt*. The vigour of the assault on the measure by George BROWN and Scatcherd threatened the life of the government, and led to the withdrawal of the bills and the resignation of Galt.

With the adoption of confederation, Scatcherd, though he was elected as a Reformer in the federal election of 1867, did not take the strongly partisan position advocated by George Brown. In addition to supporting much of the government's legislation, he defended the choice of Sir Francis Hincks* as minister of finance in 1869, an appointment strongly attacked by the Toronto *Globe*. Asserting that "all this clamor about Reform and Conservatism in Ontario amounts to very little in the Dominion Parliament," he successfully defended his moderate position against opposition that developed in the Reform organization within his constituency in 1872. He received the support of many Conservatives and, in spite of some efforts by Sir John A. Macdonald* to have him opposed, he was returned by acclamation in the general elections of 1872 and 1874. A brother, Robert Colin (1832–79), at one time mayor of Strathroy,

was also a member of parliament, and represented Middlesex North, 1876–78.

Thomas Scatcherd became an experienced and influential parliamentarian, serving on various select and standing committees including the committee of supply, of which he was chairman when he became fatally ill toward the end of the session of 1876. Though at no time a major figure, Scatcherd contributed significantly to the political life of his time.

RICHARD B. SPLANE

PAC, MG 26, A (Macdonald papers), letter book 10, pp.706, 867; letter book 18, pp.179–80. Canada, Province of, *Parliamentary debates*, 1861–65. *Globe* (Toronto), 1867, 1876. *London Advertiser*, 1867. *London Free Press*, 1867. *Ottawa Citizen*, 1876. William Horton, *Memoir of the late Thomas Scatcherd; a family record* (London, Ont., 1878). Creighton, *Road to confederation*.

SCOTT, ALFRED HENRY, bartender, clerk, and political delegate; b.*c*.1840 of English parentage; d. 28 May 1872 in Saint-Boniface, Man.

Alfred Henry Scott was a resident of the Red River Settlement in Winnipeg from 1869 to 1872. He worked as a barkeeper in the saloon of Hugh F. O'Lone, an American, and later he served as a clerk in the store of Henry McKenney, also an American.

When resistance to union with Canada began in Red River in 1869, it found the settlement divided into three camps. Some favoured union with Canada, others would accept union if it came; some wished to negotiate terms with Canada; other settlers wanted to prolong the agitation in the hope of intervention by the United States. Alfred Scott's association with the Americans, O'Lone and McKenney, gave him some influence with the last group.

A mass meeting held on 19 and 20 Jan. 1870, at Upper Fort Garry (Winnipeg), decided that a convention of delegates should be elected to consider what terms might be asked of Canada. By deft political organization on the part of O'Lone and McKenney, Scott was nominated the Winnipeg delegate at a nominating meeting duly held but attended by the American party only. The moderates led by Alexander Begg* thought it was the *only* meeting to be held, that they had been excluded, and called none of their own. For want of another nomination, Scott was then declared elected, and, despite protest by the moderates, his election was confirmed in the convention. He was later elected by the convention one of three delegates to go to Ottawa to discuss terms, the other two being the Reverend Noël-Joseph Ritchot* and Judge John

BLACK representing the French and English elements respectively. This election also was criticized, especially by Louis Riel*, who felt that one of the envoys should be a Métis. On 11 Feb. 1870, Scott, Ritchot, and Black were appointed delegates to Ottawa by the provisional government set up by the convention.

Ritchot and Scott travelled to Ottawa at the end of March, where they were arrested by agents of the Ontario government as parties to the murder of Thomas Scott*, an Ontario Orangeman executed by the provisional government. The Canadian government obtained their release and opened negotiations with the envoys. Scott played no recorded part in the discussions, but contented himself with supporting Ritchot's demands. He is known to have had a conversation with the American special agent in Ottawa, James Wickes Taylor*, but there is nothing to suggest that it was significant. After the main work was over, Scott left Ottawa towards mid-May. He visited New York to see relatives, and perhaps make American or Fenian connections. He then returned to Red River in the steps of Ritchot, who had already reported to the provisional government on the negotiations.

After a six-month illness in 1871–72, during which he was converted to Roman Catholicism, Scott became the first patient of the Hôpital Saint-Boniface. He presumably died in that institution.

W. L. MORTON

Archives des sœurs grises (Saint-Boniface, Man.), Registre de l'hôpital Saint-Boniface, 1872. Archives paroissiales de Saint-Boniface (Man.), Registres des baptêmes, mariages et sépultures. *Begg's Red River journal* (Morton), 1–148, 212, 278, 284, 305, 370, 388, 535. "N.-J. Ritchot's journal," *Manitoba: birth of a province* (Morton), 134–35. *New Nation* (Winnipeg), 18 March 1870. Morice, *Critical hist. of the Red River insurrection*, 241–42.

SCOTT, JONATHAN, Methodist clergyman, b. 5 May 1803 at Nottingham, Eng.; d. 5 May 1880 at Brampton, Ont.

Jonathan Scott was converted at Chesterfield, England, in 1816 and joined the Wesleyan Church. He became a candidate for the ministry in 1834 and was immediately sent to the Canada Conference as a missionary by the British Wesleyan Conference. Received on trial by the Canada Conference in that year, he was sent to the Grape Island Indian mission (in the Bay of Quinte) where he remained until 1836. He was then ordained and stationed at the Lake Simcoe and Coldwater Indian mission. From 1834 to 1840 he was a frequent contributor to the *Christian Guardian* on

Wesleyan missions to the Indians, criticizing the government's Indian policy under Sir Francis Bond HEAD, and defending the integrity of Indian converts.

Scott was stationed on the Goderich mission by the conference of 1839, but the appointment was immediately changed so that he might be acting editor of the *Christian Guardian* during the absence of its editor, the Reverend Egerton Ryerson*.

In 1840 the union of the Canada Conference with the British Conference of the Wesleyan Methodist Church was dissolved and Scott remained with the former. His appointment as editor was renewed each year by the conference but in 1844 it declined to reappoint him; according to John Carroll* the conference felt that Scott had worn the nib off his pen a little by long use. During Scott's editorship, the *Guardian* became a strictly religious paper avoiding political pronouncements and confining itself largely to a defence of evangelical Protestantism, more especially Methodist doctrine and polity. Much space was devoted to attacks on high church Anglicanism and on Roman Catholicism. The contrast between the paper under his editorship and that of Ryerson is quite marked.

In 1844 Scott returned to circuit work, in which he excelled. The conference of 1845 elected him secretary, in order, according to Carroll, to assuage wounded feelings over his dismissal from the editorship of the *Guardian*. He refused the appointment, however, and continued in the itinerant ministry until 1854, serving on the circuits of Stamford, Cobourg, Port Hope, Perth, and Cooksville.

He dropped from the itinerant ministry in 1854, because of his wife's ill health, and became an assistant to Dr Enoch Wood*, the superintendent of missions, at the Wesleyan Methodist Missionary Society office in Toronto. He was superannuated in 1868 and moved to Brampton, where he died.

C. GLENN LUCAS

UCA, Minutes of the Canada Conference of the Wesleyan Methodist Church in Canada, 1834–74; Minutes of the Conference of the Methodist Church of Canada, 1874–80. *Christian Guardian* (Toronto), 1834–80. Wesleyan Methodist Church in Canada, Missionary Society, *Annual Reports* (Toronto), 1834–41. Carroll, *Case and his cotemporaries*, IV, V.

SEXTON, JOHN PONSONBY, advocate, editor, and municipal official; b. 11 June 1808 in Quebec, son of John Sexton and Helen Halpen; d. in Montreal, Que., 18 March 1880.

John Ponsonby Sexton was the eldest son of

John Sexton, native of Limerick, Ireland, former officer of the 49th regiment and employee of the Crown Lands Department, Quebec. His mother was related to the Ponsonby family. He was educated at the Petit Séminaire of Quebec and studied law in Montreal where he was admitted to the bar on 9 Feb. 1829.

Sexton joined the law firm of A. Jones and practised successfully in Montreal for 11 years. In 1835 he became editor of the *Irish Advocate*, a moderate reform journal temporarily created to draw Irish support from the *Vindicator and Canadian Advertiser*, a stalwart proponent of the *Patriote* cause. Although, in the invective which followed, the *Vindicator* branded Sexton a prominent Orangeman, there is no evidence to suggest that Sexton converted to the Protestant faith. He remained an active member of the St Patrick's Society and the Irish Roman Catholic Temperance Society, and, in 1844–45, served as first vice-president of both organizations.

On 12 Sept. 1840 Sexton became Montreal's first city clerk under the new charter of 1840, at a salary of £300, winning this appointment over the recorded opposition of five of the six French Canadian members of the city council. Since the corporation had no legal department Sexton drafted most of the municipal by-laws. In 1841 the city provided him with an assistant, Richard D. Bodley. Sexton, a prescient and exacting administrator, twice persuaded the lethargic city council to appoint land assessors if the corporation was not to lose the annual tax revenue. On one occasion, the city would otherwise have lost the whole revenue from the west ward amounting to about £5,000. In 1846 Sexton's foresight saved the entire assessment of the city, an estimated £30,000. In 1849 Sexton refused to follow his Montreal merchant friends into the annexation movement.

From 1852 until 1859 he served as clerk of the Recorder's Court, a local court established to try violations of municipal laws. Upon the recommendation of the city council, Sexton was on 2 April 1859 named recorder by the governor general, Sir Edmund Walker Head*, and he held this position until his death. He served as a major in the militia of Lower Canada. On 28 Feb. 1873 he was made queen's counsel.

In St Paul's Presbyterian Church, on 15 Feb. 1834, Sexton married Jane Elizabeth Carswell, the daughter of a Montreal merchant in wine and spirits. They had one son, James Ponsonby, an author and advocate, and two daughters. Jane Sexton died on 23 Jan. 1849, at the age of 49. Ten years later, on 7 June 1859, Sexton married Lolitia Keys, the widow of Francis McDonnell.

Sexton, a competent civic administrator, has been described as "a man of learning, ability and great literary attainment and an able writer."

CARMAN MILLER

AJM, Registre d'état civil, Notre-Dame Parish, 1880; Registre d'état civil, St Paul's Presbyterian Church, 1834, 1835, 1849; Registre d'état civil, St Patrick's Church, 1859. AVM, Procès-verbaux du conseil municipal, 1–67. [Bruce and Grey], *Elgin-Grey papers* (Doughty), II, 456–58. *Le Courrier de Montréal*, 17 mars–21 mars 1880. *Le Nouveau Monde* (Montréal), 16 mars–21 mars 1880. *Pilot* (Montreal), 1–17 April 1859. *True Witness and Catholic Chronicle* (Montreal), 24 March–18 April 1859. *Vindicator and Canadian Advertiser* (Montreal), 18 Aug. 1835–10 Jan. 1838.

P.-G. Roy, *Les avocats de la région de Québec*, 404. Hector Berthelot, *Montréal; le bon vieux temps*, É.-Z. Massicotte, édit. et compil. (2v., Montréal, 1916), II, 107–10. *Histoire de la Corporation de la Cité de Montréal, depuis son origine jusqu'à nos jours . . .*, J.-C. Lamothe *et al.*, édit. (Montréal, 1903), 410–12. F.-J. Audet, "1842," *Cahiers des Dix*, VII (1942), 221, 253–54. Léon Trépanier, "Les attributs de la mairie de Montréal," *Cahiers des Dix*, XXXI (1966), 203–11.

SHAH-WUN-DAIS ("sultry heat"; better known as **John Sunday**), Methodist minister and Missisauga chieftain; b.c. 1795 near the Black River in central New York State; d. 14 Dec. 1875 at Alderville, Ont.

John Sunday was a member of the Missisauga tribe, which was scattered throughout central Upper Canada and particularly in the vicinity of Rice Lake and the mouth of the Credit River. Possibly Sunday's family was on an expedition in New York when he was born (the Black River district is opposite Kingston) or, as the border was still rather fluid in 1795, they may have lived there. Sunday said he fought in the War of 1812–14; presumably he was recruited by the British forces as an Indian auxiliary. He appears to have been recognized as a chief, and was one of the signatories of the lease for the Grape Island mission lands in 1826, but the office of chief was not very important among his people.

Urged on by the Reverend William Case*, the Canada Conference of the Methodist Episcopal Church launched a vigorous campaign in 1824 to convert the Upper Canadian Indians to Christianity and to assimilate them to British North American society. John Sunday, who, like the majority of Indians, was living in miserable conditions near the white settlements, was one of the early converts, and was quickly singled out as a potential religious leader. He was married when, in 1826, he assisted in the establishment of a model mission settlement on Grape Island in the Bay of

Shanly

Quinte, at which the Indians were induced to pursue an ordered religious life, to raise crops, and to acquire elementary academic and technical skills. Sunday, however, did not remain long on the island; under the direction of Case and his fellow-chieftain, Peter Jones*, he became an itinerant missionary to the Missisaugas and Ojibwas in Upper Canada and northern Michigan.

Sunday had acquired sufficient education and experience at the Grape Island mission by 1832 to be accepted as a ministerial candidate. He travelled extensively for several years thereafter, particularly among the Ojibwas in the Lake Superior region. Following his ordination in 1836 he visited Great Britain to stimulate interest in the Indian missions, and was presented to Queen Victoria. His addresses and his conversations with English Methodists attracted much favourable attention and helped arouse greater concern in political circles for the welfare of the Indians. Subsequently he served on several mission stations, including Alderville, where he lived after being superannuated in 1867.

Among his Methodist brethren Sunday had an outstanding reputation as a person and as a preacher. In his own tongue, he was "always effective, often eloquent"; on occasion he "rose to the grandeur of sublimity in thought and speech." Although he was never fluent in English, "the quaint originality of his remarks" was said to have been "irresistibly attractive." As a pastor he laboured faithfully for his people; when blind and near death he was still speaking to them at length, showing them "how wonderfully he had been led into the way of the Kingdom."

John Sunday's career epitomized the initial impact of Methodist missions on the scattered Indian tribes of Upper Canada. For him, as for many of his fellows, Christianity gave a new meaning to life and a measure of dignity and of material comfort, but it did not bring them fully into the white community or enable them effectively to adapt their own culture to new and changing social conditions.

G. S. FRENCH

Christian Guardian (Toronto), 22 Dec. 1875. Peter Jones, *Life and journals of Kah-ke-wa-quo-nā-by: (Rev. Peter Jones,) Wesleyan missionary* (Toronto, 1860). Methodist Church of Canada, Toronto Conference, *Minutes* (Toronto), 1876, 12–17. *The minutes of the annual conferences of the Wesleyan Methodist Church in Canada from 1824 to 1857* (2v., Toronto, 1846–63), I. Cornish, *Cyclopædia of Methodism*, I. Carroll, *Case and his cotemporaries*. G. F. Playter, *The history of Methodism in Canada: with an account of the rise and progress of the work of God among the Canadian Indian tribes, and occasional notices of the civil affairs of the province* (Toronto, 1862).

SHANLY, CHARLES DAWSON, artist, poet, and creator of ballads; b. Dublin, Ireland, 9 March 1811, the eldest son of James Shanly, a member of the Irish bar, and Frances Elizabeth Mulvany; brother of Walter* and Francis*; d. 15 April 1875, Arlington, Fla.

When Charles Dawson Shanly was five, his family left Dublin to live at Stradbally, Queens County, and, in 1825, moved to Dunboyne, County Meath. He was educated at home under the family tutor, the Reverend Henry Carpenter, and at school in Waterford, Waterford County. He entered Trinity College, Dublin, but spent a year at Penzance, Cornwall, caring for his brother William, a promising young engineer who had developed tuberculosis. There the two men devoted much time to sketching. After William died in 1833, Charles returned to Trinity College and graduated with a BA in 1834. He later studied art at the Brocas Academy in Dublin.

The ready acceptance of his poetry by a literary agent in London led him to contemplate a career as a writer in England. Instead, he came with his family to Upper Canada in 1836 and settled near Fanshawe, where Hamilton Hartley KILLALY, a Dublin friend of his father, lived. The Shanly family's 600-acre estate, "Thorndale," was only just established when the rebellion of 1837 broke out. Charles volunteered, received a commission, and served for one year.

He joined the Board of Public Works of Lower Canada as a clerk in 1840, serving under its chairman, Killaly, and remained with the board after the union of Upper and Lower Canada. However, Shanly continued writing and became editor, in 1849, of a comic magazine, *Punch in Canada*, to which he contributed poetry, satirical articles, and cartoons, all unsigned. This periodical followed the government when it was transferred from Montreal to Toronto and was published weekly until its end in 1850.

Shanly became assistant secretary to the board of works, but resigned and went to New York in 1857. He now made journalism a full-time occupation. He wrote for the *Albion, New York Leader*, and *Atlantic Monthly*, and assisted in founding *Vanity Fair*, a humorous weekly journal, admired for its wit and subtle cartoons. Shanly became its editor. His thoughtful poem, "Sword and plough," published in the early days of the Civil War, was followed by a series of clever articles, entitled "Hardee made easy," also published in *Vanity Fair*, which satirized General William J. Hardee's textbook on military tactics.

"The lilac tree" illustrates the music of his verse, but the poem most frequently quoted is "The walker of the snow." *The monkey of Porto Bello* was published in 1867, and two other witty monographs, *A jolly bear and his friends* and *The truant chicken* were apparently published in 1866. One of his close friends at this time was F. H. Bellew, the creator of "Uncle Sam."

Suffering from lung trouble, Shanly went to Arlington, Florida, in February 1875 and died there, unmarried, two months later. He was buried in Arva, Ontario, near the family homestead. He was an ardent painter, and some of his sketches, along with his portrait, are preserved in the McCord Museum in Montreal.

FRANK NORMAN WALKER

C. D. Shanly, *The monkey of Porto Bello* (New York, 1867). C. M. Whyte-Edgar, *A wreath of Canadian song* (Toronto, 1910), 25–29, contains "Blondine," "The walker of the snow," and "The lilac tree."

MTCL, Publisher's proofs of a number of C. D. Shanly's poems. PAO, Francis Shanly papers, box 95, Walter Shanly, "The Canadian Shanlys. Whence they came and how they got to Thorndale." Walter and Francis Shanly, *Daylight through the mountain, letters and labours of civil engineers Walter and Francis Shanly*, ed. F. N. Walker ([Toronto], 1957), 107, 140, 424. *Appleton's cyclopædia of American biography*, ed. J. G. Wilson *et al.* (10v., New York, 1887–1924), V, 481. *A catalogue of graduates who have proceeded to degrees in the University of Dublin ... with supplements to December 16, 1868*, ed. J. H. Todd (Dublin and London, 1869). F. N. Walker, *Sketches of old Toronto* (Toronto, 1965), 243–95.

SHARPLES, JOHN, prosperous lumberman of Quebec, shipbuilder, official, mayor, and legislative councillor; b. 1814 in Lancashire, Eng.; d. 19 Dec. 1876 at Sillery, Que.

John Sharples came from a family whose forbears had remained faithful to Catholicism. While still young, he left Lancashire to come to America. He spent the year 1822 at St Andrews, New Brunswick, then returned to England the following year; he came back to Canada only in 1827, to take up residence there once and for all. He was welcomed at Quebec by several members of his family. Indeed, in 1816 his uncle William had started the Sharples timber company, the first to trade in square timber at Quebec. Around 1850 John went into partnership with Owen Jones and William's two sons, Charles and Henry. While Henry and Owen Jones carried on business at Liverpool, England, as Sharples, Jones and Company (which became Henry Sharples and Company when Jones withdrew from the firm in 1866), Charles and John formed the company at Quebec known as C. and J. Sharples and Company. A partnership contract for a five-year period, dated 6 April 1854, specified that the capital of the company was £25,000, the sum of £5,000 being sup-

plied by John and the rest by the three other partners in proportion to their shares in the company.

Charles and John Sharples bought their lumber east of Quebec, and brought it to the coves at Sillery and Bridgewater. The company exported principally square timber, made up of white pine, red pine, oak, elm, ash, and birch; timber for construction, essentially planks, and staves were also sold to the timber merchants in England and Scotland. In 1852 John and his cousin were among the "Grand Manitous" of the Anglo-Saxon race who controlled the timber trade and shipbuilding at Quebec [*see* John GILMOUR]. From 1854 to 1871 Charles and John Sharples each built three ships. The firm became John's sole property in 1870, and took the name of John Sharples Sons and Company.

In addition, John held certain public offices: on 19 Dec. 1843 he became superintendent of cullers, a post he left in 1855. On 10 Nov. 1859 he was appointed commissioner of the port of Quebec, then president; when he resigned in May 1864, a special committee was immediately formed to inquire into the reasons for this resignation. Two years earlier his sense of civic responsibility had attracted the attention of his fellow-citizens, who had elected him mayor of Sillery. No doubt with the object of consolidating his social relationships, while seeing to his personal gain, John Sharples joined the Quebec Board of Trade (1862–76), and in May 1873 was chosen to represent the timber merchants on the council of this board. John also became director and vice-president of the Union Bank of Lower Canada, as well as of the Stadacona Fire and Life Insurance Company in 1873.

John Sharples' career reached its height on 27 Feb. 1874, when he was called upon to join the Legislative Council as representative for the division of Stadacona, in recognition of his services to society and his loyalty to the Conservative party. In the same year, while on a business trip in Europe, he learned of the death of his only daughter. The shock was so great that he does not seem to have recovered from it. He died on 19 Dec. 1876 at Sillery; the English-speaking Catholic community of Quebec mourned for one of its greatest benefactors. His sons John* (1848–1913) and William (1841–86) carried on his business under the trade name of W. and J. Sharples.

PIERRE LANDRY

ANQ, Port de Québec, 14; Quebec Board of Trade, Minute book, 6; Quebec Board of Trade, 37. PAC, MG 28, III, 11 (W. & J. Sharples Reg'd). Canada, Province of, Legislative Assembly, *Journals*, 1864, 184, 343. *L'Événement* (Québec), 20 déc. 1876. *La Minerve* (Montréal), 21 déc. 1876. *Morning Chronicle* (Quebec),

Shaw

20 Dec. 1876. *The Canadian men and women of the time: a handbook of Canadian biography*, ed. H. J. Morgan (2nd ed., Toronto, 1912), 1012. Turcotte, *Conseil législatif de Québec*, 285, 287. A. R. M. Lower, *A history of Canada; colony to nation* (4th ed., [Don Mills, Ont.], 1964), 209, 215. Ouellet, *Histoire économique*, 500. Narcisse Rosa, *La construction des navires à Québec et ses environs; grèves et naufrages* (Québec, 1897), 63–66, 70, 73, 97, 101, 105, 116–17, 142.

SHAW, JAMES, businessman and politician; b. 1798 at New Ross, Ireland, son of Richard (?) Shaw and Anne Dowsley; m. Helen Forgie of Glasgow, Scotland; d. 6 Feb. 1878 in Smiths Falls, Ont.

James Shaw was educated in Dublin, Ireland, and emigrated to Upper Canada in 1820. He was employed by the British authorities as clerk of the military settlement at Lanark-on-Clyde (Lanark) and Perth, assisting settlers to get established. After nine years he left to become an overseer, probably in the provisioning of the workers, on the section of the Rideau Canal from Smiths Falls to Bytown (Ottawa). He was a member of the Carleton and Lanark militias and had attained the rank of lieutenant-colonel when he retired in 1860. During the rebellion of 1837–38 he was stationed at Brockville with the 3rd Leeds militia.

Shaw's economic interests were varied: he opened a general merchandise store and a blacksmith shop in Smiths Falls, where he settled after working on the canal, and he assisted his sons in establishing a general merchandise store and a foundry, and also a newspaper, the *British Standard*, in Perth. He was involved briefly in banking and he invested in land and in the Brockville and Ottawa Railway.

A political career complemented his business ventures. He actively supported the Conservative party and included among his friends prominent Conservatives of the region such as William*, James*, and Alexander Morris*, George Sherwood*, Roderick MATHESON, Colonel Andrew William Playfair*, and James and Bennett Rosamond. The local political offices he held – county and town reeve and councillor of the district of Johnstown – perhaps influenced him to seek other political positions. In 1851 he successfully contested the Lanark riding and, when the constituency was divided, retained the seat of South Lanark in 1854. He lost in 1857, however, in large measure because of his moderate attitude towards Roman Catholic demands for separate schools. Shaw was a staunch Anglican and assisted in the founding of St Johns Church in Smiths Falls. He was sympathetic to the Orange Order, although not a member, and belonged to the freemasons.

Shaw was elected for the Bathurst division to the Legislative Council in 1860, and in 1867 he was appointed to the Senate, having been a supporter of confederation. Politically he was a moderate, a strong supporter of John A. Macdonald*'s conservatism, and he was influential in dispensing patronage for the area.

Shaw's business ventures proved disastrous; he lost heavily in the crash of 1857–58 because of overspeculation, and the financial difficulties of a son contributed to his business failures in the 1860s. His situation had not improved when the recession of the 1870s began, and he never recovered. The family, however, remained prominent in the area. Shaw was recalled as "Liberal in his opinions and broad in his views upon public questions," and as "a kind and sympathizing friend. . . . Full of anecdote & repartee he was a great favourite with all who knew him."

FOSTER J. K. GRIEZIC

PAC, MG 26, A (Macdonald papers); RG 8, I, A1, 130, 202; RG 9, I, B5, 1–8. Queen's University Archives, Alexander Morris papers. St Johns Church (Smiths Falls, Ont.), Burial records, entry 38, 9 Feb. 1878. *British Whig* (Kingston), 8 Feb. 1878. *Perth Courier* (Bathurst Courier, 1834–57), 1834–Feb. 1878. *Can. parl. comp.*, 1862; 1867; 1871; 1878. *Cyclopædia of Can. biog.* (Rose, 1888). Andrew Haydon, *Pioneer sketches in the district of Bathurst* (Toronto, 1925). *A summary of the proceedings of the council of the district of Johnstown and the council of the United Counties of Leeds and Grenville, 1842–1942*, comp. William Jelly (Brockville, Ont., 1943).

SHEDDEN, JOHN, cartage agent, contractor, and railway promoter; b. 4 Nov. 1825, at Kilbirnie, Ayrshire, Scotland, son of John Shedden and Jean Wyllie; d. unmarried 16 May 1873, at Cannington, Ont.

John Shedden studied at the Irvine Academy in Irvine, Ayrshire, and worked on the Glasgow and South Western Railway before emigrating to Virginia in the United States where he became a railway contractor. In 1855 he came to Canada and entered into a partnership with William Hendrie of Hamilton to form the cartage firm of Hendrie and Shedden. They were the cartage agents for the Great Western Railway and later became the agents for the Grand Trunk after its line from Montreal to Toronto was completed in late 1856. The firm introduced in Canada some of the features of cartage firms in England, such as making facilities available in several cities (in 1857 the firm had offices in Toronto, Hamilton, and London), and it improved on the service previously provided by cartage firms in Canada. It employed heavier wagons and standardized the more important forms used by the railways in moving freight. Nonetheless, the monopoly position of the firm inevitably led to complaints. A riot is said to have occurred in Montreal after meetings held to protest this monopoly, and the firm's barns were burned on two occasions.

Hendrie and Shedden dissolved their partnership in 1859 or 1860, and the latter retained the contract with the Grand Trunk. He continued to expand his company's facilities, and by 1870 he had offices in Montreal, Toronto, London, and Detroit, and owned about 400 horses. He was, however, developing other interests, particularly as a contractor and as a railway promoter.

Shedden became associated with a group of prominent Toronto businessmen, including George Laidlaw* and J. G. Worts*, who were actively promoting the construction to the areas north of Toronto of narrow-gauge railways which, it was believed, could be built more cheaply and quickly than railways with a wider gauge. Shedden had already been a contractor for several buildings in Toronto, including the Grand Trunk grain elevator, opened in 1863, and Union Station, completed in July 1873. He now became a railway contractor, in partnership with William James Mackenzie, on the narrow-gauge Toronto, Grey, and Bruce Railway, chartered in 1868 and completed from Toronto to Owen Sound in June 1873. He was also an important stockholder in the railway, and in 1870 became a director. Another narrow-gauge railway was the Toronto and Nipissing, completed as far as Coboconk in November 1872. Shedden was elected its president in 1870 and was an important stock and bondholder in the company.

Shedden did not participate actively in politics but he had close associations with the Conservative party and Sir John A. Macdonald*. He had been a director of the Toronto *Daily Telegraph* (and probably lost some money when it was discontinued in 1872), and he and C. J. Campbell signed in 1872 a note for $10,000 to Macdonald "to enable him to supply funds to the several constituencies which he hopes to carry." He had been included in 1872 in the Interoceanic Railway Company headed by David Lewis Macpherson*, which Macdonald failed to amalgamate with Sir Hugh Allan*'s Canada Pacific Railway Company. Macdonald then tried to persuade Shedden to enter a company that was being formed. Shedden was disappointed in not receiving the vice-presidency of the company and, although he "could have managed the financial part of it," he refused Macdonald's offer at the last moment because of an unspecified "difficulty."

Shedden was included in the provisional board

of directors of the St Lawrence Bank in 1872, and he was a director in a number of other firms. He died as a result of an accident at Cannington on 16 May 1873 when he was crushed between moving cars on the Toronto and Nipissing Railway line and the station platform.

Henri Pilon

General Register Office (Edinburgh), Register of births and baptisms for the parish of Kilbirnie. PAC, MG 26, A (Macdonald papers), 123, Shedden to Macdonald, 16 Dec. 1872; Alexander Campbell to Macdonald, 17 Dec. 1872; Shedden to Macdonald, 18 Dec. 1872; 125, Shedden to Macdonald, 29 Jan. 1873; letter book 17, Macdonald to C. J. Brydges, 16 Feb. 1872; letter book 19, Macdonald to Shedden, 9 Dec. 1872. PAO, Sir Alexander Campbell papers, C. J. Campbell to Alexander Campbell, 28, 30 Aug. 1872; RG 8, I-7-b-3, Toronto and Nipissing Railway, box 7; Toronto, Grey, and Bruce Railway, box 9; Toronto City Council papers, 1857, S. P. Bidder to John Hutchison, 26 Aug. 1857. York County Surrogate Court (Toronto), will of John Shedden. *Globe* (Toronto), 19 May 1873. *Mail* (Toronto), 17, 19 May 1873. *Standard dict. of Can. biog.* (Roberts and Tunnell), II, 398.

D. C. Masters, *The rise of Toronto, 1850–1890* (Toronto, 1947), 74–75, 109–14. Myles Pennington, *Railways and other ways, being reminiscences of canal and railway life during a period of sixty-seven years . . .* (Toronto, 1896), 104–7. Ross and Trigge, *History of the Canadian Bank of Commerce*, III, 214, 217. F. W. Terrill, *A chronology of Montreal and of Canada from A.D. 1752 to A.D. 1893, including commercial statistics, historical sketches of commercial corporations and firms and advertisements . . .* (Montreal, 1893), 238–39.

SHERWOOD, ADIEL, United Empire Loyalist and sheriff; b. 16 May 1779 at Fort Edward, New York, son of Thomas Sherwood and Anna Brownson; m. on 11 Oct. 1801 Mary Baldwin by whom he had seven daughters and one son; d. 25 March 1874 in Brockville, Ont.

Adiel Sherwood's parents were United Empire Loyalists who came to Quebec in 1779 when Adiel was an infant. In 1784 they settled in the future Leeds County, and Adiel later recalled that "I saw the first tree cut and the first hill of Corn and Potatoes planted by an actual settler." He probably attended a private settlers' school but had little formal education. He expressed himself well, however, and, as a young man, taught school near Elizabethtown (Brockville). About 1804, he built and operated the first tavern in Brockville. When he became sheriff he "brought [his] mercantile affairs to an end," but it is not known what these affairs comprised.

Sherwood joined the 1st Regiment, Leeds militia, as ensign at 17. He was militia paymaster from June 1813 through 1814 for the Johnstown

Shiels

and Eastern districts (eastern Ontario between the St Lawrence and Ottawa rivers). Besides issuing pay, he purchased clothing and supplies for "all classes of Militia . . . Sedentary and Embodied, the Provincial Cavalry, and Incorporated Militia." He became colonel in 1830 and retired in 1846.

In his long public career Sherwood served the Johnstown District (present-day Leeds and Grenville, and parts of Lanark and Carleton counties) as deputy clerk of the crown, branch roads commissioner, land board member, commissioner of the peace (1818–28), treasurer (1814–41), and sheriff (1829–41). He continued as sheriff for the United Counties of Leeds and Grenville from 1842 to 1864.

Sherwood was an upright and conscientious sheriff. His duties were to seize land and goods and chattels for tax arrears and to sell them at public auction, to attend the assizes and quarter sessions of the district courts, to select and summon juries for court hearings, to supervise the district (later the counties) jail and its inmates, and to bring the prisoners to court and to see that their sentences, including executions, were carried out.

After the rebellion in 1837, Sherwood investigated for the provincial government the activities of "Patriots" and of Hunter's Lodges suspected of border raids across the St Lawrence (some led by the "pirate" William Johnston*) and of the invasion at Prescott in November 1838.

Sherwood, a devout man, helped found the First Presbyterian Church in Brockville in 1811 and was an elder in it for many years. He was the first superintendent of its Sunday school (the first in Upper Canada), president of the first Bible Society in Brockville, and a member of the first Religious Tract Society of Upper Canada. When the Brockville Temperance Society was formed in 1832, Adiel Sherwood was the first president.

He was a prominent freemason. After joining the order at 21, he rose rapidly to become a mark master mason, and helped organize the Sussex Royal Arch chapter which met in his house. He became provincial junior grand warden in 1825, and grand senior warden for the year 1827–28.

When Adiel Sherwood died at 95, he was mourned as the patriarch of the United Counties. He had contributed to their development in land settlement, municipal government, and the district courts. He had participated in the founding of Ontario, and had witnessed the confederation of Canada and its expansion from sea to sea.

RUTH McKENZIE

Adiel Sherwood prepared a "Memorandum" in 1866, for William Canniff*, which the latter quoted in *History of the settlement of Upper Canada (Ontario), with special reference to the bay Quinté* (Toronto,

1869). An edited version entitled "Memoir" was printed in T. W. H. Leavitt, *History of Leeds and Grenville, Ontario, from 1749 to 1879, with illustrations and biographical sketches of some of its prominent men and pioneers* (Brockville, 1879), 18–20. The original "Memorandum" is in PAC, MG 24, 165 (Adiel Sherwood papers), which also contains a few letters. A "Memento" by Adiel Sherwood was published in the *Brockville Recorder*, 13 Feb. 1868, and reprinted 16 May 1873.

PAC, RG 5, A1, 16 Sept., 10 Nov. 1813; 21 Aug. 1821; 26 May, 26 June 1829; 19 Oct., 6, 11, 18 Dec. 1832; 18, 19, 20, 23, 30 Aug. 1833; 28 June, 17 Dec. 1838; 26 Feb. 1839; C1, 1839, no.1782; 1841, nos.1638, 2372, 2460; 1843, no.6277; 1864, no.128; RG 9, I, B4, 26, 7 Jan. 1836; RG 68, 1. *Brockville Recorder*, 15 March 1832, 31 Aug. 1854, 2 April 1874. *Recorder and Times* (Brockville), 20 Dec. 1927. *Can. biog. dict.*, I, 315–17. J. R. Robertson, *The history of freemasonry in Canada from its introduction in 1749 . . .* (2v., Toronto, 1899). H. S. Seaman, "The Rev. William Smart, Presbyterian minister of Elizabethtown, 1811–1876," *Ont. Hist.*, V (1904), 178–86.

SHIELS, ANDREW, blacksmith, poet, and magistrate; b. 12 March 1793 in the parish of Oxnam, Roxburghshire, Scotland; d. 5 Nov. 1879 at Dartmouth, N.S.

After emigrating to Nova Scotia in 1818, Andrew Shiels worked as a blacksmith at Halifax. A decade later he moved across the harbour to Dartmouth, where he owned a farm, and continued his trade at Ellenvale Tavern. By 1834 he had set up a carding mill at Ellenvale, named for his wife, Ellen, who died in 1846. Shiels later married Isabella Blair; he was the father of a large family, but most of his children died young.

A supporter of Joseph Howe, Andrew Shiels was appointed a justice of the peace for Halifax County on 20 Nov. 1848 in the commission appointed by the Reformers after the winning of responsible government. In 1857 the Court of Quarter Sessions appointed Andrew Shiels a stipendiary magistrate, and in 1860 he became a member of the commission for the relief of insolvent debtors in Halifax County.

Shiels is remembered as a colourful local character who wrapped himself in a long plaid cloak in cold weather, as a man of strong opinions active in the affairs of the community, and as a respected magistrate. At the time of his death the *Presbyterian Witness* said, "He was a fast friend and an implacable enemy." During the greater part of his life he belonged to the Presbyterian Church, but after a misunderstanding with members of the local presbytery he joined the Methodists.

Largely self-educated, Shiels read widely and had an excellent memory. He was influenced by the history, tales, and imagery of his native border country and by the poetry of Robert Burns. His popular verse appeared frequently in the Halifax newspapers for 50 years over the pseudonyms "Albyn" and "the Bard of Ellenvale." *The witch of the Westcot; a tale of Nova-Scotia, in three cantos* was an ambitious work. An historical tale in verse, it was based on the Indian massacre at Dartmouth in 1751, and in the preface he remarked on his difficulty in adapting his border vernacular to the English spoken in Nova Scotia. He also commented on the colony's apathy towards poetry, which he believed to be due to pioneering conditions. His most significant poems were those devoted to nature and those where he attempted to draw upon the history and imagery of his adopted country. He was also strong in satire.

PHYLLIS R. BLAKELEY

Following is a list of some of the writings of Andrew Shiels [Albyn]: *Dupes & demagogues: a souvenir* (Halifax, 1879); *Eye to the ermine: a dream* (Halifax, 1871); *John Walker's courtship: a legend of Lauderdale* (Halifax, 1877); *Letter to Eliza* (Halifax, 1869); *My mother: in memorium* (Halifax, 1868); *The preface, a poem of the period* (Halifax, 1876); *Retribution: a literary contribution to the Nova Scotia Department of the Philadelphia Exhibition* (Halifax, 1875); *Rusticating in reality: a Pierian paraphrase* (Halifax, 1873); *Sabbath in Dartmouth* (Halifax, 1870); *The witch of the Westcot; a tale of Nova-Scotia, in three cantos; and other waste leaves of literature* (Halifax, 1831). "To the late Honourable Simon Bradstreet Robie," *Sun* (Halifax), 7 Jan. 1858.

Woodlawn Cemetery, Dartmouth, N.S., Shiels family tombstones. *Morning Chronicle* (Halifax), 6 Nov. 1879, 8 April 1885. *Presbyterian Witness* (Halifax), 8 Nov. 1879. M. J. Katzmann (Mrs William Lawson), *History of the townships of Dartmouth, Preston and Lawrencetown; Halifax County, N.S.*, ed. Harry Piers (Halifax, 1893), 101–2. J. P. Martin, *The story of Dartmouth* (Dartmouth, N.S., 1957).

SHIVES, ROBERT, printer, publisher, and public servant; b.c. 1815 in Aberdeen, Scotland, son of Robert Shives and Martha Wiggins; d. a bachelor on 7 Jan. 1879 in Saint John, N.B.

Robert Shives, whose father was a Saint John merchant, was born during a visit by his parents to Scotland. He was raised in Saint John, and in 1827 apprenticed as a printer to the *New Brunswick Courier*. Upon completion of his apprenticeship in 1834 he went to Scotland for two years before settling permanently at Saint John.

Shives was responsible for adding another dimension to the increasingly sophisticated urban settlement of Saint John in the 1840s. From 1840 to 1843 he ran the *Amaranth*, one of the first literary magazines in the Maritime provinces. The

36 monthly editions, of approximately 30 pages each, contain a bulk of original prose and verse contributed by New Brunswickers and Nova Scotians. As well Shives carried reprints from foreign sources. From the *London Sporting Review*, for example, were drawn articles written by the ubiquitous Saint John attorney, Moses H. Perley*. A short story, "Mark Meriden," may have been from another source: it had an American setting and was written by Mrs Harriet Beecher Stowe. Partly because of the disappointment of getting less public support than he had hoped for, but mainly because of "the slenderness of the pecuniary returns" Shives stopped publishing the *Amaranth*.

Robert Shives probably continued his trade as a printer on one of the Saint John newspapers until he succeeded Moses H. Perley as immigration agent in the late 1840s or early 1850s. Shives led an active life in the community. He was elected a director of the Mechanics' Institute in 1844, was a freemason, a member of the St Andrew's Society, and held the rank of lieutenant-colonel in the provincial militia.

RICHARD RICE

Amaranth (Saint John, N.B.), January 1841–December 1843. *Daily Sun* (Saint John, N.B.), 8 Jan. 1879. *Daily Telegraph* (Saint John, N.B.), 8 Jan. 1879. *Morning News* (Saint John, N.B.), 13 Dec. 1843. *New Brunswick Courier* (Saint John, N.B.), 9 Jan. 1841, 9 Dec. 1843. *Royal Gazette* (Fredericton), 14 Feb. 1844. *Saint John Globe*, 8 Jan. 1879. *Saint John Weekly Freeman*, 11 Jan. 1879. Harper, *Hist. directory*, 47. D. R. Jack, "Acadian magazines," *RSCT*, 2nd ser., IX (1903), sect.II, 173–203.

SHORT, EDWARD, lawyer and judge; b. 10 June 1806 at Bristol, Eng., son of John Quirk Short, inspector of military hospitals, and grandson of the Reverend Robert Quirk Short, Anglican minister of Trois-Rivières; d. 5 June 1871 at Sherbrooke, Que.

Edward Short emigrated to Canada while still young, and studied with the lawyer David Augustus Bostwick at Trois-Rivières, then with Dominique Mondelet* and A. Lebourdais at Montreal. He was called to the bar on 12 Oct. 1826. He practised his profession in turn at Montreal, Trois-Rivières, Quebec (as partner of Thomas Cushing AYLWIN), and, after 1830, at Sherbrooke; in this last place he was a partner first of Ebenezer Peck, then of his brother John Short*, who later became protonotary of the judicial district. He also presided over the Court of the Sessions of the Peace for the district of Saint-François.

During the 1850 by-election in Sherbrooke County (which did not then include the town),

Short worked against John Sewell SANBORN. He opposed annexation to the United States, which Sanborn was promoting, and the annexationist movement, which he regarded as "seditious." Because of his relationships with the Anglican community, Short was the ideal candidate to save the town of Sherbrooke for the Liberals. It was therefore not surprising that the government of Francis Hincks* and Augustin-Norbert Morin* supported his candidature during the general election of 1851. Short represented the town of Sherbrooke in 1851 and 1852. On 12 Nov. 1852 he received his mandate as justice of the Superior Court (district of Saint-François) and held this post until his death. He also sat as judge on the Seigneurial Court, which was created in 1854. It was the task of this tribunal, composed of judges of the Court of Queen's Bench and of the Superior Court, to determine the real rights of the seigneurs and those the *censitaires* had to redeem as a result of the abolition of the seigneurial system. Short, a sociable man with an affable disposition, was remembered as a fair and understanding judge.

Edward Short died on 5 June 1871 at Sherbrooke. By a resolution passed on 8 June 1871, the bar of the judicial district of Saint-François agreed that they would attend his funeral as a corps and wear mourning for two months. Short Street perpetuates his name in Sherbrooke.

On 7 May 1839, at Sherbrooke, he had married Ann Brown; he had seven children, among them Robert, who also practised law at Sherbrooke, and Major Charles John, who perished through his devotion to duty in the fire that in 1889 destroyed the district of Saint-Sauveur in Quebec.

MAURICE O'BREADY

Archives judiciaires de Saint-François (Sherbrooke, Qué.), Registre d'état civil, St Peter's Church, 10 June 1806, 7 May 1839, 5 June 1871, 7 March 1881, 16 May 1889. Private archives of Mrs F. P. Cluderay (North Hatley, Que.), Short family papers. *Le Pionnier de Sherbrooke*, 9 juin 1871. P.-G. Roy, *Les juges de la province de Québec*, 501. L. S. Channell, *History of Compton County and sketches of the Eastern Townships, district of St. Francis, and Sherbrooke County* (Cookshire, Que., 1896), 40. Jean Mercier, *Autour de Mena' Sen* (Sherbrooke, Qué., 1964), 163.

SIMARD, GEORGES-HONORÉ, businessman and politician; b. 18 April 1817, in Quebec City, son of Pierre Simard and Louise Clouet; m. 3 Sept. 1844, Julie Measam (of their children three survived him); d. 27 June 1873 at Sainte-Foy, Que.

Georges-Honoré Simard received his education in Quebec City, where he began his career as a printer. He soon abandoned this trade to enter the hardware business, first with his uncle, Michel Clouet, and later with his own firm of Chinic, Simard et Méthot. He sold his interests in the firm in 1860 and later became sole proprietor of the Quebec Plaster Mills. At various times he held office in a number of companies, banks, societies, and on boards in Quebec, including president of the City Building Society, 1857–59, vice-president of the Caisse d'Économie de Notre-Dame de Québec from 1858, director of the De Lery Gold Mining Company from 1865 [see Alexandre-Réné CHAUSSEGROS], vice-president of the Shipbuilding Association [see CHAREST] in the same year, and director of the Union Bank of Lower Canada, 1867–71. In 1859, he was appointed a member, and in 1870 the chairman, of the Quebec Harbour Commissioners Board.

Simard attempted to enter politics in 1854, when he contested the Quebec City seat for the Legislative Assembly of the Province of Canada. He was defeated but ran again for the same riding in the by-election of 27 Oct. 1856 and in the general election of 1857 and was successful in both instances. Violence and political machinations surrounded the latter election, and he was unseated by petition on 16 April 1860, but in the subsequent by-election, held on 7 May, in Quebec Centre, was returned. Defeated in 1863, he served on a number of commissions for the next few years. One, appointed in 1865, was for an investigation of the failure of St Roch's Savings Bank. On several occasions he was a member of a permanent commission for the erection and maintenance of parish buildings in the Quebec diocese. In 1867 Simard was elected by acclamation to the Legislative Assembly of Quebec for Quebec Centre, and to the House of Commons for Quebec City. He retired from provincial politics in 1871 and from federal politics in 1872.

Throughout his life Simard was a successful businessman and he always maintained firm connections with the mercantile community. As a politician, he was active in Quebec interests. In the debates on a capital for the united province, he strongly supported Quebec City and when Ottawa was chosen in 1857 he bitterly attacked George-Étienne CARTIER for his compromising attitude. He was a Conservative and a loyal supporter of Cartier but, on this occasion, he voted against him.

CAROLE B. STELMACK

PAC, RG 68, 1. *L'Événement* (Québec), 1840–juill. 1873. *Morning Chronicle* (Quebec) 28 June 1873. *Quebec Mercury*, 1840–July 1873. [G.-É. Cartier], *Discours de sir Georges Cartier ...*, Joseph Tassé, édit. (Montréal, 1893). *Can. directory of parliament* (Johnson), 530. *Can. parl. comp., 1867; 1869; 1871;*

1872. P.-G. Roy, *Fils de Québec*, IV, 16–18. Rumilly, *Hist. de la prov. de Québec*, I.

SIMPSON, JOHN, government official and politician; b. 1788 in England; d. 21 April 1873 in Kingston, Ont.

Having failed in England as a farmer and a merchant, John Simpson emigrated to Augusta, Upper Canada, in 1815 with his wife Zipporah Tickell and, very likely, his six step-sons. Following the arrival of Lord Dalhousie [Ramsay*] as governor-in-chief of Canada in 1819, Simpson joined his staff as a private secretary. In 1822 the governor appointed him inspector of merchandise, collector of customs, and overseer of his majesty's locks at Coteau-du-Lac, a post on the St Lawrence where the British had built a canal and a small fort, and where customs duties on goods passing between Upper and Lower Canada were levied.

Remarkably, two years after his arrival at Coteau-du-Lac, Simpson had "gained an influence over French Canadians" and was elected to the assembly of Lower Canada for the County of York. During his term he opposed the election of Louis-Joseph PAPINEAU as speaker and generally supported his benefactor, the governor, in his quarrels with the assembly. When he stood for re-election in 1827, he was strongly opposed and, fearing electoral violence, he withdrew from the contest. Simpson's first venture into colonial politics ended in a storm of controversy when he claimed that the Roman Catholic clergy had fomented "unholy excitement" on behalf of his opponents, whom he labelled a "Revolutionary Faction."

Simpson remained collector of customs at the increasingly busy port of Coteau-du-Lac throughout the 1830s and was indirectly associated with the growing reform movement of the period through the activities of his step-son, John Arthur ROEBUCK, the agent for the Lower Canadian assembly in the British House of Commons. However, when violence broke out in November 1837, Simpson organized a group of volunteers to occupy the undefended British fort at Coteau-du-Lac, preventing it from falling to the *Patriotes*, and earned the thanks of Sir John Colborne* for his "zeal and activity." Later Simpson received rare praise from the opposite quarter. Jean-Joseph Girouard*, a *Patriote* leader for whose capture a £500 reward had been offered, surrendered to him on Christmas Day 1837, and later commended Simpson for "the generous and prudent treatment of the persecuted Canadians which he ensured in his area."

This same generous attitude which Girouard praised led Simpson into prominence and problems in 1838. It was Simpson who suggested to Lord Durham [Lambton*] that a general amnesty be granted to all political prisoners captured during the troubles except the leaders. Once the governor had accepted this idea, it was Simpson who acted as his intermediary in obtaining a signed confession of guilt from eight of the principal *Patriote* prisoners, who were banished to Bermuda by Lord Durham. Towards these men Simpson later displayed a compassionate – almost paternalistic – regard. He accompanied them from Montreal to Quebec, dining with them on the way, and arranged with Lord Durham for them to be given freedom of the island once they reached Bermuda. Following the disallowance of Durham's ordinance and the subsequent pardoning of the Bermuda exiles, Simpson sent the prisoners £100 to enable them to return from exile. The revelation of these past kindnesses by the *Montreal Herald* after the uprising of 1838 marked Simpson as "a notoriously bad character" in the eyes of the Tory establishment.

In 1841 John Simpson again entered politics. He resigned as collector of customs at Coteau-du-Lac, arranged for his son, William B., to succeed him at the post, and stood as the chosen candidate of Lord Sydenham [Thomson*] in Vaudreuil County (part of the earlier York County). After a violent contest in which "pitchforks, axes and clubs were made use of," Simpson was elected to the Legislative Assembly. The controversial contest was highly criticized by the Reform party and in 1844 Simpson chose not to risk re-election. One year later he was appointed to the Rebellion Losses Commission, on which he served until it completed its work in 1851 [*see* Philip Henry MOORE]. Even as a commissioner, he was the target of journalistic abuse; in 1851 the Conservative *Montreal Gazette* severely criticized his work on the hated commission. In later life Simpson lived in quiet retirement with his son, collector of customs at Brockville and then with his son at Kingston, where he died in his 85th year.

John Simpson was a conspicuous member of the privileged minority which dominated Lower Canada during the first half of the 19th century, but his quixotic enthusiasm prevented him from becoming a typical member of it. Possibly the best analysis of Simpson's chequered career was written by his step-son, John Arthur Roebuck: "He was a daring and sanguine man and indulged in schemes that would have terrified a more sober-minded one."

JOHN BESWARICK THOMPSON

ANQ, QBC, Procureur général, Événements de 1837–1838, no.4082. Canada, Department of Indian Affairs and Northern Development, National Historic Sites

Simpson

Service, Research Division, George Ingram, "A history of Coteau-du-Lac" (typewritten report, 1967). PAC, MG 24, A27 (Durham papers), 26, pp.631–34, 652–53; RG 1, E13, 14, p.174; RG 8, I, A1, 49, pp.62–69; A2, 1271, pp.54–55, 58–59.

Canada, Province of, Legislative Assembly, *Journals*, 1841–52. [Charles Grey], *Crisis in the Canadas: 1838–1839; the Grey journals and letters*, ed. W. G. Ormsby (Toronto, 1964), 176. Lower Canada, House of Assembly, *Journals*, 1824–37. "Les Patriotes aux Bermudes en 1838 – lettres d'exil," Yvon Thériault, édit., *RHAF*, XVII (1963–64), 107–12. "Les patriotes de 1837–1838 d'après les documents J.-J. Girouard," P.-A. Linteau, édit., *RHAF*, XXI (1967–68), 310. *News* (Kingston), 22–24 April 1873. *Life and letters of John Arthur Roebuck . . .*, ed. R. E. Leader (London and New York, 1897), 8–17. F.-J. Audet, "Les députés de la vallée de l'Ottawa: John Simpson (1788–1873)," CHA *Report, 1936*, 32–39.

SIMPSON, JOHN, businessman, politician, and public servant; b. 27 Dec. 1807, at Helmsley, Yorkshire, Eng.; d. 19 Sept. 1878, at Ottawa, Ont., and buried at Niagara.

John Simpson was a linen draper in London, England, before moving to Niagara, Upper Canada, in 1835, and setting up as a bookseller and stationer. In September 1837 he began publishing the *Niagara Chronicle* in partnership with George Menzies*, and became its sole owner in 1839. In January 1837 he had edited a volume of poems, tales, and essays by local authors, and from 1843 to 1849 he published, in some years associated with Hugh Scobie*, annual editions of *The Canadian mercantile almanack*. He continued to centre his interests in the paper, its press, and associated bookstore until he disposed of the whole undertaking in 1852. Simpson married a local lady, Miss Baker, on 12 May 1841 in St Mark's Church.

Simpson had shifted and enlarged his business interests in the late 1840s. The subscription list of the newly launched Niagara District Bank was located in the *Chronicle* office in 1845. In the following years he subscribed to the stock of the Erie and Ontario Insurance Company and a proposed Niagara Boot and Shoe Manufacturing Company. In addition, he was secretary of the Niagara and Ten Mile Creek Plank Road Company, the Niagara Permanent Building Society, the Niagara District Building Society, and the Erie and Ontario Railroad Company. Niagara's economy was declining under competition from neighbouring towns, however, and Simpson was content to be sustained by the collectorship of customs at Niagara in the years 1855–57. Early in 1857 he was projecting a large woollen mill.

Simpson's political apprenticeship began in 1846–47 when he was president of the Niagara board of police. In 1848 he was elected to the Lincoln district council and in 1851 to the town council of Niagara. He served as mayor of Niagara for four years beginning in 1852. He then entered provincial politics. In recent parliaments Niagara had been represented by the moderate Reformers Francis Hincks* and Joseph Curran Morrison*. Simpson was returned in 1857 as a Conservative, defeating Charles Curry. He was successful in the two following general elections, defeating T. McMicking in 1861 and Henry John Boulton* in 1863. A man of proven competence and party loyalty, Simpson was appointed provincial secretary in the Étienne-Paschal Taché*–John A. Macdonald* government on 30 March 1864, and continued in the cabinet until the formation of the "Great Coalition" in 1864. He then resigned on 29 June to make way for three Grit ministers, including George Brown*, to enter the cabinet. In compensation he was appointed deputy auditor general, an office he continued to hold until his death at Ottawa in 1878.

In his years at Niagara Simpson was a close associate of William Kirby* who was his election agent. A requisition to him, requesting that he stand for nomination in 1857, held 206 signatures, a veritable directory of the business community and the social register of Niagara. Throughout his career he was a member of the Church of England, and he was active in Christ Church in Ottawa.

PAUL CORNELL

John Simpson was the editor of *The Canadian forget me not for MDCCCXXXVII . . .* (Niagara, Ont., [1837]), and publisher of *The Canadian mercantile almanack . . .* (Niagara, Ont., and Toronto), 1843–49.

Niagara Chronicle, 1838–52. *Niagara Mail* (Niagara; St Catharines), 1847–64. *Ottawa Citizen*, 20 Sept. 1878. *Dom. ann. reg., 1878*. Wallace, *Macmillan dictionary*, 693. L. A. Pierce, *William Kirby, the portrait of a Tory loyalist* (Toronto, 1929).

SINCENNES (Saincennes), JACQUES-FÉLIX, shipowner, businessman, and politician; b. in Deschambault, Hampshire County (Portneuf), L.C., 7 Jan. 1818, son of Jacques Saincennes, a farmer and pilot, and Marie-Josephte Marcotte; d. at Montreal, Que., 20 Feb. 1876.

The Saint-Seine family were Acadians, who had originally come from the village of Bourguignon, near the source of the Seine in France. At the time of the expulsion of the Acadians, they settled on the north shore of the St Lawrence, and the name became first Saincennes and then Sincennes, which is the form Jacques-Félix used. At the age of 13, after six years at school, he was apprenticed to his father as a pilot and for two years plied the

St Lawrence between Quebec and Montreal. He then returned to school to finish his education and was thereafter employed as a clerk in a commercial house, before he obtained the post of purser in 1839 on a Montreal-Laprairie steamer.

Sincennes soon realized that one of the great needs of the region was a steamship service on the Richelieu River to carry produce from Chambly to William-Henry (Sorel) and on to Montreal: a 90-mile route in all. In 1845 he held a series of meetings of the Richelieu habitants, at such centres as Saint-Charles-sur-Richelieu, at which subscriptions were raised to the value of £3,715; this amount was used to build the side-wheeler *Richelieu* (the first ship built at the Sorel shipyards) and the barge *Sincennes*. The new company was called "La Société de Navigation de la Rivière Richelieu." Sincennes became the captain, in which capacity he not only transported produce, but soon performed the apparently impossible task of moving square timber from William-Henry to Chambly.

Almost immediately a rival line was formed and the first of many amalgamations took place, resulting in the Richelieu Company (La Compagnie du Richelieu), which was incorporated by statute in 1848. The founders and stockholders were all French and French was the language in which the entire business of the company was conducted until 1875. By 1848 operations had so expanded that Sincennes gave up the captaincy to conduct the shore business; he was secretary-treasurer of the company for many years, president for a decade, and a director until his death. His policy was one of continued expansion and, when competition broke out, amalgamation with his rivals. In 1856 the company launched the *Victoria* and the *Napoléon* and entered the hotly contested Montreal-Quebec run in rivalry with the Molson, Torrance, and Tate interests [see TORRANCE]. At the same time it took over the fleet of the Montreal and Three Rivers Navigation Company. In 1857 the Richelieu Company was capitalized by statute at £75,000 and in that year it paid a 32 per cent dividend. The next year the Torrance interests were incorporated into the company and David Torrance became a director, thus ending the competition.

In 1860 the expanded organization made a profit-pooling agreement with the Toronto-Montreal Royal Mail Line to prevent competition. The St Lawrence North Shore Navigation Company was taken over in that same year and the Lake St Peter Navigation Company and the Terrebonne and L'Assomption Navigation Company in 1861. By this time "in many cases the season's operations resulted in gross earnings greater than the total capital of the company," which by 1861 was $161,733. In 1862 the charter of the Richelieu Company was extended to permit operations throughout the St Lawrence and the Great Lakes. The final amalgamation with which Sincennes was involved came in 1875, after a period of rivalry, when the Richelieu Company joined with the Canadian Navigation Company (formerly the Royal Mail Line) of Sir Hugh Allan* to found the Richelieu and Ontario Navigation Company (from 1913 Canada Steamship Lines), which operated a total of 18 ships on the Great Lakes and St Lawrence and had a paid up capital of $750,000. Sincennes remained a director of the new corporation.

While establishing the Richelieu Company, Sincennes was also involved with another important shipping operation. In 1849 he and William McNaughton, whose interests lay in Ottawa valley lumber and forwarding, formed a partnership, the Sincennes-McNaughton Line (today McAllister Towing Limited). With headquarters at Sorel and Montreal, this company specialized in towing and berthing ships, as well as towing timber rafts and lumber barges on the Ottawa, Richelieu, and St Lawrence rivers, as far east as Quebec. The tugs used were of the side-wheel type. Sincennes was the president in what must have been an amiable relationship, for he and McNaughton were also engaged in various other partnerships such as the Montreal and Ottawa Forwarding Company, formed in 1865.

Sincennes took part in many other commercial and financial enterprises: in 1873, with McNaughton and others, he founded the Royal Canadian Insurance Company of Montreal and at the end of its first year became president. By 1875 the company had 300 agencies in Canada and the United States. He was, in addition, vice-president of La Banque du Peuple and was involved with companies manufacturing cotton and india-rubber goods.

In 1853 he was appointed a magistrate of the Montreal district and in 1857 made a brief entry into politics, running as a Ministerialist (Conservative) for the County of Richelieu, in which he had his residence, at Sorel. On December 28–29 by 1,204 votes to 1,169 he defeated the sitting member, Jean-Baptiste Guévremont, who appealed unsuccessfully. Sincennes, however, did not run in the next election, in July 1861.

He married twice: first, Clotilde-Héloise Douaire Bondy, by whom he had a son and three daughters; the second time, in 1866, Delphine-Denise Perrault, widow of lawyer Victor-Henri Bourgeau. There were no children by the second marriage. A man of medium stature, and faultless

Sitting on an Eagle Tail

dress, Sincennes was noted in Montreal for the regularity of his habits. When asked what he took as his motto he replied: *Esse potius quam videri*: to be rather than to seem. Although he lived in Sorel for much of his life, and was also a magistrate of this district, he spent his last years at Montreal, where his funeral service at Saint-Jacques-le-Majeur was conducted by Bishop Édouard-Charles Fabre*.

FREDERICK H. ARMSTRONG

AJM, Registre d'état civil. AJQ, Registre d'état civil. PAC, MG 30, D62 (Audet papers), 28, pp.107–8; RG 68, 240, p.49; Liber 21, p.171. Canada, Province of, Legislative Assembly, *Journals*, 1858; *Statutes*, 1857, c.170; 1862, c.69. Canada, *Statutes*, 1873, c.99. Andrew Merrilees, "A history of the Sincennes-McNaughton Line" (typescript, property of McAllister Towing Ltd, Montreal). *Montreal Gazette*, 2 Jan. 1858, 12 July 1861, 15 Feb. 1862, 21 Feb. 1876. *Le Nouveau Monde* (Montréal), 21 févr. 1876. *L'Opinion publique* (Montréal), 25 avril 1875, 2 mars 1876. *Pilot and Journal of Commerce* (Montreal), 5 Jan. 1858. *The Mercantile Agency reference book (and key) for the dominion of Canada ... Jan., 1876* (Montreal, 1876), 319, 511.

Atherton, *Montreal*, II 168, 531, 574, 577. Azarie Couillard-Després, *Histoire de Sorel de ses origines à nos jours* (Montréal, 1926), 281, 297–98, 308–12. James Croil, *Steam navigation in Canada and its relation to the commerce of Canada and the United States* (Toronto, 1898), 314–15. M. J. Patton, "Shipping and canals," *Canada and its provinces* (Shortt and Doughty), X, 539, 541–42, 551. L. C. Tombs, *National problems of Canada; the port of Montreal* (McGill University Economic Studies, 6, Toronto, 1926), 43. Turcotte, *Canada sous l'Union*, II, 384. Wood, *All afloat*, 148–50. R. W. Shepherd, "The Richelieu and Ontario fleet," *Detroit Marine Historian*, VIII (March–June 1955).

SITTING ON AN EAGLE TAIL. *See* SOTAI-NA

SMALLWOOD, CHARLES, physician, professor of meteorology, and founder of McGill Observatory at Montreal; b. 1812 in Birmingham, Eng.; d. 22 Dec. 1873 in Montreal, Que.

Charles Smallwood arrived in Canada in 1833, with an MD from University College, London, and for at least two years lived at Huntingdon, Lower Canada. There he kept a weather notebook. He was licensed to practise medicine in Lower Canada on 16 July 1834. Sometime between late 1835 and early 1841 he established a residence and presumably a medical practice at Saint-Martin (Isle-Jésus), nine miles west of Montreal.

For the years until 1856 information about Smallwood is meagre. However, a paper published by Smallwood in 1858 describes, as it was then, the weather observatory he had established at Saint-Martin in 1841, and had developed since that time. It was a small wooden building, within 20 yards of his house, with instruments inside, outside, and on an array of wooden masts. Regular instruments included barometers, thermometers, hygrometers, an anemometer, and rain and snow gauges. He took readings of these and recorded observations of the state of the sky three times daily, along with notes on natural events such as bird migrations. He built ingenious autographic recorders, some of them photographic. Dew and evaporation were measured. Ozone, measured by chemically prepared paper, was studied intensively. A copper lantern, hoisted to the top of an 80-foot mast, was connected to electroscopes and electrometers, to measure atmospheric electricity. Snow crystals were examined by microscope and by photography. With a 7-inch telescope he took astronomical observations on all favourable nights. For time-keeping, a transit telescope looked out through an opening along the ridge of the roof, and the observatory was connected by the Montreal telegraph with major cities in the United States.

After 1856 information about Smallwood's activities suddenly becomes plentiful. In that year a committee of the Montreal Natural History Society visited his observatory and subsequently forwarded a petition to parliament urging assistance for publication of his records for the preceding 15 years. When the American Association for the Advancement of Science met in Montreal in 1857, Smallwood gave the opening remarks and they are those of someone who is clearly an established member of the Montreal scientific community.

He had been elected an honorary member of the Montreal Natural History Society in 1856, and was president in 1865. His papers were usually presented to that society. Six papers and four annual weather reviews appeared in the *Canadian Naturalist* (conducted by a committee of the society) in 1857–60, nine papers and seven weather reviews in 1866–72. Perhaps his most important paper, "On some of the forms of snow crystals and the different electrical states of the atmosphere during their formation," appeared in the annual report of the society for 1855–56. The topic to which he gave most attention was ozone, especially its relation to relative humidity rather than to atmospheric electricity. Smallwood's scientific activities also brought him in 1856 an LLD from McGill University and he was appointed professor of meteorology, without salary. (A further degree of DCL was granted by the University of Bishop's College in 1864.)

In 1863 all the apparatus of Smallwood's

Smart

observatory was moved from the frame building at Saint-Martin to a stone structure built for the purpose in the McGill University grounds. The Montreal Observatory, as the establishment was renamed (later McGill College Observatory, then the McGill Observatory), remained in this building until it was demolished in 1962, and continues now in the Macdonald Physics Building. (Dr Smallwood had moved his own residence and practice, probably in 1863 but surely by 1868, to Montreal.) Magnetic-field observations were added by the observatory. The astronomical time-keeping was made available to the community; it was only succeeded as a national time service by the Dominion Observatory at Ottawa in the 1920s, and like the weather recording its time-keeping has continued to this day.

For almost six years, commencing in January 1857 and terminating with Dr Smallwood's removal to Montreal, the *Canadian Naturalist* published monthly tabulations of the Saint-Martin observations. It published others for the McGill Observatory, but only for ten months of 1864. These "abstracts" are the only detailed record of Dr Smallwood's observations, apart from record books at the McGill Observatory for 1860–62 (Saint-Martin) and 1868–72 (McGill).

Dr Smallwood had had various grants for his meteorological work but had canvassed over some 15 years for comprehensive government support for the observatory. It was finally obtained in 1871, jointly from the Signal Office of the United States War Department and the Canadian Ministry of Marine and Fisheries. The observatory became the Montreal station in the network reporting observations directly by telegraph to Toronto for use in national weather forecasting by the Meteorological Service of Canada, established in 1871.

Also in the spring of 1871, Bishop's College created in Montreal a medical faculty, toward which Dr Smallwood had been a prime mover. On 19 March he became professor of midwifery and diseases of women and children; next day the new faculty met and elected him their dean. In late May, however, he finally received word of government support for the observatory and resigned his medical positions; on 12 June the medical faculty met, but failed to dissuade him.

Just two years later, in December 1873, Dr Smallwood died after a brief illness, and was buried on Christmas Eve. He was succeeded at the observatory by his assistant, Clement Henry McLeod*.

Smallwood was a member of four foreign scientific societies: La Société Météorologique de France, the Pulkova astronomical observatory, Académie Royale de Belgique, the National Insti-

tute of the United States, and the Academy of Natural Sciences (Philadelphia). He was a governor of the College of Physicians and Surgeons of Lower Canada (founded 1847) from 1851 until at least 1865. His achievements as meteorologist become more striking when they are recognized as being an avocation, carried out while he was practising medicine, with sufficient competence to be offered a medical professorship

J. S. MARSHALL

Charles Smallwood's research and studies have been published by the Natural History Society of Montreal in: *Canadian Naturalist and Geologist* (Montreal), II (1857), 321–35; III (1858), 110–15, 352–61, 444–49; IV (1859), 81–84, 169–72, 276–80, 343–45, 383–87, 408–10; new ser., III (1868), 125–34; *Canadian Naturalist and Quarterly Journal of Science* (Montreal), new ser., IV (1869), 62–64, 112–18, 183–87, 249–56; new ser. V (1870), 10–13, 22–23; new ser., VI (1872), 334–39.

PAC, RG 1, E1, 82, p.497; RG 4, C1, 247, no.549; 393, no.149; 408, no.627; 494, no.478; 511, no.717; 512, no.805; 522, no.2231; 570, no.138; 588, no.272; 760, no.2989; 768, no.1351; 794, no.191; 796, no.58; 798, no.232; RG 19, D4a, 4, 16 March 1861. McGill Observatory (Montreal), Charles Smallwood's record book, Montreal Observatory, 1868–72; Charles Smallwood's record book, Saint-Martin, 1860–62. Natural History Society of Montreal, *Annual Reports*, 1854–81.

SMART, WILLIAM, Presbyterian minister; b. 14 Sept. 1788 at Haddington, East Lothian, Scotland, son of Alexander and Margaret Smart; m. first, Phylina Foote, 7 Nov. 1816, by whom he had a son, William (judge of Hastings County, Canada West, from 1850 to 1865), and secondly, Sarah Mallory, in 1862; d. 9 Sept. 1876 at Gananoque, Ont.

William Smart's parents moved to London, England, when he was an infant. They attended Wells Street secession church whose minister, the Reverend Alexander Waugh, became William's mentor. As a boy, William was delicate and precociously religious. He "gave himself to the Church" at 17, taught in Sabbath school, and preached at mission stations before enrolling in the London Missionary Society Seminary at Gosport, Hampshire, England. He was ordained in the Scots Church, Swallow Street, London, in April 1811.

Smart had "thought of Calcutta or some part of the East Indies" for his ministry but when a request for a missionary came from the Presbyterians of Elizabethtown, Yonge, and Augusta (three townships along the St Lawrence in Upper Canada), the interdenominational London Missionary Society recommended him.

William was welcomed in Montreal by the

Smith

Reverend Robert Easton and proceeded to Elizabethtown (Brockville) in October 1811. Within a week he organized a Sunday school, the first in Upper Canada. Until the Reverend Robert Boyd came to Prescott in 1820, Smart preached for congregations scattered from Gananoque on the west to near Cornwall on the east, and north to the Rideau River and Lakes. He preached at military posts during the War of 1812, and afterwards at the new settlement of Perth until the Reverend William Bell* arrived in 1817. Because of Smart's efforts, the First Presbyterian Church in Brockville was built in 1817; when the church burned in 1847, Smart raised funds for rebuilding.

In 1818, William Smart helped to found the Presbytery of the Canadas, a union of secessionist churches free of Scottish control. This became the United Presbytery of Upper Canada in 1829, with Smart as first moderator, and the United Synod of Upper Canada in 1831. To strengthen its claim for financial support from the government, which endowed only the Church of England and the Church of Scotland in Canada, Smart promoted the union of 1840 between the United Synod and the Presbyterian Church of Canada in connection with the Church of Scotland. However Smart (along with Boyd) withdrew in 1844 saying "the Union was one rather of form than of affection." His action displeased his congregation and he resigned from the Brockville church in 1849. For many years he did supply preaching for congregations in Leeds and Grenville counties and in Kingston.

Smart opposed the monopoly of the Church of England in clergy reserves and its control over the district schools. He believed that education should be equally available and he worked through his presbytery and synod toward these ends. Similarly, he promoted the establishment of a theological seminary to train Presbyterian ministers, but when this project failed he supported Queen's College at Kingston.

As a secessionist Presbyterian, Smart could not legally (until 1831) perform marriages. He persisted in doing so and in 1824 a charge was brought against him, but the jury returned "No bill." Smart joined the freemasons in 1820, a step which threatened to disrupt his congregation. He was grand chaplain, Provincial Grand Lodge, in 1822, 1823, and 1825. He was an early advocate of temperance and helped organize the Brockville Temperance Society in 1832.

William Smart expressed his views on the church, education, and other matters in contributions to the *Brockville Recorder* in the 1820s and 1830s, writing as "The Wanderer," "The Traveller, or Pickings by the Wayside," and "Presbuteros."

He also wrote in the *Canadian Watchman*, a religious weekly, and he and the Reverend Robert McDowall* founded the *Evangelical Herald*, a short-lived periodical published in Kingston. Towards the end of his life, Smart wrote an autobiography in the third person but it was never published. He was a man of independent mind, courageous, compassionate, and visionary.

RUTH McKENZIE

The most important source is William Smart's autobiography at UCA: "Biography of Rev. Wm. Smart, Presbyterian Church, Brockville, 1811–49." Knox College Archives, William Morris to Smart, 24 June 1840; William Rintoul to Smart, 4 Aug. 1831, 17 Nov. 1832. Methodist Missionary Society (London), correspondence, continent of America, letters written by Smart, 1811–20. UCA, William Smart, presbytery correspondence, 1819–56.

Presbyterian Church of Canada in connection with the Church of Scotland, Synod, *Acts and Proceedings* (Montreal, Toronto), 1831–44. United Presbytery of Upper Canada, *Minutes*, 1829–31. United Synod of Upper Canada, *Minutes*, 1832–38. William Bell, *Hints to emigrants, in a series of letters from Upper Canada* (Edinburgh, 1824), 90–93, 99–101, 117–18. *Brockville Recorder*, 1821–55, espcially 1821–32. *Canadian Watchman* (Kingston), 1831–32. Gregg, *History of the Presbyterian Church*. Ruth McKenzie, *Leeds and Grenville, their first two hundred years* (Toronto, Montreal, 1967), 72, 82–84, 89. J. R. Robertson, *The history of freemasonry in Canada from its introduction in 1749 . . .* (2v., Toronto, 1899). Isabel Skelton, *A man austere, William Bell, parson and pioneer* (Toronto, 1947), 19–21, 104–10, 169, 178–228, 314–15. N. G. Smith et al., *A short history of the Presbyterian Church in Canada* (Toronto, [1967]). H. S. Seaman, "The Rev. William Smart, Presbyterian minister of Elizabethtown, 1811–1876," *Ont. Hist.*, V (1904), 178–86.

SMITH, WILLIAM HENRY, surgeon, dentist, and author; fl. 1843–73.

William Henry Smith was probably born in England, most likely not before 1800, judging from the vigour of his activities in the 1840s. His parents have not been identified. Smith's writings show him as a man of education, remarkable energy and patience, and occasionally of humour. He studied surgery in London under Sir David Barry and was a pupil of G. J. Guthrie, president of the Royal College of Surgeons, who had earlier spent five years in Canada. There is, however, no evidence that Smith ever qualified as FRCS. He became surgeon to the emigrant ship *Amazon* and, perhaps in this capacity, emigrated to Canada. From the title-page and dedication date of his *Gazetteer*, we know that he had arrived in Canada West by 1843.

Smith travelled through all the settled parts of

the upper province collecting data and walking more than 3,000 miles in all weathers. The result was his first known work, *Smith's Canadian gazetteer*, published in Toronto for the author in 1846; it was compiled expressly to dispel ignorance and misinformation regarding Canada, particularly in Britain and amongst immigrants, and to encourage settlement. It comprises articles on districts, counties, townships, and communities in alphabetical arrangement, and includes tables (original data recorded nowhere else), six plates, and a folded map. Three new issues or variant states of the book appeared before 1849, when it was reissued with a new title-page and the names of London booksellers added to the imprint.

Smith was referring to Canada as his adopted country by the end of the 1840s, and he is listed in a Toronto directory for 1850–51 as "surgeon dentist." He appears to have settled in Toronto with his family for in his next work, of 1851, he lists a Mrs and Miss Smith as conducting a ladies' seminary at his own address.

Encouraged by the success of his *Gazetteer*, and with the desire further to promote settlement, Smith compiled his *Canada: past, present and future*. It was copyrighted in 1851, but publication in ten subscription parts extended into 1852. The 1,200 pages and 11 maps to be bound into two volumes are a monument of industry, for Smith had distributed thousands of prospectuses requesting information, endured long journeys to gather data, and spent years of "exertion of body and mind" to complete the work. Detailed descriptions of each county in Canada West are given, going from west to east, with commercial tables and notes on townships and settlements. An invaluable business and professional directory is added, and each volume has a geographical index. The work was acclaimed in the press of both the Canadas. Another issue bound in two volumes appeared in 1852, and a third later with additional plates.

Smith drops from sight in 1852, when the final parts of his *Canada* were issued, until 1873 when he published in Montreal his last known work, *Smith's family physician*. Its long title-page records the details of his professional training and position as a ship's surgeon. After this time our knowledge of him ceases.

Smith's *Gazetteer*, though not the first in Canada West as he claimed, and his *Canada*, are indispensable references for the period, and are still widely quoted.

WILLIAM F. E. MORLEY

W. H. Smith, *Canada: past, present and future, being a historical, geographical, geological and statistical account of Canada West* (2v., Toronto, [1851–52]);
Smith's Canadian gazetteer; comprising statistical and general information respecting all parts of the upper province, or Canada West … (Toronto, 1846); *Smith's family physician: comprising the nature, causes, symptoms and treatment of diseases …* (Montreal, 1873). *Rowsell's city of Toronto and county of York directory, for 1850–1 …* ed. J. Armstrong (Toronto, 1850).

SOTAI-NA (Sotenah; called Rainy Chief), a leading chieftain and warrior of the Blood tribe of the Blackfoot nation; b.c. 1809, a member of the Mamyowi (Fish Eaters) band, probably in what is now southern Alberta; d. 1878 in the same area.

As a young man Sotai-na was known as Makoyi-ksiksinum (White Wolf), a name he received after a battle in which he killed a Crow Indian of that name. In this fight, Rainy Chief deliberately exposed himself to danger and, with a fellow chief, Peenaquim (Seen from Afar), held off an enemy war party until his own followers could escape. Later Sotai-na became leader of a small family group of Bloods which eventually was recognized as a band in its own right. It was named Isiso-kaas (usually translated Hair Shirts but sometimes Robe Shirts or Robes with Hair on Outside) after a member of the band who wore a shirt made from the skin of a buffalo calf from which the hair had not been removed.

Sotai-na was also called Sowatsi-tapitowpi (Sitting on an Eagle Tail) and was identified under this name by James Doty who met him in 1855. Doty was searching for Blackfoot Indians, who normally hunted or traded on American territory, to sign a treaty with the American government. He described the chief as "a good friend to the Whites" but "himself and people were very poor." The chief usually traded at Hudson's Bay Company establishments and so did not become a party to the American treaty. At this time, Rainy Chief's following consisted of only 18 lodges; by 1870 this number had increased to 29 lodges and 348 people. Sotai-na's band was always poor, perhaps because he was on good terms with everyone and did not encourage the theft of horses, a source of wealth, from enemy tribes.

In spite of the fact that he was recognized as a medicine man, Rainy Chief was one of the few leaders of the Blackfoot nation to accept Christianity during the nomadic era. Most chiefs were hostile to missionary endeavours, but Rainy Chief became a friend of the Oblate father Albert Lacombe* (they first met around 1865) and believed he inherited supernatural powers from the priest. The chief permitted three of his grandchildren to be baptized by Oblate priests in 1873–74 and allowed Father Constantin Scollen* to labour in his camp during the winter of 1876–77. Scollen

Soulerin

observed that the chief was an "old man who . . . did not leave me during a month of travels; his faith and simplicity were truly touching!" At a time when the Blackfoot tribes were feared and distrusted by traders and missionaries, Rainy Chief maintained his friendship with the white people.

When the bands gathered to sign Treaty No. 7 with the Canadian government in 1877, Rainy Chief, whose winter camp was now usually near the Red Deer River, was recognized by officials as the leader of all bands which camped in the northern part of the Bloods' hunting grounds. Only two head chiefs were selected from the Blood tribe, the young and dynamic Mekaisto (Red Crow) for the south, and the older patriarch Rainy Chief for the north. The latter was chosen not only for his friendly attitude towards the whites, but also because of the strength of his position within the tribe. By signing Treaty No. 7, these Indians conceded their right to hunt in most of present-day southern Alberta. Rainy Chief was among the first of the chiefs to sign but died before his people were settled upon the reserves it provided.

Sotai-na was probably buried on a high hill or in a scaffold on a tree, the usual Blackfoot custom. He had four children; his youngest son Apawa-kaasi (White Antelope) became a minor chief of the band but was never as important as his father.

HUGH A. DEMPSEY

H. A. Dempsey, "Blood Indian bands; their identification and history," 1955, and "Interviews with Charlie Pantherbone, 1954–1955" (unpublished MSS in author's possession).

National Archives (Washington), Census of the Blackfeet Indians, Alfred Sully to E. S. Parker, 16 July 1870; H. A. Dempsey, "A visit to the Blackfoot camps by James Doty," *Alberta Hist. Rev.*, XIV, no.3 (1966), 24–25; Morris, *Treaties of Canada with the Indians*, 245–75, 368–75; "Rapport de Constantin Scollen à Mgr Vital Grandin, 15 Sept. 1874," *Missions des O.M.I.*, XIV, 35; this report has been translated and edited by Hugh A. Dempsey in "Early Alberta teacher here before Mounties," *Calgary Herald*, 1 Sept. 1955.

SOULERIN, JEAN-MATHIEU, priest, Basilian, superior of St Michael's College in Toronto, and superior general of the Basilian fathers; b. 6 June 1807 at Ailhon (department of Ardèche, France), son of Mathieu Soulerin and Marie Pigeyre; d. 17 Oct. 1879 in Annonay, France.

Jean-Mathieu Soulerin studied at the college of Annonay and entered the Basilian order in 1830. After his ordination on 20 Dec. 1834, he taught at the college of Feyzin, near Lyons, until 1842, when he became director of studies at the college of Annonay. He also studied in Paris in 1836 and 1837, and later had the benefit of summer travel in Italy, Belgium, and England.

On 15 Sept. 1852, shortly after his arrival in Canada, Soulerin and four other Basilians, two priests and two not yet ordained, opened St Mary's Lesser Seminary in Toronto at the request of Bishop Armand de Charbonnel*. In the same year, the Christian Brothers had founded another school, St Michael's College, for students at the secondary level. The bishop merged the two schools in 1853 and named Soulerin the superior of the new college.

The opportunity to attend an educational institution presided over by members of their own faith was welcomed by Roman Catholics. Almost 50 students were attending the college in its second year but a lack of funds and the bishop's dislike of having the community engaged almost exclusively in teaching hampered efforts to expand beyond the bishop's palace where it was located. However, in 1856 Soulerin succeeded in establishing the new St Michael's College on property donated in part by John Elmsley* near the University of Toronto, the site it still occupies. That same year, Soulerin's foresight led him to open St Basil's Novitiate to prepare Canadians for membership in the Basilian community.

Father Soulerin was of less than average height, shy in disposition, and strong of will. His administrative abilities were soon recognized; he was a shrewd adviser, practical in business matters, sensitive to changing conditions, and gifted in appraising men and their actions. In Toronto, he served as vicar general under Charbonnel and his successor, John Joseph Lynch*, and twice, during the absence of the former, he was administrator of the diocese, once for a period of about two years. Soulerin also assisted in the work of the diocese by caring for a parish in Weston after 1852 and by building St Basil's Church in Toronto in 1856. His appreciation of needs outside Toronto led him to send a Basilian priest to Assumption College at Windsor in 1857, and in 1863 he took over St Mary's parish and its missions in Owen Sound. He was consulted by the bishop of Hamilton, John FARRELL, and the bishop of Ottawa, J.-B. GUIGUES, and in 1857 the bishop of London, Adolphe Pinsonnault*, appointed him a vicar general. After his return to France he held this same office in his native diocese of Viviers.

Father Soulerin was elected fourth superior general of the Basilian fathers for life on 19 Jan. 1865 and returned to France in June of that year. During his years as the head of the community the work of the Basilians reached a peak in France and their order grew rapidly in America.

ROBERT J. SCOLLARD

[Jean-Mathieu Soulerin described the prospects of the Roman Catholic Church in Ontario in "Missions du Canada," *Annales de la propagation de la foi* (Lyon), XXVIII (avril 1856), 308–19. He also published *Constitutions de la congrégation de Saint-Basile* (Lyon, 1878). Father Soulerin's letters are in the archives of the Congregation of Priests of St Basil in Toronto and in Annonay, France. In Toronto, the archives are located at the residence of the superior general and Soulerin's letters are placed in chronological order under the institutions he was concerned with. In Annonay, the archives are located at the Institution secondaire du Sacré-Cœur and there are letters of Soulerin in four collections: C, Documents de la période 1839–1859 (Tourvieille); D, Documents Actorie (1859–64); E, Documents de la période 1865–1879 (Soulerin); S, Rapports avec le Canada. R.J.S.]

R. J. Scollard, *Dictionary of Basilian biography, lives of members of the Congregation of Priests of Saint Basil from its beginnings in 1822 to 1968* (Toronto, 1969), 148–50. Adrien Chomel, *Le collège d'Annonay, 1800–1880, mémoires et souvenirs* (Annonay, 1902), 184, 483–504, 511, 516–17. Charles Roume, *Origines et formation de la communauté des prêtres de Saint-Basile, contribution à l'histoire religieuse du Vivarais* (Privas, 1965), 239, 245, 273, 313, 329–40, 347, 387–88. Francis Boland, "Father Soulerin, C.S.B., founder and administrator," CCHA *Report, 1956*, 13–27. L. K. Shook, "The coming of the Basilians to Assumption College, early expansion of St Michael's College," CCHA *Report, 1951*, 59–73; "St Michael's College, the formative years, 1850–1853," CCHA *Report, 1950*, 37–52.

SOWATSI-TAPITOWPI. *See* Sotai-na

SPENCER, AUBREY GEORGE, Church of England clergyman, missionary, and bishop; b. 12 Feb. 1795 in London, Eng., a great-great-grandson of John Churchill, 1st Duke of Marlborough, and the eldest son of the Honourable William Spencer and Susan Jennison, Countess of the Holy Roman Empire; d. 24 Feb. 1872 at Torquay, Devon, Eng.

Aubrey George Spencer was educated at St Albans Abbey School, at Dr Charles Burney's private school in Greenwich, and at Magdalen Hall, Oxford. He was ordained deacon in Norwich Cathedral on 24 May 1818 by Bishop Henry Bathurst of Norwich, who also raised him to the priesthood on 24 Feb. 1819 at Welbeck Chapel, Middlesex. Spencer served as curate in Prittlewell, Essex, during 1818 and 1819; he then entered the service of the Society for the Propagation of the Gospel and was appointed as their missionary at Ferryland, Newfoundland, in 1819. He was transferred to Trinity Bay in 1820. While visiting St John's in 1821, he informed the society that the intense cold was undermining his health and that he wished to return to England for the winter. He further advised the SPG that he had written William Howley, the bishop of London, requesting an appointment to one of five vacant missions in Bermuda.

Late in 1821 Spencer informed the society that he was in Bermuda and would not be returning to Newfoundland. The governor of Bermuda, Sir William Lumley, nominated him rector of Smiths and Hamilton in February 1822 and appointed him to his council. Shortly after, Spencer married Eliza Musson, daughter of a wealthy Bermuda merchant, by whom he had one son and three daughters. In 1825 Bishop John Inglis* of Nova Scotia appointed Spencer archdeacon of Bermuda and rector of Paget and Warwick. In 1827, the same year that he published *Sermons on various subjects* (London), he was granted a Lambeth DD by Archbishop Charles Manners-Sutton and a DCL by King's College, Windsor, N.S. Bishop Inglis offered him the archdeaconry of Newfoundland late in 1829, but he refused because he felt deeply committed to the spiritual welfare and education of the blacks of Bermuda.

By letters patent from Queen Victoria dated 27 July 1839 Aubrey George Spencer was appointed first bishop of the see of Newfoundland. In Lambeth Palace chapel on 4 August he was consecrated by William Howley, by this time archbishop of Canterbury, Bishops Charles James Blomfield of London, William Otter of Chichester, and John Inglis of Nova Scotia.

When Spencer took up his post in Newfoundland he found that the small number of clergy and the depressed condition of the people had cast a shadow on the growth of the Church of England. However, with the financial help of the SPG, the church progressed steadily under the new bishop's leadership. Missions expanded rapidly and the number of clergy in Newfoundland had risen to 27 by 1842. Spencer divided the diocese into deaneries and, in cooperation with the Newfoundland and British North American School Society – whose work had been opposed by John Inglis for its low church or evangelical leanings – increased the number of church schools. Spencer established a theological training school and in 1841 planned the building of his cathedral in St John's. However his health remained precarious and in 1843 he gladly accepted the bishopric of Jamaica. His successor Edward Feild inherited a far more progressive see than had existed when Spencer assumed office.

Spencer remained in Jamaica until 1855 when his health broke completely. He thereupon retired to Torquay, Devon, where he lived until his death. During this period he worked on his last publication, *A brief account of the Church of England,*

Spike

its faith and worship: as shown by the Book of Common Prayer (London, 1867).

                                    C. E. THOMAS

A. G. Spencer, *A brief account of the Church of England, its faith and worship: as shown by the Book of Common Prayer* (London, 1867); *Sermons on various subjects* (London, 1827).

USPG, C/CAN/NFL, 4 add., Spencer to the secretary of the SPG, 4 Jan., 22 May, 15 Sept., 5 Dec. 1821; 22 Feb., 2 April 1822; 6 Jan. 1830; Spencer to G. M. Markland, treasurer of the SPG, 3 Dec. 1822, 1 Nov. 1827; C/CAN/NFL, 6 (letters concerning the building of the cathedral in St John's, Nfld.). *Times* (London), 27 Feb. 1872. Pascoe, *Two hundred years of the S.P.G.* O. R. Rowley, *The Anglican episcopate of Canada and Newfoundland* (London and Milwaukee, Wis., 1928). "Aubrey George Spencer, D.D., D.C.L., first bishop of Newfoundland, 1839–1843, second bishop of Jamaica, 1843–1872," Can. Church Hist. Soc. *J.*, X (1968), 186–93 [reprinted from the *International Magazine of Literature, Art and Science* (New York), II, no.11 (1 Jan. 1851), 157–59].

SPIKE, JAMES, printer and publisher; b. at Halifax, N.S., in 1807 (baptized 10 June), sixth child of Daniel Spike and Grace Cullimore; m. in 1831 to Elizabeth Kerr (widow of his cousin Francis Leston) by whom he had two children, and in 1842 to Mary Elizabeth Metzler by whom he had 12 children; d. 29 March 1879 in Halifax.

James Spike's mother was remotely related to the Howe family and her son seems to have learned the printing trade from them. In 1826 Spike and Joseph HOWE, then 22, bought the *Weekly Chronicle* from William Minns, Howe's step-uncle. They changed the paper's name to the *Acadian and General Advertiser* and began publication on 5 Jan. 1827. This partnership was Howe's first business venture and is the main reason Spike is remembered. Their newspaper took a moderate, even faintly progressive, stand, and Howe's editorial touch is apparent. At the end of the year Spike bought out, but never paid, his partner, and changed the name of the paper to the *Acadian*. He was evidently more a printer than a journalist for he announced he had "committed the Editorial part to a gentleman fully competent to the task." The last number of the paper in the Nova Scotia archives is dated 9 May 1834. After Spike and Howe parted, their opinions diverged towards the right and the left. With his "unassuming manners and kindness of heart" Spike seems out of place in the fierce newspaper politics of that day.

On 6 June 1838 James Spike became the first printer and publisher of the *Guardian*, the un-official voice of the Kirk of Scotland and also a good general newspaper. Ten years later he ended

his newspaper career when the *Guardian* changed publishers on 30 June 1848.

Spike was appointed city health inspector of Halifax on 16 Oct. 1854 and continued in this office until his death from cancer. In his obituaries he was most remembered for his prominence in the temperance movement.

                                    C. ST.C. STAYNER

Brunswick Street Church (Halifax), Records. St Luke's Church (Halifax), Records. St Paul's Church (Halifax), Records, 1769, 1787, 1807. *Acadian* (Halifax), 28 March, 9 May 1834. *Acadian and General Advertiser* (Halifax), 5, 12 Jan., 28 Dec. 1827. *Acadian Recorder* (Halifax), 8 July 1826, 9 July 1831, 29 March 1879, 10 March 1919. *Guardian* (Halifax), 6 June 1838, 30 June 1848. *Halifax Daily Reporter and Times*, 29 March 1879. *Morning Chronicle* (Halifax), 31 March 1879. *Novascotian* (Halifax), 13 Sept. 1827. J. A. Roy, *Joseph Howe, a study in achievement and frustration* (Toronto, 1935). J. J. Stewart, "Early journalism in Nova Scotia," N.S. Hist. Soc. *Coll.*, VI (1888), 91–122.

STAMP, EDWARD, master mariner and in-dustrialist; b. Alnwick, Northumberland, Eng., 5 Nov. 1814; d. at Turnham Green, Middlesex, 20 Jan. 1872.

Edward Stamp obtained his master's certificate in 1851. In 1854, during the Crimean War, he was captain of the steam transport *Emeu* and succeeded in bringing her undamaged through the great storm off Balaklava in November of that year, in which 18 ships were lost and 12 others dismasted. He first visited the north Pacific coast in 1857, when the ship he commanded came to Puget Sound to load lumber for Australia. Later he returned to purchase spars, ship-timbers, and lumber for two London firms, Thomas Bilbe and Company and James Thomson and Company. Some of the spars were used to make masts and yards for the steamer *Great Eastern*. When the Fraser River gold rush began in 1858, Stamp established a commission and importing business in Victoria. He also made "considerable purchases of land in Vancouver Island, Victoria & Langley," not, he explained, as a speculator, but with a view to providing for his sons.

Stamp seems always to have been interested in a variety of enterprises, and in 1859, while in Eng-land, he tried to secure a contract for a steamer service between Victoria and San Francisco. When success seemed near he was thwarted by a change of government in Britain which so delayed negotia-tions that he had to return to Victoria without securing an agreement. While in London, Stamp had formed a syndicate to establish an export lumber mill either on Puget Sound or on Van-couver Island; James Thomson and Company was the major shareholder. This firm later became

Anderson, Anderson and Company; in 1859 it was already controlled by the Anderson family, and the mill Stamp built was popularly known as the Anderson mill.

When Stamp returned to Victoria, he opened negotiations with Governor James DOUGLAS and agreed finally to place the mill on the Alberni Canal (now Alberni Inlet), on a site now within the city of Port Alberni. He was granted 2,000 acres for his mill and settlement, as well as timber limits that totalled 15,000 acres. Construction began in the summer of 1860 and the mill was completed in May 1861. The initial export shipment was to Peru. Stamp seems to have been a somewhat difficult character, and he resigned from the management of the mill in January 1863. Its future was then in doubt; in spite of the wealth of timber in the district, much of it was so large that with the equipment then available only trees close to the water could be brought to the mill, and it was running out of logs. It finally ceased operation about the end of 1864, having produced in all about 35,000,000 board feet of lumber.

Stamp now turned for a time to mining and prospecting for copper along Alberni Inlet and on Tzartus and other islands in Barkley Sound; but he soon returned to lumbering. He had a crew cutting spars at Port Neville in 1864, and in 1865, in England, he was instrumental in forming the British Columbia and Vancouver Island Spar, Lumber and Saw Mill Company, with a capital of £100,000, for the purpose of acquiring timber limits and building a sawmill on Burrard Inlet. The first site chosen was in what is now Stanley Park, but the strong currents at that point made it hazardous to dock sailing ships and the mill was actually built farther east, on the south side of the inlet. Its timber limits included many of the fine stands that then occupied the site of the city of Vancouver. When the machinery for the mill was shipped from Glasgow one box was left behind, and as a result operations could not begin until June 1867. In the interval Stamp exported spars. In the next year or two, lumber shipments were made to San Francisco, Mexico, Peru, China, and Australia. All seemed to be going well, but Stamp again had differences with his principals and he ceased to be manager on 2 Jan. 1869. Lawsuits followed and he received a judgement for $14,000. The company itself soon went into liquidation, and in February 1870 the mill was sold for a tithe of its value. Under new ownership it developed into the famous Hastings Mill, and became the nucleus around which the city of Vancouver grew up in the 1880s.

As usual, Stamp had other irons in the fire. In 1866 he had completed an office building in

Victoria and he had a ship-chandlery there. He was once again interested in a steamer service to San Francisco and also in the building of a graving-dock; finances for both ventures were promised under the terms of union by which British Columbia entered confederation. In 1871 Stamp leased buildings at New Westminster that had been used formerly by the Royal Engineers and established a fish curing business. Convinced that fish packing had a promising future, he left for England in November to organize a company that would finance salmon packing on a large scale. It was while he was on this mission that he died suddenly of a heart attack.

Stamp served as a member of the Legislative Council of British Columbia in 1867 and 1868 as representative of the Lillooet District, but he does not seem to have taken a very active part in politics. His interests centred upon shipping and manufacturing, and he deserves to rank as British Columbia's first industrialist. The mill at Alberni was the first large export mill in British Columbia and his second mill on Burrard Inlet was for many years the leading industry there.

Stamp was survived by his wife, Maria, and by four sons and a daughter. Several geographical features in the vicinity of Alberni have been named after him, including Stamp Falls Provincial Park which surrounds the falls on the Stamp River.

W. KAYE LAMB

PABC, Edward Stamp correspondence. Somerset House (London), Principal Probate Registry, 1872, will of Edward Stamp. *Colonist* (Victoria), 1858–72. *Times* (London), November–December 1854. Walbran, *B.C. coast names*, 469. F. W. Howay, "Early shipping in Burrard Inlet, 1863–1870," *BCHQ*, I (1937), 4–20. "Journal of Arthur Thomas Bushby" (Blakey Smith), Biographical appendix, 194. W. K. Lamb, "Early lumbering on Vancouver Island. Part II: 1855–1866," *BCHQ*, II (1938), 95–121.

STEEVES, WILLIAM HENRY, merchant, lumberman, and politician; b. 20 May 1814 at Hillsborough, Westmorland County (Albert County), N.B., son of Joseph Steeves and Martha Cross, and great-grandson of Heinrich Stief (Henry Steeves) who came to New Brunswick from Germany in 1765; d. 9 Dec. 1873 at Saint John, N.B.

William Henry Steeves attended public school at Hillsborough. His teacher was Duncan Shaw, a native of Scotland, a graduate of the University of Edinburgh, and a prominent early educator in the colony. Steeves always gave the impression that he had much more education than was usually acquired in New Brunswick by persons attending only public school and he attributed this

Steeves

to the teaching of Mr Shaw. He married Mary Steeves, another great-grandchild of Heinrich Stief; they had six children, two sons and four daughters.

Steeves began his business career with a small store and then became a partner of James Abel Steeves and Gilbert Martin Steeves in the firm of Steeves Brothers, a mercantile and lumber export business with headquarters at Hillsborough. He later moved to Saint John where he continued in the lumber export business and became a leader in the financial and commercial activities of the city. His brother Gilbert moved to Liverpool, England, and established a branch office to handle the company's overseas interests.

When Albert County was created in 1846, Steeves was elected as one of its first two representatives in the House of Assembly. He was re-elected at the general election of 1850, but only sat for one session. Steeves favoured reform of the government and in 1851 voted for an unsuccessful bill which would have required that all members of the Legislative Council be elected; he also voted against paying council members.

Steeves was appointed to the Legislative Council in December 1851. In 1852 he was apparently offered the position of surveyor general by the lieutenant governor, Sir Edmund Head*, who wished to appoint to the government someone from Saint John since that city was the headquarters of opposition to his advisers led by Edward Barron CHANDLER. Steeves declined the office, which finally went to Robert Duncan Wilmot*, also a Saint John critic of the government. In 1854 the compact government was defeated and Charles FISHER headed a new liberal, reform, or "smasher" administration. The governor, John Henry Thomas MANNERS-SUTTON, described this government as "formed on the principle that the direction of public affairs had been too long in the hands of men of property and liberal education." Steeves was again offered the position of surveyor general and this time he accepted. His appointment was opposed by many members of the assembly, who felt that the surveyor general should be selected from among the elected representatives. Accepting this criticism, Steeves resigned on 4 Dec. 1854.

In March 1855 he was appointed the first chairman of the newly created Department of Public Works – a position he held until 30 May 1856. He was then out of office for a short time when the government led by Fisher and Samuel Leonard Tilley* was defeated over the unpopular prohibition act. The "smasher" government was returned to power in 1857, Steeves regained his post as chief commissioner of the Department of Public Works, and kept it until 1861. He was the only member of the Legislative Council ever to hold this office. As minister without portfolio he continued in the Tilley government from 1861 until April 1865, when Tilley and his supporters were defeated over the issue of confederation.

Steeves was an advocate of railway communications and was eager to promote schemes which would benefit Saint John. For this reason he was interested in the Intercolonial Railway and the route it would follow through New Brunswick. He was a member of the delegation sent to Quebec in September 1862 to discuss the proposals of the Duke of Newcastle [Henry Pelham Clinton] for imperial aid in the construction of the Intercolonial.

A supporter of Maritime union and confederation, Steeves was a New Brunswick delegate at the Charlottetown conference in September 1864. He was also a delegate to the Quebec conference in October 1864 when the terms of confederation were discussed. In these meetings he supported Sir Leonard Tilley, but there is no record of his having made any speeches of importance. As a reward for his support of confederation, Steeves was called to the Canadian Senate in July 1867 as one of the original 12 senators for New Brunswick.

In his later years, Steeves became interested in the treatment of the insane. Probably encouraged by his brother, Dr James Thomas Steeves, a prominent Saint John physician who in 1876 succeeded John WADDELL as superintendent of the provincial insane asylum at Saint John, he supported reform and improved facilities for this institution. One obituary credits him with part responsibility for legislation providing better treatment for the mentally ill.

Although Steeves' career was not spectacular he served capably in the government of New Brunswick for many years. He consistently advocated reform and his loyal support of Sir Leonard Tilley assisted in the struggle to bring New Brunswick into confederation.

W. A. SPRAY

N.B. Museum, Hazen papers, draft of a protest regarding the Board of Works under W. H. Steeves; Steeves family, miscellaneous genealogical notes; Tilley family papers, W. H. Steeves to S. L. Tilley, 13 Jan. 1863; Webster coll., W. H. Steeves to A. R. McClelan, 10 Dec. 1852, 2 May 1855. University of New Brunswick, Graves (New Brunswick), MSS, Albert County, 32. *Daily Telegraph* (Saint John, N.B.), 10 Dec. 1873. *Morning Freeman* (Saint John, N.B.), 11 Dec. 1873. *New Brunswick Reporter* (Fredericton), 10 Dec. 1873. Fenety, *Political notes and observations*, 307–38, 405. *Can. parl. comp.*, 1872. E. C. Wright, *The Steeves descendants* (Wolfville, N.S., [1965]), 667–68. Hannay, *History of New Brunswick*, II, 170–71, 185, 201, 221, 225. MacNutt, *New Brunswick*,

353–88. E. C. Wright, *Samphire Greens: the story of the Steeves* (Kingsport, N.S., [1961]).

STEWART, FRANCES. *See* BROWNE

STEWART, JOHN, clergyman; b. in Perthshire, Scotland, *c.* 1800; d. in New Glasgow, N.S., 4 May 1880.

John Stewart was educated at Perth Academy and at the University of Edinburgh where he studied medicine for a short time but finally chose to take a degree in theology. He was licensed by the presbytery of Dunkeld on 26 June 1832, and from 1832 until 1834 taught at St George's Academy, Edinburgh. Under the auspices of the Edinburgh Ladies Association and the Glasgow Colonial Society, he immigrated to Nova Scotia, landing at Plaster Cove, Cape Breton, on 23 Aug. 1834. After a year's missionary work in Cape Breton, he was ordained by the Pictou presbytery of the Church of Scotland on 6 Oct. 1835. Thirteen days later he was inducted into the West Bay charge of Cape Breton.

In the summer of 1836 Stewart returned to Edinburgh to marry Alica Murray Drysdale. The couple left Cape Breton in June 1838 and moved to Fraser's Mountain (New Glasgow) where John Stewart was pastor until his retirement in 1869. Fluent in both English and Gaelic, he continued his missionary travels in Cape Breton and elsewhere, and was often the first missionary to visit a pioneer settlement.

A disciple of Dr Thomas Chalmers, leader of the Free Church movement in Scotland, Stewart opposed state control and patronage in his parishes. In 1844 he worked to free his own congregation, the Pictou presbytery, and the synod of Nova Scotia from the Church of Scotland. In New Glasgow most of his congregation followed him when he left St Andrew's Church and formed John Knox Free Church. As early as 25 Dec. 1839, in a letter to the Halifax *Guardian*, he advocated the union of all Presbyterian bodies, and continued to support this policy until 1875 when practically every Presbyterian church in Canada was under one organization. Stewart also gave full support to the church's missionary work in the New Hebrides and Trinidad and was the leader of missionary activities in the synod for a number of years.

Perhaps the Reverend John Stewart's greatest contribution was in the field of ministerial training. By 1848, four years after the inception of the Free Church in Nova Scotia, he and several other clergymen had organized the Free Church College in Halifax. The college, giving classes in arts as well as divinity, opened with two professors and 15 students. In 1850 the synod sent Stewart to Britain to obtain funds for the endowment of the college. He travelled and canvassed widely, returning the following year with £1,000 and a valuable library. This divinity school was one of the ancestors of Pine Hill Divinity Hall, the present United Church seminary.

E. ARTHUR BETTS

Free Church of Nova Scotia, Synod, *Minutes* (Halifax), 1844–60; *Minutes of the last session*, 1860. Presbyterian Church of Nova Scotia, *Minutes of the last session* (Halifax), 1860. Presbyterian Church of the Lower Provinces of British North America, Synod, *Minutes of the first session* (Halifax), 1860; *Minutes*, 1860–75. Presbyterian Church in Canada, Synod of the Maritime provinces, *Minutes* (Halifax), 1875–80. Presbyterian Church in Canada, General Assembly, *Acts and Proceedings* (Toronto), 1880, 61.
Guardian (Halifax), 25 Dec. 1839, 12 May 1841. *Presbyterian Record* (Halifax), June 1880. *Presbyterian Witness* (Halifax), 12 July, 4 Oct. 1851; 8, 15 May 1880. *The missionary record and ecclesiastical intelligencer for 1851 and 1852* (Halifax, 1852). Gregg, *History of the Presbyterian Church*, 344–47. John Murray, *The history of the Presbyterian Church in Cape Breton* (Truro, N.S., 1921), 54–57.

STISTED, Sir HENRY WILLIAM, soldier and administrator; b. 1817 at Saint-Omer, Pas-de-Calais, France, son of Charles Stisted and Eliza Burn; m. in 1845 Maria, daughter of Colonel Joseph Netterville Burton and sister of Sir Richard Francis Burton; d. 10 Dec. 1875 at Upper Norwood, Eng.

Henry William Stisted was born into a military family and was educated at the Royal Military College, Sandhurst. He entered the British army in 1835 as an ensign and advanced rapidly, becoming a lieutenant-colonel in 1850 and a major-general in 1864. He commanded a brigade in the Persian War in 1856–57 (receiving the CB in 1858) and the advance guard at the relief of Lucknow, India, in 1857; he was later stationed on the northwest frontier of India.

Stisted was appointed to serve in Canada in November 1866 and in January 1867 he took over command of the 1st Military District at Toronto in Canada West. As the chief imperial officer in what was to become Ontario, he was appointed provisional lieutenant governor of the new province at confederation in 1867. Although his appointment was hailed with approval in Toronto military and social circles, where he had become popular, the politicians were not impressed and George BROWN considered him "an old fool."

His most important official act was the naming of John Sandfield MACDONALD as premier. Although not in itself necessarily illogical, the

Street

choice was dictated to Stisted by Sir John A. Macdonald* in Ottawa with strong support from Senator David Lewis Macpherson*, the Conservative party organizer in Ontario. Macpherson considered Sandfield best able to form a coalition administration friendly to the dominion government. As he had written to Sir John A., he wanted it "first understood with that gentleman [Stisted] who *he* is to get to join him, letting him understand that if he attempts any tricks he will find his commission withdrawn."

Stisted remained lieutenant governor only until the appointment of William Howland*, in July 1868. He remained in Toronto until June 1869 when he became the commanding officer at Quebec. Shortly thereafter, he returned to England. He was created a KCB in 1871 and promoted lieutenant-general in 1873.

BRUCE W. HODGINS

PAC, MG 26, A (Macdonald papers), D. L. Macpherson to Macdonald, 3, 7 July 1867. *DNB.* D. B. Read, *The lieutenant-governors of Upper Canada and Ontario, 1792–1899* (Toronto, 1900), 204–6. W. T. Barnard, *The Queen's Own Rifles of Canada, 1860–1960: one hundred years of Canada* (Don Mills, Ont., 1960), 33. B. W. Hodgins, *John Sandfield Macdonald, 1812–1872* (Canadian Biographical Studies, Toronto, 1971).

STREET, THOMAS CLARK (Clarke), lawyer, businessman, and politician; b. probably in 1814, son of Samuel Street* and Abigail Ransome; d. unmarried, 6 Sept. 1872, at Chippawa, Ont.

Thomas Clark Street's father, Samuel, a United Empire Loyalist of English descent, owned, in partnership with Thomas Clark*, several grist and sawmills in the Niagara area. When Clark died in 1837, Street took these over and expanded into textile milling. His son, Thomas Clark, studied law in Toronto under Christopher Hagerman* and William Henry DRAPER, and was called to the bar in 1838. He returned to Chippawa to practise law but became more of a businessman than a lawyer. When his father died in 1844 he inherited "a liberal fortune" which he thereafter managed with considerable success. He later became a director of the Niagara Falls Suspension Bridge Company and when he died he was president of the firm. He also served as president of the Gore Bank from 1862 to 1868 and was a director of the British American Assurance Company, the Canadian Bank of Commerce, and the Bank of Upper Canada. He invested in stock, owning shares in a number of financial and transportation companies.

Like many of his business colleagues, Street invested heavily in land and mortgages. Before the secret ballot this form of business involvement was of considerable political utility. As the *Niagara Mail* in St Catharines commented in 1851 when Street first ran for office, his principal assets were "his money and his mortgages." He was elected to the Legislative Assembly for Welland in 1851 but defeated in an unusually violent contest in 1854. Elected again in 1861, he sat for Welland in the union and later the federal parliaments until his death. Street was a lifelong Conservative. In 1851 he had campaigned as an independent, calling himself a "Constitutional Reformer," but was regarded by Reformers as a Family Compact Tory.

Although his political career was long and seemingly placid and took second place to his business interests, Street was an important politician. Men like Street did not sit in parliament as mindless supporters of a particular leader; he was not dependent on his party for campaign funds, and he needed neither his sessional indemnity nor a patronage post. His own economic interests were pushed, and he often acted with independence and courage. A strong supporter of representation by population, which he advocated not for love of the measure but because of what he feared would happen without it, he refused to enter the cabinet in 1862 when asked by John A. Macdonald* because it had not accepted that policy. He also supported the unpopular bill presented by Richard William Scott* in 1863 regarding separate schools. His weight was recognized by Macdonald, who assured him in 1867 that a place was reserved for him in the Senate: "[As] vacancies will be annually occurring you can, when you are wearied of well doing in the Commons, find your way to the dignified retirement of our House of Peers."

Street was very much an aristocrat, and in 1860 "entertained [the Prince of Wales] on a scale of magnificence seldom equalled in any colony of England." A member of the Church of England, he served as trustee of the University of Trinity College in Toronto. He was a lieutenant-colonel in the Welland militia and a justice of the peace. He died in 1872 in Chippawa shortly after being re-elected to the House of Commons by acclamation. He left an estate valued at between $3,000,000 and $4,000,000, often regarded as the largest in Ontario at that time.

DONALD SWAINSON

PAC, MG 26, A (Macdonald papers), 338, 513. PAO, W. H. Merritt papers; Samuel Street papers. *Gazette* (Montreal), 1872. *Globe* (Toronto), 1861–72. *Leader* (Toronto), 1872. *Mail* (Toronto), 1872. *Niagara Mail*, 1851–61. *Can. directory of parliament* (Johnson). *Can. parl. comp.*, 1872. M. F. Campbell, *Niagara: hinge of the golden arc* (Toronto, 1958). Cornell, *Alignment of political groups.* Creighton, *Macdonald, young politician.* Ross and Trigge, *History of the Canadian Bank of Commerce*, II. Swainson, "Personnel of politics."

STUTSMAN, ENOS, lawyer, legislator, treasury and land agent; b. 14 Feb. 1826 in what is now Fayette County, Indiana, son of Nicholas Stutsman; d. 24 Jan. 1874 at Pembina, North Dakota.

Enos Stutsman was of German ancestry, his grandfather Jacob having settled in Pennsylvania in 1728. After being educated in what is now Coles County, Illinois, Enos taught school from the age of 17 to 21, then studied law, and was admitted to the bar in 1851. In the 1850s he combined a law practice with a real estate business in Des Moines and Sioux City, and was active in politics as a Democrat. He moved to Yankton, Dakota Territory, in 1858 to supervise the laying out of a townsite for the Yankton Land and Town Company. From 1862 until 1873 he was a member of the territorial legislature of Dakota representing the Yankton and later the Pembina district. Stutsman was appointed a United States treasury agent in 1866 and thereafter divided his time between Yankton and Pembina, the latter being the site of the only customs house in Dakota Territory. Four years later he became a government land agent.

During the Red River disturbances of 1869 and 1870 he was one of a group of Americans at Pembina and Fort Garry (Winnipeg) who were actively promoting the annexation of the Red River Settlement to the United States. It has been suggested by Professor W. L. Morton that his intrigues were directed towards obtaining American intervention in the disturbances and the establishment of a military post at Pembina from which he would benefit as a result of his land speculations in the area. Alexander Begg*, the diarist, records his many visits to the Red River Settlement and to Louis Riel* at this time. Along with other Americans he had easy access to Riel during the early days of the disturbances and sought to influence the Métis leader in favour of union with the United States; it seems generally agreed today that, whatever his fears for the rights of his people with the entry of Red River into Canada, Riel never seriously considered annexation. Stutsman was, along with Joseph ROLETTE, one of a group of "correspondents" at Pembina forwarding distorted accounts of the events at Red River in 1869 and 1870 to the *St Paul Daily Press*, on which Canadian papers relied for their reports about the disturbances.

Stutsman was a curious if not pathetic figure on the Dakota frontier having been born with practically no legs. He used crutches throughout his life

but was able apparently to move about the country independently by wagon or on horseback. He died a bachelor and was buried in Sioux City, Iowa.

HARTWELL BOWSFIELD

Begg's Red River journal (Morton). Stanley, *Louis Riel.* G. W. Kingsbury, "Enos Stutsman," North Dakota State Hist. Soc. *Coll.,* I (1906), 350–54.

SUNDAY, JOHN. *See* SHAH-WUN-DAIS.

SWABEY, WILLIAM, soldier, civil servant, farmer, and politician; b. 13 June 1789 in England, son of Maurice Swabey and Catherine Bird; m. 4 Aug. 1820 to Mary Ann Hobson by whom he had seven sons and four daughters; d. 6 Feb. 1872 in England.

William Swabey, a native of Buckinghamshire, spent 18 years in the British army. He rose to the rank of captain in the Royal Horse Artillery, and fought at the battle of Copenhagen, in the Iberian peninsula, and at Waterloo. In 1840, several years after his retirement from the army, Swabey and his family immigrated to Prince Edward Island. He took up residence in Charlottetown Royalty, and leased two farms, comprising about 100 acres, which he cultivated with his family's help. He used the most modern farming methods and frequently advertised surpluses of hay, wheat, and turnips.

Immediately upon his arrival in the colony, Swabey began to play an active and visible role in organizations such as the Colonial Church Society and on various committees to promote improvements. In November 1841 he was appointed to the Legislative Council by the lieutenant governor, Sir Henry Vere Huntley*, who was a personal friend. He attended one session the following spring, and then, at the urging of Huntley, resigned to run for a seat in the assembly. He contested Prince County, Second District, as a Tory in the general election of 1842 and lost; two years later, he was reappointed to the Legislative Council, where he remained until his return to England.

Swabey, who had been described at the Colonial Office as "a great Tory," transferred his support to the Reform party in the mid 1840s and went on to establish himself as its leading spokesman in the Legislative Council. This change may have been related to an alteration in the political sympathies of the lieutenant governor. Huntley, who had been called a tyrant for his use of troops to suppress Escheat disorders in 1843 [*see* John McDONALD], had broken with the Tories for reasons perhaps more personal than political. Huntley's feud with leading members of the family compact was widely known, and he left the Island as a Reform hero in 1847.

When responsible government was attained in 1851, Swabey joined the Executive Council of George COLES' Liberal government, was appointed registrar of deeds, and later became commissioner of public lands. He held these major positions, and about a dozen smaller ones, for most of the period until the Liberals were defeated in 1859. He was especially vocal on the land question and increasingly advocated a radical approach as gradualist measures failed to abolish leasehold tenure. Swabey's other major interest was education; he served 18 years on the Board of Education, actively promoted the Free Education Act of 1852, and vehemently defended its non-denominational aspect when the Bible question arose [see Coles].

William Swabey was a vigorous Liberal partisan; both his ability and his change in party affiliation made him a controversial figure – a fact amply demonstrated when he returned to England in 1861. The farewell dinner tendered to him as a Liberal, and the salute fired in his honour as a lieutenant-colonel in the militia, caused a series of bitter exchanges in the local press. The verbiage did not explain why Swabey left the Island; it is quite possible that, at the age of 72, he simply wished to retire, and to spend his last years in his native country.

IAN ROSS ROBERTSON

[PRO, CO 226/89. 201–16, is particularly important because it includes a letter from William Swabey to Dominick Daly*, 30 June 1858, which gives Swabey's account of the Bible question from 1845 to 1858. *See also*: CO 226/91, 173–75; 226/92, 11–21; 226/94, 144–51.

Prince Edward Island, Legislative Council, *Journals*, 1842, 1844–61; *Debates*, 1856–60. The debates of 1861 were not published in a bound volume; for the 1840s, the early 1850s, and 1861 consult the reports of the debates in the Island newspapers. For reports of the farewell dinner for Swabey *see*: *Examiner* (Charlottetown), 18, 25 Nov., 2, 16, 23 Dec. 1861, and *Islander* (Charlottetown), 22, 29 Nov., 13 Dec. 1861. *Also see*: *Examiner* (Charlottetown), 9 Feb. 1857. *Island Argus* (Charlottetown), 12 March 1872. *Monitor* (Charlottetown), 26 April 1859. *Patriot* (Charlottetown), 14 March 1872. *Royal Gazette* (Charlottetown), 19 April, 10 May, 21 June 1842. Robertson, "Religion, politics, and education in PEI." I. R. R.]

SWEET GRASS. *See* WIKASKOKISEYIN

SZALATNAY, MÁRK, trade unionist and revolutionary socialist; b. in Hungary; d. in Los Angeles, U.S.A., 1875.

The son of a Protestant school-teacher, Márk

Szalatnay was expelled from the University of Budapest in 1836 for propagating doctrines of the American and French revolutions. Imprisoned for four years, after agitating over grievances of the 1838 Danube River flood victims, he wrote *Traditiones communes Hungarorum et populorum Balcanicorum*, subsequently published. Szalatnay then studied in the Netherlands at Leiden and Dordrecht but returned to Hungary to support Lajos Kossuth on the outbreak of the 1848 revolution, taking part as a combatant in the defence of Komárom, held by Magyar nationalists. Following the defeat of the revolution he went to England, became associated with the Chartists, and for six years worked as secretary of the South Wales Miners' Union. He took part in numerous strikes, suffered repeated arrests, and campaigned to have the trade union movement endorse the *Manifesto of the Communist Party* of Marx and Engels. Deported to the United States as an "undesirable alien" in 1855, he worked as a cigar-maker in Baltimore and was active in trade union organization.

An ardent abolitionist, Szalatnay was seriously wounded during a protest action against a pro-slavery demonstration. Disabled, he moved with a group of fellow Hungarian workers to Montreal, where he organized a local of the International Union of Cigar Makers of America in 1865. He organized another local in Toronto in 1869 and here, in 1872, the year of the historic printers' strike and the upsurge of the nine hour day movement, Szalatnay led a strike of the cigar-makers. Arrested, imprisoned for four months, then deported to the United States, he became an organizer for the National Labor Union. During a bitterly fought strike of bakery workers in Los Angeles, in 1875, he was shot and killed by police. The hardships and hazards of his 20 years' stormy sojourn in North America he had shared with Mary Fergusson, a leader of the early feminist movement in the United States.

One of the founders of the Canadian trade union movement, an early proponent of the ideas of revolutionary socialism and international labour solidarity, Márk Szalatnay embodied in his life's work a remarkable combination of militant traditions: those of the Hungarian revolutionary democrats of 1848, of British Chartism, of the American anti-slavery movement, trade unionism, and (through his association with Mary Fergusson) the movement for women's rights. He was the first Marxist of whom there is record in the history of Canadian labour; it has been surmised that Szalatnay may have been instrumental in the publication of an excerpt from *Das Kapital* (a passage from the chapter on "The working day") in the first issue of the *Ontario Workman*, 18 April 1872, 14 years before the full work appeared in English.

STANLEY B. RYERSON

Ontario Workman (Toronto), 18 April, 10, 31 Oct. 1872. Charles Lipton, *The trade union movement of Canada, 1827–1959* (Montreal, 1966). H. A. Logan, *Trade unions in Canada, their development and functioning* (Toronto, 1948). S. B. Ryerson, *Unequal union; confederation and the roots of conflict in the Canadas, 1815–1873* (Toronto, 1968). István Szöke, *We are Canadians; the national group of the Hungarian-Canadians* (Toronto, 1954).

T

TALBOT, JOHN, schoolmaster, journalist, and merchant; b. 21 Sept. 1797, probably at Cloughjordan, Tipperary County, Ireland, second son of Richard Talbot, a soldier and promoter of immigration, and Lydia Baird; d. 22 Sept. 1874, at Robinson, Illinois, U.S.A.

John Talbot came to Upper Canada in 1818 with the group of settlers brought out by his father on the *Brunswick* on the "£10 deposit plan," whereby Richard Talbot hoped to obtain a large grant of land. The family, including John's brothers, Edward Allen* and Freeman, settled in London Township. John Talbot, after several years of wandering through Ireland, eastern British North America, and New York State, working as a schoolmaster and labourer, became a schoolmaster in London Township in 1830, and two years later opened a school in London. Perhaps as a result of his failure to secure the land grant he considered rightfully his from 1818, he became a Reformer. Early in 1836 he took over the editorship of the St Thomas *Liberal*. His uncompromising support of reform ideas and his leadership in the Reform movement in the London District made him suspect. A few days after William Lyon Mackenzie*'s abortive uprising, the authorities sought Talbot; he escaped to Detroit and his press was seized.

He remained in Detroit until 1838, went to St Louis, and finally took a teaching position in Independence, Missouri. In 1839 he opened a general store in Somerset, Ohio; here he married Mary Jane Blake and had a family of four sons and three daughters. In 1863 he was forced to sell his store owing to an overextension of credit. After a brief stay in Terre Haute, Indiana, he moved to Robinson, Illinois, where in October he began publication of the *Constitution*, which supported the Democratic party. He turned the paper over to his two surviving sons in 1872 and died two years later.

DANIEL J. BROCK and JAMES J. TALMAN

PAC, RG 1, L3, T19/26; RG 5, A1, 159. PAO, RG 1, C-I-1, 49. University of Western Ontario Library, 248/3 (Talbot family papers). "Letters of John Talbot," ed. Leslie Gray, *Ont. Hist.*, XLIV (1952), 139–64. F. W. Scott, *Newspapers and periodicals of Illinois, 1814–1879* (Illinois State Hist. Lib. Coll., VI, Springfield, Ill., 1910), 297. *History of the county of Middlesex*, 512.

TAYLOR, JOHN, paper manufacturer; b. at Uttoxeter, Staffordshire, Eng., 1 May 1809, son of John Taylor and Margaret Hawthorne; d. at Toronto, Ont., 13 May 1871.

John Taylor Sr, a Methodist, left Uttoxeter in 1821 to settle in Cherry Valley near Albany, New York, and in 1825 or 1826 came to Vaughan Township in Upper Canada. With his family he pioneered there for about nine years before beginning with his brother James to clear several lots near the forks of the Don River. The pines in this neighbourhood, according to Henry Scadding*, who accounted the Taylors "substantial and enterprising immigrants," were of "a remarkably fine growth"; one white pine is said to have produced some 5,000 board feet and to have been hollow for 12 feet up from the ground. These splendid trees encouraged the Taylors to build a sawmill near their house, and the west branch of the Don was dammed just above the forks to produce the water power.

In 1844, as communications with Toronto began to be improved, it is said that George BROWN, inaugurating the *Globe*, persuaded John Jr to start a paper-mill at the same site as the sawmill. He and his brothers, Thomas (b. 4 March 1811) and George (b. 28 Dec. 1813), incorporated as John Taylor and Brothers in 1845 and opened an office in Toronto.

The sons were now all in their early 30s; John provided the organizing leadership and technical mill-working skills, Thomas managed the office, and George looked after the farming and lumbering. The family's landholding in the Don Valley and to the north of it increased to a conservative estimate of 2,000 acres. A village of Don Mills

Taylor

grew up in the valley near their mills. In 1847 fire destroyed a substantial part of the complex of mills near Todmorden (Doncaster) and the Taylors bought them in 1855, thus acquiring (or rebuilding) a second paper-mill and later rebuilding a grist mill. In 1858 they built a third paper-mill about half-way between the other two, on the site of the present mill.

Their three mills were known as the Upper, Middle, and Lower Mill respectively, and each was run, about 1867, by a shift of some ten men. The raw materials – rags, straw, and jute (flax was probably used around 1850, and an experiment with esparto grass failed) – were cooked with soda and lime, washed, drained on an "agitated stuff chest," pressed, and dried, emerging in various forms: newsprint (for the *Globe* and other newspapers), book paper, or manilla wrapping. Paper bags were also made, but by hand. By 1877 the mills were described as operating round the clock (except for Sunday) and as supplying goods "to all parts of the Dominion from Newfoundland to the Red River." "The proprietors have earned a name not always to be found among paper manufacturers, namely that of always putting the full count of sheets in every ream (*viz.*, 480)." The next year, the firm's paper won an honourable mention at the Paris exposition.

John Taylor died in 1871, surviving by several years his wife Anne Eliza. He had experimented in making paper from straw and had applied for patents on making wood-pulp first with "a gang of saws mounted on a mandrel" and later with a "chisel-like machine ... that ... moved up and down." He had become a public figure in a minor way, as a leader of the Toronto branch of the Reform Association of Upper Canada, reconstituted in 1867, and as a member of the coterie surrounding Brown became a founding director of the Bank of Commerce in that same year. On his death, the *Globe* praised his "liberality and kindness" and his "probity"; as befitted a proper Torontonian, he was described as bearing his sufferings "with the firmness and patience which belonged to his character, and at the close he met death with Christian-like resignation."

Control of the business went to his two brothers, who renamed it Thomas Taylor and Brother, and George "inherited" John's directorship at the bank. In 1880 Thomas and George retired, Thomas dying soon afterwards on 21 April 1880 and George living until 17 May 1894. The business went to George's three sons. They called it Taylor Brothers, and advertised themselves as "Manufacturers of Printing, Colored Manilla, Roll, Hanging, and all kinds of Common Paper, Roofing and Carpet Felt, and Paper Bags."

In the 1880s and 1890s the company's business apparently began to decline, perhaps for technological reasons, perhaps because it employed no "travellers," or perhaps because of competition from Quebec firms which had opened offices in Toronto and which used wood-pulp. The Upper Mill was sold within the family in 1886 and then closed down in 1890; the Lower Mill was largely destroyed by fire in 1900; and in 1901 the defalcations of an employee forced the company into bankruptcy with liabilities of $750,000. The Middle Mill was taken over by Robert Davies, an enterprising son-in-law of George Taylor, and became the Howard Smith (Domtar) mill that stands in the valley today.

R. I. K. DAVIDSON

Globe (Toronto), 15 May 1871, 22 April 1880, 18 May 1894. *Illustrated Toronto past and present; being an historical and descriptive guide-book ...*, comp. J. Timperlake (Toronto, 1877). Ontario, Department of Planning and Development, *Don Valley conservation report* (Toronto, 1950). George Carruthers, *Paper-making* (Toronto, 1947). Ross and Trigge, *History of the Canadian Bank of Commerce*, II. J. A. Blyth, "The development of the paper industry in old Ontario, 1824–1867," *Ont. Hist.*, LXII (1970), 119–33.

TAYLOR, WILLIAM, Presbyterian minister; b. 18 March 1803 at Dennie (Denny), Scotland; d. in Portland, Maine, 5 Sept. 1876.

William Taylor was educated in Glasgow, but he was not a graduate of the university. He may have studied theology with one of the senior clergy, as was the custom in the Secession Church. He had been attracted by the fervour of that church, although his parents were members of the Church of Scotland. He was licensed to preach in 1827 and ordained in 1831. Between that date and his departure for Canada in 1833, he ministered in the Secession Chapel at Peebles.

In July 1833 he was inducted as pastor of the Montreal Secession Congregation, "the Wee Kirk in little Dublin [Lagauchetière Street]." This congregation, under the name Erskine (1864) and in a new location (1866), was still in his care at the time of his death. Taylor was a fine Hebrew and Greek scholar and zealous minister, active in social and charitable causes of Protestant Montreal. He was an earnest temperance worker and first editor of the *Canada Temperance Advocate*, printed by John C. BECKET. He was persuaded to become editor by James Court* and John Dougall*. With them, Taylor was also closely associated in the French Canadian Missionary Society. He held the editorship for only about one year, when he was succeeded by John Dougall.

Taylor's interest in aiding Negro refugees may have been the reason for the honorary DD bestowed upon him in 1851 by the now defunct Franklin College, Ohio, which was strongly abolitionist.

Taylor worked for the union of the Canadian churches adhering to the Westminster Standards, that is, the doctrines and discipline of Presbyterianism, and he hoped for the ultimate union of all Protestant denominations. He was an able speaker and skilful conciliator; hence his effectiveness before church assemblies or with smaller gatherings. Following the first major fusion, in 1861, Taylor became moderator of the new Canada Presbyterian Church, of which the Secession and Free churches were the chief constituents. It was only after confederation that he had success with the congregations in connection with the Church of Scotland. National sentiment and the practical example of Presbyterian union in the Maritime provinces softened opposition. In 1875, he had the satisfaction of seeing the dominion-wide Presbyterian Church in Canada formed.

Taylor was an advocate of cooperation among Protestant denominations – a founder of the Evangelical Alliance, of the Montreal Ministerial Association, and of the French Canadian Missionary Society (8 April 1839). On behalf of the last, in 1839 he visited Britain and Protestant communities in France in a successful search for money and men. He was a secretary of the society and its third president, 1870–74. The militancy of his Protestantism is shown by the title of one of his sermons, published in 1876 in pamphlet form under the authority of the Montreal-Ottawa Presbytery: "The Pope, the Man of Sin."

Taylor died while on holiday in Portland, Maine. He was predeceased by his wife, Mary Hamilton, and survived by three sons.

JOHN IRWIN COOPER

Erskine and American United Church (Montreal), Erskine Church records, 1833–76. McLennan Library, McGill University (Montreal), James Court, Journal of the Committee of the French Canadian Missionary Society, 1839–40. French Canadian Missionary Society, *Annual Report* (Montreal), 1842–78. Campbell, *Hist. of Scotch Presbyterian Church. In memoriam, the Rev. William Taylor, D.D.* (Montreal, 1876). E. A. McDougall, "History of the Presbyterian Church in western Lower Canada, 1815–1843," unpublished PHD thesis, McGill University, 1969, 13, 354. Guy Tombs, *One hundred years of Erskine Church, Montreal, 1833–1933* (Montreal, 1934).

TAYLOR, WILLIAM HENRY, Anglican clergyman; b. 1820; d. at Clifton, Bristol, Eng., 19 Jan. 1873.

Prior to his arrival with his wife in Rupert's Land, 5 Sept. 1850, William Henry Taylor had served for eight years in Newfoundland, where he had been ordained as a deacon. In 1847 he was listed as schoolmaster at Spaniard's Bay.

Accepted by the Society for the Propagation of the Gospel as its first missionary in Rupert's Land, Taylor was ordained priest by Bishop David Anderson* in St Andrews Church (near Lower Fort Garry), 22 Dec. 1850. By 1851 he had a "good congregation in a Licensed Schoolroom and a very regular Sunday School with fifty or fifty-two on an average." In that year he built a parsonage on a site given by the Hudson's Bay Company west of the Red along the Assiniboine River, on high ground used as a refuge from the floods. The cornerstone of a church was laid in 1853, but the flood of 1852 delayed construction so that it was not consecrated until 29 May 1855 under the name of St James. Taylor himself "laboured hard . . . both in the exterior and the interior; the painting he has done all himself." By 1854 he had established a parochial lending library of nearly 200 volumes, "one of the grand levers to elevate our people in the social and intellectual scale of society." By 1862 he also had two "nicely-conducted" schools and his congregation was increasing with increasing settlement. In 1854 he had been appointed first registrar of the diocese of Rupert's Land.

Taylor appears to have been a faithful, modest, and singularly considerate man. He secured the cooperation of the not very promising population of settlers and pensioners among whom he and his wife worked so devotedly until 1867, though his last years were marred by a quarrel over the location of a school. He and Bishop Anderson were on terms of close friendship. The Taylors lived at the bishop's house after their arrival in the settlement and the bishop and his family found shelter in their uncompleted parsonage during the flood of 1852. Bishop Robert Machray*, Anderson's successor, was less impressed by the effectiveness of the "good Mr. Taylor" as a parish priest.

Taylor wrote regularly and extensively to the SPG and his letters are of considerable interest for their descriptions of the affairs of the settlement. He played some part in the intellectual life of Red River and was in 1862 elected to the council of the short-lived Institute of Rupert's Land, established in an attempt to enrich the cultural life of the settlement.

In 1867 he and his wife were both in ill health; he retired from St James and returned to England. He had Worcestershire connections and owned a small freehold property at Clent. When he made his will in 1872 he was residing at Fearnall Heath in the parish of Claines and was curate of Martin

Hussingtree in the diocese of Worcester. He died at Clifton, Bristol, where Bishop Anderson resided after he left Rupert's Land. Taylor's wife, the sole heir to an estate of under £300, survived him. They had no children.

L. G. THOMAS

Classified digest of the records of the Society for the Propagation of the Gospel in Foreign Parts, 1701–1892 (with much supplementary information) (London, 1895), 88–234. Society for the Propagation of the Gospel in Foreign Parts, *Reports* (London), 1862–63. [W. H. Taylor], "William H. Taylor's journal, Assiniboia, 1851," ed. F. A. Peake, Canadian Church Hist. Soc. *J.* (Toronto), XII (1970), 24–36. Boon, *Anglican Church*, 87. Pascoe, *Two hundred years of the S.P.G.* M. P. Wilkinson, "The episcopate and the Right Reverend David Anderson, D.D., first lord bishop of Rupert's Land, 1849–1864," unpublished MA thesis, University of Manitoba, 1950. T. C. B. Boon, "The Institute of Rupert's Land and Bishop David Anderson," HSSM, *Papers*, 3rd ser., no.18 (1961–62), 92–114.

TERRILL, TIMOTHY LEE, lawyer, merchant, farmer, and politician; b. 12 March 1815 in Ascot Township, Sherbrooke County, L.C.; d. 26 Aug. 1879 in Stanstead, Que.

Timothy Lee Terrill's father was Joseph Hazard Terrill, commissioner of small causes for the rugged pioneer settlement of Sherbrooke. Strong and ambitious, Timothy Lee was at 16 both a champion axeman and a keen student. During the rebellions of 1837–38, Timothy Lee interrupted his law studies to join his three brothers in a cavalry troop, where he earned a lieutenancy. These studies were in the offices of his brother Hazard Bailey, in Sherbrooke and then in Stanstead. On 25 July 1840 he was admitted to the bar of Lower Canada. His law practice and commercial ventures brought him almost instant wealth. He began his political career as an annexationist in 1849, entering politics in earnest when in 1852 cholera killed his brother Hazard Bailey, Liberal member of the assembly for Stanstead. Despite John A. Macdonald*'s efforts to free Stanstead for Alexander Tilloch Galt*, Terrill was elected by acclamation in his brother's place on 23 Nov. 1852.

In 1854, Terrill, now a queen's counsel, overwhelmed the Conservative John McConnell in the July general elections. In May 1856 he became provincial secretary in the Étienne-Paschal Taché*–Macdonald government. The choice of Terrill may be explained by the fact that though he was a Liberal, he was moderate rather than radical, that he was the brother of the brilliant Hazard Bailey, and above all that he was an available English Lower Canadian – the only one in the government. After his ritual resignation Terrill was re-elected on a platform emphasizing the honour of his appointment for the Eastern Townships, and advocating progressive government by moderate men. However, Terrill resigned his executive office in 1857 when his neglected business affairs fell "into confusion and disorder"; about the same time his family, including his wife Harriet, suffered ill health, and his baby son died. He continued in the assembly, however, and in the December 1857 general elections Stanstead returned him again, on the pledge that he would continue to protect the interests of the Stanstead, Shefford and Chambly Railroad. He had helped to raise funds for this enterprise and guided through the legislature all legislation affecting it.

After several serious paralytic attacks, Terrill retired from politics in 1861. He became one of the leading agriculturalists in the townships, an officer in the Stanstead Agricultural Society, and a breeder of prize livestock. Terrill also sat on the Council of Public Instruction from 1859 until its reorganization in 1869, "assisted in the direction" of at least one railway company, and was a leading director of the Eastern Townships Bank. He suffered a paralytic attack on 25 Aug. 1879 and died the next morning.

In person and spirit, Timothy Lee Terrill epitomized the pioneer. Attached to the land, he wrested an abundant living from it; loyal to his locality, he contributed much to its political, financial, and commercial growth. Wealthy, socially prominent, and personally affable, Terrill helped the Townships gain appropriate recognition in the broader context of the United Canadas.

ELIZABETH NISH

[J. A. Macdonald], *Letters* (Johnson), I. *Sherbrooke Gazette*, 22, 29 July 1854. *Stanstead Journal* (Rock Island), 22 Feb. 1855; 5 June 1856; 5 March, 27 Aug., 22 Oct., 19 Nov., 3, 17, 27, 31 Dec. 1857; 26 Sept. 1861; 28 Aug., 4 Sept. 1879. *Political appointments, 1841–1865* (J.-O. Coté). F.-J. Audet, "Commissions d'avocats de la province de Québec, 1765 à 1849," *BRH*, XXXIX (1933), 590. Chapais, *Histoire du Canada*, VII. Cornell, *Alignment of political groups.* Dent, *Last forty years.*

TÉTREAU (also rendered Tétreault, Tetrault, and Tetrau), HUBERT-JOSEPH, Roman Catholic priest, Protestant evangelist; b. 25 Feb. 1803 at Verchères, Lower Canada, son of Jean-Baptiste Tétreau and Marie-Anne Guyon; d. 1 Dec. 1877 at Montreal.

Hubert-Joseph Tétreau studied at the college of Montreal, where he was encouraged to prepare for the priesthood. From 1822 to 1824 he taught at the seminary of Saint-Hyacinthe and at the seminary of Nicolet. He then studied theology at Quebec, and was ordained priest 8 Jan. 1826, by Bishop Bernard-Claude Panet*.

His first postings were as assistant priest to stations in the Montreal district, Varennes and Saint-Hyacinthe; next, 1826–30, as missionary in northern New Brunswick; the last 13 years of his life as a Roman Catholic were spent in the dioceses of Quebec and Montreal, his final posting as parish priest being to Les Éboulements. It was there that the break with the Roman Catholic Church occurred. For several years Tétreau had had differences with his superiors, and in October 1843 Bishop Joseph Signay* relieved him of his jurisdiction in the parish, although he did not forbid him to celebrate mass.

Tétreau settled at Sainte-Cécile-de-Milton (Shefford County), and devoted himself to the cause of French Canadian Protestantism. It cannot be established from documents that he was a regularly appointed minister in either the Baptist or the Wesleyan Church. He assisted Baptist clergy in their evangelical work and was active in door-to-door visiting and in public debate, the favourite weapons of the Protestant controversialists. He was associated with the Protestant missionaries Louis ROUSSY and Henriette Odin* Feller, not at their chief centre, Grande Ligne (Saint-Jean County) [see Charles LA ROCQUE], but in the newer missions, Saint-Pie (Bagot County), established in 1842, and Salem (Roxton Pond, Shefford County), begun about 1848. In both places he aided the Reverend Théodore Lafleur*, and, upon the opening of a school for girls in 1850 at Saint-Pie, Tétreau took charge of the primary department. When the girls' school moved in 1855 to Longueuil, and later to Grande Ligne, he did not go with it, but continued to live in the locale of his mission post.

An appreciation of Tétreau was provided by his former co-worker, Lafleur. He found Tétreau less energetic than he would have liked, but "with very decided protestant principles. . . . He often wrote short but sensible articles for our french protestant papers." When called to preach, Tétreau would give a good sermon, but might leave the impression after the service that "he had got rid of a duty which reminded him of the mass said in bygone days."

Tétreau's wife, Harriet, was buried in Montreal in July 1864. Whether the couple was then living there is not known. He spent the last years of his life in the city – from at least 1874 – and died there on 1 Dec. 1877. The funeral service was conducted (3 December) in the Baptist Church on St Catherine Street by his old mission associate, Lafleur. Burial was in the Mount Royal Cemetery.

JOHN IRWIN COOPER

[In the records of the Mount Royal Cemetery (Montreal) Tétreau's Christian name is given as "Herbert" along with the title "Reverend"; they also show his age, place of birth, and his Montreal address. The *Montreal Daily Witness*, which had a strong denominational bias, gave notice of Tétreau's death and a brief obituary; see issues of 3 and 4 Dec. 1877. Allaire's *Dictionnaire* provides a brief statement on the Roman Catholic phase of Tétreau's career, but has virtually nothing on the Protestant phase and is in error regarding his place of burial. The earliest and thus valuable biography of Henriette Odin Feller is by J. M. Cramp, *A memoir of Madame Feller, with an account of the origin and progress of the Grande Ligne Mission*, published in London probably in 1876. The standard history on French Protestantism is that of R.-P. Duclos, *Histoire du protestantisme français au Canada et aux Etats-Unis* (2v., Montréal, [1913]), see I, 291. Théodore Lafleur's *A semi-centennial, historical sketch of the Grande Ligne Mission, read at the jubilee gathering, Grande Ligne, Oct. 18th, 1885* (Montreal, [1886]), 52–53 gives an appreciation of Tétreau's close associate at Saint-Pie and later his pastor in Montreal, and is valuable because of its objectivity. Amand Parent, *The life of the Rev. Amand Parent, the first French-Canadian ordained by the Methodist Church* (Toronto, 1887), which gives a good account of the French Canadian approach to proselytizing, is indispensable to an understanding of the evangelists' frame of mind and of their techniques in controversy; see p.64, for a valuable reference to Tétreau's work. W. N. Thomson, "Réflexions historiques sur le champ de Roxton Pond, Québec" (typescript in possession of the author, 1957), an able, though brief, study, refers to Tétreau's relationship to Lafleur. Léo Traversy, *La paroisse de Saint-Damase, co. Saint-Hyacinthe* (s.l., 1964) contains a full account of Tétreau's Roman Catholic life, but is much less satisfactory on the Protestant phase; it makes a statement, which I have been unable to substantiate, that Tétreau served in Granby as a Protestant minister. W. N. Wyeth, *Henrietta Feller and the Grande Ligne Mission* (Philadelphia, Penn., 1898), adds little not in Cramp, but contains some valuable references to the mission. J.I.C.]

AAQ, Diocèse de Montréal, 5, pp.87, 89; Diocèse de Montréal, 8, p.193; Registre des lettres des évêques de Québec, 6, pp.180, 320, 367, 398; Registre des lettres des évêques de Québec, 20, p.436; Vicaires généraux, 2, p.40. Archives judiciaires d'Iberville (Qué.), Registre d'état civil, 29 mars 1868. ASQ, Séminaire, LIV, 10; Polygraphie, L, 16–17.

THIBAUDEAU, JOSEPH-ÉLIE, merchant, politician; b. 2 Sept. 1822 at Cap-Santé, Portneuf, L.C., son of Pierre-Chrysologue Thibaudeau and Émilie Delisle; d. 5 Jan. 1878 at Cap-Santé, Que.

Joseph-Élie Thibaudeau was born to a Cap-Santé merchant-politician family which included

Thibault

an older brother Isidore* and a younger Joseph-Rosaire*. Thibaudeau's life centred around Cap-Santé. He married a local girl, Félicité Larue, and when he left his business it was to represent his county in the Legislative Assembly. From 10 Aug. 1854 until after the 1857 general elections Thibaudeau was a moderate Liberal who usually supported the Liberal-Conservative coalition government. Then in 1858, as a means of embarrassing the ministry, he moved that double majority be adopted as a principle of government although since 1856, when it had actually used double majority to oust Sir Allan Napier MacNab* from leadership, the ministry had lost its Upper Canadian, therefore double, majority. Thibaudeau's motion and various amendments were defeated, but the government cunningly resigned soon after making use of strong, if not majority, disapproval of the queen's choice of Ottawa as the seat of government. George BROWN formed a new Executive Council and named Thibaudeau president and minister of agriculture. On 4 August, two days after its formation, this "Short Administration" fell. Thibaudeau was re-elected after having resigned to accept office, but never again reached the executive level. In the 1861 general elections he was defeated by Jean-Docile Brousseau*, a Bleu. This defeat ended Thibaudeau's political career. In 1863 the government of John Sandfield MACDONALD and Antoine-Aimé Dorion* appointed him registrar for Portneuf County, a post he held until his death in 1878.

Thibaudeau was a typical middle-class French Canadian even though his family had a business rather than professional tradition. His political career was not outstanding, though he was a competent and articulate representative for his constituency, the District of Quebec, and Lower Canada.

ELIZABETH NISH

Archives paroissiales de Sainte-Famille-du-Cap-Santé (Cap-Santé, Qué.), Registres des baptêmes, mariages et sépultures, 1822, 1878. Canada, Province of, *Parliamentary debates*, 1858–61. *Political appointments, 1841–1865* (J.-O. Coté). Careless, *Brown*, I. Chapais, *Histoire du Canada*, VI, VII. Cornell, *Alignment of political groups*. Dent, *Last forty years*. David Gosselin, "L'honorable Élie Thibaudeau," *BRH*, VI (1900), 62. "Les Thibaudeau," *BRH*, XXXIX (1933), 58–59.

THIBAULT (Thibaud, Thebo), JEAN-BAPTISTE, secular Catholic priest, missionary, founder of the Lake St Anne mission (Alberta); b. 14 Dec. 1810 at Saint-Joseph-de-Lévis, L.C., son of Jean-Baptiste Thibault and Charlotte Carrier; d. 4 April 1879 at Saint-Denis-de-la-Bouteillerie (Kamouraska County), Que.

Jean-Baptiste Thibault, a farmer's son, received his classical and theological education at the seminary of Quebec, where on 31 March 1833 he was admitted into the subdiaconate. On 28 April he set out for the North-West. Contrary to several of his predecessors, he had no debt to pay before his departure. Yet the Thibault family was scarcely well-to-do, if the sums of money that the bishopric subsequently sent rather often to his father are an indication.

During the voyage, the missionary was frequently shocked by the behaviour of the crew. Unable to quiet them, or to ensure the use of more acceptable language, he complained to the captain. He was sturdy, but, hampered by his timidity, he was unable to enforce respect from those who provoked him. This timidity was to be construed as pride when Thibault, feeling ill at ease with the employees, later refused the hospitality offered at the Hudson's Bay Company's trading posts. He arrived at Saint-Boniface in June 1833, and began to study the Cree and Chippewa languages. On 8 September he was ordained priest by Bishop Joseph-Norbert Provencher*.

Two years later, in the bishop's absence, Thibault showed himself to be a wise and skilful administrator of the western missions. The building of the cathedral at Saint-Boniface progressed, and the yield from the farm belonging to the mission increased. Thibault proved to be a good preacher, without being too verbose. Above all, he was good at expounding; this quality was appreciated by Bishop Provencher, who considered that Christianity should be brought to the Indians by persuasion, and not "in the Protestant fashion" by gifts. In such a manner the ministers of the different faiths accused each other of trading in souls.

In 1842, therefore, at the request of the Indians and Métis, Bishop Provencher sent Thibault as a missionary across the prairies to the Rocky Mountains. The bishop made this decision unknown to the HBC, which had refused to approve his plan; Thibault, however, met the preference of the company for Canadian rather than French missionaries. His first journey lasted six months, during which, prudently, he travelled on horseback across the plains as far as Edmonton House – the first Catholic or Protestant missionary to adopt this form of transportation. Delighted with the politeness and cordial welcome extended to him by the commandants of the company's forts, he preached the gospel to all the Canadiens, Indians, and Métis who came to him. He welcomed the Blackfeet, whom he described thus: "These

Indians . . . are very clean, and very well-disposed towards the whites; but their number, their war-like qualities, and particularly their rapacity make them the terror of their redskin enemies. They have only a very imperfect idea of the divinity." This journey, the prelude to the diffusion of Catholicism throughout the American north-west, bore fruit: Thibault conducted 353 baptisms and celebrated 20 marriages, in addition to acquiring a better knowledge of the religious needs of this vast region.

For 10 years the missionary worked discreetly, without displaying excessive zeal, and visited the meeting-places of the Indians and Métis. Thibault was probably the first Catholic missionary to make his way to several of the HBC posts and to several places where the Oblates were later to establish missions [see EYNARD; REYNARD]. However, only one foundation is acknowledged unanimously as his, the Lake St Anne mission. Crees were accustomed to stay in this spot, which they called Devil's Lake; Thibault substituted the name of St Anne. He stayed there in 1842 and 1843, but it was only in the summer of 1844 that a house was built for the missionary.

In 1852, acting on Thibault's request to return to Quebec, Bishop Provencher recalled him to Red River. When Thibault reached Saint-Boniface, however, Provencher asked him to stay there, as there was no one to minister to the region. Thibault did so, and did not return to the diocese of Quebec until 1868.

While at Quebec in the autumn of 1869, Thibault was visited by Hector-Louis Langevin*, who asked him to go to Red River as a representative of the Canadian government. Thibault was believed to have a great influence over the Métis. Some of them had just refused to allow William McDougall*, who had been appointed lieutenant governor of the North-West Territories by the Canadian government, to enter the settlement. By this action the Métis and their leader, Louis Riel*, meant to force the federal government to negotiate with them the terms of their union with Canada. Conjointly with Charles-René-Léonidas d'Irumberry* de Salaberry, Thibault was to reassure them that Ottawa intended to respect their rights and not to treat them as a conquered people, and to convince them to lay down their arms [see Sir John YOUNG]. A third delegate, Donald Alexander Smith*, was for his part to set at rest the minds of the company's directors, and to discuss with all "the people of Red River" the conditions of their entry into the dominion. The prime minister, John A. Macdonald*, judging Thibault to be "a sensible old French Canadian" and "a shrewd and at the same time a kindly old gentleman," was of the

opinion that, if he accomplished nothing in particular, at least he would not commit any blunders since he knew the region and supported the Canadian government. A reserved and prudent man, Thibault was content to remain in the background, and this was where circumstances kept him during his governmental mission.

Salaberry having remained at Pembina, Thibault, on 25 December, arrived in the west alone. By order of the recently proclaimed provisional government, Thibault was escorted to the bishop's palace at Saint-Boniface, where he was kept under surveillance so that he would not meddle in political affairs. On 6 Jan. 1870 Louis Riel and his council received Thibault and also Salaberry, who had just arrived. "Immediately we communicated our instructions to the president [Riel] and his council," Thibault recounted, "and they took them under consideration." However, no comment was received, and four days later Thibault wrote to the provisional government to ask about the conditions required by the colony in the event of its union with Canada, "in order that we can submit them," he said, "to the examination of the government that sent us." The next day the council replied to him that the documents Thibault and Salaberry had submitted did not confer on them the necessary powers to conclude an agreement. On 13 January the council expressed this opinion to Thibault and Salaberry by word of mouth. According to the commissioner D. A. Smith, Thibault ceased to be useful from then on. In general, historians agree that he had no influence on the course of events. But Smith wrote that had it not been for the steps Thibault took during the night of 19–20 January, he himself would have succeeded in settling everything at this time. During that night, as Smith has it, Thibault contributed to a closing of the ranks of the demonstrators, who that day had held public meetings which Smith's money and promises had managed to break up. Subsequently Riel's position grew stronger, and he became formally president of the provisional government, whose bases were enlarged. Then delegates were sent to Ottawa to negotiate the entry of the Red River colony into confederation [see John BLACK]. Was Thibault partly responsible for this sudden change? In his report, he said that he had had "to reason with the leaders, and with the people; always, however, by conversations with single individuals, as that seemed to me the best . . . way of effecting any good result."

Thibault stayed two more years at Red River, ministering to the parish of Saint-François-Xavier; then in 1871 he accepted the post of vicar general of the diocese. The following autumn he returned to the east for good, and was successively in charge of the parishes of Sainte-Louise (L'Islet County) and Saint-Denis-de-la-Bouteillerie.

A man of little ambition, Thibault preferred to work in a parish where he could follow the instructions of a bishop, for he did not like to direct affairs himself. Although he spent the greater part of his life in the diocese of Saint-Boniface, he was of the opinion, as early as 1856, that secular priests should withdraw from that region. As a missionary, Thibault opened up the way to the west and north in America; as a government emissary, he defended the interests of those whom he was supposed to appease.

LIONEL DORGE

AAQ, Registre des lettres des évêques de Québec, 15, p.367; Rivière-Rouge et diocèse de Saint-Boniface (Man.), III, 161. ACAM, RLL, 5, p.383; RLL, 7, p.132; 255.109. ANQ, Collection Chapais, Fonds Langevin, Jean Langevin à Hector-Louis Langevin, 5 janv. 1870, Taché à Cartier, 15 mars 1870. Archives de l'archevêché de Saint-Boniface (Man.), Documents historiques, 1861–1872. ASQ, Séminaire, XXXVIII, 7, 9. PAC, MG 17, B2, C.1/M–C.1/M10; MG 26, A (Macdonald papers), 101, pp.40831, 40833, 41082, 41083, 41086, 41198; 516, pp.614–17, 646–51, 666–69, 717–18, 939–41; RG 6, C1, 10A, p.1041. PAM, Louis Riel papers; Red River Settlement, Copies of miscellaneous letters and documents, 92.

Begg's Red River journal (Morton), 81, 82, 88–91, 239, 240–50, 268, 289, 299, 301, 454, 468, 482, 533, 535. *Canadian North-West* (Oliver), II, 907–8. [P.-J. De Smet], *Life, letters and travels of Father Pierre-Jean De Smet, S.J., 1801–1873* . . . , ed. H. M. Chittenden and A. T. Richardson (4v., New York, 1905), IV 1560. Hargrave, *Red River*, 129, 135. HBRS, XXII (Rich), 917, 921–22, 932. *James Wickes Taylor correspondence* (Bowsfield), 97. Paul Kane, *Wanderings of an artist among the Indians of North America* . . . , intro. and notes by L. J. Burpee (Master-works of Canadian authors, ed. J. W. Garvin, VII, Toronto, 1925; repub. with intro. by J. G. MacGregor, Edmonton, 1968), 261, 276. "Lettres de Monseigneur Joseph-Norbert Provencher, premier évêque de Saint-Boniface, Manitoba," *Bulletin de la Société historique de Saint-Boniface*, III (1913), 137, 138, 147, 154, 167, 173, 179, 195, 196, 234–35, 246, 247–48, 249–50, 256–57. *McLean's notes of twenty five years service* (Wallace), 123, 318–19. [A.-A.] Taché, *Vingt années de missions dans le Nord-Ouest de l'Amérique* (Montréal, 1866; New York, 1970), 4, 20, 57–58, 64–66, 86, 88, 222, 238.

Allaire, *Dictionnaire*. Morice, *Dict. hist. des Can. et Métis*, 297. Julienne Barnard, *Mémoires Chapais: documentation, correspondance, souvenirs* (4v., Montréal et Paris, 1961–64), III, 18–19, 156. F. E. Bartlett, "William Mactavish, the last governor of Assiniboia," unpublished MA thesis, University of Manitoba, 1964. J.-É. Champagne, *Les missions catholiques dans l'Ouest canadien (1818–1875)* (Publ. de l'Institut de missiologie de l'université pontificale d'Ottawa, I, Ottawa, 1949), 64–65. Georges Dugas, *Histoire de l'Ouest canadien de 1822 à 1869; époque des troubles* (Montréal, [1906]), 154; *Monseigneur Provencher et les missions de la Rivière-Rouge* (Montréal, 1889). Donatien Frémont, *Monseigneur Provencher et son temps* (Winnipeg, 1935). Giraud, *Le Métis canadien*, 1074–81. Morice, *Hist. de l'Église catholique*, I, 234; II. Alexander Ross, *The Red River Settlement; its rise, progress, and present state* . . . (London, 1856; Minneapolis, 1957), 275–300. Stanley, *Birth of western Canada*, 88–91, 93–96, 121, 146, 148; *Louis Riel*, 85. Gaston Carrière, "L'honorable compagnie de la Baie d'Hudson et les missions de l'Ouest canadien," *Revue de l'université d'Ottawa*, XXXVI (1966), 15–39, 232–57. C. J. Jaenen, "Foundations of dual education at Red River, 1811–1834," HSSM, *Papers*, 3rd ser., no.21 (1965), 35–68. G. F. G. Stanley, "Louis Riel," *Canada's past and present; a dialogue*, ed. R. L. McDougall, (Toronto, 1965), 21–40.

THOMPSON, JOSHUA SPENCER, journalist, accountant, prospector, and politician; b. at Belfast, Ireland, in 1828; d. at Victoria, B.C., on 20 Dec. 1880.

Educated in Belfast, Joshua Spencer Thompson emigrated to British Columbia in 1858, settling first in Fort Hope but later, probably in 1862, moving to Barkerville. As foreman of the Fort Hope grand jury in 1860, Thompson complained to Chief Justice Matthew Baillie Begbie* of the poor roads in the Fraser Canyon, and as secretary to two citizens' political conventions in 1860 and 1861 he spoke for Fort Hope commercial interests, condemning the abuses of the absentee government of James DOUGLAS and demanding responsible government, lower taxes, and improved roads for the colony. In 1861 Thompson was a member of the committee that met with Governor Douglas to discuss the financing of the proposed Cariboo road.

Working in Barkerville first as a clerk, accountant, auctioneer, and mining commissioner, Thompson later acquired interests in various mining claims, and in 1866 was elected to the Mining Board of the Cariboo. In 1871 he was foreman of the grand jury of Richfield, and was elected chairman of the first school board in the Cariboo. As editor of the *Cariboo Sentinel* in 1870 and 1871, Thompson became the Cariboo's most influential advocate of confederation and "that grand bond of union," the transcontinental railroad. On 20 Dec. 1871 he was elected by acclamation the first MP for Cariboo. He was re-elected by acclamation in the general elections of 1872, 1874, and 1878. In the commons Thompson opposed Chinese immigration and urged that the house devise "some means by which that great evil which threatened to overwhelm their country, namely, the unlimited immigration, might be averted." He also called for improved postal and telegraphic communications between east and west. But above all he called for the completion of the Canadian Pacific railroad. Although a Conservative supporter, he criticized both parties for delays in railroad construction.

Apart from his commercial and political activity, Thompson was active in Cariboo social life, being president of the Cariboo Literary Institute in 1866, 1867, and 1870, an officer in the freemasons brotherhood in 1871, and an actor and manager in the Cariboo Amateur Dramatic Association after 1869. He helped establish the first library and the first freemasons Grand Lodge in the Cariboo.

After Thompson's death, a San Francisco woman claimed his estate as his widow, but his relatives denied her claim, maintaining that he had never married.

JOHN A. LYON and GEORGE A. TRIPP

PABC, Joshua Spencer Thompson correspondence, 1851–61. Canada, House of Commons, *Debates*, 1871–81. I. M. L. Bescoby, "Some aspects of society in the Cariboo from its discovery until 1871," unpublished BA thesis, University of British Columbia, 1932, especially 14, 113, 123, 127, 130. F. W. Howay *et al.*, *British Columbia and the United States: the north Pacific slope from fur trade to aviation*, ed. H. F. Angus (The Relations of Canada and the United States series, Toronto, New Haven, Conn., London, 1942), 212. R. L. Reid, *Grand Lodge of British Columbia A.F. & A.M.: historical notes and biographical sketches 1848–1935* (Vancouver, B.C., n.d.), 30–33. G. M. Murray, "Cariboo M.Ps. – 1871–1951," *Northwest Digest* (Quesnel, B.C.), VII (July 1951), 3–5, 16–21.

THOMSON, SAMUEL ROBERT, lawyer; b.c. 1825 at St Stephen, N.B., the fourth son of Skeffington Thomson, Church of England rector at St Stephen; d. 19 Nov. 1880 in London, Eng.

Samuel Robert Thomson studied law with his eldest brother George, and was admitted an attorney on 5 Feb. 1846. Following his admission to the bar on 3 Feb. 1848, he practised briefly at Fredericton, then at Saint John, where he was in partnership for many years with Robertson Bayard until the latter's death. He was made a queen's counsel in 1871 or 1873. Thomson also ventured into politics: he was defeated in at least one contest for the New Brunswick assembly.

Thomson enjoyed an unusually high reputation as a barrister both in New Brunswick and abroad. His first major case was in 1860 when he served as counsel for the tenantry before the P.E.I. Land Commission which included John Hamilton Gray* for the crown, John William Ritchie* for the proprietors, and Joseph HOWE for the tenantry. Though the commission's recommendations were disallowed in London, the land question was finally resolved in favour of freehold tenure. In 1875 Thomson along with Louis H. Davies* was again retained by the tenantry to appear before the arbitration commission set up to settle the P.E.I. land claims. Perhaps the most significant tribute to his ability was that of William Henry POPE, who, though an ardent defender of the landlords' property rights, described a crucial speech by Thomson in 1860 as "the most eloquent ever delivered in the colonial building."

Before the 1875 arbitration closed, Thomson returned to New Brunswick to defend Acadians charged with murder and sedition following disturbances at Caraquet, Gloucester County, in January 1875. The incident was linked directly to the Common Schools Act of 1871 which withdrew public assistance from denominational schools. Catholic sentiment interpreted the bill as against the spirit of Article 93 of the British North America Act; the government and courts upheld that "de jure" denominational schools did not exist at confederation. Four years of unrest in the province culminated in the incident at Caraquet, in which two men were killed. Thomson, rather than an Acadian barrister, was retained, as much for his calmness in the face of the sectarian emotions roused by the case as for his ability. Though the charges were upheld at the Gloucester sessions before Chief Justice John C. Allen* in December 1875, Thomson, in a highly acclaimed manoeuvre, had the verdict quashed on technical grounds by an appeal in the New Brunswick Supreme Court the following June.

Thomson's most important case was heard before the Joint High Commission which met at Halifax in 1877 under the stipulations of the Treaty of Washington of 1871 to determine the amount of compensation the United States should pay Canada for the use of her inshore fisheries. Though Alexander Tilloch Galt*, the commissioner appointed by Great Britain, was pessimistic about the outcome of the case, he was obviously heartened by the prospect of Thomson's summing up the argument for the crown. Galt's hopes were well founded, for on 23 November the commission made an award of $5,500,000 in favour of Canada. When Thomson died, his colleagues recalled his speech as the highlight of his career.

In September 1880 Thomson contracted typhoid fever while on the Northumberland circuit. Despite growing ill health, he sailed for England on 30 October to argue a case before the Privy Council. His illness became progressively worse after his arrival in London on 9 November, and he died ten days later. His body was transferred

Thomson

to Saint John. His wife, Catherine McDonell, whom he had married less than five years before, was expecting their third child at the time of his death. Thomson died while still in the prime of his professional life. Of his career H. J. Morgan* wrote, "There was not a trial, criminal or civil, of any importance, during the past twenty years in New Brunswick in which Thomson did not take a leading part."

BERNARD POTHIER

N.B. Museum, Webster coll., Court record, Caraquet murder case, 1875. PAC, MG 27, 1, D8 (Galt papers). Queen's University Archives, Alexander Mackenzie papers (on microfilm in PAC, MG 26, B1 (Mackenzie papers, general correspondence)). *Daily News* (Saint John, N.B.), July 1876, December 1880. *Daily Telegraph* (Saint John, N.B.), July 1876. *Examiner* (Charlottetown), September–October 1860, August–September 1875. *Islander* (Charlottetown), August–October 1860, August 1861. *Le Moniteur acadien* (Shédiac, N.B.), septembre–décembre 1875. *Morning Freeman* (Saint John, N.B.), September–November 1875, June–July 1876.

Award of the Fishery Commission. Documents and proceedings of the Halifax Commission, 1877, under the Treaty of Washington of May 8, 1871 (3v., Washington, 1878). Judgement of the Supreme Court of New Brunswick in the case of Maher v. the town council of Portland (1873), reported *sub nomine Ex parte Renaud*, 14 New Brunswick *Reports* (I, Pugsley, 1876), 273, and in G. J. Wheeler, *Confederation law of Canada; Privy Council cases on the British North-America Act, 1867* ... (London, 1896), 338–62. The case was appealed to the Judicial Committee of the Privy Council in 1874, and the judgement is reported in Wheeler, *Confederation law* ... , 362–67. *Can. biog. dict.*, II. *The Canadian legal directory: a guide to the bench and bar of the dominion of Canada*, ed. H. J. Morgan (Toronto, 1878). *Dom. ann. reg., 1880–81.* Lawrence, *Judges of New Brunswick* (Stockton), 401. G. H. Lee, *An historical sketch of the first fifty years of the Church of England in the province of New Brunswick (1783–1833)* (Saint John, N.B., 1880). C. C. Tansill, *Canadian-American relations, 1875–1912* (Carnegie endowment for International Peace: Division of economics and history, pub., New Haven, Conn., London, and Toronto, 1943). Onésiphore Turgeon, *Un tribut à la race acadienne: mémoires, 1871–1929* (Montréal, 1928).

THOMSON, WILLIAM ALEXANDER, railway promoter, author, and politician; b. November 1816 in Wigtownshire, Scotland; d. 1 Oct. 1878, near Queenston, Ont.

William Alexander Thomson attended school in Wigtownshire before emigrating to the United States. He went to Buffalo, New York, then came to Upper Canada in 1834, settling in Queenston. He was active in arranging for the incorporation, financing, and development of railways in western Ontario beginning with the Fort Erie Railway (later the Erie and Niagara Railway), and then the Erie and Ontario Railway, which was purchased by the Erie and Niagara in 1863. He became president of the Erie and Niagara Railway and a senior officer of the Canada Southern Railway; the Toronto *Globe* reported that the latter appointment was "largely the result of his determination, perseverance, and energy." He was an enthusiastic advocate of western expansion, and at his death was said to have been "engaged in the promotion of railway enterprises in Manitoba."

Thomson was an unsuccessful candidate at the federal general election of 1867, standing for Niagara, but was elected to the House of Commons as a Liberal in a by-election on 19 Nov. 1872 for Welland, and was re-elected in 1874. He was prevented by ill health from being a candidate for re-election in 1878. A man of advanced views, enterprising spirit, and "a bold speculative turn of mind," Thomson was also called "a large-hearted, liberal man, of kindly and social sympathies, a loyal member of his political party, and true to his convictions."

Thomson was an effective advocate of radical agrarian economic doctrine in the years just before and after confederation. He set forth most of his ideas for the first time in 1863 in a long pamphlet entitled *An essay on production, money, and government; in which the principle of a natural law is advanced and explained.* Thomson believed that Canadian laws and institutions had been formulated to advance mercantile rather than productive interests and were not conducive to national development. He told the House of Commons in 1876: "The cause of our troubles has been that our laws have been made to suit the merchants instead of the producing classes." He recommended more public works, lower tariffs, and above all an issue of irredeemable government notes to assist farmers and other producers of real goods. Like many other radical spokesmen before and since, he tended to overstate his case and to confuse his economic theory with religious and moral doctrine. He explained: "Nature laid the foundation, Adam Smith and his successors built the columns, and, I believe, it has been given to me to place the keystone in the arch of Political Economy."

Public management of the currency, Thomson argued, could eliminate depressions, stimulate growth, help to finance government expenditures, and bring about the reign of Christian principles on earth. "The present money," he said, "never moves production, it only exchanges products." Thomson's ideas are strikingly similar to those of Canadian Social Credit theorists in the 20th century, and he even used the term "social credit" in presenting his case. He described an economic crisis as follows: "When the collapse happens, apart from the increase of human wretchedness that will arise, there will be a depreciation of fixed properties just equal to the amount of social credit withdrawn." He expressed his views often to parliament, and he proposed a series of resolutions in 1878 asking that a system of "Agricultural Banks" be established on his model. Though there is little evidence that his ideas were influential beyond a few contemporary advocates of a "national currency," he is remembered as one of Canada's first agrarian radicals and as a pioneer advocate of government monetary policy.

CRAUFURD D. W. GOODWIN

W. A. Thomson, *An essay on production, money, and government; in which the principle of a natural law is advanced and explained, whereby credit, debt, taxation, tariffs, and interest on money will be abolished; and national debt and the current expenses of government will be paid in gold* (Buffalo, N.Y., 1863). PAO, Misc. 1946, "Historical sketch of Canada Southern Railway Company." Canada, House of Commons, *Debates,* 1875–78. *Globe* (Toronto), 2 Oct. 1878. *Can. parl. comp., 1878. Can. directory of parliament* (Johnson), 570. Morgan, *Bibliotheca Canadensis,* 372. C. D. W. Goodwin, *Canadian economic thought: the political economy of a developing nation, 1814–1914* (Duke University Commonwealth-Studies Center pub., 15, Durham, N.C., and London, 1961); "A forgotten forerunner of Social Credit: William Alexander Thomson," *J. of Canadian Studies* (Peterborough, Ont.), IV (May 1969), 41–45.

THURGAR, JOHN VENNER, merchant, banker, and militia officer; b. 1797 in Yorkshire, Eng.; m. Anna Paddock by whom he had two daughters and one son; d. in Saint John, N.B., 29 Feb. 1880.

John Venner Thurgar left England at the age of 20 to apprentice with his uncle, John Lawder (Lauder) Venner, a Saint John loyalist and owner of a wine and commission business. He succeeded his uncle as proprietor in 1823 and continued at the same location at Market Wharf for 57 years. He overcame many financial obstacles, including a large original debt, a near-ruinous swindle, a disastrous fire, and several severe economic depressions. Thurgar's business steadily expanded into the United Kingdom, the West Indies, New York, and Boston.

Banking emerged as a vital part of Thurgar's career when he became the founding president of the City Bank of Saint John in 1836. Three years later, when it merged with the Bank of New Brunswick, Thurgar became a director. He was a senior director of the Bank of British North America for 25 years, director of the Equitable

and Marine Insurance companies, and Saint John agent for the New Brunswick and Nova Scotia Land Company.

Thurgar also had a life-long interest in the local militia, entering the artillery corps as a private and rising to the rank of colonel. His son, John Venner Thurgar, followed this tradition, becoming lieutenant-colonel of the 3rd batallion of the Saint John City Militia.

In November 1864, when Thurgar handed over his firm's operation to his son, the *Saint John Globe* wrote: "No man could retire from business with a cleaner record in every respect." His will, drawn up nine years later, indicated that he had amassed considerable wealth and achieved an important social position in the community. Despite the fact that he was not a Saint John "native," Thurgar had met the other requirements by which his contemporaries measured success: a thriving business and an influential marriage. For half a century, when Saint John was a vital part of the British empire, Thurgar was an important member of its commercial establishment.

RICHARD WILBUR

N.B. Museum, J. V. Thurgar papers, letter book, 1827–31; Scrapbook 13, Clarence Ward, "Old times in Saint John," clippings from *Saint John Globe,* 12 Aug. 1905. *Census of Canada, 1870–71* (5v., Ottawa, 1873), for district 174. *Royal Gazette* (Fredericton), 1835–38. *Saint John Daily Sun,* 1 March 1880, 3 Nov. 1887. *Dom. ann. reg., 1880–81,* 432. R. M. Breckenridge, *The Canadian banking system, 1817–1890* (American Economic Association pub., X, New York, 1895).

TODD, WILLIAM, merchant, lumberman, railway promoter, and politician; b. at North Yarmouth, Maine, on 10 June or 10 July 1803, one of ten children of William Todd and Hannah Worthley; m. in 1826 to Clarissa Hill by whom he had 12 children, and on 9 July 1862 to Mrs Mary Jane Haney; d. 5 Aug. 1873 at St Stephen, N.B.

William Todd Sr had built a lucrative business in the Atlantic coast–West Indies trade, but the business was destroyed by the blockade during the Napoleonic Wars, and in 1811 the Todd family, like many of their countrymen, sought a new life in the security of British North America. They settled in St Stephen, N.B., where by the age of 22 William Jr had established himself as a merchant in nearby Milltown. Within a short time he moved into the lumber business, then the principal industry of the St Croix River valley. He was an able businessman and became one of the wealthiest lumbermen on the St Croix. His business interests in both New Brunswick and Maine were extensive, making him one of the leading members of the "international community" on the St Croix. At the time of his death, Todd's estate was valued at $187,571.

Early in his career Todd became engaged in railway construction. He was president of the St Croix and Penobscot Railroad and of the St Stephen Branch Railroad (later known as the New Brunswick and Canada Railway). In addition he was a founder and director of the St Stephen's Bank and served as its president from 1849 until 1873.

Todd was a member of the Congregational Church of St Stephen and was active in the affairs of the church and the community. His interest in education is indicated by the fact that he was a founder, and for many years a director, of the Milltown Academy – one of the leading schools of the province.

In 1854, the year in which the Liberals under Charles FISHER gained control of the assembly, Todd was appointed to the Legislative Council. At the deliberations of the council he was a strong supporter of the business community in general and of the lumber industry and railways in particular. During the confederation controversy Todd did not, at least in the beginning, take a strong stand. The St Stephen area was regarded as an anti-confederation centre and several influential lumbermen, including Todd's brother, Freeman H. Todd*, opposed the union of the provinces. As late as 1866 William remained uncommitted, but during the council session of that year he was influenced by the forceful case in favour of confederation which was presented by Edward Barron CHANDLER. Finally, when the resolution supporting confederation was placed before the council, Todd voted for it.

In October 1867 he was called to the Senate, but he was unwilling to go to Ottawa and declined the appointment. He retained his seat in the Legislative Council of the province where he made his last appearance during the session of 1872.

MICHAEL SWIFT

PANB, Department of Justice, Probate Court Records, Milltown, 873/Wm. Todd. New Brunswick, Legislative Council, *Debates*, 1866; *Journals*, 1854–72. *Morning Freeman* (Saint John, N.B.), 7 Aug. 1873. *Statutory history of the railways of Canada* (Dorman). H. A. Davis, *An international community on the St. Croix, 1604–1930* (University of Maine Studies, 2nd ser., 64, Orono, 1950). G. H. Mowat, *The diverting history of a loyalist town* (St Andrews, N.B., 1932). Guy Murchie, *Saint Croix, the sentinel river; historical sketches of its discovery, early conflicts and final occupation by English and American settlers, with some comments on Indian life* (New York, 1947). William Todd, *Todds of the St. Croix Valley* (Mount Carmel, Conn., 1943).

TOPP, ALEXANDER, Presbyterian clergyman; b. at Sheriffmill, near Elgin, Elgin (now Moray) County, Scotland, 1 April 1814, the second of three sons in a family of six; d. Toronto, Ont., 6 Oct. 1879.

Alexander Topp was educated at Elgin Academy, at King's College, Aberdeen, where he obtained an AM in 1831, and at the divinity faculty of the University of Aberdeen. He was appointed assistant to the minister of the Elgin parish church in 1836 and minister in 1837. He had early identified himself with the evangelical party in the Church of Scotland, and in 1843 he sided with the Free Church movement, leading most of his congregation into the new body. He was active in organizing Free Church congregations in the north of Scotland and, in 1852, he was inducted minister of Free Roxburgh Church in Edinburgh.

Topp received a call to Knox Church, Toronto, and on 16 Sept. 1858 he was inducted its minister. He remained at Knox Church until his death, and his congregation became, under his able leadership, one of the largest Presbyterian churches in Canada. An outstanding Presbyterian leader in Canada, Topp held many high offices in the church. He was elected moderator of the Canada Presbyterian Chutch in 1868 by unanimous vote. Convener of the committee on union of the Canada Presbyterian Church from 1871 to 1875, he was also secretary of the joint union committee of the four churches which united in 1875 to form the Presbyterian Church in Canada. In 1876 he was elected moderator of the general assembly of the Presbyterian Church in Canada. He was also a member of the general assembly committees on French Canadian evangelization, the *Home and Foreign Record of the Presbyterian Church* (Toronto), and foreign missions.

Topp was closely identified with Knox College in Toronto, founded in 1844, and was a member of the board of management for 1859–65 and 1869–79, the chairman of the board 1860–62, 1871–73, and 1877–79, and a member of the senate on several occasions between 1860 and 1875. He took an active interest in the founding of the Presbyterian College in Montreal and of Manitoba College in Winnipeg in 1871.

Interested in benevolent work, Topp served as chairman of the board of management of the Toronto Home for Incurables from its inception in 1874 to 1879, and was a member of the board of management of the House of Industry in Toronto, 1866–70, and of the board of trustees, 1870–79.

Alexander Topp was awarded an honorary doctor of divinity by King's College, Aberdeen, in 1870. He died in Toronto on 6 Oct. 1879. He had married Jane Mortimer, the widow of John Clark, both natives of Aberdeen, and his only son died in 1853 at age four.

C. GLENN LUCAS

UCA, Minutes of Synod of the Presbyterian Church of Canada, 1844–61; Minutes of Synod of the Canada Presbyterian Church, 1861–69; Minutes of the General Assembly of the Canada Presbyterian Church, 1870–75; Minutes of the General Assembly of the Presbyterian Church in Canada, 1875–79. *Globe* (Toronto), 7 Oct. 1879. Knox Presbyterian Church, *Annual Report* (Toronto), XIII (1880). *Presbyterian Record for the Dominion of Canada* (Montreal, Toronto), November 1879. Toronto Home for Incurables, *Annual Reports* (Toronto), 1875–80. Toronto House of Industry, *Annual Reports* (Toronto), 1869–80. Robert Cowan, *Remember your leaders, a sermon occasioned by the death of the Rev. Alexander Topp, D.D. . . .* (Elgin, Scotland, 1879). Dent, *Canadian portrait gallery*, III, 54–55. H. M. Parsons, *Biographical sketches and review: First Presbyterian Church in Toronto and Knox Church, 1820–1890* (Toronto, 1890).

TORRANCE, DAVID, merchant, shipper, and president of the Bank of Montreal; b. 1805, New York, N.Y., son of James and Elizabeth Kissock Torrance; d. 29 Jan. 1876 at Montreal, Que.

The Torrances were a Scottish Lowland family who came from Larkhall in Lanark. Five brothers, sons of Thomas Torrance (1735–1805), emigrated to Canada via New York shortly after the turn of the 19th century. Of these, Thomas* (1776–1826) and John* (1786–1870) settled at Montreal, where they established wholesale and retail groceries, trading largely in wines and liquor; James went to Kingston, Upper Canada, where he acted as the agent for the forwarding business of the family and carried on commercial operations of his own. The first two, at least, became very prosperous as a result of the War of 1812.

David Torrance, the son of James, went to Montreal about 1821 to work in his uncle John's St Paul Street business, John Torrance and Company. Among the firm's clerks were Henry Wilkes*, the future Congregationalist minister, and John YOUNG, with whom David was to operate a Quebec City partnership, known as Torrance and Young, for some five years after 1835. On 9 Jan. 1832, David married his cousin Jane Torrance (1812–75), the eldest daughter of his uncle John, and in 1833 he became a partner in the business. In the years following he assumed an important role in Montreal commerce and with his uncle's retirement in 1853 the firm became David Torrance and Company. His partners were Thomas Cramp* and later also his own son, John Torrance Jr (1835–1908). With Cramp and another son, George William Torrance (c.1849–

1911), David also formed a second partnership in Toronto entitled Cramp, Torrances and Company. The John Torrance businesses dealt in all forms of general merchandizing, but specialized in teas; from the late 1820s the Torrances challenged the monopoly of Forsyth, Richardson and Company in tea importation. They were the first Canadian firm to deal directly with China and India, where their name was well known for over 30 years; in 1853 they began holding annual sales of teas imported directly from China. At the time of David's death Bradstreet estimated the value of David Torrance and Company in Montreal at $400,000–$500,000.

John Torrance and Company were also interested in shipping and their Montreal Tow Boat Company was to be the first to rival the Molsons in river shipping [*see* William MOLSON]. In 1825 the company gained control of the powerful steam tug *Hercules*, and over the next few years had steamers for both passengers and freight plying the Montreal-Quebec route, including the *St George*, *British America*, and the 240-foot *Canada*, the last being the largest and fastest boat in British North America. By 1831 they were also operating the *Voyageur* and the *Edmund Henry* between Montreal and Laprairie, and in 1833 they added the *Britannia*. Competition with the Molsons on the St Lawrence was at first fierce, but in 1833 both parties "agreed to unite in forming a daily line between Quebec and Montreal for the convenience of the public." At the same time passenger and barge traffic were separated. The Montreal and Quebec Steamboat Company, as the Torrance firm became known, soon had agents at Quebec, Trois-Rivières, Sorel, and Saint-François (Yamaska County) and new boats were added during the 1840s. In late 1853 the *Montreal*, which they owned with the Molsons and others, was lost off Cape Batiscan, in a snowstorm. The 1850s saw another period of competition, for by 1852 the Tate brothers had established a rival line and in 1856 the Richelieu Company (La Compagnie du Richelieu) [*see* Jacques-Félix SINCENNES] extended its operations to the Montreal-Quebec route. This rivalry resulted in both reduced fares and competitive races until 1858, when an amalgamation was arranged under which the Torrance Company was merged in the Richelieu Line, of which David Torrance became a director.

In 1870 Torrance branched into a different type of shipping, when he became involved with the new Mississippi and Dominion Steamship Company Limited, which was chartered to develop trade from Liverpool to New Orleans and Montreal. The American connection was soon discontinued and the name changed to the Dominion

Torrance

Line; the Torrance family retained its agency long after David's death.

David Torrance's other main financial interest was the Bank of Montreal. His uncle, Thomas Torrance, had been one of the original shareholders in 1817 and a year later had been elected to the Board of Directors, an office he held until his death in 1826. Thomas' brother John succeeded him and remained a director until 1857; meanwhile, in 1853, David had been elected to the board and by the time Edwin H. King* resigned from the presidency in 1873, he was second in seniority. When Senator Thomas Ryan, the senior director, refused the office of president, the board, of which David's brother-in-law, Sir Alexander Tilloch Galt*, had just become a member, elected Torrance president.

Torrance's presidency of the bank was a short one, for he died in early 1876 and was ill through most of 1875. It was also marked by the major depression which began in 1873, shortly after he was elected president. Nevertheless, profits remained steady, dividends were held at 14 per cent, a loan of $1,250,000 was made to the Grand Trunk Railway in 1873, and in 1874 the bank entered the field of investment banking by jointly underwriting an issue of Quebec provincial bonds with the London firm of Morton, Rose and Company, one of whose principals was its London agent, Sir John Rose*. Torrance's term, however, is easily overlooked, coming as it did between the brilliant presidencies of King and his own vice-president and successor, George Stephen*, later Baron Mount Stephen.

David Torrance was noted for the regularity of his attention to his work; the *Montreal Daily Witness* summed this up well in his obituary when it stated "he was a diligent merchant, and did not meddle much in public affairs, though he was a consistent Liberal in politics throughout." His only real political activity was in connection with the annexation movement in 1849, when he was treasurer of the Montreal Annexation Association and fifth of the 325 initial signatories of the Annexation Manifesto.

The Torrance family was originally Presbyterian, but became Methodist and was active in the affairs of the St James Street Methodist Church; David contributed £100 to the building fund for the second church in 1845. He became a charter member of the St James Club in 1857. Torrance was also a member of the Montreal Board of Trade, was on its council, and was a member of its committee which was active in obtaining the second act of incorporation for Montreal in 1840. In 1845 he was commissioned a captain in the 8th Battalion, Montreal militia, and

in 1847 recommissioned in the 6th Battalion, but was dismissed in 1850 for his part in the annexation movement. In addition he was prominently associated in many benevolent and philanthropic undertakings. Examples are his directorship in the High School of Montreal, which he helped establish in 1843, and his many charitable donations to the Montreal General Hospital, of which he was a governor from 1869 to 1876.

He was survived by five children and one son and four daughters predeceased him. Besides the sons who succeeded him in the business, another son, Edward Fraser Torrance, became minister of St Paul's Presbyterian Church, Peterborough, 1876–1909. David Torrance was an able businessman and a conscientious worker, who "in the days of his prosperity was as regular in attendance at the counting house as when he first started in business." His activities in business, in religion, and with most of his interests, however, seem to be very much a continuation of those of his uncle *cum* father-in-law John Torrance, who, with his brother Thomas, was the real innovator and founder of the family fortunes.

FREDERICK H. ARMSTRONG

AJM, will of David Torrance, 7 April 1875. PAC, RG 1, L3ᴸ, 194, pp.92426–52; RG 9, I, A3, 12; A5, 16, pp.437–38; C4, 1, pp.145, 150; C4, 4, p.266. Bank of Montreal Archives (Montreal), Minute book of the board of directors, 1873–76. Molson Archives (Molson's Brewery, Montreal). "The annexation movement, 1849–50," ed. A. G. Penny, *CHR*, V (1924), 237. *Bradstreet's reports of the dominion of Canada, February 1, 1876* (New York, 1876), 642. *Montreal Daily Witness*, 20 Jan. 1870, 31 Jan. 1876. *Montreal Herald*, 15 Oct. 1849, 21 Jan. 1870. *The Canadian men and women of the time: a handbook of Canadian biography*, ed. H. J. Morgan (1st ed., Toronto, 1898). Notman and Taylor, *Portraits of British Americans*, II, 228.

C. D. Allin and G. M. Jones, *Annexation, preferential trade and reciprocity; an outline of the Canadian annexation movement of 1849–1850, with special reference to the questions of preferential trade and reciprocity* (Toronto and London, 1912), 114. Atherton, *Montreal*, II, 168, 531, 574, 577. Campbell, *Hist. of Scotch Presbyterian Church*, 313–16. *Canada, an encyclopædia*, V, 443. *The centenary of the Bank of Montreal, 1817–1917* (Montreal, 1917), 50–51, 80. E. A. Collard, *The Saint James's Club; the story of the beginnings of the Saint James's Club* (Montreal, 1957), 12–13. James Croil, *Steam navigation in Canada and its relation to the commerce of Canada and the United States* (Toronto, 1898), 221, 308–10, 313–15. Merrill Denison, *The barley and the stream; the Molson story . . .* (Toronto, 1955), 90, 92, 95, 148, 152, 159–60; *Canada's first bank*, I, 162, 299; II. G. E. Jacques, *Chronicles of the St. James St. Methodist Church, Montreal, from the first rise of Methodism in Montreal to the laying of the corner-stone of the new church on St. Catherine Street* (Toronto, 1888), 68, 84, 90. L. C.

Tombs, *National problems of Canada; the port of Montreal* (McGill University Economic Studies, 6, Toronto, 1926), 36, 38.

TOWNSEND, WILLIAM H., merchant, banker, shipowner, and politician; b. 1812 in New York City, son of William and Lucinda Townsend; m. Sarah Gardner and had two children; d. 14 Oct. 1873 in Yarmouth, N.S.

Round Hill, Annapolis County, would awaken no great expectation in the soul of an ambitious young man, and when his more confident parents abandoned New York for that drowsy hamlet, the young William H. Townsend responded in story-book style and ran away from home in 1828. He chose Yarmouth, the second port in the sometime bustling commerce of Nova Scotia, as his adopted home, learned the wheelwright's trade, and six years after his arrival opened his first ship-chandlery and hardware business there.

Between 1837 and 1870 he was a director or shareholder in the Yarmouth Marine Insurance Association, the Acadian Insurance Company, the Yarmouth Commercial Insurance Company, the Atlantic Insurance Company, and the Pacific Insurance Company. During the same period Townsend launched himself into shipping ventures on an increasingly large scale, until in 1855 he became a director of the Yarmouth Steam Navigation Company which launched Yarmouth's first home-owned steamship. He became the first president of the Bank of Yarmouth in 1865 and served as president of the Exchange Bank of Yarmouth in 1869. The base of his business ventures, however, remained the steady family trade in dry goods and hardware.

His first taste of politics as warden of the short-lived Yarmouth Township apparently whetted a latent appetite; after his defeat in 1858, following a year in office, he stood for the assembly as a Conservative, and sat in opposition to the Joseph HOWE–William Young* ministry. Defeat in 1863 failed to eliminate him from the all-important confederation struggle. The sitting member resigned his seat in criticism of Charles Tupper*'s régime and, in 1866, Townsend was re-elected on the strength of a promise to bolt his party on the confederation issue.

His opposition speech was thus necessarily based on the injury dealt Yarmouth in the proposed union. He balked at rerouting trade to the west, at paying Canadian debts with high tariffs, and at the suggestion that the Intercolonial Railway would benefit any ports other than Saint John, N.B. Unlike most prominent "antis," he was opposed not only to the Quebec scheme but to any union. The temper of Yarmouth was so roused

that annexation was more to its liking, and Townsend so informed the house. Despite his disagreement with his party, he was not a supporter of the Liberals under William Annand* but a dissenting Tory, caught in the realignments on the hottest issue of his day.

Townsend was re-elected as an anti-confederate in the 1867 election, but by December 1868 he was convinced of the futility of further resistance to the John A. Macdonald*–Tupper machine. He wrote Howe urging him to take a federal post, and explaining his own reluctance to continue in opposition. Both men were old and tired and destined to die within months of one another. In 1872 Townsend's health failed, and he resigned his seat. He was dead within a year.

He was a small historical figure, despite the fact that he walked and talked with the great men of Nova Scotia legend. He was an ordinary, laconic assemblyman of that peculiar Nova Scotia type, presenting his constituents' petitions, performing his committee duties, distributing the local patronage, and leaving the oratory to others. But for the confederation agitation, he might have been forgotten outside his family and his community. As a voice of the shipping and merchant interest, and as one of the 19 who opposed Tupper's union resolution in 1866, he became of more than usual significance.

MARY ELLEN DUBÉ CLANCEY

PANS, Joseph Howe papers; William H. Townsend papers; "Yarmouth genealogy, 1761–1913," compiled by G. S. Brown. *Halifax Chronicle-Herald*, 21 March 1959. *Tribune* (Yarmouth), 1863–64, 1866–67. *Vanguard* (Yarmouth), 2 Aug. 1967. *Yarmouth Herald*, 1859, 1863–67, 1872–73. Nova Scotia House of Assembly, *Debates and proceedings*, 1855–61, 1864–67. *Directory of N.S. MLAs* (Fergusson). G. S. Brown, *Yarmouth, Nova Scotia: a sequel to Campbell's history* (Boston, 1888). J. R. Campbell, *A history of the county of Yarmouth, Nova Scotia* (Saint John, N.B., 1876). J. M. Lawson, *Yarmouth past and present: a book of reminiscences* (Yarmouth, N.S., 1902). K. G. Pryke, "Nova Scotia and confederation, 1864–1870," unpublished PHD thesis, Duke University, 1962.

TREMBLAY, PIERRE-ALEXIS, surveyor, politician, and journalist, commonly known as "Pitre" and familiarly as "Pitre à Kiki" (Kiki being the name given to his father at Charlevoix); b. 27 Dec. 1827 at La Malbaie, L.C., son of Alexis Tremblay and Josephte Duguay; d. 4 Jan. 1879 at Quebec.

Pierre-Alexis Tremblay was educated at the Petit Séminaire of Quebec, where he formed friendships with students later important in the religious world, such as the prelates Dominique* and Antoine Racine*, and the abbés Benjamin

Tremblay

Pâquet* and Pierre-Télesphore Sax. Tremblay remained closely attached to his religion, despite the trials and personal attacks to which he was to be subjected later by fervent Catholics, and even by several members of the clergy. His principles and beliefs took a concrete form both in his personal and in his public life. At the time of the disastrous fire of 1870 that ravaged the Saguenay area and ruined several thousand settlers, he travelled throughout the province and wrote many accounts of the calamity, in order to raise enough donations to cover the most urgent needs. In fact Pierre-Alexis Tremblay makes us think of a fighter, an armed knight ready to defend what he believed to be right and just. He was "tall, thin, slender. His drawn features and pale face reveal a high-strung temperament. His well-developed forehead is topped by black hair mingled with silvery streaks." A portrait of Tremblay, preserved in the archives of the Quebec provincial museum, confirms this description.

On 5 Oct. 1853 Pierre-Alexis Tremblay became a surveyor of the Saguenay region, particularly in the townships of Demeulles, Parent, Signay, Labarre, and Caron; he carried out the survey of the Rivière Péribonca and plotted the course of Lac Saint-Jean. His cherished dream, to see the fertile districts of the Saguenay opened to settlement, inevitably clashed with the ambitions of the timber merchants, who then formed "a kind of business aristocracy." Among the most important might be mentioned the Prices, who, in the county of Chicoutimi-Saguenay, "subscribed to the Conservative treasury, and enjoyed in exchange not only commercial privileges but electoral support." Tremblay was opposed to the existing system, despite the enticing offers that were made to him.

Not a man who was afraid of battle, he loved difficulties. Politics gave him ample opportunity to exercise his talents as a jouster; he concerned himself actively with politics from 1857 until his death, in the counties of Chicoutimi-Saguenay and Charlevoix. Pierre-Alexis Tremblay first stood as a candidate on the Conservative ticket, but soon left the party as a result of his opposition to confederation. As an independent, then as a Liberal, he was elected seven times to the Legislative Assembly and to the House of Commons; in 1874, when the end of the double mandate obliged him to make a choice, he decided for the federal arena. It was he who proposed secret balloting at elections, a measure which, before helping the cause of democracy, was first to work against him.

Each of the elections in which Tremblay took part would be worth describing as a good illustration of the electoral customs of the time or an accurate depiction of the political role of the clergy in the years 1870 to 1880. The Charlevoix election of 1876, in which Tremblay was defeated by Hector-Louis Langevin* after a memorable struggle, may be taken as typical. "Undue influence" was exhibited there with particular effectiveness; Tremblay and his collaborators noted several statements on this occasion and produced them before the courts and before Bishop Elzéar-Alexandre Taschereau*. The simple country-folk of Charlevoix County were unable to resist parish priests such as the one at Baie-Saint-Paul: "Document no. 3 proves that on 16 January last, the Reverend [Joseph] Sirois [–Duplessis] . . . depicted me [Tremblay] from the pulpit, me and those who supported me, as dangerous men, persecutors of religion, false prophets and false Christs, venomous serpents seeking to deceive the people. According to this reverend gentleman, if I were elected the people would be threatened with a revolution; the Pope, the bishops, the priests would be led to the scaffold and slaughtered; those who would have supported me would be guilty of all these crimes, and in death's hour they would be a prey to remorse and despair." This famous election of 1876 was an occasion for Tremblay to display his usual perseverance, which finally ensured his triumph in the Supreme Court. In September 1878, in the same county, he was elected by acclamation.

Pierre-Alexis Tremblay is perhaps less known as a journalist, even though he did contribute to several papers such as *Le Canadien*, *La Nation*, *Le National*, and *L'Événement*; it was particularly in *L'Éclaireur* that he gave his full measure as a polemicist and popular writer. The most remarkable document we have of him is probably the testament he drew up on his deathbed and addressed to the public. This text, published by the newspapers of the province, was inspired by a charity that led him to pardon all those who had offended him, and to ask forgiveness of all those whom he had hurt in the course of his eventful career. In both cases the individuals were numerous. Finally, he affirmed his fidelity and attachment to the church, despite earlier statements or attitudes which could have given rise to unfavourable interpretations.

Pierre-Alexis Tremblay died on 4 Jan. 1879, as a result of a leg infection of which the origin is unknown. His funeral took place in the cathedral at Quebec, and he was buried in St Patrick's cemetery, in the family vault of his wife, Mary Ellen Connolly. He left no children. In the spring of 1880 his body was transferred to the cemetery of La Malbaie.

NOËL BÉLANGER

The newspapers to which Pierre-Alexis Tremblay contributed are an important source for a study of him. ASHS, Dossier 86, pièces 34, 35, 36; Dossier 1638, pièces 1, 3, 10, 11; Mémoires 115 (Mlle Émilie Tremblay), par. 25, 59, 65, 70. Auguste Achintre, *Portraits et dossiers parlementaires du premier parlement de Québec* (Montréal, 1871). [Arthur Buies], *Chroniques . . .* (2v., Québec, 1873–75), I. Rumilly, *Hist. de la prov. de Québec*, I, II.

TROY, EDWARD, Roman Catholic priest; b. *c.* 1797, probably in Ireland; d. 2 April 1872 at Torbay, Nfld.

Nothing is known of Edward Troy's birthplace, family background, or education. He was ordained at Carrick-on-Suir, in the diocese of Waterford and Lismore, Ireland, by Bishop Michael Anthony Fleming* of Newfoundland; shortly afterward he sailed for Newfoundland where he landed in May 1831. He served as priest and assistant to Fleming at the chapel in St John's. His zeal and energy were soon evident. In October 1833 Troy presided at the dedication in Portugal Cove of a church whose completion the *Newfoundlander* credited to his efforts. Edward Troy became known, however, chiefly through his political activities in St John's.

The granting of an elected assembly in 1832 had only emphasized the many divisions in Newfoundland. The colony was increasingly split between the Irish Catholics, mainly fishermen and labourers, influenced by their priests, and the educated and prosperous, both Protestant and Catholic, who were primarily merchants and often English. The *Patriot* had become the newspaper of the former; the *Public Ledger*, the focus of Protestant and conservative opposition.

Troy clashed first with Governor Thomas John COCHRANE. Early in 1834 the *Patriot* published letters of "Junius," accusing the governor of bigotry and injustice. Cochrane was about to sue John V. NUGENT, co-proprietor of the *Patriot*, when Troy admitted authorship. The governor instituted a libel suit against Troy. It was dropped when Cochrane was replaced by Henry PRESCOTT. There is evidence that Cochrane thought he owed his hostile, mud-spattered send-off from St John's in November 1834 partly to an inflammatory sermon by Troy.

Troy's next antagonist was Henry D. Winton*, proprietor of the *Ledger*. In December 1833 Winton had praised Troy's moderating influence in helping to disperse a mob besieging Winton's premises because of his denunciation of Fleming's electoral intervention. But by early 1835 the *Ledger* was reporting that Troy was forbidding his congregation to subscribe to the paper, denying religious rites to Catholics who supported its political sentiments, and prohibiting trade with

them under threat of excommunication. In a sermon quoted in the *Ledger* his bent appears: "I'll put the fear of God in them, and if that does not do I'll put the fear of man in them." The risk of financial ruin and starvation was real for those who failed to obey. The *Ledger* regarded such use of religious authority as an attempt at political dominance. By spring 1835 even the official newspaper, the *Royal Gazette*, was alarmed for the freedom of the press and for the whole colonial society. When Winton was assaulted on 19 May by ruffians who cut off his ears, the governor and others blamed the crime on the repeated tirades of Troy and other priests.

In July 1836 Bishop Fleming departed for Europe, leaving Troy as vicar-general for 14 months. He now increased his attacks on Catholics whose political opinions differed from his own. Stigmatizing them as "Orange Catholics" or "Mad Dogs," he denied them even burial rites, and created an uproar and several court cases when he expelled a few from the chapel during service. In the autumn elections of 1836 Troy campaigned for candidates to the assembly. After a boisterous rally on 23 October, he and candidates William Carson*, Patrick Morris*, and John KENT were indicted for illegal and riotous assembly. Although acquitted in January 1837, they were accused by the Protestant press of a deplorable attempt to intimidate the electorate. Troy's "popular" (radical) candidates were elected, but the election was declared invalid. In the new election of May 1837, Troy instructed his people to vote for the same candidates, and participated in their successful campaigns. He even took an active part in the new assembly. On 7 July 1837 the *Ledger* noted: "we have occasionally glanced up at the reporter's box and witnessed the gaunt, stalworth [*sic*] frame and figure of the Rev. Father TROY, leaning upon his elbows and grinning ineffable delight at the proceedings of his Parliament below. . . ."

The final phase of Father Troy's political career centred on Henry John Boulton*, chief justice since 1833. The Catholic reformers thought him harsh and unfair in the exercise of his office, and he had been subjected to constant attacks, especially by the *Patriot*. In 1835 he charged its editor, Robert John Parsons*, with contempt, heard the case, and convicted him. Troy joined the Constitutional Society which sought Boulton's removal, and subscribed on Fleming's behalf to its fund to pay Parsons' fine. By December 1837 an impasse between the assembly and the Legislative Council, of which Boulton was president, and his continued judicial severity impelled the assembly to send Carson, Morris, and Nugent to England to press for his removal. Boulton crossed the Atlantic to

Truteau

defend himself. Bishop Fleming joined the assemblymen and from London wrote to Troy with news and also instructions that indicate Troy's influence with the assemblymen in St John's. Troy campaigned against Boulton by sermons and petitions displayed in the chapel for signatures. When word reached St John's in August that the British government had dismissed Boulton, Troy ordered a *Te Deum*. His actions aroused further anger and anxiety in Newfoundland. The Colonial Office had already sought Troy's removal, in 1836 and in 1837, and through the Foreign Office had got the Congregation of Propaganda to request Fleming to control the political activity of his priests. The mounting disorder in Newfoundland and the threat to its prosperity led the Foreign Office to take final steps to make Rome fully aware of Troy's actions. A decision to remove Troy from St John's was apparently made; his name disappears from newspaper reports and it seems probable that early in 1839 Fleming ordered him to Merasheen Island in Placentia Bay.

After 1839 Troy appears to have been out of favour for a while. He was not mentioned as present at the laying of the foundation stone of the cathedral in St John's in May 1841. From 1848 on he once more took part in major annual religious celebrations in St John's, and was also noted as assisting at other important services in the 1850s and 1860s such as the consecration of the cathedral in September 1855.

Father Troy's energies were channelled into parish activities. In his seven or eight years at Merasheen he built a church and presbytery. Then he moved to Torbay as parish priest for his last 25 years. There he replaced the existing wooden church with a stone one, consecrated in October 1863. In 1865 a convent and school house, with four nuns of the Presentation Order, were established at Torbay. Michael Francis Howley*, in his *Ecclesiastical history of Newfoundland*, credited him with a spreading of the Catholic faith in the area, and told of often seeing him walking the nine miles back from St John's carrying a sack of nails.

A deed of property drawn up 28 May 1870 reveals that Troy focussed much of his energy upon acquiring land in Torbay and erecting a permanent presbytery to ensure the presence of a Roman Catholic priest. Single-minded energy, discipline, sacrifice, and pride are all manifest in his chronicle of privations and achievement attached to the deed. ". . . owing to the failure of the fisheries and consequent decrease in the revenues of the Parish, I was compelled to use the poorest description of food nor could I afford to procure sugar for my table and was obliged to use molasses. . . . I was often pained when visited by priests at not being able to give them a dinner nor even a glass of wine but so anxious was I to leave a dwelling House for a Priest that I joyfully submitted to these privations." Years of work enabled him to transfer ten acres of land (Father Troy's farm), a dwelling, coachhouse, and outhouses to a group which included his brother-in-law John Delaney*, postmaster general of St John's, and his nephew Father Patrick Delaney, to be held in trust. By this time his powers were declining, but he served until his death at the age of 75.

Bishop Fleming had lauded Troy as Newfoundland's most zealous missionary. His obituary in the *Newfoundlander* paid tribute to the warmth, simplicity, and kindliness which won him the veneration of the lowly. For more than forty years he had been an energetic, ambitious pioneer of Roman Catholicism in Newfoundland.

PHYLLIS CREIGHTON

Archives of the Archdiocese of St John's, Deed of land of Edward Troy (includes autobiographical material). PANL, material gathered on Edward Troy from various files. *Newfoundlander* (St John's), 1831–43, 1837–38, 1845–70, especially 31 March, 30 April 1869; 5 April 1872. *Public Ledger* (St John's), 1833–40, especially 24, 27 Feb., 6, 17 March 1835; 25 March, 7 Oct., 22 Nov. 1836; 7 Feb., 7 July 1837. *Royal Gazette* (St John's), 1833–35, 1837–38. G.B., Parl., House of Commons paper, 1839, XXXIV, 525, pp.565–94, *Newfoundland: return to an address of the honourable the House of Commons dated 12 July 1839*; – for, *copy of any addresses received at the Colonial Office from the Legislative Council or Assembly of Newfoundland, or from public bodies of individuals in that colony, relative to the state of affairs there.* Gunn, *Political history of Nfld.* M. F. Howley, *Ecclesiastical history of Newfoundland* (Boston, 1888). "The new church at Torbay," *Newfoundland Quarterly*, XXI (April 1922), 12.

TRUTEAU, ALEXIS-FRÉDÉRIC, secular priest, canon, vicar general, superior of a religious community, and administrator of the diocese of Montreal; b. 11 June 1808 at Montreal, L.C., son of Toussaint Truteau, a contractor, and Marie-Louise Papineau; d. 28 Dec. 1872 at Montreal, Que.

Alexis-Frédéric Truteau made his first communion on 25 May 1818, and was confirmed in June 1819 by Jean-Louis Lefebvre de Cheverus, first Catholic bishop of Boston. He received a classical education at the college of Montreal, and, after completing his studies, took the clerical habit and became a teacher in the same institution. During his years of teaching he studied theology and received the various orders, finally being ordained priest on 18 Sept. 1830 by Bishop Jean-Jacques Lartigue*.

On 25 September of the same year he was appointed curate at Boucherville (Chambly County). He was summoned by Bishop Lartigue to the bishop's palace at Montreal on 27 Sept. 1831 to direct the young ecclesiastics who, for want of a seminary, were studying theology there. Being in close communion of ideas and doctrine with his hierarchical superior, he imbued his disciples with ultramontane principles. Later Abbé Truteau held the office of procurator, then in 1836 that of secretary to the bishop in place of Abbé Ignace Bourget*.

When Bishop Bourget, who succeeded Bishop Lartigue in 1840, established the chapter of his bishopric, he chose Abbé Truteau as one of the first canons. The latter were installed on 21 Jan. 1841 by Bishop Charles-Auguste-Marie-Joseph de Forbin-Janson*, who had been invited, on completing the great retreat he had just preached at Montreal, to preside over the ceremony, which was entirely new for this city. On 21 Dec. 1847, with the death of the vicar general Hyacinthe Hudon, Canon Truteau was chosen to succeed him; he was to hold this office for a quarter of a century.

In 1867, on the occasion of the anniversary of St Peter's death, he was delegated by his bishop to travel to Rome with Bishop Joseph Desautels*, the parish priest of Varennes (Verchères County), and Canon Étienne-Hippolyte Hicks. The purpose of his voyage was to work, together with his colleagues, towards the settlement of the difficulties that existed at the time between the Sulpicians and the diocesan bishop, over the breaking up of Notre-Dame parish.

In addition to his duties at the bishop's palace at Montreal, Truteau was entrusted with the direction of several religious communities, among others the Institut de la Providence, which he guided as confessor or superior for 21 years. His subordinates liked to call him "the worthy Father Truteau."

But vicar general Truteau deserves to go down in history especially for the important part he played in the Guibord affair (Joseph Guibord*, dit Archambault) as administrator of the diocese of Montreal in the absence of Bishop Bourget, who on 19 Jan. 1869 had left for Rome to attend the Vatican council. On 18 Nov. 1869 Truteau wrote to the Sulpician Benjamin-Victor Rousselot, parish priest of Notre-Dame, to tell him that, having received the day before "a letter from the bishop of Montreal" instructing him to "refuse absolution, even at the point of death, to those who belong to the Institut Canadien and are not

willing to cease to be members of it" [see Gonzalve Doutre], he could not "allow ecclesiastical burial to those of its members who died without having withdrawn from it"; he added: "You tell me that M. Guibord was a member of the Institut and that he died without having left it; therefore it is impossible for me to grant him ecclesiastical burial."

Guibord's widow, Henriette Brown, brought a legal action against the parish priest and the first churchwarden of Notre-Dame for having opposed the burial of her husband's remains in the part of the cemetery reserved for Catholics, and Truteau, as administrator, was called to give evidence before Judge Charles-Elzéar Mondelet. In his testimony on 10 and 11 Jan. 1870, he stated that "ecclesiastical burial," "being under the sole jurisdiction of the ecclesiastical authority," had had "to be refused" Guibord, "because the minor excommunication to which he had been subjected made him a public sinner," he having incurred this penalty "because he was a member of the Institut Canadien," "which was, as it still is, under the censure of the Church."

Three days later the administrator gave his hierarchical superior an account of his actions and his state of mind on that occasion: "At the court of inquiry before which I was summoned, I began by protesting that in such a matter, since it was a question of an ecclesiastical burial and not of a simple burial, I recognized as my superiors, entitled to require me to account for my conduct, only my Bishop and the Holy Father. Notwithstanding, Judge Mondelet forced me to speak, although my protest was recorded. In the end I was not sorry to answer, in order to make better known the institute's behaviour and its existence in a state of excommunication."

In the same letter vicar general Truteau made some forecasts about the outcome of this lawsuit: "If the affair is pleaded before Judge Mondelet, the Institute is likely to win the first time. But then the case will be appealed again, and all the odds will be against it." He did not live long enough to discover that if he had been accurate in the first part of his prediction, he had not anticipated the decision of the English Privy Council, which on 21 Nov. 1874 was to confirm Mondelet's judgement.

All testimonies agree that Alexis-Frédéric Truteau was an exemplary priest, zealous and sympathetic towards the suffering of others; but it must be admitted that, blindly submissive as he was to the instructions of a passionately ultramontane bishop, he lacked the suppleness and openness of mind that would have given a quite different turn to an "Affair" in which the initial refusal to bury a Catholic in a Catholic cemetery appeared to an impartial observer, Robert-Alexis Lefaivre, the French consul at Quebec, "of a severity unheard of in our century."

PHILIPPE SYLVAIN

ACAM, 420.005. Archives du ministère des Affaires étrangères (Paris), Correspondance politique des consuls, Angleterre, 50, f.33. *La Minerve* (Montréal), 12 janv., 13 janv. 1870. *L'Institut de la Providence; histoire des Filles de la Charité Servantes des Pauvres dites sœurs de la Providence* (2v., Montréal, 1925–28). [Ignace Bourget], *Mémoire pour servir à l'histoire du chapitre de la cathédrale S. Jacques de Montréal* (Montréal, 1882), 141–57.

TURCOTTE, LOUIS-PHILIPPE, historian; b. 11 July 1842 at Saint-Jean, Île d'Orléans, C.E., of the marriage of Jean-Baptiste Turcotte, farmer, and Marie-Josephte Fortier; d. a bachelor on 3 April 1878 at Quebec.

After his first years of study at the parish school, Louis-Philippe Turcotte entered the first form at the Petit Séminaire of Quebec in 1855, and left it three years later without finishing his classical education. He then worked as a clerk for one of his brothers, a Quebec businessman. On 23 Dec. 1859, while crossing the frozen river to get to Île d'Orléans, he fell into the icy water, and this accident left him infirm for the rest of his life. He retired to his parents' house at Saint-Jean and was encouraged by the parish priest, M. Antoine Gosselin, to explore the archives of the Île d'Orléans. This research enabled him to publish in 1867 his *Histoire de l'île d'Orléans*, dealing with the French period; in it he outlined the history of each parish and recounted shipwrecks in which islanders had been the victims. He then undertook the preparation of his principal work, *Le Canada sous l'Union* the first part of which was published in 1871 and the second in 1872. He followed a chronological order from 1841 to 1867 and gave a faithful but colourless account of political events. He showed no ability to draw the threads together or to express views of his own.

In December 1872 Louis-Philippe Turcotte became assistant librarian of the library of the Quebec legislature, which was directed by Léon-Pamphile Le May*. In November 1873 he was admitted to membership in the Institut Canadien of Quebec, where he held the offices of librarian (1874–77) and vice-president (1877). He had been president for two months when, on 3 April 1878, he died at Quebec.

Besides the two works already mentioned, Turcotte published in 1873, at Quebec, two short biographies, one of the Honourable René-Édouard CARON, lieutenant governor of the province of Quebec, and the other of Sir George-Étienne CARTIER. In 1875, at the Institut Canadien, he organized a celebration of the centenary of the Americans' siege of Quebec in 1775. The following year he published an account of these celebrations, as well as a study called *Invasion du Canada et siège de Québec en 1775–1776*.

Louis-Philippe Turcotte was a conscientious worker, but, lacking a certain kind of intellectual development, a proper perspective on events, and elementary qualities of style, he was able to produce only one useful work.

J.-C. BONENFANT

L.-P. Turcotte, *Le Canada sous l'Union, 1841–1867* (2v., 1re éd., Québec, 1871–72; 2e éd., Québec, 1882); *Histoire de l'île d'Orléans* (Québec, 1867); *L'honorable R.-É. Caron, lieutenant-gouverneur de la province de Québec* (Québec, 1873); *L'honorable sir G.-É. Cartier, ministre de la milice* (Québec, 1873); *Invasion du Canada et siège de Québec en 1775–1776* (Québec, 1876). *Dom. ann. reg.*, 1878, 368–69. *Annuaire de l'Institut canadien de Québec, 1878* (Québec, 1879), 75–86. Henri d'Arles, *Nos historiens* (Montréal, 1921), 125–55. N.-H.-É. Faucher de Saint-Maurice, "Louis Turcotte," *RSCT*, 1st ser., I (1883), sect.I, 111–18.

V

VALOIS, NARCISSE, tanner and city councillor; b. 12 Aug. 1811 at Vaudreuil, L.C., eldest son of Captain Narcisse Valois*, a *Patriote* of 1837, and Agathe Lalonde; d. 28 Aug. 1880 at Montreal, Que.

When he was still an adolescent, Narcisse Valois found employment at Montreal. At the time of his marriage with Ursule Ritchot, in November 1837 at Montreal, he was described as a tanner. After 1850 his establishment was situated in the west of the town, in the Saint-Antoine district, where in 1874 the parish of Saint-Joseph was set up, and where later the Canadian Pacific Railway station was built.

He was a city councillor of Montreal by 1846, and from 1853 on represented Saint-Antoine ward as councillor or alderman. He sat on the city council for more than 20 years, and during the last two (1867–69) he became once more alderman for East ward, which he had first represented in 1846. He was vice-president of the temperance society of the diocese of Montreal in 1863, and was also

Van Cortlandt

a member of the Roman Catholic School Commission during the year 1869–70.

Narcisse Valois was 69 when on 28 Aug. 1880 he passed away at Montreal, intestate according to the inventory of his possessions drawn up on 28 December by the notary Évariste-Odilon Labadie. He was buried in the crypt of the chapel of the sisters of the Holy Names of Jesus and Mary, which had been built through the good offices of his uncle, Simon Valois*, likewise a tanner. Narcisse Valois left few assets, apart from a two-storey stone building in Rue Saint-Vincent, adjoining that of his uncle Simon.

His wife, Ursule Ritchot, survived him by five years. He is known to have had one son, Jude, a commercial agent, and four daughters.

JEAN-JACQUES LEFEBVRE

AJM, Registre d'état civil. AVM, Biographies de conseillers. *Le Courrier de Montréal*, 1ᵉʳ sept. 1880. Fauteux, *Patriotes*, 390–91.

VAN CORTLANDT, EDWARD, physician, surgeon, and author; b. 1805 in Newfoundland, son of Major Philip Van Cortlandt, an officer in the War of the American Revolution, and United Empire Loyalist; d. 25 March 1875 in Ottawa, Ont.

Edward Van Cortlandt was educated in Quebec at the school run by the Reverend Daniel Wilkie*, and from 1819 to 1825 he studied medicine in Quebec under Dr William Hackett. He then went to England and, in 1827, passed the examinations at the Royal College of Surgeons in London, receiving praise from the celebrated John Abernethy and from Sir Anthony Carlisle for "the creditable manner in which he passed through the vigorous ordeal." In 1829 he was chosen over 12 competitors to be librarian to the Royal Medical and Chirurgical Society, an early indication of a bookish tendency.

Van Cortlandt returned to Canada in 1832, and on 26 December was authorized by the provincial secretary to practise medicine in Lower Canada. The succeeding year, he went to the new frontier community of Bytown (later named Ottawa), Upper Canada, on the recommendation of Dr James Skey. There he quickly established a large and lucrative practice and in 1834 served through the cholera epidemic. He contributed his services gratuitously for a time in the lower Bytown hospital of the Grey Nuns of the Cross under Élisabeth BRUYÈRE who had arrived from Montreal in 1845, and he was appointed physician and later consulting physician to their General Hospital which was established in 1851. He was coroner of the city of Ottawa, physician to the county gaol, and surgeon for some 20 years to the Ottawa Field Battery.

Edward Van Cortlandt also had a deep interest in other aspects of science, particularly geology and archeology. In 1843, when workmen building the Union Bridge came upon an Indian burial site on the Ottawa River, he carried out searches, collected artifacts, and recorded his work in a report which appeared in 1853 in the *Canadian Journal*. He published, in 1854, a little study entitled *The productions of the Ottawa district of Canada*, and, in 1860, a significant brochure entitled *Observations on the building stone of the Ottawa country*. In the latter, Van Cortlandt claims to have earlier called to the attention of Lord Elgin [James Bruce*] the location of the stone from which the parliament building was constructed. Van Cortlandt also contributed many articles to Ottawa newspapers and took part in civic movements, including a celebration of the tercentenary of Shakespeare's birth.

Van Cortlandt was a founding member of the Ottawa Silurian Society, president of the Horticultural Society, the Mechanics' Institute, the Athenaeum, and one-time secretary to the Board of Arts and Manufactures of Montreal. Almost from his arrival in Bytown he was an ardent promoter of the Ottawa region, and occasionally established exhibits of its products. He constructed a private museum of archeology and geology in the capital and opened it to the public.

Edward Van Cortlandt was a "bold surgeon and a good operator," if mannered in style. It is said that he imitated "the great Abernethy" but, "as always happens, a second edition was a failure." He was "eccentric in his manner," and was no doubt quarrelsome; about 1839 he was involved in an assault against one Lieutenant Hadden over pet animals. In the same year he pursued the impecunious Wright family for non-payment of an account in respect of Philemon Wright*'s last illness, and threatened to treat Wright's son Ruggles* the way he had Hadden. When he died in 1875, however, his obituaries stated that his "genial and warm-hearted qualities won the esteem of a large circle of acquaintances."

He married Harriet Amelia Harrington of St Andrews East (county of Argenteuil), Quebec, and they had four daughters and two sons. One daughter, Gertrude, was a writer and published *Records of the rise and progress of the City of Ottawa, from the foundation of the Rideau Canal to the present time* (Ottawa, 1858).

Edward Van Cortlandt died in 1875 and received full military honours from the Ottawa Field Battery.

COURTNEY C. J. BOND

691

Vandusen

Edward Van Cortlandt, "Notes on an Indian burying ground," *Canadian Journal*, I (1852–53), 160–61; *Observations on the building stone of the Ottawa country; being the abridgment of a lecture delivered before the Ottawa Silurian Society, the 15th November, 1859* ([Ottawa], 1860); *The productions of the Ottawa district of Canada . . .* (Montreal, 1854).

PAC, MG 12, D, T28, 14, p.12; MG 23, D1 (Chipman papers), ser.1, 26, p.207; MG 24, D8 (Wright papers), 27, ff.10674, 10727–28; 35, ff.16013–14, 16241–42; I9 (Hill collection), 3, ff.754–55; 19, ff.4697–99, 4712–15, 4723–24; 20, ff.5046–59, 5105–6; 21, ff.5456–57, 5459; 30, ff.7523; RG 8, I, D2, 1203½P, pp.128, 140, 162, 196. PRO, CO 5/1067, pp.172–73. *Ottawa Citizen*, 9 Feb., 26 April 1864, 3 Jan. 1953. *Ottawa Free Press*, 27 March 1875. *The Quebec directory, or strangers' guide to the city, for 1826 . . .*, ed. John Smith (Quebec, 1826), 44. *Quebec Mercury*, 29 Dec. 1832.

Morgan, *Bibliotheca Canadensis*, 381. Wallace, *Macmillan dictionary*, 766. C. C. J. Bond, *City on the Ottawa* (Ottawa, 1967), 37. Canniff, *Medical profession in Upper Canada*, 652–53. J. W. Hughson and C. C. J. Bond, *Hurling down the pine; the story of the Wright, Gilmour and Hughson families, timber and lumber manufacturers in the Hull and Ottawa region and on the Gatineau River, 1800–1920* (2nd ed., Old Chelsea, Que., 1965), 31. C. C. J. Bond, "Alexander James Christie, Bytown pioneer; his life and times, 1787–1843," *Ont. Hist.*, LVI (1964), 16–36.

VANDUSEN (Van Dusen), CONRAD, Methodist minister; b. 14 Dec. 1801 in Adolphustown, U.C., son of Conrad Vandusen, a loyalist veteran who had been sentenced to death by the American forces for his activities during the Revolution; d. 18 Aug. 1878 in Whitby, Ont.

Conrad Vandusen grew up in comfortable circumstances at Adolphustown, where his father owned a tavern and a store, and in Marysburgh Township (now North and South Marysburgh). He acquired a good education for that period. In his youth he was "vivacious, droll," and "distinguished for the use of *cant* or *slang* phrases," according to John Carroll* who served on a neighbouring circuit in 1830. Although his father was one of the founders of the Hay Bay chapel near Adolphustown, the first Methodist church in Upper Canada, the young Vandusen was evidently a lively fellow who, according to a later clerical observer, badly needed the restraints imposed by a marriage at 18 and his work as teacher and farmer. In 1827, however, he was converted at a camp meeting near Demorestville, Ameliasburgh Township. "He could hardly tell the hour or the place where the light of God's countenance broke in upon him. By the time, however, that he had got back to his home, he was happy and his soul overflowing with love." Immediately he began to spread the word to his neighbours.

Vandusen was soon pressed into service as a Methodist itinerant, at first as the assistant on the Whitby circuit, to which he would retire decades later. Received on trial in 1830, he was ordained into the Wesleyan Methodist Church at the conference of 1833. In subsequent years he laboured inconspicuously if not quietly on several circuits across Upper Canada, and gained an enviable reputation as an heroic but kindly minister.

In 1849, when Victoria College at Cobourg had few students and was low in funds, Vandusen was appointed governor and treasurer. Confronted with the necessity of retaining students "by the argument *a posteriori*, that is by holding onto their coat-tails," he devised an ingenious plan to build up an endowment through the sale of scholarships that would entitle the purchasers to free tuition for members of their families. It was "a natural product of a decade of speculation," but unfortunately it yielded little permanent return to the college.

Vandusen returned to his regular work as a preacher in 1852 as chairman of the mission of Newash, an Indian village near Owen Sound, and was superannuated in 1859. He continued to preach in the 1860s, mainly in the Toronto area and on the Wardsville circuit, but his attention centred increasingly on writing. In 1867, under the pseudonym of "Enemikeese," he published *The Indian chief*, in which he used the life of David Sawyer, an Indian Methodist minister, to illustrate the mistreatment of Indian tribes. The same year saw his *Practical theology*, an illuminating example of the literal way in which he and his contemporaries used biblical texts to construct a complete theology. Three years later he issued *The prodigy*, a memoir of the brilliant physician, G. E. A. Winans, and *The successful young evangelist*, a brief biography of Winans' brother, William Henry Winans. Appropriately, in 1878 he produced *The doctrine of the human soul* in which he argued, on biblical grounds, that man consists of body, soul, and spirit, and that death constitutes the birth of man's spiritual body in which his personality is preserved without physical defects and limitations.

In many ways, Conrad Vandusen exemplified the qualities of the first generation of native Canadian Methodist ministers. A tall, powerful man, famous for his endurance, he was equally notorious for his strongly conservative political attitudes and for his human touch. He had "a strong, inquiring, almost metaphysical mind" which he sought to develop by hard study, but he never attained intellectual or cultural sophistication. His preaching was vigorous and earthy: for him an indolent Christian was "like a lazy hired man, who would leave his corn-hoeing and spend his time chasing squirrels"; the Christian was not to forget that "the devil paid his servants as the cat paid the owl, over the face and eyes." His writings display some originality, but little literary skill. They are today chiefly significant for the light they throw on the climate of opinion within the Methodist community in his generation. His devoted work as minister and writer imparted a measure of comfort and a sense of purpose to the lives of many Upper Canadians.

G. S. FRENCH

Conrad Vandusen was the author of *The doctrine of the human soul; philosophy of a trinity in man, and the phenomena of death, philosophically considered, showing that death will produce no additional pang in the hour of dissolution* (Toronto, 1878); *Practical theology: a plain exposition of various subjects based upon divine revelation* (London, 1867); *The prodigy, a brief account of the bright career of a youthful genius, Dr. G. E. A. Winans, together with some interesting extracts from his correspondence and manuscripts* (Toronto, 1870); *The successful young evangelist; an account of the brief but brilliant career of Wm. Henry Winans, Wesleyan preacher . . .* (Toronto, 1870); and, under the pseudonym of Enemikeese, *The Indian chief: an account of the labours, losses, sufferings, and oppression of Ke-zig-ko-e-ne-ne (David Sawyer) a chief of the Ojibbeway Indians in Canada West* (London, 1867).

Christian Guardian (Toronto), 18 April 1860, 5 March 1879. Methodist Church of Canada, *Minutes of the Toronto conference* (Toronto, Montreal), 1879. *The minutes of the annual conferences of the Wesleyan Methodist Church in Canada, from 1824 to 1857* (2v., Toronto, 1846–63), I. William Canniff, *History of the province of Ontario (Upper Canada) . . .* (Toronto, 1872), 125. C. B. Sissons, *A history of Victoria University* (Toronto, 1952).

VanKOUGHNET, PHILIP (the name is often spelled Vankoughnet but he consistently used VanKoughnet), merchant and politician; b. probably 2 April 1790, at New Johnstown (Cornwall) in the district of Luneburg (later part of Upper Canada), son of Michael VanKoughnet, whose father was Alsatian, and Eve Empey, both loyalists; d. 7 May 1873.

Michael VanKoughnet was a large landowner and his son was educated at John Strachan*'s grammar school. With this background it is not surprising that Philip became an avid defender of the British connection. He served as a subaltern during the War of 1812 and was present at the battle of Crysler's Farm where the advance of an American force on Cornwall was stopped. A quarter of a century later, in 1838, VanKoughnet, now a lieutenant-colonel, commanded a battalion of militia at the battle of the Windmill against the American invaders who sympathized with the Canadian rebels.

VanKoughnet began his political career at an early age. He was elected to the assembly of Upper Canada for the riding of Stormont and Russell in 1816 as a staunch defender of the colonial administration. He held one of the two seats of the county of Stormont from 1820 when they were created until 1828, and again from 1830 to 1834, and his friend Archibald McLean* held the second seat during the same period.

In 1836, two years after leaving the assembly, VanKoughnet, clearly a secondary member of the Family Compact, was appointed to the Legislative Council by Sir Francis Bond HEAD, no doubt on the recommendation of Sir John Colborne* whom Bond Head had just succeeded. One week after his commission as councillor, VanKoughnet preceded Colborne in a Cornwall procession and carried a standard inscribed "Sir John Colborne and the Constitution" to assert the town's loyalty. He was not reappointed to the upper chamber after the union of 1841 and appears to have virtually retired from politics until 1857 when he re-emerged briefly. He contested the Cornwall seat unsuccessfully for the Conservatives when John Sandfield MACDONALD switched his candidacy from Glengarry to the town. The Conservative efforts succeeded in keeping Macdonald tied to the local contest but VanKoughnet lost 428 to 246.

As a merchant and landowner, VanKoughnet was involved in several projects to improve transportation in the Cornwall area. In 1831 he was a member of a commission on roads and bridges in the township of Cornwall. Two years later he was one of the commissioners appointed to put into effect an act authorizing the financing and construction of the Cornwall Canal, begun in 1834 to improve navigation on the St Lawrence from Dickinson's Landing to Cornwall, a distance of $11\frac{1}{2}$ miles.

In 1833 VanKoughnet was appointed to the newly formed 5th division of the Cornwall and Roxborough Court of Requests as one of the 11 commissioners. He held this office until the court was abolished in 1841. In 1870, after a prolonged absence from public life, he was appointed chairman of the Canadian Board of Government Arbitrators, a position he still held at his death.

In 1819 he had married Harriet Sophia Scott of Carrick-on-Suir, Tipperary County, Ireland, who predeceased him. The most distinguished of their several children was Philip M. M. S. Vankoughnet*, who died in 1869.

BRUCE W. HODGINS

Queen's University Archives, Edmund Morris papers, "Colonel, the Hon. Philip Vankoughnet, M.L.C."

Viger

Armstrong, *Handbook of Upper Canadian chronology*, 27, 35, 64, 69, 70, 73, 75. B. W. Hodgins, "The political career of John Sandfield Macdonald to the fall of his administration in March 1864: a study in Canadian politics," unpublished PHD thesis, Duke University, 1964. J. F. Pringle, *Lunenburgh or the old Eastern District, its settlement and early progress; with personal recollections of the town of Cornwall, from 1824 ...* (Cornwall, Ont., 1890), 34, 46, 66, 77–78, 155–62, 242, 260, 266–67.

VIGER, BONAVENTURE, *Patriote*; b. 14 May 1804 at Boucherville, son of Bonaventure Viger and Louise Carmel-Levasseur, and cousin of Denis-Benjamin Viger*; d. 15 Dec. 1877 at Beloeil, Que.

Bonaventure Viger is known above all for his share in the disturbances of 1837. Before that date, we have no knowledge of him. Viger, one of Louis-Joseph PAPINEAU's most loyal supporters, was "of a fiery and generous disposition." Consequently, on 16 Nov. 1837, when he learned that Dr Joseph-François Davignon and the notary Pierre-Paul Desmaray were being taken to prison in Montreal as a result of their active participation in the *Patriotes*' meetings, he had no hesitation in taking up arms to free the prisoners. Viger and a handful of men set up an ambush near Longueuil, awaiting a detachment, commanded by Lieutenant Ermatinger; they succeeded in setting Davignon and Desmaray free. This first act of hostility on the part of the *Patriotes* against the English soldiers marked the beginning of skirmishes. Subsequently, Viger took part in the battles at Saint-Denis and Saint-Charles. He was taken prisoner at Bedford, in the Eastern Townships, together with Louis-Isaac Larocque, a comrade in arms: the two of them, in an attempt to reach the American border after the defeat at Saint-Charles, had lost their way in the neighbouring woods.

Viger was incarcerated in Montreal prison on 7 Dec. 1837; he proved to be the most unruly of all the political prisoners, and numerous legends have circulated concerning him. In June 1838 he was one of eight prisoners sentenced to exile in the Bermudas. Set free in October of the same year, Viger settled in the United States, near the border, and had further brushes with the law. He rashly entered Canada, where he was again arrested. He was taken to Montreal prison on 8 June 1839, and he and two companions were charged with the murder of the loyalist Vosburgh. The affair came to an abrupt end in December 1840, when the jurors were unable to reach agreement.

After 1840 Viger lived a quiet life. On 11 Oct. 1841, at Boucherville, he married Eudoxie Trudel, by whom he had five children. In a short while his cheeses made him as famous as his other exploits.

In 1867 he was a militia captain and the coroner at Saint-Bruno de Chambly. Viger was undoubtedly a popular and legendary hero, "one of the figures whose memory playwrights and novelists were to take pleasure in preserving."

JEAN-MARC PARADIS

ANQ, Ludger Duvernay, nos.308, 317; QBC, Procureur général, Événements de 1837–1838, nos.50, 52, 54, 55, 59, 61, 62, 65, 68, 301, 355, 1485, 2871, 3082, 3100, 3180, 4103, 4145. PAC, MG 30, D62 (Audet papers), XXX. "J.-J. Girouard à sa femme," *RHAF*, XIX (1965–66), 463–64. "Les Patriotes aux Bermudes en 1838, lettres d'exil," Yvon Thériault, édit., *RHAF*, XVI (1962–63), 117–26, 439–40; XVII (1963–64), 428–30. C.-M. Boissonnault, *Histoire politico-militaire des Canadiens français 1763–1945* (Trois-Rivières, Qué., 1967). J. D. Borthwick, *History of the Montreal prison from A.D. 1784 to A.D. 1886 ...* (Montreal, 1886); *Jubilé de diamant, rébellion de 1837–1838; précis complet de cette période, rôle d'honneur ou liste complète des Patriotes détenus dans les prisons de Montréal en 1837–1838–1839; date et lieux des arrestations et autres détails intéressants et inédits sur ce sujet* (Montréal, 1898). David, *Patriotes*, 130–37. L.-P. Desrosiers, *L'accalmie; lord Durham au Canada* (Montréal, 1937). Duclos de Celles, *Patriotes of 1837*. Fauteux, *Patriotes*. Lionel Groulx, *Histoire du Canada français depuis la découverte* (4e éd., 2v., Montréal et Paris, 1960), II. S. B. Ryerson, *Unequal union; confederation and the roots of conflict in the Canadas, 1815–1873* (Toronto, 1968). L.-O. David, "Les hommes de 1837–1838," *L'Opinion publique* (Montréal), 15 févr. 1877. Léon Ledieu, "Entre nous," *Le Monde illustré* (Montréal), 5 nov. 1887. R.-L. Séguin, "Biographie d'un patriote de '37, le Dr Luc-Hyacinthe Masson (1811–1880)," *RHAF*, III (1949–50), 349–67.

VOYER, LUDGER-NAPOLÉON, soldier and writer; b. 20 April 1842 at Quebec, son of Louis Voyer, a wheelwright; d. accidentally 22 Feb. 1876 at Quebec.

Information about Louis-Napoléon Voyer's childhood is almost non-existent. We know, however, that he entered the college at Sainte-Anne-de-la-Pocatière in 1854, at the age of 12. There, under the influence of Abbé Pierre-Stanislas Vallée, a teacher at the college and an enthusiast of military history, he decided to take up a military career.

In 1858, England obtained authorization from the Canadian authorities to raise an infantry regiment in Canada, the 100th Royal Canadian Regiment of Foot. It was the first time a regiment of regular soldiers was recruited in Canada to serve imperial interests abroad. Rapidly, 1,027 men were enlisted. Voyer was one of them. On 25 July 1859 he was sworn in, thanks to the support given by "protectors in high places." He embarked at

Quebec on 9 November of the same year, bound for England.

We know little concerning the motives that prompted the youth of 17 to enlist in the British army. There are only hints. In the diary he kept from 1859 to 1870 is the following passage: "My engagement, honour, and duty take me still further away from my country. My great, my sole hope is to earn distinction, to have my name attached to some meritorious act, some glorious deed, so that it will be repeated at home, and so that my friends will speak of me with interest. . . ." If this text sheds some small light on the motives, it tells nothing about the social, family, and other reasons behind his decision. André-Napoléon Montpetit*, one of Voyer's friends, merely reports that he enlisted "despite his parents, protectors, and friends."

From 1859 to 1863 his military career abroad was uneventful. He seems to have accepted life in barracks at Parkhurst, on the Isle of Wight, and at Gibraltar calmly and patiently. He took advantage of it to improve his education by studying languages, history, and commerce, and to observe the behaviour of the British, Spaniards, and others. His personal diary of this period reveals certain traits of his personality, in particular perseverance, tolerance, a sense for observation, and a spirit of discipline. On 15 April 1863 he obtained a three months' leave to come to Canada. He was never to leave it again.

On 15 June 1863 Sir Étienne-Paschal Taché*, the minister of militia, appointed him special instructor to the Canadian militia; this appointment was confirmed on 20 July by the Duke of Cambridge, commander-in-chief of the British army. He worked as an instructor at various places: Rivière-du-Loup, Trois-Pistoles, the college at Sainte-Anne-de-la-Pocatière, Quebec, and Lévis. On 31 July 1865 he purchased his discharge from the 100th Regiment. On 9 January of the following year he was appointed captain in the 9th battalion, Voltigeurs de Québec, which had been formed earlier by drawing upon Quebec independent volunteer companies. He served as captain for four years and six months. His career as an officer at Quebec was in fact no more thrilling than his career as a soldier in the 100th Regiment.

Throughout the whole of the Fenian crisis, which alarmed the Canadian authorities unduly, he saw only garrison duty at Quebec and in the Eastern Townships.

It is not improbable that Voyer was grieved by the drab quality of his military career, for he was a man who extolled warlike virtues and idealized the life of the soldier. "Each of them," he wrote in 1865 in *Les qualités morales du bon militaire*, "when he takes up his arms receives as in trust the safety of our countryside, the tranquillity of our towns, the life, the liberty of his brothers; he becomes the sword and shield of him who has none, or who, having limbs too weak to bear them, cannot make use of them."

For Voyer, to be a soldier was not merely to serve one's country, it was also and perhaps more a means of social advancement. Thus he wrote *Les qualités morales du bon militaire* in order to "show Canadians that it is a great honour to wear military uniform." His friend Montpetit wrote that after his return in 1863 he lived all the time "with one foot in civilian society," winning people's sympathies and acquiring new protectors. The son of a wheelwright, on 2 Jan. 1869 he married Arline Laroche, "who had received her education from the Ursulines."

In 1870 his social ascent continued, thanks to his appointment as chief superintendent of the Quebec Provincial Police, an office he held until 1876. In January 1871 he was promoted major. Practically nothing is known about his duties as superintendent except that he was appreciated by his subordinates, in whom he endeavoured to instil the spirit of military discipline.

On 22 Feb. 1876 he died from a wound which he had inflicted upon himself accidentally the day before while handling a fire-arm. He left his wife and three young children aged from one month to six years.

YVES ROBY

L.-N. Voyer, *Les qualités morales du bon militaire* (Québec, 1865). A.-N. Montpetit, *Major L. N. Voyer, surintendant de la Police provinciale* (Québec, 1876).
C. P. Stacey, *Canada and the British Army, 1846–1871* (2nd ed., Toronto, 1963). G. F. G. Stanley, *Canada's soldiers; the military history of an unmilitary people* (Toronto, 1960).

W

WADDELL, JOHN, physician, superintendent of the New Brunswick Lunatic Asylum; b. 10 March 1810 at Truro, N.S., son of the Reverend John Waddell, Presbyterian minister, and Nancy Blanchard; d. 29 Aug. 1878 at Truro.

John Waddell was educated at the grammar

Waddington

school in Truro and at the Pictou Academy. In 1833 he began to study medicine under Dr David B. Lynds of Truro. He continued his studies in Glasgow and London and on 18 Oct. 1839 received a diploma from the Royal College of Surgeons. In 1840, having spent some time in Paris where he attended lectures given by the leading French scientists, he began a medical practice in Truro. In the same year he married the daughter of his former teacher, Susan Lynds, who died in 1841. He was married again in 1846 to Jane Walker Blanchard of Truro; they had two daughters and a son who died as a child.

In 1849 Dr Waddell was appointed superintendent of the New Brunswick Lunatic Asylum. His appointment was opposed by many who felt that he had no special qualifications for the job and that a native of New Brunswick should have been given the position. Waddell carried out his duties capably and held the position until he retired for reasons of health in 1876. He continually urged that the government spend more on improving the hospital. He visited asylums in Canada and the United States and attempted to introduce the latest methods of treatment. The common practice in many mental hospitals was to confine violent patients in small cells. They were bound with ropes or chains and beaten frequently by keepers who were untrained and had no sympathy for the mentally ill. Facilities in many hospitals were inadequate and the patients were crowded into wards where there was no segregation of the sexes. They were placed in solitary confinement at the least sign of violent behaviour. Waddell tried as much as possible to do away with mechanical restraints and to improve the conditions under which the insane were forced to live by urging the New Brunswick government to provide more spacious accommodation. He was aware of the value of occupational therapy and attempted to provide opportunities for some of the patients to work with their hands, particularly in the gardens of the asylum. He urged that all patients be treated equally regardless of their social status and wanted to build an institution "to which those most loved" could "with confidence" be committed if required.

Waddell was greatly respected throughout the province and his resignation was accepted with regret in 1876. "Probably no man in the province of New Brunswick was better or more generally known than Dr. Waddell, and there are few whose name and works will be held in more grateful remembrance."

W. A. SPRAY

N.B. Museum, James Brown, Journal, 1844–70, sect.C, 26. PANS, Community Records, Truro Township book, 107. *Daily Sun* (Saint John, N.B.), 30 Aug. 1878. *Daily Telegraph* (Saint John, N.B.), 30 Aug. 1878. *Morning Freeman* (Saint John, N.B.), 31 Aug. 1878. *Morning News* (Saint John, N.B.), 7–31 Dec. 1849, 4 Jan. 1850. *New Brunswick Reporter* (Fredericton), 14 Dec. 1849. New Brunswick, House of Assembly, *Journals*, 1850–76; 1881, 172–73. *Cyclopædia of Can. biog.* (Rose, 1888), 29–30. *Dom. ann. reg., 1878*, 370. Thomas Miller, *Historical and genealogical record of the first settlers of Colchester County* (Halifax, 1873), 160–62. C. T. Phillips, "Care of the insane," *Saint John Daily Sun*, 27 Feb. 1904.

WADDINGTON, ALFRED PENDERELL, writer and railway promoter; b. at Crescent House, Brompton, London, Eng., 2 Oct. 1801, sixth son of William Waddington, a merchant and banker of London and Paris, and Grace Valentine Sykes, a descendant of the Penderells who concealed Charles II in an oak tree after the battle of Worcester; d. a bachelor, at Ottawa, Ont., on 26 Feb. 1872.

Alfred Penderell Waddington received his early education in England, but after the death of his father in 1818 he joined an elder brother Thomas, who had become head of the French branch of the family, and whose sons were later prominent in public life in France. Alfred attended the École Spéciale du Commerce in Paris and then spent two years in Germany, at the University of Göttingen and in Leipzig. In 1823 he and his brother Thomas formed a company to operate a foundry, but the partnership ended in 1825. This was the first of a series of unsuccessful business ventures; "the whole of my existence for the past 20 years," Alfred wrote in 1841, "has been one continued series of disappointments, and struggles with adversity, and it would appear I am not yet at the end." At that time he was director of an ironworks at Lanvaux, near Auray, in Brittany, a position he held from 1829 until about 1845, when he moved to Épinac, in Burgundy. His favourite brother, Frederick, had helped him repeatedly, and it was he who provided funds when, attracted by the gold rush, Alfred sailed for California in May 1850. By 1854 he was a partner in the wholesale grocery firm of Dulip and Waddington, in San Francisco. The firm prospered and when the gold rush to the Fraser River began in 1858 Waddington came north to Victoria and opened a branch of the business there. At this time he was 57 years of age, and he must have been one of the oldest as well as best educated of the men who joined in the rush.

Waddington quickly adopted his new country and was soon championing its resources and involving himself in its future. The first gold discoveries had been shallow placer deposits along the banks of the Fraser in the vicinity of Hope and Yale. These were soon worked out and thousands of disgruntled men began to leave the country. In an effort to check the exodus and re-establish the good name of Vancouver Island and British Columbia, Waddington in November 1858 published *The Fraser mines vindicated, or the history of four months* (Victoria), the first book, other than official publications, printed on Vancouver Island. He soon became involved in politics, by joining Amor De Cosmos* and others in opposing the authoritarian ways and powers of Governor James DOUGLAS and the Hudson's Bay Company. In 1859 he published anonymously a pamphlet entitled *The necessity of reform: a tract for the times: addressed to the colonists of Vancouver Island* (Victoria). Early in 1860 he was elected to the House of Assembly as a representative of Victoria District, but he resigned in October 1861 to devote his time to furthering the road-building projects for which he is best remembered. In 1862 he helped draft the charter of the city of Victoria, but he declined to accept nomination as its first mayor.

In 1861 miners who had worked their way up the Fraser discovered the first of the rich gold deposits in the Cariboo country; excitement and activity mounted quickly. The new fields were far inland and the canyons of the Fraser made transportation costly and difficult. Waddington quickly became convinced that they could be reached more easily overland from the head of one of the many inlets along the coast. He had become an ardent partisan of Victoria in its rivalry with New Westminster, and undoubtedly part of the attraction of the plan was that it promised to give Victoria a virtual monopoly of the trade with the new mines.

Little was known about the hinterland of any of the coastal inlets, but Waddington decided that Bute Inlet was probably the best suited for his purpose. In September he visited the inlet and left an exploring party that returned in October with promising reports, based in large part on data gathered from the Indians. Waddington planned to establish a port at the head of Bute Inlet and to build a road from it up the valley of the Homathko River and thence eastward to the Fraser River in the vicinity of Alexandria; the distance would be about 160 miles. After negotiating with Governor Douglas during the winter, he was granted a charter in March 1862 that authorized him to build a bridle path or trail over the route proposed; this was supplemented almost at once by a further agreement authorizing the building of a road instead of the trail. Tolls were to be charged, and Waddington's concession was to be for ten years.

Work crews left for the inlet immediately, and in spite of the formidable obstacles met with in the Homathko canyon, 33 miles of road had been practically completed by the time operations ceased for the season in November. By contrast, the progress made in 1863 was discouraging. Freshets had washed out bridges and done other damage, and no way of getting the road through the rest of the canyon had been found. To make matters worse, time was beginning to run out on Waddington. Douglas had been pushing forward construction on two other roads to the Cariboo, one beginning at the head of Harrison Lake and the other going up the Fraser River from Yale. The former route was open for traffic in the summer of 1863, and it was clear that the other would be ready within a year. Yet Waddington refused to be discouraged, and in the winter of 1863–64 sold his property in Victoria to finance the next season's operations. These came to a tragic halt in April 1864 when his work parties were attacked by the Chilcotin Indians led by their chief Klattsasine*, and 19 men were killed. Frederick Seymour*, who had just succeeded Douglas as governor of British Columbia, took prompt action and the so-called "Chilcotin War" led to the apprehension of the murderers, five of whom were executed. Waddington, who had spent about $50,000 on the road project, asked for compensation, but was refused, and after vainly trying to raise funds he was obliged to abandon his scheme. In June 1865, when badly in need of a livelihood, he was appointed the first superintendent of schools of Vancouver Island, a post he filled competently until the colony was annexed to British Columbia in November 1866.

External events now prompted Waddington to revive and greatly enlarge his project. It seemed certain that a confederation of the eastern provinces of British North America was impending and that ultimately Rupert's Land and British Columbia would be included. Transportation between east and west would be essential. In addition, Waddington was much disturbed by the progress being made in the construction of a railway to California. He feared that it would divert to the United States much of the trade of the Orient, and felt that the British government should counter this by encouraging the development of a transcontinental travel route through British territory. He thought at first in terms of a traction line or tramway along the Bute Inlet–Fraser River route that his wagon road had been intended to follow, but the proposal soon grew into a plan for a railway that would continue on through the Yellowhead Pass to Edmonton and Red River. This he outlined in a pamphlet published in

Watson

Victoria in June 1867 entitled *Overland communication by land and water through British North America.*

To promote this scheme Waddington left Victoria in September 1867 for London, where, he claimed, he had already been in touch with people who were "financially of the first class and men of means." On 9 March 1868 he described his plan in a lecture to the Royal Geographical Society. It aroused some interest and prompted Sir Harry Verney to move in the House of Commons for a commission to inquire into the settling of the Red River and Saskatchewan country. A debate followed on 9 June, but the motion was withdrawn in view of the negotiations with regard to the future of Rupert's Land that were then in progress. In September Waddington published a second pamphlet, *Overland route through British North America; or, the shortest and speediest road to the east* (London), which outlined his proposals and stressed their importance in relation to trade with the Orient. At this time he was still thinking in terms of a combined land and water route, which would reduce costs by taking advantage of navigable rivers and lakes whenever these were available, but his map also showed an all-rail route. In 1869, in a new version of his plea entitled *Sketch of the proposed line of overland railroad through British North America* (London) only the all-rail route was mentioned.

In 1870 Waddington was in Ottawa, seeking support and inquiring about the possibility of securing a charter for his railway. In December he had an interview with Sir John A. Macdonald*, who mentioned liberal land grants and possible subsidies, but pointed out that nothing could be done until British Columbia entered confederation. Waddington's English backers have not been identified; by the time he saw Macdonald again, in July 1871, his chief financial support was clearly from Americans, notably George W. McMullen and Charles M. Smith, of Chicago. Macdonald took shelter in the fact that he could make no commitment, as parliament had given him no authority to do so. Waddington evidently came away from the interview convinced that all was going well, and that all he had to do was wait for parliamentary approval. He seems still to have been in this optimistic mood when he was stricken with smallpox and died in Ottawa in February 1872. But in reality there was virtually no possibility that his bid for a charter to build the Pacific railway would have been accepted. Macdonald was determined at all costs to prevent the project from falling under American control, and he may already have sensed that McMullen was in this respect a power to be reckoned with.

When describing the interview with Waddington and his associates in July 1871 Macdonald remarked that "their movement was altogether premature, and was improperly hurried by that respectable old fool Waddington." The comment was cruel, but Waddington was undoubtedly an optimistic old man in a hurry. A friend who saw him in Ottawa in June 1870 wrote: "Alfred Waddington is here working up his railroad scheme. He is quite as sanguine of success as he ever was." Chartres Brew*, the shrewd head of the British Columbia police, described him as "one of the most sanguine imaginative men I have ever met; prompt to delude himself on any matter of which he makes a hobby." He has been called the original promoter of a transcontinental Canadian railway; this he was not. The idea was being discussed long before he became attracted to it. But his pamphlets and projects did much to popularize the project, and to create the atmosphere in which its construction came to be taken for granted.

Waddington was buried in St James Cemetery, on the outskirts of Hull, Quebec. Several geographical features bear his name, the most notable being Mount Waddington (13,260 feet), the highest peak in the British Columbia Coast Range, and Waddington Canyon on the Homathko River.

W. KAYE LAMB

PAC, MG 26, A (Macdonald papers), 519. PRO, CO 60/22, 225. *Colonist* (Victoria), 1858–73. Creighton, *Macdonald, old politician*, 106–7. Ormsby, *British Columbia*, 205–6. J. P. Waddington, *Who's who in the family of Waddington* (London, 1934), 152–53, 217–29, 474. R. L. Reid, "Alfred Waddington," *RSCT*, 3rd ser., XXVI (1932), sect.II, 13–27.

WATSON, JAMES CRAIG, astronomer; b. 28 Jan. 1838 near Fingal, U.C., the eldest son of William Watson and Rebecca Bacon; d. at Madison, Wisc., U.S.A., 23 Nov. 1879.

William Watson left his farm near Fingal in 1850 and the family settled at Ann Arbor, Michigan, where James Craig entered high school and, later, the University of Michigan. His lifelong interest was in celestial mechanics, the branch of astronomy that deals with the determination and nature of the orbits of heavenly bodies. He was well suited for such work, being an exceptionally keen mathematician and a rapid, skilful computer. He had also considerable mechanical ability: he supported himself in high school and university by working as an engineer in a factory. At Michigan, his ability developed rapidly under the guidance of his teacher, the eminent astronomer Franz Friedrich Ernst Brünnow. After graduation in

1857, he was appointed assistant in the observatory (1858), professor of astronomy, and, in Brünnow's absence in 1859, acting director of the observatory. He was made professor of physics in 1860. When Brünnow left Michigan in 1863, Watson was appointed his successor as director.

Three weeks after his appointment, Watson discovered the first of the 22 asteroids that were to be associated with his name. As an aid to such discoveries, he spent many years preparing a series of ecliptic star maps, but the project was never completed. A result of his interest in asteroids was his publication *Theoretical astronomy* (1868), an authoritative treatise on orbit determination which remained a standard text for many decades. Watson also wrote *A popular treatise on comets* (1861) and numerous scientific papers. He received many awards, including three honorary doctorates.

Watson, like many astronomers of his day, participated actively in eclipse expeditions (Iowa, 1869; Sicily, 1870; Wyoming, 1878), and he also led an expedition to observe the transit of Venus (Peking, 1874). At the 1878 eclipse, he became interested in the possible existence of an intra-Mercurial planet. He believed he had observed one, and devoted considerable effort to calculations which would aid in the verification of his observation. Unfortunately, his calculations were never published, and his observation never verified.

In 1879 Watson became first director of the new Washburn Observatory at the University of Wisconsin in Madison. In this position he carried out his duties with vigour, efficiency, and care, and he showed the utmost concern for the welfare of his colleagues and students. While engaged in the supervision of the construction of the observatory, he became ill, apparently of exposure, and died suddenly on 23 Nov. 1880. He was survived by his wife, Annette Waite, whom he had married in 1860. There were no children.

In a sense, Watson's interest in asteroids transcended his death, for he left a sum of money, deposited with the National Academy of Sciences, to finance the computation of tables that would assure his asteroids would never become lost to the scientific world. To the author's knowledge, Watson's asteroids are the only celestial bodies so endowed.

JOHN R. PERCY

James Craig Watson was the author of *A popular treatise on comets* (Philadelphia and Detroit, 1861); *Tables for the calculation of simple or compound interest* . . . (Ann Arbor, Mich., 1878); and *Theoretical astronomy* . . . (Philadelphia, 1868). *DAB*. G. C. Comstock, "Biographical memoir of James Craig Watson," National Academy of Sciences, *Biographical Memoirs* (Washington), III (1895), 45–57. W. J. Hussey, "A general account of the observatory," Astronomical Observatory of the University of Michigan, *Pubs.* (Ann Arbor, Mich.), I (1912), 3–6. B. L. Newkirk, "The Watson asteroids," *Popular Astronomy* (Northfield, Minn.), XII (1904), 645.

WEE-KAS-KOO-KEE-SEY-YIN. *See* WIKASKO-KISEYIN

WENTWORTH-FITZWILLIAM, WILLIAM, Viscount Milton (an hereditary courtesy title), traveller, author, and politician; b. 27 July 1839 in London, Eng., son and heir-apparent of William Thomas Spencer Wentworth-Fitzwilliam, 6th Earl Fitzwilliam, and Frances Harriet Douglas; m. on 10 Aug. 1867 to Laura Maria Theresa Beauclerk by whom he had one son and three daughters; d. 20 Jan. 1877 at Rouen, France.

William Wentworth-Fitzwilliam was educated at Eton and at Trinity College, Cambridge. He appears to have been an intelligent, sensitive, romantic, and sociable man who was also slightly irritable and not too robust. In 1860 he visited the Red River Settlement and the trip whetted his appetite for more travel in British North America. According to a lecture he gave to a number of British scientific and literary societies in 1864, he was the initiator of a second and more important journey: "In the spring of 1862 I resolved to investigate for myself the nature of the country between the Red River Settlement and the Rocky Mountains; and to penetrate, if possible, by the shortest route to the gold regions of Cariboo. . . ." He rightly considered himself "fortunate to obtain the assistance" of a friend, Dr Walter Butler Cheadle*, who proved to be the real leader of the expedition.

Lord Milton and Dr Cheadle arrived in Quebec on 2 July 1862 and travelled to Upper Fort Garry by way of Toronto, Chicago, and St Paul, Minnesota. They wintered about 80 miles northwest of Fort Carlton, hunting and trapping. Resuming their journey in the spring, they obtained at Fort Pitt the services of a new guide, Louis Battenotte, a Métis, whom they called "the Assiniboine." They crossed the Rockies *via* Edmonton, Jasper, and the Yellowhead Pass. Because their party was small, ill assorted, without adequate food, and lacked a guide with local knowledge, they turned aside from one of the purposes of their expedition – to find a direct route to the Cariboo – and instead followed the North Thompson River to Kamloops. Generally travelling by horse, they met with great difficulties and privations, probably managing to survive only because of the resourcefulness and

Westphal

strength of Cheadle and Battenotte. On the expedition Dr Cheadle aided Milton during a number of attacks, which may have been epileptic; he also gave medical assistance at many of the posts they visited.

After reaching Kamloops on 29 Aug. 1863, Milton and Cheadle went on to Victoria, and then visited the Cariboo, going inland by the Lake Harrison–Lillooet route, and returning by the Fraser Canyon. They sailed from Victoria on 20 Dec. 1863. On their way back to England, which they reached on 5 March 1864, they visited San Francisco, Panama, and New York.

In 1865 the two travellers jointly published in London an account of their journey called *The north-west passage by land*. It was deservedly popular and went through eight editions by 1875 and another in 1901. Although Milton's name appears before Cheadle's on the title page of the book, comparison of its text with that of Cheadle's *Journal* (published in Ottawa in 1931) leaves little doubt that the latter was the main author. The *Journal* also has much detail left out in *The north-west passage by land*. The latter gives a lively, sometimes humorous, and rather roundabout account of their adventures and provides a great deal of information about the Canadian west. One well-known and gruesome incident was their finding a beheaded Indian corpse in a sitting position. By contrast, Mr O'B [Eugene Francis O'Beirne*], who fastened himself to the party, provided comic relief. With its analysis of the prospects of the prairies and British Columbia, the book helped prepare opinion in both Britain and Canada for the ending of Hudson's Bay Company rule, confederation, and the inclusion of the west in the union. Its intelligent estimate of the value of the Yellowhead Pass was vindicated by the route's being chosen for the Grand Trunk Pacific.

Lord Milton was elected an MP for Yorkshire in 1865. He was a Liberal and a supporter of such causes as abolition of church-rates, extension of the franchise, admission of dissenters to the universities, and extension of education to every child in the kingdom. He was also an active supporter of the development of British Columbia and of the Canadian west, and urged improved mail service between the United Kingdom and Victoria, B.C. In 1869, while still an MP, he published, in London, *A history of the San Juan water boundary dispute question . . .*, which remains a valuable source.

Milton resigned his seat in the commons in 1872 and travelled with his wife to New York and then to Canada. They lived for a short time in a camp on the north shore of Lake Superior called Pointe de Meuron. Here their only son was born in July 1872. A dubious story maintains that Milton lived for a time under an assumed name as a landowner in Virginia. For most of the last years of his life he was away from England for his health.

V. G. HOPWOOD

William Wentworth-Fitzwilliam, Viscount Milton, collaborated with Walter Butler Cheadle in several works describing their journey across British North America. These include: "An expedition across the Rocky Mountains into British Columbia, by the Yellow Head or Leather Pass," Royal Geographical Society, *Proceedings* (London), IX (1864–65), 17–21; *An expedition across the Rocky Mountains into British Columbia, by the Yellow Head or Leather Pass* (London, 1865); *How we crossed the Rocky Mountains into British Columbia* (n.p., 1864); and *The north-west passage by land: being the narrative of an expedition from the Atlantic to the Pacific . . . to British Columbia . . . by one of the northern passes in the Rocky Mountains* (1st ed., London, 1865; 9th ed., London, 1901). Wentworth-Fitzwilliam also wrote *A history of the San Juan water boundary dispute question as affecting the division of territory between Great Britain and the United States* (London, New York, 1869).

PABC, Milton, William Fitzwilliam, Correspondence outward, 1863, 1864. W. B. Cheadle, *Cheadle's journal of trip across Canada, 1862–1863*, intro. and notes by A. G. Doughty and Gustave Lanctot (The Canada series, ed. F. P. Grove, I, Ottawa, 1931; repr., Edmonton, 1970). "British Columbia," *Daily British Colonist* (Victoria), 21 Sept. 1863. "From British Columbia," *Daily British Colonist* (Victoria), 23 Nov. 1863. G. E. Cokayne, *The complete peerage . . . of England Scotland Ireland Great Britain and the United Kingdom extant extinct or dormant*, ed. Vicary Gibbs et al. (13v., London, 1910–40), V, 525–26. *Debrett's illustrated peerage and titles of courtesy, of the United Kingdom of Great Britain and Ireland* (London, 1883), 276. *Dod's parliamentary companion* (London), 1865–73.

WESTPHAL, Sir GEORGE AUGUSTUS ALEXANDER, admiral in the Royal Navy; b. probably in Preston, N.S. (he was christened in St George's Church, Halifax) on 27 March 1785, youngest son of George Frederick and Anna Westphal; m. in 1817 to Alicia Chambers, a widow; d. 12 Jan. 1875 at Hove, Brighton, Eng.

George Augustus Alexander Westphal entered the Royal Navy in 1798 on board the frigate *Porcupine*, then serving on the North American Station. In 1803 he was a midshipman in *Amphion* which took Horatio Nelson to the Mediterranean as commander-in-chief. Westphal was transferred to *Victory* and served in her at the battle of Trafalgar where he was severely wounded. When he was taken below to the cockpit, his head was laid on Nelson's rolled coat; some of the bullions of an epaulette became tangled in his hair and

700

were so fixed with dried blood that they had to be cut out. For the rest of his life Westphal treasured these bullions as a memento of Nelson.

Promoted lieutenant on 15 Aug. 1806, Westphal served for a short time in the West Indies but was captured by a French privateer when returning to England in a merchant ship. Although again severely wounded, he escaped from prison in Guadaloupe, made his way back to England after being picked up at sea by an American schooner, and returned to the West Indies as lieutenant first in the *Neptune* and then in the *Belleisle*, under the command of Commodore Sir George Cockburn. He served ashore at the reduction of Martinique, and, after further naval employment in European waters, returned with Cockburn to the Chesapeake where his many gallant services brought him promotion to commander on 8 July 1813. He was advanced to post-rank on 12 Aug. 1819 and in May 1822 commanded *Jupiter* which took Lord Amherst to India as governor general. Knighted on his return, Westphal served in 1832 as flag-captain to Sir George Cockburn on the North American station but was invalided early in 1834 and saw no further active service.

On the retired list, he was promoted rear-admiral on 17 Aug. 1851, vice-admiral on 10 Sept. 1857, and admiral on 23 March 1863. For the last 40 years of his life he lived at Hove, Brighton. Westphal was the longest surviving officer of those who had served at Trafalgar on the *Victory*. His brother, Philip (1782–1880), was also a Royal Navy admiral. They served together, though not on the same ship, in the operations in the Chesapeake in 1813.

PETER KEMP

St George's Church (Halifax), Register of births and children baptized by the Reverend B. M. Houseal (microfilm in PANS). *Times* (London), 14 Jan. 1875. *DNB.* John Marshall, *Royal naval biography . . .* (2v. and supps., London, 1823–30). O'Byrne, *Naval biog. dict.*

WHITE, EDWARD, Methodist minister and missionary; b. 11 Nov. 1822 in Philadelphia, Penn., son of William and Hannah White; m. in Canada West, on 22 or 23 July 1852, Sarah Jane Woodman by whom he had several children; d. 15 June 1872 at Montreal, Que.

Edward White grew up in the township of Raleigh, near St Thomas, Upper Canada. He attended the local school while working on his father's farm, and after studying at home was licensed as a local preacher at the age of 21. He earned a teacher's certificate and taught for a short time, then in 1845 began circuit work under the guidance of the Wesleyan Methodist Church of

Canada, Canada conference. By 1852 he was sufficiently advanced to be passed at the annual conference meetings in Kingston, where he was ordained the same year. White worked on the Smithville circuit until 1858 when he and three other Wesleyan Methodists were chosen for missionary work in the newly formed colony of British Columbia. Dr Ephraim Evans*, superintendent of the group, Ebenezer Robson, Arthur Browning, and White arrived in Victoria in February 1859 and received a warm welcome from local Methodists. Governor James DOUGLAS and other influential citizens, though not themselves Methodists, eagerly greeted the newcomers and offered assistance in setting up the mission.

White was assigned to Queensborough (New Westminster) in the mainland colony where conditions were rough and primitive. On 1 April in the open air outside his tent he held his first services, preaching to a congregation of "fifty men, one woman and two children." Confronted with virgin forest, overwhelmed by "the unspeakable mosquito," and suffering the usual privations of pioneer life, the undaunted missionary with his wife and two children took up his task with a will. White possessed an athletic frame and was an expert axe-man – qualities which enabled him to build a parsonage and later a church while the Royal Engineers under Colonel Richard Clement Moody* carved the proposed capital city out of the wilderness. White's small wooden building – the first Methodist church west of the Great Lakes – was dedicated on 8 April 1860 on land donated by Colonel Moody. Before long, ably assisted by his wife's sister, Emily Woodman, the missionary had established a day school, a night school for the Chinese, a Sunday school, a temperance society, and prayer groups.

After four years White and his family were named to replace Robson at Nanaimo, where the congregation included numerous Indians. Thomas Crosby*, a layman, was already there and had mastered enough of the Salish tongue to interpret for White on the circuit, which embraced Comox, Cowichan, and Saltspring Island.

By 1866 White was again in New Westminster, and he assumed the added responsibility of chairman of the British Columbia District since Dr Evans had retired. The New Westminster circuit had been enlarged to include Burrard Inlet, Chilliwack, Hope, and Yale, and as chairman White was expected to visit all stations including far-off Barkerville and the Methodist churches on Vancouver Island. Fortunately the Cariboo Road had been completed and Barnard's stage coaches were operating. Toward the end of 1869 White was again in charge at Nanaimo but by then the effects of exposure to the elements and over-exertion were beginning to show. The need for a protracted rest was evident by 1871 and White returned to Ontario.

In less than a year's time White was travelling in Britain "for health and observation" and lecturing as immigration agent for the Ontario government. Returning home from an enjoyable and successful tour, during which he had sent interesting dispatches to the Victoria *Colonist*, he paused in Montreal where he was stricken with smallpox and died.

Edward White's character as a minister of the Gospel, unselfish and zealous, is revealed in his soul-searching diaries. They show him as a "man of virility and faith." The foundations of Methodism in British Columbia were well laid by the "incredible zeal of men of this calibre."

MADGE WOLFENDEN

PABC, Edward White diaries, 1 Jan. 1859–31 Dec. 1866, 1867 (typescripts; typescript copies also held by the United Church British Columbia Archives, Vancouver); Letter of appointment, Enoch Wood to Edward White, 16 Nov. 1858 (photostat). *Colonist* (Victoria), 1859–72. *Victoria Gazette*, 12 Feb. 1859. Edgar Fawcett, *Some reminiscences of old Victoria* (Toronto, 1912). [John Sheepshanks], *Bishop in the rough*, ed. D. W. Duthie (London, 1919). E. O. S. Scholefield and F. W. Howay, *British Columbia from the earliest times to the present* (4v., Vancouver, B.C., 1914). W. D. Young, "Pioneer Methodist missionaries in British Columbia, 1859–71," unpublished BA essay, University of British Columbia, n.d.

WHITE WOLF. *See* SOTAI-NA

WIKASKOKISEYIN (also written **Wee-kas-koo-kee-sey-yin,** called **Sweet Grass**), **ABRAHAM,** chief of the Plains Cree Indians of the Saskatchewan country; place and date of birth unrecorded; d.*c.* 11 Jan. 1877 in a shooting accident on the plains, presumably at Saint-Paul-des-Cris (Alberta).

Wikaskokiseyin's mother, a member of the Crow tribe of the Missouri area, had been kidnapped during a war with the Crees, and Wikaskokiseyin was born in the Cree camp. As a young man, he was called Apistchi-koimas (Le Petit Chef). It was in his youth that he undertook the daring exploit which accounted for his later name and recognition as a brave. Alone he penetrated into Blackfoot territory where he killed one of his enemies and captured over 40 horses. Upon his return, amidst shouts of triumph, he held up a tuft of grass dipped in the blood of his victim; the whole camp took up the cry, "Sweet Grass!" By 1870 he was the principal chief in a large area of the central part of the Prairies (Alberta and Saskatchewan), and in that year he was converted to Roman Catholicism and baptized with the Christian name, Abraham, by Father Albert Lacombe*, who had founded the mission of Saint-Paul-des-Cris in 1865.

After the acquisition of the Hudson's Bay Company territory by Canada in 1870, Wikaskokiseyin communicated his concern for the condition of his people to Governor Adams George Archibald* at Upper Fort Garry (Winnipeg). "Our country is getting ruined of fur-bearing animals, hitherto our sole support," he said in 1871. "We have had great starvation the past winter, and the small-pox took away many of our people, the old, young, and children. We want you to stop the Americans from coming to trade on our lands, and giving fire water, ammunition and arms to our enemies, the Blackfeet." He requested that representatives be sent to treat with the Crees and that they receive assistance from the government.

Wikaskokiseyin was the leading spokesman for the Indians in the negotiation of Treaty No. 6 at Fort Pitt (near present-day Lloydminster), and was the treaty's first signatory at that place, 9 Sept. 1876. Although he died a few months later, his name is perpetuated in the Sweet Grass reserve established for his band near present-day Battleford, Saskatchewan.

ALLAN R. TURNER

Annales de la propagation de la foi pour la province de Québec, no.2 (juin 1877), 115–19. Canada, *Sessional papers*, V (1872), PT.7, no.22; X (1877), PT.7, no.11. Morris, *Treaties of Canada with Indians*, 168–245. *Le Métis* (Saint-Boniface), 11 janv. 1877. P. E. Breton, *The big chief of the Prairies; the life of Father Lacombe* ([Montreal, 1956]). Katherine Hughes, *Father Lacombe; the black-robe voyageur* (3rd ed., Toronto, 1920).

WILD PERSON. *See* ONISTAH-SOKAKSIN

WILKES, ROBERT, politician and businessman; b. at Tullaghan, County Leitrim, Ireland, 24 June 1832; m. Martha Cooke in 1863; d. at Sturgeon Point, Ont., 16 Aug. 1880.

Robert Wilkes' father died before 1832 and his family, in which there were six other children, was probably poor. His education in Ireland was limited and he emigrated in 1848 at 16. He came to Toronto where opportunities existed since his uncle, R. H. Brett, was "one of the leading merchants." Wilkes clerked with Brett for a time, then for Rossin Brothers, jewellers in Toronto. In 1857 or 1858 he bought Rossin Brothers, thus establishing his own wholesale jewellery firm in Toronto; he subsequently expanded to Montreal, Hamilton, and western Canada. He was sending travellers to Manitoba and British Columbia by 1872. He diversified his business interests as he grew wealthier and in 1869 he was a charter member of the Toronto, Simcoe, and Muskoka Junction Railway (later part of the Northern Railway). He became a director of the Canadian Bank of Commerce in 1871 and was one of its vice-presidents from 1874 to 1876. He served as a director of the Confederation Life Assurance Association and of the Isolated Risk Fire Insurance Company.

Wilkes was a Liberal, but an unusually unpersistent politician. He does not appear to have taken part in municipal politics, and it was not until 1872 that he contested a parliamentary riding, that of Toronto Centre. He was elected then and again in 1874, but when the latter return was voided in the same year he retired from politics.

Although Robert Wilkes himself is not memorable politically, the 1872 election in Toronto Centre in which he ran against Francis Shanly*, a railway engineer, was most revealing. George BROWN thus described the election to his wife: "The struggle . . . in Centre Toronto was the keenest & bitterest I ever knew. The amount of bribery & perjury done by our opponents was never approached in any previous contest." A Conservative observer agreed: "We had great excitement yesterday over the Central Division Election. It is said none of the old famous struggles were anything like it. The halt the lame the blind, & even the absent & the dead were brought out to vote . . . & there can be no doubt a large sum of money was spent, & probably on both sides." One of the Conservative managers has left an interesting insight into the politics of open voting: "We suffered a most mortifying defeat yesterday when victory was within our grasp, at 11 o'clock we were 201 behind, at 12 178 at 1 157 & at 2 70, we then began to work & spend money but it was too late, we were beaten by 28, half an hour more would have cleaned off the 28 & given us a good majority." The Conservative party accounts survive, and reveal a minimum expenditure of $8,807.25. The Liberals probably spent as much. When the small size of the electorate is considered (Toronto Centre had 4,148 eligible voters of whom 2,404 voted), along with the real value of an 1872 dollar, the expense and financial pressure of a 19th-century election become clear.

Wilkes was an active churchman and a member of the general conference of the Methodist Church. He retired from the wholesale business shortly before his premature death by drowning, along with two of his children, at Sturgeon Point, Ont., on 16 Aug. 1880. Wilkes had become a "wholesale merchant of great energy, who from a position of a clerk . . . raised himself to wealth. . . ."

DONALD SWAINSON

PAC, MG 24, B40 (Brown papers), 8. PAO, Sir Alexander Campbell papers, 1872; Francis Shanly papers. *Globe* (Toronto), 1880. *Sarnia Observer*, 1872. [Walter and Francis Shanly], *Daylight through the mountain; letters and labours of civil engineers Walter and Francis Shanly*, ed. F. N. Walker ([Toronto], 1957), 390. *Can. directory of parliament* (Johnson), 602. *Can. parl. comp.*, 1873. *Dom. ann. reg.*, 1880–81.

Davin, *Irishman in Canada. Hist. of Toronto and county of York*, II, 173–74. Hunter, *Hist. of Simcoe County*, I, 207. Ross and Trigge, *History of the Canadian Bank of Commerce*, II. Swainson, "Personnel of politics."

WILKINSON, JOHN, surveyor, draughtsman, and engineer; b. 2 April 1804 at Cowgill, Yorkshire, Eng.; d. 10 April 1871 at Fredericton, N.B.

John Wilkinson received his education in England where he graduated from the Institution of Engineers in London. He emigrated to New Brunswick in 1830 as manager of the Owen family property on Campobello Island. At St Andrews, N.B., on 6 June 1837, he married Mary Rebecca Curry; they had one daughter.

In 1836 Wilkinson joined Thomas Baillie*, chief commissioner of crown lands and the surveyor general, in his department at Fredericton as a surveyor and draughtsman. He served from 1840 to 1843 on the staff of the British commissioners for fixing the boundary between New Brunswick and Maine. He carried out an exploratory survey for the proposed European and North American Railway in 1847. The following year he surveyed a line for the railway between the city of Saint John and Shediac harbour, and in 1850 one for the proposed railway between Saint John and Calais, Maine. He also prepared reports for the government on surveys for railways, county boundary lines, and telegraph lines. From 1856 to 1858 he worked on an official map of the province of New Brunswick, which was published in 1859. This was the first general map of the province to include the results of admiralty surveys, boundary surveys, and the accumulated land surveys in the crown land office. He became involved in a dispute with the government over the copyright of this map and other matters, and in 1864 published a pamphlet in which he set out his side of the dispute. The government, of course, won. He later joined the provincial Board of Works as an engineer and was employed examining sites for bridges and lighthouses.

Willis

Wilkinson was an extremely careful and accurate surveyor, and his plans in the crown land office are by far the best in their extensive collection. His map of New Brunswick, according to W. F. Ganong*, was "scientifically constructed, minutely correct," and "beautifully engraved," and "must ever remain a classic of *New Brunswick Cartography*."

W. A. SPRAY

N.B. Museum, Ganong MS coll., "The province of New Brunswick," chap. 1, sect.3, 6 (unpublished MS by W. F. Ganong); Ganong MS coll., box 37; New Brunswick Historical Society papers, W. H. Steeves correspondence, items 7, 46. New Brunswick, House of Assembly, *Journals*, 1847, 1849, 1850, 1852, 1854, 1859. W. G. MacFarlane, *New Brunswick bibliography: the books and writers of the province* (Saint John, N.B., 1895), 84. MacNutt, *New Brunswick*, 325–26. A. W. Bailey, "Railways in New Brunswick, 1827–1867," unpublished MA thesis, University of New Brunswick, 1955. W. F. Ganong, "A monograph of the cartography of the province of New Brunswick," *RSCT*, 2nd ser., III (1897), sect.II, 403–4.

WILLIS, JOHN ROBERT, naturalist, teacher, and first Nova Scotian conchologist; b. 14 Feb. 1825 in Philadelphia, Pa., son of John Willis; m. in 1847 to Mary Ann Artz by whom he had six children, and in 1865 to Eliza Jane Mosely by whom he had four children; d. 31 March 1876 in Halifax, N.S.

John Robert Willis came to Halifax as a child; he was educated at the national school where he later became a successful teacher and principal. He was appointed superintendent of the new industrial school in Halifax in 1864, and a year later became secretary to the new board of school commissioners for the city. He retired from the latter post only in 1875.

Willis is remembered primarily, however, as a naturalist. A painstaking and discriminating collector and classifier, mainly of shells but also of insects and birds, he first won acclaim in 1854 when he exhibited his shells at the Nova Scotia Industrial Exhibition and won first prize. Later he sent exhibits of mollusca and pearls to an international exhibition, and to the Dublin Exhibition in 1864. His work brought him into correspondence with distinguished British, American, and Canadian scientists, among whom Sir John William Dawson* became a particular friend. With their assistance, he identified and publicized the existence of many species of shells, including European and southern types hitherto not recognized as existing as far north as Nova Scotia. He gave shell collections to local colleges, the British Museum, the Boston Society of Natural History, the Academy of Natural Sciences of Philadelphia, and the Smithsonian Institution.

In recognition of his work he was elected corresponding member of the Liverpool Natural History and Microscopical Society in 1862, of the Boston Society of Natural History in 1863, and of the Academy of Natural Sciences of Philadelphia in about 1866. He was one of the founders of the Nova Scotian Institute of Natural Science in 1862, and worked for the establishment of a provincial museum.

His shell catalogues showing localities, range, and relative importance helped American naturalists to wider, more accurate generalizations and are of historical interest since the distribution of shell forms changes with time.

PHYLLIS CREIGHTON

[John Robert Willis' own publications include the first known list of Nova Scotia shells, published in 1857 in a periodical which has not survived; a list of birds of Nova Scotia in the *Annual report of the board of regents of the Smithsonian Institution . . . for . . . 1858*; a catalogue of marine shells of Nova Scotia in the Boston Society of Natural History, *Proceedings*, VIII (1862); a catalogue of edible mollusca, from a paper read before the Nova Scotia Literary and Scientific Society, published in *Colonial Review* (Halifax), 29 Nov. 1862; and a privately printed extensive list of 193 Nova Scotia shells (November 1863). P.C.]

Dominion Illustrated Weekly, a Canadian pictoral weekly (Montreal, Toronto), 11 Oct. 1890, 247. *Unionist and Halifax Journal*, 27 Dec. 1865. "John Robert Willis, the first Nova Scotian conchologist, a memorial; his life, his list of shells of Nova Scotia, and his other published works," ed. W. F. Ganong, Nova Scotian Institute of Natural Science, *Proceedings and transactions* (Halifax), VII (1886–90), PT. IV, 404–28. Harry Piers, "A brief historical account of the Nova Scotian Institute of Science . . . with biographical sketches of its deceased presidents and other prominent members," Nova Scotian Institute of Science, *Proceedings and transactions*, XIII (1910–14), xciii–xciv.

WILLIS, JOHN WALPOLE, judge; b. in England, 4 Jan. 1793, son of William Willis and Mary Smith; d. 10 Sept. 1877 at Wick House, Wick-Episcopi, Worcestershire, Eng.

William Willis died in 1809 leaving little estate and John Walpole rose by a combination of ambition, legal talents, and charm. He published his first legal work in 1816 and was called to the bar the following year. Willis' interest in equity led to the publication in 1820 of a book that long remained an authority, and of a third work in 1827. His increasingly successful practice of the law was matched by a profitable advance into established society. These interests converged in

1823–24 when Willis was retained by the 11th Earl of Strathmore. In August 1824 their association led to his marriage to the earl's elder daughter, Mary Isabella Bowes-Lyon, aged 22.

As a successful barrister and an authority on equity, Willis might have thrived indefinitely amid the efforts of Sir Robert Peel, as home secretary, to encourage the codification and moderation of English civil law and commercial law. But marriage to Lady Mary did not guarantee solvency or harmony. She brought no great dowry. Her life with Willis in Hendon, a quiet London suburb, offered little excitement; his limited means meant that his mother and sister were forced to share their home. Lady Mary's consciousness of her rank appears to have grown, rather than diminished, following her marriage; her ambitions and the other financial and professional demands of Willis' career were propelling him forward at a forced pace.

In 1827 the Colonial Office played briefly with the idea of pressing upon Upper Canada some of the current British legal reforms and of establishing a court of chancery through which remedies could be sought in equity. The Earl of Strathmore suggested that his son-in-law could grace that new bench with authority during the period of necessary adjustment. The reform was not yet finally settled, but on some loose understanding Willis accepted an interim appointment as junior puisne judge on the province's Court of King's Bench. Willis, with the entire Hendon *ménage*, arrived in York (Toronto) on 18 Sept. 1827. He was to be in Canada only nine months – less than half of Robert F. Gourlay*'s stay – but he would cause nearly as much alarm in official circles and stir the reform-minded at a decisive moment in their organization.

Willis discovered immediately that the governor, Sir Peregrine Maitland*, and his Executive Council questioned the Colonial Office's flirtation with chancery. The attorney general, John Beverley Robinson*, and other Family Compact lawyers, including the solicitor general, Henry John Boulton*, differed over important details of the plan; Maitland's strong will, thus reinforced, gave way only slowly to Whitehall's proposals for a provincial enabling act. Robinson was prepared to accede to the proposal and even entrusted the drafting to an opposition lawyer, Dr John Rolph*, but Willis over-reached himself in attempting to force the pace of negotiations. The Reformers were anxious to bargain with the government by log-rolling – an equity court in return for a more independent judiciary. Willis abandoned his natural alliance with Robinson to consort with four lawyers who were then chief opposition

spokesmen – Rolph, William Warren Baldwin*, Robert Baldwin*, and Marshall Spring BIDWELL. Despite such advocates, Willis' bill was emasculated and finally abandoned in the Tory assembly. Meantime, the imperial law officers had advised Whitehall not to press the matter further. Thus, the junior puisne judge was forced to reassess his prospects in the less familiar field of common law and in a provincial society.

At the outset Willis and his wife had been warmly accepted into York's small circle. If Lady Mary thought her charms wasted, Willis quickly joined the round of parties and fashionable charities with the confidence that had served him at home. This goodwill, however, was soon squandered. Willis' appointment had been deeply resented by aspirants such as Robinson, Boulton, and Christopher Hagerman*, who had prepared themselves through years of service in the common law and in Upper Canada's legal system. Willis' contempt for their abilities was expressed plainly, as was his poor opinion of his two superiors on the King's Bench, Chief Justice William Campbell* and Levius Peters Sherwood*. In part Willis' cause was sound: he argued, for example, that punishment in criminal cases was inhumane by contemporary English standards. But, by flaunting his own lack of factional spirit, he made the case for equity seem like a call for purity. Neither a demagogue like the earlier Judge Robert Thorpe*, nor a firebrand like Gourlay, he, with his charm and plausibility, seemed a more formidable opponent. Moreover, Governor Maitland's wife, daughter of a duke, saw a threat to her social position from an earl's daughter. These social and professional conflicts had developed so quickly that an open conflict must arise when Willis, after being resident only a few weeks, applied, in rivalry with Robinson, for succession to the chief justice's seat.

On 11 April 1828, taking advantage of the absence of his two colleagues, Willis behaved extraordinarily while presiding over the libel trial of Francis Collins*, editor of the *Canadian Freeman*. Collins had sought the latitude customarily accorded those appearing without counsel, but Willis permitted and even encouraged him in a prolonged, irrelevant attack upon the law officers, Robinson and Boulton. On Robinson's interjection, Willis presumed to question from the bench Robinson's entire record of public office, threatening to make "a representation . . . to His Majesty's Government." As John Charles Dent* concludes, "Judge Willis seems to have been wrong in his law, wrong in his etiquette, wrong in his temper, and wrong in his construction of judicial amenities."

Willis

By now, however, an impending general election invited hyperbole and postures of convenience. Maitland hastily assured Whitehall that because no one had before protested against "the laws, or the manner in which they have been administered, I must conclude that the people are content with both." On the other hand, "the people" – including the most notable Reform lawyers – had already decided for Willis. Memory of the application of the sedition act to Robert Gourlay and Barnabas Bidwell* was fresh. Willis' legitimate concern for the laws, however, threatened to give way to demagogy – an easy trap for a man of his vanity.

On 16 June Willis displayed a sensitivity for legal technicalities that would not have served him on 11 April by declaring that the act establishing King's Bench required the presence of the "Chief Justice, together with two puisne justices." Campbell was still absent on leave, as legal and administrative officers had frequently been of necessity in the past. Willis now presumed to cast doubt upon the entire legal foundation and record of the court for the past generation. The technicality needed to be met: the Baldwins refused to pursue justice further in King's Bench. But Willis had really sought to indict a society, not a court. Public alarm and confusion might gain him much.

On 26 June, advised by the threatened law officers, Maitland and his council agreed to the "amoval" of Judge Willis; a week later, Hagerman was named to fill the post. Public meetings and messages of condolence encouraged Willis to press his case in London. Trustees, including the Baldwins, John Galt*, and their wives, offered to care for Lady Mary and the family, and Robert Baldwin undertook to act as her solicitor. But committees can only do so much, and when Lady Mary was to rejoin her husband in England, she quietly chose instead to take up residence in Montreal with an officer in the 38th Light Infantry, Lieutenant Bernard, and subsequently to elope to England, leaving her son in a maid's care.

John Willis' career and Upper Canada's fortunes might have improved from that moment. Willis, as a cause, had helped to knit together the Reformers, who in the election of 1828 won their first assembly majority and elected Bidwell as speaker. Willis appealed his removal, lost an initial round, but was rehabilitated by the Privy Council, which overruled his amoval without chance of defence; he was given a new judicial appointment in Demerara (now part of Guyana). His marriage was dissolved, and in 1836 he married Ann Susanna Kent of Wick-Episcopi, Worcestershire, by whom he had three children. In 1841 he received another judicial appointment, in

New South Wales, but again he clashed with a strong-minded governor, Sir George Gipps, and was amoved without notice; again, the Privy Council sustained his appeal on the same technicality. This time he received no new appointment. He retired to Wick House and lived privately for another 30 years.

In retirement Willis composed a summary of his colonial experiences, *On the government of the British colonies*. In it he displayed all that lack of faith in the colonies that had been implicit in his public career. Colonies, he argued like John Graves Simcoe*, only deserved recognition equivalent to English counties; as their highest political ambition they might be represented in the British parliament, but they should be administered by lords lieutenant. Whatever the convenience of the Willis incident to the Reformers of 1828, those future advocates of responsible government could not have lived with Willis for long – nor could most people.

ALAN WILSON

J. W. Willis was the author of the following works: *A digest of the rules and practice as to interrogatories for the examination of witnesses, in courts of equity and common law, with precedents* (London, 1816); *Pleadings in equity, illustrative of Lord Redesdale's treatise on the pleadings in suits, in the Court of Chancery, by English bill* (London, 1820–21); *A practical treatise on the duties and responsibilities of trustees* (London, 1827).

PRO, CO 42/381–42/387; 42/408. G.B., Parl., House of Commons, *Hansard*, XXIV (1830), 551–55; Parl., House of Commons paper, 1831–32, XXXII, 740, pp.49–58, *Upper Canada. Return to several addresses to his majesty, dated 31 July 1832 . . .* ; Parl., House of Lords, *The mirror of parliament . . . for the session . . . commencing 29th January 1828 . . .* , ed. J. H. Barrow (36v., London, 1827–37), III, 1610–11, 14 May 1829. *Papers relating to the removal of the Honourable John Walpole Willis from the office of one of his majesty's judges of the Court of King's Bench of Upper Canada* ([London?], 1829). Upper Canada, House of Assembly, *Journals*, 1829, app., "Report of the select committee on the case of Mr. Justice Willis and the administration of justice." "Willis v. Gipps [1846]," *Reports of cases heard and determined by the Judicial Committee and the lords of the Privy Council, 1845–47*, ed. E. F. Moore, V (*The English Reports*, XIII, Edinburgh and London, 1901, 379–91). DNB. "Willis-Bund of Wick Episcopi," in Bernard Burke, *A genealogical and heraldic history of the landed gentry of Great Britain* (12th ed., London, 1914), 270–71.

Craig, *Upper Canada*. Dent, *Upper Canadian rebellion*, I, 162–94. Aileen Dunham, *Political unrest in Upper Canada, 1815–1836* (London, 1927),110–15, 157. William Kingsford, *History of Canada* (10v., Toronto, 1887–98), IX, 258–79. Roger Therry, *Reminiscences of thirty years' residence in New South Wales and Victoria . . .* (2nd ed., London, 1863),

341–45. G. E. Wilson, *The life of Robert Baldwin; a study in the struggle for responsible government* (Toronto, 1933).

WILLIS, MICHAEL, Presbyterian minister, educator, and abolitionist; b. 1798 at Greenock, Renfrew, Scotland, son of William Willis, a prominent minister and theologian of the Original Associate Synod (Old Light Burghers), one of the groups deriving from the first secession of 1733 which protested the abuses of patronage in the Church of Scotland; d. at Aberlour, Banff, Scotland, 19 Aug. 1879. The name of his wife is not known.

Michael Willis obtained his MA at the University of Glasgow in 1817 and received theological training in the Divinity Hall of the Old Light Burghers. After his ordination on 23 Jan. 1821 he served the Albion Street Church, Glasgow, until in 1839 he was called to Renfield Street Church in that city. In 1835 he had been given added responsibility when he succeeded his father as professor of theology at the Divinity Hall.

Willis played a leading role in the negotiations which led to the reunion of the Old Light Burghers with the Church of Scotland in 1839. The same year he received the DD from Glasgow University. His stay in the Church of Scotland was short-lived, however, as he joined with those who separated from it in 1843 to form the Free Church of Scotland. He was sent to Canada in 1845 to represent the Free Church cause and to cement relations with those in Canada who had separated from the Church of Scotland synod in sympathy with the Free Church. While in Canada he taught on a temporary basis at the newly founded Knox College in Toronto. Two years later, upon the unanimous recommendation of the colonial committee of the Free Church of Scotland, he was appointed professor of theology in Knox College. His scholarly and administrative gifts were recognized when he was appointed its first principal in 1857. He assisted in drawing up the constitution under which the college was incorporated the following year. During his principalship Willis kept Knox College in the paths of Calvinist orthodoxy. A popular preacher and churchman, Willis visited extensively throughout the church.

Named to the senate of the University of Toronto in 1851 by the governor general, Lord Elgin [Bruce*], Willis also served as a university examiner. However, he resigned from both posts in 1863 when objections were raised against him as an examiner. The objections appear to have stemmed from his sympathy for the point of view reflected in the findings of the university commission, which had published its report early in 1863.

Willis openly supported the claims of the denominational colleges to a share of the university endowments and thereby incurred the displeasure of his synod and college, both of which were bitterly opposed to the granting of financial aid to denominational colleges. Such grants, they believed, would be destructive of the "unsectarian System of Education in Canada West." Queen's University in Kingston conferred the LLD on him in 1863.

Willis was the first and only president of the Anti-Slavery Society of Canada, founded in 1851 to find ways and means to provide relief for, and to rehabilitate, fugitive slaves from the United States. Included on the executive with Willis were George BROWN and Oliver Mowat*. Prior to his coming to Canada Willis had published a lengthy pamphlet against slavery, describing it as degrading and contrary to the will of God. He took a personal interest in the Reverend William King*'s Elgin settlement in which King attempted to prepare the Negro fugitives for productive participation in the Canadian community. Willis preached at the first communion service held for the little congregation of fugitives at Buxton.

Willis retired as principal and professor of Knox College in 1870. He was elected moderator of the first general assembly of the Canada Presbyterian Church in that year. He retired to London, England, but frequently travelled to the Continent or to Scotland as a guest preacher, and in 1877 he represented the Presbyterian Church in Canada at the first general Presbyterian council held in Edinburgh. He died in 1879 while preaching for a friend at Aberlour, Banff, Scotland.

ALLAN L. FARRIS

Michael Willis edited *Collectanea graeca et latina: selections from the Greek and Latin fathers; with notes, biographical and illustrative* (Toronto, 1865), and was the author of *A discourse on national establishments of Christianity* (Glasgow, 1833); *Pulpit discourses, expository and practical and college addresses* (London, 1873); *Remarks on the late union between the Church of Scotland and the Associate Synod in opposition to certain statements of the dean of faculty, with the documents pertaining to the union* (Glasgow, 1840); *Slavery indefensible: an essay* (Glasgow, 1847).

Presbyterian Church of Canada, Synod, *Minutes* (Toronto), session 28, 1857, 26, 54. Canada Presbyterian Church, Synod, *Minutes* (Toronto), session 2, 1862, 54–55; session 3, 1863, 26–27. Canada Presbyterian Church, General Assembly, *Acts and proceedings* (Toronto), 1870, 61. Presbyterian Church in Canada, General Assembly, *Acts and proceedings* (Toronto), 1880, 59.

Constitution and bye-laws of the Anti-Slavery Society of Canada (Toronto, 1851). *Documentary history of education in Upper Canada* (Hodgins), XVII,

Willson

171–72; XVIII, 15. *Ecclesiastical and Missionary Record for the Presbyterian Church of Canada* (Toronto), IV (1847–48), 35; VII (1851–52), 180. *First annual report, presented to the Anti-Slavery Society of Canada, by its executive committee, March 24th 1852* (Toronto, 1852). *Presbyterian Record* (Montreal), IV (1879), 263.

Hew Scott, *Fasti ecclesiae, the succession of ministers in the Church of Scotland from the Reformation* (new ed., 9v., Edinburgh, 1915–61), III, 431–32. *Our Scottish clergy; fifty-two sketches, biographical, theological, & critical, including clergymen of all denominations*, ed. John Smith (Edinburgh, 1840), 120–25. G. S. Pryde, *Scotland from 1603 to the present day* (London, 1962), 182. W. J. Rattray, *The Scot in British North America* (4v., Toronto, 1880–84), III, 823–24. William Caven, "The Rev. Michael Willis, D.D., LL.D," *Knox College Monthly* (Toronto), IV (1885–86), 97–101.

WILLSON, HUGH BOWLBY (Bowlsby, Boultby), barrister, author, journalist, and businessman; b. in Saltfleet Township, U.C., 15 Sept. 1813, third son of John Willson* and Elizabeth Bowlby, and uncle of Thomas Leopold "Carbide" Willson*; d. in New York City, 29 April 1880.

Hugh Bowlby Willson was educated at the Gore District grammar school in Hamilton and became a close friend of John RAE, headmaster of the school. From Rae and from his own father Willson received his interest in the economic ideas of Adam Smith. Politically, Willson became first a Peelite Conservative and signed with Rae a petition in January 1836 calling for a public display of loyalty to the king in opposition to the Upper Canadian Reformers. He served in the rebellion in 1837 as a lieutenant in the 3rd Regiment of Gore militia. In the 1840s, though acquainted with such Reformers as Hamilton Hartley KILLALY, William Hamilton Merritt*, and Francis Hincks*, he distrusted the Reform leadership of Robert Baldwin*. Instead, he considered himself independent of party and favoured policies for the promoting of economic development of the united province.

For a short time in 1834 Willson had been a purser on a steamer on Lake Ontario. In 1836 he began to study law and was admitted to the bar in 1841, but before practising he travelled to the West Indies for his health. He spent some time in Trinidad and wrote articles about its "natural curiosities" in the New York *Albion*.

Willson apparently had limited success as a barrister. He turned to land speculation in the late 1840s and to development of real estate in the Hamilton region, laying out a residential area in east Hamilton and villa lots in the village of Ontario (later named Winona). In 1847 he was secretary of the Upper Canada Mining Company. His attention also turned to journalism. He was always keenly interested in topical affairs and contributed articles to the *Hamilton Spectator* for many years after its establishment in 1846.

When the British parliament abandoned mercantilism in the late 1840s, Canada lost its preferred trading position and suffered a serious recession; many disgruntled merchants and politicians began to consider an alternative economic alignment to benefit the colony, annexation to the United States. To discuss the new problems facing Canada, the British American League was formed in 1849, largely by Tories. When it met at Kingston in July under the presidency of George Moffatt*, Willson was a delegate for Saltfleet Township. He spoke in favour of annexation, and withdrew from the league in September because it rejected the idea. In succeeding months he followed Luther Hamilton HOLTON and Alexander Tilloch Galt* in advocating Canadian separation from the British Empire and annexation to the United States, and in October 1849 he founded and edited the annexationist *Independent*, a Toronto weekly; Willson lost a considerable amount of money when it failed in April 1850 from lack of interest and financial support. That year he was a secretary of the Toronto branch of the annexation committee.

Willson abandoned his law practice about 1852 and became a dealer in securities in London, England, with William Shaw and Malcolm Cowan. While in England he may also have written for the London *Times*. He was appointed a commissioner to the Paris Exposition of 1855 by the Canadian government; he was again in Hamilton in that same year, and by 1857 appears to have settled there. He became the first editor of the *Hamilton Times* in 1858, resigning in 1860. It was an independent liberal paper, which succeeded the Hamilton *Banner* and strongly promoted the commercial development of Canada. Willson also wrote widely on currency and banking, and on the advantages of a written constitution for Canada, An early advocate of building the Great Western Railway, he canvassed for municipal subscriptions to the company's stock. He was also active in planning the construction of the Hamilton and Port Dover Railway (later called the Hamilton and Lake Erie).

In the early 1860s Willson resided in Quebec City as parliamentary correspondent for the Quebec *Morning Chronicle* and other newspapers; for the *Chronicle* he wrote a series of articles on Canada's defence problems which were subsequently published as a pamphlet in 1862. As a resident of Quebec City, in 1864 he described himself: "Barrister and Attorney at Law, parliamentary agent, solicitor of patents of invention, &c. &c."

Willson moved to Washington, D.C., around the close of the Civil War and married Harriot Conway Ladde of that city. He later settled in New York City but continued to follow Canadian affairs and to write for the *Hamilton Spectator*. He had sophisticated and advanced ideas on monetary theory, and was a persistent advocate of reform of the money and banking system in both the United States and Great Britain. He became deeply involved in the postwar "Greenback" controversy in the United States. In a number of pamphlets and in testimony before a congressional committee in 1879, he argued strongly that notes issued by the state should be the permanent and exclusive circulating medium. He suggested the creation of a currency board to control the issue of paper money and proposed that the amount of paper money should be related to the volume of business transactions in the country. He believed that monetary mismanagement was a principal cause of periodic depressions in Great Britain and the United States. He was also a vigorous opponent of the Bank of England and wanted the introduction of one pound notes for general circulation "of a convenient size for pocket use."

The quality of Willson's writings on money and banking was excellent and he foreshadowed a number of welcome changes which were to be introduced after his death. He kept in touch with his friend and mentor John Rae until Rae's death in 1871, and, although he does not specifically refer to Rae in his writings, he was clearly influenced by his penetrating ideas on economics. He died in New York in 1880, survived by his wife and two adopted children.

R. WARREN JAMES and JOHN S. MOIR

H. B. Willson is the author of: *Canada and the United States: [a letter] to the editor of the National Intelligencer* (Washington, 1849); *Currency; or, the fundamental principles of monetary science postulated, explained and applied* (New York, 1882); *Great Western Railway of Canada* (Hamilton, Ont., 1860); *The Great Western Railway of Canada: its proposed branches and extensions* (London, 1854); *High speed steamers; or, how to build a river boat to run thirty miles an hour* (Albany, N.Y., 1866); *Industrial crises, their causes and remedies . . . from the report of the congressional committee on depression in labour and business* (Washington, 1879); *The military defences of Canada, considered in respect to our colonial relations with Great Britain, in a series of letters published in the Quebec "Morning Chronicle"* (Quebec, 1862); *The money question considered scientifically and practically . . .* (London, 1874); *A plea for Uncle Sam's money: or greenbacks versus bank notes* (New York,

1870); *The proposed Hamilton and South-western Railway* (Hamilton, Ont., 1854); *Reports and correspondence on the "Patent Compound Rail"* (London, 1851); *The science of money considered . . .* (Washington, 1869); *The science of ship-building, considered in its relations to the laws of nature* (London, 1863).

Hamilton Public Library (Hamilton), Land papers, 1838, p.34; 1849, p.6; 1850, p.3. New York County, Surrogate's Court (New York), will of Harriot C. Willson. PAO, William Hamilton Merritt papers, H. B. Willson to W. H. Merritt, 17 Dec. 1842, 2 April 1859. "The annexation movement, 1849–50," ed. A. G. Penny, *CHR*, V (1924), 236–61. [Bruce and Grey], *Elgin-Grey papers* (Doughty), I, 446. *Hamilton Spectator*, 1, 4, 5 May 1880. *Montreal Gazette*, 19 Jan. 1836. *Canada directory . . . 1851*, ed. R. W. S. Mackay (Montreal, 1851), 108. *A supplement to the Canada directory . . . 1853*, ed. R. W. S. Mackay (Montreal, 1853). *Arthur papers* (Sanderson). C. D. W. Goodwin, *Canadian economic thought: the political economy of a developing nation, 1814–1914* (Durham, N.C., and London, 1961). Middleton, *Municipality of Toronto*, I, 241. C. D. Allin, "The British North American League, 1849," *Ont. Hist.*, XIII (1915), 74–115. *Annals of the Forty* (Grimsby), IX (1958), 66. Canadian Library Association, Microfilm committee, *News Notes* (Ottawa), September 1959.

WILMOT, LEMUEL ALLAN, lawyer, politician, and judge; b. 31 Jan. 1809 in Sunbury County, N.B., son of William Wilmot and Hannah Bliss; d. 20 May 1878 at Fredericton, N.B.

Lemuel Allan Wilmot's father was a lumberman of loyalist ancestry, and his mother, who died before he was two years old, was a daughter of Daniel Bliss*, a loyalist and member of the first New Brunswick Executive Council in 1784. William Wilmot, not particularly successful in business, moved to Fredericton in 1813 to found a Baptist church and to educate his children. There he acquired an interest in politics and was elected to the assembly in 1816; he was defeated in 1819 and 1820 but re-elected in 1823. Twice, however, he was denied permission to take his seat, for an act had been passed in 1818 to prevent clergymen from sitting in the legislature. As he was ejected from the house for the second time, he is reported to have said, "Sir, the time will come when that lad (pointing to him [Lemuel Allan]) will see that justice is done to my memory." This story and another, that Wilmot overcame a speech impediment to become a great orator, form part of a mythology that enveloped Lemuel Allan Wilmot after his death and elevated him to heroic stature.

Wilmot was educated at the Fredericton grammar school and took a partial course at King's College. In June 1825 he entered the law office of Charles Simonds Putnam; he became an attorney in 1830, was admitted to the bar in 1832, and

Wilmot

created a queen's counsel in 1838. As a lawyer and later as a judge, Wilmot impressed more by his style and oratory than by his logic and wisdom. His striking appearance, sharp gestures, and flowing language full of historical and biblical illustrations were combined with high emotion in most effective presentations. "When he drew his tall form up before a jury, fixed his black piercing eyes upon them, moved those rapid hands and pointed that pistol finger, and poured out his arguments and made his appeal with glowing, burning eloquence, few jurors could resist him."

Wilmot's admission to the bar in 1832 coincided with his marriage to Jane Ballock of Saint John. Her death the following year, "after a severe and protracted illness," may have affected Wilmot's religious attitudes. In 1833 he came under the influence of the Reverend Enoch Wood* of the Fredericton Methodist Church, and soon dedicated himself to the church. His marriage to Elizabeth Black in the fall of 1834 was closely related to this religious commitment. She was the granddaughter of the Reverend William Black*, "the father of Methodism" in the Maritimes. Wilmot never swayed from his new faith.

Almost as soon as he opened his law practice in Fredericton Wilmot turned his skills to politics. Successful in both a by-election and a general election in 1834, he took his seat in the assembly on 25 Jan. 1835. Neither his youth nor his surroundings inhibited Wilmot; in his first session he introduced resolutions and bills on subjects such as the Maine–New Brunswick boundary and the expenses of judges on circuit. By 1836 he was reputed to be able "to thrill and enchain legislatures" in four- to five-hour speeches. The subject of many was the crown lands office and its management by the commissioner, Thomas Baillie*. Apparently as a result of these speeches Wilmot was chosen to accompany William Crane* of Sackville to London in 1836 with specific demands for the surrender to the assembly of the remaining crown lands and of the revenue that Baillie had accumulated from earlier sales. Lord Glenelg [Charles Grant], the colonial secretary, agreed to all the requests and the crown lands were handed over in return for a permanent civil list. Of greater significance was Glenelg's decision that the Executive Council was to be reconstructed "to ensure the presence in the Council of Gentlemen representing all the various interests which exist in the Province, and possessing at the same time the confidence of the people at large." Glenelg was concerned not only with New Brunswick but also with the whole of British North America, and planned to use New Brunswick as the model for change. Lieutenant Governor Sir Archibald

Campbell*, horrified at Glenelg's decisions, frustrated them at every turn, so much so that Crane and Wilmot were again dispatched to London in 1837 to reaffirm their gains. The trip was unnecessary, for Campbell, whose resignation they sought, had been replaced by Sir John Harvey*, the governor of Prince Edward Island.

Wilmot returned to New Brunswick to see a civil list bill passed in the legislature and Harvey liberalize the council by the addition of assemblymen including Crane. Wilmot as yet had no claim. In the meantime he supported the governor's struggle against the old Odell-Baillie clique, which was not easily uprooted. Wilmot's objectives were limited to those outlined in the Glenelg dispatch and it is unlikely that he either accepted or even understood the full meaning of responsible government. Never a good party man even when he was the leader of the reform movement, Wilmot did not hesitate to desert his colleagues when government appointments were offered. His pursuit of office, first on the Executive Council, then on the bench, and finally as lieutenant governor, might well be classed as rapacious. One authority has suggested recently that even before he was in office Wilmot was part of a "new family compact" that controlled New Brunswick after 1837 to a far greater extent than had the old compact. As an example, when George Pigeon Bliss*, the receiver general, died leaving his accounts short by £7,000, Wilmot and other Bliss relatives prevented the crown from seizing his assets. On another occasion, Wilmot, attacked in the press for his "usual effrontery and disregard for the truth," had the journalist, John A. Pierce, committed to common jail for his "gross and scandalous libel." Pierce had been criticizing Wilmot for some time and the latter proved remarkably sensitive to attack. In 1840 the Saint John *Chronicle*, which referred to Wilmot as "That inflated bladder of wind," attacked the lieutenant governor, and it too was taken to court. Harvey had not wished to pursue the matter, but Wilmot and others insisted. This case was lost as was a final one in 1844, when Wilmot was again criticized. In a negative way he thus contributed to the freedom of the press for the courts settled the issue by ruling against assembly decisions.

From 1837 until 1843 Wilmot participated actively in the assembly. The smart phrases of the Durham *Report* and the popularization of the ideas of responsible government provided him with the necessary slogans, yet Charles FISHER of York County, the leading constitutional expert in the province, was the only New Brunswick politician who treated the subject at an elevated level. Wilmot's devotion to the principle of responsible government was questioned by his contemporaries and remains hypothetical.

Under Sir William Colebrooke*, the new governor, an election was held early in 1843. Wilmot paraded the country with statements on responsible government, yet in New Brunswick, as in the rest of British North America, these were not the sort of issues that captivated the public imagination. Colebrooke, a moderate reformer himself, and aware of the diversity in the assembly, set about to form an all-factions Executive Council that undoubtedly had the support of the majority in the assembly. It included, among others, Edward Barron CHANDLER, Robert Leonard HAZEN, Hugh Johnston* and Wilmot. Wilmot's presence required little if any soul searching. To him taking office was a logical outcome of the Glenelg approach and probably satisfied his interpretation of responsible government. There was not much consternation at the time, although a liberal historian has written: "Mr. Wilmot certainly lost prestige by his action on this occasion, as he did subsequently from the display of similar weakness."

Colebrooke's limited acceptance of the new system soon forced Wilmot out of the council. On Christmas Day 1844 William Franklin Odell*, the provincial secretary, died. Before the sun had set Wilmot was at Colebrooke's door to inform him that Odell's position must be filled by a member of the assembly holding a seat on the Executive Council. Colebrooke, unwilling to make such a concession, appointed his son-in-law, Alfred Reade. The British government later declared the appointment invalid; in the meantime Chandler, Hazen, Johnston, and Wilmot resigned from the council. The first three stated that they had resigned because of Reade's unsuitability for the position; Wilmot had two reasons. The first was "that all the offices of honour and emolument in the gift of the administration of the government should be bestowed upon the inhabitants of the province." The second was that he supported British practices "which require the administration to be conducted by heads of departments responsible to the legislature. . . ." Colebrooke formed a new council and retained it even after the assembly passed by 23 to 10 a resolution that it did not possess "the confidence of the House nor the Country at large."

Out of office, Wilmot took on the appearance of the leader of the opposition and, although his position changed from issue to issue, he regularly pressed for the initiation of money grants by the executive.

Another of his interests was King's College. Between 1839 and 1846 he introduced a series of bills for some liberalization of the college. Only in 1846 was a minor revision accepted. Later he worked closely with Charles Fisher on a total revision which resulted in the creation of the University of New Brunswick in 1860. A related issue was a non-sectarian public school system and to this he gave untiring support. "It is unpardonable that any child should grow up in our country without the benefit of, at least, a common-school education," he stated in 1852. "It is the right of the child. It is the duty not only of the parent but of the people; the property of the country should educate the country. . . ." As lieutenant governor of New Brunswick in the 1870s he assisted in the passage of a school act fulfilling many of his own aims.

The nature of the political system was, however, the overriding issue of the 1840s. An election of 1846 returned many new members, and Wilmot confidently expected an invitation into the government. It came; in fact, he was the first offered a seat in council. After "much deliberation" he accepted, if "four professing his own opinion, whom he would be prepared to nominate, were appointed in a cabinet of nine." From this distance it is difficult to determine which was the greater – Colebrooke's relief at being able to refuse or Wilmot's dismay at the rejection. Chandler, Hazen, and Johnston returned to the government, and the "new compact," without Wilmot, governed with the support of the majority.

Over the next few months Wilmot's action as *provocateur* reached its height, especially during the debate on a motion of want of confidence in 1847. On 25 March 1847 he appeared at his best and his worst in a long, colourful, but rambling speech full of high sentiment and scorching personal references. George Edward Fenety* reported the speech: "A good deal had been said about politics and political principles; but his political principles were not of yesterday – he had gleaned them from the history of his country which they were all proud to own. Would any hon. member dare to tell him that because we were three thousand miles from the heart of the British Empire, that the blood of freemen should not flow through the veins of the sons of New Brunswick?" Almost in the next breath he could turn to a slashing personal attack on Hazen. Much of the speech was responses to interjections and chatter in the house. Fisher's constitutionally sound speeches lulled to sleep those who stayed; Wilmot's appeal to the converted and unconverted filled the house and few came through the experience unaffected. The motion of 1847 was lost 23 to 12.

This exercise of 1847 was really the last of its

type for Wilmot. Sir Edmund Walker Head* became governor in 1848, with instructions to follow the dispatch of Earl Grey to Sir John Harvey of Nova Scotia requiring that the council be "men holding seats in one or other House, taking a leading part in political life, and above all, exercising influence over the Assembly." Head immediately set about to form a coalition "of the ablest Liberals with the preponderantly powerful Conservatives." Wilmot and Fisher thus joined Chandler, Hazen, John Simcoe SAUNDERS, William B. Kinnear*, and John R. Partelow*. Head had wanted Wilmot to become provincial secretary, but he refused and insisted on being appointed attorney general, the logical stepping stone to the Supreme Court. Wilmot did hasten to assure Chandler that the latter's "claims for the Bench are undoubted."

Wilmot and Fisher were accused of deserting their principles in 1848. "All hope of radical change, with the loss of two of the ablest standard bearers of the party, now vanished," lamented Fenety. "It was almost worse than useless to contend longer for equal political justice, when the leading champions of the party had joined the standard of the enemy. . . . This was the great political mistake of their lives." From this point of view, responsible government was not introduced into New Brunswick in 1848 and the major reason was the Wilmot–Fisher betrayal. Both men, however, believed they were entirely consistent with their principles. The Glenelg settlement had created a spirit of moderation which bridged the gap between 1837 and 1848. Chandler Hazen, Wilmot, and Fisher were products of a system that achieved most of the features of responsible government without the necessity of political parties. In addition, all preferred coalitions. Wilmot, moreover, was merely rejoining his colleagues of 1843 and 1844. The government formed in 1848 unquestionably had the support of the majority in the assembly and retained it until 1854.

Wilmot as attorney general (1848–1851) was a disappointment to even the most faithful. His principal achievement was an act for the consolidation of the criminal law, "a useful but not a brilliant work." Some practical changes were made to assist municipalities, and as chairman of the committee on agriculture he rendered good service. On the whole, however, Wilmot's primary function was to present and defend the position of the government in the assembly. There he frequently found himself on the receiving end of sharp barbs from former colleagues, especially William Johnstone Ritchie* of Saint John. On other occasions he took action not approved by

the government but which he seemed called upon to pursue to retain political support. Goaded by Ritchie, for instance, he pressed legislation to lower the salaries of public officials, especially those of judges. In general, it is difficult to find consistency in his stand on issues. He voted against Fisher's bill requiring members to vacate seats on accepting appointments. He supported railway construction, but saw no conflict of interest between the Intercolonial and the European and North American line to the United States. In 1850 he made the major speech at the Portland convention in support of the latter [see John Alfred POOR]; that same year he accompanied Head to Toronto to discuss the Intercolonial. Wilmot had attended the first British North American intercolonial conference at Halifax in 1849 and seems then to have become a supporter of a union. At that same conference he offered to throw the whole inshore fisheries open to the Americans in return for reciprocity, and in 1850 he and Head were in Washington to explore possibilities.

Wilmot was never defeated at the polls, but in the election of 1850 he barely scraped into the assembly. Fisher was defeated. Wilmot may well have come to view his position as precarious and have realized that he had lost touch with New Brunswick politics. Governor Head was not enamoured with him, especially after his action concerning the salaries of judges. "If the Attorney General choose to resign, because he is offended by the expression of my opinion," wrote Head to Grey, "he must do so." A defrocked Wilmot might be a menace in the house, but Head did not believe he would resign. An escape for both was provided with the resignation of the chief justice, Ward Chipman*, on 17 Oct. 1850.

"I expect My Government here to break up in a scramble for the Chief Justiceship," Head wrote a friend the same day. The scramble, with one exception, failed to take place; the exception was Wilmot. The Executive Council decided not to add to the bench, considering the three remaining judges adequate for the work. Only Fisher, Kinnear, and Alexander Rankin* dissented. The day the council made its decision, most of the members left Fredericton for their homes. That evening Wilmot composed a letter to Head: "I certainly think we have not acted wisely in the advice given by our minute today, and I am now disposed to retract the opinion therein expressed." The next day he read his letter to Head. The encounter made it clear that Head would decide "on his own responsibility and not necessarily on that of his Council," and that Wilmot would accept appointment to the bench regardless of any problems over responsibility or principle. Secretly, Head had James CARTER appointed the chief justice and Wilmot a puisne judge. In January 1851 this news was sprung on the province in a special edition of the *Royal Gazette*.

After all possible rationalizations have been considered, it remains that Head and Wilmot between them sacrificed the essence of responsible government. Yet only Fisher resigned from the council for the principle, and he had lost his seat in the assembly and had no choice. It may be that New Brunswick was not ready for responsible government; it is more likely that the system was not well served by the two men, Head and Wilmot, who had the power to make it succeed. The other members of the council served the principle no better, but they had not committed themselves to it as had Wilmot.

From 1851 until 1868 Wilmot was a judge; apparently he served well but gained little distinction. No great decisions are on the record nor are there any blotches. He remained before the public to a far greater degree than most judges, however, and his other interests brought him into prominence: the Methodist church, the militia, educational changes, and confederation.

Wilmot was the first non-conformist to hold the office of attorney general and to be appointed to the bench. For these reasons if for no others he would have been important among the dissenters, but he took his church work more seriously than any of his other endeavours. He was the main pillar of the Fredericton Methodist (now Wilmot United) Church. Following a fire in 1850 he headed a movement to construct a much larger church of modern design. He had in addition been choir director from 1845 and was superintendent of the Sabbath school for most of his adult life.

During these same years Wilmot gave frequent and popular public lectures. In Saint John in 1858 over 2,000 came to hear "The most eloquent lecture I have ever listened to." His range of subjects was quite wide. It might be "Havelock's March to Lucknow," the public school system, the evil of Darwin, or the dangers of alcohol, though he does not appear to have been a prohibitionist.

Wilmot's missionary zeal was kept for common schools. Undoubtedly he supported an education for everyone, but he wished to eliminate Roman Catholic influences from the schools. His strong anti-Catholic and anti-French positions were public knowledge. As a judge he was severely reprimanded for a speech on a priest who flogged a boy for reading the Bible. When he was lieutenant governor in the 1870s a public school act was passed – the product, according to the Catholic press, of Pope L. A. Wilmot and his half-dozen Methodist cardinals. Wilmot's view of the French had been stated firmly in 1837: "Lower Canada would [not] be tranquillised and restored to a proper state, till all the French distinguishing marks were utterly abolished, and the English laws, language and institutions, universally established throughout the Province."

As a young man Wilmot had joined the York County militia and quickly rose to the rank of major. When the Aroostook War threatened in 1838–39 Wilmot at the head of his troop was patrolling the banks of the Saint John River. That was as close as he got to battle; he remained ready, however, and was a battalion commander at the first militia camp in the province in 1862. Lieutenant Governor Arthur Hamilton Gordon* was favourably impressed and promoted him to lieutenant-colonel on 1 Jan. 1863.

Wilmot's public activity was most strikingly displayed when confederation, which he fully supported, was mooted. "Keep your eye on the Pacific," was his theme. Wilmot and Samuel Leonard Tilley*, the government leader in 1864, had come to know each other in the 1850s and had participated in a lecture series in 1860. Shortly after the Quebec conference, Tilley consulted Wilmot over an approach to the public. "You must not lay too much scope on the financial adjustments," he told Tilley. Stress the *"great future,"* and "national greatness." When Tilley was defeated by Albert James Smith* a few months later, Wilmot's position became uncomfortable. Smith reprimanded Wilmot for his strong pro-confederation statement before a grand jury. The office of chief justice twice became open and Wilmot was twice passed over, the second time for a junior judge and former antagonist, W. J. Ritchie. Even his cousin, Robert Duncan Wilmot*, who was on the Executive Council, could not assist him.

The eventual success of the confederation movement led to Wilmot's appointment as the first native-born lieutenant governor of New Brunswick. Tilley had written John A. Macdonald* on 3 Oct. 1867 requesting it, but it was not granted until nine months later, on 23 July 1868, and only after Tilley's continual pleadings. During his five years as lieutenant governor, Wilmot conducted himself well, pleasing even those who had been opposed to him. The University of New Brunswick, which owed much to him and on whose senate he served from 1860, awarded him an honorary DCL during this period.

Wilmot retired to his gardens at "Evelyn Grove," Fredericton, when Tilley succeeded him as lieutenant governor on 15 Nov. 1873. He served

Wilmot

on the commission to settle the Prince Edward Island land claims, and he was appointed arbitrator in the western Ontario boundary dispute. Before the commission got underway, he died of a heart attack on 20 May 1878.

Few New Brunswick figures are better known than Lemuel Allan Wilmot. He is bracketed with Joseph Howe, Robert Baldwin*, and Louis-Hippolyte La Fontaine* as a central personality in the struggle for responsible government. The city of Fredericton commemorates him with a church, a park, and several buildings. An examination of his career, curiously, does not reveal the reasons for this high reputation. As a politician and a judge he was not particularly notable. His legislative record was not impressive. His devotion to principles was tenuous at best, and he betrayed responsible government. How then can his eminence be explained? It seems to rest on three components.

As a public speaker Wilmot ranked with the best of his time. He thrilled audiences long after he had left the political scene and long after they had forgotten what his contribution had been. By the time he had become lieutenant governor, he was almost an institution.

Of more importance was his religion. He became prominent in his province as a non-conformist, proudly parading his religion all the way. In 1880 the Reverend John Lathern*, a Methodist clergyman and editor, wrote a eulogistic biography in which the whole of Wilmot's career was treated as a service to God, church, and country. Few New Brunswick politicians had biographies; no other was interpreted in providential terms. For over 25 years Lathern's remained the standard work on Wilmot. In 1907 James Hannay*, writing for the Makers of Canada series, started with Lathern's book as a solid foundation and erected on it the Whig-Liberal interpretation demanded by the series. Its preoccupation with responsible government as the great Canadian achievement assumed a Howe or a Baldwin in New Brunswick and Hannay obligingly produced Wilmot. Even with this sanguine approach, however, Hannay had difficulty forcing Wilmot into the mould. His humble youth and distinguished later years served admirably, but the main body of the career lacked the essential ingredients. In preparing the 1927 edition of the text, George Wilson felt it necessary to stress some of the problems in the preface and to add a 16-page appendix. The Hannay biography, nevertheless, remained unchanged. Sixty years after its publication it was still the authority.

Wilmot's reputation, in the final analysis, is decidedly inflated. He was a first-rate stump politician who failed to live up to the promise of his early career. His greatest success was in using his political influence to acquire prestigious appointments for himself – a practice that was normal in his era. His biographers, by attempting to create a man he never pretended to be, have spawned the view that he was a lesser man than he might have been.

C. M. WALLACE

[Lemuel Allan Wilmot's papers are scattered throughout other collections, and are incomplete. The following contain material on Wilmot: N.B. Museum, Edward Barron Chandler papers; Webster coll.; R. D. Wilmot, Record-books, 1868–85. PAC, MG 24, B29 (Howe papers); MG 26, A (Macdonald papers); MG 27, I, D15 (Tilley papers). PRO, CO 188 University of New Brunswick Library, Archives and Special Collections Department, Arthur Hamilton Gordon papers, 1861–66.

For printed primary sources see: New Brunswick, House of Assembly, Journals, 1835–50; Synoptic report of the proceedings, 1835–50. Globe (Saint John, N.B.), 1858–73. Morning Freeman (Saint John, N.B.), 1861–73. Morning News (Saint John, N.B.), 1839–65. New Brunswick Courier (Saint John, N.B.), 1842–62. New Brunswick Reporter (Fredericton), 1844–78.

Among printed sources G. E. Fenety's Political notes and observations is essential and his "Political notes," Progress (Saint John, N.B.), 1894, collected in a scrapbook at the N.B. Museum and PAC, are of some use. J. W. Lawrence's Judges of New Brunswick (Stockton) is also a valuable source.

Biographical notices of Wilmot appear in the following: Appleton's cyclopædia of American biography, ed. J. G. Wilson et al. (10v., New York, 1887–1924), VI; Dent, Canadian portrait gallery, III; DNB. The only two biographies of Wilmot were written by people who knew him: John Lathern, The Hon. Judge Wilmot: a biographical sketch, intro. D. D. Currie (rev. ed., Toronto, 1881), and James Hannay, Lemuel Allan Wilmot (Makers of Canada series, Anniversary ed., [VIII], London and Toronto, 1926). Hannay presents his view of Wilmot in a shorter form in his History of New Brunswick, II. Though useful, Lathern and Hannay must be approached with caution. W. S. MacNutt provides a major revision on Wilmot in New Brunswick: a history as does D. G. G. Kerr in Sir Edmund Head, a scholarly governor, with the assistance of J. A. Gibson (Toronto, 1954).

Of some use is G. E. Rogers, "The career of Edward Barron Chandler – a study in New Brunswick politics, 1827–1854," unpublished MA thesis, University of New Brunswick, 1953.

The following articles should be consulted: D. G. G. Kerr, "Head and responsible government in New Brunswick," CHA Report, 1938, 62–70; and W. S. MacNutt, "The coming of responsible government to New Brunswick," CHR, XXXIII (1952), 111–28; "New Brunswick's age of harmony, the administration of Sir John Harvey," CHR, XXXII (1951), 105–25; "The politics of the timber trade in colonial New Brunswick, 1825–40," CHR, XXX (1949), 47–65. C.M.W.]

WILSON, CHARLES, businessman, mayor of Montreal, politician; b. in April 1808 at Coteau-du-Lac (Soulanges County), L.C., son of Alexander Wilson and Catherine-Angélique d'Ailleboust de Manthet; d. 4 May 1877 at Montreal, Que.

Charles Wilson was a sort of microcosm of the Canadian population. Through his father, Alexander Wilson, a custom-house officer, he was linked with Scottish immigrants; through his mother, a d'Ailleboust, he had roots that were very "New France." And when on 19 May 1835 he married Ann Tracey, a sister of Dr Daniel Tracey*, the founder of the *Vindicator and Canadian Advertiser* (Montreal), he joined the Irish group.

He quickly made a start in business. Thanks to his intelligence and perseverance, a hardware store he set up in 1834 prospered. He subsequently became one of the directors of the Scottish Provincial Assurance Company.

Wilson was a sturdy little man, quick of gesture, and with a face framed in sidewhiskers, who established himself firmly in the life and society of Montreal; he was a Catholic who secured a prominent place, along with the Unitarian Francis Hincks*, in the St Patrick Society, which had been founded in 1834. Both of them, with Lewis Thomas Drummond*, instilled in the Montreal Irish a sense of pride and an awareness of their strength. Wilson was elected mayor of Montreal by acclamation in 1851, then again in the two following years, and on 23 Oct. 1852 was appointed member of the Legislative Council. He was thus in a position to exert on his two friends – Hincks, who had become prime minister, and Drummond, the attorney general east – a political influence not underestimated by the government's opponents.

On 24 Jan. 1852, in the debating hall of the municipal council at Bonsecours market, which had been inaugurated for the occasion as a town hall, Peter McGill*, one of Wilson's predecessors as mayor, presented him with a full-length portrait of himself by the Quebec artist Théophile Hamel*. Wilson could then measure the extent to which public opinion had evolved in his favour since 26 April 1849, when the mob had surged towards his house to shatter doors and windows: the assent given to the rebellion losses bill had provoked violent demonstrations at Montreal, and Wilson, no doubt because he was a friend of Louis-Hippolyte La Fontaine*, had not been spared.

But Wilson was fated to experience again the tribulation of unpopularity, at the time of the Gavazzi affair. Did he, on the evening of 9 June 1853, order the detachment of the 26th Scottish regiment, which had been dispatched to Zion Church to assist the hard-pressed municipal police, to open fire on the crowd as it streamed out of the temple after listening to the speech of the ex-Barnabite Alessandro Gavazzi*? The subsequent inquiry did not establish clearly who was the author of the fatal order, but Protestant journalists such as John Dougall* of the *Montreal Witness* persisted in accusing the mayor. On the morning of 2 August his full-length portrait, which hung in the hall of the municipal council, was found decapitated: in the canvas, in the place of Wilson's head, was a gaping hole, probably made with the help of a razor fastened to the end of a stick or cane! And when, in September 1855, at Bishop Ignace Bourget*'s request, Wilson received the cross of commander of the Order of St Gregory the Great from Pius IX, the Protestant press resumed its accusations against the man responsible for the "St Bartholomew of Montreal."

But Wilson had already left the mayoralty, having been replaced in this office in 1854 by Wolfred Nelson*. In May 1867 he was granted the title of senator and represented in the federal parliament the constituency of Rigaud. He died at Montreal on 4 May 1877.

PHILIPPE SYLVAIN

[Robert [Philippe] Sylvain, *Clerc, garibaldien, prédicant des deux mondes: Alessandro Gavazzi (1809–1889)* (2v., Québec 1962), II, 392–423; this work, based on an exhaustive study of the primary sources, places Wilson's actions as mayor in the context of a troubled and significant time in Montreal's history. P.S.]

Thérèse Archambault-Lessard, "Alexandre et Thomas Wilson," *BRH*, XLII (1936), 347–55.

WILSON, WILLIAM MERCER, judge and freemason; b. 12 or 24 Aug. 1813 at "Mavisbank," the family estate in Perthshire, Scotland, son of Graeme Mercer; d. 16 Jan. 1875, at Simcoe, Ont.

William Mercer was adopted by his mother's brother, and William took his name, Wilson. He emigrated to Canada in 1832 and settled at Nanticoke in what is now Haldimand County. In 1834 he moved to Simcoe and was appointed commissioner to the Court of Requests in the Talbot District. In the same year he married Jane Brown, by whom he had 10 children. She died about 1849. During the rebellion in Upper Canada in 1837–38 he commanded the Norfolk Cavalry troop, which he had organized, and joined Allan MacNab* at Scotland, following him to Chippawa where he participated in the capture of the *Caroline*. He was gazetted lieutenant-colonel of the 3rd Battalion Norfolk militia in 1848 and retired from it with that rank in 1869.

In 1838 Wilson became clerk of the peace and clerk of the court for the Talbot District and

Woods

accumulated other minor posts. He began the study of law, and in 1853 was called to the bar. His law practice flourished and he became active in local political affairs. During the 1860s he was elected reeve of Simcoe for five years and warden of Norfolk County for two years. He continued as clerk of the peace until 1858 when he was appointed crown attorney for the county. On 5 May 1868 he became judge of the county court.

Wilson's career indicates a wide variety of interests. In 1840 he had imported the first printing press into the Talbot District and founded at Simcoe the *Norfolk Observer*, which he conducted for about two years, He helped form the St Andrew's Society in 1842 and was president of it and of the Mechanics' Institute. In 1851 he was a delegate of the Provincial Agricultural Association to a meeting in London, England. Wilson's association with freemasonry began in 1840. He was initiated into Lodge no.14 (the Norfolk Lodge) at Simcoe and eight years later he was named grand senior warden of the Provincial Grand Lodge. When the Grand Lodge of Canada West was formed, independent of the Grand Lodge of England, in October 1855, Wilson became the first grand master. It was largely through his encouragement that the rival Ancient Grand Lodge under Sir Allan MacNab, which was formed from the Provincial Grand Lodge when it too broke away from the English lodge, joined the Grand Lodge of Canada in 1858. Wilson was grand master until 1860 and was again elected to this position for 1866–68 and from 1872 until his death in 1875. He had married in London, England, Susan Grace Codner by whom he had three children. She died in 1855 and he married Mary Elizabeth Dixon; they had one daughter.

ANNE E. F. SNIDERMAN

J. of Education for Ont., XXVIII (1875), 42. *Militia list for Canada West* . . . , comp. Joshua Thompson (Toronto, 1851). G. D. Maxwell, *The first one hundred years: a history of Wilson Lodge A.F. & A.M., no.86, Grand Lodge of Canada in the Province of Ontario, 1857–1957* (n.p., n.d.). B. M. Pearce, *First grand master: a biography of William Mercer Wilson, first grand master of the Grand Lodge of Canada A.F. & A.M.* (Simcoe, Ont., 1932). *Simcoe and Norfolk County; in commemoration of the Simcoe reunion of Norfolk County old boys, August 2nd to 7th, 1924* (Simcoe, Ont., 1924).

WOODS, JOSEPH, newspaper editor and proprietor, printer, and politician; b. at St John's, Nfld., in 1813, son of Joseph and Mary Woods; d. at St John's in March 1871.

Of Joseph Woods' early life we know only that he was born into an Anglican family and that his parents were converted to Methodism while he was still a child. In 1843, in St John's, Joseph Woods and William James Ward became proprietors of the *Morning Post*. The partnership was dissolved on 14 May 1846; Ward became sole proprietor of the *Morning Post* and Woods purchased the *Morning Courier* (*Courier* after 1855) from Ebenezer Winton. In addition to editing the *Courier*, Woods was compiler, printer, and publisher of the *Newfoundland Almanac*.

The *Morning Courier*, a semi-weekly established in 1844 by William Beck, carried local and foreign news but became much more political in tone with Woods as editor. As early as 1847 he declared himself in favour of the principles of responsible government. In supporting this Liberal demand Woods was an exception among Wesleyans, most of whom supported the Conservatives. He admitted that his primary goal was to gain a share of government patronage for the Wesleyans, who "generally are poor," from the Episcopalians, who "generally are rich." The Liberal press, including the *Morning Courier*, suggested to the Wesleyans that their interests would be promoted by joining the Roman Catholics in the struggle for responsible government. In the crucial 1855 general election, just before the introduction of responsible government, Woods was defeated as a Liberal candidate in the district of Burin. However, as the Liberals won a majority in the House of Assembly, the *Courier* duly received a share of much-needed printing jobs and Woods continued to give his paper a Liberal bias. Accordingly in 1861 it opposed the dismissal of John KENT's government, violently criticized the Conservative and Protestant government of Hugh William Hoyles*, but supported the coalition of Frederic Bowker Terrington Carter* and Ambrose Shea* which followed. When confederation became the issue, Woods advocated union with "*increasing warmth*" until July 1869 when he suddenly switched allegiance to the anti-confederate party led by Charles Fox Bennett*. This change created the suspicion that the *Courier* was being subsidized by Bennett. Woods said he was convinced that confederation had brought no real benefits to the mainland provinces and that Newfoundland would not suffer by remaining outside the union.

A prominent Wesleyan, Joseph Woods was a member of the Wesleyan Methodist School Society and the St John's Day School Committee. He was married and had two daughters. After his death the *Courier* and the *Newfoundland Almanac* continued to be published by his brother John on behalf of Joseph's widow and children.

ELIZABETH A. WELLS

Newfoundland, Department of Provincial Affairs, "List of affidavits of proprietorship of newspapers," 1836–1900. *Courier* (St John's), 1847–72. *Morning Chronicle* (St John's), 4 March 1871. *Telegraph* (St John's), 8 March 1871. *The Newfoundland almanac, for ... 1858 ...*, comp. Joseph Woods (St John's, 1857). *The Newfoundland almanac for ... 1877 ...* (St John's, 1876). E. C. Moulton, "The political history of Newfoundland, 1861–1869," unpublished MA thesis, Memorial University of Newfoundland, 1960. E. A. Wells, "The struggle for responsible government in Newfoundland, 1846–1855," unpublished MA thesis, Memorial University of Newfoundland, 1966.

WORKMAN, WILLIAM, merchant, businessman, and mayor of Montreal; b. May 1807, at Ballymacash near Lisburn, County Antrim, Ireland; fifth of nine children of Joseph Workman and Catherine Goudie; d. 23 Feb. 1878 in Montreal, Que.

William Workman was born to a family whose fortunes, once considerable, had apparently declined. There is no evidence concerning William's schooling; however, he had mastered the skills for employment with the Ordnance Survey of Ireland from 1827 to 1829.

His older brothers, Benjamin, Alexander, Samuel, Thomas*, and Matthew, had left Ireland before the rest of the family set sail for Canada in 1829. Soon after his arrival in Montreal, William was employed by a newspaper, the *Canadian Courant and Montreal Advertiser*, owned by his brother Benjamin and Nahum Mower. In 1830 William joined brother Thomas in the wholesale hardware house of John Frothingham. The Workmans rose quickly in the firm; by 1836 William and Thomas had become full partners, an indication perhaps that they had brought some capital into the firm. Until his retirement from the concern in 1859, it provided Workman's business base. As well as handling imported items, Frothingham and Workman manufactured some hardware in their Montreal factories which employed hundreds of men.

Workman did not confine his business interests to hardware, however. He was typical of the Montreal business community of that period in his involvement in ventures stimulated by growth and technological change. The scale of Workman's speculation in railways, land, and banking is evidence of his wealth by the early 1840s. Among his interests was the City Bank, a Montreal institution of which he was president from 1849 to 1874. His investments in railways included Canada's first railway, the Champlain and St Lawrence, completed in 1836 to connect Laprairie, on the

St Lawrence River opposite Montreal, to Saint-Jean on the Richelieu. This 14-mile railway was designed to facilitate trade between the St Lawrence and the neighbouring states; Workman was one of its directors. Attracted also to the St Lawrence and Atlantic Railroad [*see* John YOUNG], he was one of the largest shareholders when the line was taken over by the Grand Trunk in 1854. A less successful railway venture was the abortive Montreal and Bytown [*see* Alexandre-Maurice DELISLE].

Workman also invested heavily in Montreal real estate. In the early 1840s he bought a large number of lots in a fashionable west-end residential suburb, where he built his own impressive mansion, Mount Prospect, in 1842. He had considerable property elsewhere in Montreal, and with Delisle bought a sizeable tract on its western outskirts. Workman ventured also into shipping, when in 1854, with Montreal businessmen David TORRANCE, Andrew Shaw, Ira Gould, and John Kershaw, he established the Canadian Ocean Steam Navigation Company. A year later, Workman purchased two large steamboats for the St Lawrence trade.

Although business was clearly Workman's major concern for many years, after his retirement from Frothingham and Workman in 1859 he took an active interest in public affairs. As a banker, he combatted the government's proposed measures to widen its fiscal powers during the late 1860s. In 1866, he attacked Alexander Tilloch Galt*'s recommendations for tariff reductions, "these wild Balaklava dashes at fiscal legislation" which would entail "beggary or emigration" for many Canadians. As a manufacturer, Workman had favoured high protective tariffs since the late 1840s when he led the Association for the Promotion of Canadian Industry. He made no known attempts to enter provincial politics but took an interest in federal affairs after confederation. During the 1870s, perhaps goaded by his brother Thomas' attachment to the Liberals who, in William's view, were scented with "a spice of Communism," Workman wrote occasionally to John A. Macdonald* reminding him of his loyalty and contributions of "the ready" to the party. The letters were little more than importunate pleas for a Senate seat.

Workman was best known in Montreal for his municipal political activity and his local philanthropy. He was nominated for mayor in February 1868 and ran against Jean-Louis Beaudry*, a former incumbent. Workman won the contest easily after overcoming disqualification and serious allegations of corruption levelled against him by his opponent. So popular was he as

Wright

Montreal's mayor, that he was returned to the post by acclamation in 1869 and 1870.

Workman was a well-known local figure even before he became mayor. Many years earlier, he had been president of the St Patrick's Society before it became an exclusively Roman Catholic organization in 1856. Transferring his deep concern for the welfare of the less fortunate to the Irish Protestant Benevolent Society, Workman served it for years, giving money and time to its causes. He helped to establish the Montreal Protestant House of Industry and Refuge in 1864; he served as its president from 1874 to 1877 and left the institution a legacy of $20,000. To encourage thrift and saving among the city's workingmen, Workman helped to found the Montreal City and District Savings Bank in 1846 [see Marc-Damase MASSON]. He was the bank's first president, 1846–52, and a director, 1861–72.

Workman's private life was touched with much sorrow. Five children predeceased him and the loss of his only son, at age 24, was especially painful. Throughout most of his adult life, Workman was an adherent of the Unitarian church; he once confided to a friend that, as a Unitarian, he was "accustomed to vituperation from opposing Protestant sects (never from Roman Catholics)." According to one source, he later found solace in Roman Catholicism. He turned increasingly to private worship and had a family chapel added to his large mansion.

G. TULCHINSKY

PAC, MG 24 B40 (Brown papers), 4, p.778; D16 (Buchanan papers), 63, Workman; MG 26, A (Macdonald papers), 345, pp.158327–30; 346, pp.158526–30; RG 12, AI, 176, pp.137–38. [Bruce and Grey], *Elgin-Grey papers* (Doughty), IV, 1492. Canada, Province of, Legislative Assembly, *Journals*, 1851, app.UU, "Proceedings of the standing committee on rail-roads and telegraph lines; together with the minutes of evidence ordered by the committee to be printed"; 1857, app.6, "Report of the special committee appointed to inquire and report as to the condition, management, and prospects of the Grand Trunk Railway Company." Canada, Province of, *Statutes*, 1854, c.45. *Report of the committee appointed to enquire into the transactions of the Montreal and Bytown Railway Company, prepared by Mr. Loranger, by order of the committee, and unanimously adopted* (Toronto, 1856), 51. *Gazette* (Montreal), 25 Feb. 1878. *Montreal Herald*, 2 Dec. 1867; 10, 18, 21–23, 25 Jan., 18, 21, 25, 26, 28 Feb., 2 March 1868; 13 Feb. 1869; 13, 14 Feb. 1870.

Montreal directory (Mackay), 1845–46, 286; 1852, 353. Borthwick, *Montreal*, 123. Campbell, *Hist. of Scotch Presbyterian Church*, 436, 439. T. T. Smyth, *The first hundred years; history of the Montreal City and District Savings Bank, 1846–1946* (n.p., n.d.), 22. F. J. Workman, "The Workman family history" (manuscript in the possession of its author). Brian Cahill, "90-year-old papers found in cornerstone," *Gazette* (Montreal), 5 July 1955. Allan Cook, "Ancient chapel built here for spite still stands as reminder of bygone feuds," *Montreal Daily Star*, 12 Aug. 1937.

WRIGHT, WILLIAM, shipbuilder and shipowner; b. post 1800, probably in Scotland; d. a bachelor 17 Feb. 1878, probably in Liverpool, Eng.

William Wright and his younger brother Richard (b. before 1816, probably in Scotland; m. 4 May 1837 to Jane Nevins by whom he had two daughters; d. 12 Aug. 1872 in London, Eng.) made a modest beginning in the shipping industry. They apprenticed to the Saint John, New Brunswick, shipbuilder, George Thomson, for whom they may have worked after putting in their time. By the summer of 1839 they had set up their own shipbuilding yard at Courtenay Bay, Saint John. That autumn they launched three vessels, a whaling ship, a paddle steamer, and a timber ship. This was an ambitious start which placed them in the company of the best Saint John builders. During their initial eight years of operation the Wrights built 15 vessels averaging 567 tons. The first eight were either constructed for, or sold before registration to, local merchants, but five of the subsequent ships were registered, owned, and managed by the Wrights for very short periods, no doubt to take timber cargoes to Liverpool. There was considerable inducement for a shipbuilder to extend his operations to include shipowning because in delivering his vessel to be sold at Liverpool the revenue from the timber cargo could amount to a third of the cost of building the ship. In 1844 Richard started sailing as master or captain on the maiden voyages to Liverpool – at least 16 uneventful crossings of the Atlantic were a tribute to his seamanship. Not only were the masters' wages saved, but agency fees for selling the vessels or arranging freights could be eliminated.

In 1847 the Wrights moved permanently into shipowning with two of the three ships they built that year, the two ships being their first to exceed 1,000 tons. That year marked the beginning of the period in which William and Richard Wright were unrivalled in British North America as builders of the biggest class of wooden ships. Their second 15 ships averaged 1,352 tons each with not less than 3,000 tons of shipping launched yearly from their yard from 1849 until 1855. The climax in the Wrights' shipbuilding career came with their last two ships – the 2,339 ton *White Star* in 1854 and her slightly larger twin in 1855, the 2,379 ton *Morning Light*. Easily the largest British

North American sailing ships, they were built to excel on the highly competitive emigrant run to Australia. The Wrights retained 21 of the 64 shares of the *White Star* for two and a half years and full ownership of the *Morning Light*. Perhaps the principal evidence of the quality of these ships was that they far exceeded the normal life-span of North American vessels, lasting 30 and 35 years respectively.

By the end of 1857 the Wrights had increased their fleet to ten ships. William remained at Saint John for a decade, but Richard, despite toying with an invitation he apparently received from Samuel Leonard Tilley* to enter New Brunswick politics, was mainly in Liverpool after 1857. Like the majority of the large New Brunswick and Nova Scotian vessels, the Wright ships were operated not from their port of registration but from Liverpool. Their smaller ships of about 1,000 tons were generally kept on the North Atlantic. Outbound cargoes, particularly for ports in the Maritime provinces, were often difficult to obtain, but there were ready supplies of timber, oil, and cotton for the return voyages. Their larger ships were in the Far East bulk trades.

In 1857 and 1858 the Wrights ran into a cash shortage which apparently stopped their expansion temporarily. They mortgaged six ships for £51,930. This sum represented 51 per cent of the Wright tonnage and therefore the Wright fleet can be reasonably estimated to have been valued at that time at £100,000 or $400,000. During the 1860s they slowly expanded their fleet and continued the shipbroking of Saint John ships.

Perhaps in recognition that the market for wooden ships was drying up, William joined his brother at Liverpool in the spring of 1867, and their ships registered at Saint John were re-registered at Liverpool. In the two previous years they had participated in the trend into iron ships, buying three, and in 1869 they purchased their only large screw steamer.

When Richard died in 1872, the Wright fleet was at its largest, 17 ships totalling more than 23,000 tons. William thereafter reduced the number of ships to 11. At his death in 1878 the firm was inherited by his nephew George Wright Gass

who had been working in the Liverpool office. Under Gass the dilution of ownership and reduction in the number of ships were accelerated to such a point that W. and R. Wright and Company ceased at his death in 1887.

RICHARD RICE

N.B. Museum, Marriage register B (1828–39), 420; Tilley family papers, Richard Wright to S. L. Tilley, 1 Jan. 1858; Wright family deeds, 1859–1912, numerous documents including typescript of the will of Richard Wright, 5 Oct. 1871, typescript of probate of will of William Wright, 24 March 1885. Registry of British Ships, HM Customs and Excise, Custom House (Liverpool, Eng.), Liverpool Registers, 1835–90. *Commercial News and General Advertiser* (Saint John, N.B.), 16 Sept. 1839. *Liberal Review* (Liverpool), 2 Feb., 16 Aug., 4 Oct. 1879. *Liverpool Mercury*, 14 Aug. 1872. *Liverpool Telegraph and Shipping Gazette*, 28 Aug. 1863. *New Brunswick Courier* (Saint John, N.B.), 16 Jan. 1841. *Saint John Daily News*, 13 Aug. 1872. *Sea Breezes; the Ship Lovers' Digest* (Liverpool), XXIII (April 1938), 34; (May 1938), 75; (November 1938), 300–2; (December 1938), 340–41, 354; XXIV (March 1939), 466. *Times* (London), 14 Aug. 1872. F. W. Wallace, *Record of Canadian shipping: a list of square-rigged vessels, mainly 500 tons and over, built in the eastern provinces of British North America from the year 1786 to 1920* (Toronto, 1929). E. A. Woods, "Liverpool fleet lists," I, 35–38 (typescript compiled *c.* 1939, copy in Liverpool City Libraries, Liverpool, Eng.). R. S. Craig, "British shipping and British North American shipbuilding in the early nineteenth century with special reference to Prince Edward Island," in *The south-west and the sea*, ed. H. E. S. Fisher (Exeter Papers in Economic History, 1, Exeter, Eng., 1968), 21–43. Wallace, *Wooden ships and iron men*. D. M. Williams, "The function of the merchant in specific Liverpool import trades, 1820–50," unpublished MA thesis, University of Liverpool, 1963. P. R. Lindo, "The whale fishing industry of Saint John," N.B. Museum, *Hist. Bull.*, XIV, no.3 (1967). Donald Ross, "History of the shipbuilding industry in New Brunswick," essay awarded the James Simonds prize in history by University of New Brunswick, 1933 (copy in N.B. Museum). A. C. Wardle, "The ship 'Thomas' of Liverpool," Liverpool Nautical Research Society, *Trans.*, I (1944), 14–22. D. M. Williams, "Merchanting in the first half of the nineteenth century: the Liverpool timber trade," *Business History* (Liverpool), VIII (1966), 103–21.

Y

YALE, JAMES MURRAY, HBC chief trader; b.*c.* 1798 at Lachine, L.C.; d. at Saanich, near Victoria, B.C., on 7 May 1871.

James Murray Yale entered the service of the Hudson's Bay Company in 1815 and was first

stationed at Fort Wedderburn on Lake Athabasca. This post had just been built by John Clarke* in an effort to secure a foothold for the HBC in Athabasca, the great stronghold of the North West Company. It was subjected to constant harassment by the NWC's large staff at nearby Fort Chipewyan. Violence reached a climax when Archibald Norman McLeod* was in charge there; Clarke was twice arrested and Yale himself was seized in April 1817, taken to Great Slave Lake, and detained there until the autumn. In 1818 he was with Joshua Halcro* when he built Colvile House on the Peace River for the HBC.

In 1821 Yale was put in charge of Fort George on the Fraser River, and he spent the rest of his long career west of the Rocky Mountains. He was at Fort George until 1824, and later served at Fort Alexandria and at Fort St James. Unwell in 1827, he was sent to Fort Vancouver where medical attention was available. A year later he was back at Fort St James and there met Governor George Simpson*, who was on an inspection trip and was anxious to explore the Fraser River as a possible transport route to the coast. Yale accompanied him, and while Simpson travelled overland to Kamloops and returned to the Fraser down the Thompson River, Yale explored the Fraser itself from Alexandria to the mouth of the Thompson. From there he went through the main canyon of the Fraser with Simpson on a trip that was rivalled only by that of Simon Fraser* in 1808.

Yale left the party at Fort Langley, where he was to spend more than 30 years. After serving under James McMillan*, who had founded the post, and Archibald McDonald*, Yale was placed in charge of Fort Langley in 1833. In 1839 he supervised the construction of new buildings about two and a half miles upstream from the original site. These were burned in April 1840, and Yale had to rebuild the post a second time. He was appointed chief trader in 1844. Although never a chief factor he was well regarded by the company, and Fort Yale, built upstream from Fort Langley in 1848, was named after him.

By this time very few furs were being traded at Fort Langley, but Yale fought successfully against any proposal that it should be abandoned and he developed other resources that justified its continued existence. He was a pioneer in the packing of salt fish on the Fraser; his first efforts were made soon after 1830, and in 1850 some 2,000 barrels of salmon were packed at the fort. Yale also developed much the largest farms then existing on the mainland of what is now British Columbia. The crops included grain, potatoes, and vegetables; much of the produce was sent to the posts of the Russian American Company in Alaska, under the terms of its trading agreement with the HBC. Yale's chief assistant at Fort Langley for many years was Ovid Allard who later was in charge for a decade.

When the Fraser River gold rush erupted sud-

denly in the spring of 1858, Fort Langley was the only settlement on the lower river and it became a scene of great activity. It was intended at first to locate the capital of the new colony of British Columbia on the original site of Fort Langley, and the colony was proclaimed there on 19 Nov. 1858. The plan was abandoned in February in favour of New Westminster, but it had occasioned much turmoil and excitement with which Yale dealt competently. He retired in May 1859, and after a brief visit to Montreal settled on Stromness Farm, in Saanich, on Vancouver Island.

The name of Yale's wife seems not to have been recorded. They had three daughters, one of whom married a son of Sir George Simpson. A much liked character, Yale was known as "Little Yale" because of his short stature about which he was sensitive. Chief Factor James Douglas, his superior in the HBC, a big man, took a quiet delight in standing near Yale and observing his discomfiture. In his famous "Character Book" Governor Simpson devoted an entry to Yale: "A sharp active well conducted very little man but full of fire with the courage of a Lion. Deficient in Education, but has a good deal of address & Management with Indians and notwithstanding his diminutive size is more feared and respected than some of our 6 feet men."

W. Kaye Lamb

HBC Arch. A.34/2. HBRS, I (Rich), 473–74; X (Rich). "Fort Langley correspondence," ed. R. L. Reid, BCHQ, I (1937), 187–94. R. L. Reid, "Early days at old Fort Langley: economic beginnings in British Columbia," BCHQ, I (1937), 71–85.

YOUNG, JOHN, merchant, business promoter, and manufacturer; b. 30 Jan. 1808, Galston, Ayrshire, Scotland, youngest son of James Young, merchant in Galston, and Margaret Mason; d. 20 March 1873, Hamilton, Ont.

In 1825, after finishing his education in Galston, John Young opened a small hardware business in nearby Kilmarnock with his brother James. Seemingly it did not prosper, and Young soon sought other employment. In 1828 he secured a post with Pollok, Gilmour and Company, Glasgow shipowners and timber merchants [see John Gilmour], who sent him to clerk in their new Montreal branch, William Ritchie and Company. William Ritchie* decided in 1832 to open a branch in Hamilton, which, though a small community, seemed best located to capture the trade of Upper Canada's rapidly developing west. To run the new store, he chose John Young, whose ambition, ability, and, perhaps, modest capital made him an ideal manager. The business, known briefly as Young and Weir, then as John Young and Company, retailed dry goods, groceries, and hardware, sought wholesaling business in the west, and bought or solicited consignments of wheat, flour, staves, and ashes for William Ritchie and Company.

The west grew rapidly; Hamilton's population, reflecting this growth, doubled twice in five years, and Young, with his strong financial support, took full advantage of his opportunities. But then his senior partners quarrelled, and the future became uncertain. In 1840, Peter* and Isaac Buchanan*, Toronto's leading wholesalers, were establishing a Hamilton branch; to strengthen its management and remove a competitor, they asked Young to join them. He quickly accepted, for Isaac Buchanan had full financial support in Glasgow and offered the opportunity of certain expansion. In June 1840 Isaac Buchanan and Young opened Buchanan, Harris and Company, whose store Peter Buchanan described as "the largest establishment in British North America."

Young's capital in 1840 totalled $22,000. During his association with the Buchanans the business continued to grow with the west and his capital increased to well over $120,000. In the 1850s, Young and the Buchanans' Montreal partner, James Law, sought greater recognition in the firm. Increasingly heated conflict with the Buchanans ensued, and late in 1853 Young and Law withdrew from the Buchanan firms to establish Young, Law and Company in Hamilton and Glasgow, and Law, Young and Company in Montreal. Glasgow, where both men were well known in mercantile circles, was their centre for finance and buying; their Hamilton outlet, under Young, sold wholesale groceries and dry goods; and the Montreal firm, under Law, sold wholesale groceries and hardware, dealt in Upper Canadian produce, and forwarded goods to Hamilton. Prosperity during the next three years, the peak of the 1850s boom, enabled Young and Law to establish their business solidly.

Like other successful merchants in Canada, Young was anxious to develop new financial institutions. A large shareholder in the Gore Bank, he was elected to its first board in 1836. He resigned his directorship in 1837 to protest lending policy, gained re-election after the crisis of 1837–38, but resigned in the early 1840s to save his own business reputation after again failing to force the Gore to alter its policy of lending heavily to its own directors. In 1847 he took the leading part in founding the Canada Life Assurance Company; for the next 20 years he was its vice-president and then, for five years, its president.

Although Young subscribed to the abortive London and Gore Railroad Company in 1834 and,

through his connection with the Buchanans, played some part in the promotion of its successor, the Great Western, railways were not one of his central interests until 1856. Then, discontented British stockholders, seeking to consolidate the Great Western, began a revolution in the Great Western Railway Company. They asked Young, a minor shareholder untainted by previous involvement, to become vice-president of the railway and chairman of its Canadian board. He held both posts for ten years and was also a director of the Hamilton and Lake Erie Railway. In 1850, Young organized the Hamilton Gas Light Company, and for the next 23 years he was its president. He was a member of the executive of the Hamilton Board of Trade from its founding in 1845 until his death, and served as president from 1846 to 1852 and again in 1857–58.

In 1835, Young married Anne Coleman, daughter of an English gentleman farming at Paris, Upper Canada, and had several children by her. He captained a militia company in 1837. As his family, wealth, and social standing grew during the 1840s, he built Undermount, a large home on the newly fashionable mountainside of Hamilton. Outside business, his leading interest was the Church of Scotland. In 1833 he helped found St Andrew's Church in Hamilton and, in the 1850s, he contributed heavily to its building fund; for many years he was its trustee and senior elder. He helped to found in Hamilton the Mechanics' Institute, the Mercantile Library Association, and the Protestant Orphan Asylum. Young never took an active role in politics; although he was friendly with Allan MacNab*, he rejected compact Toryism and was always a moderate Conservative.

Like all businesses in Upper Canada, Young's was hard hit by the commercial crisis in 1857–58. After the crisis, Hamilton's trade failed to revive and the city's challenge to Toronto and Montreal as a wholesaling centre was over. Young, Law and Company wrote off much capital, but the firm survived, and, by 1866, Young was ready to retire from trade. Three employees, Alexander Thomson, William Birkett, and John Bell, took over the dry goods business, and the grocery business was wound up completely. Young now turned to manufacturing, taking over Joseph Wright's Dundas Cotton Mills. This transition was most unusual for someone of Young's mercantile eminence, and it must be assumed that he acted to rescue tied-up capital, probably invested originally by Young, Law and Company as short-term commercial credit which Wright could not repay. Young, Law and Company continued in being, as manufacturers instead of traders.

By 1873, Young was said to have succeeded as a

Young

manufacturer, and he remained president of Canada Life and the Gas Light Company. At the time of his death he was at the head of Hamilton's business community, a community whose growth he had done much to foster.

DOUGLAS MCCALLA

Hamilton Public Library, A. W. Roy, "Newspaper clippings scrapbook," 13. PAC, MG 24, D16 (Buchanan papers). City of Hamilton, *Directories*, 1853, 1856, 1858, 1862, 1865–66, 1870, 1871–72, 1872–73. City of Hamilton and county of Wentworth, *Directories*, 1867–68, 1868–69. Great Western Railway of Canada, *Report of the directors*, 1852, 1856–66. *Scobie & Balfour's Canadian almanac, and repository of useful knowledge* . . . (Toronto), 1850–52. M. F. Campbell, *A mountain and a city, the story of Hamilton* (Toronto, 1966). A. W. Currie, *The Grand Trunk Railway of Canada* (Toronto, 1957). C. M. Johnston, *The head of the lake, a history of Wentworth County* (Hamilton, Ont., 1958). John Rankin, *A history of our firm, being some account of the firm of Pollok, Gilmour and Co. and its offshoots and connections, 1804–1920* (2nd ed., Liverpool, 1921). Ross and Trigge, *History of the Canadian Bank of Commerce*, I. [W. J. Shaw], *A century of service; St. Paul's Church (Presbyterian), Hamilton, Ontario* (Hamilton, Ont., 1933). G. R. Stevens, *Canadian National Railways* (2v., Toronto, 1960), I. J. R. Holden, "Historical data re state and church in the county of Wentworth," Wentworth Hist. Soc. *Papers and Records* (Hamilton, Ont.), III (1902), 44–71.

YOUNG, JOHN, businessman, entrepreneur, and politician; b. 11 March 1811 at Ayr, Scotland, son of William Young, a cooper, and Janet Gibson; d. 12 April 1878 at Montreal, Que.

John Young completed studies at Ayr Academy in 1824. At 14, he became a teacher in the parish school at Coylton, a small village near Ayr. After a year, Young left Scotland for Upper Canada, arriving in 1826 and going directly to Kingston to work with a local merchant named MacLeod. In the early 1830s he moved to Montreal to the Torrances' wholesale merchanding firm. At this time the firm, established by John* and Thomas Torrance*, was also active in the steamboat business along the St Lawrence between Montreal and Quebec, and it offered Young ample opportunity to learn the Canadian import and export business and to formulate views of how St Lawrence trade could be improved.

After several years as a clerk, Young was elevated to partnership with David TORRANCE, a nephew of John. The two young men managed the family's Quebec business between 1835 and 1840. The partnership ended in 1840 and Young formed a new firm, Stephens, Young and Company, with Harrison Stephens*, a Vermonter who had been importing rice, tobacco, and other American goods to Montreal since 1832. The partners probably continued the specialized importing trade begun by Stephens, but in any case handled large quantities of western staples as commission merchants. The firm also had a general merchandising trade, and Young's prime job was to travel west to Ohio, Illinois, Indiana, and Michigan buying produce and arranging for its storage, shipment, insurance, and, often, the milling of wheat into flour. The scale of the firm's operations is not known, but they were apparently remunerative. On 31 Aug. 1846 the partnership was terminated by mutual consent and Stephens left the company, but the firm continued importing American goods. Young also formed a partnership with Benjamin Holmes* of Montreal, formerly cashier of the Bank of Montreal; their firm seems to have had extensive trade with Chicago, acting as a receiver of products and as a supplier of imported manufactured goods.

Although Young came to be known as an untiring – and tiresome – crusader for the Caughnawaga canal, and a proponent of improvements to Montreal's waterways, he was cognizant of the potential importance of railways in improving Montreal's competitive strength for the trade of the interior. He was informed about economic developments elsewhere and, as an early member of the Mercantile Library Association of Montreal, encouraged the city's business community to read business periodicals and books from Britain and the United States. With other Montrealers, Young was an early participant in the St Lawrence and Atlantic Railroad Company, authorized to build a line from Montreal to Portland, Maine, in 1845. A director from 1847 until 1851, he supported Alexander Tilloch Galt* in raising capital by placing the company's bonds with London bankers.

Young was an active supporter of Louis-Hippolyte La Fontaine* in the 1847 elections and may have helped the railway gain favourable legislation in 1849 from the new Reform ministry. To Young, the St Lawrence and Atlantic promised communication to a winter port and a probable lessening of transportation costs to the ocean. Young also favoured the Intercolonial Railway scheme of the early 1850s, by the Saint John River route.

Another railway venture supported by Young was the St Lawrence and Ottawa Grand Junction, chartered in 1850 to build a line from Lachine west to Prescott. This project was unsuccessful but Young, undismayed, dabbled in other railway ventures. In 1854, supported by Augustin-Norbert Morin*, Galt, and John Alfred POOR, associates from the St Lawrence and Atlantic, he unsuccessfully petitioned the Canadian government for a charter to build a railway to the Pacific by the Ottawa valley and the south shore of Lake Superior. Never a strong nationalist, Young preferred a transcontinental rail line south of Lake Superior, which would link with the Northern Pacific at Duluth. He rejected military or political considerations and argued that the Pacific route should be determined solely on the basis of commercial benefits. To build north of Lake Superior "for no better reason, than it must be on British territory, and on a line as far as possible from our American neighbours, seems to us to be not a little absurd."

Young also assisted Father François-Xavier-Antoine Labelle*'s efforts in the 1860s and early 1870s to build the Montreal Northern Colonization Railway to Saint-Jérôme and Ottawa. As early as 1856 he had been interested in Joseph-Édouard Cauchon*'s plans for the North Shore Railway from Quebec to Montreal. Young had been among the first to see the need for a bridge at Montreal to bring a railway from the south shore to the city's harbour and from 1845 he urged the construction of Victoria Bridge, completed ultimately in 1860 [see James HODGES]. He used his position as harbour commissioner to promote on the North Shore's behalf a new bridge over the St Lawrence. Despite objections from his fellow commissioners, the Montreal Board of Trade, and the Corn Exchange that the proposed Royal Albert Bridge was a "serious danger and obstruction to the navigation of the river and Harbour," Young in 1876, unsuccessfully, carried his minority opinion to Ottawa. Not insignificant in his long support for this railway were lots in Montreal's east end which he held for speculation.

Throughout his life, Young's favourite transportation scheme was the Caughnawaga canal. He had been delighted with the St Lawrence canals when they were opened in 1848, and he believed that to ensure their success another canal should be built from the St Lawrence to Lake Champlain. This canal, he claimed, would greatly improve Montreal's attractiveness as an *entrepôt*. After some discussion of the canal in the legislature, an engineer was appointed to recommend the best route. Then a campaign was undertaken to promote public interest and government assistance. The Montreal Board of Trade favoured such a canal but did not wish it to be built from Caughnawaga several miles upstream from Montreal for fear it would injure the city's *entrepôt* trade. The board refrained, therefore, from requesting government aid. The government, labouring under its responsibilities for canals and rail-

ways, was probably reluctant to build a controversial canal whose estimated cost was £500,000. Young believed that it could be financed privately and in 1849, with Montreal businessmen Harrison Stephens, Luther Hamilton HOLTON, William Bristow*, and William Dow*, he framed a charter, which was passed by the legislature after violent opposition. Young's company was empowered to raise £1 million and to decide on the route. Apparently his company never became operative. Further efforts to sway the Montreal Board of Trade, whose endorsement was indispensable for government aid or private investment, proved fruitless. The canal was reported by John C. Jarvis to be viable in 1855; but Young's insistence that it commence at Caughnawaga was damaging. For nearly 30 years he advocated the scheme in pamphlets, letters to newspapers, and speeches in the assembly, but he was unable to quell Montrealers' fear that the canal, which would allow vessels to sail from the Great Lakes to New York without breaking bulk, would seriously harm Montreal's trade. It is difficult to understand why Young was apparently unwilling to meet their objections, and also how he could justify another channel of trade from Montreal to the Atlantic which would compete with the lower St Lawrence and with three railways, in two of which he was himself associated.

In business, Young remained a partner in the commission house established in 1846 with Holmes. In February 1848, Joseph Knapp was brought into the firm, now Holmes, Young, and Knapp. Young continued to travel west during the winter to buy produce. This partnership ended in December 1849 and Young established a new one with James Benning, a comparative newcomer to Montreal business. Little is known of this firm. However, by 1852 Young had the means to build Rosemount, his impressive country villa, on Côte-Saint-Antoine.

Young was involved in other entrepreneurial ventures in the 1850s. One of the more remunerative was the St Gabriel Hydraulic Company. With Montreal miller, Ira Gould, Young in 1850 acquired a lease from the government for water power at the St Gabriel lock on the Lachine Canal. For an annual fee of £420, his company made immense profits by converting what had been intended as a right to use restricted amounts of canal water into a licence to use virtually unlimited quantities. In 1853 a question of abuse of the lease arose but the attorney general east, Lewis Thomas Drummond*, advised that the contract should nevertheless be observed. It is likely that Young maintained his connection with this lucrative company for many years.

Young

Young was also interested in telegraphic communications. In 1847 he became a promoter of the profitable Montreal Telegraph Company. In 1856 he sought a charter to connect Canada to Britain by telegraph. He headed a group, including Luther Holton, Theodore Hart, and Thomas Cramp*, that formed the Canadian and British Telegraph Company, chartered in 1859 to build a telegraph line via the St Lawrence River and Labrador to Britain. Young was also a leading figure in the company, composed essentially of Montrealers, including Sir George Simpson*, L. T. Drummond, Holton, and Antoine-Aimé Dorion*, that received a charter for the Transmundane Telegraph Company, to build a line west by way of Alaska to the Orient. These projects failed but in 1869 he and Galt sought to recharter the Canadian-European Telegraph Company. Despite cooperative arrangements with the Great Western Telegraph Company and Hugh Allan*'s Montreal Telegraph Company, Young's company could not raise sufficient capital. In 1872 he asked the federal government to guarantee a net dividend of 5 per cent on the $4,000,000 needed to finance the building of the line from Gaspé to Scotland.

Like many businessmen in Montreal Young was interested in politics. He viewed government essentially as an instrument for economic development, an agent for "progress" and for ensuring a favourable atmosphere for commerce. He appears to have had no strong political interests during the early 1840s when he was building up his own business. However, by the late 1840s he was favouring moderate liberalism and in 1847 he nominated La Fontaine in Montreal.

Young's interest in free trade was probably a reason for his adherence to the Liberals. From them he would have expected effective measures of tariff reform and an attempt to seek the elimination of imperial restrictions on American shipping. Soon after the end of the corn laws, Young established, in 1846, the Free Trade Association in Montreal, and with a group of local merchants, including Thomas Kay, Henry Chapman, and John Glass, he advocated removal of all restrictions on Canadian trade. In their weekly newspaper, the *Canadian Economist*, for which Young wrote many articles, the Montreal free traders set forth the benefits to Canada of free trade. Young also advanced his views before the reluctant Montreal Board of Trade, dominated by the more conservative and protection-minded merchants. He continued to uphold free trade throughout his career.

Young strenuously opposed annexation to the United States in 1849, and was one of the few Montreal merchants who refrained from signing the Annexation Manifesto. Lord Elgin [Bruce*] believed that Young wrote two letters in 1849 in the *Pilot and Journal of Commerce*, which argued against annexation on the grounds that Canada would thrive "if our commercial legislation is conducted with ordinary judgement." Young had faith in the viability of the northern economy and St Lawrence river transportation system and in the continuation of traditional Canadian trade with Britain.

Young may have expected the Liberals to be more favourable to his ideas for canal and railway development. There is no indication of the relationship between Young and La Fontaine although Young's vigorous support of him in 1847 suggests their relations were amicable. In late 1849, Lord Elgin, who regarded Young as "the most enlightened merchant and the best political economist I have met with in Canada," persuaded him to assist the British ambassador at Washington, Sir William Henry Lytton Earle Bulwer, who was attempting to secure a reciprocity treaty. After La Fontaine's resignation in 1851, Young reluctantly entered the new Francis Hincks*–Morin ministry as commissioner of public works on 28 Oct. 1851. His appointment, which was probably due to La Fontaine and Lord Elgin, was applauded even by the opposition *Montreal Gazette*, which hailed Young as a man of "intelligence, integrity, and energy" and a "credit" to the administration. A provincial election was called in December 1851 and, with a strong campaign organization, he headed the polls by a narrow majority over Conservative lawyer William Badgley*. Young was vigorously opposed by the business community because of "his determination to build a canal from Caughnawaga, to take away our trade, and to build a railway to Halifax, to overwhelm us with debt."

Young resigned from the Executive Council in September 1852 but he retained his seat for two parliaments. As minister he took special interest in measures to improve navigation on the St Lawrence River. He believed that a bi-weekly service between Montreal and Britain during the navigation season and a monthly service in winter from Britain to Portland, Montreal's Atlantic outlet, would greatly enhance the competitive position of the St Lawrence. The service began in 1853 and won widespread approval in Montreal. In his report to parliament as chief commissioner, Young displayed his familiar preoccupation with waterways and a canal from the St Lawrence to Lake Champlain.

Young left the ministry over its proposal to impose higher tolls on American than on Canadian vessels using the Welland Canal and its decision to set higher rates of duty on semi-processed and manufactured goods imported into Canada through the United States. As a free trader, Young expressed dismay at a policy which was solely an act of retaliation against the United States for its failure to adopt reciprocity.

Young's resignation also reflected his increasing chagrin over the ministry's coldness to the Caughnawaga canal. A third reason was probably his sharp disagreement with Hincks. By the summer of 1852, Hincks favoured the Grand Trunk scheme of Thomas Brassey and William Jackson. As a cabinet member, Young was unwilling to accept the Grand Trunk scheme, especially since he himself was associated in an alternate company with Galt, Holton, and David Lewis Macpherson*.

As a member of the assembly Young supported many government measures. He endorsed the bill presented in April 1853 by George Brown and Adam Johnston Fergusson Blair* to abolish rectories, and the June 1854 motion of Joseph Hartman* and Louis-Victor Sicotte* calling for measures to abolish seigneurial tenure and secularize the clergy reserves. But although an "advanced-Liberal" on some questions, Young did not identify himself with the anti-clericalism of the Rouges or the opposition of the Brownites to "Catholic power." In August 1852 he introduced and piloted through the assembly a bill to establish Collège Sainte-Marie in Montreal.

Young ran for election again in Montreal in 1854 and was careful to present himself as an opponent of the Hincks–Morin ministry, whose reputation had been damaged by revelations of trafficking in securities. He claimed to be running not as a "political man" but as a "mercantile man" interested solely in Montreal's trade. Again the Conservative *Montreal Gazette* recommended him as an "honest and straight-forward man." Young even temporarily muted his views on free trade and the Caughnawaga canal. Along with Luther Holton and Dorion, he was returned for Montreal (now a three-seat constituency) in the Rouge sweep of the city. Although nominally a Rouge, he said little in the assembly except for a few brisk contributions on his favourite subjects of transportation and tariffs.

Not a candidate in 1857, Young strongly supported Holton. It is not clear why he did not contest a seat. Perhaps his own claim that he was less a politician than a businessman can be accepted. He tried to re-enter politics in 1863 but was defeated by Thomas D'Arcy McGee* in Montreal West. After the election Charles John Brydges* and James Ferrier* of the Grand Trunk charged in the *Montreal Gazette* that Holton, Dorion, and John Sandfield Macdonald had pressured them

to support Young. Holton had no doubt that Brydges and Ferrier were the reason for Young's defeat because "they had powerful connections in contractors and persons doing occasional jobs for them, all of whom again had their circles of influence."

After 1863 Young continued his independent Liberal ways. In 1869 in a speech at Waterloo, Ontario, he attacked confederation and called for greater independence from Britain. Both Hugh Allan and Brydges wrote to John A. Macdonald* in 1869 that Young was in New York promoting the annexation of Canada and obstructing hopes of a commercial treaty with the United States. Again in 1871, Young proclaimed that confederation was only "a transition State," and although he opposed "political annexation" he called for "commercial annexation." His proposed Zollverein would include complete freedom in trade between Canada and the United States and in the use of waterways.

This heresy against Montreal Conservative interests was compounded in 1872 when Young supported the Parti National, a Liberal organization attempting to win clerical support for the Liberal party in Quebec. Montreal Conservatives spared no attempt to destroy it. Young acted as a moderate in the Parti National and influenced it to support free trade and a Pacific railway. With its help Young formed part of the Montreal Liberal team that unseated George-Étienne Cartier in Montreal East, and Young himself defeated George Alexander Drummond* in Montreal West in the federal election of 1872. Despite this auspicious beginning Young's new parliamentary career was lack-lustre and in 1873 he declined to run again.

Probably Young's most notable achievements were with the Montreal Harbour Commission. Appointed to it in 1850, he became chairman in 1853. The commission was established to supervise wharves and improve the ship channel; its functions overlapped with that of Trinity House, Montreal, which under the Navigation Acts oversaw navigation in the St Lawrence. In 1868 Trinity House was abolished and with strong pressure from Young its functions were assumed by the Montreal Harbour Commission. Young was also largely responsible for the transformation of the commission into the National Harbours Board.

Young's attitude to the harbour seems to have mixed public good and personal gain. He owned land in the east end of Montreal and consistently urged expansion of the harbour into the Hochelaga Bay region. His support for a bridge in east Montreal, via Île Sainte-Hélène, coincided with

Young

his land speculations. At the very least, Young did not let his position as commissioner interfere with his private business. He sold both land and buildings to the commission for their offices; the Montreal Sailors' Institute took office space in two different buildings which Young owned.

Yet Young's 25-year contribution to the development of the harbour far transcended any personal interest. He understood the significance of Montreal's harbour facilities in the struggle between the St Lawrence and American canal routes. Attacking what he called "the farthing-candle policy" of the Grand Trunk and the government in not developing the harbour, Young consistently called for improved facilities throughout the St Lawrence channel. The Welland and Lachine canals, buoys below Quebec, the training of river pilots, wharving, and the duty structure were all given close attention by Young. This concern with detail and his predilection for facing problems head-on seem to have been his primary assets on the commission. However, personal struggles, often at a petty level, offset his effectiveness. His attacks on Hugh Allan were typical. Whether criticizing the fresh fruit on the Allan steamships or the depth of the ship channel between Montreal and Quebec, or disputing whether he or Allan had originated the idea of steamer service between Quebec and Britain, Young's battles regularly ended in public name-calling and personalities. (In 1847 a series of articles he wrote in the *Pilot* led to a Sunday morning duel with W. S. Turner: despite two shots each, no one was injured.) Yet Young maintained business contacts with Hugh Allan and continued to curl with him and Andrew Allan*.

In this period Montreal's harbour grew to over eight miles and Young envisaged a harbour of 16 miles. By 1878, wharves extended from the Lachine Canal basin in the west to the Hochelaga Wharf. In 1851, 258 overseas ships with a tonnage of 70,910 visited Montreal; in 1874, 731 ships with a tonnage of 423,423. Young never gave up his efforts to incorporate much of the American west as well as the St Lawrence and Ottawa trade into the harbour's vortex. To facilitate trade with the north shore of the St Lawrence he envisaged a tunnel through Montreal mountain and a new railway complex at the east end of the harbour. He constantly criticized what he interpreted as selfish policies by the Grand Trunk, attacking the location of their yards in Pointe-Saint-Charles, the blight their tracks had brought to the centre of Montreal, and the inadequacy of their loading facilities. He was probably responsible for the Harbour Commission's insistence that the Grand Trunk pay its fair share of the harbour's costs.

Young was particularly interested in deepening the ship channel through the shallows of Lac Saint-Pierre. He realized that in the age of the steamships and improved oceanic communication the depth of the channel was critical. In November 1851 it was only 12′6″ but by 1854, owing to his efforts, was 16′. The Harbour Commission records for 25 years abound with evidence of Young's efforts to acquire capital to deepen the channel. He considered himself an engineer and was fond of visiting controversial points on the river to take soundings and to challenge engineers' reports. The deepening in Lac Saint-Pierre in 1866 brought charges from Young of unnecessary expense and delay. He apparently forced the Montreal Board of Trade to choose between him and his fellow commissioners. Ultimately dismissed from the Harbour Commission by Cartier for his obstreperousness in 1866, Young continued to air his case in the public press, and throughout 1867 and 1868 a correspondence was carried on in the *Gazette* between Allan and Young. However, Young would again be commissioner in 1870–72 and 1873–78.

In 1860 Young's fortunes had been at their peak and he reported that he had shipped 100,000 barrels of flour to Portland since the rail link opened. Although president of the Royal Canadian Insurance Company, Young's interests centred on his forwarding business as well as the harbour and land speculation. In 1860 he proposed a new storage complex on the Lachine Canal with facilities for 200,000 barrels of flour and 500,000 bushels of wheat. He assured a business associate that he had assembled land worth $18,000 and buildings worth $7,000. His plans included a swing bridge to link railway lines into the complex. Young had also received rights from the government to use water power from the canal to operate the elevating machinery and permission from the city of Montreal to buy streets in the area.

With investments such as these Young was able to retire from active business in 1860. During his last years he dabbled in politics, maintained his strong interest in the Harbour Commission, and spent more time with his family and his curling. In 1860 he served as Montreal chairman for the visit of the Prince of Wales, the future Edward VII. The following year he moved with his wife, Amelia Jane Tilley, and his 13 children to Scotland for two years to ensure their proper education; the old country only reinforced his Scottish scrappiness. On the return voyage Young and his family were shipwrecked off Newfoundland on the *Anglo-Saxon*. Young was the most prominent witness in the investigation and attacked both the captain's competence and the Allan Line Steamship Company, owners of the vessel. He served in 1864 as a commissioner to Washington on the reciprocity treaty; he remained active on the Montreal Board of Trade of which he was president in 1855, 1860, 1870, and 1871; he was the first president of the Dominion Board of Trade in 1871.

Perhaps as a result of financing difficulties in his transatlantic telegraph and land speculations, Young's circumstances soured in the 1860s and by 1872 he was impecunious. Rosemount, the family estate, was sold and thereafter the family moved regularly. In 1873 the Harbour Commission petitioned the federal government for permission to grant Young a pension out of its funds. Young himself wrote plaintive letters to Cartier, Hincks, and Macdonald begging assistance for his "position of urgent necessity." A year later, although still on the commission, he continued to request a pension of $20,000 from Macdonald. However, Young's Montreal enemies had no intention of permitting him to enjoy a government pension. William WORKMAN, in particular, reminded Macdonald of Young's Liberal associations, his free trade proclivities, and his failure to protect Montreal interests. He accused Young of profiting from a $400,000 Harbour Commission contract let through Young's nephew in Scotland. Instead of a pension, Young had to accept from the Liberal administration of Alexander Mackenzie* a number of patronage positions. After his short term in parliament in 1872–73 he became flour inspector for the port of Montreal and also served as chairman of the Baie Verte Canal Commission. He continued writing pamphlets in favour of free trade, canals, and railways. His last public service was in 1877 as Canadian commissioner to the international exhibition in Sydney, Australia. Afflicted by sunstroke while returning, Young died in Montreal of heart trouble 12 April 1878.

John Young was one of the best-known public figures in Montreal in the mid-19th century. He shared the assumption of his fellow merchants that the St Lawrence was potentially the most advantageous commercial outlet from the west, and their aspiration that Montreal thrive on this trade, but he had different views as to how the goal could best be achieved. He championed free trade and the Caughnawaga canal with the persistence and fervour of an evangelist. In his later years he supported the commercial annexation he had so strongly opposed in 1849.

Despite the attacks and ridicule lavished upon him by his fellow businessmen, who feared his projects and his pen, Young was in many ways representative of his class, place, and time. He was a businessman in the export-import trade, an entrepreneur in a number of railway and telegraph ventures, a land speculator, and a dabbler in other ventures. Businessmen of this type assumed that the prime role of the state was to improve the climate of enterprise by building the necessary facilities, providing assistance for others, and following the "right" policies. Young could hardly have been president of the Montreal Board of Trade several times and harbour commissioner for so many years without the support of many Montreal businessmen who recognized him as a maverick but nevertheless one of their own. The merchants of Montreal buried him with respect and since he left a meagre estate provided a lavish headstone for his grave.

G. TULCHINSKY and BRIAN J. YOUNG

[Young wrote a great deal throughout his life, for he avidly threw himself into public debate on questions of policy that vitally affected Canadian trade. He expressed his views in reports to the Montreal Board of Trade and in speeches on local public occasions. He was indeed the most prolific Montreal polemicist of his era. Young's best-known and most representative writings are: *Views of the commercial policy of Canada* (Montreal, 1853); "Montreal," *Encyclopædia Britannica* (8th ed., 21v., Edinburgh, 1853–60), XV, 521–24; *Letters to the Hon. Francis Lemieux, chief commissioner public works, on Canadian trade and navigation, and to the citizens of Montreal, on the commerce of the city and the means of its further development* (Montreal, 1855); *Reply to J. C. Trautwine, C.E., on the subject of the construction of docks at Montreal* (Montreal, 1859); *Rival routes from the west to the ocean, and docks at Montreal: a series of letters . . . in reply to letters of "A merchant," written by W. Workman* (Montreal, 1859); *On the changed opinions of the Montreal Board of Trade on the canal to connect the St Lawrence with Lake Champlain* (Montreal, 1866); *Three letters on Canadian independence* (Montreal, 1869); [   ], *Independence of Canada; Waterloo meeting; speeches of Hon. John Young, Hon. L. S. Huntington and Rudolph Laflamme, esq., Q.C., delivered at Waterloo, Oct. 2, 1869* (Montreal, 1869); [   ], *Letters, &c., first published in the "Northern Journal," during 1871, by the Hon. John Young, on various questions of public interest* (Montreal, 1872); *North Shore Railway: a brief sketch of its commercial relations and financial prospects* (Montreal, 1872); *Memorandum for contractors, prepared by the directors of the Caughnawaga Ship Canal Company* (Ottawa, 1873); *Remarks on the Montreal harbour and the Lachine Canal* (Montreal, 1875); *The origin of the Victoria Bridge* (Montreal, 1876).

Young wrote numerous letters to Montreal newspapers under his own name and also under the pseudonym "A Merchant." *Evening Telegraph and Daily Commercial Advertiser* (Montreal), 9 Aug. 1866. *Gazette* (Montreal), 12 June, 9 July 1868; 13 April 1878. *Globe* (Toronto), 28 Aug. 1863; 26 Oct. 1867; 7 May, 12 June, 9 July 1868. *La Minerve* (Montréal), 29 août 1863. *Montreal Gazette*, 16, 23–25, 30 Oct. 1844; 6 Oct. 1847; 26 May, 4 Aug. 1849; 3, 5 Nov.

Young

1851; 9 Jan., 30 Aug., 23 Sept. 1852; 13 April, 21, 31 May, 1, 3, 4, 12 June, 4 July 1853; 15, 17, 26 July 1854; 26 Oct. 1867. *Morning Courier* (Montreal), 17, 24 May, 19, 29 June, 26, 28 July, 4 Aug. 1849. See also: *Montreal Herald*, 13, 15 April 1878.

McCord Museum (McGill University, Montreal), Bagg papers, Letter books of Stanley Bagg; Jedediah Hubbell Dorwin, Antiquarian autographs. National Harbours Board (Cité du Havre, Montreal), Letter books, 24 June 1876; Minute books, 19 Sept. 1862, 10 March 1876. PAC, MG 24, E1 (Merritt papers), ser.2, 21, pp.3496–99; 22, pp.3586–89; MG 26, A (Macdonald papers), 344, pp.157516–17; 346, pp. 158526–30; Young to Macdonald, 2 March 1873; MG 27, I, D8 (Galt papers), Young to Galt, 9 Jan. 1862; RG 4, C1, 111, no.3010; 266, no.2615; RG 30, A1g, 146–58. Queen's University Archives, John Young papers, Young to T. E. Blackwell, 30 May 1860 (copy); Hugh Allan to Young, 11 Nov. 1869; Young to the secretary of state, 9 May 1872; Young to the governor general, 20 March 1873; extract from *Montreal Herald*, 1856; "The route of the Canada Pacific Railway" (speech by Young); "Cheap transportation: speech of John Young to the Chicago Cheap Transportation Convention."

[Bruce and Grey], *Elgin-Grey papers* (Doughty), I, 420; II, 565. *Canada Gazette* (Montreal, Toronto), 1846, p.3308; 1848, p.5109; 1850, p.7686. Canada, Province of, Legislative Assembly, *Journals*, 1852–53, app.Q, "Report of the commissioners of public works, for 1851"; 1857, app.6, "Report of the special committee appointed to inquire and report as to the condition, management, and prospects of the Grand Trunk Railway Company"; *Parliamentary debates*, 24, 28, 29 Nov. 1854; 20 Feb., 8, 11, 20 April 1856; *Statutes*, 1847, c.83; 1849, c.180; 1850, c.113; 1854, c.131; 1859, c.100, 101. [J. A. Macdonald], *Correspondence of Sir John Macdonald; selections from the correspondence of the Right Honourable Sir John Alexander Macdonald, G.C.B., first prime minister of the Dominion of Canada*, ed. Joseph Pope (Toronto, [1921]), 105, 108. *The origin of the ocean mail steamers between Liverpool and the St Lawrence, and the advantages of the northern routes* (Montreal, 1877). *Proceedings of the convention held at Saratoga Springs, August 21, 1849, relative to the St Lawrence and Lake Champlain ship canal; with separate reports of the Canadian and American committees* (Saratoga Springs, N.Y., 1849). *Report of the commission appointed to inquire into the affairs of the Grand Trunk Railway* (Quebec, 1861), 101. *Report of royal commission on the leasing of water-power, Lachine Canal* (Ottawa, 1887), 18, 35–36. *Report of the committee on the Montreal and Kingston section of the Canada Grand Trunk Railway* (Montreal, 1851). *Return to an address from the Legislative Assembly of the 28th ultimo [February] for copy of Mr. Jarvis' report relative to the survey of the proposed Caughnawaga canal, and the amount of the cost of such survey as submitted by the said engineer* (Toronto, 1855). *Thoughts on the last election, and matters connected therewith* (Montreal, [1854]), 7.

Can. biog. dict., II, 347–48. Dent, *Canadian portrait gallery*, III, 194–99. *Montreal directory* (Mackay), 1845–46, 197, 246; 1847–48, 269; 1852, 256–57. Morgan, *Sketches of celebrated Canadians*, 528–33. Notman and Taylor, *Portraits of British Americans*, II, 227–36. *Political appointments, 1841–1865* (J.-O. Coté), 9, 21–22, 29, 55, 83, 92, 95.

Atherton, *Montreal*, II, 675. Cornell, *Alignment of political groups*, 33, 70. R. C. Dalton, *The Jesuits' estates question, 1760–1888: a study of the background for the agitation of 1889* (Canadian Studies in History and Government series, 11, Toronto, 1968), 120. *Facts of interest in relation to the harbour of Montreal* (Montreal, 1929). J. E. Graham, "The Riel amnesty and the Liberal party in central Canada, 1869–1875," unpublished MA thesis, Queen's University, 1967, 107. P. G. MacLeod, "Montreal and free trade, 1846–1849," unpublished MA thesis, University of Rochester, 1967. Gustavus Myers, *History of Canadian wealth* (Chicago, 1914). W. J. Rattray, *The Scot in British North America* (4v., Toronto, 1880–84), II, 600–1. "Protection and free trade," *Spectator* (Montreal), 12 Jan. 1878. "Royal Albert Bridge Extra," *Canadian Illustrated News* (Montreal), 22 March 1876. G.T. and B.J.Y.]

YOUNG, Sir JOHN, Baron Lisgar, second governor general of Canada; b. 31 Aug. 1807 in Bombay, India, eldest son of Sir William Young, a director and large shareholder in the East India Company, and Lucy Frederick; d. 6 Oct. 1876 in Bailieborough, Ireland.

John Young was educated at Eton and Corpus Christi College, Oxford (BA 1829). In 1834 he was called to the bar of Lincoln's Inn but never practised law. Elected to the House of Commons first in 1831 from County Cavan (his ancestral home), he served as a Conservative MP until 1855 and held two senior Treasury offices between 1841 and 1846, during Sir Robert Peel's administration. He succeeded to the baronetcy in 1848 and was chief secretary for Ireland, 1852–55. Created GCMG in 1855, he became in that year lord high commissioner of the Ionian Islands. The theft and publication of a dispatch in which he recommended an unpopular policy about their government led to his recall, though his administration was commended. As governor general of New South Wales, 1861–67, Young, urged by the premier, nominated 15 new members to the upper house to secure passage of a regulation and was rebuked by the colonial secretary; he nevertheless completed his term. He became a KCB in 1859 and GCB in 1868.

Young was appointed governor general of Canada and governor of Prince Edward Island on 29 Dec. 1868 and assumed office on 2 Feb. 1869. Shortly after arriving in Canada, he commented publicly on Canada's independence within the empire and her freedom "to continue the present connection or in due time . . . to exchange it for some other form of alliance." There was nevertheless, he felt, greater loyalty to and respect for Britain in Canada than in Australia. He himself, however, found he now had less influence since his Canadian ministers decided measures in cabinet before they came to him whereas in New South Wales he had been consulted by ministers before council meetings.

In Young's first year in Canada the disturbance led by Louis Riel* broke out. As an appeasement he proclaimed an amnesty on 6 Dec. 1869. During the unrest the United States government barred the Canadian ship *Chicora* from the Sault Ste Marie Canal on its way west; Young made a formal protest that it carried no military supplies and that American vessels, some armed, were freely using the Welland Canal. The ban on passage was lifted.

During his term of office the Hudson's Bay Company territory of Rupert's Land was transferred to Canada, and Manitoba became a province in confederation. Originally scheduled for early 1869, the transfer was delayed by the rebellion until August 1870, and from April 1869 to that date Young had a key role as nominal lieutenant governor of Rupert's Land. During the Fenian raid into Canada in 1870, Young, according to Lord Dufferin [Blackwood*] later, by a peremptory but judicious telegram to the adjutant-general, Colonel P. Robertson-Ross*, prevented the summary hanging of captured American invaders.

When a delegation from British Columbia came to discuss confederation in June 1870, it was informed by Young personally of the desire of Canadians to have the colony join them. In 1871, the agreements for construction of the Canadian Pacific Railway to British Columbia were concluded. In that year also the Treaty of Washington was drawn up and signed. Prime Minister John A. Macdonald* represented Canada on the commission in Washington and fought diligently to protect Canadian interests. His independence annoyed the British commissioners and Lisgar (he had become Baron Lisgar on 2 Nov. 1870) added to their annoyance by communicating to them indiscreet remarks from Macdonald's correspondence with cabinet colleagues in Ottawa. Lisgar also complained to the colonial secretary of Macdonald's independence. Macdonald eventually agreed to secure Canadian approval of the unpopular Treaty of Washington if the British government would grant Canada a guaranteed loan of £4,000,000. Lisgar advised the British cabinet that a much smaller sum would suffice. Nevertheless, Macdonald considered Lisgar the ablest of all the governors general under whom he had served.

Shortly before his retirement Lisgar inadvertently failed to reserve a bill imposing discriminatory duties in Canada against tea and coffee from the United States. The Australian colonies then asked for similar rights, which the colonial secretary granted rather than risk displeasing Canada by disallowing its act. These protective tariffs meant an end to the British ideal of a free-trade empire.

Lisgar did not enjoy good health in Canada and resigned prematurely in June 1872. A man of ability, experience, and generally sound judgement, he died at his family home, leaving his wife, Adelaide Annabella Dalton, daughter of an Irish landowner, whom he had married 8 April 1835. There were no children.

CHARLES A. THOMPSON

Manitoba; birth of a province (Morton), 85. *The annual register; a review of public events at home and abroad for the year 1876* (London, 1877), 157. *Appleton's cyclopædia of American biography*, ed. J. G. Wilson *et al.* (10v., New York, 1887–1924), VI, 648. Boase, *Modern English biography*, II, 444. *Burke's peerage* (1953), 641. *The complete peerage or a history of the House of Lords and all its members from the earliest times*, ed. G. E. C. Kayne *et al.* (13v., London, 1932), VIII, 38–39. *DNB.* Edward Walford, *The county families of the United Kingdom or royal manual of the titled and untitled aristocracy of England, Wales, Scotland and Ireland* (London, 1875), 604.

British Columbia & confederation, ed. W. G. Shelton (Victoria, 1967), 202. Creighton, *Macdonald, old chieftain.* Dent, *Canadian portrait gallery*, IV, 40; *Last forty years*, II, 487–88. Morton, *Critical years*, 266; *Manitoba: a history*, 131–32, 139, 142. Joseph Pope, *Memoirs of the Right Honourable John Alexander Macdonald G.C.B., first prime minister of the Dominion of Canada* (2v., Ottawa, [1894]). R. A. Preston, *Canada and "imperial defense"; a study of the origins of the British Commonwealth's defense organization, 1867–1919* (Durham, N.C., and Toronto, 1967), 74. Stanley, *Birth of western Canada*, 134, 146.

GENERAL BIBLIOGRAPHY AND
LIST OF ABBREVIATIONS

List of Abbreviations

AAQ   Archives de l'archidiocèse de Québec
ACAM   Archives de la chancellerie de l'archevêché de Montréal
ADB   *Australian Dictionary of Biography*
AHO   Archives historiques oblates
AHSJ   Archives générales des Religieuses hospitalières de Saint-Joseph
AJM   Archives judiciaires de Montréal
AJQ   Archives judiciaires de Québec
AJTR   Archives judiciaires de Trois-Rivières
ANQ   Archives nationales du Québec
APQ   Archives de la province de Québec. Now ANQ
AQ   Archives du Québec. Now ANQ
ASGM   Archives des sœurs grises de Montréal
ASHS   Archives de la Société historique du Saguenay
ASJ   Archives de la Société de Jésus
ASJCF   Archives de la Société de Jésus, province du Canada français
ASN   Archives du séminaire de Nicolet
ASQ   Archives du séminaire de Québec
ASSM   Archives du séminaire de Saint-Sulpice de Montréal
ASTR   Archives du séminaire de Trois-Rivières
AVM   Archives de la ville de Montréal
AVQ   Archives de la ville de Québec
BCHQ *British Columbia Historical Quarterly*
BNQ   Bibliothèque nationale du Québec
BRH   *Bulletin des recherches historiques*
CCHA   Canadian Catholic Historical Association
CHA   Canadian Historical Association
CHR   *Canadian Historical Review*
DAB   *Dictionary of American Biography*
DCB   *Dictionary of Canadian Biography*

DNB   *Dictionary of National Biography*
HBC   Hudson's Bay Company
HBRS   Hudson's Bay Record Society
HSSM   Historical and Scientific Society of Manitoba
JALPC *Journal de l'Assemblée législative de la province du Canada*
JIP   *Journal de l'Instruction publique*
MTCL   Metropolitan Toronto Central Library
PABC   Provincial Archives of British Columbia
PAC   Public Archives of Canada
PAM   Public Archives of Manitoba
PANB   Provincial Archives of New Brunswick
PANL   Provincial Archives of Newfoundland and Labrador
PANS   Public Archives of Nova Scotia
PAO   Ontario Department of Public Records and Archives
PAPEI   Public Archives of Prince Edward Island
PRO   Public Record Office
RHAF *Revue d'histoire de l'Amérique française*
RSCT Royal Society of Canada *Transactions*
RUL   *Revue de l'université Laval*
SAB   Saskatchewan Archives Board
SCHÉC   Société canadienne d'histoire de l'Église catholique
SGCF   Société généalogique canadienne-française
SH   *Social History*
SHQ   Société historique de Québec
SHS   Société historique du Saguenay
SPRI   Scott Polar Research Institute
USPG   United Society for the Propagation of the Gospel
UCA   United Church Archives

General Bibliography

The General Bibliography is based on the sources most frequently cited in the individual bibliographies of volume X. It is not, therefore, a complete list of background materials for the history of Canada during the period covered by this volume.

Section I provides a description of the principal archival sources used for this volume and is divided by country. Section II has two parts, A and B: A contains printed primary sources including documents published by the various colonial, provincial, and federal governments, and the works printed in the 19th and 20th centuries that may be regarded as contemporary sources; B provides a listing of the contemporary newspapers most frequently cited by the contributors to the volume and includes an introduction listing some sources for background information on the newspapers. Section III includes various dictionaries, nominal lists, and guides to printed matter. Section IV contains secondary works, mainly written in the 20th century, including a few general histories, relevant series, and theses. Section V describes the principal journals containing material relevant to the 19th century as well as individual articles frequently cited in the text.

I. ARCHIVES AND MANUSCRIPT SOURCES

CANADA

ARCHIVES DE LA CHANCELLERIE DE L'ARCHE-VÊCHÉ DE MONTRÉAL. These archives, where documents up to 1896 can be consulted, contain photographs, maps, 634 registers divided into 17 series (mainly the correspondence of the bishops of Montreal), and some 500,000 separate items describing the dioceses, clergy, laity, institutions, missions, religious orders, etc. For a more complete description of this archives, see, *RHAF*, XIX (1965–66), 652–55; SCHÉC, *Rapport, 1963*, 69–70. A detailed inventory of several registers and files appears in *RHAF*, XIX (1965–66), 655–64; XX (1966–67), 146–66, 669–700; XXIV (1970–71), 111–42.

The following series were used in preparing vol. X:

Dossiers
255: Diocèses du Canada
.109: Diocèse de Saint-Boniface
420: Clergé
.005: Truteau, Alexis-Frédéric
901: Fonds Lartigue-Bourget
.059: Voyage à Rome de Mgr Bourget, 1869
.079: Chanoine Joseph-Octave Paré à Mgr Bourget, 1840, 1874
RCD: Registres et cahiers divers. 110 vols.
RDM: Registres des dispenses de mariages. 65 vols.
RLB: Registres des lettres de Mgr Bourget. 25 vols. A descriptive inventory of Mgr Bour-get*'s correspondence from 1837 to 1850 was published in APQ, *Rapport, 1945–46*, 137–224; *1946–47*, 81–175; *1948–49*, 343–477; *1955–57*, 177–221; AQ, *Rapport, 1961–64*, 9–68; *1965*, 87–132; *1966*, 191–252; *1967*, 123–70; *1969*, 3–146.
RLL: Registres des lettres de Mgr Lartigue. 9 vols. An inventory of Mgr Lartigue*'s correspondence from 1819 to 1840 appears in APQ, *Rapport, 1941–42*, 345–496; *1942–43*, 1–174; *1943–44*, 207–334; *1944–45*, 173–266; *1945–46*, 39–134.

ARCHIVES DE L'ARCHIDIOCÈSE DE QUÉBEC. Contains about 1,060 feet of documents, an analytical card file for all documents before 1930, and a Réper-toire général des registres officiels de l'archvêché in 6 vols., from 1659 to the present. A guide to these archives can be found in SCHÉC, *Rapport, 1934–35*, 65–73. Since the publication of *DCB*, II, the AAQ has instigated a system of alphabetical-numerical classification; it is given below but was not used in the individual bibliographies of this volume.

Series relevant to the period of vol. X include:
A: Évêques et archevêques de Québec
210 A: Registres des lettres expédiées, X–XXII. 1819–80. An inventory of Mgr Joseph Signay*'s correspondence for 1825–40 can be found in APQ, *Rapport, 1936–37*, 125–330; *1937–38*, 21–146; *1938–39*, 180–297.

C: Secrétairerie et chancellerie
CB: Structures de direction
  1 CB: Vicaires généraux, I–XIV. 1742–1867
CD: Discipline diocésaine
  515 CD: Séminaire de Nicolet, 1800–74
  61 CD: Paroisses.   Sainte-Marie de Beauce, II. 1851–1906
  71 CD: Religieux. Oblats de Marie-Immaculée, I. 1844–1913
CN: Église canadienne
  330 CN: Rivière-Rouge, 1818–70. 4 vols.
  331 CN: Diocèse de Saint-Boniface, 1850–1900
  36 CN: Colombie-Britannique, I–III. 1835–1929
CP: Église du Québec
  26 CP: District et diocèse de Montréal, II–XII. 1823–98.

ARCHIVES DE LA SOCIÉTÉ DE JÉSUS, PROVINCE DU CANADA FRANÇAIS, Saint-Jérôme (Terrebonne). These archives were founded in 1844 by Father Félix Martin*. Originally they were housed at the Collège Sainte-Marie in Montreal, and were designated by the abbreviation ACSM. In 1968 they were transferred to the noviciate of the Jesuits of the ecclesiastical province of French Canada, at Saint-Jérôme, and are now designated by the abbreviation ASJCF. In the year of their founding these archives received a rich gift from the religious of the Hôtel-Dieu in Quebec. They contain numerous documents relating to the history of the missions of the Society of Jesus in Canada [see ARCHIVES DU COLLÈGE SAINTE-MARIE, DCB, I, 686].

Vol. X of the DCB mentions several documents found in:

A section of 140 metal boxes containing about 8,000 numbered documents (personal papers or correspondence) in the form of original manuscripts or copies

Section A (documents relating to the Jesuit missions in Ontario around the Great Lakes), 1845–1924, about 8,000 numbered documents

Section B-106 (letters and fragments of letters of Jean-Baptiste Meilleur), 118 items

Section D-7 (various documents relating to the fathers of the Society of Jesus)

ARCHIVES DE LA SOCIÉTÉ HISTORIQUE DU SAGUENAY, Chicoutimi, Que. This important repository for the history of the Saguenay was organized by the Société historique du Saguenay, but also received documents from the Séminaire de Chicoutimi and the research notes on the history of the region accumulated by Mgr Victor Tremblay after 1920.

The ASHS also holds recorded and printed information, oral history, maps, photographs (43,000, as well as 65,000 negatives), a museum, and a library. The classification system uses titles for sections and numbers for each unit; there is an index. The Documents and the Dossiers cover the whole period of the history of the Saguenay from its discovery in 1535 and contain a little information on its earlier history. Since 1920 the society has been collecting oral history, "les Mémoires d'anciens." The SHS has published books and pamphlets since 1934. One of the repository's most important holdings is its collection of Publications saguenéennes which contains almost all the newspapers and periodicals published in the region. A more complete description of ASHS can be found in Victor Tremblay, "Les archives de la Société historique du Saguenay," RHAF, IV (1950–51), 3–16.

The sections used in preparing this volume were:

Documents. 5,220 originals, 93 copies
Dossiers. About 35,000 items, totalling 21,300 pages
  Price, 1810– . [Inventory in progress.]
Mémoires d'anciens. 692 memoirs, totalling 3,550 typed pages

ARCHIVES DE LA VILLE DE MONTRÉAL. The archives division of the Secrétariat municipal of the city of Montreal was created in 1913 to hold the city's administrative documents. The AVM contains 12,000 feet of documents classified into files or volumes. The section Documents administratifs is composed of all the official papers from 1796 to the present. The section Documentation contains extracts from articles in newspapers, periodicals, and other printed matter reporting on subjects or individuals relating to the administration and history of Montreal. This last section contains the correspondence (originals and copies) of several mayors and the original music of Alexis Contant*. The AVM also holds copies of material from other archives including the terrier of the Sulpiciens and documents relevant to the mission of Saint-François-Xavier of Caughnawaga. There are indexes which will soon be available on microfilm. Materials used in vol. X include:

Documentation

B: Biographies autres que celles des maires et des conseillers. Classified by numerical order with an alphabetical card file.
Biographies de conseillers. Arranged alphabetically.
Biographies de maires. Arranged alphabetically.
36: Commerces, industries
10: Banques

.4: Banque d'Épargne de Montréal
.6: Banque des Marchands
Documents administratifs, 1796– .
   Registres des procès-verbaux du comité des
   Finances
   Registres des procès-verbaux du conseil
   municipal

ARCHIVES DE LA VILLE DE QUÉBEC. The archives department of Quebec City was officially organized in 1925 under the direction of Valère Desjardins. Its most important original documents are those of the municipal administration from the time of the incorporation of Quebec in 1833 until the founding of the AVQ. The archives contains at least 1,200 cubic feet to which will soon be added a large number of municipal documents. The oldest documents, in broken series, go back as early as 1796, but complete series begin from 1814.

The archives is in the process of reorganization (classifying and preparing an inventory), but there are already several finding aids (a list can be found in the guide prepared by the AVQ) and a complete list of collections will soon be available. While the latter is being prepared, the archives is proceeding with a complete inventory of the Fonds Baillairgé, which contain 400 plans and original drawings of the buildings of Quebec by Charles Baillairgé* dated 1846–99. The AVQ plans to publish a descriptive inventory of these drawings and plans, and will make photographs and slides available.

For the period covered by vol. X the documents of the municipal administration are those of the municipal council and each of the different committees (Aqueduc, Chemins, Feu, Finances, Police, Règlements, Traverse, etc.), except from 1836 to 1840. In 1836, the corporate charter was not renewed and the city was administered for four years by justices of the peace. When the registries of the Cour municipal from 1848 are transferred to the AVQ, the full collection of documents for the period 1833–1928 will include about 600 volumes. The main groups for this period are:
   Registres des procès-verbaux du conseil muni-
   cipal, 1833–36, 1840–1928
   Registres des procès-verbaux de chaque comité,
   1833–36, 1840–1928
   Pièces justificatives présentées au conseil par
   chaque comité, 1833–36, 1840–1928
   Rapports présentés au conseil par chaque
   comité, 1833–36, 1840–1928

ARCHIVES DES SŒURS GRISES, Montreal. The documents that were at the Hôpital Général de Montréal when Madame d'Youville [Dufrost*] came there as administratrix in 1747 make up the Fonds "Charon," and are the basis of this archival repository. Subsequently, items necessary for the general administration of the community were added. The classification for this repository is alphabetical for the dossiers and chronological within each dossier. These archives contain thousands of documents, the earliest dating from 1663, and about 300 maps and plans.

The principal documents used in vol. X were:
"Ancien journal, 1688–1877"
"Chapitre des fondations, 1849"
"Chroniques de Saint-Boniface (Man.), 1843– "
"Correspondance de Saint-Boniface, 1843– "
"Registre d'admissions, vêtures et professions, 1771– "

ARCHIVES DU SÉMINAIRE DE NICOLET. Located since 1969 in a building of the seminary of Nicolet, the ASN is kept in 8 filing cabinets and 26 metal boxes. Although the oldest original document is dated 1706, the majority are from the 19th and 20th centuries. Among the most important sections are the Section Henri Vassal, which includes material on the Odanak Indian reserve (near Pierreville, Que.), and the Archives de la seigneurie de Nicolet, given to the seminary by the seigneur, Arthur St Lawrence Trigge, in 1939. The latter collection includes a large number of volumes and registers from the seigneury. The following documents were used in vol. X:
   Collection Charles-Édouard Bois, 44 vols. of
   notes and historical documents [copies at
   PAC, MG 24, B26 (Jean-Baptiste Meilleur
   collection)]
   Section de 26 Boîtes métalliques
   Section Polygraphie
   Section Séminaire (documents on the seminary
   from its founding in 1803 until its sale to the
   Quebec government in 1966)

ARCHIVES DU SÉMINAIRE DE QUÉBEC. One of the most important collections of documents in North America. The archives dates from the founding of the seminary in 1663, but Mgr Thomas-Étienne Hamel* and Mgr Amédée-Edmond Gosselin* may be considered to have founded the ASQ at the end of the 19th and the beginning of the 20th century. The ASQ contains some 1,172 feet of documents (seminary and private papers, the oldest from 1636 and the majority from 1675 to 1950), 2,000 maps, and 160 feet of engravings and photographs.

For vol. X the following were used:
Carton Laverdière. 1 carton
Fichier des anciens du séminaire

735

Fonds Henri-Raymond Casgrain. Abbé Casgrain's letters and various manuscripts that he kept. Index. mss 0400–0507

Fonds René-Édouard Caron. 13 cartons containing notarial acts and a series of manuscripts (mss 764–817, documents used in codifying the laws of Lower Canada)

Fonds Verreau. Includes Fonds Viger, hence frequently called Viger-Verreau. The collections of Abbé Hospice-Anthelme Verreau* and of Jacques Viger*, principally composed of about a hundred cartons, several large notebooks, and the series of Viger's manuscript volumes entitled "Ma Saberdache." [*See*, Fernand Ouellet, "Inventaire de la Saberdache de Jacques Viger," APQ, *Rapport, 1955–57*, 31–171.]

Journal du séminaire, 1849–1962. 15 vols.

Lettres, M, 171 items; S, 2 cartons, 188 items; T, 156 items; X, 1863–67, 384 items; Y, 127 items

Manuscrits, 26, "Journal de Mgr Méthot, 1865–1866"; 611, "Journal de Mgr M.-E. Méthot, I, 1er juill.–18 déc. 1870"; 626–27, "Journal de H. Laverdière, 16 oct. 1858–23 mars 1868"; 651, "Journal de Prosper Vincent, 1863–1865"; 676–77, "Journal de C.-F. Légaré, 25 mars 1865–17 avril 1873"; 764–817, *see*, Fonds René-Édouard Caron

Polygraphie. 324 cartons

Seigneuries, LXVIII–LIX, Laval; LXX, Acquisitions diverses

Séminaire. 274 cartons

S.M.E., Résolutions du conseil du séminaire ou Plumitifs, 1766–1950

Université, 1852–1952. 368 cartons

ARCHIVES DU SÉMINAIRE DE SAINT-SULPICE, Montreal. An important repository for the history of the Montreal region and of the Sulpicians. On his departure in 1665 Paul de Chomedey* de Maisonneuve left there the greater part of his papers, dating from 1642. This repository, divided into 49 sections, contains 190 feet of documents for the years 1586–1950, and about 1,200 maps and plans.

The following sections were used in vol. X:
Communautés religieuses
Histoire et biographies, 2e partie: biographies. 88 items arranged in chronological order. 1657–1926
Œuvres et institutions diverses

ARCHIVES DU SÉMINAIRE DE TROIS-RIVIÈRES. In 1918 the authorities of the seminary, gave Abbé Albert Tessier the task of arranging the archives of the institution. Three years later he published the first work of what would become the collection of "Pages Trifluviennes." In 1926 a fire completely destroyed the library and its contents; because of this the institution received books from Abbé H.-A. Scott, Cyrille Tessier, Édouard Bureau, and René-Montarville Boucher* de La Bruère. Then, in 1934, important gifts of documents were added including the Pierre Boucher collection and the Hart collection. The latter contains thousands of accounts, notes, and letters on Canadian economic life in the 19th century. The archives, housed at the Séminaire Saint-Joseph, is a valuable source for the political, religious, and economic history of the region. ASTR also holds numerous maps and newspapers of Trois-Rivières, the most important for the period 1865–1963. For a more complete description *see*, AQ, *Rapport, 1961–64*, 69–134.

Documents from the following sections were used in vol. X:
Fonds et papiers
Archives du diocèse de Trois-Rivières. 16 feet. The largest part is the Louis-François Laflèche collection. 8 drawers
Archives de la famille Hart. 9 drawers. Contains many documents on the Hart family, the first Jews to settle in Canada. The oldest document is dated 1760. Detailed index
Papiers J.-Napoléon Bureau. 6 inches
Correspondance, 1860–69
Trifluviana
Trifluviens du 17e au 20e siècles. 4 drawers. Arranged alphabetically
Personnages canadiens. 4 drawers
Trois-Rivières: institutions et vie sociale. 3 drawers
Commerce et industries. Hall & Baptist
Mauriciana
Le Saint-Maurice: chantiers, navigation, sport. 1 drawer
George Baptist: Correspondance, 1867–72, 1875; Pièces comptables, 1860–74
La Mauricie: territoire, histoire, missions. 1 drawer

ARCHIVES GÉNÉRALES DES RELIGIEUSES HOSPITALIÈRES DE SAINT-JOSEPH, Montreal. In process of being catalogued. This repository was previously known as Archives des Religieuses hospitalières de Saint-Joseph de l'Hôtel-Dieu de Montréal.

The principal documents used in vol. X include:
Actes de décès, 1861–90
Annales de sœur Césarine Raymond, 1756–1861
Annales de sœur Joséphine Paquet, 1860–81
Obédiences des Religieuses hospitalières de Saint-Joseph de l'Hôtel-Dieu de Montréal, 1827–76

Registres des entrées, 1787–1851. 1 vol.

Registres des procès-verbaux des vêtures et professions, 1787–1847

ARCHIVES HISTORIQUES OBLATES, Ottawa. An important repository for the history of the Oblates of Mary Immaculate in Canada from the time of their arrival in 1841. Even before 1930 Father Jean-Marie-Rodrigue Villeneuve* had begun to collect a large number of documents relating to the Oblates. In 1933, Father Léo Deschâtelets obtained from Rome copies of the writings of the order's founder, minutes of general and executive meetings, and letters from the first Oblates in Canada.

The AHO holds personal papers including the manuscript of Father Louis Le Jeune*'s *Dictionnaire* and the notes of Father Louis Babel*'s trip to Labrador. There are also many Indian language manuscripts, some written by Oblates [*see* Gaston Carrière, "Une riche collection de manuscrits en langues indiennes," *Culture* (Québec), XVIII (1957), 105–12].

In 1941, the archives began to microfilm numerous documents, which were important to the history of the Oblates in Canada, from other repositories. Now the AHO's most valuable possession is its large number of copies (typescripts, photocopies, or microfilm), which enable the researcher to find, in one location, almost all documents relating to the Oblates in Canada. The microfilm section alone comprises more than 500,000 pages and a descriptive file with about 250,000 cards. There are several indexes and also a photographic archives and a library of about 10,000 volumes including a few works printed in Indian languages and a large collection of Oblate publications, in particular *Missions des O.M.I.*, which are to the Oblates what the *Relations* were to the Jesuits.

ORIGINAL documents used in vol. X include:
Dossiers
Orégon et Colombie-Britannique, 1847–1928. 1,923 items
Fonds manuscrits
Flavien Durocher. [Pierre Cholenec], "Vie de Catherine Tekakwita appelée en algonquin Mitakwenibekwe, morte en odeur de sainteté au Sault St Louis en 1680, à l'âge de 24 ans, traduit de l'algonquin par Flavien Durocher."
COPIES held at AHO from the following repositories were used in volume X:
Archives de la Propagation de la Foi de Paris
F. 182: Ottawa, rapports des missions, 1848–76
F. 202: Vancouver, rapport des missions, 1847–1922

Archives générales des oblats de Marie-Immaculée, Rome
Dossiers
"Histoire de la mission de Notre-Dame-des-Sept-Douleurs établie au fond du lac Athabasca."
Archives paroissiales
Saint-Sauveur, *Codex historicus*
Archives provinciales des oblats de Marie-Immaculée, Montréal
Codex historicus
Dossiers

ARCHIVES JUDICIAIRES DE MONTRÉAL. Materials used in vol. X include:
Greffes: Stanley Clark Bagg, 1842–56
J.-L. Coutlée, 1867–1914
Charles Cushing, 1869–1910
Louis-Michel Darveau, 1871–74
Alphonse-Clovis Décary, 1866–98
William M. Easton, 1843–74
Isaac Jones Gibb, 1835–67
Léonard-Ovide Hétu, 1859–1903
William Ross, 1835–89
Procédures non-contentieuses
Registre d'état civil
Louis Richard, La famille Masson. 173 pages

ARCHIVES JUDICIAIRES DE QUÉBEC. Materials used in vol. X include:
Greffes: Étienne Boudreault, 1816–25
Louis-Michel Darveau, 1856–68
Edward Graves Meredith, 1876–1938
Registre d'état civil

ARCHIVES NATIONALES DU QUÉBEC. The administrators of New France took back to France, after 1763, documents relating to the government of the colony – an action contrary to international law at the time but agreed to under articles 43, 44, and 45 of the capitulation of Montreal. Only archives having a legal value for individuals remained in the country and these were to suffer many misfortunes before an official repository was created. The Bureau des Archives de la province de Québec – now the Archives nationales du Québec – was created in 1920 [*see* Gilles Héon, "Bref historique des Archives du Québec," ANQ, *Rapport, 1970*, 13–25]. Some 3,300 feet of documents are preserved there today (official and private papers, originals and copies), the majority for the period 1663–1867. In 1968, the ANQ published an *État général des archives publiques et privées du Québec* and established a new system of classification of documents. Cited in vol. X:
Archives privées. Being classified numerically
Autographes. Copies, 1/2 inch

René-Édouard Caron, 1842–76. 2 feet
  Lettres reçues
  Documents juridiques
  Divers, 1851–73
Collection Chapais, Fonds Langevin
  Sir Hector-Louis Langevin, 1826–1903. 22
    items (some originals are at PAC)
Collection Pierre-Georges Roy
Ludger Duvernay, 1805–48. 1 foot. An inventory was published in APQ, *Rapport, 1926–27*, 145–258.
Famille Chaussegros de Léry
  Alexandre-René, 1845–76. 2 inches
Famille Hale, 1842, 1847, 1930. 10 pages
Fonds Papineau-Bourassa
  Famille Papineau, 1801–1902. 40 feet
Jean-Joseph Girouard, 1822–55. 8 inches
John Heath, 1822–45, 1861. 12 pages
Port de Québec, 1779–1922. 28 vols.
Quebec Board of Trade, 1832–1932. 39 vols., 2 cartons
PQ: Province de Québec
  Éducation, 1867–1959. 2,165 feet
QBC: Québec et Bas-Canada
  Instruction publique, 1842–99. 236 vols.

BIBLIOTHÈQUES DE L'UNIVERSITÉ DE MONTRÉAL. In April 1971 the libraries of the Université de Montréal created the Service des collections particulières whose purpose was to make available to researchers the numerous valuable documents that the university had acquired through purchase and donation. At the same time the service began a series of publications. Used in vol. X:

Collection Baby. Made up of an important collection of original material gathered by François-Louis-Georges Baby* (1832–1906), and bequeathed to the Université de Montréal. Including more than 20,000 items, it covers almost every subject in Canadian history from 1602 to 1905. In 1942 Camille Bertrand began to inventory this collection and to arrange the material into two large divisions: Documents divers and Correspondance générale. Documents divers mainly consists of individual items arranged under 20 general titles in alphabetical order from A to S. The division includes 42 files, 10 boxes, 200 registers and books, and 18 folio-volumes. Correspondance générale, arranged alphabetically by names of the signatories of the letters, contains about 12,000 original letters kept in 120 boxes. The collection is too large and varied to describe here in full but the researcher may consult either the repository's 20,000 manuscript index cards or the *Catalogue de la Collection François-Louis-*

Georges Baby, rédigé par Camille Bertrand, préface de Paul Baby et introduction par Lucien Campeau (Publ. du Service des collections particulières, Bibliothèques de l'Université de Montréal, Montréal, 1971). Typescript copies of most items in the Collection Baby are held by PAC.

BIBLIOTHÈQUE NATIONALE DU QUÉBEC, DÉPARTEMENT DES MANUSCRITS, Montreal. In 1965 the Bibliothèque Saint-Sulpice (since 1967, the Bibliothèque nationale du Québec) owned enough archival material to create an autonomous manuscript department. This department now holds papers collected from 1844 by the Sulpicians and recent acquisitions. There are 2,230 feet of documents; the oldest, dated 1316, is part of the Jacques Mordret collection. The manuscript collections include mainly private and literary papers, the majority of the private papers being from the 19th century and of the literary papers from the 20th century. Besides these documents the manuscript department of the BNQ holds 6,000 maps and plans and 30,000 photographs. The collection used in vol. X was that of the Société historique de Montréal. In 1970 the Société historique de Montréal deposited at BNQ its complete collection of manuscripts, archives, documents, and books, which covers 975 feet. This collection was previously housed at the library of the École des Hautes Études Commerciales de Montréal. The main documents cited in vol. X are:

Collection La Fontaine. For a complete inventory of this collection see, *Inventaire de la collection Lafontaine*, Elizabeth Nish, compil. (Publ. du Centre d'étude du Québec, Bibliographie pour servir à l'étude de l'histoire du Canada français, 2, Montréal, 1967.)

McCORD MUSEUM, Montreal. Begun from the private archives collected between 1860 and 1919 by David Ross McCord*. The documents are kept in about 364 boxes and cover the period 1682–1970. In addition the McCord Museum holds a photographic archives which includes the celebrated Notman Photographic Archives – about 400,000 prints and negatives – a most important source for research on 19th and 20th century Canada and Canadians.

  The following collections were used in vol. X:
Stanley and Abner Bagg papers. Ledgers, letter books, account books, receipts, etc., referring to various business enterprises, especially the Lachine Canal. 1810–45.
Hale family papers. Principally the papers of Edward Hale, 1801–75. Includes private and business correspondence relating to the

British American Land Company, settlement of the Eastern Townships, rebellion of 1837, travel in Upper and Lower Canada, social and political life in Montreal, Quebec, Kingston, and Sherbrooke, etc. Index available

McGILL UNIVERSITY ARCHIVES, Montreal. Founded in 1962 and placed under the direction of Alan D. Ridge, the McGill University Archives holds documents produced and received by the administration of the university, by its researchers and professors. Certain personal papers are also found there. The repository contains 2,500 square feet of documents of which the oldest is dated 1807 and concerns the correspondence of the Royal Institution for the Advancement of Learning. Other archival repositories exist at McGill University including the McCord Museum, the McLennan Library (Rare Books and Special Collections Division), and the Osler Library.

The archives has several indexes and published inventories of limited range to aid the researcher. A more complete description of this repository can be found in Alan D. Ridge, "The McGill University Archives," *Archives, Journal of the British Records Association* (London), VIII, no.37 (April 1967), 16–23.

The following sections were used in preparing vol. X:

Board of Governor's minute books, 1829– . 19 vols.

Board of the Royal Institution for the Advancement of Learning. Minutes, 1835–56. 2 vols.

Correspondence of the principals, 1829–

Dawson family personal papers, 1849–1901. 3 cubic feet

Official papers of Sir John William Dawson, 1855–99. 54 bundles. The archives has published an inventory of the first seven bundles.

METROPOLITAN TORONTO CENTRAL LIBRARY, Toronto. The manuscript collection of MTCL contains approximately 500 feet of Canadian documents. There are several large sets of personal papers and business records and many single pieces: diaries, account books, letter books, etc. Most of the material is from the 19th century with the emphasis on pre-1850 Ontario politics.

The materials used in the preparation of vol. X include:

Anderson Ruffin Abbott papers

Robert Baldwin papers

Henry John Boulton papers

John Hillyard Cameron papers

Consumer's Gas Company papers

Denison family papers

Minute-books of the Toronto Choral Society, 1845, and the Philharmonic Society, 1846–47

Plan of Toronto, surveyed and compiled by W. S. and H. C. Boulton, Toronto [1858(?)]

Publisher's proofs of a number of Charles Dawson Shanly's poems

J. H. Richardson, "Reminiscences of the medical profession in Toronto, *1829–1905*." (typescript copy)

Vaughan Maurice Roberts papers

John Ross Robertson collection, sketches by John Arnot Fleming

Toronto, Mechanics' Institute papers

Robert John Turner legal papers relating to cases in the Court of Chancery, Upper Canada, 1837–56

NEW BRUNSWICK MUSEUM, Saint John, N.B. Established in 1930, the N.B. Museum became a provincial institution in 1942. Parent organizations, such as the Natural History Society of New Brunswick, had been acquiring manuscripts for nearly a century; these materials were transferred to the museum's Department of Canadian History in 1932 and form the nucleus of the present archives. For further information *see*: W. A. Squires, *The history and development of the New Brunswick Museum (1842–1945)* (N.B. Museum pub., Administrative series, 2, Saint John, N.B., 1945). For a further description of the collections see: New Brunswick Museum, Department of Canadian History, Archives Division, *Inventory of manuscripts, 1967.*

The following collections were especially useful in vol. X:

Brown, Hon. James (1790–1870), journal (photocopy), 1844–70

Chandler, Edward Barron (1800–80), papers, 1821–70

Chipman family, papers, 1764–1879

Ganong manuscript collection, 1686–1941, "The province of New Brunswick," unpublished MS by W. F. Ganong

Milner, Dr William Cochrane (1846–1939), collection, 1744–1930; Chandler correspondence

New Brunswick Historical Society, papers, 1811–75; Steeves, Hon. W. H. (1814–73), correspondence, 1858–1860

New Brunswick land grants, 1826–67, Gloucester County, 1830–65

Register of marriages for the city and county of Saint John, 1812–1880, in 10 vols, with an index

Tilley family, papers, 1845–1931; Correspondence between Sir Samuel Leonard Tilley and Edward Barron Chandler

Webster manuscript collection, 1610–1956, Chandler correspondence

ONTARIO DEPARTMENT OF PUBLIC RECORDS AND ARCHIVES, Toronto. A Bureau of Archives was established in 1903 and departmental status was conferred by legislation in 1923. As constituted in 1971, the department includes three branches – the archives, records services, and historical branch. The archives branch is authorized to acquire, preserve, and analyse all records of significance of the Ontario government. It also acquires, through donation or purchase, manuscripts, maps, photographs, pictures, posters, and early newspapers relating to the history of the province. Unpublished inventories, calendars, catalogue entries, guides, and other finding aids are available in the archives.

The most important materials used in the preparation of vol. X include:

Bethune (Alexander Neil) papers
Blake (Edward and family) papers
Buell (A. N.) papers
Campbell (Sir Alexander) papers
Carstairs and Reid research papers – Legislative Assembly
Cartwright family papers
Clarke (Colonel Charles) papers
Gowan (James R. and Ogle R.) papers
Hodgins (John George) collection
Jarvis-Powell papers
Jones (Solomon) papers
Macaulay (John) papers
Mackenzie-Lindsey collection
Marston collection
Merritt (William Hamilton) papers
Ridout papers
Robinson (Sir John Beverley) papers
Shanly (Francis) papers
Strachan (John) papers
Street (Samuel) papers
Toronto City Council Records
RG 1: Records of the Department of Lands and Forests
Series A: Offices of surveyor general and commissioner of crown lands
I: Correspondence
IV: Schedules and land rolls
Series C: Lands branch
I: Land grants
IV: Township papers
RG 8: Records of the Department of the Provincial Secretary
Series I-7: Office of the clerk of the Legislative Assembly
Series I-7-B: Sessional Papers
1. Indexes
2. Sessional papers (by years)
3. Railway sessional papers
RG 22: Court Records
Series 7: Courts of General Quarter Sessions

PROVINCIAL ARCHIVES OF BRITISH COLUMBIA, Victoria. Established in 1893, this is the oldest archival institution in western Canada. Its manuscript collection is rich in material on the exploration of the Pacific northwest by land and by sea and in material for the fur trade period. The official records for the colonial period (1849–71) are remarkably complete; records for the provincial period are also held. Substantial collections of private papers, some business records, and a large number of maps, including many of early cartographic interest, are held. There is an extensive collection of visual records – photographs, paintings, and lithographs. Integral to PABC's holdings is an extensive and valuable collection of some 50,000 volumes of books and pamphlets as well as printed ephemera relating to the Pacific northwest. The archives holds almost complete files of newspapers for the colonial period and selected titles for later years.

The collections of PABC have been used extensively in the preparation of this volume. The principal sources of information have been the correspondence of the employees of the HBC, both official and private, the correspondence and records of colonial governors, secretaries, and other government officials, and departmental correspondence. Several other major collections of papers have also been drawn upon often: the Archibald McDonald papers, the James Douglas papers, the Kenneth McKenzie papers, the Crease collection, and the John Sebastian Helmcken collection.

PROVINCIAL ARCHIVES OF NEW BRUNSWICK, Fredericton. Established in 1968, the PANB contains government records series from 1785 as well as several private manuscript collections, including that of the York-Sunbury Historical Society. Records and manuscripts formerly with the New Brunswick Legislative Library have also been transferred to the archives.

Materials used in the preparation of vol. X include:

Department of Justice, Probate Court records
Lieutenant governor's letter book, 1867–74
New Brunswick, Executive Council, Draft minutes, 1843–56

PROVINCIAL ARCHIVES OF NEWFOUNDLAND AND LABRADOR, St John's. Created by an act of the

Newfoundland House of Assembly in 1959, the provincial archives took over the collection and preservation of existing public archives from Memorial University of Newfoundland, which had performed the task in the previous three years. Before 1956 government documents were scattered through departmental offices.

The main holdings of the PANL consist of Newfoundland government documents. In addition the archives holds either microfilm and/or transcript copies of the British colonial records, 1689–1934, and the records of the Northern District Court, Harbour Grace, 1799–1945. With the exception of newspapers, 1810–1969, the remainder of the collection consists of miscellaneous court records, government publications, private papers, and business records. For a list of the collections held by PANL see: *A preliminary inventory of the records in the Provincial Archives of Newfoundland and Labrador*, comp. John P. Greene ([St John's], 1970).

The materials mainly used in the preparation of vol. X include:

Government documents:

Newfoundland, Department of the Colonial Secretary, Letter books, 1747–1864, 1867–1934

Newfoundland, Executive Council, Minutes, 1861–65

Newfoundland, Governor's office, Dispatches to the Colonial Office, 1824–59

Newfoundland, Sessions Court, Harbour Grace, Records, 1825–35

PUBLIC ARCHIVES OF CANADA, Ottawa. In 1873 the government of Canada commissioned Abbé H.-A.-J.-P. Verreau* to investigate the holdings of English and French archives with a view to copying documents concerning the early history of Canada. The work of transcribing and microfilming such manuscripts has proceeded since that time. The PAC also holds, and continues to acquire, extensive private and official manuscript and record collections particularly relating to the 19th and 20th centuries.

Many unpublished finding aids are available only in the archives, but between 1951 and 1967 the Manuscript Division published a series of *Preliminary Inventories*. In 1971 the first *General Inventory, Manuscripts, Volume I, MG 1–MG 10* (Ottawa, 1971) appeared launching a new series to replace the old inventories – "It reworks them, completes them and presents them in a more systematic fashion." The only section of the *General Inventory* which applies to vol. X is "MG 9, Provincial, local and territorial records."

Until the *General Inventory* is completed the following *Preliminary Inventories* will remain useful to researchers of this period:

Manuscript Group 17, Religious archives (1967)

Manuscript Group 19, Fur trade and Indians, 1763–1867 (1954)

Manuscript Group 23, Late eighteenth century papers (1957)

Manuscript Group 24, Nineteenth century pre-confederation papers (1961)

Manuscript Group 26, Prime ministers' papers (1958)

Manuscript Group 27, Political figures, 1867–1948 (1960)

Manuscript Group 28, Records of post-confederation corporate bodies (1960)

Manuscript Group 29, Nineteenth century post-confederation manuscripts, 1867–1900 (1962)

Manuscript Group 30, Twentieth century manuscripts (1966)

Record Group 1, Executive Council, Canada, 1764–1867 (1953)

Record Group 2, Privy Council Office; Record Group 3, Post Office Department (1960)

Record Group 4, Civil and Provincial Secretaries' Offices, Canada East, 1760–1867; Record Group 5, Civil and Provincial Secretaries' Offices, Canada West, 1788–1867 (1953)

Record Group 7, Governor General's Office (1953)

Record Group 8, British military and naval records (1954)

Record Group 9, Department of Militia and Defence, 1776–1922 ([1957])

Record Group 10, Indian affairs (1951)

Record Group 11, Department of Public Works; Record Group 12, Department of Transport (marine; railways and canals) (1951).

Record Group 19, Department of Finance (1954) Unpublished addenda for the above inventories are available for consultation at the PAC. Also available are typescript copies of the following unpublished inventories:

"Manuscript Group 12, War Office, Treasury, Audit Office, and others." This collection is in the process of transfer through Manuscript Groups 13 to 16. It is not known in 1971 exactly which departments will continue to be listed in MG 12 and which will be transferred.

"Record Group 6, Department of the Secretary of State."

"Record Group 31, Dominion Bureau of Statistics."

"Record Group 68, Registrar General."

For Record Group 30, which contains the papers of the Canadian National Railways and the various companies that preceded it, an inventory is in progress.

Manuscript Group 25, which contains numerous genealogies and is a holding unit for minor collections, is also in the process of revision.

The following collections, many of which contain original manuscript material, were found useful in the preparation of vol. X:

MG 9

A: New Brunswick
  12: Local Records, 1762–1894

MG 12

D: Treasury
  T28: Treasury Board out letters, various, 1761–1823

MG 17

B: Anglican
  2: Church Missionary Society, 1821–1950 (microfilm)

MG 19

A: Fur Trade: General
  2: Ermatinger family
    Series 2. Edward Ermatinger
  21: Hargrave papers
E: Red River Settlement
  1: Selkirk papers
  7: Inkster, John
F: Indians
  1: Claus papers

MG 23

D: New Brunswick
  1: Chipman, Ward, 1767–1843
    Series 1. Lawrence collection: Ward Chipman, muster master's office, 1771–85
G II: Quebec and Lower Canada: political figures
  18: Hale, John, 1799–1882
I: Colonies general
  6: Waldo, Samuel, 1764

MG 24

A: British officials and political figures
  13: Bagot, Sir Charles, 1816–43
  16: Elgin, James Bruce, Eighth Earl of, 1823–58
  17: Harvey, Sir John, 1825–41
  19: Roebuck, John Arthur, 1831–53
  20: Head, Sir Edmund, 1831–61
  25: Head, Sir Francis Bond, 1836–41
  27: Durham, John George Lambton, First Earl of, 1837–42
  40: Colborne, Sir John, 1830 [1839]
B: North American political figures and events
  1: Neilson collection, 1666–1912
  11: Baldwin, William Warren, and Robert, 1807–55

    Series 2: Related papers, 1825, 1850–55
  16: Cochran papers, 1812–54
  18: Mackenzie, William Lyon, 1818–68
  19: Chamberlin, Brown, 1818–94
  24: Rolph, Dr John, 1824, 1837–85
  29: Howe, Joseph, 1830–73
  30: Macdonald-Langlois papers, 1831–1926
  40: Brown, George, 1837, 1848–80
  50: O'Callaghan, Dr Edmund Bailey, 1840–60
D: Industry, commerce, and finance
  8: Wright papers, 1806–69
    1: Wright, Philemon, Sr, and Philemon, Jr, 1806, 1837, 1853, 1869
  16: Buchanan papers, 1813–83
  21: Baring Brothers & Co., 1818–72
  47: Robertson collection, 1766–1852
E: Roads, railways, and canals
  1: Merritt papers, 1775–1897
    Series 1: Merritt, Thomas, 1775–1836
    Series 2: Merritt, William Hamilton, 1804–62
  9: Gzowski, Sir Casimir S., 1845, 1852–71
F: Military and naval figures
  53: Clinton, Sir William Henry, 1821–29
I: Immigration, land, and settlement
  9: Hill collection, 1798–1942
  33: Keefer papers, 1817–72
  65: Sherwood, Adiel, 1836–46
  79: Anderson, Thomas B., 1846–50
K: Education and cultural development
  2: Coventry, George, 1793–1865
  19: Robertson, Peter, 1847–54

MG 26

A: Macdonald papers, 1832–91
B: Mackenzie papers, 1852–92
  2: Letterbooks, 1872–83
F: Tupper papers, 1843–1915

MG 27

I: 1867–1896
  D: Cabinet ministers
    4: Cartier papers, 1835–73
    8: Sir Alexander T. Galt papers, 1858–91
    15: Sir Samuel Leonard Tilley, 1882
  E: Members of the House of Commons and the Senate
    5: Luther H. Holton, 1864
    30: Ferguson, Thomas Roberts, 1857–1964 (copies from originals in possession of C. S. Ferguson, London, Ont.)
  F: Provincial political figures
    2: W. H. Pope papers, 1860–79
  I: Correspondence of political figures
    17: James O'Reilly, 1869, 1873
II: 1896–1921
  D: Cabinet ministers

14: R. W. Scott papers, 1843–1913

MG 28

III: Business establishments

6: Gilmour and Hughson Limited, 1845–1926

11: W. & J. Sharples Reg'd., 1854–1923

MG 29

B: Economic development and social life

13: Lowe, John, 1848–1912

F: North West Mounted Police, military units, and events

13: Denison, George Taylor III, 1847–1925

G: Arts, letters, and education

27: Morgan, Henry James, 1866–1913

MG 30

D: Education and cultural development

9: Johnson, George, 1855–1910

62: Audet, Francis-Joseph, 1918–42

RG 1

E: State records of the Executive Council

1: Minute books, 1764–1867

3: Upper Canada state papers, 1791–1841

7: Submissions to council, 1841–67

13: Blue Books, 1824–64

14: Correspondence, 1769–1874

L: Land records of the Executive Council

1: Minute books, 1787–1867

3: Petitions, Upper Canada and Canada, 1791–1867

3^L: Miscellaneous records, Quebec and Lower Canada, 1764–1842

7: Miscellaneous records, 1765–1867

RG 2

Series 1: Minutes and orders in council, 1867–1949

Series 2: Records, 1867–1930

RG 4

A: Civil secretary's correspondence, 1760–1841

1: S Series, 1760–1840

B: Miscellaneous records, 1763–1867

28: Bonds, licences, and certificates, 1763–1867

29: Militia records, 1774–1865

36: Municipal records, 1830–67
Provincial Red Book, 1845

37: Rebellion records, 1837–53

48: Exploration journals, 1830, 1833

C: Provincial secretary's correspondence, 1765–1867

1: Numbered correspondence, 1839–67

RG 5

A: Civil secretary's correspondence, 1791–1840

1: Upper Canada sundries, 1766–1840

B: Miscellaneous records, 1788–1866

C: Provincial secretary's correspondence, 1821–67

1: Numbered correspondence, 1821–67

RG 6

A1: General records, 1867–1952

C: Secretary of state for the provinces, 1867–73

1: General correspondence, 1867–73

RG 7

G1: Dispatches from the Colonial Office, 1784–1909

G9: Drafts of dispatches to the Colonial Office, 1792–1909

G10: Drafts of secret and confidential dispatches to the Colonial Office, 1856–1913

G12: Letter books of dispatches to the Colonial Office, 1799–1902

G16: Letter books, Upper Canada, 1793–1841

G17: Letter books, Canada, 1839–1910

A: Governor's internal letter books, 1839–1909

G20: Civil secretary's correspondence, 1841–1909

RG 8

I: C series

A: Correspondence of the military secretary of the commander of the forces, 1767–1870

1: Subject files, 1767–1870

2: Letter books, 1796–1870

B: Records of the Canadian command, 1785–1883

5: Militia rolls and pay lists, 1838–43

C: Records of the Nova Scotia command, 1762–1899

18: Correspondence of the commanding officer in New Brunswick, 1844–71

D: Miscellaneous records, 1757–1896

2: Order books, 1764–1894

5: Miscellaneous records relating to the Fenian raids, 1866–70

RG 9

I: Pre-confederation records

A: Adjutant General's Office, Lower Canada, 1776–1847

3: Ordres généraux, 1805–46

B: Adjutant General's Office, Upper Canada, 1795–1846

1: Correspondence, 1802–47

4: Pensions and land grants, 1814–51

5: Registers of officers, 1824–47

C: Adjutant General's Office, United Canada, 1846–69

1: Correspondence, 1846–69

4: General orders, 1846–68

6: Register of officers, 1846–69

8: Subject files, 1846–68
II: Post-confederation records
  A: Deputy minister's office, 1867–1920
    1: Correspondence, 1867–1903
RG 10
  A: Administration records, period of imperial control, 1755–1860
    1: Governor general's and lieut.-governor's offices
    8: Civil secretary as superintendent general of Indian affairs
RG 11
  Series 2: Roads and bridges (general), 1765–1856
RG 12
  A: Department of Marine
    1: Shipping registers, 1787–1933
RG 19
  A: Minister of finance
    1: Correspondence
  D: Department of the Inspector General and Department of Finance
    4: Records transferred from other departments, 1843–83
      (a) Provincial secretary, C.E., 1843–67
      Provincial secretary, C.W., 1843–67
RG 30: Canadian National Railways
RG 31:
  A1: Census records, 1825–71
RG 68
  1: Registers and plan books, 1860–1955 (indexed)

PUBLIC ARCHIVES OF MANITOBA, Winnipeg. In 1884 the librarian of the Legislative Library of Manitoba began to assemble a small collection of manuscripts. In 1952 the government named an official archivist and in 1955 the archives became by law an official repository. In 1971 the archives contained about 2,100 feet. The oldest document, relating to the North West Company, is dated about 1795. As well as original material the PAM has an excellent collection of maps and microfilm of certain John A. Macdonald papers. The archives are arranged alphabetically by person and subject. The researcher is aided by a central file for all documents and by biographical files. For a listing of PAM material see, *Public Archives of Manitoba, Preliminary Inventory, 1955.*

The following documents were used in vol. X:
Adams George Archibald, 1870–72. 2 feet, 6 inches
Church of England registers, Diocese of Rupert's Land. Microfilm
  St Andrew's Church
    Records of baptisms, 1845–72
    Records of burials, 1835–84

    Records of marriages, 1860–83
  St John's Church
    Records of baptisms, 1813–79
    Records of burials, 1821–75
    Records of marriages, 1820–82
Miss Davis' School. 10 inches
John Inkster, 1837–76. 1 inch
Alexander Morris, 1845–1911. 7 feet, 6 inches
  Ketcheson Collection, 1845–1911. 6 cartons. PAM bought this collection in 1951 from Frederick G. Ketcheson who had obtained the papers from the estate of Edmund Montague Morris, son of Alexander Morris.
    Correspondence, 1845–1911
    Telegram and letter books, 1873–77
  Lieutenant-governor's collection, 1872–88
    Correspondence, 1872–77
    Letter books, 1874–88
Red River Settlement, 1832–70
  Copies of miscellaneous letters and documents, 1832–36. 110 pages
  Red River Census, 1832–70. 5 inches
  Samuel Taylor, 1849–67. 127 pages
    Journal kept at Moose Factory, 1849–63
    Red River Settlement, 1863–67
Louis Riel papers, 1860–1926. 2 feet, 11 inches
  Correspondence and papers, 1860–1926. 550 documents, 1869–85
  Family papers, 1869–1923. 15 inches
Alexander Ross family papers, 1810–1903. 10 inches
  Correspondence and papers, 1810–1903
Settlement and pioneers, *c.*1870–*c.*1920. 9 feet, 6 inches. This section is arranged alphabetically by name and place; correspondence, newspapers, memoirs, business papers.

PUBLIC ARCHIVES OF NOVA SCOTIA, Halifax. Founded in 1857 when the Nova Scotian government decided to preserve and arrange "the ancient records and documents illustrative of the History and progress of Society in this province," thus establishing the first provincial archives in Canada. The present fireproof building was officially opened on 14 Jan. 1931, and records were transferred from various government departments. The archives also contains court papers, municipal records, family and business papers, collections of societies such as the Nova Scotia Historical Society, community and church records, microfilm copies of deeds and wills from county registries of deeds and courts of probate, and a collection of Nova Scotian newspapers. For further information *see*: C. B. Fergusson, *The Public Archives of Nova Scotia* (PANS *Bull.*, no.19, Halifax, 1963). For a further description of the collections used in the preparation of vol. X see: *Catalogue or list of manuscript documents, arranged, bound and catalogued under the direction of the commissioner of public records . . .* (Halifax, 1877; 2nd ed., 1886). Available for use at PANS are sections of an "Inventory of manuscripts" which is now being compiled for publication in 1972.

Collections of importance in the preparation of vol. X include:

Private papers:
Mather Byles Almon papers
Bliss family papers
Enos Collins papers, 1817–1860
Pierce Stevens Hamilton diary, 1861–78
John Inglis papers
James William Johnston letters
Johnstone family papers
Joseph Howe papers
Beamish Murdoch papers
Simon Bradstreet Robie papers
Sir Charles Tupper papers
Genealogies and compilations:
"Collection of genealogies of Nova Scotian families (Cumberland County)," compiled by Thornton Henry Lodge, 1954
"Pictou County cemeteries' list," compiled by Henry C. Ritchie, 1951, 1956
"Yarmouth genealogy, 1761–1913," compiled by George Stayley Brown
Official records:
Community records, Truro Township book
Halifax County death registrations, June quarter, 1874; March quarter, 1877
Pictou County death certificates for the quarter ending 31 March 1877

PUBLIC ARCHIVES OF PRINCE EDWARD ISLAND, Charlottetown. The PAPEI was created by an act of the Legislative Assembly which received royal assent in 1964 and is located in the library building of Confederation Centre. The nucleus of the collection was documents received from various government offices, and material that had been stored in Province House. Funds for the operation of the archives are provided by an annual vote of the legislature, the archives being a division of the Department of the Provincial Secretary.

Materials used in the preparation of vol. X include:

Henry Jones Cundall letter book, 27 March 1867–26 May 1871
Robert Bruce Stewart and David Stewart letter book, no.1, 16 March 1821–21 Aug. 1834
Prince Edward Island, Executive Council, Minutes, 1847–79

QUEEN'S UNIVERSITY ARCHIVES, Kingston, Ont.

During the past century the Queen's University Archives has developed as a non-governmental repository with collections of private papers and records of national significance. Its holdings include the records of Queen's University from its founding in 1841, the personal papers of noted faculty members and of Canadians prominent in literature, politics, journalism, and business, and many family and business records pertaining to eastern Ontario.

Materials used in the preparation of vol. X include:

William Macaulay papers
Alexander Mackenzie papers
Alexander Morris papers
Edmund Morris papers
Queen's University records, Correspondence series 1, Liddell correspondence
James Williamson papers
John Young papers

SASKATCHEWAN ARCHIVES BOARD, Regina and Saskatoon. Created in 1945 by a provincial statute, The Archives Act, the Saskatchewan Archives Board is a joint university and government board which supervises the Saskatchewan archives. The archival repository has two offices situated at the University of Saskatchewan, one on the Regina campus and the other on Saskatoon's. The original collections of the SAB included manuscripts and documents of the government of the North-West Territories; this collection had been assembled by an archival service existing at the University of Saskatchewan since 1935. The repository contains about 15,000 feet of documents, private and official; the oldest date back to about 1800 but the largest part cover the period 1875–1960. SAB holds an important collection of microfilmed Saskatchewan newspapers, about 1,500 maps, more than 17,000 photographs, and a large number of pamphlets. There are also microfilm copies of documents from other archives containing material on Saskatchewan. For a list of the collections and documents of this repository *see*, SAB, *Report, 1945–46* through to *. . . 1970*.

Since 1948 the archives has published a review, *Saskatchewan History*, appearing three times yearly. Among its other publications is: *Saskatchewan executive and legislative directory, 1905–1970* (1971).

The following documents were used in preparing vol. X:

Kennedy, Dan (Ochankugahe) papers. 64 articles by D. Kennedy on the history and legends of the Assiniboines (typescript copies and manuscripts)
Saskatchewan Historical Society. Secretary,

1936–46, correspondence and documents, 1862–1946, clippings. 20 feet
  37: Hon. James McKay, Biographical note compiled by R. H. Leveson-Gower, Hudson's Bay Company, October 1943
  100: Correspondence and documents *re* Cypress Hills massacre
Supreme Court of Ontario
  Regina *v* George Bennett, 1880. Judge's notes and testimony, 55 pages (photocopies; originals at the Supreme Court of Ontario, Registrar's office, Osgoode Hall, Toronto)

UNITED CHURCH ARCHIVES, Toronto. The Canadian Methodist Historical Society was organized in 1899, and the Presbyterian Historical Committee in 1917; the collections were consolidated in 1950 and the United Church Archives was constituted in its present form in 1953. Since that time, regional depositories have been established in each of the four western provinces, in Montreal, Halifax, and St John's, Nfld. Collections gathered by college librarians and private individuals have been consolidated in all of these centres. In 1967 a large collection of Methodist material relating to the Maritime provinces which had been gathered at Mount Allison University for almost a century was moved to and consolidated with a similar Presbyterian collection at Pine Hill College in Halifax.

The collection at Toronto is the largest, and includes correspondence of the home and foreign missionary societies of the denominations now within the United Church, as well as microfilm copies relating to Canada from the parent societies in Great Britain and the United States. The collection also contains the official records of the various bodies merged into the United Church and copies of almost all the denominational publications, papers of prominent individuals within these churches, some parish records for Ontario, pictures of home and overseas mission work, printed works relating to the history of the denomination, the archives of the Ryerson Press, and the official records and files of correspondence of the various boards, departments, and committees of the Canadian Methodist, Presbyterian, Congregational, and Evangelical United Brethren churches.

Materials used in the preparation of vol. X include:
John Maclean collection
Egerton Ryerson papers
Canada Presbyterian Church, Acts and Proceedings of the General Assembly, 1870–75
Canada Presbyterian Church, Minutes of Synod, 1861–69
Methodist Church of Canada, Journal of

Proceedings of the 1st General Conference, 1874, 2nd General Conference, 1878
Missionary Synod of Canada, Minutes, 1843–47
Presbyterian Church of Canada, Minutes of Synod, 1844–61
Presbyterian Church in Canada, Acts and Proceedings of the General Assembly, 1875–80
Presbyterian Church in Canada, Presbytery of Toronto, Minutes, 1875–80
United Presbyterian Church in Canada, Minutes of Synod, 1848–61
Wesleyan Methodist Church in Canada, Minutes of Conference, 1834–74
Methodist Missionary Society (London), Wesleyan Methodist Missionary Society, records (available on microfilm)

UNIVERSITY OF TORONTO ARCHIVES. Includes the manuscript and printed material produced by the operations of the university. The archives contains: general administrative records, created, for example, by offices of the president, the registrar, heads of faculties, etc.; minutes, correspondence, routine records of faculties and departments; publications by students, alumni, societies; publications about the University of Toronto; University of Toronto theses and dissertations; photographs and paintings; microfilms, tape recordings, film, etc., relating to the university. Finding aids are available within the archives, describing most of the accessioned material.

Materials used in the preparation of vol. X include:
Office of the Chief Accountant. Financial Records
  41: University quarterly accounts, September-December 1871
  109: Final report of the commission of inquiry of 1848 into the affairs of King's College and Upper Canada College
  117: King's College Council minute book, III, 1842–48
Sir Daniel Wilson's journal, Toronto, 1851–1892. (Typescript copy from original diary of the extracts pertaining to university affairs.)

UNIVERSITY OF WESTERN ONTARIO LIBRARY, London, Ont. The library is the official depository for the Archives of the Society of Friends in Canada. The deposit of their papers began in 1926 and constituted the first major set of papers in the collection founded by Dr Fred Landon* and continued by Dr J. J. Talman and Robert Lee. The Regional History Department was formally organized in 1942 with Miss Elsie McLeod (Mrs Wilfred Jury) as head. The Regional History

Collection is attempting to form a comprehensive archives on southwestern Ontario. Major holdings include court, educational, and municipal records for several counties centring on London; records of business firms; and personal, political, or literary papers of local personalities.

Major collections used in the preparation of vol. X include:

27: Ermatinger papers
28: Donnelly family papers
234: Proudfoot family papers (William Proudfoot journals, 1832–50)

ENGLAND

HUDSON'S BAY COMPANY ARCHIVES, London. The HBC archives comprise over thirty thousand volumes and files of records dating from the founding of the company in 1670. The archives as constituted at present were established in 1932, and the work of organization proceeded thereafter [see R. H. G. Leveson Gower, "The archives of the Hudson's Bay Company," *Beaver*, outfit 264 (December 1933), 40–42, 64; Joan Craig, "Three hundred years of records," *Beaver*, outfit 301 (autumn 1970), 65–70]. A publishing programme was undertaken by the Hudson's Bay Record Society [see section II], and in 1949 the HBC and PAC arranged jointly to microfilm the records. Information on the PAC copies is found in PAC *Report, 1950*, 13–14; *1952*, 16–18; *1953–54*, 21–22; *1955–58*, 44–46.

Documents from the following categories were used in the preparation of vol. X:

Section A: London office records
A.1/: Minute books of the governor and committee
A.5/: London correspondence books – outward
General series, 1753–1871
A.6/: London outward correspondence books – HBC official
A.7/: London locked private letter books, 1823–75
A.8/: London correspondence with the British government
A.11/: London inward correspondence from HBC posts
A.12/: London inward correspondence from governors of HBC territories
A.16/: Officers' and servants' ledgers, account books, etc.
A.30/: Lists of servants in Hudson's Bay, 1798–1816
A32/: Servants' contracts

A.33/: Commissioned officers' indentures and agreements
A.34/: Servants' characters and staff records
Section B: North America trading post records
B.3/a: Albany journals
B.89/a: Île-à-la-Crosse journals
B.89/b: Île-à-la-Crosse correspondence books
B.99/a: Kenogamissi journals
B.99/e: Kenogamissi reports on districts
B.113/b: Fort Langley correspondence books
B.113/c: Fort Langley correspondence inward
B.135/e: Moose District reports
B.223/b: Fort Vancouver correspondence books
B.226/a: Fort Victoria post journals
B.226/b: Fort Victoria correspondence books
B.226/c: Fort Victoria correspondence inward
B.239/c: York correspondence inward
B.239/k: Northern Department of Rupert's Land, Minutes of council
B.240/a: Fort Yukon journals
Section C: Records of ships owned or chartered by the HBC
C.1: Ships' logs
Section D: Journals and correspondence books, etc., of governors-in-chief of Rupert's Land, commissioners, etc.
D.4/: George Simpson's correspondence outward
D.5/: George Simpson's correspondence inward
Section F: Records relating to companies connected with or subsidiary to the HBC
F.4/: North West Company account books
Section G: Maps, both manuscript and published (not including maps which are attached to journals or other documents)
G.1/: Manuscript charts

PUBLIC RECORD OFFICE, London. For an introduction to the contents and arrangement of these archives see: *Guide to the contents of the Public Record Office* (3v., London, 1963–68).

The documentary series cited in vol. X include:

Admiralty
Adm. 37: Ships' muster books. Series II (1804–42)
Adm. 38: Ships' muster books. Series III (1793–1878)
Colonial Office [see R. B. Pugh, *The records of the Colonial and Dominions offices* (PRO Handbooks, 3, 1964)]
CO 5: America and West Indies, original

correspondence, etc. (1606–1807)

CO 42: Canada, original correspondence (1700–1922)

CO 60: Columbia, British, original correspondence (1858–71)

CO 188: New Brunswick, original correspondence (1784–1867)

CO 189: New Brunswick, entry books (1796–1867)

CO 194: Newfoundland, original correspondence (1696–1922)

CO 217: Nova Scotia and Cape Breton, original correspondence (1710–1867)

CO 218: Nova Scotia and Cape Breton, entry books (1710–1867)

CO 226: Prince Edward Island, original correspondence (1769–1873)

CO 305: Vancouver Island, original correspondence (1846–67)

CO 478: Vancouver Island, miscellanea (1863–65), blue books of statistics in three volumes

CO 537: Colonies, general: original correspondence: supplementary, 1759–1929

Foreign Office [see: *Records of the Foreign Office 1782–1939* (PRO Handbooks, 13, 1969)]

FO 5: General correspondence, America, United States of. Series II (1793–1905)

FO 414: Confidential print, America, North, 1711–1941. Correspondence relating to the U.S. and Canada, and to Mexico (up to 1919 only)

War Office

WO 1: Correspondence, in-letters and papers (1755–1868). Includes original dispatches, letters, and papers addressed to the secretary-at-war, 1755–95, and to the secretary of state for war, 1794–1865. Also some bundles of correspondence addressed to the commander-in-chief

WO 25: Registers, various (1660–1938). Commissions, appointments, descriptions, returns of service, etc.

WO 32: Correspondence, registered papers, general series (1855–1964)

WO 55: Ordnance office, miscellanea (1568–1923)

WO 69: Returns, Artillery records of services, etc. (1765–1906)

WO 71: Judge Advocate General's office, courts martial, proceedings (1668–1956)

Various

PRO 30/6: Carnarvon papers (1833–98)

For copies in the PAC of documents in the Colonial Office of the PRO *see* PAC, *Preliminary Inventory, Manuscript Group 11* (Ottawa, 1951).

SCOTT POLAR RESEARCH INSTITUTE, Cambridge. Established in 1920 as a centre of polar research and as a memorial to Captain R. F. Scott and his companions. Since 1957 it has been a sub-department within the Department of Geography in the University of Cambridge. The institute includes a museum, research laboratories, a library, and an extensive archives of manuscripts related to both polar regions. Around the nucleus of the Lefroy bequest (1941), which included papers of Sir John* and Lady Jane Franklin [GRIFFIN] and of Sophia Cracroft, the institute has built an important and growing collection of materials related to the exploration of northern Canada.

The following are the most important collections used in the preparation of vol. X:

MS 116/: Penny Craik gift, 1950

57/1–10: Letters from Sherard Osborn to William Penny, 1850–56

MS 248/: Lefroy bequest, 1941

121–122: Jane Franklin's two-volume journal August-September 1860, 1–5 Jan. 1861

160: Jane Franklin's journal, July-August 1846

163/3: Jane Franklin's journal notes, July-August 1860

242: Sophia Cracroft's journal at Sitka, 12 May–14 June 1870

247/73–96: Sophia Cracroft's letters home, 13 Dec. 1860–9 June 1862; 23 Jan.–18 July 1870

MS 395/: Pares loan. George Back's Arctic papers. (A large collection of journals, correspondence, notes, etc.)

MS 695/: Sophia Cracroft's letter home, February-April 1861

MS 768/: George H. Richards's private journal aboard HMS *Assistance*. 17 Aug. 1853–28 May 1854

MS 864/1: Émile-Frédéric de Bray, "Journal de bord de l'enseigne de vaisseau Émile-Frédéric de Bray à bord de la frégate anglaise 'La Resolue.' Expédition polaire de 1852–1853 envoyée à la recherche de Sir John Franklin."

MS 864/2–4: George de Bray, "Notice sur la participation de l'enseigne de vaisseau de Bray à l'expédition britannique de 1852–1854 envoyée à la recherche des navires de Sir John Franklin perdus dans les mers polaires," La Rochelle, 1926; copies of documentary and genealogical material relating to Émile de Bray

UNITED SOCIETY FOR THE PROPAGATION OF THE GOSPEL, London. Formed in 1965, the USPG is responsible for continuing the work formerly carried on by the Society for the Propagation of the Gospel in Foreign Parts (incorporated by royal charter, 1701) and the Universities' Mission to Central Africa (founded, 1857). The archives is in the process of reorganizing and reclassifying some material. Thus classifications used by Canadian archives holding USPG microfilm do not always correspond to those of the archives itself. However indexes are available at USPG and most dated references are easily transferred. For copies of USPG archives documents in the PAC *see*: PAC, *Preliminary Inventory, Manuscript Group 17* (Ottawa, 1967).

Documents from the following groups were used in preparing this volume:

Journal of proceedings of the Society for the Propagation of the Gospel. Comprises bound and indexed volumes of the proceedings of the general meetings held in London from 1701, and four appendices, A, B, C, D (1701–1860) of which only the last two (1840–60) have references to Canada.

C/CAN: Unbound letters from Canada, 1752–1860. Letters from Newfoundland, Nova Scotia, Lower Canada, and Toronto groupings were used. Nominal card index is available at USPG.

D: Original letters received from 1850, bound in volumes. Handlist of writers and places, not alphabetical, available at USPG.

E: Reports from SPG missionaries from 1856, bound in volumes. Handlist available at USPG.

II. PRINTED PRIMARY SOURCES

A. OFFICIAL PUBLICATIONS AND CONTEMPORARY WORKS

[ARTHUR, GEORGE.] *The Arthur papers; being the Canadian papers mainly confidential, private, and demi-official of Sir George Arthur, K.C.H. last lieutenant-governor of Upper Canada in the manuscript collection of the Toronto Public Libraries.* Edited by Charles Rupert Sanderson. 3 vols. Toronto, 1957–59.

[BEGG, ALEXANDER.] *Alexander Begg's Red River journal and other papers relative to the Red River resistance of 1869–1870.* Edited with an introduction by William Lewis Morton. (Champlain Society publication, XXXIV.) Toronto, 1956.

BEGG, ALEXANDER, and WALTER R. NURSEY. *Ten years in Winnipeg. A narration of the principal events in the history of the city of Winnipeg from the year A.D., 1870, to the year A.D., 1879, inclusive.* Winnipeg, 1879.

[BLACKWOOD, FREDERICK TEMPLE, and HENRY HOWARD MOLYNEUX HERBERT.] *Dufferin-Carnarvon correspondence, 1874–1878.* Edited by Cornelis Willem de Kiewiet and Frank Hawkins Underhill. (Champlain Society publication, XXXIII.) Toronto, 1955.

BRITISH COLUMBIA

Blue Books, used for 1859–70 (copies in PABC).

LEGISLATIVE ASSEMBLY

Journals of the Legislative Assembly of the province of British Columbia . . . , used for 1876–79.

LEGISLATIVE COUNCIL

Debate on the subject of confederation with Canada reprinted from the Government Gazette Extraordinary of March, 1870. Victoria.

Journals of the Legislative Council of British Columbia . . . , used for 1868–70.

[BRUCE, JAMES, and ALBERT HENRY GEORGE GREY.] *The Elgin-Grey papers, 1846–1852.* Edited with notes and appendices by Arthur George Doughty. (PAC publication.) 4 vols. Ottawa, 1937.

CANADA

HOUSE OF COMMONS

House of Commons debates, used for 1867–80.

Journals of the House of Commons of the dominion of Canada . . . , used for 1867–74.

SENATE

Debates of the Senate . . . , used for 1872–79.

Sessional papers . . . of the dominion of Canada, used for I (1867–68)–XV (1882).

CANADA, PROVINCE OF

LEGISLATIVE ASSEMBLY

Debates. See *Debates of the Legislative Assembly of United Canada.*

Journals of the Legislative Assembly of the Province of Canada . . . , used for 1841–67.

LEGISLATIVE COUNCIL

Journaux du Conseil législatif de la province du Canada, used for 1862–67.

Parliamentary debates, used for 1846–67 (microfilm project of the Canadian Library Association)

Parliamentary debates on the subject of the confederation of the British North American provinces. . . . Quebec, 1865; reprinted, Ottawa, 1961.

Sessional papers . . . of the Province of Canada, used for XVIII (1860)–XXVI (1866).

Statutes of the Province of Canada . . . , used for 1847–59.

The Canadian North-West, its early development and legislative records; minutes of the councils of the Red River Colony and the Northern Department of Rupert's Land. Edited by Edmund Henry Oliver. (PAC publication, 9.) 2 vols. Ottawa, 1914–15.

CHAMPLAIN SOCIETY. "Founded in 1905, with headquarters in Toronto, for the purpose of publishing rare and inaccessible materials relating to the history of Canada. Its publications are issued only to elected members, limited in number. . . ." Publications related to vol. X include:

XIX: *McLean's notes of twenty-five year's service* (Wallace).

XXIV: *Hargrave correspondence* (Glazebrook).

XXVII: *Loyalist narratives* (Talman).

XXVIII: [Mactavish], *Letters of Letitia Hargrave* (MacLeod).

XXXIII: [Blackwood and Herbert], *Dufferin-Carnarvon correspondence* (de Kiewiet and Underhill).

XXXIV: *Begg's Red River journal* (Morton).

XLIV: *Palliser papers* (Spry).

CHAMPLAIN SOCIETY. ONTARIO SERIES. The Champlain society was invited by the Ontario government to prepare and publish a series of documentary volumes "to preserve in printed form . . . a representative selection of the more interesting and significant records of the past. . . ." This series is sold through normal publishing channels. Publications relevant to vol. X include:

I: *Valley of the Trent* (Guillet).

V: *Town of York, 1793–1815* (Firth).

VI: *Muskoka and Haliburton* (Murray).

VII: *Valley of the Six Nations* (Johnston).

VIII: *Town of York, 1815–1834* (Firth).

COMMISSION GÉOLOGIQUE DU CANADA. *See* GEOLOGICAL SURVEY OF CANADA

Debates of the Legislative Assembly of United Canada: volume I, 1841. Edited by Elizabeth Nish. (Debates of the Legislative Assembly of United Canada, 1841–1867, published under the direction of the Centre d'Étude du Québec and the Centre de recherche en histoire économique du Canada français. General editor, Elizabeth Nish.) Montreal, 1970.

Documentary history of education in Upper Canada from the passing of the Constitutional Act of 1791 to the close of Rev. Dr. Ryerson's administration of the education department in 1876. Edited by John George Hodgins. 28 vols. Toronto, 1894–1910.

Documents relating to the constitutional history of Canada, 1759–1791. Edited by Adam Shortt and Arthur George Doughty. Ottawa, 1907; second and revised edition, in two parts, Ottawa, 1918.

Documents relating to the constitutional history of Canada, 1791–1818. Edited by Arthur George Doughty and Duncan A. McArthur. Ottawa, 1914.

Documents relating to the constitutional history of Canada, 1819–1828. Edited by Arthur George Doughty and Norah Story. Ottawa, 1935.

Dufferin-Carnarvon correspondence. See: [BLACKWOOD, FREDERICK TEMPLE. . . .]

Elgin-Grey papers. See: [BRUCE, JAMES. . . .]

FENETY, GEORGE EDWARD. *Political notes and observations; or, a glance at the leading measures that have been introduced and discussed in the House of Assembly of New Brunswick. . . .* Fredericton, 1867.

GEOLOGICAL SURVEY OF CANADA / COMMISSION GÉOLOGIQUE DU CANADA

BILLINGS, ELKANAH. *Catalogues of the Silurian fossils of the island of Anticosti, with descriptions of some new genera and species.* Montreal, London, New York, and Paris, 1866.

DOWLING, DONALDSON BOGART. *General index to the reports of progress, 1863 to 1884.* Ottawa, 1900.

Memoir 154: W. H. Twenhofel. *Geology of Anticosti Island.* Ottawa, 1928.

Report of progress from its commencement to 1863; illustrated by 498 wood cuts in the text, and accompanied by an atlas of maps and sections. (Geological Survey of Canada, director, William Edmond Logan.) Montreal, London, Paris, New York, 1863; reprinted with an introduction and appendix, 1865. [Commonly known as *Geology of Canada.*]

Report of progress for 1876–77. Montreal, 1878.

GREAT BRITAIN, PARLIAMENT, 1857 (Session II)

House of Commons papers, XV, 224, 260

Report from the select committee on the Hudson's Bay Company; together with the proceedings of the committee, minutes of evidence, appendix and index.

[HARGRAVE, JAMES.] *The Hargrave correspondence, 1821–1843.* Edited with introduction and notes by George Parkin de Twenebrokes Glazebrook. (Champlain Society publication, XXIV.) Toronto, 1938.

HARGRAVE, LETITIA. See [MACTAVISH.]

HEAD, FRANCIS BOND. *A narrative.* London, 1839. Republished as *A narrative with notes by William Lyon Mackenzie.* Edited with introduction by Sydney Francis Wise. (Carleton Library series, 43.) Toronto, Montreal, 1969.

[HOWE, JOSEPH.] *The speeches and public letters of Joseph Howe (based upon Mr. Annand's edition of 1858).* Revised and edited by Joseph Andrew Chisholm. 2 vols. Halifax, 1909.

HUDSON'S BAY RECORD SOCIETY. Initiated in 1938 by the Hudson's Bay Company after classification of its London archives, begun in 1932, had progressed to the point where publication was feasible. Membership in the society is limited. Inquiries should be directed to: the Hon. Secretary, Beaver House, Great Trinity Lane, London, E.C.4, England.

PUBLICATIONS

General editor for vols. I–XXII, E. E. Rich; for vols. XXIII–XXV, K. G. Davies; for XXVI, A. M. Johnson. 26 vols. published to date. Vols. I–XII, issued in association with the Champlain Society, Toronto, were reprinted in 1968 by Kraus Reprint Division of Kraus-Thomson Organization Limited, Nendeln, Liechtenstein.

I: [Simpson, George.] *Journal of occurrences in the Athabasca Department by George Simpson, 1820 and 1821, and report.* Edited by Edwin Ernest Rich, with an introduction by Chester Martin. 1938.

II: [Robertson, Colin.] *Colin Robertson's correspondence book, September 1817 to September 1822.* Edited with an introduction by Edwin Ernest Rich, assisted by R. Harvey Fleming. 1939.

III: *Minutes of council Northern Department of Rupert Land, 1821–31.* Edited by R. Harvey Fleming, with an introduction by Harold Adams Innis. 1940.

IV: [McLoughlin, John.] *The letters of John McLoughlin from Fort Vancouver to the governor and committee, first series, 1825–38.* Edited by Edwin Ernest Rich, with an introduction by William Kaye Lamb. 1941.

VI: [McLoughlin, John.] *The letters of John McLoughlin from Fort Vancouver to the governor and committee, second series, 1839–44.* Edited by Edwin Ernest Rich, with an introduction by William Kaye Lamb. 1943.

VII: [McLoughlin, John.] *The letters of John McLoughlin from Fort Vancouver to the governor and committee, third series, 1844–46.* Edited by Edwin Ernest Rich, with an introduction by William Kaye Lamb. 1944.

X: [Simpson, George.] *Part of dispatch from George Simpson, Esqr, governor of Ruperts Land to the governor & committee of the Hudson's Bay Company, London, March 1, 1829. Continued and completed March 24 and June 5, 1829.* Edited by Edwin Ernest Rich, with an introduction by William Stewart Wallace. 1947.

XVI: [Rae, John.] *John Rae's correspondence with the Hudson's Bay Company on Arctic exploration, 1844–1855.* Edited by Edwin Ernest Rich, assisted by Alice M. Johnson, with an introduction by J. M. Wordie and R. J. Cyriax. 1953.

XVIII: [Black, Samuel.] *A journal of a voyage from Rocky Mountain Portage in Peace River to the sources of Finlays Branch and North West Ward in summer 1824.* Edited by Edwin Ernest Rich, assisted by Alice M. Johnson, with an introduction by R. M. Patterson. 1955.

XIX: [Colvile, Eden.] *London correspondence inward from Eden Colvile, 1849–1852.* Edited by Edwin Ernest Rich, assisted by Alice M. Johnson, with an introduction by William Lewis Morton. 1956.

XXI: Rich, *History of the HBC. I: 1670–1763.* [*see* section IV]

XXII: Rich, *History of the HBC, II: 1763–1870.*

XXIV: *Northern Quebec and Labrador journals and correspondence, 1819–35.* Edited by Kenneth Gordon Davies, assisted by Alice M. Johnson, with introduction by Glyndwr Williams. 1963.

Journal de l'Assemblée législative de la Province du Canada. . . . See CANADA, PROVINCE OF, LEGISLATIVE ASSEMBLY, *Journals. . . .*

Journal de l'Instruction publique, Québec, Montréal. Monthly. I (1857)–XXIII (1879). Official publication of the Department of Public Instruction, published variously at Quebec and Montreal. It must not be confused with the *Journal of Education* which is also an official publication of the same department. They were completely independent journals, and neither was a translation of the other.

Journal of Education for Ontario, Toronto. A monthly publication which began, I (January 1848), as the *Journal of Education for Upper Canada,* it was the official publication of the province's department of education. Title changed in 1867 to the *Journal of Education for Ontario* which continued to XXX (July 1877).

751

[LANGELIER, JEAN-CHRYSOSTOME.] *List of lands granted by the crown in the province of Quebec from 1763 to 31st December 1890*. Quebec, 1891.

[Logan *et al.*] *Geology of Canada. See* GEOLOGICAL SURVEY OF CANADA.

LOWER CANADA
HOUSE OF ASSEMBLY
Journals of the House of Assembly of Lower-Canada, used for 1824–37.
SPECIAL COUNCIL
Journaux du Conseil spécial de la province du Bas-Canada, used for 1838–40.

Loyalist narratives from Upper Canada. Edited with introduction and notes by James John Talman. (Champlain Society publication, XXVII.) Toronto, 1946.

[MCCLURE, ROBERT JOHN LEMESURIER.] *The discovery of the north-west passage by H.M.S. "Investigator," Capt. R. M'Clure, 1850, 1851, 1852, 1853, 1854*. Edited by Sherard Osborn. London, 1856.

[MACDONALD, JOHN ALEXANDER.] *The letters of Sir John A. Macdonald, 1836–1857*. Edited by J. K. Johnson. —— *1858–1861*. Edited by J. K. Johnson and Carole B. Stelmack. (PAC publications, The Papers of the Prime Ministers series, I, II.) Ottawa, 1968, 1969.

[MCLEAN, JOHN.] *John McLean's notes of twenty-five year's service in the Hudson's Bay territory*. Edited by William Stewart Wallace. (Champlain Society publication, XIX.) Toronto, 1932.

[MACTAVISH, LETITIA.] *The letters of Letitia Hargrave*. Edited with introduction and notes by Margaret Arnett MacLeod. (Champlain Society publication, XXVIII.) Toronto, 1947.

Mandements, lettres pastorales et circulaires des évêques de Québec. Henri Têtu et Charles-Octave Gagnon, éditeurs. 4 vols. Québec, 1887–88. 13 vols. Québec, 1889–1955.

MANITOBA
Statutes of the province of Manitoba . . ., used for 1873–78.

Manitoba: the birth of a province. Edited by William Lewis Morton. (Manitoba Record Society publication, I.) Altona, Man., 1965.

MANITOBA RECORD SOCIETY PUBLICATIONS. General editor, William David Smith.
I: *Manitoba: birth of a province* (Morton).
III: *James Wickes Taylor correspondence* (Bowsfield).

MORRIS, ALEXANDER. *The treaties of Canada with the Indians of Manitoba and the North-West Territories. . . .* Toronto, 1880.

MURRAY, ALEXANDER HUNTER. *Journal of the Yukon, 1847–48*. Edited with notes by Lawrence Johnston Burpee. (PAC publication, 4.) Ottawa, 1910.

Muskoka and Haliburton, 1615–1875; a collection of documents. Edited with an introduction by Florence Beatrice Murray. (Champlain Society publication, Ontario series, VI.) Toronto, 1963.

NEW BRUNSWICK
HOUSE OF ASSEMBLY
Journals of the House of Assembly of the province of New Brunswick . . ., used for 1824–81.
Reports of the debates of the House of Assembly of the province of New Brunswick . . ., used for 1854–66.
Synoptic report of the proceedings of the House of Assembly of New Brunswick . . ., used for 1834–68.
LEGISLATIVE COUNCIL
Debates of the Legislative Council of New Brunswick, used for 1866.
Journals of the Legislative Council of the province of New Brunswick, used 1836–72.

NEWFOUNDLAND
Blue books, used for 1832–74 (copies in PANL).
HOUSE OF ASSEMBLY
Journal of the House of Assembly of Newfoundland . . ., used for 1834–63.

NOVA SCOTIA
HOUSE OF ASSEMBLY
Debates and proceedings of the House of Assembly . . . of the province of Nova Scotia, used for 1855–71.
Journal and proceedings of the House of Assembly of the province of Nova Scotia, used for 1836–68.
LEGISLATIVE COUNCIL
Journal of the proceedings of Her Majesty's Legislative Council of the province of Nova Scotia, used for 1836–67.

ONTARIO
LEGISLATIVE ASSEMBLY
Journals of the Legislative Assembly of the province of Ontario . . ., used for 1867–72.
Sessional papers . . . of the province of Ontario, used for III (1870–71)–XIII (1881).
Statutes of the province of Ontario . . ., used for 1878, 1879.

The papers of the Palliser expedition, 1857–1860. Edited with an introduction and notes by Irene

Mary Spry. (Champlain Society publication, XLIV.) Toronto, 1968.

PRINCE EDWARD ISLAND
HOUSE OF ASSEMBLY
Debates and proceedings of the House of Assembly of Prince Edward Island, used for 1855–79.
Journal of the House of Assembly of Prince Edward Island, used for 1825–73.
Journal of the House of Assembly of the province of Prince Edward Island, used for 1874–79.
LEGISLATIVE COUNCIL
Debates and proceedings of the Legislative Council of Prince Edward Island, used for 1856–60, 1871–73.
Debates and proceedings of the Legislative Council of the province of Prince Edward Island, used for 1874–75.
Journal of the Legislative Council of Prince Edward Island, used for 1830–73.
Journal of the Legislative Council of the province of Prince Edward Island, used for 1874–75.

PROVOST, HONORIUS. *Le séminaire de Québec: documents et biographies* (Publications des archives du séminaire de Québec, II.) Québec, 1964.

PUBLIC ARCHIVES OF CANADA
NUMBERED PUBLICATIONS
4: Murray, *Journal of the Yukon* (Burpee).
9: *Canadian North-West* (Oliver).
THE PAPERS OF THE PRIME MINISTERS SERIES
I: [J. A. Macdonald], *Letters* (Johnson).
II: [J. A. Macdonald], *Letters* (Johnson and Stelmack).
OTHER PUBLICATIONS
[Bruce and Grey], *Elgin-Grey papers* (Doughty).
Canadian directory of parliament (Johnson). [*see* section III]
Guide to Canadian ministries since confederation. [*see* section III]
Union list of manuscripts (Gordon). [*see* section III]

QUEBEC
A complete, descriptive list of Quebec government publications is found in *Répertoire des publications gouvernementales du Québec de 1867 à 1964.* André Beaulieu *et al.*, éditeurs. Québec, 1968.
Department of Lands and Forests. *See* [Langelier, Jean-Chrysostome], *List of lands. . . .*

Department of Public Instruction. See *Journal de l'Instruction publique.*
LEGISLATIVE ASSEMBLY
Journaux de l'Assemblée législative du Québec, used for 1875–80.
LEGISLATIVE COUNCIL
Journaux du Conseil législatif de la province de Québec, used for 1867–77.

[RYERSON, ADOLPHUS EGERTON.] *"The story of my life,"* by the late Rev. Egerton Ryerson, D.D., LLD., *(being reminiscences of sixty years' public service in Canada).* Edited by John George Hodgins. Toronto, 1883.
SCADDING, HENRY. *Toronto of old: collections and recollections illustrative of the early settlement and social life of the capital of Ontario.* Toronto, 1873. Republished as *Toronto of old.* Abridged and edited by Frederick Henry Armstrong. Toronto, 1966.
[TAYLOR, JAMES WICKES.] *The James Wickes Taylor correspondence, 1859–1870.* Edited by Hartwell Bowsfield. (Manitoba Record Society publication, III.) Altona, Man., 1968.
The town of York, 1793–1815: a collection of documents of early Toronto. Edited with an introduction by Edith Grace Firth. (Champlain Society publication, Ontario series, V.) Toronto, 1962.
The town of York, 1815–1834: a further collection of documents of early Toronto. Edited with an introduction by Edith Grace Firth. (Champlain Society publication, Ontario series, VIII.) Toronto, 1966.
TURCOTTE, LOUIS-PHILIPPE. *Le Canada sous l'Union, 1841–1867.* 2 vols. Québec, 1871–72; 2e édition, 1882.

UPPER CANADA
HOUSE OF ASSEMBLY
Journal of the House of Assembly of Upper Canada . . . , used for 1821–40.

The valley of the Six Nations: a collection of documents on the Indian lands of the Grand River. Edited with an introduction by Charles M. Johnston. (Champlain Society publication, Ontario series, VII.) Toronto, 1964.
The valley of the Trent. Edited with an introduction and notes by Edwin Clarence Guillet. (Champlain Society publication, Ontario series, I.) Toronto, 1957.

B. NEWSPAPERS

Various sources have been used for discovering the

753

titles and affiliations of newspapers during the period of this volume. These include: J. W. Dafoe, "Early Winnipeg newspapers," HSSM *Papers*, 3rd ser., no.3 (1947), 14–24; J. R. Harper, *Historical directory of New Brunswick newspapers and periodicals* (Fredericton, 1961); "Chronological list of Newfoundland newspapers in the public collections at the Gosling Memorial Library and Provincial Archives," compiled by Ian McDonald (copy deposited in the Reference Library, Arts and Culture Centre, St John's); Ella Naomi Tratt, "A survey and listing of Nova Scotian newspapers with particular reference to the period before 1867," unpublished MA thesis, Mount Allison University, Sackville, N.B., 1957 (copy in PANS); *Catalogue of Canadian newspapers in the Douglas Library, Queen's University*, compiled by L. C. Ellison *et al.* (Douglas Library Occasional Papers, 1, Kingston, 1969); *Early Toronto newspapers, 1793–1867: a catalogue of newspapers published in the Town of York and the City of Toronto from the beginning to confederation*, ed. E. G. Firth (Toronto, 1961); W. L. Cotton, "The press in Prince Edward Island," *Past and present of Prince Edward Island . . .* , edited by D. A. MacKinnon and A. B. Warburton (Charlottetown, [1906]), 112–21; R. L. Cotton, "Early press," *Historic highlights of Prince Edward Island*, ed. M. C. Brehaut (Prince Edward Island Hist. Soc. pamphlet, Charlottetown, 1955), 40–45; and Beaulieu et Hamelin, *Journaux du Québec*. Because this last includes such complete details on all the papers covered, full descriptions of the Quebec newspapers are not given in the following listing.

Acadian Recorder, Halifax. Published from 16 Jan. 1813 until 10 May 1930. The paper was a weekly from 1813 until 27 Aug. 1863, a tri-weekly from 5 Sept. 1863 until 1930, and a daily from 1868 until 1930.

British Colonist, Halifax. Its full name was *British Colonist: A Literary, Political and Commercial Journal*. Published from 25 June 1848 until 31 Dec. 1874 as a tri-weekly; a weekly was added in January 1849 and a daily edition later. From 11 Sept. 1851 until January 1855, the full title was *British Colonist and North American Railway Journal*.

British Colonist, Victoria. See *Colonist*

Brockville Recorder and the Eastern Johnstown and Bathurst Districts Advertiser, Brockville, Ont. Began publication on 16 Jan. 1821 as a weekly and became a daily on 10 Nov. 1873. Bought out the *Times* (Brockville) and on 1 Feb. 1918 became the *Recorder and Times*, which continued to be published in 1971.

Canadian Churchman, Toronto. See *Church*

Canadian Citizen, Ottawa. See *Ottawa Citizen*

Canadian Free Press, London, Ont. See *London Free Press*

Le Canadien, Québec. Published from 22 Nov. 1806 until 11 Feb. 1893.

Cariboo Sentinel, Barkerville, B.C. Published from 6 June 1865 to 30 Oct. 1875 although publication was suspended for several short periods. The paper was published at various times as a weekly, a semi-weekly, and a semi-monthly.

Central Canada Citizen, Ottawa. See *Ottawa Citizen*

Christian Guardian, Toronto. Published as a weekly at York (later Toronto) from 21 Nov. 1829 until 10 June 1925 when it was superseded by the *New Outlook* which ceased publication on 24 Feb. 1939. A general index of the *Christian Guardian* for the years 1829–67 is available at the United Church Archives, Toronto. A selective index for church news, general historical information, and genealogical information is in preparation for the period after 1867.

Church, Cobourg, Toronto, and Hamilton, Ont. Published as a weekly from 6 May 1837 to 25 July 1856. Began publication in Cobourg, then moved to Toronto from 11 July 1840 to 14 July 1843 when it returned to Cobourg only to move again to Toronto on 17 July 1846. Between 5 Aug. 1852 and 16 June 1853 the title was the *Canadian Churchman*. Between 3 Aug. 1855 and 25 July 1856 the *Church* was published in Hamilton.

Colonist, Victoria. Published under various titles from 11 Dec. 1858 to the present. Until 28 July 1860 the full name was the *British Colonist*; from 31 July 1860 to 23 June 1866, *Daily British Colonist*; from 25 June 1866 to 31 Dec. 1886, the *Daily British Colonist and Victoria Chronicle*; and from 1 Jan. 1887 to the present, *Daily Colonist*. The paper began as a weekly, then on 16 May 1859 a tri-weekly issue was begun. The weekly continued to 1888 as the *Weekly British Colonist*. The paper published five issues per week beginning on 31 July 1860, and after 16 Feb. 1861 became a full-scale daily.

Courier, St John's. See *Morning Courier and General Advertiser*

Le Courrier du Canada, journal des intérêts canadiens, Québec. Published from 2 Feb. 1857 to 11 April 1901.

Daily British Colonist and Victoria Chronicle. See *Colonist*

Daily Colonist, Victoria. See *Colonist*

Daily Ledger, St John's. See *Public Ledger and Newfoundland General Advertiser*

Daily Mail and Empire, Toronto. See *Mail*; *Globe*

Daily News, Saint John, N.B. See *Morning News*

Daily Telegraph, Saint John, N.B. See *Telegraph*

Eastern Chronicle, Pictou and New Glasgow, N.S. Its full name was *Eastern Chronicle and Pictou County Advocate*. Published from 1843 until 1865 as a weekly in Pictou and from 4 Jan. 1866 until 1953 as a semi-weekly in New Glasgow.

L'Événement, Québec. Published from 13 May 1867 to 31 March 1966.

Evening Standard, Victoria. See *Victoria Daily Standard*

Examiner, Charlottetown. Published from 7 Aug. 1847 until 1919 or 1920 when it was absorbed by the *Guardian* (Charlottetown). The *Examiner* was a weekly from 1847 until May 1877 when it became a daily only. A few months later the weekly edition was revived, and both editions continued.

Examiner, Toronto. Published as a weekly from 3 July 1838 until 29 Aug. 1855 when it merged with the *Globe*.

Gazette, Montreal. Began publication on 3 June 1778 and continued in 1971.

Globe, Toronto. Began as a weekly on 5 March 1844, became a semi-weekly 4 Nov. 1846, a tri-weekly, 3 July 1849, and a daily, 1 Oct. 1853. A second weekly series began 6 July 1849 and continued to 28 Jan. 1914; its title changed to *Weekly Globe and Canadian Farmer* on 5 Jan. 1877. A second semi-weekly series was published from 19 Oct. 1853 to 2 July 1855 when it became a tri-weekly which lasted until 1864. There was a second daily, the *Evening Globe*, from 19 Dec. 1861 to 20 July 1908. The *Western Globe*, published weekly in Toronto but issued from London, C.W., lasted from 16 Oct. 1845 until at least 1851. Title became the *Globe and Mail* when it merged with the *Daily Mail and Empire* (Toronto) on 23 Nov. 1936 and publication continued under this title in 1971.

Herald, Montreal. Published from 19 Oct. 1811 until 18 Oct. 1959.

Island Argus, Charlottetown. A weekly, published from 4 Nov. 1869 until it was absorbed by the *Examiner* on 25 Feb. 1881 when the name became the *Examiner and Island Argus*.

Islander, Charlottetown. Its full title was the *Islander or Prince Edward Weekly Intelligencer and Advertiser* until 21 Jan. 1853 when it became the *Islander or Prince Edward Island Weekly Intelligencer and Advertiser*. It was published from 2 Dec. 1842 until 1874 as a weekly. A new owner changed its title in 1872 to *Prince Edward Islander: A Weekly Newspaper of General Intelligence*. It was absorbed by the *Patriot* in 1874.

Journal de Québec. Published from 1 Dec. 1842 until 1 Oct. 1889.

Leader, Toronto. Began publication as a semi-weekly on 1 July 1852 and as a weekly on 7 July. A daily edition was added on 11 July 1853. The semi-weekly ceased publication in 1864 but the daily and weekly editions continued to 1878. The *Leader* absorbed several Toronto newspapers including, for a time, the *Toronto Daily Patriot and Express*.

London Advertiser, London, Ont. A daily, begun 27 Oct. 1863 as the *London Evening Advertiser and Family Newspaper*, its name changed to *London Evening Advertiser* on 23 May 1865 and to *Daily Advertiser* in the spring of 1869. On 4 Dec. 1880 its name became the *London Advertiser*. The *Weekly Advertiser* was begun in 1864, and its name had changed to *Western Advertiser* by 1873; in 1875 it combined with the *Weekly Liberal* (Toronto) to become the *Western Advertiser and Weekly Liberal* (London and Toronto), but by 1884 the title was again *Western Advertiser*.

London Free Press, London, Ont. Began publication as a weekly on 2 Jan. 1849 as the *Canadian Free Press*. A daily edition, the *London Free Press and Daily Western Advertiser*, began on 5 May 1855 and, except for a brief interruption in the late 1850s, continued in 1971. The *Canadian Free Press* continued as a weekly, probably until 6 March 1868.

Mail, Toronto. Began publication as a daily on 30 March 1872. Its name was changed to the *Toronto Daily Mail* on 2 Aug. 1880. The paper merged with the *Empire* (Toronto) to become the *Daily Mail and Empire* on 7 Feb. 1895. A weekly edition was also published. The *Daily Mail and Empire* merged with the *Globe* to become the *Globe and Mail* on 23 Nov. 1936.

Mainland Guardian, New Westminster, B.C. Published on a semi-weekly basis from 28 Aug. 1869 until 21 Aug. 1889 or later (21 Aug. 1889 issue was the last available to *DCB* for examination but does not contain a notice that it was the last issue of the paper).

Manitoba Free Press, Winnipeg. Founded on 30 Nov. 1872 as a weekly, it became a daily on 6 July 1874. On 2 Dec. 1931 its name changed to the *Winnipeg Free Press*, still published in 1971.

Mélanges religieux, Montréal. Published from 14 Dec. 1840 until 6 July 1852.

La Minerve, Montréal. Published from 9 Nov. 1826 to 27 May 1899.

Le Monde canadien, Montréal. Published between 19 Sept. 1867 and 5 July 1900.

Montreal Daily Witness. Published from 13 Aug. 1860 until 11 July 1913.

Montreal Gazette. See *Gazette*

Montreal Herald. See *Herald*

Montreal Herald and Daily Commercial Gazette. See *Herald*

Montreal Weekly Witness. Its prospectus appeared on 15 Dec. 1845 with publication beginning on 5 Jan. 1846 and continuing to May 1938.

Morning Chronicle, Halifax. Published under various titles from 24 Jan. 1844 to the present. It began as a tri-weekly, then expanded in 1877 to a daily; it was also printed as a weekly from 1844 until 1912. The name changed to the *Halifax Chronicle* on 22 Jan. 1927; on 1 Jan. 1949 the paper merged with the *Herald* and its name became the *Halifax Chronicle-Herald*, which was shortened to the *Chronicle-Herald* on 26 Dec. 1959.

Morning Chronicle, Quebec. Published from 1847 to 1888.

Morning Courier and General Advertiser, St John's. Published from 1844 to 1878 as a semi-weekly. The name was changed in 1856 to the *Courier*.

Morning Freeman, Saint John, N.B. This paper began in 1849 as a weekly under the title *St. John Weekly Freeman*. The *Morning Freeman* was added in 1851 as a tri-weekly and lasted until 1878. The weekly continued until 1884.

Morning News, Saint John, N.B. Published from 1839 until 1884 but under a great variety of titles beginning with *Commercial News and General Advertiser*. The paper was, at different times, a weekly, a tri-weekly, and a daily. Used in this volume were issues appearing as the *Morning News*, the *Saint John Daily News*, and the *Daily News*.

Morning Telegraph, Saint John, N.B. See *Telegraph*

New Brunswick Reporter, Fredericton. A weekly, published from November 1844 until December 1902. Its full title was the *New Brunswick Reporter and Fredericton Advertiser* until its last years when it was the *Reporter and Fredericton Advertiser*.

Newfoundlander, St John's. Published from 1806 until 1884 although issues are only available from 1827. The paper was a weekly, then a semi-weekly.

Newfoundland Patriot, St John's. Published from 1834 to 1878 as a weekly, although issues are available only from 1854. In 1842 the name was changed to the *Patriot & Terra Nova Herald*; in 1877, it became the *Patriot and Catholic Herald* for four issues only; in 1878, it was the *Patriot and Terra Nova Advocate*.

New Nation, Winnipeg. Published from 7 January to September 1870. It was founded by Americans living in Red River, after the *Nor'Wester* ceased publication; in March 1870 it became the organ of Louis Riel*'s provisional government.

Nor'Wester, Winnipeg. The first newspaper published in the Red River Settlement, it was founded "in opposition to the existing order." It was published from 28 Dec. 1859 to 24 Nov. 1869.

Le Nouveau Monde, Montréal. See *Le Monde canadien*

Novascotian, Halifax. Published under various names from 1824 until 1925. From 1824 until 1892 the full name was *Novascotian and Colonial Herald*, then in 1892 it became a weekly called the *Nova Scotian and Weekly Chronicle* which lasted until 13 Oct. 1922. At that time the format changed and it was the *Nova Scotian: Nova Scotia's Farm and Home Journal* until it ceased publication.

L'Opinion publique, Montréal. Published from 16 Dec. 1892 until 16 June 1893.

Ottawa Citizen. Began as a weekly in the autumn of 1844 as the *Packet*, but changed to the *Ottawa Citizen* on 22 Feb. 1851 under which title it was still published in 1971. A semi-weekly edition was added on 4 Oct. 1859, which became a daily edition on 15 May 1865. The weekly continued to 1916 with the name changing to the *Central Canada Citizen* from 1909–12, then to the *Canadian Citizen*.

Patriot, Charlottetown. Published from 8 July 1865 until the present. The *Patriot* began as a weekly and became a semi-weekly in 1867; in mid-1874 it reverted to being a weekly but in 1875 it began to feature both editions again. Later it became a daily. [This paper is sometimes said to have begun publication on 5 July 1859 because it was numbered consecutively from the *Protestant and Evangelical Witness* which began on that date and ceased publication on 1 July 1865. For various reasons, including religious affiliation and financial support, it is not strictly correct to assume that the *Patriot* was a continuation of the *Protestant*.]

Patriot, Kingston, Ont., and Toronto. Began publication as a weekly in Kingston in 1828 as the *Patriot and Farmer's Monitor*. Moved to York (Toronto) on 7 Dec. 1832. A semi-weekly edition began in November 1833 and continued to April 1852; in March 1834 the title was changed to the *Patriot*, and in 1839 to the *Toronto Patriot*. In April 1850 a daily edition was added entitled the *Toronto Daily Patriot and Express*; it continued to 1855 and was absorbed, for a time, by the *Leader* (Toronto). The weekly ceased publication in 1878.

Patriot, St John's. See *Newfoundland Patriot*

Le Pays, Montréal. Published between 15 Jan. 1852 and 26 Dec. 1871.

Pilot and Journal of Commerce, Montreal. Appeared under various titles between 5 March 1844 and 25 March 1862.

Le Pionnier de Sherbrooke. Published from 13 Oct. 1866 until 11 May 1902.

Protestant and Evangelical Witness, Charlottetown. See *Patriot*

Public Ledger and Newfoundland General Advertiser, St John's. Published from 1820 to 1882 first as a semi-weekly, then as a tri-weekly, and finally as a daily in 1859, when it became the *Daily Ledger*.

Royal Gazette, Charlottetown. Published from 1791 to the present. This paper began as a semi-monthly entitled *Royal Gazette, and Miscellany of the Island of Saint John* published by the king's or queen's printer, and subsequently it became a weekly.

Royal Gazette and Newfoundland Advertiser, St John's. Published from 1807 to 1924 as a weekly, although issues are only available from 1810. In 1926 the paper became the *Newfoundland Gazette* which continues to the present.

Saint John Daily News. See *Morning News*

St. John Daily Telegraph and Morning Journal. See *Telegraph*

Standard, Winnipeg. See *Weekly Manitoban and Herald of Rupert's Land and the North-Western Territory*

Telegraph, Saint John, N.B. This paper, begun as the *Weekly Telegraph*, was published from 27 Sept. 1862 until July 1923, when it became the *Telegraph-Journal* which still exists as a daily. It was published at various times as a weekly, a semi-weekly, and a daily under a great many titles. The titles appearing in this volume include the *Morning Telegraph*, the *Daily Telegraph*, the *St. John Daily Telegraph and Morning Journal*, and the *Telegraph-Journal*.

Telegraph-Journal, Saint John, N.B. See *Telegraph*

Times, Halifax. Published under various names from 3 June 1834 until 1880: it was a weekly entitled the *Times* from 1834 until 27 June 1848. It became the *New Times* on 3 July until 30 December when it merged with the *Courier* to become the *Times and Courier* until 1867. In that year it merged with the *Evening Reporter* and became the *Evening Reporter and Daily & Tri-weekly Times*; finally on 13 Oct. 1879 it became the *New Times and Reporter* and lasted only one more year.

Times and General Commercial Gazette, St John's. Published from 29 Aug. 1832 until 23 March 1895 mainly as a semi-weekly but at times as a weekly.

Toronto Daily Mail. See *Mail*

Toronto Daily Patriot and Express. See *Patriot*

Toronto Patriot. See *Patriot*

Victoria Daily Standard. Published from 20 June 1870 until 4 Aug. 1888 as a daily. Was replaced by the *Evening Standard* (Victoria) which continued until sometime in 1889.

Victoria Gazette. Published from 25 June 1858 until 30 July 1860. Began as a semi-weekly which continued until 24 July 1858; on 28 July became the *Daily Victoria Gazette* which existed until 26 October. On 28 October reverted to *Victoria Gazette* as a tri-weekly lasting until 26 Nov. 1859. On 5 Dec. 1859 a new tri-weekly appeared under the same title and continued to 30 July 1860. A weekly issue appeared briefly on two occasions.

Weekly British Colonist, Victoria. See *Colonist*

Weekly Globe and Canadian Farmer, Toronto. See *Globe*

Weekly Manitoban and Herald of Rupert's Land and the North-Western Territory, Winnipeg. An independent liberal paper, it was founded on 15 Oct. 1870 and remained a weekly until 1874. It became the *Standard* from 28 Nov. 1874 until 20 Nov. 1875. Publication ceased in 1882.

Western Globe, London, Ont. See *Globe*

III. REFERENCE WORKS

ALLAIRE, JEAN-BAPTISTE-ARTHUR. *Dictionnaire biographique du clergé canadien-français*. 6 vols. Montréal, 1910–34.

ARMSTRONG, FREDERICK HENRY. *Handbook of Upper Canadian chronology and territorial legislation*. London, Ont., 1967.

AUDET, FRANCIS-JOSEPH. *Les députés de Montréal (ville et comtés), 1792–1867*. Montréal, 1943.

Australian dictionary of biography. General editor, Douglas Pike. 3 vols. Melbourne, 1966–69. [Two volumes covering the period 1788–1850 were published, 1966–67, and the first volume for the period 1851–1890 was published in 1969.] In progress.

BEAULIEU, ANDRÉ, et JEAN HAMELIN. *Les journaux du Québec de 1764 à 1964.* (Les cahiers de l'Institut d'histoire, 6.) Québec et Paris, 1965.

A bibliography of the Prairie provinces to 1953. Compiled by Bruce Braden Peel. Toronto, 1956. —— *supplement.* Compiled by Bruce Braden Peel. Toronto, 1963. [New edition in progress.]

BOASE, FREDERIC. *Modern English biography, containing many thousand concise memoirs of persons who have died between the years 1851–1900 with an index of the most interesting matter.* 3 vols. and 3 supplements. Privately printed in England, 1892–1921; reprinted [London], 1965.

British Museum general catalogue of printed books. (Photolithographic edition to 1955.) 263 vols. London, 1961–66.

Canada, an encyclopædia of the country: the Canadian dominion considered in its historic relations, its natural resources, its material progress, and its national development. Edited by John Castell Hopkins. 6 vols., Toronto, 1898–1900. Also, *Index topical and personal to Canada: an encyclopædia of the country.* Toronto and London, 1900.

The Canada directory for 1857–1858; containing names of professional and business men, and of the principal inhabitants. . . . Montreal, 1857.

The Canadian directory of parliament, 1867–1967. Edited by J. K. Johnson. (PAC publication.) Ottawa, 1968.

The Canadian parliamentary companion. Published in Quebec, 1862 and 1863, in Montreal from 1864 to 1874, and in Ottawa from 1875. Appeared irregularly from 1862, then annually from 1871. Became the *Canadian parliamentary guide . . .* early in the 20th century. Editors during the period of vol. X of the *DCB* were Henry James Morgan until 1875, then Charles H. MacKintosh.

The Catholic encyclopedia, an international work of reference . . . of the Catholic church. Edited by C. G. Herbermann *et al.* 15 vols., index, 1 supplement. New York, 1907–22.

CHADWICK, EDWARD MARION. *Ontarian families; genealogies of United-Empire-Loyalist and other pioneer families of Upper Canada.* 2 vols. Toronto, 1894–98.

Classified digest of the records of the Society for the Propagation of the Gospel in Foreign Parts, 1701–1892. London, 1893.

Commemorative biographical record of the county of York, Ontario; containing biographical sketches of prominent and representative citizens and many of the early settled families. Toronto, 1907.

CORNISH, GEORGE HENRY. *Cyclopædia of Methodism in Canada: containing historical, educational, and statistical information. . . .* 2 vols. Toronto and Halifax, 1881–1903.

A cyclopædia of Canadian biography: being chiefly men of the time. Edited by George MacLean Rose. (Rose's national biographical series, I, II.) Toronto, 1886, 1888.

DENT, JOHN CHARLES. *The Canadian portrait gallery.* 4 vols. Toronto, 1880–81.

DESJARDINS, JOSEPH. *Guide parlementaire historique de la province de Québec, 1792 à 1902.* Québec, 1902.

Dictionary of American biography [to 1928]. Edited by Allen Johnson and Dumas Malone. 20 vols., index. New York, 1928–37. 2 supplements [to 31 Dec. 1940], New York 1944, 1958. New edition, comprising 22 vols. in 11, New York, 1959. *Concise DAB*, New York, 1964. In progress.

Dictionary of national biography [to 1900]. Edited by Leslie Stephen and Sidney Lee. 63 vols.; supplement, 3 vols.; index and epitome. London, 1885–1903. 6 supplements for the 20th century. *Concise DNB.* 2 vols., 1952, 1961. In progress.

A directory of the members of the Legislative Assembly of Nova Scotia, 1758–1958. With an introduction by Charles Bruce Fergusson. (PANS publication, Nova Scotia series, II.) Halifax, 1958.

The dominion annual register and review for . . . 1878. —— *1879.* —— *1880–1881.* Edited by Henry James Morgan *et al.* Montreal, 1879, 1880, 1882.

The encyclopedia of Canada. Edited by William Stewart Wallace. 6 vols. Toronto, 1935–37. *Newfoundland supplement.* Edited by Robert Harold Blackburn. Toronto, 1949.

GAUTHIER, HENRI. *Sulpitiana.* Montréal, 1926.

GREAT BRITAIN, ADMIRALTY. *The navy list . . .* (London), used for 1813, 1844–77.

Guide to Canadian ministries since confederation, July 1, 1867–January 1, 1957. (PAC publication.) Ottawa, 1957. [Revision in progress.]

Guide to the principal parliamentary papers relating to the dominions, 1812–1911. Prepared by Margaret I. Adam *et al.* Edinburgh and London, 1913.

HARPER, JOHN RUSSELL. *Historical directory of New Brunswick newspapers and periodicals.* Fredericton, 1961.

758

LE JEUNE, LOUIS-MARIE. *Dictionnaire général de biographie, histoire, littérature, agriculture, commerce, industrie et des arts, sciences, mœurs, coutumes, institutions politiques et religieuses du Canada.* 2 vols. Ottawa, 1931.

MORGAN, HENRY JAMES. *Bibliotheca Canadensis: or, a manual of Canadian literature.* Ottawa, 1867; republished, Detroit, 1968.

—— *Sketches of celebrated Canadians, and persons connected with Canada, from the earliest period in the history of the province down to the present time.* Quebec and London, 1862.

MORICE, ADRIEN-GABRIEL. *Dictionnaire historique des Canadiens et des Métis français de l'Ouest.* Kamloops, B.C., Saint-Sauveur, Qué., and Saint-Boniface, Man., 1908.

Notices nécrologiques de la Congrégation des Oblats de Marie-Immaculée. 8 vols. Paris, 1860–1939.

NOTMAN, WILLIAM, and FENNINGS TAYLOR. *Portraits of British Americans, with biographical sketches.* 3 vols. Montreal, 1865–68.

O'BYRNE, WILLIAM RICHARD. *A naval biographical dictionary; comprising the life and services of every living officer in Her Majesty's Navy, from the rank of admiral of the fleet to that of lieutenant.* London, 1849.

Patents of Canada ... [1824–1855]. 2 vols. Toronto, 1860–65.
I: *From 1824 to 1849.* 1860.
II: *From 1849 to 1855.* 1865.

Place-names and places of Nova Scotia. With an introduction by Charles Bruce Fergusson. (PANS publication, Nova Scotia series, III.) Halifax, 1967.

Political appointments and elections in the Province of Canada from 1841 to 1860. Edited by Joseph-Olivier Coté. 1st ed., Quebec, 1860. —— *from 1841 to 1865.* 2nd ed., Ottawa, 1866. —— *and appendix from 1st January, 1866, to 30th June, 1867, and index.* Edited by Narcisse-Omer Coté. Ottawa, 1918.

Political appointments, parliaments and the judicial bench in the Dominion of Canada, 1867 to 1895. Edited by Narcisse-Omer Coté. Ottawa, 1896.

PUBLIC ARCHIVES OF NOVA SCOTIA PUBLICATIONS, Nova Scotia series:
II: *Directory of N.S. MLAs* (Fergusson).
III: *Place-names of N.S.* (Fergusson).

ROY, PIERRE-GEORGES. *Les avocats de la région de Québec.* Lévis, Qué., 1936.

—— *Fils de Québec.* 4 vols. Lévis, Qué., 1933.

—— *Les juges de la province de Québec.* Québec, 1933.

A standard dictionary of Canadian biography; the Canadian who was who. Edited by Charles George Douglas Roberts and Arthur L. Tunnell. 2 vols. Toronto, 1934–38.

A statutory history of the steam and electric railways of Canada, 1836–1937, with other data relevant to operation of Department of Transport. Compiled by Robert Dorman. Ottawa, 1938.

TANGUAY, CYPRIEN. *Dictionnaire généalogique des familles canadiennes depuis la fondation de la colonie jusqu'à nos jours.* 7 vols. [Montréal], 1871–90.

Union list of manuscripts in Canadian repositories. Edited by Robert S. Gordon *et al.* Ottawa, 1968. [Revision in progress.]

WALBRAN, JOHN T. *British Columbia coast names, 1592–1906, to which are added a few names in adjacent United States territory, their origin and history with map and illustrations.* Ottawa, 1909.

WALLACE, WILLIAM STEWART. *The Macmillan dictionary of Canadian biography.* 3rd edition, revised and enlarged. London, Toronto, and New York, 1963.

WATTERS, REGINALD EYRE. *A check list of Canadian literature and background materials, 1628–1950, in two parts.* Toronto, 1959. [New edition in progress.]

WATTERS, REGINALD EYRE, and INGLIS FREEMAN BELL. *On Canadian literature, 1806–1960: a check list of articles, books, and theses on English-Canadian literature, its authors, and language.* Toronto, 1966.

IV. STUDIES (BOOKS AND THESES)

ABBOTT, MAUDE ELIZABETH [SEYMOUR]. *History of medicine in the province of Quebec.* Toronto, 1931; McGill University publication, series VIII, no. 63, 1932.

AHERN, GEORGE et MICHAEL JOSEPH. *Notes pour servir à l'histoire de la médecine dans le Bas-Canada depuis la fondation de Québec jusqu'au commencement du XIXe siècle.* Québec, 1923.

ATHERTON, WILLIAM HENRY. *Montreal, 1535–1914.* 3 vols. Montreal, Vancouver, and Chicago, 1914.
I: *Under the French régime, 1535–1760.*
II: *Under British rule, 1760–1914.*
III: *Biographical.*

AUDET, LOUIS-PHILIPPE. *Histoire du conseil de l'Instruction publique de la province de Québec, 1856–1964*. Montréal, 1964.

——— *Le système scolaire de la province de Québec*. 6 vols. Québec, 1950–56.

BECK, JAMES MURRAY. *The government of Nova Scotia*. (Canadian government series, 8.) Toronto, 1957.

BEGG, ALEXANDER. *History of the North-West*. 3 vols. Toronto, 1894–95.

BOLGER, FRANCIS WILLIAM PIUS. *Prince Edward Island and confederation, 1863–1873*. Charlottetown, 1964.

BOON, THOMAS CHARLES BOUCHER. *The Anglican Church from the Bay to the Rockies; a history of the ecclesiastical province of Rupert's Land and its dioceses from 1820 to 1950*. Toronto, 1962.

BORTHWICK, JOHN DOUGLAS. *History and biographical gazetteer of Montreal to the year 1892*. Montreal, 1892.

——— *Montreal, its history, to which is added biographical sketches, with photographs, of many of its principal citizens*. Montreal, 1875.

CAMPBELL, ROBERT. *A history of the Scotch Presbyterian Church, St. Gabriel Street, Montreal*. Montreal, 1887.

Canada and its provinces; a history of the Canadian people and their institutions. Edited by Adam Shortt and Arthur George Doughty. 23 vols. Toronto, 1913–17.

CANADIAN CENTENARY SERIES. William Lewis Morton, executive editor; Donald Grant Creighton, advisory editor.
7: Craig, *Upper Canada*.
9: MacNutt, *Atlantic provinces*.
10: Careless, *Union of the Canadas*.
12: Morton, *Critical years*.

CANADIAN GOVERNMENT SERIES. General editors, Robert MacGregor Dawson, 1946–58; James Alexander Corry, 1958–61; Crawford Brough Macpherson, 1961– .
5: MacKinnon, *Government of PEI*.
7: Hodgetts, *Pioneer public service*.
8: Beck, *Government of Nova Scotia*.
14: Donnelly, *Government of Manitoba*.

CANADIAN STUDIES IN HISTORY AND GOVERNMENT Series. Edited by James Maurice Stockford Careless, 1958–60; Kenneth William Kirkpatrick McNaught, 1960–65; Goldwin Sylvester French, 1965– .
1: Moir, *Church and state in Canada West*.
2: Thompson, *French shore problem in Nfld*.
3: Cornell, *Alignment of political groups*.
7: Gunn, *Political history of Nfld*.
8: Wilson, *Clergy reserves of Upper Canada*.
14: Ormsby, *Emergence of the federal concept*.

CANNIFF, WILLIAM. *The medical profession in Upper Canada, 1783–1850. An historical narrative, with original documents relating to the profession, including some brief biographies*. Toronto, 1894.

CARELESS, JAMES MAURICE STOCKFORD. *Brown of The Globe*. 2 vols. Toronto, 1959–1963.
I: *The voice of Upper Canada, 1818–1859*. 1959.
II: *Statesman of confederation, 1860–1880*. 1963.

——— *The union of the Canadas: the growth of Canadian institutions, 1841–1857*. (Canadian centenary series, 10.) Toronto, 1967.

CARRIÈRE, GASTON. *Histoire documentaire de la Congrégation des Missionnaires Oblats de Marie-Immaculée dans l'Est du Canada*. 9 vols. Ottawa, 1957–70.

CARROLL, JOHN. *Case and his cotemporaries; or, the Canadian itinerants' memorial: constituting a biographical history of Methodism in Canada, from its introduction into the province, till the death of the Rev. William Case in 1855*. 5 vols. Toronto, 1867–77.

CHAPAIS, THOMAS. *Cours d'histoire du Canada*. 8 vols. Québec et Montréal, 1919–34.

CHRISTIE, ROBERT. *A history of the late province of Lower Canada, parliamentary and political, from the commencement to the close of its existence as a separate province. . . .* 6 vols. Quebec and Montreal, 1848–55.

CHRONICLES OF CANADA SERIES. Edited by George McKinnon Wrong and Hugh Hornby Langton.
25: Duclos de Celles, *Patriotes of 1837*.
26: Grant, *Tribune of N.S., Howe*.
28: Colquhoun, *Fathers of confederation*.
31: Wood, *All afloat*.

CLARK, ANDREW HILL. *Three centuries and the Island, a historical geography of settlement and agriculture in Prince Edward Island, Canada*. Toronto, 1959.

COATS, ROBERT HAMILTON, and R. EDWARD GOSNELL. *Sir James Douglas*. (Makers of Canada series, anniversary edition, IX.) London and Toronto, 1926.

COLQUHOUN, ARTHUR HUGH URQUHART. *The fathers of confederation; a chronicle of the birth of the dominion*. (Chronicles of Canada series, 28.) Toronto, 1921.

CORNELL, PAUL GRANT. *The alignment of political groups in Canada, 1841–1867*. (Canadian studies in history and government series, 3.) Toronto, 1962.

CRAIG, GERALD MARQUIS. *Upper Canada: the formative years, 1784–1841*. (Canadian centenary series, 7.) Toronto, London, and New York, 1963.

CREIGHTON, DONALD GRANT. *John A. Macdonald, the young politician*. Toronto, 1952.

—— *John A. Macdonald, the old chieftain.* Toronto, 1955.

—— *The road to confederation; the emergence of Canada: 1863–1867.* Toronto, 1964.

DAVID, LAURENT-OLIVIER. *Les patriotes de 1837–1838.* Montréal, [1884].

DAVIN, NICHOLAS FLOOD. *The Irishman in Canada.* London and Toronto, 1877; reprinted Shannon, Eire, 1969.

DENISON, MERRILL. *Canada's first bank; a history of the Bank of Montreal.* 2 vols. Toronto and Montreal, 1966–67. Translated into French as *La première banque au Canada; histoire de la Banque de Montréal* by Paul A. Horguelin and Jean-Paul Vinay. 2 vols. Toronto, 1966–67.

DENT, JOHN CHARLES. *The last forty years: Canada since the union of 1841.* 2 vols. Toronto, 1881.

—— *The story of the Upper Canadian rebellion; largely derived from original sources and documents.* 2 vols. Toronto, 1885.

DONNELLY, MURRAY SAMUEL. *The government of Manitoba.* (Canadian government series, 14.) Toronto, 1963.

DROLET, ANTONIO. *La ville de Québec, histoire municipale; III: de l'incorporation à la Confédération (1833–1867).* (SHQ, Cahiers d'histoire, 19.) Québec, 1967.

DUCLOS DE CELLES, ALFRED. *The "Patriotes" of '37; a chronicle of the Lower Canadian rebellion.* Translated from the French by William Stewart Wallace. (Chronicles of Canada series, 25.) Toronto, 1916.

FAUTEUX, ÆGIDIUS. *Patriotes de 1837–1838.* Montréal, 1950.

GIRAUD, MARCEL. *Le Métis canadien. Son rôle dans l'histoire des provinces de l'Ouest.* (Travaux et mémoires de l'Institut d'ethnologie, XLIV.) Paris, 1945.

GRANT, WILLIAM LAWSON. *The tribune of Nova Scotia; a chronicle of Joseph Howe.* (Chronicles of Canada series, 26.) Toronto, 1915.

GREENHILL, BASIL, and ANN GIFFARD. *Westcountrymen in Prince Edward's Isle: a fragment of the great migration.* London and Toronto, 1967.

GREGG, WILLIAM. *History of the Presbyterian Church in the dominion of Canada, from the earliest times to 1834; with a chronological table of events to the present time, and map.* Toronto, 1885.

GUNN, GERTRUDE E. *The political history of Newfoundland, 1832–1864.* (Canadian studies in history and government series, 7.) Toronto, 1966.

HANNAY, JAMES. *History of New Brunswick.* 2 vols. Saint John, N.B., 1909.

—— *Lemuel Allan Wilmot* and *Sir Leonard Tilley.* (Makers of Canada series, anniversary edition, VIII.) London and Toronto, 1926.

HARGRAVE, JOSEPH JAMES. *Red River.* Montreal, 1871.

HARRIS, REGINALD V. *The Church of Saint Paul in Halifax, Nova Scotia: 1749–1949.* Toronto, 1949.

History of the county of Middlesex, Canada. From the earliest time to the present; containing an authentic account of many important matters relating to the settlement, progress and general history of the county; and including a department devoted to the preservation of personal and private records, etc. Toronto and London, Ont., 1889.

History of Toronto and county of York, Ontario; containing an outline of the history of the dominion of Canada; a history of the city of Toronto and the county of York, with the townships, towns, villages, churches, schools; general and local statistics; biographical sketches, etc., etc. 2 vols. Toronto, 1885.

HODGETTS, JOHN EDWIN. *Pioneer public service; an administrative history of the united Canadas, 1841–1867.* (Canadian government series, 7.) Toronto, 1955.

HUNTER, ANDREW FREDERICK. *A history of Simcoe County.* 2 vols. Barrie, Ont., 1909; reprinted, 1 vol. in 2 parts, Barrie, Ont., 1948.

Landmarks of Toronto; a collection of historical sketches of the old town of York from 1792 until 1833 and of Toronto from 1834 to [1914]. Edited by John Ross Robertson. 6 vols. Toronto, 1894–1914.

LAREAU, EDMOND. *Histoire de la littérature canadienne.* Montréal, 1874.

LAWRENCE, JOSEPH WILSON. *The judges of New Brunswick and their times.* Edited by Alfred Augustus Stockton. Saint John, N.B., 1907.

Lewis & Dryden's marine history of the Pacific northwest; an illustrated review of the growth and development of the maritime industry, from the advent of the earliest navigators to the present time, with sketches and portraits of a number of well known marine men. Edited by E. W. Wright. Portland, Ore., 1895; reprinted, New York, 1961.

Literary history of Canada: Canadian literature in English. Edited by Carl Frederick Klinck *et al.* Toronto, 1965.

LONGLEY, JAMES WILBERFORCE. *Joseph Howe* and *Sir Charles Tupper.* (Makers of Canada series, anniversary edition, VIII.) London and Toronto, 1926.

MACKINNON, FRANK [FRANCIS PERLEY TAYLOR]. *The government of Prince Edward Island.* (Canadian government series, 5.) Toronto, 1951.

MacMillan, John C. *The history of the Catholic church in Prince Edward Island from 1835 till 1891*. Quebec, 1913.

MacNutt, William Stewart. *The Atlantic provinces: the emergence of colonial society, 1712–1857*. (Canadian centenary series, 9.) Toronto, 1965.

———— *New Brunswick, a history: 1784–1867*. Toronto, 1963.

Makers of Canada series, anniversary edition. Illustrated under the direction of Arthur George Doughty and edited by William Lawson Grant. London and Toronto, 1926.
VI: Shortt, *Sydenham*.
VIII: Longley, *Howe*; Longley, *Tupper*; Hannay, *Wilmot*; Hannay, *Tilley*.
IX: Coats and Gosnell, *Douglas*.

Martin, Chester. *Empire & commonwealth, studies in governance and self-government in Canada*. Oxford, 1929.

Middleton, Jesse Edgar. *The municipality of Toronto, a history*. 3 vols. Toronto and New York, 1923.

Millman, Thomas Reagh. *Jacob Mountain, first lord bishop of Quebec, a study in church and state, 1793–1825*. (University of Toronto Studies, History and economics series, X.) Toronto, 1947.

Moir, John Sargent. *Church and state in Canada West; three studies in the relation of denominationalism and nationalism, 1841–1867*. (Canadian studies in history and government series, 1.) Toronto, 1959.

Monet, Jacques. *The last cannon shot; a study of French-Canadian nationalism, 1837–1850*. Toronto, 1969.

Morice, Adrien-Gabriel. *A critical history of the Red River insurrection after official documents and non-Catholic sources*. Winnipeg, 1935.

———— *Histoire de l'Église catholique dans l'Ouest canadien du lac Supérieur au Pacifique (1659–1915)*. 4 vols. Saint-Boniface, Man., et Montréal, 1921–23.

———— *History of the Catholic Church in western Canada from Lake Superior to the Pacific (1659–1895)*. 2 vols. Toronto, 1910.

———— *The history of the northern interior of British Columbia formerly New Caledonia [1660 to 1880]*. Toronto, 1904.

Morton, Arthur Silver. *A history of the Canadian west to 1870–71; being a history of Rupert's Land (the Hudson's Bay Company's territory) and of the North-West Territory (including the Pacific slope)*. London, [1939].

Morton, William Lewis. *The critical years: the union of British North America, 1857–1873*. (Canadian centenary series, 12.) Toronto, 1964.

———— *Manitoba, a history*. 1st edition, Toronto, 1957; 2nd edition, Toronto, 1967.

Ormsby, Margaret Anchoretta. *British Columbia: a history*. Toronto, 1958.

Ormsby, William G. *The emergence of the federal concept in Canada, 1839–1845*. (Canadian studies in history and government series, 14.) Toronto, 1969.

Ouellet, Fernand. *Histoire économique et sociale du Québec, 1760–1850, structures et conjoncture*. (Histoire économique et sociale du Canada français.) Montréal et Paris, 1966. [Translation in progress.]

Pascoe, Charles Frederick. *Two hundred years of the S.P.G.: an historical account of the Society for the Propagation of the Gospel in Foreign Parts, 1701–1900 (based on a digest of the society's records)*. 2 vols. London, 1901.

Prowse, Daniel Woodley. *A history of Newfoundland from the English, colonial, and foreign records*. London, and New York, 1895; revised edition, 1896.

Rich, Edwin Ernest. *The history of the Hudson's Bay Company 1670–1870. Volume I: 1670–1763*; *Volume II: 1763–1870*. (Hudson's Bay Record Society publications, XXI, XXII.) London, 1858–59. Another edition, 3 vols., Toronto, 1960. A copy of this work available in the PAC contains notes and bibliographical material omitted from the printed version.

Robertson, Ian Ross. "Religion, politics, and education in Prince Edward Island from 1856 to 1877." Unpublished MA thesis for McGill University. Montreal, 1968.

Ross, Victor, and A. St L. Trigge. *A history of the Canadian Bank of Commerce, with an account of the other banks which now form part of its organization*. 3 vols. Toronto, 1920–34.

Roy, Joseph-Edmond. *Histoire du notariat au Canada depuis la fondation de la colonie jusqu'à nos jours*. 4 vols. Lévis, Qué., 1899–1902.

Rumilly, Robert. *Histoire de la province de Québec*. 41 vols. parus. Montréal, 1940– .

Saunders, Edward Manning. *Three premiers of Nova Scotia: the Hon. J. W. Johnstone, the Hon. Joseph Howe, the Hon. Charles Tupper, M.D., C.B.* Toronto, 1909.

Savaète, Arthur. *Voix canadiennes; vers l'abîme*. 12 vols. Paris, n.d.

The shield of Achilles: aspects of Canada in the Victorian age/Le bouclier d'Achille: regards sur le Canada de l'ère victorienne. Edited by William Lewis Morton. Toronto and Montreal, 1968.

Shortt, Adam. *Lord Sydenham*. (Makers of Canada series, anniversary edition, VI.) London and Toronto, 1926.

SISSONS, CHARLES BRUCE. *Egerton Ryerson: his life and letters.* 2 vols. Toronto, 1937–47.

SOCIÉTÉ HISTORIQUE DE QUÉBEC. CAHIERS D'HISTOIRE 19: Drolet, *Ville de Québec.*

SOCIÉTÉ HISTORIQUE DU SAGUENAY. PUBLICATIONS. 21: Tremblay, *Histoire du Saguenay.*

STANLEY, GEORGE FRANCIS GILMAN. *The birth of western Canada: a history of the Riel rebellions.* London, 1936; Toronto, 1960.

——— *Louis Riel.* Toronto, 1963.

The storied province of Quebec; past and present. Edited by William Wood *et al.* 5 vols. Toronto, 1931–32.

SWAINSON, DONALD WAYNE. "The personnel of politics; a study of the Ontario members of the second federal parliament." Unpublished PHD thesis for the University of Toronto. 1968.

TASSÉ, JOSEPH. *Les Canadiens de l'Ouest.* 2e éd., 2 vols. Montréal, 1878.

THOMPSON, FREDERIC FRASER. *The French shore problem in Newfoundland: an imperial study.* (Canadian studies in history and government series, 2.) Toronto, 1961.

TRAVAUX ET MÉMOIRES DE L'INSTITUT D'ETHNOLOGIE, Paris. XLIV: Giraud, *Le Métis canadien.*

TREMBLAY, VICTOR. *Histoire du Saguenay depuis les origines jusqu'à 1870.* (Publications de la SHS, 21.) Chicoutimi, Qué., 1968.

WAITE, PETER BUSBY. *The life and times of confederation, 1864–67: politics, newspapers, and the union of British North America.* Toronto, 1962; 2nd edition, with corrections, 1962.

WALLACE, FREDERICK WILLIAM. *Wooden ships and iron men: the story of the square-rigged merchant marine of British North America, the ships, their builders and owners, and the men who sailed them.* London, 1924; New York, 1925; Boston, 1937.

WILSON, [GEORGE] ALAN. *The clergy reserves of Upper Canada, a Canadian mortmain.* (Canadian studies in history and government series, 8.) Toronto, 1968.

WOOD, WILLIAM. *All afloat; a chronicle of craft and waterways.* (Chronicles of Canada series, 31.) Toronto, 1914.

V. JOURNALS AND STUDIES (ARTICLES)

The Beaver. Winnipeg. Publication of the HBC. Monthly until March 1925; thereafter quarterly. I (outfit 250, 1920)– . Index for I (outfit 250, 1920)–outfit 284 (March 1954) published at unknown date.

British Columbia Historical Quarterly. Victoria. Quarterly, I (1937)–XV (1951) then semi-annually to XXI (1957–58) which is the last volume to date. Published by the Provincial Archives of British Columbia in cooperation with the British Columbia Historical Association.

Bulletin des recherches historiques. Lévis, Québec. Monthly from 1895 to 1945 from which date some issues were published together; became a quarterly in 1951 until publication was suspended in 1956; thereafter published irregularly. Journal of archaeology, history, biography, bibliography, numismatology, etc. I (1895)– . *Index:* I (1895)–XXXI (1925). 4 vols. Beauceville, 1925–26. For subsequent years see manuscript index in ANQ. In addition, a nominal index for the same years is being prepared in the *Dictionary* offices. Founded by Pierre-Georges Roy*, the *BRH* became in March 1923 the journal of the ANQ (formerly APQ and AQ).

Les Cahiers des Dix. Montréal. I (1936)– . Annual review published by "Les Dix," a group of historians who formed a legal association on 6 Aug. 1935.

The Canadian Antiquarian and Numismatic Journal. Montreal. 1 (July 1872)–13 (1886); 2nd series, 1 (July 1889)–3 (May 1894); 3rd series, 1 (1898)–13 (1916); 4th series, I (1930)– . Founded in 1872 by the Canadian Numismatic and Antiquarian Society to publish reports of its activities and the results of its research (numismatics, collecting coins and medals, archaeology, and history). Publication was suspended in 1884, 1887–June 1889, 1895–96, 1901, and 1903–7.

CANADIAN HISTORICAL ASSOCIATION/LA SOCIÉTÉ HISTORIQUE DU CANADA. Ottawa. The aims of the association are "to encourage historical research and public interest in history; to promote the preservation of historic sites and buildings, documents, relics, and other significant heirlooms of the past; to publish historical studies and documents as circumstances may permit." Publications include: annual reports, 1915– , and historical booklets.

The Canadian Historical Review. Toronto. Quarterly, I(1920)– . *General Index,* I(1920)–X(1929); XI(1930)–XX(1939); XXI(1940)–XXX(1949). Each issue includes a current bibliography of publications in English and

French – a continuation of the annual *Review of historical publications relating to Canada*, edited by George MacKinnon Wrong, Hugh Hornby Langton, and William Stewart Wallace. I(for 1896)–XXII(for 1917 and 1918). Indexes for I–X, XI–XX.

CANADIAN CATHOLIC HISTORICAL ASSOCIATION/ SOCIÉTÉ CANADIENNE D'HISTOIRE DE L'ÉGLISE CATHOLIQUE. *Report/Rapport*. Ottawa. This bilingual society, founded 3 June 1933, annually publishes French and English volumes with entirely different contents. I(1933–34)– (1965). Separate index for 1933–1957 [1960]. After 1965, the society discontinued publication of the *Report* and published instead *Study Sessions/ Sessions d'étude*.

Canadian Journal. Toronto. Publication of the Canadian Institute which became the Royal Canadian Institute in 1914. Began as the *Canadian Journal: a repertory of industry, science and art; and a record of the proceedings of the Canadian Institute*, I (1852–53)–III (1854–55). Title was modified to the *Canadian Journal of Industry, Science and Art*, new series, I (1856)–XI (1866–67) and to the *Canadian Journal of Science, Literature and History*, XII (1868–70)–XV (1876–77). Superseded by the *Proceedings of the Canadian Institute, Toronto, being a continuation of "The Canadian Journal of Science, Literature and History,"* third series, I (1879–83)–VII (1888–89). Merged for a few years with the Canadian Institute, *Transactions*, then published irregularly for a time as Canadian Institute, *Proceedings*, new series, I(1895–98). Published as Royal Canadian Institute, *Proceedings*, third series or series IIIa, I (1935–36)– .

Dalhousie Review. Halifax. Quarterly publication of Dalhousie University. I (1921–22)– .

HISTORICAL AND SCIENTIFIC SOCIETY OF MANITOBA. Winnipeg. Incorporated in 1879, the society was founded by historians and businessmen to encourage science and to make Manitoba known. Since its founding the society has had numerous publications. These include: *Report*, I (1880)–XXVII (1906); several series known as *Transactions*, 1 (Oct. 1882)–72 (Nov. 1906); new series, 1 (Nov. 1924)–5 (July 1930); 3rd series, 1 (1944–45)– (the title of these transactions varies: *Publication*, 1–2, 4–6; *Transactions*, 5–72; new series, 1–5; *Papers*, 3rd series); *Manitoba History*, I (March 1946)– . HSSM also published *Manitoba historical atlas; a selection of facsimile maps, plans, and sketches from 1612 to 1969*. Edited by John Warkentin and Richard I. Ruggles. Winnipeg, 1970. "The journal of Arthur Thomas Bushby, 1858–

1859." Edited by Dorothy Blakey Smith. *BCHQ*, XXI (1957–58), 83–160.

NOVA SCOTIA HISTORICAL SOCIETY. *Collections*. Halifax. 36 vols. to date. I (1878)– . Title *Report and Collections* was used in 1878 and in 1882–83.

Ontario History. Toronto. Originally published annually as Ontario Historical Society, *Papers and Records*, I(1899)–XXXVIII(1946). The title was changed to *Ontario History* with XXXVIII(1946). Quarterly publication began with XLI(1949) and continues to the present. Indexes can be found in three of the volumes: for I–XX in XX(1923); for I–XXXII in XXXII(1937); for XXXIII–XLIII in XLIII (1951). A cumulative index which is constantly updated can be purchased from the Ontario Historical Society.

ONTARIO LAND SURVEYORS ASSOCIATION. *Annual Report*. Toronto. Organized in 1886, the association began its publications in that year: *Proceedings of the association of provincial land surveyors of Ontario at its first annual meeting.* . . . Title varied after incorporation of the association in 1892 until 1912 when the publications began to appear as the Ontario Land Surveyors Association, *Annual Report*, which continued in 1971. General indexes are available in the 1914, 1925, 1935, 1945, 1955, 1960, and 1965 volumes. Various biographical indexes also appear in the reports of 1934, 1949, 1957, and 1965. The *Annual Report, 1964* contains an index of all papers published from 1886.

Revue de l'université d'Ottawa. Ottawa. I (1931)– . Quarterly publication of the University of Ottawa. Publishes articles in French or English on the Bible, theology, canon and civil law, history, philosophy, science, and the arts. From 1932 to 1960 the review published in its *Section spéciale* particularly specialized articles in theology, canon law, and philosophy. General indexes are published for 1931–40, 1941–50, 1951–60.

ROYAL SOCIETY OF CANADA / SOCIÉTÉ ROYALE DU CANADA. *Proceedings and transactions*. Under the patronage of the Marquess of Lorne, the society was formed in 1882 for the encouragement of literature and science in Canada. Originally the society was composed of five sections – two for literature and three for sciences. The annual *Mémoires* of Section I and the *Transactions* of Section II include historical articles. First series: I (1882–83)–XII (1894). Second series: I (1895)–XII (1906). Third series: I (1907)–LVI (1962). Fourth series: I (1963)– . There are also index volumes.

Social History, a Canadian review / Histoire sociale, revue canadienne. Ottawa. 1 (April 1968)–   . A semi-annual publication of the University of Ottawa and Carleton University. Published under the direction of an inter-disciplinary committee from various Canadian universities. Concentrates exclusively on the social history of Canada and other countries.

SOCIÉTÉ CANADIENNE DE L'HISTOIRE DE L'ÉGLISE CATHOLIQUE. *See* CANADIAN CATHOLIC HISTORICAL ASSOCIATION

SYLVAIN, PHILIPPE. "Libéralisme et ultramontanisme au Canada français; affrontement idéologique et doctrinal (1840–1865)," *Shield of Achilles* (Morton), 111–38, 220–55.

Contributors

ANDRE, JOHN. Town planner, Borough of York, Ontario.
William Bent Berczy [in collaboration with J. R. Harper].

ANDREWS, CATER WILSON. Professor of biology, Memorial University of Newfoundland, St John's, Newfoundland.
William Jackman [in collaboration with G. M. Story].

ARMSTRONG, FREDERICK H. Associate professor of history, University of Western Ontario, London, Ontario.
George Anthony Barber. John Birrell. Thomas Clarkson. Charles Hunt. Ellis Walton Hyman. Benjamin Lyman. Donald McDonald. Andrew Mercer. Charles-Séraphin Rodier. Charles Roger. Jacques-Félix Sincennes. David Torrance.

AUDET, LOUIS-PHILIPPE. Professeur à la retraite, Saint-Bruno-de-Montarville, Québec.
Pierre-Urgel Archambault. Jean-Baptiste dit Jean-Philippe Boucher-Belleville. Cyrille Delagrave. Patrick Delaney. Jean-Baptiste Dupuy. Césaire Germain. Edward Hale. Léon Kérouac. Louis Lacoste. Étienne Mayrand. Hector Peltier. François-Joseph-Victor Regnaud. Louis-David Roy.

BAILEY, ALFRED GOLDSWORTHY. Professor emeritus of history, University of New Brunswick, Fredericton, New Brunswick.
Joseph Marshall de Brett Maréchal, Baron d'Avray.

BAKER, JOHN NORMAN LEONARD. Emeritus fellow, Jesus College, Oxford, England.
Sir Robert John Le Mesurier McClure.

BARKER, DIANE M. Manuscript editor, *Dictionary of Canadian Biography/Dictionnaire biographique du Canada*, University of Toronto Press, Ontario.
Enos Collins [in collaboration with D. A. Sutherland]. *James Forman* [with P. R. Blakeley]. *John Geddie* [with P. R. Blakeley].

BARNARD, JULIENNE. Sillery, Québec.
Édouard Quertier.

BECK, J. MURRAY. Professor of political science, Dalhousie University, Halifax, Nova Scotia.
John Alexander Barry. Joseph Howe.

BÉLANGER, NOËL, PTRE. Professeur d'histoire, Université du Québec à Rimouski, Québec.
Pierre-Alexis Tremblay.

BETTS, E. ARTHUR. Archivist, Maritime Conference, United Church of Canada, Halifax, Nova Scotia.
John Stewart.

BLAKELEY, PHYLLIS R. Assistant provincial archivist, Public Archives of Nova Scotia, Halifax, Nova Scotia.
William Blowers Bliss. James Cochran. James Forman [in collaboration with D. M. Barker]. *John Geddie* [with D. M. Barker]. *Mary Eliza Herbert. Henry How. George Moir Johnston. Andrew Shiels.*

BLAKEY SMITH, DOROTHY. Formerly assistant archivist, Provincial Archives of British Columbia, Victoria, British Columbia.
Ovid Allard. Edward Graham Alston. Arthur Thomas Bushby. Robert William Weir Carrall. John Evans. Lumley Franklin. Robert Ker. William Alexander Mouat.

BOISSONNAULT, CHARLES-MARIE. Écrivain, Québec, Québec.
Joseph Painchaud.

BOND, COURTNEY C. J. Formerly head, Canadian Section, National Map Collection, Public Archives of Canada, Ottawa, Ontario.
Edward Van Cortlandt. John Gilmour.

BONENFANT, JEAN-CHARLES. Professeur de droit, Université Laval, Québec, Québec.
René-Édouard Caron. Sir George-Étienne Cartier. Jacques Crémazie. Bernard Devlin. Eugène-Philippe Dorion. Magloire Lanctôt. Louis-Siméon Morin. John Buckworth Parkin. Louis Renaud. Louis-Philippe Turcotte.

BOON, THOMAS C. B. Former archivist of Rupert's Land (Anglican Church), Winnipeg, Manitoba.
Henry Budd.

BOUCHARD, ANTOINE, PTRE. Professeur agrégé de musique, Université Laval, Québec, Québec.
Joseph Casavant.

BOVEY, JOHN A. Provincial archivist, Provincial Archives of Manitoba, Winnipeg, Manitoba.
Lord Gordon Gordon.

BOWSFIELD, HARTWELL. University archivist; lecturer in history, York University, Downsview, Ontario.
Alexander Christie. Francis Evans Cornish. Jean-Baptiste Lépine. Joseph Rolette (jr). Bernard Rogan Ross. Enos Stutsman.

BOYLAN, DOUGLAS BRUCE. Provincial archivist, Public Archives of Prince Edward Island, Charlottetown, Prince Edward Island.
Francis Kelly. Alexander Laird.

BROCK, DANIEL JAMES. Graduate student in history, University of Toronto, Ontario.
William E. Niles. John Talbot [in collaboration with J. J. Talman].

BUGGEY, SUSAN. National Historic Sites Service, Department of Indian Affairs and Northern Development, Ottawa, Ontario.
Isabella Binney Cogswell.

BURNSIDE, ALBERT. Minister, Victoria Village United Church, Toronto, Ontario.
Francis Metherall.

BURROUGHS, PETER. Chairman, Department of history, Dalhousie University, Halifax, Nova Scotia.
John Arthur Roebuck.

CAMERON, WENDY. Toronto, Ontario.
Charles Rubidge.

CARELESS, J. M. S. Professor of history, University of Toronto, Ontario.
George Bennett. George Brown. David Christie.

CARRIÈRE, GASTON, O.M.I. Historien des Oblats au Canada, secrétaire du Centre de recherche en histoire religieuse du Canada, Séminaire universitaire Saint-Paul, Ottawa, Ontario.
Flavien Durocher. Marie-Germain-Émile Eynard. Joseph-Bruno Guigues. Lucien-Antoine Lagier. Louis-Étienne-Delille Reboul.

CHABOT, RICHARD. Chargé de cours d'histoire du Canada, Université du Québec à Montréal, Québec.
Robert Nelson [in collaboration with J. Monet and Y. Roby].

CHALIFOUX, JEAN-PIERRE. Directeur, Service des publications officielles, Bibliothèque des sciences sociales, Université de Montréal, Québec.
Robert Lea MacDonnell. Andrew Robertson.

CHASSÉ, BÉATRICE. Archiviste, Archives nationales du Québec, Québec.
Antoine Légaré. John Maguire.

CLANCEY, MARY ELLEN DUBÉ. Secondary school teacher, Chester, Nova Scotia.
William H. Townsend.

COGSWELL, FREDERICK WILLIAM. Professor of English, University of New Brunswick, Fredericton, New Brunswick.
May Agnes Early (Fleming).

COLEMAN, MARGARET. Researcher, National Historic Sites Service, Department of Indian Affairs and Northern Development, Ottawa, Ontario.
Malcolm Cameron.

CONNERS, IBRA LOCKWOOD. Ottawa, Ontario.
David Fife.

COOKE, ALAN GORDON RICHARD. Assistant librarian and curator of manuscripts, Scott Polar Research Institute, Cambridge, England.
Jane Griffin (Lady Franklin). Richard King.

COOPER, JOHN IRWIN. Professor emeritus of history, McGill University, Montreal, Quebec; visiting professor, University of Guelph, Ontario.
John C. Becket. John Bethune. William Taylor. Hubert-Joseph Tétreau.

CORNELL, PAUL GRANT. Professor of history, University of Waterloo, Ontario.
John Ross. John Simpson.

COSBIE, WARING GERALD. Historian for the Toronto General Hospital, Toronto, Ontario.
William Rawlins Beaumont.

COUTU, JEAN. Professeur d'histoire de l'art, Université Laval, Québec, Québec.
Amable Gauthier.

CRAIG, G. M. Professor of history, University of Toronto, Ontario.
Marshall Spring Bidwell.

CREIGHTON, PHYLLIS. Research assistant, *Dictionary of Canadian Biography/Dictionnaire biographique du Canada*, University of Toronto Press, Ontario.
Edward Troy. John Robert Willis.

CRÊTE-BÉGIN, LOUISE. Licenciée en histoire, Sainte-Foy, Québec.
Charles-Christophe Malhiot.

CROSS, MICHAEL S. Dean of men, Victoria University; associate professor of history, University of Toronto, Ontario.
Caleb Hopkins. Daniel McLachlin.

DANSEREAU, ANTONIO, P.S.S. Archiviste, Collège de Montréal, Québec.
Jacques-Victor Arraud. Antoine Mercier.

DAVIDSON, R. I. K. Editor (social sciences), University of Toronto Press, Ontario.
George Monro. John Taylor.

DAVIS, WILLIAM L., S.J. Professor emeritus of history, Gonzaga University, Spokane, Wash., U.S.A.
Pierre-Jean De Smet.

DEMPSEY, HUGH A. Director of history, Glenbow Alberta Institute, Calgary, Alberta.
Onistah-sokaksin. Sotai-na.

DÉSILETS, ANDRÉE. Professeur d'histoire, Université de Sherbrooke, Québec.
Elkanah Billings [in collaboration with Yvon Pageau]. *Marie-Julie-Marguerite Céré de La Colombière, dite sœur Mance. Lemuel Cushing. Albine Gadbois, dite Marie de Bonsecours. George Benson Hall. Marie-Anne-Marcelle Mallet. Isidore-Édouard-Candide Masson. Luc-Hyacinthe Masson. Marc-Damase Masson.*

DEVEREUX, E. J. Associate professor of English, University of Western Ontario, London, Ontario.
John Williams McCoubrey.

DODGE, ERNEST S. Director, Peabody Museum, Salem, Massachusetts, U.S.A.
Charles Francis Hall [with C. C. Loomis].

DOLMAN, CLAUDE ERNEST. Professor of microbiology, University of British Columbia, Vancouver, British Columbia.
James Bovell.

DORGE, LIONEL. Assistant professeur d'histoire, Université du Manitoba, Winnipeg, Manitoba.
John Black. Jean-Baptiste Thibault.

DUBUC, ALFRED. Directeur, Département d'histoire, Université du Québec à Montréal, Québec.
William Molson.

DYSTER, BARRIE. Secretary, Community Aid Abroad, New South Wales, The Glebe, N.S.W., Australia.
George Duggan. John William Gamble. William Charles Gwynne. Thomas Dennie Harris. Francis Henry Medcalf. Duncan Milloy.

EDDY, EARL B. Port Credit, Ontario.
James Porter.

FALARDEAU, JEAN-CHARLES. Professeur titulaire de sciences sociales et de lettres, Université Laval, Québec, Québec.
Étienne Parent.

FARRIS, ALLAN L. Professor of church history, Knox College, University of Toronto, Ontario.
Michael Willis.

FERGUSSON, CHARLES BRUCE. Archivist, Public Archives of Nova Scotia, Halifax, Nova Scotia; associate professor of history, Dalhousie University, Halifax, Nova Scotia.
Maria Frances Ann Morris (Miller). Hugo Reid.

FERLAND, LÉONIE, S.G.M. Maison provinciale des sœurs grises, Montréal, Québec.
Scholastique Gosselin.

768

FIRTH, EDITH. Associate Head, Metropolitan Toronto Central Library, Toronto, Ontario.
William Lawson.

FLEMMING, DAVID B. Research historian, National Historic Sites Service, Department of Indian Affairs and Northern Development, Ottawa, Ontario.
Thomas Louis Connolly. Donald Charles MacLean.

FLEURY, ALCIDE. Correcteur d'épreuves, Arthabaska, Québec.
Louis-Eusèbe Richard.

FRENCH, GOLDWIN SYLVESTER. Professor of history, McMaster University, Hamilton, Ontario.
Robert Alder. James Richardson. Shah-wun-dais (John Sunday). Conrad Vandusen.

GAGAN, DAVID P. Assistant professor of history, McMaster University, Hamilton, Ontario.
George Taylor Denison.

GAGNON, JEAN-PIERRE. Étudiant gradué en histoire, University of Toronto, Ontario.
Marc-Pascal de Sales Laterrière.

GAGNON, SERGE. Professeur d'histoire, Université d'Ottawa, Ontario.
Alexis Mailloux.

GALARNEAU, CLAUDE. Professeur d'histoire, Université Laval, Québec, Québec.
Jacques Dorion.

GARON, ANDRÉ. Étudiant gradué en histoire, Université d'Ottawa, Ontario.
Thomas Cushing Aylwin. James Leslie.

GATES, LILLIAN FRANCIS. Ithaca, New York, U.S.A.
John Doel. Donald M'Leod.

GLAZEBROOK, GEORGE PARKIN DE TWENEBROKES. Formerly professor of history, University of Toronto, Ontario.
Frances Browne (Stewart). William Cawthra.

GLOBENSKY, YVON. Chef de division, Ministère des Richesses Naturelles du Québec, Québec.
Hortense Globensky (Prévost).

GODFREY, MICHAEL, LT. COMDR. R.N. (RETD). Record agent, East Molesey, Surrey, England.
James Hooper Kerr.

GOODWIN, CRAUFURD DAVID WYCLIFFE. Professor of economics, vice provost and director of international programs, Duke University, Durham, North Carolina, U.S.A.
William Alexander Thomson.

GREENHILL, BASIL, Director, National Maritime Museum, Greenwich, London, England.
Thomas Burnard Chanter.

GRIEZIC, FOSTER J. K. Assistant professor of history, St Patrick's College, Carleton University, Ottawa, Ontario.
James Shaw.

GUILLET, EDWIN C. Consultant in Canadiana to the Librarian, Trent University, Peterborough, Ontario.
John Montgomery.

GUNDY, H. PEARSON. Formerly professor of English, Queen's University, Kingston, Ontario; associate director and senior editor, McGill-Queen's University Press.
Charles Belford. Edward Jackson. Thomas Liddell.

HAMELIN, JEAN. Directeur, Département d'histoire, Université Laval, Québec, Québec.
Médéric Lanctot.

HAMELIN, MARCEL. Professeur d'histoire, Université d'Ottawa, Ontario.
Pierre Bachand.

HAMILTON, WILLIAM B. Associate professor of history of education, University of Western Ontario, London, Ontario.
Hiram Blanchard. James Cuppaidge Cochran. Isaac LeVesconte. George Rogers McKenzie.

HARPER, JOHN RUSSELL. Department of fine arts, Sir George Williams University, Montreal, Quebec.
William Bent Berczy [in collaboration with J. Andre]. *Robert Stuart Duncanson. Paul Kane.*

HECHT, IRENE W. D. Assistant professor of history, Lewis and Clark College, Portland, Oregon, U.S.A.
Israel de Wolfe Andrews.

HENDERSON, JOHN LANCELEY HODGE. Professor of history; librarian, Huron College, London, Ontario.
William Craddock Bettridge.

HERTZMAN, LEWIS. Professor of history, York University, Downsview, Ontario.
Anthony von Iffland.

HILLER, JAMES K. Lecturer, Memorial University of Newfoundland, St John's, Newfoundland.
Robert Carter. Thomas Bulley Job.

HODGINS, BRUCE W. Associate professor of history, Trent University, Peterborough, Ontario.
James Douglas Gordon. John Sandfield Macdonald. Sir Henry William Stisted. Philip VanKoughnet.

HOLLAND, CLIVE A. Research assistant, Scott Polar Research Institute, Cambridge, England.
Sir George Back. Émile-Frédéric de Bray. Sherard Osborn.

HOLMES, KENNETH L. Professor of history, Oregon College of Education, Monmouth, Oregon, U.S.A.
Donald Manson. Alexander Hunter Murray.

HOPWOOD, VICTOR GEORGE. Associate professor of English, University of British Columbia, Vancouver, British Columbia.
Robert Christopher Lundin Brown. William Wentworth-Fitzwilliam.

JAMES, R. WARREN. Director, Consumer Research Branch, Department of Consumer and Corporate Affairs, Ottawa, Ontario.
John Rae. Hugh Bowlby Willson [in collaboration with J. S. Moir].

JARVIS, JULIA. Toronto, Ontario.
William Benjamin Robinson.

JOHNSON, ALICE MARGARET. Formerly archivist, Hudson's Bay Company, London, England.
Erland Erlandson. Nicol Finlayson. John Keast Lord.

JOHNSON, J. K. Associate professor of history, Carleton University, Ottawa, Ontario.
James Rogers Armstrong. James William Cook. George Stephen Benjamin Jarvis. Donald Aeneas MacDonell. John Philip Roblin.

JOHNSON, LEO A. Assistant professor of history.

769

University of Waterloo, Waterloo, Ontario.
Andrew Norton Buell.

JOHNSTON, CHARLES M. Professor of history, McMaster University, Hamilton, Ontario.
John Farrell. Ralph Leeming. Eliakim Malcolm.

JONES, ELWOOD H. Assistant professor of history, Trent University, Peterborough, Ontario.
Abraham Diamond.

JONES, FREDERICK. Research student, Selwyn College, Cambridge, England.
William Grey.

KALLMANN, HELMUT. Chief, Music Division, National Library of Canada, Ottawa, Ontario.
Jean-Chrysostome Brauneis. James Paton Clarke. Marie-Hippolyte-Antoine Dessane. James Dodsley Humphreys.

KEMP, PETER KEMP. Head, Naval Historical Branch, Ministry of Defence, London, England.
Sir George Augustus Westphal.

KLASSEN, HENRY CORNELIUS. Assistant professor of history, University of Calgary, Alberta.
Luther Hamilton Holton.

KLINCK, CARL F. Senior professor of English, University of Western Ontario, London, Ontario.
James Lynne Alexander.

LACOURCIÈRE, LUC. Directeur, Archives de folklore, Université Laval, Québec, Québec.
Philippe-Joseph Aubert de Gaspé.

LACROIX, JEAN-MICHEL. Traducteur, *Dictionnaire biographique du Canada/Dictionary of Canadian biography*, Les Presses de l'université Laval; professeur, Département d'études anglaises, Université Laval, Québec, Québec.

LAMB, WILLIAM KAYE. Former dominion archivist, Vancouver, British Columbia.
William Irving. Sewell Prescott Moody. Edward Stamp. Alfred Penderell Waddington. James Murray Yale.

†LANDON, FRED. London, Ontario.
Linus Wilson Miller.

LANDRY, PIERRE. Licencié en histoire, Québec.
Edwin Atwater. Stanley Clark Bagg. Louis-Michel Darveau. John Sharples.

LA TERREUR, MARC. Directeur du volume X, *Dictionnaire biographique du Canada/Dictionary of Canadian Biography*; professeur d'histoire, Université Laval, Québec, Québec.
Henri-Émile Chevalier.

LEFEBVRE, JEAN-JACQUES. Ex-archiviste en chef, Cour supérieure, Palais de justice, Montréal, Québec.
Joseph-Ubalde Beaudry. Nazaire Dupuis. Isidore Hurteau. Charles-André Leblanc. Félix-Hyacinthe Lemaire. Jean-Baptiste Prat. Narcisse Valois.

LESSARD, CLAUDE. Archiviste, Université du Québec à Trois-Rivières, Québec.
Thomas Caron. Alexandre-René Chaussegros de Léry.

LÉVESQUE, ULRIC. Professeur d'histoire, Collège d'enseignement général et professionnel de La Pocatière, Québec.
John Le Boutillier.

LINDO, PATRICK RICHARD. Historical consultant, National Historic Sites Service, Department of Indian Affairs and Northern Development, Ottawa, Ontario.
Robert Leonard Hazen.

LOOMIS, CHAUNCEY C., JR. Associate professor of English, Dartmouth College, Hanover, New Hampshire, U.S.A.
Charles Francis Hall [in collaboration with E. S. Dodge].

LORTIE, LÉON. Historiographe de l'université de Montréal, Québec.
Aldis Bernard. Jean-Baptiste Meilleur.

LUCAS, C. GLENN. Archivist-historian, United Church of Canada, Victoria University, Toronto, Ontario.
John Jennings. Jonathan Scott. Alexander Topp.

LYON, JOHN A. Port Hardy, British Columbia.
Joshua Spencer Thompson [in collaboration with G. A. Tripp].

MCCALLA, DOUGLAS. Assistant professor of history, Trent University, Peterborough, Ontario.
George Percival Ridout. John Young.

MCCLOY, T. R. Chief librarian, Glenbow-Alberta Institute, Calgary, Alberta.
John Richards McKay.

MCDOUGALL, ROBERT L. Professor of English, Carleton University, Ottawa, Ontario.
Alexander Harris.

MACKENZIE, ANTHONY A. Assistant professor of history, St Francis Xavier University, Antigonish, Nova Scotia.
Edmund Murray Dodd.

MCKENZIE, RUTH. Ottawa, Ontario.
Adiel Sherwood. William Smart.

MACKINNON, CHARLES F. Archivist, Public Archives of Canada, Ottawa, Ontario.
Charles Connell.

MACLEAN, RAYMOND A. Head, Department of history, St Francis Xavier University, Antigonish, Nova Scotia.
Colin Francis MacKinnon.

MACNUTT, WILLIAM STEWART. Professor of history, University of New Brunswick, Fredericton, New Brunswick.
James Carter. Robert Gowan. John Simcoe Saunders.

MACPHERSON, K. R. Supervisor, Manuscript Division, Ontario Department of Public Records and Archives, Toronto, Ontario.
Thomas Dick. Edward George O'Brien.

MAGILL, MAXWELL LEROY. Toronto, Ontario.
Andrew Drew.

MAINER, GEORGE GRAHAM. Toronto, Ontario.
Alfred Booker. Solomon Yeomans Chesley. William Hamilton. Hamilton Hartley Killaly. Roderick Matheson. Walter O'Hara.

†MANNY, LOUISE. Newcastle, New Brunswick.
John Harley.

MARSHALL, J. STEWART. Macdonald professor of physics and meteorology; Director, McGill Observatory, McGill University, Montreal, Quebec.
Charles Smallwood.

MARTINEAU, ANDRÉ. Archiviste, Archives publiques du Canada, Ottawa, Ontario.
Terence Joseph O'Neill.

MASSEY, GEORGES. Professeur d'histoire, Université du Québec à Trois-Rivières, Québec.
George Baptist.

MASTERS, DONALD CAMPBELL CHARLES. Professor of history, University of Guelph, Ontario.
Jasper Hume Nicolls.

MATHEWS, HAZEL C. Fort Myers Beach, Florida, U.S.A.
George King Chisholm.

MATHIEU, JACQUES. Professeur d'histoire, Université Laval, Québec, Québec.
John Heath. James Hodges.

METCALF, GEORGE. Lecturer in history, King's College, University of London, England.
William Henry Draper.

MILLER, CARMAN. Assistant professor of history, McGill University, Montreal, Quebec.
Thomas Brown Anderson. Charles Drolet. John Ponsonby Sexton.

MILLMAN, T. R. Professor of church history, Wycliffe College, University of Toronto, Ontario.
Thomas Gummersall Anderson. James Beaven. Adam Elliot. William Macaulay. John George Delhoste MacKenzie.

MITCHELL, ELAINE ALLAN. Toronto, Ontario.
Angus Cameron.

MOIR, JOHN SARGENT. Professor of history, Scarborough College, University of Toronto, Ontario.
Anson Green. Hugh Bowlby Willson [in collaboration with R. W. James].

MONET, JACQUES, S.J. Professeur d'histoire, Université d'Ottawa, Ontario.
Henry Black. Thomas Edmund Campbell. Alexandre-Maurice Delisle. Batholomew Conrad Augustus Gugy. Louis Labrèche-Viger. Robert Nelson [in collaboration with R. Chabot and Y. Roby].
Edmund Bailey O'Callaghan.

MONTAGNES, IAN. Projects co-ordinator, University of Toronto Press, Ontario.
John Ellis.

MORLEY, MARJORIE G. Provincial librarian, Provincial Library and Archives of Manitoba, Winnipeg, Manitoba.
Mathilda Davis.

MORLEY, WILLIAM F. E. Curator of Special Collections, Douglas Library, Queen's University, Kingston, Ontario.
William Henry Smith.

MORTON, DESMOND PAUL. Assistant professor of history, Erindale College, University of Toronto, Ontario.
William Foster Coffin. Sir James Alexander Lindsay.

MORTON, WILLIAM LEWIS. Vanier professor of history, Trent University, Peterborough, Ontario.
George-Antoine Bellecourt. Thomas Bunn. John Arnot Fleming. Alfred Henry Scott.

MUISE, DELPHIN A. Historian, National Museum of Man, Ottawa, Ontario.
Edmund Mortimer McDonald.

MURRAY, JEAN ELIZABETH. Professor emeritus of history, University of Saskatchewan, Saskatoon, Saskatchewan.
James Nisbet.

NEATBY, LESLIE HAMILTON. Formerly professor of classics, University of Saskatchewan, Saskatoon, Saskatchewan.
François Beaulieu. Sir Henry Kellett.

NEWELL, GEORGE R. Archivist, Provincial Archives of British Columbia, Victoria, British Columbia.
William George Cox. Jerome Harper. William Henry McNeill.

NISH, ELIZABETH. Research director, Centre d'Étude du Québec, Sir George Williams University, Montreal, Quebec.
Rollo Campbell. Charles-Elzéar Mondelet. Timothy Lee Terrill. Joseph-Élie Thibaudeau.

NIX, JAMES ERNEST. Montreal, Quebec.
George Millward McDougall.

†O'BREADY, MAURICE, P.D. Sherbrooke, Québec.
William Locker Pickmore Felton. Edward Short.

ORMSBY, MARGARET A. Head, Department of history, University of British Columbia, Vancouver, British Columbia.
James Cooper. Sir James Douglas.

ORMSBY, WILLIAM G. Professor of history, Brock University, St Catharines, Ontario.
Jacob Keefer. William Rees.

OSTRY, BERNARD. Assistant under secretary of state, Department of the Secretary of State, Ottawa, Ontario.
James Ryan.

OUELLET, FERNAND. Professeur d'histoire, Carleton University, Ottawa, Ontario.
Louis-Joseph Papineau.

OUELLET, GÉRALD G. Directeur, Section des sciences sociales, École normale, Moncton, Nouveau-Brunswick.
François-Lambert Bourneuf.

PAGEAU, YVON. Professeur des sciences de la Terre, Université du Québec à Montréal, Québec.
Elkanah Billings [in collaboration with A. Désilets].

PALMER, KATHERINE VAN WINKLE. Director, Paleontological Research Institution, Ithaca, New York, U.S.A.
Philip Pearsall Carpenter.

PAQUIN, MICHEL. Chargé de recherche, *Dictionnaire biographique du Canada/Dictionary of Canadian Biography*, Les Presses de l'université Laval, Québec, Québec.
Charles-Honoré Laverdière.

PARADIS, JEAN-MARC. Professeur d'histoire, Université du Québec à Trois-Rivières, Québec.
Bonaventure Viger.

PAUL-ÉMILE, SŒUR (Louise Guay), S.G.C. Sœurs de la Charité d'Ottawa, Ottawa, Ontario.
Élisabeth Bruyère.

PEEL, BRUCE BRADEN. Librarian, University of Alberta, Edmonton, Alberta.
Pierre Falcon.

PEMBERTON, IAN C. B. Lecturer in history, University of Windsor, Ontario.
William McClure.

PERCY, JOHN R. Assistant professor of astronomy, Erindale College, University of Toronto, Ontario.
James Craig Watson.

PHELPS, MARION L. Curator and assistant archivist,

Brome County Historical Society Museum and Archives, Knowlton, Quebec.
Philip Henry Moore.

PILON, HENRI. Manuscript editor, *Dictionary of Canadian Biography/Dictionnaire biographique du Canada*, University of Toronto Press; archivist, Trinity College, University of Toronto, Ontario.
Joseph-Ignace Aumond. Frederick Henry Baddeley. Robert Bell. Edward Mulberry Hodder. John Shedden.

PINCOMBE, CHARLES ALEXANDER. Secondary school teacher, Atlantic Baptist College, Moncton, New Brunswick.
Jonathan Berry. Stephen Binney.

POTHIER, BERNARD. Historian, Canadian War Museum, National Museums of Canada, Ottawa, Ontario.
William End. Ferdinand-Edmond Gauvreau. Samuel Robert Thomson.

POULIOT, LÉON, S.J. Assistant archiviste de la Compagnie de Jésus, Saint-Jérôme, Québec.
Antoine-Olivier Berthelet. Charles Conilleau. Hippolyte Moreau. Joseph-Octave Paré.

PRESTON, RICHARD ARTHUR. W. K. Boyd professor of history, Duke University, Durham, North Carolina, U.S.A.
Henry Charles Fletcher. Sir William O'Grady Haly. Sir William Rowan.

PROVOST, HONORIUS, PTRE. Archiviste, Séminaire de Québec, Québec.
Patrick J. Doherty. Elzéar-Henri Juchereau Duchesnay. Louis Proulx.

PRYKE, KENNETH GEORGE. Associate professor of history, University of Windsor, Ontario.
Mather Byles Almon. John Boyd. Ezra A. Churchill. Alexander Keith. James Charles McKeagney. Beamish Murdoch. Jeremiah Northup.

RALSTON, H. KEITH. Assistant professor of history, University of British Columbia, Vancouver, British Columbia.
John Sullivan Deas.

RAYMOND, MARCEL. Ex-conservateur, Jardin botanique de Montréal, Québec.
Eugène Bourgeaux.

REA, J. E. Associate professor of history, University of Manitoba, Winnipeg, Manitoba.
Robert Cunningham. Edward John Horan. Alexander McLeod.

REANEY, JAMES. Professor of English, University of Western Ontario, London, Ontario.
James Donnelly.

REYNOLDS, ARTHUR G. Registrar and associate professor of church history, Emmanuel College, University of Toronto, Ontario.
Thomas Hurlburt.

RICE, JAMES RICHARD. Graduate student in history, London, England.
Edmund Hillyer Duval. Thomas Hilyard. Robert Shives. William Wright.

RIOUX, JEAN-ROCH. Professeur d'histoire, Campus intercommunautaire Saint-Augustin, Cap-Rouge, Québec.
Gonzalve Doutre.

RITCHIE, THOMAS. Research officer, National Research Council, Ottawa, Ontario.
Henry Ruttan.

ROBERTSON, IAN ROSS. Historian, Mermaid, Prince Edward Island.
Herbert Bell. Daniel Brenan. George Coles. Nicholas Conroy. Donald Currie. George Dundas. James Douglas Haszard. Sir Robert Hodgson. John McDonald. Emanuel McEachen. William Henry Pope. Edward Reilly. William Swabey.

ROBIDOUX, RÉJEAN. Professeur de français, University of Toronto, Ontario.
Octave Crémazie.

ROBY, YVES. Professeur d'histoire, Université Laval, Québec, Québec.
Pierre-Claude Boucher de La Bruère. Édouard-Élisée Malhiot. Robert Nelson [in collaboration with R. Chabot et J. Monet]. Ludger-Napoléon Voyer.

RODDICK, EDNA MADALINE. London, Ontario.
Simeon Morrill.

ROME, DAVID. Lecturer, McGill University; director, Jewish Public Library, Montreal, Quebec.
Adolphus Mordecai Hart.

ROSSER, FREDERICK THOMAS. Ottawa, Ontario.
Samuel Stearns Day. Robert Alexander Fyfe. Louis Roussy.

ROTHNEY, GORDON OLIVER. Professor of history, University of Manitoba, Winnipeg, Manitoba.
John Sewell Sanborn.

†ROUSSEAU, JACQUES. Professeur d'ethnobiologie, Centre d'études nordiques, Université Laval, Québec, Québec.
Louis-Ovide Brunet.

ROY, PATRICIA E. Assistant professor of history, University of Victoria, British Columbia.
John Deighton.

RYERSON, STANLEY BRÉHAUT. Department of political science, University of Ottawa, Ontario; Département d'histoire, Université du Québec à Montréal, Québec.
Márk Szalatnay.

SAMPSON, WILLIAM R. Assistant professor of history, University of Alberta, Edmonton, Alberta.
David Cameron. William Frederick Crate. Richard Lane. Kenneth McKenzie. Dugald Mactavish.

SAVARD, PIERRE. Professeur d'histoire, Université Laval, Québec, Québec.
Louis-Moïse Brassard. Zéphirin Charest. Hippolyte Dubord. Félix-Odilon Gauthier.

SCOLLARD, ROBERT JOSEPH, C.S.B. Periodicals librarian, University of St Michael's College, Toronto, Ontario.
Jean-Mathieu Soulerin.

SENIOR, ELINOR LAURIE. Graduate student in history, McGill University, Montreal, Quebec.
Robert Alsop. Edward Feild. Robert John Pinsent.

SENIOR, HEREWARD. Associate professor of history, McGill University, Montreal, Quebec.
D'Arcy Boulton. William Henry Boulton. Ogle Robert Gowan. Arthur Hopper.

SHUFELT, HARRY B. Knowlton, Quebec.
Edmund Leavens Chandler.

SMITH, ALLAN C. L. Assistant professor of history,

University of British Columbia, Vancouver, British Columbia.
John Nugent.
SMITH, WILLIAM DAVID. Professor of history, University of Manitoba, Winnipeg, Manitoba.
Curtis James Bird. James Ross.
SNIDERMAN, ANNE E. F. Verdun, Quebec.
Samuel Hazlewood. William Mercer Wilson.
SPENCER, STEPHEN F. Graduate student in history, University of Western Ontario, London, Ontario.
Thomas Nepean Molesworth.
SPLANE, RICHARD B. Director-General, Welfare Assistance and Services, Department of National Health and Welfare, Ottawa, Ontario.
Thomas Scatcherd.
SPRAGGE, GEORGE W. Toronto, Ontario.
James William Bridgland. William Arthur Johnson.
SPRAY, WILLIAM ARTHUR. Associate professor of history, St Thomas University, Fredericton, New Brunswick.
Henry Bliss. George Luther Hatheway. Amand Landry. William Henry Steeves. John Waddell. John Wilkinson.
SPRY, IRENE M. Associate professor of history, University of Ottawa, Ontario.
John Inkster.
SQUIRES, WILLIAM AUSTIN. Curator emeritus, New Brunswick Museum, Fredericton, New Brunswick.
Charles Frederick Hartt.
STACEY, C. P. Professor of history, University of Toronto, Ontario.
John O'Neill.
STANLEY, GEORGE F. G. Professor of Canadian studies and Curator of the Davidson Collection, Mount Allison University, Sackville, New Brunswick.
Louis Bétournay. Louis-Adolphe Casault. Marie-Anne Gaboury (Lagemodière). William Bernard O'Donoghue.
STAYNER, C. ST. C. Halifax, Nova Scotia.
James Spike.
STELMACK, CAROLE B. Editor-historian, Public Archives of Canada, Ottawa, Ontario.
Thomas Roberts Ferguson. Robert Alexander Harrison. Georges-Honoré Simard.
STOCKDALE, JOHN CHRISTIE. Professeur adjoint d'anglais, Université Laval, Québec, Québec.
Charles Heavysege. Rosanna Eleanora Mullins (Leprohon).
STORY, G. M. Professor of English, Memorial University of Newfoundland, St John's, Newfoundland.
William Jackman [with C. W. Andrews].
STORY, NORAH. Freelance writer and consultant, Toronto, Ontario.
Thomas Fisher.
STUART-STUBBS, BASIL. Librarian, University of British Columbia, Vancouver, British Columbia.
Sir Edward Belcher.
SUTHERLAND, DAVID ALEXANDER. Graduate student in history, University of Toronto, Ontario.
Enos Collins [in collaboration with D. M. Barker]. *John Holmes. James William Johnston.*

SWAINSON, DONALD. Associate professor of history, Queen's University, Kingston, Ontario.
John Hillyard Cameron. John Willoughby Crawford. John Corry Wilson Daly. Asa Belknap Foster. John Bower Lewis. Samuel Sylvester Mills. James O'Reilly. Thomas Clark Street. Robert Wilkes.
SWIFT, MICHAEL. Provincial archivist, Provincial Archives of New Brunswick, Fredericton, New Brunswick.
Edward Barron Chandler. William Todd.
SYLVAIN, PHILIPPE. Professeur d'histoire, Université Laval, Québec, Québec.
Charles-Étienne Brasseur de Bourbourg. Francis Cassidy. George Edward Clerk. Vincislas-Paul-Wilfrid Dorion. Évariste Gélinas. Horace Greeley. Charles Laberge. Charles La Rocque. Hugh Murray. Alexis-Frédéric Truteau. Charles Wilson.
SYMONS, THOMAS H. B. Associate professor of history; president and vice-chancellor, Trent University, Peterborough, Ontario.
George Ridout. John Ryerson. William Ryerson.
TALMAN, JAMES JOHN. Professor of history, University of Western Ontario, London, Ontario.
Benjamin Cronyn. Hannibal Mulkins. John Talbot [in collaboration with D. J. Brock].
TAYLOR, HUGH ALEXANDER. Director, Historical Branch, Public Archives of Canada, Ottawa, Ontario.
Francis Pym Harding.
TESSIER, YVES. Directeur de la Cartothèque, Université Laval, Québec, Québec.
Robert-Shore-Milnes Bouchette.
THOMAS, CHRISTMAS EDWARD. Research assistant, Public Archives of Nova Scotia, Halifax, Nova Scotia.
William Bullock. George McCawley. John George Marshall. Christopher Milner. Aubrey George Spencer.
THOMAS, LEWIS GWYNNE. Professor of history, University of Alberta, Edmonton, Alberta.
Edward Ermatinger. Donald Gunn. William Henry Taylor.
THOMAS, LEWIS HERBERT. Professor of history, University of Alberta, Edmonton, Alberta.
Alexis Reynard.
THOMPSON, ARTHUR NEWEY. Rector, St George's Anglican Church, Winnipeg, Manitoba.
Alexander Neil Bethune.
THOMPSON, CHARLES A. Graduate student in history, Duke University, Durham, N.C., U.S.A.
Timothy O'Hea. Sir John Young.
THOMPSON, FREDERIC FRASER. Professor of history, Royal Military College of Canada, Kingston, Ontario.
Sir Thomas John Cochrane. Robert Law. Sir Henry Prescott.
THOMPSON, JOHN BESWARICK. Research historian, National Historic Sites Service, Department of Indian Affairs and Northern Development, Ottawa, Ontario.
John Simpson.
TRACY, MINERVA. Wolfville, Nova Scotia.
John Davis. James De Mille. Charles Pedley.

TREMBLAY, VICTOR, P.D. Archiviste, Société historique du Saguenay, Chicoutimi, Québec.
William Evan Price.

TRIPP, GEORGE A. London, Ontario.
Joshua Spencer Thompson [in collaboration with J. A. Lyon].

TULCHINSKY, GERALD. Assistant professor of history, Queen's University, Kingston, Ontario.
William Workman. John Young [in collaboration with B. J. Young].

TURNER, ALLAN REAMAN. Provincial archivist, Saskatchewan Archives Board; adjunct professor of history, University of Saskatchewan, Regina, Saskatchewan.
Hunkajuka. James McKay. Abraham Wikaskokiseyin.

TURNER, WESLEY B. Assistant professor of history, Brock University, St Catharines, Ontario.
William Dixon.

USHER, JEAN MYFANWY. Historian, National Museum of Man, Ottawa, Ontario.
Modeste Demers.

VACHON, CLAUDE. Archiviste, Fédération des commissions scolaires catholiques du Québec, Québec.
Joseph-Octave Beaubien.

VÉZINA, RAYMOND. Professeur d'histoire de l'art, Université Laval, Québec, Québec.
Cornelius Krieghoff.

VOISINE, NIVE. Professeur d'histoire, Université Laval, Québec, Québec.
George Conroy. François-Magloire Derome.

WAITE, PETER B. Professor of history, Dalhousie University, Halifax, Nova Scotia.
William Garvie. John Kent. Sir John Gaspard Le Marchant. Jonathan McCully.

WALDON, FREDA F. Formerly chief librarian, Hamilton Public Library, Hamilton, Ontario.
Archibald Macallum.

WALKER, FRANK NORMAN. Toronto, Ontario.
Charles Dawson Shanly.

WALLACE, CARL MURRAY. Assistant professor of history, Laurentian University, Sudbury, Ontario.
John Adolphus Beckwith. Charles Fisher. William Hayden Needham. John Robertson. Lemuel Allan Wilmot.

WARD, NORMAN. Britnell professor of political science, University of Saskatchewan, Saskatoon, Saskatchewan.
William Henry Lee.

WATERSTON, ELIZABETH. Assistant professor of English, University of Guelph, Ontario.
William James Anderson. Robert Middleton.

WATTS, ALFRED. Judge of the Provincial Court, West Vancouver, British Columbia.
George Pearkes.

WELLS, CLAIRE. Traductrice, *Dictionnaire biographique du Canada/Dictionary of Canadian Biography*, Les Presses de l'université Laval, chargée de cours, Extension de l'enseignement, Université Laval, Québec, Québec.

WELLS, ELIZABETH A. St John's, Newfoundland.
Thomas Bennett. Edmund Hanrahan. John Munn. Joseph Noad. John Valentine Nugent. Thomas Ridley. Joseph Woods.

WHITELEY, WILLIAM HENRY. Associate professor of history, Memorial University of Newfoundland, St John's, Newfoundland.
Johann August Miertsching.

WILBUR, RICHARD. Caraquet, New Brunswick.
John Henry Thomas Manners-Sutton. John Venner Thurgar.

WILSON, ALAN. Chairman, Department of history, Trent University, Peterborough, Ontario.
John Walpole Willis.

WILSON, J. DONALD. Assistant professor of history, Lakehead University, Thunder Bay, Ontario.
William Hincks.

WINDER, C. GORDON. Professor of geology, University of Western Ontario, London, Ontario.
Sir William Edmond Logan.

WINKS, ROBIN W. Professor of history, Yale University, New Haven, Connecticut, U.S.A.
Wilson Ruffin Abbott.

WISE, SYDNEY FRANCIS. Director, Directorate of history, Canadian Forces Headquarters, Ottawa, Ontario
Sir Francis Bond Head.

WOLFENDEN, MADGE. Formerly assistant provincial archivist, Provincial Archives, Victoria, British Columbia.
Robert Burnaby. Sosthenes Maximilian Driard. Edward White.

WOOD, JOHN S. Gooderham professor of French, Victoria College, University of Toronto; translator into English of biographies in French, *Dictionary of Canadian Biography/Dictionnaire biographique du Canada*, University of Toronto Press, Ontario.

YON, ARMAND, PTRE. Professeur à la retraite, Sainte-Dorothée, Québec.
Paul-Henry de Belvèze.

YOUNG, BRIAN J. Instructor in history, University of Vermont, Burlington, Vermont, U.S.A.
John Alfred Poor. John Young [in collaboration with G. Tulchinsky].

Index

Included in the index are the names of persons mentioned in volume X. They are listed by their family names, with titles and first names following. Wives are entered under their maiden names with their married names in parentheses. Persons who appear in incomplete citations in the text are fully identified when possible. An asterisk indicates that the person has received a biography in a volume already published, or will probably receive one in a subsequent volume. A death date or last floruit date refers the reader to the volume in which the biography will be found. Numerals in bold face indicate the pages on which a biography appears. Titles, nicknames, variant spellings, married and religious names are fully cross-referenced.